CAPITALISM

CAPITALISM

A Treatise on Economics

George Reisman

Jameson Books, Ottawa, Illinois

Copies of this book may be purchased from the publisher. All inquiries should be addressed to Jameson Books, 722 Columbus St., Ottawa, IL 61350. (815)-434-7905. Fax: (815)-434-7907.

Distributed by LPC Group, Chicago. All returns to LPC Group warehouse.

Photocopying of excerpts from Jameson Books editions are licensed through the Copyright Clearance Center, 222 Rosewood Drive, Danvers, MA 01923. Call 508-750-8400 for information.

ISBN: 0-915463-73-3

Library of Congress Catalogue Card Number: 96-78105

Manufactured in the United States of America

To Ludwig von Mises, my teacher, and Edith Packer, my wife.

CONTENTS IN BRIEF

EPILOGUE

CONTENTS

PART ONE
THE FOUNDATIONS OF ECONOMICS

CHAPTER 2. WEALTH AND ITS ROLE IN HUMAN LIFE

PART TWO
THE DIVISION OF LABOR AND CAPITALISM

CHAPTER 4. THE DIVISION OF LABOR AND PRODUCTION

CHAPTER 5. THE DEPENDENCE OF THE DIVISION OF LABOR ON CAPITALISM I

PART A. THE NATURE OF THE DEPENDENCIES

PART THREE
THE PROCESS OF ECONOMIC PROGRESS

CHAPTER 12. MONEY AND SPENDING

PART B. THE PRODUCTIVITY THEORY OF WAGES

CHAPTER 16. THE NET-CONSUMPTION/NET-INVESTMENT THEORY OF PROFIT AND INTEREST

PART A. THE POSITIVE THEORY

EPILOGUE

CHAPTER 20. TOWARD THE ESTABLISHMENT OF LAISSEZ-FAIRE CAPITALISM

FIGURES

TABLES

PREFACE

This book is the product of a labor of love extending over many years. I conceived of it as an explicit project at least as far back as the spring of 1977, when I made a several-page-long list of the major points it would contain. Although I was eager to begin writing it at once, one thing after another interfered, the most important being finding a publisher for my previous book *The Government Against the Economy,* which I had only recently completed. As a result of this and a considerable variety of less important projects, I was not able actually to begin work on the present book until sometime in 1981.

In that year and the next, I completed the first draft of what are now the Introduction and first three chapters.

In 1982, my wife Edith Packer and I, together with our friend Jerry Kirkpatrick, founded what later became known as The Jefferson School of Philosophy, Economics, and Psychology (TJS). I agreed to deliver eight lectures on the institutions and functioning of a capitalist society for TJS's first summer conference, which was held the following year on the campus of the University of California, San Diego. Those lectures, which were fully written out, constituted the first draft of what are now Chapters 4 and 9 and the first part of Chapter 5.

The writing out of my lectures for succeeding TJS summer conferences in 1985, 1987, and 1989, which were also held on the UCSD campus, represented drafts of what are now chapters 11 and 13–17.[1] My 1986 TJS Fall seminar lecture was the first draft of what is now Chapter 20, which bears the same title as the lecture, namely, "Toward the Establishment of a Capitalist Soci-

ety." Thus, this book is a lasting legacy of the TJS conferences and seminars.

By 1990, my progress on the book had decisively outstripped my lecture preparations and I was using material from the manuscript as the substance of my lectures.[2] By this time, I at last had a complete draft of the book, which included an updated and expanded version of *The Government Against the Economy* as Chapters 6–8. Extensive editing, reorganization, and rewriting occupied another five years, with the result that the work that is offered now is as well organized, well-written, and clear as I have been able to make it.

I want to say that a very important element in the pleasure I have derived from the writing of this book rested on my use of a personal computer. When I wrote *The Government Against the Economy* and when I began writing this book, I experienced it as me, a fountain pen, and a yellow legal pad against the world. I fully believed, of course, that the pen is mightier than the sword and that with my pen I would ultimately prevail. But however mighty is the pen, the personal computer is far mightier. And every morning, since the fall of 1983, when I entered my office and sat down at my desk I would eagerly watch my computer as it went through its startup routine. My thought was, in effect, "Here is this wonderful, extremely powerful machine that is my ally in the work I am doing and that makes the doing of it so much easier and more enjoyable." To me, as a writer, the personal computer is the greatest of all the remarkable goods supplied by capitalism, surpassing even the personal automobile in its contribution to the ease and enjoyment of life. Without it, the writing of this book would probably not have been possible.

On a vacation early in the course of writing this book, I read a Western novel by the late Louis L'Amour. I don't remember the story itself, but one brief portion of the novel has stood out in my mind ever since and was a significant help to me in the rest of my writing. It was about the journey of pioneers traveling west in covered wagons, and described how on some days they would make so little progress that after a whole day's march, they could still see the remains of their campfires of the night before. The important thing to those pioneers, L'Amour stressed, was that each day they did make *some* progress—they always finished the day further west than they began it. This became an inspiration to me on all those days when the end result of many hours of work was that I had gotten only a few paragraphs beyond where I had finished the night before. At those times, I contented myself with the knowledge that at least I was that many paragraphs further ahead and that I was still moving "west," so to speak. In retrospect, I think of things somewhat more humorously, and say to myself, "Even if you average just half a page a day, after five or ten years it adds up."

I said that I conceived of this book as an explicit project in 1977. It was an implicit project long before that time. It is the culmination of practically a lifetime of concern that I have had for the protection of property rights and for the right of individuals personally and selfishly to enjoy all the prosperity they can peacefully achieve. I remember identifying as a boy of no more than ten or eleven years of age that what the tenants and city government of New York, which is where I then lived, were doing with the property of the landlords of that city, by means of rent control, was exactly the same in principle as what schoolyard bullies often did with my baseball or football—namely, seize it against the will of its owner and arbitrarily use it for their own pleasure, without a thought for the rights of the owner, mine or the landlords'.

From that early age, I was very much aware of a widespread contempt and hostility toward property rights and property owners—a contempt and hostility manifested in such comments as the one I heard a little later from a junior high school teacher that she did not care about the fact that there were people paying ninety percent of their incomes in taxes (which was then the maximum federal surtax rate), "because they still had a lot left." When I encountered the same attitude of contemptuous philosophic indifference to the violation of property rights in one of my own close relatives, I came to the conclusion that property rights were very much in need of defense, and that I must write a book on their behalf. I actually set out to write such a book at the time, and succeeded in putting together about one or two paragraphs.

It was clear to me that such contemptuous attitudes and the violations of property rights that they supported were contrary to everything that the Declaration of Independence and Constitution of the United States stood for, which above all was the right of the individual to the pursuit of his own happiness, which included his material prosperity and enjoyment of same. Indeed, my first serious professional ambition, which I held around the age of twelve, was to become a Constitutional lawyer, so that I might best defend that right.

I can trace my admiration for the United States' Constitution back to about the age of five. I remember early in World War II, asking my father why the United States deserved to win all the wars it had ever fought, as well as the one it was now in. He answered that the United States was the world's best country. And when I asked what made it the world's best country, he answered "the Constitution." I don't know what understanding I could have had of such an abstraction at that very young age, but I am quite sure that very early, at least implicitly, I grasped that the Constitution was a body of principles controlling the behavior of the government of the United States and defining the character of that government as good. The Constitution, I came very early to understand, made the United States the world's best country because it created a government that, totally unlike the governments of the countries of Europe and the rest of the world, did not harass its citizens, but instead left them free to pursue their happiness. This, I understood, was why both pairs of my grandparents had come to the United States and why all the immigrants, starting with the Pilgrims, had come to America. I wondered why all other countries did not adopt the Constitution of the United States.

Until the age of eleven or twelve, I took for granted that practically every American recognized the value of his country because he loved its freedom and supported the principles on which the United States was based. Based on my reading of editorials and columnists in the Hearst Press, then represented in New York by *The Daily Mirror* and the *Journal American*, I thought that now that the Nazis had been defeated, the only exceptions were a handful of communist or socialist crackpots.

I had had an inkling, at the age of ten, that this sanguine view of things might not be altogether accurate. This occurred when someone pointed out to me that the paper currency of the United States had imprinted on it a promise to pay the bearer on demand the number of dollars on the face of the bill, that until 1933 this had meant a promise to pay those dollars *in gold coin*, which was the money of the country affirmed by the Constitution, but now meant the utter absurdity of paying the bearer merely the very same kind of paper notes that he already possessed. I was astounded that such an obvious absurdity was tolerated—that it was accepted routinely, everyday, by everyone, without protest.

My cheerful confidence in the popularity of individual freedom did not begin to erode, however, until I reached junior high school. There, after a few months' attendance, I came to the conclusion that a disproportionate number of the communist and socialist crackpots I had read about were to be found among my teachers. In addition to numerous such remarks by teachers as the one I described above, I encountered teachers who openly confessed to being socialists, including one who regretted that he lived just inside the border of a conservative Republican's congressional district because if he lived across the street he could have voted for Representative Vito Marcantonio, then the most far-leftwing member of Congress. The same man described the Soviet Union as a great experiment. He and his colleagues dismissed questions that challenged any of their interpretations by referring to the presumed size of the bank account or stock portfolio of the questioner's father. I clearly remember this man's response to what I thought was an astonishing fact that all by itself proved the value of the United States and what it stood for, a fact which I happily conveyed to my classmates in the seventh grade in an oral report, and which I had learned from a motion-picture documentary shortly before. This was the fact that with only six percent of the world's population, the United States produced fully forty percent of the world's annual output of goods and services. The man's reply was yes, but so what; ten percent of the country's population owned ninety percent of its wealth.

I soon realized that no one I knew, neither other students, nor any of the adults I knew, was able to answer the leftwing arguments I was encountering daily at school. For a time, I thought, the explanation was that this was New York City. The people here have been intellectually corrupted. But the rest of the country is still full of people who support the principles of individual rights and freedom and know how to defend them. Over the next two summers, I learned that the problem was nationwide. I made this discovery as the result of my experiences at a vacation camp in Maine, where I met a wide variety of college students from all over the country who were working as camp counselors, as well as occasional local citizens. The college students too included a goodly proportion of self-confessed "social democrats." I remember one of them telling me with obvious contempt how ignorant the parents of many of the campers were. They had been to see a local production of a play by George Bernard Shaw that made their type of people its targets, and

they all loved it.

There was a flood of leftist arguments against individual rights and freedom, and nowhere were there answers being given, at least nowhere that I had found. I reluctantly came to the conclusion that the principles of individual rights and freedom enshrined in the Declaration of Independence and Constitution had largely lost their influence on the American people and that these glorious documents themselves were on the way to becoming items of merely historical interest, rather than living documents controlling the conduct of our country's government.

It quickly became obvious to me, from the arguments of my teachers and the college students I met, and from those even of my own dentist, who favored socialized medicine, that what gave rise to the contempt for property rights and property owners, and the readiness to discard everything that the United States as a country had stood for in defending those rights, was a set of *economic* beliefs. Respect for property rights, it was held, was tantamount to respecting the right of a handful of capitalist exploiters to impoverish the masses by paying them starvation wages on the one side while charging them outrageous, monopoly prices on the other. Respecting the rights and freedom of businessmen and capitalists, it was claimed, was also the cause of terrible depressions and mass unemployment, as well as the cause of unsafe food and drugs, child labor, sweat shops, poverty in old age, wars, and countless other evils. Again and again, I saw, the assault on property rights was based on ideas about economics. It was ideas about economics that were destroying the concepts of individual rights and freedom. And, thus, by the age of thirteen, I gave up my ambition to become a Constitutional lawyer and began the study of economics instead.

I undertook the study of economics for the explicit purpose of finding economic arguments in defense of individual rights, i.e., property rights. In my first year of study, with the aid of a dictionary by my side, I read substantial portions of Adam Smith's *The Wealth of Nations* and David Ricardo's *Principles of Political Economy and Taxation,* as well as the whole of a book on the history of economic thought. I started with Smith and Ricardo in the belief that their books would provide the arguments I was seeking, for they had the reputation of having been the leading defenders of capitalism in the system's heyday. Although my mature evaluation of them is that they do in fact have some very important things to say in the defense of capitalism, I was greatly disappointed in them at the time, because it seemed to me that with their support for the labor theory of value, they served merely to prepare the ground for Marx.[3] None of the other authors described in the book I read on the history of economic thought appeared to offer any serious arguments in defense of capitalism.

I turned to browsing the card catalog of the public library for any author who might be a defender of capitalism and from whom I might learn something. In my search, I came across *Capitalism, Socialism, and Democracy* by Joseph Schumpeter, and *Capitalism: The Creator* by Carl Snyder, both of which books I quickly gave up on. I considered Schumpeter valueless as soon as I came across his statement that while socialism looked better than capitalism on paper, capitalism had proved superior to socialism in practice. To me this meant that Schumpeter was saying that socialism seemed better as far as we could think and speak about it, but that somehow, for reasons that we could not understand or verbalize, capitalism turned out to be better in the real world. That was not what I was looking for, which was to know why capitalism was right *in theory*, and not just in some realm of practice that could not be understood in theory. I immediately gave up on Snyder for essentially the same reason—namely, his book appeared to be largely descriptive and statistical and to have little or nothing to say in the essential realm of conceptual understanding, i.e., of theory. I experienced great disappointment even in Thomas Jefferson, when I read that he thought that the preservation of an *agricultural* society was essential for liberty. I realized that the modern world depended vitally on such things as steel mills and all other forms of heavy industry, and I wanted authors who would defend individual rights in *that context*.

At the age of fourteen, I discovered William Stanley Jevons's *The State in Relation to Labour* and *The Theory of Political Economy.*[4] While the first of these titles began with major concessions on the side of government intervention, the substance of the book was a brilliant analysis of the destructive consequences of labor unions.[5] The second was an exposition of the theory of marginal utility, which I valued greatly, inasmuch as it seemed to provide an essential part of the answer to Marxism—enough, at least, to convince me that Marx and all of my Marxist high-school teachers were wrong in economic theory.

During this period, I had come to subscribe to a fortnightly magazine called *The Freeman.* At that time, Henry Hazlitt played a major role in writing the magazine's editorials and in determining its content. So long as he continued in that role, I found the magazine so valuable that I read every issue from cover to cover.

It was in one of the early issues of *The Freeman* that I had my first exposure to the writings of Ludwig von Mises. It was his essay "Lord Keynes and Say's Law."[6] From reading the essay, I could see that Mises knew the history of economic thought and that he was presenting a strong, self-assured position in defense of an important and relatively complicated aspect of the functioning of capitalism, a position that Say and Ricardo had taken in the early nineteenth century, which was that general business depressions could never be caused by any so-called excess of production. I knew immediately that here was a man I must read further. And, a few months later, at the age of fourteen, I borrowed his classic *Socialism* from the public library.[7] Unfortunately, the book was then beyond me and I was not able to gain very much from the parts I attempted to read. But less than a year later, with some of the money I had been given on my fifteenth birthday, I bought *Socialism* and over the coming months had one of the very greatest intellectual experiences of my life, before or since. In the intervening months since my previous attempt, my mental powers must have grown the intellectual equivalent of the several inches that boys of that age are capable of growing in such a short time, because I was now able to understand a very great deal of what I read. And what I read filled me with a sense of utter enlightenment.

Mises argued that real wages were determined by the productivity of labor, which in turn depended on capital accumulation, which was accomplished by the saving and investment of businessmen and capitalists and was undermined by progressive income and inheritance taxation. He explained the operations of the price system and showed that the businessmen and capitalists were not a law unto themselves but, in order to make profits and avoid losses, had to produce the goods the consumers wanted to buy. He showed how price controls destroyed the price system and resulted in the establishment of de facto socialism, of which Nazi Germany was the leading example. He explained why socialism had to fail economically, because of its lack of markets and consequent inability to have a price system and thus to perform economic calculations. He showed how political freedom depended on economic freedom and thus why socialism, with its utter lack of economic freedom, was necessarily a system of dictatorship. He showed how under capitalism, the privately owned means of production operated to the benefit of the great mass of nonowners of the means of production to almost as great an extent as they did to the benefit of the owners and that economic progress, based on the profit motive and saving and capital accumulation, brought about a steadily rising standard of living of the nonowners. He showed how the law of comparative advantage made room for virtually everyone, however unskilled, to participate in the great world-embracing system of division of labor and to obtain all of its essential benefits. He showed that unemployment and the consequent inability of people to participate in the division of labor was the result of government interference with the height of wage rates. He showed why the economic interests of all individuals and groups, of all countries, races, and economic classes were fundamentally harmonious and were made to conflict only by means of the adoption of the irrational ideologies of nationalism, racism, and Marxism and the policies of government intervention based upon them. He demonstrated that the existence of society—a division-of-labor society—and of all the other people who participated in it, was in the material self-interest of every individual, and thus that there was a profoundly rational, self-interested basis for social cooperation and such ethical norms as not killing or injuring other people.

These essential points were amplified and additional major arguments were added to them in his other writings then available in English, above all, *Human Action* and *The Theory of Money and Credit,* as well as *Planning For Freedom*, *Bureaucracy,* and *Omnipotent Government*, all of which I read over the next three years. In these other works Mises added vigorous defenses of the gold standard, brilliant analyses of inflation, compelling demonstrations that depressions were the result of government-sponsored credit expansion, and much else besides. Reading Mises on a random day, I would encounter such brilliant observations as that even if a chorus of people were simultaneously to say "We," it would still be individuals who were saying it, which served as an illustration of the fact that collectives and groups of any kind had no real existence apart from the individuals who comprised them; that high profits provided not only an incentive to stepped-up investment, but also the means of stepped-up investment, inasmuch as the high profits would themselves be largely reinvested; that war and division of labor were incompatible, inasmuch as war represented a situation of the baker fighting the tailor, with the result that both parties were deprived of vital supplies; that democracy was necessary as the means of making possible peaceful changes in government, so that a dissatisfied majority would not have to resort to revolution or civil war to have its way; and so on. Looking back, I do not recall a single paragraph of von Mises that did not serve as an inspiration to my own thinking, even in the cases (which were relatively few) in which I ultimately came to disagree with him.

Mises was clearly the man whose writings I had been searching for. Here at last was a great, articulate defender of the economic institutions of capitalism, who wrote with all the power that logical argument could provide and with the authority of the highest level of scholarship. (*Socialism* and *Human Action* abound with references and quotations in German, French, Latin, and Greek.[8])

One of the great good fortunes of my life, that profoundly contributed to my subsequent intellectual devel-

opment, was to be invited by von Mises to attend his graduate seminar at New York University. I received this invitation shortly after my sixteenth birthday, in the last part of my senior year in high school. It came about as the result of a meeting, arranged by The Foundation For Economic Education, between Mises, myself, and Ralph Raico, who was then a fellow student of mine at the Bronx High School of Science (Raico is now Professor of History at the State University of New York, Buffalo). After several hours of conversation, spent mainly answering our questions, Mises invited us both to come to his seminar—provided (in reference to our extreme youth) that we did "not make noise." We both eagerly accepted his invitation and began attending the very next week.

The format of the seminar was that each semester it was devoted to some topic of special current interest to von Mises, such as inflation or the epistemology of economics. It met on Thursday evenings from 7:25 to 9:05 PM, and, for most of the period in which I attended, at the Gallatin House, which was a fine old town house (once the home of the British consul) located at 6 Washington Square North, in New York's Greenwich Village. It would open each evening with Mises himself speaking from a few notes for about twenty minutes to half an hour, followed by a general, cross discussion among the various seminar members who wished to participate or who Mises occasionally called upon. Often, a portion of the discussion was devoted to some paper that a seminar participant had prepared for the occasion.

I regularly attended the seminar for about seven and a half years, through the remainder of high school, all through my college years at Columbia University, and then as an enrolled student in NYU's Graduate School of Business Administration, which was where Mises taught. I stopped attending only when I myself began to teach and had a class of my own to conduct on Thursday evenings.

At the seminar, I had the opportunity of hearing many observations by Mises that were not in his books that I had read. Equally important, I had the opportunity of asking him questions. Uncharacteristically, I did not raise any questions until after I had been in attendance for about a year and a half. Thereafter, I became a full-fledged participant, often being assigned papers to write and deliver.

My most outstanding memory of the seminar is that of Mises himself. I always experienced a heightened level of awareness when he entered the room and took his seat at the seminar table. What I was acutely aware of was that here, just a few feet away from me, was one of the outstanding thinkers in all of human history.

One of the things Mises stressed in his seminar was the importance of knowing foreign languages. One of the reasons he gave for this was the frequent inadequacy of translation. In this connection, I was very surprised to learn that he was unhappy with the translation of *Socialism*.

I accepted his injunction to learn foreign languages and because there were important writings of his own not yet translated, as well as important writings of Menger and Böhm-Bawerk, his predecessors in the Austrian school, I put the opportunity I had of studying German at Columbia College to very good use. I wholeheartedly plunged into freshman and then sophomore German and memorized every new word I came across, sometimes to the extent of fifty or a hundred words a day. I memorized the declension of every model noun and the conjugation of every model verb, in every tense, mood, and voice, for every person, and every model sentence that I found. The result was that in the Christmas vacation of my sophomore year, I dared to translate a chapter of his *Grundprobleme der Nationalökonomie (Epistemological Problems of Economics)* and then show it to him. Although he had some misgivings, he supported my application for a grant from the William Volker Fund to translate the remainder of the book over the following summer. I obtained the grant and the next summer accomplished the translation at Columbia's Butler Library. I translated four pages a day, Monday through Friday, and three more on Saturday, for ten weeks, until the whole book was done. I worked from nine in the morning until seven in the evening during the week, and from nine until five on Saturdays. When I finished, I typed the manuscript and had copies of it in the hands of the Volker Fund and Mises well before Columbia's fall semester began. I know that both he and the Volker Fund were very favorably impressed, because he urged me to translate Heinrich Rickert's *Kulturwissenschaft und Naturwissenschaft,* which he considered a major answer to logical positivism, over the next summer, and, when I applied for a grant to do it, I got an immediate favorable response. Both translations were published a few years later by D. Van Nostrand, the latter under the title *Science and History.* I have to say that translating Mises, and being well paid to do it at that, was absolutely the most fabulous thing I could think of doing at the time, and to this day, I count it as a major accomplishment of my life.

Some of the credit for my having had the courage to start the translation belongs to the late Murray Rothbard, whom I met when I entered the seminar and became close friends with over the next five years. (Other members of the seminar when I arrived on the scene were Hans Sennholz, now President of the Foundation for Economic Education, and his wife Mary; Israel Kirzner, now a Professor of Economics at New York University; Professor William H. Peterson, then of New York University,

and his wife Mary; and Percy Greaves, who later wrote *Understanding the Dollar Crisis,*[9] and his wife Bettina Bien Greaves, then and now a staff member of the Foundation for Economic Education. Prominent more or less frequent visitors to the seminar were Henry Hazlitt, then a regular columnist for *Newsweek* as well as the author of numerous books, the best known of which is *Economics in One Lesson,*[10] and Lawrence Fertig, who at the time was a columnist for the New York *World Telegram and Sun.)* Rothbard was then working on his *Man, Economy, and State* on a grant from the Volker Fund and urged me to apply, assuring me that a proposal to translate *Grundprobleme* would be considered both seriously and sympathetically.[11]

By the time I had been in the seminar for about a year, Rothbard, Raico, and I, were joined by Robert Hessen (now a Senior Fellow at the Hoover Institution in Stanford) and Leonard Liggio (who later became President of the Institute for Humane Studies). About a year after that, Ronald Hamowy (now a Professor of History at the University of Alberta in Edmonton) also joined us. We almost always continued the discussions of the seminar until past midnight, usually at Rothbard's apartment, and frequently met on weekends. We informally called ourselves "The Circle Bastiat," after the leading nineteenth-century French advocate of capitalism, Frederic Bastiat.

At one of our gatherings, in the summer of 1954, over three years before the publication of *Atlas Shrugged,* Rothbard brought up the name Ayn Rand, whom I had not previously heard of. He described her as an extremely interesting person and, when he observed the curiosity of our whole group, asked if we would be interested in meeting her. Everyone in the group was very much interested. He then proceeded to arrange a meeting for the second Saturday night in July, at her apartment in midtown Manhattan.

That meeting, and the next one a week later, had an unforgettable effect on me. In the year or more before I entered Ayn Rand's apartment, I held three explicitly formulated leading intellectual values: liberalism (in the sense in which Mises used the term, and which actually meant capitalism); utilitarianism, which was my philosophy of ethics and which I had learned largely from Mises (though not entirely, inasmuch as I had already come to the conclusion on my own that everything a person does is selfish insofar as it seeks to achieve *his* ends[12]); and "McCarthyism," which I was enthusiastically for, because I believed that the country was heavily infested with communists and socialists, whom I detested, and to whom Senator McCarthy was causing a major amount of upset. By the time I left Ayn Rand's apartment, even after the first meeting, I was seriously shaken in my attachment to utilitarianism.

Both meetings began at about 8:30 in the evening and lasted until about five o'clock the following morning. When I was introduced to her, I had no real idea of her intellectual caliber. I quickly began to learn her estimate of herself, however, when I offered her two tickets to an upcoming dinner in honor of Roy Cohn, Senator McCarthy's chief aide, at which Senator McCarthy would be present. (I was scheduled to make a brief speech at the event, and when I mentioned to one of the event's organizers that I was going to meet Ayn Rand, she asked me to extend the invitation.) Miss Rand declined the invitation on the grounds that to get involved as she would need to get involved, she would have to drop her present project (which was the writing of *Atlas Shrugged)* and do for McCarthy what Zola had done for Dreyfus. I had seen the Paul Muni movie *Zola,* and so had a good idea of Zola's stature. I don't quite remember how I experienced the comparison, but it was probably something comparable to the expression of a silent whistle. (After I came to appreciate the nature of Ayn Rand's accomplishments, a comparison to Zola would seem several orders of magnitude too modest.)

At both meetings, most of the time was taken up with my arguing with Ayn Rand about whether values were subjective or objective, while Rothbard, as he himself later described it, looked on with amusement, watching me raise all the same questions and objections he had raised on some previous occasion, equally to no avail.

I had a sense of amazement at both meetings. I was amazed that I was involved in an argument that in the beginning seemed absolutely open and shut to me, and yet that I could not win. I was amazed that my opponent was expressing views that I found both utterly naïve and at the same time was incapable of answering without being driven to support positions that I did not want to support, and that I was repeatedly being driven into supporting such positions.

Neither of the evenings was very pleasant. At one point—I don't know how we got to the subject, nor whether it occurred at our first or second meeting—I expressed the conviction that a void must exist. Otherwise, I did not see how the existence of motion was possible, since two objects could not occupy the same place at the same time. Ayn Rand's reply to my expression of my conviction was that "it was worse than anything a communist could have said." (In retrospect, recognizing that the starting point of her philosophy is that "existence exists," I realize she took my statement to mean that I upheld the existence of "nonexistence" and was thus maintaining the worst possible contradiction.)

Because of such unpleasantness, I did not desire to see her again until after I read *Atlas Shrugged.* However, I could not forget our meetings and could not help won-

dering if somehow she might be right that values really were objective after all. I was very troubled by the implications of the proposition that all values are ultimately arbitrary and subjective, as Mises claimed. It no longer seemed enough that the great majority of people happened to prefer life to death, and health and wealth to sickness and poverty. For if they happened not to, there would be nothing to say to them that could change their minds, and if there were enough of them, no way to fight them, and, worst of all, no way even morally to condemn any slaughters they might commit, because if all values really were arbitrary and subjective, a concentration-camp sadist's values would be as good and as moral as the values of the world's greatest creators.

The years between my first meetings with Ayn Rand and the publication of *Atlas Shrugged* spanned my sophomore through senior years in college. In that time, I experienced serious intellectual doubt in connection with my ability to defend capitalism. What I had learned from Mises enabled me decisively to answer practically every argument that had been raised against capitalism prior to 1930, which was more than enough to answer my high school teachers. But my college professors presented a different challenge. They were teaching Keynesianism and the doctrine of pure and perfect competition/imperfect competition. Mises, I reluctantly had to conclude, had not dealt adequately with these doctrines.[13] At any rate, these were two major areas in which I found myself unable to turn to his writings for the kind of decisive help I had come to expect from him.

The doubts I experienced in college were not in response to any kind of solid arguments, but more in response to phantoms of arguments that could not be grasped in any clear, precise way and that in fact usually bore obvious absurdities. This last was certainly true of the Keynesian multiplier doctrine and of the claim on the part of the pure-and-perfect competition doctrine that competition implied the *absence of rivalry.* Despite the absurdities, all of the faculty and practically all of my fellow students at Columbia seemed perfectly at home with the doctrines and absolutely confident of their truth.

If any one concrete can convey the intellectual dishonesty of Columbia's economics department in those days, it was this. Namely, while neglecting to provide a single copy of any of the writings of von Mises, or even so much as mention the existence of any of them in any of the assigned readings or, as far as I was aware, in a classroom, the department saw to it that literally dozens of copies of Oskar Lange's attempted refutation of Mises's doctrine on the impossibility of economic calculation under socialism were available on open reserve in the library—as an optional, supplementary reading in the introductory economics course.[14]

Economics was not the only area in college in which I experienced revulsion for Columbia's teachings. I had the same experience in the so-called contemporary civilization courses I had to take, and in history courses. I know I would have had it in philosophy courses, but I wisely dropped the one or two I enrolled in, after the first week. There were, to be sure, things I valued at college, having greatly gained from them: such as having to read the great classics of Western literature, which I would probably not have done on my own; the freshman English-composition course, which gave me the ability to write a solid essay; the German courses; and the mathematics courses. However, with the exception of three of the mathematics courses, almost all of these were in the first two years. By the time of my senior year, I had profoundly soured on Columbia University. I remember walking the campus and noting the names of the various buildings: "School of Mines," "School of Engineering," "Philosophy Hall," and so on. I remember thinking that the first two served honorable purposes, while the third served no purpose but the emission of intellectual poison.

I do not know if my college education could have damaged my intellectual development permanently. It did not have the chance. For just a few months after graduation, *Atlas Shrugged* appeared.

I obtained a very early copy and began to read it almost immediately. Once I started it, I could not put it down, except for such necessary things as eating and sleeping. I was simply pulled along by what I have thought of ever since as the most exciting plot-novel ever written. Every two hundred pages or so, the story reached a new level of intensity, making it even more demanding of resolution than it was before. I stopped only when I finally finished the book, four days after I had started it. When I finished, the only thing I could find to say in criticism, tongue in cheek, was that the book was too short and the villains were not black enough.

The first thing I got out of *Atlas Shrugged* and the philosophical system it presented was a powerful reinforcement of my conviction that my basic ideas were right and a renewal of my confidence that I would be able to expose my professors' errors.

Very soon thereafter, the whole Circle Bastiat, myself included, met again with Ayn Rand. We were all tremendously enthusiastic over *Atlas*. Rothbard wrote Ayn Rand a letter, in which, I believe, he compared her to the sun, which one cannot approach too closely. I truly thought that *Atlas Shrugged* would convert the country—in about six weeks; I could not understand how anyone could read it without being either convinced by what it had to say or else hospitalized by a mental breakdown.

The following winter, Rothbard, Raico, and I, and, I think, Bob Hessen, all enrolled in the very first lecture course ever delivered on Objectivism. This was before Objectivism even had the name "Objectivism" and was still described simply as "the philosophy of Ayn Rand." Nevertheless, by the summer of that same year, 1958, tensions had begun to develop between Rothbard and Ayn Rand, which led to a shattering of relationships, including my friendship with him.[15]

Shortly after that break, I took Rothbard's place in making a presentation in Ayn Rand's living room of the case for "competing governments," i.e., the purchase and sale even of such government services as police, courts, and military in a free market. As the result of Ayn Rand's criticisms, I came to the conclusion that the case was untenable, if for no other reason than that it abandoned the distinction between private action and government action and implicitly urged unregulated, uncontrolled government action, i.e., the uncontrolled, unregulated use of physical force. This was the logical implication of treating government as a free business enterprise. I had to conclude that government in the form of a highly regulated, tightly controlled legal monopoly on the use of force, was necessary after all, in order to provide an essential foundation for unregulated, uncontrolled private markets in all goods and services, which would then function totally free of the threat of physical force. This indeed, represented nothing more than a return to my starting point. It was what the government established by the United States' Constitution had represented, and which I had so much admired.

At that time, and in later years, I came to be influenced by Ayn Rand's ideas in numerous ways, thanks in part to the fact that over the years between 1957 and her death in 1982, I had the opportunity of frequently meeting with her and speaking with her extensively about her writings. The influence of her philosophy extolling individual rights and the value of human life and reason appears repeatedly in this book and sets its intellectual tone. To be specific, I have found her treatment of the concepts of individual rights and freedom to be far superior to that of anyone else, and I have taken it over and have applied it extensively both in Chapter 1 and as the foundation of my treatment of monopoly as inherently government created in Chapter 10. In Chapter 1, very much in the spirit of Ayn Rand, I have shown how the whole of capitalist development, including the development of the panoply of capitalism's institutions from private ownership of land to the division of labor and continuous economic progress, can be understood as "a self-expanded power of human reason to serve human life."[16] In Chapter 2, I have made her views on the role of reason in human life, on the objectivity of values, and on the integration of mind and body essential elements of my approach to the foundations of economics, that is, to man's objective need both for the constantly growing supply of wealth that capitalism produces and for the science of economics itself. Her influence pervades my critique of environmentalism in Chapter 3. It is present in my discussion of competition in Chapter 9, where I have adopted her principle of the "pyramid of ability" and integrated it with the law of comparative advantage. It appears in my critique of the doctrine of pure and perfect competition in Chapter 10, much of which was originally published in *The Objectivist* under her editorship. It is also to be found in the epistemological aspects of Chapters 11, 15, and 18, that is, in my approach to definitions, axiomatic concepts, and the epistemological errors of Keynes and his followers. Her influence is probably to be found in some measure in every chapter, at the very least insofar as it has contributed to an improved ability on my part to know what is a forceful argument and what is not. Needless to say, it is very much present in my treatment of the philosophical influences that led to the development of capitalist civilization and the current philosophical influences that are threatening to destroy it, and, of course, everywhere insofar as I deal with such essential matters as egoism versus altruism, individualism versus collectivism, and reason versus mysticism.

Looking back over the past and all that has led to the writing of this book, I cannot help but take the greatest possible pride and satisfaction in the fact that along the way, in having been the student of *both* Ludwig von Mises *and* Ayn Rand, I was able to acquire what by my own standards at least is the highest possible "intellectual pedigree" that it is possible for any thinker to have acquired in my lifetime, or, indeed, in any other lifetime.

The year and a half or more following my abandonment of the doctrine of competing governments turned out to be the most intellectually productive of my life, and to provide most of what is original in this book. The distinctive intellectual background of that period included a long-standing disagreement I had had with Rothbard concerning whether or not the rate of profit ("originary interest" in the terminology of Mises) had to fall in connection with capital accumulation. Rothbard maintained that it did, as did the overwhelming majority of economists since the time of Adam Smith. To me, such a position seemed comparable to implying the gradual extinction of the sun as the necessary accompaniment of capital accumulation. For it was only the prospect of profit that provided motivational energy to the entire economic system. And while Mises's own position on this subject was unclear, he held another doctrine of similar import. This was his doctrine of purchasing-power price premiums in the rate of interest, according to which the prospect of prices rising at any given rate added an equivalent percentage to the rate of interest,

while the prospect of prices falling at any given rate resulted in an equivalent deduction from the rate of interest. Thus formulated, an implication of this doctrine, I concluded, was that rapid increases in production that caused a rapid fall in prices would result in a negative rate of interest and thus in a lack of all incentive to lend or invest, and thus in a depression. This conclusion too was unacceptable to me. It implied the overproduction doctrine, which Mises himself, of course, totally opposed.[17]

I compiled a written list of such points, which also included numerous questions I had come to formulate in connection with my classes at Columbia and then at NYU, where I was now enrolled in the doctoral program.

By this time, in just a year and two summers, taking ten two-credit courses in the fall and ten in the spring, I had already completed all of the course work for a Ph.D., but I still had the written and oral exams and the dissertation in front of me. My original plan had been to go straight through for the Ph.D., in the shortest possible time. Now I found the prospect of the obstacles that still remained to be somewhat more daunting, and so I decided that it would be worthwhile to take a few months out and obtain an MBA degree. For this, all I needed to do was write an MBA thesis.

I decided to choose a topic that would require that I read only "good people"—i.e., sound authors. I had come to the conclusion that because the efforts of proto-Keynesians, such as Malthus and Sismondi, had been decisively defeated by the classical economists in the early nineteenth century, and because nothing like the pure-and-perfect-competition doctrine had ever even arisen in the nineteenth century, when classical economics was in vogue, there must have been something in classical economics that served to refute or thoroughly preclude such doctrines in the first place, and thus that I should turn to it once again as a source of knowledge. The thesis topic I chose was *The Classical Economists and the Austrians on Value and Costs*. This topic required that I read extensively in Menger, Böhm-Bawerk, and Wieser for the Austrian views, and not only in Smith and Ricardo, but also in James Mill, Say, McCulloch, Senior, and J.S. Mill, for the views of classical economics.

This project turned out to be a very good idea, indeed. I learned much more about the doctrine of diminishing marginal utility, including how it subsumes cases in which prices are actually determined in the first instance by cost of production.[18] In reading seven different classical authors, each one covering essentially the same ground, and doing so at the age of twenty-one and twenty-two, instead of thirteen, I was able to come to a genuine understanding of their work. This included seeing how their views on the labor theory of value and the "iron law of wages" greatly differed from those of Marx, whose views on these subjects are usually assumed to be the same as theirs, and that Ricardo's doctrine that "profits rise as wages fall, and fall as wages rise" did not, despite all appearances, actually imply a conflict of interests between wage earners and capitalists.[19] I came to see, in fact, that very little substantive difference actually existed between the views of Böhm-Bawerk and those of John Stuart Mill concerning the determination of the prices of reproducible products.[20] Very importantly, I began to see how the whole contemporary approach of "imperfect competition" versus "pure and perfect competition" was a result of the abandonment of the classical economists' recognition of the role of cost of production in the determination of the prices of reproducible goods, a recognition that Böhm-Bawerk and Wieser had retained but all others had apparently lost.[21]

What I gained from the extensive reading I had done in connection with my thesis went far beyond the subject of value and costs. In the months immediately following, I knew that I had learned a great deal that had not gone into the thesis—knowledge that I could then not yet even explicitly formulate. I felt good about my state of mind and I am pretty sure that I described my mental condition to myself as one of being "intellectually pregnant."

Back in the spring of 1958, I had succeeded in formulating to my own satisfaction a set of conditions in which capital accumulation could take place indefinitely with no accompanying fall in the rate of profit. I had tried to explain it to Rothbard, but without success. That demonstration was one element in the back of my mind, before I even got to the reading for my thesis. My exposure to principles of actual business accounting, as the result of having taken a number of courses on investments and corporation finance in the NYU program, provided another critical element besides what I had learned from my reading.

In July of 1959, it all came together. The precipitating event was my reading an extensive quotation from John Stuart Mill presenting the proposition that "demand for commodities is not demand for labour." This was a passage I had not read before. It appeared in Henry Hazlitt's newly published *The Failure of the "New Economics."*[22]

Very soon thereafter, I had a period of five successive days in which I was able to make one connection after another and to answer one question after another from my list. In essence, I had put together, and was able to hold in my mind all at the same time, an early version of what now appears in this book as Figures 16–2 and 17–1 and derive a succession of major implications from it.[23]

I saw how Mill's proposition was essential to explaining an *excess* of the demand for the products of business over the demand for factors of production by business. It was only because the demand for "commodities"—viz., consumers' goods—was not a demand for labor that the demand for consumers' goods could *exceed* the demand for labor, and thus that the demand for the products of business in general could exceed the demand by business for factors of production in general. This excess of demand for products over demand for factors of production was an essential cause of an excess of sales revenues over costs, and, therefore, of an aggregate profit in the economic system. I could see at the same time how with a given aggregate amount and average rate of profit, based on a given excess of the demand for the products of business over the demand for factors of production by business, both capital accumulation and falling prices caused by increased production could take place, with, of course, no effect whatever on the average rate of profit. I could also see other important relationships. In those five days, I was able to grasp essential portions of what are now Chapters 11 and 13–18 of this book. Virtually everything else that is in these chapters, and much that is in other chapters, is an elaboration or further implication of the discoveries I made in those five days, though in many cases, the elaboration or further implication did not occur to me until much later. Indeed, the process of tracing out the implications continues down to the present.

As I made the new connections I wrote them down, sometimes jumping out of bed to do so, lest I forget any of them. After the first five days, I had accumulated about 15 pages of notes, the most important part of which was an elaborate numerical example of the most essential points in a form consistent with the principles of business accounting. In August, I wrote a hundred-page-plus typed paper called "The Consumption Theory of Interest," which I showed to Henry Hazlitt, who, as mentioned, sometimes attended von Mises's seminar. He was generally impressed with it, and, starting with the third printing of *The Failure of the "New Economics,"* credited me with an important application I had made in the paper identifying a simultaneous breakdown of the Keynesian doctrines on consumption, employment, liquidity preference, and the rate of interest, though he did not refer to my manuscript specifically.[24]

Not long after I made my discoveries, I decided that they should be the main subject of my doctoral dissertation, which I began to do research for soon after passing my oral examination in the spring of 1960. For the sake of thoroughness, I wanted to include not only my own views, but also a critical analysis of all significant alternative views. I set out to follow the example of Böhm-Bawerk, who had done just that. Thus, in preparation for writing my dissertation, I read virtually all of Böhm-Bawerk that I had not previously read, as well as major selections from other authors whose views concerning the rate of profit/interest were prominent, such as Irving Fisher, Knut Wicksell, and Frank Fetter, as well as Smith, Ricardo, other classical economists, and Marx and Keynes.

I began writing the dissertation in May of 1961 and handed in a 625-page typed manuscript in the fall of 1962. The title was *The Theory of Originary Interest.* (At this time, I still followed Mises in describing what businessmen and accountants normally describe as profit, and which I too now refer to as profit, as "originary interest.")

In January of 1963, I learned that one of the members of my reading committee had rejected the dissertation. In order to gain his approval, it was necessary for me to eliminate well over half of the manuscript I had submitted, and write approximately thirty new pages at the beginning and thirty more new pages at the end. (On my own initiative, I replaced "originary interest" with "profit" throughout.) The last time I spoke with this committee member, he said he liked the new version much better than the original one, except for the first thirty pages; he also said he had not yet read the last thirty pages. (Sometime later, I was told that this individual had left the university to write editorials for *The Washington Post.*) My dissertation, as finally approved, carries the title *The Theory of Aggregate Profit and the Average Rate of Profit.*[25]

This situation constituted the one time in my life when I was seriously disappointed in von Mises. He told me that he found it amusing that I should receive such trouble from this particular committee member, whom he regarded as a Marxist, when what I was providing was a modernized, more scientific version of the very ideas that were the foundation of the man's own beliefs. Mises believed that because of my resurrection of the classical economists, I was indirectly resurrecting Marx. (Happily, he changed his mind on this subject two years later, after hearing my lecture "A Ricardian's Critique of the Exploitation Theory."[26] But the same essential material had been available to him in my original dissertation.)

As much of the preceding makes clear, this book is very much the product of ideas I first developed over thirty-five years ago and have been further developing and elaborating ever since. Over this period, I have published various portions of my ideas in articles. In cases in which I have been unable to improve upon formulations I presented in those articles, I have retained the formulations. Appropriate acknowledgment is made to the publications in question in notes to the portions of the text where the formulations appear.

Here I wish to express my special thanks to Libertarian Press for its permission to include the very lengthy quotation from Böhm-Bawerk's *Capital and Interest* that appears on pp. 414–416.

I have not sought permission from any publisher to quote passages in cases in which direct quotation is necessary to prove to the reader that the author in question really does hold the views I ascribe to him. Here I rely on the doctrine of fair use, which I believe provides protection against the intellectual hit and run that would be entailed in allowing authors to propound absurd and vicious ideas and then to hide behind copyright protection so that a critic could not prove what they had actually said and thus be placed at risk of being accused of having presented their views unfairly. This applies above all to my numerous quotations from various editions of the textbook *Economics* by Paul Samuelson. It also applies to my quotations from less well-known textbooks, from *The General Theory* by Lord Keynes, *The New Industrial State by* John Kenneth Galbraith, and from sundry environmentalists.

I want to acknowledge the very great contribution of my wife, Dr. Edith Packer, with whom I have now shared most of my adult life. I doubt very much that I could have undertaken, let alone carried to completion, a project of this size without her. She has provided both the necessary emotional framework and an extremely helpful intellectual framework. It was she who served as the first reader and editor of the manuscript of this book. An important part of the organization and much of the readability of my book are due to her suggestions.

Laguna Hills, California
June 1996

GEORGE REISMAN

Notes

1. These were the tape-recorded lecture series that are known as *An Introduction to Procapitalist 'Macroeconomics,' A Theory of Productive Activity, Profit, and Saving,* and *Capital, the Productive Process, and the Rate of Profit.* These titles and the one described in the next sentence of the text are available on audio cassette from The Jefferson School at PO Box 2934, Laguna Hills, Calif., 92654.

2. Thus, my 1990 TJS Fall seminar lecture "The Nature and Value of Economics" was a portion of Chapter 1. My 1991 TJS summer conference series *Wealth, Natural Resources, and the Environment* and *The Political Concept of Monopoly* was drawn from Chapters 2, 3 and 10.

3. Concerning the errors of this view, see below, pp. 473–500.

4. William Stanley Jevons, *The State in Relation to Labour* (London: Macmillan and Co., 1894); *The Theory of Political Economy,* 4th ed. (London: Macmillan and Co., 1924).

5. I happened to buy *The State in Relation to Labour* as the result of not being able to afford Jeremy Bentham's *In Defence of Usury,* a work whose title greatly appealed to me, and thus having to choose the substantially less expensive title by Jevons.

6. The essay has been reprinted in Ludwig von Mises, *Planning For Freedom,* 4th ed. enl. (South Holland, Ill.: Libertarian Press, 1980).

7. Ludwig von Mises, *Socialism* (New Haven: Yale University Press, 1951); reprint ed. (Indianapolis: Liberty Classics, 1981).

8. Happily, these have been translated in the currently available Liberty Classics reprint edition of *Socialism* cited above. As a major aid to reading *Human Action,* see *Mises Made Easier A Glossary for Human Action* prepared by Percy L. Greaves, Jr. (Dobbs Ferry, N. Y.: Free Market Books, 1974).

9. Percy Greaves, *Understanding the Dollar Crisis,* (Belmont, Mass.: Western Islands, 1973).

10. Henry Hazlitt, *Economics in One Lesson,* new ed. (New Rochelle, N. Y.: Arlington House Publishers, 1979).

11. Murray N. Rothbard, *Man, Economy, and State,* 2 vols. (Princeton, N. J.: D. Van Nostrand Company, Inc., 1962).

12. This is a conclusion that I now consider to be mistaken, because it attaches no objective meaning to the concept of self.

13. This conclusion may appear somewhat ironic in view of the fact that what is today accepted as a new and convincing major critique of Keynesianism, namely, the "rational expectations doctrine," is nothing more than arguments made by Mises and Hazlitt in the 1950s, for which they have received no credit. See, for example, Paul Samuelson and William Nordhaus, *Economics,* 15th ed. (New York: McGraw Hill Book Company, 1995), Figure 31–5 on p. 613 and the surrounding discussion. Then see Ludwig von Mises, *Human Action,* 3d ed. rev. (Chicago: Henry Regnery Co., 1966), pp. 792–793. See also below, p. 6 and p. 11, n. 15.

14. See Oscar Lange, *On the Economic Theory of Socialism,* Benjamin E. Lippencott, ed. (Minneapolis: University of Minnesota Press, 1938). See also below, my critique of Lange and his doctrine of the artificial market, on pp. 279–282.

15. When I knew Rothbard, he was a staunch pro-McCarthy, anticommunist. Later on, incredible as it may seem, he became *an admirer of the Soviet Union!* For evidence of this, see below, p. 11, n. 13.

16. See below, pp. 19, 27–28.

17. For demonstrations of why capital accumulation does not entail a falling rate of profit and of why falling prices caused by increased production do not reduce the rate of profit or interest, see below, pp. 569–580, 810–818, and 825–826.

18. On this point, see below the lengthy quotation from Böhm-Bawerk on pp. 414–416.

19. Concerning these points, see below, pp. 475–498.

20. See below, p. 218, n. 31.

21. On this subject, see below, pp. 408–417.

22. Henry Hazlitt, *The Failure of the "New Economics"* (New York: D. Van Nostrand, 1959), p. 363.

23. Figures 16–2 and 17–1 are shown facing each other on pp. 810–811.

24. See Henry Hazlitt, *The Failure of the "New Economics,"* 3d prntng. and later, p. 196, n. 6.

25. George Reisman, *The Theory of Aggregate Profit and the Average Rate of Profit,* Ph.D. diss., New York University Graduate School of Business Administration (1963; reprinted by University Microfilms, Inc., Ann Arbor, Mich.).

26. The substance of this lecture was published many years later as my essay "Classical Economics Versus the Exploitation Theory" in Kurt Leube and Albert Zlabinger, eds., *The Political Economy of Freedom Essays in Honor of F. A. Hayek* (Munich and Vienna: Philosophia Verlag, 1985). The same analysis, greatly elaborated, appears below, on pp. 473–498.

INTRODUCTION

The subject of this book is the principles of economics. Its theme is that the application of these principles to the service of human life and well-being requires the existence of a capitalist society.

The purpose of this introduction is to enable the reader to classify the present book in relation to the wider body of procapitalist economic thought and of economic thought as such.

1. Procapitalist Economic Thought, Past and Present

Procapitalist economic thought and economic thought as such are essentially synonymous. The substance of both is to be found in the same two main sources, namely, the writings of the British (and French) classical economists and the Austrian neoclassical economists. All other schools of economic thought are essentially either just prescientific gropings or nothing more than misguided criticisms of the positive truths established by the classical and Austrian schools.

Among the classical economists are, above all, Adam Smith (1723–90), David Ricardo (1772–1823), James Mill (1773–1836), and John Stuart Mill (1806–73), and the Frenchmen Jean-Baptiste Say (1767–1832) and Frederic Bastiat (1801–50). The nineteenth-century Englishmen Nassau W. Senior (1790–1864), John R. McCulloch (1789–1864), and John Cairnes (1824–75) also deserve mention as important members of this group. Important close allies of the classical school are the Manchester school, led by Richard Cobden (1804–65) and John Bright (1811–89), who were the parliamentary leaders of the British free-trade movement in the mid-nineteenth century, and the currency school, which included the English economists Lord Overstone (1796–1883) and Robert Torrens (1780–1864), and the American monetary theorists William Gouge (1796–1863) and Charles Holt Carroll (1799–1890). The classical school incorporated important economic truths previously identified by Richard Cantillon (1680–1734), David Hume (1711–76), and, above all, the French Physiocrats. The Physiocrats flourished around the middle of the eighteenth century. The leading members of the school are François Quesnay (1694–1774), Pierre Du Pont de Nemours (1739–1817), Robert Jacques Turgot (1727–81), and Mercier de la Rivière (1720–93). The great merit of the Physiocrats was to have identified the existence of natural economic laws (*physiocracy* means the rule of nature) and, on the basis of their understanding of those laws, to have reached the conclusion that the government should follow a policy of laissez faire, a term which they originated.[1]

The most important members of the Austrian school are Carl Menger (1840–1921), Eugen von Böhm-Bawerk (1851–1914), and Ludwig von Mises (1881–1973). Other important members are Friedrich von Wieser (1851–1926); F. A. Hayek (1899–1992), who was the most prominent of von Mises's students and who won the Nobel prize for economics in 1974; Henry Hazlitt (1894–1993); Murray Rothbard (1926–95), who was one of von Mises's later students; and, among the later students of von Mises who are still alive, Hans Sennholz and Israel Kirzner.[2]

Closely allied with the Austrian school on many points

are the major neoclassical English economists William Stanley Jevons (1835–82) and Philip Wicksteed (1860–1927), the major Swedish economist Knut Wicksell (1851–1926), and the major mid-nineteenth-century German economist Hermann Heinrich Gossen (1810–58), who had anticipated some of its leading doctrines in a book published in 1854. Other major economists who are more or less significantly allied with the Austrian school are the Americans John Bates Clark (1847–1938), Frank Fetter (1863–1949), Irving Fisher (1867–1947), and Frank Knight (1885–1972), who were prominent earlier in this century. The contemporary Chicago school, led by Milton Friedman, and its offshoot the Public Choice school, headed by James Buchanan, also fall into the category of allies of the Austrian school. (Friedman won the Nobel prize in economics in 1976; Buchanan, in 1986.) Other, less well-known but important contemporary or recent economists who are more or less significantly allied with the Austrian school and sympathetic to capitalism are Armen Alchian, William Allen, Dominick Armentano, Paul Heyne, Wayne Leeman, John. S. McGee, Mark Skousen, Thomas Sowell, Walter Williams, Leland Yeager, and the late W. H. Hutt (1899–1988) and Ludwig Lachmann (1906–1990). And there are many more, both here in the United States and abroad. Both the Austrian school and its allies have been heavily influenced in turn by the writings of the classical economists.

It should not be surprising that such a large number of those who are recognized as important economists are, at the same time, leading advocates of capitalism. To the extent that an economist really understands the principles governing economic life, and desires that human beings live and prosper, he can hardly fail to be an advocate of capitalism.

The classical and Austrian schools have had important allies in the field of philosophy. Ayn Rand (1905–82), in particular, must be cited as providing a philosophical foundation for the case for capitalism, and as being responsible probably more than anyone else for the current spread of procapitalist ideas. The great English philosopher John Locke, who was a leading intellectual influence on the Founding Fathers of the United States, also deserves an especially prominent mention. And the English philosophers Jeremy Bentham and Herbert Spencer must be cited as well.

The classical and the Austrian schools and their allies have developed virtually all of the great positive truths of economic science. Their ideas, especially those of von Mises, Ricardo, Smith, and Böhm-Bawerk—in that order—together with important elements of the philosophy of Ayn Rand—are the intellectual foundation and inspiration of this book, which seeks to carry the work of these extraordinary individuals a step further by integrating leading elements of it into a logically consistent whole and by incorporating the present author's own contributions.

Because the whole of this book is itself an exposition of the ideas of the classical and Austrian economists, it is not necessary (nor would it be possible) to explain at this point precisely what it is that these economists maintain, beyond a few generalities. They recognize the gains derived from the division of labor. They explain the nature, origin, and importance of money; the laws governing the determination of prices, wages, profits, and interest; and the vital role of saving and capital accumulation in raising the standard of living. They understand the benevolent nature of self-interest and the profit motive operating under economic freedom, and show how government intervention is the cause of inflation, depressions, economic stagnation, poverty, international economic conflict, and wars. In sum, they support capitalism and oppose government interference and socialism. To a great extent, the views of these authors will become clear in the pages that follow. But, because this is not a book on the history of economic thought, no systematic effort is made to explain precisely which individuals held which specific positions. The reader who is interested in acquiring that knowledge is advised to consult the bibliography, which appears at the end of this book, and to undertake the immeasurably valuable task of reading through the works listed in it.

A subject which must be dealt with here, however, is a brief account of the *differences* between the classical and Austrian schools. The leading difference concerns the theory of value and price. The classical economists, with exceptions, assigned an exaggerated role to cost of production as an explanation of prices, and, as a consequence, to the quantity of labor required to produce goods. They even went so far as frequently to maintain that wages are determined by "the cost of production of labor." Wages, they often held, tend to equal the price of the goods necessary to enable a worker to live and to raise replacements for himself and his wife.

Such an exaggerated role assigned to cost of production and quantity of labor made it possible later in the nineteenth century for Karl Marx to present himself as the logical heir of the classical economists, devoted merely to developing the implications of their doctrines. Marx was believed, and the consequence was that when the Austrian and other neoclassical economists appeared on the scene around 1870 and propounded the theory of marginal utility as the explanation of value and price, the doctrines of classical economics were abandoned to an extent much greater than necessary, to the great loss of later economic science. Only those doctrines were retained that could be supported either on the basis of the theory of marginal utility or otherwise independently of the basic classical framework. In terms of what was lost intellectually, it was a case of the classical economics baby being thrown out with the Marxist bath water. Ironically, those who threw out the baby were precisely the people who needed it most and to whom it really belonged—namely, the later advocates of capitalism.

Significantly, the abandonment of classical economics was also brought about by the growing influence of socialism. And to this extent, it was clearly a case of the abandonment being caused by classical economics' *antisocialist* implications. What I refer to was the altogether unjustified recantation in 1869 of a central pillar of classical economics by its then leading spokesman, John Stuart Mill. In response to utterly flimsy criticisms, easily capable of being answered, and apparently based on nothing more than his own growing attachment to socialist ideas, Mill abandoned the so-called wages-fund doctrine, according to which wages are paid out of savings and capital. In so doing, he cut the ground from under the entire classical perspective on the role of saving and capital in the productive process, including his own previous brilliant contributions to that perspective, and set the stage for the intellectual success of Keynesianism in the 1930s.[3]

The theory of marginal utility resolved the paradox of value which had been propounded by Adam Smith and which had prevented the classical economists from grounding exchange value in utility. "The things which have the greatest value in use," Smith observed, "have frequently little or no value in exchange; and on the contrary, those which have the greatest value in exchange have frequently little or no value in use. Nothing is more useful than water: but it will purchase scarce any thing; scarce any thing can be had in exchange for it. A diamond, on the contrary, has scarce any value in use; but a very great quantity of other goods may frequently be had in exchange for it."[4]

The only explanation, the classical economists concluded, is that while things must have utility in order to possess exchange value, the actual determinant of exchange value is cost of production. In contrast, the theory of marginal utility made it possible to ground exchange value in utility after all—by showing that the exchange value of goods such as water and diamonds is determined by their respective *marginal* utilities. The marginal utility of a good is the utility of the particular quantity of it under consideration, taking into account the quantity of the good one already possesses or has access to. Thus, if all the water one has available in a day is a single quart, so that one's very life depends on that water, the value of water will be greater than that of diamonds. A traveler carrying a bag of diamonds, who is lost in the middle of

the desert, will be willing to exchange his diamonds for a quart of water to save his life. But if, as is usually the case, a person already has access to a thousand or ten thousand gallons of water a day, and it is a question of an additional quart more or less—that is, of a marginal quart—then both the utility and the exchange value of a quart of water will be virtually nothing. Diamonds can be more valuable than water, consistent with utility, whenever, in effect, it is a question of the utility of the first diamond versus that of the ten-thousandth quart of water.

A fundamental accomplishment of this book, which makes possible almost all of its other accomplishments, is *the integration and harmonization of the ideas of the classical and Austrian economists.* This has made it possible for me to modernize and reintroduce into economic analysis several of the major doctrines of the classical economists which were abandoned unnecessarily, and thereby to add greatly increased strength to the central ideas of von Mises and the Austrian school. A leading application of the classical doctrines, of which I am especially proud, and which I hasten to name, is a radically improved critique of the Marxian exploitation theory. In my judgment, classical economics makes possible a far more fundamental and thoroughgoing critique of the exploitation theory than that provided by Böhm-Bawerk and the Austrian school, despite the prevailing mistaken belief that it implies the Marxian exploitation theory.[5] It also provides the basis for greatly strengthening the refutation of the ideas of Keynes and of the doctrine that big business implies "monopoly power."

Among the classical doctrines I have reintroduced is the recognition of saving and productive expenditure, rather than consumption expenditure, as the source of most spending in the economic system. Closely related to this, I have brought back the wages-fund doctrine and have made clear the meaning of John Stuart Mill's vital corollary proposition that "demand for commodities does not constitute demand for labor." I have reinstated Adam Smith's recognition that in a division-of-labor society the concept of productive activity must incorporate the earning of money and that because of its failure to earn money, government is a consumer. I have reintroduced Adam Smith's and James Mill's conception of the role of saving in relation to the disposition of "the gross annual produce" between consumers' goods and capital goods, and James Mill's conception of what has unjustly come to be known as *Say's* Law.[6] Along with this, I have reintroduced Ricardo's insights that capital can be accumulated not only by saving but also by anything else that serves to increase wealth, and that technological progress operates not to raise the general rate of profit but to reduce prices (and, implicitly, to increase the supply of capital goods). I have also reintroduced Ricardo's profound recognition of the distinction between "value and riches" and of the need for the concept of an invariable money as a methodological device in developing economic theories. I have even gone so far as to interpret Ricardo's proposition that "profits rise as wages fall and fall as wages rise"—a proposition that on its face appears to imply class warfare—in the light of the assumption of an invariable money. I have found that when interpreted in this light, the proposition both serves in the overthrow of the exploitation theory and points the way to a sound theory of profits. I have also found it extremely useful to revive the classical economists' conception of demand and supply as a ratio of expenditure to quantity sold, and to employ it no less than the contemporary conception of demand and supply as schedules of quantities demanded and supplied at varying prices.

I have used the classical economists' insights to develop a substantially new theory of the rate of profit and interest; a new theory of saving and capital accumulation; a radically new theory of aggregate economic accounting, which features the role of saving and productive expenditure; new definitions of such fundamental economic concepts as capital goods and consumers' goods; and a theory of wages that is also new in major respects.

The main thing I have discarded in classical economics is any notion that wages are determined by "the cost of production of labor." On the contrary, I show that the essential economic function of businessmen and capitalists is to go on raising the productivity of labor and thus to raise the standard of living of the average wage earner by bringing about a reduction in prices relative to wages—that is, to bring about a progressive rise in so-called real wages. I have not discarded the role of cost of production as a determinant of the prices of *products,* however. Ironically, here I have been inspired by Böhm-Bawerk and Wieser, who clearly recognized cost of production as being usually the direct, immediate determinant of prices in the case of manufactured or processed goods and who explained how the determination of price by cost was fully consistent with the principle of marginal utility—indeed, was a manifestation of the principle of marginal utility.[7] When all is said and done, I believe I have succeeded in grounding the work of the Austrian school in foundations supplied by the classical school—foundations, of course, which have been cleared of major errors. Among the major themes of my book that are derived from classical economics, in addition to those already described, are: production, not consumption, is the essential economic problem; production throughout is supported by capital; and the central economic figure is the businessman, not the wage earner and not the consumer. These views are in opposition both to Marx-

ism and, in part, to those of the Austrian school, which, I believe, has overemphasized the role of the consumer.

The consumers, it is true, have the power, by virtue of the pattern in which they spend their incomes, to decide which investments of the businessmen turn out to be profitable and which unprofitable, and thus, in the last analysis, to govern the pattern of investment, as businessmen compete for their favor. The consumers' valuations and the spending patterns that result from them also determine the relative prices of the factors of production—for example, the wages of skilled labor relative to the wages of unskilled labor, the prices of real estate in one location relative to those in other locations, and the relative prices of capital goods insofar as their production cannot immediately be varied in response to changes in demand. And, of course, they also directly determine the relative prices of consumers' goods, insofar as the supply of consumers' goods cannot immediately be varied in response to changes in demand.

Nevertheless, the funds of the consumers come from business and the whole of their consumption is supported by production and the productive process. The individual business is dependent on the consumers because it is directly or indirectly in competition with all the other business firms in the economic system, and it is up to the consumers to decide which business firms to buy from. But from the point of view of the economic system as a whole, it is the consumers who are dependent on business. They have the power to consume only by virtue of making a contribution to production. And whatever funds they so receive, they will assuredly spend, sooner or later, in buying from some business or other. For money qua money is absolutely useless except as a means of obtaining goods or services.

Furthermore, a major finding of this book is that while the consumers determine the *relative* prices of the factors of production, such as the wages of skilled labor relative to those of unskilled labor, the consumers do not determine the *absolute* height of the prices of the factors of production. The absolute height of the prices of the factors of production is determined by the extent of *saving*, and is the greater, the greater is the extent of saving, and the smaller, the less is the extent of saving. Consumption relative to saving, it is shown, is the major determinant of the extent to which the prices of consumers' goods (and of capital goods too) *exceed* the prices of the factors of production used to produce them—that is, it is the major determinant of the rate of profit and interest.[8]

These views do not represent any real or fundamental break with the views of the Austrian school but, on the contrary, in vital respects are supported by them. For example, it will be shown that a rise in saving and fall in consumption does not operate to raise the prices of factors of production above the prices of consumers' goods and thereby plunge the economic system into losses and a depression. What happens is merely what the Austrian school would call "a lengthening of the structure of production." Greater saving relative to consumption means that there is not only more spending for capital goods and labor to produce consumers' goods, but also, and even primarily, more spending for capital goods and labor to produce *capital goods.* The productive expenditure of the greater savings is a deduction not merely from a diminished consumption expenditure, but from an enlarged demand for capital goods, which takes the place of the diminished demand for consumers' goods. The demand for capital goods is as much a source of business sales revenues as the demand for consumers' goods. In the last analysis, what happens is that labor comes to be employed in the performance of work that is temporally more remote from its ultimate results in the form of consumers' goods.[9]

I believe that by the time the reader finishes this book, he will share my conviction that in fundamental essentials, the classical and Austrian schools are not in conflict, but represent major, complementary elements of the same great body of truth. I even believe that he will be able to read Böhm-Bawerk and John Stuart Mill on the subject of prices and costs and no longer see any fundamental or essential differences between them.[10]

One economist above all others must be singled out as *the* leading intellectual defender of capitalism, namely, Ludwig von Mises. When von Mises appeared on the scene, Marxism and the other socialist sects enjoyed a virtual intellectual monopoly. As explained, major flaws and inconsistencies in the writings of Smith and Ricardo and their followers enabled the socialists to claim classical economics as their actual ally. The writings of Jevons and the early Austrian economists—namely, Menger and Böhm-Bawerk—were insufficiently comprehensive to provide an effective counter to the socialists. Bastiat had tried to provide one, but died too soon, and probably lacked the necessary theoretical depth in any case.

Thus, when von Mises appeared, there was virtually *no systematic intellectual opposition to socialism or defense of capitalism.* Quite literally, the intellectual ramparts of material civilization were undefended. What von Mises undertook, and which summarizes the essence of his greatness, was *to build a systematic intellectual defense of capitalism and thus of material civilization.*

Point for point, von Mises developed answers to virtually all of the accusations made against capitalism—from its alleged exploitation of labor and responsibility for unemployment and depressions to its alleged respon-sibility for monopoly, wars, and racism. He developed a social philosophy of capitalism which demonstrates the benevolent operation of all of captialism's leading institutions, especially private ownership of the means of production, economic competition, and economic inequality. He expounded a procapitalist interpretation of modern economic history, and provided a devastating critique of socialism and government intervention in all of its forms. Above all, he demonstrated that a socialist economic system lacks the ability to engage in rational economic *planning* because of its lack of a price system and thus the ability to perform economic calculation. In making it possible for the more intelligent and honest members of Communist-bloc governments to understand the causes of the chaos and misery surrounding them, the writings of von Mises have played a major role in the growing worldwide efforts to abandon socialism. Nothing could be more deserved than if some of the statues of Lenin, now being removed all across Eastern Europe, were replaced with statues of this man, whose writings clearly proved the destructive consequences of socialism as far back as 1922. Indeed, statues should be erected to von Mises all across the world for saving it from socialism, and for his accomplishments in support of capitalism.

It is to von Mises, more than to any other single source, that this book is indebted. Indeed, the present book could accurately be described as "Misesianism" reinforced by a modernized, consistently procapitalist version of classical economics—it is the ideas of von Mises fused with insights derived from Ricardo and Smith.[11]

Largely thanks to von Mises, there have been other important recent or contemporary advocates of capitalism. F. A. Hayek and Milton Friedman are the two leading examples. But, in my judgment, neither they nor anyone else begins to compare to von Mises in logical consistency and intellectual breadth and depth in the defense of capitalism. Hayek, for example, finds "a comprehensive system of social insurance" to be consistent with capitalism.[12] Friedman believes that fiat money is consistent with capitalism.

Other, lesser defenders of capitalism have even more serious inconsistencies. The so-called supply-siders—Robert Mundell, Arthur Laffer, and Jude Wanniski—apparently want to achieve capitalism without facing the need to reduce government spending and eliminate the welfare state. Much worse, Rothbard, who was widely regarded as the intellectual leader of the younger generation of the Austrian school and of the Libertarian party as well, was a self-professed anarchist and believed that *the United States was the aggressor against Soviet Rus-*

sia in the so-called cold war.[13]

By way of contrast, Henry Hazlitt, a brilliant economist and journalist, had the great merit of providing what are unquestionably the best introductions to the ideas of von Mises and the classical economists that exist.[14] Hazlitt, incidentally, also shared with von Mises the honor of having expounded decades ago, as a virtual intellectual footnote to their major accomplishments, the legitimate substance of what has today become known as "the rational expectations approach"—namely, the recognition that economic phenomena such as interest rates incorporate expectations concerning inflation and thus defeat the objectives sought by the government's policy of inflation.[15]

2. Pseudoeconomic Thought

Little or nothing is known about the state of economic knowledge that may have been achieved by the ancient Greeks and Romans. Some discussions of economic matters took place among scholastic philosophers in the Middle Ages, who appraised economic activity largely from the hostile perspective of the Roman Catholic church and who, accordingly, denounced as unjust such perfectly normal economic activities as the taking of interest on loans, speculation, and, indeed, even the mere changing of prices. The scholastics contributed nothing to sound economics.

The first prominent group of writers on economic subjects were the mercantilists, who appeared on the scene in the sixteenth and seventeenth centuries, following the great intensification of commerce and trade that had taken place subsequent to the end of the Dark Ages. The main concern of the mercantilists was with the so-called balance of trade and the alleged need of governments to secure an excess of exports over imports, as the means of increasing the quantity of money in a country that lacked its own gold and silver mines.[16] The concern of the mercantilists with increasing the quantity of money led them to anticipate the essential fallacy of Lord Keynes in this century, namely, that it is necessary for the government to intervene in the economic system for the purpose of stimulating "demand" and "employment." The leading members of the mercantilist school were Louis Bodin (1530–96), Thomas Mun (1571–1641), William Petty (1623–87), Josiah Child (1630–99), and the philosopher John Locke (1622–1704).

The positive economic truths later demonstrated by the classical and Austrian schools and their allies have been opposed from a number of quarters. In the first part of the nineteenth century, there were Malthus (1766–1834) and Sismondi (1773–1842) who, in anticipation of the Marxists and Keynesians, erroneously argued that depressions were caused by overproduction and excess saving and underconsumption. (Malthus was also the author of the mistaken doctrine that increases in population necessarily tend to reduce the productivity of labor and the general standard of living—a doctrine that, apart from Adam Smith and Bastiat, was, regrettably, accepted by most of the classical economists.) In addition, there were the protectionists and the nationalists who, continuing to be committed to mercantilist ideas, attacked the classical economists' doctrine of international free trade. Foremost in this group were Alexander Hamilton (1755–1804), who, of course, was the first American secretary of the treasury, and the German Friedrich List (1789–1848).

Fundamental opposition to classical and Austrian economics came from the German historical school, whose members denied the very possibility of a science of economic laws. This group included Wilhelm Roscher (1817–94), Gustav Schmoller (1838–1917), Lujo Brentano (1844–1931), and Werner Sombart (1863–1941). (Sombart, interestingly, began his career as a Marxist and later became a leading supporter of Nazism.) The essential approach of the German historical school was propounded in the United States by Thorstein Veblen (1857–1929), John R. Commons (1862–1945), and Wesley Mitchell (1874–1948), who are known as the American institutionalist school. The leading characteristic of these schools is a distrust of deductive logic (which is the essential method used in economics for arriving at knowledge), and thus opposition to economic theory as such. They deny the possibility of universally valid economic laws, claim that each country, in each historical period, has its own economic laws, and advance historical research, the study of economic institutions, and the gathering and study of economic statistics as the only legitimate means for arriving at economic knowledge.

The socialists, not surprisingly, are entirely opposed to the fundamental economic truths propounded by the classical and Austrian schools. (This is aside from the labor theory of value and the so-called iron law of wages, which they take over from classical economics and totally distort and twist into a form that the classical economists would not support.) The leading socialists, of course, were Karl Marx (1818–83) and Friedrich Engels (1820–97). Among their most important followers were Rosa Luxemburg (1870–1919) and Rudolf Hilferding (1877–1941). Other prominent socialists, prior to or contemporary with Marx, were Henri de Saint-Simon (1760–1825), Robert Owen (1771–1858), Charles Fourier (1772–1837), Louis Blanc (1811–82), Pierre Proudhon (1809–65), and Karl Rodbertus (1805–75). It should be noted that the socialists and the other opponents of the doctrines of the classical and Austrian schools substantially overlap in their criticisms of capitalism. For example, virtually all of them share the belief that depressions are the result of "overproduction" and excess saving.

For want of a better place to classify him, mention must be made here of Henry George (1839–97), an American economist who developed certain half-truths of the classical school concerning land and land rent into a doctrine calling for the nationalization of land. Surprising as it may seem, in all other respects, George and most of his followers claim to be supporters of capitalism.[17]

Marshallian Neoclassical Economics: The Monopoly Doctrine and Keynesianism

In the present-day United States, the leading opposition within the economics profession to the ideas of the classical and Austrian schools, and to capitalism, derives from the ideas of a late-Victorian British neoclassical economist named Alfred Marshall (1842–1924), and two other figures associated with Britain's Cambridge University and heavily influenced by the ideas of Marshall: John Maynard Keynes (1883–1946) and Mrs. Joan Robinson (1903–83). Marshall superficially accepted the concept of marginal utility while opposing the fundamental approach of the Austrian school. At the same time, he abandoned the fundamental ideas of the classical school while wrapping himself in the guise of the defender of classical economics against the criticisms of the Austrian school. The result of his work, his bequest to subsequent generations of economists, was a hodgepodge of confusions, which took the place of sound economics.

Both the classical and the Austrian schools study economic phenomena from the point of view of their effects on all members of the economic system, not just on those directly involved. In contrast, Marshall advanced the doctrine known as "partial equilibrium," which is the attempt to study the behavior of individual consumers, individual firms, and individual industries divorced from the rest of the economic system. His approach was one of disintegration, resulting in the present-day existence of two allegedly separate branches of economics: "microeconomics" and "macroeconomics"—the first studying the actions of individuals apart from their relationship to the rest of the economic system, and the second studying the economic system as a whole, apart from the actions of individuals.

Marshall and his followers coupled the doctrine of partial equilibrium with a total confusion between the concepts of cost of production and supply, making it impossible to distinguish between cases in which prices are determined by supply and demand and cases in which, in the first instance, they are determined directly on the basis of cost of production. The result was the loss of the knowledge gained by the classical economists (and recognized by Böhm-Bawerk and Wieser) that prices are in fact frequently determined in the first instance directly by cost of production. The result was also the inability to grasp the contribution of the Austrian school (substantially anticipated by John Stuart Mill) that the prices which constitute the costs of production are themselves always ultimately determined by supply and demand. It is Marshall's confusions which underlie the widespread belief that economic law does not apply to the pricing of most manufactured or processed goods—that the prices of such goods are "administered prices," precisely because they are determined directly on the basis of a consideration of cost of production rather than by the combination of demand and supply.

In propounding the doctrine of partial equilibrium, Marshall introduced the perverse concept of the "representative firm"—an alleged *average* firm, some multiple of which was supposed to constitute an industry. This concept destroyed economic theory's ability to recognize even the possibility of competition. This was because if all firms in an industry were in fact perfectly equal, no basis could exist for any of them winning out in competition, or, therefore, for attempting to compete in the first place. Not surprisingly, the acceptance of the concept of the representative firm led some decades later to the conclusion (regarded at the time as a revolutionary discovery) that no reason existed for a sizable firm ever to cut its price, except in conditions in which it would pay a single-firm "monopoly" to do so. This was because its competitors, all of whom were supposed to be just as efficient as it was, would immediately match its cut. Thus, it would have little or nothing to gain by cutting—certainly not the business of its competitors.

The notion of the representative firm and the inability to see how cost of production normally acts as the direct determinant of the prices of manufactured or processed goods have served as the foundation for the widespread acceptance since the 1930s of the thoroughly malicious and destructive doctrine of Joan Robinson and Edward Chamberlin. That doctrine states that with a few, limited exceptions, such as wheat farming, the whole of a capitalist economic system is tainted by an element of monopoly. The solution for this alleged state of affairs is supposed to be a radical antitrust policy, which would fragment all large businesses, or else the nationalization of such businesses and/or government control over their prices—and further policies that would force firms in the same industry to produce identical, indistinguishable products. Since the 1930s, this doctrine and its elaboration have constituted the substance of the theoretical content of most textbooks of "microeconomics." At the same time, little or nothing of the sound price theory developed by the classical and Austrian economists is presented in these textbooks.

The abandonment of classical economics and Marshall's concentration on what later came to be called microeconomics created a temporary intellectual vacuum. In the 1930s, this vacuum was filled by Keynes, by means of the resurrection of the long-refuted fallacies of the Mercantilists, and Malthus and Sismondi, alleging that capitalism causes depressions and mass unemployment through overproduction and excess saving. On this thoroughly erroneous foundation, Keynes argued for the need for inflation and deficit-financed government spending to counteract or prevent the evils of depressions and mass unemployment. The elaboration of the Keynesian doctrines has constituted the theoretical substance of the textbooks on "macroeconomics."

Mathematical Economics

Another prominent school of economic thought is that of mathematical economics, which is characterized by the use of calculus and simultaneous differential equations to describe economic phenomena. The principal founder of mathematical economics was Léon Walras (1834–1910), a Swiss, who also independently discovered the law of diminishing marginal utility shortly after Menger and Jevons. Vilfredo Pareto (1848–1923), an Italian, succeeded Walras at the University of Lausanne and elaborated his approach.

Mathematical economics is fundamentally a matter more of method and pedagogy than of particular theoretical content. And although neither the classical nor the Austrian schools is mathematical in the above sense, there are mathematical economists who are allied with their teachings and their support of capitalism. Walras, Jevons, and Gossen are important cases in point.

Regrettably, the use of calculus and differential equations to describe economic phenomena represents a Procrustean bed, into which the discrete, discontinuous phenomena of actual economic life are mentally forced, in order to fit the mold of mathematically continuous functions to which the methods of calculus can be applied. This has consequences which represent a matter of theoretical content, as well as method.

One major consequence is the aid given to the perpetuation of a false theory of the determination of the prices of the factors of production: namely, the theory that the prices of the factors of production are directly derivable from the value of the consumers' goods they help to produce. For example, the wages of automobile workers, and the prices of auto-making equipment, steering wheels, brakes, spark plugs, and all other factors of production necessary to produce an automobile, are regarded as being derivable directly from the price of automobiles,

by means of calculating the loss in the value of an automobile that would accompany the withdrawal of a unit of any of the factors of production necessary to produce it.

Such a derivation of value, of course, must encounter the same difficulty as attempting to derive from the value of a pair of shoes a separate value for the right and left shoes—namely, the fact that the value of the combined product is capable of being alternatively attributed to *any* of the elements necessary to its production or enjoyment, and that on this basis the sum of the derived values of the factors of production must far exceed the value of the product. In the case of the shoes, for example, the loss of either shoe destroys the whole value of the pair. If the value of each shoe were derived by calculating the loss in value of the pair resulting from its removal, the sum of the value of the two shoes considered separately would be twice the value of the pair. In the case of the automobile, the entire value of the automobile would have to be attributed to each of many different components, such as each of the four wheels, the carburetor, the steering wheel, etc.

Mathematical economics creates the illusion that this problem can be solved by making believe that what are withdrawn are not discrete units of the factors of production, such as one whole shoe or one whole wheel, but infinitesimally small quantities of them. In this case, the loss in the value of the product could be regarded as a partial derivative of the reduction in the quantity of the factor of production, and the theorem would be applicable that the sum of the partial derivatives does not exceed, but is equal to the total derivative.

The area of a room, which is determined by the product of its length and width, can serve as an illustration. If the length of the room is ten feet and the width is ten feet, then the entire area of the room is lost if either the length or the width shrinks to zero. If one adopts the procedure of alternatively attributing to the length and the width the area that is lost when it is lost, then one would have to attribute a total of two hundred square feet of area lost, despite the fact that the actual area of the room is only one hundred square feet. If, however, one assumes that what is lost is not all of the length or, alternatively, all of the width, but only a small fraction of the length or width, then the difference between the sum of the two separate losses and the actual total loss diminishes. For example, if what is lost is one foot of length out of ten or, alternatively, one foot of width out of ten, the sum of the two separate areas lost is twenty square feet. The area lost by the simultaneous loss of a foot of length and width is nineteen square feet. Thus the difference between the sum of the two partial losses and the total loss has sharply diminished. It would approach zero, as the reduction in length and width became smaller.

Unfortunately for this approach, the actual problem in the real world is how does one evaluate the effect of the loss of a whole shoe or wheel, not the tip of the shoelace or the effect of a scratch on the hubcap.

The result of such distortion of the actual problem is that mathematical economics has operated to conceal the true proposition, grasped by Ricardo and endorsed by Böhm-Bawerk and Wieser, that typically it is *not* the price of the product that determines the prices of the factors of production used to produce it, but the other way around. The price of automobiles and virtually all other manufactured or processed goods is determined on the basis of the wage rates, equipment prices, and parts prices that enter into their production. However, wage rates, which are the prices that most fundamentally determine costs of production, since they enter into every stage of production, are themselves determined by the supply of and demand for labor operating throughout the economic system. The same is true of the prices of the various raw materials whose supply cannot be immediately increased or decreased in response to changes in demand. The wage rates of the different types of labor relative to one another, above all the wages of skilled labor relative to those of unskilled labor, and the relative prices of such raw materials, reflect the relative marginal utilities of these factors of production in the economic system as a whole. Thus it is mainly in this *indirect* way that marginal utility operates to determine prices.[18]

A second and even more serious consequence of mathematical economics is that it leads to an undue concentration of attention on states of final equilibrium, which are all that its differential equations are capable of describing. It thus takes attention away from the real-world *operation* of the profit motive and of the *market processes* by means of which the economic system continually tends to move toward a state of full and final equilibrium without ever actually achieving such a state. The economic system never actually achieves such a state because of continuous changes in the fundamental economic data. For example, there are changes in the state of technology, changes in the size of population, changes in the relative valuation of the various consumers' goods, changes in the relative valuation of present enjoyment versus provision for the future, and numerous other such changes which occur continuously and which operate to change the final state of equilibrium toward which the economic system is tending.[19]

The effect of the dominance of mathematical economics and of the fact that it ignores market processes has been that all the major principles which explain how prices are actually determined, and which were discovered by the classical economists, have been virtually forgotten. Among the principles lost have been recognition of the tendency toward a uniform rate of profit on capital invested throughout the economic system, recognition of the tendency toward the establishment of uniform prices for the same goods throughout the world and over time, and recognition of the tendency toward the establishment of uniform wage rates for labor of the same degree of skill and ability in the same market. These principles have virtually disappeared from contemporary economics textbooks.[20]

Third, mathematical economics has come to serve as a mechanism for the erection of a sort of exclusive "Scholars' Guild," which, as was the case in the Middle Ages, seeks to shut out all who do not first translate their thoughts into its esoteric language. Higher mathematics is no more necessary to the discussion or clarification of economic phenomena than was Latin or Greek to the discussion of matters of scientific interest in previous centuries. One can, for example, say that the amount of bread people will buy at any given price of bread depends both on the price of bread and on the prices of all other goods in the economic system. Or one can say that the quantity demanded of bread is a mathematical function of all prices in the economic system, and then write out a nonspecific mathematical function using symbolic terminology.

If one merely writes such an equation and stops at this point, all that has taken place is an act of intellectual pretentiousness and snobbery—a translation into a present-day equivalent of Greek or Latin. If, however, one goes further, and believes one can actually formulate a *specific equation*—that, for example, the quantity demanded of bread equals ten thousand divided by half the square of the price of bread minus the price of butter and the average age of grocers, then one is led into major errors. This is so because no such equation can possibly hold up in the face of changes in the fundamental economic data. New goods are introduced. People's ideas and valuations change. Their real incomes change. Population changes. The belief that an equation could be constructed that would take such changes into account is totally opposed to reality. It is tantamount to a belief in fatalistic determinism and implies, in effect, that a mathematical economist can gain access to a book in which all things past, present, and future are written and then derive from it the corresponding equation. Whatever it may be, such a view is definitely not within the scientific spirit.

3. Overview of This Book

I have divided the present book into three major parts. Part 1, *The Foundations of Economics*, explains the nature of economics and capitalism, including the role of a philosophy of reason in economic activity. It then shows that, based on his nature as a rational being, man possesses a limitless need for wealth. This, in turn, is shown to give rise to the central problem of economic life, which is how steadily to raise the productivity of human labor, that is, the quantity and quality of the goods that can be produced per unit of labor. Next, it is shown why the continuing rise in the productivity of labor is not prevented by any lack of natural resources, indeed, how man is capable of progressively enlarging the supply of useable, accessible natural resources as part of the very same process by which he increases the production of products. The part concludes with a lengthy critique of the ecology doctrine, which, it shows, represents a direct and major assault on the value of economic progress and thus on the very foundations of economics, and has replaced socialism as the leading threat to economic activity and economic progress.

Part 2, *The Division of Labor and Capitalism*, opens with a demonstration that the existence of a division-of-labor society is the essential framework for the ongoing solution of the problem of how continually to raise the productivity of labor. It then goes on to demonstrate that a division-of-labor society is a *capitalist* society, totally dependent on the operation of a price system, which in turn totally depends on private ownership of the means of production. Private ownership of the means of production is shown to be the foundation both of the profit motive and of the freedom of competition, which are respectively the driving force and regulator of the price system. This part, which incorporates almost all of my previously published *The Government Against the Economy,* develops all of the leading principles of price theory and applies them to understanding major events of the present and recent past.[21] It clearly explains the factors leading to the collapse of socialism around the world and the destructive consequences of socialistic government intervention here in the United States in the form of price controls. It shows why, necessarily lacking a price system, socialism is necessarily chaotic economically and tyrannical politically. It shows how price controls were responsible for all aspects of the energy crisis of the 1970s and how they continue to threaten the long-term viability of major industries in the United States, such as electric power and rental housing.

Very importantly, this part explains the actual, benevolent nature of capitalism, in that it shows how the existence of the division of labor profoundly influences the operation of private ownership of the means of production, economic competition, and economic inequality, in ways that render these institutions thoroughly benevolent in their effects on the average person. In essence, this part shows that beneath the division of labor it is capitalism that is the essential framework for economic progress and a rising productivity of labor, and that capitalism is characterized by a harmony of the rational self-interests of all men under freedom. The part also includes critiques of all forms of the doctrine that capitalism results in monopoly. It shows that monopoly, properly understood, is not a product of capitalism but is imposed on the economic system by government intervention. In addition, it includes an exhaustive critique of the Marxian exploitation theory. It shows that under capitalism there is no economic exploitation, that capitalists, far from exploiting wage earners and appropriating as profits what is rightfully wages, make it possible for people to live as wage earners, and to live ever more prosperously. It shows that this is because capitalists *create* wages and the demand for labor in tandem with reducing the share of sales proceeds which is profit, and go on steadily increasing the supply of goods that the wage earners can buy. It shows that socialism is the system both of the exploitation of labor and of universal monopoly.

Part 3, *The Process of Economic Progress*, centers on the explanation of the process of economic progress under capitalism. It explains the quantity theory of money and the essential role of the quantity of money in determining aggregate monetary demand, that is, total spending in the economic system. In full confirmation of Say's Law, it shows that in contrast to mere monetary demand, *real* demand—that is, actual purchasing power—is increased only by virtue of increases in the production and supply of goods. Along the same lines, it shows that real wages are increased essentially only by virtue of increases in the productivity of labor and thus increases in the supply of goods relative to the supply of labor. This part explains the vital role of capital accumulation in raising the productivity of labor and real wages. It explains the dependence of capital accumulation itself on saving, technological progress, and everything else that is necessary to economic efficiency, from freedom from government regulation at home to free trade abroad. It shows that the ultimate foundation of capital accumulation and economic progress is the existence of a capitalist society and its cardinal values of reason and freedom. Part 3 also explains the determinants of the average rate of profit and interest and the relationship between the rate of profit and interest, on the one side, and capital accumulation and falling prices caused by increased production, on the other side. It shows that capital accumulation and such falling prices do not reduce the rate of profit or interest and thus do not interfere with or retard the process of economic progress in any way.

This part contains refutations of all the leading economic fallacies concerning alleged overproduction, oversaving, and underconsumption. Under this head, it includes a chapter-length refutation of the doctrines of Keynes and critiques of virtually all other fallacies underlying demands for inflation and government spending. The part makes a consistent case for a full-bodied gold standard as the ideal monetary system, which would exist under laissez-faire capitalism and which would operate to prevent inflation, deflation and depression, and mass unemployment. It shows that all of these destructive phenomena are caused by government intervention in the economic system, not by the nature of the economic system itself—that is, not by capitalism. It shows consistently that the establishment of economic freedom, of laissez-faire capitalism, is the solution for all such problems.

Finally, the Epilogue outlines a long-term political and educational strategy for the achievement of a society of laissez-faire capitalism.

This book is useable as a textbook in virtually any economics course. Those who must conform to the arbitrary division of economics into microeconomics and macroeconomics will find that Chapters 1–10 can easily serve in the micro portion, while Chapters 11–19 can easily serve in the macro portion.[22] Chapter 20, although best read after all of the other chapters, is suitable for use in either portion.

Use of this book in any economics course will provide the most efficient means both of advancing positive economic truth and of refuting the manifold errors in the prevailing views of economics, including those in the present generation of textbooks

Notes

1. For an excellent account of the doctrines of the Physiocrats, see Adam Smith, *The Wealth of Nations* (London, 1776), bk. 4, chap. 9; reprint of Cannan ed. (Chicago: University of Chicago Press, 2 vols. in 1, 1976), 2:182–209. From now on, specific page references to the University of Chicago Press reprint will be supplied in brackets.

2. The present author was also one of the later students of von Mises. However, because of the profound influence of the classical economists on my thinking, it would be more appropriate to describe my views as "Austro-classical" rather than as "Austrian."

3. On the wages-fund doctrine and the consequences of its abandonment, see below pp. 664–666 and 864–867.

4. Smith, *Wealth of Nations*, bk. 1, chap. 4 [1:32–33].

5. For confirmation of this claim, see below, pp. 475–485. See also the whole of Chapter 14.

6. The contributions of James Mill are among the least recognized in the history of economic thought. Their best statement appears in his little known work *Commerce Defended* (London, 1808), chaps. 6 and 7, which are respectively titled "Consumption" and "Of the National Debt." The complete work is reprinted in *James Mill Selected Economic Writings*, ed. Donald Winch (Chicago: University of Chicago Press, 1966).

7. Cf. below, pp. 414–416, where Böhm-Bawerk is quoted at length on this subject.

8. Strictly speaking, the consumption in question is what I term *net* consumption. See below, pp. 725–736.

9. See below, pp. 838–856.

10. See Eugen von Böhm-Bawerk, *Capital and Interest*, 3 vols., trans. George D. Huncke and Hans F. Sennholz (South Holland, Ill.: Libertarian Press, 1959), 2:168–176, 248–256; 3:97–115. See also John Stuart Mill, *Principles of Political Economy*, Ashley ed. (1909; reprint ed., Fairfield, N. J.: Augustus M. Kelley, 1976), pp. 442–468.

11. For a related description of the ideas of von Mises, see above, pp. xlii–xliii. The ideas of Böhm-Bawerk also play an important role.

12. See Friedrich A. Hayek, *The Road to Serfdom* (Chicago: University of Chicago Press, 1944), p. 121.

13. Cf. Murray N. Rothbard, *For a New Liberty* (New York: Macmillan, 1973). In that book, Rothbard wrote: "Empirically, the *most* warlike, *most* interventionist, *most* imperial government throughout the twentieth century has been the United States" (p. 287; italics in original). In sharpest contrast to the United States, which has supposedly been more warlike even than Nazi Germany, Rothbard described the Soviets in the following terms: "Before World War II, so devoted was Stalin to peace that he failed to make adequate provision against the Nazi attack. . . . Not only was there no Russian expansion whatever apart from the exigencies of defeating Germany, but the Soviet Union time and again leaned over backward to avoid any cold or hot war with the West" (p. 294).

14. See Henry Hazlitt, *Economics in One Lesson*, new ed. (New Rochelle, N. Y.: Arlington House, 1979); idem, *The Great Idea* (1951; rev. ed. published under the title *Time Will Run Back*, New Rochelle, N. Y.: Arlington House, 1966).

15. See Henry Hazlitt, "Is Inflation Necessary?" *Freeman* 2, no. 26 (September 22, 1952), pp. 880–882, and Ludwig von Mises, *Human Action*, 3d ed. rev. (Chicago: Henry Regnery Co., 1966), pp. 776–777, 792–793. Amazingly, as an eloquent commentary on the state of contemporary economics, while the rational expectations approach has come to be regarded as a major and profound school of economic thought, the overwhelming merit of von Mises and the Austrian school still goes largely unrecognized. Thus, Samuelson and Nordhaus, in their self-proclaimed "authoritative" and "comprehensive" textbook include "Rational Expectations Macroeconomics" in their "Family Tree of Economics" and devote a full appendix to discussing it. Yet they make almost no mention of the Austrian school or von Mises; the Austrian school does not even appear in the index. See Paul Samuelson and William Nordhaus, *Economics*, 13th ed. (New York: McGraw-Hill, 1989, in particular the inside back cover). The leading members of the Rational Expectations school, incidentally, are Robert Barro, Robert Lucas,

Thomas Sargent, and Neil Wallace. (I wish to note that my references to Samuelson and Nordhaus throughout this work will be to the 13th edition rather than to the more recent 14th edition, unless otherwise stated. This is because it better represents the errors that two generations of students have had to endure at the hands of Prof. Samuelson, who, until not many years ago, was the sole author.)

16. For an exposition and critique of the doctrines of the Mercantilists, see Adam Smith, *Wealth of Nations,* bk. 4, chaps. 1–8 [2:3–209]. See also below, pp. 526–536.

17. In private conversation with the present author, Leonard Peikoff once aptly described the position of the Georgists as advocating the government allowing a person to own a piano and do anything he likes with it, except put it down without its permission.

18. For elaboration of these points, see below, the discussions of the relationship between prices and costs on pp. 200–201, 206–209, and 411–417.

19. Cf. von Mises, *Human Action,* pp. 244–250.

20. For an explanation of these principles, see below, pp. 172–201.

21. George Reisman, *The Government Against the Economy* (Ottawa, Ill.: Jameson Books, 1979). A few pages of this book, which demonstrate the limitless potential of natural resources, are incorporated in Chapter 3.

22. Logically, Chapter 11 belongs in Part 2, where it is. Nevertheless, from the point of view of the division of economics into "microeconomics" and "macroeconomics," the chapter is far more essential in a course on the latter than in one on the former.

PART ONE

THE FOUNDATIONS OF ECONOMICS

CHAPTER 1

ECONOMICS AND CAPITALISM

THE NATURE AND IMPORTANCE OF ECONOMICS

1. Economics, the Division of Labor, and the Survival of Material Civilization

Economics has been defined in a variety of ways. In the nineteenth century it was typically defined as the science of wealth or of exchangeable wealth. In the twentieth century, it has typically been defined as the science that studies the allocation of scarce means among competing ends.[1]

I define economics as *the science that studies the production of wealth under a system of division of labor,* that is, under a system in which the individual lives by producing, or helping to produce, just one thing or at most a very few things, and is supplied by the labor of others for the far greater part of his needs. The justification of this definition will become increasingly clear as the contents of this book unfold.[2]

The importance of economics derives from the specific importance of wealth—of material goods—to human life and well-being. The role of wealth in human life is a subject that will be examined in Chapter 2 of this book, but provisionally its importance can be accepted on a common-sense basis. Obviously, human life depends on food, clothing, and shelter. Moreover, experience shows that there is no limit to the amount of wealth that practi-cally all civilized men and women desire, and that the greatest part of their waking hours is actually spent in efforts to acquire it—namely, in efforts to earn a living.

Yet the importance of wealth, by itself, is not suffi-cient to establish the importance of economics. Robinson Crusoe on a desert island would need wealth, and his ability to produce it would be helped if he somehow managed to salvage from his ship books on various techniques of production. But it would not be helped by books on economics. All that books on economics could do for Crusoe would be to describe abstractly the essen-tial nature of the activities he carries on without any knowledge of economics, and, beyond that, merely to provide the possible intellectual stimulation he might feel as the result of increasing his knowledge of the society from which he was cut off. Something more than the importance of wealth is required to establish the importance of economics.

As Chapter 4 of this book will show, the production of wealth vitally depends on the division of labor. The division of labor is an essential characteristic of every advanced economic system. It underlies practically all of the gains we ascribe to technological progress and the use of improved tools and machinery; its existence is indispensable for a high and rising productivity of labor, that is, output per unit of labor. By the same token, its absence is a leading characteristic of every backward economic system. It is the division of labor which intro-duces a degree of complexity into economic life that makes necessary the existence of a special science of economics. For the division of labor entails economic phenomena existing on a scale in space and time that makes it impossible to comprehend them by means of personal observation and experience alone. Economic life under a system of division of labor can be comprehended only by means of an organized body of knowledge that proceeds by deductive reasoning from elementary principles. This, of course, is the work of the science of economics. The division of labor is thus the essential fact that necessitates the existence of the subject of economics.[3]

Despite its vital importance, the division of labor, as a country's dominant form of productive organization—that is, a division-of-labor society—is a relatively recent phenomenon in history. It goes back no further than eighteenth-century Britain. Even today it is limited to little more than the United States, the former British dominions, the countries of Western Europe, and Japan. The dominant form of productive organization in most of the world—in the vast interiors of Asia, Africa, and most of Latin America—and everywhere for most of history, has been the largely self-sufficient production of farm families and, before that, of tribes of nomads or hunters.

What makes the science of economics necessary and important is the fact that while human life and well-being depend on the production of wealth, and the production of wealth depends on the division of labor, *the division of labor does not exist or function automatically.* Its functioning crucially depends on *the laws and institutions* countries adopt. A country can adopt laws and institutions that make it possible for the division of labor to grow and flourish, as the United States did in the late eighteenth century. Or it can adopt laws and institutions that prevent the division of labor from growing and flourishing, as is the case in most of the world today, and as was the case everywhere for most of history. Indeed, a country can adopt laws and institutions that cause the division of labor to decline and practically cease to exist. The leading historical example of this occurred under the Roman Empire in the third and fourth centuries of the Christian era. The result was that the relatively advanced economic system of the ancient world, which had achieved a significant degree of division of labor, was replaced by feudalism, an economic system characterized by the self-sufficiency of small territories.[4]

In order for a country to act intelligently in adopting laws and institutions that bear upon economic life, it is clearly necessary that its citizens understand the principles that govern the development and functioning of the division of labor, that is, understand the principles of economics. If they do not, then it is only a question of time before that country will adopt more and more destructive laws and institutions, ultimately stopping all further economic progress and causing actual economic decline, with all that that implies about the conditions of human life.

In the absence of a widespread, serious understanding of the principles of economics, the citizens of an advanced, division-of-labor society, such as our own, are in a position analogous to that of a crowd wandering among banks of computers or other highly complex machinery, with no understanding of the functioning or maintenance or safety requirements of the equipment, and randomly pushing buttons and pulling levers. This is no exaggeration. In the absence of a knowledge of economics, our contemporaries feel perfectly free to enact measures such as currency depreciation and price controls. They feel free casually to experiment with the destruction of such fundamental economic institutions as the freedom of contract, inheritance, and private ownership of the means of production itself. In the absence of a knowledge of economics, our civilization is perfectly capable of destroying itself, and, in the view of some observers, is actually in the process of doing so.

Thus, the importance of economics consists in the fact that ultimately our entire modern material civilization depends on its being understood. What rests on modern material civilization is not only the well-being but also *the very lives* of the great majority of people now living. In the absence of the extensive division of labor we now possess, the production of modern medicines and vaccines, the provision of modern sanitation and hygiene, and the production even of adequate food supplies for our present numbers, would simply be impossible. The territory of the continental United States, for example, counting the deserts, mountains, rivers, and lakes, amounts to less than nine acres per person with its present population—not enough to enable that population to survive as primitive farmers. In Western Europe and Japan, the problem of overpopulation would, of course, be far more severe. Needless to say, the present vast populations of Asia, Africa, and Latin America would be unable to survive in the absence of Western food and medical supplies.

2. Further Major Applications of Economics

Solving Politico-Economic Problems

Apart from the very survival of a division-of-labor society, and all that depends on it, the most important application of economics is to provide the knowledge necessary for the adoption of government policies conducive to the smooth and efficient functioning of such a society.[5] On the basis of the knowledge it provides, economics offers logically demonstrable solutions for politico-economic problems. For example, it explains very clearly how to stop such major present-day problems as inflation, shortages, depressions, and mass unemployment, and how to turn capital decumulation into capital accumulation and a declining productivity of labor into a rising productivity of labor. In addition, economics can very clearly show how to achieve economic progress all across the world, and is potentially capable of playing an enormous role in eliminating the intellectual and economic causes both of domestic strife and of international conflict and war. As I will show, the essential nature of the policies economics demonstrates to be necessary to solve all such problems is respect for property rights and economic freedom.

Understanding History

Because it explains what promotes and what impairs the functioning of the division of labor, economics is an essential tool for understanding the world's history—the broad sweep of its periods of progress and its periods of decline—and the journalistic events of any given time. Its applications include a grasp of the causes of the decline of ancient civilization and of the rise of the modern, industrial world, both of which can be understood in terms of the rise or fall of the division of labor.

Economics brings to the understanding of history and journalism a foundation of scientific knowledge which can serve historians and journalists in much the same way as a knowledge of natural science and mathematics. Namely, it can give to historians and journalists a knowledge of what is and is not possible, and therefore a knowledge of what can and cannot qualify as an explanation of economic phenomena. For example, a knowledge of modern natural science precludes any historical or journalistic explanation of events based on Ptolemaic astronomy or the phlogiston theory of chemistry, not to mention beliefs in such notions as witchcraft, astrology, or any form of supernaturalism. In exactly the same way, it will be shown in this book that a knowledge of economics precludes any historical or journalistic explanation of events based on such doctrines as the Marxian theory of exploitation and class warfare, or on the belief that machinery causes unemployment or that depressions are caused by "overproduction."[6]

Economics can also serve historians and journalists as a guide to what further facts to look for in the explanation of economic events. For example, whenever shortages exist, it tells them to look for government controls limiting the rise in prices; whenever unemployment exists, it tells them to look for government interference limiting the fall in money wage rates; and whenever a depression exists, it tells them to look for a preceding expansion of money and credit.[7]

Implications for Ethics and Personal Understanding

Economics has powerful implications for ethics. It demonstrates exhaustively that in a division-of-labor, capitalist society, one man's gain is not another man's loss, that, indeed, it is actually other men's *gain*—especially in the case of the building of great fortunes. In sum, economics demonstrates that the rational self-interests of all men are harmonious. In so doing, economics raises a leading voice against the traditional ethics of altruism and self-sacrifice. It presents society—a division-of-labor, capitalist society—not as an entity over and above the individual, to which he must sacrifice his interests, but as an indispensable means within which the individual can fulfill the ultimate ends of his own personal life and happiness.[8]

A knowledge of economics is indispensable for anyone who seeks to understand his own place in the modern world and that of others. It is a powerful antidote to unfounded feelings of being the victim or perpetrator of "exploitation" and to all feelings of "alienation" based on the belief that the economic world is immoral, purposeless, or chaotic. Such unfounded feelings rest on an ignorance of economics.

The feelings pertaining to alleged exploitation rest on ignorance of the productive role of various economic functions, such as those of businessman and capitalist, retailing and wholesaling, and advertising and speculation, and on the underlying conviction that essentially only manual labor is productive and is therefore the only legitimate form of economic activity.[9] Feelings pertaining to the alleged purposelessness of much of economic activity rest on ignorance of the role of wealth in human life beyond the immediate necessities of food, clothing, and shelter. This ignorance leads to the conviction that economic activity beyond the provision of these necessities serves no legitimate purpose.[10] Feelings pertaining to the alleged chaos of economic activity rest on ignorance of the knowledge economics provides of the benevolent role of such institutions as the division of labor, private ownership of the means of production, exchange and money, economic competition, and the price system.

In opposition to feelings of alienation, economic science makes the economic world fully intelligible. It explains the foundations of the enormous economic progress which has taken place in the "Western" world over the last two centuries. (This includes the rapid economic progress that has been made in recent decades by several countries in the Far East, which have largely become "Westernized.") And in providing demonstrable solutions for all of the world's major economic problems, it points the way for intelligent action to make possible radical and progressive improvement in the material conditions of human beings everywhere. As a result, knowledge of the subject cannot help but support the conviction that the fundamental nature of the world is benevolent and thus that there is no rational basis for feelings of fundamental estrangement from the world.[11]

The above discussion, of course, is totally in opposition to the widely believed claims of Marx and Engels and their followers, such as Erich Fromm, that the economic system of the modern world—capitalism—is the basis of alienation. Indeed, it is consistent with the above discussion that the actual basis of "alienation" resides within the psychological makeup of those who experience the problem. Ignorance of economics reinforces feelings of alienation and allows the alleged deficiencies of the economic system to serve as a convenient rationalization for the existence of the problem.[12]

Economics and Business

Despite popular beliefs, economics is not a science of quantitative predictions. It does not provide reliable information on such matters as what the price of a common stock or commodity will be in the future, or what the "gross national product" will be in the next year or quarter.[13]

However, a knowledge of economics does provide an important intellectual framework for making business and personal financial decisions. For example, a businessman who understands economics is in a far better position to appreciate what the demand for his firm's products depends on than a businessman who does not. Similarly, an individual investor who understands economics is in a vastly better position to protect himself from the consequences of such things as inflation or deflation than one who does not.

But the most important application of economics to business and investment is that only a widespread knowledge of economics can assure the continued existence of the very activities of business and investment. These activities are prohibited under socialism. In a socialist society, such as that of the former Soviet Union, which is governed by the belief that profits and interest are incomes derived from "exploitation," individuals who attempt to engage in business or investment activity have been sent to concentration camps or executed. Business activities can endure and flourish only in a society which understands economics and which is therefore capable of appreciating their value. The value of economics to businessmen should be thought of not as teaching them how to make money (which is a talent that they possess to an incalculably greater degree than economists), but as explaining why it is to the self-interest of everyone that businessmen should be *free* to make money. This is something which businessmen do not know, which is vital to them (and to everyone else), and which economics is uniquely qualified to explain.

Economics and the Defense of Individual Rights

Knowledge of economics is indispensable to the defense of individual rights. The philosophy of individual rights, as set forth in the writings of John Locke and the Declaration of Independence and Constitution of the United States, has been thoroughly undermined as the result of the influence of wrong economic theories, above all, the theories of Karl Marx and the other socialists. The essential conclusion of such theories is that in the economic sphere the exercise of individual rights as understood by Locke and the Founding Fathers of the United States serves merely to enable the capitalists to exploit the workers and consumers, or is otherwise comparably destructive to the interests of the great majority of people. Precisely as a result of the influence of these vicious ideas, culminating in the victory of the New Deal, the Supreme Court of the United States has, since 1937, simply abandoned the defense of economic freedom. Since that time it has allowed Congress and the state legislatures, and even unelected regulatory agencies, to do practically anything they wish in this area, the Constitution and Bill of Rights and all prior American legal precedent notwithstanding.[14]

A thorough knowledge of economics is essential to understanding why the exercise of individual rights in the economic sphere not only is not harmful to the interests of others, but is in the foremost interest of everyone. It is essential if the American people are ever to reclaim the safeguards to economic freedom provided by their Constitution, or if people anywhere are to be able to establish and maintain systems of government based on meaningful respect for individual rights. Indeed, in demonstrating the harmony of the rational self-interests of all men under freedom, this entire book has no greater or more urgent purpose than that of helping to uphold the philosophy of individual rights.

The nature and importance of economics imply that study of the subject should be an important part of the general education of every intelligent person. Economics belongs alongside mathematics, natural science, history, philosophy, and the humanities as an integral part of a liberal education. It deserves an especially prominent place in the education of lawyers, businessmen, journalists, historians, the writers of literary works, and university, college, and secondary-school teachers of the humanities and social sciences. These are the groups that play the dominant role in forming people's attitudes concerning legislation and social institutions and whose work can most profit from an understanding of economics.

CAPITALISM

This book shows that the laws and social institutions necessary to the successful functioning, indeed, to the very existence, of the division of labor are those of *capitalism.* Capitalism is a social system based on private ownership of the means of production. It is characterized by the pursuit of material self-interest under freedom and it rests on a foundation of the cultural influence of reason. Based on its foundations and essential nature, capitalism is further characterized by saving and capital accumulation, exchange and money, financial self-interest and the profit motive, the freedoms of economic competition and economic inequality, the price system, economic progress, and a harmony of the material self-interests of all the individuals who participate in it.

As succeeding chapters of this book will demonstrate, almost every essential feature of capitalism underlies the division of labor and several of them are profoundly influenced by it in their own operation. When the connections between capitalism and the division of labor have been understood, it will be clear that economics, as the science which studies the production of wealth under a system of division of labor, is actually the science which studies the production of wealth under *capitalism.* Economics' study of the consequences of government intervention and of socialism will be shown to be merely study of the impairment or outright destruction of capitalism and the division of labor.

1. The Philosophical Foundations of Capitalism and Economic Activity

Economic activity and the development of economic institutions do not take place in a vacuum. They are profoundly influenced by the fundamental philosophical convictions people hold.[15] Specifically, the development of capitalist institutions and the elevation of the level of production to the standard it has reached over the last two centuries presuppose the acceptance of a *this-worldly, proreason philosophy.* Indeed, in their essential development, the institutions of capitalism and the economic progress that results represent the implementation of *man's right to life,* as that right has been described by Ayn Rand—namely, as the right "to take all the actions required by the nature of a rational being for the support, the furtherance, the fulfillment and the enjoyment of his own life."[16] Capitalism is the economic system that develops insofar as people are free to exercise their right to life and choose to exercise it. As will be shown, its

institutions represent, in effect, a self-expanded power of human reason to serve human life.[17] The growing abundance of goods that results is the material means by which people further, fulfill, and enjoy their lives. The philosophical requirements of capitalism are identical with the philosophical requirements of the recognition and implementation of man's right to life.

It was no accident that the gradual development of capitalist institutions in Western Europe that began in the late Middle Ages paralleled the growing influence of prosecular, proreason trends in philosophy and religion, which had been set in motion by the reintroduction into the Western world of the writings of Aristotle. It is no accident that the greatest era of capitalist development—the last two centuries—has taken place under the ongoing cultural influence of the philosophy of the Enlightenment.

Philosophical convictions pertaining to the reality and primacy of the material world of sensory experience determine the extent to which people are concerned with this world and with improving their lives in it. When, for example, people's lives were dominated by the idea that the material world is superseded by another, higher world, for which their life in this world is merely a test and a preparation, and in which they will spend eternity, they had little motive to devote much thought and energy to material improvement. It was only when the philosophical conviction grew that the senses are valid and that sensory perception is the only legitimate basis of knowledge, that they could turn their full thought and attention to this world. This change was an indispensable precondition of the development of the pursuit of material self-interest as a leading force in people's lives.

The cultural acceptance of the closely related philosophical conviction that the world operates according to definite and knowable principles of cause and effect is equally important to economic development. This conviction, largely absent in the Dark Ages, is the indispensable foundation of science and technology. It tells scientists and inventors that answers exist and can be found, if only they will keep on looking for them. Without this conviction, science and technology could not be pursued. There could be no quest for answers if people were not first convinced that answers can be found.

In addition to the emphasis on this-worldly concerns and the grasp of the principle of cause and effect, the influence of reason shows up in the development of the individual's conceptual ability to give a sense of present reality to his life in decades to come, and in his identification of himself as a self-responsible causal agent with the power to improve his life. This combination of ideas is what produced in people such attitudes as the realization that hard work pays and that they must accept responsibility for their future by means of saving. The same combination of ideas helped to provide the intellectual foundation for the establishment and extension of private property rights as incentives to production and saving. Private property rights rest on the recognition of the principle of causality in the form that those who are to implement the causes must be motivated by being able to benefit from the effects they create. They also rest on a foundation of secularism—of the recognition of the rightness of being concerned with material improvement.

Thus, insofar as production depends on people's desire to improve their material conditions, and on science, technology, hard work, saving, and private property, it fundamentally depends on the influence of a this-worldly, proreason philosophy.

And to the extent that production depends on peace and tranquility, on respect for individual rights, on limited government, economic and political freedom, and even on personal self-esteem, it again fundamentally depends on the influence of a this-worldly, proreason philosophy.

From the dawn of the Renaissance to the end of the nineteenth century, the growing conviction that reason is a reliable tool of knowledge and means of solving problems led to a decline in violence and the frequency of warfare in Western society, as people and governments became increasingly willing to settle disputes by discussion and persuasion, based on logic and facts. This was a necessary precondition of the development of the incentive and the means for the stepped-up capital accumulation required by a modern economic system. For if people are confronted with the chronic threat of losing what they save, and again and again do lose it—whether to local robbers or to marauding invaders—they cannot have either the incentive or the means to accumulate capital.

During the same period of time, as part of the same process, a growing confidence in the reliability and power of human reason led to the elevation of people's view of man, as the being distinguished by the possession of reason. Because he was held to possess incomparably the highest and best means of knowledge, man came to be regarded, on philosophical grounds, as incomparably the highest and best creature in the natural order, capable of action on a grand and magnificent scale, with unlimited potential for improvement. In conjunction with the further philosophical conviction that what actually exist are always individual concretes, not abstractions as such, and thus not collectives or groups of any kind, the elevated view of man meant an elevated view of *the individual human being* and his individual potential.

In their logically consistent form, these ideas led to a view of the individual as both supremely valuable—as an end in himself—and as fully competent to run his own life. The application, in turn, of this view of the individual to society and politics was the doctrine of inalienable individual rights, and of government as existing for no other purpose than to secure those rights, in order to leave the individual free to pursue his own happiness. This, of course, was the foundation of the freedom of capitalism. The same view of man and the human individual, when accepted as a personal standard to be lived up to, was the inspiration for individuals to undertake large-scale accomplishments and to persevere against hardship and failure in order to succeed. It inspired them when they set out to explore the world, discover laws of nature, establish a proper form of government, invent new products and methods of production, and build vast new businesses and brand new industries. It was the inspiration for the pioneering spirit and sense of self-reliance and self-responsibility which once pervaded American society at all levels of ability, and a leading manifestation of which is the spirit of great entrepreneurship.

Finally, the ability of economic science itself to influence people's thinking so that they will favor capitalism and sound economic policy is also totally dependent on the influence of a proreason philosophy. Economics is a science that seeks to explain the complexities of economic life through a process of abstraction and simplification. The method of economics is the construction of deliberately simplified cases, which highlight specific economic phenomena and make possible a conceptual analysis of their effects. For example, in analyzing the effects of improvements in machinery, an economist imagines a hypothetical case in which no change of any kind takes place in the world except the introduction of an improved machine. The truths established deductively in the analysis of such cases are then applied as principles to the real economic world. Consequently, the ability of economics to affect people's attitudes depends on their willingness to follow and feel bound by the results of abstract reasoning. If economics is to have cultural influence, it is indispensable that people have full confidence in logic and reason as tools of cognition.

Not only are economic activity and economics as a science dependent on a proreason philosophy in all the ways I have described, but also it should be realized that economics itself is a highly philosophical subject, potentially capable of exerting an extremely important proreason influence on philosophy. As the subject that studies the production of wealth under a system of division of labor, economics deals both with essential aspects of man's relationship to the physical world and with essential aspects of his relationship to other men. Indeed, the subject matter of economics can be understood as nothing less than the fundamental nature of human society and the ability of human beings living in society progressively to enlarge the benefits they derive from the physical world. For this is what one understands when one grasps the nature and ramifications of the division of labor and its effects on the ability to produce. In this capacity, economics overturns such irrationalist philosophical doctrines as the notion that one man's gain is another man's loss, and the consequent belief in the existence of an inherent conflict of interests among human beings. In their place it sets the doctrine of continuous economic progress and the harmony of the rational self-interests of all human beings under capitalism, which doctrine it conclusively proves on the basis of economic law.

2. Capitalism and Freedom

Freedom means *the absence of the initiation of physical force*. Physical force means injuring, damaging, or otherwise physically doing something to or with the person or property of another against his will. The *initiation* of physical force means starting the process—that is, being the first to use physical force. When one has freedom, what one is free of or free from is the initiation of physical force by other people. An individual is free when, for example, he is free from the threat of being murdered, robbed, assaulted, kidnapped, or defrauded.

(Fraud represents force, because it means taking away property against the will of its owner; it is a species of theft. For example, if a bogus repairman takes away a washing machine to sell it, while saying that he is taking it to repair it, he is guilty of force. In taking it to sell, he takes it against the will of the owner. The owner gives him no more authorization to sell it than he gives to a burglar.)

Freedom and Government

The existence of freedom requires the existence of government. Government is the social institution whose proper function is to protect the individual from the initiation of force. Properly, it acts as the individual's agent, to which he delegates his right of self-defense. It exists to make possible an organized, effective defense and deterrent against the initiation of force. Also, by placing the use of defensive force under the control of objective laws and rules of procedure, it prevents efforts at self-defense from turning into aggression. If, for example, individuals could decide that their self-defense required that they drive tanks down the street, they would actually be engaged in aggression, because they would put everyone else in a state of terror. Control over all use of force, even in self-defense, is necessary for people to be secure against aggression.[18]

An effective government, in minimizing the threat of aggression, establishes the existence of the individual's freedom in relation to all other private individuals. But this is far from sufficient to establish freedom as a general social condition. For one overwhelming threat to freedom remains: namely, aggression by the government itself.

Everything a government does rests on the use of force. No law actually is a law unless it is backed by the threat of force. So long as what the government makes illegal are merely acts representing the initiation of force, it is the friend and guarantor of freedom. But to whatever extent the government makes illegal acts that do not represent the initiation of force, it is the enemy and violator of freedom. In making *such* acts illegal, *it* becomes the initiator of force.

Thus, while the existence of freedom requires the existence of government, it requires the existence of a very specific kind of government: namely, a *limited* government, a government limited exclusively to the functions of defense and retaliation against the initiation of force—that is, to the provision of police, courts, and national defense.[19]

In a fully capitalist society, government does not go beyond these functions. It does not, for example, dictate prices, wages, or working conditions. It does not prescribe methods of production or the kinds of products that can be produced. It does not engage in any form of "economic regulation." It neither builds houses nor provides education, medical care, old-age pensions, or any other form of subsidy. All economic needs are met privately, including the need for charitable assistance when it arises. The government's expenditures are accordingly strictly limited; they do not go beyond the payment of the cost of the defense functions. And thus taxation is strictly limited; it does not go beyond the cost of the defense functions.[20]

In short, in its logically consistent form, capitalism is characterized by laissez faire. The government of such a society is, in effect, merely a night watchman, with whom the honest, peaceful citizen has very little contact and from whom he has nothing to fear. The regulations and controls that exist in such a society are not regulations and controls on the activities of the peaceful citizen, but on the activities of common criminals and on the activities of government officials—on the activities of the two classes of men who use physical force. Under capitalism, while the government controls the criminals, it itself is controlled (as it was for most of the history of the United States) by a Constitution, Bill of Rights, and system of checks and balances achieved through a division of powers. And thus the freedom of the individual is secured.[21]

Given the existence of government and its power to restrain the private use of force, the concept of freedom must be defined in a way that places special stress on the relationship of the citizen to his government. This is because the government's capacity for violating freedom is incomparably greater than that of any private individual or gang whose aggression it fights. One has only to compare the Gestapo or the KGB with the Mafia, to realize how much greater is the potential danger to freedom that comes from government than from private individuals. The government operates through open lines of communication and has at its disposal entire armies that in modern times are equipped with artillery, tanks, planes, rockets, and atomic weapons. Private gangs number comparative handfuls of individuals, operating clandestinely and equipped at most perhaps with submachine guns. Thus, freedom must be defined not merely as the absence of the initiation of physical force, but, in addition, in order to highlight its most crucial aspect, the absence of the initiation of physical force by, or with the sanction of, *the government*. The very existence of government can easily secure the freedom of the individual in relation to all other private citizens. The crucial matter is the individual's freedom in relation to the government.

Freedom as the Foundation of Security

It is important to realize that freedom is the foundation of both personal and economic security.

The existence of freedom directly and immediately establishes personal security in the sense of safety from the initiation of physical force. When one is free, one is safe—secure—from common crime, because what one is free of or free from is precisely the initiation of physical force.

The fact that freedom is the absence of the initiation of physical force also means that *peace* is a corollary of freedom. Where there is freedom, there is peace, because there is no use of force: insofar as force is not initiated, the use of force in defense or retaliation need not take place. Peace in this sense is one of the most desirable features of freedom. Nothing could be more valuable or honorable.

There is, however, a different sense in which peace of some sort can exist. Here, one person or group threatens another with the initiation of force and the other offers no resistance, but simply obeys. This is the peace of slaves and cowards. It is the kind of peace corrupt intellectuals long urged on the relatively free people of the Western world in relation to the aggression of the Communist world.

Freedom is the precondition of economic security, along with personal safety, because it is an essential requirement for individuals being able to act on their rational judgment. When they possess freedom, individuals can consider their circumstances and then choose the course of action that they judge to be most conducive to their economic well-being and thus to their economic security. In addition, they can benefit from the like choices of those with whom they deal.

Under freedom, everyone can choose to do whatever he judges to be most in his own interest, without fear of being stopped by the physical force of anyone else, so long as he himself does not initiate the use of physical force. This means, for example, that he can take the highest paying job he can find and buy from the most competitive suppliers he can find; at the same time, he can keep all the income he earns and save as much of it as he likes, investing his savings in the most profitable ways he can. The only thing he cannot do is use force himself. With the use of force prohibited, the way an individual increases the money he earns is by using his reason to figure out how to offer other people more or better goods and services for the same money, since this is the means of inducing them voluntarily to spend more of their funds in buying from him rather than from competitors. Thus, freedom is the basis of everyone being as secure as the exercise of his own reason and the reason of his suppliers can make him.

The detailed demonstration of the fact that economic freedom is the foundation of economic security is a major theme of this book. This book will show, for example, that free competition is actually a leading source of economic security, rather than any kind of threat to it, and that such phenomena as inflation, depressions, and mass unemployment—the leading causes of economic insecurity—are results of *violations of economic freedom by the government,* and not at all, as is usually believed, of economic freedom itself.[22]

The harmony between freedom and security that this book upholds is, of course, in direct opposition to the prevailing view that in order to achieve economic security, one must violate economic freedom and establish a welfare state. The existence of the social security system, in the United States and other countries, both represents a leading consequence of this mistaken belief and provides essential evidence about what is wrong with it.

In the name of economic security, the freedom of individuals to dispose of their own incomes has been violated as they have been forced to contribute to the social security system. A major consequence of this has been that an enormous amount of savings has been diverted from private individuals into the hands of the government. Had these savings remained in the possession of the individuals, they would have been invested and would thus have helped to finance the construction and purchase of new housing, new factories, and more and better machinery. In the hands of the government, these savings have been dissipated in current consumption. This has resulted from the fact that the government has an overwhelmingly greater interest in its own immediate financial needs than in the future economic security of any private individuals and thus has spent the funds in financing its current expenditures. This has meant the dissipation of these savings and thus the serious undermining of the wealth and productive ability of the entire economic system.[23]

These results have proceeded from the essential nature of the case, which is that while private individuals have an interest in their long-run future economic security, and will provide for it if they are left free to do so, the government does not have such an interest. The interest of government officials is to get by in their term of office and leave the problems of the future to their successors. Thus the violation of economic freedom necessarily results in making individuals less economically secure. Indeed, having been deprived of the existence of actual savings to provide for their future economic security, individuals are now in the position of having to depend on the largess of future legislators, who will have to turn to future taxpayers for the necessary funds. This arrangement has much more in common with the gross insecurity of living as a beggar than it has with any actual economic security.[24]

In opposition to all such delusions, this book shows that to achieve economic security, the essential requirement is precisely economic freedom.

The Indivisibility of Economic and Political Freedom

Although the emphasis of this book is necessarily on the importance of economic freedom, this fact should not be taken in any way to mean a lack of concern for political freedom. Economic freedom and political freedom are indivisible. They are, in fact, merely different aspects of the same thing. The alleged dichotomy between economic freedom and political freedom, between property rights and human rights, is groundless. Virtually every human activity employs wealth—property. To respect the right and freedom to use property is to respect the right and freedom to carry on the activities in which property is used. To deny the right and freedom to carry on such activities is to deny the right and freedom to use the property involved.

For example, the freedom of speech is implied in a farmer's right to use his pasture as he sees fit. The farmer's property rights include his right to invite people onto his land to deliver and or hear a speech. Any effort by the government to stop or prevent such a speech is an obvious interference with the farmer's property rights.

Property rights also include the right to build meeting halls and radio and television stations and to use them to propound whatever ideas one likes. Freedom of speech is fully contained in the economic freedom of the owners of property of the kind that facilitates speech to use their property as they see fit. By the same token, the freedom of speech of those who do not own such property is implied in their right and freedom to buy the use of such property from those who do own it and are willing to rent it to them. Government interference with any such speech is simultaneously an interference with the property rights of the owners of meeting halls or radio or television stations to use or rent their facilities as they see fit.

In the same way, freedom of the press is fully contained in the freedom of an individual to set his type to form the words he wants to form, and then to use his presses, paper, and ink to reproduce those words, and to sell the resulting product to buyers of his choice. Freedom of travel is contained in the property right to build railroads and highways, automobiles and airplanes, to drive one's automobile where one likes, or buy a bus, train, or plane ticket from any willing seller. It is contained in the freedom to use one's shoes to walk across the frontier.

In prohibiting the freedom of speech, press, or travel, one prohibits property owners from using their property as they wish. By the same token, in respecting property rights, one respects these freedoms. On this basis, one should observe the irony of alleged conservative defenders of property rights advocating such things as antipornography legislation—a violation of the property rights of press owners—and of alleged liberal defenders of civil liberties advocating the violation of property rights.[25]

The Rational Versus the Anarchic Concept of Freedom

The concept of freedom when employed rationally, presupposes the existence of reality, and with it the laws of nature, the necessity of choice among alternatives, and the fact that if one resorts to force, one must expect to be met by force. Of particular importance is the fact that it presupposes the necessity of having the voluntary cooperation of everyone who is to aid in an activity—including the owners of any property that may be involved. After taking for granted the presence of all this, the rational concept of freedom then focuses on the absence of one particular thing: the initiation of physical force—in particular, by the government.[26]

In sharpest contrast to the rational concept of freedom is the anarchic concept. The anarchic concept of freedom evades and seeks to obliterate the fundamental and radical distinction that exists between two sorts of obstacles to the achievement of a goal or desire: "obstacles" constituted by the ordinary facts of reality, including other people's voluntary choices, and obstacles constituted by the government's threat to use physical force. For example, by the nature of things, it is impossible for me to square circles, walk through walls, or be in two places at the same time. It is also not possible for me, in the actual circumstances of my life, to win the Nobel prize in chemistry or the Academy Award for best actor of the year, or to enter the automobile or steel business. There are all kinds of such things I simply cannot do. And among the things I could do, there are many I choose not to do, because I judge the consequences to myself to be highly undesirable. For example, I cannot arbitrarily decide to walk off my job in the middle of winter to take a vacation in the sun, without the very strong likelihood of being fired. I cannot drive down a city street at ninety miles an hour, nor can I strike or kill another, without running the risk of paying the penalty for violating the law. And then, there are things that are possible for me to do, and that I would very much like to do, but that would require the consent of other people, which consent they are unwilling to give. In this category, are such things as having my views published in *The New York Times* or having this book assigned in courses at leading "liberal" universities.

Absolutely none of these facts constitutes a violation of freedom, a denial of rights, or anything of the kind. In order for a violation of freedom to exist, it is not sufficient merely that someone be unable to achieve what he desires. What is necessary is that *the specific thing stopping him be the initiation of physical force;* in particular, the government's threat to use force against him in response to an action of his that does not represent the use of force.

The stock-in-trade of the anarchic concept of freedom, however, is to construe precisely such facts as a violation of freedom and rights. On the basis of the anarchic concept of freedom, it is claimed that freedom is violated any time there is anything that, for whatever reason, a person cannot do, from flying to the moon, to being able to afford a house or a college education that is beyond his reach, to committing murder.[27]

Ironically, the anarchic concept of freedom is implicitly accepted by conservatives and fascists, as well as by anarchists and hippies. This is evident in the arguments they advance when they seek to establish the principle that it is necessary and proper to violate freedom. For example, they argue that we do not allow a man the "freedom" to murder his mother-in-law or to speed through red lights and thereby threaten the lives of others. In propounding such arguments, the conservatives and fascists casually neglect the fact that such acts constitute the initiation of force, and are so far from representing freedom that their *prohibition* is what actually constitutes freedom.

The anarchic concept of freedom, of course, is present in the assertions of Communists and socialists that their freedom of speech is violated because they are threatened with arrest for attempting to disrupt the speech of an invited speaker by shouting him down or by speaking at the same time. This assertion by the Communists and socialists neglects the fact that their action constitutes the use of someone else's property against his will—namely, the use of the meeting room against the will of the owner or lessee, who wants the invited speaker to speak, not the disrupters. It is thus the action of the Communists and socialists which is a violation of freedom in this instance—a genuine violation of the freedom of speech.

It follows from this discussion of the erroneous claims of the Communists and socialists that a prohibition on arbitrarily shouting "fire" in a crowded theater should not be construed as any kind of limitation on the freedom of speech. Arbitrarily shouting "fire" constitutes a violation of the property rights of the theater owner and of the other ticketholders, whom it prevents from using their property as they wish. When one holds the context of the rational concept of freedom, it becomes clear that it is no more a violation of freedom of speech to prohibit such speech, than it is to prohibit the speech of disruptive hecklers, or the speech of an uninvited guest who might choose to deliver a harangue in one's living room. Violations of freedom of speech occur only when the speaker has the consent of the property owners involved and then is prohibited from speaking by means of the initiation of physical force—in particular, by the government or by private individuals acting with the sanction of the government.

Because of the confusions that have been introduced into the concept of freedom, it is necessary to set matters right in a number of important concrete instances. Thus, freedom of speech is violated not when an individual does not receive an invitation to speak somewhere, but when he *does* receive it and is stopped by the government (or by private individuals acting with the sanction of the government) from accepting the invitation or exercising it. It is violated precisely by Communist and socialist disrupters whom the police refuse to remove. Ironically, in the case of a live theatrical performance, it is violated precisely when someone arbitrarily shouts "fire." Such a person violates the freedom of speech of the actors on stage.

The freedom of the press is violated and censorship exists not when a newspaper refuses to publish a story or a column that, for any reason, it regards as unworthy of publication, but when it is prepared to publish a piece and is stopped from doing so by the government. Thus, if I want to print my views in *The New York Times,* but can neither afford the advertising rates nor persuade the publisher to give me space, my freedom of the press is not violated; I am not a victim of "censorship." But suppose I do have the money to pay the advertising rates or could persuade the publisher to print my views, and the government disallows it—*that* would be a violation of the freedom of the press; that would be censorship. It is a violation of my freedom of the press if the government stops me from mimeographing leaflets, if that is all I can afford to do to spread my ideas. Again, censorship exists not when the sponsor of a television program refuses to pay for the broadcast of ideas he considers false and vicious, but when he does approve of the ideas he is asked to sponsor and yet is stopped from sponsoring them—for example, by an implicit threat of the government not to renew the license of the television station, or arbitrarily to deny him some permission he requires in some important aspect of his business.[28]

In the same way, if I ask a woman to marry me, and she says no, my freedom is not violated. It is only violated if she says yes, and the government then stops me from marrying her—say, by virtue of a law concerning marriages among people of different races, religions, or blood types. Or, finally, if I want to travel somewhere, but lack the ability to pay the cost of doing so, my freedom of travel is in no way violated. But suppose I do have the ability to pay the cost, and want to pay it, but the government stops me—say, with a wall around my city (as existed until recently in East Berlin), a passport restriction, or a price control on oil and oil products that creates a shortage of gasoline and aviation fuel and thus stops me from driving and the airlines from flying—then my freedom of travel is violated.

What is essential in all these cases is not the fact that there is something I cannot do for one reason or another, but what it is, specifically, that stops me. Only if what stops me is the initiation of physical force—by the government in particular—is my freedom violated.

Subsequent discussions in this book will unmask the influence of the anarchic concept of freedom in the distortions that have taken place in connection with the antitrust laws—in the concepts of freedom of competition and freedom of entry, and in the related notions of private monopoly and private price control. They will also deal with the distortions to be found in the present-day notion of the "right to medical care."[29]

Here it must be pointed out that application of the anarchic concept of freedom operates as a cover for the violation of genuine freedom. If, for example, having to work for a capitalist, as a condition of earning wages and being able to live, is a violation of freedom and represents the existence of "wage slavery," as the Marxists call it, then it appears that when the Communists murder the capitalists, they are merely retaliating against the aggres-

sion of capitalists—indeed, of slave owners.[30] Similarly, if, as the anarchic concept of freedom claims, freedom of travel or movement requires the ability to be able to afford to travel or move, then a state's requirement of a year's residency, say, as the condition of receiving welfare payments, can be construed as a violation of the freedom of travel or movement. Maintenance of such alleged freedom of travel or movement then requires the continued corresponding enslavement of the taxpayers, who must pay to finance it under threat of being imprisoned if they do not.

What is essential always to keep in mind is that since freedom—real freedom—is the absence of the initiation of physical force, every attempt to justify any form of restriction or limitation on freedom is actually an attempt, knowingly or unknowingly, to unleash the initiation of physical force. As such, it is an attempt to unleash the destruction of human life and property, and for this reason should be regarded as monstrously evil.

What makes the anarchic concept of freedom so destructive is the fact that in divorcing freedom from the context of rationality, it not only seeks to establish a freedom to initiate physical force, as in the cases of "wage slavery" and the anarchic concept of the freedom of travel, but also, on the basis of the consequences of such a perverted concept of freedom, provides seeming justification for the violation of freedom as a matter of rational principle. For example, the anarchic concept of freedom of speech, which claims that hecklers can speak at the same time as a lecturer and thus prevent him from communicating his thoughts, not only serves to legitimize the violation of the lecturer's freedom of speech but also, if accepted as being a valid concept of freedom of speech, must ultimately doom the freedom of speech as a matter of rational principle. For if freedom of speech actually entailed the impossibility of communicating thought by speech, because hecklers could continually interrupt the speaker, respect for rationality—for the value of communicating thought—would then require the denial of the freedom of speech.

Such a vicious absurdity arises only on the basis of the anarchic concept of freedom. It does not arise on the basis of the rational concept of freedom. Freedom of speech rationally means that the lecturer or invited speaker has the right to speak and that hecklers and disrupters are violating the freedom of speech. The rational concept of freedom establishes freedom of speech precisely as the *safeguard of the communication of thought,* not its enemy. It is vital to keep this principle in mind today in an environment in which many university campuses have been transformed into virtual zoos, in which cowardly and ignorant administrators regularly tolerate disruptions of speech by gangs of delinquents masquerading as students. Such university administrators thereby abandon their responsibility to maintain their universities as the centers of teaching and learning that in their nature they are supposed to be. In tolerating anarchic violations of freedom of speech in the name of freedom of speech, they pave the way for the outright fascistic destruction of freedom of speech in the name of rationality.

The Decline of Freedom in the United States

In the twentieth century, freedom in the United States has been in decline. A twofold measure of this decline is the fact that, with little if any exaggeration, it is now the case that the average mugger has less to fear from the police and courts than the average successful businessman or professional has to fear from the Internal Revenue Service. In allowing common crime to go increasingly unchecked, the government has increasingly failed in its function of securing the individual's freedom in relation to other private individuals. At the same time, as the limits on its powers have been removed, it has itself increasingly violated the freedom of the individual. The government's energies and efforts have more and more been diverted from the protection of the individual's freedom to the violation of it.

To some extent, the process of the destruction of freedom has taken place under the code words of combatting "white-collar crime" instead of "blue-collar crime." The latter type of crime is genuine crime, entailing the initiation of physical force. The former type of crime incorporates some elements of genuine crime, such as fraud and embezzlement, but consists mainly of fictitious crimes—that is, perfectly proper activities of businessmen and capitalists which are viewed as crimes from the perverted perspective of Marxism and other varieties of socialism, such as charging prices that are allegedly "too high" or paying wages that are allegedly "too low."

A profreedom political party would have as the essence of its platform the replacement of the government's suppression of the activities of businessmen and other peaceful private individuals with the rightful suppression of the activities of common criminals, such as muggers, robbers, and murderers. Its essential goal would be the total redirection of the energies of the government away from interference with the peaceful, productive activities of the citizens to forcibly and effectively combatting the destructive activities of common criminals.

The extent to which this can happen, and thus the future of freedom in the United States, depends first of all on the concept of freedom being properly understood, and then on its being upheld without compromise in every instance in which freedom is violated or threatened, from the police turning their backs on campus disruptions and even open rioting and looting in major cities, to income tax audits and the ever growing array of government regulations.

All of the major problems now being experienced in the United States have as an essential element the inconsistent application or outright abandonment of the country's own magnificent original principle of a government upholding individual freedom. Every violation of that principle—every act of government intervention into the economic system—represents the use of physical force either to prevent individuals from acting for their self-interest or to compel them to act against their self-interest. It is no wonder that as the violations of freedom multiply, people are less and less able to serve their self-interests and thus suffer more and more. In order for the American people once again to succeed and prosper, it is essential for the United States to return to its founding principle of individual freedom.

The Growth of Corruption as the Result of the Decline of Freedom

Closely and necessarily accompanying the destruction of freedom in the United States has been the growing corruption both of government officials and of businessmen, who are increasingly under the power of the officials. The ability to violate the freedom of businessmen gives to the government officials the power to deprive businessmen of opportunities to earn wealth or to retain wealth they have already earned. The power of the officials is fundamentally discretionary, that is, it may or may not be used, as they decide. This is always the case with legislators contemplating the enactment of new laws. It is often the case with officials charged with the execution of a law—if they have the power to decide whether or not to enact this or that new regulation in the course of its execution, and whether or not to apply the regulation in any given case, or to what extent.

This situation inevitably creates an incentive on the part of businessmen to bribe the officials, in order to avoid the passage of such laws or the enactment or application of such regulations and thus to go on with the earning of wealth or to keep the wealth they have already earned. It is a situation in which businessmen are made to pay the officials for permissions to act when properly they should be able to act by right—by the right to the pursuit of happiness, which includes the right to the pursuit of profit.

At the same time, the government's ability to violate freedom gives it the power to provide businessmen with subsidies and to damage their competitors. This creates corruption of a much worse character, one in which businessmen are led to offer bribes not to defend what is theirs by right, but as part of an act of depriving others of what belongs to those others by right. Few businessmen are moral philosophers, and those who may have begun their practice of bribing government officials in order simply to avoid harm to themselves cannot be counted upon always to keep in mind the distinction between an act of self-defense and an act of aggression, especially when they must operate increasingly in the conditions of a virtual jungle, in which competitors are prepared to use the government against them and in which large and growing numbers of other businessmen are all too willing to gain subsidies at their expense. The result is a powerful tendency toward the destruction of the whole moral fabric of business.

The obvious solution for this problem of corruption is, of course, the restoration of the businessman's freedom and his security from the destructive actions of the government officials. When the businessman can once again act for his profit by right rather than permission, when the government has lost the power both to harm him and to harm others for his benefit, the problem of such bribery and corruption will shrivel to insignificance.[31]

3. Capitalism and the Origin of Economic Institutions

To the degree that they exist, freedom and the pursuit of material self-interest, operating in a rational cultural environment, are the foundation of all the other institutions of capitalism. And the study of these institutions and their functioning is the substance of the science of economics.

If individuals both possess freedom and, at the same time, rationally desire to improve their lives and well-being, then they have only to use their minds to look at reality, consider the various opportunities that nature and the existence of other people offer them for serving their self-interest, and choose to pursue whichever of the opportunities confronting them they judge best. They can do whatever they judge is most in their self-interest to do, provided only that they do not initiate the use of force against others.

What people do in these circumstances is spontaneously to set about establishing, or extending and reinforcing, all the other institutions, in addition to freedom and limited government, that constitute a capitalist economic system, such as private ownership of the means of production, saving and capital accumulation, exchange and money, division of labor, and the price system.

Thus, in pursuing their rational self-interest under freedom, they appropriate previously unowned land and natural resources from nature and make them into private property and thus privately owned means of production. Private property in products, including capital goods, then follows on the basis of private property in land and natural resources: the owners of land and natural re-

sources own the products that result from them, including those which they use as means of further production. In addition, of course, they can exchange their products with others for services. These others then also own products, including capital goods, and can, of course, obtain land and natural resources from their original owners by means of purchase or, in primitive conditions, barter exchange.

Being secure in their possession of property from violent appropriation by others, and rational enough to act on the basis of long-run considerations, individuals save and accumulate capital, which increases their ability to produce and consume in the future (for example, following the appropriation of land, they clear trees, remove rocks, drain, irrigate, build, and do whatever else is necessary to establish and improve farms and mines and, later on, commercial and industrial enterprises).

They also perceive the advantages of establishing division of labor and performing exchanges with others. They perceive that some individuals are more efficient than others in the production of certain goods, whether by reason of personal ability or because of the circumstances of the territory in which they live, and that an advantage is to be gained by individuals concentrating on their areas of greater efficiency and exchanging the results.[32]

They perceive the advantages of indirect exchange— that is, of accepting goods not because they want them themselves, but because others want them and the goods can thus be used as means of further exchanges. Out of indirect exchange money develops, with the result that the division of labor is enabled radically to intensify—to the point where each individual finds it to his interest to produce or help to produce just one or at most a very few things, for which he is paid money, which he in turn uses to buy from others virtually all that he himself consumes.[33]

In the context of a division-of-labor, monetary economy, the individual's pursuit of his material self-interest gives rise to the narrower principle of financial self-interest—that is, of preferring, other things being equal, to buy at lower prices rather than higher prices and to sell at higher prices rather than lower prices. These are the ways to increase the goods one can obtain by the earning and spending of money. In combination they represent the profit motive—the principle of "buying cheap and selling dear."

The individual's pursuit of self-interest also gives rise to economic inequality, as those who are more intelligent and ambitious outstrip those who are less intelligent and ambitious; and to economic competition, as different sellers seek to sell to the same customers, and as different buyers seek to buy one and the same supply of a good or service.

The combination of the profit motive and the freedom

of competition, in turn, constitutes the basis of the price system and all of its laws of price determination.

Thus, rational self-interest and the individual's freedom to act on the basis of it underlie private property and private ownership of the means of production, saving and capital accumulation, the division of labor, exchange and money, financial self-interest and the profit motive, economic inequality, economic competition, and the price system—in a word, the whole range of capitalism's economic institutions.

The combined effect of these institutions is *economic progress*—that is, the increase in the productive power of human labor and the consequent enjoyment of rising standards of living. Economic progress is the natural accompaniment of rationality and the freedom to act on it. This is so because the continued exercise of rationality creates a growing sum of scientific and technological knowledge from generation to generation. This, together with the profit motive, the freedom of competition, the incentive to save and accumulate capital, and the existence of a division-of-labor society, is the essential basis of continuous economic progress.[34]

Economic progress is the leading manifestation of yet another major institutional feature of capitalism: *the harmony of the rational self-interests of all men,* in which the success of each promotes the well-being of all. The basis of capitalism's harmony of interests is the combination of freedom and rational self-interest operating in the context of the division of labor, which is itself their institutional creation. Under freedom, no one may use force to obtain the cooperation of others. He must obtain their cooperation voluntarily. To do this, he must show them how cooperation with him is to their self-interest as well as his own, and, indeed, is *more* to their self-interest than pursuing any of the other alternatives that are open to them. To find customers or workers and suppliers, he must show how dealing with him benefits them as well as him, and benefits them more than buying from others or selling to others. As will be shown, the gains from the division of labor make the existence of situations of mutual benefit omnipresent under capitalism.[35] The division of labor, in combination with the rest of capitalism, represents a regular, institutionalized arrangement whereby the mind of each in serving its individual possessor, serves the well-being of a multitude of others, and is motivated and enabled to serve their well-being better and better.

In sum, capitalism, with its economic progress and prosperity, is the economic system of a free society. It is the economic system people achieve if they have freedom and are rational enough to use it to benefit themselves. As I have said, it represents a self-expanded power of human reason to serve human life.[36]

4. Capitalism and the Economic History of the United States

The development of all the institutional features of capitalism is well illustrated by the economic history of the United States. Of course, the United States was by no means the perfect model of a capitalist country. Negro slavery existed, which denied all freedom to blacks and prevented them from pursuing their material self-interests. This was in total contradiction of the principles of capitalism. And other important contradictions existed as well, such as a policy of protective tariffs, public canal and turnpike building, the government's claim to ownership of the western lands and its consequent ability to use land grants to subsidize uneconomic railroad building, and, very important, the government's promotion of the use of debt as backing for paper money, which repeatedly resulted in financial panics and depressions when substantial debtors failed, as, in the nature of the case, they had to.[37]

Nevertheless, the history of the United States shows a government committed in principle to upholding the freedom of the individual and, for the white population, doing so in fact to a degree never achieved before or since. And thus, following the establishment of the United States, we observe a century-long process of the appropriation of land and establishment of private property and private ownership of the means of production, as people were made free to appropriate previously ownerless territory and moved west to do so. This period represents the most important historical example of the process of establishing private property and private ownership of the means of production described in the preceding section. By and large, the settlers simply moved into what was virtually an empty continent and made major portions of it into private property by direct appropriation from nature. The private property that exists today in the United States can generally be traced back, through intervening purchases and sales, to such original appropriations from nature.[38]

The history of the United States was also characterized by the rapid development of the division of labor and the growth of a monetary economy. The largely self-sufficient pioneers of colonial times were succeeded by farmers producing more and more for the market and buying goods in the market, including all manner of equipment and other aids that greatly increased their ability to produce. The result of the rising productivity of labor in agriculture was a steady shift in population away from farming and toward towns and cities, which sprang up in the wilderness and grew rapidly as centers of an ever more prosperous commerce and industry.

The growing concentration of farmers on producing

for the market and the movement of more and more of their sons and daughters to the towns and cities to find employment constituted the actual building of a division-of-labor society. This was a process that was dictated by considerations of self-interest on the part of millions of individual people. Each individual farmer who devoted his labor to producing crops for the market did so because he judged that he would be better off with the products he could buy with the money he earned than he would be with the products he could produce for himself with the same labor. Each individual son or daughter of a farmer who moved to a town or city to find employment did so because he judged that he would be better off by doing so—that the income to be earned in a town or city exceeded the income to be made as a farmer and any allowance for the self-produced goods and other benefits associated with living on a farm. Thus, the self-interested actions of millions of individuals is what created a division-of-labor society in the United States and everywhere else that it exists.

The security of property made the American people both industrious and provident, because they knew that they could keep all that they earned and be able to benefit from all that they saved. (There was no income tax prior to 1913.) Not surprisingly, they were considered to be the hardest-working people in the world. And their consequent high rate of saving ensured that each year a substantial proportion of their production took the form of new and additional capital goods, which had the effect of increasing their ability to produce and consume in succeeding years.

The freedom of production in the United States led to an unprecedented outpouring of innovations—to the steady introduction of new and previously unheard of products and to the constant improvement of methods of production. This, along with the constant availability of an adequate supply of savings to implement the advances, produced the most rapid and sustained rate of economic progress in the history of the world.[39]

In the process, some individuals achieved enormous personal wealth and distinction. But their success was not the cause of anyone else's impoverishment. It was, on the contrary, precisely the means whereby the general standard of living was raised and all were progressively enriched. For these individuals made the innovations and built the industries that were the source of the growing volume of goods enjoyed by all.

And, overall, guiding the entire process of production in the American economy were the profit motive and the price system. The "dollar-chasing Americans," as they were called, were vitally concerned with earning money. Calculations of profit and loss governed every business decision and, therefore, practically every decision con-

cerning the production of goods and services. Because of the freedom of competition, those business firms succeeded which found ways to reduce their costs of production and offer better goods at lower prices—earning high profits by virtue of low costs and large volume.

The economic history of the United States can be understood on the basis of a single fundamental principle: *people were free and they used their freedom to benefit themselves.* Each individual was free to benefit himself, and the necessity of respecting the freedom of others necessitated that he benefit them as well if he was to have them as workers, suppliers, or customers. Because people had the freedom and the desire to benefit themselves, they went ahead and virtually all of them actually succeeded in benefitting themselves.

In 1776 the present territory of the United States was an almost empty continent, whose cities either did not exist or were little more than coastal villages. Its population consisted of approximately half a million Indians, who lived on the edge of starvation, and three million settlers, most of whom were semi-self-sufficient farmers living in extreme poverty. In less than two centuries, it was transformed into a continent containing the two hundred million richest people in the history of the world; a continent crisscrossed with highways, railways, telephone and telegraph lines; a continent filled with prosperous farms and dotted with innumerable towns and cities that were the sites of factories using methods of production and producing all manner of goods that probably could not even have been imagined in 1776.

One should ask how the United States' economy got from where it was then to where it is even now. One should ask how Pittsburgh, Cleveland, Detroit, Chicago, St. Louis, San Francisco, Los Angeles, Houston, and Dallas came to be the great cities they all were, not very long ago, and, for the most part, still are. One should ask how New York City grew from a population of twenty thousand to eight million, and how Boston and Philadelphia could increase in size thirty-five and one hundred times over. One should ask where all the means of transportation and communication, all the farms and factories, houses and stores, and all the incredible goods that fill them came from.

The answer, as I say, is astoundingly simple. What was achieved in the United States *was the cumulative, aggregate result of tens of millions of people, generation after generation, each pursuing his individual self-interest—* in the process, necessarily helping others to achieve their self-interests. And what made this possible was individual freedom.

Thus, eastern farmers realized that the land in the Midwest and West was better for many purposes than the land in the East, and that a higher income was to be made by moving there. And so they moved. Merchants realized that these farmers needed supplies and that money was to be made in supplying them. And so they opened clusters of stores and built their houses at supply points in proximity to the farmers, thus laying the base of towns and cities. They made money and expanded their operations. Others perceived the growing trade and the money to be made in improving transportation to the new regions. They built barge lines and stagecoach lines, then steamship companies and railroads, and made money.

Businessmen and inventors, often one and the same, were constantly on the lookout for the new and the better. They discovered and introduced thousands upon thousands of improvements both in products and in methods of production, with each new advance serving as the base for something still newer and still better. These businessmen and inventors built the factories and the industries that made the cities and towns. The rest of the population, always on the lookout for better jobs, recognized the advantages of employment in the new industries and the new cities and so took the ever improving, ever better-paying jobs they offered.

All this happened because it was to the rational self-interest of individuals to make it happen and because no one could use force to stop them from making it happen. The British had tried to prevent the development of the territory west of the Appalachian Mountains—to set it aside as a kind of gigantic wildlife preserve, so to speak—but the American Revolution overthrew their rule and cleared the way for the unprecedented economic progress I have described.

The rising prosperity of each generation brought about a continual doubling and redoubling of the population, as a higher and higher proportion of children survived to adulthood, and as an ever growing flood of immigrants bought, borrowed, and sometimes stole their way to the shores of what—in their awe and admiration for the United States and its freedom—they called "God's country."

In recent years, it is true, the economic glow of the United States has lost much of its luster. While advances continue in some fields, such as computerization, major areas of economic life, and the economic conditions confronting large numbers of people, have clearly fallen into a state of decline. Major industries, such as automobiles and steel, and entire industrial regions—the Northeast and the Midwest, once the backbone of the American economy—are in decline. What was once the industrial heartland of the United States is now known as the *rust belt*—a dreadful, but accurate description of its condition. Detroit, once the home of the American automobile industry and the leading industrial city in the world is now on the verge of losing its last automobile factory,

and growing portions of it are becoming uninhabited. The housing stock, industry, and downtown shopping districts of many other large cities are also in a state of profound decay. For some years, homeownership has been beyond the reach of most people, and a sharp rise in the price of electricity, heating oil, and gasoline has made the operation of homes and automobiles far more costly and has undercut people's ability to afford other goods. The supply of power plants is becoming inadequate. A growing number of bridges, highways, and commercial aircraft are in need of major overhaul or replacement. Large-scale unemployment persists.

This book makes clear that the cause of such problems is the progressive abandonment of capitalism and the undermining of its institutions over a period of several generations. This is a process that has finally assumed dimensions so great as to jeopardize the continued functioning of the economic system.

There has been a steady increase in government spending for alleged social welfare, which has been financed by a system of progressive income and inheritance taxation and by budget deficits and inflation of the money supply. These policies, in turn, destroy incentives to produce and the ability to save and accumulate capital. They have been coupled with a steadily increasing burden of government regulations restricting or prohibiting economically necessary activities and encouraging or compelling unnecessary, wasteful, and even absurd activities. For example, the production of fuel has been restricted or even prohibited by price controls and so-called environmental legislation, while the hiring and promotion of unqualified employees has been encouraged and even compelled under systems of government imposed racial and sexual quotas.

The consequence of all of this has been growing economic stagnation, if not outright economic decline, a situation punctuated by rapidly rising prices, growing unemployment, and sporadic shortages.

In recent years, it appears that there has been some recognition of the nature of our problems. Unfortunately, the recognition does not yet go deep enough nor is it yet nearly widespread enough. Thus its benefits are likely to prove elusive or at least extremely short-lived. For example, a major undermining of the OPEC cartel and partial retracement of the price of oil took place in the 1980s, mainly as a result of the repeal of price controls on oil and the easing of "environmental" regulations early in the decade. But now this improvement is in the process of being reversed, through the reimposition and further extension of "environmental" regulations. At the same time, other forms of government interference and government spending continue to grow, and federal budget deficits continue at an alarming level, which makes it likely that the government will turn either to destructive tax increases or to a no less destructive acceleration of inflation. Even the sudden collapse of socialism in Eastern Europe and the former Soviet Union provide little cause for long-term optimism about the economic system of the United States. This is because, as will be explained later, all the essentials of socialism live on in the ecology movement, and are enjoying growing influence in the United States even while socialism in the form of Marxism is in decline in most of the world.[40]

5. Why Economics and Capitalism Are Controversial

In propounding sound economic theory and thus in presenting the case for capitalism, this book cannot avoid being highly controversial. It is necessary to explain the reasons.

The Assault on Economic Activity and Capitalism

Virtually every aspect of capitalism and thus of economic activity is savagely denounced by large segments of public opinion. The pursuit of self-interest is condemned as evil, and of material self-interest as "vulgar" besides. Freedom under capitalism is ridiculed as "the freedom to starve" and as "wage slavery." Private property is condemned as theft—from a patrimony allegedly given by God or Nature to the human race as a whole. Money is denounced as the "root of all evil"; and the division of labor, as the cause of one-sided development, narrowness, and "alienation."

The profit motive is attacked as the cause of starvation wages, exhausting hours, sweatshops, and child labor; and of monopolies, inflation, depressions, wars, imperialism, and racism. It is also blamed for poisoned foods, dangerous drugs and automobiles, unsafe buildings and work places, "planned obsolescence," pornography, prostitution, alcoholism, narcotics abuse, and crime. Saving is condemned as hoarding; competition, as "the law of the jungle"; and economic inequality, as the basis of "class warfare." The price system and the harmony of interests are almost completely unheard of, while economic progress is held to be a "ravaging of the planet," and, in the form of improvements in efficiency, a cause of unemployment and depressions. At the same time, by the same logic, wars and destruction are regarded as necessary to prevent unemployment under capitalism.

Virtually all economic activity beyond that of manual labor employed in the direct production of goods is widely perceived as parasitical. Thus businessmen and capitalists are denounced as recipients of "unearned income," and as "exploiters." The stock and commodity markets are denounced as "gambling casinos"; retailers and wholesalers, as "middlemen," having no function

but that of adding "markups" to the prices charged by farmers and manufacturers; and advertisers, as inherently guilty of fraud—the fraud of attempting to induce people to desire the goods that capitalism showers on them, but that they allegedly have no natural or legitimate basis for desiring.

Despite the obvious self-contradictions, capitalism is simultaneously denounced for impoverishing the masses and for providing them with "affluence," for being a rigid class society and for being dominated by the upstart nouveau riche, for its competition and for its lack of competition, for its militarism and for its pacifism, for its atheism and for its support of religion, for its oppression of women and for its destruction of the family by making women financially independent.

Overall, capitalism is denounced as "an anarchy of production," a chaos ruled by "exploiters," "robber barons," and "profiteers," who "coldly," "calculatingly," "heartlessly," and "greedily" consume the efforts and destroy the lives of the broad masses of average, innocent people.

On the basis of all these mistaken beliefs, people turn to the government: for "social justice"; for protection and aid, in the form of labor and social legislation; for reason and order, in the form of government "planning." They demand and for the most part have long ago obtained: progressive income and inheritance taxation; minimum-wage and maximum-hours laws; laws giving special privileges and immunities to labor unions; antitrust legislation; social security legislation; public education; public housing; socialized medicine; nationalized or municipalized post offices, utilities, railroads, subways, and bus lines; subsidies for farmers, shippers, manufacturers, borrowers, lenders, the unemployed, students, tenants, and the needy and allegedly needy of every description. They have demanded and obtained food and drug regulations, building codes and zoning laws, occupational health and safety legislation, and more. They have demanded and obtained the creation of additional money, and the abolition of every vestige of the gold standard— to make possible the inflation of the money supply without limit. They have demanded this last in the belief that the additional spending the additional money makes possible is the means of maintaining or achieving full employment, and in the belief that creating money is a means of creating capital for lending and thus of reducing interest rates. The ability to create money has also been demanded because it is vital in enabling additional government expenditures to be financed by means of budget deficits and thus in fostering the delusion that the government can provide benefits for which the citizens do not pay. And when, as is inevitable, the policy of inflation results in rising prices, capital decumulation, and the destruction of credit, people demand price and wage controls, and then, in response to the shortages and chaos that result, the government's total control over the economic system, in the form of rationing and allocations.

In the face of such ideas and demands, which have swept over the country with the force of a great flood, traditional American values of individual rights and limited government have appeared trivial and antiquated—appropriate perhaps to an age of independent farmers, but by no means to be permitted to stand in the way of what a frightened and angry mass of people perceive as the requirements virtually of their self-preservation. Indeed, so complete has been the destruction of traditional American values, that the concept of individual rights has itself been made over into a vehicle serving demands for government subsidies and extensions of government power—in such forms as the assertion of "rights" to jobs, housing, education, pensions, medical care, and so on.

This book flies in the face of all such anticapitalistic ideas and demands. Its thesis implies that never have so many people been so ignorant and confused about a subject so important, as most people now are about economics and capitalism. It shows that in its logically consistent form of *laissez-faire* capitalism—that is, with the powers of government limited to those of national defense and the administration of justice—capitalism is a system of economic progress and prosperity for all, and is a precondition of world peace.

The Prevailing Prescientific Worldview in the Realm of Economics

There are a number of mutually reinforcing reasons for the prevailing mass of errors about economics and capitalism.

First, even though this is the late twentieth century, it is no exaggeration to say that in the realm of economics, the thought of most people continues to bear the essential characteristics of the mentality of the Dark Ages or of primitive peoples in general. What I mean by this is that prior to the development of a scientific worldview in the Renaissance, it was common for people even in Western Europe to interpret natural phenomena as the result of the operation of good or evil spirits. Thus, if a flood came and washed away their huts, or if their animals died of disease, polytheistic primitive peoples would think the explanation lay in the anger of a river god or some other deity. Similarly, the supposedly monotheistic Europeans of the Dark Ages would believe the explanation lay in the curse of some witch or other evil spirit. Both believed that their protection from such harm lay in securing the aid of a more powerful benevolent spirit, whether another deity or an angel, or simply the one and only deity. What was essential was that they believed that their harm

resulted from the exercise of arbitrary power by evil forces and that their security depended on obtaining the aid of a greater, stronger arbitrary power who would act on their behalf.

As the preceding discussion of the assault on economic activity and capitalism should make clear, this is precisely the worldview people continue to apply in the present day in the realm of economics. Again and again they view their economic harm as caused by the ill will of an arbitrary power—above all, "big business." And they believe that their protection depends on the good will of a bigger, tougher, stronger arbitrary power—namely, the government—which will act on their behalf. If, for example, the level of wages or prices or the quantity or quality of housing, medical care, education, or anything else is not to people's satisfaction, the explanation, they believe, is that evil businessmen are responsible. The solution, they believe, is for the government, which is more powerful than the businessmen, to use its greater power on behalf of the people.[41]

In contrast, the view of the economic world imparted by economic science is as far removed from that of the primitive mentality as is the view of the physical world that is imparted by the sciences of physics and chemistry. The worldview imparted by economics is, like that of physics and chemistry, one of operation according to natural laws which can be grasped by human intelligence. The domain of the natural laws of economics is, of course, that of the rationally self-interested actions of individuals insofar as they take place under freedom and center on the production of wealth under a division of labor.

This scientific view of economic phenomena, even though in existence since the late eighteenth century in the writings of the Physiocrats and the early British classical economists, has been prevented from replacing the primitive worldview. It has been prevented by the combined operation of the factors explained in the remainder of this section.

Economics Versus Unscientific Personal Observations

Everyone is a participant in economic activity and as such develops or accepts opinions about economic life that seem consistent with his own observations of it. Yet those opinions are often mistaken, because they rest on too narrow a range of experience, which renders them inconsistent with other aspects of experience of the same subject. Examples of this phenomenon in the everyday world of physical reality are such naive beliefs as that sticks bend in water, that the earth is flat, and that the sun revolves around the earth. In contrast with such naïveté, a scientific process of thought seeks to develop the theory of a subject based on logical consistency with *all* the valid observations pertaining to it. Thus, the visual appearance of sticks being bent in water is reconciled with the fact that they continue to feel straight when subjected to touch; the reconciliation being by knowledge of the refraction of light caused by water. The earth's appearance of flatness is reconciled with such observations as the masts of ships first becoming visible on the horizon by knowledge of the very gradual curvature of the earth. The appearance of the sun's revolution about the earth is reconciled with knowledge of the sun's relationship to other observable heavenly bodies through knowledge of the earth's rotation about its axis.

Economics suffers from an apparent conflict between personal observation and scientific truth probably to a greater extent than most other sciences. This is because of the very nature of the system of division of labor and monetary exchange. Every participant in the economic system is a specialist, aware of the effect of things on his own specialization. As a rule, he does not stop to consider their effect on other specializations as well; nor, as a rule, does he consider what their longer-run effect on him might be were he to change his specialization. As a result of this, people have come to believe such things as that improvements in production, which can in fact necessitate the shrinkage or total disappearance of employment in any particular branch of the division of labor, are economically harmful. By the same token, they have come to believe that acts of destruction, which can in fact result in an expansion of employment in particular branches of the division of labor, are economically beneficial.[42]

Closely related to the failure to look beyond one's own current specialization is the widespread confusion between money and wealth. In a division-of-labor economy everyone is naturally interested in earning money and comes to measure his economic well-being by the amount of money he earns. Thus, it is extremely easy for people to conclude that anything that enables the average person to earn more money is desirable, while anything that results in the average person's earning less money is undesirable. It takes a scientific analysis to show that while each individual is always economically best off earning as much money *as the freedom of competition allows him to earn,* people are not economically better off when average earnings increase as the result of government policies of creating money, or because the government violates the freedom of competition. Indeed, economics shows that lower monetary earnings without money creation and without violations of the freedom of competition represent a higher actual standard of living than do higher monetary earnings with them.[43] Along these lines, there are important cases in which, even in the absence of money creation, it turns out that a lower "national income" or "gross national product" signifies

a more rapid rate of increase in the production of wealth and improvement in human well-being than does a higher "national income" or "gross national product."[44]

Economics Versus Altruism

If economics merely contradicted people's unscientific conclusions based on their personal observations, its path would be difficult enough. Its problems are enormously compounded, however, by the fact that its teachings also contradict some of the most deeply cherished moral and ethical doctrines, above all, the doctrine that the pursuit of self-interest by the individual is harmful to the interests of others and thus that it is the individual's obligation to practice altruism and self-sacrifice.

Economics as a science studies the rational pursuit of material self-interest, to which it traces the existence of all vital economic institutions and thus of material civilization itself, and from which it derives an entire body of economic laws. It cannot help concluding that rational self-interest and the profit motive are profoundly benevolent forces, serving human life and well-being in every respect, and that they should be given perfect freedom in which to operate. Nevertheless, traditional morality regards self-interest as amoral at best, and, indeed, as positively immoral. It considers love of others and self-sacrifice for the sake of others to be man's highest virtues, around which he should build his life.

Thus, the teachings of economics are widely perceived as a threat to morality. And, by the same token, the anticapitalistic slogans described earlier in this section are perceived as expressions of justified moral outrage. As a result, economics must make its way not merely against ignorance, but against ignorance supported by moral fervor and self-righteousness. Without the issue being named, economists are in a similar position to the old astronomers, whose knowledge that the earth revolved about the sun not only appeared to contradict what everyone could see for himself but also stood as a challenge to the entire theological view of the universe. Economics and capitalism are a comparable challenge to the morality of altruism.

It is almost certain that economics and capitalism will be unable to gain sufficient cultural acceptance to ensure the influence of the one and the survival of the other until there is a radical change in people's ideas concerning morality and ethics, and that this change will have to be effected in fields other than economics—notably, philosophy and psychology. But even so, economics itself has an enormous contribution to make in changing people's ideas on these subjects, which every advocate of rational self-interest would be well advised to utilize.

A major reason for the condemnation of self-interest

is, certainly, beliefs about its economic consequences. If people did not believe, for example, that one man's gain is another's loss, but, on the contrary, that in a capitalist society one man's gain is actually other men's gain, their fear and hatred of self-interest could probably not be maintained. Yet precisely this is what economics proves. It proves what is actually the simplest thing in the world. Namely, that if individuals rationally seek to do good for themselves, *each* of them can in fact *achieve* his good. It proves that in a division-of-labor, capitalist society, in the very nature of the process, in seeking his own good, the individual promotes the good of others, whose self-interested actions likewise promote the achievement of his good. Economics proves the existence of a harmony of the rational self-interests of all participants in the economic system—a harmony which permeates the institutions of private ownership of the means of production, economic inequality, and economic competition. At the same time, it shows that the fear of self-interest and the consequent prohibition of its pursuit is the one great cause of paralysis and stagnation—that if individuals are prohibited from doing good for themselves, their good simply cannot be achieved.

Economics Versus Irrational Self-Interest

The teachings of economics encounter opposition not only from the supporters of altruism, but also from the practitioners of an irrational, short-sighted, self-defeating form of self-interest, as well. These are, above all, the businessmen and wage earners whose short-run interests would be harmed by the free competition of capitalism and are protected or positively promoted by policies of government intervention, and who do not scruple to seek government intervention. For example, the businessmen and wage earners who seek government subsidies, price supports, tariffs, licensing laws, exclusive government franchises, labor-union privileges, immigration quotas, and the like.

Such businessmen and wage earners form themselves into pressure groups and lobbies, and seek to profit at the expense of the rest of the public. They and their spokesmen unscrupulously exploit the economic ignorance of the majority of people by appealing to popular misconceptions and using them in support of destructive policies. Their action is self-defeating in that the success of each group in achieving the privileges it wants imposes losses on other groups that are greater than its gains; at the same time, its gains are canceled by the success of other groups in obtaining the special privileges they want. The net effect is losses for virtually everyone. For not only does each group plunder others and in turn is plundered by them, but, in the process, the overall total of what is produced is more and more diminished, as well.

For example, what farmers gain in subsidies they lose in tariffs, higher prices because of monopoly labor unions, higher taxes for welfare-type spending, and so on. Indeed, the gains of each type of farmer are even canceled in part by the gains of other types of farmers—for example, the gains of wheat farmers are lost in part in paying higher prices for other subsidized farm products, like cotton, tobacco, milk, and butter. In the same way, the benefit of the higher wages secured by a labor union is lost in the payment of higher prices for products produced by the members of all other unions, as well as in the payment of higher prices caused by subsidies, tariffs, and so on. The net effect works out to be that less of virtually everything is produced, because such policies both reduce the efficiency of production and prevent people from being employed. Virtually everyone is made worse off—those who become unemployed and those who continue to work. Because of the inefficiencies introduced, the latter must pay prices that are increased to a greater degree than their incomes, and they must also use part of their incomes to support the unemployed.

The pressure-group members may subjectively believe that they are pursuing their self-interests. The supporters of altruism and socialism may believe that the absurd process of mutual plunder carried on by such groups represents capitalism and the profit motive. But the fact is that self-interest is not achieved by pressure-group warfare. Nor is the activity of pressure groups a characteristic of capitalism. On the contrary, it is the product of the "mixed economy"—an economy which remains capitalistic in its basic structure, but in which the government stands ready to intervene by bestowing favors on some groups and imposing penalties on others.

(As used in this book, the term "mixed economy" is to be understood as what von Mises called a "hampered market economy." As he explains, an economic system is either a market economy, in which case its operations are determined by the initiative of private individuals motivated to make profits and avoid losses, or a socialist economy, in which case its operations are determined by the government. These two alternatives cannot be combined into an economy that would somehow be a mixture of mutually exclusive possibilities. Thus, the term "mixed economy" is to be understood in this book as denoting a hampered market economy.[45])

In contrast, under genuine capitalism—laissez-faire capitalism—the government has no favors to give and no arbitrary penalties to impose. It thus has nothing to offer pressure groups and creates no basis for pressure groups being formed out of considerations of self-defense.

The absurdity of the pressure-group mentality manifests itself in the further fact that it provides powerful support for the fear and hatred of self-interest emanating from altruism, and thus leads to the suppression of the pursuit of self-interest. The practitioners of pressure-group warfare are in the contradictory position of wanting to serve their own particular interests and yet, with good reason, simultaneously having to fear and oppose the pursuit of self-interest by others, since under pressure-group warfare, one man's gain actually is another's loss. The result is that while people strive to achieve their self-interest in their capacity as members of pressure groups, yet, in their capacity as citizens, they strive to create social conditions in which the pursuit of self-interest of any kind becomes more and more impossible. Because, given their mentality, they cannot help but regard the pursuit of self-interest as antisocial and thus must oppose it for everyone else.

In these ways, the irrational pursuit of self-interest represented by pressure group warfare actually represents people actively and powerfully working against their self-interest.

The practitioners of pressure group-warfare condemn economics because they do not understand it—indeed, may have made themselves incapable of understanding it. Their mental horizon is so narrow and confined that it does not extend beyond what promotes or impairs their immediate self-interest in their present investments and lines of work. They perceive the doctrines of economics entirely from that perspective. Thus, a shoe manufacturer of this type, who could not withstand foreign competition, hears economics' doctrine of free trade from no other perspective than that, if implemented, it would put him out of the shoe business. And thus he concludes that he has a self-interest in opposing the doctrine of free trade. And, for similar reasons, virtually every other doctrine of economics is opposed by the pressure groups concerned. To use the analogy to astronomy once more, it is as though people mistakenly concluded not only that the sun circled the earth and that morality itself supported the proposition, but also that their personal well-being required them to oppose any alternative explanation.

Economics Versus Irrationalism

The preceding discussion points to the most fundamental and serious difficulty economics encounters, which is a growing antipathy to reason and logic as such. Economics presupposes a willingness of the individual to open his mind to a view of the entire economic system extending over a long period of time, and to follow chains of deductive reasoning explaining the effects of things on all individuals and groups within the system, both in the long run and in the short run.[46] This broadness of outlook that economics presupposes is, unfortunately,

not often to be found in today's society. Under the influence of irrationalist philosophy, people doubt their ability to achieve understanding of fundamental and broad significance. They are unwilling to pursue matters to first causes and to rely on logic to explain effects not immediately evident.

In large part, people's reluctance to think has been the result of a two-centuries-long attack on the reliability of human reason by a series of philosophers from Immanuel Kant to Bertrand Russell—an attack which began soon after the birth of economic science. More than any other factor, this attack on the reliability of reason has been responsible for the perpetuation of the mentality of primitive man in the realm of economics.[47]

A leading consequence and manifestation of this attack has been the appearance of a series of irrationalist writers, who have come to the fore in field after field, and who have taken a positive delight in establishing the appearance of paradox and in seeming to overturn all that reason and logic had previously been thought to prove true beyond doubt. The most prominent figure of this type in economics is Keynes, who held that "Pyramid-building, earthquakes, even wars may serve to increase wealth, if the education of our statesmen on the principles of the classical economics stands in the way of anything better."[48] In other fields, renowned authorities proclaim that parallel lines meet, that electrons can cross from one orbit of an atom to another without traversing the interval in between, that an empty canvas or smears made by monkeys is a work of art, and that the clatter of falling garbage pails or a moment of silence is a work of music. And lest we should forget our recurrent example of the motion of the earth around the sun, contemporary philosophers assert that one cannot even be certain that the sun will rise tomorrow—that such a thing has no necessity, and will just "probably" occur.

The ability of such views to gain prominence already reflects an advanced state of philosophical corruption. Once established, they give the realm of ideas the aura of a dishonest game, a game that serious people are unwilling to play or to concern themselves with. At the same time, they open the floodgates to the dishonest. In the realm of economics, the establishment of such views has enormously encouraged the pressure groups and advocates of socialism, who have been enabled to propound their opposition to the teachings of economics under the sanction of an allegedly higher, more advanced "non-Euclidean economics." In addition, by depriving the intellect of credibility and substituting sophistry for science, their establishment has allowed demagogues to flourish as never before. The demagogues can count both on few serious opponents and on audiences not willing or able to understand such opponents. Thus, they have an open season in propounding all the absurd charges against capitalism that I described earlier.

Economics by itself certainly cannot reverse this epistemological current. Even more than in the case of ethics, that must come mainly from within philosophy. But economics, or any other special science, can certainly make an important contribution to that reversal by refuting the irrationalists within its own domain and by establishing the principle that within its domain intelligible natural law is, indeed, operative. In refuting the theories of Keynes and similar authors, it can show that in economics there is no basis for the advocacy of irrational theories and that reason prevails. This perhaps may help to set a pattern for the same kind of demonstration in other fields.

Economics, moreover, is uniquely qualified to demolish the apparent conflict between theory and practice which today's intellectuals experience in connection with the undeniable failure of socialism and success of capitalism. The overwhelming majority of today's intellectuals, it must be kept in mind, believe virtually every point of the indictment of capitalism described earlier in this section. Thus, from their perspective, socialism should have succeeded and capitalism have failed. They had to expect that Soviet Russia, with its alleged rational economic planning and concentration on the building up of heavy industry, should have achieved the kind of economic eminence that Japan has achieved under capitalism, and have done so long ago. At the same time, they had to expect that the United States and Western Europe should have fallen into greater and greater chaos and poverty.

Yet, despite everything they believe, and think they understand, socialism has failed, while capitalism has succeeded. Being unwilling to admit that they have been wrong in their beliefs—thoroughly, devastatingly wrong—they choose to interpret the failure of socialism and success of capitalism as proof of the impotence of the mind to grasp reality, and now turn en masse to supporting the ecology movement and its assault on science and technology.[49] In this way, ironically, the failure of socialism and success of capitalism have played an important role in accelerating the growth of irrationalism.

In presenting a correct theory of capitalism and socialism—that is, in explaining why in reason capitalism must result in a rising productivity of labor and improving standards of living, while socialism must culminate in economic chaos and a totalitarian dictatorship—economics reunites theory and practice in this vital area. It thereby reaffirms the power of the human mind and removes the failure of socialism and success of capitalism as any kind of pretext for irrationalism.

6. Economics and Capitalism: Science and Value

This is not a book on philosophy. It is not its purpose to validate the philosophy of the Enlightenment with respect to the fundamental questions of metaphysics, epistemology, or ethics. It simply takes for granted the reliability of reason as a tool of knowledge and the consequent value of man and the human individual. It leaves to philosophers the job of convincing those who do not share these convictions. Its domain is merely the principles of economics and the demonstration that capitalism is the system required for prosperity, progress, and peace.

Nevertheless, one philosophical question that must be briefly addressed here is the assertion that science and value should be kept separate and distinct—an assertion that is often made by advocates of socialism and interventionism when they are confronted with the advocacy of capitalism. This book obviously flies in the face of that demand, for it consistently seeks to forge a union between the science of economics and the value of capitalism.

Despite the prevailing view, this procedure is perfectly sound. The notion that science and value should be divorced is utterly contradictory. It itself expresses a value judgment in its very utterance. And it is not only self-contradictory, but contradictory of the most cherished principles of science as well. Science itself is built on a foundation of values that all scientists are logically obliged to defend: values such as reason, observation, truth, honesty, integrity, and the freedom of inquiry. In the absence of such values, there could be no science. The leading historical illustration of the truth of these propositions is the case of Galileo and the moral outrage which all lovers of science and truth must feel against those who sought to silence him.

It is nonsense to argue that science should be divorced from values. No one who makes this demand has ever been able consistently to practice it. What it is proper to say is that science should be divorced from *mere emotion*—that it must always be solidly grounded in observation and deduction. Irrational emotion should not be confused with dedication to values, however.

The basis of the value of capitalism is ultimately the same as the basis of the value of science, namely, human life and human reason. Capitalism is the social system necessary to the well-being and survival of human beings and to their life as rational beings. It is also necessary to the pursuit of science—to the pursuit of truth without fear of the initiation of physical force. These are all demonstrable propositions. The advocacy of capitalism by economists, therefore, should be no more remarkable, and no more grounds for objection, than the advocacy of health by medical doctors.[50]

Notes

1. For an account of the change that has taken place in the definition of economics, see Israel M. Kirzner, *The Economic Point of View* (New York: D. Van Nostrand, 1960).

2. I could also say that economics is the science which studies the production of wealth under a system of division of labor *and* monetary exchange, or under a system of division of labor *and* capitalism. (See below, p. 19, the first two paragraphs of Part B of this chapter.) Both of these statements would be correct, but they would also be redundant, because, as later discussion will show, a system of division of labor presupposes both monetary exchange and all the other essential institutions of a capitalist society. Finally, the expression goods and services could be substituted for the word wealth. This too would yield a true statement about what economics studies. But, as will be shown, a certain priority and emphasis must be given to wealth as opposed to services.

3. Secondarily and peripherally to its study of the production of wealth under a system of division of labor, economics also studies the production of wealth under the absence of division of labor. It does so insofar as by so doing it can develop its theorems under simplifying assumptions that will enable it to shed light on the operations of a division-of-labor society, and insofar as by so doing it can place the value of a division-of-labor society in its proper light, by contrasting it with non-division-of-labor societies.

4. In the second century A.D., the Roman Empire extended from Syria in the southeast to the northern border of present-day England in the northwest. It circled the Mediterranean Sea, embracing Egypt and all of North Africa, and included all of Europe west of the Rhine, as well as present-day Romania and Turkey and all of Eastern Europe south of the Danube. Goods produced in the various regions of the Empire were consumed throughout the Empire. For example, pottery made in Syria was consumed as far away as England, and tin mined in England was consumed as far away as Syria.

5. Because of its primary application to government policy, it is understandable why the subject was originally known as political economy, which was its name from the time of Adam Smith to the last quarter of the nineteenth century, when the change to "economics" took place.

6. See below, pp. 473–498, 544–548, 559–580, and pp. 603–668.

7. I am indebted to von Mises for this view of what economics has to offer historians and journalists. Cf. Ludwig von Mises, *Epistemological Problems of Economics,* trans. George Reisman (Princeton, N. J.: D. Van Nostrand, 1960), pp. 27–30, 99–102.

8. Cf. Ludwig von Mises, *Socialism* (New Haven: Yale University Press, 1951), p. 402; reprint ed. (Indianapolis: Liberty Classics, 1981). Page references are to the Yale University Press edition; pagination from this edition is retained in the reprint edition.

9. On this subject, see below, pp. 462–498.

10. For elaboration, see below, pp. 42–49 and 542–559.

11. See the writings of Ayn Rand for a consistent elaboration of the "benevolent universe premise" across the entire range of human activity.

12. For a discussion of the ideas of Marx and Engels on "alien-

ation," see below, pp. 129–130.

13. See above, the discussion of mathematical economics on pp. 8–9. See also below, pp. 158–161.

14. See Bernard Siegan, *Economic Liberties and the Constitution* (Chicago: University of Chicago Press, 1980).

15. This section was inspired by and draws heavily on the content of a lecture delivered by Dr. Leonard Peikoff in Chicago, in May 1980, under the title "The Philosophic Basis of Capitalism," before the Inflation and Gold Seminar of the US Paper Exchange/Tempor Corporation.

16. Ayn Rand, "Man's Rights," in Ayn Rand, *The Virtue of Selfishness* (New York: New American Library, 1964), pp. 124–125.

17. See below, pp. 27–28.

18. On these points, cf. Ayn Rand, "The Nature of Government," in Ayn Rand, *Virtue of Selfishness.*

19. Cf. ibid.

20. In a fully consistent capitalist society, taxation itself would be of a voluntary nature. On this subject see Ayn Rand, "Government Financing in a Free Society," in Ayn Rand, *Virtue of Selfishness.*

21. Again, cf. Ayn Rand, "The Nature of Government," in *Virtue of Selfishness.*

22. See below, pp. 343–371, 513–514, 542–594 passim, and 938–942.

23. It should be realized that even if much of the savings individuals presently pay into the social security system were invested in housing, as they likely would be, those savings would indirectly still contribute to investment in factories and machinery. This is because savings would then not have to be withdrawn from financing factories and machinery to financing housing, as is presently the case because of the vast siphoning off of personal savings caused by the social security system.

24. The problem of the economic insecurity of prospective social security recipients (and of everyone else) is compounded by the fact that an inevitable accompaniment of the welfare state is fiat money, which makes all contractual obligations stated in fixed sums of money essentially meaningless. On these points, see below, pp. 925–926 and 930–931.

25. It should go without saying that the context taken for granted in the reference to antipornography legislation is one in which all the parties involved are freely consenting adults.

26. The following discussion is essentially an application of principles set forth by Ayn Rand in criticizing the use of the word *censorship* in reference to the actions of private individuals. Cf. Ayn Rand, "Man's Rights," in Ayn Rand, *Virtue of Selfishness,* especially pp. 131–134.

27. Cf. ibid., pp. 128–130.

28. Ibid.

29. See below, pp. 375–387 and 238. The contrasting meanings of the right to medical care are discussed on p. 380. Concerning this last subject, see also George Reisman, *The Real Right to Medical Care Versus Socialized Medicine,* a pamphlet (Laguna Hills, Calif.: The Jefferson School of Philosophy, Economics, and Psychology, 1994).

30. For further discussion of the distortions introduced into the concept of freedom of labor and present in the notion of "wage slavery," see below, pp. 330–332.

31. I am indebted to von Mises for the substance of this discussion. See Ludwig von Mises, *Human Action,* 3d ed. rev. (Chicago: Henry Regnery Co., 1966), pp. 734–736.

32. Concerning the fact that the division of labor originates on the basis of differences in human abilities and in the conditions of people's natural surroundings, see von Mises, *Socialism*, pp. 292–293.

33. On the fact that money originates in the self-interested actions of individuals, see Carl Menger, *Principles of Economics* (Glencoe, Ill.: The Free Press, 1950), pp. 257–262. See also below, pp. 506–517.

34. These factors also operate to create a steadily growing supply of useable, accessible natural resources. See below, pp. 63–67.

35. See below, pp. 123–133.

36. See above, p. 19, the opening paragraph of Section 1 of Part B, of the present chapter.

37. See below, pp. 938–941.

38. In most of the world, unfortunately, the history of private property is not so simple. Again and again, owners were forcibly dispossessed by foreign invaders, by civil wars and revolutions, and by other expropriations carried out by governments. Nevertheless, one of the things that later discussion will show is that even where holdings of private property can be traced back to acts of force, the operations of a capitalist society steadily wash away these stains. Once a few generations have gone by, during which private property no longer passes by force, but by purchase, the result is virtually the same as if it had never passed by force. For a discussion of this point and also of the alleged injustices committed specifically against the American Indians in the process of appropriating land in North America, see below, pp. 317–319. See also Ludwig von Mises, *Socialism*, p. 504.

39. In the last generation, Japan, Taiwan, and South Korea have achieved even more rapid rates of economic progress than the United States did in its era of greatest progress. But the rapidity of their advance is largely the result of being able to take advantage of the enormous heritage of innovations pioneered by and bequeathed to them by the United States.

40. See below, pp. 99–106.

41. The leading manifestation of this worldview is the Marxian exploitation theory and the "liberal" political agenda that rests on it. See below, pp. 603–604.

42. The nature of these fallacies, along with most of their leading manifestations, has been brilliantly dissected by Henry Hazlitt, *Economics in One Lesson,* new ed. (New Rochelle, N. Y.: Arlington House Publishers, 1979), and by Frederic Bastiat in his *Economic Sophisms*, trans. Arthur Goddard (New York: D. Van Nostrand, 1964).

43. See below, pp. 618–663, 930–937.

44. On this subject see below, pp. 712–714.

45. See von Mises, *Human Action,* pp. 258–259. Also, see below, pp. 263–264.

46. Cf. Henry Hazlitt, *Economics in One Lesson*, pp. 15–19.

47. Among the most important and comprehensive writings on the subject of irrationalism and its destructive influence are those of Ayn Rand, virtually all of whose works shed profound light on it. See, for example, *Atlas Shrugged* (New York: Random House, 1957) and the title essay in *For the New Intellectual* (New York: Random House, 1961). See also the book of her leading intellectual disciple Leonard Peikoff, *The Ominous Parallels: The End of Freedom in America* (New York: Stein and Day, 1982). The works of von Mises also stress the destructive influence of irrationalism in all matters pertaining to economics and capitalism and are extremely valuable in this regard. See in particular, *Human Action* and *Socialism*.

48. J. M. Keynes, *The General Theory of Employment, Interest, and Money* (New York: Harcourt, Brace, 1936), p. 129.

49. See below, pp. 99–106.

50. For a philosophic demonstration of the wider union of fact and value, see the excellent essay "Fact and Value" by Leonard Peikoff in *The Intellectual Activist* 5, no. 1 (May 18, 1989).

CHAPTER 2

WEALTH AND ITS ROLE IN HUMAN LIFE

1. Wealth and Goods

Wealth is material goods made by man. It is houses and automobiles, piles of lumber and bars of copper, steel mills and pipelines, foodstuffs and clothing. It is also land and natural resources in the ground insofar as man has made them useable and accessible. Man, of course, does not make the material stuff of land and natural resources, but he certainly does create their character as wealth.[1]

Air, sunlight, rainfall, and wind are also material goods. But insofar as they come to us automatically, without any need for labor or effort on our part to cause their existence or our benefit from them, they are outside the province of economic activity and of economics. They are nature-given conditions that automatically benefit us; historically, they have been described as *free goods*. Economics deals only with those goods which are the object of economic activity, that is, which man needs to produce in some sense—goods whose existence or beneficial relationship to his well-being he needs to cause in his capacity as a thinking being, that is, on whose behalf he must expend labor or effort. Such goods are *economic goods*.[2] In saying that wealth is goods, we refer only to economic goods; we exclude free goods.

Some implications of the fact that wealth consists of goods must be named.

Wealth is not at all synonymous with money or monetary value. The wealth produced in an economic system and the total monetary value of that wealth are separate and distinct phenomena. The one can increase without the other. More wealth can exist totally apart from more money. More wealth produced in the form of ordinary commodities, like steel, sugar, automobiles, and so on, without any increase in the supply of money, is nonetheless more wealth; but in such circumstances it results in correspondingly lower prices, and no increase in the total monetary value of commodities. By the same token, more money and more monetary value can exist totally apart from more wealth. This happens almost every day under a system of fiat paper money, where the supply of money is determined by the wishes of the government, irrespective of the supply of goods. In such circumstances, the effect of the additional money is simply to raise prices.

A connection between the quantity of money and the amount of wealth would exist only if money consisted of gold or silver. Even then, it would be a highly imperfect connection. Under such circumstances, an increase in the supply of gold or silver would constitute both an increase in the supply of money and an increase in the supply of wealth insofar as more gold and silver in their capacity as industrial materials meant more wealth. A further connection would exist insofar as increases in the supply of money under such circumstances tended to exist as the by-product of general improvements in the ability to produce, that is, insofar as a larger supply of gold or silver was the result of improvements in machinery, transportation, and so forth, having wider application than merely to the mining of the precious metals. In reality, all the popular measures of the production of wealth expressed in terms of totals of money, such as Gross Domestic

Product (GDP) (formerly Gross National Product or GNP) and National Income, are nothing but indicators of the quantity of money, not the physical volume of goods produced.[3]

Stocks, bonds, and bank deposits are also not wealth. They are claims to wealth—to the plant and equipment and inventories of firms issuing the stocks or bonds or borrowing from the banks; to the houses or automobiles of the consumers who have borrowed; or, in the case of unsecured loans, to the equivalent of the goods that would otherwise be purchasable by the borrowers with their incomes.

Nor is the market value of licenses, or legal rights in any form, wealth; this includes the market value of perfectly proper legal rights such as patents and copyrights. Government licenses, such as liquor licenses, derive their market value from the privilege they confer on their holders to *restrict the production of wealth* and thereby artificially to increase the incomes of the license holders.[4] While patents on new inventions and copyrights on other new intellectual creations greatly contribute to the production of wealth by providing incentives to the development of new ideas underlying the production of wealth, neither the ideas themselves nor the patents and copyrights which protect and promote them are wealth. The ideas are preconditions to the production of wealth, but not wealth itself. And the patents and copyrights derive their market value from the fact that they make it possible for the intellectual creators of new and additional wealth to benefit from their contributions by temporarily limiting the increase in wealth that their intellectual contributions bring about. When patents and copyrights expire, the supply of wealth further increases at the same time that the market value of the patents and copyrights vanishes.[5]

Finally, the labor of people, and their persons, while also indispensable preconditions to the production of wealth are never themselves wealth, but merely preconditions to the production of wealth. This is true even in a society in which slavery exists. In such a society, the fact that slaves possess market value no more qualifies them as wealth than the fact that government licenses restricting production possess market value qualifies them as wealth. Indeed, slavery reduces the production of wealth far more than do restrictive government licenses: it attacks production at its very root by depriving people of the incentive to produce.[6]

Thus, wealth must be distinguished from the wider concept of property possessing market value. Property possessing market value that is not itself wealth exists, as we have seen, in such forms as various legal rights to wealth, such as stocks and bonds, and in various legal rights, proper or improper, to restrict or limit the produc-

tion of wealth, such as government licenses and patents and copyrights. Property that is not wealth—that, indeed, is the destroyer of wealth—but that nonetheless possesses market value is what exists in the case of slavery.

The meaning of wealth depends on the meaning of goods. More or less following Menger, the founder of the Austrian school of economics, we can define goods—economic goods—as *things which are recognized as capable of satisfying human needs, requiring the expenditure of labor or effort in order to be produced or enjoyed, and over which one has sufficient command gainfully to direct them to the satisfaction of one's needs.*[7] In other words, goods are things actually capable of benefiting us, that is, of doing us personal good, provided that we make the necessary effort to secure their benefit. Our wealth is the collection of material goods which we possess or against which we hold enforceable claims.[8]

Things which have the power to satisfy our needs but which we do not recognize as possessing that power are not goods and do not form part of our wealth. For example, before the second half of the nineteenth century, petroleum was not a good; before the twentieth century, uranium was not a good. People did not know the beneficial properties of petroleum or uranium and thus did not know how to use them for anything. Thus, at the time, such things could do them no actual good and were therefore not goods and not a part of wealth. (The only circumstance in which a thing could do us good without our being aware of its beneficial properties, and thus without our having to take action based on such awareness, would be if its benefit came to us automatically, that is, if it were a free good. For a thing to be an *economic* good, it is essential that we possess awareness of its beneficial properties.)

In the same way, even if technological knowledge exists concerning the usefulness of a given type of mineral, all of the specific deposits of the mineral which are as yet undiscovered are not goods and do not constitute wealth. They too can do us no actual good in such a case. Further, things are not goods and do not constitute wealth whose useful properties and specific locations are known, but over which we lack sufficient command to direct them to the satisfaction of our needs. For example, iron on Mars, or even fifty miles down in the Earth, is not a good and not wealth, even if we are aware of its specific location, given our present inability to gain access to it. By the same token, water in the United States is not a good to someone wandering in the Sahara. Manufactured products too are not goods to those who have no knowledge of their existence or cannot gain access to them.

Finally, things are not goods and do not constitute wealth even if their useful properties and specific locations are known and even if we have sufficient command over them to direct them to the satisfaction of our needs, if we cannot *gainfully* direct them to the satisfaction of our needs. For example, vast stretches of land in the United States which could be used to grow crops if someone decided to do so, are not actually goods and not wealth, because their potential could be exploited only by withdrawing capital and labor from other employments where the product of the capital and labor is greater. (These other employments could be more productive farmland, or nonagricultural employments whose product is more important than an addition to the supply of farm products.) The use of such land to grow crops would thus not achieve our actual good, all things considered, but would inflict a loss in comparison with what could be produced without its use. Thus, such land does not constitute a good and is not part of wealth. (It is possible, of course, that such things, presently not goods, could someday become goods and thus wealth—if, for example, the costs of exploiting them could be reduced, or if a growing population provided labor and capital that had no better alternatives to which to be applied. To some extent, such things may be valued as goods and count as wealth in the present, in anticipation of their being able to accomplish actual good in the future.)

Just as the beneficial properties of things can fail to be recognized, it sometimes happens that beneficial properties are ascribed to things which do not in fact possess them, such as the beneficial properties some people ascribe to rabbit's feet, tarot cards, and so on. We can join with Menger in characterizing such things as "imaginary goods." It is not necessary, however, for economics to devote any special consideration to such goods beyond acknowledging the fact of their existence. This is both because they constitute unimportant exceptions and because the economic principles that apply to such goods, such as the laws of price determination, are the same as that apply to genuine goods.

Again following Menger, we can divide goods into various orders, corresponding to their closeness to, or remoteness from, the satisfaction of our needs and wants. Goods that stand in a direct causal relationship to the satisfaction of our needs and wants can be described as goods of the first order. These are the things that benefit us directly and that are, therefore, directly good. For example, the food we eat, the clothes we wear. Those goods, in turn, that are necessary to the production of goods of the first order can be described as goods of the second order. For example, the ingredients and implements required to prepare a meal; the cloth, sewing machines, and thread required to produce clothes. Similarly, those goods that are necessary to the production of goods of the second order can be described as goods of the third order, and so on. The advantage of this termi-

nology is that it highlights the fact that the source of the goods-character of things is ultimately *within us.* Goods derive their character as goods by virtue of their ability to benefit human beings. Goods-character radiates outward from people to things and touches first those goods which we categorize as goods of the first order, second, those which we categorize as goods of the second order, and so on.[9]

2. Economics and Wealth

The fact that economics is a science of wealth was taken for granted by the classical economists in the nineteenth century. Economics' focus on wealth has been challenged in the twentieth century, however, and a large majority of economists now downplays its special importance in the subject.

One challenge is constituted by the frequent assertion that our economy has become a "service economy" rather than an economy which concentrates on the production of goods. The basis of this assertion is the fact that more than half of the working population is now employed in rendering services rather than producing goods.

This service-economy argument against the focus on wealth is superficial, for the following reason. Not only are agriculture, mining, construction, and manufacturing all engaged in the production of goods, but also *all of the so-called service industries center on goods.* Retailing and wholesaling—service industries—are the retailing and wholesaling of *goods.* Cleaning, repair, and maintenance services are the cleaning, repair, and maintenance of *goods.* Transportation and communications are largely transportation of, and communications concerning, *goods.* Banking, finance, insurance, and advertising are services performed overwhelmingly in connection with facilitating the production, distribution, or ownership of *goods.*

Those services that are performed not as auxiliaries to the production, distribution, or ownership of goods—services such as passenger airline travel for vacationers, personal communications, personal medical, legal, or grooming services—vitally depend on the use of goods in their rendition. There could be no passenger airline travel without airplanes and airports; no telephone service without telephones and telephone exchanges; no mail service without post offices and delivery trucks; precious few medical services without drugs, hospitals, laboratories, and all manner of equipment; precious few legal services without courthouses, law offices, law books, law schools, memo pads, and so on; and precious few grooming services without scissors, razors, hair dryers, and the like. The rendition of personal services falls within the sphere of economics insofar as the providers of such services render them *for the purpose of acquiring wealth*. As will be seen, in a division-of-labor society this refers to the rendition of such services for the purpose of earning money. Thus, the services of personal physicians, personal attorneys, barbers, and the like come within the sphere of economics insofar as they are performed for money, which is the means by which these parties obtain wealth.

It is true, of course, that there could be no wealth without the rendition of services—above all, the performance of labor. But this does not give services an equal position with wealth in economics. Although economics is concerned with services, it is so only insofar as they are necessary to the production, enjoyment, or acquisition of wealth, or depend on the use of wealth. Economics is not at all concerned with the rendition of services apart from their connection with wealth. For example, when two people hold an interesting conversation, they are rendering a service to each other. But economics is not concerned with activities of this nature except insofar as they can be connected with wealth.

It could be argued that the direct exchange of services for services also sometimes falls within the sphere of economics—for example, an exchange of French lessons for mathematics lessons, in which the rendition of each service is performed as the conscious, explicitly agreed-upon requirement of receiving the other. Even in such cases, what brings the rendition of the service within the purview of economics is ultimately a connection to wealth. This is so because what makes exchange itself a vital economic phenomenon, central to the studies of economics, is the fact that in a division-of-labor society the production and enjoyment of wealth requires it, as the means of bringing goods from their producers to their consumers.[10]

The second challenge to economics' focus on wealth is the mistaken claim that economics is a science of choices rather than a science of wealth—a science which studies the "allocation of scarce means among competing ends."[11]

This contention rests on a logical fallacy. It does not see that what gives rise to economics' study of choices and its concern with the allocation of scarce means among competing ends is the fact that people have a virtually limitless need for *wealth* but only a limited capability of satisfying that need at any given time. Thus, people must choose which aspects of their need for wealth are to be satisfied and which are not. Economics studies the determinants of human choice only insofar as they concern choices of how to spend incomes that are of necessity limited, and only insofar as they affect the attraction of capital and labor to the production of some goods rather than other goods. In other words, it studies

the issue of choices for no other reason than that it is necessary to do so as part of its study of the production of wealth under a system of division of labor.

To claim that economics is on this account a science of human choices rather than of wealth is to confuse an aspect of the science with its totality. To adopt this view is to be led to ignore all the really crucial matters that economics deals with and to seek esoteric extensions of the subject that have nothing whatever to do with its actual nature. Fortunately, those who adopt this view are highly inconsistent in its application and generally continue to devote most of their attention to the serious business of economics and leave the alleged necessity of extending the subject beyond the domain of wealth as a task to be carried out in the indefinite future.[12]

3. The Limitless Need and Desire for Wealth

The leading propositions laid down in Chapter 1 were that economics is the science that studies the production of wealth under a system of division of labor and that capitalism is the essential requirement for the successful functioning of a division-of-labor society, indeed, ultimately for its very existence. It is implicit in these propositions that the ultimate source of the importance of the division of labor and capitalism, and of the science of economics, is *wealth*. This is because, in the last analysis, the division of labor, capitalism, and the science of economics are all merely means to the production of wealth.

Nevertheless, many philosophers and religious thinkers have held that the production of wealth serves only a low order of needs of secondary importance and that concern with its production beyond the minimum necessities required for the sustenance of human life is evil, immoral, and sinful by virtue of elevating low material values to the place properly reserved only for the pursuit of noble spiritual values. If these beliefs were correct, then economics would at best be a science of secondary importance and preoccupation with it by serious thinkers would be a mark of perversity.

In the face of such attitudes, it is incumbent upon economics to justify itself by providing philosophical validation for the production of wealth being a central, continuing concern of human existence. In other words, economics must explain the role of wealth in human life beyond that of the food, clothing, and shelter required for immediate sustenance. It is necessary to show how the continuing rise in the productivity of human labor made possible by the division of labor and capitalism serves *objectively demonstrable human needs*—to show, indeed, why there is no limit to man's need for wealth. Only on the basis of an objectively demonstrable need for wealth without limit is there a full and secure foundation for the need for the division of labor and capitalism and the continuous economic progress they bring, and for the science of economics.

Human Reason and the Scope and Perfectibility of Need Satisfactions

Man's need for wealth is limitless because he possesses the faculty of reason. The possession of this faculty both radically enlarges the scope of man's needs and capacities in comparison with those of any other living entity and, at the same time, makes possible continuous improvement in the satisfaction of his needs and in the exercise of his capacities. Considered abstractly, man's possession of reason gives him the potential for a limitless range of knowledge and awareness and thus for a limitless range of action and experience. Man's mind can grasp the existence both of subatomic particles and of galaxies, and of everything in between. It observes all manner of patterns and similarities and differences, of which no other form of consciousness is capable. Thus, the potential is created for man to act over a range extending from the subatomic level to the remotest reaches of outer space, and to experience all that his mind enables him to discern and enjoy in the totality of the universe.

Material goods—wealth—are the physical means both of acting in the world (for example, automobiles and airplanes, tools and machines of all kinds) and of enjoying the experiences of which man is capable (for example—in addition to many of the goods in the preceding category—works of art and sculpture, landscaped grounds and gardens, beautiful homes and furniture). They are the instrumentalities of man's action and objects of his contemplation. The potential of a limitless range of action and experience implies a limitless need for wealth as the means of achieving this potential. Man needs wealth without limit if he is to fulfill his limitless potential as a rational being in physical reality.

This abstract principle can be illustrated in a wide variety of forms, starting with the contribution of additional wealth to the improved satisfaction of man's elementary needs for nutrition and health. Because man possesses reason, and is thus able to abstract, form concepts, and think conceptually, his mind is able to grasp connections spanning generations and continents between his material well-being and the physical state of the world. Thus, for man, functioning on the conceptual level, the satisfaction just of the needs for nutrition and health implies a practically limitless need and desire for wealth: in the form of canning and freezing facilities, a modern transportation and communications system, a farm-equipment industry, and everything that is necessary to the existence of these things, such as the steel, oil,

and coal industries, the transportation and communications equipment industries, and so on. All such wealth is necessary to an adequate quantity and sufficient variety of food to meet man's nutritional needs. Likewise, man's need for health further implies a need not only for medicines, hospitals, and all manner of diagnostic and therapeutic equipment and everything necessary to their existence, but extends even to such seemingly unrelated things as automobiles and space travel: the former made possible the ability of people to live in the fresh air of the suburbs and also the modern ambulance; the latter holds out the possibility of such things as recuperation from heart disease in an environment of reduced gravity.

Reason gives to man the ability to use wealth progressively to enhance the exercise of the capacities he shares in common with lesser species. For example, man shares with animals the capacity for locomotion. Animals can do no better than rely on their unaided legs. Man domesticates the horse, the elephant, and the camel. He produces shoes and builds roads, rafts, and sailing vessels. He goes further and invents the railroad, the steamship, and the automobile; and then the airplane and the rocketship. Similarly, man shares with the animals the capacity to see and hear. Animals can do no more than rely on their unaided eyes and ears, but man produces telescopes, microscopes, and stethoscopes; television sets and radios; eyeglasses and hearing aids; X-ray machines and computers; motion pictures and VCRs; and phonographs, compact-disk players, and tape recorders.

As noted, the fact that man is the rational being also gives him a wider range of capacities than is possessed by any of the lesser species. Because man is the rational being, he is able to pursue such activities as music, art, science, and athletics. He is able to form relationships with others which are maintained even though the parties may be separated by great distances and for long intervals of time. It is the nature of man's brain that enables him to integrate separate sounds into harmonies and melodies, to grasp representations and thus the meaning of a painting, to pursue science, to follow the system of rules of a game of sport, and to maintain an awareness of others from whom he is separated by time and distance. These are feats of which an animal's brain is incapable. In the pursuit of all of these additional activities made possible by the possession of reason, wealth either is absolutely indispensable or, at a minimum, enormously contributes to the performance and enjoyment of the activity.

Wealth contributes to music when it takes the form of musical instruments, music books and scores, concert halls and conservatories, radios, phonographs, and tape recorders. If music were deprived of the existence of these forms of wealth, the activity would be reduced to the unaided, untrained, and largely unheard singing of the human voice. In the absence of wealth in the form of brushes, paints, and canvases, of museums, schools, and books of art, art would be reduced to primitive drawings on the walls of caves. In the absence of wealth in the form of scientific equipment, laboratories, universities, and libraries, science could not be pursued. In the absence of wealth in the form of playing fields, athletic equipment, stadiums, and radio and television sets, athletic events and the enjoyment derived from them would suffer a radical decline. In the absence of wealth in the form of pens and paper, post offices, telephones, automobiles, railroads, ships, and planes, friendships and other human relationships could not be maintained over long distances.

On the basis of these observations, it is obvious that the ancient prejudice that man's desire for wealth serves his "lower" needs is absurd. Wealth is the material means of carrying on virtually *every* human activity and of serving virtually all of man's needs. It is man's means of acting in accordance with his human potential.

Moreover, even the wealth that does serve man's "lower" needs, such as, presumably, his needs for nutrition and elimination, also reflects his nature as a rational being, in ways beyond those already described. When man serves his "lower" needs, he does so in a manner that is unique to him—in a manner that reflects the distinctive nature of his consciousness. For example, when man eats, he does not do so in the manner of an animal, indifferent to his surroundings. On the contrary, he desires such things as tables and chairs, table linen, china, silverware, and so on. He is also highly sensitive to the preparation of his food and to the combinations in which it is served. When man eliminates, he desires the existence of such things as indoor plumbing and privacy. In such activities, the nature of man's consciousness requires the incorporation of psychological and aesthetic elements into the satisfaction of what in animals are merely physical needs. For man, at least in his waking hours, there is probably no such thing as a purely physical need. Man's physical needs are intimately connected with his psychology as a rational being—as a being aware of such things as patterns and harmonies and dissonances in shapes, sounds, and colors, and possessing the need to organize his activities and control the functions of his body. In everything he does, man can be aware of his own emotional responses and can distinguish between aesthetic elements which enable him to have a more enjoyable or a less enjoyable emotional response.

Thus, the aesthetic element enters into the satisfaction of virtually all of man's needs. It leads him to desire not just clothing and shelter, but clothing and shelter with style and beauty. It leads him to desire not just "transportation," but automobiles with chrome trim and whitewall tires. Matters of design and appearance feature prominently in all consumers' goods where men are free to choose.

Closely related to man's need for aesthetic satisfaction is his need for novelty and variety, which need also emanates from the rational nature of his consciousness. The lower animals do not become bored with the repetition of the same routine. Man does. The nature of man's consciousness enables him to appreciate differences of a kind of which animals show no apparent awareness, and seems to require that he periodically experience such differences. Thus, whereas animals are content to eat the same food day in and day out, man requires a variety of food. Man experiences a sense of intellectual refreshment when he breaks his routine and takes a vacation or a weekend off. He also experiences a sense of intellectual refreshment in the introduction and possession of new goods, and with the coming of style changes.

Thus, the appearance of almost every new "gadget" is an occasion for a kind of excitement: it is a thrill for a rational consciousness to see such new products appear (each in its day) as automobiles, airplanes, refrigerators, radios, television sets, pocket calculators, computers, and so on. The purchase of such goods is almost always an occasion for special pleasure, because it provides something new and valuable to experience. Even the replacement purchases of such goods are usually a source of pleasure, because further improvements have usually been made in them, and because of style changes. Changes in style, whether in automobiles, clothing, or furniture, are a source of intellectual refreshment and pleasure, because they provide a sense of the new and different.

It must be stressed that man's desire for novelty and variety stands in the service of his life. The principle is very similar to that of the pursuit of scientific knowledge, where the motive is curiosity and the effect is all manner of practical applications that could not have been foreseen in advance. In just this way people originally desired automobiles not as a practical means of transportation, but as an object of amusement. Yet this desire led to the growth of the automobile industry and to the transformation of the economic system. A similar course of development occurred in the case of electric light and power, and telephones and television sets, and now seems to be under way in the case of home and personal computers.

Even if no practical applications ever result directly from the things desired, their being desired produces practical results. For example, a great industrialist's motive in earning additional millions on top of those he already has may be merely to add to his collection of fine paintings and statues. But in pursuing this motive, the industrialist is led to introduce products and methods of production that enable the average person to obtain such things as more and better food, clothing, and transportation.

Man's life gains incalculably from the fact that his activities are not limited to the "practical," but are undertaken largely for the sheer pleasure of experiencing the new and different and the corresponding expansion of his own powers required to accomplish it. For this leads him to do things that have practical results which would otherwise be impossible for him to obtain. In effect, reason serves man's life in being free to serve itself. Although man's life may not need every particular object of his desire for novelty and variety, it very much does need the existence of his desire for novelty and variety.

On the basis of the existence of an objectively limitless need for wealth, there is no limit to man's desire for wealth. The occasional cases that exist of individuals in whom the desire for additional wealth is totally repressed are comparable in their frequency and significance to the cases of individuals in whom sexual desire is totally repressed. These cases are rare indeed. Even medieval monks, for example, thoroughly committed to the doctrine of asceticism, were torn by the temptation for material things. The truth lies with Adam Smith, who observed that "the desire of food is limited in every man by the narrow capacity of the human stomach; but the desire of the conveniences and ornaments of building, dress, equipage, and household furniture seems to have no limit or certain boundary."[13]

To translate Smith's observation into contemporary terms, we can observe as the overwhelming norm such things as that the man who has no automobile would like to be able to afford one. The man who has an automobile would like to be able to afford a newer, better one. The man who has several new automobiles of the highest quality would like to be able to afford a yacht or a plane. If he is rich enough to afford both a yacht and a plane, then he would like to be able to afford a yacht on which the plane can land, and so on. Similarly, the man who has a small house or apartment would like to be able to afford a larger one. If he has a large house or apartment, then he would like a more luxurious one—perhaps with a swimming pool or tennis court, or both; and with finely landscaped grounds. And he would probably like to have more than one house or apartment—perhaps a hunting lodge in Maine, a winter home in Palm Beach, an apartment in Paris, or, indeed, all three of them. The more one has, the more one wants.

The fact that both the need and the desire for additional wealth are limitless for all practical purposes does not mean, however, that people automatically act to satisfy that need and desire. It is certainly possible for the

need and desire for additional wealth to fail to result in the production of additional wealth, let alone in continuous economic progress. Indeed, history and most of the world around us are characterized by stagnation and poverty. The mere possession of a need or desire is never sufficient to ensure that the need or desire will be satisfied. In the absence of the influence of a rational philosophy establishing limited government and economic freedom and inculcating such convictions as that the material world has both reality and primacy, that it is intelligible, and that hard work pays, man is not able to devote himself sufficiently to the production of wealth.[14]

In such conditions, man desires more wealth than he possesses, but his desire is not strong enough or consistent enough to enable him actually to go and produce additional wealth. And if it is strong enough to induce him to increase his production, he is again and again stopped from doing so because of the initiation of physical force by others. Even when the barrier of physical force temporarily relaxes and some individuals are able to make some improvements, the absence of a rational philosophy precludes the development of science. It also precludes the establishment of sufficient freedom to make possible the development of the division of labor and the other capitalistic institutions necessary to the continuous increase in wealth.

As a result, despite the existence of both a need and a desire for additional wealth on the part of those affected, we witness such phenomena as masses of people dying of starvation, yet unable—indeed, sometimes even unwilling to expend the effort—to produce additional food. We witness primitive people delighted with the gift of mirrors and trinkets of all kinds, not to mention transistor radios and bicycles, yet continuing to live under essentially the same conditions as their remotest ancestors.

Progress and Happiness

The fact that the need and desire for wealth are limitless does not mean that when people devote themselves to satisfying that need and desire, as in the nations of modern capitalism, they go through life with a sense of endless frustration, seeking more than they can ever hope to obtain. The normal man, if he lacks an automobile, does not actively desire a yacht. He actively desires merely an automobile. His desire for a yacht lies dormant until such time as he already has acquired one or more high-quality automobiles. The limitless desire for wealth, in other words, becomes active only step by step. It manifests itself in an active desire for things that are merely one or two steps beyond our reach at the moment. It leads us to exert ourselves and extend our reach. And then, as we succeed, desires previously dormant become active, or totally new desires are formed, and we are led to exert ourselves and extend our reach still further. Thus, the limitless desire for wealth impels us steadily to advance.

Oriental philosophy and some schools of thought in the contemporary Western world claim that the fact that our desires will always be a step ahead of our possessions shows the futility of our efforts—that, instead, we should seek to rid ourselves of our desires and be content forever with some minimum of wealth. Such teachings are utterly mistaken, and their influence helps to account for the stagnation and poverty that exist in the world. They view the excess of our desires over our possessions as a source of discontent and unhappiness. Actually, this excess is the root of our ambitiousness and our rising to meet challenges. It is what impels us to progress, and, as such, is an essential element of our happiness.

It should be realized that as rational beings we are also progressive beings. Progress is the corollary of the continuous application of reason. Any individual who continues to use reason—who continues to think—necessarily comes to know more and more, and thus to be capable of accomplishing more and more. If a society is characterized by continuous thinking from generation to generation, and if its educational system works—that is, if it succeeds in transmitting to the rising generation the essentials of the knowledge discovered by all the preceding generations—then the general body of knowledge in the society is progressive, and thus the society as a whole is capable of accomplishing more and more. Progress is the natural result of the use of reason as a constant.

If our happiness depends on living in accordance with our nature as rational beings, then our happiness and progress are inseparably connected. The fact that our desires will always be ahead of our ability to satisfy them is not a cause of unhappiness. It is the inducement to the steady exercise of our reason, to our living in accordance with our nature, which is indispensable to our happiness. Our happiness does not come from the existence of desires satisfied, but from the steady upward climb itself—from the process of continuing to think and solve problems and to become capable of accomplishing more and more. In other words, progress is a source of happiness. In the lives of scientists, inventors, businessmen, engineers, and managers, progress is the obvious focal point of thinking, planning, and problem solving. It is also what necessitates that the average worker make himself capable of continuing to think and learn throughout his life, so that he can acquire the new skills necessary to adapt to the changing requirements of production. Thus, progress is what helps to elevate even the average man of modern Western civilization into a thinking, literate being possessing an intellectual life incomparably superior to that of previous eras. If happiness depends

on the possession of a sound, active mind, progress fosters happiness.

A further aspect of the connection between progress, reason, and happiness must be mentioned. As rational beings, we are able to be aware of the future: the future has reality for us in the present. To be able to look forward to a better future enables us to bear considerable hardship in the present without complaint, even cheerfully. But to look to a future of unrelieved hardship, or, worse, a future that holds out the prospect of even greater hardship, makes hardship in the present more difficult, if not impossible, to bear. Indeed, the prospect of impoverishment in the future deprives one of the ability to derive pleasure even from the possession of substantial wealth in the present, for the shadow of such a future must hang over whatever enjoyment one might have in the present. Thus, the prospect of progress, as well as the process of achieving it, contributes to our happiness.

The Objectivity of Economic Progress: A Critique of the Doctrines of Cultural Relativism and Conspicuous Consumption

According to the widely held doctrines of cultural relativism and conspicuous consumption, the concept of economic progress can have no objective meaning.[15] These doctrines hold, for example, that our preference for automobiles over horses, or for radios and television sets over jungle tom-toms, is a matter of social and cultural conditioning. It is allegedly the result only of the fact that in this particular culture it happens to have been instilled in people—for no really good reason—that it is desirable to own such goods as automobiles and television sets. Accordingly, people supposedly want to own such goods not because it really is desirable to own them in any objective sense, but merely that they may conform to what is expected of them in this culture. They allegedly want to own them as a source of *prestige* in the eyes of others.

The essential meaning of these doctrines can be grasped by realizing that what they imply is that people want to own television sets not because they want to watch the television sets, but because they want to be *seen* watching them—or because they were told to do so by the advertisers. Not the actual consumption of goods is important, we are told, but the "conspicuousness" of their consumption. Thus, the only real significance of television sets or any of the other "gadgets" of capitalist society is supposed to be their significance in the eyes of others. In a different culture people allegedly derive equal satisfaction from appearing before others with a ring through their nose, and in the society of the future (or at least as many people conceived the future until very recently) they will allegedly do so by wearing a chest full of medals proclaiming them as heroes of socialist labor.

Thus, according to these doctrines, there is no reason to believe that people's preferences in a modern, capitalist society are any better grounded than those of people in any other type of society, or that a modern, capitalist society is in any objective sense superior to any other society. There is thus allegedly no basis for believing that what has been accomplished in a modern, capitalist society is in any objective sense progress.

Now what is wrong with these doctrines is that they omit any consideration of man in relation to the physical world. For them, the most important thing in human life is the mere approval or disapproval of other people, which is thought to constitute an ultimate standard, incapable of being subjected to further evaluation. But the truth is, of course, that the primary issue in human life is man's relation to the physical world. It is there and there alone that man must live or die, irrespective of the culture in which he lives. And how man succeeds in relation to the physical world provides an objective standard by which to judge the value of cultures. The examples of automobiles and television sets can serve to illustrate this point.

It is not true that our preference for the automobile over the horse is arbitrary, based on nothing more than social and cultural conditioning. It is based on our nature both as animate beings possessing the capacity of locomotion, and as rational beings capable of enlarging all of our physical capacities. We call the automobile an advance over the horse by the same standard by which we call the domestication of the horse an advance over possessing merely our unaided legs, and by the same standard by which we value the possession of our legs themselves. Namely, it extends our range and power of locomotion. If the automobile were not an advance over the horse, then the horse would not be an advance over our unaided legs. And, on the basis of such reasoning, the very possession of legs themselves could not be considered better than not possessing them. The automobile is an advance over the horse, therefore, for the same reason that it is better to have legs than not to have them.

Similarly, we call the telegraph an advance over the tom-tom, and radio an advance over the telegraph, because they increase the efficacy of our sense of hearing. The one enables us to hear sounds coming from a greater distance; the other, sounds from a greater distance as well as a greater range of sound. Thus, we value the radio over the telegraph, and the telegraph over the tom-tom, by the same standard as we value our sense of hearing itself. We call television an advance over radio for the same reason that we value the possession of eyes and ears together over the possession of ears alone. We call color television an advance over black and white, for the same reason that

we value normal vision over being colorblind.

The advances in our goods represent extensions of our power to use our limbs, senses, and minds to accomplish results. In effect, they magnify the power of these vital attributes of our persons. They are advances by the standard of the value of these attributes, and thus by the standard of the value of our persons.[16]

It may be that there are cultures in which people regularly grow up incapable of appreciating the value of economic advances. It may be that in this culture there are some people who really do not understand what our advances are all about and who see no better reason for valuing them than that of conforming to the expectations of others. The existence of such people and of such cultures proves not that our advances are not advances, but only that there are people with a gross deficiency of understanding, and cultures that are highly destructive of the capacity for understanding.

This discussion has major bearing on the fact that in American society, the earning of wealth has traditionally been the leading source of prestige. The objective fact underlying such prestige is that the earning of wealth benefits one's life by enabling one to do more. Thus, it *deserves* to bring prestige, by the standard of human life as a value. It is a great tribute to the culture of the United States that it is to such activity that it has accorded prestige.

It must also be pointed out that the attempt to reverse cause and effect, and to take prestige as the starting point, must backfire. For example, the attempt of a socialist society to induce work by the offer of prestige, rather than material incentives, not only cannot succeed, but must bring the opposite of prestige to those who would be willing to work for it. To mine coal, drive a truck, harvest a field, work in a factory—to do virtually any of the run-of-the-mill jobs that occupy the bulk of the labor force—for the sake of prestige, would be to mark a person as nothing but a fool. He would have to be a fool to drive himself day in and day out, sweating and straining, all for the sake of nothing more than, in effect, being called a good boy.

The objective superiority of the goods of modern capitalism is not called into question by the fact that in our culture many people want to own such goods as horses, canoes, bows and arrows, and so on, and in some cases prefer units of these goods to units of more advanced goods serving the same needs. Such choices do not by any means necessarily mark these people as primitivists. There are conditions in which the horse is superior to the automobile—for example, where there are no roads. Similarly, canoes can navigate shallow waters that a motorized craft cannot. Also, the physical experience that a horse or canoe affords is different from that provided by an automobile or motorboat: they enable one to observe things more closely and more leisurely, for example.

The desire to own such goods, even though one lives in the conditions of modern civilization, is actually nothing more than a manifestation of our limitless need for wealth: a person wants one or more automobiles as his normal means of transportation, and a horse as a further refinement, as it were, of his ability to locomote. Thus, he loads his horse into a horse trailer, hitches it to his car, or, better, motor home, and drives to the edge of terrain where only horses can go. Or he simply goes for a ride on a nearby trail to experience the motion of a gallop and the wind on his face. To be able to enjoy the widest possible range of pleasurable and beneficial experiences is precisely why an individual desires to obtain the greatest possible amount of wealth. But to obtain it, and have the time to enjoy it, he must be able to accomplish everything that is not itself pleasure, or otherwise valued for its own sake, in the shortest possible time. If, for example, what a person wants is the experience of leisurely riding along a beautiful mountain stream, then he doesn't want to waste that time using a horse to cross the country to get to the mountains. For that, he wants a motor vehicle. It (together with roads) is objectively superior to the horse as a normal means of transportation. As a direct source of enjoyment, however, there is still a need for horses, even in the conditions of a modern economy. In effect, the limitless need for wealth embraces a kind of recapitulation of the goods that were prominent in less advanced conditions.

The Objective Value of a Division-of-Labor, Capitalist Society

I have shown that economic progress is not a matter of arbitrary preference, but is objectively desirable—desirable on the basis of our nature as rational beings. The goods that result are objectively improvements, and the process of acquiring them—the continuous thinking that must be done—is called for by our nature as rational beings.

The objective value of economic progress implies that the cultural values that make economic progress possible are likewise objectively better than those that stand in its way. These values, of course, are the values that underlie the division of labor and capitalism—above all, reason, science, technology, individual rights, limited government and economic freedom, and private ownership of the means of production. In the name of being able to see, hear, move, or do anything that our senses, limbs, and minds enable us to do—in short, in the name of being able to live as human beings—these values deserve to be upheld.

Indeed, the same principle that establishes the objectivity of the economic advances of modern capitalism directly establishes the objectivity of the superiority of modern capitalist civilization as such, in comparison to any other form of civilization. Here the attribute that serves as the standard is the ability to acquire and apply knowledge. Modern capitalist civilization—modern "Western" civilization—possesses this ability in greater measure than any previous civilization. In addition to knowledge of the laws of logic and the principle of causality, which were known to the Greeks and Romans and which enabled them to surpass all previous civilizations in the ability to acquire knowledge, modern Western civilization possesses not only a much more highly developed knowledge of the laws of mathematics and science but also a division-of-labor economy and, above all in its Anglo-Saxon variant, the freedoms of speech and press. As I will show in Chapter 4, a division-of-labor economy makes possible an enormous and progressive increase in the amount of knowledge that a society possesses and in the application of knowledge to production. The freedoms of speech and press also play an essential role in the increase in knowledge by guaranteeing the individual's right to disseminate knowledge without being stopped by the coercive power of the state operating in support of the ignorance, fears, or superstitions of any individual or group. Thus, capitalist civilization deserves to be upheld in the name of the value of knowledge.

It should go without saying that capitalist civilization is open to men of all races, as the brilliant success of Japan and several other Oriental nations dramatically illustrates. It is not the civilization of the white man, but of all men who wish to prosper and are prepared to adopt reason as their fundamental means of doing so. Those who view it, whether with pride or with hatred, as the civilization of the white man only, are implicitly racists, in that they view civilization and culture as being racially determined. The fact is, of course, that civilization and culture, above all, modern capitalist civilization, is a body of knowledge and values that is accessible to all of mankind.[17]

While extolling the values of capitalism, it must be stressed that nothing that has been said or that will be said in this book should be taken to imply a belief on my part that contemporary Western or American culture is perfect. Far from it. Obviously some very serious flaws mar our culture. And they have been growing.

Our culture's basic flaw is its philosophic contradictions.[18] These contradictions, in the form of irrationalist doctrines, such as that of cultural relativism, lead it to attack its virtues. Thus, we witness the spectacle of our culture flagellating itself for its successes in science, technology, and the creation of wealth. We see the spectacle of its intellectuals holding the most primitive and barbaric cultures as superior to their own, as they declare that all cultures are of equal value except their own, which is to be despised.

The spectacle is particularly gross in regard to the culture of the United States, which is the foremost capitalist country. The United States is denounced by its enemies as the leader of the evil, reactionary forces—the champion of monopoly capital and imperialism. Many of its own intellectuals join the denunciations and find nothing but evil in the history of their country and in its current policies. Yet all the flaws of the United States were flaws of being inconsistent with its own magnificent principles. Its flaw today, which is potentially deadly, is that many of its intellectual leaders have been corrupted to the point of despising those principles, above all, the principles of limited government and economic freedom, and, more recently, the values of science and technology, as well.

4. The Law of Diminishing Marginal Utility and the Limitless Need for Wealth

The principle that man's desire for wealth is limitless is fully consistent with the law of diminishing marginal utility, one of the most important and well-known principles of economics. The law of diminishing marginal utility states that *the utility or, equivalently, the importance or personal value that an individual attaches to a unit of any good diminishes as the quantity of the good in his possession increases.*

An example drawn from Böhm-Bawerk, the leading theorist of marginal utility, will illustrate the principle. Imagine that an isolated frontiersman, say, of the old American West, requires five sacks of grain, which must last him until his next harvest. He needs one sack to meet his minimum need for nutrition. Without it, he would die of starvation. He needs a second sack to be sure of having enough food to keep up his health and strength. A third sack enables him to raise some poultry and satisfy his hunger completely. With a fourth sack he can distill some brandy. With a fifth sack he can feed some parrots, from which he derives amusement.

If our frontiersman in fact possesses only one sack of grain, he will value it as highly as his very life. This is because, in this context, the possession of a sack of grain is a necessary condition of his survival; if he loses his one and only sack of grain, he will die. If, however, he possesses two sacks of grain, he will not value one sack as highly as his life, but only as highly as the maintenance of his health and strength. Because now, in this context, this is what depends on the possession of a sack of grain;

if he lost one of his two sacks, it would be his health and strength, not his life, that would be threatened. In the same way, if he should possess three sacks of grain, he will value one sack only as highly as the remaining satisfaction of his hunger. With the possession of a fourth sack, the value he attaches to any one sack falls to the importance he attaches to having brandy; with a fifth sack, it falls to the importance he attaches to feeding the parrots. Thus, the marginal utility of a good can be thought of as the utility of the last unit of a supply, giving all due allowance to the more important want satisfactions provided by the earlier units of the supply, and thus falling as the number of such earlier units increases.[19]

The law of diminishing marginal utility rests on two closely related foundations. First, because goods have the power to satisfy wants, successive units of a good that are used to satisfy a want necessarily encounter wants that are more and more satisfied. For example, if I am very thirsty, the first glass of water I drink meets a very intense need. But that glass of water helps to satisfy the need. The second glass of water I drink, therefore, goes to serve a need that is less urgent precisely because it is already partly satisfied by virtue of the first glass of water. The same, of course, is true of the frontiersman's grain, insofar as he consumes it.

The second foundation of the law of diminishing marginal utility is that insofar as we must choose which of our wants to satisfy, and act rationally in doing so, we choose to satisfy our more important wants in preference to our less important wants. Our frontiersman, for example, chooses to feed himself ahead of the parrots. Indeed, as far as we are able, we devote our goods to the satisfaction of the most important of our wants that they are capable of satisfying. Diminishing marginal utility follows from this because, with the units of the initial supply devoted to serving the most important of the wants they can serve, the only wants that remain to be served by an addition to the supply are necessarily wants that are less important than those already being served.

The concept "most important of our wants that a good is capable of satisfying" must be understood as *a variable range,* whose extent depends on the quantity of the good we possess. Our frontiersman, for example, devotes his supply of grain to its most important uses even when he feeds parrots. In the context of possessing five sacks of grain, feeding parrots is the most important use to which he can devote his *fifth* sack. While it is certainly not as important as devoting any of his first three sacks of grain to feeding himself, it is certainly more important than devoting a fourth sack of grain to feeding himself (which might be unhealthy and make him feel ill) and more important than any other use to which he can devote that fifth sack, given the existence of the other four.

We satisfy our most important wants in descending order of importance. The larger the number of units of a good at our disposal, the further down in the scale of importance we are able to carry the satisfaction of our wants. The marginal unit of a supply is devoted to the most important wants that it can serve, but these wants are necessarily less important than the wants being served by the "earlier" units of the supply. The marginal wants that a good serves should be thought of not as being unimportant, *but as being the least important of the most important wants that its supply suffices to serve.* The marginal wants are always *more important* than any of the *submarginal* wants, that is, wants whose satisfaction would require a still larger supply of the good.

It should be realized, of course, that the utility of the marginal unit of a supply determines the utility of *any* of the units of that supply at that moment. If, for example, our frontiersman were to attach a tag to one of his five sacks of grain, and label it specifically as the sack necessary to his survival, the utility of that particular sack would still be no greater than the utility of a sack specifically labeled as necessary to the feeding of his parrots. This is because irrespective of any such labeling, it is still only a question of one sack out of a supply of five. If the particular sack labeled necessary to survival were lost, the sack previously designated as reserved for the feeding of the parrots could take its place. By virtue of making this substitution, the actual loss would fall on feeding of the parrots, and that utility, therefore, would be the marginal utility of the sack in question.

As previously stated, the law of diminishing marginal utility is perfectly consistent with the fact that man's need for wealth is limitless. It is necessary to stress this point in view of the misconception spread by Galbraith that increasing wealth, and the consequent fall in the marginal utility of a unit of wealth, makes the pursuit of wealth progressively less important.[20]

One reason for the consistency between the law of diminishing marginal utility and the limitless need for wealth is the elementary fact that the *total utility* of a person's supply of wealth must go on increasing so long as wealth has any positive marginal utility to him whatever. For example, the fact that the fifth sack of grain has a lower marginal utility to the frontiersman than the fourth does not contradict the fact that five sacks of grain have a greater total utility to him than four and thus that it is better for him to own five sacks than four. So long as additional wealth has any marginal utility whatever, there is a need for more wealth.

Of course, if one considers a very narrow type of good, such as bread, say, it is possible to imagine additional units beyond a point being of negative utility, and, therefore, a larger supply being of less utility than a smaller

supply. This would be the case, for example, if the additional units either had to be eaten by people who already had all they wanted or else would simply rot and impose costs of removal and cleanup. But, for reasons explained earlier in this section, it could certainly never be the case that all or most goods, or, therefore, wealth in general, could fall into this category.

Furthermore, it should be realized that the very process of increasing the amount of wealth that is available to the average member of any society entails the opening up of *new uses for additional wealth,* which has the effect of increasing the marginal utility of additional units of wealth. The opening up of new uses for wealth occurs because essential to the ability to increase the supply of wealth is scientific and technological progress, which makes possible not only improved methods of producing goods of the kind that already exist, but also brand new kinds of goods. Thus, for example, the invention of the electric motor and the internal combustion engine, which radically increased our ability to produce and enjoy wealth, did not result in our sating ourselves with a vastly increased production of such goods as candles and ox-carts. On the contrary, as part of the same process of improvement, these inventions were accompanied by the invention of the electric light and all the electrical appliances and, of course, the automobile. In this way, increases in the ability to produce raise the marginal utility of additional wealth along with providing it.

Thus, an automobile represents perhaps a hundred or a thousand times the wealth represented by an oxcart, and, at the same time, is probably of correspondingly greater marginal utility than an oxcart. Certainly, the marginal utility of a second automobile does not represent a drop in the marginal utility of wealth to the point that would correspond to the possession of a second hundred or thousand oxcarts. Along the same lines, one might think of a two-hundred horsepower automobile as representing the material equivalent of two hundred horses. Wealth representing a two-hundredth part of an automobile has a higher marginal utility to the owner of an automobile than would the wealth representing a two-hundredth horse. Thus, the effect of a growing ability to produce is not only more wealth, but also a higher marginal utility of the additional wealth in comparison with what it would otherwise have been (if somehow the additional wealth had been able to come into existence without such technological advances). And, as these examples imply, the effect of a growing ability to produce is a tendency toward an increase in the size of the marginal unit of wealth, as well.

This last point requires elaboration. The size of the marginal unit is never something fixed and immutable. It is always a matter of context, and the context is always the circumstances and conditions with which the individual is confronted. If, for example, our frontiersman had two of his five sacks of grain stored in the same place, and that place was threatened by a fire, what would be at stake for him would be the importance of satisfying the wants dependent on the two sacks together. The two sacks together would have to be evaluated, and they together would constitute the marginal unit. As von Mises once said in a discussion with the present author, the marginal unit is whatever is the amount under consideration.

As people grow richer, the size of the marginal unit tends to increase. Not only do they deal with things like automobiles instead of oxcarts, but richer people deal with Cadillac- or Mercedes-level automobiles rather than Chevrolet- or Toyota-level automobiles. When differences in quality are considered, a house, a suit or a dress, a restaurant meal, practically everything, tends to be a larger-sized unit of wealth for a richer person than for a poorer person. When this is taken into account, it becomes clear that it is a great mistake to assume that as wealth increases, the utility of *the marginal units actually dealt with* diminishes. On the contrary, the utility of these units actually increases! Unit for unit, a Cadillac has a higher marginal utility than a Chevrolet; a large, luxurious house has a higher marginal utility than a small, modest house; and so on.

Furthermore, the fact that the utility of a marginal unit of wealth of given size diminishes as the quantity of wealth available to us increases is actually an important aspect of the desirability of increasing our wealth. What we rationally want is to be in a position in which the marginal utility of a unit of wealth of any given size more and more approaches zero, while what we deal with more and more is progressively larger-sized units of wealth. We want to be in a position in which the loss of the wealth represented by $10, say, is absolutely unimportant to us; better still, in which the loss of the wealth represented by $100, $1,000, or $10,000 is absolutely unimportant to us. The loss of wealth represented by $10 will be unimportant to us when we are rich enough to afford spending $50 or $100 for a single fine meal rather than $10 for a whole day's food—when, in other words, $50 or $100 replaces $10 as the representative of a marginal unit of food. The loss of $1,000 will be unimportant to us when we can afford to spend $50,000 for a second automobile, perhaps, rather than just $1,000 for our one and only ancient used car. The loss of $10,000 will be unimportant to us when we can afford to spend $1,000,000 for our second or third home rather than just $10,000 for our one and only small used trailer.

Thus, we rationally want more wealth in order to be able to deal with marginal units of wealth of progressively larger size, and to be less and less concerned with units of wealth of any given size. In the spirit of the welcoming party allegedly once given by American millionaires to the famous nineteenth-century English defender of capitalism Herbert Spencer, the symbolic ideal is to be able to afford to use hundred-dollar bills to light one's cigar—while dealing with mansions, yachts, and private railway cars as the significant marginal units of one's life.

5. Applications of the Law of Diminishing Marginal Utility

The law of diminishing marginal utility has important applications. It is appropriate to consider several of them here, both because they shed light on the rationality of economic activity and because, in one case at least, they provide positive confirmation of the fact that man's need for wealth is limitless.

Resolution of the Value Paradox

As explained in the Introduction, the law of diminishing marginal utility makes possible a resolution of the classical economists' paradox of value—the seeming paradox constituted by the fact that goods of apparently the lowest utility, such as diamonds, are normally more valuable in exchange than goods of apparently the highest utility, such as water. This apparent paradox was, of course what prevented the classical economists from being able to ground their theory of exchange value and prices in utility.

When people regard water as more useful than diamonds, what they have in mind is that if one had to choose between having no water or no diamonds, one would obviously choose to have no diamonds. Up to a considerable point, units of water are vastly more important than units of diamonds. But because of the operation of the law of diminishing marginal utility, a point is reached at which the utility of the *marginal* unit of water falls below the utility of the *marginal* unit of diamonds. The first gallon of water, the hundred and first, or probably even the thousand and first gallon of water, is more important than the first carat of diamonds or even the first ten or a hundred carats of diamonds taken together. But at some point, after one has all the water necessary for drinking, cooking, washing, irrigating, and so forth, the marginal utility of water falls below the marginal utility of diamonds. The extremity of the abundance with which nature provides water and the extremity of the scarcity with which it provides diamonds jointly operate to establish a far higher *marginal* utility of diamonds than of water in normal circumstances.

Thus the fact that in the normal circumstances of

civilized life people value diamonds above water is not at all paradoxical or irrational. It is perfectly consistent with considerations of genuine utility, provided the latter are properly understood—that is, in the light of the principle of diminishing marginal utility.

By the same token, the fact that people nowadays desire to possess such things as power windows on their automobiles, and are willing to pay substantial sums for what many may regard as relatively modest improvements in fashion or style, is also perfectly consistent with rational principles of behavior. It is a question of the context of how much wealth or income one has available and thus of the marginal utility to the individual of a unit of wealth or income. If one has sufficient wealth or income so that one is already able to provide for a very full satisfaction of such needs as those for food, clothing, and shelter, then, indeed, the most important use for the price of power windows or the price of a relatively modest improvement in fashion or style may well be the purchase of the power windows or the improvement in fashion or style. One must always consider what the individual's choices are in the context confronting him. If the choice is, for example, the power windows or an improvement in his hi-fi equipment, because all wants of greater importance are already provided for, then the purchase of the power windows may very well be the most important use for the money in question.

Determination of Value by Cost of Production

The law of diminishing marginal utility also makes it possible for the first time to understand the actual role of cost of production in the determination of prices. Although the classical economists mistakenly believed that cost of production provided an explanation of prices that was a logical alternative to an explanation on the basis of utility, an understanding of marginal utility makes it possible to grasp the determination of price by cost as a major instance of the operation of the law of diminishing marginal utility.

As Böhm-Bawerk and Wieser explained, there are numerous cases in which cost of production is in fact the immediate determinant of the price of a good. These are cases in which a good of relatively high direct marginal utility is produced by factors of production whose supply is abundant enough to permit their employment in the production of other goods of relatively low marginal utility. In such cases, *the marginal utility of the factors of production is determined by the utility of the least valuable of the products for whose production their supply is sufficient.* The value of the factors of production, determined in this way, then reduces the value of the products of higher direct marginal utility to the utility of their least valued product. Thus, cases in which prices are determined by cost of production actually represent a special application of the law of diminishing marginal utility. Namely, the value of all the products of the same factors of production, however high their own, direct marginal utility, is reduced to the marginal utility and value of the marginal product of those factors of production.[21]

Böhm-Bawerk's example of the frontiersman with five sacks of grain, originally used to illustrate the principle of diminishing marginal utility itself can serve, in a slightly modified form, to illustrate the present point. Thus, instead of imagining a sack of grain labeled "sack required for survival," let us imagine a quantity of biscuits, baked from flour made from this sack of grain, and labeled "biscuits required for survival." As before, the frontiersman possesses four additional sacks of grain, which are sufficient for satisfying his needs down to the point of feeding parrots. If now this supply of biscuits is destroyed, the frontiersman's life is not threatened any more than it was before, when his sack of grain labeled sack required for survival was lost.

Just as he could previously replace that sack of grain, so now he can replace the biscuits by withdrawing grain from the feeding of parrots. Thus, even though the direct marginal utility of the biscuits, like the sack of grain before them, is as high as that of his life itself, the ability to replace them, by withdrawing supplies from the feeding of parrots, reduces their actual, effective marginal utility to the much lesser marginal utility of feeding the parrots.

What is present here is that the value of the biscuits is reduced to the value of the grain which makes possible their replacement, and which in turn is determined by its marginal utility. Thus, the value of the biscuits, like the value of the sack of grain before it, labeled sack required for survival, comes to be determined by marginal utility at a point corresponding to the much lesser importance of feeding parrots. In this way, determination of the value of a product on the basis of the lesser value of the means required for producing it, represents the operation of the principle of marginal utility.

Determination of Consumer Spending Patterns

In addition, and very important, the law of diminishing marginal utility helps to explain the pattern of demand that prevails in the economic system at any given set of prices of goods. People can buy goods in many different combinations. They can buy more of some goods by curtailing their purchases of other goods. The law of diminishing marginal utility implies, however, that as people increase their purchases of any good, successive additional units of it are accompanied by diminishing marginal utility. By the same token, as they restrict their purchase of other goods, to make additional funds available for the purchase of this particular good, the remaining units they purchase of these other goods acquire greater marginal utility.

From these facts, a principle of equilibrium in spending patterns emerges, which is that beyond a point, additional units of any good are not purchased at the expense of further reductions in the purchase of other goods because the marginal utility gained would be less than the alternative marginal utility forgone. Purchases in every line are carried only to the point at which the marginal utility derived is greater than the alternative marginal utility that could be derived by devoting the price of the good to the purchase of other goods. The equilibrium that emerges is defined by the condition that the marginal utility of each good purchased in each line is greater than the marginal utility of any other good or combination of goods that could alternatively be purchased with its price in any other line. At the same time, the marginal utility of an additional unit in any line is less than the marginal utility that would have to be forgone in other lines to make possible its purchase.

For example, consumers carry their purchases of food, clothing, shelter, and entertainment only up to the point at which the marginal utility of a unit of each of these goods exceeds the marginal utility of any alternative good or combination of goods that they might purchase with the same money. They limit their purchases in each line at the point at which the marginal utility gained by the purchase of an additional unit would be at the expense of a greater loss in marginal utility by virtue of having to restrict unduly the purchase of one or more other such goods. People wish to achieve a certain balance in the different areas of their consumption. Normally, they do not want to live in penthouses if it means having to eat beans and wear rags. Nor, by the same token, do they usually want to drink champagne and eat caviar if that means having to live in a hovel. They tend to achieve an equilibrium that is characterized by the utility of the last units purchased in each line being greater than the utility of any additional units that might be purchased in other lines.

In an overzealousness for the use of mathematics, economics textbooks often describe the equilibrium of spending patterns by claiming that the marginal utility of each good comes to stand in a uniform proportion to its price. Thus, it is said, the

$$\frac{Marginal\ Utility\ of\ Good\ A}{Price\ of\ Good\ A} = \frac{Marginal\ Utility\ of\ Good\ B}{Price\ of\ Good\ B}$$

and so on for all goods and all prices. It is claimed that this mathematical equilibrium results from the fact that

wherever the equal proportionality of marginal utility to price does not exist, it pays to spend less for the goods of relatively lower marginal utility and more for the goods of relatively higher marginal utility, which raises the marginal utility of the former category and reduces that of the latter category relative to their respective prices until equal proportionality does prevail.[22]

What the use of the above mathematical formula overlooks is the fact that marginal utility often undergoes major discontinuities. For example, the marginal utility of a steering wheel in an automobile relative to the price of the steering wheel is enormous, for it is as great as the marginal utility of the entire automobile. On the other hand, the marginal utility of a mere second headlight on the automobile relative to its price is comparatively quite modest. In such circumstances, the above described mathematical doctrine implies that one should forgo the purchase of the second headlight in order to purchase a second steering wheel. This, of course, is obviously nonsensical. Equilibrium in such cases cannot be described in terms of a uniform proportionality of price to marginal utility, but only in terms of the utility of the last units purchased in any line being greater than that of any alternative additional units that might be purchased with the same money in other lines. In effect, the condition of equilibrium is that the marginal utility of good A exceeds the utility of any additional units of goods B, C, etc., which might be purchased with its price, while, at the same time, the marginal utility of good B exceeds the utility of any additional units of goods A, C, etc., which might be purchased with its price, and so on for all goods.

Say's Law

Finally, and what is most relevant to the fact that the need for wealth is limitless, the principle of diminishing marginal utility helps to explain the phenomenon of partial, relative overproduction and underproduction described by Say's Law. It thus helps to explain why any alleged general or absolute overproduction, with the supply of wealth allegedly surpassing man's need for wealth, is never actually present.[23] In so doing, it provides important confirmation of the fact that man's need for wealth has no practical limit.

To understand this point, it must be realized that increases in the ability to produce always take place in particular industries. Very often, devoting the whole or even the greater part of such increased ability to produce to an expanded production of the particular products of those industries would result in the marginal utility of the products in question falling below the marginal utility of additional quantities of other products. These other products are products whose supply could be increased by a withdrawal of capital and labor from the industries in which the improvements in the ability to produce have taken place. To the extent that the increased ability to produce is unduly concentrated in the particular industries in which it originates, the products of such industries may be said to be in a state of partial and relative overproduction, while the products of other industries are in a corresponding state of partial and relative underproduction.

For example, devoting a doubled ability to produce potatoes with the same labor to an actual doubling of the supply of potatoes, would result in a partial and relative overproduction of potatoes. At the same time, there would be an equivalent partial and relative underproduction of other goods, additional quantities of which possess a higher marginal utility than the additional potatoes and which could be produced with capital and labor used to produce the additional potatoes. The problem in such a case is not any actually excessive ability to produce, but merely the misapplication of an increased ability to produce in an undue concentration on the production of a particular good. The solution is thus simply a better balance in the production of additional goods.[24]

Further major applications of the law of diminishing marginal utility will be developed in Chapter 5, in connection with the discussions of the concept of demand and of price determination.

6. "Scarcity" and the Transformation of Its Nature Under Capitalism

Man's limitless need for wealth, combined with the respective natures of desires and goods, is responsible for the fact that the desire to consume always far outstrips the ability to produce. Desires are mental phenomena, based on thoughts and concepts. Goods are physical phenomena, requiring for their existence the performance of human labor. For all practical purposes, the referents of concepts are limitless; and to desire, one need do hardly more than imagine. But goods are always specific concretes, and each must be produced, requiring labor and effort. In essence, our desires outstrip our ability to produce by virtue of the limitless range of the mental in comparison with the physical and thus by virtue of the fact that the range of our imaginations is always incomparably greater than the power of our arms.

This relationship remains true no matter how much we may augment the power of our arms by means of tools and machinery. For at the same time, as part of the same process, we augment the power of our imaginations, in that the new knowledge required to provide the tools and machines also opens up new vistas in terms of what can be produced. For example, as already mentioned, the invention of the electric motor and the internal combus-

tion engine did not result in our sating ourselves with a vastly increased production of candles and oxcarts, but, as part of the same process of improvement, was accompanied by the invention of the electric light and all the electrical appliances and by the invention of the automobile. Thus, the desire for goods grew with the ability to produce them. It will continue to grow with further improvements in the ability to produce. If, to take an extreme example, the day should ever come when radical advances in technology make it physically possible for us to be sated with things like automobiles, the same radical advances in technology will open up the possibility of producing things like rocketships accessible to the general public and vacation homes on the moon. Thus, the desire for goods will always remain far greater than the ability to produce them.

Economists almost universally describe the condition in which the desire for wealth exceeds the amount of wealth available as one of "scarcity." Scarcity, they hold, means any limitation of wealth relative to the need or desire for wealth, irrespective of whether the limitation proceeds from the lack of wealth or the abundance of desires.

If one wishes to retain this terminology, one must say that capitalism radically transforms the nature of scarcity. For the people of precapitalistic societies, scarcity means a deficiency of wealth relative to urgent biological needs; it means supplies of food insufficient to still hunger; supplies of shelter and clothing insufficient to provide protection from the elements. Under capitalism, on the other hand, scarcity does not mean any such deficiency of wealth, but a vast and growing supply of wealth that lags behind the *desire* for wealth—a desire that always exceeds it, always grows as it grows, and that provides the impetus for its further growth. Scarcity under capitalism actually means economic ambitiousness, and is the cause of the progressive elimination of scarcity in the urgent biological sense.

For example, under capitalism, the scarcity of food quickly ceases to mean starvation. Instead it is a situation in which grain supplies have become abundant, but the point has not yet been reached where people can have all the meat they want. And then it ceases to mean even a deficiency of meat, but the fact that not enough of the meat supply is in the form of sirloin steak, and so on. Similarly, a scarcity of housing quickly comes to mean not a scarcity of dwelling space as such, but only a scarcity of ever more improved, more solidly constructed, and more luxurious dwelling space.

At each stage, the desire to advance to a higher stage makes the threat to urgent biological needs more remote. In a country in which the scarcity of food is merely a scarcity of meat, a year of bad crops does not threaten famine. It just means that less grain will be devoted to feeding meat animals, and people will end up with less meat. In a country in which the scarcity of food means a scarcity of sirloin steak, a year of bad crops means merely that people will have to switch to somewhat poorer cuts of meat, as they utilize a smaller but still abundant supply of meat animals more fully for human consumption. And as a general principle, cutting across all branches of production, the growing abundance of supplies in a capitalist society steadily prolongs and enriches human life at the same time that it further and further removes such direct threats to human life as famine and plague. Evidence for the truth of this proposition can be found in the fact that hardly anyone dies from hurricanes, tornadoes, volcanoes, earthquakes, or contagious diseases in the United States, while large numbers do so in the poor and backward countries. Our better record is the result of our greater progress in wealth—in the form of such things as better constructed buildings, better means of transportation, and better medical facilities, as well as a more abundant and varied food supply.[25] There is no fixed limit to the process by which the increasing production of wealth can further enhance and extend human life and its enjoyment.[26]

7. Time Preference and the Scarcity of Capital

In addition to the law of diminishing marginal utility, there is a second major economic principle of valuation that closely bears on the subject of scarcity, namely, that of time preference. Time preference operates to maintain the specific scarcity of savings and capital.[27]

According to the principle of time preference, an individual values goods available to him in the present more highly than goods available to him in the future, and goods available to him in the nearer future more highly than goods available to him in the more remote future. For example, he values having a house, a car, or a television set now, more highly than having it a year from now, and more highly having it a year from now than two years from now.

The principle of time preference holds that the prospective location of goods in time has a similar effect on our valuation of them as the location of things in space has on our visual perception of them. The further away from us things are in space, the smaller do they appear to us in our field of vision. The temporally more remote goods are in our field of valuation, so to speak, the smaller is the value we attach to them.[28]

Like any principle, that of time preference must be understood as applying other things being equal. For example, I would probably prefer to have a bathing suit in July rather than in January, even though July may lie

further in the future than January. In this case, other things are not equal. Much more benefit can be obtained from a bathing suit in the heat of July than in the cold of January. The appropriate application of the principle of time preference in this case is the fact that if I want to go swimming, I value the possession of a bathing suit for this coming July more highly than for the following July.

Similarly, the prospective marginal utility of a unit of a good in the future can be higher than its marginal utility in the present, if one expects to have fewer units in the future. For example, instead of eating two sandwiches now, a person can very well save one for later, because the marginal utility of a first sandwich later is greater than the marginal utility of a second sandwich now. Here the appropriate application of the principle of time preference is that a person attaches greater importance to consuming his first unit of a good today than to consuming his *first* unit tomorrow, and to consuming his second unit today than to consuming his *second* unit tomorrow. The fact that future units in a less abundant supply can have a greater marginal utility than present units in a more abundant supply does not contradict the principle of time preference, since that principle refers to the valuation of present and future units of equal supplies.

Finally, the principle of time preference is not contradicted by the fact that the prices of commodity futures are usually higher than the prices of the corresponding "cash" commodities available for immediate delivery. For example, in the month of September, the price of corn for delivery in December is always higher than the price of corn for immediate delivery, while the price of corn for delivery in the following March is still higher than that for delivery in December. Such a price structure does not mean that, other things being equal, people prefer commodities in the future to commodities in the present. On the contrary, month by month they are consuming the stocks of commodities, demonstrating that they prefer present consumption to future consumption. The ascending price structure of commodity futures is the reflection of the prospectively increasing scarcity of commodities between harvests, and/or of the need to compensate those who store supplies of commodities for future sale for the costs they incur in so doing and for tying up their capital in such investments. In the absence of such an ascending price structure, time preference would result in the unduly rapid consumption of stocks of commodities.

The Foundations of Time Preference

Time preference is implied in the very nature of valuation, and, indeed, of human life itself. All other things being equal, to want something is to want it sooner rather than later. If all other things are equal in two succeeding periods of time and a good exists which could be consumed in either period, then the very fact of the good's being valued implies that it must be consumed in the first period. If it is not consumed in the first period, then the identity of conditions implies that it also cannot be consumed in the second period. Hence, the good simply would not be consumed and, by implication, its consumption would be demonstrated not to be valued. If, however, the good is consumed in the first period, its nonconsumption in the second period does not contradict its being wanted just as much in the second period; it is simply unavailable in the second period.

The nature of human life implies time preference, because life cannot be interrupted. To be alive two years from now, one must be alive one year from now. To be alive tomorrow, one must be alive today. Whatever value or importance one attaches to being alive in the future, one must attach to being alive in the present, because being alive in the present is the indispensable precondition to being alive in the future. The value of life in the present thus carries with it whatever value one attaches to life in the future, of which it is the precondition, *plus* whatever value one attaches to life in the present for its own sake. In the nature of being alive, it is thus more important to be alive now than at any other, succeeding time, and more important to be alive in each moment of the nearer future than in each moment of the more remote future. If, for example, a person can project being alive for the next thirty years, say, then the value he attaches to being alive in the coming year carries with it whatever value he attaches to being alive in the following twenty-nine years, plus whatever value he attaches to being alive in the coming year for its own sake. This is necessarily a greater value than he attaches to being alive in the year starting next year. Similarly, the value he attaches to being alive from next year on is greater than the value he attaches to being alive starting two years from now, for it subsumes the latter value and represents that of an additional year besides.

The greater importance of life in the nearer future is what underlies the greater importance of goods in the nearer future and the perspective-like diminution in the value we attach to goods available in successively more remote periods of the future.

The Scarcity of Capital

Later discussion will show that time preference has an important bearing on the determination of the rate of profit and interest.[29] What must be stressed here is that time preference prevents the existence of profit and interest from always resulting in saving and the accumulation of additional capital. For example, assuming a constant buying power of money, if the rate of profit and interest is 5 percent, the implication is that by saving and investing $100 this year, one can have and consume $105 worth of goods next year. The reason that people do not all rush to save as much as possible, despite the fact that doing so would enable them to consume more in the future, is that they have time preference. Time preference results in people preferring an additional $100 of consumption today to an additional $105 (or whatever the figure may be) of consumption a year from now. It thus acts to limit the extent of saving and capital accumulation and to contribute to the scarcity of capital.

Time preference manifests itself in the extent to which individuals make provision for the future relative to their current consumption. An individual with an extremely high time preference will have no savings. He will consume his entire income and not use any of it to provide for his future consumption. By the same token, an individual with a very low time preference will seek to accumulate savings to a substantial multiple of his current income and consumption.

There are two dimensions to the scarcity of capital and capital goods. In one respect, capital goods are simply as scarce as our labor and ability to produce consumers' goods. To whatever extent our desire for consumers' goods, such as houses and cars, exceeds our ability to produce them, our implicit, indirect desire for things like bricks and lumber, steel sheet and tires, and the appropriate kinds of equipment used in making houses and cars, exceeds our ability to produce them. This kind of scarcity can be thought of as a horizontal scarcity of capital, in the sense that as wide as is our desire for consumers' goods relative to our ability to produce them, equally wide is our desire for the corresponding capital goods relative to our ability to produce them. Such scarcity of capital is obviously as ineradicable as the scarcity of wealth.

The second dimension of the scarcity of capital refers to the fact that goods can be produced with varying amounts of capital per unit, that is, with varying degrees of *capital intensiveness*. For example, a railroad can be constructed to go from point A to point B directly, or with various detours to avoid obstacles like lakes and mountains in between. Usually, constructing the bridges and tunnels required for the more direct route requires a greater capital investment than the longer, indirect route. In deciding which route to adopt, a railroad company must weigh the disadvantage of the larger capital investment required against the advantage of lower fuel and labor costs and reduced wear and tear on equipment in every year thereafter.

The choice of whether to employ more or less machinery in a manufacturing process is of the same nature: one must weigh the disadvantage of a larger initial outlay for the machinery against the advantage of lower labor costs in each year of the machinery's use. Whether or not it pays to improve a piece of farmland through irrigation or drainage, or to improve a mine by widening or deepening its shafts, is also similar in nature.

The extent to which our products are aged, as in the case of whiskey, beef, and woods of different growing time, is also a matter of differences in the amount of capital employed per unit of output. For example, in order for the whiskey companies to turn out a unit of eight-year-old scotch every year, they need to have capital representing units of scotch of each of eight different years of age on hand in the pipeline, so to speak. In order to turn out the same quantity of twelve-year-old scotch each year, they need correspondingly more capital—more units of partially aged scotch for every one that is fully aged. In the same way, lumber companies harvesting trees with a twenty-five-year growth cycle need growing stands of trees representing years one through twenty-four for every stand of trees they harvest today, and lumber companies harvesting trees with a fifty-year growth cycle need a correspondingly larger number of stands of trees at various stages of growth for every one they harvest today.

A similar principle applies to the use of more valuable materials in preference to less valuable materials. Any use of more valuable materials at any given stage of production is likely to reflect the performance of correspondingly more labor, or more skilled labor, prior to that stage of production, and thus a higher degree of capital intensiveness. Thus, for example, a house made of bricks requires the use of more capital than a house made of wood, insofar as more previously performed labor is required to produce bricks for a house of a given size than lumber for a house of the same size. The same applies to the extent to which products contain various previously produced components and accessories. For example, other things being equal, an automobile with automatic transmission, an air conditioner, power windows, and the like, requires a larger quantity of capital in its production than one without these things or equipped with fewer of them.

Different industries have very different degrees of capital intensiveness. A far larger amount of capital investment stands behind the average dollar that is received in the form of house rent or a mortgage payment than stands behind the average dollar received as payment for restaurant meals or haircuts. Similarly, it takes more capital investment to earn a dollar of sales in the electric utility industry than it does in the motion picture business, and more in the motion picture business than it does in the grocery business.

The extent to which capital is scarce in this second sense—in what we can call its vertical dimension—is determined by time preference. In a society characterized by relatively low time preference—that is, by a willingness to forgo present consumption to the point of making substantial provision for the future—the methods of production will tend to be relatively capital intensive: relatively capital-intensive industries, such as railroads and electric utilities, can exist, and will be larger in relation to less capital intensive industries; the railroads will be more able to build bridges and tunnels, and the factories to adopt labor-saving machinery; the farms and mines will be more improved; a wide variety of products will enjoy the benefit of the use of better-quality materials and of greater aging.

Our discussion of the causes of capital accumulation, later in this book, will show how the lower is the degree of time preference in a society, and thus the greater is its overall degree of capital intensiveness, the greater is its ability to adopt technological advances and to enjoy a cumulative process of capital accumulation.[30] What must be emphasized here, however, is that the existence of time preference prevents the scarcity of capital in its vertical dimension from ever being overcome.

Before the scarcity of capital in its vertical dimension could be overcome, capital would have to be accumulated sufficient to enable the 85 percent of the world that is not presently industrialized to come up to the degree of capital intensiveness of the 15 percent of the world that is industrialized. Within the industrialized countries, capital would have to be accumulated sufficient to enable every factory, farm, mine, and store to increase its degree of capital intensiveness to the point presently enjoyed only by the most capital-intensive establishments, and, at the same time, to enable all establishments to raise the standard of capital intensiveness still further, to the point where no further reduction in costs of production or improvement in the quality of products could be achieved by any greater availability of capital in its vertical dimension.

This would mean the maximum possible use of machinery and automation. It would mean going so far that, for example, canals would frequently be built without locks, because capital would be available simply to remove all the interfering higher elevations. By the same token, every curve and grade would have to be eliminated from railroads and highways, all the whiskey and wines produced would have to be aged to the point where no additional aging could improve them further, and even the enormous growing time of redwoods would cease to be an obstacle to their planting. Capital would also have to be accumulated to the point where no further gain attached to the expansion of the more capital-intensive industries relative to the less capital-intensive industries. This would entail a growth in industries such as housing, the electric utilities, and bridge, tunnel, and canal building up to their maximum possible limits relative to less capital-intensive industries.

Capital would have to be accumulated to the point where absolutely no project representing an economic improvement was left undone for a lack of capital, however enormous the amount of capital required. This includes projects that today belong in the realm of science fiction because of the vast amounts of capital that would be required for their execution: for example, digging tunnels not only under the English Channel, but under the various seas and even oceans of the world; making inland cities like Phoenix, Arizona, into seaports through the construction of massive canals, and thereby achieving substantial reductions in transportation costs for all time to come; virtually eliminating freight costs between cities, such as New York and Chicago, say, by constructing straight-line tunnels between them that would constitute secants relative to the earth's circumference, with the result that objects would simply be pulled by the force of gravity to the center of the tunnels and, in a frictionless vacuum, hurled to the opposite surface by the force of inertia. Indeed, it may be that some of these projects would even achieve such great cost savings as to yield a substantial rate of return on the capital that would have to be invested, but cannot be undertaken at present because, in the actual state of capital accumulation, they would strip the rest of the economic system of too much of its capital.

The accumulation of capital in its vertical dimension can never remotely begin to exhaust the uses for such capital. Its accumulation always ceases far short of that point. It is always necessary to leave undone an incalculable range of potential improvements whose execution would require a more abundant accumulation of capital in its vertical dimension than exists. Thus, capital in its vertical dimension, as well as in its horizontal dimension, remains permanently scarce.[31]

Such capital accumulation comes to an end because of time preference. Once people succeed in accumulating a certain amount of capital relative to their incomes, they feel that they have done their duty by the future and can now turn more heavily toward enjoying life in the present. Thus, they stop accumulating capital relative to their incomes, even though the accumulation of still more capital relative to their incomes would provide them with still higher incomes in the future.

A Word on Capital Accumulation and the Rate of Return

As stated, later discussion in this book will show that the gains from a lower time preference are both profoundly important and cumulative in their significance, in that they permit the adoption of technological methods of production that would not otherwise be economically feasible. It will show that the adoption of the more advanced methods of production made possible by a lower degree of time preference is itself a further source of capital accumulation, with the result that capital accumulation does not require steadily repeated reductions in time preference, but is perfectly consistent with an unchanged state of time preference, provided it is sufficiently low. A still lower time preference will be shown to result in an *acceleration* of the rate of capital accumulation.[32]

Furthermore, the fact that a lower degree of time preference accelerates the rate of economic progress will be shown to result in a positive addition both to the real and to the nominal (viz., monetary) rate of profit and interest. Thus, the almost universally held opinion among economists that capital accumulation must be associated with a falling rate of return on capital will be challenged. Capital accumulation will be shown not only not to require a falling rate of return, but, as I say, to the extent that it results in a more rapid increase in the supply of goods and money, to result in an addition to the real and nominal rate of return.[33]

Time Preference, Rationality, and Freedom

Our previous discussion of the philosophical foundations of capitalism and economic activity implies that time preference is the lower the more rational and the freer a society is.[34] The more rational people are, the more are they aware of the future: the more they can mentally project it and the greater is the reality for them of such projections; in addition, the more are they aware of themselves as self-responsible causal agents, capable of affecting the course of future events to their own advantage by means of saving. Similarly, to the degree that people are free and enjoy the security of property, they know that they can benefit from whatever provision for the future they decide to make in the present. Thus, to the degree that a society is dominated by the values of reason and freedom, the more conducive it is psychologically and politically to saving and providing for the future, which is only another way of saying that it is more conducive to a low time preference and to all that that implies about capital accumulation and economic progress.

8. Wealth and Labor

Wealth is the result of human labor. Labor is the means by which man's mind transmits his designs and purposes to matter. It is man's application of his bodily and mental faculties for the purpose of altering matter in form or location and thereby making the matter thus altered serve a further purpose. Matter thus altered by man's labor is a *product*. Production is the process of thus altering matter. A producer is one who effects such alterations.[35]

The matter which is altered in production, that is, which is the subject of man's labor, can be nature-given, such as a piece of land or ore in the ground, or itself a previously produced product, such as cotton cloth or steel sheet. Always, the performance of human labor is essential to production.

It is important to realize that in a division-of-labor society, the labor applied in production is not limited to manual labor, that is, to labor applied to materials or otherwise in physical operations. In such a society, it embraces much more, such as the labor entailed in founding, organizing, and directing business firms and in providing them with capital. Such labor achieves its effects by operating through the manual labor of others, which it renders more efficient.[36]

The concept of wealth embraces not only products but also natural resources, such as land, and mineral deposits in the ground. The physical matter of which natural resources are composed is, of course, not made by man—it is nature-given. Nevertheless, the *wealth-character* of natural resources is man-made: it is the result of human labor. It is the result of the labor that discovers the uses to which the natural resources can be put, and of the labor that enables them to be become accessible in ways in which they can be used gainfully. Thus, it is labor that establishes the character of natural resources as goods and thus as wealth. As the leading historical example of this fact, one need only consider that all of the land and mineral deposits of North America were present at the time of the American Indians. Nevertheless, hardly any of that land and mineral deposits then constituted wealth. The land and mineral deposits did not constitute wealth, because the necessary labor—mainly of an intellectual character—had not yet been performed to render them wealth.

The Scarcity of Labor and Its Ineradicability

Wealth not only is the product of human labor, but also could be produced in larger quantity if more labor were devoted to its production. Indeed, the application of more labor is the only fundamental requirement for increasing the supply of wealth. This is because more labor is the source of additional equipment and materials, including additional agricultural commodities and mineral supplies extracted from the ground. Thus, the scarcity of wealth implies a more fundamental *scarcity of labor*.

As has already been shown, and will be fully confirmed in the next chapter, the fact that the wealth-character of natural resources is the result of labor indicates that in a capitalist society, the supply of natural resources

can be indefinitely expanded and therefore does not constitute a long-run limitation on the ability to produce that is independent of the supply of labor. Indeed, as the next chapter will show, even within very short periods of time—weeks or months—the supply of raw materials can almost always be increased through the application of more labor.[37]

The fundamental scarcity of labor is manifest in the fact that virtually everyone would like to enjoy an income many times greater than the income he is presently capable of earning. For example, today an average worker may earn on the order of $20,000 per year for working forty hours a week. If such a worker had it in his power to earn $100,000 per year, he would have no difficulty in finding ways to live up to such an income. Unfortunately, to earn such an income at his present rate of pay, he would have to work more hours than there are in the week. His maximum actual ability to work is obviously vastly less than corresponds to the income he would like to have.

But this is only another way of saying that the utmost goods and services he is capable of *producing* are far less than the goods and services he would like to consume. Taken collectively, our desire to be able to spend five or ten times more than we now can afford to spend is an indication that we would like five or ten times more work performed than is now performed. In the present state of technology and productivity of labor (output per unit of labor), this is how much additional labor would need to be performed to produce the larger volume of output we would like to be able to buy.

Consider. It would be very easy for the government of the United States to arrange things so that the average worker could earn and spend $100,000 a year instead of $20,000 a year. Indeed, the governments of many countries have long ago made it possible for all of their citizens to be millionaires! To accomplish such results, all the government would have to do is print enough new and additional paper money. But there is nothing to be gained from such a procedure. It is accompanied by rising prices, which prevent the higher incomes from having any greater buying power than the smaller incomes did before. The only way that earning and spending $100,000 a year instead of $20,000 a year can represent the ability to buy five times more goods is if five times more goods are produced. Only then would prices not rise in the face of five times more spending to buy goods. But in a given state of technology and productivity of labor, this would be possible only if five times as much labor could be performed, which, of course, is itself impossible. People can work themselves to the point of utter exhaustion, and still they cannot produce more than a small fraction of all that it would be useful and desirable for them to produce. Thus, the supply of labor that people can provide falls radically short of the supply whose products they would like to have. Labor is scarce.

(It should be obvious that the scarcity of labor implies there is never any *metaphysical* reason for the existence of unemployment—that is to say, there is never any reason for it by virtue of the necessary, inescapable nature of things. Unemployment belongs strictly in the category of the man-made. Either it is voluntary and chosen by the individuals concerned, because they prefer to wait to find better terms of employment or because they simply prefer leisure; or, where it is involuntary and unchosen by the individuals concerned, it is *forcibly imposed on them.* Unemployment is forcibly imposed through the imposition of too high a level of money wage rates by the government or by coercive labor unions operating with the sanction of the government. These policies, of course, could be done away with. The causes of unemployment will be fully clear once we understand the principles governing money and spending, and the fact that under the freedom of competition, purchasing power sufficient to buy all the goods and services that can be produced in the economic system at the point of full employment is automatically generated by the process of production itself. The discussion of these important matters is reserved for later chapters.[38])

The scarcity of labor, of course, is also the result of a scarcity of personal services. Virtually everyone, if he could afford it, would like to be able to be served by maids, cooks, gardeners, personal secretaries, and so on. Each individual could probably find worthwhile uses for the labor of half a dozen or more full-time servants, without even giving the matter more than a moment's thought.

The labor that we implicitly desire to have at our disposal, whether to produce goods for us or to provide us with personal services, is, as I have said, limited only by our imaginations. And yet while nature has provided each of us with an imagination capable of forming desires on a grand scale, it has simultaneously equipped each of us with only two arms to provide for the satisfaction of those desires. Each of us is easily capable of forming desires whose fulfillment requires the labor of multitudes, and yet by the laws of arithmetic, the average member of any society can never obtain more than the labor, or products of the labor, of just *one* person. This is so because for each person who exists to consume, there can be no more than one person present to produce. Indeed, when the very young and the sick and infirm are allowed for, who can only be supported by the labor of others, it turns out that for each person who consumes there is, on average, substantially less than the labor of one person available to produce.

The preceding discussion demonstrates the existence of a fundamental scarcity of labor. The scarcity of labor is not only fundamental, however. It is also *ineradicable.*

I have already shown earlier in this chapter how increases in the ability to produce are accompanied by new and additional desires for wealth, which grow out of the very same technological advances that make possible the increases in the ability to produce. The effect of this is that the scarcity of labor is not reduced by increases in the productivity of labor. The scarcity of labor is also not reduced by any increase in the size of the population and thus the number of people able and willing to work, because the additional members of that population bring with them their own needs and desires for goods and services that are in excess of their ability to add to the supply of goods and services. Furthermore, as the productivity of labor rises and increases the workers' standard of living, the workers tend to acquire a growing desire for leisure. As a result, not only does the desire for wealth grow as the ability to produce it increases, but also the amount of labor the individual is willing to perform decreases. This represents an additional cause of the continuing scarcity of labor.

Thus, the fundamental and essential nature of economic life is this: the need and desire for additional wealth are there and the nature-given means of producing it are there; all that is lacking is the ability of human labor to transform the nature-given means of production into additional wealth.

On this foundation, the fundamental economic need of rational beings emerges as the overcoming of the limitations production imposed by the scarcity of labor. Always, what stands between man and his need for greater wealth is his limited ability to produce wealth— his limited ability and also willingness to perform labor. There is only one solution to this problem. And that is *continuously to raise the productivity of labor*—that is, continuously to increase the quantity and quality of the goods that can be produced per unit of labor, including the variety of goods. An ineradicable scarcity of labor resulting from a need and desire for labor that are always vastly greater than the supply of labor requires that the productivity of labor be rendered greater and greater. The rise in the productivity of labor is the only conceivable way in which man can obtain the progressively greater amounts of wealth that his rational and progressive nature requires.

The problem of precisely *how continuously to raise the productivity of labor,* to make possible an ever increasing production and enjoyment of goods per capita, is what I call *the economic problem.*

(Associated with the economic problem is an important but subsidiary problem, which is often mistakenly presented as the central economic problem, namely, how to allocate an existing limited ability to produce in accordance with the choices of individuals to satisfy their more important wants ahead of their less important wants. The necessity of this choice is implied by the existence of needs and wants that have no limit, in the face of a productivity of labor that at any given time is always strictly limited. Regrettably, it is this subsidiary problem that most economists have in mind when they describe economics as focusing on "the allocation of scarce means among competing ends." Closely associated with this mistaken view of the economic problem is the formulation of the fundamental problem of economic life in terms of a scarcity of *goods*. The actual fundamental problem, of course, is a scarcity of *labor* and thus how to raise the productivity of labor.)

The next chapter provides a conclusive demonstration of the limitless potential of natural resources and contains a necessary critique of the objections of the ecology movement to economic progress. Following it, Chapter 4 will explain why the focal point of the ongoing solution to the economic problem is *the division of labor.* The division of labor will be shown to constitute the indispensable social-organizational framework for the progressive increase in the productivity of labor required by

man's nature as a rational being. It will be shown to represent in its inner nature the form of society required for the efficient and progressively improving use of man's mind, body, and nature-given environment in production.

As previously indicated, subsequent chapters will then show the dependence of the division of labor on the leading institutions of a capitalist society, above all, private ownership of the means of production and the price system. They will also show the reciprocating and thoroughly benevolent influence of the division of labor on private ownership of the means of production and other essential institutions of capitalism, namely, economic inequality and economic competition. Still later chapters will show how, within the framework of the division of labor and capitalism, the productivity of labor is continuously increased on the basis of *capital accumulation*—which entails the employment of ever increasing amounts of wealth as means of further production—and the absolute dependency of this process too on the institutions of capitalism.

In effect, the remainder of this book can be summarized as demonstrating a single proposition: in every possible way, with no valid objection, *the solution for the economic problem is capitalism.*

Notes

1. See below, p. 59.
2. Cf. Ludwig von Mises, *Planning For Freedom,* 4th ed. enl. (South Holland, Ill.: Libertarian Press, 1980), p. 65.
3. For elaboration of these points, see below, pp. 673–674.
4. See below, pp. 378–380.
5. Exactly the same principles apply to the market value of trade secrets. For a discussion of why, unlike government licenses, patents and copyrights do not constitute a case of monopoly, see below, pp. 388–389. For discussion of the status of rights and relationships in general in relation to the concepts of goods and wealth, see Eugen von Böhm-Bawerk, *Whether Legal Rights and Relationships Are Economic Goods* in *Shorter Classics of Böhm-Bawerk* (South Holland, Ill.: Libertarian Press, 1962).
6. Slavery also undermines the production of wealth by undermining the accumulation of capital. On this point, see below, pp. 455–456.
7. Menger would have disputed the need to include the qualification concerning the expenditure of labor or effort in the definition of economic goods. Nor did he think it necessary to include the qualification "gainfully" in his discussion of "sufficient command" over things. Cf. Carl Menger, *Principles of Economics,* trans. and ed. James Dingwall and Bert F. Hozelitz (Glencoe, Ill.: The Free Press, 1950), pp. 51–54, 100–101.
8. Stocks, bonds, and bank deposits are such claims.
9. Cf. Menger, *Principles of Economics,* pp. 55–58.
10. See below, pp. 141–144.
11. See Israel M. Kirzner, *The Economic Point of View* (New York: D. Van Nostrand, 1960), pp. 22–29, 108–185, for an

exposition of this belief.
12. Regrettably, this criticism applies to the great von Mises and his efforts to portray economics as merely the "hitherto best developed part" of an allegedly wider science of human action known as praxeology. See Ludwig von Mises, *Human Action,* 3d ed. rev. (Chicago: Henry Regnery Co., 1966), pp. 1–10 passim. I wish to note, indeed to stress, however, that even when I have ultimately come to disagree with some position of von Mises, as in this case, I do not recall ever having read so much as a single paragraph of his writings that did not serve as the most powerful stimulus to my own thinking. Therefore, I urge everyone to give the most serious consideration to every portion of his writings.
13. Adam Smith, *The Wealth of Nations* (London, 1776), bk. 1, chap. 11, pt. 2; reprint of Cannan ed. (Chicago: University of Chicago Press, 2 vols. in 1, 1976), 1:183.
14. For a discussion of the essential elements of a rational philosophy which pertain to economic activity, see above, pp. 19–21.
15. For a presentation of the doctrine of cultural relativism by one of its leading advocates, see Melville J. Herskovits, *Cultural Relativism Perspectives in Cultural Pluralism* (New York: Random House, 1972). For a presentation of the doctrine of conspicuous consumption by one of its leading advocates, see Thorstein Veblen, *The Theory of the Leisure Class* (New York: Modern Library, 1934), chap. 4.
16. I am indebted to Ayn Rand both for the general concept of an objective code of values based on man's life as the standard and for the special application of that concept in the form of

some goods being classified as being of greater "philosophically objective value" than others. See Ayn Rand, *Atlas Shrugged* (New York: Random House, 1957), pp. 1012–1023; *Capitalism: The Unknown Ideal* (New York: New American Library, 1966), pp. 16–17.

17. See my pamphlet *Education and the Racist Road to Barbarism*, 3d and subsequent printings (Laguna Hills, Calif.: The Jefferson School of Philosophy, Economics, and Psychology, 1992), pp. 4–5. As I wrote in that pamphlet, "Reference to an objective superiority of one civilization or culture over another encounters the opposition of a profound, self-righteous hatred of the very idea. Thus, cultures may practice ritual sacrifice, cannibalism, mass expropriation, slavery, torture, and wholesale slaughter—all of this is accepted as somehow legitimate within the context of the culture concerned. The only alleged sin, the only alleged act of immorality in the world is to display contempt for such cultures, and to uphold as superior the values of Western culture. Then one is denounced as an imperialist, racist, and virtual Nazi. It should be realized that those who take this view do not regard as the essential evil of Nazism its avowed irrationalism, its love of force and violence, and its acts of destruction and slaughter. All this they could accept, and do accept in the case of other cultures, such as that of primitive tribes, ancient Egypt, the civilization of the Aztecs and Incas, the Middle Ages, and Soviet Russia. What they hold to be the evil of Nazism was its assertion that Nazi culture was superior to other cultures. Needless to say, of course, it is only on the basis of the recognition of objective values that one can seriously condemn Nazism—not for its absurd claims of superiority, but as a primitive, barbaric culture of the type one would expect to find among savages." (Ibid., pp. 7–8.)

18. The flagrant contradiction of upholding individual rights in the midst of Negro slavery has already been noted. See above, p. 28.

19. Cf. Eugen von Böhm-Bawerk, *Capital and Interest*, 3 vols., trans. George D. Huncke and Hans F. Sennholz (South Holland, Ill.: Libertarian Press, 1959), 2:143–145.

20. Cf. John Kenneth Galbraith, *The Affluent Society* (Boston: Houghton Mifflin, 1958), chap. 10. See also, in opposition, George Reisman, "Galbraith's Modern Brand of Prussian Feudalism," *Human Events* 18, no. 6, sec. 5 (February 3, 1961), pp. 77–80.

21. Again, see below, pp. 414–416.

22. See, for example, Paul Samuelson and William Nordhaus, *Economics,* 13th ed. (New York: McGraw-Hill, 1989), p. 450. See also above, the Introduction, n. 15, for an explanation of why my references are typically to the 13th edition of Samuelson and Nordhaus rather than to the more recent 14th edition.

23. For a full discussion of Say's Law, see below, pp. 559–580.

24. See below, pp. 561–569.

25. An illustration of this principle is the devastating storms which occurred in Bangladesh in 1992. Had the same storms occurred in a more prosperous country, in which people could afford concrete houses instead of thatched huts, and in which adequate sea walls could be built, the death toll would have been in the hundreds, rather than over one hundred thousand. See "Even in Bangladesh's Storms, Poverty Is Underlying Killer," *New York Times*, May 11, 1991, p. 1, p. 5. Unless otherwise noted, throughout this book all references to this publication are to the national edition.

26. For further discussion of the role of wealth in the lengthening and enrichment of human life, see below, pp. 76–78.

27. Capital is wealth employed in the production of wealth. In the context of a division-of-labor, monetary economy, it is the wealth employed by business enterprises, that is, means of production which have been purchased for the purpose of producing goods or rendering services which are intended to be sold. For further elaboration on the meaning of the concept, see below, pp. 445–456.

28. See Böhm-Bawerk, *Capital and Interest*, 2:268–273.

29. See below, pp. 743–744.

30. See below Chapter 17, in particular pp. 824. See also pp. 629–631.

31. Later discussion will show that the capitalized value of land also contributes to the ineradicable scarcity of capital. See below, pp. 856–857.

32. See below, pp. 813–824.

33. See below, pp. 813–826.

34. See above, pp. 19–21.

35. Depending on the extent of the alteration of the matter, the product may be described either as a new good or merely as the alteration of an existing good. On this point, see below, p. 130.

36. For elaboration of this very important subject, see below, pp. 462–464 and 475–485.

37. See below, pp. 63–71.

38. See below, Chapters 12–19.

CHAPTER 3

NATURAL RESOURCES AND THE ENVIRONMENT

PART A

NATURAL RESOURCES

1. The Limitless Potential of Natural Resources

The potential for economic progress is in no way limited by any fundamental lack of natural resources. Despite the claims so often made that we are in danger of running out of natural resources, the fact is that *the world is made out of natural resources*—out of solidly packed natural resources, extending from the upper limits of its atmosphere to its very center, four thousand miles down. This is so because the entire mass of the earth is made of nothing but chemical elements, all of which are natural resources. For example, the earth's core is composed mainly of iron and nickel—millions of cubic miles of iron and nickel. Its oceans and atmosphere are composed of millions of cubic miles of oxygen, hydrogen, nitrogen, and carbon, and of lesser, but still enormous, quantities of practically every other element. Even the sands of the Sahara desert are composed of nothing but various compounds of silicon, carbon, oxygen, hydrogen, aluminum, iron, and so on, all of them having who knows what potential uses that science may someday unlock. Nor is there a single element that does not exist in the earth in millions of times larger quantities than has ever been mined. Aluminum is found in some quantity practically everywhere. There are immense quantities even of the very rarest elements,

such as gold and platinum, to be found floating in trace amounts throughout the oceans, for example.

What is true of the earth is equally true of every other planetary body in the universe. Insofar as the universe consists of matter, it consists of nothing but chemical elements, and thus of nothing but natural resources.

Nor is there any fundamental scarcity of energy in the world. More energy is discharged in a single thunderstorm than mankind produces in an entire year. Nor is the supply of energy in the world reduced in any way by virtue of the energy man captures from nature. Heat from the sun provides a constantly renewed supply that is billions of times greater than the energy consumed by man. The total quantity of energy in the world remains a constant, for all practical purposes incalculably in excess of what mankind consumes, and will remain so until the sun begins to cool.

The problem of natural resources is in no sense one of intrinsic scarcity. From a strictly physical-chemical point of view, *natural resources are one and the same with the supply of matter and energy that exists in the world and, indeed, in the universe.* Technically, this supply may be described as finite, but for all practical purposes it is infinite. It does not constitute the slightest obstacle to economic activity—there is nothing we are prevented from doing because the earth (let alone the universe) is in danger of running out of some chemical element or other, or of energy.

The problem of natural resources is strictly one of *useability, accessibility, and economy.* That is, man needs to know what the different elements and combinations of elements nature provides are good for, and then to be able actually to get at them and direct them to the satisfaction of his needs without having to expend an inordinate amount of labor to do so. Clearly, the only effective limit on the supply of such *economically useable* natural resources—that is, natural resources in the sense in which they constitute *wealth*—is the state of scientific and technological knowledge and the quantity and quality of capital equipment available.

Because the supply of resources provided by nature is one and the same with the supply of matter and energy, the supply of economically useable natural resources is capable of virtually limitless increase. It increases *as man expands his knowledge of and physical power over the world and universe.*

For example, petroleum, which had been present in the ground for millions of years, did not become an economically useable natural resource until the second half of the nineteenth century, when uses for it were discovered. Aluminum, radium, and uranium also became economically useable natural resources only within the last century or so. The economic useability of coal and, more recently, silicon, has been enormously increased by the discovery of new and additional uses for them.

The supply of economically useable natural resources is increased not only by the discovery of uses for things previously thought to have no uses, or new and additional uses for things already known to have uses, but also by advances that enable man to improve his access to things—for example, to mine at greater depths with less effort, to move greater masses of earth with less effort, to break down compounds previously beyond his power, or to do so with less effort, to gain access to regions of the earth previously inaccessible or to improve his access to regions already accessible. All of these increase the supply of economically useable natural resources. All of them, of course, at the same time bestow the character of goods and wealth on what had before been mere things.[1]

Today, as the result of such advances, the supply of economically useable natural resources is enormously greater than it was at the beginning of the Industrial Revolution, or even just one or two generations ago. Today, man can more easily mine at a depth of a thousand feet than he could in the past at a depth of ten feet, thanks to such advances as mechanical-powered drilling equipment, high explosives, steel structural supports for mine shafts, and modern pumps and engines. Today, a single worker operating a bulldozer or steam shovel can move far more earth than hundreds of workers in the past using hand shovels. Advances in reduction methods have made it possible to obtain pure ores from compounds previously either altogether impossible to work with or at least too costly to work with. Improvements in shipping, railroad building, and highway construction have made possible low-cost access to high-grade mineral deposits in regions previously inaccessible or too costly to exploit.

In the light of such facts, one should consider how foolish it is to complain, for example, that today copper ores are being mined which contain only 1 percent pure copper, whereas at the beginning of the twentieth century the ores mined often contained 10 percent pure copper. With a worker in the cab of a steam shovel able to move hundreds or thousands of times more earth in the same time as a worker with a hand shovel, the volume of pure copper moved in the same time is now enormously greater, even with ores only one-tenth as pure. The resort to such ores is evidence not that we are running out of supplies, but that we have been able to create vastly greater sources of supply than ever before. The very fact that we exploit such deposits is evidence of the advances that have been made. For we would not exploit them in the absence of vast improvements in the productivity of labor.

Similarly, the development of chemical fertilizers and low-cost methods of irrigation have enabled man not only radically to improve the productivity of arable land, but actually to *make more arable land.* Today, land previously desert or semidesert has been made vastly more productive than the very best lands available to previous generations. Israel and California provide leading examples.

There is no limit to the further advances that are possible. Hydrogen, the most abundant element in the universe, may turn out to be an economical source of fuel in the future. Atomic and hydrogen explosives, lasers, satellite detection systems, and, indeed, even space travel itself, open up limitless new possibilities for increasing the supply of economically useable mineral supplies. Advances in mining technology that would make it possible to mine economically at a depth of, say, ten thousand feet, instead of the present much more limited depths, or to mine beneath the oceans, would so increase the portion of the earth's mass accessible to man that all previous supplies of accessible minerals would appear insignificant in comparison. And even at ten thousand feet, man would still, quite literally, just be scratching the surface, because the radius of the earth extends to a depth of four thousand *miles.*

As just indicated, equally dramatic advances are possible in the field of energy. These may occur through the use of atomic energy, hydrogen fusion, solar power, tidal power, or thermal power from the earth's core, or still other processes as yet unknown. Reductions in the cost of extracting petroleum from shale and tar sands have the potential for expanding the supply of economically use-able petroleum by a vast multiple of what it is today. The physical volume of petroleum present in such formations in our own Rocky Mountain states and in Canada far exceeds the liquid petroleum deposits of the Arab countries. All that is required is ways to reduce the costs of extraction.[2] Similarly, there are also vast known coal fields in the United States containing enough coal to supply present rates of coal consumption for many centuries, and already capable of doing so economically. Since most petroleum products can be made from coal, reductions in the cost of using coal for this purpose would represent the equivalent of a further enormous increase in the supply of economically useable petroleum deposits.

Because the earth is literally nothing but an immense solid ball of chemical elements and because man's intelligence and initiative in the last two centuries were relatively free to operate and had the incentive to operate, it should not be surprising that the supply of useable, accessible minerals today vastly exceeds the supply that man is economically capable of exploiting. In virtually every case, there are vast *known* deposits of minerals which are not worked, because it is not necessary to work them. Indeed, if they were worked, there would be a relative overproduction of minerals and a relative under-production of other goods—that is, a waste of capital and labor. In virtually every case, it is necessary to choose *which* deposits to exploit—namely, those which, by virtue of their location, the amount of digging required, the degree of concentration and purity of the ore, and so forth, can be exploited at the lowest costs. Today, enormous mineral deposits lie untouched which could be exploited with far less labor per unit of output than was true of the very best deposits exploited as recently as a few decades ago—thanks to advances in the state of mining technology and in the quantity and quality of mining equipment available.

So long as men preserve a division-of-labor, capitalist society and are free and motivated to think and to build for the future, the body of scientific and technological knowledge at the disposal of mankind will grow from generation to generation, as will the supply of capital equipment.[3] On this basis, man can steadily expand his physical power over the world and thus enjoy an ever greater supply of economically useable natural resources. There is no reason why, under the continued existence of a free and rational society, the supply of such natural resources should not go on growing as rapidly as in the past or even more rapidly.

The ultimate key to the economic availability of natural resources is *motivated human intelligence,* which means: *a capitalist society.* In such a society, large num-bers of the most intelligent people devote their lives to science, technology, and business. All are highly motivated to increase the supply of economically useable natural resources by the prospect of earning a personal fortune for every significant success they achieve in this regard. No greater guarantee of mankind's ability to enjoy a growing supply of natural resources could be found.

The essential principles pertaining to natural resources can be summarized as follows. What nature provides is a supply of matter and energy that for all practical purposes is infinite. Yet at the same time, nature does not provide a single particle of natural resources in the form of *wealth.* The bestowal of the character of economic goods and wealth on what nature provides is the work of human intelligence. An essential economic task of man is progressively to apply his intelligence to achieve a growing understanding of nature and to build progressively more powerful forms of capital equipment that give him growing physical mastery over nature.

In this process, advances both in knowledge and in capital equipment themselves set the stage for further advances in knowledge and in capital equipment, thereby operating to give man both ever greater understanding and ever greater physical power over nature—provided, of course, that he continues to be rational, that is, continues to think and to act long range. For example, learning arithmetic sets the stage for learning algebra, which in turn sets the stage for learning calculus, and so on. Being able to build the first primitive railroads and steel mills provides the physical capacity for being able to build more and better railroads and steel mills later on. Developing a metallurgical industry sets the stage for developing an electrical industry and appliance industry, which sets the stage for developing an electronics and computer industry, which in turn sets the stage for developing a capacity to launch spaceships, and so on. The combination of increasing knowledge and increasing physical capacities brings a growing fraction of the physical mass of the earth and, indeed, the universe more and more within man's power to serve his ends and thus continually enlarges the fraction of nature that represents economically useable natural resources and thus wealth.

Thus the portion of nature that represents wealth should be understood as a tiny fraction that began as virtually zero and even though it has since been multi-plied by several hundredfold, is still virtually zero when one considers how small is the portion of the mass of the earth, let alone of the universe, that is subject to man's control, and how far man is from understanding all aspects and potential uses of what has become subject to his control. To borrow and expand upon Ayn Rand's statement that the good is an aspect of reality in relation to man: For all practical purposes, nature in its infinity will forever remain something far more of whose good in relation to man remains to be discovered and achieved than ever has been discovered and achieved, with the essential requirements of the ongoing process being reason and capitalism.[4] Reason and capitalism achieve a progressive enlargement of the goods- and wealth-character of nature and thus a continually increasing supply of economically useable natural resources. Not only can no greater guarantee of mankind's ability to enjoy a growing supply of natural resources be found, but the underlying metaphysics of a virtually infinite nature that is confronted by motivated human intelligence, which steadily expands both man's knowledge and his physical capacities, ensures that no greater guarantee of mankind's success is necessary.

The growing threat to the supply of natural resources that people are beginning to complain of is not the result of anything physical—no more than it was when these terrible words of despair were written:

> You must know that the world has grown old, and does not remain in its former vigour. It bears witness to its own decline. The rainfall and the sun's warmth are both diminishing; the metals are nearly exhausted; the husbandman is failing in the fields, the sailor on the seas, the soldier in the camp, honesty in the market, justice in the courts, concord in friendships, skill in the arts, discipline in morals. This is the sentence passed upon the world, that everything which has a beginning should perish, that things which have reached maturity should grow old, the strong weak, the great small, and that after weakness and shrinkage should come dissolution.[5]

That passage is not a quotation from some contemporary ecologist or conservationist. It was written in the *third century*—long before the first chunk of coal, drop of oil, ounce of aluminum, or any significant quantity of any mineral whatever had been taken from the earth. Then as now, the problem was not physical, but philosophical and political. Then as now, men were turning away from reason and toward mysticism. Then as now, they were growing less free and falling ever more under the rule of physical force. That is why they believed, and that is why people in our culture are beginning to believe, that man is helpless before physical nature. There is no helplessness in fact. To men who use reason and are free to act, nature gives more and more. To those who turn away from reason or are not free, it gives less and less. Nothing else is involved.

The Energy Crisis

There has been much talk about an energy shortage. There is obviously no shortage of energy in nature and no inherent reason why mankind should not be able to continue the progress of the last two centuries and gain economical access to more and more of nature's virtually infinite supply of energy.

Even if liquid petroleum deposits were to run out in the next fifty years or so, there is no reason why, before they did, men should not be able to produce petroleum products from shale, tar sands, or coal with less labor than they presently produce them from liquid petroleum— just as they presently produce iron and copper from relatively low-grade ores with far less labor than they used to produce them from higher-grade ores. Indeed, petroleum products today can already be produced from these sources with far less labor than they could be produced from liquid petroleum deposits in the past. The power of man's mind, operating in the context of a division-of-labor, capitalist society is clearly such as to leave no doubt that comparable beneficial results could be accomplished with respect to petroleum products in the years ahead.

The energy crisis of the 1970s was purely political. In essence, it was the result of making it largely *illegal* to produce energy. In almost every foreign country, the ownership of oil and natural gas deposits, and thus the production of oil and natural gas, has been made a monopoly of the government. It is simply illegal for private citizens to produce these goods and thus their production has been restricted by all the inefficiencies of government ownership.[6] In the United States, the federal government claims ownership of the continental shelf and the majority of the land area of the Western states. On the basis of these claims, and under the guise of "concern for the environment," it has closed off many of the most promising areas for oil and gas discoveries. It has set them aside as "wildlife preserves" and "wilderness areas," and thus prohibited their development. In these ways and others, to be explained later in this book, the government made it illegal to produce energy. This is the only reason that there was an energy crisis.[7] The substantial reduction in government interference that took place in the early 1980s, above all, the repeal of price controls on oil, made the energy crisis disappear. The achievement of a fully free market in energy would ensure a resumption of the growing abundance and declining real cost of energy that characterized the Western world in the two hundred years prior to the 1970s.

Regrettably, however, the government's policy of restricting the supply of energy continues. It continues to withdraw ever more territory from exploration and development: virtually the entire continental shelf of the United States is now closed to new oil drilling and further development of Alaskan fields is in doubt. The government even prohibits the use of already existing facilities for producing energy, the two best-known cases being the Shoreham atomic power plant on Long Island, in New York State, and the Gaviota Oil and Gas Plant near Santa Barbara, California. The Shoreham plant, completed in 1984 at a cost of $5.5 billion, had the capacity to supply one-third of the power needs of the 900,000-plus homes on Long Island. Nevertheless, it was never allowed to operate beyond the test level, and as of October 1994, its nuclear reactor was actually dismantled.[8] The Gaviota plant, completed in 1987 at a cost of $2.5 billion, has the capacity to refine 100,000 barrels of oil per day. But it too has never been allowed to operate, because of environmentalist policies on the part of the State of California and the County of Santa Barbara.[9]

2. The Law of Diminishing Returns

The production of any product requires the use of at least two factors of production, for example, labor and land, or labor, a land site, a factory building, and machinery and material.[10] The combinations of factors of production, of course, can be far more complex, entailing such things as a variety of machines, materials, means of transportation, and fuels both to power the means of transportation and to provide power and light to the factories involved.

Now if all of the factors necessary to the production of a product are increased in the same proportion, such as all of them being doubled, then it is to be expected that the quantity of product produced will also be increased in that proportion, that is, in the present instance, doubled. Usually, however, it is also possible to increase the production of a product by means of increasing the quantity just of some of the necessary factors of production. For example, the quantity of output produced on a farm might be increased by increasing only the quantity of labor, or labor and equipment together, without increasing the quantity of land employed. In manufacturing, it is almost always possible to increase production within existing factories, simply by increasing the quantity of labor, materials, and fuel employed, and thus without increasing either the number or size of the factory buildings or even the quantity of machinery employed.

All such cases constitute the domain of *the law of diminishing returns,* or, as it sometimes called, the law of nonproportional returns. The law of diminishing returns states that under a given state of technological knowledge, the use of successively larger quantities of any factor of production or combination of factors of production in conjunction with a fixed quantity of any other necessary factor or factors of production eventually results in less than proportionate increases in output. For example, a repeated doubling of the labor and capital applied to a given piece of land must soon result in less than double the output being obtained from that piece of land.

If such were not the case, then the entire world's supply of food could be grown on this one piece of ground. Similarly, the entire world's supply of any given good could be produced within a single factory building. The fact that sooner or later more land and more factory buildings, more of *all* the necessary factors of production, are required for the production of more of anything, is evidence of the existence of diminishing returns. The point is reached where the application merely of more of the factors of production initially allowed to increase— the so-called variable factors of production—results in an amount of additional output that is less than proportional to the additional quantity of the variable factors of production, and, ultimately, in no additional output whatever. Sooner or later, to increase output in the same proportion as the increase in the variable factors of production, or, indeed, to increase it at all, it becomes necessary to increase the quantity of the factors of production that were initially held fixed (the so-called fixed factors of production).

This necessity results from the existence of what von Mises has called "quantitative definiteness." Everything physical has only a definite, delimited capacity to produce effects. That capacity may be exhausted at one fell swoop, or it may be approached more or less gradually. For example, the capacity of a given quantity of flour of a definite quality to produce bread is thoroughly exhausted in the production of a definite quantity of bread of a definite type. It is not possible to produce more such bread without the availability of more such flour. The application of additional labor alone in this case would not result in any additional product.

In other cases, such as loading a flatbed truck higher and higher, it is possible to increase the quantity of labor expended disproportionally and succeed in producing more of the product, in this case more cargo loaded onto a given truck. But again, sooner or later, the carrying of more cargo requires another truck, and before another truck becomes absolutely essential, the carrying of more cargo *relative to the employment of a given amount of labor* requires another truck. This last reflects the fact that disproportionate increases in the quantity of labor are required to accomplish additional increases in the amount of cargo loaded onto a given truck. In both cases, that of the flour and that of the truck, the capacity of the fixed factor of production to render service is limited and sooner or later more of the fixed factor is required for the production of more of the product and/or to maintain the productivity of the variable factor(s) of production.[11]

Table 3-1 provides a quantitative illustration of the

Table 3–1

Diminishing Returns

Quantity of Labor Employed on a Farm of 100 Acres (in man-years)	Output (in bushels)	Increase in Output	Average Output per Worker
1	100	100	100
2	190	90	95
3	270	80	90
4	340	70	85

operation of diminishing returns in the context of the application of varying amounts of labor to a farm of a given number of acres. It makes clear how more of the fixed factor of production is required to maintain the *productivity* of the variable factor(s) of production long before it is absolutely required for the production of any more of the product whatever. Thus, in Table 3-1, while more output can be produced simply by employing more labor, the use of more land is necessary to stop the productivity of labor from falling. For example, the table shows 85 units as the average output per worker resulting from the employment of 4 man-years of labor on a farm of 100 acres. At the same time, the table implies that with four such 100-acre farms, the average output per worker would be 100 units rather than only 85 units.

The only context in which the law of diminishing returns does not apply is that of technological formulas or recipes, that is, ideas. The same identical idea can be applied over and over, ad infinitum, with absolutely no loss in its ability to render service and thus no decline in the productivity of the other factors of production.[12]

Closely related to the law of diminishing returns is a parallel phenomenon which was identified by the great classical economist David Ricardo, and which operates on the basis of the pursuit of rational self-interest. This is the fact that as far as people have knowledge and the power of choice, they will choose to exploit land and mineral deposits where the productivity of their labor is greatest. As Ricardo put it, they will begin by cultivating land of the first quality and by exploiting mineral deposits of the first quality. Only when population reaches the point where all the land and mineral deposits of the first quality have been brought into production, will they resort to land and mineral deposits of the second quality, which now represents the most productive land and

mineral deposits available to them. In comparison with land of the first quality, land of the second quality will tend to be farther away from the market it serves, to be higher up on the hillsides, and to have rockier soil; mines of the second quality will also tend to lie farther away from the market they serve, and to have less pure ores and require deeper digging.

Further increases in population and the bringing into production of more and more of the land and mineral deposits of the second quality ultimately results in the need to exploit land and mineral deposits of the third quality, which at that point are rendered the most productive still available, and, after that, land and mineral deposits of the fourth, and still lower qualities. Thus, a man-year of labor performed on land of the first quality may result in an output of 100 units, while an identical man-year of labor performed on land of the second quality results in an output of 90 units, and on land of the third quality, 80 units, and, finally, on land of the fourth quality, only 70 units.[13]

The necessity of progressively resorting to land of inferior degrees of productivity operates in just the same way as the diminution of returns accompanying the employment of more and more labor on any given piece of land. Indeed, the two processes go on side by side. In the examples presented here, when it became necessary to cultivate land of the second quality, land of the first quality would be cultivated more intensively, and the additional output gained by the employment of the second man-year on land of the first quality would equal the output produced by the first man-year on land of the second quality, namely, 90. Similarly, when it became necessary to cultivate land of the third quality, land of the second quality would be cultivated more intensively, and the cultivation of land of the first quality would be further intensified. In our examples, the output of the first man-year on land of the third quality is equal to that of the second man-year on land of the second quality and to that of the third man-year on land of the first quality, that is, 80.

The Law of Diminishing Returns and the Limitless Potential of Natural Resources

The law of diminishing returns in no way contradicts the previously established proposition that there is no practical limit to the potential supply of economically useable natural resources. This is because the law of diminishing returns in application to agriculture and mining applies only *at any given time*, in the context of *a given state of technology and capital equipment*. Over time, economic progress can occur. Indeed, in a division-of-labor, capitalist society, with its rationality and its incentives both monetary and cultural for the continuous application of reason to the problems of human life, economic progress is the norm.[14]

The advancing technology and improving capital equipment which such a society makes possible can easily offset the effects of the law of diminishing returns, and by a wide margin. Quantitative definiteness continues to exist and it continues to be true that, for example, one can bake just so much bread of a given quality from a given quantity of flour, or generate just so much heat from a pound of coal. However, ways are found for the same quantity of human labor, using improved machinery and equipment, to produce and process larger quantities of flour, coal, and all other goods. Similarly, ways are found for the same quantity of human labor to farm or mine larger quantities of land, and to render larger quantities of land suitable for farming or mining. In farming, this occurs through such means as the use of tractors and harvesters and the development of improved methods of irrigation. In mining, it occurs through such means as the use of steam shovels, bulldozers, improved drills, and high explosives. In addition, as scientific and technological knowledge increases, ways are found radically to increase the productive power of each acre of farmland or mineral deposit. In farming, this occurs by such means as improving the chemical composition of the soil, the use of insecticides and herbicides, developing improved strains of seed, and, of course, once again, irrigation. In mining, it occurs by such means as finding ways to process ores previously impossible to process or too costly to process—for example, acquiring the ability to move multiton loads of ore with less effort than was previously required to move a single shovelful of ore, and learning to break elements out of different compounds or to do so at a lower cost, such as learning to break iron out of sulfide compounds as well as oxide compounds and to do so at a lower cost.

Thus, in a division-of-labor, capitalist society, a more intensive or more extensive use of land encounters diminishing returns whether in 1894 or in 1994. But in such a society, by 1994 economic progress has so improved the powers of human labor that the very poorest lands and mines currently in use are a hundred times more productive than the very best lands and mines in use in 1894, and the point to which the productivity of labor diminishes in agriculture and mining in 1994 is more than a hundred times higher than the point to which it diminished in 1894. Indeed, thanks to economic progress, it is possible today to take even extremely submarginal land—actual desert—and by piping in water and adding various chemicals to the soil, make such land vastly more productive than were the very best lands of a few generations ago, as has been accomplished in Israel and in the Imperial Valley in California. Similar examples can be found in the case of mining. Indeed, so great has been the access to better lands and the increase in yields per acre on all grades of land, that extensive acreages farmed in the past have been thrown out of cultivation and returned to forest or pasture. This was the case in large portions of the eastern United States as better lands opened up in the Midwest, and in Great Britain, as American lands became a source of supply.

With still further economic progress, such results will continue to be achieved in the future. For example, in recent years, it has been demonstrated that it is even possible to grow many crops in scientifically controlled soils and solutions in multistory buildings, in virtual factory conditions. This, of course, is a development potentially equivalent to a practically limitless increase in the supply of agricultural land. The art of genetic engineering, presently in its infancy, also holds out enormous potential. In the case of mining, it will probably one day be possible with the aid of controlled atomic and hydrogen explosions to move the most enormous masses of earth at a minimum of cost. And it will probably come within man's power someday to conduct mining and even farming operations not only under the sea, but elsewhere in the solar system, and beyond.

Thus, the leading principle continues to be that as man increases his knowledge of and physical power over the world—indeed, the universe—the supply of accessible and economically useable natural resources continues to increase, and to increase per unit of labor expended.

The discussion of the law of diminishing returns confirms the fact that the only limiting factor in production—the only fundamentally scarce agent of production—is human labor, never land or natural resources. There is always uncultivated land that could be cultivated, or already cultivated land that could be cultivated more intensively, and mineral deposits that are known but presently unexploited, or that are exploited, but which could be exploited more intensively. For example, there is all the land left as natural forest or pasture, which could easily be used to grow crops, and the enormous quantities of desert-type land which potentially could also be used for crops. As an example from the case of minerals, there are, as previously mentioned, enormous deposits of oil in the form of shale and tar sands that have never been touched. And roughly two-thirds of the oil in conventional oil fields has typically been left in the ground.

The reason for leaving such useable land and mineral deposits alone is that the labor that would be required to work them would have to be withdrawn either from better land and mineral deposits, where its productivity is higher, or from the production of other goods that are more important than the production of additional agricultural commodities or minerals. For example, to farm land that we now leave alone, we would have to withdraw labor either from better farmland, where its productivity is higher, or from the production of other goods having greater importance to buyers than the additional agricultural commodities.

For exactly the same reasons, we do not exploit each piece of land or mine to the maximum possible extent. The additional labor that would be required would have to come either from other land or mines where the operation of diminishing returns had not been carried as far, and thus where the productivity of labor is greater, or from the production of other goods having a greater importance to buyers than additional agricultural commodities or minerals. For example, to get all the remaining two-thirds of the oil out of a conventional oil field, we might have to give up the one-third normally extracted from a dozen other oil fields, because we would need so much additional labor. Or we would have to give up other goods in quantities that we judged to be more important than the additional oil.

Nevertheless, it should be clear that if we do need more agricultural commodities or minerals, we can obtain them by withdrawing labor from other lines and applying it to existing farms or mines, or to land or mineral deposits which we know to be capable of production but which we have up to now left idle because their exploitation did not pay. Thus, even in the short run, that is, without waiting for any new technological advances or discoveries, production need never be restricted by a lack of raw materials.

Of course, with economic progress, which is to be expected under capitalism, we can have more and more raw materials, not only without withdrawing labor from other lines, but along with actually making labor available for other lines. The economic history of the last two centuries, for example, shows not only a radical increase in the supply of raw materials of all types, but also a radical decrease in the proportion of labor devoted to agriculture and mining, and a corresponding increase in the proportion of labor devoted to manufacturing and the various service industries. These results can be understood simply by imagining a hundredfold increase in the productivity of labor in the production of raw materials, accompanied by a willingness to consume only a ten-times greater quantity of raw materials before giving preference to larger quantities of more highly processed goods and to larger quantities of services. In such circumstances, instead of using 100 workers in agriculture and mining to produce 100 times the output of raw materials, 10 such workers will now be used to produce 10 times the output of such goods, and 90 workers previously used to produce such goods will be released to produce more of other things.

Diminishing Returns and the Need for Economic Progress

The existence of the law of diminishing returns implies that economic progress is necessary not only for improvement in the standard of living, but also to maintain the standard of living at any given level. In the absence of economic progress, a rising population would result in diminishing returns in both agriculture and mining, because the larger supply of foodstuffs and minerals that would be required for the larger population would necessitate resorting to land and mines too poor to have been exploited before, and to the more intensive exploitation of the land and mines already in use. Even if the population did not grow, diminishing returns would still be encountered in mining, as the ores closest to the surface and otherwise easiest to work gave out. (In the case of mining, diminishing returns actually accompany the repetition of the same amount of labor over time, not just the application of additional labor at the same time.)

Thus, even with a constant population, *in the absence of economic progress, the standard of living falls rather than remains stationary.* When it does remain stationary, it does so as the result of at least enough economic progress taking place to offset the operation of the law of diminishing returns in mining.

These facts should be of significance in judging the proposals of those who desire an end to economic progress, notably the ever increasing numbers within the environmental or ecology movement who subscribe to the goal of zero economic growth. What they are asking for is not the maintenance of our present level of well-being, but growing impoverishment.[15] Furthermore, it should be realized that such impoverishment cannot be made gradual and gentle, as year-to-year diminishing returns in mining might suggest. Nor is it possible somehow to arrange for just enough economic progress to offset diminishing returns in mining.

Economic progress is not something that can be controlled or regulated in amount. If the conditions are right for it, there is no fixed limit to how much of it there can be at any time. If the conditions are wrong for it, there will be not only no economic progress, but radical economic decline.

The essential precondition of economic progress is the existence of individuals who are motivated to think and to apply the results of their thinking to the economic world. But this is also an essential precondition of the *maintenance* of any modern economic system as well. To maintain such a system, new problems must constantly be solved. Even if essentially the same problems have been solved before, in previous generations, they are new to those who must solve them in the present generation. And almost always, they will differ in at least some important respects from the problems solved in the past. All machinery and equipment eventually wear out and must be replaced. All buildings, roads, bridges, and tunnels sooner or later need total replacement or such extensive maintenance and repair as to be tantamount to total replacement. All of this requires a fresh process of thought. And this requires the existence of a large body of individuals willing and able to think.

The attempt to stifle the fresh thinking that results in economic progress must, if successful, also stop the fresh thinking that is necessary to maintain the economic system at its present level. This is because it must operate against fresh thinking as such. One cannot tell a self-activating intelligence that it can be driven by its curiosity up to the point of repeating what happens to be the old, but must not undertake the new. If the attempt is made to stifle the curiosity and discovery associated with the new, it must serve to stifle the curiosity and discovery required to replicate the old. The effect of prohibiting economic progress must be to make eager intelligence give way to passive stupidity throughout the economic system, and thus radically to undermine the economic system, not merely prevent its improvement.

3. Conservationism: A Critique

The preceding discussions imply that the doctrine of conservationism is incorrect. Conservationism regards the existing supply of economically useable natural resources as nature-given, rather than as the product of human intelligence and its corollary, capital accumulation. It does not see that what nature provides is, for all practical purposes, an infinite supply of matter and energy, which human intelligence can progressively master, in the process creating a steadily increasing supply of economically useable natural resources. It does not see that the supply of economically useable natural resources increases as man gains understanding of the world and the universe and correspondingly improves his means of production, thereby progressively enlarging the fraction of nature over which he holds physical power. It does not see that as the fraction of nature within man's knowledge and control grows, so too does his supply of economically useable natural resources. In a word, conservationism does not see that the increase in the supply of economically useable natural resources is part of the very same process by which the ability to produce as such and in general is increased.

Having no conception of the role of human intelligence in the creation of economically useable natural resources, and confusing the present supply with all the natural resources present in nature, the conservationists naïvely believe that every act of production that consumes natural resources is an act of impoverishment, using up an allegedly priceless, irreplaceable treasure of nature. On this basis, they conclude that the pursuit of self-interest by individuals under economic freedom leads to the wanton consumption of mankind's irreplaceable natural heritage, with no regard for the needs of future generations.

Once having arrived at the existence of this altogether illusory problem, the product of nothing more than their own ignorance of the productive process, the conservationists further conclude that what is necessary to solve this alleged problem is government intervention designed to "conserve" natural resources by restricting or prohibiting in various ways mankind's use of them.

Ironically, the consequence of all such restrictions and prohibitions is *waste*—the waste of the one truly scarce factor of production, namely, human labor. It is our labor and our time that are fundamentally scarce, not land or natural resources. It is our labor and our time that we fundamentally need to save, not land or natural resources. For the most part, we need to economize on land and natural resources only insofar as doing so represents a saving of our labor or time. We need to be concerned with those land sites and mineral deposits whose existence saves us labor as compared with having to produce by using inferior land or mineral deposits. For example, we value farmland in the Midwest and an oil field because their existence saves us labor in producing food and oil. Without that midwestern farmland, we would have to produce to a greater extent on less productive East Coast farmland, or cultivate other midwestern land more intensively and thus produce with a lower productivity of labor. Similarly, without that oil field, we would have to resort to more intensive, less efficient methods of extracting oil from other such fields or perhaps bring into production a less productive source of oil, such as tar sands, or even shale deposits. In both cases, the effect would be that it would take more labor to produce the same amount of goods. The existence of the midwestern land and of the oil field saves us that labor, and that is why we value both.

Sometimes, it is true, particular land sites are unique in *what* they enable us to produce. Their product cannot be perfectly duplicated by using a larger quantity of labor elsewhere. For example, real estate in downtown Manhattan, sturgeon beds providing fine caviar, vineyards serving in the production of grapes, and thus wines, of a unique flavor. At other times, no amount of labor can provide more of a good—for example, agricultural commodities between harvests. In these categories of cases, we may speak of a problem of conservation apart from the saving of labor.

But even in these cases, conservationism is thoroughly mistaken in thinking that some kind of political action is required to avoid misuse of the goods in question. This is because the market price of such goods reserves them to their most important uses and limits the rate of their consumption in conformity with the limited supply of them available. The free-market price of real estate regularly ensures that it is devoted to its most important uses. The free-market price of every agricultural commodity acts to conserve an adequate supply of it until the next harvest comes in. In exactly the same way, the free-market price of minerals operates to limit their rate of consumption between the discovery of new deposits or improved methods of extraction, to whatever extent that may be necessary. In such cases, the prospect of higher prices in the future operates to bring about higher prices immediately, which higher prices automatically limit the rate of consumption.[16] No limitation of the rate of consumption by the government is required. All the necessary limitation is effected by the free-market price, which makes all due allowance for the needs of the future. Any limitation of the rate of consumption over and above that accomplished by the free-market price merely serves needlessly to sacrifice the present to the future, which does not require such sacrifice, and thus simply to render human labor less productive.

The mistaken philosophy of conservationism currently plays a major role in the opposition to atomic power, the strip mining of coal, and the opening of new landfill areas for garbage disposal. It also underlies the many proposals for "recycling" and even the fifty-five mile an hour speed limit.

It is argued, for example, that the disposal of radioactive material from atomic power plants constitutes a major problem because the dump sites in which the material is placed will remain radioactive and therefore unuseable for other purposes for tens of thousands of years. Similarly, it is argued that the strip mining of coal should not be undertaken because once the coal is removed, the land will no longer be useable for farming or ranching, unless, at great expense, the soil layer is restored.

The supporters of these arguments simply do not realize that we do not need every last piece of land that we possess. In the United States, we have hundreds of thousands of square miles of land—deserts and mountains, for example—that as far as their contribution to human life and well-being is concerned might as well be covered with sea water. The marginal utility or importance of such land is simply zero. Even if some of it were totally lost to use forever, it would make absolutely no difference to human life and well-being. In insisting on the sacredness of every square mile of land, we place ourselves in the position of a kind of irrational miser— not a miser of money, but, if it is possible to imagine it, a miser of water in a country that is filled with lakes, rivers, and streams. It is as though we were a farmer needing, say, a thousand gallons of water a day for every purpose that water can serve, and having ten thousand gallons a day available, and yet losing sleep at night over the loss of a cupful somewhere.

Even if, out of the 3.5 million square miles of territory of the United States, atomic dump sites and surface coal mines totally and forever destroyed the usefulness of a few hundred or even a few thousand square miles for other purposes, there would be no loss to us. Even if some of the land to be used for these purposes presently has other uses, like serving as farmland or ranch land, these uses would be given up only because of the land's greater value as a dump site or mine. And its loss as farm or ranch land would be made good either by bringing other, presently unused land into production or by producing more intensively on other land. The net effect would simply be that we could have some of the additional energy that we so urgently need.

To make all this concrete and as clear as possible, let us assume that a coal-mining company wants to buy land in Wyoming that is presently a cattle ranch. It is willing to pay a price that is far higher than corresponds to the income its present owner can make from ranching. Neither the coal-mining company nor the rancher nor the great majority of other people may realize it, but this higher offer reflects the fact that this piece of land is more urgently needed for coal mining than for cattle ranching. The buyers of coal are willing to allow more in the price of coal for the use of this piece of land than the buyers of cattle products are willing to allow for it in the price of cattle products. That is why it is worth more to the coal mining company than it is to the cattle rancher. Even if the piece of land is lost forever to cattle ranching or any other use thereafter, the effect is that we can obtain urgently needed coal and energy, while the cattle the land previously supported can be fed on other land. Furthermore, because of the greater availability and therefore lower price of energy that would result from allowing the all-out development of energy sources, it is almost certain that the cattle would soon be able to be raised at a lower cost on other land than they could be if they continued to remain on the coal-bearing land.

The same principles, of course, apply to atomic dump sites. It should go without saying that, in a capitalist society, the owner of such a dump site would not be able to expose the property of his neighbors to harmful doses of radiation. He would have to own a large enough site to ensure that radiation levels at its perimeter were well within the zone of safety. (It should also go without saying that a landowner's neighbors, let alone people living at the opposite end of the country, have no right to the preservation of any special aesthetic qualities of a piece of land. Even if it were true, for example, that strip mining left the land horrendously ugly, rather than bestowing its own kind of grandeur, no one could legitimately claim that he is thereby denied the use and enjoyment of his own property, or, therefore, that he has a right to interfere.[17])

Of course, it is probably the case that in the future technology will find ways of eliminating radioactivity and restoring land at far less cost than is presently possible. Whether it does or not, however, is irrelevant. For nothing of significance depends on our having the land in question.

As matters now stand, the kind of mistaken ideas about the waste of land that have been discussed are threatening us with an enormous waste of our labor. This is because the only alternative to the energy that man-made fuels such as atomic power and strip-mined coal can provide is the minuscule amounts that human muscles can provide. Thus if we prevent the development of such man-made fuels, our ability to produce is correspondingly impaired.

As indicated, a further consequence of the conservation mentality has been a sharp reduction in the number of government permits issued for the opening of landfill areas for garbage disposal.[18] The conservationists' rationale is that the use of land for this purpose represents a "waste" of the land. The effect has been that as the existing landfill areas approach their planned capacity, a shortage of space for garbage disposal has begun to develop. In response to this shortage, citizens are denounced for a profligate lifestyle, which allegedly generates an excessive amount of garbage, and as part of the solution, parents are urged to sacrifice both their own convenience and even the comfort and health of their infants by giving up the use of disposable diapers and going back to the use of diaper services. In addition, homeowners and apartment dwellers are urged to turn a portion of their dwelling space into minirecycling centers, carefully separating newspapers, metal cans, and glass containers from ordinary refuse, to make possible the convenient collection and recycling of these items.

As the shortage of landfill space has developed, such facts as the government's restrictions on the opening of new landfill areas have been conveniently ignored in the press, which has led the public to believe that the problem is one of an actual lack of space for garbage disposal. Also ignored is the fact that the average American, with his modern, prosperous lifestyle actually generates substantially *less* garbage today than in the past, and less than the average contemporary Mexican with his much less advanced and highly impoverished lifestyle.[19] This is the result of such facts as that in modern society the twelve hundred pounds or more of coal ash that the average American family used to generate is no longer generated, thanks to the use of electricity, natural gas, and heating oil to heat homes; nor, thanks to such things as canning and freezing and modern meat packing, is there nearly as much garbage for the average family to dispose of in the form of animal and vegetable matter, such as chicken feathers, fish scales, and potato peels. And of the garbage that is generated, it turns out that the contribution made by disposable diapers is on the order of a mere 1 percent, while that of fast-food containers (another leading target of today's conservationists and "environmentalists") is closer to a tenth of 1 percent and that of all plastics combined (yet another leading target) is less than 5 percent.[20]

Confusions about waste are present in much of the concern expressed about the need for "recycling." When it is possible for a comparative handful of workers using giant steam shovels and other such machinery to move and process ores in multiton loads and thus to produce things like new tin cans and glass jars easily and cheaply, it makes little sense for the average person to spend his time ferreting through his garbage to find a few cans or jars to bring to his neighborhood "recycling center" or to set aside for pickup by a special garbage truck. It is not his throwing away the cans or jars that is wasteful, but his spending time to retrieve and deliver them, or the garbage disposal company's having to make a separate collection of them. For he certainly has better things to do with that time, and the garbage company should not be put to the needless expense of having a second truck and crew to collect items of insignificant value.

Of course, not all recycling is wasteful. Whether it is or not is indicated by the relationship between the market price of the recycled material and the cost of recycling it. If the market price of the recycled material is high enough to allow compensation for the labor involved and for a competitive rate of profit on the capital that must be invested, then the recycled material is important enough to justify the recycling. For example, the price of gold and silver is high enough to make it pay dentists to retrieve the shavings drilled from fillings, which would otherwise simply be washed down the drain. On the other hand, it normally would not pay people to save their steel or aluminum cans, because the productivity of labor in mining and processing fresh iron and aluminum ore is so high, and the price of steel and aluminum cans accordingly so low, as to make their efforts in this regard highly inefficient and unnecessary.

In this connection, it should be realized that there is nothing "wasteful" or uneconomic in the fact that we use so many cans or so many paper wrappings. As pointed out a few paragraphs back, they actually serve considerably to reduce the volume of the more unpleasant forms of garbage.[21] Furthermore, as I wrote elsewhere, if we consider how little labor it costs us—in terms of the time it takes us to earn the money we spend for it—to have things brought to us clean and fresh and new, in new containers and new packaging, and what the alternatives are for the spending of that money or the use of that time, it becomes clear that the expenditure is well made.[22]

For consider the alternatives. We could have our food and other goods wrapped in old newspapers and put in jars, bags, or boxes that we would have to carry along with us whenever we went shopping, or which we would have to make a special trip to go and fetch whenever we came on something unexpectedly that we wanted to buy. We could then use the money we saved in that way to buy a handful of other goods. Conceivably, we could use the money we saved to work a few minutes less at our jobs each day, and earn correspondingly less. But these alternatives would simply be bizarre, because neither a handful of extra goods nor working a few minutes less at our jobs each day would compensate us for the loss of cleanliness, convenience, aesthetic satisfaction, and also time saved in shopping that is provided by modern packaging.

Of course, people are free to adopt a poverty-stricken personal lifestyle if they choose. They may go about like old Russian grandmothers in Moscow, with an ever present shopping bag and herring jar, if that is what they like. They may pick through garbage pails while pretending that they live in a spaceship—"spaceship Earth," they call it—rather than in the richest country of the planet Earth. But there is absolutely no sane reason why anyone should, or needs to, live this way, and certainly not in modern America. Above all, no one should be forced by

law to comply with such peculiar values.

Not surprisingly, the attempt to force people to accept such irrational values has begun to introduce what must be described as a measure of totalitarian interference into their lives. Where recycling has become mandatory, as in New York City, there are now garbage police, whose job is to snoop into people's garbage to make sure that they are complying with the recycling requirements. Such coercion and spying are unavoidable when people are required to do something nonsensical and which they would thus not do voluntarily. It can be expected that school children indoctrinated with environmentalism will be encouraged to report neighbors and even their own parents to the garbage police.

The fifty-five mile-an-hour speed limit is also inspired by conservationism. It is supposed to avoid the waste of oil. As a conservation measure, the fifty-five mile an hour speed limit turns out to be wasteful in the same way that the compulsory recycling measures are wasteful. Namely, in a misguided effort to save oil, it wastes labor, equipment, and people's time, the loss of which is more important than the oil it saves.

The proof of this wastefulness is that all the trucking companies and most automobile owners know that by driving at fifty-five miles an hour, rather than at seventy miles an hour, say, they can reduce the amount of fuel consumed per mile and thus reduce their fuel costs. Nevertheless, despite this cost saving, they do not voluntarily choose to drive at the lower speed. The reason the trucking companies do not is that the value of the fuel saved is less than the additional wages that must be paid to truck drivers, who must spend more hours driving at the lower speed to haul the same amount of freight the same distance; in addition, a larger number of trucks may be required to haul the same amount of freight within the same period of time. The owners of automobiles do not voluntarily drive at the lower speed, because the importance they attach to the money they would save by doing so is less than the importance they attach to the time they save by driving faster.

The comparison of the money saved with the money lost, or of the importance of the money saved with the importance of the personal time lost, is the only rational criterion of waste, because it weighs *all* the relevant factors involved (such as the truckers' labor as well as the fuel), not just one factor in isolation. Furthermore, if it is kept in mind that additional oil can always be produced if necessary, by withdrawing labor from the production of other things, then it should come as no surprise that the use of this criterion leads to goods being produced with the lowest overall amount of labor, or with labor of the least value.

The fact, for example, that the fuel trucking companies can save by driving more slowly is less valuable than the extra truck drivers' labor they need at the lower speeds is an indication that the labor needed to *produce* the additional fuel is less than the labor needed to save fuel by driving more slowly. For example, saving five dollars' worth of fuel by virtue of having to pay ten dollars more in wages to truck drivers is an indication that at least twice as much labor is required to make possible the saving of the fuel than is required to produce an equivalent amount of the fuel. Indeed, since the wages paid in the production of fuel worth five dollars are *less* than five dollars, the saving of labor through the use of the fuel in question turns out to be even greater. The fact that a given amount of fuel can be made available by less labor if we produce more fuel than if we consume less fuel means that conservationism's forcing us to consume less fuel simply makes us waste our labor.[23]

Ironically, in previous decades, mistaken ideas about waste led to demands for government-sponsored development of natural resources, above all, irrigation and flood control projects. At that time, it was naïvely assumed that the mere fact that a piece of land was capable of being used productively meant that it should be used productively; otherwise, it was held, the land was "wasted." It was not realized that in view of the fundamental scarcity of labor, it is simply not possible to use all the land that is potentially useable. It was not seen that the effect of compelling the development of land that the market judges to be submarginal is to cause the waste of labor and capital—that is, the withdrawal of labor and capital from better, more productive land or from the production of other goods more urgently desired. On the basis of such ignorance, the U.S. government, under the New Deal, squandered billions of dollars on such projects as the Tennessee Valley Authority.

Conservationism has spawned the popular misconception, now taken up by the ecology movement, that the individual's freedom to pursue his self-interest is responsible for such phenomena as senseless deforestation and the wanton destruction of species. The improper, uneconomic deforestation practiced in various portions of the United States in the late nineteenth and early twentieth centuries, and the near disappearance of the buffalo, which once roamed the Great Plains of the United States in large numbers, are presented as leading examples.

These examples do not prove what the conservationists believe they prove. It was not the pursuit of self-interest under freedom that was responsible for such deforestation, but the government's *violation of the individual's freedom to establish private property.* Since the second half of the nineteenth century, the U.S. government has claimed ownership of most of the territory of the Western states, including, of course, forests and mineral deposits, and refused to allow this territory to become private property.

When, in contrast, forests are privately owned, self-interest does not normally lead their owners to cut them down without bothering to replant, which is what the logging companies were denounced for in the late nineteenth and early twentieth centuries. Indeed, a self-interested owner does not normally cut trees down without bothering to replant, any more than he cuts down wheat or corn without bothering to replant. Trees are simply a longer-term crop than wheat or corn. They are commercially grown wherever land is private property and the prospective price of trees covers the costs of planting and an allowance for a compound competitive rate of return over their growing life.

However, the fact that the western forests of the United States were owned by the government meant that the logging companies which worked them could not expect to receive the benefits of replanting. As a result, they had no incentive to go to the trouble and expense of replanting. Had the government owned the farmland, and deprived farmers of the prospect of owning the next crop of wheat or corn, no incentive would have existed for replanting those crops either. The obvious solution was to make forest lands private property. Private owners, whether logging companies or others, would have had the incentive to replant.

The near extermination of the buffalo resulted from the fact that their value to man was simply not great enough to justify the expense of the labor of preserving them. The buffalo certainly could have been raised commercially, on ranches, just as cattle are raised. But no one found it profitable to do so, because the consumers were simply unwilling to allow prices for buffalo meat and buffalo hides high enough to cover the costs of such operations. They much preferred beef and cowhides instead. Buffalo were valuable to man only so long as they were free for the taking on the open range.

In the light of such facts, their near extermination was not an act of wanton destruction, but perfectly reasonable. The only alternative would have been to compel the domestication of the buffalo and, to that extent, to force the consuming public to accept buffalo meat and buffalo hides in preference to beef and cowhides. Or else the alternative would have been to close the Great Plains, or some large part of them, to settlement, in order to maintain the open range for the sake of the buffalo. Either way, the preservation of the buffalo as a significant species would have entailed enormous waste: the waste of ranch land, labor, and capital in supporting buffalo herds instead of cattle herds, or the waste of the whole Great

Plains or some huge portion of them in being closed to development altogether. Either way, there would have been an enormous loss in terms of the ability of the Great Plains to contribute to human life and well-being.

PART B

THE ECOLOGICAL ASSAULT ON ECONOMIC PROGRESS

1. The Hostility to Economic Progress

A long-standing hostility has existed to economic progress. Prior to the 1960s, this hostility was based on the doctrines of asceticism, conspicuous consumption, cultural relativism, and on a cluster of economic fallacies to which I have given the name consumptionism. (This last is represented by such beliefs as that machinery causes unemployment and that war and destruction cause prosperity. According to consumptionism, the fundamental problem of economic life is not the creation of wealth but of the need or desire for wealth, which is thought to be naturally limited, and which allegedly has been or is about to be surpassed by the production of wealth, thereby resulting in a problem of "overproduction," depression, and unemployment.)

The doctrines of conspicuous consumption and cultural relativism have already been dealt with in Chapter 2. Consumptionism is dealt with below, in Part A of Chapter 13. As for asceticism, which claims to find value in self-denial for its own sake, there is nothing to say except that wealth is the means to better health and longer life, as well as to greater enjoyment of life. Thus, its value is logically implied in the very concept of human values, which presupposes the existence of living human beings who value their lives.[24] Moreover, as was shown in Chapter 2, wealth without practical limit is necessary for the achievement of values in the physical world on the scale made possible and required by man's possession of reason.[25] Asceticism is thus simply a doctrine of the negation of human values and human life.

In the last three decades, a powerful new opposition to economic progress has developed. This opposition emanates from the so-called ecology or environmental movement. (In what follows, I use the expressions "ecology doctrine" and "environmentalism," and "ecologists" and "environmentalists," interchangeably.) This movement has achieved such a degree of influence that it presently seems on the verge of actually being able to stop further economic progress by means of the enactment of its program into law.

Such a threat cannot be ignored. Indeed, there is no point in explaining how the division of labor makes possible economic progress, and the dependency of the division of labor on capitalism, when the value of economic progress itself has been called into question in this way. Thus, even though it is in the nature of a digression, the doctrines of the environmental movement, and their refutation, must be the subject of the remainder of this chapter.

2. The Claims of the Environmental Movement and Its Pathology of Fear and Hatred

The essential, all-encompassing doctrine of the environmental movement is that the continuation of economic progress is both *impossible and dangerous.* Insofar as it claims the impossibility of the continuation of economic progress, the movement offers nothing more than a repetition of the claims of conservationism. Indeed, it can be considered as having fully absorbed the conservation movement, with conservationism now standing merely as an aspect of environmentalism.

The argument against the possibility of economic progress continuing is, of course, based on the failure to grasp the physical nature of the world and the progressive nature of man. It should not be necessary to dwell further on this aspect of the ecology doctrine, because it has already been thoroughly refuted in Part A of this chapter. There it was shown that the problem of natural resources is strictly one of making a greater fraction of nature's virtually infinite endowment accessible and economically useable. This in turn was shown to be accomplished to the degree that man gains understanding of and power over nature through scientific and technological progress and correspondingly improved capital equipment.[26]

The Actual Nature of Industrial Civilization

Before considering the specific claims the environmental movement makes concerning the alleged dangers of economic progress, it is vital to recognize the enormous contribution that the essential vehicle of economic progress, namely, *industrial civilization,* has made to human life and well-being since its birth over two centuries ago in the Industrial Revolution.

Industrial civilization has radically increased human life expectancy: from about thirty years in the mid-eighteenth century to about seventy-five years today. In the twentieth century, in the United States, it has increased life expectancy from about forty-six years in 1900 to the present seventy-five years. The enormous contribution of industrial civilization to human life is further illustrated by the fact that the average newborn American child has a greater chance of living to age sixty-five than the average newborn child of a nonindustrial society has of living to age five. These marvelous results have come about because of an ever improving supply of food, clothing, shelter, medical care, and all the conveniences of life, and the progressive reduction in human fatigue and exhaustion. All of this has taken place on a foundation of science, technology, and capitalism, which have made possible the continuous development and introduction of new and improved products and more efficient methods of production.

In the last two centuries, loyalty to the values of science, technology, and capitalism has enabled man in the industrialized countries of the Western world to put an end to famines and plagues, and to eliminate the once dread diseases of cholera, diphtheria, smallpox, tuberculosis, and typhoid fever, among others. Famine has been ended, because industrial civilization has produced the greatest abundance and variety of food in the history of the world, and has created the storage and transportation systems required to bring it to everyone. This same industrial civilization has produced the greatest abundance of clothing and shoes, and of housing, in the history of the world. And while some people in the industrialized countries may be hungry or homeless (almost always as the result of destructive government policies), it is certain that no one in the industrialized countries needs to be hungry or homeless.[27] Industrial civilization has also produced the iron and steel pipe, the chemical purification and pumping systems, and the boilers, that enable everyone to have instant access to safe drinking water, hot or cold, every minute of the day. It has produced the sewage systems and the automobiles that have removed the filth of human and animal waste from the streets of cities and towns. It has produced the vaccines, anesthesias, antibiotics, and all the other "wonder drugs" of modern times, along with all kinds of new and improved diagnostic and surgical equipment. It is such accomplishments in the foundations of public health and in medicine, along with improved nutrition, clothing, and shelter, that have put an end to plagues and radically reduced the incidence of almost every type of disease.

As the result of industrial civilization, not only do billions more people survive, but in the advanced countries they do so on a level far exceeding that of kings and emperors in all previous ages—on a level that just a few generations ago would have been regarded as possible only in a world of science fiction. With the turn of a key, the push of a pedal, and the touch of a steering wheel, they drive along highways in wondrous machines at sixty miles an hour. With the flick of a switch, they light a room in the middle of darkness. With the touch of a button, they watch events taking place ten thousand miles away. With the touch of a few other buttons, they talk to other people across town or across the world. They even fly through the air at six hundred miles per hour, forty thousand feet up, watching movies and sipping martinis in air-conditioned comfort as they do so. In the United States, most people can have all this, and spacious homes or apartments, carpeted and fully furnished, with indoor plumbing, central heating, air conditioning, refrigerators, freezers, and gas or electric stoves, and also personal libraries of hundreds of books, records, compact disks, and tape recordings; they can have all this, as well as long life and good health—as the result of working forty hours a week.

The achievement of this marvelous state of affairs has been made possible by the use of ever improved machinery and equipment, which has been the focal point of scientific and technological progress.[28] The use of this ever improved machinery and equipment is what has enabled human beings to accomplish ever greater results with the application of less and less muscular exertion.

Now inseparably connected with the use of ever improved machinery and equipment has been the increasing use of *man-made power,* which is the distinguishing characteristic of industrial civilization and of the Industrial Revolution, which marked its beginning. To the relatively feeble muscles of draft animals and the still more feeble muscles of human beings, and to the relatively small amounts of useable power available from nature in the form of wind and falling water, industrial civilization has added man-made power. It did so first in the form of steam generated from the combustion of coal, and later in the form of internal combustion based on petroleum, and electric power based on the burning of any fossil fuel or on atomic energy.

This man-made power, and the energy released by its use, is an equally essential basis of all of the economic improvements achieved over the last two hundred years. It is what enables us to use the improved machines and equipment and is indispensable to our ability to produce the improved machines and equipment in the first place. Its application is what enables us human beings to accomplish with our arms and hands, in merely pushing the buttons and pulling the levers of machines, the amazing productive results we do accomplish. To the feeble powers of our arms and hands is added the enormously greater power released by energy in the form of steam, internal combustion, electricity, or radiation. In this way, energy use, the productivity of labor, and the standard of living are inseparably connected, with the two last entirely dependent on the first.

Thus, it is not surprising, for example, that the United States enjoys the world's highest standard of living. This is a direct result of the fact that the United States has the world's highest energy consumption per capita. The United States, more than any other country, is the country where intelligent human beings have arranged for motor-driven machinery to accomplish results for them. All further substantial increases in the productivity of labor and standard of living, both here in the United States and across the world, will be equally dependent on man-made power and the growing use of energy it makes possible. Our ability to accomplish more and more with the same limited muscular powers of our limbs will depend entirely on our ability to augment them further and further with the aid of still more such energy.

So little are these elementary facts understood that a thoroughly perverted concept of economic efficiency has come into vogue, a concept whose actual meaning is the precise opposite of economic efficiency. Economic efficiency centers on the ability of human beings to reduce the quantity of labor they need to expend per unit of output and thus to be able to produce more and more while expending the same or a smaller amount of labor. This, of course, requires the growing use of energy per capita, as I have just explained. Nevertheless, increasingly the practice today is to view economic efficiency as centering on how little energy can be consumed per unit of output, which, of course, necessarily implies an increasing need for human labor per unit of output. For example, a front-page article in *The New York Times,* of February 9, 1991, was headlined "Bush's Energy Plan Emphasizes Gains in Output over Efficiency." Although the headline meant to refer specifically to the output of energy, the article's actual position reduces to the absurdity the headline suggests, namely, that increases in the overall output of goods produced by the same amount of human labor are a contradiction of efficiency, for any such increase in production requires the greater production and use of energy per capita, which the article characterizes as inefficient. Along the same lines, a later headline in the same newspaper read "Bad News: Fuel Is Cheap."[29] Later discussion will make clear that the perversion of the concept of efficiency is philosophically consistent with the environmental movement's most fundamental values.

Now not only does the environmental or ecology movement respond to the marvelous accomplishments of industrial civilization with all of the sensibilities one might expect from a dead log, but in virtually every respect, it represents an attack on industrial civilization, on the values of science, technology, and capitalism on which that civilization rests, and on all of its material fruits, from air conditioners and automobiles to television sets and X-ray machines. The environmental movement is, as Ayn Rand so aptly characterized it, "the Anti-Industrial Revolution."[30]

Consistent with what I said earlier in connection with the values of capitalism, none of the preceding is to say that life in the modern world is without serious problems, especially in many of today's large cities.[31] It is to say, however, that the problems are not the result of economic progress, capitalism, technology, science, or human reason. On the contrary, they are the result precisely of the absence of these values. The solution to every problem, from crime to unemployment is a combination of one or more of these essential attributes of industrial civilization. Thus, for example, if rent control destroys the quality of housing in cities, if minimum wage and pro-union legislation cause unemployment, if inflation and confiscatory taxation cause capital decumulation and economic decline, if acceptance of the doctrine of determinism stops the punishment of criminals—on the grounds that they could not help it—and the crime rate soars, if people are sick and seek health, if they are poor and seek to be richer, the solution is not the destruction of industrial civilization. The solution is more of what industrial civilization rests upon. It is economic freedom—capitalism. It is recognition of the power of reason and thus the power of the individual to improve himself. And it is science, technology, and economic progress.

What the solution is not, is environmentalism.

The Environmental Movement's Dread of Industrial Civilization

The environmental movement is characterized by pathological fear of industrial civilization and of science and technology. It fears the "pollution" of water and air as the result of industrial production and the emission of its by-products. It fears the poisoning of fish, the destruction of rivers and lakes, the "pollution" of entire oceans. It fears "acid rain," the destruction of the ozone layer, the onset of a new ice age, the contrary onset of global warming and the melting of the polar icecaps and rise of sea levels. It fears the use of pesticides and herbicides out of fear of the food chain being poisoned. It fears the use of chemical preservatives and countless other alleged causes of cancer stemming from the "chemicals" produced by industrial civilization. It fears radiation not only from atomic power plants but also from color television sets, microwave ovens, toasters, electric blankets, and electric power lines. It fears the disposal of atomic wastes, all other toxic wastes, and all nonbiodegradable wastes. It fears landfills and the destruction of wetlands. It fears the destruction of animal and vegetable species that are useless or even hostile to man, and demands the preservation of each and every one. It demands the preservation or re-creation of everything as it is or was, before the arrival of man on the scene, from "old-growth" forests, stretches of prairie, and Arctic and Antarctic wastes to the reintroduction of wolves and bears into areas from which they had been eliminated.[32]

As I wrote elsewhere, as a result of the influence of the environmental movement, increasing numbers of present-day Americans and West Europeans "view science and technology in reality as they used to be humorously depicted in Boris Karloff and Bela Lugosi movies, namely, as frightening 'experiments' going on in Frankenstein's castle. And casting themselves in a real-life role of terrified and angry Transylvanian peasants, they seek to smash such science and technology."[33] For all practical purposes, the effect of environmentalism has been the creation of a horde of hysterical bumpkins in the midst of modern civilization.

As a leading manifestation of this phenomenon, a growing number of our contemporaries view atomic power as a terrifying death ray, beyond man's power to use safely. Their fear is such that they refuse to sanction even the establishment of dump sites for atomic wastes. Indeed, as previously mentioned, the government of the state of New York, itself having been overcome by the fears inculcated by the ecology movement, has dismantled the brand-new, fully constructed Shoreham atomic power plant on Long Island, a plant whose power output would have prevented the overloads and brownouts and blackouts that are now a much more real possibility in the New York City area in the years to come. It and the environmentalists seem to be totally unaware of or unconcerned with such likely consequences of the plant's dismantling as people being trapped in elevators and subways, massive food spoilage, deaths from heat stroke because of lack of air conditioning, and so on, because that plant and its power output will not exist. All that the state government and the environmentalists seem to have been aware of is their *imagining* of a large-scale radiation leak.

In indulging their fear of atomic power, the environmentalists simply disregard all the scientific and engineering safeguards built into atomic power plants in the United States, such as backup systems, automatic shutdown in the event of coolant loss, and containment buildings capable of withstanding the direct crash of a jet liner.[34] They ignore such facts as that the worst nuclear accident in American history—that of the Three Mile Island nuclear plant—actually confirmed the safety of atomic power plants in the United States. Totally unlike the more recent case of Chernobyl in the former Soviet Union, there was not a single death, not a single case of radiation overdose to any member of the public in that accident. In addition, according to studies reported in *The New York Times,* the cancer rate among residents in the area around Three Mile Island is no higher than normal and has not risen.[35]

To be sure, the case of Chernobyl was a genuine disaster. But this fact is not an indictment of atomic power, still less of modern science and technology in general. It is an indictment only of the incompetence, and indifference to human life, inherent in communism. Under communism (socialism), there is no incentive to supply people with anything they need or want, including safety.[36] In addition, under communism (socialism), the ability of the government to prosecute wrongdoing in connection with the use of means of production is necessarily compromised by the very nature of the case, inasmuch as the state itself is the owner of the means of production and therefore is itself the party responsible for any misuse in connection with them. Indeed, any prosecution by the state would have to be a prosecution of its own officials, logically entailing the prosecution of its very highest officials. This is because under the central planning that is an essential characteristic of socialism the highest officials have responsibility for every detail of economic activity. The implicit need to challenge the top leaders, of course, greatly diminishes the likelihood of such prosecutions. Thus under communism, as the result of the lack both of economic and legal incentives to provide safety, industrial accidents of all kinds are commonplace, including airplane and train crashes. This is a good reason for rejecting communism, but certainly not a rational basis for rejecting atomic power and an industrial society.

As indicated, as a result of the influence of the environmental movement, the fears of a growing number of our contemporaries are such that they refuse to sanction not only atomic dump sites but also new dump sites for the disposal of all kinds of more mundane chemicals that result as a by-product of industrial processes, such as sulfuric, hydrochloric, or nitric acid, dioxin, PVCs, and even ordinary lead or mercury. They refuse to do so out of fear of being poisoned by "toxic wastes." In addition, they stop eating one thing after another, in terror that it too is poisoned—with preservatives, pesticides, "chemicals." Increasingly, they view every man-made chemical additive to food as though it were a cause of cancer or other dread disease. More and more they turn to "natural" foods, as though millions of years of blind evolution in the selection of food were to be trusted, but the application of science and human intelligence to the improvement of food were not. The fear of "chemicals" is such that a major and once proud chemical company has felt obliged to change its slogan from "Better Things for Better Living Through Chemistry" to, simply, "Better Things for Better Living," because the very word *chemistry* has become controversial and a source of fear. Increasingly, our contemporaries also fear ordinary mechanical devices, from automobiles and washing machines on down to stepladders, and demand absolute guarantees of safety in connection with their use. All of these fears are supposedly in response to the allegedly self-destructive tendencies of an industrial society.

Yet in virtually no case has any actual *proof* of danger ever been offered. Indeed, some of the claims immediately show themselves to be absurd on simple logical grounds. For example, it is a contradiction to fear both a new ice age *and* a global warming. Since everything physical in the world is a chemical, it is absurd to fear *chemical* preservatives. Such a fear is tantamount to the fear of preservatives as such and thus fear of the very fact that food does not spoil as rapidly.

Not only is there no proof of danger from industrial civilization and science and technology, but all the proof runs entirely the other way. As I have shown, the actual effect of industrial civilization, science, and technology has been to increase life expectancy by two and a half times since the beginning of the Industrial Revolution and radically to improve human health and well-being. The environmentalists simply ignore all this. In their view, it is outweighed by "air pollution." This belief is clearly present in the words of Carl Sagan, a leading environmentalist:

> The "satanic mills" of England in the early years of the industrial revolution polluted the air and caused an epidemic of respiratory disease. The "pea soup" fogs of London, which provided haunting backdrops to the Sherlock Holmes stories, were deadly domestic and industrial pollution. Today, automobiles add their exhaust fumes, and our cities are plagued by smog—which affects the health, happiness and productivity of the very people generating the pollutants. We've also known about acid rain, the pollution of lakes and forests, and the ecological turmoil caused by oil spills. But the prevailing opinion has been—erroneously, in my view—that these penalties to health and environment were more than balanced by the benefits that fossil fuels bring.[37]

Thus, Sagan has declared that in his view it is erroneous to believe that the progressive and radical increase in life expectancy and in human health and well-being outweigh the ill effects of air pollution. For it is precisely these which are the benefits which fossil fuels have brought. The avoidance of air pollution is allegedly more important.

Interestingly, in presenting the Industrial Revolution as the cause of respiratory disease, Sagan somehow manages to forget the virtually total elimination of tuberculosis and the radical reduction in the frequency of, and mortality resulting from, pneumonia, which has been achieved by industrial civilization. Tuberculosis and pneumonia, of course, were traditionally the leading respiratory diseases. In virtually totally eliminating the one and radically reducing the other, the positive contribution of industrial civilization specifically to respiratory health overwhelmingly surpasses the negative of any respiratory diseases resulting from industrial civilization. Sagan, of course, does not even bother to specify the nature and extent of such alleged diseases. In his view, in developing industrial civilization, we have gotten ourselves into a "mess."[38]

The fear the environmental movement has of industrial civilization leads it to want to destroy industrial civilization. Thus, an essential goal of environmentalism is to block the increase in one source of man-made power after another and ultimately to roll back the production of man-made power to the point of virtual nonexistence, thereby undoing the Industrial Revolution and returning the world to the economic Dark Ages. There is to be no atomic power. According to the environmentalists, it represents the death ray. There is also to be no power based on fossil fuels. According to the environmentalists, it causes "air pollution," and now global warming, and must therefore be given up. There is not even to be significant hydropower. According to the environmentalists, the building of the necessary dams destroys intrinsically valuable wildlife habitat.

Only three things are to be permitted as sources of energy, according to the environmentalists. Two of them, "solar power" and power from windmills, are, as far as can be seen, utterly impracticable as significant sources of energy. (If, somehow, they became practicable, the environmentalists would undoubtedly find grounds for attacking them: they would denounce them for such things as the massive reflection of light from thousands or tens of thousands of acres filled with solar panels, or for maiming and killing birds with their propellers.) The third allowable source of energy, "conservation," is a contradiction in terms. Conservation is *not* a source of energy. Its actual meaning is simply using less. Conservation is a source of energy for one use only at the price of deprivation of energy use somewhere else.[39]

The environmentalists' campaign against energy calls to mind the image of a boa constrictor entwining itself about the body of its victim and slowly squeezing the life out of him. There can be no other result for the economic system of the industrialized world but enfeeblement and ultimately death if its supplies of energy are progressively choked off.

The Toxicity of Environmentalism and the Alleged Intrinsic Value of Nature

The environmental movement's blindness to the value of industrial civilization is matched only by the blindness of the general public toward the nature of the environmental movement's own actual values. Those values explain the movement's hostility to industrial civilization, including its perversion of the concept of efficiency.

They are not known to most people, because the environmental movement has succeeded in focusing the public's attention on absolutely trivial, indeed, nonexistent dangers, and away from the enormous actual danger it itself represents.

Thus, not so long ago, as a result of the influence of the environmental movement, a popular imported mineral water was removed from the market because tests showed that samples of it contained thirty-five parts per billion of benzene. Although this was an amount so small that not many years ago it would have been impossible even to detect, it was assumed that considerations of public health required withdrawal of the product.

Such a case, of course, is not unusual nowadays. The presence of parts per billion of a toxic substance is routinely extrapolated into being regarded as a cause of human deaths. And whenever the number of projected deaths exceeds one in a million (or less), environmentalists demand that the government remove the offending pesticide, preservative, or other alleged bearer of toxic pollution from the market. They do so, even though a level of risk of one in a million is one-third as great as that of an airplane falling from the sky on one's home.

While it is not necessary to question the good intentions and sincerity of the overwhelming majority of the rank-and-file members of the environmental or ecology movement, it is vital that the public realize that in this movement itself, which is so widely regarded as noble and lofty, can be found more than a little evidence of the most profound toxicity—evidence provided by leaders of the movement themselves, and in the clearest possible terms. Consider, for example, the following quotation from David M. Graber, a research biologist with the National Park Service, in his prominently featured *Los Angeles Times* book review of Bill McKibben's *The End of Nature:*

> This [man's "remaking the earth by degrees"] makes what is happening no less tragic for those of us who value wildness for its own sake, not for what value it confers upon mankind. I, for one, cannot wish upon either my children or the rest of Earth's biota a tame planet, be it monstrous or—however unlikely—benign. McKibben is a biocentrist, and so am I. We are not interested in the utility of a particular species or free-flowing river, or ecosystem, to mankind. They have intrinsic value, more value—to me—than another human body, or a billion of them.
>
> Human happiness, and certainly human fecundity, are not as important as a wild and healthy planet. I know social scientists who remind me that people are part of nature, but it isn't true. Somewhere along the line—at about a billion years ago, maybe half that—we quit the contract and became a cancer. We have become a plague upon ourselves and upon the Earth.
>
> It is cosmically unlikely that the developed world will

choose to end its orgy of fossil-energy consumption, and the Third World its suicidal consumption of landscape. Until such time as Homo sapiens should decide to rejoin nature, some of us can only hope for the right virus to come along.[40]

While Mr. Graber openly wishes for the death of a billion people, Mr. McKibben, the author he reviewed, quotes with approval John Muir's benediction to alligators, describing it as a "good epigram" for his own, "humble approach": "'Honorable representatives of the great saurians of older creation, may you long enjoy your lilies and rushes, and be blessed now and then with a mouthful of terror-stricken man by way of a dainty!'"[41]

Such statements represent pure, unadulterated poison. They express ideas and wishes that, if acted upon, would mean terror and death for enormous numbers of human beings.

These statements, and others like them, are made by prominent members of the environmental movement.[42] The significance of such statements cannot be diminished by ascribing them only to a small fringe of the environmental movement. Indeed, even if such views were indicative of the thinking only of 5 or 10 percent of the members of the environmental movement—the "deep ecology," Earth First! wing—they would represent toxicity in the environmental movement as a whole not at the level of parts per billion or even parts per million, but at the level of *parts per hundred,* which, of course, is an enormously higher level of toxicity than what is deemed to constitute a danger to human life in virtually every other case in which deadly poison is present.

But the toxicity level of the environmental movement as a whole is much greater even than parts per hundred. It is certainly at least at the level of *several parts per ten.* This is obvious from the fact that the mainstream of the environmental movement makes no fundamental or significant criticisms of the likes of Messrs. Graber and McKibben. Indeed, John Muir, whose wish for alligators to "be blessed now and then with a mouthful of terror-stricken man by way of a dainty" McKibben approvingly quotes, *was the founder of the Sierra Club,* which is proud to acknowledge that fact. The Sierra Club, of course, is the leading environmental organization and is supposedly the most respectable of them.

There is something much more important than the Sierra Club's genealogy, however—something which provides an explanation in terms of *basic principle* of why the mainstream of the ecology movement does not attack what might be thought to be merely its fringe. This is a fundamental philosophical premise which the mainstream of the movement shares with the alleged fringe and which logically implies hatred for man and his achievements. Namely, the premise that *nature possesses intrinsic value*—that is, that nature is valuable in and of itself, apart from all contribution to human life and well-being.

The antihuman premise of nature's intrinsic value goes back, in the Western world, as far as St. Francis of Assisi, who believed in the equality of all living creatures: man, cattle, birds, fish, and reptiles. Indeed, precisely on the basis of this philosophical affinity, and at the wish of the mainstream of the ecology movement, St. Francis of Assisi has been officially declared the patron saint of ecology by the Roman Catholic church.

The premise of nature's intrinsic value extends to an alleged intrinsic value of forests, rivers, canyons, and hillsides—to everything and anything that is not man. Its influence is present in the Congress of the United States, in such statements as that made by Representative Morris Udall of Arizona: to wit, that a frozen, barren desert in Northern Alaska, where substantial oil deposits appear to exist, is "a sacred place" that should never be given over to oil rigs and pipelines. It is present in the supporting statement of a representative of the Wilderness Society that "There is a need to protect the land not just for wildlife and human recreation, but just to have it there."[43] It has, of course, also been present in the sacrifice of the interests of human beings for the sake of snail darters and spotted owls.

The idea of nature's intrinsic value inexorably implies a desire to destroy man and his works because it implies a perception of man *as the systematic destroyer of the good, and thus as the systematic doer of evil.* Just as man perceives coyotes, wolves, and rattlesnakes as evil because they regularly destroy the cattle and sheep he values as sources of food and clothing, so on the premise of nature's intrinsic value, the environmentalists view man as evil, because, in the pursuit of his well-being, man systematically destroys the wildlife, jungles, and rock formations that the environmentalists hold to be intrinsically valuable. Indeed, from the perspective of such alleged intrinsic values of nature, the degree of man's alleged destructiveness and evil is directly in proportion to his loyalty to his essential nature. Man is the rational being. It is his application of his reason in the form of science, technology, and an industrial civilization that enables him to act on nature on the enormous scale on which he now does. Thus, it is his possession and use of reason—manifested in his technology and industry—for which he is hated.

Indeed, the doctrine of intrinsic value implies that man is to regard himself as profaning the sacredness of nature by virtue of his very existence, because with every breath he draws and every step he takes he cannot help but disturb something or other of alleged intrinsic value. Thus, if man is not to extinguish his existence altogether, he is obliged by the doctrine of intrinsic value to mini-mize his existence by minimizing his impact on the rest of the world, and to feel guilty for every action he takes in support of his existence.

The doctrine of intrinsic value is itself, of course, only a rationalization for a preexisting hatred of man. It is invoked not because one attaches any actual value to what is alleged to have intrinsic value, but simply to serve as a pretext for denying values to man. For example, caribou feed upon vegetation, wolves eat caribou, and microbes attack wolves. Each of these, the vegetation, the caribou, the wolves, and the microbes, is alleged by the environmentalists to possess intrinsic value. Yet absolutely no course of action is indicated for man. Should man act to protect the intrinsic value of the vegetation from destruction by the caribou? Should he act to protect the intrinsic value of the caribou from destruction by the wolves? Should he act to protect the intrinsic value of the wolves from destruction by the microbes? Even though each of these alleged intrinsic values is at stake, man is not called upon to do anything. When does the doctrine of intrinsic value serve as a guide to what man should do? Only when *man* comes to attach value to something. Then it is invoked to deny him the value he seeks. For example, the intrinsic value of the vegetation et al. is invoked as a guide to man's action only when there is something man wants, such as oil, and then, as in the case of Northern Alaska, its invocation serves to stop him from having it. In other words, the doctrine of intrinsic value is nothing but a doctrine of the negation of human values. It is pure nihilism.

It should be realized that it is logically implicit in what has just been said that to establish a public office such as that proposed in California, of "Environmental Advocate," would be tantamount to establishing an office of Negator of Human Valuation. The work of such an office would be to stop man from achieving his values for no other reason than that he was man and wanted to achieve them.

Of course, the environmental movement is not pure poison. Very few people would listen to it if it were. As I have said, it is poisonous only at the level of several parts per ten. Mixed in with the poison and overlaying it as a kind of sugarcoating is the advocacy of many measures which have the avowed purpose of promoting human life and well-being, and among these, some that, considered in isolation, might even achieve that purpose. The problem is that the mixture is poisonous. And thus, when one swallows environmentalism, one inescapably swallows poison.

Given the underlying nihilism of the movement, it is certainly not possible to accept at face value any of the claims it makes of seeking to improve human life and well-being, especially when following its recommendations would impose on people great deprivation or cost. Indeed, nothing could be more absurd or dangerous than to take advice on how to improve one's life and well-being from those who wish one dead and whose satisfaction comes from human terror, which, of course, as I have shown, is precisely what is wished in the environmental movement—openly and on principle. This conclusion, it must be stressed, applies irrespective of the scientific or academic credentials of an individual. If an alleged scientific expert believes in the intrinsic value of nature, then to seek his advice is equivalent to seeking the advice of a medical doctor who was on the side of the germs rather than the patient, if such a thing can be imagined. Obviously, congressional committees taking testimony from alleged expert witnesses on the subject of proposed environmental legislation need to be aware of this fact and never to forget it.

Not surprisingly, in virtually every significant case, the claims made by the environmentalists have turned out to be false or simply absurd.

The Alleged Pollution of Water and Air and Destruction of Species

The ecologists claim that economic progress and the industrial civilization that underlies it have been responsible for polluting the water and air and wantonly destroying animal and vegetable species, thereby endangering human life. To answer the ecologists' claims in these areas, it is only necessary to recall a few facts that are known to everyone.

First, as concerns the relationship between industrialization and water quality: it is obvious that the actual safety of drinking water is in direct proportion to a country's degree of economic advancement. One can safely drink the water virtually everywhere in the United States. One can do so in the major cities of Western Europe. But in travelling to poorer areas, such as Mexico, most of the rest of Latin America, and most of Asia and Africa, it is necessary to take precautions. (The recent cholera epidemic in Peru, with its chemically untreated, "natural" water supply provides a tragic testimony to the truth of the preceding statements.) Certainly, if one travels in the African or Vietnamese jungles, or even in the Canadian wilderness, one had better boil the water or use purification tablets. Even in a beautiful blue Canadian lake—the kind for which environmentalist posters used to depict an American Indian shedding a tear—there can be dead, decaying animals emitting morbific germs into the water one may happen to drink. The safety of water supplies obviously depends on chemical purification plants, pipelines, and pumping stations—in a word, on modern industry. While some rivers, lakes, and streams in the industrialized countries may be dirtier today than in the past, supplies of safe drinking water have never been greater, thanks to modern industry. (And, no doubt, many or most of the presently dirty bodies of water too would be clean and safe, if they were made subject to private property rights. In that case, individuals would have the incentive to make them clean and safe by being able to charge for water and such benefits as fishing rights.)

Second, as concerns the relationship between industrialization and air quality, the obvious fact is that although air quality in large towns and cities is poorer than that in the open country, and always has been, it is far better today than in the past—precisely because of economic progress. Before the advent of modern industry, the open streets served as sewers. In addition, in any large town or city, a heavy concentration of horses created an enormous pollution problem from the dropping of vast quantities of manure and urine. The development of the modern iron and steel industry eliminated the sewage problem with low-cost iron and steel pipe; the development of the automobile industry eliminated the pollution from horses. Central heating, air conditioning, indoor plumbing, and modern methods of ventilation have made further major contributions to improving the quality of the air in which people live and work.

And although in the earlier years of the Industrial Revolution the process of economic improvement was accompanied by coal dust in towns and cities (which people willingly accepted as the by-product of not having to freeze and of being able to have all the other advantages of an industrial society), subsequent advances, in the form of electricity and natural gas, have radically reduced this problem. The substitution of atomic power plants for coal and oil-fired plants would make a further major contribution to air quality, because they emit no particulate matter of any kind into the atmosphere. Atomic power, however, is the form of power most hated by the environmentalists.[44] As shown previously, the virtual elimination of tuberculosis and the radical reduction in the frequency of, and mortality rate resulting from, other respiratory diseases, such as pneumonia, provide further eloquent testimony to the actual contribution of industrial civilization to air quality.

Third, as concerns man's alleged wanton destruction of other species: man is responsible for the existence of many species of animals and plants in their present numbers and varieties. For example, man is responsible for the existence of the overwhelming majority of the cattle, sheep, hogs, chickens, goats, horses, and cats and dogs that are alive, and for the existence of most of the specific breeds in which they exist. There would certainly be no such things as Holstein cattle, thoroughbred racehorses, miniature schnauzers, toy poodles, or Persian cats, in the absence of man. The population of all varieties of domestic animals would be radically reduced without the existence of man to feed them, promote their health, and protect them from their natural enemies. In the same way, man is responsible for the fact that grain, vegetables, flowers, and grass grow where otherwise there would be only weeds. Man is responsible for the existence of all manner of specific strains of plant life, from American Beauty roses to varieties of zucchini.

Furthermore, as we have seen, despite the misconceptions spawned by conservationism and the ecology doctrine, where forest land is privately owned, man is also responsible for the existence of many trees and forests, which the profit motive leads him to regard as a long-term crop.[45] In addition, of course, man also plants trees as objects of beauty to enhance his surroundings. Practically all of the trees in many portions of Southern California and other arid areas were planted and are maintained by man for just this reason.

Man is clearly not the destroyer of species. He enormously promotes the existence of those species that are of benefit to him. He seeks to destroy only those species that are harmful to him, including those that are harmful to the species whose existence he tries to promote. Thus, he seeks to extirpate such species as the smallpox virus, rats, fleas, rattlesnakes, coyotes, wolves, and mountain lions.

Sometimes, of course, cases arise in which his activity threatens the existence of species that are not hostile and that have been useful to him, such as the American buffalo and, nowadays, certain varieties of whales. In these cases, the species are not domesticated and raised commercially because the usefulness of the animal is not great enough to justify the expense involved.[46]

It might be of some value if a few members of every species could be preserved as objects of study or curiosity and perhaps as a future source of genes for use in genetic engineering. From this point of view, it would be a welcome event if the story line of some low-budget films became a reality and a scientific expedition were to come upon a preserve of dinosaurs somewhere. Those who consider such objectives important, and there certainly appears to be no lack of such people, are free to raise money to establish wildlife preserves. Nevertheless, from a practical point of view, it is obvious that man's life would simply not be significantly affected by the passing of such species as the buffalo or the endangered whales. The mere fact that the loss of a species may be irreplaceable from a genetic point of view, and that at some point in the future it might conceivably be regretted for this reason, is not a logical basis for arguing that it must not be allowed to occur. If this line of argument were accepted, people could never clean their garages or

throw anything away, for who knows, the clutter might contain a letter from George Washington or a winning lottery ticket. Furthermore, the ecology movement, ironically enough, strongly opposes any human use to which such an enlarged future gene pool might be put: it is totally opposed to genetic engineering. The sense of moral imperative it projects in seeking not to permit the loss of any species derives from its mistaken notion that species possess intrinsic value.

The disappearance of species has been going on since the beginning of life on earth. It appears to be no more rapid now than at any other time. Furthermore, to whatever extent it occurs as the result of human activity, it is still simply part of the process of nature. Man himself is part of nature. Any species that he may destroy in the course of his activities cannot in reason be regarded any differently from the countless species destroyed by any other natural process.

If one wishes to judge matters from an ethical perspective, the only valid perspective is that of man himself—that is, a perspective which takes for granted the supreme value of human life and well-being and man's right to do everything in his power to promote his life and well-being. From this point of view, one cannot regard man's activities in relation to nature with anything but awe and admiration. In the territories embraced by modern Western civilization, he has not only succeeded in these activities, but succeeded with surpassing brilliance. For he has transformed his environment to promote his survival and well-being. He has transformed enormous areas that were originally hostile or at best indifferent to his survival into virtual gardens—into thriving areas of agriculture, industry, and commerce. In so doing, he has changed the balance of nature radically in his favor.

In view of these facts, the environmentalists' claims that the effect of man's productive activities in an industrial society on water, air, and species represents any kind of danger to human life and well-being are patently absurd. All of the isolated negatives the environmentalists point to, such as smog in some cities, or dirty rivers, lakes, or beaches in various places, have occurred in the context of the most radical improvements in human life, health, and well-being, including the most radical improvements in the quality of the water people drink and otherwise use, in the quality of the air they live and work in, and in the whole balance of nature. Nevertheless, the environmentalists proceed as though problems of filth emanated from industrial civilization, as though filth were not the all-pervasive condition of human life in preindustrial societies, and as though industrial civilization represented a decline from more healthful conditions of the past. If it is filth and squalor one wants to complain about, one should go to virtually any of the countries of the so-called third world, which are not industrialized. There one will find filth and squalor—"pollution"—of the worst kind: human excrement and, indeed, human corpses floating downstream and contaminating the rivers through which they pass.

Moreover, as previously indicated, what would overcome most of the isolated negatives in the industrial societies, apart from the wider use of atomic power, would be the extension of private ownership of the means of production, especially of land and natural resources. The incentive of private owners is to use their property in ways that maximize its long-run value and wherever possible, to improve their property. Consistent with this fact, ways should be sought for extending the principle of private ownership to lakes, rivers, beaches, and even to portions of the ocean. Privately owned lakes, rivers, and beaches, would almost certainly be clean lakes, rivers, and beaches. Privately owned, electronically fenced ocean ranches would guarantee abundant supplies of almost everything useful that is found in or beneath the sea. Certainly, the vast landholdings of the U.S. government in the Western states and in Alaska should be privatized.

Of course, what leads the environmentalists to make their claims concerning water and air pollution and the destruction of species is not any actual concern with human life and well-being. Human life and well-being, it cannot be repeated too often, are not their standard of what is good; instead, it is the alleged intrinsic values found in nature.

The Alleged Threat from Toxic Chemicals, Including Acid Rain and Ozone Depletion

Almost all of the other claims of the environmentalists, which for the most part are more recent, do not fare any better than their claims concerning water and air pollution and the destruction of species. In virtually every case, they too have turned out to be false or simply absurd.

Consider, for example, the recent case of Alar, a chemical spray used for many years on apples in order to preserve their color and freshness. Here, it turned out that even if the environmentalists' claims had actually been true, that the use of Alar would result in 4.2 deaths per million over a 70-year lifetime, all that would have been signified was that eating apples sprayed with Alar would then have been less dangerous than driving to the supermarket to buy the apples!

Consider: 4.2 deaths per million over a 70-year period means that in any one year in the United States, with its population of roughly 250 million people, approximately 15 deaths would be attributable to Alar! This is the result obtained by multiplying 4.2 per million times 250 mil-

lion and then dividing by 70. In the same one-year period, approximately 50,000 deaths occur in motor vehicle accidents in the United States, most of them within a few miles of the victims' homes, and undoubtedly far more than 15 of them on trips to or from supermarkets. Nevertheless, because of irresponsible, sensationalist newspaper and television reporting of the ecologists' claims concerning Alar, a panic ensued, followed by a plunge in the sale of apples, the financial ruin of an untold number of apple growers, and the virtual disappearance of Alar.

Before the panic over Alar, there was the panic over asbestos. According to *Forbes* magazine, it turns out that in the forms in which it is normally used in the United States, asbestos is one-third as likely to be the cause of death as being struck by lightning.[47]

Then there is the alleged damage to lakes and forests caused by acid rain. While the phenomenon of acid rain certainly exists (largely as the result of governmental insistence on the construction of smokestacks two hundred feet or more tall), it turns out, according to *Policy Review,* that the acidification of the lakes and surrounding forests has been the result not of acid rain, but of the cessation of logging operations in the affected areas and thus the absence of the alkaline runoff produced by such operations. This runoff had made naturally acidic lakes and forests nonacidic for a few generations.[48] Furthermore, according to the final report of the U.S. government's National Acid Precipitation Assessment Program, the direct major cause of acidification appears to be simply one hundred fifty million tons a year of bird droppings.[49]

Besides these cases, there were the respective hysterias over dioxin in the ground at Times Beach, Missouri; TCE in the drinking water of Woburn, Massachusetts; the chemicals in Love Canal, in New York; and radiation at Three Mile Island, in Pennsylvania. (The last has already been shown to be groundless.) According to Professor Bruce Ames, one of the world's leading experts on cancer, the amount of dioxin that anyone would have absorbed in Times Beach was far less than the amount required to do any harm and, indeed, the actual harm to Times Beach residents from dioxin was less than that of drinking a glass of beer.[50] (The Environmental Protection Agency itself subsequently reduced its estimate of the danger from dioxin by a factor of fifteen-sixteenths.[51]) In the case of Woburn, according to Ames, it turned out that the cluster of leukemia cases which occurred there was statistically random and that the drinking water there was actually above the national average in safety, and not, as had been claimed, the cause of the leukemia cases.[52] In the case of Love Canal, Ames reports, it turned out upon investigation that the cancer rate among the former residents was no higher than average.[53] (It is necessary to use the phrase "former residents" because the town lost most of its population in the panic and forced evacuation caused by the environmentalists' claims.) Overall, Ames writes, "There is no convincing evidence from epidemiology or toxicology that pollution is a significant source of birth defects and cancer. . . . the epidemiologic studies of Love Canal, dioxin in Agent Orange, Contra Costa County refineries, Silicon Valley, Woburn, and the use of DDT provide no convincing evidence that pollution was the cause of human harm in any of these well-publicized exposures."[54] The reason is that the amount of actual exposure was simply far too small to be harmful.

Before these hysterias, there were allegations about the death of Lake Erie and mercury poisoning in tuna fish. All along, Lake Erie has been very much alive and was even producing near record quantities of fish at the very time its death was being announced. The mercury in the tuna fish was the result of the natural presence of mercury in sea water; and evidence provided by museums showed that similar levels of mercury had been present in tuna fish since prehistoric times.

And now, in yet another overthrow of the environmentalists' claims, a noted climatologist, Professor Robert Pease, has shown that it is impossible for chlorofluorocarbons (CFCs) to destroy large quantities of ozone in the stratosphere because relatively few of them are even capable of reaching the stratosphere in the first place. He also shows that the celebrated ozone "hole" over Antarctica every fall is a phenomenon of nature, probably in existence since long before CFCs were invented, and results largely from the fact that during the long Antarctic night ultraviolet sunlight is not present to create fresh ozone.[55]

The Dishonesty of the Environmentalists' Claims

The reason that one after another of the environmentalists' claims turn out to be proven wrong is that they are made without any regard for truth in the first place. In making their claims, the environmentalists reach for whatever is at hand that will serve to frighten people, make them lose confidence in science and technology, and, ultimately, lead them to deliver themselves up to the environmentalists' tender mercies. The claims rest on unsupported conjectures and wild leaps of imagination from scintillas of fact to arbitrary conclusions, by means of evasion and the drawing of invalid inferences. It is out and out evasion and invalid inference to leap from findings about the effects of feeding rats or mice dosages the equivalent of a hundred or more times what any human being would ever ingest, and then draw inferences about the effects on people of consuming normal quantities. Fears of parts per billion of this or that chemical causing single-digit deaths per million do not rest on science, but on imagination. Such claims are based neither on exper-

iments nor on the concept of causality.

No one ever has observed, or can or will observe, such a thing as two groups of a million people identical in all respects except that over a 70-year period the members of one of the groups consume apples sprayed with Alar, while the members of the other group do not, and then 4.2 members of the first group die. The process by which such a conclusion is reached, and its degree of actual scientific seriousness, is essentially the same as that of a college students' bull session, which consists of practically nothing but arbitrary assumptions, manipulations, guesses, and plain hot air. In such a session, one might start with the known consequences of a quarter-ton safe falling ten stories onto the head of an unfortunate passerby below, and from there go on to speculate about the conceivable effects in a million cases of other passersby happening to drop from their hand or mouth an M&M or a peanut on their shoe, and come to the conclusion that 4.2 of them will die.

Furthermore, as indicated, in contrast to the procedures of a bull session, reason and actual science establish causes, which, in their nature, are *universal*. When, for example, genuine causes of death, such as arsenic, strychnine, or bullets, attack vital organs of the human body, death is absolutely certain to result in *all but* a handful of cases per million. When something is in fact the cause of some effect, it is so *in each and every case* in which specified conditions prevail, and fails to be so only in cases in which the specified conditions are not present, such as a person's having built up a tolerance to poison or wearing a bulletproof vest. Such claims as a thousand different things each causing cancer in a handful of cases are proof of nothing but that the actual causes are not yet known—and, beyond that, an indication of the breakdown of the epistemology of contemporary science. (This epistemological breakdown, I might add, has radically accelerated since the 1960s, when the government took over most of the scientific research in the United States and began the large-scale financing of statistical studies as a substitute for the discovery of causes.)

In making their claims, the environmentalists willfully ignore such facts as that carcinogens, poisons, and radiation exist in nature. Fully half of the chemicals found in nature are carcinogenic when fed to animals in massive quantities—the same proportion as applies to man-made chemicals when fed in massive quantities. (The cause of the resulting cancers, according to Professor Ames, is actually not the chemicals, either natural or man-made, but the repeated destruction of tissue caused by the massively excessive doses in which the chemicals are fed, such as saccharin being fed to rats in a quantity comparable to humans drinking eight hundred cans of diet soda a day.[56]) Arsenic, one of the deadliest poisons, is a naturally occurring chemical element. Oleander, one of the most beautiful plants, is also a deadly poison, as are many other plants and herbs. Radium and uranium, with all their radioactivity, are found in nature. Indeed, all of nature is radioactive to some degree. If the environmentalists did not close their eyes to what exists in nature, if they did not associate every negative exclusively with man, if they applied to nature the standards of safety they claim to be necessary in the case of man's activities, *they would have to run in terror from nature.* They would have to use one-half of the world to construct protective containers or barriers against all the allegedly deadly carcinogens, toxins, and radioactive material that constitute the other half of the world.

It would be a profound mistake to dismiss the repeatedly false claims of the environmentalists merely as a case of the little boy who cried wolf. They are a case of the *wolf* crying again and again about alleged dangers to the little boy. The only real danger, of course, is to listen to the wolf.

Direct evidence of the willful dishonesty of the environmental movement comes from one of its leading representatives, Stephen Schneider, who is well-known for his predictions of global catastrophe. In the October 1989 issue of *Discover* magazine, he is quoted (with approval) as follows:

> ". . . To do this, we need to get some broad-based support, to capture the public's imagination. That, of course, entails getting loads of media coverage. So we have to offer up scary scenarios, make simplified, dramatic statements, and make little mention of any doubts we may have. This 'double ethical bind' we frequently find ourselves in cannot be solved by any formula. Each of us has to decide what the right balance is between being effective and being honest."

Thus, in the absence of verification by sources totally independent of the environmental movement and free of its taint, all of its claims of seeking to improve human life and well-being in this or that specific way must be regarded simply as lies, having the actual purpose of inflicting needless deprivation or suffering. In the category of malicious lies fall all of the environmental movement's claims about our having to abandon industrial civilization or any significant part of it in order to cope with the dangers of alleged global warming, ozone depletion, exhaustion of natural resources, or any other alleged danger. Indeed, all claims constituting denunciations of science, technology, or industrial civilization which are advanced in the name of service to human life and well-being are tantamount to claiming that our survival and well-being depend on our abandonment of reason. (Science, technology, and industry are leading products of reason and are inseparable from it.) All such claims should be taken as nothing but further proof of the environmental movement's hatred of man's nature and man's life, certainly not of any actual significant danger to human life and well-being.

The Alleged Threat of "Global Warming"

Currently, the leading claim of the environmentalists is that of "global warming." It is alleged that man's economic activities, above all the burning of fossil fuels, are increasing the amount of carbon dioxide in the atmosphere. This will supposedly raise the average mean temperature of the world by several degrees over the next century and will cause a rise in sea levels because of melting ice.

It should be realized that despite the sensationalist claims of James Hansen of NASA, made during the heat wave of the summer of 1988, that global warming was at hand, weather satellites showed no evidence of global warming in the 1980s.[57] According to *The New York Times,* "Few scientists believe that greenhouse warming can now be detected amid the normal swings of climate."[58]

If one did not understand its underlying motivation, the environmental movement's resort to the fear of global warming might appear astonishing in view of all the previous fears the movement has professed. These fears, in case anyone has forgotten, have concerned the alleged onset of *a new ice age* as the result of the same industrial development that is now supposed to result in global warming, and the alleged creation of a "nuclear winter" as the result of man's use of atomic explosives.

The words of Paul Ehrlich and his incredible claims in connection with the "greenhouse effect" should be recalled. In the first wave of ecological hysteria, that "scientist" declared:

> At the moment we cannot predict what the overall climatic results will be of our using the atmosphere as a garbage dump. We do know that very small changes in either direction in the average temperature of the Earth could be very serious. With a few degrees of cooling, a new ice age might be upon us, with rapid and drastic effects on the agricultural productivity of the temperate regions. With a few degrees of heating, the polar ice caps would melt, perhaps raising ocean levels 250 feet. Gondola to the Empire State Building, anyone?[59]

The 250-foot rise in the sea level projected by Ehrlich as the result of global warming has been scaled back somewhat. According even to McKibben, the "worst case scenario" is now supposed to be 11 feet, by the year 2100, with something less than 7 feet considered more likely.[60] According to a United Nations panel, it is supposed to be 25.6 inches.[61] (Even this still more limited projected rise did not stop the U.N. panel, allegedly composed of scientists, from calling for an immediate 60 percent reduction in worldwide carbon dioxide emissions to try to prevent it.[62])

Perhaps of even greater significance is the continuous and profound distrust of science and technology that the environmental movement displays. The environmental movement maintains that science and technology cannot be relied upon to build a safe atomic power plant, to produce a pesticide that is safe, or even to bake a loaf of bread that is safe, if that loaf of bread contains chemical preservatives. When it comes to global warming, however, it turns out that there is one area in which the environmental movement displays the most breathtaking confidence in the reliability of science and technology, an area in which, until recently, no one—not even the staunchest supporters of science and technology—had ever thought to assert very much confidence at all. The one thing, the environmental movement holds, that science and technology can do so well that we are entitled to have unlimited confidence in them is *forecast the weather*—for the next one hundred years!

It is, after all, supposedly on the basis of a weather forecast that we are being asked to abandon the Industrial Revolution or, as it is euphemistically put, "to radically and profoundly change the way in which we live"—to our enormous material detriment. We are being asked to begin with a curtailment of energy consumption sufficient to achieve a global limitation on carbon dioxide emissions, indeed, a curtailment sufficient to achieve an immediate 60 percent reduction in such emissions. (It is significant, of course, that any global limitation on carbon dioxide emissions, let alone a 60 percent reduction, implies that the economic development, and hence increased energy consumption, of the vast presently backward regions of the world would have to be accomplished at the expense of the equivalently reduced energy consumption of the more advanced countries.)

Very closely connected with the demand for reduced carbon-dioxide emissions and energy consumption is something else that might appear amazing. This concerns prudence and caution. As we have seen, no matter what the assurances of scientists and engineers, based in every detail on the best established laws of physics—about backup systems, fail-safe systems, containment buildings as strong as U-boat pens, defenses in depth, and so on—when it comes to atomic power, the environmental movement is unwilling to gamble on the unborn children of fifty generations hence being exposed to harmful radiation. But on the strength of a weather forecast, it is willing to wreck the economic system of the modern world—to literally throw away industrial civilization. (Any significant limitation on carbon dioxide emissions would be utterly devastating, let alone the enormous immediate reduction urged by that U.N. panel.)

The meaning of this insanity is that industrial civilization is to be wrecked because this is what must be done to *avoid bad weather*. All right, very bad weather. If we destroy the energy base needed to produce and operate the construction equipment required to build strong, well-made, comfortable houses for hundreds of millions of people, we shall be safer from the wind and rain, the environmental movement alleges, than if we retain and enlarge that energy base. If we destroy our capacity to produce and operate refrigerators and air conditioners, we shall be better protected from hot weather than if we retain and enlarge that capacity, the environmental movement claims. If we destroy our capacity to produce and operate tractors and harvesters, to can and freeze food, to build and operate hospitals and produce medicines, we shall secure our food supply and our health better than if we retain and enlarge that capacity, the environmental movement asserts.

There is actually a remarkable new principle implied here, concerning how man can cope with his environment. Instead of our taking action upon nature, as we have always believed we must do, we shall henceforth control the forces of nature more to our advantage by means of our *inaction*. Indeed, if we do not act, no significant threatening forces of nature will arise! The threatening forces of nature are not the product of nature, but of *us!* Thus speaks the environmental movement.

In answer to this insanity, it must be stressed that even if global warming turned out to be a fact, the free citizens of an industrial civilization would have no great difficulty in coping with it—that is, of course, if their ability to use energy and to produce is not crippled by the environmental movement and by government controls otherwise inspired. The seeming difficulties of coping with global warming, or any other large-scale change, arise only when the problem is viewed from the perspective of government central planners.

It would be too great a problem for government bureaucrats to handle (as is the production even of an adequate supply of wheat or nails, as the experience of the whole socialist world has so eloquently shown). But it would certainly not be too great a problem for tens and hundreds of millions of free, thinking individuals living under capitalism to solve. It would be solved by means of each individual being free to decide how best to cope with the particular aspects of global warming that affected him.

Individuals would decide, on the basis of profit-and-loss calculations, what changes they needed to make in their businesses and in their personal lives, in order best to adjust to the situation. They would decide where it was now relatively more desirable to own land, locate farms and businesses, and live and work, and where it was relatively less desirable, and what new comparative advantages each location had for the production of which goods. Factories, stores, and houses all need replacement sooner or later. In the face of a change in the relative desirability of different locations, the pattern of replacement would be different. Perhaps some replacements would have to be made sooner than otherwise. To be sure, some land values would fall and others would rise. Whatever happened individuals would respond in a way that minimized their losses and maximized their possible gains.[63] The essential thing they would require is the freedom to serve their self-interests by buying land and moving their businesses to the areas rendered relatively more attractive, and the freedom to seek employment and buy or rent housing in those areas.

Given this freedom, the totality of the problem would be overcome. This is because, under capitalism, the actions of the individuals, and the thinking and planning behind those actions, are coordinated and harmonized by the price system (as many former central planners of Eastern Europe and the former Soviet Union have come to learn).[64] As a result, the problem would be solved in exactly the same way that tens and hundreds of millions of free individuals have solved much greater problems, such as redesigning the economic system to deal with the replacement of the horse by the automobile, the settlement of the American West, and the release of the far greater part of the labor of the economic system from agriculture to industry.

This is not to deny that important problems of adjustment would exist if global warming did in fact come to pass. But whatever they would be, they would all have perfectly workable *solutions.* The most extreme case would be that of the Maldive Islanders, in the Indian Ocean, all of whose land might disappear under water. The population of the Maldive Islands is less than two hundred thousand people. In 1940, in a period of a few days, Great Britain was able to evacuate its army of more than three hundred thousand soldiers from the port of Dunkirk, under the threat of enemy gunfire. Surely, over a period of decades, the opportunity for comfortable resettlement could be arranged for the people of the Maldives.

Even the prospective destruction of much of Holland, if it could not be averted by the construction of greater sea walls, could be dealt with by the very simple means of the rest of Europe, and the United States and Canada, extending the freedom of immigration to Dutch citizens. If this were done, then in a relatively short time, the economic losses suffered as the result of physical destruction in Holland would hardly be noticed, and least of all by most of the former Dutchmen.

For densely populated, impoverished countries with low-lying coastal areas, like Bangladesh and Egypt, the obvious solution is for those countries to sweep away all of the government corruption and underlying irrational laws and customs that stand in the way of large-scale foreign investment and thus of industrialization. This is precisely what needs to be done in these countries in any case, with or without global warming, if their terrible poverty and enormous mortality rates are to be overcome. If they do this, then the physical loss of a portion of their territory will not entail the death of anyone, and, indeed, their standard of living will rapidly improve. If they refuse to do this, then nothing but their own irrationality should be blamed for their suffering. The threat of global warming, if there is really anything to it, should propel them into taking now the actions they should have taken long ago.[65]

Indeed, it would probably turn out that if the necessary adjustments were allowed to be made, global warming, if it actually came, would prove highly beneficial to mankind on net balance. For example, there is evidence suggesting that it would postpone the onset of the next ice age by a thousand years or more and that the higher level of carbon dioxide in the atmosphere, which is supposed to cause the warming process, would be highly beneficial to agriculture by stimulating the growth of vegetation.[66] Growing seasons too might be extended.[67]

Furthermore, any loss of agricultural land, such as that which is supposed to take place in low-lying areas as the result of higher sea levels, would be far more than compensated for by vast quantities of newly useable land in central Canada and in Russia. In addition, there would be the major contribution made by the preceding clearing of the Amazon and other jungles. (The clearing of these *jungles*—not "tropical rain forests," as they are euphemistically called nowadays—and the concomitant elimination of their poisonous snakes and other hostile beasts, and replacement with farms and ranches, is an enormous boon from the point of view of human life and well-being.[68])

Whether global warming comes or not, it is certain that nature itself will sooner or later produce major changes in the climate. To deal with those changes and virtually all other changes arising from whatever cause, man absolutely requires individual freedom, science, and technology. In a word, he requires the industrial civilization constituted by capitalism. What he does not require is the throttling of his ability to act, by the environmental movement. If it really were the case that the average mean temperature of the world would rise a few degrees in the next century as the result of the burning of fossil fuels and of other modern industrial processes, the only appropriate response would be along the lines of being sure that more and better air conditioners were available.

(Similarly, if there were in fact to be some reduction in the ozone layer, the appropriate response, to avoid the additional cases of skin cancer that would allegedly occur from exposure to more intense sunlight, would be to be sure that there were more sunglasses, hats, and sun-tan lotion available.) In absolutely no case would the appropriate response be to seek to throttle and destroy industrial civilization. Primitive man, the ideal of the environmentalists, was incapable of successfully coping with climate changes. Modern man, thanks to industrial civilization and capitalism, *is* capable of successfully coping with climate changes. To do so, it is essential that he ignore the environmentalists and not abandon the intellectual and material heritage that elevates him above primitive man.

Why Economic Activity Necessarily Tends to Improve the Environment

It is important to realize that when the environmentalists talk about destruction of the "environment" as the result of economic activity, their claims are permeated by the doctrine of intrinsic value. Thus, what they actually mean to a very great extent is merely the destruction of alleged intrinsic values in nature such as jungles, deserts, rock formations, and animal species which are either of no value to man or hostile to man. That is their concept of the "environment." If, in contrast to the environmentalists, one means by "environment" *the surroundings of man*—the external material conditions of human life—then it becomes clear that all of man's productive activities have the inherent tendency to *improve* his environment, indeed, that that is their essential purpose.

This becomes obvious when one recalls that the entire world physically consists of nothing but chemical elements. These elements are never destroyed. They simply reappear in different combinations, in different proportions, in different places. Apart from what has been lost in a few rockets, the quantity of every chemical element in the world today is the same as it was before the Industrial Revolution. The only difference is that, because of the Industrial Revolution, instead of lying dormant, out of man's control, the chemical elements have been moved about, as never before, in such a way as to improve human life and well-being. For instance, some part of the world's iron and copper has been moved from the interior of the earth, where it was useless, to now constitute buildings, bridges, automobiles, and a million and one other things of benefit to human life. Some part of the world's carbon, oxygen, and hydrogen has been separated from certain compounds and recombined in others, in the process releasing energy to heat and light homes, power industrial machinery, automobiles, air-

planes, ships, and railroad trains, and in countless other ways serve human life. It follows that insofar as man's environment consists of the chemical elements iron, copper, carbon, oxygen, and hydrogen, and his productive activity makes them useful to himself in these ways, his environment is correspondingly improved.

All that *all* of man's productive activities fundamentally consist of is the rearrangement of nature-given chemical elements for the purpose of making them stand in a more useful relationship to himself—that is, for the purpose of improving his environment.

Consider further examples. To live, man needs to be able to move his person and his goods from place to place. If an untamed forest stands in his way, such movement is difficult or impossible. It represents an improvement in his environment, therefore, when man moves the chemical elements that constitute some of the trees of the forest somewhere else and lays down the chemical elements brought from somewhere else to constitute a road. It is an improvement in his environment when man builds bridges, digs canals, opens mines, clears land, constructs factories and houses, or does anything else that represents an improvement in the external, material conditions of his life. All of these things represent an improvement in man's material surroundings—his environment. All of them represent the rearrangement of nature's elements in a way that makes them stand in a more useful relationship to human life and well-being.

Thus, all of economic activity has as its sole purpose the improvement of the environment—it aims exclusively at the improvement of the external, material conditions of human life. Production and economic activity are precisely the means by which man adapts his environment to himself and thereby improves it.

So much for the environmentalists' claims about man's destruction of the environment. Only from the perspective of the alleged intrinsic value of nature and the nonvalue of man, can man's improvement of his environment be termed destruction of the environment.

The environmentalists' claims about the impending destruction of the "planet" are entirely the result of the influence of the intrinsic value doctrine. What the environmentalists are actually afraid of is not that the planet or its ability to support human life will be destroyed, but that *the increase in its ability to support human life* will destroy its still extensively existing *"wildness."* They cannot bear the thought of the earth becoming fully subject to man's control, with its jungles and deserts replaced by farms, pastures, and forests planted by man, as man wills. They cannot bear the thought of the earth becoming man's garden. In the words of McKibben, "The problem is that nature, the independent force that has surrounded us since our earliest days, cannot coexist with our numbers and our habits. *We may well be able to create a world that can support our numbers and our habits,* but it will be an artificial world. . . ."[69]

The influence of the doctrine of intrinsic value and of its implicit hatred of mankind is present in the usage of the very word *pollution.* More and more, "pollution" is used to mean any change in the state of nature caused by man. It is only from this perspective that one can label as "pollution" such things as the possible changes in the chemical composition of the earth's atmosphere which may result as the by-product of man's productive activity. Consider. Somewhat more carbon dioxide in the atmosphere or less ozone in the stratosphere (assuming these things were in fact the result of human productive activity) does not make the atmosphere dirty. It merely makes it somewhat different, requiring a somewhat different response on the part of human beings in order most efficiently to adapt to their environment. It is of a radically different character from pollution in the legitimate sense of, say, the discharge of human fecal material into drinking water. Its being subsumed under the concept of "pollution" serves as a vehicle to attack productive activity.

Closely related to the misuse of the word *pollution* is the practice of describing the chemical emissions into the atmosphere entailed in industrial production, as using the atmosphere as "a garbage dump." The meaning of the word "garbage," according to *The American College Dictionary,* is "1. refuse animal and vegetable matter from a kitchen. 2. any foul refuse; vile or worthless matter." To use the term to describe chemical emissions is an unwarranted extension of the term having no other purpose than to attack productive activity and man's life. Ironically, garbage is precisely that allegedly good "biodegradable" material the environmentalists are so fond of. A further irony is that precisely when human beings *eliminate* garbage, by burning it and thus reducing it to mere carbon and gases, they are denounced for dumping garbage—into the atmosphere.

Like the use of the word *concupiscence* in an earlier age to describe sexual desire, the use of the word *pollution* to describe essential aspects of the productive activities of an industrial society represents an attempt to defame an entirely proper human capacity by means of using an evil sounding name for it.

3. The Collectivist Bias of Environmentalism

As I have said, the ecology movement could not have nearly the following and the influence it does if its basic ethical perspective were known. Thus, most of the time it asserts that it actually has the welfare of people in mind, and that it is in the name of human well-being that it

attacks technology and economic progress. When it does this, it proceeds as though despite all the best efforts of scientists, engineers, and businessmen to improve human life and well-being they systematically fail, at least in the long run. Here, as in the case of alleged global warming, the movement apparently claims to be able to see from the vantage point of its allegedly superior wisdom that the true road to human well-being requires that mankind not attempt to travel the road to well-being—that it renounce action based on science and technology. Only then, allegedly, by virtue of its renunciation of such activity, and by virtue of its inaction, will mankind avoid self-destruction.

In proceeding in this way, the ecology movement adopts the tactic of taking for granted all the benefits of economic activity and proceeds as though they existed independently of such activity. It then concentrates all of its attention on a few relatively minor phenomena of a negative kind that it traces to economic activity and that it regards as the sum and substance of such activity, such as the emission of certain chemicals into the atmosphere and the consequent creation of smog or, more recently, alleged global warming. Thus, for example, it treats automobiles and power plants as though they were a threat to human life and well-being rather than the enormous source of improvement that they actually are. It proceeds as though people could continue having efficient transportation and electric power and light while being deprived of the means required for their existence: the oil fields, pipelines, and power plants whose construction it fights tooth and nail.

In this process, the ecology movement refers to "conservation" as though it were some kind of magical method of achieving radical reductions in energy use without sacrifice. It claims, for example, that the loss of millions of barrels of oil per day can easily be offset by such means as simply doubling the number of miles per gallon obtained by the average automobile Americans drive. (In its view, evidently, people have up to now simply been too foolish to realize that they could get along just as well with automobiles that would cut their cost of fuel in half. Or, allegedly, if the buyers of cars have realized it, each and every manufacturer and potential manufacturer of automobiles has been too foolish to realize the enormous competitive advantage he would enjoy by meeting the public's demand for such fuel-efficient cars. Or, if the manufacturers have realized it, they have not provided such cars, because each and every automobile manufacturer and potential automobile manufacture is allegedly part of a "monopolistic conspiracy" or otherwise just arbitrarily refuses to provide the market with such cars. In this way, the environmental movement contemptuously dismisses as of no significance such differences in automobiles as size, weight, and power of acceleration, and the public's demonstrated preference for larger, heavier, and more powerful automobiles that obtain fewer miles per gallon, over smaller, lighter, less powerful automobiles that obtain more miles per gallon.)

In its masquerade as fighter for human welfare, the technique of the ecology movement consists of an appeal to collectivism and hysteria, in order to create the impression of an overthrow of the harmony-of-interests doctrine of classical economics and the existence of a conflict of interests between the individual and the rest of society.

The truth is that the necessary tendency of economic activity to improve the environment, which was described at the end of the preceding section, is powerfully reinforced by the existence of freedom and free exchange. Freedom and free exchange create an inherent harmony of the rational self-interests of people. When the actions of individuals are free and do not represent the use of force, their effect is necessarily to benefit everyone involved. This is because each individual acts to benefit himself and must at the same time benefit those whose cooperation is to be secured, or else he will not receive it. In addition, no one standing outside the transaction can be harmed, because any evidence of harm to the person or property of others is grounds to prohibit the action as an act of force and violation of freedom. For example, under freedom, if I decide to construct a building, I do so because I judge that I can serve my own interests by doing so. At the same time, I can find workers and suppliers to help me build it and a buyer or tenants to use it, only by making it to the self-interest of all of these parties to deal with me. In addition, the construction of my building must not endanger other, surrounding buildings or passersby; if it does, I am guilty of an initiation of physical force against the property or persons of others, and thus grounds exist to stop me. As a result, the inherent tendency of my action is to produce improvement for others as well as myself, and thereby to improve general well-being.

The stock in trade of the ecologists, however, is to find cases in which perceptible negative consequences to others appear when the actions of large numbers of individuals are cumulated, and then incredibly to exaggerate the importance of those negatives by techniques of hysteria, in the process obliterating all concern for the rights and responsibilities of individuals. The ecologists conclude by arguing that no individual should be allowed to act without first proving that his action will have no adverse "impact" on the "environment."

Thus, for example, ecologists consider such phenomena as the clearing of large areas of land for the establishment of farms. Such clearing of land may sometimes have the effect of raising the water level downstream and thereby causing flooding, as allegedly occurred along the Mississippi River as the result of the settlement of the Midwest. Likewise, they consider the fact that the movement of large numbers of people into the same area may result in traffic congestion. And in exactly the same way, they consider the effects of hundreds of millions or billions of people burning fossil fuels, using CFCs, and so on, which actions allegedly result in global warming and ozone depletion.

In their treatment of all such cases, the ecologists show themselves to be collectivists. They are prepared to hold individuals responsible for negative effects that are not the responsibility of individuals qua individuals, that is, for negative effects which are not caused by any individual, but which are the result of the combined actions of the members of the group to which the individual belongs. Such negative effects, not being the responsibility of any individual, should properly be regarded as the equivalent of acts of nature, and individuals should be left free to respond to them in the way most to their advantage. Instead, the ecologists seek to paralyze the individual by harnessing him to the collective—to prohibit him from acting in all cases in which noticeable negative consequences flow from the actions of the collective to which he belongs. And then, of course, instead of allowing the negative effects to be dealt with by the free actions of individuals, the ecologists can see no other solution than that of collective action, in the form of government planning.

In such cases, the ecologists mistakenly assume that they have the right to prohibit the actions they find displeasing. Actually, however, they do not. The fact that the separate, independent actions of vast numbers of people may result in significant negative consequences to someone by virtue of their cumulative effect is simply not the responsibility of any of the individuals concerned. It should not be a basis for prohibiting his actions. To prohibit the action of an individual in such a case is to hold him responsible for something for which *he* is simply not in fact responsible. It is exactly the same in principle as punishing him for something he did not do.

The harm that results from the cumulative actions of the whole category of individuals, without any of the individuals qua individuals being responsible, should, as I say, be regarded as having the same status as harm caused by acts of nature. That is, such phenomena as floods downstream possibly resulting from the actions of tens or hundreds of thousands of separately acting individuals, each of whom as an individual causes no perceptible harm to anyone, should be regarded in exactly the same way as floods that result when few or no human beings are present upstream. Exactly the same is true of the similar phenomena, or alleged phenomena, of global warming, ozone depletion, and acid rain. As the result, or alleged result, of the actions of vast numbers of individuals, each of whom has no individual responsibility for them, they should be regarded in exactly the same way as one would regard global warming, ozone depletion, or acid rain existing totally apart from modern economic activity. That is, they should be regarded as phenomena of nature, for which no individual human being is responsible and to which individual human beings must be left free to respond.

Those who are adversely affected in such cases should not blame anyone, but should simply be left free to take steps to protect themselves by engaging in the appropriate form of productive activity. In the case of downstream flooding, this might consist of building dikes or flood-control channels; in the case of traffic congestion, it might consist of building more roads, or moving elsewhere.[70] The kind of responses appropriate to the alleged cases of global warming, ozone depletion, and acid rain have already been explained, in the preceding section. The all-encompassing appropriate answer to the ecologists in all the cases they bring forward of this kind is simply that under capitalism, man will deal with the negative forces of nature resulting as by-products of his own activity in precisely the same successful way that he regularly deals with the primary forces of nature.

Furthermore, it must never be forgotten that the harm done in these cases is necessarily minuscule in comparison with the good achieved. The ecologists use the technique of weighing the full harm against the actions of each individual alone. For example, they argue that an individual farmer should not be allowed to clear his land because if hundreds of thousands do so, flooding may be caused downstream. The fact is, the individual farmer accomplishes a substantial amount of good and no perceptible damage. If one wants to look at the damage caused by all the farmers together, it must be compared with the enormous good accomplished by all the farmers together.

The development of the Midwest, for example, obviously represented a far greater gain to virtually everyone than the occasional greater flooding in the New Orleans area, which may have been its result, represented a loss. (It represented a gain even to the people who lived in the areas subject to occasional greater flooding.) Yet the logic of the environmental movement, had it been present and guided government policy in the nineteenth century, could well have prohibited the development of the Midwest and required the American people to remain bottled up behind the Appalachian Mountains. (One can easily imagine a nineteenth-century campaign of ecological hysteria centering not only on the fear of such allegedly horrifying results as higher flood levels along

the Mississippi, but also on the pollution of many rivers and lakes, and on the disturbance of the habitat of this or that species. The impending near extinction of the buffalo would probably have been considered sufficient by itself to stop the settlement of the Midwest, if the environmental movement had existed at the time.)

Precisely the same principles apply to the cases of global warming, ozone depletion, and acid rain. Each individual who uses an automobile, electricity, and so on, derives immense benefits from doing so and causes absolutely no perceptible harm to anyone. The same is true of the manufacturers of automobiles and is probably true even of the very largest individual electric utilities and chemical companies, in connection with the creation of acid rain. The prohibition or curtailment of such activities for the sake of preventing global warming, ozone depletion, or acid rain is fully comparable to prohibiting or curtailing the development of the Midwest for the sake of preventing floods at New Orleans. It is the attempt to stop production and its immense benefits for the sake of avoiding the relatively minuscule negative effects of the by-products of production. It is comparable to prohibiting the use of machinery and the achievement of all its benefits for the sake of avoiding such a thing as short-run technological unemployment.

Of course, it is possible in productive processes for individual producers to cause *perceptible* negative effects on others. Even if this is not so in the case of acid rain, it was certainly so in the days when power plants and steel mills generated large quantities of soot which fell in the surrounding territory, and which the very tall government-mandated smokestacks that result in acid rain were designed to overcome.

In such cases, an important principle is that of who holds prior established rights. For example, if a steel mill begins operations in the open countryside, where the surrounding land is simply unused, and the landowners make no complaint over a period of several years or more, it appears reasonable to say that the steel mill acquires a right to continue its operations. The same, of course, would certainly be true if the steel mill made a mutually agreeable payment to the owners of the surrounding land as compensation for the negative effects of its operations. In either case, the price at which the surrounding land sells would tend to be cheaper in reflection of the negative consequences caused by the existence of the nearby steel mill. On the basis of such considerations, the owners of the surrounding land would have no justifiable basis for complaint. Justifiable grounds for complaint exist in cases in which an action of a producer creates some new negative effect, which has not become an established right, and which was not reflected in the price that the present owners of the surrounding land paid for it. In such cases, the only proper way in which the producer can proceed is by buying the right to do so from the owners of the affected surrounding land.[71]

In the absence of modern technology, the existence of densely populated areas necessitates considerable, individually perceptible mutual impositions by the inhabitants on the health, cleanliness, and property of one another. In the absence of low-cost iron and steel pipe, for example, there is virtually no alternative to using the open streets as sewers. In the absence of the automobile, there is no alternative to the streets being filled with horse droppings. In the absence of heating oil, natural gas, and electric power, there is no alternative to the soot produced by wood or coal-burning fires which falls on neighboring properties as well as on one's own.

If people are to live in towns and cities in such circumstances, they must put up with such problems. However, thanks to economic progress, it becomes economically and financially feasible to reduce the extent of these impositions. This comes about as the result of the continual widening of technological alternatives, reductions in cost, and fall in prices relative to incomes that economic progress represents.[72] It is in this spirit that one should fundamentally understand such public health measures as the requirement of sewer hookups as a precondition to housing construction. It is in this spirit that one should understand such measures as the city of London's requiring some years ago the gradual replacement of coal-burning furnaces with natural gas and electric furnaces. Measures of this kind, though they were better carried out by organs other than local governments, namely, by associations of private property owners, are consistent with the principle of individual rights. Furthermore, they are fully in the spirit of economic progress. They thus have nothing in common with the kind of measures characteristically advocated by the environmental movement.

The ecologists employ the technique of confusing the effects of the actions of specific individuals with effects that can be caused only by cumulating the actions of large numbers of individuals to downplay the importance of positive individual contributions. For example, the Sierra Club has argued against government approval of the search for oil in Northern Alaska on the grounds that if oil were found there, it would represent only a 200-day supply, which is too little to justify the project, according to the Sierra Club. In a mailing to its members, the executive director of the Sierra Club declared:

Imagine! The supporters of drilling in the Refuge are

willing to ravage a fragile ecosystem. To build airfields, pipelines and roads where caribou, polar bears and wolves, golden eagles, swans and snow geese make their home. To destroy a wilderness—perhaps North America's greatest wilderness—forever denying the right of future generations to marvel at its majesty. And why. For *a 19% chance that they will find a 200-day supply of oil!*[73]

Thus, if an individual oil field succeeds in adding 200 days' worth of oil to the world supply, it is allegedly too small to be worth developing. Presumably, each oil field must be capable of dramatically increasing the entire world's supply—adding at least several years' worth all by itself—if it is to be allowed to be developed. The implication of this position is that no one is to be allowed to act unless his action all by itself can have absolutely stupendous positive consequences, and is virtually certain to achieve them. Since the world supply of anything is almost always produced by large numbers of producers, each of whom produces a relatively small percentage of the total supply, the adoption of this standard easily serves to prohibit increases in production by practically every private individual or firm.

The leadership of the Sierra Club almost certainly knows that a 19 percent chance of finding oil is almost four times the chance that is present in most exploratory efforts and that oil in the area concerned is actually found seeping out of the ground. It is not so illogical as seriously to believe that roads and pipelines would be constructed without definite proof having first been obtained that substantial quantities of oil were actually present in the region. Nor is it so illogical as to believe that future generations will be able to go and marvel at the "majesty" of the area without the benefit of roads and airfields to bring them to it (that is, if the area were not a frozen barren desert and thus actually had majesty worth travelling to see). And the Sierra Club is almost certainly capable of realizing that if, as might be expected, the field contributed to production over a 20-year period and added just a 10-day supply to the otherwise existing supply of oil in each of those years, that would represent an almost 3 percent increase in the world supply of oil in each of those years. It is capable of realizing that such an increase in supply is approximately equal to the reduction in supply caused by Iraq's invasion of Kuwait and the consequent embargo imposed against Iraq, and that it would likely have as much effect in reducing the price of oil as the Iraqi invasion had in increasing it. The Sierra Club's leadership undoubtedly is aware of all of these things.

Nevertheless, it attempts to trivialize the importance of the project by setting an impossible standard of what must be produced in order for the project to be considered worthwhile.[74] Having trivialized the project in this way, it can then rank the project below the alleged value of maintaining absolutely undisturbed the wildlife in the region and the existing state of the mere ground itself, to neither of which anyone attaches any actual value.

Thus a major technique of the environmentalists is to *confuse the individual with the collective*—to hold the individual responsible for the negative effects resulting from the actions of the whole category of individuals to which he belongs and to demand that his positive actions be on a scale great enough dramatically to benefit the whole of society.

Confusion of the individual with the collective, indeed, of the individual with the cosmic, is present also in the environmentalists' scare tactics. For example, Carl Sagan writes: "The typical temperature *difference* averaged over the whole world between an ice age and an interglacial is only 3° to 6°C (equivalent to 5°F to 11°F). This should immediately sound an alarm: A temperature change of only a few degrees can be serious business."[75]

Of course, Dr. Sagan and every housewife knows how easy it is to bring a pot of water to a boil, let alone to raise its temperature by a mere few degrees. On this basis, he apparently believes that raising the temperature of the hundreds of millions of cubic miles of the earth's atmosphere and oceans and thus the surface of the whole earth a few degrees is a comparably easy matter, which we are readily capable of doing if we do not employ him and his colleagues to take charge of our lives.

Indeed, as should now be clear, the mentality of collectivism permeates environmentalism. It contributes to the notion of a "fragility of nature" in all of its immensity comparable to the fragility of an individual's possessions or an individual's life. As we have seen, it plays a vital role in the existence of the belief that there is an "environmental crisis," in projecting that only incompetent governmental action is available to deal with the changing environmental conditions allegedly caused by man's productive activities, and not the intelligent actions of individual human beings. That is, it is totally ignorant of the intelligent actions of individuals coordinated by the price system, as the means of solving such problems. Indeed, the very notion of an "environmental crisis" is the result of a preexisting mentality of collectivism. If not for the prevalence of the mentality of collectivism, human productive activity would have gone on just as smoothly and successfully as before, with individuals being happily and legitimately unconcerned with avoiding the effects resulting from the actions of the collectives of which they are members and easily dealing with such effects as and when they arose.

Environmentalism and Irrational Product Liability

Confusions—inspired by collectivism—concerning the responsibility of individuals also arise in other important

areas, which may or may not be connected with environmentalism. Thus, for example, an individual criminal is held not to be responsible for his actions. Instead, responsibility is held to lie with "society" and with other individuals, who somehow convey negative social attitudes to such individuals, such as lack of respect for their race or national origin.

The fallacy of such misplaced responsibility is present in the case of product liability, when large manufacturers who are aware that statistically so many accidents of a certain kind will occur per hundred thousand or million units of their product are held to be morally responsible for those accidents, especially if it is possible to take steps to prevent or mitigate them and they do not do so. To illustrate the logic of this view, one might imagine a fruit company that imports tens or hundreds of millions of bananas. Some percentage of the peels from these bananas will end up in places where people can slip on them and suffer serious injury. Never mind who thoughtlessly threw away the banana peels or who was responsible for watching where he walked. If it is known that statistically one person will break his neck or arm as the result of every X million bananas imported, the logic of this view implies that the fruit company somehow has responsibility for the injuries people suffer as the result of slipping on banana peels. (Presumably, it should be obliged to work on a nonskid banana peel.)

While the example of banana peels may seem far-fetched, because no one has gotten around to bringing suit on this basis, it is difficult to distinguish the logic of it from cases which have been brought and won by the plaintiffs. For example, the Ford Motor Company was held responsible for the fact that in a certain category of collision the fuel tank of its Pinto automobile was apparently capable of exploding. On this view, the responsibility of the individual(s) who caused the accident was dropped from view, and it was assumed that because statistically there could be a certain percentage of such accidents, the manufacturer was responsible: he allegedly should not only have known about such a statistical probability but also have taken steps so that people would not suffer such grave injury in the accidents for which somehow none of them allegedly bore responsibility.

The logic of holding an individual responsible for the actions of others is also present in legislation requiring soft-drink manufacturers to charge return deposits on cans and bottles, which they would normally not seek to have returned and on which, therefore, they would not charge such deposits. The manufacturers are viewed as responsible for the actions of their customers, who simply leave the cans or bottles lying on the ground.

The effect of imposing such wrongly increased liability on producers is to increase costs and prices for everyone. And because of the grave uncertainties created wherever the sums in question are substantial, to prevent the introduction of new products, and sometimes, as in the case of the manufacture of small private airplanes, cause even the discontinuation of existing products. Irrational product liability is an important ally of the ecology movement in its campaign to end economic progress and reduce the standard of living.

Environmentalism and the Externalities Doctrine

The influence of the environmental movement has been promoted in the science of economics by a pernicious doctrine known as the theory of "external costs and benefits" or, sometimes, simply the theory of "externalities."[76]

The externalities doctrine must be understood against the background of the fact that economists realized early that the pattern of spending adopted by consumers determines the pattern of spending adopted by businessmen, whose products must sooner or later serve to satisfy consumers. They saw, for example, that if consumers spent more money for shirts and less for shoes, businessmen would be impelled to spend more money in producing shirts and less in producing shoes. The economists recognized in this the operation of a profoundly benevolent principle enabling people to obtain what they wanted by virtue of the ways in which they spent their money.

The supporters of the externalities doctrine are not satisfied with the fact that the spending pattern of consumers determines the spending pattern of businessmen. They add the further arbitrary demand that the individual should be able to lay claim to compensation for all the benefits his action causes to the rest of mankind and should be liable for all the costs it imposes on the rest of mankind, even though the benefits and costs in question are not subjects of purchase and sale in the normal context of the individuals concerned. From the perspective of the externalities doctrine, it is a flaw of capitalism whenever an individual's action provides any kind of benefits to others for which he is not compensated, or imposes any kind of costs on others for which he does not compensate them. It calls upon the government to enter the scene and set matters right by deciding who owes what to whom and then effecting the necessary redistribution of wealth and income.

The alleged environmental damage caused by economic progress is regarded as falling under the heading of external costs, and it is urged that those responsible be held liable for damages. For example, it is argued that everyone whose car or factory emits any chemical into the air should be made to pay a share of whatever damages may be caused by the total volume of emissions of that chemical.

It is believed by many economists, including some who are usually staunch defenders of capitalism, that many of the demands of the environmental movement could be satisfied in this way within the framework of a capitalist society. They regard the demands of the externalities doctrine as fully consistent with the principles of capitalism, indeed, as representing a more-perfect implementation of those principles. In their eyes, the demand for compensation for all the benefits one causes is merely the principle of being paid for one's work; the demand for liability for all the costs one imposes on others appears to them as an implication of the principle of accepting responsibility for one's actions.

The externalities doctrine is a further confusion respecting the responsibilities of individuals. Even apart from imposing responsibility on individuals for results that individuals qua individuals do not cause, the error of the externalities doctrine is that it states matters far too broadly. A moment's reflection will show that one should *not* be compensated for *all* the benefits one causes, nor be made liable for *all* the costs one imposes. One should be compensated only for those benefits one gives to others which those others freely contract to receive. One should be liable for damages to others only insofar as one's action causes demonstrable physical harm to the persons or property of specific, individual others.

The broader standard of the externalities doctrine is an invitation to chaos and tyranny, for it opens the door to all kinds of arbitrary claims. According to the logic of the doctrine, beautiful women and the owners of beautiful homes and gardens should demand compensation for the pleasure the appearance of their persons or property brings to others without charge. Even the senders of unsolicited merchandize through the mail should also be able to demand compensation, if their merchandise confers any benefit on the recipients. Indeed, on the basis of the externalities doctrine, it is arguable that people are liable for payment for all the benefits that now come to them freely in the form of the work of all the inventors and authors whose discoveries or creations are not eligible for patent or copyright protection, starting with such contributions as fire and the wheel. Whether or not these payments are to be made to the descendants of the inventors or innovators, to the government, or to some other party, is a separate question. The principle holds that payment must be made for benefits received.

Whatever it may hold about the specific claims of the descendants of inventors and innovators, the doctrine implies that every living inventor or innovator should be prepared to meet demands for compensation by those displaced by the competition he inaugurates. For example, the doctrine implies that Henry Ford should have been made to pay for the support of unemployed blacksmiths and horse breeders, as though the latter had a right to go on in their routine irrespective of Ford's improvements and irrespective of the voluntary choices of the buyers of means of transportation.

It is a distortion of sound principles and totally inappropriate to call for payment for every benefit bestowed or to demand compensation for every cost imposed. It is in the nature of a division-of-labor, capitalist society to bestow enormous benefits for which people do not have to pay. Indeed, in such a society perhaps 99.9 percent or more of everyone's standard of living comes to him as an "external benefit" provided by the thinking of others past and present. It is also in the nature of such a society to impose various costs of a minor and transitional nature in the process of improving the methods of production and raising the general standard of living. The externalities doctrine implicitly represents a two-pronged attack on a division-of-labor, capitalist society: its logic would deprive people of the benefits such a society freely gives them, by making them pay the equivalent of those benefits. And, by making those who are the source of the benefits bear unnecessary and unjust costs in the process of bringing them about, it would operate to prevent the achievement of the benefits in the first place.[77]

There is no better place than the this to observe that in addition to being used in support of environmentalism, the externalities doctrine is used as a fundamental justification for government activity beyond defense against the initiation of physical force. It is argued that insofar as important benefits are obtainable without individuals having to pay for them, a free market cannot function successfully. A typical case advanced to illustrate this claim is that of lighthouses, which, once they exist, benefit all the ships passing in the night, whether the ships' owners have helped to pay for the lighthouses or not. It is argued that in this case, the possibility of avoiding payment and getting by as a "free rider" on the strength of the contributions of others will result in large numbers of shipowners refusing to pay for lighthouses and thus in either preventing their construction altogether or making their construction and operation less adequate. More broadly, as a general principle, it is argued that in such circumstances vital services will not be performed, or will be performed inadequately, because too many people will be hoping to take advantage of a "free ride."

The substance of the free-rider argument is the gratuitous assumption that people lack sufficient rationality to act in their own interest in cases in which they cannot receive corresponding direct payment, and hence must be forced to act in their own interest in such cases. The clearest contradiction of this belief is the success of the activities carried on by countless private charities. In their case, individual donors give without expecting to receive any corresponding material payment, direct or indirect. Although the free-rider doctrine's supporters are focused on such cases as lighthouses, the logic of the doctrine implies that all charitable activities should be performed by the government. The doctrine also implies that in every case in which there are benefits of any description which are not paid for, the government is to be put in a position in which it can demand a blank check, since no one can actually determine what voluntary payments made by the citizens on their own would be "adequate."

The truth is that private citizens are capable on their own of providing for necessary activities for which it may not be possible to arrange the normal system of payment for goods or services received. This is true even in cases requiring the cooperation of millions of individuals. There is no reason why in such cases individuals could not agree to contribute to the financing of a project on a contingency basis, namely, on the basis of a sufficient number of other individuals making the same pledge. Whether it is a matter of a hundred ship owners concerned with constructing a lighthouse or a million property owners concerned with building a dam to prevent flood damage (or perhaps installing catalytic converters on their automobiles to reduce smog), there is no reason why an arrangement could not be made whereby the individual pledges his contribution on the condition of an equal or otherwise comparable contribution being pledged by a certain percentage of other such individuals. For example, the individual ship owner or property owner might agree to pledge a definite sum on the condition that half or two-thirds of the other ship owners or property owners made the same or a comparable pledge. Only when it was established that the necessary number of pledges had been made, would the pledges of the various individuals become binding. In such cases, there might be a class of free riders, but they would certainly not stop the activity from proceeding. (To some people, of course, such a procedure may appear cumbersome. Nevertheless, it is an insignificant price to pay for maintaining consistent respect for the rights of the individual.)

Finally, although the payment for a good or service in such circumstances might be less than it would be if somehow the usual circumstance prevailed of receipt of the benefit being directly contingent on payment being made, it by no means follows that the amount of benefit provided would be any less under private control than under government control. Government is inherently wasteful. As a result, it needs to spend much more money than a private organization to provide the same amount of goods or services. True, if it spends still more than that, it may provide more of the good or service than would be provided privately. But no objective basis exists for showing that it should provide more. In fact, the one outstanding objective fact in the situation is that in taking responsibility for activities beyond defense against the initiation of force, the government does something it should not do: namely, it initiates physical force against people.[78]

4. The Economic and Philosophic Significance of Environmentalism

The American people must be made aware of what environmentalism actually stands for and of what they stand to lose, and have already lost in economic terms as the result of its growing influence. They must be made aware of the environmental movement's responsibility for the energy crisis and the accompanying high price of oil and oil products, which is the result of its systematic and highly successful campaign against additional energy supplies.[79] They must be made aware of its consequent responsibility for the enrichment of Arab sheiks at the expense of the impoverishment of hundreds of millions of people around the world, including many millions here in the United States. They must be made aware of its responsibility for the vastly increased wealth, power, and influence of terrorist governments in the Middle East, stemming from the high price of oil it has caused, and for the resulting need to send an American army to the region. In the absence of the environmental movement, the war in the Persian Gulf would not have been necessary. For in that case, the Iraqi dictator would not have been able to achieve a significant military build-up: he would not have had the oil revenues to finance it.

The American people must be made aware of how the environmental movement has steadily made life more difficult for them in prohibiting, or increasing the cost, of one economic activity after another. They must be shown how, as the result of its existence, people have been prevented from taking such necessary and relatively simple actions as building power plants and roads, extending airport runways, and even establishing new garbage dumps. They must be shown how the history of the environmental movement is a history of destruction: of the atomic power industry; of oil fields, oil refineries, and oil pipelines; of coal mines; of metal smelters and steel mills; of the Johns Manville Company and the asbestos industry; of logging companies, sawmills, and paper mills; of cranberry growers and apple growers; of tuna fishermen—to name only those which come readily to mind. They must be shown how the environmental movement has been the cause of the wanton violation of

private property rights and thereby of untold thousands of acres of land not being developed for the benefit of human beings, and thus of countless homes and factories not being built. They must be shown how as the result of all the necessary actions it prohibits or makes more expensive, the environmental movement has been a major cause of the marked deterioration in the conditions in which most people now must live their lives in the United States—that it is the cause of families earning less and having to pay more, and, as a result, being deprived of the ability to own their own home or even to get by at all without having to work a good deal harder than used to be necessary.

Ironically, while claiming to be concerned about the "environmental impact" of everyone's actions, the environmental movement is utterly unconcerned about the *economic* impact of its own actions. It demands that before human beings be allowed to act, they first prove an impossibility: namely, that their actions will bring no harm to any species, indeed, any geologic rock formation, anywhere on earth, for an indeterminately long period of time. It itself, however, is to be free to act without any concern whatever for the consequences of its actions on the lives and well-being of human beings.

The environmental movement does not care to know that the rise in the price of oil and all other increases in the cost of living that it has brought about necessarily have a negative impact on human health as well as on happiness, and have actually cut short an undetermined number of human lives. This is because as a consequence of having to meet higher costs of living, there are always at least some people who are put in the position of having to do without, or at least postpone, such things as medical checkups and necessary repairs on their automobiles, home heaters, or wiring systems, and who, because of this, suffer injury or even death from illnesses or accidents they might otherwise have avoided.

This kind of result is the effect of all legislation which increases costs. Such legislation always has negative economic consequences which are not immediately obvious. For it embraces the consequences of millions of people having to respond to some degree of straightening of their financial circumstances and corresponding decline in their standard of living.[80]

Even more insidious, legislation that increases costs, or in any way reduces economic efficiency, has a *cumulative* negative effect on the standard of living, which results from the fact that it reduces the ability of the economic system to accumulate and maintain capital. This is the result of the vast diversion of capital from normal, productive uses to uses required by law to be in compliance with the ever swelling array of "environmental" regulations—for example, the vast sums of capital that must be unnecessarily expended to remove asbestos from buildings, to replace underground gasoline storage tanks at service stations, or to prevent the escape of ordinary chemical fumes from dry cleaning establishments. Capital diverted in this way is drawn not only from the production of consumers' goods but also from the production of subsequent capital goods. This last reduces the ability of the economic system to produce more capital goods than it uses up in production and thus its ability to increase the supply of capital goods, on which depends its ability to increase production in the future, including the future supply of capital goods. Carried far enough, by means of enough wasteful and destructive environmentalist regulations, the reduction in the production of capital goods may be so great as to make impossible even the replacement of the capital goods used up in production. If that happens, the subsequent ability to produce declines, including the subsequent ability to produce capital goods.[81]

In sum, the American people need to be shown how the actual nature of the environmental movement is that of a *virulent pest,* consistently coming between man and the work he must do to sustain and improve his life.

If and when such understanding develops on the part of the American people, it will be possible to accomplish the appropriate remedy. This would include the repeal of every law and regulation in any way tainted by the doctrine of intrinsic value, such as the endangered species act. It would also include repeal of all legislation requiring the banning of man-made chemicals merely because a statistical correlation with cancer in laboratory animals can be established when the chemicals are fed to the animals in massive, inherently destructive doses. And it would include abolition of the Environmental Protection Agency, which is one of the foremost practitioners of pseudo-science in the United States today and the leading instrument of the economic destruction that is practiced in the name of environmentalism. The overriding purpose and nature of the remedy would be to break the constricting grip of environmentalism and make it possible for man to resume the increase in his productive powers in the United States in the remaining years of this century and in the new century ahead.

As I will show in the remainder of this chapter, the philosophic significance of environmentalism is more profound than its economic significance, which is certainly great enough. The cultural acceptance of a doctrine as irrational as environmentalism makes clear that the real problem of the industrialized world is not "environmental pollution" but *philosophical corruption and moral depravity.*

As an indication of the depths of the depravity into which contemporary society has fallen, I offer the following excerpt from a recent news story. I believe that the actions described in this news story rival in absurdity, and far exceed in viciousness, those described in the ancient report that the Roman Emperor Caligula had made his horse a member of the Roman senate.

A New York commodities dealer pleaded guilty in Federal District Court today to destroying 86 acres of wetlands on his hunting retreat and was ordered to pay a $1 million fine and $1 million as restitution.

The dealer, Paul Tudor Jones 2d, was also banned from hunting migratory wildfowl through 1991—"restitution for the birds," said Judge Frederick Smalkin, who sentenced him.

. . . Under the plea bargain, he was fined $1 million, ordered to pay $1 million in restitution to the National Fish and Wildlife Foundation and ordered to restore the 86 acres, said Jane Barrett, assistant United States attorney. Mr. Jones was placed on 18 months' probation and barred from developing 2,500 of his 3,272-acre estate. Wetlands are critical because they filter pollutants and provide wildlife habitats.[82]

The meaning of this news story is that the rightful owner of a piece of property has been wantonly deprived of his property—the substance of it—and then outrageously humiliated by a gang of smirking tormentors, indistinguishable in the nature of their behavior from hoodlums robbing an innocent man on the street. For what else does it mean to seize the power to determine the use of someone else's property, without his consent and without compensation, and then punish *him* for daring to use what is in fact absolutely his right to use, and no one else's, and, in the process, as a calculated act of outrage, make *him* pay compensation—for his use of his own property—to birds. The only difference between this and the activities of ordinary hoodlums is that the hoodlums in this case wear the robe of a U.S. district judge and occupy the office of an assistant U.S. attorney.

5. Environmentalism, the Intellectuals, and Socialism

Environmentalism is the enemy not only of industrial civilization, individualism, and capitalism, but also of technology, science, human reason, and human life. It must be fought in the name of these values. Those who should be leading the fight against it are the intellectuals. They, presumably, are men of the mind and thus automatically advocates of reason, human life, and all the fundamental human values that are obviously based on reason, such as science and technology.

Unfortunately, of course, it is not working out that way. If the intellectuals were opposed to environmentalism, it would never have achieved the following it has.

It would probably be nonexistent; if it existed, it would be utterly disreputable. The fact is that the great majority of today's intellectuals, who should be fighting for human values, either do not know enough to do so, or have become afraid to do so, or, still worse, have themselves become the enemies of human values and are actively working on the side of environmentalism.

It is important to explain how this has happened.

I believe that to an important extent the hatred of man and distrust of reason displayed by the environmental movement are a psychological projection of many contemporary intellectuals' self-hatred and distrust of their own minds, which have been made much more acute as the result of the visible worldwide collapse of socialism, and the fact that they, as the advocates and apologists of socialism, have been responsible for the destruction it has wrought. As the parties responsible for socialism—for a system which has brought poverty and tyranny to every country upon which it was imposed, from Soviet Russia and the East European nations to mainland China, Indochina, Ethiopia, Angola, and Cuba—they have certainly been "a plague upon the world." And if socialism had in fact represented reason and science, as most intellectuals cannot help but continue to believe, there would be grounds to distrust reason and science. For then, reason and science would have been responsible for scores of millions of murders.

Of course, it is not reason and science that have been responsible for those murders. What have been responsible are the vicious, irrational ideas and immoral character of the majority of the last several generations of intellectuals. Although it is never spoken of, the undeniable fact is that the hands of several generations of Western intellectuals are covered with blood: intellectually and morally, they have been accessories, either before the fact or after the fact, to the mass murders committed by the socialist regimes.

Socialism, international and national, Marxist and Nazi, with all of its wanton destruction and mass murder, was not an accident visited upon mankind from heaven. It was the product of the leading *ideas,* moral and economic, of generations of Western intellectuals. Karl Marx and Friedrich Engels, and all of the intellectuals who elaborated and disseminated their theories, were responsible for socialism's coming to power in Russia and China and everywhere else that the rule of the Communists extended. And all those intellectuals who thereafter refused to know what was going on in those countries, who denied the facts, excused them, or outright lied about them—they bear responsibility for socialism's having remained in power.

And wider than these groups, and fundamentally just as responsible, have been all the hordes of intellectuals who consistently evaded the ideas of the major theoretical defenders of capitalism and critics of socialism, by ignoring or otherwise refusing to take those ideas seriously. As the result of this evasion, even the very name of Ludwig von Mises, who was the greatest defender of capitalism and critic of socialism of all time, is still unknown to the great majority of intellectuals.

The great majority of intellectuals never bothered to try to understand the intellectual case for capitalism: namely, the economic theories not only of von Mises but also of the Austrian and British classical economists in general, and the political philosophy of John Locke and the Founding Fathers of the United States, and, more recently, the philosophy of Ayn Rand. For the most part, the intellectuals either ignored the intellectual case for capitalism or found it to be an object of amusement, and ridiculed it. Yet such ideas as the law of comparative advantage and the harmony of the rational self-interests of all individuals and groups, which the advocates of capitalism espoused, would have prevented the rise both of Marxism and of Nazism, and the existence of both world wars—if the intellectuals had taken the trouble to understand them.[83]

Thus, I believe, it is certainly not without cause that the "mainstream" of today's intellectuals has lost confidence in reason. The "intellectual mainstream" has practiced a long-standing policy of massive and willful evasion, in refusing to know what it could have known. It has carried evasion to the point of creating for itself an entirely illusory, make-believe notion of rationality, which has now come crashing down. The intellectual mainstream has so far removed itself from reality that insofar as it turns to introspective evidence for the reliability of reason, it encounters the fact that on the basis of virtually everything it believes, *socialism should work.* As I stated previously, it believes that on the basis of every principle it knows, socialism is ethically and economically superior to capitalism.[84] And when, at last, the intellectual mainstream is confronted with inescapable, overwhelming evidence of the failure of socialism, rather than admit it has been profoundly, devastatingly wrong, it decides that it has no other choice than to throw up its hands, and take the failure of socialism as the final, convincing proof of the failure of reason. And then, I believe, in appraising what it perceives as its long-standing *adherence to reason* in supporting socialism in the face of rising rivers of blood, it comes to the conclusion that reason can be a devastatingly destructive force, and that those who have adhered to reason are worthy of hatred.

Today's intellectual mainstream, in other words, has very good reason for doubting its mind and hating itself. And thus it is not surprising to see that just as the failure of Marxian "scientific" socialism has become more and more apparent, the ranks of the "greens," who hate science and technology, have more and more swelled.

But while the greens have come to hate science and technology, they continue to love socialism. Their conception of a "postindustrial" world is entirely socialistic.

Indeed, it should be realized that the environmental movement has the potential for bringing about the achievement of socialism on a global basis, despite all of the enormous setbacks socialism has recently suffered around the world. The establishment of worldwide socialism is implied in efforts to limit global carbon-dioxide emissions and other global chemical emissions. The setting of such global limits and their allocation among the various countries of the world imply the existence of a worldwide central planning authority with respect to a wide variety of essential means of production. Such an authority would be necessary to determine which countries were to receive the right to burn how much oil or coal, and to carry on how much of virtually any industrial process that emitted chemicals held to be dangerous global pollutants. A global central planning authority is implicit in all potential international efforts to combat alleged global problems. For what is necessarily present in all such efforts is the attempt to organize mankind into a collective unit that acts as one and does so with consistency and coordination, i.e., is centrally planned.

Not surprisingly, one of the most prominent theorists of the environmental movement, Barry Commoner, offers a specific bridge between the doctrines of the socialists and those of the ecologists. The bridge is in the form of an attempted ecological validation of one of the earliest discredited notions of Karl Marx—namely, Marx's prediction of the progressive impoverishment of the wage earners under capitalism. Commoner attempts to salvage this notion by arguing that what has prevented Marx's prediction from coming true, until now, is only that business firms have been subsidized by society at the expense of the environment. In effect, says Commoner, the exploitation of the workers has been mitigated by capitalism's ability—temporarily—to exploit the environment. But now this process must come to an end, and the allegedly inherent conflict between the capitalists and the workers will emerge in full force. In Commoner's own words:

> Marx believed that as capital accumulated, the amount of its fixed forms (productive machinery)—which is related to what he called the "organic composition of capital"—would increase. This is the denominator in the profit equation, and Marx believed that as this denominator grew, the rate of profit would fall. To counteract this trend, the capitalists would need to make increasing inroads on the share of production that goes to the workers. The working class would become increasingly impoverished, and the growing conflict between capitalist and worker would lay

the grounds for the revolutionary change that is the political outcome of the Marxist analysis. . . .

> In a curious way, an explanation of why Marx's prediction has failed to materialize—that is, until now—emerges from the improved understanding of economic processes that is one product of the recent concern with the environment. . . . Since no one has to pay for it, there is nothing to keep pollution from happening. And, as we now well know, the cost is borne by society as a whole. As I pointed out in *The Closing Circle,* "A business enterprise that pollutes the environment is therefore being subsidized by society; to this extent, the enterprise though free is not wholly private." I pointed out as well that this arrangement leads to ". . . [a] temporary cushioning effect of the 'debt to nature' represented by environmental degradation on the conflict between entrepreneur and wage earner, which as it now reaches its limits may reveal this conflict in its full force. . . . In this sense the emergence of a full-blown crisis in the ecosystem can be regarded, as well, as the signal of an emerging crisis in the economic system."[85]

Thus, according to Commoner, Marx will be proved right after all—on the basis of such things as the accumulation of carbon dioxide in the atmosphere and of beer cans on the beach. These will allegedly compel the world to adopt a social system in which much less is produced in total and in which the members of one group can gain only at the expense of the loss of the members of other groups. In that world, apparently, Commoner will feel at home. It will be a world in which men do not join together to subdue nature for their mutual and increasing benefit, but an impoverished, static world in which men must fight one another for scraps of bread, for the alleged sake of appeasing nature.

Along these lines, it should be realized that the belief in the need for global limits on carbon dioxide and other chemical emissions and thus in the need for international allocation of permissible emissions implies that every country is an international aggressor to the degree that it is economically successful (and thus, of course, that the United States is the world's leading aggressor). For the consequence of its success is held to be either to push the volume of allegedly dangerous emissions beyond the safe global limit or to impinge upon the ability of other countries to produce, whose populations have more urgent needs. Thus, in casting the production of wealth in the light of a danger to mankind, by virtue of its alleged effects on the environment, and thereby implying the need for global limits on production, the ecology movement attempts to validate the thoroughly vicious proposition, lying at the very core of socialism, that one man's gain is another's loss.[86]

Another important illustration of the profoundly socialistic sympathies of the greens is provided by a recent publication of the Sierra Club. This is a collection of essays entitled *Call to Action, Handbook for Ecology,*

Peace and Justice. The book is dedicated to "the people of El Salvador" and has a preface by Jesse Jackson. It contains articles with such titles as "Share the Wealth" and "Co-ops: An Alternative to Business as Usual." Very significantly, and capturing the essence of the book, the editor declares in the foreword that "[T]he political and economic system that destroys the Earth is the same system that exploits workers. . . ."[87]

The environmental movement, of course, also advocates socialism on a much less grandiose scale than that of a worldwide central planning authority. For example, it also advocates socialism in the form of "bio-regionalism," which represents socialism on the scale of self-sufficient local regions allegedly distinguished by their biological characteristics.[88] Indeed, it is to be expected that the environmental movement will increasingly revert to the advocacy of such utterly naïve forms of socialism, which Marx labeled utopian.

Such forms of socialism are more consistent than is Marxism with the movement's thoroughgoing irrationalism and also with the irrationalist origins of socialism itself. Socialism was originally founded on hatred for reason, science, technology, and the industrial civilization that rests on them. It began as an irrational reaction against the emergence of modern capitalism—as part of a wider "romantic" reaction against the Enlightenment as a whole. But in the nineteenth century, the prestige of capitalism's underlying values was beyond challenge. The major contribution of Marx to socialism was to separate himself and his supporters from the then existing main body of the socialist movement, which he labeled utopian, and to wrap the socialist program in the mantle of reason and science. Henceforth, socialism was to be in the vanguard of science, enlightenment, and progress. The unraveling of that effort, which is now taking place across the world and which is manifest in the collapse of Communist regimes, means that socialism should be expected to revert to its irrationalist origins, which is precisely what it is doing in the rise of the environmental movement.

Thus, the green movement is the old red movement, deprived of its pretensions to rationality and seeking to evade its guilt by turning on reason itself, as though reason were responsible for the failure of socialism and for all the horrors that have been committed as the result of socialism. The green movement, in other words, is the red movement stripped of the veneer of reason and science and bent on the destruction of reason and science rather than take the trouble to learn what reason and science actually are. The green movement is the red movement no longer in its boisterous, arrogant youth, but in its demented old age.[89]

The only difference I can see between the green movement of the environmentalists and the old red movement of the Communists and socialists is the superficial one of the specific reasons for which they want to violate individual liberty and the pursuit of happiness. The Reds claimed that the individual could not be left free because the result would be such things as "exploitation," "monopoly," and depressions. The Greens claim that the individual cannot be left free because the result will be such things as destruction of the ozone layer, acid rain, and global warming. Both claim that centralized government control over economic activity is essential. The Reds wanted it for the alleged sake of achieving human prosperity. The Greens want it for the alleged sake of avoiding environmental damage and for the actual, admitted purpose of inflicting human misery and death (which was also the actual, but unadmitted purpose for which the Reds wanted it). Both the Reds and the Greens want someone to suffer and die; the one, the capitalists and the rich, for the alleged sake of the wage earners and the poor; the other, a major portion of all mankind, for the alleged sake of the lower animals and inanimate nature.

Thus, it should not be surprising to see hordes of former Reds, or of those who otherwise would have become Reds, turning from Marxism and becoming the Greens of the ecology movement. It is the same fundamental philosophy in a different guise, ready as ever to wage war on the freedom and well-being of the individual. In seeking to destroy capitalism and industrial civilization, both movements provide ample potential opportunity for those depraved individuals who would rather kill than live, who would rather inflict pain and death than experience pleasure, whose pleasure comes from the infliction of pain and death.

Unfortunately, there is no lack of such individuals. There are serial murderers in the world. History tells us of mobs that cheered at the sight of human beings being torn to pieces by wild beasts in the arena, and of other mobs that cheered at the sight of "witches" and heretics burning alive at the stake. In our own time, there have been Hitler, Stalin, and Mao, and an array of lesser such gangsters, each with a whole army of sadistic murderers at his beck and call. In every case but that of the serial murderers, there has been some kind of philosophical justification for the murders, such as the security of the State, the will of God, the achievement of Lebensraum, or the establishment of communism and a future classless society. Each of these alleged values supposedly justified the murder of living human beings. As the Communists were so fond of saying, "The end justifies the means." And now there are the leaders of the ecology movement, whose alleged end is the preservation of such things as wildlife, jungles, and rock formations for their own sake, and for whose alleged sake they look forward to throttling and destroying industrial civilization and decimating mankind.

Whatever may have been the delusions of religious fanatics and the advocates of racial or class warfare concerning the actual nature of their values, such delusions must wear exceedingly thin in the case of the environmental movement. It is transparently obvious that no one in the world can actually value such things as rock formations, jungles, and dangerous wildlife for their own sake. At best, that would be comparable to valuing pebbles on Mars or gas clouds on Jupiter for their own sake. But what some people can value, unfortunately, is the sight of other human beings suffering. *This* was the value which the Communists and the Nazis sought, which religious fanatics have sought, which serial murderers seek, and which the leaders of the environmental movement seek.

The kind of potential murderers that are to be found in the ranks of the environmental movement are, for the most part, probably not personally violent in any apparent way. In eras that are philosophically and culturally better than our own, they might even pass their entire lives quietly, in modest obscurity, causing harm to no one. In such a better era, Hitler might have passed his days as an obscure paperhanger, Himmler as a chicken farmer, and Eichmann as a factory worker or office clerk. Lenin would probably have been just a disgruntled intellectual, and Stalin perhaps an obscure cleric. But in the conditions of a collapse of rationality, frustrations and feelings of hatred and hostility rapidly multiply, while cool judgment, rational standards, and civilized behavior vanish. Monstrous ideologies appear and monsters in human form emerge alongside them, ready to put them into practice. The ecology movement is just such a movement, with just such a potential. Its expressions of approval for such images as that of a terrified human being, being eaten alive by alligators, is an invitation to torturers and murderers looking for a rationale to call for the exercise of their blood lust.

In my view, the open irrationalism of environmentalism and ecology marks them as nothing but the intellectual death rattle of socialism in the West, the final convulsion of a movement that only a few decades ago eagerly looked forward to the results of paralyzing the actions of individuals by means of "social engineering" and now seeks to paralyze the actions of individuals by means of prohibiting engineering of any kind. If such comparisons are possible, I think the Greens are actually a cut below the Reds and will fade much more quickly from the scene, because of their open irrationality. In the case of socialism and the Reds, there was for many years at least room for some doubt on the part of many people. It was possible for many years for people to believe that the purpose of the human sacrifices being called for on the part of the rich and the capitalists was to raise the level of the average human being by bringing justice and prosperity to the wage earners, who had allegedly been victimized by the injustices and economic evils of capitalism.

But with environmentalism and the Greens, the first thing to be sacrificed, with scarcely a moment's concern, is the standard of living of the wage earners and the average human being. Indeed, from the perspective of environmentalism, their very existence for the most part represents "surplus population," which prevents the existence of allegedly more important members of animal species. Thus the livelihood of wage earners is to be sacrificed en masse, without a thought, whenever the preservation of any "endangered species" is in question. Everything wage earners buy is to be made more expensive by restricting the production of energy and by imposing one unnecessary cost after another in efforts to escape imaginary terrors.[90] Environmentalism and the Greens stand for human sacrifice without even the pretense of human beneficiaries. They stand for sacrifice— for destruction—pure and simple. They reveal far more clearly than did socialism and the Reds the actual nature of the doctrine of altruism—of human sacrifice.[91]

However justified today's intellectual mainstream is in doubting its mind and hating itself, it has absolutely no basis for blaming its self-doubt and self-hatred on reason. What it took as reason in advocating socialism was never reason, but contemptible ignorance; what it apparently takes as having been loyalty to reason in its adherence to socialism was never loyalty to reason, but willful, defiant ignorance. The roots of the intellectuals' abandonment of reason are to be found not in the collapse of socialism, but in their previous support of socialism.

In the days of a generation or more ago, when the intellectual mainstream still projected confidence in reason, what it took reason to mean in the realm of politics and economics was that a comparative handful of men— an intellectual elite—would arrogate to themselves a monopoly of thought: they would deny the rationality and the independence of the great mass of mankind, and treat everyone as clay for them to mold. Everyone would be compelled to live his life in compliance with their central plan. This was the meaning of socialism and its "social engineering."

Naturally, this project failed miserably. Its failure was certainly not the failure of reason, however. On the contrary, it was the failure of a monumentally *irrational* idea: namely, that the independent exercise of reason by the great mass of mankind could be prohibited in the economic realm, and that somehow, on the strength of a tiny, insignificant fraction of mankind's collective intelligence, economic success could be achieved for all. Whatever sort of "fatal conceit" this may have been, to use the expression of Professor Hayek, it was not any conceit of reason.[92] At its base, the entire project was marked by the most profound contempt for reason—for the reason of all of mankind but that of the intellectual elite, which was to rule mankind under socialism.

Today, the intellectuals apparently think they have learned their lesson. They are through with engineering—*all* of engineering—and through with reason, because they think they know how badly the seemingly best-laid rational plans can run amuck. They now believe that man's acting on nature on a foundation of reason and science is as dangerous as their acting on man on a foundation of "reason" and "science"—on what, in a state of virtual dementia, they choose to believe is reason and science, namely, Marxism and other variants of collectivism. Thus, for example, they believe that the engineering of atomic power plants and dams is as dangerous as the engineering of people that they so long supported in countries such as the former Soviet Union. This is how they act. This is how their behavior can be understood.

The lesson the intellectuals should have learned from the failure of socialism, and still could learn if they finally chose to end their ignorance and read the authors I have mentioned, above all, Ludwig von Mises and Ayn Rand, is the precise opposite of the one they claim to have learned. The correct lesson is that *it is human reason that one must respect,* namely, the reason of the *individual* human being. The substantive meaning of this proposition is that one must respect *individual rights,* as understood by John Locke and the Founding Fathers of the United States, and that the social system which one must uphold, as representing the consistent implementation of respect for individual rights, is *laissez-faire capitalism.* If the intellectuals understood this lesson, then they would understand that what it is dangerous to violate is laissez faire in the realm of *human beings.*

The obvious fact is, of course, that man can successfully control nature for the benefit of his life. But the essential politico-economic requirement of his doing so is that the government must not attempt to control man. The individual man or woman is the possessor of reason and the being of ultimate value, each to himself or herself, whose rights must be fully respected. It is these individually sovereign beings who must be free to act upon nature. When they are free, they form and intensify the associations that constitute a division-of-labor society. They create capitalism. They are then capable of acting upon nature with all of the progressively growing success demonstrated in the Western world over the last two centuries or more.

However, because today's intellectual mainstream does not fundamentally distinguish man from inanimate nature—on such explicit philosophical grounds as determinism—the inference today's intellectuals have apparently drawn from the failure of socialism is the lunatic notion that it is dangerous to violate laissez faire in the realm of *nature.* Instead of arriving at the insights of the British classical economists into the natural economic harmonies prevailing among free, rational beings and requiring the absence of government intervention, they believe they have gained insights into alleged natural harmonies prevailing among wild animals and inanimate objects. They call these alleged harmonies "ecosystems," and they believe that the existence of "ecosystems" requires the absence of intervention by rational human beings in nature. In a manner reminiscent of economists arguing against government intervention into the affairs of human beings, they argue against *human* interference with nature and its alleged ecosystems.

Ironically, in arguing in this way, the ecology movement not only seeks the perpetuation of all the horrors of socialism, but also turns out to embody the substance of what was once an unjust caricature of the defenders of capitalism. For it adopts as its actual policy what its intellectual predecessors ridiculed the defenders of capitalism for supposedly believing, namely, that man should not intervene in nature for fear of unleashing unknown forces. That was what the advocates of socialism and government intervention repeatedly accused the defenders of capitalism of believing when the latter stood on the grounds of economic law and its harmonies as an argument against government interference in the economic system. In taking this position, the advocates of capitalism, of course, never advocated a policy of "do nothing," as their socialist and interventionist critics claimed. On the contrary, they have always advocated that *the government* do nothing, so that the *individual citizens* could be free to do what was necessary to achieve their prosperity.

The defenders of capitalism argue both against government interference into the affairs of men and in favor of human interference in nature. The two are merely different sides of the same coin: namely, individuals must be free of government intervention precisely in order for *them* to be able effectively to intervene in nature. It is the individual citizens, not the government, who are the controllers of nature. Whether the government prohibits its citizens from acting on nature on the grounds that it must have a monopoly of such activity, or on the grounds that such activity is simply dangerous, the substance and the consequences are identical: namely, paralysis, poverty, and death. The socialists at least kept up the pretense that they wanted to achieve human values more efficiently than free individuals could. The environmentalists make clear that their actual purpose in alleging the harmonies of "ecosystems" and arguing against human intervention in nature is the destruction of human values.

In the ecology movement, the Left has reduced itself to a mass of terrified ignoramuses, fearful of all "newfangled" technology. It reveals itself as a virtual Ma and Pa Kettle of the intellect; a remnant from the Dark Ages, having managed to survive all this time on some kind of intellectual wildlife preserve, to borrow an expression of Ayn Rand's. What irony it is, that even as this is what the Left has become, its members continue to have the audacity to criticize the advocacy of capitalism and economic freedom as "reactionary." The more consistent elements of the ecology movement openly urge a return to the Pleistocene—to the Stone Age—in order to live in an alleged harmony with nature. Yet, at the very same time, in the political arena, advocates of some measure of freedom and capitalism, who espouse recognizable elements of the social philosophy formed in the eighteenth century, in the Age of Reason, and found in the United States Constitution, are ridiculed as "dinosaur Republicans"—because they presumably wish to return to the Age of Reason.

It is high time this travesty ended. Its foundation was the Marxist doctrine that socialism was the politico-economic system called for by human reason and thus that movement toward it represented an improvement in human conditions, and, moreover, that mankind was impelled toward progress by automatic historical forces. All of these notions, of course, are totally false and are now discredited in the eyes of the world. Socialism is a vicious, destructive system. Movement toward socialism is movement toward tyranny, poverty, and death. On the other hand, *capitalism* is the politico-economic system actually called for by human reason. Its rising production and improving standards of living represent economic progress. Movement toward capitalism, or toward a more consistent form of capitalism, is what represents progress in the political realm. And, of course, neither movement toward capitalism nor toward socialism, that is to say, neither progress nor decline, is inevitable. Each depends on the influence of ideas: progress, on the influence of rational ideas; decline, on the influence of irrational ideas.

In the environmental movement, the Left now clearly reveals itself to be the most reactionary movement in the history of the world, a movement whose "moderates" seek a return to the economic conditions of a century ago, and whose logically consistent elements openly seek a return to the economic conditions of the Middle Ages or, indeed, of the Stone Age. If ever there were a group of

people who, in the words of a well-known "liberal" of the last generation, needed to be "dragged, kicking and screaming, into the twentieth century"—into the modern world—it is today's Left: the Greens of the ecology movement.

The transformation of the socialist movement into the ecology movement creates the opportunity for the defenders of capitalism to reclaim their rightful place as the true representatives of science, progress, and enlightenment, and to make sure that wherever intelligent people who value reason are found, they will increasingly enroll under the banners of capitalism.

Furthermore, the advocates of capitalism should now proudly proclaim that they turn to the thinkers of earlier centuries of the modern era for inspiration—to thinkers such as Adam Smith and John Locke—rather than to most of today's intellectuals. Thanks to the Left's transformation into the ecology movement, they can now claim, with obvious justification, the same kind of modernity in doing so that men of the Renaissance could claim in looking to the thinkers of antiquity for inspiration rather than to their ignorant contemporaries.

It can readily be conceded that Adam Smith and John Locke and the Founding Fathers of the United States rode in horse-drawn carriages and wore powdered wigs, and that contemporary intellectuals fly in jet planes and wear the fashions of today. But those men were the source of essential ideas on which the Industrial Revolution and our present level of technological and economic development rest. When they rode in horse-drawn carriages, they were thinking the thoughts that made possible the jet planes of today. Today's intellectuals, although they fly in jet planes, are thinking thoughts which are incompatible with the continuation of industrial civilization. This is now blatantly obvious in their support of the ecology movement and in their growing denunciations of economic progress and transparent efforts to stifle it and undo it. They should certainly not be given any form of credit for the technological and economic achievements of the age in which they live, and which they are in fact out to destroy, and then, on the basis such error, be regarded as superior in any way to the thinkers of earlier centuries who made possible the accomplishments of our own. The nature of their souls and the intellectual level of their philosophy are well expressed in the call "Back to the Pleistocene!" a call which if they do not make themselves, they are certainly not at pains to dispute or capable of disputing. In other words, contemporary intellectuals, with few exceptions, are not at all "modern" or advanced, but backward and primitive, far, far behind intellectuals of earlier generations whom they delight in ridiculing.

The future course of civilization hinges on the extent

to which the advocates of capitalism and reason can take the intellectual offensive against an opposition that is now nothing more than a rapidly decomposing intellectual corpse. Their ultimate victory appears to be assured, provided only that they keep their philosophy alive.

6. Environmentalism and Irrationalism

While the collapse of socialism is an important precipitating factor in the rise of environmentalism, there are other, more fundamental causes as well. Philosophical-cultural forces are at work in the rise of environmentalism which are of the same fundamentality and significance as built modern civilization.[93] Only now, centering on a negative appraisal of the reliability of reason, they are working in reverse, to bring about the destruction of modern civilization.

Environmentalism is the product of a growing loss of confidence in reason long predating the collapse of socialism. It is the leading manifestation of a rising tide of irrationalism that is engulfing our culture. As previously mentioned, over the last two centuries the reliability of reason as a means of knowledge has been under a constant attack led by philosophers from Immanuel Kant to Bertrand Russell.[94] The growth of irrationalism has been manifested in a series of developments each of which has contributed to the rise of environmentalism. Among them have been the loss of the concept of economic progress, the growth of irrational skepticism, a growing decline and outright perversion of education, and the cultural devaluation of man.

The Loss of the Concept of Economic Progress

An important intellectual confusion in the decades prior to the appearance of the ecology movement, which helped to pave the way for it and continues to sustain it, was the loss of very concept of economic *progress.* Somewhere along the line, the seemingly synonymous, but in fact very different, concept of economic *growth* took its place. Only after this change had occurred could the ecology doctrine succeed.

Growth is a concept that applies to individual living organisms. An organism grows until it reaches maturity, then it declines, and sooner or later dies. The concept of growth is also morally neutral, equally capable of describing a negative as a positive: tumors and cancers can grow. Thus the concept of growth both necessarily implies limits and can easily be applied negatively.

In contrast, the concept of progress applies across *succeeding generations of human beings.*[95] The individual human beings reach maturity and die. But because they possess the faculty of reason, they can both discover new and additional knowledge and transmit it to the rising generation, which then starts out in life in possession of a larger body of knowledge than did the present generation. If the new generation continues to think, it succeeds in further enlarging the sum of human knowledge and thus it too passes on a larger body of knowledge to its successors than it inherited. And so it can continue from generation to generation, with each succeeding generation receiving a greater inheritance of knowledge than the one before it and making its own fresh contribution to knowledge. This continuously expanding body of knowledge, insofar as it takes the form of continuously increasing scientific and technological knowledge and correspondingly improved capital equipment, is the foundation of continuous economic progress.

Progress is a concept unique to man: it is founded on his possession of reason and thus his ability to accumulate and transmit a growing body of knowledge across the generations. Totally unlike growth, whose essential confines are the limits of a single organism, progress has no practical limit. Only if man could achieve omniscience would progress have to end. But the actual effect of the acquisition of knowledge is always to lay the foundation for the acquisition of still more knowledge. Through applying his reason, man enlarges all of his capacities, and the more he enlarges them, the more he enlarges his capacity to enlarge them.[96]

The concept of progress differs radically from the concept of growth in that it also has built into it a positive evaluation: progress is movement in the direction of a *higher, better, and more desirable state of affairs.* This improving state of affairs is founded on the growing body of knowledge that the possession and application of human reason makes possible. Its foundation is the rising potential for human achievement that is based on growing knowledge.

While it is possible to utter denunciations of too rapid "growth" as being harmful, it would be a contradiction in terms even to utter the thought of too rapid *progress,* let alone denounce it. The meaning would be that things can get *better* too quickly—that things getting better meant they were getting worse.

Irrational Skepticism

A major foundation of the ecologists' irrationalism that is of long standing is the conviction that whatever we may think we know today about anything, can turn out to be wrong tomorrow, because of the discovery of something new which totally invalidates all of our presumed knowledge about it. This doctrine, which is now increasingly popular, has been a virtual stock in trade of philosophy courses and of higher education in general for several generations. It is on this premise that the ecologists believe and project that every technological advance is a potential thalidomide.[97] All of their wild conjectures about mass destruction are reinforced by this premise, of which they are already convinced, in advance of, and apart from, the facts of any particular case.

Such skepticism rests on ignorance of the science of epistemology and on the fallacy of equivocation. It does not understand how man achieves knowledge—how he validates his conclusions and can therefore be rationally confident of them. It assumes, in effect, that all claims to knowledge are equal—the proved and the unproved—and that because some claims to knowledge turn out to be false, any claim to knowledge can turn out to be false. For example, it believes that the very fact that people ardently believed in Ptolemaic astronomy at one time, and were later proved wrong by Copernicus and Galileo, itself raises the possibility that Copernican and Galilean astronomy will someday be proved wrong.[98]

The truth is that knowledge is knowledge and continues to be knowledge for all time to come. It is not overthrown by later discoveries, but is supplemented and expanded by them. The physics of Archimedes was not overthrown, but expanded by the physics of Newton. The geometry of Euclid is as true today as ever, though we now know much more about mathematics than Euclid did. The truths in the writings of Adam Smith are as true today as when he first wrote them, though our knowledge of economics has been greatly expanded by Ricardo, the Mills, Böhm-Bawerk, von Mises, and others. All of technological and economic progress is a confirmation of the fact that the discoveries of later generations *add* to the discoveries of previous ones rather than refute them. If new discoveries constantly refuted previous discoveries, as the skeptics claim, progress of any kind would simply be impossible. Progress rests on the fact that knowledge is a growing sum, in which the contributions of succeeding generations are added to those of previous generations.

Similar reasoning applies to the possibility of accidents, which the ecologists fear so greatly. Despite man's best efforts, accidents sometimes occur. A dam may burst, a building may collapse, a drug may turn out to be unsafe. But by the nature of the case, accidents are the exception—a departure from the normal. Moreover, they are steadily tending to be reduced in frequency and severity as man's knowledge and prosperity grow. Indeed, each accident, if its causes are studied and analyzed, itself tends to prevent a repetition of that accident. Thus, the actual record of man (when he chooses to use his reason) is a steady increase in safety. Few things could be more obvious than that the food, drugs, dams, buildings, bridges, ships, trains, and factories of the twentieth century are incomparably safer than those of the nineteenth century. Apart from the influence of grow-

ing irrationality, progress in safety has continued decade by decade in the twentieth century. (The irrationality I refer to is not only the phenomenon of narcotics use, but also destructive government interference through such means as inflation, confiscatory taxation, and stifling regulation. Such policies can prevent the necessary replacement or maintenance of facilities, let alone their improvement.)

The Destructive Role of Contemporary Education

It is sometimes observed that most of today's high school and college graduates have very little education in science and mathematics and thus do not understand and cannot properly appreciate modern technology. There is considerable merit in these observations, but the problem goes much deeper. Namely, from the earliest grades, *the prevailing methodology of contemporary education systematically encourages the irrational skepticism I have just described.*

To explain how this is the case, I must briefly digress into the history of philosophy.

At the end of the eighteenth century, Immanuel Kant foisted on the intellectual world a distorted version of what reason is, namely, a faculty divorced from knowledge of the real world and limited to awareness of a world of mere appearances created by the human mind itself.[99] Both in reaction against the Kantian version of reason and on the direct foundation of it, as early as the first quarter of the nineteenth century, reason was being popularly denounced by intellectuals of the "Romantic" era as "a false secondary power by which we multiply distinctions."[100]

The Romantics' reaction against the Kantian version of reason can be understood in part in exactly the same way as Ayn Rand has described the later reaction of the Existentialists against it, namely, if "*this* is reason, to hell with it!"[101] Romanticism, however, also follows on the direct foundation of Kantianism, which holds that man's mind is incapable of actually knowing reality and thus that "'to attain a knowledge of the real, we must go out of consciousness.'"[102] According to W. T. Jones, a leading historian of philosophy:

> To the Romantic mind, the distinctions that reason makes are artificial, imposed, and man-made; they divide, and in dividing destroy, the living whole of reality—"We murder to dissect." How, then, *are* we to get in touch with the real? By divesting ourselves, insofar as we can, of the whole apparatus of learning and scholarship and by becoming like children or simple, uneducated men; by attending to nature rather than to the works of man; by becoming passive and letting nature work upon us; by contemplation and communion, rather than by ratiocination and scientific method.[103]

The Romantics held that "we are nearer to the truth about the universe when we dream than when we are awake" and "nearer to it as children than as adults."[104] The clear implication of the philosophy of Romanticism is that the valuable portion of our mental life has no essential connection with our ability to reason and with the deliberate, controlled use of our conscious mind: we allegedly possess it in our sleep and as children.

In its essentials, the philosophy of Romanticism is *the guiding principle of contemporary education.* Exactly like Romanticism, contemporary education holds that the valuable portion of our mental life has no essential connection with our ability to reason and with the deliberate, controlled use of our conscious mind—that we possess this portion of our mental life if not in our sleep, then nevertheless as small children. This doctrine is clearly present in the avowed conviction of contemporary education that *creativity* is a phenomenon that is separate from and independent of such conscious mental processes as *memorization* and the use of logic. Indeed, it is an almost universally accepted proposition of contemporary pseudoscience that one-half of the human brain is responsible for such conscious processes as the use of logic, while the other half is responsible for "creativity," as though, when examined, the halves of the brain revealed this information all by themselves, perhaps in the form of bearing little labels respectively marked "Logic Unit, Made in Hong Kong" and "Creativity Unit, Made in Woodstock, New York." Obviously, the view of the brain as functioning in this way is a *conclusion,* which is based on the philosophy and thus interpretative framework of the doctrine's supporters.

Now, properly, education is a process by means of which students *internalize* knowledge: they mentally absorb it through observation and proof, and repeated application. Memorization, deduction, and problem solving must constantly be involved. The purpose is to develop the student's mind—to provide him with an instantaneously available storehouse of knowledge and thus an increasingly powerful mental apparatus that he will be able to use and further expand throughout his life. Such education, of course, requires hard work from the student. Seen from a physiological perspective, it may be that what the process of education requires of the student through his exercises is an actual *imprinting* of his brain.

Yet, under the influence of the philosophy of Romanticism, contemporary education is fundamentally opposed to these essentials of education. It draws a distinction between "problem solving," which it views as "creative" and claims to favor, and "memorization," which it appears to regard as an imposition on the students, whose valuable, executive-level time, it claims, can be better spent in "problem solving." Contemporary education thus proceeds on the assumption that the ability to solve problems is innate, or at least fully developed before the child begins school. It perceives its job as allowing the student to exercise his native problem-solving abilities, while imposing on him as little as possible of the allegedly unnecessary and distracting task of memorization.

In the elementary grades, this approach is expressed in such attitudes as that it is not really necessary for students to go to the trouble of memorizing the multiplication tables if the availability of pocket calculators can be taken for granted which they know how to use; or go to the trouble of memorizing facts of history and geography, if the ready availability of books and atlases containing the facts can be taken for granted, which facts the students know how to look up when the need arises. In college and graduate courses, this approach is expressed in the phenomenon of the "open-book examination," in which satisfactory performance is supposedly demonstrated by the ability to use a book as a source of information, proving once again that the student knows how to find the information when he needs it.

With little exaggeration, the whole of contemporary education can be described as a process of encumbering the student's *mind* with as little knowledge as possible. The place for knowledge, it seems to believe, is in external sources—books and libraries—which the student knows how to use when necessary. Its job, its proponents believe, is not to teach the students knowledge but "how to acquire knowledge"—not to teach them facts and principles, which it holds quickly become "obsolete," but to teach them "how to learn." Its job, its proponents openly declare, is not to teach geography, history, mathematics, science, or any other subject, including reading and writing, but to teach "Johnny"—to teach Johnny how he can allegedly go about learning the facts and principles it declares are not important enough to teach and which it thus gives no incentive to learn and provides the student with no means of learning.

The results of this type of education are visible in the hordes of students who, despite years of schooling, have learned virtually nothing, and who are least of all capable of thinking critically and solving problems. When such students read a newspaper, for example, they cannot read it in the light of a knowledge of history or economics— they do not know history or economics; history and economics are out there in the history and economics books, which, they were taught, they can "look up, if they need to." They cannot even read it in the light of elementary arithmetic, for they have little or no internally automated habits of doing arithmetic. Having little or no knowledge of the elementary facts of history and geography, they have no way even of relating one event to another in terms of time and place.

Such students, and, of course, the adults such students become, are chronically in the position in which to be able to use the knowledge they need to use, they would first have to go out and acquire it. Not only would they have to look up relevant facts, which they already should know, and now may have no way even of knowing they need to know, but they would first have to read and understand books dealing with abstract principles, and to understand those books, they would first have to read other such books, and so on. In short, they would first have to acquire the education they already should have had.

Properly, by the time a student has completed a college education, his brain should hold the essential content of well over a hundred major books on mathematics, science, history, literature, and philosophy, and do so in a form that is well organized and integrated, so that he can apply this internalized body of knowledge to his perception of everything in the world around him. He should be in a position to enlarge his knowledge of any subject and to express his thoughts on any subject clearly and logically, both verbally and in writing. Yet, as the result of the miseducation provided today, it is now much more often the case that college graduates fulfill the Romantic ideal of being "simple, uneducated men."

Contemporary education is responsible for the growing prevalence of irrational skepticism. The students subjected to it do not acquire actual knowledge. They have no firm foundation in a base of memorized facts and they have not acquired any solid knowledge of principles because their education has avoided as far as possible the painstaking processes of logical proof and repeated application of principles, which latter constitutes a vital and totally legitimate form of memorization. Such students go through school "by the seat of their pants." They are forever "winging it." And that is how they go through life as adults. It is impossible for them to have genuine understanding of anything that is beyond the realm of their daily experience, and even of that, only on a superficial level. To such people, almost everything must appear as an arbitrary assertion, taken on faith. For their education has made them unfit to understand how things are actually known. Their failure to memorize such things as the multiplication tables in their childhood, makes it impossible for them to understand whatever directly depends on such knowledge, which, in turn, makes it impossible for them to acquire the further knowledge that depends on that knowledge, and so on. With each passing year of their education, they fall further behind.

Ironically, their failure to memorize what it is appropriate to memorize ends up putting them in a position in which to pass examinations, they have no other means than out-of-context memorization—that is, memorization lacking any foundation in logical connection and proof. Because they have never memorized fundamental facts, and thus have no basis for developing genuine understanding of all that depends on those facts, they are placed in the position in which to pass examinations they must attempt to memorize out-of-context conclusions. It is because of this that a growing proportion of what they learn as the years pass has the status in their minds of arbitrary assertions. They are chronically in the mental state of having no good reason for most or almost all of what they believe. Thus, in their context of actual ignorance masked by pretended knowledge, they are prime targets for irrational skepticism. To them, in their mental state, doubt of everything can only seem perfectly natural.

Such students, such adults, are easy targets for a doctrine such as "environmentalism." They are totally unprepared intellectually to resist any irrational trend and more than willing to leap on the bandwagon of one that caters to their uncertainties and fears. Environmentalism does this by blaming the stresses of their life on the existence of an industrial society and holding out the prospect of an intellectually undemanding and thus seemingly stress-free pastoral existence, one which is allegedly "in harmony with nature."

The destructive work of contemporary education carried on against the development of students' conceptual abilities from the earliest grades on is compounded, as their education advances to the higher grades, by the teaching of a whole collection of irrationalist doctrines that constitute the philosophical substance of contemporary liberal arts education.

Among them, besides irrational skepticism and the recent addition of environmentalism, are collectivism in its various forms of Marxism, racism, nationalism, and feminism; and cultural relativism, determinism, logical positivism, existentialism, linguistic analysis, behaviorism, Freudianism, and Keynesianism.

These doctrines constitute a systematic attack on reason and its role in human life. All the varieties of collectivism deny the free will and rationality of the individual and attribute his ideas, character, and vital interests to his membership in a collective: namely, his membership in an economic class, racial group, nationality, or sex, as the case may be, depending on the specific variety of collectivism. Because they view ideas as determined by group membership, these doctrines deny the very possibility of knowledge. Their further effect is the creation of conflict between members of different groups: for example, between businessmen and wage earners, blacks and whites, English speakers and French speakers, men and women. And, of course, when collectivism becomes the guiding political principle of a country, the results are unmitigated disaster, ranging from impoverishment to mass murder.[105]

Determinism, the doctrine that man's actions are controlled by forces beyond his power of choice, denies the very possibility of rational thought being capable of guiding human life and achieving human happiness. Existentialism, the philosophy that man is trapped in a "human condition" of inescapable misery, obviously teaches exactly the same conclusion.

Cultural relativism denies the objective value of modern civilization and thus undercuts students' valuation not only of it, but also of the technology and science necessary to build such a civilization, and the valuation of human reason itself, which is the ultimate foundation of modern civilization. It also undercuts people's willingness to work hard to achieve personal values in the context of modern civilization. The doctrine blinds people to the objective value of such marvelous technological advances as automobiles and electric light, and thus further prepares the ground for the sacrifice of modern civilization to such nebulous and, by comparison, utterly trivial values as "unpolluted air."

Logical positivism denies the possibility of knowing anything with certainty about the real world. Linguistic analysis regards the search for truth as a trivial word game. Behaviorism denies the existence of consciousness. Freudianism regards the conscious mind (the "Ego") as surrounded by the warring forces of the unconscious mind in the form of the "Id" and the "Superego," and thus as being incapable of exercising substantial influence on the individual's behavior. Keynesianism regards wars, earthquakes, and pyramid building as sources of prosperity. It looks to peacetime government budget deficits and inflation of the money supply as a good substitute for these allegedly beneficial phenomena. Its practical effects, as the present-day economy of the United States bears witness, are the erosion of the buying power of money, of credit, of saving and capital accumulation, and of the general standard of living.

Such doctrines, as I say, constitute the philosophical substance of what now passes for a liberal arts education. If one wishes to use the expression "intellectual mainstream," and borrow for a moment the environmentalists' alleged concern with the cleanliness of streams and such, these doctrines may justifiably be viewed as intellectual raw sewage comparable to what can be seen bobbing up and down in a dirty river. They and the methodology of contemporary education have totally fouled the "intellectual mainstream." The kind of education I have described—if it can still be called education, consisting as it does of an unremitting assault on the rational faculty and every rational value—is responsible for the hordes of graduates turned out over the last decades who have had no conception of the meaning and value of the Constitution and history of the United States, of the meaning and value of Western civilization itself, or in-

deed, as we shall see, of the meaning and value of membership in the human race. It has been responsible for the decline in the quality of government in the United States, as, unavoidably, many such miseducated graduates have found their way into the halls of Congress and the state legislatures, and into major offices in all the other branches of government, and, of course, into all the various branches of the news media and publishing. I believe it has even been responsible for the widespread use of drugs, inasmuch as living in the midst of modern civilization with a level of knowledge as meager as that imparted by contemporary education, must be a source of chronic and profound anxiety, urgently calling for relief. To many, drugs may seem to provide that relief.

The "intellectual mainstream" has been at war with the surrounding capitalist society for over a century and a half. Today, the rise of environmentalism, and of feminism and the new racism, on university campuses and elsewhere, makes clear that the contemporary intellectual mainstream is also at war with the wider intellectual tradition of Western civilization as well. Environmentalism denounces Western civilization for extolling man above nature.[106] Feminism and the new racism denounce it as "sexist" and "racist," the alleged product of white male genes.[107] Contemporary education, despite the existence of individual exceptions, is thus reduced in its essentials to the activities of a clutch of nonentities engaged in a two-front war with the surrounding material civilization of capitalism and with the intellectual heritage of all of Western civilization.

Clearly, as Ayn Rand observed over thirty years ago, "the intellectuals are dead." And matters have now reached the point where the most urgent task confronting the Western world is to find replacements—"new intellectuals," who, unlike the alleged intellectuals of today, will be committed to the value of human reason.[108] Unless such intellectuals can be found, and in sufficient number, the world coming into existence before our very eyes will be very much like the one H. G. Wells described in his science fiction story *The Time Machine*. In Wells' story, set in the far future, the human race has divided into two degenerate branches: the hideous, subterranean Morlocks, who feast on human flesh, and the pretty, surface-dwelling Eloi, who in totally vacuous innocence serve as food for the Morlocks.[109]

It is sometimes difficult to avoid believing that, figuratively speaking, as a result of irrationalist philosophy and its inculcation through contemporary education, these degenerate branches of the human race already exist, in the form of the leaders of the environmental movement and those who offer it no resistance or even rush to join it, oblivious to the obvious destruction that awaits them. For it would seem that contemporary education has resulted in the creation both of monsters and of vast numbers of people so mentally enfeebled and so deprived of even an elementary sense of manhood that they have no wish or capacity to resist the monsters. Almost every day, such people hear open calls for the radical curtailment of energy consumption—*their* energy consumption—and they do not react. They buy bestselling books by environmentalists and read such passages as, "The environmentally sane standard of living for a population our current size would probably be somewhere between that of the average Englishman and of the average Ethiopian—each lives unreasonably."[110] In other words, they read an open declaration by a leading environmentalist that if environmentalism has its way, *their* standard of living would be somewhere between poverty by American standards and outright famine! Again, they do not react. Of course, they do not even react against calls for mass death.

I believe that the reason the masses of people do not respond with outrage against environmentalism is partly the fact that their education has left them unable to take ideas seriously. They hear and read such pronouncements and have the reaction that, like so much of what they were taught in school, the pronouncements do not mean what they say. In addition, and even more important, their education, reinforced by the experience of growing up in a welfare state, has left many of them with a mentality similar to that of small children, who, lacking all knowledge of how wealth is created, sometimes appear to believe that "money grows on trees." Very many of our contemporaries, almost certainly the overwhelming majority of the rank and file of the environmental movement, believe that the availability of goods is automatic and indestructible, and that they have a corresponding automatic right to goods. For the most part, they have little or no knowledge of history, and even the very best educated among them have absolutely no real knowledge of economic theory. They simply have no conception of the process of creating wealth or what its requirements are. They have absolutely no concept of what a remarkable productive achievement the economic system of the present-day industrial world actually is and that it is capable of being destroyed.

They are not, of course, so incredibly ignorant as to believe that human beings all over the world live as people do in the United States or the other industrial countries, or that even in these countries people have always lived as they now do. And they certainly do not believe that everyone even in the present-day United States lives well. But to the extent that they have any explanation of differences in the standard of living, it centers on the notion of a *distribution* of wealth. There are poor people in America and elsewhere in the world,

they believe, because of "social injustice"—that is, because of an unfair distribution of wealth. And that is the basis on which they explain the lower standard of living of earlier periods, especially the nineteenth century.

Thus, like small children, they believe that automobiles, television sets, and everything else exist automatically, that, in effect, they just grow on trees. Moreover, they believe that these trees, unlike the trees of nature, will always exist, no matter what is done to them, and that, in the absence of "social injustice," they will always be able to obtain from them all of the goods they now enjoy.

On this basis, they feel free to support the delivery of one blow after another to the economic system—ever more taxes, ever more regulations—in the expectation that they themselves will never suffer as a result of such actions. All that will happen, they believe, is that they will succeed in shaking loose some more goods, or, nowadays, more and more, succeed in putting an end to this or that irritant or annoyance. The only ones ever to suffer, they believe—if anyone ever actually suffers—are rich businessmen.

All of this is an essential part of the intellectual environment in which the ecology movement has flourished. In this intellectual environment, it is perfectly possible for people to proceed as though, for example, the only connection between their lives and the existence of oil companies is that the oil companies contribute to the pollution of beaches, or, with their pipelines, prevent the migration of one or another species of cute, precious animals. It is perfectly possible for them to carry such blindness to the level of economic activity as such, and to believe that the only practical effect of economic activity is "pollution," and that in stopping economic activity all they will stop is "pollution."

It is in this way that they are ripe for the remarkable conclusion, described earlier, that the threatening forces of nature are created by us and that we could do better without our material means for dealing with nature than with them. They feel free to abandon industrial civilization in the unstated conviction that if and when it is abandoned, they will still be able to keep essentially all the goods they now enjoy, and in addition will have such benefits as cleaner air, the preservation of assorted cute animals, and the avoidance of such allegedly impending calamities as frighteningly bad weather. Nothing, they believe, will be required of them but some token loss, such as having to sort their garbage for recycling, or to form carpools, which is not so bad, they feel, because it provides new bases for such good things as "sharing" and camaraderie.

Thus, in what may prove to be the greatest tragedy in all of human existence, we see at the end of more than two centuries of man's most dazzling success, the proliferation of heirs who as adults possess less than the mentalities of children. We see a culture of reason and science being transformed before our very eyes into one which more and more resembles a culture of primitive man.

Only the emergence of a large number of "new intellectuals" prepared to fight against environmentalism and irrationalism and for reason and capitalism can assure that twenty-first-century man will be man in a sense worthy of the name.[111]

The Cultural Devaluation of Man

The popular acceptance of environmentalism is explainable in all of its aspects on the basis of the irrationalism inculcated by the contemporary educational system and the consequent cultural decline of reason.

The cultural decline of reason is what has created the growing hatred and hostility on which environmentalism feeds, as well as the unreasoning fears of its leaders and followers. To the degree that people abandon reason, they must feel terror before reality, because they have no way of dealing with it other than by reason. By the same token, their frustrations mount, since reason is their only means of solving problems and achieving the results they want to achieve. In addition, the abandonment of reason leads to more and more suffering as the result of others' irrationality, including their use of physical force. Thus, hatred and hostility increase as rationality decreases.

The closely related readiness of people to accept the doctrine of intrinsic values is also a consequence of the growing irrationalism. An "intrinsic value" is a value that one accepts without any reason, without asking questions. It is a "value" designed for people who do what they are told and who do not think. A rational value, in contrast, is a value one accepts only on the basis of understanding how it serves the self-evidently desirable ultimate end that is constituted by one's own life and happiness.

As was implicit in earlier discussion, along with destroying confidence in science and technology, the rising tide of irrationalism and growing loss of confidence in reason means loss of the philosophical basis of the valuation of man. For reason is man's fundamental distinguishing attribute and a culture's view of reason determines its view of man.[112] Thus, as a further result of the assault on reason and loss of confidence in it, the philosophical and cultural status of man has been in decline. This decline was evident well before the emergence of environmentalism. It was evident in such phenomena as the acclaim given to the "antihero" in literature, to works of art and sculpture that were grotesque, twisted representations of human beings, and to books describing man in such terms as "the naked ape" or "the trousered ape." In the last generation, as the growth of irrationalism has further accelerated and the effects of the process have more and more reached the general public, confidence in the reliability of reason, and thus the philosophical status of man, have declined so far that now virtually no basis is any longer recognized for a radical differentiation between man and animals. This explains why the doctrine of St. Francis of Assisi and the environmentalists concerning the equality between man and animals is now accepted with virtually no opposition. (Indeed, newspaper and television reporting of animal deaths has taken on a tone once reserved for the human victims of airplane crashes and similar tragedies. This was evident, for example, in the reporting of the Exxon-Valdez oil spill in Alaska and later in that of the oil spills in the Persian Gulf caused by Saddam Hussein. Numbers of dead animals and birds were reported in the same tone of tragedy as numbers of human casualties are reported.)

To the environmentalists, and the closely related supporters of "animal rights," the possession of reason does not seem significant—because they consider reason to be unreliable; indeed, they regard it as a trap and a snare and hate it. With man's distinctive attribute thus held to be unworthy of special valuation, man himself necessarily appears unworthy of special valuation. Thus, as the environmentalists see matters, they are advocates of a universal brotherhood of all species and all elements of the "environment." In their eyes, there are, in effect, blacks, caucasians, orientals, giraffes, snail darters, flies, spotted owls, and mountainsides, all with equal rights in the "environmental family."[113] The assertion of man's rights above those of any other species or inanimate object is, in their view, a form of racism and Nazism—of "speciesism"—in which man seeks to treat other parts of the brotherhood of nature as concentration camp inmates.[114]

This trend is directly and powerfully reinforced insofar as people are increasingly unaware that there ever was such a thing as the Age of Reason and what it stood for, and that there existed, and still do exist, philosophers of reason. Furthermore, people increasingly lack the intellectual capacity to acquire even the slightest understanding of what such thinkers have to say. For example, a book written in the eighteenth or nineteenth century is beyond the power of many of today's college students and recent graduates to read; they think of it as having been written in "old English." Worst of all, the introspective experience of the growing hordes of such miseducated people does not provide very powerful testimony on behalf of reason or the value of man. Nor does their external behavior, which increasingly incorporates such practices as the use of narcotics. To someone who can barely read, let alone write or even speak coherently, despite years of schooling, a view of man as a heroic being, if comprehensible at all, must appear to be from another planet. Such people are intellectually far more at home with the animals of the forest than with the man of the Renaissance and the Enlightenment. They fulfill to the letter the ideal of the Romantics.

The environmentalists do not realize that, apart from man, the allegedly beautiful and harmonious "Nature" that they extol is in reality merely a place in which one thing eats another—alive. If man were nothing more than an animal, he would be entitled to act toward the rest of nature in exactly the same way as all other living things act, namely, to use it for no other purpose than as a means of serving his own survival. But man's possession of reason elevates him above the rest of nature. By virtue of it, man has a range of knowledge and awareness incomparably surpassing that of every other species. And with the aid of goods that his reason makes it possible for him to produce, he comes to surpass all other species in virtually every physical respect as well. Thus, with the aid of goods such as automobiles, airplanes, ships and submarines, telescopes and microscopes, radio and radar, and bulldozers and steam shovels, he can outrace any animal, fly higher and faster than any bird, move in water deeper and faster than any fish, and see and hear further and in more detail and exert incomparably greater force than any other living being.

The possession of reason not only elevates man above the rest of nature in the inherent conflict of species for survival. *Within the human race, it also creates a harmony of rational self-interests* by virtue of making all men potential cooperators in the division of labor and thereby enabling each to serve his own self-interests better by living in peace with his fellow men and enjoying the benefits of the exercise of their reason as well as his own.[115] Thus, it is man's possession of reason that is the foundation for an objectively demonstrable brotherhood of *man,* and for the respect that each human being should accord every other human being. It is man's possession of reason that is the only basis for the existence of the concept of rights. Rights are precisely the social conditions of existence rational beings require their fellow creatures to acknowledge for the sake of the proper survival of all. The essential such social condition is that others not initiate the use of physical force against the individual. Only on the basis of respect for individual rights can human beings reap the benefits of the operation of each other's motivated intelligence.[116] To put this another way, rights are fundamental *utilitarian* principles, with human life and well-being as the standard of what constitutes utility.[117]

The only proper ethical standpoint is one which, on the basis of man's possession of reason, asserts the harmony of the self-interests of human beings and the absolute priority of human life and well-being over that of any lesser species.

It is only in the name of the special value of man that individual rights can be upheld and such evils as racism and Nazism be opposed. The attempt, for example, to introduce the concept of "speciesism" as something akin to racism totally cuts the ground from all genuine opposition to racism. If man had the same status as cockroaches, what possible difference could it make if two beings the equivalent of cockroaches applied for a job, say, and the employer chose one and rejected the other because he had a prejudice in favor of one color of cockroach over another? Racism can only be opposed on the grounds that it is a denial of what the victim is entitled to as *a human being,* namely, among other things, recognition of his achievements and qualifications irrespective of his skin color—i.e., justice. The environmentalists are able to get away with such a concept as "speciesism" only because hardly anyone any longer stops to think of the meaning of words, but reacts to mere sounds and the tone of voice in which they are uttered. To the unthinking, "speciesism" sounds similar to racism in that it purports to attach significance to membership in some kind of category, and when it is uttered with the same tone of condemnation as that used in connection with racism, it sounds as though it must be an equivalent evil.[118]

When the environmentalists disregard the special status conferred on man by the possession of reason, they do not thereby elevate flies, snail darters, and mountainsides to the level of man, but rather reduce man to the level of those things. If man is regarded as no better than flies, that is how he will be treated—that is how he is treated in every irrational culture.

Indeed, the doctrine of the environmentalists and the animal rights advocates implies nothing less than that *a human being deserves to be killed for killing a fly*—or for walking on grass or for leaving his footprints in the sand. Each of these things—flies, grass, sand—is alleged by the environmentalists to have a right either to life or to its preexisting condition.[119] If capital punishment is to be used to defend such an alleged right to life or preexisting condition, then the conclusion follows inescapably that human beings are to be killed for such things. And what if capital punishment is not to be used? Are human beings then to be imprisoned or flogged for the violation of such alleged rights of flies, etc.? If they are not, is there then to be no punishment at all for the violation of such alleged rights? If the violation of such alleged rights is not to be punished, does that mean that there is also to be no punishment for the violation of a human being's right to life? In proclaiming an equality of species and of the "environmental family," environmentalism is not merely mistaken. It reveals itself as psychopathic.

In this light, one may wish to consider such statements as: "It is an intensely disturbing idea that man should not be the master of all, that other suffering might be just as important. And that individual suffering—animal or human—might be less important than the suffering of species, ecosystems, the planet."[120] The reader may find it difficult to distinguish some of the above thoughts from the utterances of a psychopath who, in the process of torturing his victim, declares that the victim's suffering is "less important than the suffering of species, ecosystems, the planet." The reader may encounter similar difficulties in differentiating these words as well:

> To cap his argument, White [Lynn White, the leading environmentalist theologian] even dared to defend the rights of life-forms undeniably hostile to his own species, like the smallpox virus, *Variola*. . . . The implication was that a thoroughgoing Christian sense of morality must include smallpox, just as St. Francis included man-eating wolves. Perhaps White hoped for a latter-day saint who could instruct *Variola* in cosmic courtesy. More likely, he simply recognized that in killing people the smallpox virus was only performing its appointed role in the eco-system God created.[121]

Of course, these words cannot actually be psychopathic. After all, if they were, such prestigious publishers as Random House and the University of Wisconsin Press could not possibly have published them. Could they? Furthermore, how could anyone object to the teachings of those who "love" so much that they love the enemies of man, and love man fully as much as they love wastelands, ferocious beasts, and vermin?

Contrary to the environmentalists, man and man alone introduces conscious purpose and the perception of order and harmony into the world, and is the source of all value to himself. All of these concepts center entirely on his furtherance, fulfillment, and enjoyment of his life. Man and man alone is capable of having purposes, and must have them if he is to live, since he can live only by means of thinking, planning, and acting on a long-range basis.[122] The perception of order and harmony comes into the world as man comes to understand the world and how to use that understanding to serve his life. In the process of serving his life, man gives value to nature and to other species of life, as means of serving his life. Always, he is the center and the source of all value and purpose and of the perception of order and harmony.

Of course, the members of other species may be presumed to be of value to themselves, in that they act to survive. However, insofar as their survival clashes with any human value, conflict exists between them and man, and man must—deserves to—prevail. The standard of man's values is *man's* life. All presumed other standards of value may be safely left to other forms of life, to represent them as best they can.

Regrettably, large numbers of our contemporaries apparently have so little self-esteem that it appears sufficient to them merely to assert the existence of any kind of will or value seeking that is contrary to their own and they are prepared to abandon their own values. Thus, there are growing numbers of people who abstain from wearing furs or eating meat out of deference to the desire of lower animals to go on living. Such people value themselves and the enhancement of their own lives below the lives of lower animals. They place their own value not only below that of the lower animals whose furs they might wear or whose flesh they might eat, but also below the value that lower animals attach to themselves. That is, they accord less value to themselves relative to lower animals than all the animals that hunt accord to themselves relative to other lower animals. A lion or leopard values himself above a zebra or gazelle. But the environmentalists and advocates of animal rights value themselves below cattle and sheep and as less worthy of enjoying cattle and sheep than lions and leopards. The logically consistent expression of their view is that of McKibben and White, which calls for surrender to suffering and disease.

True enough, the environmentalists do not always put it this way. What they often say is something along the lines that because man is higher than the animals his behavior must be better than theirs—that, in effect, he must become their benevolent keeper. In other words, the human race is to become a kind of Mother Theresa to the lower animals. This is altruism at the very bottom of the pit. Man, the being who can reach the stars, is to sacrifice his ascent to the heavens for the sake of animals who cannot rise from the mud, and this is how he is to be better than them. Exactly the same point applies to the nonsensical claim that the role of human beings is to serve as "stewards" of the animal kingdom and of inanimate matter, as though the highest creature on earth existed for the sake of the lowest and of inanimate matter.[123]

To be sure, in serving his own life, man may extend the hand of a form of friendship to members of such species as cats and dogs, which in some ways resemble small children and which typically respond to him with what can only be described as joy and love. Indeed, the love people feel for such friendly creatures may provide a basis for overcoming the growing lunacy of animal rights. Whoever loves a dog, for example, should think of his dog's pleasure in chewing on a steak bone, say, and ask himself if he does not, after all, value his dog's pleasure above the life of the cow that provided the steak bone? And then he should ask if this is not perfectly right in view of the fact that the dog is capable of recognizing and responding to him with love, while the cow is little more than an object, whose greatest contribution to human life and well-being is to serve as a source of milk, meat, and leather? Finally, he should ask himself if it is not also perfectly right that while his dog chews on the steak bone, he, the man, eats the steak itself because he values his own pleasure even more highly than that of his dog?

It is worth noting here that a frequent tactic of the environmentalists in promoting the notion of animal rights is to depict all animals as the equivalent of loving and adorable pets which man somehow viciously chooses to hunt down and terrorize. Amazingly, one environmentalist television "documentary" attempts to depict grizzly bears as the equivalent of puppies or kittens on the basis of the behavior of a young grizzly cub. It casually neglects the fact that an adult grizzly is a terror to man and, incidentally, to cats and dogs.

The producers of such "documentaries" also casually show wild jungle cats terrifying weaker animals and actually eating them alive—animals whom their cameramen, being present on the scene, might have saved from such brutality. At the same time, they and the rest of the environmental movement endlessly berate man for his killing of animals that are not conscious of their fate and that, if necessary, he renders unconscious before killing, as, for example, seal pups. (It should not be necessary to say that the fact that in such cases typically a small number of human beings kills animals on a vastly larger scale than is the case in the animal kingdom itself is a reflection of the existence of the division of labor, not of wanton, pointless killing. Those who work as seal hunters and so forth, act on behalf of the enormously larger number of people who consume the products the animals make possible.) Surely, even if human beings were no better than lions or leopards, an individual human being would have as much right to the skin of a seal as a lion or leopard has to the flesh of a gazelle. But human beings are incomparably better, more efficient in serving their needs, and deserve incomparably more of everything than any animal does.

The environmentalists and the advocates of animal rights need to learn the value of man and of themselves as the possessors of reason. Perhaps if they were to acquire the education they thus far have apparently lacked, they would succeed in learning their own value.

Man—rational man—not only is capable of creating an economic system which can produce an ever rising standard of living, but, precisely because he is rational—because he is man properly so called—also *deserves* such an economic system and all of the marvelous goods it can bring. In this spirit, the twenty-first century should be the century when man begins such great undertakings as the colonization of the solar system. It should not be a century in which he returns to the Dark Ages. It is the intention of every page and every word of this book to make sure that it is the former alternative which prevails.

Notes

1. See above, pp. 39–41. Most of this section previously appeared in my book *The Government Against the Economy* (Ottawa, Ill.: Jameson Books, 1979), pp. 15–19.

2. In recent years, considerable progress has been made in reducing the costs of extracting oil from tar sands, to the point where such oil now accounts for approximately one-fourth of Canada's annual production of crude oil. The recoverable oil from the deposits in Alberta alone is estimated to be 300 billion barrels, versus 265 billion barrels estimated for Saudi Arabia. See *New York Times*, December 28, 1994, p. C5.

3. See below, pp. 123–128, for an explanation of how the division of labor provides the framework for continuous economic progress. See also below, pp. 176–180, for an explanation of how, within the framework of a division-of-labor society, the profit motive achieves continuous economic progress, and pp. 622–642, for an explanation of the process of capital accumulation.

4. See Ayn Rand, *Capitalism: The Unknown Ideal* (New York: New American Library, 1966), p. 14.

5. In W. T. Jones, *The Medieval Mind*, vol. 2 of *A History of Western Philosophy*, 2d ed. (New York: Harcourt, Brace, and World, 1969), p. 6.

6. See below, pp. 303–304, for the reasons why government ownership of an industry causes inefficiency.

7. See below, pp. 234–237.

8. "Dismantling of the Shoreham Nuclear Plant Is Completed," *New York Times*, October 13, 1994, p. B6. See also "New Chapter for Shoreham: New York Files to Take Plant," ibid., June 29, 1990, p. B3. Remarkably, the environmentalist destroyers of the Shoreham plant attack its owner, the Long Island Lighting company (Lilco), for having high power rates, as though their policies had nothing to do with those rates. It appears, moreover, that Lilco's acquiescence in its own total elimination has been obtained by a $9-billion takeover offer from New York State, which is to be financed by the sale of municipal bonds in that amount. If this offer is consummated, it will repeat the pattern previously evident in the government's takeover of the American railroad industry, namely, first, the government's destruction of an industry's or company's profitability, followed by the comparative relief of socialization at a price that at least provides some measure of compensation. Following an official statement of the takeover offer, which would entail a purchase price of Lilco's stock at $21.50 a share, the firm's stock rose 25 cents to $17.375 a share on the New York Stock Exchange. (*Wall Street Journal*, Western ed., October 28, 1994, p. A9.)

9. See "Mideast Crisis Puts New Spotlight On an Idle Oil Plant in California," *New York Times*, September 1, 1990, p. 1.

10. The expression "factors of production" can be understood as synonymous with the expressions "means of production" or "physical elements of production." As will be seen, in the context of a division-of-labor economy, in which all productive activity is vitally dependent on the earning of money, use of the expressions implicitly requires that the physical goods or services representing the factors of production be purchased for the sake of making subsequent sales. On this point, see below, pp. 442–456.

11. Cf. Ludwig von Mises, *Human Action*, 3d ed. rev. (Chicago: Henry Regnery Co., 1966), pp. 127–131.

12. See ibid.

13. Cf. David Ricardo, *Principles of Political Economy and Taxation,* 3d. ed. (London, 1821), chaps. 2 and 3; reprinted as vol. 1 of *The Works and Correspondence of David Ricardo*, ed. Piero Sraffa (Cambridge: Cambridge University Press, 1962).

14. See above, n. 3 of this chapter. See also above, pp. 45–46, and below, 106.

15. For elaboration of this point, see below, pp. 313–316.

16. For elaboration of these propositions, see below, pp. 191–192 and 206–209.

17. Of course, if the property in question were of truly outstanding beauty, it would have greater economic value as a tourist attraction than in any ordinary economic use such as coal mining. All that would be necessary to ensure its use in this capacity would be that it be privately owned. In this way, all possible competing uses would be free to find expression in competing bids to the owner, with the one most highly valued by the consumers thereby being free to outcompete the ones less highly valued by the consumers.

18. Cf. Llewellyn H. Rockwell, "Government Garbage," *Free Market* 8, no. 2 (February 1990), pp. 2, 8. See also Peter Passell, "The Garbage Problem: It May Be Politics Not Nature," *New York Times*, February 26, 1991, pp. B5, B7.

19. Rockwell, "Government Garbage."

20. Ibid.

21. Today's conservationists and environmentalists, of course, have a preference for "biodegradable" garbage, such as decaying animal and vegetable matter, which rots and smells. They prefer this to the inert kind, such as aluminum or styrofoam, which appears to remain in its original condition for an indefinitely long time. The basis of their preference appears to be that they object to the existence of permanent evidence of modern technology and concomitant mass consumption.

22. The last sentence of this paragraph and the next two paragraphs are taken, with a few minor changes, from *The Government Against the Economy*, pp. 19–20.

23. Of course, the essential objection to the policy of conservationism is not strictly that it compels us to perform more labor, though that is almost always true, but that it compels us to expend means of production of greater value to achieve a saving of lesser value. There are cases in which we must expend two or more hours of low-paid labor to save one hour or less of high-paid labor, or many hours of labor to save a quantity of extremely valuable material. The comparative market prices involved determine which is the appropriate course of action. See below, pp. 206–209 and 212, for further explanation of this principle.

24. Cf. Ayn Rand, *Atlas Shrugged* (New York: Random House, 1957), pp. 1012–1013; *The Virtue of Selfishness* (New York: New American Library, 1964), pp. 1–34.

25. See above, pp. 43–45.

26. See above, pp. 63–66.

27. The destructive government policies I refer to are prounion and minimum-wage legislation, the welfare system, farm subsidies, rent controls, and laws prescribing such things as the number of people who may occupy an apartment or the minimum floor space, window area, and so forth which must exist per occupant. Prounion and minimum-wage legislation deprive people of the opportunity of obtaining employment by making labor artificially more expensive and thus reducing the quantity of it demanded below the supply available. The welfare system eliminates the necessity of being self-supporting and thus of learning the skills necessary to become so and thus the possibility of advancing from there. Farm subsidies make the price of food higher than it would otherwise be. Rent controls create shortages of rental housing by enlarging the quantity of rental housing demanded and reducing the supply available, thereby making it impossible for some people to find housing. Laws prescribing minimum levels of housing amenities have the effect of pricing housing beyond the reach of some people. In the absence of such laws and of rent controls, some amount of housing would be available for and within the financial reach of every working person. For elaboration of all these points, see below, pp. 172–294 passim, 580–594, and 655–659.

28. Chapter 4 will show how the invention, production, and application of machinery all depend on the division of labor. See below, pp. 123–128.

29. *New York Times*, May 25, 1992, p. 1.

30. Cf. Ayn Rand, *The New Left: The Anti-Industrial Revolution* (New York: New American Library, 1971).

31. See above, pp. 48–49.

32. An excellent book that refutes most of the specific claims of the environmentalists is Jay Lehr, ed., *Rational Readings on Environmental Concerns* (New York: Van Nostrand Reinhold, 1992). Portions of this chapter, previously published as a pamphlet *The Toxicity of Environmentalism*, appear as the summary to the book.

33. George Reisman, "Education and the Racist Road to Barbarism," *Intellectual Activist* 5, no. 4 (April 30, 1990), pp. 4–7; reprinted as a pamphlet (Laguna Hills, Calif.: The Jefferson School of Philosophy, Economics, and Psychology, 1992).

34. For a comprehensive discussion of the safety of nuclear power, see Petr Beckmann, *The Health Hazards of Not Going Nuclear* (Boulder, Colo.: Golem Press, 1976).

35. *New York Times,* September 20, 1990, p. A15.

36. For elaboration of this point, see below, pp. 275–278. See also pp. 172–180, for an account of the contrasting operations of capitalism.

37. Carl Sagan, "Tomorrow's Energy," *Parade,* November 25, 1990, p. 10.

38. Ibid., p. 11.

39. It should be realized that it is no answer to this fact to point to cases in which the loss of energy may appear to be compensated for by a change in the kind of equipment or materials used—for example, obtaining the same illumination, despite the consumption of less electricity, by means of using specially designed lamps. By their nature, cases of this kind entail greater costs. If they did not, there would be no need for the conservationists to urge, let alone attempt to compel, the adoption of

such things. The significance of the higher costs is that less wealth is available for other purposes. Thus, conservation provides energy for one use only by depriving people of energy needed for other uses and, in provoking their efforts to compensate for this loss, may well deprive them of wealth required for other purposes.

40. *Los Angeles Times Book Review*, Sunday, October 22, 1989, p. 9.

41. Bill McKibben, *The End of Nature* (New York: Random House, 1989), p. 176.

42. Another example is that of Christopher Manes, the author of *Green Rage: Radical Environmentalism and the Unmaking of Civilization* (Boston: Little, Brown, 1990). He and the Earth First! organization he supports regard famine in Africa and the spread of AIDS as environmentally beneficial developments. The founder of Earth First!, David Foreman, has described mankind "as a cancer on nature," and has said, "I am the antibody" (in *New York Times Book Review*, Sunday, July 29, 1990, p. 22). Another representative of Earth First! writes: "Only a very few of human pathogens are shared by other partners on our planet. Biological warfare will have no impact on other creatures, big or small, if we design it carefully" (in *Forbes*, October 29, 1990, pp. 96–97). And Paul Ehrlich, one of the oldest and most prominent leaders of the environmental movement, who is supposedly entirely respectable, criticizes the "preoccupation with death control," by which he means, "preoccupation with the problems and diseases of middle age." In his view, such preoccupation, and its consequent lengthening of human life expectancy, "will lead to disaster." (Ehrlich, *The Population Bomb* [New York: Ballantine Books, 1968], p. 91).

43. *New York Times,* August 30, 1990, pp. A1, C15.

44. The alleged danger of radiation is not a valid objection to atomic power. The radiation emission of an atomic power plant located next door to one's house is equal to about two percent of the radioactivity one normally receives from all other—almost entirely natural—sources. On this point, see Beckmann, *Health Hazards*, pp. 112–113. Nor are the alleged dangers of storing atomic wastes a valid objection. Nature itself has always stored such highly radioactive elements as radium and uranium without significant danger to human life.

45. See above, p. 75.

46. In the case of whales, domestication might be feasible if the establishment of electronically fenced ocean "ranches" were allowed and if some part of the existing population of whales could be made private property. In the case of the buffalo, it appears that to a modest extent they now are raised commercially.

47. *Forbes*, January 8, 1990, p. 303.

48. Cf. Edward C. Krug, "Fish Story," *Policy Review*, no. 52 (Spring 1990), pp. 44–48.

49. See *Fortune*, February 11, 1991, p. 145.

50. See March 18, 1988 broadcast of ABC's "20/20." See also Bruce Ames, "What Are the Major Carcinogens in the Etiology of Human Cancer?" in V. T. De Vita, Jr., S. Hellman, and S. A. Rosenberg, eds., *Important Advances in Oncology 1989* (Philadelphia: J. B. Lippincott, 1989), pp. 241–242.

51. See *New York Times*, August 15, 1991, pp. 1, A14.

52. "20/20"; Ames, "Major Carcinogens," p. 242.

53. "20/20"; Ames, "Major Carcinogens," p. 244.

54. Ames, "Major Carcinogens," p. 244.

55. *Orange County Register*, October 31, 1990, p. B15. See also Rogelio A. Maduro and Ralf Schauerhammer, *The Holes in the Ozone Scare* (Washington, D. C.: 21st Century Science Associates, 1992), pp. 11–40, 98–149.

56. Cf. Ames, "Major Carcinogens," pp. 243–244.

57. See "No Evidence of Global Warming in 1980's Is Detected by Satellites," *New York Times,* March 30, 1990.

58. Ibid., December 13, 1989, p. A18. See also Lehr, *Rational Readings on Environmental Concerns*, pp. 393–437.

59. Ehrlich, *Population Bomb,* p. 61.

60. Cf. McKibben, *End of Nature*, p. 111.

61. See "Scientists Warn of Dangers in a Warming Earth," *New York Times,* May 26, 1990.

62. Ibid.

63. See below, Chapter 6, especially pp. 209–211 and 212.

64. On the operations of the price system and the vital role it plays in genuine economic planning—that is, the economic planning of private individuals and business—see below, pp. 137–139 and 172–294 passim.

65. The process of rational reform would be greatly accelerated, if students from such countries, when attending universities in the United States, were taught the virtues of capitalism rather than Marxist propaganda.

66. On these points, see *New York Times,* January 16, 1990, p. C1, and ibid., September 18, 1990, p. B5.

67. See ibid., December 13, 1989, p. A18.

68. The ecologists, of course, denounce it, on the grounds that it destroys various plant and animal species and contributes to global warming through destroying forests. They also claim that after the land has been cleared and the existing soil nutrients are exhausted, the land becomes desert. In answer to this last, they have apparently never heard of the Atherton tablelands in Australia, which were originally jungle and which are now, and for many years have been, beautiful and thriving farmland. Nor, apparently, do they take into account the ability to replenish soil nutrients through the use of chemical fertilizers.

69. McKibben, *End of Nature*, p. 170. Italics mine.

70. Nature, to be sure, does not produce anything directly comparable to traffic congestion, but it does produce all manner of obstacles in the way of travel, such as forests, rivers, and mountains. Thus, traffic congestion is abstractly comparable to nature's obstacles to travel.

71. Of course, it would be possible for the owners of surrounding land at some later time to buy back this right. This would occur in cases in which the increase in the value of their land once free of the negative effects caused by the present producer outweighed the value to that producer of continuing his present operations. In such cases, the owners of the surrounding land would be able to offer him a price that made the surrender of his previously acquired right financially worthwhile.

72. The fall in prices relative to incomes that economic progress achieves is, of course, present when incomes rise faster than prices, which is the way the phenomenon is experienced when accompanied by inflation of the money supply. On the subject of how real incomes rise, see below, pp. 176–180. See also pp. 618–622 and 655–659.

73. Letter signed by Michael L. Fisher is undated (but appeared sometime in 1990), p. 3. Emphasis his.

74. Exactly the same practice, it is worth noting, was followed by the administration of former Governor Jerry Brown of California, which argued that oil fields off a certain portion of the state's coast should not be developed because they would provide the nation as a whole with only a ten-day supply of oil.

75. Carl Sagan, "Tomorrow's Energy," p. 10.

76. For an exposition of the doctrine, see Paul Samuelson and William Nordhaus, *Economics,* 13th ed. (New York: McGraw-Hill, 1989), pp. 770–775.

77. It is worth noting that in a division-of-labor, capitalist society everyone normally does *earn* his standard of living, even people of average and below average ability. But he earns it very easily. The essential thing that is required of the great majority of people is merely the expenditure of the mental effort required to learn the new skills made necessary by the work of the innovators. Thus, someone with the muscles and brawn of a caveman, or a blacksmith, is enabled to enjoy a standard of living that includes such things as automobiles and television sets, merely by being willing to acquire an elementary education, to learn some new skills throughout his life when others introduce further advances, and, above all, to respect the rights of such others to their greater gains. For elaboration on the economic position of the average person under capitalism, see in particular Chapters 9 and 14, below.

78. For a further critique of the externalities doctrine, in particular the external-benefits doctrine, see below, pp. 335–336.

79. For a full account of how the environmental movement, in conjunction with the U.S. government, has been responsible not only for the high price of oil and oil products but also for virtually every other aspect of the energy crisis, see above, pp. 66–67 and 172–264 passim, but especially pp. 234–237.

80. These principles were clearly understood both by the U.S. Federal Appeals Court for the District of Columbia Circuit and by the U.S. government's Office of Management and Budget under the Bush administration. The Court cited research demonstrating that one additional death may result from reduced incomes caused by each $7.5 million of additional expense imposed by government regulation. On this basis, the Office of Management and Budget blocked the enactment of a costly set of environmental regulations proposed by the Department of Labor which ostensibly sought to promote workers' health and safety. The Office found that the regulations were so expensive that their enactment would cause more deaths than they would avoid. See "Citing Cost, Budget Office Blocks Workplace Health Proposal," *New York Times,* March 16, 1992, p. A13.

81. For elaboration of the principles involved in the present discussion, see below, pp. 622–642.

82. "Marsh Destroyed, Owner Is Fined," *New York Times,* May 26, 1990.

83. The law of comparative advantage is explained on pp. 350–356. The doctrine of the harmony of interests is demonstrated in almost every chapter of this book, but see especially Chapters 6, 9, 11, 13, and 14.

84. See above, pp. 35–36.

85. Barry Commoner, *The Poverty of Power* (New York: Alfred A. Knopf, 1976), pp. 252, 254. For a refutation of all aspects of the Marxian exploitation theory, see below, pp. 473–498 and 613–666.

86. If the influence of the ecology movement continues to grow, then it is perfectly conceivable that in years to come, the very intention of a country to increase its production could serve as a cause of war, perhaps precipitating the dispatch of a U.N. security force to stop it. Even the mere advocacy of economic freedom within the borders of a country would logically—from the depraved perspective of the ecology movement—be regarded as a threat to mankind. It is, therefore, essential that the United States absolutely refuse to sanction in any way any form of international limitations on "pollution"—that is, on production.

87. Cf. Brad Erickson, ed., *Call to Action, Handbook for Ecology, Peace and Justice* (San Francisco: Sierra Club Books, 1990), p. 5.

88. See, for example, Kirkpatrick Sale, *Dwellers in the Land* (San Francisco: Sierra Club Books, 1985). This book is marked by total ignorance of history and of every proposition of economics.

89. Cf. Ayn Rand, "The Left: Old and New," in Ayn Rand, *The New Left.*

90. The costs merely of complying with the environmental movement's demands for the cleanup of toxic waste sites is estimated at between $300 billion and $700 billion over the coming few years. See "Experts Question Staggering Costs of Toxic Cleanups," *New York Times,* September 1, 1991, p. 1. (The cost of complying with other antipollution regulations is currently $115 billion per year. [Ibid., p. 12.]) Even using the EPA's far-fetched methods of estimating risk, the maximum number of cancer cases which can be linked to public exposure to hazardous wastes is approximately 1,000 per year. (Ibid.) All reasonable protection against such wastes can frequently be secured for as little as one-half of one percent of the costs presently mandated by law and by the EPA. (Ibid.) Thus, hundreds of billions of dollars have been and are to be squandered to appease the imaginary terrors of the environmentalists.

91. On the nature of altruism and self-sacrifice, see Ayn Rand, *Atlas Shrugged* and *Virtue of Selfishness.*

92. Cf. F. A. Hayek, *The Fatal Conceit: The Errors of Socialism,* W. W. Bartley III, ed. (London: Routledge, 1988).

93. See above, pp. 19–36.

94. See above, pp. 35–36.

95. I am indebted for this vital distinction to von Mises. It was an observation he made in his seminar at New York University.

96. This proposition bears an essential similarity to the theory of capital accumulation presented below on pp. 622–642.

97. Thalidomide, of course, was the drug that was prescribed as a tranquilizer for pregnant women and that turned out to cause major damage to fetuses.

98. On these points, see the article of Leonard Peikoff, "Maybe You're Wrong," *Objectivist Forum* 2, no. 2 (April 1981), pp. 8–12.

99. See Ayn Rand, *Introduction to Objectivist Epistemology,* 2d ed. enl., ed. Harry Binswanger and Leonard Peikoff (New York: New American Library, 1990), pp. 77–82.

100. In W. T. Jones, *Kant to Wittgenstein and Sartre,* vol. 4 of *A History of Western Philosophy,* 2d ed. (New York: Harcourt, Brace, and World, 1969), p. 102.

101. Ayn Rand, "The Cashing-in: The Student Rebellion," in Ayn Rand, *Capitalism,* p. 235.

102. Ayn Rand, *Objectivist Epistemology*, p. 81.

103. Jones, *Kant,* p. 102.

104. Ibid., p. 104.

105. See below, Chapter 8 passim.

106. For example, McKibben writes: "Perhaps the ten [sic] thousand years of our encroaching, defiant civilization, an eternity to us and a yawn to the rocks around us, could give way to ten [sic] thousand years of humble civilization, when we choose to pay more for the benefits of nature, when we rebuild the sense of wonder and sanctity that could protect the natural world." (McKibben, *End of Nature*, p. 215.) According to this passage, the ten thousand years in which man has risen from the cave and which embrace the totality of man's civilization were a mistake—they were "encroaching, defiant." In the next ten thousand years, McKibben hopes, the wildlife, the weeds, and the rock formations that constitute nature will be protected from us, because we will have abandoned anything resembling Western civilization.

107. On the new racism and its hostility to Western civilization, see my essay "Education and the Racist Road to Barbarism."

108. See Ayn Rand, *For the New Intellectual* (New York: Random House, 1961) p. 67.

109. See H. G. Wells, *The Time Machine* (London, 1895); reprinted in *Treasury of World Masterpieces: H. G. Wells* (New York: Octopus Books, 1982.)

110. McKibben, *End of Nature*, p. 202.

111. An essential requirement of becoming such a "new intellectual" is, of course, to read and understand the works of Ayn Rand, Ludwig von Mises, and the British classical and Austrian economists, as well as the political philosophy of John Locke and the Founding Fathers of the United States. The importance of all of these works was explained above, in the Introduction to this book. In addition, a thorough knowledge of history and extensive reading of the great classics of literature and philosophy, as well as familiarity with mathematics and natural science at what used to be the college level, are also requisite. In other words, to be a "new intellectual," one must have an education similar in kind to that which intellectuals used to have, plus be thoroughly familiar with the philosophy of Objectivism, the writings of von Mises, classical and Austrian economics, and the political philosophy on which the United States was established.

112. See above, pp. 19–21.

113. It is interesting to recall here some previously quoted words of Graber, whose implications I did not develop at the time: "I, for one, cannot wish upon either my children or the rest of Earth's biota. . . ." The philosophical meaning of these words is that Graber sees no fundamental distinction, requiring separate classification, between his own children and flies and earthworms.

114. The term *speciesism* appears, among other places, in Roderick Frazier Nash, *The Rights of Nature* (Madison, Wisc.: University of Wisconsin Press, 1989) pp. 5, 138, 142, 153. This book is impregnable against all arguments falling in the category of reductio ad absurdum inasmuch as it enthusiastically supports almost every imaginable absurdity that is present in the doctrine of animal rights. For example, it states, approvingly: "The ecologist noted that smallpox, as part of the biotic community, was a product of evolution as were wolves and whales and redwood trees. According to the biocentric reading of environmental ethics, there was no logical reason for discriminating against the virus just because it was small and harmful to humans" (p. 85). Interestingly, the author pretends throughout to be a fervent supporter of John Locke and the doctrine of natural rights. Yet at no point in his book is there a discussion of the connection between human reason and rights or of the proreason, proman context in which John Locke wrote. The word *reason* does not even appear in the book's index. Although publication of such a philosophically disgraceful book by a university press should not be surprising in today's environment, it should still provoke outrage.

115. See below, Chapter 4. See also von Mises, *Human Action,* pp. 143–176 on the nature of human society, and below, Chapter 9 passim.

116. Cf. Ayn Rand, "Man's Rights," in *Virtue of Selfishness*; and the discussion of rights in *Atlas Shrugged,* pp. 1061–1063.

117. This observation, of course, has bearing on the dispute between those defenders of capitalism who support the doctrine of natural rights and those who describe themselves as utilitarians. If rights are understood in the context of taking man's life as the standard of useful action, there need be no conflict.

118. Interestingly, exactly the same kind of process of lack of thought has resulted in the term "discrimination" becoming one of opprobrium. It is perfectly proper, in fact absolutely necessary to human survival, to discriminate between food and poison, between tigers and pussycats, between danger and the lack of danger. What is not proper is to ignore an individual's achievements and superior qualifications because of his racial membership. Such behavior represents a failure to discriminate on the basis of fundamentals—namely, what the individual has accomplished—in favor of discriminating on the basis of a triviality, namely, his mere racial membership. It is to deny credit to the individual for what is within his power, while condemning him for what is not in his power. It is for this reason that discrimination based on race is wrong. But today's unthinking mentalities hear the word "discrimination" uttered with condemnation and then believe that any form of discrimination is evil, including discrimination in favor of the competent over the incompetent.

119. "I am quite seriously proposing that we give legal rights to forests, oceans, rivers and other so-called 'natural objects' in the environment—indeed, to the natural environment as a whole." (Christopher D. Stone, a University of Southern California law professor in Nash, *Rights of Nature*, p. 121. Stone argued this position before the U.S. Supreme Court with the support of the Sierra Club. His views were endorsed by Justice Douglas. [Ibid., pp. 128–131].)

120. McKibben, *End of Nature*, p. 182.

121. Nash, *Rights of Nature*, p. 95.

122. Cf. Ayn Rand, *Virtue of Selfishness,* pp. 11–16.

123. People can, of course, legitimately be concerned with the avoidance of unnecessary cruelty to animals. Much more importantly, they can legitimately be concerned with the avoidance of unnecessary suffering on the part of their fellow human beings. The proper course for those who truly are concerned with eliminating unnecessary human suffering is not to immolate themselves, but, first and foremost, to support capitalism and its underlying philosophy and economic theory, and, no

less, to pursue their own rational self-interest. For elaboration see below, pp. 332–335, and above, n. 111, which provides a list of the major philosophical and theoretical sources in defense of capitalism. Practically the whole of this book is a demonstration of how the pursuit of rational self-interest operates to the interest of all. Long before the reader reaches the end of this book, it should be overwhelmingly clear to him, if he has read with any significant degree of understanding, how the self-interested activities of businessmen and capitalists accomplish far more economic benefit for the poor, and thereby alleviate far more suffering and hardship, than the work of the most devout practitioners of self-sacrifice and charity ever has accomplished or ever could accomplish. These results, of course, are not the motive of the businessmen's and capitalists' activities—selfish profit is the motive—but they are the necessary, inevitable effect of those activities, provided only that the businessmen and capitalists are left free to pursue their profit and thus to carry on their activities.

PART TWO

THE DIVISION OF LABOR AND CAPITALISM

CHAPTER 4

THE DIVISION OF LABOR AND PRODUCTION

1. The Division of Labor and the Productivity of Labor

Human life and well-being depend on the production of wealth. The production of wealth vitally depends on the division of labor, that is, a system of production in which the labor required to support human life and well-being is broken down into separate, distinct occupations. As we have seen, under a system of division of labor, the individual lives by producing, or helping to produce, just one thing or at most a very few things, and is supplied by the labor of others for the far greater part of his needs.

The division of labor raises the productivity of labor in six major ways, and thereby achieves a radical increase in the efficiency with which man is able to apply his mind, his body, and his nature-given environment to production.

It increases the amount of knowledge used in production by a multiple that corresponds to the number of distinct specializations and subspecializations of employment. This makes possible the production of products and the adoption of methods of production that would otherwise be impossible.

It makes it possible for geniuses to specialize in science, invention, and the organization and direction of the productive activity of others, thereby further and progressively increasing the knowledge used in production.

It enables individuals at all levels of ability to concentrate on the kind of work for which they are best suited on the basis of differences in their intellectual and bodily endowments.

It enables the various regions of the world to concentrate on producing the crops and minerals for which they are best suited on the basis of differing conditions of climate and geology.

It increases the efficiency of the processes of learning and motion that are entailed in production.

It underlies the use of machinery in production.

The Multiplication of Knowledge

To understand how the division of labor represents a multiplication of the knowledge used in production, it is only necessary to realize that in a division-of-labor society, such as our own, there are as many distinct bodies of knowledge used in production as there are distinct specializations and subspecializations of employment. Steel producers, for example, have a different body of knowledge from that of auto producers. Wheat farmers have a different body of knowledge from both of these and even from that of other farmers, such as vegetable growers or dairy farmers. The bodies of knowledge of all such specializations enter into the process of production in a division-of-labor society, and each individual is enabled to obtain products reflecting the total of such knowledge. Thus, steel producers give the benefit of their knowledge to the whole rest of society; in return, they are able to receive from the rest of society the benefit of the specialized knowledge held by all other categories of producers. And so it is with the members of every specialization.

This is a result of enormous importance, and its significance needs to be carefully considered. What a division-of-labor society represents is *the organization of the same total sum of human brain power in a way that enables it to store and use vastly more knowledge than would otherwise be possible.*

To grasp this point fully, we must consider the contrasting case of a non-division-of-labor society, such as exists in most of Asia, Africa, and Latin America. In those areas, where the overwhelming majority of people live as virtually self-sufficient farmers, each family knows essentially what all the others know about production. To confirm this fact, one might imagine an effort to compile all the knowledge entering into production in such places. One might imagine a corps of interviewers who obtain a grant from the U.S. government to go out and write down all that the rural farm families of these areas know about production. After interviewing the first such family in each area, very little additional information would be gained from interviewing the hundreds of millions of other such families. What this means, in essence, is that the sum total of the knowledge used in production in a non-division-of-labor society is limited to what the brain of just one or two individuals can hold. Any one farmer, or farmer plus his wife, in those areas holds practically all of the knowledge that is used in production in the entire society.

To put it mildly, such a situation is a case of wasteful duplication. It is the wasteful duplication of the mental contents of the human brain—the wasteful use of man's ability to store and use knowledge. In this respect and in this sense, a division-of-labor society is indispensable to the efficient use of the human mind in production. To the degree that production is divided into separate specializations, with separate bodies of knowledge, the same total of human brain power is enabled to store and use more knowledge, to the benefit of each and every individual member of that society. This is the meaning of the proposition that the division of labor represents the multiplication of the knowledge used in production. It multiplies such knowledge to the degree that specializations and specialized bodies of knowledge exist. And it multiplies correspondingly the benefits that man is able to derive from the use of his mind.

The enlarged body of knowledge that a division-of-labor society makes possible is the precondition for producing products and adopting methods of production that require more knowledge than any one person, family, village, or tribe can possess. To illustrate this fact and be able to appreciate its importance, let us consider the amount of knowledge required to produce a relatively simple product, such as a ballpoint pen, which almost everyone uses practically every day in our society.

To make the pen, far more knowledge is required than is possessed by the producers of the pen. They can begin with the purchase of plastic, ink, pen points, and various

types of machinery. What they know is how to produce such pens from this stage on. But others must know how to produce the plastic, the ink, the points, and the equipment. Still others must know how to produce the petrochemicals, from which the plastic comes; the various chemicals from which the ink is made; the metals from which the points are produced; and the components for the equipment.

At further stages of remove from the pen, yet still others must know how to refine petroleum, how to explore for it, drill for it, and store and transport it; how to produce the drilling and refining equipment, the parts and materials to make that equipment, and so on. Tracing now the chemicals for the ink, the metals for the points, and the components for the pen-making equipment further back, we are led into the chemical industry, the mining industry, and the machine tool industry. At practically all stages, we encounter the construction industry, which had to erect the various factories involved; the electric power industry, which provides the factories and machines with light and power; and the transportation industry, which moves the various products and means of production to where they are required. And these industries lead us back to the industries producing the materials and equipment they in turn require.

We find that the production of a seemingly simple product like a ballpoint pen is not so simple after all. It is closely tied to the production of most of the rest of the economic system in a virtual spider web of complexity, with threads running back and across to almost every other branch of industry in ways that are too complex even to be completely and accurately *named* by anyone, let alone actually understood in the way required for production. This "simple" product is the result of vastly more knowledge applied to production than any one individual, family, village, or tribe could ever hope to acquire.

A division-of-labor society is obviously indispensable for the production of all the wonderful products introduced over the last two centuries, from steam engines to rocketships. By the same token, it is equally indispensable for the ability to use modern, efficient methods of production in making goods that can be produced in modest quantities with little or no division of labor—for example, being able to use tractors and chemical fertilizers to help produce wheat.

The Benefit from Geniuses

Closely related to the multiplication of the knowledge used in production is the fact that the division of labor makes possible a radical and progressive increase in the benefit derived from the existence of geniuses. In the absence of a division-of-labor society, geniuses, along with everyone else, must pass their lives in producing their own food, clothing, and shelter—assuming they are fortunate enough to have survived in the first place. Perhaps their high intelligence enables them to produce these goods somewhat more efficiently than do other people. But their real potential is obviously lost—both to themselves and to the rest of society.

In contrast, in a division-of-labor society geniuses are able to devote their time to science, invention, and the organization and direction of the productive activity of others. Instead of being lost in obscurity, they become the Newtons, the Edisons, and the Fords of the world, thereby incalculably raising the productivity of every member of the division-of-labor society.

The effect of a division-of-labor society is thus not only to increase the total of the knowledge that the same amount of human brain power can store and use, but *also to bring that knowledge up to a standard set by the most intelligent members of the society.* The average and below-average member of a division-of-labor society is enabled to produce on the strength of the intelligence of the most intelligent. Thus, in a division-of-labor society, people even of minimal intelligence are enabled to produce and obtain such goods as automobiles and television sets—goods which on their own they would not even have been able to imagine.

And in each succeeding generation, geniuses are able to begin with the knowledge acquired by all the preceding generations, and then make their own, fresh contributions to knowledge. In this way, the knowledge and productive power of a division-of-labor society are able progressively to increase, reaching greater and greater heights as time goes on.

Concentration on the Individual's Advantages

In a division-of-labor society, not only productive geniuses, but everyone is enabled to concentrate on the kind of work for which he is best suited by virtue of his intellectual and bodily endowment. This principle applies to artistic and musical geniuses, to individuals with the kind of rare talents required to perform surgical operations or to be a champion athlete, on down to people whose special advantage may consist merely of such attributes as the possession of relatively keen eyesight or relatively great physical strength.

As with productive geniuses, those with the potential ability to be great artists or musicians, great surgeons or athletes, or outstanding creators or performers of any kind, would not be able to realize their potential in the absence of a division-of-labor society. Because even if they managed to be born and reach adulthood, their time would be taken up with growing their own food and making their own clothing and shelter. In a division-of-

labor society, on the other hand, such individuals can realize their potential. And all the rest of mankind gains from it—from being able to enjoy the art and music they create, from being able to live because of the surgical operations they perform, and from being able to have the pleasure of observing the feats they accomplish.

In a division-of-labor society, *every* productive advantage that individuals possess tends to be put to use and to raise the productivity of labor. Imagine, for example, the case of just two people: Robinson Crusoe and Friday. Assume that Crusoe is particularly skillful in fishing, but not very skillful in hunting. Assume that with Friday, it's just the opposite: he is very skillful in hunting, but not particularly skillful in fishing. To make the case more concrete, imagine that it takes Crusoe 1 day to catch 10 salmon, and 2 days to hunt a deer; while Friday requires 2 days to catch 10 salmon, but only 1 day to hunt a deer. If the two men work independently of each other, without dividing labor, then in 3 days each will have caught 10 salmon and hunted 1 deer. Their combined output will be 20 salmon and 2 deer. But if they divide labor, with Crusoe concentrating on fishing, and Friday on hunting, then in exactly the same time, their combined output will be 30 salmon and 3 deer—that is, 50 percent more. For in 3 days Crusoe can catch 30 salmon, while Friday can hunt 3 deer.

In a society of millions, hundreds of millions, or however many people, each person tends to concentrate on the specific things for which he is intellectually and physically best suited. And thus the production of everything tends to be carried on in the most efficient way it can be carried on in the circumstances. The production of everything tends to be carried on by those who can do it relatively best.

Geographical Specialization

A special aspect of individuals concentrating on what they do best is the more efficient utilization of land and natural resources. What an individual does best depends not only on his intellectual and bodily endowments, but also on the external conditions of nature that confront him. An individual living in a tropical climate, say, is able to grow tropical fruits or vegetables far more easily than someone living in a temperate climate, if the latter can grow them at all. An individual living close to rich deposits of iron ore, say, is able to mine such ore far more easily than someone not living close to such deposits, if the latter can mine iron ore at all.

Thus, a major aspect of the gains provided by the division of labor is that it raises the productivity of labor in the exploitation of land and natural resources. For what many people do best and are led to concentrate on is precisely the exploitation of advantages afforded them by climate and by their proximity to special types of land and natural resources.

The result of specialization along these lines is that every geographical area can obtain products that depend on the special advantages of other areas. Each area that possesses special advantages concentrates on those advantages to some degree and produces more of the products in question than its own inhabitants consume. The difference is exchanged for the products of other areas, which possess different advantages. The effect is that every area can obtain the benefit of the special advantages of every other area. Thus, the people of the whole United States can be supplied with iron ore from Minnesota, coal from Pennsylvania, oil from Texas, wheat from Kansas, corn from Iowa, and oranges from Florida. And, of course, the gains are international: the whole world can benefit from Brazil's advantages in coffee growing, Saudi Arabia's oil deposits, and the advantages of the various American states just described.

Furthermore, the ability of each area to exploit its own advantages vitally depends on its incorporation into the division of labor. For example, very little iron ore could be smelted without coal to provide fuel. By the same token, very little coal could be mined without iron and steel to make possible the production of the necessary equipment. The exploitation of every natural resource is enormously improved by virtue of access to the resources of other areas.

Economies of Learning and Motion

The division of labor increases the efficiency of the processes of learning and motion that are entailed in production.

First, under the division of labor, the individual who learns an occupation is able to apply his learning repeatedly, because he devotes his full working time to that occupation. The effect of this repetition is that he becomes extremely proficient in the use of his knowledge. In effect, he subconsciously automatizes the knowledge—he learns it so well that he no longer has to think things out step by step, as one does before one has the necessary experience or after one has been away from a field for a long time. A worker who is constantly practiced in his work can obviously accomplish a great deal more in the same time than one who is not. Outside the division of labor, on the other hand, even in cases in which people might be able to acquire sufficient knowledge to accomplish something, they would most likely not have sufficient occasion to use that knowledge to become proficient in its use.

A good example of this, drawn from the context of our own society, is the case of a professional repairman versus a do-it-yourself homeowner. A good professional plumber, say, can usually spot the source of a plumbing problem very quickly, decide exactly what needs to be done, reach for the appropriate tools and supplies, and do it. The inexperienced homeowner, on the other hand, who tries to repair his own plumbing, must probably first read a book about how to do it, and then, assuming he has correctly diagnosed the problem and obtained all the necessary tools and supplies, fumble about trying to do it. Even if, later on, he needs to make the same repair again, the homeowner will probably experience many of his original difficulties, because probably so much time will have gone by that he will have forgotten much of what he learned the first time he made the repair.

This example illustrates the second way that the division of labor increases the efficiency of the learning process in connection with production: it increases the ratio of the time spent in using knowledge to the time spent in acquiring it. Our plumber spends a given amount of time learning how to make a given repair, and then makes that repair over and over again. The homeowner spends a given amount of time learning how to make a given repair, and then hardly ever uses the knowledge he has acquired. The learning time put in by the plumber is obviously much more fruitful. The same principle, of course, applies to all specialists in comparison with nonspecialists, and is the reason that it pays specialists to acquire vastly more knowledge about their work than it can ever pay nonspecialists to acquire.

Finally, the division of labor increases the efficiency of the learning process in connection with production by making education and communications—indeed, all the activities concerned with storing and transmitting knowledge—into specializations. These, like all other specializations, also tend to be carried on by those best suited for them. In this way, the diffusion of knowledge of all kinds, including, of course, all that pertains to production, tends to become more efficient.

Thus, the division of labor increases the degree to which knowledge of production is assimilated and therefore the proficiency with which it is used, the yield to the time spent in acquiring it, and the efficiency with which it is disseminated. These advantages, of course, are obviously closely related to the multiplication of knowledge that was discussed at the beginning of this investigation of the ways in which the division of labor raises the productivity of labor.

The division of labor also achieves a large increase in production simply by eliminating unnecessary motion in production. The tendency under the division of labor is to concentrate work of the same type in the same place, and, depending on the volume of work that can be so concentrated, to break it down into the simplest possible steps, consisting of the smallest possible number of separate motions.

For example, most factory-made products are produced under an arrangement whereby the typical worker remains in just one place and performs just one kind of operation in the course of his working day. Typically, he performs just one step in the making of just one component or part, or joins just one component or part to one other component or part. The advantages of such a system are that it eliminates the time that would otherwise be lost in walking back and forth from one place to another to do different kinds of work, in constantly picking up and putting down different types of tools, and in constantly having to finish up and perhaps clean up what one has been doing and warm up to what one is about to do.[1]

Repetitious factory work is a further and important example of the division of labor's enhancement of the yield to learning. It represents the yield to learning being raised so high that people can live by virtue of knowing merely how to perform a few simple motions. Under the division of labor, the intelligence of businessmen, capitalists, industrial engineers, and managers, achieves the isolation, concentration, and coordination of small, distinct steps in production, which then constitute highly productive jobs for people even of very limited intelligence. Because of the productive efforts of the first group, highly sophisticated products, such as automobiles and even computers, can be produced by members of the second group—by people who otherwise could hardly even conceive of such products, let alone produce them.

The Use of Machinery

Finally, the division of labor raises the productivity of labor by constituting the foundation for the use of machinery in production. It does so, first of all, by creating a sufficient fund of knowledge in a society to make the production of machinery possible. As explained in the discussion of the multiplication of knowledge, the division of labor is indispensable to the production of all products requiring the existence of an extensive body of knowledge—a body of knowledge greater than can be held by any one individual or family, or even village or tribe. Virtually all machinery is in this category.

The division of labor is equally indispensable to the existence of machinery in providing the extensive and widely scattered range of materials necessary for the production and use of most machines, such as iron, copper, lead, tin, leather, rubber, timber, coal, oil, and so on. In the absence of division of labor among the different regions of the world, it would be virtually impossible to obtain the materials required for the production and use of machines.

In addition, also as explained earlier, the division of labor makes science and invention into specializations carried on by geniuses, which, of course, greatly facilitates the invention of machinery. And, in reducing jobs wherever possible to a small number of distinct motions repeated over and over again, it enormously simplifies the problems of *designing* a machine or special tool to help do the work. As a result, machines and tools have frequently been invented by intelligent, ambitious workers who gave careful thought to the exact nature of the operations they performed every day and who thus discovered how their work might be aided by the application of some special mechanical device or implement.

Lastly, by concentrating a large volume of work of the same type in the same hands, the division of labor makes the use of machinery and specialized tools *economically worthwhile*. For example, it pays a plumber to acquire not only all kinds of knowledge about plumbing, but also all kinds of specialized plumbing tools that it would not pay a homeowner to acquire. In the same way, it pays a large-scale manufacturer to use all manner of machinery that it would not pay a small-scale manufacturer to use. This is because machinery and specialized tools are often very expensive. If their use is to be economical, they must be used fairly often, so that their high cost can be spread over a large number of units of output. Where this is not possible, it is probably cheaper to produce by hand. In concentrating work of the same type in the same place, the division of labor operates to ensure that the use of machinery pays. It increases the productive yield to specialized machinery just as it does to specialized knowledge, and thus makes its acquisition and employment worthwhile.

The above connections between the division of labor and the use of machinery make it possible to understand why the Industrial Revolution began in England in the late eighteenth century. At that time, England already possessed the highest degree of division of labor ever achieved and was also the world's greatest commercial nation. It thus possessed or had access to the necessary fund both of knowledge and of materials required for the construction of machines. By the same token, it also possessed conditions favoring the invention and design of machines and the conditions in which their use would pay.

Far more importantly, because the use of machinery is utterly dependent on the division of labor, it follows that the division of labor must indirectly be credited with all the magnificent advances in human life and well-being that have taken place over the last two centuries or more and that have been the result of the use of machinery. These advances, ranging from improvements in sanitation to high-speed travel by jet aircraft, and eloquently summarized by the radical lengthening of life expectancy, were described at length in the preceding chapter.[2]

2. The Division of Labor and Society

All of the preceding discussion of the division of labor can be summarized by saying that the division of labor increases the efficiency with which man is able to apply his mind, his body, and his nature-given environment to production. It expands his capacity to store and use knowledge, which knowledge it raises to a standard set by the most intelligent members of society. This standard in turn tends to rise higher and higher in each succeeding generation, as creative geniuses again and again enlarge the stock of technological knowledge. The division of labor also increases the degree to which knowledge of production is assimilated, the yield to the time spent in acquiring it, and the efficiency with which it is disseminated.

It increases the efficiency with which man applies his body to production inasmuch as it enables everyone to concentrate on whatever he is relatively best suited for by virtue of his bodily endowment. It also eliminates unnecessary motion in production. And, finally, it makes possible the addition of machine and mechanical power to the power of human muscles. This last enables man to accomplish physical results that would otherwise be unthinkable.

Similarly, by means of geographical specialization the division of labor increases the efficiency with which man applies his nature-given environment to production. And it does so even more by the use of ever improved machinery and methods of production that flow from the heightened and progressively increasing efficiency that it lends to man's use of his mind and body. This enables man to obtain progressively more from his environment.

On the basis of all of the foregoing considerations, it should be obvious that from the perspective of the production of wealth and all that depends on the production of wealth, a division-of-labor society is the form of society that is appropriate to man's nature. While man always possesses the faculty of reason, a division-of-labor society is necessary if he is to use his rationality efficiently in production. It is necessary if he is to actualize the productive potential provided by his possession of reason.

It should be equally obvious that the existence of a division-of-labor society is to the material self-interest of every individual. Whoever, in the words of von Mises, prefers wealth to poverty and life and health to sickness and death, is logically obliged to value the existence of a division-of-labor society and all that it depends on. For

it is the essential foundation of all significant wealth and of the vital contribution made by wealth to man's life and health. Take away a division-of-labor society, and production shrivels to the level of medieval feudalism, with its consequently recurring famines and plagues and resulting average life expectancy of twenty-five years— years, it should never be forgotten, whose passage was marked with cold, hunger, exhaustion, and pain. Apart from the amelioration provided by Western aid in the form of food and medicines, such continues to be the miserable condition of human life today in all that vast part of the world that is not integrated into the division of labor.

Thus, the widely held notion that life in society requires the sacrifice of the individual's self-interest is totally mistaken in regard to a division-of-labor society. That notion applies only to societies characterized by force and plunder, not to a division-of-labor society. A division-of-labor society represents the mutual cooperation of individuals for the purpose of achieving their own individual ends. The radical and progressive increase in the productivity of labor it brings about makes it possible for everyone to achieve his ends incalculably better within its framework than outside of it.[3]

These considerations have major implications for ethics. They imply that the ethical principle of respect for the persons and property of others is not something that is arbitrarily enjoined upon the human race by an outside authority, but has a rational basis in the requirements of the individual serving his own material self-interest. In order for the individual to enjoy the benefits of the division of labor, he needs the existence of other people who participate in the division of labor with him. He also needs those others to be secure in their persons and property—that is, to be free from the initiation of force and the threat of the initiation of force—and thus to be motivated and able to work and produce as efficiently as possible, so that there will be the most abundant and best possible supply of goods available for him to buy. Thus, it is to his self-interest that others, as well as himself, be secure from such threats as murder, assault, and robbery, and that others, as well as himself, be free.[4] These principles apply to *all* other human beings the world over who might potentially associate with him in the division of labor and thus contribute to his material well-being by enlarging and improving the supply of goods available for him to buy. Thus, the gains from the division of labor constitute an objective foundation for the existence of good will on the part of each individual toward the rest of mankind.

Furthermore, it can be stated categorically that these principles are in no way lessened, let alone contradicted, by the existence of free economic competition. On the contrary, as later chapters will demonstrate, they are powerfully reinforced by the existence of such competition. The effect of free economic competition is to improve the organization and efficiency of the division of labor. It is both to provide everyone with the opportunity to work and produce in the area in which he is best suited and to increase the output per unit of labor, especially on the part of individuals of lesser ability. Thus it enables everyone to enjoy a higher and continually rising standard of living.[5]

3. Rebuttal of the Critique of the Division of Labor

Because of the dependency of human life and well-being on wealth, and of wealth on the division of labor, it should now be obvious that in the name of the value of human life and well-being, a division-of-labor society is itself a cardinal value, and should be upheld with all the means at our disposal. Indeed, every individual who decides that he is better off working for money and buying the things he wants, rather than attempting to produce for himself, acts to build or maintain the division-of-labor society as he thereby positions himself in it; and in this way he affirms its value. A division-of-labor society is formed and maintained precisely on the basis of such self-interested actions of individuals.[6]

Despite the fact that man's vital interests depend on it, the division of labor has been attacked, most notably by Marx and Engels, who blame it for making work boring and unpleasant, for "alienating" the worker from his work, and for making him narrow and one-sided rather than broad and well rounded in his interests and capacities. Socialism, they boast, will abolish the division of labor and turn work into a pleasure.[7]

These accusations are nonsensical. Work in a routine factory job may well be boring and unpleasant for many people. This is particularly likely to be so in the case of people who have the potential for doing much more intellectually demanding work but who, for psychological reasons, are unwilling to challenge themselves and acquire the necessary skills. Yet even so, routine factory work is far less boring and unpleasant than the work of primitive farmers, which preceded it, and from which tens of millions of people in the Western world willingly fled to take factory jobs. Even now, large numbers of housewives consider it less boring than housework, which consists of little more than a wide variety of boring jobs. A dull job performed for money is almost always less dull than one performed merely for the sake of a given physical result, because the money can be exchanged for so many different things and thus at least ties the work to interesting possibilities.

Furthermore, if a fuller measure of capitalism existed,

even the otherwise most monotonous, repetitious types of factory work would be given an important measure of challenge and excitement through the establishment of piecework and competition among individual workers and, perhaps, among assembly-line teams. Under such conditions work becomes perceived as the direct, immediate means of putting money into one's pocket. Workers then go at the otherwise dullest kinds of jobs with enthusiasm. Physically, the dullest kind of job can be no duller than pulling the handle of a slot machine over and over again, which multitudes eagerly do in gambling casinos, in the hope of winning a jackpot. In a factory operating under the piecework system, each such operation brings a guaranteed small jackpot, as it were.[8]

It is also significant that a free market operates to offer premium wage rates for any jobs that most people find relatively dull and unappealing, and, by the same token, to reduce the wage rates of jobs that most people find relatively exciting and attractive.[9] Consistent with this fact, to the extent that intellectually overqualified people presently in relatively dull jobs decided to do what was necessary to find more demanding, more interesting, and, at the same time, higher-paying jobs—higher paying because of the higher skill requirements—the effect would be that everyone who had to remain in the relatively dull jobs would be compensated by receiving higher wages. The effect of the establishment of the higher wages in turn would be to provide an inducement to employers to seek ways to make such jobs more interesting, in order to attract workers without having to offer such higher wages. (Of course, the increase in the supply of labor in the more-skilled fields, into which the previously overqualified workers moved, would operate to reduce wage rates in those fields.)[10]

The charge that factory work is "alienating" rests on a view of the average factory worker as being incapable of intellectually understanding the importance of his particular work to the final product. It assumes that to take personal pride in his work, a worker has to be in the position of a medieval cobbler and oversee the process from raw material to finished product. It does not see that a worker can conceptually understand that, for example, the welds he performs help to keep an airplane in flight or an automobile in operation. The charge of alienation does not see that in a division-of-labor society a worker can take pride in the fact that he contributes to the production of magnificent products whose very existence would appear absolutely miraculous to any medieval cobbler.

Finally, it is in a division-of-labor society that the average worker, for the first time in all of human history, has the opportunity of actually becoming something of a Renaissance man, if that is what he chooses to be. The division of labor has raised the productivity of labor so high that today the average member of a division-of-labor society has both substantial real wealth at his disposal and substantial leisure in which to enjoy it. The average worker today can easily afford an extensive personal library—in paperback—of books on science and philosophy. He can afford an extensive collection of fine musical recordings and prints of the greatest works of art. He has the leisure to engage in all kinds of athletic activities, including year-round swimming if he lives in a sizable town or city. In short, he has open to him in no small measure precisely the kind of life that the ancient Greeks thought could be enjoyed only by a slave-owning aristocracy. Further improvements in the productivity of labor under the division of labor will place still more wealth and leisure at the average worker's disposal.

In addition, the proportion of truly interesting and challenging jobs in the economic system has steadily increased with the progress of the division of labor, and will continue to increase in the future, if the division of labor and capitalism are preserved. Today, a far larger proportion of the population than ever before works in the professions, in management, and in various mechanical and skilled trades that have sprung up and grown with the intensification of the division of labor. These jobs are in addition to those of the custom craftsmen that came into existence with the first revival of the division of labor in early modern times, and that the enemies of the division of labor like to contrast with factory work—forgetting that before the factories, very few people held such jobs as craftsmen and that the overwhelming majority were half-starving, illiterate peasants. Computerization and automation, if allowed to proceed, will make possible substantial further improvements along these lines.

Furthermore, Marx and Engels were wrong because the wealth and leisure and the resulting education and level of knowledge that a division-of-labor society makes possible are powerful forces working *against* feelings of "alienation." While it is true that alienation—a sense of lack of belonging and lack of control in one's life—is a growing problem in present-day society, it is not because of, but *in spite of* the existence of the division of labor. The wealth the division of labor makes possible enables us to gain control over our physical circumstances. Our houses are not blown down by every strong wind. We do not starve when the rain does not fall or when the locusts come. We do not, as a common occurrence, see our children and loved ones or our friends and neighbors dead and dying around us. We do not live in the constant fear of disaster, disease, and death. Yet that is the normal state of life in non-division-of-labor societies. By the same token, when a disaster does strike us from which

we cannot escape, we are at least able to understand it as a natural phenomenon, and not as the visitation of the wrath of some mysterious power. Wealth and education are the physical and intellectual means of being in control of our lives, and therefore of not being alienated. Both depend on the productivity of a division-of-labor society.

Marx and Engels were correct about one thing, however: socialism, if it were ever imposed on a global basis, would abolish the division of labor. The division of labor that socialist regimes inherit from a preceding era of capitalism can endure, in a crippled, highly inefficient state, only so long as an outside capitalist world exists which is large enough, and foolish enough, to subsidize the socialist regimes with such things as free food and the proceeds of government-guaranteed loans, and which provides a continuous market for the purchase of emergency supplies.[11] Recent revelations about the poverty of Eastern Europe and the former Soviet Union fully confirm these propositions.

A division-of-labor society is a *capitalist* society.

4. Universal Aspects of Production

While the division of labor is the hub of production under capitalism, and creates the need for the science of economics, there are other important aspects of production as well. These aspects are present in one form or another both under capitalism and all other imaginable forms of economic activity, such as feudalism and that of Robinson Crusoe on a desert island. They may be described as universal aspects of production. It behooves economics as a science to take notice of them. Thus we shall consider here the general concepts of production, product, producer, labor, land, and capital goods, and also the concept of consumption with respect to its multifaceted relationship to production. Later on, in Chapter 11, we will show how the existence of the division of labor profoundly modifies the whole concept of productive activity, including these other aspects.[12]

Physically, production can be defined as man's alteration of matter in form or location, in accordance with conscious design, in order to make the matter thus altered serve a further purpose. (In a division-of-labor society, as we shall see, the concept of production becomes more complex. It incorporates, as a necessary feature, the earning of money, and comes to include the rendition of services performed for money.[13]) When the matter thus altered undergoes some significant physical, chemical, or biological change—such as the making of flour from wheat, metal from ore, or wine from grape juice—man may be said to produce a distinct product, and a new good may be said to result. Where the alteration is relatively minor, or consists of a mere change in location—for example, removing stains from clothing or carrying water from one place to another—production takes place, but a distinct product does not result; no new good is produced. A product is matter that has been altered in one or more of the above ways (e.g., flour), or the *alteration* in matter that we perceive as essentially unchanged (e.g., the removal of a stain). A producer in the physical sense is one who effects such alterations.

All production, of course, entails the performance of human labor. Labor is the means by which man's mind transmits his designs and purposes to matter. It is man's application of his bodily and mental faculties for the purpose of altering matter and thereby making it serve a further end.

By the same token, all production also entails the presence of preexisting matter, which is to be altered. The ultimate source of this matter is always nature. The name which economists have traditionally given to nature's contribution to production is land. "Land" includes land as we normally think of it, namely, pieces of ground, *plus* all the natural resources within it and all the trees and plants and animals that are naturally present upon it— i.e., present without man's intervention. It also embraces bodies of water and their contents, air, and, eventually no doubt, even outer space, insofar as these things are employed in production. Land and labor together are sometimes referred to as the original factors of production. (The description of land as an original factor of production can be misleading, however, insofar as man is responsible for whatever wealth-character it possesses.[14])

Materials of production which are themselves products or otherwise the result of the previous performance of labor, plus tools, implements, and machines, and buildings used in production (and land too, insofar as it has been improved by the previous performance of labor), have traditionally been called capital goods. It must be stressed, however, that this description can at most be allowed to stand only in the context of a non-division-of-labor economy. As will be shown later, the division of labor exerts such a profound influence on virtually every aspect of economic activity that its existence requires that many materials of production, and even many tools and machines be categorized as consumers' goods rather than capital goods—for example, the materials required for serving meals in the home, and all sorts of tools and machines found in homes, such as knives and forks, hammers and screwdrivers, washing machines, sewing machines, and automobiles. In a division-of-labor society, the concepts of capital and capital goods, like that of production, come to incorporate as a necessary feature the purpose of earning a money revenue or income.[15]

Products produced are continuously used up, worn out, or simply deteriorate through the action of nature, as when they rust or rot. The using up, wearing out, or deterioration both of products and nature-given goods (such as mineral deposits) is *consumption,* in its physical sense. And a consumer in this sense is one who uses goods up, wears them out, or in whose possession they deteriorate.

Production and consumption are related in a double way. On the one hand, every product produced is subsequently consumed. On the other hand, every product reflects *a prior consumption in the process of its own production.* The production of bread, for example, entails the consumption of flour and other ingredients, and of the pots, pans, oven, and building which are employed in its production. There is no product the production of which does not entail consumption. Even the cave man, in producing the very first products, had to consume nature-given goods. And all production above the cave man level entails a consumption of previously produced *products.* The materials consumed in production come, for the most part, to be themselves products, and even where the materials remain nature-given goods, as in mining, products are nonetheless consumed in the form of the wearing out of tools, implements, machinery, buildings, and other installations, at least some varieties of which are employed in all branches of production without exception once economic activity advances beyond the most primitive level.

The recognition that consumption is entailed in the very process of production itself, led the classical economists to distinguish between two, and sometimes three, very different kinds of physical consumption, which they called, respectively, productive, unproductive, and reproductive consumption. Retaining these terms, I define them as follows:

Productive consumption: consumption for the purpose of production. For example, the consumption of flour and ovens for the purpose of baking bread, as above; the consumption of steel and stamping equipment for the purpose of producing automobiles; the consumption of cloth and sewing machines for the purpose of making clothing.

Unproductive consumption: consumption *not* for the purpose of production. For example, the eating of bread, the driving of an automobile for pleasure, the wearing of clothes.

Reproductive consumption: that variety of productive consumption in which the product produced can play the same role in further production as the goods consumed in its own production, or can be employed in the production of such products. The consumption of seed in the production of wheat and the wearing out of trucks in making deliveries to truck factories are obvious examples of reproductive consumption. The same phenomenon is no less present, however, in the wearing out of oxcarts in the construction of a railroad. For though physically very different, oxcarts and railroads play the same role in production, in that both are means of transport. The using up of steel in the manufacture of iron mining equipment is likewise reproductive consumption, as is the subsequent wearing out of the iron mining equipment. For iron mining equipment indirectly serves in the production of steel, which, in turn, serves in the production of iron mining equipment.

The concepts of productive and, especially, reproductive consumption are closely related to a proper concept of capital goods. Capital goods, in the physical sense, are goods productively or reproductively physically consumed. For example, the flour and ovens, steel and stamping equipment, cloth and sewing machines, and the seed, trucks, oxcarts, and steel and iron mining equipment, as above. As we shall see, in the context of a division-of-labor, monetary economy, in which anything that is used in the production of a product to be sold can make possible its own replacement by way of exchange—that is, by using the sales proceeds its products bring in, to purchase its replacement—the concepts productive consumption and reproductive consumption become synonymous.[16] And the concepts capital goods and capital come to be inseparably connected with the question of whether or not the goods are purchased, or the sums of money are expended, for the purpose of bringing in subsequent sales revenues.[17]

The aggregate of capital goods in the possession of an individual can be described as his *capital*. And capital can be defined as *wealth reproductively employed*—that is, as wealth employed in the production of wealth. (In the context of a division-of-labor economy, capital is wealth employed in the earning of money.)

It is obvious that if the supply of capital goods is to be maintained, a substantial proportion of production must be devoted to their production in order to replace the supplies undergoing productive consumption. If the proportion of labor and capital goods devoted to the production of capital goods is large enough to more than offset productive consumption, then capital accumulation takes place—i.e., the supply of capital goods grows. If the proportion is insufficient, then capital decumulation takes place.[18]

The supply of capital goods is of vital significance to production because it is a major determinant of the productivity of labor—i.e., the output per unit of labor. A larger supply of capital goods per capita operates to raise the productivity of labor, and a smaller supply to reduce it. More capital goods make it possible to produce not only more of various products, but products whose production would otherwise be completely impossible.

For example, while a plow enables a farmer to grow more food than he could grow without it, a blast furnace of some sort is necessary in order to produce any steel at all. A growing supply of capital goods is indispensable to the adoption of more advanced technologies and to the continuing rise in the productivity of labor.[19]

As previously indicated, the existence of division of labor operates to raise the productivity of labor in large measure by virtue of increasing the supply of capital goods per capita.[20] This is actually the effect of division of labor in all the ways that it serves to increase production, insofar as the products are capital goods. In particular the most important sources of gain from the division of labor—namely, the multiplication of knowledge, the benefit from the existence of geniuses, and geographical specialization, all of which are indispensable to technological progress and the use of machinery and ever-improved machinery—make their contribution to the productivity of labor mainly by means of bringing about capital accumulation.[21]

The present discussion of the role of division of labor in capital accumulation indicates that in addition to the proportion of total production in which capital goods are produced being a determinant of their supply, and thus of the productivity of labor, there is a further, equally important factor: namely, the general efficiency with which labor and existing capital goods are used. The more efficient an economic system is in the utilization of its labor and existing supply of capital goods, the greater will be its ability to accumulate additional capital goods. This is because a greater efficiency in the utilization of labor and existing capital goods means that with any given supply of capital goods it can produce a larger total product, including a larger supply of capital goods for any given proportion of its productive efforts that it devotes to the production of capital goods. The effect of this, in turn, is that the proportion of its output which it needs to have in the form of capital goods in order to make possible the replacement of the capital goods consumed in production—its maintenance proportion, so to speak—is correspondingly reduced. To whatever extent the economic system was already devoting to the production of capital goods a larger proportion of its efforts than was required for mere replacement, this reduction in the maintenance proportion further widens the margin by which it accumulates capital.

This point can be illustrated by considering the conditions of a self-sufficient farmer, whose own product is the source of the capital goods he uses in further production. If such a farmer can use one bushel of crop in the form of seed to produce an output of two bushels of crop, then in order to maintain his stock of seed and produce the same-sized crop in the next year, the farmer must employ half of his output as seed. If he becomes more efficient, and can produce three bushels of crop for every one of seed, then he requires only one-third of his output to replace his stock of seed. If he continues to devote half or more of his output to seed, he is now enabled to accumulate capital and increase his production, or to do so more rapidly than before.

The exact same principle applies to the accumulation of capital goods in a complex division-of-labor economy such as our own. Just as in the case of the self-sufficient farmer, the physical source of capital goods for us is the product of our economic system. For taking a division-of-labor economy as *a whole,* it resembles the situation of the self-sufficient farmer in that there is nothing outside of it to provide capital goods. The physical source of capital goods in a division-of-labor economy, as with a self-sufficient farmer, is always its own output.

It is worth noting that production with capital goods always represents an indirect, more time-consuming process of production as compared to production without capital goods. For labor must first be applied to the production of the capital goods and only then to the production of consumers' goods. The greater lapse of time between the performance of labor and the achievement of its ultimate result is, of course, compensated for by the larger size of the result and by the fact that in many cases results of the same kind could simply not be ob-tained otherwise. The use of labor in a hand-to-mouth process of production—for example, to pick fruits and nuts growing wild in the forest—is the most direct, least-time-consuming method of production one might imagine. Yet the product of such a process of production is insignificant in comparison with processes of production in which labor is used first to produce tools and implements; and if labor were not first used to produce materials as well, no products could be produced beyond the crudest, most primitive type.[22] The division of labor is intimately bound up with the question of the time factor involved in production insofar as one group of workers begins its production with capital goods produced by previous groups of workers. Such temporal succession in the stages of division of labor can be described as the division of labor in its vertical aspect.

In any discussion of universal aspects of production, some mention must be made of the law of diminishing returns, which has application under all economic conditions. However, inasmuch as this law has already been explained in the last chapter, it is not necessary to explain it again.[23] It is only necessary to stress that it is the framework provided by the division of labor and capitalism, and the resulting continuous ability to achieve technological progress and accumulate capital, that makes it possible to counteract and more than counteract the influence of the law of diminishing returns.

Notes

1. These particular advantages of the division of labor are sometimes lost sight of in misguided efforts to make unskilled factory jobs more interesting. One such recent effort in the automobile industry failed with a loss of over $800 million in just eighteen months. This was a case in Sweden, in which assembly lines were abolished and replaced by work groups of ten to fifteen members with responsibility for building vehicles on their own. See "Saab Is Closing Plant After Venture's Loss," *New York Times,* February 9, 1991.

2. See above, pp. 76–78.

3. On the contribution of the division of labor to the self-interests of the individual, see Ludwig von Mises, *Human Action,* 3d ed. rev. (Chicago: Henry Regnery Co., 1966), pp. 143–176. See also idem, *Socialism* (New Haven: Yale University Press, 1950), pp. 289–358; reprint ed. (Indianapolis: Liberty Classics, 1981). Page references to *Socialism* are to the Yale University Press edition; pagination from this edition is retained in the reprint edition.

4. See von Mises, *Human Action,* pp. 170–174.

5. On these points, see below, p. 144 and pp. 343–371 passim.

6. Cf. above, pp. 27–31. Also cf. von Mises, *Human Action,* pp. 143–144.

7. Karl Marx, *Economic and Philosophic Manuscripts of 1844;* Karl Marx and Friedrich Engels, *The Holy Family: A Critique of Critical Criticism* (1845); *The Communist Manifesto* (1848);

Friedrich Engels, *Anti-Dühring* (1878).

8. The piecework system is often mistakenly attacked on the grounds that it operates perversely. To wit: it is argued that the incentives the piecework system provides result in increased production, which, if great enough relative to the demand for the product, in turn results in the piece rates being cut and thus in workers earning less money than they did before. The error in this argument is essentially the same as that which is present in the doctrine of overproduction and in criticisms of Say's Law. See below, pp. 561–564, in particular the analysis of the hypothetical case of the potato growers who double their production and earn less as the result of doing so. See also p. 568 and pp. 655–656. The ultimate effect in all such cases is to raise the general standard of living, including the standard of living of those who might initially lose by the process of improvement.

9. For the explanation of this fact, see below, p. 195.

10. For a discussion showing how the consistent implementation of procapitalist policies, namely, a free market in labor and a 100-percent-reserve gold standard, would create a wide range of readily available employment opportunities, see below, p. 594. In such conditions, people would have an incentive to develop the ability to do a variety of jobs and to move between those jobs.

11. On the necessary failure of socialism and its incompatibility with the division of labor, see below, pp. 135–139 and 267–282

passim.

12. Much of the material in this section originally appeared in my article "Definitions Pertaining to Production and Consumption," *Il Politico* 32, no. 1 (March 1967).

13. See below, pp. 442–462 passim, and above, 41–42.

14. See above, pp. 39–41 and 63–66.

15. See below, pp. 442–447.

16. See below, pp. 444–445.

17. See below, pp. 445–447.

18. See below, pp. 622–629.

19. On this point, see below, pp. 631–632.

20. See above, pp. 127–128.

21. For a discussion of increases in production as a source of capital accumulation, see below, pp. 629–631 and 634–636.

22. Cf. Eugen von Böhm-Bawerk, *Capital and Interest*, trans. George D. Huncke and Hans F. Sennholz (South Holland, Ill.: Libertarian Press, 1959), 2:77–118.

23. See above, pp. 67–69.

CHAPTER 5

THE DEPENDENCE OF THE DIVISION
OF LABOR ON CAPITALISM I

THE NATURE OF THE
DEPENDENCIES

Chapter 4 explained how the division of labor is essential to the existence of a high and rising productivity of labor. This and the next three chapters demonstrate the dependence of the division of labor on the fundamental economic institutions of a capitalist society. These institutions, of course, are private ownership of the means of production, saving and capital accumulation, exchange and money, economic competition, economic inequality, and the profit motive and the price system. By the end of Chapter 8, the dependence of the division of labor on the institutions of capitalism will have been established so thoroughly that the proposition will appear unexceptionable that in the long run the division of labor itself is an institution of capitalism.

1. Dependence of the Division of Labor on Private Ownership of the Means of Production

Private ownership of the means of production is the most fundamental of the institutions of capitalism, along with freedom and the pursuit of material self-interest. It underlies a division-of-labor society in a direct way and in a variety of indirect ways.

The direct dependence of the division of labor on

private ownership of the means of production is based on the very nature of the gains provided by the division of labor. These gains, above all the multiplication of knowledge and the benefit from the existence of geniuses, fundamentally derive from the fact that individuals possess separate, independent minds, which permit, indeed, require them to have separate independent knowledge and to make separate, independent judgments and decisions. In a division-of-labor society, each person benefits from the fact that other people possess knowledge which he does not, and an intelligence separate from and often greater than his own. His benefit requires that others be able to acquire and apply their knowledge on their own initiative, without having to await his orders, approval, or permission, which, in the nature of the case, he would be unable to give in any rational way, since he necessarily lacks the knowledge that would be required to do so.

Now, in order for people to act and produce on any significant scale, they must possess material means of action and production: they must possess wealth. In order for them to act and produce separately and independently from one another, *they must hold wealth separately and independently from one another*—that is, there must be private property, including private ownership of the means of production.[1]

In essence, private property and private ownership of the means of production are fundamental and essential to a division-of-labor society because the separate, independent thinking and acting of individuals is fundamental and essential to it, and because they are the material requirement of such separate, independent thinking and acting.[2]

Socialism and Collectivism Versus Economic Planning

Just as capitalism—private ownership of the means of production—is indispensable to the existence of a division-of-labor society, so, by the same token, socialism and collectivism are incompatible with the existence of a division-of-labor society.[3] The truth of these propositions is confirmed by the collapse of socialism in Eastern Europe and—how wonderful the words sound—the *former* Soviet Union. Despite extensive Western aid, economic conditions in the Communist bloc were so bad for so long that finally all hope of improvement under socialism has been abandoned and attempts are now underway to institute private ownership of the means of production and establish a price system.

The incompatibility of socialism and collectivism with a division-of-labor society would long since have been blatant if the capitalist countries had not continuously rescued the Soviet Union and its allies from famine, with massive supplies of grain sent for free or on government-guaranteed credit that was never intended to be repaid. Even the grain *purchases* made by the Soviet Union and its allies ultimately depended on the aid of Western governments, which guaranteed investments made in the development of natural resources and in the construction of factories in the Soviet Union and other Communist-bloc countries. These investments, particularly those in the development of natural resources, in which the quality of the product does not enter as a decisive factor, were the foundation of most of the exports of the Soviet Union and the Communist bloc and thus of their ability to obtain funds with which to make purchases from abroad. In the absence of such Western aid, a series of famines—the necessary consequence of the massive inefficiencies of socialism—would have led to a flight from the cities and resettlement of practically the whole of the surviving population of the Communist countries on farms, in an effort of people to secure a food supply. This would have meant the end of all significant division of labor in those countries and their reversion to the economic conditions of feudalism.

It should be realized that collectivism openly demands that everyone think and act as a unit. It leaves no room for the vast differentiation and individuation of knowledge on which a division-of-labor society rests. The propaganda of socialism fully displays this absurdity when it pretends that under socialism all economic decisions will be arrived at democratically. In order for people intelligently to vote on all economic decisions, everyone would have to have all the necessary knowl-edge pertaining to all economic decisions, which is clearly impossible in a division-of-labor society. It would mean, for example, that the voters would have to decide such questions as whether a new steel mill should be built in Gary, Indiana, or somewhere else, what kind of steel mill it should be, how large it should be, and so on. In the face of hundreds or thousands of such questions arising every day, the voters would have to devote their lives to nothing else, and still they would be almost entirely ignorant about the matters raised in each case.

Socialism is not rescued from its incompatibility with a division-of-labor society by substituting the dictatorship of an alleged expert or body of experts for the democracy of the ignorant masses. For now, instead of demanding that everyone know everything about production, it demands that one person or several people—the Supreme Dictator or the members of the Central Planning Board—know everything about production. The very expression "central planning" describes the essence of this absurdity. It means that one consciousness must be able to see and plan the entire economic system, either alone or in consultation with one or more other such all-seeing consciousnesses. For central planning means the planning of the entire economic system as an indivisible whole.

Socialism is incompatible with a division-of-labor society because in all of its versions it is incompatible with a division of *the intellectual labor* required in the planning of the conduct of the economic system. When it attempts such an intellectual division of labor, as it necessarily must, the result is contradictory partial planning. This is a state of affairs in which separate ministries, industries, regions, and even individual factories and farms plan in discoordination and at cross purposes. In a word, it is economic chaos.[4] As a result of this chaos, the whole division of labor disintegrates—or would in the absence of aid from capitalist countries. For people are subjected to a chronic inability to obtain vital supplies from others and thus must attempt to produce them themselves.

The lack of vital supplies includes all manner of things. There are not only shortages of food, but also shortages of such things as lubricants, electric power, and raw materials and component parts of all kinds, and, of course, labor and all kinds of consumers' goods.[5] It is in response to such conditions that Soviet factories found it necessary to attempt to manufacture even their own screws and nails. Thus, for example, without any awareness of the fact that the conditions he described were hostile to the division of labor, an admirer of the Soviet system wrote:

> There is considerable evidence that Russian plants do for themselves many things—like producing screws with

slow-speed machinery—which could be better done by others—in this case, specialized screw manufacturers using high speed equipment. But this desire to be independent of others, in part at least, grows out of the Soviet effort to operate its plant capacity at a pace rarely achieved under capitalism except in wartime. In fact, the sort of barter deals just discussed are not too different from those which take place in a capitalist economy under the impact of *wartime shortages.*[6]

In describing such conditions, another observer wrote:

> For a Soviet factory—or a Soviet research institute—the best response to unreliable business partners is self-sufficiency. When the planners decided to build the giant Fiat factory, they decided to make it almost entirely self-sufficient. Except for electrical equipment, window glass and tires, every part used in Zhiguli—every nut, bolt, seat cover and piston ring—is made in the factory itself. Gersh Budker's Institute of Nuclear Physics in Novosibirsk couldn't buy the instruments it needed, so the scientists there began to make their own. This kind of self-reliance is expensive and inefficient. Yet no amount of planning can provide the trust and reliability that could substitute for it.[7]

The fact is that such results are inescapable under so-called central planning. They can be avoided only by means of capitalism and its price system.

Happily, at long last, it appears that after more than seventy years of abject failure, the concept of central planning is now being abandoned in the former Soviet Union. The process of abandonment of the concept appears to be well underway even in Communist China. Hopefully, within the next few years, these and all other socialist countries will have made the transition to private ownership of the means of production and capitalism.

Capitalist Planning and the Price System

Division of labor in the planning process is possible only under capitalism. This is because of the existence of the price system, which is unique to capitalism. Under capitalism each individual plans his own particular sphere of economic activity. But he plans on the basis of a consideration of prices—the prices he will receive as a seller and must pay as a buyer.

The consideration of prices is what integrates and harmonizes the plans of each individual with the plans of all other individuals and produces a fully and rationally planned economic system under capitalism. For example, a student changes his career plan from actor to accountant when he contemplates the vast difference in income he can expect to earn. A prospective home buyer changes his plan concerning which neighborhood to live in when he compares house prices in the different neighborhoods. And businesses change their plans concerning product lines, methods and locations of production, and every other aspect of their activities, in response to profit-and-loss calculations.

All of these changes represent the adjustment of the plans of particular individuals and businesses to the plans of others in the economic system. For it is the plans of others to purchase accounting services rather than acting services that cause the higher income our student can expect to earn as an accountant rather than as an actor. It is the plans of others willing and able to pay more to live in certain neighborhoods, and less to live in certain others, that determine the relative house prices confronting our home buyer. It is the plans of its prospective customers, of all competing sellers of its goods, and of all other buyers of the means of production it uses or otherwise depends on, that enter into the formation of the prices determining the revenues and costs of any business firm and thus what it finds profitable or unprofitable to produce.

Now the fact that capitalism even *has* economic planning, let alone the only possible kind of rational economic planning, is almost completely unknown. Practically everyone under capitalism has been in the position of Molière's M. Jourdan, who spoke prose all his life without ever knowing it. The overwhelming majority of people have not realized that all the thinking and planning about their economic activities that they perform in their capacity as individuals actually *is* economic planning.[8] By the same token, the term "planning" has been reserved for the feeble efforts of a comparative handful of government officials, who, having prohibited the planning of everyone else, presume to substitute their knowledge and intelligence for the knowledge and intelligence of tens of millions, and to call *that* planning. This is an incredible state of affairs, one which implies the most enormous ignorance on the part of the great majority of today's intellectuals, from journalists to professors.

The dependence of the division of labor on the price system points the way to its *indirect* dependence on the institution of private ownership of the means of production. The price system rests on the profit motive and the freedom of competition. Operating in conjunction with one another, these are the elements that drive and regulate the price system—that determine the formation of all individual prices and their integration into a system. The profit motive and the freedom of competition, in turn, vitally depend on the institution of private ownership of the means of production.

It is necessary to explain here the nature of both of these sets of dependencies: that of the price system on the profit motive and the freedom of competition and, in turn, that of the profit motive and the freedom of competition on private ownership of the means of production.

The profit motive—financial self-interest—makes everyone be concerned with the revenue or income he earns and the costs or expenses he incurs. As stated, precisely this is what harmonizes and integrates the economic plans and the economic activities of all the separate businesses and individuals who make up a division-of-labor society. While the principles describing just how this occurs are the subject matter of price theory and are explained at length in the next three chapters of this book, this much can be stated now, as a brief, advance indication: Namely, the profit motive provides powerful incentives for the steady expansion and improvement of production and, at the same time, operates to keep the relative size of all the various industries and occupations in proper balance. It makes production accord with the will of the ultimate buyers—the consumers—and ensures that the production of each individual good takes place in a way that is maximally conducive to production in the rest of the economic system. The profit motive is what balances the demand and supply of each product and ensures the most rational and efficient distribution of each product over space and time—among all the markets that compete for it—and its delivery into the hands of those individuals who, within the limits of their wealth and income, need or desire it the most. The profit motive ensures the most rational and efficient allocation of capital and of every type of labor and material among its possible alternative uses, and makes the economic system respond to changes in economic conditions in the most rational and efficient manner possible.

Thus, the profit motive is what prevents any sort of "anarchy of production" and, instead, creates economic order and harmony out of the activities of all the different individuals who comprise the economic system. It is what enables capitalism to be an economic system that is rationally and cohesively planned by each and every individual who participates in it.

If the profit motive is the engine which drives the price system, competition and the freedom of competition are the built-in regulator which provide the essential context in which that engine operates. What this means is that in seeking to serve his financial self-interest, every seller under capitalism must be aware that there are other sellers or potential sellers who might sell to his customers and thus that he must accordingly limit the prices he asks. By the same token, every buyer under capitalism must be aware that there are other buyers or potential buyers who might buy from his suppliers and thus that he must set the prices he offers accordingly.

Now while the profit motive and the freedom of competition are the elements that drive and regulate the price system, as stated, they themselves in turn rest on the foundation of private ownership of the means of production.

Private ownership of the means of production is what makes the profit motive operative in the formation of prices, the prices both of means of production and of products. Furthermore, private ownership of the means of production underlies the very existence of the incentives of profit and loss, in that it is private property, above all in the form of private ownership of the means of production, that is the substance of what is gained or lost by producers. Without the ability to accumulate holdings of private property, there would be nothing for producers to gain except the ability to enlarge their immediate consumption, and nothing at all for them to lose, because losses can be losses only of preexisting property. With private ownership of the means of production there is not only the incentive of profit and loss to use the means of production profitably but also the vitally important fact that an individual's control over the means of production is increased or decreased to the extent that he uses them profitably or unprofitably.

This last results from the fact that those owners who use the means of production profitably are in a position to save and reinvest, in proportion to the extent of their profits. To the extent that their sales proceeds exceed their costs, they obtain the funds not only to replace the means of production with which they began but to more than replace. They are thus enabled to enlarge their control over the means of production. By the same token, those owners of the means of production who suffer losses correspondingly lose control over the means of production. Their losses mean that their sales proceeds are less than their initial outlays and thus that they lack the funds to replace the means of production with which they began.

Thus private ownership of the means of production is what gives the profit motive virtually all of its economic influence: it enables the profit motive both to be operative in the formation of the prices of means of production and products and to direct the use of the means of production. At the same time, it enables success or failure in earning profits to determine the extent of one's control over means of production in the future. And, of course, it is what gives the profit motive its strength.

As to economic competition: private ownership of the means of production underlies economic competition, in that economic competition presupposes separate, independent producers, who, in order to be separate and independent, must hold the wealth they use in production separately and independently from one another. Thus competition among producers presupposes private ownership of the means of production. Furthermore, the freedom of competition, like virtually all other freedoms, is an aspect of property rights: it is the freedom of owners of means of production to employ their means of production in any branch of industry they choose.[9]

In addition to its dependence on the profit motive and freedom of competition, the price system, of course, also depends on the institutions of exchange and money. Prices are sums of money exchanged for units of goods or services. The very phenomenon of exchange presupposes the separate ownership of the things exchanged. Exchange is a mutual transfer of property between two parties, with the property of each being given as the condition of receiving the property of the other. A collectivist monopoly on production, which is the essence of socialism, is incompatible with the means of production being exchanged or, therefore, having prices. Capital goods cannot be bought or sold because all capital goods are owned by the same party: the state. At the same time, the leading purpose of socialism is supposed to be the removal of labor from the status of a commodity that is bought and sold in the market; and, indeed, labor cannot be bought and sold under socialism except on the terms arbitrarily dictated by a universal monopoly employer: the state. Thus, private ownership of the means of production is essential for the existence of markets and of market prices of the means of production.[10] It is essential both for the very existence of a market in capital goods and thus for prices of capital goods, and for the existence of employer competition in the market for labor and thus for wage rates greater than the barest minimum of subsistence.

Closely related to the above, the price system further depends on the institution of saving and capital accumulation, in that the prices of the means of production are not paid by the consumers, who purchase only the ultimate final products, but by businessmen. All the materials and supplies, all the tools, equipment, and labor services used in production are purchased and paid for by businessmen, almost entirely out of accumulated capital, not by the ultimate consumers out of consumption spending.[11] The prices of all the means of production, therefore, depend on saving and capital accumulation. And, as indicated previously, saving and capital accumulation vitally depend on the institution of private ownership of the means of production and its security. In order for people to save and accumulate capital, to improve the productive property at their disposal in any way, or even just to maintain it, they must have the expectation of benefitting from such action. They can rationally have that expectation only if that wealth—those means of production—are securely their private property.

Thus, through each of these four roots—the profit motive, competition, exchange and money, and saving and capital accumulation—the price system is grounded in the institution of private ownership of the means of production.

Further dependencies of a division-of-labor society on the institutions of saving and capital accumulation, exchange and money, economic competition, and also economic inequality—all of them leading features of capitalism—can now be explored.

2. The Dependence of the Division of Labor on Saving and Capital Accumulation

Even before the development of money and monetary exchange, saving and capital accumulation are vital to the development of the division of labor. They are necessary to release people's labor from the immediate production of food, so that they can turn to the production of other things, including tools for producing food. In the absence of any saving and capital accumulation whatever, everyone's labor would have to be devoted almost exclusively to securing his next meal. With saving and capital accumulation, even if only in the form of stores of food, people can turn their attention to the production of other things. For example, primitive hunters or fishermen who have accumulated stocks of food can live off them while they set about constructing huts and also better means of hunting and fishing, such as bows and arrows and boats and nets.

The ability to carry on the production of things other than immediate food supplies is an obvious precondition of the development of the division of labor, in that without it there would be the production of essentially just one thing, in which virtually everyone would be engaged, namely, food for the next meal. Probably there would be some division of labor even at that level—for example, some members of a tribe might concentrate on chasing animals, while others concentrated on the actual killing of them. But a precondition of people specializing in the production of distinctly different products is the ability to carry on the production of such products, and here saving and capital accumulation are necessary in the case of every product whose production entails the lapse of more time than transpires between two meals. They are necessary insofar as people must have that second meal (or whatever else they normally consume) before their labor results in the consumers' goods they help to produce. Their ability to consume before their product is produced is possible only to the extent that savings exist.

As indicated, the accumulation of capital is also vital in raising the productivity of the labor of food producers, so that not everyone's labor is required in the production of food. It is only to the degree that fewer people are required to produce the food needed by all, that more people can devote their labor to things other than food, and thus the division of labor develop. The relationship between the productivity of labor in food production and the division of labor is reciprocal. To the degree that the productivity of labor in food production rises, more people can be spared for other branches of production. The effect of the expansion of these other branches in turn is a higher productivity of labor in food production, because food producers are thereby enabled to work with the aid of more and better products of other branches of production—for example, farmers can work with the aid of more of the products of manufacturing.

Saving and capital accumulation, of course, are no less vital in the context of a monetary economy, as has already been shown. Closely connected with the fact that they are the source of the demand for factors of production is the fact that their existence is what enables producers to be paid within a reasonable period of time after the completion of their work. In the absence of savings and capital in terms of money, any significant division of labor would be impossible, because it would then be necessary for many producers to wait years, decades, generations, or even centuries before being paid.

Consider the case of automobile workers today. At present, like most other workers, they are paid after the completion of a week's work. Yet far more than a week goes by between the performance of the auto workers' labor and the time the auto companies are paid for the cars those workers help to produce. What makes this possible is the fact that the auto companies possess capital. They pay the wages of their workers week after week out of capital, and only months later do they recover the outlays of any given week in sales revenues.

Indeed, even most of the sales revenues of the auto companies are paid out of savings and capital. Most new-car buyers buy on installment credit. Under this arrangement a bank or some other financial institution advances them the funds to buy their car, and they then pay off over a period of two to four years. In the absence of this capital and the capital of the auto companies, auto workers would have to wait in excess of two to four years before being fully paid for their work. And the same would be true of all the suppliers of the auto companies, such as the steel and tire companies, and the like. They would all have to wait to receive the installment payments from the car buyers.

In the absence of capital in the hands of steel and tire producers as well as auto producers and companies financing automobile purchases, the period for which companies and workers would have to wait to be paid would be increased still further. The workers employed by the steel and tire companies, and the suppliers of the steel and tire companies, such as iron mining concerns and rubber plantations, would all have to wait the full period of time waited by the auto workers *plus* the period of time that presently elapses between the payments by the steel

and tire companies and the receipt of sales revenues by these companies. The consequence of a still further lack of capital, this time by the iron mining concerns and rubber plantations, would, of course, be to make the plight of the employees and suppliers of these concerns even worse. And so it would be with every further stage of remove from the production of automobiles.

The full magnitude of the time factor in production becomes clear if we begin to look at the equipment and buildings used by an industry. For example, the auto industry's equipment probably lasts on the order of a generation; its factory buildings, on the order of two or three generations. If the auto industry did not possess capital funds to pay for that equipment and those buildings, the suppliers of the equipment and the construction contractors involved would have to wait to be paid out of the sales revenues earned by the auto companies over a period of from one to three generations.

In the absence of capital in the hands of the equipment makers and construction contractors as well, it would be their employees and suppliers who would have to wait this period of time to be paid. These workers and suppliers would also have to wait the additional time that transpires within these industries in the making of the equipment and the construction of the buildings. Indeed, those involved in the production of such things as construction equipment and in the building of factories for producing machinery and construction equipment would be confronted with periods of waiting time that extended beyond their life spans and their children's life spans. This would be the case, for example, where the steel girders used to erect an auto plant that will last fifty years come from a steel mill that is itself fifty years old and was constructed with materials produced in a previous plant that at that time was fifty years old. Here a time span of a hundred and fifty years is involved between the performance of labor and the payment by an ultimate consumer.[12]

In the absence of capital in the hands of business enterprises, there would simply be no way for heavily time-consuming processes of production to exist. Even substantial savings in the hands of workers would not be sufficient. We might imagine a few workers with enough savings to enable them to work for a few years before they were paid, but we certainly cannot imagine an economic system in which there are workers willing to work and not be paid in their lifetimes, indeed, in which payment would not occur even in the lifetimes of their children or grandchildren.

In order for the division of labor to exist in an extensive temporal succession, in which groups of workers produce tools or materials taken up by other, succeeding groups, in processes extending over long periods of time, it is absolutely essential that there be capital funds, so that each group can be paid within a reasonable time after completing its work. The existence of capital funds introduces a necessary *division of payments,* so to speak, that corresponds to the temporal division of labor.

In the absence of capital funds, there is only one source of payment—the ultimate, final consumers, whose outlays lie months, years, generations, even centuries in the future. With the existence of capital funds, there is immediate payment, however far in the future the expenditures of the ultimate, final consumers may lie. Only because of the existence of capital funds can the division of labor exist in an extensive temporal succession.

And, as will be shown later in this book, the greater is the accumulation of capital funds relative to consumer spending, the greater is the employment of labor serving the achievement of temporally remoter ends. This means, the greater is the accumulation of capital funds relative to consumer spending, the more does labor in the present serve consumption in the future, and the more is consumption in the present served by labor performed in the past. As will be shown, the effect of labor being able to be employed for temporally more remote ends is to accelerate the rise in its productivity.[13]

The existence of division of labor in the form of a temporal succession of producers can be termed the vertical aspect of the division of labor. It is important to realize that saving and the provision of capital it makes possible also vitally contribute to the division of labor in what may be termed its horizontal aspect—that is, the extent to which it can be carried at any given stage of production. The extent to which the division of labor can be carried at any given stage of production depends on the scale on which production is carried on at that stage. For example, if automobiles are produced on a scale of only one or two a day in a given establishment, there is obviously room for far less division of labor than if they are produced on a scale of hundreds or thousands a day in a given establishment. In the former case, it is impossible to make a full-time job, or anything approaching a full-time job, of any individual operation that requires only a small amount of labor per unit of output. But in the latter case, it becomes possible to make full-time jobs of individual operations requiring quite small amounts of labor per unit of output.[14]

What is important to realize here is that in order for production to be carried on, on the larger scale, *more capital is required.* To be able to produce automobiles on a scale of hundreds or thousands per day rather than one or two per day, vastly more capital is required. In this way, more capital becomes the precondition for the extension of the division of labor in its horizontal, as well as vertical, aspect.[15]

Thus, saving and capital accumulation lay the groundwork for the division of labor in four ways. They make possible the production of goods other than the food required for the next meal. They raise the productivity of labor in food production, so that people can be spared for other branches of production, which makes possible further increases in the productivity of labor in food production. They make possible a division of payments, so that the time which elapses between the performance of labor and the receipt of payment by the producers is relatively short, no matter how long is the time which must elapse between the performance of labor and payment by the ultimate, final consumers. Finally, they provide the foundation for larger-scale production and thus the basis for carrying the division of labor further at any given stage of production.

3. The Dependence of the Division of Labor on Exchange and Money

The division of labor presupposes the ability to make exchanges, and the existence of an extensive division of labor presupposes the existence specifically of money and monetary exchange. The necessity of exchange and money is implied by the fact that in a division-of-labor society each person produces or helps to produce just one or at most a very few things, and is dependent for his consumption on the goods and services produced by a vast number of others. In these circumstances, some mechanism must exist whereby the products of each can be channelled to others and the products of others channelled to each. Exchange is that mechanism. A division-of-labor society requires exchange on a massive scale, as a constant, major feature of economic life. In a division-of-labor society, all or practically all of everyone's production must leave him through the process of exchange, and all or practically all of everyone's consumption must come to him through the process of exchange.

But a special kind of exchange is required to make this possible. The direct, barter exchange of goods for goods is not sufficient. In order for exchange to take place under such conditions, a so-called double coincidence of wants must exist—that is, each of the two parties must possess what the other desires and desire more what the other possesses. This condition very often, indeed, usually, cannot be realized. For example, a producer of ball bearings, steel girders, or sulfuric acid desires food possessed by grocers or farmers. Yet few or no grocers or farmers desire ball bearings, steel girders, or sulfuric acid. If exchange were confined to barter, producers of such goods could not live by producing them, and so people would not produce them. The economic system would thus have to get along without such vital goods.

Indeed, hardly anyone could live by producing the goods or services he now produces, because hardly anyone produces things that are consumed to any significant extent by those who supply him. (The reader should consider to what extent the goods or services he produces or helps to produce are consumed by those who regularly supply him.)

And even where people might be engaged in producing things that would be desired by their suppliers, it would still be impossible to effect many valuable exchanges. For example, the producers of television sets, or the builders of houses, desire bread and shoes; and the producers of bread and shoes desire television sets and houses. Putting aside such obvious problems as the particular houses probably being in the wrong location for the bread and shoe producers, there is the very serious problem of how could the producers of bread and shoes *make change* for the producers of television sets and houses when the latter wished to purchase a loaf of bread or pair of shoes? Would they require them to accept hundreds or thousands of loaves of bread or pairs of shoes? Also, how could the producers of the television sets or houses pay their employees? With a fraction of a television set per hour? With a piece of a house per week? With the change they received in the form of loaves of bread or pairs of shoes?[16]

It might be thought that a series of indirect exchanges could provide a solution—that if the goods for which a product was exchanged were not of the kind desired by those from whom one wanted goods oneself, then one could reexchange these goods for goods that were in fact desired by those from whom one wanted goods oneself. But this could not actually provide a solution. A producer of ball bearings or sulfuric acid would probably acquire quantities of goods that ball bearings or sulfuric acid helped to produce. (A producer of steel girders, however, would immediately confront a problem of indivisibilities, in that he could not acquire a fraction of a building or bridge.)

Putting the problem of indivisibilities aside, it would be necessary to engage in an enormous series of exchanges, spanning who knows what distances and time intervals, if one were to assemble the various goods that even just a few of the producers desired from whom one wished to obtain goods oneself. To obtain the things he now does, the producer of ball bearings, for example, would have to reexchange the products he received for his ball bearings for the collections of goods desired by all the various suppliers of the consumers' goods he now obtains, from his grocer and landlord to his physician and travel agent. He would also have to reexchange them for the collections of goods desired by all the various suppliers of the means of production he uses in producing

ball bearings, namely, all his suppliers of materials, equipment, fuel, and labor services. The same would be true of the producers of virtually *all* goods, whose output now goes to people other than those from whom they receive goods and who are supplied by people other than those whom they supply. The problem here is that the *costs* of indirect exchanges, in terms of the time and effort that would have to be spent in effectuating them, would be too great to make the system practicable.

Thus, an economic system operating under the constraints of barter exchange would obviously offer only very limited opportunities for division of labor and would thus be extremely primitive. In essence, to live in such an economic system, one would either have to be a farmer or produce the kinds of things that could be readily exchanged with farmers, such as blacksmithing services.

What is required for the existence of a division-of-labor society is the existence of *money* and *monetary exchange*. Money is a good readily acceptable in exchange by everyone in a given geographical area, and is sought for the purpose of being reexchanged.[17] Of course, one of the properties of money, which helps to make it universally acceptable, is its divisibility into small units.

With money, those for whom the individual produces and those by whom he is supplied can be, and almost always are, different and distinct parties. With money, a process of indirect exchange takes place about which no one need be concerned—it takes place virtually automatically and without cost. Each produces for others, though not the others by whom he is supplied. The individual produces for anyone who has money to offer, and then uses the money to buy from anyone who has the goods he wants. With the existence of money, the producers of ball bearings, steel girders, and so on sell them for money to whoever wants them and has money to offer for them, and then they turn around and spend the money in buying food or whatever else they may wish, from whomever they choose. Everyone works in his particular specialization, is paid money, and buys from all manner of people who do not at all consume the goods or services that he himself produces.

With money, the producers of television sets and the builders of houses can easily obtain items as small as a loaf of bread or pair of shoes, because they sell their products for sums of money, which in turn are divisible into parts as small as the price of a loaf of bread or a pair of shoes. The employees of these producers are likewise easily paid out of capital funds.

In these ways, money radically enlarges the opportunities for specialization. It makes specialization possible not merely in a comparative handful of cases, but universally.

Closely related to the previous discussion of the price

system, the use of money also solves another problem that would otherwise be insoluble and prevent the existence of a division-of-labor society. Namely, it makes it possible to perform economic calculations and thus economic comparisons. Without the use of money, a productive process would show only a variety of physical means of production at the beginning and some physical product at the end. For example, it would show at the beginning quantities of building materials, equipment, and goods exchanged for labor services, and at the end a finished building.

In such circumstances, it would be impossible to determine if the product represented a gain or a loss of wealth, because one would be comparing quantities of different kinds, with no common denominator in terms of which to add them or subtract them.[18] One could not even answer such usually simple questions as which represents the higher wage or price? This is because, without the use of money, these questions would have to be posed in such forms as, which is more, a dozen eggs plus a loaf of bread plus a pair of shoes or two shirts plus a blender? But with the use of money, producers are able to compare the money value of their outputs with the money value of their inputs. They can also compare the costs of using different methods of production, the profitability of the different branches of production, and the remuneration of the various occupations. All of this is vital if production in the various branches of the division-of-labor system is to be properly coordinated and not collapse into chaos.

Guidance by monetary calculations and comparisons, in contrast, provides an objectively valid standard for economic behavior.[19] This is because following this standard enables the individual actually to increase the wealth at his disposal. For example, if the purchasing power of money has not significantly declined in the interval, selling a building or any other product for a larger sum of money than the sum of money one has previously expended to produce it, means that one really does increase one's command over goods and services, for one now has the means of buying a larger quantity of them than before. Similarly, using a lower-cost method of production in place of a higher-cost method, buying anything at a lower price rather than a higher price, and earning a higher profit or wage rather than a lower profit or wage—all of these things in fact serve to increase the quantity of goods and services one can obtain in the market.

Thus, the existence of money is vital to the existence of a division-of-labor society, in that it makes possible economic calculations and thus economic comparisons serving as an objectively valid standard of economic behavior, as well as radically widens the possibilities for specialization.

On the basis of what has been shown concerning the importance of money, it should be obvious what ignorance and injustice underlie the utterance that money is "the root of all evil." It would be far more correct and reasonable to argue that money is the root of all good. It is an essential root of the division of labor and of all the benefits to human life that flow from the division of labor.[20] The destruction of money would mean nothing less than the destruction of the division of labor and thus of modern material civilization. It would mean radical depopulation and utter impoverishment for whoever remained alive.[21]

The notion that money is the root of all evil finds expression in the alleged moral ideal propounded by the Communists of "from each according to his ability to each according to his need" and in the accompanying resentments against the necessity of earning money and against the great prominence accorded to the earning and spending of money in a capitalist society.[22]

Those who hold the antimoney mentality, and who yearn for goods simply to be "free" for the taking, have apparently not stopped to consider what the alternatives to money are. The alternatives can only be either the absurdly cumbersome procedures of barter, which would make the acquisition of goods far more difficult or altogether impossible, or, worse, having to go naked into the forest to hunt and gather what little nature offers to human beings without any mechanisms of exchange at all—namely, a handful of nuts and berries (if others have not appropriated them first), or else the establishment of a totalitarian socialist dictatorship that is economically chaotic.

In a capitalist society on the other hand, by the relatively simple process of earning and spending money, the individual integrates his activities into a division of labor that has come to embrace the entire world and that stretches back in time to the point when man first began to employ previously produced goods in all of his productive activities. Thus, by earning money an individual is able to buy products that represent the application of the intelligence and knowledge of enormous numbers of other human beings both living and dead. He is thereby enabled to obtain goods in a way that is incomparably easier and more rewarding than any conceivable alternative.

Ironically, the earning of money could be substantially easier and less worrisome for many people than it now is, if only the enemies of capitalism had not in their ignorance succeeded in making it unnecessarily difficult. They have made it more difficult by such means as the imposition of minimum wage laws and prounion legislation. In raising wage rates above the free-market level, such measures have the effect of reducing the quantity of labor demanded below the supply available and thus of preventing people seeking to earn money from becoming employed and thereby earning it. In the absence of such measures, not only would employment and thus the earning of money be readily possible for everyone, but also costs of production and prices would be correspondingly lower. This last would mean that the buying power of the money earned more easily as the result of lower wage rates would be increased. Thus, the lower wage rates needed to secure full employment and the consequent ease of earning money would not imply any corresponding reduction in the goods a worker could obtain by virtue of his labor. Indeed, the goods the average worker could obtain would almost certainly be greater, precisely because of everyone who wanted to work being able to work and thus not having to be supported by others. Moreover, the productivity of labor would certainly rise more rapidly in the absence of government-supported labor-union efforts to sabotage it, such as preventing or delaying the introduction of labor-saving machinery. As a result, not only would the earning of money be substantially easier and less worrisome, but it would also be substantially more rewarding in terms of the goods it brought.[23]

4. The Dependence of the Division of Labor on Economic Competition

As explained in Chapter 4, a major source of the gains from the division of labor is that the production of everything tends to be carried on by those who are able to do it best. Economic competition is the process of establishing who is able to produce things best.

The significance of economic competition for the division of labor is actually even wider than this statement may suggest. It is the process that establishes not only which individuals are best suited in the eyes of the market for all the various occupations, from wealthy businessman on down to janitor, but also which products are best suited for any given market, and which technological methods are best suited for the production of any given product. (This last embraces, for example, such choices as machine versus handicraft production, larger-scale production versus smaller-scale production, using copper versus using aluminum as a material, or coal versus oil as a fuel, producing in one geographical location rather than in another, and so forth.) Thus, economic competition is the process of determining the organization of a division-of-labor society with respect to the choice of products for markets and the technological methods of producing any given product, as well as of

persons for occupations.

Economic competition is necessary because the most efficient form of organization of a division-of-labor society is not automatically known. Also, it is subject to constant change, as new products and methods of production are discovered and old ones must be abandoned, as individuals' personal knowledge and preferences change, as capital is accumulated or decumulated, as the size and composition of the population changes, as new mineral deposits are found or old ones exhausted, and as soil and climate conditions change. In a free market, those who have differing opinions about which product is best suited for given customers, which method is most appropriate for producing a given product, or who is best qualified for a given job, come forward and submit their goods, their investments, and their talents to the judgment of the markets in which they seek to operate, and succeed or fail according to the judgment of those markets. (The judgment of a market, of course, is never final, in that individuals are always free to make further appeals to it, and again and again succeed in swaying it to their side when they have something better to offer.)

Thus, economic competition, far from representing any kind of antisocial phenomenon, as its critics claim, is a highly positive social phenomenon. It is an essential mechanism of organizing production under the division of labor, and thus an essential mechanism for improving the efficiency of the social cooperation which the division of labor represents.[24]

Consistent with our earlier discussion of the price system, economic competition, or, more correctly, the *freedom* of such competition, is necessary to a division-of-labor society in a further respect as well. Namely to prevent it from being put at the mercy of the arbitrary demands of particular categories of producers.

By its very nature, a division-of-labor society vitally depends on the work done by various small minorities of people constituting particular categories of producers. In many cases, as the result of the government's intervention into economic activity, coupled with its refusal to enforce ordinary laws protecting individual rights, such minorities have been able to coerce the rest of the society into meeting their arbitrary demands, on pain of a breakdown of the economic system. One has only to think of the consequences of prolonged strikes in such fields as transportation, steelmaking, coal mining, electric power production, and even garbage collection—and the terms on which such strikes are almost always settled.

The existence of such cases is the result of violations of the freedom of competition by or on behalf of labor unions. In practically every country, the unions have succeeded in having laws enacted that greatly restrict the employment of workers taking the place of strikers. For example, for many years, striking workers in the United States were held by law virtually to *own* their jobs, which had to be held open for them even though they refused to work, on pain of the employers having to pay triple back wages to the strikers in damages. (At the time of writing, efforts are underway in Congress to reimpose such conditions.) In addition, where replacement workers for strikers are legally allowed to work, the unions are able to practice violence and intimidation against which there is little or no legal recourse. For it is almost impossible to obtain legal protection against so-called mass picketing, which is inherently intimidating, and the police and district attorneys rarely enforce the laws against assault and battery and property damage when it comes to union violence.[25] The recent strike against *The Daily News* in New York City, in which some newsstands were actually set on fire in efforts to intimidate vendors into not selling the newspaper, and in which no arrests were made, is a glaring illustration of this fact. For further illustration, one has only to recall any of dozens of news pictures of mobs of burly workers blocking factory gates during a strike and the reports of slashed tires, shootings, and bombings that so frequently accompany strikes, and the fact that rarely if ever does any legal action take place against the perpetrators. In these ways, the unions and the government have succeeded in prohibiting freedom of competition in the labor market and thus in compelling the entire rest of society to give in to whatever arbitrary demands the unions in various critical branches of production may choose to make.

While this is a subject that requires a much fuller discussion, it can be said that the freedom of competition would be a sufficient guarantee against arbitrary demands by business firms as well as wage earners—even in cases in which the result of competition might be the establishment of just one company in a particular branch of production, such as one electric power company or one gas company in a given town. The freedom of competition would permit the entry of a new electric or gas company if the existing one's rates became excessive, and this fact would operate as a powerful check on the rates charged by the existing company. Also, in cases such as these, it is almost certain that different suppliers would compete with one another in terms of offering the customers in a given area long-term contractual guarantees concerning rates and service, so that when a company did succeed in becoming the sole supplier, it would operate under the terms of such a contract and not be able to impose arbitrarily high rates even temporarily. Under such an arrangement, an excessive rate or price would certainly not mean one that was arbitrarily increased by

a supplier, but, at most, one that failed to reflect improvements in efficiency made by other, potential suppliers. But even this situation could not long exist, if others possess the legal freedom of entry into the field.[26]

5. The Dependence of the Division of Labor on the Freedom of Economic Inequality

A division-of-labor society depends on the institution of economic inequality, insofar as the latter results from the process of economic competition or, more broadly, from individuals freely engaging in production and exchange, whether they are in competition with one another or not.

Economic inequality inexorably emerges from the freedom of the individual to pursue his own prosperity and to keep as his own whatever he achieves. It emerges simply because not everyone is equally intelligent, talented, ambitious, or hardworking, or saves as great a proportion of his income. In effect, it emerges as the consequence of different individuals enacting different degrees of economic causation.[27]

A division-of-labor society depends on economic inequality in the sense that it depends on individuals being free and motivated to produce. The abolition of economic inequality would mean the abolition of all connection between an individual's efforts and his income. It would be tantamount to the abolition of causality in the receipt of income.

To understand why this would be the result, imagine that a group of just ten people were formed whose members agreed to share equally all the income earned by each of them. Now imagine that a member of this group found a way to increase the income he earns by some given amount. Since he has to turn it over to the group and share it equally with the other nine members of the group, the personal benefit which he would obtain would be only *one-tenth* of that amount.[28]

If the group consisted of a thousand people, then any individual who increased or decreased the income he earned by any given amount, would personally experience a gain or loss of only one *one-thousandth* of that amount: he would personally gain or lose only one dollar for every one thousand dollars by which he increased or decreased the income of the group. If, as the egalitarians desire, the group consisted of the whole population of the United States or of the world, then for any given amount by which an individual increased or decreased the income of the group, he would increase or decrease the income available to him personally by only *one 250-millionth or one 5-billionth of that amount.*

It is obvious that once the size of the egalitarian group becomes substantial—probably anything much in excess of ten—no significant connection can exist between what an individual produces and what he receives. And, what is also very important, no significant connection can exist between what an individual produces and what *any other particular individual receives.*

In a group as small as ten, say, especially if it consists of close friends and relatives, an individual might rationally consider the effect of his actions on the income available to the other members of the group and give it substantial weight in deciding how much to produce. But in any large group, the individual loses the power significantly to affect the income available to any other individual, as well as losing the power significantly to affect the income available to himself. In a group of a thousand, a million, or a billion, nothing the average individual does can significantly affect the income received by his wife and children or parents and friends; even their combined share is an insignificant part of the group's total income. Nothing he does can have any significant effect on the income of the group as a whole or, therefore, on any given proportion of that income, for he is only one among many, and his production, a small part of the total production. In collectivizing his product and spreading it over a large group, egalitarianism destroys the ability of the great majority of individuals to achieve results that are of significance *to anyone.*

The average person is capable of accomplishing results that are large in relation to himself, and large in relation to his immediate family. But very few people are capable of accomplishing results that are large in relation to significantly greater numbers of people. It is as though egalitarianism, seeing that individuals had legs easily strong enough to support their own weight, demanded that each individual's legs had to support the weight of the whole human race as the requirement for his being permitted to walk. To make it the job of the individual to improve his own life and well-being only insofar as he equally improves the life and well-being of everyone else in the country or the world is a demand that is fully comparable.

If implemented, it would give everyone the incentive to do as little as possible. In the same way that doubling one's production, if that were possible, would increase one's own income by only one 250-millionth, if egalitarianism were practiced on a national scale—or by one 5-billionth, if it were practiced on a world scale—and thus would not be undertaken, so getting away with not producing at all would reduce one's own income only by that amount.[29] Increasing one's production would not be of perceptible benefit to anyone, and decreasing it would not be a perceptible loss to anyone. As a result, everyone would have the incentive to do nothing.

It should be obvious that equality of income implies *forced labor*—because, as shown, it eliminates the earning of income as an incentive to work. If people are to work without income as the incentive, the only remaining means of getting them to work is force.

It is true that there are other positive incentives for working besides income—such as the enjoyment of the work itself. But for the great majority of jobs, this factor exists in a form that is closely related to the earning of income and is largely felt only after the work is completed and the satisfaction of supporting oneself can be experienced. For example, no one digs ditches, hauls garbage, mines coal, works on an assembly line or in an office, or is even president of a bank, for the sheer love of his work, apart from all connection with the income it brings him. And even in the cases in which the work all by itself may really be a source of pleasure—for example, in the arts and sciences—this would not be sufficient to induce the amount of work that is presently done and that only the earning of income elicits. For example, I personally very much enjoy lecturing on economics and would want to continue my teaching career even if I were a millionaire and did not need the income from it. But instead of teaching two or three classes every term, I might want to teach only one class every other term. In the absence of personal material incentives, the only way of inducing any significant amount of work is by means of force.

There is an exception to the inability of individuals to achieve perceptible results in relation to large groups. This is the case of individuals of unusually great ability. A great scientist, inventor, or businessman is capable of increasing production so greatly that the whole world can experience a perceptible benefit. Yet this exception certainly does not represent a case in which economic equality would be practicable. On the contrary, precisely this case presupposes the possibility of *very great economic inequality.*

No scientist, inventor, or businessman should be imagined to be motivated to devote his life to raising the standard of living of the world by one, two, five, or x percent in order that he may, as part of the process, raise his own standard of living by one, two, five, or x percent. That would be an absurdly bad bargain: to work so hard and achieve so much for the rest of the world and so little for oneself.

The main value that a scientist achieves is the intellectual satisfaction of making his discoveries. In his case, this may stand in the place of any very great material reward. But inventors generally require the prospect of substantial material rewards, or they will not devote the time and effort or go to the expense that is necessary to make an invention. And as for businessmen, who are the ones who actually implement the work of scientists and inventors—who search out and perfect the inventions, and who often set the scientists and inventors to work in the first place—their work takes place for virtually no other reason than as the means of accumulating a personal fortune, and, indeed, is possible for the most part, only to the extent that they have already accumulated one. This last follows from the fact that only to the degree that businessmen possess capital are they able to implement their ideas—that is, to buy or build the necessary factories and machines, purchase the necessary materials and supplies, and hire the necessary workers. Ford, Rockefeller, and Carnegie, for example, could raise the standard of living of the world only in the course of accumulating their fortunes, and only on the basis of the fortunes they had already accumulated.[30]

Thus, the whole foundation of individuals of exceptional ability being able to act on a scale that raises the standard of living of everyone is the existence of enormous economic inequality, in the form of their being able to accumulate personal fortunes both as the incentive and as the means for raising the general standard of living.

The demand for economic equality turns out to be opposed to causality in a double respect: in respect both to the incentives for production and to the means of production. It would deprive the average person of the incentive to produce by depriving his productive effort of virtually all effect on his own or any other individual's standard of living. It would deprive the exceptionally able person of the incentive to produce by making the effect of his productive effort on his standard of living too small and by depriving him of the material means of achieving very great productive effects in the first place.

It should be realized that economic inequality plays a vital role in connection with the institutions of saving and capital accumulation and economic competition. The highest incomes in a capitalist society are those earned by successful businessmen. Insofar as such incomes represent the earning of high rates of profit on capital invested, the greater part of them tends to be saved and reinvested as the means of accumulating a fortune. Fortunes are earned by earning a high rate of profit on a rapidly growing capital—a capital which grows rapidly because most of the high rate of profit is constantly reinvested.[31] High incomes are also frequently of the kind that must be regarded as temporary or exceptional by their recipients—for example, the incomes of authors of best-selling books and of successful professional athletes and movie stars. If such people want to enjoy the benefit of their currently high incomes over the course of their whole lives, during most of which they will probably not earn comparably high incomes, they must save a very substantial portion of them.[32]

It is for these reasons that a close, observable relationship exists between relatively high incomes and high rates of saving out of income, and that attempts to restrict economic inequality must substantially reduce saving and capital accumulation.

The role played by economic inequality in connection with economic competition is that it profoundly influences the areas in which people choose to compete. For example, the fact that Mr. A the engineer earns substantially more than Mr. B the mechanic ensures that Mr. A will not compete against Mr. B for the job of a mechanic, even though he might make a much better mechanic. The inequality of income leads people to compete only in the areas of those of their talents that pay the most, and to abstain from competing in the areas of their talents that pay less. It operates, when necessary, to enable the less able actually to outcompete the more able, and thus it guarantees the less able a place in the economic system.[33]

Economic inequality, of course, can also be the product of government coercion, as occurs under feudalism and socialism, or as the result of any other arrangement under which the government grants privileges or imposes arbitrary burdens.[34] This latter sort of economic inequality is of a radically different character and is not only totally unnecessary, but also positively inimical, to a division-of-labor society. This is the case because the government's establishment of such inequalities deprives producers of a more or less considerable part of their product or income and directly infringes their freedom to produce in the first place. In so doing, it deprives producers both of the incentive to produce and even, in varying measure, of the very possibility of producing. It deprives them of the very possibility of producing insofar as it establishes arbitrary economic inequality by means of monopolistic restrictions against their entry into various lines of production. It also deprives them of the very possibility of producing insofar as it appropriates their incomes and thereby reduces their ability to save and invest, which deprives them of the ability to purchase the means of production. At the same time, in giving their product or income to others or in bestowing monopolistic privileges on others, the government rewards nonproducers or less efficient producers. Thus, economic inequality based on government coercion is economically destructive.

The fact that economic inequality can be the result of coercion is the reason why I did not describe it earlier in this chapter as an institution to which private ownership of the means of production is essential, as I did in the cases of the price system, the profit motive, economic competition, saving and capital accumulation, and ex-

change and money. Private property and private ownership of the means of production are essential only to
earned inequalities of wealth and income—that is, to
inequalities arising out of differences in the ability and
willingness to produce and save, where the freedom to
own and use property is essential. By the same token,
unearned inequalities of wealth and income—that is,
inequalities forcibly imposed by the government—represent a violation of property rights and thus of the
institution of private property and private ownership of
the means of production. For they entail depriving people
of their property or the freedom to use their property,
including, of course, their means of production.[35]

Thus it should be understood that at a fundamental
level the case for economic inequality that I have presented is not at all a case for economic inequality per se,
but only for the economic inequality that results from the
existence of individual freedom and respect for individual rights. (Such inequality, of course, includes that
which is based on inherited wealth insofar as the wealth
was accumulated by means of production and saving
under free competition and then must be maintained by
the heirs in the face of free competition.[36])

In connection with the distinction between the sources
of economic inequality, it is worth noting that economic
inequality that is founded on economic freedom is accompanied by much less in the way of visible inequality
than is economic inequality founded on the initiation of
physical force. This is because, as I will show in Chapter
9, the economic inequality that is based on economic
freedom, serves to raise the standard of living of all.[37] As
a result, under economic freedom, even the poorest strata
of society consume substantial and progressively increasing quantities of wealth. Thus, the inequality that
prevails is not one of a contrast between those who are
starving, half-naked, and living in hovels, and those who
are fat, clad in furs, and living in castles, as is the case
under feudal inequality, for example. Rather it is an
inequality between those who are rich enough to drive
Chevrolet or Ford automobiles, and those who are rich
enough to drive Cadillacs or Rolls Royces. Under modern capitalism, everyone who works is well-fed, comfortably housed, and attractively dressed. Indeed, it often
takes an expert to distinguish between the clothing worn
by a well-dressed secretary and that worn by a million-
airess.

Failure to realize that the economic inequality that
results from economic freedom and capitalism is less
extreme than the economic inequality that is based on the
initiation of physical force, sometimes leads to the absurd conclusion that forcible restrictions on the freedom
of economic inequality can promote prosperity. Thus one

compares the extreme inequality of semi-feudal societies
such as Saudi Arabia, with the lesser inequality of relatively free societies such as the United States, and attributes the greater prosperity of the latter to their greater
equality rather than to their greater freedom. The fact is,
of course, that it is greater freedom which is responsible
both for greater prosperity and for a less extreme degree
of economic inequality, while forcible restrictions on the
freedom of economic inequality only serve to undermine
prosperity.[38]

Egalitarianism and the Abolition of Cost: The Example of Socialized Medicine

In addition to encouraging people to do nothing, egalitarianism also leads them to demand everything. It is
tantamount to the abolition not only of causality in the
earning of income, but also of cost in the spending of
income. To make something free to the individual and
chargeable to the group as a whole, is to make the
consumption of the individual virtually costless—both
to himself and to every other individual.

Socialized medicine provides an excellent illustration
of this principle. When visits to doctors are made free to
the individual and chargeable to the taxpayers collectively, then each individual perceives the benefit of his
going to a doctor, while he and every other taxpayer
experiences a personal cost equal to the cost of the visit
divided by the number of millions of taxpayers. In such
circumstances, every individual is encouraged to take
advantage of the situation and, as a result, the overall cost
to everyone actually ends up greatly increasing.

What happens is this: A doctor's visit that might cost
an individual fifty dollars, is passed on to, say, one
hundred million taxpayers, to each of whom it costs a
hundred-millionth of fifty dollars. But now, perhaps, two
hundred million people each want to make five times as
many visits to doctors, and so the total cost to everyone
ends up being vastly greater than it would otherwise have
been. Furthermore, the absence of cost to the individual
patient is responsible for an enormous increase in the
amount of medical tests, hospitalizations, and surgeries
performed, which add even more to the cost of the
system. And, of course, there is the substantial overhead
cost added by the need for a large bureaucracy to admin-
ister the system.

Ironically, even though they pay vastly more, people
end up obtaining *less* actual medical service than before.
In large measure, the effect of the system is simply to
make doctors' and other medical fees rise and to create
shortages of doctors' time and hospital beds—as manifested in crowded waiting rooms and reduced time with
the individual patient, and in waiting lists to enter hospitals. A large portion of the additional medical tests,

hospitalizations, and surgeries is actually unnecessary, and serves to prevent or delay the meeting of genuine medical needs. The measures adopted to deal with these problems, such as controlling doctors' fees and their methods of treatment, and thereby thoroughly bureaucratizing the field, ultimately make medicine unattractive as a profession and deter talented individuals from entering it. In addition, they frequently serve to deny necessary treatment to people, since the government has no rational method of determining what is the appropriate treatment in the individual case.

In what is perhaps the supreme irony of the system, in efforts to control costs, the government ends up actually *opposing advances in medical technology*. It comes to regard such procedures as the implantation of artificial hearts as a major threat to its budget. This is with good reason, since, by the logic of socialized medicine, everyone who needs it is entitled to demand a procedure as soon as it becomes recognized as practicable. The result of this is that the normal, free-market incentives which work to reduce costs before something becomes available to a mass market are not present under socialized medicine. Thus, for these reasons, advances in medical technology become feared and arrested under socialized medicine.

In addition, in further cost-containment procedures, the government begins to restrict or prohibit whole categories of procedures, from cosmetic surgery to bypass operations. Such procedures are excluded from the socialized system on the grounds that they are "nonessential" or "too costly relative to the benefits obtained" (benefits for the government). Thus, people who under private medicine could have obtained such procedures by spending their own money for them are denied the ability to obtain them. They are denied this ability because taxes to pay for the medical care of others, and simply to squander, drain them of the necessary financial resources. The possibility of obtaining the necessary procedures, of course, can also end up being prohibited outright, if the socialized system achieves a complete monopoly and decides not to perform the procedures or not to make them available to specific categories of individuals.

Along these lines, the government begins to deny medical care to those whom it regards as only "marginally valuable to society," such as the aged. From the perspective of the government's budget, medical care for the aged is a poor investment: the cost is high and the remaining ability of the aged to pay taxes is relatively small in view both of the limitation of their remaining years and of their possibly diminished capacity, or total lack of capacity, for working and earning taxable income. Thus it should not be surprising that under socialized

medicine in Great Britain, for example, bypass operations are made difficult to obtain for people over fifty-five years of age, and an elderly person who breaks a hip is likely to die before being able to obtain corrective surgery.

Thus, in an irony with truly ominous implications, the same system of socialized medicine which began in the United States largely as a means of financing the medical bills of the aged has the long-run potential of turning the aged into sacrificial victims. It has the potential not only of depriving them of all the advances in medical care that they could have obtained in a free market and of making them share in the general decline in the quality of medical care that must result from socialized medicine, but also of placing them in a position of helplessness, in which they are the mercy of a system which attaches little value to their lives.

The fact that socialized medicine has such results should not come as a surprise. It is a profound mistake to believe that there is such a thing as any form of free lunch from the government in the first place. And only someone very foolish indeed should be surprised that when the government buys him lunch it is not eager to increase its expenses on his behalf and thus is not willing to buy him a steak for lunch. He should not be surprised that the government will much more likely end up placing him on short rations, in order to have more funds left over for paying the bills for those whose needs it considers to have a higher "social priority." Thus, anyone who wants his medical care to be free by virtue of having the government pay for it, should not expect very much or very good medical care. He should rather expect his medical care and treatment to resemble that of the general care and treatment of an unfortunate child whose life has been entrusted to uncaring and potentially cruel stepparents. The state will likely prove just such a guardian of the aged. A child, of course, does not usually select such stepparents. The aged of today, in a state of knowledge below that which should be expected of children, are selecting such a guardian for themselves.[39]

It should be realized that the collectivization of medical costs—an essential feature of socialized medicine—has existed for many years in the United States. It was brought into existence not only by the medicare and medicaid programs that date from the mid-1960s but also by unsound private medical insurance practices imposed by government intervention, and which date back to World War II. Like medicare and medicaid, and socialized medicine in general, most private medical insurance plans of the last fifty years give medical care the appearance of being free or substantially free to the user, and thus substantially increase the demand for it and its cost.

Such private insurance came into being as a substitute for socialized medicine and was greeted as a means of forestalling the enactment of socialized medicine. It was extended to a significant part of the population first through a World-War-II decision by the price-control authorities that while ordinary, take-home wages were subject to controls, employer-financed medical insurance for employees was not. And then, following the war, in the remaining years of the 1940s and in the 1950s, it was extended to the great bulk of the population by the contract demands of coercive labor unions, which most nonunion employers felt obliged to meet, as part of their efforts to remain nonunion. The growth of such insurance was also fostered by the fact that from the beginning employer contributions to medical insurance on behalf of employees was made tax exempt, while the payment of the same amount of compensation directly to employees has been fully taxable to the employees.

Government Intervention, Democracy, and the Destruction of the Individual's Causal Role

Essentially the same kind of destruction of causality as results from the establishment of equality of income or an equal sharing of costs among the entire population results from all governmental usurpations of power and responsibility. When, for example, the government comes to decide the manner in which individuals provide for their old age, or to decide matters pertaining to education, it destroys the ability of the individual to choose for himself.

The fact that the government may be subject to the verdict of democratic elections only serves to highlight this fact. Instead of signifying that nothing is wrong, because the government is still subject to the will of the people, the fact is that the power of the *individual* to determine his own life is submerged in that of an enormous mass of voters. True enough, under democracy if a majority of a voting population ranging from several hundred to a hundred million or more (depending on the level of the election—local, state, or federal) votes against an existing policy, the policy will likely be changed. But this does not mean, as the supporters of government intervention often argue, that the government is still "controlled by us." As far as any individual is concerned, the government is totally out of control.

For example, when it comes to the use of savings in the so-called individual retirement accounts that the government supervises (let alone the use of savings siphoned off into the social security system), instead of the individual being able to decide for himself that he wants to use a portion of his savings to make the down payment on a home, he must wait until tens of millions of other citizens have become ready to join with him to bring about this possibility. In the same way, instead of an individual set of parents being able to decide to send their child to an elementary school that is close to their home, they may have to wait until that possibility is established by means of a national election.

Thus, to the extent government intervention exists, even under democracy, the individual by himself is prevented from accomplishing what he wants to accomplish. His power to act as an individual causal agent is destroyed. For government control under democracy still means collectivization of the power to make decisions. And thus from the perspective of any individual the result for all practical purposes is as much a loss of the freedom of choice and the power to act as exists under dictatorship. Only limitation of the powers of government can secure individual freedom and the ability of the individual to act as a causal agent. Violations of individual freedom by democratic majorities are as much violations of individual freedom and the ability of the individual to act as those imposed by dictators.

Summary

The preceding sections have shown why the division of labor is entirely dependent on the institutions of capitalism. Section 1 showed how it depends on private property and private ownership of the means of production as the basis for enabling people to act and produce separately and independently of one another. Such independence is essential if people are to be able to take advantage of the fundamental facts underlying the gains from the division of labor, namely, that individuals possess separate, independent minds and separate, independent knowledge. This section showed that socialism and central planning are incompatible with the necessary intellectual division of labor that must exist in order to have rational economic planning. It showed why the existence of the price system is essential for such planning and both why the price system depends on the profit motive and the freedom of competition and why these two institutions in turn depend in turn on private ownership of the means of production. The section also showed why the price system depends on exchange and money and saving and capital accumulation and why they too are dependent on the institution of private ownership of the means of production.

Subsequent sections explained the direct dependence of the division of labor on the institutions of saving and capital accumulation, exchange and money, competition, and the freedom of economic inequality. Saving and capital accumulation were shown to provide the essential basis for making possible the production of goods requiring more or less considerable lapses of time between the performance of labor and the appearance of the resulting product. Saving and capital accumulation were also shown to be responsible for initially raising the productivity of labor to the point where labor could be spared from food production for the production of other things, and then for making it possible for wage earners and suppliers to be paid within a reasonable period of time after the performance of their work, and, finally, to provide the foundation for larger-scale production and thus the basis for carrying the division of labor further at any given stage of production.

Exchange and money were shown to be essential to the channelling of goods from their producers to their consumers. The existence specifically of money and monetary exchange was shown to be essential to overcoming the problem posed under barter of the need for the existence of a double coincidence of wants as the precondition of an exchange. In overcoming this problem, the existence of money was shown to make possible a radical widening of the extent of the division of labor. Money was further shown to be vital to the existence of a division-of-labor society in making possible economic calculations and comparisons. The gross injustice of regarding money as the root of all evil was pointed out, along with other common errors found in the antimoney mentality.

Economic competition was shown to perform the vital function of determining the ongoing organization of a division-of-labor society with respect to the choice of which persons are to hold which occupations, which products are to be produced for which specific markets, and which technological methods of producing any given product are to be used. Economic competition, or at least the freedom of such competition, was also shown to be necessary to prevent a division-of-labor society from being placed at the mercy of the arbitrary demands of various vital industries or occupations.

Finally, the existence of economic inequality, resulting from unequal degrees of achievement, was shown to be essential to individuals being able to act as causal agents in accomplishing results, whether within a division-of-labor society or outside of a division-of-labor society. The alternative to such economic inequality was shown to be forced labor, as the only means of inducing people to work in the absence of economic incentives. In addition, such economic inequality was shown to play a major role in promoting saving and capital accumulation and in making it possible for the less able to compete with the more able. The imposition of equality in the meeting of costs was shown to be tantamount to the abolition of cost from the perspective of the individual user of a good or service. The destructive consequences of such impositions were explained, using socialized medicine as

an example. And then, government intervention in general, even under democracy, was shown to represent the destruction of the individual's ability to act as a causal agent, inasmuch as it requires that before the individual can accomplish what he wants to accomplish, he must first join with perhaps millions or tens of millions of others to make it possible.

PART B

ELEMENTS OF PRICE THEORY: DEMAND, SUPPLY, AND COST OF PRODUCTION

Before proceeding to the substance of price theory, it is necessary to deal with matters which occupy the major portion of most of today's courses and textbooks on the subject, namely, the concepts of demand and supply, and, in particular, their representation as curves. This material is included in this book in part for the benefit of economics instructors who are obliged to present a geometric analysis using such curves. It is offered in the hope that if they are otherwise inclined to adopt this book, they will not have to turn elsewhere in order to expose their students to such curves.

Frankly, while I believe that the ability to understand and visualize downward sloping demand curves, and vertical lines as representing supply, is of some significant value, I do not attach very great weight to geometrical analysis in economics. I share with von Mises the conviction that the substantive relationships of economics must all be explained by an essentially verbal analysis and that the drawing of such curves is mere byplay as far as real economic analysis is concerned.[40] I present my substantive, verbal analysis of price theory in the next three chapters of this book. Indeed, I believe that geometrical analysis using demand and supply curves masks some major confusions. The clearing up of these confusions is an important objective of the remainder of this chapter and is the main justification for including the extended discussions of the derivation of supply curves and of the prevailing confusions between the concepts of supply and cost of production. On a positive note, in the following pages I explain the various meanings that are attached to the words demand and supply, demonstrate why price and quantity demanded vary inversely, and present what is genuinely valuable in being able to visualize demand and supply curves.

The connection of the following discussions to my theme that the division of labor depends on the institutions of capitalism is perforce indirect. As I have already indicated, the division of labor depends on the existence of the price system both for its successful functioning and, indeed, for its very existence. The following discussions are preliminary to the detailed demonstration of that proposition.

1. The Meaning of Demand and Supply

Perhaps no proposition of economics is more frequently uttered than that prices are determined by demand and supply. Yet in the history of economics, and to an important extent even at the present time, the concepts of demand and supply have had more than one meaning, which can make the above proposition highly ambiguous.

According to the classical economists, demand is to be understood predominantly as an amount of expenditure of money, such as $1 billion, while supply is to be understood as an amount of a good or service offered for sale. On this basis, prices are to be conceived as formed by *the ratio* of the demand to the supply, with demand as the numerator and supply as the denominator, and to vary in direct proportion to the demand and in inverse proportion to the supply. The classical view of price determination by demand and supply is expressed in the formula

$$P = \frac{D}{S},$$

where P is the price, D is the demand, and S is the supply.[41]

The classical economists also frequently defined demand as "the will combined with the power of purchas-

ing."[42] Here demand is to be understood in terms of the goods or services one is actually able to obtain by virtue of the expenditure of money. While certainly not inconsistent with the view of demand as an expenditure of money, this is a different concept of demand. To avoid confusion, it is best to describe demand in this second sense as *real* demand, with the word "real" denoting the fact that the quantity of goods or services one can obtain for the money expended are essential.

As used in contemporary economics, the concepts demand and supply mean *the set of quantities buyers are prepared to buy or sellers to sell at varying prices, arranged in descending (ascending) order, all other things being equal.* Viewed in this light, the concepts refer to hypothetical schedules, which when diagrammed, appear as curves. Illustrations of such hypothetical schedules and curves appear in Table 5–1 and Figure 5–1 respectively.

In the usage of contemporary economics, the entire set of prices in Table 5–1, ranging from $10 down to $3, together with the entire set of quantities demanded at those prices, ranging from 100 up to 500, represents *one demand schedule—the* demand—for the good in question. Strictly speaking, the concept of the demand schedule embraces prices ranging from zero to infinity, proceeding by the smallest possible increments in price, and all of the quantities demanded at all of these prices. The demand schedule presented in Table 5–1, therefore, represents only a few selected points on the actual demand schedule.

When diagrammed, as in Figure 5–1, the demand schedule appears as the demand curve *DD.* (In Figure

Table 5–1			
Hypothetical Demand and Supply Schedules			
Price	Quantity Demanded	Quantity Supplied	Quantity Demanded II
$10	100	500	250
9	125	325	300
8	160	275	400
7	200	200	500
6	250	150	600
5	325	100	725
4	400	50	850
3	500	0	900

5–1, in accordance with the usual practice, price is shown on the vertical axis, where it is labeled *P*, and quantity, on the horizontal axis, where it is labeled *Q*.) The curve results from drawing a line through the various point values derived from Table 5–1. Ideally, the curve would be drawn by plotting all the point values derived from a complete demand schedule. The demand curve of Figure 5–1, of course, represents a limited range of the demand schedule, and most of its values are derived by interpolation between the few selected values that were present in Table 5–1.

In the same way, the entire set of prices and of quantities supplied, ranging from $10 and 500 units down to $3 and 0 units, together with all prices and quantities supplied above and below these limits, represents *one supply schedule—the* supply—of the good in question. When diagrammed in Figure 5–1 on the basis of the selected data appearing in Table 5–1, the supply schedule appears as the supply curve *SS*.

Accordingly, in the usage of contemporary economics, a change in demand or supply does not refer to a change in the quantity demanded or supplied within a given demand or supply schedule, or along a given demand or supply curve. For example, the increase in the quantity demanded from 100 to 125, accompanying the fall in price from $10 to $9 is not described as an increase in demand, but merely as an increase in the quantity demanded within a given demand schedule or along a given demand curve. A change in demand or supply is

said to occur only when there is *a change in the schedule or curve.* For example, the column labeled "Quantity Demanded II" in Table 5–1 is said to represent an increase in demand. Here, the quantities demanded are greater *at the same set of prices.* A change in demand or supply is held to mean a change in the quantities demanded or supplied at the same set of prices, or, equivalently, a change in the prices accompanying the same set of quantities demanded or supplied.

The demand curve *D′D′* in Figure 5–1 is an illustration of a shift in the demand curve. In contrast with the curve *DD*, it shows larger quantities demanded at the same prices, and higher prices offered for the same quantities. It is drawn higher and to the right of *DD*. By the same token, a fall in demand would be illustrated by a movement from *D′D′* back to *DD*.

In the view of contemporary economics, determination of price by demand and supply means *determination of price by the intersection point of demand and supply curves.* A rise in demand is held to increase both price and quantity supplied by virtue of the higher demand curve intersecting the given supply curve at a point up and to the right on the latter. Similarly, a fall in demand is held to decrease both price and quantity supplied by virtue of the lower demand curve intersecting the given supply curve at a point down and to the left on the latter. Likewise, an increase in supply, is held to decrease price and increase quantity demanded, while a decrease in supply is held to increase price and reduce quantity

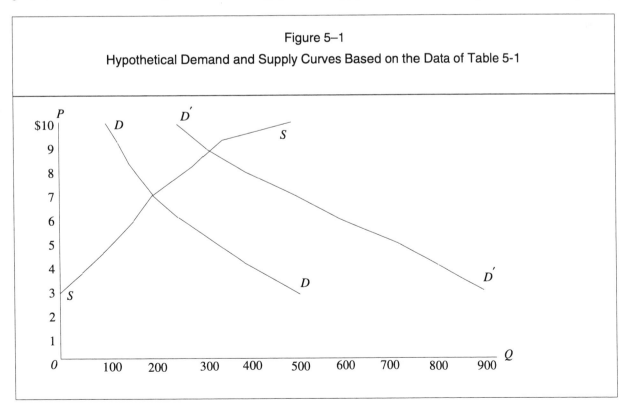

Figure 5–1

Hypothetical Demand and Supply Curves Based on the Data of Table 5-1

demanded. (To show an increase in supply in Figure 5–1, the reader can draw in a new supply curve, down and to the right of *SS*, and more or less parallel to it, which would intersect either *DD* or *D'D'* at a point down and to the right of the intersection point given by *SS*. Movement from that curve back up to *SS* could then be used to depict the effects of a fall in supply.)

The classical and contemporary concepts of demand and supply are in agreement concerning the direction of price changes resulting from changes in demand or supply: on both views, price varies in the same direction as changes in demand and in the opposite direction of changes in supply. Moreover, it should be noted that when the demand schedule or curve of contemporary economics *changes,* the change coincides with a change in demand according to the classical concept as well. For what is implied is a change in the expenditure of money for any given quantity of a good supplied. For example, on demand curve *DD*, the price corresponding to a quantity demanded of 400 is $4; on demand curve *D'D'*, the price corresponding to this same quantity demanded is $8. Thus, in the first case, demand in the classical sense is $1,600 (400 x $4) and in the second case, it is $3,200 (400 x $8). Whenever, there is a movement of the demand curve, a corresponding change in expenditure is implied for any given quantity of the good. This is implied by the geometry of the situation, because expenditure for the good equals any given quantity of it times the corresponding price indicated by the demand curve; insofar as the demand curve changes and thus the price

corresponding to the given quantity changes, the expenditure for the good must change to the same extent.

The classical and contemporary concepts of demand and supply come closest together in the usage of the Austrian school. In the view of the Austrian school, supply fundamentally means a given quantity of a good or service available for sale.[43] Thus, in essence, the Austrian school retains the meaning given the concept of supply by the classical economists. In geometrical terms, when the Austrian economists describe price as determined by demand and supply, they have in mind the kind of demand curve represented by *DD* in Figure 5–1, but a supply curve constituted by a vertical line drawn upward from the point on the horizontal axis (the quantity axis) that represents the given amount of supply available. This is shown in Figure 5–2.[44]

In the Austrian view of things, depicted in Figure 5–2, the sellers are presumed merely to be prepared to sell their given supply of goods at the best price they can obtain, from zero on up.[45] This is because in the context of a division-of-labor economy, the sellers normally possess goods in such great quantities that most of their supply has zero marginal utility—zero personal value—to them. As a result, on the Austrian view, prices that are determined by supply and demand are determined on the basis of the valuations of "the marginal pair of buyers" alone.[46]

What this means is that the marginal utility attached to the price of any good that is purchased must simultaneously be below the marginal utility of the last unit of the good purchased and above the marginal utility of one

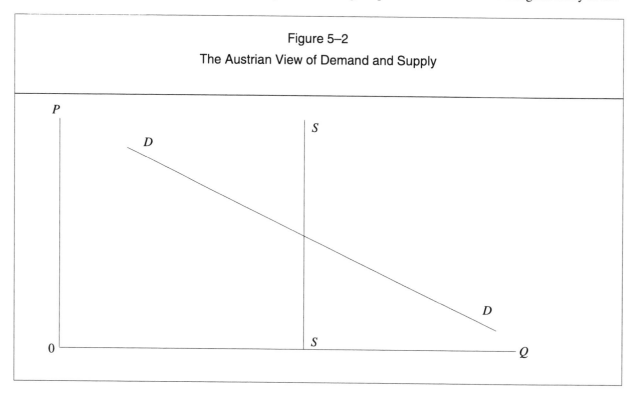

Figure 5–2

The Austrian View of Demand and Supply

additional unit more of the good that potentially might be purchased. For example, it implies that if a supply of one million shirts of a given kind is to be met with a quantity demanded of shirts that is also one million, then the price of a shirt must be such that the marginal utility of the price of the shirt is simultaneously below the marginal utility of the one millionth shirt and above the marginal utility of a potential one millionth and first shirt. The marginal utility of the price of the shirt must, in effect, be sandwiched between the utility of the marginal pair of shirts, that is, simultaneously below the utility of the marginal shirt and above the utility of the potential first submarginal shirt (that is, of one potential additional shirt more).

This is the necessary condition of equalizing the quantity demanded of *any* good with any given supply of that good that is to be sold. The marginal utility attaching to the price being below the marginal utility of the good in question is the condition of all the buyers of the good finding its purchase to be the source of a gain and hence worthwhile. By the same token, the marginal utility attaching to the price of the good being above the marginal utility of a potential additional unit of the good is the condition of it not being worthwhile for anyone to attempt to purchase an additional quantity of the good, and thus of the quantity of the good demanded not being greater than the given supply available. Whenever a case exists in which a given quantity of a good or service is to be sold in a free market, its price will tend to be determined within the limits set by the valuations of the marginal pair of buyers—that is, the marginal utility attached to the good by the buyer of the marginal unit and the marginal utility attached to the good by the potential buyer of one additional unit more, that is, the first submarginal unit.[47]

In this book, the concepts of demand and supply will be used both in their classical and contemporary—especially Austrian—significations. The classical concept of demand as an amount of expenditure of money will be found to be extremely useful when dealing with questions pertaining to the operation of the economic system as a whole. In that context, it can be related, via the quantity theory of money, directly to the quantity of money in the economic system, which will be shown to be its main determinant.[48] The fact that economy-wide, aggregate demand in the classical sense is determined primarily by the quantity of money in the economic system makes it essentially independent of changes in aggregate supply in the classical sense, which latter can be understood as operating in the face of a given aggregate demand and thus to result in inversely proportionate changes in the general price level. In dealing with demand at the level of individual industries and companies,

however—where in essence it is a matter of explaining the adjustment of a part of the economic system to the rest of the economic system—this book will make use of the contemporary, Austrian concept of demand. This procedure will not be found to be in any way inconsistent with the use of the classical concept of demand at the level of the economic system as whole. Rather, it will be found to reflect the fact that at the level of individual industries and companies *competitive elements* are present which are mutually canceling at the level of the economic system as a whole.

The difference in treatment ultimately comes down to the fact that at the level of the individual industry or company, demand in the classical sense cannot be taken as independent of supply in the classical sense. Changes in supply at this level represent changes in competitive conditions among the various firms and industries, which cause changes in the pattern of expenditure for their various goods and services. This is because a change in the supply of any one good, such as automobiles or copper, means a change in its supply relative to the supply of other goods and a change in its price relative to the prices of other goods. If the supply of the good in question increases, say, and does so in the absence of increases in the supply of other goods, the marginal utility of this particular good may fall precipitously because of its additional supply, thus leading to the amount of money spent to buy it being reduced. For example, while people almost certainly would like to have an additional supply of automobiles, they want them along with more and better housing and clothing, more travel and entertainment, and so on. Until they can have more of all of these things, they will not be prepared to accept merely an additional supply of automobiles except at disproportionately lower prices.[49] On the other hand, in many circumstances the lower price of the given good may enable it to compete more effectively with other goods serving the same purposes, as we shall see very shortly. To the extent that this is so, the amount of money spent to buy it will increase. Thus, while demand in the classical sense can be taken as independent of supply in the classical sense at the level of the economic system as a whole, it cannot be so taken at the level of the individual industry or firm. Hence, at this level, it is necessary to resort to the contemporary, Austrian concept of demand.

2. The Law of Demand

A fundamental proposition of economics, applicable both to the classical and to the contemporary, Austrian concept of demand, is *the law of demand*. This is the fact that *other things being equal, the quantity demanded of a good is the greater, the lower is its price, and the smaller, the higher is its price.*

At the level of the economic system as a whole, the law of demand follows directly from the fact that the need and desire for wealth has no limit and that a fall in the prices of goods and services is all that is necessary to enable any given expenditure of money to purchase a larger quantity of goods and services. The fall in prices expands the buying power of any given amount of expenditure and is potentially capable of making it sufficient to purchase any volume of aggregate supply, however large.[50]

At the level of the individual industry or company, however, a fall in any given price always means much more than the fact that the average of prices is now lower relative to the willingness and ability to spend money and thus that the same aggregate expenditure can buy a larger total of goods. As stated, it also means a change in the prices of individual goods and services relative to one another.

For example, an increase in the supply and fall in the price of cotton means a fall in the price of cotton relative to the price of wool and other goods that cotton can more or less satisfactorily be substituted for. As a result, the purchase of cotton becomes competitively favored over their purchase. For now, in purchasing it, one can accomplish the common objective for which cotton, wool, and all the other relevant substitutes are means, and do so without having to forgo as large a quantity of alternative goods as previously. A lower price of cotton relative to the price of wool means that if one buys cotton instead of wool, one still obtains clothing (albeit, of course, with the specific advantages or disadvantages associated with cotton) and can now do so while forgoing a smaller quantity of alternative goods than before relative to the quantity one must forgo to obtain clothing made of wool. This change results in an increase in the quantity demanded of cotton at its lower price, and a decrease in the quantity demanded of wool and of the other goods for which cotton is a substitute, at their given prices. In other words, the quantity demanded of cotton increases, and the demand for wool and the other goods for which cotton is a substitute decreases.

In the literature of contemporary economics, such a change in the quantity demanded of a given good as its price falls is described as "the substitution effect." This effect is equally present, of course, when the price of a good increases relative to the prices of the goods for which it can be substituted or which can be substituted for it.

As will become clear, the substitution effect is actually just a special case of the operation of the law of diminishing marginal utility. And I turn now to a demonstration of how the existence of diminishing marginal

utility explains why, other things being equal, the quantity of a good people are prepared to buy is greater at a lower price than at a higher price.[51]

The reason is that in order to purchase a good, people must attach greater marginal utility to the good than they attach to the price of the good. A lower marginal utility is attached to a lower price than to a higher price. This is because the price of a good is the measure of the alternative goods that must be forgone in order to purchase it. A lower price of any given good means that to be able to buy an additional quantity of it, the quantity of alternative goods that must be forgone in order to have the funds available to make its purchase is correspondingly reduced (assuming their prices are unchanged). Since, other things being equal, a smaller quantity of alternative goods represents a lower marginal utility than a larger quantity of alternative goods, this means that the marginal utility represented by a lower price is less than the marginal utility represented by a higher price. (The lower marginal utility of a smaller quantity of goods compared with that of a larger quantity of goods follows on the basis of all that was established about man's limitless need for wealth. If more wealth is better than less wealth, it must have more utility, and less wealth must have less utility.) Thus a lower price of a good means that in purchasing it, the marginal utility one forgoes in the purchase of other goods is less.

As a result, the marginal utility attached to a lower price tends to stand below the marginal utility of a larger number of units of a good than does the marginal utility attached to a higher price. The consequence is that the purchase of a larger number units is made advantageous at a lower price.

As illustration, imagine that an individual attaches marginal utilities of 40, 30, 20, and 10 to four successive units of given good. Imagine also that to the sum of $100 he attaches a marginal utility of 50, and to the sums $80, $60, $40, and $20, he attaches marginal utilities of 35, 25, 15, and 5, respectively. Thus, at a price of $100, he will not buy any of the good, because the marginal utility of its price, 50, stands above the marginal utility even of the very first unit of the good, which is 40. But at a price of $80, the marginal utility of the price, now 35, stands below the marginal utility of the first unit of the good. And thus this individual will buy one unit of the good. And for every further $20 reduction in the price, he will buy one additional unit, up to a total of four, because the lower marginal utilities attached to these lower prices stand below the marginal utilities of the successive units of the good.[52]

The role of the different alternative amounts of wealth that different prices represent can be seen in the following example, which deals with the hypothetical demand for radios. If the price of a radio is $100, then the purchase of a radio implies that one must forgo the purchase of whatever else that $100 might have bought— that is, an additional quantity or improvement in the quality of alternative goods that one consumes. In order to buy the radio, one must attach a marginal utility to it that is greater than the marginal utility one attaches to the $100 in any alternative line of spending. Those who buy radios at the price of $100 do attach a higher marginal utility to them than to the expenditure of the $100 in any other line or lines. Those who buy two, three, or more radios at the price of $100 attach a marginal utility to each of them that is above the marginal utility they attach to any other, alternative goods the $100 price could buy. By the same token, those who buy no radios at the price of $100, or who buy one radio but not two, or two but not three, and so on, do not buy the radio in question because they attach a marginal utility to it that is below the marginal utility they attach to the purchase of alternative goods with the $100 in question.

If, however, the price of radios fell to $90, say, then the quantity/quality of alternative goods that would have to be forgone in order to make possible the purchase of a radio would be correspondingly reduced. This would mean a reduction in the marginal utility that had to be forgone in order to purchase a radio. This lower, alternative marginal utility would now tend to stand below the marginal utility of an additional quantity of radios. In the face of having to forgo alternative goods purchasable with only $90 instead of $100, in order to secure a radio, there would be people who previously judged the marginal utility of a first, second, or third radio, or whichever, to be less than the marginal utility of its price, who would now decide that it was greater than the marginal utility of its price.

In this way, a lower price of any good, whether it has direct substitutes or not, acts to favor its purchase.

Indeed, as stated, the substitution effect is merely a special case of the operation of the law of diminishing marginal utility. When the price of one substitute falls relative to that of another, as is the case when the price of cotton falls and the price of wool stays the same, what creates the competitive advantage is precisely the fact that the marginal utility of the alternative goods which must be forgone in order to purchase the one becomes less relative to the alternative goods which must be forgone in order to purchase the other. This is what favors the cotton, namely, that by buying cotton rather than wool, one can still meet the common purpose, in this case having cloth or clothing, and yet have greater marginal utility in terms of other things than if one buys wool, because now one gives up less of other things to buy cotton.[53]

There is another major aspect of the competition that is present at the level of individual goods and services. A fall in the price of any given good, whether cotton, radios, or whatever, also means that to whatever extent people were already prepared to be purchasers of the good, they can now purchase the quantity they would otherwise have purchased, for a smaller expenditure of money. This means they will have correspondingly more money left over for the purchase either of more of that good or more of other things that they desire. For example, if one otherwise would buy 10 yards of cotton at $2 per yard, a fall in price to $1.50 per yard makes possible the purchase of the same 10 yards for only $15 instead of $20. This makes an additional $5 available for buying either additional cotton or additional quantities of other goods.

In contemporary economics textbooks, such availability of additional funds is called "the income effect." The income effect derives its name from the fact that the funds made available by the fall in price of something one already buys is viewed as similar to an increase in income with the price of the good unchanged.[54] Thus, the additional $5 made available as the result of the fall in the price of cotton that we have just imagined is viewed as the equivalent of a $5 increase in income with the price of cotton unchanged.

The so-called income effect also operates in accordance with the law of diminishing marginal utility. When, for example, the price of cotton falls, it is considerations of marginal utility that determine how the additional funds made available will be used in the purchase of additional goods. The additional funds will be used to purchase those additional goods which have the highest marginal utility.

Thus, the effect of a fall in the price of anything on the quantity of it demanded can be viewed as the combined effect of two things. One is an increase in available funds that results from the saving in purchasing the quantity of the good that would have been purchased without the fall in price. The other is the enhancement of the good's competitive position in relation to other goods.

These other, competing goods must be understood not only in the narrow sense of substitutes serving the same particular needs or wants, such as wool versus cotton, but also in the broader sense of goods in general, or combinations of goods, that compete in terms of their marginal utility for the expenditure of the same funds. A lower price of television sets, for example, is capable of drawing funds in competition with goods serving physically dissimilar needs or wants, such as housing or automobiles. This is because a lower price of television sets relative to housing or automobiles means that the marginal utility forgone in buying a television set is that much lower relative to the marginal utility forgone in buying housing or an automobile. This enhances the competitive position of television sets vis-à-vis housing and automobiles.

The operation of the law of diminishing marginal utility, both in and through the substitution and income effects and otherwise, is responsible for the existence of the law of demand, namely, that, other things being equal, the quantity of a good that is demanded moves in the opposite direction of its price. In the last analysis, the operation of the law of demand, and of the underlying principle of diminishing marginal utility, is tantamount to the fact that a lower price makes possible the acquisition of more wealth, which is always desired.

The Concept of Elasticity of Demand

Elements of the preceding discussion point the way to what has become an exceptionally prominent concept in contemporary economics, namely, that of *the elasticity of demand.* The elasticity of demand is typically defined as the percentage change in the quantity demanded of a good divided by the percentage in its price. As its name indicates, the concept seeks to measure the "stretch" or "shrinkage" in the quantity of a good or service demanded relative to changes in its price.

Three categories of demand are distinguished according to their degree of elasticity: elastic, inelastic, and unit elastic demands. Each is judged by the effect of a price change on total expenditure for the good (or, equivalently, on the total revenue derived from its sale). If expenditure (revenue) changes in the opposite direction of price, the demand is said to be elastic at that point—the stretch or shrinkage in the quantity demanded outweighs the change in price. In the case of an elastic demand, more is spent in buying the good at a lower price than at a higher price, and when the price rises, less is spent in buying the good. Here the change in the quantity demanded outweighs the change in the price.

If, on the other hand, expenditure (revenue) changes in the same direction as the price, the demand is said to be inelastic at that point—the stretch or shrinkage in the quantity demanded is insufficient to offset the change in price. In the case of an inelastic demand, more is spent in buying the good at a higher price than at a lower price, because of the relative lack of stretch or shrinkage in the quantity demanded.

Finally, if expenditure (revenue) for the good remains the same when the price changes, the demand is said to be unit elastic at that point, which means that the change in quantity demanded accompanying the change in price precisely counterbalances the change in price. When demand has unit elasticity, the change in quantity demanded is *inversely proportionate* to the change in price—

for example, a halving of price is accompanied by a doubling of quantity demanded, a cut to a third is accompanied by a tripling, and so on.

By far the most important example of unit elastic demand, and, at the same time, perhaps the only example that is not essentially accidental and passing, is *economy-wide, aggregate demand.* As previously stated, the volume of expenditure in the economic system as a whole tends to be the same so long as the quantity of money in the economic system is the same. Any increases or decreases in expenditure for particular goods or services are accompanied by equivalent decreases or increases in expenditure elsewhere in the economic system.

For example, an increase in expenditure for cotton, resulting from the operation of a strong substitution effect accompanying a lower price of cotton, is accompanied by a decrease in expenditure for wool and other substitutes. A possible resulting increase or decrease in the expenditure for clothing as a whole in such circumstances (depending on the marginal utility of additional clothing in comparison with the marginal utility of additional quantities of other things) would tend to be accompanied by a counterbalancing decrease or increase in the expenditure for things other than clothing. In the same way, a possible decrease in the expenditure for cotton, resulting from the existence of a weak substitution effect when its price falls, tends to be accompanied by an equivalent increase in the expenditure for other goods that is made possible by the availability of additional funds stemming from the fall in the price of cotton.

The principle here is that while competitive elements entailed in the substitution and income effects cause the expenditures for the products of individual industries and companies to vary in response to supply and price changes, nevertheless, in the very nature of the case, these elements, being competitive, cancel out when the level of analysis is raised to that of the economic system as a whole. Competition for expenditure takes place only *within the economic system,* among the various industries and firms that make up the economic system. It does not take place between the economic system and anything outside of the economic system.

Now a total expenditure for goods that is constant essentially so long as the quantity of money in the economic system is constant, is one in which price changes are necessarily accompanied by inversely proportionate changes in quantity demanded. Geometrically, the aggregate demand curve has the property that the area under the curve (found by multiplying the quantity demanded times the price) is a constant. The curve is asymptotic to both axes.[55] Such a demand curve is shown in Figure 5–3.

Turning now to the very different case of elastic demands, important examples of an elastic demand are

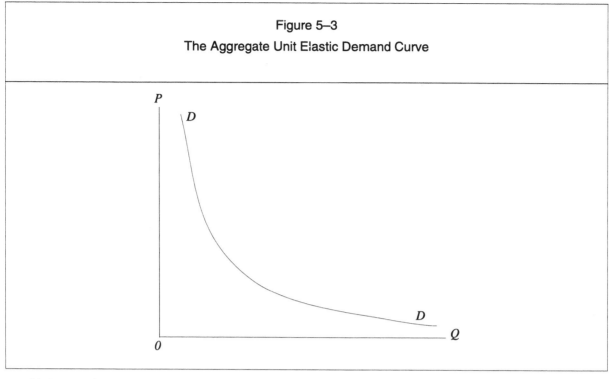

Figure 5–3
The Aggregate Unit Elastic Demand Curve

provided by goods which are presently luxuries, beyond the reach of most people, and which price reductions would bring within their reach. Equally important examples are provided by goods which can easily substitute for other goods or be substituted for by other goods.

An example of the first kind was the automobile in the first decades of the twentieth century. Television sets and personal computers are more recent examples of the same type. In these cases, price reductions succeeded in opening up a mass market to the good, which resulted in the expenditure for the good being greater at the lower price than at the higher price. Possible examples of the second type, representing varying degrees of substitutability, are provided by the case of cotton versus wool, previously considered, beef versus chicken and pork, and steel cans versus aluminum cans and plastic and glass containers. The degree of substitutability, of course, is vastly greater between the products of companies within the same industry, such as the steel cans of U.S. Steel and the steel cans of Nippon Steel.

Examples of an inelastic demand arise in cases in which a good has achieved the status of a low-cost necessity. In such cases, in a prosperous country, price reductions are not likely to expand the quantity demanded very significantly, since the good is already probably being consumed at or close to the limit of its usefulness. At the same time, the quantity demanded will diminish only slightly, or even not at all, in the face of moderate price increases, since people will continue to be able to afford the good in virtually unchanged quanti-

ties and it will still be less expensive than the substitutes for it. Such goods as bread, wheat, potatoes, and salt are in this category.

The demand for a good will tend to be inelastic to the degree that the substitutes for it are poor or more expensive than it is. It will also tend to be inelastic in cases in which it is employed as a factor of production in combination with other, complementary factors of production and in which its price constitutes only a small portion of the total cost of producing the product or products in question. In the latter instance, a rise in its price raises the overall cost of production and price of the product(s) in a much smaller proportion. The consequent reduction in the quantity demanded of the product and thus of it, corresponds to this much smaller relative increase in the price of the product(s).

Both sets of conditions appear to describe the demand for a great many goods, such as ordinary nails and screws, silver and mercury, gasoline and heating oil, and most components or parts. Nails and screws, for example, both have poor substitutes and their price constitutes such a small fraction of the overall cost and price of the products into which they enter—houses in particular—as hardly to be noticeable. Thus their price could double or triple and produce very little effect on the quantity of them demanded.

The degree of inelasticity of demand for goods tends to diminish to the degree that time is available for making adjustments. For example, a rise in the price of heating oil will be accompanied by a greater reduction in quantity demanded as time goes by and a larger proportion of furnaces are equipped to burn alternative fuels.

The concept of elasticity of demand helps to make possible the comprehension of such phenomena as the effect of labor-saving improvements in machinery on employment. From the perspective of the economic system as a whole, such improvements in machinery neither cause unemployment nor additional employment. They enable the same total amount of labor to produce a larger quantity of goods. But from the perspective of individual industries, such improvements in machinery can sometimes result in additional employment and sometimes in less employment. It depends on the elasticity of demand for the particular products.

If a labor-saving improvement in machinery occurs in an industry that is confronted with an elastic demand, the effect will be more employment in that industry and correspondingly less employment in other industries. The saving of labor per unit of product results in a reduction in cost of production and selling price that is accompanied by a more than proportionate increase in the number of units of the product demanded.[56] At the same time, the larger expenditure for the product in question necessitates a reduction in expenditure for other products in comparison with what such expenditure would otherwise have been. Thus, for example, labor-saving improvements in the automobile industry earlier in this century resulted in a vast increase in the number of people employed in the automobile industry. At the same time, they resulted in a vast decrease in the number employed in raising horses and growing oats—goods which experienced a major reduction in demand as the result of the growth of the automobile industry.

If a labor-saving improvement takes place in an industry that is confronted with an inelastic demand, the effect will be less employment in that industry and correspondingly more employment in other industries, which experience a rise in demand as the result of the release of funds from the industry where the labor-saving improvement occurred. For example, labor-saving improvements in agriculture are typically accompanied by a reduction in the number of people employed in agriculture and a corresponding increase in the number employed in industry and commerce. This is in response to less money being spent to buy farm products, and more being spent to buy the products of the rest of the economic system.

Regrettably, the major application of the concept of elasticity in contemporary economics has been in connection with a false theory of monopoly. The practical usefulness of the concept has been thought to lie with enabling ordinary private businessmen, who somehow allegedly possess monopoly power, to decide whether it is more profitable to produce a smaller quantity of a good

for sale at a higher price rather than a larger quantity available for sale at a lower price.[57]

Two variants of the concept of elasticity have been developed, which are known as "income elasticity" and "cross elasticity" of demand. By income elasticity is meant the percentage change in the quantity demanded of a product divided by the percentage change in people's incomes. By cross elasticity is meant the percentage change in the quantity demanded of a product divided by the percentage change in the price of one of its substitutes or complements—for example, the percentage change in the quantity demanded of aluminum divided by the percentage change in the price of copper, or the percentage change in the quantity demanded of automobiles divided by the percentage change in the price of gasoline or automobile insurance.

In the face of the construction of such concepts as income and cross elasticity, and of attempts actually to derive concrete measurements of the elasticity of demand, it must be pointed out that there is no such thing as any kind of constancy of elasticities. Elasticities of demand bear no resemblance to such physical measurements as electrical conductivity, specific gravity, or tensile strength, which scientists and engineers can determine for the various elements and compounds. For example, it is simply not the case that as there is a definite electrical conductivity of copper, there is a definite elasticity of demand for copper—or for anything else.

The elasticity of demand varies over the length even of a given demand curve for a good. For example, the demand for automobiles is highly elastic in the zone in which a change in their price either brings them within or places them beyond the reach of a mass market. But once the price of automobiles is low enough to achieve a mass market, further reductions in their price will be accompanied by less elastic responses in the quantity demanded. The demand for automobiles may very well become inelastic. It is possible that a given demand for a good could go through various zones of elasticity, depending on such things as its relationship to the price of various alternative goods at different points. It is possible to imagine a good that becomes a worthwhile substitute for a variety of other goods as its price declines, with its demand alternating between elasticity and inelasticity as it absorbs the market of a competing good and then must await a fall to a substantially lower price to come within range of competing against a further good.

Beyond this, *there is no constancy of demand curves themselves.* Movement along any given demand curve implies changes in the demand curves of a wide variety of other goods. Every time a fall in the price of a good increases the quantity of it demanded by virtue of making it a more worthwhile substitute for other goods, the demand curves for those other goods fall. Every time a fall in the price of a good inaugurates the income effect, the demand curves for countless other goods rise. Changes occur mutatis mutandis every time the price of a good rises.

Demand curves change because of changes in the prices of complementary goods as well as substitute goods. For example, a rise in the price of gasoline reduces the demand for automobiles and for the labor and other factors of production used to produce automobiles. In effect, a rise in the price of any complementary good— that is, any good which must be used in conjunction with other goods to accomplish a definite purpose—represents a rise in the price of accomplishing the overall purpose. In the face of this rise in the overall price, there is a reduction in the quantity demanded of all of the complementary goods required for accomplishing the desired purpose. Since the individual prices of all of the complementary goods but one are unchanged, the fall in quantity demanded of them represents a fall in demand pure and simple. Obviously, the same point applies with the necessary changes to the case of a fall in the price of a complementary good.

Demand curves change because of changes in the price of any other good whatever insofar as the effect is a change in the expenditure for that other good. For a change in the expenditure for any good means offsetting changes in expenditure for other goods. Demand curves also change because of changes in the quantity of money and the level of money incomes, changes in knowledge, tastes, and preferences, and the discovery or invention of new substitutes or complements. All such changes entail changes in elasticities of demand along with changes in the demand curves. The belief in any kind of measurable constancy of demand curves or of elasticities of demand is a manifestation of the philosophical determinism and arrogance of mathematical economics described earlier.[58]

Seeming Exceptions to the Law of Demand

The downward sloping demand curve rests on the bedrock of fundamental economic principles. The fact that, other things being equal, people will buy more of something at a lower price than at a higher price is not contradicted by zones of demand curves in which the quantity demanded does not increase even though the price decreases. In such cases, either a greater decrease in price is what is required to expand the quantity demanded further, or else the good is already purchased to the point of satiety—thanks to the price already being low enough so that the marginal utility attaching to the price is below the marginal utility of the last unit of the good for which any useful employment whatever can be

found. In these cases, of course, the effect of a fall in price is still to increase the quantities demanded (and the demands) of all manner of other goods, for whose purchase the lower price of the good in question makes the necessary funds available.

A seeming exception to the law of demand exists in cases in which the demand for a good depends in part on its already possessing a recognized high value in exchange. For example, the demand for gold and silver as a store of value, and ultimately for use as money, depends upon the fact that in their capacity as ordinary commodities they are already highly valuable. It is for this reason, that when people wish to hold buying power in the form of stocks of physical commodities, they turn to gold and silver rather than other metals: the comparatively high value of the precious metals means that they can be used to hold a given store of value in a smaller bulk, which is easier and less expensive to store and transport.

Similarly, the fact that precious metals, diamonds and other precious stones, and various furs already possess a high value as commodities adds to their suitability for being given as gifts: in addition to their physical properties, their existing high value bestows on them the ability to symbolize the importance of the recipient to the giver. In such cases, it is true, if the price of the good fell below a certain point, part of the demand for it would disappear. But this does not mean that people prefer to pay more, other things being equal, rather than less. In these cases, the decline in value would represent a loss of one of the good's useful properties. The case is comparable to the demand for anything else being less when one or more of its useful properties is impaired. So long as the good retains sufficient value to serve the purposes for which a high value makes it qualified to serve, then, within that zone, the quantity demanded varies inversely with the price in the normal, uncomplicated way. When and if the price declines to the point that the good ceases to be able to serve the purpose that depends on a high value, the case must be understood in terms of the good having been rendered of lower quality.

Thus, the fact that part of the demand for such things as precious metals, precious stones, and various furs would disappear if their value were substantially lower should not be regarded as a contradiction of the law of demand. It is no more a contradiction of it than the fact that, say, grapes which are unsuitable for being made into good wine are less in demand than those which are suitable for being made into good wine, or that cattle incapable of breeding are less in demand than cattle which are capable.

Cases of so-called snob appeal are also essentially similar. If one wishes to be in the company mainly of wealthy people, then restaurants and hotels that only wealthy people can normally afford derive a further, useful property in the minds of some people by virtue of that fact. One may agree or disagree with these people's assessment of what is or is not useful or desirable, but one must recognize that their behavior does not contradict the law of demand. So long as the price charged is within the zone of being high enough to restrict the clientele in this way, the normal relationship between price and quantity demanded prevails. And when the price charged falls below this zone, the usefulness of the good is reduced from the perspective of these buyers.

Finally, the law of demand is in no sense contradicted by observations of the fact that over time higher prices are frequently accompanied by increases in the quantity of a good that is demanded. Such results are precisely the effect to be expected from increases in demand—that is, of an upward shift of the demand curve. Increases in demand for this or that good or service can, of course, occur at any time. However, since the abandonment of the gold standard in the United States in 1933, substantial and practically universal increases in demand have become the norm, because of rapid increases in the quantity of money. It should not even be necessary to mention such obvious facts but for the existence of attempts to derive demand curves on the basis of alleged empirical observations.

The Derivation of Supply Curves

While the case for the downward sloping demand curve can be taken as unexceptionable, the same is most certainly not true of the case for the upward sloping supply curve that is presented as typical by contemporary economics textbooks.

It might appear that such a case could be made by working the law of diminishing marginal utility in reverse. For example, it could be argued that a farmer who owns five horses will need a higher price to be willing to part with his second horse than with his first horse, and a still higher price to part with his third horse than with his second, and so on. For as the number of horses remaining in his possession decreases, the marginal utility he attaches to each remaining horse increases. And since the marginal utility he attaches to the price he receives for a horse must exceed the marginal utility he attaches to any horse he sells, the rising marginal utility of his diminishing supply of horses could be taken to imply a need for a rising price of horses as the condition of his offering a larger quantity of them for sale. The same principle could then be applied to all other suppliers of horses and to suppliers of all other goods. On this basis, a case might be thought to exist for assuming that just as demand curves slope downward, so supply curves slope upward.

The law of diminishing marginal utility may well play a significant role in this way in the determination of supply curves in conditions in which the supplies of goods are capable of being used by the suppliers themselves. But, as already pointed out, in the conditions of a

Table 5–2 Hypothetical Total and Partial Demand Schedules			
Price	Total Quantity Demanded	Quantity Demanded in Market I	Quantity Demanded in Market II
$10	100	60	40
9	125	75	50
8	160	100	60
7	200	125	75
6	250	150	100
5	325	200	125
4	400	250	150
3	500	300	200

division-of-labor economy, goods are produced in such enormous concentrations that for all practical purposes they can be viewed as possessing zero marginal utility for their producers. For example, the pin maker, shirt maker, or automobile producer who turns out tens or hundreds of thousands or even millions of units of his product, can attach marginal utility only to an insignificant fraction of his supply. On this basis, Böhm-Bawerk pointed out that it is more reasonable to regard him as attaching no marginal utility whatever to his supply, and thus as being willing to accept any price for his product that he can obtain, from zero on up, as determined by the competition of the buyers.[59] This, of course, is the basis of Böhm-Bawerk and the Austrian school regarding the supply curve as essentially a vertical line, representing a given amount that the sellers are prepared to sell, irrespective of price.[60]

Nevertheless, it is possible, with some difficulty, to derive upward sloping supply curves. This can be done by conceiving of them as reflecting the competition for a given overall physical supply that arises from the existence of two or more competing demand curves that represent alternative uses for the same supply. To make this point clear, it is necessary to begin by representing the demand schedule previously shown in Table 5–1, as the summation of two lesser, partial demand schedules. These lesser, partial demand schedules can be under-

stood as the demand for a given good, such as wheat or gasoline, that exists in two distinct geographical markets, such as New York and Chicago, or the demand that exists for wheat or crude oil in two distinct employments, such as the baking of bread versus the making of crackers or the production of gasoline versus the production of heating oil. In reality, of course, the number of partial markets would be far greater, but for the sake of simplicity, we confine ourselves to the consideration of just two, which is adequate to illustrate the principle.

In Table 5–2, the column "Total Quantity Demanded" is identical with the column labeled "Quantity Demanded" in Table 5–1. However, this column is now presented as representing the sum of the quantities demanded at the various prices in Markets I and II, respectively, which are shown in the third and fourth columns of the table.

Figures 5–4 and 5–5 are derived from Table 5–2. Figure 5–4 shows the total demand curve, formed by pairing the prices shown in the first column of Table 5–2 with the quantities demanded in the second column. This results, of course, in the replication of the demand curve DD, previously depicted in Figure 5–1. Figure 5–4 differs from Figure 5–1 only in that a given amount of supply is now assumed to exist, namely, 200 units. This results in the drawing of a vertical supply curve SS, ascending from the quantity 200 on the horizontal axis. The implied equilibrium price of $7 is shown by the

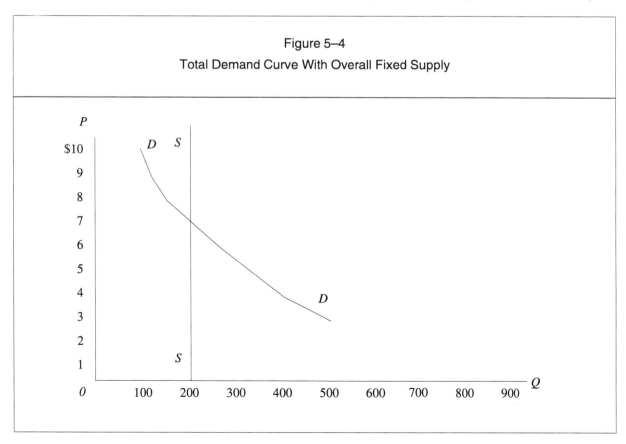

Figure 5–4
Total Demand Curve With Overall Fixed Supply

intersection of this supply curve with the demand curve *DD*.

The upper portion of Figure 5–5 shows the demand curves in the two partial markets, Market I and Market II, which when summed, yield the demand curve of Figure 5–4. As can be inferred from Table 5–2, in a state of equilibrium the price both in Market I and in Market II is $7, with Market I purchasing 125 units, and Market

II, 75 units, of the total supply of 200 units. Nevertheless, it is possible to imagine one of the markets, say, Market II, purchasing varying parts of the total supply, from none of it whatever, all the way on up to the entire 200 units. The various possibilities for the division of the supply between Market II and Market I are shown in Figure 5–5 in the diagram immediately below the diagram for the

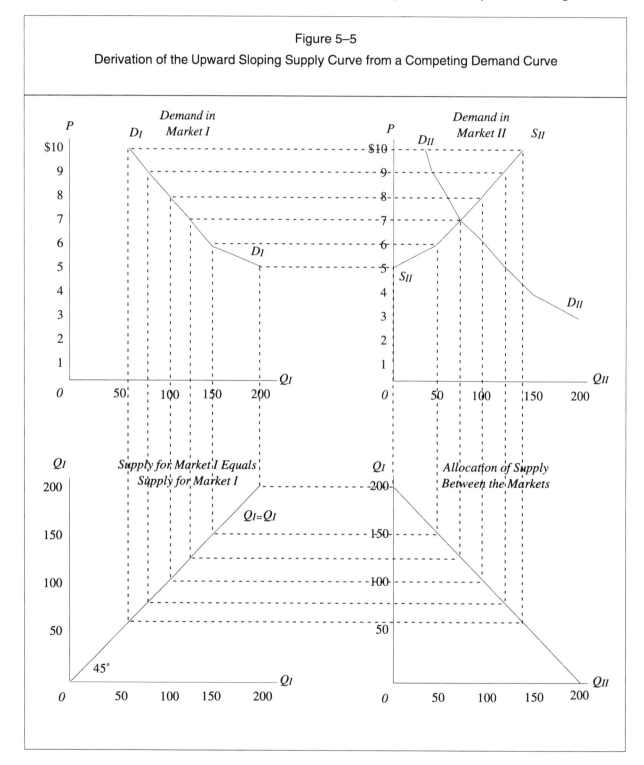

Figure 5–5

Derivation of the Upward Sloping Supply Curve from a Competing Demand Curve

Market II demand curve, that is, in the diagram labeled "Allocation of Supply Between the Markets." The allocation line is drawn as the base of an isosceles triangle, with the vertical and horizontal axes forming legs of equal length. Where the allocation line crosses the vertical axis, which is labeled Q_I, the entire supply of 200 units is shown as going to Market I and none at all as going to Market II. Where the allocation line crosses the horizontal axis, which is labeled Q_{II}, the entire supply of 200 units is shown as going to Market II and none at all to Market I. The various intermediate points on the allocation line show the various other possible combinations of supplies going to the two markets.

The diagram in the lower left-hand corner of Figure 5–5, labeled "Supply for Market I Equals Supply for Market I," has the purpose merely of showing the supply for Market I on the horizontal rather than on the vertical axis, which is where it is shown in the "Allocation of Supply Between the Markets" diagram. This is accomplished by drawing a 45 degree line through the origin. Every point on this line represents an equal distance along both axes.

Thus, on the basis of these four interrelated diagrams in Figure 5–5, it is possible to see that the greater is the supply in Market II, the smaller is the supply that remains in Market I. At the same time, corresponding to every given supply in Market I, there is a definite price in Market I, determined by the demand curve in Market I. The price paid for the supply in Market II, must match the price paid in Market I. And since the larger is the supply in Market II, the smaller is the supply that remains for Market I, the higher must be this price.

In this way, it is possible to trace out an upward sloping supply curve in Market II. We begin in the upper right-hand diagram with a supply in Market II of zero units. Reading down along the dashed line to the lower right-hand diagram, this implies a supply available for Market I of all 200 units. Reading now along the dashed line across to the lower left-hand diagram and then up to the upper left-hand diagram, it is clear that with a supply of 200 units, the price in Market I will be $5. This is the price at which the quantity demanded in Market I equals 200 units. If the price offered in Market II is not above $5, the implication is that Market II has no way to bid supplies away from Market I. Reading the dashed line across from the upper left-hand diagram to the upper right-hand diagram, it is clear that a price of $5 and a supply of zero units can be considered as a point on the supply curve in Market II. This is shown in the diagram for Market II.

The remaining points on the supply curve in Market II are derived by the same method, as shown by additional dashed lines. Examination of the set of diagrams shows that in order for a supply of 50 units to be attracted to Market II, which would leave 150 units for Market I, a price of $6 must be paid. For only at that price is the quantity demanded in Market I reduced to 150 units, thereby releasing 50 units of supply for Market II. Similarly, examination of the diagrams shows that in order for a supply of 75 units to be attracted to Market II, leaving only 125 for Market I, a price of $7 must be paid, since only at that price will the quantity demanded in Market I be reduced to 125 units, and 75 units be released for Market II. In the same way, a price of $8 in Market II will attract 100 units to that market, for at a price of $8 in Market I, the quantity demanded is reduced to 100 units and thus 100 units of the total supply are made available for Market II. A price of $9 in Market II will attract 125 units, for at that price the quantity demanded in Market I falls to 75 units, thereby releasing 125 units of the total supply for Market II. Finally, a price of $10 in Market II will attract 140 units, because at that price, the quantity demanded in Market I is only 60 units, thereby releasing 140 units of the total supply to Market II. Connecting these various points constitutes the drawing of the supply curve for Market II.

In effect, the supply curve in Market II is upward sloping by virtue of the fact that bringing additional supplies into Market II requires riding up the demand curve of Market I, so to speak, as the condition of outbidding Market I for progressively greater supplies. The principle is that the greater is the supply in Market II, the smaller is the supply and thus the higher is the price in Market I. It is the rising price in Market I, in the face of dwindling supplies in that market, that necessitates that larger supplies in Market II be accompanied by rising prices, in order to outcompete the buyers in Market I.

The supply schedule underlying the supply curve for Market II can be derived by means of subtracting from the total supply of 200 units available for both markets the quantities demanded at the various prices in Market I. This is done in Table 5–3.

It would be possible, of course, to apply the above procedure to derive an upward sloping supply curve for Market I from the demand curve in Market II. An upward sloping supply curve in any given partial market can be understood as resulting from the downward sloping demand curve(s) in one or more other markets that are in competition for the same overall given total supply.

Limitations of Geometrical Analysis

It should be obvious that the procedure followed for deriving an upward sloping supply curve is extremely cumbersome even when confined to just two partial markets. To apply the procedure to three partial markets would require the use of solid geometry, to show how a

Table 5–3

Derivation of an Upward Sloping Supply Schedule
from a Downward Sloping Demand Schedule

Price	Quantity Demanded in Market I	Total Supply	Quantity Supplied in Market II
$10	60	200	140
9	75	200	125
8	100	200	100
7	125	200	75
6	150	200	50
5	200	200	0
4	250	200	0
3	300	200	0

definite supply in any given market implied various definite pairs of supplies in the other two markets. The simultaneous relationships between four or more partial markets simply cannot be shown by geometrical methods.

What is implied here is a limitation on the usefulness of supply and demand curves and of geometry in general in economic analysis. True enough, one may think in such terms as, say, fifty partial markets, each with its own demand curve, and with a larger supply in any one market causing diminished supplies in each of the remaining forty-nine partial markets and a corresponding riding up along the demand curves of those forty-nine partial markets. But at this point, even though the analysis makes reference to supply and demand curves, the references and the analysis itself have become purely verbal.

A case such as this clearly shows why the substantive relationships of economics must all be explained by an essentially verbal analysis. Geometry is capable of relating two, or at most three, elements at the same time, and can neither make qualitative distinctions among them nor consider any further aspects pertaining to them without regarding what it previously considered to be one element alone, now to be two or more elements—something which rapidly exhausts and then utterly surpasses its capacity for analysis. In contrast, a verbal analysis is capable of proceeding both in far greater breadth and in far greater depth. The relatively simple set of verbal principles concerning price determination presented in Chapters 6 through 8 of this book, will make it possible to grasp the competition that goes on for limited total supplies between any number of partial markets. Those principles will also make it possible to understand in a far more meaningful way than is possible by the mere visualization of the intersection point of two curves the market *processes* by means of which prices are actually determined.

Contemporary economics, for the most part, is not troubled by the needless complexities and limitations created by an excessive reliance on the use of geometry, because, for all practical purposes, when it comes to price theory, its intellectual horizon is narrowly limited to that of *partial equilibrium*.[61] In effect, the problems of relating what goes on in different partial markets do not arise for contemporary economics, because it is concerned only with what happens in one given market at a time. It does not derive the upward sloping supply curve it presents as typical from any consideration of competition among various partial markets, but from the operation of the law of diminishing returns.

The procedure of contemporary economics is to take the prices of the factors of production as given from the point of view of the individual business enterprise. It then assumes that as the enterprise increases its output from existing plant and equipment, it encounters diminishing returns—less output per unit of the additional factors of production—which implies that larger quantities of the additional factors of production are needed to produce equal additional units of the product. Given the prices of the factors of production, this means rising marginal costs per unit. ("Marginal costs" are the addition to total costs accompanying the production of a given additional quantity of the product. With plant and equipment taken as fixed, they are the cost of additional labor, materials, and fuel. It is these costs which are assumed to increase per unit of additional output.) The supply curve of an industry is then assumed to consist of a summation of all such individual supply/marginal-cost curves of the constituent firms. Indeed, it is assumed to consist of a mere multiplication of the supply/marginal-cost curve of any one of the various allegedly interchangeable "representative firms" of which the industry is assumed to consist, by the number of such firms.[62]

Confusions Between Supply and Cost

Ironically, resort to the law of diminishing returns as the basis for upward sloping supply curves turns out to be inapplicable to actual price formation in the cases in which it might appear to be most plausible—namely, agriculture and mining. These are cases in which diminishing returns occupy a prominent position and are reinforced by the closely related phenomenon of the need to resort to progressively inferior grades of land or mines in order to expand production under a given state of technology. Nevertheless, precisely in these cases, output comes in large discrete bursts, because it is seasonal and depends on the harvests, or because it can be increased or decreased only by substantial discrete increments as, for example, accompany the adding on or elimination of shifts of mine workers or the working or not working of this or that seam of mineral deposit.

In these cases, the concept of supply that is relevant to price formation is the Austro-classical concept of a fixed quantity, with price being determined by the competition of the buyers for that quantity. When the law of diminishing returns is taken as the basis of supply curves and thus of price formation in an industry, via the concept of marginal cost, the result is conceptual chaos of such magnitude that its sorting out is best left for a separate discussion.[63]

The derivation of the upward-sloping supply curve from a rising marginal-cost schedule is only one aspect of the confusions contemporary economics suffers from in connection with the relationship between the concepts of cost of production and supply. In agriculture and mining, it confuses cases in which price is actually determined by demand and supply with determination by cost of production in the form of "marginal cost." In manufacturing, wholesaling, and retailing, it confuses cases in which prices are actually determined in the first instance by cost of production—the *full* cost of production—with determination by demand and supply. Indeed, this is its most serious confusion in that it totally obscures the very existence of cases in which price is directly determined on the basis of cost, by making them appear to be merely another instance of price determination falling under the general rubric of demand and supply.

Thus, contemporary economics admits the existence of cases in which the supply curve is horizontal, as in Figure 5–6 or, indeed, even downward sloping, as in Figure 5–7. In such cases, however, it continues to proceed as though prices were determined by demand and supply, merely because one can show demand curves intersecting such supply curves.

The case of horizontal supply curves is actually extremely common—probably more common than that of upward sloping supply curves. It describes the willingness and ability of sellers to supply a variable quantity at a given price. It is typical in retailing, wholesaling, manufacturing, and the service industries. For example, at the prices posted on its menu, a restaurant is prepared to serve a number of meals ranging from zero on up to the maximum number it can prepare in its kitchen. The same kind of wide-ranging variability in quantity is true of the number of haircuts a barbershop is willing to provide at the price it posts for haircuts, of the number of television sets an appliance store is willing to sell at the prices it posts, and of the quantity virtually any manufacturer is willing to sell of his product at the price he posts. One can express this phenomenon by saying simply that the supply curve is horizontal, and one can then bring the case under the formula that the price is determined by demand and supply, merely because there is a demand curve and a supply curve, and they have an intersection point.

Nevertheless, it should be obvious that the alleged

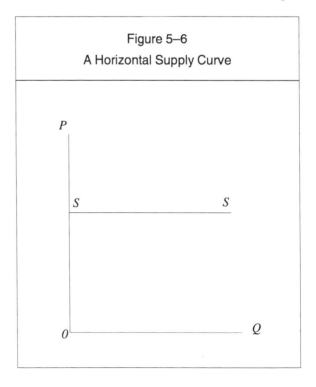

Figure 5–6
A Horizontal Supply Curve

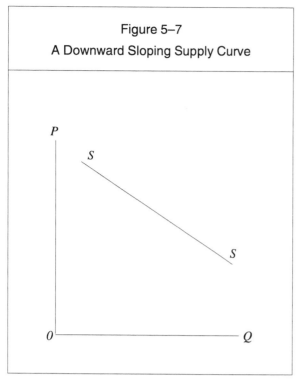

Figure 5–7
A Downward Sloping Supply Curve

determination of price by demand and supply is totally superficial in cases of this kind. The price is actually determined by the decisions of the sellers. Their asking price, together with the demand curve, determines the quantity of the good that is demanded, and the quantity of the good demanded then determines the quantity supplied at the asking price. The critical question is, *what determines the asking prices of the sellers?* The answer, as we shall see, is consideration by the sellers of the cost of production of the item—either their own cost of production or that of competitors or potential competitors. Normally, we shall see, cost of production turns out to be the immediate determinant of the prices of manufactured or processed goods—of any goods or services whose quantity can be immediately expanded or contracted in response to changes in demand by such means as the ability temporarily to decrease or increase inventory levels and, before the inventories are depleted or accumulate unduly, to increase or decrease production from existing plant capacity.[64]

Cases of this kind may appear to represent a direct contradiction of Böhm-Bawerk's proposition that prices are determined by the competition of buyers for limited supplies. For these are cases in which price is determined by the competition of sellers prepared to offer highly variable supplies.[65] Actually, there is no contradiction between the two patterns of price formation. They pertain to different situations—one to cases in which supply is a given quantity for a longer or shorter period of time, and

the other to cases in which supply can be varied in immediate response to changes in demand. Furthermore, it cannot be stressed too strongly that the bridge between the two cases has been provided by none other than Böhm-Bawerk himself, in his demonstration that determination of value and price by cost of production is itself merely a special case of the operation of the law of diminishing marginal utility.[66]

At most, cost of production is a determinant of prices only in the first instance. When one investigates the nature of costs, they are always revealed as constituted by prices of factors of production. These prices are themselves determined by demand and supply, or on the basis of costs that reflect the operation of demand and supply at a further stage of remove. Ultimately, prices determined on the basis of costs are determined on the basis of demand and supply—but on the basis of demand and supply operating in broad factor markets, not the market for the individual product itself. Thus, for example, in saying that the price of new automobiles is determined by cost of production, rather than demand and supply, what is actually meant is that it is determined in the first instance by cost of production; but the wage rates, real estate prices, and many of the raw materials prices—*all* the prices into which the cost of production of an automobile is ultimately resolvable—are determined by demand and supply.[67]

Downward sloping supply curves represent cases in which cost per unit declines as the level of production expands. The charging of lower prices in the face of higher levels of demand, which make possible operation on an expanded scale, is also clearly a case in which prices are set in the first instance on the basis of a consideration of costs of production—specifically, the ability to use declining costs to gain a decisive advantage over potential competitors by charging prices too low for their operations to be profitable, but which are not too low for one's own operations to be profitable.

The confusions of contemporary economics are such that it is largely unaware that in the cases of horizontal and downward sloping supply curves, it actually is dealing with situations in which cost of production is the immediate determinant of prices. Insofar as it is aware that these cases are different, it regards the resulting prices *as standing virtually outside the operation of normal economic law*—as representing "administered" prices, set more or less arbitrarily by one or another type of wielder of "monopoly power," on the basis either of evil motives or at least peculiar motives. These confusions are the result of the fact that contemporary economics has lost the ability to understand determination of price by cost. It cannot deal with cases in which prices are set on the basis of a consideration of the full costs of production, together with an allowance for earning the going rate of profit, rather than on the basis merely of marginal costs.[68]

Putting aside all the confusions that have characterized their use, it is an obvious fallacy to believe that demand and supply curves can ever be derived from empirical observation. Any price and quantity demanded and supplied that one can observe is necessarily only a single point on a demand and supply curve. And, it could, conceivably, be a point on any one of a virtually infinite number of such curves! For through a given point, there is no limit to the number of lines that can be drawn—even if, as in the case of the demand curve, they must possess a negative slope.

Whenever a new price and quantity demanded and supplied are observed, it is inescapable that at least the demand curve or the supply curve has changed, and more than likely that both have changed. If neither had changed, the change in price and quantity would not have been possible. The conclusion to be drawn from this is that when different prices and quantities are observed over time, absolutely no rational basis exists for believing that what is being observed is movement along any given curve.

As previously explained, it should also be apparent on this basis that observations of rising prices associated with rising quantities demanded over time are perfectly consistent with the law of demand. The combination is explained simply by increases in the demand schedule—most likely, nowadays, as the result of an increase in the quantity of money.

The Circularity of Contemporary Economics' Concept of Demand

Contemporary economics' concept of demand en-counters a problem of circularity. It explains each individual price on the basis of demand and supply. But the demand curve in each case *presupposes* all other prices in the economic system: it is constructed on the assumption of their existing and remaining unchanged. Yet if the formation of those other prices is to be explained on the basis of demand and supply curves, then the price of the good in question, which is supposedly first to be explained by demand and supply curves, must already be presupposed. Fortunately, the classical concept of demand, when taken in conjunction with the law of diminishing marginal utility, provides a way out of this circularity.

The classical concept of demand makes it possible to understand the absolute level of prices on the foundation of the quantity theory of money, which will be explained in Chapter 12. At the same time, the law of diminishing marginal utility shows that the relative prices of all goods and services that exist in some definite, given supply at any given time, are determined by their relative marginal utilities.[69] For example, the prices of wheat, crude oil, skilled and unskilled labor, the various improved and unimproved land sites, and so forth are all determined in such a way that the marginal utility attaching to the price in each case is below the utility of the marginal unit of the good in question and above the utility of a potential additional unit of the good in question. This means that the prices of these goods relative to one another reflect their relative marginal utilities. In this way, the prices of goods and services in limited supply can be explained without the error of circular reasoning. And because prices determined by cost of production are based on such prices, all prices can thus be explained without falling into the error of circular reasoning.[70]

Notes

1. See Ayn Rand, "What Is Capitalism?" in *Capitalism: The Unknown Ideal*, ed. Ayn Rand (New York: The New American Library, n.d.), pp. 9–12. See also Leonard Peikoff, *Objectivism: The Philosophy of Ayn Rand* (New York: New American Library, 1992), pp. 380–384.

2. A division-of-labor, capitalist society is, of course, characterized by the existence of medium and large-sized business enterprises, in which large numbers of individual wage earners produce under the direction of businessmen and capitalists. But the formation and extent of all such enterprises is itself the product of the separate, independent thinking and acting of all the individual participants. The individual stockholders decide the extent to which it is advantageous to pool their capitals and employ other people; the individual wage earners decide the extent to which working for such an enterprise is to their advantage compared with working on their own, as businessmen, and with working for any other such enterprise.

3. My discussion of this subject is completely indebted to the writings of von Mises and Hayek. See Ludwig von Mises, *Socialism* (New Haven: Yale University Press, 1951), pp. 111–142, 211–220, 516–521; reprint ed. (Indianapolis: Liberty Classics, 1981); idem, *Human Action*, 3d ed. rev. (Chicago: Henry Regnery Co., 1966), pp. 689–715. See also F. A. Hayek, *The Road to Serfdom* (Chicago: University of Chicago Press, 1944), pp. 48–50.; *Individualism and Economic Order* (Chicago: University of Chicago Press, 1948), pp. 33–56, 73–91, 119–208.

4. For a detailed discussion of the economic chaos of a socialist

state, see below, pp. 269–275, and the references cited in the preceding note of this chapter.

5. See Hedrick Smith, *The Russians* (New York: Quadrangle/New York Times Book Company, 1976), pp. 60–61.

6. The quotation is from Henry H. Villard, *Economic Development* (New York: Reinhart & Co., 1959), p. 171. Italics supplied.

7. Robert Kaiser, *Russia* (New York: Atheneum, 1976) p. 338.

8. For elaboration on the nature of economic planning under capitalism, see below, pp. 269–275, and 172–294 passim.

9. On the indivisibility of property rights and all other rights, see above, p. 23.

10. This insight, of course, is one of the greatest contributions of von Mises. See above, n. 3.

11. For elaboration of this fundamental fact, see below, pp. 682–699.

12. The truth is that to some extent the consumers' goods that are paid for in the present can be traced back to the performance of labor in the remotest periods of antiquity, indeed, to the point when man first began to use previously produced goods in the production of all goods. However, the extent to which goods of the present owe their existence to labor performed in the past diminishes in geometric progression. See below, pp. 820–824 and 852.

13. See below, p. 824. See also Eugen von Böhm-Bawerk, *Capital and Interest,* 3 vols., trans. George D. Huncke and Hans F. Sennholz (South Holland, Ill.: Libertarian Press, 1959), 2:79–118.

14. For a precise, arithmetic illustration of this point, see below, p. 360.

15. On the relationship between the accumulation of capital and the division of labor, cf. Adam Smith, *The Wealth of Nations* (London, 1776), bk. 2, Introduction; reprint of Cannan ed. (Chicago: University of Chicago Press, 2 vols. in 1, 1976).

16. Cf. Henry Hazlitt, *Time Will Run Back* (New Rochelle, N. Y: Arlington House Publishers, 1966); originally published as *The Great Idea* (New York: Appleton-Century-Crofts, 1951) p. 155.

17. For an account of the origin and evolution of money and the contemporary monetary system, see below, pp. 506–517.

18. Cf. von Mises, *Socialism*, p. 121.

19. And, as von Mises has shown, it provides the *only* such standard. See *Socialism*, pp. 113–128, 131–135.

20. For a brilliant defense of the moral value of money and of the proposition that money *is* the root of all good, see Ayn Rand, *Atlas Shrugged* (New York: Random House, 1957), pp. 410–415.

21. Knowledge of the dependence of the division of labor on the existence of money sheds major light on the causes of the collapse of the Roman Empire, which took place following a century-long process of the destruction of money through inflation. See below, p. 950. The whole of Chapter 19 and much of Chapter 12 make clear the potential for inflation and destruction inherent in the present monetary system.

22. For a brilliant critique of the doctrine of from each according to his ability to each according to his need, see Ayn Rand, *Atlas Shrugged,* pp. 660–670.

23. On these points, see below, pp. 613–664 passim, and 580–589.

24. Cf. Ludwig von Mises, *Socialism*, pp. 319–321.

25. The passage of the Norris-La Guardia Act in 1932 eliminated the possibility of gaining federal court injunctions against mass picketing.

26. For a detailed discussion of these points, see below, pp. 420–421.

27. Of course, economic inequality can also result from differences in luck, but such differences are of relatively minor importance in comparison with the kind of differences described above and are certainly not of sufficient importance to detract in any way from the significance of these differences.

28. The discussion in this and the next several paragraphs was inspired by Henry Hazlitt's *Time Will Run Back*, pp. 88–91.

29. See ibid.

30. For a demonstration of how the accumulation of great fortunes is a case of one man's gain being other men's gain, see below, pp. 327–328.

31. For further explanation of why incomes that represent high rates of profit are heavily saved, see below, pp. 741–743.

32. See Milton Friedman, *A Theory of the Consumption Function* (Princeton, N. J.: Princeton University Press, 1957).

33. For elaboration of this point, see below, pp. 355–356.

34. On the feudalistic-type economic inequalities necessarily prevalent under socialism, see below, pp. 288–290.

35. See above, p. 23., for an explanation of why almost all violations of freedom entail violations of property rights. See also below, pp. 331–332, for a demonstration of the fact that the economic advantages of the feudal aristocracy vis-à-vis the serfs rested on a foundation of government power, not economic power, and were the result of a violation of property rights rather than of the use of property rights.

36. For further discussion of inheritance, see below, pp. 306–308.

37. See below, pp. 326–330 for a comprehensive demonstration of this fact.

38. *The New York Times* of January 8, 1994, reported an instance of this error with some degree of fanfare, on its first business page, as though it represented a scholarly finding.

39. For a free-market solution to the growing problems in the area of medical care, see below, pp. 378–380. See also George Reisman, *The Real Right to Medical Care Versus Socialized Medicine* (Laguna Hills, Calif.: The Jefferson School of Philosophy, Economics, and Psychology, 1994.) This pamphlet is a discussion of all aspects of the cause and cure of the current crisis in medical care.

40. See von Mises, *Human Action,* p. 333.

41. See John E. Cairnes, *Some Leading Principles of Political Economy Newly Expounded* (1874; reprint ed., Fairfield, N. J.: Augustus M. Kelley, 1967), pp. 22–29.

42. See John Stuart Mill, *Principles of Political Economy,* Ashley ed. (1909; reprint ed., Fairfield, N. J.: Augustus M. Kelley, 1976), p. 445.

43. See Böhm-Bawerk, *Capital and Interest,* 2:244–245.

44. No significance should be attached to the fact that the demand curve in Figure 5–2 is drawn as a straight line. It is drawn that way merely for the sake of convenience and is in accordance with the present-day practice of drawing such curves.

45. Ibid.

46. Ibid.

47. See ibid.

48. See below, pp. 219–221 and 503–506.

49. See above, pp. 53–54, and, below, pp. 566–568.

50. Indeed, it will subsequently be shown in detail that more aggregate supply itself creates equivalently more aggregate real demand precisely in this way. See below, pp. 559–564, especially Figure 13–3, on p. 561.

51. For an explanation of the law of diminishing marginal utility, see above, pp. 49–51.

52. In case the reader is wondering what would happen if the marginal utility attached to a unit of the good and to its price were the same, the answer is, nothing. The precondition of a purchase is the valuation of what is received in exchange above the valuation of what is given in exchange. Actually, as determinants of purchases, marginal utilities should be thought of in terms of ordinal rather than cardinal numbers. On this subject, see von Mises, *Human Action,* pp. 119–127.

53. Insofar as it is businessmen who buy cotton instead of wool, they will not be the parties who have the gain in marginal utility described here. Those who have the gain in marginal utility will be the consumers of cotton clothing. Precisely as a result of this fact, the consumers will favor the purchase of cotton clothing, and because of this the businessmen will buy more cotton and less wool. The change in the businessmen's purchases is thus dictated by the effects of changes in marginal utility on the consumers.

54. On the fallacies entailed in viewing a saving of expense as actually the same as an increase in income, see below, pp. 456–459.

55. To anticipate later discussion under the heading of Say's Law: given the quantity of money and volume of spending in the economic system, what determines the price level and the goods and services the aggregate demand is actually capable of purchasing at any given time is nothing other than the aggregate supply of goods and services. In this way, it is aggregate supply that determines the aggregate *real* demand. See above, n. 50 of this chapter for further reference.

56. The saving of labor and increase in employment must be understood in terms of the overall, total quantity of labor directly or indirectly required in the production of the product. In the case of automobiles, for example, this means the labor required in the production of the iron ore and steel sheet, all the various parts and the materials required to produce them, and the equipment used at all the various stages, as well as the labor required in the auto plants. If a reduction in the overall quantity of labor required per unit of a product can be assumed to result in a corresponding reduction in the unit cost and price of the product, then a more than proportionate increase in the quantity of the product demanded results in an increase in overall employment in the production of the product.

57. See below, pp. 408–409.

58. See above, p. 9.

59. See Böhm-Bawerk, *Capital and Interest,* 2:244.

60. See above, p. 154.

61. See above, p. 7.

62. See, for example, Paul Samuelson and William Nordhaus, *Economics,* 13th ed. (New York: McGraw-Hill, 1989), pp. 540–545. See also above, pp. 7–8, for a critique of the doctrine of the representative firm.

63. See below, pp. 425–437, which are a critique of contemporary economics' doctrine of "pure and perfect competition."

64. See below, pp. 200–201.

65. This was the kind of case Ricardo considered typical. See *The Works and Correspondence of David Ricardo*, 11 vols., ed. Piero Sraffa (Cambridge: Cambridge University Press, 1952–73), 8:276–277. The essential passage from Ricardo is quoted below, on p. 414.

66. See above, p. 52, and below, pp. 414–416, for the previously referenced lengthy quotation from Böhm-Bawerk on this subject.

67. See below, p. 201.

68. See below, pp. 425–437 passim.

69. More correctly, insofar as they themselves are not consumers' goods, their relative prices are determined by the relative marginal utilities of their final products to the ultimate consumers.

70. See below, pp. 200–201, 209.

CHAPTER 6

THE DEPENDENCE OF THE DIVISION OF LABOR ON CAPITALISM II: THE PRICE SYSTEM AND ECONOMIC COORDINATION

PART A

UNIFORMITY PRINCIPLES

The dependence of the division of labor on the price system centers on the coordinating function of prices. The price system coordinates the various branches of the division of labor in a variety of essential respects. It keeps the various branches of industry, and thus the production of the various products, in proper balance with one another by appropriately adjusting their relative size. It does the same with respect to the relative size of the various occupations. It also achieves a harmonious balancing of the supplies of the various products produced with respect to their distribution in terms of place and time. These results are accomplished by the operation of a series of principles that I call uniformity principles, which are described and elaborated in the first four sections of this part.

1. The Uniformity-of-Profit Principle and Its Applications

The best way to begin to understand the functioning of the price system, and thus the full nature of the dependence of the division of labor on capitalism, is by understanding the following very simple and fundamental principle. Namely, *there is a tendency in a free market*

toward the establishment of a uniform rate of profit on capital invested in all the different branches of industry. In other words, there is a tendency for capital invested to yield the same percentage rate of profit whether it is invested in the steel industry, the oil industry, the shoe business, or wherever.

Profit, of course, is the difference between sales revenues and costs. The rate of profit on capital invested is the amount of profit divided by the amount of capital invested.[1]

The reason for the tendency toward a uniform rate of profit on capital invested is that, other things being equal, investors naturally prefer to earn a higher rate of profit on their capital rather than a lower one. The higher is the rate of profit they earn, the larger is the amount of profit they earn per year and thus the more rapidly they can augment their wealth through saving and, at the same time, the more they can afford to consume. As a result, wherever the rate of profit is higher, and all other things are equal, investors tend to invest additional capital. And where it is lower, they tend to withdraw capital they have previously invested. The influx of additional capital in any initially more profitable industry, however, tends to reduce the rate of profit in that industry. This is because its effect is to increase the industry's production and thus to drive down the selling prices of its products. As the selling prices of its products are driven down, closer to its costs of production, the rate of profit earned by the industry necessarily tends to fall. Conversely, the withdrawal of capital from an initially less profitable industry tends to raise the rate of profit in that industry, because less capital means less production, higher selling prices on the reduced supply, and thus a higher rate of profit on the capital that remains invested in the industry.

To illustrate this process, let us assume that initially the computer industry is unusually profitable, while the motion-picture industry is earning a very low rate of profit or incurring actual losses. In such conditions people will obviously want to invest in the computer industry and to reduce their investments in the motion-picture industry. As investment in the computer industry is stepped up, the output of computers will be expanded. In order to find buyers for the larger supply of computers, their price will have to be reduced. Thus, the price of computers will fall and, as a result, the rate of profit earned in producing them will fall. On the other hand, as capital is withdrawn from the motion-picture industry, the output of that industry will be cut, and the reduced supply it offers will be able to be sold at higher prices, thereby raising the rate of profit on the investments that remain in the industry.

In just this way, initially higher rates of profit are brought down and initially lower rates of profit are raised up. The logical stopping point is a uniform rate of profit in all the various industries.

Keeping the Various Branches of Industry in Proper Balance

This principle of the tendency of the rate of profit toward uniformity is what explains the amazing order and harmony that exists in production in a free market. It was largely the operation of this principle that Adam Smith had in mind when he employed the unfortunate metaphor that a free economy works as though it were guided by an invisible hand.

In the United States production is carried on by several million independent business enterprises, each of which is concerned with nothing but its own profit. Knowing this, and knowing nothing about economics, one might easily be led to think of such conditions as an "anarchy of production," which is how Karl Marx described them. One might easily be led to expect that because production was in the hands of a mass of independent, self-interested producers, the market would randomly be flooded with some items, while people perished from a lack of others, as a result of the discoordination of the producers. This, of course, is the image conjured up by those who advocate government "planning." It is the view of most advocates of socialism.

The uniformity-of-profit principle explains how the activities of all the separate business enterprises are harmoniously coordinated, so that capital is not invested excessively in the production of some items while leaving the production of other items unprovided for. The operation of the uniformity-of-profit principle is what keeps the production of all the different items directly or indirectly necessary to our survival in proper balance. It counteracts and prevents mistakes leading to the relative overproduction of some things and the relative underproduction of others.

To understand this point, assume that businessmen make a mistake. They invest too much capital in producing refrigerators and not enough capital in producing television sets, say. Because of the uniformity-of-profit principle, the mistake is necessarily self-correcting and self-limiting. The reason is that the effect of the overinvestment in refrigerator production is to depress profits in the refrigerator industry, because the excessive quantity of refrigerators that can be produced can be sold only at prices that are low in relation to costs. By the same token, the effect of the underinvestment in television set production is to raise profits in the television set industry, because the deficient quantity of television sets that can be produced can be sold at prices that are high in relation to costs. The very consequence of the mistake, therefore, is to create incentives for its correction: The low profits—or losses, if the overinvestment is serious enough— of the refrigerator industry act as an incentive to the withdrawal of capital from it, while the high profits of the television set industry act as an incentive to the investment of additional capital in it.

Moreover, the consequence of the mistake is not only to create incentives for its correction, but simultaneously, to provide the means for its correction: The high profits of the television set industry are not only an incentive to investment in it, but are themselves a *source* of investment, because those high profits can themselves be plowed back into the industry. By the same token, to the extent that the refrigerator industry suffers losses or earns a rate of profit that is too low to cover the dividends its owners need to live on, its capital directly and immediately shrinks, and it is thereby made unable to continue producing on the same scale.

In this way, the mistakes made in the relative production of the various goods in a free market are self-correcting.

With good reason, the operation of profit and loss in guiding the increase and decrease in investment and production has been compared to an automatic governor on a machine or to a thermostat on a boiler. As investment and production go too far in one direction, and not far enough in another direction, the very mistake itself sets in motion counteracting forces of correction. Moreover, the greater the mistake that is made, the more powerful are the corrective forces. For the greater the overinvestment and overproduction, the greater the losses; and the greater the underinvestment and underproduction, the greater the profits. Thus the greater the incentives and the means (or loss of means) to bring about the correction. In this way, the mistakes made in a free market are not only self-correcting, but self-limiting as well: the bigger the mistake, the harder it is to make it.

Further, in a free market, most of the mistakes that might be made in determining the relative size of the various industries and the relative production of the various goods are not made in the first place. This is because the prospect of profit or loss causes businessmen to weigh investment decisions very carefully in advance and thus to avoid mistakes as far as possible from the very beginning. In seeking to avoid losses, businessmen necessarily aim at avoiding overinvestment and overproduction. In seeking to make the highest possible profits, they necessarily aim at providing the market with those goods in whose production they do not expect other businessmen to invest enough. This last fact, incidentally, makes each businessman eager to invest sufficiently in his own industry, lest the opportunities he does not seize be seized by others instead.

In addition, the free market performs a constant process of selection with respect to the ownership of capital. Capital gravitates, as it were, to those businessmen who know best how to employ it and is taken away from those who do not know how to employ it. For those who invest in providing goods that are relatively more in demand make high profits and are thereby able to increase their capitals, and, consequently, their influence over future production; while those who invest in producing goods that are relatively less in demand earn low profits or suffer losses, and are correspondingly deprived of capital and of influence over future production. At any given time, therefore, capital in a free market is mainly in the hands of those who are best qualified to use it, as demonstrated by their past performance in investing. For this reason, too, most of the mistakes that might be made in determining the relative production of the various goods are avoided in the first place in a free market.

The Power of the Consumers to Determine the Relative Size of the Various Industries

The uniformity-of-profit principle explains not only how a free market prevents and counteracts mistakes in the relative production of the various industries, but also how the consumers in a free market have the power of positive initiative to change the course of production. All the consumers need do to cause production to shift is to change the pattern of their spending. If the consumers decide to buy more of product A and less of product B,

the production of A automatically becomes more profitable and that of B less profitable. Capital then flows to A and away from B. The production of A is thus expanded, and that of B contracted, until, once again, both A and B afford neither more nor less than the general or average rate of profit.

Of course, businessmen do not sit back and passively wait for the consumers to shift their demand. On the contrary, businessmen seek to anticipate changes in consumer demand and to adjust production accordingly. In addition, of course, they constantly seek to introduce whatever new or improved products they believe will attract consumer demand once the consumers learn of the product. Businessmen will produce anything for which they believe the consumers will pay profitable prices, and they will cease to produce anything for which the consumers are unwilling to pay profitable prices. In this sense, business is totally at the disposal of the consumers—the consumer is king, as the saying goes. In total opposition to the misguided efforts of the Marxists to contrast production for profit with "production for use," the fact is that production for profit *is* production for use. It is production for the use of the consumers, as determined by the value judgments of the consumers themselves. It is the way production for use takes place in the context of a division-of-labor society, in which the producers produce for the needs of others, whose needs are conveyed to them by means of profit and loss.

i. The "Consumer Advocates" Versus the Consumers

It should not be difficult to see that the real advocates of the consumers—their virtual agents—are businessmen seeking profit, not the leaders of groups trying to restrict the freedom of businessmen to earn profits. Such groups, called, ironically, the "consumer movement," seek to force businessmen to produce things the consumers do not want to buy, like seat belts and air bags in automobiles before they are sufficiently improved in comfort and reliability and reduced in cost to be attractive to many people. At the same time, the so-called consumer movement seeks to prohibit businessmen from producing things the consumers do want to buy, like breakfast cereals that are enjoyable to eat, and full-sized automobiles. As von Mises has pointed out, inasmuch as what is produced in a free economy is, in the last analysis, the result of the free choices of the consumers, the demands of the consumer advocates are comparable to efforts arbitrarily to overturn the results of a free election when one does not like the outcome. The dictatorial character of such demands should be obvious.[2]

Of course, whenever they can be gotten to admit that it is actually the choices of the consumers they wish to overturn, not any arbitrary decisions of businessmen, the "consumer advocates" are almost certain to argue that they are nonetheless justified in their activities, on the grounds that they merely force the consumers to act "for their own good." Here the "consumer advocates" lose sight of the fact that the fundamental basis of achieving the individual's good is his guidance by his own judgment. They show absolutely no respect for the character of the consumers as rational beings, who must be persuaded by facts and logic, not compelled as though they were brutes, in the name of something allegedly more valuable than their free judgment and their dignity as rational beings.

It may well be the case that using seat belts saves lives and that if left to their own free choice, the consumers would not have used them as fast as they have been made to use them through compulsion. But what saves infinitely more lives than seat belts is the acceptance of the principle that each human being, as the possessor of reason, is valuable and competent and should be free to run his own life and pursue his own happiness. The use of any specific case as the pretext for overturning this principle opens the floodgates to unlimited destruction through the use of physical force to overrule people's judgment and thus to prevent them from achieving their well-being or to compel them to act against their own well-being. Ayn Rand has rightly compared the use of force in the name of achieving a man's good to an attempt to give him a picture gallery at the price of cutting out his eyes.[3]

ii. Consumer Safety and Pressure Group Warfare

The fact of the matter is that the consumers cannot even properly be described as irrational in refusing to use seat belts, so long as their use had (or has) the effect of making every automobile trip a physically uncomfortable experience. It cannot reasonably be claimed that the remote possibility of an accident automatically outweighs any possible physical discomfort that would have to be experienced on every trip in order to safeguard against it. Let the use of seat belts be made comfortable enough, their cost low enough, and knowledge of their benefits widespread enough, and there is no doubt that consumers will freely use them, because in such circumstances they really would benefit from their use. But when compulsion is introduced into the picture, it is an entirely different story.

Thus, even if the "consumer advocates" have succeeded in compelling the use of seat belts—by means of the threat of fines and possibly jail terms for failure to use them—what remains is the fact that the consumers have been compelled to endure what in their judgment is a chronic physical discomfort (and/or too high a cost). This cannot be justified if one values the free judgment

of the human mind and thus elementary human dignity. In sharpest contrast, under freedom, such an affront would not only have been avoided, but it might well have been avoided *while people still gained the benefit of seat belts*. When based on compulsion, the use of seat belts does not have to be comfortable and sufficiently economical—it is simply compelled, whether the consumers like it or not. When based on freedom, the use of seat belts does have to be comfortable enough and economical enough, because the consumers have to both like using them and value them above their price if they are to buy them. On a free market, these are the kind of seat belts the consumers would have to have obtained.

Only a free market can rationally decide such questions as whether or not seat belts, and now air bags, should be installed in automobiles. In a free market, if air bags, for example, represented a major advance in automobile safety, one of the consequences would be that their presence would so reduce the costs of insurance companies in the settlement of injury claims that the insurance companies would be in a position significantly to reduce the premiums of whoever owned a car which had one. This saving in insurance premiums, coupled with the personal benefits of reduced likelihood of serious injury, would then be weighed by the consumers against the cost of having air bags installed, or the additional cost of buying an automobile that came with an air bag in comparison with one that came without an air bag. The greater the reduction in physical injuries, and the financial costs associated with them, that air bags achieved, and the lower the cost of installing air bags, the greater would be the demand for air bags. Depending on these data, the potential quantity of air bags demanded would exist on a continuum ranging from none at all, in the event the advantages were deemed insufficient by everyone relative to the additional cost, down through high-cost luxury add-on or option, down through widely chosen add-on or option, down through standard feature on some or most new models, down through standard feature on all new models.

Things are very different in a hampered market economy, such as today's so-called mixed economy, with its pressure-group warfare. In such conditions, each pressure group seeks to violate the rights of others for its own benefit, either for its own aggrandizement or in order to make good the depredations of others that have been inflicted on it. Thus, the automobile insurance industry—itself made to bear the skyrocketing medical costs caused by government intervention into health care (insofar as it must pay the medical bills of the victims of automobile accidents), bled white by jury awards based on the notion that any large corporation is fair game for anything, and the victim of government interference to the point of being rendered incapable of controlling the automobile repair costs it must pay—forms into a pressure group and joins the "consumer advocates" in demanding that the automobile industry install air bags. It acts in the hope that the reduction it expects to have in its own costs will serve as a reprieve. As cover, it waves the banner of consumer safety, while making no mention of the higher prices that consumers will have to pay for automobiles. Ironically, at the same time, on the basis of their own accumulated grievances, automobile owners join in demands for rate rollbacks for the insurance companies.

And while this goes on, the "consumer advocates" lead an ignorant public to believe that the costs imposed on the automobile industry in the name of safety, fuel economy, pollution control, and whatever are somehow just at the expense of the automobile companies and have nothing whatever to do with raising the cost of production and price of automobiles. The fact is, of course, that such legislation has already added several hundred dollars to the cost of the average new automobile that is sold in the United States. The paradoxical effect of this has actually been to work to *reduce* automobile safety! To the extent that new automobiles are made more expensive than they need to be, people are compelled to operate their cars longer. Since older cars as a rule are not as safe as new cars, this means that people are forced to drive in automobiles that are not as safe as they would be in the absence of automobile safety legislation and allied legislation. Thus, the introduction of physical force into the issue of automobile safety (and anywhere else in the market) actually has the perverse effect of operating to reduce safety.[4]

The Impetus to Continuous Economic Progress

The uniformity-of-profit principle explains how the profit motive acts to make production steadily increase in a free market. It explains how the profit motive becomes an agent of continuous economic progress.

In order to earn a rate of profit that is above average, it is necessary for businessmen to anticipate changes in consumer demand ahead of their rivals, to introduce new and/or improved products ahead of their rivals, or to cut the costs of production ahead of their rivals. I say, "ahead of their rivals," because as soon as any innovation becomes general, then, in accordance with the uniformity-of-profit principle, no special profit can be made from it. For example, the first firms that produced shoes by machinery rather than by hand, or put zippers in clothing, or found a way to sell a cigar for ten cents, or whichever, were able to make above-average rates of profit by doing so. But once such things became general, no special profit could any longer be made from them. They became the ordinary standard of the industry and were taken for

granted. Sooner or later, virtually every innovation does become general. This implies that for any firm to continue to earn an above-average rate of profit, it must *repeatedly* outdistance its rivals; it must work as an agent of continuous economic progress.

Perhaps one of the most dramatic examples of this is provided by the career of the first Henry Ford. When the Ford Motor Company began, in the early part of the twentieth century, the automobile was a rich man's toy. Extremely primitive models by our standards were selling for about $10,000—in the very valuable money of the time.[5] Henry Ford began to find ways to improve the quality of automobiles and at the same time cut the costs of their production. But it was not possible for Ford to make a single improvement or a single cost reduction and stop there, because it was not long before those innovations were generally adopted in the industry and, indeed, superseded. Had Ford stood pat, it would not have been long before his once profitable business was destroyed by the competition. In order for Ford to go on making a high rate of profit, he had to continuously introduce improvements and reduce costs ahead of his rivals.

The same is true in principle, in a free market, of any individual or firm that earns an above-average rate of profit over an extended period of time. What was good enough once to make a high rate of profit, ceases to be good enough as soon as enough others are able to do the same thing. In order to go on earning an above-average rate of profit, one must continue to stay ahead of the competition. By the same token, any business that stands pat is necessarily finished in a free economy, no matter how great its past successes. For the technological advances of any given time are further and further surpassed as time goes on. Think how absurd it would be in virtually any industry to try to make money today by producing with the most advanced, most profitable technology of 1900, 1940, or even 1980, and not bothering to adapt to the changes that have taken place since then.

It is necessary to explain in more detail how the competitive quest for an above-average rate of profit expands the total of production.

If a firm is a leader in the improvement of production, it expands its sales revenues and profits at the expense of the sales revenues and profits of other firms that are less quick to improve. This is because it has something better or equally good but less expensive to offer than they do; and so buyers shift their purchases to it, thereby enlarging its sales revenues and profits and diminishing the sales revenues and profits of other firms.

(It is important to realize that this same result—the innovative firm's gain in sales revenues and profits accompanied by a decline in the sales revenues and profits of others, who are less innovative—occurs even in the exceptional case in which a business cuts its costs of production and yet keeps its selling price absolutely unchanged. In this case, it does not attract sales revenues from other sellers in the same industry, but it almost certainly attracts sales revenues and profits from sellers in different industries. Because to the extent that it saves, and reinvests its extra profit anywhere in the economic system, it will bring about an increase in production. This new production in some other line of business will take sales revenues and profits away from whichever sellers buyers now abandon in order to be able to purchase this new production. For example, imagine that a maker of razor blades, say, finds a way to cut his costs, and yet chooses not to cut his selling price at all. He will not reduce the sales revenues and profits of other razor blade manufacturers, but to the extent that he saves, and invests his profit in the production of some other product—whether it is an after-shave lotion, chocolate bars, or anything—he will increase the supply of that product and take sales revenues and profits away from somewhere else in the economic system, because to buy this additional product of his, people will have to restrict their expenditures for other things.)

Now the combination of an innovator's higher profits and others' lower profits or outright losses is what then impels these others to improve their production, too. These others may simply want to cash in on the high profits of the innovator and so duplicate his innovation for that reason. Or they may be in the position of *having* to duplicate his innovation in order merely to stay in business.

It cannot be stressed too strongly that under the freedom of competition, innovations must be adopted not only to make exceptional profits, but to be able to make *any profits whatever.* They must be adopted merely to be able to remain in business at all. This is true because sooner or later, as the result of the freedom of competition, virtually all cost cuts are translated into price cuts, and whoever does not produce with the lower-cost method cannot cover his costs. Even in our present-day, highly inflationary environment, in which wages rise every year and prices hardly ever fall, it is necessary for all producers to adopt cost-cutting improvements. They must adopt them in order not to have to raise prices in full proportion to the increase in wages and so be in the untenable position of requiring price increases greater than their competitors' in order to stay in business.

As indicated, there is probably no business in the United States today that would still be in business had it not adopted major innovations over the last generation and probably even over the last decade. It is not possible for a business to sell at the same prices as others and yet produce at substantially higher costs—not when its selling prices are governed by their lower costs. Nor is it possible for a business to sell a substantially poorer product than others at the same price they are asking for a better product. The penalty for falling too far behind either in efficiency or in quality of product is going out of business. The only way to avoid this penalty is by adopting the innovations before it is too late.

The fact that sooner or later competitors do adopt innovations not only enables them to increase their own profitability, or at least to restore it and thus to survive (which of these it is depends on how much sooner or later they adopt them), but it also takes away the special profits of the innovators. The fact that the special profits of innovating do tend to disappear, because competitors catch up, is what necessitates that everyone who wants to go on making an exceptional rate of profit over an extended period of time introduce repeated innovations. If he is to prevent the loss of all his special profits to competitors who are catching up, he must make fresh advances over them. In this way, the combination of the profit motive and the freedom of competition leads successful producers to seek continuous improvements. That is the only way they can sustain an exceptional rate of profit; they cannot rest content merely with their past successes.

In connection with the freedom of competition, it should be realized, moreover, that the ranks of businessmen are open to everyone, including penniless newcomers. Those who have a valuable idea, but lack the funds to implement it themselves, can offer a partnership to others who do have capital; and further capital can be borrowed. In a capitalist society, there is an enormously large number of possible sources of financing for any new idea. It is equal to the number of individuals or combinations of individuals who possess the amount of capital required. For example, if a million dollars is the sum required, there are as many potential sources of financing as there are individuals or combinations of individuals who possess a million dollars or more.

This situation guarantees that every new idea has many possible chances for being implemented. If the innovator does not possess the necessary capital himself, he can turn to as many separate sources of financing as there are individuals or groups who do possess the necessary capital. It is not necessary for him to convince everyone, a majority, or even a significant-sized minority of his fellow citizens that his idea is valuable before he can put it into practice. If he owns the necessary capital himself, he can go ahead without convincing any other person at all. If he does not own the necessary capital himself, then he needs to convince only a minority consisting of possibly just one other person, and in no case of more than a relative handful of people who in combination possess the necessary capital.

The importance of this fact cannot be overestimated. Not only are new ideas always the product of individual minds, known at first to just one individual member of the whole human race, but also, no matter how sound or important they are, their value is often not recognized for a considerable time by the overwhelming majority of other people. To confirm this fact, one has only to recall the difficulties even of such giants of progress as Columbus, Pasteur, Edison, Ford, the Wright brothers, and Goddard in obtaining recognition and support for their profoundly important innovations. Columbus had to spend years attempting to raise funds for his voyage, and was very lucky finally to succeed in doing so. Pasteur's theory that germs cause diseases was denounced by the French Academy of Sciences as a fraud. Edison's claim that he could produce electric light was denied by most of the physicists of his day. Ford and the Wright brothers were widely regarded as cranks. Goddard's ideas on rocketry and space flight were dismissed with contempt by such prominent publications as *The New York Times*. In the absence of a wide range of chances for new ideas being tried, the great majority of valuable innovations are unlikely to be tried, and, in the face of that prospect, unlikely even to be arrived at in the first place. In order for new ideas to flourish, it is essential that a sufficient number of opportunities for their implementation exist so that innovators can above all find ways around the prevailing "mainstream" views—that is, the views of the then current "experts." As von Mises often pointed out, the "experts" are always experts merely on the state of knowledge up to their time, never on the subject of new knowledge, which in the nature of the case has not yet entered the "mainstream" and is often at odds with the "mainstream."

Thus, in connection with the operation of the uniformity-of-profit principle, a capitalist society provides the incentive of profit to introduce continuous innovations and the incentive of avoiding losses to adopt the innovations of competitors. At the same time, it opens the possibility of introducing innovations to everyone in the entire society and provides an enormous number of possible sources of financing for innovations. It is impossible to imagine an economic system that could be more conducive to economic progress.

As for the translation of this process of innovation into terms of physical increases in production, it is probably self-evident that the introduction of new and/or improved products constitutes an increase in production or is a source of an increase in production. One has only to think of such cases as the automobile replacing the horse and buggy, or the automobile with the self-starter replacing the hand-cranked automobile, or such cases as the tractor bringing about a vast increase in the production of agricultural products, or the electric motor bringing about a vast increase in the production of all kinds of manufactured goods. It may be less obvious, however, how the day-by-day attention of businessmen to costs, and their constant efforts to reduce the costs of production, are an equally important source of the increase in production. Still less obvious is the role in increasing production that is played by correct anticipations of changes in consumer demand. Therefore, let us briefly consider the contribution of these factors to increasing production.

Reducing the costs of production means, for the most part, that one finds a way to produce the same amount of a good with less labor. This acts to increase production because it makes labor available to produce more of this good or more of other goods, somewhere else in the economic system. The saving of labor is clearest in the case in which the businessman achieves the cost reduction by employing labor-saving machinery. But even if the cost reduction is achieved by finding a way to use less of some material or a less costly material, labor will also be saved. If less of a material is required, less labor is required to produce the smaller quantity of the material. If a less costly material is required, it is probable that labor will be saved, since it is probable that the less costly material is less costly because less labor is required to produce it. To this extent, then, saving costs means saving labor and, therefore, making the means available for increasing production.

Even if a saving in the quantity of labor is not involved in a cost reduction, the ability to produce something with a less costly material, or with less costly labor for that matter—say, unskilled labor in place of skilled labor—still brings about a net increase in total production. What happens in these cases is that the more costly material or labor is released to expand the production of something else which is comparatively important, while the less costly material or labor that replaces it is withdrawn from the production of something else which is comparatively unimportant.

The principle here is perhaps best illustrated by the case of employing nurses and other aides for many of the tasks that would otherwise have to be performed by doctors. What is gained is the added work that can only be performed by doctors and which otherwise would have been impossible for lack of availability of doctors' time. What is lost is only the work that the nurses or whoever might have performed as secretaries, bookkeepers, or whatever. Every substitution of less costly labor for more costly labor is comparable to this case in its effect. The same applies to the substitution of less costly for more costly materials. In this way, a net economic gain, equivalent to an increase in production, takes place, because the production of something more important, that is, something with higher marginal utility, is increased at the expense of the production of something less important, that is, something with lower marginal utility. As far as labor goes, the ability to substitute unskilled for skilled labor and achieve equal results can also be viewed as the equivalent of increasing the intelligence and ability of workers, which in the very nature of the case must increase production.[6]

The correct anticipation of changes in consumer demand is also a necessary part of the process of increasing production. To understand this point, it must be realized that increases in production are one of the most important causes of wide-ranging changes in the pattern of consumer spending. For example, the steady improvements in agriculture and the consequent drop in the proportion of people's income that has had to be tied up in buying food has made possible a continuously growing demand for the whole range of industrial goods. Similarly, the introduction and development of the automobile brought about far-reaching shifts in demand: it made possible the development of the suburbs and a whole host of new businesses from gas stations to motels; expanded the demand for other businesses, such as ski resorts; reduced the demand for passenger railroads and horses; and virtually destroyed the businesses of buggymaking and blacksmithing. Every improvement in production exercises a similar, if less dramatic, effect on the demand for other goods.

In order for these shifts in demand to be accompanied by corresponding shifts in production, it is necessary for wide-ranging changes in the investment of capital to occur. Thus, to continue with the examples of agriculture and the automobile, capital had to be diverted from agriculture to industry, from cities to suburbs, from railroads, horsebreeding, buggymaking, and blacksmithing, to automaking, gas stations, motels, and ski resorts. To the extent that the appropriate shifts of capital did not occur, or occurred with undue delay, the benefit from the improvement in production was lost. For example, to the extent that capital was not shifted out of farming rapidly enough—as a result of government farm subsidies or the inertia of many farmers—the effect of the improvements in agriculture was limited to a relatively unwanted increase in agricultural production and correspondingly less of an increase in much more desired industrial production. Similarly, to the extent that capital would not have been shifted rapidly enough out of buggymaking and horsebreeding, the benefits from the automobile would have been held down: capital would have been wasted in buggymaking and horsebreeding which could have been employed with infinitely greater benefit in any

of the new or expanding industries brought about by the automobile. In all such cases, to fail to make the appropriate shifts of capital is to lose some or all of the benefit of the improvement in production. For this reason the correct anticipation of changes in consumer demand is an integral part of the process of increasing production.

I have established that the effect of the quest for an above-average rate of profit in the face of the operation of the uniformity-of-profit principle is to bring about the steady improvement and enlargement of production. The inescapable implication of this fact is a powerful tendency for prices to fall from year to year. It is necessary to reconcile this implication with the fact that based on the experience of almost everyone now living the reality appears to be that prices rise virtually every year.

The fall in prices that the profit motive has actually achieved can be clearly seen if prices are calculated not in terms of depreciating paper money, but in terms of *the amount of labor that the average worker must perform in order to earn the means of buying any given quantity of goods.* Today, the average worker performs perhaps forty hours of labor in a week and is able to obtain the goods that constitute his present standard of living. As we look back in time, however, we see that the hours of work that had to be performed were greater, and the goods constituting the average worker's standard of living were less. Thus, as time has gone on, and the average worker has come to receive more and more while working less and less, the quantity of goods he can obtain for each hour of his labor has increased. To say the same thing in different words, *the amount of labor he must perform in order to obtain a unit of goods has steadily decreased.* In this sense, prices—calculated in terms of the quantities of labor that must be performed in order to buy goods—actually have fallen steadily as the result of the operation of the profit motive.

The fact that in terms of paper money, prices have risen is the result of the fact that while prices of goods really do tend to fall because of the operation of the profit motive, the value of the paper money tends to fall still faster. When falling prices are expressed in a standard that itself falls even more rapidly (which is the case with paper money), they have the appearance of having risen. The following illustration will make this point obvious. In the early 1970s a primitive four-function pocket calculator sold for about $400. At the same time, a fairly primitive video tape recorder sold for about $2,400. Thus, at that time, it took 6 pocket calculators to represent the price of one video tape recorder. Today, the price of a much improved video tape recorder is about $400— which certainly represents a radical drop. But today, the price of a comparable pocket calculator is only about

$10. Thus, today, it takes *40* pocket calculators to equal the price of a video tape recorder instead of only 6. When the lower price of the video tape recorder is expressed in terms of pocket calculators, it appears to have risen instead of fallen, because the price of the pocket calculators has fallen so much more.

Exactly this principle applies to the rise in prices in terms of paper money. While the profit motive operates to reduce the prices of the mass of commodities and does in fact succeed in reducing them when expressed in any kind of reasonably fixed standard of value, the value of paper money falls even more rapidly and so gives the appearance that things have become more expensive instead of less expensive.

This result can be further understood if we realize that paper money is actually among the cheapest goods in the world to produce in the first place. It starts out with a virtually zero cost of production. If its production were open to the freedom of competition, so that anyone in possession of the appropriate paper and printing plates was allowed to manufacture it, its value would quickly be driven down to the value of goods with a comparable cost of production, such as pieces of note paper and pins. Indeed, its value would even be less, because it would not have the actual physical utility of such goods, and the need to carry vast quantities of it to buy other goods would destroy its usefulness as money. In other words, under the freedom of competition, the profit motive would soon make paper money absolutely worthless. All other goods would be worth an infinite quantity of it.

The value of paper money is not destroyed this quickly, because its creation is a monopoly privilege of the government. But even so, as we shall see, the government has powerful incentives to increase the quantity of paper money at a substantially more rapid rate than the scientists, inventors, businessmen, and savers and investors are able to increase the supply of goods.[7] The result is that while the productive work of these most intelligent and ambitious members of society may succeed in an average year in increasing the supply and thus tending to reduce the prices of goods by, say, three, four, five percent, or whatever, the government is easily able to outstrip their performance and increase the quantity of money and volume of spending in the economic system by a larger amount, with the result that prices rise instead of fall.

To summarize the discussion of the price system thus far: The desire of businessmen to earn profits and avoid losses, and to earn higher profits in preference to lower profits, brings about a tendency toward a uniform rate of profit on capital invested in all the different branches of industry. The operation of this tendency counteracts,

delimits, and largely prevents mistakes from being made in the relative production of the various goods. Because of it, consumers have the power of positive initiative to shift the course of production simply by changing the pattern of their spending; because of it, businessmen are made to act virtually as the consumers' agents. The operation of the tendency toward a uniform rate of profit requires that high profits be made by continuously introducing productive innovations in advance of competitors. These innovations are the base of a continuous increase in production, whether they take the form of new and improved products, reduced costs of production, or correct anticipations of changes in consumer demand. As such, they operate continuously to raise the average standard of living. They steadily enlarge and improve the goods available while reducing not only the amount of work that must be performed in order to produce any given quantity of goods but also the amount of work that must be performed in order to buy any given quantity of goods. In other words, they make possible progressively improved products at prices corresponding to progressively falling real costs of production.

On the basis of the foregoing, we must conclude that the profit motive and the price system of capitalism have been responsible for virtually all of the economic progress of the last two hundred years or more. They have ensured the maximum possible effort to introduce innovations and to extend their application as rapidly as possible, with the result that in comparatively short periods of time revolutionary improvements have become commonplace. Because of this and because of the rapid adaptation they assure to all changes in economic conditions, they have rendered every crisis, from natural disasters, to wars, to absurd acts of government, a merely temporary setback in a steady climb to greater prosperity.

Profits and the Repeal of Price Controls

What we have learned about the free market can be applied to a number of cases in which the free market does not or for a time did not exist in our country. A brief consideration of these cases will both illustrate the principle of the tendency of the rate of profit toward uniformity and provide a demonstration of the value to be gained by extending the free market.

Consider the case of government farm subsidies. Let us imagine that the government stopped buying up farm products to be stored or given away, and at the same time reduced taxes by the amount of money it saved in abolishing the farm subsidy program.

The effect would be a drop in the demand for farm products. But since the taxpayers would now have the money previously used to pay the subsidies, there would be a rise in the demand for a host of other products—

products which the taxpayers judged would satisfy the most important of their needs or wants which previously had had to go unsatisfied, such as an extra room added on to a house, a newer or better car, extra education, and so on, depending on the needs and desires of the various individuals concerned. The immediate effect of this shift of demand would be to depress prices and profits in farming and to raise them in these various other industries. The further consequence would be a withdrawal of capital and labor from farming and their transfer to the production of these other goods.

The movement of capital and labor out of farming would take place until the rate of profit in farming was raised back up to the general level, and the rate of profit earned on the various goods in additional demand by the taxpayers was brought down to the general level. Until this result was achieved, incentives would exist for a further movement of capital and labor out of farming and into these other fields. When the process was finally completed, therefore, the rate of profit earned in farming would be on a par with the rate of profit earned everywhere else. In accordance with the uniformity-of-profit principle, it would simply not be possible for the rate of profit in farming to be permanently depressed.

It follows from this analysis that in the long run those who remained in agriculture would tend to earn, on average, the same level of income they had earned before the repeal of the subsidies. Even the incomes of ex-farmers would, on average, come to be on a level comparable to what they had been initially. This would be the case as soon as the former farmers acquired industrial skills on a level comparable to those they had possessed in agriculture and so could take appropriate advantage of the new employment opportunities created by the expansion in the demand for industrial goods. The one permanent difference that would now exist and which would be of benefit to everyone, farmers and ex-farmers included, would be that the taxation of everyone's income would be smaller and everyone would be enabled to buy more of the goods he himself desired. Instead of everyone being forced to spend a part of his income, through the government, for the purchase of farm products to be uselessly stored or given away, he would be able to spend that part of his income for industrial goods of value and importance to his life. And those goods would be produced by the capital and labor previously employed in producing the farm products.

In sharpest contrast to the beneficial effects the uniformity-of-profit principle brings to the abolition of farm subsidies, are the further harmful effects it leads to if farm subsidies are retained. Insofar as the subsidized prices are above the costs of producing additional agricultural

output by more than is necessary to provide the going rate of profit, the incentive is created to increase production. The incentive is created to increase production all the way to the point that any further increase would have to be carried out under conditions of such diminishing returns and need to resort to land of inferior quality, that higher costs of production would finally offset the receipt of the artificially higher farm product prices and bring the rate of profit in agriculture down to the general level in this way. To reach this point, the government would have to purchase and store truly immense quantities of agricultural commodities. It would not only run out of grain elevators, as it did, but also probably run out of caves and the holds of mothballed ships, to which it has actually turned for use as supplementary storage facilities. And, not to be overlooked, its budget would be thrown substantially further out of balance.

To avoid these consequences, the government is led to seek ways to limit the increase in production its policy of farm subsidies makes profitable. Thus, it restricts the number of acres that can be planted. It may require that the growers have a special license in order to grow a crop. To a large extent the effect of this policy is to allow inefficient, high-cost producers to go on producing while prohibiting production by more efficient, low-cost producers. In a free market, the low-cost producers would expand production, drive the price down, and force the high-cost producers out of business. But this cannot happen when the price is prohibited from falling and the government restricts production.[8] This added policy of restricting production, of course, represents a blatant infringement of the right of people to use their own property as they see fit. And it has even taken such bizarre forms as imposing fines on farmers for growing food to feed to their own animals. The rationale for this outrage is that such food production makes it possible for the farmers in question to avoid buying feed and thus with the same feed production reaching the market imposes on the government the need to make additional purchases to maintain the price of crops used as feed. Thus individual liberty is sacrificed in order to hold down government expenditures which are absurd in the first place. In effect, the government begins by playing the role of a fool and ends by becoming a tyrant.

As a result of farm subsidies, until very recently a major portion of agricultural output was worse than wasted—it was used to sustain Communist regimes around the world through being given away to them for nothing under such programs as "Food for Peace," or in exchange for funds provided to the Communist regimes by private banks under loans whose repayment was guaranteed by the U.S. government. In sustaining these regimes, which would otherwise have fallen many years ago from a lack of food supplies caused by the inherent nature of socialism, the farm subsidy program perpetuated the need for large-scale defense spending, in order to be able to provide security against the permanent policy of aggression of such regimes. It thereby operated to multiply the burden of taxation far beyond its own, direct cost.

A related consequence of the existence of agricultural surpluses which would otherwise rot, and which the government's restrictions on production have served merely to diminish, not eliminate, has been the encouragement of public dependency and unemployment in the United States. These are results of the food stamp program, which provides large numbers of American citizens with the ability to obtain free food, and thus acts as a major public welfare program, enabling many people to live without working.

I chose the example of farm subsidies mainly to illustrate how the free market reacts when the profitability of an industry is initially rendered low. Farm subsidies, however, represent a form of price controls different from the kind we shall predominantly be concerned with in the first half of this book. Farm subsidies are a way the government achieves artificially high prices. They are an illustration of legal minimum prices—that is, prices below which the government prevents the producers from selling. They are comparable in their effects to minimum-wage legislation. They cause unsaleable surpluses—which, in the case of labor, means unemployment. We will deal with such price controls further and at length in the second half of this book, in the discussion of unemployment and depressions. The kind of price controls that we want to focus on first, because they are most directly relevant to the subject of the dependence of the division of labor on capitalism, are controls designed to keep prices artificially low—that is, legal maximum prices or ceiling prices, namely, prices above which one is not allowed to sell.

Thus let us take as a second major illustration of the effects of the repeal of price controls, the consequences that would follow if rent controls were repealed.

To simplify this discussion, let us assume that the entire supply of rental housing in a given locality has been under controls. In this case, the first effect of the repeal of controls would simply be a jump in all rents. As a result of the jump, however, rental housing would again become profitable—in fact, as a result of previously inadequate building due to rent controls, extremely profitable. However, it is impossible that the rental housing industry should be permanently more profitable than other industries. The high rate of profit would be the incentive, and would itself provide much of the means,

for expanded investment in the rental housing industry. There would be a building boom in rental housing. As a result, the supply of rental housing would be stepped up and the rents and the profitability of rental housing would begin to fall and would go on falling until the rate of profit in rental housing was no higher than the rate of profit in industry generally. The long-run effect of the repeal of rent controls, therefore, would simply be an increase in the supply of rental housing. Rents themselves in the long run would be no higher than corresponded to the costs of constructing and operating apartment houses, with profits only enough to make the industry competitive, by providing the going or average rate of profit.[9]

Exactly the same effects would follow the repeal of price controls on crude oil, natural gas, or any other good. There would be a temporary surge in price and profit, followed by expanded production and a reduction in price and profit to the point where the price corresponded to the good's production cost and allowed only enough profit to make the good's production competitive. The repeal of the price controls on domestically produced oil and oil products in the United States in 1981 provides an excellent illustration of this proposition. After a temporary surge in its profitability, followed by a major expansion in domestic production and fall in the price of oil and oil products, the American oil industry ceased to be extraordinarily profitable.

Of course, it should not be forgotten that once a price control is repealed, the dynamic effects of the uniformity-of-profit principle take over. As we have seen, if someone wants to make an above-average rate of profit on a free market, he must strive to reduce his costs of production and improve the quality of his products, and repeatedly succeed in doing this ahead of his rivals. This means that in the absence of controls, costs and prices tend steadily to *fall*—if not in terms of a depreciating paper money, then nevertheless in terms of the time people must spend to earn the money to buy goods. Once controls are repealed and a free market established, the free competitive quest for high profits causes prices to fall further and further below the point at which they were controlled, while the quality of goods rises higher and higher.

It should be obvious that the repeal of rent controls would act to end New York City's housing shortage and make possible an enormous improvement in the quantity and quality of housing for the average person in New York City, and continuing improvements thereafter. It should be equally obvious that the repeal of price controls on crude oil and on natural gas, if not sabotaged by such measures as the government's physically closing off the sources of an expanded supply of energy, act to set the stage for growing supplies of these goods and thus for a return to America's traditional abundance, indeed, growing abundance, of energy supplies.

In sum, it should already be clear, even at this stage of our knowledge, that the problems we have experienced in these areas have been the result of government controls and that the solution lies with the extension of economic freedom and thus, among other things, of the ability of the profit motive and the price system to operate to achieve their benevolent consequences. More broadly, the solution lies with the intensification of the capitalist elements that have traditionally characterized the economic system of the United States, and which have been increasingly restricted.

Of course, the ability of the profit motive and the price system, and other essential elements of capitalism, such as saving and capital accumulation, to achieve continuous economic progress, should not be thought to be hindered in any fundamental way by a possible lack of natural resources. Nor should such economic progress be thought to be dangerous or undesirable by virtue of "harming the environment." I have already demonstrated in Chapter 3 how capitalism operates continuously to increase the supply of economically useable natural resources along with the supply of products. In the same place, I have also shown how the inherent nature of production is to make the chemical elements provided by nature, and which constitute the totality of the physical world, stand in an improved relationship to man—that is, to improve his environment.[10]

The Effect of Business Tax Exemptions and Their Elimination

The uniformity-of-profit principle sheds light on the effect of business tax exemptions and their elimination. For example, for many years prior to 1975, the U.S. oil industry, along with other extractive industries, was able to deduct from its taxable income a depletion allowance based on the value of the oil it extracted, and thus to reduce its overall effective rate of taxation. The effect of the depletion allowance was not to make the oil industry permanently more profitable than other industries, however.

It is true that the initial effect of such a tax advantage is to raise an industry's after-tax rate of profit relative to that of other industries. But the higher after-tax rate of profit then results in the attraction of additional capital to the industry, and itself provides such additional capital, with the result that the industry's rate of profit falls back toward the general, average after-tax level. The effect is that the industry is larger, its production is greater, and the price of its product is lower. It does not permanently earn a higher rate of profit.

This principle applies even if the industry is totally tax exempt. Then the effect is simply that the industry's expansion is carried that much further, but not that its rate of profit remains permanently above the going or average rate. The total exemption from the federal income tax of bonds issued by state and local governments provides an excellent illustration of the principle. Because of their tax exemption, these bonds are purchased to the point that the rate of return they afford is on a par with the after-tax rate of return of bonds that are fully subject to the federal income tax.

By the same token, of course, repeal of a tax exemption, once it has been incorporated into the pattern of investment, is tantamount to a reduction in an industry's rate of profit. If its effect is to reduce the industry's rate of profit below the general rate, then the consequence will be a withdrawal of capital and a reduction in the size of the industry, until the smaller industry that remains can once again earn the going rate of profit—by charging a higher price for its product. (If the rate of profit of the industry is not pushed below the going or average rate, because of the presence of some factor such as an increase in the demand for the industry's product, the effect will be that the industry will grow less than it otherwise would have, and the price of its product will not fall to the same extent that it otherwise would have.)

In the 1970s, in the midst of a widely proclaimed "energy crisis," the U.S. government, in addition to imposing price controls on oil, acted to further restrict oil company profits, and thus oil industry investment, by punitively increasing their rate of taxation precisely by first reducing and then totally abolishing the customary depletion allowance on crude oil. The effect was a further blow to domestic oil production.

Additional Bases for the Uniformity-of-Profit Principle

Before leaving the uniformity-of-profit principle, it must be pointed out that in addition to changes in the selling prices of products resulting from changes in the amount of capital invested in an industry, other factors also operate to establish a uniform rate of profit among the different branches of production. One of these has already been indicated in the discussion of the effects of repealing or maintaining farm subsidies. There it was pointed out that as agricultural output is increased, unit costs rise as the result of the operation of the law of diminishing returns and the need to resort to land of inferior quality. The same factors operate on unit costs in the case of mining. And obviously they operate in reverse when it is a question of reducing the production of agricultural commodities or minerals. Thus, in cases of this kind, the investment of additional capital operates to reduce the rate of profit by virtue of bringing about a combination of lower selling prices and higher unit costs of production, not simply lower selling prices alone. By the same token, the withdrawal of capital in such cases operates to raise the rate of profit by virtue of a bringing about a combination of higher selling prices and lower unit costs of production, not simply higher selling prices alone.

A second, similar factor, which is of relevance throughout the economic system, is a possible rise or fall in the prices of the factors of production used in an industry, as the capital invested in the industry, and thus its level of output, increases or decreases. As later discussion will show, factors of production such as labor and many raw materials exist at any given time in a given supply. The prices of such factors of production are determined by the combination of their given supply and the prevailing demand.[11] Thus insofar as changes in capital investment change the relationship between the demand for such factors of production and their supply, they change the prices of such factors of production.

Thus, for example, if the demand for one product rises and the demand for another product falls, and if the labor or raw materials used in the production of the products cannot be transferred from the one to the other, then changes in the prices of these factors of production will occur. For example, if the demand for a product made of iron rises and the demand for a product made of cotton falls, no part of the supply of cotton can be used to meet the additional demand that will result for iron ore. Nor can the land that produces cotton be used in the production of additional iron ore. As a result, the effect will be a rise in the price of iron and a fall in the price of cotton. Similarly, if the demand for a product requiring one type of labor skill rises while the demand for a product requiring a different type of labor skill falls, the result will be a rise in the wage rate of the one kind of labor and a fall in the wage rate of the other kind of labor.

In all such cases, the industry whose product is in greater demand and whose rate of profit has been elevated above the average, will, as before, experience an influx of capital investment. In these circumstances, the effect of the additional capital investment will be not only to increase the supply and reduce the selling price of the product, but also to raise the demand relative to the supply of one or more of the factors of production the industry uses. This will raise the price of those factors of production and thus the industry's unit cost of production. Thus, in this case too, the industry's rate of profit will fall toward the general level both because of a fall in its selling price and a rise in its costs.

By the same token, the industry whose product is in decreased demand and whose rate of profit has been depressed below the general level, will, as before, experience an efflux of capital. The effect will be both to reduce the supply of its product and the demand for one or more of the factors of production it uses. Thus, while the selling price of its product tends to rise, the prices that constitute its costs of production tend to fall. Its rate of profit, therefore, tends to be restored to the general level as the result of both of these phenomena.

It should be realized that this discussion implies that the uniformity-of-profit principle operates even in circumstances in which it is physically not possible to increase the production of a product because one or more of the necessary factors of production simply does not exist. For example, if there is an increase in demand for a particular wine, which must be made from grapes that can be grown only on a small quantity of land on which very special growing conditions exist, the first effect will be a rise in the price of the wine and in the rate of profit to be made in producing the wine. As usual, additional capital will now tend to be invested in producing the item, but the effect of the additional investment in this case will simply be to raise the price of the grapes and the vineyards. The rate of profit in this case will be brought down to the general level without an increase in supply and fall in the price of the product. It will be brought down by virtue of the rise in the prices of the factors of production and in the amount of capital that must be invested in order to earn any larger amount of profit. The winery will not be able to go on making an above-average rate of profit, because it will have to pay a correspondingly higher price of grapes. The vineyard, that receives the higher price of the grapes, will not be able to go on making a higher rate of profit, because the value of the vineyard will increase to the point that its larger amount of profit, earned on the more valuable grape crop, is divided by a correspondingly larger amount of capital that must be invested in order to purchase such a vineyard. If, of course, the demand for the wine later falls, the result will be a fall in the price of the grapes and in the value of the vineyard, which will once again tend to establish a rate of profit on a par with the general rate.

Still another factor working to establish a uniform rate of profit is changes in the percentage of capacity at which plant and equipment are operated, or, for short, changes in the operating rate of firms. Indeed, it is possible, within limits, that this factor can work even in the absence of changes in the price both of the product and of the factors of production used to produce it.

Whenever there is an increase in demand for the product of an industry which possesses unused plant capacity, the effect is to make that industry operate at a higher level of capacity. By the same token, the effect of a decrease in demand is to cause the industry to operate at a lower level of capacity. Even if the price of the product does not change, the change in the extent to which plant capacity is utilized makes the average profit margin in the industry vary in the same direction as the change in demand. This is because utilizing plant capacity at a higher rate spreads such fixed costs as depreciation quotas over more units of product and thus reduces unit costs. Thus the profit per unit and the average profit margin increase. Furthermore, in causing a higher operating rate at unchanged selling prices, the rise in demand also causes a rise in the rate of capital turnover, inasmuch as a larger physical volume of goods sold at the same prices represents greater sales revenues. While sales revenues are markedly greater, the size of the capital invested in the plants operating at higher rates increases only by the necessary increase in working capital—that is, the capital invested in such things as inventory and work in progress. This means that the increase in capital almost certainly takes place in much smaller proportion than the increase in sales revenues. Thus, on the strength both of a higher profit margin and higher capital turnover ratio, the rate of profit on capital invested in the industry necessarily increases as the demand for its products rises.[12] Of course, for the same reasons as just given, but working in reverse, the rate of profit on capital invested in an industry necessarily falls when a fall in demand causes operation at a lower level of capacity.

On the basis of such facts, a rise in the demand for a product may be accompanied by an above-average rate of profit simply by virtue of a rise in the operating rate of the industry, without a rise in the selling prices of its products. In response to this higher rate of profit, additional capital is invested, and the effect of the additional investment is to reduce the rate of profit of the industry, back toward the general level, merely by virtue of the consequence being a reduction in the rate of capacity utilization. Similarly, the withdrawal of capital from an industry with a below-average rate of profit can restore the rate of profit merely by virtue of raising the operating rate of the plant and equipment that remains. This mechanism of adjustment can exist in an industry which normally maintains the same selling prices so long as it operates within some defined range of capacity, and which experiences a pronounced tendency toward a rise or fall in its average rate of operations due to changes in demand. Before the rise in demand is such as to outstrip its ability to meet it at the prevailing prices of its products, it adds to its capacity and meets the now higher level of demand with additional capacity. The advantage to the firms which do this is that it forestalls the possibility of competitors or potential competitors seizing the opportunity of meeting the additional demand. In that case, not only would the rate of profit of the firms which undertake the expansion come back down, but their share of the

market would be reduced as well. Likewise, before a declining demand goes too far, it may be accompanied by decisions not to replace plant and equipment otherwise coming due for replacement.

Thus, changes in demand may result in changes in the rate of profit leading in the usual way to changes in investment and a resulting movement of the rate of profit back to the going rate without the necessity of changes in the price of the product.[13]

It must be stressed that the uniformity-of-profit principle describes a *tendency,* never an actually existing state of affairs. This is because before a uniform rate of profit can be achieved in all branches of production, new changes occur, requiring a different pattern of investment of capital in the economic system if such uniformity is to be achieved. And before the relative size of the various industries can be adjusted to conform with that pattern, still further changes occur, requiring yet another pattern of investment of capital, and so on without end. Thus, the economic system never comes to rest in an actual state of final equilibrium, whose existence is an essential condition of the existence of a uniform rate of profit. The economic system is merely tending toward such an equilibrium, which is itself constantly changing.[14]

The final equilibrium toward which the economic system tends constantly changes because of continuous changes in such phenomena as the state of technology and supply of capital equipment, population and its distribution in terms of age and sex, climate and weather conditions, usefulness of various areas for mining, and so on.[15] The uniformity-of-profit principle is nonetheless fully real. Its reality is confirmed by the fact that definite changes *must* occur in order to prevent its realization. Among the most important of such changes, of course, is, as we have seen, the continuous innovation required to stay ahead of competitors, whose emulation of one's earlier improvements would, in fact, drive one's profits down to the average rate if one did not continue to innovate.

Permanent Inequalities in the Rate of Profit

In addition to the fact that there is constant change in the final state of equilibrium toward which the economic system tends, there are factors operating to create permanent inequalities in the rate of profit even in a state of unchanging final equilibrium. In a sense, inequalities in the rate of taxation can be described as such a factor, in that in order to earn equal after-tax rates of profit, the more-heavily-taxed industries will require a higher pretax rates of profit than the less-heavily-taxed industries.

If a branch of business is subjected to any other form of legal disability, in particular, if it is simply made altogether illegal, then that fact will operate to make it earn a permanently higher rate of profit than other branches of business. This is because no one will engage in that line of business unless, over and above the going or average rate of return, the profits provide compensation for the risk of incurring the legal penalties imposed. Thus, the illegalization of such activities as gambling, prostitution, and narcotics, for which, however regrettably, a substantial portion of the population is ready to pay, has the ironic effect of enabling those who are prepared to engage in them and who, in addition, are willing to break the law, to earn premium incomes.

Apart from all government intervention, there is also the fact that in many cases the profits earned must compete with the wages and salaries that the businessmen involved could have earned by working elsewhere, as employees. This phenomenon is especially important in the case of small, unincorporated business firms, in which much or even all of the physical labor performed is performed by the owners. When expressed as a percentage of the capital invested, the profits of such firms tend to constitute a far higher percentage than the profits of larger-sized firms, in which comparable labor is performed by paid employees. Thus, for example, a drug store chain, with pharmacists and branch managers who are paid employees, will tend to earn the same rate of profit as the average department store chain, automobile company, or steel company. But a small, independently owned drug store, in which the owner performs the labor of a pharmacist and manager, will tend to earn a rate of profit that is high enough to include compensation that is comparable to what the owner could earn in these capacities if he worked as the paid employee of a chain. The same principle, of course, applies to all other small businesses in which the owner performs labor that elsewhere is performed by paid employees.[16] It is possible that because of the satisfaction derived from owning one's own business, the profits in these cases, while substantially higher in terms of a rate of profit, nevertheless fall somewhat short of fully compensating for the wages or salary that could be earned working elsewhere.

A permanent inequality in the rate of return on capital invested can exist between the rate of profit in the narrower sense and the rate of interest.

Whenever the rate of profit is spoken of, without qualification, it should be understood as reflecting profit *gross* of interest payments—that is, prior to deduction of interest payments. The prospective rate of profit in this sense is what determines whether or not it is worthwhile to pay any given rate of interest. For example, in deciding whether or not it pays to borrow a million dollars at a 10 percent rate of interest, a businessman will wish to know what rate of profit he can make by investing that million. It will pay to borrow only if the prospective rate of profit is somewhat greater than 10 percent.

The rate of profit in this sense, or, as it is often called, the rate of return on capital invested, can be calculated in any given case simply by adding interest payments back to profits net of interest, and then dividing by the total of the invested capital that is owned by the business itself plus the borrowed capital the business uses. By the same token, a rate of profit in the narrower sense can be found by dividing the profit net of interest exclusively by the invested capital that is owned by the business itself.

The following example makes these distinctions clear. If a business borrows $1 million at a 10 percent rate of interest, and already has $1 million of invested capital of its own, and earns a profit gross of interest of $220 thousand, its rate of profit—its overall rate of return on the total capital invested of $2 million—is 11 percent. At the same time, its rate of profit in the narrower sense of profit net of interest, divided only by its own invested capital, is 12 percent.

We should view the relationship between the rate of profit in the narrower sense and the rate of interest in the light of the following: Equity investors and lenders, or, in a corporate structure, stockholders and bond and noteholders, come together as classes of partners, each with special ownership rights, and jointly invest their capitals in enterprises. The lenders agree to receive a fixed and limited return on their capitals on condition that the capital of the equity investors serve as a buffer between them and any below-average profits or outright losses which the enterprise as a whole might suffer. The equity investors agree to allow their capital to serve as such a buffer, and have claim to everything the enterprise may earn after meeting its contractually fixed obligations to the lenders. The total investment in the enterprise may then earn the average rate of profit, an above-average rate of profit, or a below-average rate of profit, including an outright loss. As a rule, any above-average rate of profit earned on the investment as a whole will accrue to the equity-capital investors; and when considered as a part of the rate of return on the equity capital, will magnify this rate of return to the degree that the equity capital represents a smaller percentage of the total capital, i.e., to the extent that it is leveraged. To the extent that the investment as a whole fails to earn as much as the average rate of profit, the failure is borne first by the equity investors, who may not only earn no return whatever, but may also lose the full amount of their capitals, and only then by the lenders. And this reduction in the rate of return to the equity capitalists will be magnified to the degree that the equity capital represents a smaller fraction of the total capital, that is, to the extent that it is leveraged.

As these remarks suggest, while the rate of profit gross of interest is the determinant of the rate of interest, it is not necessary that the two be equal. It is likely that the greater degree of certainty and safety attaching to loan capital and its return will depress that return somewhat below the average rate of profit inclusive of interest. Indeed, in conditions of rapid economic progress and keen competition in the process of improvement, the rate of profit in the narrower sense tends to be significantly and permanently higher than the rate of interest. In such conditions, the general rate of profit on capital as such may be relatively high, for reasons to be explained in Chapter 16. Yet high rates of profit are available only to those who are capable of introducing improvements or at least rapidly adapting to them. All others, if they are prudent, will be content to accept a much lower and, for them, much more secure rate of return, in the form of interest.

In the light of the preceding discussion, the frequent complaint that one can borrow money only to the extent that one already has it, appears absurd. Nothing could be more natural or reasonable than that one must have money in order to borrow money. This is because if one is to acquire the funds of others at a fixed, limited rate of return, one must have the means of ensuring that these funds and the promised return are protected. In essence, all loans are margin loans. Only to the extent that the borrower himself possesses capital can he provide a margin of safety on a larger total capital. It is thus no less absurd to complain that people cannot borrow funds except to the degree that they already possess funds than it would be to complain that one cannot speculate on the stock exchange beyond the degree that one can provide the necessary margin. Every entrepreneur must himself be a capitalist or he must find a capitalist who is willing to be his partner in entrepreneurship. In every venture in which lenders have capital there must also be equity capital. To secure more borrowed capital, there must be more equity capital.

2. The Tendency Toward a Uniform Price for the Same Good Throughout the World

A second principle of price determination, similar and closely related to the uniformity-of-profit principle, and which also plays a major role in coordinating the division of labor, is that *in a free market there is a tendency toward the establishment of a uniform price for the same good throughout the world.*

The basis of this principle is the fact that any inequality in the price of the same good between two markets creates an opportunity for profit. In order to profit, all one need do is buy in the cheaper market and sell in the dearer market. The very fact of doing this, however, acts to reduce the inequality in price. For the additional buying raises the price in the cheaper market and the additional selling lowers it in the more expensive market. The process tends to continue until the inequality in price between the two markets is totally eliminated and a uniformity of price achieved.

The reason that uniform prices among different geographical markets are not actually established is mainly the existence of transportation costs. The existence of these costs means that before a price discrepancy between two markets becomes profitable to exploit, it must exceed these transportation costs. These costs, however, then set the limits which geographical price discrepancies do not tend to exceed. Or, to put it positively, the price of the same good tends to be uniform throughout the world except for transportation costs between markets.

(In the case of goods sold by a single seller, such as those with brandnames or under patent protection, the principle may take the form that the wholesale price in the market that imports tends not to exceed the retail price in the market that exports, plus transportation costs. So long as the good is publicly available to all comers at the retail level in any given country, its wholesale price in a free market cannot for long be greater elsewhere by more than the costs of transportation. Thus, for example, in a free market, while American pharmaceutical manufacturers might charge less for various patented drugs in Mexico than in the United States, because of the lower incomes and thus smaller demand for drugs in Mexico, they would not be able to do so for very long by more than corresponded to this variant of the principle.)

The significance of the principle of the tendency toward a geographic uniformity of prices is very great. Its operation explains, for example, why local crop failures in a free market do not result even in significant scarcities, let alone famines. The effect of a failure of the local grain crop, say, is to begin raising the price of grain in the local market. Once the local price of grain exceeds prices in outside markets by more than transportation costs, it becomes profitable to buy in those outside markets and sell locally. The effect is that the reduction in the local supply is almost entirely made good by drawing on the production of the rest of the world. Consequently, instead of a disastrous reduction in the local supply and an enormous rise in the local price, there is a modest reduction in the world supply and a modest rise in the world price of grain.

A good analogy to what happens is provided by the physical principle that water seeks its level. Imagine that you have just filled an ice tray—the kind in which water is able to flow around and underneath the plastic or metal insert that marks off the separate compartments for the ice cubes. If you now remove water from one compartment of the tray, you will not reduce the water level in that compartment by the amount of water you take from it. You will reduce the water level in that compartment and in the whole tray very slightly, because the loss from the one compartment will be spread over the whole tray.

In just the same way, if half the wheat crop of France were lost, the supply of wheat in France would not fall by half. On the contrary, the supply in France and in the whole world might fall by 2 or 3 percent—or however much of a decline the French loss represented in the world supply.

Water seeks its level by virtue of the force of pressure. It moves from places of higher pressure to places of lower pressure. Commodity supplies seek their level by virtue of the attraction of profits. They move from places of lower prices to places of higher prices, in the process equalizing prices as the movement of water equalizes pressure.

It should be realized that the principle of the tendency toward a geographical uniformity of prices is not only descriptively analogous to a law of physics, but, as far as the ability of governments to act is concerned, has the same *existential status* as a law of physics. (And so, incidentally, do all the principles of economics.) [17] That means it is impossible even for the world's most powerful governments to annul its operation. Governments can frustrate its operation, but even in the cases in which they do so, they cannot annul its operation. The existence of the principle is confirmed by the very attempts to frustrate it, because to frustrate it, definite means must be adopted, which are necessary only because the principle exists, and is working. For example, governments may adopt tariffs, or they may prohibit imports or exports altogether, and in that way stop the equalization of prices. But why must they resort to such measures? The answer is because the principle does exist and is at work even in a controlled economy. Controls of a specific kind are needed to counter it. There is no difference here between economics and the example of water seeking its level. We can make ice trays in which each compartment is totally insulated from the others. That does not contradict the principle that water seeks its level. It confirms it, because the insulation is required only because water does seek its level, and for some reason one wishes to stop it from doing so. It is the same way with all economic laws and government attempts to frustrate them.

Why the Arab Oil Embargo Would Not Have Been a Threat to a Free Economy

The principle that in a free market there tends to be a uniform price for the same good throughout the world has major application to the Arab oil embargo of 1973–74. The principle shows that if the United States had had a free market in oil when the Arabs imposed their embargo, our oil supplies could not have been seriously jeopardized.

Let us think back to the time of the embargo, and imagine that everything else is the same except that the United States has a free market in oil.

The Arabs now launch their embargo. The immediate effect is that a large part of the oil supplies of the northeastern United States—the major importing region and the one dependent on the Arabs—is cut off.

In a free market, no sooner would this have happened, than the price of oil and oil products in the Northeast would have begun to rise. Once prices in the Northeast came to exceed those in the rest of the country by more than the costs of transportation, supplies would have moved from the rest of the country to the Northeast. The effect would have been largely to replenish supplies in the Northeast and to reduce supplies somewhat in the rest of the country. The reduction in imports from the Arabs, in other words, would have been spread over the whole country instead of being concentrated in the Northeast, where it threatened to cripple the economy of the region. In this way, its impact would have been minimized. Prices in the Northeast would have been held down by the inflow of the new supplies, and those in the rest of the country raised up by the shipments to the Northeast.

In fact, the higher level of oil prices in the Northeast and in the country as a whole would have acted as a magnet to supplies of oil from outside the country. The same motives that would have impelled a Southern or Midwestern oil producer to send additional supplies to New York or Boston would also have impelled a Venezuelan or Nigerian producer to do so. In fact, additional imports could have come from the most remote places. As the rise in prices in the Northeast pulled up prices in the rest of the country, it could very well have become profitable to start shipping additional supplies to the West Coast from oil-producing areas like Indonesia, thereby freeing more of domestic production for supplying the Northeast.

Indeed, the United States could have gone on benefitting from Arab oil! This would have occurred simply as a result of expanding the import of refined petroleum products made from Arab oil in places not subject to the Arab embargo. For example, if the Arabs continued to supply Spanish refineries, say, and the price of refined products had risen in the United States, those refineries would have diverted more of their output to the United States.

It thus becomes apparent that within a fairly short time

an embargo by the Arabs against oil shipments to the United States would have had very little effect on the supply of oil in the United States. To the extent that the United States had been importing Arab oil, it would, for the most part, merely have changed importers, and, for much of the rest, it would even have continued to benefit indirectly from Arab oil, in the form of importing refined products made from Arab oil in non-Arab countries.

The reason the Arab embargo did threaten us was the existence of our price controls on oil and oil products. These price controls had been imposed by President Nixon in August of 1971, as part of a temporary general price freeze, and then remained in force after almost all of the other price controls were removed. Thus, when oil supplies to the Northeast were cut off by the embargo, price controls prohibited the people in the Northeast from bidding up oil prices. The people in the Northeast were therefore made powerless to bring about the shipment of additional supplies from the rest of the country. In the same way, price controls prohibited the people of the United States as a whole from biding up prices, with the result that it was not possible to bring about stepped-up imports from non-Arab sources. The effect of our controls was to cause the reduction in imports from the Arabs to be experienced with full force at its initial point of impact and to make it impossible to obtain replacement imports. Our price controls paralyzed us—they made it impossible for us to take the actions needed to deal with the situation.

Indeed, because of our price controls, we were not only prevented from finding replacement imports for the loss of Arab imports, but were forced to lose imports from non-Arab sources as well! This happened because other countries in the world, such as West Germany, became better markets in which to sell oil than the United States. As a result, our non-Arab foreign suppliers were led to sell more of their oil to those countries and less to us. Because of our price controls, we tied our hands in the international competition for oil, and made it possible for countries far poorer than ourselves to outbid us for oil we had normally consumed.

There is more to say about why a free American economy would have had nothing to fear from an Arab embargo.

In late 1973 and early 1974, the Arabs were apparently threatening to cut off oil supplies to the world. There was near panic over whether they would do so. There seemed to be no solution except either to give in to their demands, whatever they might be, or go to war with them.

If we had had a free economy, the only lasting effect of any embargo the Arabs might have launched against the rest of the world would have been to strengthen our oil industry at the expense of their oil industry.

To understand this point, let us assume that the American economy had been free of all price controls in 1973 and that the Arabs had launched their embargo with the serious intention of cutting off their supply of oil to the world. Let us assume that the worst fears people had at the time came true and that the Arabs simply stopped selling oil to anyone, in an effort to blackmail the world into doing their bidding.

The effect, of course, would have been a skyrocketing of the price of oil.

But observe. The Arabs wouldn't have gotten the benefit of the higher price, because *they* wouldn't have been selling any oil.

The benefit of the higher price of oil would have gone to the non-Arab producers, mainly to the producers in the United States.

The American oil companies in that case really would have made fabulous profits. They might have made profits at a rate fast enough to double their capitals in a single year, or less. They would have made the kind of money the Arabs made.

In the face of the Arabs' withdrawal from the market, a tendency would have set in to reestablish the United States as an oil exporter, because Western Europe and Japan would have had to turn to us. However much prices skyrocketed here, they would have skyrocketed still more there. Instead of our high prices pulling oil in, we would have begun to ship oil out, in response to their still higher prices. Billions of dollars would have begun to flow from Western Europe and Japan to the United States, not to Iran or Saudi Arabia.

With vast profits starting to pour in from the rest of the world and, of course, from American buyers too, huge sums would have become available for every kind of oil and energy project in the United States. It would not have taken long, with such profits, for the domestic oil industry to have been entirely rejuvenated and established on an enormously larger scale than ever before, and who knows what other new sources of energy along with it.

Now consider the Arabs. While the American oil producers would have been making money hand over fist, the Arabs would have been starving for lack of income. In this context, it would have been virtually certain that the Arab alliance would soon have broken up. The less fanatical Arab countries would soon have resumed the sale of oil in order to cash in on the profits. Probably, in very short order, all of them would have begun selling again. So, in fact, the supply of oil in the world would almost certainly not have been drastically reduced for very long, despite whatever intentions the Arabs may originally have had. And, therefore, the United States would not, in fact, have had to switch for very long, if at all, from the role of an oil importer to the sudden role of an oil exporter. But to whatever extent the Arabs had delayed in resuming the sale of oil, the effect of their action would have been to impoverish themselves while enormously enriching the oil industry in every other country, especially the United States.

In the years that followed, the American oil industry would have been bigger and richer. American oil production and the production of other forms of energy in the United States would have been expanded because of the additional profits that American firms had earned. Very possibly, a year or two after the embargo, the price of oil would have fallen below its level in the period before the embargo, because of expanded American production. The oil industry at that point might have run at losses for a while. The American firms would have been able to cover their losses out of the profits the Arabs had handed them. The Arabs would not have been able to cover their losses as easily. Consequently, the effect of the whole process would have been a larger American oil industry and, quite possibly, a smaller Arab oil industry.

This is what economic freedom would have accomplished.

The question might be raised of just how high oil prices could have gone during the Arab embargo if we had not had price controls. It is impossible to answer such a question with any accuracy. Perhaps for a brief period we might have had very high prices of oil and oil products. While they lasted, such prices would certainly have represented a hardship for many people, the author of this book included. But later we would have had lower prices than we had, thanks to a larger domestic oil industry and energy industry in general. Indeed, the preceding discussions make clear that the rise could not have been very great for very long, and that in a short time, oil prices would have begun to fall, just as has turned out to be the case since the repeal of the price controls. Furthermore, as we will see, even while a high price lasts, the real problem is not the high price, but the scarce supply. No one's hardship is alleviated by a low price for goods he cannot buy, which is always the effect of price controls. If we in fact have a scarcity, and consumption must be restricted, then, as will be shown, the high price is necessary and positively beneficial, because it leads people to restrict their consumption in the ways that are least damaging to themselves.

The policy of price controls on oil during the embargo, therefore, cannot even be said to have sacrificed our long-run economic well-being to our short-run economic well-being. It sacrificed both our long-run and our short-run economic well-being.

Tariffs, Transportation Costs, and the Case for Unilateral Free Trade

The existence of tariffs modifies the operation of the principle that the price of a good tends to be the same throughout the world in exactly the same way as does the existence of transportation costs. Namely, it allows the prices of goods to differ between two markets by a wider margin, equivalent to the existence of additional transportation costs—that is, by the sum of transportation costs between the two markets plus the amount of the tariff. Now, only when the price of a good in one market comes to exceed its price in another market by more than the sum of transportation cost plus tariff, does it pay to buy in the cheaper market and sell in the dearer market. This, of course, operates to drive the discrepancy in price to the point where it no longer exceeds the sum of transportation cost plus tariff.

The fact that tariffs have the same effect on price differentials between markets as do transportation costs, and can be analyzed as the equivalent of additional transportation costs, implies that a country must benefit from a policy of free trade even if it adopts that policy *unilaterally,* with its citizens having to go on selling their goods in countries that continue to maintain tariff barriers. For a policy of unilateral free trade is analytically equivalent in its effects to a fall in inbound transportation costs while outbound transportation costs remain the same.

In the nature of the case, the inhabitants of a territory must benefit from the fact that the cost of transporting goods to them is as low as possible. The fact that it is lower than the cost of transporting goods from them to other areas can make no difference. If, for example, they were fortunate enough to live in a territory toward whose coast the predominant winds blew or the ocean current flowed and which, accordingly, found itself with correspondingly low inbound transportation costs, they would benefit from that fact, even though inbound transportation costs were thereby rendered less than outbound transportation costs. The fact that it is not equally less costly for their goods to reach others does not take away the advantages to them of others' goods being able to reach them more cheaply. It would be the height of absurdity on their part to demand that inbound freight be rendered artificially more costly, say, by requiring inbound ships to carry extra ballast, in order to equalize the transportation costs of inbound and outbound freight.

The situation is exactly the same with regard to a policy of unilateral free trade or a country having tariffs lower than the tariffs of the countries with which it trades. To insist that one's own country have tariffs so long as the countries its citizens sell to have tariffs, or have tariffs that are as high as the tariffs of those countries, is to demand the equivalent of raising inbound transportation charges merely because they happen to be lower than outbound transportation charges.[18]

3. The Tendency Toward Uniform Prices Over Time: The Function of Commodity Speculation

In a free market there is a tendency toward the equalization of the price of a good in the present with the expected price of that good in the future. For example, there is a tendency for the price of wheat or crude oil or whichever, today, to be equal to the expected price of wheat or crude oil or whichever next month, six months from now, or next year. This principle applies to any good that is capable of being held in storage.

The basis of this principle is the familiar fact that any discrepancy in price creates an opportunity for profit, the exploitation of which reduces the discrepancy. If, for example, wheat is expected to be more expensive six months from now than it is today, then speculators begin to buy wheat at today's comparatively low price for the purpose of storing it and later selling it at the comparatively high price that is expected to exist in the future. The effect of their action is to raise the price of wheat in the present, and, by enlarging the supply available in the future, reduce the price of wheat in the future. As a result, the present and expected future prices are brought closer together.

The present and expected future prices will never actually be equalized, for two important reasons. First, there are costs of storing any commodity. In addition, since every business must yield the going rate of profit, if it is to continue in existence, it is necessary to earn as good a rate of profit in storing commodities as in any other line of business. Consequently, the actual relationship between present and future prices is that they tend to differ by no more than the costs of storage plus an allowance for the going rate of profit on the capital that must be invested in the storage.

The practical significance of this principle can be seen in the following example. Assume that the wheat harvest is one-twelfth below the size of the average annual harvest. It is therefore necessary to stretch what would normally be an eleven months' supply of wheat over twelve months. If the price of wheat did not rise at harvest time, the consumption of wheat and wheat products would go on at the usual rate, requiring a more severe restriction of consumption later on. Imagine that the price did not rise until after ten months had gone by, during which consumption had occurred at the usual rate. In that case, two months would be left to go until the next harvest, and it would be necessary to stretch the remaining supplies, equal to only one month's usual consump-

tion, over that period. By the rise in price being delayed this long, one month's supplies would have to be made to do the work of two, instead of eleven months' supplies doing the work of twelve. The rate of consumption would have to be cut in half instead of merely by one-twelfth. It is the same in principle for all shorter periods during which the rate of consumption is excessive. Always, an excessive rate of consumption in the earlier months must be balanced by a more severely reduced rate of consumption in the later months.

The existence of speculation on future prices prevents such calamities and minimizes all such imbalances in the rate of consumption. Speculators anticipate the future prices of commodities and buy or sell the commodity in question for the purpose of profiting from every discrepancy between the present price and the prices they expect to exist in the future. In our example, the activity of the commodity speculators would serve to bring about the minimum necessary restriction in the rate of wheat consumption. For if they see that in the absence of their activity prices will reach famine levels in the future, or levels reflecting a severe scarcity, or even any level whatever that exceeds the present price by more than the costs of storage and the going rate of profit, they begin to buy the commodity in question for the purpose of profiting from the future high price. Their additional buying raises the price of the commodity in the present and thus restricts the rate of its consumption. Later, as the future unfolds, the goods in the hands of the speculators constitute a larger supply and serve to reduce prices in comparison with what they would otherwise have been. The activity of the speculators therefore serves to transfer supplies from a period in which they are less urgently needed, as indicated by their lower price, to a period in which they are more urgently needed, as indicated by their higher price. In this way, it brings about the optimum rate of consumption of limited supplies.

Speculative activity, of course, is not limited to anticipating just future scarcities. Rather, it seeks in general to balance consumption and production over time by accumulating stocks of commodities and regulating their rate of consumption. If it is anticipated, for example, that a future harvest will be larger than originally forecast, and thus that the price of wheat in the future will be lower than originally expected, the activity of the speculators will bring about a lower price immediately. In anticipation of the lower future price, some of the speculators will begin to sell their holdings of the commodity now, in order to find a more profitable employment for their capitals. As a result of their sales, the price begins to fall right away. As a consequence of the lower price, the rate of consumption in the present is expanded. In this case, the effect of speculative activity is to permit present consumption to expand in the knowledge that larger future production than originally expected necessitates the holding of smaller present stocks.

Much speculative activity occurs on organized commodity exchanges. However, only a relatively small number of basic commodities are traded on the exchanges—principally various agricultural commodities and nonferrous metals. For the rest, speculation is largely limited to those who are engaged in the actual production or use of the commodity.

It should be realized that every businessman is a commodity speculator when he decides what size inventory to hold of his product or materials and whether it is a good time to increase or decrease the size of his inventory. For he is basing his decision on a comparison of present prices and the prices he expects to exist in the future. In the same way, every consumer engages in commodity speculation when he decides to buy more or less than his normal requirements on the basis of a comparison of present prices with the prices he anticipates in the future.

The speculative activities of businessmen and consumers serve to equalize present and future prices in additional ways than the one we have considered. For example, if, in anticipation of higher prices, businessmen simply hold back on selling their inventories, they are decreasing the supply available in the present and increasing the supply available in the future, which, of course, acts to narrow the discrepancy in price. By the same token, if businessmen or consumers step up their purchases in the present, in anticipation of higher prices in the future, then, to that extent, their demand for the item in the future will be less because it will already have been provided for. In this case, a larger present demand and smaller future demand act to reduce the discrepancy in price.

Like almost every economic activity that goes beyond manual labor, commodity speculation is frequently denounced. Because speculation transmits the higher prices expected to exist in the future to the present, it is denounced as the cause of the higher prices. What is overlooked in this accusation is that the supplies accumulated as a result of speculation must ultimately be used, and at that time they necessarily act to reduce prices—because either they are put on the market and sold, thereby increasing the supply of the commodity, or, by sparing their owners the need to purchase, they reduce the demand for the commodity. Moreover, if the speculators are mistaken—if they raise the present price and there is no independent cause of a higher price in the future— *they* pay the penalty for their mistake: they have bought at high prices and must later sell at low prices; or they have stocked up at high prices when they might later have

bought at low prices; or, in holding back their supplies in the hope of selling at higher prices, they end up having to sell at lower prices than they could have obtained by not holding back.[19]

It is necessary to point out that the connection between present and expected future prices is broken in conditions of increases in production and declines in price. In such conditions, the ability to reduce prices in the present by selling out of accumulated stocks reaches its limit once those stocks have been reduced to their necessary minimum. At that point, if prospective future prices are lower still, no mechanism remains which is capable of driving present prices down any further and thus coming back into correspondence with the prospective future prices. (There is no basis for a decline in demand in cases in which the item needs to be used in the present, such as food. There is also no basis for any general or widespread decline in demand insofar as the falling prices that are expected to result from increased production will enable people's incomes to go further, for this gives them the prospect of being better off in the future. In these conditions, people are in a continually better position to buy.) Thus it becomes possible for prospective future prices to fall below present prices by almost any amount. This in fact is regularly the case with respect to agricultural commodities in the months preceding the harvest. Their prospective prices during the coming harvest are almost always sharply below their current prices, precisely because of the inability to make significant further sales out of accumulated stocks, which stand at their low point in the period before the harvest. And the very fact that the stocks do stand at a low point is also responsible for the prices in the months just prior to the harvest standing at a high point.

The connection between present and future prices is established mainly by the accumulation of stocks to take advantage of prospective higher prices in the future. Declines in present prices based on the anticipation of lower future prices occur in a context in which the holding of significant supplies for the future is still necessary, but in which it is possible for the magnitude of the supplies held to be less.

Rebuttal of the Charge That the Oil Shortages of the 1970s Were "Manufactured" by the Oil Companies

Our knowledge of speculation can be applied to the charge that the oil shortages of 1973–74 and 1979, were "manufactured" by the oil companies. This was an accusation which was repeated again and again in the press and on television in those years. The accusation represents a classic case of economic ignorance, and is thus well worth analyzing.[20]

The proof offered that the oil companies were artificially creating the oil shortage was the allegation that their storage depots were full of oil. I remember one television news story in the 1973–74 crisis, filmed at an oil company tank farm, in which the reporter pointed to the tanks, said he had personally seen that they were full, and, therefore, that there could be no real shortage of oil, but just an "artificial" one created by the oil companies.

The reporter, his editor, station, and network evidently forgot, or did not know, the major news item of the time, which was the prospect that in the coming months the United States would be deprived of a significant part of its customary imports of oil, while having to meet the possibility of a long, severe winter. The tanks and storage depots most certainly *should* have been full, *in anticipation* of that terrible prospect. Any fullness of the tanks and depots was not, as the news media claimed, a proof of the abundance of oil, but of its *prospective scarcity*. (The reader should imagine what it would mean if the day ever came when he thought it necessary to fill every spare inch of his kitchen with food. His large stockpile would not be a proof of the abundance of food, but of the prospective scarcity of food.)

Apparently, the media were simply unaware of the need to hold supplies of oil for future sale. For it appears that they would have been satisfied with the genuineness of the shortage only if their reporters had visited the tank farms and found them empty. By that time, however, it would have been too late: millions would have died from the lack of oil.

The unfortunate fact was, however, that the oil company storage depots and tank farms were *not* full. The media erroneously inferred from their observation of a large quantity of oil at some tank farms that there must be a large supply of oil in the country. Their logic was the same in principle as that of someone travelling to an impoverished country like India and seeing a few warehouses full of food, and then concluding that there is a large quantity of food in the country. In reality, because of price controls, the stocks of crude oil, gasoline, and residual fuel oil in the United States in the period from October 31, 1973, to April 1, 1974—the time of the oil crisis—were all substantially less in most months than their respective averages had been for that period of the year over the preceding five years; distillate fuel (home heating oil) was the only major oil product whose stock had been increased. Overall, that is, if one simply adds up the number of barrels of crude oil and of the various kinds of oil products, stocks were significantly lower in all but two months, when they were very slightly higher.[21]

The fact that stocks of oil in storage were actually below average in 1973-74 should not be surprising. Such a result is to be expected from price controls. It is implied in our example of the deficient wheat harvest in which the price does not rise. It is only necessary to realize that price controls not only induce buyers to buy up commodities too rapidly for supplies to last, but also induce sellers to sell them too rapidly. Sellers are led to sell too rapidly because it is more profitable to sell goods at the fixed, controlled price in the present rather than in the future. By selling in the present, a seller saves storage costs and can earn profit or interest by investing the sales proceeds. If he is going to have to sell at the controlled price, it pays him to sell as soon as possible and simply put the money in the bank if necessary.[22]

The only reason that stocks of distillate oil were built up in the crisis period was that the government ordered it. Distillate stocks had declined sharply in early 1973, as the result of price controls, with the result that shortages began to appear even then. The government feared vastly worse shortages in the winter of 1974: it feared the prospect of people freezing to death.

It should be understood that if we had not had price controls, any build-up in stocks of oil that would have occurred, would not have caused a shortage, even though it reduced the supply of oil currently available. In the absence of price controls, the build-up would have raised the current price of oil. At higher prices, people would have economized on their use of oil products to whatever extent it was necessary to reduce current consumption. Of course, higher prices would also have pulled in supplies from other markets, making the necessary reduction in current consumption that much less. As will be shown in later discussion, anyone able and willing to pay the higher current prices would have been able to buy whatever oil products he wished. There would have been no shortage in the sense of people being able and willing to pay the asking price of oil but unable to obtain it. Thus, even if there had been a build-up of stocks of oil, as the media claimed, it could not have caused a shortage of oil in the absence of price controls.

In charging the oil industry with "manufacturing" the oil shortage by holding large stocks of oil, the media displayed ignorance in four respects. First, they were ignorant of the fact that, with the exception of distillate, stocks of oil were not actually large, but significantly below normal. Second, they were ignorant of what large stocks of oil would have signified had they existed (or, in the case of distillate, what the large stock did signify)—i.e., proof not of abundance, but of prospective *scarcity*. Third, they were apparently ignorant even of the fact that it is necessary to hold stocks of oil in the first place, for their attitude was, it seems, that so long as oil was on hand, there could be no problem of a lack of it. Fourth, they did not know that in the absence of price controls, no accumulation of a stock could cause a shortage in the current market.

In their treatment of the oil shortage, the media functioned on the level of men without the ability to think conceptually. They proceeded as though they were unable to make distinctions between quantities that are perceptually large, that is, between a tank farm full of oil, and an adequate national supply. They proceeded as though they were unable to think beyond the range of the immediate moment, that is, to realize the need to hold supplies for future sale. They proceeded as though they were incapable of understanding connections among concrete events, namely, the connection between the prospect of the loss of imports and the need to build up stocks of oil. They proceeded, in short, as though they had never heard of, and were incapable of grasping, a single principle of economics. Only because they functioned at this incredibly low mental level, was it possible for the media to assert that the oil shortage was "manufactured" by the oil companies.

I will have much more to say about this accusation in the pages that follow. I will show that it is correct to say that the oil shortage was "manufactured" and "artificial," only if one realizes that it was manufactured by the government, through price controls, not by the oil companies and their perfectly natural and praiseworthy desire to earn profits.

4. The Tendency Toward Uniform Wage Rates for Workers of the Same Degree of Ability

In a free market there is a tendency toward an equalization of wage rates for workers of the same degree of ability.

The basis of the tendency toward equality is the fact that men prefer to earn a higher income rather than a lower income, and therefore seek higher-paying jobs in preference to lower-paying jobs. The movement of labor into the higher-paying fields and out of the lower-paying fields reduces wage rates in the higher-paying fields and raises them in the lower-paying fields. The stopping point is an equality of wage rates.

This is not to say that forty- or fifty-year-old workers suddenly give up their work of many years to change to a brand-new occupation in response to a 5 or 10 or even 20 percent difference in wages. No. In view of the costs and the various other problems such workers would have to incur in the learning of new skills, it would not pay them to switch occupations except in cases of extremely large differences in wages—brought about, for example, by their previous jobs being rendered obsolete through technological progress.

The movement of labor from occupation to occupation in response to less-than-gross differences in wage rates is accomplished in a different way. It is accomplished by virtue of the fact that each occupation continually loses members through death or retirement and must continually be resupplied with young workers. Changes in the flow of young workers into the various occupations produce the same effect as an actual movement of labor between occupations. Where the number of young workers entering an occupation exceeds the number of old workers dying or retiring, the supply of labor in that occupation rises. Where the number of young workers entering an occupation is less than the number of old workers leaving, the supply of labor in that occupation falls.

Now by the time young people are ready to begin preparing themselves for a career, there are very marked differences in their ability and willingness to learn. And, for this reason, the labor force necessarily assumes a hierarchical structure, with the tendency toward an equalization of wage rates being operative only within the respective levels of this structure, not throughout the structure as a whole.

Those with the greatest ability and willingness to learn are potentially capable of performing practically any job. For example, the young man who is capable of learning to be a surgeon is also certainly capable of learning to be a printer. In turn, the young man who is capable of learning to be a printer is also certainly capable of learning to work on an assembly line. Everyone, in other words—the potential surgeon, the potential printer, and the potential assembly line worker—is capable of learning the work of the assembly line worker. But only the potential surgeon and the potential printer are capable of learning the work of the printer. And only the potential surgeon alone is capable of learning the work of the surgeon.

In conformity with the principle contained in this example, let us think of the young people ready to prepare for a career as divided into three broad groups: those capable of entering the professions, those capable of learning to do skilled work, and those capable of learning to do no more than unskilled work.

Such a division of the potential labor force necessarily prevents any tendency toward a general equalization of wage rates. No matter how high the wage rates of the professions may climb in relation to those of skilled and unskilled labor, it is simply impossible for young people who lack the necessary capacity, to go into the professions instead of skilled or unskilled labor. Similarly, no matter how high the wages of skilled labor may climb in relation to those of unskilled labor, there is, again, no way for the young people who lack the necessary capacity, to enter the field of skilled labor instead of unskilled labor. On the other hand, the wages of skilled labor *are* limited in relation to those of professional-level labor. For as soon as the wages of skilled labor begin to exceed those of professionals, it is possible for young people capable of the professions to enter the field of skilled labor. In the same way, the wages of unskilled labor are limited in relation to those of skilled labor. For as soon as the wages of unskilled labor begin to exceed those of skilled labor, it is possible for young people capable of skilled labor to enter the field of unskilled labor.

It is because of this hierarchical division of the total pool of human talent—of the fact that ability can flow downward to lower channels, but not upward to higher channels, so to speak—that we observe in actual life that the wages of professionals markedly and permanently exceed those of skilled workers, while those of skilled workers, in turn, markedly and permanently exceed those of unskilled workers. And we observe that the wages of the highest-paid skilled workers cannot get very far ahead of the wages of the lowest-paid professionals, nor the wages of the highest-paid unskilled workers very far ahead of the wages of the lowest-paid skilled workers.

This explains inequalities in wages. Let us return to the question of why wage rates for any given level of ability tend to be equal.

Let us consider the wage rates of a number of skilled occupations, for example, the various building trades, such as carpenters, electricians, and plumbers, and other skilled occupations, such as printers, draftsmen, mechanics, and locomotive engineers. All of these occupations, and others of a similar nature, require the same basic level of intelligence and education on the part of the workers. As a result, they are all potentially capable of being performed by the same people. All of them, in effect, can be supplied with labor that is drawn from a pool of human talent on the same basic level. Because of men's preference for a higher income over a lower income, this pool of talent naturally runs more heavily into those occupations which offer higher wages and less heavily into those which offer lower wages. As a result, there is a tendency toward an increase in the supply of labor in the better-paying kinds of skilled work and a decrease in the supply of labor in the poorer-paying kinds of skilled work. Since the effect of the increases in the supply of labor in the initially higher-paying fields is to reduce wages in those fields, while the effect of the decreases in the supply of labor in the initially lower-paying fields is to raise wages in those fields, the discrepancies in wages among the different kinds of skilled labor are narrowed, and thus these wage rates tend toward equality.

In exactly the same way, there is a tendency toward a uniformity of wages among the various unskilled or low-skilled occupations, such as assembly line workers, machine tenders, truck and bus drivers, clerks, steve-

dores, and so on. There is a tendency toward a further uniformity of wage rates among the various professions, such as doctors, lawyers, scientists, engineers, professors, and so on. In these cases, too, the original pool of talent flows into the various channels on its level in accordance with the wages to be made; and, in flowing more or less heavily, lowers or raises those wages, thereby reducing the discrepancies among them and driving them toward equality.

There are, of course, important differences in wages of a permanent nature even within the three broad groups of workers that I have delineated. At each level, there is a tendency for some particular occupations to earn more than others—for example, for doctors to earn more than professors, and for stevedores to earn more than clerks. There are also important differences in earnings within each occupation, especially at the professional level. For example, there are always some doctors or lawyers who earn five or ten times as much as the average of their profession, and there are some printers or mechanics who earn significantly more than others.

These differences are due in part to the existence of further categories of division in human ability. There are those who have the ability and willingness to learn how to be a doctor or lawyer, and others who have the ability and willingness to learn how to be a great doctor or lawyer. In other cases, willingness and ability to learn is not the sole criterion of division. Other factors have to be added. For example, in many types of work, especially unskilled work, it is necessary to possess a significant degree of physical strength. Those who have it are in a narrower category than those who do not and, accordingly, tend to be higher paid. In other cases, workers are differentiated by the special development of other physical or psychological potentials—such as muscular coordination, an ear for music, special visual acuity, and so on. In the case of great athletes, opera singers, musicians, and actors—all the really star performers—the combination of special characteristics is such as to make the labor of these persons virtually unique. As a result, when they are in demand, their earnings do not have any fixed limit in relation to the earnings of others, because no one is able to increase the supply of what they are offering.

For the rest, the differences in wages within the various broad groups are the result of the fact that considerations other than money income are associated with each job. There are such considerations as how interesting or uninteresting is the work, how pleasant or unpleasant are the conditions of the work, how safe or dangerous is it, how regular is the employment, how long and how expensive is the special preparation required, and, perhaps, still other, similar considerations. Considerations of this kind explain, for example, why scientists tend to earn less, and tax lawyers more, than is commensurate with their respective levels of ability. In the one case, the work itself may be the highest pleasure in life to those who perform it; in the other, it is more likely to be experienced as painfully dull. As a result, those with the necessary ability to be scientists are willing to enter the field even to the point of accepting substantially lower wages in comparison with what they could earn elsewhere. By the same token, people would cease to enter such a field as tax law as soon as that field no longer offered significant monetary advantages over other fields they might enter. The principle that emerges is that any occupation which offers advantages other than income tends to offer correspondingly lower wages, while any occupation that imposes special disadvantages of any kind tends to offer correspondingly higher wages. These discounts and premiums in wages balance the special advantages and disadvantages of the various occupations.

In sum, in a free market there are at least three principles of wage determination at work simultaneously. One is a tendency toward a uniformity of wages for labor of the same degree of ability. A second is a tendency toward unequal wage rates for labor of different degrees of ability—primarily intellectual ability, but also other abilities as well. And a third is a tendency toward the inclusion of discounts and premiums in wages as an offsetting element to the special advantages or disadvantages of the occupations concerned. The combined operation of these three principles helps to explain the full range of the various wage rates we observe in actual life.

Now, as far as it operates, the principle of the uniformity of wage rates is similar in its consequences to the uniformity-of-profit principle. That is, it serves to keep the various occupations supplied with labor in the proper proportions. Too many people do not rush into carpentering and not enough go into printing, say, because the very effect of such a mistake is to reduce the wages of carpenters and raise those of printers. This acts to delimit and counteract the mistake. In addition, the operation of this principle gives to consumers the ultimate power to determine the relative size of the various occupations. If, to continue with the same example, the consumers buy more printed matter and fewer products made of wood, then the effect of the change is to cause the demand for printers to rise and that for carpenters to fall. As a result, the wages of printers rise and more young men are induced to become printers, while the wages of carpenters fall and fewer young men become carpenters.

It should be realized, as this example of the printers shows, that in seeking to earn the highest wages, the individual worker is seeking to do the kind of work the consumers most want him to do. This is true of every individual who seeks to take the best-paying job he can find at any given level of ability or who seeks to raise his level of ability. For what enables any job to pay more is only the fact that the consumers want its products sufficiently. Let them decide to reduce their demand for its products, and the wages it pays will tend to fall, while if they raise their demand for its products, the wages it pays will tend to rise still higher.

In a free market, within the limit of his abilities, each person chooses that job which he believes offers him the best combination of money and nonmonetary considerations. In so doing, he simultaneously acts for his own maximum well-being and for that of the consumers who buy the ultimate products his labor helps to produce.

Equal Pay for Equal Work: Capitalism Versus Racism

The uniformity-of-wages principle must be understood as implying the existence of a powerful tendency under capitalism toward equal pay for equal work. Despite the prevailing belief that capitalism arbitrarily discriminates against such groups as blacks and women, the fact is that the profit motive of employers operates to eradicate all differences in pay not based on differences in performance. Where such differences persist, they are the result of government intervention or private coercion that is sanctioned by the government.[23]

Where the profit motive is free to operate, if two kinds of labor are equally productive, and one is less expensive than the other, employers choose the less expensive, because doing so cuts their costs and raises their profits. The effect of choosing the less expensive labor, however, is to raise its wages, since it is now in greater demand; while the effect of passing by the more expensive labor is to reduce its wages, since it is now in lesser demand. This process goes on until the wages of the two kinds of labor are either perfectly equal or the remaining difference is so small as not to be worth caring about by anyone.

As illustration of the fact that even very small differences in wage rates could not be maintained under capitalism, consider the following example. Assume that white workers of a certain degree of skill are paid $5 per hour. Assume that black workers of identically the same degree of skill can be hired for just 5 percent less, that is, for just 25¢ an hour less. Assume that a factory must employ 500 workers of this degree of skill. With a 40-hour week, over a 50-week year, this slight difference in hourly wage rates results in a saving of labor cost and a corresponding extra profit per year of $250,000 if the factory owner employs 500 blacks rather than 500 whites (for 25¢ x 500 x 40 x 50 = $250,000).

Even in the case of a small establishment employing

only 10 workers, the annual saving in labor cost, and thus the extra profit attaching to the employment of blacks, would be $5,000 (since 25¢ x 10 x 40 x 50 = $5,000)—enough for the owner to afford a new car every other year or to make significant improvements in his business.

It is doubtful that there are many employers so bigoted as to be willing to indulge their personal prejudice in favor of whites at a cost of $250,000 per year, or even $5,000 per year. The clear implication is that even slight differences in wage rates would make the employment of blacks in preference to whites virtually irresistible. Not only would a 5 percent differential in wages not be sustainable, but neither would a 2 percent or even a 1 percent differential. Every such differential would lead employers to hire blacks in preference to whites, and would thus bring about a further rise in the wage rates of blacks and a further fall in the wage rates of whites, until a virtually perfect equality was achieved.

Indeed, profit-seeking employers *qua* profit-seeking employers are simply unconcerned with race. Their principle is: of two equally good workers, hire the one who is available for less money; of two workers available for the same money, hire the one who is the better worker. Race is simply irrelevant. Any consideration of race means extra cost and less profit; it is bad business in the literal sense of the term.

It should be realized that one of the great merits of capitalism is that by its very nature employers are virtually compelled to be oblivious to race. The freedom of competition under capitalism ensures this result. For even if, initially, the majority of employers were so fanatically bigoted as to be willing to forgo extra profits for the sake of their prejudice, they would be powerless to prevent a minority of more rational employers from earning these extra profits. ("Rationality" in this context means not passing moral judgment against a person on the basis of his racial membership and not allowing such a judgment to outweigh the desire for profit. Such a judgment represents a logical contradiction in that morality pertains only to acts open to choice, while a man's racial membership is not open to his choice. The irrationality is then compounded by the sacrifice of one's own objective good—the earning of a profit—for the sake of the irrational judgment.) Because of their higher profits, the more rational employers would have a relatively greater income out of which to save and expand their businesses than the irrational majority. Moreover, since they operated at lower costs, they could afford to charge lower prices and thus increase their profits still further by taking customers away from the irrational majority. The result of these factors would be that the more rational employers would tend to replace the less rational ones in economic importance. They would come to set the tone

of the economy, and their attitudes would be transmitted to all other employers, who would seek to emulate their success. In this way, capitalism virtually guarantees the victory of rationality over racial bigotry.

This discussion also provides a rebuttal to the accusation that under capitalism the skills and abilities of groups such as blacks are not utilized. For it follows that the unhampered profit motive leads employers to place the members of all groups in the highest positions for which their skills and abilities qualify them. Consider the following example. Assume that a skilled lathe operator must be paid $15 per hour, and that black workers who have been taught this skill in a trade school are presently employed as janitors at $5 per hour. The black workers would almost certainly be willing to change their jobs for a raise to, say, $10 an hour. Any employer who hired them as lathe operators at $10 per hour would thereby add $5 to his profits for every hour of their work, as compared with employing whites. Over the course of a year composed of 50, 40-hour weeks, his extra profit would amount to $10,000. And this would be on the labor of just one man.

It is obvious that under capitalism, if the skills and abilities of blacks or any one else are being wasted in low-skilled, low-paying jobs, it is to the financial self-interest of employers to change the situation, indeed, to seek out such workers, and in many cases even to incur substantial costs in training them. And it follows that the greater the extent to which a group's skill or ability is wasted, the greater is the profit to be made by rectifying the situation. For example, if a black with the ability to do the work of a $100,000-a-year company vice president is working as a $20,000-a-year clerk, it is even more to the interest of an employer to seek him out and rectify the situation than in the case of the lathe operator working as a janitor. In this case, the employer could double the black worker's salary to $40,000, and at the same time add $60,000 to his own profits by employing him in a capacity commensurate with his skill and ability.

Of course, just as in the initial case, the wages and salaries of blacks brought into the more skilled and higher-level jobs would more and more tend to match those of the white workers performing these jobs. Because as employers competed for blacks, their wages would rise, while, in order to be competitive with the black workers, the white workers would have to accept reductions. Indeed, once the first few blacks or members of other groups in a comparable situation are brought into an occupation in which they were previously unrepresented and succeed in proving their ability by actual satisfactory performance, a dynamic effect ensues. The breaking of the taboo, followed by the visible proof of its lack of rational foundation, changes the way in which such individuals are viewed. The demand for their services then greatly increases. (The history of major league baseball provides an excellent illustration. Once the taboo on the admission of blacks was broken with the employment of the very able Jackie Robinson, all barriers to the admission of blacks soon fell.)

In connection with the fact that free competition with members of so-called minority groups can entail a fall in the wage rates of the average member of the groups already established, most notably, white male workers, it should be realized that any such reductions in wage rates would take place as part of a process operating to raise the *real wages*—the actual standard of living—of the average member of *all* groups. For it would be accompanied by reductions in the prices of consumers' goods greater than any reduction in after-tax money incomes experienced by the average member of the groups already established. This conclusion is conclusively demonstrated in later chapters of this book.[24]

Of course, none of the above developments can occur if they are stopped by the initiation of physical force. If, for example, the local Ku Klux Klan is able to burn down the factory of an employer who employs blacks instead of whites, because it knows it will go unpunished by the law; or if local government officials are capable of suddenly finding all kinds of violations of building, health, and safety codes on the part of such an employer, to the point of crippling his operations, then employers will not seek to take advantage of the lower wages of blacks, and thus the wages of blacks will not be raised to parity with those of whites of equal skill.

Although not motivated by racial prejudice, what is also capable of aborting the advance of blacks (and women), particularly at the higher levels of employment, is a system of taxation that takes away the greater part of the additional profits that might be made by defying custom and making the necessary innovations of bringing them into fields of employment in which they were previously not represented. Indeed, industries whose profits are limited by the government, such as public utilities, or whose output is purchased on a cost-plus basis, such as that of defense contractors, have no financial incentive whatever to make such innovations. And, of course, in an environment in which destructive government regulations can be unleashed at any time on virtually any business, or in which valuable government favors or outright government subsidies can be obtained—in an environment, therefore, in which it does not pay to have enemies, or to offend any significant group, or, as the saying goes, in which it does not pay "to rock the boat"— businessmen will not be very quick to make such controversial innovations in employment.[25] Ironically, such measures as equal-employment-opportunity laws directly rule out the very possibility of employing blacks or

women at lower wages for the same work as whites or men. They thus directly prevent businessmen from finding the employment of blacks or women in the higher positions to be unusually profitable—profitable enough to begin defying traditions and customs based on nothing more than empty stereotypes.

Later discussion will show the especially destructive effects of minimum-wage and prounion legislation on blacks, in aborting the very possibility of their gaining significant advancement.[26]

The uniformity-of-profit principle implies that along with equal pay for equal work, capitalism operates to supply the members of all groups on equal terms in their capacity as consumers. As a demonstration of this fact, assume that blacks had to pay monthly rents just 5 percent higher than those of whites, while the landlord's costs were the same in both cases. This 5 percent premium would constitute a major addition to a landlord's profits. If a landlord's profit margin—his profit as a percentage of his rents—were normally 10 percent, a 5 percent addition to his rents would constitute a 50 percent addition to his profits. Even if his profit margin were initially as high as 25 percent, a 5 percent addition to his rents would constitute a 20 percent addition to his profits.

In response to such premium rates of profit, housing construction for blacks would be stepped up, and a larger proportion of existing housing would be rented to them. The effect of this increased supply of housing, of course, would be to reduce the rental premium paid by blacks. And because a mere 1 percent premium would mean significant extra profits in supplying blacks with housing, even a premium of this small size could not be maintained. Thus, blacks would pay no higher rents than whites, and obtain housing equal in quality to that obtained by whites.

Likewise, assume that merchants in black neighborhoods charged higher prices than the same goods would bring in other neighborhoods, while the merchants' costs of doing business were the same in both places. The higher prices in such a case would constitute a clear addition to profits. With higher profits to be made in black neighborhoods than white neighborhoods, merchants considering the location of new stores would choose the black neighborhoods. The influx of new stores, of course, would lower selling prices in the black neighborhoods; and the process would go on until the prices and the profits to be made in those neighborhoods were no higher than elsewhere. (Regrettably, today it is often the case that retail prices in black neighborhoods are substantially higher than for the same goods in white neighborhoods and, at the same time, merchants are moving out of the black neighborhoods rather than moving in. This situation is the result of the existence of higher costs of operation in the black neighborhoods—caused by such phenomena as higher rates of burglary, pilferage, and arson—coupled with the inability in many cases to raise prices sufficiently to cover such higher costs, which inability results from the fact that prices are limited by competition with stores in surrounding areas. The obvious solution is to reduce the crime rate. Despite all the rhetoric to the contrary, the economic self-interest of the average black is allied with that of the merchants who supply him, not with that of the criminals who impoverish and destroy the merchants.)

Moreover, under laissez-faire capitalism racial segregation would disappear, even though it would be legally permissible on private property. It would disappear because it is fundamentally incompatible with the requirements of profit-making and because it is irrational.

The businessman seeking profit is vitally dependent on the patronage of customers. This dependency is expressed in such popular sayings as "the customer is king" and "the customer is always right." Blacks are customers, and, as they rose economically, would be more and more important customers. It is absurd to believe that businessmen would want to turn customers away by denying them access to their premises or by humiliating them with such requirements as separate drinking fountains. The businessman's desire for profit makes him put aside all such malice. It does not matter that he personally may not like blacks. All he has to like is their money. Competition with other businessmen for the patronage of blacks then does the rest.

It might be objected that despite the willingness of businessmen to abolish segregation when doing so is profitable, the attitudes of white customers might prevent such action from being profitable. For example, it would obviously not be profitable to gain five poor black customers and lose ten good white ones as a result of desegregating.

Cases such as this could exist, in places such as the deep South of previous generations. But they could exist only in an ever-diminishing sphere. Even in the deep South of the past, there were many whites who positively desired equal treatment for blacks, and many more who did not oppose it strongly enough to withdraw their patronage from a business which desegregated. As a result, in the absence of government intervention, and the threat of private violence sanctioned by local governments, there would have been many businessmen in the South who would have found that, while they might lose some white customers by desegregating, they would by no means lose all, and would gain more black customers

than they lost whites. This would have been certain to occur in areas where the population was relatively concentrated—that is, lived in cities or large towns—and in which the proportion of blacks was relatively high. In such areas, a businessman who desegregated would have been able to count on a relatively large black market to more than compensate him for his loss of white customers. For example, imagine a mass merchandiser, such as Sears, in a Southern town where there were two other such stores. If this store abolished segregation, it would certainly not have lost all of its white customers. Not that many Southern whites were so bigoted that they would have refused to shop there just because the store no longer humiliated blacks. Desegregating, however, would have enabled this store to gain a large number of black customers from the other two stores, for the blacks would have flocked to where they were treated as human beings. Desegregation would thus have been profitable for this store.

This case would have been repeated throughout the South. From practically the first day of freedom from government intervention and government sanctioned private coercion, there would have been voluntarily unsegregated stores, restaurants, hotels, and other establishments. The existence of these unsegregated establishments in their midst would then have acted to change the attitude even of those whites who had initially refused to deal with them. They would have seen with their own eyes that others were not contaminated by contact with blacks and that they would not be either. Thus, as time went on, fewer and fewer whites would have been prepared to withdraw their business from establishments which desegregated. The result would have been that businessmen would have had less and less to lose by desegregating; and the rising earning power, and thus growing buying power, of blacks would have given them more and more to gain. Finally, segregation would have come to be regarded as eccentric and then have ceased to exist altogether.

In this way, even such barriers as racially restrictive covenants in real estate would have been overcome. Property free of such restrictions, and therefore open to a wider market, would have become more valuable than property which carried them. Such covenants would have fallen into disuse and have been eliminated by voluntary consent.

Thus, even in areas such as the deep South, the extension of the economic freedom of capitalism to racial matters would have meant a significant measure of immediate integration, followed by an accelerating growth in integration. And it would all have been achieved voluntarily, in the pursuit of self-interest, in a spirit of mutual good will.[27]

5. Prices and Costs of Production

In a free market the prices of products tend to be governed by their costs of production.

This principle follows directly from the uniformity-of-profit principle, and we have already glimpsed it in discussing the long-run consequences of repealing price controls. The uniformity-of-profit principle implies that the prices of products tend to equal their costs of production plus only as much profit as is required to afford the going rate of profit on the capital invested. If prices exceed costs by more than this amount of profit, then there is a tendency toward expanded production and lower prices (and possibly higher unit costs). If they fail to exceed costs by as much as this amount of profit, then there is a tendency toward reduced production and higher prices (and possibly lower unit costs). The stopping point is, as I say, where prices equal costs of production plus the amount of profit required to yield the going rate of profit on the capital invested.

Now there are two ways that cost of production governs prices. One way is indirectly—through variations in the supply of the good, as above. The other way is directly—through the decisions of the sellers of the good in setting their prices.

Let us consider first the cases in which the role of cost is indirect—for example, all or most agricultural commodities. In any given year, the price of wheat, or potatoes, or cotton, or whatever, is determined simply by supply and demand. Over a period of years, however, the price of such a good tends to gravitate about its cost of production. This is because whenever the price begins to exceed cost by more than what is required to afford the average rate of profit to the industry, additional capital will be invested, supply will be expanded, and the price and profit will decline. If the price fails to provide the average rate of profit to the industry, capital will be withdrawn, supply will be reduced, and the price and profit will be restored. What ties price to cost in such a case is variations in supply.

However, there is a vast category of cases in which the connection between price and cost is far more direct. This is the case of most manufactured or processed goods. In these cases, the sellers typically maintain inventories of their goods and have plant capacity available to produce more. In such a situation, a rise in demand, provided it is not too large, is met out of inventories, and before the inventory is exhausted, production is stepped up from plant capacity held in reserve. Similarly, when a fall in demand occurs, inventory is temporarily allowed to build up, and production is cut back. Provided the changes in demand are not of major proportions, there is little or no change in price. It can be observed, for example, that the price of bread, automobiles, newspapers, restaurant meals, paper clips, and countless other goods does not change with every change in demand. A change in demand must be fairly substantial to raise or lower the price of these goods. In cases in which the demand changes are not too substantial, they are simply accompanied by corresponding changes in production, while the price of the product remains the same.

In cases of this kind, it is not correct to say that the price of the product is determined simply by supply and demand. On the contrary, the price of the product determines the quantity of the product the buyers buy, and the quantity that the buyers buy determines the quantity the sellers produce and sell.

The prices themselves in these cases are set by sellers on the basis of a consideration of costs of production. It is not that each seller sets his price on the basis of his own costs. But some seller in an industry—usually, the most efficient large firm and one that is in a position to expand its production significantly from existing capacity—sets its price on the basis of a consideration of costs, and the other firms are forced to match its price. The other firms cannot exceed its price, because it has the additional production capacity required to supply many of their customers if they should try to sell at higher prices. Nor, as a rule, can the other firms undercut its price, because it is the lowest-cost, most efficient producer, and sets its price accordingly.

The cost of production on the basis of which such a firm sets its price is not primarily its own cost of production, but the costs of production of its less efficient competitors or, if it has no current competitors, the costs of production of potential competitors. It sets its price in such a way as to prevent its competitors from earning too-high profits, because it does not want them to accumulate the capital that would enable them to become more efficient and to expand at its expense. Nor does it want to invite new firms into its field. It wants to avoid creating a situation in which it makes it possible for others to make inroads into its business, which, once started, might lead to its own downfall. It therefore tries to set its price in such a way as to prevent this, which means it tries to set its prices not very far above their costs—as a maximum. At the same time, of course, it strives to reduce its own costs of production even further, so as to be able to expand its own profits and to be able comfortably to meet any price reductions inaugurated by competitors that in the meanwhile may have grown more efficient. It is only when the demand for the product becomes so strong that it is not possible to meet it at a price determined in this way, that the price rises to permit high profits to all in the field.

In the case of manufactured and processed goods,

therefore, the direct determinant of price is cost of production.[28]

However, as should already be clear from Chapter 5, if we examine costs of production, we find that they are reducible to two things: to the physical quantities of the means or factors of production employed to produce a good and to the prices of those factors of production.[29] For example, the cost of producing an automobile equals the quantity of each type of labor employed in turning out a car times the wage rates of that labor, plus the quantity of steel used times the price of that steel, and so on. Now the prices of these factors of production are themselves directly determined either by supply and demand or by cost of production. For example, the wage rates are determined by supply and demand, while the price of steel is determined by cost of production.[30] Now the costs of producing steel and all the other elements of an automobile whose prices are determined by cost are themselves resolvable in the same way as the cost of producing an automobile. That is, they in turn are based on prices directly determined by supply and demand and prices directly determined by cost of production.

It should be observed that as we keep pushing the matter back and back, the cumulative role of prices directly determined by supply and demand becomes greater and greater. In the case of our automobile, the production cost of an automobile ultimately depends on the wages of auto workers, the wages of steel workers, the wages of iron miners, and so on, all of which are determined by supply and demand. And, along the way, the prices of some of the materials, such as the copper and zinc the auto companies may have to buy, the raw rubber the tire manufacturers buy, the scrap metal the steel producers need—these prices, too, are directly determined by supply and demand. Ultimately, therefore, as far as it rests on prices, cost of production itself is determined entirely by supply and demand.

Consequently, when prices are determined by cost of production, what they are ultimately determined by is still supply and demand, but supply and demand operating in a wide context—that is, by supply and demand operating in the context of the labor market and in certain broad commodity markets, not in the relatively narrow market of the individual product itself.[31]

The analysis of cost of production into elements which are themselves determined by supply and demand brings us full circle. We began the analysis of price determination in Part B of Chapter 5 with a discussion of supply and demand, and now we must return to supply and demand, in order to explain prices determined on the basis of cost of production. For, as we have seen, insofar as cost of production rests on prices, those prices are ultimately determined by supply and demand. Thus, if

we want an ultimate explanation of prices determined by costs, we must explain prices determined by supply and demand. This will be our task, at a more advanced level than before, in the next part of this chapter, as we complete the presentation of the free market's laws of price determination.

PART B

ALLOCATION PRINCIPLES

1. The General Pricing of Goods and Services in Limited Supply

The determination of price by supply and demand applies to all goods and services whose supply is a given fact and therefore limited for a longer or shorter period of time to come. As we have seen, it also applies *indirectly* (via determining the prices that constitute their costs of production) to products whose supply can be immediately varied in response to changes in demand.

It is necessary to consider a kind of catalog of goods and services in limited supply, in order to understand concretely the range of application possessed by the principle of supply and demand.

The most important item in this list is, of course, human labor, which is always limited by the number of people able and willing to work. Furthermore, the labor of each person is limited by his need for rest and relaxation. And, as the general level of real wages—that is, the quantity of goods a worker can buy with his money wages—goes up, the fewer are the hours that people are prepared to work. This occurs because to the degree that people can earn a higher standard of living from any given number of hours of labor, their need for the additional real income that extra hours could provide is less intense. In addition to this, of course, the supply of skilled labor is always still further limited, and that of professional-level labor even more so; and, at any given time, the supply of labor in each occupation and each location is very narrowly limited.

After labor services come materials whose supply is temporarily limited, such as agricultural commodities between harvests. Housing and buildings of all kinds are in a state of temporarily limited supply, because considerable time is always required before their supply can be increased through new construction. Any material, any product whatever, is capable of being in limited supply temporarily, if the demand for it outruns the ability to supply it from existing facilities at a price based on cost of production.

Land sites are in the category of goods in limited supply on a long-run basis, insofar as there is anything special or unique about them that makes them superior to other land, such as their superior location or superior fertility.[32]

In a few cases, the products of such land sites are also in the category of goods in limited supply on a more or less permanent basis: for example, wines of a special flavor that can be produced only from grapes grown on a soil of a very limited extent, or caviar found in sturgeon beds located only in a few places.

Goods such as paintings and statues by old masters, first editions, rare coins, and so on, are in the category of goods in limited supply on an absolutely permanent basis, because their production is necessarily past.

Finally, all second-hand goods are in a state of limited supply.

The prices of all goods and services in limited supply are determined in an essentially similar way in a free market and have a similar significance. One basic determinant is *the quantity of money* in the economic system. As previously indicated, the quantity of money determines aggregate demand.[33] It can do this, of course, only in determining at the same time the demand for the various individual goods and services. We will not go too far wrong if we assume that once the economic system becomes adjusted to a change in the quantity of money, the effect of the change is to change the demand for everything more or less to the same degree. For example, in the long run, if the quantity of money doubles, and everything else remains the same (including such things as the rate at which the money supply increases and is expected to go on increasing), the demand for each individual good and service in the economic system should also tend to double. With a doubled quantity of money, we should expect that eventually the demand for shoes, baseballs, zinc, skilled and unskilled labor, and all other goods and services should all just about double. This means that, in the long run at least, we can regard the quantity of money as acting more or less equally on the price of everything.[34]

The second major determinant of the prices of goods and services in limited supply is *the value judgments of the consumers with respect to the various goods and services on which they spend the quantity of money.* The value judgments of the consumers determine, in effect, how the aggregate demand that is made possible by any given quantity of money is distributed among the products of the various industries and among all the different goods and services in limited supply. The value judgments of the consumers determine, for example, how much is spent for shoes versus shirts, and indirectly, therefore, how much is spent for leather versus cloth, cowhides versus cotton, and grazing land versus cotton land; similarly for the labor services at each stage. In

determining the relative spending for all the different consumers' goods, each with its own requirements for labor of specific types, the consumers determine how much is spent in the economy as a whole for each type of labor in relation to every other type of labor, both in terms of specific occupations and in terms of wide groups of occupations, such as skilled labor versus unskilled labor. The same applies to all other goods and services in limited supply, such as diamonds versus wheat, real estate in New York City versus Des Moines, Iowa, and so on. In this way, the value judgments of the consumers ultimately determine the prices of all goods and services in limited supply in relation to one another. It is the value judgments of the consumers that ultimately determine how much more professional-level labor must be paid relative to skilled labor, and how much more skilled labor must be paid relative to unskilled labor.

In sum, the quantity of money determines the absolute height of the prices of goods and services in limited supply, and the value judgments of the consumers determine their relative heights. The value judgments of the consumers are, of course, judgments with respect to *marginal quantities,* and one may say that the relative prices of goods and services in limited supply are determined by their relative marginal utilities, or, in the case of factors of production, the relative marginal utilities of their final products to the consumers.[35]

2. The Pricing and Distribution of Consumers' Goods in Limited Supply

For our purposes, the most important characteristic of the price of a good in limited supply is the fact that *in a free market it always tends to be set high enough to level down the quantity of the good demanded*—that is, the quantity of it that buyers are seeking to buy—*to equality with the limited supply of it that exists.*

For the sake of simplicity, consider the case of a rare wine, for example. It may be that, potentially, millions of people would enjoy drinking this wine and would be prepared to buy tens of millions of bottles of it every year. But because of the limitation of the special soil on which the necessary grapes can be grown, no more than, say, ten thousand bottles of the wine can be produced in an average year. What happens in this case is that the price of the wine rises to such a point that the great majority of potential buyers are simply eliminated from the market. They look at the high price and say to themselves, "This wine is simply too expensive for me, however delicious it may taste." In fact, in the knowledge that this would be their decision, the very existence of such a wine would probably never even be called to the attention of the great majority of people. As for those who do buy the wine, the high price probably makes almost all of them restrict the amount of it that they consume. At fifty dollars a bottle, say, even millionaire wine lovers probably drink it much less often than they would at, say, ten dollars a bottle.

The case of apartment rentals is essentially the same. In a free market, rents go high enough to level down the quantity of rental space demanded to, or somewhat below, equality with the limited supply of it that exists. The only difference is that in an economy like that of the United States, no one need be excluded from the rental market entirely. Everyone is always able to afford to rent *some* space, even if it is only half of a room he must share with someone else.[36]

Always, a free-market price acts to level the quantity demanded of any good or service in limited supply down to equality with the supply that exists.

This characteristic of a free-market price has a major implication. *It implies that shortages cannot exist in a free market, even in cases of the most severely limited supply.* That is because, however limited the supply may be, a free-market price always rises high enough to level down the quantity demanded to equality with the supply available. In a free market, limited supplies do not cause shortages, but high prices. At the high price, there is no shortage.

In order further to prove this point, let us take an extreme example—one that is very unfair to the free market, namely, the case of the gasoline shortage of 1973–74. In a variety of ways, the government was responsible for vastly reduced supplies of gasoline, especially in the Northeast. Let us start with these artificially low supplies of gasoline and imagine that at that point the government had simply repealed its price controls on gasoline.

Whoever went through the experience should think back to the sight of service stations faced with multiblock-long lines of cars waiting for gasoline. Let us imagine a service station that has 1,000 gallons of gasoline in its own tanks and is confronted with a line of cars whose drivers are seeking 2,000 gallons of gasoline for their tanks. This is a case of 1,000 gallons of gasoline available, 2,000 gallons demanded. Even in this case, a free market would have equalized the quantity demanded with the supply available. If the owner of the gas station had been free to set his own price, he would have set a price high enough to make those drivers reduce the quantity they demanded by 1,000 gallons. Such a price undoubtedly existed. If the reader doubts this, he should imagine the gas station owner simply auctioning his gasoline off to the highest bidders. As the price at the auction rose, more and more bidders would have restricted the quantities they bid for, and some would have

dropped out of the bidding altogether. At some point, the quantity of gasoline demanded would have been cut back to equality with the 1,000 gallons available. It makes no difference, of course, if instead of conducting an auction, the service station owner had simply set his price where such an auction would have set it. In either case, people who previously were prepared to buy 2,000 gallons of gasoline would have found that they could not afford more than 1,000 gallons and would have limited their purchases accordingly.

In fact, things would have gone further than this. A service station owner not restricted by price controls would have considered not only the demand of the drivers of the cars presently in line, but also the demand of all the drivers of the cars that might have shown up later in the day, or the next day, or any time before his next deliveries were to arrive. He would not have been willing to sell gasoline to someone presently in line if he expected that someone else would show up later willing to pay more. The price he set, in other words, would have corresponded to the price set in an auction market that extended over time and represented future bidders as well as present bidders.

The effect of the owner's pricing gasoline in this way would have been not only further to reduce the quantity demanded on the part of those presently in line, thereby reducing the waiting line further, *but actually to make gasoline available at all times at his service station.* Since all other service station owners would also have been pricing gasoline in the same way, motorists would soon have realized that gasoline was in fact available whenever they wished it and in whatever quantity they wished it—provided they were willing to pay the price. There would have been no shortage and motorists would have known that they did not have to fear a shortage; they would have ceased to be afraid to drive with less than a full tank of gasoline. (It should be realized that this is largely a description of what actually happened later on. Shortages ended in the spring of 1974 because the controls on oil prices were substantially relaxed, and totally eliminated as far as imported oil was concerned.)

Of course, in the case of a good like gasoline, a rise in price to the free-market level not only restricts the quantity demanded, and eliminates the need to hoard, but also pulls in supplies from other geographical areas. As we will see, it also causes oil refineries to step up the production of gasoline at the expense of other petroleum products, if necessary. And, in the long run, it increases the total production of oil products. In these ways, a free market not only balances the demand and supply of gasoline, but does so at the point of large and, indeed, continuously growing supplies.

However, the crucial point here is that even in the case

of goods in strictly limited supply, there are no shortages, no waiting lines, in a free market. Whoever has the price is always able to buy as and when he wishes, and as much as he wishes.

There is a further very important point that follows from our discussion. This is the fact that in the context of limited supplies, it is not only to the self-interest of the sellers that prices rise when conditions make it necessary, but, no less, to the self-interest of the *buyers*. It is simply not true, as most people seem to believe, that the interests of buyers are always served by low prices. On the contrary, *it is to the self-interest of buyers of goods in limited supply that prices be high enough to exclude their competitors from the market.*

To grasp this point in the clearest possible way, imagine an art auction, with two bidders for the same painting. One of them is willing to go as high as $1,000; the other, as high as $2,000. The man whose limit is $2,000 would certainly like to pay as little as necessary. He would be glad to pay just $100, or less, if he could. But given the fact that someone else at the auction is prepared to bid up to $1,000, it would be very foolish for this man to insist on paying any preconceived figure below $1,000. If he arbitrarily insisted on bidding any amount below $1,000, the effect of his action would simply be to allow the painting to go to his rival. If he bid exactly $1,000, and refused to bid any more, he would make it a matter of accident to whom the painting went—if the other bidder bid the $1,000 first, it would probably go to that other bidder. In either case, by refusing to outbid the other bidder, he would prevent himself from getting the painting he wants and which he really values above the other bidder's maximum of $1,000 for the painting.

There is absolutely no difference as far as this man is concerned if, instead of his having to appear personally at an auction and outbid his rivals, the art dealer who possesses the painting anticipates the strength of his bid, and simply sets a price on the painting in his gallery that is high enough to deter other potential buyers and thus to reserve it for him. From the standpoint of the rightly understood self-interests of this man, it is a positively good thing that the art dealer asks more than $1,000, because if he did not, someone else would buy the painting and it would be gone by the time our man got around to trying to buy it.

The only difference between the cases of the art auction and the art dealer and that of all other commodities in limited supply is simply one of size. Instead of it being a unique painting that is put up for auction or for sale and which is of interest to a relatively small number of bidders or potential buyers, it is more common to have millions of units of the same good offered in the market and sought after by large numbers of bidders or potential buyers. Just as in the case of the painting, in all these cases, too, the fact that a price is high enough to level down the quantity of the good demanded to equality with the limited supply of it that exists is very much to the interest of all those buyers who are willing and able to pay that price. That price is their means of eliminating the competition for the good from other bidders or potential buyers not willing to pay as much. It is their means of being able to secure the good for themselves. In our example of the wine, for instance, the price of fifty dollars a bottle—if that is the price necessary to level the quantity demanded down to equality with the supply available—is in the interest of everyone who values the wine at or above fifty dollars. If the price were any lower, the wine would be within reach of other potential buyers, who did not value it so highly, and it would, therefore, to that extent, not be available to those who did value it so highly. In the same way, whatever price of a square foot of rental space, or any other good, is required to level the quantity demanded down to equality with the supply available, that price is to the interest of all those who value that space or that good at that price or any higher price. If the price were any lower, they would simply lose their ability to secure the good for themselves—the good would be bought up by those not able or willing to pay as much, and to that extent it would be unavailable to those who did value it sufficiently.

There are two possible misunderstandings of what I am saying that I want to anticipate and answer before going any further.

First, I want to stress that the ability to outbid others for the supply, or part of the supply, of a good is by no means the exclusive prerogative of the rich. The fact is that absolutely everyone exercises this prerogative to the extent that he earns an income or has any money to spend at all. Even the very poorest people outbid others, and the others whom they outbid can include people who are far wealthier than themselves. Of course, this is not true in a case such as our example of the rare wine, where the entire supply is obviously consumed by those who are quite well-to-do.

But it is true in a case such as rental space, or housing in general, where everyone succeeds in obtaining some part of the supply. In a case of this kind, a wealthier family will obtain a larger share of the supply than a poorer family, but what stops it from obtaining a still larger share is the fact that the poorer family outbids it for part of the supply. For example, a wealthier family may rent an eight-room apartment, while a poorer family rents only a four-room apartment. The reason that the wealthier family does not rent a nine-room apartment is the fact that the poorer family is able and willing to pay more for its fourth room than the wealthier family is able and willing to pay for a ninth room.

This competition, of course, does not take place at an actual auction, but the result is exactly the same as if it did. If, for example, apartments are renting at some given figure per room, such as $300 a month, and the poorer family decides it can afford a four-room apartment, while the wealthier family decides it cannot afford a nine-room apartment, the implication is that the poorer family values a fourth room above $300, while the wealthier family values a ninth room below $300. In effect, the poorer family outbids the wealthier family for the marginal room. If this poorer family wants to be sure of obtaining its four rooms, it is just as important to it that rents be high enough to level the quantity of space demanded down to equality with the supply available, as it is to the richer family.

If the price were any lower than the necessary equilibrium price, then while some poorer families might be able to afford a fifth room, wealthier families would just as often be able to afford a ninth room. And as often as poorer families succeeded in grabbing off a fifth room at the expense of a wealthier family's eighth room, a wealthier family would succeed in grabbing off a ninth room at the expense of a poorer family's fourth room. The same results apply to any good that is universally consumed: an artificially low price permits the "rich" to expand their consumption at the expense of the "poor" just as often as it permits the poor to expand their consumption at the expense of the rich.

Thus, the setting of prices at levels high enough to achieve equilibrium between the quantity demanded and the supply available is to the rational self-interest of everyone, irrespective of his income. Moreover, a harmony of interests exists in a free market even in those cases in which the price totally excludes some people from the market for particular goods. It exists on a remoter plane. For example, the price of Rembrandt paintings excludes the author of this book from the market for those paintings entirely and without question. Nevertheless, it is to my self-interest that if someone must be excluded, it be me, and not an industrial tycoon. For if his vastly greater contribution to production did not enable him to live at a better level than I do, I would be in serious trouble. To put this another way, if an industrial tycoon can have his art collection and other super-luxuries, then I can have all the food I want, a house, an automobile, and so on, and more and better all the time. If I were to be able to compete on equal terms with him for the super-luxuries, he would have no motive to conduct production in such a way that I am assured of all the necessities and lesser luxuries.

In order to avoid a second possible misunderstanding about the interest buyers have in prices being sufficiently high, I want to stress that I am *not* saying that people should simply welcome higher prices and be glad to pay them. Obviously, rising prices impose major hardships on large numbers of people, and they cannot simply look on stoically and be glad of their ability to pay those prices. However, there are two separate things here that must be very carefully distinguished, namely, the fact of the rise in prices and the cause of the rise in prices.

Our example of the art auction will serve to make this distinction clear. Assume that the losing bidder, whose maximum bid was previously $1,000, is now placed in a position in which he is able to bid as high as $1,500. In order to outbid him, our man will now have to bid above $1,500, whereas before he only had to bid above $1,000. Obviously, this is not a pleasant development for our man. But nevertheless it is still to his interest to bid a price that is sufficiently high to secure him the painting. Our man should, indeed, still value the opportunity to outbid his rival. His sorrow should be directed only at that which now makes it more difficult for him to do so.

In the same way, even in periods of rising prices people should, indeed, still value the opportunity to outbid their rivals and the fact that sellers set prices high enough to achieve this objective for them. Their anger should be directed only at that which makes it more and more difficult for them to accomplish this overbidding. What they should be angry about is not the existence of a market economy and the way the market economy works *but at the presence in the market of a vast gang of dishonest bidders and dishonest buyers,* a gang that bids and spends dollars created out of thin air in competition with their earned dollars. As later discussion will show, the source of these dollars created out of thin air is none other than the government. And the dishonest gang consists of it and of everyone else who demands and receives such fiat money.[37]

In other words, it is inflation and the pressure-group demands for inflation that the victims of rising prices should denounce, not the market economy or the opportunity it affords them for outbidding their rivals. It is the entry of newly created money into the economy that they should seek to stop, not the registry of that newly created money in the form of higher prices. Instead of, in effect, calling for the closing of the market, they should simply call for an end to the government's inflation of the money supply, and thus for the establishment of a *fully free* market—a market free of this as well as the government's imposition of price controls.

On the basis of the way their prices are determined, the distribution of consumers' goods in limited supply—

in the sense of who actually ends up with them—always tends to take place in a free market in accordance with two criteria: the relative wealth and income of the various potential buyers and the relative intensity of their need or desire for the good in question. The wealthier a buyer is, the more of any good he can afford to buy—obviously. But wealth is not the sole criterion of distribution. Where two buyers possess the same wealth, the one who needs or desires a good more intensely will be willing to devote a larger proportion of his wealth to its purchase, and he will therefore be able to outcompete an equally wealthy buyer who values the good less intensely. And, of course, in many cases a buyer who possesses a sufficiently strong desire will be able to outcompete a wealthier buyer, sometimes even a substantially wealthier buyer. In our example of the wine, for instance, a wine connoisseur of relatively modest means might very well be willing to pay prices that a millionaire would not. Or, because of their relative preferences, some poorer families might outcompete some wealthier families not just for a marginal room, but for an equal-size apartment by devoting a sufficient proportion of their income to rent.

In a free market, therefore, consumers' goods in limited supply are distributed in accordance with purchasing power directed by needs and desires, or, equivalently, in accordance with needs and desires backed by purchasing power. Everyone consumes these goods in accordance with a combination of his means and his needs and desires.

3. The Pricing and Distribution of Factors of Production in Limited Supply

All that we have learned about the prices of consumers' goods in limited supply applies to the prices of factors of production in limited supply, that is, to the prices of materials, labor, machinery, and anything else that is bought for business purposes and that is in limited supply.

The price of a factor of production in limited supply is also determined in such a way that the quantity of it demanded is levelled down to equality with the limited supply of it that exists, just like a consumers' good in limited supply. What pushes the price to the necessary height is, once again, a combination of the self-interests of the sellers and the buyers. The immediate buyers, directly concerned, are, of course, businessmen. Businessmen desire a factor of production not for the satisfaction of their own personal needs or wants, but in order to secure the means of producing goods for profit. Nevertheless, it is just as much against the interests of businessmen to try to pay too little for a factor of production as it is for a consumer to try to pay too little for something

he buys. Like a consumer, a businessman must be willing to pay prices that are high enough to secure him the things he wants. This means that he must be willing to pay prices that outbid what other businessmen are prepared to offer for the same part of the supply. (It follows that the doctrine that self-interest drives employers arbitrarily to pay subsistence wages is as absurd as the belief that self-interest drives the bidder at an art auction to offer scrap-paper prices for a valuable painting. Employers who would arbitrarily decide to pay too-low wages would simply enable other employers to hire away their labor. The employer who wants labor must be willing to pay wages that are high enough to make that labor too expensive for all its other potential employers.[38])

The only complication that is introduced by the price of a factor of production in limited supply is that it does double duty, so to speak. It not only levels down the quantity of the factor that is demanded to equality with the supply available, but, indirectly, the quantity of all the various products of the factor as well.

Let us consider first a simple case, such as cigarette tobacco, whose only product is cigarettes. The price of cigarette tobacco not only levels down the quantity of cigarette tobacco that is demanded, but, as a major part of the cost of producing cigarettes, it carries through to the price of cigarettes and also levels down the quantity of *cigarettes* demanded. The price of cigarette tobacco thus adjusts the demand for cigarettes to the supply of cigarette tobacco. Observe just how this happens. As the price of cigarette tobacco rises, the cost of producing cigarettes rises, which, in turn, raises their price. As the price of cigarettes rises, the quantity of cigarettes demanded falls. In fact, it is this fall in the quantity demanded of cigarettes, as their price rises, that necessitates a fall in the quantity demanded of cigarette tobacco, as its price rises. As the price of cigarette tobacco rises, businessmen purchase less of it because they know that they cannot sell as many cigarettes at the higher prices that are necessary to cover the resulting higher costs of production. In this way, therefore, the price of cigarette tobacco levels down the quantity demanded both of cigarettes as well as cigarette tobacco to equality with the supply of cigarette tobacco available.

Nothing is changed if we now consider the somewhat more complicated case of wheat or any other factor of production that has a variety of products, such as skilled labor. As the price of wheat rises, the cost of production and prices of all products made from wheat—such as bread, crackers, macaroni, whiskey, and wheat-fed cattle and chickens—also rise. The rise in the prices of wheat products reduces the quantity of the various wheat products demanded, and this reduces the quantity demanded of wheat. Again, as the price of wheat rises, businessmen cut back their purchases in anticipation of the fact that they will not be able to sell as many wheat products at the higher selling prices necessary to cover the higher cost of wheat. In this way, therefore, through its effect on the cost of production and the selling prices of all the various wheat products, the price of wheat equalizes not just the quantity of wheat demanded, but also the quantity demanded of all wheat products as a group, with the supply of wheat available.

There is a further important similarity between what is accomplished by the price of a factor of production in limited supply and the price of a consumers' good in limited supply. If we look at the whole range of products of such a factor as forming a single group, we can observe the same essential principle of distribution with respect to the factor that we previously observed with respect to a consumers' good in limited supply. Namely, the benefit of the factor, as conveyed by its various products, is distributed to the various individual consumers in accordance with their relative purchasing power and in accordance with their relative desire for products of that type. For example, the benefit of the supply of wheat is distributed to the ultimate consumers in accordance with a combination of their relative wealth and relative preferences for products made of wheat. Other things being equal, richer buyers obtain the benefit of more of the supply of wheat than poorer buyers. Not that richer buyers eat more bread—they probably eat less of it—but they eat more meat, which requires the use of far more wheat to make possible its production pound for pound (in the feeding of cattle) than does bread. In the same way, a buyer with a relatively strong preference for wheat products, such as a buyer who especially likes steak and scotch, is able to obtain a larger share of the benefit of the wheat supply than a buyer of equal wealth who values these things less.

The benefit of the supply of crude oil, skilled and unskilled labor, and all other factors of production in limited supply is distributed to the ultimate consumers in just the same way.

Thus far, it is evident that the prices of factors of production in limited supply have the same characteristics and the same significance as the prices of consumers' goods in limited supply. The great difference between them pertains to the fact that there is an added dimension to the distribution of the factors of production. Not only is the benefit of a factor of production distributed to different persons, in accordance with their relative wealth and relative preferences, but the factor itself must be distributed to *different concrete uses in production.* Its benefit goes to the persons only by means of those specific uses. For example, consumers do not buy the benefit of wheat or skilled labor as such, but the various

specific products of wheat or skilled labor. The supply of the factor must be distributed among its various specific products—in order to produce them.

This distribution of a factor of production among its various products is the result of a further process of mutual bidding and competition among the consumers. Only this time, it is not merely one consumer bidding against another consumer, *but the different needs, desires, or purposes of one and the same individual consumers bidding against each other, as well.* For instance, there is a competition for wheat between its use for baking bread, its use for making crackers, its use for making whiskey, feeding meat animals, and so on. There is a competition for crude oil between its use for making gasoline, its use for making heating oil, and so on. And there is a competition for the labor of each ability group among all of its various possible employments. Since the same individual consumers consume most or all of the various products of these factors of production, the competition is, as I say, ultimately largely one between the competing needs, desires, or purposes of the same individuals.

In order to grasp the nature and the importance of this competition, let us consider the question of why just so many bushels of wheat—to continue with that example—are devoted to each of its specific uses. Why aren't a million bushels, say, withdrawn from making crackers and added on to baking bread? The reason this does not occur is that the consumers of the quantity of crackers requiring the million bushels in question are perfectly willing and able to pay a price for the crackers that makes it profitable to cracker manufacturers to produce them at the current price of wheat. The consumers of the crackers, in other words, are willing to allow the producers of the crackers to pay the present price of wheat. But suppose that a million bushels of wheat were used to produce additional loaves of bread. In order to find customers for the additional bread, its price would have to be reduced. In fact, in a country like the United States, where, as a rule, even the very poorest people can already buy all the bread they desire to eat, the price would probably have to be cut so drastically as to induce people to feed the extra bread to pigeons. Conceivably, the extra bread might not be saleable at any price. In any case, it is clear that the bakers of bread would not be able to buy any additional wheat except at a lower price of wheat. And that means that the bread industry, in effect, bids less for the million bushels of wheat in question than the cracker industry. The cracker industry gets the wheat by outbidding the bread industry. And this happens because ultimately the consumers of crackers are outbidding the consumers of bread for the benefit of that wheat.

For the same reasons, the reverse situation does not

occur either—that is, a million bushels of wheat are not withdrawn from the bread industry and added on to the cracker industry. For the consumers of the present quantity of bread are willing to pay prices for that quantity that allow the bread industry to be profitable at the present price of wheat. But the consumers of crackers would only be willing to buy a larger quantity of crackers at a lower price. In order for crackers to be profitable at a lower price, the price of wheat would have to be lower. As a result, the only way the cracker industry could buy an additional quantity of wheat would be at a lower price of wheat than the bread industry is willing to pay for it. Thus, the bread industry outbids the cracker industry for this particular quantity of wheat. Again, ultimately it is the consumers of the one product outbidding the consumers of the other product for the benefit of the quantity of wheat in question. And since it is the same people who consume both products, it is really one kind of need, desire, or purpose of the same individuals outcompeting another.

In exactly the same way, any other such transfer of wheat from one use to another is prevented by the fact that in its changed employment the quantity of wheat in question could only be employed profitably at a lower price than in its present employment. In other words, the present employments outbid the potential changed employments, and thus they get the wheat. And the reason they outbid them is because of the fact that the ultimate consumers are willing to allow more for the use of wheat in its present employments than in its changed employments.

In this way, the distribution of wheat to its various uses is determined by a process of competition among those uses, which in turn reflects a process of competition among the needs, desires, and purposes of one and the same individual consumers.

We can substitute any factor of production for wheat, and the results will be the same. If we ask why a million man-hours of unskilled labor are not withdrawn from one industry and added on to another, the answer again is that the consumers are willing to pay product prices in its present employments that enable businessmen to employ that labor profitably at its going wage rate; if the labor were shifted, however, the consumers would only buy the resulting products at prices that would require lower wage rates for their production to be profitable. These products, therefore, are unable to compete for the necessary labor. They are unable because of the choices and value judgments of the consumers, which enable the existing employments to outbid them.

A principle which emerges from our discussion is that *in a free market a factor of production in limited supply always tends to be distributed to its most important employments, as determined by the value judgments of the consumers themselves.* In our example of the distri-

bution of wheat, it was more important for the million bushels to be employed in producing crackers that people wanted—as demonstrated by their willingness to pay for them—than additional bread that people did not want or wanted less. It was more important for a million bushels to be retained in producing bread that was desired than to be added on to producing crackers that were less strongly desired—as manifested, this time, in the willingness of consumers to allow more for wheat used to produce bread than for wheat used to produce additional crackers.

It is this way in every case. A factor of production in limited supply is employed in those uses that can afford to pay the highest prices for it. And that is determined by the willingness of the consumers to pay prices for the resulting final products. Every factor of production in limited supply is distributed to those employments where the consumers are willing to allow the most for it in the prices of the goods they buy. That is, it is distributed to those employments which the consumers regard as the most important to their own well-being.

It must be stressed that the concept "the most important employments of a factor of production" is *a variable range* that expands or contracts with the supply of the factor of production available. What it means is the most important employments *for which the supply of the factor suffices.*[39] For example, if the supply of the factor is extremely limited, the most important employments for which the supply suffices might be as important as life itself. If the supply is very great, the most important employments can extend downward to include many luxury uses. The case of wheat again provides a good example. In a country like India, or medieval France, devoting wheat to its most important employments means, essentially, producing as much bread as possible to ward off starvation. In a country like the present-day United States, devoting wheat to its most important employments ranges downward through totally satisfying the desire for products such as bread and pasta, heavily satisfying the desire for such things as cakes and cookies made from wheat, substantially satisfying the desire for alcoholic beverages made from wheat, and partly satisfying the desire for wheat-fed meat.

A second major principle follows from this discussion. Namely, the price of every factor of production in limited supply, and thus the prices of all of its various products, is determined by the importance attached to the *least important of the employments for which its supply suffices;* that is, by the importance attached to its *marginal* employments. In our example of wheat, for instance, the price of wheat in the present-day United States is determined by the importance attached to the use of wheat in feeding meat animals—its marginal employment in the context of our economy. This results from the fact that the price of wheat has to be low enough to permit its use to be profitable in *all* of its employments. If it is to be used in feeding meat animals, its price has to be low enough to make that use profitable at prices consumers are willing to pay for wheat-fed meat. However, there is only one uniform price of wheat in the same market at the same time. As a result, the bread industry pays no more for wheat than the cattle-raising industry. And because the price of bread is determined by its cost of production, the price of bread in the United States is actually determined not by its own importance, which may be as great as the stilling of hunger, but by the relatively low importance attaching to the use of wheat in producing meat.

Or, to take another example, the price of surgical instruments, on which countless lives may depend, is not determined by the importance of the needs they serve directly. It is not even determined by the importance attached to the marginal employments of iron and steel, but by the importance attached to the marginal employments of the ability groups of the labor that produces iron, steel, and surgical instruments. For the price of the surgical instruments is determined by their cost of production. And the wage rates which constitute that cost are low enough to make the employment of the different ability groups of labor profitable in their marginal employments. To put it another way, the price even of surgical instruments is no higher in relation to the wages of the ability groups of labor employed to produce them than the marginal products of such labor, which may be a quantity of razor blades or even magazines or chocolate bars or who knows what.

To summarize our discussion of factors of production in limited supply, we have seen that all the principles apply that we developed in relation to consumers' goods in limited supply, plus two others: First, that factors are distributed to their most important employments through a process of the different needs, desires, and purposes of the same individual consumers bidding against one another. And second, that the prices of the factors are determined with respect to the *least important* among the employments for which their supply suffices. Determination of price by cost, we have seen, therefore, ultimately means determination with respect to the consumers' value judgments concerning the *marginal products* of factors of production.[40]

4. The Free Market's Efficiency in Responding to Economic Change

On the basis of the way their prices are determined, every change in the demand or supply of a factor of production in a free market tends to be dealt with in the most rational and efficient manner possible—that is, in a way that maximizes gains and minimizes losses.

To understand why this is so, imagine that the demand for one product in the economic system rises, while the demand for another product falls. For the sake of simplicity, assume for the moment that the two products are produced with the same factors of production. Washing machines and refrigerators are a good illustration of such products, because both of them require just about the same overall proportions of skilled and unskilled labor in their production, use largely the same materials, and can probably be produced in the very same factories without great difficulty. If the demand for one of these products increases while the demand for the other decreases, there will probably be little or no change at all in the demand for factors of production that cannot be matched by an immediate corresponding shift in their supply. Essentially, all that occurs in this case is that more of the same kinds of factors are employed in one capacity, and less in another. In accordance with a change in consumer demand, the production of the one item is expanded while the production of the other item is contracted. In this case, there is obviously no tendency toward a change in the prices of the factors of production.

But now let us consider a more complicated case, which will bring out an important new principle of the free market. Assume that a change in fashion occurs which dictates that the average person own one extra wristwatch, and which, at the same time, encourages him or her to own one less suit or dress. I choose this example because the labor used to produce clothes cannot be transferred to the production of watches, due to the enormous skill differences involved. Here, therefore, we have a case of changes in the demand for factors of production that cannot be matched by offsetting shifts in their supply. Let us see what happens in such a case in a free market.[41]

The wage rate of watchmakers and the cost of production and price of watches, of course, will rise; while the wage rate of garment workers and the cost of production and price of clothing will fall. However, the effects will not be confined to these initial areas of impact. A rise in the wages of watchmakers will begin to attract other workers into the field, say, some workers who would have gone into instrument making, optics, jewelry making, and so forth—that is, whatever fields employ labor of a kind that can be used to make watches. A fall in the wage rates of garment workers, on the other hand, will begin to push some of these workers out of that field and into other fields. As a result, a tendency develops toward widening and diffusing the initial impact of the change in demand.

As workers leave fields such as instrument making and optics to go into watchmaking, the wage rates and thus the production costs and product prices in these fields will begin to rise. Thus, the rise in demand for watches will raise not only the cost and price of watches, but also the cost and price of instruments, optical goods, and so forth—all products that use the same kind of labor as watchmaking. Conversely, as workers leave the garment industry and begin to enter other fields for which they possess the necessary skills, the wage rates, production costs, and product prices in those fields will begin to decline.

The question we want to ask is: what *principle* determines which industries among those that employ the same kind of labor as watchmaking actually release additional labor for watchmaking, and to what extent? And which industries among those potentially capable of absorbing the labor released from the garment industry actually absorb it, and to what extent? To arrive at the answer, we must realize that at the higher prices of the various goods that use the same kind of labor as watches, the consumers will reduce their purchases of those goods. It is these decisions of the consumers to restrict their purchases, that determine which of the industries release labor for watchmaking and to what extent. For example, if the consumers decide to go on buying an unchanged quantity of optical goods at their higher price, but a reduced quantity of jewelry and various instruments, none of the labor will come from the optical goods industry, and all of it will come from the jewelry and instrument industries. Obviously, the labor will come from these various industries in accordance with whatever proportions the consumers decide to curtail their purchases of the various products at their respectively higher prices.

Clearly, what occurs in this case is an indirect bidding for the use of labor between the buyers of wristwatches and the buyers of all other products employing the same kind of labor. The buyers of wristwatches cause a bidding up of the price of the wider category of labor that produces both wristwatches and all the other products I have named. As a consequence of this intensified bidding for labor, the buyers of these other products—jewelry, instruments, optical goods, and so forth—are confronted with higher product prices and so must restrict their purchases. To the degree that they restrict their purchases, they release labor to the watch industry and make possible its expansion.

Now to the extent that the consumers are rational, the products whose purchase they discontinue at the higher prices will be the *least important* among the ones they previously purchased. That is, the consumers will discontinue their previously *marginal purchases*. For each consumer who buys these various products will cut back his purchases in the way that hurts him least in his context and in his judgment. Thus, if he needs eyeglasses, he will certainly go on buying a pair of eyeglasses, but perhaps forgo the purchase of a telescope for his hobby, say. If he was previously in a position to buy several pairs of eyeglasses and a telescope and some jewelry, then, when he is confronted with higher prices for all of them, he may decide to go ahead with the telescope but cut back on an extra pair of sunglasses and some jewelry. The effect on the quantities demanded of these goods in the whole economy is, of course, simply the aggregate of all such individual decisions. In this way, it can be seen that in a free economy the labor released for watchmaking will come from its previously marginal employments—that is, from the employments where all the various individual consumers in the market judge they can best spare it.

By the same token, the labor released from the garment industry will be absorbed in those employments which are the most important of the employments for which the supply of that type of labor did not previously suffice; that is, it will be absorbed in the most important of its previously submarginal employments. This conclusion follows from the fact that the workers released will be seeking to earn the highest incomes they can and that these incomes will be found in producing those goods for which the consumers are willing to allow the highest prices over and above the allowance for the other costs entailed in producing them. The displaced garment workers will enter whatever fields can absorb them with the least fall in wage rates. These are the fields whose products the consumers are willing to buy in additional quantities at the least fall in prices. They offer the displaced garment workers the highest wages now available to them. I have not attempted to enumerate these other employments because the skills involved are so common that the labor released would probably be absorbed to some degree in a vast number of industries. For example, some of the former garment workers might end up as office workers, taxi drivers, metal workers, or who knows what.

Everything we have seen concerning the source of labor for additional watches applies in principle to the source of any factor of production in limited supply for an expansion of the production of any good. Always, the process is one of an intensified bidding for the factor by businessmen acting as agents of the consumers of one or more of its particular products against businessmen acting as agents of the consumers of its other products. This bidding drives up the price of the factor, the costs of using it in production, and the prices of all of its various products. Supplies of the factor are always released, in accordance with the choices of the consumers, from the production of its previously marginal products—from the products where the consumers decide they can best spare it. In the same way, everything we have seen concerning the absorption of labor released from the garment industry applies to the absorption of any factor in limited supply released from any industry. Always, the factor is absorbed in the most important of its employments previously unprovided for, in accordance with the judgment of the consumers, as manifested in what they are willing to pay the most for.

The identical reasoning that we have applied to changes in the demand for a factor of production in limited supply applies to changes in the supply of such a factor. If the overall supply of a factor should increase, the addition goes to provide for the most important of the employments of the factor previously unprovided for. For example, an increase in the supply of wheat in the present-day United States would be used to expand the production of such things as wheat-fed meat and aged whiskey. If the supply of a factor should decrease, the reduction is taken out on the least important of the employments previously provided for. In the case of wheat in the context of the present-day United States, this would mean a reduction in the production of such things as wheat-fed meat and aged whiskey. In other words, an increase in the supply of a factor goes to the most important of its previously submarginal employments; a decrease is taken out on its previously marginal employments.

The principle that emerges from this discussion is that *in a free market if a factor of production is in reduced demand or additional supply, the portion of it that becomes newly available is channelled to the most important of its previously submarginal uses; if the factor of production is in additional demand or reduced supply, the portion of it that is no longer available is taken from the least important of its previous uses, that is, from its previously marginal uses.* In other words, as stated, every change in the demand or supply of a factor of production in a free market is dealt with in a way that maximizes gains and minimizes losses; which is to say, it is dealt with in the most rational and efficient manner possible.

A Rational Response to the Arab Oil Embargo

The above principle has major application to such economic disruptions and pretenses for price controls as the Arab oil embargo. It enables us to understand in yet another respect how a free market would have minimized the impact of any reduction in the supply of oil that the Arabs might have been able to impose on us, and would minimize any other such disruption that might occur in the future.

If we had had a free market, the price of crude oil and the production costs and prices of all oil products would have risen during the embargo. The consumers would have decided where the reduction in the use of crude oil was to be effected and to what degree, by the extent to which they cut back on their purchases of the various oil products at the higher prices. Where the use of an oil product was important, consumers would have paid the higher price, and oil would have continued to be used for that purpose. Only where the use of an oil product was not worth its higher price, would the use of oil have been cut back or discontinued. For example, consumers would have paid a higher price for the gasoline required to drive to work and for the heating oil required to keep them warm. They would not have been as ready to pay higher prices for the gasoline required for extra shopping trips or for heating oil to keep their garages warm.

The crucial point is that in a free market the more important employments of oil would have outbid the less important ones, and the reduction in the supply of oil would have been taken out exclusively at the expense of the *marginal* employments of oil—that is, at the expense of the least important employments for which the previously larger supply of oil had sufficed.

But, of course, we did not have a free market. We had price controls. Price controls prevented the more important employments of crude oil from outbidding the less important employments. They prevented the most vital and urgent needs for oil from outbidding the most marginal. For example, during the oil shortage 1973–74 one could read stories in the newspapers about truck drivers not being willing to deliver food supplies to southern Florida for fear of being unable to obtain fuel for the return trip up the length of the Florida peninsula. There was even a story about the operation of oil rigs off the Louisiana coast being threatened as the result of an inability to obtain supplies of certain oil products needed for their continued functioning.

Now it is simply insane that such vital activities should suffer for a lack of oil—that even the production of oil itself should be threatened. In a free market, this could never happen. Such vital uses of oil would always be able to outbid any less urgent employment for all the oil they required. But under price controls even these most vital employments were prohibited from outbidding any other employment that could pay the controlled price.

Price controls simply paralyze rational action. In effect, they bring together at an auction for the use of oil a trucker needing fuel to deliver food supplies and a housewife needing gasoline to take an extra shopping trip to the supermarket, and they prohibit the trucker from outbidding the housewife. They bring together oilmen needing lubricants for their wells and homeowners seeking oil to heat their garages, and they prohibit the oilmen from outbidding the homeowners. In a word, price controls make it *illegal to act rationally.*

---

5. The Economic Harmonies of Cost Calculations in a Free Market

We can now understand even more fully than was possible earlier how in a free market the production of each good is carried on in a way that is maximally conducive to production in the rest of the economic system. For we are now in a position to understand more fully how the concern with costs of production promotes the production of other goods every time it leads to the substitution of lower-priced factors of production in limited supply for higher-priced ones, such as the use of unskilled labor where skilled labor was previously required, or the use of a less expensive quantity of aluminum where a more expensive quantity of copper was previously required, and so on. All we have to do is keep in mind that the less expensive factors in limited supply *are* less expensive because the importance of their marginal products to the consumers is less. To substitute less expensive factors for more expensive ones, therefore, is to make it possible for the consumers to obtain products to which they attach greater marginal importance at the expense of products to which they attach smaller marginal importance. For the more expensive factors are released to uses of greater importance than those from which the less expensive factors are withdrawn.

Thus, the fact that in a free market production is carried on at the lowest possible cost that businessmen can achieve means that the production of each thing is carried on not only with the least possible amount of labor, but with *those specific types of labor and other factors of production in limited supply whose use represents the least possible impairment of the satisfaction of alternative wants.*

We can observe the operation of this principle in every cost calculation that businessmen make. To take some examples, let us assume that a railway company is contemplating the extension of its line across a body of water or that an electric company is contemplating the construction of additional generating capacity. In these cases, and in practically every other case, alternative methods of production are possible. The railway could build a bridge across the water, it could tunnel under the water, build a ferry, or, perhaps, detour around the body of water. In each instance, a variety of further alternatives are possible, such as where to construct the bridge, what materials and design to use, and so on. In the same way, the electric company could build a coal-powered plant, a water-powered plant, an oil or gas-powered plant, or an atomic-powered plant. Again, major variations are possible in each of these alternatives.

Now each method of production and each variant of any given method requires some different combination of factors of production in limited supply. Each of these factors of production has its own alternative uses in various other employments. For example, the bridge requires workers with the special skills required to build bridges. These workers could be employed in building bridges elsewhere or in building skyscrapers, or, of course, in a variety of lesser jobs. The tunnel requires the special skills of sandhogs. These men may first have to be trained, and then a long period of time will go by during which they are unavailable to produce a different variety of goods than the bridge builders. Again, different methods require different combinations of materials that may themselves be in limited supply or require different combinations of labor skills or limited materials in their own production.

The point here is that the selection of any given method of production has its own unique impact on the rest of the economic system in terms of withdrawing factors of production from possible alternative employments. The fact that businessmen select the lowest-cost methods of production means that they try to produce each good with the least overall impairment of the production of alternative goods. Because to produce at the lowest cost means to use that combination of factors of production in limited supply that has the lowest total marginal significance in alternative employments.

Not only is the production of each good harmoniously integrated with the production of all other goods in a free market, but so too, not surprisingly, is the consumption of each good. As we have seen, insofar as any good is produced by factors of production in limited supply, its price reflects the competitive bidding of the consumers of all the products of those factors. For example, the price of bread in a free market reflects the competitive bidding of the consumers of all wheat products for the use of wheat; the price of gasoline in a free market reflects the competitive bidding of the consumers of all oil products for the use of crude oil; and so on. Going still further, the price of wheat and wheat products relative to the price of oil and oil products reflects the competitive bidding of the consumers of all wheat products relative to the competitive bidding of the consumers of all oil products. Indeed, the prices of all factors of production in limited supply and of their respective products reflect the relative utilities of the respective marginal products to the ultimate consumers. The consumer buyers of any of these products, therefore, when they take account of their prices, are led to pay the same regard to the rest of the economic system as businessmen when they make cost calculations.

More on the Response to the Oil Embargo

The above facts about the harmonious integration of the production and consumption of each good into the rest of the economic system also have application to how a free market would have responded to the Arab oil embargo.

If we had had a free market, the response to the reduction in the supply of oil would have been based on the exercise of the intelligence and judgment of each and every individual businessman and consumer in the economic system.

As the price of oil and oil products rose, each individual businessman and consumer would have decided where and to what extent to cut back on the use of oil by consulting his own individual circumstances. Those businessmen would have cut back who had lower-cost alternatives available. For example, businessmen with the alternative of switching to coal or shipping by rail or barge instead of truck would have done so. And more and more would have done so, more and more rapidly, as the price of oil and oil products rose higher, because the comparative savings in doing so would have become greater. In the same way, some firms might have concentrated their production in fewer days to conserve fuel. Some might have concentrated production more heavily in plants in warmer parts of the country. Some might have reduced or stopped production entirely, because of an inability to sell as many goods at the higher prices necessitated by higher costs of fuel and transportation. The point is that there would have been as many *individual* responses as there were separate business firms and even subunits within business firms. The response in each case would have been based on a consideration of costs and alternatives in the individual case.

Similarly, each individual consumer would have decided where and to what extent to cut back on the basis of the individual circumstances confronting him. What would have decided in each case was the importance of the particular oil product, as determined by the individual consumer's personal needs and desires dependent on that product, and the extent of his wealth. For example, no one to whom time was essential would have been forced to reduce his driving speed. Nor would a wealthy person have been forced to give up driving his Cadillac. By the same token, no one whose only means of getting to work was an automobile would have gone without gasoline. He would have chosen to go without other things first and to spend the money he saved from somewhere else, to buy the necessary gasoline. Anyone in such a position would have been assured of all the gasoline he required, because he would certainly have been willing and able to pay more for gasoline for the purpose of getting to work than most other people would have been willing to

pay for it for any lesser purpose. To obtain gasoline for getting to work, one would merely have had to outbid other people seeking gasoline for pleasure trips, marginal shopping trips, and so on.

More broadly, since more gasoline can always be produced from crude oil made available by producing less of other oil products, an individual needing gasoline to get to work would merely have had to outbid other people requiring the use of *crude oil* for any lesser purpose than one comparable to that of getting to work. For example, he would have been able to obtain gasoline by outbidding even people far richer than himself who previously used oil to heat their swimming pools, or, perhaps, who previously consumed vegetables or flowers grown in hothouses with the aid of large quantities of oil.

The specific ways in which oil would have been economized are far too numerous to name. It is impossible even to learn them all. They would have depended on an enormous number of individual circumstances, in many cases known only to the individuals directly involved, whoever and wherever they might have been.

The essential fact is that oil would have been economized in ways that affected each individual as little as possible. Each individual—businessman and consumer—would have dealt with the problem in the way best suited to his own business or personal context, and at the same time his efforts would have been harmoniously integrated—through the price of oil and oil products—with the like efforts of everyone else. Each would have acted on the basis of the price of oil and oil products, and the circumstances and judgments of each would have determined just how high those prices would have had to go before the quantity of oil and oil products demanded was levelled down to equality with the reduced supply of crude oil available. In other words, *in a free market, the oil crisis would have been met by the conscious planning of each individual, harmoniously integrated with that of every other individual.*

Of course, this is not what occurred—because of price controls. All considerations of individual context were dropped. The intelligence and planning of the individuals were paralyzed, as we have already seen. The government's solution was a sledgehammer approach that disregarded all individual circumstances and context. It arbitrarily curtailed the use of oil and oil products for whole categories of employments. For example, it declared that the airline industry would operate on 80 percent of its previous year's fuel, that farmers would have to make do with so much less propane, and that everyone would have to drive at no more than fifty-five miles per hour and set his thermostat at no more than sixty-eight degrees. This absurd approach simply ignored which industries and which specific firms and individuals could really afford to cut back on oil, and just where. It disregarded such elementary facts as that lower truck speeds would require proportionately more trucks and man-hours to haul the same amount of freight, so that to arbitrarily save a few gallons of gasoline, whole trucks and untold man hours to operate them would be wasted. It disregarded the fact that thermostat settings of sixty-eight degrees in some places and for some people can be tantamount to freezing and cause pneumonia. But more of such consequences of price controls soon enough.

Appendix to Chapter 6: The Myth of "Planned Obsolescence"

A popular fallacy—advanced in full contradiction of the uniformity-of-profit principle and its implications for economic progress—holds that businessmen engage in the practice of "planned obsolescence," that is, they allegedly plan for their products to wear out more rapidly than is necessary, in order to create an additional, replacement demand for them.[42] According to Vance Packard, one of the leading popularizers of this fallacy: "Even the best of products, of course, wears out sometime. Therefore a company cannot be legitimately criticized for estimating the death date of its product. It is vulnerable to criticism, however, if it sells a product with a short life expectancy when it knows that for the same cost, or only a little more, it could give the customer a product with a much longer useful life. In such situations one may properly wonder about the company's motives."[43]

Despite the prevalence of such beliefs, the fact is that in all cases in which a more durable product can be produced at the same cost of production as a less durable one, the profit motive acts as an inducement to produce the more durable product. Indeed, the profit motive acts as an inducement to produce the more durable product even when its cost of production is substantially greater, provided that the extra durability is sufficiently great.

A simple example will demonstrate why this must be so. Assume that there are two light bulbs costing $1 each to produce. One lasts 10 times as long as the other. The manufacturers are presently producing the less durable bulb and selling it at a price of $1.25. Assume that they are presently selling 100 million of these bulbs per year and that if they introduced the longer-lasting bulb, they would sell only 10 million of them per year. The question must be asked: Is it less profitable to sell 10 million longer-lasting bulbs than 100 million of the present bulbs?

The supporters of the planned obsolescence doctrine believe that the answer is yes. But the answer is no.

At present, the manufacturers have sales revenues of $125 million—$1.25 per bulb times 100 million bulbs. They have a total cost of $100 million—$1 per bulb times 100 million bulbs. Their present profit, therefore, is $25 million. Now assume that they introduce the 10-times-longer-lasting bulb. Such a bulb could certainly be sold for 5 times as much as the present bulb. (If it is, the customer is far better off, for he pays only *half* as much per unit of service life of a bulb as he did before. In fact, he gains at any price below 10 times as much). A price 5 times as high is $6.25. This price times 10 million bulbs sold, gives sales revenues of $62.5 million. The manufacturers' total costs are now $1 per bulb times 10 million bulbs, or $10 million. Profits, therefore, go to $52.5 million—more than doubling from their present level!

Manufacturers can increase their profits by introducing the longer-lasting product even if its unit cost is higher, provided that the higher cost is less than proportionate to the product's longer life. For example, even if the 10-times-longer-lasting bulb cost 9 times as much to produce, or $9, the manufacturers could still increase their profits substantially. If they offered the bulb at a price of $12, which would still represent a saving to the consumers, they could increase their profits by $5 million. They would have sales revenues of $120 million and total costs of $90 million, leaving them with a $30 million profit instead of a $25 million profit.

As a rule, the only time it would not pay to introduce a longer-lasting good is if it has a higher cost which is more than in proportion to its longer life. For example, it would be absurd to introduce a 10-times-longer-lasting bulb which cost 50 times as much to produce. There are exceptions to this rule, however. In some cases, the convenience of not having to replace a product as often could be so significant as to outweigh a cost more than in proportion to its longer life. Thus, a light bulb lasting 10 times as long and which could be profitable only at a price of 11 times as much, might be successful simply because it would save time in changing bulbs, reduce the risk of falling from ladders, and so on. On the other hand, an automobile which would last twice as long and which had to be sold at twice the price would not make economic sense. Such an automobile would require that people tie up twice the sum of money (and, if they bought on credit, pay twice the interest) and not derive any compensating advantage. A 2-times-longer-lasting automobile would only make sense if it could be sold profitably at a price significantly less than double, perhaps 1.8 or even 1.7 times the price of the present car. (Interest rates would play a major role in determining how large the saving had to be.)

What the above examples demonstrate is that not only consumers but also manufacturers derive a gain from the introduction of longer-lasting products, provided only that such products are not disproportionately more expensive to produce. The fact that manufacturers might sell a smaller number of units of longer-lasting goods because of the reduced need to replace them, is altogether irrelevant. Any profits which they must forgo as a result of reduced volume can easily be made up in the price of the quantity they continue to sell, together with a major increase in their profits. To understand the principle involved, it is only necessary to realize two things. First, as an upper limit, the price of the longer-lasting product can be raised approximately in proportion to its greater durability. Second, only a relatively small price increase is required to make up for the profits lost on the quantity no longer produced. Any price in between these limits represents both a saving to the consumer and additional profits to the producer.

To make this clear, let us return to our example of the light bulbs. If the present light bulb is sold for $1.25, a 10-times-longer-lasting one could be sold at a potential upper limit of $12.50. At any price lower than $12.50, the consumers have a clearcut gain. While the manufacturer's volume is cut to one-tenth of its initial level, the profit he loses is only 25¢ on each bulb. Since he no longer sells 9 bulbs for every one which he continues to sell, he must be compensated to the extent of $2.25 in the price of the longer-lasting bulbs. If the longer-lasting bulb costs $1 to produce, then the manufacturer needs a price of only $3.50 to make as much profit on one-tenth the quantity of bulbs as he did on the initial quantity. At any price greater than $3.50, his profits increase. Any price greater than $3.50 and less than $12.50 thus represents a gain to both the consumers and the producers. (If the longer-lasting bulb costs $9 to produce, the manufacturer must have a price greater than $11.50 to come out ahead.)

Consider wider illustrations. Profits are only a small percentage of sales—5 percent, 10 percent, on rare occasion 20 percent. Assume profit is 20 percent of sales—for example, a manufacturer has costs of 80, profits of 20, and sales of 100. If his physical volume were to be cut in half, while his unit cost and selling price remained the same, he would have costs of 40, profits of 10, and sales of 50. His profits could be restored to 20, however, if he could raise his price by 20 percent, thus raising his sales revenues from 50 to 60. If the halving of his sales volume is the result of a doubling of his product's life, there can be no doubt about his ability to raise his price by 20 percent—the upper limit by which he could raise it is 100 percent. Observe. In this case, the manufacturer only

needs a price rise in excess of 20 percent to come out ahead, while the conditions of the case permit a price rise as high as 100 percent. Suppose the manufacturer's sales volume is reduced to a third of its initial level, as a result of his introducing a product which lasts 3 times as long. The potential upper limit of his price increase is now 200 percent. But all he needs to come out ahead is a price increase of 40 percent—40 percent more on a third of his initial volume will give him the same profits he made on the other two-thirds, if his initial profit margin was 20 percent. Similarly, if his volume is cut to a fourth of its initial level, as a result of quadrupling his product's life, then while the upper limit of the price rise goes to 300 percent, the manufacturer only needs a price rise in excess of 60 percent to come out ahead.

If we change the assumed profit margin to 10 percent, then a mere 10 percent rise in price restores profits when volume is cut to a half of its initial level, a 20 percent rise restores profits when volume is cut to a third of its initial level, and so on. With a 5 percent profit margin, a 5 percent rise in prices restores profits when volume is cut to a half, and a 10 percent rise in prices restores profits when volume is cut to a third of its initial level, and so on. The upper limits by which prices might be raised in these cases, however, continue to be 100 percent, 200 percent, and ever more, to the degree that volume is cut as a result of the introduction of longer-lasting products.

The principle which emerges is the following. The consumers are willing to pay an increase in price equal to as much as one less than the multiple of durability times the product's initial price. (For example, if the product is made 10 times more durable, the consumers are willing to pay an increase in price equal to 9 times the product's initial price.) To come out even, however, the manufacturers require a price increase equal merely to one less than the multiple of durability times the product's initial *profit margin*—for example, 9 times 20 percent, 9 times 10 percent, or 9 times 5 percent. Between a multiple of the initial price and an equal multiple of the initial profit margin is an enormous field for mutual gain to both consumer and producer. This field is so great that any necessary writeoffs of existing plant and equipment could easily be compensated for along with profits forgone on lost volume.[44]

Perhaps the best and simplest way to regard longer-lasting products in comparison with less-durable products is in terms of the comparative costs of producing equivalents. If one better light bulb lasts 10 times as long as a present light bulb, it is the equivalent of 10 of the present light bulbs. If the cost of production of both types of bulb is $1, then what we have is a $1 cost of production versus a $10 cost of production of the same equivalent. If the cost of production of the better bulb is $9, then we have a case of $9 versus $10 as costs of production of the same equivalent. The issue of whether or not manufacturers will introduce longer-lasting products can thus be seen to reduce to the question of *whether or not they prefer lower-cost methods of production to higher-cost methods of production.* They will introduce longer-lasting products whenever the longer-lasting products represent a reduction in the cost of producing equivalents. And they will do so with a rapidity and enthusiasm in direct proportion to the cost reductions to be achieved. To ask if *GE* would introduce a 10-times-longer-lasting light bulb, or *GM* a 2-times-longer-lasting car, having the same unit cost of production as the present light bulb or car, is to ask the equivalent of: Would *GE* introduce a light bulb costing one-tenth as much to produce? Would *GM* introduce a car costing half as much to produce? The answer to both questions is obviously yes.

Thus far, I have deliberately understated the case. I have assumed that the reduction in the quantity of a good demanded would be in full proportion to its greater durability. In fact, this would usually not be so. If a 10-times-longer-lasting light bulb or a 2-times-longer-lasting automobile can be sold at less than 10 or 2 times the price, the quantity demanded will not fall to a tenth or a half, but to some amount greater than a tenth or a half. (Indeed, in some cases, the quantity of the good demanded might even increase, if the demand for it is sufficiently elastic.) The reason, of course, is that in terms of a unit of service life the good is made less expensive and thus tends to be used in larger quantity. This tendency of the quantity demanded to fall less than in proportion to the product's greater life would be powerfully reinforced in every case in which the producer of the longer-lasting product was faced with competitors producing the shorter-lived product. In all cases of this kind, the firm introducing the more durable product would have the entire existing market of its competitors as a potential field for its own expansion. It thus might very well succeed in increasing its physical volume by a substantial multiple.

The fact is that business does not produce less-durable goods in preference to more-durable goods, but the contrary. Nor does it foist undesired fashion changes on the public, or dribble out over time improvements which it has the ability to introduce all at once. These beliefs rest on the fallacy that profitability depends exclusively on the physical volume of goods sold. In fact, in all these cases, any profits lost as a result of diminished volume, could more than be made up by a relatively modest rise in price on the remaining volume. Consumers would benefit at the same time, because they would save the expense of buying unnecessary units.[45]

Despite the fact that the profit motive leads businessmen to try to produce the highest-quality, longest-lasting products per dollar of cost, it can, of course, be the case that over time the quality of products deteriorates and their life shortens. This is because the beneficial effect of the profit motive can be outweighed by the contrary effect of government interference. For example, prounion legislation can deprive firms of the ability to fire careless workers. Taxation can deprive them of the funds to buy the quantity and quality of the labor, materials, and machinery they would otherwise employ in producing a given quantity of goods. Above all, price and wage controls can lead to a deterioration in the quality and life of products by creating shortages of means of production and by eliminating all the normal, competitive incentives to high-quality production.[46] The essential point is not that deterioration in the quality and life of products cannot exist, but that the profit motive always acts to improve the quality and lengthen the life of products insofar as it is allowed to operate.

It is conceivable that the objection might be raised to the preceding analysis that it is mistaken in assuming that manufacturers of more-durable products are in a position substantially to increase the prices of such products and thus make up for any reduction in physical volume they might suffer. The objection might be made that freedom of competition would quickly put prices at the same level as they were to begin with. The answer to this objection is that under capitalism whoever introduces a significant improvement in production normally enjoys patent protection, which would secure his ability to obtain the higher price for a sufficient period of time to make the improvement worthwhile.

The doctrine of planned obsolescence is merely one more groundless assault on the profit motive and the pursuit of self-interest. If it does not represent "planned error"—that is, outright malice—it represents such a degree of thoughtlessness as to constitute reckless disregard of facts and logic.

Notes

1. The rate of profit on capital invested should not be confused with the concept of profit margin. A profit margin is profit taken as a percentage of sales revenues, not capital invested. Because of technical factors centering on the periods of time which must elapse between outlays of capital and receipts of sales revenue, different industries tend to earn permanently unequal profit margins, even though they tend to earn equal rates of profit on capital invested. Thus, for example, a retail grocery business, which has a substantial portion of its capital invested in merchandize of the kind that is sold within days of purchase, or even on the very same day, may have annual sales revenues equal to five times its capital. A steel mill, on the other hand, may have annual sales revenues that are merely equal to its capital. An electric utility may have annual sales revenues that are equal to only half of its capital. Because of these very different rates of capital turnover—i.e., ratio of sales to capital—namely 5:1, 1:1, and ½:1, very different profit margins must exist if equal rates of profit on capital invested are to exist. Thus, the profit margin in the retail grocery business would have to be just 2 percent; that of the steel mill, 10 percent; and that of the electric utility, 20 percent, in order for all of them to earn a rate of profit on capital invested of 10 percent.

2. Cf. Ludwig von Mises, *Socialism* (New Haven: Yale University Press, 1951), p. 535; reprint ed. (Indianapolis: Liberty Classics, 1981). Page references are to the Yale University Press edition; pagination from this edition is retained in the reprint edition.

3. See Ayn Rand, *Capitalism: The Unknown Ideal* (New York: New American Library, 1965) pp. 15–16.

4. See above, p. 118, n. 80, for a reference to the fact that the validity of this principle has found important recognition within the U.S. government.

5. At that time, $10,000 represented approximately 500 ounces of gold. To estimate the equivalent in terms of today's money, one should multiply 500 oz. of gold by the currently prevailing price of gold.

6. For elaboration and related discussion of these points, see below, pp. 206–214.

7. See below, pp. 925–927.

8. Cf. Henry Hazlitt, *Economics in One Lesson,* new ed. (New Rochelle, N. Y.: Arlington House, 1979), pp. 114–115.

9. I must point out that it is an error to assume that the repeal of rent controls would create any kind of insuperable problems of short-run hardship. Indeed, I will demonstrate later on that even before sufficient time went by to make possible the construction of any additional new housing, the overall effect of the repeal of rent control would be to improve the conditions of more people than it worsened and to impose no greater hardship on those who had to give up their rent-controlled apartments than was already being experienced, and had been experienced for many years, by just as many other people precisely as the result of rent controls. On this point, see below, pp. 252–254.

10. See above, pp. 63–66 and 90–91.

11. See below, pp. 201–202.

12. See above, n. 1 of this chapter, for an explanation of the relationship between the rate of profit on the one side, and the rate of capital turnover and the profit margin on the other.

13. Of course, the absence of price changes is possible only if the changes in demand are within certain limits. If increases in demand are so great as either completely to outstrip the ability of the industry to meet them from existing capacity, or to require the use of older, substantially less efficient, higher-cost capacity, product prices must rise. It is only a question of by how much. Similarly, if the fall in demand is so substantial that one or more firms finds that the quantity of their products demanded is insufficient to enable them to operate even their most efficient lowest-cost capacity at an adequate rate, while other firms are still using substantially less efficient, higher-cost capacity, then it will be to the interest of such firms to cut prices below the operating costs of others' less efficient capacity. This will enable their efficient capacity to displace the others' less efficient capacity. The price cut in these circumstances will be profitable to the firms which make it, because continued operation of high-cost capacity by others is thereby made unprofitable, with the result that the price-cutting firms secure substantial additional business that is profitable to them. See below, p. 436, for the application of this point to a critique of the doctrine of pure and perfect competition and the Marshallian doctrine of the representative firm.

14. Cf. Ludwig von Mises, *Human Action*, 3d ed. rev. (Chicago: Henry Regnery Co., 1966), p. 245.

15. Ibid.

16. It is standard practice in contemporary economics to consider the portion of the profits of small businessmen which is comparable to the compensation they could earn as wage earners as though it actually were wages. For a critique of this practice, see below, pp. 459–462.

17. This has already been indicated in connection with the uniformity-of-profit principle. See above, p. 185.

18. For an analysis of the actual process of adjustment in wages and prices that would follow the adoption of a policy of unilateral free trade or unilateral tariff reduction, and of the consequences if other countries simply refused to allow the goods of the country in question into their territory while it pursued a policy of free trade, see below, pp. 535–536.

19. The fact that speculators must lose in the absence of an independently caused rise in the demand for and price of the commodity they speculate in is confirmed by the following supply-and-demand diagram. The diagram shows that initially, in the absence of speculators, the price of a commodity is p_0, resulting from the demand DD and the supply SS. The general public buys the entire supply, equal to quantity $0A$, at the price

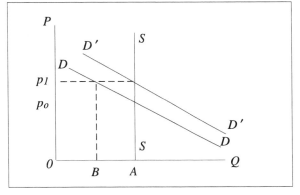

p_0. Now speculators appear on the scene, and when their demand is added to that of the general public, the total demand for the commodity rises from DD to $D'D'$. The result is that the price rises from p_0 to p_1. At the higher price, the general public reduces its purchases from the full supply, $0A$, to the part of the supply represented by $0B$. The speculators buy up the part of the supply represented by AB. If the speculators bought the quantity AB all at once, they would have to pay a price of p_1 for it. In the absence of an increase in demand on the part of the general public, the speculators would then have to sell back their supply at a price of p_0, if they sold it back all at once. The fact that they would probably buy the quantity AB in increments and sell it back in increments changes nothing fundamental, because the purchase and sale of each increment is described by exactly the same analysis. In addition, there is the further problem of a likely movement of the quantity supplied to somewhere to the right of the line SS, in response to the rise in price. For further discussion of why speculators must lose in the absence of an independent cause of higher future prices, see below, pp. 224–225.

20. Indeed, in 1991, the attorneys general of several states renewed the accusation in new lawsuits that they brought against various oil companies.

21. See George Reisman, *The Government Against the Economy* (Ottawa, Ill.: Jameson Books, 1979), pp. 29–30, Table 1.

22. For an important exception to the principle that sellers are led to sell too rapidly, see below, pp. 225–226.

23. The substance of the following discussion concerning the opposition between capitalism and arbitrary discrimination has been excerpted, with minor modification, from my pamphlet *Capitalism: The Cure for Racism* (Laguna Hills, Calif.: The Jefferson School of Philosophy, Economics, and Psychology, 1992). The pamphlet originally appeared as a six-part article in *The Intellectual Activist* in 1982.

24. See below, pp. 367–371, 584–585, and 663–664. See also *Capitalism: The Cure for Racism,* pp. 6–8.

25. On these points, see George Reisman, *Capitalism: The Cure for Racism,* pp. 12–14. What is described here is government-inspired bureaucratic management taking the place of profit management. On this subject, see Ludwig von Mises, *Bureaucracy* (1944; reprint ed., New Rochelle, N. Y.: Arlington House, 1969), pp. 64–73. See also below, pp. 304–305.

26. On this subject, see below, pp. 382–385.

27. For an account of the precise nature of all the government intervention that has blocked the benevolent operation of capitalism on behalf of blacks in their capacity both as wage earners and as consumers, not only in the South but also in the North, see George Reisman, *Capitalism: The Cure for Racism,* pp. 10–28. See also below, pp. 375–376 and 382–385.

28. This accords with the views of the great classical economist David Ricardo. See David Ricardo, *Principles of Political Economy and Taxation,* 3d ed. (London, 1821), chap. 30 especially; reprinted as vol. 1 of *The Works and Correspondence of David Ricardo,* ed. Piero Sraffa (Cambridge: Cambridge University Press, 1962).

29. See above, p. 168.

30. Wage rates are explainable in terms of supply and demand analysis even in cases in which they are imposed arbitrarily by labor unions or governments. For in such cases, an essential part of the process is an artificial restriction of the supply in the face of a given demand.

31. As previously indicated, this analysis of the relation between cost of production and supply and demand is the work of the great economist Eugen von Böhm-Bawerk, one of the founders of the Austrian school of economics. Very similar ideas are also propounded by John Stuart Mill, the last major representative of the British classical school. Cf. Eugen von Böhm-Bawerk, *Capital and Interest,* 3 vols. (South Holland, Ill.: Libertarian Press, 1959), 2:168–176 especially, but also 2:248–256 and 3:97–115; John Stuart Mill, *Principles of Political Economy,* Ashley ed. (1909; reprint ed., Fairfield, N. J.: Augustus M. Kelley, 1976), pp. 442–468. As previously noted more than once, a lengthy quotation from Böhm-Bawerk, expressing the substance of his views on the relationship between cost of production and prices appears below, on pp. 414–416.

32. Submarginal land, such as most deserts and mountains, is limited from a mathematical point of view, but stands beyond the limit of the supply of economically useable land. Its limitation in this latter sense provides it with no economic value, for it has zero marginal utility.

33. See above, pp. 152–169 passim, especially p. 158, and below, pp. 219–220. See also below, pp. 503–505.

34. While the economic system is in process of adjusting to a change in the quantity of money, the demand for the various goods and services is affected unevenly. Cf. von Mises, *Human Action,* pp. 412–414; idem, *The Theory of Money and Credit,* new ed. (1953; reprint ed., Irvington-on-Hudson, N. Y.: The Foundation for Economic Education, 1971), pp. 137–141. Von Mises argues that there are also permanent effects on the relative demands for the various goods and services, and thus on their relative prices.

35. See above, p. 169.

36. Of course, government intervention can deprive people of the ability to rent space they can afford to rent, by declaring such space to be substandard and its rental illegal. Such government intervention causes homelessness. See below, pp. 384–385.

37. See below, pp. 503–526 and 895–963 passim.

38. For elaboration of this vital fact and of its significance, see below, pp. 613–618 and 618–664 passim.

39. Cf. above, pp. 49–50.

40. This insight is one of the great contributions of Böhm-Bawerk. See above, p. 52 and the present chap., n. 31.

41. The results that will be derived from the present case could also be derived from the case of opposite changes in the demand for products of iron and products of cotton that was used earlier in connection with establishing additional causes of the tendency toward a uniform rate of profit. See above, p. 184.

42. This appendix, with minor revision, is drawn from the author's article of the same title which originally appeared in *Il Politico* 38, no. 3 (September 1973). It appears by permission of the publisher.

43. Vance Packard, *The Waste Makers,* Giant Cardinal ed. (New York: Pocket Books, Inc., 1963), p. 49.

44. For a demonstration of this fact, see my above-referenced article from which the present discussion is drawn, pp. 485–486.

45. For elaboration on these points, see ibid.

46. On these destructive effects of price controls see below, pp. 219–264 passim.

CHAPTER 7

THE DEPENDENCE OF THE DIVISION OF LABOR ON CAPITALISM III: PRICE CONTROLS AND ECONOMIC CHAOS

PART A

PRICE CONTROLS AND SHORTAGES

1. Price Controls and Inflation

Knowledge of the dependence of the division of labor on capitalism deepens profoundly with an understanding of the destructive consequences of price controls, which are the subject matter of the present chapter.

Price Controls No Remedy for Inflation

Price controls are advocated as a method of controlling inflation. People assume that inflation means rising prices and that it exists only when and to the extent that businessmen raise their prices. It appears to follow, on this view, that inflation would not exist if price increases were simply prohibited by price controls.

Actually, as we shall see later in this book, in Chapters 12 and 19, this view of inflation is utterly naïve. Rising prices are merely a leading *symptom* of inflation, not the phenomenon itself. Inflation can exist, and, indeed, accelerate, even though this particular symptom is prevented from appearing. Inflation itself is not rising prices, but an unduly large increase in the quantity of money,

caused, almost invariably, by the government. In fact, a good definition of inflation is, simply: an increase in the quantity of money caused by the government. A virtually equivalent definition is: an increase in the quantity of money in excess of the rate at which a gold or silver money would increase. These two definitions are virtually equivalent, because without government interference in money over the course of our history, the supply of money today would consist mainly or even entirely of precious metals and fully backed claims to precious metals. The increase in the supply of such a money would almost always be quite small and at all times would be severely limited by the high costs of mining additional quantities of the precious metals. Rising prices as a chronic social problem are a consequence of the government's overthrow of the use of gold and silver as money and putting in their place irredeemable paper currencies whose quantity can be increased without limit and virtually without cost.

Because it is necessary to approach the subject of price controls with clear ideas about why prices chronically rise in the world around us, it is necessary to anticipate here some of the discussion of later chapters and to show in no uncertain terms that the quantity theory of money—viz., the increase in the quantity of money—is the only valid explanation of the phenomenon.[1]

The truth of the quantity theory of money follows

from the best known principle in the theory of prices, which is that prices are determined by demand and supply and vary directly with demand and inversely with supply. By *demand* in this context is to be understood the willingness combined with the ability to spend money, and by *supply,* the existence of goods combined with the willingness to sell them. Demand manifests itself in the spending of money; supply, in the quantity of goods sold.[2]

When people complain of "inflation," what they have in mind is not an isolated rise in some prices here and there, offset by a fall in prices elsewhere, but a rise in prices in general, that is, a rise in the general consumer price level. The general consumer price level is the weighted average of all consumer prices.

It follows from the law of supply and demand that the general consumer price level can rise only if the aggregate demand (the total spending) for consumers' goods rises, or the aggregate supply (the total quantity sold) of consumers' goods falls. Indeed, the general consumer price level can be conceived of—as it was by the classical economists—as an arithmetical quotient, with demand (spending) as the numerator and supply (quantity of goods sold) as the denominator, for the average of the actual prices at which things are sold *is,* literally, nothing more than the total spending to buy them divided by the total quantity of them sold. In effect, in any given year, some definite mass—however measured—of houses, cars, soap, matches, and everything else in between, exchanges against some definite overall expenditure of money to buy them, and the result, the arithmetical quotient, *is* the general consumer price level.[3]

Rising prices in the United States are obviously not the result of falling supply, since supply has been growing in practically every year. The same is true of the countries of Western Europe, Japan, and even many of the Latin American countries. There can be no question, therefore, but that the rise in prices in these countries can be the result only of an increase in aggregate demand. Moreover, in the few cases in which supply appears to have fallen, such as Chile and Uruguay in the late 1960s and early 1970s, the rise in prices was enormously out of proportion to any possible decrease in supply in those countries. In those countries above all, demand grew.[4]

An increase in aggregate demand is the result of an increase in the quantity of money in the economic system. When new and additional money enters the economic system, whether it is newly mined gold in a country using gold as money, or newly created paper currency or checkbook money, as in the present-day United States, that money will be spent, and those who receive it in the sale of their goods and services will respend it. The additional money will be spent and re-

spent in every year of its existence, thereby raising aggregate demand and spending in the economic system to a correspondingly higher level. Indeed, the more rapidly new and additional money enters the economic system, the more rapidly the previously existing quantity of money tends to be spent, because people progressively lose the desire to hold balances of such money.[5] (For example, who wants to hold Argentine pesos? Who wants to hold U.S. dollars as much today as a generation ago?) Aggregate demand and spending thus begin to rise more than in proportion to the increase in the quantity of money. The rise in aggregate demand is what bids up the prices of all goods and services in limited supply, and is what enables price increases initiated by sellers, whether businessmen or labor unions, to take place as a repeated phenomenon. In the absence of the rise in aggregate demand, price increases initiated by sellers would reduce the amount of goods and services that could be sold. This loss of sales volume, and the mounting unemployment that goes with it, would soon put an end to such price increases.[6]

Once the truth of the quantity theory of money is recognized, the government's responsibility for rising prices follows immediately. Under the conditions of the last seventy-five years or more, the government has had virtually total control over the quantity of money. It has deliberately brought about its rapid increase. Since the inauguration of the New Deal in 1933, the quantity of money in the United States has been increased by more than 58-fold, from little more than $19 billion to well over $1,100 billion at the end of 1993. Since 1955, the rate of increase has shown a pronounced tendency to accelerate, despite the absence of any major war. Today, rates of increase are considered "normal" and even "modest" that a generation ago would have been considered huge.[7]

Inflation Plus Price Controls

The imposition of price controls to deal with inflation does not stop inflation. Rather it *combines* with inflation to produce a different and worse set of consequences than would inflation alone. It is as illogical—and as self-destructive—as would be an attempt to deal with expanding pressure in a boiler by means of manipulating the needle in the boiler's pressure gauge. The last two chapters have shown, in effect, that prices are equivalent to an instrument panel on the basis of which everyone plans his economic activities and which enables the plans of each individual to be harmoniously adjusted to the plans of all other individuals participating in the economic system. When price controls are imposed, the gauges on this instrument panel are frozen. Not only do the gauges no longer record the fact of inflation, which still continues and probably accelerates because the government need no longer fear rising prices, but the gauges also no longer reflect any other aspects of the state of supply and demand, which people must be able to take into account if their actions are to be coordinated with one another. Thus, economic activity under the division of labor becomes discoordinated and chaos ensues. It follows, and every page of this chapter will confirm it, that a government which imposes price controls is in process of destroying the economic system of its own country.

2. Shortages

We have seen that the price system of capitalism—the free market—constitutes a rational, ordered system of social cooperation; indeed, that it is a truly awe-inspiring complex of relationships in which the rational self-interest of individuals unites all industries, all markets, all occupations, all production, and all consumption into a harmonious, progressing system serving the well-being of all who participate in it.

All of this is what price controls destroy.

The one consequence of price controls that is the most central and the most fundamental and important from the point of view of explaining all of the others, and which most directly threatens the ability to produce under the division of labor, is the fact that *price controls cause shortages.*

A shortage is an excess of the quantity of a good buyers are seeking to buy over the quantity sellers are willing and able to sell. In a shortage, there are people willing and able to pay the controlled price of a good, but they cannot obtain it. The good is simply not available to them. Recalling the gasoline shortage of the winter of 1974 should make the concept real to everyone who experienced it. The drivers of the long lines of cars all had the money that was being asked for gasoline and were willing, indeed, eager, to spend it for gasoline. Their problem was that they simply could not obtain the gasoline. They were trying to buy more gasoline than was available.

The concept of a shortage is not the same thing as the concept of a scarcity. An item can be extremely scarce, like diamonds, Rembrandt paintings, and so on, and yet no shortage exist. In a free market, as we saw in the last chapter, the effect of such a scarcity is a high price. At the high price the quantity of the good demanded is levelled down to equality with the supply available, and no shortage exists. Anyone willing and able to pay the free-market price can buy whatever part of the supply he wishes; the height of the market price guarantees it, because it eliminates his competitors. It follows that however scarce a good may be, the only thing that can explain a shortage of it is a price control, not a scarcity. It is a price control that prevents the price of a scarce good from being raised by the self-interest of the buyers and sellers to its free-market level and thus reducing the quantity of the good demanded to equality with the supply of the good available.

Of course, if a price control on something exists, and a scarcity of it develops or grows worse, the effect will be a shortage, or a worsening of the shortage. Scarcities can cause shortages, or worsen them, *but only in the context of price controls.* If no price control existed, the development or worsening of a scarcity would not contribute to any shortage; it would simply cause the price to be higher.

It should be realized that a shortage can exist despite a great physical *abundance* of a good. For example, we could easily develop a severe shortage of wheat in the United States even with our normally very abundant supplies, or even much larger supplies. This is because the quantity of wheat demanded depends on its price. If the government were to roll back the price of wheat sufficiently, it would create a major increase in the quantity demanded—not only a larger quantity demanded for export, but a larger quantity demanded for raising cattle and broilers, making whiskey, and perhaps for many other employments for which one does not presently think of using wheat, because of its price. In other words, no matter how much wheat we produced, we could have a shortage of it, because at an artificially low price we could create a demand for an even larger quantity.

It should be held in mind, therefore, that shortages are not a matter of scarcity or abundance. Scarcity need not cause them; abundance is no safeguard against them. Shortages are strictly the result of price controls. Price controls are the only thing that allows scarcities to cause shortages; and they create shortages even when there is no scarcity, but abundance.

Indeed, the true relationship between scarcities and shortages is the *reverse* of what is usually believed. While scarcities per se do not cause shortages, *shortages cause scarcities.* That is, no matter how abundant are the supplies with which we begin, we have only to impose price controls, create shortages, and we will soon bring about growing scarcities. As an example of this, consider the fact pointed out in the last chapter that in the oil crisis oilmen needing oil products to keep their wells running were prohibited from outbidding homeowners needing oil to heat their garages. It is obvious what such a situation is capable of doing to the subsequent supply of oil.

The fact that it is shortages that cause scarcities will be a recurring theme of this chapter.

In a free market shortages are a virtual impossibility.

The closest thing that exists to them is that sometimes people may have to wait in line for the next showing of a popular movie. The typical case in a free market is that a seller is in a position to supply more than his present number of customers. There are very few stores or factories in a free market that are not able and eager to do more business. Even goods and services in limited supply are priced in such a way that the sellers are usually able and willing to do more business. For example, the wine shops have some reserve inventory of the rare wines. Landlords have a certain number of vacancies. There is even some limited degree of unemployment in most occupations. This is because, in a free market, the prices of goods and services in limited supply are set somewhat above the point that would enable the sellers to sell out entirely and the workers to be 100 percent employed. The reason prices are set in this way is because the sellers, including the workers, believe that by waiting before they sell, they can find better terms. They are holding out, waiting for the right customers or the right job.

3. Price Controls and the Reduction of Supply

The preceding discussion showed how price controls create shortages by artificially expanding the quantity of a good demanded. To the degree that the controlled price is below the potential free-market price, buyers judge that they can afford more of the good with the same monetary wealth and income. They judge that they can carry its consumption to a point of lower marginal utility. In this way, the quantity of the good demanded comes to exceed the supply available, whether that supply is scarce or abundant.

Price controls also reduce supply, which intensifies the shortages they create.

a. The Supply of Goods Produced

In the case of anything that must be produced, the quantity supplied falls if a price control makes its production unprofitable or simply of less than average profitability.

It is not necessary that a price control make production unprofitable or insufficiently profitable to *all* producers in a field. Production will tend to fall as soon as it becomes unprofitable or insufficiently profitable to the highest-cost or *marginal* producers in the field. These producers begin to go out of business or at least to operate on a smaller scale.

For example, the price controls on oil held down the supply of oil. They did not totally destroy the supply of oil, but they did discourage the development of high-cost domestic sources of supply. They also made the more intensive exploitation of existing oil fields unprofitable,

which fields can be made to yield from one-third to two-thirds more oil over their lives by the adoption of such methods as thermal or chemical flooding, sometimes known as "tertiary recovery." At the same time, in restricting the profits from the lower-cost oil deposits, price controls held down both the incentives to discover and develop new such deposits and the capital necessary to the oil companies for expanded oil operations of any type. Thus, it should not be surprising that following the repeal of price controls on oil in 1981, a major surge in domestic drilling and production occurred—despite the fact that the government imposed a confiscatory "windfall-profits tax" that deprived the oil companies of a major part of the benefit of the repeal of the price controls. For now domestic oil production became more profitable.

Rent controls on housing that has already been constructed provide a similar example of the destruction of supply. As inflation drives up the operating costs of housing—namely, such costs as fuel, maintenance, and minor repairs—more and more landlords of rent-controlled buildings are forced to abandon their buildings and leave them to crumble. The reason is that once the operating costs come to exceed the frozen rents, continued ownership and operation of a building become a source merely of fresh losses, over and above the loss of the capital previously invested in the building itself.

This destruction of the housing supply starts with the housing of the poor and then spreads up the social ladder. It starts with the housing of the poor because the operating costs of such housing are initially so low that they leave relatively little room for economies. For example, there are no doormen to eliminate and therefore no doormen's salaries to save. Also, the profit margins on such housing (that is, profits as a percentage of rental revenues) are the lowest to begin with, because the land and the buildings are the least valuable and therefore the amount of profit earned is correspondingly low. As a result, the housing of the poor is abandoned first, because it provides the least buffer between rising operating costs and frozen rents.

b. The Supply of Goods in a Local Market

A price control reduces supply whenever it is imposed in a local market and makes that market uncompetitive with other markets. In such a case, the local market is prevented from drawing in supplies from other areas, as was the Northeast and the United States as a whole during the Arab oil embargo.

The Natural Gas Crisis of 1977

In exactly the same way, in the winter of 1977, price controls on natural gas prevented areas of the United

States that were suffering freezing weather from bidding for additional supplies from the producing regions in the South and Southwest. Natural gas shipped across state lines was controlled by the Federal Power Commission at a maximum of $1.42 per thousand cubic feet. Natural gas sold within the states where it was produced, and thus outside the jurisdiction of the FPC and free of price controls, was selling at $2.00 per thousand cubic feet, with lower costs of transportation besides. It was therefore much more profitable to sell natural gas in the states where it was produced, such as Texas and Louisiana, than in such states as New Jersey or Pennsylvania.

Indeed, in the absence of government controls over the physical distribution of supplies, price controls would have resulted in still less gas being shipped outside the producing states and more being sold inside, in accordance with the difference in price and profitability. This process would have gone on until enough additional gas was retained within the markets of the producing states to make its price in those markets actually fall below the controlled interstate price by an amount equal to the costs of transportation; only at that point would it have paid producers to ship their gas out of state. The shortage in the rest of the country, of course, would have been correspondingly more severe. As I say, government controls over the physical distribution of natural gas prevented this outcome; the government simply forced the gas producers to sell a major part of their output in the interstate market. But the government's allocation formulas did not take into account the extremely cold winter of 1977, and its allocations proved inadequate to keep people from the threat of freezing. Price controls then prevented the people of the affected regions from obtaining the additional supplies they urgently needed.[8]

The Agricultural Export Crisis of 1972–73

A price control not only prevents a local market from drawing in supplies from elsewhere, but it can also cause a local market that normally exports, to export excessively. In this case, as supplies are drawn out, the price control prevents the people in the local market from bidding up the price and checking the outflow.

This phenomenon occurred in the United States in 1972 and 1973. Our price controls on wheat, soybeans, and other products made possible an unchecked exportation that jeopardized domestic consumption and led to an explosion of prices each time the controls were taken off, in President Nixon's succession of on-again, off-again "phases" of price controls.

In this instance, the fall in the value of the dollar in terms of foreign currencies played a critical role. When President Nixon imposed price controls in August of 1971, he also took steps to devalue the dollar by 10 percent. Over the following two years, the dollar continued to fall in terms of foreign currencies and in 1973 was formally devalued a second time. The fall in the dollar's foreign exchange value meant a lower price of dollars in terms of marks, francs, and other currencies. Since the prices of our goods were frozen, a lower price of dollars meant that all of our goods suddenly became cheaper to foreigners. As a result, they began buying in much larger quantities—especially our agricultural commodities. As they began buying, domestic buyers were prevented by price controls from outbidding them for the dwindling supplies. As a result, vast accumulated agricultural surpluses were swept out of the country, and domestic food supplies were threatened, which is why prices skyrocketed each time the controls were taken off.

Price Controls as a Cause of War

The fact that price controls jeopardize supplies in markets that export leads to embargoes against further exports, as occurred in this country in the summer of 1973, when we imposed an embargo on the export of various agricultural commodities. In addition, price controls in markets that must import make such markets helpless in the face of embargoes imposed by others, as we were made helpless in the face of the Arab oil embargo. It follows that to the degree that countries impose price controls, they must fear and hate each other. Each such country must fear the loss of vital supplies to others, as the result of excessive exportation, and the deprivation of vital supplies from others, as the result of their embargoes and its helplessness to cope with them. Each such country makes itself hated by its own embargoes and hates the countries that impose embargoes against it. Our embargo on agricultural products in 1973 did not endear us to the Japanese. And there was actual talk of military intervention against the Arabs. Simply put, price controls breed war. A free market is a necessary condition of peace.

c. The Supply of Goods Held in Storage

A price control reduces supply whenever it is imposed on a commodity of the kind that must be stored for future use. The effect of a price control in such a case is to encourage a too rapid rate of consumption of the commodity and thus to reduce supplies available for the future. As we have seen, buyers are led to buy too rapidly by the artificially low price, and sellers are led to sell too rapidly, since the fixity of the controlled price does not enable them to cover storage costs and earn the going rate of profit in holding supplies for future sale.

If the buying public and the professional speculators were unaware of the impending exhaustion of supplies, the effect of sellers placing their supplies on the market right away would be to depress the current market price below the controlled price. This process would go on until the current market price fell far enough below the controlled price, so that once again it would have sufficient room to rise in the months ahead to be able to cover storage and interest costs. The resulting structure of prices would guarantee the premature exhaustion of supplies.

An elaboration on the example of the deficient wheat harvest will make these points clear.[9] Assume that in a year of normal wheat supplies, the price of wheat begins at $1.00 per bushel in the harvest month, when supplies are most abundant, and then rises a few cents per month, to cover the costs of storage and interest, and reaches a peak of $1.20 in the month immediately preceding the next harvest. Now assume that when the harvest is one month's consumption below normal, the price of wheat should begin at $1.30 in the harvest month and gradually ascend to something over $1.50 in the month preceding the following harvest, in order to reduce the quantity of wheat demanded to equality with the smaller total supply available. Assume further that a price control limits the price of the deficient wheat crop to no more than $1.20 in any month. In this case, when the deficient crop comes in, its value cannot remain even at $1.20 for very long, because it has no prospect of ever getting above $1.20; as a result, it will be sold more heavily. It will tend to be sold until the price in the harvest month is driven down to $1.00, and from there the price will gradually ascend in the succeeding months toward $1.20. This structure of prices will encourage the same rate of consumption as prevailed in years of normal supplies, and will threaten famine conditions at the end of the crop year.

Hoarding and Speculation Not Responsible for Shortages

Under conditions such as those described above, the buying public sooner or later becomes aware of the fact that supplies will run out. At that point, demand skyrockets, as the buyers scramble for supplies. As soon as this occurs, and it may be very early, the larger supplies that sellers are encouraged to place on the market under price controls are not sufficient to depress the market price below the controlled price, because they are snapped up by the speculative buying of the public, which is aware of the shortage to come. (In our example of wheat, the whole supply would tend to be carried off at the controlled price of $1.20 per bushel as soon as the public becomes aware of the inevitable shortage of wheat to come.) The consequence of the speculative buying of the public is that the item disappears from the market right away; it is hoarded.

The hoarding of the buying public is not responsible for the existence of shortages. The public hoards *in anticipation* of shortages caused by the price controls. The public's speculative demand cannot even be blamed for hastening the appearance of a shortage. That too must be blamed on price controls, because in the absence of the controls the additional demand of the public would simply raise prices; at the higher prices, the rise in the quantity of goods demanded would be cut back; prices would rise to whatever extent necessary to level down the quantity demanded to equality with the supply available.

Speculation on the part of the suppliers of goods is likewise blameless for the existence of shortages. Contrary to popular belief, price controls do not give suppliers a motive to withhold supplies, but, as we have seen, an incentive to unload them too rapidly.

There is, of course, an important exception to the principle that price controls give sellers an incentive to sell their supplies too rapidly. This is the case in which the sellers are able to look forward to the repeal of the controls. In this case, a price control makes it relatively unprofitable to sell in the present, at the artificially low, controlled price, and more profitable to sell in the future, at the higher, free-market price. In this case, sellers do have a motive to withhold supplies for future sale.

Even in this case, however, it is still the price control that is responsible for the existence of any shortage that develops or intensifies. In this case, the price control discriminates against the market in the present in favor of the market in the future; it prevents the market in the present from competing for supplies with the market in the future. Furthermore, in the absence of a price control, any build-up of supplies for sale in the future would simply be accompanied by a rise in prices in the present, which would prevent the appearance of a shortage, as we have seen repeatedly in previous discussion.

Finally, it should be realized that the withholding of supplies in anticipation of the repeal of a price control does not imply any kind of antisocial or evil action on the part of the suppliers. Price controls, as we have seen, lead to inadequate stocks of goods; in many cases, it is probable that the build-up of stocks in anticipation of the repeal of controls merely serves to restore stocks to a more normal level. Even if the build-up of stocks does become excessive, its effect later on, when the stocks are sold, is merely to further reduce the free-market price in comparison with what that price would otherwise have been. In any event, all ill-effects that may result are entirely the consequence of price controls.

Rebuttal of the Accusation That Producers Withhold Supplies to "Get Their Price"

The preceding discussion applies to the accusation that producers withhold supplies in order to "get their price." This accusation was levelled against the oil companies during the oil crisis and, again, during the natural gas crisis. It will undoubtedly be levelled anew if price controls are imposed in the future.

Once more, the fact is that price controls generally cause sellers to sell too rapidly, and not to hold even normal stocks. Where the anticipation of the controls being removed does lead to the withholding of supplies, the fault is not that of the sellers, but of the existence of controls in the present. It is simply absurd to tell producers that soon they will be permitted to sell at the free-market price while for the present they must pay fines or go to jail if they attempt to sell at as good a price. Responsibility for the withholding of supplies in such a case lies with those who impose price controls and whose support of price controls makes their imposition possible. For no other result can be expected. To blame the producers and the profit motive in such a case is comparable to blaming the rocks and the laws of physics for the damage done by a delinquent who throws the rocks against windows. In acting to make profits, the producers are doing nothing more than acting in accordance with their nature—their *moral* nature as rational beings who wish to live by means of production and exchange.

Although this did not happen in the oil or gas crisis, and is unlikely ever to happen so long as the great majority of businessmen remain ignorant of sound economic theory and lack moral courage, it would be perfectly proper if sellers really did withhold supplies to "get their price"—that is, not merely to take advantage of the higher free-market price they expect to follow the government's removal of controls, but to withhold supplies *in a deliberate attempt to force repeal of the controls.* Such a withholding would be a kind of strike; more correctly, it would be a refusal to work under conditions of forced labor. By putting an end to price controls, it would be an action in the public interest in the true sense of the term.

It should be realized in connection with this discussion, that in a free market the speculative withholding of supplies is not a means by which sellers can arbitrarily enrich themselves. It is not possible, as widely believed, for sellers arbitrarily to raise prices by withholding supplies and then to sell the supplies they have withheld at the higher prices they themselves have caused. Any attempt to do this would necessarily cause losses to the sellers who tried it. First of all, when these sellers put their supplies back on the market, they would push prices back down by as much as they had first increased them, and in the meanwhile they would have incurred additional costs of storage and have had to forgo the profits or interest they could have earned by selling sooner. In addition, so long as the high prices lasted, other sellers would be encouraged to place on the market whatever

stocks they could spare, so that when the first set of sellers returned to the market they would find their normal market already partly supplied, and thus would end up having to sell at prices lower than they could have received had they not attempted to raise prices in the first place. The only way the speculative withholding of supplies can be profitable in a free market is when it takes advantage of a prospective rise in price that is independently caused, which, of course, means, not caused by the speculators themselves.[10]

In the specific case of the oil crisis the withholding of supplies turned out to be entirely mythical. Reports of large numbers of fully loaded tankers standing offshore to "get their price" had no more foundation in fact than the stories about full tank farms and storage depots.[11] As concerns the natural gas crisis, the charge was ultimately withdrawn by one of the principal original accusers, President Jimmy Carter's then Interior Secretary Cecil D. Andrus. According to *The New York Times*, the secretary "said today that a series of studies had produced no evidence that oil companies were withholding natural gas from offshore leases. . . . The interior secretary insisted today that he had had no part in raising those charges and contended instead that they were initially leveled by reporters. . . . Mr. Andrus also made it clear today that the question of withholding was now closed. 'I'm not going to continue to chase a rabbit,' he said."[12]

Price Controls and the "Storage" of Natural Resources in the Ground

Price controls have a particularly destructive effect on the supply of natural resources. Unlike products, natural resources in the ground are imperishable and have zero storage costs. This means that it is possible to consider reserving their use to much more remote periods of the future than is the case with regard to products. The consequence is that under price controls a tendency exists to withhold natural resources from current exploitation even though their current exploitation might be profitable. The reason is that their future exploitation—following the repeal of price controls—is expected to be sufficiently more profitable to justify waiting. In this way, price controls on natural resources act to bring about a twofold restriction of supply: they prevent the development or exploitation of high-cost deposits by making them unprofitable and they postpone the development or exploitation of low-cost deposits by making their development or exploitation in the present less profitable than it will be in the future.

The question may be raised of why price controls would not encourage the more rapid exploitation of low-cost natural resources if the controls were expected to exist permanently. To answer this question, it is only necessary to realize what "permanently" would have to mean in this context. "Permanently" would have to refer to a period of at least a decade and, more probably, at least a generation. For suppose the effect of a price control is to hold the real value of a resource to half of what it would be in the absence of controls. This means the owners of the resource can look forward to the prospect of a doubling of its real value whenever controls are repealed. Since they incur no storage costs of any kind by waiting, even if they had to wait *twenty-five years* for price controls to be repealed, their gain would work out to something on the order of 3 percent per annum compounded. Such a rate of return, in *real terms* (which means, adjusted for losses in the purchasing power of money), is by no means insignificant in a period of inflation, when it is common for many or most investments to show losses in real terms.[13] In such conditions, it might pay to wait even for the prospect of a considerably lower positive real rate of return. Of course, if price controls undervalue a resource less severely, the inducement to postpone exploitation is less powerful. But it does not take very much undervaluation to make the owners of the resource prefer to wait five or ten years for the repeal of a control if they have to.

On the basis of these considerations, it is not surprising that the repeal of the price controls on crude oil was followed by a substantial increase in the supply of low-cost oil as well as by additional supplies available only at higher costs.

d. The Supply of Particular Types of Labor and Particular Products of a Factor of Production

A price control reduces supply if it is applied to the wages of any particular occupation or to the wages paid by any particular industry while wages in other occupations or industries are left free. In these cases, the workers in the controlled occupation or industry simply leave to take better-paying jobs at uncontrolled wages elsewhere; and new workers do not enter the occupation or industry. The controlled occupation or industry is made uncompetitive and loses its labor force. For example, if the government were to control just the wages of steel workers, say, the effect would be that steel workers would start going into other industries in response to higher, uncontrolled wages in those industries. Young workers would stop becoming steel workers. Exactly the same would happen if the government controlled just the wages of carpenters, say.

A price control reduces supply whenever it applies to some products of a factor of production, but not to other products of that factor. In this case, the production of the controlled products is curtailed, because it is more profitable to use the factor of production to produce the uncontrolled products. For example, if the price of milk is controlled, but cheese is not, then the production of cheese will be more profitable than the production of milk. As a result, raw milk will be used more heavily to produce cheese, and less milk will be available for drinking. In other words, the supply of milk for drinking will fall. In view of the continuing popularity of rent control, it is worth pointing out that exactly the same principle applies specifically to apartment houses. Apartment houses can be viewed as a factor of production with multiple possible uses, namely, use as rental housing or use as condominium or cooperative housing. If rent controls are imposed, then landlords will convert their housing to condominiums or co-ops if they are free to do so, because the effect of rent controls is to reduce the profitability of using apartment buildings for rental housing in comparison with that of using them for condominium or cooperative housing. Of course, their decision to do so evokes the same kind of outbursts of self-righteous irresponsibility and irrationalism that we observed a few paragraphs back in connection with the blame heaped on producers for withholding supplies in the face of price controls and the prospect of imminent relief from the price controls.

e. Price Controls and the Prohibition of Supply

Sometimes, the question is raised as to what argument one could give to a consumer to convince him to be against price controls; especially what argument one could give to a tenant to convince him to be against rent controls. Our discussion of how price controls reduce supply indicates a very simple argument to give to any consumer against any price control. This is that if he wants something, he must be willing to pay the necessary price. It is a natural law—a fact of human nature—that a good or service can only be supplied if supplying it is both worthwhile to the suppliers and as worthwhile as any of the alternatives open to them. If the price is controlled below this point, then it is equivalent to a prohibition of supply. To command, for example, that apartments be supplied at rents that do not cover the costs of construction and maintenance, and the going rate of profit, is equivalent to commanding that buildings be built out of impossible materials like air and water rather than steel and concrete. It is to command construction in contradiction of the laws of nature. In the same way, to command that oil be sold less profitably in New York than in Hamburg, say, or that natural gas be sold less profitably in Philadelphia than in Houston, is equivalent to commanding that these materials become drinkable and that water become burnable, for it is no less an act in contradiction of the nature of things.

Now it is simply absurd for a consumer who wants a

good, to support a measure which makes its supply impossible. And that is what one should tell him. That is what the consumers themselves should tell the legislators as soon as the latter become busy trying to enact price control laws for the consumers' alleged benefit. These would-be benefactors of the consumers prohibit the consumers from making it worthwhile for businessmen to supply them. They destroy the businessmen. In doing so, they destroy the consumers' ability to find agents to act on their behalf. Such legislators are capable of reducing the consumers to the point where if they want anything, they will have to produce it themselves, because price controls will make it unprofitable for anyone to supply it to them. Already, rent control has "benefitted" tenants to the point that it is has become increasingly necessary if one wants an apartment to own it oneself: one must buy a "co-op" or a condominium. Price controls made it extremely difficult, and at times absolutely impossible, to buy oil or natural gas. If the legislators go on "benefitting" the consumers long enough with their price controls, they will benefit them all the way back to the economic self-sufficiency that was the leading characteristic of feudalism. They will have destroyed the division of labor.

The Destruction of the Utilities and the Other Regulated Industries

It may be thought that price controls on genuine monopolies, such as government-franchised electric utilities, are an exception to the principle that price controls reduce, indeed, prohibit, supply. In fact, they are not. On the contrary, they have been an excellent illustration of it.

In the absence of inflation these controls are largely without effect, for then they do not actually impose below-market prices. At such times, they are set at a level that, if anything, is almost certainly higher than would have prevailed in a free market. This is the case because they are set high enough to provide the going rate of profit, and then some, to legally protected monopolists, whose costs of production are almost certainly above the costs of production that would prevail in a free market with its legally open competition. But when they exist in conjunction with inflation, the price controls on these monopolies begin to operate as genuine price controls. This occurs because inflation drives up the production costs of the monopolies, while the regulatory authorities either refuse to allow rate increases or allow only insufficient rate increases. In this way, the utilities, and all the other regulated industries, become unprofitable. At first, they merely cease to grow rapidly enough, because their reduced profitability throttles their ability to generate additional capital—that is, they lack the profits to plow back and they lack the profits to provide an incentive to

the investment of sufficient additional outside capital.

When the reduced profitability of these industries is understood to be permanent, or when the policy of the regulatory agencies inflicts actual losses on them in terms of making it impossible for them to replace worn-out equipment at the higher prices caused by inflation, then these industries go into actual decline. They do not have the means of replacement, and their owners withdraw capital to whatever extent they are able in the form of taking dividends.

We are already very far along in this process. Areas such as New York City and much of the state of Florida, for example, have been skirting for many years on the edge of power disasters. Almost every year there is a question of whether generating capacity will be adequate to meet the demand in such places. So-called brownouts, and even blackouts, are not uncommon. Problems of this kind would undoubtedly be far more common and severe if it were not for the relatively depressed state of the American economy in recent years.

The situation of an inadequate supply of power is the result of the restricted profitability of the utilities, caused by price controls. It is compounded, of course, by the ecology movement's policy of harassment of energy producers. Both causes have prevented the construction of sufficient additional generating capacity to keep pace with demand.[14]

At the present time, the traditionally regulated industries, such as the electric utilities, the railroads, and telephone service, are the principal victims of price controls, along with rental housing in various towns and cities. Although the situation by and large is probably much improved in comparison with that of the late 1970s, when conditions in these industries appeared more critical—and the oil and natural gas industries were in a state of growing crisis as well, thanks to price controls—these industries are still capable of being destroyed by price controls. And, since the rest of the economic system is vitally dependent on them, their destruction would be disastrous for the entire economy.

Indeed, despite the improvements brought about in the 1980s under the Reagan administration, one must still regard the future with a high degree of pessimism. The public's state of knowledge of economics has not significantly improved. Thus, the causes of the improvements in the situation are not understood. Even those who were responsible for the improvements—through such measures as the repeal of the price controls on oil, the easing of "environmental" restrictions, and the abandonment, at least for the time being, of the policy of accelerating inflation—apparently do not know enough to take credit for their good work, despite the fact that it would be very much to their political advantage to do so. Instead, the improvements are regarded as essentially accidental and are more or less taken for granted.

Thus, the continued existence even of the remaining price controls holds out the specter of growing power shortages, a disintegrating railroad network, and deteriorating telephone service. The potential for destruction is especially great in the case of electric power, where the effects of price controls are compounded by the actions of the ecology movement. So long as these industries are subject to price controls, and so long as the potential exists for significant inflation, all of these industries are capable of being reduced to the level of rent-controlled housing in the slums of New York City. The only difference will be that if they suffer comparable devastation, they will carry down with them the rest of the economic system. These problems will become apparent if and when a policy of accelerating inflation is resumed.

4. Ignorance and Evasions Concerning Shortages and Price Controls

The fact that price controls are the cause of shortages has been known to all economists at least since the time of Adam Smith. Nevertheless, this elementary knowledge is either unknown or simply evaded by the great majority of today's presumably educated political and intellectual leaders.

These people do not have any idea of the connection between price controls and shortages. In their view, shortages are the result of some kind of physical deficiency in the supply or of an innate excess of needs. They simply do not have any knowledge of the role of price in balancing demand and supply. As a result, it is common to hear them blame shortages on such things as poor crops, an alleged depletion of natural resources, even that old standby the "greed" of consumers. Their level of knowledge is typified by a provision of the rent control law that governed New York City for many years. According to this law, rent controls could not be lifted until the vacancy rate in apartments had first climbed to a certain substantial level. In other words, only when the shortage that rent controls created and maintained was over, could rent controls be lifted.

The same point of view was expressed by a former mayor of New York, Abraham Beame, when still in office. When asked to comment on an economic regeneration plan for New York City that had urged the repeal of rent control, he "refused to endorse the rent control proposal, saying, 'we still have a vacancy rate of less than 5 percent and we still have a housing shortage.'"[15]

To find a parallel for this kind of reasoning, one would have to find a badly overweight person, say, who was firmly resolved to go on a diet just as soon as he lost twenty pounds, or an alcoholic who was firmly resolved to stop drinking just as soon as he sobered up. Of course, these are not perfect analogies, because the overweight person and the alcoholic at least know the causal connections and are evading them. In the case of the government officials and the intellectuals responsible for rent control, most of them do not even know the causal connection. They are too ignorant even to be guilty of evasion in this particular instance.

The confusion of our public officials extends to the point that when they are confronted with the fact that the repeal of a price control would actually end a shortage, they then deny the very reality of the shortage: they view the shortage as "artificial" or "contrived." For example, during the natural gas crisis the then Governor of Pennsylvania, Milton Schapp, declared before television news cameras that if price controls were lifted and the gas shortage came to an end through the appearance of additional supplies, the very appearance of the additional supplies would prove that the shortage had been "contrived." The governor simply did not know that a higher price increases supply by enabling a local market successfully to compete for supplies with other markets, and, of course, that it leads to an expansion of the total supply by making production more profitable. He also did not know that the supply available for vital purposes can be increased by enabling those purposes to outcompete marginal purposes, and that the elimination of shortages eliminates the need to hoard supplies, which supplies then also appear on the market.

Inflation and the Appearance of High Profits

In an important respect, the ignorance that surrounds the effect of price controls is made possible by the fact that inflation raises the apparent or, as economists say, the nominal rate of profit that businesses earn. It does not increase the real rate of profit—the rate in terms of the actual physical wealth that business firms gain—(in fact, quite the contrary), but it does increase the rate of profit expressed in terms of the depreciating paper money.

To understand what is involved, it must be realized that the costs which enter into the profit computations of business firms are necessarily "historical"—that is, the outlays of money they represent are made prior to the sale of the products. This follows from the fact that production always takes place over a period of time. Materials and labor must usually be bought weeks or months before the resulting products are ready for sale, and sometimes even further in advance. Machinery and factory buildings are bought many years, even decades, before their contribution to production comes to an end. Thus the costs of business enterprises in producing their products represent outlays of money made weeks, months, years, or even decades earlier.

Now to whatever extent inflation occurs, the sales revenues of business firms are automatically increased: the greater spending that inflation makes possible is simultaneously greater sales revenues to all the business firms that receive it. Since costs reflect the given outlays of earlier periods of time, the increase in sales revenues caused by inflation necessarily adds a corresponding amount to profits.

A slightly different way to grasp the same basic idea is to realize that the total outlays business firms make for productive purposes at any given time are a reflection of the quantity of money in existence at that time, while the sales revenues they will subsequently take in for the products resulting from those outlays, will be a reflection of the quantity of money in existence later on. It follows that the more rapidly the quantity of money grows, the greater must be the ratio of sales revenues to costs of production and to capital previously invested. This, of course, implies a corresponding rise in the general rate of profit on capital previously invested. The rate of profit in the economy is raised to progressively higher levels the more rapidly the quantity of money, spending, and sales revenues rise.

It cannot be stressed too strongly, however, that the rate of profit that rises is purely nominal, that is, it is strictly in terms of money. All that is happening is that the more rapidly money is increased, the faster is the rate at which *money* is gained. If there are different monies, increasing at different rates, then the nominal rate of profit is higher in the monies that increase more rapidly. For example, it is higher today in U.S. dollars than in Swiss francs, and higher in Argentine pesos than in U.S. dollars. (The same principle and example apply to interest rates, since the most important determinant of interest rates is the rate of profit that can be earned by investing borrowed money in business.)

The rise in the nominal rate of profit does not imply any increase in the *real* rate of profit, that is, the rate of gain in actual wealth, because the same rise in spending that raises sales revenues and profits in the economy also raises the level of prices. The extra profits are almost all necessary to meet higher replacement costs of inventory and plant and equipment, and the rest are necessary to meet the higher prices of consumers' goods that the owners of businesses were previously able to buy in their capacity, say, as stockholders receiving dividends. Indeed, the real rate of profit firms earn actually *falls* while the nominal rate of profit rises. One major reason it does so is because the additional nominal profits, while mainly necessary for the replacement of assets at higher prices, are *taxed*, as though they were real profits. Thus firms

are placed in a position in which, after paying taxes, they are actually worse off as the result of the rise in the nominal rate of profit.

A good illustration of these facts is the case of a hypothetical merchant who normally buys $100 worth of goods on January 1 and sells them at the end of the year for $110. If a rapidly increasing quantity of money increases total spending in the economy by 10 percent over the year, this merchant will tend to sell his goods for $121 instead of $110, that is, also by 10 percent more. Consequently, his nominal profit will be increased from $10 to $21. However, the same increase in the quantity of money and volume of spending that enlarges our merchant's sales revenues and profit also raises the replacement cost of his inventory. Instead of being able to replace his inventory for $100, as he was able to do in the past, he will now have to replace it at a cost of $110. Thus, the whole increase in the merchant's profit is purely nominal, not real. While his profit rises from $10 to $21, fully $10 of this additional profit is required merely to replace inventory at higher prices. This leaves the merchant with $11 that he can use for other purposes. But these $11 will probably buy no more than $10 used to buy, because the increase in the quantity of money and volume of spending has probably raised the prices of the things the merchant can buy outside of his business. Thus, the $21 profit the merchant now has represents no more in terms of actual wealth and ability to buy goods than the $10 profit he used to have.

Indeed, as I have said, our merchant will actually be *worse off* as a result of his higher nominal profit. Because, apart from other reasons that will be presented later in this book, he must pay additional taxes on the additional nominal profit, and must restrict his consumption or new investment in order to do so.[16] To understand this point, assume a tax rate of 50 percent on profits. Thus, initially, when our merchant made $10 in profit, he paid $5 in taxes and had $5 left to himself, which he could either consume or add to his business. When his profit rises to $21, his taxes rise to $10.50. Of the $10.50 left over, fully $10 are required to replace inventory at higher prices. Therefore, the merchant is left with a mere *50¢* that he can consume or use to expand his business, whereas he initially had $5, and at a lower level of prices as well.

Exactly the same principles as apply to the profit of our hypothetical merchant apply to the profits of all real-life merchants, and to the profits of businessmen in general, because the same kind of increase in nominal profits as occurs on inventories also occurs in the case of depreciable assets, such as buildings and machinery.[17]

It is in this light that the consequences of the attitude that profits are "too high" must be considered. The fact is that in the context of inflation the seemingly high rates of profit that firms earn represent a decline in real profits and, quite possibly, the total elimination of real profits. In such circumstances, to argue that because a rate of profit is high by historical standards it is high in any meaningful sense, is to display the utmost ignorance. To limit an industry's profits in any way in such circumstances is simply to invite its destruction.

But precisely that is what is being done or has been done to the electric utilities, the railroads, the telephone companies, and the oil and natural gas industries. And it is what has been done to the rental housing industry in New York City for over half a century. For many years, for example, the government of New York City was proud of the fact that it guaranteed to landlords under rent control the right to earn a *6 percent* rate of return on their initial investments, made, in most cases, before World War II. Six percent, reasoned the city officials, was a "fair" rate of return. What honest landlord could want more? The city officials neglected the fact that since the landlords' original investments were made, replacement costs had increased many times over and that a 6 percent return on the construction costs of decades earlier had to represent a disastrously losing proposition.

Amazingly, when landlords began to stop keeping up their properties as a result of such loss-making conditions, *they* were the ones accused of "milking" their properties—as though the city or the tenants had originally constructed the buildings and the landlords were now trying to squeeze out of them whatever they could. (And then, as punishment, the city refused to grant rent increases even when called for by its own criterion of providing a 6 percent return.) The simple truth is that the city government of New York, with the support and participation of hundreds of thousands of ignorant tenants, has milked the rental housing industry to the point of virtually totally destroying it. Today, in New York City, the point has been reached where if one wishes a place to live, one must buy it. As already pointed out, the same fate may well be in store for other, more important industries in this country that labor under price controls.

The Destructionist Mentality

What is at root in these cases of wholesale industrial destruction is not ignorance alone, but a mentality that makes itself ignorant. It is a mentality that shows up in the cavalier assumption that the problems an industry experiences as the result of price controls, rising costs, mounting taxes, and harassment by the ecology movement are all somehow the result of "its own inefficiency." This mentality is unaware that inefficiency is itself an inevitable consequence of government interference. If an industry is deprived of the prospect of profits, if its operations are encumbered with endless bureaucratic regulations, then it has no incentive or even possibility to be efficient.[18] It is absurd to blame an industry's inefficiency on anything but government interference; in a free economy, profit and loss incentives and the freedom of competition operate steadily to increase efficiency.

The ignorance that underlies the destruction of our economic system is made possible by a protective shell of envy and resentment. People take the attitude that somehow the utilities, the landlords, the oil industry, or whoever, are "already rich enough," and that they'll be damned if they'll let them get any richer. So, on with the price controls. That is the beginning and the end of their thinking on the subject, and they just don't care to think any further. They are eager to accept high nominal profits as a confirmation of their view that the industries concerned are "rich enough," and to let it go at that.

However, the simple fact is that none of these industries is rich enough, and in preventing them from becoming richer, or even staying as rich as they are, people foolishly harm themselves. None of these industries is rich enough for the simple reason that we really do not have enough power plants, enough good apartment buildings, or enough oil wells and oil refineries. Speaking for myself, *as a consumer,* I must say that I would like the power companies, the landlords of New York City, the oil industry, and so on, all to be worth many more billions than they are presently worth. I would benefit from that fact. If the utilities had more power plants, my supply of electricity would be better assured and I would not be subject to the power interruptions that I am now subject to. If the landlords of New York City had more and better buildings, tenants and possible prospective tenants, such as myself, would be able to have a better apartment. If the oil industry had more wells and refineries, I would have a more abundant and secure supply of oil products.

If one thinks about it, I believe, nothing could be more absurd than consumers in a capitalist economy attacking the wealth of their suppliers. That wealth serves *them*— they are the physical beneficiaries of it. All of the wealth of the utilities, the landlords, the oil companies—where is it? It is in power plants and power lines, apartment buildings, oil wells and oil refineries. And whom does it actually, physically, serve? It serves the consumers. It serves *us*—all of us. We have a selfish interest in the preservation and increase of that wealth. If we deprive an electric utility of a power plant, we deprive ourselves of power. If we deprive our landlords of more and better buildings, we deprive ourselves of apartments. If we deprive the oil industry of wells and refineries, we deprive ourselves of gasoline and heating oil.

This harmony of interests between the consumer and

the producer under capitalism is one of the great, profound insights of von Mises.[19] Because of it, even if businessmen become cowardly and do not fight for their own interests, we, as consumers, must fight for them, and thereby for ourselves. For we have a selfish interest in being able to pay prices that make it profitable for businessmen to supply us. It is to our self-interest to pay utility rates, rents, oil prices, and so on, that enable the producers in these fields to keep their facilities intact and growing, and that make them want to supply us. And I must say, in view of the principles we have already learned, that we do not have to worry about being charged unfairly in a free market, because any high profits that might be made from us are simply the incentive and the means to an expanded supply, and are generally made only because of special efficiency on the part of the producers who earn them.

A Defense of Inventory Repricing

In early 1974, when inflation was proceeding more rapidly than now, supermarkets began to raise the prices of the goods already on their shelves, which had initially been marked with lower prices. Because the stores had purchased those goods at prices which had not yet risen, it was assumed that it was some kind of monstrous injustice for them to charge higher prices. The higher prices, it was argued, merely bloated the profits of the supermarkets and were the cause of a higher cost of living for consumers.

What those who spread this argument chose to ignore was that the *replacement* costs of the merchandise had risen and that if the supermarkets had not raised their prices, they would not have had the means of replacing their inventories. They would have been in exactly the same position as our hypothetical merchant if he had not raised his prices.[20] Assume that our merchant held to his old prices and thus continued to take in only $110, while his replacement cost rose from $100 to $110. His nominal profit that year, based on historical cost, would have remained at $10 and, after paying taxes, he would still have had $5. The only problem would have been that even if he allowed absolutely no dividend for his own consumption, he would have had no more than $105 available for replacing his inventory, while the sum he required for replacement was $110. He would have had to reduce the size of his operations. Exactly this would have been the position of the supermarkets if they had been unable to raise their prices in anticipation of higher replacement costs.

It follows that the consumers who wanted cheap goods at the supermarkets' expense would have gotten fewer goods and, if this process were kept up long enough, eventually no goods at all. And, paradoxically, at what-

ever point the control on the nominal rate of profit was finally abandoned, they would have had to pay higher prices than if the control had never been imposed, because prices would then have had to rise on the basis of a decrease in supply as well as on the basis of an inflation-caused increase in demand.

In confirmation of the fact that little or nothing has been learned since 1974, the identical line of argument was raised against the oil companies in the fall of 1990, when they increased the prices of their refined products on the basis of the sharply higher current price of crude oil, which had been caused by Iraq's invasion of Kuwait. Fortunately, the critics were not able to impose price controls on the oil industry in 1990, as they had in 1971.

The Campaign Against the Profits of the Oil Companies

In early 1974, every release of a quarterly earnings report by an oil company was an occasion for *The New York Times* to run a story headlined as a staggering increase in oil company profits. Day after day, one would read a headline in that newspaper that the profits of oil company X were up 60 or 70 percent or more over the same quarter the year before. This rise in profits was constantly mentioned in conjunction with the rise in the price of gasoline and other petroleum products, which had also risen on the order of 60 or 70 percent over the same period of time. It was constantly implied—by *The New York Times*, by *Time* magazine, and by a host of television news commentators—that the rise in oil company profits was responsible for the rise in the price of oil products. And because the rise in these prices was presented as the cause of practically the whole problem of inflation, the impression was created that the oil companies were out to destroy the country with their insatiable greed for profits. By the same token, of course, the oil companies were depicted as eminently deserving to be throttled with price controls.

The evasions, distortions, and misrepresentations in this case were enormous. I think they are worth going into because they are a classic illustration of how the supporters of price controls argue and what they are capable of.

First of all, the supporters of controls evaded two facts that should have been known to everyone: They evaded the fact that the rise in the price of oil products in the United States was the result of a rise in the world price of crude oil brought about by the Arab embargo and the Arab-sponsored cartel, that is, that it was the result of a rise in the oil companies' *costs* of obtaining imported oil. In addition, they evaded the fact that since August of 1971 the prices of oil and oil products produced or sold in the United States had been totally controlled by the

U.S. government, and were currently controlled at levels far below the world-market prices of these goods; indeed, at levels which, until the end of the crisis period, did not even allow the oil companies to pass on more than a part of the higher cost of imported oil. The truth is that our price controls made the importation of foreign oil highly *unprofitable,* which is one of the major reasons we suffered from a shortage of oil at the time. Furthermore, while *The New York Times* and the other news media were spewing headlines about the enormous rise in oil company profits, they neglected to mention that the profits of the oil companies on oil production within the United States increased only on the order of about 6 percent during the crisis period. This was in line with the increase in the physical volume of domestic production in the period. Profits on domestic production did not and could not have increased any more than that because the selling prices of the oil companies were all rigidly controlled by the government, in line with their costs of production.

The real facts, therefore, are that during the oil crisis the American market was a very unprofitable market for the importation of foreign oil and a not very profitable market for the production of domestic oil or oil products. Nevertheless, the news media constantly pointed to a sharp rise in oil company profits and claimed that it was responsible for the rise in prices.

To be sure, there was a substantial increase in oil company profits *on a percentage basis.* Technically, the media were correct in reporting profit increases of 60 and 70 percent or more. But in representing these profit increases as the cause of higher American oil prices, the media committed four distinct acts of dishonesty or misrepresentation.

First, the media neglected to inform the public that these higher profits were not earned on the production or sale of oil or oil products *in the United States.* In many cases, over half the rise in profits came from inventory profits on stocks of oil and oil products held abroad, where price controls did not apply, and from profits on foreign-exchange holdings. The inventory profits were the same in principle as the jump in profits of our hypothetical merchant or of the supermarkets that raised prices in anticipation of higher replacement costs. These inventory profits earned abroad reflected nothing more than that the oil companies possessed some inventories acquired before the rise in the world-market price of crude oil, and were able to sell the inventories at the higher prices corresponding to the higher replacement price of crude oil. The extra profits earned on the inventories merely served to enable the oil companies to maintain their level of operations, just as was the case with the supermarkets.

The profits on foreign-exchange holdings were similar. The oil companies are largely international and hold such currencies as Swiss francs and German marks, as well as U.S. dollars. During the oil crisis, the price of the dollar fell in terms of these currencies. This meant that the francs and marks held by the oil companies were suddenly equivalent to a larger number of U.S. dollars. This increase in the dollar value of their foreign-exchange holdings was included in the reported profit gains of the oil companies.

The rest of the increase in oil company profits was the result of higher profits on foreign operations other than profits on inventory or currency holdings, and higher profits on other lines of business, such as the chemical business, in which a number of oil companies were involved and which had a good year at the time. All of these facts about the sources of higher profits were simply ignored.

The second dishonesty of the media was that they did not point out that even with the 60 or 70 percent increase—from whatever sources—the profits of the oil companies were only restored to the same level in relation to sales revenues at which they had existed in 1968. It was not pointed out that the intervening years had been poor ones for the oil industry and that the sharp percentage increase in its profits was largely the result of measuring the increase against an unusually low base. I remember one case in particular, in which the headline in *The New York Times* blared "2-Month Earnings Soar at Occidental."[21] It turned out, if one read the article very, very carefully, and did some arithmetic that the reporter and the editor had apparently not bothered to do, that the soaring earnings represented an increase in profits from about *seven-tenths of 1 percent of sales revenues to about 5½ percent of sales revenues,* which latter figure was still below normal for the oil industry in previous years. Of course, with this type of misrepresentation, it would be possible to write headlines about infinite increases in profits. All one would need would be to find firms that earned some profits in the current period but which had earned zero profits or incurred losses in the period with which it was compared. The percentage increase would be infinite.

Closely related to this kind of dishonesty was a further misrepresentation. In all of the countless times that the news media mentioned 60 to 70 percent increases in profits in conjunction with 60 or 70 percent increases in product prices in the petroleum industry, they never once, to my knowledge, mentioned that profits are only a small percentage of prices—5 percent, 10 percent, rarely much more than 10 percent. This applies both to the petroleum industry and to practically every other industry. Accordingly, it was never pointed out that any given percentage increase in profits must necessarily represent a much smaller percentage increase in prices. If profits are initially 10 percent of a price, a 70 percent increase in profits does not equal a 70 percent increase in price, but only a *7 percent* increase in price. If, as in the case I mentioned, profits are initially seven-tenths of 1 percent of the price, even a 1,000 percent increase in profits would not mean some kind of fantastic increase in price, but a rise merely on the order of a few percent. Thus, even if the oil companies had earned their higher profits in the United States, which they did not, and even if those higher profits had been the cause of a rise in oil prices, which they were not, they could not have been of any significance as a cause of higher oil prices. Nevertheless, by the news media's constant conjunction of their roughly equivalent percentage increases, it was made to appear that the rise in profits of the petroleum industry is what accounted for the rise in the prices of petroleum products.

Finally, just as the media regularly associated the percentage increases in profits with the percentage increase in the price of oil products, they just as studiously avoided ever mentioning the rate of profit on capital in connection with the rise in the consumer price index. Such a connection would have shown that the oil industry was far from being very profitable in real terms. The reasons are as follows. During the oil crisis, the consumer price level was rising at an annual rate of 13 percent, while the United States' most profitable, most successful major oil company was earning only 18 percent a year on its capital. This meant that while $100 invested in that company would grow to $118 in a year, it would take $113 at the end of the year to buy what the $100 had bought at he beginning of the year. This meant that the real rate of gain of the owners of that company was less than 5 percent a year—it was $5 divided by $113. A real rate of profit of less than 5 percent for the country's most profitable, most successful major oil company is quite low. And, of course, most oil companies were earning substantially lower real rates of profit. Any oil company whose nominal rate of profit was below 13 percent, say, 8, 10, or 12 percent, was actually losing money in real terms! But, as I say, one never found the media dealing with the real rate of return of the oil companies.

It may be asked where I obtained my knowledge of the facts I have cited. The answer, strangely enough, is the general news media themselves, especially *The New York Times*. The facts appeared there. They simply received no stress, or they weren't integrated. They were buried in a mass of articles whose headlines and general tenor created exactly the opposite impression. Or they appeared at different times, in different stories. For example, as I have indicated, figures were reported showing dollar totals of profits and sales revenues; it was simply left to the reader to perform the necessary long division in order to compute profits as a percentage of sales revenues. Likewise, while the percentage increase in profits over the previous year was carried in headlines, only occasionally, in an almost offhand reference, would one find a mention of the actual nominal rate of profit on capital invested. And, while the rate of increase in the consumer price level was featured prominently, it was never mentioned in connection with nominal profit rates, so that one would know what to make of those rates.

One would also read statements, buried deep in articles denouncing oil company profits, that, according to oil company officials or other sources, the rise in profits was largely the result of inventory profits earned abroad and gains on foreign-exchange holdings. The statements were never disputed. They were simply ignored, as being of no significance. And, of course, it was certainly reported in the press that all of the prices charged by the oil companies were controlled by the government and that the Arabs had brought about a radical increase in the world price of crude oil, which, of course, meant higher costs to the oil companies. Yet, these two facts of fixed prices and radically higher costs, facts which were obviously incompatible with the oil industry being very profitable, were simply ignored in the articles reporting the profit increases, as I pointed out earlier.

The kind of distortions committed in the media's treatment of the profits of the oil companies will almost certainly be committed in the future, in attempts to impose or continue controls on other industries. The reader should be on guard against them and should hold in mind, in addition to the need for nominal profits to allow for the replacement of assets at higher prices, such further important matters as the source of the alleged profits under attack, their size in relation to sales revenues, the basis of comparison used in showing their change, and the relation between percentage changes in them and percentage changes in selling prices.

In connection with the distortions present in recent attempts—that is, in 1992 and 1993—to blame the sharp rise in the cost of medical care over the last decades on the high profits made on a few patented drugs, the reader should also keep in mind the substantial losses incurred in the numerous unsuccessful research and development efforts that take place. He should also realize that the attacks made on the large size of the pharmaceutical companies' outlays for advertising and promotion ignore the fact that much of the outlays for promotion represent the distribution of large quantities of free samples of new medications to physicians, who in turn give the samples to their patients without charge. Thus, alongside the accusation that the pharmaceutical industry charges too much for its products, this accusation turns out to represent an attack on the pharmaceutical industry for giving away too many of its products for free. Finally, the reader should realize that the attacks made on the pharmaceutical industry for spending large sums on the development of new drugs that do the same job as already existing drugs sold by other firms, represent the contradiction of attacking the industry both for the high profits to be made from successful drugs and for the competitive quest that serves to bring those high profits down by means of others being able to offer competing alternatives. Such attacks are attacks on the very nature of the profit system.

How the U.S. Government, Not the Oil Companies, Caused the Oil Shortage

Let us try to keep in mind all that we have learned about shortages, and look further at the ignorance and evasions displayed during the oil shortage. I am concentrating on the oil shortage because it had such a dramatic effect on practically everyone in the United States and is so illustrative of all of the problems associated with price controls, including the kind of inappropriate mental attitudes that are connected with them.

There were two very popular explanations of the oil shortage that went around at the time, both of which tried to blame it on the oil companies rather than on price controls. According to one of these explanations, the oil companies had created the shortage in order to be able to obtain permission to build the Alaskan oil pipeline, which had been delayed for many years by the lawsuits of the ecology movement. According to the second explanation, the oil companies had created the shortage in order to eliminate the independent gas stations, to which they were reportedly observed denying supplies.

The first observation which must be made against both of these claims is that they do not see that shortages can result only from a price that is too low and must disappear as the price rises. To repeat once again, no matter how physically limited is the supply of a good or how urgent the demand for it, no shortage can possibly exist at the price established in a free market. For the free-market price will be high enough to level the quantity of the good demanded down to equality with the supply that exists—all the while, of course, acting to expand the supply that exists. Even if one could establish—which one certainly cannot—that the oil companies had conspired to reduce the supply of oil, still, one could not blame them for the shortage. Had they reduced the supply of oil, they would have sold it at a higher price, and at the higher price there would have been no shortage. In order to blame the oil companies for the *shortage,* one would have to show that the oil companies *deliberately charged too low a price for their oil.* That would be the only conceivable way that they could have caused the

shortage. But that is absolutely absurd. It was not the oil companies that were responsible for too low a price, but the government, with its price controls. The government stood ready to fine or possibly even imprison anyone selling oil or oil products at prices that would have eliminated the shortage.

The interests of justice, however, require that I show not only that the oil companies could not have caused the shortage, but also that they were not responsible for anything acting to raise the price of oil in the absence of price controls.

Observe. The oil companies were not responsible for the nationwide and worldwide increase in aggregate demand that acted to drive up all prices, including, of course, the price of oil. Nor were the oil companies responsible for any decrease in the world supply of oil. Both were exclusively the result of government actions. All governments, that of the United States included, were and are bent on reckless expansions of the money supply that act to raise the demand for everything and the price of everything. And it was governments that were responsible for the restriction in the supply of oil—not only the governments that are members of the international oil cartel or that participated in the Arab embargo, but also the U.S. government.

The U.S. government, acting largely under the influence of the ecology movement, restricted the supply of oil in the following ways: (1) It prevented exploration for and development of oil reserves in vast areas of territory arbitrarily set aside as "wildlife preserves" or "wilderness areas." It even delayed the development of the vital North Slope Alaskan oil fields for many years, on the grounds of alleged concerns over the "environmental" effects of the pipeline required to transport the oil to Alaska's south coast. (2) It prevented the development of offshore wells on the continental shelf. (3) It prevented the construction of other oil and gas pipelines, of new refineries, oil storage facilities, and facilities for handling supertankers. Where it did not totally prohibit these activities, it greatly increased their cost by creating enormous delays—a policy that was enthusiastically joined by the other levels of government. (For example, the plan for an oil pipeline from Southern California to Texas was abandoned, with a loss of over fifty million dollars, because the necessary permissions could not be obtained from the more than *seven hundred and fifty* federal, state, and local government agencies involved.) (4) The U.S. government imposed price controls on oil. (5) It acted further to restrict oil company profits, and thus oil industry investment, by punitively increasing their rate of taxation through first reducing and then totally abolishing the customary depletion allowance on crude oil. (6) It deterred investment in the oil industry through threats of antitrust actions forcing the breakup of existing companies, and through threats of nationalization.

In addition, the U.S. government was responsible for an enormous artificial increase in the demand for oil, over and above the increase caused by its policy of inflation. It caused this artificial increase in demand in the following ways: (1) Since the mid-1960s, it controlled the price of natural gas, thereby undermining the growth of that industry. The demand for fuel that normally would have been supplied by natural gas therefore overflowed largely into an expanded demand for petroleum, which is its closest substitute for most purposes. (2) Under the influence of the ecology movement, the government prevented the construction of atomic power plants and restricted the mining of coal, policies which it continues to pursue. In these ways too, it forced, and continues to force, the demand for fuel to rely more heavily than necessary on oil supplies. (3) Again under the influence of the ecology movement, the government forced electric utilities to shift from the burning of coal to the burning of oil and it forced automobile manufacturers to produce engines requiring far higher gasoline consumption per ton-mile.[22]

In sum, the government and the ecology movement have done everything in their power to raise the demand for and restrict the supply of oil.

It should be realized that it was only these actions of the U.S. government that made possible the dramatic rise in the price of oil. The U.S. government bears a far greater responsibility than the Arab cartel. *It* is the party that made it possible for the cartel to succeed. All that the cartel did was to take advantage of the artificial increase in demand and restriction of supply brought about by the U.S. government. Had the U.S. government not restricted the expansion of the domestic petroleum industry and forced up the demand for oil, the supply reductions carried out by the cartel would not have had such a significant effect on the price. Because in that case, such supply reductions would have been at the expense of far less important wants than actually turned out to be the case. With the larger domestic supply of oil and competing fuels that a free market would have produced, the marginal utility of any given amount of oil would have been far less. The loss of any given amount of oil by virtue of the supply reductions carried out by the cartel would therefore have been much less serious. As a result, the cartel would not have been able to raise the price nearly as much by virtue of any given amount of supply reduction. In such circumstances the cartel members would probably not have found it worthwhile to reduce the supply at all. In order to achieve a rise in the price of crude oil of the magnitude that actually occurred, the cartel members would have had to reduce their own

production over and above the amount by which they actually did reduce it, by a further amount equal to the sum of the reduced supply and increased demand for oil caused by the policies of the U.S. government.

Furthermore, in the absence of our price controls, any rise in the price of oil achieved by the cartel would have worked to the advantage of the American oil industry at the expense of the oil industry in the countries belonging to the cartel. This alone would have been enough to frustrate the plans of the cartel. For in this case, the effect of the cartel's restriction of supply would have been to hand the American oil industry the profits and the capital required for an expansion of supply. The cartel would then either have had to allow the price of oil to fall or else it would have had to restrict its own production still further, which would have meant that the American oil companies would have earned the high price of oil on a larger volume of production and have had still greater profits available for expansion, thereby creating still worse problems for the cartel in the future.

It should be obvious that it is impossible for any cartel to succeed that is confronted with a major competitor able to profit from its policies and expand his production. The Arab cartel was able to succeed only because the U.S. government did its utmost to prevent the cartel's competition—the U.S. oil industry—from earning high profits and expanding. Although it was certainly not their intent, in imposing and then perpetuating price controls on oil and oil products, a majority of the highest elected officials in the United States—three presidents (from Nixon to Carter) and a majority of the members of the U.S. House and Senate during those three administrations—behaved as though they owed their election to voters in the member countries of the Arab cartel—as though they were elected in places like Saudi Arabia and Iran rather than in states and districts within the United States. For it was certainly not an American constituency that their actions served, but the interests of the Arab cartel.

In the absence of the U.S. government's destructionist policies, the Arab cartel would probably never even have been formed in the first place, because the conditions required for its success would have been totally lacking. It is not accidental that following the repeal of our price controls on oil in 1981 and the easing of price controls on natural gas and the "ecological" restrictions on the development of oil reserves, the price of oil dramatically declined, despite all efforts to prevent it on the part of the OPEC cartel. If the United States were to abolish all the remaining controls on the production of energy, the OPEC cartel would be completely broken, and the real price of energy would resume the descent it enjoyed from the start of the Industrial Revolution until the enactment of price controls in 1971. Such a policy, of course, would entail removing the prohibitions on the construction of atomic power plants and the restrictions on the strip mining of coal. It would also entail the privatization of the vast landholdings of the federal and state governments in Alaska and the other Western states and of the continental shelf, so that oil and gas reserves could be freely developed.

In sharpest contrast to the actions of the U.S. government, at every step of the way the oil companies sought, and have continued to seek, to expand the production of crude oil and oil products in order to keep pace with the growing demand for oil. They have consistently sought to develop new sources of supply, such as the Alaskan and offshore fields, and to construct new refineries and improved harbor facilities. In other words, they have done everything in their power to keep the price of oil and oil products as low as economically possible. Any other policy would have been against their interests.

This last point must be stressed. In a free market, the oil companies' *profit motive* is tied to achieving as great a supply and as low a price as possible. Consider first the interests of the firms that are predominantly petroleum refiners. Their capital is invested primarily in refineries, pipelines, tankers, delivery trucks, and the like, rather than in deposits of crude oil in the ground. These firms clearly have an interest in the greatest possible supply and lowest possible price of crude oil. For the price of crude oil is their *cost*. These firms have the same interest in an abundant supply and low price of crude oil that every producer has in an abundant supply and low price of his raw material.

By the same token, consider the interests of the producers of crude oil. Their interests lie with the greatest possible efficiency of refining operations and the lowest possible price of refined petroleum products. Because the lower the prices of refined products, the greater the quantity of them demanded and therefore the greater the quantity demanded of crude oil: the price of crude oil can benefit by part of any cost savings in refining. This mutual tension between the interest of refiners and producers of crude oil makes it necessary for each group to try to improve its own production. If the existing producers of crude oil lag behind, they can expect competition from the refiners, who can develop their own supplies of crude oil or expand their existing crude oil operations. If the existing refiners lag behind, they can expect competition from the producers of crude oil, who, for their part, can undertake refining operations or expand their existing refining operations.

In addition, both groups can expect competition from total outsiders if they fail to exploit any significant opportunity for improvement. And, of course, within each group, whichever individual firm succeeds in improving production ahead of its rivals will almost certainly gain at their expense. For example, if one particular refiner improves his efficiency and cuts his costs, he will have higher profits and will thus be able to accumulate additional capital. It will almost certainly pay him to use his additional capital to expand his production, and to create a market for his additional production by lowering his prices. His lower costs will still enable him to have high profits even at lower prices, and his lower prices will both attract new customers to the industry and take away some customers from rivals who cannot afford to sell at such low prices. Exactly the same considerations, of course, apply to the producers of crude oil.

For these reasons, it was no accident, but logically necessary, that the oil companies have all along sought to expand their production. It was the operation of these very principles that brought the oil industry into existence in the first place and developed it from virtually nothing into the productive giant it later became and still is today.

To argue, therefore, that the oil companies were responsible for the oil shortage is an absurdity compounded by a triple injustice. It is an absurdity in that, as we have seen, it implicitly accuses the oil companies of charging too low a price for their oil. This is something they would never do. And the critics of the oil companies, who constantly accuse them of seeking to charge prices that are too high, should have a sufficient respect for logic not to accuse them simultaneously of causing shortages by charging prices that are too low. (Of course, the critics do not know that they are guilty of a contradiction, because they have no idea either of what causes shortages or what determines the price of oil.) The accusation embodies a triple injustice in that it evades: (1) the fact that it was the government's price controls that kept the price too low and so created the shortage, (2) the fact that the government and the ecology movement did practically everything they could to restrict the supply and expand the demand for oil, and (3) the fact that by the nature of the profit motive the oil companies have always worked to expand the supply of oil and reduce its price.

To argue in addition that the oil companies created the shortage for the purpose of being able to build the Alaskan pipeline is to pile on still further absurdities. The obvious truth—given the price controls—is that the construction of the pipeline would have mitigated the shortage somewhat, had it not been so long delayed. To argue that its construction was the *motive* for the shortage is not only to display the utmost ignorance about the causation of shortages and callous indifference to the most elementary questions of justice, it is also to display a lack of comprehension of the law of causality in relation to the physical world. Because according to this argument, the pipeline was something that only the oil companies wanted; the consumers of oil products, allegedly, could have gotten along quite well without the pipeline. Oil products, according to the mentality behind this argument, simply come from oil companies. The oil companies, it is believed, are perfectly capable of producing oil products without oil fields or oil pipelines. The oil companies desire oil fields and oil pipelines, one gets the impression, not because they are necessary to production—production is causeless—but in order to disturb the caribou and the grizzly bears and to pollute the air.

This denial of the elementary physical connection between products and the means of producing them, I must point out, is not an isolated phenomenon confined to the arguments about the Alaskan oil pipeline. It is simply a further manifestation of the same mentality we have already encountered in consumers who denounce the wealth of their suppliers—consumers who will be damned if they'll let the utility that supplies them own the power plants necessary to do so, or their landlord own a decent building. This mentality pervades the whole ecology movement. It is the mentality of all of its members insofar as they both prevent the development of energy supplies and denounce the producers of energy for not producing enough.[23]

Let us turn to the second version of the argument that the oil companies were responsible for the shortage: the claim that they created it for the purpose of eliminating the independent gas stations by denying them supplies.

It may very well be the case that the oil companies did cut off or discriminatorily reduce supplies to the independents, as widely reported. My own personal experience does not confirm this, but I am willing to believe it—not because it was reported in the press, but because it would have been a logical consequence of the shortage. Given the existence of the oil shortage, every oil company that owned gas stations had the following choice: either it could reduce supplies to its own gas stations, where its own capital was invested and stood to suffer loss if the stations had to close or restrict operations; or it could reduce supplies to gas stations owned by others, where it was other people's capital that was invested and would suffer loss. Naturally, if an oil company—or anyone else—is confronted with the choice of having to lose its own capital as a result of some absurd government action, or allowing the loss to fall on the capital of someone else, it will choose the latter. And there is no moral reason why it should not. It is no one's moral obligation to offer up his wealth to the government's destructionist policy so that he may suffer his "fair share" of the damage it inflicts.

I must point out that if it were not for the controls and the shortage, the oil companies and the independents would have enjoyed a perfectly harmonious, mutually profitable relationship, as they always did in all the years before the controls and the shortage. An oil company *benefits* from the existence of independent stations willing to sell its gasoline, and has absolutely no reason to try to undermine them, but every reason to try to promote them. Its benefit is that it can sell more gasoline without having to supply the capital necessary to buy or build gas stations. Even if the oil company owns some of its own gas stations, it still benefits from selling to independents—in just the same way that a company like Häagen Dazs or Carnation benefits by being able to sell its ice cream through retail outlets it does not own. The benefit is wider marketability of the product. An oil company benefits by selling to independent stations even if they are in direct competition with stations it owns, because it is better that *it* supply the competing stations than that some other oil company do so—if that happened, it would still have the same competition, but it would sell less gasoline. In the absence of price controls, even the physical scarcity of oil would not have stopped the oil companies from selling to the independents. They would have been glad to sell whenever an independent was in a position to pay a price higher than their own stations could afford.

The Conspiracy Theory of Shortages

I cannot help noting that this whole argument about the oil companies being out to eliminate the independents (or even just being out to build the Alaskan pipeline), and allegedly staging a nationwide, worldwide crisis to do it, introduces a strange element into the discussion. That is the element of alleged secret plots, dark conspiracies, evil forces, and all the rest of that syndrome.

Strange to say, this kind of argument is much more prevalent than one might imagine. It is present in implicit form whenever anyone asserts that a shortage, whether of oil or anything else, is "contrived." This view of things is not only ignorant of all the consequences of price controls, but it implies the existence of a secret conspiracy. It assumes that price controls themselves create no problems, but that the problems are created by the evil of private firms who combine together secretly and arbitrarily to produce the consequences we have seen can result only from price controls.

In view of all that we have proved about shortages in general and about the oil shortage in particular, I believe I am justified when I say that these arguments really deserve no greater intellectual respectability than the fear some unfortunate people have of Martians or the evil eye. Certainly, they should not be taken seriously by the media or by public officials, as, unfortunately, they have been. It is the intellectual and moral responsibility of the media and the public officials to stop engaging in slander based on ignorance and fear, and to acquire the enlightenment provided by economic science.

Rebuttal of the Charge That Private Firms "Control" Prices

A rather vicious argument has been advanced as a justification for the imposition of price controls. This is the argument that private firms already "control" prices, only they "control" them in their own selfish interest. Instead, it is urged, the government should control prices, for it will do so in the "public interest."

This argument was repeatedly presented in television commercials during the campaign for the 1976 Democratic presidential nomination by one of the leading contenders, Representative Morris Udall. Representative Udall repeatedly asserted that he believed that instead of the price of oil being "controlled" by the oil companies, in their selfish interest, it should be controlled by the president (i.e., Morris Udall), in the public interest.

The reason that Representative Udall and others believe that private firms "control" prices is that they can observe the producers of manufactured or processed goods, and also retailers and many wholesalers, engaged in the *setting* of prices. For example, these businessmen (or their employees, acting under their instructions) can be observed sending out price catalogs and price lists, and also posting prices on signs and writing them on tags. To set prices in this way is, according to Representative Udall and others, to "control" prices. The essential characteristic of a controlled price, on this view, is that someone sets it. It is considered secondary and inconsequential *who* sets it—whether a private businessman or a government official. Indeed, since prices do not create themselves, it is difficult to understand how, on this view, any price can avoid being described as "controlled."

The distinction seems to be that a price is not considered controlled if it is formed in markets so broad—like the organized exchanges for common stocks and commodity futures—that it is difficult to trace from precisely whom any given price quotation emanates; such price quotations have the appearance of being formed independently of any definite individual. If, on the other hand, price quotations emanate regularly from the same, easily identifiable source—such as a steel mill's published price at which it stands ready to ship steel, or a candy store's sign announcing the price at which it stands ready to sell candy bars—the price is declared to be "controlled." (Often, the word "administered" is used as a synonym for "controlled.") The supporters of this idea rarely mention the fact that they believe candy stores and

barbershops and the like are engaged in "price control"—they confine their attacks to large firms, like steel companies and oil companies, where they can count on envy and the existing hostility to big business—but that is the logic of their position.

The viciousness of this doctrine is that it evades and seeks to obliterate the fundamental and radical distinction between private action and government action.[24] Private citizens, and this, of course, includes private corporations, have no authority to resort to physical force against other people. If they do, they are in violation of the law and will be punished. Private action, therefore, is essentially voluntary in character—that is, it can only occur by peaceful means, with the mutual consent of all involved. Government action is totally different. The government has legal authority to resort to physical force—e.g. to arrest, fine, imprison, and even execute people. All government actions rest on this authority. There is no such thing as a law (or a ruling, edict, or decree) that is not backed by the threat of physical force to assure compliance.

Let us see what difference these facts make to whether prices are set by private firms or by the government. When prices are set by private firms, they are set with regard to the mutual self-interest of the buyer and seller, including the need to take into account the threat of competition or potential competition. Thus, a seller must ask prices that are not only high enough to enable him to stay in business and make the best possible profit he can, but, simultaneously, that are low enough to enable his customers to afford his goods and too low for other sellers or potential sellers to try to take away his market.

When the government sets prices, its prices are backed by the threat of physical force, and are necessarily against the mutual self-interests of buyers and sellers. The government invariably tries to sacrifice either the seller to the buyer (by imposing prices that are too low), or the buyer to the seller (by imposing prices that are too high). In the one case, it succeeds in destroying the sellers, leaving the buyers without suppliers. In the other case, it succeeds in destroying the buyers, leaving the sellers without customers (or the workers without employers).

This is the difference that is made by whether prices are set by private firms or by the government. This is the difference that Congressman Udall's usage of the term "price control" evades and seeks to obliterate.

Private firms do not and cannot control prices because they have no power to resort to physical force. Only the government can control prices—i.e., only the government can use force to set prices in violation of the mutual self-interests of buyers and sellers. Price control means not the setting of prices, but the setting of prices *by the government*.[25]

FURTHER EFFECTS OF PRICE CONTROLS AND SHORTAGES

1. Consumer Impotence and Hatred Between Buyers and Sellers

Once price controls result in shortages, their destructive effects are greatly increased. The combination of price controls and shortages not only deprives the consumer of the power to make it profitable for sellers to supply the goods he wants, but of all economic power of any kind over the seller. Instead of being a valued customer, whose patronage or lack of patronage makes a difference to the seller's profit or loss, the buyer is reduced to the status of absolute insignificance, totally at the seller's mercy. His position is much worse, in fact, than if he were dealing with a protected legal monopolist.

Consider. If a shortage exists, and a buyer is dissatisfied with his supplier, he dare not leave him, because he has nowhere else to go. In a shortage, even if there are many other suppliers of the same good, each of them has his own waiting line or waiting list, and, as a result, the dissatisfied customer of any one supplier cannot count on actually being supplied by any other supplier. The other suppliers, therefore, do not represent a real alternative for him in a shortage. Consequently, no matter how many sellers of a good there may be, price controls and shortages place each of them in the position of being the only one. In addition, just as in the case of a protected legal monopolist, these sellers are immune from potential competition. (The threat of potential competition, in a free market, would keep in check the occasional sellers who were in the position of being sole suppliers.) Potential competition is ruled out because the industry is forced to operate at a rate of return that is not competitive, and perhaps even at an outright loss. As a result, no outside firm would want to enter such an industry.[26]

The situation for the customer is worse than if he were dealing with a protected legal monopolist, because under price controls and shortages, the seller who surpasses a customer's limits of tolerance and succeeds in driving him away *does not lose anything by doing so.* This is because for each customer who is driven away, there is a multitude of others eager to take his place. The seller simply sells to someone else who otherwise would not have been able to buy or not buy as much as he desired. This goes beyond the conditions faced by a protected legal monopolist, because such a monopolist does not have a reserve of unsupplied potential customers willing to buy on just as good terms as his present customers. If

such a monopolist drives away his present customers, he can find new ones only at lower prices. A protected legal monopolist who has any sense, therefore, will not do this. He will value his customers, because he knows that he cannot afford to lose them without harming himself. But under price controls and shortages, the seller is free to regard his customers as absolutely valueless—as being instantaneously replaceable by others drawn from waiting lines or waiting lists without any loss to himself.

By the nature of the case, shortages lead sellers to regard customers not only as valueless, but as a positive nuisance—as a source of trouble and expense, not a source of livelihood. This occurs because, in fact, under a system of shortages and waiting lines, that is just what customers become. Under such a system, when a seller renders a customer some service or goes to some expense on his behalf, he is no longer doing it for the sake of gaining or keeping the customer's business and thereby earning his own livelihood, because having the customer's business no longer depends on performing the service or incurring the expense. The seller can have the customer anyway, or, if not that customer, then any one of ten or a hundred or a thousand other customers. If the seller is to continue to provide the service or incur the expense for the sake of the customer, he can only do so out of a sense of altruistic duty, not out of the sense that in serving the customer he serves himself.

Thus, price controls and the shortages they create take the profit out of serving the customer and the loss out of not serving him. They break the harmonious union of the self-interest of buyer and seller that prevails in a free market and replace it with an altruistic relationship between the two. In this relationship, the customer is reduced to impotent pleading for the customary service and customary quality that the seller no longer has any economic motive to supply. Indeed, all of the seller's motives, both economic and noneconomic, now work in the direction of reducing the quality of his product and the service associated with it.

The seller's economic motive lies with reducing quality and service because by doing so he reduces his costs and perhaps his own labor, and he does not have to fear any reduction in his revenues. For the same reason, employees feel free to work less hard in serving customers. Their poor performance no longer threatens their employer's revenue, and so he is no longer motivated to make them produce high quality products and to treat customers properly. (Thus, even under price controls, there is a tendency for customers to get what they pay for. To the extent that they pay prices below the potential free-market prices, they tend to receive products that are below the level of the products they would have received in a free market.)

The fact that price controls inflict actual harm on the sellers, and the fact that this harm is inflicted for the avowed purpose of benefitting the buyers, introduces a noneconomic element into the attitude of many sellers. They see themselves as being sacrificed for the benefit of their customers, and they may actually come to hate their customers as a result of it. In some cases it is possible that they may derive actual pleasure from the reduction in quality and service that they impose on their customers.

Price controls and shortages, in fact, launch a spiral of mutually reinforcing hatreds between buyer and seller. The buyer arbitrarily demands the quality and service he is accustomed to, even though he is not paying the necessary price any longer. The seller has no economic reason to comply with these demands, but, on the contrary, has both economic and psychological reasons not to. The buyer then views the seller as an omnipotent tyrant whom he must beg for favors or threaten with reprisals in order to obtain what he wants. The seller views the buyer as a hysterical petty chiseler seeking values without payment. To the degree that the accustomed quality and service are not forthcoming, the buyers become more shrill and insistent in their demands, and the sellers become correspondingly more resistant.

This principle—of deterioration of quality and service accompanied by mutual hatred between buyer and seller— was illustrated to some extent in the gasoline shortage of early 1974. Suddenly, service station attendants who had always cleaned windshields and eagerly volunteered to check under the hood ceased to do so. Whereas before they had always been courteous and polite, seeking to encourage as much repeat business as possible, they now became surly and rude. The customer, who had always been king at the gas station, as everywhere else, suddenly became a useless pest waiting in line to have his tank filled and causing unnecessary labor to gas station attendants. The breakdown of the normal harmony of interests between buyer and seller, and its replacement with open hostility, was strikingly illustrated in a *New York Times'* "Quotation of the Day." (I quote first the statement quoted by *The Times* and then its description of the person and circumstances surrounding the quotation. I omit the individual's name, in order to spare him possible embarrassment.) "'If he's that stupid, he waits in line an hour and doesn't know the rules, I let him get to the pump—and then I break his heart.'— . . . a service station attendant in Elizabeth, N.J., where gasoline rationing rules went into effect yesterday."[27] (For the benefit of readers who may be unfamiliar with the circumstances, what the attendant let unsuspecting motorists wait in line an hour to find out was that they were there on the wrong day: their license plates ended with an odd number when they should have ended with an even number, or vice versa.)

The shortage of gasoline did not last long enough to make hatred between motorists and service station attendants become a regular feature of life. With the ending of the oil shortage in the spring of 1974, normal relations were restored, and the conditions of early 1974 were soon largely forgotten. A more enduring and, therefore, probably more significant example is afforded by the relations between landlords and tenants in places like New York City, which has had almost continuous rent control since early in World War II. In New York City mutual hatred between landlords and tenants is commonplace. It has become the norm. Nothing is more frequent than complaints about things landlords do not do, unless it is complaints about things they are trying not to do. For example, depending on the particular circumstances, landlords do not provide, or are trying to avoid providing, such services as doormen, painting, repairs, and even heat. Tenants regard all of these things as theirs by right, and hate the landlords for not supplying them or trying not to supply them. Landlords, on the other hand, often regard the tenants as people who want to live without paying the proper rent. And, in many cases, while they watch the real value of their investments shrink to zero, they observe tenants able to afford expensive automobiles and adopt a style of life that is above their own— made possible by the low, controlled rents they pay. In such circumstances, there are landlords who derive positive enjoyment from such things as providing no heat, as well as save money by it.

Of course, it should be realized that there are also many cases—and undoubtedly a far greater number—in which the controls simply make it impossible for a landlord to provide many things, even if he wants to for the sake of keeping up his building, such as a new boiler or wiring system or any major repair or improvement. The controls often make these things impossible by leaving the landlord with too little capital to make the necessary investments. In the long run, controls must produce a progressive elimination of services even if landlords have the best will in the world.

How Repeal of Rent Controls Would Restore Harmony Between Landlords and Tenants

The hatred between landlords and tenants would disappear in a rental market that was free of controls. Such a market would restore economic power to the tenants: it would give tenants the power to make landlords serve them out of self-interest.

Consider how a free market would bring this about.

The first effect of the establishment of a free rental market would be a jump in the previously controlled rents. This jump in rents would eliminate the shortage of rental housing. Immediately, even before any increase in the supply of rental housing could occur, the rise in rents would level the quantity of living space demanded down to equality with the limited supply that exists. In fact, the quantity of living space demanded would be reduced to a point somewhat below the supply that exists: landlords would have some vacancies on their hands at free-market rents. Precisely these vacancies are what would restore to tenants their economic power over landlords. At free-market rents, each tenant would be able to choose from a large number of apartments available in his price range. If he did not like the service his present landlord gave him, he would simply move when his lease expired. He would not be in the position of having to regard his present apartment as the only one in the world, and feel obliged to stay no matter how bad conditions in it became. By the same token, his landlord would no longer be able to count on easily replacing him. At free-market rents, his landlord would not have a waiting list of potential tenants, but vacancies on his hands. If he were to act in such a way as to make too many tenants move, he would either be unable to replace those tenants or he would have to reduce his rents below the general market in order to attract replacements. In this way, a landlord who did not satisfy his tenants would suffer financial loss. The landlord's self-interest would once again make him want to gain and keep tenants. Landlords would once again begin to compete with each other in terms of improved quality and service. They would have to, because they would need tenants once again, while tenants would no longer need any particular one of them.

2. The Impetus to Higher Costs

A major consequence of price controls and shortages is that they increase costs by means of creating various inefficiencies.

For example, in those cases in which goods come in a variety of models and price ranges, such as television sets, cars, lawn mowers—most goods—they create an incentive for producers to eliminate the more economical models while cutting corners in the production of the more expensive models. The reason this occurs is that, on the one hand, the buyers are able and willing to pay the higher prices of the more expensive models rather than do without the good altogether, and, on the other hand, corner cutting can generally be carried out more easily and with less serious results on the upper end of a product line than on the lower end. The process is actually a disguised way of raising prices and restoring profits. But it is a very uneconomic way of doing so, because, as a result of it, many buyers end up having to

pay more for more expensive models that they don't really need or want than they would have had to pay in a free market for the models they really do want. For example, someone seeking a sixteen-inch black-and-white television set may end up having to buy a nineteen-inch color set, because that's all that's available. At the same time, the buyers who do want the better models find they are not as good any more.[28]

This process is a corollary of the decline in quality and service discussed in the previous section. And as soon as a shortage becomes severe enough, quality and service are cut to the point that buyers are offered models that would never appear in a free market in any price range. What happens is that sellers are led to cut corners in order to make relatively small savings to themselves and which have a great impact on the buyers. For example, situations can exist in which it is advantageous to a seller to save a few cents in manufacturing costs that later imposes many dollars in repair costs on the buyer. The harm inflicted on the buyers does not cause the sellers any economic loss, because at the controlled price there is a surplus of buyers eager to buy even a very inferior product.

In the same way that price controls and shortages make it impossible for a consumer to select his model on the basis of cost, they also make it impossible for a businessman to select his *methods of production* on the basis of cost. For one or more of the factors of production he requires may simply be unobtainable, because a price control has created a shortage of it. Under price controls, businessmen must select those methods of production for which the means happen to be available, and not necessarily those which have the lowest costs. The inability to find the right factors of production, of course, also frequently results in a decline in the quality of products as well, and should be viewed as a further and major cause of declining quality. The very deterioration of quality and service is itself a powerful source of higher costs both to businessmen and consumers, as I have already indicated. If, for example, a machine is produced or serviced in an inferior way, then even if its price remains the same, it will cause higher costs of maintenance and repair and may have to be replaced sooner. The same obviously applies to many consumers' goods. If a television set lasts only half as long and has to be repaired twice as often, it is a lot more expensive to own, even though its price remains the same.

Shortages of supplies and the mere threat of shortages themselves directly raise the costs of production. The effect of a shortage of a factor of production is to delay production. This causes the capital invested in all the other, complementary factors of production that depend on it, to have to be invested for a longer period of time than would otherwise be necessary. For example, a shortage of building-nails causes capital to be invested in half-finished houses and in piles of lumber for an unnecessary period of time. Since interest must be paid on capital for the full time it is invested, the effect of all such delays is to raise the interest cost of production. Similarly, the mere anticipation of shortages of supplies leads businessmen to hoard supplies of all types. This requires that production be carried on with a larger capital investment—in the additional stocks of supplies and in facilities for storing them. And this, of course, in turn, means extra interest costs and extra costs on account of the storage facilities. Finally, there is the loss of the valuable time of executives in searching for sources of supply and in performing all the paperwork required to comply with the government's price controls and any associated regulations, such as rationing.

It should be noted that shortages and the threat of shortages also directly raise costs to consumers. Consumers too suffer effects analogous to wasted investment and the need for more investment. For example, consumers who could not obtain gasoline could not use their cars or enjoy their country homes until such time as they could obtain gasoline. To that extent, the money they had spent for these complementary consumers' goods represented a kind of wasted investment. In addition, of course, consumers too are led to hoard supplies and thus to tie up larger sums of money in stocks of goods and, quite possibly, incur additional costs on account of acquiring extra storage facilities—for example, extra home freezers, if there should be the threat of a food shortage. Finally, one must mention the wasted man-hours spent in waiting lines during every shortage, which, while not a money cost, are nonetheless a real hardship and burden and can well be at the expense of actual working time.

To some extent, the rise in production costs that price controls and shortages bring about may come out of profits. But it certainly does not always do so—as, for example, when it is a case of concentrating on the production of more expensive models that have correspondingly higher controlled prices. Moreover, it is possible for most or even all of the rise in costs not to come out of profits—at least, not out of nominal profits. For the government may very well follow a policy of allowing prices to rise insofar as the producers can prove a rise in costs. This was the case to a large extent in World War II. During World War II, most defense contracts were written on a cost-plus basis—that is, the government paid defense contractors their costs plus a percentage of their costs as profit. The same principle seems often to have been applied in setting the price controls on civilian goods. This procedure, it should be realized, is tantamount to the positive encouragement of extra costs, because it makes the incurrence of extra costs the way to raise profits. It thereby totally perverts the profit motive from being the driving force of greater efficiency to being a driving force of greater inefficiency.

By their very nature, price controls pervert the operation of the profit motive. One must charge to their account not only all of the actual inefficiencies they create, but all of the potential improvements in efficiency they prevent. Price controls create a situation in which it is no longer necessary to reduce costs or improve quality in order to raise profits. In a free market, the price every firm receives is the very best it can obtain under the prevailing state of the market. A firm has the legal right to ask a higher price than this in a free market, but does not ask such a price because it would drive away too many customers: its customers would turn to competitors, and new competitors would probably appear; or, even if there were no close competitors, its customers would simply buy too much less of its type of product to make a further rise in price worthwhile.

Thus, in a free market, a firm must accept the fact that its price is limited by forces beyond its control. In order to increase its profits, it cannot simply raise its price—it must reduce its costs of production or improve the quality of its products to attract new buyers. That is final. There is simply no other choice. But under price controls, the price a firm receives is not something that is imposed upon it by an unyielding external reality, to which it has no choice but to adapt its own conduct. The price it receives can be changed in its favor—if only it can prevail upon the officials in charge of the price controls to relax them, or if it can find ways of evading them. Thus, the firm's focus necessarily switches. Instead of being focused on reducing costs and improving quality as the ways of increasing profits, it becomes focused on ways to have the price controls relaxed or to evade them. This alone represents a radical change in the way a firm directs its talents and energies.

Furthermore, as we have seen, firms lose the incentive to reduce costs or improve quality. Price controls and the shortages they create place *these things* beyond a firm's power. Even if it wanted to, a firm has no power to reduce its costs or improve its quality when shortages prevent it from obtaining the appropriate means of producing its products or cause the quality of those means to deteriorate. But, of course, even if it had the power, there is simply no reason under price controls and shortages for a firm to reduce its costs or improve the quality of its products. There is no reason to improve the quality of its products, because its customers will snap up goods of lower quality than it now offers. It has no reason to reduce its costs (except at the expense of quality) in an environment in which customers are eager to pay prices that would cover substantially higher costs and in which, besides, it has little or no prospect of profiting from any improvements in efficiency it might achieve.

This last is the situation of every price-controlled firm in a period of inflation, insofar as its suppliers are still free to raise their prices or to impose higher costs by virtue of declines in the quality of their products or services. Such phenomena will raise the costs and destroy the profitability of a firm that must operate under price controls, no matter what it does to control its costs by means of becoming more efficient. To the extent that it succeeds in retarding the rise in its costs through greater efficiency, the price-control authorities will use that very fact to deny its need for a price increase. The only effect of achieving greater efficiency in such a situation is to postpone the day that one is permitted to obtain relief by raising one's prices. In other words, normal cost reductions, based on improvements in efficiency, simply cease to pay, even if they are still within the firm's power to make. The only cost reductions that pay under price controls are the ones that can be made effortlessly, namely, cost reductions at the expense of quality—the kind of cost reductions that would not pay in a free market.

In sum, price controls and shortages thoroughly pervert or destroy the operation of the profit motive. In place of profit incentives to improve quality and reduce costs, they make it possible to profit by means of reducing quality and allowing costs to rise. For they destroy the resistance of buyers to declining quality and to higher prices to cover higher costs. Indeed, they often necessitate declining quality and positively encourage higher costs insofar as they entail cost-plus pricing.

The Administrative Chaos of Price Controls

It should be realized that the willingness of the government to allow higher controlled prices on the basis of higher costs of production introduces a significant complication into the administration of price controls. The complication arises because different parts of the supply of the same good will have different costs of production. As a result, the government must set a *number* of controlled prices on the identical good, depending on the particular cost of production incurred to produce the particular batch of goods in question. This procedure is generally accompanied by further procedures, all of which help to make price controls an administrative nightmare.

What the government does is to allow producers to sell to distributors (or to further processors) at varying prices, corresponding to their varying costs. The distributors, however, are required to sell to the ultimate consumers at a *uniform* price, based on an average of the varying costs to them as a group. By itself this procedure would threaten some distributors with financial ruin while

offering other distributors the prospect of correspondingly higher profits. For all distributors must sell at the same price, while their costs may be significantly above or below the average on the basis of which that price is set. In order to deal with this problem, the government must assign to each distributor his "fair share" of low-cost and high-cost goods, or force the distributors to agree to some scheme of mutual compensation.

This sort of situation existed in the oil industry when it was under price controls. Oil produced from wells that had been in operation prior to the imposition of price controls in August of 1971, was classified as "old oil" and controlled at a price of $5.25 a barrel. Oil produced from wells brought into production subsequent to that date was called "new oil" and was controlled at approximately twice that price. Those firms that were supplied mainly with "old" oil were forced to compensate the firms that had to rely mainly on "new" oil, or on imported oil, which, since early 1974, was not subject to controls at all and (prior to the Iranian revolution of 1979), sold for about $14.50 a barrel. The compensation arrangement resulted from the fact that all the oil companies had to sell at essentially the same prices to consumers, and the consumer prices were based on an average of the price of old, new, and imported oil. Under this arrangement, some oil companies were forced to turn over hundreds of millions of dollars, called "entitlements," to other oil companies.

The entitlement system was not only administratively chaotic, but actually represented an expropriation of the wealth of American oil companies for the benefit of the Arabs. Under it, the profits that were made by refiners that bought "old" oil at $5.25 a barrel were transferred largely to those refiners that bought Arab oil at $14.50 a barrel. This meant that money that should have gone to purchase American oil was instead used to finance the purchase of Arab oil. It was literally a system for keeping money out of the hands of American producers and putting it into the hands of the Arabs.[29]

3. Chaos in the Personal Distribution of Consumers' Goods

In the last chapter, we saw that, in a free market, consumers' goods in limited supply are distributed to the individual consumers in accordance with a combination of their relative wealth and income, on the one side, and the relative strength of their needs and desires for the goods, on the other.[30] Price controls and shortages totally disrupt this principle of distribution. What they substitute is not another principle, but merely the rule of the random, of the arbitrary and the accidental—the rule of chaos.

One should think back to the gasoline shortage and consider what determined the distribution of gasoline. It was a matter of luck and favoritism. Gasoline went to those who happened to be on the spot when deliveries were made to gas stations, or who had the time to waste waiting hours in line or following gasoline delivery trucks around. It went to those who happened to be friendly with service station owners or the employees of service stations. Both the wealth and the needs of the buyers were made irrelevant. The country's most productive businessmen were placed on an equal footing with welfare recipients: the value of their higher incomes was simply nullified. It was just a question of who arrived first or who had the right friends. By the same token, people whose very livelihood depended on gasoline were in no better position to obtain it than people wanting it for the most marginal purposes. Again, it was just a question of who got there first or who had the right friends.

Rent-controlled apartments are distributed in just the same way. If meat were placed under price control, it would not be long before it too was distributed in this way. The distribution of any good subjected to price controls becomes chaotic just as soon as the controls produce a shortage.

4. Chaos in the Geographical Distribution of Goods Among Local Markets

We already know that price controls prevent an area that has an urgent need for a product from obtaining it by bidding up its price in competition with other areas. When price controls are joined by shortages, a further major element of chaos is introduced. Under the combination of price controls and shortages, not only is the price of a good prevented from rising, but also, paradoxically, it is prevented from *falling.*

Where a shortage exists, an increase in the supply of a good, or a decrease in the demand for it, does not reduce the price; *it merely reduces the severity of the shortage.* Where a shortage exists, an additional supply merely makes it possible for someone to buy at the same—controlled—price who previously could not do so; likewise, a decrease in demand merely means a reduction in the number of those contending for the supply who must go away empty-handed. The price does not fall in such circumstances because it is already too low, as a result of price control.

The significance of the fact that prices can neither rise nor fall is that if price controls and shortages exist in various local markets, producers are in a position to sell a larger quantity in every such market without any reduction in the price in that market or, therefore, in the

profitability of sending supplies to it. All that they have to do is find an additional supply of the good to send. What this situation makes possible, in essence, is that producers can send their goods practically anywhere, in widely varying proportions, and it doesn't matter to them. If they send too little to some areas, the price controls in those areas prevent prices and profitability from rising and halting the drain. Meanwhile, in the areas into which they are sending too much, shortages prevent prices and profitability from falling and stemming the inflow. In a word, the geographical distribution of a good simply becomes random and chaotic, disconnected from the consumers' needs and purchasing power.

Consider the following case, based on the experience of the gasoline shortage. The price control on gasoline created a shortage in the whole northeastern region of the United States. Almost every state and locality in that region had its own individual shortage. In this context, it largely ceased to matter to the oil companies how their gasoline was distributed among the various areas in the region. Suppose, for example, that they sent a million gallons less a month to New Jersey and a million gallons more a month to Connecticut. It didn't matter to them. The price of gasoline in New Jersey and the profitability of sending it there could not rise even if New Jersey received hardly any gasoline at all. Price controls prevented it. At the same time, the price of gasoline in Connecticut and the profitability of sending it there could not fall—until the shortage in Connecticut was totally eliminated. Of course, just the reverse could have occurred. A million gallons less a month could have been sent to Connecticut, and a million gallons more a month could have been sent to New Jersey. Price control would have prevented any rise in the price and profitability of sending gasoline to Connecticut; and, so long as it existed, the shortage would have prevented any fall in the price and profitability of sending gasoline to New Jersey.

This indeterminacy introduced by price controls explains how some areas can suffer relatively mild shortages, and other areas very severe shortages, and how their positions can easily be reversed. The significance of this is that price controls not only create shortages, *but make it a random matter how the burden of those shortages is distributed.* In the gasoline shortage, for example, it would have been possible for the various areas to share the burden of the overall shortage in any proportions. All might have suffered more or less equally, or some particular areas might have borne almost the entire shortage, while others suffered almost none at all, or any intermediate situation might have existed. The actual chaos that did exist fully accords with this principle.

Precisely how the burdens are distributed is the result of accident. In the gasoline shortage, the main accidental factor was that the Northeast happened to be the region most heavily dependent on imports, and so it bore the far greater part of the nationwide burden—given the fact that price controls prevented the people of the region from bidding up the price of gasoline and thus making the shipment of replacement supplies profitable. Within the Northeast, further accidental factors played a role, such as the very time of the year when the controls were imposed. To understand this last point, imagine that the controls are imposed in the summertime. In the summer, there is a large demand for gasoline in many resort areas. As a result, the wholesale price of gasoline in these areas is at a seasonal high in relation to the wholesale price in many city areas. It is high enough to cover such special summertime costs as may be entailed in having to bring in supplies from more distant refineries than is necessary at other seasons, when the local demand in the resort areas is smaller. The imposition of controls freezes this seasonal price relationship and carries it forward to the fall and winter, when there is a different pattern of demand, and when there should be a different set of gasoline price relationships to reflect it. Given the perpetuation of the summertime price relationships, what happens is that gasoline continues to be heavily supplied to the summer resort areas—perhaps to the point of pushing the price there somewhat below the level permitted by the controls. As a result, no shortage whatever exists in these resort areas. The entire shortage is concentrated in the cities. If the controls are imposed in the wintertime, instead of the summertime, then, of course, the reverse situation develops.

Further chaos in distribution can be caused by such things as small bureaucratic adjustments in the price controls. For example, it is quite possible that after the controls are imposed, the officials in charge may make some minor adjustments here and there, such as for the purpose of rectifying the kind of seasonal problems I have just described. In doing this, they can unleash major movements in supply which they may not be aware of causing. Imagine, for example, that they decide to permit, say, a penny a gallon rise in the price of gasoline in one particular major city. If this small rise makes this particular city a relatively more profitable market than other markets, the various distributors will want to sell more heavily in this city; and as long as a shortage exists in the city, they can do so without any reduction in the newly increased price and profit margin. The effect will be that this particular city will tend to be supplied very heavily, perhaps to the point of totally eliminating its local shortage, while supplies will simply disappear from other markets to the same extent.

Frankly, it is impossible to know all the different factors that might suddenly unleash major movements in

supply. The essential point is that under price controls and shortages, movements in supply have no effect on price and profitability until a local shortage is totally eliminated, at which point the local price and profitability will begin to fall and the further movement of supplies to that area will stop. Short of that point, massive movements of supply are possible in response to very small differences in profitability. Anything that can create such differences can cause such movement.

5. Chaos in the Distribution of Factors of Production Among Their Various Uses

The discussion of random geographical distribution applies equally to the distribution of factors of production in limited supply among their various uses. If a shortage exists of all the different products that a factor of production is used to produce, then there is a ready and waiting market for more of each such product. More of each such product can be sold without causing any reduction in its price or profitability, until the shortage of that particular product is totally eliminated. All that it is necessary for producers to do is find a way of getting more of any such product to the market.

In this situation, the allocation of a factor of production among its various uses becomes utterly chaotic. A factor of production can be withdrawn from the production of any of its products and added on to the production of any other of its products. The price and profitability of the product in reduced supply cannot rise to halt the decrease in supply. The price and profitability of the product in expanded supply cannot fall to stop the increase in supply, until its particular shortage has been totally eliminated.

Again, the oil shortage provides an excellent illustration of the principle. During the oil shortage there was a shortage of all the different oil products: gasoline, heating oil, jet fuel, propane, kerosene, etc. In these circumstances, it essentially ceased to matter to the oil refineries what they produced. If they took a million barrels of crude oil away from the production of gasoline and added it on to the production of heating oil, they could sell the additional heating oil with absolutely no reduction in its price or profitability, because of the shortage of heating oil. And if they did the reverse—if they took a million barrels of crude oil away from the production of heating oil and added it on to the production of gasoline—they could sell the additional gasoline with absolutely no reduction in its price or profitability, because of the shortage of gasoline. Of course, the price and profitability of the product being cut back could not rise—its price was controlled.

The result was that the production of the various oil

products was made random and chaotic. Practically any combination of products was possible. The only limits were those set by the possible total elimination of particular shortages. For example, gasoline production might have been expanded at the expense of heating oil production up to the point where the gasoline shortage came to an end and any further increase in the supply of gasoline would have forced a reduction in its price. At that point, the whole burden of the combined shortage of gasoline and heating oil would have been borne by heating oil. Or, of course, the reverse could have occurred. Heating oil production might have been expanded at the expense of gasoline production up to the point of eliminating the shortage of heating oil and throwing the whole burden of the combined shortage on gasoline production.

Either of these extremes or any intermediate situation was possible, and not just with regard to gasoline and heating oil, of course, but with regard to all oil products. Any of them might have been produced up to the point of no shortage, or any of them might have suffered a drastic reduction in production. Moreover, the position of the various products could suddenly have been reversed—with the relatively abundant ones suddenly becoming short, and the short ones suddenly becoming relatively abundant. Furthermore, if we add in the existence of geographical chaos, the situation could have been different in different parts of the country at the same time—for example, a severe shortage of gasoline and little or no shortage of heating oil in New Jersey and just the opposite in Connecticut.

The chaos that existed during the oil shortage fully accords with this description. And the same kind of random, accidental factors determined what actually did occur as in the case of geographical chaos. For example, the time of the year when the controls happened to be imposed played an important role in determining to what extent the overall oil shortage fell on heating oil or on gasoline. Controls imposed in the summertime tend to cause relatively abundant supplies of gasoline and a severe shortage of heating oil. This is because they impose the freeze at a time when the price of gasoline is high in relation to the price of heating oil, with the result that it is profitable to go on producing gasoline and not profitable to step up the production of heating oil even after the summer ends.

Conversely, controls imposed in the wintertime tend to cause a relatively abundant production of heating oil and a severe shortage of gasoline. Since our controls were originally imposed in August of 1971, it is not surprising that the first major petroleum product to develop a shortage was heating oil, which occurred in the late winter and early spring of 1973, months before the Arab embargo. (Subsequently, the government took special steps to assure the supply of heating oil, and thereafter the burden of the oil shortage fell more heavily on gasoline and the other petroleum products.)

As in the case of geographical chaos, bureaucratic adjustments in the controls can cause sudden major shifts in supply among the various products of a factor of production. By making the production of any one particular product of a factor of production somewhat more profitable than the others, for example, the officials administering the controls can bring about a sudden expansion in its production up to the point of totally eliminating its particular shortage, while, of course, correspondingly worsening the shortages of other products of the factor in an unpredictable way. And if they suddenly reduce the profitability of a particular item, they can make the supply of it disappear and other items show up in its place, again, in an unpredictable way.

Anything that produces even slight changes in the relative profitability of the various products of a factor of production, whether a bureaucratic change in the price-control regulations, or anything else, can produce major changes in supply when shortages exist. As just one example, imagine that the uncontrolled price of some of the chemical additives used to make gasoline changed. If the prices of these chemicals rose, the profitability of gasoline might suddenly be reduced below that of other oil products. Since the price of gasoline could not rise as its supply was cut back, while the price of other oil products would not fall as their supply was increased, it would now pay to shift as much crude oil as possible away from gasoline production to the production of all other oil products. Conversely, if the price of the chemical additives fell instead of rose, then gasoline production would suddenly become more profitable, and a massive increase in gasoline production would probably occur at the expense of the production of all other oil products.

A principle that emerges from this discussion is that *price controls and shortages create tremendous instability in supply.* The supply of everything subjected to controls is subject to sudden, massive, and unpredictable shortages.

Hoarding

The chaos in supply caused by controls has a further important consequence, one that I have already noted in other connections, but which deserves some additional elaboration and stress here. This is the fact that shortages and the fear of shortages cause hoarding. If a person cannot count on being able to buy something when he wants it, because, overnight, it may disappear from the market, then he had better try to buy it when he can, so that he will have it available when he needs it. The effect of this is that price controls and shortages artificially expand the demand for everything even more. Price controls not only expand the quantity of goods demanded by virtue of artificially holding down prices, but also by virtue of creating shortages and then the need to hoard, to cope with the shortages. The demand price controls create for the purpose of hoarding is a demand that does not exist even potentially in a free market—i.e., it is not even a submarginal demand—because it would serve no purpose whatever in a free market. But under price controls and shortages, hoarding becomes a matter of survival and greatly adds to demand.

The effect of this is that the irrationality of price controls goes beyond even what I have previously described. In the second part of the last chapter, I explained how price controls prevent the most vital and urgent employments of a factor of production from outbidding its most marginal employments. I explained, for example, how they prevented truckers delivering food supplies from outbidding housewives wanting gasoline for marginal shopping trips; how they prevented the operators of oil rigs needing oil products from outbidding homeowners seeking oil to heat their garages. Actually, the situation is even worse. Under price controls, the most vital and urgent employments of a factor of production are prevented from outbidding not only its most marginal employments, but, from the standpoint of a free economy, employments that could not even qualify as submarginal; that is, employments for hoarding purposes.

Under price controls and shortages it is entirely possible for people to be unable to get to work, to be without food, or even to freeze to death, not only because they are prohibited from outbidding the marginal employments of the oil, or whatever factor of production it may be, but because products are being hoarded by other people in fear of this very kind of possibility happening to them. The consequence is that price controls and shortages not only sacrifice men's well-being and very lives to the unearned, fleeting gains of other men, but, very largely, to a hoarding demand created by price controls themselves. In effect, men are sacrificed to the controls themselves.

6. Shortages and the Spillover of Demand

The effect of a shortage of any particular commodity is to cause the unsatisfied demand for that commodity to spill over and add to the demand for other commodities.

We have already had a glimpse of this principle earlier in this chapter, in our discussion of people ending up having to buy more expensive models of goods as the result of the unavailability of less expensive models. For example, as we saw, the man who wants a sixteen-inch black-and-white television set may end up having to buy a nineteen-inch color set, because there is a shortage of the sixteen-inch sets and he cannot obtain one; so he settles for this substitute.

This principle applies not only to close mutual substitutes, such as different models of the same good, but also to goods which are totally dissimilar in their nature and function. For example, if our prospective buyer of a television set cannot find any model television set that satisfies him, he will eventually decide to buy some other kind of good. He may decide to buy a suit or to apply the sum he wanted to spend for a television set to the purchase of a better car or to any one of thousands of things or combinations of things. In this way, the money that price controls prevent from being spent in one channel is diverted to another channel.

This diversion of demand, it should be realized, takes place almost immediately. For example, even if our prospective television set buyer decides to add the price of the set to his savings, in the hope of being able to find the set later on, still, the demand for other things will rise almost immediately. This is because he will almost certainly deposit his savings in a bank, which will lend them out. As a result, a borrower will be put in the position of being able to buy something with the money our man had wanted to use for a television set.

The effect of this diversion or spillover of demand depends on whether or not price controls apply to the second-choice goods that people turn to. If these goods too are controlled, then the effect tends to be a worsening of the shortages of these goods. I will not elaborate on this consequence, however, until we begin our discussion of universal price controls, in the next part of this chapter. If price controls do not apply to the second-choice goods, then the effect of the spillover of demand is simply to drive the prices of uncontrolled goods still higher and to make the profitability of their production in comparison to that of the controlled goods still greater.

This principle concerning the effects of the spillover of demand in a partially price-controlled economy has a number of important implications.

Why Partial Price Controls Are Contrary to Purpose

First, the principle shows that "selective" or partial price controls, that is, price controls imposed merely on certain goods only, are contrary to any rational purpose the government might have in imposing them.[31] The government imposes controls on the goods which it believes are the most vital. It imposes the controls because it believes they will enable people to obtain these goods who otherwise could not have obtained them because of too high a price. The government leaves uncontrolled those goods whose production it considers to be relatively unimportant. The effect of this policy, however, is to destroy the production of the very goods the government regards as vital, while encouraging the production of the goods it considers unimportant. This occurs because the price controls restrict or altogether destroy the profitability of producing the controlled goods. At the same time, the shortages the price controls create cause demand to spill over into the markets for the uncontrolled goods and thereby make their production still more profitable.

For example, the government might control the price of milk on the grounds that it is a vital necessity, and leave uncontrolled the price of ice cream and soft drinks on the grounds that they are trivial "luxuries," not worthy of its attention. The effect of this policy is to reduce the profitability of milk production in comparison with these and all other uncontrolled goods. As a result, it brings about a fall in the production of milk; this, together with the increase in the quantity demanded of milk resulting from its too low price, creates a shortage of milk. The effect of the shortage of milk is to cause the unsatisfied demand for milk to spill over into the markets for uncontrolled goods, including, of course, ice cream and soft drinks, whose relative profitability is then further enhanced.[32] The effect of the government's action, therefore, is to destroy the production of milk, which it regards as necessary and vital and wants people to have, and to promote the production of such goods as ice cream and soft drinks, which it considers unimportant.

Clearly, it would be less illogical if the government imposed controls on the things it considered unimportant and whose production it did not mind seeing destroyed, and left free the production of goods it considered vital. Nevertheless, governments do not do this, and again and again—in the early stages of a war, for example—they impose controls that undermine the production of necessities, while the so-called ash-tray industries and the night clubs and the cabarets flourish. For temporarily at least, these lines of business are left uncontrolled, on the grounds of being unimportant, and are therefore able to benefit from the spillover of demand caused by the shortages of necessities.

How Price Controls Actually Raise Prices

A second implication of the principle that shortages cause a spillover of demand and a rise in the prices of uncontrolled goods is that selective or partial controls cannot hold down the general price level. The expectation that they can is based on the erroneous belief that the problem of inflation consists in the rise of this or that group of prices and can be solved by prohibiting a particular group of prices from rising. The fact is that such controls hold down the prices of some goods only by making the prices of other goods rise all the more.

Indeed, the effect of partial price controls is actually to *raise* the general price level. Partial controls have this effect, because while they leave aggregate demand and spending unchanged, they reduce the efficiency of production and, therefore, the aggregate amount of production and thus supply. We have seen that they can destroy vital industries, such as the electric power industry and the oil industry, on which the production of all other industries depends. In the course of destroying an industry, they reduce the quality of its products and the service associated with them, thereby raising maintenance and replacement costs for the buyers of the products. We saw also that controls cause resort to unnecessarily expensive models and methods of production, and lead to a system of cost-plus pricing. And we have seen that they create utter chaos in the geographical distribution of the products of a controlled industry and in the combination of the various products that such an industry produces; this disrupts all subsequent production that depends on these industries, and thus reduces aggregate supply. In all these ways, therefore, partial price controls actually raise the general price level.

The Absurdity of the Claim That Price Controls "Save Money"

A third, closely related implication is that the supporters of price controls are badly mistaken in claiming that any particular price control "saves people money," and in arguing that the repeal of any given control will "cost" people this or that amount of money. This may be true in the short run for some individuals, who are lucky enough to obtain the goods they desire at below-market prices. But it is never true in the aggregate. In the aggregate, a control saves people money only in the sense of making them spend less for the controlled goods. At the same time, it makes them spend more for the uncontrolled goods. In the aggregate, they do not spend any less money. They do, however, receive fewer goods. Clearly, whatever saving or gain some buyers may have by virtue of controls is always at the expense of a greater loss to other buyers.

Indeed, in view of the fact that controls tend to destroy the controlled industries, the only kind of long-run "saving" they can achieve for anyone, including the people who might temporarily gain from them, is a rather bizarre one. It consists in preventing a person from spending the money he wants to spend for the goods he wants to buy. In this sense, the drivers who could not obtain gasoline at the controlled prices "saved money" on gasoline. Instead of having the gasoline they desperately wanted and which they valued far above the controlled price, they had money left over to spend on other things which they wanted much less. Such savings are obviously absurd and contrary to purpose. They are comparable to making a person save money by not buying food or medicine, or anything he values more, so that the may have money for something he values less—if he is alive to spend it. Yet this is the only kind of "saving" that controls can achieve in the long run, and it is the only kind of saving they achieve right from the very beginning for whoever suffers from the shortages they create.

As will be shown in the next part of this chapter, total or universal controls—price controls on all goods—may be said to "save people money" in an even more bizarre way than partial controls. By virtue of creating a shortage of everything, and thus making money simply unspendable, universal controls enable people to save money in the sense of having it available for such purposes as papering their walls or lighting their fires with it. And as production declines under universal controls, and the volume of spending that can take place at the controlled prices accordingly drops further, the money that people "save" in this absurd way grows greater.

It follows from our discussion that in the aggregate the repeal of price controls would not cost people anything. If universal controls exist and are repealed, people would spend more money, but this greater spending would represent an exchange of otherwise useless paper for valuable goods, whose production would be greatly increased as a result of the repeal of the controls. If partial controls exist and are repealed, then the effect is a shift in the pattern of spending away from the previously uncontrolled goods to the newly uncontrolled goods. The prices of the former would tend to drop while the prices of the latter would tend to rise. But since the effect of the repeal is an increase in total production and supply, the general price level must tend to fall. For the same total demand with a larger total supply means a lower price level. The repeal of any partial control, therefore, must always tend to *reduce* the general price level by virtue of its effect of increasing production. It is only the repeal of a control, therefore, not the imposition of a control, that can truly be said to save people money.

Applications to Rent Controls

The principle that shortages cause the unsatisfied demand for controlled goods to spill over into the market for uncontrolled goods and to raise their prices has special application to rent controls as they have existed in places like New York City over most of the period in which they have been in force.

Such rent controls are partial price controls in an even more restricted sense than we have considered up to now.

They are partial controls not only in the sense that they apply only to specific goods, but also in the further sense that they apply only to part of the supply even of these goods. For example, in New York City all housing completed since January 1974 is totally exempt from rent controls. Prior to August 1971, all housing completed since February 1947 had been free of controls, and certain still earlier housing, considered "luxury housing," had also been exempted. (All this previously uncontrolled housing is now subjected to controls in the form of government limitations on annual rent increases.) Perhaps even more important has been the fact that while rents have been controlled in New York City, they have generally been uncontrolled in the surrounding suburban counties and in most of the rest of the country. Nor have the prices of houses been controlled anywhere.

As a result of the fact that rent control has had only partial application, large numbers of people in New York City have been able to escape its effects. Those who could afford them have been able to find uncontrolled apartments or, in many cases, buy houses, co-ops, or condominiums in the city. Those who could not afford to live in New York City have been able to find places to live outside the city.

i. Internal Passports and Compulsory Assignment of Boarders

Before considering further the effects of the diversion of demand caused by partial rent controls, it will be well to project the consequences of controls applied to all of these alternatives. In other words, let us project the consequences of a fully price-controlled housing market on a regional and national scale. We will see that some of the potentially most disastrous effects of rent controls have been avoided because of the relatively limited scope of the controls.

If the entire housing market were controlled, housing would be artificially cheap in all of its forms and everywhere. The quantity demanded of all types of housing would therefore exceed the supply. This would be true all across the country. As a result, there would be a shortage of living space and no way around it. People would simply be unable to find space in New York City, and they would be unable to find it in the surrounding counties or anywhere else in the country. There would be people desperate for living space with absolutely no way to obtain it. They would need apartments and houses but with no better chance of finding them than they had of finding gasoline at the height of the gasoline shortage.

What might happen in such circumstances? The answer is two things worth thinking about: *The government would contemplate the restriction of the internal freedom of migration. And it would contemplate the assignment of boarders to private homes and apartments.*

As to the first point, it would soon become obvious that in the circumstances of a pervasive housing shortage, the influx of additional people into any area would have the effect of making the local housing shortage worse. Each area would therefore become anxious to keep out as many new arrivals as possible on the grounds of their worsening the local housing shortage. Each area would try to set up barriers to in-migration and try to prevail upon the federal government to keep people where they were. As to the second point, the argument would be made that people cannot be left to sleep in the streets and that in the "housing emergency," or whatever it might be called, it was necessary for those fortunate enough to have space, to share it with those not fortunate enough to have space.

This state of affairs has actually existed in many countries. For example, it was no accident, but precisely for reasons such as these, that the government of Soviet Russia deliberately restricted the number of inhabitants of its various cities and controlled the internal movement of the Russian population through a system of internal passports.[33] The Communist sympathizers and apologists who boasted about how inexpensive housing was in the Communist countries—extremely limited and wretched housing, it should be noted—did not realize that precisely this was what created a nationwide housing shortage in those countries. They did not realize that the low rents they were so proud of virtually necessitated restrictions on the internal movement of people—even apart from all other factors working in the same direction in the Communist countries. In addition, of course, as the result of the low rents and the consequent housing shortage, families could not take their privacy for granted in the Communist countries. Millions of families were forced to live in communal apartments. Often, two families had to share a single room, separated from each other only by a curtain—just as depicted in the movie *Ninotchka.*

Fortunately, in the areas of the United States where rent control has existed, such as New York City, people have been able to escape such disastrous effects, because the controls have been confined to a very limited part of the overall housing market. But, even so, the consequences have been severe.

ii. How Rent Controls Raise Rents

Let us pass over quickly the consequences of partial rent controls as they affect the part of the housing supply subjected to them, and then focus on the consequences as they affect the part of the housing supply that is left free of controls.

We know that controls create a shortage of the housing to which they apply because people scramble for apart-

ments at artificially low rents. We know that this fact, coupled with the lack of capital on the part of landlords that results from restricted profits, causes the quality of such housing to decline, in the process unleashing a spiral of mutually reinforcing hatreds between tenants and landlords. Ultimately, as the costs of operating buildings continue to rise, because of inflation, the effect of rent control is to cause widespread abandonments of buildings by their owners. Such abandonments have been going on for many years in New York City. As a result of rent control, there are growing areas in New York City—in the South Bronx, for example—that have been reduced to the status of a primitive village, with people living without electricity and having to fetch their water from public fire hydrants. (Such facts are reported every so often in *The New York Times.*)

As for the uncontrolled rental housing, we know that the shortage of rental housing that is under controls causes the unsatisfied demand for such housing to spill over and enlarge the demand for uncontrolled rental housing. This phenomenon and its consequences must be examined more closely.

The controls on rents bring space within the reach of people who otherwise could not have afforded it. That is their purpose and that is what they achieve. But to whatever extent the controls make it possible for some people to obtain space who otherwise could not have obtained it, they simultaneously *reduce* the space that is available for other people, who could have afforded to rent that space in a free market. These other people, of course, must then make their demand for space in a market that is less well supplied. The result is that rents on uncontrolled space in the area rise.

As far as the market is concerned, in addition to causing a diversion of the demand for housing, *partial rent controls are equivalent to a reduction in the supply of rental housing.* They take part of the rental housing stock off the market by giving it to people who could not afford the market rents. This leaves less of a supply of rental housing for the market and, consequently, increases rents on the diminished supply that is available for the market.

Perhaps the best and clearest way to understand these points is to think once again of the conditions of an auction. So imagine that an auctioneer is holding up two units of the same good. Imagine further that there are three bidders for these units. One bidder, imagine, is willing to bid a maximum of $300 for one of these units, if necessary. Another bidder is willing to go as high as $200, if necessary. The third bidder, assume, can afford to bid no more than $100—that is his maximum limit in the bidding. In a free market, the price at which these two units will be sold will be above $100 and below $200.

The price will have to be above $100 to eliminate the weakest bidder. It will have to be below $200, in order to find buyers for both units. It will tend to be the same for both buyers because there is usually no way to discriminate between them. Let's assume the actual price turns out to be $150: too high for the weakest bidder, yet low enough for both of the other bidders.

The weakest bidder has been excluded from this market. What must happen if we begin to feel sorry for him? Suppose people begin to feel so sorry for him that they get a law passed that orders the auctioneer to give him one of the units of the supply at a price he can afford—say, $50. In that case, he gets his unit at $50. But now, as a result of this, instead of the auctioneer having two units to auction off in the market, he has only one; the supply available for the market has fallen. And this one unit will now have to sell at a price somewhere above *$200* and below $300—say, $250. It has to be high enough now to eliminate *the middle bidder* instead of the weakest bidder. All that has happened is that one party has gotten part of the supply at an artificially low price and has caused the price on the remaining supply to go high enough to eliminate another party. The party eliminated could have afforded the market price if it were determined by the full available supply. But he cannot afford the market price *as determined by the artificially reduced supply*. Deprived of the supply that would have been available to him in a free market, his demand is diverted into a competition with the other remaining bidder, which competition, in the nature of the case, he must lose.

This auction example does not differ in any essential respect from the case of partial rent controls. Partial rent controls give part of the supply of housing to some people at below-market rents. To whatever extent these people could not have afforded as much space in a free market as they obtain under rent control, they leave that much less space available in the uncontrolled market. Consequently, rents in the uncontrolled market must rise that much higher—in order to level down the quantity demanded to equality with the reduced supply that is left for the market. For example, if the total rental housing supply in a city is one million rooms, and rent control results in giving half of those rooms to people who could not have afforded them at free-market rents, then rent control correspondingly deprives other people of those rooms who could have afforded them at free-market rents. In the process it makes the rents on the uncontrolled half-million rooms rise so high that that diminished number of rooms is all that people will be willing and able to rent in the uncontrolled segment of the market. In other words, rent control makes the open-market rents balance demand and supply at a supply of half a million rooms instead of a million rooms. People are

eliminated from the market who could have afforded market rents *as determined by the full supply of rental housing*. These people cannot afford market rents *as determined by the artificially reduced supply of rental housing that results from rent control*. Just as in the auction example, when deprived of the supply that would have been available to them in a free market, their unsatisfied demand is made to spill over into a competition with buyers who are able to outbid them for the reduced supply.

Obviously, the larger is the proportion of the housing stock under rent control, the higher must be the rents on the correspondingly diminished supply that remains for the open market. If this principle is understood, it should not be surprising that, for example, New York City, which has the largest proportion of rental housing under controls of any major city in the United States, also has, for that very reason, the highest rents in the nation on housing that is available for the open market.

The fact that partial rent controls act to raise rents on the uncontrolled part of the housing supply is reinforced by the fact that they increase the *costs* of providing rental housing. This occurs because the existence of controls on some housing today implies that the housing that is presently free of controls may later on be brought under controls. The threat of being brought under rent controls in the future makes it necessary for landlords of presently uncontrolled buildings to recover their investments more rapidly. For example, instead of looking forward to recovering their investments over a fifty-year period, say, the threat of rent control being imposed may make them want to recover their investments over a ten-year period, or even a five-year period, to be safe. This represents a great jump in the costs of providing new rental housing, and helps to explain why high rents on uncontrolled buildings do not result in corresponding new construction.

Insofar as rent control comes to be regarded as a regular institution, to be imposed at any future time the government may desire, the effect is to make today's tenants in uncontrolled buildings pay for the spoils of tomorrow's prospective beneficiaries of rent control. This artificial increase in the costs of new housing, it should be realized, is also one of the reasons why today's so-called luxury housing is often inferior in many respects to housing constructed in earlier decades. The reason is that it is not genuine luxury housing, but rather cheap housing that must be rented at luxury rates in order to offset the prospective losses that are expected to be caused by rent controls in the future.

Ironically, even if, however unlikely, rent controls were not expected to be extended to housing that is currently free of them—indeed, if they were expected ultimately to be repealed—partial rent controls would still prevent the premium rents on uncontrolled housing from being eliminated by means of the construction of new housing. In a free market, it is true, rents tend to equal the costs of constructing and maintaining housing plus only as much profit as is required to yield the going rate of profit. Under partial rent controls, however, the rents on the uncontrolled portion of the market tend permanently to exceed this level, and exceed it the more, the larger is the proportion of the housing stock under controls. It is not only that the larger the portion of the housing stock under controls, the smaller is the supply remaining for the market, which is sufficient reason for the rents on the uncontrolled supply to be correspondingly high. But also the premium profits which such rents might be thought to offer for the construction of new housing are largely nullified by the consequences of the potential repeal of rent control no less than by the prospect of the extension of rent control. Consider. If the supply of uncontrolled housing were increased to the point that the rents on such housing were no higher than costs plus an allowance for the going rate of profit, the danger would exist that if rent controls were ever repealed, rents in the open market would then be driven below cost plus the going rate of profit. For the repeal of rent controls would throw back on the market all of the housing diverted from the market to tenants paying below-market rents. If open-market rents were already no more than equal to cost plus the going rate of profit, this increase in the supply available for the market would drive them below that point.

Thus, so long as they are in force, partial rent controls raise rents on uncontrolled housing, whether landlords expect them to be extended to the uncontrolled housing or to be removed from the housing to which they presently apply.

It follows from the preceding discussion that when partial rent controls are repealed, not only do rents in the open market fall, but the construction of new housing becomes much more profitable at any given level of open-market rents. For the repeal of the partial controls reduces the threat of new housing later on being subjected to controls, and thus extends the period of time over which investments in housing can be recovered. At the same time, the repeal eliminates any fear hanging over the market concerning the possible adverse effects of repeal on profitability. Thus, unless the decline in open market rents is quite drastic, the effect of the repeal of partial rent controls is not only lower open-market rents, but also a surge in the construction of new housing at those lower rents.

The repeal of partial rent controls and the decline in

open market rents that it brings is also accompanied by further substantial reductions in the costs of providing new rental housing, apart from that of a longer period of depreciation and correspondingly smaller annual depreciation charges. The decline in open-market rents on newly constructed buildings and thus in the market value of such properties is accompanied by a decline in the amount of taxes that such buildings must pay at the prevailing rates of property tax. Further declines in property tax on such buildings can occur by virtue of a fall in property tax *rates,* which is made possible by the rise in rents and property values, and thus property tax collections, in the case of the housing that had previously been controlled.

It is implicit in what I have just said, incidentally, that another of the destructive effects of rent control is a rise in property tax rates. This results from the destruction of the rent-controlled properties' ability to pay rising taxes in pace with inflation. Thus, the rates are increased on the properties left free of controls and on owner-occupied housing. Also, as the property tax declines as a source of revenue, local sales taxes and income taxes are imposed. They too, and all the unpleasantness that accompanies them, must be laid at least in part at the door of rent control.

iii. The Case for the Immediate Repeal of Rent Controls

The fact that partial rent controls increase the rents on uncontrolled housing is not recognized by the general public. The result is that the higher do partial controls drive rents, the more necessary do people believe rent controls to be; the more desperately do they cling to the existing controls and the more eager they are to urge the extension of the controls. They fear that the repeal of the existing controls would raise all rents to the level of the presently uncontrolled rents, and they believe that the uncontrolled rents are enormous because they are not controlled.

Our discussion shows that the best solution to the problems created by rent controls would be the *immediate* and total abolition of rent controls, accompanied by constitutional guarantees against their ever being reimposed. This would both immediately reduce rents in the open market and bring about the greatest and most rapid possible increase in the supply of rental housing.

Calling for the immediate abolition of rent control raises the question of what is to become of many of the people who presently live in rent-controlled apartments and who would have to move if rent control were all at once repealed. (In order to have some term to describe these people, let us refer to them as the "beneficiaries" of rent control—provided it is understood that they are beneficiaries in a short-run sense only, and not genuine beneficiaries.)

Our previous discussion provides the answer to the question of what would happen to these people. In essence, the answer is that *they would simply have to change places with an equally large but generally unrecognized class of victims of rent control.*

Two facts about the immediate repeal of rent control must be kept in mind: not only would it raise rents to the beneficiaries of rent control, but also, as we have seen, it would simultaneously reduce rents in the open market, because the space presently occupied by the beneficiaries of rent control would be added to the supply in the open market.

What would happen in response to these changes in rents is two related sets of developments, the one affecting the beneficiaries of rent control, the other the victims. Let us consider the effects on the beneficiaries first.

In the face of a jump in their rents, some of the beneficiaries of rent control might have to share apartments or even single rooms with other people, in order to economize on rent. Others might have to move in with relatives. Still others might decide to move to remoter areas of the city, where rents were cheaper, or to leave the city altogether. It should be observed that none of the former beneficiaries of rent control would have to sleep in the street as the result of the rise in the rents they had to pay; they would simply have to occupy less space or live in less favorable locations. These points must be stressed, in view of the hysteria that is often evoked in projecting the allegedly dire fate of these people as the result of the repeal of rent control.[34]

Now consider the fact that the apartments vacated by the former beneficiaries of rent control would not remain empty, but would practically all be occupied. For the rents on those apartments, though too costly for the rent-control beneficiaries, would represent a decline in the rents charged in the open market, and would thus come within the reach of new tenants. To use the same figures as in our auction example earlier in this discussion, assume that initially a beneficiary of rent control was paying a controlled rent of $50, while rents in the open market were $250. Now, with the repeal of rent control and the addition of the previously rent-controlled apartments to the supply available in the market, rents in the market fall from $250 to $150. A rent of $150 is too expensive for the former rent-control beneficiaries. But it represents a reduction in rents in the open market and brings apartments within reach of people who could not afford them at the $250-a-month rents caused by partial rent controls.

Let us focus on the new tenants who would occupy the previously controlled apartments. Let us try to figure out who they would be and where they are now. These are people who could afford their own apartments in the city at $150 a month, but not at $250 a month. At $250 a month, they find it necessary to share apartments (or single rooms), to live with relatives, or to live in remote areas of the city or out of town altogether. In other words, they find it necessary to do all of the things the beneficiaries of rent control might have to do if rent control were repealed. Perhaps some readers of this book may know some of these victims of rent control, though they probably have not thought of them in that light before. The victims are young people who must live with roommates, young couples who must live with in-laws, families that cannot afford to live in the city, and so on. These people represent the class of rent-control victims, though they are almost all unaware of that fact and see no connection between rent controls and their own plight. They are fully as numerous as the class of rent-control beneficiaries, and they are already suffering the same kind of hardships as the rent-control beneficiaries would suffer if rent control were repealed.

In fact, these victims of rent control are suffering vastly *more* hardship than the beneficiaries of rent control would suffer. For if rent control were repealed, the total supply of housing would quickly begin to expand and its quality would improve. In places like New York City, the supply would increase almost overnight, because the abandonment of buildings would cease, and many previously abandoned buildings would be restored. The hardship of the former beneficiaries of rent control would be temporary, because rental housing would once again become an expanding, progressing industry. As time went on, more and more of the former beneficiaries of rent control would be better off than they ever could have been under rent control. In the long run, everyone would be better off. The real answer to the question of what would happen to the present beneficiaries of rent control if rent control were repealed, therefore, is this: In the short run and at the very worst, they would suffer no more, and probably less, than what the victims of rent control have already been suffering for many years. In the long run, what would happen to them is simply more and better housing.

Furthermore, it should be stressed that in the long run, the very idea of someone being a beneficiary of rent control is a self-contradiction. The gains of the beneficiaries of rent control are made possible by the consumption of their landlords' capital. The tenant who is able to afford a better car, say, or an extra vacation, because of the artificially low rent he pays, is buying that car or vacation at the expense of part of a new apartment building somewhere, and ultimately he is buying it at the expense of the upkeep of the very building in which he lives. The day comes when he wants to move and finds no decent place to move to, because he and millions of others like him have consumed the equivalent of all the new apartment buildings that should have been built. For they have consumed their landlords' capitals and destroyed the incentives for building. Finally, the day comes when they have consumed the equivalent of a new boiler or wiring system or plumbing system that their own building needs, and their landlord has neither the means nor the incentive to try to replace it. Then they live in cold, in darkness, and without running water. This is already the fate of tens of thousands of people in Harlem and in the South Bronx, as I have indicated. There is no reason why it could not happen to all rent-controlled housing in the country, given further inflation and more time. The only "gains" from rent control are the gains of consuming the capital invested in housing and then being left without housing. People do it because the housing belongs to the landlords, not to them. But in the long run, the loss is theirs, because they are the physical beneficiaries of the stock of housing. When they destroy the property of the landlords, they destroy the property that serves them.

How Repeal of Our Price Controls on Oil Reduced the Price Received by the Arabs

A further application of the principle that partial controls raise prices of goods that are free of controls concerns oil prices. It follows from this principle that our price controls on oil, which were in force from 1971 to 1981, raised the price received by the Arabs, and that their repeal immediately operated to reduce the price received by the Arabs. It follows further that a major effect of repeal was to undo the diversion of billions of dollars a year away from our oil industry to the Arab oil industry. The effect of this, in turn, was an expansion in the American oil industry and a still further drop in the world price of oil received by the Arabs. In other words, it follows that the dramatic decline in the world price of oil experienced in the 1980s can be directly traced to the repeal of price controls on oil in the United States.

In 1980, domestically produced crude oil in the United States was controlled at an average price of approximately $10 per barrel. Imported crude oil was uncontrolled and sold at about $34 per barrel, which was the price the Arabs received. Since the spring of 1974, the prices of the various oil products produced in the United States, such as gasoline, heating oil, and so forth, had been controlled on the basis of the weighted average of the uncontrolled price of imported oil and the controlled price of domestically produced oil. Since about half of our crude oil was imported and half was domestically

produced in 1980, the prices of oil products were set on the basis of an average cost of crude oil of approximately $22 per barrel. Roughly speaking, the prices of oil products were set high enough to cover not only this weighted average cost of crude oil, but all the other costs of producing and distributing oil products and a more or less competitive rate of profit on the capital invested in refining and distribution. Such product prices did not differ radically from prices that would have existed had the free market price of crude oil been $22 per barrel.

In order to see how this arrangement benefitted the Arabs and how its repeal brought back billions of dollars a year to our oil industry that had been diverted to their oil industry by price controls, all we have to do is think through the consequences of repealing our controls. Following repeal of our controls, the price of domestically produced oil immediately had to rise above $10 a barrel. But the effect also had to be that the price of imported oil, and, therefore, the price received by the Arabs, fell below $34 a barrel. To understand just why, imagine for the moment that the price of domestically produced oil simply rose all the way to $34—the same price as the Arabs had been receiving. If that happened, the cost of producing oil products would have had to be based on an average price of $34 a barrel of crude oil rather than on the previous average of $22 a barrel. The prices of oil products would therefore have had to be raised correspondingly. But observe. At such higher prices, the quantity of oil products that could be sold would have been less, and, therefore, the quantity of crude oil that could be sold would also have been less. The only way to counteract this loss in sales would be if the prices of oil products did not rise by so much. The only way that that was possible was if the average price of crude oil did not rise by so much. But this implied that the price received by the Arabs actually had to *fall*. For in a free market our oil must sell for just as much as theirs; yet, we have just seen that their price of $34 was too high for an *average* cost of crude oil—it would significantly have reduced the quantity of oil products and thus of crude oil that could be sold. Thus, our price could not have met theirs at $34 a barrel. Our price and their price had to come together at some lower average figure.

Observe further. In order for the *same* quantity of crude oil to be sold in this country as was sold prior to the repeal of price controls, it would have been necessary for the Arabs' price to meet ours *at $22 a barrel—the previous average price of crude oil*. For any higher price than $22 required a rise in the price of oil products, which had to reduce the quantity of oil products that could be sold in this country and therefore the quantity of crude oil that could be sold in this country.

Indeed, one may raise the question of why the effect

of repeal was not actually to leave the price of oil products unchanged in the United States and simply reduce the price of Arab crude oil and raise the price of our crude oil to the previous average price of $22. The reason these results did not occur was because one of the effects of decontrol was a reduction in *oil imports* into the United States. The price of $34 for imported oil prevailed throughout most of the world. The price of imported oil could not fall to $22 here while it was any higher elsewhere. What happened was that as the price of imported oil fell in this country, in the direction of $22, less of it was sent here and more of it was sent to other markets. The result was that the United States reduced its import of oil and the price of imported oil settled at an amount above $22. For a time, bolstered by cutbacks in their own production, the Arabs were able to maintain the world price at $29 per barrel.

But subsequently, in the face of the pressure of growing supplies of crude oil produced in the United States, the world price of oil collapsed, despite all efforts of the Arab-led OPEC cartel to maintain it.

Thus, temporarily, the consequence of repeal was a rise in the average price of crude oil in the United States and a rise in the price of petroleum products in the United States. But the rise in price to American consumers was much less than the rise in price to American producers; much of the rise in price received by our oil companies was financed by a fall in the price received by the Arabs and other foreign suppliers. For example, when the price of crude oil temporarily settled at $29 per barrel, the cost base of oil products for American consumers was increased by $7 per barrel (from $22 to $29), while the price received by our oil companies was increased by $19 per barrel (from $10 to $29). The rise in price received by our oil companies was financed in part by a $5 drop in the price received by the Arabs and the other foreign suppliers (from $34 to $29).[35]

Furthermore, as shown, this rise in domestic prices was merely a short-run effect, for oil production in the United States became substantially more profitable. Domestic oil production immediately begin to expand, and as it did so, the world price of oil began to fall sharply. Temporarily it declined to as low as $10. Currently, despite years of continued inflation, the price is approximately $18 per barrel.[36]

The preceding analysis can be presented in simpler, more dramatic terms in the light of the auction example I have used to explain why partial rent controls raise rents on the portion of the supply that remains uncontrolled.[37] Thus, one can conceive of the supply of oil consumed in the United States between 1971 and 1981 (the respective years in which the price control on crude oil was imposed

and finally repealed) as consisting essentially of two units: the half produced in the United States and the half produced outside, by OPEC and other foreign suppliers. The U.S. government compelled the half produced in the United States to be sold at a below-market price and thus more or less considerably to come within the reach of otherwise submarginal buyers, leaving correspondingly less of the supply of domestically produced crude oil available for the market. In effect, it compelled Exxon, Chevron, and Texaco to sell their unit of oil to the submarginal buyer for less than $100, which left only one unit of supply available for the market, namely, the unit produced by Qadafi, the Ayatollah Khomeini, and Saddam Hussein, which unit could then be sold for a price of between $200 and $300. That was the essence of the situation. More precisely, in reducing the supply of American oil that a free market would have made available to American buyers, it forced American citizens into a competition for the remaining supply of oil in the market, a needless competition that many American citizens necessarily lost, and from which America's enemies in the Middle East greatly profited.

As I have indicated, such a policy might have been understandable if the U.S. government had been run by officials in the service of Libya, Iran, and Iraq. What its existence actually demonstrated, of course, was not that our officials were traitors in the service of foreign powers, but that they were men and women who, while intending to serve the American people, were intellectually unqualified to do so and, as a result, wreaked great harm upon them.

Given such incredible ignorance and destructiveness on the part of the U.S. government, it should not be surprising to learn of a further unnecessary tragedy inflicted on many American oil producers when the price control on domestically produced crude oil was finally repealed. Not content with simply repealing its price control and desisting from further acts of destruction against the oil industry, the U.S. Congress, acting on malice and greed, decided to confiscate a major part of the profits of American oil producers that resulted from their ability to receive a higher price of crude oil. In 1981, it enacted the so-called windfall-profits tax on crude oil as an accompaniment of the decontrol of oil prices. This was an act of malice in that its deliberate, overriding purpose was to limit as far as possible the ability of the oil companies to profit from the rise in price—for no other reason than simply that they should not profit. It was also an act of mindless greed insofar as its primary purpose having been accomplished, its subsidiary purpose was the enrichment of the U.S. Treasury without knowledge of, or concern for, the consequences.

The effect of this tax was that instead of billions of dollars of revenue simply being diverted from the Arab oil industry back to the American oil industry, a major portion ended up being diverted to the U.S. Treasury. The effect of this in turn was that the American oil industry lacked an equivalent number of billions of dollars of internally generated funds with which to undertake its expansion. Instead, it had to turn to outside sources of funds and borrow heavily. Then, when the collapse in oil prices came, instead of losing back what would have been previously earned "windfall" profits, American oil producers lost borrowed money. And thus many of them went bankrupt who, in the absence of the windfall-profits tax, would not have gone bankrupt, because they would merely have lost back previously earned profits.

A major consequence of this unnecessary tragedy is that the American oil industry today is smaller and less capable of expansion than it would otherwise have been, and thus less capable of further reducing the price of oil.

PART C

UNIVERSAL PRICE CONTROLS AND THEIR CONSEQUENCES

1. The Tendency Toward Universal Price Controls

Price controls tend to spread until all prices and wages in the economic system are controlled—i.e., partial price controls lead to universal price controls.

Universal price controls existed in Nazi Germany. The equivalent of universal price controls exists under socialism, as for example in the former Soviet Union and its satellites. Universal price controls existed in the United States in World War II. They also existed very briefly under President Nixon, when he imposed a ninety-day freeze on all prices and wages in August 1971. They could easily come into existence again in this country, and this time on a long-term basis, in response to any significant worsening of inflation.

The reason partial price controls lead to universal price controls is their destructiveness. We have already seen how partial price controls destroy the industries to which they apply, while causing the uncontrolled industries to flourish. If the government wants to prevent the destruction of the industries it initially brings under controls, it has only three alternatives: It can repeal its controls on those industries, it can subsidize their losses out of the treasury, or it can control the prices that constitute their costs of production. If the government refuses to repeal its initial controls, and if it is unable or unwilling to pay the necessary subsidies, then its only

alternative is to extend its price controls to the prices that constitute the costs of the industries concerned. But then the same story repeats itself, and the government finds that it must bring under controls the prices that constitute the costs of these industries, too, and so on, with the list of controlled prices steadily lengthening.[38]

For example, consider the case of the oil industry when it was under price controls. The combination of controlled selling prices and rising costs of exploration and development resulting from inflation, meant that the domestic oil industry was progressively being destroyed and was ultimately headed for extinction. In order to prevent these outcomes, the government either had to repeal the price controls on oil (which, fortunately, it did), or subsidize the oil industry to the extent of billions of dollars a year to offset the rise in its costs, or extend its controls to include the prices that constitute the oil industry's costs, such as the price of steel pipeline and the wages of oil field workers. If it had decided to control these prices, then it would have had to go still further. It would have had to extend its price controls not only further backwards, but in every direction. For example, if it had controlled the price of steel pipeline, then it would have had to extend its controls to all other steel products, such as I-beams, steel sheet, steel cans, and so on, as well as to the price of iron ore, coke, the wages of steel workers, and so forth. If it did not, the effect of its price control on steel pipeline would simply have been to make that one steel product less profitable than the others, and so to destroy its production.

Similarly, if the government had controlled the wages of oil field workers, it would have had to control wages in other occupations, into which the oil field workers might have gone, or into which potential oil field workers might have gone. Obviously, the government would quickly have had to seek to control all wages, because all the different occupations are interconnected. Finally, as the government controlled wages and other prices that constitute costs, it would have had to extend its controls forward to whatever remaining products may have previously escaped controls. Otherwise, the controls on costs would merely have served to make such products more profitable and thereby encouraged their production at the expense of the controlled products.

In this way, price controls have the potential to spread through the economic system like a cancer travelling through the human body's lymphatic system. All that it takes for this to occur is for controls to reach the point that the government, while still convinced that the controls are necessary, becomes unable or unwilling either to tolerate their effects or to use subsidies to mitigate their effects, and thus turns to the extension of controls to deal with the problems created by the controls already in force.

2. Universal Price Controls and Universal Shortages

The first point which must be understood concerning universal price controls is that they create universal shortages, in which the shortage of each good compounds the shortage of every other good. Under universal price controls, not only does a shortage exist of each good, but also the excess demand for each good spills over and adds to the excess demand for every other good. As illustration, consider again the case of the man who wants a television set but cannot find one at the controlled price. If television sets are the only controlled good, he can find his second choice, a new suit, say. But now, under universal price controls, the suit will probably be as hard to find as his television set. As a result, he must be prepared to settle for his third choice, or, indeed, for his fourth, fifth, or still lower choice, if it is all that is available to him. Eventually, in fact, he will be willing to settle for *any* good that is of greater physical utility to him than the otherwise useless paper money—that is, he will be willing to settle for virtually anything at all.

It should be realized that paper money is of less physical utility than the least valuable good. It does not even make good wallpaper or provide a good fire. The only reason that people do not rush to trade it in for matches or pins or any other physically more useful commodity is that they expect to be able to obtain still more valuable goods for it later on—perhaps later that day, the next day, the next week, or whenever. Price controls and shortages undermine this expectation. They destroy the desire to hold money and eventually make people willing to accept virtually anything in exchange for it.

In these conditions, our man's unsatisfied demand for a television set is *simultaneously* an unsatisfied demand for a new suit and *simultaneously* an unsatisfied demand for goods of still lower choice—it is an unsatisfied demand for anything and everything. And so it is with the unsatisfied demand of everyone else. Thus, it comes about not only that there is an excess demand in the entire economic system, but also that the whole of it is poised ready to strike at whatever goods may be available from any industry. The excess demand facing each industry comes to be not only the unsatisfied demand of those for whom its products are the first choice with the money in question, but also the unsatisfied demand of those for whom its products are the second, third, fourth, and still lower choices. In this way, the excess demand of the whole system comes to exert its pressure against every point in the system. In addition, this excess demand is everywhere further compounded by an enormous hoarding demand for each good.

This discussion, it should be realized, is an actual *description* of conditions as they existed in Soviet Russia. In Soviet Russia, there was a shortage of *everything*. The only exceptions were goods they managed to produce that were of negative utility, such as pots that ruined the taste of food, or clothes that shrank out of all relation to their original size. Apart from such exceptions, everything was chronically in the same state of shortage as gasoline was in this country in early 1974 and in the spring of 1979. In his book *The Russians,* Hedrick Smith, who for some years was the head of *The New York Times'* Moscow Bureau, tells of waiting lines up to a mile long; and of one, to sign up to buy rugs (a once-a-year event in Moscow), that was comprised of between ten and fifteen thousand people lined up four abreast in the winter snow and that lasted for two solid days and nights. Smith reports that Russian women normally spent fourteen hours a week waiting in line just to buy food. He writes that women normally carried shopping bags called "just-in-case bags"—meaning bags for just in case they happened to find something that was for sale and worth buying. The briefcases that Russian men were generally seen carrying served the same purpose.[39] I cannot resist quoting one passage because it so eloquently describes the condition of a willingness to buy anything:

> Yet despite such ordeals the instinctive reaction of a Russian woman when she sees a queue forming is to get in line immediately—even before she knows what is being sold. Queue-psychology has a magnetism of its own. Again and again, I have been told by Russians that anyone's normal assumption on seeing people up front hurrying to get in line is that there must be something up there worth lining up for. Never mind what it is. Get in line first and ask questions later. You'll find out when you get to the front of the line, or perhaps they'll pass back word before then. A lady lawyer told me she once came upon an enormous line stretching all through the Moskva Department Store, and when she asked those at the end of the line what was on sale, "they said they didn't know or else snarled at me and told me not to interfere. I walked up 20 or 30 yards asking people and no one knew. Finally, I gave up asking."[40]

Shortages of this type come to exist whenever universal price controls are in force for any extended period of time.

Excess Demand and Controlled Incomes

It is necessary to deal with a difficulty that many people have in understanding how excess demand can exist under universal price controls. Many people reason in the following way: The main source of demand for consumers' goods, they say, is incomes, especially wages. But under universal price controls, everybody's wages, interest, dividends, and so on are controlled. Therefore, people ask, how can demand be rising and a problem of excess demand be created?

The answer to this question is that excess demand is created by virtue of an expansion in the quantity of money, and that the limitation of incomes is irrelevant.

In order to understand this point as clearly as possible, consider the case of a hypothetical small economy with $10,000 of total spending, 1,000 units of supply, and a general price level of $10 per unit. Assume that the $10,000 of spending in this economy is the result of $10,000 of incomes. Assume further that when price controls are imposed in this economy, incomes are frozen at a total of $10,000. Nevertheless, demand in this economy can grow progressively more excessive—in the following way. Assume that the government decides to spend $1,000 out of newly created money. The price of what the government buys is controlled at $10 a unit. Consequently, the government buys 100 units of the economy's supply. This leaves 900 units of supply for the citizens. These 900 units are controlled at a price of $10 per unit. This means that the most it is possible for the citizens to spend in buying them is $9,000. Nevertheless, the citizens want to spend $10,000—their incomes. Clearly, the citizens have $1,000 of unspendable income. What has happened is that the government's spending of $1,000 out of newly created money has displaced $1,000 of spending by the citizens and has made $1,000 of the citizens' incomes back up on them as surplus, unspendable funds.

This phenomenon can grow progressively worse from year to year. We have just seen the government spend $1,000 and the citizens spend $9,000. This means that businesses have taken in $10,000 of sales revenues and in the second year are again able to pay out $10,000 of incomes. But now, these $10,000 of incomes are added on to $1,000 of surplus unspendable income from the year before. This year, therefore, the citizens would like to spend $11,000 rather than $10,000. If the government again spends $1,000 out of newly created money, the citizens will again be able to succeed in spending no more than $9,000. Thus, there will now be an excess demand of $2,000, and in the third year it will be $3,000, and so on. In this way, the shortages grow worse from year to year. It is not too long before people are ready to buy anything.

This example, incidentally, helps to show why price controls do not create severe shortages in the very moment they are introduced. When the controls are first imposed, the existing prices are the proper prices. In fact, they may even have been raised somewhat in anticipation of the controls being imposed. It takes time for these prices to become outmoded—both by continuing inflation and by all the other forces acting to bring about changes in supply, demand, and cost. The longer the controls remain in force, the more serious their consequences become, because the more out of line do the controlled prices become in relation to the potential free-market prices that would exist if the controls were repealed.

3. The Destruction of Production Through Shortages

The government's purpose in imposing universal price controls is to assure an adequate rate of profit to the vital industries it initially brings under controls. For this reason it imposes controls on the prices that constitute the production costs of these industries. It extends controls to the selling prices of all other industries in order to restrain their rate of profit in relation to that of the controlled industries.

It should be realized that it is perfectly possible under universal controls for all industries to be guaranteed not only approximately equal rates of profit, but rates of profit that by historical standards are relatively high in nominal terms. This is possible because the government controls all the prices that constitute costs, including wages, which are the fundamental element in costs. Nevertheless, no matter how high the nominal rate of profit the government allows, vital industries are still destroyed, and production is disrupted far more seriously than under partial price controls.

What destroys production under universal controls is the consequences of the shortages they create.

In Part B of the present chapter, we saw a variety of ways in which shortages disrupt production under partial controls. I will briefly recount them because all of them apply under universal controls.[41] (It should be recalled in this recounting, by the way, that anything that acts to raise costs implies a decline in production.[42])

(1) Shortages make buyers impotent and thereby remove the incentives of sellers to provide good quality and service. As a result, quality and service decline and the costs of maintenance and replacement increase.

(2) Shortages of means of production, such as a material, often force sellers to reduce quality and service and make it necessary to resort to more expensive substitute methods of production.

(3) Shortages encourage sellers to concentrate on the production of unnecessarily expensive models as a disguised way of raising prices.

(4) Shortages create a positive incentive to using more expensive methods of production if the government allows the pass-through of higher costs and makes the incurrence of higher costs a source of higher profits.

(5) Shortages result in delays in production.

(6) Shortages cause hoarding and the construction of additional storage facilities.

(7) Shortages cause the waste of time in searching for supplies.

(8) Shortages create chaos in the geographical distribution of a good among local markets—for example, gasoline during the oil shortage.

(9) Shortages create chaos in the distribution of a factor of production among its various uses in production—for example, crude oil in the production of the various oil products.

Under a system of universal price controls and universal shortages, these elements of chaos apply to all industries, instead of just a few industries. In addition, they apply more strongly to each industry than if that industry were the only industry under price controls, or if price controls were confined to it and just a few others.

First of all, the excess demand confronting each industry is far greater than under partial price controls, because it is compounded by the excess demand for all other products, as we have seen. The greater severity of the shortage of a product under universal controls creates correspondingly more severe problems in connection with that product. As just one illustration, consider the case of cotton and cotton products. If the prices of cotton and cotton products were the only controlled prices in the economic system there would be a problem of using too much cotton to produce shirts, say, and not enough to produce other cotton products, or vice versa. Because, similarly to what we saw earlier in this chapter in the case of crude oil, there would be a shortage of each cotton product.[43] Thus more of any one cotton product, such as shirts, could be produced at the expense of the others without reducing its price and profitability, until its particular shortage was totally eliminated. Yet if shirts, cotton, and the other cotton products were the only controlled goods, the increase in shirt production would be limited by the fact that people could spend their money on other goods. Beyond a point, people would be willing to buy additional shirts only at prices that made any further increase in shirt production unprofitable, however low the price of raw cotton might be controlled.

But if *everything* is controlled, and people find no other goods available on which to spend their money than shirts, there is no reason why they would not buy enough shirts to have two or three new ones to wear every day, if there were that many available. People would be willing to go on buying more shirts just so long as extra shirts had a physical utility greater than that of paper money. They would be willing to buy them as a source of cleaning rags, buttons, pins, or whichever, that otherwise might be unobtainable. They would buy them merely to hold as a store of value for the future, because holding them would be better than holding the otherwise unspendable paper money.

The principle that emerges is that under universal controls *it becomes practically impossible to eliminate the shortage even of an individual good by means of expanding its production,* because each good is confronted with the excess demand of the whole economic system.

There is a second reason why the elements of chaos connected with partial controls must apply more strongly under universal controls. This is the fact that *each industry must suffer the consequences of shortages in its capacity as a buyer.* Indeed, it must suffer them in everything it buys. For example, under universal controls, not only does chaos reign for the customers of the oil industry, but the oil industry itself now encounters the same chaos in its own purchases of pipeline, drilling equipment, trucks, tankers, and labor services. Whatever problems the oil industry had before are now intensified. And, of course, in accordance with the principle we just developed, the excess demand confronting the oil industry is radically expanded by the spillover of unsatisfied demand from every other fuel and chemical for which petroleum products could substitute; it is also expanded by the sheer desire of people to own any storable physical good in preference to unspendable paper money.

Not only do universal price controls spread chaos through the whole economic system, and intensify it at every point, but they add a wholly *new dimension* to the chaos, that we have not previously encountered. Namely, *they create chaos in the allocation of capital and labor,* the two elements of production required by every industry. This chaos exists because the shortages of consumers' goods create a ready and waiting employment for more capital and labor in every industry. As a result, the distribution of capital and labor among the various industries is made random. Capital and labor are made to stand in the same relation to all the different industries that we have seen crude oil or raw cotton stand in relation to their respective products. What this means is that capital and labor can be withdrawn from any industry and placed in any other industry, and there is no effect on the rate of profit anywhere. If capital and labor are withdrawn from any industry, price controls prevent prices and profits in that industry from rising. If additional capital and labor are invested in any industry, shortages prevent prices and profits in that industry from falling— all that happens is that the shortage in the industry is reduced. For example, if capital and labor are withdrawn from making paper and transferred to making pots, price controls prevent the price and profitability of paper from rising, while shortages prevent the price and profitability of pots from falling.

The consequence of this state of affairs is that production from industry to industry becomes utterly chaotic.

Not only can any product of crude oil be randomly expanded at the expense of any other product of crude oil, not only can any product of cotton be randomly expanded at the expense of any other product of cotton, but any product anywhere in the economic system can be randomly expanded at the expense of any other product anywhere else in the economic system. The chaos is total.

Let us consider the significance of this. Assume the consumers would prefer to have more shoes and fewer shirts. Under price controls, they cannot bid up the prices of shoes and increase the profitability of shoe production. At the same time, as a result of universal shortages, they will not decrease their purchase of shirts, because they have no alternative use for the money. In fact, in this situation it is perfectly possible that capital and labor could be withdrawn, unchecked, from shoe production, which the consumers want more of, and added on, unchecked, to shirt production, which they want less of—that is, that the *exact opposite* of the consumers' wishes could occur. For if this perverse result did occur, price controls would prevent the price and profitability of shoes from rising to stem the withdrawal of capital and labor from the shoe industry. At the same time, the existence of a shortage would prevent the price and profitability of shirts from falling to stem the inflow of capital and labor into the shirt industry.

Indeed, this perverse result is not only possible, but fully as likely as that the consumers will get the result they want. Under universal price controls, there is no longer any connection between the consumers' preferences and business firms' profits or losses. In an economy in which there are universal shortages, the consumers are ready to buy *anything*. And that makes it possible for businessmen to produce *anything*. I leave it to the reader's imagination to think of what kind of deterioration in quality and service can take place in this kind of situation, and of all the other inefficiencies that can exist.

It should already be clear that the extent to which this perverse process can be carried, of consumers getting goods they want less at the expense of goods they want more, has no limits under universal price controls. No matter how bad the shortage of a particular good becomes as the result of a decrease in its production, price controls prevent its production from becoming more profitable. No matter how much the production of a particular good is increased, its shortage is so severe that practically no amount of additional production will eliminate it, because its shortage reflects the spillover of unsatisfied demand from the whole economic system.

In this way, universal price controls have the effect of flooding people with shirts, while making them go barefoot, or inundating them with shoes, while making them go shirtless; of giving them enormous quantities of writing paper, but no pens or ink, or vice versa; of giving them food, but no clothing, or clothing, but no food; of giving them toothpaste, but no soap, or soap, but no toothpaste; indeed, of giving them any absurd combination of goods. Moreover, at any moment, the positions of the goods can be reversed, with the relatively abundant ones suddenly disappearing, while the ones previously impossible to find suddenly appear in comparative abundance.

These conditions are not a mere theoretical projection. They were the normal, chronic conditions of Soviet Russia ever since the Communist Revolution. There was no connection in Soviet Russia between production and the desires of the consumers, and practically everything produced for the individual consumers in Soviet Russia was, in the words of Hedrick Smith, "simply junk".[44]

This kind of chaos in production is the source of drastic declines in production.

Merely giving consumers unbalanced combinations of goods is itself equivalent to a major decline in production, for it represents just as much of a loss in human well-being. For example, imagine that a dozen shirts represents the same physical volume of production as three new pairs of shoes, in terms of the capital and labor that must be employed to produce them. Suppose further that what a person wants each year is a dozen shirts plus three pairs of shoes. If he ends up having to settle for two dozen shirts and go barefoot, he is much worse off than if he could have gotten eight shirts and two pairs of shoes, or even just four shirts and one pair of shoes. The same overall volume of physical production becomes equivalent to a smaller volume of physical production by virtue of its being improperly proportioned among people's different wants and needs.

However, this kind of chaos in production does not merely cause chaotic combinations of consumers' goods. It also causes chaotic combinations of capital goods. And in so doing, it reduces the economic system's overall physical ability to produce.

An economic system's ability to produce does not depend merely on the quantity of its capital goods, but, no less, on *the proper apportionment of that overall quantity among the various specific types of capital goods*. If, for example, the steel industry is unduly expanded at the expense of the coal industry, say, the economic system's subsequent ability to produce will be impaired: not only the extra steel mills, but part of the *existing* steel mills may be inoperable for lack of fuel. In the same way, if the coal industry is unduly expanded at the expense of the steel industry, not only the new coal mines, but part of the previously existing coal mines may be inoperable because of a lack of steel products such as structural supports and drills. An economy's overall ability to produce must be thought of in terms analogous to the functioning of an organism. It depends on the smooth coordination and adjustment of all of its parts. Like a human body, whose total performance cannot exceed the power of its brain, heart, lungs, or any other vital organ, the overall performance of an economic system cannot exceed the power of any one of a large number of vital industries. If some are unduly expanded at the expense of others, the effect is to reduce the functioning of the whole. Indeed, every malproportion has serious consequences.

Consider the devastating effects on production not only of disproportions among whole major industries, like steel and coal, but of disproportions within the output of individual industries—for example, the production of too many trucks to haul farm products and of not enough tractors to harvest them. Consider the effects on production of disproportions in the production of just a few key products here and there—like ball bearings, lubricants for machinery, spare parts, even ordinary screws, and so on. A shortage of any one of these items, or a shortage of one special type of these items, such as ball bearings of a particular size, must cause a widespread paralysis and the grossest inefficiencies in production. And, of course, improper geographical distribution of these or any other inputs has equally devastating consequences for production; for the mere existence of a thing is of no value if its location prevents the producers who need it from obtaining it. The same is true if anything is unavailable for production because it is being hoarded. These declines, of course, are all further compounded by the declines that result from producers just not having to care any longer about the quality of their products or about economies in producing them.

Again, this chaos is not a mere theoretical projection, but an actual description of the chronic conditions of Soviet Russia. In Soviet Russia, hydroelectric stations were built without generators and without the existence of industries to supply; wheat could not be harvested because the necessary tractors had not been built, or, if they had been built, they lacked spare parts, or were in the wrong place, or quickly became inoperable; factories could not operate because they lacked materials; new buildings and new machines were worthless, because of shoddy construction due to lack of care or lack of the necessary materials.[45]

Now the declines in production resulting from all of these causes tend to be *self-reinforcing and cumulative*. For in the course of production, capital goods are physically consumed; i.e., materials and fuel are used up, and machinery and buildings wear out. If production is to be maintained, the capital goods consumed in production must be replaced. The only source of replacement, however, is production itself; i.e., the capital goods consumed in production in an economic system can be replaced only out of that system's production. But if that production declines sufficiently, because of economic chaos, then it will not be possible to reproduce the capital goods consumed in production. As a result, the stock of capital goods will fall. Once that happens, production must decline further, because it will be carried on with fewer capital goods. If the smaller supply of capital goods is used as inefficiently as was the larger supply, because of continuing chaos in production, it will not be possible to replace the smaller supply of capital goods either. Thus, once again production will decline. This process, of less production causing fewer capital goods causing less production, can go on until the economic system is carried back all the way to the level of barbarism.

To make this process more concrete, just think of the fact that in the course of production such things as steel mills, cement factories, freight cars, and so on are wearing out and must be replaced. The only way to replace them is out of the economy's current production. If that production declines sufficiently, because of economic chaos, then it will not be possible to replace them. The result will be that in the future, production will have to be carried on with fewer steel mills, cement factories, and so on. And then even the smaller number of steel mills, etc., will not be able to be replaced, because, given the continuation of chaos, the output that is obtained from them will be too low.[46]

Special consideration must be given to the shortage of labor that universal price controls create. For the labor shortage introduces a second powerful factor making for a self-reinforcing, cumulative decline in production.

Under universal controls, every industry is eager to employ more labor, because whatever extra products it can produce with more labor will be snapped up by goods-hungry buyers. In addition, the labor shortage is intensified by the declines in efficiency that price controls create, because these declines in efficiency mean that it takes more labor on the average to produce a unit of goods. As a result of the labor shortage, employers are even led to "hoard" labor, that is, keep it on the payroll in idleness or semi-idleness in order to have it available when they need it. This, of course, only intensifies the labor shortage.

What is of special importance is that the labor shortage not only exists because of an excess demand for labor, but it also very soon becomes compounded by a *falling supply* of labor. The supply of labor begins to fall as a result of the shortages of consumers' goods. *These shortages destroy the incentive to work.* As people accumulate surplus, unspendable income, it begins to occur to them that they need not earn money they cannot spend. They lose the incentive to advance, because earning more money is useless to them. They cease to care about being fired, because not only can they immediately find another job if they wish it, but the loss of income they cannot spend does not affect them. They begin to do their jobs badly. They become willing to settle for lower-level, less demanding jobs that pay less. They quit their jobs altogether and live off their forced savings for extended periods before taking another job. All of these things represent a decline in the supply of labor. Of course, they also cause a major decline in production and thus in the supply of consumers' goods. This decline in the supply of consumers' goods resulting from the decline in the supply of labor makes the shortages of consumers' goods still worse and thereby further reduces the incentives to work, which, of course, causes even worse shortages. And so it goes, until in fairly short order production must come to a total halt.

Again, it is worth noting that the economy of Soviet Russia was characterized by a labor shortage, in which factory managers "hoarded" labor in order to be sure of fulfilling their quotas under the official economic plan. The shortages of consumers' goods in Russia also contributed to the labor shortage.[47]

The Prosperity Delusion of Price Controls: The World War II "Boom"

Something that is truly remarkable about universal price controls is that, at least in their earlier stages, they can create a delusion of prosperity, even while production is becoming chaotic and on is the road to collapse. The reason for this is that under universal price controls any businessman can find a ready and eager market for any merchandise, no matter how poorly it is produced. All he has to do is produce something of greater physical utility than paper money. In the process, he can even make large nominal profits, simply by virtue of the government having controlled at an appropriate level the prices that constitute his costs. By the same token, the labor shortage makes it possible for any worker to obtain immediate employment in any occupation for which he is even remotely qualified. To those who confuse going through the motions of production with real production, and who confuse the earning of mere paper money with the acquisition of real, physical wealth, this situation looks like prosperity. What they see is that business is humming, everyone is employed who cares to be, and everyone is making money.

Just this situation characterized the United States during World War II. The combination of massive inflation to pay for the war, and universal price controls to hide

the symptoms of the inflation, quickly produced widespread shortages, including a labor shortage. Most people mistook this situation for prosperity.

Nevertheless, despite a superficial appearance of prosperity, the real standard of living of the American people fell drastically during World War II. It fell to a level far below the worst years of the depression. In the worst years of the depression, three-fourths of the American labor force were employed, and everyone who was working could buy anything he wanted commensurate with his earnings. During World War II, *no one* could buy a new car, a new house, or a new major appliance of any kind: the government prohibited their production altogether. In addition, many of the most common, everyday goods simply became unobtainable or obtainable only with great difficulty—such as chocolate bars, chewing gum, sugar, meat, nylon stockings, gasoline, rubber tires, and so on. The goods that were obtainable badly deteriorated in quality—everyone recognized the difference between what they called "prewar quality" and "wartime quality."

People believed they were prosperous in World War II because they were piling up large amounts of unspendable income—in the form of paper money and government bonds. They confused this accumulation of paper assets with real wealth. Incredibly, most economic statisticians and historians make the same error when they measure the standard of living of World War II by the largely unspendable "national income" of the period.

The controls did not last long enough in this country to wreck the economic system. Their effect was further mitigated by the fact that we entered the war with mass unemployment and a large amount of idle plant capacity. The absorption of these factors into production made it possible to offset much of the wastes and inefficiencies resulting from the controls. They constituted a kind of temporary reserve fund, as it were, out of which much of the costs of the controls were met.

Also, during the war, people were highly motivated by considerations of patriotism, and were not only willing to tolerate the hardships imposed by the war, but actually to work harder and longer. Many of them reasoned that if the soldiers at the front could risk their very lives in the defense of civilization, they could do with fewer goods and put in an extra effort at work. Finally, no one regarded the controls as a permanent institution—everyone looked forward to a quick end to the war and to the opportunity to spend after the war.

Such things, however, can at best only delay the full consequences of universal controls. In the circumstances of the present and of the foreseeable future, moreover, no such mitigating factors are present.

4. Socialism on the Nazi Pattern

In an effort to deal with the chaos it creates through price controls, the government adopts further measures: *it seizes control over production and distribution.*

For example, during the oil shortage of 1973–74 a new government agency—the Federal Energy Administration (now the Department of Energy)—was established. This agency had the power to tell the various oil companies how much of each of the various petroleum products they were to produce and to which industries, firms, and regions they were to distribute those products. Thus, government officials decided how much refining capacity should be devoted to producing gasoline, how much to producing heating oil, jet fuel, propane, kerosene, and so forth. In the process, government officials decided which industries dependent on the various petroleum products would obtain supplies, and to what extent. They decided the distribution of each individual petroleum product among its various uses, such as how much gasoline would go to truckers, how much to bus lines, and how much would be left for passenger automobiles. They decided which firms in each industry would get how much of the product allotted to that industry. For example, in the airline industry, they decided that each airline would get 80 percent of the jet fuel it had consumed in the previous year. They decided which geographical areas would get how much of each product. For example, the decided how much gasoline went to New Jersey and how much to New York. And they were about to decide how much gasoline and heating oil went to each individual consumer—for example, the plan to give every licensed driver over eighteen a fixed monthly ration of gasoline by issuing coupons with the picture of George Washington on them.

In addition, government officials made it their business to look into the methods of production employed by the users of oil products. For example, they began to try to force electric utilities to switch from burning oil to burning coal, in order to reduce oil consumption. (Often, these were the same utilities that only a short time before the same government had forced to convert to oil, under the influence of the ecology movement.) As part of this process, they reduced highway speed limits, which must be viewed as an interference with methods of production insofar as it applies to trucks and buses or any form of travel for business purposes.

All of these further interferences were an unavoidable response to the chaos in the oil industry, given the fact that the government was not prepared to abandon its controls over oil prices. Price controls and shortages had made the output of the oil industry and the subsequent distribution of that output utterly chaotic. The government took control of production and distribution in the oil industry in an effort to deal with this chaos.

Now under a system of universal price controls, such as existed in World War II, the government is led to seize control over the production and distribution of *every* commodity. The government thus comes to decide not only all prices and wages, but how much of each item is produced, by what methods, in what locations, and to whom it is distributed. The government fully controls all the inputs that each firm receives, how it combines those inputs into outputs, and what it does with the outputs.

There is only one appropriate name to describe this state of affairs of full government control over production and distribution. And that is *socialism.* In seizing control over all production and distribution, the government fully socializes the economic system.

The reason the system must be called socialism is because, in fact, *the government exercises all of the powers of ownership.* The meaning of ownership is the power to determine the use and disposal of property. If the government determines what a firm is to produce, in what quantity, by what methods, and to whom it is to sell its output and at what prices, then it is the government that determines the use and disposal of the firm's property. The government, therefore, becomes the real owner of the firm—the de facto owner. The nominal owners recognized by the law—that is, the firm's stockholders (and also the board of directors chosen by the stockholders, and the managers appointed by the board of directors)— are reduced to the status of government functionaries, compelled to carry out the government's orders. The fact that the stockholders may be allowed to continue to draw dividends is irrelevant. The status of these stockholders is essentially no different than if the government had openly nationalized their property and given them government bonds on which they received interest.

This system of de facto socialism, carried out under the outward guise and appearance of capitalism, in which the legal forms of private ownership are maintained, has been aptly characterized by von Mises as socialism on the German or Nazi pattern.[48] The Germans under Ludendorf and Hindenburg in World War I, and later under Hitler, were the foremost practitioners of this type of socialism. (The more familiar variant of socialism, in which the government openly nationalizes the means of production and establishes socialism de jure as well as de facto, von Mises calls socialism on the Russian or Bolshevik pattern, after *its* leading practitioners.

It cannot be emphasized too strongly that Nazi Germany was a socialist country and that the Nazis were right to call themselves National *Socialists*. This is something everyone should know; yet it appears to have been overlooked or ignored by practically all writers but von

Mises. In Nazi Germany, the government controlled all prices and wages and determined what each firm was to produce, in what quantity, by what methods, and to whom it was to turn over its products. There was no fundamental difference between the Nazis and the Communists. While the Communists in Russia wore red shirts and had five-year plans, the Nazis in Germany wore brown shirts and had four-year plans.

There is a further point that must be made about the use of the term "socialism." Socialism means *an economic system based on government ownership of the means of production*. On the basis of this definition, not only must Nazi Germany, a country usually not recognized as socialist, be categorized as socialist, but other countries, usually thought of as *being* socialist, must *not* be categorized as socialist—for example, Great Britain, Sweden, and Israel when they were under the rule of so-called labor governments.

In these three countries, the economic system has always been characterized by private ownership of the means of production—not only de jure, but de facto private ownership. This private ownership, to be sure, has labored under all sorts of restrictions and prohibitions, but still it has been private ownership, and production in these countries has been carried out primarily at the initiative of private owners for the sake of private profit. The philosophy of the ruling political parties of these countries may have been socialism and socialism may have been their ultimate goal, but their actual practice, up to now, has not been socialism. The correct description of these economies is von Mises's expression "hampered market economy," and that description applies to the economy of the United States, too. For the sake of brevity, such an economy can be referred to as a "mixed economy," provided it is understood that what is meant is an economy based on private ownership of the means of production but more or less severely hampered by an extensive list of socialistically motivated acts of government intervention.

In this last connection, it should be realized that the existence of isolated socialized industries, such as the postal service and the railway network, does not warrant characterizing a country as socialist. So long as such industries operate in the context of a market and market prices based on a foundation of private ownership of the means of production and the profit motive, they represent, in effect, merely a blemish on an otherwise capitalist body. The existence of such industries belongs under the heading of socialistically motivated acts of government intervention and properly serves to categorize the economy of a country as a hampered market economy, but not as a socialist economy.[49]

The only truly socialist countries in the world today are Communist China and the other remaining members of the Communist bloc, such as Cuba and North Korea. Perhaps several of the East European countries, the surviving "republics" of the former Soviet Union, and possibly some of the so-called third-world countries should also continue to be classified as socialist. But no other countries are in fact socialist. Indeed, to the extent that growing market activity now exists in virtually all of the East European countries and the various former Soviet Republics, the classification even of these countries as socialist becomes increasingly dubious. More and more, their status appears to be that of primitive market economies, in which economic activity takes place in the absence of clearly defined or legally protected private property rights, but nevertheless on the basis of individual initiative, motivated by private profit. Hopefully, within the next few years, no existing country will warrant being described as socialist. Indeed, it appears that in at least one major province of Communist China, de facto private ownership of the means of production and a market economy more advanced than those of most former members of the Communist bloc, have already come into existence.

Notes

1. The quantity theory of money is elaborated at length on pp. 503–506. The demonstration that it is the only possible valid explanation of a sustained, significant rise in prices occupies the whole of pp. 895–922.

2. See above, p. 152.

3. This equation and its implications are developed and elaborated below, pp. 505–506 and 897.

4. Actually, I will show later that falling supply can practically never be the cause of a sustained significant rise in prices and that at no time can it be the cause of the full *complex* of symptoms that people complain of in discussing inflation, such as the enormously greater number of prices rising compared

with the number of prices falling and the effects on the relationship between debtors and creditors. In addition, I will show that falling supply is itself usually a consequence of rapid inflation. Concerning these points, see below, pp. 897–907.

5. For the explanation of this phenomenon, see below, pp. 519–526.

6. On these points, see below, pp. 895–922, which show conclusively why the quantity theory of money is the only valid explanation of an inflationary rise in prices, and why any element of truth in any alternative explanation of rising prices serves only to confirm the quantity theory of money.

7. Statistics of the money supply are published every Friday in

The New York Times and *The Wall Street Journal.* Historical statistics are available from the Board of Governors of the Federal Reserve System, Washington, D.C. The Federal Reserve Bank of St. Louis regularly publishes data showing the trend of growth in the money supply on a short-term and long-term basis.

8. For a further, related discussion of the effects of price controls on natural gas, see George Reisman, *The Government Against the Economy* (Ottawa, Ill.: Jameson Books, 1979), pp. 130–132.

9. Cf. above, p. 191.

10. On these points, see John Stuart Mill, *Principles of Political Economy,* Ashley ed. (1909; reprint ed., Fairfield, N. J.: Augustus M. Kelley, 1976), pp. 706–709. See also above, p. 192 and pp. 217–218, n. 19

11. For the rebuttal of those fallacies see above, pp. 192–194.

12. *New York Times*, April 28, 1978, pp. 1, D9.

13. The explanation of why inflation reduces or altogether eliminates the real rate of return on capital is provided below, pp. 930–938.

14. Indeed, as previously pointed out, the hysteria of the ecology movement has caused the government of the State of New York to deprive its citizens of the benefit of an actually existing, brand new major atomic power plant—the Shoreham plant on Long Island. See above, pp. 66–67.

15. *New York Times*, January 29, 1977, p. 22.

16. For a discussion of the various ways in which inflation reduces the real rate of profit, see below, pp. 930–937.

17. See below, pp. 931–933. In the case of inventories, there is some relief in that it is possible for businesses to choose to calculate their costs for tax purposes on the basis of the cost of the inventory acquired last rather than first—i.e., the so-called "Lifo" system (last in, first out) rather than the customary "Fifo" system (first in, first out). In the case of fixed assets, however, there is no such palliative.

18. See Ludwig von Mises, *Bureaucracy* (1944; reprint ed., New Rochelle, N. Y.: Arlington House, 1969), passim.

19. See Ludwig von Mises, *Socialism* (New Haven: Yale University Press, 1951), pp. 40–42, 500–504; reprint ed. (Indianapolis: Liberty Classics, 1981). See also below, pp. 296–300, which greatly elaborate on the points just made.

20. See above, pp. 228–230.

21. *New York Times*, April 11, 1974, pp. 49, 55.

22. Reported improvements in fuel economy are largely the result of compelling manufacturers to produce smaller, lighter-weight cars.

23. It is closely associated with what I described earlier as the Eloi mentality. See above, pp. 110–112.

24. Cf. above, pp. 23–26.

25. For a rebuttal of the closely related charge that a free economy lacks freedom of competition and freedom of entry, see below, pp. 375–376. For further discussion of the concepts of freedom and freedom of competition and a refutation of the related tissue of fallacies that constitute the doctrines of "oligopoly," "monopolistic competition," and "pure and perfect competition," and of the charge that a free economy lacks "price competition," see below, pp. 425–437. See also the discussion of the concept of freedom on pp. 21–27, above.

26. As will be seen, under universal price controls, it is possible for the controls to build in a substantial rate of profit. Even so,

potential competition would not be a factor, because in the context of universal price controls, the shortages are so severe that even if new suppliers could enter any given industry, the effect would not be to eliminate the shortage faced by the customers of that industry. At the same time, the effect would be to make shortages elsewhere in the economic system more severe. On these points, see below, p. 257.

27. *New York Times*, February 5, 1974.

28. These results are reinforced by the fact that the more economical models, being more popular and therefore selling faster, tend to carry lower profit margins in a free market than do the higher priced models. For example, $1 million of capital invested in a fast-moving inventory of low-priced models may generate $2 million of sales revenue in a year, while the same sized capital invested in a slow-moving inventory of high-priced models may generate only $1 million of sales revenue in a year. In order to earn the same rate of profit on capital, say 10 percent, when invested in either inventory, it is only necessary to have a 5 percent profit margin on the low-priced models, while a 10 percent profit margin is required on the high-priced models. If price controls are imposed and costs rise by any given percentage, the reduction in profit margins will be more severe in the case of the low-priced models. For example, a 5 percent rise in costs will just about totally eliminate profits on the low-priced models, while it will roughly halve them on the high-priced models. This too tends to cause the discontinuance of low-priced models ahead of high-priced models.

29. For a more forceful demonstration of this point, see below, pp. 254–256.

30. See above, pp. 205–206.

31. I am indebted to von Mises for this point and for the example used to illustrate it. See Ludwig von Mises, *Human Action,* 3d ed. rev. (Chicago: Henry Regnery Co., 1966), pp. 762–764; *Socialism,* pp. 532–534; *Planning For Freedom,* 4th ed. (South Holland, Ill.: Libertarian Press, 1980), pp. 73–75.

32. The additional expenditure on the uncontrolled goods is equal to the funds that the sellers of milk are prevented from receiving by virtue both of the artificially low, controlled price of milk and the reduced production of milk.

33. Because the Soviet Union was always nothing more than an illegitimate extension of Russia—the Russian Empire—I follow the practice of referring to it simply as Russia or Soviet Russia, though in view of the recent breakup of this empire, it is sometimes necessary to distinguish Russia from the former Soviet Union as whole.

34. Of course, the government is capable of forcing people to sleep in the streets, by prohibiting landlords from providing housing in the limited size and quality people can afford. Where they are local, such prohibitions are accompanied by a spillover effect of their own, which makes conditions worse in areas free of such restrictions. On these points, see below, pp. 384–385.

35. It should not be forgotten, of course, that a major portion of the increase in price paid to the American oil companies was not actually received by them but was taken by the government in the form of the so-called windfall-profits tax.

36. This is written in the fall of 1993.

37. See above, pp. 250–252.

38. See above, n. 31 of this chapter, the reference to von Mises.

39. See Hedrick Smith, *The Russians* (New York: Quadrangle

Books, 1976), pp. 62–65, and Robert G. Kaiser, *Russia* (New York: Atheneum, 1976), pp. 46–48.

40. Smith, *Russians,* p. 65.

41. See above, pp. 239–247.

42. On the significance of cutting costs and, by implication, of raising them, see above, pp. 179 and 212.

43. See above, pp. 245–246.

44. See Smith, *Russians,* pp. 60–61.

45. See Kaiser, *Russia,* pp. 315–356. See also Hedrick Smith,

The New Russians (New York: Random House, 1990), p. 210.

46. For a discussion of the role of economic efficiency in capital accumulation, see below, pp. 629–631 and 634–636.

47. See Kaiser, *Russia*, pp. 16, 324; Smith, *Russians*, p. 267.

48. See Ludwig von Mises, *Human Action*, pp. 717–719, 758–759, 764; *Socialism,* pp. 533–534; *Planning For Freedom,* pp. 4–5, 22–27, 30, 72–78; *Omnipotent Government* (1944; reprint ed., New Rochelle, N. Y.: Arlington House, 1969), pp. 55–58.

49. See von Mises, *Human Action*, pp. 258–259, 716.

CHAPTER 8

THE DEPENDENCE OF THE DIVISION OF LABOR ON CAPITALISM IV: SOCIALISM, ECONOMIC CHAOS, AND TOTALITARIAN DICTATORSHIP

PART A

THE CHAOS OF SOCIALISM

1. Socialism

From this point on, our discussion of the consequences of price controls becomes a discussion of the consequences of *socialism.*

In studying the consequences of socialism, it does not matter whether we study an economy that has arrived at socialism through price and wage controls or one that has arrived at socialism openly, through the explicit nationalization of all industry. Nor does it matter whether socialism has been brought about peacefully, through lawful processes and the observance of democratic procedures, or by means of a violent revolution; it also does not matter whether the professed goal of socialism is universal brotherly love or the supremacy of a particular race or class. Economically, the system is the same in all these cases: *The government owns the means of production and it is the government's responsibility to decide how they are to be used.* Consequently, everything I will have to say about socialism will apply to all variants of socialism: to the socialism of the Nazis, to the socialism of the Communists, and to the socialism of the Social Democrats, such as the late Norman Thomas. What I

have to say will apply to any economic system actually based on government ownership of the means of production. Of course, it will not apply to countries such as Great Britain, Israel, and Sweden, which, though governed for extensive periods by political parties espousing the philosophy of socialism, did not implement socialism as their actual economic system. Of course, it may apply to one or more of those countries in the future. Most importantly, it will apply to the economic system of the United States, should price controls once again be imposed and made universal and the government seize control over production and distribution in this country, which is more than possible at some point in the years ahead, given the profoundly inflationary nature of our present monetary system.

2. The Essential Economic Identity Between Socialism and Universal Price Controls

The most important principle to grasp about socialism is that *its economic consequences are essentially the same as those which result from universal price controls.* If socialism is introduced in response to the chaos created by universal price controls, its effect is to perpetuate that chaos; if it is introduced without the prior existence of universal price controls, its effect is to inaugurate that very chaos. This, of course, is ironic insofar as the government uses the chaos created by price controls as the grounds for its socialization of the economic system. Nevertheless, socialism and universal price controls are fundamentally the same in their economic nature and therefore produce the same effects. It is for precisely this reason that Soviet Russia has so consistently provided such excellent examples of the consequences that follow from universal price controls: Among these examples have been restrictions on the internal freedom of migration and the compulsory sharing of housing, shortages so severe that they result in mile-long waiting lines and people being ready to swoop down on whatever may happen to be available, and, above all, gross inefficiencies in the production and use of capital goods, which radically reduce the overall ability to produce.[1]

The essential economic identity between socialism and universal price controls consists in the fact that *both of them destroy private ownership of the means of production and its offshoots the profit motive and the price system.*

Price controls destroy private ownership of the means of production in the very fact of destroying the right to bid and ask prices. In a division-of-labor economy, in which buying and selling are indispensable to production and all other economic activity, the right to bid and ask prices is a fundamental, indispensable right of ownership. Without it, all other rights of ownership are meaningless. For example, the right to own a factory is meaningless if the owner is prohibited from charging or paying the prices required to keep his factory in existence. Essentially, price controls are fully as destructive of the rights of ownership as socialism itself. And, of course, when price controls are compounded by shortages, the government's response to the consequences is to seize total control over the means of production and establish *de facto* socialism.[2]

Furthermore, *what makes price controls produce the chaos they do is precisely the fact that they interfere with the property rights of businessmen.* Specifically, they prohibit businessmen from using their capitals in the ways that would be most profitable to themselves. If they did not interfere with the right of businessmen to use their capitals in the most profitable way, then they could produce none of their chaotic effects. Try to imagine the government *not* interfering with the businessman's property rights and profit motive, and yet the consequences of price controls developing. Think back to the preceding chapter and recall the following elements of chaos that we saw resulting from price controls: shortages and the destruction of vital industries; the impotence of consumers accompanied by hatred between buyer and seller; the impetus to higher costs; chaos in the personal distribution of goods to consumers; chaos in the geographical distribution of goods among various local markets; chaos in

the distribution of a factor of production among its various products; chaos in the distribution of capital and labor among the various industries.

Consider. All of these elements of chaos result from just one thing: *interference with the businessman's property rights and profit motive.* For example, would businessmen voluntarily sell their goods too cheaply and thus cause shortages? Obviously not. Their property rights must be violated and they must be forced to do so. Would businessmen abandon the production of vital goods if they were free to charge profitable prices for them? Obviously not. Would they drive away customers offering them profitable business? Again, no. Would they run up the costs of production if those costs came out of profits (as they would have to in the absence of price controls and shortages)? Clearly not. Would businessmen saturate some markets at low prices, while starving others offering them high prices? Would they use a factor of production to produce some products to excess at low prices, while producing not enough of other products offering them high prices? Would they overinvest in some industries at low profits or loses, while underinvesting in other industries offering high profits? Again, the answer is clearly no to all of these questions. What makes businessmen behave in these ways is that their property rights are violated and they are thus prevented from doing what is profitable to themselves.

The wider principle that emerges is that the entire price system and all of its laws and harmonies depend on one essential fact: *the observance of private property rights and thus the freedom of businessmen to act for their own profit.* It is private property rights and the profit motive that are the foundation and the motive power that underlie and drive the entire price system. It is they which underlie and actuate all of the benevolent economic laws we observed in our study of the free market, such as the uniformity-of-profit principle, the various principles of price and wage uniformity, the cost-of-production principle, the principle that prices are set high enough to limit demand to the supply, and the principle that factors of production are channelled to their most important employments. All of these laws and all of their benevolent consequences are the result of just one thing: private property rights and the profit motive.

Now socialism destroys all property rights. And with them it destroys the operation of the profit motive and the entire price system.

Socialism produces the same chaotic effects as price controls, *because it destroys the same thing as price controls,* namely, the one and only source of economic order and harmony in the world: private property rights and the profit motive.

The essential fact to grasp about socialism, which

explains why it is essentially identical to price controls, is that *it is simply an act of destruction*. Like price controls, it destroys private ownership and the profit motive, and that is essentially *all* it does. It has nothing to put in their place. Socialism, in other words, is not actually an alternative economic system to private ownership of the means of production. It is merely a *negation* of the system based on private ownership.

3. The Myth of Socialist Planning—The Anarchy of Socialist Production

Of course, socialism is not usually perceived simply as a negation. The first economist fully to grasp the destructive nature of socialism was von Mises, and he has not had many followers.[3] Much more often, socialism is perceived as a source of economic order and harmony. In fact, the most popular synonym for socialism is "economic planning." The belief in socialism's ability to plan is why a government turns to socialism when confronted with the chaos created by price controls. Indeed, the belief in socialism's ability to plan may be one of the reasons for instituting price controls in the first place—namely, as a deliberate step leading directly to socialism. Certainly, the belief in socialism's ability to plan has been a major factor in the popularity of socialism. Without it, it would be difficult for socialism to find supporters.

Nevertheless, a socialist government is helpless to bring order out of the chaos created by price controls. And if price controls do not exist when it assumes power, then it proceeds to create the same chaos as price controls by the very fact of socializing the economic system. For the great joke of socialism, of "planning," as it is called, is that it *cannot plan;* it *destroys* planning and substitutes chaos.

In order to understand why socialism cannot plan, we must look again at capitalism. This will enable us to form an idea of what is required for economic planning and, therefore, why socialism is incapable of it.

The reader should recall that *under capitalism each individual engages in economic planning.*

I must stress this fact and I am going to give a very extensive list of examples of it, because it is very important and because socialist propaganda has created exactly the opposite impression in the minds of most people. It has created the impression that what individuals do under capitalism is run about like chickens without heads in an "anarchy of production," and that rational action—planned action—is a prerogative of government. The truth is that each individual under capitalism is engaged in economic planning almost continuously. Unfortunately, as pointed out in Chapter 5, most of us are in the position of M.

Jourdan—the character in the Molière play—who spoke prose without ever knowing it.[4] We are all engaged in economic planning under capitalism, practically every day, but hardly any of us realize it—least of all, today's intellectuals. Let us see in just what ways we practice economic planning.

An individual is engaged in economic planning when he plans how much of his wealth and income to save and invest and how much of it to consume; when he plans where to invest it and in what ways to consume it. He is engaged in economic planning, for example, when he plans to put his money in a bank or in the stock market, and in which specific shares in the stock market; when he plans to buy more clothes or a new stereo; even when he plans to drive to work or take the train, instead.

Every businessman under capitalism is engaged in economic planning when he plans to expand or contract the production of any item; when he plans to introduce a new product or discontinue an old product; when he plans to change his methods of production or retain his existing methods; when he plans to build a new factory or not to replace an existing one; when he plans to change the location of his business or let it remain where it is; when he plans to buy new machinery or not; to add to his inventories or not; to hire additional workers or let some of his present workers go.

Every wage earner under capitalism is engaged in economic planning when he plans to seek new employment or to retain his present employment; when he plans to improve his skills or rest content with the ones he has; when he plans to do his job in one particular area of the country, or in one particular industry, rather than in another.

In short, every one of us under capitalism is engaged in economic planning every time he plans any aspect of his personal finances or business affairs. We are engaged in economic planning every time we *think* about a course of action that would benefit us in our capacity as a buyer or seller.

It is simply amazing that all of this planning could be overlooked, and that the socialists have been able to proceed as though capitalism lacked planning. Capitalism *has* planning—the planning of each and every person who participates in the economic system.

Let us observe another, equally important fact, briefly described in Chapter 5: Namely, that the planning of capitalism—which, as I say, takes place on the part of everyone—is based on prices.[5]

Prices have a twofold function in the planning of capitalism. First, *they enable the individual planner of capitalism to perform economic calculations*. That is, they enable him to compute the money cost and/or money revenue of various modes of conduct. If the planner is a businessman, he weighs a money cost against a money revenue. If he is a consumer, he weighs a money cost against a personal satisfaction. If he is a wage earner, he weighs a money revenue against his personal efforts. *These economic calculations provide a standard of action for the planner under capitalism.* They tell businessmen to produce the products and use the methods of production that are anticipated to be the most profitable. They tell consumers to consume in the ways that, other things being equal, occasion the lowest cost. And they tell wage earners to work at the jobs that, other things being equal, pay the highest wages. Thus, prices are an indispensable guide both to the planning of production and to the living of one's personal life under capitalism.

The second, corollary function of prices is that *they coordinate the plans of each individual under capitalism with the plans of all other individuals.* That is, prices serve to make each individual adjust his own plans to the relevant plans of all other individuals in the economic system. In this way, *capitalism and the price system bring about a harmoniously integrated planning of the entire economic system.* Our whole discussion of the free market's price system demonstrated this process of coordination and mutual adjustment. It is only necessary to say the following, by way of summary of that discussion: Namely, that concern with money revenue makes one adjust to the plans of the prospective buyers of one's goods or services and to the plans of all competing—and even potentially competing—sellers of those goods or services. And that concern with money costs makes one adjust to the plans of all other buyers seeking either the things one buys, the factors of production from which they are made, or alternative products of those factors of production—and to the plans of sellers in their capacity as individuals having definite personal values and preferences. The desire to earn a money revenue leads one to produce things that the buyers want and that are not being produced excessively by other sellers. The desire to limit costs leads one to economize on things to the degree that other buyers value them, or value the factors of production on which they depend, or the alternative products of those factors of production; and also to economize to the degree that the goods or services in question can be provided only at some special inconvenience to the sellers engaged in producing them.

Now socialism, in destroying the price system, destroys the possibility of economic calculation and the coordination of the activities of separate, independent planners. It therefore makes rational economic planning impossible and creates chaos.

As an illustration of the consequences, consider the problems confronting a socialist government in trying to plan the production of a simple item, such as shoes. Shoes can be produced in varying quantities, in various styles or combinations of styles, and by various methods or combinations of methods, such as by machine or by hand, including the choice between using various proportions of machine or hand production in different parts of the overall process. They can be produced from different materials or combinations of materials, such as leather, rubber, and canvas, and in different geographical locations, again, in both instances, in varying proportions. Under capitalism, all of these choices are determined on the basis of economic calculations. Thus, shoe production as a whole tends to be carried to the point where further production would make the shoe industry relatively unprofitable in comparison with other industries; the styles are those which the consumers are willing to make profitable; the methods of production, the materials used, the geographic locations are all the lowest cost except insofar as they provide special advantages for which the consumers are willing to bear the extra cost.

Under socialism, the lack of economic calculation makes it impossible to make any of these choices on a rational basis. The extent of attempted shoe production is determined arbitrarily—most likely on the basis of some official's judgment about how many pairs of shoes are "necessary" per thousand inhabitants, or some such criterion. Style is determined arbitrarily—according to what suits the tastes of those in charge. The methods, materials, and locations planned must be selected arbitrarily. And then—for reasons that will soon become clearer—the actual carrying out of production, as opposed to what is called for in the plans, may very well have to be undertaken on the accidental basis of the means of production that happen to be available.

Now it must be stressed that the decisions about all of these choices—quantity, styles, methods, and so on—are important not only from the standpoint of the consumers of shoes, *but, no less, from the standpoint of the production of all other goods.* It must be borne in mind that shoe production, or the production of any good whatever, requires factors of production which are thereby made unavailable for other purposes. Shoe production requires labor that could be employed elsewhere. It requires leather or other material that either might be employed elsewhere or which is produced by labor that could certainly be employed elsewhere. In the same way, the tools or machines required, or the labor and the materials used to make them, have alternative employments. Moreover, each of the different choices respecting shoe production makes a *different* combination of factors of production unavailable for alternative employments. For example, shoes produced by hand reduce the number of handicraft workers available for other purposes. Those produced by machine reduce the number of machine makers and the amount of fuel available for other purposes. Shoes produced in Minsk leave less labor available for other purposes in Minsk than if they were produced in Pinsk, and so on.

It is, therefore, clearly not enough, as most socialists appear to believe, for a socialist government—having inherited or stolen the technology of shoe production—to simply decide how many shoes to produce, determine on a style, quality, method, and locations for production, and then give the orders to produce them. In planning the production of shoes, or any other individual item, a socialist government is logically obliged to consider its effect on the production of *all other items in the economic system*. It is logically obliged to try to plan the production of shoes, or any other good, in a way that least impairs the production of other goods. In drafting its plans for shoe production, a socialist government is obliged to consider the extent of shoe production in relation to the production of all other goods using the same factors of production. It is obliged to consider such questions as whether shoe production might be expanded with factors of production drawn from the production of some other good, and whether the production of that other good might be maintained by drawing factors of production from a third good, and so on.

For example, it must consider whether it would be advisable to use more labor in Minsk for shoes and less for making clothing, say, and perhaps to expand clothing production in Pinsk, at the expense of some third good. It must consider *all* of the industries using *any* of the factors of production used in the shoe industry. It must consider what depends on the output of those industries and what alternative factors of production are available to those industries. Indeed, it must go even further. It must consider all of the industries using the alternative factors of production. It must consider what depends on *their* products, and what further alternative factors of production may be available to *them*. And so on. And at each step, it must consider the possibility of expanding the overall supply of the factor of production in question, and, if so, by what means, where, and at the expense of what.

To make these problems real, let us continue with the example of shoes. In order to plan shoe production rationally, it would be necessary for a socialist government to consider all of the alternative employments of each of the factors of production used to produce shoes. Let us start just with leather. A socialist government would have to consider the alternative employments of leather, such as upholstering furniture and providing belting for machinery. It would have to consider the consequences of having more or less furniture and machinery versus more or less shoes. It would have to consider alternatives to the use of leather in upholstering furniture and making belting for machinery—for example, various fabrics, and plastic and steel. It would have to consider the alternative uses for the various fabrics and for the plastic and steel, or for the factors of production used to produce them. It would have to consider what depended on those alternative uses, and what substitutes were available for them. It would have to consider whether the total supply of leather, its substitutes, or the substitutes for its substitutes, should be expanded, and, if so, by what means, where, and at the expense of what. Then, of course, the socialist government would be obliged to repeat the same procedure for all of the other factors of production employed to produce shoes, or which potentially could be employed to produce shoes.

All of this raises the insuperable difficulty of socialist planning: *Namely, under socialism, it is necessary to plan the production of the entire economic system as an indivisible whole.* That would be the only rational procedure.

But the planning of the economic system as an indivisible whole is simply impossible.

It would require a superhuman intellect to be able to grasp the physical connections among all the various industries and to be able to trace the consequences of alterations in any one industry on all the others. What would be required for the rational planning of a socialist economy would be the existence of an omniscient deity willing to descend from heaven and assume the management of the socialist economy.

This deity would have to be able to hold in mind at one time a precise inventory of the quantities and qualities of all the different factors of production in the entire economic system, together with their exact geographical locations and a full knowledge of the various technological possibilities open to them. That is to say, it would have to be able to hold in mind at one time all of the millions of separate farms, factories, mines, warehouses, and so forth, down to the last repair shop, together with a knowledge of the quantity and quality of all the machines, tools, materials, and partly-finished goods that they contained, and exactly what they were potentially capable of accomplishing and when.

It would then have to be able to project forward in time all of the different new combinations of factors of production that might be produced out of the existing factors, together with where and precisely when they would come into existence and the technological possibilities that would then be open to them. It would have to be able to make this projection for an extended period of time— say, a generation or more—in order to avoid the possibly wasteful production of machines and buildings lasting that long.

And then, out of all the virtually infinite number of different possible permutations and combinations of what might be produced, it would have to pick one that on some undefined and undefinable basis it considered "best," and then order it to be undertaken. That would be its economic plan. *That* is what would be required even to begin to duplicate what capitalism accomplishes through the price system.

For observe. Under capitalism, different individuals in combination—that is, when their knowledge is added together—*do know* the precise quantities, qualities, locations, and technological possibilities open to all the various factors of production in the economic system. And everybody's production is based on the sum of all of this knowledge, because the knowledge is reflected in the prices of all the various factors of production and products. For example, the price of wheat at any given time reflects the knowledge of each owner of wheat concerning the amount, quality, and location of the wheat he owns; it also reflects the knowledge of each user of wheat about the technological possibilities open to wheat. All of this knowledge enters into the supply and demand and hence the price of wheat. It is the same with every other good: its price reflects the sum of existing knowledge about the amount of it available, the technological possibilities open to it in production, and every other relevant consideration. And the future supply, locations, and production possibilities of factors of production are taken into account in the anticipation of their future prices.

The deity needed for the planning of socialism would require intellectual powers even surpassing those I have described. For under socialism any unanticipated event, such as a train wreck, an early snowstorm, a warehouse fire, an unexpectedly bad harvest—even unanticipated favorable events, such as the opposite of all of these—is a calamity, for it requires *the replanning of the entire economic system.* For example, if a tank train carrying a shipment of oil is destroyed, how is the socialist economy to decide where to take out the loss? It would have to look at all of the different uses for oil, all the possible remote consequences of its withdrawal from this or that area of production, and it would have to look at all of the alternative employments of factors of production that might be used to replace the lost oil, and all the permutations and combinations entailed in that, and then decide. By the same token, if, as a result of good fortune, a socialist economy had fewer wrecks of tank trains than anticipated, it would have to replan the entire economic system to find the right use for the extra supply of oil.

Capitalism, on the other hand, as we have seen throughout, responds easily and smoothly to unforeseen changes in economic conditions. Such changes simply bring about a change in the structure of prices and thus generate the most efficient response on the part of all concerned. Thus, the wreck of a tank train—to continue with that example—acts to raise the price of oil a little. The rise in price diminishes the consumption of oil in its marginal employments and simultaneously encourages its production—and, of course, at the least possible expense to other productive activities. The reason capitalism responds so smoothly and efficiently is that every individual in the economic system is involved in planning the response. Each individual acts on the basis of his knowledge of his own personal or business context, and the actions of all the individuals are harmoniously integrated through the price system.[6]

The essential problem of socialism is that it requires economic planning to take place without benefit of a division of intellectual labor. It requires that one man (the Supreme Director), or each of several men (the Supreme Board of Directors), hold in his head and utilize the knowledge that can be held and utilized only by millions of separate individuals freely cooperating with one another on the basis of private ownership of the means of production and its offshoots the profit motive and the price system. The essential economic flaw of socialism is that in destroying these basic institutions of capitalism, it destroys the foundations of the intellectual division of labor that is indispensable to rational economic planning.

As I say, therefore, the planning of the economic system as an indivisible whole—by single individuals—let alone its continuous replanning in response to every unforeseen change, is simply impossible. The ruler of socialism, after all, is simply not an omniscient deity.

As a result, although it is called "central planning," socialism can never have anything even approaching a rationally integrated plan for the entire economic system. In reality, the actual planning of socialist countries is undertaken by separate government ministries, each responsible for different industries or regions. Even the individual factories undertake part of the planning process. The plans of these separate ministries and individual factories are only superficially integrated into an economy-wide plan. In this sense, the actual planning of socialism must be called "decentralized planning." There is no alternative to decentralized planning, because it is simply impossible for any one individual to try to plan everything. Decentralized planning exists as soon as two or more people assume separate responsibilities in the planning process.

However, the decentralized planning of socialism necessarily causes chaos. Because without a price system—without the foundation and mainspring of the price system, i.e., private ownership of the means of production and the profit motive—the individual planners must operate at cross purposes. First of all, there is nothing to stop their various discoordinated plans from presupposing the availability of the same factors of production. In such conditions, the execution of any plan necessarily absorbs factors of production whose absence then makes the execution of other plans impossible. For example, if the shoe industry is planned by one ministry, the clothing industry by a second ministry, the steel industry by a third ministry, and so on, there is nothing to prevent all of these industries from drafting mutually contradictory plans. There is nothing to prevent them from basing their plans on the availability of the same labor, or the same material, fuel, transport facilities, or whatever. In such a case, to whatever extent one industry succeeds in obtaining the factors of production necessary to execute its plan, it simultaneously wrecks the plans of other industries.

Observe what is involved here. Because planning under socialism is necessarily both decentralized and lacks coordination, the production of each of the various goods can be expanded more or less randomly at the expense of destroying the production of other, more important goods. *This is exactly the same chaos that prevails under universal price controls and universal shortages.*

Furthermore, to whatever extent individual industries or factories are given discretion in the plans, the products that are produced can very well be unsuited to the needs of other industries that depend on them, and in that way wreck the plans of these other industries. For example, the plan for agriculture can be wrecked by the poor quality of tractors that break down too often or aren't suited for the terrain. Under socialism, suppliers do not have any incentive of profit and loss in meeting the requirements of their customers. Nor are they subject to any form of competition. Each branch of industry under socialism is a protected legal monopoly that is totally disinterested in the requirements of its customers. This, too, is exactly the same situation we observed in the case of price controls and shortages. And it applies, as I say, not only at the consumer level, but at the producer level as well.

Under socialism, each industry, as well as each consumer, is at the mercy of disinterested monopoly suppliers. To understand what this is like, first recall our discussion of the problems at service stations and in the relations between tenants and landlords resulting from price controls on gasoline and from rent controls.[7] Now observe that similar or even worse problems exist around us in the present-day United States in practically every case in which the government is the supplier. For example, think of the services provided by municipal bus lines and subway systems, the public schools, the motor vehicle bureau, and the Post Office. All of these operations are notorious in the utter indifference and contempt they

display toward customers and in the low quality and lack of dependability of their services. These characteristics are the result of the fact that these operations are government owned and therefore operate without the incentives of profit and loss; in addition, they are generally immune from the threat of competition. Because of the lack of profit and loss incentives, it doesn't matter to them whether they gain customers or lose customers—whether they perform fast and efficient service or slow and inadequate service.

Now imagine the steel industry being owned by the government and run in the same way, and the customers of the steel industry having to contend with its performance. The industries needing steel would not be able to make their plans with very great confidence.[8] Moreover, since they too would be owned by the government, they would not particularly *care* about not receiving the quality and service or even the kind of products they were supposed to. The effects on *their* customers, in turn, and on the plans of their customers, would be compounded.

For example, an industry waiting for a new factory, say, called for by its plan, would have to contend with the indifference and bad service of a construction industry suffering from the indifference and bad service of the steel industry. And so it would go, with the plans of each industry wrecked by the lack of incentives and poor performance of every other industry further back in the chain of supply. It is for these very reasons, which are tantamount to the conditions of chronic shortages, that suppliers in the Soviet Union were so unreliable that, as previously pointed out, each factory there strove as far as possible to be self-sufficient and thus independent of suppliers.[9]

To think of socialism as a "planned economy" is absurd. It is, in fact, an "anarchy of production"—a true anarchy of production.

The Soviet Quota System

The fact that socialism is an anarchy of production could not be better illustrated than by the famous Soviet "quota system." Socialist planning in Soviet Russia assigned to each farm and factory a specified physical production goal, called its "quota"—for example, so many bushels of wheat or so many pounds of nails. And each farm or factory was encouraged *to exceed its quota.*

Now this situation is identical to the one we discussed under a system of universal price controls and universal shortages, for it means that there is a ready and waiting employment for more factors of production in every branch of production, with the result that any branch is capable of expanding at the expense of any other, more important branch. This, of course, is a system of pure chaos. The Soviet quota system, moreover, illustrated the anarchy of socialist production in another major respect as well. The central planning authority did not even attempt to issue really precise production quotas because of the enormous additional detail that would have been required. For example, at times it did not even attempt to specify the number of each particular size nail or screw and so forth that was to be produced. It simply ordered the production of so many pounds or mere units of nails or screws or whatever, overall. As a result, depending on whether the orders were in terms of weight or mere number of units, the factories concerned were led to try to concentrate on items that were giant sized and enormously heavy, or pin sized and very large in number. For these were the ways most easily to meet and exceed the quotas. The disastrous results for subsequent production can be imagined.

The quota system and its stress on meeting and exceeding quotas is an inevitable consequence of the fact that socialism cannot rationally plan. It results from the fact that a socialist government wants to expand production, but is unable to trace the connections among the different industries. It is unable to determine—and is not even aware that it is necessary to determine—the effects of producing more of any one item on the ability to produce other items. A socialist government sees the particular product it wants to produce in each case, but, because it lacks a price system, it has no concept of the cost of producing that product or, therefore, of what other products it must forgo in the process. As a result, it simply gives orders to produce as much as possible of everything.

Socialism is simply unable to determine costs and is not concerned with costs. It should be realized how much more profound this lack of concern with costs is in a socialist economy than in the case of isolated socialized enterprises operating in an economy that is based on private ownership of the means of production. Today, for example, the Post Office is not overly concerned with costs, because there is no one in the Post Office who stands to make a profit by reducing costs or suffer a loss by allowing them to run up. In the context of a socialist economy, the problems of the Post Office, or any other enterprise, would be far more profound. In that case, it could not even know what its costs were, because of the absence of a price system. As a result, the Post Office, and every other enterprise under socialism, would be operated totally in the dark, with an unknown impact on the rest of the economic system.[10]

Shortages of Labor and Consumers' Goods Under Socialism

Because this will be an important matter for consideration in Part B of this chapter, it should be realized that socialism's inability to determine costs and consequent lack of concern with costs produces exactly the same kind of *labor shortage* as exists under universal price controls. A labor shortage exists under socialism both because of a socialist government's desire to produce more of everything and because of its inefficiency in how it produces anything in particular. The latter circumstance increases the amount of labor required to produce each good. In addition, of course, shortages of consumers' goods contribute to the labor shortage. The extent of the labor shortage is such that factory managers routinely hoard labor, that is, keep it on the payroll, in idleness, merely to have it available as and when the need for it may arise.[11]

A few words must be said specifically about the reasons for the existence of shortages of consumers' goods under socialism, especially since it is often claimed by socialists who have some familiarity with economics that such shortages could be avoided by a socialist society. Shortages of consumers' goods exist under socialism even without inflation. They exist as a result of the following factors. First, the chaos in the production and geographical distribution of the various goods: at any time, goods can cease being produced, or cease being sent to particular localities. This can occur because particular plans are fulfilled that snatch away the necessary factors of production or perhaps the very consumers' goods themselves from other plans. Second, when this happens, the managers of the local stores and warehouses of the socialist society have no incentive and no authority to raise prices. Nor do they have the incentive or authority to try to anticipate such events and build up stockpiles—that would be speculation. In the same way, they have no incentive or authority to bring in supplies from other areas (or send supplies to other areas)—that would be another form of activity possible only under capitalism, namely, arbitrage. In addition, all of the moral and political pressures of a socialist society work against prices being raised.

A basic moral postulate of socialism is that goods should be free to whoever needs them, or, if not free, then at least as inexpensive as possible. The political pressures of socialism are likewise overwhelmingly against price increases (a fact that in the Poland of the 1970s and 1980s was repeatedly confirmed by rioting and even by changes in the top officials on occasions when price increases were imposed). The reasons for such political pressures are exactly the same as those which make rent control so popular in New York City, namely, whoever succeeds in buying at the low price sees his benefit and applauds the government officials responsible; on the other hand, those who are victimized by the shortage the too-low price creates rarely see any connection between the too-low price and their inability to obtain the goods they want; they view the low price as being in their interest, too, and hope to be able to buy at that price.

All of these circumstances create shortages of consumers' goods under socialism, which, of course, are worsened by the desire to hoard that necessarily accompanies them. On top of all this, the socialist government can issue additional money to the consumers and typically does so, which, of course, further intensifies the shortages by expanding aggregate demand in the face of a given level of prices.

4. Further Economic Flaws of Socialism: Monopoly, Stagnation, Exploitation, Progressive Impoverishment

The most fundamental fact about socialism is that *government ownership of the means of production constitutes an attempt to make intelligence and initiative in production a monopoly of the state.*

Production depends on the possession of means of production. If the means of production are monopolized by the state, because it arbitrarily claims to own them all, then no one is free to produce on his own initiative and to regard his own intelligence and judgment as the ultimate authority for his action. In a socialist economy, no one can produce without the permission, indeed, without the orders, of the state.

This attempted monopoly of intelligence and initiative is the cause of socialism's anarchy of production. Socialism simply *prohibits* all of the independent planning of millions of free, self-interested individuals that is required to run an economic system in a rational and ordered way.

There are additional, corollary consequences of socialism's monopoly character that must be stressed, namely, *the necessary technological backwardness of socialism and the utter powerlessness of the plain citizen under socialism.*

To understand these points, compare the conditions of socialism with those of capitalism. Under capitalism, whoever sees a profitable opportunity for action is free to act on his own initiative. He is powerfully motivated to do so by the prospect of the profit he can make. At the same time, he is restrained from rash action by the risk of losing his own money. In addition, his action constitutes a challenge to the established ways of doing things. For if what he is doing is in fact an improvement over present products or methods of production, then those producing the present products or practicing the present methods must copy his or be driven out of business. And, as we have seen, competition is powerfully promoted by the fact that if an innovator lacks capital of his own, he can turn to any one of hundreds or even thousands of

independent sources of financing by offering to share his profits with potential backers. Thus, under capitalism, every new idea has an enormous number of possible chances for being implemented.[12]

Because of its freedom of initiative, its incentives to use that initiative, and its freedom of competition, the products and methods of production of capitalism tend to be literally the very best that anyone in the entire society can think of, and to improve further as soon as anyone can think of any still better idea. We saw all this, of course, back in Chapter 6.[13]

Under socialism, on the other hand, individual initiative is paralyzed by the fear of punishment. Prison replaces profit for the man who would seek to implement an idea on his own initiative, for it is against the law under socialism to act outside the government's "plan." If an individual does manage to think of some improvement under socialism, he must submit it to the government. If he does so, he will at most have only a handful of chances for approval of his idea. In addition, whatever officials he turns to in the government will have no economic incentives to adopt his idea, whatever its possible merit. They will be inclined to reject it, in order to spare themselves the difficulties and uncertainties that are always entailed in implementing an innovation—such as the need to find new suppliers of raw materials, obtain new workers, or discharge or relocate present workers. The officials will not want to run the risk of the innovation being judged a failure and thus arousing the displeasure of those in a position to do them harm. At the same time, if the innovation were somehow to succeed, by whatever arbitrary standard success is judged under socialism, the effect on the officials would likely be merely the difficulties of establishing the new arrangements and then having their assigned production quotas increased. These are the conditions that prevailed in the former Soviet Union.[14] Under such circumstances, very few new ideas are thought of, fewer still are implemented, and virtually none at all are of benefit to the plain citizen.

The complete and utter powerlessness of the plain citizen under socialism can hardly be exaggerated. Under socialism, the plain citizen is no longer the customer, "who is always right," but the serf, who must take his rations and like it. For no official of a socialist government stands to make a profit by supplying him better or suffer a loss by supplying him worse. These officials both lack the incentive of profit and loss and need not fear any competition from the initiative of outsiders. Thus, the plain citizen is economically powerless against them.

It is not even necessary to speak of the absence of any improvements for the plain citizen. Even if it had the ability, socialism has *no reason* to supply the plain citizen even with such goods as already exist and to which he may have grown accustomed in the preceding era of capitalism. Indeed, it has no reason to supply him with *anything more than is necessary to prevent an uprising.* Consider a simple example. Assume there is a neighborhood somewhere that needs a grocery store. Under capitalism, this need represents a profitable opportunity for someone. Whoever sees it and has no better opportunity available simply opens a grocery and proceeds to make money, at the same time satisfying the neighborhood's need.

Under socialism, on the other hand, the residents of the neighborhood can obtain a grocery only by petitioning the economic planning board for one. Even if the residents actually went so far, which is itself highly doubtful, the officials of the board would have no compelling reason—no personal material incentive—to comply with their request. They would certainly be far less likely to do so than officials in the United States who presently accede to requests for traffic lights at dangerous intersections, which is often only after repeated deaths have occurred. It is for these very reasons, incidentally, that even Moscow, the leading city of socialism, is grossly lacking in retail and service establishments; residents living in outlying suburbs must often travel all the way to the center of the city to obtain even such things as food supplies.[15]

To take a second example: if ten million citizens of a socialist state are without shoes and must go barefoot, this does not and cannot mean any more to the officials of the socialist state than it means to the officials of New York City that everyday hundreds of thousands of New Yorkers are subjected to inhuman, cattle-like conditions in the city's municipalized subway system. No government official is motivated seriously to work to do anything about such conditions, because he has no profit/loss incentive to improve them. He will not grow richer by improving them. He will not grow poorer by leaving them alone.

The closest a government official could come to having an incentive to make an improvement anywhere is if he were running for election and the outcome of the election depended on that improvement. Then, until the clamor died down, he might attempt to do something to make that particular improvement—at the expense, of course, of sacrificing other areas, where fewer complaints would be generated. Such an occasional, narrow political incentive, however, is as nothing compared with capitalism's freedom of individual initiative motivated by the incentives of profit and loss. This immensely powerful combination of freedom and incentive under capitalism is continually applied to improving all aspects of economic life, the overwhelming majority of which can never even be the subject of an election. For example,

that specific neighborhood's getting a grocery store cannot be the focus of a mayoral election, much less a national election. It would simply be lost in the shuffle of far too many other matters. The same is usually true even of such larger matters as ten million people going barefoot or hundreds of thousands being treated like cattle. These are likely merely to have the status of particular dissatisfactions among innumerable other dissatisfactions and thus require no special urgency of response on the part of government officials.

Furthermore, under socialism, for reasons to be explained in Part B of this chapter, there are no free elections, and thus even the occasional democratic political incentive does not arise. Under socialism, the closest a government official comes to having an incentive to improve conditions is when the populace is on the point of revolt and it is more expedient to make some show of improvement rather than crush the protest with force.

In contrast to the politicians, democratic or totalitarian, the people who really do work to improve the economic conditions of the general public, who—literally—stay up nights thinking of ways to provide them with such things as grocery stores, more and better shoes and means of transportation, and everything else they may possibly want, are *capitalists,* who are continually motivated by the prospect of making or losing a fortune and who can act on their own initiative. Capitalists know not only that they will profit from improving conditions but also that if they fail to make improvements, others can make them and that the resulting competition will cause those who have not made the improvements to lose the wealth they now own.

The simple fact is that under socialism, the consumers must accept whatever the government decides to give them, however meager and inadequate that may be. For the rest, they are helpless, and whatever pleas they might make fall on deaf, indifferent, and often hostile ears.

The paralysis of initiative and incentives under socialism knows no limit—it extends to death itself. For example, if one asks how it is that Russia under socialism could periodically be threatened by famine despite the fact that it possessed the world's richest farm land, in the Ukraine, and was a major wheat exporter even under the Czars, the answer is that the individual Russians were prevented—by physical force—from taking the actions necessary to save their lives. Russian peasants, however ignorant they may have been, were not so ignorant that they did not know that to eat they must grow food; nor did they lack the knowledge to grow sufficient food. They could have grown not only enough to feed themselves, but the urban population of the country as well, and far more. The urban population could have produced things of value to the peasants, and they could mutually have exchanged and both have lived far removed from the threat of starvation.

The reason they did not is quite simple: The Soviet government arbitrarily declared the whole of the Soviet Union to be its property, and refused to allow the peasants to farm for their own profit or the urban population to produce for its own profit. It threatened, quite literally, to kill anyone who tried to do so. Thus, a Russian peasant may have looked at virgin forest land that he could have cleared and made his farm, and which would have fed himself and ten others. He may have looked, but he would not have lifted a finger, because he would have been killed for trying. People starve to death under socialism because the actions they would have to take to prevent starvation would bring them a more immediate death from the government. It is that simple.

It follows from the powerlessness of the plain citizens that *the government of a socialist country is not and has no reason to be interested in anyone's values but those of its rulers.* This principle applies both to technological developments and to the whole of production. The only kind of technological developments that a socialist government is interested in are those which are of value to its rulers: above all, improvements in weapons production and in the kinds of things that add to the rulers' prestige, such as "sputniks"—or pyramids. Of course, even these, or their base, it must steal from capitalist countries, because it is impossible significantly to develop military technology, or any other aspects of technology of special interest to the state, while repressing civilian technology. For example, the tank and the military airplane could not have been developed in the absence of the automobile. Radar and rocketry could not have been developed in the absence of radio. But the automobile and radio would never have been introduced under socialism. They could not because the motive that inspires the introduction of such goods is pleasure and profit—the personal, selfish pleasure of the consumers and the private profit of the producers—not collectivistic duty and altruistic sacrifice.[16]

The only kind of production a socialist government is interested in is the production of weapons, spectacles, and monuments, which enhance the power and prestige of the rulers—and of just enough consumers' goods to prevent mass starvation or, perhaps, a revolt, either of which would weaken its power. Ironically, in *Das Kapital,* Karl Marx refers to capitalists as "blood-sucking," "vampire-like" "exploiters." It is clear, however, that it is not capitalists, but the rulers of socialism who are the genuine "blood-sucking," "vampire-like" "exploiters" of labor. Minimum physical subsistence is the most they will ever voluntarily give to the masses, for they have absolutely no reason to give more. Over seventy years of

communism in the Soviet Union served to confirm this principle. But in the long run they cannot even provide this much. For, as should be apparent, as a result of its "anarchy of production," socialism "cannot even maintain its slaves in their slavery": the workers of socialism "sink deeper and deeper into poverty"—to borrow some other of Marx's choice clichés and apply them truthfully for once.

If anyone doubts that the standard of living under socialism tends to sink below the level of minimum physical subsistence, let him consider where the citizens of the former Soviet Union would be right now without American wheat. Let him consider how many of them would die from the famine that would then result. Let him consider how many of them would already have died from the numerous famines that have been averted only because of the existence of an outside capitalist world to turn to for grain supplies. The citizens of the former Soviet Union averted famines and countless other disasters only because an outside capitalist world existed to provide them with all sorts of supplies to make good the errors of their chaotic economy. Their system was able to drag itself out for over seventy years only by means of the direct or indirect aid of the United States and other Western governments, which was responsible even for most of their ability to export and thus to pay for some of their imports.[17]

As previously stated, without the aid of capitalist countries, socialism must revert to feudalism, for it could not feed an extensive urban population. Such urban population as it might begin with would be destroyed by famines or flee to the countryside to avoid such destruction. These results must ultimately occur even if socialism were to begin with the present economy of the United States, the inheritance of more than two centuries of capitalism. For the chaos of socialism would so reduce production as to make it impossible to replace the existing stock of capital goods. Then, as a result of fewer capital goods, production would drop again, and the supply of capital goods would thus decline still further. Socialism would find itself caught in the vicious circle I described in the last chapter, of less production causing fewer capital goods causing less production.[18] The day would come when, no matter how high the level at which it began, it could not feed the population. Socialism is an utterly destructive and self-destructive economic system.

The overwhelming inefficiencies of socialism shed light on what otherwise might be a puzzling phenomenon, namely, the inability of the former Soviet Union, despite its alleged concentration on the production of capital goods for most of its history, significantly to increase its per capita production of consumers' goods, or, indeed, to accumulate any very great amount of additional capital goods. If the apologists for the Soviet Union were to be believed, the reason for its miserably low production of consumers' goods was its concentration on the production of capital goods—on the "building up of heavy industry." Now it would be possible, perhaps, to explain the lack of consumers' goods for a few years on the grounds that the means for producing them have been devoted to the production of capital goods, instead. If, however, capital goods have in fact been accumulated, the effect is to make possible an increase in the production both of capital goods *and* consumers' goods, because the possession of more capital goods raises the overall ability of an economic system to produce.

If, with a greater overall ability to produce, an economic system still does not produce more consumers' goods, the explanation cannot be that it is continuing to devote some given high proportion of its efforts to the production of capital goods. If the production of capital goods is to be the explanation at all, it must be that the economic system devotes *a larger and larger proportion* of its growing ability to produce to the production of capital goods. In the case of Soviet Russia, which had had little or no increase in the average standard of living since 1913 (indeed, as we have seen, would have suffered from famines in the absence of an outside capitalist world to turn to), this would imply that by the 1970s or 1980s, something on the order of ninety-nine and forty-four one-hundredths percent of its output must have been in the form of capital goods, and be increasing further every year— that by then Soviet Russia must have been purer in its devotion to the production of capital goods than Ivory is in soap; that it must have been one enormous factory from Leningrad to Vladivostok.

Yet, curiously, with all this implied devotion to the production of capital goods, the Soviet Union could not generate sufficient capital of its own to build an automobile or truck factory or natural gas pipeline. Again and again, it had to turn to the United States, to Japan, and to Western Europe—even to Italy, which was the source of its most important automobile factory.

The truth is, a socialist country can never accumulate much capital, even under the most favorable circumstances of outside aid, because its inefficiencies are so great. The greatest efforts it devotes to the production of capital goods are always in danger of being more than offset by the *low productivity of those efforts,* to the point that it cannot even replace the capital goods it consumes in production, and thus must decumulate capital. The former Soviet Union, and every socialist country, was in the position of a farmer who is so inefficient that for every bushel of seed he uses up in production, he can barely produce a bushel of crop. With such inefficiency, no matter how great the concentration on the production of capital goods, very little indeed can remain after allowing for the minimum subsistence of the producers as well as the replacement of the capital goods consumed in production.

Capital accumulation under socialism is possible only at the cost of human life, on the scale imposed by Stalin. Stalin ordered the production of capital goods at the expense of the production of the food and clothing and other necessities required to sustain the lives of the producers. To build hydroelectric stations, steel mills, and armaments factories, he consumed the lives of tens of millions of human beings. These are facts which Gorbachev should have kept in mind when he simultaneously condemned Stalin for being a tyrant and credited him for the development of the Soviet economy. *Under socialism, economic development is possible only under the kind of tyranny and mass murder practiced by Stalin.* It is the exchange of human lives for piles of steel and concrete, which in turn, as the source of weapons for military aggression to further extend the power of socialism's rulers, are useful only for further destruction. When the mass murder lets up, the result is "the years of stagnation" for which Gorbachev denounced the Brezhnev era.

Of course, when left entirely to its own inefficiencies, without an outside capitalist world to turn to, socialism cannot maintain either the capital it inherits from capitalism or what it has accumulated through mass murder. Its inefficiencies are then so great, its production so limited in comparison with the capital goods being used up, wearing out, or deteriorating with age, that with or without mass murder it decumulates capital and retrogresses—to the economic conditions of feudalism and the Dark Ages.

In such circumstances, the economic self-destructiveness of socialism would not be reduced even if a socialist society abandoned its quest for war-making power and thus did not maintain a large-scale military establishment. Its economic self-destructiveness rests on the fundamental chaos and inefficiencies of the system. Socialism can accomplish nothing, including the maintenance of a significant military establishment, without the support of an outside, capitalist world, which continuously provides it with vital supplies. In the absence of the maintenance of a military establishment, its chaos and inefficiencies would render it no less dependent on an outside, capitalist world. Thus, in the absence of the necessary support from the capitalist world, socialism must collapse with or without the maintenance of a military establishment.

5. Socialism's Last Gasp: The Attempt to Establish a Socialist Price System and Why It Is Impossible

Von Mises's demonstration of the chaotic consequences of socialism's lack of a price system has not gone entirely unnoticed. While practically all socialists continue to denounce the "wages system" and to extol what they call "production for use" above the hated "production for profit," a handful of academic socialists who are conversant with economics have recognized the devastating power of von Mises's criticisms.

According to these socialists, it was a minor oversight of all other socialists to have failed to understand the operations of the price system and to have sought to destroy it, and thus to destroy all of civilization along with it, for over a century. Fortunately, however, before socialism could destroy civilization, the material productive forces have come to the rescue and made von Mises see the problem, and his criticisms have now led this handful of academic socialists to recognize what must be done to avert disaster. I do not exaggerate. Oskar Lange, formerly of the University of California and the University of Chicago and later deputy premier of Communist Poland, wrote:

> Socialists have certainly good reason to be grateful to Professor Mises, the great *advocatus diaboli* of their cause. For it was his powerful challenge that forced the socialists to recognize the importance of an adequate system of economic accounting to guide the allocation of resources in a socialist economy. Even more, it was chiefly due to Professor Mises's challenge that many socialists became aware of the very existence of such a problem. . . . a statue of Professor Mises ought to occupy an honorable place in the great hall of the Ministry of Socialization or of the Central Planning Board of the socialist state. . . . a socialist teacher might invite his students in a class on dialectical materialism to go and look at the statue, in order to exemplify the Hegelian *List der Vernunft* [cunning of 'reason'] which made even the stanchest of bourgeois economists unwittingly serve the proletarian cause.[19]

The alleged solution to the economic problems of socialism offered by Lange and the others (whom we must view as a kind of self-styled vanguard of the vanguard of the proletariat, trying to teach the vanguard not to act as a barbarian horde) is known as "liberal socialism" or, sometimes, "market socialism." It consists in the construction of a mythical economic system that is analogous to the centaur of Greek mythology, the beast that was supposed to be half man, half horse. That system is *capitalism's price system appended to the body of socialism.* Socialism is to have free-market prices for all goods and services. It is to have wages, interest, and profits. The hated "wages system," that Marx spent his life attacking, is to be retained. Production is to be "production for

profit," not, as all socialists have always said previously, "production for use." In this way, socialism is allegedly to be able to have all the advantages of capitalism, plus more; for it will simultaneously pocket all of the profits that under capitalism would go to the capitalists. Profits will serve as a "parameter," that is, as a guide to what to do—though, of course, no one will actually profit from doing what he is supposed to do.

This doctrine, incidentally, was presented for consideration in Soviet Russia under Khrushchev. It was known as "Libermanism," after a Russian professor of that name. The proposed role of profits was described with great fanfare at the time, in practically the very words I have used. "Libermanism" has not been heard from since, and with good reason, as we shall see.

Now the way socialism is to achieve a price system is by dividing the socialist economy up into separate sections or firms. Each will be assigned a balance at the government's central bank. The government will set prices for all goods and services. At least on paper, these firms will then buy from and sell to each other; they will also sell to consumers and pay wages. They will pay interest on capital to the government's central bank and even to other enterprises, and they will record profits and losses.

There is really nothing astonishing in any of this. It is similar to socialism on the German or Nazi pattern, in that seemingly separate, independent enterprises will exist. Lange, Liberman, and the others simply want to convert Russian-style socialism into something more closely resembling German-style socialism.

They go further. They claim that many or most of the controls of German-style socialism can be abolished. They claim that a price system can be developed within the context of their German-style socialism, that would make it unnecessary for the government to engage in specific allocations of physical factors of production. They claim, in effect, that all the government need do is allocate capital in money terms to different enterprises or individuals, tell them to invest and produce in the lowest-cost, most profitable way, and then everything will take place as under capitalism except that the government will rake in the profits. There allegedly need be no problem of shortages as a result of the government's prices being set too low, or unsalable surpluses as a result of its prices being set too high; for as soon as such shortages or surpluses appear, it is claimed, the government can raise or lower the prices concerned and thus achieve a balance between supply and demand.

Now the absurdity of what Lange, Liberman, and the others propose can be grasped most simply by starting with the existence of capitalism and then imagining two alternative things to occur: (1) the government imposes price and wage controls, (2) the government obtains the power to expropriate any firm's or individual's capital and turn it over to any other firm or individual at its discretion. After we look at the consequences of each of these measures separately, we can consider their operation in conjunction; and that will describe what to expect from any attempt at a "price system" under socialism.

According to Lange, Liberman, et al., a socialist government could have a price system and make it work by varying prices in response to changing conditions of supply, demand, and cost. In the case of price controls imposed on an existing capitalist system, the individual capitalists have a powerful personal incentive to try to push the government to change its controls every time there is a change in supply, demand, or cost. It is absurd to believe, however, that the government could be made to change its controls in the same way that the capitalists would have changed their prices in a free market.

To make this as concrete as possible, what Lange, Liberman, and the others are implying—though apparently without being aware of it—is that the government could control the price of oil and gasoline and apartment rents and so forth, and would then vary its controls every day in just the same way as a free market would have varied its prices. Now if this were really so, we must ask why the U.S. government did not listen to the oil companies and raise the controlled price of oil and gasoline during the oil shortages of 1973 and 1979, or why the New York City rent-control authorities have never listened to the landlords and raised the controlled rents in the face of the shortage of rent-controlled housing? We must ask why price controls are imposed in the first place, for what purpose could they serve if they were really to duplicate the prices charged in a free market?

The fact is that government price-control officials do not and cannot control prices in the way a free market would have set them. For the basis of the free market's prices is the *self-interests* of the different individuals concerned, acting in an environment of freedom of competition. A gas station owner, an oil company, a landlord, and so on, sets his price on the basis of what is most profitable *for him,* given the same endeavor of all others in setting their prices and in choosing whether or not to pay his. *Self-interest, operating under the freedom of competition, is the driving force of price determination under capitalism. Government control of prices thwarts this driving force.*

While price controls thwart this driving force, the socialization of the economic system destroys it utterly, and more besides.

There is one, indispensable control that socialism must have, even under the most relaxed imaginable variant of the German-style socialism envisioned by Lange, Liberman, et al.; and that is *the right to withdraw capital at any time from any enterprise and make it available to any other enterprise.* This minimum control on the allocation of capital is inescapably implied in the very nature of government ownership: if the government is to be the owner, the enterprises and those in charge of them can have no right to regard the capital at their disposal as theirs for one moment longer than the government wishes it.

To grasp the significance of this fact, let us forget about price controls for the moment. Let us return to an existing capitalist system, and assume that all the government does is obtain the power to expropriate the capital of any firm or individual and turn it over to any other firm or individual at its discretion. This is the equivalent to what it must be able to do, as a minimum, under the most "liberal" variant of so-called market socialism. Thus, for example, one year, it uses this power to halve or totally eliminate the capital of the General Motors Corporation and build up the capital of other enterprises. The next year, it gives the real estate of Manhattan Island to a different group of owners. In the following year, it dispossesses the farmers of New Jersey and turns their farms over to others. The government can do this in the same way that a private business today can close down some branches and open others, or fire existing managers and replace them with new ones—for the property is the government's, not that of the private firms or individuals any longer.

Now this measure would totally destroy all the incentives of ownership.

Nevertheless, it is to people in such a position that "market socialism" in its logically consistent form wants to entrust the supreme management of the socialist economic system. "Market socialism" wants the socialist government to place capital in the hands of firms and individuals who will have absolutely no incentives of ownership, and then to give them discretion as to its investment. It wants the government to delegate its responsibility for investment to them, by giving them capital and then telling them to go and make believe they are capitalists. As I have said, it expects that then everything will work as under capitalism except that the state will be able to claim all of the profits.

If this system were actually implemented, those to whom the socialist state entrusted the use of its capital at any time would be in the position of owners of capital at the pleasure of the state. Their powers of discretion in investment would be genuine powers of ownership, but they would last no longer than the state desired. They would be in the position of people facing the constant threat of expropriation. They would, in effect, be property owners, but they would be less secure in their possession of property than were the owners of fields along the coast of Europe in the era of the Viking raids. It is obvious that the self-interest of people in such a position is very different from that of capitalists under capitalism. Not being secure owners of property, they are not in a position to think of enhancing its value on a long-range basis. Their horizon extends no further than the immediate moment. If they are given significant discretion in its use, their self-interest lies with personally consuming as much of the capital entrusted to them as possible, or converting it to some concealable form, such as gold or jewels. If the socialist state effectively thwarts this motive, it succeeds merely in securing the services of people who are disinterested in the most literal sense of the term.

To grasp the nature of this disinterest, simply think again of our example of the General Motors Corporation, the owners of Manhattan real estate, the New Jersey farmers, and so on. Under "market socialism," all of them have the threat of impending expropriation hanging over their heads. Their self-interest is to consume or conceal as much of their property as possible. We may assume that to prevent this, the government issues orders severely punishing such acts, and that it thereby actually succeeds in stopping them. Now what? Now, the "market socialists" believe, these property owners will be willing to simply go to work for the state with the same zeal with which they would have worked for themselves, and will continue in loyal service until the day the state expropriates them and turns their property over to a new set of owners. Then this new set will do the same thing.

It should be clear that what all of the abstruse talk of the "market socialists" about the "parametric" function of profits in a socialist society boils down to is this: It is profitable to a man to clear and cultivate a field, to develop a business, to construct a factory, which is why under capitalism he does it. Under socialism he will allegedly still do it, not because it is profitable *to him,* but because it is "parametrically" profitable—that is, profitable *to his expropriators.* If traditional socialism requires that an omniscient deity assume command of the socialist economy to make it work, "market socialism" requires the descent of Jesus of Nazareth, Francis of Assisi, and all the other saints of altruism, who will, in the meantime, assume the garb of hard-nosed, calculating businessmen. "Market socialism" is the same old line of "from each according to his ability, to each according to his need," but dressed up in the ludicrous guise of the businessman's quest for profit.

I have not mentioned the opportunities for corruption that a system of "market socialism" would create, nor, having now mentioned them, will I dwell on them. It is clear, however, that under such a system vast personal fortunes could rotate, as it were, among succeeding sets of government favorites who were awarded the right to invest the capital of the economic system.

It is really a nonessential under "market socialism" whether the government explicitly controls prices or not. It could delegate this responsibility to the individual enterprises if it wished. If it did, it might achieve an economic system at the level of, say, Turkey under the arbitrary, despotic rule of the sultans, when no one could be secure in the possession of any property—when no one dared to improve his house or fields, let alone build a factory, for fear of having them seized by the government.

If the government does control prices, as Lange and the others actually suggest, it is absurd to believe that the enterprises to whom it entrusts capital will be zealously besieging the price-control office with requests to raise or lower them so as to balance demand and supply; or, of course, that the price-control office would have any more reason to listen to their requests than when price controls are imposed on an existing capitalist system.

It is obvious that socialism cannot rationally entrust its management to people who either have no incentive at all or an incentive to grab what they can while the opportunity exists. And, in fact, none of the so-called market socialists is actually consistent enough to go very far in his proposals. Without ever explicitly mentioning it, and certainly without ever stressing the fact, they all take for granted that the state will give precise orders to each enterprise concerning what industry or industries it is to operate in, what products it is to produce, how many factories it is to have, and where, and what kind and how many machines it is to have. The discretion they are actually willing to allow is in the relatively minor and very narrow area of how best to use the existing quantity and quality of plant and equipment assigned, for the purposes assigned.

But this brings "market socialism" back to all of the problems of socialist "planning" that it claims to have solved. For in this case, the state must still decide the relative size of the various industries, the quantity and composition of their output, their basic methods of production, and their physical location. And, as we have seen, it has no rational way of deciding these things, for it must attempt to plan the totality of the economic system as an indivisible whole while being simply incapable of comprehending the specific details of the economic system and their myriad interrelationships.

The limited discretion the "market socialists" want to

allow would only introduce further disruption into the already anarchic conditions of socialist production. For it would allow enterprises on their own initiative to snatch away materials, supplies, and labor from other enterprises in ways that could not be controlled by the government planners, and which would thus disrupt even such limited, partial planning as they are able to accomplish on behalf of projects of special priority. Imagine, for example, the government of Soviet Russia trying to build a tank factory, only to find that it could not do so because some of its own enterprises had snapped up all the supplies of some vital material or part. It is for this very reason, I am sure, that "market socialism"—even of the very timid variety actually recommended by Lange and the others—was never tried in any socialist country, is unlikely ever to be tried, and, if tried, would soon be abandoned.

The only solution for the problems of socialism is, as von Mises saw over seventy years ago, the restoration of capitalism.

Indeed, the debate over market socialism is now closed and the correctness of von Mises's position definitively established. It is established by the recognition on the part of socialist regimes all across the world that it is necessary to establish private ownership of the means of production. It is established by the overwhelming fact that all across the world the cry is raised "no more socialism" and efforts are underway in almost every socialist country to establish capitalism.

In echo of these momentous developments, it is gratifying to read the words of a lifelong socialist and admirer of the Soviet Union, Robert Heilbroner, who now says, "Fifty years ago, it was felt that Lange had decisively won the argument for socialist planning. . . . It turns out, of course, that Mises was right. . . . From what we know now [which von Mises knew in 1922] about how anarchic the planning process was, the wonder is not that the Soviet economy has given out but that it went on as long as it did."[20] Heilbroner also declares: "At a recent meeting near Washington, Soviet economists from the prestigious Academy of Sciences disputed the 'pessimistic' conclusions of the C.I.A. that the Soviet G.N.P. was today only between one-half and one-third as high as that of the United States, and that Soviet citizens enjoyed the equivalent of Portuguese or Greek living standards. The Soviet experts maintained that a truer measure put the Soviet G.N.P. at one-seventh of the American—a figure that yields a per-capita standard of living in the Soviet Union which is approximately that of China."[21]

PART B

THE TYRANNY OF SOCIALISM

1. The Tyranny of Socialism

The chaos of socialism is equalled only by the tyranny of socialism. In abolishing economic freedom, socialism abolishes political freedom. In abolishing property rights, it abolishes civil rights. In a word, socialism means the establishment of a totalitarian dictatorship.

It must be stressed again that when I refer to socialism, I am referring to *all* variants of socialism—the socialism of the allegedly respectable socialists, such as the Social Democrats, as well as the socialism of the Nazis and Communists. I stress this fact because a widespread misconception prevails that somehow the "good" socialists could achieve socialism by peaceful means and thereafter preserve political freedoms and civil liberties. That is not so, and it has never been so. And no one should make the mistake of thinking that countries like Great Britain, Israel, and Sweden have been or are exceptions. As we have seen, these countries have not in fact been socialist countries, but "mixed economies."[22]

In every instance in which socialism has actually been enacted, as, for example, in Nazi Germany, Soviet Russia, Communist China, Communist Cuba, and all the other Communist-bloc countries, its totalitarianism has been manifest. It is only necessary to show why the violent, bloody means that have been employed to achieve socialism, and the perpetual reign of terror that follows thereafter, are no accident, but are caused by the very nature of socialism; why, in other words, socialism is a thoroughly evil end, necessitating evil means for its achievement, and necessarily producing the most evil consequences.

2. The Necessity of Evil Means to Achieve Socialism

Let us begin by considering the means employed to achieve socialism. We observe two phenomena that are not unrelated. First, wherever socialism has actually been enacted, as in the Communist-bloc countries and Nazi Germany, violent and bloody means have been used to achieve it and/or maintain it. And, second, where socialist parties have come to power but abstained from wholesale violence and bloodshed, as in Great Britain, Israel, and Sweden, they have *not* enacted socialism, but retained a so-called mixed economy, which they did not radically or fundamentally alter. Let us consider the reasons for these facts.

Even if a socialist government were democratically elected, its first act in office in implementing socialism would have to be an act of enormous violence, namely, the forcible expropriation of the means of production. The democratic election of a socialist government would not change the fact that the seizure of property against the will of its owners is an act of force. A forcible expropriation of property based on a democratic vote is about as peaceful as a lynching based on a democratic vote. It is a cardinal violation of individual rights. The only way that socialism could truly come into existence by peaceful means would be if property owners *voluntarily donated their property to the socialist state.* But consider. If socialism had to wait for property owners to voluntarily donate their property to the state, it would almost certainly have to wait forever. If socialism is *ever* to exist, therefore, it can only come about by means of force—force applied on a massive scale, against all private property.

Further, in the case of the socialization of the entire economic system, as opposed to that of an isolated industry, no form of compensation to the property owners is possible. In the case of an isolated nationalization, the government can largely compensate the former owners by taxing the rest of the property owners to some extent. If the government seizes all property, however, and simply abolishes private ownership, then there is just no possibility of compensation. The government simply steals everyone's property lock, stock, and barrel. In these circumstances, property owners will almost certainly resist and try to defend their rights by force if necessary, as they properly should.

This explains why it takes the Communists to achieve socialism, and why the Social Democrats always fail to achieve socialism. The Communists, in effect, know that they are out to steal all of men's property from them and that if they expect to succeed, they had better come armed and prepared to kill the property owners, who will attempt to defend their rights. The Social Democrats, on the other hand, are held back by fear from taking the steps that would be necessary to achieve socialism.

In sum, the essential facts are these. Socialism must commence with an enormous act of theft. Those who seriously want to steal must be prepared to kill those whom they plan to rob. In effect, the Social Democrats are mere con men and pickpockets, who engage in empty talk about pulling the "big job"—socialism—someday, and who flee before the first sign of resistance by their intended victims. The Communists, on the other hand, are serious about pulling the "big job." They are armed robbers prepared to commit murder. This is why the Communists are able to implement socialism. Of the two, only the Communists are willing to employ the bloody means that are necessary to implement socialism.

3. The Necessity of Terror Under Socialism

If socialism is not to be achieved by open force, the only other way it can be achieved is behind people's backs—i.e., by fraud—which is the method of price and wage controls. This was the route chosen by the Nazis.

But however socialism may be achieved, whether by open force or by fraud, its maintenance requires a reign of terror. It requires an environment in which people cannot trust even their friends, an environment in which they are afraid to express any ideas of their own, or even to ask questions. It requires precisely the kind of environment that existed in Nazi Germany and is characteristic of every Communist country.

In order to begin to understand this point, let us consider merely the requirements of enforcing price and wage controls in an economy that is falling under the rule of de facto socialism. Let us imagine our own economy suffering from universal price controls and universal shortages and observe what would be required just to enforce the price-control regulations and prevent the development of a black market so large as to make the price controls largely meaningless.

Imagine, therefore, that we have a fully price-controlled economy, and that enough time has gone by to create shortages of practically everything. Imagine that we have gasoline shortages, meat shortages, power shortages, shoe shortages—shortages of all goods. In these conditions, every seller would have a powerful self-interest in charging higher prices than the law allowed, and every buyer would have a powerful self-interest in offering to pay such higher prices as a means of outbidding others, in order to obtain a larger supply for himself. How could the government stop the buyers and sellers from pursuing their mutual self-interests and transacting business above its ceiling prices?

Obviously, there would have to be penalties imposed for selling above the ceiling prices. But what kind of penalties? If a seller stood to make the equivalent of an extra twenty or thirty thousand dollars a year, say, by defying the price-control regulations, an occasional small fine would certainly not be a sufficient deterrent. And probably even the smallest neighborhood shops would stand to take in far more than that amount of extra income by defying the regulations. If the government were serious about its price controls, therefore, it would be necessary for it to impose severe penalties—penalties comparable to those for a major felony.

But the mere existence of such penalties would not be enough. The government would also have to make it actually dangerous to conduct black-market transactions. It would have to make people fear that in conducting such a transaction they might somehow be discovered by the police, and actually end up in jail. In order to create such fear, the government would have to develop an army of spies and secret informers. For example, the government would have to make a storekeeper and his customer fearful that if they engaged in a black-market transaction, some other customer in the store would report them. Because of the privacy and secrecy in which many black-market transactions could be conducted, the government would have to make anyone contemplating a black-market transaction fearful that the other party might turn out to be a police agent trying to entrap him. The government would have to make people fearful of their long-time associates, even of their friends and relatives, lest even they turn out to be informers.

And, finally, in order to obtain convictions, the government would have to place the decision about innocence or guilt in the case of black-market transactions in the hands of an administrative tribunal. It could not rely on jury trials, because it would be unlikely that many juries could be found willing to bring in guilty verdicts in cases in which a man might have to go to jail for several years for the crime of selling a few pounds of meat or a pair of shoes above the ceiling price.

In sum, therefore, the requirements merely of enforcing price-control regulations would be the adoption of essential features of a totalitarian state, namely, the establishment of the category of "economic crimes," in which the peaceful pursuit of material self-interest is treated as a criminal offense, and the establishment of a totalitarian police apparatus replete with spies and informers and the power of arbitrary arrest and imprisonment. Clearly, the enforcement of price controls requires a government similar to that of Hitler's Germany or Stalin's Russia. If the government is unwilling to go to such lengths, then, to that extent, its price controls prove unenforceable and simply break down. The black market then assumes major proportions.

Now observe that in a socialized economy, a black market also exists. Only in this case, its existence entails the commission of further crimes. Under de facto socialism, the production and sale of goods in the black market entails the defiance of the government's regulations concerning production and distribution, as well as the defiance of its price controls. For example, the goods themselves that are sold in the black market are intended by the government to be distributed in accordance with its plan, and not in the black market. The factors of production used to produce those goods are likewise intended by the government to be used in accordance with its plan, and not for the purpose of supplying the black market. Under a system of de jure socialism, such as existed in Soviet Russia, all black-market activity necessarily entails the misappropriation of state property. From the point of

view of the legal code of a socialist state, most black-market activity must be regarded as theft of state property. For example, the factory workers or managers in Soviet Russia who turned out products that they sold in the black market were considered as stealing the raw materials supplied by the state.

Observe further. In a socialist state, the government's economic plan is part of the supreme law of the land. We have already seen in Part A of this chapter how chaotic the so-called planning process of socialism is. Its further disruption by workers and managers siphoning off materials and supplies to produce for the black market, is something which a socialist state is logically entitled to regard as an act of *sabotage*. And that is how the legal code of a socialist state does regard it. Consistent with this fact, black-market activity in a socialist country often carries the death penalty. In Nazi Germany, people were beheaded for it. In Soviet Russia, they were shot for it.

Even apart from possible indulgence in black-market activity, every socialist official who has responsibility for production necessarily leads a dangerous life. On the one hand, any use of factors of production in a way different than that specified by the state's economic plan lays such an official open to a charge of sabotage. On the other hand, it is generally impossible for the state's economic plan to be very precise, as we have seen; and so some discretion must be used. Since a socialist economic system functions in a state of continuous chaos and chronic crisis, it is very easy for any given official to be singled out and blamed for some disaster caused by socialism's anarchy of production. It becomes an essential talent under socialism for an official to be able to know how to cover himself and always to have scapegoats of his own at hand. From the top to the bottom, an incredible game of buck passing, favor trading, and mutual blackmail takes place. Ever-shifting alliances and factions are formed for mutual protection. And, periodically, victims are sacrificed: usually, subordinate officials here and there; sometimes, entire factions in giant purges.

The fundamental fact driving socialism to a reign of terror is the incredible dilemma in which the socialist state places itself in relation to the masses of its citizens.[23] On the one hand, the socialist state assumes full responsibility for the individual's economic well-being. It openly avows this responsibility—this is the whole source of socialism's popular appeal. On the other hand, in all of the ways I have shown, the socialist state makes *an unbelievable botch of the job*. It makes the individual's life a nightmare. Every day of his life, the citizen of a socialist state must spend time in endless waiting lines. For him, the problems Americans experienced in the gasoline shortages of the 1970s are normal; only he does not experience them in relation to gasoline—for he does not own a car and has no hope of ever owning one—but in relation to simple items of clothing, to vegetables, even to bread. Even worse, as we will see, he is frequently forced to work at a job not of his choice and which he therefore must certainly hate. And he lives in a condition of unbelievable overcrowding, with hardly ever a chance for privacy. To put it mildly, such a man must seethe with resentment and hostility.

Now against whom would it be more logical for the citizens of a socialist state to direct their resentment and hostility than against that very socialist state itself? The same socialist state which has proclaimed its responsibility for their life, has promised them a life of bliss, and which *in fact* is responsible for giving them a life of hell. Indeed, the leaders of a socialist state live in a further dilemma, in that they daily encourage the people to believe that socialism is a perfect system whose bad results can only be the work of evil men. If that were true, who in reason could those evil men be but *the rulers themselves,* who have not only made life a hell, but have perverted an allegedly perfect system to do it?

It follows that the rulers of a socialist state must live in terror of the people. By the logic of their actions and their teachings, the boiling, seething resentment of the people should well up and swallow them in an orgy of bloody vengeance. The rulers sense this, even if they do not admit it openly; and thus their major concern is always to keep the lid on the citizenry.

Consequently, it is true but very inadequate merely to say such things as that socialism lacks freedom of the press and freedom of speech. Of course, it lacks these freedoms. If the government owns all the newspapers and publishing houses, if it decides for what purposes newsprint and paper are to be made available, then obviously nothing can be printed which the government does not want printed. If it owns all the meeting halls, no public speech or lecture can be delivered which the government does not want delivered. But socialism goes far beyond the mere lack of freedom of press and speech. It totally *annihilates* these freedoms. It turns the press and every public forum into a vehicle of hysterical propaganda in its own behalf, and it engages in the relentless persecution of everyone who dares to deviate by so much as an inch from its official party line.

The reason for these facts is the socialist rulers' terror of the people. To protect themselves, they must order the propaganda ministry and the secret police to work 'round the clock. The one, to constantly divert the people's attention from the responsibility of socialism, and of the rulers of socialism, for the people's misery. The other, to spirit away and silence anyone who might even remotely suggest the responsibility of socialism or its rulers—to spirit away anyone who begins to show signs of thinking

for himself. It is because of the rulers' terror, and their desperate need to find scapegoats for the failures of socialism, that the press of a socialist country is always full of stories about foreign plots and sabotage, and about corruption and mismanagement on the part of subordinate officials, and why, periodically, it is necessary to unmask large-scale domestic plots and to sacrifice major officials and entire factions in giant purges.

It is because of their terror, and their desperate need to crush every breath even of potential opposition, that the rulers of socialism do not dare to allow even purely cultural activities that are not under the control of the state. For if people so much as assemble for an art show or poetry reading that is not controlled by the state, the rulers must fear the dissemination of dangerous ideas. Any unauthorized ideas are dangerous ideas, because they can lead people to begin thinking for themselves and thus to begin thinking about the nature of socialism and its rulers. The rulers must fear the spontaneous assembly of a handful of people in a room, and use the secret police and its apparatus of spies, informers, and terror either to stop such meetings or to make sure that their content is entirely innocuous from the point of view of the state.

Socialism cannot be ruled for very long except by terror. As soon as the terror is relaxed, resentment and hostility logically begin to well up against the rulers. The stage is thus set for a revolution or civil war. In fact, in the absence of terror, or, more correctly, a sufficient degree of terror, socialism would be characterized by an endless series of revolutions and civil wars, as each new group of rulers proved as incapable of making socialism function successfully as its predecessors before it.

The inescapable inference to be drawn from this discussion is that the terror actually experienced in the socialist countries has not been simply the work of evil men, such as Stalin, but springs from the nature of the socialist system, and at least in those socialist countries which are not committed to the abandonment of socialism, *is still going on at this very moment.* (As of the fall of 1994, this is certainly the case in China, Cuba, North Korea, Laos, Cambodia, and Vietnam. Despite claims of commitment to the abandonment of socialism, it may very well still be the case both in portions of the former Soviet Union and in some of the former East European satellites.) Stalin could come to the fore because his unusual willingness and cunning in the use of terror were the specific characteristics most required by a ruler of socialism. He rose to the top by a process of socialist natural selection: the selection of the worst.[24] His heirs resorted to the same techniques. As well-known examples, consider the invasions of Hungary and Czechoslovakia, the use of drugs to destroy the sanity of dissidents, and, above all, the vast network of forced labor camps in the Soviet Union. And, of course, even in the last years of socialism, there was no way of knowing what was not reported to the outside world, which almost certainly was a good deal worse than what was reported. Indeed, most of the territory of the Soviet Union was inaccessible to foreigners, and contacts with Soviet citizens were severely limited by the Soviet government.[25] The Soviet government pursued this policy of secrecy only because it had a great deal to hide. The policy of secrecy has now apparently been abandoned by the successor regime, and it is to be hoped that the full truth of the atrocities committed in the Soviet Union under socialism will emerge in the years to come.

Under the Soviet regime, the Russian people experienced all the hostility and resentment I have described, but they were so fearful and behaved so contemptibly that they channelled it against each other rather than against socialism and its rulers. Hedrick Smith wrote: ". . . Soviet society in general is peopled by mini-dictators inflicting inconvenience and misery on the rest of their fellow citizens, often, it seems, as a way of getting back at the system for the hardship and frustration they themselves have suffered."[26] He quotes a Russian scientist: "'Put a Russian in charge of a little plot of ground or a doorway somewhere, and he will use his meager authority over that spot to make life hard on others.'" Smith notes that he has heard Russians describe this phenomenon as "a mass settling of scores on a personal level."[27]

This is the psychological and moral climate of a socialist society—a society blinded by terror and reduced virtually to the punishment of all by all. It is terror and universal hatred that socialism and its rulers require lest they be blasted from power.[28]

If Stalin's heirs did not find it necessary to be fully as brutal as Stalin himself, it was only because they were able to coast on the environment of fear and the habit of unquestioning obedience that he created. But in the prolonged absence of fresh demonstrations of terror on the scale applied by Stalin, and as the result of the relaxation inspired by Gorbachev, more and more resentments surfaced and came to be focused on the government. Thus, the stage was set for the collapse of socialism.

It was to be expected that to avoid such collapse, the Soviet government would return to its traditional policy of all-out repression. Fortunately, the attempt to do this failed—in the aborted coup of August 1991. However, similar, more successful attempts by the remnants of the Communist apparatus cannot be ruled out and may well take place in the future.

The only alternative both to renewed repression and to an unending series of civil wars and revolutions, as successive socialist governments attempt the impossible and are driven out in a storm of hatred, is to abandon socialism in favor of capitalism. Whether or not Russia and the other portions of the former Soviet Union will find the will to make such a historic change, or even be allowed to make it by a citizenry that is intellectually still committed to socialism, remains to be seen. Thus far, the economic reforms enacted constitute but the faintest beginning of such a change.

In Eastern Europe, where the end of fear of Soviet invasion led to the quick loss of the satellites, the prospects for establishing capitalism appear to be better. This is especially true in what was formerly East Germany, where the unified German government is in a position to provide genuine guarantees of property rights. Hopefully, at least Hungary, Czechoslovakia, and Poland, and the Baltic states of Lithuania, Latvia, and Estonia, which were so recently part of the Soviet Union, will also be able to succeed in establishing capitalism. The nature of the requirements for establishing capitalism in a formerly socialist country will be explained at the end of this chapter.

4. The Necessity of Forced Labor Under Socialism

Socialism necessitates a system of forced labor—slavery. Forced labor is implied in the very idea of socialist planning. If the state is to plan the production of all commodities, it must also plan the skills that the workers will possess who are to produce those commodities, and where those workers are to live and work. It is incompatible with socialist planning for private individuals to have the freedom to acquire the skills *they* want and to live where *they* want. Such freedom would alone make socialist planning impossible.

Of course, socialism cannot plan in any case. Nevertheless, forced labor remains an essential feature of socialism. As shown in Part A of this chapter, the economic conditions of socialism are the same as those which prevail under universal price controls and universal shortages. Accordingly, socialism is characterized by a labor shortage, in which there is a ready and waiting employment for more labor in the production of virtually every good. The labor shortage under socialism results from the fact that a socialist government wants to expand production, but is unable to trace the connections among the different industries; it is unable to determine the effects of producing more of any one item on the ability to produce other items.

As a result, as we have seen, it establishes a quota system, as in Soviet Russia, in which it tries to encourage the maximum possible production of *each* item. This creates a need for additional labor and all other factors of production in every industry and factory. The labor shortage is compounded by all of the inefficiencies of socialism, which cause a larger amount of labor to be required to produce each unit of a good. Finally, the shortages of consumers' goods under socialism act to reduce the supply of labor by destroying the incentive to work and earn money, leading people to stop working.[29]

In the face of such conditions, if the government is unwilling to abandon socialism (or price controls, however the case may be), its only alternative is *to freeze people into their jobs, order them into those jobs and those geographical areas where it considers their work vital, and extract work from them by the threat of physical force.* The government must freeze people into their jobs to stop them from quitting in response to the shortage of consumers' goods. It must order them into specific jobs in specific areas for the same reasons it finds it necessary when a shortage exists to allocate crude oil or any other factor of production to the production of specific products in specific places, namely, to avoid the chaos of products it considers vital not being produced because other products it considers less important are produced instead. It must extract work by the threat of force because, with the money that jobs offer no longer a value to the workers, it lacks adequate positive incentives to offer them.

This, of course, is a system of slavery.

Forced Labor in the Soviet Union

It is necessary to consider the extent to which forced labor existed in the Soviet Union.

First and foremost, over the life of the Communist regime untold millions of people suffered and died in concentration camps—the infamous Gulag system. In the Stalin years, the camps may have held as many as 20 to 30 million slave laborers.[30] Even as late as the Gorbachev era, the camps contained hundreds of thousands if not a million or more slave laborers. Second, forced labor existed insofar as all people living on collective farms—as much as 40 percent or more of the Soviet population—were prohibited from moving away from those farms without the permission of the collective farm managements. In addition, at harvest time, all available urban workers could be forced into the countryside to help bring in the harvest. (Observe, incidentally, that the collective farming system was so inefficient that 40 percent of the population was insufficient to bring in the harvest. In the United States, by way of comparison, less than 4 percent of the population is more than sufficient for agriculture.) Third, every graduate of a university or technical school in the Soviet Union was compulsorily assigned to a job for a period of two to three years following graduation. Fourth, every remaining worker in the Soviet Union was compelled to have a labor book that detailed all of his previous employment, including com-

ments by the government officials who were his former employers, reasons for changing jobs, and so on. This book had to be presented to each new government employer. Employment could not be obtained without it. The new government employer then kept the book so long as the worker was employed at that particular job. Theoretically, since Khrushchev, the government employer was supposed to return the labor book at the worker's request. Nevertheless, this system certainly discouraged the worker's leaving any given job against the government employer's wishes, and was, in fact, a forcible deterrent to changing jobs. In addition, it was illegal in the Soviet Union to be unemployed.[31]

If the severity of forced labor in Soviet Russia under Stalin's successors was not as great as it was under Stalin, the explanation was largely a more flourishing black market. In the latter part of the Brezhnev era, for example, the black market was estimated to account for about 20 percent of the Soviet Union's economy.[32] In addition, for many years following Stalin it was legal for the members of collective farms to farm small plots of up to an acre on their own account and to sell the produce in the cities for whatever prices it could bring. These small plots accounted for less than 3 percent of the cultivated land in the Soviet Union and produced about 30 percent of its agricultural output.[33] This agricultural output and the black market made it worthwhile for people to work and earn money; within limits they provided people with something to spend the money on.

Notice, however, how the mitigation of forced labor and, indeed, the very survival of the socialist system, depended on the extent to which socialist principles were violated. Strictly, according to socialist principles, there should have been no black market and no quasi-private farming plots. But it was only by permitting them that the system could survive. For the rest, the fact that forced labor was not as severe as it was under Stalin was the result of a willingness on the part of Stalin's successors to tolerate enormous rates of labor absenteeism and a general breakdown of what the regime called "labor discipline."[34] (To illustrate how pervasive these problems were, Hedrick Smith described a popular comedy routine in Russia, in which three workers sneaked away from their jobs to get haircuts. They received miserable service because their barbers had sneaked off too. The barbers, in turn, could not obtain the things they wanted, because the dentist, repairman, and grocer they were seeking were the very customers left sitting in their chairs.[35])

The Imposition of Forced Labor in the United States

It must be stressed that a system of forced labor could be imposed even in the United States. This could happen either as a result of the open socialization of the economic system, or, as is much more likely, as part of a program of *de facto* socialization carried out in response to the chaos created by price controls. None of our traditions, none of our past record of freedom, would be enough to stop it.

It should be realized that such slavery was actually instituted during World War II in countries with very similar traditions as the United States. It was imposed in Great Britain, Australia, and even Canada. During World War II, workers in those countries could not quit or change their jobs without government permission, and they could be ordered to work wherever the government required them. Similar legislation was proposed to the Congress of the United States by President Roosevelt in his State of the Union Message of January 1944.[36] Fortunately, the legislation did not pass. But had the United States been at war longer and the effects of the labor shortage become more severe, as a result of the continued operation of inflation and price controls, it is very likely that such legislation would have been enacted even here. For the only alternative, given the continuation of price controls, would have been chaos in the allocation of labor and the massive stoppage of work.

Thus, if we someday adopt socialism in this country, no matter what its form, we must expect the same consequences as existed in the Soviet Union.

5. Socialism as a System of Aristocratic Privilege and a Court Society

Once the government assumes the power to determine the individual's job, it obtains the power to decide whether he must spend his life working in a coal mine in a remote village somewhere, or in the comparative comfort of one of its offices in the capital. It obtains the power to decide whether he will pass his life as an obscure nobody living in poverty, or enjoy a flourishing career, celebrated in his field, and living in comparative opulence.[37] This, of course, goes along with the government's power over the distribution of consumers' goods—a power which every socialist government naturally possesses. In accordance with its powers of distribution, a socialist government decides what kind of house or apartment the individual is to occupy, what kind of clothing he is to wear, what kind of food he is to eat, whether or not he is to own an automobile, and so on.

In Soviet Russia, for example, the government assigned different grades of housing based on rank in the government or Communist Party. On the same basis, it decided who could and who could not buy an automobile. It even maintained special stores that were closed to the general public and which exclusively served high

government and party officials and their favorites in the arts and sciences. These stores carried many kinds of Western imports, from clothing to tape recorders, and the limited supplies of whatever worthwhile goods as were produced in the Soviet Union itself. While such things as meat were unavailable throughout most of the Soviet Union for months on end, the privileged customers of these stores were supplied with caviar.[38]

The existence of a system of naked aristocratic privilege is not a contradiction of the principles of socialism, but their natural outgrowth. It follows directly from socialism's fundamental moral and political premise, which is that the individual does not exist as an end in himself, but as a means to the ends of "Society." Since Society is not an independent entity with a will and voice of its own, the alleged ends of Society are necessarily ends determined by the rulers of the socialist state. This means that under socialism the individual is actually nothing more than a means to the ends of the *rulers*. It is difficult to imagine a system that could be more aristocratic and servile in nature.

The existence of a system of aristocratic privilege does not contradict the slogan "from each according to his ability, to each according to his need."[39] The rulers of socialism can and do assert that they and their favorites have "special needs." Moreover, that slogan was intended by Marx to be achieved only under "socialism in its higher phase"—that is, after generations of socialism had changed human nature. If one thinks seriously about the meaning of the phrase "a change in human nature," one must realize that it is a contradiction and therefore impossible. A change in human *nature* is as absurd an idea as a change in the nature of water or lead. Men will be able to practice the principle "from each according to his ability, to each according to his need," when water is able to flow uphill and lead to float. Meanwhile, while it is waiting for human nature to "change," a socialist state is free to adopt any system of distribution it pleases. Moreover, it cannot, as a matter of practice, adopt a system of economic equality, because, as previously explained, such a system is tantamount to the destruction of causality in production—it renders the individual incapable of accomplishing results perceptibly affecting his or his loved ones' well-being and thus would have the consequence of immediately bringing production to an end.[40]

What positively generates the system of aristocratic privilege under socialism is the fact that the only values that actually count in a socialist society are the values of its rulers. It should be recalled from Part A of this chapter that the absence of competition and profit-and-loss incentives in supplying the consumers makes the plain citizens economically impotent under socialism. Production thus takes place exclusively in accordance with the values of the rulers. What the rulers value is what contributes to their military strength, their prestige, and their amusement. The goods required by the masses for survival enter into the rulers' valuations only to the extent that the rulers need subjects and do not wish to lose too many of them.

The nature of the rulers' values determines the nature of the incentives and inequalities of a socialist society. It is not true that a socialist society exists entirely without incentives. That would be true only if it tried to practice consistently the absurd ideal "from each according to his ability, to each according to his need." In actual fact, a socialist society does have some incentives. But the incentives are geared entirely to the achievement of the values of the rulers. There are no incentives to the achievement of the values of the plain citizens.

The kind of incentives and inequalities that prevail under socialism are similar to those which prevail in an army. In an army there are incentives for privates to make corporal and for everyone to advance to a higher grade. But all the incentives in an army are geared to achieving the objectives of the supreme commander. The objectives of the supreme commander are the ultimate ends, definitely not the improvement of the life of the privates. Indeed, neither in an army nor under socialism is the improvement of *anyone's* actual life the goal. The goal is always some impersonal achievement, whether victory in the battle with the neighboring country or victory in the battle of the new dam or truck factory, which is just how the socialists in Soviet Russia described their construction projects.[41] The closest socialism ever comes to making the improvement of life its goal is its alleged concern with the improvement of the life of unborn future generations. But no sooner does the generation of the grandchildren arrive, than socialism's concern switches to the grandchildren of the grandchildren.[42]

Socialism is essentially a militaristic-aristocratic type society. It rests on a base of starving serfs, comprising the great majority of the population, who live at or below the level of minimum physical subsistence and whose only function in life is to toil for the values of the rulers. Workers with special skills of value to the rulers may be somewhat better off, if that is what is necessary to make them deliver their skills and if it is practicable to offer them such incentives. But they too are essentially just serfs—they too work under force, and what they receive is subsistence or sub-subsistence, plus a small bonus for their skill. Above the serfs come various grades of officials and favorites, who help the rulers to exploit the serfs or who provide the rulers with weapons of war, the means of gaining greater prestige, or simply amusement. In this category are all the production managers, all the lower and middle party and police officials, the propagandists, the intellectuals, the scientists, the artists, the athletes. These are the tools, the henchmen, the flunkies, and the simple court favorites of the socialist society. Finally, at the very top, come the supreme rulers themselves—the men who have outmaneuvered and outgunned all of their rivals. These are the Neanderthals whose powerlust and gluttony socialism elevates to the ultimate end of human existence.

A few further words need to be said in reference to the middle strata of a socialist society, especially its intellectuals. As a result of a socialist state's twin powers over the individual's work and consumption, everyone's life comes to depend unconditionally on the good graces of every government official with power or influence. In such circumstances, not only are people stopped by terror from criticizing anything the government or any government official does, but a competition breaks out in the positive *praise and adulation* of the government and its officials. As illustration of the lengths to which such self-abasing flattery can be carried, it should be remembered that educated Germans proclaimed that Hitler spoke with God, the "Führer of the Universe"; and that educated Russians praised Stalin as "the leader genius," the sight of whom made them want "to howl from happiness and exaltation."[43]

The same sort of thing continued to go on in Soviet Russia almost to the very end, though, since the time of Khrushchev it was more subdued. In Soviet Russia, no one was able to rise in his field without the backing of influential friends in the Party. Major advancement, including the highly coveted privilege of travelling abroad and thus being able to buy foreign goods simply unavailable in Soviet Russia, required serving as an informer for the KGB—the secret police. In the Soviet Union, men betrayed friends and relatives for the meanest material gains: to be able to buy such things as a Western refrigerator, Western furniture, even a Western toilet.[44]

Ironically, the American sympathizers of the Soviet Union, who continue to work for the establishment of a similar regime here, frequently write books and plays denouncing corporate executives under capitalism for allegedly selling their souls for material advantage. The socialist society that these authors and playwrights yearn for is a society in which the only way that intellectuals can advance is by means of displaying the most abject servility to Neanderthals, who, in the absence of a capitalist world outside, could offer them no more than a few extra scraps of food wrung from some poor serf. It is pitiable, but that is evidently the path that many of today's intellectuals find most secure and the reward they find commensurate with their abilities, since a socialist society is what they are striving to bring about.

Such intellectuals should not be thought of, however, as motivated by a desire to sell their souls merely for a crust of bread or a toilet. They describe themselves as nonmaterialists, and what they seek is primarily a non-material reward. The nature of that nonmaterial reward makes a crust of bread or a toilet appear far too generous as a measure of their worth. For, as we have seen in the discussion of environmentalism, what they are motivated by is simply the nihilistic desire to destroy human achievement. Their nonmaterial reward is to be the impoverishment and suffering of all.[45]

6. From Forced Labor to Mass Murder Under Socialism

There is a further consequence of forced labor under socialism that must be considered, namely, its potential for developing into mass murder. To understand how this can happen, we must contrast forced labor under socialism with forced labor under different conditions.

Slavery existed in ancient Greece and Rome and in the Southern United States before the Civil War, and was, of course, a moral abomination. Nevertheless, abominable as slavery was, there was an important factor in these cases which restrained the slave owners and the overseers in their treatment of the slaves. That was the fact that *the slaves were private property.* A private slave owner was restrained in his treatment of his slaves by his own material self-interest. If he injured or killed his slave, he destroyed his own property. Of course, out of ignorance or irrationality, this sometimes happened; but it was the exception rather than the rule. Private slave owners were motivated to treat their slaves with at least the same consideration they gave to their livestock, and to see to it that their overseers acted with the same consideration.

But under socialism, the slaves are "public property"—the property of the state. Those who have charge of the slaves, therefore, have no personal economic interest in their lives or well-being. Since they are not owners of the slaves, they will not derive any personal material benefit if the slaves are alive to work in the future, nor suffer any personal material loss if the slaves are not alive to work in the future. In such conditions, slave labor results in mass murder. The officials in charge of the slaves are given orders to complete certain projects as of a certain time. Quite possibly, they are threatened with being reduced to the status of slaves themselves, if they fail. In these circumstances, the slaves are treated as valueless natural resources. Brutal punishments are inflicted on them for trifling reasons, and they are worked to the point of exhaustion and death. The slaves of socialism are slaves, but they are no one's property and therefore no one's loss.

In this way, slave labor under socialism results in mass murder. In just this way, tens of millions of people have been murdered.

Of course, the economics of slavery under socialism is not a sufficient explanation of mass murder. Those who participate in the system must be utterly depraved. But observe how socialism creates the conditions in which depravity flourishes—the conditions in which depravity can express itself, is freed of the restraints of better motives, and is positively nurtured and encouraged. For it is socialism that delivers men into slavery. It is socialism that removes the restraint of self-interest from those in charge of the use of any form of property. And it is socialism that creates an environment of hatred and sadism. In such conditions, the most depraved and vicious element of the population finds a place for its depravity and viciousness and steps forward to run the labor camps and the whole socialist society.

7. From Socialism to Capitalism: How to Privatize Communist Countries

The worldwide discrediting of socialism and the desire to replace it with capitalism raises the vital question of precisely how to establish private ownership of the means of production in the socialist countries. The purpose of this section is to explain not only how state property can initially be placed in private hands, but, even more importantly, what is required for private ownership of the means of production to be made genuine and effective.

The advantages of private ownership of the means of production are so overwhelming that it is actually of secondary importance precisely who the initial private owners are and how their ownership is established. Whatever the specific method or methods of establishing private ownership of the means of production, the institution will function to the benefit of everyone—owners of the means of production and *nonowners* of the means of production alike.[46] It will do so, however, only to the degree that the individual private owners possess *full and secure rights of ownership.*

The security of property rights means that the owners must be secure both against the possibility of any form of new confiscation by the state and against successful challenge to their ownership by other private individuals claiming to be the rightful owners. To understand the necessity of the security of property rights, the reader should imagine how his behavior would be affected if he were contemplating buying a home that he could not be certain would be his for very long. He would not be prepared to pay very much for it, and, after he bought it, he would not be prepared to put very much into it. Indeed, his incentive would probably be to let the house run down and even to sell off such things as the appliances for the sake of obtaining cash or other assets that would be more securely his. Without the security of property rights, the situation of all would-be owners of factories, farms, mines, and stores in the present-day socialist countries must be exactly the same. Such owners would be in essentially the same position as the state employees described earlier who were supposed to act as capitalists under "market socialism."[47] The absolute security of the owners' property rights is essential if people are to be willing to pay proper prices for the various properties and then to stay on and improve them rather than milk them for whatever they can.

An essential aspect of the rights of ownership is the right freely to buy and sell property. This aspect of property rights is especially important in the transition from socialism to capitalism. The combinations of assets of the various enterprises of socialism and thus the combinations of assets of the enterprises that will initially exist under capitalism will almost certainly need radical change. It will be essential for the market to have the freedom literally to redefine all enterprises by changing the combinations of their assets. This means, there must be the freedom both to break up existing enterprises by selling off their assets in the manner of "corporate raiders" and to combine their assets through such devices as mergers and acquisitions.

As I say, these freedoms are essential. For a major foundation of the efficiency of capitalism—ironically, increasingly overlooked in the supposedly capitalist United States—is the ability to create business firms that possess *the right combinations of assets.* This ability is essential if firms are to be able to produce the right products by the most efficient methods. It must be present at all times, if the economic system is to be able to adjust to changing conditions. It is acutely necessary in the context of putting right the combinations of assets that a socialist government is likely to have thought appropriate for the various enterprises. It would be essential not only for such things as combining manufacturers with the right parts makers, and retail outlets with the appropriate warehouse facilities, but also for changing the uses made of all kinds of existing factories and land sites.

Nothing less than a radical overhaul of the entire apparatus of production inherited from socialism will be necessary if the economic system is to become efficient. Many factories will have to be closed and such of their assets as are still useable, devoted to production in different locations. Most other factories will have to undergo major changes in what they produce and the methods

by which they produce. The output of innumerable factories will have to go to different users. The use that is made of innumerable land sites will have to change. All of this requires the freedom to buy and sell and to breakup and combine the assets of firms.

Along the same lines, the market would need the absolute freedom to hire and fire the managers of enterprises. This freedom too is necessary at all times and acutely necessary in the conditions of a transition from socialism to capitalism. Any managers inherited from socialism are likely to need replacement. Many of the initial managers under capitalism will also need replacement. To be effective, the transition from socialism to capitalism will need to be followed by a fall into obscurity of numerous former top managers and rise from obscurity of numerous new managers. Nothing must be allowed to impede the business takeovers and buyouts that are an essential part of this process.

In addition, of course, there must be the absolute freedom to hire and fire ordinary workers. Socialism is characterized by a massive misallocation of labor, just as it is characterized by massive misallocation of capital. This too must be put right if production is to become efficient.

A vital aspect of the transition from socialism to capitalism, that is implicit in all that has just been said and is clearly called for by the nature of capitalism, is the freedom of every enterprise to enter into the industry of every other enterprise, and, of course, the freedom of everybody to form new enterprises. In other words, the full freedom of competition must exist.

In the light of these requirements, the specific methods of establishing private ownership of the means of production can now be considered.

The simplest and most obvious method is that wherever former owners of property or their descendants are still alive, the properties should be returned to those from whom they were stolen, or to their descendants.

In Eastern Europe, this method is somewhat complicated by the fact that many of the private property owners who were dispossessed by the Communists were themselves beneficiaries of expropriations carried out not long before by the Nazis. Here the solution clearly is to return the properties to the earlier owners dispossessed by the Nazis, or to the descendants of those owners.

To the difficulty of settling claims as between two or more private claimants is added the fact that the method of returning property to former owners becomes less and less adequate, the longer is the period of time during which socialism has existed and the more ruthless were the means employed to establish socialism in the first place. This is because it becomes correspondingly more difficult to locate specific individuals with valid claims to ownership. (In many cases, everyone with a valid claim may simply have been murdered.) The major part of the problem, however, is the fact that as time has passed, numerous new plants and machines have been constructed, which no one can now claim on the basis of property rights existing before the establishment of socialism. These observations are particularly applicable to the former Soviet Union, where socialism existed for over seventy years and where over twenty million people were murdered by the Communist regime. The mass murders committed by the Nazis may pose a similar problem to the location of heirs.

In view of these facts, I propose three methods of privatization. First, as far as possible, property should be returned to those from whom it was stolen, or to their descendants. Second, in the case of agricultural land where it is not possible to locate former owners or their descendants, the land should be made the individual private property of those who now work it. That is, all the collective farms and state farms should be broken up into separate, individual private farms. Formulas could be devised allowing for differences in the amount of land individuals received based on differences in the time they had been compelled to work the land. Those who had suffered such forced labor for a longer period, would receive more of the land than those who had suffered it for a shorter period. Individuals who would otherwise receive parcels of land too small to farm might simply receive cash.

Third, in the case of all other property—factories, mines, shops, and so forth—the appropriate principle would be to place the assets on the open market for competitive bidding. Foreigners should be actively encouraged to participate in this bidding and, indeed, the bidding should be carried on in Western currencies and in gold. Foreigners should have the same full rights of ownership as citizens: they should be allowed to buy and sell property of all kinds, to form companies, and to remit dividend and interest payments to their own countries to whatever extent they wish.

Active foreign participation in the bidding creates the possibility of the average citizen of the socialist countries deriving an important immediate benefit from privatization. Namely, as the proceeds from the sale of assets came in, each individual citizen could receive his individual share of the proceeds—that is, the proceeds of the government's sales could be divided up among the citizens. Thus, during the period of liquidation of state assets, the average citizen could receive one or more checks payable in Western currencies. He could use the proceeds to buy essential consumers' goods that could be imported from the outside world because the means would be present to pay for those imports. This would help to tide

him over during the difficult period of transition during which his country's economic system was being reorganized and he was unemployed or not in a position to earn a significant amount by working. In this way, for the first and only time—in the process of its liquidation—collective ownership of the means of production would turn out to provide some actual benefit to the citizens: in the moment of its being liquidated for Western cash, it would enable them to obtain something of value to their lives.

It should be observed, incidentally, that the benefit to the average citizen would be the greater, the greater was the prospective security of property. Because to the extent that newly acquired property rights were expected to be upheld, the higher would be the prices that foreigners would be prepared to pay for the assets being offered for sale, and thus the greater would be the proceeds accruing to the average citizen of the formerly socialist country. Economic morality would be rewarded. (The ability of foreigners freely to remit dividends and interest payments is an important aspect of this morality and also an important foundation of the foreigners' willingness to bid up the prices of the assets offered for sale, and thus of the ability of the average citizen of the formerly socialist country immediately to benefit from privatization.)

The next chapter will show why it is of absolutely no consequence that much of the property of the formerly socialist country would be owned by foreigners—why there are no negatives to offset the positives I have just described, but only the further positives resulting from the operation of private ownership of the means of production once it is in place. Furthermore, once the transition to capitalism was accomplished and the average citizen of the formerly socialist country was in a position to begin saving and investing on a significant scale, not only would he begin to accumulate capital within his own country, but the capital market of the entire world would be open to him, and he could invest abroad just as others had invested in his country. This is an aspect of what can be called capitalist internationalism.

In order to secure the best prices for assets being sold off, a corps of professional auctioneers and brokers should be employed, who would receive a commission based on a percentage of the sales proceeds.

The principle of distributing the proceeds from the sale of assets equally among the citizens could be modified to give greater compensation to victims of labor camps and survivors of those who have been murdered by the Communist regime. However, the primary compensation for such crimes should probably be left until after the transition to capitalism has been completed and it is thus possible to provide more substantial compensation.

There are, of course, other possible methods of establishing private property. One would be simply to make the various existing enterprises the private property of their present managements. Another would be to turn the various enterprises over to their present employees. Obviously, the two methods could be combined, with the present managers receiving a certain percentage of the ownership and the present employees a further percentage. To some extent, these methods are actually in use.

If, following the establishment of private property in these ways, there really was security of property and full rights to buy and sell assets and shares, to hire and fire managers and workers, and to compete in all branches of industry, these methods would ultimately be effective in establishing private ownership of the means of production. As time went on, all the necessary changes could take place, including changes in ownership, which would be effected by the market, and an efficient economic system would emerge. However, the appropriation of enterprises by their Communist-appointed managers will necessarily carry with it the taint of the old regime and all of its injustices, and is likely also to be accompanied by a continued large-scale ability to use political pull, based on previously established relationships with government officials. Thus, private ownership of the means of production begun in this way will be tainted by injustice, past and present, and by corresponding inefficiency. This would be a legitimate source of resentment and would constitute a potential threat to the continuation of such ownership.

Turning the ownership of each establishment over to the workers of that establishment would at best arbitrarily favor some workers over others. Those workers who happened to work in highly capital-intensive industries, such as electric-power production or steel making, would obtain ownership of far more capital than workers who happened to work in less capital-intensive industries, such as clothing factories and restaurants. The same point would apply within each industry, insofar as some plants were more modern and efficient than others. It is very pertinent, of course, that as the result of socialism's protracted gross inefficiencies, the value of many factories and other productive establishments would turn out to be altogether nonexistent.

The problem of workers benefitting or failing to benefit by virtue of the accidental circumstances of where they worked would also exist in agriculture. The workers of collective farms with abundant, rich soil would receive more than the workers of collective farms with relatively meager, poor soil. In agriculture, however, apart from the return of former owners or their descendants, there does not appear to be an alternative to the workers' coming to own the land. Of course, the workers on the relatively poorer lands could be given the option of sharing in the proceeds of the sale of other assets rather than accept land they had been forced to work.

To the extent that workplaces do become the property of the workers employed in them, it must be stressed that it is vital that the workers of each plant be free both to sell their ownership shares while keeping their jobs and to leave their jobs while keeping their shares. In this case, ownership and employment would eventually become almost entirely separate, as under capitalism. The ability to hold ownership and employment separately is essential for the free movement of capital and labor between industries. In its absence, workers would be reluctant to leave their employment, because they would then lose their capital, and they would be afraid to admit new workers into their firm or industry, because they would then have to correspondingly dilute their ownership. There would be no possibility of transferring capital from one industry to another, since the workers of the industry from which the capital came would simply lose it. Furthermore, the rapid separation of ownership and employment is necessary to overcome a bias that might otherwise exist against improvements in efficiency if workers as owners were in a position to reject improvements that might cost them their jobs.[48]

Thus, at its worst, turning ownership over to the workers could mean a state of affairs in which the movement of labor and capital between the various branches of industry was made impossible. In addition, it could mean a situation in which the workers of each industry, by virtue of their possession of a monopoly on employment in their industry, were in a position to practice extortion on the rest of the economic system as the price of providing their services. Obviously, these are conditions which should be avoided at all costs.[49]

Provided that the essential requirements of security of property, the separation of employment and ownership, and the unrestricted freedoms to buy and sell, hire and fire, and compete, are observed, what remains is to accomplish the transition to private ownership as quickly as possible. Reasonable but strict time limits must be set for the location of former owners or their heirs, and it must be firmly established that thereafter no new claims will be heard on their account. This is an essential part of establishing the security of property. All of the assets in the hands of the state must likewise be disposed of within a strict time limit, so that no one in the market need labor under any uncertainty about what properties will be available and when and thus what plans he can and cannot make. This is essential to making the economic system as efficient as possible as soon as possible.

In the absence of the establishment of private ownership of the means of production, all other reform is meaningless. For example, decontrolling prices without first establishing private ownership of the means of production and its corollary the freedom of competition, simply means giving arbitrary, monopolistic power to lesser government officials in charge of individual industries and enterprises. It is comparable to giving the postmaster general or the local postmaster the right to set postal rates. Without private ownership of the means of production, there can be no market economy or free market. Divorced from private ownership of the means of production, such notions are a contradiction in terms. Nor, of course, can there be lasting or meaningful reform in the political realm. As shown earlier in this chapter, political freedom cannot exist without private ownership of the means of production both in such specific forms as printing presses and lecture halls and in general, throughout the economic system, in order to secure the

individual's livelihood from the power of the state. If the present, avowedly anticommunist regime in Russia does not soon succeed in establishing large-scale private ownership of the means of production, it will be certain to begin taking on all of the odious features of the Communist regime it has replaced. Indeed, one authority claims that 150,000 people are in jail even now in Russia for having engaged in black market activity.[50]

For the rest, it is essential that public opinion come to be based on an understanding of the importance of private ownership of the means of production and why its existence is in the material self-interest of everyone. Such understanding is essential to the long-run security of property. To further promote such understanding is a leading purpose of the next chapter.

Notes

1. On these points, see above, pp. 249–250, 257, and 260–262 passim.

2. See above, pp. 263–264.

3. See Ludwig von Mises, *Socialism* (New Haven: Yale University Press, 1951), pp. 111–142, 211–220, 516–521; reprint ed. (Indianapolis: Liberty Classics, 1981); idem, *Human Action*, 3d ed. rev. (Chicago: Henry Regnery, 1966) pp. 689–715. Von Mises's leading supporter on this issue is F. A. Hayek, to whom I am also greatly indebted in the following discussion. See his *The Road to Serfdom* (Chicago: University of Chicago Press, 1944), pp. 48–50; and *Individualism and Economic Order* (Chicago: University of Chicago Press, 1948), pp. 33–56, 77–91, 119–208.

4. See above, p. 137.

5. See above, ibid.

6. See above, pp. 172–214 passim, but especially pp. 209–214.

7. See above, pp. 239–240.

8. Cf. Robert Kaiser, *Russia* (New York: Atheneum, 1976), p. 338.

9. See above, pp. 136–137.

10. This point, of course, was made repeatedly by von Mises. See the references to him above, in n. 3 of this chapter.

11. See Kaiser, *Russia*, p. 324.

12. See above, pp. 176–178.

13. Ibid.

14. See Kaiser, *Russia*, pp. 330–335.

15. See Hedrick Smith, *The Russians* (New York: Quadrangle/New York Times Book Company, 1976), p. 59.

16. By the same token, the ability of the civilian economy to benefit from government-sponsored weapons research, such as that of the U.S. government in World War II or the U.S. space program in the 1960s, presupposes the existence of a capitalist economic system. It is only the existence of capitalism's profit motive and freedoms of individual initiative and competition that makes it possible to put such research to civilian use. This explains why there were significant civilian benefits in the United States from such research, but not in the Soviet Union, despite the Soviets' early and substantial lead in space research. Needless to say, moreover, in the absence of the need for

weapons research in a capitalist economy, all of the major scientific and engineering talent that is employed in it, would be employed in other lines of research, and with far greater efficiency, because that research would be privately supported. Thus, for example, in the absence of the development of the atomic bomb, while atomic power would probably not have come as soon, other fundamental advances with other major derivatives would probably have come sooner—it is a case of what Bastiat and Hazlitt refer to as the seen versus the unseen. (See Henry Hazlitt, *Economics in One Lesson,* new ed. [New Rochelle, N. Y.: Arlington House, 1979].) Indeed, with growing government control over research—its seizure of so much of the funds that would otherwise support private research and its politicizing of so much of research—the alternative private research that might have been may simply never be.

17. On this point, see above, pp. 136–137.

18. See above, pp. 258–262. For a detailed explanation of the dependence of capital accumulation on economic efficiency and, more fundamentally, on economic freedom, see below, pp. 634–636.

19. Oskar Lange, *On the Economic Theory of Socialism,* Benjamin E. Lippincott, ed. (Minneapolis: University of Minnesota Press, 1938), pp. 57–58.

20. Robert Heilbroner, "Reflections After Communism," *New Yorker,* Sept. 10, 1990, pp. 92, 94.

21. Ibid., p. 94.

22. See above, pp. 263–264.

23. Cf. Frederic Bastiat, "The State," in Frederic Bastiat, *Selected Essays On Political Economy*, trans. Seymour Cain (New York: D. Van Nostrand, 1964), pp. 140–151. Bastiat's essay was originally written in 1848. Also cf. Hayek, *Road to Serfdom,* p. 107.

24. Cf. Hayek, *Road to Serfdom,* pp. 134–152.

25. See Kaiser, *Russia,* pp. 87, 141–142; Smith, *Russians,* pp. ix–x, 3–6, 11–22.

26. Smith, *Russians,* p. 265.

27. Ibid. Along exactly the same lines, in his more recent book, Smith relates the widely told story of the Russian who is asked by God to wish for something that he would like God to do for

him, on the understanding that whatever God does for him, he will do twice as much for his neighbor. After hearing this offer, the Russian asks that God pluck out one of his eyes, so that his neighbor can lose both eyes. See Hedrick Smith, *The New Russians* (New York: Random House, 1990), p. 204.

28. Smith and Kaiser, incidentally, were both aware of the fundamental insecurity of the Soviet regime. See Smith, *Russians*, pp. 253–254; Kaiser, *Russia*, pp. 10–12, 21–23, 172–174, 451–453, 459, 473.

29. See above, pp. 258–262 and 273–275.

30. See, for example, David J. Dallin and Boris Nicolaevsky, *Forced Labor in Soviet Russia* (New Haven: Yale University Press, 1947), pp. 84–87.

31. Concerning these various points, see G. Warren Nutter, *The Strange World of Ivan Ivanov* (New York: World Publishing Co., 1969), pp. 87–89; Kaiser, *Russia*, pp. 336–337; Smith, *Russians*, pp. 267, 285; ibid., *New Russians,* pp. 190–191.

32. See Kaiser, *Russia*, pp. 111–113, 341–343; Smith, *Russians*, pp. 82–85, 92–93.

33. See Nutter, *Strange World,* pp. 99–100; Smith, *Russians*, pp. 200–201; Kaiser, *Russia*, pp. 46–47.

34. See Smith, *Russians*, pp. 222–225; Kaiser, *Russia*, pp. 339–340.

35. Cf. Smith, *Russians*, p. 223.

36. See *New York Times,* January 12, 1944, p. 12.

37. Cf. von Mises, *Socialism*, pp. 185–191.

38. See Kaiser, *Russia*, pp. 175–181, 192, 328; Smith, *Russians*, pp. 7–8, 25–52, 355–360, 464–467.

39. For a critique of this slogan and its underlying moral philoso-phy, see Ayn Rand, *Atlas Shrugged* (New York: Random House, 1957), especially pp. 660–672 and 1009–1069; also *The Virtue of Selfishness* (New York: New American Library, 1964), pp. 1–34.

40. See above, pp. 145–146.

41. See Smith, *Russians*, pp. 219–221, 230–232, 334, 338–343. For a novel that makes real the feeling of life under socialism, see Ayn Rand, *We The Living* (New York: Random House, 1959).

42. Cf. Ayn Rand, *Capitalism: The Unknown Ideal* (New York: New American Library, 1966), p. 21.

43. Ludwig von Mises, *Omnipotent Government* (1944; reprint ed., New Rochelle, N. Y.: Arlington House, 1969), p. v; idem, *Bureaucracy* (1944; reprint ed., New Rochelle, N. Y.: Arlington House, 1969), p. 106.

44. See Alexander Solzhenitzyn et al., *From Under the Rubble* (Boston: Little, Brown and Company, 1974), pp. 246–248; Kaiser, *Russia*, pp. 360–380; Smith, *Russians*, pp. 25–52, 109–110, 464–467.

45. See above, pp. 99–106.

46. The benefit of private ownership of the means of production specifically to nonowners is dealt with below, pp. 296–326 passim.

47. See above, pp. 279–282.

48. Any requirement that ownership of capital and employment be united constitutes syndicalism. See the critique of syndicalism presented by von Mises in *Socialism*, pp. 270–275.

49. See above, pp. 144–145.

50. Yuri Maltsev, "Putting Rouge on a Corpse," *Washington Times,* January 22, 1992.

CHAPTER 9

THE INFLUENCE OF THE DIVISION OF LABOR ON THE INSTITUTIONS OF CAPITALISM

PART A

PRIVATE OWNERSHIP OF THE MEANS OF PRODUCTION

1. The General Benefit from Private Ownership of the Means of Production

The influence of the division of labor on the institution of private ownership of the means of production is almost universally ignored. Typically, people think of privately owned means of production in terms that would be appropriate only in a non-division-of-labor society. That is, they think of them in the same way that they think of privately owned consumers' goods—namely, as being of benefit only to their owners. They believe that before the nonowners can benefit from the means of production, they must first become owners.[1]

This belief underlies the popularity of all forms of "redistributionism" and socialism.[2] People believe that so long as wealth remains concentrated in the hands of a relatively small number of capitalists, the capitalists alone benefit from it. For the great mass of noncapitalists to benefit, it is believed, the wealth of the capitalists must first be taken away and given to the noncapitalists, or be held by the government and used for the collective good of all.

Closely related to these ideas, of course, is the be-lief—held virtually as a self-evident axiom—that capitalism is a system which operates only in the interests of the capitalists, and that the defenders of capitalism must therefore either be capitalists themselves or be in the pay of the capitalists, or else simply be perverse enemies of the great majority of mankind. So deeply rooted are such convictions that it is often thought to be a sufficient refutation of the arguments of an advocate of capitalism to intimate the size of his bank balance or stockholdings.[3]

Similarly, in reporting election results, the news media routinely explain voting patterns on the basis of the voters' wealth and income status. They take it for granted that only wealthy, upper-income voters will favor "conservative," i.e., procapitalist policies, and that poorer, lower-income voters will automatically favor "liberal," i.e., anticapitalist policies.

Even the alleged friends of capitalism often share the conviction that private ownership of the means of production and capitalism serve only the capitalists: very often their notion of how to fight the spread of communism is first to create more capitalists. Only then, they believe, will there be a sufficient number of people with an interest in opposing communism.

The Benefit of Capital to the Buyers of Products

The first thing that must be realized is that in a division-of-labor society, all private property that is in the form of means of production—i.e., of capital—serves everyone, *nonowners* as well as owners. In a division-of-labor society, the means of production are not used in producing for their owners' personal consumption, but *for the market*. They are used in producing goods that are *sold*. The physical beneficiaries of this private property—and it is the far greater part of the capitalists' wealth—are all those who buy the products it helps to produce. In other words, it is the general buying public who are the physical beneficiaries of the capitalists' capital.

Consider, for example, the question of who are the physical beneficiaries of the auto plants of General Motors. That is, who physically receives the products of these plants? Is it the stockholders and bondholders of General Motors? Of course not. The number of GM's cars that is produced for the capitalists who own GM is relatively insignificant. Almost 100 percent of General Motors' auto output goes to people who do not own a single share of its stock or a single one of its bonds. The same is true of every other business enterprise.

Indeed, the proportion of General Motors' auto output that is purchased by stockholders or bondholders of any enterprise—by capitalists of any description—out of the proceeds of profit or interest income, is relatively small when compared with the proportion that is purchased by wage and salary earners. The far greater part of the automobiles purchased from GM and almost all other auto manufacturers is purchased by wage and salary earners. Wages and salaries, not profits and interest, are the source of the overwhelming bulk of consumption expenditure throughout a capitalist economy. It is wage and salary earners who consume the overwhelming majority of the automobiles, television sets, housing, furniture, food, and clothing, and almost every other consumers' good that is produced.

Thus, the overwhelmingly greater part of the physical benefit derived from the privately owned means of production in a capitalist economic system goes to nonowners of the means of production—to wage and salary earners.

It cannot be stressed too strongly: the simple fact is that in a division-of-labor society, one does not have to own the means of production in order to get their benefit. One has only to be able to buy the products. In a division-of-labor society, one gets the benefit of means of production *owned by others*—every time one appears in the market as a customer. Indeed, it is of the very essence of a division-of-labor society that one obtains the benefit of others' means of production, just as one obtains the benefit of others' labor and knowledge, and that this occurs by means of the purchase of products in the market. It is only in a non-division-of-labor society, in which there is little or no production for the market, in which the producer and the consumer are almost always one and the same person, that privately owned means of production benefit only their owners, or virtually only their owners.

Implicitly, it is such a society that the enemies of capitalism have in mind. They have not yet woken up to the fact that capitalism is a division-of-labor society. They are unaware that in a division-of-labor society, the means of production serve everyone who buys products, and that thus, under capitalism, *there is a general benefit from the capital owned by the capitalists*—a benefit which everyone shares in his capacity as a buyer of products, even if he himself does not own any means of production or capital.

This general benefit, it should be realized, applies to all of the means of production, not merely to those which are employed in the direct production of consumers' goods. The benefit of the steel mills that produce the steel that enters into GM's cars goes to the buyers of the cars, along with the benefit of the auto plants, as does the benefit of the iron mines that contribute to the production of that steel, and the benefit of the factories that produce iron-mining equipment. The benefit of the land that grows wheat goes to the buyers of bread, as does the benefit of the tractors used in the growing of wheat, and the benefit of the factories which produce those tractors, along with the benefit of the flour mills that make the wheat into flour, and of the bakeries that finally turn out the bread.

Furthermore, if we are to acknowledge the truth, we must recognize that the general buying public, composed overwhelmingly of wage and salary earners, not only obtains the benefit of all of the means of production owned by the capitalists, but exercises real and decisive power over the ways in which those means of production are employed. As was shown in Chapter 6 of this book, it is the general buying public which determines, by its pattern of buying and abstention from buying, which products it is profitable to produce and which it is unprofitable to produce. The buying public thus places the capitalists in a position in which, to make profits and avoid losses, they must produce what it wants to buy, and abstain from producing what it does not want to buy.[4] In a division-of-labor, capitalist society, it is ultimately the consumers—composed, it cannot be stated too often, overwhelmingly of wage and salary earners—who determine not only the pattern of production, including the relative size of the various industries, but even the specific methods of production used in every industry. For the demand of the consumers determines the relative prices of the factors of production, such as the wages of skilled versus unskilled labor, or the price of copper versus the price of aluminum, and thus which methods of production are more economical in any given case.[5]

The power of the consumers under capitalism is such that businessmen and capitalists are constantly on the lookout for ways in which they might supply the consumers better. For example, a businessman or capitalist who has invested in a clothing store or clothing factory, in a restaurant, or in the manufacture of breakfast foods, or who is contemplating such an investment, is vitally interested in improving the clothing or the food he sells. He is interested not because he values the satisfaction of others' needs for its own sake, but because he values his own wealth. The only way to increase his wealth, or prevent the competitive improvements introduced by others from decreasing it, is for him to serve his customers better and more efficiently. This, of course, applies to all branches of production that are privately owned and subject to the freedom of competition. It dictates the behavior not only of producers of consumers' goods, but also of suppliers at all stages of production, such as those who sell cloth to the clothing factories, and raw material to the factories which make cloth. For the businessmen who sell to consumers seek to buy means of production that will enable them to produce products of the kind the consumers most want, and to do so at the lowest possible costs of production. The suppliers of these businessmen in turn are obliged to purchase means of production that produce products that best satisfy these criteria. The same principle guides the suppliers of these suppliers, and so on through all stages of production. In other words, the whole system operates so as to produce the best possible products for the final buyers, the consumers, and to do so at the lowest possible costs.

Indeed, as we have seen, even without being bidden, businessmen and capitalists are constantly on the lookout to anticipate any unmet needs of the consumers and to supply those needs. For example, let there be a new residential real-estate development somewhere, and profit-seeking businessmen race to provide the new inhabitants with all the stores they may require, from appliance stores to xerography centers. Let there be any need or desire whatever for whose satisfaction a sufficient number of consumers are willing to pay profitable prices, and, as soon as they become aware of it, as soon as they have discovered it by a process of actively searching out its existence, businessmen and capitalists race to meet that need or desire. This, of course, is in sharpest contrast to conditions under socialism, where, in the nature of the case, no incentives exist for the rulers to serve the general public.[6]

Thus, under capitalism, privately owned means of production are employed for the benefit of all, nonowners as well as owners. They are employed for the benefit of all who buy the ultimate products of the means of production—the consumers' goods—which to the far greater extent represents wage and salary earners. And thus it should be clear that capitalism, the system of

self-interest, works to the interest of all. It is a system of the harmony of self-interests. It is a system in which each, together with any means of production he may own, serves the self-interest of others who in the meanwhile, together with any means of production they may own, serve his self-interest. It is a system in which the individual, and his means of production, serve the self-interests of all those others who *pay* for his products or services, whether those others own means of production or not, which preponderantly they do not to any great extent.

The Benefit of Capital to the Sellers of Labor

It is implicit in much of what I have just said, that there are, in fact, two aspects to the general benefit from the existence of the capitalists' capital. The first of these is the one I have already explained: that of the buyers of products, ultimately consumers' goods, benefitting from the capital directly or indirectly used in the production of those products. The second is in connection with the fact that capital constantly appears in the market as a demand—expenditure—by the capitalists for means of production, including labor. The capitalists begin their productive activities with outlays of money for labor, materials, and equipment. The revenues they subsequently take in from the sale of the products they produce are then almost entirely reexpended in the form of fresh outlays for labor, materials, and equipment. These outlays of the capitalists for labor are what make possible the purchase of products by noncapitalists. They are the incomes of the wage and salary earners.

Thus, there is a twofold benefit to the nonowners from other people's private property in the form of means of production—of capital: Namely, *it is the source of the supply of what the nonowners buy and of the demand for what the nonowners sell.*

It should be obvious that the more economically capitalistic the economic system is, in the sense of the capitalists expending a larger proportion of their sales revenues for means of production and a smaller proportion on their own consumption, the higher will be the income and consumption of wage and salary earners in comparison with the consumption of the capitalists. In other words, the more the capitalists abstain from consumption, in order to accumulate or maintain their capitals, the larger the share of the economic system's output of consumers' goods that goes to wage and salary earners, and the smaller the share that goes to capitalists.[7]

The Direct Relationship Between the General Benefit from Capital and Respect for the Property Rights of Capitalists

There is a conclusion that follows from all this which will appear highly paradoxical to many people, because it totally contradicts all they have been mistakenly led to believe—by the educational system, by the media, and by our culture in general—but which is nonetheless perfectly logical and correct. That is, *the more the private property rights of capitalists are respected, the greater are the benefits to noncapitalists.* Because to the extent that their rights are respected, the capitalists are encouraged to save and accumulate capital; their own consumption is small in relation to their capital and grows only as their capital grows. In each year the demand for labor and for capital goods is correspondingly larger—because of the capitalists' greater saving—and the share of consumers' goods purchased by wage earners is likewise correspondingly larger.

The profound significance of a greater demand for capital goods relative to consumers' goods, which results from the capitalists' security of property and greater saving, for capital accumulation, for the productivity of labor, and thus for real wages will be explained in Chapter 14.[8] The vital significance of a higher degree of capital intensiveness—that is, a higher ratio of accumulated savings and capital to current consumption expenditure—for the ability to implement technological advances, and thus to raise the productivity of labor and real wages, will be explained in Chapters 14 and 17.[9]

Also, of course, the more the property rights of the capitalists are respected, the more powerfully do the incentives of profit and loss operate to make the capitalists satisfy the demand of the consumers, because the profits of doing so are correspondingly less diluted by taxation. At the same time, the losses of failing to do so are not offset by reduced tax payments on other profits, since, to the extent that the property rights of the capitalists are respected, there are no tax payments on other profits. Thus losses are experienced with their full impact. Nor, when property rights are respected, are losses compensated for by subsidies of any kind. (The existence of subsidies is incompatible with the property rights of those who are forced to pay taxes to provide them.) In addition, respecting the property rights of the capitalists means leaving them legally free to enter any branch of production they wish. Thus it means the freedom of competition and therefore, in this way too, the full effect of profit and loss incentives in bringing about new and improved products and in improving the methods of producing already existing products and thereby continually reducing costs of production and prices.

Respecting the property rights of capitalists also means not imposing on them arbitrary requirements that raise costs of production and thus prices, such as compulsory bargaining with labor unions, zoning laws, government building codes, regulations for alleged product safety, and the regulations imposed by the ecology movement.

All of these regulations are actually at the expense of the consumers, in that anything which raises costs of production ultimately raises prices.[10] Still worse, as I will show in Chapter 14, all governmentally imposed cost increases and the inefficiencies they represent have a cumulative negative effect on the ability to accumulate capital and thus to raise the productivity of labor and real wages.[11]

But what is most important of all in the long run, and subsumes all the other benefits, is that if the capitalists' property rights are sufficiently respected, then from year to year *the total production of consumers' goods available to everyone tends to grow and thus the purchasing power of everyone's income tends to rise.* In other words, there is not only a general benefit from private ownership of the means of production, but *a progressively increasing general benefit.* This should be obvious merely on the basis of what was shown back in Chapter 6 about the effects of the uniformity-of-profit principle in bringing about economic progress. As indicated, however, later discussion will show how the stimulus to economic progress provided by the uniformity-of-profit principle combines with the saving and productive expenditure of the capitalists to achieve a steadily growing supply of capital goods, a rising productivity of labor, and thus rising real wage rates, and that this progress is the more rapid, the more the property rights of the capitalists are respected.[12]

The conclusion should already be obvious that an individual is far better off as a nonowner of the means of production under capitalism than he is as an equal owner under socialism. For in his capacity both as a wage earner and as a consumer he obtains the benefit of the means of production owned by others. In a division-of-labor, capitalist society, others' means of production are the source both of the demand for his labor and of the supply of the goods he buys. And his benefit in both capacities is the greater, indeed, becomes progressively greater, the more the property rights of those others are respected.

Of course, nothing I have said means that under capitalism the mass of people must be nonowners of means of production. It may be that everyone would own some means of production, if not directly, then indirectly, through such forms as stock or bond ownership, ownership of mutual-fund shares, and ownership of life-insurance policies. It is absolutely certain that everyone who chooses to save under capitalism can accumulate a substantial amount of personal savings representing either means of production or such assets as homes financed by means of mortgages. Nevertheless, the fundamental gain of the mass of people comes from means of production owned by others, above all, by large capitalists. This gain is the source of real incomes high enough to make possible significant saving on the part of the average person.

2. The Capitalists' Special Benefit from Private Ownership of the Means of Production

The preceding section showed the general benefit—the progressively increasing general benefit—that everyone, capitalist and noncapitalist, derives from the institution of private ownership of the means of production in a division-of-labor society.

It is now necessary to consider the *special benefit* derived by the capitalists from their ownership of capital. Obviously, no matter what the gains that their capital provides to noncapitalists, it is better to be a capitalist than a noncapitalist, and better still to be a wealthier capitalist than a poorer capitalist. What needs to be answered now is the question of what precisely is the nature of these special gains that the capitalists derive from their capital that is over and above the gains that everyone else derives from it.

There is undoubtedly a temptation to answer that the capitalists earn profits or interest on their capital, which the rest of society does not, and that that is their special benefit. This answer is mistaken. It is true that only the capitalists earn the profits and interest on their capital. However, to the extent that they save and invest their profits and interest, the profits and interest provide the same kind of general benefit as their original capital—that is, the saved profits and interest represent additional means of production serving the general buying public and are the source of additional wage payments. Thus, the profits and interest that the capitalists earn are actually *not* the measure of the special benefits they derive from their ownership of the means of production.

There are two gains that the capitalists obtain which others do not. The first is the portion of their profits and interest that they do not save and invest, but *consume*. Even this overstates their special gains to the extent that their consumption includes such things as the support of universities, libraries, hospitals, and opera companies, because here again are general benefits. The second is the *psychological value* that the possession of capital has. To the extent that an individual possesses capital, he has the potential of consuming it. He thus has the psychological security of knowing that he could consume it if he had to or wanted to.

Now so long as the institution of private ownership of the means of production remains secure, this advantage of owning capital usually remains strictly psychological. That is to say, the potential the capitalists have of consuming their capital usually remains just that—a potential. The capital itself is generally not consumed, but left

invested; and upon death, it is passed to heirs.

In part, this is because capitalists who are in business regard the possession of their capital as essential to their livelihood. Significant-sized capitalists, moreover, whether they are in business or not, are likely to regard the possession of their capital as being the means by which they can live for the remainder of their lives and provide for their children and grandchildren. (In today's conditions, significant-sized capitalists can be taken to mean those with a capital of, say, $2 million or more.) As a result of these facts, the major instances in which the consumption of capital occurs is when the rate of profit or interest that is earned falls to the point that it cannot provide the standard of living the capitalists feel they can afford on the basis of their accumulated capital.[13] In such circumstances, they encroach upon their capital. Even then, they generally do so only to a relatively modest degree, because they require the great bulk of their capital as the means of providing for their future needs and wants.[14]

On the basis of this and previous discussion, it should be clear that if the institution of private ownership of the means of production is secure, the *actual* consumption of businessmen and capitalists, whether out of current profits or interest or out of capital accumulated out of past profits or interest, is minor in comparison with wages and the consumption of wage earners. This is especially true of the consumption of the significant-sized businessmen and capitalists, who own the great bulk of the capital of the economic system and earn most of the profits and interest in the economic system. In fact, in a country with the degree of security of property that was historically enjoyed in the United States, the consumption of the significant-sized businessmen and capitalists, including whatever great mansions and ocean-going yachts and caviar and champagne they might consume, would most likely amount to not much more than about 10 percent of the total consumption taking place in the economic system. This is because the mansions and yachts, and the suppers of caviar and champagne, in their hundreds and thousands pale into insignificance alongside the consumption of wage and salary earners in their tens of millions enjoying ordinary houses and automobiles and even just hamburgers and Coca Cola.[15]

Implications for Redistributionism

The above facts about the capitalists' special benefit from the institution of private ownership of the means of production have an important bearing on the appraisal of demands for the redistribution of wealth and income, and for socialism, insofar as socialism is advocated as a method of redistribution. For after all is said and done, it is something on the order of a mere 10 percent of the overall, total consumption of the economic system that turns out to be the grand prize for which the redistributors and socialists have been clamoring all these years! *This* is the great fund of wealth by means of which they have expected to abolish all poverty, cure disease, and achieve utopia; and for the sake of which they have been ready to overturn existing society, seize private property, and shed rivers of blood—all in magnificent obliviousness to the fact that capitalism itself gratuitously provides such wealth *over and over again every few years,* through economic progress and an accompanying 2 or 3 percent annual rate of improvement in the productivity of labor. Indeed, if the approximately 10 percent of total consumption that is accounted for by the consumption of the significant-sized capitalists is divided by the approximately 90 percent of consumption that already takes place on the part of the rest of the population, the resulting 11 percent ratio would be made good for rest of the population over and over again approximately every four to five years, through economic progress.[16]

These points need to be emphasized, in order to understand the actual nature of the demands for redistribution and socialism. The conclusion that follows from them is that even if the redistributors and socialists could succeed in expropriating the capitalists' wealth without causing the destruction of that wealth or of its productivity—which, of course, they cannot—the utmost that they could obtain for the benefit of the average person that he would not already have *is his share of the approximately 10 percent of total consumption that is accounted for by the consumption of the significant-sized capitalists.* And this, of course, would be a one-time-only, nonrepeatable benefit. This would be the limit of the "benefit," because anything beyond it would represent capital decumulation.[17]

Obviously, even if it could be obtained, such a benefit would not be worth making into the leading objective of a political philosophy and movement, let alone fighting a revolution for. But the fact is, of course, that no such benefit can be obtained. The attempt to seize the 10 percent can only inflict injury on those intended to benefit from the seizure. It must deprive them both of all the vastly greater future gains they would have had from the further operation of capitalism, and of the continued enjoyment of the gains they have already obtained from the operation of capitalism up to that time. For the capitalists cannot be forcibly prevented from consuming without losing interest in the management of their capital, and in its accumulation in the first place. Their capital is valuable to them only insofar as it serves as a source of actual or potential consumption for them or their heirs. To the extent that their ability to consume is forcibly restricted, the value of their capital to them is destroyed.

For example, a forced limitation of a capitalist's consumption to some fixed amount, such as $50,000 per year, would make all that portion of his capital valueless to him that was beyond what was required to provide the income needed for such consumption. If, for example, he had $5 million of capital and the rate of return on capital were 5 percent, so that $1 million of capital was sufficient to provide the income needed for the maximum permitted consumption, he could well lose interest in the management of $4 million of his capital, and in the accumulation of such capital in the first place. For the $4 million would arguably no longer be able to contribute anything to his life and well-being. Indeed, even if for reasons of financial security he always wished to possess capital equal to some definite greater multiple of his annual consumption than implied by the assumed 5 percent rate of return, such as 40 times his maximum permitted annual consumption of $50,000, he would have no motive to be interested in possessing any capital beyond $2 million in this case, and thus would still lose interest in the management of the other $3 million of his assumed capital, and in the accumulation of such capital in the first place.

All efforts to limit the consumption of capitalists must result in the destruction of incentives to accumulate and maintain capital. If the limits were set very high, at a level of consumption that the great majority of capitalists could never expect to reach, the effect would be to destroy the incentives of the most successful capitalists. As the limits were lowered, the effect would be to destroy the incentives of more and more capitalists. Whatever the level of interference, any possible per capita gains to the general public from obtaining funds the capitalists otherwise would have consumed must be far more than offset through declines in the incentive to improve and even maintain production. If, for example, the public attempts to reap the gains of limiting a capitalist's consumption to, say, $50 million a year, so that only a bare handful of capitalists is affected, namely, multibillionaires, the possible gains to the treasury are absolutely minimal, while the losses in terms of innovation and the growth of major new industries are substantial. If the effort is made to capture any substantial part of the capitalists' overall consumption, the disincentives to capital accumulation and the management and maintenance of capital are such that the socialization of the means of production would have to follow as a logical next step. Because in the absence of capitalists caring about their capital, the only party left to care would be the state. But, of course, for the reasons explained in the last chapter, socialism would also mean the collapse of production.

Essentially similar reasoning applies to proposals to limit the after-tax income of capitalists to some fixed amount, such as was advocated earlier in this century by

Eleanor Roosevelt and the labor union leader Walter Reuther. The enactment of such a proposal would first be accompanied by a decumulation of capital, to the extent that the capitalists considered their existing capital sufficient to enable them to consume in excess of their statutorily limited income. For example, a limitation of after-tax income to $50,000 a year would not stop capitalists from consuming in excess of $50,000 a year so long as they judged their capital to be sufficient to provide such consumption. In the words of von Mises, "If one eliminates the capitalist's role as receiver of interest [profit], one replaces it by the capitalist's role of consumer of capital."[18] Such a limitation of income would obviously have to be followed by a limitation of the capitalists' consumption and then, for the reasons just explained, by the government taking over the management of their capital as well.

The destructiveness of redistributionism is evident in the decline of the American economic system that has taken place in recent decades. The redistributors have succeeded in depriving the significant-sized capitalists of perhaps as much as half of what they would otherwise have consumed, and the American economic system of perhaps as much as half of the capital that such capitalists would otherwise have accumulated and used to the advantage of everyone. This conclusion is supported by the fact that in the nineteenth century and the first few decades of the twentieth century, the ratio of total accumulated capital in the United States to the so-called national income of the United States (viz., the sum of all wages and salaries and profits and interest earned in the country), was on the order of five or six to one. However, as the redistributors gained ground in imposing and expanding the welfare state and enacting policies of confiscatory taxation, government budget deficits, and inflation to pay for it—all of which policies undermine the ability to accumulate capital—this ratio, which is typically called the capital-output ratio, has fallen to three to one.[19]

The reduction in the ratio of capital to national income represents a reduction in the overall degree of capital intensiveness of the American economic system.[20] As I will explain in Chapters 14 and 17, reduction in the degree of capital intensiveness signifies a reduced ability to implement technological advances.[21] A second, closely related result that redistributionism has caused and that operates against economic progress, is a reduced demand for capital goods relative to the demand for consumers' goods. This is the necessary consequence of taxing away funds that would otherwise have been saved and productively expended, that is, expended for business purposes, and using those funds instead to finance consumption expenditures by the government or those to whom the

government gives money. The reduction in the demand for capital goods relative to the demand for consumers' goods causes a reduction in the production of capital goods relative to the production of consumers' goods. It thereby reduces the ability of the economic system to increase or even to maintain its supply of capital goods.[22]

These destructive results stand alongside of and reinforce the destructive results of redistributionism that can be understood in the light of the uniformity-of-profit principle, namely, the effects of depriving businessmen of the financial incentives and means that the freedom to earn and keep the profit one earns provides for improving and expanding production. Thus, it should not be at all surprising that as a result of the destructiveness of redistributionism, the economic system of the United States is now stagnating. In effect, for the sake of denying wealthy capitalists a portion of their luxuries—for the sake of depriving them of an amount of consumption equal perhaps to 5 percent of the total consumption of the economic system—the average American wage earner has been deprived of the benefits of economic progress and the annual improvement in his standard of living, which would have added up to far more than that 5 percent within a very few years and would have done so over and over again. Further substantial implementation of redistributionism will almost certainly result in an annual rate of decline in the standard of living of the average American wage earner.

The destructive effects of redistributionism on capital accumulation have been evident all along in the very size of what the redistributors have expected to accomplish and have believed to be available as the means of accomplishing it. As they have depicted matters, what is available for raising the standard of living of the masses is not the small percentage of the output of consumers' goods that the capitalists personally consume, *but the whole of the capitalists' existing wealth.* The propaganda of the redistributors and socialists has always depicted the capitalists as rich fat men, whose larders are overflowing, while the plates of the poor are empty. It has demanded that the capitalists' wealth be shared for purposes of mass *consumption.* Since, in reality, the wealth of the capitalists is overwhelmingly in the form of factories and other capital goods, this has all along been a blatant demand for capital decumulation. The poor are to be benefitted by consuming the capital that underlies the productivity of labor and the payment of wages, and without which production must plunge. Thus, practically on its face, redistributionism has been a policy of destruction.

It is important to bear in mind that no undue emphasis should be placed on the consumption of the capitalists constituting any definite percentage of total consumption at any definite time, such as 10 percent. The essential point is that their consumption will be the smaller, and their saving and demand for labor and capital goods the greater, the more fully are their property rights respected and secure. This is what in the long run guarantees the highest possible percentage of consumption stemming from wages and the lowest possible percentage stemming from profits and interest. Thus, if at some point it were found that the consumption of the capitalists relative to that of wage earners were far higher than what I have indicated, it would not at all follow that any kind of case for redistributionism then existed. On the contrary, such a situation would almost certainly largely be the result precisely of the threat of redistribution. The remedy would be the abandonment of all such threats and the establishment of the security of property. Then, a greatly intensified process of competition in saving would take place among the capitalists, in which those who consumed the least and saved the most came to own an ever increasing portion of the capital of the economic system and more and more determined the consumption and saving of all capitalists taken together.[23]

I have already demonstrated the destructiveness of redistributionism insofar as it is a demand for the socialization of the economic system. Its destructiveness will become further evident as we consider the lesser measures that the redistributors have advocated for implementing their program: namely, government ownership of isolated industries and the progressive taxation of incomes and inheritances, and, in non-division-of-labor societies, land reform. In the discussion immediately following, we will consider government ownership of isolated industries.[24]

Destructive Consequences of Government Ownership

The government's ownership of a business supposedly makes every citizen an equal owner of that business, and in this way supposedly benefits him. Thus, every American is supposed to be an approximately one 260-millionth owner of the U.S. Postal Service, Amtrak, the national parks, and so on.

Yet, one need hardly do more than name such examples, in order to understand the destructiveness of government ownership. The citizen's share in government enterprises does him no good whatever. The fact that the enterprise is government owned merely means that it is operated without benefit of profit-and-loss incentives and the freedoms of individual initiative and competition.[25] The result is almost always gross inefficiency, high costs, poor service, and low quality of products. In fact, in one major case—the government's ownership of enormous areas of the Western states and of Alaska—the

effect of government ownership is largely to deprive the citizen of all possible economic benefit from the existence of the property. For much of the property is set aside as "wildlife preserves" and "wilderness areas," and its economic development is either totally prohibited or made extremely difficult and severely limited.

The average American is far better and more economically served by the privately owned telephone companies and airlines than he is by the U.S. Postal Service, Amtrak, and all the various municipally owned subway and bus lines. He is much better off dealing with them, even if he does not own a single share of their stock, than in dealing with the government enterprises, which are supposed to be his. For in dealing with the private enterprises, he obtains not only the benefit of the existence of their capital, but also the benefit of the employment of their capital *under the incentives of profit and loss and the freedoms of individual initiative and competition*, with the result that they are highly motivated to serve him and to serve him progressively better.

The adverse consequences of government ownership are, of course, enormously compounded when it goes beyond the case of isolated industries to embrace the entire economic system. Then, in addition to the far more serious problems created directly by the lack of profit-and-loss incentives and the freedoms of individual initiative and competition, there are the problems created by the destruction of the price system, which, as we saw in the last chapter, means the disintegration of the economic system into chaos.

Putting aside for the moment the consequences of a socialized economic system, as opposed to isolated socialized industries, it is worth noting that government ownership does not normally provide the alleged citizen-owners with any of the *special benefits* of ownership that exist under private ownership of the means of production. Government ownership does not give the alleged citizen-owner the psychological security that the possession of capital gives to a capitalist. Because, unlike the capitalist, *he cannot sell his share in a government enterprise*. He is born with his share and must die with it. *Nor*—except in the most unusual cases—*does he receive dividends on his share*. In no sense does his alleged ownership provide him with any actual or potential means for consuming and thus for enriching his life. Thus, in no way does it provide him with the distinctive benefits that private ownership of the means of production bestows.[26]

In the case of government ownership of industry, the citizen's share not only normally brings him none of the special gains of ownership, but, on the contrary, is almost always a *liability* to him, in that government enterprises almost inevitably incur deficits, which he, the average citizen must make good through his taxes. Government-owned enterprises incur deficits precisely because it is the taxpayers who must make them good, under coercion. The administrators of the enterprises do not suffer any losses out of their own pockets, nor are they appointed or removable by those who do suffer the losses—the taxpayers. At best, they are appointed and removable by elected officials. When it becomes one of the powers of government to own and operate business enterprises, these officials owe their election and their prospects for reelection to promises to favor some groups at the expense of other groups—namely, large and vocal groups at the expense of small and quiet groups. The individual taxpayer is smaller and quieter than any group, and thus he ends up as the principal victim of pressure-group warfare. The politicians and the bureaucrats they appoint are free to use the government enterprises to provide costly vote-buying "services" and to have them operate with inefficient methods of production, which also buys votes by providing lucrative contracts or employment for pressure-group members; and he, the taxpayer, must keep still and simply cover the losses.[27]

Thus, the average citizen is a loser in his dealings with government enterprises not only in his capacity as a consumer, but also, however ironically, in his capacity *as an owner*—in the very capacity in which he was above all supposed to benefit. He is a loser both ways. And, of course, the magnitude of his loss grows exponentially as the economic system approaches full socialization.

Government ownership is sometimes supported on the grounds that it keeps the use of property free, whereas private ownership would result in the imposition of charges. This argument comes up most clearly in such cases as government ownership of beaches and parks, but it is present in the support for government ownership of every kind. And, indeed, the case for government ownership in such instances is about as valid as would be an argument for government ownership of all other land based on such considerations. Thus, one might argue that if the government socialized all land, people could obtain food without having to pay for it. They would merely have to go into the forest and collect the nuts and berries that grew there, without having to pay anyone for the right to do so.[28] Of course, there would be nothing to eat but nuts and berries and no more of them than nature provided, with the result that most people would die of starvation.

In contrast, when the land becomes private property, the owners collect charges for its use, or for the products of its use. But those charges serve merely to make it worthwhile for the owners to apply their intelligence and labor to the improvement of their property, with the result that yields progressively improve and increase. Thus the payment of charges results in progressively growing supplies that continually raise the standard of living of those who pay them. Exactly the same is the case with beaches and parks. Private ownership would entail charges, but it would also be the foundation of progressive improvement in the benefits derived from the existence of beaches and parklands, because the charges would serve to introduce the incentives of profit and loss and the phenomena of individual initiative and competition. That is, it would serve to bring about the application of human intelligence and the progressive improvement that the use of intelligence makes possible. As a result, instead of the nonowners paying no charges and obtaining little more than nothing, they would pay something and obtain more and more.[29]

Profit Management Versus Bureaucratic Management

A major factor bearing on the superiority of privately owned enterprises over government-owned enterprises is the fact that the former are characterized by what von Mises calls *profit management,* while the latter are characterized by what he calls *bureaucratic management.* In the absence of government interference, the ability to construct separate balance sheets and income statements for the constituent parts of an enterprise makes it possible for private enterprises to delegate substantial authority to subordinate managers, such as branch and division managers. Because their activities can be appraised on the basis of their separate profit-and-loss performance, such subordinate managers can be allowed to exercise major discretion within the framework of the one, overall guiding business directive which is simply to make profits and avoid losses. What is of the greatest importance, is that they can be given discretion in the spending of money, which they can be trusted to spend wisely, because they have a powerful incentive to hold down costs in order to show a greater profit on the operations for which they are responsible. In effect, such managers are made junior partners, which thereby extends throughout the firm not only the incentives provided by private ownership of the means of production but also a corollary freedom of individual initiative.[30]

In contrast, *bureaucratic management* necessarily characterizes government-owned enterprises, owing to the inherent lack of profit-and-loss incentives at their very base, which incentives can be provided only by private ownership. Such enterprises—for example, a police department—very often do not and cannot sell their products, which by itself makes the construction of any kind of income statements for subordinate units out of the question. And even where they can sell their products, as in the case of a post office, the lack of profit-and-loss incentives at the very base of their operations rules out any form of profit management at subordinate levels. Thus, government enterprises must be conducted bureaucratically—that is, in accordance with detailed rules and regulations rigidly prescribing every procedure and leaving virtually nothing to the discretion of the officials, who otherwise would have no reason to limit expenditures.[31] Indeed, when one considers that government is always the agency that resorts to the use of physical force against people, and that spends public funds obtained by taxes, the bureaucratic restriction of the discretion of its officials appears positively desirable. Bureaucratic management is actually the form of management that is *appropriate* to the conduct of government affairs.[32]

The appropriateness of bureaucracy to government is an argument for the strict limitation of the functions of government, and thus the confinement of bureaucratic management to the sphere in which it is necessary to restrict the use of physical force. When the functions of government are not thus limited, bureaucratic management spreads to private enterprise. For then government interference undermines the strength of profit-and-loss incentives, makes business firms dependent on the decisions of government bureaus, and forces them to employ former bureaucrats in leading positions in order to be able to deal with the government bureaus.[33]

Thus, business firms become less and less subject to the power of profit-and-loss incentives and more and more come to resemble the bureaus that determine their fate. For example, under affirmative-action laws and environmental-protection laws, it is out of the question to leave anything to the discretion of lower-level business managers, lest the well-being of the whole firm be jeopardized by the inadvertent violation of some government regulation. Under such conditions, the lower-level business managers must be as careful to "go by the book" as any government bureaucrat.[34]

The "Successful" Nationalizations of Oil Deposits: A Rebuttal

The leading exceptions to the principle that the citizen loses even in his capacity as an owner of government enterprises occur when such an enterprise has the good fortune to own low-cost mineral deposits and at the same time enjoys substantial monopoly privileges in selling outside the country. This is the position of the nationalized oil industries in various Arab countries.

These industries were established and developed by private oil companies, who continue to play a major role in their operation. Their success is principally the result of the fact that the government of the United States has granted them extensive monopoly privileges in the world market by severely hampering the activities of their major competitors—namely, the American producers of

oil and other forms of energy—in all the ways I explained in Chapter 7.[35] In the absence of these measures by the U.S. government, the price of oil would not have risen any more than most other prices, and the inefficiencies of government ownership would have prevented the Arab countries from earning any very great profits, despite the high quality of their oil reserves. Further progress in the production of energy in a free United States would eventually have inflicted losses on such inefficiently run outfits.

As matters stand, the free telephones, free medical care, and so on, that the citizens of Kuwait, say, are able to enjoy, thanks to the dividends their government pays from its oil profits, and the lesser benefits that the citizens of other thinly populated Arab countries obtain—all this is paid for at the expense of the impoverishment of everyone else in the world who must pay the artificially enhanced price of oil. Scores of millions of people in the non-oil-producing countries are that much closer to starvation and death because the oil industries of the Arab countries are nationalized and enjoy monopoly privileges.

To summarize much of our discussion in this section: What we have seen is, first of all, that insofar as the capitalists' special benefit from the ownership of the means of production takes the form of an enhanced consumption, it is quite small in relation to the size of overall consumption, and thus that nothing of great significance could be gained by the average person from its seizure, even if it were possible to seize it. And then we have seen that the attempt to seize it must backfire in a radical decline in production and the overall volume of goods available, because the capitalists' incentive to accumulate and maintain their capitals would be destroyed and the ensuing socialization of the economic system would also cause collapse. We have seen that redistributionism is destructive practically on its face, in that it is a call for the wholesale consumption of the capitalists' capital, and we have seen its destructive role in the present economic stagnation of the United States. And, finally, we have seen that the socialization of isolated industries causes losses to the average person both in his capacity as a buyer of the products of the socialized industries and in his capacity as an alleged owner of the socialized industries. That is, we have seen that in addition to depriving the buyers of the benefits of profit-and-loss incentives and the freedoms of individual initiative and competition in the industries' operation, socialization also fails to deliver the special benefits of ownership that exist under capitalism. This is the case inasmuch as the citizen cannot sell his alleged shares, and, instead of receiving dividends, almost always ends up paying higher taxes to cover the socialized enterprises' losses. We have also seen that the socialization of business, and growing government interference, are responsible for the bureaucratization of business, even of business that still remains privately owned.

3. The General Benefit from the Institution of Inheritance

It is necessary to consider the benefits of two particular forms of the institution of private property and private ownership of the means of production which have come under special attack, namely, the institution of inheritance and, in Section 5, the private ownership of land. These institutions are denounced even by people who in other respects consider themselves supporters of private property and private ownership of the means of production.

As in the case of the broader institution of private property and private ownership of the means of production as such, the institution of inheritance is perceived as being of benefit only to the owners of the property involved—in this case, those who are fortunate enough to be heirs—and not as being of benefit to anyone else. Indeed, the interests of the nonheirs are usually perceived as lying with the confiscation and redistribution of inheritances, and thus with the more or less complete abolition of the institution.

Despite the popularity of this view, the fact is that in a division-of-labor society, substantial inheritances are overwhelmingly in the form of means of production, precisely because the far greater part of the wealth of the bequestors—capitalists—is in the form of means of production. If such inherited wealth remains invested—and it almost always does when it is received in a large amount—its existence is to the benefit of everyone. In order to benefit from its existence, one need not be an heir; one need merely be a buyer of the products it helps to produce and whose supply is increased because of it. One need merely be a wage earner, whose labor is in additional demand and whose wages are higher because of it.

The institution of inheritance powerfully promotes the accumulation of capital. It provides a motive to people to maintain their capital, and even to go on accumulating additional capital, as long as they live—for the sake of their heirs. Its effect is that substantially more capital exists than would exist without it. Everyone in a division-of-labor society benefits from the existence of this additional capital, whether he himself is an heir or not. He benefits both in his capacity as a buyer of products and in his capacity as a wage earner. He benefits in the former capacity because the generation of additional capital raises and goes on raising the productivity

of labor and thus the supply of goods available for all to buy. He benefits in the latter capacity because, at the same time, it increases the share of total consumption that is enjoyed by wage earners in comparison with nonwage earners. Rational self-interest dictates that everyone, nonheirs as well as heirs, uphold the institution of inheritance. From the point of view of the nonheirs, the rationale is that it enables their employers to pay them more and their suppliers to supply them with more, and, indeed, to supply them progressively better—at prices that are lower and lower relative to the wages they earn. This last is the effect of the greater relative demand for and production of capital goods and the higher degree of capital intensiveness that the institution of inheritance achieves.[36]

As previously pointed out, however startling it may seem, the simple fact is that in a division-of-labor society one benefits from the property of others when those others are one's employers or suppliers, because the effect of their property is a greater means of buying what one sells and of producing what one buys. The institution of inheritance enhances these sources of gain.

Indeed, the preceding observations have somewhat understated the case for the institution of inheritance from the point of view of the nonheirs. While it is true that most large inheritances do remain invested, the institution of inheritance promotes capital accumulation even in the cases in which the heirs consume some or all of what they receive—as an elderly widow or minor children must often do, or as spendthrift heirs simply choose to do. For even in these cases, the capital is first accumulated, and because estates are constantly being built to be left to heirs, there is *permanently* more capital. Even in these cases, in which all or most of an inheritance is consumed by the heirs, there is the capital that exists in the inheritance "pipeline," so to speak, and which would not exist in the absence of the institution of inheritance.

It is necessary to realize that inherited wealth can easily be lost through unwise investments on the part of the heirs. In a division-of-labor society, wealth is never invested just once, for all time; it must constantly be reinvested, under ever-changing conditions. Materials and labor services are fully used up in the production of a single batch of products and must be replaced immediately thereafter if production is to continue. Machinery and factory buildings, while much longer lasting, are also constantly in process of wearing out; they too must be periodically replaced. On the other hand, as time goes on, new products and new methods of production are introduced and all those other dynamic changes occur that take place in connection with economic competition. These changes make it impossible for the heirs to continue with a routine established by the parent or grand-parent who built their fortune. They must constantly *reacquire* their wealth through their own successful investments, investments which must win the approbation of the buyers of the products concerned, under the freedom of competition.

To the extent the heirs lack the ability to make the right investment decisions, but nonetheless attempt actively to manage their funds themselves, they risk the loss of their entire fortune. If they recognize their lack of business ability, or if it has been recognized for them by the bequestors of their wealth, they must be content with a sharply reduced rate of return on their capital, which is the necessary accompaniment of making investments recognized as having a high degree of safety of principal. And from that low rate of return must usually be deducted management or trustees' fees.

The effect of these facts is that unless one or more of the heirs possesses extraordinary ability, the relative significance of any given fortune in the economic system tends steadily to diminish as time goes on. For even if the heirs do not lose it outright through poor investments, and even if they are content to live within the income afforded by the low rate of return they earn on their capital, their fortune is unable to grow in pace with the new capital being accumulated by more-talented investors earning higher rates of return and therefore able to save and accumulate capital more rapidly. Moreover, the significance of any given fortune is further diminished by a tendency toward its constant subdivision among a growing number of descendants, as one generation succeeds another.

In just this way, the wealth of the present-day Astors and Vanderbilts, once among the greatest fortunes in the country, is now not nearly so large in relation to the rest of the American economic system; and that of any given individual Astor or Vanderbilt is no greater than what hundreds of thousands of individuals have accumulated purely by their own efforts, all within the present generation. Even the much more recent and initially much greater fortunes of the Rockefellers, Fords, and Mellons show the same tendencies toward decline in their relative significance.

The Destructive Consequences of Inheritance Taxes

The inheritance tax, especially on large inheritances, where it is often confiscatory, is practically a pure tax on capital. To the extent it exists and is actually carried out—that is, to the extent the so-called loopholes are closed, so that the tax cannot be avoided—the long-run effect is to reduce the accumulation of capital by reducing the building of estates in the first place. It is pointless for people to accumulate fortunes, intended to be be-

queathed to heirs, which, upon their death, the government confiscates and prevents from reaching the heirs. The effect of confiscatory inheritance taxes is to cause the builders of estates to consume their income more heavily and not to bother earning part of the income they might otherwise be capable of earning at any given time. For their motivation both to save and to earn the income out of which saving can occur is reduced.

Inheritance taxes which are not so high as to prevent heirs from substantially benefitting from the accumulation of estates do not deprive the builders of estates of the motive to earn and save. By the same token, they do not achieve the egalitarian objectives of the supporters of the inheritance tax. Nevertheless, even these more-modest inheritance taxes reduce capital accumulation to the extent that they are paid with funds that otherwise would have remained invested. Any inheritance tax whatever reduces capital to the extent that it is paid with funds that otherwise would have remained invested.

The specific way that this occurs is that the heirs or the executors of estates find it necessary to sell part of the estate to pay the taxes. This siphons funds from the buyers of these portions of the estates into the government's treasury. If the heirs had not had to sell, the buyers of these portions of the estates would have had to use their funds essentially for the purchase of new capital assets, which would have existed alongside of and in addition to the inherited wealth of the heirs. Instead, as matters stand, the funds of the buyers are diverted from the purchase of such additional capital assets into the purchase of part of the heirs' existing capital assets, and from there to the government's treasury and its expenditures. The result is less accumulated capital.

This remains the result even if the government were to use the proceeds of the inheritance tax exclusively for such alleged capital purposes as the building of roads, bridges, canals, and tunnels, the making of river and harbor improvements, and the like. For even if government expenditures for such purposes really did represent capital formation, which they do not, they would be at the expense of that much less private capital formation, so long as they were financed by the inheritance tax.[37]

The fact is, however, that most government spending is avowedly for purposes of consumption—such as welfare payments and expenditures for military preparations. And what is for alleged capital purposes is almost always carried out with enormous waste and inefficiency in comparison with what private enterprise would achieve if it were responsible for the same undertaking.

Thus, when they do the least damage conceivable, inheritance taxes represent a diversion of capital into financing activities that are necessary or useful to a country's ability to produce, but which are carried on inefficiently under government ownership. Such activities should not be carried on by the government in the first place; if they are carried on by the government, they should not be financed by an inheritance tax or by any other tax that significantly reduces capital accumulation. Finally, the use of the inheritance tax to finance such expenditures as welfare payments and outlays for defense, which is what, for the most part, it is actually used for, is nothing but an unmitigated assault on the foundations of a country's standard of living.

In every case, an inheritance tax reduces the demand for labor that business firms are able to make and thus either the wage rates or volume of employment that they are able to offer. Simultaneously, it reduces the economic system's overall degree of capital intensiveness, and thus its ability to implement technological advances.[38] Equally important, it reduces the demand for capital goods relative to the demand for consumers' goods and thus the economic system's degree of concentration on the production of capital goods, and, consequently, the ability of the economic system progressively to raise the productivity of labor and real wages.[39] An inheritance tax always represents a diversion of funds from capital to consumption and is thus a force working against both economic progress and the share of total consumption in the economic system that goes to the employees of business firms, whose wages are paid out of capital.[40] Thus, inheritance taxes are against the interests of everyone, nonheirs as well as heirs.

4. The General Benefit from Reducing Taxes on the "Rich"

The progressive personal income tax, the corporate income tax, and the capital gains tax all operate in essentially the same way as the inheritance tax. They are all paid with funds that otherwise would have been saved and invested. All of them reduce the demand for labor by business firms in comparison with what it would otherwise have been, and thus either the wage rates or the volume of employment that business firms can offer. For they deprive business firms of the funds with which to pay wages.

By the same token, they deprive business firms of the funds with which to buy capital goods. This, together with the greater spending for consumers' goods emanating from the government, as it spends the tax proceeds, causes the production of capital goods to drop relative to the production of consumers' goods. In addition, of course, they all operate to reduce the degree of capital intensiveness in the economic system and thus its ability to implement technological advances.[41] The individual and corporate income taxes, and the capital gains tax, of course, also powerfully reduce the incentive to introduce new products and improve methods of production. In all these ways, as will be shown at length in Chapters 14 and 17, these taxes, along with the inheritance tax, undermine capital accumulation and the rise in the productivity of labor and real wages, and thus the standard of living of everyone, not just of those on whom the taxes are levied.

What makes it difficult for people to recognize the fact that everyone would benefit from reductions, or, better still, the total abolition of all of these taxes on the so-called rich—made possible, of course, by equivalent reductions in government spending—is not only massive ignorance of economics, especially of the general benefit from private ownership of the means of production, but also collectivistic habits of thought inspired by Marxism and its doctrine of class interest. By this last, I mean that when it comes to matters of economics, most people tend to think of themselves essentially as members of the class of wage earners rather than as separate individual wage earners, and to think of their interests as indistinguishable from the interests of other wage earners.

Thus, an individual wage or salary earner knows that he would certainly be better off if his own taxes were reduced by some given amount than if the taxes of a millionaire or some large corporation were reduced by that same amount. As far as it relates just to himself, that conviction is absolutely correct. I, for example, would be much better off if my taxes were reduced by, say, a thousand dollars a year than if the taxes of some contemporary John D. Rockefeller or the taxes of General Motors were reduced by a thousand dollars a year. Where most wage earners go wrong is in generalizing from what is true of a reduction in their own, individual taxes, in comparison with an equal reduction in the taxes of businessmen and capitalists—the "rich"—to conclusions about the effects on them of reducing the taxes of *other* wage earners, in comparison with the same amount of reduction in taxes on businessmen and capitalists.

In considering, for example, whether the taxes of businessmen and capitalists as a class should be reduced by some massive sum, such as $100 billion, or whether the taxes of wage earners as a class should be reduced by that sum, almost everyone mistakenly assumes that the interest of the individual wage earner lies with the tax reduction going to the wage earners, as though all wage earners shared a common class interest against all capitalists. This, however, is a fallacy, which becomes apparent as soon as one objectively analyses the situation from the perspective of the individual wage earner. Then it becomes clear that much more is involved than the matter of a reduction in the taxes of the rich or an equal reduction in the individual wage earner's own taxes. For example, while it is certainly true that I gain more from my own taxes being cut by $1,000 rather than the taxes of a Henry Ford or a Bill Gates, it is absolutely false to believe that I gain more from the taxes of my random fellow wage earners—call them Henry Smith and Bill Joneses—being cut by $1,000 each rather than the taxes of Ford and Gates being cut by $1,000 each.

What is actually involved in the question of a reduction in taxes on businessmen and capitalists as a class in the amount of $100 billion, versus an equal reduction in the taxes of wage earners as a class, is two separate, further questions, that represent constituent elements of this question. There is first the question of the benefit to an individual wage earner of his own taxes being cut by $1,000, versus the taxes of any businessman or capitalist being cut by $1,000. We know the answer to this question: it is more to the individual wage earner's interest that his own taxes be cut. But then there is a second question. Namely, which is more to an individual wage earner's self-interest: a reduction in the taxes of businessmen and capitalists in the remaining amount of $99,999,999,000, or a reduction in the taxes of wage earners other than himself in the same remaining amount, that is, of 99,999,999 other individuals very much like himself perhaps, but not himself, each getting a reduction of $1,000?

In other words, put aside the question of a cut in the individual wage earner's own taxes of a $1,000 versus a $1,000 cut in the taxes of businessmen or capitalists. Consider only the effect on his self-interest of a cut in the taxes of all other wage earners besides himself—all of the Henry Smiths and Bill Jonses of the country—in the combined amount of $99,999,999,000, versus an equivalent cut in the taxes of businessmen and capitalists—all of the Henry Fords and Bill Gateses of the country. A $99-billion-plus cut in the taxes of all those other wage earners will make each of them better off, but what will it do for him, for the particular, individual wage earner we are focusing on? To what extent will his fellow wage earners save and invest their tax cut and so raise the demand for his labor? To what extent will his fellow wage earners increase the demand for capital goods and the rate of business innovation and thus bring about improvements in the quantity and quality of the products he buys and thereby increase the buying power of the wages he earns?

It is obvious that the individual wage earner benefits far more from tax reductions on businessmen and capitalists, the so-called rich, than from equivalent tax reductions on his fellow wage earners, and that this is true of each and every individual wage earner, for any wage earner could take the place of the particular individual we have focused on. A tax reduction on businessmen and capitalists will promote capital accumulation, far, far

more than a tax reduction on the mass of the individual wage earner's fellow wage earners. The average businessman and capitalist will save and invest the taxes he no longer has to pay, in far greater proportion than would the average wage earner.[42] He will be induced to introduce more improvements in products and methods of production, which are also a major cause of capital accumulation, and is a process in which wage earners qua wage earners play little or no role.[43] (This is not to say that wage earners are never responsible for innovations. They often are. But as soon as they are, they typically become businessmen. Fundamentally, it is always the prospect of higher profits that stimulates innovations, not the earning of higher wages. It is the prospect of higher profits that leads employers to offer incentives to wage earners to make innovations.) And, on the basis of what has previously been pointed out, the greater saving of the businessmen and capitalists will promote innovation by virtue of making the economic system more capital intensive.[44] Thus the individual wage earner has far more to gain from the taxes of businessmen and capitalists being reduced than from the taxes of his fellow wage earners being reduced.

The gains from this aspect of the matter are so substantial that they almost certainly outweigh the fact that having them precludes the ability to have the benefit of one's own taxes being reduced by a sum such as a thousand dollars a year. This is merely to say that the gains to an individual wage earner of his own taxes being cut by a sum such as $1,000 a year are far less than the gains to him of the taxes of businessmen and capitalists being cut by an immensely larger sum such as a $100 billion a year—that is, by an amount that equals the potential $1,000 tax cuts of all the millions of *other* wage earners in the economic system, which, in the hands of those fellow wage earners, would have been of little or no value to him.

As I have shown, the individual wage earner gains from cutting the taxes of businessmen and capitalists in part because the effect of their sharply increased saving is significantly to raise the demand for labor and thus, quite possibly, significantly to raise his own wage income.[45] But far more importantly, the effect of cutting the taxes of businessmen and capitalists rather than of wage earners will be a substantial rise in the demand for capital goods relative to the demand for consumers' goods and a substantial rise in the rate of innovation, including under the latter head, it is worth pointing out, the ability of upstart new firms to grow rapidly and thus to challenge old, established firms.

The effect of this combination is continuing capital accumulation and thus a continually rising productivity of labor. The effect of this, in turn, is a continually growing supply of consumers' goods relative to the supply of labor, and thus prices of consumers' goods that are progressively lower relative to the wages of labor, which means progressively rising real wage rates, so that in not too many years the average wage earner is far ahead of where he would have been on the strength of a cut in his own taxes.[46]

Starting with tax cuts for the so-called rich—based on equivalent reductions in government spending—is the only hope for the resumption of significant economic progress, indeed, for the avoidance of economic retrogression and growing impoverishment. Because of this, it is actually the quickest and surest road to any major reduction in the tax burden of the average wage earner. It holds out the prospect of the average wage earner being able to double his standard of living in a generation or less. The average standard of living would double in a single generation if economic progress at a rate of just 3 percent a year could be achieved. Such economic progress would also mean a halving of the average wage earner's tax burden in the same period of time—if government spending per capita in real terms were held fixed, for then he would have double the real income out of which to pay his present level of taxes. And then, of course, once all the taxes that most stood in the way of capital accumulation and economic progress were eliminated, further reductions in government spending and taxation could and should take place that would be of corresponding direct benefit to wage earners, that is, show up in the reduction of the taxes paid by them.

Ironically, an aspect of this approach exists in, of all places, Sweden! What has enabled Sweden to have one of the world's highest burdens of taxation and, at the same time, to remain a modern country, more or less advancing, is the fact that the tax burden in Sweden falls far more heavily on the average Swedish wage earner than it does on Swedish business, whose tax burden is actually less than that of business in many other Western countries. (For example, when allowance is made for the fact that Swedish companies can automatically deduct 50 percent of their profits as a tax-free reserve for future investment, the effective corporate income tax rate in Sweden turns out to be below that in the United States: 26 percent versus 34 percent.[47]) If Swedish business had had to bear the burden of taxation borne by Swedish wage earners, the Swedish economy would long since have been in ruins.

This is certainly not to argue for taxation of American workers at a level comparable to the taxation of Swedish workers, or for any increase in the taxes paid by American workers whatever. It is to argue for reductions in government spending sufficient both to eliminate the budget deficit and to make possible substantial tax cuts

on businessmen and capitalists, the so-called rich. It is to argue that as soon as the resulting economic progress begins to increase the real revenues of the government, further tax cuts of the same kind occur, in order further to accelerate economic progress. It is to argue for the achievement first of the total elimination of the inheritance tax, the capital gains tax, the corporate income tax, and the progressive portion of the personal income tax, all taken together, and then, once that has been achieved, for the continuing reduction in the remaining personal income tax, until the personal income tax is totally eliminated. The essential mechanism for achieving these results is a combination of economic progress and continuing reductions in government spending. This is how radically to reduce the taxes of everyone. It is the only way.

Of course, many people will characterize the line of argument I have just given as the "trickle-down theory." There is nothing trickle-down about it. There is only the fact that capital accumulation and economic progress depend on saving and innovation and that these in turn depend on the freedom to make high profits and accumulate great wealth. The only alternative to improvement for all, through economic progress, achieved in this way, is the futile attempt of some men to gain at the expense of others by means of looting and plundering. This, the loot-and-plunder theory, is the alternative advocated by the critics of the misnamed trickle-down theory.

5. Private Ownership of Land and Land Rent

The private ownership of land and natural resources is an aspect of the institution of private property and private ownership of the means of production that has been condemned by economists who in other respects were supporters of capitalism, most notably Henry George. Their case against private ownership of land and natural resources rests on the theory of land "rent" developed by David Ricardo, a theory which, as I will show, is grossly deficient in its failure to incorporate the actual effects of private ownership of land and natural resources. Thus, it is with an exposition of Ricardo's theory of land rent that our discussion must begin.

To understand Ricardo's theory, it is helpful to realize that Ricardo lived in late eighteenth and early nineteenth century England. It was a common practice in the England of that time for farmers to rent the land they worked from aristocratic landowners. Ricardo focused on the portion of such rents that were paid not as compensation for the use of the buildings or any kind of improvements that had been made on the land, but, as he put it, "for the use of the original and indestructible powers of the soil."[48] This abstract portion of the rents actually paid and received, Ricardo held, existed even when the land was farmed by its owner. In that case, he maintained, some part of the value of the produce was attributable not as compensation for any cost incurred, nor as a rate of profit on capital invested, but as a payment for the use of the so-called original and indestructible powers of the land itself.

Ricardo explained the origin and determination of land rent in the following way. In a country with an abundance of land of the first quality—that is, best quality—and that is thinly populated, land will yield no rent. In such conditions, people can obtain the best land merely by appropriating it from nature. They are therefore not under the necessity of paying anything for its use. They will pay for the use of buildings or improvements made upon the land, but nothing for the use of the land itself.

Land rent commences, says Ricardo, when the population of the country grows to the point where all land of the first quality has been brought under cultivation, and it becomes necessary to resort to land of the second quality. On land of the second quality, the same quantity of labor and capital produces less than on land of the first quality. It produces less because the soil is simply inferior or because part of the labor and capital must be expended in transporting the produce a greater distance to market or in first making improvements that land of the better quality already possesses naturally.

The rent that will be paid, according to Ricardo, depends on the difference in the productivity of labor and capital on the two grades of land. If, for example, the same labor and capital produce 100 units of product or $100 of product value on land of the first quality, and only 90 units of product or $90 of product value on land of the second quality, then people will be willing to pay a rent of 10 units or $10 for the right to produce on land of the first quality. They will be willing to pay 10 (whether physical units of product or dollars, it is indifferent here) for the use of first-quality land because their labor and capital produce 10 units more on that land than on land of the second quality, which is their next-best alternative. If they can rent land of the first quality for just the smallest amount less than 10, they have a gain in renting it. And thus their competition will drive its rent to 10. At that point, the product or income obtained by labor and capital becomes no greater on land of the first quality than it is on land of the second quality, because rent absorbs the difference.

If the population of the country grows further, to the point where all the land of the second quality has been brought under cultivation and resort must be had to land of the third quality, then, says Ricardo, rent will commence on land of the second quality and will increase on land of the first quality. For example, if the same labor and capital that produce 100 on land of the first quality, and 90 on land of the second quality, produce 80 on land of the third quality, then when it becomes necessary to resort to land of the third quality, land of the second quality will begin to yield a rent of 10, while the rent on land of the first quality will rise to 20.[49] Again, the reason is that so long as the rent remains below these amounts, there is an advantage in bidding up the rent, because even after paying it, the same labor and capital will earn more on the first two grades of land than on land of the third quality.

The land-rent theory is intimately bound up with Ricardo's and the other classical economists' ideas on diminishing returns and population growth. The law of diminishing returns held that successive equal doses of labor and capital, when applied to a given piece of land, yield smaller and smaller increments of product.[50] In effect, having to apply labor and capital to land of the second quality is comparable in its results to the application of a second dose of labor and capital on land of the first quality, and similarly for the extension of cultivation to still lower grades of land.

Ricardo's and the other classical economists' views on population entered in explaining the limits that exist to the formation of land rent at any given time. According to Malthus, whose views on population Ricardo largely accepted, population tends to grow up to the limit of the food supply. Taken in conjunction with the land rent theory, this means that population tends to grow until the land that must be cultivated is of such an inferior degree of fertility that it yields barely enough to enable its cultivators to survive and rear the number of children required to replace them. At that point, all output on better grades of land that is in excess of what is required for such minimum subsistence shows up as "land rent."

If, for example, we assume that 80 units of product represents subsistence, then, as we have just seen, a rent of 10 would be reached on land of the second quality, and 20 on land of the first quality. This would represent a kind of equilibrium. Rent could not grow further, because population could not grow further—an additional population could not be sustained, because yields would be too low to support it. (Eighty units of agricultural output, remember is assumed to represent minimum subsistence. Land of the fourth quality yields less than subsistence, say, 70 units.)

To develop further the case thought to exist against private ownership of land, we must consider what allegedly would happen if some improvements in production were now made—improvements that would increase the output of labor and capital on all the different grades of land. For example, suppose that with the use of the same labor and capital, first-quality land could now yield 110 units of product; second-quality land, 100 units of product; and third-quality land, 90 units of product. For a time, everyone would be better off. But then, precisely as a result of the greater prosperity, more children would survive to adulthood, population would grow, more land would need to be cultivated, and it would become necessary to resort to land of the fourth quality, which now yielded 80 units of product and could therefore support its cultivators.

The great mass of people, who lived by their labor, would end up no better off than they had been before. From their point of view, the long-run effect of the improvements would simply be that a larger number of them survived at the edge of subsistence. Land of the fourth quality, which before could not be cultivated, because it yielded less than subsistence, would now yield subsistence and would be cultivated. Rent would commence on land of the third quality, which previously yielded no rent, and would increase on all the higher grades of land. Thus, the increase in yields on all the different grades of land previously cultivated would end up in the pockets of the landowners as additional rent, while the great mass of people toiled on at subsistence.

It was on the basis of this analysis that Ricardo and many other classical economists concluded both that the "natural" or equilibrium level of wages is subsistence and that rent tends to constitute a larger and larger proportion of the total income of a country as the country grows in wealth and population.[51] (The alleged tendency of wages toward subsistence was widely believed to be so inescapable that the proposition gained the name *"the iron law of wages."*) In fairness, it must be pointed out that Ricardo sometimes admitted that in an improving country wages might stay ahead of their so-called natural level for an indefinite period of time.[52] But he could not free himself from thinking of subsistence as representing the natural equilibrium.

Ricardo's views are understandable if one keeps in mind when he lived, and that his knowledge of history referred to the centuries prior to the Industrial Revolution. The five hundred years from 1250 to 1750 strongly appeared to confirm his view that economic improvements benefit primarily the landowners, while leaving the position of the masses unchanged. Those five hundred years represented a period of significant improvement when considered from beginning to end. Yet the standard of living of most people was hardly touched. The major beneficiaries by far were the landowning aristocracy and those merchants and artisans who enjoyed their patronage. By the end of the period, the landowning aristocrats could afford magnificent homes, fine furniture, fancy clothing, and gilded coaches. But the mass of people still

could not afford new clothing, meat, or, often, even enough bread to still their hunger.

While Ricardo himself did not advocate the nationalization of land or the confiscatory taxation of land rent, others did.[53] His theory led people to view landowners as receiving the greatest incomes in the society and doing the least to earn them—as passively sitting back and pocketing the fruits of progress and other people's labor, by virtue merely of the growth of population. It should not be surprising that demands were soon made that these apparently unearned gains be used for the good of all.

These views on land and land rent exert an important, if not generally recognized, influence on public opinion in the present-day United States. They provide much of the intellectual basis for proposals that have been made to nationalize the American oil industry, and for the so-called windfall profits tax that was enacted when price controls on domestic crude oil were removed. For essentially the same analysis respecting the formation of rent applies to mining, and the extractive industries generally, as applies to agriculture. Thus, the rise in the world price of crude oil is widely seen as the result of a growth both in world population and in average oil usage per capita pressing upon limited reserves of oil. The owners of the reserves are perceived as undeserving beneficiaries of this process. The objective of the nationalization proposals and of the windfall profits tax is to seize these allegedly undeserved gains and use them for the alleged general welfare.

These views on land and land rent play a major role in perpetuating the U.S. government's enormous landholdings in the Western states and in Alaska. In many of the Western states, the federal government owns over half the land; in Alaska, it owns about 99 percent. It is thought that in government hands the land serves everyone, while in private hands it would merely provide unearned income to its owners. These views also influence public opinion in its appraisal of conditions in other countries. It is taken for granted that a precondition of overcoming poverty in many of the backward countries is "land reform," by which is meant the confiscation and redistribution of all significant-sized landholdings. The economic intent of these proposals is to give to small cultivators the allegedly unearned rents now going to the large landowners.

In this last connection, it must be pointed out that the Communists and socialists are more consistent than the advocates of land reform. Land reform would transfer land rents to a larger number of people than had received them before, but would leave the basic conditions complained of unaltered: those cultivators to whom the better grades of land were given would earn more for the same labor than those to whom the poorer grades were given.

And those working the poorest grades of land would receive no benefit at all. Nor would the dwellers of towns and cities receive any benefit. The Communists and socialists, on the other hand, advocate the nationalization of the land, rather than its redistribution, and thus the use of the land rents for the alleged benefit of the whole society.

How Private Ownership of Land Reduces Land Rent

The inference, so easily drawn from Ricardo's theory, that private ownership of land enables landowners passively to sit back and pocket the fruits of economic progress and other people's labor, is utterly mistaken. The truth is exactly the opposite: namely, private ownership of land is an essential foundation of economic progress, and the more it is respected, the more rapid is economic progress. Thus, it is precisely private ownership of land that prevents land rent from constituting an ever growing share of income. For private ownership of land operates to increase the productivity of land and thus reduce its scarcity value and rent.

We can begin to understand the effect of private ownership of land on land rent if we look again at the case of economic progress and a rise in yields on all grades of land. Only this time, let us consider a far more rapid rate of progress than before, the kind of rate of progress that results from the incentives and ability to increase production that is made possible by unrestricted private ownership of land and which is therefore rapid enough to outstrip the growth in population. For the sake of simplicity, let us assume that the rate of increase in output per worker in agriculture is twice the rate of increase in population. Thus, by the time that population doubles, the same absolute number of workers employed in agriculture is capable of producing quadruple the agricultural output.

In this case, there can be a doubled *per capita* consumption of agricultural commodities without the employment of any additional workers in agriculture whatever. If, as is entirely possible, a doubled per capita consumption of agricultural products is all that the public is prepared to pay prices for that are profitable to the producers, then the effect would in fact be that the number of workers employed in agriculture is no larger than before. Because the doubling of population would mean a doubling of the total number of workers in the economic system, the implication of agriculture continuing to employ only the same number of workers would be that the size of agriculture relative to the rest of the economic system is cut neatly in half. And with this halving of the relative size of agriculture would be a halving of the size of agricultural land rents relative to the total income of the economic system.

In terms of physical agricultural produce, agricultural land rents would quadruple: Where before there were three workers respectively producing 100, 90, and 80 on land of the first three qualities, there would now be three workers respectively producing 400, 360, and 320. Therefore, in terms of physical produce, land rents would now be 80 plus 40, instead of 20 plus 10, or four times as large.[54] That is, they would maintain the same proportional relationship to the four-times larger agricultural produce. What is different, however, and this is vital, is that agriculture itself would now be only half of its former size relative to the rest of the economic system, and thus those land rents as a percentage of the incomes earned in the economic system would be cut in half. And their relative significance would be halved again and again, every time the same set of developments was repeated.

Of course, it is not necessary that when the productivity of labor in agriculture doubles relative to the increase in population, the per capita consumption of agricultural commodities also doubles. It might increase by less than double or by more than double. If it increased by less than double, then a smaller absolute number of workers would be needed in agriculture than before, and thus the relative decline in agriculture and in the economic significance of land rent would be all the greater. Indeed, in this case, there would also be a need for less land under cultivation than before (and for the less intensive cultivation of the land that remained in production). For example, it might be that instead of the doubled population wanting to buy, at prices profitable to the sellers, the 1080 units of agricultural output now produced on the first three grades of land (400 + 360 + 320), they only wished to buy the 760 units now produced merely on the first two grades of land. This would still represent a significant increase in the per capita consumption of agricultural commodities, namely, a little over 40 percent. For 760, the output now produced on the first two grades of land is more than 2.8 times as large as the output previously produced on the first three grades of land (100 + 90 + 80, which equalled only 270), and thus, when divided by a doubled population, represents per capita consumption at a level 1.4 times as great. Yet it would also mean the withdrawal of land of the third quality from production. And this, in turn, would mean a further decline in land rents, this time even as a proportion of the physical volume of agricultural produce. In terms of the physical produce, land rent would now be $40/760$ instead of $30/270$, that is, about 5 percent instead of about 11 percent.

It makes no fundamental difference if the increase in the per capita consumption of agricultural commodities is so great that to provide it, it is necessary to increase the absolute number of workers directly or indirectly contributing to the production of agricultural commodities, so long as there continues to be a substantial enough decline in the *relative* number of workers so employed. In this case, even though more labor is directly or indirectly applied to each unit of land, and even though the amount of land under cultivation may be increased through the resort to land of relatively inferior quality, still the relative decline in the size of agriculture outweighs any increase in the proportion of agricultural produce which constitutes rent. Moreover, it should be realized that even when it is necessary to resort to additional land, it is possible for land rent as a proportion of the physical volume of the produce not to increase, or, indeed, even to decrease. This will be the case insofar as it becomes possible to make previously submarginal land the equivalent of land of above-marginal quality. To the extent that this occurs, the need to resort to additional land does not mean a need to resort to land of relatively inferior quality.

Under the kind of economic progress I have just described, which has been characteristic of the Western world since the Industrial Revolution, there is no tendency either toward a fall in real wage rates to subsistence or toward a rise in the economic significance of land rent—that is, no tendency toward a rise in the share of so-called national income constituted by land rent. On the contrary, under these conditions, real wages go on rising further and further above subsistence and the share of national income constituted by land rent is radically reduced.[55] And this is true despite rapid increases in population. Indeed, as will be shown later in this chapter, in the context of a division-of-labor, capitalist society, the very increase in population itself tends to become a major source of the productivity of labor outstripping the increase in population.[56]

Historically, the rate of economic progress in Britain and North America began to accelerate markedly starting around 1750, and by the early nineteenth century was far outstripping increases in population and the consequent operation of the law of diminishing returns and the need to resort to inferior grades of land. In the course of the nineteenth century similar developments occurred in various countries on the European continent.

A succession of radical improvements, continuing right down to the present time, has enormously increased the productivity of labor and the yields per acre on all grades of agricultural land. As I pointed out previously, the poorest land cultivated in the Western world today is vastly more productive than the very best land in use a couple of generations ago, let alone in Ricardo's day. Modern technology, it is worth repeating, is able to make mountains and deserts into land that is far more productive than the very best lands cultivated not many decades ago.[57]

This same process, of converting previously submarginal land into very high-quality land, was exemplified in a different form by the improvements in ocean and overland transportation that took place throughout the nineteenth century. Before the days of low-cost ocean transport, practically all of the land of North America had to be considered submarginal from the point of view of Britain and Western Europe. Before the days of the railroad, most of the land of the American Midwest had to be considered submarginal from the point of view of the Eastern United States as well as the rest of the world. But with these improvements, the land of the American Midwest emerged as an enormous addition to the supply of very-best-quality land. In the Eastern United States, in places like New York, Vermont, and Massachusetts, there are actually substantial tracts of land that at one time were farmed, but have since been put back to forest, because they were displaced by the competition of far superior Midwestern lands. Similar developments occurred in Great Britain in the nineteenth century, where substantial acreages that had been farmed were turned to pasture.

The resulting sharp decline in the economic significance of land rent can be seen by comparing the locus of wealth in Great Britain in 1850 with its locus in 1750. In 1750, the locus of wealth in Britain was great landed estates. In 1850, it was far and away industry and commerce. This change in the locus of wealth was the result of the continual shrinkage in the relative size of agriculture and the corollary continual enlargement of the rest of the economic system, then principally consisting of manufacturing and commerce.

The same course of development that has been described with respect to agriculture took place, of course, with respect to mining as well. Since the Industrial Revolution, the poorest-quality mines in commercial operation at any given time have tended to be far more productive than the very best-quality mines in operation a generation or two before. And the proportion of the labor force employed in mining, and the relative economic significance of mining and mining rents, has sharply declined.

This rapid rate of increase in agricultural and mining productivity has not been a mysterious accident. It is the result, as I have said, precisely of the private ownership of land and natural resources. The private ownership of land and natural resources gives each individual owner the incentive to improve his property, to use it for the benefit of the market, and to go on seeking ways to increase its efficiency and yield. Competition among the various private owners leads to the rapid widespread adoption of whatever improvements are introduced and requires that anyone wishing to go on earning a high rate of profit introduce still further improvements.

In other words, the combination of the incentive to save and accumulate capital, the profit motive, and the freedoms of individual initiative and competition that private ownership establishes, operates to increase the yield of agricultural and mining property rapidly and steadily, and thus to *reduce* land rent! Private ownership increases the productivity of land, which counteracts diminishing returns and the need to resort to inferior grades of land. In this way, *private ownership of land reduces land rent.*

To present the same idea in still different words, a growing significance of land rent is the reflection of an increasing scarcity of the better grades of land. Private ownership of land, on the other hand, provides the incentives and the means for making each piece of land more productive and for bringing into production every piece that is better than what is presently in use. It is thus the most powerful force operating in favor of abundance and against any growing scarcity of the better grades of land. Thus, it works to reduce land rent and its economic significance.

This principle—that private property is what reduces the significance of land rent—is confirmed if we examine the historical facts. The beginning of the more-rapid rate of progress in agriculture and mining coincides with a *vast extension of the institution of private property in land.* In the century and a quarter or so following 1750, practically the whole of the territory of the United States east of the Mississippi River and extending several hundred miles to the west of it became private property. In addition, the second half of the eighteenth century was the major period of the *enclosure movement* in Great Britain. This was a movement that established private property in land where before there had been communal property. The enclosure movement converted village-owned pastures and forests into separate private property holdings; it also consolidated into larger, compact units the small, scattered strips of land that many villagers had previously farmed. The result was the large-scale creation of modern private farms in Britain. This was followed by the rise of scientific farming: selective animal breeding, the development of newer and better strains of seed, and the application of more modern tools and implements.

Furthermore, both in Britain and on the continent of Europe, the power of feudal laws and customs was broken in other respects as well. Property which had previously been prohibited from being sold, or even leased on a long-term basis, because it was viewed as having to provide support for an unbroken line of future aristocratic descendants rather than being the private possession of any living individual aristocrat, was now allowed to be sold or leased on long term. This made possible the transfer of such property to more efficient hands. Also, the corollary of the abolition of serfdom on the European continent—which did not take place in most countries until after the French Revolution—was that landowners could now fire unnecessary workers. (Serfdom had not only prohibited workers from leaving the feudal estates of their birth but also prohibited the feudal "owners" from removing them.[58]) Thus, the abolition of serfdom gave landowners a powerful incentive to seek more efficient methods of production, which incentive had previously been lacking because of feudalism's violation of the right to fire along with the right to quit.

In all these ways, it was the extension of private ownership over a vastly greater area that brought about continual doublings and redoublings of the productivity of labor in agriculture and mining. Thus it was private property in land and natural resources that made it possible for a steadily declining fraction of the labor force to supply a growing population ever more abundantly with agricultural commodities and minerals, and which thus reduced the scarcity of productive land and thereby the economic significance of the income derived from such land.

In our own day, the principle that private property reduces land rent is dramatically confirmed by the oil situation. As explained previously, the U.S. government's ownership of vast land areas in the Western states and in Alaska operates to keep vast amounts of oil off the market. The same is true of its ownership of the continental shelf. If these areas were privately owned, or open to the establishment of private ownership, the most profitable use to which they could be put would be to develop them and extract and sell the oil they contained. The effect would be vastly more oil on the market and thus a lower price of oil. The effect of this, in turn, would be a reduction in the so-called mining rents derived from owning oil deposits and a reduced significance attaching to the ownership of oil deposits. This result would be achieved the more strongly, the more the territory throughout the world that was privately owned. For then the greater would be the volume of oil deposits under the control of people who had an incentive to develop them and extract and sell the oil they contained.

The result would also be achieved the more strongly, the more the property rights of the existing private owners of oil deposits, and of all other forms of energy deposits, were respected. If, for example, the owners of existing privately owned oil deposits are not forced to operate under price controls, rising taxes, or the threat of confiscation through nationalization or antitrust "divestitures," they will invest more and produce more oil. By the same token, if the property rights of the owners of natural gas deposits, coal mines, and uranium mines are not infringed, they will produce more of these forms of energy, which, of course, compete with oil and whose more abundant production would keep down the price of oil and any mining rents derived from the ownership of oil deposits.

Thus, private property and respect for the rights of its owners is what holds down and actually reduces the significance of land rent. However paradoxical it may seem, the objections and criticisms that Ricardo's followers raised against private ownership of land should have been directed against the *absence* of private ownership of land and against violations of the rights of existing private owners. For it is the absence of private property, and the violation of property rights in land, that hold down the supply of agricultural and mineral products and thus bring about a scarcity of the better grades of land and mineral deposits and so increase the significance of land rent. It is precisely government intervention at home and the worldwide nationalization of oil deposits that have made possible the emergence of a new aristocratic class of officials and sheiks, who derive enormous revenues through absolutely no productive contribution on their part. Abolish that intervention and open more land to private ownership, and the rents derived from the ownership of oil deposits will be radically reduced.

It is worth pointing out in connection with the fact that private property is the basis for the reduction of land rent, that efforts to tax away the land rents that do exist under private property only serve to increase land rents. For in reducing the income that can be derived from the ownership of a piece of land, they reduce the incentive of landowners, and the means available to landowners, to improve their methods of production and thus to bring about reductions in land rent. Thus, such taxation deprives the average wage earner of an essential defense against the consequences of rising population, which, in the absence of rapid and continuing progress in agriculture and mining, would be the unleashing of the law of diminishing returns against him, and all that that implies.

In addition, of course, it should always be kept in mind, on the basis of the discussion of natural resources in Chapter 3, that the increase in the supply of agricultural and mineral products that private ownership of land achieves is not at the expense of the future. On the contrary, the increase is progressive and can go on virtually without limit, so long as man expands his knowledge of and power over the physical world in which he lives, which is precisely what private ownership of land and natural resources gives him the incentive to do.[59]

Land Rent and Environmentalism

Knowledge of the role of private ownership of land and natural resources in preventing any tendency toward a progressive growth in land rents and decline in real wages toward an equilibrium of subsistence confirms the critique of environmentalism made in Chapter 3. We have already seen the role played by environmentalism in the rise in mining rents in connection with petroleum, and the consequent enrichment of Arab sheiks and terrorist governments at the expense of the rest of the population of the world.[60] It is necessary to realize that in general, as a matter of principle, the environmental movement is bent on stopping further increase in, indeed, on reducing, the productivity of labor in agriculture and mining, and thereby, whether it is aware of the fact or not, on driving down real wage rates and raising land rents. This is the meaning of its systematic efforts to stop the use of pesticides, herbicides, and chemical fertilizers, and of its further systematic efforts to stop the conversion of previously submarginal land and mineral deposits into highly productive land and mineral deposits—notably its efforts to stop the economic exploitation of "rainforests," "wetlands," the Arctic, Antarctica, and the ocean floors, as well as much of the American West and Alaska. The measure of its success must be the rise in the economic significance of land and mining rents and a decline in the level of real wages toward subsistence.

The environmental movement openly declares its hostility to the Industrial Revolution, which masses of unthinking people take to mean opposition merely to black smoke belching from factory chimneys. It should be clear from this analysis that the fact is that even if environmentalism does not succeed in removing modern technology from the world, it can easily succeed in recreating pre–1750 conditions for the masses of people in the presently advanced countries, merely through throttling further rapid progress in agriculture and mining. The environmental movement is often characterized as elitist. It is elitist. Economically, it is a latter-day movement of feudal aristocrats, seeking the existence of a privileged class able to pocket the benefits of the economic progress that has taken place up to now, while denying those benefits to the broad mass of the public. It is a movement of monopolists, typified by the mentality of homeowners of the type who, having gotten "theirs," seek to stop all further development of land in their area. It is the movement of neofeudal mentalities who desire a world of broad open spaces for themselves, spaces that are essentially ownerless, and who care nothing for the plight of crowded, starving masses, who are to be denied the benefit of access to those open spaces, which are to be closed to all development. Essentially it is the old story of the feudal lords who are to have vast forests set aside for their enjoyment, while the serfs dare not remove a log for their fires or kill an animal for their meal.[61]

The Violent Appropriation Doctrine

It is necessary to consider the argument that the institution of private property in land is tainted insofar as present titles can be traced back to the violent dispossession of previous owners.

As noted in Chapter 1, this argument has its clearest application to conditions in Europe, in the course of whose long and bloody history probably many violent transfers of ownership can be found in connection with almost any particular piece of land.[62] It is doubtful that even on its own terms the argument has much application to the United States. To be sure, in the process of appropriating land, occasional injustices were committed against Indians. These injustices, however, arose only in those isolated cases in which individual Indians could claim legitimate rights of private ownership which the white settlers violated, such as having established a farm which white settlers appropriated. There was no injustice present in the settlers disregarding the claims of the Indian tribes to political sovereignty over territory, nor in their disregarding the collectivist claims of the tribes to economic ownership. By the principles set forth in the Declaration of Independence, governments are instituted among men to secure their inalienable individual rights and deserve to be overthrown when they become destructive of that end. If this was true of the relatively enlightened despotism of the British under George III, it was infinitely truer of the barbaric governments of the Indian tribes and their arbitrary claims to land ownership.

In the United States, the settlers found an almost empty continent, whose relative handful of inhabitants almost all lived by hunting and who had few or no fixed settlements, nor, therefore, any solid basis for claiming title to the land, over which they merely roamed. And, even so, the settlers frequently paid the Indian tribes for the relinquishment of their claims to rights of hunting and camping. In this sense, they purchased Manhattan Island and many other, far more substantial pieces of territory from the Indian tribes. Thus, in the United States, it is true to say that the historical record of the overwhelming majority of property holdings is free of violent appropriation—that practically all property holdings can be traced back through voluntary purchases and sales to a point of peaceable appropriation from nature on the part of their very first owners.

Moreover, it should be realized that in any case in which a division-of-labor, capitalist society supersedes a non–division-of-labor society, it is logically illegitimate to view matters in the light of forcible expropriation. The conditions of a non–division-of-labor society are necessarily those of recurring conflict and warfare, with successive waves of newcomers again and again forcibly displacing the previous inhabitants. This is the necessary outcome of population growth and the operation of the law of diminishing returns within the narrow constraints of a society of hunters, nomads, or self-sufficient farmers. In such circumstances, as soon as population growth reaches the limit of the ability of a group's present territory to support it, its members must range further afield, in the quest for additional hunting grounds, pastures, or agricultural land. And thus they come into conflict with the members of other groups who seek the same territory or who already occupy it, and whose survival likewise depends on its possession. It is only the establishment of a division-of-labor, capitalist society, with its potential for continuing increases in production, that removes these economic causes of conflict and makes possible a harmony of interests among men. It is only within such a society that property rights or any other rights can be secure.

It should also be realized that in any conflict between a division-of-labor, capitalist society and a non–division-of-labor-society, such as existed between the society of the American settlers and those of the Indian tribes, the former possesses an overwhelming and decisive *moral* superiority over the latter, which absolutely entitles it to victory. This superiority is the fact that the division-of-labor society possesses the ability to *assimilate* all of the members of the non–division-of-labor society, and to enable them and their heirs to enjoy greater wealth and longer life, along with those who are already members of the division-of-labor society. But the non–division-of-labor society cannot assimilate the members of the division-of-labor society—it cannot even support all of its own members. Thus, while the division-of-labor society of the American settlers had the ability to offer the Indians the life of the settlers upon assimilation, the non–division-of-labor society of the Indians offered only the prospect of starvation and death if the settlers were to attempt to assimilate with it. The conflict between the settlers and the Indians was a conflict between a society easily capable of absorbing an additional million members, and a society capable of sustaining no more than a million members (despite the availability of most of the land mass of the North American continent), for that was the population limit that the Indians were apparently unable to go beyond, before encountering a shortage of hunting grounds. If any failing can be charged to the settlers, it was their failure sufficiently to seek to assimilate the Indians. But this was probably the result of the refusal of the Indians to be assimilated.[63]

Furthermore, it must be stressed that in any case— even aside from that of conflict between a division-of-labor society and a non–division-of-labor society—the legitimacy of the institution of private property and of the title of its present owners does not in any way depend on the absence of violent appropriations in the past. Private property in Britain and France, for example, and the title of its present owners, is fully as legitimate as it is in the United States, despite a record of violent appropriations in the past. The reason for this is that in a division-of-labor society, such as Britain and France represent, there is a powerful force at work which steadily operates to wash away all stains of past violence. This is the fact that in such a society production is carried on for the market and that property is gained or lost to the degree that one produces to the satisfaction of the market.[64]

To illustrate this principle, let us assume the existence of a society in which every piece of property has been violently seized from its previous owners. But let us also assume that from this point forward there is an end to violent appropriation, because the law now recognizes the last group of violent appropriators as the legitimate owners. Henceforth, acts of violent appropriation occur in violation of the law and are prosecuted and severely punished, and thus, from this time forward, property which is not passed by inheritance must be acquired by no other means than by voluntary purchase and sale.

Thus, from this point on, the owners of property are secure in their possession and have the incentive to improve their property and its ability to produce. In the context of a division-of-labor society which grows up around them, the incentive to increase production means the incentive to produce more for the market, in order to be able to earn the money to buy the things one wants in the market. An essential means of increasing production for the market is the increasing use of capital in the form of money, so that one's production can have the benefit of products previously produced by others and the benefit of services voluntarily performed by others. Capital must be used in order to purchase such things as animals, tools, building materials, equipment, and labor services, which are essential to being able to increase production for the market. There is no alternative to making such purchases if one wishes to be able to earn the money one would like to earn.

In the very process of raising capital, however, it becomes necessary either to sell land or to borrow against it. Such sales of land are obviously an important way in which land passes into the hands of people who have no necessary connection with violent appropriators.

Furthermore, the necessity of using capital—of making purchases in order to make sales—creates the possibility of financial losses. Such losses are certain to occur for many landowners as the widespread efforts of land-

owners to increase production for the market result in lower prices. Only the more efficient landowners—those with lower costs—can be profitable in the face of such lower prices. The less efficient ones suffer losses.

Thus, the newly established security of property and its incentives to save and invest and increase production result in market competition among the landowners. In this competition, some of the landowners succeed and grow richer, while others fail and lose their land. They lose their land either because they have borrowed against it, and their losses prevent them from meeting the interest and principal payments, or simply because to offset financial losses and continue producing with the aid of capital—of the means of production that can only be obtained with the expenditure of capital—it becomes necessary to sell more land. Ultimately, of course, a landowner who continues to sell at losses must lose all of his land.

Thus land more and more passes into the hands of those who acquire it on the basis of their success in serving the market, and is retained only by those who are successful in serving the market.

Moreover, the purchase of land, of course, is not limited to those who have been previous owners of land. It is open to everyone, including (very importantly in the context of the transition from feudalism to capitalism) former serfs and the descendants of serfs. Under these conditions, anyone, irrespective of his class of origin, or that of his ancestors, will be in a position to acquire land who earns the money necessary to buy it or who offers good prospect of efficiently using the land he acquires. (This second condition is a principal basis for being able to borrow money to buy land.) The money with which to buy land can, of course, be earned in any area of the economy, whether the accumulation of profits in manufacturing or commerce or the saving up of wages in any line of employment, whether in industry or in agriculture. And, as indicated, money to purchase land can be borrowed on the basis of demonstrated ability and good prospects for its profitable use.

Thus, the basis of acquiring and retaining property becomes the ability to produce efficiently for the market.

Initially, of course, the power to spend in the market of a country that recently experienced a forcible appropriation of property will reflect that forcible appropriation. To the extent that those who have appropriated others' property, or the heirs of these appropriators, are richer, their power to spend is greater, and production for the market is, accordingly, production that serves them. But to the extent that the members of this group are not themselves as adept in producing for the market as those who have not seized property, or whose ancestors have not seized property, property begins to gravitate away from the members of this group and toward the members of the second group. Soon, a substantial amount of property is held not by those who have seized property, or by their heirs, but by those who have supplied the wants of this group. And now *their* spending emerges as a growing factor in the market. And insofar as property is retained by descendants of forcible appropriators, it is so by virtue of their success in serving the market.

As more time passes, property is increasingly held not by those who seized it, nor by their heirs, but simply by those who are most adept at supplying the wants of others who have money to spend, who, for their part, possessed the same ability. In this way, the significance of the violent seizure of property in the past is steadily diminished and all property comes to be held by those who have fully earned their right to it.

How rapidly this cleansing process takes place depends on how free the market in land is allowed to be. The main obstacle delaying the process is *entail legislation*—i.e., laws that restrict the passage of property to a specific line of descendants, and which prohibit its sale, forfeiture in payment of debts, or even long-term lease, to parties outside this line of descendants. Such legislation (which existed in Europe even after the French Revolution) was enacted to preserve the holdings of aristocratic families in the face of the market forces just described. Of course, entail legislation is itself a gross violation of property rights—it denies the property rights of the living in the name of the alleged property rights of the unborn.

The Demand for Land Reform

The doctrine that present titles are invalid because of past acts of violence in the appropriation of property, is often associated with demands for "land reform." Land reform is a demand that property be forcibly transferred from its present owners to a new group of owners. The connection to the violent-appropriation doctrine exists whenever this new group is alleged to be descended from earlier possessors whose rights the ancestors of the present owners allegedly violated.

It should be realized that no amount of past violence in the appropriation of land can justify land reform. Land reform is simply a new, fresh act of violent transfer of land. It is one thing for the actual victim of a dispossession, or his children or grandchildren, to demand to be put back in the possession of the property that was forcibly taken from him. But if for any reason these individuals are denied justice, it becomes a fresh injustice to later on dispossess an owner on the grounds that his ancestors, or the ancestors of some previous seller, lacked just title. In order for justice to be done, there must be a time limit on the recognition of claims for the redress of past injustices.

If this were not the case, no one could be secure in his property. At any time, parties could step forward claiming dispossession of their ancestors by the current owner's ancestors or by the ancestors of some previous seller of the property. And claims of any one group of alleged victims could in turn be superseded by the claims of still another group of alleged victims able to trace the dispossession of its ancestors further back. In a country like England, for example, the same piece of ground might be contended for by those able to trace the dispossession of their ancestors to the War of the Roses, or, alternatively, to the Norman Conquest, or to the still earlier invasions of the Danes, Saxons, Romans, and even Picts and Celts.

It would certainly be a gross injustice to ask anyone to work and save to improve his property, and then take it from him on the basis of such claims. For justice to be done, conditions must be such that people can work and save to improve their property. And for such conditions to exist, property rights must be put beyond challenge as quickly and as completely as possible. This means, as a minimum, a strict time limit on the recognition of claims based on past injustices.

Once private property rights are made secure, not only are the effects of past injustices washed away, but, as should already be clear, the land of a country is quickly put to its most efficient uses. It is important to stress this point in dealing with the issue of land reform. As the advocates of land reform describe matters, the system of land ownership they seek to overthrow is highly inefficient and has no economic basis. According to them, the actual unit of agricultural production is almost always a small farm, a large share of whose output its peasant operator must turn over as rent to a wealthy landowner who has done nothing to earn it. "Land reform"—the forcible transfer of ownership to the peasant operators—is then urged not only as the means of rectifying past injustices, but also as the means of providing powerful incentives for the improvement of production. As owners, it is argued, the peasant operators will have the incentive to increase their production—something which they now lack, because the increase would allegedly be appropriated by the wealthy landowners.

What must be realized here is that if the "land reformers" were right in their description of the facts, a free market in land would automatically and peaceably operate to transfer ownership to the small operators. For if, as owners, the small operators would have greater incentives and would produce more, and there is no economic basis for the present, large-scale ownership of land, then the present owners would have a powerful incentive to *sell out* to the small operators. This is because if the same piece of land presently owned as a single unit would produce more when subdivided into a multiple of smaller property holdings, its total market value would also be greater when subdivided into such holdings. The situation would be perfectly analogous to what happens right now in the United States, as cities expand into surrounding farm or ranch land. The farmers or ranchers who own units of several hundred or several thousand acres find it profitable to subdivide and sell out their holdings in units as small as a quarter or eighth of an acre, or even less, to a larger number of home owners.

If, indeed, small units of ownership were in fact more efficient, the owners of large holdings would have exactly the same kind of incentive to sell out to small owners. And it is worth noting that the small owners would not have to be able to pay for their purchases right away, any more than home buyers need to be able for their purchases right away. The small owners could buy their holdings on credit—with mortgages on their property. This arrangement would probably be advantageous to the present, large owners even if they were the ones who had to hold the mortgages, because for twenty or thirty years they would receive far more as interest and principal payments from land used efficiently than they could otherwise receive as rent from land used inefficiently. This excess of funds received over twenty or thirty years would more than compensate them for the loss of all future rents—in exactly the same way that receipt of a sufficiently high price in the present would more than compensate them for the loss of every subsequent year's receipts.[65]

Thus, even if the advocates of land reform were correct in their claim that the system they want to overthrow is inefficient, all that would be necessary to achieve greater efficiency is not "land reform"—not the forcible expropriation of property—but *the establishment of a free market in land*. If the more efficient system is the breakup of large landholdings into small units, then this is what a free market in land will accomplish—without force or violence, and to the mutual self-interest of all concerned.

But the fact is that the breakup of large landholdings that the land reformers want to achieve by no means typically represents an improvement in efficiency. Often, it is precisely the large landholdings that are the more efficient arrangement and are the product of the market as far as it is free. This appears generally to be the case in instances in which large plantations produce and export such crops as bananas, sugar, pineapples, or coffee. Here the unit of production is not a farm of a few acres but perhaps the whole plantation, or at least some substantial portion of it. The large landholding is necessary

in order to utilize expensive modern equipment, such as tractors, which would be uneconomical if they had to be applied within the limits of separate farms consisting of only a few acres each.

In all cases of this kind, land reform represents a serious reduction in agricultural efficiency—over and above the disincentives its prospect creates for saving and any form of improvements to be undertaken by those likely to be expropriated by it. For it represents a forced reduction in the scale on which agriculture is undertaken, and thus a loss of the benefits of large-scale production.

The advocates of land reform are actually oblivious to all such concerns. Their real goal is not greater efficiency in agriculture, but to enable the largest possible number of people to survive by means of subsistence farming. They want each family to be able to live by having its own few acres. And when there are more families, each will presumably have a little bit less land to farm, as the result of a further land reform if necessary.

If one thinks seriously about land reform as a solution to poverty in the backward countries, it becomes clear that it is actually *incompatible* with the real solution. The real solution to poverty in the backward countries requires not that more people there be able to squeeze by a little bit more easily as farmers, but that the populations of those countries become *integrated into the international division of labor.* If the people of most of Asia, Latin America, and Africa are ever to enjoy a high standard of living, it will not be as farmers on a few acres each, but as workers in the same kind of division-of-labor society as presently exists in the United States, Western Europe, and Japan.

Thus, land reform seeks the solution to poverty in totally the wrong direction. It actually operates to prevent the real solution from being achieved. In forcing the breakup of large plantations producing for the export market, it cuts backward countries off from such connection to the international division of labor as they have managed to achieve. In disrupting the exports of these countries, it deprives them of the ability to import from the more advanced countries, and thus deprives them of the ability to obtain technologically more advanced goods than they can produce for themselves. At the same time, of course, in reducing the production of goods for export and thus raising the prices of the goods affected, it operates to reduce the real wages of workers in the more advanced countries, since the buying power of their wages is correspondingly reduced.

Even more fundamentally, the forcible restriction of the scale on which agriculture is undertaken and the constant threat of renewed confiscations that land reform represents operate to prevent permanently the rise in the productivity of agricultural labor that is indispensable to building a division-of-labor society. It should be remembered that labor can be spared for industry and commerce only to the degree that it is possible for a fraction of the working population to produce the food required by the whole. Land reform operates to keep down the productivity of the fraction required in agriculture and thus to keep up the size of that fraction. It thus works to prevent the development of industry and commerce and the establishment of a division-of-labor society in the countries in which it exists.

The solution to the agricultural problems of the backward countries is not land reform, but the establishment of a fully free market in land and thus, for the first time in those countries, the full recognition of private property rights in land. That will eliminate all vestiges of feudalism and feudal inefficiency and make possible the progressive improvement of agricultural production.

Our discussion of land reform has application to conditions in El Salvador in recent years. In that country, the government of the United States spearheaded a drive for land reform, even under the auspices of the avowedly conservative Reagan administration. It made land reform a precondition of American aid.

While the official policy of the U.S. government is, and was, supposed to be noninterference in the internal affairs of other countries, this policy was somehow forgotten in the case of land reform in El Salvador. (It has been scrupulously observed, however, in connection with almost all of the nationalizations of industries, including the expropriations of the property of American nationals, that have occurred throughout the world. It has also been observed in connection with Communist atrocities. But the same State Department that helped to lose China and Cuba to communism did not remember the policy of noninterference in connection with land reform in El Salvador.)

It is almost impossible to know the details of what actually happened in El Salvador as a result of land reform, because the representatives of the press lack the knowledge of economics that is required for intelligent reporting on the subject. Nevertheless, reports did come through that the so-called Right in El Salvador, whatever that designation may mean, denounced land reform as a violation of free enterprise and blamed it and the related nationalization of banks for destroying the economy of the country and fomenting the unrest on which the Communists thrived. In view of what has been established in principle concerning land reform, it would seem that such claims deserve thorough investigation. There is a strong likelihood that they are correct.

If they are correct, our government's policy of having made land reform a precondition of American aid would

be ironic in the extreme. It would mean that before we were willing to aid El Salvador in a defense against communism, we required that its government violate private property rights on a massive scale and create the chaos which the Communists needed in order to thrive. (Later, if the Communists had won their revolution, which, until the recent fall of communism in Eastern Europe and the Soviet Union, was the likely outcome, the State Department could have issued a white paper explaining why their victory was inevitable.)

In connection with the subject of land reform, it is necessary to mention the fact that the American military occupation under General MacArthur forced the policy on Japan after World War II. Large landowners were forced to sell at prices set by the government, and rapid inflation of the currency quickly made their compensation almost valueless.

On the basis of all that has been established concerning land reform, it should be clear that this policy must be condemned, even though it is almost universally regarded as having been a major element in establishing American "democracy" in place of Japanese feudalism. The only appropriate policy, the only one consistent with the American principle of individual rights, would have been the establishment of a free market in land—i.e., the abolition of all aspects of entail legislation and any elements of legal privilege for the large landowners, but not their expropriation.

The effect of land reform in Japan has been to hold down the efficiency of Japanese agriculture and to impose a drain on the rest of the Japanese economy, which is obliged to subsidize the inefficient agricultural sector. In Japan today, landholdings are typically no more than two or three acres and are operated on a part time basis, by people whose main employment is in industry.

This highly inefficient arrangement has not resulted in a catastrophe, because at the time it was instituted Japan was already a highly industrialized nation able to import most of its food supplies, and over the years it has greatly increased its ability to import food. The effect of land reform in Japan has thus worked out to be equivalent to that of the destruction of agriculture within the territory of a city, as it were. It has not been disastrous, because the role of agriculture was relatively small to begin with and the losses inflicted on it could easily be made good by a rapidly expanding industrial economy, through imports. Japan's food supply would be affected far more seriously by land reform in the United States, Canada, Australia, Brazil, or Argentina than by land reform in Japan, because these are the places on which it actually depends for most of its food supply. The effect of the Japanese land reform would be virtually nil if not for the protectionist measures against the import of foreign rice. These force Japanese consumers to bear the burden of the land reform as far as the consumption of rice is concerned.

It must be noted that Japan's postwar industrial success is the result of following policies with respect to industry that are the opposite of land reform. Property rights in industry have been respected far more highly in Japan than in the Unites States—as manifested in sharply lower rates of taxation on profits and interest. This, of course, has resulted in much higher rates of saving, capital accumulation, and economic progress in Japan than in the United States. Furthermore, since the early postwar years, inflation in Japan has been at a significantly lower rate than in the United States. This is also very important in regard to a country's real rate of taxation of profits and interest, since the greater the rate of inflation, the higher are the artificially inflated profit and interest incomes subject to taxation and thus the greater is the actual taxation of such incomes.[66]

To summarize our discussion of land reform, we have seen how in a division-of-labor, capitalist society the stain of violent appropriations of land in the past is steadily washed away through the operation of market processes. In close connection with this, we have also seen how land reform represents a fresh act of injustice and is economically disruptive and against the interests not only of existing landowners, but also of everyone else in the long run. For land reform seeks to perpetuate agricultural inefficiency and thus to keep down the real income of all buyers of the agricultural products concerned. By the same token, it operates to prevent the development of the division of labor in the countries in which it exists by making impossible the release of labor for industry and commerce. Thus, in the long run, it holds down the real income even of those who are supposed to be benefitted by it. Whatever legitimate objectives the advocates of land reform might have would be achieved by the establishment of a free market in land, not by land reform.

6. Private Property and Territorial Sovereignty

The principles we have established concerning private ownership of the means of production have implications for the extent of the territorial sovereignty of countries.

In history books and discussions of current affairs, one frequently encounters such statements as: The motive of country A in going to war with country B was to obtain the latter's coal mines—or steel industry, or whatever. It is taken as virtually self-evident in these discussions that the citizens of a country gain to the extent that their country's territory is enlarged to contain more natural resources and more branches of industry.

Our discussion of the general benefits derived from privately owned means of production in a division-of-labor society shows that this belief is false. We have seen that an individual does not need to own property in order to benefit from it, so long as he is able to buy its products. In the same way, *a country does not require sovereignty over a territory for its citizens to be able to obtain all the economic benefits that that territory can offer.* For the most part, they obtain those benefits merely by being able to buy the products of that territory.

For example, in order for the citizens of Germany to obtain the economic benefits of the natural resources and industries of Alsace-Lorraine, it is absolutely unnecessary that Germany own Alsace-Lorraine or that fellow German nationals own those resources and industries. An individual German who wants something from that region obtains it by paying for it. What difference can it make to him whether the producers of the good he buys salute the French or the German flag? Or the Burgundian flag? What difference can it make to him whether they sing the "Marseillaise" or "Deutschland Über Alles"? How are the goods, or their price, affected by such matters?

The only rational political-economic interest that the citizens of a country have in the territory of other countries is that that territory be *under a free government.* (And that, of course, is their first and foremost real interest with regard to the territory of their own country as well.) If a country is under a free government—i.e., a government that is limited to defending the individuals in its territory from the initiation of physical force—then its territory offers to the entire world every economic benefit that can possibly be derived from it. Not only can all the world buy its products, but all the world is free to try to improve the development of its natural resources and industries. For in such a country, foreigners have the same right as nationals to own land, invest capital, and to live and work. Thus the products available for purchase from such a country are as good and as inexpensive as it is possible for them to be in the circumstances. Anyone anywhere in the world who sees a way to make them still better or cheaper is free to go ahead and try to do so.

There is absolutely no rational economic basis for any country to seek sovereignty over the territory of any other country that has a free government. For its citizens already derive all the economic benefits they could derive if it were under the sovereignty of their own government. Indeed, if their own government is less free than that of the foreign country under consideration, they would almost certainly derive *less* benefit from the foreign country's territory if it were brought under the sovereignty of their own government. As an extreme example, the citizens of Soviet Russia would have died of starvation if the territory of the United States had come under the sovereignty of the former Soviet Union and shared its economic chaos.

The major implication of this discussion is that in a world made up of free countries, there would be absolutely no rational economic basis for war or imperialism. It would make no difference to anyone what the extent of the territory controlled by his own government was. He would be perfectly free to buy and sell anywhere, to invest anywhere, and to live and work anywhere, irrespective of whose flag flew over the territory. Thus, there could be no rational economic motive for the citizens of any country to seek an extension of their own country's sovereignty, and thus no economic grounds for war.[67]

A rational economic motive for interfering with the sovereignty of other countries arises only insofar as they lack free governments. And then, the only rational economic purpose of such interference is to establish a free government. For example, if there is an area rich in low-cost natural resources, but anyone who tries to develop them has his property confiscated and runs the risk of being murdered, then the rest of the world is deprived of the benefit of those resources. Its interests would be served by the establishment of a free government in that area.

It must be acknowledged that the British Empire in the nineteenth century by and large served as just such an instrument. It was the means of establishing relatively free governments in many areas of the world that would otherwise have remained in a state of anarchy or despotism. Its existence served to open vast territories to economic development that benefitted the entire world. It was not only the citizens of Great Britain who gained by the entry of those territories into the world market, but people everywhere. Every buyer of rubber and tin everywhere in the world benefitted from the fact that British rule made possible the development of the Malayan rubber plantations and tin mines and thus a more abundant and less expensive supply of rubber and tin. Every buyer of cotton, flax, linen, jute, and all the other products of India benefitted from the fact that British rule made possible the development of the production of these things in India. This is not to excuse the racist attitudes that were often displayed by the British in their colonies, nor any of the injustices they committed in the course of colonial rule, but it is to acknowledge the genuinely great accomplishment that their empire represented.

A Defense of Foreign "Exploitation" of Natural Resources

It is necessary to point out that foreign development and export of a country's natural resources in no way represents a loss to the native population of that country. It is not economic "exploitation" in any evil or improper sense. For example, the fact that the British developed the tin mines of Malaya and then exported the tin throughout the world was no more a loss to the Malayan population than it is a loss to the people of Minnesota that the iron mines of their state were developed by businessmen from New York and Chicago, who in turn have exported the iron throughout the rest of the United States and the world as a whole.

The belief that such activity represents "exploitation" is based on the premise that natural resources are rightfully the collective property of the population of the territory in which they are found. Those who hold this view then observe that only the private owners are paid for the extraction of the resources sent abroad, and that much of the money received for the resources remains abroad. On this basis they conclude that a territory's property is being taken from it without compensation.

The answer to this view is that land and natural resources do not properly belong to the people of a territory collectively, but to specific private individuals and companies. For all the reasons I have shown, private ownership is the key to the development of natural resources and thus to the general population of the world being able to benefit from their existence. Collective ownership means nondevelopment or, at best, inefficient development and therefore less general benefit from the existence of natural resources.

The inefficiencies of collective ownership operate to prevent much or any gain from being realized by the countries that enact collectivization—at least where the collectivized resource deposits must compete with privately owned deposits whose operators are not prevented from expanding their activities. Furthermore, whatever the citizens of a given area might gain by the collective ownership of a natural resource in their territory is always at the expense of the greater loss of others. There is not only the loss of the private owners, whose property is collectivized; there is also the loss of the buyers of the resource and its products, for whom the resource is made less abundant and more expensive. In addition, there is the loss of sellers of other products and resources whose sales revenues and incomes are diminished because buyers have less funds available to buy their products because of the necessity of paying more for the higher-priced collectivized resources. (For example, the gains of the members of OPEC were at the expense of the greater loss of the buyers of oil and of the sellers of other products for which the demand was diminished because of the high price of oil.) The net effect of collective ownership and its inefficiencies is that while some sellers may take in more money, other sellers take in equivalently less money, and at the same time the same total expenditure of money, which constitutes the revenues of all sellers combined, buys less. Thus reduction in production is the net loss to the world.

And, finally, to the degree that collective ownership is carried further, any gains associated with it from the point of view of the citizens of any particular territory are lost back in the form of less abundant supplies and higher prices for everything that depends on natural resources found in all other territories where collective ownership exists. Thus, whatever the citizens of Malaya or Minnesota might gain by collectivizing the tin or iron mines of their country or state would not only be more than offset by the losses of others, but it would also be offset by less abundant supplies and higher prices of all the things consumed by Malayans or Minnesotans insofar as those things were also produced under conditions of collective ownership of the natural resources involved. The consequence of collective ownership of natural resources applied as a general principle is that everything would be more expensive to everyone. And many of the collectivized resource deposits would not even be able to operate at all for a lack of other resources or of products made from those resources. For example, some of the collectivized tin mines could be made inoperable by the inefficiencies of collectivized iron mines, which resulted in the cost of tin-mining equipment being made too high. The inefficiencies of collectivized iron and tin mining together would operate to reduce the availability of equipment for extracting oil and coal; the inefficiencies in the production of these latter would also work against the production of iron and tin, and so on.

It should be realized that in fact the foreign development and export of natural resources is a source of gain not only to the general population of the world, through bringing about a more abundant and less expensive supply of the resource, but also to the *general population of the specific territory in which the resource is found*. For it means foreign investment in the area and thus a greater demand for local labor and therefore higher local wage rates. It also means the ability of the local population to obtain imports from other countries, because to the extent that it produces products that are exported, its wages are paid with funds earned abroad. The imports obtainable with these funds include not only products made from natural resources found throughout the rest of the world, but also products of modern technology that it would otherwise be impossible to obtain in the area.

If the local population would like to see foreign in-

vestors spend locally a greater proportion of the revenues they earn abroad by exporting natural resources from the area, then the basic thing they must do is respect the rights of foreign investors. Foreign investors will spend more locally—in the form of increasing their investments—if they judge that investment in the area is profitable, which, in the long run, presupposes that it is secure from depredations by the local government and the local population.

It should also be realized that the profitability of foreign investment depends on the ability of the investors to withdraw their funds whenever they wish. It is one thing for an investor living in London or New York to be willing to invest his money in Malaya or Minnesota. It is a different thing to require, in effect, that he live there in order to be able to enjoy the profits from his investment. Yet that is the effect of laws that interfere with the remission of dividends and interest abroad. Outsiders will readily invest in an area that offers the prospect of high profits if they know that they are free to enjoy their profits elsewhere and free to withdraw their funds to take advantage of the possibility of still more profitable investment opportunities elsewhere.

To the extent that they possess free governments, backward countries naturally offer a very powerful attraction for outside investors—namely, their low wage rates. To the extent that foreign investment can raise the productivity of labor in the backward countries toward the level at which it exists in the more advanced countries, those low wages represent lower costs of production and thus higher profits in comparison with investment in the more advanced countries. If foreign investors judge that their investments are secure in such a country, it is able to attract a veritable flood of investments. And the high profits earned on those investments are plowed back to create still more local investment. On just this basis, we can observe spectacular rates of economic progress today in such countries as Taiwan, South Korea, and Singapore. The rapid progress of Japan, too, was explainable until not too many years ago on the basis of the constant reinvestment of high profits earned on the basis of relatively low wages.

The effect of all this additional investment, of course, is to *raise* local wage rates more and more, and to bring the economy and general standard of living of the area to a higher and higher level, until what began as a backward country is transformed into a fully modern country with a very high standard of living. This has already happened in Japan, where wages are now among the highest in the world and are comparable to those in the United States. The same process is well underway in the other countries named.

Moreover, it should be realized that as local wages rise, the ability of the local population to save and invest on its own increases, and thus that more and more businessmen can come from the ranks of the local population. In other words, the conduct of local business automatically comes to include a growing proportion of natives. And some of the native businessmen, of course, can themselves choose to operate internationally. In this and all other respects, the local area comes to be fully integrated into the world economy. Again, Japan, South Korea, and Taiwan are outstanding examples of this process.

Thus, if they possessed free governments, many of the backward countries of the world could be very rapidly developed into fully modern countries. What prevents this is their belief that foreign investors are their enemies and should be expropriated. This stops foreign investment and perpetuates the backwardness of these countries.

To avoid possible misunderstanding, there is no intent to imply here that the problems of the backward countries are purely political. More fundamentally, they are philosophical and cultural. In many cases the influence of irrational ideas is so great that even the establishment of a free government would not be able to produce very dramatic results. The establishment of a free government achieves dramatic results only in a culture which, among other things, is prepared to accept science and technology and individual self-responsibility. As I pointed out earlier in this book, this in turn rests on the acceptance of causality, the efficacy of the human mind, and human free will. Only on such a foundation is it possible to develop such vital economic attitudes as: improvement is possible, hard work pays, and the individual has a responsibility to save. At the deepest level, the development of a modern economic system depends on the cultural acceptance of the reliability and efficacy of human reason.[68]

There is a peculiar consequence of the collectivist view of natural resources that deserves mention. I call it the "Argentine delusion," since it is especially prominent in that country. It manifests itself in such statements as: "We are a rich country, but a poor people." And: "We have tremendous wealth. None of our problems are real or fundamental. They're just psychological."

I heard these comments some years ago, when I was in Buenos Aires to give a series of lectures. What the people who made them were referring to is the fact that Argentina is a country of about one million square miles in territory, lying in a latitude comparable to that of the United States, and full of rich farm land and all kinds of mineral deposits. These people believed that somehow this automatically made Argentina rich, and that nothing could change that fact—not high taxes, not destructive labor unions, not extreme protectionism, not even hyperinflation.

The comments were made to me in Buenos Aires, where these people lived and worked. It is obvious that the speakers would have felt very differently if Buenos Aires had been a separate country, politically independent of the rest of Argentina. In that case, they would not have thought of counting the alleged wealth of Argentina as "theirs" in any sense. Yet if Buenos Aires had been a separate country and maintained mutual free trade with the rest of Argentina, including the ability of individuals in the two areas to come and go as they wished and to do business on the same terms as before, the real benefit of all those resources to the citizens of Buenos Aires would have been exactly the same.

The truth is that Argentina's natural resources do not make her a "rich country." They might make some individual Argentines or foreigners rich—i.e., whoever their private owners are or would be—but the only ways in which they could make the average Argentinean rich would be insofar as their development increased the demand for Argentine labor and thus raised Argentine wage rates, and insofar as their use in production increased the supply and lowered the price of various products. This latter benefit, of course, would be enjoyed not only by the citizens of Argentina but by all buyers of the products concerned throughout the world, no matter what their nationality.

Unfortunately, the policies of the Argentine government prevent both domestic capital accumulation and foreign investment, and thus make the more extensive development of Argentina's natural resources impossible. Thus, in the delusion that they are somehow automatically rich, irrespective of the policies that their government follows, the Argentine people are likely to remain relatively poor. Given their mentality, the natural resources of their country are actually a *liability* to them: in being regarded as an automatic guarantee of wealth, no matter what their government does, the resources make it that much easier for them to allow the bad policies to go on.

Buenos Aires and the other cities of Argentina might actually be more prosperous as independent city states, devoid of all territorial sovereignty over natural resources, than as part of Argentina, with all of its alleged wealth. In such a case, they might realize that the only thing they had to rely on was the industry of their people and that everything they received had to be paid for, even if it came from the surrounding territory. The loss of the delusion of automatic wealth because of territorial sovereignty over natural resources might make them address their problems seriously and thus establish conditions in which people would be more highly motivated to work and save than is now the case. If that were so, then they could obtain whatever natural resources and agricultural products they required either from the surrounding territories or from anywhere else in the world that offered better terms. Then, perhaps, with a new mentality that recognized the value of a free government, they might look about and see the opportunities awaiting if the neighboring countryside were opened up to free development. They might then reextend their sovereignty into the neighboring countryside and, in effect, reconstitute Argentina on the basis of a free government. Then and only then—under a free government, with full respect for private property rights—would the resources of Argentina finally realize their potential as a source of prosperity, both to the citizens of Argentina and to people all around the world.

The point here, of course, is not to urge the actual breakup of Argentina, even temporarily, but only to highlight the need to shatter the collectivist delusion of automatic wealth through sovereignty over natural resources, and the need to establish a free government in Argentina and in every other country where this collectivist delusion exists.

This section has shown that just as it is not necessary for people to own means of production in order to get the benefit of them, so long as they are free to buy the products of the means of production, so it is not necessary for a country to have sovereignty over any foreign territory so long as its citizens are free to purchase the products of that territory. Indeed, it has shown that the only legitimate interest of the citizens of one country in the territory of another is that it have a free government and thus that its land and natural resources be open to settlement and development by all and that they and their products be purchasable by all. In that way the whole rest of the world derives the maximum possible benefit from the territory of a country without having to have the least degree of sovereignty over it. Thus, a world comprised of capitalist countries would lack any rational economic motive for extensions of sovereignty or for wars of aggression.

In connection with this discussion, the doctrine was refuted that the development and exportation of natural resources by foreigners constitutes an exploitation of the people of a country. It was shown, on the contrary, that such activity is the basis of a higher demand for the labor of a country's citizens and the ability of its citizens to import products of other countries' natural resources as well as products of modern technology. It was also shown how the freedom of foreign investment would operate rapidly to modernize backward countries and raise their standard of living, if only the governments of those countries would allow investors to profit from the existence of low wages in those countries.

PART B

ECONOMIC INEQUALITY

1. Economic Inequality Under Capitalism

The influence of the division of labor on the institution of economic inequality is almost totally ignored. The views that are typically expressed concerning economic inequality would be plausible only if they referred to a non-division-of-labor, precapitalist society. Thus, typically, people take for granted the validity of such statements as "the rich get richer and the poor get poorer," and the more fundamental proposition that "one man's gain is another man's loss."

Now these propositions rest on the assumption that the total wealth that exists in the world, or which can be produced, is a fixed, static sum. Only on that assumption could it be true that one person's gain necessarily implied an equivalent loss by others. Only then could it be true that an increase in the wealth of the rich necessarily implied a corresponding decrease in the wealth of the poor.

Yet this assumption of a fixed, static amount of wealth that can be produced is clearly incorrect in the context of a division-of-labor society. In such a society, a growing body of technological knowledge, manifested in ever improved tools and machines and in man's growing power over the physical world in which he lives, makes possible a continuous increase in the sum total of what is produced. Where the total of what can be produced expands, it is simply false to conclude that one man's gain implies another man's loss, or that the greater wealth of the rich implies the greater poverty of the poor.

Indeed, these propositions are false even in the context of a non-division-of-labor society, so long as conditions are present that make possible an increase in the total of what is produced. To take the simplest and most obvious kind of case, imagine that initially Robinson Crusoe and Friday are each able to gather 10 coconuts a day on their desert island. And now Crusoe, say, devises a pole that enables him to bring down coconuts from higher up in the trees, so that from now on he is able to gather 20 coconuts a day. Crusoe's gain is certainly not Friday's loss. In fact, his gain is almost certain to be followed by Friday copying his new method and thus being able to gather more coconuts of his own. In other words, Crusoe's gain will bring about a gain to Friday, as well.

This little example, it should be realized, also illustrates the absurdity of viewing matters in terms of a "distribution" of wealth and income and then complaining that the "distribution" is unfair insofar as it is unequal. When Crusoe increases his production from 10 coconuts a day to 20 coconuts a day, his "share" of the "national income" of his island rises from one-half to two-thirds. Now Crusoe receiving half of the island's income is just, according to the egalitarians. But his receiving two-thirds is inherently unjust, according to them. Yet Crusoe's larger "share" is nothing but the result of his increasing his production.

In opposition to the egalitarians, it should be realized first of all that there is no actual *distribution* of wealth or income here—that a "distribution" exists only in a purely mathematical sense. What actually exists is separate individuals producing different amounts of wealth. When we add up their separate outputs, we reach a sum, and can mathematically express each individual's production as a percentage or "share" of the total and in this sense speak of a "distribution" of wealth and income. But there is no actual distribution in the sense of someone handing out more to Crusoe and less to Friday. In the same vein, there is no one who makes Crusoe "overprivileged" and Friday "underprivileged." What each has is the result of what each produces. And, of course, to have what one produces, however great, is a matter of right, not privilege.

It follows from this discussion that what egalitarianism implies is that it is unjust for one person to produce more than another, even if that other not only does not lose, but in fact gains as a result of it. Egalitarianism rests on a mentality that actually ignores production and the ability to increase it. In the manner of a backward child, it assumes that everything comes miraculously from some kind of father, who distributes it this way or that way—fairly, if equally; unfairly, if unequally. It wants the government to compel the father to distribute wealth equally or for the government itself to become the father and distribute it equally.

Now it cannot be stressed too strongly that in a division-of-labor society, one person's gain is not only not other people's loss, but is *other people's gain.*

The most fundamental and important instance of this kind, however much it may shock the egalitarians, who typically depict business as the domain of "robber barons," is *precisely the building of great business fortunes.* Both in their origin and in their use, these fortunes are a source of gains to everyone who participates in the economic system.

Such fortunes originate in the earning of a high rate of profit on capital, almost all of which is constantly reinvested, so that the high rate of profit rapidly com-

pounds. The fortunes emerge as the sum of the reinvestments of these compound profits over a period of many years. For example, to go from an initial investment of, say, $100 thousand to $100 million, requires that one earn a very high rate of profit on the $100 thousand, save and reinvest almost all of it, and then repeat the same process over and over again for a considerable number of years. Only in this way, through the combination of earning a high rate of profit and saving and reinvesting the far greater part of it over a protracted period of time, can one possibly transform a sum such as $100 thousand into $100 million. This is a matter of simple financial arithmetic.

Now as explained in Chapter 6, to earn a high rate of profit requires that one be a leader in the introduction of new and better products, in improving the methods of producing existing products, or in meeting changes in consumer demand inaugurated, for the most part, by economic progress.[69] And, as also shown in Chapter 6, because competitors copy innovations as fast as they can and try wherever possible to supersede them, with the result that the profits from any given innovation tend steadily to disappear and be replaced by losses, the earning of a high rate of profit over a long period of time requires that one *repeatedly* be a leader in innovation. *Thus, the high profits out of which great fortunes are accumulated are the result of repeatedly introducing improvements in production.*[70]

These improvements, of course, represent better and less expensive goods for the general buying public. They thus represent a rise in the real income of everyone—everyone benefits in his capacity as a buyer. This is what I mean by the statement that in their origin great business fortunes are a source of gains to all.

What I refer to in the statement about the general gains great business fortunes represent in their use is simply the fact that the fortunes are invested: they represent factories, machines, inventories and work in progress, and the means of paying wages and salaries. Here again they are the base of additional goods coming to market and thus of gains to all buyers; in addition, they provide greater financial means for people to be buyers—insofar as they are the source of a greater demand for labor and thus of additional payments of wages and salaries.

Thus, *in a division-of-labor, capitalist society, the accumulation of a great fortune is the mark of great contribution to general human well-being.*

This principle is readily confirmed by an examination of the history of great fortunes in the United States. To take two leading examples from the age of the so-called robber barons, both Henry Ford and John D. Rockefeller began their careers in industries that were relatively small and backward. They devoted their lives to searching out and implementing all manner of improvements in those industries, on the basis of which they earned very high rates of profit, almost all of which they saved and reinvested. At the end of their lives, the industries in which they worked were enormously improved and expanded because of their efforts, and their wealth was embodied in the means of production of those industries.

Thus Ford increasing his capital from approximately $25,000 in 1903 to approximately $1 billion at the time of his death in 1946, was the result, and, indeed, the measure, of his introduction of one major improvement in automobile production after another, such as the use of moving assembly lines and interchangeable, mass-produced parts, and his use of the profits he made thereby to pay for the construction and equipping of one major automobile plant after another, each embodying the improvements he introduced. Similarly, Rockefeller's fortune was founded on the introduction of improvements transforming the petroleum industry from the backward, inefficient production of kerosene into the highly modern, efficient production of a whole range of petroleum products previously unheard of. It was also based on his pioneering in the ability to use petroleum deposits that were previously unuseable—by virtue of the development of such innovations as refineries capable of chemically cracking petroleum molecules. Rockefeller's billion was the measure of the improvements he introduced and of his continuous reinvestment of the profits resulting from those improvements. It was embodied in a host of modern oil refineries and pipelines, which did not exist before him and might very well never have come into existence without him.

Andrew Carnegie and Commodore Vanderbilt played comparable roles in the building of the American steel and railroad industries. Many great industrialists made great fortunes. As far as the fortunes were made in a free market, the essential principle underlying all of them was a process of repeated productive innovation and the reinvestment of the far greater part of the resulting profits. As the result of such fortune building, the American people obtained an increasingly more modern and more efficient economic system, from which they all greatly benefitted in their capacity as consumers and as wage earners. From the perspective of the general public, whatever people may have mistakenly believed, the *objective* significance of the fortunes was new and better products, new industries, and lower prices relative to wages. The gains of the great industrialists—the so-called robber barons—were overwhelmingly the gains of everyone who bought their products—or even the products of competitors, who were forced to meet the standard they set. Their gains were also the gains of everyone whose wages were increased by the additional

demand for labor their savings created. Their wealth represented an enormous net increase in the total wealth of the economic system and was the source of a correspondingly great increase in the standard of living of the average person, since it served to increase the production and supply of products he could buy and the demand for the labor he wished to sell. These men were among the greatest innovators and accumulators of capital of all time, and everyone benefitted enormously from their success. They were neither robbers nor barons, but in the highest rank of capitalist producers, whose great self-enrichment was the measure of their enrichment of the general public. They did not steal their wealth but created it, in the process greatly enriching others, not impoverishing them. They were in fact among the greatest benefactors of mankind in all of history.

Consistent with the preceding discussion, in appraising the so-called distribution of wealth—that is, distribution in the sense of who owns what percentage of the total capital that is invested in the economic system—one should keep in mind the following essential facts. Namely, in a division-of-labor, capitalist society there are basically two elements determining such "distribution." These are the relative amounts of income people earn and the relative degrees to which they save and invest those incomes.

In the case of large accumulations of wealth, the relative amount of income one earns typically reflects the relative rate of profit one earns on one's capital. Basically, those individuals have the greatest accumulated wealth who earn the highest rates of profit and save and invest the greatest percentage of their profits. Thus, for example, an individual who earns a 25 percent annual rate of profit and saves and reinvests 80 percent of his profit increases his capital at a 20 percent compound annual rate. In contrast, an individual who earns a 3 percent annual rate of profit and consumes all of it does not increase his capital at all. By the same token, an individual who earns a zero rate of profit and consumes at an annual rate of 3 percent of his capital steadily depletes his capital; and if he incurs actual losses, he depletes it all the faster.[71] Thus, it should be clear that relative rates of growth or decline in accumulated wealth are the result of a combination of relative rates of profit and relative degrees of saving out of profits.

In both of these respects, the accumulation of wealth under capitalism is the measure of contribution to the economic well-being of the rest of society.

To the degree that businessmen and capitalists earn relatively high rates of profit, it is because they are in the forefront of introducing better products and better methods of production and in reshaping the economic system to adapt to changes in demand originating mainly in economic progress.[72] To the degree that they save and invest a higher percentage of those profits, then along with increasing the economic system's degree of capital intensiveness and thus receptiveness to technological progress, they increase both the demand for capital goods relative to the demand for consumers' goods and wage payments relative to the personal consumption spending of businessmen and capitalists as a class.[73] The higher relative demand for capital goods leads to a correspondingly greater concentration on the production of capital goods in the economic system and thus to a more rapidly growing supply of capital goods, which is a critical factor in raising the average productivity of labor and thus real wages.[74] And the increase in wage payments relative to the personal consumption spending of businessmen and capitalists enables wage earners to enjoy a larger proportion of the overall consumption spending that does take place, which also serves to raise real wages.[75] In all these ways, inequality in the so-called distribution of wealth is an essential aspect of a high and rising absolute amount of wealth that is available to the average person under capitalism, in particular to the average wage earner.[76] It is thus the measure of the individual's relative productive contribution to general economic well-being.

Mutuality of gains—one man's gain being other men's gain—is inherent in the very nature of a division-of-labor, capitalist society. It is inherent, first of all, in the fact that in such a society, cooperation takes place by means of exchanges, which are strictly voluntary and entered into only in the expectation of gain by both parties. In an exchange, each party gives only in order that he may receive something he values more. Unless both parties expect to gain by it, an exchange does not take place.

The objective foundation underlying mutual gains from exchange as an everyday, common occurrence—as a virtually omnipresent phenomenon—is the division of labor. Its existence ensures that gains are in fact available for all. For the division of labor raises the average productivity of labor and allows it and the total of what is produced to go on rising, without limit. At the same time, of course, it places every individual in a position in which he must exchange the overwhelmingly greater part of his goods or services for all the things that he himself does not produce and which others produce.

The progressive rise in the productivity of labor and the mutual gains from exchange are two aspects of the process by which one man's gain becomes the gain of others in a division-of-labor society. A third aspect, present, as we saw, even in the context of Robinson Crusoe and Friday on their desert island, is the copying of others'

success. This last aspect is present in a division-of-labor society in the competitive quest for high profits, which constantly operates to deprive every innovation of its special profitability and to require fresh innovation as the means of maintaining a high rate of profit. It is equally present in the competition of wage earners for higher-paying jobs. As explained in Chapter 6 of this book, it is the element that, in the absence of further changes, operates to drive the rate of profit on capital invested toward uniformity in all branches of industry and the rate of wages for all workers of the same degree of skill and ability toward uniformity in the same labor market.

Indeed, as the example of Crusoe and Friday and their coconuts suggests, and as the tendencies toward uniform rates of profit and uniform wages for workers of the same degree of ability suggest, economic inequality in a division-of-labor, capitalist society can be understood as resting on an inequality in productive ability that is dynamic in several senses. The inequality in productive ability is dynamic in one sense in that those of outstanding ability succeed in steadily raising the productivity and real remuneration of those of lesser ability. It is dynamic in a second sense in that at each level of ability, it reflects uneven contribution or adaptation to the process of improvement. Finally, it is dynamic in that there are no legal barriers to individuals crossing over from one level of ability to another.

Thus, businessmen and capitalists have greater income and wealth than wage and salary earners. But their innovations and capital accumulation raise the productivity and remuneration of the wage and salary earners, and do so continually. Among businessmen and capitalists and among each grade of wage and salary earners, there are further inequalities that reflect uneven contribution or adaptation to the process of improvement. That is, there are businessmen and capitalists who earn very high rates of profit because they introduce innovations or adopt them relatively early, and there are others who earn low rates of profit or suffer losses because they lag too far behind in the adoption of innovations. Similarly, there are wage earners who earn relatively high wages because they adapt their skills relatively quickly to the kinds of labor being demanded for the implementation of the improvements introduced by the businessmen and capitalists, and, by the same token, there are wage earners who earn relatively low wages because they fail to adapt their skills quickly enough to the process of improvement. Finally, wage earners are always legally free to become businessmen and capitalists, and unsuccessful businessmen and capitalists are always being reduced to the ranks of the wage and salary earners. Indeed, there is constant movement up and down within and between all economic strata.

On the basis of all of the foregoing, it should be clear that the economic inequality that exists in a division-of-labor, capitalist society is an inequality in which the greater success of some is the cause not of the failure of others, but of their success too. It is in its most important respects simply an inequality of success and progress—an inequality in which some are merely further ahead than others on the road of improvement. The inequality of such a society is an inequality in which the "rich" and the "poor" *both* grow richer, and in which the classification of any given individual as belonging to the class of the "rich" or the "poor" is constantly subject to change by virtue of his own efforts and abilities.

This discussion, of course, provides the answer to those who make such complaints as that under capitalism 10 percent of the population owns 90 percent of the "wealth" (i.e., the capital) of the country. Even if the claim were accurate, there would be absolutely nothing wrong with such a situation. It would not be the result of wealth being unfairly "distributed." It would be the result of some people contributing more to production than others—in the more important cases, introducing a series of major improvements into production, and then saving and investing very heavily out of the higher incomes they earned. The 90 percent of the wealth that is not only owned but also *created and earned* by the 10 percent who own it (or by their parents or grandparents), would then serve the 90 percent of the population that did not contribute as much to production. Because of the freedom of the 10 percent to create and earn the wealth and income they do, there is incalculably more wealth: there is more saving and the means of production that exist at any given time are more efficiently used, both of which facts are causes of the continuous further increase in the supply of means of production—of capital goods—that, as we have seen, are used to produce overwhelmingly for the benefit of the 90 percent of the population that allegedly owns only 10 percent of the wealth of the economic system.

For the 90 percent to seek to steal the wealth of the 10 percent is to destroy the creation of the wealth that serves them. It is to begin with no concept of the production of wealth and how it is accumulated, but instead with the myth of the "distribution fairy," and from there to go to envy and resentment, from there to theft, and with theft, to the destruction of the incentives to saving, efficiency, and the accumulation of capital. The result is that those whose heads are empty of the knowledge of how wealth is produced and accumulated come to live in a world that is physically empty of the production and accumulation of wealth. Once having become maliciously ignorant thieves, they go on to end as starving wretches.

2. Critique of the Marxian Doctrine on Economic Inequality

On the basis of what has been established concerning the nature of economic inequality in a capitalist society, it is now possible to grasp the enormity of the injustice that Marxism and its supporters have perpetrated in connection with this subject.

According to Marxism, the inequality between capitalist and worker is essentially no different than the inequality that prevailed in earlier periods of history between master and slave or between lord and serf. All of history, declares Marxism, is the record of one continuous class struggle that has been carried on in different forms and under different guises. In the Ancient World, it was between master and slave; in the Middle Ages, between lord and serf; today, it is allegedly between capitalist and worker. The worker of capitalism, says Marxism, is also a slave—a "wage slave." And the capitalist is an "exploiter" even more ruthless than the feudal lord or ancient slave owner. For capitalism, says Marxism, cannot even "assure an existence to its slave within his slavery," but compels the worker to sink ever deeper into poverty and starvation.[77]

Mankind's only salvation from exploitation and class conflict—its only hope for elevation into a new world of peace and harmony—Marxism declares, is the establishment of socialism. Socialism, it claims, holds out the promise of a classless society, free of all exploitation and conflict—a society of perfect equality. In achieving the equality of wealth and income, it will allegedly complete the work of the so-called bourgeois revolutions of the eighteenth and early nineteenth centuries that established representative government and political equality.[78]

These doctrines permeate the contemporary educational system—in history books, in so-called social-science courses, in literature courses, in every field and in every way in which it is possible to inculcate them.

Every aspect of the Marxian doctrine on inequality is false and vicious.

The Marxian doctrine claims to see as essential the mere existence of inequalities in wealth and income, absolutely irrespective of their nature and cause. It ignores the radical, day-and-night difference between economic inequality under capitalism and economic inequality under serfdom and slavery. Specifically, what it ignores is the fact that under capitalism economic inequality rests on *differences in productive contribution,* which contribution operates to the benefit of all. Those who have more under capitalism have it because they contribute more to production (or because their parents or grandparents did), and their contributions enable everyone else to have more also. In other words, the greater wealth and income of the capitalists and of the higher-paid wage and salary earners is *earned,* and the process of earning it is the source of *general benefits.*

The greater wealth and income of a feudal lord or of a slave owner, on the other hand, was of an entirely opposite character. It was obtained not by means of any productive contribution on his part, but by means of *physical force*—essentially by theft and extortion. As such, his gain really was the loss of others: what a robber steals, his victim loses.

The Marxists seek to evade having to acknowledge the difference between a capitalist and the owner of serfs or slaves by means of an equivocation on the use of the word "force." The owner of serfs or slaves obviously uses force or the threat of force against them. But, ask the Marxists, isn't the fact that reality compels a man to work if he would eat, not also a kind of force? And isn't it force that, for all practical purposes, a worker must work for a capitalist, unless he is in the exceptional position of having a substantial amount of savings of his own? Thus aren't the workers "forced" after all to work for the capitalists?

Such ideas are expressed in a more subtle form by John Kenneth Galbraith in his book *The New Industrial State*:

> The worker in a Calcutta jute mill who loses his job—like his American counterpart during the Great Depression—has no high prospect of ever finding another. He has no savings. Nor does he have unemployment insurance. The alternative to his present employment, accordingly, is slow but definite starvation. So though nominally a free worker, he is compelled. The fate of a defecting southern slave before the Civil War or a serf before Alexander II was not appreciably more painful. The choice between hunger and flogging may well be a matter of taste.[79]

The essential point Galbraith seeks to make in this passage is that the distinction between freedom and slavery is nominal if a worker must work in order to avoid starvation. This idea is absolutely vicious. It is straight out of the world of *1984*: it claims literally that freedom is slavery. It is a repetition of the apologetics for slavery offered in the South before the Civil War and more recently by the supporters of Soviet Russia.

The difference between freedom and slavery is as sharp as day and night, even when a worker must work to avoid the pain of hunger. For even in this case it is not the capitalist employer who *causes* the worker's hunger. On the contrary, he provides the means of *satisfying* the worker's hunger. The worker works for the capitalist always in order to receive a positive—his wages. The difference between a free worker and a slave can always be seen in this: A slave is someone who is kept at his work against his will: by chains, whips, and guns—i.e., by physical force applied by other people. In the absence of

such things, he would run off. A free worker, on the other hand, is someone who works of his own choice and who, more likely, can be *kept from* his work only by means of physical force. The worker in Galbraith's Calcutta jute mill, for example, is not kept there by the threat of being shot if he leaves, as is the case of a worker in a Communist or Nazi labor camp. On the contrary, from Galbraith's description, it is probable that it would take the threat of being shot to keep that worker away from his job.

A worker is a slave not because he must choose to work as the means of eating, but when he chooses *not* to work and is compelled to do so nevertheless—by means of physical force. Of course, very few people can choose not to work at all for very long. But no matter how poor they are, they can always choose not to work for any *particular employer,* whenever any other employer offers them better terms. This fact, that while people must work in some capacity, they can choose *in which particular capacity,* Galbraith and the Marxists choose to ignore, by focusing on the case of unemployment and the unavailability of alternative jobs.

The existence of unemployment and the lack of alternative jobs is itself the consequence of violations of freedom and capitalism—specifically, violations such as prounion and minimum-wage legislation, which keep money wages artificially high relative to the demand for labor.[80] Yet even though mass unemployment exists, it does not prevent individuals from having alternative employment opportunities at some time or other in their lives. And the ability to choose among these alternatives is vital. Its importance to the individuals concerned is demonstrated by the fact that to deprive them of it, chains, whips, and guns are required.

So much then for the attempt to portray capitalist employers as slave or serf owners, on the basis of an equivocation between forced labor and the necessity of working imposed by the nature of reality.

By the same token, it should also be realized that slave and serf owners qua slave or serf owners did not at all derive their incomes in the manner in which a businessman or capitalist derives his. They did not, for example, derive their incomes by virtue of owning land or capital—the means of production. They derived their incomes by means of the initiation of force—by extortion and theft. It is necessary to clear up this confusion particularly in regard to feudal aristocrats, who, it is often assumed, held their position on the basis of their ownership of large tracts of land.

The feudal nobility were in fact not landowners at all in the proper sense of the term. Their position was more analogous to that of hereditary commanders of military bases. As mentioned earlier in this chapter, a feudal nobleman did not have the right to sell his alleged property, or to pledge it as security for debt, or to contract away its use on a long-term basis. For the theory of feudal landholdings was that the land was intended to serve an unbroken line of succeeding generations of noblemen. Each of these would use it in part to maintain himself and his family at a level dictated by custom, and, for the rest, to maintain vassals, with whom he would appear at the side of the king or some other higher nobleman when called upon to do so. And the king himself was not to regard his domains as his private property, serving his personal pleasure, but as serving the purposes of the state.

The feudal nobleman both lacked essential rights of a private property owner and possessed powers that are absolutely no part of the rights of a private property owner. For all practical purposes, *he was the local government*: he combined in his person the powers of policeman, judge, and lawmaker. His workers were legally prohibited from leaving his estate. By the same token, no other nobleman was allowed to bid for the services of his workers.

Thus, a feudal nobleman did not earn his income in the manner of a landowner or capitalist, who must compete for labor, and who holds his position only by being able successfully to compete as a seller in the market for products as well. Rather, he derived his income in his capacity as a virtual slave owner and as a tax collector.

Consequently, every aspect of Marxism's attempt to confuse economic inequality under capitalism with economic inequality under earlier systems is false. The greater income and wealth of the businessman and capitalist is the result of their positive productive contribution, which increases the income and wealth of everyone else as well; while the greater income and wealth of the owner of slaves or serfs is based on force and is thus at the expense of the income and wealth of everyone else. It is economic inequality based on positive productive contribution and resulting in general benefit, versus economic inequality based on force and resulting in others' corresponding loss. That is the difference between economic inequality under capitalism and economic inequality under slavery and serfdom.

Ironically, the difference between the economic inequality of capitalism and that of slavery and serfdom is no less the difference between the economic inequality of capitalism and the economic inequality of *socialism.* Socialism, we have seen, is itself, both in fact and by its very nature—both economically and morally—a system of aristocratic privilege and of systematic exploitation of the masses by a ruling elite. It renders the ordinary citizen economically powerless by establishing the state as a universal monopoly employer and, at the same stroke, by destroying the incentive or profit and loss and the freedoms of individual initiative and competition in the production of goods. Morally, it demands that the individual live not as an end in himself, as he does under capitalism, but as a means to the ends of "Society," which, of necessity, means that he live as a means to the ends of the rulers, who divine the ends of "Society."[81]

In no sense is socialism some kind of extension into the economic sphere of the noble principles associated with the words political democracy, or, more accurately, political freedom—as many people believe in naively repeating this popular Marxist theme. On the contrary, it constitutes the total destruction of all political freedom along with all economic freedom. As I have shown, socialism is necessarily a system of totalitarian dictatorship.[82]

Thus, virtually every evil that the socialists allege of capitalism on the score of economic inequality, while not true of capitalism, is true of socialism. By the same token, the end of exploitation and the achievement for the first time in human history of a society based on the peaceful, harmonious cooperation of all men, which the socialists allege will come with the arrival of socialism, has already come—to the extent of the arrival and continued existence of *capitalism.*

Economic Inequality and the Law of Diminishing Marginal Utility

The attempt is sometimes made to support the advocacy of economic equality on the basis of the law of diminishing marginal utility. Such writers as Oscar Lange and other socialists argue that any given-sized unit of wealth has a higher marginal utility to whoever has fewer such units.[83] They argue, for example, that $1,000 has a higher marginal utility to a man who is worth only $10,000 than to a man who is worth $100,000. It follows, they believe, that if $1,000 were taken from the man with $100,000 and given to the man with only $10,000 an increase in total marginal utility would result.

In their view, the law of diminishing marginal utility implies that some kind of gain in utility can be achieved so long as anyone has more than someone else and his wealth can be transferred to a party who has less: the marginal utility of the wealth gained by the poorer person will allegedly be greater than the marginal utility of the wealth lost by the richer person. Perfect equality of wealth and income appears to them to be a norm requisite for maximizing "utility"—in a country or in the world. Needless to say, this argument serves as an important rationalization for the progressive income and inheritance tax and for other forms of confiscation of wealth and income.

It is difficult to say which is the greater defect of this

argument: the lightness with which it takes the matter of property rights and the speed with which it is prepared to violate them, or its confusion concerning the nature of marginal utility. The argument assumes that all that has to be established is that something is wanted or needed by someone more than by its owner, and that that is sufficient to justify forcibly taking it from its owner and giving it to the nonowner.

That this is what the argument assumes is highlighted if we put aside any question of inequality of wealth or income for the moment, and consider the vast range of other cases in which something can have a higher marginal utility to someone who does not own it than to the person who does own it. Thus, for example, if anything, whether a painting or a puppy, is owned by someone who does not appreciate it or therefore value it as highly as someone else would who does not own it, the argument of the socialists concerning diminishing marginal utility implies that a prima facie case exists for taking the property from its owner and giving it to the other party. For this change in ownership too will allegedly result in an increase in total marginal utility. Thus, the argument implies not only that a poor person has a right to the property of those who are better off than he is, and who therefore need it less. It implies equally that anyone who would value something more highly than its present owner, whether on the basis of his education, character, or whatever, as much as on the basis of the smallness of the number of units he owns, has a right to it at the expense of the owner.[84]

The supporters of this view, it should be clear, have no regard for rights of any kind, but merely for needs and desires. They have never outgrown the chaotic world of small children, who frequently act on the principle that whoever needs or wants something has the right to take it away from its owner, irrespective of the owner's wishes. The only difference between them and such children is that they think it must be clear that they, or some other beneficiary, need the goods *more* than the owner before they seize them and that they use the government to seize the goods rather than seize them personally.

This brings us to the other fundamental defect of the argument for economic equality on the basis of the law of diminishing marginal utility. This is the fact that it divorces the concept of marginal utility from individual people and assumes that it pertains to a kind of collective organism, of which the individuals are mere cells serving as centers of pleasure and pain for the organism. It is only on this basis that it can be assumed that the loss of a thousand dollars by one person and the gain of a thousand dollars by another person represents any kind of overall net gain. The argument assumes that the individuals are mere cells of *"Society,"* which allegedly feels only a

relatively small loss when the richer person's wealth is diminished and a relatively great gain when the poorer person's wealth is increased.

Of course, the problem with this view of things is that people are not cells of some greater organism. Each *individual person* is an organism. Thus, each individual person constitutes a separate base and standard for judging utility. It is only *to the individual human being* that there can be utility, marginal utility, or any other kind of value.[85]

It is true that *to one and the same person* $1,000 would be of higher marginal utility if all he had was $10,000 than if he had $100,000. But it is a non sequitur and completely false to imply that the marginal utility of $1,000 to this individual is increased if, when *he* has $100,000, $1,000 is taken away and given to *someone else,* who has only $10,000. It is absurd to think that the eleventh $1,000 in the hands of someone else is of greater marginal utility to a person than the one-hundredth $1,000 in his own hands. And if it is not the marginal utility to *this person,* the man who has the $100,000, that is increased, then there is no universal, objective, or valid sense in which marginal utility could be increased by "redistribution." Exactly the same point applies to "redistribution" in favor of those who appreciate and value things more highly on the basis of factors other than the smallness of the number of units they possess. It is no satisfaction to someone whose painting has been stolen that now it is in the collection of someone who looks at it more often and with greater pleasure than he, the owner, would. The most intense pleasure of the thief is of no account to the owner.

The fundamental philosophical issue that is present here is the conflict between altruism and egoism. Altruism demands that we regard the needs of others as though they were our own. If we were starving, we would value a bowl of rice as highly as our lives. Asiatic coolies and others *are* starving, and thus, according to altruism, we should be as concerned as if we ourselves were starving. Nevertheless, in fact, we value our last scoop of ice cream or bar of chocolate above their first bowl of rice, which rice we could buy for them with the price of the ice cream or chocolate, if we chose.

According to altruism, such a state of affairs is a moral abomination, and we deserve to feel profoundly guilty for allowing it to exist. Many of us, no doubt, do feel guilty for a while, when the plight of the coolies or other impoverished, suffering group is called before us; but our guilt rarely lasts so long or goes so deep that we are led to give up very much for the sake of such groups. We find that giving charitable assistance is also of diminishing marginal utility, just like any other activity, and we leave off at a point where the importance we attach to the satisfaction of others' needs is far less than if those needs were our own. There is good reason for this. The basic fact is that we are separate, independent organisms, and our survival, well-being, and enjoyment require that each of us devote his abilities to providing for himself.

This does not mean that we are unconcerned with the needs of others. There are some others, such as spouses, children, parents, and close friends, whose existence and well-being are very important to our happiness. We are very much concerned with the needs of these others, and often attach as much or even more importance to providing for their needs as for our own, because we regard their existence and happiness as vital to our own. For example, most parents would rather go hungry themselves than allow their children to go hungry.

Apart from this small number of other people, however, there is no connection between our lives and well-being and the lives and well-being of others that is of such a nature as would justify our expending any major portion of our energies or wealth for their sake. It is true that because of the harmony of rational self-interests that prevails under freedom, and which this book repeatedly demonstrates, we also derive major benefits from the existence, success, and prosperity of others whom we do not know or have any personal relationship with, and, indeed, potentially could each derive enormous benefit if the whole human race were successful, prosperous, and happy. Nevertheless, in the very nature of the case, the good will that we can reasonably feel for the rest of our countrymen and the whole rest of the human race that is founded upon their actual or potential success and prosperity *precludes their being a drain upon us.* This is because our benefit comes from the work and saving they do, which are the source of their success and prosperity along with contributing to our own. To the extent that others are successful and prosperous, of course, they do not need our charity.

Of course, the reasons for desiring to see other people in a state of well-being go beyond purely economic considerations. As rational beings, we practice induction. When we see another human being, we see another creature who in the most fundamental essentials is like us. When such a being is successful and happy, we see a confirmation that we can be successful and happy, and so we feel better as a result. By the same token, when we see another human being who is suffering and in pain, though he has done nothing to deserve it, we see evidence that we ourselves can be threatened, and thus we feel badly. As a result, when people are the victims of natural disasters beyond their control, such as earthquakes or floods, charity can be given in the name of the positive value of seeing them restored to their normal success. By its very nature, however, such assistance both has a

selfish basis and is limited and temporary. It does not represent a blank check. It does not elevate the needs of others into any kind of mortgage on our lives or imply that we must make any form of sacrifice of our own well-being in order to serve them. On the contrary, it is given in the name of our own values and as part of the process of pursuing our own happiness.[86]

In giving such assistance, the values involved for us are the same in nature as those which are involved in literature and drama, where we desire to see "happy endings"—that is, human success—and feel depressed at the vision of human failure. And just as our desire to see the success of human values does not lead us to spend more than a limited amount of time and money on novels, plays, and motion pictures, and so forth, so it does not lead us to devote more than a limited amount of time and money to charitable activities. Just as we find that after a point the marginal utility of all kinds of other goods outweighs the marginal utility of another novel or movie, we find that it also outweighs the marginal utility of charitable contributions.

In the present-day world, the apparent need for charitable assistance enormously dwarfs the self-interest of people in providing it. Over three-quarters of the world's population live in or not far removed from a state of hunger. Even in the richest countries, there are large numbers of people who are unemployed, or who, even if they are employed, are still apparently unable to pay the cost of an education, an illness, or a modest home. If one looks back at the past, the situation was even worse: there were far fewer prosperous people, and those who were considered prosperous had much less.

Charity is obviously impossible as a solution to a problem of poverty on this scale. It can never be to the self-interest of people to attempt the support of so many others to such an extent. Even if, somehow, they were willing to try, they could not succeed.

Nevertheless, most moralists have proceeded as though charity were the solution. And they have vilified people to the extent they were able to prosper and devoted their wealth to the enjoyment of their own lives. They have attempted to make people feel guilty for their success and enjoyment and have tried to take it away, through governmental "redistributions" of wealth and income. The influence of such moralists is entirely destructive. So-called redistribution impoverishes even those whom it is intended to benefit, as should by now be abundantly clear.[87]

The fact that neither private charity nor governmental coercion is the solution to poverty does not mean that there is no solution and that the alternative is simply to accept a world of suffering. On the contrary, we can have a world in which a high and rising degree of human well-being is the overwhelming norm everywhere. In such a world the cases requiring charity would be so reduced in frequency that they could be provided for within the limits of people's rational self-interest.

The solution to the present problem of massive, overwhelming poverty is nothing other than *the science of economics.* As should be increasingly clear, economics is a science which can make possible the construction of a social and political system in which human success is a feature of normal, everyday life everywhere. It is truly *the humanitarian science,* and only those who have studied it well and who are prepared to implement its teachings deserve to be called friends of mankind. The most important charity which the true friends of mankind can pursue is to disseminate knowledge of this vital subject as widely and as deeply as they know how.

The solution to poverty that economics offers is, of course: *the freedom of the individual*—i.e., laissez-faire capitalism—a system in which each pursues his own good and, at the same time, is necessarily led to promote the good of those with whom he deals, as the condition of obtaining their voluntary cooperation. *This* is the *engine* for transforming poverty into prosperity. In its effectiveness in overcoming poverty, it surpasses the futile gestures of traditional, altruist morality, which has been handed down unchanged in all essentials since the Middle Ages, on the same scale as the rest of modern civilization surpasses that of the Middle Ages. It is the difference between a rocket ship and an oxcart. Indeed, when one considers the nature of the demands for sacrifice, pain, and suffering, it is the difference between a rocket ship and a medieval torture chamber.[88]

It should be realized that the use of the law of diminishing marginal utility to support the demand for economic equality, is closely related to the doctrine of "external benefits," in that both rest on the obliteration of the individual human being as the base and source of values, and feel free to talk of "utility" or "benefits" apart from the context of specific individuals.[89] The only difference is that the doctrine of external benefits goes a step beyond the egalitarian version of diminishing marginal utility. Thus, according to its logic, if a painting is stolen from the private collection of a millionaire who does not appreciate it very highly, and is stolen not merely by someone who appreciates it more, but by someone who exhibits it to multitudes of others, many of whom also appreciate it more, then what is present is not only the alleged gain in marginal utility that exists by virtue of the painting falling into the hands of the more-appreciative thief, but also the further alleged gain of the more-appreciative multitude's enjoyment. This last is an alleged "external benefit" of the theft. What is overlooked by the

external-benefits doctrine, of course, is that, like the enjoyment of the thief, the enjoyment of such a multitude, especially if its members are knowing accomplices to the theft, represents absolutely no value, indeed, a negative value, to the victim of the theft, and thus can claim no objective status, certainly no positive moral status.

Precisely such considerations must be raised against the use of the external-benefits doctrine to justify taxation for the sake of such programs as public education. It can be granted that education benefits not only its recipients but also all who come into contact with its recipients. This fact, however, does not justify the support of education by taxation or imply that a free market provides inadequately for education. The combined benefit of education both to its recipients and to those who come into contact with its recipients does not have any existence apart from the lives and purposes of definite, individual human beings. An individual millionaire, for example—the prospective victim of an education tax—can legitimately value his own yacht above all the effects, direct and indirect combined, of other people's children receiving an education at the price of his not receiving his yacht.

True enough, if education lived up to its inherent potential of typically producing civilized adults, instead of, as is the case today, growing hordes of illiterate, semi-savage delinquents, it would indeed represent a major benefit to everyone. It would be the basis of a civilized, flourishing society. And in such circumstances, many people, especially many millionaires, would value the support of education above the purchase of some further personal luxuries. This in fact is why millionaires have traditionally been generous benefactors of education. In so doing, they would serve their own selfish values. They would provide to some significant extent both for the value they attached to living in a civilized society and to passing on such a society to their children, and for the value they attached to their own direct personal enjoyment in the form of such things as yachts.

The external-benefits doctrine, of course, ignores such facts. When it talks of the free market, it takes for granted that the participants are unthinking brutes incapable of understanding or appreciating the wider benefits resulting from such things as education and thus unwilling to support such activities voluntarily. Then, in a still greater affront to the humanity and the human dignity of the individual, it urges the government totally to disregard the choices, the judgment, indeed, the very existence of the mind and person of the individual, and to proceed simply to seize his wealth for use in the support of "external benefits."

What the supporters of the external-benefits doctrine need to realize is that a free market, in the sense of the arena of all voluntary financial transactions, provides all the funds to which education and all other activities entailing "external benefits" are properly entitled, consistent with the understanding and values of the citizens. Even more importantly, they need to realize that an essential precondition of the existence of any objective value of external benefits is that those who are to finance them not be regarded as sacrificial victims. An indispensable precondition of the pleasure or enjoyment or any other kind of value to others being a value to an individual is respect on the part of those others for his individual rights and his free judgment, including, of course, his free judgment with respect to the use of his own property. Nothing represents an external benefit to an individual if his sacrifice is required to achieve it. No gain to others is a gain to an individual insofar as those others regard him as a sacrificial animal. Thus, the external-benefits doctrine, as an attempt to wring benefits for others from sacrificial victims, by means of force, destroys the very foundation of the existence of benefits to others being a value to an individual. The doctrine is thus a self-nullification.

Further, when applied to education, the doctrine is a twofold self-nullification. For it introduces into the very foundation of education the preschool principle of uncivilized small children that the mere fact of wanting something entitles one to seize it, irrespective of the will—irrespective of the mind—of the owner. Education supported on the principles of the external-benefits doctrine is the self-contradictory monstrosity of education without respect for the human mind. It is the self-nullification of education that is visible above all in today's system of public education.

Economic Inequality and the Normal Curve

The widely-used economics textbook by Samuelson and Nordhaus claims that economic inequality cannot be explained on the basis of inequalities of ability. It declares: "People differ enormously in their abilities . . . . However, these personal differences provide us with very little of the answer to the puzzle of income dispersion."[90] In support of this claim, the authors observe: "Abilities are much more equally distributed than are incomes . . . . While human traits seldom differ by more than a factor of 3, high incomes today are more than 100 times greater than the lowest."[91]

The meaning of these words is that economic inequality has little or nothing to do with ability, inasmuch as the "distribution" of income does not follow the pattern of distribution of ability. Abilities, Samuelson and Nordhaus point out, such as those measured by IQ tests, follow the pattern of frequency distribution described by the normal curve.[92] The normal curve is a bell-shaped curve whose mean value, represented by the apex of the curve, is the most frequently occurring value. Additional properties of the normal curve are that the deviations above and below the mean occur both equally and with more rapidly diminishing frequency the greater is their departure from the mean. In a normal distribution, over 99 percent of all occurrences lie within the limit of plus or minus three standard deviations from the mean value. Thus, for example, in the case of IQs, the most frequently occurring IQ is 100, and approximately as many people have IQs above 100 as below 100, with more than 99 percent of the population having IQs between 50 and 150, that is, between values respectively equal to half and one-and-a-half times the mean value.

Apparently, according to the logic of Professors Samuelson and Nordhaus, what would be necessary for intelligence to be the explanation of inequalities of income would be if the earnings of those with IQs of 150 were only three times as high as those with IQs of 50, rather than one hundred or more times as high—in other words, if the earnings of geniuses were only three times those of morons, rather than a hundred or more times those of morons. In that case, inequalities of income would show the same pattern of dispersion as inequalities of intelligence. Indeed, it is logically implicit in the position of Professors Samuelson and Nordhaus that for inequalities in income to be based on inequalities in intelligence and ability—that is, to meet the requirement of similarly conforming to the normal curve—either morons must be capable of performing such activities as brain surgery one-third as frequently as brain surgeons perform it, or the work that morons can do must be one-third as valuable as the work brain surgeons do—and similarly in comparison with others whose abilities are greater and rarer even than those of brain surgeons. If neither of these conditions is met, that is, if morons cannot perform such activities as brain surgery at all and if brain surgery and the like are substantially more than three times as valuable as the work morons can do, then according to Professors Samuelson and Nordhaus, inequalities in income cannot be based on inequalities in intelligence and ability; they allegedly cannot, because if they were, they would be normally distributed, just as are the inequalities in intelligence and ability.

Of course, none of the above is a claim on my part that intelligence is the only factor which determines the relative income and wealth of individuals. (Nor is it to say that what is today considered intelligence necessarily embraces all aspects of intelligence or gives them their proper weight.) In order for greater intelligence to result in the earning of higher income and greater wealth, it must be accompanied by such factors as rationality, ambition, hard work, and forethought, and, in addition, the valuation of more income and wealth above alternative goals. If it is accompanied by the necessary further factors, however, then its influence on the earning of income and wealth is very different from the pattern represented by the normal curve.

First of all, its effect when present in this combination is clearly *exponential*, not linear. That is, each additional few points of intelligence, or, better, productive ability (however that might be precisely gauged) should be expected to yield exponentially increasing results. Those of average ability, represented by IQs of 100, should be expected to earn substantially more than twice as much as morons, represented by IQs of 50. Productive geniuses who revolutionize the work of hundreds of thousands of individuals and the consumption of hundreds of millions, should be expected to earn and accumulate many thousands of times the wealth and income of the average person, which, in fact, is what they do. In connection with productive geniuses, moreover, it should be recognized how crucial is that extra measure of intelligence and ability which separates them from individuals who are merely very bright, and which gives the geniuses the ability to conceive of the new and original, not merely repeat what others have done, which is all that even the merely very bright can do.

Secondly, the very nature of productive ability in a division-of-labor society accounts for the fact that deviations from the mean value of wealth and income are not nearly so great on the negative side as they are on the positive side. This is precisely because the success of men of exceptional ability so radically increases the wealth and income of all individuals of lesser ability. Thus, while productive geniuses may earn a thousand or more times what the average individual earns, productive morons, to coin a phrase, earn many times more than one one-thousandth of what a person of average ability earns. This, as I say, is because of how much is added by the productive geniuses to the results of all individuals of lesser ability. This also helps to explains the pattern of income distribution diagrammed by Professors Samuelson and Nordhaus.[93]

The kindest words one can say on behalf of the normal-curve argument propounded by Professors Samuelson and Nordhaus is that its supporters simply have no serious appreciation of the role of intelligence and ability in the creation of wealth. Indeed, so profound is their apparent ignorance on this score, that it suggests an alternative for what might otherwise stand as the obvious hypothesis for explaining the propounding of such an absurd doctrine. The obvious hypothesis, of course, is a readiness to grab at anything that to the unthinking appears capable of tarnishing capitalism and the success of its leading producers. But the enormous degree of ignorance present in the normal-curve argument suggests the possibility that the deeper-lying explanation of wanting to tarnish capitalism and its producers in the first place may be simply some form of compartmentalized imbecility.[94] But whether it is a form of imbecility that causes malice against capitalism and successful individuals, or such malice that causes the imbecility, is a question that may be left to others to decide. What is important here is merely to recognize the actual relationship between inequalities of income and wealth, on the one side, and inequalities of intelligence and ability, on the other. This relationship is that inequalities of intelligence and ability operate exponentially, not linearly, in the earning of income and wealth and that the greater intelligence and ability of some is a source of gain to all.

3. The "Equality of Opportunity" Doctrine: A Critique

The advocates of economic equality have a fallback position, which they also frequently use as a camouflage, namely, the doctrine of "equality of opportunity." They do not, they say, advocate anything so foolish or so extreme as the imposition of actual economic equality. All they advocate, they say, is that everyone have an equal chance—that, as they put it, all the runners begin the race from the same starting line. On this basis, they feel free to advocate the confiscation of inheritances, public education through the postgraduate level, and laws preventing private discrimination on the basis not only of such factors as race, religion or national origin, but also age, medical condition, and physical handicap.

The supporters of the equality-of-opportunity doctrine view opportunities as fundamentally external to the individual—in effect, as various dishes carried by waiters on trays, which, under capitalism, are arbitrarily served to some and withheld from others. They want the government to seize control, they say, not of the distribution of wealth and income, but merely of the distribution of these dishes, as it were—that is, of the opportunities to earn wealth and income—and so give everyone an equal chance.

To most people, this doctrine sounds eminently fair and reasonable. But, in fact, it is as much against the nature of reality as is the doctrine of the out-and-out equality of wealth and income. This becomes clear as soon as we look beyond the inheritance of wealth and begin to consider other external factors that affect the opportunities an individual has.

For example, consider such factors as the intelligence of a child's parents, their education and vocabulary, their system of values, and their love for him and treatment of him, not to mention their level of income and the kind of material life they lead and thereby expose him to while he is growing up. It is certainly arguable that differences in these factors confront a child with differences in opportunities that are certainly of no less significance for his future life, including his ability to earn wealth and income, than those which are based on the wealth he may or may not inherit.

To create equality of opportunity with respect to these factors, nothing less would be necessary than to *abolish the institution of the family and to raise all children in government orphanages, where they could all be brought up in exactly the same way.* This, of course, was the idea of Plato, and it was supported by many socialists in the nineteenth century and earlier in this century.

But even this would not be enough to achieve equality of opportunity. Because even if all of these environmental factors could be made the same, there would still remain enormous differences in the intellectual and physical endowment of the child himself, based on his genetic inheritance. A highly intelligent, strong, and beautiful child, for example, automatically has enormous advantages over a stupid, weak, and ugly child who is given the same upbringing. How can such different children, and the adults they later become, be given equality of opportunity?

One possible answer to this question is that the government should concentrate more heavily on the upbringing of the less fortunate, thus, perhaps raising their intelligence, improving their strength, and possibly even their looks. But no amount of such extra effort by the government can significantly make up for what nature has denied. Thus, another possible answer is that the government should insist that such differences simply be disregarded. The first answer manifests itself today in large-scale government support for special programs for the education of the retarded and the handicapped; the second, in those antidiscrimination laws, such as California's, which prohibit discrimination in employment based on medical condition or physical handicap.

Another possible answer is that, failing the government's ability to create equality of opportunity by raising up the less fortunate, it should tear down the more fortunate. If it cannot make the stupid intelligent, the weak strong, and the ugly beautiful, it can find a way to hamper or destroy intelligence, strength, and beauty, and so achieve equality of opportunity by making everyone stupid, weak, and ugly. It may be difficult to find anyone who would openly advocate such a policy, but it does follow logically from the goal of equality of opportunity.

There is a fourth conceivable answer: the government should attempt to determine the genetic endowment of children. It should enact a program of eugenics, and attempt to breed children who would all possess the same

characteristics at birth. Then, with the same upbringing, the demand for equality of opportunity could, apparently, at last be satisfied.

These absurd and vicious implications of the equality of opportunity doctrine should make one begin to wonder what kind of ideal "equality of opportunity" really is. In reality, it is not a legitimate ideal at all. It appears to represent justice only on the basis of a thoroughly confused view of the nature of opportunities and the causes of human success.

Let us consider what opportunities actually are, and then establish some important facts about them.

An opportunity is merely *an occasion on which successful action is possible.* It is a situation that an individual can take advantage of to his gain.

What needs to be realized about opportunities is, first of all, that *there is no scarcity of them*; they arise again and again. The second thing that needs to be understood is that what is important in connection with them and deserves to be fought for, as a matter both of justice and universal self-interest, is not that vicious absurdity "the equality of opportunity," but *the freedom of opportunity.* What the freedom of opportunity means and why it is so important will be explained shortly. Finally, what needs to be understood about opportunities is that they can be and regularly are *created* by individuals. Indeed, opportunities are themselves products of human thought and action. Just how they are is something that will also be explained shortly.

Let us consider the abundance of opportunities. An opportunity exists every time there is the possibility of improving oneself in any way. If one is penniless and there is an unfilled job available that one has the ability to fill, one has the opportunity of ending one's pennilessness. If one has a job, and there is any better job available that one has the ability to fill, one has the opportunity to improve one's position further. If there is any skill that one does not possess, but is capable of acquiring, then one has the opportunity of expanding one's skills.

In fact, in the nature of the case, the economic opportunities potentially open to the individual far exceed his ability to exploit them, with the result that he must *choose* among them, selecting some and rejecting others. This follows from the fact that there is always room for improvement in the satisfaction of man's wants, and that the basis for carrying out such improvement is the performance either of more labor or of more productive labor. In other words, built into the fact that man's wants can always be satisfied more fully or better is the opportunity for the performance of more labor as the means of satisfying them more fully or better, and the opportunity for improving the productivity of his labor.

Indeed, on the basis of what has been established

earlier in this book, in Chapter 2, it follows that in the nature of things *there are potentially limitless opportunities both for increasing employment and for raising the productivity of labor*, for there are virtually limitless possibilities for improvement in the satisfaction of man's wants. Indeed, the potential opportunities for employment always dwarf man's ability actually to work, which is a major reason why he must be concerned with raising the productivity of his labor.[95]

People may wonder, of course, how it can be true that there are virtually limitless employment opportunities and yet, at the same time, the world in which we live is characterized by chronic mass unemployment and the experience of millions is that they have no opportunity for work. There is a simple reconciliation of these facts. Namely, misguided laws and social institutions deny man the freedom of exploiting the opportunities for employment that the nature of reality offers him, and so force unemployment upon him. The problem of unemployment is the result of the violation of *the freedom of opportunity*—i.e., the violation of man's freedom to exploit the opportunities that reality offers him. The freedom of opportunity means, to be precise, *the ability to exploit the opportunities afforded by reality, without being stopped by the initiation of physical force.*

People are unable to find work not because there is no work for them to do in reality, but because government and labor-union interference, based on the initiation of physical force, prices their labor beyond the reach of potential employers. This interference is, specifically, the inflation of the money supply (which sets the stage for a later financial contraction and depression) coupled with so-called prolabor legislation. The precise ways in which such interference serves to cause unemployment are explained later in this book.[96] For now, however, it may be helpful to realize that if, for example, employers have the financial ability to pay a trillion dollars a year in payrolls and there are 100 million workers able and willing to work, those payrolls would be capable of employing all those workers at an average annual wage of $10,000 per year. But to the extent that the government and the unions keep in force an average annual wage greater than $10,000, the payroll funds are rendered incapable of employing that many workers. The result is that corresponding unemployment is caused and can be made to continue to exist indefinitely. Thus, as this example indicates, unemployment and the lack of employment opportunity are not the result of any fundamental or "metaphysical" lack of employment opportunity, but of the government's violation of the freedom of opportunity with respect to employment. In essence, first, the government creates the boom-bust cycle, and then, when the bust comes, it and the coercive labor

unions it sanctions prohibit businessmen and wage earners from offering and accepting the lower wage rates that would enable them sufficiently to exploit the limitless employment opportunities that reality offers, to the point of establishing full employment.

As shown elsewhere in this book, the violation of freedom of opportunity is also what underlies the problems described under the head of racial discrimination. Their solution, too, would follow from the establishment of freedom of opportunity.[97]

I stated that opportunities are themselves products. What I mean by this is the following. In any given instance, an opportunity is the result of a combination of external circumstances and the skills and abilities an individual possesses, such that he is able to exploit the circumstances to his advantage. An opportunity is a product in the sense that the skills and abilities an individual possesses are the result of his successful exploitation of previous, lesser opportunities.

It must be realized that opportunities are never a matter merely of external circumstances that are served up on a plate, as it were. They always depend on what the individual himself brings to the external circumstances in the way of skills and abilities. These skills and abilities in turn are never the automatic result of the individual's genetic inheritance. They are the cumulative product of what the individual has done with his life up to that point. They reflect his initial choices to use his genetic inheritance to deal with external circumstances in ways that developed certain skills and abilities, and then further choices to use those skills and abilities to deal with further external circumstances in ways that developed still further skills and abilities, and so on up to the present moment.

For example, a child who chooses to use his mind to learn arithmetic thereby creates an indispensable precondition for the potential opportunity to learn algebra. Unless and until he learns arithmetic, there can be no possibility of any opportunity for him to learn algebra. If he does learn arithmetic and then, when he is confronted with the opportunity of learning algebra, successfully exploits it too, he creates a necessary internal basis for the further opportunity of learning calculus. And so on.

It is similar with regard to employment. The individual who exploits the opportunity to become a worker in a factory thereby creates a possible basis for his later on becoming a foreman there. If he becomes a foreman, he creates a possible basis for later promotion to a higher managerial position, and so on. Of course, he will have to expand his abilities in each of these jobs and possibly acquire other skills off the job, as well—perhaps by going to night school, for example. The principle is that opportunity presents itself as the rungs of a ladder. Each rung is open only to those who have climbed within reach by ascending previous rungs.

Once things are viewed in this light, the notion of the advocates of "equality of opportunity," that opportunities are a matter of environmental circumstances, or environmental circumstances combined with genetic inheritance, appears absurdly inadequate. It is actually ludicrous to think that what a person does is the outcome merely of his environment and genes. In between the environment and the genes is a lifetime of choices, each of which has a vital bearing on the individual's ability to deal with his environment and to make further choices. In between the environment and the genes is the whole life of the person as a being who functions on a level above that of an automaton.

It is not necessary that people make the choices that develop their skills and abilities at any precise moment. There is considerable leeway. And it is never completely too late to start. For example, someone can learn to read even in old age and then begin rapidly to build on that foundation.

In a free society—with its superabundance of opportunities, with no fixed deadline on the process of developing one's skills to better exploit them—all talk of inequality of opportunity must be judged as just so much whining and excuse-making. In such a society, everyone, whatever his starting point in life, is able to raise himself very far, if that is what he chooses to do. He can miss many, many opportunities, and still there will be more. He can begin improving his ability to exploit them at any time, and start moving up from that moment.

It is true that in such a society if two individuals were born equal in every respect, except that one had richer parents than the other, and if they both actively and constantly chose to develop their skills and abilities from birth on, the one with the richer parents would probably always be ahead of the one with the poorer parents. But far from representing any kind of embarrassment to a free society, it is perfectly just that things be this way. The advantages of the individual with the richer parents would not prevent the one with the poorer parents from rising, and rising not only very high, but without any fixed limit. It is simply the case that wealth *is* beneficial, and if everything else is *in fact* the same, it makes a difference. But what else is wealth for if not to provide benefits? (And, more fundamentally, what are parents for, if not to provide every possible benefit to their children? One of the ugliest consequences of the equality-of-opportunity doctrine is that it actually causes some parents deliberately to do less for their children than they otherwise would, on the grounds that other parents are unable to do as much, and thereby willfully to default on their responsibilities as parents.) Furthermore, as ex-

plained in the discussion of the institution of inheritance, everyone, nonheirs as well as heirs, benefits from the capital that is accumulated in order to be passed on to heirs. The nonheir is thus able to achieve more than he would have in the absence of the institution of inheritance, even if that is less than what someone else can achieve who is both equally capable in every respect and has the benefit of an inheritance.

The way this principle applies in the present instance is not only that the nonheir has the benefit of a more abundant supply of products and a greater demand for his labor by virtue of the existence of capital accumulated because of the institution of inheritance, but also that he can benefit specifically in his potential capacity as a businessman and capitalist himself. In the example of the two boys who grow up with equal ability while one has the advantage of money, that advantage can enable the one without the money to make his own fortune, even if it is a smaller fortune than the one who begins with the money. For example, suppose the two of them become partners in business. If neither of them had capital, both would be equal partners, because they are equally talented. But neither of them would be able to get very far, or at least not nearly as soon, because of their lack of capital. If one of them has the necessary capital to contribute to their business, he will have more than a 50 percent share in their partnership, but the one with the smaller share will also be better off now. He will have, say, 40 percent or 30 percent of a business that now earns two, three, or five times more profits because of the capital contributed to it, with the result that his absolute share is greater. He must have more than he otherwise would have had, or he will not enter into the partnership.

Now, of course, the real fact is that individuals are not born perfectly equal in all respects but the wealth of their parents, and they do not make the same choices in connection with developing their skills and abilities. Time and again, there are individuals born to poorer parents, to parents badly deficient not only in wealth, but in education, knowledge, and even character; individuals whose own endowment at birth or in childhood is not only not exceptional, but possibly deficient in some important respects. Yet, over the course of their lives, these individuals manage to far outstrip in their accomplishments practically everyone else, despite their having begun under such seemingly insuperable disadvantages.

What enables them to do this is making the choice and the effort to exploit as far as they can whatever opportunities present themselves for self-improvement. Once they begin to do this, they actually do begin to improve themselves. And now, when they face the world, they are better equipped than before. And because they are better equipped, there are more opportunities for self-improvement open to them than there were before. They seize these further opportunities, thereby further improving themselves and their subsequent ability to act and to seize opportunities. And so on, year after year.

What happens is that these individuals engage in a personal, internal process very similar to capital formation in the economy of a country. They use the means at their disposal to *build* the personal attributes—intellectual, psychological, moral, and physical—required for further success. And then they use the personal attributes they have constructed thus far to further construct such attributes. It is similar in principle to the process of a poor farmer scrimping and straining to obtain an additional supply of seed; of then using the larger supply of seed to produce a bigger crop the following year, from which a much greater supply of seed can be obtained for the year after that, and so on. Or to the economy of a whole country working very hard and saving very heavily to be able to make iron and steel available for the construction of the first railroads and steel mills, and then with the aid of those first railroads and steel mills being able to produce more of practically everything, including more and better railroads and steel mills.

Concentration on building up the means of further action, whether internal and personal or external and material, produces exponentially increasing results. Each success serves to increase the capabilities for further action, which makes possible still greater success. Those who concentrate heavily on these efforts rapidly improve, while those who neglect them stagnate or decline. It is on these principles that we can understand both such things as how Japan, so poor and backward a generation or two ago, can now be within sight of economically overtaking the United States and how Demosthenes the ancient Athenian, who began as a stutterer, could become a great orator, and how, again and again, in a free society, poor boys grow up to become rich and famous.

The secret of the success of the poor boys is contained in that old but very accurate expression that is so seldom heard today: *the self-made man.* Those poor boys *build themselves into the kind of men capable of achieving great success.* (While custom and tradition apply the principle to "boys and men," it should go without saying that the principle applies no less to girls and women. There are self-made women, as well as men.)

The following example, perhaps, can help in understanding how by building themselves into the right kind of men they outstrip even those with the greatest advantages at birth. Thus, imagine two boys—one the newborn son of a highly educated millionaire; the other, the newborn son of a poor, uneducated coal miner. To most people, it seems that the millionaire's son has such great advantages that he can never be overtaken. But this is not

so. And the reason why not can be seen in terms of a few conceptual snapshots, as it were, of the two boys at different stages of their development.

At birth, neither of them is capable of very much of anything. All of their capabilities remain to be developed. The millionaire's son is not capable of jumping out of his crib and using his father's millions to make more millions. If he is ever to have that ability, he will first have to develop it.

By age six or seven, say, the two boys have developed certain attitudes toward acquiring knowledge, and other important attributes, too, of course. But, for simplicity's sake, we will focus just on this aspect and its possible ramifications. If the poorer boy recognizes the value of knowledge and the necessity of making his best effort to acquire it, while the richer boy does not, the poorer boy has gained an advantage that can become of growing significance over the years. By age fourteen or fifteen, perhaps, the poorer boy has acquired an important body of knowledge that the richer boy has not. He understands algebra, trigonometry, and something of physics and chemistry. The richer boy has no real understanding of these subjects. By age twenty or twenty-two, the poorer boy is capable of working as an engineer, say, and making a significant contribution to the profits of anyone who employs him. The richer boy, on the other hand can only be employed either in a menial capacity or at the expense of his father, who must continue to support him under the guise of giving him a salary, or who must provide for some associate to pay a fictitious salary, and compensate that associate in some form.

By age thirty, if he is really talented, the poorer boy has developed some significant ideas which have earned him some significant sums of money and have enabled him to start his own business. He now possesses a capacity for earning money which exceeds the richer boy's. The richer boy may still have vastly more money and earn a larger absolute amount, but the poorer boy is in a position to earn it now at a much faster rate. For the poorer boy's money is under his own, intelligent control and can earn a high rate of profit. The richer boy's money is either in his own, incompetent hands, in which case he can rapidly lose it, or it is in the hands of others who are more competent but who pay him only a relatively modest rate of interest or dividends. As the years go by, with the poorer boy earning a 50, 75, or 100 percent annual rate of profit, and plowing back almost all of it, while the richer boy earns a 3, 4, or 5 percent rate of interest or dividends and consumes almost all of it, the poorer boy becomes the richer man.

This, in briefest essence, is how it actually happens that in a free society penniless newcomers are able, again and again, to overtake and surpass even those with the greatest inherited wealth.

It cannot be stressed too strongly in this connection how critical is the element of *freedom of opportunity.* In order to succeed, the poorer boys must have the freedom to earn the highest rates of profit they can and to keep those profits. They must also be free of government controls and regulations, which can easily prevent them from ever getting started, by placing innumerable bureaucratic obstacles in their way—such as causing unnecessary delays, requiring unnecessary staffs of lawyers, accountants, and clerks that they are unable to afford, and by diverting their valuable time and efforts from serious work to contending with the arbitrary power and sheltered incompetence of government officials.

Education and the Freedom of Opportunity

Now it is also true that the success of the poorer boys depends on their being able to obtain education. But this certainly does not mean that a case is made for public education of any kind. The kind of men and boys I have described grasp very early the value of acquiring knowledge and make it their business to find opportunities for acquiring it. Public education, on the other hand, by removing all incentives of profit and loss and all possibility of genuine competition in education, and by thus sheltering inefficiency and incompetence while making improvement almost impossible, creates a system of instruction so poor that compulsion is the only means of keeping most of the students in attendance. And because people, including children, are not automatons programmed by a combination of genes and their environment, the system of forcing books and lectures on unwilling minds simply does not work.

For the kind of men and boys I have described, public education is unnecessary. What is necessary, or, more correctly, would be extremely helpful to them, and would be far more efficient and effective for everyone, is *the freedom of education,* combined with the availability of private, voluntarily supported merit scholarships and also the freedom of working and earning money to pay for education. People do not generally realize the extent to which the present system of public education destroys the freedom of opportunity with respect to education. By making educational innovations virtually impossible through government controls on curricula, faculty qualifications, and teaching methods, and requiring that competition take place against a subsidized competitor who does not charge, countless educational innovations that might have been made have not been made. People have been prohibited or prevented from exploiting the opportunities they perceive for improvement in education. The further opportunities that those improvements would have constituted for students have thus been prevented

from coming into being. We have a situation today where the law both prevents better, more economical forms of education from being offered and prevents students from earning the means of paying for education, by making it almost impossible for anyone under the age of eighteen to obtain any kind of meaningful job. Our present system is one of systematic opposition to the freedom of opportunity with respect to education.

Everyone's Interest in the Freedom of Opportunity

In general, on an increasing scale, people are prevented from exploiting the opportunities open to them, and thereby prevented from creating further opportunities that would be available not only to them but to those with whom they dealt. I have just shown how this is the case in education. On the basis of what we have seen earlier in this chapter, it is also obvious that in preventing the acquisition of fortunes, our present system prevents the opportunities from coming into being that those fortunes would have afforded to workers and suppliers in the form of a demand for labor and capital goods, and to customers, in the form of more and better products produced.

These observations bring out a further important principle pertaining to opportunities that is consistent with our wider, previous discussions both of economic inequality under capitalism and with the synergistic nature of a division-of-labor society in general, especially of private ownership of the means of production: namely, each person's successful exploitation of the opportunities open to him creates further opportunities not only for himself, but also for those with whom he deals. In other words, with respect to opportunities too, one man's gain is the gain of others. The losses caused by the violation of freedom of opportunity represent losses to everyone. This is true ranging from the consequences of aborting the earning of great fortunes and the development of major industries all the way down to the level of licensing laws aborting one man's opportunity to be a cab driver and another's opportunity to find a cab, or immigration laws aborting one person's opportunity to be a gardener or a maid and other people's opportunity of obtaining such services.

The notion of "equality of opportunity," however innocent it may sound at first, is actually vicious and absurd. In its logically consistent form, it implies the destruction of the institution of the family, the implementation of a governmental program of eugenics, and the elimination or destruction of every personal attribute that represents an advantage of one person over others.

In a positive vein, what has been shown is that what is actually important in connection with opportunities is the establishment of a free society and its corollary *the freedom of opportunity*. In such a society, the individual is free to exploit the virtually limitless opportunities offered by the combination of his nature and the nature of the world. He must pick and choose among them. And he progressively creates better and better opportunities for himself by successfully exploiting the best of the opportunities available to him at any given time.

In such a society, the notion of equality of opportunity reveals itself as absurdly irrelevant, as nothing more than an excuse for not taking advantage of the opportunities one has and for not creating better ones. In such a society, everyone can rise no matter what his starting point or present position, and again and again people of the most humble origins overtake and surpass those who began with seemingly insuperable advantages.

What is required for everyone to be able to succeed and, at the same time, represents full justice, is not equality of opportunity, but freedom of opportunity. The successful exploitation of opportunities that freedom makes possible is the basis of each individual being able to rise and create better opportunities not only for himself, but also for those with whom he deals.

PART C

ECONOMIC COMPETITION

1. The Nature of Economic Competition

In a division-of-labor society, competition is of a radically different character than it is in the animal kingdom. In the animal kingdom, competition is over a limited, nature-given supply of means of subsistence. For the lions in the jungle, for example, there are only so many zebras or gazelles in the surrounding territory. Once the population of lions grows to stand in a sufficiently high ratio to that of the surrounding species that it eats, the individual lions are placed in competition with one another for survival. For each lion that succeeds in obtaining a supply of food, the survival of some other lion is jeopardized. For there is simply not enough to go around. In these conditions, those lions that have the keenest senses, that can run fastest and furthest, and that are the strongest, catch their prey and survive, while those that are less well endowed in these respects fail in the chase and perish. This is truly "the law of the jungle" and "the survival of the fittest."

The competition that exists in a division-of-labor, capitalist society, on the other hand, is so radically different that it is actually of a diametrically opposite character. It is not competition over any limited, nature-given

supply of means of subsistence. On the contrary, it is *a competition in the positive creation of new and additional wealth*. Ford and General Motors, IBM and Apple, and so on, are not competing in the seizure of a fixed supply of automobiles or computers provided by nature. They are competing in the positive creation of automobiles and computers—of ever more and better automobiles and computers. While animals in the jungle chase prey, which they seize with their teeth and claws, producers under capitalism chase dollars, which they gain from willing customers only by virtue of sending after the dollars more and better goods—goods which they have created.

Man does not obtain his automobiles, computers, food, or anything else that he requires, as a gift from nature. He must produce them. His possession of reason and his organization of production into a system of division of labor enable him steadily to increase the total of the wealth he produces. Unlike the lions in the jungle, man increases the size of the animal herds that serve him (to return to that example); he domesticates them; he studies their requirements for health and nutrition and so on; he grows food for them and studies the requirements for the health and nutrition of the crops that feed them; he progressively expands and implements such knowledge, with ever increasing benefit to himself. And similarly with regard to each and every other source of his material well-being.

Economic competition takes place *within this context*—the context of unlimited potential improvement in man's material well-being, based on his possession of reason and the organization of production into a system of division of labor. Because of this, what economic competition is about is not the means of subsistence, but, as pointed out in Chapter 5, the selection of products for markets, of technological methods for producing any particular product, and of persons for specific occupations.[98] That is, it is not at all about one human being's survival causing another human being to perish for lack of subsistence. Rather it is about one product serving a given market instead of another product serving that market, about whether this or that technological method will be used to produce a given product, and to what extent, and about which individuals are to perform which jobs in the economic system. Throughout, it is a competition for the patronage of customers (including employers) and for the services of workers—a competition which can be won only to the degree that one renders labor more productive and so operates to raise the general standard of living by producing more and better products. Economic competition is the process of achieving an ever more efficient organization of the division of labor. It is not in opposition or in contrast to social cooperation, as so many people have believed; on the contrary, it is precisely the process of steadily reorganizing the system of social cooperation—the division of labor—in terms of who is to produce what and by what methods, so as steadily to raise the productivity of labor and increase the quantity and quality of products produced and pouring onto the market.[99] Indeed, it is the mechanism whereby a veritable growing flood of goods is produced and poured onto the market, raising the standard of living of everyone further and further above "subsistence."

In this competition there are no genuine, long-run losers—only winners. Everyone benefits from the ever-increasing wealth that economic competition creates. Even those who at first sight appear to be losers turn out to be winners, and usually fairly quickly. Consider, for example, the effect of the competition of the automobile on blacksmiths, horsebreeders, and buggymakers. These "losers" in this competition suffered only a very temporary loss—in the period in which it was necessary for them to adapt their skills to the requirements of other jobs. Once they did this, the only permanent effect on them of the competition they "lost" was that, along with everyone else, they too obtained the benefit of the automobile in their capacity as consumers, including, of course, the benefit of having all manner of products transported by means of trucks rather than horse-drawn wagons. In exactly the same way, the farmers using horses and mules, who lost out in competition to other farmers using tractors and harvesters, did not die of starvation, but merely ended up in different jobs. Only now, along with everyone else, they were able to obtain their food cheaper and had money left over for the purchase of larger quantities of other things—other things that could now be produced because the labor required for their production was no longer required in the production of food, thanks to the successful competition of tractors and harvesters.[100]

It is vital to realize that there is *room for all* in the competition of a division-of-labor society.[101] To "lose" in such competition does not mean to be cast out of the productive system and to perish. It means only to have to relocate to some other point in the productive system—to produce some different product, to work in some different occupation; or, perhaps, to continue in the same occupation and learn to produce one's present product differently. The effect of making such adjustments is almost always that one ends up benefitting *even from the very improvement in production that caused one's initial "loss"*—in the same way as occurred in the examples just given of the blacksmiths et al. and of the backward farmers.

The so-called weak in particular gain from the process of economic competition. Consider all those millions who might have perished from hunger or malnutrition, or from disease or accident; who suffer from some impairment of vision or hearing; who lack the muscles or the agility to live in the jungle or the forest. And now consider the effect on them of competition among farmers and farm-equipment manufacturers; among pharmaceutical makers and manufacturers of diagnostic equipment; among the makers of eyeglasses and hearing aids; among the producers of every labor-saving device and life-enhancing product. Can anyone fail to see that such competition is what enables the weak to survive?[102]

Economic competition is not a process by which the success of the biologically fit brings about the extermination of the biologically weak. On the contrary, it is the process by which the success of better products and more efficient methods of production promotes the survival and well-being of *all*. It is a process in which *the success of the more able raises the productivity and improves the standard of living of the less able.* For the competitive success of the more able is merely their achievement of positions in which *they,* rather than the less able, take charge of production. *The less able remain in the productive system and are more productive because they work under the direction of the more able.* They work in the enterprises founded and run by the more able. In those enterprises, they produce the new and improved products made possible only by virtue of the work of the more able, and they work with the aid of the progressively more productive methods of production, again, made possible only by the work of the more able. Economic competition is thus the process of improving the efficiency of social cooperation under the division of labor, and thereby of promoting the survival of every member of the human species.[103]

An important aspect of the benefits of economic competition can be understood in the light of the beneficial effects that typically result from competition in such fields of human endeavor as athletics and the arts. Thus, for example, without competition, an individual can pursue such an activity merely as a pleasurable pastime, engaging in it as it suits him, with no strong dedication to improving his performance and raising it to the maximum level of which he is capable. But now let him enter into competition in his chosen activity. The immediate effect is that he is confronted with a standard that is set by the performance of his competitor or competitors. To succeed in the competition, he must exceed that standard.

It follows that for all those competitors whose performance does not presently measure up to the standard set by the leading competitor, competition creates the need to raise their level of performance—to make it exceed the performance of the presently leading competitor. To the extent that one or more of the initially lagging competitors is inspired to surpass the initially leading competitor, the effect is to confront that individual too with a standard that he must now aspire to match and exceed. The effect of competition is thus a kind of upward ratcheting of standards accompanied by continual efforts to match and exceed the rising standards, thereby setting still higher standards, until everyone is led to exert his utmost best efforts and turn in the absolute best performance of which he is capable. In other words, competition brings out the very best in the participants.

It is the same in the economic world. Here, each company must take the quality of the goods produced by its competitors, and the prices charged by its competitors for their goods, as a standard for the quality of its own goods and for the prices it must charge. It must make its performance match and, if possible, exceed theirs. Thus, economic competition is a process by which producers are led to exert themselves to their utmost best.

Now what could be more wonderful or more beneficial than an arrangement which leads individuals to exert their very best efforts for the sake of their own and their customers' material well-being and very survival? Exactly this is what economic competition accomplishes. Exactly this is why capitalism has succeeded in so radically improving the material conditions of everyone who lives under it and in so radically lengthening life expectancy. People live and prosper under capitalism in large measure for no other reason than that economic competition drives them to put their heart and soul into doing so.

In the next section, we will consider in more detail the matter of the short-run losses that various people can experience in connection with economic competition. Following that, I will explain more fully why there is room in the competition of a division-of-labor society even for people who are less efficient than others in every respect. I will show precisely why and how even such people can have a secure place in a division-of-labor society. I will also explain further why, by the very same token, such people not only need not fear the competition of those who are more able than themselves, but derive incalculable benefits from their existence. Where appropriate, I will apply the principles derived from our discussion to the questions of international competition and free international trade. One of the major themes throughout will be that the hardships usually blamed on competition are not the result of competition, but of government intervention infringing the freedom of competition.

2. The Short-Run Loss Periods

In order to understand the problem of short-run losses and why, in a free economy, it would not be a very great one, let us consider the inherent difficulties of adjusting to the effects of competition that are experienced by three different groups of people: unskilled workers, skilled workers, and businessmen or others with invested fortunes. Between them, these groups embrace everyone directly affected.

When competition makes obsolete the job of an unskilled worker, there is no intrinsic reason for his short-run loss period to be longer than a few weeks or months. For that is the period of time required to acquire a comparable level of skill, and thus to earn a comparable level of income, in some other unskilled job. From that point on, an unskilled worker should be back to where he was in his capacity as an income earner, and he should now be in a position to benefit in his capacity as a consumer—a buyer—from the very improvement in production that displaced him.

This, of course, assumes the existence of some other job for him to take. But as explained in Chapter 2, there are always far more potential jobs out there, waiting to be done, than we are capable of doing. If the government does not intervene and so prevent the exploitation of employment opportunities that the nature of reality provides in superabundance, there will indeed be other jobs available. And in modern conditions, in which even the very poorest workers can afford the cost of a bus ride that will take them practically anywhere in the country within days, alternative employment opportunities can be drawn from the entire length and breadth of the land. The intrinsic difficulties in the way of people adjusting to the temporary job losses caused by competition are now less than ever, and diminish with every further improvement in transportation and communications.

The temporary losses suffered by skilled workers are necessarily longer lasting than those of unskilled workers. If a skill is made obsolete that required two or three years to learn, then it will probably take that much time for such a worker to acquire a comparable level of skill in some other line of work and thus, once again, to earn a comparable level of income. But even so, if the worker does reestablish his level of skill and income, then, from that point on, he too benefits from the very improvement that initially cost him his job. For he has now drawn even in his capacity as an income earner and, because of the improvement, is ahead in his capacity as a consumer. For example, a typesetter displaced by automated typesetting equipment would come out a permanent net gainer from the lower-cost books, newspapers, and magazines that that improvement made possible. He would have this permanent net gain once he acquired a comparable level of skill and thus of income in some other line of work, perhaps two or three years later.

Now I have stressed the fact that in a free society individuals end up gaining even from the improvements that initially make them lose their jobs. It should not be forgotten, of course, that they also benefit from the overwhelmingly greater number of improvements that do not make them temporarily lose their jobs, but which purely and simply benefit them in their capacity as consumers. For example, the typesetter just referred to benefits purely and simply from the effects of competition in the production of food, housing, clothing, transportation, and everything else to which he is related merely as a consumer.

For every individual, such improvements are always in the great majority, for the simple reason that he works in only one industry at any one time, while competition affects all industries. His job is potentially threatened only by the competition which goes on within his industry, or between his industry and one or more other industries. It is not threatened by any of the competition that goes on in all the rest of the economic system—by all the competition that goes on within and between all the other industries and that does not directly relate to his one industry. Such competition merely improves his position as a consumer. In essence, if the economic system can be thought of as consisting of one-hundred industries, the individual benefits purely and simply from the effects of competition in and between the ninety-nine industries to which he is related merely as a consumer. When it comes to his own industry, he may lose his job and have to change his employment, after which he benefits in his capacity as a consumer even from the improvement that initially cost him his job.

Thus, the position of the individual in a capitalist society is that over the course of his lifetime competition improves the production and lowers the cost of practically everything, and introduces many totally new and previously unheard of products, with the result that the standard of living of the average person steadily rises. But from time to time the nature of the competition is such that the individual must change his job. At that point, his standard of living may temporarily decline. The fall in his standard of living is from an upward sloping line, so to speak; and as soon as he acquires a comparable level of skill in another type of work, his standard of living is raised to a point further up the line than it ever was before—in part, precisely because of the very improvement that displaced him.

The picture that emerges of an individual's life under capitalism, in connection with competition, is one of steady improvement punctuated by a few brief periods of setback. The impact of such periods of setback could, of course, be minimized by the possession of savings. It could also be greatly reduced in most cases by forethought, in the form of paying attention to the factors affecting the existence of one's job and making preparations for obtaining a new job before the loss of one's present job. This would mean learning a new skill while one still had one's old job. For individuals willing to exercise such forethought, the main negative impact of competition, if, indeed, it can even still be called a negative impact, would be merely that it required them to do fresh thinking.

Indeed, in most cases, fresh thinking is practically all that competition need require of a person. For example, the great majority of the blacksmiths, horsebreeders, and buggymakers who were displaced by the automobile did not have to wait to lose their jobs. It took over twenty years for the automobile substantially to displace the horse even in the United States, the country where the automobile made its most rapid progress. Thus most of those workers were in a position to see well in advance what they needed to do, before they lost their existing jobs. Such conditions are typical, and for many workers the impact of competition on their employment is in fact little more than that they need to learn new skills.

In a free economy, the only case of a loss period that is necessarily long and major is that of wealthy individuals who lose an invested fortune as the result of competition. The owner of a harness factory or horsebreeding farm in the early decades of this century, who lost the equivalent perhaps of a million dollars or more when his investment became obsolete, was far less likely to be able to accumulate such a sum a second time than were his workers to adapt their skills to the requirements of other jobs. For it is incomparably more difficult to earn a fortune than to learn a new job—even a highly skilled one.

Of course, even this is not impossible. There are numerous instances of individuals who have made and lost several fortunes. But for many people, especially those whose wealth has come to them through inheritance rather than their own abilities, it is simply out of the question to earn back a fortune.

Let us concentrate now on the effects of competition on this group, precisely because it is the only group whose members must probably suffer a major and prolonged loss as the result of free competition. The question we must consider is whether even the members of this group can legitimately claim to be harmed by competition.

The first thing we must realize is that the effect of competition on this group is certainly not to cause the extermination of its members, but merely their fall from a relatively high position in the economic system to the ranks of the average. We must also keep in mind that the position of the average member of the society is steadily rising because of competition. Thus, it is only a question of time before the standard of living of a former millionaire would rise to the point where it was higher in his position as an average worker than it used to be when he was a millionaire.

This last statement is not only a theoretical inference, but also an accurate description of the actual historical facts of capitalism. The average worker in the United States today is materially far better off than a millionaire of a century ago—than even the world's very richest people of that time or of any other time much before the beginning of the present century. He has at his disposal all kinds of goods they simply did not have, such as automobiles, airplanes, electric light, indoor plumbing, radios, telephones, television sets, phonographs, tape-recorders, motion pictures, air-conditioners, refrigerators, freezers, antibiotics, modern anesthetics, and all the other advances of modern medicine. No one in the world had any of these things much before the beginning of the present century—not Queen Victoria, not Napoleon, not Louis XIV, not any of the Roman Emperors or Egyptian Pharaohs. The only respect in which these immensely wealthy individuals of the past can be described as better off than the average wage earner under capitalism today is that they had access to personal servants, which he, of course, does not. But servants to carry chamber pots and harness horses do not begin to compare to indoor plumbing and automobiles, which today's wage earner does have.

Furthermore, until about twenty-five years ago, when we still had a substantially freer economy than we do now, the rate of economic progress was sufficiently rapid so that it was not unreasonable to expect that by the time an average individual reached the end of his life, he himself would actually live better than a millionaire did when he, the average person, was a boy or a young man.

Of course, even under conditions of full capitalism, many or even most people who lose a fortune cannot live long enough for further competition and progress to give them a higher standard of living as an average person than they previously had as a millionaire. If they lose their fortune when they are sixty-five or even forty-five years old, it is virtually impossible that they will live long enough for economic progress to restore the equivalent of all that they have lost. And even if they lost their fortune, say, at age twenty-one and did perhaps live long enough, finally—say, some forty or fifty years later—to have a standard of living as an average person higher than they had had as a millionaire in their youth, the period of gain would be too short compared with the period of loss

for us to be able to say that competition had on the whole raised their standard of living in their lifetimes. Thus, even though competition and economic progress operate to raise the standard of living of the average person above that of millionaires of previous generations, they often do not do so rapidly enough to enable those who lose fortunes to improve their standard of living on net balance in their lifetimes.

Even so, there is no legitimate argument that can be raised against economic competition. Those who lose a fortune cannot logically regard competition as their enemy. For we must consider the foundation on which their fortune rested. If it was acquired legitimately, i.e., through production and trade, it could only have been so by virtue of their or their parent's or grandparent's previous success in the process of competition. To have a million dollars or more almost certainly requires that someone have earned an exceptional rate of profit that he kept plowing back over a period of years. That exceptional rate of profit represented successful competition. Thus, the fortunes that are lost because of competition were first acquired because of competition. One cannot reasonably denounce the process of competition for taking away what one could not have had without it in the first place.

This point applies in a double way. Not only is competition responsible for the existence of any fortune with which one legitimately begins, but it is also responsible for the *purchasing power* of that fortune and of every other sum of money one will ever possess. Virtually all of the products that can be bought are the result of the process of competition. The millionaire who loses the ability to buy a Rolls Royce and caviar and champagne, and who ends up having to settle for a Chevrolet and hamburgers, could not have had *any* of these things without the process of competition. To denounce competition as the source of his loss ignores the foundation of virtually everything he has or ever could have. (The same point, of course, applies to a worker who might be tempted to denounce competition for a decline in his income. The purchasing power of any income he ever earned or will earn is created by the competition of producers. There would be almost nothing for him to buy without it. And the previously higher money income he earned was itself the result of his own previously more successful competition.) Thus, an accurate description of the millionaire's loss, or anyone else's loss in connection with competition, is not to say that the phenomenon of competition has caused him any kind of actual loss or harm, but that competition both before and after his financial loss has benefitted him incalculably. It is just that after his financial loss, competition, while still benefitting him incalculably, benefits him somewhat less than it did before, and will require some period of time to benefit him even more than it did at its previous peak of benefit to him. Always, the effect of economic competition on the standard of living of everyone is positive—enormously positive.

The Enemies of Competition as the True Advocates of the Law of the Jungle

It should be realized that it is those who denounce competition who are the true advocates of the law of the jungle. They want to preserve their or others' accustomed standard of living by means of prohibiting or restricting competition. The only way they can accomplish such a goal is by means of *the initiation of physical force*. For competitors will not stay back or stop their competition voluntarily.

For example, if the owner of a harness factory wanted to preserve his standard of living by stopping the competition of the automobile, it would not be sufficient for him merely to send a polite letter to Henry Ford explaining the hardship he was suffering on account of Ford's activities and requesting, therefore, that Ford stop or restrict his business. Ford would obviously disregard such a request, since it is overwhelmingly to his self-interest to go on with his business and increase it.

If our harness factory owner were seriously out to stop Ford's activities, the only way he could do so would be by means of force. Either he would have to employ private criminals to stop Ford, by such means as wrecking his factories and threatening his workers, or he would have to have a law passed, which would stop him by the threat of seizing his property or putting him in prison. One way or another, force would have to be his only recourse, because there is no way that Ford or any other competitor would voluntarily give up the means of making his own fortune in order to preserve the fortune of someone else. Such activity on the part of the harness-factory owner—who is in the position usually regarded as that of a victim of "the law of the jungle"—is the real law of the jungle in its human setting. For it is the attempt to live by means of force, rather than production and exchange. All those who denounce economic competition implicitly support such behavior, and in this sense are advocates of the law of the jungle.

In contrast, economic competition itself has now been clearly established as *the opposite* of the law of the jungle. It is a uniquely human mode of survival: the achievement of success by offering progressively better goods and services to others, who have alternatives for spending their money and who must be voluntarily induced to spend it in any particular way—who are induced because they are offered something better. Economic competition is both the product and the agent of man's ongoing use of his mind to improve his life—the product of the minds of those who have something newer and better to offer, and the agent compelling all others to do the thinking necessary to be able to follow if they are to retain the voluntary patronage of their customers. It is not the law of the jungle, but of *progressing civilization*—the basis not of the survival of the biologically fittest, but of everyone, at a higher and higher level.

3. Economic Competition and Economic Security

Our discussion has important implications for the relationship between economic competition and economic security, which need to be developed.

Usually, competition is perceived as one of the foremost threats to the individual's economic security, because it can cause him to lose his present job. We are now in a position to see that in actuality *the freedom of competition is an essential basis of economic security*—that it is so in terms both of the individual's ability to obtain physical goods and services in exchange for the money income he earns and to earn a money income in the first place.

It should be realized that in its most fundamental, physical sense, economic security means the ability to obtain the goods and services on which one's life and well-being depend. It means that when one is hungry, one can obtain food, that when it is cold and raining, one has a warm, dry house to stay in; and so on. In its fundamental, physical sense, economic security obviously depends on the ability to produce. The ability to produce and physically have goods depends on the freedom of competition. The freedom of competition is thus a fundamental basis of physical economic security.

This point can be highlighted by a brief consideration of the medieval guild system, whose absurdity it makes manifest. The guilds existed in order to give their members economic security. The means chosen by the guilds for achieving economic security was the prohibition of all economic competition both by outsiders and among their own members. Thus, the bakers' guild sought security by prohibiting improvements in the production of bread; the cobblers' guild, by prohibiting improvements in the production of shoes; the tailors' guild, by prohibiting improvements in the production of clothing, and so on, industry by industry, occupation by occupation.

The effect of all this misguided seeking of security was that everyone remained much poorer and therefore much less physically secure than he needed to be. People were deprived of bread and made insecure against hunger because of the activities of the bakers' guild. They were deprived of shoes and clothing and made insecure against the elements because of the activities of the cobblers' and tailors' guilds, and so on. And those so deprived included the members of all of the guilds. Each guild operated to perpetuate the poverty and insecurity of the whole society—that of the population standing outside the guild system, that of the members of all other guilds, and even that of its own members (for it should be recalled how people benefit even from the improvements that initially displace them). Thus, the guilds operated in a veritable self-contradiction: they professed a desire for security and yet in fact perpetuated insecurity. Much the same, of course, is true of modern-day labor unions, which are similar to the guilds in essential respects.

The focus of the guilds, to be sure, was not on the physical basis of economic security in the production and availability of goods, but on the ability of their members to have jobs and earn money income. In this respect too, their policy operated contrary to purpose, in that they themselves created the very insecurity with respect to employment and income that they feared and complained of. (Again, the same point applies to modern-day labor unions.)

The following example will demonstrate this point. Someone loses his job because competition makes it obsolete. This individual must now find a new job. This means that he must turn around and enter the labor market of some other industry or occupation *as a new competitor.* As such, what he requires is precisely *the freedom of competition.* If the whole economic system has the freedom of competition, the hardships accompanying his loss of his original job need not be very great at all. He is free to compete anywhere else in the entire economic system and will obviously pick whichever industry or occupation he feels is most advantageous for him, given his abilities, including his ability and willingness to learn. The freedom of competition also ensures the availability of an abundance of jobs. It does so because, as will be explained in detail later in this book, it makes wages, costs of production, and prices low enough so that whatever the amount of spending of money that exists in the economic system, it will be sufficient to employ everyone seeking work and to buy all that they are capable of producing.[104] Thus, under the full freedom of competition, the problems of finding alternative employment are minimal.

But now consider what must happen as restrictions on the freedom of competition are introduced. Now, alternative employment opportunities begin to be closed off. The consequences of losing one's present job thus become more severe. At the same time, with every further restriction of the freedom of competition, pressures are created leading to still more such restrictions. Because, with every reduction in the alternative opportunities for employment, more and more workers must crowd into the industries and occupations still open to them. In these

industries and occupations their products and services are in artificial oversupply, and their wages must suffer correspondingly. In addition, their productivity declines because an artificial scarcity exists of the complementary means of production that must be obtained from the restricted industries and occupations. To compensate for such decline in the productivity of labor, wage rates in the remaining free industries must fall still further.

Thus, as conditions grow worse in the remaining free areas, more and more of them are led to demand restrictions of their own—as a matter of self-defense. And then at last there is simply no place for an unemployed worker to go. By then almost everyone lives in mortal terror of losing his job, and opposes everything that might have that effect.

It is clear that it is largely the existence of the restrictions on competition that makes them seem so necessary. *They* are the cause of the terrifying insecurity that grips so many people at the prospect of losing their job and makes them so desperately fear competition. Competition is terrifying *when one is not allowed to compete.* People are terrified of losing the competition concerning their present jobs, because if they lose it, they are *prohibited from competing for alternative employment.* The prohibitions on their competing elsewhere are what make them cling so desperately to the jobs they have.

The belief that the freedom to compete is a threat to economic security is completely wrong. The freedom to compete is *a precondition of economic security.* The belief that it is a threat is an illusion based largely on the lack of the freedom to compete. Furthermore, it is this belief that is a real source of economic insecurity, precisely because it leads to the restriction of competition.

As a further illustration of these principles, let us return briefly to the matter of the short-run loss periods connected with competition. Hostility to competition leads to the imposition of seniority, rather than merit, as the criterion for promotion and pay increases. This artificially lengthens the short-run loss periods associated with competition. A level of skill and income that in fact should take only a few weeks or months, or, perhaps, in the case of skilled workers, two or three years, to achieve may be stretched out to ten or twenty years by the seniority system. As a result, a worker who may lose a relatively modest stake in terms of genuinely necessary experience, which he could reacquire with relatively little difficulty in another job, is made to lose a major stake in seniority, which he can reacquire only with tremendous difficulty. Such workers are obviously placed in a position in which the loss of their present jobs is made into a much worse threat than it would be under the freedom of competition and its concomitant absence of the seniority system.

4. The Law of Comparative Advantage

Now let us consider just why there is not only room but also actual *need* for everyone in the competition of a division-of-labor society, even for those who are less capable than others in every respect.

There is, first of all, the fundamental economic fact that the need and desire for goods and services are virtually unlimited, while the ability to produce goods and services is always strictly limited.[105] Thus, there is a need for all the productive ability that exists—even for productive ability on the most modest scale.

A good example of how the need for productive ability translates into a need for productive ability on a more modest scale is the case of a one-man business which begins to grow. Originally, the owner had time to do everything, from making all of the most important decisions to sweeping the floor. But now, as his business begins to grow, it is physically impossible for him to do all these things. It pays him to begin to employ others to do jobs which he might be better able to do than they, but which he simply lacks the time to do. Thus, even though he might be a better secretary than the secretary he employs, and better at sweeping floors than the janitor he hires, it pays him to employ these people in order to be able to carry on a larger scale of activity. Their presence enables him to concentrate on the performance of tasks in which his superiority is greater and more important, such as thinking about what needs to be done in his business.

This brings us to the law of comparative advantage, or, as von Mises calls it, the law of association. This law holds that *human cooperation in a division of labor is mutually advantageous even when one party is productively superior to the other in every way, because it allows the superior party to concentrate on those areas of his superiority which are greater and more important—i.e., on his areas of comparative advantage.* By the same token, the inferior party concentrates on those areas in which his inferiority is less or less important, which represents *his* comparative advantage.[106]

Although originally advanced by Ricardo to show that international free trade and division of labor are mutually advantageous even if one country could produce every single good without exception with less labor than its trading partners, the principle of comparative advantage is all-pervasive, which is why von Mises calls it the law of association. It is found not only in the case of the boss and his secretary or the boss and the janitor, but also in such other everyday cases as the physician and his X-ray technician, the architect and his draftsman, the engineer and the mechanic, and so on. These are all cases in which one party could almost certainly do the work of the other in less time than the other does it, but in which it does not pay him to do it, because it would mean time away from his own work, in which his superiority is greater. In the light of this principle, it is clear that even a productive genius as great as Edison can benefit from being able to employ the humblest cleaning lady, despite the fact that he could almost certainly clean his office in the barest fraction of the time it takes her to clean it. Employing the cleaning lady enables him to devote whatever time he would otherwise have to devote to cleaning, to inventing, where his productive superiority over the cleaning lady is incalculably greater than it is in cleaning, however great it is there.

In the case of international trade, a good example of the principle of comparative advantage would be the following. Assume that with modern technology and mechanized picking, the United States can grow coffee in hothouses with less total labor, including the labor of building and maintaining the hothouses, than is required to grow it in the open air in Brazil, where it must be picked by hand. Specifically, imagine that the labor required to produce x bags of coffee in the United States is 1 million man-days, while in Brazil it is 2 million man-days. Assume further, however, that in the United States it is possible to produce y automobiles with .5 million man-days of labor and that the same quantity of automobiles requires 5 million man-days of labor in order to be produced in Brazil. These assumptions are shown in Table 9–1.

Will the United States grow its own coffee and undersell Brazil even on coffee, merely because it can produce it with less labor than Brazil? The answer is no. It will pay the United States and Brazil each to concentrate on their areas of *comparative advantage* and to trade. The United States will not devote 1 million man-days to producing its own coffee. Instead, it will devote perhaps an additional .5 million man-days to producing automobiles—its area of comparative advantage—and exchange them for the quantity of coffee it would have cost 1 million man-days to produce at home. The effect will be that the United States gets its coffee and saves the labor of .5 million man-days, with which it produces additional products, to be enjoyed in addition to the coffee.

The Brazilians will gladly give x bags of coffee for y of automobiles, because in doing so, they obtain for 2 million man-days of labor devoted to growing coffee a quantity of automobiles that would have cost them 5 million man-days of labor to produce. Thus, division of labor and trade are still mutually advantageous. The absolute advantage of the United States in growing coffee is irrelevant, because it gains much more by concentrating on automobile production, in which its absolute advantage is far greater.

Table 9–1		
The Absolute Advantage of the United States over Brazil		
Labor Required In (country)/ to Produce (product)	United States	Brazil
x of Coffee	1 million man-days	2 million man-days
y of Cars	.5 million man-days	5 million man-days

It should be realized, incidentally, that to the degree that the United States does concentrate on cars, and Brazil on coffee, *the total combined production that both countries obtain from the same amount of labor increases.* If there is no concentration, and each country simply produces its own coffee and its own automobiles, then the United States produces x of coffee with the labor of 1 million man-days, and y of cars with the labor of .5 million man-days. Brazil produces a further x of coffee with the labor of 2 million man-days, and a further y of cars with the labor of 5 million man-days. The combined output of the two countries, obtained from the labor of 1.5 million man-days in the United States and 7 million man-days in Brazil, is $2x$ of coffee plus $2y$ of cars.

But now, if the United States gives up growing coffee and switches the labor previously employed in producing coffee to producing cars, it can produce $3y$ of cars. If Brazil gives up automobile production and switches the labor previously employed in producing cars to producing coffee, it can now produce $3\frac{1}{2}x$ of coffee. The total combined production of the two countries obtained from the same total labor thus increases from $2x + 2y$ to $3\frac{1}{2}x + 3y$—just by virtue of employing the labor along the lines of comparative advantage.

Production increases because the United States gives up the production of a good in which its superiority is 2:1, in order to expand the production of a good in which its superiority is 10:1; at the same time, Brazil gives up the production of a good in which its inferiority is 1:10, in order to expand the production of a good in which its inferiority is 1:2.

Not only does the total of what is produced increase, but also each of the two countries necessarily gains by following the law of comparative advantage. The ability of both countries to gain rests not only on the fact that the total of what is produced is greater and thus that more is available to be had by both countries, but also on the following consideration: Namely, because the United States can produce $2y$ of cars with the same labor as it requires to produce x bags of coffee, it will be willing, if necessary, to offer as many as something just short of $2y$ of automobiles for x bags of coffee. So long as it can obtain its coffee for less than $2y$ of automobiles, it obtains it for less labor than it would have had to expend in producing the coffee. At the same time, Brazil is prepared to accept for x bags of coffee anything more than $.4y$ of automobiles, since by devoting the labor required to produce x bags of coffee to producing automobiles, it could produce only $.4y$ of automobiles. (This follows from the fact that it takes Brazil 2 million man-days to produce x bags of coffee and 5 million man-days to produce y of automobiles. Two million man-days is .4 times 5 million man-days, and if the product of the 5 million man-days is y of automobiles, the product of 2 million man-days is $.4y$.) Hence, Brazil comes out ahead so long as it can obtain anything more than $.4y$ of automobiles for x bags of coffee. Thus, within the broad limits of anything less than $2y$ of automobiles for x bags of coffee and anything more than $.4y$ of automobiles for x bags of coffee, both the United States and Brazil are able to gain from the arrangement.

International Competition and Free Labor Markets

The introduction of money into the preceding example will help to reinforce the conclusion that it is economically worthwhile for each country to concentrate on its areas of comparative advantage, and will make possible wider applications of the principle.

Assume simply that wage rates in the United States are more than double what they are in Brazil—say, triple. In this case, even though it takes only half the labor to grow coffee in the United States as in Brazil, it will be *one-and-a-half times more expensive* to do so—because of our higher wage rates. Thus, on a dollars-and-cents basis, the United States would be led not to grow coffee. We would concentrate on producing automobiles, where our cost would be three-tenths of Brazil's (after allowing for the effect of our three-times higher level of wage rates applied to our one-tenth the quantity of labor).

The question may be asked of how we know that our wages will be more than twice as high as Brazil's and thus that it will pay us to leave coffee growing to Brazil? We know because it follows logically that if American wages are not more than twice as high as Brazil's, economic forces will soon make them so. All we need do is assume that initially our wages are no higher than Brazil's, and then see what happens.

In other words, what we are assuming now is the nightmare case of the Brazilian protectionists. For in this case, with wage rates the same in the United States as in Brazil, it *is* cheaper to produce everything in the United States, and the United States could undersell Brazil even on coffee. But what will happen under these conditions? The answer, which the protectionists claim to know all too well, is that Americans won't buy anything from Brazil, while Brazilians will try to buy everything from the United States. That is exactly right.

But what is the consequence of this? The consequence is that money leaves Brazil and enters the United States. In Brazil, the effect will be less spending—less demand—for labor and goods. In the United States there will be somewhat more demand for labor and goods. (I say somewhat more, because being a much larger economy, the transfer of any given sum of money will represent a much smaller percentage increase here than it does a decrease there.)

If the freedom of competition exists in Brazil, wages and prices in Brazil will come down as the result of the drop in demand, while in the United States, they will rise somewhat. They will continue falling in Brazil and rising in the United States until the change in relative wages, costs, and prices between the two countries makes Brazil the cheaper country for the United States and other countries to buy from as often as the United States and other countries are cheaper for Brazil to buy from. Only then will money stop flowing out of Brazil and her wages, costs, and prices stop falling. Since our productivity-of-labor advantage in coffee is relatively modest, our cost advantage there will be among the first to disappear as Brazilian wage rates fall and ours rise.

It follows from this discussion that *there is room for every country in the world market.* However backward it may be in its methods of production, it can still be competitive in whatever it sells, provided only that its relative money wage rates compensate for its deficiencies in the productivity of labor.

To further bear this out, imagine, for example, that the labor of one country was uniformly half as productive as that of another—i.e., twice the labor was required to produce every good. Such a country would nevertheless have the same costs of production and be able to sell profitably at the same prices as the more productive country, provided only that its wage rates were half as great. For half the wages per hour times double the number of hours equal the same costs of production. In the same way, if its productivity of labor were a third, a fifth, or a tenth as great, it would have the same costs of production and be able to sell profitably at the same prices as any more advanced country, provided only that its wages were a third, a fifth, or a tenth as great as those of its more productive competitor. The principle that emerges is that *every country can be internationally competitive provided that its relative level of money wage rates corresponds to its relative productivity of labor.*

The mutual gains that accompany every country's presence in the world market stem from the fact that the differences in the productivity of labor are not uniform: there is comparative advantage. A country with half the productivity of labor and thus half wage level almost certainly does not have half the productivity of labor in the production of each and every good, but just as a kind of weighted average. In the production of many goods, it has less than half the productivity of labor; in the production of many others, it has more than half the productivity of labor. In the cases in which it has less than half the productivity—i.e., requires more than twice the labor to produce a good—its wage level of one-half prices it out of the market and it imports; but in every case in which it has more than half the productivity—i.e., requires less than twice the labor to produce a good—its wage level of one-half puts its costs below those of its competitors and it exports. In this way, each country tends to curtail the production of some things and expand the production of others, and thus to participate in the international division of labor in accordance with the principle of comparative advantage. The very fact of each country's expansion of its areas of comparative advantage then makes possible still further economies associated with division of labor and production on a larger scale.

In each country that enters into free trade, prices fall relative to wages, which increases the buying power and standard of living of the average wage earner in that country. Where it is necessary for wage rates to fall in order for a country to become competitive, the prices of domestically produced goods and services tend to fall in the same proportion. Some of these goods and services are now cheaper than foreign-produced goods and services and so are exported. But some foreign-produced goods and services are still below domestically produced goods and services and so are imported. The ability to get these foreign-produced goods and services represents a fall in prices greater than the fall in wages.

As illustration, consider again the case of the two countries one of which, on average, is half as productive as the other. If wage rates in the less productive country are initially 60 percent of the wage rates of the more productive country, they must fall by one-sixth in order to become only 50 percent as great. This fall in domestic wage rates reduces domestic costs of production and prices by one sixth. Thus, as far as domestically produced goods are concerned, the wage earners in the country have not lost any buying power, because prices are lower by as much as their wages. Where they gain is from the fact that now imported goods will be available to them which continue to be lower in price than domestically produced goods. These goods are the goods that require more than twice the labor to produce at home than abroad, and which thus continue to be more expensive to produce at home despite the fall in domestic wage rates to half the level of the foreign wage rates. At the same time, of course, the fall in domestic wage rates to half the foreign level gives the country concerned a cost advantage in all those cases in which its productivity of labor is anything more than half as great as the foreign country's— that is, in which it requires less than twice as much labor to produce a good. The proportion of its labor force which is no longer employed in producing the goods that are now imported will be employed in producing goods of this latter description instead, which are exported and which are the source of benefit to the wage earners of the foreign country.

The preceding examples bring to light a split vision on the part of protectionists. In the backward countries, the protectionists claim that free trade will be ruinous because of the higher productivity of the more advanced countries. In the more advanced countries, they claim that free trade will be ruinous because of the low wages of the backward countries—that to have free trade with the low-wage countries is to "import their standard of living." The truth is, of course, that the higher productivity of labor of the more advanced countries tends to be counterbalanced by their higher wages, and the lower wages of the backward countries tends to be counterbalanced by their lower productivity of labor. This is what tends to occur on a weighted-average basis. In all the individual cases that deviate from the average, i.e., in which one or the other country retains a cost advantage, we have the mutual gains from comparative advantage.

The source of problems in international trade is the persistence of wage rates that are too high in relation to a country's productivity of labor. If a country has two or five times the average productivity of labor of its trading partners, then it can be competitive with wage rates two or five times as high as theirs, but not with wage rates,

say, two-and-a-half or six times as high as theirs. By the same token, the countries with the low productivities of labor can be competitive with wage rates of a half or a fifth, but not two-thirds or one-fourth those of their trading partners.

In a labor market subject to the freedom of competition, such undue differences in wage rates could not persist. The unemployment resulting from them would drive down wage rates and costs and restore the country's international competitiveness and the full employment of its workers as well. But where labor unions, minimum-wage laws, and other government interference prevent wage rates from falling, or from falling sufficiently, the problem of unemployment remains and tends to grow worse. More and more companies that have kept their prices competitive, and paid the higher wages at the expense first of funds for capital improvements, and then at the expense of dividends and funds for capital replacement, must finally cut back or go out of business altogether. This is exactly what has occurred in the United States in the automobile industry, the steel industry, and in many other branches of industry.

Government intervention in the form of confiscatory taxation, inflation, and deficit spending has deprived American business of the capital funds required for raising the productivity of labor. Labor legislation and the resulting union wage scales and union work rules, and all manner of government regulations have also operated to prevent the rise in the productivity of labor, or actually to reduce it. Meanwhile, foreign competitors, in countries with policies less hostile to capital accumulation and with less labor union and regulatory interference, have rapidly improved their productivity of labor. This combination of circumstances is what has made vast segments of American industry unable to compete at today's relative wage levels, which were inherited from an era of great relative superiority in America's productivity of labor. (All this, of course, is usually ignored. The most popular explanation of the problem is such trivialities as the alleged bad judgment of the American automobile companies in continuing to produce large cars after critics of the American standard of living had made known their preference for small cars. References to alleged cycles of inevitable decline are another popular explanation.)

The actual solution to the United States' lack of competitiveness (and to all of our other politico-economic problems, as well) would be to abolish all the government interference and establish laissez-faire capitalism. That would end the destruction of the American economic system and allow it to rebuild and resume the rise in the productivity of labor. But this almost certainly will not be done. What most likely will be done is that foreign competition will be severely restricted. The effect of that will not only be that the American people will lose many of the benefits of international division of labor. It will also contribute to future wars.

Countries like Japan, with huge populations and small territories, vitally depend on being able to export manufactured goods in order to be able to import food and raw materials. If we close them out of major export markets, we threaten their vital interests. We give them grounds for enmity and an economic rationale for war, as a means either of forcing open markets or of seizing the food- and mineral-producing territories they are prevented from earning the foreign exchange to buy from, and making them into captive markets.

Of course, for now and for the foreseeable future, the Japanese are not capable of being a military threat to us. Interestingly, however, as if to remedy this, the same U.S. Congress which has tried to restrict Japanese exports to this country has also urged Japan to increase her military expenditures.

A major implication of this whole discussion is that one of the requirements of free international trade, and thus of world peace, is free labor markets within countries. That is what is necessary to keep a country's wage level in a proper relationship to the wage levels of its competitors, and so enable it to have free trade without fear of mass unemployment developing because it is too widely undersold. A further implication is that since labor legislation and the coercive labor unions it spawns are incompatible with the establishment of the necessary relative wage levels, they are incompatible with free trade and thus, in the long run, with friendly international relations and world peace. It should be obvious that this consideration alone demands the abolition of such legislation.

Comparative Advantage Versus the Infant-Industries Argument

Recognition of the gains from comparative advantage can serve as the basis for a refutation of the so-called infant-industries argument. The infant-industries argument is the claim that new industries require tariff protection until such time as they have become established and are in a position to stand on their own. Thus, according to this argument, the means for developing new industries is to concentrate on industries in which one is currently relatively inefficient and would not pursue on the basis of following the law of comparative advantage. Then, by means of the employment of coercion in one's favor—namely, protective tariffs—one will somehow be able to grow more efficient and later on be able to operate in the industry under conditions of free competition.

The economic error of the infant-industries argument is that it fails to see that the quickest way to become efficient in new industries is to acquire the capital necessary to become efficient in them. The quickest way to do that is to concentrate on those areas in which one can earn the highest income and thus be in a position to save and invest to the greatest possible extent, which means: to follow the law of comparative advantage. As illustration, imagine that I as an individual want to go into business for myself, but at present, because of my lack of capital, the only way I can do so is at the level of buying a frankfurter pushcart, which will enable me barely to earn a living. If I am in a position to earn a substantially higher income by virtue of working for someone else, and thus to save and invest much more heavily, it should be obvious that the most effective way to establish myself in business is to work for someone else until such time as I have accumulated the capital necessary to go into business for myself on an efficient basis, with a reasonable prospect of earning a higher income than I can by working for someone else—i.e., that I wait until such time as my comparative advantage in the face of my greater capital, leads me to go into business for myself.

Exactly the same common-sense principle applies to the conduct of a whole country. Thus, the fact that in the early years of the United States, comparative advantage meant that the United States should concentrate on agriculture, while Great Britain concentrated on manufacturing, implied that concentration on agriculture was actually the fastest route to efficient industrialization in the United States. The higher incomes earned by concentration on agriculture provided the ability to save and invest far more heavily than would have been possible on the basis of premature industrialization brought about by coercion. Concentration on agriculture was the foundation for the development of industry on an efficient basis, and thus for the far greater development of industry. To the extent that the United States, or any other country, has employed the coercion of tariffs and other government intervention to promote the development of unprofitable industries, its policy has actually served to retard the industrial development of the country, because it has served to make its people earn lower incomes than they could have earned and thus to be less capable of saving and accumulating the capital necessary for the development of industry.

Any gains that may have resulted to particular industries as the result of this policy were at the expense of greater losses to other industries, whose development was thereby prevented. The truth of this proposition can be clearly seen if we imagine that the government were to encourage my purchase of the previously mentioned frankfurter stand, by means of giving me some kind of monopoly privilege in connection with the sale of frankfurters. Anything I might gain in this way would be at the expense of an equivalent loss to my customers. At the same time, I would be producing less than I could have been producing had I worked in another line. In addition, there would be less production on the part of whoever might have been in the business of selling frankfurters and who is now forced to find some less remunerative line of work because of my monopoly privilege. In exactly the same way, diverting part of the capital and labor of the whole country from efficient employment in agriculture to inefficient employment in industry, represents an equivalent economic loss. To whatever extent the reduced production is disguised by the coercive transfer of wealth, the loss of the victims is as great as the gain of the recipients. What remains is the reduction in production and thus in the ability to save and invest, and thus in the ability to develop industry.

Consideration of the law of comparative advantage provides the answer to those who complain about the alleged dangers to a country of being "overspecialized" and about its alleged need to diversify its economy to avoid such "overspecialization." The fact is that the gains from efficient specialization far outweigh any possible losses arising from lack of "diversity." This is obvious in the case of any individual. Thus, for example, a man works regularly as a house painter or truck driver. He does this rather than attempt to alternate between several employments, because he earns more income this way. Such specialization represents his comparative advantage. He gains even though occasionally the circumstances of the market cause the demand for his specialty to fall sharply. Despite such periods, he is far better off concentrating on his specialization. Any possible loss of income he might be spared in such periods by "diversifying" and dividing his time between more two or more regular employments, are far outweighed by the reduction in income he would have to experience in the much lengthier periods of normal demand for his specialty.

A government policy of forced diversification for the purpose of avoiding periods of slack international demand in the areas of its citizens' specializations, is comparable to forcing an individual who judges it best for him to be a house painter or truck driver, or whichever, to divide his time between two or more employments to avoid the occasional loss of income in his area of specialization. It represents forcing people to do that which they judge on net balance to be overwhelmingly against their interest, and which in fact is against their interest. This is the result even though the government does not force a given individual to pursue two or more lines of work at the same time, but instead, for the sake of its citizenry collectively diversifying, uses such coercive means as protective tariffs and subsidies to force various portions of its citizenry to pursue full-time lines of work or branches of industry that are less remunerative to them as individuals than the lines of work or branches of industry they would have chosen on their own.

How the Less Able Can Outcompete the More Able in a Free Labor Market

The principle that wage differences compensate for productivity differences applies within the labor market of each country, as well as internationally. It shows how less efficient individuals can be fully competitive with more efficient individuals in seeking employment. All they have to do is accept wage rates that are lower to the degree that their productivity is lower. For example, a man who can lay only twenty bricks per hour can be fully competitive with workers who can lay forty bricks per hour, provided only that he be willing to accept half the hourly pay they receive. For then the cost to an employer per brick laid is the same.

Indeed, less productive individuals can, and regularly do, *outcompete* more productive individuals for jobs simply by virtue of their wages being lower to a greater degree than their productivity is lower. All other things being equal, the worker who can lay twenty bricks per hour and asks five dollars an hour outcompetes the worker who can lay forty bricks an hour but asks fifteen dollars an hour. The first man's cost per brick laid to an employer is only twenty-five cents ($5/20), while that of the second man is thirty-seven-and-a-half cents ($15/40).

The law of comparative advantage guarantees a job for everyone—a job in which he outcompetes all other contenders for that job, no matter how modest his abilities—provided only that the labor market is free to bring about the appropriate adjustments in relative wages.

As the wage rates of less capable people fall relative to those of people who are more capable, the less capable are able to match or exceed in more and more employments what a more capable person is able to offer an employer per dollar of cost. When the wages of a less capable person are half those of a more capable person, he is the more economical employee in every job in which his productivity is more than half as great as that of the more capable person. When his wages are only a third of the wages of a more capable person, he is the more economical employee in every job in which his productivity is merely more than a third as great as that of the more capable person, and so on.

By the same token, the relatively higher wage rates of those who are more capable operate to reserve their talents and abilities for those specific employments in which their relative productivity is great enough to offset their higher wage rates. Our man with the three-times higher wage, for example, is the more economical employee in any occupation in which his relative productivity is more than three times as great as that of the less capable person. He is, of course, also the more economical employee in any occupation that the less capable person is simply incapable of performing at all and which at the same time is in sufficient demand to pay him the high wage he receives. The higher wage rates of more capable people, derivable from those employments whose requirements they alone can satisfy, or in which their relative productivity is otherwise sufficiently high, operate to keep such people *out of the portions of the labor market served by the less capable people.*

For example, an engineer or doctor capable of laying even a hundred bricks an hour would not dream of working as a bricklayer, nor could anyone dream of employing him as one, given his ability to earn, say, fifty or a hundred dollars an hour as an engineer or doctor. His relative productivity advantage as a bricklayer may be as great as five to one (that is, a hundred bricks an hour to twenty bricks an hour), but his advantage as a doctor or engineer gives him an income so high that, given the availability of workers who can lay twenty bricks an hour for only five dollars, he would need to have an unattainable relative productivity advantage of ten or twenty to one before such an occupation as bricklaying could afford him an income comparable to what he earns as an engineer or doctor. (This is putting aside the fact that he would almost certainly want a good deal more income as a bricklayer, to compensate for the greater unpleasantness and much lower social standing of the job.)

It is no exaggeration to say that at the appropriate level of relative wage rates, people with abilities no greater than those of a janitor are able to outcompete everyone else in the entire economic system—even the world's most talented people. They not only are capable of doing so, they actually *do so*—for such jobs as janitor: by being willing to accept the income of a janitor.

Thus, on the basis of the law of comparative advantage, there is room even for the least talented individuals in the productive system of a division-of-labor society. Even they have a contribution to make, and one that is of benefit to others who are more talented. Namely, by taking over tasks in which their productive inferiority is relatively small, they enable those who are more talented to concentrate on areas where their productive superiority is greater and more important.

Competition for jobs is not the enemy of such people. They can compete successfully for jobs appropriate to their abilities, provided they are free to accept the necessary wage rates. Indeed, free competition is precisely what they need in order to be successful in getting the jobs they want.

The enemy of such people is the misguided attempt to give them wages they are unable to earn. That attempt—principally in the form of minimum-wage laws and pro-union legislation—is tantamount to *prohibiting* such people from competing. It prohibits them from competing by the one means that can compensate for their low productivity, namely, sufficiently low wage rates.

In the name of a misguided humanitarianism, people are stopped from competing, and the results are blamed on *competition!* The poor and weak, we are told, have no jobs and no income, because they have been overrun by the competition of the strong that casts them adrift and leaves them to perish. The actual fact, of course, is that the poor and the weak have not been harmed by the competition of the more able, but by *the police,* who are sent in by the "humanitarians" to enforce the laws to stop them from competing where they could successfully have competed.

The "humanitarians"—today's so-called liberals—are responsible for millions of low-skilled people, most notably, black teenagers, being prohibited from competing. Despite the "humanitarians'" alleged concern for human welfare, their ignorance of economics has led them to enact government policies that condemn millions to unemployment and a lifetime of poverty on the welfare rolls. Had these people been free to take a low-paying job, on the other hand, most of them would have gained some skills and experience that would have fitted them for better paying jobs later on. Many of them would have seen the need for further education and have gotten it.

Furthermore, it should be realized that the policy of attempting to enforce wage rates above the market level operates to *reduce* wage rates elsewhere. The higher wage rates imposed reduce the volume of jobs offered. The result is that workers who could have worked in such jobs cannot find employment in them and thus must seek work elsewhere. Thus, the supply of workers in other lines is increased, and wages elsewhere are put under pressure to fall. Because of this, every time labor unions succeed in artificially increasing the wages of skilled workers, they increase the supply of labor seeking employment in less-skilled jobs, and thus operate to reduce wages in the less-skilled areas artificially. It follows that in an economic system free of all government interference with wage rates, the wages of the unskilled would not have to be as low to establish full employment for them as is presently the case. The least capable members of the economic system not only could be employed under free competition, but could be so on more favorable terms than is the case under restrictions on the freedom of competition.

5. The Pyramid-of-Ability Principle

The law of comparative advantage explains the nature of the productive contribution of the less able to the more able. Now we must consider the incalculably greater productive contribution of the more able to the less able. In effect, having considered the contribution of the cleaning lady to Edison, let us consider the contribution of Edison to the cleaning lady. The principle we are now about to consider is *the pyramid-of-ability principle,* which is the name given to it by Ayn Rand, who was the first to identify it explicitly.[107]

The principle can be stated as follows: *To the degree that those who are more able occupy the higher positions in a division-of-labor society, the productivity of those in the lower positions is increased.*

For example, if a better-qualified person becomes foreman in a factory, the workers under him will produce more than if a poorer-qualified person became foreman. If a better-qualified person becomes company vice president or president, all those working under him will produce more than if a poorer-qualified person got the position. If two people both want to be an automotive engineer, and the better qualified succeeds, while the less qualified ends up as an auto mechanic, the better-qualified one can raise the productivity of the poorer-qualified one by designing a better car for him to work on. If their positions were reversed, this would not be possible.

More broadly and fundamentally, if there is the freedom to invent new and better products and new and better methods of production, and to start and expand new lines of business that produce or implement them, the productivity of all who help to produce the goods or services concerned, or who use them in production, or who are simply enabled to buy them by virtue of the work they presently do, is raised. It is raised by the activities of the inventors, businessmen, and investors who made those improvements possible.

The division of labor itself, as it exists within every factory and workplace, is a marvelous example of how the activities of those who are more capable raise the productivity of those who are less capable. As explained in Chapter 4, their work of breaking the production of a product into a series of small, simple, repetitious steps, which they then concentrate and coordinate, allows people of very little ability to produce highly complex products, such as automobiles and television sets. The contribution of the more able to the productivity of the less able can be gauged by the fact that in a division-of-labor society even janitors, merely by the effort of pushing a broom, can actually obtain automobiles, television sets, and almost all the other products of modern technology—products which on their own they could never even imagine.

It follows from this discussion that in "losing" the competition for the higher positions in a division-of-labor society, those who are less qualified do not in fact lose, but win. Their productivity of labor and standard of living are raised by the greater success of those who are more able than they. Were they to somehow force their way into the higher positions, they would lose. For they would destroy the productivity of labor of all those who would be under them and thus the possibility of obtaining the goods they wanted.

For example, I would like to have the income of the president of General Motors, which is a substantial multiple of my own. If by some means, despite my total lack of knowledge and experience or even interest in the automobile industry, I could force my way into his job, I would certainly reduce the production of General Motors by an enormously greater amount than corresponds to any additional income I would receive. For I would be disrupting the work of hundreds of thousands of people and causing the misuse of billions of dollars of capital. Perhaps, if this were the only instance of its kind in the whole economic system, I might still have a substantial gain for myself—provided I didn't have to trust my own life to GM products; the enormous loss I caused would fall almost entirely on others. But now suppose someone else similarly unqualified has become president of the airline I fly; or he's the surgeon who will operate on me; and so on. As this sort of action becomes more widespread, it becomes impossible for anyone to gain from it. Everyone suffers losses—those who succeed in getting the positions they don't deserve and can't obtain under the freedom of competition, along with all whom they victimize. In this way, they would actually end up losing by virtue of trying to obtain the gains they don't deserve.

Freedom of Competition and the General Gain from the Existence of Others

The pyramid-of-ability principle and the law of comparative advantage can be integrated into a wider principle that subsumes them both. Namely, that *each person gains from the existence of other people who participate with him in the division of labor.* If they are less productively capable than he, his gain from them is described by the law of comparative advantage. If they are more productively capable than he, his gain from them is described by the pyramid-of-ability principle.

In either case, looking down the scale or up, the individual gains from the existence of others who participate with him in the division of labor. *The great precondition of his gain is the freedom of competition: that everyone should have the legal right to enter every occupation and every industry.* That is the condition which simultaneously guarantees him the widest possible scope for his own talents as a producer and operates to assure that everything he buys will be produced by those who are best suited to produce it, in an environment of constant progress and improvement. The freedom of competition is the true basis of his economic security and the diametric opposite of the law of the jungle. It gives a place in the system of division of labor to everyone, and tends to put everyone in the particular place for which he is best suited, with the result that the productivity and standard of living of all are increased and go on increasing. So far from being the law of the jungle, the freedom of economic competition emerges as the true principle of the universal brotherhood of man.

6. The Population Question

With the notable exceptions of Adam Smith and Frederic Bastiat, the classical economists taught, in sympathy with Malthus, that population growth represents a threat to the average standard of living. As explained in connection with the discussion of private ownership of land and "land rent" earlier in this chapter, their belief was that the larger number of people, the larger the amount and poorer the quality of land and mineral deposits that must be worked to support them, and, at the same time, the more intensive the exploitation of each piece of land and mineral deposit worked, resulting in diminishing returns. For both reasons, they held, increases in population and in the number of workers tend to be accompanied by less than proportionate increases in the supply of food and minerals.

The clear implication of this doctrine is that there is an inherent conflict of interests among people as their numbers increase. It is tantamount to the claim that man is in the position of the lions in the jungle after all. The lions are at the point of a scarcity of food supply; man allegedly approaches it with every increase in his numbers. Indeed, Malthus was the inspiration for Darwin, whose writings were in turn the inspiration for the doctrine of conflict of interests presented under the name Social Darwinism.[108] A garbled form of Malthusianism is a root of the ecology movement's hostility to population growth.

The fact is, however, that the classical economists' ideas on the effects of population growth are valid *only for a stagnant, non-division-of-labor society*. (This was essentially the kind of society to which all but the most recent experience of the human race referred at the time that Ricardo wrote, which was in the early nineteenth century. He wrote too soon to know that he lived at the beginning of a radically new era in human history. Thus, it is understandable that neither he nor his followers were

able decisively to break with this pessimistic view.) In such a society, everyone lives in the same way—namely, as a self-sufficient farmer. In such a society, the existence of more people does mean the need for more and more land of progressively inferior quality and an ever worsening problem of diminishing returns. In such a society, it does mean the need to start farms higher and higher up the sides of hills or mountains, to extend farming to rockier patches of soil, or down into marshlands, and to subdivide existing farms among more and more people—all with the result of declining yields per unit of labor expended.

But this is not at all what the existence of more people means in a division-of-labor society. *In a division-of-labor society, a larger population means a greater, more intensive division of labor.*

Adam Smith alluded to this fact when he wrote that "the division of labor is limited by the extent of the market."[109] The meaning of this proposition is that the extent to which the division of labor can be carried in the production of anything depends on the volume in which it is to be produced. If, for example, automobiles are to be turned out at a rate of, say, 10 or 20 a day in a given location, then it is impossible that a step which takes 5 minutes to perform on any one car could be anyone's full-time job. The daily volume of automobile production would have to be increased to approximately 100 in a given location before such an operation could be made into a full-time job. (One hundred times 5 minutes equals 8.33 hours, which represents a full-time job.) The daily volume of automobile production would have to be increased to approximately 1 thousand in a given location, before an operation requiring only 30 seconds could be made into a full-time job, and so on. (One thousand times 30 seconds also equals 8.33 hours.) Thus, the larger the volume to be produced—the larger the market to be served—the further can the division of labor be carried.[110]

Markets, however, are not made possible by nonproducing consumers, as Adam Smith well knew, but only by producers.[111] And without a larger total number of producers participating in the division of labor overall, a more intensive division of labor in the production of any one good would require drawing labor away from the production of other goods, and thus correspondingly reducing the extent of division of labor elsewhere. The only way to have a greater division of labor overall is by virtue of a larger population of participating producers. This alone permits the division of labor to be extended in some areas without being correspondingly reduced in other areas. Thus, when we refer to the connection between the division of labor and population, or the division of labor and markets, it must be kept in mind that what is always referred to is a larger population of *producers,* and of overall markets that are larger by virtue of the existence of more producers.

Keeping this in mind, let us consider some further illustrations of the connection between the division of labor and the size of the population. Consider, for example, why large cities have so many specialized shops and restaurants, which are rarely found elsewhere. The reason is that the large population of such a city constitutes so vast a market that the statistically most infrequent tastes and interests are present in a great enough absolute quantity to make their accommodation possible.

For example, on any given evening perhaps only one person in ten thousand would like to eat Indian food. If the whole surrounding territory has only fifty thousand inhabitants, such a restaurant almost certainly could not survive, for it would have only five customers on an average evening. Its survival in such conditions would require patrons willing to pay very high prices. Only then could it be worthwhile for anyone to operate such an establishment. But in a large city or metropolitan area, with a surrounding population of ten million, say, there will be a thousand people, on average, wanting such food every evening. As a result, several such restaurants can exist and prosper.

The same principle applies to specialized book stores, equipment stores, and so on. It also explains why it is in large cities that one finds such cultural institutions as museums, opera companies, symphony orchestras, and so on, which appeal to refined and, in terms of their frequency of occurrence, relatively uncommon tastes. Only large cities have a sufficiently large market to provide a sufficient level of attendance for such institutions.

The advantages of a large population can be observed by considering the size of the population necessary for the existence of an economical-sized medical school, say, and for the existence of medical specializations. The principles observed in these cases will apply throughout the economic system.

Thus, as a hypothetical illustration, let us assume that an efficient-sized medical school produces 100 new doctors per year. This number, let us assume, is a number that represents enough students to keep the cost of lectures and demonstrations within reason on a per student basis, and yet not so many students that they cannot obtain sufficient individual consultations and so forth with the faculty. Let us assume further that the average graduate of this medical school will practice medicine for 40 years after graduation. This means that ultimately there will be 4,000 graduates of this school in practice at any one time. Finally, let us assume that the average frequency of diseases and accidents, and so on, that require medical attention is such that in order to keep the average doctor more or less fully occupied, there have to be 1,000 people for every doctor. These assumptions imply that a population of *4 million* is necessary to provide a market large enough to support one efficient-sized medical school.

But this is by no means the end. For suppose that only one doctor in a thousand is a brain specialist. With a total of only 4,000 thousand doctors, there would be just 4 brain specialists. That is hardly enough to support much specialized research in brain diseases, a specialized journal of brain diseases, graduate programs or seminars in brain diseases, and so forth. A population of *4,000* brain specialists, however, would make these things possible. But that implies an underlying population not of 4 million, but of 4 billion people.

This same kind of radical step-up in the size of the population necessary to make further specialization possible occurs throughout production. Consider again the case of automobile production, where it was pointed out that for a full-time job to be made out of one specific step that requires 30 seconds per car, volume would have to be approximately 1,000 cars per day in a given location. Only this time, let us assume that the worker doing this job could be helped by a machine specifically designed for that purpose. If the total market for automobiles is limited to 1,000 per day, then there is room for only one such machine. Obviously, it would be impossible to have any regular employment in producing such machines. But suppose the market for automobiles is not 1,000 thousand per day, but 50,000 thousand per day, so that 50 such machines are required. Now it may be possible to have some people regularly employed just in the production of these machines, who will produce them with greater experience and expertise. Of course, their division of labor could not go very far: only a very few such machines would need to be produced in any one year. If there is a specific operation in building such a machine which takes a whole month, say, it is doubtful that even that operation could be anyone's full-time job, because it occurs so infrequently. A vastly larger market would be required to carry the division of labor to the point where even very large-sized steps in the production of these machines could be made into full-time jobs. It is doubtful if markets could ever be achieved that were so large that all possibilities for carrying the division of labor further in the production of specialized machines and tools would be exhausted.

Now it is necessary to realize how important are the gains a larger market provides not only in allowing the existence of further specializations and subspecializations, but also simply in allowing existing specializations and subspecializations to be carried on, *on a larger absolute scale.* Our medical school example can illustrate this point very well.

Some kind of very small market, say a few hundred people, is necessary to allow one person to specialize as some sort of primitive doctor. A larger market of several million, that permits the existence of several thousand doctors, also permits them all to be trained in a medical school and creates the subspecialization of brain specialist. A still larger market increases the absolute number of brain specialists. And here we can easily see something that is vitally important. Namely, if the market is big enough to support 400, or better still, 4,000 brain specialists, rather than just 4, the likelihood of some important discovery being made about brain diseases is substantially increased. For there will be 400 or 4,000 highly intelligent and experienced people thinking about the problems involved, instead of just 4. And whatever any one of them discovers, can, of course, be quickly communicated to all the rest—through the journals, seminars, and so on that their number is large enough to support.

Again, exactly the same principle applies throughout production. The larger the size of the market, the greater is not only the number of the scientific and engineering specializations and subspecializations, but also the absolute size of all of them—and, equally important, the larger the absolute number of intelligent, innovative individuals prepared to go into the various lines of business. Thus, throughout the economic system, the chances of new discoveries and inventions being made, being quickly communicated throughout the fields concerned, and then being implemented are greatly increased. And thus the rate of economic progress accelerates.

The potential gains of this kind from a larger-sized population in a division-of-labor society can be thought of in terms of a doubled population having a doubled number of Edisons and Fords and the like. Indeed, in a division-of-labor society, a doubled population even with just one-tenth more of such innovators would probably be easily capable of overcoming any problems of diminishing returns and poorer-quality land and mineral deposits, and of doing so by an ever widening margin. It would do so through the greater technological progress that the existence of a larger number of such outstanding individuals would make possible. For the existence of each additional productive genius serves to raise the productive power of the whole human race. Because essentially what he supplies is *ideas.* Ideas can be used by everyone who has need of them without in any way diminishing their ability to serve others. They are an inexhaustible gift.[112]

What we have here in the existence of a larger population in a division-of-labor society is a further step-up in productive power along the lines of the multiplication of knowledge used in production and the raising of the level of such knowledge to a standard set by the most intelligent.[113] For now we have *a larger absolute number of the most intelligent,* which is bound to mean a more rapidly rising standard of knowledge used in production.[114]

Thus, the effect of population growth in a division-of-labor society is radically different than in a non-division-of-labor society. In a division-of-labor society it means a greater, more intensive division of labor, including the larger absolute size of the various specializations and subspecializations concerned with making new discoveries and implementing them in the form of new products and better methods of production—in a word, it means a greater absolute number of productive geniuses, whose work operates to raise the standard of living of everyone. These advantages enable a division-of-labor society easily to overcome any problems that would otherwise be associated with the need to produce more food and minerals for a larger population.

Worldwide Free Trade

The fact that a larger market provides important gains, in the form of a more intensive division of labor and a larger absolute size of the various specializations and subspecializations, implies the desirability of worldwide free trade. Under worldwide free trade, every producer would be able to regard the entire world as his market. Production could be carried on in each locality on the vastly greater scale commensurate with a world market. Thus, the division of labor could reach its maximum possible extent consistent with the existing size of the world's population and the proportion of it already incorporated into the division of labor within the various national boundaries.

One may believe that already, even with substantial trade barriers, the scientific and engineering professions of all the various countries are essentially integrated, and that knowledge flows freely among them, with the exception, of course, of the Communist and other totalitarian countries. This is probably true. But what cannot flow freely, so long as there are trade barriers, is the *implementation* of scientific and technological progress—in the form of improvements in products and methods of production. If we want that, we need access to all the business talent to be found in the world, which means: we need to establish the right of every businessman everywhere to sell his goods everywhere. So long as that is missing, the benefit of the existence of much business talent is largely lost, because it is kept out by tariffs and other trade barriers. In other words, people are deprived of the benefit of the existence of talented foreign businessmen. And, of course, they are deprived of the benefit of all the economies of larger-scale production that free trade would make possible.

Free Trade and the Economic Superiority of the United States over Western Europe

The gains from free trade and the consequent access to a larger market can be illustrated by comparing the economic history of the United States with that of Western Europe. The fact that since the enactment of the Constitution there has always been free trade among the various states of the Union made the United States into a much larger free-trade area than Western Europe, in terms of population as well as land area. Because of its substantially greater population than any single West-European country, American businessmen were able to produce on a larger scale, with greater division of labor and more efficiency, than their West-European counterparts. A businessman anywhere in the United States could regard the whole territory and population of the United States as his market, and businesses were able to be built up accordingly. In Europe, on the other hand, tariffs and other trade barriers increasingly tended to restrict the markets of businessmen to the much smaller territories and populations of their respective countries.

By the same token, the American people had free access to the greater absolute volume of business talent to be found among its own greater population, while the people of most European countries were increasingly confined to the smaller absolute volume of business talent to be found among their smaller populations. These facts help to explain the more rapid rate of economic progress that prevailed in the United States than in Western Europe until fairly recently.

The fact that in recent decades West-European countries have greatly reduced their tariffs and other trade barriers against one another, under the aegis of the Common Market, has contributed to their rapid rate of economic progress in this period. Now, to a substantial degree, businessmen in any one member country can regard the populations of all the rest as part of his market. The combined population of these countries, counting that of the newer members, exceeds the population of the United States. The result has been an intensification of the division of labor within Western Europe and a much greater ability of the citizens of each member country to gain access to the talents of businessmen in the other member countries.

International Free Trade and Domestic Laissez Faire

The advantages of the United States from internal free trade and the gains from freer trade within Western Europe would be dwarfed by those derived from fully free trade on a world basis. But free foreign trade ulti-

mately requires a policy of laissez faire domestically. We have seen how in preventing necessary adjustments in relative wage rates government interference in the labor market causes free trade to result in mass unemployment, which leads to the abandonment of free trade. Similarly, government subsidy programs are incompatible with free trade: a government cannot, for example, try to raise the price of wheat in its country above the world-market level and at the same time allow the free importation of foreign wheat.

Some economists have held that external free trade *is* compatible with government intervention domestically, if governments abandon much of their political sovereignty to a supranational authority, which would impose a uniform policy of intervention. For example, the problem of wheat subsidies could be solved, it is held, if all countries in the trading area had the same subsidy program. To some degree, the European Common Market represents a relinquishing of national sovereignty to the organs of the Common Market. The ultimate success of the Common Market is widely thought to rest on the prospects for the political unification of Western Europe.

However, no uniform policy of government intervention can deal with such matters as the major differences between the productivity of labor in different areas. A uniform minimum wage between the United States and Taiwan, for example, would mean the virtually total destruction of the Taiwanese economy if it were set at the present American level, or, for all practical purposes, the total absence of a minimum wage in the United States if it were set at a level that would not destroy the Taiwanese economy.

Furthermore, the long-run effect of government intervention is to break up the unity of *existing* political entities, not to promote the formation of still larger political entities. For the existence of government intervention is an invitation to pressure-group warfare. Groups form to use the government as an instrument serving their short-run interests at the expense of the interests of the rest of society. In such an environment, such groups often come to be formed on the basis of such factors as regional ties, ethnic origin, and common language. Each such special group feels the need to control the use of government power in order to promote its own interests at the expense of other groups, and to protect itself from the depredations of other groups. In such conditions, growing conflict and hostility develop among the various groups, culminating in violent clashes and, ultimately, in demands for political separation. Thus, at the very same time that some people are calling for a United States of Europe, others are demanding the breakup of the existing countries of Europe. In Great Britain, there are the Scottish and Welsh nationalists; in Spain, the Basque and

Catalan separatists; in Belgium, the Flemish separatists; and in other countries, similar such groups.

Thus, international free trade and the gains to be derived from the international division of labor ultimately require the existence of domestic free trade—of laissez-faire capitalism. This is necessary to avoid both the surrender of national sovereignty and the pursuit of policies promoting the development of ethnic conflicts that lead to the rupturing of nations. With domestic laissez faire, there are no obstacles of any significant kind to the establishment of international free trade. There is no unemployment problem caused by free trade, because wage rates are free to adjust as necessary; no problem of protecting the recipients of subsidies, because there are none; and no problems of uniform government regulation, because there is no government regulation.

The Birth Rate

It has been shown that in a division-of-labor society a larger-sized population, far from reducing the average standard of living, actually increases it. This demonstration by no means implies, however, that the ideal arrangement would be the highest possible birth rate, or that birth-control measures operate to hold down the standard of living. There is an important difference between a larger-sized existing population, made up of self-supporting adults, and a rapidly growing population, composed of a high proportion of dependent children. The latter represents a reduction in the standard of living of those who must support the children.

Too-rapid population growth caused by a too-high birth rate is almost impossible, however, in a society which is not dominated by religious fanaticism and in which parents are financially responsible for the costs of raising their own children, and are free to practice birth control. For then, the parents simply consider the costs they will have to bear, and act accordingly. The only way a problem of population growth can be created in these circumstances is insofar as the government taxes the general public to pay for the costs of raising children. Then, people can have children at little or no cost to themselves; the cost is borne by the taxpayers. Welfare allowances geared to family size, so-called family assistance allowances, and public education are examples of measures of this type.

7. Free Immigration

It is necessary to address the issue of free immigration, which is closely related to the subject of population growth. This section will show that free immigration is in the long-run material self-interest of the citizens of a capitalist country.

The words *capitalist country* must be stressed. To the extent that a country has a welfare system, tax-supported hospitals and schools, public housing, and so on, and the immigrants come to take advantage of these offerings, the effect is a corresponding loss to the present inhabitants of the country, who have to pay the costs. The above proposition applies to a country insofar as it is *without* these and other welfare-state-type programs—a country in which the immigrants must be self-supporting and themselves pay for whatever they receive. By the same token, the freedom of a country implies the absence of economic disabilities imposed on immigrants: there are no minimum-wage laws or prounion legislation to prevent them from gaining employment, and no legal obstacles to their starting businesses, buying land, and so on.

Under such conditions, the freedom of immigration must ultimately prove economically beneficial to everyone. Because among the immigrants and their descendants will be individuals of great talent, capable of achieving great things in a free country, but who would be stifled and be able to contribute little or nothing in the lands of their origin. In effect, the freedom of immigration into a free country from countries that are less free or unfree is a vital means of *unlocking human talent and increasing the gains from the pyramid of ability.*

As a simple example, one should consider what would have been the effect on Andrew Carnegie, and not just on the American but on the world steel industry, if he had been prevented from immigrating to the United States and confined to the less free environment of Scotland and Great Britain. One should consider what would have been the effect on the development of the helicopter if Sikorsky had been prevented from immigrating to the United States from Russia. Is it likely that the Russians would have seen the value of his ideas before they had been proved by actual repeated demonstration in the United States?

Indeed, we should consider the effects if the *ancestors* of any American industrial innovator had had to remain in their native lands, and thus that person have been born and spent his life in a country like Italy, Poland, Russia, or Germany, or even France or Great Britain, instead of the United States. Probably most of the innovators would have been stifled or at least significantly held back.

The historical advantage noted in the previous section, of the people of the United States having access to more business talent than the people of any European country, was due to America's policy of greater economic freedom in general combined with her policy of free immigration in particular. The latter gave the United States a larger population from which to draw such talent, while the former ensured that in the larger population *a greater frequency of such talent would be manifested,* because freedom is the essential condition for the development and flowering of such talent. The combination of free immigration and general economic freedom thus results both in more people *and,* at the same time, as an inextricable part of the same process, *a rate of economic progress that is not only rapid, but also further accelerated by virtue of the immigration.* Simply put, free immigration into a free country accelerates economic progress, *because talent requires freedom in order to flourish. Free immigration into a free country brings talent to freedom, and so enables more of it to develop and contribute to economic progress.* The acceleration of economic progress it achieves ultimately far outstrips whatever short-run problems may accompany an increase in immigration.

Refutation of the Arguments Against Free Immigration

It is necessary to refute the arguments advanced against the freedom of immigration and the population growth it causes.

It is claimed that the larger population resulting from free immigration creates the need to resort to inferior grades of land and mineral deposits and is accompanied by diminishing returns. This argument has already been answered both in our discussions of population growth and in our discussion of private ownership of land.[115] Here it is only necessary to add a further point which applies particularly when the population growth results from immigration. Namely, that the immigration can be accompanied by the importation of additional raw materials along with the additional people.

Imagine, for example, that workers of the British steel industry immigrated to the United States and became steel workers here. This would not mean that the iron ore they required must be taken from the Mesabi range in Minnesota. Very probably, it would simply mean that iron ore that used to go from Labrador to Britain will now go from Labrador to the United States.

This example points up the fact that those who fear population growth are thinking in terms of a non-division-of-labor society, in which people work the land and in which more people in a territory means more working of the land in that territory. Actually, immigration into towns and cities has no necessary connection with the extent to which the land and mineral deposits of the surrounding territory must be worked, because the towns and cities can draw their raw materials from anywhere in the world. The notion that more people in a country must mean a higher ratio of labor to land in that country, and thus diminishing returns, simply does not apply in a division-of-labor society.

It is also claimed that a larger population must reduce the productivity of labor because it means a higher ratio of labor to capital goods, or, what is the same thing, less capital goods per worker. Those who advance this argument believe that population growth and increases in the supply of capital goods are independent processes. Capital accumulation, they believe, is determined simply by saving, which allegedly has no connection with the growth of population.

The fact is that a larger number of people working and producing *is itself the cause of a larger supply of capital goods.* A larger number of people working and producing in conjunction even with an unchanged supply of capital goods results in an increase in total production. This no one can deny. It is only necessary to realize that what is produced in an economy is not only consumers' goods, but also *capital goods.* Labor and existing capital goods are used to produce both consumers' goods *and* capital goods, and, as we shall see in later chapters, they do so in accordance with the relative demands for the two types of goods.[116]

The implication of this is that if there is any single, one-time increase in the number of people working and producing, it automatically tends to be followed by a growth in the supply of capital goods per worker and thus in output per worker at least back to their original levels. This is because the larger number of workers produces more capital goods with which that same larger number of workers then works in the next period, and with the aid of which it enjoys a higher productivity. The further effect is another increase in production in the following period—both of consumers' goods *and* of capital goods, until the original levels of capital goods per worker and the productivity of labor are equalled and, indeed, surpassed.

Thus, it should be clear that no reasonable case exists against any single dose of immigration or population increase based on the argument that it reduces the amount of capital goods per worker. For the additional labor itself results in progressively more capital goods.

In the case of a continuous increase in the supply of labor, it could be argued that just as the first group of additional workers brings about an increase in the supply of capital goods, a second group arrives on the scene, so that the ratio of capital goods to labor does not increase and may even fall further. Yet even this, more sophisticated version of the reduced-capital-per-worker argument against immigration and population growth cannot stand. This is because if the productivity of labor were threatened by a relative excess of labor and a relative deficiency of capital goods, the effect would be a drop in the demand for labor, and thus in the wage earners' demand for consumers' goods, and a rise in the demand for capital goods. The effect of this, in turn, would be a higher relative production of capital goods and a lower relative production of consumers' goods. The larger number of workers of each year would find sufficient additional capital goods available because they would be produced by *a larger proportion of the labor and capital goods of each year,* as well as by a growing volume of labor and capital goods from year to year.

And, as time went on, the positive effects of the unlocking of more human talent would occur. The effect of this would be an increase in the output of capital goods (and consumers' goods) that can be obtained from any given quantity of labor working in conjunction with any given quantity of capital goods. Even if it occurred on a strictly delimited, once-and-for-all basis, the effect of this in turn would be a more rapid rate of increase in the production both of capital goods and consumers' goods, with each year's larger output of capital goods serving as the base for the following year's further increase in the production both of capital goods and of consumers' goods.[117]

Thus, a capitalist economy with the freedom of immigration turns out in the long run to have a more rapid rate of capital accumulation than one without it. For it has both a larger relative production of capital goods and uses capital goods more efficiently in the further production of capital goods than one without the freedom of immigration. The effect of this more rapid rate of capital accumulation is a correspondingly faster rate of economic progress, which soon makes up for the reduction in the proportion of output going to the consumption of wage earners.

If one wants to form a more precise, quantitative estimate of the relationships involved, let us assume that free immigration, together with any increase in population coming from those already present, results in an overall rate of population growth of 3 percent per year. This is a rate last seen in the United States in colonial times. It would be sufficient to double the population every twenty-five years.

In order for a 3 percent larger number of workers each year to be as well equipped as the workers would be without population increase, something on the order perhaps of an additional 9 to 12 percent of national income—more accurately, current net output—would need to be devoted to saving and capital accumulation. This figure is generous. I arrive at it on the basis of the fact that in the nineteenth century and the first few decades of the twentieth century, the period in which the American economy was relatively free, the long-term historical ratio of reproducible capital to national income was about three or four to one.[118] Thus, a 3 percent increase in capital to accompany the 3 percent increase in the number of workers and so maintain a three or four to one ratio of capital to output per worker, would repre-

sent no more than something on the order of 9 to 12 percent of national income in conditions in which the degree of capital intensiveness was substantially higher than it is today.

Having to obtain this 9 to 12 percent of national income from the share of national income previously going to wage earners, would represent something on the order of a one-time reduction in wages of about 13 to 17 percent, if, as is typical, wages initially constitute about 70 percent of national income. This magnitude of reduction in wages, however, greatly overstates the magnitude that would actually follow the establishment of free immigration. This is because it is predicated on going from *zero* population increase to an annual rate of 3 percent increase. In reality, the effect would be more likely to be to go from a $1\frac{1}{2}$ percent annual increase without freedom of immigration to perhaps a 3 percent annual increase with it. The additional capital required would thus actually equal only $4\frac{1}{2}$ to 6 percent of national income, rather than 9 to 12 percent; and the one-time wage reduction would be on the order of $6\frac{1}{2}$ to $8\frac{1}{2}$ percent rather than 13 to 17 percent.

If the freedom of immigration were introduced following the establishment of greater economic freedom in other respects, this short-run negative effect would probably go largely unperceived, since it would be more than offset by other, positive developments. But, in any case, if the effect of the freedom of immigration and the pool of talent it unlocks is to enable the productivity of labor to increase by just an additional 1 percent a year, then, as soon as this happens, within seven to nine years the initial loss is made good and thereafter the process results only in gains.

A third argument raised against the freedom of immigration is that its effect would be to reduce the wages of unskilled workers relative to those of skilled workers. This result would occur to the extent that such factors as their lack of knowledge of the language, and the possibly lower educational standards of the poorer countries from which they came, led the immigrants to enter the economic system more heavily at the unskilled end of the labor market than at the skilled end.

Now this argument would have weight only if it could be shown that the influx of unskilled workers substantially increased the short-run reduction in the standard of living of the present unskilled workers, over and above the reduction just discussed. This cannot be shown, because by the time the influx of immigrants is able to have a significant depressing effect on the relative wages of unskilled workers, it also exerts a significant positive effect on the absolute standard of living of everyone.

Consider. If the freedom of immigration means an

additional increase in the number of workers of about 1½ percent a year, then whatever the proportions of skilled and unskilled labor among the immigrants, in any one year it can change the proportion among workers as a whole only very slightly. As a hypothetical illustration, if initially half the workers are skilled and half are unskilled, while among the immigrants only one-third are skilled and two-thirds are unskilled, the effect in one year is to change the overall composition of the labor force to a little more than 49¾ percent skilled, and a little less than 50¼ percent unskilled. (This conclusion follows by applying a rate of increase of 2 percent to the unskilled half of the population and a rate of increase of 1 percent to the skilled half of the population, and then expressing the results as percentages of the combined total.[119])

Furthermore, this change in the relative composition of the labor force does not go on indefinitely, because as time passes more and more of the earlier immigrants move up the ladder into skilled jobs. And among their children, the proportion of skilled and unskilled workers will be about the same as among the original population.

But what is most important is that with each passing year in which the proportion of unskilled workers becomes more pronounced, until it finally levels off at its new equilibrium, more and more of the earlier immigrants have had time to achieve positions from which they can begin making contributions that raise the general standard of living. Thus, after ten years, say, while the overall proportion of unskilled labor has risen in our hypothetical example from 50 percent to about 52½ percent, there will be immigrants who have established their own businesses and introduced important innovations having a growing impact on the rest of the economic system and operating to raise the standard of living of everyone. And with each passing year, this effect will become more pronounced. (The figure of 52½ percent results from applying to the half of the population that is initially unskilled a compound rate of increase of 2 percent for ten years, and to the half of the population that is initially skilled a compound rate of increase of 1 percent for ten years, and then taking the former result as a percentage of the combined result.)

Thus, the effect of the change in the proportions of skilled and unskilled labor operates perhaps to postpone somewhat the restoration and increase in the standard of living of the unskilled workers. At the same time, it accelerates the restoration and increase in the standard of living of the skilled workers. For what happens is that while the unskilled workers, with their relatively lower wages, are unable to buy as many of the goods and services of the skilled workers, the skilled workers are able to buy correspondingly more of the goods and

services of the unskilled workers.

Thus, overall, the effect of free immigration is that the immigrants enjoy a substantial gain immediately, while the original population gains after a period of time, which is shorter for skilled workers and longer for unskilled workers. Within the span of a single generation it is likely that almost everybody will have gained and from that point on will gain more and more. For by then, the immigrants and their children will have been making important contributions for some time, and will continue to do so, while further changes in the proportion between skilled and unskilled labor will probably have come to a halt.

The fourth and final objection to the freedom of immigration is a noneconomic argument to the effect that it means turning the country over to foreigners and thus destroying its language and culture.

The fact is that for a capitalist country the *opposite* is true. The freedom of immigration is the principal means of extending the language and culture of such a country. For the immigrants come voluntarily, in order to take advantage of freedom and to benefit themselves. They come with the knowledge that they are now in a better country than the one they left behind, and so are well-disposed to learning its language and absorbing its culture. And because they come from many different lands, each with its own language, the language of the new country is the logical common ground for them to choose in dealing with one another. Learning it is also virtually indispensable for practical success, since almost all of the existing wealth of the country is in the hands either of its native inhabitants or of earlier immigrants who have learned the language to be able to deal with the native inhabitants. It was in just this way that English came to be the language of tens of millions of people who originally did not speak English; people who, along with learning English, made the most important parts of Anglo-Saxon culture their own, such as the idea of the rule of law and the sanctity of private property.

The immigrants, of course, do not merely absorb their new country's culture. They help to make it better. They contribute to it not only all their business, scientific, and artistic achievements, and what is valuable in their own heritage, but, perhaps most important of all, a constantly renewed sense of personal ambition and personal achievement. They are a fresh inspiration in every generation.

The fact that while two hundred years ago English was the native language of perhaps 12 million people out of a world population of 1 billion, and is today the native language of over 350 million people out of a world population of about 4 billion, is due principally to the existence of the freedom of immigration into the United

States. The ability of the United States to become the leading economic and military power in the world would not have been possible without its freedom of immigration, which both attracted the numbers and powerfully contributed to their per capita productivity. Had the United States adhered to its policy of free immigration—along with the rest of its freedom—it is probable that today it would have a population approximately twice as large and a standard of living at least twice as high as the population and standard of living it presently has. As such, it would so far surpass any combination of external powers as to be absolutely unassailable.

Free Immigration and International Wage Rates

The discussion of free immigration that has just been presented implies the necessity of modifying an important proposition of economics—namely, the proposition that the movement of workers from lower-paying to higher-paying jobs brings about an equalization of wage rates. This proposition must be limited to a context in which the jobs are performed *under the same degree of economic freedom and cultural rationality.* The movement of workers from lower-paying jobs in less free, less rational countries to higher-paying jobs in a freer, more rational country does not equalize wage rates, but increases the differences still further, because the productivity of labor in the freer, more rational country will tend to grow all the more rapidly relative to the productivity of labor in the other countries, thanks to the unlocking of human talent and the capital formation that is brought about in the freer, more rational country. Thus, free immigration contributes to the emergence of virtually two different worlds, as population moves from politically created wastelands into countries in which freedom and rationality make possible continuous economic progress.

It should now be clear that the freedom of immigration into a capitalist country is to the long-run economic self-interest of all of its inhabitants. It enables more talent to flourish and thus increases the rate of economic progress in that country, through the greater operation of the pyramid-of-ability principle.

Capital Export

Closely related to the subject of freedom of immigration is the subject of capital export. Just as the immigration of labor is feared, on the grounds that it will reduce the ratio of capital to labor in the country experiencing the immigration, so the export of capital to foreign countries is also feared, on exactly the same grounds. The ratio of capital to labor, and thus the productivity of labor and real wages, will allegedly be reduced either by the im-

migration of labor or by the exportation of capital. Thus, for example, at the time of writing, objection is widely voiced to the prospective export of capital from the United States to Mexico, as the result of the impending establishment of greater freedom in the economic relations between the two countries. (It is rather ironic that most of those who fear the export of capital from the United States also fear the import of capital into the United States—from Japan, for example. It seems that the enemies of economic freedom have two fears in connection with the movement of capital: its movement out of a country and its movement into a country.)

The answer to the fears concerning the export of capital is essentially the same as the answer to the fears concerning the immigration of labor. Namely, that it too is the source of more rapid capital accumulation, including, ultimately, more rapid capital accumulation in the countries that export capital. Capital is exported only because it can be employed more productively abroad than at home. That is why it is more profitable to export the capital than to keep it at home. But the fact that capital can be employed more productively abroad than at home—that the same capital has a larger product abroad than at home—implies that the production of capital goods, no less than the production of consumers' goods, will be larger than before. For capital goods no less than consumers' goods are the product of capital goods and labor. Anything which serves to increase production in general serves to increase the production of capital goods.[120] Thus, the freedom of the Japanese to export capital to the United States, and the freedom of the United States to export capital to Mexico, makes possible the production of more goods—more capital goods as well as consumers' goods—with the same total labor and capital goods than would otherwise be possible. Thus such freedom increases the overall rate of capital accumulation.

Insofar as capital is exported to develop the exploitation of foreign natural resources and to take advantage of special climate and growing conditions found abroad, its beneficial effect on the capital-exporting country is obvious. For now raw materials and other products become available to the domestic market of the capital-exporting country that would not otherwise be available or available as economically. The effect is an immediate rise in the standard of living of the capital-exporting country. The effect is also a rise in the standard of living of all other countries that obtain the benefit of the expanded and improved production of minerals and agricultural commodities, through their import of such commodities.

The export of capital for the purpose of developing foreign manufacturing is similarly advantageous. Once again, an expanded and improved supply of products becomes available wherever these products are sold. If the major market for these products is the capital-exporting country, then its citizens have the most benefit from the larger supply of products.

As far as the expanded production that results from the export of capital—whether to develop foreign natural resources, foreign agriculture, or foreign manufacturing—is an expanded production of capital goods, the effect is, as I say, a further increase in the ability to produce, everywhere that the additional capital goods become available. For now these capital goods are added to the supply of capital goods otherwise existing and thereby raise the productivity of labor. The result of this higher productivity of labor is a greater ability to produce, including a greater ability to produce capital goods. Thus still more capital goods become available, followed by a still greater ability to produce, followed by an even greater supply of capital goods, and so on. This process is capable of continuing indefinitely, causing the supply of capital goods, the ability to produce, and the standard of living to go on rising further and further, and thus to be higher everywhere throughout the world than they would otherwise have been.[121]

An essential foundation of the permanently higher rate of capital accumulation attendant on the freedom of capital export is the intensification of the international division of labor that freedom of capital export brings about. Freedom of capital export is the means of bringing previously undeveloped or backward territories into the international division of labor and thereby enabling any given quantity of labor and capital goods to produce more, including, of course, more capital goods, by virtue of the intensification of the division of labor that is achieved.

Economic history, precisely the economic history of the United States and Mexico, provides a clear demonstration of the consequences of capital export. A major portion of the present-day United States—Texas and the whole of the Southwest and California—once was a part of Mexico. The economic development of this vast area was made possible by substantial capital export from the Eastern United States. However, although its original foundation was capital exported from the Eastern United States, most of the capital that is today invested in this region did not actually come from the Eastern United States. Rather it was accumulated out of the increasing production of the region itself (or out of goods obtained in exchange for that increasing production). Thus, the capital exported from the Eastern United States provided the foundation of the capital accumulation of the former Mexican territories but not the substance of it. A major by-product of the increasing production of the region, of course, was a growing supply of products in the Eastern United States, which, as far as they were capital goods, made an important contribution to all aspects of economic progress in the Eastern United States. In other words, the fact that Texas and California and the other states that once were part of Mexico have developed as they have, has greatly contributed to capital accumulation, production, and the standard of living in the rest of the United States. Had the United States of the nineteenth century attempted to retain all of its capital east of the state of Texas, in order to avoid the allegedly harmful consequences of exporting capital to "Mexican territory," the effect would have been a United States that in succeeding decades was far poorer than it turned out to be.

Today, there may be the opportunity to export capital to the remaining territory of Mexico. To the extent that the United States is free, the process of the economic development of the remainder of Mexico could only be accompanied by further improvement in the economy of the United States. The development of this remaining part of Mexico, it if can actually take place, would have the same impact on the economy of the United States as the development of Texas and California.

It should be evident that in the nature of the case there is no inherent reason for the export of capital to be accompanied by unemployment. Many people, of course, must change their jobs as the result of such a process, but in a free economy the overall effect is no reduction of employment, but merely a rise in the productivity of labor and standard of living.[122]

8. The Harmony of Interests in the Face of Competition for Limited Money Revenues

Going beyond the various aspects of international economic competition, the case for the freedom of economic competition in general becomes stronger still when one considers its benevolent effects in the context which might be thought most hostile to it, namely, the context of a fixed, invariable quantity of money and volume of spending in the economic system. In such a context, each person's gain of sales revenues and money income would imply a corresponding loss of sales revenues and money income by someone else. I will show that in such a context the effect of economic competition is necessarily to reduce prices by an amount sufficient to compensate, indeed, more than compensate, for the loss of money revenue or income in the rest of the economic system. This demonstration will constitute a further validation of the principle that in a division-of-labor, capitalist society, one man's gain is not another man's loss, but other men's gain.

Thus, for the sake of further reinforcing the case for freedom of competition by confirming it even in these rather extreme circumstances, let us imagine an economic system in which gold is money and all the gold has been mined, so that no further increase in the quantity of money is possible.[123] If the quantity of money were to be become fixed in this way, then, as Chapter 12 will show, there would be no basis for a rising volume of spending in the economic system, nor, therefore, for a rising volume of sales revenues and money incomes earned. This is because the increase in all of these depends on the increase in the quantity of money.[124]

For the sake of convenience, let us assume that the fixed quantity of money generates a volume of total spending and therefore of total sales revenues in the economic system equal to 1,000 units of money per year, year in and year out. Let us further assume, for the sake of simplicity, that the 1,000 of sales revenues earned each year constitute 1,000 of net incomes to the sellers. If one likes, each of the 1,000 units of money spent and received can be conceived of as equal to $5 billion or more of our present money, so that the economic system we are imagining could be physically as large as our own is now.

Let us also assume that this hypothetical economic system is initially composed of two groups of producers which are equal both in the number of their members and in the productive ability of their members. Thus, initially, each of these two groups produces half of the total output of the economic system. Because equal outputs command equal prices and exchange for equal revenues, we are justified in inferring that the sales revenues and incomes of the two groups are initially equal at 500 units of money each.

Now, to show the benevolent effects of competition, let us imagine that over a period of years, while both groups remain the same in terms of the number of their members, the members of one of the groups succeed on average in doubling the productivity of their labor, while the members of the other group merely maintain the productivity of their labor. The effect of this will be that one of the groups doubles its production while the production of the other group remains unchanged. This, in turn, means that one of the groups will now account for two-thirds of the output of the economic system while the other group now accounts for only one-third of the output of the economic system.

On the principle that equal outputs command equal prices and sell for equal revenues, we can infer that the members of the group that has doubled its production will now earn two-thirds of the total sales revenue and income of the economic system while the members of the other group will now earn only one-third of the total sales revenue and income of the economic system. Because total sales revenue and income are fixed at 1,000, the consequence is that the revenue and income of the

group that has doubled its output increases from 500 to 667, while the revenue and income of the group whose output remains unchanged decreases from 500 to 333. These changes are in accordance with the changed relative contributions of the two groups to the total product of the economic system in the face of a fixed 1,000-monetary-unit value of that product.

Thus, the picture may appear to be one of a conflict of interest between the members of the two groups. The totality of sales revenue and income is strictly limited and the members of the one group gain sales revenue and income only by equivalently depriving the members of the other group of sales revenue and income.

Here one must keep in mind the fact that the nature of the competition is not a grabbing off of a limited supply of something from nature by means of the exercise of greater physical strength and agility, but the earning from willing consumers of a greater share of money revenue and income by means of the enlargement of the supply of goods produced in exchange for that revenue and income. A number of benevolent consequences follow from this fact that are crucial, and they can be seen at their clearest precisely in the present case.

The first such consequence is that totally unlike the conditions in the animal kingdom, where the success of the strong deprives the weak of means of subsistence, the success of the more productive never deprives the less productive of the ability to earn at least some revenue and income. In the present case, the relatively less productive group still earns a full one-third of the sales revenue and income of the economic system, corresponding to its one-third contribution to total production. It would not matter by how much it fell behind in its relative contribution to total production, it would still earn revenue and income in proportion to whatever it did produce.

For example, if the members of the more productive group increased their productivity ninefold instead of twofold, the consequence would be that their relative production would rise from 1:1 to 9:1, instead of to only 2:1. Under these conditions, the members of the group that did not increase its productivity, instead of accounting for a third of the output of the economic system and earning a third of the revenue and income of the economic system, would account for only a tenth of the output of the economic system and earn only a tenth of its revenue and income. In other words, its members would earn 100 of revenue and income. This 100 is still something, and so long as the members of this group produce anything at all, they will still account for some positive proportion of the output of the economic system and earn a corresponding proportion of the revenue and income of the economic system.

And here is where we find the second benevolent consequence of the nature of economic competition that is brought out in the present analysis—a consequence that may appear astonishing. This is the fact that precisely to the same extent that the money income of the group that does not increase its productivity declines, *so too do the prices it must pay in order to obtain goods.* And thus its real income—its ability to obtain goods for the money it earns—does not fall at all!

Consider. The doubling of production by the members of the one group—let us call it Group *A* from now on—represents two things simultaneously: First of all, of course, a rise in its production relative to that of the other group—which from now on we call Group *B*—from 1:1 to 2:1. This is what is responsible for its proportion of total production rising from a half to two-thirds and for the proportion of Group *B* falling from a half to one-third. In virtue of the fact that total sales revenues and income are fixed at 1,000 units of money, it is responsible specifically for the revenue and income of Group *A* rising from 500 to 667 and for that of Group *B* falling from 500 to 333. But the second thing that the doubling of production by Group *A* is responsible for is an increase in the total production of the economic system in the ratio of 3:2. For a doubling of one-half of the output of the economic system plus the remaining initial one-half of the output of the economic system totals to three-halves of the initial output of the economic system.

Now, given the fact that the total expenditure to buy the output of the economic system is frozen at 1,000 units of money—which is why the total sales revenues and incomes of the economic system are frozen at 1,000 units of money—it follows that the purchase of three-halves the output entails a fall in prices to two-thirds of their initial level. *This fall in prices to two-thirds of their initial level is precisely equal to the fall in the revenue and income of the members of Group B,* inasmuch as the ratio of the 333 of revenue and income that the members of Group *B* now earn to the 500 of revenue and income that they initially earned is also equal to two-thirds. (At the same time, of course, the proportion of the total physical output of the economic system that is produced by the members of Group *B*, in falling to a third from a half, also falls precisely to two-thirds of its initial level. For when one divides a third by a half, the result is two-thirds.) Thus, while the members of Group *B* suffer a one-third decline in their money revenues and incomes as the result of the greater production on the part of the members of Group *A*, they simultaneously experience a one-third reduction in the prices they pay, and thus no reduction whatever in their actual buying power or so-called real incomes.

Could this amazing result be some kind of strange coincidence?

To find out, let us consider the results if the members of Group *A* were in fact to succeed in increasing their production ninefold instead of only twofold. In this case, the members of Group *A* would account for nine-tenths of the output of the economic system and earn 900 of the fixed 1,000 of total sales revenue and income. At the same time, the members of Group *B* would now account for only one-tenth of the output of the economic system and would accordingly earn only 100 of the fixed 1,000 of total sales revenue and income. In falling to one-tenth of the output of the economic system from one-half of the output of the economic system, the proportion of Group *B*'s production to that of the economic system as a whole falls to one-fifth of its initial level, for that is the ratio of a tenth to a half. And, of course, the revenue and income of Group *B*, in falling to 100 from 500, falls to a fifth of its initial level.

To find out if our previous finding was a coincidence, we need only determine the extent to which prices fall in the present instance. If they too fall to one-fifth of their initial level, then we can be sure that more than a coincidence is involved.

It turns out that prices do fall precisely to a fifth of their initial level. This results from the fact that in increasing its production by a multiple of nine, Group *A* now produces an output equal to nine-halves of the initial output of the economic system. When added to the output of Group *B*, which is equal to one-half of the initial output of the economic system, the result is a total production that is equal to ten-halves of the initial output of the economic system. The fact that in the conditions of the case the ten-halves of the initial total output must be sold for the same fixed 1,000 of sales revenues requires that prices be two-tenths as great, which, of course, means that they are one-fifth as great. Thus, once again, the percentage fall in the revenues and incomes of the members of Group *B* is precisely matched by the percentage fall in the prices of the goods they buy, and thus, once again, the members of Group *B* suffer no decline in their real incomes.

The mathematical necessity of prices and the revenue and income of the members of Group *B* falling by the same percentage, and thus the real incomes of the members of Group *B* remaining the same, can be established as a universal principle. To do this, it is only necessary to state matters algebraically. Thus, let the initial output of Group *A* be expressed as O_A and that of Group *B*, as O_B. The total initial output of the economic system as a whole will then be represented simply as the sum of $O_A + O_B$. The initial proportion of total output produced by Group *B* will then be $\dfrac{O_B}{O_A + O_B}$. The initial relative production of the two groups in this case need no longer be equal. It could be anything.

Now let us imagine that the members of Group A find a way to increase their production by any amount. Call it X. As a result of this increase in output by Group A, the proportion of total output produced by Group B falls to $\dfrac{O_B}{O_A + X + O_B}$ from $\dfrac{O_B}{O_A + O_B}$. When the former expression is divided by the latter, the two O_B terms constituting the numerators cancel out and the result is $\dfrac{O_A + O_B}{O_A + X + O_B}$. This is the measure of the fall in the sales revenues and incomes earned by the members of Group B. It is the ratio of their new, lower proportion of total production to their previous, larger proportion of total production.

It turns out that the fall in prices that results from Group A's increase in its production by amount X is also precisely equal to $\dfrac{O_A + O_B}{O_A + X + O_B}$. For the numerator of this expression is the initial volume of total production and the denominator is the larger volume of total production that results from Group A's increase in its output by amount X. When production is $O_A + O_B$, the price level is the fixed 1,000 of spending divided by this volume of production. When production is increased to $O_A + X + O_B$, the price level falls to the fixed 1,000 of spending divided by this larger volume of production. The ratio of this new, lower price level to the initial price level is thus found by dividing $\dfrac{1,000}{O_A + X + O_B}$ by $\dfrac{1,000}{O_A + O_B}$. When this division is performed, the two 1,000 terms constituting the numerators cancel out, and the result stands as the ratio of the second denominator to the first, which is exactly the same as the ratio of Group B's new, lower sales revenue and income to its initial sales revenue and income.

The principle that has now been established is that under the conditions of a fixed quantity of money and volume of spending, the increase in production by any group acts equally to reduce the price level as well as the sales revenues and incomes of the members of the rest of the economic system.

We are not yet through with amazing results, however. The result of free competition and the inequality of revenue and income that results from it is that prices end up falling *by more* than the revenue and income of the members of Group B. This is because of the fact that in the process of competition the members of Group B will almost certainly succeed in increasing their production to some extent. They will be strongly aided in doing so by the operation of the pyramid-of-ability principle.

Thus, for example, imagine that Group A represents 10 percent of the producers and Group B, 90 percent. Assume that initially Group A produces 10 percent of the total product of the economic system and Group B, 90 percent of the total product of the economic system. Now imagine that under the freedom of competition, the members of Group A, who represent the most intelligent, ambitious, and hardworking individuals in the economic system, succeed in increasing their production by a multiple of nine. At the same time, imagine that the members of Group B succeed in doubling their production. (This doubling occurs as the result of the members of Group B having to compete with the members of Group A and thus improve their own performance, of being able to learn from the success of the members of Group A, and of being able both to work under the direction and with the aid of products and methods of production devised by members of Group A.)

As the result of these respective increases in production, the members of Group A now produce an amount equal to nine-tenths of the initial output of the economic system, for they have increased their output, initially equal to one-tenth the output of the economic system, by a multiple of nine. At the same time, the members of Group B now produce an amount equal to 1.8 times the initial output of the economic system, for they have doubled their nine-tenths of the initial output. Thus total production in the economic system as a whole is now 2.7 times its initial amount. The proportion of the total output produced by the members of Group B is now two-thirds— $1.8/2.7$. It was initially nine-tenths. The fall in the proportion of output produced, and therefore of revenue and income earned, by the members of Group B is found by dividing two-thirds by nine-tenths. The result is $20/27$. Given 1,000 monetary units of total revenue and income in the economic system, the earnings of the members of Group B fall from 900 to 667.

Despite this fall in their money sales revenues and incomes, the members of Group B come out far ahead in this case in real terms. In fact, their real incomes precisely double, in full proportion to their increase in production. This is evident in the fact that total production in the economic system increases by a multiple of 2.7 and thus that prices fall to $10/27$ of their initial level. When the $10/27$ price level is divided into the $20/27$ money-revenue-and-income level of the members of Group B, the result is that the buying power—that is, the real revenues and incomes—of the members of Group B exactly doubles, just as their production.

Indeed, it should be obvious that it can be shown algebraically, as a general principle, that if Y is the amount of increase in the production of Group B, while X is the amount of increase in the production of Group A, then the real income of Group B increases in the ratio of $\dfrac{O_B + Y}{O_B}$, at the same time that the real income of Group

A increases in the ratio of $\dfrac{O_A + X}{O_A}$. This result follows

from the fact that the change in a group's real income is equal to the change in its money income divided by the change in the price level. In an economy with an invariable money, the change in a group's money income is equal to the change in its relative contribution to production. Thus the change in the money income of Group B is equal to the ratio of its current relative contribution to production to its initial relative contribution to production. Its current relative contribution to production is $\dfrac{O_B + Y}{O_A + O_B + X + Y}$. Its initial relative contribution to pro-

duction, of course, was $\dfrac{O_B}{O_A + O_B}$. When the first fraction

is divided by the second, the result is $\dfrac{O_B + Y}{O_B} \times$

$\dfrac{O_A + O_B}{O_A + O_B + X + Y}$. When this expression is divided by

the change in the price level, which also equals

$\dfrac{O_A + O_B}{O_A + O_B + X + Y}$, the result simplifies to $\dfrac{O_B + Y}{O_B}$. Ex-

actly the same procedure establishes the fact that the real income of Group A changes in the ratio of $\dfrac{O_A + X}{O_A}$.

Thus, the entirely benevolent nature of economic competition and the economic inequality that results from it has now been demonstrated in the context of an invariable money. It should scarcely be necessary to say that the only difference that is made by an increase in the quantity of money more or less in pace with the increase in the volume of production is that in those conditions the money revenue and income of the members of any Group B would not decline and would actually tend to increase to the extent that the members increased their production. Under these conditions, of course, prices would no longer tend to decline.

It should also scarcely be necessary to say that in the course of economic progress, the members of any Group B would have to be prepared to change their occupations. They could not, for example, rationally expect to go on producing horses and buggies once members of Group A have introduced the automobile. Their same or greater production would have to be in the context of their making the necessary adjustments in what they produced.

Notes

1. Cf. Ludwig von Mises, *Socialism* (New Haven: Yale University Press, 1951), pp. 40–42; reprint (Indianapolis: Liberty Classics, 1981). Page references are to the Yale University Press edition; pagination from this edition is retained in the reprint edition.

2. For a discussion of its influence on the mentality of destructionism, see above, pp. 230–231.

3. Cf. von Mises, *Socialism*, pp. 500–504.

4. See above, p. 174. This, of course, is a leading theme of von Mises.

5. See above, pp. 201–212.

6. See above, pp. 275–278 and 288–290.

7. For elaboration of the significance of this fact, see below, pp. 477–480. See also below, pp. 632–634.

8. See below, pp. 622–642, especially pp. 622–629. So intimately connected is the present discussion with that just referenced, that it would almost certainly be worthwhile to reread it after having read that material.

9. See below, pp. 631–632 and 824.

10. Even if a rise in costs comes out of above-average profits earned by the producers, and thus does not raise the price of the product they are selling, it still operates to make that price higher than it would have been in the long run, because now competition will not be able to reduce the price to the extent that it otherwise would have. In addition, whatever portion of that profit would have been used for reinvestment, either in this particular branch of production or anywhere else in the economic system, is now no longer available. Thus production will

be held back in the lines which are deprived of this additional capital and prices will be made higher than they otherwise would have been in this respect too.

11. On this point, see below, pp. 634–636. See also above, pp. 98–99.

12. See below, pp. 622–642. See also below, pp. 462–473 and 480–482, which explain the productive functions of businessmen and capitalists. The meaning of productive expenditure, incidentally, is expenditure for the purpose of making subsequent sales; it is the expenditure of business enterprises for business purposes. See below, pp. 444–445, for elaboration.

13. This is apart from instances in which business or investment losses are incurred, which the capitalists certainly strive to avoid but which are capable of wiping out one's entire capital, and more.

14. Matters are different when an individual acquires a possibly substantial sum of wealth that he does not regard as essential to his livelihood or to the provision for his future needs and wants. In such cases, he probably goes through that wealth fairly quickly. Even though the wealth in question may be thought of as capital to the extent that it is temporarily invested and earns a rate of return, the behavior of such individuals should not be thought of as at all typical of that of capitalists. Insofar as individuals behave in such a way, they certainly are not capitalists for very long.

15. The figure of the significant-sized capitalists' consumption being approximately 10 percent of total consumption is easily consistent even with the sum of all profit and interest incomes

being 30 percent of national income, while the sum of all wage and salary incomes is 70 percent of national income (national income being the sum of both such categories of incomes). It is consistent if the significant-sized capitalists own approximately 75 percent of the capital of the economic system and earn approximately 75 percent of the profit and interest incomes, and then save half of their incomes and consume half of their incomes. On these assumptions, the incomes of the significant-sized capitalists represent 75 percent of 30 percent of national income, that is, 22.5 percent of national income; their consumption of half of their incomes thus represents a consumption of 50 percent of 22.5 percent of national income, that is, 11.25 percent of national income. When that 11.25 percent is divided by the almost 90 percent of national income that can be assumed to be expended for consumption as distinct from net investment, the result is a consumption expenditure on the part of the significant-sized capitalists that is not much more than 10 percent of total consumption expenditure.

16. For a discussion of the same subject from the perspective of the very limited extent to which wage rates in particular might conceivably be raised, see below, pp. 650–653.

17. And, indeed, if it could be gained, a significant portion of the 10 percent would come at the expense of such things as support of education, the arts, and other charitable activities.

18. Ludwig von Mises, *Human Action*, 3d ed. rev. (Chicago: Henry Regnery Co., 1966), p. 531.

19. See Simon Kuznets, "Long-Term Changes in the National Income of the United States of America Since 1870" in Simon Kuznets, ed., *Income and Wealth of the United States* (Baltimore: The Johns Hopkins Press, 1952), pp. 82, 86. See also Paul Samuelson and William Nordhaus, *Economics,* 13th ed. (New York: McGraw-Hill Book Company, 1989), p. 860.

20. The degree of capital intensiveness is indicated by the ratio of accumulated capital to national income as well as by the ratio of accumulated capital to current consumption expenditure mentioned earlier in this chapter. This is because national income and consumption expenditure are necessarily always very closely related—indeed, are almost equivalent concepts. (Concerning the relationship between national income and consumption, see below, pp. 699–706.) For additional measures of the degree of capital intensiveness, see below, p. 631.

21. See above, the preceding page, n. 9.

22. For elaboration, see below, pp. 622–629.

23. For elaboration of this point, see below, pp. 737–739.

24. For a discussion of the destructive consequences of inheritance and income taxes, see below, pp. 306–310. See also pp. 636–639, 653–655, and 826–829. For a critique of land reform, see below, pp. 317–322. For further critiques of redistributionism, namely, of its role in the interpretation of the economic history of capitalism and as a leading aspect of welfare statism, see below, pp. 642–663.

25. On the significance of profit-and-loss incentives, see above, pp. 172–183, especially 176–180. Concerning the lack of individual initiative and the freedom of competition under government ownership, see above, pp. 275–278.

26. The destruction of the special gains of ownership is actually a consequence of redistributionism in general, and one that is especially noteworthy in the context of a non-division-of-labor society. For as soon as it is realized that redistributionism is to be a *system*, not only do people stop accumulating or maintain-

ing wealth, thus leaving very little for the recipients of "redistributions" to receive, but also what the recipients do receive can give them no pleasure, in that they know that they themselves will in turn suffer expropriation.

27. Even if the taxpayers have the power, in their capacity as voters, to remove the elected officials, they are unlikely to be able to use that power. Obviously, there is no question of such power insofar as relatively small numbers of high-income taxpayers are plundered by majorities. Insofar as tens of millions of taxpayers are made to foot the bill for the losses of nationalized enterprises, the losses of any given such enterprise are rendered too small to impel the individual taxpayer to action. A hundred million taxpayers who must pay $10 or $20 more in taxes to cover the losses of this or that government enterprise are no match in terms of motivation and organization for the pressure-group members, who as individuals gain very substantially from the government enterprise's losses.

28. Amazingly, none other than Adam Smith appears to hold this view. See below, pp. 476–477, where I quote him precisely to this effect.

29. This discussion is closely related to the critique of the doctrine that money is the root of all evil, which I presented earlier. See above, pp. 143–144.

30. Cf. Ludwig von Mises, *Bureaucracy* (1944; reprint, New Rochelle, N. Y.: Arlington House, 1969), pp. 20–39.

31. Ibid., pp. 40–63.

32. Ibid.

33. Ibid., pp. 64–73.

34. As further illustration of the bureaucratization of business, see above, pp. 196–199, where government-made obstacles to the operation of profit management are described as standing in the way of the achievement of fair treatment of blacks.

35. See above, pp. 234–237 and 254–256.

36. For the proof of these points, see below, pp. 618–642, especially 622–629 and 631–632. See also p. 824.

37. The reason such expenditures, when undertaken by the government, do not represent capital formation is explained below, on pp. 454–455.

38. Again, see below, pp. 631–632 and 824.

39. See below, pp. 618–642, for a comprehensive explanation of how capital accumulation is achieved and how it raises real wage rates.

40. See below, pp. 622–629 and 632–634.

41. Once more, see below, pp. 622–629 and 824.

42. See above, p. 147. See also, below, pp. 741–743.

43. For an explanation of how innovation, and anything else that increases efficiency, is a source of capital accumulation, see above, the example of the more efficient farmer, on pp. 132–133, and below, pp. 629–631 and 634–636.

44. Yet once again, see below, pp. 631–632 and 824.

45. Even if the effect is not to raise wage rates, but, in raising the demand for labor, to reduce or eliminate unemployment, that too operates to increase the funds available to the average wage earner—by virtue of reducing what he must pay to support the unemployed.

46. See below, pp. 618–642.

47. Cf. Touche Ross & Co. AB, *Tax & Investment Profile Sweden* (New York: Touche Ross International, 1985), pp. 5–6, 34.

48. David Ricardo, *Principles of Political Economy and Taxa-*

tion, 3d ed. (London, 1821), chap. 2; reprinted as vol. 1 of *The Works and Correspondence of David Ricardo*, ed. Piero Sraffa (Cambridge: Cambridge University Press, 1962), pp. 67–69. (Where appropriate, from now on, specific page references to the Sraffa edition will be supplied in brackets.)

49. Ibid., pp. 70–71.

50. See above, pp. 67–69.

51. Cf. Ricardo, *Principles of Political Economy and Taxation*, chap. 5, [p. 93].

52. Ibid. [pp. 94–95.]

53. See ibid., chap. 24, [pp. 203–204].

54. Hopefully, it is not necessary to say that these numbers are to be understood merely as representative, not as describing the actual total agricultural output or total produce rent of the country. To do that, they would need to be multiplied perhaps by a factor of several hundred thousand or several million, depending on the number of units of land involved.

55. Interestingly, Ricardo was very much aware of these possibilities. See *Principles of Political Economy and Taxation*, chap. 2 [pp. 78–83].

56. See below, pp. 358–367.

57. See above, p. 69.

58. Justification for the use of quotation marks around the word "owners," if not already understood, will become clear in the next part of this chapter. See below, pp. 331–332.

59. See above, pp. 63–71.

60. See above, pp. 66–67, 98. and 234–237.

61. For a discussion of how the rise in land rents caused by environmentalism comes at the expense of the demand for labor, see below, pp. 667–668.

62. See above, Chapter 1, n. 38.

63. The problems in the way of assimilation are a matter that needs historical investigation. They evidently continue even down to the present time, with the continued existence of Indian "reservations." The logically necessary intertribal warfare of the Indians, and all other primitive peoples, is also a matter worthy of historical investigation and dissemination to the public, which is increasingly under the sway of doctrines extolling the life of primitive peoples and attacking the life of modern, Western man.

64. Cf. von Mises, *Socialism*, pp. 55, 375.

65. What is present here, of course, is the operation of time preference, which renders a given sum in the present more valuable than a larger sum in the future. See above, pp. 55–58.

66. See below, pp. 931–933.

67. On these points, cf. von Mises, *Human Action*, pp. 684–688, 823–824; *Socialism*, pp. 225–226.

68. See above, pp. 19–21.

69. See above, pp. 176–180.

70. See above, ibid.

71. For an explanation of the significance of different rates of consumption by businessmen and capitalists relative to their capitals in connection with the determination of the average rate of profit and interest in the economic system, see below, pp. 737–739.

72. See above, pp. 176–180.

73. For an explanation of the connection between capital intensiveness and receptiveness to technological progress, see below, pp. 631–632. See also p. 824.

74. See below, pp. 622–629.

75. See below, pp. 632–634.

76. See below, pp. 618–642.

77. Cf. *The Communist Manifesto*, translated by Samuel Moore, chap. 1 (1844; reprint ed. (Chicago: Henry Regnery Company, Gateway, 1954), pp. 37–38. Henceforth, page references to the Gateway Edition will appear in brackets.

78. Cf. ibid., chap. 2 [pp. 56–57].

79. John Kenneth Galbraith, *The New Industrial State,* 2d ed. rev. (New York: New American Library, 1971), p. 141.

80. For elaboration, see below, pp. 580–594.

81. See above, pp. 275–278 and 288–290.

82. See above, pp. 267–282 passim.

83. Cf. Oskar Lange and Fred M. Taylor, *On the Economic Theory of Socialism* (Minneapolis: University of Minnesota Press, 1938), pp. 102–103.

84. I am indebted for this identification to my wife, Dr. Edith Packer.

85. Cf. Ludwig von Mises, *Human Action*, pp. 41–44; Ayn Rand, *Atlas Shrugged* (New York: Random House, 1957), pp. 1012–1013; idem, *Capitalism: The Unknown Ideal* (New York: New American Library, 1965) pp. 7, 12–13.

86. Cf. Ayn Rand, "The Ethics of Emergencies" in *The Virtue of Selfishness* (New York: New American Library, 1964), pp. 46–56.

87. See above, pp. 300–303.

88. The specific works that need to be disseminated are, above all, those of Ludwig von Mises and, though a philosopher rather than an economist, Ayn Rand. These, of course, should be reinforced by the writings of the classical economists and of Austrian economists other than von Mises.

89. On the doctrine of external benefits and external costs, see above, pp. 96–98.

90. Samuelson and Nordhaus, p. 649.

91. Ibid.

92. Ibid.

93. Ibid.

94. This latter hypothesis is supported by the profound mental weakness displayed above all by the supporters of environmentalism. See above, pp. 107–112. See also above, pp. 332–336.

95. See above, pp. 42–45 and 59–61.

96. See below, pp. 580–594 passim and 938–942.

97. See, above, pp. 196–199 and, below, pp. 382–384. See also George Reisman, *Capitalism: The Cure for Racism*, pamphlet (New York: *The Intellectual Activist*, 1982); reprinted (Laguna Hills, Calif.: The Jefferson School of Philosophy, Economics, and Psychology, 1992).

98. See above, p. 144.

99. Cf. von Mises, *Human Action*, pp. 273–276; *Socialism*, pp. 319–321.

100. For a confirmation of the above analysis in terms of the operation of Say's Law, see below, 561–569.

101. Cf. von Mises, *Human Action*, pp. 159–164; *Socialism*, pp. 294–295.

102. Cf. Ayn Rand, *Atlas Shrugged*, pp. 1063–1065.

103. See again the last two notes to von Mises and the preceding reference to Ayn Rand.

104. See below, pp. 559–594.

105. Again, see above, pp. 42–45 and 59–61.

106. Cf. von Mises, *Human Action*, pp. 159–161.

107. Cf. Ayn Rand, *Atlas Shrugged*, pp. 1064–1065.

108. Cf. von Mises, *Socialism*, pp. 315–319.

109. Cf. Adam Smith, *The Wealth of Nations* (London, 1776), bk. 1, chap. 3; reprint of Cannan ed. (Chicago: University of Chicago Press, 2 vols. in 1, 1976), 1:17–25. See also Frederic Bastiat, *Economic Harmonies*, trans. W. Hayden Boyers (New York: D. Van Nostrand & Co., 1964), pp. 561–567.

110. It is important to recall that the extension of the division of labor in this way requires the availability of more capital. There must be the appropriate additional supplies of plant and equipment and materials, as well as the larger number of workers. See above, p. 141.

111. Cf. below, pp. 542–580 passim.

112. Cf. von Mises, *Human Action*, p. 128; Ayn Rand, *Atlas Shrugged*, pp. 1064–1065.

113. See above, pp. 123–125.

114. For an account of how more rapid technological progress contributes to capital accumulation, see below, pp. 629–631.

115. See above, pp. 358–362 and 313–316.

116. On these points, see below, pp. 622–629 and 709.

117. For a discussion of the causes of capital accumulation and how it is promoted by anything which increases the efficiency of production, see below, pp. 634–636.

118. Cf. *Income and Wealth of the United States,* p. 82. (Raymond Goldsmith indicates a significantly lower range. See ibid., p. 297.) In contrast with the previous estimates cited of the ratio of capital to national income in that period, which estimates included the value of land in capital, capital is here presented simply as the value of structures and producers' equipment, exclusive even of the value of business inventories. However, it is doubtful that the inclusion of business inventories would make the capital-output ratio significantly larger.

119. The use of these percentages is based on the fact that two-thirds of an increase of 1½ percent of the population as a whole is 1 percent of the population as a whole and 2 percent of half the population. Likewise, one-third of the 1½ percent increase in the population as a whole is ½ percent of the population as a whole and 1 percent of half the population.

120. On this essential point, see below, pp. 634–636.

121. See below, ibid.

122. I deal with the vital subjects of unemployment and the determinants of the average worker's standard of living—his real wages—throughout Chapters 13 and 14, below. See also pp. 938–942.

123. Actually, of course, the quantity of gold that has been mined is probably as small compared with the quantity that remains to be mined as is the quantity of most other minerals that has been mined compared with the quantity of them that remains to be mined. As I have shown, in reality, the useable, accessible supply of everything, even including gold, can be indefinitely increased by virtue of man enlarging his knowledge of and physical power over the world and the universe. See above, pp. 63–66.

124. See below, pp. 503–506 and 517–526.

CHAPTER 10

MONOPOLY VERSUS FREEDOM OF COMPETITION

1. The Meaning of Freedom and of Freedom of Competition

If there is anything for which capitalism is more strongly denounced than its competition, it is its alleged *lack* of competition and tendencies toward monopoly. These denunciations stem in large part from a failure properly to understand the meaning of freedom of competition and of monopoly. The terms are usually understood in the light of the anarchic rather than of the rational concept of freedom.[1]

According to the rational concept of freedom, of course, freedom means *the absence of the initiation of physical force*—in particular, on the part of the government. Viewed in a positive light, freedom is the freedom to *do* whatever one is otherwise capable of doing, unconstrained by the initiation of physical force.

Applied to the realm of competition, if a man possesses only a few thousand dollars of capital or no capital at all, freedom of competition for him does not mean the ability to enter into competition with General Motors. It *does* mean the ability to do whatever he is capable of doing with the few thousand dollars of capital he has (or with his abilities unaided by any capital)—without being stopped by the government. It means, for example, that if he can afford to buy a taxicab or a liquor store and judges that that is what is best for him to do, he will not be stopped from doing it by licensing laws. It means that if he is capable of working at a job and can find an employer willing to hire him, he will not be stopped from working by minimum-wage laws or by laws giving co-

ercive powers to labor unions—in both of which cases a part of the supply of labor is forced into unemployment by wages rates being forcibly raised above the market level. And if a man (or a company) does have the capital required to compete with General Motors, and wishes to compete, freedom of competition means for him that he will not be stopped by a tariff or by antitrust laws preventing mergers and the growth of big business. It means, for example, that Toyota and Nissan will not be stopped and that if U.S. Steel, Exxon, Boeing, or IBM want to enter the automobile business, they will not be stopped.

Freedom of competition does not mean that one is automatically able to compete—that one automatically has the necessary knowledge, capital, or whatever else may be required to compete. It means only that insofar as one *does have the means of competing,* one will not be stopped from exercising those means by the initiation of physical force.

The fact that freedom of competition does not guarantee that one will be able to compete—the fact that freedom in general does not guarantee that one will be able to do whatever it is one would like to do, because freedom does not by itself supply the necessary means—does not reduce freedom to the status of a trivial luxury capable of being enjoyed only by the wealthy, as the Marxists claim. Freedom, including the freedom of competition, is a vital necessity for everyone. It means, in essence, *the freedom of opportunity*—the freedom to exploit the opportunities one already has, and so later on be capable of enjoying greater opportunities.[2] It means, for example, that an impoverished black youth is able to take a low-paying job, if that is the best he can find, and then with the experience and skill he gains from that job go on to something better. It means that he is able to keep the income he earns from that job and, if he wishes, save it to buy a taxicab or any other kind of business he can afford and so further increase his ability to earn money. Freedom, thus understood—as the freedom of opportunity—is vital to everyone.[3]

Not only does everyone need freedom for himself, but he also needs freedom for others because he enormously benefits from their freedom. Everyone in the world is vastly more prosperous because Thomas Edison and Henry Ford and all the other great inventors and industrialists had the freedom to implement their ideas and bring their products to the market. The general gains from the freedom of lesser men are no less real.[4] For example, there is a gain to everyone who uses such services as those of barbers and tailors if those best able to provide such services are free to provide them. The freedom of all is a condition in which every industry can be carried on by those best suited in the world to conduct it. It is a condition in which each can be supplied by the best choice of suppliers. This, indeed, is the meaning of the freedom of competition: *that every industry and occupation should be legally open to everyone who judges that he is equipped to succeed in it and who wishes to try and that then the buyers should be free to choose among them.*

High Capital Requirements as an Indicator of Low Prices and the Intensity of Competition

In connection with this discussion, it should be realized that the existence of high capital requirements as a condition for being able to compete does not constitute a "barrier to entry" in any legitimate sense, despite the frequency of the claim that it does. The fact that in present conditions it may take a billion dollars or more to build a competitive-sized automobile factory or steel mill does not represent a violation of the freedom of entry or competition. On the contrary, it is the result of the fact that in order to be profitable, it is necessary to produce at low costs, thanks precisely to the freedom of competition. The high capital is necessary only in order to produce on a large scale and with the use of capital-intensive methods of production, both of which are means of achieving low costs of production. If the achievement of low costs of production were not necessary, then neither would be the substantial sums that must be invested to reduce costs. High capital requirements would not exist.

What makes it necessary to achieve low costs of production is the fact that others, who employ large sums of capital and who thereby achieve low costs of produc-

tion, sell at correspondingly low prices, which makes it impossible to succeed in the business while producing at the high costs resulting from the lack of sufficient capital. In the simplest possible terms, the high capital of General Motors and the other major automobile companies does, indeed, stop people with capitals as limited as those of neighborhood grocers from producing automobiles. This is as it should be. In order for people to be able to succeed in the automobile business with such limited capitals, automobiles would have to be produced without the aid of substantial machinery or the use of such things as moving assembly lines (which require a very large volume of output). As a result, they would have to be produced at an extremely high cost, comparable to the cost that existed in the early years of the industry. And thus they would have to sell at correspondingly high prices.

It also follows from this discussion that in order to achieve the competitive advantages of the possession of a large capital, a firm *must* sell at prices that reflect its low costs of production. If it does not, then it opens the door to firms with smaller capitals and higher costs of production, that can then succeed in the business and possibly accumulate the capital necessary themselves to achieve the lower level of costs. Thus, high capital requirements are the result of the freedom of competition, which results in low costs of production and low prices, and which necessitates the possession of a substantial capital where that is the means of achieving low costs and low prices.

High capital requirements are an illustration of the principle that under the freedom of competition and the freedom of entry the only way one keeps others out of a field is by producing better and more economically. Where the freedom of competition and the freedom of entry are violated, on the other hand, it is the better, more economical producers, including those with larger capitals, who are kept out—by means of the initiation of physical force.

2. The Political Concept of Monopoly and Its Application

Consistent with the concepts I have expounded of freedom in general and of freedom of competition in particular, is what I call *the political concept of monopoly.* According to the political concept of monopoly, *monopoly is a market, or part of a market, reserved to the exclusive possession of one or more sellers by means of the initiation of physical force by the government, or with the sanction of the government.*

Monopoly exists insofar as the freedom of competition is violated, with the freedom of competition being understood as the absence of the initiation of physical force as the preventive of competition. Where there is no initiation of physical force to violate the freedom of competition, there is no monopoly. The freedom of competition is violated only insofar as individuals are excluded from markets or parts of markets by means of the initiation of physical force. Monopoly is thus a market or part of a market reserved to the exclusive possession of one or more sellers by means of the initiation of physical force. It is thus something *imposed* upon the market from without—by the government. (Private individuals—gangsters—can initiate force to reserve markets only if the government allows it and thereby sanctions it.)

Thus, monopoly is not something which emerges from the normal operation of the economic system, and which the government must control. That mistaken view is based on the *economic concept* of monopoly, which will be considered later in this chapter. The economic concept of monopoly is the corollary of the anarchic concept of freedom and its implication that private individuals can violate the freedom of speech or press by their mere refusal to provide others with the material means for spreading their ideas and can violate the freedom of competition by virtue merely of their possession of larger capitals and superior abilities.[5] Rationally understood, monopoly is external to the normal operation of the economic system and is, as I say, imposed by the government or with the government's sanction. It is, as it was originally understood, an exclusive grant of government privilege, such as was extended by English monarchs in earlier centuries to the British East India Company and to various guilds of producers or merchants.

As subsequent discussion will show, the leading examples of monopoly rationally understood, that is, according to the political concept of monopoly, are exclusive government franchises, licensing laws, tariffs, the operation of minimum-wage and prounion legislation, government-owned or government-subsidized enterprises, a socialist society, and, however surprising, the antitrust laws.

Monopoly Based on Exclusive Government Franchises

Exclusive government franchises reserve markets to the exclusive possession of the holders of the franchises, and do so by means of the government's initiation of force. Leading examples of this category of monopoly are electric, gas, and water service, cable television, local telephone service, and, in many localities, local bus service. In each case, no one but the holder of the government's franchise is legally allowed to sell the service in question in the particular market. Anyone else who might wish to sell the service in that market is stopped by law and the threat of physical force that stands behind the law. Since the provision of such service does not represent an act of force, stopping its provision by means of the use of force represents an *initiation* of force—an act of aggression—on the government's part.

In connection with monopoly in the form of exclusive government franchises, what is essential is not the fact that there is only one supplier. There might well be just one supplier in these cases under the freedom of competition. What is essential to monopoly is that physical force is initiated in order to keep out of the market sellers who might otherwise wish to be in it—that the determination of the fact that there is just one seller, and which particular one seller, is made by means of the initiation of physical force, not by the freedom of competition. Under the freedom of competition, Alcoa was for many years practically the only seller of aluminum ingot in the United States. Nevertheless, it was *not* a monopoly, according to the political concept of monopoly. This was because its position did not rest on the initiation of physical force, but on its ability and willingness to produce and sell its aluminum at prices that were profitable to it, but yet too low for any potential competitor to be profitable.

It is possible, indeed, likely, that economies of scale associated with most or all of the cases presently falling under the category of exclusive-government-franchise monopoly would make possible a situation similar to that of Alcoa. Like the case of Alcoa, a single electric or gas company providing service in a given area would not constitute a monopoly, if, in order to be in that position, it offered its customers lower rates than any other potential supplier offered. What would be crucial is that under the freedom of competition, precisely this is what it would have to do, if it wished to be the sole supplier. Indeed, in order to become the sole supplier, it would almost certainly have to offer its customers *contractual guarantees* concerning its rates, so that they would not have to fear temporary arbitrary increases in the period in which competitors did not yet have the time required to enter the field. In other words, to become the sole supplier of gas or electricity and so forth, under the freedom of competition, a firm would have to offer a long-term, contractually guaranteed price that was below what its potential competitors were prepared to offer.

To guard against possible misunderstanding, it is necessary to say explicitly that exclusive *private* franchises, such as the right to own and operate a Coca Cola bottling plant, or a McDonald's hamburger restaurant, do not represent any kind of initiation of force. The name and formula of Coca Cola and the name, supplies, and counseling provided by McDonald's are the private property of these concerns, and thus they have the right to determine who is and who is not to receive the use of that property. It would be an initiation of force—theft—for anyone to use that property against their will.

The government, on the other hand, should not own any property whose use it may give to some and withhold from others, because it is properly nothing more than the agent of the people—of each and every person equally. Apart from what is required for such things as police stations, courthouses, and military bases, which are necessary for the carrying out of its rightful and strictly delimited functions, it certainly should not, and for the most part does not, own the land of the country. The citizens individually and in private voluntary associations are properly the owners of the land and all that is upon it. They alone have the right to determine who can and who cannot use their private property. In denying anyone the right to undertake economic activity, the government simply initiates the use of force.

Licensing Law Monopoly

Licensing laws create monopolies by virtue of initiating force to reserve markets to the exclusive possession of the license holders. Examples of monopoly based on licensing laws are the occupations of accountant, barber, beautician, contractor, dentist, lawyer, liquor store owner, optician, pharmacist, physician, psychologist, teacher, and taxicab driver. Only the holders of the licenses are legally allowed to pursue the field in question. All others are excluded by means of the initiation of physical force.

Of course, licensing laws are defended, on the grounds that they are necessary to public health or safety, or some other such high purpose. But the fact is, they keep out of fields suppliers who otherwise would be in them—suppliers with whom the public would be glad to deal voluntarily, without any form of force or fraud being present. Their effect is always to deprive the buyers of services they could have had, to raise the price of the services they are allowed to receive, to elevate the incomes of the license holders, and to depress the incomes of those who are excluded from the licensed fields and forced to crowd into other, less-well-paying fields.

It may well be the case that licensing sometimes does serve, as its supporters often claim, to raise the minimum level of competence and expertise in a field and thus to guarantee to the buyers a higher level of service than they would have received in its absence. But even if this is true, it is not by any means an advantage to the buyers. It merely means, in many cases, that buyers are forced to buy a higher level of service than they want or need and, if they cannot afford the higher level of service, are forced to do without the service they could have had. The result on this score is comparable, in essence, to a law that would require that the minimum quality of automobiles on the road be no less than, say, that of a five-year-old Chevrolet of average quality. While such a law would undoubtedly raise the average quality level of the cars that remained on the road, it would also operate to prevent many people from driving—namely, those who could not afford anything beyond the quality of the cars they presently drove and whose cars were below the quality of the average five-year-old Chevrolet.

In just this way, medical licensing—the field in which licensing might be thought to be more necessary and proper than in any other—has the paradoxical effect of depriving the poor of medical care altogether.

In the absence of medical licensing, it would not be the case that barbers and butchers would be able to compete as doctors, any more than they can compete in the automobile or steel industry. Competition would establish educational, performance, and other requirements. And it would still be fraud to claim a degree, or any other form of private certification, that one did not have. The new competition in medicine would come from people who today must be content to be registered nurses, pharmacists, paramedics, biologists, and so forth, but who could become qualified to practice important aspects of medicine presently monopolized by the licensed physicians, and do so with a high degree of competence.

These people are present in the ranks of those arbitrarily rejected by today's monopolistically restricted medical schools, or who are deterred from even trying for admission to today's medical schools. They would be able to provide medical care to many who today cannot afford medical care, and even if the medical care they provided was less complete than that provided by most of today's practitioners, it would certainly still be far superior to no medical care at all. Moreover, in serious cases beyond their competence, they could make referrals to doctors of greater expertise than themselves. At the same time, in necessary cases, the poor would be better able to afford the services even of the more qualified doctors, since those services too would be rendered less expensive by the new competition. For many people who had had to use them would also turn to the less expensive services of the new competitors to varying degrees. This would operate both to reduce the price of the more qualified doctors' services, bringing them more within reach of the poor, and to make their time more available to the poor, since it would no longer be in as great demand by the middle class and the wealthy.

In many cases, licensing actually serves no legitimate purpose whatever. It is nothing more than a pretext for imposing arbitrary requirements on prospective suppliers, its only real purpose being to keep the supply down and the price up. For example, requiring barbers and beauticians to take year-long courses on dermatology can have no other purpose but to discourage people from becoming barbers or beauticians and thus to keep up the price of the services of those who do become barbers or beauticians.

Where, as in medicine, and even in home building, there is a legitimate purpose in licensing, that purpose can be achieved without licensing. People want to know with whom they are dealing. That is why they attach so much importance to brandnames and why customer good will is so important. In dealing with doctors and home builders—especially if they could not take for granted the approval of an allegedly all-wise, all-knowing government, bestowed through the conferral of a license—people would insist on an established reputation or on strong endorsements from those with established reputations and whose judgment they trusted. And, of course, insurers (and in home building, lenders as well) could impose their own, additional requirements. Indeed, it is even possible to imagine that the very same employees of the present medical licensing boards, and the very same building inspectors who now work for the government, would stay on as employees of private certification agencies and continue to perform all the legitimate substance of the work they presently perform.

There would be one essential difference, however, that would constitute a fundamental and major improvement. That would be that no one would be compelled to accept the judgment of government officials or of any other group of people. With private certification, not only would the supply of a service be greater and the price correspondingly lower, but, no less important, there would permanently be more chances for new ideas being tried, and thus improvements would come far more rapidly than is possible today. Under private certification, not only would there almost certainly be more than one certification agency in any given occupation, but the individual would always have the right to step outside the system and decide entirely for himself. It would not be necessary, as is now the case, that before trying a new cure for a disease, or a new method of constructing a building, a person would have to wait upon the pleasure of any group of government officials to approve it. If, to take a particularly outrageous example, a person has heart disease, or has suffered a stroke, he could freely buy medications whose effectiveness has already, long-since been proved in Western Europe, to the satisfaction of large numbers of American doctors. Neither he nor his physician would have to fear the licensing power either of a state's medical licensing board or of the federal government's Food and Drug Administration. If an individual is dying of cancer, and cannot be cured by methods endorsed by the present medical establishment, he could freely accept the responsibility of turning to something different.

It is no doubt true that under the freedom of competition, some individuals would act irresponsibly and at the first opportunity turn to quacks. The existence of such people, however, is no reason for denying freedom to everyone else, who would use it to great advantage. Moreover, under freedom, stupidity of choice serves as its own punishment!

If the misuse of freedom by the ignorant and the foolish is what is feared, then a better case can be made for the licensing of politicians and government officials than of doctors or the members of any other profession or trade. This is because here, when people turn to charlatans, the consequences are suffered by all. But, of course, there can be no such thing as the licensing of politicians and government officials, for who would license them, but other politicians and government officials? And what could be more dangerous than to allow politicians and government officials to have such power?

The existence of freedom carries with it the possibility that people will make wrong and even foolish choices. But there is no alternative. That possibility exists *with or without freedom*. The great advantage of freedom is that each individual has the right to make his own choices and need not be bound by the ignorance or stupidity of others. The alternative to freedom is settling matters by force, and here the ignorant and the stupid have the greatest chance to control the outcome and to compel all to go with them. Indeed, the use of force is the only way that those who are knowledgeable and intelligent can be made to follow the lead of those who are ignorant or stupid. The choice, in other words, is not one between people making foolish choices on their own when they live under freedom and wise choices when they live under the control of government officials. The real choice is between at least those who are intelligent and wise making wise choices under freedom, and thereby setting an example for all others to follow, and those who are intelligent and wise being compelled to follow the will of the ignorant and stupid when the initiation of physical force takes the place of freedom.

The premise of a free country is that the citizens are intelligent enough to run their own affairs and, in the time left over from their own affairs, the affairs of their government as well. Citizens who are not qualified to pass judgment on the qualifications of their doctor or building contractor (or on the qualifications of the experts whose advice they accept) are even less qualified to pass judgment on matters of foreign policy or domestic policy. This is certainly not a plea to deprive such citizens of the right to vote—for the reasons just explained (though it certainly can be taken as a good argument for limiting the questions that people have the power to decide by vote, that is, as an argument for limited government). On the contrary, it is a plea simply that people retain and enlarge their freedom of choice in the economic area and, by the natural method of gaining from their right choices and suffering from their wrong choices, be led to make all of their decisions as conscientiously and as wisely as they can.

Before leaving the subject of licensing monopoly, it is necessary to observe that probably far more important than breaking the licensing monopoly presently enjoyed by physicians would be breaking the licensing monopoly presently enjoyed by hospitals. People justly complain of the enormous costs of hospital stays. These costs could be radically reduced by allowing the freedom of competition in hospital care. The cost of hospital stays to patients is enormously higher in many cases than corresponds to the actual cost to the hospitals of providing their services. A thousand dollars a day for a hospital stay is often far out of line with the hospital's own costs that are necessary to provide the service together with an allowance for a competitive rate of profit. Under the freedom of competition, physicians and profit-seeking hospital administrators would be free to cash in on the high profits that could be made by opening their own hospitals. They would be free to concentrate on offering the presently most profitable types of care. The effect would be a decline in the price of such hospital stays to a point corresponding to the actual costs of providing them together with an allowance for the going rate of profit. At the same time, the freedom of competition would permit hospitals to cut their costs of operation and thus to bring rates down to levels reflecting still lower levels of actual cost.[6]

Today there is a great deal of justified outrage over the enormous and ever increasing cost of medical care, and, in response, people assert a right to medical care. But their idea of a right to medical care is a right consistent with the anarchic concept of freedom, that is, an alleged right which is to be implemented without regard to the willingness of others to cooperate. The government is to take money from the taxpayers, at the point of a gun, to implement this alleged right to medical care and it is to hold a gun to the heads of physicians and hospitals to make them supply medical care on the terms and by the methods it imposes. This is a total corruption of the concept of rights. It is, as Ayn Rand would describe it, the assertion of an alleged right to enslave.[7]

What needs to be done to solve the medical crisis is to understand the concept of the right to medical care consistently with the rational concept of freedom and the political concept of monopoly. The right to medical care rationally means *the right to all the medical care one can afford to buy and chooses to buy from any willing provider.*

The medical crisis exists because of a repeated pattern of violation of the right to medical care properly understood. Individuals want to buy medical services from willing providers whom the government excludes from the medical professions by licensing laws. It violates the right of these individuals to buy, and of these providers to sell, medical care. Thus the government monopolizes the medical profession on behalf of its license holders. This makes medical care scarcer and more expensive. The government practices the same policy of exclusion and monopolization in the case of hospitals, again making medical care scarcer and more expensive. The government does exactly the same thing in the case of medications, through the Food and Drug Administration, which creates a systematic monopoly of the drugs and treatment methods it approves by forcibly excluding from the market all other drugs and methods of treatment.

The violations of freedom and individual rights practiced by the government in the pursuit of its policy of medical monopoly are powerfully reinforced by its policy of violating freedom and individual rights in forcing some citizens to pay for the medical care of others. In the face of pervasive monopoly, the policy of pouring ever more taxpayer money into medicine simply represents steadily enlarging the demand in the face of an artificially restricted supply, with the inevitable result that prices continually rise. This process is further powerfully compounded by the fact that medical care is made substantially or even entirely free to large numbers of recipients, who then have no reason to limit the amount of it they use, which, of course, leads to correspondingly large government expenditures to pay for it and to higher rates for paying patients, to whom a substantial part of the burden is shifted.[8]

The solution to the medical crisis is not the implementation of a vicious alleged right to medical care whose actual meaning is a right to enslave, but the implementation of the rational right to medical care. That is, to *end the government's policy of medical monopoly* (and, of course, its policy of forcing some citizens to pay the medical bills of others). It is to make the government recognize the citizen's actual right—his rational right—to obtain medical care from any willing provider and thus to stop the government's forcible exclusion of willing providers from the market.[9]

Tariff Monopoly

Protective tariffs represent the use of force to make foreign producers sell their goods at a higher price than domestic producers and/or less profitably than domestic producers. As such, they represent legislation on behalf of monopoly, in that they attempt to reserve the market, or a larger share of the market, to the exclusive possession of domestic producers.

Protective tariffs (and licensing laws) highlight the fact that monopoly, according to the political concept, is not limited to the case of sole producers protected by the initiation of physical force. It applies equally to cases of *very large numbers* of producers whose market is protected by the initiation of physical force. A tariff monopoly can serve to protect tens of thousands of small, inefficient domestic producers against foreign competition. For example, a protective tariff on wheat in France has the effect of giving a monopoly of the French wheat market, or of a larger share of that market, to French wheat growers. The monopoly of these producers is no less a monopoly merely because of their large number. The market, or their part of the market, is reserved to them by means of the initiation of force. More efficient foreign producers are correspondingly denied the freedom of competition.

The Monopolistic Protection of the Inefficient Many Against the Competition of the More Efficient Few

Both tariffs and licensing laws make possible monopolies shared by large numbers of inefficient, high-cost producers. Such monopolies are no less monopolies when the more efficient, lower-cost producers who are forcibly kept out are small in number—even when there is only just *one* very large, more efficient, lower-cost producer who would otherwise gain the market that is presently monopolized.

The New York City taxicab industry provides a good example of the monopolistic protection of the inefficient many against the competition of the more efficient few.

The number of taxicabs in New York City that can cruise the streets for hire has been forcibly limited since 1937, at slightly below 12,000. Since that time, it has been a legal precondition of operating such a taxi, that one possess a small metal medallion, issued by the city government of New York and affixed to the hood of the cab. To operate a taxicab, one must not only know how to drive and be able to afford to buy a cab. One must possess a further item as well: the precious medallion, which signifies the government's permission that one can do what one already can do. If one does not possess this medallion—this fifth wheel of taxi driving, in terms of its actual physical relationship to the ability to operate a cab—one is in violation of the law and subject to arrest. In this way, the city government of New York reserves the market for taxicabs that cruise the streets, to the exclusive possession of its license holders and excludes all others by the initiation of force.

These medallions, it should be noted, now sell for a price well in excess of $100,000 each. The price of a medallion is the measure of the additional annual income that is to be made by virtue of operating a taxicab at the higher level of rates caused by the licensing requirement and the consequent artificial scarcity of cabs. More precisely, the price of a medallion is the discounted present value of the additional income that is to be made year after year thanks to the monopoly privilege conferred by the possession of the medallion. It is equal to the principal that is necessary to make the additional annual income yield the going rate of profit and interest. If, for example, the additional annual income derived from owning a taxicab with a monopoly privilege is $10,000, while the going rate of profit and interest is 10 percent per year, then $100,000 appears as the value of possessing that privilege year after year. In effect, $100,000 is the amount of capital necessary to make the $10,000 additional income stand as a 10 percent rate of return on capital. The price of the medallion is $100,000, because any lower price would make it possible to earn an above-average rate of profit by owning such a taxicab.

If the licensing requirement for taxicabs were abolished, more cabs would cruise the streets and their competition would drive rates down. In the face of lower rates and the elimination of the extra income presently conferred by the possession of a medallion, the pressure to reduce the costs of operating a taxicab would intensify. This would strongly favor fleet operation over individual operation. It would mean the replacement of thousands of very small, relatively inefficient cab companies, consisting of a single cab and owner-driver, by a relatively small number of much larger, more efficient taxicab companies operating substantial fleets of cabs. The fleets would enjoy such competitive advantages as the ability to keep their cabs on the road for three successive shifts a day, seven days a week; the presence of resident mechanics to minimize down-time for repairs; and the possession of spare cabs, to take the place of those out of operation for repair. Such advantages would enable them to gain vastly greater use from each cab in any given year, and not to be put out of operation—as would an owner driver—by the breakdown of any given cab.

The probable effect of fleet competition would be a decline in taxicab rates to the point where it was simply not economically possible to operate a cab as an individual owner-driver. In this way, the freedom of competition would operate, in this instance, to replace a large number of small relatively inefficient producers with a relatively small number of large, efficient producers.

It is true that it is possible to obtain the economies of fleet operation in New York City even under present circumstances, and that there presently already are some substantial fleets. But the system of monopoly privilege eliminates the *pressure* for cost reductions and thus the adoption of the economies fleets provide. It makes it possible to operate successfully even with relatively inefficient methods. It also stops the fleets from expanding in any other way than by buying additional medallions and thus raising their price still further. In these ways, the system of monopoly privilege in the New York City taxicab industry protects the inefficient many against the competition of the more efficient few.

A similar phenomenon existed in many parts of Europe with respect to the competition of department stores and chain stores, and may still exist in some places. In order to protect large numbers of small merchants from their competition, the establishment of these stores was discouraged or simply prohibited. Here again was a case of monopoly in favor of the inefficient many against the more efficient few.

The implication of this discussion is that monopoly exists, and the freedom of competition is violated, not because there happens to be just one seller in a market, when all have the legal right to enter, but when there are millions in the market, and all *but one* are allowed to enter, with that one otherwise able and willing to enter. In such a case, the market is reserved to the exclusive possession of all but that one. It is monopolized against him. It is monopolized against him even if his entry were to result in his displacing all of the many who are in the market now and thus in his becoming the sole seller. For example, a monopoly would exist in the automobile market even if it were comprised of thousands of small automobile companies and everyone in the world were allowed to enter it with the single exception of the original Henry Ford! Such exclusion of Ford would constitute a monopoly, in violation of the freedom of competition. It would constitute a monopoly even if Ford's entry were to mean that he would then become the sole seller of automobiles, which fact would *not* constitute a monopoly.

In every case, whether a particular monopoly represents the initiation of force to protect one firm against the competition of many firms or many firms against the competition of a few firms or even just one firm, its effect is to protect the less efficient against the more efficient and to raise the price to the buyers of the good or service in comparison with the price that would exist under the freedom of competition.

Monopoly Based on Minimum-Wage and Prounion Legislation: The Exclusion of the Less Able and the Disadvantaged

Minimum-wage and prounion legislation operate to reserve labor markets to the exclusive possession of the reduced number of workers who can be employed at the higher wage rates such legislation establishes. Minimum-wage and prounion legislation forcibly exclude from the market the additional number of workers who could be employed at the lower wage rates that the freedom of competition would establish. Such legislation also tends to reserve labor markets to the exclusive possession of *the more skilled workers,* by virtue of impairing the ability specifically of the less skilled workers to compete through the acceptance of lower wage rates. For as we saw in the last chapter, the acceptance of lower wage rates is the essential means by which those who are less skilled are able to compete with those who are more skilled.[10]

Minimum-wage and prounion legislation undermine the ability of the less skilled to compete with the more skilled in two ways. As in the case of the bricklayers able to lay different numbers of bricks per hour, with every forced increase in the wages of less skilled labor relative to the wages of more skilled labor, the ability of the less skilled to compete with the more skilled who are already present in the occupation is reduced.[11] Thus, for example, being able to accept a wage rate of five dollars an hour allows the worker who can lay only twenty bricks per hour to compete with a worker who can lay forty bricks per hour and who earns ten dollars an hour. Requiring that the worker who is capable of laying only twenty bricks per hour be paid more than five dollars an hour destroys his ability to compete.

In addition, with every forced increase in wage rates, the jobs of the less skilled become attractive to a larger number of more skilled workers, who otherwise would not have considered them. This is because standing outside of almost every occupation is a continuum of more skilled workers who could perform that occupation more efficiently than the people who presently perform it. In a free labor market, they do not attempt to perform it because the wages they receive in their present occupations are higher than those they could obtain in the less skilled occupation, even with their advantage in efficiency. But with every forced increase in the wages of the relatively less skilled occupation, such as results from minimum-wage or prounion legislation, the field is made more attractive to the more skilled workers.

Thus, for example, to the extent that a bricklayers' union could impose a minimum scale above five dollars an hour, the effect would be not only to undermine the ability of the twenty-brick-an-hour workers to compete with the more skilled, more efficient bricklayers already in the field, but to attract into the field *an additional number* of more skilled, more efficient bricklayers who presently work in other fields. For as the union raised the minimum hourly pay scale, the average cost per brick laid would also rise, and as that happened, bricklaying would become a more attractive occupation to workers presently employed elsewhere. For example, a thirty-cent cost per brick laid would mean that a worker capable of laying forty bricks an hour could earn twelve dollars an hour as a bricklayer instead of ten dollars an hour, which is the rate corresponding to a twenty-five cent cost per brick laid. In the same way, a thirty-five cent cost per brick laid would mean that such a worker could now earn fourteen dollars an hour, and so on.

In these ways, the effect of minimum-wage and pro-union legislation is not only to reduce the number employed, but to exclude specifically those who are less skilled. Thus, such legislation monopolizes labor markets specifically against this group.

It should be realized that prounion legislation has this effect even though it tends also, or even predominantly, to raise the wage rates of more skilled workers as well as those of less skilled workers. In bringing about a rise in the wages of more skilled workers, prounion legislation operates against the interests of less skilled workers in two respects. First, it operates against the interests of the less skilled or less efficient workers within whatever higher-skill category it raises wage rates. If, for example, it raises the wage rates of carpenters or plumbers, it operates to prevent the less skilled or less efficient carpenters or plumbers from being competitive through the acceptance of lower wages than the more skilled or more efficient carpenters or plumbers, for it establishes a minimum scale that is above the wage rates that are necessary for these workers to be competitive. Second, it operates to reduce wage rates and/or cause unemployment among groups of wage earners in skill categories below the ones in which it forces wage increases. This latter effect comes about because of a spillover of the workers who are displaced, into lower-skill fields.

For example, the lower-skilled carpenters or plumbers who are displaced must turn elsewhere for employment. They must turn to fields with lower skill requirements on the whole than carpentry or plumbing, such as driving a taxicab or waiting on tables. Their turning to such other fields increases the supply of labor in those fields and tends to cause a fall in wage rates in them. If the fall in wage rates in those other fields is allowed to occur, then the effect is that the less skilled carpenters and plumbers, and the other workers already in the occupations they enter, must take lower wage rates than they could have had under the freedom of competition. In other words, the monopoly legislation raises the wage rates of some workers and reduces the wage rates of others. If, however, prounion or minimum-wage legislation prevents a fall in wage rates in those other fields, then the effect is greater unemployment in those fields. And that unem-

ployment will tend to be concentrated among the least skilled people capable of performing those jobs. For the displaced carpenters and plumbers, if they are able to apply their presumably greater capacity for acquiring skill to the new occupations they turn to, will render some of those already in those fields less skilled by comparison. These others will then become the workers unemployed in those fields. And they, in turn, if they do not themselves simply join the ranks of the unemployed, will have to turn elsewhere, with a repetition of the same results on a still lower rung of skill.

In these ways, prounion legislation and minimum-wage legislation tend in the last analysis to do the most harm to the least skilled members of the economic system. At every stage, it is the less skilled against whom the labor markets are monopolized by minimum-wage and prounion legislation.

Minimum-wage and prounion legislation do not handicap exclusively the less skilled. In creating an artificial surplus of workers and the necessity of choosing among them, they also create an opportunity for the play of such factors as personal favoritism, cronyism, and racial and other forms of group prejudice. With the ability to compete by means of lower wage rates eliminated, wherever there are no discernible differences in skill among the applicants for jobs, it is such factors that tend to determine the decision of who will be employed. (And insofar as the decision of who is employed is made by labor unions rather than employers, such factors can easily outweigh differences in skill.)

Factors of this kind would not play a role in a labor market governed by the freedom of competition. In such a labor market, competition would reduce wage rates to the point where all could be employed, including those who labored under any form of social prejudice and who would be employed at a somewhat lower wage than others—to the extent necessary to offset the prejudice.

It should be realized that the freedom of competition makes it possible for people to overcome the handicap not only of a lower degree of skill, but also of such a thing as being the victims of prejudice. From an economic point of view, racial or ethnic prejudice can be taken as the equivalent of a mistaken and, indeed, irrational presumption that the members of some group are uniformly of a lower degree of skill than the members of other groups. In a free labor market, the existence of prejudice by itself—in the absence of the initiation of physical force by the government or by private groups acting with the sanction of the government—would not stop the employment of the members of the disadvantaged group. They would be employed, but, temporarily, at wage rates somewhat lower than other workers doing the same kind of work. The discount in their wages would compensate for their presumed lack of ability.

As we saw in Chapter 6, to the extent that in fact the members of this group were as good workers as the members of other groups, any discount in their wages would serve to make their employment particularly profitable, thereby creating an incentive for their greater employment, and thereby tending to *eliminate* any discount in their wages. We also saw that the same principle would apply to the entry of the members of any group against which prejudice exists into the higher levels of employment.[12] In addition we saw that this sequence of developments cannot occur if it is stopped by the initiation of physical force, such as that practiced by bigoted local governments in the arbitrary exercise of their powers, or by organizations acting with the sanction of such governments, such as the Ku Klux Klan.[13]

In the Northern United States, racial prejudice does not appear to have been a major policy of local governments, and equal pay for equal work has long since become the rule of the market in the occupations where blacks are already accepted. Here what has held blacks back is precisely such measures of allegedly enlightened and liberal government intervention as minimum-wage and prounion legislation. This legislation works against blacks in particular not because that is the motive or intent of its authors, but because blacks, for historical reasons, are disproportionately represented in the ranks of the unskilled, and are thus disproportionately forced into the ranks of the unemployed by this legislation. Furthermore, minimum-wage and prounion legislation causes blacks not only to be unemployed, but to remain permanently low skilled. It condemns them to a lifetime of unemployment and poverty, in which they cannot gain their first job because, given their existing low level of skills resulting from such factors as lack of education, they would have to accept wages below the legally prescribed minimum. And because they cannot obtain their first job, they are prevented from raising their level of skills through experience gained on the job, and thus becoming capable of being employed later on at a wage greater than the minimum wage. As things stand, unable to develop their skills through employment, they remain permanently incapable of performing work even as valuable as the minimum wage. And so they must remain permanently unemployed.

However surprising and however paradoxical it may appear, the fact is that the whole panoply of government intervention constitutes virtual monopoly legislation against the poor and the disadvantaged.[14] Precisely they are the ones whom it excludes from the market. The effect of this monopoly legislation against the poor and disadvantaged is to throw them into unemployment and keep them from

ever demonstrating their abilities in the higher levels of employment. Thus, it both perpetuates their lack of skills and maintains the existence of prejudice against them.

An important phenomenon paralleling the exclusion of the poor and the disadvantaged from the labor market by the kinds of government intervention discussed here is, of course, their exclusion from the market for medical services, as the result of government licensing requirements, which was described earlier in this section. A further major example of the harm done to the poor by government intervention is their exclusion from the housing market, and its manifestation in the growing phenomenon of homelessness. Zoning laws, government building codes, the compulsory withdrawal of land from development, laws that compel home builders to deal with labor unions and thus to suffer the artificially high wage rates and inefficiencies imposed by the unions, rising property taxes, rent control, urban renewal—all of these are ways in which the government causes either an increase in the cost of building and operating housing or a decrease in the existing supply of housing. The people who can least afford the higher costs imposed are, of course, the poor. Efforts to deal with this problem through rent control destroy the profitability of maintaining the rental housing of the poor in particular, since such housing offers the least margin for absorbing the rising costs resulting from inflation and the growing volume of government regulation. The result is that such housing is the first to be abandoned by landlords, and the poor are then left to live without running water, heat, or plumbing. At the same time, urban renewal prides itself on physically tearing down the "blighted" areas that represent much of the housing of the poor.[15]

Homelessness (in the cases in which the homeless are not psychotic and actually prefer to live in the streets) is a consequence of the above factors coupled with government health and safety requirements setting minimum standards for housing. In a growing number of cases, the poor are simply unable to afford housing that meets the government's standards. The government then forcibly dispossesses them from housing that it considers substandard. At that point, they simply have nowhere to go—they are homeless. Just as in the case of medical licensing, the government's action is analogous to passing a law—in the name of a high sounding phrase like public safety—banning all cars from the road that are more than five years old. Such a law would primarily stop poor people from being able to have a car. The minimum standards for housing do the same for housing.

Ironically, the low quality of the housing occupied by the poor is in large part the direct result of government efforts to impose minimum standards. The imposition of these standards in any given locality and the corresponding expulsion of the poor from that locality serves to make the housing problems in surrounding localities all the worse, as a larger number of poor people are forced to compete for the diminished supply of housing that still remains open to them. Because of minimum standards imposed by various localities, poor people who might have had some kind of apartment to themselves, are forced to live elsewhere, under still worse conditions—perhaps in someone's garage. If the housing market were free of government interference, they would not have to live in a garage, or even in the housing they are presently driven from before they get to the garage—but in housing considerably better than that and tending to get better still, with all the improvements a free economy is capable of achieving over time in housing and all other lines. Instead, however, they are driven into the streets.

Government-Owned and Government-Subsidized Enterprises as Monopoly

Government-owned and government-subsidized enterprises represent monopoly, in that markets or parts of markets are reserved to their exclusive possession by means of the initiation of physical force. Government-subsidized enterprises, of course, are a category which includes all government-owned enterprises, inasmuch as the initial resources of government-owned enterprises are provided by the government and their subsequent losses are covered by the government.

The funds of all enterprises supported by the government are obtained by means of the initiation of force against the taxpayers, who certainly do not pay taxes voluntarily for such purposes. At the same time, the subsidies make possible those enterprises' possession of markets, or parts of markets, to which other suppliers are denied access. Competitors of the subsidized enterprises cannot gain their markets even if they are more efficient and offer better products, for the subsidized enterprises are enabled to sell their products at a loss, and even to give them away free of charge. Thus, government-subsidized enterprises are monopolies: their markets are reserved to them on a foundation of the initiation of force against the taxpayers, which then makes possible their ability to retain their markets despite the economic superiority of competitors.

The monopoly position of government-owned enterprises, and other government-subsidized enterprises, can be buttressed by the initiation of force against parties other than the taxpayers—above all, the initiation of force directly against competitors or potential competitors. The government-owned postal service in the United States is an example of this phenomenon. Here, in order to limit its losses, the government prohibits important

categories of competition, such as the delivery of first class mail, which apparently would be highly profitable to competitors at the government's present rates. It simply declares most of the roads of the United States to be "post roads," and then prohibits the carrying of private first-class mail over the post roads. Whoever would carry such mail would be in violation of the law, and would face the threat of fines and imprisonment.

An even more important example of monopoly than the postal service, in the category of government-owned or government-subsidized enterprises, is the public education system. The total absence of tuition charges in the public elementary and secondary schools, and the substantially lower tuition charges in the public colleges and universities, which tax-financed subsidies make possible, enable the public education system to retain the far greater share of the education market despite its clear inferiority in comparison with private schools.

As the result of the subsidies the government system receives and thus its ability to charge prices below cost—indeed, no price at all—it is not sufficient that a private school or college simply be perceptibly better in order to induce customers to give it their patronage rather than the public system. To take advantage of the superiority of the private schools, students or their parents must be prepared to pay the *full* tuition in order to gain what is merely an *improvement* on what is offered in the public system for nothing or for very little. In effect, they are placed in a position in which to choose a private school or college, they must pay the full price for what, from their perspective, is not the full product, but only a qualitative increment in the full product, because they already have the basic product from the public system for nothing or for very little.

In these conditions, before people will switch from the public schools and colleges to the private schools and colleges, they must regard the mere superiority of the private school or college as so great that it justifies paying the whole price of the education. In effect, this requires that to obtain a customer, a private school or college must be able to offer a doubled product for just one tuition. To be competitive with the subsidized school system, it must offer one part of its product, equal to what the government provides, for free. It can earn tuition revenue only on the other part of its product, which must be judged to be of such importance as to justify the payment of the whole tuition. And it must produce this doubled product at no greater cost than the tuition it is able to charge for the mere part of it—indeed, at an even lower cost, to the extent it wants to have a profit.

This is *unfair* competition. It is unjust, immoral competition. It is competition based on the initiation of force. It is not the competition of a free market, but the practice of monopoly—the excluding of competitors by means of the initiation of force.

In the long run, public education does not, as its supporters believe, make it possible for students to obtain education who would otherwise not obtain education. On the contrary, it serves to deny education to students who would otherwise have obtained it.

In making it impossible for private schools to be commercially successful, it prevents all those improvements in quality and efficiency from coming into being that would take place in education under the competitive quest to make profits and avoid losses, and which would eventually bring a much higher quality education within the reach of all than is now available even to the wealthiest. In addition, it precludes any significant competitive barrier to deterioration in the education it itself offers.

Because it is financed by subsidies, public education has the potential to decline in quality all the way to the point where it becomes clear to most people that what it offers is no longer worth even a zero price. Only at that point does private education achieve a decisive competitive advantage in the mass market and threaten the public school system and its bureaucracy with economic extinction.

Thus, the consequence of public education is the prevention of improvements in education and, ultimately, the destruction of such education as exists. For these reasons, its ultimate effect is to deprive people of education who could have obtained it, not to promote education.

What public education accomplishes is that education is supplied without the benefit of the incentive of profit and loss in an environment of freedom of competition. If education had to operate in the same basic economic context as the automobile industry or grocery business, a powerful incentive would exist to improve quality and reduce costs. For this would be the way to increase profits. Any school or chain of schools that introduced any perceptible improvement in education would have a substantial increase in its profits. Students and their parents would want to deal with it, not its less efficient competitors: it would be giving them more for their money. Similarly, if it succeeded in cutting its costs and could operate profitably at a lower level of tuition, it would also enjoy a large expansion in business, as a larger part of the market came to prefer to deal with it, because its tuition charges were now lower than its competitors'.

In response to the competitive pressure of the loss of business to the schools which improved their quality and efficiency, all the other schools would be compelled to improve their quality and efficiency, or else be driven out of business. As the schools in this latter group caught up,

it would no longer be possible for the schools that had introduced the improvements to continue to make exceptional profits. To go on making exceptional profits, they would now have to introduce further improvements, with the same ultimate results. Thus, the basis would exist for continuous improvements in quality and efficiency, for the benefit of the buying public. All of this is simply the operation of the uniformity-of-profit principle applied to education.[16]

But, of course, with public education, there is no incentive of profit and loss. There is nothing to be gained within the system by introducing improvements; nor is there anything to be lost within the system in failing to match the performance of others. A loss of students, whether it results from an improvement in the performance of other schools or from a decline in the performance of one's own school, does not mean a loss out of the school superintendent's pocket or out of the pocket of anyone who sits on the local school board. At the same time, the public schools' shield of a zero or minimal tuition charge greatly reduces the volume of any additional business that any private school could obtain by virtue of improving its quality or reducing its costs within the range of what is presently feasible. As matters stand, the potential market for commercially successful private education is confined to an extremely narrow one, constituted by the children of the very well-to-do, who can afford to pay the whole price of an education for an incremental improvement.

Commercial private education is seriously hampered by the existence of costly legal requirements mandating such things as a school's provision of a cafeteria, gymnasium, library, and so forth, and limiting its ability to adopt more economical educational methods in still other respects as well—for example, requirements concerning class size, the ratio of full-time faculty to students, the minimum education of faculty, and the number of hours of in-class instruction. Its development is still further hampered by the fact that the present hostile environment fosters the tradition of noncommercial private education, in which even private education is largely subsidized—by wealthy individuals and religious organizations. In this environment, commercial private education is faced with obstacles that may simply be too great for it to overcome. It is greatly limited both in its ability to reduce costs and improve quality and in the additional market it can gain should it manage, despite all obstacles, somehow to do so. Thus, under present conditions, it is virtually impossible for it to develop the momentum of progressive improvement that would characterize it under the freedom of competition. Indeed, under present conditions, it is next to impossible for it to attract the kind of talent that would be capable of achieving major improvements in the first place. For those who are capable of accomplishing something are not prepared to waste their time in futile efforts to move an uncomprehending bureaucracy.

The position of private education today, and that of education as a whole, is analogous to what the position of the automobile industry would be if the production of all the low- and medium-priced models were in the hands of the government, which subsidized their production to the point of giving these models away for nothing—indeed, of compelling every adult to accept one for nothing—while the privately owned portion of the automobile industry were confined to the production of very expensive models, and essentially prohibited from cutting its costs. In such circumstances, the only significant force that could operate in favor of the growth of the private automobile industry would be the total collapse in the quality of the government's automobiles. Just so, the only significant factor operating in favor of the growth of private education today is the continuous decline in the quality of public education.

In addition to public education and the postal service, government ownership of railroads, bus, and subway lines, and enterprises producing electric power, such as the Tennessee Valley Authority, represents cases of monopoly. The market of these enterprises too is reserved by the initiation of force against the taxpayers in order to provide subsidies that enable them to sell at prices below those that private competitors must charge. Government-owned roads and highways must also be placed in this category.

The Antitrust Laws as Promonopoly Legislation

However surprising it may seem, the *antitrust laws constitute promonopoly legislation.* They reserve markets to the exclusive possession of all but those who in a state of freedom of competition would occupy them. They monopolize markets precisely against the most capable and efficient firms, which, in their absence, would be able to be in those markets, and which instead, because of their existence, are today forcibly excluded from them. They prevent the capable newcomer from entering an industry—for example, they would almost certainly operate to prevent General Motors from entering the steel industry in any significant way. They prevent the capable firms within an industry from acquiring the markets of the less capable ones by absorbing them in mergers, by buying them out, or by driving them out. Ironically, while endless complaints are made about such things as high capital requirements and lack of technological knowledge as "barriers to entry," no voices are raised to complain about the antitrust laws' forcible exclusion from markets of precisely those firms which

do have the capital and the technological knowledge required to enter them. In serving forcibly to exclude from markets precisely those firms which have the ability to enter and compete in them, the antitrust laws constitute a major violation of the freedom of entry and the freedom of competition. As such, they are among the most important instances of promonopoly legislation.

In the last analysis, what has prevented the antitrust laws from being identified as promonopoly legislation, and has allowed them to be regarded as antimonopoly legislation instead, is the irrationalist mentality underlying the anarchic concept of freedom. This irrationalist mentality places the unreal world of arbitrary desires above the real world of competence and ability. Its concept of the violation of freedom is frustration of arbitrary desires by facts of reality. It does not see as a violation of freedom the frustration of competence and ability by the initiation of physical force. Thus it holds that the existence of such things as high capital requirements are a violation of freedom of competition and a support of monopoly, but does not see as a violation of freedom of competition and a support of monopoly the forcible exclusion from markets of those who do possess the necessary capital and otherwise meet the requirements of reality. Precisely such forcible exclusion from markets is the essence of the operation of the antitrust laws.

The misguided economic rationale behind the antitrust laws will be dealt with later in this chapter.

Socialism as the Ultimate Form of Monopoly

The most extreme form of monopoly imaginable is socialism. A socialist society represents monopoly carried to its ultimate limits. The government of such a society forcibly appropriates all the means of production and thereafter forcibly reserves the entire market of its country to its own exclusive possession. Whoever attempts to compete with it is automatically held to be guilty of the crimes of misappropriating state property and of sabotaging the national economic plan, since the means of production he must use have arbitrarily been declared to be the property of the state and to be required for use in the state's national economic plan.[17] Concentration camps and firing squads are held in constant readiness to deter such competitors and protect the state's monopoly.[18]

3. Further Implications of the Political Concept of Monopoly: High Costs Rather than High Profits

In addition to the fact that monopoly can represent the protection of the inefficient many against the competition of the more efficient few or even just one, it follows from much of the preceding discussion that monopoly does not have any necessary connection with high profitability. There are, of course, instances of monopoly which can be associated with high profitability. Monopolies based on exclusive government franchises would be a leading case if they were not at the same time subjected to rate controls. Licensing monopolies are also cases in which profits tend to be artificially high.

But the monopolies made possible by tariff protection, government subsidies, and the antitrust laws often do not result in any exceptional profitability on the part of the monopolists. (And the monopolies based on minimum-wage and prounion legislation, of course, relate to wage income rather than profit income.) These are cases in which monopoly is established primarily for the purpose of protecting high-cost producers. The same is often true in the case of licensing monopolies as well: for example, the cases of the New York City taxicab industry and the small merchants of many European countries who obtained protection against the competition of department stores and chain stores. In many of these cases, the monopolists would be in the position of having to accept exceptionally low profits or even sustain losses in the absence of the government's help. In the case of government subsidies, they are enabled to afford to go on sustaining losses. Such monopolists turn to the government precisely because their profits would otherwise be exceptionally low or negative. Thus the high monopoly prices that result in these cases serve as much or more to cover the monopolists' high costs, due to inefficiency, as to provide an exceptionally high rate of profit. And, of course, in the case of government-subsidized enterprises, the monopoly prices charged may actually be very low or even zero.

Patents and Copyrights, Trademarks and Brandnames, Not Monopolies

Patents on new inventions, copyrights on books, drawings, musical compositions, and the like, and trademarks and brandnames, do *not* constitute monopolies. True enough, they reserve markets, or parts of markets, to the exclusive possession of the owners of the patents or copyrights, or trademarks or brandnames, and they do so by means of the use of physical force inasmuch as it is against the law to infringe on these rights.

None of these rights represent monopoly, however, because none of them is supported by the *initiation* of physical force. In all of these cases, the government stands ready to use physical force in defense of a preexisting property right established either by an act of personal creation or by the fact of distinct identity. A new invention, or book, drawing, or song, and so forth is the product of a definite individual or group of individuals and belongs to him or them on the same basis that a farmer's crop or a corporation's product belongs to him or it—namely, the right of having created it. A trademark or brandname belongs to its creator on the same basis as his own name—in order to distinguish the distinct identity of the individual and his actions from that of all other individuals and their actions, and thus to be able to assign individual responsibility for the good or bad that is done.

The fact that the government is ready to use force to protect patents and copyrights is fully as proper as that it stands ready to use force to protect farmers and businessmen in the ownership of their physical products and to come to their rescue when they are set upon by trespassers or attacked by robbers. In both cases, it does nothing more than protect the rights of producers to their products. In protecting trademarks and brandnames, it does nothing more than when it protects individuals from impersonation by others. It acts to enable them to be recognized for the good or bad they do, and thus to gain or lose accordingly.

The existence of patents and copyrights, and trademarks and brandnames, like all other protection of property rights, serves to increase the supply of goods and services—by making it possible for those who are the cause of the increase to benefit from the improvements they make. It thus serves to reduce prices and to increase everyone's buying power as time goes on.[19]

It is true that at any given time, taking for granted the existence of the most recent batch of improvements, introduced in the expectation that those responsible would benefit from them, it might be possible to achieve a temporary acceleration in the increase in the supply of goods and services by abolishing patents and copyrights. Such a temporary increase would be comparable in its ultimate significance to the abolition of the property rights of any other group of producers, such as storekeepers and manufacturers, and allowing mobs to sack their shops and warehouses. A very short-lived gain would be followed by a permanent loss of future supplies—in this case, further new inventions and new ideas. This is because no one would invest years of effort and perhaps millions of dollars of capital in the development of a new invention only to find that as soon as he brought it to market, a competitor who purchased a working model would have the benefit of all that effort and capital just for the price of the working model, and that he, the innovator, would probably be unable to profit from his efforts because of the rapid fall in the price of the product that would follow in such a situation. Ultimately, the prevalence of such conditions would cause not only the cessation of further economic progress, but also actual economic decline, as the result of the inability to offset the operation of the law of diminishing returns in mining and agriculture, something which it is possible to do only on the basis of continuing technological progress.[20]

The same basic principle would apply to the abolition of trademarks and brandnames, which would result in producers losing the incentive to increase or even maintain the quality of their goods, inasmuch as their goods would be rendered indistinguishable from those of everyone else, and consumers would thus have no way of singling them out for purchase. For example, imagine what conditions would be like if every soft-drink manufacturer could call his product "Coca Cola" if he wished, or if every computer manufacturer could sell his machines as made by IBM. All the efforts of Coca Cola and IBM, and of every other producer who tried to distinguish his product by its superior quality, would be wasted, because the buying public would have no way of distinguishing his product from the rest and thus no way of giving it the preference it deserved. Thus, there would no longer be any special profit in producing a superior product. The result would be that no one would attempt to produce a superior product. By the same token, no loss would attach to producing inferior products that were rendered indistinguishable, with the result that major declines in the quality of products would ensue.

Thus, contrary to monopoly, patents and copyrights, and trademarks and brandnames, operate to increase supplies and reduce prices, while their abolition would result in the opposite. Indeed, their existence must be considered *a requirement of the freedom of competition,* and their abolition as constituting the establishment of monopoly! Their existence upholds the fundamental freedom of individuals to be secure in their property and to compete on that basis. Their abolition would reserve markets to the dull and incompetent by means of the initiation of force against the intellectual property of those who had new ideas and something better to offer. Their abolition would thus serve to establish the monopoly of the dull and incompetent by forcibly depriving the intelligent and competent of the benefit of their intelligence and competence, and thereby forcibly excluding them from the market.

Because patents and copyrights protect intellectual property, their duration must necessarily be limited. It must be long enough to make it worthwhile to bring new products and new creations to the market, and yet not so long that the thinking of later generations is progressively hobbled by ever growing royalty payments to the descendants of inventors and authors. The present law of seventeen years for patent protection and the lifetime of the author plus fifty years for copyright protection seems to provide just about the proper balance between the rights of the creators of today and those of the thinking men and women and the creators of the future.[21]

All Monopoly Based on Government Intervention; Significance of Monopoly

According to the political concept of monopoly, all monopoly is based on government intervention, which restricts the freedom of entry and competition. The significance of monopoly is that it forcibly bars from the market sellers who would otherwise be capable of being in the market. It thus restricts the range of choice buyers have in suppliers and compels them to deal with less efficient suppliers and to accept higher costs and poorer quality than a free market would require them to accept.

I have shown how monopoly in the form of licensing laws is a principal cause of the growing crisis in medical care, and that to solve the crisis in medical care it is essential to assert the rational right to medical care, that is, the right to medical care from *willing providers.* This means demanding the abolition of all aspects of medical monopoly imposed by the government, which is what keeps people from willing providers of medical care.

I have shown how monopoly in the form of minimum-wage and prounion legislation operates systematically to exclude the less able and the disadvantaged from employment by depriving them of the means of competing through offering to work for lower wages. I have also shown how monopoly in the form of government-owned and government-subsidized enterprises retards economic progress and can destroy economic progress previously achieved, and that this is particularly true in the case of public education today. And, of course, I have shown how protective tariffs and antitrust legislation constitute monopoly.

On the basis of what I have shown, the program of the announced enemies of monopoly should not be, as it has been for many years, the breakup of big business or the government's growing control over big business. Rather, it should be the progressive elimination of government intervention into the economic system. This is what violates the freedom of competition and constitutes monopoly. Political progress should no longer be measured by the ever increasing hobbling of competence and ability by the threat of physical force, but by the steady disappearance of the initiation of force and thus the progressive opening up of the world to competence and ability. Such should be the profreedom, antimonopoly politics of the future. It should stand alongside of, and be an integral part of, the advocacy of economic progress and an industrial society.

4. The Economic Concept of Monopoly

In sharpest contrast to the political concept of monopoly is the economic concept of monopoly. The economic concept of monopoly holds that monopoly emerges from the normal operation of the economic system—not on the basis of the initiation of physical force, but on the basis of mere economic circumstances, and that it nonetheless produces evils of such magnitude that the government must suppress or control it by means of force.

According to the economic concept of monopoly, monopoly exists whenever there is only one supplier of a given good in a given territory. That supplier is said to have a monopoly and to be a monopolist. The economic concept of monopoly considers the "oneness" of the seller to be the essential fact, and makes no distinction between cases in which such a seller has achieved his position by virtue of providing better goods and services at lower prices than anyone else, or has achieved it by means of physical force. No matter how he has achieved his position, it is assumed that it is a position which automatically and inherently gives him the power to inflict great evil. At the same time, the only consideration that the economic concept of monopoly gives to cases in which markets are served by more than one seller is insofar as it can construe them as somehow essentially similar to markets served by only one seller. It gives absolutely no consideration to markets in which large numbers of sellers are present all of whom are protected against the competition of more efficient outsiders. It does not consider this case to constitute monopoly in any sense.

The economic concept of monopoly can be construed in such a way that it embraces hardly anything or almost everything, depending on how broadly or how narrowly one defines a good. For example, if one considers the good "beverage," then all suppliers of water, milk, fruit juice, coffee, tea, cocoa, and soft drinks qualify as competing producers. If one considers the narrower good "soft drink," or the still narrower good "cola" beverage, then the number of suppliers correspondingly diminishes. Finally, if one considers the specific good "Pepsi Cola," or "Coca Cola," the case appears as one of monopoly, for there is ultimately just one supplier of each of those goods, namely, the Pepsi Cola Company or the Coca Cola Company. On a sufficiently narrow definition, almost everything appears as a case of monopoly.

The economic concept of monopoly has been the dominant concept for several generations. Even the classical economists held an important aspect of it, in believing that monopoly can arise in the market itself. As the classical economists used the term, monopoly applied to goods whose supply—for any reason—was incapable of further increase. Such goods—for example, wines produced on land of a special quality that exists only in a very limited extent, and paintings and statues by old masters—even though produced or sold by a substantial number of suppliers, were held to represent monopolies.

Indeed, all cases in which prices were determined by the competition of buyers for a fixed, limited supply were held to represent monopoly prices.[22] Competitive prices were held to be those established by the competition of the sellers, based on the possibility of an increase in supply through additional production.[23]

In the later nineteenth century and the first three decades of the twentieth century, the economic concept of monopoly in its present form was in vogue. But the concept was usually used in such a way as to imply that monopoly was a comparatively rare phenomenon—limited essentially to the cases of public utilities and local public transportation, which were thought to constitute "natural monopolies," in the sense of offering major economic advantages by virtue of being provided by a single source. In this category were electric, gas, water, sewage, and telephone service, and subway, bus, and trolley car lines. Cases in which towns or cities happened to be served by only one railroad, or in which villages were too small to have more than a single general store, were also identified as monopolies. Apart from such cases, the rest of the economic system was assumed to be characterized by "free competition."

In the decades between the end of the Civil War and the start of World War I, growing fears were expressed about the potential spread of monopoly to all branches of industry, coming about through the continued growth of big business, especially as exemplified in the trust movement and the waves of mergers that accompanied it. Despite these fears, monopoly was still thought to be relatively rare in actual practice, for it was unusual for any firm, however large, to have achieved a full 100 percent of the business of any given industry.

Since the 1930s, the economic concept of monopoly has come to be interpreted in ways that make almost the entire economic system fall under the heading of some form of monopoly or other. What has made possible this vast extension of the concept is the introduction of the concepts of "oligopoly" and "monopolistic competition."

"Oligopoly" is supposedly characterized by the existence of a relatively small number of sellers in a given market. The U.S. Bureau of the Census uses so-called four-firm and eight-firm concentration ratios, according to which markets are classified as oligopolistic depending on the percentage of domestic sales of an industry made by the four or eight largest domestic firms in the industry. "Oligopoly" is held to exist in cases in which the four largest firms account for as little as 5 or 10 percent of the industry's sales.[24] Depending on the circumstances, an oligopolist is held to behave either exactly as a "monopolist" would behave in terms of the price he charges and the output he produces, or to occupy some middle ground between a monopolist and a "pure competitor."[25] In the former case, oligopolists are held to be guilty of "collusion" by the mere fact of anticipating one another's responses to changes in price.[26]

The concept of "monopolistic competition" is supposed to describe cases in which there are a large number of sellers of only slightly dissimilar products. This concept clearly implies that an element of monopoly is present to whatever extent one product is *different* from another. The unique elements of the product constitute its "monopolistic" aspect. At the same time, such products are in competition with one another. Hence, the notion of "monopolistic competition." According to this notion, the Pepsi Cola and Coca Cola companies are, indeed, monopolists, but, at the same time, competitors.

The concepts of "monopolistic competition" and "oligopoly" are actually indistinguishable, both in theory and in practice. As examples of "monopolistic competition," Samuelson and Nordhaus cite the competition between Pepsi Cola and Coca Cola, Newports and Kools, and Hondas and Toyotas—examples which would equally well fit under the heading of "oligopoly," because of the large market shares of these firms.[27] Indeed, even small retail establishments, such as restaurants, drug stores, and dry-cleaners—more popular examples of "monopolistic competition"—can also be classified under "oligopoly," since there are only a few specimens of any of these categories in any given neighborhood or small town or city. Similarly, cases in which products may be physically identical, such as the cold rolled steel sheet produced by "oligopolistic" steel firms, are nonetheless likely to be accompanied by important differences in such things as terms of financing, delivery schedules, customer assistance, and so forth provided by the particular supplier.

In any case, these two concepts of "oligopoly" and "monopolistic competition" embrace virtually all industries except the few that are called "pure monopoly." All that is now believed to remain in the realm of free competition—or "pure" or "pure and perfect competition," as it has come to be called—is little more than wheat farming and the production of other agricultural commodities. These are the cases in which an enormous number of individually insignificant producers turn out perfectly homogeneous products and thereby satisfy the leading requirements of such "competition." Of course, when one allows for the existence of government farm-subsidy programs and the limitations on agricultural production the government imposes, in order to limit the costs of the programs, it turns out that even most of agriculture no longer can properly be classified as falling under the head of genuine competition, but must be described as controlled by government-organized cartels.

The virtual disappearance of full-bodied competition from the intellectual horizon of contemporary economics—a disappearance caused by the adoption of fundamentally flawed concepts—has led to efforts to reconstruct economic history, so that it can simultaneously conform both with the state of contemporary economic theory and with the generally accepted observations made in the past as to the prevalence of competition. Accordingly, the myth has grown up of the existence of a past golden age of competition before the Civil War, when, allegedly, "pure and perfect competition" was the norm. Only since then, the story goes, have we fallen from grace. This reconstruction of economic history in turn is used as a basis for explaining away much of the procapitalist economic thought of the early nineteenth century. It is claimed that the economists of that time were living in a world of pure and perfect competition and developed economic theories applicable to that world, and that, accordingly, their system of thought does not apply to the economic world that has come into being since their time.

The fact is, of course, that there never was an economic world characterized by the existence of vast numbers of sellers competing in the same market. It may be that prior to the Civil War, when each small town still had to be largely self-sufficient, because of a still undeveloped transportation network, the total number of iron foundries, meat packing establishments, and so forth, in the United States as a whole substantially exceeded the number that existed some decades after the Civil War. But this reduction in the total number of producers in many industries in the country as a whole was accompanied by a substantial increase in the number of producers in those industries *in actual competition with one another in any given market*. Improvements in transportation, in the form of railroad building and the growing use of steam-powered steel ships, made possible a radical increase in the area over which any given productive establishment was able to compete. Thus, at the same time that hundreds or even thousands of small, inefficient plants in an industry were being replaced with a much smaller number of large-scale, efficient plants, the number of firms actually competing in any given market increased rather than decreased.

It should not be necessary to say that no serious economic defense of any aspect of capitalism was ever based on the assumptions of so-called pure and perfect competition. The classical economists' theory that prices are determined by the costs of production did not presuppose any specific minimum number of producers. It presupposed only the ability of producers to increase supplies by increasing production. Indeed, their theory of prices can be taken as regarding precisely what contemporary economics denounces as "oligopoly" and "monopolistic competition," as the normal state of affairs, in which both competition and the determination of price by cost take place.

Now that the meaning of the economic concept of monopoly has been explained, it is possible to turn to an analysis of the alleged significance of the concept. As will be shown, the consequences of monopoly are alleged to range from the most dire and extreme, in the earlier formulations of the doctrine, to what must be regarded as absolutely trivial, in the formulations presented by contemporary economic theory when it cries "monopoly" because of the absence of "pure and perfect competition." (It must be remarked that the triviality of the consequences of "monopoly" is not evident to the economists who support the pure-and-perfect-competition doctrine, although even they now have some awareness of the actual facts.[28])

5. The Alleged Tendency Toward the Formation of a Single Giant Firm Controlling the Entire Economic System: A Rebuttal

The Marxian doctrine on monopoly is that capitalism is characterized by the progressive concentration of the means of production in fewer and fewer hands. In the words of Marx himself:

> Success and failure both lead here to a centralization of capital, and thus to expropriation on the most enormous scale. Expropriation extends here from the direct producers to the smaller and the medium-sized capitalists themselves. It is the point of departure for the capitalist mode of production; its accomplishment is the goal of this production. *In the last instance, it aims at the expropriation of the means of production from all individuals.* With the development of social production the means of production cease to be means of private production and products of private production, and can thereafter be only means of production in the hands of associated producers, i.e., the latter's social property, much as they are their social products. However, this expropriation appears within the capitalist system in a contradictory form, as appropriation of social property by a few . . . .[29]

The meaning of this passage is that if left unchecked and allowed to run its full course, capitalism is headed for the day when one company and one individual or small clique of individuals will become the sole owner of the world. Ford and General Motors will merge with Toyota and Honda; General Electric, IBM, and AT&T will merge; U.S. Steel and Bethlehem will merge, as will Exxon, Mobil, and Texaco. And the combinations resulting from these mergers will combine into still larger combinations, which ultimately will sweep up all remaining independent concerns into one Supercombine that owns all the capital in the world.

This is the well-known scenario of the bigger fish swallowing the smaller fish, and in turn being swallowed by still bigger fish, until only one gigantic fish remains. This process of the growing concentration of capital is supposed to be inevitable, and is what allegedly makes the coming of socialism inevitable. The growing concentration of capital under capitalism supposedly constitutes the creation of *the structural framework of a socialist society.* Seen in this light, all that socialism represents is a mere changing of the Board of Directors of the Supercombine. Instead of the Board being composed of men who will operate the social apparatus of production in the narrow interest of a handful of dominant individuals and families, it will be composed of men of nobler character, who will operate the apparatus of production in the interest of all members of society. (To illustrate this analysis, one may imagine that on the last day of capitalism there is a board of directors of the Supercombine that is subservient to the grasping, fist-pounding General Bullmoose—the cartoon character in the old L'il Abner comic strip by Al Capp. And then, on the first day of socialism, that board is replaced by the likes of such warm-hearted and public-spirited souls as Ralph Nader, Jane Fonda, and Tom Hayden, who will proceed to run the world for the benefit of all mankind.)

Of course, argue the socialists, it is not necessary to wait for capitalism actually to run its full course. Socialism can come into being sooner, and spare the world much suffering. What is important, say the socialists, is that the coming of socialism is in accordance with inexorable principles of economic development: socialism is hatched out of the womb of capitalism, as it were.

This view of the inherent tendency of capitalist development underlies support for the antitrust laws. It is believed that the antitrust laws are necessary in order to forestall the adoption of socialism. In the eyes of their supporters, they forcibly prevent the growing concentration of capital and, at the same time, the growth of "monopolistic abuses" and dissatisfaction with capitalism.

The same view underlies all the rather sinister books and articles that periodically appear and which describe in detail alleged cabalistic schemes of wealthy individuals and families to gain control of the economic system through devices ranging from interlocking directorates of corporations to intermarriages of heirs and heiresses.

Incompatibility With the Division of Labor—Socialism as the Only Instance of Unlimited Concentration of Capital

Now any fear that there is a tendency in capitalism toward the concentration of all ownership in the hands of one man or one corporation, or any other such narrow group, is absurd. Such a development would contradict the very nature of the gains derived from the division of labor and its corollary the division of knowledge. It would thus be against the self-interests of everyone, including even the handful of capitalists who were supposed to gain from it.

The truth is that such a state of affairs exists only under *socialism*. It is established and maintained only by the initiation of physical force. Nothing less than a Communist revolution, which forcibly seizes all the means of production and places them in the hands of the state, is capable of accomplishing it, and nothing less than the continued existence of a thoroughly repressive regime is capable of maintaining it. Despite its ownership of all the means of production in the Soviet Union, the Soviet government was able to prevent the development of competition only by means of the most repressive measures: to limit, let alone stop, the competition of the black market, it found it necessary to resort to draconic penalties, imposed by administrative tribunals, on the basis of evidence supplied by secret informers. There can be no doubt that had the Soviet government abandoned its repressive measures merely to the point of allowing its citizens to homestead unoccupied land in Siberia and produce there whatever they might be capable of producing, its monopoly position would have been completely broken. Indeed, such economic concentration as characterized the Soviet Union must be maintained not only by the resort to physical force, but also by the prevalence of a spirit of *self-sacrifice* on the part of the ruling group.

To illustrate this last point, let us imagine that in the separation between the Russian government and the Russian Communist Party, the latter had been allowed to take with it, as its own private property, all of the inhabited land of Russia and all of the factories, farms, mines, and stores that it possessed until recently in its capacity as the effective government of Russia. It would have retained title, we may assume, as the Catholic Church and the feudal lords retained title in earlier centuries to the vast properties they had originally obtained on the basis of the initiation of physical force.

If this had happened and the members of the Communist Party wished to act on behalf of their own material self-interests, or even merely to increase the wealth of the Communist Party Corporation, their first step would have been to place much or even most or all of their property into the possession of others. They would have sold out to them on credit if necessary.

They would have done so because if they consulted their own material self-interests, they would have realized how far they were from being omniscient and even how far they were from possessing the knowledge required to grow a sufficient quantity of grain to avoid starvation. By placing a major portion or even all of their property in the ownership of others, its effective employment could be so greatly increased, so much more could be produced, that the Communist Party as a private corporation would soon have found itself materially much better off owning 20 or 25 percent of a greatly expanded Russian economy than 100 percent of the then existing Russian economy. And as time wore on, its relative significance in the Russian economy would have continued to decrease, though its absolute wealth might have continued to increase.

None of this is to advocate in the least that Russia should have been or should be desocialized in this manner. The Communist Party and its members have no right to anything. It is merely to make the point that anyone truly following his self-interest knows that it is to his self-interest that there exist other people able to act and produce without being dependent on the use of his property and thus on obtaining his consent—that is, that there exist other people capable of acting and producing without being limited by the limits of his knowledge. (Along these lines, of course, an essential advantage resulting from the end of socialism is the reestablishment of markets for all goods and services and thus of the price system, economic calculation, and economic planning—vital features which socialism lacks.[30])

Indeed, although it has taken a different form, what is going on today in the former Soviet Union and throughout the Communist and formerly Communist worlds is precisely the growing realization that an all-embracing economic monolith is not in the interests even of those who are in charge of it. The great mass of present and former members of the Communist Parties around the world, extending high up into the ranks of the various central committees, will all be far more prosperous under capitalism than under socialism, even though they have been the ones in charge of the monolith. Finally, they appear to have come to understand this fact, and for some time have been seeking ways to dismantle socialism and establish capitalism, and to varying degrees are succeeding in doing so.

The entire experience of socialism confirms the fact that monopoly is a political phenomenon, not an economic phenomenon.

Inherent Limits to the Concentration of Capital Under Capitalism

In order to show further why there is no tendency toward an ever increasing concentration of capital under capitalism, it is necessary first of all to elaborate on the fact that beyond a point concentration of capital runs counter to the division of knowledge.

No businessman or team of businessmen is capable of

possessing the knowledge required to succeed in more than a few industries. There is simply too much to know. For this reason, there is the phenomenon of *bad mergers*—acquisitions that do not fit into a company's areas of expertise and which thus turn out to reduce profits rather than add to them. Such ill-fated acquisitions must later be "spun off"—divested—if they are not to constitute a continuing drain on the profits of the company's sound operations.

It is not possible—in the absence of government intervention that seriously undermines normal profit-and-loss incentives—to overcome this problem through the formation of conglomerates, with separate divisions each under the control of businessmen with the necessary knowledge of the particular area of specialization. A businessman with confidence in his own ability to succeed in an industry he knows and understands, and in which his income is determined exclusively by his own success or failure, would not be willing to exchange such a position for one in which he receives a much smaller share of the profits of a conglomerate, which are the outcome of the success or failure of many others, whom he is unlikely to consider as capable as himself.

Similar considerations operate to frustrate the combination of firms even within the same industry. Imagine, for example, an industry composed of 10 firms, each presently doing 10 percent of the industry's business, and owned by individuals each of whom expects that under his management his firm will grow to the point of doing 40 percent or 50 percent of the industry's business. It is not possible to merge such firms. To make the merger appear worthwhile in comparison with the anticipated gains from remaining independent, each of the 10 would have to be given 40 percent or 50 percent of the stock of the resulting combination—or 4 or 5 times the value of the combination in all.

It is not necessary, of course, that all of the firms in an industry hold such an optimistic view of their prospects. So long as there are *any* firms who believe they will enjoy a substantial increase in the share of the industry's business they will do if they remain on their own, it is probably not possible to offer them terms that would make merging appear worthwhile.

Furthermore, it should be realized that when mergers take place that are *successful*—that is, succeed in realizing important economies—a major consequence is the formation of new and additional capital. The stockholders in such a combined enterprise enjoy higher incomes, can save more, and the value of their shares of stock is increased. The result is that these stockholders are now in a position to finance the launching of new firms—not, most likely, in the same industry in which the merger has occurred that underlies the increase in their wealth, but

in other industries. Yet if successful mergers take place throughout the economic system, a consequence will be the formation of new firms throughout the economic system, and thus in most or even all of the industries which have experienced mergers. In effect, successful mergers in the oil, steel, and cement industries, say, result in the formation of additional capital which makes possible the launching of new firms in, say, the automobile, aluminum, and chemical industries. Later on, successful mergers in one or more of these industries, or in other industries, result in the formation of additional capital that makes possible the launching of new firms back in the oil, steel, and cement industries.[31] Thus, the very process of successful mergers is itself the source of the formation of new firms and thereby operates to limit the concentration of capital.

In addition, it should be realized that an enormous number of new small firms is started every year in a capitalist economy with or without the aid of capital generated by the process of successful mergers. Over the years, some of these firms enjoy great success and grow into medium and even giant-sized firms. One has only to think of the present-day American computer industry or the present-day Japanese and Korean automobile and steel industries. The continuous formation and success of new companies makes it possible for mergers to go on as a regular phenomenon, without being accompanied by any actual increase in the overall degree of concentration of capital in the economic system. While the merged firms represent more capital in the hands of fewer firms, the growth of new firms represents more capital outside the hands of the merged firms. Thus, the proportion of the total capital of the economic system in the hands of the merged firms does not grow.[32]

Government Intervention as Limiting the Formation of New Firms

It must be pointed out that the formation and growth of new firms would take place on a much greater scale than at present precisely under conditions of laissez-faire capitalism. A major potential source of the formation of new firms in virtually every industry is key executives of the existing firms who believe that they could do better on their own. If not for the personal income tax, such executives would be able to accumulate far more personal wealth in their present positions. In the absence of restrictions on stock trading based on "inside" knowledge, their accumulations of personal wealth would be greater still.[33] In such conditions, it would be possible to start even new domestic automobile and steel companies requiring an initial investment of a billion dollars or more. A group of a half-dozen or a dozen key executives of existing automobile or steel firms might well have a collective personal net worth of several hundred million dollars. On the basis of that equity, combined with their knowledge and experience, they would be in a position to raise any necessary additional capital from outside sources, such as banks or a public stock offering. This potential competition, of course, is aborted by the government intervention—most notably, the progressive personal income tax—which prevents the accumulation of the necessary personal wealth by these individuals. And then, of course, the very same people who advocate such government intervention denounce capitalism for the fact that no one has the capital to start such new firms!

Taxes and other government regulations undermine the formation and growth of new firms also by virtue of the amount of time and effort they require firms to devote to the paperwork and other regulatory procedures that are imposed. Small firms just starting out simply cannot afford the staffs of accountants, lawyers, lobbyists, and others that are necessary to cope with the burden of government regulation. The established, large firms are in a much better position to do so. Here again are important instances of promonopoly policy, this time, on behalf of the established, large firms.

The Incentives for Uneconomic Mergers Provided by the Tax System

Besides preventing the formation and growth of new firms, the tax laws have also encouraged mergers that lack a genuine economic basis. Until 1981, firms that had been profitable in their existing lines of business were given an incentive to branch out into different lines of business in which they did not possess any special competency, as a means of reducing the tax burden of their major shareholders. Paying out the profits from their existing lines of business in the form of dividends would have imposed a federal income tax rate of 50 percent on stockholders in the top bracket. On the other hand, using those profits to buy the assets of another firm served to increase the company's assets and the price of its common stock. Upon selling their stock at a higher price (provided it had been held for a year or longer), stockholders had only to pay the capital gains tax of 20 percent. Such an arrangement, which had prevailed for many years, obviously favored giving stockholders their profits in the form of capital gains rather than dividends, and, as a means of accomplishing this, the use of profits for acquisitions which otherwise would not have been made.

By the same token, such considerations provided an incentive to the owners of successful small and medium-sized concerns to sell out to larger firms rather than continue on and attempt to grow further on their own. To enjoy the fruits of their success by paying themselves large dividends, they would have had to pay the 50 percent federal income tax. But by selling their shares, either for cash or in exchange for shares in the acquiring company, they could obtain capital-gains treatment on whatever portion of their firm's profits they wished to enjoy.

And, of course, the tax laws provide an incentive for acquiring firms which have accumulated losses over the years. When such a firm is acquired, its losses are subtracted from the profits of the acquiring firm, and thus the corporate income tax that must be paid by the acquiring firm is correspondingly reduced.

The preceding remarks are not intended in any way to provide an argument for raising the capital gains tax or for restricting the ability of businesses to reduce their shareholders' tax burden through mergers or through buying firms that have accumulated losses. Anything which serves to reduce the taxes paid by business firms and their stockholders serves to increase substantially the supply of capital funds available and thus to promote capital accumulation and economic progress. The achievement both of this vital end and of the elimination of the incentive to uneconomic mergers would be served if income tax rates were reduced below the capital gains tax rate. The incentive to acquire loss-making concerns merely for tax purposes would be eliminated entirely, and the incentive and means for accumulating capital would be increased enormously, if the whole system of income taxation were simply abolished.

In Defense of "Insider Trading"

In connection with market processes limiting the concentration of capital, I have made favorable reference to stock trading by corporate executives based on their inside knowledge. Inasmuch as a great deal of scandal has become attached to the phenomenon of "insider trading"—as though it represented some sort of heinous crime—it is necessary to say something further, in defense of the phenomenon.

There is absolutely nothing wrong with insider trading, even in situations in which corporate executives might sell the stock of their own company short (provided, of course, that they did nothing to cause the negative developments that could be expected to reduce the price of their company's stock). Insider trading does not make the "insiders" rich at the expense of any shareholder who continues to hold his shares. If the insiders profit by buying in advance on their inside knowledge of favorable developments, the effect is simply that the stock price starts to rise sooner. Whoever has decided to hold the stock gains that much sooner. Some who were planning to sell the stock, upon seeing the rise caused by the insiders' buying, may be persuaded to hold it instead; people in this group enjoy gains they would otherwise not have had. Whoever had made up his mind to sell his shares is enabled to sell them at a better price, thanks to the demand for them coming from the insiders.

The only parties who have any possible basis for complaint are those who do not have any strong conviction about the company's future prospects and who are induced to sell at the higher price the insiders bring about, and those who were planning to buy and who must now do so at a higher price. The complaint of people in the first group is that they accepted what they thought was a good price at the time and somehow have a right to the same gains they would have had if they had known better or had had more confidence in the company's future. The demand that the insiders must work for the "stockholders" actually means that those who see the value of becoming stockholders, or of increasing their holdings, must work for the benefit of those who do not see the value of continuing to be stockholders. It is a demand that they work for the least committed, least loyal of the stockholders, who upon the first opportunity cease to be stockholders and who are no longer stockholders when the inside news finally becomes public knowledge. There is no good reason why the interests of the insiders should be sacrificed to the interests of such people. As for the buyers who pay a higher price, their only complaint can be that their gain is less than it might have been. But many of them may well be buyers in the first place only because they observe the rise in the stock price brought about by the insiders' buying.

If the insiders sell in advance on the basis of their inside knowledge of negative developments, they are not responsible for the loss that is suffered by those who continue to hold the stock. That loss would come in any case, when the bad news finally became public knowledge. Only it would come more precipitously and dramatically, rather than being preceded by declines caused by the insiders' selling. As matters stand, the insiders' selling and the lower price it causes provides a clue to other stockholders to begin selling and to potential buyers to abstain from buying. Those who decide to buy in any case, are enabled to buy at a lower price.

The opposition to insider trading is actually based on nothing more than malicious envy—envy of those who profit by knowing what they are doing, by those who lack knowledge and who demand profit nonetheless. Ironically, their claims are upheld with righteous indignation by the very people who regard all stock market activity as pure gambling and all the gains made in the stock market as unearned and undeserved. Indeed, if the gains of the insiders, who know what they are doing, must be transferred to those who do not, the latter will not be able to keep those gains for very long. For they will have no basis on which to argue for the retention of their unearned, accidental gains from society as a whole. If knowledge is not an adequate basis for earning a profit that others do not earn, the mere accident of owning the right stock at the right time can hardly be such a basis. The attacks on insider trading proceed from a fundamentally anticapitalistic perspective. Their purpose is not to benefit any alleged group of victims, but to defame and ultimately destroy capitalism.

6. Economically Sound Mergers

Despite the fact that government intervention today encourages many economically unsound mergers, conditions often exist in which mergers are economically sound. By making possible an increase in the scale of a company's operations, they often achieve important economies of the kind previously described in the discussion of the gains from the division of labor, and which, appropriately, are termed economies of scale.[34] For example, by virtue of concentrating a larger quantity of work of the same type in the same place, they make it possible for smaller individual steps in the production of a product to come to have to be performed with such frequency that they can constitute the full time jobs of workers. For example, 100 automobile companies each turning out 10 automobiles a day, cannot make full-time, eight-hour-a-day jobs out of individual steps in producing an automobile that require less than 48 minutes of labor time. But a single automobile company, turning out 1,000 automobiles a day in the same factory, can make full time jobs out of individual steps requiring as little as .48 minutes of labor time. This represents the establishment of a substantially higher degree of division of labor and achieves important economies of learning and motion.

Similarly, larger-scale production frequently makes it possible to adopt machine methods which would be uneconomic on a smaller scale of production. For example, it probably does not pay for two companies to install machines of the kind that they will each use only 40 percent of the time. Still less would it be likely to pay four companies to install machines of the kind that they would each use only 20 percent of the time. But one company, producing twice or four times the volume would use such machines 80 percent of the time, at a correspondingly lower unit cost of the machine's services. Thus the adoption of machine methods is favored by a larger scale of operations.

Mergers can achieve important economies in cases in which companies carry complementary product lines, which can easily be sold by the same sales force. For example, if many of the customers of steel companies frequently need both steel sheet and iron castings, it is probably more economical for both products to be provided by one company than for each of two companies to provide only one of the products.

Mergers can also achieve important economies in connection with advertising and the raising of capital. For example, newspaper and television advertising are more economical if what is advertised is available throughout the area reached by the advertising. On this basis, it pays chain stores to engage in advertising which would not pay neighborhood shops. Larger firms, resulting from mergers, are also able to carry on their financing on a larger scale. As a result, other things being equal, they can borrow money at lower interest rates, since the lender can spread the administrative costs of making the loan over the larger sum lent. Similarly, sufficiently large firms, with sufficiently large financial requirements, can justify listing on a stock exchange and thus obtain the more economical access to capital that that makes possible.

Perhaps the single most important gain achieved by mergers is the ability of more competent individuals to gain control over the management of additional capital. If there are two firms each with the same capital, but one is run by more competent people than the other, the extension of the management of the former to the assets of the latter, will result in the combined firm producing more than was produced by the two individual firms separately. Even apart from economies of scale, two railroads merged under the management of Vanderbilt, or two oil refineries merged under the management of Rockefeller, resulted in more than twice the respective production of the two outfits in isolation, simply because the acquired assets were managed better in the hands of their new owner. It should be obvious from this point in particular that the economies provided by mergers can go far beyond the economies of scale achieved in individual larger-sized factories or other productive establishments. There is very good reason for a more competently run firm to own far more than just one optimum-sized plant in its industry. Its ownership of additional such plants results in more being produced from them than would be the case if they were owned by less competently run firms. It is necessary to stress this point in view of the widespread belief that economies of scale provide the only economic justification of mergers.[35]

The Trust Movement

The preceding discussion helps to explain an important part of the economic history of the late nineteenth and early twentieth centuries—the phenomenon of the so-called trust movement. The trusts were the earliest method devised for accomplishing corporate mergers.

Prior to the Civil War, the formation of corporations was an extremely difficult and costly process. A special act of a state legislature was necessary. Corporations were confined largely to railroading and insurance. In the years following the Civil War, with recognition of the growing need for large aggregations of capital, requiring the participation of such a large number of investors as to make traditional partnership arrangements unwieldy and impractical, the process of incorporation was radically simplified and the ability to incorporate was made easily available to everyone.

In the period following the Civil War, corporate law did not immediately provide a mechanism whereby one corporation could be combined with another one. The trusts were a device for accomplishing that purpose. Under a trust arrangement, the stockholders of separate corporations turned their shares over to trustees, who then had the power to vote the shares and run the corporations. By assembling the shares of two or more corporations in the hands of the same trust, it was possible to operate the corporations as a single unit and thus achieve a merger.

Despite the sinister connotations of the word, the trusts played a major role in improving the efficiency of the economic system, and thus in raising the general standard of living. Their success in rapidly increasing production was instrumental in bringing about a generation of steadily falling prices in the years 1873–1896. (The fall in prices came to an end with major discoveries of gold in Alaska and Australia, and the development of processes which made possible the commercial exploitation of a vastly increased portion of South Africa's deposits.) In every case, the rise of the trusts was associated with a vast increase in production and improvement in the quality of products. The era of the trusts was the era of America's most rapid economic progress and the transformation of the country into the world's foremost industrial producer and economic power. The development of the trusts was indispensable to these achievements.

The fact that the actual result of the trusts was more production and lower prices, not less production and higher prices, which is the result one would expect if the trusts had been the monopolists their critics claim them to have been, is confirmed even in the adverse decision of the U.S. Supreme Court in 1911, which broke up the Standard Oil Trust. In its decision, the Court admitted: "Much has been said in favor of the objects of the Standard Oil Trust, and what it has accomplished. It may be true that it has improved the quality and cheapened the costs of petroleum and its products to the consumer. But such is not one of the usual or general results of a monopoly; and it is the policy of the law to regard, not what may, but what usually happens. Experience shows that it is not wise to trust human cupidity where it has the opportunity to aggrandize itself at the expense of others."[36] Ironically, of course, the leading "evidence" that is usually cited on behalf of the terrible effects of the trusts and of private "monopoly" in general is precisely the alleged record of the Standard Oil Trust!

Apart from the special business talent that was characteristic of the men who formed the trusts, and the advantages to be had by virtue of that talent being in charge of a larger volume of capital, a fundamental economic factor that favored the formation of the trusts—indeed, made their formation vital—was the major improvements in the transportation system that had been going on for several decades, and which sharply accelerated following the Civil War. The decades following the Civil War were a period of enormous railroad building, and also of the rapidly growing use of steam-powered steel ships. These developments brought about a radical reduction in transportation costs and the ability to transport quickly and economically, to practically everywhere in the country and to much of the world, goods whose transportation prior to that time had been extremely expensive and for all practical purposes simply out of the question as far as most locations were concerned.

These improvements in transportation favored larger-scale manufacturing and processing. They meant that the lower manufacturing and processing costs of larger-scale plants would outweigh transportation charges over a wider radius, and thus that the adoption of larger-scale manufacturing and processing methods was now economic in a vast number of situations in which it had not previously been economic. The following hypothetical example will serve as an illustration.

Imagine that in a small-scale plant, manufacturing cost is $10 per unit of product, while in a large-scale plant, thanks to the operation of the kind of factors explained above, manufacturing cost can be brought down to only $1 per unit, provided the facility operates at a sufficient percentage of its capacity. Assume that initially, however, transportation costs are 50¢ per mile per unit. Under these conditions, transportation charges more than offset the manufacturing cost advantage of the larger-scale plant in every case in which it is located more than 18 miles further away from the market it must serve than is the smaller-scale plant. The total cost per unit of providing the product from a smaller-scale plant located on the spot, and thus without its having to incur transportation charges, is $10 per unit—its manufacturing cost. But that is exactly the total cost of providing the product from a larger-scale plant located only 18 miles away, when one adds to its $1 manufacturing cost per unit,

transportation charges of 50¢ per mile times 18 miles. Indeed, in every case in which the larger-scale plant is located more than 18 miles further away from the market than is the smaller-scale plant, the closer, smaller-scale plant actually has the cost advantage. The smaller-scale plant located, say, 5 miles from the market it must serve, has a total, delivered cost of $12.50 per unit. The larger-scale plant located, say, 30 miles from that same market has a total, delivered cost of $16 per unit.

In such circumstances, it is doubtful that the larger-scale plant can compete successfully against smaller-scale plants even when it is located in the same immediate vicinity. This is because it must find the volume of business necessary to enable it to operate at a sufficient level of its capacity within too small a radius. It may well be the case that when confined to such a narrow radius, the volume of business it can attract is so small that at the low level of operation it is able to achieve, even its manufacturing cost turns out to be no lower than that of the smaller-scale plant. Indeed, a larger-scale plant that must operate at, say, only 5 or 10 percent of its capacity, may well have higher manufacturing costs than a smaller-scale plant operating at 80 or 90 percent of its capacity.

Such results are not unlikely. Any inability to find a sufficient volume of business within the narrow radius enjoined by the high transportation charges diminishes the manufacturing-cost advantage of the larger-scale plant and forces it to find its market still closer to its gates, which then compounds the problem of finding a sufficient volume of business. For example, if the larger-scale plant could find sufficient business within an 18-mile radius to operate at no more than 25 percent of capacity, even though it charged prices corresponding to manufacturing costs at an 80 percent or 90 percent operating rate, its manufacturing cost per unit would be substantially greater than $1—perhaps $4. In that case, to operate economically, it would actually have to find a sufficient volume of business to support 25 percent operation within a radius of 12 miles, not 18 miles, for its actual manufacturing cost advantage over the smaller-scale plant is reduced to $6 per unit from $9 per unit. If it cannot do that, then the same story repeats itself, and it is driven to having to find an adequate market even closer to its gates, at a still lower percentage of capacity, and at correspondingly higher manufacturing costs per unit. The probable outcome is that it cannot operate economically at all.

But now imagine that, thanks to radical improvements in railroading and ocean shipping, transportation cost is reduced to a mere 1¢ per mile per unit. Under these new conditions, the larger-scale plant has an advantage in total, delivered cost per unit extending over a radius of 900 miles! Wherever its distance from the local market is less than 900 miles further away than the small-scale plant, it has the lower total delivered cost. In these circumstances, the larger-scale plant will almost certainly find a sufficient volume of business so that it can operate at a level of capacity high enough to achieve its manufacturing economies. Indeed, probably at least several such plants will be required.

The much maligned trusts were precisely the means of achieving the replacement of high-cost, small-scale plants with much lower-cost, large-scale plants. They accomplished this by merging large numbers of small firms, with small-scale facilities, into a smaller number of larger firms, with large-scale facilities. They built the larger-scale facilities by pooling the profits and replacement funds of the smaller concerns, and as they built them, they dismantled and closed down the outmoded small-scale facilities. For example, Standard Oil is reported to have acquired 123 refineries, of which it dismantled at least 75, while producing a greatly increased volume of oil products in only 20 separate facilities.[37] In accomplishing such results, the trusts brought into being large-scale manufacturing and processing centers serving national and world markets at radically reduced costs and prices. For example, they developed Cleveland as the major oil-refining center, Pittsburgh as the major steel-producing center, and Chicago as the major meat-packing center.

The historical distortions surrounding the trusts totally ignore their actual accomplishments and substitute for the facts nothing more than the implications of moral and economic doctrines that are themselves totally unfounded—above all, the implications of the vicious doctrine that one man's gain is another man's loss. On the basis of this depraved doctrine, the trusts are damned *a priori*, precisely by virtue of their great success.

7. The Predatory-Pricing Doctrine

An economic doctrine that has played a major role in the condemnation of the trusts and in the fear of big business in general is the doctrine of predatory pricing. According to this doctrine, a large firm, because it is "big and rich," and possibly operates in many different markets at the same time, can afford losses which a small firm cannot, because the latter is "small and poor." On this basis, it is held to be in the interest of the large firm temporarily to slash its price and sell at a loss, in order to force the small firm also to sell at a loss. Because it can afford the loss while the small firm cannot, the argument goes, it will be able to drive the latter out of business, and, as soon as it has done so, raise its price to a higher level than ever before. New competitors will be kept out, the doctrine claims, by the fear of being ruined by a repetition of predatory price cutting. Thus, it is held,

the predatory large firm succeeds in unconscionably gouging the helpless public, which, in simple innocence, has taken the large firm's lure of a temporarily lower price as children sometimes take candy from an evil stranger, only to suffer greatly later on from its mistake, when its only protection, the small and poor firm, has been eliminated.

The belief in the validity of this doctrine is so powerful that all the achievements of big business in reducing prices and improving quality are regarded as having no reality. They are all seen as being merely a prelude to this kind of gouge. Conditions will be normal, the doctrine's adherents believe, only when big business and the rich do what it is absolutely certain that their nature impels them to do and, indeed, makes them enjoy doing, namely, make life miserable for everyone else.

Despite the evident psychological bias that underlies its acceptance—namely, envy carried to the point of unreasoning fear and hatred of others' success—it is necessary to examine the predatory-pricing doctrine as though it were advanced in all good faith and honesty. Proceeding in this way, a series of major difficulties with the doctrine must be pointed out.

First, it should not at all be taken for granted that the large, rich firm is even in a position to impose a price reduction below the small firm's costs. At the lower price it asks, there will be an increase in the quantity of the good demanded. The large firm can make the lower price effective only if it is in a position to supply this additional quantity demanded. Whether or not it can do so depends on how elastic the demand for the product is in response to the price reduction—i.e., on how much the quantity of the product demanded expands—and also on how much unused productive capacity the firm has on hand and that is available for the particular market concerned. If its capacity is insufficient to meet the larger quantity demanded, it has no means of compelling its small competitor to sell at the lower price it asks. For in this case, customers who come to it in order to obtain the lower price must be turned away. They will have to deal with the smaller firm. Indeed, it is even possible that the effect of the large firm's action could actually be to *raise the price received by its small competitor*. This will occur insofar as its lower price attracts a new and additional quantity demanded which is met with supplies that are now made unavailable for satisfying the firm's regular quantity demanded. In this case, the item actually becomes scarcer for the firm's regular customers, and they will now have to turn to the smaller firm, where their competition will actually drive up the price.[38]

If the large firm does have the capacity to meet the additional quantity demanded at the lower price, and thus to satisfy a substantial portion of the customers of the smaller firm as well as all of its own customers, then, of course, it can impose the lower price. The smaller firm will have to meet it if it wishes to keep its customers.

But even so, to the degree that the demand for the product is elastic, the large firm must go to the expense of possessing this necessary additional capacity. And then, of course, if it should actually succeed in closing down the small competitor and thereupon raise its price, which is its presumed plan all along, it must continue to maintain this additional capacity even though it no longer uses it in production. This can be an expensive proposition.

A further, much greater difficulty arises. If it is the case that as soon as the small competitor is driven out, the large firm can sharply increase its price, while so long as the small competitor remains in business the price is held below the level of his costs, then usually unrecognized but nonetheless extremely powerful interests are created on behalf of the continued existence of the small competitor. The obvious interests, of course, are those of the small competitor himself, who wants to stay in business, and those of the industry's customers, who pay much less so long as he is in business, and so much more as soon as he is driven out of business. A less obvious interest in the continued existence of the small competitor is that of *the industry's suppliers* and that of *the producers of products that are complementary to the industry's products.*

If, for example, a predatory-pricing policy were to be followed in the oil industry (as many believe was actually the case in the late nineteenth century and the early years of the twentieth century under Rockefeller's Standard Oil Company), the consequence would be that the business of the suppliers of oil rigs, drills, pipeline, and tank cars would sharply increase every time a small competitor existed who was being driven out by Standard Oil, and sharply decrease every time Standard Oil succeeded in driving him out. The same would be true of the business of the automobile industry and its suppliers, which is increased by a low price of gasoline and reduced by a high price of gasoline. The obvious question arises, if Standard Oil were to follow such a policy, why shouldn't the suppliers of the oil industry and the producers of products complementary to oil products, like automobiles and steel, deliberately subsidize a small competitor of Standard Oil, for the very purpose of making Standard Oil sell at a sharply lower price?

Going still further, if it is the case that the large firm has only to be confronted with a small firm in order to slash its price, people are placed in a position in which they can use that very knowledge to profit by forming small competing firms. All they have to do is first go out and take a substantial short position in the stock of the large firm, and in the product it sells. They can do so in the knowledge that they have the power to drive down the price of its stock along with the price of its product while it proceeds against their new company by means of slashing the product's selling price and its own profits. And as a kind of frosting on the cake, as it were, as soon as they have taken their short positions, they can publicly advertise the formation of their new company and urge everyone to delay his purchases of the product in anticipation of the sharply lower prices their entry will precipitate. This will immediately reduce the business of the large firm, enable the owners of the new firm to profit right away on their short positions, and when their firm actually appears in the market, the quantity of the product demanded may be so increased, thanks to the postponement of purchases, that the large firm may not even be able to meet it. The result of this last is that for a time the small firm may even be able to sell at prices that are highly profitable despite all the efforts of the large firm.

Of course, apart from all of these considerations, there is the very simple and obvious question of why all the customers are ready to deal with the large firm if they know that as soon as it succeeds in driving the small firm out, it will sharply increase its price. In reality, buyers take steps to protect themselves from arbitrary price increases. In addition to the simple refusal to give all their business to such a firm, a further major protection is *prices that are set by contractual agreement.* Such prices can altogether eliminate the ability even of firms that constitute the sole source of supply to profit from arbitrary price increases. I will say more about this shortly.

There is yet a further and particularly vital matter that the predatory-pricing doctrine ignores and which must now be pointed out. This is the fact that to the extent that the big and rich firm is larger in the same market, it must take the price cut and the resulting loss *on a correspondingly larger volume than the small and poor firm.* It cannot cut the price only to the customers of the small firm, because that leaves the small firm free to cut price by a much smaller amount to an equal number of customers of the large firm. If the small firm is not to be able to sell to anyone except at the low price imposed by the large firm, the large firm must make that low price available to all of its own customers as well as to the customers of the small firm. This means that if—to introduce an element of personality into the example— "Big John" (viz., Rockefeller), who does 90 percent of the business in a given market, wants to cut price in order to inflict a loss on "Little Joe," who does 10 percent of the business in that market, he must suffer the resulting loss on his *90 percent* share in contrast with the latter's 10 percent share. Assuming that he has the same unit costs, this means nothing less than that he must take a loss that is *nine times as large!* It is difficult to see the advantage constituted by nine times the wealth and nine times the business if money is lost at a rate that is nine times as great.[39]

Indeed, when matters are seen in this light, it even turns out that the smaller, poorer firm may be in a better position to withstand losses than the larger, richer firm. If, for example, while Little Joe's market share was only one-ninth as great as that of Big John, his capital was more than one-ninth as great—say, two-ninths as great—then he would actually be in a position to sustain losses for a longer time than Big John! And if Little Joe is an innovator and produces a superior product at the same cost as Big John's product, or has lower units costs of production than Big John for an equally good product, then his position is virtually impregnable. In this case, by cutting price Big John can suffer immense losses, while Little Joe merely earns lower profits, and Big John must suffer even greater losses before he can impose any loss whatever on Little Joe. (Such a situation is very often the case in reality, though it is hardly ever considered by the supporters of the predatory-pricing doctrine or, for that matter, by almost anyone else in contemporary economic theory.)

Of course, Big John's larger capital can often be expected to give him economies of scale which Little Joe does not possess. In recognition of this fact, the predatory-pricing doctrine's supporters may wish to modify their position that it is greater wealth and size in and of itself that enables the larger firm to sell at lower prices. They may wish to say that Big John can afford to sell at lower prices because he has lower costs, which permit him to continue to be profitable even while Little Joe earns no profits, or, indeed, suffers losses. There is certainly nothing objectionable in Big John selling at lower prices in such a case. But even here, it should be realized that in selling at lower prices, the more efficient, larger firm must still at least *reduce* its own profits by a multiple of any loss it inflicts on its small competitor, which makes it extremely unlikely that it could pay to cut prices for the purpose of driving the small competitor out.

For example, let us imagine that Big John has a cost per unit of 80¢, while Little Joe has a cost per unit of 90¢ and needs a price of $1 per unit in order to earn a competitive rate of profit on his capital. If Big John sets his price at $1 per unit, and sells 9 units for every 1 that Little Joe sells, then he makes $1.80 in profit for every 10¢ that Little Joe makes. If now, he slashes his price below Little Joe's cost, to 85¢, say, then for every 5¢ of loss he inflicts on Little Joe, he reduces his own profits by 15¢ per unit times 9 times the number of units, viz., by $1.35. The damage he does himself in this case, in terms of the reduction in his own profit, is 27 times the loss he inflicts on Little Joe. To describe the situation in more conservative terms, the reduction in his own profit is still 9 times the reduction in Little Joe's profit, which goes from plus 10¢ to minus 5¢. But however it is described, this hardly seems to qualify as an intelligent method of doing business. On the contrary, it seems to have more in common with a policy not merely of shooting flies with an elephant gun, but of perversely singling out for such shooting, flies that reside on one's own nose! From the perspective of the smaller firms in competition with such absurdly managed large firms, it would simply be a case of "the bigger they come, the harder they fall."

Furthermore, in order to drive Little Joe out of competition, or, more correctly, Little Joe's plant capacity, Big John must sell not merely below the latter's total costs, but below his *operating costs* (together with an allowance for earning a competitive rate of profit on the working capital that must be tied up in meeting the operating costs). Little Joe's operating costs are his costs merely on account of such things as labor, materials, and fuel. Such costs as depreciation on plant and equipment and interest paid on capital borrowed for investment in plant and equipment do not enter. So long as Little Joe, or whoever else may come to own Little Joe's plant, can sell merely for more than these costs plus an allowance for earning a competitive rate of profit on the working capital that must be tied up in meeting them, it pays him to remain in operation. To whatever extent Big John charges a price that is higher than this, Little Joe or his successor is also able to recover a portion of the original investment in the plant and equipment.

To drive out Little Joe, Big John must not only set his price below this level, but he must also hold it at this low level *for as long as Little Joe's plant capacity lasts.* Even if Little Joe himself should be driven out of business, because he is unable to meet interest or principal payments, say, continued operation of his capacity will pay the creditors who take over his assets, or those to whom the creditors sell the assets. This is the case, because, as stated, this way they will at least be able to earn the rate of profit on the working capital—and more besides, to whatever extent Big John charges a price that more than equals the costs of operating Little Joe's plant plus allowance for a competitive rate of profit on the working capital that must be tied up. (From the perspective of a later owner who acquires Little Joe's plant at the bargain prices of a bankruptcy sale, practically all such additional proceeds may constitute profit.[40])

If Big John does not want to wait until Little Joe's capacity has worn out before he raises his price, he may consider buying Little Joe out. Given the enormous financial burden of holding his own price down for so many years, while waiting for Little Joe's capacity to wear out, it would certainly be much more sensible to buy Little Joe's capacity even at a premium price—above what Little Joe himself had paid for it. Of course, if this is what Big John were to be accused of, it would represent a dramatic reversal of the predatory-pricing doctrine. Now, instead of being accused of eliminating his competitors by charging ruinously low prices, he would be accused of eliminating them by buying them out at premium prices for their assets.[41]

But neither method can actually pay Big John if his goal is to profit by imposing arbitrarily high prices. This is because both methods imply that later on, once Little Joe's capacity is out of the way by one method or the other, it is absolutely *necessary* for Big John to charge a premium price merely in order to recoup the reduction in profits he has sustained or the premium price for Little Joe's assets that he has paid. But any premium price he charges in the future, after Little Joe's capacity is out of the way, will only serve to attract *new competitors*, to whom the premium price will offer the prospect of a premium rate of profit. Because of its highly self-destructive nature, and for all of the other reasons explained, these competitors cannot be kept out by the fear of still more predatory pricing. The fact is that the permanent, long-run price that Big John can obtain is limited by the costs of production—the full costs—of potential new entrants, together, of course, with an allowance for the competitive rate of profit on their capital.[42] These costs set an objective limit above which the price cannot be maintained in the absence of legal protection from competition—namely, that provided by monopoly according to the political concept. As a result, Big John cannot in fact later on charge the premium price that is necessary to recoup the profits he must forgo or the additional expense he must incur.

Thus, even if Big John were able to succeed in driving out his smaller rival or rivals, he would have very little to gain by doing so. His gain would merely be their share of the market, at selling prices not significantly higher than the selling prices that prevailed before he began his effort to drive them out. In terms of our previous example, all that he could gain by years of selling his own 9 units at a loss, or at least at a profit of much less than 20¢ per unit, while he was keeping Little Joe's capacity out of operation, is a profit of an additional 20¢ on the extra unit he was finally able to supply in place of Little Joe. For his price could not significantly exceed the $1 that prevailed before he cut in order to drive Little Joe out.

More Than One Firm in an Industry as the Normal Case

A major implication of the preceding discussion is that it normally does not pay a firm to attempt to gain the entire market even of the particular industry in which its comparative advantage lies. In the great majority of cases, of course, it is simply not possible for a firm to gain the entire market of its industry—it is not in a position to outcompete all the other firms, and there are other firms in its industry whose interests are not served by merging with it. But even apart from these factors, even if the firm in question is the most efficient in its industry, once it achieves a certain relative size, whether 60 percent, 80 percent, or 90 percent of the industry's market, gaining the remaining share of the market simply does not constitute enough of a prize to make it worthwhile.

If the remaining, relatively small share of the market is all that is to be gained, it does not pay the large firm to cut its price and reduce its profits on its much greater volume. Its actual interest will lie with the highest price it can obtain that is consistent with its small competitors (and potential competitors) not being able to make enough profit to accumulate the capital required to become more efficient and thus to offer it serious competition. In other words, its interest will lie with setting its price not too far above the full costs of its less efficient competitors or potential competitors, and making the highest possible profits it can by reducing its own costs of production as far below theirs as possible. So long as no one else can make substantial profits at the price it charges, it has no incentive to reduce its price further for the sake of gaining their small volume of business. Its policy will be to allow its small competitors to survive on the most favorable terms short of their rapidly accumulating capital. It will reduce its price only insofar as it perceives a likelihood of the costs of production of its competitors or potential competitors falling. (Sooner or later, in a free economy, this will happen, and it will have to reduce its price. But then, if it manages to retain a cost advantage by having further reduced its own costs of production—which it is motivated to do—it will cut only to the point of once again preventing others from rapidly accumulating capital.)

The exception to this rule of the large firm not disturbing its less efficient small competitors is the case in which, by charging a price below their costs, a vast expansion in the total market of the industry can take place, from which it will be able to benefit substantially. If, for example, at a selling price of 85¢ rather than $1, the quantity demanded of the industry as a whole expands by a factor of two or three, and Big John is meanwhile able to achieve further economies of scale and reduce his unit cost to 75¢ or even 70¢, then, indeed, it will pay him to undercut his small rivals and drive them out of business (or buy them out). But his motive here is not to gain the piddling volume of his small competitors, in order then to jack up his price to a higher level than ever before. On the contrary, it is to gain the vast increase in the market of the industry as whole, which can only be done by charging *a permanently lower price*.

But even in this case, becoming the sole producer would not pay if the large firm's cost advantages are of a kind that can be patented and thus shared with other producers in exchange for royalty payments. For then, the firm could make additional profits on 100 percent of an expanded market without having to accumulate by itself all the capital required to supply the market.

If the only substantive gain from price cutting is the volume of business presently carried on by one's competitors, then it follows that it is more efficient *small* firms that have much more to gain by following an aggressive pricing policy than more efficient large firms. A large firm, with 90 percent of the market, has only the 10 percent share of its rivals to gain. But a small firm, with 10 percent of the market, has the *90 percent* share of its rivals to gain. Such a small firm will be much more intent on expanding its share of the market than the large firm.

Thus, this discussion has demonstrated further inherent limits to economic concentration under capitalism, even within a given industry.

And in the light of this discussion, it should come as no surprise that historical research has now established that the old Standard Oil Company (for which, of course, the "Big John" of our examples was a stand-in) *never actually engaged in a policy of predatory price cutting.*[43]

"Predatory Pricing" in Reverse: The Myth of Japanese "Dumping"

It is ironic in the extreme, that after generations of claims about the predatory-pricing powers of the Big Johns of the world versus the helpless Little Joes of the world, the enemies of capitalism have now done a complete about-face. Now, at least in the case of Japan, they claim to fear the predatory-pricing powers of Little Joes against Big Johns. This new doctrine is manifest in the claims that the economic success of Japanese firms, that only a few decades ago were economically insignificant in comparison with their American counterparts, is the result of Japanese "dumping"—i.e., selling below cost, i.e., "predatory pricing." Yes, now we are asked to believe that the piddling Toyota and Nissan corporations of the 1950s and 1960s, and the piddling Nippon Steel Corporation of the same period, and their piddling counterparts in numerous other industries, have driven out of business or come close to driving out of business one American industrial giant after another. Poor General Motors, poor U.S. Steel, poor whoever—so the story goes—they could not stand the losses inflicted on them

by year after year of "dumping" by Japanese firms that were only a fraction of their size.

No, it may be said, not dumping on the part of small Japanese firms acting on their own, but dumping made possible by subsidies provided by the Japanese government, guided by its nefarious *Ministry of International Trade and Industry*.

Such a tale of Oriental intrigue would deserve to fail even as a Charlie Chan story. What it overlooks, of course, is that the resources at the disposal of the Japanese government have been entirely dependent on the success of Japanese business, which has not operated at losses in its export trade but at very high profits, based on a combination of low costs of production and high quality of products. The Japanese firms may often have sold below the costs of their unionized and otherwise hamstrung American competitors, which came more and more to be managed by incompetents whose leading skill lay in such things as pacifying government regulators rather than in successfully running a business. But rarely if ever did they sell below their own costs.

Only to a fascistic-type mentality imbued with a belief in government omnipotence can it seem reasonable to attribute the success of the Japanese economy to the guidance and subsidies of a government ministry.[44] The truth is, to whatever extent the Japanese government has diverted Japanese businesses from the path they would have followed strictly on the basis of profit-and-loss considerations and has provided them with subsidies, the success of Japanese business has been less than it otherwise would have been. This is the case because such interference only serves to make firms earn lower profits than they otherwise could have earned and makes it possible for inefficient producers to survive by covering their losses on the basis of taxes taken from the profits of efficient producers. Given the enormous success of the Japanese economic system, such interference, while it may have existed to some extent, could not have been very significant. The success of the Japanese economy is attributable to those elements of it that are consistent with freedom and profit making, not to violations of freedom, not to the earning of lower profits rather than higher profits, and not to the payment of subsidies to cover losses.[45]

The Chain-Store Variant of the Predatory-Pricing Doctrine

The predatory-pricing doctrine must be examined further insofar as it is the case that the larger firm is larger by virtue of its presence in more than one market—for example, chain stores that compete with local merchants, or conglomerates that compete with smaller firms in a variety of different industries. In such cases, of course, if the larger firm were to slash its price for the purpose of making its smaller rival run at a loss, it would not have to suffer a reduction in its own revenues and profits in proportion to its overall greater size, but only in proportion to its greater size in the particular market concerned.

Here, the argument goes, the large firm is able to cover its losses in the particular market out of the profits it earns in all its other markets. It is able to bring overwhelming resources to bear, and thus not only to drive out its small rivals in one market at a time, but also to keep out all potential new entrants by the mere threat of dipping into its vast treasury and inflicting losses on them.

It was popular at one time to accuse the A&P Company, which for many years was the largest retail grocery chain in the United States, of having followed this policy against neighborhood grocers. The accusations seem to have died down in the years since the company lost that eminent position as the result of a competition that the supporters of the predatory-pricing doctrine must judge to be virtually incapable of having occurred.

An essential fact that must be pointed out in cases of this kind is that the far greater part or, indeed, almost the whole of the profits and capital of the "big, rich firm" is *irrelevant* to its ability to sustain temporary losses in driving its smaller, poorer rivals out of business. The truth of this proposition can be understood by imagining that on the one side is A&P, with *$1 billion* of total capital invested in a thousand stores nationwide, and on the other side a small grocer and his wife, with perhaps only $50,000 of capital invested in their one little store.

This case, of course, is similar to the cases we have already considered, insofar as in slashing its price A&P will have to suffer a reduction in revenues and profits perhaps twenty times as great as the reduction in revenues and profits it can impose on the small store. (This ratio is implied in the fact that A&P's assumed overall total of $1 billion of capital is supposed to be invested in a thousand stores. The resulting $1 million average investment per store is twenty times larger than the assumed investment of the small grocer and his wife. To the extent that the larger investment implies a larger volume of business, the losses of A&P must be a multiple of the losses of the small competitor.)

The special fact that must be recognized in the present case, however—a fact that would be critical even if in the particular local market the two firms had invested the same amount of capital and did the same volume of business—is that almost all of A&P's billion and the profits it may make in its other 999 stores are *irrelevant* to what it can afford to lose in this particular location. To demonstrate this conclusion, it is only necessary to assume for the moment that A&P can actually succeed in driving out its small rival or rivals and thereafter keep

out all new rivals by the mere threat of ruining them. If it really could do this, it would forever after earn a premium profit in this one location. But precisely that is the point—it would be a premium profit *in only one location*. Such a premium profit is surely quite limited—perhaps an additional $100,000 per year, perhaps even an additional $500,000 per year, but certainly nothing remotely approaching the profit that would be required to justify the commitment of A&P's total financial resources.

And now the question arises, just how much is it worth temporarily losing in order to secure such an extra profit? The temporary loss must be regarded as an additional investment, made for the purpose of later on adding to profits.

True enough, A&P *has* $1 billion in capital, and its total annual profits may be on the order of $100 million or even $200 million or more. But it could never pay to temporarily lose—to invest—sums of such magnitude for the sake of earning an extra $100,000 or $500,000 a year, even if these latter sums could be earned every year thereafter forever. Each individual branch of a business must be judged on the basis of its own profitability and must be profitable in its own right, if the investment in it is to be justified. The measure of how much it pays temporarily to lose in order to increase profits later on, is provided by the going rate of profit on capital in the economic system. If the going, average rate of profit or interest is, say, 10 percent a year, then a $500,000 annual amount of profit or interest can be made by the investment of $5 million. This sum—$5 million—is then the upper limit of what it pays temporarily to lose, in order to eliminate competitors in this one location. By the same token, if the extra permanent annual profit in this one location will only be $100,000 then the most it pays temporarily to lose in eliminating competitors is $1 million.

These sums—$5 million and $1 million—are the respective capitalized or present values of $500,000 and $100,000 a year forever, if the annual rate of return on capital is 10 percent. To the extent that it is necessary to lose sums larger than these in order to secure the $500,000 or $100,000 higher profits every year, the effect is that the firm ends up earning *a below-average rate of profit on its capital* in this investment. It earns less on the capital in question than it readily could have earned. The investment is a bad investment.

It cannot be stressed too strongly: all of A&P's billion of capital and all of its tens or hundreds of millions of total annual profits beyond these $5 million or even just $1 million of capital are simply irrelevant to its ability to make a worthwhile investment in this case. A&P cannot afford to regard more than these strictly limited sums as available for a temporary loss. If it loses any more than these sums, its investment is a poor one even if it succeeds in its alleged goal of driving out and keeping out everyone else and becoming the "monopoly" supplier in the area. This is because in such conditions it would end up earning a below-average rate of profit despite its having secured a local "monopoly." For example, if it temporarily loses $2 million in order thereafter to earn an additional $100,000 a year in profits forever, and actually succeeds in earning such profits while the going rate of return is 10 percent, the result is that it ends up earning only a 5 percent rate of return when it could have earned a 10 percent rate of return. Exactly the same result applies if it temporarily loses $10 million in order to end up earning an additional $500,000 a year forever.

An equally important implication of these facts is that everyone contemplating an investment in the grocery business who has an additional $5 million or even just $1 million to put up *is on as good a footing as A&P* in attempting to achieve such additional profits. For it simply does not pay to invest additional capital beyond these sums. In other words, the predatory-pricing game, if it actually could be played in these circumstances, would be open to a fairly substantial number of players—not just the extremely large, very rich firms, but everyone who had an additional capital available equal to the limited capitalized value of the "monopoly gains" that might be derived from an individual location.

And this very circumstance helps to explain why a policy of predatory pricing cannot be pursued, even in limited areas, one at a time. For what must happen if a company such as A&P were to attempt it? It loses, let us imagine, $500,000 in eliminating the competitors who were on the scene when it made its initial appearance in the area. Now, if the capitalized value of becoming the sole seller is $1 million, it can afford to lose only an additional $500,000; if the capitalized value is $5 million, it can afford to lose an additional $4.5 million. But in either case, what is its position in comparison with any outside entrant who has his full $1 million or $5 million available?

Such an outsider is now in a position in which, from the point of view of ending up with an investment that at least yields the going rate of return, he can afford to lose more than A&P for the prize of becoming the sole seller. Of course, if he pursues this policy, he in turn will find himself in the same position in relation to still another outsider—all of which means that there is no way of actually securing the kind of premium profits imagined in this example, and that all that can result from the attempt is the pouring of money down a bottomless well. As we have seen before, whoever would attempt it, would find himself in the position of having made a larger-than-necessary capital investment, which he would

later *need* to recover through higher-than-necessary prices and more than a competitive rate of profit, but would be unable to recover in the actual conditions of the market. The capital he expended in the effort to achieve the illusory extra profits would place him in the same position as someone who had constructed his store or bought the land for it at an unnecessarily high price. This is certainly not a formula for growing rich.

Contract Pricing

As I have said, it should not be thought that after having gone to the expense of driving its initial rivals out of business in a particular market, a very large firm might be able to secure premium profits by a policy merely of threatening to lose whatever sums might be required to inflict losses on potential new competitors and thus keep them out by sheer intimidation, with the result that it would not be put to the actual expense of major losses very often. If it is going to charge prices higher than those at which outsiders would be profitable, it will often be put to the test, and suffer accordingly—usually to a considerable multiple of whatever losses it may be able to inflict on its smaller competitors. In fact, it is often extremely easy to overcome any such attempt at intimidation. Apart from everything else I have described, all that would need to be done is for a competing supplier to sell his product *under long-term contract.*

Such a competitor can offer a price that is equal to his cost plus an allowance for the going rate of profit. And he can offer it for the life of his plant. (If he already has a plant and were the object of predatory price cutting, it would pay him, if necessary, to enter such an agreement at any price above his operating costs plus allowance for the going rate of profit on his working capital.) The contract can give the buyers the right not to buy from him—if the alleged predator firm or anyone else is currently charging prices low enough to make dealing with them more attractive. In this case, all that need be required of the buyers is that they pay a relatively modest penalty charge for the units they do not take—a charge just sufficient to cover the supplier's costs of being in the business and earning the going rate of profit on the capital he must tie up.

Such a charge would exclude any cost of materials or direct labor, since no product would actually change hands, and all but a skeleton level of administrative overhead. In terms of our earlier example of Big John and Little Joe, a new Little Joe, contemplating entry into the field against Big John, could make a contract in which he agrees to sell a unit of his product at $1 for the life of his capacity, and to accept a fee of, say, 20¢ for each unit not bought. The 20¢, or whatever the comparable figure might be, would cover Little Joe's depreciation charges, the cost of maintaining a minimal organization in being, and the profit on the capital invested in the plant, which might have to function sometimes on a standby basis only. (If Little Joe is already in the business, then, depending on his operating cost, it might be worth his while to agree if necessary perhaps to a price as low as 90¢ or even 85¢, and a penalty charge of as little as 10¢ or even 5¢, since his investment in plant has already been made and it represents the lesser loss to accept such terms than simply to go out of business.)

Under such an arrangement, the small competitor's position is made secure, and the buyers are able to place a permanent upper limit on the price they have to pay. If Big John is to obtain their business, he must offer a price that is lower than Little Joe's by more than the penalty charge, which means that he ends up financing the penalty charge. (He ends up financing it, because once his price falls below Little Joe's by the amount of the penalty charge, the buyers save in the lower price as much as they pay in the penalty charge.) If Big John does not wish to price that low in order to obtain their business—if he wants their business at a price close to Little Joe's full price—the only way to obtain it is by offering it on a *permanent* basis. This means that Big John will have to offer long-term contracts with a specified price. In that way, upon the expiration of the life of Little Joe's capacity, he might obtain the latter's business if his long-term contract price is lower than little Joe needs to make replacement worthwhile. But, for the reasons explained, it is unlikely that it will pay Big John to reduce the price on his vastly greater volume in order to obtain Little's Joe's modest share of the market.

At the retail level, contract pricing might take the form of customers joining a buyers' club, for which they pay a flat fee that defrays the seller's costs of staying in business and that guarantees them the right to buy the item at a low price. It is worth noting in addition that at the retail level elements of consumer tastes and preferences enter which almost always establish niches of small competitors that are impossible to dislodge even with substantially lower prices that are permanent. For example, there are all kinds of small stores that have stayed in business through offering greater convenience and more personal service and so forth, despite much lower prices being charged by the chain stores and department stores. Starting from this relatively secure base, such stores are in a position to take away a substantial volume of business from the chains and department stores, should the latter significantly increase their prices.

The Predatory-Pricing Doctrine and the Inversion of Economic History

As previously indicated, the implication of the pred-

atory-pricing doctrine is that real costs and prices both in retailing and everywhere else have tended to increase because of the alleged monopolistic character of the chain stores and of big business in general. In the view of the predatory-pricing doctrine, the development of chain stores and big business does not have any basis in greater economic efficiency, but serves only as a means of raising prices. The implication of the doctrine is that from the point of view of the consumers, the days when all that existed were local general stores, whale oil, and blacksmith shops were the good old days. These days have passed because those suppliers were put out of business by predatory pricing. Now all that exists is price gouging.

It is difficult to imagine a view of things more at odds with the facts. But this is the view implied by the predatory-pricing doctrine. It totally ignores the efficiencies of the chain stores and of big business in general, and that the firms which became big did so by providing better products at lower costs of production. Typically, such firms did not start out as big businesses, but *became* big businesses on the basis of the high profits they earned by virtue of their greater efficiency and which they constantly plowed back. And those firms which began as the result of mergers of already existing firms grew much further—both in terms of the quantity and quality of their output and in terms of their efficiency and capital investment. It is impossible to reconcile the actual economic expansion—the constant increase in capital invested and the constant fall in real costs and prices—throughout the domain of big business over the last five generations, with the contention that big business achieves high profits by means of high prices based on diminished production.

The Myth of Predation With Respect to Suppliers

A notion similar to the predatory-pricing doctrine is the belief that large firms are in a position to deprive their small competitors of access to vital supplies. By means of threatening to withdraw their own business, or by means of bribery, they allegedly induce such suppliers either to refuse to deal with the small firm or to do so only on terms that are unprofitable to it.

The fallacy present in this belief is essentially similar to that which exists in the predatory-pricing doctrine. It overlooks the fact that if the large firm seriously wished to pursue such a policy, it would have to make dealing with it rather than the small competitor more profitable to *every actual and potential supplier* to whom the small competitor might turn, and to offer more to them not only than the small competitor is currently capable of doing, but also is potentially capable of doing in the future.

It must be realized that the small competitor only needs to find *one* supplier, and that to stop him from doing so, the large firm must close off *every* actual and potential supplier. Moreover, to whatever extent the small firm offers the prospect of becoming larger and thus of offering more business to a supplier as time goes on, it is the profit on that volume of business that the large firm must exceed in its offers.

Furthermore, when one takes into account the fact that the purpose of the large firm in driving out the small firm is supposed to be to sharply increase the price of the product, the position of the small firm must be regarded as all the more secure. This is because the prosperity of the industry's suppliers then depends on the continued existence of competitors to the large firm. As previously explained, if the large firm were actually to be capable of succeeding in raising the price, the effect would be a smaller quantity of the product demanded and thus less demand for the product or service of the suppliers. In other words, the suppliers' market depends on the continued existence of the small firm in these conditions. And that is why, indeed, they can be assumed to be an actual *ally* of the small firm, rather than a partner in its destruction.

While the multiple of cost to the large firm is increased to the degree that its small competitor has access to a larger number of suppliers or potential suppliers, it should not be assumed that if there are only few suppliers or potential suppliers, this represents any kind of advantage to the large firm. On the contrary, even if there were only some definite, delimited number of suppliers or potential suppliers who would need to be secured against the small firm, the large firm would be unable to take comfort in that fact. The consequence would be that any one of the suppliers or potential suppliers with sufficient capacity to meet the requirements of the small firm would be in a position to demand a lion's share of whatever additional profits might be earned by virtue of the absence of the small competitor and the consequent alleged ability to charge substantially higher prices. In other words, since the large firm's extra profit would depend on the cooperation of *all* of the suppliers and potential suppliers, *each of them* would be in a position to demand the greater part or almost all of the presumed extra profits.

The Myth of Standard Oil and the South Improvement Company

In the light of the above, one can regard the story of Standard Oil and the South Improvement Company as a historical fable, at least as far as the interpretation goes that is usually placed upon it. According to a typical account, in a widely used textbook of economic history:

In 1870 Standard Oil was producing about 10 per cent of the country's output of refined oil. This quickly increased to 20 per cent by an ingenious and notorious scheme involving the South Improvement Company in 1872. Refiners associated with the South Improvement Company were to receive rebates, presumably for acting as "eveners" in the oil traffic pool formed at the same time among the Pennsylvania, New York Central, and Erie Railroads. The open rate on crude oil by rail from the oil regions in western Pennsylvania to Cleveland was to be 80 cents per barrel, and the open rate on refined products from Cleveland to New York City was to be two dollars ($2.00) per barrel. Thus the combined open rate was $2.80. The open rate was the same to all shippers, but the members of the South Improvement Company were to receive a secret rebate of 90 cents (40 cents on crude and 50 cents on refined products). In addition to a rebate on all their own shipments, members of the South Improvement Company were also to receive the same rebate on all petroleum shipped by their competitors. Thus the harder their competitors worked, the more money Rockefeller and his associates would make....

Armed with this contract, Standard representatives bought out most of their competitors. Within three months twenty-one of twenty-six Cleveland refiners went out of business. Their plants were either junked or put into use by Standard Oil producers. Although the agreement was signed between the railways and the South Improvement Company the scheme never actually went into operation so far as railway rates were concerned. Yet it was fully effective in achieving its purpose: the elimination of competition.[46]

The meaning of these passages is that Standard Oil somehow managed to obtain an arbitrary discrimination in railroad rates in its favor, for the purpose of eliminating its competitors. Interestingly, the passages note that at the time Standard was not even a particularly large firm (it had only 10 percent of the market), and the railroads did not actually increase rates to Standard's competitors, but cut them to Standard. Apart from a reference to "acting as 'eveners,'" the meaning of which is left unexplained and which is dismissed contemptuously, no explanation is offered of why the railroads would do such a thing. It is apparently thought to be sufficient merely to conjure up an aura of big business and sinister machinations, and to let it go at that.

Without having investigated the historical facts, but approaching the matter with a framework of a knowledge of economic principles, I am confident that if the actual facts were known, an entirely different interpretation would have to be placed upon the episode than the one in the above passages. My confidence is comparable to that of a natural scientist upon hearing a tale of some miracle. He knows automatically that a rational explanation is to be found.

If the episode occurred at all (and the admission that "the scheme never actually went into operation" indicates that perhaps even this should be questioned), then I would offer the following hypothesis. Namely, that Standard Oil devised a plan for regular large-scale shipments of oil and oil products which substantially reduced the railroads' costs of transportation and, at the same time, gave promise of a substantial increase in the total volume of shipments. In return, Standard deservedly received the rebate. It received a rebate on its competitors' shipments as well, insofar as its transportation plan made it possible for the railroads to save money on their shipments by tying them into Standard's plan. The basis for the buyout of most of its Cleveland competitors was probably the fact that the transportation plan could be made more effective by making their volume directly subject to its control. On the basis of prospective major cost savings in transportation, Standard was able to buy out the competitors at prices profitable to them.[47]

8. Marginal Revenue and the Alleged "Monopolistic Restriction" of Supply

The doctrine of an alleged tendency toward a growing concentration of capital in fewer and fewer hands—whether it is to be achieved by means of mergers or by means of predatory price cutting—can now be judged to have been laid to rest. Yet the economic concept of monopoly advances another claim, that is less sweeping, but still quite serious. This is the doctrine that to the degree that a firm is large relative to the size of the market it serves, it is motivated to restrict its production to a quantity of product that is less than what in some sense it "should produce."

The following example provides an illustration of this doctrine in its comparatively more reasonable form. Thus, let us imagine an industry in which there is only a single firm—an out-and-out "monopolist," according to the economic concept of monopoly. At present, this firm produces an output of 100 units of product, which it sells at a price of $15 per unit. Its cost of production is $8 per unit. Thus, its sales revenues are $1,500, its total cost is $800, and its profit is $700. The firm is considering the question of whether or not it should produce and sell a second 100 units of its product. If it does, it will have to reduce its selling price to something less than $15. Let us imagine that $9 will be the price necessary to attract buyers for a total of 200 units. We can assume that the firm's cost of production per unit will remain at $8.

I have chosen to assume that the price will have to be $9 and that the cost per unit will remain $8 because these figures imply that the production of the second 100 units, if considered in their own right—that is, independently, apart from the effect on anything else—is *profitable*. The second 100 units will bring in sales revenue of $900 and will be produced at a cost of $800. Thus, they will bring in a net profit of $100, which can reasonably be assumed to constitute a sufficient amount of profit to constitute

the going, competitive rate of profit on the capital which must be invested in their production. Consequently, by the ordinary standard of profitability, this second 100 units should be produced.

Nevertheless, argue the supporters of the economic concept of monopoly, our firm will find it unprofitable to produce them. This is because it must consider something besides the profitability of producing the second 100 units in their own right. It must also consider the effect on its profits of having to sell the quantity it is already selling, namely, the first 100 units, at the reduced price of $9. This aspect of the situation represents a $600 *reduction* in its profits. This is because instead of selling those first 100 units at a price of $15, and thereby bringing in sales revenues of $1,500, it now must sell those first 100 units at a price of only $9 and thus earn sales revenues of only $900. Given its total cost of $800 to produce the first 100 units, this means that the profit it earns on them falls from $1,500 minus $800 to $900 minus $800, viz., by $600.

This fact, it is held, far outweighs the fact that the sale of the second 100 units nets a profit of $100, for the gaining of this $100 profit requires the simultaneous reduction of $600 in the profits already being earned on the first 100 units. And thus, the effect of expanding its production from 100 to 200 units is, for this "monopoly" firm, to reduce its overall, total profit from $700 to $200—an overall, net reduction of $500 in its profits. As a result, it is held, it will not produce the second 100 units. It will prefer instead to keep its output at 100 units and its price at $15. And the buying public will thus be correspondingly deprived. Table 10–1 summarizes all the relevant data.

The table includes the headings "Marginal Revenue" and "Marginal Revenue per Unit." Marginal revenue is *the change in total revenue that accompanies a change in quantity produced and sold*. In this case, it is $300. In selling 200 units at $9 per unit, instead of 100 units at $15 per unit, our firm would end up increasing its total sales revenue by only $300, because the $900 received for the second 100 units of its product would be accompanied by a $600 reduction in the revenues received for the sale of its first 100 units. Marginal revenue per unit is simply the total marginal revenue, in this case $300, divided by the additional number of units, in this case 100 units.

The relevant consideration for our firm in deciding whether or not to increase its production—and, indeed, for any firm that must reduce the selling price of its product in order to sell a larger quantity of it—is not, it is held, whether the new selling price exceeds the unit cost of the additional products by enough to provide a competitive rate of profit. The relevant consideration is,

				Table 10–1				
			Marginal Revenue and the Alleged Incentive of a "Monopoly" Firm to "Restrict" Its Production					
Quantity	Price	Total Revenue	Marginal Revenue	Marginal Revenue per Unit	Unit Cost	Total Cost	Profit
100	$15	$1,500	—	—	$8	$800	$700
200	$9	$1,800	$300	$3	$8	$1,600	$200

allegedly, whether or not *the marginal revenue per unit*, rather than the price, exceeds the unit cost of the additional output. The marginal revenue per unit takes into account the drop in price on the quantity that is already being sold. In the present case it is $3, reflecting the combined effect of receiving a selling price of $9 on the increase in quantity sold from 100 to 200 units and having to accept a price reduction of $6 on the initial 100 units.

This belief, that marginal revenue, rather than price, is the relevant item for a firm to compare with its cost in deciding whether or not to expand output can be called *the marginal-revenue doctrine.*

It is on the basis of the marginal-revenue doctrine that it is held that to the degree that a firm is large relative to the market it serves, it is correspondingly less motivated to expand its production. To the degree that the firm is large, it is argued, the more will its marginal revenue per unit accompanying any increase in its production fall short of the selling price that accompanies that additional production. For it will experience the fall in price that is associated with its additional production on a correspondingly larger initial quantity. Thus, the more strongly will it be motivated not to expand its production, despite the fact that by the standard of the profitability of the additional output considered in its own right, output should be expanded.

A "monopolist," it is held, has the least incentive to expand, for he must experience the price reduction on the full quantity of the product presently sold. But a firm that initially produces and sells only half, or even a tenth, of the total output of an industry, can also have a powerful incentive not to expand its production, according to the marginal-revenue doctrine.

This last claim can be illustrated by imagining that the initial output of the industry is 10 times larger than previously assumed—1,000 units instead of 100. Our firm produces 100 units out of the 1,000 and is contemplating whether or not it should produce 200 units. If the production of this second 100 units for our firm, which at the same time is the production of an eleventh 100 units for the industry as a whole, should necessitate a reduction in the selling price of the industry's product to $9, then, it is argued, everything would be just as before from the perspective of our firm. It would allegedly not expand its output because doing so would require too great a reduction in the selling price of the quantity it was already selling.

From the point of view of the supporters of the marginal-revenue doctrine, the only difference between this case and the first case is that the demand curve of the industry is now less elastic. In the first case, it takes a doubling of the output of the industry to necessitate a price reduction of 40 percent. In the present case, it takes an increase in the industry's output of only 10 percent to necessitate a price reduction of 40 percent. The percentage change in the quantity demanded of the industry's product relative to the percentage change in the price of the product necessary to achieve that percentage change in quantity demanded—which is the definition of elasticity—is one-tenth as great in the present case.

However, given the *same* elasticity of demand for the product of the industry as a whole, it follows from the marginal-revenue doctrine that the smaller the size of the firm relative to the industry, the greater will be its incentive to increase its production. If we retain the assumption that our firm initially produces 100 units out of an industry total of 1,000, and that the elasticity of demand for the product of the industry as a whole is no lower than it was in our first example, then a 10 percent increase in the industry's supply, brought about by a doubling of our one particular firm's supply, will cause perhaps only a 4 percent reduction in the industry's selling price—viz., from $15.00 to $14.40. (The assumption here is that a 10 percent increase in the industry's supply necessitates a price reduction only one-tenth as great as a 100 percent increase in the industry's supply—in this case, 4 percent instead of 40 percent.[48]) Thus, in this case, it supposedly pays the firm to double its output, for it now takes in $2,880 in sales revenues (200 x $14.40) and, with total costs of $1,600, it earns a substantially increased profit of $1,280 instead of $700.

Given the elasticity of demand for the product of the industry, the elasticity of demand for the product of an individual firm, it is held, is inversely proportionate to the smallness of its size in the industry as a whole. To the degree that the firm is small, what appears as a large relative increase in its own production is nevertheless a small percentage increase in the production of the industry as a whole, and thus results in a reduction in selling price that is correspondingly small. For instance, in the present example, a 100 percent increase in the firm's own output constitutes a mere 10 percent increase in the output of the industry as a whole and necessitates a reduction in selling price only in accordance with the 10 percent increase in the overall supply of the industry, not a doubling of the supply of the industry. If the firm initially represented 1 percent of the industry instead of 10 percent, then, it is argued, a doubling of its supply would constitute only a 1 percent increase in the industry's supply and would thus be accompanied by the still more modest price reduction accompanying this much lesser increase in the industry's supply. And thus the incentive of the firm to increase its production would be greater still. It is on this basis that contemporary economic theory has long preceded the environmental movement in subscribing to the cliché that "big is bad and small is beautiful"—at least when it comes to business.

It should be observed, however, that there is an important and paradoxical difference between the contemporary economist's and the ecologist's attachment to this cliché. What the contemporary economist is actually criticizing the large firm for is *its failure to produce still more and thus to become larger still*. What he is applauding the small firm for is its presumed readiness to produce more and thus to become larger. There are two elements of paradox present in this. First, if the large firm did produce all that it is supposed to produce—if, for example, in our initial illustration the firm did produce the 200 units and accept the price of $9—it would then be denounced as a monopoly. Thus, it is denounced as a monopoly if it does produce the extra 100 units, and denounced as monopolistically restricting supply if it doesn't produce the extra 100 units. It is in the same position as the poor Russian worker under the Soviet regime, who was guilty of spying if he came to work early, sabotage if he arrived late, and of having a capitalist watch if he came on time. Second, if it is the case that the large firm will not produce the extra units, and the small firm or new entrant will, then the whole alleged problem simply disappears. The large firm ceases to be

relatively so large, as it holds its production steady and small firms expand or new entrants appear. As far as it exists, such behavior on the part of the large firm would simply be one more reason why there is normally more than one firm in an industry.

The marginal-revenue doctrine is usually not presented in such relatively simple and therefore clear terms as it has been presented here. In particular, no special stress is normally laid on the production of the additional units being profitable in their own right. Thus, the implications of that fact are rarely if ever considered. It is simply established that there are circumstances in which a large firm, especially a "monopolist," could gain more by producing less. But because it has stressed this aspect, the preceding exposition suggests a profound and very obvious difficulty with the marginal-revenue doctrine.

This difficulty can be seen clearly even in the seemingly strongest case in favor of the marginal-revenue doctrine, namely, that of the so-called out and out monopolist, in which there is just one seller. The difficulty is that unless this firm produces a product which others are simply physically unable to produce, or, more likely, are forcibly prevented from producing by the government (rightly so in the case of patents and copyrights), its actual choice is not such as between producing and selling 100 units at a price of $15 or 200 units at a price of $9, but between 100 units at a price of *$9* or 200 units at a price of $9. Apart from the exceptions just mentioned, so long as the second 100 units are profitable in their own right, *they will be produced*. The only question is whether they will be produced by the firm that is already producing 100 units or by another firm. In the latter case, the first firm ends up selling at $9, but only 100 units instead of 200 units.

The principle here is that where competition is physically possible and is peaceful—that is, in which the same or a similar good is capable of being produced by others without violation of anyone's intellectual property rights—and is legally free, the decision of any seller or group of sellers to produce less, or not to produce at all, cannot lastingly establish a selling price that is above the cost of production, plus allowance for the going rate of profit, of potential competitors. Under such conditions, it is impossible for anyone to charge prices significantly higher than would be required for a potential new entrant into the industry to make a competitive rate of profit—except in the case of temporary scarcity, and except to the extent that one's product may be of premium quality over his.

If one does charge a price above the point an outsider needs to be profitable, the outsider enters, and, for the reasons explained in the preceding section, one cannot then reverse field and resort to the policy of driving him out by means of ruinous prices. One simply loses volume and must accept the lower price he will charge. *The upper limit to one's price, therefore, is set by the cost of production of potential new entrants.* If one goes higher than their cost plus an allowance for the competitive rate of profit they would require, one loses more and more volume, until one is finally driven out oneself or accepts the fact that one cannot exceed this limit in price.

One's price may certainly be lower than this limit, and will be whenever one has a lower cost of production than the outsiders and it is more profitable to charge a lower price. But it cannot be higher. As previously stated, the cost of production of potential new entrants constitutes an objective given that limits one's price. One's only choice is to sell either a smaller volume at that cost-limited price or a larger volume at that cost-limited price or a still larger volume at a lower price. But one cannot get a higher price.

If one allows for the time that may be required for new firms to enter a field, one can say that irrespective of the elasticity or inelasticity of the demand for the product of an industry as a whole, *the elasticity of the demand for the product of any individual firm,* however large, *is virtually infinite if it charges a price above outsiders' costs plus allowance for the going rate of profit.* At such a price, or just below it, it can potentially sell the full quantity demanded at that price. Above such a price, it will sell little or nothing.

In the face of competitors already in the field, the pressures for a price limited by outsiders' costs are all the more intense. The pricing of the whole group of present producers must be limited by this consideration even if they were formed into a single combination. Acting separately and independently, however, the acceptance by any of them of the need to make his price conform to the cost of production places the others under a powerful immediate pressure to limit their price in the same way. For whoever charges more than the cost-limited price will immediately lose substantial volume to those who do not (unless his product is of such premium quality over theirs as to justify the premium price he charges).

To state matters further in terms of the concept of elasticity of demand, one must say that under the freedom of competition the elasticity of demand for the product of any individual company or group of companies at a price above outsiders' costs plus allowance for the going rate of profit, is determined by the sum of the elasticity of demand for the product of the industry as a whole *plus the elasticity of supply of competitors and potential competitors.* That is, at such a price, the quantity of the firm's product that is demanded falls not only in accordance with the amount by which quantity demanded from the industry falls, but also by the amount by which the supply

provided by competitors and potential competitors increases, for their sales will be made at its expense. And thus, while the demand curve facing the industry as a whole may be almost perfectly inelastic, or, indeed, actually be perfectly inelastic, the demand curve facing any individual firm in the industry tends to be perfectly elastic at a price above outsiders' costs plus allowance for the going rate of profit.[49]

Competitors' and Potential Competitors' Costs—Ultimately, Legal Freedom of Entry—as Setting the Upper Limit to Prices in a Free Market

The implication of the preceding discussion is that in a free market, prices of products are normally determined by cost of production—if not one's own cost of production, then at least that of competitors or potential competitors, which cost product prices must not exceed by more than an amount of profit sufficient to provide the going rate of profit. It is further implicit in the preceding discussion that *legal freedom of entry is the essential foundation of competitive price determination.* For it is legal freedom of entry that is necessary to make possible the threat of new entrants, whose costs determine the upper limit to almost every industry's prices.

In contrast, the elasticity or inelasticity of demand—that is, the extent of the willingness of buyers to pay higher prices for smaller quantities of the product—usually does not enter into the determination of prices, and, as will be demonstrated later in this section, plays only a limited role even in the cases in which it does enter.[50] The demand for many goods is extremely inelastic, meaning that if it were possible to achieve even modest reductions in their supply, sharply higher prices could be obtained. All kinds of spare parts, manufacturing components, inexpensive supplies, and necessities fall into this category. Imagine how much every buyer of spark plugs, fan belts, fuel pumps, carburetors, nails, screws, paper clips, bread, and table salt would be willing to pay even for the marginal unit he now buys, if he had no choice. Certainly, it would be a substantially higher price than he does pay in most such instances. Every spare part, if priced on the basis of its own marginal utility, would be worth the full value of the product it restores to operation: e.g., the marginal fan belt or carburetor would have the value of the marginal automobile. And even in the cases in which the present marginal unit might not bring a higher price, a very slight reduction in supply would so elevate the importance of the marginal unit as to bring about a sharply higher price.

Imagine for the moment that because of a very slight reduction in its production and supply, the amount of table salt annually consumed had to be reduced by as little as 1 percent, indeed, by just .1 percent, of what is presently consumed. Consider how high the price of table salt would have to rise from its present level to make buyers economize on their use of table salt even to this extremely modest extent—to be careful to get more of the salt on the food rather than elsewhere on the plate or on the table cloth. The price of table salt might very well have to go up by a factor of five or ten times or more, to make people conscious of this need to economize on its use, given how cheap it now is.

It should be obvious that what the buyers would be willing to pay for table salt—or any of the other goods mentioned—if its supply were the least bit smaller, is totally irrelevant to the price they actually do have to pay for it in all normal circumstances. Its actual price is set within the much lower limit determined by the cost of production plus competitive profit of potential new producers. And were there only one seller of table salt rather than the comparatively small number that presently exist, and he were subject to the legal freedom of competition, its price would be determined no differently.

Perhaps the most powerful factor operating to keep prices in line with cost of production, irrespective of the elasticity of demand for the product, is the existence of formal or informal contractual arrangements. Prices set by contract are routinely ignored in economic theory, except as an alleged impediment to the adjustment of prices to the currently prevailing market forces. Nevertheless it is vital to recognize the role of contractual arrangements in removing the relative inelasticity of demand as a factor influencing price determination and in making cost of production the determinant of price.

Because of the ability to enter into contractual agreements, buyers can safely rely on small numbers of sellers—indeed, even just one seller—to serve as their source of supply, no matter how inelastic the demand for the good in question may be. The prices set under the contracts are cost-limited prices, in that they are limited at least by the costs of other potential suppliers, and are normally below the prices required by those other potential suppliers for the latter to be sufficiently profitable. (That is why the contracts are made with the particular suppliers they are made with, and not with other, merely potential suppliers.) Although limited by cost, such prices can easily be made to reflect the operation of current market forces, by being allowed to vary with one or more of the prices that enter into the supplier's current costs, and which he is not in a position to determine. For example, a contractually determined price of electric power might contain a provision for variability with the price of coal; a contractually determined price of components or supplies might contain a provision for variability with the price of the principle raw materials used in their production.

The setting of prices by contract, on the basis of cost,

prevents the possible inelasticity of demand for the product from being a factor in setting prices because the sellers are unable to obtain any higher price on whatever quantities they have agreed to sell under contract. Indeed, it may well be the case that the contractual arrangement gives buyers the right to purchase a variable quantity at the contractual price, with the result that, in effect, there are buyers who hold *options* on additional supplies at contractually set prices. In the face of such contractual arrangements, it may simply be impossible for the seller or sellers to reduce the market supply at all. And to the extent that it may still be possible for them to do so—only temporarily, of course—they are placed in a position in which the major beneficiary of their action would not be themselves, but *the buyers who have the right to buy at contractually fixed prices.*

To illustrate these points, let us consider once more our example of the ability to sell 200 units at a price of $9 and 100 units at a price of $15. Let us imagine that the firm producing the first 100 units has decided to forestall the entry of an outside firm and itself to produce and sell all 200 units at the price of $9. Thus, it is the sole supplier of the full competitive quantity at the competitive price.

Contract pricing prevents this firm from deciding from time to time to cut production back to 100 units in order to raise the price back up to $15. Even if only half of its output—100 of its 200 units—is sold at a contractual price of $9, it loses any motivation to cut back its production. If it did decide to produce 100 instead of 200 units, then, even without any competitor entering the field, the effect would be that it would sell 100 units at $9 instead of 200 units at $9, because those 100 units would be bought by the contract holders at a price of $9. Contract pricing operates to make the demand curve facing this firm perfectly elastic even in the immediate moment. Because of contract pricing, its choice in the immediate moment is reduced to whether it should sell 100 units at $9 or 200 units at $9.

And if for any reason this firm did produce only 100 units, the only possible beneficiaries of the resulting market price of $15 would be the firm's customers who held contractual rights. They would buy the product at the contractually fixed price of $9 and would be able to sell it at the higher open-market price of $15. In these conditions, it bears repeating, even the short-run interest of our firm is to produce and sell 200 units rather than only 100 units. (It should be observed that if our firm decided to produce any intermediate amount of output, between 100 and 200 units, it would gain any higher price only on the quantity it produced in excess of 100 units, while its customers who had contracts gained the rise in price on their 100 units. The profits earned by the customers on their 100 units could be used to finance a new competitor or new sources of supply under their own, direct control. The result would be that if our firm did decide to reduce its production below 200 units, it would set the stage for being faced with a new competitor or with a permanent reduction in the quantity demanded from it because its customers developed their own sources of supply—or it would end up having to sell a still larger portion of its output under contract. Or some combination of all three possibilities would result. In any event, the firm would not be able to repeat the procedure and would probably find it inadvisable to resort to it in the first place.)

This example illustrates the fact that in a free market, with substantial portions of output sold under contract, there need be no danger even of short-run arbitrary increases in price—even in situations of the most highly inelastic industry demand and in which there is just one supplier. Thus, even if there were just one producer of table salt, it would probably not be possible for him even temporarily to take advantage of the inelasticity of demand for table salt. His customers—grocery-store chains and wholesale jobbers who distribute to small retail grocers—would almost certainly obligate him to deliver at a contractually set price, limited by the cost of production of other potential producers, a quantity of table salt that, at their option, actually exceeds the quantity that is demanded from them at a normal retail or wholesale price of table salt. In such circumstances, even in this extreme case it would be impossible for the supplier to restrict the supply and raise the price.

Indeed, the fact that the price of table salt and of other goods with a comparably inelastic demand does not periodically shoot up in an effort to exploit the high inelasticity of demand can probably be explained only by the existence of contractual arrangements. For even when such goods are supplied by ten or twenty suppliers, in the absence of extensive formal or informal contractual arrangements, any one of the suppliers would probably be physically capable of reducing the industry's supply by the relatively tiny amount necessary to make its price skyrocket. Contractual arrangements, however, tie the price to cost on such a volume of output that no producer is in a position to reduce the supply below what the market demands at the cost-determined price, or would find it profitable to do so even if he were temporarily capable of doing so. Typically, a reduction in production by any one producer can be offset by an increase in production by others. And even if it cannot, it would not pay him.

The role of cost of production, rather than elasticity of demand, in the determination of prices is further evident in such cases as an excise tax increase on ciga-

rettes. Cigarettes are a good that is faced with a highly inelastic demand and which is produced by only a handful of firms. When the excise tax on cigarettes is increased, the price of cigarettes is correspondingly increased. At the higher price there is very little reduction in the quantity of cigarettes demanded, and the tobacco industry's pretax sales revenues sharply increase. The tobacco industry raises its price when the excise tax is increased because that is a factor raising the costs of doing business of all producers and potential producers.

In the absence of such a factor that increases costs to everyone, the tobacco industry would not be able to raise its price, despite the fact that if it could succeed in doing so all the firms would have sharply higher sales revenues and profits. By the same token, if the excise tax on cigarettes is reduced, or some other development occurs which broadly reduces the cost of providing cigarettes, the price of cigarettes must be correspondingly reduced.

The reason is that the existence of exceptionally high profits not based on any special advantage in cost of production or premium in quality would be an invitation for the entry of one or more new cigarette companies, including all kinds of house brands marketed by retailers. The ability of a tobacco company to retain the volume of business it does with many of its major customers, such as wholesalers and supermarket and drugstore chains, is contingent on the price it charges being reflective of the cost of production on the part of such other potential producers. It is clear that this is a case in which price is governed by cost of production, not by the elasticity or inelasticity of the demand for the product.

It is implicit in the present discussion that a major factor that directly ties the prices of products to their cost of production is *the potential competition which can take place between producers at different stages of the productive process*. If, for example, the tobacco companies were to raise or keep up the price of cigarettes without any objective foundation in the form of higher costs for all potential competitors, their action would be contrary to the interests both of their customers—wholesalers and retailers of cigarettes—and of their suppliers—most notably, the tobacco growers. The higher price they charged would be perceived as an unnecessarily higher cost of doing business by the cigarette wholesalers and large retailers, who would be on the lookout for lower-cost sources of supply. At the same time, when passed forward to the consumer, the higher price would result in some reduction in the quantity demanded of cigarettes and thus in some reduction in the demand for and price of cigarette tobacco. Thus, tobacco growers would have a powerful interest in the reduction in the price of cigarettes to the consumer, in order to restore the demand for and price of their tobacco leaf. If the tobacco companies want to avoid giving the tobacco wholesalers and retailers a motive to move backward, and the tobacco growers a motive to move forward, into cigarette manufacturing, they must keep the price of cigarettes below the level of outsiders' costs plus allowance for the competitive rate of profit. The same principle applies, of course, to producers at different stages in the productive process in all other industries.[51]

Ricardo and Böhm-Bawerk on Cost of Production Versus the Elasticity of Demand

The much-maligned doctrines of the eminent classical economist David Ricardo on the subject of cost of production as a determinant of prices should be taken as the basis for the critique of the marginal-revenue doctrine rather than support for Marxism. In a letter to Malthus, he writes in criticism of Say:

> He certainly has not a correct notion of what is meant by value, when he contends that a commodity is valuable in proportion to its utility. This would be true if buyers only regulated the value of commodities; then indeed we might expect that all men would be willing to give a price for things in proportion to the estimation in which they held them, but the fact appears to me to be that the buyers have the least in the world to do in regulating price—it is all done by the competition of the sellers, and however the buyers might be really willing to give more . . . they could not, because the supply would be regulated by the cost of production . . . .[52]

This and similar passages are perfectly correct if understood not as presenting a universal and primary proposition, but one which is descriptive of conditions in the case of reproducible goods for which the demand is highly inelastic. In such cases, the valuations of the buyers are, indeed, clearly rendered irrelevant. The freedom of competition prevents the sellers from exploiting the inelasticity of demand and obtaining a price that would come up to the marginal valuation of the product by the buyers (or their marginal valuation of a slightly reduced supply). Competition sets the price at the much lower point corresponding to the cost of production of the item.

Observe. There is no necessary implication here that cost of production can make anything *more valuable* than corresponds to its marginal utility, but only that it can make something *less valuable* than corresponds to its direct marginal utility. Understood in this way, Ricardo's doctrine is perfectly reconcilable with the views of Böhm-Bawerk, despite the latter's espousal of the seemingly totally contradictory proposition that "price is actually limited and determined by the valuations on the part of the buyers exclusively."[53]

In advancing this proposition, Böhm-Bawerk has in mind merely *the personal, subjective valuations* of the sellers. These he rightly dismisses as a determinant of prices, on the grounds that in modern conditions of division of labor, in which goods are produced in quantities far beyond any possible personal requirements of their producers, the marginal utility of almost the whole supply of most goods is virtually zero to the sellers.[54] Determination of price by cost of production, however, is something very different than its determination by the personal, subjective valuations of the sellers. Indeed, Böhm-Bawerk himself demonstrates precisely how determination of price by cost of production is fully consistent with determination by the marginal utility of products to buyers, and is actually *an essential aspect* of that determination.

Because so many who claim to be Austrian economists have apparently never read Böhm-Bawerk on this vital point, I quote him at length:

> Up to this point in our discussion the law of the value of production goods was developed subject to the simplifying hypothesis that every group of means of production admits of utilization only to one very definite purpose. That hypothesis is in real life only very rarely in agreement with the facts. It is preeminently production goods, far more than consumption goods, which are characterized by egregious heterogeneity. The overwhelming majority of them will be capable of service in several productive fields, some are adaptable to thousands of such productive services. Examples are iron, coal, and above all, human labor. Of course, we have to take these factual circumstances into account in conducting our theoretical investigation. We must observe what modifications, if any, affect the law that the value of a group of goods occupying remote orders is governed by the value of their product.
>
> Let us alter the order of the presuppositions of our ypical example accordingly. Someone possesses a rather large supply of means of production of second order (G_2). From each of these groups he can produce at will a consumption good of the category A, or one of category B or finally, of category C. He desires, of course, to take advance measures toward balanced provision for his various wants, and will therefore draw simultaneously on various parts of his supply of means of production to produce consumption goods of all three categories. And he will produce amounts in each in accordance with his needs. If there is genuinely balanced provision, the quantities produced will be so regulated that needs of approximately equal importance depend upon the last specimen in each category, and that thus the marginal utilities are approximately equal. In spite of that it is not impossible that there will be differences—possibly even quite considerable differences—in the marginal utilities because, as we already know, the gradation of concrete wants occurring in any one category is not always either uniform or continuous. The first stove in my room will afford me a very considerable utility, say one we might designate with an index of 200. A second stove will afford no utility at all. I shall most emphatically call a halt in providing stoves when I have a single specimen with its

marginal utility of 200, even though in other areas provision for needs may see a dropping off of the average of marginal utility to as little as 120 or even 100. And so it is permissible and necessary, if our example is to be true to nature, to assume that the marginal utility of a specimen will be different in each of the categories A, B and C. Let us call it 100 for A, 120 for B and 200 for C.

Now the question arises, "What is the value, under these circumstances, of a group of means of production, G_2?"

We have had so much practice with selective decisions of a similar nature that we can give the answer without hesitation. The value will be equal to 100. For if one of the available groups of means of production should be lost, the owner would naturally shift the loss to the least sensitive area. He would not curtail production in category B where he would be sacrificing a marginal utility of 120, and certainly not in category C where the sacrifice would go as high as 200. He would quite simply produce one specimen fewer of category A where the reduction in well-being is only 100. Let us express it in general terms. *The value of a unit of means of production is governed by the marginal utility and the value of that product which has the least marginal utility among all those products for the making of which the unit means of production could have justifiably been used.*

All the relations which we had declared to be plainly in force with regard to the value of means of production and their products under the simplifying assumption of only a single possible disposition, are therefore generally valid as between the value of means of production and value of its least valuable product.

And what is the situation with respect to the other categories of products, B and C? That question brings us to the origin of the "law of costs."

If under all circumstances the marginal utility attainable by a good within its own category were determinative, then the categories B and C would have to receive a value divergent not only from that of category A, but also from the value of its costs G_2. B would then have a value of 120, C a value of 200. But here we are confronted with one of the cases where, through substitution, a possible loss in one category is transferred to another, and as a result, the marginal utility of the latter becomes determinative for the other as well. Thus, if a specimen of category C is lost, it is not necessary to forgo the marginal utility of 200 which the specimen would have delivered directly. Instead, it is possible to convert one unit of the means of production G_2 into a new specimen C, and in its place rather produce one specimen fewer in that category in which the marginal utility, and hence the loss in utility is least. And indeed that possibility becomes a reality. The category in question in our example is the category A. Because of the opportunity which production offers for substitution, a specimen C is therefore not valued in accordance with its own marginal utility of 200, but in accordance with the marginal utility of the least valuable related product, the product A; its value is therefore 100. The same applies, naturally, to the value of category B, and would apply generally to every category

of good which is "productionally related" to A, and of which the direct marginal utility is also greater than that of category A.

This leads to some important consequences. The first is that in this way the value of goods having a higher individual marginal utility occupies the same rank as the value of the "marginal product";[55] and *hence also the same rank as the means of production from which both emanate. The identity which exists in principle between "value" and "costs" therefore obtains in this instance as well.* But it is to be carefully noted that here the coinciding is brought about in quite a different way from that which was followed in the case of costs and marginal product. In the latter instance the two coincide because the value of the means of production accommodates itself to the value of the product. The value of the product is the determinant factor, the means of production is the factor that is determined. In our present case it is the other way around, and it is the value of the *product* that must do the accommodating. Ultimately it accommodates only to the value of another product. But initially it accommodates also to the value of the means of production from which it emanates and which brings about its substitutional connection with the marginal product. The transmission of value proceeds, so to speak, along a broken line. First it goes from the marginal product to the means of production, fixes the value of the latter, and then ascends in the opposite direction from the means of production to the other products which it is possible to produce from them. In the end product, then, the products of higher immediate marginal utility derive their value from their means of production. Let us translate the abstract formula into terms of concrete practice. Good B or good C is, in general, a product of higher immediate marginal utility. If now we consider what good B or good C is worth to us our first response is, "Just exactly as much as the means of production are worth to us from which we can at any moment replace the product." If we then inquire further and ask how much the means of production themselves are worth, we arrive at the marginal utility of the marginal product A. But on innumerable occasions we can spare ourselves this further inquiry. Time and again we already know the value of the goods that comprise the cost, without any necessity for working it out from its foundation and proceeding onward from case to case. And on all these occasions we simply determine the value of products by their costs, and in doing so we are taking advantage of an abbreviation which is as accurate as it is convenient.

And now the whole truth about the celebrated law of costs is revealed. It is indeed quite correct to say that costs govern value. Only it is imperative to remain aware of the limits within which this "law" is valid and of the source from which it derives its virtues. *In the first place* it is only a *particular* law. It is valid only so long as the possibility is present of furnishing, through production, substitute specimens in any quantity and at any time they are desired.[56] If there is no possibility of substitution, then in the case of each product, value must be determined by its immediate marginal utility in its own category. In that case its value no longer coincides with that of the marginal product and of the intermediate means of production. Therein lies the explanation of the empirically established principle that the law of costs is valid only for the goods that are "reproducible at will," and that it is a law of only approximate validity. For it does not bind the goods over which it holds sway to slavishly meticulous adherence to costs. On the contrary, it permits fluctuations above and below such costs, depending on whether production at the moment lags behind demand or outstrips it.

A second and still more important consideration is that even where the law of costs is valid, those costs are not the final, but only an intermediate cause of the value of goods. In the last analysis, they do not give value to their products, but *receive* it from them. That is clear as crystal in the case of production goods for which there is only one productive use. Surely no one will wish to deny that it would be erroneous to assert that Tokay wine is valuable because Tokay vineyards possess value; everyone will concede that the truth is the other way around, and those vineyards have a high value because their product is highly valued. It is just as hopeless to deny that the value of a quicksilver mine depends on that of the quicksilver, the value of a wheatfield on that of wheat, the value of a brickkiln on that of brick, and not vice versa. Only because of the manysidedness of most cost goods is it possible for the situation to present the opposite appearance. As the moon reflects the light of the sun upon the earth, so do the manysided cost goods reflect the value which they receive from their marginal product on their other products.[57]

What Böhm-Bawerk has shown in these passages is that when the price of goods such as fan belts, or anything else whose own, direct marginal utility is extremely high, is determined on the basis of cost of production, precisely then is its value determined on the basis of marginal utility—the marginal utility of the means of production used to produce it, as determined in other, less important employments. The buyer of a fan belt, or whatever, does not pay a price corresponding to the value he attaches to his car, but a much lower price corresponding to the marginal utility of the materials and labor required to produce fan belts or whatever—a marginal utility that in turn is determined by the marginal utility of products other than fan belts or whatever. As Böhm-Bawerk develops the law of diminishing marginal utility, it is no more surprising that the price of vital components and parts, or any necessity, is in conformity with its cost of production rather than its own direct marginal utility than it is that the marginal utility of the water on which our physical survival depends is no greater than the utility of the marginal quantity of water we use. Determination of price by cost is merely a mechanism by means of which the value of supramarginal products is reduced to the value of marginal products. The only complication is that the marginal products in this case are physically different and lie in other lines of production.

Views on costs very similar to those of Böhm-Bawerk

are expressed by Friedrich von Wieser, another leading member of the early Austrian school of economists. Wieser flatly declares "... on the whole, the cases where costs directly determine value predominate."[58]

It should be clear that the notion that cost of production has no significant explanatory role in economics does not come from Böhm-Bawerk and Wieser. It comes from Jevons. It was Jevons who held that the only possible connection between cost of production and price was through the intermediary of variations in supply and that every price is actually determined by the specific demand for and supply of the individual good in question.[59]

The principle actually elaborated by Böhm-Bawerk leads to the surprising conclusion that in one important respect the direct determination of price by cost, rather than by supply and demand, goes even beyond what Ricardo maintained. Namely, it exists even in cases of products like vintage wines, which are capable of being produced only in limited quantities. Ricardo described the prices of such goods as an exception to the general principle and as being determined by supply and demand rather than by cost of production.[60] It is true that the price of vintage wines is not determined by their cost of *production*. It is no less true, however, that the retail price of such wines is also not determined by the supply and demand for them retail store by retail store.

The actual fact, which is in accordance with the essentials of Böhm-Bawerk's view, is that supply and demand and marginal utility determine the *wholesale* price of such wines—often at an actual auction, where the bidders are the major distributors, whose bids are limited by the prices they expect the ultimate consumers will be willing to pay. The wholesale price that is determined thus reflects the full range of consumer demand for the wine, not just the demand at any one retail location. The wholesale price, in turn, is then normally the immediate determinant of the retail price at all the individual retail locations. (The retail price, of course, may differ somewhat from location to location, depending on special circumstances). In effect, determination of price by cost is simply determination by supply and demand and by marginal utility *operating across the whole of the relevant market or markets, not just the narrow market immediately concerned.* Cost is what communicates to the narrow, individual market the state of supply and demand and marginal utility in these broader markets.

If contemporary economists had a greater familiarity with the writings of Ricardo and Böhm-Bawerk, they might not find themselves in the embarrassing position of writers such as Samuelson and Nordhaus, who, after devoting chapter after chapter to developing a theoretical analysis that is entirely dependent on the concept of marginal revenue, are surprised to find that it is largely irrelevant to the real world and that they have no theory to explain the actual facts of pricing. Thus, in describing the actual pricing decisions of businesses, Samuelson and Nordhaus must write:

> Here is where the surprise comes:
>
> Armed with the information about sales and costs, you will almost surely never set your price by an *MR* [marginal revenue] and *MC* [marginal cost] comparison. Rather, you will generally take the calculated average cost of a product and *mark it up* by adding a fixed percentage—5 or 10 or 20 or 40 percent of the average cost. This cost-plus-markup figure then becomes the selling price. Note that if all goes as planned, the price will cover all direct and overhead costs and allow the firm a solid profit.
>
> Investigators of actual business pricing policies have testified that corporations often do follow the above-described practice of quoting prices on a "cost-and-markup" basis. Case after case shows that markup pricing is the norm in imperfectly competitive markets.[61]

It is one of the great tragedies of contemporary economic theory that it has lost sight of the role of cost of production as the direct determinant of prices of most manufactured or processed goods *precisely under normal conditions of free competition,* which contemporary economists such as Samuelson and Nordhaus erroneously call "imperfect competition." If a firm can assume that its own costs of production are no higher than its competitors' or potential competitors', then in setting its prices in conformity with its costs—that is, above its costs only by enough to earn the going rate of profit—it ensures that it is not likely to be undersold to any great extent, or to attract newcomers to its field. If it can assume that its own costs are significantly below those of its competitors, then, as already explained, it will want to set its price not too far above its competitors' costs, as a maximum, so that they are not in a position to accumulate much capital and expand at its expense, and also in order not to provide an incentive for others to enter the industry. (If a firm's costs are above those of its competitors, then except to the extent its product may be of premium quality over theirs, it must simply match the prices they set. It will continue to do so, so long as it is less unprofitable for it to remain in business than to withdraw from the field.) Only in the exceptional conditions in which the quantity demanded at a price determined by cost outruns the ability to produce from existing capacity, does the price lose its connection with cost of production and rise to a point determined by the demand for and limited supply of the specific product, that is, become governed by the direct marginal utility of the product. Even then, the demand and price are usually restrained by the prospect of return to normal conditions in the not too distant future.

In the absence of knowledge of the connection between prices and costs, and on the basis of the prevailing fallacy that the price of each and every product must be determined by the specific demand for and supply of the product—by its own independent marginal utility—contemporary economics is driven to the expectation that without the presence of a vast number of individually insignificant firms, sellers will be in a position to exploit the product's elasticity of demand. Largely, on this basis, it denounces most branches of industry as "imperfectly competitive," because they allegedly do not possess a sufficiently large number of sellers to avoid this.

In essence, it is on this basis that it regards big business per se in a way that should be reserved for one or a few firms operating under monopolistic legal protection against competition, but not when operating under the freedom of competition. And then, of course, in the last analysis, it finds that its theory simply does not fit the facts and that it has no applicable theory. Yet it retains the notion that most of the economic world is "imperfectly competitive" and that big business is inherently "monopolistic."

Pricing Under Patents and Copyrights

Patents and copyrights place the producers who hold them in a position in which they alone decide the quantity of their product that is produced—or at least the quantity of it that is produced by means of their method of production. So long as the patent or copyright lasts, others are simply prevented from producing the good, or, at least, producing it by means of the patent or copyright holder's method of production.[62] Nevertheless, as previously explained, patents and copyrights are in no sense a violation of the freedom of competition, but a vital safeguard of it. They protect the intellectual property rights on the basis of which free competition takes place.[63] Moreover, in most cases, they do not fundamentally or radically alter the connection of prices with costs of production that has been explained in the preceding pages and in Chapter 6.

What patents and copyrights protect comes under the heading of something new that is more efficient: namely, new, more efficient methods of producing goods that are already being produced and new, more efficient methods of satisfying needs that are already being satisfied in other ways, by different goods. (Of course, patents and copyrights can exist on products and methods of production which do not represent any form of improvement—for example, a copyright on a book no one wants to read or buy, or a patent on a method of production that is more expensive rather than less expensive to use. In such cases, as soon as the fatal flaws are recognized, the patents and copyrights do not protect anything. From that point on, no one seeks to produce such products or use such methods of production. Nor would anyone do so, if they lacked patent or copyright protection. In this sense, patents and copyrights serve to protect only things which represent improvements, which people would appropriate and put to use if not prevented by the patent or copyright from doing so.)

Insofar as patents and copyrights protect more efficient methods of producing a good that is already being produced, viz., methods of reducing its cost of production, the price of the good is still limited by the cost of producing it by the older, less efficient methods. The patent or copyright merely operates to prevent the price of the good from being reduced immediately to correspond to the lower level of cost made possible by the new method of production.

Ultimately, the price will drop to that point—when the patent or copyright expires—and, most likely, it will drop to some significant extent almost immediately, because the holder will want to take advantage of his lower costs to expand the quantity he sells. But even if the price does not drop at all for the time being, the reinvestment of profits made by virtue of the cost-cutting improvement will operate to increase production and reduce prices somewhere else in the economic system.

As an illustration of this last point, the reinvestment of the profits made by virtue of cutting the cost of producing razor blades, say, in the production of other goods, such as shaving cream and after-shave lotion perhaps, operates to expand the supply and reduce the prices of these other goods. Such a case would be likely to arise in an industry like razor blades, where the demand was highly inelastic and a firm that already accounted for the great bulk of the market would find it unprofitable to cut its price, no matter how substantially it had reduced its cost of production—until it was confronted with the ability of others to produce at the lower cost. What is crucial, of course, is that because of the system of patents and copyrights, the incentive exists to go on developing and introducing improvements in production, and thus for cost of production and price to go on falling in the long run.

If what the patent or copyright protects is an improvement in the methods of satisfying a need that previously had been satisfied by other goods less effectively, then the price of the new good is still limited by the prices and costs of production of the older goods that satisfy the need less effectively. Here, the patent or copyright enables the holder to obtain a premium in the price of his product in comparison with the prices of the older goods serving the same need—a premium that corresponds to the degree of improvement that is perceived as attaching to the use of his product rather than the older products. It is implicit in the nature of such a premium that the

source of the patent or copyright holder's income is the provision of a positive value that the buyers regard as worth more than the premium in price. And thus, once again, there is an immediate gain to the buyers, namely, the extent to which they value the improvement above the premium in price that they pay for it. Eventually, of course, when the patent or copyright expires, the buyers will buy the improved product at no higher price than the original product (except to the extent that its cost of production may be higher), and their gain will be correspondingly greater.

Precisely the newness of patented or copyrighted products typically leads to the practice of setting their prices on the basis of cost of production, though with the addition of a substantially greater-than-usual profit margin. Because patented and copyrighted products are necessarily new, and their potential markets, therefore, largely unknown and undeveloped, the producers of such products more often than not have little or no reliable basis for estimating the elasticity of demand for their products. In such circumstances, it is highly reasonable to price the product in some standard way that is both generous to the producer and yet, at the same time, does not elevate the price too greatly to the buyer, and then attempt to make very high profits by selling the largest possible volume at the price so determined. This is the typical procedure, for example, in the publishing industry, the recording industry, and the motion picture industry, all of which have the perfect legal right to charge whatever price they wish for their unique copyrighted products, but nonetheless appear to follow a defined pricing pattern in which high profits are made not through inordinately high prices, but through high volume at prices that are not all that far above the total cost of production per unit.

Thus, the rewards of innovation that are protected by patents or copyrights typically turn out to be a relatively modest part of the price of the product—perhaps just an additional 10, 20, or 30 percent added to what would constitute a normal profit margin. Financial success comes when this relatively modest additional part of the price is multiplied by a substantial number of units. A very high rate of return on capital then results from the multiplication of the high profit margin by a high capital turnover ratio.

The same principle seems to apply in the pharmaceutical and computer software industries, with the principal difference being that the combination of relatively high costs of research and development and relatively narrow markets often necessitates the charging of much higher prices, in order to cover the resulting high unit costs. In such cases, unexpectedly large quantities demanded, which, of course, serve to reduce unit costs correspondingly, tend to be followed by price reductions, in efforts to reach wider markets and to forestall potential competition from comparable products and methods of production that could be developed without infringement of the patents or copyrights in question.

In such price reductions, a process takes place in which the proceeds of an extremely high profit margin and rate of profit are reinvested in order to earn a larger amount of profit on the strength of a lower profit margin and rate of profit applied to a greater volume of sales and quantity of capital invested in the production of the good (or more advanced versions of the good). As stated, the existence of such a process also helps to guard against others being tempted to enter into competition through the development of comparable new products or methods of production of their own, which even patent or copyright protection cannot prevent. This last objective, of course, is further secured to the extent that as the result of its reinvestment, the firm is able to achieve reductions in unit costs and improvements in product quality stemming from the adoption of more capital-intensive methods of production. This serves further to increase the capital requirement of any potential competitor and thus further to reduce the likelihood of the actual appearance of such a competitor. The practice of reinvesting a substantial portion of any very high rate of profit in the further production of the extremely profitable product, and then earning a lower rate but larger amount of profit in the production of that good, makes sense for any business. It is the way to transform a temporary bonanza into greater and more lasting success.

In connection with patented life-saving drugs, it is necessary to explain the benevolent role that can be played by the ability to practice price discrimination between classes of buyers with substantially different levels of income. In the case of patented life-saving drugs, every potential buyer whose life depends on the drug can be assumed to be willing, if necessary, to pay his entire life's savings to obtain the drug. Because of this, it may appear that the price of such a drug would necessarily be set at a point at which the marginal buyer at least, would have to pay away his life's savings. If the price were set in this way, then only buyers with income and wealth substantially greater than that of the marginal buyer would be able to avoid paying away their life's savings or something close to it, while all those potential buyers with income and wealth below that of the marginal buyer would simply die for lack of the ability to afford the drug.

Fortunately, where price discrimination can be practiced, it is more profitable for the drug company in such a case both to charge substantially less to the marginal buyer and, at the same time, to offer its product at a substantially still lower price to the broadest possible class of buyers with wealth and income less than that of the marginal buyer. Indeed, it is entirely possible that no buyer will have to pay away his life's savings, thanks to the existence of a variety of different prices geared to individuals of substantially different wealth and income.

Thus, for example, the full price of a year's supply of the drug might be, say, $20,000 in money of 1993's buying power. At that price only a small minority of individuals could afford it without being bankrupted. If, however, the drug company can control the distribution of the drug to patients by means of the cooperation of physicians and hospitals, perhaps in conjunction with offering somewhat different versions of the drug, it is in a position to charge such a price only to those who can afford it, while offering a substantially lower price to the broad mass of people who otherwise could not afford it. And it could offer a substantially still lower price to physicians and hospitals who purchased the drug on behalf of charity patients. Where price discrimination is possible, it pays to offer the lower prices to gain access to additional segments of the market. At the same time, the existence of the lower prices for lower-income individuals operates to prevent the price paid by individuals in higher-income segments of the market from approaching the limit set by their marginal valuation of the drug when what is at stake is their very lives.

Today's sometimes outlandishly high price of patented prescription drugs is the result, I believe, of a combination of the existence of a system of collectivized medical costs, and the inability to practice price discrimination.[64] To the extent that the market for medical care comes to be made up of buyers for whom price is no object, because they are covered by the kind of private medical insurance policies that have prevailed for the last several decades, or by government programs, the price that it is profitable to charge is correspondingly increased. This is because to that extent the higher price does not operate to reduce the quantity of the drug demanded. Thus the incentive is created to charge a higher price. At the same time, various prohibitions against price discrimination serve to prevent the offering of lower prices to those who lack private insurance and are outside of the government programs. Today, if a drug company offered a lower price to anyone, the government and many or most of the private insurance companies would almost certainly demand that they too obtain the benefit of the lower price. (This observation, made with respect to the domestic market of the United States, is confirmed by the recent furor caused by newspaper reports of the availability of lower drug prices in Mexico, a foreign country.) Thus, the offering of a lower price to any segment of the market, at least within the present-day

United States, does not pay. And thus the result is that everyone in the United States is confronted with artificially higher drug prices.

In addition, of course, when discussing today's drug prices, one should not overlook the role that is played in raising drug prices by arbitrary FDA regulations that delay and inhibit the introduction of new drugs. Such regulations are responsible for the average new drug that is introduced having a development cost, and thus price, far in excess of what market conditions require.

Contract Pricing and Radical Privatization

The fact that prices can be set contractually, and thus eliminate all possibility of the exercise of arbitrary power by private individuals in setting their prices, has major bearing on the potential for future privatization. Because of it, it is possible to imagine a day when virtually every good or service but the administration of justice and national defense is provided by unregulated, profit-seeking private businesses.[65] For example, it is possible to imagine such things as electricity, water, and gas being carried from various points of supply over major trunk lines and various major branch lines, and large individual users, such as major factories or apartment complexes, and associations of small users, such as neighborhood associations of property owners, entering into contracts with the suppliers who offered the best terms. Different suppliers would periodically connect or disconnect their major branch lines with or from local networks of wires and pipeline owned by the large individual users or property owners' associations. Essentially the same principles, of course, apply to sewage lines and to telephone service as well, except that in the case of telephone service, modern technology has or soon will make it possible to connect any two points economically without the use of wires. The ability to transmit to and from a given space satellite either is or soon will be all that is required to link any two locations.

(Despite the rationalizations offered on behalf of the present system of exclusive government franchises and rate controls, or outright government ownership, there is no reason to fear continuous large-scale disruption because of tearing up of streets to lay wire or pipe. Any modern city with five or ten main avenues could, if necessary, easily support five or ten major branch lines of each type running underneath—with just one of each kind per avenue. Any local area parallel to any of these major branch lines could easily be connected just by running a single minor branch line to it from the major branch line, and be disconnected merely by shutting off that minor branch line.)

Property owners and voluntary associations of property owners could obtain fire-protection services on a contractual basis, after examining competing bids. Such protection would undoubtedly be required by insurers and mortgage lenders, and might even be provided under their auspices.[66] Private fire fighters could (and should) be authorized to put out fires on the property of individuals who did not subscribe to their services, whenever it appeared to be a matter of life or limb or a danger existed to the property of a subscriber or other requestor of protection. In such cases, it could be made the legal obligation of the property owner(s) in question to pay for the service under a preestablished, publicly known and legally sanctioned set of rates. In cases in which individuals had subscribed to a fire-fighting service, but it was slow to arrive, with the result that it became necessary to use the services of another fire-fighting company, the delinquent fire-fighting service could be legally obliged to pay the bill, plus, perhaps, a preestablished penalty charge. Of course, preestablished cross-billing arrangements would almost certainly exist between fire-fighting companies for cases in which it was necessary for one such service to call upon the assistance of other such services.

Pricing under long-term contract makes it possible to see the day when highways, bridges, and tunnels will be privately owned and operated and supported by tolls, unregulated by the government—even in situations in which only one such road, bridge, or tunnel is feasible. Today, it may be difficult to imagine such an arrangement. This is because one starts in the middle, with a vast population already dependent on the existence of the facility. One then projects the existence of the facility under private ownership, with the owners free to charge whatever tolls they wish. Naturally, in such a situation, the owners would be able to practice a form of extortion against everyone else in the vicinity. But had the facility been private from the beginning, before the area came to be dependent on it, its owners would have had to provide contractual guarantees of permanently reasonable rates *as the precondition* of any subsequent development that would create a dependence on the facility.

In the overwhelming majority of cases, of course, there is more than one route connecting any two points, and very often many routes. Almost always there is the potential for at least several routes and the potential for more routes than currently exist. In such cases unregulated private ownership could probably be adopted even without any provision for long-term contractual guarantees. In perhaps the worst imaginable case, such as a single company somehow being given ownership of all the major bridges and tunnels entering Manhattan Island, the result could not be nearly as serious as the disruption which occurs whenever there is a major transit strike by labor unions. Such a company might charge substantially higher tolls, which would reduce the flow of traffic in and out of the city through its facilities, but by no means threaten the lifeblood of the city, as does a transit workers' or garbage collectors' strike. Unlike the striking unions, such a company would not be able to resort to physical force to stop competition. And such a company would have competition from the very first, if it set its tolls too high.

Its tolls would be limited not only by the economization on transportation into and out of the city that would take place in response to its higher tolls, but also, from the very first, by the costs of providing ferry service and bringing in more supplies by ship or helicopter. Such competition could begin immediately, if necessary, even if it meant having to use small private boats. But within a very short time, regular large-scale ferry boat service could be in operation if the tolls were high enough to make it attractive. And the same technological expertise which made it possible for the United States Army Corps of Engineers to construct temporary bridges spanning major rivers in Europe in World War II, would make it possible for private enterprise, using improvements in such technology that have been developed since then, to construct substantially better temporary bridges just as fast or faster.

The fact is that New York City and many other major cities are desperately short of transportation facilities as the result of government ownership, with its gross inefficiencies and high costs of construction and maintenance and the policy either of not charging tolls at all or charging tolls that are inadequate in the face of the limited capacity of the facilities. In such a situation, the establishment of private ownership, whether in the hands of just one company or however many companies, might very well be accompanied by a substantial increase in tolls. But this would be followed by a desperately needed increase in the supply of transportation facilities. Within in a few years, permanent new bridges would exist, along with additional tunnels and roadways. Such high tolls as might exist on the present facilities would provide the incentive and, no doubt, to some considerable extent, the means of financing the new facilities, as profits made on the present facilities were reinvested. The net effect would be a radical improvement in the state of transportation and, once the supply of transportation facilities became adequate, tolls that reflected no more than the costs of construction and maintenance plus an allowance for the going rate of profit. At the same time, the costs of construction and maintenance would tend to be the most economical possible and to go on falling in real terms.

Private Streets

Two problems must be discussed in connection with the kind of radical privatization described above. The first is that of the efficiency of toll collection, especially if private ownership were to be extended to secondary roads and even to city streets. The second is that of the principle of eminent domain, which can be related to almost all of the above areas of privatization.

It would obviously be absurd to stop traffic every block or two in order to collect a toll. A similar problem arises even on major highways, such as the freeways in Southern California, where there is an entrance and exit every one or two miles. Conventional methods of toll collection in such circumstances would be extremely costly as well as time consuming. Fortunately, modern technology is or very soon will be capable of dealing with the problem easily and efficiently. Computer scanning equipment will be capable of reading an automobile's identification at the point of entry and exit from any given body of roadway and thus provide the input for an itemized monthly bill of toll charges. Even so, in the case of residential, neighborhood streets, with little or no through traffic, in which the streets serve merely for people to get to and from major thoroughfares, it may well be found that it is sufficient for local property owners' associations to maintain the streets and finance them by means of dues charged under some form of covenant arrangement among the property owners.

If the owners of thoroughfares also own the property on either side of them (which is a reasonable assumption in the case of city streets or local roads), and seek business from the passing traffic, then their interests would probably be served by the absence of tolls, in order to encourage the passage of traffic by their establishments. Such toll-free thoroughfares would be appropriate for people going shopping. But they will necessarily be relatively slow moving. Toll thoroughfares will be appropriate for through traffic. Here the tolls will limit the traffic and thus make possible more rapid movement. At the same time, they will make the provision of such thoroughfares worthwhile, since the property owners on either side will not be able to gain from the passing traffic itself. The tolls charged on these thoroughfares, of course, will be limited by the fact that slower moving toll-free thoroughfares remain available as an alternative.

Eminent Domain

It is usually taken for granted that the ability to construct roads, railroads, pipelines, and so forth, depends on the existence of the principle of eminent domain, according to which the government has the right to take private property against the will of its owner when its use is necessary for such purposes. The existence of eminent domain is thought to be required in order to prevent a comparative handful of property owners, or even a single individual owner, from arbitrarily and capriciously making the construction of such vital facilities either alto- gether impossible or at least uneconomic, by means of preventing the completion of a route or causing it to take a grossly distorted path.

The principle of eminent domain presents an apparent dilemma. On the one hand, it is presented as a necessary safeguard of the possibility of rational action that de- pends on the cooperation of large numbers of individuals any one or small number of whom is capable arbitrarily of frustrating all the rest. On the other hand, it appears to constitute a clear violation of the principle of individual rights and thus to have no place in a capitalist society. The apparent dilemma is heightened by the fact that the basis of the existence of individual rights is precisely the provision of safeguards for rational action. Rights protect individuals from the initiation of physical force in order that they can then be free to follow the judgment of their own minds. Moreover, it is necessary to uphold the individual's rights precisely against majorities, and above all against overwhelming majorities.

In an intellectual and cultural environment rational enough to establish a society approaching consistent capitalism, the principle of eminent domain could almost certainly be dispensed with. There would still be irratio- nal, capricious individuals, to be sure, but their number would almost certainly not be great enough to constitute a significant barrier to the accomplishment of any im- portant cooperative venture. Occasionally, perhaps, it might be necessary to have an extra bend in a road, or to make a detour here and there in the course of a pipeline, in deference to the principle of individual rights even when individuals chose to exercise their rights capri- ciously. Such instances would be minimized not only by the relatively small number of capricious property own- ers in such a society, but also by the fact that in such a society, rights-of-way for roads, railroads, pipelines, and so forth would be acquired far in advance of the time of actual construction. In the absence of eminent domain, the laying out of such rights-of-way far in advance would be understood to be a precondition for an area's future development. Thus the problem posed by capricious individuals arbitrarily refusing to sell their property or the right of passage through it would be minimized. Communities would be formed with provision for such rights-of-way included in the deeds of the buyers who later might be affected. Where such provision had failed to be made, still, sellers would usually not be asked to part with their property immediately, but only, in effect, to sell an option on its later purchase or use, probably a generation or more in the future. With the necessity of planning long range for the acquisition of rights-of-way, prospective buyers could wait and buy such rights from more reasonable heirs if necessary.

In the present intellectual and cultural state of society, the principle of eminent domain is probably necessary, though not in its present form. One can easily imagine groups of "environmentalists" buying up strips of land in the path of every possible right of way for all kinds of vital roads and pipelines, for no other purpose than to prevent economic development, and succeeding by means of a refusal to sell at any price. A legitimate basis for the principle of eminent domain in such a case can be found in the same source as the legitimate basis for not accord- ing full rights to children, or, perhaps closer to the mark, the insane.

Happily, apart from the possible case of the "environ- mentalists," the far greater part of the seeming dilemma posed by eminent domain could be eliminated as a prac- tical matter even now. All that would be necessary would be the adoption of two very simple measures. The first is to restrict the role of eminent domain to its traditional sphere in the United States, which is precisely such projects as road and pipeline construction, in which a vast stretch of property is required for an indivisible use. (In recent years the principle of eminent domain has come to be extended to the seizing of private property from some owners in order to turn it over to other owners who then employ it in essentially the same way, such as the operation of a department store or the use of the land for residential housing. This is a purely arbitrary redistribu- tion of property, and potentially constitutes a far worse problem than any arbitrary refusal of individuals to sell their property.)

The second necessary measure is to *provide sufficient payment to those whose property is sought.* The over- whelming majority of property owners will be glad to sell if they receive a price for their property that is significantly higher than what they could otherwise ob- tain for it, and which more than compensates them for any loss of income they may suffer by having to part with it. It is one thing to announce that a road is scheduled to pass through someone's living room, and that his house is to be taken from him at half its actual value. It is something very different if he will be offered two or three times the current value of his house. In the latter case, instead of dreading such economic developments, people would actually vie for the privilege of having their prop- erty become the scene of them. This explains the radical difference between people's reactions that presently ac- company receiving a letter from the government notify- ing one of plans to build a road through one's property and, say, a letter from an oil company notifying one that it is likely that one's property contains a petroleum deposit and that the company is interested in drilling wells on it.

This reform, which is immediately practicable, would

remove from the actual operation of the principle of eminent domain almost all of its vicious character. It would reduce the principle to forcing people to take what almost any rational person would be more than glad to take. Thus, the element of actual force would virtually disappear. And this indeed is how the phrase "just compensation" should be interpreted in applying the Fifth Amendment protection of the United States Constitution "nor shall private property be taken for public use without just compensation."

Such an interpretation would provide a powerful incentive to limit resort to the power of eminent domain and to guarantee that where it was used, the project had major economic value indeed. Furthermore, it should be obvious that the actual limitation of the principle of eminent domain in this way would be much more likely if accompanied by the privatization of the areas in which it was employed. Businessmen are used to paying for what they receive, not taking it, as the government does. And the government is more likely to act as an impartial judge when an outside, private party requests the use of eminent domain, rather than one of its own branches.

Once such a reform had been made, a constitutional amendment could be enacted totally abolishing eminent domain as of, say, fifty years from the date of the amendment's enactment. This would provide sufficient time to assemble rights of way for all necessary projects thereafter on a strictly voluntary basis.

9. Cartels

Cartels are associations of independent producers of a good who agree to limit their production of it in order to obtain a higher price on the resulting smaller supply. The prevailing belief is that cartels are an evil of capitalism, serving to establish arbitrarily high prices to consumers, and would be a characteristic feature of the economic system in the absence of government intervention to prevent their formation.

The fact is that apart from the handful of cases such as diamonds, in which there are very few physical sources of supply, the only time cartels can succeed under capitalism is when they serve *merely to reduce the extent of losses,* i.e., raise a price from a point of more severe losses to a point of less severe losses or modest profits. This is because, in addition to the problem of deciding which producers must curtail production how much, which is difficult enough in itself (as frequent newspaper reports about the OPEC oil cartel attest), profitable cartels have two further problems, which tend to make their continuation impossible.

There is first the problem of controlling the reinvestment of the profits. If the firms are profitable and want to reinvest their profits, the industry will expand and the cartel's price will crash in efforts to find buyers for the additional output. At the same time, the independent reinvestment of the profits may well enable some of the firms to be profitable at the lower prices, while those firms which did not reinvest—or reinvest as much or as skillfully—suffer major losses. In order to prevent the breakdown of the cartel in this way, it would be necessary for the cartel to control its individual members' reinvestments—something which the mere formation of a cartel is not sufficient to accomplish. Second, and more importantly, a profitable price attracts outside entrants to the field, which not only makes the cartel's price crash, but also deprives the cartel's members of volume they could have had. It is the same case we saw in the last section in connection with attempts to produce less in order to sell at a higher price. If the higher price is profitable to outside producers, the effect is that one ends up selling less at a price that is no higher than the costs of such outsiders plus an allowance for the going rate of profit, when one could permanently have sold more at that price.[67] Furthermore, while it is possible to imagine cartels enjoying a brief period of premium profitability by means of jacking up prices, it should be realized that pricing under contract operates to make even this impossible after it happens once or twice in a field—assuming that it actually does happen.

However, if a cartel exits that is not particularly profitable, these two problems of controlling the reinvestment of profits and attracting the entry of outsiders do not arise, and thus the cartel may succeed. In such a case, there are no significant profits to reinvest and thus there is no problem of having to cut the price to sell an expanded output. And there is nothing to attract outside entrants into the field. In the light of these facts, the following passage from a prominent antitrust textbook should not be surprising: "We even have evidence suggesting that large firms caught engaging in illegal collusion earn *lower* profits than other large firms. Perhaps collusion is most commonly attempted in situations where some adversity has depressed profits below a normal level."[68]

In such circumstances, it is difficult to see what objection can be made to the formation of a cartel. It is a voluntary association that harms no one and may actually benefit everyone, by virtue of preventing unnecessary losses to producers and thereby enabling them to maintain a level of capacity that will be present to prevent prices from shooting upward when demand for the product revives, as it generally does sooner or later.

As indicated, the one area in which profitable cartels can be formed with a strong likelihood of continued success is in the field of mining, in cases in which the known, commercially exploitable deposits are few in number. In such cases, the formation of a unified group of producers is a matter of relative ease and, more importantly, the entry of outsiders in response to a higher price is impossible, because the necessary deposits are simply not available to them. The leading examples of this kind are diamonds and mercury.

Even in such cases, it must be kept in mind that the prices that can be charged are still limited by the cost and price of various substitutes, which, however imperfectly, can be used in place of the item for various purposes. For example, man-made diamonds are a substitute for natural diamonds as a cutting tool in many industrial processes. It is even possible that additional deposits of the item exist, which would be capable of commercial exploitation at a sufficiently high level of prices. Quantities of mercury found naturally in sea water are an example. The price charged by the cartel must take such competition or potential competition into account and must be lower than the price that would make significant competition from such quarters profitable.

Moreover, the progressive nature of the economic system under capitalism creates an unremitting downward pressure on the real price charged even by such a cartel. Improvements in the efficiency of producing substitutes and the development of new substitutes, along with the progressive reduction in the real costs of exploiting submarginal deposits, make it necessary for such a cartel to continue to improve its own efficiency of production in order to be able to maintain its profitability in the face of declining real prices for its product. Thus, since the start of the Industrial Revolution, the price of the average diamond, the price of an ounce of mercury, and of almost any other good that a free market would subject to cartelization has substantially fallen generation by generation relative to the income of the average person, along with the fall in the real price of virtually all other goods that have been in existence over the same period of time. Diamond rings and thermometers, for example, have become progressively more affordable. If the producers of the cartelized goods had not improved their efficiency over the decades, their profits would long since have disappeared and they would no longer be in existence, because in that case their customers would have turned to alternative sources of supply that had grown progressively cheaper in real terms. It is as necessary for the diamond or mercury cartel to operate with modern methods of production as it is for producers in any other branch of industry, and to go on improving those methods so long as the producers of substitutes can improve their methods of production, so long as new substitutes can be developed, and so long as the real costs of exploiting submarginal deposits can be reduced.

What is true of the price of such a cartelized good is that at any given time it is higher than would be the case if the same known physical quantity of the good were found in widely scattered deposits. The effect of this higher price is to slow down the rate at which the limited known supplies are consumed. Thus, von Mises is correct in describing the higher prices charged by the cartels as tantamount to a form of conservation.[69] Only after the fact of improvements in the production of substitutes or in the ability to exploit submarginal deposits is the price (relative to people's incomes) reduced and the rate of consumption increased. Over time, of course, the improvements in methods of extraction introduced by the producers of the cartelized good themselves operate to increase the economically useable supply that their mines provide.

Cartels and Government Intervention

Cartels as an economic problem are the result of government intervention, and where they are formed or maintained on this basis, they represent part of the genuine and very serious problem of monopoly. Three leading instances of such cartels are the largely unacknowledged cartelization of major portions of agriculture in the present-day United States, the OPEC cartel in oil, and the cartels of Imperial Germany before World War I. The U.S. government's enforced restriction of agricultural output for the purpose of reducing its outlays under the farm subsidy program has already been dealt with.[70] So too has the OPEC cartel and the vital dependence of its success on the policies of the U.S. government, above all, price controls on oil and environmental legislation.[71] Thus, it is only necessary here to deal with the case of the Imperial German cartels.

As von Mises shows in *Human Action*, the German cartels in the decades prior to World War I—the classic case of widespread cartelization of industry—were the result of Bismarck's *Sozialpolitik*. This policy of social security and allegedly prolabor legislation raised production costs in Germany relative to those in other countries, which had not adopted such legislation. In the absence of further measures, the result would have been that German manufacturers could not have sold profitably either at home or abroad. The consequence of that would have been both mass unemployment and the inability to pay for imports of vitally needed foodstuffs and raw materials which could not be produced domestically.

To prevent these consequences, the German government enacted protective tariffs and encouraged the formation of domestic cartels, which could thus sell at high prices in the German market. The extra, monopoly profits thus reaped in the domestic market permitted the subsidization of German exports, which could then be sold abroad at competitive prices, which were below those at home—a phenomenon described by foreign manufacturers as "dumping."[72] (Although von Mises does not mention it, a further necessary aspect of the German government's policy was an increase in the quantity of money, in order to make possible the larger total expenditure necessary to employ the same number of workers at higher wage rates and to buy the same-sized domestic product at higher prices.) The overall effect of *Sozialpolitik* on the German workers, of course, was that their real, take-home wages were reduced, inasmuch as domestic prices had to rise by enough to cover all the additional costs imposed on employers—the costs not only in the form of higher wage rates, but also in the form of contributions to the social insurance programs.

Thus, it should be clear that the Imperial German cartels were the result of government intervention designed to offset the destructive consequences of prior government intervention. They were not the product of capitalism or the free market.

10. "Monopoly" and the Platonic Competition of Contemporary Economics

After having devoted so many pages to the discussion of the alleged significance of the economic concept of monopoly—ranging from the alleged tendency toward the formation of a single giant firm controlling the entire economic system, on down through the alleged gouging of buyers left and right in this or that particular circumstance, by this or that particular means—it may be found somewhat astonishing that in the hands of contemporary economic theory, the economic concept of monopoly has been absolutely trivialized. Indeed, the substance of the objection that is raised when contemporary economic theory sounds the cry of "monopoly" is actually nothing more than *a condemnation of business for refusing to sustain unnecessary losses*. This fact is not obvious, but it is the unmistakable implication of contemporary economics' doctrine of "pure and perfect competition." This doctrine is a central element of contemporary economic theory and is the standard by which it and the Antitrust Division of the Department of Justice decide whether an industry is "competitive" or "monopolistic," and what should be done about it if they find that it is not "competitive."[73]

"Pure and perfect competition" is totally unlike anything one normally means by the term "competition." Normally, one thinks of competition as denoting a rivalry among producers, in which each producer strives to match or exceed the performance of other producers. This is not what "pure and perfect competition" means. Indeed, the existence of rivalry, of competition as it is

normally understood, is *incompatible* with "pure and perfect competition." If that is difficult to believe, consider the following passage in a widely used economics textbook: "By way of contrast, intense rivalry may exist between two automobile agencies or between two filling stations in the same city. One seller's actions influence the market of the other; consequently, pure competition does not exist in this case."[74]

While competition as normally, and properly, understood rests on a base of individualism, the base of "pure and perfect competition" is collectivism. Competition, properly so-called, rests on the activity of separate, independent individuals who own and exchange private property in the pursuit of their self-interest. It arises when two or more such individuals become rivals for the same trade. The concept of "pure and perfect competition," however, proceeds from an ideology that obliterates the existence of individuals, of private property, and of exchange. It is the product of an approach to economics based on what has aptly been characterized as the "tribal premise," viz., the collectivist view that the individual human being is a cell in a greater organism: Mankind, the State, the Nation, or the Tribe.[75]

The tribal premise dominates contemporary economic theory, and is accepted not only by the enemies of capitalism, but even by its supporters. The link between the concept of "pure and perfect competition" and the tribal concept of man, is a tribal concept of property, of price, and of cost.

According to contemporary economics, no property is to be regarded as really private. At most, property is supposedly held in trusteeship for its alleged true owner, "society" or the "consumers." "Society," it is alleged, has a right to the property of every producer and suffers him to continue as owner only so long as "society" receives what it or its professorial spokesmen consider to be the maximum possible benefit. As another supporter of the "pure-and-perfect-competition" doctrine declares in his textbook: "At any point in time a society possesses a pool of resources either individually or collectively owned, depending upon the political organization of the society in question. From a social point of view the objective of economic activity is to get as much as possible from this existing pool of resources."[76]

According to the tribal concept of property, "society" has a right to 100 percent of every seller's inventory and to the benefit of 100 percent use of his plant and equipment. The exercise of this alleged right is to be limited only by the consideration of "society's" alleged alternative needs. Thus, a producer should retain some portion of his inventory only if it will serve a greater need of "society" in the future than in the present. He should produce at less than 100 percent of capacity only to the extent that "society's" labor, materials and fuel, which he would require, are held to be more urgently needed in another line of production.

The ideal of contemporary economics—advanced half as an imaginary construct and half as a description of reality, with no way of distinguishing between the two— is the contradictory notion of a private-enterprise, capitalist economy in which producers would act just as a socialist dictator would wish them to act, but without having to be forced to do so.[77] In accordance with this "ideal," contemporary economics tears the concepts of price and cost from the context of individuals engaged in the free exchange of private property, and twists them to fit the perspective of a socialist dictator. It views the system of prices and costs as the means by which producers in a capitalist economy can be led to provide "society" with the optimum use and "allocation" of its "resources."

A price is viewed not as the payment received by a seller in the free exchange of his private property, but as a means of *rationing* his products among those members of "society" or the "sovereign consumers" who happen to desire them. Prices are justified on the grounds that they are a means of rationing, superior to the issuance of coupons and priorities by the government. Indeed, rationing itself has been described by Nobel Laureate George Stigler as "non-price rationing," prices allegedly being the form of rationing that exists under capitalism.[78]

Similarly, a cost, according to contemporary economics, is not an outlay of money made by a buyer to obtain goods or services through free exchange, but the value of the most important alternative goods or services "society" must *forgo* by virtue of obtaining any particular good or service. A typical textbook formulation is:

> The social cost of using a bundle of resources to produce a unit of commodity X is the number of units of commodity Y that must be sacrificed in the process. Resources are used to produce both X and Y (and all other commodities). Those resources used in X production cannot be used to produce Y or any other commodity. To illustrate with a simple example, think of Robinson Crusoe living alone on an island and sustaining himself by fishing and gathering coconuts. The cost to Crusoe of an additional fish is measured by the number of coconuts he has to forgo because he spends more time fishing.[79]

On the basis of this concept of cost, contemporary economics holds that the only relevant cost of production is "*marginal* cost." As a rule, and roughly speaking, for the concept can only be approximated, "marginal cost" is held to be the cost of the labor, materials, and fuel required to produce an additional unit of a product. Their value is supposed to represent the value of the most important alternative goods or services that "society" forgoes in obtaining this additional unit.[80] (Marginal cost

depends on the context. It is always the *extra* cost that must be incurred from a given, present starting point, and varies with this starting point. For example, the extra cost of producing an automobile is typically the cost of labor, materials, and fuel, because normally one may take for granted the existence of the automobile factory and its equipment. But if the production of an additional automobile requires an additional automobile factory, then, in that context, the marginal cost of an automobile would include the whole cost of the factory as well. By the same token, if the automobile has already been produced and is sitting in the auto company's lot, the marginal cost becomes merely the cost of shipping it. If it has already been shipped to a dealer and is in his lot, the marginal cost is hardly anything at all.)

It must be stressed that the concept of "marginal cost" normally *excludes* the cost of existing factories and machines. The reason for this exclusion is that these assets are "here," they were paid for in the past and, therefore, their cost does not constitute an additional cost from the present moment forward. Accordingly, their cost is not regarded as a concern of "society" in the present.

Marginal cost is supposed to be the measure of the value of alternative goods forgone, because the prices of the factors of production that remain to be purchased and which constitute marginal cost are supposed to be determined by the value of the alternative goods whose production must be forgone. For example, the prices (wages) of the labor, materials, and fuel required to produce and ship an additional automobile are supposedly determined by the value of the refrigerators, television sets, or whatever other goods cannot now be produced because the factors of production required to produce them will be used to produce an additional automobile instead.[81]

All prices, according to this collectivist, tribal view, should be *scarcity prices*, that is, prices determined by the necessity of balancing a limited supply against a comparatively unlimited demand.

Supply, in the context of this doctrine, means the goods that are *here*—in the possession of sellers—and the potential goods that the sellers would produce with their existing plant and equipment, if they considered no limitation to their production but "marginal cost." *Demand* means the set of quantities of the goods that buyers will take at varying prices. Every price is supposed to be determined at whatever point is required to give the buyers the full supply in this sense and to limit their demand to the size of the supply.

The essence of this theory of prices is the idea that every seller's goods and the use of his plant and equipment belong to "society" and should be free of charge to "society's" members unless and until a price is required to "ration" them. Prior to that point, they are held to be *free goods*, like air and sunlight; and any value they do have is held to be the result of an "artificial, monopolistic restriction of supply"—of a deliberate, vicious withholding of goods from "society" by their private custodians. After that point, however, the value they may attain is limited only by the importance that buyers attach to them.

On this view, every price is supposed to be an index of the intensity of "society's" need or desire for a good—an index of the good's "marginal social utility." Production should be carried to the point of price equals marginal cost, it is argued, because only then is production at an optimum. So long as price is greater than marginal cost, it is claimed, "society" is in a position to obtain a good that it values more at the expense of other goods that it values less. For the price of the good is held to be the measure of its value, while the marginal cost is allegedly the measure of the value of the alternative goods that must be forgone in order to make the factors of production available for an expanded production of the good in question. By the same token, if the price of the good is less than its marginal cost, then "society" would supposedly gain by curtailing the production of the good in question and expanding the production of other goods that employ the same factors of production.

In the words of Samuelson and Nordhaus: "Only when prices of goods are equal to marginal costs is the economy squeezing from its scarce resources and limited technical knowledge the maximum of outputs."[82] "Price," they declare, in the previous edition of their textbook, "is the signal that consumers use to indicate how much they value various goods. Costs, and particularly marginal costs, are the indicators of how much of society's valuable resources each good's production utilizes: scarce land, sweaty labor, and other resources that could produce other goods."[83]

But, despite all this, what does the "imperfect competitor"—viz., the "monopolist," the "oligopolist," or the "monopolistic competitor"—do, according to Samuelson and Nordhaus?

> Does it produce goods up to the point where their social cost—as measured by *MC* [Marginal Cost]—is equal to what the last unit of the good is worth to society—as measured by market *P* [Price] resulting from consumer money votes? No. The imperfect competitor is contriving to keep its output a little scarce. It is contriving to keep *P* above *MC* because in that way it sets *MR = MC* [Marginal Revenue equal Marginal Cost] and thereby maximizes its profit. So society does not get quite as much of A's [the "imperfect competitor's"] good as it really wants in terms of what that good really costs society to produce.[84]

The following series of examples will help to illustrate the alleged crime of the "imperfect competitor."

We can begin by imagining a simple fishing village.

The fishing fleet goes out and returns with an enormously successful catch. The catch is so large that it exceeds the ability of the local canning and freezing plants to process it and the local human and cat population to consume it before it spoils. In these circumstances, the rationing theory of prices holds that fish are a free good; they are not scarce; their marginal social utility is zero. Hence, no just basis exists for a price being charged for fish; they should be given away for nothing.

The fishermen, we can be sure, have a different view of things. They face ruin with a price of fish that is too far below their costs, let alone zero. (And, incidentally, if the fishermen are ruined, the long-run effect will be a smaller-sized fishing fleet, a smaller long-run average catch of fish, and a higher long-run average price of fish to the buyers.) If the fishermen can come to an understanding among themselves, they will throw back part of their catch in order to make the remaining supply command a positive price that is not too far below their costs or is modestly above their costs. If they succeed in doing so, however, the tribal-rationing theory denounces them for a "monopolistic restriction of supply."

Exactly the same type of crime is held to be committed every time an inventor, or any other intellectual creator, earns something by virtue of the ideas he has created—indeed, so much as covers any part of the costs he has incurred in developing his work. As von Mises points out, the ability of ideas—of formulas, recipes, and techniques of all kinds—to render service is potentially unlimited.[85] The only physical limit to their ability to render service at any given time is the availability of the physical factors of production. On this basis, the rationing theory of prices must view ideas as inherently *free goods* and the existence of any prices being charged for their use as the result of a "monopolistic restriction of supply."

This conclusion follows because if the physical factors of production are available in any desired quantity to produce more of a product, in accordance with a given idea, then the supply of the product can be increased and its price will fall. This can continue until the price falls all the way to the point that it covers only the cost of the physical factors of production together with the going rate of profit on the capital invested in the physical factors of production. If the lack of the necessary physical factors of production is what limits the production of a product, then the price of the limiting physical factor or factors of production will rise to reflect the high price of the product. Either way, nothing will remain for the service rendered by the idea.

If and to the extent that something does remain for the use of the idea, it is held to be the result of an "artificial scarcity" having been created in the use of the idea. The owner of the idea, whether it is patented, copyrighted, or is a trade secret, restricts its use below the limit set by the availability of the physical factors of production, in order to secure a price for the use of his idea (or an allowance for the use of his idea in the price of the product it serves to produce). In effect, like the fishermen who throw back some fish, he holds down the number of times his idea is used in order to secure a price on the use of it that he does allow.[86]

Finally, and, for present purposes, most importantly, the same kind of crime is held to take place in connection with the use of existing plant and equipment. According to the tribal-rationing theory, fixed costs, notably, the depreciation cost of plant and equipment and interest paid on capital invested in plant and equipment, are only properly recoverable as and when the use of the plant and equipment becomes "scarce." Any allowance in the price of the product for fixed costs, other than in the case of the use of the plant and equipment being "scarce," is also supposed to rest on a "monopolistic withholding of supply."

This notion can be illustrated by assuming the existence of plant and equipment with some definite capacity to produce—for example, the capacity to produce one million units of product per month. This capacity to produce can be construed as representing a supply of one million service-units of plant and equipment. If the quantity demanded of the product that the plant and equipment helps to produce is less than a million units a month at any price greater than the marginal cost of a unit, then, according to the tribal-rationing doctrine, no just basis exists for any allowance for plant and equipment being charged in the price of the product. This is shown in Table 10–2, where it is assumed that marginal cost is constant at $8 per unit and that, even at a selling price as low as $8 per unit, the quantity demanded of the product is less than a million units.

Under the assumptions made in Table 10–2, if the product were to be sold at a price of $10, the quantity of the product demanded would be only 500,000 units. If the owners of the plant and equipment kept the price at $10 and went on supplying only 500,000 units, then they would be in the position of receiving an allowance of $2 in the price of the product for a service-unit of plant and equipment (viz., the product's selling price of $10 minus the marginal cost of $8). This, it is held, would be "inefficient"—viz., unjust, according to the perspective of collectivism. With a supply of 1 million service-units of plant and equipment and a requirement for only 500,000 such service-units, there is no scarcity of service-units to justify such a price, it is held. Efficiency and justice, it is claimed, demand that the implied allowance for a service-unit of plant and equipment be reduced.

Now this will be accomplished if the price of the product is cut from $10 to $9. But, as Table 10–2 shows, even at a price of $9, the quantity of the product demanded, and thus the number of service-units of plant and equipment required, grows only to 600,000. The service-units of plant and equipment are still not scarce. Even if the selling price of the product is reduced all the way to $8—the marginal cost—and the implied allowance for plant and equipment is correspondingly reduced all the way to zero, the quantity of the product demanded—and thus the quantity of service-units of plant and equipment required—still grows only to 700,000. Thus, the tribal-rationing theory concludes, plant and equipment in this case simply are not scarce and therefore deserve no allowance in the price of the product.

Such an allowance would be deserved only if at a price above $8, the quantity demanded of the product, and thus the requirement for service-units of the plant and equipment, were greater than a million units. In that case, the plant and equipment's service-units would be scarce and deserve an allowance in the product's price. The allowance would be necessary to reduce the quantity of the product demanded to a million units. Such an allowance could be anything, it is implied. It need have no fixed limit. It would be whatever is required to reduce the

Table 10–2			
The Implications of Price Equal Marginal Cost for the Recovery of Fixed Costs			
Quantity of Product Supplied and Demanded	Price	Marginal Cost	Implied Allowance in Product Price for Use of Plant and Equipment
500,000	$10	$8	$2
600,000	$9	$8	$1
700,000	$8	$8	$0

quantity of the product demand to equality with the limited capacity available to produce it. Thus, if at a price of $8, 5 million units of the product were demanded and a corresponding requirement for 5 million service-units of plant and equipment existed, and it took a price of $50 to reduce the quantity of the product demanded—and the requirement for service-units of plant and equipment— to a million units, that supposedly would be perfectly acceptable. (In actual practice, of course, one may be certain that most proponents of the doctrine would soon be crying for price controls, if the selling price came to exceed the full costs by any substantial amount.)

As stated, in all circumstances in which the owners of plant and equipment recover any part of their investment, short of the services of their plant and equipment being in a state of scarcity, they are accused—just like the fishermen and the owners of intellectual creations—of monopolistically withholding a part of their supply from the market in order to obtain a price on the portion they do allow to enter the market. Automobile plants, steel mills, and all other lines of business which are able to recover their fixed costs at less than capacity operation, are denounced for monopolistic restrictions of supply. This is the implicit substance of all the attacks made against "oligopoly" and the alleged refusal of "oligopolists" to cut prices in the face of a decline in demand. (Similarly, the attacks made against "monopolistic competition" can be understood as attacks on the ability to profit from a "contrived scarcity" of the services of intellectual creations, such as a product's distinctive features and its brand name.)

Proponents of the tribal-rationing theory may not agree with my claim that their doctrine calls for no recovery of fixed costs short of capacity operation. They almost always assume that marginal cost continuously rises, starting from a very low percentage of capacity operation, and that in the relevant range of operations, it already exceeds average variable cost.[87] (Average variable cost can be understood as the average cost per unit on account of labor, materials, and fuel.) On these assumptions, an equality of price with marginal cost is compatible with some or even full recovery of fixed costs, short of the point of 100 percent capacity operation of the whole firm or even single factory. For in this case, when price is equal to marginal cost, it is equal to the marginal cost only of the present marginal unit; it simultaneously exceeds the lower marginal costs of all the earlier units. Out of that excess can come coverage of fixed costs.

Unfortunately for the proponents of the tribal-rationing theory, marginal cost does not continuously rise. The law of diminishing returns, which is the basis presented for the assumption that it does, is not in fact an adequate

basis for such a conclusion.[88] The law of diminishing returns implies merely that *at some point* more plant and equipment is required if the output per unit of labor and other variable factors of production is not to decline.[89] It is entirely consistent with the law of diminishing returns that prior to full capacity operation of a plant, or a level of operation not far short of full capacity operation, marginal cost is constant. Indeed, this is the typical case in manufacturing and processing. To confirm this conclusion, one need only imagine a dress factory, say, with rows of workbenches and sewing machines. So long as there are empty workbenches and idle sewing machines, there is no reason for assuming that the employment of additional labor, and the use of additional materials and fuel, will be accompanied by diminishing returns.

A reasonable basis for assuming a rise in marginal cost as output levels increased would be if the firm owned machinery (or whole factories) of different ages, representing earlier and later models, and thus of marked differences in efficiency. It might be imagined that, say, 20 percent of its capacity was in the form of the newest and most efficient machines, which enjoyed the lowest marginal cost per unit; that a further 60 percent of its capacity was in the form of somewhat older and less efficient machines, which necessitated production at a higher marginal cost; and that its final 20 percent of capacity was in the form of still older, still less efficient machines, which necessitated production at a still higher level of marginal cost. Similarly, it might well be the case that the addition of a third shift would entail a higher level of marginal costs, because of the need to pay a somewhat higher level of wages in off hours. But none of these cases implies continuously rising marginal cost. They imply a marginal cost that rises in two or three steps and at each step stays constant over the range of that step.

In such conditions, the only modification or, more correctly, elaboration, that needs to be made to the statement that the rationing theory of prices requires the achievement of capacity operation before fixed costs can justly begin to be covered is that capacity operation must be achieved *for the particular grade of capacity concerned.* For example, in order for the fixed costs on the most efficient 20 percent of our dress company's machinery to justly begin to be covered, according to the rationing theory of prices, that factory must be operating at a level equal to at least 20 percent of capacity. If it is, the service-units representing that grade of capacity are in a state of scarcity. By the same token, the only way that fixed costs on the machines representing the next 60 percent of capacity can justly begin to be covered, according to the rationing theory of prices, is if the factory is operating at a level equal to at least 80 percent of its capacity. At that point, the service-units representing this grade of capacity are in a state of scarcity.

It thus turns out, upon analysis, that the tribal-rationing theory can be understood as an attempt to apply the Ricardian land-rent doctrine to the determination of the value of the services of plant and equipment. It should be recalled that according to Ricardo, rent commences on land of the first quality only when all of it is under cultivation and it becomes necessary to resort to the cultivation of land of the second quality, and that rent commences on land of the second quality (and correspondingly increases on land of the first quality) when all of it, in turn, comes under cultivation and it becomes necessary to resort to land of the third quality.[90]

The essential point remains that compensation for produced capital goods is being made to depend on an absolute scarcity of their services and that any attempt by their owners to obtain compensation short of such a scarcity is denounced as a monopolistic restriction of supply. In our example of the dress factory, which certainly represents a typical case when modified to have three grades of capacity, the tribal-rationing theory holds that efficiency and justice demand that the firm earn nothing toward the replacement of the great bulk of its machinery whenever it operates below 80 percent of capacity. (And to earn anything toward the replacement of the factory itself, it would probably have to operate at a full 100 percent of capacity—unless it were fortunate enough short of that point to have some machinery in operation of such inefficiency that "rents" on its more efficient capacity were high enough to leave something over for the replacement of the plant itself.) If despite the absence of these conditions the firm does earn something on the bulk of its capacity, it is denounced for monopolistically restricting the services of its plant and equipment and the supply of its products.

The Doctrine of Pure and Perfect Competition

To understand the view of competition held by contemporary economics, all one need do is take such alleged monopolistically contrived scarcities as those just described, as the standard of the kind of evil that competition is supposed to prevent. If one follows this procedure, one can grasp the nature of "pure and perfect competition" and how it is a product of the tribal view of property, of price, and of cost.

Competition in contemporary economics is viewed as the means by which prices are driven down either to equality with "marginal cost" or to the point where they exceed "marginal cost" only by whatever premium is necessary to "ration" the benefit of plant and equipment operating at full capacity.

This is not competition as it exists in reality. The competition which takes place under capitalism acts to regulate prices simply in accordance with the full costs of production and with the requirements of earning a rate of profit. It does not act to drive prices to the level of "marginal costs" or to the point where they reflect a "scarcity" of capacity. The kind of "competition" required to do *that*, is of a very special type. Literally, it is out of this world. It is "pure" and "perfect."

No one has ever defined "pure and perfect competition"—the procedure is merely to present a list of conditions which it requires. A fairly full list of these conditions is presented by Professor Clair Wilcox (who is not an advocate of capitalism) as if it were a definition of "pure and perfect competition." He writes:

> The requirements of perfect competition are five: First, the commodity dealt in must be supplied in quantity and each unit must be so like every other unit that buyers can shift quickly from one seller to another in order to obtain the advantage of a lower price. Second, the market in which the commodity is bought and sold must be well organized, trading must be continuous, and traders must be so well-informed that every unit sold at the same time will sell at the same price. Third, sellers must be numerous, each seller must be small, and the quantity supplied by any one of them must be so insignificant a part of the total supply that no increase or decrease in his output can appreciably affect the market price . . . . Fourth, there must be no restraint upon the independence of any seller or buyer, either by custom, contract, collusion, the fear of reprisals by competitors or the imposition of public control. Each one must be free to act in his own interest without regard for the interests of any of the others. Fifth, the market price, uniform at any instant of time, must be flexible over a period of time, constantly rising and falling in response to the changing conditions of supply and demand. There must be no friction to impede the movement of capital from industry to industry, from product to product or from firm to firm; investment must be speedily withdrawn from unsuccessful undertakings and transferred to those that promise a profit. There must be no barrier to entrance into the market; access must be granted to all sellers and all buyers at home and abroad. Finally, there must be no obstacle to elimination from the market; bankruptcy must be permitted to destroy those who lack the strength to survive.[91]

To summarize these conditions: uniform products offered by all the sellers in the same industry, perfect knowledge, quantitative insignificance of each seller, no fear of retaliation by competitors in response to one's actions, constant changes in price, and perfect ease of investment and disinvestment.

To understand the alleged need for all these conditions and what they would mean in reality, it is necessary to project them on a concrete example. This is usually not done at all, and is never done fully—if it were, neither the theory of "pure and perfect competition" nor the rationing theory of prices could be propounded. So I shall use an example of my own, which will not be of a kind used by their supporters, but which will express accurately the meaning of these theories.

Imagine a movie theater with 500 seats. The picture is about to go on; the projectionist, the ushers and the cashier are all in their places. "Society" has the alleged right to the occupancy of 500 seats. If they are not all occupied for this performance, no future satisfaction can be obtained by any storing up of the use of the seats for a future time. The seats, the theater, the film, the necessary workers are "here." "Society," supposedly, "has them" and now it demands the full benefit from its alleged property.

If the film is not run, the only thing that "society" can save is the electric current which might be made available elsewhere, or the coal which must be consumed to generate the current. The costs of the theater, the film, the workers are all "sunk costs"—"water over the dam," as the textbooks say—and, since "bygones are bygones," the only thing which counts for "society" now is the cost of the electric current.

The theater, according to the tribal-rationing theory, should charge an admission price which will guarantee the sale of 500 tickets for the performance. If droves of people are standing in line for admission, it should raise the price to whatever point is required so that only 500 people will be able to afford it. If all the people in line have identical incomes, the same medical disabilities, and natures of equal sensitivity, such a price, supposedly, will mean that the 500 people who want to see the film most, will see it. If they are unequal in these respects, that is already supposed to be an "imperfection" in the justice of the "market mechanism."

If, however, there are few people standing in line, the theater should begin reducing its admission price. It must keep on reducing its admission price until it has attracted 500 customers. If an admission price of only 2¢ is required to get this many customers, then, supposedly, that is what should be charged, provided only that the revenue brought in at the box office covers the cost of the electric current.

If the theater persists in charging its standard price of, say, $5, at which it sells less than 500 tickets, then, according to the tribal-rationing doctrine, it is guilty of "administering" its price and, of course, of "monopolistic restriction of supply." It is engaged in a process of "price control"—in violation of the "laws of supply and demand"—and in creating an "artificial scarcity" of seats by "monopolistically" withholding a portion of its supply from the market to maintain a high price on those seats for which it does sell tickets.

If the theater cannot sell 500 tickets even at 1¢ per ticket, then, according to this theory, it must either open its doors for free or cancel the performance. In this case,

a theater seat is, allegedly, a free good—it is no longer "scarce" in relation to the demand for it, and so there is no longer any need for a price because there is no longer any need to ration theater seats. If there are 100 people who want to see the movie and who are prepared to make it worth the theater owner's while, he should perhaps run the film—contemporary economics would hold—provided he sells the remaining 400 tickets at whatever price is required to unload them, including zero. This, however, would be another "imperfection" in the "market mechanism"—*price discrimination*. The "ideal solution" in such a case, it is alleged, would be to have the government nationalize the theater, charge nothing and subsidize the loss.[92]

In the process of adjusting its price to attract customers, the theater must not, of course, send anyone out in the street to tell people about the movie it is playing or the price it is charging. That would be another "imperfection"—advertising. Advertising, according to this theory, is a wasteful and vicious means of "demand creation"—it makes the "consumers" act differently than they really want to act. So, as the theater is reducing its price, it must be careful not to be too obvious about it. Simply changing the price in the cashier's window should be enough.

However, while advertising by the theater is an "imperfection," "perfection" requires that all potential customers of the theater possess perfect and instantaneous knowledge of its price changes and of the picture it is showing. It is another "imperfection" in the operation of the "market mechanism" if people about to enter other theaters, or riding in their automobiles, or making love, do not receive instantaneous communication of the price changes, so that they may speedily alter their plans. And, presumably, it is an "imperfection" if they have not already seen all the movies many, many times—to be perfectly informed about them.

Because the theater owner wants to "maximize his profits," he will not act in accordance with the theory's tribalistic precepts. However, he *would*, it is argued, if knowledge *were* perfect and automatic, if people *did* race back and forth between theaters in response to penny price differences, and if a number of further conditions were also fulfilled. If, for example, there were 401 identical theaters in the same neighborhood, all showing the same movie, and all in the same position with regard to empty seats, then, it is argued, the cunningly clever, "profit-maximizing" businessman would reason as follows: "At my standard price of $5, I can sell only 100 tickets today. But if I charge $4.99999 . . . 9 (it is a standard assumption of the theory that all economic phenomena are mathematically continuous and thus capable of treatment by calculus), I can sell all 500 tickets. For in response to this insignificant price change, which is infinitely close to my present price, I could attract away one customer from each of the 400 other theaters. This would be very good for me, and none of the other theater owners would really notice the loss of just one customer, and thus no one would match my lower price. So that is what I will do."

The same thought, however, will be racing simultaneously, it is assumed, through the heads of the other 400 theater owners, and so everyone's price will be trimmed just so much, and no one will end up with any additional customers drawn from other theaters. Each theater may attract *one percent* of an additional customer who otherwise would not have gone to the movies, but that is all.

The same process is repeated at the infinitesimally lower price, as each theater owner seeks to "maximize his profit," led by the idea that his insignificant price change will draw an unnoticed amount of business from each of many competitors, who will not reduce their prices in response to *his action.* This process of infinitely small price reductions is supposedly performed with infinite rapidity—presumably through the "automatic market mechanism"—and so, instantaneously, the price is brought down to the point where everyone's theater either is jammed to capacity or must close its doors.

According to the theory of "pure and perfect competition," the large number of sellers is the main condition required to drive prices either to "marginal cost" or to the point where they reflect a "scarcity" of the capacity that is "here." If the individual seller were a significant part of the market and were in a position to handle a major part of the business done by his competitors, then, supposedly, he would never cut his price because he would know that as a result of *his action* others will lose so much business that they will have to match his cut and that he will thus be left basically only with the lower price. When there are a large number of small sellers, every price cut is also matched, but, the argument is, *not because of one's own price reduction,* but because the other sellers are led to cut their prices independently, guided by exactly the same thought.

The significance of all sellers having an *identical* product is supposed to lie in the greater responsiveness of customers to price changes. If each theater is playing a different movie, customers are not likely to shift their business among the various theaters in response to infinitesimal price differences, and so a theater owner will have less incentive to trim his price. The significance attached to perfect knowledge is similar.

This portrait of the economic world of perfection is not yet complete, however. There remain two other major requirements if "society" is to derive the maximum benefit from its "scarce resources." It must be possible, as Professor Wilcox puts it, for investment to "be speedily

withdrawn from unsuccessful undertakings and transferred to those that promise a profit. There must be no barrier to entrance into the market . . . ." This condition would be achieved if movies were shown in tents, with projectors using candle light instead of electricity. Then, whenever demand changed, theater owners would merely have to unfold or fold up their theaters, and light or blow out their candles.

This would be "perfection," but not quite in its full "purity." For in addition, "the market price," as Professor Wilcox says, "uniform at any instant of time, must be flexible over a period of time, constantly rising and falling in response to the changing conditions of supply and demand." This would be achieved if, after leaving the theater and going to a restaurant for dinner, one were not given a menu, but were seated in front of a ticker tape—and were offered a futures contract on dessert; and if afterward, on leaving the restaurant and walking back to one's apartment, one would not know whether one could afford to live there that night, or whether the rentals of penthouses had collapsed. Only then would the world be "purely perfect."

Implications of Marginal-Cost Pricing

It should be obvious that the "purely perfect" world of pure and perfect competition would be an utter chaos. If prices had to constantly be set equal to marginal cost, not only would firms routinely be prevented from charging prices high enough to cover their fixed costs, but many firms would routinely be prevented from charging *any price at all!* Consider how many cases there are like movie theaters. Consider how often not only movie theaters, but also athletic stadiums, concert halls, and opera houses have empty seats. Consider how often airplanes, trains, and buses travel with empty seats. What is the marginal cost of admitting or carrying one more customer in these cases? What is the marginal cost of providing electricity or telephone service? What is the marginal cost of using any invention one more time? A price equal to marginal cost in any of these cases would have to be zero or not very far above zero.

The supporters of the pure-and-perfect-competition doctrine may or may not be aware of the frequency with which their doctrine calls for a price of zero or almost zero, but they are prepared to deal with such cases. According to Samuelson and Nordhaus, in their treatment of "ideally regulated pricing" in connection with public utilities:

> If $P = MC$ [price = marginal cost] is such a good thing, why shouldn't the regulators go all the way and make the monopolist lower P until it is at the intersection point of the DD [demand] and MC curves [viz., where price equals marginal cost] . . . ?

Actually, requiring $P = MC$ or *marginal-cost pricing* is the ideal target for economic efficiency. But one serious problem arises. A firm that has declining cost and produces where price equals marginal cost, will be incurring a chronic loss. . . .

Firms of course will not operate for long when they are running at a loss. Hence the ideal regulatory solution requires the government to subsidize the decreasing-cost producer, presumably by funneling tax revenues to the firm.[93]

Thus, in the view of Samuelson and Nordhaus, and of the so-called mainstream of contemporary economics that they represent, in cases in which marginal-cost pricing entails a chronic loss, it is still the ideal; the loss should be supported by a permanent government subsidy. This is in the name of "economic efficiency"—efficiency by the absurd standard that all that counts for efficiency is providing "society" with something it allegedly values more at the expense of something it allegedly values less, irrespective of who is sacrificed, of what coercion is involved to provide the taxes to cover the losses, of the notorious inefficiencies of government subsidies (and government ownership), and irrespective of the utter short-sightedness of using marginal cost as the criterion and assuming that anyone could be benefitted by a policy that makes it impossible for an economic activity to sustain itself.

In the allegedly ideal world of price having to be set equal to marginal cost, there would be a radical reduction of productive capacity relative to the supply of labor and materials, and an even more radical reduction in capacity in cases in which marginal cost is zero or close to zero. In such a world, of course, there could be virtually no private research and development whatever, because of the zero marginal cost of using the results of research and development and thus the alleged obligation to charge nothing for its use. (Presumably, according to Professors Samuelson and Nordhaus, the government would conduct all research and development on the basis of tax revenues—in the name of "efficiency.") As for fixed productive capacity of any kind, after a series of losses, its supply would be cut back to the point where whatever capacity remained would be operated at 100 percent often enough so that it could be replaced. At those times, the price of the product or service would be high enough and the profits great enough to compensate for the losses incurred when having to sell at marginal cost.

This would be a world largely incapable of making adjustments to changes in demand through changes in supply. To the degree that less capacity existed, increases in demand would more quickly run up against a physical inability to expand supply. Such a world would be full of major production bottlenecks. In such a world, the government would actually lack the power to provide any substantial subsidies—it would be impoverished along with the citizens who had to support it.

To term such a world "economically efficient," as such writers as Samuelson and Nordhaus repeatedly do, is to adopt a standard of efficiency by which the economy of Soviet Russia was more efficient than that of the United States. In Soviet Russia, of course, there was less of everything than in the United States, but what there was, was used more fully. In Soviet Russia, the citizen wore his single suit everyday (assuming he was rich enough to own a suit). In the United States, the citizen has long had the idle capacity of several suits. Just so, with regard to plant and equipment. Under capitalism, the normal state of production requires the possession of extra machines and plant capacity in every industry, to meet every foreseeable change in demand. This is not a "waste," not any more than the fact that the consumers under capitalism own more clothes than the ones they happen to be wearing. But such a desirable state of affairs would not be possible if producers had to sell at prices equal to marginal cost whenever they operated short of the full capacity of the plant and equipment concerned.

Ironically, what the "pure-and-perfect-competition" doctrine seeks is *the abolition of competition among producers*. Its "ideal" is a state in which producers are unable to take business away from other producers. If a producer is operating at full capacity, he cannot meet the demand of a single additional buyer, let alone compete for that demand. He cannot compete for additional business if he is operating merely at the full capacity of a given grade of plant and equipment and his idle capacity is of a kind whose operating cost is greater than the currently prevailing price. And if he is not producing at full capacity even of a given grade of plant and equipment and is charging a price equal to his "marginal cost," he still cannot compete for the business of any additional buyers because he is forbidden to "differentiate" his product or to advertise it. Thus, the normal competition of capitalism—the competition of producers for customers, based on an ability to expand production—would give way to a competition of consumers for meager, essentially fixed supplies of goods, in which the only way anyone could have more of a good would be by virtue of someone else having less of it. The only relief from this state of affairs would be when a higher price succeeded in covering the higher marginal cost associated with additional production.

Such competition, a competition largely resembling that of animals for a fixed stock of prey, is what the pure-and-perfect-competition doctrine regards as ideal. However ironic it may be, the pure-and-perfect-competition doctrine seeks to establish as the competitive ideal precisely conditions resembling the law of the jungle.

When it denounces capitalism for a lack of competition, what it is denouncing is the fact that under capitalism, competition is the diametric opposite of the law of the jungle: it is a competition of producers in the production of wealth, not of consumers in the consumption of wealth.

The doctrine of "pure and perfect competition" marks the almost total severance of economic thought from reality. It is the dead end of the attempt to defend capitalism on a collectivist base.

Ironically, that attempt took hold in economics in the late nineteenth century (and has been gaining influence ever since) through the efforts of Victorian economists to refute the theories of Karl Marx on the subject of value and price. The rationing theory of prices was advanced as the alternative to the Marxist labor theory of value. The irony is that the "pure-and-perfect-competition" doctrine is *to the left of Marxism.*

Marxism denounced capitalism merely for the existence of profits. The "pure-and-perfect-competition" doctrine denounces capitalism because, as shown, businessmen refuse to suffer unnecessary *losses.* The argument of the supporters of "pure and perfect competition" is not that businessmen make excessive *profits* through any kind of "monopoly," but that they are "monopolistic" in refusing to sell their products at a *loss*—which they would have to do if they treated their plant and equipment as costless natural resources that acquired value only when they happened to be "scarce."

The fact that the pure-and-perfect-competition doctrine is, indeed, essentially an attack against business for refusing to accept unnecessary losses is borne out by the well-known study of Prof. Arnold Harberger.[94] In an attempt to measure the so-called deadweight welfare loss from "monopoly" in manufacturing in the United States, Harberger found that it turned out to be extremely small. Samuelson and Nordhaus write:

> Harberger's finding shocked the economics community. He found the welfare loss from monopoly was slightly less than 0.1 percent of GNP. In today's economy, it would total about $5 billion. One economist quipped that, if we believe this study, economists would make a larger social contribution fighting fires and eradicating termites than attempting to curb monopolies.

> Many studies have refined and criticized Harberger's original findings. . . . After reviewing all these subsequent analyses, a careful recent survey concludes:

> "It appears that the deadweight welfare loss attributable to monopolistic resource misallocation in the United States lies somewhere between 0.5 and 2 percent of gross national product, with the estimates nearer the lower bound inspiring more confidence than those on the high side."[95]

Thus, despite all expectations, it now appears to be an established fact that the problem of monopoly is a relatively small one by any standard. This, of course, does not stop Samuelson and Nordhaus, or the writers of all the other textbooks dealing with "microeconomics," "industrial organization," and "antitrust policy" from continuing just as before in making "monopoly" versus "pure and perfect competition" the sum and substance of their theoretical analysis. They report findings such as Harberger's and then proceed to ignore them.

But there is a simple reconciliation between the "empirical" findings concerning the insignificance of the "monopoly" problem and the overwhelming preoccupation with it on the part of contemporary economic theory. This is the fact that a critical assumption of the so-called empirical studies appears to be that *marginal cost can be assumed to be equal to total average cost plus an allowance for earning the competitive rate of profit.* At any rate, this is how Samuelson and Nordhaus's graphical depiction of the measurement problem shows matters.[96]

Now if one takes marginal cost as this high, and thus uses as the measure of monopoly merely what amounts to *profits earned at above-average rates,* then indeed, the measure of monopoly will be small. (And even then, it will be far overstated, for it will include for the most part above-average rates of profit made by virtue of reducing costs of production, improving the quality of products, and successfully anticipating changes in consumer demand. Only a modest portion of above-average profits results from actual monopoly privilege.) The reason that, despite the insignificance of monopoly profits when computed in this way, they loom so large in contemporary economic theory is precisely the fact that, whether it is aware of it or not, contemporary economic theory is actually concerned with "monopoly" as the means of avoiding losses. This is what it sees everywhere and denounces everywhere, while the "empirical" studies, such as Harberger's, automatically preclude such measurement by virtue of their assumption that marginal cost is equal to total average cost plus an allowance for earning the going rate of profit.

The Alleged Lack of "Price Competition"

The "pure-and-perfect-competition" doctrine distorts the facts of reality to a greater extent than did the traditional critiques of capitalism. Those critiques recognized that competition is a fundamental element of capitalism, but they denounced it. Capitalism, they claimed, is ruled by the "law of the jungle," by the principles of "dog eat dog" and "the survival of the fittest." The "pure-and-perfect-competition" doctrine proceeds from the same base as these earlier critiques, and is in full agreement with them in their objections to such characteristics of the process of competition as the continuous improvement in products, the variety of products, advertising, and the existence of idle capacity. Both schools regard all these characteristics of competition as a "waste" of "society's scarce resources."

But the "pure-and-perfect-competition" doctrine regards these characteristics as "imperfections" and attacks capitalism on the grounds that capitalism *lacks* competition. Every industry, it asserts, is "imperfectly competitive" (with the barely possible exception of wheat farming). Every industry is guilty of "monopolistic competition" or "oligopoly."[97]

The competition that capitalism is accused of lacking—as a result of "monopolistic competition" and "oligopoly"—is called *price competition*. The nature of price competition, as contemporary economists see it, is indicated in the following quotation: "Analytically, the crucial thing about an oligopoly is the small number of sellers, which makes it imperative for each to weigh carefully the reactions of the others to his own price, production, and sales policies. The result is a strong pressure to collude to avoid price competition or to avoid it without formal collusion."[98]

Capitalism is accused of lacking price competition on the following grounds: if there are few sellers in a market, any seller who cuts his price must take into account the fact that the other sellers will match his cut—so he may be better off if he refrains from price cutting; thus prices will not be driven down to the level of "marginal cost" or to the point where they "ration" the benefit of "scarce" capacity.

Consider the denial of facts entailed in the accusation that capitalism lacks price competition. Every decade, since the beginning of the Industrial Revolution, commodities have become not only better, but also cheaper—if not always in terms of paper money (the value of which has been repeatedly reduced by the inflationist policies of governments), then in terms of the labor and effort that must be expended to earn them. What is it that has made producers lower their prices for the last two hundred years? Obviously, it is *price competition*.

Price competition exists even in the midst of inflation. Even under inflation, every firm is still interested in improving the productivity of the labor it employs. To the extent a firm succeeds in doing so, it is able to hold its price increases below the wage increases it must pay. Other firms in the same line of business which have not succeeded in raising the productivity of the labor they employ, or not to the same extent, must nevertheless keep their price increases in line with these price increases. The result is that if these firms wish to remain as profitable as before, ultimately, indeed, even to remain profitable and in business at all, they must further increase the productivity of the labor they employ. They simply cannot afford to fall too far behind. *This*, of course, is *price*

competition. It is a phenomenon known to virtually every businessman, but it is essentially unknown to contemporary economists, because of their arbitrary definition of price competition as the process of equalizing price with marginal cost. Their arbitrary definition simply blinds them to the existence of actual price competition. All that they look for in the world is what complies with their absurd definition; they have eyes for nothing else.

Actual price competition is an omnipresent phenomenon in a capitalist economy. But it is completely unlike the kind of pricing envisioned by the doctrine of "pure and perfect competition." It is not the product of a mass of short-sighted, individually insignificant little chiselers each of whom acts to cut his price in the hope that his action will not be noticed by any of the others. The real-life competitor does not live in a rat's world, hoping to scurry away undetected with a morsel of the cheese of thousands of other rats, only to find that they too have been guided by the same stupidity, with the result that all have less cheese.

The competitor who cuts his price is fully aware of the impact on other competitors and that they will try to match his price. He acts in the knowledge that some of them will not be able to afford the cut, while he is, and that he will eventually pick up their business, as well as a major portion of any additional business that may come to the industry as a whole as the result of charging a lower price. He is able to afford the cut when and if his productive efficiency is greater than theirs, which lowers his costs to a level they cannot match.

The ability to lower the costs of production is the base of price competition. It enables an efficient producer who lowers his prices, to gain most of the new customers in his field; his lower costs become the source of additional profits, the reinvestment of which enables him to expand his capacity. Furthermore, his cost-cutting ability permits him to forestall the potential competition of outsiders who might be tempted to enter his field, drawn by the hope of making profits at high prices, but who cannot match his cost efficiency and, consequently, his lower prices. Cost efficiency is the foundation of the ability to take business away from others in the field, insofar as one's own cost reductions exceed theirs. Thus price competition, under capitalism, is the result of a contest of efficiency, competence, ability.

Price competition is not the self-sacrificial chiseling of prices to "marginal cost" or their day-by-day, minute-by-minute adjustment to the requirements of "rationing scarce capacity." It is the setting of prices—perhaps only once a year—by the most efficient, lowest-cost producers, motivated by their own self-interest. The extent of the price competition varies in direct proportion to the size and the economic potency of these producers. It was firms like Ford, General Motors, and A & P, and, more recently, the major Japanese producers—not a microscopic-sized wheat farmer or sharecropper—that have been responsible for price competition. The price competition of the rapidly growing Ford Motor Company early in this century reduced the price of automobiles from a level at which they could be only rich men's toys to a level at which even a low-paid laborer could afford to own a car. Later on, the price competition of General Motors was so intense that firms like Kaiser and Studebaker could not meet it. The price competition of A & P was so successful that the supporters of "pure and perfect competition" have never stopped complaining about all the two-by-four grocery stores that had to go out of business. And in recent years, the price competition of firms such as Toyota, Nissan, Sony, Mitsubishi, and Nippon Steel has set a pace that even the very best of American producers have found difficult to follow.

Price competition, it must be observed, frequently forces some of the sellers in an industry to sell at a price that is equal to or not far above *their* marginal costs, yet, at the same time, is substantially above the marginal costs of the more efficient, more competitively capable firms. This is part of the process by which the more efficient firms gain the business of the less efficient firms, which will be unable to replace their assets and thus unable to continue in business on the present scale. Indeed, the more efficient firms typically sell at prices *below* the marginal costs of a substantial portion of the capacity of the less efficient firms. Such prices are what keeps that less efficient capacity from serving the market, and thus competitively reserves the market to the more efficient firms.

Considerations of this kind explain why, when an industry is confronted with a substantial drop in the demand for its product, the result is a fall in price even though the demand for the industry's product is relatively inelastic and the industry is made up of few firms. What accounts for a price reduction that is consistent with rational self-interest in such circumstances is an inequality in the marginal costs of the different firms in connection with the capacity they had employed prior to the drop in demand. If the drop in demand idles capacity with a relatively low marginal cost of operation, while other firms continue to supply the market with capacity that has a relatively high marginal cost of operation, then it becomes to the self-interest of the firm with the lower-cost capacity to cut the price in order to make way in the market for its capacity. Cutting the price below other firms' higher marginal costs is the means of eliminating the higher-cost capacity of those firms from the market. This is genuine competition in adverse circumstances.

Such competition takes place throughout the economic system in every recession. Yet contemporary economic theory is virtually incapable of comprehending how it can exist—that is, how prices can fall in the face of a drop in demand, or, indeed, under any other circumstances—apart from the conditions of "pure and perfect competition." What blinds its vision here is its inheritance from Alfred Marshall of the notion of "the representative firm."[99] It typically regards "an industry" as consisting of a mere multiplication of so many interchangeable, identical "representative firms." It thus proceeds on the assumption that all the firms in an industry have exactly equal efficiency and equal costs. In such conditions, there is obviously no basis for competition: no one can have any rational basis for expecting to succeed by competing. The moment anyone cuts his price, the other producers, who are assumed to be equally efficient, cut theirs in response. The result is that the only possible gain for a producer in cutting his price is the gain that would exist if there were only one producer. On this basis, contemporary economics concludes that what it calls "oligopoly" is essentially the same in its effects as "monopoly." For it appears to it that it will pay an "oligopolist" to cut his price only when it would pay a "monopolist."[100]

Competition, centering precisely on an *inequality* in the productive efficiency of firms, is the means by which continuous progress and improvement are brought about, in terms both of falling real prices of products and ever better products. Indeed, nothing could be more pure and perfect—in the rational sense of these terms—than the competition that takes place under capitalism. As the result of this competition, generation after generation, in industry after industry, one massive improvement in production succeeds another, and the best of the products of the past cease to be good enough for the present. At the same time, everything becomes more and more affordable to more and more people. This is what the whole of Part C of the preceding chapter and, indeed, the whole of this book has shown.

The ideal of the "pure-and-perfect-competition" doctrine, however, is a totally stagnant economy—the "static state," as it is called—in which production and consumption consist of an endless repetition of the same motions.[101]

It is in the name of this "ideal" that the supporters of "pure and perfect competition" attack the constant introduction of new or improved products, the ever-growing variety of products, and the advertising required to keep people abreast of what is being offered.

And only from the standpoint of this "ideal" can one declare that idle capacity is a "waste"—for only in a "static state" would there be no need for any unused capacity.

The supporters of "pure and perfect competition" are aware of the fact that their doctrine is inapplicable to reality. This does not trouble them. Their view is expressed by Professor Wilcox, who casually observes: "Perfect competition, thus defined, probably does not exist, never has existed, and never can exist. . . . Actual competition always departs, to a greater or lesser degree, from the ideal of perfection. Perfect competition is thus a mere concept, a standard by which to measure the varying degrees of imperfection that characterize the actual markets in which goods are bought and sold."[102]

This "concept" divorced from reality, this Platonic "ideal of perfection" drawn from nonexistence to serve as the "standard" for judging existence, is one of the principal reasons why businessmen have been imprisoned, major corporations broken up and others prevented from expanding, and why economic progress has been retarded and the improvement of man's material well-being significantly undercut. This "concept" is at the base of antitrust prosecutions, which have forced businessmen to operate under conditions approaching a reign of terror.

The doctrine of pure and perfect competition is a leading manifestation of the influence of irrationalism and mysticism in contemporary economics. It can be taken as an illustration of the proposition that while unreality and nonexistence as such can have no consequences, those who are confused enough to advocate them, do. It belongs hopefully to the last, and certainly to the most convoluted and absurd phase of the denunciations of capitalism as a system of monopoly.

11. A Further Word on Cost of Production and Prices

The discussions of the marginal revenue and pure-and-perfect-competition doctrines make clear that the reaction to classical economics' exaggeration of the explanatory role of cost of production as a determinant of prices has gone too far, in two respects.

First, cost of production operates to set many prices far below what they would be if they were determined on the basis of the direct marginal utility of the good concerned. This, of course, is the case with respect to some necessities and virtually all components and spare parts used in manufactured goods.

Second, cost of production operates to establish prices at a point that is above what they would be if producers did in fact have to regard their plant and equipment and intellectual property as not deserving to command an allowance in the price of the product because their renditions of service were not scarce. The fact that producers do not have to regard their plant and equipment in this way is, of course, what makes it possible for prices to be below the direct marginal utility of the specific goods concerned, because producers then have the productive capacity on hand immediately to make more of the goods available. And the fact that they do not have to regard their intellectual property in this way is what underlies their incentive and ability to go on introducing further productive innovations, which steadily reduce prices in real terms.

Thus, prices are very often lower than one would expect on the basis of the direct marginal utility of the product. At the same time, they are typically higher than corresponds to the marginal utility of the full available supply of the means of producing the product—viz., the full available supply of renditions of service that the plant and equipment and, even more, the knowledge of the requisite methods of production, is capable of providing. In both cases, prices are pulled toward cost of production—the full cost of production.

In the first case, they are pulled in a downward direction; in the second case, in an upward direction. In the first case, cost of production communicates the marginal utility of the means of production in other employments and pulls the marginal utility and price of products in specific industries down to conform with that wider marginal utility. In the second case, cost of production on the part of potential outside entrants, together with an allowance for the going rate of profit, sets the upper limit to which producers can raise the price of their product without encouraging outside competition—except insofar as their products possess premium quality. It thus limits the extent to which prices can exceed a correspondence to the marginal utility of the full available supply of means of production. As stated, and it cannot be too strongly stressed, such excess of price is an essential foundation for the cheapness of price in comparison with the direct marginal utility of many goods and for the progressive decline in prices in real terms.

Notes

1. For a discussion of the rational and the anarchic concepts of freedom, see above, pp. 23–26. See also above, p. 238.

2. On the subject of freedom of opportunity, see above, pp. 337–343.

3. For a critique of the contrasting notion of an "equality of opportunity," see above, ibid.

4. Cf. above, p. 342, the discussion of the synergistic nature of the freedom of opportunity.

5. For a critique of the notion that the freedoms of speech and press can be violated in this way, see above, pp. 23–26.

6. Strictly speaking, in order for the freedom of competition to reduce hospital rates to a level corresponding to the necessary costs of providing hospital care, together with a competitive rate of profit, and then to reduce those necessary costs, more would be required than freedom from licensing. Freedom from other forms of government regulation that artificially increase costs would also be necessary. This is because today's outlandish hospital rates do not rest on a foundation of exorbitant profits, but on a foundation of artificially created costs caused by government intervention in medical care. The freedom of competition that escape from licensing is to make possible must be understood as allowing the competitors to avoid all such artificial costs. Such costs include the practice of so-called defensive medicine in order to avoid irrational malpractice suits.

7. Cf. Ayn Rand, *The Virtue of Selfishness* (New York: New American Library, 1964), p. 129.

8. See above, pp. 148–150.

9. This theme is elaborated, along with an explanation of all aspects of the cause and cure of the current crisis in medical care in my pamphlet *The Real Right to Medical Care Versus Socialized Medicine* (Laguna Hills, Calif.: The Jefferson School of Philosophy, Economics, and Psychology, 1994.)

10. See above, pp. 355–356.

11. See above, ibid.

12. See above, pp. 196–199.

13. See above, ibid.

14. For an account of its destructive effects on blacks in particular, see George Reisman, *Capitalism: The Cure for Racism*, a pamphlet (1982; reprint ed., Laguna Hills, Calif.: The Jefferson School of Philosophy, Economics, and Psychology, 1992), pp. 13–21.

15. See ibid., pp. 21–23.

16. On the uniformity-of-profit principle, see above, pp. 172–187, especially pp. 176–180.

17. See above, p. 284.

18. For a demonstration that the existence of socialism serves to confirm the fact that monopoly is a political phenomenon, not an economic phenomenon, see below, pp. 392–393.

19. For elaboration of this point, see below, pp. 417–420.

20. See above, pp. 70–71.

21. For a discussion of the principles underlying the limitation of patent and copyright protection, see Ayn Rand, "Patents and Copyrights" in Ayn Rand, ed., *Capitalism: The Unknown Ideal* (New York: New American Library, 1966), pp. 126–128.

22. Cf. David Ricardo, *Principles of Political Economy and Taxation*, 3d ed. (London, 1821), chaps. 17 and 30; reprinted as vol. 1 of *The Works and Correspondence of David Ricardo*, ed. Piero Sraffa (Cambridge: Cambridge University Press, 1962), pp. 249–250, 384–385. (Where appropriate, from now on, specific page references to the Sraffa edition will be supplied in brackets.)

23. Ibid. See also chap. 1 [p. 12].

24. See Richard Caves, *American Industry: Structure, Conduct, Performance*, 4th ed. (Englewood Cliffs, N. J.: Prentice-Hall, Inc., 1977), p. 8.

25. See Paul Samuelson and William Nordhaus, *Economics*, 13th ed. (New York: McGraw-Hill Book Company, 1989), pp. 605–611.

26. Ibid., pp. 607–608.

27. Ibid., p. 612.

28. See, for example, ibid., p. 584, and below, pp. 432–434.

29. Karl Marx, *Capital*, 3 vols. (Moscow: Foreign Languages Publishing House, 1962), 3:430. Italics supplied.

30. See above, pp. 135–139 and 267–282 passim.

31. As later discussion of saving and capital formation will make clear, the extent to which successful mergers, or anything else which serves to increase real wealth and capital, are accompanied by an increase in the monetary value of invested capital in the economic system as a whole, depends on the rate of increase in the quantity of money. What is essential here is only that successful mergers result in the formation of more new capital in real terms, and thus in the basis for the formation of new and additional firms.

32. It must be noted that this conclusion is not contradicted by statistics alleging a growing concentration of the capital of the American economic system in the hands of the 200 or 500 largest corporations. At the same time that this phenomenon has been going on, foreign trade has become of greater importance and the capital of America's major trading partners has increased much more rapidly than that of the United States. Thus, the ratio of the capital controlled by the 200 or 500 largest American corporations to the total capital employed in serving the American market has sharply fallen over the last generation!

33. For a defense of insider trading, see below, pp. 395–396.

34. See above, p. 127.

35. For an example of this error, see Samuelson and Nordhaus, *Economics*, pp. 571–572.

36. *Ohio v. Standard Oil Co.*, 49 Ohio, 137 (1892).

37. Cf. John S. McGee, "Predatory Pricing: The Standard Oil (New Jersey) Case," *The Journal of Law and Economics*, October, 1958, p. 144.

38. The situation here is similar to the case of partial price controls raising prices on the uncontrolled portion of the supply. See above, pp. 250–252 and 254–256.

39. Cf. Wayne Leeman, "The Limitations of Local Price Cutting as a Barrier to Entry," *Journal of Political Economy*, August, 1956, pp. 331–332.

40. Cf. ibid., p. 330.

41. In fact, Rockefeller did buy out small competitors at premium prices, but not in order later on to charge higher prices—rather, in order to achieve the economies of larger-scale operations. In this way, the small competitors shared the gains of merging and achieving economies of scale. See John S. McGee, "Predatory Pricing." See also Leeman, "Limitations of Local Price Cutting," p. 332.

42. Leeman, "Limitations of Local Price Cutting," pp. 332–333.

43. Cf. John S. McGee, "Predatory Pricing," especially p. 168.

44. This is the same mentality of state worship as is present when people credit government-sponsored research efforts with bringing about major advances in the production of civilian goods, in the process ignoring the essential context of the existence of a capitalist economic system with its profit motive and freedoms of individual initiative and competition, without which no civilian use would ever be made of any such research. (On this subject, see above, p. 277, especially n. 16.) It is the same mentality that is present above all in that combination of unsurpassed ignorance and arrogance that blithely ignores the economic planning that takes place every day under capitalism on the part of millions and tens of millions of private business firms and individuals, and regards economic planning as a capacity unique to the state, which is utterly incapable of planning an economic system and characteristically bungles whatever lesser planning it may undertake. (Concerning this subject, see above, pp. 137–139 and 269–273.)

45. For further analysis pertaining to the post–World War II success of the Japanese economy in comparison with the American economy, see below, pp. 622–629, where the United States can be thought of as the stationary economy depicted in Figure 14–4 on p. 624, and Japan as the progressive economy depicted in Figure 14–5 on p. 625. That analysis explains the role both of relative rates of saving and relative degrees of economic freedom in bringing about capital accumulation and economic progress. See also pp. 831–834.

46. Dudley Dillard, *Economic Development of the North Atlantic Community* (Englewood Cliffs, N. J.: Prentice-Hall, 1967), pp. 409–410.

47. An investigation of the actual facts concerning Standard Oil's dealings with the railroads, undertaken by someone who understands the principles of sound economics, would make an excellent subject for a doctoral dissertation and subsequent book.

48. In reality, it is likely that the elasticity accompanying ten 10 percent increases in supply would not be uniformly one-tenth of the elasticity of a doubling of supply, but would show some variation, with some of the 10 percent increases in the industry's supply being accompanied by lesser or greater price reductions, which, nevertheless, would cumulatively add up to a 40 percent reduction in price accompanying a doubling of supply.

49. Interestingly, Samuelson and Nordhaus show some modest awareness of the fact that potential increases in competitors' output can increase the elasticity of demand facing a given firm. See Samuelson and Nordhaus, 13th ed., pp. 609–610. They seem utterly unaware, however, of the critical role played by outsiders' costs.

50. See below, pp. 417–420.

51. Application of the principle to the oil industry was present in the discussion, back in Chapter 7, of the injustice of blaming the oil industry for the oil shortage or for any increase in the scarcity of oil. See above, p. 236.

52. *The Works and Correspondence of David Ricardo,* 11 vols., ed. Piero Sraffa (Cambridge: Cambridge University Press, 1951–1973), 8:276–277.

53. Eugen von Böhm-Bawerk, *Capital and Interest,* 3 vols., trans. George D. Huncke and Hans F. Sennholz (South Holland,

Ill.: Libertarian Press, 1959), 2:245.

54. Ibid., 2:244–245.

55. Böhm-Bawerk uses the term "marginal product" here to refer to a distinct product of a different type, not, as is the practice in contemporary economics, to the gain or loss of a product of a given type attributable to the presence or absence of a unit of a factor of production.

56. It must be pointed out that the existence of inventories, which can be drawn down in response to an increase in demand, before additional production succeeds in increasing supplies, and which can be temporarily built up in response to a decrease in demand, before production is cut back, makes it unnecessary that production be adjusted instantaneously to changes in demand. The extent to which demand is postponable also introduces a measure of flexibility in how quickly production must be adjusted to changes in demand in order to maintain a connection between prices and costs.

57. Böhm-Bawerk, *Capital and Interest,* 2:173–176. (The permission granted by Libertarian Press to quote this very long passage is gratefully acknowledged.) See also *Capital and Interest,* 3:Excursus 8, and Böhm-Bawerk's untranslated article "Wert, Kosten, und Grenznutzen," *Jarhbuch für Nationalökonomie und Statistik,* Dritte Folge, 3:328.

58. Friedrich von Wieser, *Natural Value* (London and New York: The Macmillan Company, 1893), p. 181n. See also Wieser's Ursprung und Hauptgesetze des Wirtschaftlichen Werthes (Vienna: 1884), pp. 150–151.

59. See W. S. Jevons, *The Theory of Political Economy,* 4th ed. (London: Macmillan and Co., 1924), p. 165.

60. Ricardo, *Principles of Political Economy and Taxation,* chap. 1 [p. 12].

61. Samuelson and Nordhaus, *Economics,* p. 614.

62. It will be found that the substance of what is said here concerning patents and copyrights applies equally to trade secrets. The only difference is that in the case of trade secrets there is no fixed time limit within which competitive advantages must fall into the public domain. That time may come sooner or later than is the case under patents and copyrights.

63. See above, pp. 388–389.

64. On the subject of collectivized medical costs, see above, pp. 148–150.

65. These and any other possible exceptions all pertain to the use of physical force, which is the essential feature of government power. This is the one activity which, insofar as it cannot be entirely eliminated, must be tightly controlled and regulated, so that the only force used is the appropriate minimum necessary for defense and retaliation against the initiation of force. In a fully free society, government would be the only controlled and regulated institution.

66. Insurers and mortgage lenders would undoubtedly also require adherence to various safety precautions in the construction and maintenance of the properties they insured or lent money on.

67. See above, pp. 408–414.

68. Richard Caves, *American Industry,* p. 59.

69. See Ludwig von Mises, *The Free and Prosperous Commonwealth,* trans. Ralph Raico (Princeton: D. Van Nostrand Company, 1962), pp. 92–93; reprinted under the title *Liberalism: A Socio-Economic Exposition* (Kansas City, Kans.: Sheed Andrews and McMeel, Inc., 1978). The original, German-lan-

guage title of the book was *Liberalismus*.

70. See above, pp. 180–182.

71. See above, pp. 234–237.

72. See Ludwig von Mises, *Human Action*, 3d ed. rev. (Chicago: Henry Regnery, 1966), pp. 366–368.

73. Much of what follows originally appeared in my article "Platonic Competition," *The Objectivist* 7, nos. 8 and 9 (August and September 1968); reprinted as a pamphlet (Laguna Hills, Calif.: The Jefferson School of Philosophy, Economics, and Psychology: 1991). References have been updated where possible.

74. Richard H. Leftwich and Ross D. Eckert, *The Price System and Resource Allocation*, 9th ed. (Chicago: The Dryden Press, 1985), p. 41.

75. See Ayn Rand, *Capitalism: The Unknown Ideal*, p. 7. See also von Mises, *Human Action*, pp. 41–46.

76. C. E. Ferguson, *Micro-economic Theory*, 5th ed. (Homewood, Ill.: Richard D. Irwin, Inc., 1980), pp. 173–174.

77. For an account of the origins of this alleged ideal, see von Mises, *Human Action*, pp. 689–693.

78. George J. Stigler, *The Theory of Price*, rev. ed. (New York: The Macmillan Company, 1952), p. 83.

79. Ferguson, *Micro-economic Theory*, p. 173.

80. Cf. Samuelson and Nordhaus, *Economics*, pp. 514–515, 526, *passim*.

81. Ibid., pp. 514–515, 524–527, 656–665.

82. Ibid., p. 552.

83. Paul Samuelson and William Nordhaus, *Economics*, 12th ed. (New York: McGraw-Hill Book Company, 1985), p. 518.

84. Ibid.

85. See von Mises, *Human Action*, p. 128.

86. Cf. ibid., pp. 364–365. Regrettably, as the passages cited here will show, von Mises, the greatest of the economic defenders of capitalism, in this instance himself implicitly accepts the tribal-rationing theory and its application.

87. See, for example, Samuelson and Nordhaus, 13th ed., p. 517, Figure 22–2 and the accompanying discussion.

88. See ibid., pp. 514–516, for a standard textbook presentation of the law of diminishing returns as the basis for continuously rising marginal cost.

89. On the nature of the law of returns, see von Mises, *Human Action*, pp. 127–131.

90. See above, pp. 308–311.

91. Clair Wilcox, "The Nature of Competition," reprinted in Joel Dean, *Managerial Economics* (Englewood Cliffs, N. J.: Prentice-Hall, Inc., 1951), p. 49. An essentially identical list of requirements appears in the much more recent textbook *The Price System* by Leftwich and Eckert, pp. 39–41.

92. For confirmation of this point, see below, in the next subsection, the discussion of Samuelson and Nordhaus's notion of "ideally regulated pricing" in connection with public utilities.

93. Samuelson and Nordhaus, 13th ed., p. 590.

94. See Arnold C. Harberger, "Monopoly and Resource Allocation," *American Economic Review* (May 1954), pp. 771–787.

95. Samuelson and Nordhaus, 13th ed., p. 584. In a footnote on p. 584, they attribute their quotation to "F. M. Scherer, *Industrial Market Structure and Economic Performance* (Rand McNally, Chicago, 1980), p. 464."

96. See Samuelson and Nordhaus, 13th ed., p. 583, the diagram in Figure 24–6. On page 524 it is stated that cost includes the "opportunity cost" constituted by the possibility of earning a rate of return on one's capital. These "costs" are counted in what is labeled *"AC"* [average cost] in Figure 24–6.

97. See above, pp. 390–391.

98. George Leland Bach, *Economics*, 6th ed. (Englewood Cliffs, N. J.: Prentice-Hall, Inc., 1968), p. 361. (Bach expresses the same view in the eleventh edition of his book, published in 1987, pp. 376–377, but not as succinctly.) See also the discussion of "Collusive Oligopoly" in Samuelson and Nordhaus, 13th ed., pp. 607–609.

99. See Alfred Marshall, *Principles of Economics*, 8th ed. (New York: The Macmillan Company, 1920), pp. 317, 342, 377, 459–460, 805, 809n.

100. Cf. Samuelson and Nordhaus, 13th ed., the previously referenced discussion of "Collusive Oligopoly" on pp. 607–609.

101. For a valuable discussion of the influence of this "ideal" on contemporary economics, see von Mises, *Human Action*, pp. 250, 350–357.

102. Clair Wilcox, "The Nature of Competition," p. 49, immediately following his alleged definition—the list of conditions quoted earlier.

CHAPTER 11

THE DIVISION OF LABOR AND THE CONCEPT OF PRODUCTIVE ACTIVITY

THE ROLE OF MONEYMAKING IN PRODUCTIVE ACTIVITY

1. The Division of Labor and Productive Activity

The existence of the division of labor exerts an influence on the nature of productive activity that is no less profound than its influence on the institutions of private ownership of the means of production, economic inequality, and economic competition. An understanding of this influence is sorely lacking in the present-day world, however. Unfortunately, most people hold a concept of productive activity that would be appropriate only in a non-division-of-labor society.

The Doctrine That Only Manual Labor Is Productive

The notion of productive activity that the majority of our contemporaries hold is that productive activity is *manual labor*. Productive activity and manual labor are seen as virtually interchangeable concepts. For evidence of this proposition, consider the distinction drawn in the United States by the Internal Revenue Service between "earned income" and "unearned income." "Earned income" is held to be wages and salaries. Profits, interest, and dividends, on the other hand, are held to be "unearned income." The basis of the distinction is that the

first two are perceived as being received by virtue of the performance of labor. The last three are perceived as being received without the performance of labor.

Exactly the same ideas are held by the labor unions, who believe that their members, who are almost all manual workers, are the people truly responsible for production and thus the rightful recipients of all income. It is on this basis that the unions feel entitled to appropriate every last dollar of profits that they possibly can for wage increases. In their view, the profits rightfully belong to their members in the first place.

The view that productive activity and manual labor are one and the same is an essential doctrine of Marxism and is held by every socialist government. It is in the name of this proposition that the Marxists have sought to expropriate private property and establish socialism, so that the "unearned income" can be given back to its alleged rightful owners, the manual workers. Marxism also provides intellectual inspiration for the labor unions and the tax authorities. It is the leading source of their conviction that they are appropriating unearned income for the benefit of those who are entitled to it.

But the notion that only manual labor is productive long predates Marxism. It was propounded by the classical economists in most respects, and, more than that, it is a reasonable conclusion if one's only experience is that of the conditions of a non-division-of-labor society. In a non-division-of-labor society, where production means, essentially, the growing of food, the making of clothing, and the building of shelter, on a household basis, the producers are those who do these things, and the nonproducers are those who do not. In a non-division-of-labor society there is no room for any category of producer much beyond that of toiler in the field or at the loom.

The doctrine that only manual labor is productive—a mental inheritance originating in the primitive conditions of earlier times and then frozen, as it were, by virtue of a failure to consider the radically new conditions established by the development of the division of labor—underlies the condemnation of an immense proportion of the productive activity of a capitalist society. Because of its influence, many people have no conception of perhaps what half of the present-day economic system is for. In addition to its most serious consequence of excluding the activities of businessmen and capitalists from the category of productive activity, the manual-labor doctrine excludes many other important productive activities performed in a capitalist society. Thus, retailing and wholesaling are widely perceived as having nothing to do with production, but serving merely as a pretext for adding on "markups" to the prices charged by manufacturers and farmers. Advertising is routinely considered to be nonproductive, indeed, to be inherently fraudulent. The stock and commodity exchanges are regularly denounced as mere "gambling casinos," with virtually no connection to productive activity. The banking and financial system in general is regarded with similar suspicion.

The manual-labor doctrine rests on an ignorance of the requirements of a division-of-labor society and is far too narrow in its view of what constitutes productive activity. A proper concept of productive activity must make room for the activities of businessmen and capitalists, retailers and wholesalers, and advertisers, and of the stock, bond, and commodity exchanges and financial system in general.[1]

In another respect, however, the manual-labor doctrine leads to a view of productive activity that is actually far too broad. For it regards as productive activity *all* activity that represents manual labor. Thus, it leads to the very popular notion that there is no basis for distinguishing between the labor of unpaid housewives and that of paid housekeepers who perform the same work. Both are held to be equally productive on the grounds that both perform the same manual labor. It also leads to the very popular view (contrary to the teachings of Adam Smith on this subject) that there is no basis for regarding the labor of government employees as inherently unproductive, inasmuch and insofar as they perform the same type of physical work as the employees of private business.

The appropriate concept of productive activity for a

division-of-labor society has a variety of characteristics which distinguish it from the concept of productive activity appropriate to a non-division-of-labor society. The aspect which can most easily be explained in a way that is fully self-contained is the connection between productive activity and *moneymaking*. As a result, this aspect will be our starting point in the elaboration of a proper concept of productive activity. It will take us into the distinction between production and consumption in the context of a division-of-labor society, between capital goods and consumers' goods, producers' labor and consumers' labor, and producers' loans and consumers' loans. It will make us aware of the existence of a category of spending—*productive expenditure*—that our investigations in later chapters of this book will show to be larger than consumption expenditure and to be the source of most consumption expenditure, and yet whose very existence is almost entirely overlooked in contemporary economics.[2]

The application of the concept of productive expenditure to economic analysis will take place to an important extent later in this chapter, in the critique of the conceptual framework of the Marxian exploitation theory and the validation of the productive activity of businessmen and capitalists. Productive expenditure and the closely related concepts of capital goods and producers' labor will also turn out to be the foundation of the system of aggregate economic accounting that I develop in Chapter 15, and an essential basis of the theory of aggregate profit and the average rate of profit that I present in Chapter 16.

2. Productive Activity and Moneymaking

In a division-of-labor economy, the earning of money becomes an essential aspect of productive activity. This is because in order to live in such an economy, one must obtain the goods and services of other people. Those goods and services are not given away for free, nor, to any significant extent are they, or could they be, obtained through barter. To obtain the goods and services of others, one must possess *money*. Thus, if one's productive activity is to be appropriate to life in a division-of-labor society, that is, to be the means of obtaining the goods and services of others, it is essential that it be moneymaking. Only then, does one's activity make it possible for one to share in the benefits of a division-of-labor society. However productive an activity may be in a purely physical sense—that is, result in physical products—it is not productive in the context of a division-of-labor economy unless it is carried on for the purpose of earning money. If it is not carried on for the purpose of earning money, it does not provide the means of obtaining the goods and services of others, and it thus renders one's activity incapable of providing for the support of one's life in the context of a division-of-labor society. Without the earning of money, one must attempt to produce and live at a level somewhere between that of Robinson Crusoe and the inhabitants of Tobacco Road.

Thus, in the context of a division-of-labor society, productive activity can appropriately be defined, just as it often is in practical life, as *activity the purpose of which is the earning of money.*

I refer to purpose rather than to the actual fact of whether or not money is earned, because purpose is more fundamental. An activity is productive or economic so long as moneymaking is its purpose, even if, in a given instance, it fails to make money, or actually loses money. The principle is the same as applies to a carpenter, say, who is nonetheless a carpenter, even though, on occasion, the actual result of his action may not be the result he intended and may even be destructive of some of his material; or to a musician, who, on occasion, strikes a sour note. By the same token, the accidental receipt of money resulting from the performance of an activity would not be sufficient to render it productive—any more than, say, the accidental typing of a word by a monkey playing with a typewriter would qualify as writing. The *purpose* of moneymaking is the essential element.

To avoid a possible misunderstanding, it must be pointed out that common criminal activities, such as robbing banks, do not qualify as productive activity, even though the ostensible purpose of such activities may be the bringing in of money. The *earning* of money, as opposed to its mere receipt, implies the existence of voluntary trade, which precludes the obtaining of money by force or fraud.

In addition, activities which can be proven to be inherently destructive of innocent human life, such as, presumably, the manufacture and sale of narcotics, are not to be classified as productive, even if the money is obtained from the customer without the use of force or fraud. This is because the concept of productive activity ultimately rests on the promotion of human life and well-being and must always be consistent with that ultimate purpose.[3]

It must also be noted that the standard of human life and well-being implies that the paid manufacture of weapons of defense can come under the heading of productive activity. For example, American defense contractors, who produce weapons to defend a division-of-labor, capitalist society against foreign aggression, perform an invaluable service on behalf of the protection of innocent human life. The fact that they are paid for their goods and services qualifies their activity as fully productive in the sense appropriate to life in a division-of-labor society.

The main concern of this discussion, of course, is not the moral aspects of productive activity, but the economic aspects. And returning now to the economic aspects, it should be clear that manual labor is, indeed, too broad a standard for gauging productive activity. Manual labor is not productive if it is not performed for the purpose of earning money. In such a case, it does not enable the worker to obtain the goods and services he requires from others. Thus, his labor is not productive in the sense required by life in a division-of-labor society.

The recognition of this fact implies that the labor of housewives, for example, is not productive, while the physically identical labor of paid housekeepers is productive. Even though the physical labor of the two is the same, there is an essential difference between the two cases, in that because the labor of the housekeeper is paid, it is a source of her being able to obtain the goods and services of others, while because the labor of the housewife is unpaid, it is not a source of her being able to obtain the goods and services of others.

Consumptive Production

In a division-of-labor society an activity that is physically productive but is not carried on for the purpose of earning money is not only not to be classified as productive, but actually represents *consumption.*

In a division-of-labor society, the physically productive activity of every individual begins with the use of means of production—materials, tools, equipment, and so forth—produced by others, and for which money has had to be expended. These means of production are physically used up or worn out in the course of production. Sooner or later, they must be replaced, which will require fresh outlays of money. If their use does not bring in money, they cannot be replaced, except by means of an outside source of funds. They certainly cannot be replaced by virtue of the nonmoneymaking activity in question. Thus, the activity in question is a *consumptive production,* in that it uses up the means of production with which it begins and does not make possible their replacement.

The activities of housewives and home hobbyists provide countless instances of consumptive production. For example, it is certainly an act of physical production when a housewife makes her own clothes, or when a hobbyist makes his own furniture. It is an act of physical production when a housewife bakes a cake or prepares a meal, and even when one simply makes a sandwich or butters a piece of bread. But all of this production is a consumptive production in that the production requires the using up of materials and the wearing out of tools, equipment, or implements, all of which must sooner or later be replaced, while the product disappears without bringing in the money necessary for their replacement.

3. Productive Expenditure and Consumption Expenditure

The above discussion of consumptive production implies that it is necessary to distinguish between two fundamentally different types of expenditure: *productive expenditure* and *unproductive expenditure*—which latter represents *consumption expenditure.*

Productive expenditure is *buying for the purpose of subsequently selling* (and, implicitly, at a profit, for there can be no other reason to buy for this purpose).

Unproductive expenditure is buying *not* for the purpose of subsequently selling. It is buying for any other purpose than subsequently selling.

Productive expenditure is synonymous with *reproductive expenditure,* for it is money which is both laid out and brought back by virtue of productive expenditure.

Though all expenditure represents a using up of funds at hand, the term "consumption expenditure" can be employed as a synonym for unproductive expenditure, and the term "consumer" can be reserved exclusively for those who make unproductive expenditures—insofar as they make them. This is because, in the context of the whole process of which it is a part, productive expenditure does not constitute a using up of money, while unproductive expenditure does constitute a using up of money. Funds that are productively expended subsequently return, usually with the addition of a profit. Funds that are unproductively expended, as a rule, either do not return at all or return only in a smaller amount, and thus are simply consumed. Funds that are productively expended are advanced against the receipt of a larger sum of money, while funds that are unproductively expended simply disappear from their owner's possession. In the one case, there is replacement and increase. In the other, simply decrease.

For example, both a restaurant and a housewife buy roast beefs. The restaurant cooks the roast beef, serves it, and is paid for it by its customers, who physically consume it. In this way, its expenditure is returned to it and, most likely, with the addition of a profit. In the context of the entirety of the process, the restaurant has not consumed its funds, but has obtained additional funds, which are available for other purposes, such as expanding its business or enabling its owner to make consumption expenditures. The restaurant's expenditure is both self-sustaining, in that it subsequently makes possible the purchase of a second, replacement roast beef, and more

than self-sustaining, in that it subsequently makes possible the purchase of additional goods besides.

The housewife, on the other hand, cooks the roast beef, serves it, and, of course, is not paid for it. The roast beef simply disappears in the physical consumption of her family, and with it, all trace of the housewife's expenditure. Her money is simply used up and gone forever. Her purchase of a roast beef does not provide any funds for the subsequent purchase of a second roast beef, but simply annihilates, as it were, the funds expended. Her purchase, once made, is not thereafter self-sustaining, but on each new occasion must be sustained by the infusion of fresh funds from outside sources. If a second roast beef is to be purchased to replace the first, and then a third to replace the second, and so on, the funds must be obtained from an outside source, such as, typically, a job held by the housewife's husband.[4]

Similarly, both a housewife and a laundromat buy washing machines. In the course of their use, both machines undergo wear and tear and natural deterioration. Eventually, they will have to be scrapped, at which time they will command prices much below their initial purchase price. Every time the laundromat's machine is used, however, it is paid for this use. And out of the payments thus received, it obtains the money to pay for repairs of the machine and, when the day arrives, for a new machine. Plus, it normally earns a profit on the machine, and the laundromat's owner, therefore, like the restaurant's owner, can purchase more than just a replacement.

The housewife does not receive any payment for the use of her machine. Both repair bills and the difference between the price of a new machine and the eventual scrap value of her present machine have to be met from outside sources of revenue. Her washing machine is used up more slowly but just as certainly as her roast beef, and with it, again, disappears, if not the whole, at least the major part of her expenditure for it.

From a physical standpoint, to be sure, the washing machine is productively consumed, in making clothes clean. It differs in this respect from the roast beef dinner, which is unproductively physically consumed (though not from the raw roast beef, which is productively consumed in being cooked.)[5] But it makes no difference. This is because the products of the washing machine, the cleaned clothes, are unproductively physically consumed without bringing in any money—as they would for a laundry or laundromat. At most, recognition of the fact that the housewife's washing machine has a physical product might cause us to say that the housewife's expenditure for the machine, instead of disappearing bit by bit with each operation of the machine, disappears bit by bit each time the clothes it cleans get dirty again.

It happens, of course, that productive expenditures are sometimes accompanied by losses, while consumption expenditures occasionally result in gains. But, as previously noted, these are accidental phenomena, not following from the nature of the activity, and do not necessitate any change in the classification of any given expenditure.

The great, practical difference between productive expenditure and consumption expenditure is that an individual grows richer through productive expenditure and poorer through consumption expenditure. Two people, both beginning with identically the same sum of money (we might imagine two brothers sharing equally in an inheritance), the one productively expending his funds, the other unproductively expending his funds, will almost necessarily arrive at opposite stations in life. The one will be richer; the other will be impoverished.

4. Capital Goods and Consumers' Goods

Closely paralleling the concepts of productive expenditure and consumption expenditure are the concepts of producers' goods and consumers' goods.

Producers' goods or, what is a synonymous expression, capital goods, are goods purchased *for the purpose of making subsequent sales.*

Consumers' goods are goods purchased *not* for the purpose of making subsequent sales.

The distinction between capital goods and consumers' goods is exclusively one of the purpose for which the goods are purchased—*for* business purposes or *not* for business purposes—and not at all a matter of their physical characteristics. The roast beef purchased by a restaurant and the washing machine purchased by a laundromat are both capital goods. Exactly the same kind of roast beef and washing machine purchased by a housewife are consumers' goods.

The reason that the purpose for which they are purchased is the crucial distinction has already been indicated. Physically, the roast beef and the washing machine are consumed, whether purchased for business purposes or purchased not for business purposes. In both cases, there is, in this instance, a physical production that takes place in which the goods are consumed: the raw roast beef is consumed in producing a cooked one, and the washing machine is consumed in producing cleaned clothes. And thus, both for the housewife and for the business enterprises, there is even a productive consumption in the physical sense.

But beyond the physically productive consumption comes a physically unproductive consumption: the cooked roast beef is eaten and the cleaned clothes get dirty in the wearing. At this point, all trace of the goods purchased by the housewife has simply disappeared from

her possession. (In the case of durable goods, such as the washing machine, all trace of the relevant *portion* of the good's life has disappeared.) But by this same point, or earlier, the restaurant and laundromat have obtained the means of replacing, and more than replacing, the goods they have purchased. The goods they have purchased, when one allows for their replacement by way of purchase, with funds earned from their very own employment, are *not* consumed—they are replaced by virtue of their own use, together with a surplus.

The roast beef of the restaurant and the washing machine of the laundromat, by virtue of being purchased for the purpose of making subsequent sales, and then by way of using the resulting sales proceeds to make replacement purchases, are *reproductively employed.* The restaurant's roast beef and the laundromat's washing machine are, as it were, employed in the production of roast beefs and washing machines, or their equivalent in other goods, as wheat seed is employed in the production of wheat. And thus in the fullest sense they represent wealth employed in the production of wealth, and are capital goods, even though from a strictly physical standpoint, a roast beef cannot be used to produce roast beefs, and a washing machine cannot be used to produce washing machines.

Actually, it is not necessary that the restaurant or laundromat use its proceeds to buy specifically a second roast beef or a second washing machine, or even a good playing the same role in production as a roast beef or a washing machine. What counts is that, because he earns revenue by the use of the roast beef or washing machine, the restaurant's or laundromat's owner is enabled to obtain the *equivalent,* and more than the equivalent, of his roast beef or washing machine by the time it is physically consumed, while a housewife is not in this position. Whether that equivalent takes the form of a new roast beef or washing machine, of goods employed in a different line of business, or even of consumers' goods, the essential fact remains that he is engaged in a process whose inherent tendency is to preserve and increase his initial wealth rather than decrease it.

Classification of Capital Goods and Consumers' Goods Not Based on Physical Characteristics

The principle that goods are capital goods or consumers' goods depending only on the purpose for which they are purchased, and not on their physical characteristics, needs to be illustrated with additional examples. Thus, a box of breakfast cereal purchased by a grocer or a restaurant is a capital good; one purchased by a housewife is a consumers' good. Knives and forks and tables and chairs purchased by a restaurant are capital goods; those purchased for (nonbusiness) use in the home are consumers' goods. A house purchased in order to be rented out is a capital good; one purchased in order to be occupied by its owner is a consumers' good. A lathe purchased by a business enterprise is a capital good; one purchased not for moneymaking purposes, for instance, by a hobbyist, is a consumers' good. A bulldozer purchased by a construction company is a capital good; a bulldozer purchased by a government, say, for use in constructing military airfields or dams for flood-control projects, is a consumers' good—as, indeed, would be a bulldozer factory that was not operated for profit-making purposes. Freeways, public school buildings and their fixtures, nonprofit hospitals and their equipment, courthouses, military bases, fire houses and fire trucks, government river and harbor improvements—all these are consumers' goods, because they are not operated for the purpose of earning money, and thus do not make possible their own replacement when they have been physically consumed.

The acquisition of every good, except the crudest, most primitive kind, presupposes an outlay of money. Money must be spent not only if one wishes to acquire a good ready-made, but even if one wishes to produce the good oneself. All physical production worthy of the name can begin only after an outlay of money has been made to provide the means with which to produce. Without money to buy food, an oven, knives, forks, dishes, tables and chairs, and a structure within which to cook and serve, neither a housewife nor a restaurant could do more perhaps than serve wild berries on a stone, in a cave. Without money to buy steel, concrete, and the use of construction equipment, and to hire labor, neither a construction company nor a government could do more perhaps than build a dam that would compare unfavorably with those built by beavers.

While an expenditure of money is at the base of all physical production in a division-of-labor society, only the activity of *business enterprises* is so designed as to recoup this expenditure. It cannot be too strongly stressed that because of this only business activity is self-sustaining. The activity of all others, however massive and durable the goods they may employ, however complex and elaborate their physical production may be, is not designed to recoup this expenditure. The goods of these others, therefore, are all on the path toward disappearing from their possession without leaving a trace. They either reach a point of unproductive physical consumption within their possession—as, for example, the housewife's roast beef dinner and her clean wash; or they simply pass from their possession—as, for example, government gifts of surplus wheat. In either case, having made an unproductive expenditure, the party who made it has less and less to show for it until absolutely nothing

at all would remain, were it not for the infusion of fresh funds received from outside sources.

Government a Consumer

A government dam or road or factory, therefore, is consumed just as fully and in the same sense as a housewife's roast beef or washing machine; and for this reason, like these, they are consumers' goods, not capital goods. And in the same sense as the housewife, the government is not a producer, but a consumer, who is dependent on producers. All of its physical production, like hers, is, in the last analysis, a consumptive production. It is a production which cannot replace the means with which it began and which ultimately leaves no trace in the government's possession; it is a production which leaves the government poorer by the amount of funds it has expended. In order to continue the activity, resort must be had to an external source of funds—in the government's case, the taxpayers or the printing press.

Producers' Labor and Consumers' Labor

The distinction between capital goods and consumers' goods applies equally to labor. Labor employed for the purpose of (its employer) making subsequent sales is producers' labor. Labor employed *not* for the purpose of (its employer) making subsequent sales is consumers' labor.[6]

It must be stressed that the distinction between producers' labor and consumers' labor is always from the perspective of the employer, not the employee. From the perspective of the employee, all labor is productive which is performed for the purpose of earning money. Those whose work is consumers' labor earn money no less than those whose work is producers' labor, and they are productive in the sense appropriate to life in a division-of-labor society. The same is true, of course, of those who produce consumers' goods. They too earn money and are productive in producing consumers' goods. The distinction both between capital goods and consumers' goods, on the one side, and between producers' labor and consumers' labor, on the other, is from the perspective of the buyer—in the one case the customer for the good, in the other, the employer of the labor.

Thus, for example, a maid employed by a hotel is producers' labor. The same maid employed by a housewife is consumers' labor. In the one case, the payment of the maid's wages is a source of subsequent revenue to her employer, which enables the employer to continue the payment of her wages and to purchase other things besides. In the other case, the payment of the maid's wages is simply a use of the revenue of her employer, with the means for each fresh payment of wages having to be supplied by an outside source of funds. The owners of a hotel grow richer by the employment of a maid—for her work helps to bring in paying guests—while a housewife grows poorer by the employment of a maid; that is the practical difference.

Further to illustrate the concepts: a secretary employed by a business enterprise is producers' labor; one employed by a government bureau or private nonprofit organization is consumers' labor, as is one employed by a wealthy individual to handle social engagements.[7] A welder employed by a private shipyard is producers' labor; one employed by a naval shipyard is consumers' labor. A musician employed by a night club owner or concert promoter is producers' labor; one employed by a bride's father to play at her wedding is consumers' labor. All government employees, from judges to public school teachers, whether their services are necessary and beneficial or not, are consumers' labor. The payment of their wages uses up the government's revenue rather than providing the government with the means of earning revenue. The fact that the government must turn to taxes to maintain its operations is the result precisely of the fact that its expenditures do not generate the revenue to sustain them.

Producers' Loans and Consumers' Loans

The same fundamental distinction that applies to expenditures, goods, and labor applies also to loans. Loans taken out for the purpose of the borrower making subsequent sales are producers' loans. Loans taken out *not* for the purpose of the borrower making subsequent sales are consumers' loans.

Again, the great practical distinction is that producers' loans, by virtue of bringing in sales revenues, provide the funds required for their own repayment, and usually more besides. Consumers' loans, on the other hand, must be repaid by means of an outside source of revenue, because the expenditure of the funds which are borrowed does not serve to bring in funds.

Government Borrowing

It should be obvious that government borrowing is in the category of consumer borrowing. But there is a vital difference between the borrowing of private consumers and the borrowing of the government. Namely, when private consumers borrow, it is they as individuals who are responsible for repaying. When the government borrows, the responsibility for repayment is that of the taxpaying public, including, insofar as they too are taxpayers, the *lenders!* Indeed, if as is very often the case, the government chooses to repay by means of inflating the money supply, the lenders can easily end up paying for the greater part of the government's borrowing.

There are sound reasons for private individuals to

borrow as consumers—namely, to be able to have the enjoyment of goods sooner rather than later. By being able to borrow the price, or the better part of the price, of a house or automobile, an individual can obtain the enjoyment of the good years sooner than he could if he first had to save up the full price himself. But in the case of government borrowing, any such possible advantage is more than outweighed by the injustice of imposing an unchosen obligation on individual citizens to repay who may attach little or no value to the purpose for which the funds are spent. Indeed, government borrowing obligates individuals to repay who may be too young to have a voice, or not even have been born, at the time the decision to borrow is made. It is thus incompatible not only with the free choice of individuals but also with the theory of representative government, because it obligates people who cannot be represented when the decision to borrow is made—at least not by representatives of their own choosing.

Capital Goods and Consumers' Goods Internally Produced; Other Revenues

In defining capital goods and consumers' goods, it was necessary deliberately to define them in a way that, strictly speaking, is too narrow. This was required in order to exhibit their distinguishing characteristic in the strongest possible light, free of all considerations that might divert attention from the essential point.

Taken strictly, those definitions imply that every capital good and every consumers' good must itself be purchased. That, of course, is not necessary, and no such idea was intended to be conveyed. In fact, a number of the illustrations offered contradict such a view.

Many capital goods and consumers' goods are not themselves purchased, but are produced, with means of production that have been purchased. For example, in the illustration concerning the restaurant and housewife, the *cooked* roast beef as well as the raw roast beef was a capital good in the one case and a consumers' good in the other, even though only raw roast beef was purchased. By the same principle, not only the boxes of breakfast cereal purchased by a grocer or a restaurant are capital goods, but also those in the inventory of the manufacturer of breakfast cereals, who purchases only the means of producing them, not boxes of breakfast cereal themselves. Again, on the same principle, a privately owned steel mill is a capital good even though it itself may not be purchased, but only the means of constructing it. By the same token, public schools and government roads and dams are consumers' goods, even though such things are almost never purchased ready-built.

To be more exact, the definitions of capital goods and consumers' goods must be broadened as follows:

Capital goods are goods purchased for the purpose of making subsequent sales, and, by extension, goods produced, with means of production that have been purchased, for the purpose of making subsequent sales.

Consumers' goods are goods purchased *not* for the purpose of making subsequent sales, and, by extension, goods produced, with means of production that have been purchased, *not* for the purpose of making subsequent sales.

Thus both concepts embrace internally produced semi-finished and finished inventories and internally constructed facilities.

The definitions presented not only of capital goods and consumers' goods, but also of productive expenditure and consumption expenditure, producers' labor and consumers' labor, and producers' loans and consumers' loans, might be taken to imply the presence or absence of the purpose of earning *sales revenues exclusively* as the decisive point of differentiation. Such a restriction is not intended. Although sales revenues are the revenues earned in the overwhelming majority of cases, there are numerous and important instances in which businesses earn rental revenues—for example, landlords and car rental companies—or interest revenues, as is the case with banks and other financial institutions. Indeed, probably every business earns some interest revenue. There are also cases in which businesses earn royalty or commission revenues—for example, research laboratories and professional agents, respectively.

No less than in the case of sales revenues, it is the presence or absence of the purpose of earning revenues of these types that serves as the differentiating point. The words "subsequently selling" and "making subsequent sales" must be understood as embracing these kinds of revenues as well as sales revenues. The expenditures of a landlord for the purpose of earning rental revenues, of a bank for earning interest revenues, and so on, are productive expenditures. The goods they purchase for that purpose, the labor they employ, the loans they take out are capital goods, producers' labor, and producers' loans respectively.

Capital and Wealth

I have already defined capital as wealth reproductively employed.[8] In a division-of-labor society, capital is *the wealth employed by business enterprises.*

There is, of course, wealth employed outside of business enterprises. Such wealth includes the houses and furnishings of individuals, their personal stocks of food and clothing, their automobiles and appliances, and so forth. It also includes a country's highways and dams and river and harbor improvements, insofar as they are owned

by the government, and all other assets owned by the government. Such wealth may be termed "consumers' wealth," in contrast to capital, which is the wealth employed by business enterprises. So long as it is wealth, consumers' wealth has not yet been consumed, but it is in the process of being consumed. In the nature of the case, it is poised for being used up and its owner's purpose does not prepare it for making possible its own replacement. It is thus on the road to being consumed and is properly described as consumers' goods.

Jewelry, precious metals, and the land sites of owner-occupied houses usually represent a substratum of consumers' wealth which is not consumed beyond a certain point. To be sure, there is typically a maintenance cost which must be incurred in connection with all three—cleaning and repairing the jewelry, storing and insuring it and the precious metals, keeping up the appearance of the land site. But the materials from which the jewelry is made—gems and precious metals—are physically imperishable and always retain at least some substantial portion of their original value. Land sites too are physically imperishable (unless they become submerged under water), and so long as the area remains inhabited, they too almost always retain at least some substantial portion of their original value.

Capital Value and Investment

The goods owned both by business enterprises and by consumers reflect prior expenditures of money, either for the goods themselves or for the means of producing them. The prior expenditure reflected in the possession, say, of a quantity of roast beef that is owned either by a restaurant or a housewife is simply the price per pound that has been paid for it times the number of pounds in question. The prior expenditure reflected in the possession of a durable good, such as a washing machine owned either by a laundromat or a housewife, is the price that has been paid for it less a cumulative allowance for wear and tear and obsolescence known as depreciation. The prior expenditure reflected in the possession of a good one has produced or has had produced is the sum of the prices times the respective quantities of the means of production physically consumed to produce it, less, if it is a durable good, a cumulative allowance for depreciation.

For example, the prior expenditure reflected in an inventory of dresses in the possession of a dress manufacturer (or, as far as the items are applicable, in the possession of a housewife who makes her own clothes) would be the sum of the following, for each dress: the price paid per yard of cloth times the number of yards used up in making the dress, the wage rates paid to cutters and sewing machine operators and so forth times the respective number of hours of their labor spent in making the dress, the prices—under some accounting systems—paid for the various tools and machines employed times the respective fractions of their useful lives expended in making the dress, plus all other sums similarly expended to make the dress. (Depending on the particular accounting system used, the prior expenditure reflected in the inventory of dresses might not incorporate an allowance for the fraction of the useful lives of the tools and machines expended. Such expenditures might show up simply in a cumulative periodic depreciation charge against the assets concerned and in a corresponding charge against sales revenues. This is even more likely to be the case in connection with depreciation accounting for a factory or any other kind of building used in a business.)

The prior expenditure reflected in the possession of goods—whether productive expenditure in the possession of capital goods, or consumption expenditure in the possession of consumers' goods—is known in accounting as their *book value.* This concept is of no practical importance for the ordinary consumer, but it is of great importance for business enterprises. It is the necessary base for calculating profits and losses. For example, to have a profit, the dress manufacturer must sell his dresses for more than their book value and the depreciation charged against the book value of the factory and plant and equipment used to produce the dresses (insofar as this depreciation does not enter into the book value of the dresses themselves.) The concept of book value is the basis of constructing both balance sheets and income statements.

Book value can be said to reflect a putting of money into goods. The putting of money into goods for the purpose of making subsequent sales is *investment.* The book value of any aggregate of goods in which money has been invested, i.e., of capital goods, is the book value of capital, that is, of wealth reproductively employed.[9] Under a system of commodity money, such as a gold standard in which physical gold serves as actual money in the form of coins passing from hand to hand or coins or bullion providing full backing for the paper currency or checking deposits in use, the concept of capital would also include the money held by business enterprises. This is because in such a case the money would be both actual wealth, inasmuch as it was a physical commodity, and it would be reproductively employed. As wealth reproductively employed, it would be capital.

Now just as the concept of property possessing market value was shown to be wider than the concept of wealth, so the concept of capital value refers to more than the value of wealth reproductively employed, that is, to more than the value of capital goods or capital.[10] By the same token, the concept of investment refers to more than

investment in capital goods. The concepts of investment and capital value also respectively refer to investment in, and the accompanying purchase or acquisition value of, such intangible assets as stocks and bonds, mortgages and other types of loans, and patents and copyrights. One can invest in such intangible assets, and their purchase or acquisition value constitutes capital value.

Nevertheless, intangible assets no more constitute capital than they constitute wealth. Investment in *capital* occurs only when business enterprises buy either tangible goods or labor of the kind that is vested in tangible goods. (Of course, such investment is carried forward when capital goods are productively physically consumed, to the products produced—for example, the dress manufacturer's investment in cloth is carried forward to the dresses made out of the cloth.) The value of capital is the value of the tangible goods purchased by or produced within business enterprises, plus, insofar as it itself constitutes actual wealth, the money they hold. It is, to this extent, their cash and the value of their raw, semifinished, and finished inventories, of their furniture and fixtures, plant, equipment, and all other tangible property, including, of course, their land. The objective expression of the value of these capital assets is their accounting book value, which derives from their purchase prices.

In the following pages of this book, whenever investment is spoken of, it should be understood that in the absence of qualification, what is meant is always investment in *capital.*

The most important respect in which capital value in the economic system differs from the value of actual capital goods is the result of the use of savings to finance such things as home mortgages and consumer installment loans. Because owner-occupied housing and personal automobiles and the like are not capital goods, the mortgage loans and installment loans that finance them, while representing investment and the existence of capital value from the perspective of the lenders, do not represent investment in capital goods. Such investments, to be sure, represent a significant part of the total savings and capital value of the economic system.

Matters are complicated somewhat by the use of the expression "investment *of capital*" to signify the purchase of such assets. Insofar as the money invested were itself a physical commodity and thus represented wealth reproductively employed in being invested, the expression would be a perfectly legitimate one, though it would still be necessary to realize that what the capital had been invested in, in such cases would not itself represent capital, but only intangible assets possessing capital value. Of course, today money is not a physical commodity; it is not even in part a claim to a physical commodity.

Nevertheless, common usage regards the investment of fiat money as the investment of capital. For the sake of avoiding departures from common usage that would serve little practical purpose, I will follow it, even though what is being invested in the case of fiat money is not actual wealth, but at most an intangible asset that can easily be exchanged for wealth.

Consistent with this discussion, I follow the common practice of regarding anyone who invests money in intangible assets as a capitalist, even though such assets do not themselves represent actual capital but merely possess capital value. Insofar as such capital value represents the financing of the purchase of consumers' wealth, such as homes and personal automobiles, I will take it into account whenever necessary in close connection with my treatment of the degree of capital intensiveness of the economic system. For the accumulated savings of the economic system are invested not only in capital but also in intangible assets, above all, home-mortgage loans, which represent claims against consumers' wealth.[11]

It would be possible to adopt a somewhat different approach to the meaning of investment than that taken above. It could be argued that all putting of money into goods is investment, whether the purpose is or is not to make subsequent sales. In this case, it would be necessary to distinguish between productive and unproductive investment. One would then show the derivation of capital from productive investment, and consumers' wealth from unproductive investment.

The objection I have to this approach is that it would shatter the customary distinction between consumption and investment. Perhaps half or even more of consumption expenditure would then turn out to be investment expenditure, at the same time that it was consumption expenditure. This is because under such a procedure, the purchase of houses, automobiles, and all other consumer durable goods would have to be classified as investment expenditures. So too would the purchase of materials of production by consumers, such as all food needing further preparation.

Thus, it seems expedient to restrict the concept of investment in the way I have done, and not to introduce the concept of unproductive investment.

Productive Expenditure and Capital Value

While capital value reflects prior productive expenditure, not all productive expenditure results in capital value, because not all productive expenditure is invested. Productive expenditure for such things as advertising, lighting and heating, and the labor of administrative and clerical employees does not directly bring any tangible physical goods into the possession of a firm. Such things are neither tangible goods themselves, nor in any direct way are they vested in tangible goods, in the manner of the cloth and the services of a sewing machine operator that go into a dress. As a result, it is a common practice in accounting to treat such productive expenditures as *expense items.* That is, such productive expenditures are written off—expensed—as they are made, and thus do not show up in capital value.

Some accounting systems, however, seek to capitalize as many productive expenditures as possible, and do add the outlays for advertising, lighting and heating, administrative labor, and so forth to a firm's capital value, if possible in the form of its investment in inventory. The outlays are then subtracted later on, typically when the goods to which they are judged to contribute are sold. At that time, the outlays form a part of "cost of goods sold"—along with the outlays for materials and direct, manufacturing labor and, in some cases, along with depreciation.

Common Confusions About Capital Goods

There are three currently popular definitions of capital goods. All of them are physicalistic, i.e., assume that the distinguishing characteristic of capital goods lies either in their physical nature or in their relationship to physical production. According to what is perhaps the definition most favored among professional economists, capital goods are tools, implements, machinery, and durable goods. According to what seems to be the most popular definition among laymen, capital goods are the same as the above, but with the durable goods more or less limited to factory and office buildings. According to the third definition, capital goods are all previously produced factors of production, which would include the materials employed in production along with the components of the layman's definition.

Like the misconceptions concerning productive activity in general, these definitions are both too broad and too narrow. They are too broad in that they all embrace consumers' goods to varying degrees, and too narrow in that they fail to embrace many capital goods.

Those who hold these definitions seem strangely unaware in propounding them that production in its physical sense is almost an omnipresent phenomenon, and is undertaken by consumers with the aid of means of production that in principle, and sometimes in actual concretes, are no different than those employed in any factory. Strictly speaking, it is an act of physical production when one cuts the food on one's plate and raises it to one's mouth on the prongs of a fork. As already discussed, the activities of a housewife constitute acts of physical production. Certainly, cooking, cleaning, washing, baking, and, a few generations ago, the making even of clothes and soap in the home, are all instances of physical production.

And this production, no less than the production that takes place in giant factories, entails the use of materials, tools, implements, machinery, buildings, and other installations. The food in one's refrigerator is a material—indeed, so is a slice of bread in one's hand which one intends to butter. Household hammers and screwdrivers are tools; can openers, knives, and forks are implements; sewing machines, washing machines, automobiles, vacuum cleaners, toasters, television sets, tape recorders, and record players are machines; the home, in which so much physically productive activity takes place, is a building employed in production; a wash line is an installation. Indeed, there are very few consumers' goods which do not fit under these or other categories connected with physical production. And the few that do not fit, such as stocks of clothing and certain types of furniture and fixtures owned by consumers, are almost all embraced by the category of durable goods.

All three of these definitions, as soon as they are accompanied by any attempt to apply them to reality, lead to a progressive reduction in the goods classified as consumers' goods and a progressive increase in the goods classified as capital goods. Indeed, this change in classification is well under way.

It has long since, if not always, been taken for granted that government river and harbor improvements and the pieces of construction equipment owned by a government are capital goods, simply because their connection with physical production is so obvious. What has prevented the less spectacular means of production that are found in the home from being classified as capital goods seems to be only the fact that the classical economists succeeded in fairly well establishing the idea that housewives do not produce.

Of course, in recent generations, this last idea has come to be held in an erroneous way. Instead of having the conscious realization that housewives do not produce only in the sense that they do not earn money, and why this fact is decisive, one proceeds as though housewives did not produce even in the physical sense. This then acts as a sort of blinders, which prevent one from perceiving the kind of physical means of production housewives employ. Furthermore, in the present day, the idea that housewives do not produce is widely disputed. For example, it is often presented as a shortcoming of the statistics of gross national product, or gross domestic product, that they do not include an allowance for the work performed by housewives in the home.

The stage is well set, therefore, for a "revolution" in economics on this subject. That is, at practically any moment someone could come along, write a book or article forcefully making people aware that housewives do physically produce and employ machinery and the like, and then, without a knowledge on anyone's part that the earning of money is the crucial criterion, succeed in almost totally destroying the concept of consumers' goods by discovering that they are all "capital goods."

For the time being at least, the physically productive activities of the housewife and the physical nature of the goods she employs have not sufficiently impressed themselves on the minds of observers. As a result, the main breaches in the concepts of consumers' goods and capital goods have been in the somewhat related areas of durable goods and government activity.

Nonprofit universities refer to their building funds as "capital funds." Government officials wish to remove expenditures for roads, schools, dams, and the like from the ordinary budget and place them in a separate "capital budget." (This has long been the practice in New York City, for example.) Government statistics of gross product and national income treat the purchase of houses to be occupied by their owners as "investment." Few economists see any theoretical reason why the treatment now accorded to owner-occupied houses in these statistics should not be extended to personal automobiles, household furniture, and all major household appliances. The more consistent wish to add stocks of personal clothing to the list. Only the weakening forces of custom and tradition, established by the classical economists, stand in the way of a major collapse in classification here.

The belief that the government employs capital goods has been greatly reinforced both by the inclusion of durable goods in the concept of capital goods and by what must be called an eagerness to perceive in its case the fact that it is physically productive. And the idea that the government employs capital goods then lends strong support to the notion that it is a producer. If, for example, a government schoolhouse is a capital good, then it follows naturally that government school teachers must be productive in the same sense as was previously thought to be reserved to the participants in private business.

Indeed, we have been told that to deny the proposition that government officials are productive, to hold instead that their salaries and their activities simply represent consumption, is to labor under the influence of a collection of old wives' tales known as "the conventional wisdom." [12] Not surprisingly we have also been told from the same quarter, that there is no essential difference between government deficits and corporate "deficits"—i.e., between consumers' loans and producers' loans.

The current concepts of capital goods, however, are not merely overblown, to the point where they destroy any firm concept of consumers' goods. As stated, they also do not even embrace all capital goods. The first two definitions I cited ignore materials, which certainly must be included when purchased by business enterprises. The second and third appear to ignore such goods as furniture and fixtures, because they are not integrally connected with physical production, but which must be termed capital goods when purchased by business enterprises. All three leave no room for finished inventories, which are also capital goods when owned by business enterprises, despite the fact that they do not serve in any further physical production undertaken by the firms that own them, or, perhaps, in any further physical production whatever.

Answers to Misconceptions of the Concepts Presented

A number of questions frequently arise concerning the application of the concepts presented to specific cases—questions which reflect serious misconceptions of the concepts. The nature of the misconceptions, the questions, and the answers to them, are as follows:

i. Productive Consequences of Consumption Do Not Make Consumption Into Production

It is a fact that if a person did not eat some minimum amount of food, wear at least some kind of clothing, and have some type of shelter in which to sleep, he could not physically work and thus could not earn money. On this basis, the question is asked: Shouldn't the expenditure for such goods, to the extent that they contribute to one's ability to work and earn money, be termed a productive expenditure, and such goods themselves, capital goods?

The answer is no. In order for any action to be productive, either monetarily or physically, it is not sufficient that the action have productive consequences. The action must be undertaken for the *purpose* of production. For example, in driving one's car, one wears it out. Eventually, as a result of one's action, it will be scrap iron, and then it will most likely contribute to the production of steel. Nevertheless, this fact does not make one a steel producer. It does not make one's expenditure for the car a productive expenditure and the car a capital good. The scrap iron, even though the result of the process of driving one's car, is not the *product* of driving one's car. It is a fresh, original, *unproduced* factor of production, just like iron ore in the ground. In the same way, the fact that eating, wearing clothing, and possessing a shelter result in one's being alive, and thus capable of working and earning an income, is not sufficient to render these things acts of production. Like the scrap iron, a person's ability to work, based on the fact that he is alive, is a fresh, original, unproduced factor of production, not a product.

The decisive point in establishing whether an expenditure is a productive expenditure, or whether a good is a capital good, is the *purpose* for which the expenditure is made or the good bought, not the consequences it has. Food, clothing, shelter, and the like are consumers' goods, and the expenditure for them a consumption expenditure, even insofar as their consequence is an ability to work and earn money—because working and earning money are not their purpose. On the contrary, the ability to buy such goods is the purpose of working and earning money.

The essential point can be reinforced by the following considerations. If it were the case that expenditures for the goods and services necessary to enable one to stay alive and thus be able to work were regarded as productive expenditures, the effect would be that one would have to deduct these expenditures as costs from the income one earned as normally understood. One would then regard one's net income—the measure of one's gain from working—as the difference between one's income as normally understood and the cost of one's subsistence. Thus, for example, if a wage earner makes, say, $300 per week, and his cost of "subsistence" is calculated as $200 per week, he would calculate his net income—the measure of his gain from working—as $100 per week. This shows the fallacy of the whole procedure. The fact that of the worker's $300 wage, $200 is necessary to cover the cost of his subsistence, does not at all reduce his gain from working from $300 to $100. His gain from working is *$300. The greatest, most important part of a person's gain from working is that it enables him to stay alive.* A worker who works even to receive merely a subsistence wage has an enormous gain from his work: he gains the preservation of his life, a value greater than which there is none. The fact that the portion of one's wage that covers subsistence is itself a gain—the most important gain one earns—means that it is inappropriate to deduct subsistence as a cost. And on this basis it is inappropriate to regard the expenditures for the means of subsistence as productive expenditures, even though they are essential to one's ability to work. Their purpose is not the earning of income, but the support of one's life.

ii. Consumption Expenditures Imposed by Work Are Still Consumption Expenditures

A second, closely related question is this: Isn't a maid employed by a working mother to look after a young child an instance of producers' labor, in that the mother could not go to work and thus could not earn money if she did not employ the maid?

Again, the answer is no. The mother does not employ the maid for the purpose of earning money, but for the purpose of meeting a need of her personal life—namely, caring for her child. To be sure, she is unable to meet this need herself as a result of the fact that she leaves the house to go to work, but that is irrelevant. Earning an income does not take place in a vacuum. It is integrated into the rest of one's life, and compels a person to meet certain of his needs or desires by making expenditures he would not have to make if he did not have to earn an income. For example, many people who work, automatically have a higher food bill because they have to eat their lunches out. They probably have a transportation expense of getting to and from work. Possibly their work requires that they live in an area which has a cold climate, and in which, therefore, they must buy extra winter clothing and pay high fuel bills.

Though all of these expenditures are *imposed* by the earning of an income, they are still consumption expenditures, because their purpose is the direct satisfaction of one's needs or desires, not the earning of money. The working mother does not employ a maid to make money, any more than the man who must eat his lunches out because he works, eats out to make money. The commuter on the way to work does not pay his fare to make money, but because he wants to avoid walking, or to be able to live in the suburbs, just as the man whose job is in a cold area does not buy extra winter clothing or pay high fuel bills to make money, but to keep warm.

iii. A Smaller Consumption Expenditure Is Still a Consumption Expenditure

A third frequently asked question is this: In view of the fact that the purchase of a house typically means a saving of expense in comparison with renting, shouldn't it, for this reason, be considered a productive expenditure, and the house itself, a capital good? Likewise, if the purchase of a washing machine by a housewife makes it possible for her family to reduce its expense for laundry, shouldn't the expenditure for the washing machine be considered a productive expenditure and the washing machine itself, a capital good?

Once more, the answer is no. These questions rest on the idea that the saving of a consumption expenditure is a source of income. The saving on rent or laundry is supposed to be an extra income which the purchase of the house or washing machine brings in and which makes that purchase a productive expenditure and the house or washing machine a capital good.

The saving of a consumption expenditure, however, is not a source of income. It simply means that a smaller consumption expenditure takes the place of a larger one. The smaller consumption expenditure is still a consumption expenditure. And thus the conclusion contained in the question is false. If, for example, a person buys a house and has a monthly expense of $1,000 for mortgage payment, fuel, repairs, and the like, instead of, say, a $1,200-per-month rent bill for comparable living quarters, it is not true that his income is thereby increased by

$200 per month. What is true is that instead of consuming $1,200 per month for shelter, he now consumes $1,000 per month for shelter—in addition to having expended his down payment on the house for consumption. The $1,000 per month and the down payment are consumed because the house does not bring in any money revenue. It physically depreciates and must be maintained and eventually replaced by funds supplied from outside sources. Both the house and what is spent for it are simply used up and gone—consumed. In exactly the same way, if the purchase of a washing machine enables a family to reduce its expense for laundry from, say, an average of $20 per week to an average of $10 per week, what has occurred is that the family now consumes $10 per week for laundry instead of $20 per week. For its outlays, too, do not make possible the means of their being repeated, but depend on an outside source of funds for their continuation, and thus represent consumption. The case is exactly the same in principle as if the family had simply found a lower-priced laundry.

It is true that a reduction in consumption expense allows any given, *already existing* money income to go further. In this respect it achieves the equivalent of a rise in income in terms of *buying power* (assuming, of course, that what the reduced expenditure buys really is the equivalent of what the larger expenditure bought before). But the reduced expenditure does not itself bring in any income. Its ability to achieve the equivalent of a rise in income in terms of buying power presupposes the existence of an income *which it itself does not bring in.* A correct description of things would be to say that while the ability to obtain equal satisfactions for a reduced expenditure of money achieves the equivalent of a rise in income in terms of buying power—assuming that an income already exists—the reduced expenditure itself is still a consumption expenditure.

The idea that a reduction in consumption is the earning of income totally perverts the meaning of consumption by making it into its exact opposite. It seeks to wipe out the difference between spending money and making it; as though because one tended to use up one's funds and grow poorer less rapidly, one thereby earned funds and grew richer.

The difference between consumption expenditures and productive expenditures can be seen precisely in terms of the profound difference that exists in the respective ways in which they contribute to buying power. The only way that consumption expenditures can contribute to buying power is through their *reduction,* i.e., through their comparative nonexistence, not through their positive presence. Their positive presence is always merely a using up of buying power provided by other sources.

Productive expenditures, on the other hand, contribute to buying power through their positive presence, for it is their positive presence that brings in revenue and income. This is no less true in cases in which reductions take place in the productive expenditures required to produce a given product—i.e., in which the production of the product becomes more efficient and thus less costly. The reduced productive expenditures to make that product bring in sales revenues and are made for that purpose, and using the funds saved in producing that particular product to make other productive expenditures will now bring in still more sales revenues. Thus, for example, if a home builder or washing machine manufacturer finds a way to reduce his unit costs, his lesser outlays are still the source of his revenues and are still made for the purpose of bringing in those revenues, and if he devotes the savings in his outlays to fresh productive expenditures—in increasing his production of homes or washing machines or in branching into different lines of business—his sales revenues will further increase.[13]

Thus, consumption remains consumption, even when it is carried on in a more economical fashion.[14]

iv. Government Expenditure Is Consumption Expenditure Even When It Serves to Increase the Capacity of the Citizens to Pay Taxes

Certain government expenditures, such as for highways and education, if not made with the grossest inefficiency, have the potential for contributing to the productive capabilities of the citizens, and thus to their ability to work, earn income, and pay taxes. On this basis, the question is sometimes asked if such government expenditures could not be construed as productive expenditures—at least if the expenditures were made by the government for the purpose of bringing in tax revenues.

The answer is no, even in the event that the government really did make expenditures for the purpose of increasing the tax base and thus its tax revenues. So long as the highways are not self-supporting toll roads, so long as the education is provided for free or at only a nominal charge, the activities represent consumption. The very fact that taxes must be resorted to in order to support them fully confirms this fact. Taxes are not a revenue earned in production and exchange. They are not paid in exchange for the use of roads or for instruction—i.e., as the condition of receiving these things. What actually brings about their payment is the threat of being imprisoned if one does not pay them.

In providing such things as highways and education for free, the government is as much a consumer as would be a private individual who had the peculiar habit, let us imagine, of making gifts of encyclopedias to bright children. His gifts could well increase the capacity of the recipients later on to work and earn money. But the gifts would still leave him that much poorer. For him, they would still be consumption. Nothing would be changed if this individual combined his habit of gift giving with a program of systematic burglaries carried out against victims who had first been fattened up, so to speak, by the receipt of such gifts—victims whose capacity to earn incomes and thus to yield more ample caches to burglars was increased by the gifts. (The analogy is accurate insofar as the government's collection of taxes constitutes the appropriation of property against the will of its owners.)

To put the matter as succinctly as possible, the government is no less a consumer, merely because its activities have the effect of increasing the ability of the citizens to pay taxes and thus to support its consumption.

Similar considerations apply to the classification of government employees engaged in the collection of taxes. Such employees are not to be classified as producers' labor even though their work directly serves to bring in money to the government. So long as taxes are collected under the threat of physical force for nonpayment, they cannot be described as the result of any kind of productive activity on the part of the government or its agents. They are obtained as the result of coercion pure and simple. In such circumstances, the concepts of production, productive expenditure, and producers' labor simply do not apply. They are no more applicable than is the concept of capital goods to burglary tools, which also very likely serve to bring in more money than they cost. Consistent with what I have already pointed out, all concepts pertaining to production and productive activity of any sort preclude the obtaining of wealth by means of force. Expenditures made for the purpose of carrying out the use of force belong in a separate, third category, that is neither productive expenditure nor ordinary consumption expenditure—namely, that of *destructive* expenditure. True enough, when such expenditure is made for the purpose of bringing in money, the funds of the perpetrator are not decreased, but the funds of the victims certainly are. Moreover, to the degree that such expenditures exist and serve to victimize people, the effect is to diminish the incentives and the means for producing wealth. Thus the gains of the perpetrators result in more than equivalent losses to others. This is obviously a process far more at odds with the preservation and increase of wealth than is consumption.

In a very different, but nevertheless related vein, workers employed as part of a charity organization's fund-raising efforts are to be classified as consumers' labor rather than producers' labor, despite the fact that money is brought in by their activities. This is because the money brought in is charitable donations, not payments made in exchange for the receipt of goods or services. The payment of the salaries of such employees no more represents a productive expenditure than does a student's payment for the stationary on which he writes letters to his parents asking for money. The expenditure in both cases is a consumption expenditure which, fortunately for those who make it, is as a rule substantially more than defrayed by the charity of the recipients of the appeal.

Of course, the workers who are employed by a charity, whether as fund raisers or in any other capacity, are themselves productive in the sense appropriate to life in a division-of-labor society, inasmuch as they earn money. However, they earn money as consumers' labor, not as producers' labor.

v. "Human Capital" Is Not Capital

The last question to be considered here primarily concerns education. Is education, and other improvements in people's personal capacities that enable them to produce more efficiently and thus to earn a higher income, a form of capital? Is it, as many economists describe it, "human capital"?

If an education is obtained for the purpose of earning money, as is the case with vocational education, then the expenditure could, indeed, plausibly be termed a productive expenditure. Nevertheless, the fact that as productive expenditures, the outlays would have to be deducted as costs from wage incomes leads me to conclude that they should still be treated as consumption expenditures. This is because treating them as productive expenditures, which give rise to costs, would in turn require thinking of wages as analogous to sales revenues and having to regard the income of wage earners as a form of profits earned on the receipt of wages. That is to say, that merely because they had paid something in order to learn their trade, one would suddenly have to regard carpenters, plumbers, electricians, and the like as earning profits on their wages rather than as simply earning wages. At the same time, such productive expenditures and costs would have absolutely no bearing on the amount or rate of profit earned by actual businesses. Thus, radical conceptual change would be required in order to deal with a relatively small set of concretes, which concretes would have no bearing on the amount or rate of profit that is of actual concern. To avoid such a fruitless procedure, it is far simpler for all practical purposes to regard such productive expenditures of wage earners as consumption expenditures. The only exceptions should be cases in which the individuals involved actually do function as businesses, such as champion professional athletes who employ trainers and coaches and the like, and whose incomes really can be regarded as profits earned on business sales revenues.

Beyond this, even if one were to regard such expenditures as productive expenditures, it would still be an error to consider improvements in an individual's personal capacities to be a form of capital or any other kind of wealth. They are preconditions to the production of wealth or to the greater production of wealth, but not themselves wealth.[15] An essential characteristic of wealth in general, and of capital in particular, is its *alienability*. The possession of wealth and capital makes it possible for an individual to live without having currently to exercise his productive abilities—to live by means of selling off part of his wealth or capital and consuming the proceeds. It is not possible to do this with so-called capital that is part of one's very person. Such "capital" is inseparable from one's person and thus cannot be sold off. In this respect it differs radically from wealth and capital, and should not be placed in the same category.

The concept "human capital" would overcome this objection in a society that sanctioned slavery. A slave owner could regard greater personal capacities in his slaves as representing additional capital to him. But even then the concept of human capital would be improper—not only on all the grounds that make slavery improper, but also on the specifically economic grounds that neither human labor nor the persons of human beings constitute wealth.[16] And since capital is a specific form of wealth, they do not constitute capital. Indeed, as I have stated before, slavery is an institution hostile to the production of wealth by virtue of depriving the slaves of the incentive to produce it. And because of this, slavery is also hostile to the formation of capital. This last will become clear after I have shown that capital accumulation depends on all the factors that promote the production of wealth in general.[17]

In addition, there is a further major and specifically economic objection to the concept of human capital in the form of slaves. This is the fact that a society that sanctions capital in the form of the existence of other human beings thereby deprives itself of capital in the true sense of wealth reproductively employed. Such immoral and fictitious capital *displaces* actual capital. This is because people want to possess capital in some determinate ratio to their level of consumption, not in an infinite ratio. Thus to the extent that they think themselves rich on the basis of the ownership of slaves—which means that they think themselves rich merely because of the existence of workers—they feel no need to accumulate and possess genuine capital, that is, capital in the form of actual wealth. As illustration of the consequences, consider the difference in conditions between the North and South prior to the Civil War. A Northern manufacturer regarded his capital as his factory and machines, and his inventory of materials and finished products. He did not count as any part of his capital the persons of his employees. The Southern plantation owner, on the other hand, considered himself rich by virtue of the mere presence of his workers, who were his slaves. Thus he did not consider it necessary to accumulate substantial capital in the form of nonhuman means of production, because he thought he already had capital—in the possession of his slaves. The institution of slavery thus operated to deprive the South of the accumulation of actual capital, because people believed that their ownership of other people constituted their capital. The results of this deprivation of actual capital in the antebellum period contributed to the South lagging far behind the North in economic development for generations to come.

Adam Smith on "Productive and Unproductive Labor"

It is appropriate to acknowledge here the contribution of Adam Smith to the grasp of the essential connection between productive activity and moneymaking and the decisive role this connection plays in the distinction between production and consumption. To be sure, Smith commits the error of holding that in order for an activity to be productive, it must produce tangible physical goods, as though that were essential to its earning of money. He also made the error of including acquired personal abilities in the concept of capital.[18] In the very passages in which he makes the error of holding the need for the production of a tangible physical good, however, the essential role of moneymaking, as enabling the activity to be self-sustaining and a source of profit stands forth very clearly. It is worth quoting him:

> There is one sort of labour which adds to the value of the subject upon which it is bestowed: there is another which has no such effect. The former, as it produces a value, may be called productive; the latter, unproductive labour. Thus the labour of a manufacturer adds, generally, to the value of the materials which he works upon, that of his own maintenance, and that of his master's profit. The labour of a menial servant, on the contrary, adds to the value of nothing. *Though the manufacturer has his wages advanced to him by his master, he, in reality, costs him no expense, the value of those wages being generally restored, together with a profit, in the improved value of the subject upon which his labour is bestowed. But the maintenance of a menial servant never is restored. A man grows rich by employing a multitude of manufacturers: he grows poor by employing a multitude of menial servants.*[19]

And, very importantly, in regard to the activities of government:

> The labour of some of the most respectable orders in the society is, like that of menial servants, unproductive of any value, and does not fix or realize itself in any permanent subject, or vendible commodity, which endures after that labor is past, and for which an equal quantity of labour could afterwards be procured. The sovereign, for example, with all the officers both of justice and war who serve under

him, the whole army and navy, are unproductive labourers. They are the servants of the public, and are maintained by a part of the annual produce of the industry of other people. Their service, how honourable, how useful, or how necessary soever, produces *nothing for which an equal quantity of service can afterwards be procured. The protection, security, and defence of the commonwealth, the effect of their labour this year, will not purchase its protection, security, and defence for the year to come.*[20]

Smith did not realize that the labor of "menial servants" can contribute to the earning of revenue by their employer, and thus to the subsequent payment of their wages. This is the case, for example, with the employment of maids by a hotel or waiters by a restaurant. Nor did he realize that the employment of "manufacturers"—workers producing tangible physical goods—need not always be a source of revenue to their employer. It is not in such cases as workers employed in a shipyard owned by the navy.[21] For the same reasons, he did not see that an employer can increase his wealth by the employment of "menial servants" and consume his wealth in the employment of "manufacturers."[22] He did not see that the question of whether or not tangible physical goods are produced is simply irrelevant to the question of whether labor should be classified—in our terminology—as producers' labor or as consumers' labor.

Nevertheless, in comparison with his grasp of fundamental truths in connection with the tie of productive activity to moneymaking, Smith's errors are relatively minor, and do not significantly detract from the value of his accomplishments. Sadly, however, Smith's contributions here are almost completely overlooked nowadays. This is only in part because of his confusion concerning the need for the production of a tangible physical good to qualify an activity as productive. The main reason, I will show, has to do with the much more important matters discussed in Part C of this chapter.[23]

5. Critique of the Concept of Imputed Income

The concepts of income and cost pertain to receipts and outlays of money. As the preceding section made clear, this essential fact can easily be overlooked. For example, this was the case when one regarded the saving of an expenditure—the absence of a cost—in the purchase of a home or washing machine as the earning of an income.[24] For many years, I myself overlooked the essential connection of income and cost with the receipt and expenditure of money. I did so until I became aware of the requirements of explaining aggregate profit in the economic system as an excess of the money sales revenues of business over the money outlays of business that later on show up as costs deducted from the sales revenues. Solving the problem of how business in the aggregate could regularly and consistently sell for more money than it bought placed me under the necessity of looking for a *monetary source* of the surplus and of focusing on matters for the first time strictly in terms of money outlays and money revenues. When I saw the fruitfulness of this approach, I began to recognize the great importance of not confusing actual receipts and outlays of money with any form of fictional outlays and receipts of money.[25]

Contemporary economics, in contrast, continually ignores the vital connection of income and cost with the receipt and outlay of money. It does so insofar as it propounds the doctrines of "imputed income" and "opportunity cost."[26] The doctrine of imputed income openly and systematically avows that the absence of a cost constitutes income. The doctrine of opportunity cost, on the other hand, holds that the absence of an income constitutes a cost. Contemporary economics thus deals in nonexistent incomes and costs, which it treats as though they existed. Its formula is that money not spent is money earned, and that money not earned is money spent.

As I have indicated, these doctrines stand in the way of developing an understanding of the determinants of aggregate profit and the average rate of profit in the economic system. In addition, they turn out to be riddled with contradictions and absurdities.

I have already described the procedure of the imputed-income doctrine in some detail in the case of owner-occupied housing. This procedure is explicitly and officially endorsed by the U.S. government in its compilation of statistics of national income and gross national product. The rationale for the procedure is to be able to perform an alleged measurement of production which would otherwise be omitted from the statistics. In the words of an official U.S. government publication:

> The imputation for the rental value of owner-occupied homes is made to provide comparable treatment between rented and owner-occupied housing. It assumes that home ownership is a business producing housing services which are sold to the homeowner in his capacity as tenant. These sales are estimated in terms of the sum for which the particular type of home could be rented, and the expenses of the home owners are deducted to obtain imputed net rent. The imputed gross total becomes a part of sales to persons, or consumer expenditures, and imputed net rent becomes a part of the rental income of persons.[27]

To make clear the meaning of this quotation, we need only recall the example I presented of the individual who instead of renting a house for $1,200 a month buys a comparable house and incurs monthly expenses of $1,000 in keeping it up. The homeowner's $200 a month saving of expense is treated as a $200 increase in his monthly income. The only difference between the government's procedure and that of my example is that the government's procedure counts the depreciation on the house in the

homeowner's costs rather than any repayment of principal on the mortgage, which is appropriate if one holds the bizarre context.

The nature of the government's procedure and all the twists and turns it involves can be grasped by taking seriously the claim that a homeowner has an additional income of $2,400 per year by virtue of owning his home and thereby saving an expense of $200 a month in comparison with renting. If this claim is taken seriously, the question immediately arises of what has become of this $2,400 of alleged additional income? If it has been received as income, it must show up either as an addition to the individual's consumption expenditure or to his savings or, in some measure, to both. But where is it? For his consumption expenditure and the change in his savings add up only to his income in the normal sense of money actually received or due. The "solution" is to claim that not only does the homeowner receive $2,400 per year in income he doesn't receive, but that he also consumes this $2,400 per year in paying—to himself—the very rent he was originally supposed to be spared! He does not and yet simultaneously does, it is alleged, incur $200 per month of housing expense.

This "solution," when worked out in detail, entails a whole host of fictions and contradictions. The first is that the $1,200 which, by the very conditions of the case, are not paid in rent, are paid in rent. They are allegedly paid in rent by the homeowner to himself. This gives rise to the further fiction that the homeowner is a landlord, and that he is so precisely in a respect in which he cannot be—namely, with regard to the house which he himself occupies and which he therefore withholds from the rental market. From the fiction that the homeowner is a landlord follows the still further fiction that his $1,000 monthly expense for mortgage interest and so forth is a business expense, and thus the still further contradiction that a nonbusiness expense is a business expense. It is by subtracting this nonbusiness business expense of $1,000 from the nonrental rental, nonrevenue revenue of $1,200 that the nonincome income of $200 per month is arrived at, which is allegedly consumed in housing expense in contradiction of the fact that by the nature of the case this $200 is not consumed in housing expense. And, as one last touch of the absurd, this phantom income of $200 is raised to the status of a phantom who is his own grandfather. There could be no phantom income of $200 if there were no phantom revenue of $200 in excess of the phantom business expense. This extra phantom revenue, however, can only exist if there is first a phantom consumption of $200. But there can be no phantom consumption of $200 unless there is first a phantom income of $200. But, of course, in dealing with phantoms, one need not quarrel over any contradictions in the order of their descent.

The absurdities to which the doctrine of imputed income leads in the effort to measure production that is not brought to market are limited only by the extent of its application. Thus, if one applies it to housewives, and asks how much a man would have to pay to obtain from the market the same services his wife provides for free, one can easily come to the startling conclusion that the income attributable to the average housewife is higher than the income of her husband, despite the fact that she does not earn an income, while he does.

The application of the imputed-income doctrine to the services of housewives is frequently advocated by textbooks dealing with "macroeconomics." They typically consider it a deficiency of the gross product statistics (GNP or now GDP) that the statistics do not allow for the value of services performed in the home. For example, Samuelson and Nordhaus write: "Consider also do-it-yourself work done in the home—cooking meals or insulating walls. Because the values added are not bought or sold in markets, they never enter into the goods and services of the GNP . . . . An estimate of NEW ["net economic welfare"] will need to include the value of similar do-it-yourself activities."[28]

An imputed value of housewives' services was actually calculated by a major New York City bank in the 1960s, which arrived at a figure that exceeded the income of the average working husband. The bank made its calculation by applying the wage rates of cooks, housekeepers, chauffeurs, maids, governesses, nurses, and so forth to the hours the average housewife is supposed to spend in each of these respective activities, and then adding up the result. (Much more recently, in 1992, legislation was proposed in Congress to compel the Department of Commerce to include such an allowance in the calculation of gross domestic product. Inclusion would reportedly add $1.46 trillion a year to the GDP.[29])

If one were to ask how the average husband is supposed to be able to pay for these services that are allegedly beyond his income, one would be driven to the counterbalancing absurdity that the average housewife supports her husband—she turns over to him her earnings in these capacities so that he may be able to buy her services from her. This bookkeeping procedure accords perfectly with that which is used in the case of the imputation for owner-occupied housing, in which the imputed income is allegedly used to finance the alleged additional consumption that makes its own alleged existence possible. Here the wife's imputed income finances the husband's alleged additional consumption.

Curiously, the devotees of the imputed-income doctrine omit an imputed value of the wife's *sexual* services from their calculations. Were they to include it, they would no doubt discover that her income exceeds her husband's by an even more substantial margin, for the prices of call girls' services are much higher than those of cooks and housekeepers, and so forth. And on a national basis, the national income and gross domestic product of the country would most likely be doubled at least, with sex emerging as far and away the nation's largest industry, and sexual intercourse as the most important component of the index of industrial production, which economists might then follow with far more rapt attention than they do the output of steel and automobiles. Though logical consistency requires such an imputation, it has not been attempted or even suggested. The supporters of the imputed-income doctrine are willing to regard wives as interchangeable with hired cooks and housekeepers and thus to obliterate the nature of marriage in this respect, but they are unwilling to go the whole route and claim that wives are prostitutes—and husbands their customers, enabled to afford their services by living off the proceeds of their wives' prostitution.

When applied in the attempt to measure "net economic welfare," the doctrine of imputed income can easily make beggars into millionaires. Consider the expenses one saves by not being blind and thus not having to hire a nurse, or by virtue of not having cancer, or not needing a psychiatrist. When such savings are added to a person's income, in the attempt to measure his economic welfare, he can easily turn out to "earn" $100,000 a year—even though he may not be able to afford to *buy* a cup of coffee.

Consider how easy it is to raise one's income when it consists of such fictions. A wife who buys a $2,000 fur coat instead of a $5,000 fur coat, avoids an expense of $3,000. She thus allegedly secures the equivalent of a $3,000 raise for her husband. And if the husband could elevate his wife's tastes sufficiently, to the point where she would set her heart on a $15,000 fur coat, her expenditure of $2,000 would allegedly secure for him the equivalent of a $13,000 raise—enough to pay both for the coat for her and for a small sports car for him besides.

At the base of all these absurdities is the failure to realize the importance of earning *money* as the means of living in a division-of-labor society. As a result of this failure, contemporary economics does not consider the earning or nonearning of money to be a significant matter. As a further result, it does not know how to distinguish between production and consumption. It regards consumption as though it were production, merely because the physical aspect of production is present—failing to see that such production is a consumptive production.

In addition, contemporary economics considers as one of its main tasks the *measurement* of total production and total welfare in the economic system, and believes that such measurement can be performed by adding up the number of dollars for which goods and services exchange or might be exchanged. The notion that the expenditure or potential expenditure of money in an economic system, is a measure of the goods and services which are produced in that economic system is totally mistaken. What the aggregate expenditure of money in an economic system reflects, and thus indirectly measures, is nothing but *the quantity of money* in the economic system!

As we shall see when we come to the discussion of the quantity theory of money in the next chapter, it is the quantity of money, not the volume of physical production, that determines the volume of spending in the economic system. Essentially, increases in the production of goods and services are accompanied by a rise in the total spending for goods and services only insofar as they are accompanied by an increase in the quantity of money. Otherwise, the increase in production results in a fall in prices, with basically no greater total expenditure of money taking place.

Money is important *within the economic system,* as the means of individuals exchanging their goods and services and as the basis of their performing economic calculations. It has no significance as a measure of the production of the economic system as a whole. Contemporary economics fails to see the real significance of money—in the activities of individuals—and focuses instead on the illusory significance of money as a measure of aggregate production.

This is not to say that a system of aggregate economic accounting is of no value. As will be shown later in this book, it is of very great value, but as a means of improving understanding of the functioning of the economic system, not as a system of measuring the production of the economic system.

6. Critique of the Opportunity-Cost Doctrine

An opportunity cost is an imputed cost—a cost which does not actually exist in the sense of an expenditure of money being made, or having been made, but which is treated as though it existed. An opportunity cost is said to exist by virtue of the failure to earn a revenue or income that otherwise might be earned or might have been earned. It represents the absence of a revenue or income, just as imputed income represents the absence of a cost.

The treatment of the subject by Samuelson and Nordhaus is typical:

> . . . the economist generally includes more items in cost than do accountants or businesspeople. Economists include

all costs—whether they reflect monetary transactions or not; business accounts generally exclude nonmonetary transactions.

> We have already encountered . . . examples of true economic costs that do not show up in business accounts. The return to an owner's effort, the normal return on contributed capital to a firm, a risk premium on highly leveraged owner's equity—these are all elements that should figure into a broadly conceived set of economic costs but do not enter business accounts. . . .

> The notion that can help us understand this distinction between money costs and true economic costs is the concept of *opportunity cost.* The opportunity cost of a decision consists of the things that are given up by taking that particular decision rather than taking an alternative decision.[30]

The opportunity cost of a decision is subsequently described as "the value of the best available alternative."[31] Practically every elementary textbook of economics, including Samuelson and Nordhaus, offers an example of the following kind to illustrate the concept of opportunity cost and explain the need for it.

An accountant informs the owner of a neighborhood hardware store that he has made a profit of $50,000 during the preceding year. Naturally, the owner may be quite pleased with having made such a profit. But this, interjects the textbook author, shows how little this businessman and his accountant know of economics. Have they considered, he asks, that by selling the hardware store and investing the proceeds elsewhere, the store owner could make $15,000 per year in interest, and, by going to work for someone else, make $45,000 in wages or salary? These forgone opportunities or passed-up alternatives, the textbook author then argues, must be counted as costs of the owner's business, just as much as the store's payment for merchandise and the labor of hired help, if its actual profit is to be computed. And thus, the textbook author concludes, far from having the $50,000 profit that the store owner and his accountant naïvely believed he had, the store owner has incurred a $10,000 *loss.* In the words of Samuelson and Nordhaus, in reference to their particular variant of this example: "Thus, while the accountant might conclude that such a typical small business was an economically viable enterprise, the economist would pronounce the firm an unprofitable loser."[32]

Now the need for the concept of opportunity cost is simply supposed to be to make the store owner aware of the fact that he might be financially better off by selling out and going to work for someone else. But if this is so, there is no reason why it cannot be stated very simply that one can be financially better off making a larger income in the form of interest and wages than a smaller income in the form of profit. One is better off making a combined $60,000-interest-and-wage income than a $50,000-profit income. In order to make this point, there is no need to deny that the store owner's profit is a profit, and to call it a loss instead. And there is no reason for the store owner to think he has done badly merely because he might have done better. There is certainly no grounds, as Samuelson and Nordhaus believe, to challenge the accountant's judgment that the enterprise is viable. It is indeed viable. It recovers in sales all the outlays it expended to bring in those sales, and a profit besides. Thus it is self-sustaining and more than self-sustaining. It is not a "loser"—not of a single dollar of the capital with which it began the year's operations.

The doctrine of opportunity cost is not required for ascertaining how one might do better. Its sole contribution is obfuscation, not perception. Consider its implications.

Our store owner, if we are to believe such authors as Samuelson and Nordhaus, has lost $10,000. Nevertheless, he has gone through the year consuming $40,000 and adding $10,000 to his net worth. He has bought a car and taken a vacation, and, at the same time, added $10,000 to his bank account. If he in fact had had a loss of $10,000, this would not have been possible. Consuming $40,000, while losing $10,000, would have meant a decline in his net worth of $50,000. How can this discrepancy of $60,000 between the facts and the implications of the opportunity-cost doctrine be reconciled? How can the $10,000 increase in the store owner's net worth, which in fact occurs, be reconciled with the $50,000 decrease in his net worth which the opportunity-cost doctrine implies?

The solution to this puzzle is a second step into unreality, a second fiction to balance the first. It is that in addition to incurring the loss he never incurred, the store owner is alleged to receive income he never received! For not only does he have a $10,000 loss, it is claimed, but he also earns $15,000 in interest and $45,000 in wages. His $50,000-profit income is, it is claimed, in reality[!] a $10,000 loss accompanied by $60,000 in interest and wage income! And thus, paradoxically, the very interest and wage incomes which were *not* earned, and the failure of which to earn supposedly gave rise to the need for counting them as costs, are treated as being earned! They are held to be simultaneously not earned and earned.

What is involved in this juggling must be spelled out more fully. The store owner forgoes $60,000 in interest and wage income by virtue of remaining in his present business. This $60,000 which he does not make is treated as an outlay of his business, despite the fact that no such outlay exists. This nonexistent outlay then causes a nonexistent loss. The nonexistent loss, however, contradicts the change in the store owner's net worth. To reconcile this contradiction, the store owner is then credited with a nonexistent interest and wage income equal to his nonexistent payment of interest and wages. He allegedly now earns the interest and wage income he doesn't earn and which, in not being earned, created the whole alleged problem in the first place. He supposedly pays the interest and wages he doesn't pay, to himself, so he now receives from himself the interest and wages he doesn't receive.

An analogy to this procedure would be the following. One gains ten pounds, but might have gained twenty pounds. This is then taken to mean that one has lost ten pounds. When one's alleged loss of weight cannot be reconciled with the fact that one is now ten pounds too large for one's clothes, one's oversize is explained on the grounds that one's clothes have shrunk the equivalent of twenty pounds. Or: one marries a pretty woman, but might have married a very beautiful woman. This is then taken to mean that one has married an ugly woman. When the woman's alleged ugliness cannot be reconciled with the fact that she is pretty, her prettiness is then explained on the grounds that she has had plastic surgery.

The opportunity-cost doctrine leads to further absurd implications. It follows from this doctrine that it can be more advantageous to have losses than profits. Our store owner allegedly suffers a $10,000 loss because he forgoes $60,000 in interest and wage income in making his $50,000 profit. But suppose that instead of being the owner of a hardware store, he were only a poor pushcart vendor or street-corner newspaper dealer. His profit in such a case might be only $20,000. Yet if the interest he had to forgo on his tiny capital and the wages he had to forgo on his very limited talents amounted to only $15,000, the opportunity-cost doctrine would claim he had made a profit of $5,000. Obviously, it is much better to suffer the $10,000 "loss" than to make this $5,000 "profit."

It follows from the opportunity-cost doctrine that precisely to the degree that one is confronted with profitable ways to invest one's capital, and precisely to the degree that one's services are in great demand, one's income must be less—in a word, that one must suffer by virtue of possessing the very qualities that create one's success. For example, it follows from this doctrine that companies reduce their profits by having successful research departments. The effect of these research departments is to create profitable alternative opportunities for investment. According to the opportunity-cost doctrine, to the degree that they do this, they must raise the costs of these firms and thus reduce their profits. For example, if an innovative computer company or pharmaceutical company is able to make a rate of profit of 30 percent on some product, that profit must allegedly be reduced to 1 percent if its research department develops some other product which could afford a 29 percent rate of profit on the same capital. And if the new product could yield 31 percent, then the company's rate of profit must allegedly still be cut to 1 percent, because then the profit on the original product would constitute the opportunity cost. And if the company's research department develops two truly spectacular products, the one yielding a 50 percent rate of profit, the other a 49 percent rate of profit, again its rate of profit must allegedly be cut from 30 percent to 1 percent on the capital in question. Conclusion? The first step for a company to take if it wants to raise its rate of profit is to close down its research department.

Similarly, it follows that the president of General Motors must suffer from the fact that Ford and Chrysler would like to employ him, for to the degree that they become aware of his talents, it serves to raise his opportunity costs. He would allegedly make a higher income if no other auto firm were interested in him. Conclusion? Raise your income by striving to give the impression to potential employers that you are incompetent. If you can succeed in this endeavor sufficiently, you will make more money, the opportunity-cost doctrine implies, even if your "mere" accounting income falls, provided it doesn't fall by as much. And, of course, the best and quickest way to raise one's income is simply to make oneself blind to all alternative possibilities for investment and employment, and thus to remove them as opportunities, thereby totally eliminating all "opportunity costs."

Yet another manifestation of the absurdity of this doctrine can be seen if it is applied to the stock market. Imagine that an individual is considering investing a million dollars, and must decide between two stocks, *A* and *B*. Both stocks are currently selling at $10 per share. The individual decides on stock *A*. It goes to $20 per share. In the same period, however, it turns out that stock *B* goes to $30 per share. If one believes the opportunity-cost doctrine, this is grounds for leaping from the nearest skyscraper—one has lost a million dollars. Conversely, imagine that stock *A* drops to $3 per share, while stock *B* drops to $1 per share. In this case, if one believes the opportunity-cost doctrine, one has made $200,000 and can afford to buy a Rolls Royce.

The criticisms I have made of the opportunity-cost doctrine should by no means be interpreted to mean that I deny the relationship between the cost of producing an individual good and the value of the alternative products which can be produced with the same factors of production. On the contrary, I fully acknowledge that costs of production are influenced by the value of alternative products which must be forgone if the product in question is to be produced. Indeed, previous portions of this book were devoted actually to demonstrating just how

this process takes place.[33] For example, insofar as it depends on the price of wheat, the cost of producing bread is determined on the basis of the value buyers attach to other wheat products, such as meat produced from animals fed with wheat—products which cannot be produced because the means of producing them are devoted to the production of bread and are thus unavailable to produce those alternative products.[34]

But these costs of production are *money costs* of production. The actual *money price* of wheat (and of all other factors of production that exist in a given supply) is determined by a process of bidding that emanates from all the different uses and users of the factor of production. The price of the factor emerges as the result of the bidding of different *sums of money* by the various users and potential users. This process does not at all represent the concoction of any kind of make-believe costs. The costs are actual, in the full business and accounting sense.

The supporters of the opportunity-cost doctrine generally recognize the process by which money costs are determined, then confuse the alternative opportunities whose competition in bidding gives rise to the money costs with the phenomenon of cost itself, and thereafter ignore the necessity of a money outlay actually being present. In other words, they identify a cause of the determination of money costs, confuse the cause with the effect, and proceed to ignore the effect, which is nonetheless essential.

The first part of this chapter was dedicated to dealing with those errors in connection with the concept of productive activity that define it too broadly, by failing to take into account the vital importance of moneymaking. The second part of this chapter, of course, will deal with the deadly errors of defining the concept of productive activity too narrowly and excluding from it such vital activities as those of businessman and capitalist, retailer and wholesaler, and so forth.

The imputed-income and opportunity-cost doctrines constitute a kind of bridge between the two types of errors. In leading people to perceive the existence of productive expenditures, wages, and costs where there are in fact no productive expenditures, wages, or costs, and to deny the existence of profits where profits do in fact exist, they encourage an utter misconception of the foundations and mutual interrelationships of these phenomena. In particular, they blot out the essential role of businessmen and capitalists in the making of productive expenditures and the payment of wages, and proceed as though productive expenditure and wages could exist without businessmen and capitalists. In so doing, they thoroughly distort the nature of the activities of businessmen and capitalists and the relationship between those activities and the respective heights of wages and profits. Thus, they play a major role in preventing a just conception of the productive role of businessmen and capitalists and in making the Marxian exploitation theory appear plausible. This will become clear in what follows.

PART B

THE PRODUCTIVE ROLE OF BUSINESSMEN AND CAPITALISTS

1. The Productive Functions of Businessmen and Capitalists

As previously observed, the productive role of businessmen and capitalists can be understood only within the context of a division-of-labor society. While in a non-division-of-labor society, manual workers alone are productive, because there is nothing more to production in such a context than the physical making of goods, in a division-of-labor society new aspects, new dimensions, of productive activity appear. Moneymaking is only one such aspect, though an essential one, to be sure. In addition, the productive role of businessmen and capitalists emerges. Their productive role is to raise the productivity of manual labor, and thus its real remuneration, precisely by means of *creating, coordinating, and improving the efficiency of the division of labor.*[35]

Businessmen and capitalists create division of labor in founding and organizing business enterprises, in providing capital, and in making productive expenditures. They coordinate the division of labor among the various firms and industries by the very fact of seeking to make profits and avoid losses; they coordinate the division of labor within each individual firm insofar as they perform the functions of management. They improve the efficiency of the division of labor both by means of their competitive quest to earn the highest possible rate of profit, and to avoid losses, and by means of providing capital and seeking to maximize the efficiency with which capital goods, no less than labor, are employed.

Each of these aspects of the productive role of businessmen and capitalists requires elaboration.

Creation of Division of Labor

Business firms are the central units of a division-of-labor society. The division of labor exists both between the various individual business enterprises and within each individual business enterprise that comprises the labor of more than one person. Each business firm is more or less specialized in its production. Frequently, its activities are confined to a single industry; rarely do they extend to more than several industries. The cases in which firms do participate in more than a few industries will generally be found to be the result of artificial incentives created by the tax laws.[36] In absolutely no case, does any firm come even remotely close to engaging in all branches of production. Thus, each firm represents more or less specialized productive activity vis-à-vis the rest of the economic system. Furthermore, within each firm, there are separate divisions, departments, sections, and branches, all representing further aspects of the division of labor.

In these ways, business firms are the central units of a division-of-labor society, representing division of labor both in their external relationships to other business firms and in their internal organization.

It follows that in founding and organizing business firms, businessmen and capitalists create division of labor—they construct the building blocks of the division-of-labor society.

The provision of capital by businessmen and capitalists is no less essential to the existence of the division of labor. As explained in the discussion of the dependence of the division of labor on saving, the provision of capital is indispensable to the existence of any significant vertical division of labor. This is because it makes possible the existence of a necessary division of payments in the productive process. In its absence, the only source of payments to producers would be the ultimate consumers, with the result that many groups of producers would be compelled to wait intolerable lengths of time between the completion of their contribution to production and their receipt of payment. This is the problem of the auto workers and steel firms having to wait to be paid until the cars they help to produce are sold, or, if the cars are sold on credit, as they often must be, until the installment payments come in. It is the problem of the steel workers and the iron-mining concerns having to wait all this length of time plus the additional length of time that elapses between their contribution to production and the payment for the automobiles, and so on, with the problem growing worse and worse, the further back in the chain of production one stands. It is the problem of the equipment and construction industries and their workers having to wait decades for payment, and even generations and centuries, insofar as equipment and buildings are used in the production of further equipment and buildings.[37]

In contrast, the provision of capital makes possible payment to producers at numerous points in the productive process, and thus within a reasonable period of time following the performance of their contribution to production. Indeed, in a modern economic system the great majority of wage earners are paid out of the capital of the firms which employ them. This makes it possible for them to be paid in most cases not only far in advance of payment by the ultimate consumers, but also even well before the business firms at the next stage of production pay for the products to which their labor contributes. For example, steel workers are paid not only years in advance of the payment for automobiles by the ultimate consumers but also well in advance of the payment for steel by the auto companies. Wages are paid out of the capital of the firm that employs the wage earners in every instance in which payment must be made to the wage earners after a shorter interval of time than that in which payment is received by the firm for the goods or services to which their labor contributes. This, of course, occurs in the typical case in which wages are paid after a week's work and payment from the customer for the goods or services to which the wage earner's labor contributes is payable to the firm as late as thirty days later, without penalty.

There is a closely related point of great importance. Namely, later portions of this book—of this chapter—will show how the saving and productive expenditure of businessmen and capitalists are responsible for the existence of the entire demand for labor in the production of products for sale—both for first creating that demand and then increasing it relative to the demand for consumers' goods.[38] It will be shown that to the degree that businessmen and capitalists save and productively expend, they increase the proportion of "national income" that is constituted by wages and the proportion of consumption expenditure that takes place out of wages in contrast to other forms of income, notably, profits and interest. Indeed, it will be shown later in this chapter that it is the saving and productive expenditure of businessmen and capitalists that make possible the very existence of a class of wage earners separate and distinct from the sellers of products, and thus of the existence of the division of labor insofar as it depends on the existence of wage earners.[39]

It should not be forgotten that the provision of capital also vitally contributes to the division of labor in its horizontal aspect—that is, the extent to which it can be carried at any given stage of production. This is because greater division of labor at any given stage of production requires the existence of larger-scale production, which in turn requires the existence of greater amounts of capital.[40]

Thus, in founding and organizing business enterprises, in providing capital, and in making productive expenditures, businessmen and capitalists create division of labor.

Coordination of the Division of Labor

Businessmen and capitalists are responsible for the coordination of the division of labor among the various branches of production by virtue of their striving to make profits and avoid losses. As the discussion of the price system showed earlier in this book, in striving—other

things being equal—to make the highest possible rate of profit, businessmen and capitalists are led to counteract the mistake of relative underinvestment and relative underproduction. This is the mistake of failing to carry investment and production in specific industries far enough relative to investment and production in the rest of the economic system. For example, the mistake of failing to carry investment and production in the automobile industry far enough relative to investment and production in the housing industry, or investment and production in the manufacture of nails far enough relative to investment and production in the lumber industry. By the same token, in seeking to withdraw their capital from industries suffering losses or earning below-average rates of profit, businessmen and capitalists are led to counteract the mistake of relative overinvestment and relative overproduction—that is, the mistake of carrying some branches of production too far relative to the other branches of production. To be sure, the desire to make profits and avoid losses leads businessmen and capitalists to strive to avoid making mistakes representing either kind of discoordination in the first place.

In these ways, the profit motive of the businessmen and capitalists operates as the great engine maintaining coordination and balance among all the different branches of the division of labor. It is what prevents the division of labor from degenerating into any sort of "anarchy of production."[41]

The coordinating function of businessmen and capitalists is present not only among the different branches of production, and the various individual firms which comprise them, but also within each individual firm. Insofar as businessmen and capitalists exercise the functions of management, which to some extent they do inescapably in deciding the activities and organization of their enterprises, they are engaged in a further process of coordinating the division of labor. It is the essence of management to direct the activities of subordinates—individuals and groups of individuals comprising subordinate units—in such a way as to achieve the cohesive, overall goals of the enterprise at large. This is precisely the coordination of the elements of division of labor within the enterprise.

Of course, as I explained in Chapter 9, as far as the economic system is free of government interference, the managerial activities of the businessmen and capitalists represent profit management as opposed to bureaucratic management. The latter is the nature of management in government enterprises. It appears in private enterprises only to the extent that they are subject to government interference.[42]

By now one should be able clearly to appreciate just

why comprehension of the division of labor is the key to understanding the productive activities of businessmen and capitalists. If one ignores the division of labor, and focuses instead on the conditions of production in a society of self-sufficient farmers or hunters, there is no specific productive activity for businessmen and capitalists to perform. There is no division of labor to coordinate and no division of labor to create in the first place, and thus there is no possibility of grasping that precisely these are the productive functions of businessmen and capitalists. Nor, of course, on such a view is it possible to grasp the vital productive role of businessmen and capitalists in improving the efficiency of the division of labor.

Improvements in the Efficiency of the Division of Labor

The discussion of the price system earlier in this book, in particular that of the uniformity-of-profit principle, also makes very clear how the profit motive of businessmen and capitalists brings about a progressive improvement in the methods of production and in the quantity and quality of the products produced.[43] We saw major confirmation of this principle in the discussion of the nature of economic inequality in a capitalist society, in particular in connection with the building of great industrial fortunes.[44]

It is only necessary to recall the fact that under the freedom of competition of capitalism, to earn an exceptional rate of profit a producer must introduce a better product or a more efficient method of producing an already existing product. And, further, that the effect of the freedom of competition is subsequently to erode any special profit made in this way, as the improvement becomes more and more widely adopted by others and becomes the normal standard of the industry, with the result that to go on earning an exceptional rate of profit, it is necessary to introduce *repeated improvements* in production.

Later discussion of saving and capital accumulation in Chapter 14 of this book will show how the saving and productive expenditure of businessmen and capitalists result in a growing supply of capital goods and thus in the achievement of a further indispensable precondition for a rising productivity of labor. That discussion will also show how the efficiency that the profit motive leads businessmen and capitalists to achieve in the utilization of the capital goods already existing at any given time further powerfully promotes capital accumulation and the rise in the productivity of labor.[45]

Thus, in these ways—namely, the introduction of continuous improvements in products and methods of production and the achievement of capital accumulation both through saving and productive expenditure and the

efficient use of already existing capital goods—the activities of businessmen and capitalists bring about a progressive improvement in the efficiency of production under the division of labor.

2. The Productive Role of Financial Markets and Financial Institutions

The fact that in a division-of-labor society, production begins with an outlay of capital, and is thoroughly dependent upon the availability of capital, underlies the productive role of financial markets and financial institutions—namely, of the stock and bond markets, the banking system, and financial markets and financial institutions in general. The essential productive role of these markets and institutions is to promote the investment of savings and the efficiency of the investment of savings, as well as the overall degree of saving, and thereby to raise the demand for and productivity of labor and the general standard of living. Essentially, it is similar to the productive role of businessmen and capitalists themselves insofar as they provide capital and are responsible for a growing supply of capital goods.

The existence of financial markets and financial institutions makes it possible for individuals to earn a rate of return on capital without having to employ that capital in businesses of their own. It makes it possible for them to invest in businesses owned and operated by others, and to earn a rate of return on capital in the form of interest and dividends rather than in the form exclusively of profit. For many people, the existence of these markets and institutions provides the only opportunity of earning a rate of return on their savings.

In the absence of financial markets and financial institutions—of lending and borrowing and of investing for dividends—the only way that individuals could earn a rate of return on their savings would be by investing them in businesses under their own management. The possibility of investing in the enterprises of friends or close associates in the form of lending or accepting a partnership in which one plays no role in the management already represents the existence of a primitive, highly circumscribed form of financial market. Such limited possibilities may be of significant value to those to whom they are open, but they are obviously of substantially less value than the existence of full-fledged financial markets and the vastly greater opportunities for investment that the latter afford. Moreover, they are of no value for the great majority of individuals, whose friends and close associates are unable to offer the prospect of worthwhile investments.

Thus, in the absence of financial markets and financial institutions, for the great majority of people, if not for everyone, the only means of earning a rate of return on their savings would be investment in businesses under their own management. Yet there are many individuals for whom it would be highly disadvantageous to have to run a business of their own, given the alternative of being employed for wages that are higher than the profits they could hope to make in business for themselves. This in fact is the case for the great majority of people today, who can work as employees in fairly well-paying positions, but who, if they had to live by being in business for themselves would earn much less, or even lose the capital they invested.

Then, of course, there are many other people who possess savings, but who are completely unqualified to run a business, such as almost all underage orphans and many widows. In addition, there are still other people who possess savings and who might be financially more successful in business than in their present occupations, but who are simply unwilling to devote the necessary time to business activity. In this category are probably a significant number of professionals, such as doctors, lawyers, engineers, and professors.

Still another, partly overlapping group is constituted by all those people who possess savings and have successful businesses of their own, but who cannot employ all of their savings efficiently within the limits of their own businesses. In this category are many professionals in private practice, large numbers of small businessmen, and a significant number of large businessmen. For example, a doctor in private practice often easily accumulates far more savings than he can employ efficiently in his practice. The owners of many successful stores and shops are in the same position. If such people are unable or unwilling to open branches or enter into additional lines of business, or cannot do so efficiently, then they simply cannot employ all of their savings, or, at least, cannot employ them efficiently.

On the basis of these facts, it should be obvious that the absence of financial markets and financial institutions would mean that to an important extent individuals who had savings would have no incentive to invest them. Individuals in such a position would thus have no alternative but to hold their savings in the form of hoards of money or accumulations of consumers' goods, such as jewelry, housing, and works of art. The consequence would be that their savings would not serve to make possible a demand for capital goods or for labor. The result of the lesser demand for capital goods would be that the extent to which the economic system concentrated on the production of capital goods would be correspondingly less. And thus the ability to achieve a production of capital goods sufficient to make possible capital accumulation would be correspondingly less. The

effect would almost certainly be economic stagnation at an extremely low level of productivity of labor. The standard of living of the average worker would also suffer from the fact that savings that are hoarded or held in the form of accumulations of personal consumers' goods do not contribute to the demand for labor and the payment of wages, as do savings that are invested.

In contrast, the existence of financial markets and financial institutions, and the rate of return they provide, greatly encourages the investment of all such savings. The fact that financial markets and financial institutions exist thus raises the relative demand for and production of capital goods and thereby powerfully contributes to capital accumulation and a rising productivity of labor. At the same time, it raises the relative demand for labor and payment of wages.[46]

In addition, and also very important, the existence of financial markets and financial institutions enables individuals who have the opportunity of investing in their own businesses, to invest more productively in businesses owned by others. This, too, powerfully contributes to capital accumulation and the rise in the productivity of labor and the general standard of living. It does so, above all, by making possible the existence of the large aggregations of capital necessary for such undertakings as electric utilities, railroads, and, indeed, most large-scale modern industries. In this way, the surplus capital accumulated by such people as doctors and shopkeepers can be employed far more effectively than in further enhancements of such things as office furniture or perhaps a store's inventory.

The effect of this change in the pattern of investment made possible by the existence of financial markets and financial institutions is that with the same degree of demand for capital goods and concentration on the production of capital goods, the economic system is able to produce far more. This is because now it has capital goods in the form of electric power plants and the like, rather than in the form of such things as minimally useful additional office furniture. The effect of the greater ability to produce that this change in the pattern of investment makes possible is a larger supply not only of consumers' goods, but also of *capital goods*. For the existence of electric power plants, railroads, steel mills, and so forth contributes as much to the production of a larger supply of capital goods as it does to the production of a larger supply of consumers' goods. Thus, in this way too—by bringing about a higher productivity of capital goods—the existence of financial markets and financial institutions powerfully contributes to capital accumulation and the rise in the standard of living. And, as we shall see in later discussion of capital accumulation, the effect of a higher productivity of capital goods is a continuing one, making possible a permanently higher rate of capital accumulation.[47]

To an important extent the existence of financial markets and financial institutions encourages not only the investment or more efficient investment of savings already made but also an increase in the rate of saving itself. In enabling individuals who otherwise could not have earned a rate of return on their savings now to earn one, or to earn a higher rate of return than they otherwise could have, it increases the overall rate of saving.

It is important to realize that this does not occur to any great extent by increasing the incentive to save. Most people would desire to have savings even in the absence of any rate of return—simply as a means of providing for future needs that they could not expect to provide for otherwise. And to the extent that people already have savings for such reasons, the effect of the ability to earn a rate of return, or a higher rate of return instead of a lower rate of return, may be as much to motivate them to consume more in the present as it is to give them an incentive to save more in the present. This is because counterbalancing the fact that each dollar saved today will now turn into more dollars in the future is the prospect of the higher future income that will be available as the result of the higher rate of return on the savings one already has. The prospect that one will be better off in the future than in the present operates as an inducement to consume more and save less in the present. Thus, the overall effect of being able to earn a rate of return, or a higher rate of return, on the incentive to save may well be neutral or close to neutral.

Nevertheless, the ability to earn a rate of return does powerfully promote saving. It does so insofar as it enables individuals whose consumption would otherwise be at the expense of their accumulated savings to consume without decumulating their savings. For example, the fact that an individual with accumulated savings of, say, one million dollars can earn a rate of return (in real terms) of 2 or 3 percent a year enables this individual to consume twenty or thirty thousand dollars a year without depleting his savings.

In the absence of his ability to earn a rate of return, the greater part of the savings accumulated by an individual would later on be decumulated, as they came to be used for current consumption. Instead, the ability to earn a rate of return serves to enable an individual with accumulated savings to consume out of income rather than his accumulated savings.[48] In so doing, it makes possible a far higher overall rate of saving and correspondingly greater degree of capital accumulation and demand for labor.

Once again, it must be emphasized how the productive role of such a segment of the economic system as financial markets and financial institutions can be understood only within the context of a division-of-labor society, and only after one has understood the role of capital in production in such a society. It is absolutely impossible to understand it, if one's context is essentially limited to that of Robinson Crusoe producing on a desert island and standing outside the division of labor and the use of money. In that case, one simply cannot appreciate the fact that in a division-of-labor economy production must begin with outlays of money, and that the productivity of labor depends both on the relative production of capital goods and on their productivity, both of which are greatly increased by the existence of financial markets and financial institutions and the greater saving, investment out of saving, and more efficient investment that they make possible.

The Specific Productive Role of the Stock Market

A widespread misconception is that the stock market is somehow divorced from genuine productive activity except insofar as it is the source of funds going directly to corporations in exchange for newly issued stock. On this view, the overwhelming bulk of stock market activity, which consists of the trading of already outstanding shares, makes little or no contribution to the productive process.

It should be realized that the ability of stockholders to sell their shares provides a major inducement to the purchase of those shares in the first place. If it were not for the existence of the stock market and its continuous trading in already issued stock, any purchaser of newly issued stock would be faced with the prospect of not being able to sell his stock, or of being able to do so only with great difficulty. Such a prospect would greatly discourage the initial purchase of stock from the issuing corporations and would thus greatly reduce the availability of capital to those corporations. The existence of the stock market and its continuous trading in outstanding shares makes it possible for the individual investor to liquidate his investment at virtually any time, even though the funds initially supplied to the corporation itself may be invested in assets that have a productive life of several decades or more and cannot be recovered from business operations in any less time than that, and, indeed, will most likely be permanently retained by the business enterprise in which they have been invested.

Furthermore, it should be realized that the sale of already issued stock can be, and very often is, the source of funds for investment in the actual physical assets of a business by the individual shareholders who sell their holdings. For example, the owner of a drug store or restaurant who owns stock in IBM or General Motors, say, may very well decide to sell his shares, or use them as collateral on a loan, in order to raise money to expand his own business activities. In this way, the stock market provides a source of funds for investment in physical assets of business through the trading in already out-standing shares.

The determination of the price of stock in the market for already outstanding shares plays a major role in deciding whether or not it is worthwhile for the present stockholders to have their corporation issue additional shares. Other things being equal, the higher is the price of a share of its stock, the smaller is the percentage of the corporation that must be given up in order to raise any given sum of money, and thus the more likely is it that it will be worthwhile for the present stockholders to have the corporation sell additional stock. By the same token, the lower is the price of its stock, the less likely is it to be worthwhile for the present stockholders to have their corporation sell additional shares. For example, if a corporation has 1 million shares of stock outstanding, and the price of its stock is $10 per share, then in order to raise a million dollars through the sale of new stock, it must sell an interest to outsiders that will amount to one-eleventh of itself—i.e., 100,000 shares out of a new total outstanding of 1.1 million shares. If the price of the corporation's stock were $100 per share, however, then it could raise an additional million dollars by selling to outsiders less than 1 percent of itself—i.e., only 10,000 shares out of a new total of 1 million shares plus 10,000 shares. By the same token, if its stock had a market value of only $1 per share, it would have to sell 50 percent of itself in order to raise a million dollars. On this basis, it should be obvious that the stock market plays a decisive role in determining whether or not a corporation will find it worthwhile to issue new stock.

In connection with this point, it must be said that the stock market makes it possible for firms that demonstrate their success to obtain capital at a much faster rate than they could if they had to rely exclusively on the reinvest-ment of their profits. A firm's demonstration of the ability to earn a high rate of profit on its existing capital operates to raise the price of its outstanding shares and thus to make it possible and worthwhile for the firm to obtain substantial additional capital from the sale of additional stock. In this way, the firm can obtain control over larger sums of capital more rapidly than would otherwise be the case. Indeed, if it increases its equity in this way, the firm correspondingly increases its capacity to borrow and can thereby raise still more capital if it wishes. By these means, successful small businesses are enabled to grow into large businesses and play a more important role in the economic system more rapidly than they otherwise could. At the same time, as an important consequence,

they are enabled to challenge the existing large firms all the more rapidly.

Finally, it must be pointed out that the existence of the stock market serves to penalize poor management and to offer a protection against the abuse of stockholders by corporate managements. The effect of poor management, or of the abuse of stockholders, is a low price of the firm's stock relative to the value of the firm's assets. This situation invites an outside takeover of the firm, the firing of its present management, and, very often, the sale of some or all of its assets to other firms which are capable of putting them to better use. Apart from anything else, the mere fact of changing circumstances, and the inabil-ity of many corporate managements to keep pace with the changes, repeatedly necessitates the breakup of ex-isting corporations, as the land sites their facilities oc-cupy and often the facilities themselves and much of their equipment become more useful in other employments than in their present employments.

Regrettably, in the present-day United States, this important function of the stock market, of serving to bring about the redeployment of the physical assets of business firms in different hands and often for different purposes, is threatened by government intervention de-signed to protect incompetent managements from the threat of outside takeovers. With the narrow-minded perspective that is typical of opponents of the free mar-ket, the enemies of corporate takeovers can see only that some existing "jobs" are eliminated. They do not see the new employment opportunities that are created in other firms, accompanying the availability of the capital assets that have been sold to them. They are unaware that the very fact that the assets of a firm are worth more in being sold off than in being retained is virtual proof that their employment elsewhere will be more productive and thus will contribute to a more rapid rate of capital accumula-tion and a higher productivity of labor. They do not even see that corporate takeovers, followed by the selling off of assets, are a powerful remedy for previous ill-conceived mergers, whose existence, along with all other mergers, the enemies of capitalism never tire of denouncing.

3. The Productive Role of Retailing and Wholesaling

The productive contribution of retailing and whole-saling becomes apparent as soon as one realizes that in a division-of-labor society, the supply of every product originates in a great concentration, in the hands of a relatively small number of producers. In order for any benefit to be derived from these supplies, they must be moved into the hands of the vast body of consumers which, from the perspective of any one branch of pro-duction, is constituted by the producers and their dependents in all the other branches of production. Retailing and wholesaling, along with exchange and money, are the means whereby goods are moved in this way.[49] Thus, the existence of retailing and wholesaling is essential to the solution of a problem that exists only in a division-of-labor society, in which the producers of any given item are different individuals than the overwhelming majority of its consumers.

The failure to appreciate the value of retailing and wholesaling rests on the failure to keep in mind the existence of the division of labor and then to approach the subject of production and consumption as though all that were required to consume was physically to produce. In such a view of the economic world, dominated by the image of conditions in a pre-division-of-labor society, it appears that retailing and wholesaling are useless appendages to what really counts: i.e., the mere physical production of goods. On such a view, what is accomplished by retailing and wholesaling appears to be nothing but the addition of "markups" by useless "middlemen" to the prices charged by manufacturers and farmers, which prices are all that the consumers justly ought to be made to pay.

In the reality of a division-of-labor society, however, retailing and wholesaling play an essential role in the benefit derived from physical production. They are responsible for a major reduction in the amount of time and money that would otherwise need to be spent in obtaining goods, and for an equally major increase in the variety and quality of goods available.

In the absence of retailing and wholesaling, either the consumers would have to go to the producers or the producers would have to come to the consumers. The difficulty of the consumers going to the producers is evident if one simply imagines what it would be like to assemble the ingredients of an ordinary breakfast. A person would have to drive out to the countryside to buy bacon, eggs, and milk. And, if he wanted choice among his suppliers, he would have to drive to more than one farm for each item. In all probability the cost just of fuel and wear and tear on his automobile would be far greater than any "markups" added by retailers and wholesalers. In addition, we must consider the fact that all the time he had to spend in such activities would mean that he would have that much less time available either for earning a living or for leisure.

These points would apply even if individual consumers got together and formed groups for the purpose of purchasing supplies. For example, one might imagine a group of neighbors or fellow employees getting together to send representatives to the producers for the purpose of purchasing in bulk and coming back with supplies for all members of the group. They might agree that every

week one of their number would make a series of trips for all of them. They might pool their resources and buy a small truck to be used for this purpose. Perhaps the activity would become the full-time employment of one or two of them. But all of this sort of activity would simply represent consumers' attempting to do for themselves what retailers and wholesalers can do for them with far greater efficiency.

Comparable difficulties would exist if the producers were to attempt to come to the consumers.

In the circumstances of an economy in which towns and cities are surrounded by large numbers of family farms that are relatively unspecialized, the local farmers can regularly bring a wide variety of farm products into the towns and cities and sell them in farmers' markets. However, to the degree that an economic system is characterized by a higher degree of division of labor, this becomes unfeasible. For one thing, the degree of specialization of the various farms and agricultural districts increases, because of the greater efficiencies in production that such specialization achieves. Thus each agricultural district now tends to concentrate on the production of just one or a very few items. For example, one area concentrates on dairy farming, another on growing grain, a third on growing apples, a fourth on raising citrus fruits, and so on. At the same time, because of further efficiencies in production, there is the development of large-scale processing and manufacturing facilities. For example, most of the meat packing and flour milling in the United States now take place in a relatively small number of locations; canned goods, frozen foods, and a wide variety of baked goods, are also produced in plants in a relatively small number of locations. The same is true of clothing and furniture manufacture, automobile and appliance manufacture—of the production of most goods. These developments are incompatible with the existence of any wide range of nearby, local producers. Thus, it is more and more out of the question for the producers to come to the consumers. It would be one thing for a dairy farmer on Long Island to bring his butter and cheese into New York City. It is out of the question for a dairy farmer in Wisconsin to do so—or for a meat packer in Cincinnati or a biscuit manufacturer in Chicago to do so. Even more fantastic would be the prospect of a coffee grower in Brazil attempting to do so. (These difficulties, of course, would apply equally to consumers attempting to go to the producers.)

If products had to meet the requirement of being available directly from the producers, whether at the farm or the factory, or in local producers' markets, the producers for the most part would have to be local, correspondingly small and less efficient, and perhaps altogether incapable of producing the product desired. A possible exception would be cases such as automobiles, in which the items produced were of sufficient value to justify the manufacturer setting up his own specialized distribution network. (In actual practice, however, even in such cases the distribution network is almost always made up of independent retailers, who buy from the manufacturer rather than being part of the manufacturing firm itself. For example, automobile dealers are independent business firms, not part of the automobile companies themselves. This type of arrangement exists because the auto firms and other major manufacturers find it more efficient. They do so for such reasons as not having to invest as much capital of their own as would otherwise be required and because of the greater incentives ownership provides to the dealers.)

Another possible exception to the rule that the producers can no longer come to the consumers is the case of a manufacturer's mail-order business. Mail order in general, however, is a feasible method only in cases in which one does not need to physically examine the specific goods before buying them and can wait a more or less extended period of time for receipt of the goods (which last typically precludes perishable goods other than those sent by express, at a substantially higher cost). In the case of buying by mail order directly from a manufacturer, the additional requirement must be met that the customer is willing to go to the trouble of expending the time and effort to place the particular order, a circumstance which militates against buying any large number of inexpensive items from a host of separate manufacturers. The disproportionately high cost of advertising relatively inexpensive items that are offered singly or together with only a small number of other such items also militates against the use of mail order. Because of these facts, many mail-order businesses are retailers, which carry the merchandize of a large number of manufacturers. This enables the firms to advertise a large number of items at the same time, thereby saving on advertising costs and thus making it possible to charge lower prices for the products. At the same time, it enables the customer to order a variety of items at one time, thereby saving him substantial time and effort, not to mention expense.

Exactly the same advantages that are present in mail-order retailing are present in the more usual form of retailing through stores, plus, of course, the further advantages of being able physically to examine the goods one is buying and, as a rule, to take possession of them immediately. Retailing and wholesaling make it possible for producers to specialize in the production of an extremely narrow range of goods, such as just paper clips or just rubber bands, just spinach or just lettuce. Because of retailing and wholesaling, the producers of such isolated goods avoid the enormous wastes that would be entailed in attempting to advertise and sell them one at time to the consumers. They avoid such absurdities as having to place newspaper ads describing the availability and price just of paper clips or just of spinach, and of having to have a special sales representative and rent a special space to sell just this one item.

This discussion provides the appropriate basis on which to judge retailing and wholesaling. True enough, the costs of retailing and wholesaling and the profits of retailers and wholesalers must be added to the prices charged by manufacturers and farmers to arrive at the prices charged to the ultimate consumers. But, in the great majority of cases, the prices charged by manufacturers and farmers at their factories or farms are far from the total of what consumers would actually have to pay if the services of retailers and wholesalers were not present. In the great majority of cases, the consumers would then have to pay an addition to the prices charged by manufacturers and farmers at their production sites that would be far higher than the addition attributable to retailing and wholesaling. They would have to pay an addition that would cover the costs either of their inefficiently going to the producers or of the producers inefficiently coming to them. And, of course, in most cases, the prices charged by the producers even at their production sites would have to be substantially higher, because of the higher costs of production when markets must be local and small and the volume of production correspondingly limited; and, in still many other cases, the products would simply be completely unavailable. Thus, in comparison with the alternatives that would exist in the absence of retailing and wholesaling, it is obvious that retailing and wholesaling reduce the cost of goods to consumers, not increase them.

Retailing and wholesaling represent division of labor in the process of distribution. Instead of each group of consumers having to have a few volunteers or one or two hired hands, instead of each producer having to have his own distribution network—instead of the enormously wasteful duplication of labor and facilities that these things would entail—a relatively small number of retailers and wholesalers bring together in convenient locations to buyers the goods of an enormous variety of producers, and almost always at a far lower cost than would be possible for the consumers or producers acting on their own. A retail store frequently carries the products of dozens or even hundreds of different manufacturers or farmers, and usually of competing producers of the same product. Every such store means the saving of expense to consumers of not having to send their own purchasing agents, trucks, and so forth out to the dozens or hundreds of manufacturers or farmers whose products the retail store carries. It means the saving of expense to producers of not having to send out their own salesmen and establish their own distribution outlets wherever they sought to sell their goods. Each retail store almost always buys in larger quantity, greater variety, and more efficiently than could any group of consumers. And it holds the products it buys in constant readiness to meet the demands of its customers at their convenience. At the same time, the existence of retail stores (and retail mail-order houses) makes it possible for producers to reach far more consumers than they could possible do on their own, and to do so far more economically than they could do on their own. Thus, as I say, retailing and wholesaling reduce the cost and increase the variety of goods available to consumers, as well as make them available far more conveniently.

A few special words need to be said in connection with the economies achieved by the existence of wholesalers. The existence of wholesalers permits a radical reduction in the number of transactions that would otherwise have to exist between retailers and manufacturers. Imagine, for example, the existence of a thousand retailers in a given territory who each carry the products of a hundred different manufacturers—for example, small newsstands that sell cigarettes, candy, paperback books, magazines, and a variety of other such items. If each of these retailers had to deal with each of the manufacturers, there would be a hundred thousand different transactions. There would be a hundred thousand combinations of salesmen's visits, letters, phone calls, and so on. Each transaction would be for a relatively small amount of merchandise.

Now, in contrast, imagine the existence of a wholesaler, who stands between the retailers and manufacturers. In this case, there need be only a thousand large transactions between the retailers and the wholesaler, in which each retailer orders the goods of the hundred manufacturers all at the same time from the wholesaler's representative, and an additional hundred very large transactions between the wholesaler and the manufacturers, in which the wholesaler orders all at the same time merchandise from each manufacturer that is sufficient for all one thousand retailers. This means a total of only eleven hundred combinations of salesmen's visits, letters, phone calls, and so on, instead of a hundred thousand. And this, in turn, means a major reduction in transactions costs, and probably also in manufacturing costs, insofar as it permits manufacturers more easily to estimate the volume of production they need to prepare for. It also means that merchandise can be stored much more economically. The wholesaler can store merchandise in a warehouse, in a low-rent district, rather than each retailer having to store substantial amounts of merchandise on his premises, which are typically in a higher-rent district, or in his own separate storage facility, which would entail further diseconomies of the kind associated with unnecessary duplication.

It is necessary to consider the complaints often voiced about the seeming injustice that exists when the retail price of a good rises at the very same time that the price received by the farmers or manufacturers who physically make the good falls. For example, the retail price of eggs or potatoes may go up at the very same time that the price of eggs or potatoes received by farmers goes down.

Despite the incredulity often expressed by the news media over such events, there is actually nothing in them that should be surprising or that implies that retailers or wholesalers are somehow exploiting the producers and consumers. This becomes clear when it is realized that the price of a good to its producer constitutes only a portion of the total costs of bringing the good to the consumer. Particularly in the case of inexpensive bulky goods, like potatoes, or goods which require special handling and packaging, like eggs, the price of the good to the producer may well account for less than half of the total cost of bringing the good to the consumer, because other costs, such as transportation and packaging, play a such a large role.

In such cases, even though from a strictly physical point of view the product is hardly changed when it reaches the consumer from what it was when it left the producer, the price to the producer represents no greater proportion of the total cost than, say, the price of steel represents in the cost of an automobile. In such cases, a fall in the price of the good to the producer may very well be accompanied by a rise in other components of its total cost that are more than offsetting and thus raise its total cost and necessitate a rise in the retail price of the good. On the basis of the uniformity-of-profit principle, it can be stated with certainty that reductions in the price of goods to producers accompanied by increases in the price of those goods to the ultimate consumers cannot in any circumstances lastingly serve to increase the profits of retailers and wholesalers to a point significantly above what corresponds to the general or average rate of profit. Any increase in the profitability of retailing or wholesaling above the general level would provide the incentive and means for increased investment in those lines and thus a reduction in their profitability back to the general level.[50]

It should be realized that any notion of a constant tendency for prices to producers to fall while retail prices rise is an illusion resulting from continuous inflation of the money supply coupled with the greater volatility of many producer prices in comparison with retail prices. The continuous inflation of the money supply results in a tendency for all prices to rise. Many producer prices, however (particularly those of agricultural commodities), being highly volatile, frequently rise more rapidly than retail prices. These more rapid increases in producer prices are then followed by periods in which producer prices fall back, while retail prices go on rising. The periods of more rapid increases in producer prices are strangely overlooked by those who complain of the fall in producer prices. Over time, there is no tendency for the rise in retail prices to outstrip the rise in producer prices—unless, for some improbable reason, at the same time that inflation goes on, improvements in the productivity of labor at the producer level continually outstrip improvements in the productivity of labor in retailing and wholesaling and thereby retard the rise in producer prices relative to the rise in prices at the retail level. Even in this case, of course, there would be no tendency for the profits of retailing and wholesaling to rise permanently relative to those of any other segment of the economic system.

4. The Productive Role of Advertising

The fact that in a division-of-labor society the individual produces or helps to produce just one or, at most, a very small number of goods, and is supplied by others with almost everything that he consumes, also underlies the productive role of advertising. Since, in almost every instance, the consumers are separate, distinct persons from the producers, they do not possess any direct, automatic knowledge of what goods are available to them, or of where and from whom and on what terms they are available. The productive role of advertising is to supply this knowledge. In the absence of advertising, the resulting lack of knowledge would be equivalent to a radical reduction in the physical amount of production. This is because the goods and services that people would then be unaware of might as well simply not have been produced, inasmuch as they would be incapable of doing people any actual good in such circumstances.

Furthermore, even when people already know what goods are available and where and on what terms, advertising still has the effect of increasing the amount of benefit that is derived from the same amount of physical production. Advertising accomplishes this by increasing the awareness people have of the availability of various goods and by thus inducing them to try goods they would not otherwise have tried, or tried as soon, which they then discover that they prefer to goods they were previously consuming and would otherwise simply have gone on consuming.

To illustrate this point, we can consider precisely the kind of case that is frequently advanced in order to deny the value of advertising. For example, toothpaste brand

A begins to advertise and, as a result, attracts customers who previously used brands *B, C, D*, etc.[51] Perhaps, because of the increase in its sales volume, the unit cost of manufacturing brand *A* falls, thereby offsetting, or even more than offsetting, any additional unit cost incurred as the result of the advertising. Now, however, brands *B, C, D*, etc., begin to advertise. And they win customers from brand *A*. Even if, as the critics of advertising assume, each brand ends up with essentially the same number of customers when all of them advertise as when none of them advertised, and now has higher total costs as the result of the additional cost incurred in order to advertise, and thus must correspondingly raise its price—even so, advertising still provides a major benefit.

This is because now, as the result of advertising, large numbers of individuals use brands that they like better than the brands they had been using and would have gone on using in the absence of advertising. Even though brand *A* may end up with no more customers in toto than it had to begin with, the customers it has gained prefer brand *A* to the various other brands, while the customers it has lost prefer the brands to which they have switched, to brand *A*. In other words, even though every brand may end up with the same number of customers it had in the first place, the customers for each brand are now *different individuals*, who are better satisfied. In this way, because of advertising, there is an increase in the amount of benefit derived from the same physical amount of production.

In this particular case, of course, the selling price of the product would end up being somewhat higher because of the increase in total cost as the result of advertising. But this is no more of an objection against advertising than it would be an objection against the addition of flavoring or any other improvement in toothpaste, such as improved cavity-fighting capabilities, which when they were added increased the total cost and thus the price. It is no objection because the higher cost and higher price are necessary in order to provide worthwhile benefits.

Because of the extent of the ignorance surrounding advertising, it must be pointed out that any addition to total cost that advertising might be responsible for is always strictly limited. It is never the case that producers can go on increasing their advertising budgets endlessly, with the first to make the latest increase being spurred on by the prospect of enlarging his sales volume at the expense of his rivals who have not yet made that increase, with the ultimate result being an endless rise in total costs and prices for products finally consisting of little more than advertising puffery.[52]

There is such a thing as diminishing returns to advertising. Once a certain degree of awareness of a product is established, additional advertising serves to increase awareness less and less. Any producer spending excessively for advertising will find himself at the mercy of other producers, who advertise adequately, but less than he does. This is because these producers can then advertise their lower prices, made possible by lower total costs resulting from the avoidance of excessive advertising.

Despite the existence of cases in which advertising provides important benefits in conjunction with a rise in the cost and price of products, its usual effect is to *reduce* prices. It does so by encouraging new competition and the introduction of new and improved products. It encourages new competition by enabling new entrants into an industry to gain exposure in the eyes of the consuming public. In the absence of extensive advertising of new products, people's main guide to what to consume would be personal experience, which necessarily would favor the established firms, since they are the only existing firms with which people have had experience. Extensive advertising, however, allows new entrants into an industry to gain entree into people's awareness alongside of the established firms.[53]

The effectiveness of advertising in this regard is closely related to the fact that large-scale advertising is usually equivalent to a firm posting a bond with the public, as it were, guaranteeing the value of its product. The equivalence to a bond is based on the fact that advertising usually pays only if, after it induces people to try the product, the product itself is good enough to induce them to buy it again and to recommend it to others. It generally does not pay to advertise products which people will buy only once and then advise others against buying. Products which turn out not to represent a sufficient benefit to the public to induce repeat purchases and recommendations to others usually end up causing a loss of the advertising budgets expended on them.[54] On this basis, people are right to place confidence in highly advertised products. The advertising not only calls the product to their attention, but also signifies that the producer is willing to risk his money in the conviction that they will like his product.

Advertising reduces prices and promotes the introduction of new and improved products by shortening the period of time required for a product to gain a mass market and thus achieve the economies of large-scale production. In the absence of advertising, good products, it is true, can eventually gain a mass market on the strength of word-of-mouth recommendations; but advertising allows this to happen sooner.

This shortening of the period of time required for a product to establish its market, which advertising achieves, is the more important, the greater are the outlays that must be made in paying for such things as the research and development costs of a product. The longer the period of time that must elapse between the making of these outlays and their recovery in the sale of the product, the greater must be the sums ultimately recovered, in order to provide the going rate of return on the capital invested in these outlays.

For example, if $10 million must be invested in outlays for research and development, and 10 years must elapse before those outlays can be recovered in the sale of the product, then, with a going rate of return on capital of 10 percent per year, the sales revenue that needs to be brought in to compensate for these outlays is approximately $26 million—i.e., $10 million times 1.1^{10}. If, on the other hand, advertising can secure a mass market for the product within, say, 1 year, then the sales revenue necessary to compensate for the research and development outlays is only $11 million—that is, $10 million times 1.1^1. In this way, advertising reduces the price that it is necessary for a product to sell for in order to yield the going rate of return on its research and development outlays. It thus encourages the making of research and development outlays and the introduction of new products.

In the absence of advertising, there would be products that it would not pay to develop, even if they had the potential eventually to achieve a mass market. This would be because the time required to achieve that mass market would then be so great that the ultimate reduction in manufacturing costs made possible by a mass market would be offset by the increased amount of profit required to provide the going rate of return on the capital invested in the product's research and development outlays. In such cases, a mass market would never actually materialize because the price of the product necessary to provide profitability even in a mass market would be too high for the existence of such a market. In greatly reducing the time required to achieve a mass market, and thus the price that is necessary in order for a product to be profitable in such a market, advertising makes possible the profitable existence of such markets.

In general, and to repeat, advertising promotes research and development outlays and the introduction of the new products that depend on them, by reducing the extent to which such outlays need to be recovered in the price of the product. It does so by means of establishing a larger market sooner rather than later, thereby permitting the recovery of such outlays to take place sooner rather than later and thus with the accompaniment of a correspondingly smaller amount of profit.

Finally, it must be stressed that advertising never dictates what people consume. Advertising influences consumption only in the limited sense that it can make people aware of things that they then decide—on the basis of their own needs and their own experience with the things advertised—that they like or do not like. Successful advertising is advertising that makes people aware of things which have the power to serve needs that preexist in them. If what is advertised serves no preexisting need in the consumer, then it has no foundation for success.

This explains the well-known fact that it pays to advertise extensively only products that are capable of generating some significant sales even with relatively little advertising. These are the products that advertising can be effective in helping to sell. For example, publishers increase the advertising budgets of those titles that do best with their initial advertising budgets; those are the titles that advertising can help most.

The rule for success is to advertise products of the kind that when tried will be liked and recommended by the buyers. The advertisers have no power over what it is that when tried will be liked and recommended. The advertising of automobiles and electric light in competition with the horse and buggy and candles was highly successful, because people had only to try these new goods in order to appreciate their merit. On the other hand, no amount of advertising of the horse and buggy and candles could have maintained the demand for those goods in the face of the competition of the automobile and electric light.[55]

The notion that the consumers simply do what the advertisers tell them implies an inability to recognize any objective foundation in the choices consumers make. It suggests an intellectual void on the part of the critic of advertising, of such dimensions as to imply that he is an utter stranger to life in the modern world, incapable of understanding the most elementary connections between modern material goods and his own life and well-being.[56]

PART C

BUSINESSMEN AND CAPITALISTS: CLASSICAL ECONOMICS VERSUS THE MARXIAN EXPLOITATION THEORY

1. The Association Between Classical Economics and the Marxian Exploitation Theory

The leading source of the denial of the productive role of businessmen and capitalists and of the hostility to profits and interest is the Marxian exploitation theory. The essential claim of this theory is that all income naturally and rightfully belongs to the wage earners, but that under capitalism the wage earners receive only bare, minimum subsistence, while everything over and above this is expropriated by the capitalist exploiters in the form of profits, interest, and land rent, or, in the terminology of Marx, "surplus-value."

In his development of the exploitation theory (which I will describe in detail in Part A of Chapter 14), Marx employs two leading doctrines that are closely identified with classical economics: namely, the labor theory of value and the iron law of wages. I have already referred to the iron law of wages in connection with my discussion of Ricardo's theory of land rent. It is the doctrine that, broadly speaking, asserts an inescapable connection between wages and minimum subsistence. The labor theory of value claims that the prices of commodities are determined by the respective quantities of labor required to produce them. I will explain both of these doctrines, in the form in which they were propounded by the classical economists, at length, in Sections 4 and 5 of this part. In particular, I will focus on the views of Smith and Ricardo, the two foremost representatives of the classical school, to whom Marx is assumed to be particularly indebted. On the basis of my discussions in these sections, it will be obvious later on, in Chapter 14, that what Marx meant by the labor theory of value and the iron law of wages are two very different sets of ideas than what the classical economists meant, and are in fact gross distortions of what the classical economists meant.

Nevertheless, mainly because of the prominent role played by "the labor theory of value" and "the iron law of wages," however different their actual content in the two systems of thought, classical economics is almost universally assumed to lead inexorably to the Marxian exploitation theory.

My reason for writing this part, and presenting it here, is that subsequent chapters in this book depend vitally on leading doctrines I have taken over from the classical economists and reintroduced in a modernized form, doctrines which have been abandoned or forgotten precisely because of the mistaken belief that classical economics inevitably leads to the Marxian exploitation theory. As a result, in order to demonstrate the consistency of my profound intellectual indebtedness to classical economics with my unswerving support of capitalism, it is necessary for me to explain the actual nature of the relationship between classical economics and the Marxian exploitation theory, which, I will show, is ultimately one of the most intense opposition.

Consistent with the ultimate opposition that I will demonstrate between classical economics and the exploitation theory, is the fact that I have already reintroduced two abandoned or forgotten doctrines of classical economics with very positive results for the defense of capitalism: in Chapters 6 and 10, the role of cost of production in determining the prices of most manufactured or processed goods, and, in Part A of this chapter, the essential role of moneymaking in productive activity and the various concepts pertaining to what constitutes production or consumption.[57] My demonstration that considerations of cost of production rather than elasticity of demand are decisive in price determination under the freedom of competition, played an essential role in my refutation of the profoundly anticapitalistic marginal-revenue, cartel, and pure-and-perfect-competition doctrines in Chapter 10. My elaboration of the concepts pertaining to the connection between moneymaking and productive activity earlier in this chapter have served, among other things, to demonstrate that government spending and government borrowing are inherently consumption, rather than any part of the productive process. This, of course, all by itself implies the need for strict limits on government spending and for the outright prohibition of government borrowing.

Nevertheless, it is certainly true that the Marxian exploitation theory is largely the product of major errors in classical economics, particularly, as I will show, in the writings of Adam Smith. The relationship between classical economics and the exploitation theory represents a tangle of irony and tragedy.

One irony is that while various errors and confusions in classical economics really did contribute to the exploitation theory, the most fundamental and important of these errors and confusions have gone unnoticed and unidentified. These are the errors and confusions pertaining to *the conceptual framework of the exploitation theory,* which assumes that all income due to the performance of labor is wages and that profits are a deduction from what is naturally wages. They have gone unnoticed and unidentified because the validity of this framework is taken for granted—as being literally unexceptionable and therefore unobjectionable. It is assumed to be correct by the opponents of Marx as much as by Marx; this includes Böhm-Bawerk, the leading critic of the exploitation theory, as will be obvious once I have explained the essentials of his critique of the exploitation theory.

A second and greater irony is that the basis for demolishing both the conceptual framework of the exploitation theory and later the whole of the specific substance of the exploitation theory, is provided precisely by essential elements of classical economics. That is, classical economics makes it possible to understand such propositions as why profits, not wages, are the original and primary form of income and that precisely because of the work of businessmen and capitalists, wages can rise out of all connection with minimum subsistence—literally without limit.[58] I will venture to say, not by the end of Chapter

14, but by the end of the very next section of this chapter, the reader will be able to see how classical economics can be placed so squarely in opposition to the Marxian exploitation theory as literally to serve as the latter's nemesis rather than as its foundation. (Of course, I do not maintain that the classical economists were themselves aware of the implications I am claiming for their doctrines. The development and demonstration of these implications are major accomplishments for which I myself must claim original credit.)

The tragedy of the relationship between classical economics and the exploitation theory has not only been that errors and confusions in classical economics have supported the exploitation theory and thereby the assault on capitalism and advancement of the cause of socialism. That would have been bad enough. The further tragedy and irony has been that because this support was perceived as necessary and inescapable—as based on the essential nature of classical economics—the opponents of the exploitation theory—that is, the defenders of capitalism from the late nineteenth century on, who had the most to gain from the knowledge provided by classical economics—felt obliged to discard virtually the whole of it insofar as it could not immediately be validated on the basis of the neoclassical principle of diminishing marginal utility, or otherwise independently of classical economics' basic framework.

Thus, along with "the labor theory of value" and the "iron law of wages," they discarded such further features of classical economics as the wages-fund doctrine and its corollary that savings and capital are the source of almost all spending in the economic system. (The wages-fund doctrine held that at any given time there is a determinate total expenditure of funds for the payment of wages in the economic system, and that the wages of the employees of business firms are paid by businessmen and capitalists, out of capital, which is the result of saving; not by consumers in the purchase of consumers' goods.[59]) Two generations later, the abandonment of the wages-fund doctrine and with it, classical economics' perspective on saving and capital, made possible the acceptance of Keynesianism and the policy of inflation, deficits, and ever expanding government spending. In similarly paradoxical fashion, and with just about the same time lag, the abandonment of the classical doctrine that cost of production, rather than supply and demand, is the direct (though not the ultimate) determinant of the prices of most manufactured or processed goods led to the promulgation of the doctrines of "pure and perfect competition," "oligopoly," "monopolistic competition," and "administered prices," with their implicit call for a policy of radical antitrust or outright nationalizations to "curb the abuses of big business." Thus, along these two further paths, the errors of classical economics in support of the exploitation theory have served in the assault on capitalism and to advance the cause of socialism. But this time, it was with the implicit support of those who had abandoned classical economics because of its service in the advancement of socialism, and who now, precisely because of that abandonment, were themselves making possible the advancement of socialism, however much they may have believed themselves to be incapable of acting in such a destructive way.

Indeed, so strong has been the conviction on the part of the defenders of capitalism that classical economics is permeated with support for Marxism, that even to suggest such a classical doctrine as that cost of production can be a direct determinant of price, is to invite one's own censure for allegedly being sympathetic to Marxism—as well as for allegedly being ignorant of all that economics has taught on the subject of prices since 1870. Not surprisingly, in the great majority of cases, this hostility to classical economics on the part of the defenders of capitalism has kept them from any serious study of it.

The essential purpose of this part is to show how classical economics can easily cast off all the aspects of it which contributed to the exploitation theory, while leaving all of its essential and valuable features that were abandoned or forgotten because of its association with the exploitation theory, not only undamaged, but placed in a condition in which they can serve radically to advance the cause of sound, procapitalist economics in the present day. In effect, the purpose of this part is to rescue the classical-economics baby from the Marxist bath water with which he was thrown away, and then, to the extent I have not already done so, raise him up to be the great procapitalist fighting man that it is in his nature to become.

What precise features of classical economics need revision, or outright discarding, will become clear in the next four sections of this part, that is, Sections 2–5. The first of these, a critical analysis of Adam Smith's support of the conceptual framework of the exploitation theory, will go a long way toward proving the claim I made in the Introduction to this book that "classical economics makes possible a far more fundamental and thoroughgoing critique of the exploitation theory than that provided by Böhm-Bawerk and the Austrian school." Based largely on the results of correcting Smith's errors, Section 3 will name and, to the extent necessary, describe the five major aspects of classical economics in need of revision or discarding in order to transform it into the nemesis of the exploitation theory. Two of these aspects, the labor theory of value and the iron law of wages, will then be examined separately and in detail in Sections 4 and 5 of this part.

2. Correcting the Errors of Adam Smith: A Classical-Based Critique of the Conceptual Framework of the Exploitation Theory

The ideas of Adam Smith on the subject of productive activity are among the best and the worst in the literature of economics. As previously shown, Smith's *Wealth of Nations* provides a major contribution to the understanding of the concept of productive activity in its grasp of the essential connection between productive activity and moneymaking and the role of this connection in the distinction between production and consumption.[60] Thus, it is not surprising that Smith is the enemy of government spending and government borrowing and that historically his views have been a leading source of fiscal conservatism.[61]

But in his discussion of other aspects of the concept of productive activity, Smith's errors are monumental and overwhelming. For in truth, Smith can justly be called the father of the Marxian exploitation theory. Decades before the birth of Marx, he proclaimed the view of businessmen and capitalists, and of capitalism as a system, as parasitically feeding off the labor of the wage earners. Adam Smith, who, more than any other economist, is viewed by the public as the champion of capitalism, was thus in fact the father of the idea that capitalism deserves to be overthrown and replaced by socialism.

Smith's Confusion Between Labor and Wage Earning

A hint of Smith's errors in support of the exploitation theory is present even in one of the passages I quoted favorably in the first part of this chapter: "Thus the labour of the manufacturer adds, generally, to the value of the materials which he works upon, that of his own maintenance, and of his master's profit." There is a clear suggestion in these words that the labor of the manual worker creates the employer's profit.

This notion is propounded much more forcefully in earlier portions of *The Wealth of Nations*. There, Smith unmistakably expounds the view that the only productive parties in the economic system are wage earners. He clearly regards businessmen, capitalists, and landowners as having no productive function, and as existing as parasites upon the labor of the wage earners.

He begins with the—essentially correct—view that human labor is the fundamental productive agent: "Labour was the first price, the original purchase money that was paid for all things. It was not by gold or by silver, but by labour that all the wealth of the world was originally purchased . . . ."[62] He then goes on to regard *labor and wage earning as synonymous,* and to hold that *all income which is due to the performance of labor is wages, and that all who work are wage earners.*

He considers and quickly rejects the possibility that profits might be an income attributable to the performance of labor by businessmen and capitalists:

> The profits of stock, it may perhaps be thought, are only a different name for the wages of a particular sort of labour, the labour of inspection and direction. They are, however, altogether different, are regulated by quite sufficient principles, and bear no proportion to the quantity, the hardship, or the ingenuity of this supposed labour of inspection and direction. They are regulated altogether by the value of the stock employed, and are greater or smaller in proportion to the extent of this stock. Let us suppose, for example, that in some particular place, where the common annual profits of manufacturing stock are ten per cent. there are two different manufactures, in each of which twenty workmen are employed at the rate of fifteen pounds a year each, or at the expence of three hundred a year in each manufactory. Let us suppose too, that the coarse materials annually wrought up in the one cost only seven hundred pounds, while the finer materials in the other cost seven thousand. The capital annually employed in the one will in this case amount only to one thousand pounds; whereas that employed in the other will amount to seven thousand three hundred pounds. At the rate of ten per cent. therefore, the undertaker of the one will expect an yearly profit of about one hundred pounds only; while that of the other will expect about seven hundred and thirty pounds. But though their profits are so very different, their labour of inspection and direction may be either altogether or very nearly the same.[63]

Thus, Smith believed, as have so many economists who have come after him, that because profits vary with the amount of capital employed, they cannot be caused by the labor of the businessmen or capitalists—that, instead, they are caused in one way or another by capital itself. I shall deal with this idea shortly. But even here it must be stated that it is blatantly false to maintain, as did Smith, that profits "bear no proportion to the quantity, the hardship, or the ingenuity of this supposed labour of inspection and direction."

The rate of profit is *not* the same for all enterprises. The amount of profit a firm earns is by no means proportional merely to the quantity of capital it employs. The *ingenuity* of the "supposed labour of inspection and direction" is decisive. Some firms have losses, because insufficient ingenuity is supplied. Others earn an extraordinarily high rate of profit, because more than the ordinary degree of ingenuity is supplied. It is equally true, contrary to Smith, that profits vary with the *quantity and hardship* of the "labour of inspection and direction." Those firms whose owners "burn the midnight oil," as the saying goes, generally do better than those whose owners take a more relaxed attitude. But even if all firms did earn the same rate of profit on their capital, their profits, as we shall see, would still be the result of what Smith calls the "supposed labour of inspection and direction."

It is even true that profits vary with the quantity and hardship of the businessmen's and capitalists' ordinary physical labor. This latter variation is imperceptible in the case of large firms, but it is very evident in the case of small concerns. The neighborhood hardware store, for example, typically earns a much higher rate of profit than a large corporation, precisely because the quantity and hardship of the owner's physical labor bulks so large in its operations. In all such cases, accountants report the full income of the businessmen and capitalists as profit, and then economists, applying the doctrines of opportunity cost and imputed income, arbitrarily deny that that portion of the profit which obviously does correspond to the owner's labor *is* profit. They call it wages insofar as wages are what the businessman would receive if he performed similar labor for someone else, or would have to pay to someone else to have similar labor performed for him. Only by first subtracting from profit what in fact is a part of profit, is the obvious variation of profit with the physical labor of businessmen and capitalists eliminated.

The Conceptual Framework of the Exploitation Theory

Having dismissed the possibility that profits could be a labor income, and regarding whatever income might be due to labor as necessarily being wages, Smith arrives at what I consider to be the essential conceptual framework of the exploitation theory. This framework is *the belief that wages are the original and primary form of income, from which profits and all other nonwage incomes emerge as a deduction with the coming of capitalism and businessmen and capitalists.* The framework and its supporting beliefs easily lead to the assertion of the wage earner's right to the whole produce or to its full value. Thus, Adam Smith opens his chapter on wages, with the following words:

> The produce of labour constitutes the natural recompence or wages of labour.
>
> In that original state of things, which precedes both the appropriation of land and the accumulation of stock, the whole produce of labour belongs to the labourer. He has neither landlord nor master to share with him.
>
> Had this state continued, the wages of labour would have augmented with all those improvements in its productive powers, to which the division of labour gives occasion.

And he continues, a little further on:

> But this original state of things, in which the labourer enjoyed the whole produce of his own labour, could not last beyond the first introduction of the appropriation of land and the accumulation of stock. It was at an end, therefore, long before the most considerable improvements were made in the productive powers of labour, and it would be to no purpose to trace further what might have been its effects upon the recompence or wages of labour.

As soon as land becomes private property, the landlord demands a share of almost all the produce which the labourer can either raise or collect from it. His rent makes the first deduction from the produce of the labour which is employed upon the land.

It seldom happens that the person who tills the ground has the wherewithal to maintain himself till he reaps the harvest. His maintenance is generally advanced to him from the stock of a master, the farmer who employs him, and who would have no interest to employ him, unless he was to share in the produce of his labour, or unless his stock was to be replaced to him with a profit. This profit makes a second deduction from the produce of the labour which is employed upon land.

The produce of almost all other labour is liable to the like deduction of profit. In all arts and manufactures the greater part of the workmen stand in need of a master to advance them the materials of their work, and their wages and maintenance till it be compleated. He shares in the produce of their labour, or in the value which it adds to the materials on which it is bestowed; and in this share consists his profit.[64]

In these passages, Smith actually advances two views that upon examination are astonishing, and which I shall immediately consider in the next two subsections.

Smith's Failure to See the Productive Role of Businessmen and Capitalists and of the Private Ownership of Land

First, he advances the view that the division of labor, and the consequent rise in the productivity of labor, has no connection with the activities of businessmen and capitalists, nor with the institution of private property in land, and might have developed just as well in their absence. This is the meaning of the passage just quoted, "Had this state continued, [i.e., the absence of the appropriation of land and the accumulation of 'stock'—viz., capital], the wages of labour would have augmented with all those improvements in its productive powers, to which the division of labour gives occasion."

In this and the next passage previously quoted, Smith expresses the belief that the only effect of the activities of businessmen and capitalists and of the existence of private ownership of land is that it denies to the wage earners the ability to keep the whole produce of their labor or its full value. He appears totally unaware of all the ways in which the division of labor vitally depends on the activities of businessmen and capitalists and thus could not have developed without them—namely, on their function of creating, coordinating, and improving the efficiency of the division of labor.[65] He appears equally unaware of the vital contribution to the division of labor made by the institution of private ownership of land, which was demonstrated in earlier portions of this book.[66] Indeed, he is particularly harsh in his views of landowners. He writes:

As soon as the land of any country has all become private property, the landlords, like all other men, love to reap where they have never sowed, and demand a rent even for its natural produce. The wood of the forest, the grass of the field, and all the natural fruits of the earth, which, when land was in common, cost the labourer only the trouble of gathering them, come, even to him, to have an additional price fixed upon them. He must then pay for the license to gather them; and must give up to the landlord a portion of what his labour either collects or produces. This portion, or what comes to the same thing, the price of this portion, constitutes the rent of land, and in the price of the greater part of commodities makes a third component part.[67]

In this passage, Smith completely overlooks the incalculable contribution to the productivity of labor in agriculture and mining made by the incentives to efficiency and capital accumulation that private ownership and the security of private property provide. He overlooks the fact that the development of the division of labor itself—insofar as it depends on labor being made available for industry and commerce—depends on the rise in the productivity of labor in agriculture and mining brought about on this foundation. In the absence of private ownership of land and the rise in the productivity of labor it brings about in agriculture and mining, the manpower would simply be unavailable for the development of any significant division of labor in industry and commerce, because almost all workers would be required for the production of food.

Smith's error here rests perhaps on a confusion of the privileged position of the British landed aristocracy of his day, which enjoyed a virtual sinecure through such means as entail legislation and protective tariffs, with that of genuine private landowners who possess full rights of ownership and are subject to the full freedom of competition. Otherwise, it is extremely difficult to understand how he could see as the essential consequence of private ownership the charging of prices for what had previously been free, rather than the enormous improvement in the land and its productive powers. This is as naïve an error as it is possible to make with respect to private ownership of land.[68]

The Primacy-of-Wages Doctrine

The second, possibly even more astonishing notion that Smith advances in the passages quoted above is what I call the primacy-of-wages doctrine. This is the doctrine that in a precapitalist economy—the "early and rude state of society"—in which workers simply produce and sell commodities, and do not buy in order to sell, the incomes the workers receive are wages. Wages are the original income, according to Smith. All income in the precapitalist society is supposed to be wages, and no income is supposed to be profit, according to Smith, because workers are the only recipients of income. At the same time, of course, Smith advances the corollary doctrine that profit emerges only with the coming of capitalism and businessmen and capitalists, and is a deduction from what is naturally and rightfully wages.

The primacy-of-wages doctrine and the notion that profits and the other nonwage incomes are a deduction from what is naturally and rightfully wages constitute the conceptual framework of the exploitation theory. They are the starting point for Marx's detailed development of the exploitation theory.

In a precapitalist economy, production, says Marx, is characterized by the sequence C-M-C. In this state of affairs, a worker produces a commodity C, sells it for money M, and then buys other commodities C. In this state of affairs, there is no exploitation, for there are no profits, no "surplus-value"; all income is, supposedly, wages. Surplus-value—profit—emerges only with the development of capitalism, according to Marx. Here the sequence M-C-M′ applies. Under this sequence, the capitalist expends a sum of money M in buying materials and machinery and in paying wages. A commodity C is produced, which is then sold for a larger sum of money, $M′$, than was expended in making it. The difference between the money the capitalist expends and the money he receives for the product is his profit or surplus-value.[69]

Profits, then, according to both Smith and Marx, come into existence only with capitalism, and are a deduction from what naturally and rightfully belongs to the wage earners.

This is not yet the exploitation theory itself, only the conceptual framework of the exploitation theory. The exploitation theory proper, of course, builds on two further doctrines, also largely supplied by Adam Smith—with a major assist from David Ricardo—and then grossly distorted by Marx: namely, the labor theory of value and the "iron law of wages."

A full critique of the exploitation theory, to be sure, needs to deal both with the labor theory of value and with the iron law of wages, and ours shall do so in due course. First, however, what it is essential to show is the enormity of the errors involved in the conceptual framework of the exploitation theory—in the doctrines of the primacy of wages and of the deduction of profits from wages.

A Rebuttal to Smith and Marx Based on Classical Economics: Profits, Not Wages, as the Original and Primary Form of Income

As indicated, classical economics itself provides the basis for demonstrating the enormous errors in the conceptual framework of the exploitation theory. Classical economics implies that it is false to claim that wages are the original form of income and that profits are a deduction from wages. This becomes apparent as soon as we define our terms along classical lines:

"Profit" is the excess of receipts from the sale of products over the money costs of producing them—over, it must be repeated, *the money costs* of producing them.

A "capitalist" is one who buys in order subsequently to sell for a profit. (A capitalist is one who makes productive expenditures.)

"Wages" are money paid in exchange for the performance of labor—not for the products of labor, but for the performance of labor itself.

On the basis of these definitions, it follows that if there are merely workers producing and selling their products, the money which they receive in the sale of their products is *not* wages. "Demand for commodities," to quote John Stuart Mill, "is not demand for labour."[70] In buying commodities, one does not pay wages, and in selling commodities, one does not receive wages. What one pays and receives in the purchase and sale of commodities is not wages but *product sales revenues.*

Thus, in the precapitalist economy imagined by Smith and Marx, all income recipients in the process of production are workers. But the incomes of those workers are not wages. They are, in fact, *profits.* Indeed, *all* income earned in producing products for sale in the precapitalist economy is profit or "surplus-value"; no income earned in producing products for sale in such an economy is wages. For not only do the workers of a precapitalist economy earn product sales revenues rather than wages, but also those workers have *zero* money costs of production to deduct from those sales revenues.

They have zero money costs precisely because they have not acted as capitalists. They have not bought anything in order to make possible their sales revenues, and thus they have no prior outlays of money to deduct as costs from their sales revenues. Having made no productive expenditures, they have no money costs.

The profit-difference between sales revenues and zero money costs of production is the full magnitude of the sales revenues. If, for example, one sells a product for $1,000 and has costs of $500, resulting from previous outlays of $500 made in order to bring in the sales revenues, then one's profit is $500. If one sells a product for $1,000 and has costs of only $100, resulting from previous outlays of only $100 made in order to bring in the sales revenues, then one's profit is $900. If, going further, one has sales of $1,000 and costs merely of $10, resulting from previous outlays merely of $10 to bring in the sales, then one's profit is $990. If, going still further, one has sales of $1,000 and costs of just $1, resulting from previous outlays of just $1 to bring in the sales, then one's profit is $999. If, finally, one's sales are $1,000, and one's costs are zero, resulting from zero previous outlays to bring in the sales, then one's profit is $1,000—

the full magnitude of the sales revenues.

Precisely, this last is the situation of the workers in Smith's "early and rude state of society" and under Marx's "simple circulation." Those workers, selling their commodities, not their labor, earn sales revenues, not wages. And precisely because they are not capitalists, and are not employed by capitalists, there is no buying for the sake of selling, and thus there are no money costs to deduct from those sales revenues.

To state matters in Marxist terminology, the M of Marx's simple circulation is, in effect, an M' that has not been preceded by any M to bring it in. This is because in the absence of capitalists, there is no productive expenditure and thus no such prior M. Only with capitalistic circulation does an M appear to be deducted from M'. Hence the full magnitude of the M of Marx's precapitalist, simple circulation is profit.

Thus, in the precapitalist economy, only workers receive incomes, and there are no capitalists and no money capital. But all the incomes that the workers receive are *profits* and none are wages. In the precapitalist sequence C-M-C, *everything* is "surplus-value"—100 percent of the sales revenues and an *infinite* percentage of the zero money capital. In the sequence of capitalistic circulation M-C-M', a smaller proportion of the incomes are "surplus-value."

This same conclusion, that in the precapitalist economy all income is profit, and no income is wages, can be arrived at by way of Ricardo's badly misunderstood proposition that "profits rise as wages fall and fall as wages rise."[71] The wages paid in production, according to Ricardo, are paid by capitalists, out of savings and capital, not by consumers. If, as in the precapitalist economy, there are no capitalists, then there are no wages paid in production, and if there are no wages paid in production, the full income earned in Ricardo's framework must be profits.

Smith and Marx are wrong. Wages are not the primary form of income in production. Profits are. In order for wages to exist in the production of commodities for sale, it is first necessary that there *be capitalists*. The emergence of capitalists does not bring into existence the phenomenon of profit. Profit exists prior to their emergence. The emergence of capitalists brings into existence the phenomena of productive expenditure, wages, and money costs of production.

Accordingly, the profits that exist in a capitalist society are not a deduction from what was originally wages. On the contrary, the wages and the other money costs are a deduction from sales revenues—from what was originally all profit. The effect of capitalism is to create wages and to reduce the relative amount of profits. The more economically capitalistic the economy—the more the buying in order to sell relative to the sales revenues—the higher are wages relative to sales revenues, and the lower are profits relative to sales revenues.

Thus, capitalists do not impoverish wage earners, but make it possible for people to *be* wage earners. For they are responsible not for the phenomenon of profits, but for the phenomenon of wages. They are responsible for the very existence of wages in the production of products for sale.

Without other people existing as capitalists, the only way in which one could survive in connection with the production and sale of products would be by means of producing and selling one's own products, namely, as a profit earner. But to produce and sell one's own products, one would have to own one's own land, and produce or have inherited one's own tools and materials or the money to buy them. Relatively few people could survive in this way. The existence of capitalists makes it possible for people to live by selling their labor rather than attempting to sell the products of their labor. Thus, between wage earners and capitalists there is in fact the closest possible harmony of interests, for capitalists create wages and the ability of people to survive and prosper as wage earners.

And if wage earners want a larger proportion of income in the form of wages and a smaller proportion of income in the form of profits, they should want a higher economic degree of capitalism—that is, in the terminology of Marx, more M relative to M'. For precisely this represents productive expenditure, wages, and costs being higher, and profits being lower, relative to sales revenues. To achieve such change, what the wage earners require is more and bigger capitalists.

Historical confirmation for the theory I am propounding can be found in F. A. Hayek's Introduction to *Capitalism and the Historians*. There we find such statements as: "The actual history of the connection between capitalism and the rise of the proletariat is almost the exact opposite of that which these theories of the expropriation of the masses suggest. . . . The proletariat which capitalism can be said to have 'created' was thus not a proportion of the population which would have existed without it and which it degraded to a lower level; it was an additional population which was enabled to grow up by the new opportunities for employment which capitalism provided."[72]

The correct theory, as well as the actual history, is the exact opposite of the doctrine of the primacy of wages.

Curiously, even Adam Smith himself comes close to grasping the true state of affairs, when he writes:

> His [the wage earner's] employers constitute the third order, that of those who live by profit. It is the stock that is employed for the sake of profit, which puts into motion the

greater part of the useful labour of every society. The plans
and projects of the employers of stock regulate and direct
all the most important operations of labour, and profit is the
end proposed by all those plans and projects. But the rate
of profit does not, like rent and wages, rise with the prosperity, and fall with the declension, of the society. On the
contrary, it is naturally low in rich, and high in poor
countries, and it is always highest in the countries going
fastest to ruin.[73]

Here the employers, previously depicted as parasitical
and virtually functionless, suddenly emerge with plans
and projects regulating and directing all the most important operations of labor, for the sake of profit. And not
only that, but the rate of profit is held to be lower to the
degree that capitalists exist and have accumulated capital. And earlier, Smith has said that "the demand for those
who live by wages, it is evident, cannot increase but in
proportion to the increase of the funds which are destined
for the payment of wages."[74] And now we are told that
the employers' capital is the main source of such funds.

But instead of drawing the correct conclusion that the
existence of capitalists creates and raises wages and
reduces the proportion of total income—viz., national
income—which is profit, Smith simply draws a further
mistaken anticapitalistic conclusion, namely, that because the rate of profit is lower in a more highly capitalistic economic system, "The interest of this third order,
therefore, has not the same connexion with the general
interest of the society as that of the other two [viz., the
wage earners and landowners]."[75]

Now in fact, in the context in which the rate of profit
would be lower in a more highly capitalistic economic
system, it would only be the *nominal* rate of profit that
would be lower, not the real rate of gain of wealth, which
would actually be higher. The interests of the businessmen and capitalists are certainly not opposed to this. And
it must be pointed out, incidentally, and will be demonstrated later in this book, that capital accumulation does
not cause or presuppose a continually falling rate of
profit, but is consistent with an unchanged rate of profit
that is sufficiently low. The effect of a still lower rate of
profit will be shown to be an *acceleration* in the rate of
capital accumulation and economic progress.[76] Furthermore, it will be shown that there are limits to the fall in the
rate of profit, set in part by the more rapid accumulation of
capital and wealth themselves that a higher economic degree of capitalism achieves. This is because in achieving a
higher rate of capital accumulation and thus more rapid
increases in production, a higher economic degree of capitalism tends to be accompanied to an important degree by
a more rapid increase in the supply of commodity money,
which is an almost inevitable accompaniment of more rapid
increases in production in general. This in turn adds to
something to the rate of profit.[77]

However, the central stumbling block for Smith was
his utter confusion of a product sales revenue with the
payment of wages. His confusion on this point was so
great that he could write: "In some parts of Scotland a
few poor people make a trade of gathering, along the
sea-shore, those little variegated stones commonly known
by the name of Scotch Pebbles. The price which is paid
to them by the stone cutter is altogether the wages of their
labour; neither rent nor profit make any part of it."[78] Had
Smith grasped the obvious fact that the price of the stones
is *a sales revenue,* not a wage payment, he would have
understood the fact that workers who sell products, earn
sales revenues and profits, not wages; and that if they
have expended no funds for the purpose of producing
those products, the sales revenues they earn are entirely
profit. These realizations might have enabled him to
grasp the incalculably important positive productive contribution that businessmen and capitalists make to the
economic well-being of wage earners. Had Adam Smith
understood these facts, the subsequent history of the
world would have been very different.

Further Rebuttal: Profits Attributable to the Labor of Businessmen and Capitalists Despite Their Variation With the Size of the Capital Invested

In a precapitalist economy, the income of labor is
profit, and profit is thus obviously a labor income. In a
capitalist economy, too, profit is an income earned by
labor—by the labor of businessmen and capitalists.

An earlier portion of this chapter has described the
labor of businessmen and capitalists as consisting in the
creation, coordination, and improvement in the efficiency
of the division of labor.[79] We have seen that the very fact
that the labor of businessmen and capitalists is centered
on the division of labor is the reason for its almost total
omission from the purview of economists and of people
generally, inasmuch as they fail to hold in mind the
context of the division of labor and its requirements.

We have also seen how the confusion of labor with
wage earning, together with the influence of the opportunity-cost and imputed-income doctrines, has led economists arbitrarily to reclassify profits as wages—precisely
in cases in which business and accounting practice clearly recognize income resulting from the performance of
labor as profit. (The case of a hardware store owner's
profit being reclassified as wages should be recalled.[80])
Repeating the error of Adam Smith, the practice of
economists has been simply to deny application of the
term profit to income earned by virtue of the performance
of labor and to reserve the word for describing income
received on other grounds, principally the mere ownership of capital. Consistent with this practice, most of
what the classical economists called profit, and the gen-

eral public and businessmen and accountants still call profit, has come to be called interest by the last several generations of economists.

What underlies the notion that profits are an income based on the ownership of capital rather than on any performance of labor by businessmen and capitalists is the fact, pointed out by Adam Smith, that profits tend to vary with the size of the capital invested, even though the labor of the businessmen and capitalists is "altogether or very nearly the same." Smith was absolutely correct in showing the variation of profits with the size of the capital invested. Where he was incorrect was in his inference that this fact precluded profits from being attributable to the labor of businessmen and capitalists. The truth is that profits are both an income fully attributable to the labor of businessmen and capitalists *and* tend to vary with the size of the capital invested.

The variation of profits with the size of the capital invested is perfectly consistent with their being attributable to the labor of businessmen and capitalists because such labor tends to be predominantly of an intellectual nature—a work of thinking, planning, and decision making. At the same time, *capital stands as the means by which businessmen and capitalists implement their plans*—it is their means of buying the labor of helpers and of equipping those helpers and providing them with the materials of work. Thus, the possession of capital serves to multiply the efficacy of the businessmen's and capitalists' labor, for the more of it they possess, the greater is the scale on which they can implement their ideas. For example, a businessman who thinks of a better way to produce something can apply that better way on ten times the scale if he owns ten factories or ten stores than if he owns only one. The fact that in the one case the same labor on his part leads to ten times the profit as in the other case is perfectly consistent with the whole profit still being attributable to his labor.

The well-known compound variation of profits with the passage of time is also perfectly consistent with the fact that they are the product of the businessmen's and capitalists' labor. The relationship of profits to the passage of time derives from the fact that profits vary with the size of the capital invested in any given period of time. If one can earn profits in proportion to one's capital in any given period of time, then if investment for a longer period is to be competitive, one must earn the profits that one could have earned in the shorter period plus the profits one could have earned by the reinvestment of one's capital and its profits.

Closely related to the preceding point is the fact that the attribution of profits to the labor of businessmen and capitalists is also perfectly consistent with their simultaneously reflecting such a thing as the general state of time

preference in the economic system (i.e., the preference, other things being equal, for the enjoyment of goods in the nearer future rather than in the more remote future).[81] As Chapter 16 will show, time preference is a factor operating to determine the general or average rate of return on capital.[82] But the individual businessmen and capitalists then earn or do not earn this general or average rate of return, or a higher or lower rate of return, on the basis of their own individual productive accomplishments.

It should be realized that wages, too, which no one disputes are attributable to the labor of the wage earners, vary with things other than the expenditure of labor by the wage earners—for example, with the state of technology and the supply of capital equipment, and with the demand for and supply of labor. In order for an income to be attributable to labor, it is by no means necessary that the performance of labor be the only factor determining its size. The wages of the average worker in the United States, for example, are higher than those of the average worker in practically every other country because of a higher productivity of labor in the United States. This higher productivity rests on the greater extent of capital accumulation in the United States, which, in turn, is traceable to the greater degree of economic freedom and cultural rationality that has traditionally prevailed in the United States in comparison with other countries. Nevertheless, each individual American worker is still responsible for his own earnings. This is merely a restatement of the principle that income is attributable to labor even though it varies with other factors as well.

Nevertheless, precisely this principle is what Adam Smith contradicts in ruling out profits as an income due to the performance of labor. The principle he adopts is that one cannot attribute a greater effect to an agent if the means which the agent employs are greater and more potent.

His argument actually comes to this: One man pulls the trigger of a pistol, another the firing pin of a cannon; one man digs with an ordinary shovel, another with a steam shovel; one man gives orders to a squad of soldiers, another to an army; one man directs a small concern, another a large concern. In each case, the amount of labor performed by the individual in question may be presumed to be equal. According to the principle of Adam Smith, because the amount of labor is equal in each case, the product or result attributable to the labor is equal in each case.

This, of course, is false, and is a contradiction of Smith's own doctrine that labor is the sole cause of wealth. This last, sound doctrine rests on the principle that the effect is always to be attributed to *the guiding and directing intelligence that is present,* irrespective of the magnitude and potency of the means employed. (And irrespective of the presence of all other external circumstances necessary to the outcome, including the existence of such physical phenomena as gravitation and air pressure as well as the existence of the kind of economic and cultural phenomena I described a few paragraphs ago.) If this were not the standard, then it would be impossible to attribute to human beings anything beyond what they could directly and immediately accomplish with their bare hands. One could not only not say that a worker using a steam shovel digs a hole, one could also not say that a worker using an ordinary shovel digs a hole. Indeed, if one applies Smith's principle that variation of the outcome with the magnitude and potency of the means employed precludes its attribution to labor, then his whole argument against profits' being due to labor can be parodied as follows:

> The holes that are dug, it may perhaps be thought, are only a different name for the products of a particular sort of labour, the labour of digging. They are, however, altogether different, are regulated by quite sufficient principles, and bear no proportion to the quantity, the hardship, or the ingenuity of this supposed labour of digging. They are regulated altogether by the means employed for digging, and are greater or smaller in proportion to the extent of those means. Let us suppose, for example, that in some particular place, there are two different men, one of whom sets about digging with his bare hands; the other of whom employs a shovel. The one man will expect a hole of only very small dimensions, while the other will expect a hole of much larger dimensions. But though the holes that are dug are so very different, their labour of digging may be either altogether or very nearly the same.

The variation of profits with the size of the capital in no way contradicts the fact that profits are a labor income. Equal labor does *not* produce equal products. It produces unequal products when unequal means are employed. It is always labor which produces, however, because it is labor which supplies the guiding and directing intelligence in production.

It must stressed: guiding and directing intelligence, not muscular exertion, is the essential characteristic of human labor, and the basis for attributing all production to labor. As von Mises says, "What produces the product are not toil and trouble in themselves, but the fact that the toiling is guided by reason."[83]

On this basis, *all* labor is the "labour of direction." It is because the man directs the tool, that he, and not the tool, produces the product. The tool, whether an ordinary shovel, a steam shovel, dynamite, or an atomic explosive, does not produce, but is the *means* by which the man who employs it produces—in precisely the same sense that it is not a gun which can commit murder or an automobile which can commit manslaughter, but the man who pulls the trigger of the gun or the man who drives the automobile.

A Radical Reinterpretation of "Labor's Right to the Whole Produce"

Guiding and directing intelligence in production is supplied by businessmen and capitalists on a higher level than by wage earners—a circumstance which further reinforces the primary productive status of profits and profit earners over wages and wage earners.

The socialists, indeed, have so little conception of the essential role of guiding and directing intelligence in production, that while they claim the product for the manual workers in one breath, they complain in the very next breath of the manual worker's "alienation" from the product. The manual worker does not know, see, or touch the final product, they complain. Capitalism, they say, confines the worker to a narrow task. It limits his horizon to the job immediately at hand—to a tiny step in his firm's overall productive operations.[84]

Now although the division of labor and capitalism are not in fact responsible for "alienation," it is true that the manual worker is necessarily concerned with only a small step in his firm's overall productive operations. For this very reason, it is absolutely impossible that he could be responsible for its products—that the products could legitimately be said to be *his* products. The socialists evidently believe that a product emerges out of *chaos*—as a result of the fortuitous interaction of the operations of people engaged in unintegrated, totally isolated steps in its production. They simply do not see the role of businessmen and capitalists in coordinating and improving the efficiency of the division of labor—or in creating the division of labor in the first place.

The fact that profits are an income attributable to the labor of businessmen and capitalists, and the further fact that their labor represents the provision of guiding and directing intelligence at the highest level in the productive process, requires a radical reinterpretation of the doctrine of labor's right to the whole produce. Namely, that that right is satisfied when first the full product and then the full value of that product comes into the possession of *businessmen and capitalists,* for *they,* not the wage earners, are the fundamental producers of products. The employees of the firm are accurately described by the common expression "help." They are the helpers of the businessmen and capitalists in the production of *their*—the businessmen's and capitalists'—products. It should be obvious that thus understood, the realization of labor's right to the whole produce is exactly what occurs in the everyday operations of a capitalist economy, inasmuch as it is businessmen and capitalists who are the owners first of the products and then of the sales proceeds received in exchange for the products.

By the standard of attributing results to those who conceive and execute their achievement at the highest level, one must attribute to businessmen and capitalists the entire gross product of their firms and the entire sales receipts for which that product is exchanged. Such, indeed, is the normal standard in fields other than economic activity. For example, one attributes the discovery of America to Columbus, the victory at Austerlitz to Napoleon, the foreign policy of the United States to its President. These attributions are made despite the fact that Columbus could not have made his discovery without the aid of his crew, nor Napoleon have won his victory without the help of his soldiers, nor the foreign policy of the United States be carried out without the aid of the employees of the State Department. The help these people provide is perceived as the means by which those who supply the guiding and directing intelligence at the highest level accomplish *their* objectives. The intelligence, purpose, direction, and integration flow down from the top, and the imputation of the result flows up from the bottom.

By this standard, the products of the old Ford Motor Company and Standard Oil Company are to be attributed to Ford and Rockefeller. (In many cases, of course, the product must be attributed to a group of businessmen and capitalists, not just to a single outstanding figure.) In any event, labor's right to the full value of its produce is fully satisfied precisely when a Ford or Rockefeller, or their lesser known counterparts, are paid by their customers for *their* products. The product is theirs, not the employees'. The help the employees provide is fully remunerated when the producers pay them wages.

Implications for the Incomes of "Passive" Capitalists

The fact that profits, not wages, are the original and primary form of income, and that labor's right to the whole produce is satisfied when businessmen and capitalists receive the sales proceeds, leads to a very different view than Adam Smith's of the payment of incomes to capitalists whose role in production might be judged to be passive, such as, perhaps, most minor stockholders and many recipients of interest, land rent, and resource royalties. Adam Smith has committed the double confusion of putting the wage earner in the place of the seller of products, and thus of businessmen and capitalists, and of lumping the active businessmen and capitalists in with the passive capitalists. He believes, in effect, that the workers on Henry Ford's assembly line pay him his profit and pay the dividends and interest to the other suppliers of the firm's capital. The fact is, of course, that it is businessmen and capitalists such as Ford who pay both the men on the assembly line *and* any passive recipients of dividends and interest, etc.

If the payment of such incomes did represent an exploitation of labor, therefore, it would not be an exploi-

tation of the labor of wage earners. The wage earners are totally out of the picture. The incomes of the passive capitalists are paid by *businessmen*—by the active capitalists—not by the wage earners. They are not a deduction from wages, but from the profits of the active capitalists. If any exploitation were present here, it would be the active capitalists, not the wage earners, who were the exploited parties. What this would mean in practice is that individuals like Ford and Rockefeller would be exploited by widows and orphans, for it is such people who largely make up the category of passive capitalists.

In fact, however, the payment of such incomes is never an exploitation, because their payment is a source of gain to those who pay them. They are paid in order to acquire assets whose use is a source of profits over and above the payments which must be made. Furthermore, the recipients of such incomes need not be at all passive; they may very well earn their incomes by the performance of a considerable amount of intellectual labor. Anyone who has attempted to manage a portfolio of stocks and bonds or investments in real estate should know that there is no limit to the amount of time and effort that such management can absorb, in the form of searching out and evaluating investment possibilities, and that the job will be better done the more such time and effort one can give it.

In the absence of government intervention in the form of the existence of national debts, loan guarantees, and insurance on bank deposits, the magnitude of truly passive income in the economic system would be quite modest. This is because most forms of investment require the exercise of some significant degree of skill and judgment. Those not able or willing to exercise such skill and judgment would either rapidly lose their funds or would have to be content with very low rates of return in compensation for safety of principal and, in many cases, would have to bear the expense of the deduction of management fees by trustees or other parties.

It should also be realized that in a laissez faire economy, without personal or corporate income taxes (a real exploitation of labor) and without legal restrictions on such business activities as insider trading and the award of stock options, the businessmen and active capitalists are in a position to own an ever increasing share of the capitals they employ. With their high incomes they can progressively buy out the ownership shares of the passive capitalists.

In this way, under capitalism, those workers—the businessmen and active capitalists—who do have a valid claim to the ownership of the industries *in fact come to own them.* Again and again, penniless newcomers appear on the scene and by virtue of their success secure a growing influence over the conduct of production and ultimately obtain the ownership of vast personal fortunes. An ironic consequence of Adam Smith's errors in this area, to be counted among all the other absurdities of socialism, is that the socialists want to give the ownership of the industries *to the wrong workers!* And to do so, they want to destroy the economic system which gives it to the right workers. They want to give it to the manual laborers, while capitalism gives it to those who supply the guiding and directing intelligence in production.

Not surprisingly, the socialists and their fellow travelers, the contemporary "liberals," denounce capitalism's giving ownership to the right workers. They denounce it when they denounce large salaries and stock options for key executives.[85]

Acceptance of the Conceptual Framework of the Exploitation Theory by Its Critics

The enormous flaws in the conceptual framework of the exploitation theory have completely escaped the attention of the theory's critics. Instead, the critics have devoted their attention entirely to the doctrines of the labor theory of value and the iron law of wages. This has been the case because, as I have already pointed out, the critics share that very same conceptual framework. They too accept the notion that wages are the original and primary form of income and that profits (which they often call originary interest) represent a deduction from wages. Where they differ from Marx is in arguing that profits represent a just, rather than an unjust, deduction from wages.

Thus Böhm-Bawerk, the leading critic of the exploitation theory, argues that profits are a justified deduction from wages on the grounds that the capitalists pay the workers in advance of the sale of the products that the workers produce. This fact, in conjunction with the operation of time preference, Böhm-Bawerk holds, enables and entitles the capitalists to pay wages that represent a discounted present value of the wage earners' future product. Later, when the product is completed and sold, the capitalists sell it at its full, then present value.

A leading example of Böhm-Bawerk's views is his famous illustration of five workers cooperating in the production of an engine that requires five years to complete, from the making of tools for the mining of iron ore to the assembly of the various components that make up the engine. In this example, Böhm-Bawerk assumes that the completed engine will sell for $5,500 and that the five workers each perform labor of equal quantity and skill. The only difference between the workers is that the worker who completes his work at the end of the first year must wait four years to receive his share of the proceeds, while the worker who completes his work at the end of the fifth year will be paid immediately, with all the other workers having to undergo waiting times between these two extremes.

The fact of unequal waiting times, says Böhm-Bawerk, will lead the workers to make an unequal division of the engine's value. The worker who completes his work at the end of the first year, and who must therefore wait four years to be paid, will receive more than the mere one-fifth of its value that his equal labor would otherwise entitle him to. Instead of $1,100, he will receive, Böhm-Bawerk imagines, $1,200. By the same token, the worker who completes his work at the end of the fifth year, and who thus need not wait at all to be paid following completion of his work, will receive only $1,000. The other three workers will receive various amounts between these two limits.[86]

This, Böhm-Bawerk says, is an unequal division of the engine's value that the workers themselves would make because of the fact that present goods are subjectively more valuable than future goods of the same kind and number. Because of this fact, an equal sum received immediately upon completion of work is more valuable than the same sum that is not to be received until one to four years later. If the workers received the same sums of money, those who performed their labor earlier and who had to undergo correspondingly more waiting time would receive a subjectively smaller value than the workers who performed their labor later and who thus had to undergo less or even no subsequent waiting time at all. On this basis, Böhm-Bawerk argues, $1,200 received four years after the completion of one's work is no more than the equivalent of $1,000 received immediately upon completion of one's work.[87]

Having thus set the stage, Böhm-Bawerk now introduces a capitalist. The existence of the capitalist makes it possible for each of the five workers to be paid immediately upon completion of his work. Because of this, in Böhm-Bawerk's view, the just wage of each of these workers, is $1,000—the same as that of the worker who completes his work last and who by the workers' own presumed standards of justice would have been paid only $1,000.[88]

In this way, according to Böhm-Bawerk, profits emerge as a just deduction from what would otherwise rightfully all belong to the wage earners. The capitalist pays to the worker who completes his work at the end of the first year the sum of $1,000, which is the present equivalent of the $1,200 that worker would otherwise have had to wait four years to receive. He pays $1,000 to the next worker, who completes his work at the end of the second year and who would otherwise have had to wait three years to receive $1,150. And so on. Thus, the capitalist pays to the first four workers the present, discounted value of their share in the future product, takes over from them the activity of waiting, and, ultimately, when what began as a prospective future product becomes an actual present good, sells that good at its full undiscounted, present value. In sum, in buying the labor to produce a product worth $5,500 with wage outlays totaling $5,000, the capitalist has paid the present, discounted value of a future good, the rights to which he thereby acquires, and which then ripens, as it were, into a present good in his possession that sells at its full, undiscounted, present value.

For all of its ingeniousness, Böhm-Bawerk's exposition concedes the notion that the starting point of analysis is a valid claim of wage earners to the full value of the product and that profits are a deduction from what was originally all the income of wage earners. These concessions are totally unwarranted. To be accurate, his account would have had to describe the five workers as initially producing separately, on a hand-to-mouth basis, with no possibility of mutual cooperation in the production of any such time-consuming product as an engine. Each of the workers would also have had to be described as selling a product and earning a profit income, not a wage income, and as having to own or produce his own tools and materials in order to do so. The possibility of living by the sale of one's labor in the process of producing products for sale would have had to be described as nonexistent in the face of the absence of capitalists. The role of the businessman/capitalist would then have had to be described as creating and organizing the vertical division of labor among these workers that is necessary for the production of such a time-consuming product as an engine, and of making it possible for them to live as wage earners. The engine itself would have had to be presented as the product primarily of the businessman and capitalist, who provides the guiding and directing intelligence in its production. It would also have had to be pointed out that the proportion of profits in the value of the engine is lower than the proportion of profits in the production of the hand-to-mouth goods produced by the manual workers on their own, and that the proportion constituted by wages is correspondingly higher.

Böhm-Bawerk, of course, did none of these things. Instead, along with his attempt to demonstrate the justice of the deduction of profits from wages, he concentrated his fire on the labor theory of value.[89] And because the labor theory of value was generally perceived as the essential element both in the exploitation theory and in classical economics, the unfortunate consequence of Böhm-Bawerk's critique was to do as much damage to the prestige of classical economics as to the prestige of Marx.

3. Necessary Revisions in Classical Economics

I have shown that while Adam Smith is the father of the Marxian exploitation theory—in providing its con-

ceptual framework—essential propositions of classical economics can be applied to the total demolition of that framework. This is true in particular of J. S. Mill's proposition that "demand for commodities is not demand for labour" and Ricardo's proposition that "profits rise as wages fall and fall as wages rise."[90] (Ricardo's proposition, of course, must be taken on the understanding that it is capitalists, not consumers, who pay wages.)

There are five revisions that need to be made in the body of classical economics to transform it from a source of support for the exploitation theory into a source of complete and total opposition to the exploitation theory. Three of these I have already made.

The first revision, accomplished in the last section, is the consistent application of Mill's and Ricardo's propositions. From this comes the recognition that in the conditions of the "early and rude state of society" assumed by Adam Smith, all income is actually profit, not wages. The further recognition also follows that wages come into being with the emergence of capitalists, and are the greater relative to profits, the more economically capitalistic is the economic system. By "economically capitalistic" is meant the extent to which buying for the purpose of selling—productive expenditure—takes place relative to sales proceeds. In other words, wages are higher and profits are lower precisely to the degree that Marx's "M" is larger relative to his "M'."

The second necessary revision is the recognition of the positive productive functions of businessmen and capitalists and of the fact that they are the fundamental producers of products, inasmuch as they provide the guiding and directing intelligence in production at the highest level—and of the further fact that the variation of profits and interest with the size of the capital invested in no way contradicts these incomes being attributable to the labor of businessmen and capitalists. The result of this revision is the realization that labor's right to the whole produce is satisfied everyday in a capitalist economy—when businessmen and capitalists receive the proceeds from the sale of *their* products. This revision too was accomplished in the present chapter, largely in the last section.[91]

The third necessary revision, accomplished in Chapter 9, is consistent recognition of the role of private ownership of land in raising the productivity of labor in agriculture and mining. This leads to the conclusion that private ownership of land underlies the growth of the division of labor, by making labor available for industry and commerce. It also leads to the conclusion that private ownership of land operates to reduce the economic significance of land rent and thus to enlarge the relative share of "national income" that takes the form of wages, and, still more importantly, to help make possible a continuous rise in the purchasing power and thus the real income of the average wage earner.[92]

All of these revisions are in accord with the fundamental spirit of classical economics, which stands in defense of private property rights and proclaims the harmony of the rational self-interests of all men. The first and third revisions and their derivatives merely represent making classical economics more self-consistent, while the second fills in a major conceptual gap in the classical system, which was largely ignorant of the productive functions of businessmen and capitalists and largely ignored the essential aspect of guiding and directing intelligence in labor.

The fourth and fifth revisions concern two further doctrines of classical economics, which, as I have shown, usually bear the weight of the accusation that it supports the exploitation theory—namely, the labor theory of value and the "iron law of wages." For after laying down the conceptual framework he has borrowed from Adam Smith, it is these two doctrines that Marx applies to explain the extent of the alleged deduction of profits from wages. (Usually, Marx uses the term "surplus-value" in place of profits, as a catchall for all incomes other than wages.)

In the next section, I will show that the labor theory of value, as propounded by Ricardo—the classical economist who is most closely associated with it—can easily be restated in a way that not only lends no support to the exploitation theory, but, indeed, helps to provide still further criticisms of the exploitation theory. I will show that it is only the so-called iron law of wages that needs to be thoroughly discarded, and that precisely a proper understanding of the labor theory of value provides one of the leading bases for discarding it.

4. The Labor Theory of Value of Classical Economics

The labor theory of value of the classical economists held that the relative quantities of labor required to produce goods is usually the major determinant of their relative exchange values. The labor in question is all the labor directly or indirectly necessary to the production of a good. For example, in the case of an automobile, this would be the labor performed not only in the auto plants, but also in the production of the steel necessary to make the automobile, and in the production of the iron ore necessary to produce the steel. It would also include the relevant portion of the labor required to make the automaking machinery and to build the automobile factory, the relevant portion of the labor required to make the steelmaking equipment and to build the steel mill, and so on. (The relevant portion of the labor in these last cases would be construed as the fraction of the total labor required to produce these things that corresponds to the

production of just one automobile. For example, if ten million man-hours were required to construct a machine that would last for ten years and that would do nothing but contribute to the production of one million automobiles in each of those years, then the relevant portion of that labor entering into the production of one automobile as the result of the use of that machinery would be one man-hour.)

According to the classical economists, the relative prices of, for example, automobiles, motorcycles, bicycles, and roller skates would then reflect the respective relative quantities of labor required to make these goods. If, for example, it required, all in all, a thousand man-hours to make an automobile, a hundred man-hours to make a motor cycle, ten man-hours to make a bicycle, and one man-hour to make a pair of roller skates, then the relative values of these goods would be in the same ratios—namely, 1,000:100:10:1. Under a system of commodity money, the labor theory of value would apply to the determination of actual, absolute prices, as well as relative exchange values. Thus, if the monetary unit were an ounce of gold, and it required all in all, say, a hundred man-hours to produce an ounce of gold, then the money price of the automobile we have just considered would be 10 ounces, that of the motorcycle 1 ounce, that of the bicycle .1 ounce, and that of the roller skates .01 ounce.

Now I want to say that I myself believe that the quantity of labor required to produce a good is almost always a very important factor determining its price. The best evidence for this proposition is the fact that the use of labor-saving machinery makes goods more affordable. The greater the extent to which machinery reduces the quantity of labor required to produce goods, the less expensive do goods become. Such a result would not be possible if the quantity of labor required to produce goods did not have a significant connection with their price.

Harmonization of the Labor Theory of Value With Supply and Demand and the Productive Role of Businessmen and Capitalists

The recognition of the role of the quantity of labor required in the production of goods as an influence on their price does not preclude the recognition of a variety of other factors as well, nor does it imply that the quantity of labor required in production is always an influence on price. Indeed, properly understood, recognition of the role of the quantity of labor is compatible with the recognition both of supply and demand as the determinant of prices and of the role of businessmen and capitalists in raising the standard of living of the average wage earner!

To combine these three elements of understanding—that is, the quantity of labor required to produce goods, supply and demand, and the productive role of businessmen and capitalists—all we need do is this: First, realize that the reduction in the quantity of labor required to produce goods makes it possible for the same total quantity of labor in the economic system to produce a larger supply of goods, and thus to increase the supply of goods relative to the supply of labor. Next, realize that this, in turn, implies a fall in prices relative to wage rates, and thus a rise in the buying power and standard of living of the average worker. Then, realize that what brings all this about is precisely the productive activities of the businessmen and capitalists! They, together with scientists and inventors, whose work they continuously seek out and inspire, bring about the steady reduction in the quantity of labor required to produce goods, thus the steady increase in the supply of goods relative to the supply of labor, and thus a steady fall in prices relative to wage rates—viz., a steady rise in real wages. Furthermore, this relationship between the reductions achieved by businessmen and capitalists in the quantity of labor required to produce goods, and the rise in real wages, can be understood in a precise, quantitative way, using the classical economists' concepts of demand and supply as a ratio of expenditure to quantity sold.[93]

For example, a halving of the quantity of labor required to produce the average good in the economic system, would permit a doubling of the production of goods with the employment of the same total quantity of labor, and thus result in a halving of prices on the assumption that the quantity of money and volume of spending to buy goods in the economic system remained the same. Since there is no increase in the supply of labor present, the existence of a constant quantity of money and a correspondingly fixed aggregate demand for labor implies that the average level of money wage rates remains the same while the prices of goods fall in half, because the same total spending for labor continues to purchase the same total supply of labor.

What we have here, in fact, is precisely the state of affairs that Adam Smith thought would have been possible only under the continuation of his "original state of things," viz., the absence of private ownership of land and the accumulation of capital, but which in fact is possible only with the presence of these things, under capitalism. As previously quoted, Smith wrote: "Had this state continued, the wages of labour would have augmented with all those improvements in its productive powers, to which the division of labour gives occasion. All things would gradually have become cheaper. They would have been produced by a smaller quantity of labour . . . ."[94] This steady rise in real wages owing to the steady reduction in the value of the commodities that the wages purchase *is exactly what happens under cap-*

italism—as the result of businessmen and capitalists continuously finding ways to reduce the quantity of labor required to produce any given unit of goods and thus to increase the supply of goods relative to the supply of labor.

Other Classical Doctrines and the Rise in Real Wages

It should be realized that this account of the rise in real wages brought about by the businessmen and capitalists incorporates not only the role of quantity of labor required in the production of goods as a factor determining their prices, and the classical concepts of demand and supply, but no less the so-called wages-fund doctrine and Ricardo's doctrine of the distinction between "value and riches." It incorporates the wages-fund doctrine in its implication of a distinct and given demand for labor.[95] It incorporates the doctrine of the distinction between value and riches in its perception of the rise in real wages as proceeding not from a rise in money incomes, which represents merely an increase in an aggregate monetary value, but from a fall in prices, which is the natural consequence of a greater ability to produce—viz., of greater "riches."[96] Along the very same lines as the distinction between value and riches, it should also be realized that our assumption that the quantity of money and volume of spending remain the same is consistent with the procedure of the classical economists, especially Ricardo, of assuming the value of money to be constant as far as changes on the side of money itself are concerned, and thus all changes in prices to reflect changes on the side of goods other than money.[97]

Classical Economics' Limitations on the Labor Theory of Value

The classical economists, Ricardo in particular, were well aware of the limitations of the labor theory of value as an explanation of prices.

i. Exclusion of Scarce Goods

According to Ricardo, there was a substantial category of goods to which the labor theory of value did not even apply. Thus, he wrote:

> There are some commodities, the value of which is determined by their scarcity alone. No labour can increase the quantity of such goods, and therefore their value cannot be lowered by an increased supply. Some rare statues and pictures, scarce books and coins, wines of a peculiar quality, which can be made only from grapes grown on a particular soil, of which there is a very limited quantity, are all of this description. Their value is wholly independent of the quantity of labour originally necessary to produce them, and varies with the varying wealth and inclinations of those who are desirous to possess them.[98]

In order for the labor theory of value to be made

consistent with Austrian economics and the case for capitalism, it is necessary explicitly to enlarge the list of exceptions whose value is determined by their "scarcity alone." The necessary enlargement must include all the items whose prices I described back in Chapter 6 as being determined by supply and demand rather than cost of production, either on a permanent or temporary basis.[99] The most important addition to the list of exceptions, of course, is the value of human labor itself, both skilled and unskilled. This exception, it should be noted, is clearly called for by classical economics itself insofar as the latter upholds the wages-fund doctrine, according to which wage rates are determined by the ratio of the wages fund (viz., the demand for labor) to the supply of labor. Indeed, practically all of these additions to the list of items whose price is not determined either by cost of production or by quantity of labor required in their production, would have been fully acceptable to Ricardo, who, in fact, explicitly notes them.[100] As we shall see in the next section, only in the case of labor would Ricardo have registered any objection—an objection that is confined to special circumstances and then is thoroughly confused.[101]

ii. Ricardo's Recognition of the Time Factor as an Independent Determinant of Relative Value

Where the labor theory of value applies, according to Ricardo, is in the production of "such commodities only as can be increased in quantity by the exertion of human industry, and on the production of which competition operates without restraint."[102] And even in these cases, Ricardo points out, not only is the connection often confined to long-run, equilibrium prices rather than to the market prices that prevail at any given moment, but the long-run equilibrium prices themselves are subject to the operation of another very important factor. He introduces this factor with a section heading in his chapter "On Value," namely, the heading of Section 4, which reads, "The principle that the quantity of labour bestowed on the production of commodities regulates their relative value considerably modified by the employment of machinery and other fixed and durable capital."[103]

The modification Ricardo has in mind is the principle that *"commodities which have the same quantity of labour bestowed on their production will differ in exchangeable value if they cannot be brought to market in the same time."*[104] He illustrates the principle with the following example:

Suppose I employ twenty men at an expense of 1000 pounds for a year in the production of a commodity, and at the end of the year I employ twenty men again for another year, at a further expense of 1000 pounds in finishing or perfecting the same commodity, and that I bring it to market at the end of two years. If profits be 10 per cent., my commodity must sell for 2310 pounds; for I have employed 1000 pounds capital for one year, and 2100 pounds capital for one year more. Another man employs precisely the same quantity of labour, but he employs it all in the first year; he employs forty men at an expense of 2000 pounds, and at the end of the first year he sells it [his commodity] with 10 per cent. profit, or for 2200 pounds. Here, then, are two commodities having precisely the same quantity of labour bestowed on them, one of which sells for 2310 pounds—the other for 2200 pounds."[105]

A more extreme illustration of the same point is the case of aged wine or whiskey. To earn a 10 percent compound annual rate of profit in the production of whiskey that takes eight years to age, $1,000 of capital paid out as wages must result in a product that sells for approximately $2,000, while to earn the 10 percent annual rate of profit in the production of a commodity in which only one year elapses between the outlay of capital and the sale of the commodity, the commodity need sell for only $1,100. Here is a case in which two equal capitals employ two equal quantities of labor, and yet the one product has an equilibrium price of almost twice that of the other product—because of the influence of the different periods of time for which the rate of profit must be compounded.

Ricardo's examples concerning the effect of the use of machinery and buildings are too complex to bear quoting. But the following, I think, clearly represents his meaning. Imagine two cases in which $1,000 of capital is expended in the payment of wages to the same quantity of labor. Once again, assume that the annual rate of profit is 10 percent. In the one case, the product is an item that will be sold one year later. In the other case, it is a machine that will be used in production over a period of ten years. The item to be sold one year after the outlay of wages will have to sell for $1,100 in order to earn the 10 percent rate of profit. But the machine will have to bring in over the course of its life a sum of at least $1,500. One hundred dollars must be recovered in each of the ten years in the form of depreciation on the machine. Beyond that, in each of the ten years the further sum of $50 must be earned as profit on the average capital outstanding in the machine, which is $500. Thus, in the one case the same quantity of labor results in the production of a product worth $1,100, while in the other it results in the production of a series of services worth $1,500.[106]

In a letter to his follower and popularizer J. R. McCulloch, Ricardo named the essential point as follows:

Strictly speaking then the relative quantities of labour bestowed on commodities regulates their relative value, when nothing but labour is bestowed upon them, and that for equal time. When the times are unequal, the relative quantity of labour bestowed on them is still the main ingredient which regulates their relative value, but it is not the only ingredient, for besides compensating for the labour, the price of the commodity must also compensate for the length of time that must elapse before it can be brought to market. All the exceptions to the general rule come under this one of time . . . .[107]

In the same letter, he even went so far as to write: "I sometimes think that if I were to write the chapter on value again which is in my book, I should acknowledge that the relative value of commodities was regulated by two causes instead of by one, namely, by the relative quantity of labour necessary to produce the commodities in question, and by the rate of profit for the time that the capital remained dormant, and until the commodities were brought to market."[108]

iii. Ricardo's Implicit Recognition of Changes in the Rate of Profit as a Further Determinant

Ricardo, in fact, implicitly acknowledges *changes in the rate of profit* as still a further cause of variations in the relative value of commodities. This fact is not as clear as it might be, because he constantly couples a change in the rate of profit with a change in wages. He reasons in a context in which the total monetary value of consumers' goods is fixed and is equal to a sum of total profits and total wages. In this context, every change in the amount of profits is necessarily accompanied by an equivalent opposite change in the amount of wages. At the same time changes in the amount of profits produce changes in the average rate of profit. As a result of this, when total wages rise and total profits and the average rate of profit fall, the effect is to raise the price of some commodities and lower the price of other commodities, even though there has been no change in the quantity of labor required to produce any of them. In Ricardo's words: "Every rise of wages, therefore, or, which is the same thing, every fall of profits, would lower the relative value of those commodities which were produced with a capital of a durable nature, and would proportionally elevate those which were produced with capital more perishable. A fall of wages would have precisely the contrary effect."[109]

To understand this point, let us imagine an economic system with a fixed quantity of money and a fixed total volume of spending for consumers' goods of 1,000 units of money per year. Let us further imagine that initially total wages are 800 units of money per year and total profits are 200 units of money per year. The wages on average are paid one year in advance of the sale of the consumers' goods the wage earners help to produce. We can assume that total capital in the economic system is the 800 units of money expended in paying wages, and thus that the average rate of profit in the economic system is 25 percent (the 200 amount of profit divided by the 800 amount of wages, which represents the capital em-

ployed). Now wages rise to 900 and profits fall to 100. The rate of profit accordingly falls to approximately 11 percent ($100/900$).

Ricardo's conclusion becomes apparent if we consider the effect on the prices of goods in which the outlay of wages takes place less than one year in advance of the sale of the resulting product and the effect in cases in which the outlay of wages takes place more than one year in advance of the sale of the resulting product. Thus, imagine a good which initially requires an outlay of 8 of wages and which is sold six months later at a price of 9, which will be the case when the annual rate of profit is 25 percent and thus the semiannual rate of profit is 12.5 percent. The wage outlay for this good now rises to 9. Since the annual rate of profit has fallen to $1/9$, the semiannual rate of profit is $1/18$. The price of this good therefore rises from 9 to 9.5, for it now equals a wage outlay of 9 plus a profit of $1/18$ x 9. But at the same time, the price of a good in whose production the wages must be paid two years in advance of the sale of the good, will actually fall. Here the fall in the rate of profit will outweigh the rise in wages. For example, when the rate of profit was 25 percent, a good requiring an outlay of 8 of wages and selling two years later, would have to sell for 12.5. Now the outlay of wages is 9, but the good only sells for a little over 11, or to be precise, $9 \times (10/9)^2$.

Thus, as noted, Ricardo is aware of the fact that a change in the rate of profit results in a change in relative prices, with no change in the relative quantities of labor required to produce the various goods. The rate of profit, along with the relative periods of time that must elapse between outlays of capital and the sale of the resulting products, is a determinant of the relative value and prices of commodities, according to Ricardo.

In my judgment, Ricardo's development of the influence of time and the rate of profit on the relative value and prices of commodities is in some respects more insightful even than Böhm-Bawerk's. Certainly, after reading Sections 4–6 of his chapter "On Value," there is every reason to believe that he would have been fully in accord with all of the essential points of Böhm-Bawerk's critique of the exploitation theory, especially as presented in *Karl Marx and the Close of His System*.[110] For the substance of Böhm-Bawerk's critique in that essay is merely that the fact that the value of commodities varies with the period of time for which profits compound on capital makes it impossible that they should vary exclusively in accordance with the quantity of labor expended to produce them.

iv. Differences in Wage Rates Between Countries and Occupations as Still Further Factors

In the case of foreign trade, Ricardo departs even

further from a view of the relative quantity of labor as the only determinant of relative value. He says, flatly: "The same rule which regulates the relative value of commodities in one country does not regulate the relative value the commodities exchanged between two or more countries."[111]

The kind of problem that emerges for a strict labor theory of value in connection with foreign trade is that, with due allowance for costs of transportation, the same commodity tends, as we have seen, to have the same price throughout the world.[112] This is so, irrespective of the quantity of labor that must be employed to produce the commodity in different countries. For example, the price of a bushel of wheat is, let us say, three dollars. This is the price both to farmers in India and to farmers in the United States, even though the relatively backward methods of production in India may mean that it takes fifty or a hundred times the labor to produce a bushel of wheat in India than it does in the United States.

This case suggests yet another element entering into the determination of relative prices—namely, *relative wage rates*. The cost of production of wheat in India and the United States can be equal despite the fifty- or hundred-to-one difference in the quantity of labor required to produce wheat in the two countries, if wage rates in the United States are that much higher than in India.[113] Furthermore, the inequality of wage rates for different grades of labor, such as skilled versus unskilled labor, leads products produced with the same quantity of labor in the *same country* to have different costs of production and thus different prices. For example, the watches produced with a thousand hours of skilled watchmakers' labor are far more costly than the quantity of cotton or wheat produced with a thousand hours of the labor of farm hands.

Ricardo himself did not recognize the role of relative wage rates in determining relative costs and relative prices within a given country. But his disciple John Stuart Mill clearly did. The latter wrote:

> . . . if wages are higher in one employment than another, or if they rise and [*sic*] fall permanently in one employment without doing so in others, these inequalities do really operate upon values. . . . When the wages of an employment permanently exceed the average rate, the value of the thing produced will, in the same degree, exceed the standard determined by mere quantity of labour. Things, for example, which are made by skilled labour, exchange for the produce of a much greater quantity of unskilled labour; for no reason but because the labour is more highly paid.[114]

It should be realized, of course, that differences in wage rates are not a fundamental explanation of differences in the value of products, for they themselves ultimately rest on the comparative valuations made by the consumers of the various products produced with the different kinds of labor.[115]

Furthermore, it should also be realized that just as there are differences in the quantity of labor required to produce the same good among different countries, so there are also differences in the quantity of labor required to produce the same good within any given country. This is the case insofar as economic progress takes place in a country. The effect of economic progress is that the portions of the supply of a commodity produced with the more recently adopted methods of production tend to be produced with less labor per unit than the portions of the supply that are produced with older methods of production. In such conditions, the competition of the newer, more efficient methods of production tends to reduce the price of the commodity to a point where it corresponds to less than the quantity of labor required to produce it under the older methods. At the same time, because the newer methods are as yet only partially adopted, the price of the product tends to correspond to more than the quantity of labor required to produce it under the newer methods. In such cases, the price of the commodity can be described as gravitating downward, toward correspondence with the quantity of labor required to produce it under the newest, most efficient method of production, as the use of that method becomes more and more widespread. But under conditions of continuous economic progress, the price will never actually reach that point, because before any one method of production can be fully adopted, still more efficient methods of production come to be adopted.

In cases of the kind just described, the effect is inequalities in the rate of profit among different producers of the same product. Those who produce with the more recent methods of production earn above-average rates of profit, while those who produce with the older methods of production earn below-average rates of profit or suffer outright losses. However, it is also a common occurrence for products to be produced with different quantities of labor in the same country because of differences in the degree of skill among wage earners within the same occupation. For example, in many occupations there are some workers who are capable of producing twice as much as other workers even though both work with the same kind of machinery and tools. In cases of this kind, the departure of the price of the product from the quantity of labor required to produce it will be compensated for by inequalities in wage rates. Just as in the case of inequalities in the productivity of labor between countries, the workers who are twice as efficient in a given occupation in a given country will tend to be paid double the wage rates of the less efficient workers. As in the case of foreign trade, the price of the product will correspond to labor cost, but not to labor quantity.

The Actual Significance of Quantity of Labor in Classical Economics

Thus, in the hands of the classical economists, the labor theory of value was a theory which held that the relative quantity of labor required in the production of goods was usually, but not always, the major determinant of their relative prices. A variety of other factors was recognized as operating alongside of relative quantity of labor as determinants of relative prices. And in some circumstances the relative quantity of labor was held not to be a determinant at all. When the classical economists' ideas on the determination of prices are all put together, it works out that in order for the quantity of labor required in production to be the *sole* determinant of the prices in whose formation it plays a role, a whole series of very special assumptions would have to be realized.

First, the tendency toward a uniform rate of profit on capital invested, which was discussed earlier in this book, would not only have to realize itself in the achievement of an actual uniform rate of profit in all branches of production, but also it would have to operate in conditions in which every branch of industry had the same ratio of capital invested to sales revenues, i.e., the same capital turnover ratio.[116] On these two assumptions, the uniformity-of-profit principle would imply uniform *profit margins*. That is, there would not only be a uniform rate of profit on capital invested, but also a uniform ratio of profit to *sales revenues* in every branch of production. This is because if capital invested were everywhere in the same ratio to sales revenues, then profits would have to be a uniform percentage of sales revenues in order to be a uniform percentage of capital invested. Uniform profit margins, in turn, would imply a uniform relationship between prices and costs of production everywhere. Everywhere prices would stand in the same ratio to costs of production—for example, if the uniform profit margin were 10 percent, then everywhere prices would stand in the ratio of 100 to 90 in relation to costs of production.

If the further special assumption were realized that in every branch of production the costs of production broke down in the same proportion between labor costs and costs on account of materials and machinery (and any other items purchased from other business firms), then a uniform relationship between prices and costs of production would imply a uniform relationship between prices and *a series of prior wage payments*. For example, if everywhere half the cost were for wages and half for materials and machinery, etc., then a price of 100 for a consumers' good would correspond to 45 of wage payments in the direct production of the consumers' good, plus an additional 20.25 of wage payments in the production of the 45 worth of capital goods used in the production of the consumers' good, plus a further 9.1125 of

wage payments in the production of the 20.25 worth of capital goods used to produce those capital goods, and so on. (Forty-five is half of 90 percent of the 100 value of the consumers' good; 20.25 is half of 90 percent of 45; 9.1125 is half of 90 percent of 20.25.) The price of every good, in other words, would correspond to a uniformly diminishing series of prior wage payments. It would equal the sum of those prior wage payments each multiplied by the rate of profit, stated as a percentage of cost, compounded for the number of years by which the particular stage was removed from the sale of the ultimate consumers' good.

If, finally, the still further assumption were realized that there is only one uniform grade of labor in terms of skill and efficiency, with one uniform wage rate, then it would follow that product prices would everywhere tend to be proportional to the quantity of labor required to produce the various goods. For then, wage costs would always be in the same proportion to the quantity of labor purchased. With a uniform wage rate, a wage payment of 10, for example, represents the purchase of twice the quantity of labor as a wage payment of 5. In these circumstances, prices would be proportional to costs, to wage costs specifically, and to the quantities of labor purchased by the wage payments that underlie the wage costs.

Any deviation from any of these assumptions upsets any strict correspondence between price and quantity of labor, even in the cases in which quantity of labor does play an actual role in price determination. And this, I believe, is the real nature of the relationship between prices and the quantity of labor developed by the classical economists.

5. The "Iron Law of Wages" of Classical Economics

The shortcoming of the classical economists' theory of value was not their recognition of the very important role played by the quantity of labor required in production. It was, to a great extent, their failure to understand the role of marginal utility and consumer demand in determining the relative wage rates of different grades of labor and the relative prices of various other factors of production whose supply cannot be varied in immediate response to changes in demand.[117]

Much more serious, by far, was their failure clearly to understand that in a free and rational society wage rates have absolutely no tendency to conform to the cost of "subsistence" or to the quantity of labor required to produce "subsistence." This alleged connection—the so-called "iron law of wages"—was believed by the classical economists to exist mainly on the basis of a combination of the law of diminishing returns and the ideas they accepted from Malthus on population growth.

Diminishing Returns and the Malthusian Influence

As already explained in the discussion of the Ricardian theory of land rent, the classical economists often expressed the belief that if wages rose above the subsistence level, the effect would be an increase in population and thus the need to resort to land of inferior quality and to cultivate land already under cultivation more intensively, in order to provide food for the additional population.[118] The consequence of this would be a diminution in the size of the product attributable to the performance of additional labor, or, as most contemporary economists would describe it, a fall in the marginal productivity of labor. This, in turn, would raise the cost of necessities to the workers and ultimately make it impossible for them to purchase anything but the bare minimum of necessities. At that point, population would stop growing because of the sheer economic inability of the average pair of parents to raise more than two children to adulthood.

In this way, subsistence was seen as marking the *equilibrium* level of real wages. When real wages were above subsistence, population grew, and then diminishing returns reduced real wages toward the subsistence level. If real wages fell below the subsistence level, people died of starvation, population fell, the poorest lands were thrown out of cultivation, and the remaining lands were cultivated less intensively. The result was that returns to labor increased, the price of necessities fell, and real wages moved up toward the subsistence level. In the words of Ricardo:

> The natural [viz., equilibrium] price of labour is that price which is necessary to enable the labourers, one with another, to subsist and to perpetuate their race, without either increase or diminution.[119]

> The market price of labour is the price which is really paid for it, from the natural proportion of the supply to the demand; labour is dear when it is scarce and cheap when it is plentiful. However much the market price of labour may deviate from its natural price, it has, like commodities, a tendency to conform to it.

> It is when the market price of labour exceeds its natural price, that the condition of the labourer is flourishing and happy, that he has it in his power to command a greater proportion of the necessaries and enjoyments of life, and therefore to rear a healthy and numerous family. When, however, by the encouragement which high wages give to the increase of population, the number of labourers is increased, wages again fall to their natural price, and indeed from a re-action sometimes fall below it.

> When the market price of labour is below its natural price, the condition of the labourers is most wretched: then poverty deprives them of those comforts which custom renders absolute necessaries. It is only after their privations have reduced their number, or the demand for labour has increased, that the market price of labour will rise to its natural price, and that the labourer will have the moderate comforts which the natural rate of wages will afford.[120]

For the most part, Ricardo's statements in these passages are actually unobjectionable, given the conditions of a precapitalist society. In such primitive conditions, the connection he makes between wages and minimum subsistence is entirely consistent with the laws of supply and demand.

What is objectionable is such statements as: "With the progress of society . . . one of the principal commodities [food] . . . has a tendency to become dearer from the greater difficulty of producing it."[121] If true, it would mean that food could be produced most easily by our caveman ancestors and has been becoming progressively more difficult to produce ever since. Obviously, the opposite is true.

Ricardo's Reservations

Although he clearly endorses the principle that wages have a tendency to conform to their "natural" rate, it is equally clear that Ricardo had some serious reservations. For just a few paragraphs later, he writes:

> Notwithstanding the tendency of wages to conform to their natural rate, their market rate may, in an improving society, for an indefinite period, be constantly above it; for no sooner may the impulse which an increased capital gives to a new demand for labour be obeyed, than another increase of capital may produce the same effect; and thus, if the increase of capital be gradual and constant, the demand for labour may give a continued stimulus to an increase of people.[122]

Furthermore, it turns out that subsistence, in Ricardo's view, does not really mean subsistence at all. It means rather that level of real wages above which the average working family is willing to bring up more than two children, and below which it is willing to bring up less than two children. "Subsistence," in other words, turns out to mean whatever level of real wages results in an equilibrium working population and thus in no tendency of real wages to fall because of population increase or rise because of population decrease. In Ricardo's words:

> It is not to be understood that the natural price of labour, estimated even in food and necessaries, is absolutely fixed and constant. It varies at different times in the same country, and very materially differs in different countries. It essentially depends on the habits and customs of the people. An English labourer would consider his wages under their natural rate, and too scanty to support a family, if they enabled him to purchase no other food than potatoes, and to live in no better habitation than a mud cabin; yet these moderate demands of nature are often deemed sufficient in countries where "man's life is cheap" and his wants easily satisfied. Many of the conveniences now enjoyed in an English cottage would have been thought luxuries at an earlier period of our history.[123]

And, further, along the same lines:

> The friends of humanity cannot but wish that in all countries the labouring classes should have a taste for comforts and enjoyments, and that they should be stimulated by all legal means in their exertions to procure them. There cannot be a better security against a superabundant population.[124]

In these two passages Ricardo's usage of the concept of "subsistence" is actually compatible even with describing the standard of living of the average worker *in the present-day United States* as subsistence. This would be the case if, with a fall in real wage rates below the present level, the average present-day American working family would decide to reduce the number of children it had to a point below the level necessary to keep up the present number of workers.

It should be realized that the observation of economic history from the perspective of the late eighteenth and early nineteenth centuries strongly supported the belief that the equilibrium level of real wages is subsistence—subsistence in the full-bodied sense of extreme poverty characterized by chronic hunger and malnutrition. This was because, again and again, the operation of the law of diminishing returns, coupled with population growth, had in fact brought wages down to actual minimum subsistence whenever, for a brief time, they had gotten above it. Prior to the nineteenth century, history had not yet provided any actual examples of the standard of living of the great mass of workers rising very far above the level of minimum physical subsistence and remaining there for very long. The Industrial Revolution was as yet too young. It was simply too soon for observers such as Ricardo to realize that the progress they were observing around them represented a radical break with all of previous human history.[125]

Adam Smith's Mistaken Belief in the Arbitrary Power of Employers Over Wage Rates

A further element in the writings of the classical economists, on the basis of which they propounded the "iron law of wages," was their belief that employers possess arbitrary power over wage rates. Adam Smith believed that wages are the outcome of an unequal struggle between wage earners and employers, in which employers possess the allegedly decisive advantage of being able to hold out for a longer period of time. He writes:

> What are the common wages of labour, depends every where upon the contract usually made between those two parties, whose interests are by no means the same. The workmen desire to get as much, the masters to give as little as possible. The former are disposed to combine in order to raise, the latter in order to lower the wages of labour.
>
> It is not, however, difficult to foresee which of the two parties must, upon all ordinary occasions, have the advantage in the dispute, and force the other into a compliance

with their terms. The masters, being fewer in number, can combine much more easily; and the law, besides, authorises, or at least does not prohibit their combinations, while it prohibits those of the workmen. We have no acts of parliament against combining to lower the price of work; but many against combining to raise it. In all such disputes the masters can hold out much longer. A landlord, a farmer, a master manufacturer, or merchant, though they did not employ a single workman, could generally live a year or two upon the stocks which they have already acquired. Many workmen could not subsist a week, few could subsist a month, and scarce any a year without employment. In the long-run the workman may be as necessary to his master as his master is to him, but the necessity is not so immediate.[126]

The apparent result of this alleged state of affairs, according to Smith, is that employers are in a position arbitrarily to drive wages as low as they like short of the point of depriving themselves of a supply of workers—i.e., to the level of minimum physical subsistence. In Smith's words:

> But though in disputes with their workmen, masters must generally have the advantage, there is however a certain rate below which it seems impossible to reduce, for any considerable time, the ordinary wages even of the lowest species of labor.
>
> A man must always live by his work, and his wages must at least be sufficient to maintain him. They must even upon most occasions be somewhat more; otherwise it would be impossible for him to bring up a family, and the race of such workmen could not last beyond the first generation.[127]

In fairness to Adam Smith, it should be pointed out that on the very next page of *The Wealth of Nations,* he comes close to grasping the actual principle on which wages are determined in a free market—namely, the competition of employers for labor that is always inherently scarce—but he regards the case as atypical.

> There are certain circumstances, however, which sometimes give the labourers an advantage, and enable them to raise their wages considerably above this rate [subsistence]; evidently the lowest which is consistent with common humanity.
>
> When in any country the demand for those who live by wages; labourers, journeymen, servants of every kind, is continually increasing; when every year furnishes employment for a greater number than had been employed the year before, the workmen have no occasion to combine in order to raise their wages. The scarcity of hands occasions a competition among masters, who bid against one another, in order to get workmen, and thus voluntarily break through the natural combination of masters not to raise wages.[128]

What Adam Smith says about the conditions of an increasing demand for labor applies in principle equally to conditions of a constant or even falling demand for labor. Even in the face of such a demand for labor, the quantity of labor demanded will exceed the supply of labor available if wage rates are sufficiently low. At that point the scarcity of labor is once again felt, and the result is a competition of employers for labor. Moreover, as will be shown in Chapter 13, any fall in wage rates necessary to achieve full employment, is the cause of lower costs and more production, both of which operate to reduce prices and thereby to prevent the fall in wage rates from entailing a fall in the average worker's actual standard of living.[129]

Ricardo's Confusions Concerning the "Iron Law of Wages"

In contrast to Adam Smith, who held that employers have arbitrary power over wages, Ricardo comes to the opposite mistaken conclusion, namely, that arbitrary power over wage rates resides with *the wage earners.* They allegedly have the ability to make employers grant wages above the level corresponding to the state of supply and demand for labor, and in so doing to reduce the rate of profit.

Consistent with this, nowhere does Ricardo present high profits as being made on the basis of subsistence wages. On the contrary, in Ricardo's view, when wages reach subsistence, profits *fall,* as the consequence of an effort to offset the fall in the wage earner's standard of living. What drives wages to subsistence, according to Ricardo, is not the arbitrary payment of low wages by employers, but, as we have seen, the rise in the price of food and other necessities caused by population growth and the operation of the law of diminishing returns. At that point, according to Ricardo, wages must be increased, to keep pace with the higher price of necessities, and this rise in wages reduces profits.

Ricardo claims that this rise in wages occurs apart from the operation of the supply and demand for labor:

Independently of the variations in the value of money, which necessarily affect money wages, but which we have here supposed to have no operation, as we have considered money to be uniformly of the same value, it appears then that wages are subject to a rise or fall from two causes:

1st. The supply and demand of labourers.

2dly. The price of the commodities on which the wages of labour are expended.[130]

A few pages later, proceeding as though he has somehow established this alleged second cause, he reminds his readers that in addition to being regulated by supply and demand:

. . . we must not forget, that wages are also regulated by the prices of the commodities on which they are expended.

As population increases, these necessaries will be constantly rising in price, because more labour will be necessary to produce them. If, then, the money wages of labor should fall [as the result of rising population and thus a

larger supply of labor], whilst every commodity on which the wages of labour were expended rose, the labourer would be doubly affected, and would be soon totally deprived of subsistence. Instead, therefore, of the money wages of labour falling, they would rise . . . .[131]

The fact that the ultimate power over wage rates in Ricardo's view rests with the wage earners becomes clear in the following passages, in which he attempts to defend his position that a rise in the price of necessities must result in a rise in wages:

It may be said that I have taken it for granted that money wages would rise with a rise in the price of raw produce, but that this is by no means a necessary consequence, as the labourer may be contented with fewer enjoyments. It is true that the wages of labour may previously have been at a high level, and that they may bear some reduction. If so, the fall of profits will be checked; but it is impossible to conceive that the money price of wages should fall or remain stationary with a gradually increasing price of necessaries; and therefore it may be taken for granted that, under ordinary circumstances, no permanent rise takes place in the price of necessaries without occasioning, or having been preceded by, a rise in wages.

The effects produced on profits would have been the same, or nearly the same, if there had been any rise in the price of those other necessaries, besides food, on which the wages of labour are expended. *The necessity which the labourer would be under of paying an increased price for such necessaries would oblige him to demand more wages;* and whatever increases wages necessarily reduces profits.[132]

Thus, in the last analysis, according to Ricardo, wages rise because the wage earners need higher wages in order to keep pace with the rise in the price of necessities.

Now this doctrine of wages rising to offset the alleged rise in the price of necessities is, of course, entirely wrong. It appears to be the result of nothing more than a desire on Ricardo's part to soften the harshness of the fact that his analysis ties real wage rates to subsistence by way of the operation of population changes and the law of diminishing returns.[133] According to that analysis, the only way that wages can recover to subsistence when conditions drive them below it is "after their [the wage earners'] privations have reduced their number." Only then, will "the market price of labour . . . rise to its natural price." The mechanism would be the operation of the law of diminishing returns in reverse, as the population and thus the supply of labor diminished because of such horrible events as famines and plagues. Instead of accepting his own analysis, Ricardo postulates a rise in wage rates to alleviate the wage earners' suffering without any reduction in the supply of labor.

Furthermore, it is actually inconceivable for any price (or wage) to rise without either the demand rising or the supply falling.[134] Inasmuch as Ricardo's context here, is an alleged rise in wages without a fall in the supply of labor, it is necessary to conclude that at least implicitly he assumes that when wages fall to the subsistence level, there will somehow be an increase in the demand for labor that will be responsible for raising wage rates in the face of higher prices of necessities.

Ricardo's apparent belief in a kind of deus ex machina of a rising demand for labor to raise wage rates in the face of rising prices of necessities, is what leads him to the conclusion that there is a tendency toward a falling rate of profit, which, fortunately, is interrupted by improvements in the production of necessities.

> The natural tendency of profits then is to fall; for, in the progress of society and wealth, the additional quantity of food required is obtained by the sacrifice of more and more labour. This tendency, this gravitation as it were of profits, is happily checked at repeated intervals by the improvements in machinery connected with the production of necessaries, as well as by discoveries in the science of agriculture, which enable us to relinquish a portion of labour before required, and therefore to lower the price of the prime necessary of the labourer.[135]

Ricardo expresses essentially the same thought in connection with foreign trade, but with more obvious radical connotations:

> It has been my endeavour to show throughout this work that the rate of profits can never be increased but by a fall in wages, and that there can be no permanent fall of wages but in consequence of a fall of the necessaries on which wages are expended. If, therefore, by the extension of foreign trade, or by improvements in machinery, the food and necessaries of the labourer can be brought to market at a reduced price, profits will rise. If, instead of growing our own corn, or manufacturing the clothing and other necessaries of the labourer, we discover a new market from which we can supply ourselves with these commodities at a cheaper price, wages will fall and profits rise; but if the commodities obtained at a cheaper rate, by the extension of foreign commerce, or by the improvement of machinery, be exclusively the commodities consumed by the rich, no alteration will take place in the rate of profits. The rate of wages would not be affected, although wine, velvets, silks, and other expensive commodities should fall 50 per cent., and consequently profits would continue unaltered.[136]

This last paragraph appears to suggest the Marxian notion that improvements in production simply pass the wage earners by, because they are followed by a corresponding reduction in wages. It is possible to argue for this interpretation on the basis of other passages in Ricardo as well.

Nevertheless, while this interpretation is logically consistent with much of what Ricardo says, it is not his actual meaning. His actual meaning is that the fall in wages here should be understood as a limited one, eliminating an extraordinary increase in wages to compensate

for the rise in the price of necessities beyond the point of minimum subsistence. Once this limited fall in wages takes place, the effect of further improvements in production *is to raise real wages through the mechanism of falling prices unaccompanied by any further fall in money wages.* His actual meaning is essentially the same as the doctrine developed in Chapter 14 of this book under the name "The Productivity Theory of Wages." Support for this interpretation appears on the very next page following the passage last quoted. Here it is pointed out how improvements in production generally do not operate to raise the rate of profit, but to reduce prices and thereby to benefit *all classes.*

> The remarks which have been made respecting foreign trade apply equally to home trade. The [economy-wide, average] rate of profits is never increased by a better distribution of labour, by the invention of machinery, by the establishment of roads and canals, or by any means of abridging labour either in the manufacture of in the conveyance of goods. These are causes which operate on price, and never fail to be highly beneficial to consumers; since they enable them, with the same labour, or with the value of the produce of the same labour, to obtain in exchange a greater quantity of the commodity to which the improvement is applied; but they have no effect whatever on profit. On the other hand, every diminution in the wages of labour raises profits, but produces no effect on the [average] price of commodities. One is *advantageous to all classes, for all classes are consumers;* the other is beneficial only to producers; they gain more, but everything remains at its former price. In the first case they get the same as before; but everything on which their gains are expended is diminished in exchangeable value.[137]

The Actual Meaning Ricardo Attached to "A Fall in Wages"

Indeed, the kind of fall in wages and rise in profits Ricardo usually has in mind turns out *not* to mean a fall in the wage earner's standard of living—in fact, it is fully compatible with a *rise* in the wage earner's standard of living. The most formidable evidence for this view occurs in Section 7 of his chapter "On Value." There he makes it clear that he is talking of changes in wages and profits in the conditions of a monetary unit of invariable "inner" value, that is, a monetary unit such that all variations in prices are the result of changes on the side of production and supply, not changes on the side of money and demand.

Ricardo's theoretical stand-in for such a monetary unit is a fixed aggregate quantity of labor employed in the production of commodities. However, his conclusions can be understood just as well, and far more easily, on the assumption of a fixed aggregate monetary demand—viz., expenditure—for the output of the economic system. (A fixed volume of spending for output would represent a monetary unit of invariable "inner" value, in that all changes in prices would reflect only changes on the side of output—that is, production and supply—not changes on the side of money and spending. This is because with the amount of monetary demand—spending—being the same, the only way that prices could rise would be by virtue of a fall in output, and the only way that prices could fall would be by virtue of a rise in output. All changes in prices would thus proceed from the side of output, not from the side of money. Money would be of invariable inner value in the sense that even though prices changed and thus the value of money changed, the changes took place from the side of output, not from the side of money.[138]) He states:

> It is not by the absolute quantity of produce obtained by either class, that we can correctly judge of the rate of profit, rent, and wages, but by the quantity of labour required to obtain that produce. By improvements in machinery and agriculture the whole produce may be doubled; but if wages, rent, and profit be also doubled, these three will bear the same proportions to one another as before, and neither could be said to have relatively varied. [To understand this point, imagine that the money value of the aggregate product of the economic system is constant at 1,000 monetary units, which is the total of the spending to buy it. Now imagine that production and the supply of goods sold double and thus that prices halve. If wages, rent, and profits all continue at the same respective monetary magnitudes as before, then, in Ricardo's view none of them has changed, even though the buying power of each of them has doubled.] But if wages partook not of the whole of this increase; if they, instead of being doubled, were only increased one-half; if rent, instead of being doubled, were only increased three-fourths, and the remaining increase went to profit, it would, I apprehend, be correct for me to say that rent and wages had fallen while profits had risen; for if we had an invariable standard by which to measure the value of this produce we should find that a less value had fallen to the class of labourers and landlords, and a greater to the class of capitalists than had been given before. We might find, for example, that though the absolute quantity of commodities had been doubled, they were the produce of precisely the former quantity of labour. Of every hundred hats, coats, and quarters of corn produced, if

> The labourers had before 25
> The landlords 25
> And the capitalists 50
>   100:

> And if, after these commodities were double the quantity, of every 100

> The labourers had only 22
> The landlords 22
> And the capitalists 56
>   100:

> In that case I should say that wages and rent had fallen and profits risen; though in consequence of the abundance of commodities the quantity paid to the labourer and landlord would have increased in the proportion of 25 to 44. Wages are to be estimated by their real value, viz., by the quantity of labour and capital employed in producing them, and not by their nominal value either in coats, hats, money, or corn. Under the circumstances I have just supposed, commodities would have fallen to half their former value, and if money had not varied, to half their former price also. If then in this medium, which had not varied in value, the wages of the labourer should be found to have fallen, it will not the less be a real fall because they might furnish him with a greater quantity of cheap commodities than his former wages.[139]

What Ricardo means to say in the passages just quoted is that production doubles and prices halve. With total money income constant at 1,000 units of money, aggregate wages and aggregate rents fall from 250 each to 220 each, while aggregate profits rise from 500 to 560. Even though the 220 each of wages and rent now buy as much as 440 would have bought initially, wages and rent still fall in terms of an invariable money. Their fall in terms of such a monetary unit will not be any the less an actual monetary fall because they enable the wage earner and landlord to buy a greater quantity of the less expensive commodities than did their former wages and rents.

What must be stressed is that while this is certainly a fall in wages in Ricardo's meaning of the term, it has nothing whatever to do with an approach of wages to subsistence. What contemporary economists would call real wages sharply increase in this case. (What Ricardo means by real wages, in contrast, is total money wages in the conditions of an invariable money. And he regards the goods the wage earners can actually buy as merely being nominal wages.)

Hopefully, it is now clear that Ricardo does not in fact argue that the capitalists arbitrarily set wages at the level of minimum subsistence, and that, indeed, the core of his analysis is actually fully compatible with real wages steadily rising and doing so *precisely on the basis of the activities of the capitalists,* whose savings create the demand for labor and capital goods and who are responsible for the steady rise in the productivity of labor and thus for a steady fall in prices relative to wages. Hopefully, it is also clear that in the writings of Ricardo, if and when wages do fall to subsistence, not only is the cause held to be the combination of population growth and the operation of the law of diminishing returns rather than any greed on the part of employers for higher profits, but also the effect is held to be a *reduction* in the rate of profit, not an increase.[140] Profits, according to Ricardo, are definitely not the result of any arbitrary imposition of subsistence wages, which is what Marx alleges them to be.[141]

Classical Economics' Mistaken Denial of the Ability to Tax Wage Earners

However inconsistently, insofar as the classical economists believed that the equilibrium level of real wages was minimum subsistence, they were led to the conclusion that wage earners cannot be made to pay a significant amount of taxes. After all, if wages are merely equal to subsistence, what is there to tax? Thus, for example, Ricardo writes: "Dr. [Adam] Smith uniformly, and I think justly, contends, that the labouring classes cannot materially contribute to the burdens of the State. A tax on necessaries, or on wages, will therefore be shifted from the poor to the rich . . ."[142]

This view is entirely false. We saw in Chapter 9 that taxes on the "rich"—on businessmen and capitalists—are overwhelming borne by the wage earners in the form of a lower demand for labor and a lower productivity of labor, which latter is caused by a lower demand for capital goods relative to consumers' goods and reduced incentives to improve production.[143] The truth is that wage earners always end up bearing the major burden of taxes; they bear the burden whether the taxes are levied on them directly or on businessmen and capitalists.

The truth of this proposition does not depend on real wages initially being above subsistence, as happens to be the case today, when they exceed subsistence many times over. If, as in most of history and in most countries even now, real wages are at the level of subsistence, an increase in taxes in any form operates to reduce them below subsistence. It does so either by directly reducing the wage earners' spendable income, if it takes the form of an additional income tax they must pay, or the buying power of their incomes, if it is an additional sales tax they must pay. If it is an additional tax on the "rich," it reduces the demand for labor and thus the wage earners' pretax incomes; it also reduces the supply of goods produced and available for them to buy, and thus raises the prices they must pay. The wage earners simply cannot escape the burden of the tax.

If real wages are initially at the subsistence level, the effect of any tax increase is that wage earners are literally taxed to death. Wages then recover to the subsistence level from a point below the subsistence level insofar as a reduced population makes it possible to produce agricultural commodities and minerals under conditions of a higher productivity of labor. At that point, the higher productivity of labor resulting from the depopulation offsets the burden of the tax.

If a modern, division-of-labor economy should ever be driven to the point of subsistence wages, and then taxes be further increased, real wages would not recover as the result of depopulation. The depopulation would further reduce the productivity of labor, by reducing the extent of the division of labor. A collapse of society would ensue.

---

6. Marxian Distortions of Classical Economics; The Final Demolition of the Exploitation Theory

In the last two sections of this chapter, I have shown the actual nature of classical economics insofar as it is alleged to underlie the Marxian exploitation theory. Indeed, precisely on the foundation of classical economics, I have demolished the conceptual framework of the exploitation theory. I have shown how the labor theory of value of classical economics—at least as developed by Ricardo, who was the leading theorist of the school—stands merely as a partial principle, alongside of a variety of other principles of price determination, and can actually be used to express the essential productive contribution of businessmen and capitalists to the rise in real wages by virtue of continuously raising the productivity of labor and thereby making goods more and more abundant relative to labor. I have shown that in the hands of Ricardo even the so-called iron law of wages of classical economics does not actually lend very much support to the exploitation theory. Thus, the notion that classical economics implies Marxism is at best highly superficial. In essentials, the opposite is true, as my critique of the conceptual framework of the exploitation theory on the basis of classical economics should make clear.

In Chapter 14, I will explain in detail Marx's very different version of the labor theory of value and "iron law of wages." A reading of that material, in the light of the account of the classical economists' views that has been presented in this chapter, will make it obvious that Marx's views represent gross distortions of the classical economists' ideas on these subjects.

Chapter 14 will complete the vital work of refuting all remaining aspects of the exploitation theory. It will provide a systematic critique of the Marxian version of the iron law of wages—that is, the notion that employers have the power arbitrarily to set wage rates at minimum subsistence. It will hunt down the numerous manifestations of this doctrine in the prevailing political-economic ideology of the twentieth century and one by one subject them to a thoroughgoing critical analysis, from which they will be unable to recover in the mind of any rational reader who takes the trouble to study and understand the analysis.

Chapter 14 will follow an extensive explanation of the nature of aggregate demand, in chapters expounding the quantity theory of money, Say's law of markets, and the cause and remedy for mass unemployment. Following this necessary preparatory work (which, of course, is enormously valuable in its own right), the critique of the

Marxian version of the iron law of wages will be provided primarily in the form of the presentation of a totally different, positive theory of wages—one that is fully compatible with the essential doctrines of classical economics. This theory of wages, I call, by the title of Chapter 14, *The Productivity Theory of Wages*.

Notes

1. The productive role of commodity speculation and the commodity markets has already been explained. See above, pp. 191–192.

2. Most of the material that explains these matters in the next three sections originally appeared in my article "Definitions Pertaining to Production and Consumption," *Il Politico* 32, no. 1 (March 1967).

3. In today's environment of blatant irrationalism and open hostility to science and technology, it must be stressed that *proof* of inherent destructiveness must be shown before an activity is to be disallowed the title of productive. There is no such proof to disqualify even alcohol, tobacco (in forms other than cigarettes), and gambling, when resorted to in moderation. Still less is there any reason to challenge the productivity of the manufacture and sale of such substances as coffee, saccharin, red meat, white flour, white bread, sugar, cow's milk, table salt, and so on, the claims of assorted cultists and food faddists to the contrary notwithstanding.

4. Cf. James Mill, *Commerce Defended* (London, 1808); reprinted in *Selected Economic Writings of James Mill*, ed. Donald Winch (Chicago: University of Chicago Press, 1966) p. 128.

5. The meaning of the terms productive, unproductive, and reproductive consumption in the physical sense was explained above, on pp. 131–132.

6. These concepts appear in the writings of Adam Smith and his followers under the names "productive and unproductive labor." Unfortunately, the classical economists were highly inconsistent in their use of these terms and frequently employed them to refer to a very different distinction, namely, the distinction between labor employed in the production of tangible, material goods and labor employed not in the production of tangible, material goods. (See below, the quotations from Adam Smith on p. 456.) Apart from this inconsistency, Adam Smith and James Mill can be acknowledged as the originators of the basic distinctions I have employed in this discussion. Cf. Adam Smith, *The Wealth of Nations* (London, 1776), bk. 2, chap. 3; reprint of Cannan ed. (Chicago: University of Chicago Press, 2 vols. in 1, 1976), 1:351–371. (Where appropriate, from now on, specific page references to the University of Chicago Press reprint will be supplied in brackets.) Cf. also James Mill, *Commerce Defended*, chaps. 5 and 6 (pp. 105–139) in *Selected Economic Writings of James Mill*.

7. In case anyone wonders about the classification of government employees engaged in tax collections or employees of private charities who are engaged in fund raising, see below, pp. 454–455.

8. See above, p. 132.

9. See above, ibid.

10. See above, p. 40.

11. On occasion, I will include accumulated savings in the methods I offer for measuring the degree of capital intensiveness of the economic system. See below, for example, Chapter 14, n. 71.

12. John Kenneth Galbraith, *The Affluent Society*, 3d ed. (Boston: Houghton Mifflin, 1976), pp. 110–111.

13. It should go without saying that productive expenditures made for the purpose of reducing costs of production, such as many of those made by a company's research and development department, are productive expenditures. They too are made for the purpose of bringing in sales revenues. Their only distinction is that they seek to do so with a greater profit than would otherwise be the case. All the expenditures made by business enterprises for business purposes are productive expenditures.

14. Subsequent discussion in the next section of this chapter, concerning the closely related doctrine of imputed income, will make still clearer the absurd results implied in the notion that a saving of expense is the equivalent of actually earning an income.

15. See above, p. 40.

16. Ibid.

17. See below, pp. 634–636.

18. Cf. *Wealth of Nations*, bk. 2, chap. 1 [1:298].

19. Ibid., bk. 2, chap. 3 [1:351]. Italics supplied.

20. Ibid., [1:352]. Italics supplied.

21. See above, 446–447.

22. Smith's confusions here are noted by Cannan. See *Wealth of Nations*, bk. 2, chap. 3 [1:351].

23. See below, pp. 473–475.

24. See above, pp. 453–454.

25. I present my theory of aggregate profit and the average rate of profit, below, in Chapter 16, and many of the leading applications of the theory in Chapter 17.

26. Much of the material in this and the next section of this chapter originally appeared in my article "Cost and Revenue: An Economist's Defense of the Accounting Concepts," *Il Politico* 33, no. 4 (December 1968).

27. United States Department of Commerce, Office of Business Economics, *National Income 1954 Edition* (Washington, D. C.: U.S. Government Printing Office, 1954), p. 46.

28. Paul Samuelson and William Nordhaus, *Economics*, 13th ed. (New York: McGraw Hill Book Company, 1989), pp. 117–118.

29. See *Glamour*, March 1992, p. 114.

30. Samuelson and Nordhaus, *Economics*, p. 524.

31. Ibid., p. 525.

32. Ibid.

33. See above, pp. 162–165. See also above, p. 201 and pp. 206–209.

34. See 208–209.

35. Many of the essential points, together with their specific

formulations, that I make in this section and below, on pp. 475–485, previously appeared in my essay "Classical Economics Versus the Exploitation Theory" in Kurt Leube and Albert Zlabinger, eds., *The Political Economy of Freedom Essays in Honor of F. A. Hayek* (Munich and Vienna: Philosophia Verlag, 1985), pp. 207–225. They were originally presented in a lecture I delivered under the title "A Ricardian's Critique of the Exploitation Theory" at the University Club of New York City, on January 26, 1965, before a group of members and friends of von Mises's seminar.

36. For a discussion of how the tax laws have fostered uneconomic concentration, see above, p. 395.

37. Cf. above, pp. 140–141.

38. See below, pp. 477–480, 632–634, and 683–685 passim.

39. See below, pp. 478–480.

40. On this point, see above, p. 141.

41. Concerning all these points, see above, pp. 173–174.

42. On the nature of profit management and bureaucratic management, see above, pp. 304–305. For a thorough discussion of the subject, see Ludwig von Mises, *Bureaucracy* (1944; reprint ed., New Rochelle, N. Y., 1969).

43. See above, pp. 176–180.

44. See above, pp. 327–328.

45. See below, pp. 622–631 and 634–636.

46. On these points, see below, pp. 622–629 and 632–634.

47. See below, pp. 634–636.

48. Cf. Ludwig von Mises, *Human Action*, 3d ed. rev. (Chicago: Henry Regnery Co., 1966), p. 531.

49. On the vital role of exchange and money, see above, pp. 141–144.

50. See above, pp. 172–173.

51. Cf. George Leland Bach, *Economics,* 6th ed. (Englewood Cliffs, N. J.: Prentice-Hall, Inc., 1968), pp. 353–354. The antiadvertising example there serves as the prototype for the proadvertising example presented here. Bach expounds essentially the same hostility to advertising in his eleventh ed., 1987, but with less clarity and forcefulness.

52. Cf. ibid. for an exposition of this fallacy.

53. See Yale Brozen, "Is Advertising a Barrier to Entry?" in Yale Brozen, editor, *Advertising and Society* (New York: New York University Press, 1974), pp. 79–109.

54. Cf. von Mises, *Human Action*, p. 321.

55. Cf. ibid.

56. On the objective foundations of the value of wealth, see above, pp. 42–49. For further reading on the subject of advertising, see Jerry Kirkpatrick, *In Defense of Advertising* (Westport, Conn.: Quorum Books, 1994). This book constitutes a thoroughgoing philosophic analysis and defense of virtually all aspects of advertising.

57. See above, pp. 200–201, 414–417 and 441–456.

58. On this last point and the demolition of the whole of the specific substance of the exploitation theory, see below, pp. 618–663 and 664–666. See also above, p. 464.

59. In this instance, of course, the abandonment of an essential classical doctrine was also the result of the prosocialist sympathies of John Stuart Mill, as well as the mistaken ideas of the late nineteenth-century defenders of capitalism. See above, pp. 3, and below, pp. 664–666. For a defense of the wages-fund doctrine, see below, ibid. For a critique of the notion that consumers pay wages in buying products, see below, pp. 683–685.

60. See above, the quotations from Smith on p. 456.

61. In connection with his opposition to government borrowing, see his discussion of public debts, in *Wealth of Nations*, bk. 5, chap. 3 [2:441–486].

62. *Wealth of Nations,* bk. 1, chap. 5 [1:35].

63. Ibid., chap. 6 [1:54–55].

64. Ibid., chap. 8 [1:73–74].

65. On the productive activity of businessmen and capitalists, see above, pp. 462–464.

66. See above, especially p. 304 and pp. 310–317. See also above, pp. 27–31, 63–71, 135–139, and 303–304.

67. *Wealth of Nations*, chap. 6 [1:56].

68. See above, p. 304.

69. Cf. Karl Marx, *Capital*, trans. from 3d German ed. by Samuel Moore and Edward Aveling; Frederick Engels, ed.; rev. and amplified according to the 4th German ed. by Ernest Untermann (New York: 1906), vol. 1, pt. 2, chap. 4; (reprinted, New York: Random House, The Modern Library), pp. 163–173.

70. John Stuart Mill, *Principles of Political Economy*, Ashley ed. (1909; reprint ed., Fairfield, N. J.: Augustus M. Kelley, 1976), pp. 79–88.

71. David Ricardo, *Principles of Political Economy and Taxation*, 3d ed. (London, 1821), chap. 6 passim; reprinted as vol. 1 of *The Works and Correspondence of David Ricardo*, ed. Piero Sraffa (Cambridge: Cambridge University Press, 1962), pp. 110–111, passim. (Where appropriate, from now on, specific page references to the Sraffa edition will be supplied in brackets.)

72. F. A. Hayek, *Capitalism and the Historians* (Chicago: University of Chicago Press, 1954), pp. 15, 16.

73. Smith, *Wealth of Nations*, bk. 1, chap. 11 [1:277].

74. Ibid., chap. 8 [1:77].

75. Ibid., bk. 1, chap. 11 [1:277–278].

76. On this point, see below, pp. 813–817.

77. See below, pp. 762–767 and 825–826.

78. *Wealth of Nations*, bk. 1, chap. 6 [1:58].

79. See above, pp. 462–464.

80. See above, pp. 459–462.

81. On the nature of time preference, see above, pp. 55–58.

82. See below, pp. 743–744.

83. *Human Action*, p. 142.

84. See the rebuttal of the alienation charge, above, pp. 129–130.

85. It is important to realize that large salaries and bonuses for key executives can be justified even in conditions of recession or depression, insofar as they are earned for sharply cutting costs, including laying off large numbers of unnecessary employees. As illustration of this principle, one should consider how desirable it would be for the U.S. Postal Service to become privately owned and for the new key executives to earn tens of millions of dollars in salaries and bonuses by virtue of massive firings of unnecessary or unproductive employees that would result in annual savings of hundreds of millions of dollars. Fortunately, this kind of process is what does occur in private business when necessary. Thus, the current complaints about the injustice of executives earning high incomes in the midst of layoffs likely are fundamentally unfounded.

86. Cf. Eugen von Böhm-Bawerk, *Capital and Interest*, 3 vols., trans. George D. Huncke and Hans F. Sennholz (South Holland, Ill.: Libertarian Press, 1959), 1:263–271.

87. Ibid., 1:266.

88. Ibid., 1:269.

89. Cf. ibid., 1:241–307; see also "Karl Marx and the Close of His System" (New York, 1898); reprinted as "Unresolved Contradiction in the Marxian Economic System" in *Shorter Classics of Eugen von Böhm-Bawerk* (South Holland, Ill.: Libertarian Press, 1962), pp. 208–287.

90. See above, pp. 478–480.

91. See also above, pp. 462–464.

92. See above, pp. 313–316.

93. This relationship is elaborated in great detail below, pp. 618–622. For elaboration of the classical economists' concepts of demand and supply, see above, pp. 152–155.

94. Adam Smith, *Wealth of Nations,* bk. 1, chap. 8 [1:72].

95. For elaboration of the meaning of the wages-fund doctrine, see above, p. 474, and below, pp. 664–666.

96. Cf. Ricardo, *Principles,* chap. 20 [pp. 280–281].

97. Cf. ibid., chap. 1, sec. 6 [pp. 43–51]. See also below, pp. 536–540.

98. Ricardo, *Principles,* chap. 1, sec. 1 [p. 12].

99. See above, pp. 201–202.

100. See Ricardo, *Principles,* chap. 4 [pp. 88–92], which deals with the distinction between market price and natural price (viz., equilibrium price). See also chaps. 2 and 3 [pp. 67–87], which deal with land and land rent, including the rent of mines, and chap. 24 [pp. 201–204], concerning taxes on houses.

101. See below, pp. 494–495.

102. Ricardo, *Principles of Political Economy and Taxation,* chap. 1, sec. 1 [p. 12]. This description clearly seems to exclude human labor.

103. Ibid., [p. 30].

104. Ibid., [p. 37]. Italics supplied.

105. Ibid.

106. In fact, the machine would have to bring in a total of $1,650 to allow for the fact that a year goes by between the outlay of the $1,000 of wages and the beginning of the machine's useful life.

107. *Works and Correspondence of David Ricardo,* 8:193.

108. Ibid., p. 194.

109. Ricardo, *Principles,* chap. 1, sec. 5 [pp. 39–49].

110. See above the reference to *Shorter Classics of Böhm-Bawerk,* in which this essay is reprinted.

111. Ricardo, *Principles,* chap. 7, [p. 133].

112. See above, pp. 187–188.

113. We have, of course, already encountered this principle in connection with the operation of competition and the law of comparative advantage. See above, pp. 351–354.

114. John Stuart Mill, *Principles of Political Economy,* p. 460.

115. See above, pp. 201–202 and 208–209.

116. Concerning the tendency toward a uniform rate of profit, see above, pp. 172–173.

117. On these subjects, see above, pp. 201–212.

118. See above, pp. 311–312,

119. Ricardo, *Principles,* chap. 5 [p. 93].

120. Ibid., [p. 94].

121. Ibid., [p. 93].

122. Ibid., [pp. 94–95].

123. Ibid., [pp. 96–97].

124. Ibid., [p. 100].

125. I made the same observation earlier, when first introducing Ricardo's theory of land rent. See above, p. 312. See also above, p. 358.

126. Smith, *Wealth of Nations,* bk. 1, chap. 8 [1:74–75].

127. Ibid., [1:76]. For a critique of the doctrine of alleged arbitrary power by employers and the inference that in the absence of government interference they will set wage rates at minimum subsistence, see below, pp. 613–618.

128. *Wealth of Nations,* bk. 1, chap. 8, [1:77].

129. On this point, see below, pp. 584–585.

130. Ricardo, *Principles,* chap. 5 [p. 97].

131. Ibid., [p. 101].

132. Ibid., chap. 6 [p. 118]. Italics supplied.

133. As I have pointed out, the alleged rise in the price of necessities as any kind of permanent, inescapable phenomenon is, of course, itself also entirely wrong. See above, p. 492.

134. See below, pp. 897–907, where this point is elaborated and applied to various alleged explanations of the rising prices caused by inflation.

135. Ricardo, *Principles,* chap. 6 [p. 120].

136. Ibid., chap. 7 [p. 132].

137. Ibid., [p. 133]. Italics supplied.

138. For a discussion of the subject of invariable money, see below, pp. 536–540.

139. Ricardo, *Principles,* chap. 1, sec. 7 [pp. 49–50].

140. A critique of Ricardo's doctrine of the tendency toward a falling rate of profit appears below, pp. 799–801.

141. For an account of Marx's theory of wages, see below, pp. 607–610.

142. Ricardo, *Principles,* chap. 16 [p. 235].

143. See above, pp. 306–310. See also below, pp. 622–642.

PART THREE

THE PROCESS OF ECONOMIC PROGRESS

CHAPTER 12

MONEY AND SPENDING

1. The Quantity Theory of Money

The quantity theory of money holds that the volume of spending in the economic system, for goods, for labor, or any other broad economic category of things, is determined primarily by the quantity of money that exists in the economic system. To state the theory in the simplest possible terms: the amount of money that is *spent* is determined primarily by the amount of money that *exists*. The quantity theory of money can be expressed in terms of the following simple equation, which relates the quantity of money to aggregate demand in the sense of the volume of spending:

$$M \times V = D ,$$

where M is the quantity of money in the economic system, D is the aggregate demand, as manifested in a definite total expenditure of money in the economic system, and V is the average number of times a unit of the money supply is spent in the period (i.e., the so-called velocity of circulation of money).

For example, as these words are written, the money supply in the United States is approximately $1,150 billion. The so-called gross domestic product (GDP) (formerly gross national product or GNP), which is the most commonly used measure of aggregate spending, is approximately $6,700 billion.[1] The implied average number of times a dollar is spent in a way that counts in GDP is thus approximately 5.8.

The money supply embraces all directly spendable money—all commonly used means of payment. In the context of modern economic conditions, this includes paper currency, coin, and, quantitatively most important nowadays, checking-account balances (including balances transferable by telephone or computer). As of the end of 1993, the money supply of the United States amounted to $329 billion of coin and currency, including $8 billion of outstanding traveler's checks, and $799 billion of checking account balances. The total money supply, therefore, amounted to $1,128 billion.[2]

GDP currently consists almost 90 percent of consumption expenditures: $4,585 billion reported as personal consumption expenditures, $1,169 billion of government expenditures for goods and services, almost all of which is consumption, and a further substantial portion of the $284 billion reported as investment in residential structures, but which in fact is consumption.[3] Thus, out of a current GDP of approximately $6,700 billion, well over $5,700 billion represents one form or another of consumption expenditure.

Because it is comprised overwhelmingly of consumption spending, GDP can be taken as an approximate measure of aggregate *consumer* demand in the economic system. The velocity of circulation figure which relates GDP and the money supply could be termed GDP velocity or consumption velocity, since it reflects the number of times the average dollar of the money supply is spent in a way that counts in GDP, which essentially means: is spent for consumption. However, because of the virtual equivalence of GDP and consumption spending with national income, it happens that this measure of velocity is called income velocity.[4] In any case, for the sake of greater accuracy, the above formula relating the quantity of money and aggregate demand should be rewritten as

$$M \times V = D_C,$$

where D_C is the aggregate demand for consumers' goods, as manifested in a definite total expenditure of money to buy consumers' goods.

For many purposes, it is necessary to use a larger measure of total spending than GDP or consumption. Total aggregate demand for all products, consumers' goods or capital goods, is one such measure; that plus all wage payments (a concept I refer to as Gross National Revenue—GNR) is another; total spending of all kinds, including for stocks, bonds, and other securities, is yet a third.[5] When these measures of aggregate demand are used, a correspondingly different figure for velocity of circulation results. The best known is called transactions velocity, which relates the quantity of money to the total of spending of every description.

The relationship between the quantity of money and the volume of spending in the economic system (whether that volume is conceived of relatively narrowly, as consisting merely of consumption spending, or more broadly) can begin to be understood by grasping the following simple and obvious connection between more money and more demand. Namely, an increase in the quantity of money raises demand because when the new and additional money comes into existence, its owners spend it. Those upon whom the new money is spent, in turn, respend it. The additional money is spent and respent over and over again, so long as it continues in existence. And in this way it raises the amount of spending that takes place in any given year.

It is probably easiest to visualize this process in the conditions of a gold standard, in which gold coins are money. Thus imagine that we are back in the old West, and some miners discover gold. They take their gold to the mint and have it manufactured into coins. Then they spend the coins in a frontier town. The merchants on whom they spend them turn around and subsequently respend them. And so it goes, with the new coins being spent and respent over and over and thus raising the aggregate demand of any given year.[6]

Nothing essential in the process is changed, except for the way that new and additional money comes into existence, if we substitute present-day paper currency and checkbook money for the gold coins of the old West. Thus, suppose that the U.S. Treasury is running short of money. It calls up its banker, the Federal Reserve System, and asks for a loan. The Federal Reserve receives some securities from the Treasury—bonds, Treasury bills, or whichever—and credits the Treasury's checking account with the proceeds of the loan. The Federal Reserve could print currency for the Treasury and the Treasury could simply spend the currency. But under modern conditions the Treasury wants to make payments by check, not by currency. So the Federal Reserve credits the Treasury's checking account, and new and additional money has come into existence at the stroke of a pen (or the touch of a few computer keys).

Having received a credit to its account, the Treasury can now write additional checks. It sends out, let us assume, a batch of social security checks. The recipients of these checks take them to their banks. They can either cash them or deposit them in their own checking accounts. It does not matter which they do. If they cash them, the banks will have to take the checks to the Federal Reserve System and obtain currency for the checks. Then the situation from this point on is literally a matter of the printing of money. The currency the social security recipients get they will spend, and those on whom they spend it will respend it, and so on. New and additional paper currency will pass from hand to hand, just as in our earlier example new and additional gold coins passed from hand to hand.

But suppose the social security recipients deposit the checks in their checking accounts. In this case, they are in a position to write additional checks of their own and they now spend their social security payments in this way instead of spending currency. Those to whom they write checks in turn deposit the checks in their checking accounts, and subsequently write checks of their own. In this case, checking deposits pass from hand to hand instead of currency. In all essentials, the process is identical with the spending of currency.

Of course, at any time, the recipient of a check is free to cash it and obtain currency, just as the owner of currency is free to deposit it and write checks. The point is that money is created equally by the expansion of the currency or the checking deposits of the Federal Reserve System. It circulates equally in the form of the passage of currency or the passage of checking balances from hand to hand.

Unlike gold and silver, however, the paper and checkbook money of the government can be created virtually without limit and without cost. While gold and silver are rare in nature and typically require laborious mining operations in their supply, the quantity of paper and checkbook money is not limited even by the supply of paper—additional zeros can be printed on the same paper. The cost of printing any piece of paper money, whether a dollar bill or a hundred dollar bill, is only a fraction of a cent. The cost of crediting the Treasury's checking account with a billion dollars is not much greater. *As a result, there is nothing intrinsic to paper or checkbook money that operates to preserve its value.*

Paper and checkbook money can be created by the government in any quantity, for any purpose, for all practical purposes, effortlessly and costlessly. The power to create it constitutes an unlimited power to buy up the people's wealth and depreciate the value of money. I will show later on to what extent the government has already used this power. (From now on, incidentally, for the sake of brevity of expression, I will generally use the words "paper money" as standing both for currency and checkbook money.)

The Quantity Theory of Money as the Explanation of Rising Prices

The quantity theory of money explains the persistent rise in prices experienced in the United States and all other countries over the last two generations or more. In the simplest possible terms, the value of money, like the value of anything else, is determined by its quantity. The greater the quantity of any good, the lower is the value of that good. The greater the quantity of money, the lower is the value of money. A lower value of money, of course, means higher prices of goods.

The same thought can be expressed more precisely by means of our equation for aggregate demand. However, we must add to that equation the further equation for expressing the general consumer price level in terms of the relationship between the aggregate demand for consumers' goods and the aggregate supply of consumers' goods. The demand/supply equation states that

$$P = \frac{D_C}{S_C}$$

where P is the general level of consumers' goods prices, in the sense of the weighted average of the prices at which consumers' goods are actually sold, D_C, is the aggregate demand for consumers' goods, as manifested in a definite total expenditure of money to buy consumers' goods, and S_C is the aggregate supply of consumers' goods, as manifested in a definite total quantity of consumers' goods produced and sold.

As used in the above equation, and everywhere throughout this book, unless indicated otherwise, the term demand means the willingness combined with the ability to spend money, as manifested in the expenditure of a definite amount of money. Similarly, supply means the existence of goods combined with the willingness of their owners to sell them, as manifested in the sale of a definite quantity of goods.[7]

The above formula shows that the general consumer price level is merely *the arithmetical quotient of a numerator divided by a denominator. Demand is the numerator, and supply is the denominator.* It is important to learn to think of the price level in just these terms,

namely, as the arithmetical quotient of a numerator—demand—divided by a denominator—supply.

Let us use some concrete numbers in our formula, to make it more real. Thus, consider initially the price of a single good, say, the price at which packs of cigarettes are sold in a given supermarket in a given week. We want to know what is the average price at which packs of cigarettes in that supermarket were sold last week. To find the answer, we must divide the number of packs sold into the total expenditure to buy those packs, that is, the supply into the demand. If, for example, one thousand packs were sold for one thousand dollars, then the average price at which a pack was sold was one dollar. In exactly the same way, we could calculate the average price at which a pair of shoes was sold last week in a given shoe store, and similarly for any good in any period of time.

All we need do is realize that exactly the same principle applies to the general consumer price level in the sense of the weighted average of the prices at which consumers' goods are sold in the economic system as a whole. At this level of analysis, we must conceive of cigarettes, shoes, and all other goods as representing varying quantities of an abstract unit of goods in general and thus as capable of being added up into an aggregate supply. Whatever the concrete difficulties we might encounter in attempting to implement this concept, the basic idea is very clear and we repeatedly rely on it in our thinking. For example, no one has any doubt that the aggregate production and supply of consumers' goods in the United States today is far greater than it was a century or even a generation ago, or that it is far greater than the aggregate production and supply of consumers' goods in contemporary Great Britain, say.

Thus let us conceive of an economic system in which the total spending for consumers' goods during the year is a trillion (i.e., one thousand billion) dollars, and in which the abstract quantity of consumers' goods that is sold is one billion units. In this case, it is clear that the general consumer price level must be one thousand dollars per unit. It equals the division of the demand by the supply. The essential point to grasp here is that the general consumer price level reflects the exchange of some definite overall quantity of consumers' goods, in whatever units stated, against some definite overall expenditure of money to buy those consumers' goods. As I stated in Chapter 7, in any given year, some definite mass of consumers' goods—houses, cars, soap, matches, cigarettes, shoes, and everything else—exchanges against some definite overall expenditure of money. The mass of consumers' goods goes up against the total expenditure of money to buy them, and the result, the arithmetical quotient, is the general consumer price level.[8]

An expanding quantity of money operates to raise the general consumer price level by virtue of raising aggregate demand relative to aggregate supply. Aggregate demand rises while aggregate supply stays the same, or it rises more rapidly than aggregate supply. For example, while aggregate supply rises 2 percent in a year, aggregate demand rises by 6, 8, or 10 percent, with the result that the general consumer price level rises by 4, 6, or 8 percent in the year.

A system of *fiat paper money,* that is, a system in which the monetary unit is a mere piece of paper stamped as such by government officials—a system in which pieces of paper are not a claim to anything beyond themselves and thus themselves possess ultimate debt-paying power—such a system virtually guarantees that prices will rise. Under such a system, the increase in the quantity of money is limited only by the self-restraint of government officials. As will be shown, these officials have great incentives to increase the quantity of money and are under constant pressure to increase it. Hence, the quantity of money increases at a rate sufficient to increase aggregate demand more rapidly than aggregate supply, with the result that prices rise.

In contrast, it must be noted that under a system of *commodity money,* that is, for all practical purposes, a system in which the monetary unit is defined as a definite physical quantity of gold or silver, there is no inherent bias toward rising prices. The annual increase in the supply of gold and silver is always extremely limited because of the rarity of these metals in nature and the great cost of mining them. The greatest ingenuity of man has never been able to increase their supply very rapidly for very long. As a result, the use of a gold or silver money can never be accompanied by a sustained rapid rise in demand, or, therefore, in prices. Even when the New World was discovered and the accumulated treasure of the Aztecs and Incas was seized by Spain and added to the money supply of Europe, and many new discoveries of gold and silver were made, it took an entire century in most of the countries of Europe for prices to double or triple.

In normal circumstances, under a precious metals monetary system, the increase in the quantity of money is largely an accompaniment of the general increase in the ability to produce; it is the result of improvements in such fields as machinery, the means of transportation, and the sciences of engineering, metallurgy, and chemistry. Indeed, in normal circumstances a gold or silver money is accompanied by constant or even *falling* prices, because the limited increase in demand that larger supplies of gold and silver make possible tends to be offset, or more than offset, by equal or greater increases in the supply of other goods. The quantity of money grows, but usually not at a more rapid pace than production in general, indeed, quite possibly at a slower pace. In the latter case, the general consumer price level falls. This last fact is well illustrated by the economic history of the United States: prices actually fell in almost every year in the generation preceding the discovery of the California gold fields in 1848, and again in the generation from 1873 to 1896.

2. The Origin and Evolution of Money and the Contemporary Monetary System

It is necessary to explain how the present monetary system of paper and checkbook money, and the government's unlimited power to create money, came into being, and, before that, how the precious metals came to be money, and, still earlier, how money of any kind originated.

Money evolved out of barter. What made it evolve was the actions of individuals in serving their self-interests. As explained in Chapter 5, in conditions of barter, exchanges are confined to situations in which a double coincidence of wants exists, that is, a situation in which each of two people holds opposite valuations with respect to goods they possess, with each valuing the good in the possession of the other more highly than the good that is in his own possession. For example, A who possesses a chocolate bar prefers the pack of cigarettes possessed by B, while B prefers A's chocolate bar to his (B's) pack of cigarettes. When, as was frequently the case, a double coincidence of wants was not present, no exchange could take place.[9]

Some of our more intelligent ancestors who encountered the problem of the lack of a double coincidence of wants invented the practice of *indirect exchange,* which others soon copied.[10] What this means is that they exchanged the goods they possessed and wished to exchange, for other goods which they themselves did not desire but which the individuals whose goods they sought did desire.

For example, the owner of a boat who desired a team of horses owned by someone who did not desire a boat, exchanged the boat for goods that the owner of the horses did desire, or which people possessing such goods desired. Perhaps he would exchange his boat for an ox that the owner of the horses desired; perhaps he first had to exchange it for a quantity of iron or wheat or whatever before he could obtain the ox desired by the owner of the horses. (The complications of this example, incidentally, would be multiplied thousands of times over in the case of anyone who would attempt to live as a specialist in a barter economy. Such an individual would have to go through a comparable process of multiple exchanges in order to obtain practically any good or service he desired, unless his own good happened to be the kind frequently sought by large numbers of people. As we have seen this is why significant division of labor is impossible in a barter economy.[11])

Thus, people began to exchange their goods for other goods which they sought neither as articles of personal consumption nor as means of further production, but as means of effecting further exchanges. In this way, *media of exchange* began to develop.

In this process, certain goods naturally come to be more widely preferred as media of exchange than others. Other things being equal, the larger the number of users of a good as an ordinary commodity and the more frequent their use of it, the more it would be preferred as a medium of exchange. For once in possession of such a good, the likelihood of finding someone who possessed what one desired and who was willing to accept this good would be substantially greater than the likelihood of finding someone who possessed what one desired and who was willing to take either one's original good or any other good.

It is on this principle that in societies of nomads, cattle emerge as a kind of money. Practically all nomads want more cattle, as the means of supporting larger families and larger numbers of servants. As a result, anyone who wants something from nomads is more likely to be able to obtain it if he can offer them cattle. It was on the same principle that in the years immediately following World War II, cigarettes emerged as a medium of exchange in the black markets of various European countries. The large number of people seeking cigarettes to smoke made cigarettes a logical good even for nonsmokers to seek in exchange for their goods. Once in possession of cigarettes, the likelihood of finding someone in possession of the goods one wanted was greatly increased.

The example of cigarettes contains a further principle. Namely, the process of certain goods being selected as media of exchange in preference to others tends to be self-reinforcing and cumulative. As soon as nonsmokers become willing to accept cigarettes, because of the large number of smokers to trade with, the effect is to increase the ability of cigarettes to serve as a medium of exchange, because now they are more widely acceptable than before. It is in this way that the acceptability of the most preferred medium or media of exchange tends to go on increasing, until it or they are universally acceptable— i.e., have developed into money. Money is merely a medium of exchange whose use has grown to the point where it is directly and readily exchangeable against all other goods in a given geographical area.

In different periods of history, in different places, a variety of goods have served as media of exchange.

Among them have been cattle, sheep, hides, furs, cocoa, tobacco, salt, sea shells, beads, iron, copper, and, of course, gold and silver. Everywhere, however, the rise of civilization was accompanied by the triumph of gold and silver over all other contenders for the office of money.

This was no accident. The rise of civilization entails fixed settlements, trade over great distances, and economic activity spanning long periods of time. Such developments make the use of animal or vegetable products as media of exchange unsuitable. Such things are all perishable and relatively expensive for dwellers in fixed settlements to transport or store. In comparison with them, practically any of the metals is superior because of its imperishability and lower costs of storage. The metals are also divisible and recombinable, something that is totally impossible in the case of animals, sea shells, beads, and the like. The precious metals have the further decisive advantage of representing a comparatively high exchange value in a small bulk. As a result, it is less costly to transport or store a given amount of exchange value in the form of gold or silver than in the form of iron, copper, tin, or any other base metal.

Furthermore, in comparison with precious stones, the precious metals have the advantage of uniformity, in that each quantity of a definite purity is perfectly substitutable for any other equal quantity of the same purity. This makes it far easier to appraise pieces of precious metal. The ability to divide and recombine units of precious metal also enormously widens the market for any given quantity. These circumstances greatly reduce the difference between the retail price, at which one must buy, and the wholesale price, at which one must sell. In the case of precious metals, this difference is relatively insignificant. In the case of precious stones, it is very considerable.

Thus, the precious metals came to be money because they are the most suitable commodities for most people to save.[12] Their desirability as a means of saving—as a so-called store of value—made them acceptable to large numbers of people as a means of payment, namely, to those who wanted to save them. A process occurred in which for some time those who held part of their savings in gold or silver originally had to buy gold or silver with an earlier existing money, such as the iron coins of the early Roman Republic, and then, when they wished to use the gold or silver to make purchases, sell the gold or silver for the existing money. But as the number of people who wished to hold precious metals as a store of value reached a certain critical proportion of the population, individuals who possessed precious metals increasingly found that they could exchange them directly with other individuals who possessed the goods they desired and who, for their part, wished to add to their own gold or silver holdings. The willingness of a significant number of people to accept the precious metals in exchange led others, who did not wish to hold the precious metals as a store of value, also to accept them in exchange—in the knowledge that they could reexchange them with those who did. This, of course, increased the acceptability of the precious metals as media of exchange and on that basis made them still more acceptable as media of exchange.

The holding of precious metals as a store of value and their growing use as media of exchange represented an additional demand for them over and above the demand for them as ordinary commodities. This additional demand could be met only with increasing difficulty, because of the comparative rarity of these metals in nature. The result was a rise in the value of the precious metals, which further reinforced their suitability as a store of value and medium of exchange. Thus, the precious metals more and more supplanted previously existing moneys. The culmination of the process was the establishment of gold and silver as money throughout the civilized world.

The growing demand for precious metals as a store of value and as a medium of exchange operated to prevent the kind of sudden substantial changes in value to which most other commodities are subject. For now changes in the supply of the precious metals did not have to be taken out of, or added on to, merely a relatively narrow commodity usage, but the increasingly broad usage as a store of value and medium of exchange as well. The demand for these purposes tends to be more stable than an ordinary commodity demand. Furthermore, the existence of a large accumulated stock of precious metals relative to their annual production operated greatly to mitigate the effect of changes in their annual production on their overall supply. For example, a 10 percent increase or decrease in the annual production represents approximately only a 1 percent increase or decrease in the total supply if the accumulated stock is on the order of nine or ten times the annual production. In addition, the extent to which the precious metals are used as ordinary commodities relative to their use as a store of value and medium of exchange is much smaller than could ever be the case with base metals such as iron or copper, and therefore, their value is correspondingly more stable.

Because of the relative stability of their value, the precious metals came to be a preferred medium in which to write contracts and state debts. In turn, the development of a class of people with obligations payable in the precious metals made them eager to exchange their goods and services for the precious metals, so that they would have the means of meeting their obligations. This, too, obviously contributed to the development of the precious

metals into money.

Coinage—the certification of the weight and fineness of specific pieces of the precious metals—followed their widespread use as a store of value and medium of exchange. Coinage performed the valuable function of sparing people the need to weigh and test individual pieces of metal. Instead, they could simply visually inspect the coins and count them out in making payment. Interestingly, the names of leading monetary units originally meant nothing other than definite weights of precious metal. For example, an English pound (in France, a livre; in Italy, a lire) meant an actual pound's weight of pure silver on the troy scale. The original English penny contained an actual penny's weight—one 240th of a troy pound—of pure silver.

In the Western World, gold and silver coins were money from the time of the early Roman Republic down to the twentieth century. (The period of the Dark Ages represented a hiatus, in which the economic system operated at an extremely primitive level, virtually without money and with hardly any division of labor.)

In modern times, starting very slowly, and gradually accelerating in the sixteenth and seventeenth centuries, and then more rapidly accelerating in the eighteenth and nineteenth centuries, the use of paper money developed. Paper money came into existence as transferable claims to gold and silver coins that were payable on demand to the holders of the paper. The practice developed of people leaving gold and silver on deposit with smiths, for safe keeping. In exchange, they were issued receipts. When these receipts were issued for specific sums, such as one pound, and, at the same time, were transferable, they were the ancestors of our present-day paper currency. When they were issued in a form that allowed the owner of the deposit to draw drafts on (i.e., write orders to) the smith specifying the amount to be paid to a specific individual, they were the ancestors of our present-day checking accounts. The smiths themselves, of course, were the ancestors of modern bankers.

Over the course of centuries, as the result of steadily increasing government intervention in their favor, paper currency and checks gradually displaced gold and silver in active circulation—to the point where, today, several generations of people have grown up with the experience of government paper as a universally acceptable medium of exchange. Today, everyone is willing to accept paper money in payment for his goods because he has had the constantly repeated experience, and thus has the expectation, that everyone else is willing to accept it and thus that he can use it to obtain whatever goods or services he wishes.

In the United States, a critical step in the displacement of the precious metals by paper occurred in the Civil War, as the result of the government's issuance of greenbacks and then the enactment of the National Bank Act of 1863. Prior to the Civil War, the federal government was held to be constitutionally prohibited from issuing paper money, as were the states. Thus, from the enactment of the Constitution down to the Civil War, the only governmentally issued money in the United States was gold and silver coin. Banknotes—that is, privately issued paper currency—as well as checkbook money, were the liability of thousands of separate private banks. Because of the vast number of different kinds of banknotes, each with a different appearance, size, and color—in other words, a variation comparable to that between the stock certificates of today's corporations—the circulation of banknotes was strictly limited. Large manuals, comparable to today's *Moody's* or *Standard and Poor's* were required to keep track of the financial condition of the various banks issuing the notes, with the result that outside of the immediate locale of the issuing bank, banknotes were accepted only by experts or at a steep discount. Only gold or silver coin were universally acceptable. These facts underlay a substantial demand for gold or silver coin as a means of exchange.[13]

The greenbacks and the National Bank Act changed that. The National Bank Act placed a prohibitive tax on the issuance of private banknotes and instead made possible the issuance of national banknotes. Those banks which joined the newly created national banking system were entitled to issue national banknotes, which were backed partly by gold and partly by government securities. These notes had a uniform size, color, and appearance. Though technically issued by the separate national banks, they were actually a government paper currency. The establishment of redeemability of the greenbacks into gold in 1879 further strengthened the movement toward paper money.

The effect of a government paper currency redeemable in gold was that the demand for actual gold coin fell. People regarded the paper as equivalent to gold—as "as good as gold"—and increasingly used the paper in place of gold. Decade by decade following the Civil War, the quantity of gold coin in actual circulation steadily diminished. The gold was deposited in the banking system. The smaller banks redeposited it with the larger banks. By the time of World War I, almost all of the country's gold supply was held by the banking system, most of it by a small number of very large banks in New York City.

The Federal Reserve System was established in 1913. During World War I, an amendment to the Federal Reserve Act required that the banks turn over their gold to the Federal Reserve Banks, in exchange for checking deposits with the Federal Reserve Banks. Thus, practically all of the country's gold came into the possession of the government during World War I. In 1933, under the New Deal, the government seized the remaining privately held gold at the same time that it abolished the domestic redeemability of the dollar—i.e., the right of holders of paper money to redeem their paper at the rate of one dollar for approximately one-twentieth of an ounce of gold.

The government's rationale for the seizure of privately held gold during World War I was its alleged need to be able to increase the quantity of money at a more rapid rate than would otherwise have been possible. This was held to be necessary to finance the war effort. On the basis of a mechanism to be explained shortly, and whose operation rested on government intervention, the private banking system had gained the ability to use gold in its possession—that is, its gold reserves—to support a quantity of paper-money claims to gold approximately four times as great. Substituting checking deposits with the Federal Reserve System for gold reserves left this four-to-one ratio on the part of the private banking system intact and, at the same time, made possible a vast expansion in bank reserves. Because now the Federal Reserve System could use the gold in *its* possession to increase the reserves of the banks in approximately a four-to-one ratio to its gold holdings. Thus, the same amount of gold was enabled to support approximately sixteen dollars of paper claims to gold instead of only four dollars of paper claims to gold. (This process is known as the pyramiding of reserves.)

In 1933, the government's rationale for the seizure of the remaining privately held gold was that its plan to increase the official price of gold above the then-prevailing $20.67 per ounce would otherwise create a corresponding "windfall profit" for private owners of gold. The more fundamental and by far the more important motive, however, was, once again, the desire to be able to increase the supply of money more rapidly than would otherwise have been possible. At an official price of $35 per ounce—the price prevailing from 1935 to 1968—the same physical quantity of gold was made capable of supporting correspondingly more paper dollars.

Contrary to the fears of some people at the time, the paper money did not immediately become worthless, even though it was no longer redeemable in gold. This was because several decades had gone by during which people had come to think of the government's paper as money. Two generations had grown up observing the general use and acceptability of paper money. It was the paper, not the gold, that they observed everyone being willing to accept, and which, therefore, they themselves desired as the means of making purchases. Thus, even though paper money lost its redeemability in gold, without which it could never have come into existence in the first place, almost all of the demand for it remained, with the result that it did not go out of existence with the loss of that redeemability.

In the later thirties and during World War II, the U.S. government came into possession of a vastly larger quantity of gold, as the gold holdings of the European nations were run down by their policies of rapid inflation, their need to import vital supplies from the United States, and the desire of their citizens and governments to have a haven secure from foreign conquest. Together with the rise in the official price of gold from $20.67 to $35 per ounce, these enlarged gold holdings made it possible for a time for the U.S. government to go on increasing the quantity of paper money as rapidly as it wished. This could go on so long as the gold reserves owned by the U.S. government were larger than the gold reserves it was legally required to have—in other words, so long as it possessed *excess gold reserves*. For example, if the Federal Reserve System has outstanding $50 billion of currency and checking deposits (the latter category held by banks as reserves) against which it is legally required to hold, say, $15 billion in gold reserves, but it actually possesses $25 billion in gold reserves, it is in a position to expand the currency and reserves of the banks by an additional two-thirds before its gold reserve requirement becomes an effective limit on its ability to create money.

Thus, the U.S. government was in a position to create money during World War II and for approximately two decades following World War II, even though it was nominally on a form of gold standard. Finally, however, once the reserves of the banks and the paper currency were expanded sufficiently, the gold reserve requirement had to become effective. Indeed, the date of its becoming effective was accelerated by the government's policy of trying to maintain a quasi-free-market price of gold of $35 per ounce, which it did in order to try to make good the claim that internationally the dollar was "as good as gold." (Under the Bretton Woods agreement of 1945, the dollar was to be internationally convertible to gold and was to be the principal monetary reserve behind most other currencies.)

The U.S. government lost a major portion of its gold reserves in attempting to maintain the $35-an-ounce price in the London gold market, which was reopened in 1951. In this market, governments and private individuals from around the world were free to buy and sell gold. (American and British citizens were excluded from the market, however. It had been illegal for American citizens to own gold for monetary purposes since 1933.) Whenever the demand for gold threatened to outrun the supply at a price of $35 per ounce, the U.S. government simply dipped into its gold reserves and supplied what-

ever amount of gold was necessary to maintain the $35-an-ounce price. As time went on, however, it became necessary to supply ever larger amounts of gold to keep the price at the $35 level.

The policy of attempting to maintain the $35-an-ounce price was doomed from the beginning, because so long as the supply of money grows more rapidly than the supply of gold, a fixed price of gold means that gold tends to become cheaper and cheaper compared with other goods whose price the more rapidly growing quantity of money tends to raise. The consequence must be a steadily growing industrial demand for gold. The growing industrial demand for gold would alone have eventually absorbed the government's gold reserves. But the process was accelerated by the fact that people recognized in advance what the ultimate result must be, and so began buying gold in anticipation of its ultimate rise in price. Such additional buying was denounced at the time as "speculative runs," but it was nevertheless perfectly reasonable in view of the underlying circumstances.

By 1965, the government's loss of gold had reached the point where it became necessary to abolish the gold reserve requirement that until then had been imposed on the Federal Reserve System. This became necessary in order for the expansion in the supply of dollars to continue. In 1968, the government abandoned the policy of selling gold to maintain the $35-an-ounce price on the London gold market. In 1971, it abandoned its obligation to redeem dollars held by foreign governments or central banks. Since that time, the price of gold has greatly increased, reaching a peak of approximately $800 an ounce in early 1980. As these words are written, it is approximately $400 an ounce.

Since 1975, it has once again become legal for American citizens to own gold for monetary purposes. It has also become legal once again to write contracts that make debts payable in terms of gold. (This last provision still lacks real substance, however, since it is far from certain that the courts would enforce such contracts. Also, taxes would be incurred on the dollar income resulting from a rise in the price of gold.)

The Potential Spontaneous Remonetization of the Precious Metals

For reasons to be explained in Chapter 19, a policy of inflation destroys the real profitability of the traditional forms of investment, such as bonds, stocks, and family businesses. The monetary value of such investments tends not to keep pace with the rise in prices. This makes it necessary for people who want to preserve the buying power of their wealth to seek out assets whose price will rise in pace with prices in general and whose costs of maintenance and storage are minimal. In the circumstances of most people, gold and silver are the ideal candidates—for the very same reasons that made them the leading store of value in earlier periods of history.

Thus, as inflation becomes perceived as a serious problem, a growing demand for gold and silver develops as an "inflation hedge"—i.e., as a store of value. Once this demand reaches a certain level, the stage becomes set for a *spontaneous remonetization of the precious metals.* For, just as in the process by which the precious metals became money in the first place, once enough people want to own gold and silver as an inflation hedge and thus are willing to accept them in exchange for their own goods and services, others become willing to accept them too, even though they themselves do not wish to hold them as an inflation hedge or store of value. Conditions exist, in other words, for a growing acceptability of the precious metals, to the point at which they become universally acceptable, i.e., become money again.

It should be realized that the remonetization of the precious metals would be greatly accelerated if they were allowed to compete with paper money freely. There exist large quantities of gold and silver coins minted both when they served as actual money and more recently as "restrikes," that is, reproductions of the older coins.

The way the freedom of competition would accelerate the remonetization of the precious metals can perhaps best be understood by thinking back to the year 1965, when silver coins were still in actual circulation in the United States. At that time, a $10 roll of silver quarters and a $10 bill could be used interchangeably to buy a quantity of groceries, say. By the mid-1980s, that same quantity of groceries cost about $30 in paper money. But the roll of silver quarters physically contained about seven ounces of pure silver. This means that at a market price of silver of $6 per ounce, which prevailed in the mid-1980s, the $10 roll of quarters had a market value of $42 based on its silver content. Thus, the purchase price of $30 for a given quantity of groceries represented less than *three-fourths* of a roll of silver quarters, or, looked at in terms of the face value of the quarters, less than *$7.50* in terms of silver coins. If merchants had been legally allowed to discriminate between paper money and precious-metal coins, they would have sold the same quantity of groceries either for $30 in the paper money or for less than $7.50 in the silver money.

The same principle applies even more strongly in the case of our old gold coins. Prior to 1933, the United States had gold coins, known as double eagles, which had a face value of $20 and contained just under an ounce of pure gold. At today's price of gold of almost $400 per ounce, a new automobile that sells for $12,000 in paper money would sell for about *$600* in gold coin. (At the current market price of gold bullion of almost $400 per ounce, thirty $20 gold coins, each containing an ounce of gold, simultaneously represent $600 in gold and $12,000 in paper.)

Such facts would make it very obvious to the general public precisely where the problem of rising prices lay—namely, in the paper money. And this knowledge, in turn, would operate to reduce the demand for paper money and increase the demand for precious-metal money. People would want to have their pensions payable in gold or silver. Creditors would want the money due them to be stated in gold or silver. This, of course, would further increase the demand for precious metals and decrease the demand for paper money. In an environment of prices steadily rising in paper money, but constant or, more likely, falling in precious metal-money, the demand for paper money would soon be wiped out altogether. Just as people prefer a better soup or automobile to a poorer soup or automobile, they prefer a better money to a poorer money. Under free competition, the only way paper money could stay in circulation would be by being made redeemable in the precious metals.

This discussion may appear to contradict Gresham's Law. It shows that under free competition "good money drives out bad money," while Gresham's Law states that "bad money drives out good money." There is no contradiction when it is realized that Gresham's Law applies to circumstances in which the freedom of competition is prohibited. What drives out good money is the fact that businessmen are prohibited from accepting it at its actual value. This is the case today. Any buyer who wished to buy with gold or silver coins today would be required to use them as though they were worth no more than the paper money. To buy a $12,000 automobile with double eagles, the buyer would be required to pay six hundred such coins, for this is the quantity that is required to have a face value of $12,000. In other words, he would be required to part with gold that had a market value of *$240,000,* in order to buy something worth only $12,000. The buyer using silver coins in our groceries example would be required to part with three rolls of quarters, having a market value of $126, in order to buy $30 worth of goods. Under such conditions it is not difficult to understand why the better money ceases to circulate as money. People will not sacrifice what is better when it is treated equivalently to what is poorer. But when what is better can be treated as better, as when gold and silver coins can circulate at their bullion value, then, indeed, good money drives out bad.

The Government and the Banking System

It is impossible to understand the extent to which the government has increased the quantity of money without understanding how the government has encouraged the creation of money by the private banking system.

What we must deal with here is how the government has encouraged the existence of what von Mises calls "fiduciary media."[14] Fiduciary media are *transferable claims to standard money, payable by the issuer on demand*, and accepted in commerce as the equivalent of standard money, but for which no standard money actually exists. The larger part of our money supply today consists of fiduciary media in the form of checking deposits.

Standard money in contrast is money that is not itself a claim to anything further. It possesses ultimate debt-paying power, in that when it is received no further claim to be paid is present. Under a gold standard, standard money is gold. Any paper money that exists is a claim to it. Under a system of irredeemable paper money—fiat money—the irredeemable paper money is the standard money. In the present conditions of the United States, the standard money consists of the supply of Federal Reserve notes and, for all practical purposes, the checking deposit liabilities of the Federal Reserve System, which are fully equivalent to the notes. It is essentially the same as what is referred to as "the monetary base," which is the sum of currency in circulation outside banks plus bank reserves.

An analysis of the composition of the present U.S. money supply will make the concept of fiduciary media clearer. As previously stated, the total U.S. money supply at the end of 1993 was $1,128 billion, and of this, $799 billion were in the form of checking deposits held at the various banks.

Now, checking deposits are not standard money. They are a liability—*a debt*—of the various banks. They are a promise of the banks to pay standard money on demand to their depositors. They circulate as the equivalent of standard money so long as no one questions the ability of the banks to meet that promise. Against these $799 billion of checking deposit liabilities the banks held on the order of $60 billion of standard money as reserves—partly in the form of currency in their actual possession, mainly in the form of deposits with the Federal Reserve System.[15] Thus, $799 billion of checking deposits were backed by $60 billion of standard money. The difference—$733 billion—represents fiduciary media. Fiduciary media are the portion of checking deposit liabilities of the banks not covered by standard money.

Fiduciary media under present conditions come into existence in either of two ways. One way is the lending out of standard money that has been deposited in checking accounts. The other way is the creation of new and additional checking deposits without benefit of new and additional standard money. Let us consider an example of each, as illustrated in Figure 12–1, which shows so-called T–accounts for the public and the banking system.

Figure 12–1 shows an individual who deposits $100 of standard money into his checking account. In doing this, the individual does not part with the use of his money, because he can spend the checking deposit itself. He is minus currency in the amount of $100 but plus a checking deposit in the amount of $100, which is shown on the very next line. His action represents merely a change in the form in which he holds his money. It is equivalent in principle to exchanging a ten dollar bill for

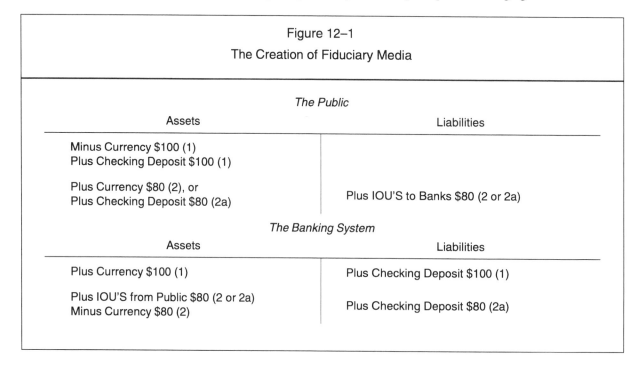

Figure 12–1

The Creation of Fiduciary Media

The Public

Assets	Liabilities
Minus Currency $100 (1) Plus Checking Deposit $100 (1)	
Plus Currency $80 (2), or Plus Checking Deposit $80 (2a)	Plus IOU'S to Banks $80 (2 or 2a)

The Banking System

Assets	Liabilities
Plus Currency $100 (1)	Plus Checking Deposit $100 (1)
Plus IOU'S from Public $80 (2 or 2a) Minus Currency $80 (2)	Plus Checking Deposit $80 (2a)

two fives. This transaction is labeled (1) in the T-account of the public and in the T-account of the banking system. The banking system is simultaneously plus $100 in currency and plus a checking deposit liability of $100, which entries are shown on opposite sides of the T-account.

If the bank now lends out any part of the $100 of standard money that has been deposited, it necessarily increases the total quantity of money in circulation, because the depositor still has his $100 that he can spend by writing checks, and the borrower from the bank now has whatever it lends him. A transaction in which the bank lends out $80 is labeled (2) in the T-account of the public. The public is shown both to receive $80 of currency and to become indebted to the banking system in the amount of $80. (Again, these entries are shown on opposite sides of the T-account.) The same transaction is also shown from the point of view of the banking system, where it is also labeled (2) and describes how the banking system is plus $80 in IOUs from the public and, on the next line, minus currency in the amount of $80. The essential point is that the spendable funds of the public equal the sum of the $100 they have deposited into a checking account plus whatever part of that $100 they then borrow from the banking system. For both the funds they have deposited and the funds they borrow represent spendable money.

The second way in which fiduciary media are created arises because of the popularity of payment by check. The borrower in our example would probably not want currency; he would probably want to make payments by check. As a result, instead of lending him currency, the bank would credit his checking account with the proceeds of the loan. Observe. Here we have a new and additional checking deposit coming into existence without benefit of any additional quantity of standard money on hand. This transaction is labeled (2a) in the T-accounts. It shows the public as simultaneously plus $80 in a checking deposit and, as before, plus $80 in indebtedness to the banking system. The banking system is shown as plus $80 in IOU's from the public, as before, and plus $80 in checking deposit liabilities instead of being minus $80 in currency. Again, just as when the bank lent currency, there are $80 of additional spendable money.

Now, the supporters of fiduciary media are quick to point out that fiduciary media are not without backing of any kind. They are backed, they say, by the loans and investments banks make in creating them and by the capitals of the banks. For example, when a bank creates a checking deposit of $80 for a borrower, the bank's assets also grow by $80—the $80 now owed to the bank by the borrower. And the borrower may have had to put up collateral worth more than $80. In addition, the bank has its own capital that is lent out or invested, and this

provides further backing, it is argued. As a result, the $733 billion of presently outstanding fiduciary media are backed by assets totaling more than $733 billion.

And, of course, an alternative way of looking at fiduciary media is that of the fractional-reserve principle. For example, instead of viewing the present $799 billion of checking deposits as representing $60 billion backed 100 percent by standard money and $733 billion backed by no standard money, one can view each dollar of checking deposits as backed by a uniform fraction of standard money—in our case, by $60/799$ of a dollar of standard money. The remaining $733/799$ of each dollar of checking deposits could be viewed as backed by the loans and investments of the banks. Whichever way we view them, fiduciary media are a kind of debt money. They are a debt of the banks, backed by debt, but circulating as money.[16]

The great problem of fiduciary media is that they set up money and debt like a house of cards or row of dominoes that any breeze can knock over. Observe. The safety and value of the fiduciary media are supposed to depend on the value of the assets behind them. What is overlooked by the supporters of fiduciary media, however, is that the value of the assets behind them depends on the continued existence of the fiduciary media themselves. To grasp this point clearly, let us assume that there is a failure of a single large bank that has issued fiduciary media. Such a failure could result from the failure of business enterprises to which the bank had made loans. The effect of the bank failure is actually to *reduce* the quantity of money in the economic system by the amount of that bank's checking deposits. Checking deposits held at a bank that has failed lose the character of money. They cease to be accepted as the equivalent of money in trade. Their status becomes that of an uncertain claim against the bank—a claim that may or may not be paid, to some unknown extent, at some future time.

Now, if the quantity of money actually falls, then, the quantity theory of money tells us, the demand for goods must fall. And as demand falls, the money revenues of businesses and the money incomes of individuals fall, because they are constituted by demand. As their revenues and incomes fall, the ability of people to pay debts falls, including, of course, their debt to banks. At the same time, the effect of a reduced quantity of money is to reduce the market value of assets that banks hold as collateral, such as stock-market collateral and the value of the property on which they hold mortgages. It is very easy, therefore, for the failure of one bank that has issued fiduciary media to cause the failure of several others—because the wiping out of its fiduciary media endangers the money value of their assets, on which their fiduciary media rest.

Indeed, once started, the process of bank failures tends to gain momentum: an initial failure wipes out money, which reduces the ability to spend money and thus to earn money and repay debts. The reduction in the ability to repay debts reduces the income and assets of banks and this in turn causes more bank failures and wipes out more money, with the effect of still greater declines in spending, sales revenues and incomes, asset values, and thus the ability to repay debts. Once begun, the process can lead, and again and again in our history has led, to periods of major deflation following periods in which the money supply was first inflated in the form of fiduciary media. The last such period of deflation was 1929 to 1933, following the expansionary period of World War I and the 1920s. In that period, the quantity of money fell by more than 25 percent and the volume of spending, as gauged by GDP, fell by almost 50 percent. Today there is even more massive deflationary potential than in 1929 because a much longer, far greater expansion of fiduciary media has occurred than in the years prior to 1929.

It must be said immediately, however, that no one should expect the deflationary potential of our day to be realized, because today, unlike 1929, the Federal Reserve System has unlimited power to expand the quantity of standard money. It will almost certainly do so to whatever extent is necessary to prevent a reduction in the quantity of money. Normally, when a bank fails nowadays, arrangements are made for it to be taken over by another bank, without loss to its depositors. In recent years there have been a few cases of losses to depositors who held over the insured amount of $100,000, but in no case has this occurred at a major bank. Indeed, when Continental Illinois National Bank, one of the country's major banks, was in danger of failing some years ago, the Federal Reserve and FDIC (Federal Deposit Insurance Corporation) made clear their willingness to make available however many billions of dollars might be necessary to prevent the failure.

This means that the government's policy of money creation—of inflation—will continue and almost inevitably accelerate. Nevertheless, the Continental Illinois case still confirms the existence of the domino effect I have described. It was rescued precisely in order to avoid that effect. Its failure would have precipitated runs on other financially troubled banks. A substantial volume of checking deposits would have been wiped out, correspondingly reducing the quantity of money and volume of spending in the economic system. The consequence would have been the onset of a major depression, accompanied by waves of bank failures.

Economists who have recognized the inherent danger of fiduciary media, and who believe that there is no advantage to a country in a quantity of money that

expends any more rapidly than gold and silver, have come to the conclusion that the ideal monetary system would be a *100-percent-metallic-reserve system.* Under this system, all paper currency and checking deposits would be 100 percent backed by gold or silver. The advantage of such a system would be that not only would it be immune from inflation, but, unlike the fractional-reserve gold standard of the nineteenth century and the first decades of this century, it would also be immune from *deflation.* Because once gold or silver money comes into existence, it *stays* in existence. It is not wiped out by the failure of any debtor. Under such a system, financial failures do not become cumulative self-reinforcing waves. Such a system would offer the maximum of monetary stability.

The 100-percent-reserve system is logically urged only for checking deposits and banknotes (currency), *not* for savings deposits or time deposits. There is a crucial difference in that savings and time deposits do not represent spendable money as such. When an individual makes a savings deposit or a time deposit, he temporarily gives up the use of his money. He cannot spend the savings or time deposit as such. If he wants his money, he must go and withdraw his deposit or wait until it matures. He must obtain actual money. When a bank lends the proceeds of a savings or time deposit, therefore, it is *not* engaged in the creation of money, but merely in the transfer of a given amount of money from a lender—that is, the savings or time depositor—to a borrower. Under the 100-percent-reserve system, therefore, banks would continue to lend out savings and time deposits, just as now. For the rest, they would earn money by charging fees for the storage of precious metal, its transfer from checking account to checking account, the issue of banknotes, and whatever other services they might perform.[17]

The supporters of the 100-percent-reserve principle divide into two groups. There are those who advocate its imposition by law. Those among this group who are committed to the principle of individual rights and laissez-faire capitalism justify this by claiming that the creation of fiduciary media is tantamount to counterfeiting and is fraudulent. They claim that it is the same in principle as accepting goods in a warehouse, issuing receipts for the goods, and then selling the goods; or selling more tickets to a theater performance than there are seats.[18]

The second group holds that if the issuance of fiduciary media is conducted openly, without deception—that is, if it is no secret to the owners of banknotes and checking deposits that the backing for them is debt—one cannot outlaw the practice. These supporters of the 100-percent-reserve principle advocate its achievement by means of a policy of *free banking*—that is, merely the total absence of all government intervention in banking. This view is well expressed in a passage quoted in von Mises's *Human Action* from the nineteenth-century French economist Cernuschi. It was made in reference to fiduciary media in the form of banknotes, but it applies equally to fiduciary media in the form of checking deposits as well. Cernuschi said: "I want to give everybody the right to issue banknotes so that nobody should take any banknotes any longer."[19]

In what follows, I content myself with providing an elaboration of the position of the second group of the supporters of the 100-percent-reserve principle—namely, the view that in an economy that was free of government interference in money and banking, the creation of fiduciary media would be legal, but for all practical purposes would not take place. This view is supported by such facts as that any granting of fiduciary media would place the customers of the banks that granted them in a position to expand their purchases from the customers of banks that did not grant them or granted them less rapidly, because such customers would have relatively more money to spend. The effect would be an adverse clearing balance against the expanding, or more rapidly expanding banks, which would thus lose reserves to the sounder banks.

The problems of the expanding banks would be further compounded by the existence of a growing demand for gold and silver coin on the part of the public. In conditions in which gold and silver coins are extensively used as money, this would occur as the by-product of any increase in the overall quantity of money. It would occur for much the same reasons as an increase in the demand for twenty dollar bills, say, when there is an increase in the quantity of money in the form of hundred dollar bills or ten dollar bills. Indeed, just as some of the hundreds or tens would be brought to banks for exchange into twenties, so, in an economic system in which gold or silver coin was extensively used, any increase in the supply of paper currency or checkbook money would necessarily be accompanied by the exchange of part of it for additional gold and silver coins, simply in order for people to maintain proper proportions among the different kinds of money they used. Such redemptions of currency and checkbook money, would, of course, represent an additional pressure on the banks' reserves if they pursued a policy of increasing the supply of paper or checkbook money.

Moreover, in a banking system totally unprotected and unsupported by the government—a banking system without any form of government controls, government inspections, examinations, assurances, guarantees, or endorsements—people would realize that when they made deposits in banks that did not hold a 100 percent reserve, they were in fact taking some risk of loss. They would realize that what they were doing was granting credit, not holding money, and that if they wanted to grant credit, they had better learn how to read a bank's balance sheet, how to evaluate it, and how to distinguish between good and bad banks. Those not prepared to do this, and whose real intention was to hold money, would realize that if that is what they wanted to do, they should hold deposits at 100-percent-reserve banks. The transferable deposits of fractional-reserve banks would cease to be regarded as money. They would be regarded as credit instruments, to be held only by those prepared to grant credit, not by people desiring to hold money.

All along, however, the government has sought to encourage the existence and growth of fiduciary media. The government has acted in the belief that the mere expansion of bank credit—i.e., the creation and lending out of fiduciary media—could create real capital goods and thus generate prosperity. From the beginning, the government was urged on and applauded by businessmen seeking lower rates of interest—seeking what they call "easy money." What actually happened, of course, was not prosperity, but the trade cycle.[20]

In the eighteenth and nineteenth centuries, fiduciary media were encouraged by the existence of government-supported central banks, such as the Bank of England and, in this country, the First and Second Banks of the United States. So long as the central banks were and are able to go on creating reserves, banks are rescued from the loss of reserves they would otherwise experience as the result of an adverse clearing balance with other banks. They are able to obtain fresh reserves, and in an even larger quantity. To the extent that the government or its central bank is able to substitute the use of its paper currency for gold and silver coin, it also reduces the pressure on reserves of a greater need for currency to keep pace with the overall growth in the quantity of money taking place. For the government can manufacture whatever additional paper currency it may wish, to replace lost reserves, while it cannot manufacture additional gold and silver coin as it may wish.

Again and again, when banks did fail, the government stepped in and allowed them to suspend payment in specie, in flagrant violation of their agreement to pay their depositors specie on demand. This prevented the wiping out of fractional-reserve banks and enabled such banks to return to issue still more fiduciary media. Restrictions on the formation of new banks and on the expansion of more conservatively managed existing banks—the latter in the form of restrictions on branch banking—also served to promote the existence of fiduciary media. This was the result insofar as the effect of the free competition of such banks, if it had been allowed, would have been a greater problem of adverse clearing balances for banks expanding their issue of fiduciary media. In addition, all government measures that built confidence in the banking system, such as imposing minimum capital requirements, double liability for bank stockholders, and bank examinations, also importantly aided in the promotion of fiduciary media in the eighteenth and nineteenth centuries.

In this century, the government has encouraged the expansion of fiduciary media principally through the Federal Reserve System. The Federal Reserve System has supplied the banking system with vastly larger reserves of standard money in the form of Federal Reserve notes and deposit credits than it could possibly have acquired if its reserves had had to be in a standard money of gold, as was the case before World War I. This more rapid growth in bank reserves of standard money has been a necessary foundation for the more rapid growth in checking deposits, because the deposits banks can create are always tied to the amount of standard-money reserves at their disposal. With more reserves, they can support more deposits, and so they create more deposits.

In addition, the government, again operating largely through the Federal Reserve System, has made it possible for any given volume of reserves to support a larger volume of deposits. It has done this by virtue of following one of the avowed objectives of the Federal Reserve's foundation, which was to act as a "lender of last resort" to the commercial banks. The Federal Reserve System stands ready to lend standard money to the banks or buy assets from them whenever they require. This permits the banks to hold such assets as the Federal Reserve will lend money on or buy, in place of holding actual standard-money reserves. The result is an expansion of deposits relative to reserves, because when the banks acquire these assets, the sellers usually take the proceeds of their sale and bring them back to the banking system in the form of fresh deposits. For example, if a bank buys a Treasury bill, say, or commercial paper, in the knowledge that it can obtain standard money from the "Fed" by means of these assets, the seller of the asset now has standard money. He will almost certainly deposit this standard money in some bank. The effect is that the banking system now ends up with more deposits and with just as much standard money as it had initially. Thus, the same reserves of standard money now support a larger volume of deposits.

Finally, the government has further promoted the existence of fiduciary media in this century through such measures as deposit insurance, increased governmental supervision of banks, and increased control over the nature of the loans and investments banks can make. All of these measures promote confidence in fiduciary media by virtue of the government's word rather than by virtue of the fact of financial soundness. If not for these and other such measures that I have described, some of them going back even before the nineteenth century, banks would have to hold far larger reserves in relation to checking deposits to instill the same degree of confidence.

In all of these ways, therefore, the government has been responsible for the creation of fiduciary media. It is against this background that the imposition of legal minimum reserve requirements by the Federal Reserve System must be viewed. For example, currently the Federal Reserve requires that on checking deposit liabilities in excess of $51.9-million, banks hold an amount equal to a minimum of 10 percent of such deposits as a reserve, in the form of currency on hand or checking account balance with the Federal Reserve.[21] This requirement exists in a situation in which current market conditions would enable the banks to get by with a smaller percentage of reserves. The preceding discussion makes it clear, however, that it would be a profound mistake to conclude from these facts that government intervention operates to impose higher reserve requirements than would a free market. For the imposition of the reserve requirements takes place in a context in which generations of government intervention, including the intervention directly carried out by the Federal Reserve System, has radically reduced the reserves that are required in current market conditions, which market conditions fully reflect the government's intervention. The Federal Reserve's minimum reserve requirements merely serve to prevent the banks' reserve ratios from declining quite as far as all the other government intervention has made it possible for them to do.

On the basis of its responsibility for the creation of fiduciary media, the government must bear the responsibility for the boom-bust pattern of our economic history. In addition, of course, its promotion and support of fiduciary media have played a major role in the rapid increase in the quantity of money that has taken place in recent decades. Today, by virtue of the government's unlimited ability to create standard money and to supply it to banks in need of it, and by virtue of its commitment to do so, fiduciary media can be considered as practically the equivalent of standard money created by the government itself, that is, as part of the overall supply of fiat money.

In the light of recent developments, this last statement must be qualified with respect to checking deposits held in smaller banks. As the result of substantial losses, and spurred on by recent legislation, the Federal Deposit Insurance Corporation has increasingly refused to make good depositors' losses on bank accounts in excess of $100,000, which is the current legal limit of its obligation. However, in the case of large banks, where a substantial number of depositors would be involved, the policy of the FDIC still appears to be that of making good all losses of depositors, irrespective of the amount.[22] Moreover, the Federal Reserve System is still in a position to rescue any bank it wishes, simply by providing the necessary funds either as a loan or as a purchase of assets.

Today, money is created in the first instance primarily by means of the so-called open market operation of the Federal Reserve System. That is, the Federal Reserve System enters the government securities market and buys outstanding government securities with standard money that is newly created, virtually out of thin air. When the sellers of the securities deposit the proceeds in their banks, the banks obtain additional deposits and equivalent additional reserves of standard money. On the basis of their additional reserves, they in turn create additional fiduciary media, whose redeemability in standard money is, of course, virtually guaranteed by the government, with the limited exception just mentioned. Government deficits are a constant source of new government securities, and for all practical purposes can be viewed as being financed directly by the Federal Reserve System, just as in the example of the social security checks earlier in this chapter.

Apart from ceasing all of its intervention in favor of fiduciary media, including its issuance of paper currency, there is one further important and totally legitimate step the government could take, short of prohibiting fiduciary media outright on the grounds of fraud. This is to follow the example of President Andrew Jackson's specie circular and refuse to accept checks or private banknotes that are not 100 percent backed by gold or silver. To accept such checks or banknotes places the government in a position in which it can be construed as granting credit to the banks in question—in which, according to the supporters of fiduciary media, it *is* granting credit to those banks, inasmuch as it knowingly accepts claims that do not represent actual money, but largely debt. The government has no business granting credit to anyone. By all the ordinary principles of laissez faire, it should not be in business of any kind; it should not be a lending agency of any kind. The only way it can unequivocally avoid granting credit is if, insofar as any money is due it, it requires payment in specie or in notes or deposits that are 100 percent backed by specie. When it receives such money, it is fully and finally paid; in that case, no question can arise of its granting credit. Such a policy by the government would all by itself do a great deal to restrain the issuance of fiduciary media. Added to con-

sistent abstention from all other acts favoring fiduciary media, it could well make their issuance virtually impossible.

3. The Quantity of Money and the Demand for Money

The volume of spending in the economic system is determined not only by the supply of money—the quantity of money—but also by the *demand* for money. The demand for money refers to the extent to which people desire to hold balances of money relative to the receipts they take in and the sums they pay out. People need to hold money in order to make purchases and pay bills in the future. Under varying circumstances, they choose to make a larger or a smaller demand for money. The greater is the demand for money, the greater are the balances of money that people wish to hold relative to their receipts and expenditures. The smaller is the demand for money, the smaller are the balances of money that people wish to hold relative to their receipts and expenditures.

It should be obvious from these statements that the so-called velocity of circulation of money is determined by the demand for money. The greater is the demand for money, the lower is the velocity of circulation of money. The smaller is the demand for money, the higher is the velocity of circulation of money.

The reason for this relationship between velocity and the desire to hold money can be understood by considering the case of any given individual who owns money. Imagine an individual who owns $1,000 in the form of currency or a checking-account balance. If this individual feels that he needs to hold, say, $700 out of his thousand in order to make purchases or pay bills in the period starting one week from the present, then the most he can afford to spend out of his thousand dollars this week is $300. If, however, he should decide that he only needs to hold, say, $600 for the period starting a week later, then, this week, he could afford to spend $400 out of the thousand he owns. Clearly, the individual's ability to spend the money he owns is the greater, the less of it he needs or desires to hold for the future; and is the smaller, the more of it he needs or desires to hold for the future.

It follows that anything that occurs which makes individuals decide to reduce the cash they hold for the future will increase spending and therefore velocity. By the same token, anything that occurs that makes individuals decide that they need to increase the cash they hold for the future will reduce spending and therefore velocity.

To quantify the relationship between the demand for money and the velocity of money more precisely, a so-called income velocity of 4 reflects the fact that people want to hold balances of money equal to $\frac{1}{4}$ of their annual incomes and consumption expenditures. The higher income velocity of 6 reflects a lower demand for money balances, equal to only ⅙ of people's annual incomes and consumption expenditures. The lower income velocity of 3 reflects a higher demand for money balances, equal to ⅓ of people's annual incomes and consumption expenditures. Whenever the demand for money falls, people step up their expenditures out of their existing cash holdings, and thus velocity rises. Whenever the demand for money rises, people cut back on their expenditures, in an effort to increase their cash holdings, and thus velocity falls.

The demand for money is determined by a variety of factors. One of the most important, and, indeed, the most fundamental, is the security, or lack of security, of property. Where property is insecure—where it is subject to arbitrary confiscation by the government or to plunder by private gangs—saving and provision for the future will be low, because people will not be in a position to count on benefitting from it. But such saving and provision for the future as does occur will largely take the form of holding precious metals and gems—items easily concealable and easily transportable. A gold money in such circumstances has a very low velocity of circulation.[23]

By the same token, under conditions in which property is secure from confiscation and plunder, the demand for gold for holding will be less, and thus the velocity of circulation of a gold money will be greater. The same result is aided by the development of financial markets and financial institutions, which make it easier and more profitable for people to invest their savings rather than hold them in the form of precious metals or precious stones.

Interestingly, the effect of lack of security of property is very different on a paper money than on a gold money. In conditions in which a government loses the power to stop private plunder or itself becomes a looter, people switch their savings from assets denominated in the government's paper to precious metals and precious stones. They lose the desire to hold such paper, because it becomes more and more likely that the government will sharply reduce its value by rapidly increasing its supply. Thus, the velocity of a paper money tends to rise in such circumstances.

The velocity of money can also be increased by such developments as improvements in transportation, which reduce the time money is in transit and correspondingly increase the speed with which it is available for respending. The development of clearing houses reduces the amount of money that is required to perform a given volume of transactions: instead of all of the transactions needing to be effected by means of the transfer of money, only the settlement of the net amounts owed or owing,

after the canceling of offsetting debts by the clearing process, needs to be effected by means of the actual transfer of money. The money set free by the clearing process is thereby made available for spending for other things. Thus, the total spending that the same quantity of money can effect is increased.

What is especially worthy of note is the fact that in the context of an economic system with developed financial institutions and financial markets, *saving* operates to raise the velocity of circulation of money. (This may be the cause of some surprise, in view of the popular fallacy that confuses saving with hoarding.) There are two reasons for this. First, under such conditions funds that are saved are likely to be made available for spending sooner than funds that are held for consumption. For example, the part of his paycheck that an individual deposits in his savings account is available for lending by the bank almost immediately. However, the part of his paycheck that he retains in his possession in the form of cash that he plans to spend on consumers' goods in the coming days or weeks prior to his receipt of his next paycheck will enter into the hands of others only over the length of this considerably longer period. Second, to the extent that the availability of additional savings contributes to credit being readily available, it becomes possible for individuals and business firms to substitute to some extent the prospect of obtaining such credit for the holding of money as the means of providing for their future need for funds. To this extent, they reduce their cash holdings and thus bring about a rise in the velocity of circulation of money.[24]

It should be realized that in the conditions in which the velocity of circulation of a gold money rises, there is unlikely to be any fall in the purchasing power of gold as a result. This is the case because the rise in velocity here is the accompaniment of a process that sharply increases the physical ability to produce—above all, the growth of saving and the channelling of those savings into productive investment. In addition, a further factor that must be mentioned, which is especially relevant in appraising the effects of the development of clearing procedures, is that the productive process also tends to become more complex at the same time that the demand for gold holdings falls. Because of the intensification of the division of labor, which is inextricably bound up both with the growth of saving and investment and the increase in production, a tendency exists toward an increase in the number of payments needed in the production and distribution of ultimate consumers' goods. For example, instead of a farmer selling his food to a consumer, he sells it to a food processor, who sells to a wholesaler, who in turn sells to a retailer. Possibly several processors and wholesalers are involved. The intensification of such specialization and its requirement for additional acts of exchange more or less keeps pace with the decline in the desire to own balances of gold. Consequently, while the total of spending of all types combined rises relative to the quantity of gold, it does not follow that spending *specifically for consumers' goods* rises relative to the quantity of gold. In other words, the velocity that actually rises is the so-called transactions velocity, but not necessarily income velocity, or certainly not to the same degree. (Furthermore, it should not be assumed that either the fall in demand for gold holdings or the growth in complexity of the productive process necessarily goes on indefinitely.)

Changes in the Quantity of Money as the Cause of Changes in the Demand for Money

There is a further source of changes in the demand for money—a source that would probably not be present at all under a 100-percent-reserve gold standard, but which exerts an extremely powerful influence under a fractional-reserve gold standard and under a system of fiat paper money. This is *rapid changes in the supply of money itself.*

Under a 100-percent-reserve gold standard, the supply of money increases no more rapidly than the supply of gold, which increase is almost always quite modest.[25] Equally important, for all practical purposes, the supply of money can never *decrease* under a 100-percent-reserve gold standard. The gold that people take to the grave with them in such things as dental fillings is dwarfed by the current production of gold. The occasional ship or plane that goes down carrying gold, which gold cannot then be found or salvaged, is also not enough to make a difference. Thus, as stated before, once a gold money comes into existence, it *stays* in existence. It is not wiped out by the failure of any debtor.

Under a fractional-reserve gold standard, on the other hand, there are periods in which the money supply can be increased relatively rapidly, by means of the issuance of fiduciary media. In these periods, the increase in the supply of money corresponds not only to the increase in the supply of gold, but also to the decrease in the ratio of gold reserves. And then, of course, when banks fail and their fiduciary media lose the character of money, the money supply can sharply decline.

Under a system of fiat paper money, the money supply can be increased at any rate the government desires. For reasons to be explained later in this book, a powerful tendency exists under this kind of monetary system for the increase in the quantity of money to accelerate.[26] The only intrinsic limit to such acceleration is the total destruction of the demand for the money, at which point the money ceases to be accepted in payment and loses its character as money. Examples of the process of an accelerating increase in the quantity of money carried to the point of the destruction of the fiat money concerned are the continental currency of the United States in the American Revolution, the French assignats during the French Revolution, the German mark following World War I, and the currency of nationalist China following World War II.

The connection between changes in the quantity of money and the demand for money is simply this: *the more rapidly the quantity of money increases, the lower tends to be the demand for it; the less rapidly the quantity of money increases, the higher tends to be the demand for it.*[27] In conditions in which the quantity of money actually decreases, the demand for money becomes all the greater. To state the relationship in terms of the velocity of circulation of money, the more rapidly the quantity of money increases, the higher tends to be the velocity of circulation of money; the less rapidly the quantity of money increases, the lower tends to be the velocity of circulation of money. In the face of a decrease in the quantity of money, velocity tends to be lower still.

We can find some immediate confirmation of this principle if we ask which currencies people prefer to own and why—for example, Argentine pesos, English pounds, or U.S. dollars? Obviously, the peso is the least desirable of the three currencies to own, and the dollar the most desirable. The reason the peso is the least desirable of the three to own is that it is the one whose quantity is most rapidly expanded and which therefore loses purchasing power the fastest. As a result, no one wants to own more than the barest minimum of pesos necessary to transact business in Argentina. The dollar, on the other hand, is the most desirable of the three to own, because its quantity is expanded the least rapidly and it therefore retains its purchasing power better than the others. Accordingly, among these three countries, the velocity of circulation of money is highest in Argentina and lowest in the United States. It is also higher in the United States today than it was in the United States in previous decades, when the increase in the supply of dollars was less rapid.

There are four avenues by which changes in the quantity of money affect the demand for money. Perhaps the most widely recognized is its effect on prices and the prospects for changes in prices. As was implicit in the previous paragraph, once an expanding quantity of money creates the expectation of rapidly rising prices in the future, people conclude that it pays to buy goods right away, before their prices rise further. They come to the conclusion that the continued holding of cash balances must cause them a substantial loss of purchasing power, and so they attempt to reduce their holdings of money. Conversely, the anticipation of a fall in prices in the future, resulting from a contraction in the quantity of money and volume of spending, increases the desirability of owning money. In such circumstances, it pays people to postpone purchases in order to take advantage of lower prices in the future.[28]

A second, closely related connection between changes in the quantity of money and the velocity of money concerns the ability to substitute holdings of other assets for holdings of money. If the quantity of money is rapidly increasing, it pays to hold other assets, such as inventories of various commodities, rather than money itself. In such circumstances, these other assets are a better source of meeting future needs for cash than the holding of money, because they can easily be sold for more money than they cost. This principle applies not only to businessmen holding inventories of commodities that they produce, but also to consumers. As inflation accelerates, it pays even the ordinary consumer to hold commodities as a source of future cash rather than cash itself—above all, gold and silver or less rapidly inflating foreign moneys.

Conversely, if the quantity of money decreases rather than increases, not only does the holding of commodities represent a financial loss while the purchasing power of money in contrast rises, but people also want to hold money even in place of such things as short-term securities and savings and time deposits. This is because in such circumstances—namely, a deflation and depression—people cannot be sure of converting these near moneys into actual money, since the issuer of the securities or the bank where one has the deposit may go bankrupt first. These are major reasons why periods of deflation—i.e., of a decrease in the quantity of money/volume of spending—are periods of an intensified desire to hold money, and, therefore, of a drop in the velocity of money.

The two remaining reasons why increases in the quantity of money tend to increase velocity, and why decreases in the quantity of money tend to reduce it, pertain to the effects of changes in the quantity of money on the availability of credit and on interest rates.

The desire to hold money—especially on the part of business firms—is largely determined by the prospective availability of credit. If credit is expected to be available easily and profitably when funds are required, the perceived need and thus the desire to hold money will be correspondingly less. If credit is expected to be unavailable or available only with great difficulty and at a loss when funds are required, the perceived need and thus the desire to hold money will be correspondingly greater. In effect, as we have seen, prospective credit that is readily and profitably available serves as a substitute for the holding of money.

Now the increase or decrease in the money supply is a major factor determining the availability of credit at any given time. When the money supply is increasing, a very large portion of the increase usually enters the economic system in the form of new loans, with the result that credit is made easier. This is particularly true when the increase in the quantity of money takes the form of additional fiduciary media. It is what people have in mind when they talk of "easy money." Conversely, when the money supply decreases, as in a depression accompanied by bank failures and the wiping out of fiduciary media, the decrease results in a sharp reduction in the availability of credit.

Thus, an expansion of the money supply reduces the perceived need to hold money through its effect on the current and prospective availability of credit. In an economy which has become accustomed to "easy money," or which offers the prospect of "easy money," businessmen will consider it safe to operate with lower money balances than they would otherwise. They will expect to be able to obtain a larger portion of the money they will later require, through credit at the time. Consequently, they will invest more fully, either in the purchase of physical assets or in the purchase of securities. And since those who receive this money will tend to behave in the same way, what occurs is an increase in the total volume of spending, lending, and trading of all kinds in relation to the quantity of money; that is, there is an increase in the velocity of money.

On the other hand, in a deflationary period, when the quantity of money is falling and credit is virtually unobtainable, businessmen find it necessary to hold relatively large money balances in order to be sure of being able to meet their obligations when they come due. In these conditions, there is a corresponding reduction in the velocity of circulation of money.[29]

The final avenue that connects changes in the quantity of money and the velocity of circulation of money is by way of the rate of interest. As we know from Chapter 6, the basic determinant of the rate of interest is the rate of profit.[30] And as Chapter 16 will show, to this must be added the fact that an expanding quantity of money, in raising total spending and total sales revenues from year to year, raises the nominal rate of profit.[31] This rise in the nominal rate of profit brings about a rise in the nominal rate of interest. The rate of interest rises because the higher rate of profit permits business borrowers to offer a higher rate of interest, and their mutual competition for loans forces them to do so. Also, insofar as loanable funds are supplied by those who have the alternative of directly investing in business and earning profits, a rise in the rate of profit makes such lenders require a higher rate of interest as the condition of their finding it worthwhile to continue lending.

Here I must briefly digress, because the connection I have just described between the increase in the quantity of money and the rate of interest is the opposite of that which is usually believed to exist. The usual belief is that an increase in the quantity of money entering the loan market reduces the rate of interest. In view of the prevalence of this belief, some further comments on my part are in order.

An increase in the quantity of money can reduce the rate of interest only temporarily. As soon as the new and additional money is borrowed and spent, it begins to raise sales revenues and profit margins, and thus the rate of profit. The rise in the rate of profit then raises the rate of interest. To prevent the rate of interest from rising in the face of the higher rate of profit, an acceleration in the rate of credit expansion would be necessary. The effect of such an acceleration would be a still more rapid rate of increase in the volume of spending and thus in business sales revenues, with the result that profit margins and the rate of profit would rise still higher, which, of course, would operate all the more powerfully to raise the rate of interest. To prevent the rate of interest from rising at this point, an even more rapid rate of credit expansion would be required, which would cause yet a still higher rate of profit, and so on. Thus, the use of credit expansion to prevent the rise in the rate of interest that results from an increase in the quantity of money would quickly entail such enormous rates of increase in the quantity of money as to destroy the monetary system.

For example, starting with a rate of profit of 4 percent and a rate of interest of 3 percent, credit expansion might temporarily reduce the rate of interest to, say, 2.75 percent. But once the new and additional money succeeds in raising sales revenues and profit margins, the rate of profit rises to, say, 4.25 percent. To keep the rate of interest at 2.75 percent in the face of this higher rate of profit, requires more credit expansion than before. If it is forthcoming, then the rate of profit rises perhaps to 4.5 percent, which means that still more credit expansion will be required if the rate of interest is to be held at 2.75 percent. Since the difference between the rate of profit and the rate of interest steadily widens, making borrowing more and more profitable, exponentially increasing amounts of credit expansion would be required to prevent the rate of interest from rising. To avoid rapid destruction of the monetary system, there is no practical alternative but to allow the rate of interest to follow the rate of profit on up as the quantity of money increases. In pattern, the rise in interest rates in the United States over the thirty-five years following World War II is explainable on the basis of a progressively more rapid rate of increase in the quantity of money, taking place in large measure in the form of credit expansion.

The mistaken notion that increases in the quantity of money reduce the rate of interest is largely the result of thinking of the rate of interest as "the price of money" and then applying the principle that increases in supply reduce prices. A more accurate description of the rate of interest than the price of money is *the difference between the money that is borrowed and the money that is repaid.* Thus, for example, one should think of the payment of a 10 percent rate of interest on a one-year loan of a thousand dollars not as a price for the borrowing of the thousand dollars, but as the difference between the eleven hundred dollars that will have to be repaid and the thousand dollars that is borrowed. If one thinks of interest this way, then it is not surprising that interest rates turn out to be higher rather than lower as the consequence of an increasing supply of money. Because to the extent that more money exists and is spent and earned at the time of repayment than at the time of borrowing—which is the necessary consequence of an increasing quantity of money—correspondingly more money is available to be repaid and is thus likely to have to be repaid than would otherwise be the case.

Thus, the effect of a more rapidly increasing quantity of money and volume of spending has been shown to be to raise the rate of interest after temporarily reducing it. As a result, it is possible to return to considering the connection between the increase in the quantity of money and the velocity of circulation of money that exists by way of the rate of interest.

The rise in the nominal rate of interest that results from a more rapid rate of increase in the quantity of money and volume of spending is significant in drawing out of cash holdings sums that it would not pay to invest at lower rates of interest. It does this by decreasing both the size of the principal and the period of time for which it must be invested in order to make lending worthwhile.

For example, at a 2 percent annual rate of interest, it would probably not pay in present conditions to lend $100,000 for a period as short as a week, because the interest that could be earned would amount only to about $40. (Two percent of $100,000 is $2,000, which, when divided by 50 weeks, equals $40.) If we assume that the minimum amount of interest that must be earned by a significant-sized business firm merely to cover the bookkeeping and related costs of a financial transaction, and thus make it worthwhile entering into, is $100, then the smallest-sized sum that it pays such a firm to lend out for a period as short as a week is $250,000, if the annual interest rate is 2 percent. (Two percent of $250,000 is $5,000, which, when divided by 50 weeks, equals $100.) At a 2 percent annual rate of interest, it would not pay to lend a sum as small as $100,000 for a period of less than two and a half weeks. However, at a 4 percent annual rate of interest, it pays to lend a sum as small as $125,000 for a week, and it pays to lend $100,000 for a period as short as a week and a quarter. At still higher rates of interest, the minimum-sized sum that it pays to lend out for a given short period, such as a week, becomes still smaller, and the minimum period of time for which it pays to lend any given-sized sum, such as $100,000, shortens further.

Thus, as the rate of interest rises, it becomes profitable to lend out progressively smaller and shorter-term sums. Consequently, these sums are drawn out of cash holdings and into the stream of spending. Since there are always such sums in the possession of various firms, the effect of a rise in interest rates—itself caused by a more rapid increase in the quantity of money—is to elevate the velocity of money throughout the year. By the same token, of course, a fall in the rate of interest brought about by a reduction in the rate of increase in the quantity of money operates to decrease the velocity of money.

(In order to avoid a possible erroneous inference, I must point out that a reduction in the rate of profit and interest that might result from a higher rate of saving should *not* be presumed to increase the demand for money and thus reduce the velocity of money. This is because, as we saw earlier in this section, the greater availability of savings and thus credit, operates itself to reduce the demand for money. The same observation, of course, applies mutatis mutandis to increases in the rate of profit and interest caused by decreases in the rate of saving. In other words, the relationship between the rate of interest and the demand for money applies only insofar as the rate of interest is determined by changes in the quantity of money and volume of spending, not insofar as it is determined by the rate of saving.

I must also point out that it is of no relevance that the effect of increases in the quantity of money is not only to add to the rate of interest, but also progressively to increase the size of the minimum sum for which it is worthwhile to lend, at least in comparison with what it otherwise would have been. This is because the increase in the minimum-sized sum does not affect the *proportion* of the money supply that it pays to lend for given short periods of time at any given rate of interest. Other things being equal, an economic system with a doubled quantity of money and a doubled minimum-sized sum for which lending is worthwhile will tend to have the same proportion of its money supply available for short-term lending at any given interest rate as an economic system with the original quantity of money. If, however, its interest rate is higher, because of a more rapid rate of increase in the quantity of money, it will tend to lend out a larger proportion of its money supply. Therefore, its velocity of circulation will be higher.)

Thus, in the four ways I have explained, increases in

the quantity of money raise the velocity of money, and decreases in the quantity of money decrease it.

Let us turn to the historical statistics of the money supply and its velocity of circulation for verification of this relationship. These statistics are shown in Table 12–1.

In viewing the statistics, of course, we should not expect the relationship to hold with immediacy. Very importantly, the influence of earlier changes in the quantity of money can continue to be felt for a time after the direction of change in the quantity of money has been reversed. Thus, a period of inflation which begins after a sustained period of deflation, and in which people's expectations continue to be influenced by their experience of deflation, will not be accompanied by an immediate rise in the velocity of circulation of money. On the contrary, it will be accompanied initially by a *fall* in the velocity of circulation of money. This will be the case in such an environment because people will want to take the opportunity of an increased availability of money to build up their cash reserves, as a precaution against renewed deflation. Only after a period of time has gone by, and the memory of the deflation has given way to the continuing experience of inflation, will the demand for money start to fall and velocity to rise.

By the same token, after a period of sustained inflation, the immediate effect of a slowdown in the rate of increase in the quantity of money may well be a further rise in the velocity of circulation of money. This will be the case if people believe that the inflation will soon resume on as great or greater a scale than before and hence become willing temporarily to operate with even lower cash holdings than before.

It is also possible that velocity may drop in the face of an undiminished rate of increase in the supply of money, indeed, even in the face of an accelerated rate of increase in the supply of money. This result can occur if the realization of people's expectations concerning inflation presupposes a more rapid rate of increase in the quantity of money than actually takes place. In such circumstances, they will have reduced their demand for money unduly in the light of the facts. Thus, they will need to increase their demand for money.

The data in Table 12–1 can be broken down into four main periods: 1914–29, 1929–45, 1945–82, and 1982 to the present. The first of these periods runs from just prior to the outbreak of World War I in Europe to the start of the Great Depression. The second runs from the start of the Great Depression to the end of World War II; the third, from the end of World War II to the most severe postwar recession; the fourth spans the subsequent recent years.

Since reliable GDP/GNP statistics are unavailable prior to 1929, it is not possible to compute values for

Table 12–1

Money Supply, Consumer Demand (GNP/GDP), and Velocity of Circulation
in the United States, Selected Years, 1914–1993

Year	Money Supply (in billions)	Consumer Demand (GNP/GDP in billions)	Velocity
1914 Je.	$11.5	N. A.	
1920 Je.	23.7	N. A.	
1921 Je.	20.8	N. A.	
1925 Je.	24.9	N. A.	
1929 Dec.	26.4	$103.1	3.9
1933 Je.	19.2	55.6	2.9
1939	36.2	90.5	2.5
1945	102.3	211.9	2.1
1950	116.2	284.8	2.5
1955	135.2	398.0	2.9
1960	144.2	503.7	3.5
1965	171.3	681.2	4.0
1970	219.6	976.4	4.4
1975	294.8	1506.0	5.1
1980	414.9	2633.1	6.3
1981	441.9	2957.8	6.7
1982	479.9	3069.3	6.4
1983	527.1	3405.7	6.5
1984	558.5	3765.0	6.7
1985	620.1	4014.9	6.5
1986	725.4	4240.3	5.8
1987	750.8	4526.7	6.0
1988	787.8	4861.8	6.2
1989	794.1[*]	5250.8	6.6
1990	826.1	5522.2	6.7
1991	899.3	5677.5	6.3
1992	1026.6	5945.7	5.8
1993	1128.4	6343.3	5.6

[*]Data are for GDP starting with 1989.

Sources: Board of Governors of the Federal Reserve System, *Banking and Monetary Statistics 1914–1941* (Washington, D. C.: Board of Governors of the Federal Reserve System, 1943), p. 34; idem, *Banking and Monetary Statistics 1941–1970* (1976), pp. 5, 17–19; idem, *Annual Statistical Digest 1971–1975* (1976), p. 49; idem, *Federal Reserve Bulletin*, December 1981, pp. A13, A52; February and November 1985, pp. A13, A51; October 1986, pp. A13, A51; March 1989, pp. A13, A53; April 1992, pp. A14, A51; October 1994 pp. A14, A51. *National Income and Product Accounts of the United States 1929-1965* (Washington, D.C.: U.S. Department of Commerce, 1966), pp. 2–3.; *Survey of Current Business,* July 1972, p. 7. From 1939 on, money supply data are for December of each year.

velocity in the first period, as we are able to do for all the years from 1929 on simply by dividing the money supply into the GDP or GNP. Nevertheless, we can infer a rise in velocity over the course of the 1920s from all the reports depicting the era as a period of great financial boom. To qualify for such a description, it seems certain that the increase in spending over the period had to exceed the 27 percent cumulative increase in the money supply between June of 1921 (the reporting date following the reduction in the money supply in the depression of that year) and December of 1929. For that increase works out to be only slightly more than 2.8 percent per year on a compound annual basis.

Velocity rose in the twenties on the foundation of a combination of the sharply increased money supply of World War I and an aggressively easy money policy on the part of the Federal Reserve System from June of 1921 to the end of 1925. From June of 1921 to June of 1925, the money supply increased at a compound annual rate of slightly more than 4.6 percent. Also very important in explaining the rise in velocity in the 1920s was the widely held conviction that the Federal Reserve System, by virtue of its ability to increase the supply of currency and member-bank reserves, had the power to prevent depressions and achieve permanent prosperity. In this environment, the demand for money fell and business firms became relatively illiquid.

The far more modest rate of increase in the quantity of money in the late 1920s presaged a fall in velocity. From June of 1925 to June of 1929, the money supply increased at a compound annual rate of approximately only 1.1 percent.[32] The fall in velocity began by the end of 1929, and intensified thereafter. The disastrous monetary contraction of the period 1929–1933 can be explained on the basis, first, of an undue increase in the quantity of money, coupled with the conviction that the Federal Reserve System would prevent any future depression. These factors reduced the demand for money and raised the velocity of money to levels that could not be sustained in the absence of a continued rapid increase in the quantity of money. This continued rapid increase in the money supply did not occur. When, as a result, the demand for money finally increased and velocity correspondingly fell, the effect was reduced spending, hence reduced revenues and incomes, and thus a decreased ability to repay debts.

This last, in turn, resulted in bank failures and an actual decrease in the quantity of money, as fiduciary media were wiped out under the fractional-reserve monetary system of the time. The decrease in the quantity of money caused a further decrease in spending and, concomitantly, a further decrease in revenues and incomes, and thus an even greater reduction in the ability to repay

debt, with the result of still more bank failures and a still greater reduction in the quantity of money. The cumulative fall in the money supply between 1929 and 1933 was approximately 27 percent! (This put the money supply in 1933 below where it had been in 1921.)

In the face of a declining quantity of money, velocity fell still further, as it became urgently necessary for business firms to raise cash to be sure of being able to pay their debts and as the expectation grew that investments made in the present could not only be made cheaper in the future, once wage rates and other costs fell, but, if made in the present, would incur an actual financial loss. The prospect of falling prices accompanied by the prospect of being unemployed in the future led consumers, too, to retrench on current spending. In the face of lack of profitable investment opportunities caused by declining sales revenues, their retrenchment in consumption spending largely meant a reduction in spending as such. Because of these factors, velocity fell from 1929 to 1933—from 3.9 to 2.9.

Our table shows, of course, that the velocity of circulation continued to fall from 1933 to 1945, despite very major increases in the money supply from 1933 on. But this is not difficult to explain. The disastrous deflation of the early thirties, in which, as just noted, the money supply fell by more than 25 percent, in which credit was unobtainable by virtually all but the strongest enterprises, in which thousands upon thousands of firms went bankrupt, was an experience that guaranteed a very high degree of financial conservatism for many years to come. As a result, even though the money supply began to increase again after 1933, funds were used to an uncommon degree to build liquidity; that is, firms chose to operate with unusually large money balances. They acted out of fear of the recurrence of deflation. This explains the continuing fall in velocity during the remainder of the thirties.

In World War II, velocity fell because of wartime government controls that limited demand. During the war, the government imposed all-round price and wage controls and instituted a system of consumer rationing. This necessarily limited the amount of spending in the economic system, because no one could spend a sum larger than the controlled prices times the limited quantities of goods available to him. At the same time, of course, the money supply was sharply increased. The combination of a governmentally limited demand and a sharply rising money supply mathematically necessitated a falling velocity of circulation.

By the early postwar years, the memory of the Great Depression and the fear of its recurrence had substantially receded, and from this period on the velocity of circulation began to rise. As in the late twenties, the years

1955 to 1960 experienced only a modest rate of increase in the quantity of money—approximately only 1.3 percent per annum. Indeed, in the early sixties, there was even a stock market crash—the most severe since 1929. But this time, the government saw to it that the quantity of money did not decrease but increased more rapidly. And thus by 1965 we see velocity reaching levels in excess of the 1929 peak.

From 1960 on, the rate of increase in the quantity of money accelerated in every five year period until 1985. From 1960 to 1965, the five-year rate of increase was 18.8 percent; from 1965 to 1970, 28.3 percent; from 1970 to 1975, 34.2 percent; from 1975 to 1980, 40.7 percent; and from 1980 to 1985, 51 percent. Not surprisingly, the velocity of circulation of money went on increasing over most of this period. It reached a peak of 6.7 in 1981.

The increase in the velocity of circulation from the end of World War II until 1981 is exactly what we would expect on the basis of our theoretical knowledge. It was an effect of the increase in the quantity of money that had been going on since 1933 and which tended to accelerate over time, with no sign of major interruption. By the end of the 1970s the demand for money in the United States had fallen to a point where it reflected a growing expectation that the country might soon experience a Latin-American style inflation.

This expectation did not materialize, however. And since 1982, velocity has receded from its 1981 peak. This result, too, is what we should expect on the basis of our theoretical knowledge. For 1980 and 1981, what occurred for the first time in the post–World War II era was precisely *a major interruption in the accelerating rate of increase in the quantity of money*. In those two years, the Federal Reserve System made a sharply reduced rate of growth in the money supply its highest priority. It supplied additional reserves to banks only at a ruinously high discount rate of 16 percent. People who had been counting on a rapidly accelerating increase in the money supply—who had further overextended themselves when such an increase failed to materialize, in the belief that it very soon would, in conformity with the pattern established in all the previous recessions experienced since the end of World War II—were caught short and had to scramble for funds.

In response to their desperate demand for funds, the government brought about an increase in the money supply of 8.5 percent in 1982 and 9.8 percent in 1983 (following an increase of 6 percent in 1980 and 6.5 percent in 1981), but only at interest rates so high as to make most borrowing unprofitable and only in order to prevent what otherwise would certainly have been the start of a major depression. Even so, the consequence of the change in government policy was the most serious

recession—the first actual depression, according to some observers—since the 1930s. A further consequence was that since that time the U.S. government has been viewed as being unwilling to allow a continuous acceleration in the rate of increase in the quantity of money. The effect of this has been an increase in the demand for dollars and a consequent tendency toward a decline in the velocity of circulation of dollars. (In the early 1980s, a major factor cushioning the effects of the increase in the demand for money for holding was the rapid increase in so-called money-market-mutual-fund accounts. These are interest-bearing savings accounts that closely resemble checking accounts in that their holders have the right to write up to three checks per month against them. Between December of 1978 and December of 1982, these accounts grew from a little over $10 billion to $230 billion.[33])

Ironically, the effect of the increase in the demand for money inaugurated by the government's policy of restricting the growth in the supply of money earlier in the decade was to enable the government to resort to a renewed acceleration of the increase in the supply of money in 1985 and 1986, with rates of increase of in those years of 11.1 percent and 16.9 percent, respectively.

Given the prevailing still relatively low state of demand for money that has resulted from decades of inflation, such rapid rates of increase in the money supply are necessary to prevent the greater demand for money corresponding to moderate increases in the money supply from resulting in a decline in total spending in the economic system and thus launching a depression. This conclusion is confirmed by subsequent events. In the remainder of the decade the rate of increase in the money supply was sharply reduced: in 1987 it was 3.4 percent; in 1988, 5 percent; in 1989, 1 percent; in 1990, 4 percent. The five-year rate of increase in the money supply between 1985 and 1990 ended up as 33 percent—the first five-year increase since 1960 that was less than the previous five-year increase. Not surprisingly, in late 1990, and in 1991 and 1992, the economic system seemed poised for a major depression.

In an effort to overcome the slide toward depression, in 1991 the increase in the quantity of money was stepped up to almost 9 percent. In 1992, it was in excess of 14 percent, and in 1993, more than 10 percent. Because these increases in the quantity of money took place in an environment of largely deflationary psychology, the result was a substantial fall in the velocity of circulation of money over the years 1991–93, namely, from 6.7 in 1990 to 5.6 in 1993, as shown in Table 12–1. Finally, in late 1993, because of the sharply increased quantity of money and the consequent ability of sales revenues and profits to increase from year to year, along with the rise in liquidity constituted by the lower velocity of circulation, the widespread fears of impending depression gave way. In the current year, 1994, there are growing fears of a resumption of more rapidly rising prices. The Federal Reserve System shares these fears, and in the present year has once again sharply reduced the rate of increase in the quantity of money—to a little over 2 percent on an annual basis (i.e., from $1,128.4 billion at the end of December 1993, to $1,149.4 billion in mid-October of 1994).[34]

What is certain is that if the rapid rates of increase in the money supply that prevailed from 1991 through 1993 were to be continued, the demand for money would once again sharply decline, in which case rapid increases in the quantity of money would be joined by a substantial rise in the velocity of circulation of money, with the result that very rapid increases in spending would ensue. On the other hand, it is no less certain that if the present, modest rate of increase in the money supply were to remain in force, a major increase in the demand for money would take place, such as began in 1990. This would result in a large-scale monetary contraction—that is, a major deflation/depression. To put it mildly, the present monetary situation is highly unstable, possessing as it does the potential both for major inflation and for major deflation. Under present monetary conditions, the economic system is poised between both dangers, with the government undertaking to prevent the one only by means of unleashing the other and then hoping to be able to change course quickly enough to overcome the momentarily greater danger by enlarging and setting against it the momentarily smaller danger.

It should never be forgotten that this deadly alternative would not exist if the policy of inflation had not been resorted to in the first place. Even now, I do not think that the alternative is inescapable, and in Chapter 19 I will present a solution for stopping inflation without precipitating a depression—a solution that is fully consistent both with a sharp increase in the demand for money and consequent major decline in the velocity of circulation, and yet, at the same time, with no decrease, indeed, an increase, in the volume spending in the economic system expressed in dollars.[35] As I will also show in Chapter 19, in the absence of once and for all ending the policy of inflation, the problem must remain substantial, as a minimum. More likely, it will grow worse.[36]

4. The Demand for Money: A Critique of the "Balance of Payments" Doctrine

Knowledge of the demand for money sheds light on the questions of the "balance of trade" and the "balance of payments." These are matters in connection with which arguments have been advanced, and generally accepted, to the effect that the vital self-interest of countries requires restrictions on the freedom of international trade. Worse, on the foundation of the belief that countries benefit from an excess of exports over imports, or of receipts from abroad over outlays to abroad, and are harmed by the opposite type of excess, the implication arises, in the clearest possible terms, that the self-interests of countries are necessarily opposed to one another. For, in the nature of the case, it is impossible for a country to have an excess of exports over imports, or receipts from abroad over outlays to abroad, without other countries having an equivalent excess of the opposite kind. Thus, each country, in pursuing what is believed to be its economic self-interest is perceived as bent at the same time on a policy that causes harm to other countries. In this way, the doctrine of the balance of trade or balance of payments serves as a leading cause of international conflict and, ultimately, of war. Few things, therefore, can contribute more to world peace than its overthrow. In accordance with this objective, I will first present the substance of the doctrine and then turn to a critique of it.

The balance of trade is the difference between the money received by the citizens of a country in exchange for exports of goods to foreign countries and the money expended by the citizens of that country in exchange for imports of goods from foreign countries. The balance of payments is an essentially similar, but more comprehensive concept. It is the difference between the total of a country's receipts from abroad and the total of its outlays to abroad. Under the heading of receipts are included not only receipts from the export of goods, but also receipts from the sale of services to foreigners, such as shipping, insurance, and the hosting of tourists. Dividends and interest received from abroad, the proceeds from the sale of securities, such as stocks and bonds, to abroad, and the proceeds of borrowings and the repayment of debts from abroad are also included. By the same token, outlays to abroad include, along with outlays for imports, the purchase of services from foreigners, dividends and interest paid to them, remissions of gifts by individuals to abroad, government foreign aid, the purchase of securities from abroad, and the granting of loans and repayment of debts to abroad.

For historical reasons that will be made clear shortly, an excess of exports over imports is mistakenly called a favorable balance of trade, while an excess of imports over exports is mistakenly called an unfavorable balance of trade. Similarly, an excess of the total of all categories of receipts from abroad over the total of all categories of outlays to abroad is mistakenly called a favorable balance of payments, while an excess of the total of all categories of outlays to abroad over the total of all categories of receipts from abroad is mistakenly called an unfavorable balance of payments.

From the perspective of the history of economic thought, the concepts of the balance of trade and the balance of payments can be taken as interchangeable. This is because when the concept of the balance of trade became prominent, with the writings of the Mercantilists in the seventeenth and eighteenth centuries, commercial dealings with foreign countries were essentially limited to imports and exports. There was as yet no significant international capital market, and the international exchange of services was also not significant.

In order to understand the importance attached to these concepts historically, it is necessary to consider the context in which the Mercantilists wrote and the ideas they advanced in connection with these concepts. The Mercantilists lived in a time when gold and silver constituted the money of all countries. Countries which did not possess gold and silver mines, which was the situation of most of the European nations of the period, could obtain an additional supply of money only from abroad. Insofar as the money was to be obtained by trade, an excess of exports over imports was the only possible means.

Obtaining an additional supply of money in a country was originally thought to be important as a means of financing future foreign wars. It was thought that the additional money would be available for taxation when it became necessary for the king to finance foreign military ventures, which would require the spending of precious metals abroad, and that it was possible and necessary to heap up sufficient "treasure" in a country to cover all or at least a substantial part of the cost of such ventures. Increasingly, however, a wider economic perspective entered in. It came to be held that a growing quantity of money obtained from an excess of exports over imports would provide an economic stimulus to production and employment in the country by virtue of increasing the volume of spending, and could lower interest rates by providing a larger quantity of money for lending. For all of these reasons, an excess of exports over imports was held to represent a "favorable" balance of trade.

In exactly the same way, an excess of imports over exports was perceived as reducing the quantity of money in a country. This, it was thought, not only impaired the ability of the country to finance future foreign wars, but reduced spending, production, and employment in the country, and raised its interest rates as well, which further contributed to its economic woes. For all of these reasons, an excess of imports over exports was called unfavorable.

On the Mercantilist view of things, in the absence of

government intervention to secure a favorable balance, the balance of trade (payments) was determined on an essentially accidental basis. It was the fortuitous outcome of the unrelated actions of everyone who happened to sell to abroad or buy from abroad. Any individual action which increased exports was thought to improve the balance of trade correspondingly. Any individual action which increased imports was thought to harm the balance of trade correspondingly. On the mercantilist view of things, imports had the potential of completely draining a country of its money supply—if, for a period of years purchases from abroad happened to exceed receipts from abroad by a wide enough margin. Indeed, the only justification of imports was thought to be either their absolute necessity in meeting important needs that otherwise could not be supplied or in bringing about subsequent exports that would constitute an improvement in the overall balance of trade. (The latter was thought to be the case insofar as imports were in the form of raw materials or equipment advantageous to the production of subsequent exports.)

The element of "heaping up treasure" to finance future foreign wars is no longer prominent. Among other things, it was shown to be incapable of making any significant contribution to the end sought, since the size of money holdings is always quite modest relative to the volume of expenditures which must be made. The actual source of wartime military expenditures abroad is always, overwhelmingly, the proceeds of current exports and borrowings from abroad. The plans of kings and emperors for accumulating precious metals within the borders of their countries turned out, on calculation, to be sufficient for supporting the war expenses of no more than a few weeks or months.

But apart from this element, Mercantilism has a very contemporary ring to it. It bears a close similarity to the ideas of Keynes and his followers in its concern with finding a source of economic "stimulus," and in its fear that in the absence of such stimulus, the economic system must languish in unemployment and poverty. Its views on the ability of a larger quantity of money to reduce interest rates are also practically indistinguishable from those of Keynes.

Mercantilism's treatment of the balance of trade (payments) as being the fortuitous outcome of the unrelated actions of individuals is also shared by most contemporary writers and commentators on the subject. It is manifested in such attitudes as that the American balance of payments is unfavorable because Americans are buying too much specifically from the Japanese, or, even more specifically, too many automobiles and electronics products from the Japanese. At other times, the specific sources of the trade or payments imbalance of the United

States has been held to be such things as the purchase of imported wines from France, tourism by Americans in foreign countries, American lending abroad, the stationing of American soldiers abroad, and the giving of foreign aid.

The presumption is that if each or any of these outlays was not present, total outlays would be equivalently reduced and thus the difference between outlays and receipts correspondingly improved. On the basis of the view that the problem of an unfavorable balance originates in this way, the remedy that appears to follow is the imposition of restrictions or prohibitions on the particular dealings in question. Thus, depending on what is being singled out at the moment, Americans have variously been urged to buy less French wine, take their vacations at home, reduce their lending abroad, and, most recently, not to buy Japanese products. Needless to say, corresponding laws and regulations have been proposed and enacted.

Of course, by the same token, any particular source of receipts from abroad is capable of being singled out for praise, on the grounds of its corresponding contribution to the country's balance of trade or payments. For example, in the 1960s, the members of a prominent rock 'n roll group were made Members of the Order of the British Empire on the basis of their alleged contribution to Britain's balance of payments through their receipt of large concert fees and recording royalties earned in the United States and Continental Europe. Of course, an obvious implication of the view that any given receipt from abroad represents a corresponding improvement in a country's trade or payments balance is the subsidization of exports. Export subsidies—the taxpayers' loss—are thought to be the basis of a gain to the nation.

The Balance of Payments Doctrine and Fiat Money

Now the first thing which should be realized about the concepts of the balance of trade and the balance of payments is that whatever plausibility they may have had in the days when a country's money supply depended on gold obtained from abroad, they no longer possess even that plausibility. Indeed, it is highly ironic, but nowadays expenditures for the importation of *gold itself* are believed to add to a country's balance of payments deficit. (For example, an important motivation in the decision of the U.S. Congress to order the minting of a new American gold coin a few years ago was the belief that it would help the United States' balance of payments to some extent by giving American citizens an alternative to buying imported gold coins, such as the Canadian Maple Leaf and the South African Krugerrand.)

Over two centuries ago, Adam Smith wrote, for reasons that will soon become apparent, "Upon every ac-count, therefore, the attention of government never was so unnecessarily employed, as when directed to watch over the preservation or increase of the quantity of money in any country."[37] When one realizes that today, the whole concern over the balance of trade and the balance of payments is over an alleged outflow of *irredeemable paper money,* this concern must be judged utterly absurd.

Even if it were the case that an unfavorable balance of payments meant a corresponding reduction in the quantity of money in a country, absolutely nothing could be more easily replaced than a loss of fiat money. All that is required is additional paper and ink, and not even that—just some additional credit entries on the ledgers of the banks. Indeed, to some extent every year there is an outflow of currency from the United States. For there are people living in many foreign countries whose currencies depreciate far more rapidly than the dollar, and who therefore prefer to have holdings of dollars rather than holdings of their own currencies—who want to have dollars in safety deposit boxes or even hidden under their mattresses. Indeed, there is an important demand almost everywhere for dollars to be used as an international currency, that is, in financing trade among most foreign countries. To that extent, there is a demand for dollars in the form of checking deposits as well. But these phenomena do not cause any actual reduction in the supply of money in the United States. They merely cause a somewhat lesser rate of increase. That is, the quantity of money in circulation in the United States does not increase by the full magnitude of the increase in the supply of dollars, but by an amount which is less to the extent that part of the increase is taken by foreigners, in exchange for goods and services they supply us. It is difficult to see how there is anything at all that is "unfavorable about this." It achieves the equivalent of a lesser degree of inflation in the United States and provides the American economy with real goods and services in exchange for intrinsically worthless pieces of paper.

But what is truly ironic is that the far greater part of what is recorded as an unfavorable balance of payments does not even represent any actual outflow of money—not even fiat money! On the contrary, it is constituted by *an increase in short-term foreign lending* to the citizens of the country, or to its government. For example, when foreigners take the dollars they have earned in selling goods or services in the United States, or simply go out and exchange their own money for dollars, and then deposit the proceeds in American banks or their overseas branches, which then remit them to the United States, or when foreigners buy U.S. treasury bills or commercial paper—*that increase in short-term liabilities to foreigners is said to constitute an unfavorable balance of payments to the United States!*

It is no less difficult to understand what is unfavorable about this than about an outflow of fiat currency. The dollars that the foreigners deposit in banks here or abroad are lent out and spent in the United States, and the same is certainly true of the funds they use to purchase U.S. treasury bills or commercial paper.[38] Indeed, such short-term foreign lending should be regarded as an indication of the *strength* of a country's economic system, in that it shows that foreigners consider the country to be a worthwhile place to invest their money. The same point, of course, applies even more strongly to intermediate and long-term foreign investment.

Foreign lending and investment contribute to domestic capital formation and thus, as later chapters of this book will show, to the rise in the productivity of labor and real wages—developments that are as favorable to a country as can be imagined. And, in passing, it should be realized that, at least until recently, foreign lending and investment in this country have helped greatly to alleviate the drain of capital funds that would otherwise have resulted from our massive government budget deficits. They have also prevented the pressure that would then exist to finance those deficits through the more rapid creation of money. There is nothing "unfavorable" about this.

Obviously, the receipt of funds in connection with foreign short-term lending and investing should very definitely be counted among a country's international receipts. Its omission creates the appearance of an imbalance in a country's international accounts when in fact there is none. And it makes what in reality is a perfectly favorable development appear unfavorable. To this extent, the doctrine of the balance of payments represents a fiction as well as an absurdity.

This leads to a wider problem in the concept of the balance of trade and payments—namely, that it is not seen that the various items in the accounts are not independent, but rather are mutually interconnected. For example, the so-called unfavorable balance of trade (the excess of imports over exports) that the United States has experienced in recent years is precisely the result of the excess of receipts by the United States over outlays in the vital area of lending and investing.

This latter excess has been largely due to the fact that in the early and mid-1980s the United States came to be considered the outstanding country in which to invest. This was the result of an apparent determination on the part of its government to restrain the growth in the money supply, to provide a more favorable tax treatment of profits, and to reduce the extent of its own interference in the economic system. All this was coupled with the existence of historically very high rates of interest.

As the result of a massive inflow of foreign funds seeking dollars for investment purposes, the exchange value of the dollar rose sharply in terms of other currencies. This rise in the foreign-exchange value of the dollar, in turn, made American goods correspondingly more expensive for foreigners to buy, inasmuch as foreigners first had to buy more expensive dollars in order to buy American goods, and, by the same token, made foreign goods correspondingly cheaper for Americans to buy, inasmuch as a dollar now bought more of foreign currencies and thus more of foreign goods. Thus, the foreign investment resulted in an excess of imports over exports. It provided both the financial means of purchasing imports without making corresponding exports and, at the same time, a financial incentive, in the form of a high foreign-exchange value of the dollar, leading the economic system to do precisely that.

Indeed, it is in the very nature of foreign investment that it be accompanied by a so-called unfavorable balance of trade in the country receiving the investment. What the foreign investment contributes is *physical wealth* from abroad. In the country receiving the wealth, this means an importation of goods without a corresponding exportation of goods. Only in this way can there be a net inflow of wealth.

Perhaps the clearest illustration of how foreign investment means an "unfavorable" balance of trade can be found in the economic development of a wilderness area. Thus, imagine, for example, that there is a stretch of coastline somewhere that contains oil deposits. To exploit the oil deposits, wells must be drilled, a refinery and storage tanks constructed, piers and warehouses built, and so forth. All of this must come from outside the area—from abroad. Its coming represents a great investment. But it is simply impossible that there can be corresponding exports while the area is in process of development. Its development is possible only so long as it is able to obtain funds with which to pay for imports of all kinds *without as yet having to make corresponding exports.* Yet, incredibly, while the area's development is going on, its balance of trade is called "unfavorable," because it imports more than it exports. What would allegedly not be unfavorable is if the area did not receive the imports that make its development possible.

The same principles, of course—the same actual favorableness of the "unfavorable" balance of trade—apply to a great nation that already is very highly developed, but is undergoing still further development. They also apply to a case in which the influx of wealth from abroad serves to offset the consumption of capital at home by a voracious government.

Such an excess of imports over exports does not in the least cause unemployment. And the truth of this statement is confirmed by the fact that precisely in the period of its massive trade deficits, the unemployment rate in the United States has been among the lowest of any major nation. As should already be clear, the purchase of the imports does not represent any significant carrying out of money from the United States or any reduction in total, overall spending for goods and services in the United States. On the contrary, the imports represent new and additional wealth brought into the United States, where they are added to the supply of domestically produced goods and made available for purchase by the same total expenditure of money that would otherwise take place. In other words, the American public obtains more for its money. The real wealth in the economic system is increased and the rise in prices is correspondingly retarded. (The reduction in exports that foreign investment in the country achieves by means of raising the foreign-exchange value of the country's money contributes to the same result. For a portion of the country's output which otherwise would have been exported is made available for purchase domestically instead.)

The following example shows the actual nature of what takes place. Thus, imagine that there is a German business firm that exchanges two million marks for one million dollars. The German firm places these million dollars in a bank, in a time deposit. The bank lends them out to an American business firm, which now expends them in the United States in the purchase of such things as plant and equipment, materials, and labor services. The firm's employees, in turn, spend their wages in buying various consumers' goods from other American businesses. Observe. There is no reduction in the number of dollars in the American economy, nor any reduction in spending for goods and services in the American economy. All that is different in the American economy is that the seller of the million dollars to the German firm now has two million marks and thus the means of importing two million marks' worth of goods into the American economy. In other words, there is the same money and spending as before, but more goods in the American economic system for the same volume of aggregate spending to buy.

Let us take another example. A Japanese automobile company sends a shipload of cars to the United States, for which it is paid a sum of dollars. It must use most of these dollars to buy yen, in order to have the funds to maintain its operations in Japan. Some of the dollars, however, it saves and deposits in American banks or uses to buy American securities. These dollars are spent in the United States, just as in the previous example. Most of the dollars that are exchanged for yen will be used by Japanese to import from the United States. The rest of the dollars are used to invest in the United States and, of

course, are expended here in the process. Again, the full supply of dollars turned over to the foreigners comes back as purchases within the United States. But what occurs is that *the supply of goods in the United States is correspondingly larger*: it is larger to the extent that the United States' import of automobiles exceeds its export of goods purchased with the dollars coming into the hands of foreigners. This last is the result insofar as the foreigners invest their dollars in the United States rather than import from it.

The rise in the foreign exchange value of a country's money that foreign investment in the country causes not only does not cause unemployment in that country, but actually tends to be accompanied by *less* unemployment. This is because the demand for labor is made overwhelmingly out of capital, which foreign investment increases. Foreign investment enlarges the capital funds in the possession of the average business firm in the country and thus puts it in a better position to employ labor. True enough, the rise in the foreign-exchange value of the country's money encourages imports and reduces exports, but it does not reduce the quantity of money or volume of spending in the country and actually tends to increase the volume of spending for labor and capital goods. What it does, to say it yet again, is increase the overall supply of goods in the country.

It is perfectly true that there are individual industries, such as automobiles and steel in the United States today, which are presently suffering large-scale unemployment because of their inability to meet foreign competition. If foreign competition were prohibited, these industries would suffer less unemployment. But unemployment in the rest of the economic system would grow more than correspondingly, or else wage rates in the rest of the economic system would have to fall. This is because the purchase even of the same quantity of domestically produced automobiles and steel as are presently purchased, under foreign competition, would require the expenditure of substantially larger sums of money at the higher prices that would then prevail. This would imply a reduction in expenditure for the output of the rest of the economic system, given the supply of money and the volume of aggregate spending in the economy. The reduction in expenditures elsewhere in the economic system would be all the greater, to the extent that the quantity of domestically produced automobiles and steel purchased at the higher prices was increased. In addition, the loss of foreign investment would operate to reduce the aggregate demand for labor in the United States. Thus, the additional employment offered by the auto and steel industries would be more than offset by the reduction in employment that the rest of the economic system could offer.

Thus, in sum, an end to the so-called unfavorable

balance of trade would come about as the result of the end of net foreign investment in the United States. It would be accompanied by a spurt in the level of prices, reflecting a reduced supply of goods available for sale. It would also mean that the full burden of the federal budget deficits would fall on the American economy. And it would tend to be accompanied by a higher overall rate of unemployment, not a lower one. Unfortunately, government policies in the United States may well have the effect of ending net foreign investment and thus of producing these highly undesirable consequences.

It is worth pointing out, as a final irony in the misconceptions surrounding the balance of payments and the balance of trade, that by any rational standard what is called a favorable balance of trade can in fact be fully as much unfavorable as an allegedly unfavorable one is favorable. A country that desires to achieve an excess of exports over imports has only to give money to its prospective customers, and they will import more and it will export more. This is exactly the kind of "favorable" balance of trade achieved by foreign aid. It can be duplicated on a small scale by any businessman who is willing to employ a doorman to give money to passersby on the condition that they spend the money in his shop.

The Balance of Payments Doctrine Under an International Precious Metal Standard

It is necessary to give some consideration to the balance-of-trade and balance-of-payments doctrines under an international gold standard. For in one form or another, this was the monetary system of the world until fairly recently, and could well become so once again. It will be seen that here, too, one of the most important things to keep in mind is that the individual items in the balance are not independent and fortuitous, but mutually interconnected.

Under a system in which the money supply of the various countries consisted of the precious metals, all of the beneficial effects of foreign investment explained above would be equally present. Instead of resulting in a higher foreign exchange value of a country's money, however, foreign investment would operate to enlarge the recipient country's money supply somewhat and, in so doing, make its prices higher than they would otherwise have been and thereby encourage imports and discourage exports. The resulting excess of imports over exports would once again be the physical mechanism by which foreign capital was transmitted to the country. And once again, the effect on overall employment would be positive, not negative, because of the greater availability of capital funds in the country.

In addition, further important principles would apply. A tendency would exist for the money supply of each individual country to follow the country's proportion of the world's production and trade. A country whose economy represented 10 percent of the world's economy would tend to possess 10 percent of the world's money supply within its borders. A country whose economy represented 20 percent of the world's economy would tend to possess 20 percent of the world's money supply within its borders, and so on. This is because money is demanded for making purchases and paying bills. The larger the relative size of a country's economy, the larger would tend to be its relative sales revenues and purchases to the same extent, and thus the larger its relative need for and ability to obtain holdings of money.

In such conditions, if the world supply of precious metals grew at a rate of, say, 2 percent per year, a country whose economy grew at the same rate as the world's economy and which, therefore, continued to constitute the same proportion of the world's economy, would tend to experience a 2 percent annual rate of increase in its money supply. The principle is that the money supply of an individual country would grow at the same rate as the world's money supply if its economy grew at the same rate as world's economy. By the same token, countries whose economies grew at a faster rate than the world's economy and whose relative share of the world's economy, therefore, tended to increase, would experience a rate of growth in their money supplies more rapid than the rate growth in the world's money supply. At the same time, those countries whose economies grew at a rate slower than that of the world's economy would experience below-average rates of increase in their money supplies, or even decreases in their money supplies.

These facts have an obvious bearing on the balance of payments positions of the various countries. Other things being equal, the more rapidly growing is the economy of a country relative to that of the rest of the world, the greater will tend to be its importation or the less will tend to be its exportation of the precious metals. This is because it will require within its borders a correspondingly larger proportion of the world's supply of precious metals. Thus, the more "favorable" or the less "unfavorable" will tend to be its balance of payments. Conversely, the less rapidly growing is the economy of a country relative to that of the rest of the world, the less will tend to be its importation or the greater will tend to be its exportation of the precious metals—that is, the less "favorable" or the more "unfavorable" will tend to be its balance of payments.

To take a major historical illustration, the rapid growth of the British economy relative to that of the rest of the world in the eighteenth and nineteenth centuries operated to produce a rising demand for money in Great Britain and a "favorable" balance of trade for Great Britain. At the same time, the stagnation and thus the relative decline of the economies of countries like India and China operated to produce a decline in the demand for money in those countries and an outflow of the precious metals.

The relative rates of growth in the economies of the different countries is not the only principle governing their balance-of-payments positions under a world precious metals standard. An equally important factor is the extent to which a country possesses or lacks precious-metal mines. Those countries in which the precious metals are mined in substantial quantities would regularly experience an "unfavorable" balance of payments. They would regularly export precious metals in exchange for the importation of ordinary commodities. By the same token, the countries in which there was little or no mining of the precious metals would regularly experience a "favorable" balance of payments: they would import precious metals in exchange for ordinary commodities.

These results would take place because of differences in the buying power of the precious metals between the two types of countries. In the countries in which the precious metals were mined, the supply of money would tend to be unduly high, and thus prices would tend to be higher than elsewhere in the world. This would make the importation of goods more attractive, since imports would be relatively cheap, and, at the same time, the exportation of goods other than the precious metals, less attractive, since such exports would be relatively more expensive than the goods people could buy elsewhere. An outstanding historical illustration is provided by the discovery of the California gold fields in 1848. The great local abundance of gold relative to ordinary commodities resulted in such phenomena as the price of a single egg being as high as a dollar for a time (a *gold* dollar of one-twentieth of an ounce of gold, which today represents the value of a substantial number of paper dollars). Thus, it was cheaper to buy almost everything outside of California. In this way, the gold originating in California found its way to the rest of the country and the rest of the world.

The same principle always applies, though when effective means of transportation exist, the disparity in prices need not be very great: the newly mined gold will be carried off rapidly and sufficient quantities of ordinary goods will be brought in rapidly, so that prices in the gold-mining areas will tend to exceed prices elsewhere by little more than the costs of transportation.

Alongside these two principles, and always limiting their operation, is a third principle, which is that, other things being equal, *the balance of trade and payments of all countries always tends toward balance.* That is, given the relative size of a country's economy in the world economy, and given the total quantity of money in the world's economy, there is a tendency for the receipts and outlays of money of all countries respectively to equalize.

This principle exists by virtue of the effects of changes in the quantity of money in the different countries. Countries whose money supply increases through an excess of receipts over outlays experience a tendency toward rising prices, while countries whose money supply decreases through an excess of outlays over receipts experience a tendency toward falling prices. The resulting changes in prices makes the countries which have experienced an inflow of money relatively less favorable markets and those which have experienced an outflow of money relatively more favorable markets. Thus, the inflow and outflow of money is ultimately stopped. In other words, the balance of trade and payments comes into balance.

Whether the balance of trade and payments of a country were in balance or not in balance, there would always be a sufficient quantity of precious metals in every country to buy all that it is capable of producing and to employ all of its inhabitants who are able and willing to work. As later chapters will show, this is strictly a question of the prices and wage rates in that country. At the appropriate level of prices and wages, any given quantity of money and volume of spending is capable of purchasing the entire supply of goods that a country can produce and of employing its entire supply of labor.[39] Indeed, as the present discussion makes clear, the problem a country experiences of an outflow of precious-metal money accompanying a decline in its relative economic position in the world is the result of its *not having increased its production sufficiently.* What is required to stop such an outflow of precious metals is precisely an increase in its ability to produce.

In this connection, the potentially extremely destructive role of monopoly labor unions must be mentioned. Such unions play a major role in retarding the rise in the productivity of labor in a country and thus in bringing about a decline in its relative position in the world economy. This decline means, as a minimum, a slower rate of increase in the supply of precious metals in the country. This, in turn, means that full employment can be achieved only at a lower level of money wage rates than would otherwise be necessary—possibly at a level of money wage rates which represents an absolute fall. But the unions are unlikely to be willing to accept the relatively lower wage rates, and almost certainly not an absolute fall in wage rates. Thus, unemployment develops. And so long as the unions retard the rise in the domestic productivity of labor, while it goes on rising more rapidly abroad, the problem of unemployment worsens.

This point, of course, has application to current conditions in the United States, even though the country is not on a gold standard of any kind. In a world of multiple fiat moneys, changes in the relative size of the economies of the various countries are still reflected in corresponding changes in the proportion of the world's money supply circulating within their borders. Only now, the change is effected partly by changes in the foreign exchange value of the various currencies and partly by changes in their respective quantities. The more rapidly production increases in one country relative to the others, the higher, other things being equal, becomes the value of its currency relative to the value of foreign currencies. By the same token, the more rapidly production increases in a country relative to other countries, the more rapidly can that country increase its quantity of money without depreciating the value of its currency relative to the value of foreign currencies. Thus, the fraction of the world's quantity of money that exists within the territory of a country is still determined by the size of its economy relative to the economy of the rest of the world.

It follows, even under the present system of multiple fiat moneys, that to the extent that labor unions in the United States have retarded the rise in the productivity of labor in the United States relative to that in foreign countries, they have caused a fall in the fraction of the world's money supply that circulates in the United States. It further follows that to the extent that they insist on continuing to receive wage rates conforming to a previous, higher relative productivity of labor in the United States, the effect must be unemployment.

These results exist in dramatic form in such major American industries as automaking and steel, where labor unions have greatly retarded the rise in the productivity of labor, at the same time that the productivity of labor in these industries in important foreign countries has sharply increased. The rise in the relative productivity of labor abroad has enabled foreign competitors to undersell American producers even while paying rapidly rising wage rates. The only thing that has prevented the unions from causing mass unemployment in the United States is the fact that many branches of industry in the United States are nonunion and have thus been in a position to absorb additional workers.[40]

Inflation as the Cause of a Gold Outflow

I have already explained how the gold standard of the eighteenth and nineteenth centuries and the earlier part of this century was a fractional-reserve gold standard. Under such a gold standard, the world supply of money can be increased by the creation of fiduciary media in any given country. (This includes, of course, fiduciary media created by governments in issuing claims to gold in excess of their actual gold holdings.) So long as the fiduciary media are accepted in commerce as the equivalent of gold, an increase in their supply appears on the market as though it were an increase in the supply of gold.

From this point on, the effects are largely analogous to those resulting from the discovery of additional gold mines in a country. The increase in the world's supply of money is initially concentrated in the country in which the additional fiduciary media are created. The effect is a disproportionate enlargement of that country's money supply relative to the money supply of other countries. On the foundation of this larger money supply, the inhabitants of the country step up their expenditures, including, of course, their expenditures to abroad. At the same time, prices in the country rise relative to prices in other countries. In addition, the appearance of the additional fiduciary media on the loan market operates to reduce interest rates in the country relative to interest rates abroad. For all of these reasons, an unfavorable balance of payments develops, as a substantial portion of the additional money supply begins to move abroad. Indeed, in the absence of the simultaneous creation of fiduciary media abroad, the only portion of the additional money supply which the country in question could retain would be the proportion corresponding to its proportion of the world's economy. That means, for example, that if it represented 5 percent of the world's economy, it could retain only 5 percent of the additional supply of money it created.

Here the analogy to the discovery of additional gold mines ends. For a country's additional fiduciary media are not in fact additional gold. And the additional money supply that foreigners will usually wish to hold is not the expanding country's additional fiduciary media, but a corresponding quantity of *gold*. Thus, the effect is that a loss of gold reserves ensues in the expanding country.

Of course, the loss of gold reserves resulting from the creation of fiduciary media is the less severe to the degree that the policy is pursued at the same time by other countries. To the extent that all countries expand fiduciary media at the same time, each will tend to have mutually offsetting claims against the gold reserves of the others. The policy can also be carried further to the extent that a country's fiduciary media are sought for holding in other countries, as was the case with the U.S. dollar in the decades following World War II, and, to a lesser extent, in the years following World War I.

Despite its actual cause, the gold outflow that occurs in such circumstances is typically blamed on the actions of the citizens, who, it is alleged, are spending too much for this or that category of import, travelling outside the country excessively, or lending abroad on too great a scale—as previously described.

Blaming the unfavorable balance of payments on the citizens and attempting to restrict their outlays to abroad (or stimulate their receipts from abroad) overlooks entirely the fact that the problem is the result of *a lack of demand for the additional money* in the country in which it originates. There is simply no basis for the citizens of the country wanting to retain the additional quantity of money all within its borders. And so long as this is the case, efforts to restrict their outlays to abroad for this or that specific purpose, such as French wines, tourism, or securities purchases, are absolutely futile. Their futility can be illustrated by imagining the case of someone who receives a $500 check on his birthday and who wants to spend the money on a new suit, say. If this person is prohibited from buying the suit, the result will certainly not be that he then simply adds the $500 to his cash holding. On the contrary, he will buy something else. If his second-choice expenditure, too, is prohibited, he will buy his third choice, and so on. If he is totally blocked from spending the additional $500 for any purpose, he will reduce his other receipts of money by $500, for there is no purpose in earning money he cannot spend. In no case can he be made to add the $500 to his cash holding until he perceives a need to do so.

It is the same in international trade. If Americans are blocked from spending money for French wines, foreign vacations, or foreign securities, they will spend it for other things from abroad. This result is guaranteed, because so long as the additional money remains in the United States, it operates to make American prices higher than prices elsewhere, and does so to the degree that the additional money is retained in the United States, with the result that the more powerful is the encouragement of imports and, at the same time, the greater is the discouragement of exports. Thus, no sooner is one avenue of outlay to abroad blocked, than another is opened up, or receipts from abroad decline.

It should be realized that a corollary of the present discussion is that when the citizens of a country do have a demand for its existing quantity of money, no amount of outlays to abroad will for very long deprive them of any part of that quantity of money. Thus, for example, if, under an international gold standard, Americans want to hold their present quantity of money and American tourists happen to spend an additional billion or five or ten billion dollars touring Europe, that additional outlay will not reduce the quantity of money in the United States. Instead, it will automatically result in the generation of additional receipts from abroad, or in a reduction in other expenditures to abroad. It will do so in the same way and for the same reason that an individual who decides to buy some item that he likes does not finance the purchase of that item by reducing his normal cash holding.

For example, if someone normally needs to carry fifty dollars in his wallet and comes upon something he likes that costs forty dollars, which he decides to buy, that individual will not then decide to walk around with only ten dollars. He will quickly move to restore his cash holding, by withdrawing money from his savings account, say, or he will reduce his purchases of other items so that he can replenish his cash holding out of his next pay check. Indeed, to the extent that individuals know in advance that they will step up their expenditure for something, they first take steps to increase their receipts or to reduce their other expenditures. In any case, only in the most immediate and temporary sense are purchases made at the expense of running down cash holdings, unless the cash holdings were initially excessive.

To demonstrate, in as dramatic a way as possible, that outlays abroad are not made at the expense of running down cash holdings, when the cash holdings are not initially excessive, let us take the highly unpopular case of government outlays for foreign aid (which the present writer, of course, totally opposes). Let us imagine that a new foreign aid bill is passed and, as part of it, an army of tax collectors is dispatched into the streets to seize money from every passerby and from every shopkeeper and businessman. The money, we can imagine, is then loaded into armored cars, rushed to nearby airports, and then flown to various foreign capitals. Will this foreign aid be at the expense of the cash holdings of the American people? Will the American people now walk around and conduct their businesses with cash holdings diminished by the amounts the tax collectors have taken from them?

If one looks at matters subsequent to a span as short as a few days, the answer to these questions is no. The American people would immediately have to take steps to replenish their cash holdings. This is because at the prevailing level of wages and prices, their former cash holdings are necessary if they are to buy the things which they want to buy and to conduct their businesses on the scale on which they want to conduct them. Precisely their efforts to replenish their cash holdings would result in a rapid return of the funds that had been taken from them.

There would be substantial withdrawals of cash from banks, reductions in the expenditure for many items, and the widespread holding of sales by businessmen, as methods of raising cash. The effect of these actions would be a rise in interest rates and fall in the prices of various commodities in the United States. Meanwhile, in the foreign capitals, opposite results would be taking place. There, the presence of the additional cash would operate to reduce interest rates and raise commodity prices. The effect would be that the cash would probably be loaded back onto the very same planes on which it had arrived and be returned to the United States on practically the very same day it had left.

The loss to the American people would take the form not of a reduction in their cash holdings, but of a diminution in the quantity of goods they were able to buy: the recipients of the foreign aid would have the funds to buy more goods, while Americans had to buy less goods. Also, the indebtedness of the American people would be increased, which they would have to repay by further restricting their consumption in favor of the recipients of the foreign aid. Of course, to some extent, instead of buying less, the American people would also have to sell more, in order to replenish their cash holdings. In other words, the foreign aid measure and the initial loss of currency it entailed would automatically be financed by a combination of a decrease in imports and increase in exports. It would not be financed by any significant loss of currency.

Considerations such as these fully confirm the observation of Adam Smith, quoted earlier in this section, that "the attention of government never was so unnecessarily employed, as when directed to watch over the preservation or increase of the quantity of money in any country."

A final analogy will help to bring into focus what is wrong with the whole balance of payments approach.

Thus, if we had nothing better to do with our time, we might construct a "balance of food account." This would show all sources of food entering a family's refrigerator and all uses of the food taken from that refrigerator. The food entering the refrigerator, of course, would be the counterpart of receipts; the food taken from the refrigerator, of outlays. The change in the quantity of food in the refrigerator, of course, is always equal to the difference between the receipts of food entering the refrigerator and the withdrawals (outlays) of food leaving the refrigerator.

We might then appoint a government official to stand guard over the refrigerator and spend his time worrying about the food balance. We can imagine him watching the food in the refrigerator diminishing, and blaming it on excessive outlays for snacks or parties, or perhaps insufficient receipts from the nearby supermarket. We can imagine him rejoicing at the increase in the amount of food in the refrigerator when a bag of groceries is unpacked and put away. We can imagine him projecting plans and issuing regulations concerning what alleged excesses on the food-outlays side must be controlled and what alleged deficiencies on the food-receipts side must be overcome, in order to secure a stable or growing stock of food.

And, finally, we might imagine trying to explain to this good civil servant that the amount of food in the family's refrigerator is not in fact the result of the hap-penstance difference between receipts and outlays of food, but of deliberate decisions by the family to build up or run down its stock of food, which decisions determine the food receipts and outlays in such a way as to achieve the desired change in the stock of food. Thus, for example, if we observe the stock of food increasing, the explanation is not that food receipts exceed food outlays, but that the family has decided to give a party, say, and has gone out and done the necessary extra shopping. Similarly, if we observe the stock of food decreasing, the explanation is not that the amount of food being withdrawn from the refrigerator exceeds the amount being put into it, but that the family has decided to go away for a vacation and thus to use up the food it has without replacing it.

In sum, what needs to be explained is that the change in the stock of money in people's pockets, like the change in the stock of food in their refrigerators, is fully within their control and that their decisions about changes in the stock determine the relationship between the receipts and outlays, not that the relationship between the receipts and outlays determines the change in the stock.

Unilateral Free Trade and the Balance of Trade

The analysis of the balance of trade/payments that has been given above sheds light on the effects of adopting a policy of unilateral free trade or unilateral tariff reduction.

Under an international gold standard, the adoption of such a policy would temporarily be accompanied by an "unfavorable" balance of trade/payments in the country concerned. This is because the immediate effect of the country's elimination or reduction of trade barriers would be that foreign goods suddenly became cheaper, while domestically produced goods remained at their initial prices. Thus, the demand for imports would increase and there would be no immediate change in the quantity demanded of exports. Accordingly, under an international gold standard there would be an outflow of gold.

However, this very loss of gold and thus the reduction in the quantity of money in the country would operate to reduce wages and prices in the country, and to increase them in the countries to which the gold was sent. These changes, in turn, would make the country's producers more competitive both in the domestic market of their country and in the international export market. The effect would be that some part of the domestic market initially lost to imports would be regained and at the same time an expansion of exports would take place.

Thus the country would end up both importing more and exporting more. Its citizens would be as fully employed as they were before. The only difference would be that more of them would be employed in export industries and fewer of them in industries producing for the domestic market. The net gain of the citizens would be that the additional imports they obtained represented more and better goods than they could produce with the same labor devoted to producing for the domestic market. By the same token, the citizens of foreign countries would gain more from the additional exports of the country in question than they lost by devoting part of their labor to producing the additional imports for that country. In other words, both the citizens of the country in question and the citizens of the countries it dealt with would enjoy greater benefits from the operation of the law of comparative advantage.[41]

An essential requirement of being able to adapt to the consequences of a temporary outflow of money is the absence of labor legislation. This is because it is vital that the wage and price level of the country be free to fall to the extent necessary for the country to become sufficiently competitive to have full employment. Precisely this is what such legislation prevents.

The present discussion provides the opportunity to deal with the question of what would happen if one country pursued a policy of free trade, while all other countries absolutely prohibited the importation of its goods.

In such a case, under an international gold standard, the country would experience an outflow of gold until its wages and prices fell so low, and those in other countries rose so high, that its citizens simply wished to purchase nothing whatever from abroad.

The existence of such a case is virtually impossible, however. As wages and prices in the country concerned fall, its goods become an ever more powerful attraction to foreign buyers. Thus, it is almost unthinkable that it would not at some point increase its exports. To whatever extent it is able to do so, then its citizens—and the citizens of foreign countries—gain the benefit of greater operation of the law of comparative advantage.

It should be obvious that if unilateral free trade is viable under the conditions of an international gold standard, and, indeed, even under conditions in which, in addition, other countries follow policies of the most extreme protectionism, then it should certainly pose no great difficulties under the conditions of a fiat money, in which there cannot even be any significant outflow of money.

5. Invariable Money

Under the head of money, it is essential to deal with the concept of *invariable money*, whose meaning and vital role in economic analysis I will at once proceed to explain.

When prices change, people usually take for granted that the change is the result of something taking place on the side of goods. When prices rise, they say that goods are becoming more expensive; when prices fall, they say that goods are becoming cheaper.

This presumption was overthrown when economists realized that money itself is subject to the same forces of supply and demand as are goods. This realization meant that changes in prices can reflect changes taking place on the side of money as well as changes taking place on the side of goods. Indeed, precisely this is the case whenever there is inflation or deflation. During an inflation, it is not actually goods which are becoming more expensive, but *money* which is becoming cheaper. During a deflation, it is not actually goods which are becoming cheaper, but money which is becoming dearer. The rise in prices during an inflation is the result of expressing them in a medium that is itself of declining value; the fall in prices during a deflation is the result of expressing them in a medium that is itself of rising value. This point has already been made clear in the example of expressing the lower price of video tape recorders in terms of pocket calculators, whose price has fallen even more, which produces the result of the price of video tape recorders appearing to rise rather than fall.[42]

That example, and its underlying theoretical insight, should not be thought of as esoteric in any way. They help to shed a great deal of light on, among other things, the respective roles of a system of fiat paper money and the businessman's profit motive in the causation of the rising prices we see almost all around us. It is a fact that prices are rising. But it is no less a fact that the profit motive of the businessman tends constantly to reduce prices. The two facts are reconciled by the third fact that we currently express prices in terms of a monetary unit whose own value falls more rapidly than businessmen are able to cut costs and reduce prices. Our present monetary unit is, of course, a mere piece of paper, whose cost of production is virtually zero to begin with, whose quantity can be expanded without limit, and which is in fact rapidly expanded. Thus, prices rise even though, if expressed in a monetary unit whose own value did not decline, they would show a pronounced fall.[43]

The variability of the value of money coming from the side of money does not apply only to a fiat paper money, however. It applies even to a pure gold or silver standard—that is, to a 100-percent-reserve gold or silver standard. The supply of gold and silver tends to increase, which, other things being equal, operates to reduce their value, i.e., to raise the prices of all other goods. Of course, the increase in the supply of precious metals tends to take place in conjunction with an increase in the supply of goods and services in general and thus tends not to result in an actual rise in prices. Moreover, because the increase in the supply of precious metals is relatively slow and steady and the supply virtually incapable of any significant sudden decrease, the demand for the precious metals would tend to be highly stable under a 100-percent-reserve, precious-metal standard. But even so, the increase in the supply of precious metals would still operate to make the fall in commodity prices less than it would otherwise be, i.e., to raise commodity prices in comparison with what they would have been in the absence of any change in the supply of the precious metals.

When economists realized that even a gold money is regularly subject to forces that tend to change its value from the side of money, they launched a search for a money of *invariable value*—that is, for a money under which changes in prices would reflect exclusively changes operating on the side of goods, not money. These efforts, and the recognition of their importance, were carried furthest by Ricardo, who declared:

> If then, I may suppose myself to be possessed of a standard so nearly approaching to an invariable one, the advantage is that I shall be enabled to speak of the variations of other things without embarrassing myself on every occasion with the consideration of the possible alteration in the value of the medium in which price and value are estimated.

> To facilitate, then, the object of this inquiry, although I fully allow that money made of gold is subject to most of the variations of other things, I shall suppose it to be invariable, and therefore all alterations in price to be occasioned by some alteration in the value of the commodity of which I may be speaking.[44]

Ricardo believed that in order for gold to be an invariable standard of value, the principle requirement that it would have to fulfill is always to require the same quantity of labor in its production. Even then, he held, it would not be perfect as an invariable standard of value, because changes in the rate of profit and in the period of time elapsing between the performance of labor in the production of gold and the exchange of that gold in the market could alter its value from its own side.[45]

In my judgment, Ricardo's discussions of an invariable standard of value and his applications of the concept, while essentially brilliant, are badly flawed and needlessly obscured by his constant intermingling of the labor theory of value. Thus, in place of Ricardo's criteria for an invariable monetary standard, I offer my own, whose nature has been indicated in previous pages of this book. Namely, what would be required for gold to be an invariable standard of value would be *a fixed, constant aggregate expenditure of gold for products*—e.g., a fixed aggregate expenditure for products of one billion ounces of gold per year.[46] This would be consistent with a fixed quantity of gold money and a fixed velocity of circulation

of that money in relation to products. The latter requirement, of course, would be consistent with an essentially fixed demand for gold for holding.

Under these conditions, price changes on the aggregate level—that is, changes in the weighted average or general level of prices—would reflect changes taking place on the side of the production and supply of products exclusively. Indeed, the implication of a fixed aggregate expenditure is that the aggregate demand curve for products would be such that all changes in the aggregate supply of products produced and sold would result in *inversely proportionate* changes in the weighted average of product prices. That is, if production and supply doubled, prices would halve. If they tripled, prices would be cut to one-third, and so on. This follows because an unchanged aggregate expenditure means that it is represented by the number "one." Whatever the increase in production and supply, it is always divided into one. Hence, the price level is always the reciprocal of production and supply. In the technical language of economists, the aggregate demand curve would have unit elasticity, which is to say that quantities of products demanded would change in inverse proportion to prices.

Changes in demand, of course, would, still take place in the economic system, but only at the level of individual industries and companies. At the aggregate level, they would always be mutually offsetting. If expenditure for product X increased, then expenditure for product Y, or for a group of products denoted as Y, would have to decrease equivalently. Thus changes in demand would be a factor determining relative prices only, not the general level of prices. All changes in the prices of individual goods would reflect changes specific to those goods, including the evaluation of those goods, not changes operating on the side of money.[47]

Invariable Money and the Velocity of Circulation

The concept of an invariable money should not be confused with the assumption of an invariable velocity of circulation of money other than that of an invariable velocity of circulation confined to the demand for products only. It is consistent with substantial variations in overall total expenditures relative to the same total quantity of money and thus with substantial variations in broader measures of velocity, such as transactions velocity and "total revenue velocity," which last would relate the combined sum of expenditures either for products or for labor to the quantity of money.[48] This is because changes in the demand for securities and in lending and borrowing operations need have no effect on changes in the aggregate demand for products inasmuch as the sellers of securities and the recipients of loans can simply take the place of the buyers of securities and the grantors of loans in making purchases of products.[49] In the same way, a rise in the demand for labor that is made possible by a fall in the consumption expenditure of employers enables wage earners to make a demand for products in place of their employers and thus also does not reduce the demand for products. The same is true even of taxation insofar as it transfers the ability to buy products from the taxpayers to the government or to other individuals to whom the government gives the tax proceeds.

Thus the aggregate demand for products can remain the same on the foundation of a fixed quantity of money in the economic system, while other forms of expenditure increase or decrease.

The Contribution of the Concept of Invariable Money to Economic Theory

The concept of an invariable money is an invaluable tool of economic analysis. (It should go without saying that as an analytical tool, it should not be confused with any kind of objective to be established by government intervention in the economic system. It is a method to be used in thinking about the economic system, not a political goal to be imposed upon it.) A few paragraphs ago, I recalled its value in reconciling the benevolent nature of the profit motive with the existence of rising prices. It should also be recalled how an analysis based on the assumption of an invariable money served to reconcile the benevolent nature of economic competition with reductions in money income on the part of less capable competitors. For it showed how competition operates to reduce prices to the same extent as it operates to reduce the incomes of the less capable competitors and, indeed, to a greater extent.[50]

Applying the concept of an invariable money permits the separate analysis of the effects of changes operating on the side of the production and supply of goods and services, and changes operating on the side of money and the monetary demand for goods and services. Its application thus makes possible the adoption of a procedure analogous to that of mechanics, which takes as its analytical starting point the existence of a vacuum and then proceeds to develop its basic laws in a context in which there is no friction and in which, therefore, it can conceptually isolate the effects of the forces operating on objects. Indeed, the assumption of an invariable money is and must be made at least implicitly by everyone who thinks about economic phenomena insofar as his theorizing is based on the assumption of all other things being equal, which, of course, is the necessary starting point of all economic analysis. Among the most important of the other things that must be held equal in economic analysis is the quantity of money and the aggregate spending for the goods and services of business that it supports. In-

stead of leaving the assumption to mere implication, however, it should be made explicitly and adhered to unless and until it is necessary to relax it.

Accordingly, my typical procedure in the chapters that follow will be to begin with the assumption that the quantity of money and aggregate volume of spending in the economic system for the goods and services of business are fixed. With the aid of this analytical context, we will be in a position to trace out in isolation the effects of all phenomena acting on the production and supply of goods—for example, such phenomena as an increase in the productivity of labor resulting from the adoption of improved machinery or any other cause, or an increase in the supply of labor, whether an increase in the number of workers employed or an increase in the number of hours or days worked by the average employed worker. We will be able to examine the effects of all such changes on prices, wage rates, average money incomes, and the average standard of living. Then, in a separate analytical procedure, we will trace out the effects of an increase in the quantity of money and volume of spending in the economic system. Finally, in a manner similar to the addition of separate vectors in mechanics, we will add the results of the two separate analytical procedures in order to arrive at a complete description of what occurs in the world around us.

I will name now some of the leading findings that this method will reach. It will validate the proposition known as Say's Law of Markets, that aggregate real demand—that is, what any given aggregate monetary demand can actually buy—is determined by aggregate supply. It will confirm the corollary proposition of the classical economists that a general or absolute overproduction is impossible—that the only kind of overproduction that can exist is a partial, relative overproduction in some portions of the economic system, which is always counterbalanced by a precisely equivalent partial, relative underproduction elsewhere in the economic system. In close connection with these points, our method will show that the falling prices caused by increased production do not constitute deflation, in that they are not accompanied by the other leading symptoms of deflation, namely, a greater difficulty of repaying debts and a decline in the general profitability of business. It will show that deflation properly so called is always a phenomenon operating on the side of money, in the form of a reduced supply and/or increased demand for money and thus in a reduction in aggregate expenditure.

Economic analysis based on the context of an invariable money will show not only that unemployment can be eliminated by means of a fall in wage rates and prices but, at the same time, that the restoration of full employment achieved in this way tends to be accompanied by a rise in the *real* wages of the average worker—that is, by a rise in the goods and services he is actually able to buy with his money wages. Here, such analysis shows, is a major case in which money wages fall and nevertheless real wages rise—in which, indeed, the fall in money wages is the precondition of the rise in real wages. Economic analysis based on the context of an invariable money will show that real wages are determined primarily and overwhelmingly by the productivity of labor, while the average level of money wages is determined primarily by the quantity of money.

This method of economic analysis will lead to the further conclusion that the rate of increase in the quantity of money and volume of spending in the economic system adds a roughly equivalent increase to the average nominal rate of profit and interest, while the rate of increase in the volume of production and supply of goods adds a roughly equivalent increase to the average real rate of profit—that, for example, a 2 percent annual increase in the quantity of money and volume of spending in the economic system add approximately 2 percent to the nominal rate of profit, while a 2 percent annual increase in the volume of production and supply add approximately 2 percent to the real rate of profit. Analysis on the basis of an invariable money will also make it possible to grasp the determinants of the nominal rate of profit *other* than the rate of increase in the quantity of money.

In addition, economic analysis based on the context of an invariable money will make it possible for the first time to grasp the actual relationships between saving, on the one side, and capital accumulation, real wages, and the rate of profit, on the other, and to discern causes of capital accumulation which otherwise must remain concealed—notably, technological progress and anything else which operates to increase production. It will show, among other things, that the value of technological progress in connection with capital accumulation is as a *source* of capital accumulation, not as a use of capital goods accumulated by saving. It will show that nominal net saving, i.e., saving out of money income, is possible as a permanent phenomenon only on the basis of an increasing quantity of money and would disappear if the increase in the quantity of money were to come to an end. It will show that the real significance of saving is to be found at a level beyond that of money income, namely, in the proportion of gross revenue saved and productively expended versus the proportion consumed, and in the ratio of accumulated nominal capital to consumption. It will show that capital accumulation does not in any way necessitate or imply a falling rate of profit, and that even nominal net saving also does not imply a falling rate of profit in the context in which it continues indefinitely,

namely, that of an expanding quantity of money.

A major theme which develops on the basis of the analytical framework of an invariable money is that of the distinction between monetary value and real wealth, or, as Ricardo put it, the distinction between "value and riches."[51] It will become apparent how mistaken it is to assume that wealth and the monetary value of wealth necessarily move together. For again and again, it will become clear how production and real wealth can increase at the same time that alleged monetary measures of that production and wealth, such as national income or gross domestic product (gross national product), show no increase or actually decrease, and, by the same token, how alleged monetary measures of production and wealth can increase while the production and wealth involved actually tend to decrease.

Thus, we have already seen how competition among workers can reduce the money incomes of broad categories of workers and yet still be the basis of a rise in the general standard of living, including the standard of living of the workers whose money incomes are reduced. Going even further, we will see how capital accumulation and improvements in machinery are capable of being accompanied by reductions in the money income of all wage earners taken together, and yet at the same time still be the basis of a rise in the standard of living of the average wage earner.[52] Indeed, we will see that the whole mentality, which is so typical of the labor unions, that the way to raise the standard of living is to raise money wages is completely mistaken when applied to the economic system as a whole. It will become clear that the rise in the general standard of living always takes place from the side of forces tending merely to reduce prices, and not to increase money incomes, indeed, tending sometimes to reduce money incomes. We will see also that forces operating to increase average money incomes can, at the same time, be the source of a fall in real incomes, and that this is true not only of the undue increase in the quantity of money, viz., inflation, but also of taxes paid for with funds that otherwise would have been expended to buy capital goods, and of government budget deficits similarly paid for. Such taxes and deficits, we will see, operate to raise pretax nominal profits and, at the same time, to undermine capital formation and reduce the ability to produce and thus the general standard of living.[53]

Perhaps among the greatest instances of the distinction between value and riches is the one we have seen in the preceding chapter. I refer, of course, to the fact that in Adam Smith's "early and rude state of society," all income would be profit and the rate of profit would be infinite, while at the same time the level of production and general standard of living would be barbarously low.

Under the assumption of an invariable money, advance from such a state of affairs would be accompanied not only by a fall in the nominal rate of profit, but also by a fall in the size of nominal national income (national income being taken as the sum of profits plus wages). For as productive expenditure grew, not only would wages rise at the expense of a fall in profits, but so too would the expenditure for capital goods and thus costs on account of the expenditure for capital goods. In other words, the fall in profits would exceed the rise in wages, as what had been profits became both wages and a demand for capital goods. Yet real wealth and prosperity would be the greater and all the more rapidly progressing, the further this process was carried.

While the distinction between value and riches—between the effect of things on money income and their effect on the actual standard of living—is at its sharpest in the context of an invariable money, it also appears again and again in the world around us. The explicit assumption of an invariable money is essential to understanding the nature of economic phenomena by thinking through the full consequences of their operation and not stopping at the point merely of recognizing their positive or negative effect on money income. When this is done, the benevolent nature of the pursuit of material self-interest under economic freedom, and the destructive nature of government violations of economic freedom, stand forth in unparalleled clarity and completeness.

Notes

1. The time of writing is the fall of 1994. The figure for the money supply comes from *The New York Times*, October 28, 1994, p. C13, while the estimate for the GDP is based on the data reported for the second quarter of 1994 in *The Federal Reserve Bulletin*, October 1994, p. A51.

2. See ibid., p. A14. This measure of the money supply is reported as M_1. Other, larger measures add to M_1 such totals as time and savings deposits, certificates of deposit, Treasury Bills, and so forth. These further items are easily convertible into money and represent highly liquid assets. But they are not directly spendable as such. One cannot, for example, walk into a store and spend directly out of one's savings-account passbook, as one can spend out of one's checkbook. Such assets can be thought of as near moneys, but they are not in fact money themselves. Concerning a recent important development pertaining to this subject, see below, p. 965 n. 100.

3. See ibid., p. A51. Both government expenditures—virtually in their totality—and private expenditures for owner-occupied housing must be categorized as consumption because, as previously explained, they are not made for the purpose of bringing in subsequent sales revenues. Hence, they lack the ability to replace the funds expended in carrying on the activity. Those funds are used up and gone—consumed. If they are to be replaced, it must be from an outside source of revenue: taxes or money creation in the case of the government, a job or business in the case of private individuals. See above, pp. 442–456.

4. The reasons for this equivalency with national income are explained below, on pp. 700–702 and on p. 712.

5. The concept of Gross National Revenue is elaborated below, on p. 712.

6. See below, pp. 519–526, for a whole series of further connections between more money and more demand.

7. These definitions, of course, accord with the usage of the British classical economists, which was explained in Chapter 5. The demand/supply formula was also present implicitly in Chapter 6, in my exposition of the theory of price formation for goods and services in limited supply, and more or less explicitly in Chapter 7, in my discussion of price controls and inflation.

See above, pp. 152, 202, and 220.

8. See above, p. 220.

9. See above, pp. 141–142.

10. In most of its essential features, this discussion of the origins and evolution of money follows the writings of Menger. Cf. Carl Menger, *Principles of Economics,* trans. and ed. by James Dingwall and Bert F. Hoselitz (Glencoe, Ill.: The Free Press, 1950), pp. 257–271, 280–285.

11. See above, p. 142.

12. Menger did not emphasize this advantage of the precious metals. As a result, his account of why the precious metals in particular became money is highly deficient. See Menger, *Principles,* pp. 265–268.

13. Gold and silver rarely circulated at the same time, because of government interference in the form of bimetallism, that is, the imposition of a price control on one or the other of the two moneys. Prior to 1834, the government compelled merchants to accept gold coin as the equivalent of only 15 ounces of silver to one ounce of gold, while in the bullion market gold was worth about 15.5 ounces of silver. The result was that gold did not circulate in this period. From 1834 on, the government required that silver coin be accepted at the rate one ounce of silver equals one-sixteenth of an ounce of gold, while in the bullion markets it was more valuable. The result was that silver coins disappeared from circulation.

14. Cf. Ludwig von Mises, *The Theory of Money and Credit*, new ed. (1953; reprint ed., Irvington-on-Hudson, N. Y.: Foundation for Economic Education, 1971), p. 133; idem, *Human Action*, 3d ed. rev. (Chicago: Henry Regnery Co., 1966), pp. 432–434.

15. *Federal Reserve Bulletin*, October 1994), p. A13.

16. Charles Holt Carroll, a nineteenth-century monetary theorist, aptly described the phenomenon as "the organization of debt into currency." See his *Organization of Debt Into Currency, and Other Papers*, ed. with an Introduction by Edward C. Simmons (1964; reprint, New York: Arno Press and The New York Times, 1972).

17. Until the mid-1970s, only commercial banks could offer checking accounts. Now more than half of total checking

accounts are held at other types of financial institutions, such as savings banks and savings and loan associations.

18. See Murray Rothbard, *What Has Government Done to Our Money?* (Novato, Calif.: Libertarian Publishers, 1979), pp. 22–24. In support of this view, see also below, pp. 957–958.

19. Cf. von Mises, *Human Action,* p. 446.

20. The best explanations of the trade cycle are to be found in von Mises, *Human Action,* pp. 398–586, 780–803, and Charles Holt Carroll, *The Organization of Debt Into Currency.*

21. *Federal Reserve Bulletin*, October 1994, p. A10.

22. On this subject, see *New York Times,* March 26, 1992, pp. C1–C2.

23. For the sake of brevity, in what follows I generally refer to gold and gold money, but, of course, my discussion applies equally to silver and silver money.

24. The destructive effects of fiduciary media become apparent in the light of this principle. See the discussion of the effects of credit expansion on the demand for money, below, p. 256. See also below, pp. 938–940.

25. Compared with rates of increase in the supply of paper money, even the gold added by the Spanish conquest of the new world and later by the California gold fields was relatively modest. See below, p. 920.

26. See below, pp. 942–950.

27. Cf. von Mises, *Theory of Money and Credit,* pp. 227–229; *Human Action,* pp. 426–428.

28. For reasons that I will explain in the next chapter, in connection with the discussion of Say's Law, falling prices caused by increases in production, rather than by decreases in the quantity of money and volume of spending, do not operate to increase the demand for money or, therefore, to reduce the velocity of circulation of money. Only those price reductions emanating from decreases in the quantity of money and/or volume of spending cause a rise in the demand for money. See below, pp. 574–576.

29. Chapter 19 explains why credit expansion is followed by periods of credit contraction and thus of deflation and depression. See below, pp. 938–941. See also von Mises, *Human Action,* pp. 538–586.

30. See above, pp. 186–187.

31. See below, pp. 762–774.

32. This calculation is based on data supplied in *Banking and Monetary Statistics 1914–1941,* p. 34.

33. Cf. *Federal Reserve Bulletin*, December 1982, p. A14; December 1983, p. A13. See below, p. 965 n. 100, concerning the more recent role of money-market mutual funds.

34. The calculation of the most recent rate of increase in the money supply is based on year-end data appearing in *Federal Reserve Bulletin*, July 1994, p. A14, and weekly money supply figures as reported in *New York Times*, October 17, 1994.

35. See below, pp. 959–962.

36. See below, pp. 942–950, especially pp. 946–949.

37. Adam Smith, *The Wealth of Nations* (London, 1776), bk. 4, chap. 1; reprint of Cannan ed., (Chicago: University of Chicago Press, 2 vols. in 1, 1976), 1:458.

38. For the most part, the foreigners' bank deposits are saving or time deposits, or take the form of the purchase of certificates of deposit.

39. See, for example, below, pp. 542–594 passim.

40. For further discussion of the destructive effects of labor unions, see below, pp. 655–659.

41. For a discussion of the law of comparative advantage and its relationship to international competition and to competition in general under capitalism, see above, pp. 350–356.

42. See above, pp. 179–180.

43. Cf. above, ibid.

44. David Ricardo, *Principles of Political Economy and Taxation,* 3d ed. (London, 1821), chap. 1; reprinted as vol. 1 of *The Works and Correspondence of David Ricardo,* ed. Piero Sraffa (Cambridge: Cambridge University Press, 1962), p. 46. Subsequent page references to the Sraffa edition will appear in brackets.

45. Ibid. [pp. 43–46].

46. In most contexts, but not all, the fixed aggregate demand for products can be taken as pertaining simply to newly produced products. For a leading exception, however, see below, pp. 578–579. Those pages contain an analysis in which the demand for products must be extended to include the demand for previously produced products.

47. The assumption of an invariable money in my sense, that is, of a fixed aggregate expenditure for products, appears implicitly throughout much of Henry Hazlitt's *Economics in One Lesson* and Bastiat's "What Is Seen and What Is Not Seen," and is a major source of the great analytical strength of those works. See Henry Hazlitt, *Economics in One Lesson,* new ed. (New Rochelle, N. Y.: Arlington House, 1979) and Frederic Bastiat, *Selected Essays on Political Economy,* trans. Seymour Cain (New York: D. Van Nostrand, 1964), pp. 1–50.

48. For discussion relevant to the concept of total revenue velocity, see below, pp. 706–707.

49. Indeed, if anything, such transactions are part of a process that actually serves to increase the demand for products. See above, the discussion of the effect of saving on the velocity of money, on p. 518.

50. See above, pp. 367–371.

51. Cf. Ricardo, *Principles of Political Economy and Taxation,* especially chap. 20.

52. Ironically, Ricardo himself was led astray from his principle when he came to cases entailing a change in the aggregate demand for labor. Thus, he came to the mistaken conclusion that the adoption of machinery is against the interests of wage earners if it reduces the aggregate demand for labor and that war is in the interests of wage earners insofar as taxation diverts funds from expenditure for luxury goods to an additional demand for labor. Cf. ibid., chap. 31. See the analysis of Ricardo's errors on these points, below, on pp. 639–641 and 647–650.

53. See below, pp. 826–830. This point applies to the so-called balanced budget multiplier doctrine of the Keynesians, concerning which, see below, pp. 712–715.

CHAPTER 13

PRODUCTIONISM, SAY'S LAW, AND UNEMPLOYMENT

PART A

PRODUCTIONISM

The identification that the fundamental problem of economic life is how steadily to increase the ability to produce in the face of a limitless need and desire for wealth, is one of the great achievements of the British classical economists.[1] This identification, together with its implications for the understanding of the effects of such phenomena as the use of machinery, advertising, a rise in the birthrate, foreign trade, imperialism, war, and government spending, I term *productionism*.[2]

Productionism is intimately bound up with a series of further propositions which the classical economists advanced, or which are clearly implied in their teachings. We have already examined a number of these propositions, among them: the central importance of the division of labor in raising the productivity of labor; the law of comparative advantage, which, together with the limitless need for wealth, guarantees a place for everyone in the division of labor, provided only that the freedom of competition exists; and the quantity theory of money. We have seen the clear implication of the quantity theory of money that depressions are caused by government sponsorship of a fractional-reserve banking system, which increases the quantity of money unduly, thereby artificially reducing the demand for money and raising its velocity of circulation, thus setting the stage for a subsequent financial contraction, deflation of the money supply, and depression. In Part B of this chapter, we shall see how production and supply, and only production and supply, create purchasing power and thus demand in its real sense—i.e., in the sense of the goods and services a monetary demand can actually buy. This is the classical economists' proposition that has come to be known as Say's Law of Markets.[3] In close connection with Say's Law, we shall come to understand the corollary proposition that the existence of a general overproduction—i.e., of an excess of aggregate supply over aggregate demand—is an impossibility. In Part C of this chapter, we shall also see how mass unemployment is the result of government intervention, not the workings of a capitalist economy itself.

While the present chapter shows how the productive process generates an aggregate real demand that is equal to aggregate supply and grows precisely as aggregate supply grows, subsequent chapters will show how the productive process also generates an aggregate monetary demand that in the absence of government interference is sufficient to buy the aggregate supply at a profit—that is, how the productive process itself inherently operates to make production financially profitable to the businessman of average skill and ability. Along the way, we shall see how, as the classical economists put it, "what is saved is spent," indeed, is the source of most spending in the economic system, and more, underlies both a growing aggregate real demand for goods and services and a growing aggregate monetary demand for them. All of these doctrines of classical economics are closely related to productionism in the sense both of supporting it and being supported by it.

The one proposition connected with productionism which will be advanced and which may appear as a significant departure from the central ideas of the classical economists, but which actually is entirely consistent with them at the most fundamental level, is that real wages and thus the average worker's standard of living are determined by the productivity of labor. This proposition, indeed, is actually nothing more than the idea behind Say's Law applied to wages: real wages are determined by production, just as the real demand for goods is determined by production. Thus throughout, productionism and its related propositions are integrally connected to classical economics.

Productionism Versus the Anti-Economics of Consumptionism

In the twentieth century, there has been a growing influence of irrationalist philosophy, which denies the reliability and efficacy of human reason and which disregards the profound influence that the possession of reason exerts on every aspect of human life. According to such philosophy, there is little to distinguish man from the lower animals. Indeed, as we have seen, man is depicted as "the trousered ape"; porpoises, it is asserted, may possess intelligence comparable to man's; snail darters, we are told, have equal rights with man.[4] Thus, at bottom, man, it is held, is just another animal. On such a view of man, it follows that man's needs and desires must be as limited as those of an animal and thus fundamentally incapable of extending beyond the range of minimum necessities. The fact that man's desires obviously do extend beyond the range of an animal's is held to be the result of "social and cultural conditioning" and the work of advertisers; at the same time, the desires are denounced as "unnatural," "artificial," and "created." Thus, the basic economic premise is advanced that the need and desire to consume are essentially fixed and given, and that the ability to produce threatens constantly to outrun them.

This premise, together with its leading implications, I call *consumptionism*. It is the doctrine that the fundamental problem of economic life is how to increase the need and desire to consume in the face of an ability to produce that exceeds them. Consumptionism proceeds as though the problem of economic life were not the production of wealth, but the production of *consumption*.

The consumptionist premise must be characterized as nothing less than the premise of *anti-economics*. This is because, as we shall see, point by point, it leads to a total inversion of the conclusions of sound, rational economic science.

While directly implied by irrationalist philosophy, the consumptionist premise also results from the error of considering the effects of things only on those most directly concerned, and neglecting the effects on the rest of the economic system.[5] Very importantly, among the leading practitioners of this error are businessmen who are in the habit of being concerned exclusively with the effects of things on their own industry.

In the context of an individual industry, the emergence of a need or desire for the product of the industry that is strong enough to outrank the need or desire for the products of other industries will channel spending to this industry from other industries. For example, if people developed a greater desire for automobiles, say, to the point that they were willing to cut back on their expenditures for housing or clothing, say, the demand for automobiles would increase. Conversely, if they developed a greater desire for housing or clothing, to the point that they were willing to cut back on their expenditure for automobiles, the demand for housing or clothing would increase. To unthinking businessmen in the industry experiencing the increase in demand—businessmen who do not stop to consider the accompanying offsetting decrease in the demand for the products of other industries—it appears simply that an increase in the need or desire for their product has increased the demand for their product. Because they are unaware of the offsetting effects on the demand for the products of other industries, such businessmen then come to the conclusion that what is required to increase the aggregate, economy-wide demand for products is an increase in the overall, economy-wide need for products, and that what is responsible for the slack demand for products in a depression is a lack of need for products. Thus, such businessmen are led to the same conclusion that is arrived at on the foundation of irrationalist philosophy, namely, that the ability to produce exceeds the need and desire to consume and that the problem of economic life is not the production of wealth but of the consumption of wealth.

Of course, what is overlooked by all such observers, whether businessmen or others, is that every increase in the demand for the product of a particular industry that is based on the need or desire for its product intensifying and thus pushing ahead of the needs and desires for the products of other industries and coming to the forefront, must be accompanied by an equivalent decrease in the demand for the products of other industries.

When this is borne in mind, it becomes clear that the need and desire for goods count in demand only insofar as they operate to determine *to which of various possible competing alternatives demand is directed*. Yet to those myopically concerned only with a particular industry, it mistakenly appears that because any given industry, at one time or another, could experience an increase in demand by virtue of the need or desire for its product gaining in priority relative to the need and desire for the products of other industries, that *all industries might gain in this way at the same time*. This is a case of adding up as additional demands what are in fact a series of mutually exclusive alternatives, each of whose individual existence is predicated on an equivalent decline in demand in the rest of the economic system. This is a glaring example of what logicians call "the fallacy of composition," that is, invalidly generalizing from what occurs in part of a system to the system as a whole.

When the actual nature of the relationship of the need and desire for goods to demand is kept in mind, it also becomes clear that any increase in the overall volume of mere need and desire—unaccompanied by an increase in the production and supply of goods—is irrelevant to the economy-wide, aggregate demand for goods. The mere need and desire for goods are always vastly in excess of demand in the economy as a whole, as was shown at length in Chapter 2. For example, I have a desire for luxurious houses or apartments in Paris, Rome, and Palm Beach, but I can barely make a *demand* for the one relatively modest home that I do occupy. If demand in fact depended merely on the need and desire for goods, and greater demand followed from the existence of a greater need and desire for goods, then the proportion of the world's demand for goods that emanates from India and China would far exceed the proportion that emanates from the United States and Japan. Nevertheless, despite the fact that the populations of India and China far exceed those of the United States and Japan, and the unmet needs and desires of the average Indian and Chinese exceed those of the average American or Japanese by the magnitude of the formers' lower standard of living, the demand for goods in the United States and Japan enormously exceeds the demand for goods in India and China. The explanation of this difference in demand is the difference in the ability to produce and supply goods, which, as we shall see in Part B of this chapter, is the cause of corresponding differences in *purchasing power*, which must be joined to need and desire in order to create demand. The United States and Japan are greater demanders of goods because they are greater producers, therefore, possess greater purchasing power, and can satisfy their needs and desires to a correspondingly greater extent.[6]

Thus consumptionism flourishes both because of the growing prevalence of an irrationalist view of man and his needs and desires and because of the widely practiced fallacy of looking at the effects of things only on those who are most directly concerned.

In this environment, economists, largely under the influence of Lord Keynes, and, still more, the hordes of intellectuals who have no familiarity with economics, have returned to the view of economic life that was advanced by the predecessors of the classical economists, the mercantilists. Instead of taking the need and desire to consume for granted and focusing on the ways and means by which production might be increased, the problem of economic life is now often believed to be how to expand the need and desire to consume so that consumption may be made adequate to production. Much of what passes for economic thinking in the twentieth century takes production for granted and focuses on the ways and means by which consumption can be increased. It proceeds, as I have said, as though the problem of economic life were not the production of wealth, but the production of consumption. It was in this spirit that Keynes declared: "Pyramid-building, earthquakes, even wars may serve to increase wealth . . . ."[7]

Because of the prevailing influence of consumptionism and the major economic errors inspired by it, my procedure here will be to present those errors, one after another, accompanied by the answers of sound economics, based on the philosophy of productionism.

1. Depressions and Alleged "Overproduction"

According to the "overproduction" doctrine, it is possible for the aggregate supply of goods produced in the economic system to exceed the aggregate demand for them, that is, to exceed the need and desire for goods—which is the sense in which the concept "demand" is understood by the doctrine's supporters. The demand for goods, it is claimed, may simply not be adequate to the rising level of production made possible by economic progress. According to the overproduction doctrine, the need or the desire for the growing volume of goods is simply lacking. People allegedly need and desire only so much, and not an ever increasing amount. Thus when production increases, producers are allegedly put in the position of producing more than the buyers are willing to buy, with the consequence that a depression results.

(Sometimes the supporters of the overproduction doctrine offer a variant of the doctrine. They claim that while the need and desire to buy the growing volume of goods may be present, the *ability* to buy them is lacking because people do not possess a correspondingly larger quantity of money. Here, instead of confusing demand with need, they confuse the ability to buy goods with the ability to spend money. As we shall see, the ability to buy goods—purchasing power—does not depend on the quantity of money and the ability to spend money, but on the volume of production and supply.[8])

The overproduction doctrine can be understood graphically, in terms of Figure 13–1, which is titled "The

Consumptionist View of the Economic World." There, in the upper portion of the figure, the consumptionists' notion of a fixed aggregate demand is depicted by the vertical line *DD*, which claims that buyers are unwilling or unable to purchase a quantity of output greater than corresponds to point *A* on the horizontal axis. No matter how low prices go, the buyers allegedly will not buy more than an amount equal to *A*. Yet at the point of full employment, the economic system is capable of producing the larger quantity of output indicated by point *B* on the horizontal axis. The vertical line *SS*, drawn directly up from point *B*, shows aggregate supply at full employment. The extent to which *B* exceeds *A*, in other words the horizontal distance *AB*, is the measure of the alleged excess of supply over demand—the measure of alleged "overproduction."

In sharpest contrast to consumptionism, productionism posits an aggregate demand curve for output that has no limit, that is capable of buying all that could ever be produced. This aggregate demand curve is shown in Figure 13–2. It is derived not only from the proposition that man's need and desire for wealth have no fixed limit, but also from the quantity theory of money. In Figure 13–2, the demand curve *DD* represents a given total expenditure of money to buy products, corresponding to

a given total quantity of money in the economic system. The curve shows that the same expenditure of money can buy any volume of goods, depending only on the price level. At half the price level, it can buy twice the quantity of goods; at a fourth, eighth, or tenth of the price level, it can respectively buy four, eight, or ten times the quantity of goods; and so on, without limit. The curve is asymptotic—that is, it never crosses the horizontal or vertical axis. It is also unit elastic.[9] (Of course, under a system of commodity money, to the extent that an aspect of increases in the production and supply of goods is an increase in the quantity of the commodity serving as money, the productionist aggregate demand curve shifts up and to the right. This diminishes the extent to which prices need to fall.)

While I will expand on the critique of the overproduction doctrine at considerable length in Part B of this chapter, it should already be obvious, in the very nature of the productionist aggregate demand curve and its foundations, that a general overproduction—an overproduction in the economic system as a whole—is an impossibility. It is also appropriate to note at this point the inherent absurdity of the overproduction doctrine. In blaming depressions and their accompanying impoverishment on overproduction, the doctrine implies that people

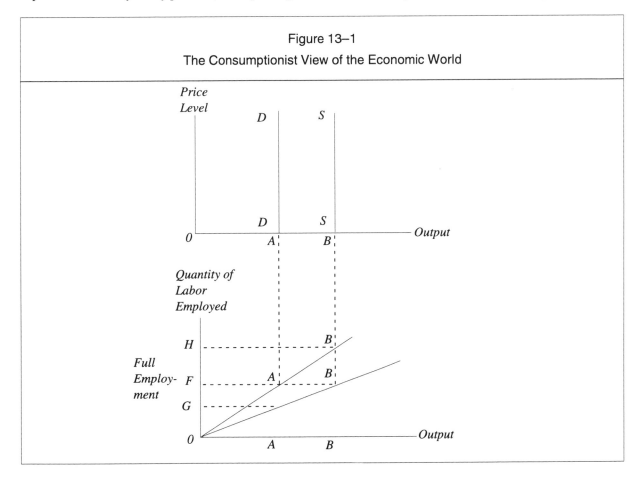

Figure 13–1

The Consumptionist View of the Economic World

cannot afford homes or apartments because they have built too many of them, that they cannot buy food because they have grown too much, that they cannot purchase cars or appliances because they have manufactured too many, in a word, that they are poor because they are rich.

2. Machinery and Unemployment

If one begins with the assumption that the buyers will buy just so much, then it follows that if now that given quantity of goods can be produced with less labor, because of the adoption of labor-saving machinery, then there will be correspondingly less work available for people to do, and thus that improvements in machinery cause unemployment. This is the essential nature of the belief that machinery causes unemployment—the process by which the conclusion is reached.

Figure 13–1 describes the consumptionist's thought process in terms of diagrams. The lower diagram shows the relationship between the quantity of labor employed (and performed), which is measured on the vertical axis, and the quantity of output produced, which is measured on the horizontal axis. Given the state of technology and the quantity and quality of machinery and other means of production available per worker, the greater the quantity of labor that is employed, the greater is the quantity of output produced. Hence, the relationship is described by a line that slopes upward to the right.

Initially, this relationship, which in contemporary eco-nomics textbooks is rather pompously called a "production function," is such that at the point of full employment—point F on the vertical axis—the output of the economic system is A, as indicated by the dashed line running from F to A. Looking upward, along the vertical dashed line running from A to the upper diagram, whose horizontal axis is exactly the same as that of the lower diagram, one sees that with an output of A, the aggregate supply initially does not exceed the allegedly fixed aggregate demand DD that is shown in the upper diagram. The aggregate supply SS corresponding to full employment under these conditions would supposedly lie directly beneath the aggregate demand DD, being perfectly concealed by it. Thus initially there is no alleged problem of "overproduction."

Now, however, comes an improvement in machinery, as the result of which any given quantity of labor can produce a larger output than before. The effect of the improved machinery is described by a new "production function," which is lower and further to the right than the original one, showing that any given quantity of labor now produces more than before, or, equivalently, that any given output can now be produced by less labor. At the point of full employment specifically, the same quantity of labor now produces the output B rather than A. This allegedly causes supply to exceed demand in the upper diagram, creating exactly the situation of alleged "overproduction" that we saw earlier. A continuation of the dashed line from FA to FB, and then a new vertical dashed line running upwards from point B, trace the new

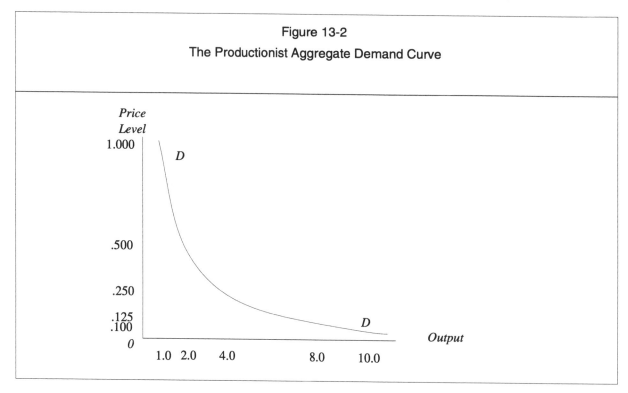

Figure 13-2
The Productionist Aggregate Demand Curve

relationship between full employment and output.

Since businessmen will not continue to produce in excess of the demand, it is argued that production will fall back from B to the initial level of A. But now, because of the use of improved machinery and the consequent movement of the "production function" down and to the right, the output A is produced with a smaller quantity of labor than F. It is produced with quantity G of labor, which is the point found by locating A of output on the new, lower production function and then reading across to the vertical axis, as indicated by the dashed lines. FG is the measure of the unemployment supposedly caused by the use of improved machinery.

In just this way, the effect of improved machinery is allegedly to reduce the supply of work available for people to do. In effect, according to the consumptionists, because there is a need and desire for just so much output, there is a need for just so much work to produce that output, and to the extent that machinery can perform more of that work, there is correspondingly less work for people to do. Thus, supposedly, machinery causes unemployment by virtue of consuming part of the allegedly fixed amount of work to be done in the world corresponding to the allegedly fixed quantity of output that is demanded.

Now the actual effect of the adoption of labor-saving machinery, of course, is to cause not unemployment but a higher standard of living. In the economy as a whole, the effect of the adoption of labor-saving improvements is that the same number of workers end up producing a vastly increased quantity of goods and obtain the benefit of those goods in their capacity as consumers. Improvements in machinery of the labor-saving variety are an essential prerequisite of labor becoming available for increasing the production of goods previously considered luxuries and for working with improvements in machinery of the kind that make possible altogether new products.

There is no problem of a lack of demand for these additional goods. As we know from Chapter 2, the need and desire for goods always far outstrips the ability to produce goods and increases further as that ability increases. We also know that the productionist aggregate demand curve shows that even any given quantity of money and volume of spending is potentially capable of buying an unlimited quantity of goods at lower prices. If one visualizes the productionist aggregate demand curve being superimposed on the upper diagram in Figure 13–1, and taking the place of the consumptionist aggregate demand curve, then it is obvious that no matter how great the output becomes at the point of full employment, it will be demanded. At the same time, the standard of living of the average worker rises as the result of the adoption of labor-saving machinery, because the effect

of such machinery is always to increase the supply of goods relative to the supply of labor and thus to reduce prices relative to wage rates. This increases the buying power of wages and in this way the standard of living of the average wage earner.[10]

All of these propositions are confirmed by the leading facts of modern economic history. Since the beginning of the Industrial Revolution, the productivity of labor has increased by an order of magnitude of at least one hundred times. The unemployment rate is not on the order of 99 percent, as the argument that machinery causes unemployment implies, but is essentially no higher now than it was in the eighteenth century. In essence what has happened is simply that the same number of workers produces vastly more and enjoys a correspondingly higher standard of living. Indeed, not only do the same number of workers find employment, but an enormously larger number. Thanks to the rise in the productivity of labor, and thus the standard of living, achieved by the Industrial Revolution and its machinery, population figures have greatly increased. And essentially the same proportion of this much larger population finds employment as was the case before the start of the Industrial Revolution.

The basic effect of the adoption of machinery, or better machinery, on employment is simply that *the pattern of employment is changed,* in accordance with the change in the relative size of the various industries that results. Thus, insofar as labor-saving improvements are adopted in industries producing necessities, or any other goods of which relatively little more is wanted, employment in those industries falls. The leading example is agriculture. But in the very nature of the case, because less labor is needed in those industries and the funds which paid the wages of that labor can now be spared, funds are released for the employment of additional labor in industries producing other goods, previously beyond people's reach. Moreover, the fall in prices of the goods produced with less labor releases funds for a larger volume of consumer spending elsewhere in the economic system.

In cases in which the introduction of labor-saving machinery takes place in the production of goods previously considered luxuries and makes it possible for such goods to come within the reach of a large number of buyers with funds to spare from other purchases, the effect is to increase employment in the industry in which the labor-saving improvement is introduced. As previously pointed out, a good example of this kind is the automobile industry earlier in this century. In 1900, automobiles were as expensive as yachts are today, and only a handful of people could afford them. However, after productive geniuses such as Henry Ford and Alfred Sloan succeeded in radically reducing the quantity of labor required to produce an automobile, and thus brought the automobile within reach of millions of buyers, the automobile industry became the largest employer of labor in the United States.[11] On a lesser scale, the same pattern occurred in the radio and television set industries and throughout the appliance industry. The video-tape recorder and personal computer industries provide more recent examples.

Because labor-saving machinery raises real wages, it places people in a position in which they can afford to choose additional leisure. Only in this, strictly *voluntary* sense, can it be said to reduce the total amount of employment. On the other hand, as I have indicated, it also enables a larger population to survive, whose members must work. In this sense, it can be said to increase the total amount of employment. Apart from the voluntary choice of additional leisure that it makes possible, and the increase in number of people alive and needing to work that it causes, machinery has no effect on the overall volume of employment, but only on the pattern in which the same total volume of employment is distributed among the different branches of industry. Its overwhelmingly outstanding effect is to raise the productivity of labor and the average standard of living.[12]

3. Alleged Inherent Group Conflicts Over Employment

As we have already seen in the argument against machinery, the notion of a fixed demand for goods implies the notion of a correspondingly fixed demand for the labor to produce them. If it were true that people desired to buy just so many goods, or could afford to buy just so many, then there would exist in the world just so much work that employers could offer—namely, the amount of work required to produce that limited quantity of goods, and nothing more. As we have seen, it is precisely on this basis that it is believed that machinery causes unemployment: it allegedly appropriates part of the limited stock of work to be done from people and transfers it to machines.

The notion of a limited demand for goods and a correspondingly limited amount of work to be done in producing them also shows up in the belief that there is an inherent conflict between men and women when both seek employment, and between whites and blacks, immigrants and natives, Protestants and Catholics, and all other such groups. Such statements as "married women shouldn't work because they take away jobs from men," or "immigration needs to be restricted so that native Americans can have jobs," rest on the idea that there are only so many "jobs" to go around and that to the extent that more of them are held by the members of any one group, there are that many fewer of them remaining for the members of other groups.

Figure 13–1 serves to depict the process of reaching such conclusions in much the same way as it depicts the process of reaching the conclusion that the use of machinery causes unemployment. Starting with the assumption that point F on the vertical axis in the lower diagram represents full employment and results in an output of A on the prevailing "production function," it is now only necessary to assume that because of the entry of additional people into the labor market, the point at which full employment exists rises from F to H. If H marked the actual level of employment, then output would once again be B, this time on the original "production function." (This becomes apparent if one follows the dashes from point H on the vertical axis over to the original production function. The corresponding output will lie at the same point as in the case when improvements in machinery moved the production function to the right.) In the upper diagram of Figure 13–1, this would once again mean an alleged overproduction measured by the excess of B over A. Once again, production would supposedly have to return to A so that supply ceased to exceed demand. Thus, the volume of employment would supposedly return to F, the old full employment point. With employment once again at F, the inescapable implication is that for everyone in the group of new workers, FH, who has gained employment, someone else in the original group, OF, has lost employment.

(Exactly the same analysis, it should be noted, applies to the case of workers seeking to increase their hours of work. They too allegedly deprive others of work. They allegedly appropriate more than their "fair share" of that allegedly scarce commodity "work.")

The existence of a limitless need and desire for wealth obviously precludes the existence of any fundamental conflict among groups for limited job opportunities. Just as in the case of machinery, if the productionist aggregate demand curve is substituted for the consumptionist aggregate demand curve, then once again it is clear that the market can accommodate all the additional output that can be produced by any additional number of workers. And this too is confirmed by the leading facts of modern economic history. Just as the hundredfold or more increase in the productivity of labor has not resulted in 99 percent unemployment, or any increase in the unemployment rate whatever, consumptionism to the contrary notwithstanding, so the vast increase in the number of people seeking employment that the Industrial Revolution and its machinery have made possible has not resulted in any displacement of workers. Far more people are alive. Far more people seek work. And far more people work. It is that simple because there is need and desire for all the output that any number of workers can produce, and any given quantity of money and volume of spending is capable of buying that output, however large.[13] The same principles, of course, apply to any increase in the hours of work that individuals might wish to perform, though as a rule individuals choose to work less as the result of a rising productivity of labor and the consequent rise in living standards.

Furthermore, as we have seen, under capitalism the effect of the employment of a larger number of workers is to raise the real income of the average worker by virtue of extending the division of labor and enabling the occupations concerned with the discovery and application of new knowledge to be carried on, on a larger scale, thereby raising the productivity of labor.[14] In Part C of this chapter, we will see that even though the achievement of full employment may entail a fall in the average level of money wage rates, the effect is still to raise the average level of *real* wage rates (that is, what the money wage rates can actually buy) and thus the actual standard of living of the average worker. In the next chapter, we will see that the effect of married women working is simply to raise the real income of their families.[15]

While there is no foundation for group conflicts over employment under capitalism and a free labor market, it is important to realize that such conflicts can be artificially created by means of government interference that sets wage rates too high and thereby creates a problem of permanent mass unemployment.[16] In conditions in which the overall total number of jobs is artificially limited by making it impossible for wage rates to fall and thus increase the quantity of labor demanded, it is true that the members of any one group can gain employment only at the expense of the employment of members of other groups. The obvious solution, of course, is not to try to prevent the competition of members of other groups but to abolish the government's interference with wage rates.

4. Make-Work Schemes and Spread-the-Work Schemes

The belief in a scarcity of work to be done in the world leads to the belief that what it is necessary to make is not more goods (that, it is claimed, only causes unemployment) but *more work*. According to the supporters of this idea, while scientists and inventors and greedy businessmen are off plundering the community's precious stock of work to be done, with their ceaseless striving for improvements in efficiency, union leaders, government officials, and every good union man must perform the vital function of making work—by, for example, respectively requiring the employment of electricians whose full time jobs consist of nothing more than turning the

lights on and off once a day, by employing people in public works projects, and by doing things more slowly and less efficiently whenever possible.

The effect of "making work" is obviously to hold down the standard of living by reducing output per worker. Indeed, the effect of make-work projects is likely to be not that the same output is produced by a larger number of workers, but that a smaller output is produced by the same number of workers. For there is nothing present in any make-work scheme that increases the overall quantity of labor demanded. That would require lower wage rates—given the quantity of money and volume of spending in the economic system. Thus, the effect of make-work schemes is that for every extra useless worker who is employed and adds little or nothing to output, some other, far more productive worker is forced into unemployment. In other words, the effect of make-work schemes is that less-efficient workers take the place of more-efficient workers, less is produced, and the standard of living is reduced. (It should be realized, of course, that the reduction in employment can be shifted to other industries. Thus if a plumbing repair is made to use the services of an unnecessary tile setter, say, the effect is not that the tile setter takes the place of the plumber. He may take the place of an auto worker, a travel agent, a farmer—a worker anywhere in the economic system where demand is now less because funds have been tied up in paying the wages of the tile setter and in buying the artificially more expensive product that is the result of his employment.)

Somewhat similar to make-work schemes, and put forward in response to the same alleged problem of a scarcity of work to be done in the world, are spread-the-work schemes. Here the existence of a given amount of work to be done is taken for granted and the attempt is made to "spread it around"—"fairly." Thus if the average work week were forty hours and at the same time one worker in four were unemployed, the advocates of spread-the-work would call for a reduction in the work week to thirty hours, in the belief that then everyone could be employed at three-quarters time, rather than three-fourths of the workers at full time.

While the effect of make-work schemes is to shift the burden of unemployment to workers who are presently employed in an efficient manner, in order to make way for workers who will be employed inefficiently, the effect of spread-the-work schemes is not only likely to be very similar, but also very likely to increase the overall amount of unemployment as well, depending on what happens to wage rates.[17]

If no attempt is made to raise hourly wage rates, then those who already have full-time jobs must suffer a reduction in their weekly wages to whatever extent their hours are reduced as the result of spreading the work. More likely than not, at the same time some decline in production will occur and some rise in unit costs and prices will take place, even though the hours worked in the economic system as a whole are the same as before. This result is likely because the workers who were without jobs were likely to have been less efficient than the workers with jobs, inasmuch as employers, as far as they have any choice in the matter, prefer to let go of their poorer workers before their better ones. Thus, by and large, it is the better workers who were able to retain their jobs and the poorer workers who were unemployed. To this extent, "spreading the work" entails substituting hours worked by less efficient workers for hours worked by more efficient workers. In this way, it reduces overall output and raises production costs and prices, even if it leaves the total hours worked the same.

However, the total number of hours worked is unlikely to remain the same. This is because in an effort to compensate the workers who already have jobs and now must accept shorter hours as a result of spreading the work, the attempt will almost certainly be made to raise hourly wage rates. To the extent the attempt succeeds, the total number of hours of labor demanded falls. Indeed, in the face of a fixed aggregate monetary demand for labor—fixed total payrolls in the economic system—(which it is reasonable to assume as a central case if the quantity of money and volume of spending are fixed), *the decrease in hours demanded is in inverse proportion to the rise in hourly wage rates.* Thus, in the case of a reduction in the work week from forty hours to thirty hours, accompanied by a fully compensating rise in average hourly wage rates in the ratio of four to three, the effect would be that total hours demanded and worked in the economic system would fall in the ratio of three to four, that is, by an additional 25 percent!

This would mean that to whatever extent some of the previously unemployed obtained jobs, the effect would be that those who already had jobs would lose them outright. The latter would not merely work thirty hours instead of forty: in order to make room for the unemployed, they themselves would be thrown into unemployment. Indeed, in these circumstances, the previously unemployed could find employment *only* to the extent that those who had jobs lost them or at least reduced their hours below thirty per week. This is because the rise in hourly pay to compensate for the shortening of hours totally nullifies any ability of shorter hours to serve as the basis for spreading the work. Thus any employment gained by the previously unemployed must come at the expense of a further reduction in the employment of those who presently are employed.

5. War and Government Spending

According to consumptionism, war has a variety of economically beneficial consequences that promote employment. It creates an enormous additional need for wealth during the war—in the form of tanks, planes, ammunition, and so on. In addition, the destruction it entails creates the need for replacing what is destroyed. And, finally, the cutback in normal civilian production that takes place during the war supposedly operates to create a kind of bank account for postwar demand: the limited need and desire for goods that people would normally have, and which cannot be satisfied during the war, supposedly accumulates and is available after the war to help prolong the alleged prosperity the war brings, by providing for the release of "pent-up" demand. In all these ways, according to consumptionism, war serves to move the allegedly fixed aggregate demand curve of Figure 13–1 to the right, and thus makes possible greater employment.

An aspect of these absurdities that is worth pointing out is that the consumptionist values the *absence* of wealth rather than wealth. For example, after World War II, he believed that the relative absence of houses, automobiles, and refrigerators in Europe was an asset of the European economy because it represented a large supply of unused consumer desire, thereby supposedly ensuring a strong consumer demand. By the same token, he believed that the relative abundance of these goods in the United States was a liability of the American economy because it represented a depleted supply of consumer desire, thereby supposedly ensuring only a weak consumer demand. Prosperity depends on the absence of wealth, and poverty follows from its abundance, the consumptionist concludes, because that priceless commodity, consumer desire, more limited in supply than diamonds, is produced by the absence and consumed by the presence of wealth.

In contrast to all such absurdities, productionism recognizes that the need for wealth is always superabundant and thus that the last thing in the world that is necessary is to create more need for wealth by destroying existing wealth. It is wealth, not the need for wealth, that must be created, and this is what war wastes and destroys. The actual economic effect of war is to divert production from civilian goods to war goods, which have no economic benefit. It is also to cause people to work longer and harder, and people who otherwise would not have found it necessary to work, such as many housewives and teenagers, to go to work—all in an effort to offset the drop in the standard of living that the diversion of output to the war effort causes. Similarly, the postwar replacement of wealth needlessly destroyed in war is at the expense of new and additional wealth that otherwise could have been enjoyed in addition to the wealth needlessly destroyed, and at the expense of leisure that people could otherwise have afforded to choose. The same is true of the wartime need to postpone the production of civilian goods. Had the production of those goods not had to be postponed, new and additional wealth could have been produced and enjoyed in subsequent years, and people could also have afforded to choose more leisure.

Nor does war promote prosperity by means of the postwar application of scientific or technological advances made in connection with the war effort. Like the output of war goods, which are at the expense of the output of civilian goods, the scientific and technological advances made in connection with war are at the expense of the advances that would have taken place had the labor of scientists and engineers not had to be diverted from peacetime pursuits to the war effort. While the most that is gained from the war effort are some derivative peacetime applications—mere by-products of the war effort— what is lost are the kinds of advances that would have resulted from the full, focused application of scientific and engineering talent to peacetime advances. In the nature of the case, the loss is greater than the gain, and thus, on net balance, war detracts from scientific and technological progress. Indeed, as we have already seen, so far from it being the case that a focus on the technology of war can serve as the foundation for technology of value to the lives of human beings, that the reverse is true. Those countries which have been free to devote their efforts to improving human life and well-being, such as the United States (at least for most of its history), have, as a by-product of their peaceful, civilian scientific and technological pursuits, developed the foundation for far more powerful military technology than countries bent on war and aggression.[18]

Finally, war does not promote prosperity by making possible the replacement of factories and machines that have been destroyed, with more advanced factories and machines.[19] The physical foundation for the construction of new factories and machines is existing factories and machines. The destruction of factories and machines destroys the physical ability to produce newer, more advanced factories and machines.

These propositions are in no way contradicted by the postwar experience of Germany and Japan. The physical ability of postwar Germany and Japan to rebuild was enormously facilitated by the fact that the factories and machines of the United States had escaped physical destruction. Had the United States been bombed to the extent that Germany and Japan had been bombed, the rebuilding would have taken many more years, if, in-

deed, it would have been possible at all. The ability of these countries to recover was also facilitated to the extent that their existing factories and machines had escaped damage and thus were available to serve in production, including not only the production of more advanced factories and machines but also goods to exchange for more advanced factories and machines.

The fact that in the years since World War II, Germany and Japan have in many cases built factories that are more modern than those used in the United States does not at all prove how fortunate they were to have been the scene of massive bombing raids and how unfortunate we were to have escaped bombing. Their success is the result of the fact that starting with whatever capital goods were available to them, they produced substantially as much as they could, and devoted a proportion of their productive efforts to the production of capital goods that was more than sufficient to replace the capital goods used up in production. This increased the capital goods at their disposal and enabled them to increase their production further. And out of the larger production, they again devoted a proportion sufficient more than to replace the capital goods consumed in production, and by a wide margin. Repeating this process over decades is the essential explanation of their great economic success.

Starting with far more capital goods, the United States was in a much better position to add further to its supply of capital goods than Germany or Japan. But the destructive policies of its government prevented it from doing so. Government policies such as confiscatory taxation (especially of profits and interest), chronic budget deficits, inflation of the money supply, prolabor legislation, and ever growing regulation in general, have stood in the way of saving and capital accumulation to a much greater extent in the postwar United States than in postwar Germany or Japan. This is the essential reason for their much more rapid rate of economic progress since World War II.[20]

It is true that World War II was accompanied by the elimination of mass unemployment in the United States. Part C of this chapter will explain why this was the case, in a way that is perfectly consistent with the philosophy of productionism. It will show that it was not the war as such that brought about full employment, nor any increase in the need for wealth that is associated with war, but a change in the relationship between wage rates and prices on the one side and the quantity of money and volume of spending in the economic system, on the other. It will show how the necessary change in this relationship, and thus full employment, could have been achieved without the war, and how government intervention in the labor market prevented its achievement. It will also show that despite the existence of full employment, and the illusion of prosperity, the war was actually a period of impoverishment far worse than the worst years of the depression of the 1930s. It will show that full employment with prosperity was achieved only after the war ended, and the labor and capital that had been devoted to the war effort once again became available for the production of peacetime, civilian goods.

The fact that war is economically destructive does not mean, of course, that there is no legitimate basis for war. When war is necessary for the defense of individual freedom, it is justified. What must never be forgotten is simply that even when it is justified, war is always a great expense, not a source of prosperity.

Consumptionists see additional peacetime government spending, whether for public works or for social welfare, as a source of prosperity comparable to war, but without entailing loss of human life. Such spending, they believe, is as beneficial to employment as would be a policy of calling in the artillery or airforce to destroy buildings after they had been evacuated. For it too allegedly increases the demand for goods and thus the need for labor, by virtue of the government performing the supposedly valuable service of exchanging its consumption for the people's products. In view of the fact that until recently, the enemy in any war we were likely to become involved in would directly or indirectly have been the Soviet Union, whose social system even now still evokes substantial support among intellectuals, this alleged method of promoting prosperity has become much more favored than war.

Of course, since there is in fact no lack of demand for goods or need for labor, the actual effect of government spending to promote employment is to divert production from the goods and services that people voluntarily choose to buy, to goods and services that they do not value sufficiently to buy. In the process, it also reduces their overall ability to produce. This last occurs as the result both of reducing their incentive to work and produce, through higher taxes to pay for the additional spending, and their freedom to produce, through a growing array of regulations enforced by many of those added to the government's payroll. Thus, production is diverted away from goods and services of value to taxpayers to such things as the production of goods and services for welfare recipients, the provision of "education" to other people's children, and the production of farm products to rot or to be given away. In addition, it is diverted to providing for the wants of millions of government employees whose function is nothing other than to restrict the freedom of the taxpayers.

In the nature of the case, all government spending inspired by consumptionism must be highly wasteful.

This follows from the fact that its essential purpose is not the achievement of any positive value in exchange for the expenditure, but merely to promote employment. If the government desires something as a positive value, such as a new courthouse or police station, then, just like any other buyer, it would want to obtain the best product it could for as little money as possible. In such a case, the government would implicitly want its product to be produced as efficiently as possible, as the basis for obtaining it for as little money as possible. For all practical purposes, this would mean that it would want its product produced with as little labor as possible, inasmuch as that is the essential nature of efficient production. However, if the government's goal is to increase spending and employment, then what it wants is not the most and best product for the least money, produced with the least amount of labor possible, but a product for the *most* money, produced with the greatest amount of labor possible. In fact, the product itself altogether ceases to matter. It can be no product at all or the most absurd product, such as pyramids—as Keynes would be among the first to admit. For the value, according to consumptionism, is not the product gained but the expenditure made and the employment that is allegedly created.[21]

Of course, all of the wasteful and destructive economic consequences of war and government spending can be reversed by the coming of peace and by the dismantling of the government programs. (The dismantling of the civilian programs, of course, can be undertaken at any time.) The effect would be a reduction in the labor and capital devoted to producing for the government's purposes, or for the purposes of those to whom the government gives or pays money, and an equivalent increase in the labor and capital devoted to producing for the purposes of private citizens. Indeed, insofar as the reduction in government spending took the form of a reduction in welfare payments to the able bodied, the effect would be an increase in the number of people working and an increase in the total volume of goods produced. This is because the former welfare recipients would now have to support themselves instead of being supported by others. An increase in the total volume of goods produced would also be the effect insofar as military personnel and other government employees rejoined the private, civilian labor force and thus the ranks of producers' labor, in contrast to their present status of consumers' labor.[22] In addition, in the case of the firing of government personnel who presently carry out the regulations hampering productive activity, the further effect would be that the efforts of the citizens would be made correspondingly more productive.

Ironically, it follows from these facts that, given some time to adjust, the effect would be that even the former welfare recipients and government employees would come out far ahead of where they were when they were on welfare or working for the government. For once they learned the habit of working, or of working in the far more efficient, competitive conditions of private business rather than in the sheltered environment of the government, and doing so, moreover, in the face of a reduced burden of taxation and regulation, they would produce and enjoy far more than they can presently wring from others by force.

6. Population Growth and Demand

In addition to war and government spending, consumptionism claims that a larger number of people, each with his or her limited quota of needs and desires, increases the total demand for goods and thus helps to eliminate the alleged excess of the ability to produce over the need and desire to consume. The existence of a larger number of people, the consumptionist tells businessmen, makes it possible for business to find someone upon whom to unload its otherwise superfluous goods. Business will prosper because its supply of goods will find a counterpart in an adequate supply of desire for goods. These beliefs are the foundation for the talk about "baby booms" and the additional demand for goods of all kinds that is automatically supposed to result from them.

Of course, when these alleged economic benefits of the larger population are put forward, there is no discussion of the additional people entering the labor market and seeking employment. The consumptionist premise, which leads to the larger population being viewed favorably from the perspective of its effects on demand, must lead to it being viewed unfavorably from the perspective of its effects on the supply of labor. For, as we have seen, it follows on the consumptionist premise, that to the extent that the larger population's members gain jobs, correspondingly fewer additional jobs are available for others. Thus, what is supposed to be the cause of prosperity here, according to consumptionism, is that the additional people exist *only as consumers*, not as producers—that is, that they exist as parasites. *That* will be their alleged contribution to employment and prosperity. In that way, they will supply the need for goods, which is allegedly scarce, but not goods, which are allegedly superabundant.

In opposition to these absurdities, the productionist recognizes that the birth and upbringing of children always constitutes an expense to the parents. In raising children, the parents must spend money on them which they otherwise would have spent on themselves. Of course, the parents may, and hopefully will, consider the money better and more enjoyably spent on their children;

but still, it is an expense. And if they have a large enough number of children, they will be reduced to poverty. This is a fact that anyone can observe in any large family that does not possess a correspondingly large income. The presence of children does not make the parents spend more than they otherwise would have, but only spend *differently* than they otherwise would have. They buy baby food, toys, and bicycles instead of more restaurant meals, a better car, or costlier vacations. There is no stimulus given to production. Production is merely differently directed, to the different distribution of demand.

In reality, the only increase in production that could take place would be as the result of the parents working longer or harder to be able to support their children while still maintaining their own previous standard of living. Furthermore, when the children grow up, the additional market that they are supposed to constitute for houses and automobiles and the like will materialize only to the extent that they themselves are able to produce the equivalent of these things and thereby earn the money with which to purchase them. Thus it will only be by virtue of their production, and not by virtue of their desire to consume, that they will be able to constitute an additional market.

7. Imperialism and Foreign Trade

The same considerations that make the consumptionist believe that a larger population at home is desirable, by virtue of its possession of a larger stock of needs and desires for goods, make him believe that it is desirable to secure the needs and desires of the vast, impoverished populations of backward foreign countries. To the consumptionist, such countries appear as virtual treasure houses of unused consumer desires. He counts the numbers of their inhabitants and the lack of goods of each person, and arrives at what he considers to be staggering sources of demand.

Such ideas undoubtedly influenced the economically ignorant politicians of many European countries before World War I, particularly those of Germany, in embarking upon policies of imperialism and colonial conquest.[23] Instead of denouncing the economic ignorance of those politicians, many historians accept exactly the same false premises of consumptionism, and thus routinely explain World War I as having been caused by conflicts among the advanced countries of Western Europe for so-called markets in the backward nations. According to such historians, each of the European powers allegedly had a problem of overproduction at home and was thus in need of foreign markets as an outlet for its allegedly surplus goods. So valuable were these alleged foreign markets supposed to be to the European countries, that, according to such historians, it is understandable that they were considered worth fighting for. More recently, the same logic was applied to the United States' involvement in Vietnam. It was claimed that we were there in order to be sure of having access to the vast "markets" of Southeast Asia.

Contrary to consumptionism and the ignorant politicians and historians that it influences, hordes of impoverished beggars do not constitute markets. Countries, and individuals, constitute markets not to the extent that they have needs and desires for goods, but to the extent that they produce and supply goods. Only to this extent are they in a position to earn the wherewithal to purchase goods and thus to constitute markets. It is for this reason that the United States and Japan are vastly greater markets than India and China, as I previously pointed out, and that Beverly Hills is a vastly greater market than Watts.

It should be realized that the same problem arises for the consumptionist in connection with the policy of imperialism, and foreign trade in general, as arises in connection with a larger population at home. Namely, the consumptionist (and imperialist) values foreign countries only as sources of alleged demand, by which, of course, he means needs and desires. At the same time, he fears them as sources of supply. To the extent that they become sources of supply, such as Hong Kong, Taiwan, South Korea, and Japan, he fears them as depriving domestic producers of markets and thus workers at home of jobs. The consumptionist believes that the gains from foreign trade are in the exports, not the imports. His view of a beneficial relationship with foreign countries is that they should provide us with their needs and desires, so as to provide an outlet for our allegedly excess goods, not that they should provide us with goods. He believes that the object of foreign trade should be to have the maximum possible excess of exports over imports. His ideal is that his country should only export and not import at all, or import only to the extent that doing so is vitally necessary or contributes to the production of a more than compensating quantity of additional exports.[24] Obviously, the notion that an excess of exports over imports constitutes a "favorable balance of trade" is entirely consistent with consumptionism and draws much of its support from it.[25]

Thus, the idea of the consumptionist and the imperialist is that a country benefits by virtue of actually *giving its goods away for free*—by working and sending them out and by receiving back as little as possible. And more, that this privilege is worth fighting for. Indeed, so perverse is the consumptionist view of things that it leads to absurdity heaped upon absurdity. By the logic of those who hold it, the military presence of the United States in Vietnam was to be explained on the grounds that the

people of Southeast Asia were too clever to be willing to accept our goods for free. We allegedly had to use force to make them accept such an arrangement, allegedly so harmful to them and so beneficial to ourselves. According to the consumptionist, the privilege of supplying impoverished beggars—that is, of working for nothing—is so valuable that if it is not actually worth dying for, it is at least understandable why it should appear to be so, to those not restrained from the pursuit of material self-interest by the possession of more noble sensibilities. This is what consumptionist historians and moralists believe.

It needs to be pointed out that the actual benefit of international trade is in the imports, not the exports. The citizens of a country gain in the conduct of international trade by virtue of the fact that the goods and services brought in by international trade surpass the goods and services that the labor and capital employed in producing exports could produce for the domestic market. Thus, to recall the example of automobiles and coffee from Chapter 9, the United States gains in its trade with Brazil by virtue of obtaining more coffee through the production of automobiles for export than it could by using the same amount of labor to produce coffee. At the same time, Brazil gains by virtue of obtaining automobiles and other manufactured goods in far greater quantity through the export of coffee than it could obtain by attempting to use the same amount of labor to produce such goods in Brazil. Or, equivalently, the countries gain by obtaining the same amount of goods with the use of less labor, and thus have labor left over to produce more of other things.[26]

International trade does not cause unemployment but, like machinery, a higher productivity of labor and standard of living. As in the case of machinery, the effect on employment is merely a change in the pattern of employment. Fewer workers are employed in the industries in which foreigners enjoy a comparative advantage and hence in which the country imports, and more workers are employed in the industries in which the given country enjoys a comparative advantage and hence in which it exports.[27] Overall, the effect is the same volume of employment but more goods.

8. Parasitism as an Alleged Source of Gain to Its Victims

The consumptionist's views on the allegedly beneficial effects of war, government spending, population growth, and imperialism rest on the idea that one benefits producers by the mere fact of consuming their products. This gives the producers the work to do of making possible one's consumption. Such an idea is obviously absurd. Only the use of money lends it the least semblance of plausibility. If it were true, then every slave who ever lived should have cherished his master's every whim the satisfaction of which required of him more work. A slave should have been grateful if his master desired a larger house, an improved road, more food, more parties, and so on; for the provision of the means of satisfying these desires would have given him correspondingly more work to do.

The belief that the consumption of the government, or of private nonproducing consumers at home or abroad, benefits and helps to support the economic system is on precisely the same footing as the belief that the consumption of the master benefits and supports the slave. It is a belief the absurdity of which is matched only by the injustice it makes possible. It is the means by which parasitical pressure groups, employing the government as an agent of plunder, seek to delude their victims into believing that they are benefitted and supported by those who take their products and given them nothing in return.

The only economic benefit that one can give to producers consists in the exchange of one's own products or services for their products or services. It is by means of what one produces and offers in exchange that one benefits producers, not by means of what one consumes. To the extent that one consumes the products or services of others without offering products or services in exchange, one consumes at their expense.

The use of money makes this point somewhat less obvious but no less true. Where money is employed, producers do not exchange goods and services directly, but indirectly. The buyer exchanges money for the goods of a seller. The seller then exchanges the money for the goods of other sellers, and so on. But every buyer in the series must either himself have offered goods and services for sale equivalent to those he purchases, or have obtained his funds from someone else who has done so.

The fact that in a monetary economy everyone measures his benefit by the amount of money he obtains in exchange for his goods or services is interpreted by the consumptionist to imply that the mere spending of money is a virtue and that economic prosperity is to be found through the creation and spending of new and additional money—i.e., by a policy of inflation.

The fact is that for everyone who spends newly created money and thus obtains goods and services without having produced equivalent goods and services, there must be others who suffer a corresponding loss. Their loss takes the form either of a depletion of their capital, a diminution of their consumption, or a lack of reward for the added labor they perform—a loss precisely equal to the goods and services obtained by the buyers who do not produce.

The consumptionist's advocacy of consumption by those who do not produce, to ensure the prosperity of those who do, is a pathological response to an economic world which the consumptionist imagines to be ruled by pathology. The consumptionist has always before him the pathology of the miser. His reasoning is dominated by the thought of cash hoarding. He believes that one part of mankind is driven by a purposeless passion for work without reward, which requires for its fulfillment the existence of another part of mankind eager to accept reward without work. This is the meaning of the belief that one set of men desire only to produce and sell, but not to buy and consume, and the inference that what is required is another set of men who will buy and consume, but who will not produce and sell. In the consumptionist's world, the producers are imagined to produce merely for the sake of obtaining money. The consumptionist stands ready to supply them with money in exchange for their goods—he proposes either to take from them the money he believes they would not spend, and then have someone else spend it, or to print more money and allow them to accumulate paper as others acquire their goods.

Hoarding is not the only phenomenon upon which the consumptionist seizes. Where nothing in reality will serve, the consumptionist is highly adept at bringing forth totally imaginary causes of economic catastrophe. Invariably, the solution advanced is consumption by those who have not produced, for the sake of those who have. Always, the goal is to demonstrate the necessity and beneficial effect of parasitism—to present parasitism as a source of prosperity to its victims. This is the meaning of his beliefs about the allegedly beneficial effects of make-work schemes, war and government spending, a growth in the population of idle consumers, and fighting for the privilege of supplying beggars around the world.[28]

9. Advertising as Allegedly Fraudulent but Economically Beneficial

The consumptionist views advertising as attempting to induce people to buy goods for which they have no real need. At the same time, precisely on the basis of this belief, he regards advertising as a method of stimulating demand in the economic system and thus helping to overcome the alleged deficiency of demand.

The fact is that advertising does not create consumer desire where no desire for additional goods would otherwise have existed. It is not the case that, in the absence of advertising, people would be at a loss as to how to spend their money. Advertising is not required, and would not be sufficient, to rouse vegetables into men. What advertising does, by making people more aware of the alternatives available to them, is lead them to consume differently and in a better way than they otherwise would have. Advertising is a tool of competition, and, as such, for every competing product whose sale is increased by it, there is another competing product whose sale is decreased by it. The only exceptions are insofar as advertising contributes to the increase in production—for example, by making people aware of the existence of products which they judge to be important enough to be worth expending extra effort to earn the money to purchase. Such cases are a further illustration of the fact that it is only the increase in aggregate supply that increases aggregate demand.

The consumptionist's attitude toward advertising brings into clear relief some further corollaries and implications of his basic premise. His estimate of advertising, like that of war and destruction, is ambivalent, and necessarily so. On the one hand, he approves of it, on the grounds that by creating consumer desires, it creates the work required to satisfy those desires. However, this very belief, that advertising creates desires where absolutely no desires would otherwise exist, also makes him condemn advertising. For if it were true that, in the absence of advertising, men would be perfectly content with very little, the desires created by advertising must appear to be only superficial and basically unnecessary and unnatural.

And this, of course, as previously explained, is precisely how the consumptionist regards such desires. In his eyes, all desires men have for goods, beyond what is necessary to make possible bare physical survival and a vegetative existence, represent an unnatural taste for "luxuries." These desires the consumptionist considers to be inherently unimportant. Their only justification is the creation of work. The consumptionist's conception of the greater part of economic activity, therefore, is that it represents senseless motion, with deceit and deception required to make people desire goods for which they have no need, in order to enable them to pass their lives in the production of those very same goods.[29]

In reality, of course, people's desire for "luxuries" is necessary and natural, for it is nothing but the desire to satisfy their inherent needs (including the need for aesthetic satisfaction) in an ever more improved way. It is from the importance that attaches to the satisfaction of the desire for "luxuries" that the importance of the work required to produce them is derived, and not vice versa. Indeed, however paradoxical it may appear, it is only from the perspective of productionism that one can understand the actual importance of consumer desires—namely, as the ever-present end and purpose of all production, not as a means serving production absurdly regarded as an end in itself.

10. Misconception of the Value of Technological Progress

Just as he believes in the need to create uses for an expanding supply of consumers' goods, so the consumptionist believes there is a problem of finding "investment outlets" for an expanding supply of capital goods. Here he looks to technological progress as providing a possible solution to this alleged problem. Its contribution is supposed to be the enlargement of the "supply of investment outlets" or "investment opportunities."

The fact is that the value of technological progress does not lie in the creation of "investment outlets" or "investment opportunities" for an expanding supply of capital goods. If the concept of capital goods is properly understood, as denoting all goods that the buyer employs for the purpose of producing goods that are to be sold, then, as has already been shown in Chapter 2, it is clear that there is no such thing as a lack of "investment outlets" or "investment opportunities" for capital goods. So long as more or improved consumers' goods are desired, there is need of a larger supply of capital goods. As shown, capital goods are scarce both in their horizontal and vertical dimensions.[30]

For example, ten million automobiles of a given quality require the employment of twice the quantity of capital goods—twice the quantity of steel, glass, tires, paint, engines, and machinery—in their production as do five million such automobiles. If the quality of the automobiles is to be improved, or if the efficiency of their production is to be increased by the adoption of more capital-intensive methods of production, then a larger quantity of capital goods is required for the production of the same number of automobiles. For example, a given number of cars of Chevrolet quality, with their greater number of accessories and larger size and greater need for materials, require a larger quantity of capital goods in their production than the same number of cars of Volkswagen quality; the same number of cars of Cadillac quality require still a larger supply of capital goods; and the same number of cars of Rolls-Royce quality require yet an even more enlarged supply. Greater capital intensiveness is entailed not only in shifting from such lower-quality models to such higher-quality models, but also insofar as more capital-intensive methods of production are to replace less capital-intensive methods of production in the manufacture of any of these given models. To this extent, too, a larger supply of capital goods is required.

The identical principle applies to houses of different size and quality. A given quantity of eight-room houses of a given quality requires the employment of a larger supply of capital goods than the same number of seven-room houses of the same quality. A given number of brick houses requires a larger supply of capital goods than the same number of wooden houses of the same size; the bricks or any more expensive material constitute a larger supply of capital goods because a larger quantity of labor is required to produce them. The principle applies to food and clothing, to furniture and appliances, to every good. So long as more of any consumers' good is desired, so long as not every consumers' good that is produced is of the very best-known quality, and produced by the most capital-intensive methods, there is a need for a larger supply of capital goods.

It is not the case that in the absence of technological progress, the supply of capital goods would continue to expand but find no "investment outlets." It is not the case that what we have to fear from a lack of technological progress is a flood of capital goods surpassing every possible use for capital goods, and that then we will be at a loss as to how to employ our expanding supply of capital goods. Before such a situation could exist, every car produced would have to be the equivalent of the finest-known-model Rolls Royce; every house would have to be a palatial mansion; every suit of clothes would have to be fit for the Prince of Wales. This is because so long as any such possibilities remained unmet, there would be a need for the additional capital goods that would enable them to be met. Before such a situation could exist, capital intensiveness would have to be carried to its utmost limits in terms of reducing costs and improving the quality of goods in every respect. Among other things, this would mean that every known machine that can save labor would be in use in every possible case, that bridges and tunnels would eliminate every major detour across land or around water, that the roads and railroads would be straight and level, and that all major inland cities technologically capable of having access to the sea would have it. Clearly, whatever problems the world may face, such a situation is not one of them. Clearly, whatever our worries may be, such a situation deserves no place among them. On the contrary, what we have to fear from a lack of technological progress is not that we will be overrun with a supply of capital goods that surpasses all worthwhile uses for capital goods and that we shall then be at a loss for what to do with our still expanding supply of capital goods, but that we will *not* have an increase in the supply of capital goods, that we will not be able to exploit any considerable portion of the virtually limitless "investment outlets" that already exist, within the framework of known technology.

The value of technological progress consists in the fact that it enables us to *obtain* a larger supply of capital goods, and not that it solves the problem of what to do with a larger supply.[31] The technological advances that made possible the canal building and railroad building of the nineteenth century and the development of the steel industry were valuable, not because they absorbed capital goods, as the consumptionist believes, but because they made possible the *accumulation* of capital goods. The consumptionist does not realize that capital goods can be increased in supply only by means of an increase in their production, and that precisely this is what technological progress makes possible. Had the technological advances that made possible the first railroads in the 1830s not taken place, the supply of capital goods required for the expanded and improved railroad building of the 1840s would not have been obtainable; or, if obtainable, only at the price of the expansion of some other industry. Had no technological advances been made in railroading in the 1840s, the supply of capital goods in the 1850s would have been less, both for railroads and for all other industries. And so it would have been decade by decade, had the technological advances made in railroading or in any other industry not taken place.

For capital accumulation to continue for any period of time, technological progress is indispensable. Only it can make possible continued increases in production, and only continued increases in production can make possible continued capital accumulation. The consumptionist is not aware that the very thing that he considers to be the solution to his imagined problem is the source of what he imagines to be the problem. The absurd implication of his belief is that somehow, in the absence of technological progress, a supply of capital goods could have been accumulated out of the level of production of a preindustrial economy that would have been sufficient to build the railroads and steel mills of the nineteenth-century United States, but, thank heaven, the technology of railroad building and steel-mill construction came along in the nick of time to find uses for those capital goods. It is on this basis, under the name of the doctrine of "secular stagnation," that the consumptionist explains why large-scale capital accumulation did not depress the rate of profit in the nineteenth century, but allegedly did in this century.[32]

Nor is the consumptionist aware that when he advances technological progress as the solution to the problem of what to do with more capital goods, he is confronting himself with the problem of what to do with the larger supply of consumers' goods, that even he admits results from technological progress. The consumptionist is faced, in addition to other quandaries, with the dilemma of explaining how it is that technological progress can raise the rate of profit by, as he puts it, "increasing the demand for capital," while at the same time, as he admits, it increases the production of consumers' goods, which, he maintains, lowers the rate of profit by causing "overproduction," falling prices, and "deflation."

The textbook of Samuelson and Nordhaus provides a typical instance of this contradiction on the part of the consumptionists. In one place it declares:

> But what happens as society invests in more and more capital goods? As a nation transfers more and more of its consumption toward capital accumulation? As production becomes more and more roundabout or indirect?

> The answer is that we would expect the law of diminishing returns to set in. As we add more fishing boats and nets or power plants or steel mills or chemical factories or computers or trucks, the extra product or return on even more roundabout production begins to fall. The first few fishing boats or nets yield many fish, but too many fishing boats simply deplete the fish stock. Eventually, as capital is accumulated, the rate of return on the investments would fall from, say, 20 percent per annum to 10 percent or even to 2 percent.

> Unless offset by technological change, therefore, rapid investment would produce diminishing returns, which would drive down the rate of return on investment. But then, why have rates of return on capital not fallen markedly over the course of the last 150 years, even though our capital stocks have grown manyfold? Because innovation and technological change have created profitable new opportunities as rapidly as past investment has annihilated them.[33]

Yet while here they claim that technological progress raises the rate of return, elsewhere in their book, they say: "The opposite of inflation is deflation, which occurs when the general level of prices is falling. . . . Sustained deflations, where prices fall steadily over a period of several years, are associated with periods of deep depression, such as the 1930s or the 1890s."[34]

It is obvious that on this definition, technological progress must cause "deflation," for clearly it operates to increase production and supply and therefore to reduce prices. Deflation, of course, entails a reduction in the rate of profit, or rate of return. Thus, Samuelson and Nordhaus are in the position of alleging that technological progress both raises and lowers the rate of return.

This unfortunate dilemma of the consumptionists is resolved by realizing that technological progress does not increase "the demand for capital" or the rate of profit. Rather, as already indicated, it increases the supply of capital goods, which reduces their prices and thus the costs of production. In increasing the productivity of labor, it also reduces costs of production. Thus the fall in prices of consumers' goods is preceded by a fall in costs of production, which prevents it from resulting in a fall in the rate of profit.[35]

Finally, it must be observed that the notion that technological progress raises the rate of profit is as mistaken as the notion that it causes deflation and thus reduces the rate of profit. Fundamentally, *technological progress is neutral with respect to the general or average rate of profit.* It raises the rate of profit of those firms that introduce appropriate technological advances or are relatively early in their adoption. But at the same time, it reduces the rate of profit of those firms that fail to introduce such advances and suffer from the greater competition of the firms that have introduced them. If, for example, a pharmaceutical company could offer an affordable pill that would prevent cancer, it would make enormous profits. At the same time, however, various other firms, probably in a wide variety of different industries, would suffer an equivalent reduction in sales revenues and profits, at least in comparison with what they would otherwise have been. And then, if some other pharmaceutical company were to be able to offer a pill at a comparable price that not only prevented cancer but also heart disease, the pill that prevented only cancer would almost certainly incur losses. The belief that technological progress raises the general or average rate of profit is simply another instance of the fallacy of composition, based on the failure to consider the effects of things on all parties in the economic system.[36] The only way in which technological progress can contribute to raising the general or average rate of profit is under a system of commodity money, such as a gold standard. In that case, as I will show, it raises the rate of profit insofar as its by-product is a more rapid rate of increase in the quantity of money and volume of spending.[37]

11. Increases in Production and Alleged Deflation

The preceding leads to the final point that must be considered here, which is not a manifestation of the consumptionist premise exclusively, but which is closely allied to it in that it implies that increases in production are responsible for depressions. This is the belief that increases in production cause deflation unless they are accompanied by equivalent increases in the quantity of money and volume of spending in the economic system.

As evidenced by the quotation from Samuelson and Nordhaus in the text above, the consumptionists, and many people who in other respects are not consumptionists, believe that falling prices in and of themselves, irrespective of their cause, represent deflation. Just as "inflation" is used as a synonym for rising prices, "deflation" is used as a synonym for falling prices. But deflation, of course, is also used as a synonym for depression. Thus, increases in production are regarded as inherently tending to produce depressions, unless, either by accident, or by virtue of the plan of the government, the quantity of money and volume of spending in the economic system grow as rapidly, and thus prevent prices from falling.

In this way, what comes to be feared is both the increase in the supply of goods and the lack of increase in the quantity of money. And what comes to be advocated, at least implicitly, is both the destruction of wealth and the inflation of the money supply—as the means of preventing "deflation."

It should be obvious that anyone who holds these ideas must be fearful of allowing the quantity of money in the economic system to be governed by the quantity of gold. For he has no guarantee that under a gold standard, the quantity of money will increase as rapidly as the supply of ordinary goods.[38]

Part B of this chapter shows why falling prices caused by increased production are of a radically different character than falling prices caused by a decrease in the quantity of money and volume of spending, and thus do not deserve to be stigmatized as "deflation." It shows that none of the negative consequences associated with genuine deflation, such as a generally greater difficulty of repaying debt or a wiping out of general business profitability, accompany falling prices caused by increased production.

12. Consumptionism and Socialism

The consumptionist premise is influential not only in all the ways I have described, which are certainly important enough in their own right, but also in an important indirect way. By this I mean that while most people who hold the consumptionist premise are content to live with its paradoxical implications to the extent that they are aware of them, many are not. The latter accept all of the absurd implications of consumptionism as applying only to the capitalist economic system in which they live. Their view is that it is *under capitalism* that improvements in production cause impoverishment; that war, destruction, parasitism, and fraud cause prosperity; and that conflicts exist within and between nations. Such an absurd and discordant system, they believe, deserves to be overthrown, and replaced with an allegedly more rational system. To them, socialism appears, or at least did appear, as a system of reason and order, in which these paradoxes and conflicts can be harmoniously resolved.

The contribution of the collapse of socialism to the spread of irrationalism, which I have referred to in connection with the rise of such doctrines as environmentalism, can be understood in part in the light of the influence of consumptionism. To consumptionists the collapse of socialism means that reason simply does not apply to the economic organization of mankind. They had been convinced of the absurdity and evil of capitalism, but had looked to socialism as the solution. Now, after almost three generations, they are coming to see that socialism means slavery and poverty. And thus, they conclude, the economic world is inherently and inescapably riddled with paradox and evil.

Some major loose ends remain to be tied up in connection with consumptionism. Above all, there is the bundle of fallacies known as Keynesianism, which represents a convoluted variant of consumptionism. I will deal with Keynesianism in Chapter 18. Of lesser prominence, but still quite significant, is the widespread fallacy that depressions are caused by too much wealth in the form of inventories. I will deal with this fallacy in an appendix following the end of this chapter.

PART B

SAY'S (JAMES MILL'S) LAW

1. Monetary Demand and Real Demand

While productionism shows that the need and desire for goods, and for the labor to produce them, have no limit, Say's Law shows that under the freedom of competition *the process of production itself creates purchasing power equal to what is produced*—that, in the typical formulation of Say's Law, "supply creates its own demand."

There are two senses in which the word demand can properly be used in the context of the present discussion. One, is the mere expenditure of money. We may call this "monetary demand." The other, is "real demand"—that is, the quantity of goods and services that the monetary demand, whatever it is, is capable of actually buying. Real demand is the monetary demand adjusted for the wage and price level. It should be observed that, depending on wages and prices, a smaller monetary demand can represent a larger real demand than does a larger monetary demand. For example, a monetary demand of 100 at one time can buy more than a monetary demand of 200 at another time, if, when the monetary demand is 200, prices are more than double what they are when the monetary demand is 100.

Real demand can be thought of also as the classical economists frequently described demand, namely, as *the will combined with the power of purchasing*. We have seen that the will to purchase can be taken for granted. All that is required to enlarge demand is the power of purchasing. And all that is required to enlarge the power of purchasing, as we shall see, is an increase in production. In the words of Ricardo, the desire to consume "is implanted in every man's breast; nothing is required but the means, and nothing can afford the means but an increase in production."[39]

Increases in production and supply create purchasing power and real demand. They do so by virtue of reducing prices. This enables any given monetary demand to buy correspondingly more—to buy all that is produced and offered for sale.[40]

Indeed, increases in production and supply are, as the classical economists held, the *only* thing that can increase real demand. In the words of James Mill, "The production of commodities creates, and is the one and universal cause which creates a market for the commodities produced."[41] This proposition becomes obvious as soon as we realize that increases in monetary demand that take place without increases in supply operate only to raise prices. The only way that increases in monetary demand can possibly represent increases in *real* demand is insofar as they are accompanied by increases in supply. Thus, increases in monetary demand alone are not sufficient to constitute increases in real demand. But increases in supply, unaccompanied by any increase in monetary demand, are fully sufficient to increase real demand.

To confirm these results, let us consider the price level formula developed in the previous chapter, namely, that the general consumer price level P is equal to D_C, the monetary demand for consumers' goods, divided by S_C, the supply of consumers' goods produced and sold. Thus:

$$P = \frac{D_C}{S_C}.$$

Observe. On the basis of this formula, if all that happens is that monetary demand rises, then the numerator in the formula increases while the denominator stays fixed. The effect is a corresponding rise in prices. If, for example, the monetary demand doubles, and that is all that happens, then the price level doubles. At the doubled price level, the doubled monetary demand buys no more than the original monetary demand. It is not the least bit larger as a *real demand*. The larger monetary demand is fully dissipated in the payment of higher prices and thus represents no increase in real demand whatever.

The only way that a larger monetary demand can represent a larger real demand, is, as stated, insofar as it is accompanied by an increase in supply. If, for example, when the monetary demand for consumers' goods doubled, the supply of consumers' goods produced and sold also doubled, *then* the doubled monetary demand would represent a doubled real demand. For the doubled supply would prevent prices from rising and thus enable the doubled monetary demand actually to purchase twice as much. An increase in supply is an absolutely indispensable condition of a larger monetary demand representing a larger real demand.

Further, the increase in supply, if any, determines to precisely what extent a larger monetary demand represents a larger real demand. If, for example, while the monetary demand doubled, supply increased only in the ratio of three to two, then real demand instead of doubling would increase only in the ratio of three to two. Our price level formula shows that in this case prices would be four-thirds as great (the doubled monetary demand divided by three-halves the supply). At four-thirds the price level, the doubled monetary demand buys only three-halves as much. All increases in monetary demand in excess of the increase in supply are dissipated in higher prices and thus do not represent increases in real demand.

Finally, an increase in supply increases real demand *without* an increase in monetary demand. The price level formula shows that an increase in supply makes the *same* monetary demand into a larger real demand—by virtue of reducing prices. For example, a doubling of production and supply in the face of an unchanged monetary demand, causes prices to halve. At the halved price level, the unchanged monetary demand buys twice as much. Thus, the increase in supply is not only necessary to the increase in real demand, it is also *sufficient* for the increase in real demand.

The principle is that under the freedom of competition, *more supply is the necessary and sufficient condition for an increase in real demand*. Its presence is what holds down prices in the face of a rising monetary demand, and reduces prices in the face of an unchanged monetary demand. In either case, it is what enables the monetary demand actually to buy more—that is, to become a larger real demand. In other words, more monetary demand without more supply just means higher prices and thus no additional real demand—it is not sufficient to create additional real demand. It takes more supply to make a larger monetary demand into a larger real demand. Thus, more supply is *necessary* for the creation of more real demand. But more monetary demand is not necessary to create a larger real demand. More supply will do it with the same monetary demand, by way of reducing prices (and, if it's a larger supply of labor that is in question, wages). *Thus, more supply is both necessary and sufficient to the creation of more real demand.* Supply, not more money, is what counts for real demand. More money is neither sufficient nor even necessary for more real demand. Again, only more supply creates more real demand.

Figure 13–3 presents not only the productionist aggregate demand curve, which we have already seen in Figure 13–2, but also the *relationship* between aggregate real demand and aggregate supply. It shows that while the quantity of goods demanded with a fixed quantity of money and volume of spending is potentially unlimited, the quantity of goods actually purchased—that is, the aggregate real demand that the volume of spending represents—is determined by supply. In the face of a given total expenditure of money to buy goods, under the freedom of competition it is supply that determines the price level and thus how much the given expenditure actually buys. For example, in the face of the same quantity of money and volume of spending, a doubling of production and supply from *SS* to *S'S'* is what results in a halving of prices and thus in a doubling of the quantity of goods that the same quantity of money and volume of spending can buy. In the same way, a four, eight, or tenfold increase in production and supply in the face of a given quantity of money and volume of spending is what would result in prices falling to a fourth, eighth, or tenth of their initial level and thus in corresponding increases in the quantity of goods that the same quantity of money and volume of spending could buy. (This is shown by the various supply lines *S" S"*, *S'''S'''*, *and S''''S''''*.) Thus, under the freedom of competition and the ability of prices to fall, the larger is the supply, the larger is the quantity of goods demanded for any given total expenditure of money. In this way, more supply creates more purchasing power, more real demand—that is, more demand in the sense of the willingness combined with the ability to purchase goods.

There is no inherent limit to aggregate real demand. It depends only on the willingness and ability of people to produce. If they are willing and able to produce more, and free to compete, then, given the quantity of money

and the monetary demand—that is, the volume of spending—the price level will drop correspondingly and the real demand will be increased correspondingly. In this sense, the formulation of Say's Law that "supply creates its own demand" is absolutely correct.

Of course, as I previously pointed out, more production and supply do not have to operate in the context of a fixed quantity of money and volume of spending, that is, in the context of an invariable money. Indeed, under a commodity money, any substantial increase in production and supply in the economy as a whole will almost certainly include an increase in the production and supply of the monetary commodity. It will thus almost certainly be accompanied by an increase in the volume of spending in the economic system, that is, by an increase in monetary demand as well as in real demand. In other words, as supply in Figure 13–3 moves out to the right, it is reasonable to expect that over time the aggregate monetary demand curve *DD* would also shift upward and to the right. Thus, we might associate with the various higher supply lines respectively higher monetary demand curves. However, while this almost certainly would happen, it is not essential that it happen. For, as we have seen, the increase in production and supply is sufficient for the increase in aggregate real demand.

2. The Referents of Say's Law and Its Confirmation by Cases Apparently Contradicting It

The major misunderstandings of Say's Law arise be-

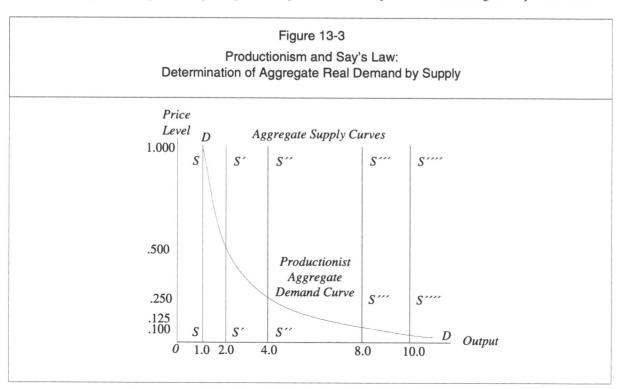

Figure 13-3

Productionism and Say's Law:
Determination of Aggregate Real Demand by Supply

cause of a failure to keep in mind that it refers both to real demand and to aggregate demand—that is, to real demand in the economy as a whole, not to the expenditure of money to buy goods and certainly not to the expenditure of money to buy the goods of any particular industry. When these referents are forgotten, it is easy to think that Say's Law is contradicted by everyday experience. Because then one interprets Say's Law as claiming that any time anyone has an additional supply of something, he will automatically be confronted with an additional expenditure of money by his customers to buy it. One then holds this interpretation up to the light of experience and finds repeated examples in which the ruin of producers can clearly be traced to an increase in the supply of the goods they bring to the market. And one concludes on this basis that Say's Law is not only false but absurd.

In order to overcome such misunderstandings, let us consider a typical case that on the surface flatly appears to contradict Say's Law, at least when it is misinterpreted in this way. I will show how such cases not only do not contradict Say's Law, but actually confirm it.

Thus, let us consider a kind of good with which people in every industrial country are already very well supplied and want little or no more of. Potatoes are a good example. Let us imagine that because of improved methods of production, the average potato grower is able to double his output, and thus that twice the supply of potatoes is brought to the market.

Just for the moment, let us put aside the use of money, and, adopting a procedure often used by the classical economists, imagine that our potato growers live in a barter economy. Thus, when they bring their potatoes to the market, they do not exchange them for money, but directly for the various other goods they require.

Even in a barter economy, our potato growers will fare very badly. A doubling of the supply of potatoes will lead to a very sharp drop in the amounts of other goods that a bushel of potatoes can be exchanged for. If a bushel of potatoes exchanges for any amount of goods less than half of what it used to exchange for, the potato growers as a group will actually be worse off than they were before they increased their production. Because in such a case the total quantity of goods they receive in exchange for their doubled supply of potatoes will be less than it was before. In other words, the doubled supply of potatoes will result in a reduction in the real demand for potatoes in such a case.

For ease of arithmetic, let us assume that the doubled supply of potatoes results in a fall of the price of potatoes expressed in terms of other goods—that is, the barter ratios of other goods to potatoes—to one-third of what it was initially. Of course, nothing essential would be changed if we assumed a price of a fourth or a fifth, or any other price less than one-half of the initial price. The essential thing is that we have a case in which an increase in supply makes the producers of the commodity concerned collectively worse off than they were before the increase in their supply. At one-third the price per bushel, a doubled supply of potatoes brings in only two-thirds as much in terms of other goods as did the smaller, initial supply.[42]

Thus, here we have a case which as much as any provides a seeming refutation of Say's Law. As part of it, we can imagine the complaints of the potato growers to the effect that here is their larger supply but where is the larger demand that Say's Law claims the larger supply must bring?

Well, let us find the larger demand, because it really does exist. Only it is not a larger demand for potatoes. We can find it by starting with the reduction in demand for potatoes. The producers of goods other than potatoes—goods such as shoes, shirts, houses, hardware, and whatever—turn over to the potato growers only two-thirds the shoes, shirts, etc., that they used to turn over to them. (That is, they pay one-third the price of potatoes times twice the quantity of potatoes.)

But now, we must ask, what do the producers of goods other than potatoes do with the portion of their goods that they no longer exchange for potatoes? The answer is, *they exchange them among themselves*. The producers of shoes are able to devote one-third of the shoes they previously exchanged for potatoes, to the purchase of shirts, houses, hardware, and so on. Likewise, the producers of shirts are able to devote one-third of the shirts they previously exchanged for potatoes, to the purchase of shoes, houses, hardware, and so on. And it is the same for all other producers of goods other than potatoes.

In other words, while the "other-goods" demand for potatoes does fall (that is, the demand for potatoes in terms of goods other than potatoes), the "other-goods" demand *for other goods* equivalently rises. There is less demand for potatoes in terms of other goods but equivalently more demand for other goods in terms of other goods. When both changes in demand are added together, we see that there is no reduction in aggregate demand in the economic system, despite the reduction in the demand for potatoes.

Say's Law, of course, promises an *increase* in aggregate demand, not an unchanged aggregate demand. Where is the increase?

The increase in aggregate demand is constituted *precisely by the increase in the supply of potatoes*. In a barter economy, potatoes are, in effect, the currency used by potato growers to purchase other goods. A doubling of the supply of potatoes brought to market constitutes a doubling of the demand for other goods in terms of

---

Table 13–1

How an Increase in Aggregate Supply Creates a
Precisely Equal Increase in Aggregate Real Demand

---

1. The "other-goods" demand for potatoes is down by one-third.

2. The "other-goods" demand for other goods is up by an equivalent amount, as the customers of the potato growers use their savings from the purchase of potatoes in exchange with one another.

3. The potato demand for other goods is increased by an amount precisely equal to the increase in supply of potatoes brought to the market.

---

potatoes. And the producers of goods other than potatoes experience this doubled potato demand in the form of doubled potato receipts.

Thus, if we add together *all* the changes in demand accompanying an increase in supply, we find that there is indeed an increase in demand precisely equal to the increase in supply—even though it may very well be the case that there is a decrease in the demand for the particular good whose supply has increased. There is an increase in *aggregate*, economy-wide demand precisely equal to the increase in supply. These facts are shown in Table 13–1, which summarizes our example of the potato growers.

It is obvious from the table that aggregate demand increases precisely to the same extent as the increase in the supply of potatoes. For the first two items—the fall in the other-goods demand for potatoes and the equivalent rise in the other-goods demand for other goods—precisely offset one another. This leaves item three, the increase in the potato demand for other goods, as representing a net increase in aggregate demand to the same extent. Of course, the increase in the potato demand for other goods is nothing but the increase in the supply of potatoes that is brought to market. Thus, the increase in aggregate real demand in this case is precisely equal to the increase in the supply of potatoes.

Obviously the same conclusion applies to any other case that might be imagined. In a barter economy, when the supply of a given good increases, it does not matter if, as a result, the quantity of other goods offered in exchange for it decreases. Real demand in the economy as a whole still increases precisely to the same extent as the increase in the supply of this good. For the decline in the other-goods demand for it is offset by an equivalent rise in the other-goods demand for other goods, while the increase in its supply that is brought to market constitutes a further increase in the demand for other goods. Thus, when all three elements of the change in aggregate demand are added up, the result is necessarily equal to

the increase in the supply of the given good that is brought to market.[43]

It should be clear, moreover, that even though the producers of a particular good may suffer as the result of the supply of their good being increased, the total gains in wealth in the economic system outweigh the losses precisely to the extent of the greater production of wealth. For example, while the potato growers are worse off, the producers of goods other than potatoes are better off in doubled measure. They receive not only the goods no longer received by the potato growers, but the additional supply of potatoes as well. The increase in the supply of potatoes represents the amount by which their gain exceeds the potato growers' loss.

If we return now to the conditions of a monetary economy, we will soon see how the potato growers are able to deal with their situation and to share in the benefits of the higher productivity of labor in potato growing.

We can assume that in a monetary economy, the doubled supply of potatoes results in the money price of potatoes falling to one-third of its initial level. The effect of this, of course, is that the average potato grower takes in only two-thirds as much money as before. Just as in the case of barter, he is clearly worse off than he was before the increase in potato production.

But now we must ask what people do with the money they no longer spend for potatoes. The answer, of course, is that they spend it for other things—shoes, shirts, etc. The producers of these other goods thus enjoy larger money revenues and incomes than before.

There is no increase in aggregate monetary demand in this case; just a decrease in the monetary demand for potatoes matched by an equivalent increase in the monetary demand for goods other than potatoes. But there is nevertheless an increase in aggregate *real* demand. And, again, it is precisely equal to the increase in the supply of potatoes.

For the same aggregate monetary demand now buys

all that it used to buy, *plus* the additional supply of potatoes. It is a larger aggregate real demand to precisely the same extent that the larger supply of potatoes represents a greater aggregate supply. If, for example, (allowing for the relatively small size of the potato industry in the economic system as a whole) the doubled supply of potatoes represents a 1 percent increase in aggregate supply, then the increase in aggregate real demand is also 1 percent, because the monetary demand buys 1 percent more goods in all than it did before.

Thus, Say's Law does not claim in any sense that an increase in the supply of a good means that its producers can be assured of a greater demand for *that* good and thus of greater immediate prosperity for themselves. It claims that an increase in supply is the source—the only source—of an increase in aggregate, real demand, that is (it cannot be repeated too often or stressed too strongly), of *real demand* in *the economic system as a whole*.

3. Partial, Relative Overproduction

It is necessary to show how the potato growers, too, ultimately come out ahead as the result of the increase in the ability to produce. In the course of this discussion, I will also show why the only kind of overproduction that can exist is *a partial, relative overproduction*—that is, overproduction in some industries counterbalanced by precisely equivalent underproduction in other industries—never a general, absolute overproduction in which the economic system as a whole overproduces.

Before economic theory can be brought to the rescue of the potato growers, it may be necessary to point out once more that this sort of case has been chosen deliberately, in order to present the opposition to Say's Law in the strongest possible light. For it is certainly not true as a general proposition, and I had no intention of implying that it is, that in every instance in which an industry succeeds in increasing its production, its producers suffer. In many cases, the producers in such an industry gain from the very outset, and gain more at first than they do later on from the improved ability to produce. If, for example, we had been dealing with a kind of good whose price would fall less than in proportion to the increase in its supply, then its producers would have been immediately better off as the result of increasing their production. But in that case, producers in other industries would have been placed in a temporarily worsened position. For example, early in this century, when the automobile was still a luxury good that only very few could afford, every improvement in the productivity of labor in producing automobiles so expanded the market for automobiles that the sales revenues and income of the automobile industry steadily grew as it increased its production

and reduced its prices. But in this case, there were short-run losses suffered by blacksmiths and horsebreeders and the like.

I would also like to point out that the fact that an industry as a whole may lose when its output is increased does not necessarily mean that everyone in that industry loses. For example, even in our case of the potato growers, if the doubling of production were the result, say, of one-fifth of the potato growers finding a way to increase their production by a factor of six, while the other four-fifths of the potato growers went on producing an unchanged amount of potatoes, this innovative one-fifth of the industry would earn doubled revenues at the one-third price, while the industry as a whole earned diminished revenues. Of course, in this event, the reduction in revenues would be all the more severe for the four-fifths of the industry that did not improve its ability to produce.[44]

But let us focus on the case as initially laid out, in which all the potato growers become twice as efficient and all lose as the result of it. This is the case that most strongly seems to contradict Say's Law.

Let us begin with the respective situations of the potato growers and producers in the rest of the economic system following the doubling of the supply of potatoes. The revenues and incomes of the potato growers are badly depressed—they are only two-thirds of what they originally were. At the same time, however, the revenues and incomes of producers in the rest of the economy are somewhat elevated, thanks to the spending of funds no longer spent in buying potatoes. (Since the funds no longer spent to buy potatoes are now spread over the whole rest of the economic system, which, of course, is vastly larger than the potato industry, the percentage increase in revenue and income outside the potato industry is far less than the percentage decrease in revenue and income in the potato industry.)

The effect of the resulting sharp disparity in income between potato growers and people elsewhere in the economic system will be that some of the potato growers, observing the higher incomes to be made elsewhere, will give up potato growing and move into other lines. As they do so, the supply of potatoes is reduced—it falls to something less than double. It is still larger than it was initially, but it is less than twice as large as it was initially. At the same time, of course, the supply of goods other than potatoes is increased as former potato growers now add their efforts to the production of other goods.

The consequence of these developments is that the price of potatoes rises above one-third of its initial price, while the prices of other goods fall somewhat. As a further consequence, the incomes of the remaining potato growers begin to recover, while the incomes of producers in the rest of the economic system begin to recede from their elevated levels.

Because the average remaining potato grower is able to grow two bushels with the same ease that he was originally able to grow only one, he will be just as well off in his capacity as an income earner as he originally was, when the price of potatoes rises to *one-half* of its initial height. Producing and selling twice the bushels at half the price will give him the same revenue and income that he had initially, when he had only his original number of bushels to sell.

Let us assume that the rise in the price of potatoes from one-third of its initial level to one-half of its initial level is accomplished when potato production is cut back from double its original amount to three-halves of its initial amount. (Obviously, we could assume any figure for potato production that was less than double and more than the initial amount. There is *some* intermediate amount of potato production that gets the price up to one-half and thus restores the incomes of the remaining potato growers. Three-halves is simply a convenient number to work with as representing this amount.)

Given the assumption that each potato grower produces double, a drop in potato production from double to three-halves is achieved when one-fourth of the initial number of potato growers leave the industry. The three-fourths of the initial number who remain, each producing double, then account for the three-halves level of potato output.

When this situation is achieved, the remaining potato growers derive the same benefit from the increase in the productivity of labor in potato growing as producers in the rest of the economic system. And so do the former potato growers, for, by this time, they should have been able to acquire levels of experience and skill in other lines of work sufficient to enable them to earn incomes equal to those they initially earned in potato growing.

In this situation, the average member of each group—the remaining potato growers, the former potato growers, and the group composed of everyone else in the economic system, who has no present or past employment in potato growing—earns the same amount of money revenue and income as he originally earned, and, at the same time, benefits from the lower price of potatoes. Everyone gains from the fact that he now receives three-halves the potatoes for three-fourths the expenditure of money, and thus has one-fourth the money he previously expended on potatoes left over to purchase additional quantities of other goods—goods whose physical production, it must be stressed, is now possible because of the availability of one-fourth of the initial number of potato growers to produce them.

These results are presented in Table 13–2, which is titled "Say's Law and the Process of Economic Adjustment." The table assumes that total revenue and income in the economic system as a whole are constant at 500 monetary units, and that initially the potato growers collectively earn a revenue and income of 5 monetary units. (Each such monetary unit could be taken as representing a billion dollars some years back, or ten billion dollars today. It makes no difference which, just so long as the size is held fixed at some definite amount and is

Table 13–2					
Say's Law and the Process of Economic Adjustment					
	Revenue and Income of Potato Growers	+	Revenue and Income of Rest of Economy	=	Revenue and Income of Economy as a Whole
I. Initial Equilibrium (Price = 1)	5	+	495	=	500
II. Doubling of Potatoes (Price = 1/3)	3.33	+	496.67	=	500
III. New Equilibrium (Quantity = 3/2; Price = 1/2)	3.75	+	496.25	=	500

large enough so that the example can be understood as referring to the economic system as a whole. Of course, for the sake of simplicity, the example greatly overstates the relative size of the potato industry, which is certainly much less than 1 percent of the economic system.)

Condition I in the table exists before the increase in the supply of potatoes. Condition II exists immediately following the increase in the supply of potatoes. In Condition II, the initial number of growers are each producing on average double the supply, and the price of potatoes is ⅓. Double the supply times ⅓ the price accounts for the decline in total revenue and income in potato growing to 3.33 from 5—a drop of ⅓. Revenue and income in the rest of the economic system are up equivalently, from 495 to 496.67. Revenue and income in the economy as a whole remain unchanged.

Condition III comes about after enough potato growers have left the industry to bring the price of potatoes up from ⅓ of its initial level to ½ of its initial level. At this point, because the average potato grower is producing double with the same effort that he previously produced his initial quantity, he earns the same revenue and income and is monetarily just as well-off as before the increase in the supply of potatoes.

Condition III further implies that we end up with ¾ the initial number of potato growers remaining in the industry, inasmuch as ¾ the growers times twice the output per grower equals 3⁄2 the output, which is the amount assumed to be required to bring the price of potatoes up from ⅓ to ½ of its initial level and so restore the income of the average remaining grower. Three-fourths the initial number of growers, each on average earning the same money revenue and income as he did initially, is what explains why the total revenue and income of the potato industry is now 3.75, that is, is ¾ of 5.

The ¼ of the initial growers who leave the industry increase the supply of goods other than potatoes. A further consequence of their change in occupation is that while revenue and income in the potato industry are partially restored in rising to 3.75 from 3.33, the increase in revenue and income in the rest of the economic system is equivalently diminished. Revenue and income in the rest of the economic system come to rest at 496.25, down from the 496.67 of Condition II.

As we have seen, the net upshot of all of this is that the average potato grower, former potato grower, and nonpotato grower from the beginning, now receives 3⁄2 the potatoes at ½ the price, for ¾ the expenditure of money. And the average person in all groups now has ¼ the funds he previously expended for potatoes, to purchase other things, which other things can physically be produced with the ¼ of the labor released from potato growing.

Now let us take this final state of affairs, in which potato production has been cut back to three-halves of its initial level, and the production of other goods correspondingly expanded, and use it as the *standard* for appraising the earlier situation, in which potato production had been doubled while the production of all other goods remained the same. In other words, we use Condition III as the standard for describing Condition II. From the perspective of this standard, it is clear that a *doubling* of the production of potatoes constituted *an overproduction of potatoes.* By the same standard, however, it is equally clear that going on with an unchanged production of other goods represented an *underproduction* of goods other than potatoes.

An appropriate description of things would be to say that more production in the economic system is always desirable and thus that a doubling of the productivity of labor in potato growing is desirable. However, it is a poor use of such an improvement in productivity if it takes the form merely of doubling the production of potatoes, in view of the fact that labor can be withdrawn from potato growing to increase the production of other things. Such a large increase in the supply of potatoes is much less needed than increases in the supply of other things. If the initial effect of the improvement in productivity is a doubling of the supply of potatoes, a mistake is being made. Losses and lower wages for potato growers, and higher profits and wages for producers of other things, will rectify this mistake and ensure that the effect of the higher productivity of labor in potato growing is an adequate increase in the production of other goods. Until this mistake is rectified, there is an overproduction of potatoes and a corresponding underproduction of other goods.

Thus, a doubling of the supply of potatoes represented a *partial* overproduction: it was an overproduction in one part of the economic system, while some or all parts of the rest of the economic system were correspondingly underproducing. The doubling of potatoes represented a *relative* overproduction, in that it made potato production too large in relation to production in the rest of the economic system.

In the case of a good like potatoes, it is possible that there is an absolute limit to the need, just as there appears definitely to be an absolute limit to the need for table salt. However, even if the production of potatoes, or any other good, surpassed its particular absolute limit of need, its overproduction would still be relative in the sense that the particular industry had expanded at the expense of the more necessary expansion of other industries. Its problems would be solved by the movement of capital and labor to other industries, to bring about their expansion. (In this connection, it should always be kept in mind that there is a need for improvements in the productivity of labor even in the production of goods with which we may actually be sated, such as table salt, because then those particular goods can be produced with less labor and the labor released can be used to expand production elsewhere.)

In the overwhelming majority of cases, and possibly even in the case of potatoes as well, however, production never comes close to absolutely sating the need for the good. In all cases of this kind, the expression "relative overproduction" takes on a further meaning. For the relative overproduction of such a good could be eliminated *without any reduction whatever in the absolute amount of its production.* It could be eliminated *if the production of other goods could be sufficiently increased.*

For example, when such things as automobiles or houses are said to be overproduced, the problem is never that the need of the buyers for that kind of product is sated. The problem is that even though the buyers would still like more of this kind of good, they would like more of other goods first. If they could have sufficiently larger quantities of other goods as well, then they would like larger quantities of this good, too.

For example, almost everybody would like, if not a second automobile, then at least the equivalent of a second automobile in the form of a higher quality automobile, and, indeed, the higher-quality equivalent of a third, fourth, and fifth automobile—and, indeed, probably several such automobiles. People would gladly buy more and better automobiles if their purchasing power increased sufficiently. With doubled real incomes they would probably easily absorb a doubled production of automobiles.

Our discussion of Say's Law implies that the only thing that can give people doubled real incomes is a doubling of production. If production doubles while money incomes remain the same, prices fall in half, and the same money incomes are able to buy double. If people's money incomes double, the only thing that can keep prices the same and thus enable their doubled money incomes to buy double is a doubling of production. Thus, a *general* doubling of the ability to produce would create doubled real incomes and thus, in all probability, a demand for a doubling of automobile production.

But, now, suppose that the *only* improvement in production is a doubled ability to produce automobiles. A doubled ability to produce automobiles does not represent a doubling of real income, but an increase in real income of perhaps only 10 or 15 percent, depending on the portion of their incomes that people presently spend on automobiles. If, for example, people are presently spending 10 percent of their incomes on automobiles, and now a way is found to double automobile production, this would constitute only a 10 percent increase in their

real incomes. For the increase that is constituted by a doubling of something that represents 10 percent of people's real incomes can itself represent no more than a 10 percent increase in their real incomes.

In this context, the automobile industry would fare very badly if it in fact doubled its production. Even though people would like a doubled production of automobiles, they can hardly be expected to devote *100 percent* of their additional real incomes to the purchase of automobiles. Yet that is what would be required in this case for the auto industry alone to expand production and for the whole of the increase in production to be desired in the form of additional automobiles.

With the 10 percent higher real incomes generated by the improvement in automobile production people would probably want some increase in automobile production, more or less on the order of 10 percent, but they would almost certainly want to devote the great bulk of their additional purchasing power to the purchase of goods other than automobiles. They would want more and better housing, more and better clothing, to eat out more often, to take more and better vacations, and so on. Before they can reasonably double their consumption of automobiles, they must be able to increase their consumption of all kinds of other goods commensurately. To obtain the purchasing power necessary to do that, there must be improvements in production not only in the automobile industry, but in many other branches of industry as well.

Then, in the same way that people want to spend most of the money they save in the price of an automobile on goods other than automobiles, they will also want to spend some of the money they save in the purchase of housing, food, clothing, entertainment, etc., on automobiles. In this way, the auto industry can find an additional demand equal to a doubled supply of automobiles. For just as its improved ability to produce creates a demand for the products of other industries, so their improved ability to produce creates an additional demand for its product.

If improvements occur on a wide-ranging enough basis, then people will want substantially more of practically everything, or at least improved versions of practically everything. The appearance of a problem of overproduction arises only when and insofar as an increase in the ability to produce is overly concentrated in a particular industry or industries. In that case, an industry's problem is that its improvement creates a limited amount of additional real income most of which people want to devote to other uses, besides the purchase of its additional output. What this industry needs is more improvements in production elsewhere, so that the growth in real income will be great enough to make possible the purchase of its additional output. If that does not happen, then what is necessary is the transfer of capital and labor out of this industry and into other industries so that a properly balanced, properly proportioned increase in production can take place throughout the economic system.

People's behavior here is guided by the law of diminishing marginal utility. They want to use their additional real income in a way that keeps marginal utility in balance in all the various lines of consumption.[45] Insofar as labor and capital can be directly or indirectly transferred from a given industry to other industries, with the result that an improvement in the productivity of labor in that industry can be made to show up as an increase in the output of other industries, failing to readjust the pattern of production to conform to the pattern of relative marginal utilities would constitute a disproportionate and wasteful use of the additional productive ability. It would represent concentrating what in fact is an improvement in the ability to produce in general within the narrow confines of the particular industry in which the improvement originates. So long as such a condition exists, there is a state of partial, relative overproduction, counterbalanced by a state of partial, relative underproduction elsewhere.

As a final, extreme confirmation of the fact that there cannot be a general, absolute overproduction, but only partial, relative overproduction, let us imagine a sudden universal doubling of the ability to produce. Everywhere, in each and every industry, the same labor is suddenly enabled to produce double. If each and every industry in these circumstances in fact began to produce double, it would be found that many industries were overproducing, but that to precisely the same extent many other industries were underproducing. If we had a doubled ability to produce and thus a doubled level of real income, we would not want double of each and every good. In the case of some goods, we would want only the same quantities, or only moderately larger quantities—certainly, much less than double the quantity. In the case of some things, we might actually want smaller quantities, as we gave up the consumption of inexpensive cheap, goods in favor of more expensive, higher-quality goods. But precisely as this last statement suggests, in the case of more expensive, higher-quality goods and in the case of virtually all goods previously considered to be luxuries, we would want more than double the quantity.

Thus, while we would want probably just the same quantity of table salt and matches, and possibly smaller quantities of things like chopped meat and cheap cars, we would want correspondingly more than double of such things as sirloin steak and restaurant meals, higher-quality automobiles, better homes, swimming pools, ten-

nis courts, yachts, and so on. If the doubled ability to produce initially took the form of a doubling of everything, then the first kinds of goods would be overproduced, but the rest would be correspondingly underproduced. And what we would want is a shift of labor and capital from the overproducing industries to the industries that were underproducing. Once that occurred, we would obtain the full benefit of our doubled ability to produce, for then it would be properly proportioned to our wants. Until then, much of the improvement in the ability to produce would be wasted in producing too many more of some goods while the production of other goods was not increased sufficiently. The only overproduction would be an overproduction on the part of some industries, that was fully matched by an equivalent underproduction on the part of other industries. The overall doubling of production as such would certainly not constitute an overproduction.

Say's Law and Competition

Our discussion of Say's Law—in particular, the example of the potato growers—confirms an important point established in Chapter 9 in connection with economic competition, where it was argued that there are no genuine long-run losers under the freedom of competition. The example of the potato growers confirms this point, in that it shows how the potato growers end up benefitting even from an improvement in production whose initial effect is to depress their standard of living and take away their jobs. For once the necessary number of potato growers leave the industry and relocate elsewhere, the effect on them is that, along with everyone else, they simply get their potatoes cheaper and have the income left over to buy more of other goods, which physically can be produced because the labor required for their production is no longer tied up in potato growing.

I would like to make a modification in the potato growers example in order to make it illustrate the way in which I think competition normally operates within an industry. In my original example, of course, I assumed simply that every potato grower doubled his production and that, as a consequence, all suffered. This represented a case of competition in which all the competitors are perfectly equal and, in the circumstances of an inelastic demand for the product—that is, a situation in which the price falls more than in proportion to the increase in supply—all temporarily suffer as the result of expanding their production. It is important to realize that in most cases, the competitors are *not* all equal. At first, only a small number are able to increase their production. Only gradually does the increased ability to produce spread throughout the entire industry. The effect of this is to enable those who introduce the improvement to gain from doing so, and to force a gradual withdrawal from the industry of those who do not introduce the improvement.

For example, let us imagine that initially only 10 percent of the potato growers are able to double their production. This represents an increase in the total supply of potatoes of only 10 percent. Given the nature of the demand for potatoes, the price will fall more than in proportion to the 10 percent increase in supply. Let us assume that it falls by 20 percent. In that case, the 10 percent of the growers who have doubled their output will greatly prosper. They will sell a doubled quantity at 80 percent of the initial price, and will thus earn 1.6 times their initial revenue and income. The entire burden of the fall in revenue and income that is experienced by the industry as a whole in selling 1.1 times the quantity at 80 percent of the initial price is experienced by the part of the industry that has not increased its production. That part of the industry simply sells its initial quantity at 80 percent of the initial price.

A withdrawal of capital and labor from potato growing will now take place on the part of producers who have not improved their productivity. And as more and more of the remaining growers adopt the more productive method, more and more of those who have not adopted it will withdraw from the industry. It is entirely possible that in this way, almost every producer who adopts the improved method will experience an increase in his individual revenue and income compared to what it was initially, while the industry as a whole continues to suffer a drop in revenue and income, with the entire drop being experienced by the producers who do not adopt the improvement. It is entirely possible that this could go on until the seventy-fifth percentile of growers doubles its output, just as the last of those who have not doubled their output leave the industry. In that case, even the last of those who adopt the improvement will experience a great gain as compared with not adopting it, and will never be worse off in their ability to earn revenue and income with the improvement than they were without it.

I think that this is the usual way in which competition operates. It rewards those who adopt improvements and puts the entire burden of an inelastic demand on those who do not adopt the improvements. The progressive adoption of the improvement finally eliminates the financial gains to be had by adopting it, except in comparison with not adopting it. Meanwhile the relocation of producers who did not adopt it into other lines enables them to restore their incomes. And, as previously explained, everyone ends up benefitting in his capacity as a consumer from the lower price of the product and the ability to obtain more goods for his money.

4. Say's Law and the Average Rate of Profit

Our discussion of Say's Law and the impossibility of a general overproduction can be reinforced by introducing alongside the price-level formula presented earlier, a second simple arithmetical formula—this time for the determination of the average level of money wage rates. Putting this new formula alongside our previous formula for the general consumer price level will enable us to see how increases in production can depress the profits of particular industries, but never the rate of profit in the economic system as a whole. The conjunction of these two formulas will also enable us later on to understand many other important economic phenomena, such as the cause and cure of mass unemployment and the determination of real wages.[46]

The formula for wages is simply this: the average money wage rate earned by those who are employed is equal to the aggregate demand for labor divided by the aggregate supply of labor. The aggregate demand for labor is to be understood as manifested in a definite total expenditure of money to employ labor in the economic system, that is, in total payrolls of a definite size, such as $1 trillion per year. The aggregate supply of labor is to be understood as manifested in a definite total quantity of labor sold, that is, in a definite number of units of labor employed, such as 100 million workers. Thus, for example, with an aggregate demand for labor of $1 trillion per year and an aggregate supply of labor of 100 million workers, the average annual wage rate per worker that results is $10,000. (Typically the period of time in view is a year, and the number of units of labor employed is in terms of number of employees. Thus, the average money wage rate earned is typically described in terms of annual earnings per worker. However, different periods of time than a year could be selected, and the number of units of labor supplied could also be stated in terms of the number of hours or days of labor rather than the number of employees.) Algebraically, the formula is

$$W = \frac{D_L}{S_L}$$

where W is the average money wage rate per unit of labor employed, D_L is the aggregate demand for labor, as manifested in a definite total expenditure of money to employ labor in the economic system, that is, in total payrolls of a given size, and S_L is the aggregate supply of labor, as manifested in a definite total quantity of labor employed.

Now, under a simplified view of things, total wages paid in the economic system can be taken as total costs of production, while the total spending to buy consumers' goods can be taken as total sales revenues. The simplified view of things rests on the assumption that all business firms are vertically integrated over the entire length of the production process—for example, that General Motors owns its own steel mills, iron mines, facilities for producing iron mining equipment, and so on, and that all other companies are in a similar position. On this assumption, the only cost of production that firms would have is wages, for that is the only outlay firms would make to outside parties, since they themselves would supply all of the materials and equipment at all stages of the process leading to the production of their ultimate products. By the same token, the only source of sales revenues that firms would have would be the consumers of the ultimate, final products. As we shall see, making the assumption of the complete vertical integration of business yields results for the theory of profit that are universally applicable, because the omission of spending for capital goods results in an equal understatement of sales revenues and productive expenditure, thereby leaving the difference between them unchanged.[47] (Of course, a full analysis must include the demand for capital goods in order to be able to relate the rate of profit to all the major phenomena in the economic system that depend on that demand.[48])

As should be apparent, in the circumstances of full vertical integration of business enterprises, total profits in the economic system would equal the aggregate demand for consumers' goods minus the aggregate demand for labor—that is, the spending to buy consumers' goods, which would constitute the sales revenues of business firms, minus the total wages business firms paid, which would constitute their total costs of production. For example, if we imagine the aggregate demand for consumers' goods to be 500 units of money, while the aggregate demand for labor is 400 units of money, then total profits in the economic system would be 100 units of money.

The following formula shows this simple relationship:

Aggregate Profits in the Economic System $= D_C - D_L$.

Now the use of this formula enables us to understand more fully why any overproduction must be a partial, relative overproduction, accompanied by an equivalent partial, relative underproduction elsewhere. For the first thing that should be clear is that *the monetary profitability of the economic system as a whole is absolutely independent of its level of physical production!* So long as the demand for consumers' goods in the economic system is 500 and the demand for labor is 400, profits in the economic system are 100. If twice as much or ten times as much, or any multiple whatever, is produced and sold at one time than at another time, aggregate profits under these conditions are still 100, and the relationship of profits to sales, costs, and, by implication, capital, is

still the same.[49]

Under these conditions, more production reduces the general consumer price level, but to precisely the same extent it causes a reduction in the level of unit costs. In effect, the larger output is divided into a given amount of consumer spending to produce lower prices, and into a given amount of total wage payments to produce lower unit costs. Total profit in the economic system is still the same because it is the difference merely between the two numerators—the demand for consumers' goods and the demand for labor—which are unchanged.

What we want to do now is to see how increases in production, while absolutely neutral with regard to profitability in the economic system as a whole, can have very major effects on the profitability of individual industries, accompanied by corresponding opposite effects on profitability in the rest of the economic system.[50]

Thus, let us now break up the economy-wide, aggregate demands for consumers' goods and labor into two portions: that of any particular industry or group of industries, and that of all the rest of the economic system taken together. As before, let us suppose, for example, that there is an individual industry that initially represents 1 percent of the economic system. If we assume that the economy-wide aggregate demands for consumers' goods and labor are 500 and 400 respectively, then this particular industry can be assumed to spend a total of 4 units of money in paying wages and to take in 5 units of money in sales revenues from consumers. The rest of the economic system combined, of course, then spends 396 units of money in paying wages and takes in 495 units of money in sales revenues from consumers. All this is described in Table 13–3, in the form of a matrix, in the portion headed "Initial State of Affairs."

It is certainly possible for this one industry to suffer lower profits, or even outright losses, as the result of an expansion of its production. For confirmation of this fact, we need look no further than to the example of the potato growers, the essential features of which are reproduced in the table in the form of a second matrix, which is labeled "Case 1." The only difference between Case 1 and the potato growers example is the introduction of the assumption that the industry spends 4 units of money in paying wages. The fall in its sales revenues from 5 to 3.33 when it doubles its production is thus responsible for a fall in the industry's profits from 1 to (.67), that is, for a loss of .67. However, it should certainly come as no surprise that profits in the rest of the economic system are increased to precisely the same extent, as sales revenues there rise from 495 to 496.67 while wage payments remain at 396. (Apart from the introduction of wage payments, the situation is identical with that of Table 13–2, under roman numeral II.) Thus, there is no fall in the economy-wide, aggregate amount of profit, nor therefore any reason for supposing a fall in the economy-wide average rate of profit.

Case 2 in the table depicts an increase in the given industry's production that is brought about not by a rise in its productivity but by the investment of additional capital that is withdrawn from other industries. Thus, as the result of the shifting of capital funds, the given industry is assumed to increase its expenditure on labor from 4 units of money to 8 units of money. In the nature of the case, however, this is at the expense of the rest of

the economic system cutting back its expenditure for labor from 396 units of money to 392 units of money. The result is that the particular industry doubles its production, while the rest of the economic system correspondingly reduces its production. Of course, unfortunately for the industry's investors, the consumers will buy the doubled output of this industry only for an expenditure of money that is less than doubled, that is, less than 10. This is implied by the fact that its selling price must fall, at least to some extent, in order to find buyers for the doubled quantity of its output. Thus, this

Table 13–3

Production and Profitability in the Individual Industry and in the Economy as a Whole

Initial State of Affairs				
	A Given Industry	+ The Rest of the Economy	=	The Economy as a Whole
Sales	5	+ 495	=	500
Costs (Wages)	4	+ 396	=	400
Profit	1	+ 99	=	100

CASE 1:	State of Affairs Following the Expansion of the Given Industry by Means of an Increase in Its Productivity (A Potato-Industry-Type Case)			
	A Given Industry	+ The Rest of the Economy	=	The Economy as a Whole
Sales	3.33	+ 496.67	=	500
Costs (Wages)	4.00	+ 396.00	=	400
Profit	(.67)	+ 100.67	=	100

CASE 2:	State of Affairs Following the Expansion of the Given Industry at the Expense of the Rest of the Economic System			
	A Given Industry	+ The Rest of the Economy	=	The Economy as a Whole
Sales	7	+ 493	=	500
Costs (Wages)	8	+ 392	=	400
Profit	(1)	+ 101	=	100

CASE 3:	State of Affairs Following the Expansion of the Given Industry by Means of an Increase in Its Productivity (A Luxury-Industry-Type Case)			
	A Given Industry	+ The Rest of the Economy	=	The Economy as a Whole
Sales	6.67	+ 493.33	=	500
Costs (Wages)	4.00	+ 396.00	=	400
Profit	2.67	+ 97.33	=	100

industry has doubled its total costs, but less than doubled its total revenue and total profits. Its profits, therefore, fall as a percentage of its costs and sales, and of its capital as well, which we may regard as having also doubled. Thus, for this particular industry, profitability declines as it expands its production.

Once again, however, to precisely the same extent, profitability in the rest of the economic system must rise! If, for example, this particular industry now takes in only 7 in revenue, say, which is the specific assumption made in Table 13–3, while it incurs total costs of 8, then the rest of the economic system takes in total sales revenues of 493, while incurring total costs of 392. Thus, the rest of the economic system earns 101 in profits, while this industry suffers a loss of 1. What the table shows is that to the same extent that sales revenues fail to keep pace with total costs in the given industry, they expand relative to total costs in the rest of the economic system. This is mathematically inescapable, so long as total sales revenues and total costs in the economic system as a whole remain constant. Thus, while profits in the given industry fall by 2, from +1 to -1, they rise by 2 in the rest of the economic system, namely, from 99 to 101.

Table 13–3 presents one other case, Case 3, which assumes that a given industry increases its productivity in the face of an elastic demand for its product, rather than an inelastic demand. It is described as "A Luxury-Industry-Type Case," in contrast to Case 1, which is described as "A Potato-Industry-Type Case." Just as in Case 1, the industry is assumed to find a way to double its output by virtue of increasing its productivity. In Case 3, however, instead of the doubled output causing the price to fall by two thirds, it is assumed that the doubled output causes the price to fall by only one third. Thus the industry's expenditure of 4 for labor is now accompanied by sales revenues 6.67. This represents an increase in its profits from 1 to 2.67. But just as the fall in the profit of the given industry in the previous cases did not represent a fall in the economy-wide amount of profit, so now the rise in the profit of the given industry does not represent a rise in the economy-wide amount of profit. The rise in the industry's profitability is the result of the improvement in its competitive position relative to other industries. By virtue of being able to offer its goods less expensively, it leads large numbers of buyers to shift their expenditures from other industries to it. Its additional products find such favor that the reduction in price attracts additional buyers more than in proportion. The obvious result, which the table shows, is that the increase in the given industry's profitability is at the expense of an equivalent decrease in the profitability of the rest of the economic system.

Thus, in all cases, the change in sales revenues, costs,

and profits of the given industry, whether in the downward or upward direction, is shown to be accompanied by opposite changes in the sales revenues, costs, and profits of the rest of the economic system. This, as I say, is the inescapable implication of the aggregate demands for consumers' goods and labor remaining the same. The table shows that while profitability in the particular industry can fall as the result of an overexpansion in its production *relative* to the rest of the economic system, profitability in the rest of the economic system correspondingly rises. It makes clear that the proposition that there can be no fall in general profitability, no matter how great the increase in production, is perfectly consistent with the fact that profitability in any given industry or group of industries can be reduced by an increase in its production. The reconciliation is that profitability in any given industry is determined by its *competitive* status, which changes in the industry's production relative to that of other industries can profoundly influence. At the same time, however, as I have said—and it cannot be stressed too strongly—the general profitability of the economic system as a whole is independent of the level of physical production. It is independent of all competitive factors—which, in the nature of the case, are always mutually offsetting. What aggregate profit depends on, basically, *is consumption spending minus wages;* from the perspective of the economy as a whole, the level of physical production acts only on the general price level and on the buying power of wages, not on profitability.

To say the same thing in different words: the determinants of aggregate profits and the average rate of profit in the economy as a whole are different than the determinants of the amount and rate of profit of any individual industry. The determinants of the former comprise above all the difference between the demand for consumers' goods (sales revenues) and the demand for labor (costs). Changes in the magnitude of production and in the price and wage level are simply irrelevant, so long as these two aggregate demands are the same. At the level of the economic system as a whole, the phenomenon of competition is not operative. Its effects on profits and losses are mutually offsetting. But at the level of individual companies and industries the effects of competition on the rate of profit are decisive. Insofar as increases in production place the marginal utility of an industry's product at a competitive disadvantage with the marginal utility of the products of other industries, its profitability is reduced or even wiped out altogether. By the very same token, however, the profitability of the rest of the economic system is equivalently increased. There is no effect on the aggregate amount or average rate of profit in the economic system as a whole.

Production and the Fallacy of Composition

If we keep the preceding discussion in mind, then it is possible to grasp more fully the nature of the mistakes underlying the consumptionist belief in the possibility of a general, absolute overproduction. Apart from the underlying mistaken philosophy that man's true, legitimate needs do not differ significantly from those of an animal, is, above all, the fact that it is possible for *any* given industry, at one time or another, to be in the position of incurring losses as the result of overexpanding relative to the rest of the economic system. Absolutely any industry could find itself in the position of our given industry and incur losses as the result of expanding its production.

The actual cause of its losses, of course, would be its *relative* overproduction, and there would exist at the same time a precisely equivalent relative underproduction in the rest of the economic system. But the businessmen in the industry concerned would be correct in concluding that the cause of their particular problem of low profits or losses was that they had carried their production too far. Not being philosophically inclined or familiar with classical economics, they would be neither aware of nor concerned with the effects of their action on the profitability of other industries. In looking only at their own particular industry, they would conclude, and again and again do conclude, that losses result simply from excessive production. And then, when there is a general business depression, and practically all industries suffer losses, they, and most other observers, conclude that the explanation is that *all* of the industries are overproducing. Their fallacy is the same as that which leads many businessmen to the mistaken conclusion that need is synonymous with demand and that what is needed for more demand is more needs because an increase in the need for any particular product relative to the need for other products that are currently being purchased can increase the demand for that product.[51]

The fallacy, of course, is the fallacy of composition—i.e., the error of assuming that what is true of part of a system is automatically true of the system as a whole. This fallacy is what makes the overproduction doctrine seem plausible. The fallacy of composition arises again and again in economics because of a failure to think out the implications of events in particular industries for the rest of the economic system. It arises because of a failure to realize that every given industry is in a state of competition with the rest of the economic system—either having its sales revenues and profits competed away by the rest of the economic system or itself competing sales revenues and profits away from the rest of the economic system. The fallacy of composition plays a prominent role in the consumptionist belief that a general, absolute overproduction is the cause of depressions insofar as that belief rests on an invalid generalization from the conditions of a particular industry to the economy as a whole. To repeat, any particular industry might at some time or other suffer low profits or losses as the result of a problem of partial, relative overproduction. But when it does, the rest of the economic system earns correspondingly higher profits as the result of a precisely equivalent partial, relative underproduction. It is the fallacy of composition par excellence to conclude that when all industries suffer losses, as is the case in a general business depression, it is the result of a general overproduction.

A general business depression has absolutely nothing to do with the level of production in the economic system. Less production would do nothing to alleviate depressions. It would only reduce the general standard of living. To whatever extent the profits of particular industries might be increased by reduced production in those industries, the profits of other industries would only be further reduced. And, as I say, the general standard of living would be reduced. Depressions are not the result of anything on the side of production or supply. *They are a monetary phenomenon.* That is, they originate on the side of money and spending—on the side of monetary demand, not production and supply. They are the result of a sudden contraction in aggregate spending for goods and labor, which makes the repayment of debt more difficult, reduces the general profitability of business, and precipitates mass unemployment. As the previous chapter showed, and as Chapter 19 will show more fully, this contraction, in turn, is the result of a preceding artificial monetary expansion caused by government interference in the economic system. In sum, it is the contraction in spending, brought on by a previous inflationary boom, that causes all the leading symptoms of a depression. The cause is *not* the increase in production.

5. Falling Prices Caused by Increased Production Are Not Deflation

A major implication of the fact that increases in production do not reduce the general rate of profit is the fact that *the falling prices caused by increases in production do not represent deflation.*

The fact that the falling prices resulting from increasing production are not accompanied by a decline in the general or average rate of profit represents an enormous departure from the conditions of a genuine deflation. In a genuine deflation, business profits are almost universally depressed, if not eliminated altogether. But we have seen that the aggregate profit of the economic system can be represented by the difference between the spending of consumers to buy products and the wages paid by business to produce them, and that so long as those magnitudes, and thus the difference between them, remain the same, the aggregate profitability of business is totally unaffected by the physical volume of goods and services produced and sold. Thus, when production increases, prices fall. That is perfectly true. But the general rate of profit does not.

By the same token, when prices fall because of an increase in production, there is nothing present that would cause any general increase in the difficulty of repaying debts, which is the most prominent symptom of a genuine deflation. A fall in prices resulting from more production in the face of constant sales revenues does not mean that there is any greater difficulty of earning any given sum of money. If, over a period of years, an increase in production, let us say a doubling, is achieved by virtue of business firms becoming more efficient, then the conditions of the case imply that the mathematically average business firm produces twice the output just as easily as it previously produced its original output. True enough, a unit of output sells for only half the price. But, by the conditions of the case, the average business firm *has twice the units to sell*. Its sales revenues in money are, therefore, just as great as they were before, and no more difficult to earn. Whatever money it is obliged to repay, does not come to it with greater difficulty than was originally the case.

It is certainly true that individual firms and whole industries could find it more difficult to repay their debts as prices fell. These would be the firms that did not improve their efficiency while their competitors did, and the industries that were relatively overexpanded. These firms and industries would suffer a decline in sales revenues and profits, and probably incur outright losses. But for every firm and industry in this position, there are other firms and industries that enjoy correspondingly increased sales revenues and profits and a correspondingly enhanced ability to repay their debts. Namely, the firms that introduce improvements ahead of their competitors, and the industries that are relatively underexpanded. There is no *overall pressure on debtors here—nothing present that operates against debtors as a class*.

Thus, it is simply incorrect to think of falling prices per se as "deflation." The falling prices caused by more production share only one symptom of deflation—namely, the fall in prices itself. They do not share two further, essential symptoms of deflation—namely, the sudden reduction or total elimination of business profitability and the increased difficulty of repaying debts.

What accounts for the combination of these three symptoms of deflation together is not any increase in production or supply, but *a decline in monetary demand*—a contraction of spending—which occurs as the result of a drop in the quantity of money or at least a slowing down of its rate of increase. A drop in total spending reduces prices. That is one of its effects. In addition, and totally unlike an increase in production and supply, it also reduces total business sales revenues. This reduces the availability of funds with which to repay debts. It makes it more difficult for the average seller to earn any given sum of money, because there is simply less money to go around. In addition, and again totally unlike an increase in production and supply, a drop in total spending reduces the general rate of profit, because while sales revenues fall immediately as a consequence of a decline in spending in the economic system, total costs of production in the economic system fall only with a time lag. For example, depreciation cost continues to reflect the larger volume of spending on account of plant and equipment that existed in the past.

Thus, deflation is a monetary phenomenon, not a phenomenon originating on the side of production. It should be thought of as a contraction in the volume of spending in the economic system, precipitated by a decrease in the quantity of money or slowing down of its rate of increase. For this is the underlying phenomenon that produces the *cluster* of symptoms that constitute deflation, not merely the one, isolated symptom, the fall in prices, that deflation shares with increases in production.

It is nothing less than absurd, indeed, vicious, to equate deflation with increases in production on the basis of their sharing this one, isolated symptom of falling prices while being of an absolutely opposite nature in connection with their effect both on the average rate of profit and on the general ability to repay debts. It is the wiping out of profitability and the sudden increase in the difficulty of repaying debts that is the substance of the evil produced by deflation. This has absolutely no connection with increases in production and the fall in prices brought about by increases in production. To view the fall in prices brought about by increased production as the same as deflation and depression is gratuitously to confuse the enormous economic good that is constituted by increases in production with the evil that is constituted by depressions. It is difficult to imagine a more profound or devastating error.

The Anticipation of Falling Prices

The question arises of whether the anticipation of falling prices caused by increases in production could have deflationary effects—i.e., could the prospect of steadily falling prices lead people to increase their demand for money in anticipation of being able to buy more cheaply later on? And, if so, wouldn't this be equivalent in its effects to a reduction in the quantity of money? And thus, on these grounds, shouldn't increasing production be called deflationary after all?

The answer to these questions is no. The prospect of falling prices *caused by increases in production*, rather than by decreases in the quantity of money and volume of spending, does not operate to increase the demand for money. And thus it does not operate to reduce the velocity of circulation of money and the volume of spending in the economic system.

The first thing that must be pointed out is that even if the prospect of falling prices caused by increases in production did increase the demand for money, which it does not, the increase would be of an essentially one-time nature. Once the increase in the demand for money took place, further increases in production and the falling prices they caused would take place with no further increase in the demand for money.

For example, let us suppose that there is a given, fixed quantity of money in the economic system and that initially the aggregate demand for consumers' goods is 500 monetary units and the aggregate demand for labor is 400 monetary units, as in our previous example in connection with Say's Law and the rate of profit. We can assume that initially production and prices are both constant from year to year. And now we assume that production begins to rise and prices to fall from year to year and, for the sake of argument, in response to the fall in prices and the prospect of the fall continuing, the demand for money rises. If it occurred, the rise in the demand for money would have the effect of reducing the monetary demand for consumers' goods and labor. For the sake of illustration, let us assume that the effect would be to reduce the demand for consumers' goods and labor by 10 percent, namely, from 500 and 400 respectively to 450 and 360 respectively. From this point on, it is clear, production would increase and prices would fall with no further increase in the demand for money and no further fall in the monetary demands for consumers' goods and labor.

Under no conditions could the prospect of falling prices be assumed to cause a continuing, endless increase in the demand for money. At most the prospect of some rate of fall in prices could plausibly be argued to result in some defined, delimited rise in the demand for money, which would then result in some delimited drop in expenditures and thus be satisfied. The only reasonable basis for a further rise in the demand for money based on the anticipation of falling prices caused by increases in production would be if the rate of increase in production and fall in prices *accelerated*. In that case, it might plausibly be argued that there would be a one-time further increase in the demand for money and a one-time further fall in the aggregate demands for consumers' goods and labor.

Thus, even if the argument alleging deflationary effects were correct, which it is not, it would still be essentially false. For at most, it would apply only to a transition phase. Thereafter, once the additional demand for money was satisfied and the volume of spending in the economic system stabilized at a lower level, production could go on increasing and prices go on falling at any given rate with no further increase in the demand for money, exactly as I have described.

As I say, however, there is no basis for assuming that falling prices caused by increased production bring about a rise in the demand for money. Insofar as the increasing production and falling prices are the result of improvements in the productivity of labor, the falling prices do not lead to a postponement of consumption and thus do not increase saving at the expense of consumption. This is because they are the accompaniment of the average person having a higher real income and thus being better off in the future than in the present, which prospect gives him as much motivation to consume more as the prospective increase in the buying power of money gives him to postpone consumption and save more.[52] Inasmuch as the two incentives are thus mutually offsetting, there is no overall tendency for consumption spending to fall, or saving to increase, as the result of falling prices caused by increases in production—not insofar as the increases in production and fall in prices are the result of a higher productivity of labor.

When increases in saving do occur, the demand for money does not increase, but, if anything, decreases. This is because, as we shall see after we have studied their determinants, the average rate of profit and interest in the economic system is always both positive and sufficiently high—in the absence of monetary contraction—to make it worthwhile to invest savings that are available for any significant period of time rather than hoard them. In such an environment, as we saw in the last chapter, the effect of an increase in saving is actually to reduce the demand for money, both because funds that are saved are normally available for spending sooner than funds that are held for consumption and because savings are the source of credit, the prospective availability of which reduces the need to hold money.[53]

Thus, the falling prices brought about by increased production do not result in a rise in the demand for money or have deflationary effects. Indeed, it should be realized that under a system of gold or silver money, an increasing ability to produce on any kind of broad, substantial scale almost certainly means the production of a larger quantity of these metals and, insofar as it represents an increase in a country's ability to produce relative to the rest of the world, the attraction of a larger proportion of the world's supply of such precious metal money to its shores. The larger quantity of money caused in these ways by an increased ability to produce implies a *growing volume of spending,* not a diminished volume of spending. Indeed, on a commodity money system, only an increasing ability to produce can bring about a growing quantity of money and rising volume of spending in the long run. Thus, under a commodity money system, the falling prices that are caused by increases in production actually take place in a context in which there is almost certainly an increase in the quantity of money and volume of spending.

What this means is that when prices fall because of increases in production, there is almost certainly some increase in the quantity of money and volume of spending taking place at the same time, as part of the increase in production itself, or at least on the foundation of the increase in production itself (the latter as far as matters pertain to international trade and the relative size of a country's production in the world economy, and hence its ability to garner part of the increase in the world supply of money). Thus, to whatever extent prices fall because of an increase in production, the fall is almost certainly not in full proportion to the increase in production, but only in proportion to the amount by which the increase in production exceeds the rise in monetary demand that takes place at the same time and in connection with it. For example, in conditions in which prices might fall perhaps 2 percent per year because of increasing production, the fall would almost certainly reflect a condition of the kind in which the quantity of money and volume of spending increased on the order of, say, 1 to 3 percent per year while the supply of goods increased on the order of, say, 3 to 5 percent per year.

Thus, falling prices caused by increased production are so far removed from deflation and financial contraction that they are actually part of a process in which the quantity of money and volume of spending grow from year to year. And, as we already have reason to know, this increase in the quantity of money and volume of spending both adds to the rate of profit and interest and, in increasing the sales revenues of the average seller in the economic system, correspondingly reduces the difficulty of earning the money that is required to repay debts. For example, in a context in which prices fall 2 percent per year because production increases 5 percent per year while the quantity of money and volume of spending increase 3 percent per year, the average seller in the economic system enjoys a 3 percent per year increase in his sales revenues. The position of the average seller—that is, a seller who has increased his production in accordance with the economy-wide increase of 5 percent per year—is that the supply of goods he has available to sell at the 2 percent per year lower prices is 5 percent per

year greater. Thus his sales revenues are 3 percent per year higher. In this case, the average seller would actually have considerably less difficulty in earning the money with which to repay his debts than when he borrowed the money. This is because, other things being equal, after he borrowed he would be able to earn 3 percent more money per year than the amount he earned at the time he borrowed, with no greater difficulty on his part.

Hopefully, on the basis of all of the foregoing, it is now even clearer than before that the existence of falling prices accompanied by a contraction in spending and the other symptoms of deflation and depression is not the result of increases in production. We have seen that the relationship between the prospect of falling prices and a greater demand for cash holdings pertains to falling prices caused by a decrease in the volume of spending, not to falling prices caused by increases in production. The decrease in the volume of spending in turn is the result either of a decrease in the quantity of money or a reduction in the rate of increase in the quantity of money, the latter in an environment in which the demand for money has first been artificially reduced by virtue of more rapid increases in the quantity of money.[54] In such a situation, the desire to hold cash balances increases and the velocity of circulation of money falls, in accordance with the principles explained in Chapter 12.[55]

In sum, the particular nature of the cause of the fall in prices is essential for the effect on the demand for money. Only those price reductions emanating from monetary contraction cause a rise in the demand for money.

Economic Progress and the Prospective Advantage of Future Investments Over Present Investments

Similar to the question of whether the prospect of falling prices resulting from increased production causes a rise in the demand for money is a question pertaining to the effects of prospective improvements in machinery on the profitability of investing in the machinery of today. Thus, to the extent that there is economic progress, the machines of the future will be more efficient than those of the present and therefore today's machines will be at a competitive disadvantage in comparison with them. The question that arises is whether this circumstance might operate to depress current investment by creating the prospect of losses or, at any rate, lower profits than could be obtained by delaying investment, and whether it might thus operate to cause an increase in the demand for money as well as to inflict losses on the producers of plant and equipment, who would have to cut their prices in the present in order to be competitive with the plant and equipment of the future.

The answer is that if economic progress took place only once, or were just about to take place for the first time, then it would be true simply that the machines of the present would be at a competitive disadvantage with the machines of the future, with the result that a rise in the demand for money might ensue and the new machines of the present might have to be sold at a loss if their competitive disadvantage were major. Observe, however, that the increase in the demand for money would exist only until the expected more advanced machines arrived on the market, and the loss would be borne only by the machines which did not embody the progress. The arrival of the more advanced machines would put an end to any increase in the demand for money. They would be in demand and would not sell at a loss. More importantly, it should be realized that if improvements in machinery are a repeated occurrence and are expected, there is no increase in the demand for money and no problem of the owners or producers of machinery incurring losses because of the prospective introduction of more efficient machines in the future.

This is because in such conditions, while the machines of next year may be expected to be more efficient and at a competitive advantage over the machines of this year, the machines of this year are, for their part, more efficient and at a competitive advantage over the machines of last year and previous years. Because of their greater efficiency and higher productivity, the machines of this year account for a disproportionately large share of total production, when compared to the machines of last year and previous years.

For example, if the average machine lasts twenty years, and the machines in use at any given time range in age from brand new to twenty years old, the current year's machines, being relatively more efficient and more productive, will account for more than one-twentieth of the production of the economic system and will earn more than one-twentieth of the total revenues attributable to machinery. If not for the prospective introduction of still more efficient machinery in the years to come, the machines of this year would be *extraordinarily profitable.* The fact that they, in turn, will be superseded means merely that a part of what would otherwise represent extraordinary profits must be set aside to compensate for the time when they will be of below-average efficiency. In other words, the effect of continuous economic progress is not to make the machinery of the present continuously unprofitable or less profitable, because the machinery of the future will be better, but to require a system of *more rapid depreciation in the earlier years of a machine's life,* when it possesses above-average efficiency. Its competitive advantage in the early years of its life compensates for its competitive disadvantage in the later years of its life.[56]

Similar observations apply to the case of inventory

and the fear that business would always have to sell its inventories at a loss, because of continuously falling costs and prices. The fact is that to the same extent that older inventories must be sold at a loss, newer inventories can be sold at a correspondingly enhanced profit. This proposition can be demonstrated for the case of any given rate of increase in production and any given ratio of inventories to sales. If, for example, production were to double from period to period, and half of current production were always to remain in and constitute inventory, then in any given period sales would represent half of the production of the current period plus half of the production of the previous period, which was half as great. Thus, two-thirds of current revenues would be attributable to half of the production of the current period and one-third of current revenues would be attributable to half of the production of the previous period. To the same extent that the half of the production of the previous period brought in deficient revenues, the half of the production of the present period that is currently sold would bring in additional revenues. Thus, the general rate of profit would not be affected. What is present here is nothing fundamentally different from the fact that businesses are profitable despite the fact that they run clearance sales on which, considered in isolation, they incur a loss; the losses on the clearance sales are compensated for by the profits on regular operations.

I have said that if economic progress took place only once, or were just about to take place for the first time, then it would be true simply that the machines of the present would be at a competitive disadvantage with the machines of the future, with the result that a rise in the demand for money might ensue and the new machines of the present might have to be sold at a loss. This is actually an overstatement of matters, because unless such a situation were pervasive, that is, applied to the greater part of the economic system at the same time, the decline in expenditure to buy the machines even of a fairly substantial number of industries would almost certainly not represent a decline in expenditure in the economy as a whole. The funds not expended for the machines in question would be made available for other purposes and be expended elsewhere. The only way that spending in the economic system as a whole would be reduced is if economic progress throughout the economic system, or at least in the greater part of the economic system, were about to take place for the first time or, what would be very similar, were about to undergo some significant acceleration. Only in such unusual cases, would spending in the economic system as a whole temporarily fall, awaiting the appearance of the improved machines.

While such a case is unlikely in connection with

improvements in machinery, it has important application to the labor market in the context of mass unemployment, as I will show in Part C of this chapter. Specifically, in the conditions of the prospective fall in wage rates and prices, and thus in the costs of investments, that mass unemployment entails, not only does an increase in the demand for money ensue, but government intervention that prevents wage rates and prices from falling lengthens its duration and thus lengthens and deepens the depression. This is because it prevents the restoration of demand that would occur upon the costs of investments made in the present coming down to a level competitive with their prospective cost in the future.[57]

Falling Prices and Accumulated Stocks

The case of goods such as housing and automobiles, that is, goods with substantial accumulated stocks and important markets for such accumulated stocks, may appear to represent a partial exception to the principle I have advanced that falling prices caused by increased production do not reduce the aggregate or average ability to repay debts because the fall in prices is accompanied by an inversely proportionate increase in the supply of goods.

In the case of goods with substantial accumulated stocks, the rate of increase in production and the rate of increase in the quantity of accumulated stock, while always ultimately tending to be equal, can be substantially different for more or less protracted periods of time, whenever the rate of increase in production changes. For example, if after being stationary for many years, the production of new houses should begin to increase at a compound-annual rate of 5 percent, the rate of increase in the accumulated stock of housing will be much less than 5 percent for many years. Indeed, if the accumulated stock of housing is initially 50 times as large as the annual production of new housing, the first 5 percent increase in the production of new housing will constitute an increase in the stock of housing of only .1 percent, that is, 5 percent divided by 50. Only after 50 years of a 5 percent compound-annual rate of increase in new housing construction, would the accumulated stock of housing also increase by 5 percent per year.[58]

If, under these conditions, the price of housing fell on the order of 5 percent per year starting as soon as the annual production of housing began to increase at 5 percent per year, the result would be that for 50 years the price of housing would fall more than in proportion to the increase in the accumulated stock of housing. A further implication would be a severe decline in the aggregate monetary value of the housing stock and, of course, in the ability of the average homeowner to repay his mortgage out of the proceeds of the sale of his house.

In answer to the possibility of this kind of argument, it is necessary to point out that in cases in which the accumulated stock is so significant, the price of a good should not be expected to fall in proportion to the rate of increase in its production, so long as the rate of increase in its production is so much larger than the rate of increase in the accumulated stock of the good. A 5 percent annual increase in the production of housing should not be expected to reduce the price of housing on the order of 5 percent, so long as all that it represents is a .1 percent increase in the total accumulated stock of housing. Such a situation would imply an extremely inelastic demand for housing.[59]

A more reasonable estimate for the extent of the fall in the price of housing under such conditions must allow for the fact that alongside the money expended in constituting the demand for new housing is the money expended in constituting the demand for already existing housing. Of course, even under an invariable money, the combined sum of these two demands is capable of undergoing change in the face of a change in the production and accumulated stock of housing. This is because people can shift the expenditure of funds either away from housing to other things, or to housing from other things. For the sake of ease of analysis, however, let us assume that the overall expenditure for housing, newly produced and already existing combined, remains the same. Under these circumstances, if the average homeowner were in the habit of moving every year, the annual expenditure for housing would initially be on the order of 50 times the annual expenditure for new housing, inasmuch as the total quantity of housing sold in a year would be 50 times the production of new housing. In this case, an increase in the housing stock of .1 percent would result in a decrease in the price of housing also on the order of .1 percent. In such circumstances, the fall in the price of housing would be precisely counterbalanced by the increase in the supply of housing, and the aggregate value of the housing stock would remain absolutely unchanged.

In reality, of course, the average homeowner does not move as often as every year. For the sake of argument, let us assume that he moves only once every 5 years (which is probably too conservative an assumption). In this case, if the existing housing stock is initially 50 times as large as the current year's production of housing, the overall funds expended for housing will be on the order of 10 (i.e., 50/5) times the funds expended for new housing, which is still an enormously greater magnitude and, as I say, probably too conservative an estimate. In this case, if the aggregate demand for housing remained the same in the face of a supply of housing sold in the market that consisted of the sum of one-fifth of the existing housing stock plus production of new housing that was

5 percent larger than the previous year's production of new housing, the initial fall in the price of housing would be on the order of .5 percent. For in this case, the initial overall increase in market supply would be on the order of .5 percent, inasmuch as the 5 percent increase in the current production of housing must be divided by the previous year's market supply that was 10 times as large as the previous year's current housing production.

In this case, there is some modest tendency toward a fall in the aggregate value of the housing stock that will go on over a protracted period of time. But what is highly significant in this or any such case is that even with total demand for the item being fixed, there is a pronounced tendency for *the regular business sellers*, as opposed to those who sell their previously purchased goods (whether consumers or businesses), actually to enjoy *growing sales revenues in the period of adjustment*. This is because the increase in supply is concentrated in their hands. And thus, from year to year they claim a growing proportion of the total funds expended to buy such goods. For example, starting with an aggregate demand for housing that is 10 times the size of the demand for new housing, the proportion of that aggregate demand that is claimed by new housing will go on increasing so long as the supply of new housing goes on increasing relative to the overall housing stock and thus the market supply of housing.[60]

The principle that emerges from this discussion is that as the result of increasing production, or a more rapid rate of increase in production, the proportion of any given economy-wide aggregate demand that is claimed by current production, as opposed to previously produced goods, goes on increasing until the rate of increase in the supply of previously produced goods catches up. Thus, from the perspective of *business*, the effect of increases in production and the falling prices they cause is analogous to the effect of the economy of one country growing relative to that of others. Namely, it attracts a growing proportion of the quantity of money and volume of spending of the economic system to the segment that is increasing relative to the rest of the system.

As for the value of the preexisting stock, what is present is only some measure of increase in the normal kind of loss of value that follows the purchase of goods. And this loss of value, I must point out, is mitigated, even if not entirely overcome, by the increase in the quantity of money and volume of spending that accompanies large-scale increases in production as a virtually inevitable by-product. Thus, even in the face of a growing population, there is almost certainly no reduction in the ability of the average member of the economic system to earn any given sum of money and thus to repay debts. (And, as we shall see very shortly, even if the growth in

population and the supply of labor did bring about modestly falling wage rates, the effect would be of no long-run significance.) Moreover, in the case of housing or any other expensive durable good, where the demand is entirely dependent on saving, it is likely that the achievement of economic progress or more rapid economic progress would be founded at least in part on an increase in the proportion of economy-wide aggregate demand that is devoted to the purchase of such goods. This would be the case insofar as the process of economic progress was inaugurated by a rise in the degree of saving.[61]

Thus, it is virtually impossible that economic progress or more rapid economic progress, would ever for very long be accompanied by any actual reduction in the aggregate nominal value of the stock of housing, automobiles, or any other such goods; rather, it would be accompanied by a continuing rise, and probably from the very beginning. It is equally impossible that it would cause the difficulty that the average member of the economic system experiences in repaying his debts to be any greater than whatever difficulty he normally experiences in repaying debts for such things as the purchase of automobiles or major appliances. For example, even if it were the case that the price of houses fell on the order of 5 percent a year, so long as the money income of the average homeowner remained the same, or fell only modestly, his difficulty in repaying mortgage debt would be no greater than is the difficulty of automobile purchasers, say, in repaying automobile installment debt, which debt is typically repaid out of income rather than the rapidly declining resale value of used cars.

In addition to all of the foregoing, it is necessary to realize that at least in the very important case of housing, the source of increases in supply is not confined to new production. This is because it is possible to varying degrees also to increase the supply represented by the preexisting stock—for example, through all manner of home improvements. To the extent that this occurs, the resale value of older units of the supply is maintained, for they themselves participate in the increase in supply. If our hypothetical 5 percent annual rate of increase in the housing supply were achieved mainly in this way, the price of a base unit of housing might fall on the order of 5 percent a year from the very beginning and there would be no necessary fall in the aggregate value of the accumulated stock of housing even under the assumption of the most rigidly fixed aggregate monetary demand for housing; at the same time, the resale value of older units of the housing stock would be maintained.

Falling Prices Resulting from a Larger Supply of Labor

I turn now to the final variant of the fallacy that falling

prices caused by increases in supply constitute deflation. This concerns the fact that a growing supply of labor tends to reduce wage rates. It might be thought that to the extent that wage earners have debts, a fall in their wage rates brought about in this way would constitute a leading symptom of deflation. This would not be so, however, for a number of reasons.

First of all, insofar as the larger supply of labor represents the employment of more married women or more offspring of the initial workers, there is no decline in the income of the average working *family*. There is just the fall in prices of goods that results from the greater production. Thus there is an increase in the real income of the average working family and, therefore, almost certainly an increase in its ability to repay any given amount of debt.[62] Insofar as the larger supply of labor is the result of immigration, then, it is true, there is a reduction in the income of the average working family already present and a correspondingly greater difficulty for such a family in repaying debts. But, by the same token, there is an increase in the income of the immigrant families and a correspondingly reduced difficulty of repaying debts as far as they are concerned. There is no greater difficulty of repaying debts on the part of the average working family as such. Such a general greater difficulty could occur only to the extent that the aggregate demand for labor fell. As we know, the only explanation for such a fall taking place suddenly and dramatically is a decrease in the quantity of money and/or an increase in the need to hold money, which latter follows from a decrease in the quantity of money or reduction in its rate of increase.[63]

Finally, it should be realized that if a fall in wage rates resulting from a growing supply of labor were accompanied by a greater difficulty of repaying debts, the difficulty would not be lastingly alleviated by a more rapid increase in the quantity of money that would prevent the fall in wage rates. As subsequent discussion will show, if the rate of increase in the quantity of money were stepped up to keep pace with the rate of increase in the supply of labor, the result would be a rise in the nominal rate of profit and interest by the same percentage. This means, for example, that if a 2 percent annual increase in the supply of labor were operating to reduce wage rates on the order of 2 percent a year, a 2 percent annual increase in the quantity of money and volume of spending, which would make possible a 2 percent annual increase in the demand for labor and thus prevent wage rates from falling, would ultimately add 2 percentage points to the average rate of profit and interest in the economic system. In other words, if the average rate of profit and interest would otherwise be 4 percent, now it would be 6 percent.[64] Thus, while workers would not experience

a fall in their money wages any longer, they would have to pay a correspondingly higher rate of interest on their debts. This, together with the reduced ability of prices to fall, which must result from the same more rapid increase in the quantity of money, would deprive them of any advantage of avoiding the fall in their money wages.

In reality, as we have seen, in a progressing economy, the quantity of money, volume of spending in general, and demand for labor in particular do all increase. As the result of the rise in the productivity of labor (and thus, one can presume, an increase in the quantity of money per capita), they increase not only absolutely but also relatively to the size of the population. And thus it is virtually impossible for falling wage rates to be the norm in such an economy. At the same time, however, the more rapid rate of increase in the quantity of money does serve correspondingly to raise the rate of profit and interest, including the rate of interest that wage earners must pay on any debts they incur, and it does serve correspondingly to diminish the rate at which prices fall. Thus while increases in the supply of labor do not actually serve to make wage rates fall from year to year, wage earners derive no permanent advantage from that fact.

PART C

UNEMPLOYMENT

1. The Free Market Versus the Causes of Mass Unemployment

It is now necessary to explain how mass unemployment can exist despite all that I have shown in Chapter 2 and in the first two parts of this chapter. That is, how it can exist despite a limitless need and desire for wealth and consequent inherent and ineradicable scarcity of labor, despite all the truths of productionism that follow from these facts, and despite the fact that, as Say's Law shows, all that is necessary for the creation of real demand is supply. Moreover, as I will show in Chapter 16, the process of production itself generates the monetary profitability that makes production financially worthwhile. It is necessary to show how mass unemployment is possible despite the existence of this fact as well.

There is a simple explanation that is perfectly consistent with all of these facts. It is that *unemployment is caused by an improper relationship between money wage rates and the demand for labor in the economic system.* Specifically, the average money wage rate is too high relative to the aggregate demand for labor. And since the aggregate demand for labor is determined by the quantity of money and the degree of saving in the economic system, one can say that the problem of unemployment is the result of money wage rates that are too high in relation to these magnitudes, as well.[65]

This explanation of unemployment is apparent in the formula I presented for the determination of the average level of money wage rates earlier in this chapter. Namely, that the average money wage of workers employed equals the aggregate demand for labor divided by the aggregate supply of labor, with the aggregate demand for labor being understood as manifested in a definite total expenditure of money to employ labor in the economic system, that is, in total payrolls of a given size, and the aggregate supply of labor being understood as manifested in a definite total quantity of labor employed. The formula, of course, is

$$W = \frac{D_L}{S_L}.$$

And an illustration of it is

$$\$10,000 \text{ per worker} = \frac{\$1 \text{ trillion}}{100 \text{ million workers}}.$$

The formula shows that with any given aggregate demand for labor, there is no limit to the number of workers that can be employed. All that is necessary is an appropriate level of money wage rates. For example, while a trillion dollar aggregate demand for labor employs 100 million workers at an average annual wage per worker of $10,000, that same aggregate demand for labor could employ 200 million workers if the average annual wage per worker were $5,000 instead of $10,000. By the same token, it could

employ only 50 million workers at an average annual wage of $20,000 per worker. The principle is that with a given aggregate demand for labor in the economic system, the number of workers that can be employed varies in inverse proportion to the average money wage rate per worker. Given the aggregate demand for labor as some definite amount of money, the division of that sum by any given average wage rate implies an inversely proportionate quantity of labor demanded.

When the demand for labor is diagrammed, as in Figure 13–4, the result is essentially the same as the productionist aggregate demand curve of Figures 13–2 and 13–3. Just as before, the demand curve is asymptotic, unit elastic, and potentially capable of purchasing an unlimited supply. And just as in Figure 13–3, under the freedom of competition what determines the actual quantity demanded and supply purchased, as opposed to the unlimited potential quantity demanded and supply purchased, is nothing but the supply that exists and whose owners want to sell it. Supply in this sense determines the quantity actually demanded—a quantity equal to itself—by virtue of its effect on the wage level, just as before it did so by virtue of its effect on the price level. Thus, as before, it "creates its own demand," so to speak.

Figure 13–4 shows that one and the same aggregate demand for labor is capable of being accompanied by full employment in the face of any magnitude of supply of labor seeking employment. The supply of labor seeking employment is what is depicted by the vertical line SS. Although only one supply of labor seeking employment

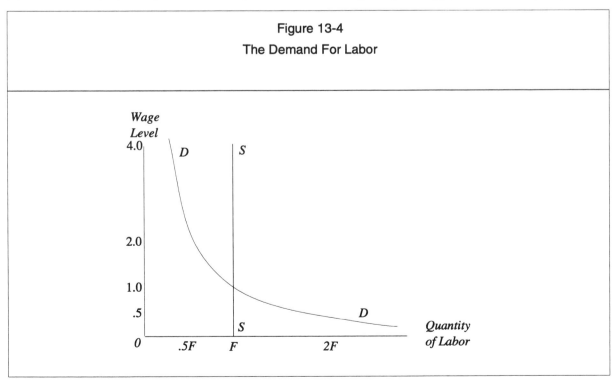

Figure 13-4
The Demand For Labor

is depicted in Figure 13–4, it is clear that the line *SS* could be placed anywhere to the right and still be accompanied by full employment. This is because no matter how much the supply of labor seeking employment increases, the quantity of labor demanded becomes equal to it, provided only that the level of wage rates falls correspondingly. The supply of labor seeking employment becomes synonymous with the supply of labor employed by virtue of the necessary fall in wage rates, which serves to enlarge the quantity of labor demanded to equality with the supply of labor seeking employment.

Figure 13–4 also shows that with a given demand for labor and any given supply of labor seeking employment, it is possible to have not only full employment but also, alternatively, either mass unemployment or a labor shortage of varying degrees of severity. Which of these possibilities actually exists depends strictly on the relationship between the wage level and the demand for labor. At the wage level 1.0 on the vertical axis, the quantity of labor demanded along the aggregate demand curve *DD* is equal to the supply of labor seeking employment, which is represented by the line *SS*. Hence, at that wage level, full employment exists. Accordingly, on the horizontal axis I have marked the point directly below the intersection of *DD* and *SS* with the letter *F*, to indicate that that point represents full employment.

However, at the doubled wage level 2.0 on the vertical axis, which causes the quantity of labor demanded to be cut in half, namely, to *.5F* on the horizontal axis, mass unemployment equal to 50 percent of the supply of labor seeking employment exists. On the other hand, at the halved wage level of .5 on the vertical axis, which causes the quantity of labor demanded to be doubled, to *2F* on the horizontal axis, a severe labor shortage exists, with twice as many jobs being offered as there are workers to fill them.

To make the same point in terms of the example of a trillion dollar aggregate demand for labor and a supply of 100 million workers seeking employment: while an average annual wage rate of $10,000 per year achieves full employment for this supply of labor, an average annual wage rate of $20,000 per year results in a 50 percent unemployment rate, and an average annual wage rate of $5,000 per year causes a labor shortage so severe that there are two jobs offered for every worker available to fill a job.

Thus, the difference between full employment, unemployment, and a labor shortage is a matter of differences in wage rates relative to the demand for labor. Depending on the height of wage rates, one and the same aggregate demand for labor is consistent not only with an unlimited potential quantity of labor demanded and thus with full employment no matter how large is the supply of labor

seeking employment, but also, as we now see, both with mass unemployment and, alternatively, with severe labor shortages. If wage rates are too high relative to the demand for labor, unemployment is the result. If they are too low, a labor shortage is the result.

Because of its great importance, a few further observations are in order concerning the aggregate demand for labor. Its constancy, indeed, its tendency to grow over time, is implied by the quantity theory of money. Its relationship to the demand for consumers' goods—and the wider relationship of the total demand for factors of production, that is, the demand for labor plus the demand for capital goods, to the total demand for goods, that is, to the demand for consumers' goods plus the demand for capital goods—is determined by the degree of saving in the economic system. Its relationship to the demand for capital goods is also determinate, but even in conditions in which the demand for labor might fall as the result of a rise in the demand for capital goods, the result is not against the interests of the average wage earner, as I have already indicated.[66] Furthermore, as we shall see, in the conditions of a depression and then of recovery from a depression, there is every reason for believing not merely that the demand for labor would remain constant in the face of a fall in wage rates, but that it would actually increase when the fall in wage rates took place and decline in the face of a failure of wage rates to fall![67]

Earlier in this book, I demonstrated the following points. The self-interest of buyers and sellers automatically operates to set prices and wages sufficiently high so that no shortages exist—so that, as I put it, quantities demanded are levelled down to equality with the supplies available. The setting of prices in this way is to the self-interest of buyers as well as sellers, and of poor buyers as well as rich ones. Shortages are created by government intervention into the economic system in the form of price controls, specifically, maximum price controls establishing legal ceilings, above which one is not allowed to sell. Shortages are exacerbated by the government's policy of inflation, which operates to raise the demand for the goods and services that are under price controls and which also creates the conditions in which price controls are imposed in the first place.[68]

I will now proceed to show that the case of mass unemployment is essentially similar. In a free market the self-interest of buyers and sellers operates to set wage rates low enough to allow the quantity of labor demanded to expand to the point of equalling the supply of labor seeking employment and thus to prevent or quickly eliminate unemployment. This process is to the self-interest of wage earners as well as employers.[69] Mass unemployment, like shortages, is the product of the government thwarting the operation of the market participants' self-interest through a policy of price controls—this time, various forms of minimum wages establishing legal floors, below which one is not allowed to buy or sell labor. In addition, mass unemployment is precipitated by the government's policy of inflation—at the point where the inflation results in monetary contraction.

In a free labor market, the existence of unemployment automatically tends to reduce money wage rates to the level required to achieve full employment. This is because it is to the self-interest of the unemployed workers to offer to work for lower wages than those presently employed, in order to obtain jobs. At the same time, it is to the self-interest of employers to confront their present employees with the alternative of accepting a cut in wages or else replacement by presently unemployed workers. Thus, the competition of the unemployed workers for jobs and the self-interest of employers operate to bring down wage rates. The effect of the fall in wage rates, in turn, is to stretch the funds available for the employment of labor and thus to create new and additional job opportunities. For it increases the purchasing power of payrolls and thereby enables more workers to be employed with the same-sized payrolls. In this way, what may appear as a competition among workers for a given number of jobs has the effect of increasing the total number of jobs employers offer. (As we have seen, what is present here is actually nothing but Say's Law in the form of an additional supply of labor creating a corresponding additional real demand for labor by virtue of increasing the buying power of payroll funds.)

Of course, even with a fixed aggregate monetary demand for labor, the fall in wage rates would not produce proportionately more employment in each and every company or industry, but only in the economy as a whole. Just as with any other increase in production, people do not want proportionately more of each and every good with the increase in production due to the achievement of full employment, but very different additional quantities of the various goods. Hence, the reemployed workers are employed in different proportions among the various industries and companies than those who are already employed.

It is appropriate to observe here that while my analysis is carried on in terms of aggregates and averages, it is vital that the *individual* wage rates of all specific occupations and industries, in all their particular locations, be free to fall to the varying extents that are necessary. While isolated wage rigidities will not prevent the achievement of full employment, their effect is to require greater than necessary reductions in wage rates elsewhere and to cause unnecessary disproportions in the relative production of the various goods, and inefficiencies in the methods of production that are used. This is because those who are prevented from being employed in the lines where wage rates do not fall, or fall less than they would in a free market, must crowd into other lines, thereby further reducing wage rates in them. At the same time, production is artificially curtailed in the lines that maintain high wage rates (and high prices) and artificially expanded in the lines that bear a greater-than-necessary reduction in wage rates and prices. Insofar as this is the case with respect to the production of capital goods, the effect is that the supply of some capital goods is artificially held back, while the supply of others is artificially expanded. The effect is necessarily a lower productivity of labor as compared with what would exist with the appropriate proportions of the various capital goods.

Full Employment, Profitability, and Real Wages

It is important to realize two further points. First, consistent with the discussion of Say's Law and the average rate of profit earlier in this chapter, it should be understood that the fall in wage rates and prices needed to eliminate unemployment does not reduce the average rate of profit in the economic system. Increases in production do not reduce the average rate of profit whether they result from increases in the productivity of labor or from increases in the supply of labor, as in the present case. To show this, we can use the same example as before, in which the assumption of the full vertical integration of business was made for purposes of simplification. Thus, if the aggregate demand for consumers' goods in the economic system were fixed at 500 monetary units and the aggregate demand for labor at 400 monetary units, the amount of profit in the economic system would essentially be fixed at 100 monetary units, and thus, the amount of capital invested remaining the same, the average rate of profit in the economic system would remain the same.[70]

This would be so irrespective of the number of workers employed for the 400 monetary units and irrespective of the resulting supply of goods produced and sold for the 500 monetary units. The fall in selling prices would not reduce the rate of profit because it would be preceded by a fall in unit costs to the same extent, based on the fall in wage rates. To state matters in an equivalent but more precise way, to whatever extent a larger output, in having to be divided into 500 of demand for consumers' goods, would reduce prices, that same larger output, in having to be divided into 400 of demand for labor, would reduce unit costs. At the same time, to whatever extent profit per unit was reduced, the increase in the number of units would precisely offset it, inasmuch as the fall in prices, unit costs, and profit per unit are all in inverse proportion to the increase in production and supply. The realization that nothing is present to reduce the rate of profit in the process of achieving full employment is necessary in order to answer critics of the free market, above all, Keynes and his followers, who claim that the process causes a fall in the rate of profit and interest to a level so low that investment ceases to be worthwhile and the demand for money rises without limit.[71]

The second point that should be realized, and which is no less important, is that the fall in wage rates that is necessary to achieve full employment does not imply a fall in the standard of living of the average worker—that, indeed, even in the short run, it would almost certainly result in a *rise* in his actual standard of living, and would unquestionably do so in the long run. The reason is that the fall in wage rates would be accompanied by a fall in the prices of consumers' goods to the same extent, thereby leaving the purchasing power of the average worker's wages—his so-called real wages—unchanged. In addition to this, the achievement of full employment would mean the elimination of the burden of supporting the unemployed, whether they are supported through charitable contributions or through taxation. This is a burden which is always borne almost entirely by those who are employed, even when taxes to support the unemployed are levied on profits or interest.[72] As a result, the fall in the prices of consumers' goods would tend to be *greater* than the fall in the average worker's "take-home" pay, thereby increasing the buying power of his take-home pay.

The conclusion that the fall in prices would be as great as the fall in wages follows on the basis of the formulas for the general level of wages and consumer prices. These formulas, once again, are

$$W = \frac{D_L}{S_L}$$

and

$$P = \frac{D_C}{S_C}.$$

The conclusion follows on the basis of the continued assumption that the aggregate demands for labor and consumers' goods remain unchanged, coupled with the further assumption that the productivity of labor remains unchanged as the number of workers employed increases and full employment is achieved. The productivity of labor in the present context means the output of consumers' goods produced and sold per unit of labor employed. If it remains constant as the number of workers employed increases, then a larger supply of labor employed means proportionately more consumers' goods produced and sold.

On these assumptions, the employment of more work-

ers requires an inversely proportionate fall in wage rates. But the employment of more workers also results in a directly proportionate increase in the supply of consumers' goods produced and sold. Since the increase in the supply of consumers' goods produced and sold is in the same proportion as the increase in the supply of labor employed, it results in a reduction in prices that is in the same proportion as the reduction in wages, given that the aggregate demand for consumers' goods as well as the aggregate demand for labor is fixed.

For example, in the face of a constant demand for labor, the employment of ten-ninths the workers, to eliminate an unemployment rate of 10 percent of the labor force, causes wage rates to fall to nine-tenths of their initial height. Because the productivity of labor is unchanged, it also results in an increase in the supply of consumers' goods produced and sold that is in the ratio of ten-ninths. In exactly the same way that ten-ninths the supply of labor reduces wage rates to nine-tenths of their initial height in the face of a constant demand for labor, so ten-ninths the supply of consumers' goods reduces the prices of consumers' goods to nine-tenths of their initial height in the face of a constant demand for consumers' goods. Stated algebraically, using an asterisk to denote the fixity of the demands, we have:

$$\frac{9}{10} W = \frac{D_L{}^*}{\frac{10}{9} S_L}$$

and

$$\frac{9}{10} P = \frac{D_C{}^*}{\frac{10}{9} S_C}.$$

Thus, the fall in prices is in the same proportion as the fall in wage rates.

Identically the same conclusion, that the fall in prices is as great as the fall in wage rates, follows on the view of cost of production as the determinant of prices. This is because if the productivity of labor remains the same, then a fall in wage rates implies a corresponding fall in the fundamental—labor—costs of production, and thus in prices.

I have said that the average worker's standard of living actually rises, by virtue of the elimination of the burden of supporting the unemployed, which has the effect of making the fall in his "take-home" pay less than the fall in prices. The following example illustrates this point. Thus imagine that in a state of mass unemployment, the average employed worker earns $400 per week and contributes $20 a week toward the support of the unemployed. As a result, his actual take-home pay is $380. Now, as implied by a 10 percent fall in average wage rates, imagine that the elimination of unemployment requires a drop of $40 a week in his wages, which is accompanied by a 10 percent drop in the general consumer price level. His wage of $360 now buys all that a wage of $400 did before. However, this worker must actually be better off now than he was before. Because even though he used to earn $400 a week, only *$380* of it was actually his to dispose of. For such a worker, therefore, the elimination of unemployment is accompanied by a fall in his take-home wages not from $400 to $360, but from $380 to $360, while prices fall in proportion to the fall in his gross wage rates from $400 to $360. In other words, while prices fall by one-tenth, our worker's take-home pay falls by only one-nineteenth. Thus, he is able to buy significantly more with his $360 of take-home pay than he used to be able to buy with his $380 of take-home pay.

There is really nothing surprising in the conclusion that the average previously employed worker comes out ahead, even though he earns less money. The conclusion does not depend on the choice of any specific set of numbers. It is implied in the very nature of things. Imagine, for example, a desert island which is inhabited by ten people. If one of them does not work and yet is to live, he must be supported by the labor of the other nine. If that individual now goes to work and supports himself, the standard of living of the other nine must certainly be improved, because now they will be able to keep for themselves the portion of their output which they used to turn over to him.

Exactly the same situation prevails in a modern economic system. What makes it difficult for most people to realize this is that almost everyone normally judges the economic effect of things exclusively in terms of their effect on money income and does not stop to consider their effect on prices. As a result, people are easily misled by the fact that the effect of the competition of a larger number of workers for jobs is a fall in the average money wage rate. What needs to be done to make one's thinking correspond to the facts, which are so obvious in the case of a desert island, is to realize that in the context in which the employment of more workers means lower wages, the sale of the products of those additional workers means proportionately lower prices. And thus the result is that the saving of the expense of supporting the unemployed works out to be a net gain.

What we have here, in other words, is another instance of the vital distinction that so often needs to be drawn between money value, on the one side, and actual physical wealth and the general standard of living, on the other. The two can go different ways in the context of the economic system as a whole, and we must not be misled into thinking that merely because something may operate

to reduce the average money income that is earned, it therefore operates to reduce the physical wealth that is obtained and the standard of living that is enjoyed.

Some economists argue that a condition of restoring full employment is a *drop* in real wages—a fall in prices that is less than the fall in wage rates.[73] The basis for this conclusion is the belief that the employment of more workers will be accompanied by the operation of the law of diminishing returns, as more labor is applied in conjunction with a given, existing quantity of plant and equipment. As reemployment occurs, plant and equipment will have to be worked more intensively. It will also be necessary to bring back into use older, less efficient plant and equipment that was idle during the depression. As a result of these circumstances, it is held, the increase in output will be somewhat less than proportionate to the increase in the supply of labor employed, and thus the fall in prices will be less than proportionate to the fall in wage rates.

In addition, it is held, there must be a recovery in profits, which are all but wiped out in the depression. And thus, for this reason, too, it is argued, the fall in prices will be less than proportionate to the fall in wage rates. Indeed, to cast this argument in terms of our supply and demand formulas and the discussion of the relationship between profits and net investment that will come in Chapter 16, it could be argued that recovery requires an increase in the proportion of workers employed in the production of plant and equipment, which proportion was sharply reduced during the depression. As a result, some significant part of the output of the reemployed workers will be retained within business enterprises and not show up in the current supply of consumers' goods, thus further limiting the fall in prices relative to the fall in wage rates.

Now the first thing that must be observed in connection with these arguments is that even if they were correct, all they would imply is that the fall in money wage rates necessary to eliminate unemployment would be accompanied by a fall in real wage rates no further than to approximately the level prevailing before the depression. The arguments about diminishing returns and the restoration of profitability imply that during the depression, the real wages of those fortunate enough to retain their jobs are artificially increased by virtue of those workers being able to work only with the newest, most productive plant and equipment, and by virtue of the consumption of capital. Thus the arguments imply that with recovery, and the elimination of those factors, the real wages of those who had retained their jobs merely fall back to a more normal level.

Secondly, it should be realized that even if these

arguments were correct, the fall in real wages accompanying the restoration of full employment would be of a temporary nature only. It is not possible for real wages to be elevated permanently on the basis of unemployment and capital decumulation. The restoration of full employment and the end of capital decumulation—the resumption of positive capital accumulation—means that as time goes on, better and better grades of plant and equipment will spread to the whole labor force, whose productivity will be raised correspondingly, with the effect of raising the average level of real wage rates to the same extent.[74] And, because full employment represents the use of a substantially larger labor force as compared with mass unemployment and thus makes possible a significantly greater division of labor, it will itself help to make possible the on-going rise in the productivity of labor that is attributable to a greater division of labor.[75]

Thus, even if real wages did have to fall with the restoration of full employment, the fall in money wage rates would still be to the long-run material self-interest of the average wage earner. This is so because not only would unemployment be eliminated, thereby eliminating the burden of supporting the unemployed, but also the assumptions of the case imply that the fall in real wages is necessary to the maintenance and increase in the supply of capital goods, and to the division of labor being carried to a greater extent, which also promotes capital accumulation.[76] These developments are necessary to increases in the productivity of labor and thus real wages in the future. Higher real wages today, obtained at the cost of capital decumulation or the failure to accumulate substantial additional capital goods that otherwise could have been accumulated, and at the closely related expense of the extent to which the division of labor is carried, cause real wages in the future to be lower or to increase by less.

However, the argument that diminishing returns and the restoration of profitability imply a fall in real wages, is by no means correct even in application to the short run. It overlooks both the elimination of the burden of supporting the unemployed and the fact that the approach to full employment is probably accompanied by a *rise* in the average productivity of labor, despite the operation of the law of diminishing returns in connection with a given stock of plant and equipment. This is because the increase in production takes place mainly in accordance with the increase in the employment of *direct*—i.e., "blue-collar"—labor, and thus tends to be more than in proportion to the increase in the *total* supply of labor employed.

As illustration of this point, imagine that in a state of mass unemployment, for every ten direct, blue-collar

workers working, there are ten overhead, "white-collar," administrative-type workers working. Now, with full employment, there are twenty direct workers working for every ten overhead-type workers working. Thus, putting aside diminishing returns for the moment, *output doubles with less than double the labor*—with only three-halves the total labor employed. The principle that the overall average productivity of labor rises with recovery from a depression is not affected if, because of the operation of the law of diminishing returns, output increases somewhat less than in proportion to the increase in the employment of direct workers, which would fully satisfy the conditions of the law of diminishing returns. Nor is it affected by the probable need to employ some additional overhead-type workers along with the additional direct workers. It holds so long and insofar as the unemployment is more heavily concentrated in the blue-collar ranks than in the white-collar ranks (which is usually the case) and output increases basically in accordance with the increase in blue-collar employment.[77]

Furthermore, the rise in the average productivity of labor that occurs is compatible with prices falling less than costs, to allow a recovery in profitability, and yet as much as or even more than wages, which also fall by less than costs. For example, wages might fall by 10 percent, costs by 15 percent (because of the increase in the average productivity of labor as well as the fall in wage rates), and consumers' goods prices by 12 percent. The fall in prices here is less than the fall in costs, which allows an increase in profitability, and yet greater than the fall in wages. Indeed, this very sort of phenomenon can be seen to have taken place in the recovery from the recession of 1982 in the United States. In that recovery, the reduction in unemployment was accompanied by the first rise in real wages to have taken place in many years.

But even if real wages did have to fall to make possible the restoration of full employment, then, as I have shown, the process would still be to the long-run self-interest of the employed workers, not to mention the self-interest of the unemployed workers, who would once again have jobs.

It should be realized that the fall in prices that accompanies the fall in wage rates in the process of eliminating unemployment greatly mitigates any greater difficulty in repaying debts that might be experienced by workers whose wages fall. And when the effect of the elimination of the burden of supporting the unemployed is taken into account, it is probable that in most cases, any greater burden of repaying debt is more than offset.

This conclusion can be understood in the light of our example of the fall in the wages of the average worker from $400 per week to $360 per week. Let us imagine that such a worker has to make debt payments and meet other fixed obligations, such as a lease, that average $100 per week. In that case, the funds he initially had available for meeting his other expenses were $300 per week—actually, $280 per week, when the burden of supporting the unemployed is taken into account. Now, with the fall in his income to $360 per week and the elimination of the burden of supporting the unemployed, he has $260 a week to spend as he wishes. This sum, of course, is $20 less than the amount he initially had available for purposes other than meeting fixed obligations. However, with the fall in prices of 10 percent, the buying power of these $260 is the equivalent of significantly more than that of the initial $280—in fact, it is equal almost to that of $289 in terms of the initial, lesser buying power of money, for at nine-tenths the prices, the buying power of any given sum is ten-ninths as great, and ten-ninths of $260 is approximately $289.

Moreover, even the fixed obligations of the workers are not permanently fixed. Within one to three years, practically all apartment leases come up for renewal, and in that time these fixed obligations come to be restated in accordance with the lower prevailing level of prices. In addition, within this time, many debts are paid off, such as most installment loans, and are replaced with smaller debts that represent equivalent buying power. Even mortgage payments can be reduced to correspond to the fall in prices, once a homeowner refinances his home at a lower rate of interest or sells his present house and buys another, equivalent house at a lower price. (As this last observation suggests, perhaps the only case of significant loss of buying power for wage earners occurs not in their capacity as wage earners but as homeowners, whose equity may be sharply reduced or wiped out by the fall in the price of houses. Of course, this loss in many cases is the loss merely of an equity that was created by preceding inflation.)

Finally, whatever additional debt burden, if any, the fall in wage rates might place on wage earners who already had jobs, it certainly does not place any additional debt burden on all wage earners taken together—those who were unemployed before the fall in wage rates, as well as those who had jobs. Before the fall in wage rates, the incomes of the unemployed workers were zero, which meant that they had absolutely no earnings with which to pay their debts. The fall in wage rates of the workers already employed is the foundation of a rise—the coming into being—of the wage rates of the workers who were unemployed and is the basis of their being able to pay their debts. Any greater debt burden on wage earners as a whole is not imposed by a fall in wage rates, which, in eliminating unemployment, at most serves to increase the debt burden of some wage earners while reducing that of others, but by a fall in the aggregate

demand for labor, which, of course, is also what precipitates mass unemployment. A fall in the aggregate demand for labor means a reduction in the total of the wages paid in the economic system, and, in the face of a given magnitude of debts on the part of wage earners, necessarily makes the repayment of those debts more difficult. Thus, the actual damage to the ability of wage earners as a group to pay their debts is done before the fall in wage rates. It is the result of a financial contraction.[78]

The fall in wage rates, as I say, at most merely redistributes the greater debt burden. And, as I have shown, in the process it actually improves the economic situation of the wage earners to whom the debt burden is transferred, by virtue of bringing about full employment and thus the elimination of the burden imposed on these workers of having to support the unemployed, while at the same time reducing the prices these workers must pay. And then, of course, following the fall in wage rates and prices, with the passage of time and the replacement of expiring debt contracts with new ones made in accordance with the lower level of prices, the greater debt burden is eliminated altogether. In addition, the greater division of labor and resumption of capital accumulation or more rapid capital accumulation that goes with full employment in a free market operates progressively to raise the productivity of labor and real wages. In sum, when unemployment exists, a fall in wage rates is a necessary and benevolent phenomenon that eliminates the unemployment and operates to raise the general standard of living.

A case in which the fall in wage rates necessary to eliminate unemployment might actually reduce the average level of real wages in a country is that of a relatively small country whose citizens are confined to the narrow labor market of their own country by other countries' immigration barriers. To the extent that the fall in wage rates in such a country achieves full employment by reducing the costs of production and prices of its exports, it is the real wages of workers in other countries that are increased. In this case, however, there is present not only the at least partially offsetting beneficial effect of eliminating the burden of the unemployed, but also the incentive to additional foreign investment in the country that is provided by its lower level of wage rates. And, of course, the workers of the country benefit from all wage reductions in foreign countries insofar as they lead to lower prices of imports into the country.

This case appears to fit present conditions in Ireland, for example, where there is a substantial unemployment rate. Ireland could achieve full employment by means of a fall in its wage rates, which in large part would make its exports more competitive and so expand employment in its export industries. However, for the reasons explained, the effect would be a fall in real wages in Ireland until such time as wage reductions abroad and the resulting decline in the price of imports into Ireland came into play.

This case has bearing on the conditions within particular industries and regions in countries of any size. Always the effect of wage cuts and the resulting reductions in costs of production and prices is to raise the real wages of the workers who buy the product. The rise in the real wages of the workers who help to produce the product depends on the fall in wage rates and costs of production and prices in the industries whose products these workers themselves buy.

Government Interference

It should be obvious from our discussion of how the free market operates to establish full employment that what is responsible for unemployment is government interference with the operations of a free market, specifically, interference of the kind that prevents unemployed workers and employers from pursuing their self-interest. Such interference, in the form of attempts to increase or maintain the level of money wage rates, forcibly holds the level of money wage rates too high relative to the aggregate demand for labor and thus prevents the number of jobs offered from coming up to equality with the number of jobs sought. Minimum wage laws and laws giving labor unions the power to force employers to accept artificially high union pay scales are leading examples. These laws push up or keep up wage rates and make the existing aggregate demand for labor inadequate to employ all the workers seeking employment. Unemployment insurance and welfare allowances that are high enough to be competitive with the wages that workers can earn also contribute to unemployment, by virtue of taking away the incentive to seek work.

The effect of these kinds of interference is greatly compounded by further government interference of the kind described in the last chapter, which has the effect of causing monetary contractions and thus actual reductions in the aggregate demand for labor on a large-scale. When this happens, a fall in money wage rates is made necessary in order to maintain the previous level of employment. But government interference with wage rates and with the incentives to work prevents the necessary fall, and so turns the reduction in the aggregate demand for labor into a cause of permanent mass unemployment.

The government interference that causes monetary contraction is, of course, the previous adoption of a policy of inflation—i.e., an increase in the money supply at a rate more rapid than the increase in the supply of precious metals—above all, the policy of encouraging credit expansion and the creation of fiduciary media.[79] The effect of this policy is to cause demand of all types, including the demand for labor, to increase to a level that can be sustained only by the continuation, indeed, only by the acceleration of the inflation. When the inflation is stopped, significantly slowed, or even merely fails to accelerate sufficiently, a contraction in spending develops.

In effect, inflation operates like a narcotic, whose stimulative effect requires increasing doses. If the narcotic is cut off, or available only in lesser quantity, or even just in insufficiently increased quantity, there is a crash. Inflation has these effects because it induces people to overextend themselves financially, in the expectation of gaining from the effects of further inflation.[80]

As we have seen, once underway, a monetary contraction can be accompanied, and greatly intensified, by an actual deflation of the money supply—that is, by an actual reduction in the quantity of money. This occurs as the result of a substantial number of borrowers becoming unable to repay debts to banks. Inflation and credit expansion had encouraged them to borrow heavily, in the expectation of gaining from the fall in the value of money caused by inflation, and from the rate of profit and rise in prices continuing to outstrip the rate of interest they had to pay, which was artificially held down by credit expansion.[81] When this turns out no longer to be the case, people find that they are saddled with debts that they cannot pay.[82] Their default on debts to banks then destroys the solvency of various banks, with the result that such banks cannot honor their deposits. Insofar as the deposits in question are checking deposits, the effect is a reduction in the quantity of money. Checking deposits held at a solvent bank are a means of payment, just as much as currency and coin. Checking deposits held at an insolvent bank have more in common with Czarist bonds. They cannot be used in making payments. As a result, as banks fail, the quantity of money is actually reduced.[83]

As we know, this causes a further contraction in spending, greater difficulties in repaying debts, and still more bank failures. Potentially, the process could go on until all of the debt-backed money supply—all the fiduciary media—had been eliminated, and all that remained was standard money—that is, money that is not a claim to anything else, but is itself the means of final payment, such as gold coin or bullion on a gold standard.[84] This appears to have been on the verge of happening in the banking crisis of 1933.

Knowledge of the fact that unemployment can be eliminated by virtue of a fall in wage rates and prices, and that government interference is what prevents this, implies that there is absolutely no necessity for any kind of "trade-off" between inflation and unemployment, as is claimed by the supporters of the so-called Phillips curve.[85] In a free market, full employment is achievable precisely by means of a *fall* in wage rates and prices. The Phillips curve analysis, however, is so imbued with the spirit of government intervention and Keynesianism that it is blind to the very possibility of this occurring. In effect, in terms of the most elementary supply-and-demand analysis, it fails to see how increases in quantities bought and sold can be achieved from the side of supply, at lower prices. It assumes that increases in quantities bought and sold originating on the side of supply are simply impossible and that only increases originating on the side of demand are possible. Only in that way can it arrive at the notion that a reduction in the unemployment rate must be accompanied by rising prices. As we shall see, where government interference makes it impossible to eliminate unemployment by means of a fall in wage rates and prices, it is also not possible to eliminate unemployment by means of increases in demand—that is, by means of increases in the quantity of money and volume of spending in the economic system.[86]

2. Unemployment and the 1929 Depression

We now know that monetary contraction is the precipitating cause of mass unemployment, which is then perpetuated by government interference in the labor market, which prevented the fall in wage rates necessary to eliminate the unemployment. In the early 1930s, the United States did not have a federal minimum wage law. And the labor unions, although already extremely powerful in the construction and railroading industries, were not nearly as widespread as they were later to become. Nor were the incentives to avoid seeking work nearly as powerful as they were later to become. Nevertheless, in this period, the federal government, under President Hoover, actively intervened against a fall in wage rates, and at a series of White House conferences obtained the agreement of the leading businessmen of the country not to reduce wage rates. Hoover, along with a majority of the businessmen of the time, naïvely believed that a fall in wage rates was equivalent to a fall in total wage payments and would thus result in a reduction in consumer spending and a deepening of the depression.[87] This mistaken belief was the reason he intervened against falling wage rates. Hoover's intervention was reinforced by the influence of the philosophy of altruism insofar as that philosophy played a role in the decisions of businessmen. For altruism too implies that employers should not take advantage of the existence of unemployment to reduce wage rates.[88]

The effect of such interference was that the fall in wage rates took place at a much slower rate than in any previous depression. Average wage rates dropped less than 2.5 percent in 1930 and only about 6.5 percent in 1931.[89] In contrast, they had dropped 19 percent in one year in the depression of 1920–21, which was extremely short-lived as a result.[90]

The effect of the failure of wage rates to fall was an unnecessary deepening of the depression, requiring a much greater fall in wage rates to restore full employment than would have been necessary if they had been allowed to fall right away. This was the case because businessmen who contemplated investments in plant and equipment and inventory accumulation had to realize that until wage rates fell, the level of construction costs and inventory acquisition costs was substantially higher in the present than it was likely to be in the future, with no compensating advantage of lower costs in the present compared with the past.[91] As a result, businessmen had a powerful incentive to postpone such investments—and did postpone them. Investment spending for plant and equipment and the net change in business inventories fell by 37 percent in 1930, by 45 percent in 1931, and by 83 percent in 1932![92]

This collapse in investment spending and inventory holdings, because of the failure of wage rates to fall, caused a virtual wiping out of business profitability. The wiping out of business profitability ensued because the collapse in plant and equipment spending meant a corresponding reduction in business sales revenues in the economic system, while depreciation costs, reflecting the plant and equipment spending of many prior years, could hardly fall at all. Similarly, the drop in spending for inventory and work in progress also meant a corresponding decline in sales revenues in the economic system. But cost of goods sold continued to reflect the higher outlays for inventory and work in progress made in previous years, and thus fell only with a lag.[93] As a result, with sales revenues reduced far more than the costs deducted from those sales revenues, profits were slashed in tandem with the fall in investment.

With the decline in sales revenues and profits came a corresponding diminution of the ability of business firms to repay debt. Thus, as a further result, bank failures were precipitated which otherwise need not have occurred. The deflation of the money supply caused by these bank failures, of course, resulted in further declines in the volume of spending, and thus in more unemployment and in a need for a still greater decline in wage rates if full employment were to be restored.

In creating the prospect that investments made in the present would be at a major competitive disadvantage with investments made in the future, the effect of the failure of wage rates to fall, or to fall sufficiently, was to block a major source of the inherent profitability that exists in a free economy in the form of virtual "springs to profitability," as it were, whose nature I will explain later in this book. Had wage rates fallen to their equilibrium level, so that there would have been no problem of investments made in the present being at a competitive disadvantage with investments made in the future, then, as we shall see, the very fact of the absence of profitability, or its unduly low rate, would itself have provided an impetus to an increase in the degree of capital intensiveness in the economic system and thus to stepped up investment and thereby the restoration of profitability. It could not do so, however, in an environment in which more-capital-intensive investments made in the present were also likely to turn out to be losing propositions in competition with more-capital-intensive investments made in the future.[94]

It should be observed, of course, that an important implication of the fact that until wage rates fall to their equilibrium level, investment spending is postponed, is that when wage rates do fall to their equilibrium level, *the demand for labor actually increases.* This is because at that point investment spending is restored. An important implication of this increase in the demand for labor, in turn, is that it is actually a mistake to look at the level of total payroll spending in the depths of a depression and to assume that the fall in wage rates necessary to achieve full employment must be such as to permit the full number of workers to be employed with that level of payroll spending. Actually, the necessary fall in wage rates is substantially less than this, because the fall in wage rates to the point of full employment will be accompanied by a rise in total payroll spending in conjunction with the decline in the demand for money that occurs as the result of the restoration of the competitiveness of investments made in the present with investments made in the future.

With the restoration of investment spending, of course, comes a restoration of general business profitability as well. For business sales revenues now rise relative to depreciation costs and cost of goods sold. Thus, the fall in wage rates to their new equilibrium level is the foundation not only of the restoration of full employment, but also of investment spending and general business profitability.[95]

3. Unemployment, the New Deal, and World War II

I have explained how government interference in the early 1930s prevented a fall in wage rates from eliminating unemployment and thus deepened the depression and greatly intensified the problem of unemployment. The

monetary contraction which represented the onset of the depression was also the product of government interference, as I have shown.[96] Specifically, it was the product of the expansionary monetary policy of the Federal Reserve System and foreign central banks in the 1920s, which built on a base laid by the massive inflations of World War I. This led to a rise in the velocity of circulation of money, which could be sustained only by the continuation—indeed, ultimately, only by the acceleration—of inflation and credit expansion. It also led to the incurrence of an even greater increase in the volume of debt, because inflation in the form of credit expansion holds interest rates at an artificially low level relative to the higher rate of profit and the rise in prices it causes. It thus encourages people to contract larger volumes of debt relative to their already artificially increased revenues, incomes, and asset values.[97] In addition, the process of inflation and credit expansion leads to numerous malinvestments—investments whose profitability is created and exists only so long as the inflation and credit expansion continue or accelerate.[98] Finally, the potential for the actual deflation of the money supply was also created by government interference—interference in support of fractional reserve banking, in order to make credit expansion possible. This form of interference spanned generations, as previously explained.[99] Having thus created all the necessary potential for a monetary contraction, that potential was actualized by the Federal Reserve's return to a very modest 1.1 percent compound annual rate of increase in the money supply between June 1925 and June 1929.[100]

Starting in 1933, with the New Deal and the overthrow of the gold standard, the government was able to inaugurate a policy of permanent inflation. Since 1933, the quantity of money and the total volume of spending in the economic system—including, of course, payroll spending—has increased significantly in almost every year. Despite the rise in payroll spending, mass unemployment continued in the United States until the country's entry into World War II. It did so, because the far more powerful labor-union movement created under the New Deal was able to increase wage rates at a substantial rate even in the midst of mass unemployment, with the result that the larger payrolls achieved by inflation could not employ correspondingly more labor or, indeed, enough additional labor to make any major headway in eliminating unemployment. (The rates of increase in average annual wages paid by private employers for the years 1934 to 1937 were 5.7 percent, 4.9 percent, 5.6 percent, and 8.3 percent respectively.[101]) Thus, while approximately 12 million workers were reported as unemployed in 1932, and 12.8 million in 1933, the numbers for 1934–1940 were not radically reduced. Indeed, when the substantial numbers of workers employed by the government in various artificial work-relief programs are added to the number of workers reported as openly unemployed, the unemployment record turns out to be as follows: 1933: 13.5 million; 1934: 12.7 million; 1935: 12.1 million; 1936: 11.4 million; 1937: 9.3 million; 1938: 12.5 million; 1939: 11.5 million; 1940: 9.9 million.[102]

The increase in union power began with The Norris-La Guardia Act of 1932, passed in the final year of the Hoover administration. This act prohibited the granting of federal court injunctions against mass picketing and other forms of union coercion. It was followed by the National Industrial Recovery Act of 1933, which was subsequently declared unconstitutional but whose provisions dealing with labor were reinstated in the Wagner Act of 1935. This legislation compelled employers to recognize labor unions and to bargain with them. These laws were the basis of the unionization of such major industries as steel, automobiles, coal, rubber, clothing, meatpacking, and cement. Their result was to compel even most nonunion employers to match union wage increases, lest they too be unionized and end up not only having to pay the higher union wages but also lose much of their ability to determine methods of production. The Fair Labor Standards Act of 1938 established a federal minimum wage. Thus, prounion legislation and minimum wage legislation substantially raised wage rates in the midst of mass unemployment and thereby prevented the larger payrolls produced by inflation from substantially reducing, let alone eliminating, unemployment.

Furthermore, insofar as the additional employment which resulted in connection with the policy of inflation was employment on government projects, or in providing the materials and equipment for such projects, it did not represent any real solution to the unemployment problem, as I have indicated. Indeed, it represented an actual *loss* to the workers producing in the rest of the economic system, who had to support it. The workers in the rest of the economic system had to supply goods and services to the workers newly employed in connection with government projects—substantially more goods and services than would have had to be provided if those workers had remained unemployed. This is because they had to supply them with a higher standard of living than the newly employed workers would have received had they remained unemployed. In addition, they had to supply them with materials and equipment with which to work, which would not have been required had those workers remained unemployed. But all that the workers in the rest of the economic system could receive from those newly employed workers was *the government projects,* which were undertaken not because of any actual value on their part but because of a desire to create

employment. In the circumstances, the projects could not constitute compensation to those whose goods and services had to pay for them. In effect, a broken circle existed: part of the output of those already employed—a greater part than before—was turned over to those newly employed, but the output of the newly employed went to the government and thus could not constitute compensation to those already employed. In effect, it was a case of Mr. A giving employment to Mr. B, and sending the bill to Mr. C. The last individual, Mr. C—the mass of the general public—necessarily lost by such an arrangement.

(As an example of this phenomenon that I give to my students, I ask them to imagine that our class constitutes an economic system and that the students in the front row are unemployed. I assume the role of the government and offer to employ those students in doing various jobs for me. In a closed economic system, the rest of the class is the only possible source of goods and services for these reemployed students. Thus, in one way or another it will be billed for their employment. I point out how much greater its bill will be if I employ the previously unemployed students in a project that requires the use of substantial materials and equipment, such as building a house for me.)

Thus, to the extent that it exists, the effect of government-caused reemployment is to reduce the standard of living of those already employed. This is in sharpest contrast to the effect of reemployment achieved by the competition of a free market, which is to eliminate the burden of supporting the unemployed. In a free market, an unemployed worker gets a job and supports himself. Under government make-work schemes, the previously unemployed worker becomes a greater burden than before.

The problem of mass unemployment came to an end with the country's entry into World War II. This happened not because, as the consumptionists believe, the war created new and additional needs and desires for wealth. As I have shown, for all practical purposes the need and desire for wealth are always infinite. It did not even happen because the war was largely financed by a massive creation of new and additional money. In a context in which monopoly labor unions and other government intervention prevent unemployment from being eliminated by a fall in wage rates, the same forces operate to cause a rise in wage rates in the face of a rising demand for labor and thus to make the rising demand for labor incapable of eliminating the unemployment.

Why Inflation Cannot Achieve Full Employment

As I have just indicated, in a context of powerful monopoly labor unions, inflation of the money supply, by itself, cannot achieve full employment. This is because it removes the brake on union demands for higher wages. Its very existence makes it possible for the unions to pursue their policy of raising wage rates, even in the midst of mass unemployment, because it puts them in the position of being able to do so without fear of causing still greater unemployment of their members. For, with inflation, employers have the necessary funds to pay higher wage rates to an unchanged number of workers, and buyers of products have the necessary funds to buy an unchanged quantity of output at the higher prices corresponding to the higher wage rates. In addition, the unions are encouraged in their demands because, as we have seen, the spending of a larger quantity of money operates to increase nominal profits. The rise in profits operates as a red flag to the unions, signalling an automatic justification in their eyes for a rise in wage rates. Finally, as soon as the increase in the quantity of money and volume of spending begin to raise prices—whether because they encounter goods available only in limited quantity, whose prices must rise in the face of an increased demand, or because they lead to a rise in wage rates and thus costs of production, in the ways just described—the unions feel entitled to demand wage increases to keep pace with the price increases. For these reasons, in a context in which a fall in wages and prices is prevented from achieving full employment, a policy of inflation by itself also cannot achieve full employment.

Inflation Plus Price and Wage Controls

What made it possible for World War II to be accompanied by the restoration of full employment was not even the drafting of more than twelve million men into the armed forces, though this did make some contribution. For insofar as these men had jobs and were supporting, or helping to support, families before our involvement in the war, their disappearance from the labor market necessarily caused large numbers of women and youths to enter the labor market in order to serve as substitute breadwinners. The reason there was a larger total number of jobs available when these groups entered the labor market was the combination of a policy of massive inflation coupled with *wage and price controls.*

The effect of this combination was that when inflation raised the demand for labor and products, wage and price controls prevented a corresponding rise in wage rates and prices. Thus, the larger volumes of spending for labor and products were able to purchase larger quantities of labor and products. Indeed, very quickly, mass unemployment and a situation of unsalable goods was transformed into an actual *shortage* of labor and products. In this way, the war did solve the unemployment problem. It did so in accordance with the same principle on which the problem could have been solved *without a war*—namely, a fall in wage rates and prices relative to the volume of spending for labor and goods.

This relative fall could have taken place in peacetime, without inflation, by means of free competition serving to reduce wage rates and prices absolutely in the face of a slowly increasing quantity of money. Instead, it took place in wartime, by means of the combination of inflation and wage and price controls, which achieved the necessary relative fall in wage rates and prices by means of a rapid increase in the quantity of money coupled with forcible restraint on the ability of wage rates and prices to rise.

Thus, the war was not at all necessary to achieve full employment. Its only economic contribution was that it served to nullify the destructive peacetime government interference in the labor market that had prevented the achievement of full employment, namely, the fixing of wage rates too high in relation to the demand for labor. It did this in the course of unleashing far greater, far more destructive government interference in the economic system and in people's lives generally, which is the inevitable accompaniment of any major war. How much simpler it would have been to achieve full employment by openly repealing the peacetime government interference in the labor market and avoiding the war. One may think of the government's peacetime interference in the labor market as the equivalent of forcing someone to wear a pair of shoes that is several sizes too small and thus extremely painful. The obvious, simple way to solve the problem is to stop forcing the person to wear that pair of shoes and to let him choose his own pair of shoes. War as a means of eliminating unemployment, through the combination of inflation and price controls, is comparable to the government making the wearer's feet fit the wrong pair of shoes by means of chopping off part of his feet. And to this, of course, must be added all the grosser dismemberments and destruction of life and property that are the literal accompaniment of war.

World War II as the Cause of Impoverishment in the United States

The fact that World War II was accompanied by the restoration of full employment does not mean, as is so often believed, that it was a period of prosperity. While some people were rendered materially better off, the immense majority were severely impoverished. As we have already seen, as the result both of the wholesale prohibition of major categories of civilian production, in order to concentrate on war production, and of shortages of practically all civilian goods that were still allowed to be produced, the standard of living of the average American family during World War II was reduced to a point far below its level in the worst years of the depression.[103]

As in the case of government make-work schemes in peacetime, any additional employment achieved by the government in wartime is at the expense of the great majority of people who are already employed. From their perspective, such additional employment is always a case of their having to pay the bill for the additional employment, in terms of the part of their output that they turn over to the reemployed or provide to them in the form of materials and equipment, and for which they receive no compensating output because the goods and services of the reemployed are of minimal economic value or altogether economically useless, which last is certainly the case when the output is war goods.

An additional aspect of the reduction in the standard of living of the great majority of the American people was the fact that people worked longer and harder during the war and, as I have indicated, many people found it necessary to work who otherwise would not have found it necessary to work, such as many housewives, high school students, and retirees. As shown, despite all extra work, the average family received much less than it did before the war. This was the inevitable result of the economic system being made to produce for the war. If roughly half the net output of the economy goes for the war, as it did in World War II, then the most that can remain for the producers is roughly half of the net product of their labor. Such a situation means that the average family must have less and work more, in order not to have too much less.

As we have also seen, during the war most people did not realize how much worse off they actually were, because people usually measure their well-being in terms of the money they earn or their property is worth. The massive creation of money during the war increased practically everyone's money income and the money value of his assets. People simply didn't stop to think that much of the money they earned was unuseable for anything but the purchase of government bonds, or the accumulation of savings accounts invested in government bonds. In addition, as I explained in my discussion of universal price controls in Chapter 7, the very existence of shortages contributed to a delusion of prosperity during the war. Under shortages, nothing more is required of a businessman than that he succeed in delivering to the market some semblance of what his product is supposed to be, because the buyers will snap up practically anything that has greater utility than the otherwise unspendable paper money. By the same token, anyone can quickly find employment who fulfills even the most minimal requirements of a job.[104]

And, finally, it should never be forgotten that the full employment of World War II was accompanied by a profound threat to the freedom of employment, owing to the chaotic conditions that always accompany a shortage of labor. This threat, of course, was expressed in President Roosevelt's proposal of forced labor in the United States, in his 1944 State of the Union Message.[105]

Prosperity Based on the Return of Peace

While the war was accompanied by full employment under conditions of impoverishment, full employment under conditions of *prosperity* was made possible only by *the return of peace*. The restoration of peace made possible a radical reduction in government spending and thus in the portion of the output of the economic system absorbed by the government. It put an end to the government's massive printing of money to buy up output and correspondingly reduce the output remaining to the citizens, who had produced the output. Between 1944, the last full year of the war, and 1946, the first full year of peace, federal government spending was reduced from $100 billion (which equalled more than half of the net national product of the time) to $38 billion, and approximately eight million soldiers and sailors were discharged.[106]

The reduction in government spending made possible a corresponding increase in private spending to the extent that taxes were slashed and the funds previously going to the purchase of government bonds likewise became available for private use. The government's spending for tanks, planes, and artillery shells was replaced by private spending for passenger automobiles, houses, and all kinds of other civilian goods, whose physical production was made possible by the fact that labor and capital were no longer required to produce the war goods. Of course, the returning soldiers and sailors also greatly contributed to the rise in the standard of living of the average family, insofar as their labor did not merely take the place of the labor of other family members but was added to it or represented more productive labor. This made possible an increase in the total volume of production. The abolition of wage and price controls following the end of the war eliminated the shortages and inefficiencies they had caused, and thus it too powerfully contributed to an increase in the overall volume of production and rise in the standard of living.

The end of wage controls was not accompanied by any substantial increase in unemployment. This was because the return to peace made possible a vast increase in private employment and rise in the general standard of living not only in the ways I have described, but also by virtue of increasing the capital funds in the possession of business firms. Thus, when government spending fell and demand shifted from war goods to peacetime goods, business did not simply shift a given amount of capital funds from war production to peace production. On the contrary, the total amount of capital funds in its possession increased, as the result of sharp reductions in its tax burden and in the drain of funds into the purchase of government bonds. Thus, business was in a position to increase its overall demand for labor and capital goods. The return to peace, therefore, meant a rise in wage payments relative to consumer spending, and a rise in the demand for, and production of, capital goods relative to consumers' goods. Our discussion of the determinants of real wages and the general standard of living in the next chapter will show that no development could be more conducive to raising the general level of real wages and to enabling them to go on rising.[107] In this context, major increases in wage rates, both nominal and real, could take place without causing unemployment or higher prices. At the time, and thereafter, the unions followed their normal, relatively conservative policy of seeking increases in real wages only modestly above those provided by the market. Such increases can, of course, gradually produce a substantial rate of unemployment over a period of years, and should not, therefore, be dismissed as unimportant. But the contribution of the labor unions to an immediate problem of mass unemployment is generally in the context of a depression, when the demand for labor sharply falls and the unions refuse to allow corresponding reductions in money wage rates.

A Rational Full-Employment Policy

Governments all over the world are concerned with policies designed to achieve or maintain full employment. To achieve this end, they typically enact policies of inflation, public works, featherbedding, and, indeed, war. But this chapter points to a far more rational policy. Namely, the establishment of a free market in labor, so that wage rates can be adjusted to correspond with the state of the demand for labor and thus make any given monetary demand for labor—any given amount of payroll spending—sufficient to provide full employment. It and the chapter before it also point to the adoption of a 100-percent-reserve gold standard, so that no financial contraction need ever occur and thus no precipitation even of temporary mass unemployment. Such contraction would not occur, because there would be no preceding inflation or credit expansion to set the stage for it by artificially increasing the velocity of circulation of money, promoting the incurrence of debt, and creating money of the kind whose supply can subsequently be decreased by the failure of debtors.

This policy would guarantee full employment in a context of the highest possible productivity of labor. The policies presently pursued by governments are all highly destructive, in serving to reduce the productivity of labor. In addition, for the most part, they are not even capable of actually increasing the overall volume of employment but merely the employment of some at the expense of the employment of others. Unlike those policies, this policy would operate to the benefit of everyone.

The achievement of a free market in labor and a 100-percent-reserve gold standard would mean the elimination of one of modern life's greatest anxieties: the fear of losing one's job and not being able to find another, and thus of being deprived of the ability to support oneself and one's family. With a free market in labor and a 100-percent-reserve gold standard, *there would always be jobs available*. And they would be available without having to wait for any large-scale decline in wage rates. Thus, there would always be a readily available way to earn money. The loss of any given job would cease to be the life-threatening calamity it now so often is and would at most be the source of some temporary unpleasantness.

Appendix to Chapter 13: Inventories and Depressions

An accumulation of business inventories which is excessive in relation to prospective sales volume is almost always associated with the beginning of a depression or recession.[108] The basis of the association is usually explained in the following way: Businessmen find that their inventories are excessive and begin to liquidate them. In order to liquidate them, they attempt to expand their volume of sales while at the same time reducing their volume of production. In reducing their volume of production, they cut back orders with their suppliers and lay off workers. The effect of these cutbacks is to make it more difficult for business firms to expand their sales volume. For the firms that supply other firms find their orders cut. And the firms that sell to consumers find that many of their customers are unemployed. Thus, inventories continue to be excessive, and further production cutbacks are undertaken, leading to a repetition of the same results.

On the basis of this view, it is easy to conclude that the wealth which the excess inventories constitute is an obstacle to production, employment, and prosperity—that its existence drives economic activity to lower and lower levels, until, by one means or another, it is finally consumed. And, indeed, most people apparently do draw this conclusion. It is generally believed that only the elimination of the wealth constituted by the excess inventories can set the stage for a restoration of production and employment; only then, supposedly, will there be a purpose to be served by maintaining production and employment. This belief is propounded in virtually all financial publications and in practically all economics textbooks. They allege that excess inventories are a cause of depressions and that recovery from a depression begins when inventories have been reduced to the point where additional sales physically require additional production.

The following quotation from a story in the financial section of *The New York Times* some years ago clearly expresses this idea:

> He [the Assistant Secretary of Commerce for Economic Affairs] cited, in particular, as a probable cause of continued downturn, the fact that businesses continued to add to their inventories in the fourth quarter. . . . The inventory position of businesses is important because, to the extent that businesses have more inventory on hand than they really need, they cut their production schedules until they have sold the excess.[109]

Similarly, a widely-used economics textbook argues that businesses are "ready to start up again," after they have reached "a position where inventories are short."[110]

It should be held in mind that these statements and countless similar statements are made not in reference to the production of particular products, but in reference to economic activity in general. They do not say that the production of this or that particular item will be decreased or increased depending on whether its inventory is excessive or deficient. They claim that the *general level* of economic activity is inversely related to the size of inventories—that the presence of excess inventories is a general economic depressant, and that a shortage of inventories is a general economic stimulant.

Now such ideas have absurd implications. They imply that *the existence of wealth is a cause of poverty* and, further, that *prosperity could be achieved through the destruction of wealth.* These implications are inescapable, for if, in fact, the existence of excess inventories were an obstacle to production and employment, the wealth they represent would be a cause of poverty. And it would follow that production, employment, and prosperity could be restored by burning down warehouses and destroying the excess inventories.

The supporters of the excess-inventory doctrine, of course, are rarely consistent enough to draw such logical inferences from their premises. Instead of recommending arson, they recommend government spending. The government, they urge, should give people money to buy up quantities of goods, thereby reducing inventories and, it is held, restoring the need to produce. Whether they recommend arson or government spending, however, what is essential is that they perceive the physical wealth constituted by excess inventories as an obstacle to pros-

perity and call for its removal.

What I will show is that the existence of excess inventories relative to sales volume, while certainly a cause of unemployment in particular lines of work, is *not* a cause of general unemployment or depressions, even though it is almost always closely associated with these phenomena. I will show that the reason for the *association* of excess inventories with depressions is that both are the effects of the same underlying cause: namely, an inflation of the money supply. I will show that inflation—i.e., an increase in the quantity of money caused by the government—brings about a wasteful accumulation of inventories *at the expense of other, more efficient forms of wealth,* thereby reducing the overall quantity of wealth. When inflation stops or is significantly slowed, these losses are revealed. The existence of the excess inventories themselves, however, then serves to help make good for the losses which have occurred in other forms of wealth.

The connection I will demonstrate between excess inventories and the impoverishment of depressions can be described by the following analogy: Imagine a miraculous kind of typhoon that came and pulled out all the lumber in houses and left it neatly stacked in lumber yards. The existence of this lumber would have two connections to the state of economic well-being. On the one hand, the greater the quantity of such lumber, the more damaging the preceding typhoon must have been. On the other hand, the existence of the lumber would be a means to repair the damage, and if more lumber could be brought into existence through means other than the typhoon, the restoration of prosperity would be so much the easier. This, I will show, is the nature of the excess inventories that exist at the onset of a depression. They are the effect of a process of impoverishment, but are themselves a cause acting in the direction of prosperity. The real problem is not that they are excessive, but, from the standpoint of making up for the damage done, *deficient.* In addition, as part of this demonstration, I will show that the decline in the spending of money that takes place with the onset of a depression is not the result of the existence of excess inventories, but of other factors associated with inflation and its cessation or slowing down. In other words, I will show that all of the adverse or seemingly adverse consequences usually attributed to excess inventories are merely associational and not caused by the inventories, and that the effect of the existence of the inventories themselves is entirely to the good.

Inventories and Capital

The underlying fallacy in the doctrine that excess inventories cause depressions and general unemployment becomes obvious when one considers the situation of an imaginary Robinson Crusoe on a desert island. If Crusoe is able to salvage a year's supply of canned goods from his ship, he has an excess inventory of food. Does this mean that if he is an industrious person and does not want to spend a year stagnating on his beach, until the need to obtain additional food is forced upon him by the exhaustion of his inventory, he should throw the canned goods back into the ocean? Common sense and economic science must answer no.

The possession of the excess inventory of food does not prevent Crusoe from working. It simply spares him the necessity of directly and immediately producing additional food. During the year in which he does not have to devote his labor to picking berries or killing animals with his bare hands, he can produce other goods, which without the inventory of food he would not have had the time to produce. Above all, he can produce tools, implements, and materials which will enhance his ability to produce food and other goods after his initial inventory is exhausted.

The excess inventory of food is not an obstacle to Crusoe's employment and production. On the contrary, it is the *source* of his employment in the production of other things. It is a fund which supports him while he works and thus makes possible the production of other things. As the inventory of food is consumed, other forms of wealth are produced. Indirectly, by way of supporting his labor, the excess inventory of food is transformed into tools, implements, materials, and supplies of goods that are ready for final consumption, none of which wealth is excessive in any sense.

Were it not for this excess inventory, certainly, Crusoe's production would be curtailed, both in the present and in the future. In the present, he would be limited to the attempt to produce the barest supply of food. And in the future, his production would not have the advantage of the tools, implements, and materials which are made possible by the excess inventory of food. The time which he could devote to employment in the abstract would be no less, but he would have no employment insofar as it contributed to or depended on the use of tools, implements, and materials whose production only the excess inventory of food could make possible.

The underlying fallacy in the doctrine that excess inventories cause depressions is that it does not see production in its full context. It does not see excess inventories as a base for the production of tools, implements, plant and equipment, and other inventories which are not excessive. It does not grasp how one type of wealth can be transformed into another type by means of its consumption serving as the support for the other's production.

The principles pertaining to Crusoe's economy per-

tain equally to the more complicated, monetary economy of today.

An inventory is a source of sales receipts. A firm which possesses an excess inventory possesses to that extent a source of revenue which does not have to be devoted to the reproduction of the inventory. The money gradually coming in from the sale of the excess inventory over time is available to be spent by the firm for other purposes or to be lent to other firms. It can be used to finance construction projects, the purchase of machinery, or the production of inventories of other goods. What is certain is that the money will not be hoarded merely because it is not required to reproduce the same inventory. Not spending to reproduce a particular inventory is not, as is naïvely assumed, not to spend at all.

A canning firm with an excess inventory will reduce its expenditures to produce inventories of canned goods, just as Crusoe with an excess inventory of food will not labor to produce food. But this does not mean that the *overall* expenditures of the canning firm or of those to whom it lends will be reduced, any more than it means Crusoe does not work because he does not work at producing food.

Moreover, it is not a contradiction to argue that firms with excess inventories may employ the revenues those inventories bring in to expand the plant facilities for producing the very goods inventories of which are said to be excessive. It is altogether possible, for example, that an automobile firm might employ the revenues from its excess inventory for the purpose of installing additional facilities for the production of automobiles. For its present inventory is not excessive in the absolute sense that there are not enough potential buyers of cars—at lower prices there would be. It is only excessive in the sense that present costs, using present plant and equipment, are too high to make the rapid sale of the inventory profitable at the lower prices that would be necessary to sell it quickly. If, however, the inventory can be used to finance the installation of lower-cost plant and equipment, it is altogether possible that subsequently the firm's regular production and sales might be profitable at such an expanded volume that what is presently considered to be an excessive inventory in relation to sales, would at that time be considered a deficient inventory.

The *causal* as opposed to the associational relationship between inventories and depressions is not merely different from what is generally believed, it is *the exact opposite*. In a depression and in the period which precipitates a depression, inventories are excessive only in relation to sales volume. As an asset item, however, they are *deficient*. They are deficient in the sense that if they were sufficiently larger, the mass bankruptcy of business enterprises, which is an outstanding feature of a depression, could not possibly take place. An inventory is an *asset*. No firm has ever or will ever go bankrupt because its assets are too large. Bankruptcies result from assets— from inventories—*not being large enough.*

To the degree that an enterprise possesses a large inventory, it is necessarily in a sounder financial position. Its assets exceed its liabilities by that much more. Its owners are richer. It represents a safer investment for creditors. It itself is more in a position to grant credit to others. To argue that it could go bankrupt because it possessed excessive inventories is to argue that Rockefeller could go bankrupt because he owned too many oil wells.

An inventory is wealth. Whoever possesses an inventory obtains the money he needs by the sale of goods out of his inventory, and, if necessary, can always borrow against the inventory. A rich man is not someone with a great hoard of money, but someone with a large ownership of physical assets, of which inventory is a major form. To be wealthy does not mean to have a vast hoard of paper *dollars* in some strongbox. It means owning a store full of valuable goods, a lot full of automobiles, a warehouse full of merchandise.

By definition, wealthy people do not go bankrupt so long as they continue to be wealthy. And they continue to be wealthy to the degree that they own physical assets such as inventories.

What is true is that an enterprise can be plunged into bankruptcy if it holds an excessive inventory *that is financed by the incurrence of debt.* But then the cause is not the inventory, but the debt. If the firm had a larger inventory and the same debt, it would be less likely to be bankrupted, while if it had a smaller inventory and the same debt, it would more surely be bankrupted.

The possession of excess inventories is not only incompatible with the bankruptcy of those who possess them, but of others, who do not possess them. The existence of excess inventories guarantees a state of genuine credit ease. The owners of such inventories are ready lenders to those seeking capital. Businesses do not go bankrupt when credit is easily obtainable. They go bankrupt when credit is difficult to obtain. And it becomes difficult to obtain when capital, of which inventories are a leading form, is deficient and funds must be retained in the enterprises which earn them in order to maintain current or prospective operations.

In sum, if inventories were truly excessive, there could not possibly be a credit contraction or mass bankruptcies. Those who truly possess excessive inventories do not appear in the market with a desperate need for funds; they more likely appear as lenders rather than as borrowers. And because—to the degree that their inventories are excessive—they afford strong security on any loans they have taken out, they are not pressed by their creditors; if they are asked to repay their debts, they have the means of doing so. It is firms with an asset-inventory deficiency which have an urgent need for money; it is such firms which are unable to repay their debts and which go bankrupt. But even many of these firms would not go bankrupt, if other firms possessed excess inventories and were therefore in a position to extend them credit.

Rather than calling for the elimination of excess inventories, it would be far more logical to argue that what is needed to end a depression is precisely an *accumulation* of inventories. For it is additional capital that is required, and to whatever extent additional inventories could be brought into being without first entailing a loss of other forms of capital, they would constitute additional capital. A policy of deliberate consumption of inventories, on the other hand, only destroys the means of supporting employment and production and of extending credit. Such a policy can only intensify a depression.

"Excess" Inventories, Malinvestment, and the Deficiency of Inventories

None of these observations is contradicted by anything in anyone's experience. For example, it might be thought that the large inventories held by the automobile industry in the recession of 1974–75 were a cause of that recession. This is not true. The only connection between the inventory of the automobile firms and the recession was that the capital to produce this inventory had been invested at the expense of other employments which could have put it to better use. Had the auto industry not proceeded with the production of this inventory, capital funds would have been available to construct other things, such as power plants, houses, and, perhaps, lower-cost manufacturing facilities for automobiles. Instead, this capital was wasted to a significant degree by having been invested in an inventory of automobiles. But given the malinvestment of capital in producing automobiles, it is far better that the inventory of automobiles existed than that it did not exist. This is so because the sale of cars out of inventory made it possible for much of the malinvested capital to be recovered. Revenues the auto industry took in from the sale of its inventory could be made available for financing these other things, thus helping to rectify the initial mistake.

And if, given the same degree of malinvestment, the inventories of the auto firms had been larger than they were, the severity of the recession would have been less. Imagine, for example, that by some miracle, the auto industry had awakened one morning in 1975 to find everything else the same except that instead of having an inventory equal to three or four months' sales, it had an inventory twice as large. This would have represented a vast increase in the wealth of the automobile industry and of the whole economy. The auto industry, of course, would have cut back its rate of production still further. It might even have suspended current production altogether. But it would have had the financial means of continuing to pay its workers and suppliers enough to retain their services until such time as normal production resumed, and it would have had the means of infusing substantial sums of capital into all other industries. Home building could have revived, improved manufacturing facilities could have been constructed in a host of industries, more bridges and tunnels could have been built, and so on—all with funds flowing in from the sale of automobiles that did not have to be reproduced. And the suppliers and workers of the auto industry would have participated to a significant degree in the opportunities created by this genuine capital boom. The steel industry, for example, would have turned out more steel for construction and machinery while it turned out less steel for automotive use. And many of the auto industry's workers would have been employed in producing bulldozers, cranes, trucks, locomotives, farm machinery, and the like.

As matters stood, the inventories of the auto industry and all other industries were grossly insufficient to finance all the power plants, pipelines, factories, machines, homes, and so forth, that had been neglected as the result of the malinvestment of capital due to inflation in the years preceding the 1974–75 recession.

Inflation and Credit Expansion as the Cause of Malinvestment in Inventories

Inflation is responsible for the malinvestment of capital in inventory at the expense of other forms of wealth in the following way. As the additional money constituted by inflation comes to be spent and respent, the sales revenues of businesses rise and prices rise. After a while, the continuation of this process comes to be anticipated. Businessmen come to believe that they will be able to sell inventories of goods into a steadily rising demand and at higher prices. Thus, they begin to accumulate inventory. The accumulation of inventory is greatly facilitated—indeed, would probably not be possible otherwise—by the fact that much of the expansion of the money supply enters the economy in the form of new loans. Because this additional money appears on the market as an additional supply of loanable funds, it drives down the rate of interest or prevents the rate of interest from rising to the height it would achieve as the result of inflation alone. This means that it becomes possible to

borrow money at relatively low rates of interest and use it to finance the wasteful accumulation of inventories.[111]

Such conditions characterized the American economy in the 1970s. Interest rates were below the rate at which prices were rising. Thus, it was possible to make money merely by stockpiling inventory.

This stockpiling of inventory is very aptly characterized by the analogy I used earlier of a typhoon that pulled the lumber out of houses and stacked it in lumber yards. The inventories, of course, do not result from the literal disassembly of already produced goods. They do result, however, at the expense of the production of other goods. Thus, piles of inventory accumulate at the expense of factories, machines, houses, and so forth, that could have been produced, if the means of producing them had not been diverted to producing inventories instead. The net result is as though these goods were destroyed and their remains thrown into piles of inventory. Inflation and credit expansion are indeed a kind of typhoon.

Why "Excess" Inventories and Monetary Contraction Are Associated

When inflation is stopped or significantly slowed down, the uneconomic nature of the investments in inventory is revealed. First, interest rates rise, because the depressing effect on the rate of interest of inflation-financed loans is removed. And then the rise in sales revenues and prices begins to abate, because the quantity of money no longer increases or increases much less rapidly. Thus, the profit is taken out of the wasteful inventory investments, and, unless the inflation is quickly resumed, these inventories must be sold on the market at a loss.

The cessation or slowing down of inflation thus reveals widespread losses of capital in the form of unproductive inventory investments. In addition to revealing losses, the cessation or slowing down of inflation increases the need of business firms to hold cash. This effect explains why the liquidation of inventories in depressions is accompanied by "cash hoarding" rather than equivalent spending in support of other forms of capital accumulation.

During inflation, and so long as inflation is expected to continue rapidly enough, businessmen are induced to operate with unduly low levels of cash in relation to the financial size of their operations. Cash holdings fall as a percentage of assets, liabilities, revenues, and expenditures. Among the reasons is the fact that inflation in the form of credit expansion leads businessmen to believe that credit will be easily available when they need it. At the same time, they come to expect to be able to sell their inventories easily and profitably. On the basis of such convictions, they come to regard their existing levels of cash as unnecessarily large and as better placed in income-earning assets. Thus, cash holdings come to be drawn down. Since the cash does not disappear from the economic system, but is merely transferred in exchange for something to someone else, who will also tend to be less conservative in his attitude toward cash holdings, what happens is an expansion in the volume of spending, lending, borrowing, and trading of all kinds, in relation to the quantity of money. When inflation stops or is significantly slowed down, however, the basis of the low cash holdings is removed, because credit turns out not to be available or to be available only at a much greater cost and with much greater difficulty than had been expected. And inventories turn out not to be as readily and profitably saleable as believed. Thus, when inflation stops or is significantly slowed down, business enterprises must begin to rebuild their cash holdings.

This necessary rebuilding of cash holdings is why there is a reduction in the general rate of spending in the economy and why the liquidation of excess inventories in the aftermath of an inflation, does not provide an equivalent financial support for other business activities. Namely, practically all firms are trying to retain a larger proportion of the funds they take in, in the form of cash. The sellers of the excess inventories use part of their proceeds to rebuild their own cash positions; and of the funds that these sellers do make available to others, as loans, for example, a portion is retained by the recipients in the form of replenished cash holdings. And it is the same with the liquid funds realized in any other way. Thus, the rate of spending slows down. It cannot be stressed too strongly that it is not the excess inventories that are the cause of the reduced volume of spending. On the contrary, both the excess inventories and the reduced volume of spending are the consequence of the distortions created by the preceding inflation and credit expansion.

What has been shown is that the relationship between excess inventories and depressions is one of association, not causation. Excess inventories and depressions are both the result of a process of inflation—specifically, of an inflation that enters the economy in the form of loans granted out of newly created money, that is, of credit expansion. The excess inventories represent impoverishment only in their origin—insofar as they are the result of the diversion of capital from other, more important employments. In their consequence, however, the effect of the existence of these inventories is to help make good for the losses entailed in their accumulation. And these losses would be all the more easily made good, if, with the same degree of malinvestment, the excess inventories were greater. In this sense, inventories in a depression are deficient, not excessive.

The existence of assets can never be the cause of bankruptcies. The existence of wealth can never be the cause of poverty. The possession of excess inventories that is associated with depressions does not contradict these principles in the slightest.

Notes

1. Concerning the fundamental problem of economic life, see above, pp. 42–51 and 54–61.
2. Most of what follows in this part derives from my article "Production Versus Consumption," *Freeman* 14, no. 10 (October 1964), pp. 3–12; reprinted as a pamphlet (Laguna Hills, Calif.: The Jefferson School of Philosophy, Economics, and Psychology, 1991).
3. In reality, Ricardo and especially James Mill propounded it with far greater clarity and consistency than Say. In my judgment, the law should actually be called James Mill's Law.
4. See above, p. 112.
5. For a brilliant analysis of this error and of its consequences, see Henry Hazlitt, *Economics in One Lesson,* new ed. (New Rochelle, N. Y.: Arlington House Publishers, 1979). See also Frederic Bastiat, "What Is Seen and What Is Not Seen" in Frederic Bastiat, *Selected Essays on Political Economy,* trans. Seymour Cain (New York: D. Van Nostrand, 1964).
6. On the subject of the confusion of need with demand, cf. Hazlitt, *Economics in One Lesson,* chap. 3.
7. John Maynard Keynes, *The General Theory of Employment, Interest, and Money* (New York: Harcourt Brace, 1937), p. 129. I previously quoted this passage as an illustration of irrationalism in economics, above, p. 35.
8. See below, pp. 559–561.
9. This last is because with a fixed total expenditure of money, the variation of quantity demanded with the price level is inversely proportionate. On the meaning of unit elasticity, see above, p. 158.
10. For a full explanation of the vital role of the productivity of labor in determining real wages, see below, pp. 618–622.
11. Cf. above, p. 159.
12. Cf. the brilliant analysis of the effects of machinery in Hazlitt, *Economics in One Lesson,* chap. 7.
13. See above, pp. 59–61. See also below, pp. 559–561.
14. See above, pp. 358–360 and 362–364.
15. See below, pp. 663–664.
16. Concerning the causes of unemployment, see below, pp. 580–589.
17. On the subject of spread-the-work, cf. Hazlitt, *Economics in One Lesson,* chap. 8.
18. See above, p. 277.
19. On this subject, cf. Hazlitt, *Economics in One Lesson,* chap. 3.
20. For elaboration of the principles involved, see below, pp.

622–642, especially pp. 622–629 and 634–639.

21. Cf. Hazlitt, *Economics in One Lesson*, chap. 4.

22. For an explanation of the nature of producers' and consumers' labor, and why government employees must be classified as the latter, see above, pp. 446–447.

23. As we shall see, consumptionist views on the benefits of a policy of imperialism go hand in glove with the balance-of-trade and balance-of-payments doctrines and thus with the latters' own militaristic implications, which were pointed out in the previous chapter. See above, p. 526.

24. In cases in which consumptionists recognize the necessity of imports, such as minerals that cannot be found domestically, they may still denounce the imports—as somehow representing the "exploitation" of the backward countries that provide them. A logical connection between consumptionism and such denunciations is provided by the affinity of consumptionism with socialism, which will be explained below, on p. 559. Concerning the actual nature of the effects of foreign "exploitation" of natural resources on the local populations, see above, pp. 323–326.

25. On the subject of the balance of trade and payments, see above, pp. 526–536.

26. See above, p. 351. See also Hazlitt, *Economics in One Lesson*, chap. 9.

27. See above, pp. 351–354.

28. The wording of this and the following two sections has been little changed from my article "Production Versus Consumption."

29. For an exposition of this view by one of its most prominent contemporary supporters, see John Kenneth Galbraith, *The Affluent Society* (Boston: Houghton Mifflin, 1958), pp. 154, 159.

30. See above, p. 56.

31. See below, pp. 629–631.

32. See Alvin Hansen, *A Guide to Keynes* (New York: McGraw-Hill Book Company, 1953), pp. 25–35. Hansen, who was the leading proponent of the doctrine of secular stagnation was also the teacher of Paul Samuelson, the author of the textbook so often quoted in these pages to illustrate errors in economic theory. (For example, see the very next note.)

33. Paul Samuelson and William Nordhaus, *Economics*, 13th ed. (New York: McGraw-Hill Book Company, 1989), pp. 721–722.

34. Ibid., p. 306.

35. For elaboration of this point, see below, pp. 817–818. See also below, pp. 569–580.

36. For another instance of the fallacy of composition in connection with consumptionism, see above, pp. 543–544.

37. See below, pp. 762–767.

38. Not surprisingly, Prof. Samuelson has missed few opportunities to belittle the gold standard over the course of the fourteen editions of his book.

39. David Ricardo, *Principles of Political Economy and Taxation*, 3d ed. (London, 1821), chap. 21; reprinted as vol. 1 of *The Works and Correspondence of David Ricardo*, ed. Piero Sraffa (Cambridge: Cambridge University Press, 1962), pp. 291–292. Italics supplied.

40. All of these propositions, of course, presuppose a normal context, that is, a context in which business firms have not been led into a state of illiquidity by a preceding inflation or credit expansion and now realize their need to rebuild liquidity. In such conditions, monetary demand falls. Its stabilization and renewed increase requires a fall in wage rates and prices sufficient to accommodate the fall in the velocity of circulation of money that is the necessary accompaniment of the rebuilding of liquidity. The problem of adjustment can be compounded by a fall in the quantity of money, in which case a further reduction in wage rates and prices is necessary. For further discussion of these points, see below, pp. 580–589 and 938–940.

41. James Mill, *Commerce Defended* (London, 1808), chap. 6; reprinted in *Selected Economic Writings of James Mill*, ed. Donald Winch (Chicago: The University of Chicago Press, 1966), p. 135.

42. I choose the fraction one-third for the new price of potatoes simply because it is the first fraction with one as the numerator that is less than a half, and is thus probably the easiest fraction to work with.

43. It should be realized that it is no objection to Say's Law to question the assumption that the "other goods" no longer offered for the given good are equivalently exchanged against themselves. To whatever extent they might not be, the corollary effect would be that the supply of such other goods brought to market would be equivalently less. Thus, to whatever extent the rise in aggregate demand turned out to be less than the increase in the supply of the given good, it would be less only to the extent of the accompanying decrease in the supply of other goods. The proposition would remain that the increase in aggregate demand was precisely equal to the increase in aggregate supply, whatever it was.

44. I elaborate on this point below, on pp. 568–569.

45. See above, pp. 53–54.

46. Concerning mass unemployment, see below, pp. 580–582. Concerning the determination of real wages, see below, pp. 618–622.

47. See below, p. 725, for confirmation of this statement.

48. For such an analysis, see below, pp. 719–859, which provide a full elaboration of the theory of aggregate profit and interest. See also below, pp. 622–642, which explain the vital role of the demand for capital goods in the process of capital accumulation and raising the productivity of labor.

49. Even though there is no demand for capital goods in the conditions of full vertical integration, there could still be capital—in the form of capitalized wage payments. For example, if a sum such as $1 million is paid to wage earners to construct a durable asset, or to produce inventory, that $1 million is capitalized in the asset accounts of the firm that pays the wages.

50. See below, p. 576, for an explanation of why broad-based increases in production under a commodity money system actually tend to be accompanied by a *higher* rather than a lower average rate of profit.

51. See above, pp. 543–544.

52. For a comprehensive explanation of how improvements in the productivity of labor are the essential cause of rising real wages, see below, pp. 613–663.

53. See above, p. 518.

54. Closely related to this last are cases in which an increase in the demand for money results from the demand for money having first been artificially reduced in expectation of an *accel-*

eration in the rate of increase in the quantity of money. In cases of this kind, the demand for money increases if the expected acceleration in the rate of increase in the quantity of money does not take place.

55. See above, pp. 519–526.

56. The need for accelerated depreciation of business plant and equipment as the result of more rapid economic progress should not be taken to imply any tendency toward a substantially smaller accumulated value of net plant and equipment in the conditions of an invariable money, still less, any reduction in the degree of capital intensiveness in the economic system. On the contrary, it is accompanied by an increase in the degree of capital intensiveness. For an explanation of the reasons why, see below, pp. 786–787.

57. See below, pp. 589–590. See also Ludwig von Mises, *Human Action*, 3d ed. rev. (Chicago: Henry Regnery Co., 1966), pp. 568–569.

58. From that point on, the stock of housing in any given year would consist of the new housing production of that year and of 49 prior years, with each succeeding year's housing production being 5 percent greater than that of the year before. In the next year, each of the 50 terms representing a year's housing production would increase by 5 percent, with the result that the total stock of housing would increase by 5 percent.

59. Today's depressed housing market in places such as California should not be ascribed to an inelastic demand for housing. Rather it is the result of a fall in the demand for housing following decades in which credit expansion artificially encouraged housing construction and then experienced major interruption. The problems of the housing market in California are also greatly compounded by the fact that the state has been rendered economically uncompetitive by the policies of its government, which have included higher taxes and more regulation than competing states, as well as numerous measures deliberately designed to discourage economic progress.

60. Ultimately, the supply of new housing will stand to the total stock of housing not in the ratio of 1:50, but in the substantially higher ratio of $1.05^{50} \div \sum_{n=1}^{n=50} 1.05^n$.

61. On the role of saving in the demand for expensive durable goods, see below, p. 694. On the relationship between saving and economic progress, see below, pp. 622–629.

62. See below, pp. 663–664.

63. See above, pp. 513–514 and 519–526. As we will see, there can also be reductions in the aggregate demand for labor in conjunction with increases in the aggregate demand for capital goods. But such reductions are relatively slow and modest in the overall economic system, and when they occur are the basis of a more rapidly growing ability to produce, including a growing ability to produce or import the precious metals, and thus of an expanding quantity of money and growing demand for labor. On this subject, see below, pp. 639–641.

64. See below, pp. 762–767.

65. Concerning the role of saving in the demand for labor, see above, pp. 478–480, and below, pp. 632–634, 683–685, 694–696, and 725–736. Finally, on the relationship between the demand for labor and the demand for capital goods and why decreases in the demand for labor caused by increases in the

demand for capital goods are not against the interests of the average wage earner, see below, pp. 639–641.

66. See above, the last reference in the preceding note.

67. On this subject, see below, p. 590.

68. See above, Chapters 6–8.

69. We have already seen how it is to the advantage of poor wage earners, above, on pp. 382–384.

70. The legitimacy of generalizing about the rate of profit from the results of the assumption of the full vertical integration of business was explained earlier in this chapter, on p. 570, when the assumption was first introduced. At that time, it was also explained how capital can exist even in the absence of a demand for capital goods. See above, the preceding page, n. 49.

71. See below, pp. 864–878, for a detailed exposition of Keynes's theories. Following that exposition, I show that the effect of a fall in wage rates necessary to achieve full employment is actually to increase the rate of profit rather than merely leave it unchanged. See below, pp. 879–884, especially pp. 883–884.

72. For an explanation of why taxes levied on profits or interest are a burden to wage earners, and the magnitude of that burden, see above, pp. 306–310. See also below, pp. 826–829.

73. This is the view of von Mises, for example. See *Human Action*, pp. 776–777.

74. As I will show in the next chapter, a rising productivity of labor is the only possible cause of a sustained, significant rise in average real wages, which, other things being equal, vary in direct proportion to the average productivity of labor. See below, pp. 618–622 and 646–653.

75. See above, pp. 358–360. The greater division of labor contributes to the rise in the productivity of labor not only directly, but also indirectly, insofar as it brings about a greater production of capital goods. On this subject, see below, pp. 634–636, where it is shown how anything that serves to increase production in general, increases the production and accumulation of capital goods.

76. On this last point, see the preceding note.

77. Unemployment tends to be more heavily concentrated in the blue-collar ranks, probably because, by and large, such workers tend to be easier to replace than the administrative-type workers.

78. In order for any major problem of greater difficulty of paying debt to be caused by a fall in the aggregate demand for labor, the fall in the aggregate demand for labor must itself be major. As we are already in a position to know, the explanation of such a fall is a general financial contraction brought on by a decrease in the quantity of money and/or increase in the demand for money for holding, which last is itself caused by a cessation or slowdown in the rate of increase in the quantity of money. On this subject, see below, the next two notes.

79. On the nature of inflation, see above, pp. 219–220 and 503–506, and below, pp. 895–907. On the role of fiduciary media and credit expansion in the precipitation of monetary contractions, see above, pp. 511–517 and 519–526. See also below, pp. 938–941.

80. See above, pp. 519–526.

81. See above, pp. 520–522, and below, pp. 938–940.

82. Also present here is the phenomenon known as "credit crunches," which also are the result of credit expansion. On this aspect, see below, pp. 939–940.

83. See above, pp. 513–514.

84. See above, ibid.

85. On the subject of the Phillips curve, see Samuelson and Nordhaus, *Economics*, pp. 328–335.

86. See below, the next section, especially pp. 591–592.

87. See Murray N. Rothbard, *America's Great Depression* (Princeton, N. J.: D. Van Nostrand & Co., 1963), pp. 187–190, 236–239.

88. It is appropriate here to recall the words of Adam Smith, who wrote, "I have never known much good done by those who affected to trade for the public good." (See Adam Smith, *The Wealth of Nations* [London, 1776], bk. 4, chap. 2; reprint of Cannan ed. [Chicago: University of Chicago Press, 2 vols. in 1, 1976], 2:478.)

89. See U.S. Department of Commerce, Bureau of Economic Analysis, *The National Income and Product Accounts of the United States, 1929–1976 Statistical Tables* (Washington, D. C.: U.S. Government Printing Office, 1981), pp. 238 and 253. These pages provide the data on the basis of which the calculations in the text have been made.

90. See Rothbard, *America's Great Depression*, p. 183.

91. On the significance of the qualification concerning compensating advantage, see above, pp. 576–578.

92. See *National Income and Product Accounts of the United States, 1929–1976 Statistical Tables*, p. 1, for the data used to make these calculations.

93. As should be evident from this discussion, there are determinants of aggregate profit other than the difference between consumption expenditure and wage payments, notably, net investment. For elaboration, see below, pp. 744–750 See also pp. 700–706, which deal with the nature of net investment.

94. On the subject of springs to profitability, see below, pp. 778–787, especially p. 784.

95. The restoration of investment spending, when wage rates fall to their equilibrium level, is guaranteed by the operation of the aforementioned springs to profitability.

96. See above, pp. 511–517 and 519–526.

97. On these points, see below, pp. 938–940. See also below, pp. 935–936.

98. On the subject of malinvestment, see below, pp. 935–936. See also below, pp. 597–598.

99. See above, pp. 515–516.

100. See above, p. 524.

101. See *National Income and Product Accounts of the United States, 1929–1976 Statistical Tables,* pp. 238 and 253 for the data underlying these calculations. The calculations use the data for private industries in line 3 of the tables.

102. Data for the number of workers reported as openly unemployed are from U.S. Department of Commerce, Bureau of the Census, *Historical Statistics of the United States Colonial Times to 1970* (Washington, D. C.: U.S. Government Printing Office, 1975), p. 126. Data for the number of workers employed in the various government work-relief programs are from the *National Income and Product Accounts of the United States, 1929–1976 Statistical Tables* p. 253.

103. See above, pp. 258–262, especially p. 262.

104. See p. 262.

105. See above, pp. 287–288.

106. See *National Income and Product Accounts of the United States, 1929–1976 Statistical Tables*, pp. 3, 23, and 254. My calculations of federal government spending include "government transfer payments to persons."

107. See below, pp. 622–629 and 632–634.

108. This appendix is a revised version of my article "Inventories and Depressions," *Il Politico* 31, no. 2 (June 1966).

109. *New York Times,* January 17, 1975, p. 47.

110. George L. Bach, *Economics,* 8th ed. (Englewood-Cliffs, N. J.: Prentice-Hall, 1974), p. 171.

111. For a numerical illustration, see below, p. 935.

CHAPTER 14

THE PRODUCTIVITY THEORY OF WAGES

PART A

THE MARXIAN EXPLOITATION THEORY

1. The Influence of the Exploitation Theory

The Marxian exploitation theory has been and continues to be among the most influential economic doctrines in the world. Despite the global collapse of socialism, it continues to be the prevailing theory of wages. Its truth in the explanation of the determination of wage rates is taken for granted both by the overwhelming majority of intellectuals and by the great mass of ordinary citizens in all countries of the world. It is for this reason that I find it necessary to begin my discussion of wage rates with an account of this theory.

According to the exploitation theory, capitalism is a system of virtual slavery, serving the narrow interests of a comparative handful of "exploiters"—the businessmen and capitalists—who, driven by insatiable greed and power-lust, exist as parasites upon the labor of the masses. This view of capitalism has not been the least bit shaken by the steady rise in the standard of living of the average person that has taken place in the capitalist countries since the beginning of the Industrial Revolution. The rise in the standard of living is not attributed to capitalism, but precisely to the *infringements* that have been made upon capitalism. Thus, people attribute economic progress to labor unions and social legislation, and to what

they consider to be improved personal ethics on the part of employers. By the same token, they tremble at the thought of unions not existing, of a society without minimum-wage laws, maximum-hours legislation, and child-labor laws—at the thought of a society in which no legal obstacles stood in the way of employers pursuing their self-interest. In the absence of such legislation, people believe, wage rates would return to the minimum-subsistence level; women and children would labor once more in the mines; and the hours of work would be as long and as hard as it is possible for human beings to bear—all for the benefit of the businessmen and capitalists, precisely as Marx maintained.

As I have indicated, the exploitation theory has been and continues to be a guiding force in the thoughts and actions not only of the various Communist and socialist parties around the world, but also in those of the great majority of people who regard themselves as anticommunists and antisocialists. It is believed to be correct by almost everyone, not as a description of present-day conditions, to be sure, but as a description of the workings of *laissez-faire* capitalism—of capitalism free of all government intervention into the economic system, of capitalism as displayed in its essential nature in the nineteenth century.

Thus, the exploitation theory is almost universally accepted as the basis for the interpretation of modern economic history. Even the great majority of anticommunists and antisocialists believe that economic conditions in the nineteenth century were bad for the average person because of the unrestrained greed of the capitalists. By the same token, the subsequent improvement in economic conditions is almost universally believed to be the result of government intervention that limits the operation of that greed.

The belief in the essential correctness of the exploitation theory as applied to laissez-faire capitalism underlies the advocacy of the so-called mixed economy and the welfare state—of virtually the whole economic program of the present-day "liberals." Among the measures enacted and maintained in force as the result of its influence are not only maximum-hours, minimum-wage, prounion, and child-labor legislation, but also progressive income and inheritance taxes and social-welfare spending, such as that for public housing, public education, social security, and socialized medicine. It is believed that none of these measures is at the expense of the workers, but only of the capitalists. Their cost, it is believed, comes exclusively at the expense of the capitalists' profits—from "surplus-value." From the point of view of the workers, it is thought, the measures represent nothing but a source of gains: less work, higher wages, and more housing, education, income security, medical care, and so forth.

In effect, these measures are perceived merely as giving back to the workers some of the wealth allegedly exploited from them by the capitalists. Indeed, the validity of the exploitation theory is so taken for granted that "liberal" politicians routinely campaign on the assumption that no possible basis can exist for opposing their allegedly humanitarian projects except membership in the class of the "rich"—that is, of the capitalist exploiters—or else some utterly perverse desire to prevent the great mass of people from being benefitted at no cost to themselves.

Thus, the influence of the exploitation theory is to be found not in any support it may provide for a Communist revolution, but in the perception it offers of the allegedly evil nature of capitalism and the need to control that allegedly evil nature, which perception is held by the overwhelming majority of people, especially by the overwhelming majority of today's intellectuals. In this essential respect, the influence of the exploitation theory is as great as ever. Indeed, the exploitation theory is the leading manifestation of the prescientific, demonological worldview that I described in Chapter 1 as continuing to be prevalent in economics.[1] The alleged good and evil arbitrary powers that are supposed to rule the economic world according to that view are, first and foremost, the businessmen and capitalists of the Marxian exploitation theory, who, of course, are the allegedly evil powers, and the government of the "liberals" and the socialists, which is the allegedly good power.

The remaining sections of this part present an exposi-

tion of the substantive content of the exploitation theory, the conceptual framework of the exploitation theory having already been presented and refuted in Chapter 11.[2] That substantive content is the Marxian version of the labor theory of value and the Marxian version of the iron law of wages, both of which represent profound distortions of the classical economists' ideas on these subjects, as a comparison with the relevant portions of Chapter 11 will clearly confirm.[3] Because Chapter 11 has already presented in great detail a mutually exclusive version of the labor theory of value, it will not be necessary in this chapter to present any further critique of this aspect of the exploitation theory. The mere presentation of the Marxian version of the labor theory of value will be enough to refute it, in the light of the material previously presented in Chapter 11. However, the same cannot be said for the iron law of wages, and thus Part B of this chapter incorporates a critique of the Marxian version of the iron law of wages, mainly in the form of the positive exposition of the mutually exclusive theory of wages that I call the productivity theory of wages and after which I have titled both Part B and the present chapter as a whole.

While the productivity theory of wages can be interpreted as a flat-out alternative to the ideas of the classical economists on the subject of wages, I believe that it is actually the theory of wages that is consistent with the essential core of classical economics. For example, it is very closely related to Say's Law, in that just as Say's Law explains real demand as determined by production and supply, so the productivity theory of wages explains real wages as also determined by production and supply—specifically, by the production and supply of goods relative to the supply of labor.[4] It is also closely related to the classical economists' ideas on saving and capital accumulation and to their doctrine of the wages-fund theory.[5] In addition, of course, as I have already indicated, it is consistent both with Ricardo's doctrine on profits and with his views on the labor theory of value, both of which I have shown to be in actual opposition to the exploitation theory.[6]

2. Marx's Distortions of the Labor Theory of Value

Marx twists the labor theory of value into a form in which Smith and certainly Ricardo would not have supported it. He proceeds as though the quantity of labor required to produce a good were the *sole, exclusive* determinant of its price, ignoring all the repeated statements by Ricardo in particular to the contrary.[7] He seems never to have heard of categories of goods whose prices are determined by supply and demand, nor of the time factor, the rate of profit, and differences in wage rates as factors influencing prices. He writes:

> A use-value, or useful article, therefore, has value only because human labour in the abstract has been embodied or materialized in it. How, then, is the magnitude of this value to be measured? Plainly, by the quantity of the value creating substance, the labour, contained in the article. The quantity of labour, however, is measured by its duration, and labour-time in its turn finds its standard in weeks, days, and hours.[8]

In answer to the objection that his theory implies that commodities should be more valuable the more idle and unskillful the workers are who produce them, Marx states that he is speaking of "socially necessary" labor-time. "The labour-time that is socially necessary," he explains, "is that required to produce an article under the normal conditions of production, and with the average degree of skill and intensity prevalent at the time."[9]

The phenomenon that is actually referred to with these words is market *competition*. But competition and its effects are quickly forgotten. For competition is responsible for the fact that, in the same market at the same time, equal quantities of products of the same type sell for the same price, irrespective of the very different amounts of labor that may have been expended to produce them. In the very next paragraph, in full contradiction of what he has just said about socially necessary labor time, Marx declares:

> Commodities, therefore, in which equal quantities of labour are embodied, or which can be produced in the same time, have the same value. The value of one commodity is to the value of any other, as the labour-time necessary for the production of the one is to that necessary for the production of the other. "As values, all commodities are only definite masses of congealed labour-time."[10]

The problem created for Marx's version of the labor theory of value by the existence of skilled labor is disposed of with equal sleight of hand, a few pages later. This problem is the fact that the products of a given amount of skilled labor tend to be worth more than the products of the same number of hours of unskilled labor—a circumstance which represents a direct contradiction of the proposition that the value of all commodities is in proportion simply and only to the relative quantities of labor required to produce them. Marx writes: "Skilled labour counts only as simple labour intensified, or rather, as multiplied simple labour, a given quantity of skilled labour being considered equal to a greater quantity of simple labour. . . . For simplicity's sake we shall henceforth account every kind of labour to be unskilled, simple labour; by this we do no more than save ourselves the trouble of making the reduction."[11]

Thus, with these difficulties out of the way, Marx feels free to develop his own peculiar, absolutist version of the labor theory of value—a version which recognizes nothing but the quantity of labor as the determinant of exchange ratios and prices. A few samples of his virtual obsession with the notion of "congealed labour" follow:

> The equation, 20 yards of linen = 1 coat, or 20 yards of linen are worth one coat, implies that the same quantity of value-substance (congealed labour) is embodied in both; that the two commodities have each cost the same amount of labour or the same quantity of labour-time.[12]

> Therefore, 10 lbs. of tea = 40 lbs. of coffee. In other words, there is contained in 1 lb. of coffee only one-fourth as much substance of value—labour—as is contained in 1 lb. of tea.[13]

> In this sense, every commodity is a symbol, since, in so far as it is value, it is only the material envelope of the human labour spent upon it.[14]

Thus, in Marx's view, the exchange value of commodities is determined by their congealed labor content. Every commodity is perceived as containing so much labor that has entered into its production. The value of every commodity relative to the value of every other commodity, i.e., their mutual exchange ratio, is then seen as nothing but a ratio of their respective congealed labor contents. The price of every commodity is seen as nothing but the ratio of the labor required to produce a unit of it to the labor required to produce a unit of gold. If, for example, an article sells for ten dollars, it can only be, according to Marx, because it takes ten times the labor to produce a unit of it as it does to produce the quantity of gold defined as one dollar.

Marx, in other words, presents what I call an absolutist version of the labor theory of value—a version which, totally unlike that of the classical economists, holds that the quantity of labor required to produce something is always the determinant of its value and is the sole and exclusive determinant of its value. Marx's "congealed labour" can only be understood as some kind of alleged pulsating sweat-content that is immanent in commodities, and that allegedly gives off some kind of charged field, so to speak, whose interaction with the similarly charged fields of other commodities supposedly determines exchange ratios and prices, and does so in proportion to the respective pulsating sweat-contents—that is, to the respective "congelations" of "labour."

Implications for Value Added and Income Formation

Marx's absolutist version of the labor theory of value provides a remarkably simple explanation of the determination of "surplus-value"—i.e., of the extent of the alleged deduction of profits from wages that the exploitation theory fallaciously claims. (Marx, of course, mistakenly believes that surplus-value—profit—comes into existence only with the appearance of businessmen and capitalists, under "capitalistic circulation."[15])

His absolutist version of the labor theory of value implies that the total of the value added at any stage in production, and thus the total of the income earned in that stage of production—that is, the sum of profits and wages together—must be due to the performance of fresh labor at that stage of production. This is because any product that is produced contains all of the labor that went into producing the materials required for its production. It also contains an appropriate share of the labor that entered into producing the machines and factory buildings that were used in its production. (On this last point, Marx says, for example, "Suppose a machine to be worth 1000 pounds, and to wear out in 1000 days. Then one thousandth part of the value of the machine is daily transferred to the day's product."[16]) If the product is to be worth more than the nonhuman means of production—the materials and plant and equipment—used up or otherwise productively consumed in producing it, then it must, according to Marx's absolutist version of the labor theory of value, be the product of a larger number of hours of labor than entered into those means of production. This is possible only to the extent that fresh labor is applied in transforming the materials, with the aid of the machinery and factory buildings, into the product. In Marx's own words:

> We have seen that the [nonhuman] means of production transfer value to the new product, so far only as during the labour process they lose value in the shape of their old use-value. The maximum loss of value that they can suffer in the process, is plainly limited by the amount of the original value with which they came into the process, or in other words, by the labour-time necessary for their production. Therefore the means of production can never add more value to the product than they themselves possess independently of the process in which they assist. However useful a given kind of raw material, or a machine, or other means of production may be, though it may cost 150 pounds or, say, 500 days' labour, yet it cannot, under any circumstances, add to the value of the product more than 150 pounds. Its value is determined not by the labour-process into which it enters as a means of production, but by that out of which it has issued as a product. In the labour-process it only serves as a mere use-value, a thing with useful properties, and could not, therefore, transfer any value to the product, unless it possessed such value previously.[17]

But, we are told:

> It is otherwise with the subjective factor of the labour-process, with labour-power in action. While the labourer, by virtue of his labour being of a specialised kind that has a special object, preserves and transfers to the product the value of the means of production, he at the same time, by the mere act of working, creates each instant an additional or new value.... The substitution of one value for another, is here effected by the creation of a new value.[18]

In accordance with this view, Marx introduces his distinction between "constant capital" and "variable capital." The constant capital, representing the portion of capital invested in materials, machinery, and factory buildings, allegedly conveys to the product only the value it itself represents. It is in no way value creating. In this sense it is "constant." The variable capital, however, that is, the portion of the capital invested in the payment of wages—in the purchase of "labour-power"—is value creating. In this sense it is "variable." In Marx's words:

> That part of capital then, which is represented by the means of production, by the raw material, auxiliary material and the instruments of labour, does not, in the process of production, undergo any quantitative alteration of value. I therefore call it the constant part of capital, or, more shortly, *constant capital.*

> On the other hand, that part of capital, represented by labour-power, does, in the process of production, undergo an alteration of value.... This part of capital is continually being transformed from a constant into a variable magnitude. I therefore call it the variable part of capital, or shortly, *övariable capital.*[19]

The "variable capital," then, is variable in the sense that in employing fresh labor, it alone makes it possible for the product to contain more hours of labor than the materials and other constituents of the constant capital. And thus the value of the product can be greater than the value of the nonhuman means of production used up or otherwise productively consumed in producing it.

Now to the extent that the value of a product exceeds the value of the nonhuman means of production, income exists in the form of profits plus wages. Profit, of course, is the excess of the value of the product over the value of all of the means of production required to produce it, including the fresh labor applied at the current stage of production. It is the excess of the value of the product over the total costs of production. The value merely of the nonhuman means of production used up or otherwise productively consumed in order to produce a product is equal to all the costs of production *but wages.* Thus, when this amount is subtracted from the value of the product, the difference is profits *plus wages.* That is, sales – (cost – wages) = profits + wages.[20] For example, if the value of a product is $100 and the costs of producing it are $80, the profit earned is $20. If, of the $80 of total costs, the costs on account of capital goods are $45, while the costs on account of labor are $35, then the difference between the value of the product and the value of the capital goods alone is equal to $100 – $45, which is $55. This $55 in turn is equal to the sum of the profit of $20 plus the wage cost of $35. That the difference between the value of the product and the value of the capital goods alone is equal to the sum of the profit plus the wages can be seen directly, by recognizing that $100 – $45 is equal to $100

– ($80 – $35), which, of course, equals the $20 of profit plus the $35 of wages.

In just this way, fresh labor is perceived as adding to the value of the nonhuman means of production consumed in producing the product the sum of wages and profits together. The sum of the wages and the profits together earned at any given stage of production is held to be in proportion to the fresh labor added at that stage.

It should be realized that, according to Marx's view, if there were a fully automated factory, requiring the performance of virtually no fresh labor to transform materials into a product, the value of the product could not exceed the value of the materials plus the depreciation on the machinery and factory. Similarly, according to Marx's view, there is no way of explaining the well-known fact that older wine or whiskey has a higher value than younger wine or whiskey, even though no additional labor is performed in the aging process.

3. Marx's Version of the Iron Law of Wages

Now, according to Marx, what determines the division of the value added—allegedly all by the performance of fresh labor—between wages and profits is a further application of his absolutist version of the labor theory of value. This time Marx applies his absolutist version of the labor theory of value to the determination of the value of labor itself, and, in so doing, provides his own peculiar version of the so-called iron law of wages. The value of labor, or "labour-power," as Marx calls it, is allegedly determined *by the quantity of labor required to produce labor!* The meaning of this proposition is explained by Marx in the following words:

The value of labour-power is determined, as in the case of every other commodity, by the labour-time necessary for the production, and consequently also the reproduction, of this special article. So far as it has value, it represents no more than a definite quantity of the average labour of society incorporated in it. Labour-power exists only as a capacity, or power of the living individual. Its production consequently presupposes his existence. Given the individual, the production of labour-power consists in his reproduction of himself or his maintenance. For his maintenance he requires a given quantity of the means of subsistence. Therefore the labour-time requisite for the production of labour-power reduces itself to that necessary for the production of those means of subsistence; in other words, the value of labour-power is the value of the means of subsistence necessary for the maintenance of the labourer.[21]

In elaboration, Marx writes:

The value of labour-power resolves itself into the value of a definite quantity of means of subsistence. It therefore varies with the value of these means or with the quantity of labour requisite for their production.

Some of the means of subsistence, such as food and fuel, are consumed daily, and a fresh supply must be provided daily. Others such as clothes and furniture last for longer periods and require to be replaced only at longer intervals. One article must be bought or paid for daily, another weekly, another quarterly, and so on. But in whatever way the sum total of these outlays may be spread over the year, they must be covered by the average income, taking one day with another. If the total of the commodities required daily for the production of labour-power = A, and those required weekly = B, and those required quarterly = C, and so on, the daily average of these commodities = ($E365A+52B+4C+&c.)/365. Suppose that in this mass of commodities requisite for the average day there are embodied 6 hours of social labour, then there is incorporated daily in labour power half a day's average social labour, in other words, half a day's labour is requisite for the daily production of labour-power. This quantity of labour forms the value of a day's labour-power or the value of the labour-power daily reproduced. If half a day's average social labour is incorporated in three shillings, then three shillings is the price corresponding to the value of a day's labour-power. If its owner [viz., the wage earner] therefore offers it for sale at three shillings a day, its selling price is equal to its value, and according to our supposition, our friend Moneybags, who is intent upon converting his three shillings into capital, pays this value.[22]

It should be observed that when Marx and his followers denounce capitalism for treating labor "like a commodity," what they really mean, as these passages make plain, is that they believe that under capitalism the value of labor is determined in the same way as the value of *products*—i.e., by the quantity of labor required to produce it. It should also be observed where Marx stands literally and intellectually in resorting to the use of such expressions as "our friend Moneybags" in referring to the capitalist employer.

Marx repeats some of the qualifications of Ricardo about the meaning of "subsistence." He says:

. . . the number and extent of his [the wage earner's] so-called necessary wants, as also the modes of satisfying them, are themselves the product of historical development, and depend therefore to a great extent on the degree of civilisation of a country, more particularly on the conditions under which, and consequently on the habits and degree of comfort in which, the class of free labourers has been formed. In contradistinction therefore to the case of other commodities, there enters into the determination of the value of labour-power a historical and moral element. Nevertheless, in a given country, at a given period, the average quantity of the means of subsistence necessary for the labourer is practically known.[23]

Nevertheless, Marx's version of the iron law of wages fundamentally differs from that of the classical economists. This is because Marx assumes that wages are somehow directly determined by "subsistence," totally apart from any connection to population growth and the operation of the law of diminishing returns. (According to the classical economists, of course, what created the alleged tendency of wages toward subsistence was precisely population growth and the ensuing operation of the law of diminishing returns.[24]) Wages are supposedly put at subsistence directly—by the arbitrary will of the capitalists. And, at bottom, despite the passage quoted, when Marx speaks of subsistence, he usually means it in a strict, biological sense. In his view, if employers can get away with it, they will pay wages sufficient to cover only the cost of the commodities *vitally necessary to the worker's survival*—and not even that. He declares:

> Capital cares nothing for the length of life of labour-power. All that concerns it is simply and solely the maximum of labour-power, that can be rendered fluent in a given working day. It attains this end by shortening the extent of the labourer's life, as a greedy farmer snatches increased produce from the soil by robbing it of its fertility.[25]

In *The Communist Manifesto,* Marx declares:

> The average price of wage-labor is the minimum wage, i.e., that quantum of the means of subsistence, which is absolutely requisite to keep the laborer in bare existence as a laborer. What, therefore, the wage-laborer appropriates by means of his labor, merely suffices to prolong and reproduce a bare existence.[26]

He even states that "The constant tendency of capital is to force the cost of labour back towards zero."[27]

In reading Marx, it is difficult to avoid reaching the conclusion that, in his view, if the capitalists could operate without restraint of any kind, there would be a section in the financial pages of the newspapers that does not presently appear—namely, a listing of the prices of such wage earners' necessities as potatoes, bread, and loincloths, and the rentals of cardboard shanties and mud huts. The capitalists, supposedly, would then periodically adjust wages to conform with the changes in these prices.

The Rate of Exploitation Formula

Marx's essential idea that fresh labor adds all value and yet is paid in accordance only with the labor required to "produce" it—that is, produce its necessities—gives rise to his formula for the expression of the degree of exploitation of the worker by the capitalist. I quote him at length:

> We have seen that the labourer, during one portion of the labour-process, produces only the value of his labour-power, that is, the value of his means of subsistence. Now since his work forms part of a system, based on the social division of labour, he does not directly produce the actual necessaries which he himself consumes; he produces instead a particular commodity, yarn for example, whose value is equal to the value of those necessaries or of the

money with which they can be bought. The portion of his day's labour devoted to this purpose, will be greater or less, in proportion to the value of the necessaries that he daily requires on average, or, what amounts to the same thing, in proportion to the labour-time required on average to produce them. If the value of those necessaries represents on an average the expenditure of six hours' labour, the workman must on an average work for six hours to produce that value. If instead of working for the capitalist, he worked independently on his own account, he would, other things being equal, still be obliged to labour for the same number of hours, in order to produce the value of his labour-power and thereby to gain the means of subsistence necessary for his conservation or continued reproduction [viz., for his continued ability to work]. But as we have seen, during that portion of his day's labour in which he produces the value of his labour-power, say three shillings, he produces only an equivalent for the value of his labour-power already advanced by the capitalist; the new value created only replaces the variable capital advanced [viz., the wages paid]. It is owing to this fact, that the production of the new value of three shillings takes the semblance of a mere reproduction. That portion of the working day, then, during which this reproduction takes place, I call *"necessary"* labour-time, and the labour expended during that time I call *"necessary"* labour. Necessary as regards the labourer, because independent of the particular social form of his labour; necessary, as regards capital, and the world of capitalists, because on the continued existence of the labourer depends their existence also.

> During the second period of the labour-process, that in which his labour is no longer necessary labour, the workman, it is true, labours, expends labour-power; but his labour, being no longer necessary labour, he creates no value for himself. He creates surplus-value which, for the capitalist, has all the charms of a creation out of nothing. This portion of the working day, I name surplus labour-time, and to the labour expended during that time, I give the name surplus labour. It is every bit as important, for a correct understanding of surplus-value, to conceive it as a mere congelation of surplus-labour-time, as nothing but materialised surplus-labour, as it is, for a proper comprehension of value, to conceive it as a mere congelation of so many hours of labour, as nothing but materialised labour. The essential difference between the various economic forms of society, between, for instance, a society based on slave labour, and one based on wage labour, lies only in the mode in which this surplus-labour is in each case extracted from the actual producer, the labourer.

> Since, on the one hand, the values of the variable capital and of the labour-power purchased by that capital are equal, and the value of this labour-power determines the necessary portion of the working day; and since, on the other hand, the surplus-value is determined by the surplus portion of the working day, it follows that surplus-value bears the same ratio to variable capital, that surplus-labour does to necessary labour, or in other words, the rate of surplus-value $\frac{s}{v} = \frac{surplus\ labor}{necessary\ labor}$. Both ratios, $\frac{s}{v}$ and $\frac{surplus\ labor}{necessary\ labor}$

express the same thing in different ways; in the one case by reference to materialised, incorporated labour, in the other by reference to living, fluent labour.

> The rate of surplus-value is therefore an exact expression for the degree of exploitation of labour-power by capital, or of the labourer by the capitalist.[28]

Marx's doctrine is thus actually the essence of simplicity. Fresh labor adds the entire amount by which the value of a product exceeds the value of the nonhuman means of production consumed in producing the product. But that labor is not paid in accordance with the number of hours for which it works, but in accordance with the smaller number of hours of labor required to produce the necessities that give the worker the capacity to work. To the extent that the workers work more hours than corresponds to the hours required to produce their necessities, they perform surplus labor, which is the foundation of surplus-value.

To express the idea even more simply, the consumption of necessities produced by only six hours of labor gives a worker the ability to perform twelve hours of labor. The capitalist is thus allegedly enabled to buy a working day of twelve hours at a wage corresponding to the six hours of labor required to produce the necessities that make possible the twelve hours of labor. The capitalist is therefore able to add twelve hours of labor to the value contained in the nonhuman means of production that must be consumed in order to produce his product, and he obtains that labor for a wage corresponding to only six hours of labor. In other words, he allegedly obtains twelve hours of labor, and the value added by twelve hours of labor, for a wage corresponding only to six hours of labor. This is the alleged source of his profit and of all other forms of "surplus-value." It is allegedly unpaid labor time. In Marx's own words:

> Let us examine the matter more closely. The value of a day's labour amounts to 3 shillings, because on our assumption half a day's labour is embodied in that quantity of labour-power, i.e., because the means of subsistence that are daily required for the production of labour-power, cost half a day's labour. But the past labour that is embodied in the labour-power, and the living labour that it can call into action; the daily cost of maintaining it, and its daily expenditure in work, are two totally different things. The former determines the exchange-value of the labour-power, the latter is its use-value. The fact that half a day's labour is necessary to keep the labourer alive during 24 hours, does not in any way prevent him from working a whole day. Therefore, the value of labour-power, and the value which that labour power creates in the labour-process, are two entirely different magnitudes; and this difference of the two values was what the capitalist had in view, when he was purchasing the labour-power. The useful qualities that labour-power possesses, and by virtue of which it makes yarn or boots, were to him nothing more than a conditio sine qua non; for in order to create value, labour must be expended in a useful manner. What really influenced him was the specific use-value which this commodity possesses of being *a source not only of value, but of more value than it has itself.*[29]

The following example makes the substance of Marx's entire system clear. (It should be noted that this example is virtually identical with the one extensively employed by Marx himself, except for the use of dollars rather than English shillings, and for the assumption that a unit of money represents just one hour of "congealed labor-time" rather than two such hours.[30])

Assume as a universal principle that for every hour of labor "congealed" in a product, there corresponds $1 of product value. (This would imply, according to Marx, that on a gold standard, 1 hour of labor was required to produce the quantity of gold defined as $1.) Assume in particular that the production of a certain quantity of cotton yarn begins with a quantity of raw cotton that is itself the product of 40 hours of labor. The money value of this raw cotton is, accordingly, $40. Assume further that the machinery by means of which, and the factory building in which, the yarn is produced lose a portion of their useful life in the processing of this particular batch of raw cotton which represents an additional 8 hours of labor. (In order to better understand this last assumption, we might assume that the machinery and factory building have required 8 million hours of labor to construct, and have a useful life such that they can contribute to the processing of a million batches of raw cotton such as the one they presently process. In that case the machinery and factory building contribute 8 hours of labor to the production of each of one million batches of yarn.) The monetary value of the contribution of the machinery and factory building to the batch of yarn is, accordingly, $8.

Thus, in this example, we have a "constant capital" used up representing 48 hours of congealed labor in all, and therefore $48 of monetary value. These 48 hours of labor congealed in the constant capital now pass over into the product, the cotton yarn. The cotton yarn is the product of all the labor that has entered into the constant capital used up to produce it and, in addition, is the product of the fresh, additional labor that is applied within the cotton mill itself. We assume with Marx that the quantity of this fresh, additional labor is 12 hours. On these assumptions, we end up with a quantity of cotton yarn that is the product of 60 hours of labor in toto—48 hours contributed by way of the constant capital used up to produce it and 12 hours more contributed by the fresh, additional labor that is employed in the cotton mill to process the raw cotton with the aid of the plant and equipment constituted by the mill. The monetary value of the resulting cotton yarn is, of course, $60.

The difference between the monetary value of the cotton yarn and the monetary value of the constant capital used up to produce the yarn is $12, precisely corresponding to the 12 hours of fresh, additional labor performed. The $12 represent the sum of all incomes earned at this stage of the process of production. They are the sum of the profits (and all other forms of "surplus-value") and the wages together. For they equal the $60 value of the product minus the $48 of costs of nonhuman means of production, that is, the costs other than wages. And thus, by the formula that *sales – (cost – wages) = profits + wages,* $60 of sales minus $48 of costs other than wages equals $12 of profits plus wages.

And now we come to see just how, according to Marx, profits and all other forms of "surplus-value" are deducted from the value supposedly added by the labor of the wage earners. The alleged "secret of profit making," to use Marx's expression, is that for the 12 hours of fresh, additional labor, and thus for the addition of $12 of monetary value to the constant capital that is used up, the capitalist pays a wage that corresponds not to the time the worker works, *but to the time required to produce the necessities the worker requires in order to be able to work*—the necessities he requires in order to be able to deliver his "labour-power." If the worker can perform 12 hours of labor by means of consuming necessities produced in only 6 hours, then the capitalist buys his 12 hours of labor for a wage of only $6. In this way allegedly, he obtains a product containing 60 hours of labor and worth $60, at a cost of only $54. He incurs a cost of $48 on account of constant capital that is used up and a further cost of only $6 for the performance of the 12 hours of labor. The "secret" is that he allegedly receives 6 hours of labor—the labor the worker performs in excess of what is equivalent to providing for his subsistence, i.e., the so-called surplus labor—that he, the capitalist, does not pay for. What he allegedly pays for is only the labor equivalent to what is required to produce the wage earner's necessities, i.e., the so-called necessary labor. In this way, says Marx,

> Every condition of the problem is satisfied, while the laws that regulate the exchange of commodities have been in no way violated. Equivalent has been exchanged for equivalent. For the capitalist as buyer paid for each commodity, for the cotton, the spindle and the labour-power, its full value. He then did what is done by every purchaser of commodities; he consumed their use-value. . . .

> By turning his money into commodities that serve as the material elements of a new product, and as factors in the labour-process, by incorporating living labour with their dead substance, the capitalist at the same time converts value, i.e., past, materialized, and dead labour into capital, into value big with value, a live monster that is fruitful and multiplies.[31]

4. Implications of the Exploitation Theory

It should be clear from the preceding discussion that the Marxists are deadly serious when they speak of "wage slavery" and describe all of history as a "class struggle" in which today's wage earners are the counterpart of the slaves and serfs of previous ages and in which today's businessmen and capitalists are the counterpart of the slave owners and feudal aristocrats of former times.[32] Marx's theory of "surplus-value" explains profit and the other nonwage incomes as the result of precisely the same facts that make possible the gains of a slave owner. The source of a slave owner's gain is the fact that a slave can perform more labor than is required to provide for his own subsistence. The excess goes to the benefit of the slave owner. Precisely that is held to be the source of the capitalist's profit and of every other form of "surplus-value."

The exploitation theory also implies that the workers are men without a country and "have nothing to lose but their chains," as *The Communist Manifesto* declares.[33] According to the exploitation theory, all economic progress simply passes the workers by. The effect of economic progress is to make available new and better goods and to reduce the prices of existing goods. But, according to the exploitation theory, the effect of reductions in the prices of goods purchased by the wage earners is a corresponding reduction in wages and increase in the portion of the worker's labor time appropriated for the creation of surplus-value. In the words of Marx:

> The value of commodities is in inverse ratio to the productiveness of labour. And so, too, is the value of labour-power, because it depends on the value of commodities. . . . [S]urplus-value is, on the contrary, directly proportional to that productiveness. It rises with rising and falls with falling productiveness. The value of money being assumed to be constant, an average social working day of 12 hours always produces the same new value, six shillings, no matter how this sum may be apportioned between surplus-value and wages. But if, in consequence of increased productiveness, the value of the necessaries of life fall, and the value of a day's labour be thereby reduced from five shillings to three, the surplus-value increases from one shilling to three. Ten hours were necessary for the reproduction of the value of the labour-power; now only six are required. Four hours have been set free, and can be annexed to the domain of surplus-labour. Hence there is immanent in capital an inclination and constant tendency, to heighten the productiveness of labour, in order to cheapen commodities, and by such cheapening to cheapen the labourer himself.[34]

Thus, according to Marx, the wage earners are deprived of the ability to buy any larger quantity of the goods whose prices fall and, by the same token, of the ability to set aside funds for the purchase of goods they did not previously purchase. Thus, all economic progress allegedly operates exclusively to the benefit of the "exploiters."

The exploitation theory implies not only that all economic progress passes the workers by, but, still worse, that the workers actually fall into a deepening state of impoverishment. In the words of *The Communist Manifesto:*

> Hitherto, every form of society has been based, as we have already seen, on the antagonism of oppressing and oppressed classes. But in order to oppress a class, certain conditions must be assured to it under which it can, at least, continue its slavish existence. The serf, in the period of serfdom, raised himself to membership in the commune, just as the petty bourgeois, under the yoke of feudal absolutism, managed to develop into a bourgeois.

> The modern laborer, on the contrary, instead of rising with the progress of industry, sinks deeper and deeper below the conditions of existence of his own class. He becomes a pauper and pauperism develops more rapidly than population and wealth. And here it becomes evident that the bourgeoisie is unfit any longer to be the ruling class in society, and to impose its conditions of existence upon society as an over-riding law. It is unfit to rule, because it is incompetent to assure an existence to its slave within his slavery, because it cannot help letting him sink into such a state that it has to feed him, instead of being fed by him.[35]

The theoretical basis for the doctrine of progressive impoverishment is a combination of two alleged circumstances that are supposedly unique to capitalism: an allegedly limitless greed for surplus-value on the part of capitalists, which supposedly arises from the nature of production for the sake of monetary gain, and an alleged tendency toward a declining rate of profit, which latter supposedly requires a rising rate of exploitation in order to limit the decline. In connection with the first of these circumstances, Marx writes:

> As capitalist, he is only capital personified. His soul is the soul of capital. But capital has one single life impulse, the tendency to create value and surplus-value, to make its constant factor, the means of production, absorb the greatest possible amount of surplus-labour.

> Capital is dead labour, that vampire-like, only lives by sucking living labour, and lives the more, the more labour it sucks. The time during which the labourer works is the time during which the capitalist consumes the labour-power he has purchased of him.[36]

> It is, however, clear that in any given economic formation of society, where not the exchange value but the use-value of the product predominates, surplus labour will be limited by a given set of wants which may be greater or less, and that here no boundless thirst for surplus-labour arises from the nature of production itself. Hence in antiquity overwork becomes horrible only when the object is to obtain exchange value in its specific independent money form; in the production of gold and silver.[37]

The doctrine of a falling rate of profit is implied in the exploitation theory on Marx's assumption that economic progress and capital accumulation are accompanied by a growth in so-called constant capital relative to "variable" capital. In Marx's own words:

> Suppose 100 pounds are the wages of 100 labourers for, say, one week. If these labourers perform equal amounts of necessary and surplus labour, if they work daily as many hours for themselves, i.e., for the reproduction of their wage, as they do for the capitalist, i.e., for the production of surplus-value, then the value of their total product = 200 pounds, and the surplus-value they produce would amount to 100 pounds. The rate of surplus-value, $\frac{s}{v}$, would = 100 percent. But, as we have seen, this rate of surplus-value would nonetheless express itself in very different rates of profit, depending on the different volumes of constant capital c and consequently of the total capital C, because the rate of profit = $\frac{s}{C}$. The rate of surplus-value is 100 percent:
>
> If c = 50, and v = 100, then $p' = \frac{100}{150} = 66\frac{2}{3}\%$;
>
> " c = 100, and v = 100, then $p' = \frac{100}{200} = 50\%$;
>
> " c = 200, and v = 100, then $p' = \frac{100}{300} = 33\frac{1}{3}\%$;
>
> " c = 300, and v = 100, then $p' = \frac{100}{400} = 25\%$;
>
> " c = 400, and v = 100, then $p' = \frac{100}{500} = 20\%$.

> This is how the same rate of surplus-value would express itself under the same degree of labour exploitation in a falling rate of profit, because the material growth of the constant capital implies also a growth—albeit not in the same proportion—in its value, and consequently in that of the total capital.[38]

Not surprisingly, in his chapter on counteracting influences concerning the tendency toward a falling rate of profit, Marx provides "Increasing Intensity of Exploitation" and "Depression of Wages Below The Value of Labour-Power" as section headings 1 and 2.[39] He declares: "The tendency of the rate of profit to fall is bound up with a tendency of the rate of surplus-value to rise, hence with a tendency for the rate of labour exploitation to rise."[40] For, as Marx's example above indicates, a rise in the rate of "surplus-value" can correspondingly offset the alleged negative effects on the rate of profit of a rise in "constant capital" relative to "variable capital."

In Marx's view, the inherent greed of the capitalists, and the tendency of the rate of profit otherwise to fall, leads the capitalists to seek to extend the working day to the maximum possible limit, as a principal means of raising the rate of "surplus-value." In effect, the capitalists see the workers lolling about after work in pubs or amusing themselves on playing fields, expending energy that the food provided by the capitalists has made possible. Instead of allowing that energy to be wasted in such idleness, the capitalists will allegedly capture it in the factories, in the production of commodities, where it can add to the magnitude of "surplus-value." They allegedly accomplish this by reducing hourly wages, thereby compelling the workers to work longer hours to earn subsistence. The result is a corresponding rise in the amount and rate of "surplus-value," and an accompanying offset to the fall in the rate of profit. If, for example, the working day can be extended to eighteen hours from twelve hours, while the worker still requires necessities produced in only six hours, then the rate of surplus-value is increased from 100 percent to 200 percent. For $\frac{s}{v} = \frac{surplus\ labor}{variable\ capital} = \frac{18-6}{6} = 200$ percent. Thus, the rate of profit can allegedly be doubled, or at least maintained in conditions in which it would otherwise have been cut in half.

Marx describes the "greed for surplus-labour" in the following words:

> "What is a working day? What is the length of time during which capital may consume the labour-power whose daily value it buys? How far may the working day be extended beyond the working time necessary for the reproduction of labour-power itself?" It has been seen that to these questions capital replies: the working day contains the full 24 hours with the deduction of the few hours of repose without which labour-power absolutely refuses its services again. Hence it is self-evident that the labourer is nothing else, his whole life through, than labour-power, that therefore all his disposable time is by nature and law labour-time, to be devoted to the self-expansion of capital. Time for education, for intellectual development, for the fulfilling of social functions and for social intercourse, for the free-play of his bodily and mental activity, even the rest time of Sunday (and that in a country of Sabbatarians!)—moonshine! But in its blind unrestrainable passion, its were-wolf hunger for surplus-labour, capital oversteps not only the moral, but even the merely physical maximum bounds of the working day. It usurps the time for growth, development, and healthy maintenance of the body. It steals the time required for the consumption of fresh air and sunlight. It higgles over a meal-time, incorporating it where possible with the process of production itself, so that food is given to the labourer as to a mere means of production, as coal is supplied to the boiler, grease and oil to the machinery. It reduces the sound sleep needed for the restoration, reparation, refreshment of the bodily powers to just so many hours of torpor as the revival of an organism, absolutely exhausted, renders essential. It is not the normal maintenance of the labour-power which is to determine the limits of the working day; it is the greatest possible daily expenditure of labour-power, no matter how diseased, compulsory, and painful it may be, which is to determine the limits of the labourers' period of repose.[41]

The greed for "surplus-value," claims Marx, leads the capitalists to appropriate the labor of women and children in exactly the same way as, he alleges, they appropriate the additional hours of labor of the adult males. Namely, they reduce wage rates and thereby make it necessary for a wage earner's entire family to perform labor in order to earn enough for the family to obtain subsistence. In this way, once again, the expenditure of energy made possible by the food the capitalists enable the workers to buy is allegedly captured in the production of commodities and thus in the generation of "surplus-value." Now, in exchange for a wage enabling the worker to buy the products of the same 6 hours of "necessary labor," or perhaps just a little more, the capitalist allegedly obtains the equivalent perhaps of 48 hours of total labor, as the labor of the adult male is joined by the full-time labor of his wife and children. And thus the rate of surplus-value can rise to 700 percent. For $\frac{s}{v} = \frac{surplus\ labor}{variable\ capital} = \frac{48-6}{6} = 700\%$.

Marx describes this alleged phenomenon in the following passages of *Das Kapital*, in which he blames machinery for making such exploitation possible:

> In so far as machinery dispenses with muscular power, it becomes a means of employing labourers of slight muscular strength, and those whose bodily development is incomplete, but whose limbs are all the more supple. The labour of women and children was, therefore, the first thing sought for by capitalists who used machinery. That mighty substitute for labour and labourers was forthwith changed into a means for increasing the number of wage-labourers by enrolling, under the direct sway of capital, every member of the workman's family, without distinction of age or sex. Compulsory work for the capitalist usurped the place, not only of the children's play, but also of free labour at home within moderate limits for the support of the family.

> The value of labour-power was determined, not only by the labour-time necessary to maintain the individual adult laborer, but also by that necessary to maintain his family. Machinery, by throwing every member of that family on to the labour market, spreads the value of the man's labour-power over his whole family. It thus depreciates his labour-power. To purchase the labour-power of a family of four workers may, perhaps, cost more than it formerly did to purchase the labour-power of the head of the family, but, in return, four days' labour takes the place of one, and their price falls in proportion to the excess of the surplus-labour of four over the surplus-labour of one. In order that the family may live, four people must now, not only labour, but expend surplus-labour for the capitalist. Thus, we see, that machinery, while augmenting the human material that forms the principal object of capital's exploiting power, at the same time raises the degree of exploitation.[42]

No absurdity escapes Marx in applying his doctrine that the capitalists arbitrarily pay the worker a wage conforming to the labor time needed to produce his minimum subsistence. Thus, according to Marx, still a further means of increasing the rate of "surplus-value" is "the intensification of labor"—what the labor unions nowadays describe as a "speedup." The intensification of labor represents the performance of more labor in a given time, and supposedly increases surplus-value both by reducing the labor time required to produce the worker's necessities and by representing the equivalent of a lengthening of the hours of work as well.[43] It allegedly becomes of particular importance after the enactment of laws limiting the length of the working day.[44]

And, beyond this, yet still another alleged method of raising the rate of "surplus-value," according to Marx, is a cheapening of the worker's diet.[45] If the workers could be forced to substitute potatoes or rice for more expensive food, the so-called necessary labor time would be reduced and "surplus-labor-time" correspondingly increased.

This then is the exploitation theory—a doctrine so contorted in its development and so grotesque and absurd in its implications that it deserves to evoke laughter in the very act of being expounded. Nevertheless, instead of being greeted with laughter, the doctrine has been taken with the utmost seriousness and, as I have shown, stands as the intellectual foundation of the whole economic and social program of twentieth century "liberalism." Above all, the mentalities that have posed as liberal "intellectuals" in the last century and a quarter—that is, as serious thinkers—have taken the validity of the theory absolutely for granted and as the starting point of their economic and social programs.

According to them, if not prevented by government intervention, the capitalists would, indeed, set wage rates at the point of minimum subsistence and the hours of work at the maximum possible limit, in order to maximize their profits. But government intervention, they believe, especially in the form of prounion legislation, can serve to decree higher wage rates, and all that occurs is that "surplus-labor-time" and "surplus-value" are reduced, thereby equivalently benefitting the wage earners at the expense of the capitalist exploiters' profits. In exactly the same way, the "liberal intellectuals" believe that the government's and the unions' decree of shorter hours also serves merely to reduce "surplus-labor-time" and "surplus-value," again allegedly benefitting the wage earners at the expense of the capitalist exploiters' profits. And, of course, identically the same analysis is present in their arguments for child labor legislation and laws compelling improvements in working conditions.

With the exploitation theory as their foundation, the

"liberal intellectuals'" contribution to the life of their times has been to set about busying themselves both with the critique of the capitalist society in which they have lived, and with the concoction of all manner of schemes and programs for overcoming the various evils that the exploitation theory in its flights of fancy absurdly and maliciously attributes to capitalism. They have bent art and literature, history and journalism, even philosophy and science, as well as politics, law, and government to conform with the exploitation theory and its ludicrous implications.

When the absurdities of the exploitation theory are fully understood, as they ought to be by the end of this chapter, it will be clear that never in all of human history has a greater bunch of pompous ignoramuses with pretensions to knowledge behaved more destructively and self-destructively—made themselves more a spectacle of downright fools meriting the utter contempt of all mankind—than have the "liberal intellectuals" of the last four or five generations. Their lack of genuine liberalism will be seen to be surpassed only by their lack of genuine intellect.

In the next part of this chapter, my first order of business will be to thoroughly overturn the Marxian version of the iron law of wages—that is, the belief, so central to the exploitation theory, that wages are determined by the arbitrary power of businessmen and capitalists, or at least would be if not for the existence of such measures as prounion legislation and minimum-wage and maximum-hours laws. I will then explain how real wages—the goods and services that a worker's money wages can actually buy—are determined by the productivity of labor, that is, by the output per unit of labor prevailing in the economic system. The remainder of the part will constitute a refutation of all aspects of the exploitation theory which may thus far have escaped direct criticism. As I have indicated previously, the refutation will be accomplished primarily simply by means of developing the implications and underlying foundations of the fact that real wages are determined by the productivity of labor.

PART B

THE PRODUCTIVITY THEORY OF WAGES

1. The Irrelevance of Worker Need and Employer Greed in the Determination of Wages

The Marxian version of the iron law of wages—that is, the doctrine of the alleged arbitrary power of employers over wages—appears plausible because there are two obvious facts that it relies on, facts which do not actually support it, but which appear to support it. These facts can be described as "worker need" and "employer greed." The average worker must work in order to live, and he must find work fairly quickly, because his savings cannot sustain him for long. And if necessary—if he had no alternative—he would be willing to work for as little as minimum physical subsistence. At the same time, self-interest makes employers, like any other buyers, prefer to pay less rather than more—to pay lower wages rather than higher wages. People put these two facts together and conclude that if employers were free, wages would be driven down by the force of the employers' self-interest—as though by a giant plunger pushing down in an empty cylinder—and that no resistance to the fall in wages would be encountered until the point of minimum subsistence was reached. At that point, it is held, workers would refuse to work because starvation without the strain of labor would be preferable to starvation with the strain of labor.

What must be realized is that while it is true that workers would be willing to work for minimum subsistence if necessary, and that self-interest makes employers prefer to pay less rather than more, both of these facts are *irrelevant* to the wages the workers actually have to accept in the labor market.

Let us start with "worker need." To understand why a worker's willingness to work for subsistence if necessary is irrelevant to the wages he actually has to work for, consider the analogous case of the owner of a late-model car who decides to accept a job offer, and to live, in the heart of New York City. If this car owner cannot afford several hundred dollars a month to pay the cost of keeping his car in a garage, and if he cannot devote several prime working hours every week to driving around, hunting for places to park his car on the street, he will be willing, if he can find no better offer, to give his car away for free—indeed, to pay someone to come and take it off his hands. Yet the fact that he is willing to do this is absolutely irrelevant to the price he actually must accept for his car. That price is determined on the basis of the utility and scarcity of used cars—by the demand for and supply of such cars. Indeed, so long as the number of used cars offered for sale remained the same, and the demand for used cars remained the same, it would not matter even if every seller of such a car were willing to give his car away for free, or willing even to pay to have it taken off his hands. None of them would have to accept a zero or negative price or any price that is significantly different from the price he presently can receive.

This point is illustrated in terms of the simple supply and demand diagram presented in Figure 14–1. On the

vertical axis, I depict the price of used cars, designated by P. On the horizontal axis, I depict the quantity of used cars, designated by Q, that sellers are prepared to sell and the buyers to buy at any given price. The willingness of sellers to sell some definite, given quantity of used cars at any price from zero on up (or, indeed, from less than zero by the cost of having the cars taken off their hands) is depicted by a vertical line drawn through that quantity. The vertical line SS denotes the fact that sellers are willing to sell the specific quantity A of used cars at any price from something less than zero on up to as much as they can get for their cars. The fact that they are willing to sell for zero or a negative price has nothing whatever to do with the actual price they receive, which in this case is the very positive price P_1. The actual price they receive in a case of this kind is determined by the limitation of the supply of used cars, together with the demand for used cars. In Figure 14–1, it is determined at point E, which represents the intersection of the vertical supply line with the demand curve. The price that corresponds to that juncture of supply and demand is P_1. The fact that the sellers are all willing if necessary to accept a price less than P_1 is, as I say, simply irrelevant to the price they actually must accept. The price the sellers receive in a case of this kind is not determined by the terms on which they are willing to sell. Rather, *it is determined by the competition of the buyers for the limited supply offered for sale.* (This, of course, is the kind of case Böhm-Bawerk had in mind when he declared that "price is actually limited and determined by the valuations on the part of the buyers exclusively."[46])

Essentially the same diagram, Figure 14–2, depicts the case of labor. Instead of showing price on the vertical axis, I show wages, designated by W. Instead of the supply line being vertical to the point of the sellers being willing to pay to have their good taken off their hands, I assume that no supply whatever is offered below the point of "minimum subsistence," M. This is depicted by a horizontal line drawn from M and parallel to the horizontal axis. Thus, the supply curve in this case has a horizontal portion at "minimum subsistence" before becoming vertical. These are the only differences between Figures 14–1 and 14–2.

Figure 14–2 makes clear that the fact that the workers are willing to work for as little as minimum subsistence is no more relevant to the wages they actually have to accept than was the fact in the previous example that the sellers of used cars were willing to give them away for free or pay to have them taken off their hands. For even though the workers are willing to work for as little as minimum subsistence, the wage they actually obtain in the conditions of the market is the incomparably higher wage W_1, which is shown by the intersection—once

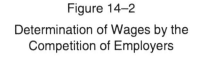

Figure 14–1

Determination of Price by the
Competition of the Buyers

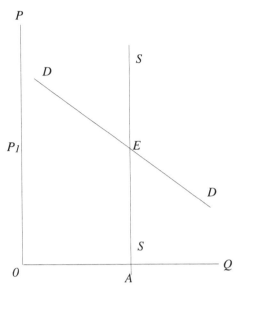

Figure 14–2

Determination of Wages by the
Competition of Employers

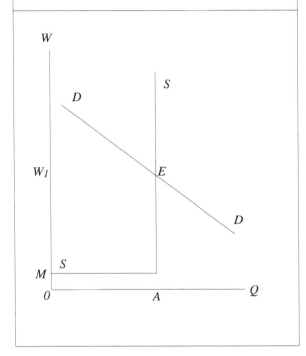

again at point *E*—of the demand for labor with the limited supply of labor denoted by point *A* on the horizontal axis. Exactly like the value of used cars, or anything else that exists in a given, limited supply, *the value of labor is determined on a foundation of its utility and scarcity, by demand and supply—more specifically, by the competition of buyers for the limited supply*—not by any form of cost of production, least of all by any "cost of production of labor."[47]

It also quickly becomes clear that "employer greed" is fully as irrelevant to the determination of wage rates as "worker need." This becomes apparent as soon as the case of the art auction is recalled that I presented in Chapter 6 in order to demonstrate the actual self-interest of buyers.[48] There I assumed that there are two people at an art auction, both of whom want the same painting. One of these people, let us now call him Mr. Smith, is willing and able to bid as high as $2,000 for the painting. The other, let us now call him Mr. Jones, is willing and able to go no higher than $1,000.

Of course, Mr. Smith does not want to spend $2,000 for the painting. This figure is merely the limit of how high he will go if he has to. He would much prefer to obtain the painting for only $200, or better still, for only $20, or, best of all, for nothing at all. What we must recall here is precisely how low a bid Mr. Smith's rational self-interest allows him to persist in. Would it, for exam-

ple, actually be to Mr. Smith's self-interest to persist in a bid of only $20, or $200?

It should be obvious that the answer to this question is decidedly no! This is because if Mr. Smith persists in such a low bid, the effect will be that he loses the painting to Mr. Jones, who is willing and able to bid more than $20 and more than $200. In fact, in the conditions of this case, Mr. Smith must lose the painting to the higher bidding of Mr. Jones, if he persists in bidding any sum under $1,000! If Mr. Smith is to obtain the painting, the conditions of the case require him to bid more than $1,000, because that is the sum required to exceed the maximum potential bid of Mr. Jones.

This case contains the fundamental principle that names the actual self-interest of buyers. That principle is that a buyer rationally desires to pay not the lowest price he can imagine, but *the lowest price that is simultaneously too high for any other potential buyer of the good, who would otherwise obtain the good in his place.*

This identical principle, of course, applies to the determination of wage rates, as I also indicated in Chapter 6.[49] The only difference between the labor market and the auction of a painting is the number of units involved. Instead of one painting with two potential buyers for it, there are many millions of workers who must sell their services, together with potential employers of all those workers and of untold millions more workers. This is because just as in the example of the art auction, the essential fact that is present in the labor market is that the potential quantity demanded exceeds the supply available. The potential quantity of labor demanded always far exceeds the quantity of labor that the workers are able, let alone willing, to perform.

For labor, it should be recalled, is scarce. It is the most fundamentally useful and scarce thing in the economic system: virtually everything else that is useful is its product and is limited in supply only by virtue of our lack of ability or willingness to expend more labor to produce a larger quantity of it. (This, of course, includes raw materials, which can always be produced in larger quantity by devoting more labor to the more intensive exploitation of land and mineral deposits that are already used in production, or by devoting labor to the exploitation of land and mineral deposits not presently exploited.[50]) As I have shown, for all practical purposes there is no limit to our need and desire for goods or, therefore, for the performance of the labor required to produce them. In having, for example, a need and desire to be able to spend incomes five or ten times the incomes we presently spend, we have an implicit need and desire for the performance of five or ten times the labor we presently perform, for that is what would be required in the present state of technology and the productivity of labor to supply us with such increases in the supply of goods. Moreover, almost all of us would welcome the full-time personal services of at least several other people. Thus, on both grounds labor is scarce, for the maximum amount of labor available to satisfy the needs and desires of the average member of the economic system can never exceed the labor of just one person, and, indeed, in actual practice, falls far short of that amount because of the existence of large numbers of dependents.[51]

The consequence of the scarcity of labor is that *wage rates in a free market can fall no lower than corresponds to the point of full employment*. At that point the scarcity of labor is felt, and any further fall in wage rates would be against the self-interests of employers because then a labor *shortage* would ensue. Thus, if somehow wage rates did fall below the point corresponding to full employment, it would be to the self-interest of employers to bid them back up again.

These facts can be shown in the same supply and demand diagram I used to show the irrelevance to wage determination of workers being willing to work for subsistence. Thus, Figure 14–3 shows that if wage rates were below their market equilibrium of W_1, which takes place at the point of full employment, denoted by E—if, for example, they were at the lower level of W_2—a labor shortage would exist. The quantity of labor demanded at the wage rate of W_2 is B. But the quantity of labor

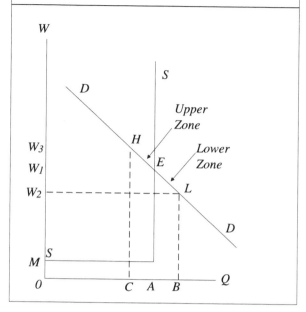

Figure 14–3
Employer Competition Versus
Labor Shortage

available—whose employment constitutes full employment—is the smaller amount A. Thus, at the lower wage, the quantity of labor demanded exceeds the supply available by the horizontal distance AB.

The shortage exists because the lower wage of W_2 enables employers to afford labor who would not have been able to afford it at the wage of W_1, or it enables employers who would have been able to afford some labor at the wage of W_1 to now afford a larger quantity of labor. To whatever extent such employers employ labor that they otherwise could not have employed, that much less labor remains to be employed by other employers, who are willing and able to pay the higher wage of W_1.

For the sake of simplicity, we can assume that at the artificially low wage of W_2 the entire quantity AB of labor is employed by employers who otherwise could not have afforded to employ that labor. (Of course, under the conditions of a shortage, it is a random matter who actually ends up as the employer. But this is inconsequential in the present context. All that is essential to the argument is that any part of the quantity AB of labor end up in the hands of employers who otherwise could not have afforded it.) The effect of this is to leave an equivalently reduced quantity of labor available for those employers who could have afforded the market wage of W_1. The labor available to those employers is reduced by AC, which is precisely equal to AB. This is the inescapable result of the existence of a given quantity of labor and some of it being taken off the market by some employers at the expense of other employers. What the one set gains, the other must lose. Thus, because the wage is W_2 rather than W_1, the employers who could have afforded the market wage of W_1 and obtained the full quantity of labor A are now able to employ only the smaller quantity of labor C, because labor has been taken off the market by employers who depend on the artificially low wage of W_2.

The employers who could have afforded the market wage of W_1 are in identically the same position as the bidder at the art auction who is about to see the painting he wants go to another bidder not able or willing to pay as much. The way to think of the situation is that there are two groups of bidders for quantity AB of labor: those willing and able to pay the market wage of W_1, or an even higher wage—one as high as W_3—and those willing and able to pay only a wage that is below W_1—a wage that must be as low as W_2. In Figure 14–3, the position of these two groups is indicated by two zones on the demand curve: an upper zone HE and a lower zone EL. The wage of W_1 is required for the employers in the upper zone to be able to outbid the employers in the lower zone.[52]

The question is: Is it to the rational self-interest of the employers willing and able to pay a wage of W_1, or higher, to lose the labor they want to other employers not able or willing to pay a wage as high as W_1? The obvious answer is no. And the consequence is that if, somehow, the wage were to fall below W_1, the self-interest of employers who are willing and able to pay W_1 or more, and who stood to lose some of their workers if they did not do so, would lead them to bid wage rates back up to W_1. The rational self-interest of employers, like the rational self-interest of any other buyers, does not lead them to pay the lowest wage (price) they can imagine, but the lowest wage that is *simultaneously too high for other potential employers of the same labor who are not able or willing to pay as much and who would otherwise be enabled to employ that labor in their place.*

The principle that it is against the self-interest of employers to allow wage rates to fall to the point of creating a labor shortage is illustrated by the conditions which prevail when the government imposes such a shortage by virtue of a policy of price and wage controls. In such conditions, employers actually conspire with the wage earners to evade the controls and to raise wage rates. They do so by such means as awarding artificial promotions, which allow them to pay higher wages within the framework of the wage controls.

The payment of higher wages in the face of a labor shortage is to the self-interest of employers because it is the necessary means of gaining and keeping the labor they want to employ. In overbidding the competition of other potential employers for labor, it attracts workers to come to work for them and it removes any incentive for their present workers to leave their employ. This is because it eliminates the artificial demand for labor by the employers who depend on a below-market wage in order to be able to afford labor. It is, as I say, identically the same in principle as the bidder who wants the painting at an auction raising his bid to prevent the loss of the painting to another bidder not able or willing to pay as much. The higher bid is to his self-interest because it knocks out the competition. In the conditions of a labor shortage, which necessarily materializes if wage rates go below the point corresponding to full employment, the payment of higher wages provides exactly the same benefit to employers.

On the basis of the preceding discussion, and also discussion in Parts B and C of Chapter 13, it should be clear that average money wage rates are determined neither by worker need nor by employer greed, but, basically, by the quantity of money in the economic system and thus the aggregate monetary demand for labor, on the one side, and by the number of workers willing and able to work, on the other—that is, by the ratio of the demand for labor to the supply of labor. It should also be clear that in a free labor market, money wage rates can fall no lower than corresponds to the point of full employment.

Two points should be realized in connection with the principle that it is against the self-interest of employers to allow wage rates to fall below the point that corresponds to full employment. First, the operation of the principle does not require that full employment be established throughout the economic system before wage rates cease to fall. On the contrary, the principle applies to each occupation and, still more narrowly, to each occupation within each geographical area. For example, the wage rates of carpenters in Des Moines can fall no further than corresponds to the point of full employment of carpenters in Des Moines. Any further fall would create a shortage of such carpenters and thus would be prevented or quickly reversed, even though there might still be major unemployment in other occupations or in other geographical areas.

Second, the operation of the principle need not be feared as possibly serving to bring about the establishment of subsistence wages through the back door, so to speak. By this, I mean that so long as unemployment exists, there is room for wage rates to fall without the creation of a labor shortage. And in a free market, wage rates would in fact fall in such circumstances. This is because in such circumstances, the self-interest of the employers, and also of the unemployed, would operate to drive them down. It should not be thought, however, that the fall in wage rates in these circumstances meant that the conditions of supply and demand were capable of accomplishing the human misery that Marxism attributes to the alleged arbitrary power of businessmen and capitalists.

It should be recalled that we saw in Chapter 13 that a drop in wage rates to the full employment point does not imply any drop in the average worker's standard of living. That is, it does not imply any reduction in the goods and services he can actually buy—any reduction in his so called real wages—because the elimination of unemployment that the fall in wage rates brings about means more production and a fall in costs of production, both of which mean lower prices. Indeed, we saw that it is likely that real wages actually rise with the elimination of unemployment, even in the short run, because not only do prices fall as much as, or even more than, wages, but also the burden of supporting the unemployed is eliminated, with the result that disposable, take-home pay drops less than gross wages and less than prices.[53] When these facts are kept in mind, it is clear that insofar as market conditions require a fall in wage rates, they are, if anything, at the same time operating to raise the average worker's standard of living further above subsistence, not drive it down toward subsistence.[54]

2. Determination of Real Wages by the Productivity of Labor

With the Marxian version of the iron law of wages now out of the way, it is possible to turn to the exposition of the productivity theory of wages proper. Chapter 13's analysis of what happens to real wages when money wages fall in the course of eliminating unemployment provides a good beginning, because it points the way to an understanding of the role of the productivity of labor in determining real wages. In Chapter 13, we saw that despite the fall in money wage rates, real wage rates—on a gross basis—stayed the same. (On a net basis, of course, they increased, because of the elimination of the burden of supporting the unemployed.)[55]

Real wages stayed the same in the analysis of Chapter 13 because the productivity of labor remained the same. This was responsible for the fact that the employment of additional workers resulted in an equal proportional increase in the production and supply of consumers' goods and thus, in the face of constant demands for consumers' goods and labor, in a fall in the prices of consumers' goods in the same proportion as the fall in wage rates. This left the purchasing power of wages—real wages—unchanged. In other words, with a constant productivity

of labor, increases in the supply of labor and consumers' goods take place in the same proportion and cause equal reductions in wage rates and prices in the face of constant demands for labor and consumers' goods, leaving real wages the same.

We shall now see that not only in the case of the elimination of unemployment through a fall in wages and prices, but in all cases, *real wages are determined primarily by the productivity of labor*—i.e., by the output of goods and services per unit of labor. This conclusion follows from the very nature of real wages.

Real wages—the goods and services the worker can buy with his money wages—are, in the first instance, determined by the relationship between wages and prices. They can be expressed as the ratio of wages to prices. The higher are wages relative to prices, or equivalently, the lower are prices relative to wages, the more can the worker's money wages buy. All this is expressed in the formula

$$Average \ Real \ Wage \ Rate = \frac{W}{P}$$

where W is the average money wage rate, and P is the general consumer price level.

We can understand how the productivity of labor operates to determine real wages if we once again employ the formulas for money wages and the price level, namely:

$$W = \frac{D_L}{S_L}$$

and

$$P = \frac{D_C}{S_C}.$$

In these equations, of course, D_L is the aggregate demand for labor, as manifested in a definite total expenditure of money to employ labor in the economic system, that is, in total payrolls of a given size; S_L is the aggregate supply of labor, as manifested in a definite total quantity of labor employed; D_C is the aggregate demand for consumers' goods, as manifested in a definite total expenditure of money to buy consumers' goods; and S_C is the aggregate supply of consumers' goods, as manifested in a definite total quantity of consumers' goods produced and sold.

We can begin by holding everything constant but the productivity of labor, which, for the sake of simplicity, we can assume doubles over the course of some period of time. Thus, we assume that the money supply is the same and therefore that the aggregate monetary demands for labor and consumers' goods are the same. We also assume that the size of the population and the number of workers employed are the same. As I say, everything is assumed to be the same except the productivity of labor, which is assumed to double. This is *Case 1*.

Using asterisks to denote fixity or lack of change, we see the results of *Case 1* in the following equations:

$$\frac{D_L^*}{S_L^*} = W^*$$

$$\frac{D_C^*}{2S_C} = \frac{P}{2}.$$

The result of prices halving while money wages remain the same is a doubling of average real wages. For inasmuch as

$$\frac{W}{P} = Average\ Real\ Wage\ Rate,$$

it follows that

$$\frac{W^*}{\frac{1}{2} \times P} = 2 \times Average\ Real\ Wage\ Rate.$$

Case 1 shows that with the demand for and supply of labor the same, average money wage rates remain the same. It also shows, and this is critical, that the effect of a doubling of the productivity of labor, given the employment of the same number of workers, is a doubling of the supply of consumers' goods produced and sold. Indeed, since the productivity of labor is the output per unit of labor, it can be expressed by the following equation:

$$Productivity\ of\ Labor = \frac{S_C}{S_L}.$$

The meaning of this equation is that the productivity of labor is reflected in the ratio of the supply of consumers' goods produced and sold to the supply of labor employed. The higher is the productivity of labor, the greater is the supply of consumers' goods produced and sold relative to the supply of labor employed. With S_L fixed, a doubling of the productivity of labor means a doubling of S_C. That is, if the supply of labor employed is the same and the productivity of labor doubles, the supply of consumers' goods produced and sold doubles. In equation form,

$$2 \times Productivity\ of\ Labor = \frac{2S_C}{S_L^*}.$$

Now, in the face of an unchanged demand for consumers' goods, the doubling of the supply of consumers' goods has the effect of halving the prices of consumers' goods and thus of doubling the buying power of the unchanged average money wage rates—that is, of doubling average real wage rates. Stating matters somewhat more broadly, the doubled productivity of labor doubles

real wages by virtue of doubling the supply of consumers' goods relative to the supply of labor and thereby halving the prices of consumers' goods relative to wage rates.

We see much more in *Case 1* than the fact that when the productivity of labor doubles, real wages double. Obviously, the general principle that is present in *Case 1* is that *real wages vary directly with the productivity of labor*, whatever it may be. This is because if the productivity of labor had increased by a factor of five or ten, rather than by a factor of two, and that had been the only change, then prices would have fallen to a fifth or a tenth, instead of to half, while money wage rates stayed the same. And thus real wage rates would have increased by a factor of five or ten, instead of two, precisely in accordance with the increase in the productivity of labor. This is because at a fifth or tenth of the initial price level, the same money wages would buy five or ten times more, respectively. (By the same token, to take an example of a fall in the productivity of labor, if the productivity of labor had halved, and that had been the only change, then the supply of consumers' goods would also have halved, and prices would have doubled while money wage rates remained the same. In this case, real wages would have halved, in accordance with the halving of the productivity of labor.)

Now that we have seen the effect of a rise in the productivity of labor in the context of a constant quantity of money and thus constant monetary demands for labor and consumers' goods, it is important to consider the effect of an increase in the quantity of money and the monetary demands for labor and consumers' goods. Once again, for the sake of simplicity, we assume that the magnitudes which increase neatly double. To isolate the effect of their increase we now assume that both the productivity of labor and the number of workers employed remain the same. This is *Case 2*, whose implications are shown in the following equations:

$$\frac{2D_L}{S_L^*} = 2W$$

$$\frac{2D_C}{S_C^*} = 2P.$$

In this case, where the supply of labor employed is unchanged and there is no increase in the productivity of labor, there is also no increase in the supply of consumers' goods. Hence, where the supply of consumers' goods is shown, it is accompanied by an asterisk. All that occurs in this case is that, in the face of unchanged supplies of labor and consumers' goods, the doubling of the quantity of money, and the consequent doubling of the aggregate demands for labor and consumers' goods, succeeds in doubling both wage rates and prices, with the result that average real wages remain absolutely unchanged, for

$$\frac{2W}{2P} = Average\ Real\ Wage\ Rate\ ^*.$$

What is important about *Case 2* is that it shows that, in sharpest contrast to an increase in the productivity of labor, a rise in money wages by itself does *not* represent any rise in real wages. The rise in money wages here is the result of an increase in the quantity of money, which operates to raise prices fully as much as wages, thus leaving real wages unchanged. In *Case 2*, the doubling of the quantity of money and the aggregate demands for labor and consumers' goods serves to double prices along with wages, leaving the real wages of the average worker absolutely unchanged. Obviously, the result of unchanged real wages would apply to *any* increase in the quantity of money and the aggregate demands for labor and consumers' goods. So long as wages and prices both increase in the same proportion, whether by two or by two hundred, or by any other number, the higher wages buy no more than did the lower wages of the past.

Now that we have considered the effects of an increase in the productivity of labor and in the quantity of money separately, in *Cases 1* and *2*, it is time to consider a case in which both factors operate side by side. This we do in *Case 3*. In this case, we assume that over a period of years *both the productivity of labor and the quantity of money double*, and that these changes once again respectively result in a doubling of the supply of consumers' goods produced and sold and in a doubling of the monetary demands for labor and consumers' goods. The substance of this case appears in these two equations:

$$\frac{2D_L}{S_L^*} = 2W$$

$$\frac{2D_C}{2S_C} = P^*.$$

When the results of these two equations are combined, the effect on average real wages is shown to be

$$\frac{2W}{P^*} = 2 \times Average\ Real\ Wage\ Rate.$$

Thus, in *Case 3*, we find that once again average real wages double. They double because in contrast to *Case 2*, the doubling of money wages is accompanied by a general consumer price level that is unchanged. What makes it possible for the general consumer price level to remain unchanged, in the face of a doubled quantity of money and a doubled aggregate demand for consumers' goods, is *the doubling of the productivity of labor*. This causes the supply of consumers' goods to double as the demand

for them doubles, and so leaves their price level unchanged. In effect, the doubled quantity of money and the doubled aggregate monetary demand for labor that it causes come up against an unchanged supply of labor and thus double average money wage rates, but thanks to the doubled productivity of labor, the doubled quantity of money and the doubled monetary demand for consumers' goods that it causes come up against a doubled supply of consumers' goods and thus leave the average of consumers' goods prices unchanged. (It should be realized that the doubling of the productivity of labor also leaves average unit costs unchanged despite the doubling of wage rates, for the doubled wage per worker is spread over double the number of units produced per worker.)

The essential point to realize is that *the source of the rise in real wages is always the rise in the productivity of labor*, not the increase in the quantity of money and the consequent increase in money wage rates. What is also very important to realize is that *the way the rise in the productivity of labor raises real wages is not by raising money wages, but by reducing prices!*

It is the increase in the quantity of money that increases money wages, not the increase in the productivity of labor. The increase in the productivity of labor increases money wages only insofar as it serves to increase the production of the monetary commodity under a system of commodity money, that is, only indirectly, insofar as it is the cause of an increase in the quantity of gold or silver money. Apart from this, the rise in the productivity of labor operates to reduce prices even in conditions such as those of *Case 3*, in which prices do not actually fall.

In such a case, it operates to reduce prices not in comparison with what they were, but in comparison with what *they otherwise would have been*. The fact that prices are unchanged in *Case 3*, even though the quantity of money and the demand for consumers' goods has doubled, thereby tending to make prices double, is the result only of the fact that the doubling of the productivity of labor simultaneously operates to cut prices in half. Prices are unchanged only as the result of being halved from the doubled level that the increase in the quantity of money and the monetary demand for consumers' goods would otherwise have made them reach.

The essential role of the productivity of labor in determining real wages is no less present if we further increase the complexity of our analysis to allow for changes in the supply of labor. If the productivity of labor remains constant, while the supply of labor employed increases, and, at the same time, the quantity of money and the aggregate monetary demands are constant, then money wages and prices both fall to the same extent, leaving average real wages unchanged. Indeed, we have already considered precisely this case in our discussion of the elimination of unemployment.[56]

If, when the supply of labor employed increases, the productivity of labor also increases, while the quantity of money and the aggregate monetary demands stay the same, then prices fall more than wages, for the supply of goods increases to a greater extent than the supply of labor. In this case, real wages rise once again, in accordance with the rise in the productivity of labor. For example, if both the supply of labor and the productivity of labor were to double, while the quantity of money and the respective aggregate monetary demands for labor and consumers' goods were to remain unchanged, then average money wage rates would fall to one-half of their initial height, reflecting the doubling of the supply of labor, while the general consumer price level fell to one-fourth of its initial height, reflecting the quadrupling of the supply of consumers' goods that ensues when twice the workers each on average produce double. Thus, once again, average real wages would double, in conformity with the doubling of the average productivity of labor.

The case which has actually occurred in the world in most periods since the end of the Dark Ages, and in a very pronounced way in the last two hundred years, is that the supply of labor, the productivity of labor, and the quantity of money and the respective aggregate monetary demands all increase at the same time. In this case, depending on the extent of the increase in the quantity of money and the aggregate monetary demands, money wage rates may still fall, while prices fall further; or money wage rates may remain constant, while prices alone fall; or money wage rates may increase, while prices fall, remain constant, or even rise—depending on how great is the increase in the quantity of money and the aggregate monetary demands for labor and consumers' goods. In all these possible cases, real wages will still be found to vary precisely with the variation in the productivity of labor, for it is the productivity of labor that determines the supply of consumers' goods relative to the supply of labor, and thus the prices of consumers' goods relative to wage rates.

The essential role of the productivity of labor in determining real wage rates can now be shown more abstractly, by means of the following simple algebraic derivation.

We already have established the following equations:

(1)
$$Average\ Real\ Wage\ Rate = \frac{W}{P},$$

(2)
$$W = \frac{D_L}{S_L},$$

and

(3)
$$P = \frac{D_C}{S_C}.$$

If we now substitute equations (2) and (3) into equation (1), we obtain

(4)
$$Average\ Real\ Wage\ Rate = \frac{D_L}{S_L} \div \frac{D_C}{S_C}.$$

Next, by the arithmetical rule of inverting and multiplying when dividing by a fractional expression, we obtain

(5)
$$Average\ Real\ Wage\ Rate = \frac{D_L}{S_L} \times \frac{S_C}{D_C}.$$

On the basis of the fact that quantities can be multiplied in any order, equation (5) is equivalent to

(6)
$$Average\ Real\ Wage\ Rate = \frac{S_C}{S_L} \times \frac{D_L}{D_C}.$$

The supply of consumers' goods relative to the supply of labor, is, of course, the expression of the productivity of labor. The demand for labor relative to the demand for consumers' goods can be called the "distribution factor," for want of a better description. It represents the extent to which wage payments are the source of consumption expenditure versus other sources of consumption expenditure, such as dividend and interest payments. Thus we have, finally,

(7) $Average\ Real\ Wage\ Rate = The\ Productivity$
       $of\ Labor \times The\ Distribution\ Factor.$

which expresses the fact that real wages are the product of the productivity of labor times the "distribution factor."

A moment's reflection shows that the productivity of labor is by far the more important determinant of real wages, for it has no fixed limit. It can be increased to whatever extent the human mind is capable of improving the capital equipment by means of which labor produces. The distribution factor, on the other hand, has a maximum potential limit of less than one (inasmuch as there must be some consumption on the part of the owners and creditors of business firms or they would have no motive to conduct production), and has probably been fairly close to its limit in the United States and Great Britain since the middle of the eighteenth century.[57] As will be shown in subsequent discussion, the distribution factor is the more favorable to wage earners, the higher is the economic degree of capitalism, i.e., of saving and productive expenditure relative to sales revenues.[58]

Thus, we have traced the influence of the productivity of labor on real wages first in isolation and then alongside the operation of changes in the quantity of money and the respective monetary demands for labor and consumers' goods, as well as changes in the supply of labor. Whatever the other factors present, the one that always explained the change in average real wages was the productivity of labor. And now, finally, we have seen the decisive role of the productivity of labor set forth as an algebraically derived general principle.

3. The Foundations of the Productivity of Labor and Real Wages: Capital Accumulation and Its Causes

The productivity of labor is not the ultimate explanation of real wages; it itself has causes. In the first instance, of course, it depends on the quantity and quality of the equipment and materials with which the average worker works, i.e., on the supply of capital goods per worker. Without the appropriate capital goods, products either cannot be produced at all or can be produced only with the expenditure of far more labor per unit of product. For example, automobiles cannot be produced at all without a preexisting supply of various metals and tools for shaping metal. Without moving assembly lines and all manner of complex equipment, their production requires far more labor per unit of output than with such facilities.

The supply of capital goods, I will show, is the result of the joint operation of two further causes: (1) *the economic degree of capitalism*—in particular, the extent to which this results in the economic system concentrating on the production of capital goods relative to the production of consumers' goods; (2) *the efficiency of the economic system in using existing capital goods*. (This latter cause, as we shall see, subsumes technological progress.) I will also show that these two causes in turn depend, still more fundamentally, on respect for property rights and the consequent security of private property, and on the degree of rationality in a society—in short, on the values of freedom and reason.

Saving as a Source of Capital Accumulation

As I have indicated previously, in describing it as the ratio of Marx's M to his M', the economic degree of capitalism refers to the proportion of sales revenues and incomes in the economic system that is *saved and productively expended*—that is, used in the purchase of capital goods and labor by business firms, as opposed to being expended for consumers' goods. It is the measure of the extent to which people act capitalistically, i.e., buy for the sake of subsequently selling (implicitly, of course, at a profit). In determining the proportions in which money is spent to buy capital goods relative to consumers' goods, saving and productive expenditure determine the proportions in which the economic system devotes its existing ability to produce to the production of capital goods relative to the production of consumers' goods.

As an illustration of this last point, the extent to which a firm with consumers' goods divisions and capital goods divisions divides its efforts between the two types of products depends on the relative demands for these products. For example, General Motors will devote a larger proportion of the labor of its employees and of its existing capital goods to the production of capital goods, like diesel locomotives and trucks, and a smaller proportion to the production of consumers' goods, like passenger automobiles, if the demand for diesel locomotives and trucks rises relative to the demand for passenger automobiles.[59]

The operation of this principle does not require that firms have both capital goods divisions and consumers' goods divisions. A rise in the demand for capital goods relative to the demand for consumers' goods will favor firms and industries that produce capital goods relative to firms and industries that produce consumers' goods. Through the operation of the uniformity-of-profit principle, this will bring about a shift of capital and labor from the production of consumers' goods to the production of capital goods. For example, to take the case of an industry in which some firms concentrate on the production of capital goods and others on the production of consumers' goods, a rise in the demand for factory and office buildings relative to the demand for residential housing will favor the branches of the construction industry that concentrate on factory and office buildings. As a result, a larger part of the construction industry will tend to devote itself to this type of construction. Similarly, a rise in the demand for the machinery and equipment used by business firms relative to the demand for home appliances will favor the producers of the former relative to the producers of the latter, and thus will have a similar effect on how existing means of production are employed. And, of course, the total capital invested in industries producing capital goods can be increased by the withdrawal of capital from other industries where it had been devoted to the production of consumers' goods.

Thus, in addition to firms with both consumers' goods and capital goods divisions being induced to concentrate more heavily on the production of capital goods, the operation of the uniformity-of-profit principle causes labor and capital to be withdrawn from firms and industries exclusively devoted to the production of consumers' goods and transferred to firms and industries exclusively devoted to the production of capital goods, if the demand for capital goods rises relative to the demand for consumers' goods.[60]

As explained in Chapter 4, the proportion of its efforts that an economic system devotes to the production of capital goods is vital in determining whether or not it accumulates capital goods.[61] Capital goods are constantly being consumed in production (and, indeed, by virtue of mere exposure to nature): materials and supplies are used up; machinery, factories, and buildings and installations of all kinds wear out or run down. If these capital goods are to be replaced, they must be replaced out of production itself. Just as a farmer must replace the seed he consumes in the planting of his crop, out of the crop itself, so in a modern economic system, the steel mills and cement factories, the inventories of wheat and flour, and so on—*all* the factories, equipment, materials, and supplies—that are consumed in production must be replaced out of production. In other words, if the supply of capital goods is merely to be maintained intact—if the productive consumption of capital goods is to be offset— it is necessary to devote some definite, and more or less considerable, proportion of the existing means of production to the production of capital goods.

What this means, for example, is that some proportion of the output of steel mills and cement factories and so forth must be devoted to the production of steel mills and cement factories and so forth, in order to keep up the number and productive capacity of such plants. By the same token, some proportion of the economic system's production must take such forms as the production of steel sheet to replace the supply of steel sheet consumed in the production of automobiles, and of iron ore to replace the supply of iron ore consumed in the production of steel sheet.

The proportion of existing means of production that must be devoted to the production of capital goods in order to offset their productive consumption I call *the maintenance proportion*. If the proportion of existing means of production devoted to the production of capital goods equals the maintenance proportion, then the economic system produces as large a supply of capital goods as it consumes and thus succeeds in maintaining its supply of capital goods intact. If the proportion of existing means of production devoted to the production of capital goods exceeds the maintenance proportion, then the economic system produces more capital goods than it consumes and thus succeeds in increasing its supply of capital goods. If the proportion of existing means of production devoted to the production of capital goods falls short of the maintenance proportion, then the economic system produces a smaller supply of capital goods than it consumes and thus suffers a reduction in its accumulated stock of capital goods. Assuming a constant population and supply of labor, in the first case the economic system is *stationary;* in the second, it is *progressive;* in the third, it is *retrogressive*. In the first case, because the supply of capital goods remains the same, the productivity of labor and the general level of real wages remain the same. In the second case, because of capital accumulation, the productivity of labor and the general level of real wages increase. In the third case, because of capital decumulation, the productivity of

labor and the general level of real wages decrease.[62]

Figure 14–4 illustrates the nature of a stationary economic system. In Figure 14–4, I assume that the existing supply of capital goods and labor—namely, *1K* of capital goods plus *1L* of labor—can be used to produce varying combinations of capital goods and consumers' goods ranging from *2K* of capital goods and *0C* of consumers' goods, at one extreme, to *0K* of capital goods and *2C* of consumers' goods, at the other extreme. These extremes are the values that would result if 100 percent of the existing supply of capital goods and labor were devoted to the production of capital goods, and 0 percent to the production of consumers' goods, and vice versa.

For the sake of simplicity, I assume that all the capital goods in existence at the beginning of a year are productively consumed in that year. Thus, by implication, I further assume (also for the sake of simplicity) that the maintenance proportion is one-half, for the replacement of *1K* of capital goods out of an output that is equivalent in size to *2K* of capital goods is, of course, half of that output. Figure 14–4 represents a stationary economic system, because in each year the relative production of capital goods *is* one-half, precisely equal to the maintenance proportion, while the relative production of consumers' goods is, of course, also one-half. Thus, the supply of capital goods remains stationary.

Figure 14–4 illustrates the previous proposition that the relative production of capital goods and consumers' goods is in accordance with the relative *demands* for capital goods and consumers' goods. The downward sloping arrows in Figure 14–4 trace the transformation of existing capital goods and of labor into their products—namely, further capital goods, shown on the left, and consumers' goods, shown on the right. The proportions shown in Figure 14–4, of 50 percent and 50 percent in the relative production of capital goods and consumers' goods in each year, are in response to the fact that the demands for capital goods and consumers' goods in each year are 500 and 500 respectively. (These numbers can be thought of as abstract monetary units. As I stated in Chapter 13, each such unit could be taken as representing a billion dollars a few years back, and ten billion dollars today. It makes no difference which, just so long as the size is held fixed at some definite amount and is large enough so that the example can be understood as referring to the economic system as a whole.) It is in response to these demands of 500 and 500, which each represent one-half of an assumed total aggregate monetary demand of 1,000 each year for capital goods and consumers' goods taken together, that the utilization of existing capital goods and labor is 50 percent for the production of capital goods and 50 percent for the production of consumers' goods.

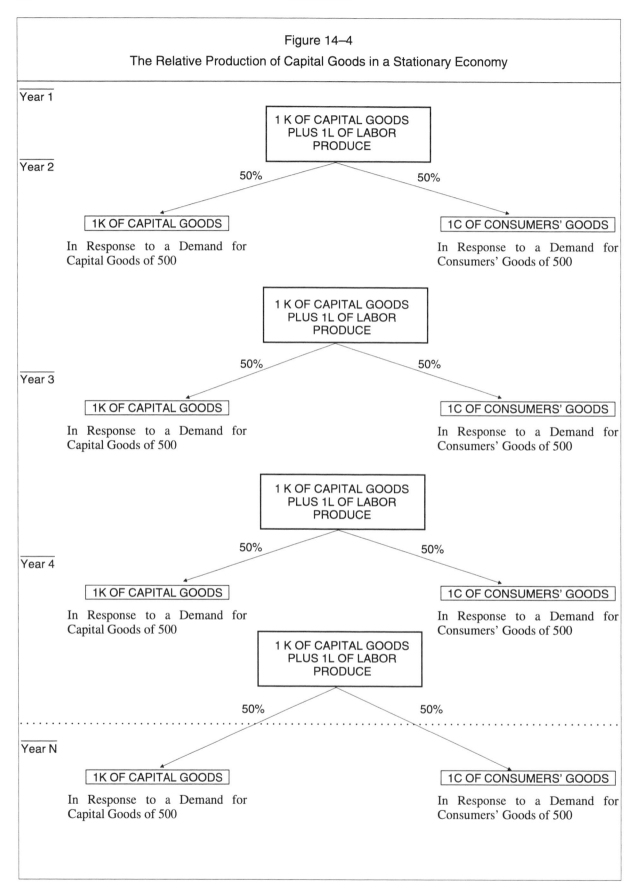

Figure 14–4

The Relative Production of Capital Goods in a Stationary Economy

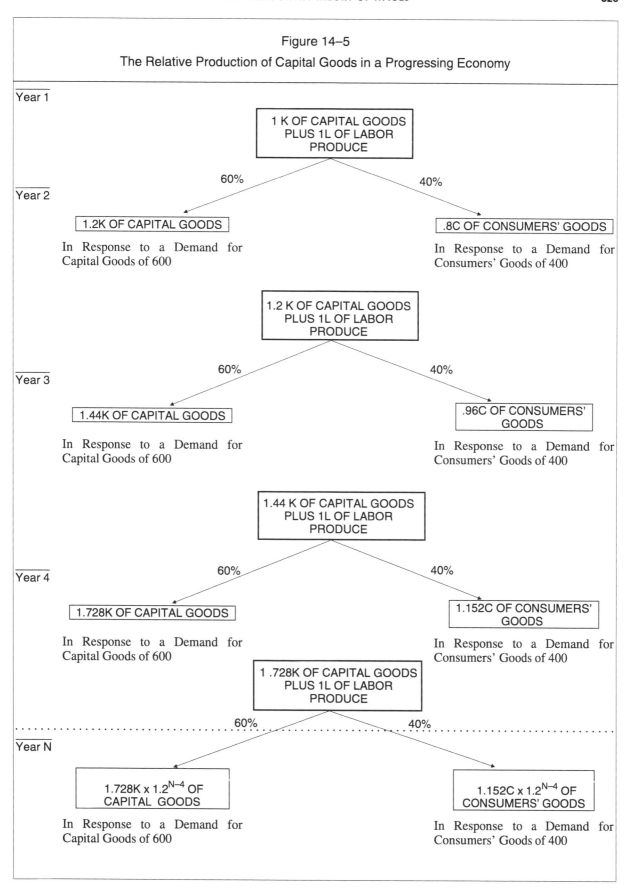

Figure 14–5

The Relative Production of Capital Goods in a Progressing Economy

In Figure 14–4, the capital goods and labor of each year are devoted to the production of capital goods and consumers' goods which become available for sale at the beginning of the following year. It is the relative demands for capital goods and consumers' goods in the following year, assumed to be correctly anticipated in the present year, that govern the relative disposition of capital goods and labor in the present year. Thus, the *1K* of capital goods plus *1L* of labor which exist in *Year 1*, produce *1K* of capital goods and *1C* of consumers' goods which become available for sale and are sold at the beginning of *Year 2*, each for 500. Thereupon, the producers in *Year 2* begin a new round of production, with the aid of the *1K* of capital goods that has been purchased for 500 and with the aid of a fresh *1L* of labor. In the course of production in *Year 2*, the fresh *1K* of capital goods is, of course, productively consumed in producing another fresh supply of *1K* of capital goods and *1C* of consumers' goods, which become available for sale and are sold at the beginning of *Year 3*—once again for 500 units of money each. The downward sloping arrows show a $50/50$ relative production of capital goods and consumers' goods in *Year 2*, this time in response to the $500/500$ relative demands for capital goods and consumers' goods that are made at the beginning of *Year 3*.

In *Year 3*, exactly the same story is repeated as takes place in *Year 2*, and will thereafter continue to be repeated indefinitely—down to *Year N*. Year in and year out, production begins with *1K* of capital goods and *1L* of labor; the capital goods are productively consumed in producing a fresh supply of *1K* of capital goods, along with a supply of *1C* of consumers' goods—in response to the relative demands for capital goods and consumers' goods of $500/500$.

Figure 14–5 depicts the conditions of a *progressing* economic system. As in Figure 14–4, the initial supply of capital goods, in Year 1, is assumed to be *1K*. But the labor and capital goods of *Year 1* are utilized very differently in Figure 14–5 than in Figure 14–4. In Figure 14–5, they are devoted *60* percent to the production of capital goods, instead of only 50 percent; and only *40* percent to the production of consumers' goods, instead of 50 percent. As a result, the supply of capital goods available to serve in production at the start of *Year 2* is *1.2K* instead of only *1K*. By the same token, the supply of consumers' goods is *.8C*, instead of *1C*. The 20 percent larger supply of capital goods in *Year 2*, in comparison with the supply in existence at the start of *Year 1* in Figure 14–5, is the result of devoting 20 percent more resources to the production of capital goods than is necessary for the mere maintenance of their supply.

This change in the proportions in which capital goods and consumers' goods are produced is, of course, the result of the change in the proportions in which they are demanded. In every year in Figure 14–5, the demand for capital goods and the demand for consumers' goods are 600 and 400 respectively, instead of 500 and 500 respectively, as was the case in Figure 14–4. The $60/40$ relative demand for capital goods and consumers' goods underlies their production in the $60/40$ ratio.

Now, as I have indicated, this change in the relative demands for capital goods and consumers' goods has its foundation in greater *saving*. For the source of the demand for capital goods, indeed, for all of productive expenditure, including the demand for labor, is saving. The demand for capital goods depends on the funds expended to buy capital goods not being expended to buy consumers' goods instead. That is, people who possess the necessary funds must abstain from consuming them— they must *save* them and employ them in productive expenditure for capital goods if the demand for capital goods is to be increased relative to the demand for consumers' goods. Precisely this represents the role of saving in capital accumulation. Namely, the degree of saving determines the relative demand for and production of capital goods.[63] I will have more to say about the role of saving, shortly, following the elaboration of the analysis depicted in Figure 14–5.

In Figure 14–5, I introduce the further assumption that the total productive ability of the economic system is *in proportion to the supply of capital goods*. Thus, when the supply of capital goods increases by 20 percent in *Year 2* in comparison with *Year 1*, the total ability of the economic system to produce also increases by 20 percent. As a result, the limiting combinations within which capital goods and consumers' goods can be produced are increased from *2K* of capital goods, *0C* of consumers' goods at one extreme, and *0K* of capital goods, *2C* of consumers' goods at the other extreme, to *2.4K* of capital goods, *0C* of consumers' goods at the one extreme and *0K* of capital goods, *2.4C* of consumers' goods at the other extreme. (The extremes, of course, are the products that would result from the use of the existing *1.2K* of capital goods and *1L* of labor in proportions of 100 percent and 0 percent in the respective production of capital goods and consumers' goods or, alternatively, consumers' goods and capital goods.) Because the $60/40$ relative production of capital goods and consumers' goods is maintained, the actual total product of *Year 2* is *1.44K* of capital goods and *.96C* of consumers' goods, which are the supply of goods available at the start of *Year 3*. (These are the results found by respectively multiplying .6 and .4 times the alternative limiting production extremes of *2.4K* and *2.4C*.)

Thus, *1.44K* of capital goods is the supply of capital goods available with which to carry on production in

Year 3. And because production in *Year 3* is thereby carried on with a 20 percent larger supply of capital goods than was production in *Year 2*, the total productive ability of the economic system in *Year 3* increases by 20 percent *once again,* with the result that, under the prevailing 60/40 relative production of capital goods and consumers' goods, the supply of capital goods and consumers' goods available for sale at the beginning of *Year 4* is *1.728K* of capital goods and *1.152C* of consumers' goods—a 20 percent increase over the respective supplies at the start of *Year 3*. (These are the results found by respectively multiplying .6 and .4 times the new limiting production extremes of *2.88K* and *2.88C*, which are the products of *1.44K* of capital goods and *1L* of labor devoted 100 percent to the production of capital goods or, alternatively, 100 percent to the production of consumers' goods.)

Indeed, in the conditions depicted in Figure 14–5, production and the supply of capital goods will go on increasing by 20 percent *in every year,* with the 20 percent larger supply of capital goods in each year increasing the ability to produce in comparison with the preceding year by a further 20 percent, including the ability to produce capital goods. Thus, in Figure 14–5, in *Year N,* the supplies of capital goods and consumers' goods are shown as their respective amounts in *Year 4* times 1.2 compounded for the number of years elapsing between *Year 4* and *Year N,* namely, N–4, which is the exponent used in the compounding.

The *dynamic* effects of changes in the relative demand for and production of capital goods cannot be overemphasized. Obviously, what is essential for capital accumulation to take place is that the supply of capital goods produced exceed the supply of capital goods productively consumed, and that for this to happen, the proportion of its efforts which an economic system devotes to the production of capital goods must exceed the maintenance proportion. This, of course, will occur only if the demand for capital goods relative to the demand for consumers' goods is sufficiently great, which in turn requires that the degree of saving be sufficiently high.

But increases in the supply of capital goods do *not* depend on *continuous increases in the relative demand for and relative production of capital goods.* Once the relative demand for capital goods rises to the point that their relative production exceeds the maintenance proportion, so that capital accumulation takes place, the productive ability of the economic system is increased, *including its ability to produce capital goods.* This greater ability to produce capital goods then results in *a further accumulation of capital goods*—provided only that the higher relative demand for and corresponding relative production of capital goods is maintained and

that the maintenance proportion does not rise.

In other words, once an economic system devotes a sufficiently large proportion of its efforts to the production of capital goods, it can go on accumulating capital goods on the strength of the larger supply of capital goods produced in the year before. For example, once the first railroads and steel mills were brought into existence on the basis of saving and a greater relative production of capital goods, the very existence of these additional capital goods made possible a further increase in the supply of capital goods. For once in the possession of these capital goods, the total ability of the economic system to produce was increased, and this included its ability to produce *further capital goods* no less than consumers' goods. Given the possession of the first railroads and steel mills, it became easier to produce railroads and steel mills, and virtually all other capital goods, than it was before, without them. On the basis of the greater productive ability made possible by their existence, the continuation of the *same,* higher relative production of capital goods had to result in a further increase in the supply of capital goods. Thus, once in possession of the first railroads and steel mills, it became possible to produce more, bigger, and better railroads and steel mills, and then, with the aid of these, to produce still more, still bigger, and still better railroads and steel mills, and so on and on, decade by decade—and, of course, to produce more capital goods of all kinds, for the principle applies throughout the economic system, to the ability to produce in general. Thus, to have continuous capital accumulation and economic progress, it is not necessary to go on raising the relative demand for capital goods and the relative production of capital goods, but only to maintain *a sufficiently high* relative demand and relative production.

This fact has major implications for the role of saving in capital accumulation. It implies that in an economic system with a given quantity of money and thus a given overall volume of spending for capital goods and consumers' goods combined, continuous increases in saving and decreases in consumption expenditure would not be necessary for the existence of capital accumulation, provided that the existing degree of saving, and thus the existing demand for capital goods relative to consumers' goods, were sufficiently high.

Given a relative demand for and production of capital goods that already exceeds the maintenance proportion, and total output that increases in proportion to the increase in the supply of capital goods, the effect of further increases in saving and the relative demand for and production of capital goods would be as *force to acceleration* is in the world of physical phenomena: that is, they would achieve *a more rapid rate* of capital accumulation and economic progress. For example, demand for and production of capital goods in a $^{70}/_{30}$ ratio to consumers' goods, rather than the $^{60}/_{40}$ ratio assumed in Figure 14–5, would result in *1.4K* of capital goods and *.6C* of consumers' goods in *Year 2*, *1.96K* of capital goods and *.84C* of consumers' goods in *Year 3*, and *2.744K* of capital goods and *1.176C* of consumers' goods in *Year 4*—that is, an annual increase in production, and thus in the supply of capital goods and the ability further to increase production and the supply of capital goods, of 40 percent instead of 20 percent. (The figures of *1.4K* of capital goods and *.6C* of consumers' goods for *Year 2* result from the multiplication of the respective limiting extremes of *2K* and *2C* by .7 and .3 respectively. Similarly, the *1.96K* of capital goods and *.84C* of consumers' goods that would be available at the start of *Year 3* are respectively 70 percent and 30 percent of the increased limiting extremes of *2.8K* of capital goods or *2.8C* of consumers' goods that could alternatively be produced with the aid of an existing *1.4K* of capital goods and *1L* of labor, devoted 100 percent to the respective production of capital goods or, alternatively, consumers' goods. Likewise, the figures of *2.744K* of capital goods and *1.176C* of consumers' goods for *Year 4* are the result of multiplying .7 and .3 times the further increased respective limiting extremes of *3.92K* or *3.92C* that could be produced with the aid of an existing *1.96K* of capital goods and *1L* of labor, devoted 100 percent to the respective production of capital goods or, alternatively, consumers' goods.)

The rates of increase in production and in capital supply that I am assuming are, of course, unrealistically high, and substantially exceed even the record rates established by Japan and other East Asian countries in the last generation. This is the result of the simplifying assumptions I use.[64] Nevertheless, the essential point remains true that the greater the degree to which the relative demand for and production of capital goods surpasses the proportion required for the mere maintenance of the supply of capital goods, the more rapidly does the economic system tend to progress. For then, each year the production of capital goods exceeds the supply of capital goods consumed in production by a correspondingly wider margin. The production of each succeeding year then takes place with the aid of that much more of a larger supply of capital goods than did the production of the year before. And each year, by virtue of raising the productivity of labor that much more, the more enlarged supply of capital goods makes possible the production of a correspondingly still more enlarged supply of capital goods, as well as consumers' goods, in the following year.

In making the claim that production can increase in proportion to the supply of capital goods, I may appear to be in contradiction of the law of diminishing returns. Actually, I am not. It is true that there can be diminishing returns to capital goods. However, this is not a necessary fact. Diminishing returns to capital goods are implied as a necessary fact only in the context of the employment of increasing quantities of capital goods of *a definite physical type* relative to labor. An increase in the supply of capital goods as such, however, does not mean an increase in the supply of some one, homogeneous factor of production employed. On the contrary, it can encompass the most radical changes in the technological methods of production. It can mean the substitution of steel for iron, titanium for steel, petroleum for coal, atomic power for petroleum, and so on. An increase in the supply of capital goods *as a genus* stands outside the context assumed by the law of diminishing returns insofar as its employment is accompanied by changes in the technological methods of production that are implemented. It is no more possible to speak of a necessary diminution of returns to capital goods as a genus than it is possible to speak of a necessary diminution of returns to human intelligence.

Indeed, even if one considers the case of a homogeneous capital good, such as iron ore of a given quality that has been mined, the law of diminishing returns can have no application insofar as the products made possible by a larger supply of iron ore may be steam engines instead of windmills, and then diesel engines and electric motors instead of steam engines, and so on, in one line of production after another. There can be diminishing returns to capital goods, but there need not be; in fact, there can even be increasing returns to capital goods as the result of advances in technology.

Only in the sustained absence of further technological progress must an additional supply of capital goods afford a less than proportionate increase in total productive power. Only in such circumstances does the additional supply of capital goods mean at some point increasing the supply of capital goods of the same types relative to labor. And this, as we shall see, results first in a slowing up and then in a complete cessation of the accumulation of additional capital goods, unless the proportion of the existing supply of factors of production devoted to their production should increase.

In connection with the above, it should be realized that even increases in the supply of capital goods of the same types relative to labor do not result in diminishing returns insofar as it is a question of extending the application of improved methods of production to a larger proportion of the labor force. For example, if initially 5 percent of automobile factories are operating with the aid of moving assembly lines, the extension of the use of moving assembly lines to 10 percent, 20 percent, and ultimately, 100 percent, of the automobile factories will not result in diminishing returns. Diminishing returns set in only with the employment of more capital goods (of a given type) in conjunction with a given worker or group of workers, such as a given assembly-line team. Then, sooner or later, the result must be a less-than-proportionate increase in output.

As this fact indicates, it is consistent with this discussion that increases in the relative demand for and production of capital goods could be accompanied by an acceleration in the rate of capital accumulation and economic progress that itself took place at a decelerating rate. This would be the case insofar as the lapse of time was required to produce capital goods of different, technologically more advanced types than those presently in existence. Thus, for example, when the relative demand for and production of capital goods rose from a $^{60}/_{40}$ ratio to consumers' goods, to a $^{70}/_{30}$ ratio, the increase in productive ability could be in a lesser proportion than 1.4 to 1.2 insofar as the resulting $1.4K$ of capital goods were of the same kind as the $1.2K$ of capital goods that would otherwise have been produced and, in addition, had to be employed more heavily with the same, limited units of labor.

Technological Progress as a Source of Capital Accumulation

This brings me to the role of technological progress in capital accumulation. In order for the supply of capital goods to go on increasing on the basis of previous growth in the supply of capital goods, it is necessary that at some point further technological progress take place. In the conditions described in Figure 14–5, further technological progress is what ultimately keeps up the process of capital accumulation after the achievement of the rise in the relative production of capital goods from 50 percent to 60 percent and its resulting initial increase in the supply of capital goods. Further technological progress is what is ultimately required to offset the operation of the law of diminishing returns and thus for the existence of constant returns to a growing supply of capital goods. It is what is necessary for the process of a 20 percent larger supply of capital goods resulting in a 20 percent greater ability to produce and thus in a further 20 percent increase in the supply of capital goods with a consequent still further 20 percent increase in the ability to produce, to go on indefinitely.

In the prolonged absence of technological progress, the larger supply of capital goods from one year to the next would sooner or later result in an increase in total productive ability in the economic system that was less

than in proportion to the increase in the supply of capital goods. For the law of diminishing returns would set in. For example, in the absence of further technological progress, the increase in the supply of capital goods, say, in *Year 8* in comparison with *Year 7,* could well be accompanied by a less than proportionate increase in the ability to produce in *Year 8* in comparison with *Year 7.* On the basis of a 20 percent increase in the supply of capital goods in *Year 8,* production might increase by only 15 percent, say. This would mean that the subsequent increase in the supply of capital goods available for *Year 9* would also be only 15 percent. This lesser increase in the supply of capital goods in *Year 9* could, in turn, well be accompanied by an increase in the overall ability to produce that was less than in proportion to it, say, only 10 percent. Thus, the growing supply of capital goods would encounter diminishing returns, and as a result, the supply of capital goods would eventually stop growing, because the additional production out of which further capital accumulation takes place would be steadily diminishing.

In the absence of technological progress, the point must *always* sooner or later be reached where additional supplies of capital goods would increase the ability to produce by diminishing amounts, with the result that capital accumulation would eventually peter out, no matter how great the relative production of capital goods. In effect, in the absence of technological progress, the diminishing additional output per unit of additional capital goods would imply a falling average productivity of capital goods—that is, a falling ratio of output to the supply of capital goods. Since the supply of capital goods would still have to be replaced out of production, the further implication would be a corresponding rise in the proportion of output required to replace the capital goods consumed in production—viz., in the maintenance proportion. The maintenance proportion would tend to rise all the way to the point of equalling the relative production of capital goods, however high the latter might be. At that point, both capital accumulation and the increase in production would cease.

Technological progress, however, offsets the operation of the law of diminishing returns and makes possible the existence of long-term constant returns to a growing supply of capital goods. Exactly as I showed in connection with the limitless potential of natural resources, the law of diminishing returns continues to apply in a given state of technology, but not under the conditions of an improving state of technology.[65] And thus, because of the offset it constitutes to the law of diminishing returns, technological progress provides a parallel in the world of economic phenomena to the absence of friction in the world of physical phenomena. By virtue of its ability to achieve constant returns to a growing supply of capital goods, technological progress stands in the same relationship to the ability of a larger relative production of capital goods to bring about capital accumulation as the absence of friction does to the ability of force to achieve acceleration in the world of physical phenomena. By virtue of technological progress, a one-time increase in the relative production of capital goods is capable of achieving an indefinitely long series of subsequent increases in the supply of capital goods. In effect, technological progress makes it possible for an increase in the relative production of capital goods to launch economic progress along a kind of inertial path, as it were.

Now, seen in this light, technological progress stands revealed *as a fundamental source of capital accumulation.* Without it, capital accumulation either cannot continue at all or can do so only by virtue of continuous increases in the relative demand for and production of capital goods, and in no case can be very substantial. If, for example, there had been no technological progress over the last two centuries, there could have been virtually no capital accumulation over this period. However high the relative production of capital goods in an economy whose technology was characterized by sailing ships and horse-drawn wagons, it would still have been simply impossible to produce any significant part of the capital goods that can be produced today, from the standpoint both of quantity and quality.

This is why, in Chapter 13, I ridiculed the secular-stagnationist variant of consumptionism as I did. It is simply absurd to believe that saving—the determinant of the relative production of capital goods—could somehow by itself provide the means of building modern steel mills and a modern railroad network and that fortunately these capital-using technologies appeared on the scene to provide uses for all the capital allegedly being generated by the process of saving. The truth is, as previously stated, that it is technological progress which is indispensable to the very existence of virtually all of the growing supply of capital goods that becomes available to implement further technological progress. It was precisely earlier technological advances in steel making, railroad building, and so forth, that underlay the growing supply of capital goods required to make possible the implementation of more advanced technologies in steel making, railroad building, and so forth later on. In effect, the technological advances of each decade played a crucial role in providing the growing supply of capital goods required to implement the technological advances of the following decade. Over the course of a period such as a generation or more, it should be obvious that it is the process of technological progress itself that is indispensable to the provision of the capital goods required for the

implementation of technological progress.

Regrettably, while the role of technological progress as a major, indispensable source of capital accumulation should now be obvious, the prevailing view in contemporary economics is that saving alone is the source of capital accumulation and that the role of technological progress is to provide "outlets" for the expanding supply of capital goods allegedly generated all by saving, and thereby to keep up the rate of profit.[66] In other words, the prevailing view is that underlying the consumptionist doctrine of secular stagnation.[67]

Even when technological progress appears to be recognized, more or less in passing, as being responsible for capital accumulation, its essential role in connection with capital accumulation is still seen as that of keeping up the rate of return in the face of capital accumulation allegedly caused by saving. For example, Samuelson and Nordhaus write: "As a result of technological progress, capital per worker, output per worker, and wages per worker grow over time, yet the real interest rate does not decline. If no invention had occurred, perhaps Marx would have been proven correct in his prophecy of the falling rate of profit. But invention increases the productivity of capital and repeals the law of the falling rate of profit. In the race between diminishing returns and advancing technology, technology has won by several lengths."[68] Thus, even though the role of technological progress in capital accumulation appears to be acknowledged in the opening words of the quotation, the acknowledgment is of no substance, and matters stand just where they stood before, with the essential role of technological progress seen as that of keeping up the rate of profit in the face of capital accumulation caused by saving. Indeed, when Samuelson and Nordhaus say that "as a result of technological progress, capital per worker . . . grow[s] over time, yet the real interest rate does not decline," they should almost certainly be understood as meaning *not* that technological progress causes the growth in capital per worker, but that it is responsible for the fact that the growth in capital per worker caused by saving can go on without the real rate of interest declining.

This interpretation is also consistent with the fact that they, along with most other contemporary economists, regard the contribution of technological progress to the increase in production as *separate from and independent of* any contribution to capital accumulation. They see technological progress as contributing only to the increased production of *consumers'* goods. Indeed, when the importance of technological progress to the increase in the production of consumers' goods is recognized, it is taken as the basis for *minimizing* the importance ascribed to capital accumulation! For example, Samuelson and Nordhaus declare: "Thus of the 2.1 percent-per-year increase in output per worker, about .25 percentage points is due to capital deepening, while an astounding 1.85 percent per year stems from T. C. [technological change]." Elsewhere in their book, Samuelson and Nordhaus make clear that by "capital deepening," they mean capital accumulation. This is when they describe capital deepening as "a rise in the capital-labor ratio," i.e., as an increase in the supply of capital goods per worker.[69]

Thus, Samuelson and Nordhaus, along with most other contemporary economists, end up in a position in which they fail to see not only the role of technological progress as a source of capital accumulation, but also the greater part of the role of capital accumulation itself in raising the productivity of labor. They believe that technological progress raises the productivity of labor directly, without any need for a corresponding additional quantity of capital goods.[70] I will show the error of this last view in the very next section of this chapter.

The Reciprocal Relationship Between Capital Accumulation and Technological Progress

It is necessary to stress that the ability of the economic system to implement advances in technology depends on the supply of capital goods it already possesses, which crucially depends on the economic degree of capitalism and on the closely related concept of capital intensiveness. Capital intensiveness in the economic system can be conceived of in terms of the ratio of the total value of accumulated capital in the economic system to—alternatively—aggregate sales revenues, wage payments, or consumption expenditures.[71] It is the greater, the higher are these ratios.

The economic degree of capitalism and the degree of capital intensiveness in the economic system operate, as it were, as a kind of long-range "radar net" for technological progress—with cumulative long-run consequences for capital accumulation and the ability to implement technological advances, in that they determine which kinds of technologies can be picked up and implemented at any given time.

The fact that the ability of an economic system to implement technological advances depends on its existing supply of capital goods can be illustrated by a close analogy from the conditions of our lives as consumers. Thus, for example, a Mercedes 450 SE represents a more advanced technology in automobiles than, say, a Chevy Nova. If we ask what it is that stops people from implementing this more advanced technology, the answer is obviously not that they lack the necessary technological knowledge of how to drive a Mercedes. They already know perfectly well how to drive one. What stops them from doing so, obviously, is the fact that they lack the

wealth—the means—to implement this more advanced technology. They simply cannot afford to buy the Mercedes.

In just the same way, there are more advanced technologies in business that businessmen already know how to employ or could easily learn to employ, but which they cannot afford to adopt, because they lack the capital. For example, as von Mises used to say in his seminar, every farmer in India who has seen American movies showing tractors and harvesters knows that he too could benefit from the use of such equipment. Again, what stops him is not that he doesn't know how to operate such devices (he could easily learn), but that he lacks the capital to purchase them. And, of course, as Say's Law shows, what makes him lack the purchasing power to buy the necessary capital goods is precisely the inability of the economic system physically to produce them or to produce them in sufficient quantity. The possession of capital—more fundamentally, the physical ability of the economic system to produce capital goods—is thus vital to the ability of the economic system to implement more advanced technologies.

An outstanding example of this fact in our own economy is that the implementation of the technology involved in the production of space rockets and communications satellites, and all that may subsequently depend on them, would not be possible if there did not already exist a highly developed electronics industry, chemical industry, computer industry, transportation system, metallurgical industry, and electrical industry, and all the other industries necessary to the existence of these industries. The mere technological knowledge alone would not be sufficient to make possible the actual production of space rockets and communications satellites.

The fact that as the result of a higher economic degree of capitalism an economic system possesses a higher relative production of capital goods and is more capital intensive means that it is able to implement technologies that it otherwise would not have been able to implement. Its greater relative production of capital goods and greater capital intensiveness provide it with the necessary capital. For example, in the nineteenth century, Great Britain was the world's most capital-intensive economy. It possessed the capital necessary to implement such highly capital-intensive technologies as railroading, and even to provide other countries with the means of doing so. If the British economy had had no greater capital intensiveness than, say, the economy of Italy, it would have been impossible for Britain to undertake railroading. The only possible source of the necessary capital would have been stripping other industries of their vital capital, and thus to end up actually reducing production overall. But with a sufficient degree of capital intensiveness in the British economic system, the capital necessary for the first railroads was available without disrupting production elsewhere. Thus, Britain could have railroads and even provide them to others.

Now once the first railroads were built, the effect, of course, was to increase the economic system's overall ability to produce—to produce not just consumers' goods but also further capital goods, including the means for more, bigger, and better railroads. As previously stated, once the first railroads, steel mills, and so forth came into existence, it became easier to build more and bigger and better railroads, steel mills, and so forth, because their production could be undertaken with the aid of the first railroads, steel mills, and so forth. In other words, the achievement of a higher degree of capital intensiveness, like the closely related achievement of a higher relative production of capital goods, made possible an increase in production which was itself the source of a second increase in the supply of capital goods. Thus, the effects of greater capital intensiveness were and are cumulative. In any given period of time, greater capital intensiveness permits the adoption of technologies that otherwise could not be adopted. And then, the increase in production that results from the adoption of those technologies provides still more capital goods in the future, so that still more advanced technologies can be adopted—without the necessity of further increases in the degree of capital intensiveness.

On this basis, it should be clear that the relationship between capital accumulation and the ability to implement more advanced technologies is *reciprocal.* Technological progress is both a vital, indispensable source of capital accumulation and, at the same time, the ability to implement advances in technology depends on the existing supply of capital goods and, more fundamentally, on the relative production of capital goods and degree of capital intensiveness in the economic system.[72] Technological progress is not implemented in a vacuum. A country which already annually produces, say, one-half of a ton of steel per capita is able to implement more advanced technological processes of production both in steel making and probably in all other branches of production than one which only produces a quarter of a ton per capita, and that country is able to implement more advanced technological processes of production than a country which only produces one-eighth of a ton of steel per capita; and it is the same with respect to the ability to produce in innumerable other lines of production, from aluminum and its products to zirconium and its products.

To take one final example, imagine, as was quite possibly the case, that all the technological knowledge required for the construction of the steel mills and oil refineries of the kind constructed in the 1960s existed in 1920. Nevertheless, it would not have been possible to construct such steel mills and oil refineries at that time, at least not economically, if for no other reason than that it would have made too great a demand on the then existing supply of steel and petroleum products. Because the supply of capital goods was increasing, it was, however, possible to construct more advanced facilities for steel making and petroleum refining in the decade of the 1920s than had been possible in the previous decade. With the aid of the larger production of capital goods made possible by these more advanced facilities, it was then possible in the decade of 1930s to construct still more advanced facilities for the production of steel and petroleum than had been possible in the 1920s; and with the aid of the then still larger supply of capital goods made possible by these still more advanced facilities, it became possible in the next decade to implement further improvements in the production of steel and oil until, two decades later, it became possible to construct steel-making and petroleum-refining facilities of the type built in the 1960s.

As the preceding words suggest, it is not necessary that further technological progress occur concurrently in order to maintain the returns to additional capital goods. Probably, even in the present-day United States, several years could go by without further technological progress taking place, and the returns to additional capital goods would remain undiminished. In the case of a backward country, such as India, most likely decades could go by, and the returns to a larger supply of capital goods would not diminish, even though no new technological knowledge came into existence. This is because the growing supply of capital goods would make possible the implementation of already known technologies which it had not been possible to implement before because of a lack of a sufficient supply of capital goods. However, sooner or later, further technological progress is always necessary to maintain the productivity of capital goods.

What it is crucial to recognize in connection with real wages, which is our central concern in this chapter, is that capital accumulation and a rising productivity of labor depend on *a combination of technological progress and a sufficiently high economic degree of capitalism,* which latter is responsible both for a sufficiently high relative demand for and production of capital goods and for a sufficiently high degree of capital intensiveness.[73]

The Economic Degree of Capitalism, the Wage "Share," and Real Wages

It is important to realize in addition that the economic degree of capitalism determines real wages not only by virtue of its connection with capital accumulation and the productivity of labor, but also by virtue of its connection with the so-called distribution factor—i.e., the relationship between the demand for labor and the demand for consumers' goods, and thus the proportion of consumer spending originating in wage payments.

The wages paid by business firms are paid by the business firms, not by the consumers, who buy the ultimate product of business firms. The wages are a part of *productive expenditure, not consumption expenditure.*[74] The higher the economic degree of capitalism—i.e., the larger the proportion of sales revenues and incomes saved and productively expended—the higher is not only the demand for capital goods relative to the demand for consumers' goods, but also the higher is the demand for labor relative to the demand for consumers' goods. For example, if the owners of a given firm, with sales revenues, let us say, of $1 billion, pay themselves an annual dividend of $50 million instead of $100 million, and thus save and productively expend $950 million instead of only $900 million, their firm's demand for labor, as well as for capital goods, is bound to be larger. And it will be all the more enlarged relative to their own consumption expenditure, which is fully halved in this case. It should be obvious that to the extent that such behavior prevails in the economic system as a whole, the same conclusions apply. Thus, a rise in the economic degree of capitalism acts in a double way to raise real wages. It raises the wage share of consumption along with raising the productivity of labor. Both members of the equation determining real wages are increased.

The full contribution of the economic degree of capitalism to real wages can be described in terms of a simple equation that represents all of the essential elements of aggregate monetary demand. Thus,

$$\frac{M}{M'} = \frac{D_L + D_K}{D_C + D_K}.$$

The only new item in the equation is D_K, which is the aggregate demand for capital goods, D_L being the by-now-familiar aggregate demand for labor, and D_C the by-now-equally-familiar aggregate demand for consumers' goods. M and M', of course, respectively represent the aggregate productive expenditures made by business and the aggregate sales revenues of business. The equation expresses the fact that these are the respective sums of D_L plus D_K and D_C plus D_K.

The twofold positive effect of a rise in the economic degree of capitalism on real wages can be illustrated in terms of this equation. Thus let us begin with an economic degree of capitalism of .8, reflecting an aggregate demand for capital goods of 500, an aggregate demand for labor of 300, and an aggregate demand for consum-

ers' goods of 500. The figure of .8 for the economic degree of capitalism equals the result of substituting the assumed numbers in the above equation. The assumed value of 500 for the demand for capital goods is, of course, substituted both in the numerator and in the denominator, inasmuch as the demand for capital goods is equally a part both of productive expenditure and of sales revenues. (For the most part, the numbers assumed merely repeat the numbers assumed in Figure 14–4. All that is added is the assumption that the aggregate demand for labor is 300—Figure 14–4 made no assumption about the demand for labor.) Thus, we have:

$$\frac{800M}{1,000M'} = \frac{300D_L + 500D_K}{500D_C + 500D_K}.$$

In these initial conditions, the 500 of demand for consumers' goods comes from the wage earners' consumption expenditure of their 300 of wages and the further consumption expenditure of 200 by businessmen and capitalists, out of such sources as dividend and interest payments.

Now let us observe the effect of a rise in the economic degree of capitalism to, say, .95. This comes about as the result of businessmen and capitalists becoming more future-oriented and thus reducing their consumption expenditures from 200 to 50, while correspondingly increasing their saving and productive expenditures from 800 to 950. We further assume that of the 150 of additional saving and productive expenditure, 100 is an additional demand for capital goods and 50 is an additional demand for labor, which the wage earners will add to their expenditure for consumers' goods. Thus, the aggregate demand for capital goods is now 600, just as in Figure 14–5, and the aggregate demand for consumers' goods is now 400, also just as in Figure 14–5. (The demand for consumers' goods falls only by 100, rather than by the 150 reduction in the consumption expenditure of businessmen and capitalists because part of the effect of the businessmen and capitalists consuming less is an increase of 50 in wages, which enables the wage earners to increase their consumption by that amount. Thus, total consumption is reduced only by 100, from 500 to 400. In the new circumstances the wage earners consume 350 and the businessmen and capitalists, 50.)

Inserting these numbers in the equation, we obtain

$$\frac{950M}{1,000M'} = \frac{350D_L + 600D_K}{400D_C + 600D_K}.$$

Here then, is a rise in the economic degree of capitalism and, as the direct result of it, a rise in the relative demand for and production of capital goods, which serves progressively to raise the productivity of labor and thus real wages, and, in addition, a rise in the so-called distribution factor in favor of wage earners, from 300/500 to 350/400. Thus, as the economic degree of capitalism rises, we observe a twofold source of higher real wages, namely, the source of a rise both in the productivity of labor and in the "distribution factor." Of course, the rise in the productivity of labor is potentially capable of continuing without fixed limit, thanks to the ability of capital accumulation to continue without fixed limit, on the strength of a rise in the relative demand for capital goods. In contrast the potential rise in the "distribution factor" is of a one-time, nonrepeatable nature and is extremely limited.

Other Factors, Above All Economic Freedom and Respect for Property Rights, as Sources of Capital Accumulation

In addition to the relative production of capital goods and technological progress as determinants of the supply of capital goods, and thus of the productivity of labor, there is, as mentioned, the general efficiency with which existing capital goods are employed—viz., *the productivity of existing capital goods*. By the productivity of capital goods, I mean, of course, the ratio of output to the supply of capital goods. Technological progress is obviously a major contributor to this factor and is subsumed under it. But it is not the only thing that contributes to it. In Chapter 4, I pointed out how the division of labor itself, in all the aspects in which it increases production in general, operates to increase the production and supply of capital goods.[75] Wider still, as Ricardo pointed out, increases in the supply of capital goods can be achieved by *anything* that operates to increase the overall ability to produce. In Ricardo's words, "Capital is that part of the wealth of a country which is employed with a view to future production, and may be increased in the same manner as wealth."[76]

This means that capital accumulation can also result from such things as the adoption of free international trade, since free trade enables the same quantity of labor and capital goods to produce more, including more capital goods.[77] Indeed, it can result from the adoption of freedom of immigration. Freedom of immigration results directly in an increase in the total ability to produce—by virtue simply of adding to the supply of labor. In so doing, it adds to the ability to produce capital goods no less than to the ability to produce consumers' goods. In a free, capitalist economy, it also ultimately results in a permanently higher productivity of capital goods and correspondingly lower maintenance proportion in the economic system, thanks to a larger absolute number of gifted people being available and motivated to pursue careers in science, invention, and business, and thereby to accelerate the rate of technological progress. In addition, it

makes it possible to carry the division of labor further throughout the economic system and thus to achieve the improvements in the production and supply of capital goods that result on this score as well.[78]

As I indicated in Chapter 4, in the example of the isolated farmer who must use part of his crop as seed, the more efficient an economic system is in the utilization of its existing supply of capital goods—the higher the productivity of its existing capital goods—the greater is its ability to accumulate additional capital goods.[79] This is because a greater efficiency in the utilization of existing capital goods means that with any given supply of capital goods it can produce a larger total product, including a larger supply of capital goods for any given proportion of its productive efforts that it devotes to the production of capital goods. The effect of this, in turn, is that the proportion of its output which it needs to have in the form of capital goods in order to make possible the replacement of the capital goods consumed in production—its maintenance proportion—is correspondingly reduced. To whatever extent the economic system was already devoting to the production of capital goods a larger proportion of its efforts than was required for mere replacement, this reduction in the maintenance proportion further widens the margin by which it accumulates capital, and thus the rate at which it accumulates capital.

To illustrate this point, one need only imagine that in Figures 14–4 and 14–5, it became possible to produce with *1L* of labor and each *1K* of capital goods used in conjunction with *1L* of labor not merely *2K* of capital goods or, alternatively, *2C* of consumers' goods, but *3K* of capital goods or *3C* of consumers' goods. Under these conditions, the maintenance proportion of the economic system would no longer be 50 percent, but only 33⅓ percent. For a mere one-third of an output equivalent to *3K* of capital goods would be sufficient to replace the *1K* of capital goods productively consumed in producing that output. As a result, the economic system would become capable of accumulating capital even in the conditions of Figure 14–4—merely by continuing to devote half of its productive effort to the production of capital goods, for a 50 percent relative production of capital goods exceeds a maintenance proportion that has been reduced to 33⅓ percent. In these circumstances, the supply of capital goods in *Year 2* of Figure 14–4 would be *1.5K* instead of merely *1K*. In *Year 3*, continuing with a 50 percent relative production of capital goods and the same higher productivity of capital goods, the supply of capital goods would grow to *2.25K*, and so on. (The figure of *2.25K* results from multiplying .5 by *4.5K*, which latter would be the output of *1.5K* of capital goods and *1L* of labor operating under the conditions of the higher productivity of capital goods and devoted 100 percent to the production of capital goods.) In Figure 14–5, of course, the effect of the improvement in efficiency and consequent reduction in the maintenance proportion to one-third would be a still more rapid rate of capital accumulation than had previously been possible with a 60/40 relative production of capital goods and consumers' goods, and one that would be correspondingly larger than the now enormously rapid rate achievable even with a 50 percent relative production of capital goods.

Nothing can be more vital than to realize that the fundamental source of capital accumulation is *economic freedom*—not only in connection with international trade and immigration, but across the board.

First, of course, it cannot be stressed too strongly that the demand for labor and capital goods, and, consequently, the wage share of consumption, the relative production of capital goods, and the closely related concept of the degree of capital intensiveness in the economic system, all depend on saving and provision for the future, as opposed to current consumption. Saving and provision for the future, in turn, depend on the freedom to enjoy one's property: they depend on respect for property rights and the consequent security of property. This is an indispensable basis of the motive to save and provide for the future.[80] If individuals could not count on benefitting from their saving and provision for the future, because the government or private bands could be expected to seize their wealth before they could enjoy it or its fruits, they would not save and provide for the future, or would do so to a far lesser extent. And to whatever extent they did continue to do so, they would do so in secret—in ways that could easily be concealed from the envious eyes of others, such as hoarding gems or precious metals, and thus in ways that would not provide material means for raising the productivity of labor.

However, as the preceding discussion of this section has shown, economic freedom and respect for property rights promote capital accumulation in ways beyond providing an environment in which people are motivated to save and invest, and thus to secure a sufficiently high relative production of capital goods and a sufficiently high degree of capital intensiveness. They do so no less *by virtue of increasing the output per unit of capital goods in the economic system and thus reducing the maintenance proportion* and allowing any greater actual relative production of capital goods to achieve capital accumulation.

Raising the productivity of capital goods is the result of economic freedom and respect for property rights not only in connection with international trade and immigration, which has already been shown, but also with respect

to other, wider phenomena. For example, the searching out and implementation of technological advances by businessmen comes under this heading. This is because such activity depends on the motive of profit and loss and on the freedom of competition, both of which, in turn, presuppose the existence of private ownership of the means of production.[81]

As we have seen, the incentive of profit and loss and the freedom of competition underlie all the benevolent effects of the operation of the uniformity-of-profit principle and, indeed, underlie and drive the entire price system.[82] As we should now be able to understand, these benevolent effects of the uniformity-of-profit principle are dynamic. That is, they consist not only in raising the productivity of labor in the present, but also in permanently raising the productivity of existing capital goods and correspondingly reducing the maintenance proportion, and thereby powerfully contributing to capital accumulation and the continuing rise in the productivity of labor that comes from capital accumulation. Thus, the operation of the uniformity-of-profit principle is a leading source of capital accumulation. For so long as businessmen are inspired continually to introduce productive innovations of all kinds as the means of earning a premium rate of profit in the face of economic competition, the productivity of capital goods will be elevated and remain elevated.

The enormous contribution of the price system to capital accumulation becomes obvious when one recalls the destructive effects of socialism. We have seen that when private ownership of the means of production and the price system are destroyed by socialism, economic chaos results and thus the productivity of the existing supply of capital goods becomes so low and the maintenance proportion so high that capital accumulation becomes impossible, except at the price of mass murder, and even then only with the aid of an outside, capitalist world to provide vital supplies.[83]

Furthermore, we have also seen, in contrast, that the more fully are property rights respected, the more powerfully do the incentives of profit and loss and the freedom of competition operate. This is because, to that extent, profits are not taxed away, nor are subsidies of any kind given by the government, and all industries are legally open to everyone. Thus, the incentive of profit and loss and the freedom of competition can operate with corresponding lack of diminution. Full respect for private property rights implies the maximum incentive to cut costs and increase output per unit of input, and thus to achieve the maximum possible efficiency in the use of existing capital goods.[84] (The freedom of profits from taxation, of course, also operates powerfully to increase the economic degree of capitalism and thus the relative production of capital goods and degree of capital intensiveness in the economic system, because most of the profits left in the hands of business firms are plowed back into the purchase of capital goods and the payment of wages.)

Of course, even more fundamental than economic freedom as the foundation of capital accumulation is the degree to which a society values *human reason*. As I explained in Chapter 1, the prevalence of a substantial degree of rationality is required for the existence of economic freedom and respect for property rights. This is because it is the foundation of the view of man and the human individual as supremely valuable and as competent to run his own life, and thus as possessing individual rights which the government must respect. The degree of rationality also further underlies the willingness to save and provide for the future in that only the exercise of reason can make the future appear real in the present, which is necessary if people are to provide for it. Also it is the influence of reason and the acceptance of causality and human free will that makes it possible for people to come to regard themselves as self-responsible causal agents able to provide for the future and with an obligation to do so. And, of course, it is the acceptance of reason and causality that underlie all scientific and technological progress.[85]

Thus, the ultimate foundations of a rising productivity of labor and rising real wage rates are *freedom and reason*.

It should be obvious that this discussion fully confirms the thesis previously advanced in the critique of the exploitation theory in Chapter 11, that the parties crucially responsible for the rise in real wages are *businessmen and capitalists*. It is they who are constantly on the lookout for more efficient methods of production and who provide the capital funds that ensure a sufficient relative production of capital goods and degree of capital intensiveness, and that constitute the demand for labor. As far as it relates to wage earners, the effect of their activities is entirely to raise real wages: it is to raise the demand for labor relative to the demand for consumers' goods and, far more importantly, continually to raise the productivity of labor through the accumulation of capital, the latter resulting from the combination of a greater relative production of capital goods and higher degree of capital intensiveness and the highest possible productivity of capital goods.

The present discussion has also fully confirmed the thesis of Chapter 9, that private ownership of the means of production and respect for property rights are to the self-interest of everyone, not just the owners of the means of production. In underlying the profit motive, competi-

tion, and saving and productive expenditure, and in making possible their fullest and most efficient functioning, private ownership of the means of production and respect for property rights make possible the rapid accumulation of capital and thus the continuous and rapid rise in the productivity of labor and real wage rates, and at the same time assure the highest possible share of consumption originating in wage payments.

Thus, what this discussion has confirmed is that private ownership of the means of production, respect for property rights, and economic freedom are in the interest of wage earners no less than businessmen and capitalists.

Unfortunately, it is one of the great ironies—and injustices—of history that while businessmen and capitalists and the institutions of capitalism have created the modern standard of living of the average wage earner, and are capable of raising it further without any fixed limit, the great majority of mankind has believed, largely under the influence of Marxism, that profits and interest are derived from the impoverishment of the wage earners, and that the institutions of capitalism represent legalized theft and plunder. The ultimate irony—and justice—of this state of affairs is that to the degree that these vicious and destructive beliefs are put into practice, those who hold them impoverish themselves. The greater their ignorance and envy, and the legalized looting and plunder that result, the more do they push themselves into poverty.

The Undermining of Capital Accumulation and Real Wages by Government Intervention

It is essential to realize the extent to which government intervention undermines capital accumulation, and with it the demand for labor and the productivity of labor, and thus real wages and the general standard of living.

The progressive personal income and inheritance taxes, and the corporate income and capital gains taxes, are paid mainly with funds that would otherwise have been saved and productively expended. Thus, their effect is to reduce the demand for capital goods and the demand for labor by business enterprises, and thus to reduce the economic degree of capitalism and the degree of capital intensiveness in the economic system. Consumption expenditure of the government and of those to whom it gives money replaces expenditure for capital goods and labor by business enterprises, and thus consumption expenditure of the employees of business enterprises. In accordance with this change in demand, the existing ability of the economic system to produce is diverted from the production of capital goods to the production of consumers' goods, and from the production of consumers' goods that the employees of business would have bought to the production of the consumers' goods that the government and its employees and dependents buy. Such taxes threaten not only the economic system's ability to progress, but even its ability to produce sufficient capital goods to replace those that are used up in production—i.e., to remain stationary.

These taxes also greatly undermine the incentives to introduce improvements in efficiency in the economic system, as do government subsidies, antitrust laws, pro-union legislation, environmental legislation, and government regulation in general. In all these ways, government intervention operates to reduce output per unit of capital goods and thus to retard capital formation by this means too. The taxes reduce the rewards of economic success and thus discourage the efforts necessary to achieve it. At the same time, subsidies perpetuate inefficient methods of production by sustaining their practitioners. Thus, the taxes and the subsidies hold down the productivity of capital goods.

Furthermore, in depriving innovative small firms of the profits that would make possible their expansion, or more rapid expansion, most of these taxes also substantially reduce the force of competition in the economic system. They create a protective shelter around established firms that have already accumulated substantial capital and are now made more or less immune from the threat of new competition, since the potential competitors are prevented from accumulating capital, or from doing so as rapidly as they might have.[86] Essentially the same analysis applies to government regulation insofar as it is more difficult for small firms to comply with it, as when the regulations give an advantage to firms able to afford the employment of staffs of lawyers and accountants.

The antitrust laws stand in the way of business mergers that would achieve important economies and thereby render production more efficient. For example, the larger firm that results from a merger can often provide a sufficient volume of production to justify the purchase of machinery that the smaller firms which preceded it could not, or makes it possible to eliminate wasteful duplication in the use of existing equipment. In such ways, mergers make possible a more efficient use of capital. Preventing them prevents such more-efficient use of capital. In so doing, it retards capital formation.

Similarly, prounion legislation, in making it possible for the unions to prevent or delay the introduction of labor-saving machinery and more-efficient work practices, holds down the total output that otherwise could be produced in the economic system by the same quantity of labor working with the existing quantity of capital goods. In so doing, it holds down the size of the output that is available to meet whatever relative demand may exist for capital goods. So-called environmental legislation likewise provides numerous examples of reducing

output per unit of capital goods, such as depriving the capital and labor employed in the energy industry of its most productive uses by closing off vast territories to the very possibility of exploration and development, and imposing all manner of regulations on business in general that require the employment of additional capital and labor to accomplish a given result. All such regulations needlessly reduce output per unit both of labor and of existing capital goods, while correspondingly increasing costs per unit.[87] Indeed, in some cases business firms must invest once in order to produce their products, and the equivalent of a second time in order to be in compliance with the government regulations inspired by the pathological fears of the environmentalists.

Every government regulation, of whatever description, that needlessly raises costs, correspondingly reduces the output of the economic system and thus the efficiency with which existing capital goods are employed. This conclusion follows from the proposition established back in Chapter 6 that reductions in unit cost underlie increases in output in the economic system, by virtue of releasing labor and capital to produce more either of the good whose unit cost is reduced or of other goods.[88] The corollary of this proposition is that increases in unit cost operate to reduce output in the economic system. Both propositions also follow from the fact that with any given magnitude of aggregate productive expenditure, average unit cost in the economic system as a whole varies in inverse proportion to output.

Indeed, given any definite magnitude of aggregate productive expenditure, the only way that average unit cost in the economic system can increase is by virtue of aggregate production correspondingly decreasing, for average unit cost in the economic system as a whole *is* aggregate productive expenditure divided by aggregate output. By the laws of mathematics, with a numerator that is fixed, the only way that a fractional expression can increase is by virtue of a corresponding decrease in the denominator, which in this case is aggregate output. Thus, any government regulation that raises average unit costs in the economic system is accompanied by a corresponding reduction in aggregate output.

The consequence of any lesser overall ability to produce is, of course, a reduced ability to produce capital goods, as well as consumers' goods. More precisely, the effect of all such regulations is to reduce the ratio of output to the capital goods consumed in producing that output, and therefore to make the maintenance proportion unnecessarily high. When placed together with the taxes described a few paragraphs back, the combined effect is a lower relative production of capital goods and a higher maintenance proportion, with a corresponding two-sided reduction in the portion of output available for new capital formation. Indeed, that portion can be eliminated altogether, and stagnation or outright capital decumulation made to take the place of capital accumulation.

Government budget deficits and social security, like the taxes I have described, also operate to reduce saving and productive expenditure. To the extent the deficits are financed by borrowing from the public (as opposed to the printing of money), they represent a diversion of savings from use as capital to the financing of the government's consumption. To the extent they are financed by the creation of money, they operate to create both additional nominal profits, on which businesses must pay taxes, and to raise the replacement cost of capital assets. Thus, they operate to make it more difficult or even impossible to replace capital assets. And in still other ways, inflation-financed deficits undermine capital formation.[89] Social security leads people to reduce their provision for the future, in the belief that their needs will be provided for by the government. Meanwhile the government consumes their social security contributions. Thus, in this way too, capital accumulation is undermined.[90]

In the face of such an assault on the foundations of capital formation, it should hardly be surprising that the present-day United States has fallen from its previous position of unchallenged economic eminence. The United States is a country whose economic foundations have been sapped by wave after wave of socialistically motivated assaults on capital formation. In this century, there has been the Progressive Era and the Square Deal, then the New Deal, the Fair Deal, and the Great Society, all bent on fundamentally altering the nature of the American economic system and, unfortunately, succeeding in doing so. Until these policies, and the envy- and resentment-filled mentality on which they are based, are reversed, the United States will continue on its path of decline.

What is required to restore economic progress and rising real wages in the United States is nothing less than radical reductions in government spending, taxation, and government regulation of business. Specifically, what is necessary is to begin phasing out the progressive personal income and inheritance taxes, the corporate income tax, the capital gains tax, the social security system, and the whole of the welfare state, which makes the revenues raised by these destructive taxes appear necessary, and, at the same time, to move toward a gold standard and the end of the arbitrary creation of money. Such a program, coupled with an equally massive reduction in government regulation, would enormously increase not just the incentive and means to save, which would be important enough, but *all* of the incentives to produce and compete. People would work harder and produce more in the knowledge that more of what they earned was theirs to

keep. More new companies would be started and be able to grow rapidly and challenge the established firms, if they could plow back most of their profits. All firms would improve in efficiency if they were free of restrictive regulations. The rate of innovation and technological progress would increase. Thus, along with a sharp rise in the relative production of capital goods, the productivity of capital goods would greatly increase and the maintenance proportion correspondingly decrease. This combination of a higher relative production of capital goods and reduced maintenance proportion would assure a sharply higher rate of capital accumulation. It would thus restore a rising productivity of labor and rising real wages. (And, of course, real wages would increase on the strength of a rise in the demand for labor made possible by the reduction in government spending, taxes, and deficits.) This is clearly the path to the long-term economic recovery of the United States (or any other country). The effect would be to lift the United States out of the stagnation of the last generation and restore it to rapid economic progress—to rapidly rising real wage rates and a rapidly rising general standard of living.

Regrettably, so powerful is the grip of ignorance and envy, that no amount of economic decline by itself seems likely to awaken the present generation of Americans to the fact that they, their twentieth-century political heroes, and their present chosen leaders might in any way be responsible for the decline through the economic policies they support and sustain, and that what is required is the radical reversal of those policies. Following the completion of my economic analysis, the final chapter of this book will attempt to develop a concrete, long-range political-economic program and strategy for achieving the necessary changes.

Happily, a leading implication of the analysis of capital accumulation I have presented here is that it is never too late for such a program. For what I have shown is that while no amount of existing capital goods and prosperity, however great, is a guarantee of the maintenance of those capital goods and prosperity, so too it is possible even for the very poorest of countries to rise, or for a country to resume its rise no matter how great its fall from former prosperity. All that is necessary is that it become more efficient in the use of whatever capital goods it continues to possess, and devote a proportion of them and of its labor to the production of further capital goods that is greater than the maintenance proportion. It is highly unlikely that the economic decline the United States may experience in the coming decades will place it below the level of Japan in 1950. But even if that were the case, it would still be possible for the United States rapidly to reverse the damage and, before too long, to exceed its former peak and go on advancing from there. To do so, it would simply have to turn once again to the philosophy of economic freedom on which it was built. That would ensure both the necessary efficiency in the use of whatever capital goods existed and a sufficient concentration on the production of further capital goods.

The Nonsacrificial Character of Capital Accumulation Under Capitalism

It should be obvious that the analysis of this chapter implies that capital accumulation under capitalism takes place *nonsacrificially,* and was in the interest of the average wage earner even in the earliest years of the Industrial Revolution. (This, of course, is in sharpest contrast to conditions under socialism, where capital accumulation, if it can be achieved at all, must be achieved at the cost of human life.[91])

Capital accumulation under capitalism was not inaugurated by any temporary fall in the standard of living of the average wage earner. It did not come about as the result of any sudden major rise in the demand for capital goods coming at the expense of a reduction in the demand for labor and thus at the expense of consumption expenditure on the part of wage earners. On the contrary, it was inaugurated by a rise in the economic degree of capitalism, combined with a rise in the efficiency with which existing capital goods were employed. The effect of the higher economic degree of capitalism was *a rise in the demand for labor alongside the rise in the demand for capital goods.* Thus, a higher degree of capital intensiveness in the economic system was achieved as part of a process which raised wage payments relative both to consumption and to total sales revenues in the economic system. In addition, the Industrial Revolution represented the greatest increase in the efficiency of production and in the use of existing capital goods in all of human history. This in turn meant the greatest decrease in the maintenance proportion in all of human history. To this extent, capital accumulation was not the result of any actual reduction in consumption, however temporary, on the part of *anyone*—even businessmen and capitalists. For, to this extent, capital accumulation was made possible out of an increase in production.

In limited circumstances, to be sure, there can be a fall in the demand for labor and rise in the demand for capital goods. Indeed, when Ricardo became aware of this possibility, he mistakenly concluded that his previous views concerning the beneficial effects of machinery were mistaken and "that the opinion entertained by the labouring class, that the employment of machinery is frequently detrimental to their interests, is not founded on prejudice and error, but is conformable to the correct principles of political economy."[92] Marx, of course, also assumed that capital accumulation originating in a reduced demand for

labor was necessarily against the interests of the wage earners. It can now be seen that the actual effect of such a change in demand, to whatever extent it occurs, is ultimately to reduce prices to a greater extent than wage rates and thus to raise real wage rates—that, in other words, Ricardo and those who follow him in this have committed the error, so clearly identified by Ricardo himself, of confusing "value" and "riches," that is, of confusing a reduction in the monetary demand for labor with a decline in the real wealth obtained by wage earners.[93] This conclusion can be demonstrated both on the basis of the determination of prices by cost of production and on the basis of the determination of prices by supply and demand.

If the rate of profit remains the same, a reduced demand for labor reduces wage rates, costs of production, and prices all to the same degree. This follows from the fact that the price of every product can be expressed as a sum of wage payments made at the various stages of production, with each such wage payment multiplied by one plus the rate of profit raised to a power corresponding to the time which elapses between the making of the wage payment and the sale of the ultimate consumers' good.[94] For example, the price of a loaf of bread can be expressed as the sum of the wages paid per loaf of bread to workers engaged in wheat growing, flour milling, and baking (and all the other stages of production that stand behind the baking of bread), with each such wage payment multiplied by one plus the rate of profit raised to a power corresponding to the time which elapses between the payment of the respective wages and the sale of the loaf of bread. Thus, if the rate of profit remains the same, while wage rates fall, it follows that prices must fall in proportion to the fall in wage rates. However, precisely the fact that the fall in demand for labor and in wage rates is the result of a rise in the demand for capital goods and thus in the relative production of capital goods and hence in the productivity of labor, means that unit costs, and therefore prices, must fall to a greater degree than wage rates. For the corollary of the rise in the productivity of labor is a corresponding reduction in the quantity of labor required to produce a unit of goods. Thus, unit costs of production and prices fall because of the operation both of the fall in demand for labor and the rise in the productivity of labor, while wage rates fall only because of the fall in demand for labor. The net upshot is that this case merely constitutes yet a further confirmation of the proposition that real wages are determined by the productivity of labor.

In terms of demand-and-supply analysis, the reduced demand for labor and enlarged demand for capital goods both reduces the demand for consumers' goods (inasmuch as the wage earners have equivalently less to spend for consumers' goods) and, as I will show in Chapter 17, by enlarging the demand for capital goods relative to the demand for consumers' goods, serves to lengthen the "average period of production."[95] The result is that, once again, the prices of consumers' goods fall in proportion to the fall in demand for labor and wage rates. At the same time, however, the higher productivity of labor, which results from the greater relative production of capital goods, increases the supply of consumers' goods. Thus, prices fall more than wage rates because both prices and wage rates fall in proportion to the fall in the demand for labor, while prices also fall in proportion to the resulting increase in the supply of consumers' goods.

A few further words are required to show why supply-and-demand analysis supports the fact that prices must fall in proportion to wage rates—apart from their further fall in proportion to the increase in the supply of consumers' goods. Strictly speaking, a fall in the demand for labor brought about by a rise in the demand for capital goods must decrease the demand for consumers' goods by a lesser percentage than it decreases the demand for labor. This is the case insofar as the demand for consumers' goods is initially larger than the demand for labor. Thus, for example, if the demand for consumers' goods is initially 500 units of money and the demand for labor is initially 400 units of money, an equal decrease in the demand for labor and consumers' goods of 100 units of money reduces the demand for labor by 25 percent, and the demand for consumers' goods by only 20 percent. Nevertheless, the prices of consumers' goods still tend to fall by 25 percent.

What reconciles the unequal percentage changes in demand with the outcome based on the cost-of-production analysis is, as I have indicated, a lengthening of the average period of production, which necessarily results from the demand for capital goods rising at the expense of the demand for labor and thus, indirectly, at the expense of the demand for consumers' goods. The nature of a lengthening of the average period of production, and its influence on prices in the face of the demand for consumers' goods falling proportionately less than the demand for labor can be understood in terms of the example of twelve-year-old scotch replacing eight-year-old scotch in the market. A 20 percent reduction in expenditure for scotch would easily be capable of being accompanied by a reduction in the price of scotch of 25 percent, indeed, of far more than 25 percent, if twelve-year-old scotch now sold for 20 percent less than eight-year-old scotch used to be sold for. Just so, a lengthening of the average period of production means that in general, goods with a longer average time span in their production come to take the place in the market of goods with a shorter average time span in their production. In

this way, a lesser percentage fall in demand for consumers' goods is capable of being accompanied by price reductions of a greater percentage than itself.

To place this analysis in the actual context of the rise in the economic degree of capitalism, what it means is that the demand for labor may recede somewhat from the peak to which a higher economic degree of capitalism has raised it. But then, of course, on the basis of the more rapid rate of capital accumulation and increase in the productivity of labor that is brought about by the greater relative production of capital goods and higher degree of capital intensiveness, real wages quickly recover from any temporary setback and go on further and further surpassing any previous peak. And, of course, in the process, the demand for labor, and with it average money wage rates, would also almost certainly be rising, as the result of the increase in the quantity of money that would almost inevitably accompany increasing production under a commodity money standard.

To understand just how rapidly any such temporary decline in real wages could be made good, it is only necessary to realize that over a 10 year period, a 2 percent addition to the annual rate of economic progress raises real wages by approximately 22 percent and that a 3 percent addition raises them by approximately 34 percent. (At the approximately 6 percent annual rate of economic progress that has taken place in Japan and other East Asian countries over the last several decades, the rise in real wages over the course of a decade is 79 percent. Over the course of three decades, it is over 579 percent.)

Indeed, it is virtually impossible that the inauguration or intensification of capital accumulation and economic progress in a capitalist country could ever result in a reduction in average real wages that would not be made good very quickly. This is because the basic effect of a higher economic degree of capitalism is to raise the demand for labor, as well as the demand for capital goods, relative to consumption and total sales revenues in the economic system. At the same time, the higher economic degree of capitalism is itself part of an even wider process which has as another major effect a rise in the productivity of capital goods and corresponding fall in the maintenance proportion.

The conclusion concerning the very limited extent and temporary nature of any fall in real wages as the result of capital accumulation and economic progress appears all the stronger, when one takes into account the fact that any rise in demand for capital goods at the expense of the demand for labor that might take place, despite the fundamental background of a rise in the demand for both, would not take place suddenly and dramatically, all at once, but only gradually, over a period of years. Thus each succeeding year over which the process occurred would benefit from the operation of forces already in place that were working to bring about a rise in real wages. Indeed, in the case of the Industrial Revolution in England, the process of capital intensification and the corresponding rise in the ratio of the value of accumulated capital to wage payments, appears to have taken place and been largely completed in the century and a half or more *prior* to 1775—the year usually taken as marking the beginning of the Industrial Revolution. This was manifested in the fall in the rate of interest on long-term government bonds in England to 3 percent as early as 1757.[96] Thus, under no circumstances could the Industrial Revolution have been responsible for any fall, however temporary, in the average worker's real wages in England.

What did hold down the standard of living of the average English worker at the time was twenty-five years of almost uninterrupted war with France between 1790 and 1815. The taxes and loans to pay for the war deprived business firms of the ability both to pay wages and to buy capital goods and thereby worked against both the so-called wage share of national income and the productivity of labor. Wartime inflation and the subsequently resulting postwar deflation and depression further substantially contributed to the undermining of capital accumulation and the rise in real wages.[97]

Only in a socialist country, such as Soviet Russia, with its gross inefficiencies and impossibly high maintenance proportion, can a process of capital accumulation or, more accurately, alleged capital accumulation, not be accompanied by rising real wage rates starting at virtually the same time.[98]

On the basis of the foregoing, it is necessary to disagree completely with such alleged defenses of capitalism as the following statement of de Jouvenel's: "[O]ne may ask whether the 'hard times' so bitterly evoked, and for which capitalism is arraigned, were a specific feature of capitalist development or are an aspect of a rapid industrial development (without outside help) to be found as well under another social system. Does the Magnitogorsk of the 1930s compare so favorably with the Manchester of the 1830s?"[99] In this passage, de Jouvenel displays the grossest ignorance of the actual nature of capitalism's economic development, equates nineteenth-century capitalist Great Britain with twentieth-century Communist Russia, and implies that socialism is capable on its own of achieving capital accumulation. It is difficult to imagine compressing a larger number of more profound errors into such a small number of words.[100]

While capitalism and the Industrial Revolution operated from the very first to raise the standard of living of the average worker, even they could not succeed in raising the standard of living of workers who refused to abandon occupations made obsolete by the process of improvement, as was the case with the English handloom weavers, for example. As the progressive application of machinery driven by man-made power drove the price of cloth ever lower and enabled the average wage earner in Britain, and in all the countries to which Britain exported cloth, to enjoy rising real wages insofar as they could now afford to buy more and better cloth and clothing, the handloom weavers, in blind obstinacy, carried on in the weaving of cloth by hand. As a result, for them, the falling price of cloth meant falling earnings.

Such occurrences were not the fault of capitalism and the Industrial Revolution, but of the refusal of workers to change occupations (and, of course, of any legal factors that may have prevented them from changing their occupations.) If such workers had changed their occupations, and thus reestablished their capacity to earn an income, the effect would have been that they, along with everyone else, would have benefitted even from the very improvements that initially had cost them their jobs, as did American horsebreeders and blacksmiths as the result of the coming of the automobile. The case of the handloom weavers, and all other such workers, is the same in principle as that of the potato growers, which I presented in connection with the exposition of Say's Law in the last chapter.[101] In the absence of government intervention, there is absolutely no need for it to have any other outcome than a beneficial one for all concerned. Capitalism should not be blamed either for the existence of government intervention that prevents workers from making rational choices concerning their occupation, or, in the absence of government intervention, for the refusal of workers to make rational choices concerning their occupation.

Appendix to Section 3: An Analytical Refinement Concerning the Rate of Economic Progress

The extremely rapid rate of reciprocating capital accumulation and increases in production present in Figure 14–5 is the result specifically of the assumption that it is possible to have a progressing economy in which all capital goods are productively consumed in a single year. In reality, of course, this is not possible. This is because there are numerous capital goods, such as virtually all major factories and office buildings, whose construction time is significantly longer than a year. Construction times for railroads, bridges, tunnels, highways, dams, and so forth are typically even longer than those for factories and office buildings. Also, given the great expense of producing these various types of capital goods, and most types of machinery as well, it is essential that they be used for periods substantially longer than a year.

Thus, in reality, the accumulated stock of capital goods in existence at the beginning of any given year substantially exceeds the portion of that stock which is productively consumed within the year.

These facts can be allowed for in our analysis by introducing the assumption that while *1K* of the opening stock of capital goods in any given year is productively consumed in producing an output lying between the extremes of *2K, 0C* and *0K, 2C*, there must be an accumulated stock of capital goods in existence at the beginning of the year that is, for example, five times larger, namely, *5K*. Under this assumption, the 20 percent increase in the production of capital goods in *Year 1* of Figure 14–5 would not constitute a 20 percent increase in the accumulated stock of capital goods available at the start of *Year 2*, but only a 4 percent increase, namely, an increase in the ratio of *5.2K: 5K.*

Furthermore, if the addition to the supply of capital goods were all in the form of work in progress, such as construction in progress, the larger supply of capital goods in existence at the beginning of *Year 2* would not serve to make the output of *Year 2* larger than that of *Year 1*. The increase in output would have to await the completion of projects extending beyond a year.

To keep matters as simple as possible with this more complicated context, let us momentarily assume that no increase in production can take place until 5 years have elapsed, by which time the 20 percent larger relative production of capital goods in each year will have resulted in increasing the accumulated stock of capital goods from *5K* to *6K*. Under this assumption, the 20 percent increase in the overall ability to produce that is made possible by a 20 percent increase in the supply of capital goods will not take place until *Year 6*, rather than *Year 2*. And then that 20 percent increase in the ability to produce, assuming that it is devoted 60 percent to the production of capital goods, will result in an increase in the accumulated stock of capital goods to *6.24K* at the start of *Year 7*. (This is because *1.44K* of capital goods are now produced, while *1.2K* of the *6K* are productively consumed.)

Assuming once more that the additional supply of capital goods is all in the form of work in progress and that 5 years of such capital accumulation must go by before production can increase in proportion to the larger stock of capital goods, it will not be until *Year 11* that the overall ability to produce increases by a second 20 percent.

In other words, while the fundamental principle is still present that increases in the supply of capital goods increase the ability to produce capital goods and thereby constitute the basis for continuing capital accumulation, the operation of that principle is slowed down by the need to build up an additional capital stock over a period of years. The regularly recurring 20 percent increases first in the stock of capital goods, then in production, and then again in the stock of capital goods because of the preceding increase in the ability to produce, now take place over 5-year intervals instead of from year to year. The effect of this, of course, is to reduce the annualized rate of economic progress from 20 percent to 4 percent.

To carry the analysis yet another step closer to the details of reality, we must recognize that the greater part of the increases in the supply of capital goods that occur in less than 5-year intervals serve to increase the overall ability to produce also in less than 5-year intervals. Thus, perhaps in *Year 3*, for example, when the supply of capital goods has reached *5.4K*, the overall ability to produce might now be increased by a few percent in comparison with that of *Year 1*. And it would almost certainly further increase by an additional few percent in *Years 4* and *5*. (To the extent such increases in production take place prior to *Year 6* rather than all being concentrated in *Year 6*, the increase in production in *Year 6* would, of course, be correspondingly less than 20 percent.) The average annual rate of increase in the supply of accumulated capital and in production would still be on the order of 4 percent rather than 20 percent, though somewhat more rapid than in the case in which the increase in production occurs only in 5-year intervals, because now there is compounding over shorter intervals of time.

This establishes the basic pattern of the relationship between my simplifying assumptions and the complex conditions of actual reality.

4. The Productivity Theory of Wages and the Interpretation of Modern Economic History

Now that the productivity of labor and thus real wages have been shown to be determined by capital accumulation, which in turn has been shown to rest on a foundation of respect for property rights and individual freedom—and ultimately, at the deepest level, on the influence of reason in a country's culture—it is possible to see that the productivity theory of wages provides a full alternative to the Marxian interpretation of modern economic history. According to the Marxian interpretation of economic history, which is generally taken for granted, the standard of living of the average worker in the nineteenth century was low because the capitalists had unchecked freedom to exploit him.

The Cause of Low Wages and Poor Working Conditions in the Past

The productivity theory of wages explains the low real wages and low standard of living of the nineteenth century not on the basis of any "exploitation of labor" by the capitalists, but on the basis of a *low productivity of labor,* inherited from centuries of feudalism, which low productivity of labor the activities of the businessmen and capitalists immediately began to raise.

To understand how low the productivity of labor was in the past, all one has to do is to look around at the goods commonly available today in the United States and other Western countries, and consider just how recent was their introduction. As we go back in time, the automobiles, airplanes, air-conditioners, computers, telephones, television sets, tape recorders, radios, phonographs, motion pictures, refrigerators, freezers, electric lights, antibiotics, antiseptics, and anesthesias all disappear. So do motor trucks, tractors and harvesters, electric power plants, steamships, and railroads. So do electric motors, steam engines, and power tools and power-driven machinery of every description. Not only do so many of the goods we take for granted simply disappear, but whatever goods remain must be produced laboriously, by hand—by human muscle power aided only by animals and, at best, by the power of wind and falling water.

In the absence of all of these goods and of all the modern methods of production, it should certainly not come as a surprise that the average standard of living was miserably low. By modern standards, the standard of living even of the world's richest people of two hundred years ago, or even just one hundred years ago, was extremely low. It was simply not possible for people to have goods that did not exist. And of the goods that did exist, it was simply not possible for most people to have very many of them, when, for example, each piece of wood used to build a house had to be sawed by hand and everything else that entered into the construction or furnishing of a house had to be made by hand; when every piece of clothing that a person wore, and every piece of food that he ate, had to be produced in the same way, that is, with the aid of virtually no power-driven machinery of any kind.

The low productivity of labor of earlier generations provides a full and sufficient explanation of the low standard of living of those generations. It also explains the long hours of work, child labor, and the bad working conditions. Long hours and child labor existed because the low productivity of labor—the low output per hour of labor—meant that a minimal standard of living could be achieved only by the performance of a correspondingly large number of hours of labor, to compensate. People worked long hours because the low productivity of labor rendered the output of a shorter working day, of the length we are accustomed to think of as desirable, inadequate to provide the minimum supply of goods people considered it necessary to have. Children worked

alongside of adults because the low productivity of labor rendered even the long hours of the adults insufficient to produce the minimum supply of goods people considered it necessary to have.

Working conditions were very poor in large part because the low productivity of labor meant that the means of making them better simply did not exist. For example, it was absolutely impossible to give workers the benefit of electric light or air conditioning or modern plumbing on the job, when such things had not even been invented. For the rest, working conditions were very poor because the low productivity of labor made it impossible to improve them except at the expense of driving the workers' low standard of living still lower.

In this connection, it must be understood that there are two types of improvements in working conditions among those that are possible within any given existing state of technology: namely, those improvements which pay for themselves, through making production more efficient, and those which do not pay for themselves. Improvements in working conditions of the kind which pay for themselves, through bringing about sufficient increases in efficiency, are adopted by employers not only voluntarily, but with exactly the same eagerness as leads them to adopt any other improvement in efficiency, such as better machinery.

Improvements in working conditions of the kind which do not pay for themselves represent an increase in the cost of employing workers. If such improvements are not to be equivalent in their effects to a forced increase in nominal wages—that is, to cause unemployment, higher prices, and a burden of supporting the unemployed— they must be accompanied by an equivalent reduction in that part of the cost of employing labor which the worker receives directly for himself, i.e., his take-home wages. In either case, such improvements in working conditions are at the expense of the average worker's standard of living off the job. In the latter case, his take-home wages are reduced. In the former case, if he is lucky enough to keep his job, the prices he must pay are increased, and he must help to support those who become unemployed as the result of the rise in employment costs. If his standard of living is already very low, then it follows that improvements in working conditions that reduce it still further are likely to be *against* the actual self-interests of the workers and to be rejected by them in the labor market. What this means is that when asked to choose between jobs offering better on-the-job conditions but correspondingly lower take-home pay, and jobs offering poorer on-the-job conditions but correspondingly higher take-home pay, the workers will choose the jobs offering the poorer on-the-job conditions and higher take-home pay. To this extent, working conditions are poor because in the prevailing conditions of a low productivity of labor, the wage earners judge that they cannot afford to have them any better.

How Real Wages Rose and the Standard of Living Improved

The productivity theory of wages explains how all aspects of the workers' conditions improved. The starting point was a growing degree of rationality and a growing respect for property rights in society. These resulted in the achievement of a sufficiently high relative production of capital goods, the discovery and adoption of technological advances, and a general improvement in the efficiency of use of capital goods, all of which brought about capital accumulation and a rising productivity of labor. At the same time, of course, the sufficiently higher relative production of capital goods was accompanied by a rise in the demand for labor relative to the demand for consumers' goods—both changes being the reflection of a higher economic degree of capitalism. This, too, contributed to a rise in real wages, even if on an essentially nonrepeatable basis.

The direct effect of a rising productivity of labor was a rise in the average worker's real wages. As people's real wages rose, a further effect was that they could afford to reduce their hours of work. For as the real earnings from jobs requiring the accustomed number of hours rose, so did the real earnings from jobs requiring fewer than the accustomed number of hours. For example, in the earliest years of the Industrial Revolution, the productivity of labor was still so low that many people needed to work eighty hours a week in order to earn enough to support a family. A generation or two later, a doubled productivity of labor not only doubled the real earnings that could be obtained from a job of eighty hours a week, but, at the same time, made it possible to obtain substantially larger real earnings from jobs requiring seventy or sixty hours a week than it had originally been possible to obtain from jobs requiring eighty hours a week. Although jobs requiring eighty hours a week still offered more than jobs requiring seventy or sixty hours a week, the jobs requiring seventy or sixty hours a week now offered *enough* for most people to be able to afford to take them.

As more and more workers could afford the relatively lower earnings from jobs with shorter hours, and came to desire such jobs, *the competition of the labor market operated to reduce the number of hours in the average work week.* Whenever employers had to compete for labor, the offer of shorter hours was a powerful means of recruiting the labor they sought. And as the shorter week became more and more widespread, it became necessary for those employers who had not yet offered it, to do so, in order retain the labor they already had.

In addition, another powerful competitive factor favored the adoption of a shorter work week. Namely, the desire of workers for a shorter week operated to make it *more economical* to employers to offer a shorter week. This was because to the extent that workers wanted a shorter week, they became willing to accept jobs offering shorter hours at wage rates that were lower *more than in proportion to the shorter hours.* For example, to the extent that they strongly desired a sixty-hour week, say, in place of an eighty-hour week, they became willing to accept jobs requiring a sixty-hour week at wages less than three-fourths of the wages of jobs requiring an eighty-hour week. This meant that an employer who offered the shorter week would have correspondingly lower unit costs of production than employers who offered the longer week. This represented a cost reduction over and above any reduction that could be achieved by virtue of the workers' being able to produce more per hour with a shorter week, which in itself was no doubt significant.

There should be nothing surprising or disturbing in any of this. The statement that the desire of workers for shorter hours leads to a discount in the wage rates for shorter hours is only another way of saying that the labor market tends to impose *premium wage rates* for jobs requiring hours that the market regards as excessive. Just as today premium rates for overtime imposed by the government discourage the use of overtime, so the premium rates that the market comes to generate for jobs with relatively long hours discourage the offer of such jobs. And the more strongly the workers prefer to work shorter hours, the greater are the relative discounts in the wage rates that can be offered in connection with jobs requiring shorter hours, and the greater are the relative premiums in the wage rates that must be offered in connection with jobs requiring longer hours. Thus, to the extent that the workers come to be able to afford and to desire shorter hours, the greater is the encouragement to the offer of shorter hours.

This, not legislation, is the actual process by which the hours of work have been reduced over the span of the last two hundred years—first, from eighty hours a week to seventy or sixty hours a week, then to fifty hours a week, and then to forty hours a week. Future generations of capitalism, with further doublings and redoublings of the productivity of labor, could well see real wages raised to such a point that people would be able to earn vastly more in thirty, twenty, or even ten hours a week than they now can earn in forty hours a week, with the result that the average person might someday have a real income substantially higher than that of a present-day physician, say, while working the hours of a present-day college professor.

The rise in the productivity of labor was also responsible for the progressive reduction in child labor. For as people's real wages rose, another effect was that they could afford to keep their children home longer. Thus, child labor diminished—not as the result of legislation, but as the result of rising real wages brought about by a rising productivity of labor.

Although the connection just made is actually very simple, it cannot receive enough stress or elaboration. With the exception of orphan children, those who decided whether or not children would work, and, if so, to what extent, were the children's parents. As soon as parents began to decide that they no longer needed as much help from their children, because their own real wages were now higher, they began to keep their children home longer, and thus to reduce the amount of child labor.

Thus, as the productivity of labor and the real wages of the parents rose, the age at which children went to work steadily increased. In the preindustrial seventeenth century, humanitarians contemplated ways in which orphan children of the age of three might be taught some simple skill, so that they might be enabled to contribute to their own support and thereby survive, in the face of the very meager charitable contributions that were all that the extremely poor society of the time could provide. In the earliest years of the Industrial Revolution, there were children who went to work at the age five or six. In the early nineteenth century, the starting age rose to seven or eight; later in the century, to nine or ten. By the beginning of the twentieth century, it was more often eleven or twelve. Today, it is typically not until the completion of a high-school or college education, and in a significant number of cases, a postgraduate education.

In addition, the rise in the productivity of labor was responsible for the improvement in working conditions that has taken place over the last two hundred years. As already indicated, one aspect of the rising productivity of labor was the very coming into being of goods that could constitute an improvement in working conditions in the first place, such as electric light and air conditioning. Another aspect was that as the productivity of labor rose in the production of goods capable of improving working conditions, and reduced their cost, the instances in which improvements in working conditions paid for themselves through greater efficiency increased. This was because any given improvement in efficiency was now weighed against a reduced cost of achieving it. A further aspect of the rise in the productivity of labor was that the higher real wages it achieved enabled workers more and more to afford to take jobs offering relatively better working conditions at the cost of relatively lower take-home pay. This was because jobs with relatively

lower take-home pay now offered far more than had jobs geared to the utmost in take-home pay in the past.

Thus, working conditions improved by virtue of the same process of competition in the labor market as reduced the hours of work. As workers came to be increasingly able to afford better conditions at the price of lower take-home pay, employers who offered the combination of better conditions together with take-home pay lower by enough to offset their cost, gained an increasingly powerful competitive advantage in recruiting workers. For as real wages rose because of the rising productivity of labor, the marginal utility that wage earners attached to the specific amount of real income required to achieve a given improvement in working conditions progressively fell. Once it fell below their rising valuation of the better working conditions, the effect was a growing relative discount in the wages of jobs with better working conditions, and a growing relative premium in the wages of jobs with poorer working conditions, which premiums and discounts more and more exceeded the cost of providing the improvements. Thus, the offer of better conditions was made more and more economical to employers. In the present-day United States, for example, the premium in take-home wages that would have to be paid to induce most workers to work in a factory without modern plumbing so far exceeds the cost of having such plumbing as to make its absence almost unthinkable. Or, to say the same thing in different words, the offer of an amenity such as modern plumbing makes possible to employers a saving in take-home wages that far outweighs its cost. The same principles, of course, apply to the presence or absence of such things as air-conditioning, cafeterias, recreational facilities, child-care centers, and so on, and to job safety, which is an important aspect of working conditions.

It needs to be pointed out that government policies promoting inflation and credit expansion, and thus the boom-bust cycle, especially when compounded by policies that interfere with the fall in money wage rates in the depression phase, can impede the market's ability to shorten hours and improve working conditions. To the extent that a situation is created in which money wage rates need to fall to reestablish full employment, and have not yet done so, or are prevented from doing so, reductions in labor cost may instead be achieved by a lengthening of hours in the face of the same weekly wages and at the expense of working conditions. In a free labor market, the workers would choose a fall in money wage rates as the means of reducing labor costs, and, as I have shown, would end up with no reduction in their real wages, because of the resulting fall in prices.[102] But to the extent that that is made impossible, they become willing to accept the equivalent of substantially lower real wages in the form of longer hours and poorer conditions rather than become unemployed and earn no wages. This constitutes a further argument against inflation and credit expansion and government interference with wage rates.

It is appropriate to consider here the fable of the company towns. Though I have not been able to find it in the writings of Marx himself, the doctrine of company towns claims that, not content with the payment of outrageously low wages, the capitalist exploiters also frequently built company towns for the purpose of charging the workers outrageously high prices. It is difficult to understand why the capitalists would go to the trouble of investing substantial sums in the construction of whole towns in order to squeeze extra profits from the workers if they have arbitrary power over wage rates, as the Marxists believe. Because if they really did have such power over wage rates, it would be far simpler for the capitalists just to cut wages by an amount equal to the profit they allegedly make by virtue of owning the company town. This would give them the same amount of profit or "surplus-value" and a substantially higher rate of profit, because they would avoid having to tie up the substantial amount of capital needed to build and operate a town.

Of course, the capitalists do not have arbitrary power over wage rates, and to induce workers to work for them they must offer the workers a combination of wage rates, working conditions, and—as far as competition with capitalists in other areas goes—living conditions (including access to housing and retail stores) that is superior to any other such combination that the workers believe is available to them. If they do not, they will lose their workers. The obvious reason that the capitalists sometimes built company towns was that doing so enabled them to offer a combination of these elements that was of greater value to the workers than if the same amount of capital had been invested in the payment of wages exclusively. In the case of companies operating in relatively isolated areas, which offer few amenities and little of value to spend money on, the payment of the maximum possible wage rates is of less value to the workers than the offer of a combination of lower wage rates together with such amenities as housing and stores. This is why company towns were built. This is why they are still occasionally built today. For example, American companies operating in places like Saudi Arabia or the North Slope of Alaska provide the equivalent of company towns. Such towns represent a major positive value to the workers and are essential for attracting sufficient workers.

The fact that prices in the stores of a company town

may often be higher than prices in better-located, more-populous areas is indicative not of unusual profits being made in such stores, but of the high costs of supplying such remote and isolated locations. If high profits were the explanation, there would soon be other suppliers in the vicinity. The fact that occasionally a worker might become excessively indebted to the stores in a company town is of no more significance than the fact that people can and do become excessively indebted without company towns. The complaints against company towns deserve no more credence than any other aspect of the exploitation theory.

5. A Rise in the Productivity of Labor as the Only Possible Cause of a Sustained, Significant Rise in Real Wages

It needs to be understood not only that the rise in the productivity of labor has been the cause of the rise in real wages and the average wage earner's standard of living over the last two hundred years, but also that the rise in the productivity of labor is the *only possible* such cause. For let us consider the alternatives.

Any rise in *money wage rates*, by itself, is inherently incapable of raising real wage rates (with one relatively minor exception to be explained shortly). This becomes clear when we examine the possible sources of a rise in money wage rates.

The Futility of Raising Money Wage Rates by Means of an Increase in the Quantity of Money or Decrease in the Supply of Labor

A rise in money wage rates can be achieved either by an increase in the demand for labor or by a decrease in the supply of labor. The most obvious source of a rise in the demand for labor is an increase in the quantity of money. But, as we have already seen, while increases in the quantity of money operate to raise the demand for labor and thus money wage rates, they also operate at the same time to raise the demand for consumers' goods and thus the prices of consumers' goods, and to the same extent. Thus, the rise in money wage rates brought about by a larger quantity of money does not constitute a rise in real wages. Indeed, when increases in the quantity of money exceed the relatively modest rate of increase in the supply of precious metals, they constitute inflation and begin to produce all of the problems associated with inflation. Among these problems is a slowing down of capital accumulation or outright capital decumulation, as will be shown in Chapter 19 of this book. This, of course, holds down the rise in the productivity of labor and real wages, or actually causes them to decline.[103]

A rise in money wage rates brought about by a reduction in the supply of labor also does not represent any rise in real wages, but the contrary. We have already seen that this is the case when the supply reduction represents nothing more than forced unemployment for the purpose of achieving or maintaining a higher level of money wage rates. For then, there is the problem of fewer workers employed producing fewer consumers' goods, which must be sold at correspondingly higher prices, and the further problem of having to support the unemployed. By the same token, a long-term reduction in the size of the population, and thus in the number of people able and willing to work, would raise money wage rates, but it would also reduce the extent of the division of labor, and thus operate to reduce the productivity of labor and therefore to raise prices even more than wage rates.[104]

The demand for labor could rise by virtue of a decrease in the desire of people to hold money, which would manifest itself in a rise in the so-called velocity of circulation of money—that is, in a more rapid rate of spending of any given quantity of money. However, as I have shown, such a phenomenon, when significant, is itself the result of rapid increases in the quantity of money. Moreover, like any increase in the quantity of money, it tends to raise prices at least to the same extent as it tends to raise wages.[105]

The Futility of a Rise in the Demand for Labor Coming at the Expense of the Demand for Capital Goods

It is conceivable that the demand for labor could rise without either an increase in the quantity of money or a decrease in the desire to own money. It could rise by virtue of a drop in the demand for capital goods. While this would raise nominal wage rates, it would reduce real wage rates, for it would raise prices by more than wages. This case is simply the converse of the case of a fall in the demand for labor and rise in the demand for capital goods, which I have already considered.[106]

Thus, in this case, the rise in demand for labor would raise wage rates, unit costs, and prices to the same extent, and the accompanying reduction in the relative production of capital goods and productivity of labor would raise unit costs and prices beyond the rise in wage rates. In terms of supply-and-demand analysis, the rise in demand for labor would result in a virtually equivalent rise in the magnitude of demand for consumers' goods, as the wage earners consumed their additional incomes. This, together with the shortening in the average period of production that is entailed in the rise in the demand for consumers' goods relative to the demand for capital goods, would raise the prices of consumers' goods in proportion to the rise in wage rates. The reduction in the productivity of labor and thus in the supply of consumers'

goods would raise prices beyond the rise in wage rates.

Indeed, because of the accompanying reduction in the ongoing *rate* of capital accumulation, and thus the compounding effect on the productivity of labor, the rise in prices relative to wages, and thus the fall in real wages, would become greater and greater with the passage of time.

Of course, it is not necessary that the supply of consumers' goods fall in comparison with what it was in the past, as the result of the decline in the demand for capital goods. The fall could take the form of the increase in the supply of consumers' goods being less than it otherwise would have been. This as a minimum must be the effect of a rise in the demand for labor coming at the expense of the demand for capital goods. In either event, in every year in which the relative demand for capital goods remained lower in order to make possible a higher relative demand for labor and consumers' goods, the reduction in the actual or potential supply of consumers' goods would become greater. The result of this would be that the rise in prices relative to wages, and the consequent reduction in real wages, would become greater, at least in comparison with what they otherwise would have been.

The present discussion should not be taken to imply that the demand for labor should never rise at the expense of the demand for capital goods or that it is always desirable for the demand for capital goods to rise at the expense of the demand for labor. In a free market, the demand for labor could rise at the expense of the demand for capital goods if the consumers decided they preferred a larger quantity of goods whose production entailed a relatively greater amount of wage payments and smaller expenditures for capital goods at the expense of goods of the opposite description. Such a case would not represent a fall in real wages, but a rise in comparison with the real wages that would exist if the change in consumer demand were not met and thus output was wasted in the form of goods consumers wanted less. A fall in real wages is entailed only insofar as the demand for labor is increased at the expense of the demand for capital goods as the result of government or labor-union coercion.

Moreover, it is important to realize that when a rise in the demand for capital goods at the expense of the demand for labor can serve to raise the productivity of labor (which, of course, is the typical case), there is always the question of by how much and starting at what point in the future. Here both the law of diminishing returns and the height of the rate of profit and interest play a decisive role in limiting the degree of capital intensiveness in the economic system and thus in limiting the demand for capital goods relative to the demand for labor.[107] The essential point of this discussion, however, is that forced increases in the demand for labor coming at the expense of the demand for capital goods reduce real wages.

The Futility of Raising the Demand for Labor by Means of Taxation

The demand for labor, and thus nominal wage rates, might be increased in still another way. The government could levy taxes that individuals paid with funds they otherwise would have used to purchase consumers' goods. The government could then expend these taxes in the expansion of its own payroll, with the effect of equivalently increasing the economy-wide, aggregate demand for labor. While those who had to pay the taxes would consume less by the amount of the taxes, the recipients of the government's additional wage payments would consume more by the amount of the taxes. Thus the total demand for consumers' goods in the economic system would remain the same, with the government's employees enabled to consume in the place of the taxpayers. Only the aggregate demand for labor would change: it would increase.

If the government's additional demand for labor came at a time of full employment, the effect would be an increase in money wage rates on a pretax basis. It it came at a time of unemployment, the effect could be an increase in overall employment in the economic system.

Essentially this case led Ricardo to call into question his previous convictions about the economic ill-effects of war and government spending. In the same chapter in which he commits his previously discussed error—of arguing that a rise in the demand for capital goods that takes place at the expense of the demand for labor is against the interest of the average wage earner—he also argues that the rise in the demand for labor in the present case is to the interest of wage earners. He writes:

> Independently of the consideration of the discovery and use of machinery, to which our attention has been just directed, the labouring class have no small interest in the manner in which the net income of the country is expended, although it should, in all cases, be expended for the gratification and enjoyments of those who are fairly entitled to it.
>
> If a landlord, or a capitalist, expends his revenue in the manner of an ancient baron, in the support of a great number of retainers, or menial servants, he will give employment to much more labour than if he expended it on fine clothes or costly furniture, on carriages, on horses, or in the purchase of any other luxuries.
>
> In both cases the net revenue would be the same, and so would be the gross revenue, but the former would be realized in different commodities. If my revenue were 10,000l., the same quantity nearly of productive labour would be employed whether I realized it in fine clothes and

costly furniture, etc., etc., or in a quantity of food and clothing of the same value. If, however, I realised my revenue in the first set of commodities, no more labour would be *consequently* employed: I should enjoy my furniture and my clothes, and there would be an end of them; but if I realised my revenue in food and clothing and my desire was to employ menial servants, all those whom I could so employ with my revenue of 10,000l., or with the food and clothing which it would purchase, would be to be added to the former demand for labourers, and this addition would take place only because I chose this mode of expending my revenue. As the labourers, then, are interested in the demand for labour, they must naturally desire that as much of the revenue as possible should be diverted from expenditure on luxuries to be expended in the support of menial servants.

And then, very significantly, Ricardo adds:

> In the same manner, a country engaged in war, and which is under the necessity of maintaining large fleets and armies, employs a great many more men than will be employed when the war terminates, and the annual expenses which it brings with it cease.[108]

Here again, in assuming, irrespective of context, that the wage earners are always "interested in the demand for labour," Ricardo commits the error he himself warned against, namely, confusing "value" and "riches," or money income and real wealth.[109] Even in the very strongest case for Ricardo, namely, that capitalists and landlords voluntarily decide to spend less in purchasing consumers' goods and equivalently more in employing consumers' labor—i.e., labor employed not for the purpose of making subsequent sales (which is necessarily the kind of labor demanded when "a landlord, or a capitalist, expends his revenue in the manner of an ancient baron, in the support of a great number of retainers, or menial servants")—there is no gain to wage earners as a class, and almost certainly a significant loss.[110]

This is because the effect of an increase in demand for labor in the form of an increment of demand for consumers' labor is correspondingly to decrease the proportion of the supply of labor employed as *producers' labor,* that is, the proportion employed by business firms, for producing products to be sold. This is true even in the case of unemployment, inasmuch as any unemployed workers who end up becoming employed as consumers' labor could have become employed as producers' labor—at least if money wage rates were free to fall. Since all producers' labor is employed directly or indirectly in the ultimate production of consumers' goods, the effect of this reduction in the proportion of the supply of labor employed as producers' labor is correspondingly to reduce the production and supply of consumers' goods and thereby to raise their prices in full proportion to the additional demand for labor and any increase in money wage rates that is present in this case. The following example, based on our formulas for the wage and price level, will make this point clear.

I assume that initially the demand for labor in the economic system is 400 monetary units, consisting entirely of a demand for producers' labor. Now, because capitalists and landlords change their pattern of consumption to favor the purchase of consumers' labor rather than consumers' goods, a demand for consumers' labor emerges equal to 100 monetary units. Thus, the total demand for labor in the economic system rises to 500 monetary units, an increase of 25 percent. The effect of this is that if the economic system already enjoyed full employment, the average wage rate in the economic system would also be increased by 25 percent in comparison with its initial level, in accordance with the rise in the aggregate demand for labor in the ratio of 500 to 400. Indeed, whether the economic system already had full employment or not, the average level of money wage rates at which full employment can now exist is 25 percent higher than it would otherwise have been. That is, wage rates can now be 25 percent higher than the level to which they otherwise might have had to fall to achieve full employment.

Nevertheless, no one can gain from such a rise in the demand for labor and in wage rates. The reason is that one-fifth of the labor of the economic system is now employed as consumers' labor, which leaves only four-fifths to be employed as producers' labor. This is the new pattern of employment, because the 100 monetary units of demand for consumers' labor is one-fifth of the now larger total demand for labor of 500 monetary units. By the same token, the 400 monetary units of demand for producers' labor, which used to constitute the entire demand for labor, now constitutes only four-fifths of the demand for labor and thus employs only four-fifths of the labor of the economic system.

Given a constant productivity of labor, four-fifths of the supply of labor working as producers' labor produces only four-fifths the output of consumers' goods. In the face of an unchanged aggregate demand for consumers' goods—which, as we have seen is the case here—four-fifths of the supply of consumers' goods results in prices of consumers' goods that are five-fourths of what they used to be. Thus, in this case, *prices rise just as much as wages*. That is, both rise in the ratio of 5 to 4.

They do so because, as I say, to precisely the same extent that wages are increased by the additional aggregate demand for labor that is constituted by the additional demand for consumers' labor, a corresponding proportion of the labor force is bid away from employment as producers' labor. The result of this is that the production and supply of consumers' goods ultimately falls in in-

verse proportion to such rise in the demand for labor, and, as a result, the prices of consumers' goods rise in direct proportion to it. The rise in prices here can, of course, also be understood on the basis of a rise in the costs of production that is brought about by the additional demand for labor and rise in wage rates. Other things being equal, higher wage rates cause correspondingly higher costs of production and thus, given the rate of profit, correspondingly higher prices of consumers' goods.

To grasp the supply and demand aspects of the case algebraically, all we need do is state the aggregate demand for labor D_L as the sum of the wages paid by business plus the wages paid by consumers, that is, as the sum of the demands for producers' labor and consumers' labor. Thus, where w_b is the wages paid by business, that is, the demand for producers' labor, and w_c is the wages paid by consumers, that is, the demand for consumers' labor,

$$D_L = w_b + w_c \, .$$

The rise in the aggregate demand for labor and in wage rates is in the ratio of $\dfrac{w_b + w_c}{w_b}$. At the same time, the fall in the proportion of the supply of labor employed by business is in the inverse ratio $\dfrac{w_b}{w_b + w_c}$. Given the same productivity of labor, this last ratio is also the measure of the reduction in the supply of consumers' goods produced, which, accordingly, must be expressed as

$$\frac{w_b}{w_b + w_c} \times S_C \, .$$

Inasmuch as the general consumer price level P is equal to $\dfrac{D_C}{S_C}$, when this reduced supply of consumers' goods is divided into the demand for consumers' goods, D_C, what we see is that

$$\frac{D_C}{\dfrac{w_b}{w_b + w_c} \times S_c} = \frac{w_b + w_c}{w_b} \times P,$$

which last expression shows that prices rise to precisely the same extent as wage rates.

Thus far, I have assumed that the productivity of labor remains the same. The fact is that the productivity of labor will almost certainly decrease, thereby bringing about a rise in product prices more than proportional to the rise in wage rates, since the supply of products produced will fall in greater proportion than the supply of labor employed by business. This is because the labor which is transferred from the employ of business to the employ of consumers will come at the expense of manufacturing and industries supporting manufacturing, where economies of scale prevail, which now cannot be exploited as fully. This is the case inasmuch as the origin of the rise in the demand for labor is supposed to be precisely a drop in the demand for luxury products of manufacturing.

If the rise in demand for labor is brought about by taxation, the negative effects are far more serious. First of all, in this case, the change in demand represents a virtual deadweight loss to whoever must pay the taxes.[111] To continue with Ricardo's assumption that it is only capitalists and landlords whose demand for consumers' goods is replaced by a demand for consumers' labor, the situation now is that these parties are compelled to give up the purchase of various luxuries in order to pay for various government expenditures. In place of the "fine clothes and costly furniture" they would have bought for themselves, they now obtain the dubious benefit of the existence of "large fleets and armies," or some peacetime equivalent. Furthermore, because the funds are obtained by taxation, that is, involuntarily, by force, and thus the change in the pattern of demand does not reflect the free choice of the owners of the funds, it cannot be expected that the owners will pay the taxes simply at the expense of their consumption expenditure. Indeed, the major effect of any such tax—any tax whatever that is aimed at the income or consumption of businessmen and capitalists (including, of course, "landlords")—is to reduce saving, the relative demand for and relative production of capital goods, and thus the accumulation of capital, the productivity of labor, and real wages. It is also to reduce the incentive to improve products and methods of production and thus the productivity of capital goods, thereby raising the maintenance proportion, all of which compounds the destructive effects on capital accumulation and the productivity of labor.[112] Finally, it is to reduce the wage "share" of national income, further adding to the reduction in real wages. A similar "boomerang" effect exists in connection with efforts to limit the consumption of businessmen and capitalists.[113]

Ricardo assumed that the additional tax fell on the consumption of capitalists and landlords rather than wage earners. In reality, the tax would more likely fall on the consumption of wage earners. Only to the extent that it did, would the destructive effects on saving and capital accumulation be mitigated.[114] However, even if the tax fell entirely on the consumption of wage earners, it would still do substantial damage.

This is because even if the effect of the government's larger payroll were more employment, the great majority of wage earners, who are already employed and who must pay the tax, must forego part of their own consump-

tion in order to finance the consumption of the additional government employees. Like the capitalists and landlords in the case already considered, they receive little or no compensation for their reduced consumption by virtue of the activities of those government employees. To the contrary, the government's additional employees may very well render their lives more difficult, through imposing additional regulations and controls on them, on the suppliers they buy from, or on the employers they work for or might work for.

If the government's additional demand for labor comes at a time of full employment and so raises the average money wage rate in comparison with what it was before, the standard of living of the wage earners is likewise reduced. For in this case, there is a rise in the prices of consumer goods as great as the rise in wage rates, and, over and above this, a rise in taxes. Thus, the average worker finds that his take-home pay does not keep pace with the rise in prices. The consequences here can be understood in terms of our previous example of the rise in demand for labor from 400 monetary units to 500 monetary units. If the 100-monetary-unit rise in taxes and the demand for labor is paid for by taxes on wage earners, then wage earners as a class are in the position that their after-tax wages are no higher than they used to be, while prices are now 25 percent higher. For in this case, while total wages are 500 monetary units, the taxes paid out of wages are 100 monetary units. Thus, there are still just 400 monetary units in total after-tax wages to be paid to the same total number of workers. At the same time, prices are 25 percent higher, both on the foundation of 25 percent higher wage rates and labor costs and on the foundation that only four-fifths of the previous labor is available to produce consumers' goods, which are thus produced in only four-fifths the quantity and therefore sell at five-fourths the price. Indeed, even the average government worker is worse off now than he was before. On an after-tax basis, he, too, ends up earning no more than he used to earn, while having to pay higher prices. And even if the government workers were previously unemployed, they are worse off in comparison with what they could have had if they had been reemployed privately and thus have added to the total of output, instead of having to share in the restricted output of others. To whatever extent wage earners are taxed to pay for the government's additional payroll spending, these effects are present.

The Limited Scope for Raising Real Wages Through a Rise in the Demand for Labor

What all of the discussion in this section leads to is the conclusion that the only way in which a rise in the demand for labor and in money wage rates can in fact benefit wage earners is if and to the extent that people decide to consume less and to save and productively expend more for labor. When, for example, consumption out of dividend and interest payments falls and the funds thereby saved are used by business firms to employ labor, there is a rise in the demand for labor and in wage rates, but no rise in the general consumer price level. Thus, there is a rise in real wage rates.

The consumer price level remains the same in this case because both the aggregate demand for and supply of consumers' goods remain the same. The overall demand for consumers' goods remains the same inasmuch as the additional consumption expenditure of the wage earners resulting from their higher wages merely takes the place of an equivalent reduction in the consumption expenditure of businessmen and capitalists, which is the foundation of the rise in wages and the consumption of the wage earners. At the same time, in contrast to the previously considered case of a rise in the demand for consumers' labor, here there is no bidding away of part of the supply of producers' labor in favor of consumers' labor as an accompaniment of the rise in wages, and thus no reduction in the supply of consumers' goods produced. Thus, with both the supply of and the demand for consumers' goods remaining the same, the result is that the general consumer price level remains the same. At the same time, of course, the rise in the demand for labor raises wage rates. Thus, real wage rates rise.[115]

Precisely this case, which is characterized by a change in demand from consumption to saving and productive expenditure, represents a rise in the so-called distribution factor in favor of wage earners. It is an aspect of a rise in the economic degree of capitalism. And because of this, it is necessary to refine the expression of the distribution factor. It is now clear that stating it simply as the demand for labor relative to the demand for consumers' goods is too broad. It must be stated as the demand for labor *specifically by business enterprises*—that is, the demand for producers' labor—relative to the demand for consumers' goods. This refinement was not necessary so long as the only demand for labor under consideration was the demand for labor by business. Now that the demand for labor by consumers has been introduced, however, and has displayed very different characteristics, the refinement in definition is necessary.

What is present in cases of a rise in the distribution factor is a fall in *net consumption*, which, as I indicated in the last chapter, and will explain more fully in Chapter 16, is consumption in excess of wage payments, made possible by consumption out of such sources of funds as dividend and interest payments.[116] A fall in net consumption, I will show, operates to reduce the general or average rate of profit and interest in the economic system,

and this explains why in cases of this kind the rise in costs of production constituted by the rise in wage rates does not operate to raise the general consumer price level— namely, it is offset by a fall in the rate of profit.[117]

The ability of a fall in net consumption to bring about a rise in real wages by means of raising the demand for labor and thus changing the distribution factor in favor of labor is strictly limited, however. Moreover it is operative only in an environment of security of property, in which people voluntarily choose to consume less and save more. In the present-day United States, net consumption on the part of all private individuals combined almost certainly equals substantially less than 10 percent of national income. This can be inferred by starting with the fact that normally less than 30 percent of national income represents profits and interest, or any other income that is not wages or salaries. Of this 30 percent, half or more can be assumed to be siphoned off in federal, state, and local corporate and personal income taxes. Something on the order of half of the remaining 15 percent of national income in the form of profits and interest can be taken as representing saving out of such incomes.[118] Thus, an amount equal most probably to something on the order of 7.5 percent of national income remains as private net consumption.[119]

It follows that even the total disappearance of today's private net consumption and the use of all of the resulting additional savings to make an additional demand exclusively for labor, would be capable of raising the demand for labor, and thus average wage rates, only the order of 10 percent. The figure of 10 percent results from dividing the 7.5 percent of national income that can be taken as today's private net consumption, by the approximately 70 percent of national income that is typically in the form of wage or salary payments. Of course, whatever the precise figure for it might be, the rise in the demand for labor and in wage rates would be on a one-time, non-repeatable basis only.

In fact, however, the disappearance of private net consumption could never take place, because, as we have seen, businessmen and capitalists have no motive to save and accumulate capital except as a means of ultimately contributing to their own consumption. Thus, their consumption cannot be eliminated without destroying the economic system. Nor can it even be significantly reduced by means of force without inflicting major damage on the economic system.[120] Net consumption is at a minimum precisely in a society in which property rights are fully respected and in which a high degree of rationality leads people to be future oriented and adopt a low time preference. In such conditions, the motive to accumulate for the future rather than to consume in the present is at a maximum. The attempt to use force to bring about a still further fall in net consumption (or to use force to cause a fall in net consumption under any conditions) results in property becoming insecure and thus in the loss of incentives to accumulate and maintain capital. As we have seen, this destructive process entails a reduction both in the relative production of capital goods and degree of capital intensiveness and in the productivity of capital goods.[121] Depending on the extent of the use of force, the consequences range from the slowing of capital accumulation and rise in real wages to outright capital decumulation and falling real wages. In all cases, the effect is to reduce real wages, at least in comparison with what they would otherwise have been.

Nevertheless, as the result of the existence of improper government activity on a large scale, there is today a significant potential source of a fall in net consumption and rise in the demand for labor by business relative to the demand for consumers' goods. This is *a reduction in government spending and thus in budget deficits and in the taxes that fall on saving and productive expenditure*. If government spending and the funds the government takes to finance that spending were reduced, more funds would be left to business enterprises to expend in meeting payrolls and in buying capital goods. The effect would be a significant one-time rise in the ratio of demand for labor by business to demand for consumers' goods. Of course, far more significant for the long-term rise in real wages would be the accompanying rise in the relative production of capital goods and in the degree of capital intensiveness. These, together with the greater incentives to technological progress and efficiency that would come from reduced government regulatory activity and reduced taxation, would bring about a sharply higher rate of capital accumulation and thus a sharply higher rate of increase in the productivity of labor. Thus, real wages could be increased at first in significant part on the basis of a rise in the demand for labor and then, thanks to the continuing stimulus given to capital accumulation and the productivity of labor, go on increasing without limit.[122]

The potential for raising real wage rates through a rise in the demand for labor by business relative to the demand for consumers' goods—viz., through a rise in the distribution factor—is always highly limited, even in conditions in which the demand for labor by business relative to the demand for consumers' goods is very modest. In such conditions, increases in the demand for labor by business are accompanied by substantial increases in the supply of labor drawn from the ranks of manual workers who are not wage earners. For example, imagine a society in which the demand for labor is 100

units of money while the demand for consumers' goods is 1,000 units of money. Imagine also that only one manual worker in ten is a wage earner. In these conditions, a doubling of the demand for labor is likely to be accompanied by approximately a doubling of the proportion of manual workers who are wage earners.

As a result, in these conditions, the rise in demand for labor does not raise money wage rates correspondingly. In addition, because the increase in the supply of wage earners does not mean any overall increase in the amount of labor actually performed in the society, it is not accompanied by any corresponding increase in the supply of consumers' goods. Thus, while wage rates stay basically the same, there is also no fall in the prices of consumers' goods caused by an increased supply of labor, and thus real wages cannot rise in proportion to the rise in the demand for labor. In terms of our formula showing real wages as determined by the product of the distribution factor times the productivity of labor, the rise in the distribution factor in these circumstances is accompanied by an apparent decline in the productivity of labor. The decline in the productivity of labor must be termed apparent because it signifies only that as manual workers change their status from non–wage earners to wage earners, the supply of consumers' goods produced increases to a much lesser extent than does the supply of wage earners. The main significance of the distribution factor in this context is that of a gauge of the proportion of the manual workers who are wage earners.

Of course, as such, the rise in the distribution factor indirectly does represent some significant rise in real wage rates. In bringing about a rise in the proportion of manual workers who are employed as wage earners, it is the basis of an increase in the division of labor and thus of a rise in the productivity of labor. As a result, while the supply of consumers' goods produced does not rise in proportion to the number of workers who are wage earners, it does rise relative both to the total number of workers and to the number who are wage earners, and thus prices do decline relative both to money incomes in general and to wage rates in particular. However, what is responsible for the improvement is the rise in the productivity of labor, not the rise in the distribution factor itself.[123]

Increases in the distribution factor signify directly corresponding increases in real wage rates only insofar as the proportion of manual workers who are wage earners can be assumed to be fixed. This assumption is perfectly reasonable in the conditions of modern, industrial economies, in which almost all manual workers are already employed as wage earners. In this case, increases in the distribution factor signify increases in wage rates in the face of unchanged prices of consumers' goods. But in this case their potential for raising real wage rates is even more limited, for the reasons explained.[124]

6. Critique of Labor and Social Legislation

It is now possible to turn to a critique of the doctrine that labor and social legislation have been responsible for the rise in the average worker's standard of living.

Redistributionism

It should be obvious that the belief that economic conditions in the past were poor because of an unjust "distribution" of wealth and income, and were improved by the imposition of a more just distribution of wealth and income, is completely wrong. In the early years of capitalism, and in all of history preceding capitalism, there was virtually nothing to redistribute. The workers of the early nineteenth century did not lack automobiles and television sets because the capitalists were keeping the whole supply to themselves. There simply were no automobiles or television sets—for anyone. Nor did the workers of those days lack sufficient housing, clothing, and meat because the capitalists had too much of these goods. Very little of such goods could be produced when they had to be produced almost entirely by hand. If the limited supplies of such goods that the capitalists had could have been redistributed, the improvement in the conditions of the workers would hardly have been noticeable. If one person in a thousand, say, is a wealthy capitalist, and eats twice as much and has twenty times the clothing and furniture as an average person, hardly any noticeable improvement for the average person could come from dividing the capitalist's greater-than-average consumption by 999 and redistributing it. At the very best, a redistribution of wealth or income would have been useless as a means of alleviating the poverty of the past.

Worse than that, it would have been positively harmful for the well-being of the average person. As I have shown, the overwhelming bulk of the wealth of the capitalists is in the form of capital goods, on which the productivity of labor depends. A policy of seizing the wealth of the capitalists, to improve the consumption of the masses, is actually a policy of capital decumulation, which must destroy the foundations of the productivity of labor and thus real wages.[125]

As I have shown, redistributionism through a policy of taxation of the capitalists' incomes and estates reduces the incentive and means for capital accumulation. It reduces saving and productive expenditure and thus the economic degree of capitalism, and with it both the demand for capital goods relative to the demand for consumers' goods and, however ironically, the wage "share" of national income. At the same time, it reduces the incentive to search out and implement technological advances, and the incentive to be efficient in the use of capital goods. Thus it reduces the productivity of capital goods and raises the maintenance proportion. In other words, it does everything possible to impair the increase in the supply of capital goods and thus the increase in the productivity of labor. It does everything possible to hold down the rise in real wages, and actually to reduce real wages.[126]

The truth is that what made possible the rise in real wages and the average standard of living over the last two hundred years is precisely the fact that for the first time in history the redistributors were beaten back long enough and far enough to make large-scale capital accumulation and innovation possible. What distinguishes eighteenth and nineteenth century Britain and America is precisely the respect shown for property rights. It was this that provided the indispensable foundation for the accumulation of capital and the rise in the productivity of labor and real wages. To the extent that the redistributors have subsequently been able to reimpose their philosophy, the rise in real wages and the average standard of living has been less than it otherwise would have been.[127]

As I have shown, the major victims of redistributionism are always the wage earners. Taxes imposed on profits and interest are paid largely with funds that otherwise would have been used to purchase labor services and capital goods. Taxes imposed on inheritances fall almost entirely on funds that otherwise would have been used in this way. In contrast, there are the taxes imposed directly on wage earners, which cannot be passed on to anyone insofar as they are imposed on workers in all industries and all occupations. To the extent that taxes are imposed on wages in this way, they simply reduce the benefit the average worker derives from the labor he performs. They make the conditions of the average wage earner equivalent to what they would be if the productivity of labor were lower. (The effects of a consumers' sales tax are essentially similar.) However, insofar as taxes are imposed on profits, interest, and inheritances, they not only make the conditions of the workers equivalent to what they would be if the productivity of labor were lower, but have the further effect of retarding or altogether stopping any further rise in the productivity of labor, and thus of making the worsened conditions longer lasting or even permanent. Indeed, such taxes have the potential for plunging the economic system into capital decumulation and economic retrogression, by virtue of bringing about a relative production of capital goods and productivity of capital goods insufficient for the replacement of existing capital goods. Thus, as I have shown, from the point of view of the long-run interests of the wage earners, taxes falling on profits, interest, and inheritances are actually *worse* than taxes falling directly on wages.[128]

It is necessary to deal briefly with the special fallacies present in the belief, so prominent in the labor-union movement, that profits can be converted into additional wage payments. The labor unions have only to see significant profits, and immediately they believe that a source of additional wage payments exists, which can serve to raise the wage rates of their members.[129]

The fact is that, apart from all the other considerations I have raised against the redistribution doctrine, profits as such are not actually available for redistribution. Profits are not, as most people appear to believe, a separable part of sales revenues that goes to the businessmen and capitalists, and which potentially could go elsewhere. All of the sales revenues go to the businessmen and capitalists, who in turn expend the far greater part of those revenues in the purchase of capital goods and labor. The separable part of sales revenues that goes to the personal use of the businessmen and capitalists is not profits but *dividend* payments, and the draw of funds by partners and proprietors. Profits themselves are actually an accounting abstraction—the difference between sales revenues and historical costs, that is, costs derived from previous outlays for labor and capital goods, made years in the past in many cases. They are *not* the difference between sales revenues and current outlays for labor and capital goods.

Profits can exist with no portion of sales revenues going to the personal disposition of the businessmen and capitalists; they can exist with 100 percent of sales revenues being used to purchase capital goods and to pay wages. For example, a firm could have sales revenues of a million dollars a year and expend the equivalent of the whole of its sales revenues in the purchase of capital goods and the payment of wages, and still have a profit—possibly, a very substantial profit. It would have a profit to the degree that the costs it deducted from its sales revenues were less than a million dollars. Its costs would be less than a million dollars, insofar as the million it spent in each year for capital goods and labor was for the purchase of durable equipment or for the accumulation of inventory.

If, for example, half of its outlay in each year were for equipment that would last ten years, and another quarter of its outlay represented the accumulation of inventory, its total costs deducted from sales revenues in that year on account of expenditures made for capital goods or labor in that year would amount to a mere $300,000, and thus its profit to as much as $700,000. This is because of its $500,000 of outlay for equipment, only $50,000 would show up as depreciation cost that year. And of its remaining $500,000 of outlay, only the $250,000 that does not go for inventory accumulation would show up as a cost

that year. Thus, its total costs on account of expenditures made in that year for capital goods and labor would be no more than $50,000 plus $250,000, or $300,000 in all.

To calculate the firm's overall, total costs in that year, one would, of course, have to add depreciation costs resulting from expenditures for plant and equipment made in prior years. If this amounted to another $100,000, say, then its profit would still be $600,000, even though in the same year that its sales revenues were a million dollars, it expended a full, equivalent million in the purchase of factors of production.

In this case, if a labor union demanded the payment of the profit as additional wages, the only possible source of the funds would have to be a reduction in the firm's expenditure for capital goods, or, however absurd, its existing expenditure for labor! Or the funds would have to come from outside the firm, which would entail a reduction in wage payments and the demand for capital goods elsewhere.

Not only in this case, but in every case without exception, the only significant funds which can be added to the payment of wages in any given firm are funds which are withdrawn from the purchase of capital goods in that firm, or from the purchase of capital goods or payment of wages in other firms. As I have shown, funds used to finance the personal consumption expenditure of businessmen and capitalists are not only not significant relative to wages, but also cannot even be obtained as a source of additional wage payments without damage to the economic system on a vastly greater scale. This last is because so long as the businessmen and capitalists retain their capital, they have the power to go on consuming with little or no diminution, while if they lose that power, they lose the incentive to accumulate and maintain capital.[130] We already know the destructive effects of forcibly increasing the demand for labor at the expense of the demand for capital goods.[131]

Furthermore, the notion of converting profits into the payment of wages is held in ignorance of the fact that a substantial portion of profits exists as the result of nothing more than the increase in the quantity of money and volume of spending in the economic system. Such profits reflect the fact that productive expenditure and sales revenue in the current period are greater than the productive expenditure of the past, on which the costs deducted from sales revenues in the current period are based. The growth in productive expenditure from year to year naturally takes the form of rising wage payments and increasing spending for capital goods. At the same time, the rising sales revenues it causes in each year generate profits because, as I say, the costs of each year reflect productive expenditures of the past, which were smaller.[132] Thus, to the extent that profits reflect merely the growth in spending, they already provide all the benefit to wage earners that they can possibly provide. This is because they are already expended as wage payments or in the purchase of capital goods. To ask that because they are profits they be paid instead as wages, is to ask for the payment of the same sum twice over to the benefit of wage earners.[133]

And the same is true of real profits, insofar as they reflect merely the increase in the physical volume of wealth in the possession of business firms. This increase in wealth represents additional capital goods, which are used in further production, and additional consumers' goods sold to wage earners. The full benefit of this additional wealth already goes to wage earners. The profit merely marks the increase in such wealth. It is not available in any way further to increase the benefits to wage earners.

On the basis of our previous discussion both of the cause of higher real wages and of the effects of redistributionism, it should be clear that the attempt of the labor unions to convert profits to wages by means of force cannot raise the average worker's standard of living and must actually tend to reduce it. As I have shown, it is in part an attempt to raise the wages paid to one set of workers at the expense of the wages paid to another set of workers, by virtue of requiring funds to be withdrawn from the payment of wages in some firms in order to be added on to the payment of wages in other firms. And for the rest, it is an attempt to raise wages and consumption at the expense of the demand for capital goods. Insofar as it may succeed in reducing profits, it does so only as the accompaniment of a reduction in the rate of economic progress and thus in the increase in real wages. It slows the increase in production, which reduces both the real profits of business and the rise in real wages.[134]

Labor Unions

This brings me to the general subject of the effect of labor unions on real wages and the wage earners' standard of living.

The productivity theory of wages implies that the labor unions (and the public at large) have an utterly wrong idea of how the average level of real wages and the average standard of living are increased. The goal of the unions is to increase the money incomes of their members. And that, of course, is the goal of practically every individual with respect to his own wages. But I have shown that almost all of the ways of accomplishing a rise in the general or average level of money wages cause either no increase in real wages and the general standard of living or actually *reduce* real wages and the general standard of living—by bringing about unemployment or a lower productivity of labor. I have shown

that the general level of real wages and the average standard of living are simply not raised to any significant sustainable extent by virtue of the average worker earning more money, but only by virtue of the productivity of labor rising and prices falling. I have also shown that the only major way that everyone can earn more money is by virtue of an increase in the quantity of money, which raises prices as much as wages, and that in that case only a rise in the productivity of labor makes it possible for prices to rise less than wages and so enables the rise in wages to represent an increase in real wages.

I now must reconcile the perception of individuals, that the way to raise their standard of living is by earning more money, with the productivity theory of wages, which shows that the general standard of living does not rise by virtue of the earning of more money, but by virtue of the rise in the productivity of labor and the consequent fall in prices relative to wages.

When an individual increases the productivity of his own labor, whether by becoming more efficient in a given job or by raising his level of skills to the point of being able to perform a more demanding job, the likely result is that he will increase his money income. What enables the individual to increase his money income in this way is partly the fact that, at the same time that he is increasing his productivity, the quantity of money and volume of spending in the economic system are also probably increasing. But this is not the major reason for people concluding that greater productivity means correspondingly more money income. A close connection between the individual's improvement in his productive ability and an increase in his money income would exist even if the quantity of money and the volume of spending in the economic system remained constant. It would exist insofar as the improvement in the productivity of the individual's labor is an improvement *relative to the productivity of labor of his competitors in the rest of the economic system.*

In considering the relationship between the improvement in his productivity and the increase in his money income, the individual is usually not aware that what is decisive for his being able to earn a higher money income is the rise in his productive ability *relative* to productive ability in the rest of the economic system. He experiences the improvement in his productive ability as an absolute improvement, not a relative improvement. In his mind, he does better and so he is paid better.

Nevertheless, what actually enables the improvement in his abilities to result in bringing him a higher money income is that it is an improvement relative to the abilities of other people. If everyone improved his productive ability at the same time and to the same extent, no one would earn any more money than before—except to the extent that there was an increased ability to produce the commodity used as money. There would be an increase in the supply of goods relative to the supply of labor, real wages and the standard of living would rise, but the improvement would be achieved through a fall in prices in the face of unchanged wages, not through a rise in wages.

As an illustration of the fact that the greater productive ability of an individual results in a greater money income for him only insofar as it represents a greater *relative* productive ability, consider the following case. An individual who works in an office or a factory wants to be promoted to manager and thereby earn a higher income. If all that happens is that he improves his performance and now surpasses all of the other candidates for the job, he will most likely be promoted and earn the higher income. But suppose that one or more of the other candidates improve their performance just as much as he improves his. Then his improvement is definitely no guarantee of his being promoted and earning a higher income. The improvement in his performance, the improvement in the performance of all of the competitors, will still tend to raise the general standard of living, through its effect on the supply of goods and services available to the firm's customers, but it will not tend to raise the income of any of the competitors themselves, except insofar as the improvement in the performance of one them *surpasses* the improvement in the performance of the others or enables their performance as a group to surpass the performance of other such groups.

This last points to the fact that the same principle applies between firms and industries. Insofar as an improvement in the productive ability of some or all individuals within a given firm creates a competitive advantage for that firm, the result might be that some or even all of its employees now earn more money. But in that case, the firms in the industry that lag behind, and their employees, suffer corresponding reductions in revenue and income. If all the firms in an industry are inspired to become more productive, it might be that they all increase their revenues and incomes. But then they do so in competition with other industries, whose firms and employees suffer corresponding reductions in revenue and income. Once again, we are driven to the fact that the only way that everyone in the economic system can earn more money is insofar as there is a larger quantity of money and thus greater volume of spending in the economic system as a whole. More production by itself does not produce this result.

In fact, as I have already shown, there are numerous cases in which, when everyone does increase his ability to produce, the average member of the group actually earns less money. The example of the potato growers, in the discussion of Say's Law, was precisely such a case.[135] The same sort of situation exists in cases often cited by labor-union supporters, in which the adoption of piecework stimulates all of the workers to improve their efficiency and results in such an increase in the supply of the product and fall in its price, that the wage per piece falls to the point where most, or even all, of the workers in the occupation earn less than before. In such a case, there is still, of course, an improvement in the general level of real wages and the average standard of living. But before the pieceworkers can participate in it, some of them must leave the field and find other jobs, just like the potato growers. What is present in this case is that piecework so increases the productivity of labor in the particular occupation, that a temporary relative overproduction of the product and oversupply of labor exists in this particular line, accompanied, of course, by a corresponding underproduction of products and undersupply of labor elsewhere. The adoption of labor-saving machinery frequently produces such results.

The efforts of individuals to improve their well-being by earning more money are perfectly reasonable and actually harmonious, even in circumstances in which the existence of a given quantity of money and a given volume of spending for consumers' goods and labor would imply that to the extent that any individual or group succeeds in earning more money, other individuals or groups must earn correspondingly less money. I demonstrated this back in Chapter 9, in showing that the fall in prices would be sufficient to provide higher real incomes to all, provided they made the necessary changes in occupation.[136]

The principle I established there was that everyone gains in real terms, in accordance with the increase in his productivity, but only those gain in monetary terms whose productivity rises by more than the average, that is, rises *relative* to the productivity of the average producer. Naturally, to the extent that a simultaneous increase in the quantity of money and volume of spending goes on, a corresponding general rise in money incomes takes place.

This then is the nature of the connection between the productivity of labor of the individual and the money wages of the individual. It appears to the individual that his gain is in the form of more money, because he considers the effects of an improvement in the productivity of his labor on the assumption of *all other things being equal*—specifically, the productivity of the labor of others being equal and the buying power of money being equal. This is perfectly understandable, in that an individual has very substantial control over the productivity of his own labor, while he has virtually no control over the general productivity of labor in the economic system as a whole, and virtually no control over the buying power of money. As far as matters are up to him, the general or average productivity of labor in the economic system, and the buying power of money, go on being whatever they are—all that changes is his own individual productivity. On this basis, it appears to him that the way he improves his standard of living is by earning more money, for in such circumstances, a rise in the productivity of his own labor will bring him more money, which will enable him to buy correspondingly more.

Thus, the earning of a higher money income is the reasonable way for an *individual* to attempt to raise his standard of living. And insofar as individuals seek to increase their money incomes through production and exchange, in an environment of freedom of competition, the effect of their actions is to increase their real incomes whether they succeed in earning higher money incomes or not. In such conditions, win, lose, or draw in terms of money, they all win in real terms, because what is fundamental and essential is not that the individual earns more money, but that, in the quest to earn more money, he produces more goods. That is the actual basis on which the standard of living of everyone rises, whether given individuals in a given case end up earning the same, more, or less money.

Unfortunately, most people, and especially the supporters of labor unions, view the earning of more money as the fundamental and essential phenomenon and mistakenly assume that everyone could be made better off simply by the earning of more money. Insofar as individuals act in a private capacity, this mistaken belief results in no direct harm. But when they act in a public and collective capacity and seek to elevate money wages by means of force, through the coercive methods of labor unions or otherwise, then the result is very harmful indeed. This is because, as I have shown, the earning of a higher money income is simply *not* a reasonable way to attempt to raise the *general or average* standard of living.

When the unions seek to raise the standard of living of their members by means of raising their money incomes, their policy inevitably reduces to the attempt to make the labor of their members artificially scarce. The unions do not have much actual power over the demand for labor. But they often achieve considerable power over the supply of labor. And their actual technique for raising wages is to make the supply of labor, at least in the particular industry or occupation that a given union is concerned with, as scarce as possible.

Thus, whenever possible, unions attempt to gain control over entry into the labor market. They seek to impose apprenticeship programs, or to have licensing require-

ments imposed by the government. Such measures are for the purpose of holding down the supply of labor in the field and thereby enabling those fortunate enough to be admitted to it, to earn higher incomes. Even when the unions do not succeed in directly reducing the supply of labor, the imposition of their wage demands still has the effect of reducing the number of jobs offered in the field and thus the supply of labor in the field that is able to find work.

If the unions were confined to just one or a small number of industries, and did not have the power to determine wage rates in the rest of the economic system, their achievement of higher wages in particular industries would not cause unemployment in the economic system as a whole. The workers displaced from the unionized industries would be able to find work—at lower wages—in the nonunion industries. The effect of unions in these circumstances would be the creation of an artificial inequality of wages—higher wages in the unionized fields, based on an artificially imposed scarcity of labor in those fields, accompanied by correspondingly lower wages in the nonunion fields, based on an artificially imposed oversupply of labor in those fields.[137]

A further consequence of this process would be some significant reduction in the average productivity of labor in the economic system. This is implied by the fact that the artificially imposed pattern of employment would be equivalent to the pattern of employment that would result if the workers in the economic system possessed fewer skills, or less potential for developing skills, than they actually do. If those people denied entry into occupations had never had the ability to gain entry in the first place, the result would be equivalent to the unions' keeping them out. The lesser degree of ability implied is the basis for inferring a lower general productivity of labor. The further implication of this is that even if the powers of the unions did not go beyond those of this case, their effect would be not simply to reduce the standard of living of some workers by as much as they raised the standard of living of other workers, but to reduce the standard of living of some workers by *more* than they raised the standard of living of other workers—in other words, to bring about a net reduction in the overall average level of real wages. This is because what is involved in this case is not only that some wage earners earn higher wages while others earn correspondingly lower wages, but also that the supply of goods produced is less—to the extent that a forced reduction in the exercise of skills is present.[138]

The artificial wage increases imposed by the labor unions result in unemployment when the unions have the power to raise wage rates throughout the economic system, or when the wage increases they achieve in particular fields take place alongside the existence of minimum-wage laws. A rise in wage rates throughout the economic system creates unemployment in virtually every line of work, and leaves no avenue open for workers displaced from any one branch of production to find work in another.

To achieve such a system-wide increase in wage rates, it is not necessary that the entire economic system actually be unionized, or even that the greater part of the economic system actually be unionized. It is sufficient merely that some substantial portion of the economic system be unionized and that the potential exist for the nonunion portions easily to become unionized. If it is possible for unions to be formed easily—if, as in the present-day United States, all that is required is for a majority of workers in an establishment to decide that they wish to be represented by a union—then the wages imposed by the unions will be effective even in the nonunion fields. Employers in the nonunion fields will feel compelled to offer their workers wages comparable to what the union workers are receiving—indeed, possibly even still higher wages—in order to ensure that they do not unionize. The nonunion employers will be likely to believe that if they do not pay wages comparable to union wages, then they will be faced with a union and, as a result, not only union wages, but the loss of major management prerogatives concerning the efficiency of production, and thus experience an even greater increase in costs than is incurred merely by matching union wages.

Furthermore, even if the wage increases caused by the unions are not universal, they will still certainly result in unemployment if they take place alongside the existence of minimum-wage laws and public welfare assistance. Widespread wage increases closing large numbers of workers out of numerous occupations put extreme pressure on the wage rates of whatever areas of the economic system may still remain open. These limited areas could absorb the overflow of workers from other lines at low enough wage rates. But minimum-wage laws prevent wage rates in these remaining lines from going low enough to absorb these workers. So too does the existence of public welfare assistance, inasmuch as people are not willing to work at such low wages if they can obtain a comparable income without working.

In these ways, labor unions cause unemployment—and unnecessarily low wages for those who work in whatever lines remain open to free competition.

From the perspective of most of those lucky enough to keep their jobs, the most serious consequence of the unions is the holding down or outright reduction of the productivity of labor. With few exceptions, the labor unions *openly combat the rise in the productivity of labor.* They do so virtually as a matter of principle. They oppose

the introduction of labor-saving machinery on the grounds that it causes unemployment. They oppose competition among workers. They force employers to tolerate feather-bedding practices, such as the requirement that firemen, whose function was to shovel coal on steam locomotives, be retained on diesel locomotives. They impose make-work schemes, such as requiring that pipe delivered to construction sites with screw thread already on it, have its ends cut off and new screw thread cut on the site. They impose narrow work classifications, and require that specialists be employed at a day's pay to perform work that others could easily do—for example, requiring the employment of a plasterer to repair the incidental damage done to a wall by an electrician, which the electrician himself could easily repair.[139]

To anyone who understands the productivity theory of wages, it should be obvious that the unions' policy of combatting the rise in the productivity of labor renders them in fact a leading enemy of the rise in real wages. However radical this conclusion may seem, however much at odds with the prevailing view of the unions as the leading source of the rise in real wages over the last hundred years or more, the fact is that in combatting the rise in the productivity of labor, the unions actively combat the rise in real wages. The unions and the public do not realize this because they do not even realize that the productivity of labor is the key to real wages. Instead, they believe that the source of a higher standard of living for the workers is higher money wages, which the unions certainly do seek. But, as we have seen, the unions' efforts along these lines are totally misdirected. The truth is that, while claiming to have the purpose of raising the workers' standard of living, the unions are dedicated to the active combatting of the rise in real wages, along with the creation of artificial inequalities in wages and of unemployment.

Consider, for example, the typical union attitude toward an improvement in machinery, such as computer-controlled typesetting equipment. The unions believe that such an improvement should be opposed, on the grounds that it will cause unemployment of typesetters and tend to reduce their wages. They have absolutely no conception that the improvement actually raises real wages—not immediately of the present typesetters perhaps, *but of all the wage earners throughout the economic system who are buyers of books and other printed matter.* The unions simply do not grasp that the rise in real wages comes about through a lower price of the product, and that it is the real wages of the workers who buy the product, not the workers who produce it, that improvements in productivity raise.

The ignorance of the unions and the public concerning the role of productivity is such that they believe that whenever there is a rise in the productivity of labor in a given industry, the workers in that industry are automatically entitled to a corresponding increase in wages. They simply do not understand that the improvement operates to raise the real wages of the workers who *buy* the product, and that it is perfectly reasonable and appropriate that the money wages of the workers who produce the product fall in many cases as the result of the improvement—because their labor is temporarily placed in a position of relative oversupply as a result of it.

Indeed, the naïve notions of the unions and the public concerning productivity imply that in industries such as computers and pocket calculators, where increases in productivity have occurred on the order of a hundredfold or more, wages should now be a hundred times or more higher than they were a decade or two ago. By the same token, in other occupations, in which there has been little or no increase in productivity, such as waiting on tables, it follows, on this view, that wages should be no higher now than in the past—indeed, in this particular case, no higher now than centuries ago, when the last improvement in the productivity of labor took place (which was probably the invention of the tray).

Of course, an industry-by-industry determination of wages based on productivity is absolutely absurd. So long as the workers of any industry can be employed in other industries—so long, for example, as the workers who today work as waiters can be employed to produce computers or calculators, or to take the jobs of other workers who can be so employed—their wages must be commensurate with the wages of such workers. And the fact is that their wages do stay commensurate, because where the productivity of labor rises, the basic effect is not to raise the money wages of the workers who produce the product, but to reduce the price of the product, which serves to raise the real wages of all workers who buy the product, including those in occupations in which there is no rise in the productivity of labor. And insofar as the rise in the productivity of labor does not succeed in reducing prices, because of an increase in the quantity of money and volume of spending, the effect of the larger quantity of money is to raise the demand for and wages of all types of labor—in the long run, basically in the same proportion, so that once again, wages remain commensurate in all the various occupations open to the same kind of workers. In other words, improvements in the productivity of labor do not raise real wages occupation by occupation, through higher incomes, but, as we have seen, throughout the economic system, by means of lower prices—prices that, as a minimum, are lower in comparison with the level to which increases in the quantity of money and volume of spending would otherwise have raised them.

In sum, far from being responsible for improvements in the standard of living of the average worker, labor unions operate in more or less total ignorance of what actually raises the average worker's standard of living, and are responsible for artificial inequalities in wage rates, for unemployment, and for holding down the average worker's standard of living.

Minimum-Wage Laws

It should already be clear that minimum-wage laws cause unemployment. It should also be clear that the extent to which they do so depends on the extent of union activity in the economic system. The more the unions close off employment opportunities, the greater is the number of workers forced to seek employment elsewhere, and thus the greater is the downward pressure on wage rates elsewhere. Thus, the greater is the number who will be unemployed as the result of a minimum-wage law, which, in effect, closes the gates in the occupations still free from the imposition of union wage-scales against the workers streaming in from the branches of production subject to union wage-scales.

An important implication of these facts is that the problem of low wages, which a minimum-wage law is intended to remedy, would be far less serious in the absence of the ability of labor unions to impose their artificially high pay-scales. If the power of the unions to impose such pay-scales ceased to exist, wages in the portion of the economic system that presently manages to remain free of union pay-scales would be higher, because fewer workers would need to seek employment in these industries, since they would be able to be employed in what are now the industries subject to union pay-scales.

As a consequence of the unemployment they cause, minimum-wage laws deny many people the opportunity of acquiring work experience and the skills they might have acquired by means of working. In the absence of minimum-wage laws, many of the people who would have become employed at lower wages would not have had to earn such wages for the rest of their lives, but could have qualified themselves, through experience and skills acquired by working, for higher paying jobs later on. By aborting such individual processes of development, a minimum-wage law tends to exert a lifelong depressing effect on people. It both stops them from working and prevents them from becoming qualified for anything better than the kind of low-skilled jobs to which a minimum-wage law tends to apply. As I have shown, these results are particularly true today of black teenagers, who are denied not only the possibility of employment by the minimum-wage laws, but also the possibility of gaining the on-the-job experience and improvement in their skills that employment would have provided. These teenagers are condemned to a life of poverty on the welfare rolls, largely because of minimum-wage legislation.[140]

Although the avowed purpose of minimum-wage laws is to help unskilled workers, by providing them with a better income, their actual effect is to achieve the exact opposite. A minimum-wage law prevents less-skilled individuals from successfully competing with more-skilled individuals. It operates precisely against the least-skilled and most-disadvantaged members of society. As I have shown, in a labor market free of government interference, less-skilled individuals can successfully compete with more-skilled individuals by being willing to work for lower wages.[141] In raising the wages of less-skilled workers relative to those of more-skilled workers, a minimum-wage law deprives the less-skilled workers of their ability to compete. It reduces their ability to compete with higher-skilled workers in the same occupation and operates to attract higher-skilled workers into the occupation from other occupations. This last observation, of course, applies equally to wage increases caused by unions. Part of the problem of unemployment in any given industry stems from the attraction to that industry of higher-skilled workers from outside the industry, as a result of wages in that industry being elevated relative to wages in other industries. This compounds the unemployment caused by the reduction in job offerings in the industry that a higher wage rate brings about.[142]

Thus, minimum-wage laws cause unemployment, a lifelong depressing effect on the earnings of many of those forced into unemployment, and harm in particular the least-skilled, most-disadvantaged members of society.

Maximum-Hours Legislation

Although it is generally taken for granted that the effect of maximum-hours legislation is to enable the workers to work less while enjoying the same income—with the cost taken out of the employers' profits—the actual effect of such legislation is correspondingly to reduce the real wages of the workers. This conclusion can easily be shown in terms of our familiar equations for average money wage rates and the general level of consumers' goods prices. Thus, taking the context of the present day, I assume the passage of a law reducing the work week from its present forty hours to thirty hours. I also assume that the respective demands for labor and consumers' goods remain the same, because of the existence of a fixed quantity of money. On these assumptions—using an asterisk to denote the fixity of the demand for labor, and stating the supply of labor in terms of hours worked—our equation for average money wage rates shows:

$$\frac{D_L^*}{\frac{3}{4}S_L \ (in \ terms \ of \ hours)} = \frac{4}{3} Average \ Hourly \ Money \ Wage \ Rate.$$

That is, average hourly wage rates increase in the ratio of four to three, as the result of dividing the fixed demand for labor by three-fourths the supply of labor in terms of hours.

At first thought, this may appear to fulfill one of the most ambitious hopes of the union leaders who seek to shorten the work week and who, in order to avoid any reduction in weekly earnings, demand a rise in hourly earnings sufficient to compensate for the shorter hours. In the formulas, the assumption of a constant demand for labor implies that hourly earnings would indeed rise in inverse proportion to the fall in the hours worked and thus that weekly earnings would remain unchanged. But before concluding that this situation would fulfill the hopes of the union leaders, let us consider the effect on the prices of consumers' goods, namely:

$$\frac{D_C^*}{\frac{3}{4}S_C} = \frac{4}{3}P.$$

This equation shows that three-fourths the labor performed shows up in three-fourths the supply of consumers' goods produced and sold, and thus, in the face of an unchanged demand for consumers' goods (indicated by the use of an asterisk), in a rise in their price in the ratio of four to three. Thus, prices rise in the same proportion as hourly wage rates. And because weekly wage rates are unchanged (again indicated by the use of an asterisk), inasmuch as

$$\frac{4}{3}Average \ Hourly \ Money \ Wage \ Rate \times \frac{3}{4}Hours \ Worked$$

$$= Unchanged \ Average \ Weekly \ Money \ Wage \ Rate,$$

the net result is

$$\frac{Average \ Weekly \ Money \ Wage \ Rate^*}{\frac{4}{3}P} = \frac{3}{4}Average \ Weekly \ Real \ Wage \ Rate,$$

which means that the rise in consumers' goods prices in the ratio of four to three implies *a fall in average weekly real wages in the ratio of three to four.* Thus, there is a reduction in real weekly earnings in exactly the same ratio as the hours worked! Not surprisingly, to the degree that he produces less, the average worker receives less. When he does three-fourths the work, he receives three-fourths the real wages, even if his money wages remain unchanged, for then the supply of goods is three-fourths as great and prices are four-thirds as great.

The principle here is that if less work is done, fewer goods will be produced and goods will be rendered correspondingly scarcer relative to the number of workers, and thus their prices will rise relative to the incomes of the workers—i.e., real wages will decline. This principle applies to every reduction in the hours of work, whether from forty to thirty, as might be contemplated in our day, or from sixty to fifty, or even from eighty to seventy, as occurred in previous generations. Always, less work per worker means less output relative to the supply of labor and thus higher prices relative to wages, and, therefore, a corresponding decline in real wages.

There is certainly no harm in such a drop in real wages, provided the workers can afford it, and value the additional leisure more highly than the real wages they must forgo in order to achieve that leisure. As I have shown, that situation will exist if the productivity of labor has risen sufficiently, in which case the labor market itself operates to bring about a shortening of hours. But there can be great harm from *forced* reductions in the hours of work imposed by maximum-hours laws. These laws force workers to accept lower real wages than they judge they need to have. Their effect is to force poor people to become still poorer, in the misguided belief that their poverty can be alleviated at someone else's expense. Maximum-hours laws did not help to raise the standard of living. Insofar as they took effect concurrently with the rise in the productivity of labor and the consequent reduction in hours achieved by the operations of the labor market, they were superfluous. Insofar as they took effect in advance of the necessary rise in the productivity of labor and the operations of the labor market, they were destructive.

My analysis of the effects of maximum-hours laws, and of labor-union wage demands to offset them, has assumed that the demands for labor and consumers' goods remain constant in the face of higher wages and prices. These assumptions would not be able to hold up in a context of free international trade in which the various countries used the same money. In such a context, there would be movements in the supply of money from country to country, in response to changes in relative wages and relative prices among the various countries. A rise in wages and prices in any one country relative to wages and prices in other countries would be accompanied by a fall in the quantity of money and volume of spending in that country, and a rise in the

quantity of money and volume of spending in other countries, as buyers sought to take advantage of the less expensive markets. The effect would be to cause large-scale unemployment in that country.

To avoid such unemployment, it is likely that a forced shortening of hours would not be accompanied by anything like an inversely proportionate rise in hourly wage rates in the country in which the shortening occurred. More likely, hourly wage rates would show very little increase in that country. Indeed, *they would tend to increase across the world* in inverse proportion to the fall in the *world supply* of labor constituted by the lower hours in this particular country. If, for example, hours are reduced in the ratio of three to four in a country that represents 10 percent of the world economy, this would represent a reduction in the world supply of labor and consumers' goods, not of 25 percent but of only 2½ percent. In this case, hourly wages, and prices, would rise not in the ratio of four to three, but on the order of 100 to 97½, on a world basis. Thus, in the country in which it occurred, the reduction in hours would be accompanied by an almost equivalent decline in weekly money earnings, with prices nearly stable. However, the essential result—the decline in real wages—would, of course, still be the same as before.

The same essential analysis applies insofar as a country has obligated itself to maintain a fixed exchange rate between its currency and the currency of other countries. In this case, if wages and prices in the country were to rise significantly relative to those in other countries, the country's currency would be turned in, in exchange for foreign currencies, which people would now want in greater quantity, in order to be able to buy relatively more cheaply. To be able to meet the demand for foreign currencies at the fixed exchange rate, the country's government would have to contract the supply of its own currency, in order to reduce such demand. Thus the result would be much the same as under a single international money.

Child-Labor Legislation

The abolition of child labor is certainly something that is highly desirable, just as is the shortening of the hours of work. But, like the shortening of hours, it is desirable only when it can be afforded. In order for this to happen, it is necessary first that the productivity of labor rise to the point where parents no longer need the labor of their children to help make ends meet. As I have shown, as that point is approached, child labor gradually disappears, simply by virtue of the decisions of more and more parents to keep their children home longer and longer.

The abolition or reduction of child labor by law, rather than by the voluntary decisions of parents in a progressing economy, ignores the precondition of the productivity of labor being high enough to enable the parents to afford its reduction or abolition. As a result, child-labor laws have had the perverse effect of rendering poor families still poorer, and, in so doing, of jeopardizing the health and well-being of the very children they were intended to protect.

In essence, their effect can be understood by imagining the conditions of an isolated family on a desert island, such as Swiss Family Robinson. The family needs the labor of its children if it is to survive or achieve some minimal degree of well-being. Now a social worker comes to the island to observe the family and he decides that he does not like the fact that the children are working. He later returns with a policeman and forcibly prevents the children from working. The actions of this social worker could certainly not be said to promote the lives and well-being of the family members in general or of the children in particular. He would simply force that family to be poorer and more wretched than it needed to be, including its children. This is the effect of a child-labor law on a desert island. Its effect in society is no different. This is because in society too, the real income of a family depends on the amount of work its members perform. And when they perform work that may appear excessive by the standards of those who are more affluent, it is usually because they have a real need to do so.

Child-labor laws do not deserve credit for the abolition of child labor. The abolition of child labor was an accomplishment of capitalism and the rise in the productivity of labor it achieved. As in the case of maximum-hours laws, insofar as child-labor laws merely ratified the abolition of child labor already being achieved by the market, they were superfluous. Insofar as they went ahead of the market, and imposed reductions in child labor beyond what parents judged their families could afford, they were destructive. Along with depriving poor families of urgently needed income, they had the effect of forcing children to work at lower wages and in poorer conditions than they needed to. This was the result of closing off major categories of relatively desirable employment opportunities, such as were provided by larger employers, and leaving open only lower-paying, less desirable employment opportunities.[143]

A question can arise concerning a possible role for child-labor laws in curbing the actions of parents who do not in fact require the labor of their children, but who would send their children to work out of indifference to their well-being. There certainly are such parents, and a strong case can be made for compelling them to provide better for their children—on the grounds of the right of a child to be supported by his parents to the extent that

his parents have the means of supporting him.

Nevertheless, in an otherwise free society, child-labor laws are not the appropriate means for dealing with this problem, because their scope cannot be limited to such cases. They necessarily have the effect of forcibly interfering with families who are not indifferent to the well-being of their children, but who send their children to work out of economic necessity. To the extent that there is immigration from poor countries, to the extent that there are any significant numbers of poor people who have not yet been sufficiently assimilated into the economic system, there will be poor families who depend on some contribution from their children that would be inappropriate in the context of families that are better off. The destructive consequences of child-labor laws in such cases far outweigh the possible good they might accomplish in prohibiting this one manifestation of parental indifference. As a general principle, it is necessary to realize that even where the particular goal the government seeks to accomplish may be legitimate, its intervention can easily introduce worse evils than it seeks to remedy. This is particularly true as concerns the relations between parents and children.

Forced Improvements in Working Conditions

The same perversity of result—that of harming the very people whom one intends to help—occurs no less in the case of government-sponsored improvements in working conditions. This, of course, includes improvements in working conditions imposed by labor unions in a position to resort to force without fear of prosecution, or which enjoy such legal privileges as the government compelling employers to deal with them.

Insofar as improvements in working conditions do not pay for themselves, their coming into being is equivalent, from the point of view of employers, to a rise in wage rates. It is an increase in the cost of employing workers. (Where the improvements pay for themselves, then, as previously explained, their implementation comes about in the same way as any other improvement in efficiency, such as the adoption of better machinery.)

A forced increase in wage rates, or, as in this case, the equivalent of a forced increase in wage rates, causes unemployment, higher production costs, reduced production, and higher prices. It thus leaves the average worker in the economic system in the position of having to accept a reduction in his real take-home pay, even if he is among those fortunate enough to escape the unemployment. This is because even if he keeps his job, he is confronted with higher prices caused by the additional costs imposed by the forced improvements, while his take-home wages remain the same. Indeed, as we have seen, to the extent that unemployment is caused, the average worker's take-home pay is actually reduced, by his having to use some portion of his wages to support the unemployed.

If unemployment is not to result, then it is necessary that wage rates fall by enough to compensate for the cost of the forced improvements in working conditions, so that employers do not experience a rise in the cost of employing workers. In either case, the cost of the improvements is at the expense of the real income of the average worker. In the case in which unemployment is created, he earns a reduced take-home money wage (after allowing for his support of the unemployed), and, at the same time, must buy at higher prices, to cover the cost of the forced improvements. In the other case, in which unemployment is avoided, he earns take-home wages that are reduced by enough to offset the cost of the forced improvements, and must buy at the same prices. In either case, the so-called improvements are at the expense of the workers, who cannot afford them.

When this fact is recognized, it becomes clear that "improvements" which must be forced upon the market have no right to be called improvements at all. They appear to be improvements only so long as one does not see that they have to be paid for by the very class of people whose poverty is the source of constant complaint, and whose members are unwilling to bear such costs. In reality, they represent no more of an improvement than forcing a poor person to eat steak instead of hamburger would represent an improvement, given the fact that he must pay for it and thus have less left over for other things, which he regards as more important to have than the out-of-context improvement in his food.

The fact that it is workers who end up bearing the cost of forced improvements in working conditions does not always mean that it is the particular workers whose conditions are improved who bear the cost in the form of lower real take-home wages. It can happen that the higher costs of employing workers in a particular occupation or industry are met by a withdrawal of funds from the payment of wages or the purchase of capital goods elsewhere in the economic system. In such a case, it is the wages of other workers that will tend to fall. In the short run, the wages of the workers who have the benefit of the improvements will be lower only in the sense that the cost of the improvement in their working conditions could just as well have been given to them in the form of higher take-home wages. Their take-home wages are lower in comparison with what they might otherwise have been. In the long run, however, if the freedom of competition exists, there will be a tendency for the take-home wages of these workers to fall, as workers from other lines, where wages have been reduced, move in to compete with them. In addition, to the extent that a reduction in the demand for capital goods is involved, the supply of goods produced in the economic system will be less, and prices higher, and will be so progressively insofar as a permanent fall in the relative demand for and production of capital goods is present. The essential point here is that wage earners as a group must suffer as the result of forced improvements in working conditions.

7. The Employment of Women and Minorities

The productivity theory of wages provides the analytical framework necessary for understanding the economic effects of the employment of women and minorities under the freedom of competition.

A large segment of public opinion fears such employment on the grounds that it causes unemployment of white-male workers and reduces the wages of white-male workers.[144] It should already be understood that to the extent that the competition of women and minority-group members succeeds in reducing the wages of white-male workers, it does not result in unemployment. On the contrary, it enables any given aggregate demand for labor to employ a larger total number of workers, and thus enables the women and minority-group members to work alongside the white-male workers. In a free labor market, absolutely no unemployment need result from the employment of women or minority-group members.

The productivity theory of wages also shows that the fall in the money wages of the white-male workers that follows from free competition does not mean a fall in their *real* wages. The larger supply of goods resulting from the employment of the women and minority-group members means lower prices. (The lower wages that result also mean lower costs of production.) If the productivity of labor remains the same, the increase in output is precisely in proportion to the increase in the supply of labor employed. And thus, given constant aggregate demands for labor and goods, the fall in prices is fully in proportion to the fall in wages.

If this were all that happened, every married couple would certainly have a considerable gain as the result of the wife going to work. The fall in wages of the husband would be compensated for by the wages earned by the wife, and at the same time prices would fall, so that the actual buying power of the couple would rise. To illustrate this point, imagine that all workers are married and that initially no married women work. Now imagine that all married women work. Thus, the number of workers employed is doubled, and the average money wage per worker is halved. But production too is doubled and prices fall in half. The position of the average couple would be that it earned the same money income and bought at half the prices. Its real income would be doubled.

The actual fact is, however, that the free competition of women and minority-group members, just like the free competition of immigrants, must ultimately operate to *raise* the average productivity of labor, because it means the presence in the productive system of a larger absolute amount of talent. If there are women and minority-group members with the potential to be better foremen or company vice presidents, and so on, than some of the white males holding these jobs, then the effect of their obtaining them under free competition must be to raise the productivity of the workers under them. If the absolute number of productive geniuses is increased in proportion to the employment of women and minority-group members, or even if it is increased only half or a quarter as much, there must be a substantial rise in the average productivity of labor. This is the operation of the pyramid of ability principle.[145]

Thus, under the freedom of competition, the employment of women and minority-group members is actually to be welcomed from the point of view of the material self-interests of white male workers.

It must be stressed, however, that this conclusion applies only under the freedom of competition. It does not apply insofar as minimum-wage and prounion legislation result in a freezing of the overall number of jobs available. Nor does it apply insofar as a system of sexual, racial, or ethnic quotas favors the advancement of less-able women and minority-group members over more-able white male workers. In such conditions, all of the negative results of violations of the freedom of competition are to be found, namely, unemployment, a reduced productivity of labor, and group conflict.

8. The Productivity Theory of Wages and the Wages-Fund Doctrine

The productivity theory of wages incorporates essential features of the classical economists' doctrine of the "wages-fund." As result, it is necessary to explain the wages-fund doctrine and to answer the unjustified criticisms that served to bring it down in the last century and which could otherwise now be directed against the productivity theory as well.

The wages-fund is simply what we have been calling the aggregate demand for labor, i.e., total payrolls. The classical economists recognized it, together with the supply of labor, as determining the level of average wage rates. They also recognized that the demand for consumers' goods is separate and distinct from the demand for labor, and that the prices of consumers' goods are determined by the demand for consumers' goods together with the supply of consumers' goods.[146] Indeed, Cairnes, the last major classical economist, was able to go so far as to

recognize explicitly that "real wages will advance with the productiveness of industry in producing such real wages—in producing, that is to say, the commodities of the laborer's consumption."[147] Nevertheless, the classical economists never succeeded in developing the wages-fund doctrine into the productivity theory of wages. They did not so much as get to the point of carrying out the analysis I presented in Section 2 of this Chapter-part, let alone systematically apply to the determination of the productivity of labor and real wage rates the further critical elements of the theory that I presented in Sections 3 – 6.[148]

The explanation is that they were generally pessimistic concerning the prospects for wage earners, mainly because of their failure to realize that a division-of-labor, capitalist society is able to overcome the operation of the law of diminishing returns.[149] As a result, they did not see much potential for a rise in the productivity of labor, and thus did not give much consideration to its ability to raise real wages. Cairnes himself wrote, as late as 1874, "Nothing is more certain than that taking the whole field of labor, real wages in Great Britain will never rise to the standard of remuneration now prevailing in new countries—a standard which after all would form but a sorry consummation as the final goal of improvement for the masses of mankind."[150]

Because, as I say, the productivity theory of wages incorporates essential features of the wages-fund doctrine, it is necessary to deal with the objection that is certain to be raised against it, which is that the wages-fund doctrine was refuted in the nineteenth century. Both the substance of the arguments raised against the wages-fund doctrine and the basis for the conviction that it was refuted can be found in the quotation from John Stuart Mill that appears below. For most of his life, Mill had been a leading supporter of the doctrine, but in these famous passages he recants his previous support. Mill's recantation, given his eminent status as the intellectual leader of classical economics in his day, was immediately seized upon as constituting an irrefutable and irrevocable overthrow of the doctrine. Mill writes:

> It will be said . . . supply and demand do entirely govern the price obtained for labour. The demand for labour consists of the whole circulating capital of the country, including what is paid in wages for unproductive labour. The supply is the whole labouring population. If the supply is in excess of what the capital can at present employ, wages must fall. If the labourers are all employed, and there is a surplus of capital still unused, wages will rise. This series of deductions is generally received as incontrovertible. They are found, I presume, in every systematic treatise on political economy, my own certainly included. I must plead guilty to having, along with the world in general, accepted the theory without the qualifications and limitations necessary to make it admissible.

The theory rests on what may be called the doctrine of the wages fund. There is supposed to be, at any given instant, a sum of wealth, which is unconditionally devoted to the payment of wages of labour. This sum is not regarded as unalterable, for it is augmented by saving, and increases with the progress of wealth; but it is reasoned upon as at any given moment a predetermined amount. More than that amount it is assumed that the wages-receiving class cannot possibly divide among them; that amount, and no less, they cannot but obtain. So that, the sum to be divided being fixed, the wages of each depend solely on the divisor, the number of participants. . . .

But is there such a thing as a wages-fund, in the sense here implied? Exists there any fixed amount which and neither more nor less than which, is destined to be expended in wages?

Of course there is an impassable limit to the amount which can be so expended; it cannot exceed the aggregate means of the employing classes. It cannot come up to those means; for the employers have also to maintain themselves and their families. But, short of this limit, it is not, in any sense of the word, a fixed amount.

In the common theory, the order of ideas is this: The capitalist's pecuniary means consist of two parts—his capital, and his profits or income. His capital is what he starts with at the beginning of the year, or when he commences some round of business operations; his income he does not receive until the end of the year, or until the round of operations it completed. His capital, except such part as is fixed in buildings and machinery, or laid out in materials, is what he has got to pay wages with. He cannot pay them out of his income, for he has not yet received it. When he does receive it, he may lay by a portion to add to his capital, and as such it will become part of next year's wages-fund, but has nothing to do with this year's.

This distinction, however, between the relation of the capitalist to his capital, and his relation to his income is wholly imaginary. He starts at the commencement with the whole of his accumulated means, all of which is potentially capital: and out of this he advances his personal and family expenses, exactly as he advances the wages of his labourers. . . . If we choose to call the whole of what he possesses applicable to the payment of wages, the wages-fund, that fund is co-extensive with the whole proceeds of his business, after keeping up his machinery, buildings and materials, and feeding his family; and it is expended jointly upon himself and his labourers. The less he expends on the one, the more may be expended on the other, and *vice versa*. The price of labour, instead of being determined by the division of the proceeds between the employer and the labourers, determines it. If he gets his labour cheaper, he can afford to spend more upon himself. If he has to pay more for labour, the additional payment comes out of his own income; perhaps from the part which he would have saved and added to capital, thus anticipating his voluntary economy by a compulsory one; perhaps from what he would have expended on his private wants or pleasures. There is no law of nature making it inherently impossible

for wages to rise to the point of absorbing not only the funds which he had intended to devote to carrying on his business, but the whole of what he allows for his private expenses, beyond the necessaries of life. The real limit to the rise is the practical consideration, how much would ruin him or drive him to abandon the business: not the inexorable limits of the wages-fund.

In short, there is abstractedly available for the payment of wages, before an absolute limit is reached, not only the employer's capital, but the whole of what can possibly be retrenched from his personal expenditure: and the law of wages, on the side of demand, amounts only to the obvious proposition, that the employers cannot pay away in wages what they have not got. On the side of supply, the law as laid down by economists remains intact. The more numerous the competitors for employment, the lower, *ceteris paribus,* will wages. . . .

But though the population principle and its consequences are in no way touched by anything that Mr. Thornton has advanced, in another of its bearings the labour question, considered as one of mere economics, assumes a materially changed aspect. The doctrine hitherto taught by all or most economists (including myself), which denied it to be possible that trade combinations can raise wages, or which limited their operations in that respect to the somewhat earlier attainment of a rise which the competition of the market would have produced without them,—this doctrine is deprived of its scientific foundation, and must be thrown aside. The right and wrong of the proceedings of Trade Unions becomes a common question of prudence and social duty, not one which is peremptorily decided by unbending necessities of political economy.[51]

It should be obvious that the whole basis of Mill's recantation is demolished by our analysis in Section 5 of the present part of this chapter. There we examined the ability of the demand for labor to increase at the expense of net consumption (viz., the personal consumption expenditure of the businessmen and capitalists) or at the expense of the demand for capital goods. We saw that the ability of the demand for labor to increase at the expense of net consumption is extremely limited and, moreover, cannot be forced. We also saw that an increase in the demand for labor coming at the expense of the demand for capital goods is against the long-run self-interests of the wage earners.

Thus, the fact remains that the only possible basis of a sustained, significant rise in average real wages is a rise in the productivity of labor and that this depends on the economic degree of capitalism and the productivity of capital goods (which depends on technological progress), both of which, in turn, depend on economic freedom—i.e., capitalism in the political sense—and the cultural influence of rationality. We have seen, and will see further, that all the essential tenets of classical economics in general and the wages-fund doctrine in particular concerning the role of saving in determining both capital accumulation and the demand for labor are absolutely correct. The fact remains, despite Mill's socialistic inclinations, that capitalism, not government intervention and socialism, is the only possible basis of a high and rising standard of living for the average worker.

9. The Productivity Theory of Wages Versus the Marginal-Productivity Theory of Wages

The productivity theory of wages should not be confused with the similarly named *marginal-productivity theory of wages.* The marginal-productivity theory begins with the premise that the value of factors of production (whether labor, land, materials, machinery, or capital in the abstract) is derived in every case from the value of the product produced—for example, that the value of flour is derived from the value of bread, and the value of wheat from that of flour. It rests on the further assumption that it is possible to determine a *physical product* that is uniquely attributable to a factor of production in every given case. It then takes the monetary value of that physical product and calls it the *marginal-value product* of the factor of production.

The reason for the use of the word "marginal" is that the theory is concerned with the determination of the physical and value products of *incremental quantities* of factors of production. For example, it seeks to determine the number of bushels of wheat that are attributable to the employment, say, of a *tenth* farm worker, all other conditions remaining the same. It arrives at such a determination by taking the difference between what is produced, all other things being equal, with the presence of that worker, and what is produced without him (assuming that it is actually possible to do this). If, for example, 10 workers on a given farm, with given equipment, produce 1,000 bushels of wheat per year, while 9 workers on the same farm, with the same equipment, produce only 925 bushels of wheat per year, it is said that the tenth farm worker is responsible for the production of 75 bushels of wheat. Seventy-five bushels of wheat are held to be the marginal-physical product of labor on this wheat farm, given the employment of ten workers on the farm. The marginal-*value* product of labor is then held to be determined by multiplying the marginal-physical product by the price of wheat. If that price is, say, $1 per bushel, then, it is held, the marginal-value product of a worker is $75.

The wages of every given type of labor, and the price of every material, semi-finished good, piece of equipment, land site, and so forth, is held to be determined by the combination of a schedule of diminishing marginal-value products, which allegedly represents the demand for the factor of production, and the supply of the factor

of production in question. The wage of every worker and the price of every nonhuman factor of production, it is held, tends to equal the marginal-value product corresponding to the quantity of the factor of production that is used in production. Thus, if the supply of farm labor is such that production on a farm will be carried to the point of using ten workers, the wages of those workers will be $75 each. If the supply of such labor were less, the wages of those workers would be greater; if it were greater, the wages of those workers would be less.[152]

The productivity theory of wages, in contrast, takes a different view. It is fully compatible with the recognition given by Austrian economics to the fact that the importance of means derives from the importance of the ends which they serve, and thus that ultimately the value of factors of production must derive from the value of the products they produce. However, it does not hold that in each and every individual case this is so. The productivity theory of wages recognizes that in many, indeed, probably the great majority of individual cases, it is simply not possible to establish a marginal-physical product that could be relevant to the determination of the actual value of factors of production.

Even in such a rather simple and contrived case as that of wheat farmers, a serious problem can arise. For example, what if while the output of 10 workers on the farm is 1,000 bushels, that of 9 workers is only 875 bushels? In this case, the marginal-physical product of the tenth worker would be 125 bushels of wheat. If each of the 10 farm workers is to be paid in accordance with the principle of marginal productivity, the total wages paid would exceed the value of the product produced. They would be 10 times 125, or 1250, times the price of the product. Nothing whatever would be left for profit or even to allow for the value of other factors of production.

This kind of problem can be sidestepped so long as the discussion is confined to cases like wheat farming. This is because in such cases the answer can be made that a factor of production will be used in a zone of diminishing returns. Farm workers will be employed to the point where the marginal-physical product of the last one will be low enough so that the payment of wages is not so great as to leave nothing over for the value of the other factors of production and for profit. This is the answer given by Rothbard, for example.[153] However, even in such cases as farm workers, this answer is dubious, if the assumption is to be maintained that all other things are truly equal. For then, it is quite possible that one less worker means that some important piece of equipment must lie idle, thereby causing a sharp drop in production.

The problems become even more obvious if we apply the methodology of the marginal-productivity theory to materials and components, which must be done insofar as the value of labor is allegedly derived through the intermediary value of materials or components. Thus, the marginal-productivity theory implies that the price of automobile parts, for example, is determined on the basis of the portion of an automobile's utility that is lost if the part in question is not present. In a case of this kind it is glaringly obvious that the sum of the value of the parts would end up far exceeding the value of the product, if the marginal-productivity theory were correct. This is because if one asks how much of a car's utility or value depends on its having a steering wheel, any one of its four wheels, or accelerator pedal, fuel pump, carburetor, and so on, the answer, over and over again, is the whole value, or at least the far greater part of the value, of the automobile. In the same way, the utility of a television set, or virtually any product, vitally depends on the presence and functioning of a number of parts. In all such cases, if the value of the parts is to be determined by the loss of utility of the product that follows from the absence of the part, the sum of the values of the parts must far exceed the value of the product.

As I showed in Chapter 10, the truth is that in such cases the value of the parts is *not* derived from the value of the product. On the contrary, the value of the parts, and, as a rule, the value of the product itself, is determined on the basis of cost of production. For example, even though the whole utility of an automobile depends on the functioning of its carburetor, one virtually never has to pay a price for a carburetor corresponding to its contribution to the utility of an automobile. One pays the far lower price corresponding to the cost of producing the carburetor. And the price of the automobile itself is, as a rule, actually determined on the basis of the prices of the components, machinery, and so forth together with the wages that must be paid in order to produce it—i.e., on the basis of its cost of production. The truth is that in the great majority of cases, including all the cases of materials, components, and parts, the buyer does not pay a price that comes up to the utility of the particular product in question, but a far lower price, determined on the basis of the product's cost of production. Although it may seem paradoxical, this fact represents the actual operation of the principle of marginal utility, which itself implies that in the first instance the prices of most products are determined on the basis of their cost of production.[154]

The productivity theory of wages, as opposed to the marginal-productivity theory of wages, regards wages and the productivity of labor as the fundamental determinants of costs of production, including the prices of materials, components, and machinery, and, by way of determining costs of production, as the determinants of the prices of consumers' goods in most cases. It regards

wage rates themselves, however, (and the prices of land and of raw materials whose supply cannot be quickly adapted to changes in demand) as reflecting the valuations of the consumers of the final products.

But even in stating this last proposition, one must be careful not to concede too much to the role of consumer demand. As I will conclusively demonstrate in the next chapter, the demand for most labor in the economic system is constituted by productive expenditure—that is, expenditure by business enterprises for the purpose of producing products for sale. It comes out of capital, which has had to be saved, not out of consumption expenditure. Given the quantity of money, and thus the total, overall ability to spend, the demand for labor employed by business enterprises varies *inversely* with consumption expenditure, not directly. The influence of the consumers on wages is basically that of determining the relative wages of different groups of workers—above all, the wages of skilled workers relative to those of unskilled workers, and the wages of professional-level workers relative to those of these two groups. And the same applies to the influence of consumer demand on the prices of land and raw materials. The actual causal sequence is that consumer demand determines the prices of the fundamental factors of production relative to one another and these prices in turn then help to determine the prices of most products, including most consumers' goods, relative to one another. (Those products whose value is not determined in this way are determined in value on the basis of their own, direct marginal utility.)[155] The value of means of production is most certainly not derived from the value of the products on a case-by-case basis.

Aside from its naïveté in assuming such derivation, the marginal-productivity theory of wages suffers from the further serious defect of placing the emphasis on the income a worker earns, to the neglect of the prices he must pay for the goods he buys. A sound theory of wages must, as I have shown, concentrate not merely on what determines the money wages of the average worker, but on what determines the *relationship* between those wages and the price of goods. This the so-called marginal-productivity theory of wages totally neglects, in addition to failing in the attempt to explain money wage rates.

The Productivity Theory of Wages and the Effect of Diminishing Returns

The marginal-productivity theory of wages is valuable in one respect, namely, that it calls attention to the law of diminishing returns and to the fact that its operation has an important bearing on real wage rates. Here I will incorporate the operation of the law of diminishing returns into the productivity theory of wages. I have largely neglected to do this up to now, because, apart from explaining why capital accumulation would come to an end in the face of the operation of the law of diminishing returns not offset by technological progress, I have gone on the assumption of continuous technological progress—technological progress caused in part by the increase in the supply of labor itself.[156]

In the absence of technological progress and the capital accumulation it makes possible, a doubling of the supply of labor results in less than a doubling of the supply of consumers' goods—for the sake of illustration, let us say 1.9 times the supply of consumers' goods. Thus the second half of the now larger supply of labor adds an output of consumers' goods of only .9 times the original output. Because both halves of the now larger supply of labor are interchangeable, each of the two halves of the now larger supply of labor will end up with real wages of .9 times the original real wages. Thus, the original workers will experience a 10 percent decline in their real wages. This 10 percent decline in the original amount of real wages represents an equivalent increase in "rents" in the economic system. This is because the inability of production to double is the result of the greater scarcity of land and natural resources, the real income derived from which, and the real value of which, accordingly increases. (Strictly speaking, along with the 10 percent decline in the real wages of the original workers, businessmen and capitalists will experience a 10 percent decline in their real profits and interest derived from investments other than in land or natural resources.)

In terms of money, if the demand for consumers' goods were originally 500 units of money, then in the absence of an increase in the quantity of money, it would tend to remain at 500 units of money. Thus, prices would fall in the inverse ratio of the increase in the supply of consumers' goods, namely, to $10/19$ their original height. If the demand for labor were originally 400 units of money and remained at 400 units of money, the wage earners would be worse off because the doubling of the supply of labor would imply a halving of wage rates, while prices fell by less than half, to $10/19$. However,

under these assumptions they would be worse off only on the order of 5 percent, namely half the money wage rate divided by $10/19$ the price level, which equals a real wage of $19/20$, i.e., a real wage that is $1/20$ or 5 percent less. What the marginal productivity theory helps to stress is that real wages in such a case would not fall merely by 5 percent but by 10 percent, that is, in proportion to the fall in the marginal productivity of labor, which is as .9 to 1. What makes real wages fall this much in the analysis of the productivity theory of wages is that a fall takes place in the *demand for labor* on the order of 5 percent. Thus the average *money* wage rate falls by more than half, which, when combined with the fall in prices of less than half, adds up to a fall in average real wages of 10 percent.

What makes the demand for labor fall is a rise in the funds absorbed in connection with "rents" for land and natural resources. In an economic system such as our own, in which the literal renting of land and natural resource deposits plays a minor role, the absorption of funds in connection with such "rents" should be thought of ultimately in terms of a rise in the magnitude of net consumption attendant on the rise in the capitalized value of the land and natural resources. Thus, under the operation of the law of diminishing returns and an invariable money, when the supply of labor increases, wage rates decrease not only because of a larger supply of labor but also because of a smaller demand for labor, as funds are shifted away from the demand for labor, first to bidding up the capitalized value of land and natural resources and then to greater net consumption based on such greater capitalized values. Prices, of course, fall by less than wage rates on two counts: the fact that the supply of goods increases by less than the supply of labor, and the fact that the demand for labor falls.

This analysis, of course, has bearing on the destructive effects of environmentalism. It shows that policies of prohibiting or restricting the application of technological advances to land and natural resources must serve to reduce real wage rates in part by reducing the demand for labor as well as by means of holding down the increase in the supply of consumers' goods.[157]

Notes

1. See above, p. 32.

2. See above, pp. 475–485.

3. See above, pp. 497–498.

4. On Say's Law, see above, pp. 559–580.

5. On these subjects, see below, pp. 622–642 passim, and 664–666.

6. See above, pp. 478–480 and 486–491.

7. For these statements, see above, pp. 487–490.

8. Cf. Karl Marx, *Capital*, trans. from 3d German ed. by Samuel Moore and Edward Aveling; Frederick Engels, ed.; rev. and amplified according to the 4th German ed. by Ernest Untermann (New York: 1906), vol. 1, pt. 1, chap. 1; (reprinted, New York: Random House, The Modern Library), p. 45. Hereafter this work will be cited as *Capital*, vol. 1. References to the Modern Library Edition will appear in brackets.

9. Ibid. [p. 46].

10. Ibid. The sentence in quotation marks is from an earlier work by Marx himself.

11. Ibid., sec. 2 [pp. 51–52].

12. Ibid., sec. 3, pt. A, subsec. 2(b) [p. 61].

13. Ibid., pt. C, subsec. 1 [p. 77].

14. Ibid., chap. 2 [p. 103].

15. See above, pp. 477–478.

16. Marx, *Capital*, vol. 1, pt. 3, chap. 8 [p. 227].

17. Ibid. [p. 229].

18. Ibid. [pp. 231–232].

19. Ibid. [pp. 232–233].

20. The profits should be taken as gross of interest or any other nonwage income.

21. Marx, *Capital*, vol. 1, pt. 2, chap. 6 [pp. 187–188].

22. Ibid. [pp. 191–192].

23. Ibid. [p. 190].

24. See above, pp. 491–493.

25. Marx, *Capital*, vol. 1, pt. 3, chap. 10, sec. 5 [pp. 291–292].

26. *The Communist Manifesto,* trans. Samuel Moore, chap. 2; (1848; reprint ed. Chicago: Henry Regnery Company, Gateway, 1954), p. 43. Subsequent page references to the Gateway Edition appear in brackets.

27. *Capital*, vol. 1, pt. 7, chap. 24, sec. 4 [pp. 658–659].

28. Ibid., pt. 3, chap. 9, sec. 1 [pp. 239–241].

29. Ibid. chap. 7, sec. 2 [pp. 215–216].

30. Cf. ibid., chap. 7, sec. 2 [pp. 208–218], and chap. 8 [pp. 221–226].

31. Ibid., chap. 7, sec. 2 [p. 217].

32. Cf. *The Communist Manifesto,* chap. 1 [pp. 13–15].

33. Ibid., chap. 2 [p. 50], chap. 4 [p. 82].

34. *Capital*, vol. 1, pt. 4, chap. 12 [pp. 350–351].

35. *The Communist Manifesto*, chap. 1 [pp. 37–38].

36. *Capital*, vol. 1, pt. 3, chap. 10, sec. 1 [p. 257].

37. Ibid., sec. 2 [p. 260].

38. Karl Marx, *Capital*, 3 vols. (Moscow: Foreign Languages Publishing House, 1962), 3:207–208.

39. Cf. ibid., pp. 227, 230.

40. Ibid., p. 234.

41. *Capital*, vol. 1, pt. 3, chap. 10, sec. 5 [pp. 290–291].

42. Ibid., pt. 4, chap. 15, sec. 3, subsec. a [pp. 431–432].

43. Cf. ibid., subsec. c, especially the reference to "the increased yield of relative surplus-value through the heightened productiveness of labour" [pp. 447–449, especially p. 448].

44. Ibid.

45. Ibid., pt. 7, chap. 24, sec. 4 [pp. 658–659].

46. See Eugen von Böhm-Bawerk, *Capital and Interest*, 3 vols., trans. George D. Huncke and Hans F. Sennholz (South Holland, Ill.: Libertarian Press, 1959), 2:245. See also above, pp. 162–163.

47. On the treatment of labor as existing in a given delimited supply, see above, pp. 201–202 and 206–209.

48. See above, pp. 204–205.

49. See above, p. 206.

50. On this point, see above, p. 59. See also above, pp. 63–70.

51. On the scarcity of labor, see above, pp. 42–45 and 58–61.

52. Although the diagram indicates that with a below-market wage, labor would be lost only by marginal employers—employers in the upper zone—the labor lost could actually be on the part of employers willing and able to pay even more than employers in the upper zone: employers having the most vital and urgent need for labor combined with the greatest ability to pay for labor. In this connection, one should recall the fact that under price controls on oil, the resulting shortage threatened the most vital and urgent uses for oil, such as the continued operation of oil rigs. On this point, see above, p. 211.

53. See above, pp. 584–585.

54. In individual cases, of course, real wages may be reduced. But to that extent, they are increased all the more elsewhere.

55. See above, pp. 584–585.

56. See above, ibid.

57. Evidence for this conclusion is provided by the relatively low rates of interest prevailing in Great Britain and the United States since that time, at least when the influence of inflation, taxation, and budget deficits is put to the side. For an explanation of why low rates of interest indicate a low proportion of total consumption on the part of businessmen and capitalists and a correspondingly high proportion on the part of wage earners, see below, pp. 725–744.

58. The concept of the "economic degree of capitalism" was introduced above, on pp. 478–480.

59. Passenger automobiles produced for rental car fleets, of course, are capital goods. By the same token, trucks produced for a government's post office are consumers' goods. On these points, see above, pp. 444–446.

60. For a discussion of the uniformity-of-profit principle, see above, pp. 172–173.

61. See above, pp. 132–133.

62. Most of the major elements of my analytical framework can be found in James Mill's remarkable essay *Commerce Defended* (London, 1808); reprinted in *James Mill Selected Economic Writings*, ed. Donald Winch (Chicago: University of Chicago Press, 1966) especially pp. 128–131. See also above, pp. 132–133.

63. The ratio of accumulated savings to total sales revenues, wage payments, and consumption expenditures is also of importance in the process of capital accumulation inasmuch as these ratios are largely measures of the degree of capital intensiveness in the economic system. On the significance of capital intensiveness, see below, pp. 631–632. See also below, p. 824.

64. For elaboration of this point and for the pattern of bringing

the analysis closer to the complexities of actual reality, see below, pp. 641–642.

65. See above, pp. 69–70.

66. For an explanation of what is responsible for the failure to see the role of technological progress in capital accumulation and the belief that saving alone is the source of capital accumulation, see below, p. 709.

67. For a critique of the secular-stagnation doctrine, see above, pp. 556–558.

68. Paul Samuelson and William Nordhaus, *Economics*, 13th ed. (New York: McGraw-Hill Book Company, 1989), pp. 858–859.

69. Ibid., pp. 864, 967.

70. For further discussion of the error of not perceiving the role of technological progress as a cause of capital accumulation and of understating the role of capital accumulation in economic progress, see below, pp. 776–778. There it will be shown that this error is present in the work of Robert Solow, the leading economic theorist of the Clinton administration, who, ironically enough, has been lauded for his alleged contributions in this area. See also below, p. 709.

71. More broadly, as pointed out earlier in this chapter in n. 63, it can be conceived of as the ratio of the total of accumulated savings relative to any of these magnitudes. Accumulated savings embrace both the value of capital in the strict sense of wealth reproductively employed and savings lent at interest to finance the purchase of consumers' wealth such as homes and personal automobiles. (On this subject, see above, pp. 449–450.) In addition, capital intensiveness can be conceived of in terms of the ratio of the total value of accumulated capital (or accumulated savings) to national income and net national product, both of which differ relatively little from aggregate consumption expenditure. For examples of such usage, see above, pp. 302 and 364, and below, pp. 759–762. See also below, pp. 699–706 and 712, which provide a demonstration both of the equality of national income and net national product and of their inherent closeness to consumption.

72. For elaboration of the role of the economic degree of capitalism and the degree of capital intensiveness in determining the ability to implement technological advances, see below, p. 824.

73. To see how the economic degree of capitalism underlies the degree of capital intensiveness, see below, pp. 725–762, which show how net consumption and productive expenditure bear on the degree of capital intensiveness. Net consumption, it will be clear, is equivalent to the difference between M and M' in the context of an invariable money.

74. For elaboration of this point, see below, pp. 682–699.

75. See above, p. 132.

76. David Ricardo, *Principles of Political Economy and Taxation*, 3d ed. (London, 1821), chap. 20; reprinted as vol. 1 of *The Works and Correspondence of David Ricardo*, ed. Piero Sraffa (Cambridge: Cambridge University Press, 1962), p. 279. Subsequent references to the Sraffa edition appear in brackets. For extensive quotations from Ricardo on the subject of capital accumulation, see below, pp. 819–820. See also, above, pp. 132–133.

77. See above, pp. 351–354 and 360–361.

78. On the contribution of free immigration to capital accumu-
lation, see above, pp. 363–364. On the contribution to capital accumulation made by the freedom of capital export, which is closely related to the freedom of immigration, see above, pp. 366–367.

79. See above, pp. 132–133.

80. Cf. above, pp. 298–299. There, the same conclusions reached in the present discussion of real wages are arrived at starting from the perspective of the benefit of private ownership of the means of production to nonowners of the means of production.

81. Concerning these last connections, see above, pp. 137–139.

82. On the uniformity-of-profit principle and its effects, see above, pp. 172–174 and 176–180. On the necessity of private ownership of the means of production for the existence of the price system, see the preceding note and, above, pp. 267–275 and 279–282.

83. See above, pp. 277–278.

84. See above, p. 299.

85. Cf. above, pp. 19–21.

86. Cf. Ludwig von Mises, *Bureaucracy* (1944; reprint ed., New Rochelle, N. Y.: Arlington House, 1969), pp. 13–14.

87. See above, pp. 98–99. The hampering of the energy industry is an example of the wider phenomenon of the environmental movement's systematic thwarting of efforts to overcome the operation of the law of diminishing returns in agriculture and mining. On this point, see above, pp. 316–317.

88. See above, pp. 178–179.

89. On the subject of the undermining of capital formation by inflation, see below, pp. 930–937.

90. Concerning social security, see above, pp. 22–23.

91. See above, pp. 277–278.

92. Ricardo, *Principles of Political Economy and Taxation*, chap. 31 [p. 392]. See his whole discussion of the subject in the first portion of his chap. 31 [pp. 386–392].

93. Cf. Ricardo, *Principles of Political Economy and Taxation*, chap. 20 [pp. 273–288].

94. See above, p. 491. See also above, pp. 200–201.

95. See below, pp. 820–824 and 852–854.

96. Cf. T. S. Ashton, *The Industrial Revolution* (New York: Oxford University Press, 1969), pp. 8–9.

97. On these points, see T. S. Ashton, "The Standard of Life of the Workers in England, 1790–1830," in F. A. Hayek, ed., *Capitalism and the Historians* (Chicago: University of Chicago Press, 1954).

98. Once more, see above, pp. 277–278.

99. Bertrand de Jouvenel, "The Treatment of Capitalism by Continental Intellectuals," in F. A. Hayek, ed., *Capitalism and the Historians*, p. 102. While de Jouvenel's essay clearly fails as a defense of capitalism, the same cannot be said, happily, of most of the other essays in the book, notably, the introductory essay by Hayek, the two by T. S. Ashton, and the one by W. H. Hutt. These essays refute in historical terms most of the popular myths held about early nineteenth-century capitalism in England.

100. In contrast to de Jouvenel, for an accurate description of matters, see Ayn Rand, "What Is Capitalism?" in Ayn Rand, ed., *Capitalism: The Unknown Ideal* (New York: New American Library, 1966), p. 21.

101. See above, pp. 561–564.

102. On this point, see above, pp. 584–585.

103. See below, pp. 930–937.

104. See above, pp. 358–360.

105. See above, pp. 519–526.

106. See above, pp. 639–641.

107. On the role of the rate of return in limiting the degree of capital intensiveness, see below, p. 758. See also below, pp. 778–784. In connection with the operation of the law of diminishing returns, it should be realized that while the economic system as a whole can take for granted the availability of the same supply of labor, irrespective of almost any decrease in the demand for labor and increase in the demand for capital goods, the same is certainly not true for any individual firm. An individual firm that would spend less for labor and more for capital goods, would almost certainly lose a good portion of its workers to other firms, and thus would not be able to produce as much, despite its possession of more capital goods. Such considerations obviously greatly limit the demand for capital goods relative to the demand for labor.

108. Ricardo, *Principles of Political Economy and Taxation*, chap. 31 [pp. 392–393].

109. As we shall see, the same basic errors as Ricardo made on this subject are propounded in contemporary textbooks of economics in the form of the so-called balanced-budget multiplier doctrine. According to this doctrine, the government can raise the national income and the pretax income of the average citizen by virtue of raising taxes and its expenditures by an equal amount. See below, pp. 714–715.

110. For discussion of the concept of consumers' labor and all other such categories, such as producers' labor, and consumers' goods and capital goods, see above, pp. 442–447.

111. See above, pp. 591–593.

112. See above, pp. 296–310 and pp. 622–642. See also below, pp. 737–744 and 826–831.

113. See above, pp. 300–301.

114. See above, pp. 308–310.

115. To the extent that the increase in demand for labor here is accompanied by an increase in the supply of labor employed by business, the rise in wage rates is less. But then, precisely because there is an increase in the supply of labor employed by business, there is an increase in the supply of consumers' goods produced and sold and thus a corresponding fall in the general level of the prices of consumers' goods. Thus, real wages still increase.

116. See above, pp. 569–570, and below, pp. 725–736.

117. See below, pp. 725–736, especially pp. 735–736, for an understanding of how a lower rate of net consumption results in a lower rate of profit.

118. Cf. U.S. Department of Commerce/Bureau of Economic Analysis, *The National Income and Product Accounts of the United States, 1929–1976 Statistical Tables* (Washington, D. C.: U.S. Government Printing Office, 1981), pp. 23–24, 34–36, 195–196; for subsequent years, cf. idem, *Survey of Current Business,* especially the July issues.

119. In Chapter 9, I argued that today the consumption expenditure of the significant-sized capitalists, namely, those with a capital of $2 million or more, is probably on the order of 5 percent of the total consumption of the economic system. (See above, pp. 302.) This is an amount that is less than 5 percent of national income to whatever extent saving out of income makes national income exceed consumption expenditure, which today is certainly not by very much. The excess of total private net consumption over the consumption expenditure of the significant-sized capitalists is accounted for by the consumption expenditure of all the smaller-sized capitalists, including, of course, wage earners in their capacity as savers who earn and consume interest.

120. See above, p. 301.

121. See above, pp. 298–300 and 636–639.

122. As the degree of capital intensiveness in the economic system increased in consequence of the reduced depredations made upon businessmen and capitalists and their ability to save, private net consumption would show a tendency to rise (not in its rate, but simply in its absolute amount) thanks to the resulting increase in accumulated capital. To properly understand the significance of this development, one should think of it simply as the undoing of the decline in the degree of capital intensiveness of the economic system that I described in Chapter 9 as having accompanied the forcible reduction in the personal consumption of significant-sized capitalists from something on the order of 10 percent of total consumption to something on the order of 5 percent of total consumption. (See above, p. 302.) Of course, even with the restoration of private net consumption, both the distribution factor and the demand for capital goods relative to the demand for consumers' goods would continue to be substantially higher than under the policy of government depredations and spending. It would be a question of total private net consumption increasing perhaps from its present level of about 7.5 percent of national income to about 15 percent of national income. Over the same period of time, the government's taxation of profits and interest would have fallen by approximately twice as much, leaving the difference to constitute a permanent increase in the demand for capital goods and labor by business. A further substantial permanent increase in the demand for capital goods and labor by business would result from the elimination of government budget deficits, inasmuch as the government's reduced consumption and borrowing would be accompanied by correspondingly more funds being made available to business firms with which to buy capital goods and pay wages.

123. It should be realized that only insofar as the rise in demand for labor serves directly or indirectly to raise wage rates relative to profit incomes can it serve as the basis for inducing non–wage earners to become wage earners.

124. See above, pp. 621–622.

125. See above, pp. 296–303.

126. See above, pp. 296–310 and 618–642.

127. Cf. Ludwig von Mises, *Human Action,* 3d ed. rev. (Chicago: Henry Regnery Co., 1966), pp. 840–851.

128. See above, pp. 308–310 and 618–642.

129. For elaboration of the following analysis, see my article "Are Profits Available for the Payment of Additional Wages?," *Il Politico* 29, no. 3 (June 1964), pp. 564–572.

130. See above, pp. 300–301.

131. See above, pp. 647–648.

132. See below, pp. 762–767. The present discussion presupposes knowledge of relationships that are not fully demonstrated until the first part of Chapter 16. Thus, to be fully clear, it should probably be reread after reading pp. 719–787.

133. The call for such a double payment was implicit in the previous example, inasmuch as all of the profit of $600,000 already had its counterpart in spending for capital goods or labor.

134. Under a commodity money standard, as a by-product of this process, it also reduces the rate of increase in the supply of commodity money, which reduces both the nominal rate of profit and the rise in nominal, that is, money, wages.

135. See above, pp. 561–564.

136. See above, pp. 367–371.

137. It should be realized that unions cause lower wage rates or unemployment in complementary fields, by means of reducing the demand for the services of those fields. For example, when a carpenters' union secures higher wage rates for carpenters, it thereby increases the construction cost and thus the price of houses. This reduces the quantity demanded of houses and thus the demand for the services of plumbers, electricians, workers who produce wallboard, and so on. These groups of workers must then either suffer unemployment or accept lower wage rates as the result of the carpenters' union-imposed wage increase.

138. Less is produced insofar as the supply of goods consumers want more is held down while the supply of goods they want less is increased. Less is also produced insofar as union restrictions lead to imbalances in the supply of various complementary means of production.

139. See Henry Hazlitt, *Economics in One Lesson,* new ed. (New Rochelle, N. Y.: Arlington House, 1979), chap. 8.

140. See above, pp. 375–376 and 382–384.

141. See above, pp. 355–356.

142. See above, pp. 382–383.

143. For an historical account of the destructive effects of child-labor legislation, see Robert Hessen, "The Effects of the Industrial Revolution on Women and Children" in Ayn Rand, ed., *Capitalism: The Unknown Ideal.*

144. See above, pp. 548–549.

145. See above, pp. 357–367 passim.

146. Cf. John Stuart Mill, *Principles of Political Economy,* Ashley ed. (1909; reprint ed., Fairfield, N. J.: Augustus M. Kelley, 1976), pp. 343–344, 79–88; John E. Cairnes, *Some Leading Principles of Political Economy Newly Expounded* (1874; reprint ed., Fairfield, N. J.: Augustus M. Kelley, 1974), pp. 149–213; James Mill, *Elements of Political Economy*, 3d ed., rev. and cor. (1844; reprint ed., Fairfield, N. J.: Augustus M. Kelley 1965), pp. 131–135.

147. Cairnes, *Political Economy*, p. 282.

148. This is not to say that the classical economists were unaware of those elements. On the contrary, my analysis of capital accumulation as being determined both by the relative demand for capital goods and by the productivity of capital goods is based largely on their writings. See above, p. 669, n. 62, and the quotation from Ricardo on p. 634, earlier in this chapter . See also below, pp. 819–820.

149. Cf. above, pp. 491–497.

150. Cairnes, *Political Economy*, p. 283.

151. Cf. John Stuart Mill, *Principles*, pp. 992–993, where these passages appear as the entire quoted content of "Bibliographic Appendix O."

152. For a typical textbook presentation of the theory, see Samuelson and Nordhaus, *Economics*, 13th ed., chap. 27.

153. See Murray N. Rothbard, *Man, Economy, and State,* 2 vols. (New York: D. Van Nostrand & Co., 1962), 1:406–408.

154. Cf. above, pp. 200–201 and 209–209. Also cf. the lengthy quotation from Böhm-Bawerk on this point, on pp. 414–416.

155. See above, pp. 201–202 and 206–209.

156. However, see above, the preceding page, n. 107, where I indicate that the law of diminishing returns plays a major role in determining the allocation of capital between the demand for labor and the demand for capital goods.

157. Cf. above, pp. 316–317.

CHAPTER 15

AGGREGATE PRODUCTION, AGGREGATE SPENDING, AND THE ROLE OF SAVING IN SPENDING

In order to understand many crucial matters in economics, it is essential to have a clear understanding of the subject of aggregate production and aggregate spending, and of the role of saving in spending. The purpose of this chapter is to provide such an understanding. In the course of providing it, I show that what is saved is not only spent rather than hoarded, but is the source of *most* spending in the economic system, and that the greater is the degree of saving, the higher and more rapidly rising tend to be both total production and total spending as a direct result.

Of necessity, much of the discussion that follows centers on the concept of gross national product (GNP), by which is meant the total of what is produced in the economic system in any given period of time, such as, typically, a year. In this chapter, I use the traditional expressions gross national product and GNP, rather than the recently introduced expressions gross domestic product and GDP, because the authors I quote all use them. For all practical purposes, GNP and GDP are the same. The only difference is that GNP includes the economic contribution of nationals living abroad and excludes that of foreigners residing within the country, while GDP reverses this procedure.

Spending Not a Measure of Output

Before proceeding further, an important preliminary matter that must be dealt with is the fact that the total of the money which is exchanged for goods and services in the economic system is not in any sense a *measure* of the total output of the economic system. The expenditure of money to buy any given good or service relative to the expenditure to buy any other given good or service can be taken as a measure of the *relative* amounts of wealth or production involved. For example, the expenditure of $30,000 to buy a Cadillac, versus the expenditure of $15,000 to buy a Chevrolet, can be taken as an indication that the Cadillac represents twice the wealth as the Chevrolet. But the total expenditure of money to buy all the goods and services produced in the economic system is not a measure of those goods and services in any sense. If, for example, the total annual output of the American economic system should sell for $20 trillion rather than $10 trillion, that is in no sense an indication that the production of the economic system has doubled. As was shown in Chapter 12, such a development is likely to be merely an indication that *the quantity of money* in the economic system has doubled. The quantity of money, not the physical volume of output, is the determinant of the total volume of spending in the economic system. Only under a system of commodity money, i.e., a gold or silver standard, is there any kind even of indirect connection between production and spending, and then it is only insofar as the ability to produce more or less in general results in an ability to produce more or less gold and silver in particular—i.e., only insofar as the ability to produce determines the quantity of money in the economic system. (These observations, of course, do not detract in any way from recognition of the importance of earning money and of the connection between moneymaking and productive activity, which, as we have seen, are essential features of a division-of-labor society.[1])

The fact that the money exchanged for the output of the economic system is not a measure of that output is confirmed by the resort to price indexes in an effort to convert so-called nominal GNP—i.e., GNP in terms of mere expenditure—into a measure of output, that is, into a measure of so-called real GNP. When nominal GNP doubles, say, it is recognized that this in no sense necessarily means that total production has doubled. It may mean merely that the same amount of production is sold at twice the prices. The attempt is then made to convert nominal GNP into a measure of real GNP by means of dividing it by the rise in prices. Thus, it is held, in this particular case, because the doubled nominal GNP is offset by doubled prices, there is no rise in real GNP; but if nominal GNP should triple, say, while prices double, then, it is held, real GNP has increased in the ratio of three to two.

Shortcomings of Price Indexes

It should be realized that even the application of price indexes does not enable GNP to serve as any kind of precise measure of total production. For one thing, price indexes either make no allowance for changes in the quality of products or an allowance that is necessarily highly subjective and more or less arbitrary. Thus, for example, if one enters into a price index the price of "an automobile," irrespective of whether it is an automobile of 1993 or 1933, one obviously omits something very important, namely, the enormous improvement in automobiles during this time. In so doing, one is led to overstate the price in the later year in comparison with the earlier year. If, however, one attempts to take into account the improvement in automobiles, any allowance one makes is necessarily highly subjective and more or less arbitrary, in that there is no way of knowing just how much more a buyer is getting for his money in 1993 in comparison with earlier years and thus no way of knowing by just how much one should adjust the price of today's automobiles before entering it into the price index. The problem, of course, applies to practically all goods, inasmuch as the quality of almost every good changes over time, for better or for worse.

In addition, the problem arises of how to *weight* the changes in individual prices over time. Obviously a change in the price of a relatively minor good, such as carrots, on which people spend only a very small portion of their incomes, cannot be counted as heavily as a change in the price of a major good, such as housing, on which people spend a very substantial portion of their incomes. The change in the price of housing will be entered in the index with a much greater weight than the change in the price of carrots. It will enter with a weight that is greater to the degree that the fraction of total income spent for housing is greater than the fraction of total income spent for carrots. The problem, however, is that the way the expenditure of income is divided between the different goods does not remain the same over time. The consequence is that different overall price indexes will result depending on which year's expenditure pattern is chosen for determining the relative weights to be assigned to the different price changes. Consider for example, the different weights that must be assigned to changes in the price of personal computers and VCRs depending on whether one takes 1987 or 1977 as the base year.

These problems, of course, are problems apart from the question of converting nominal GNP into a measure of real GNP. They are problems of price indexes as such, irrespective of the purpose for which they are used. In the last analysis, it is difficult to see how the use of price indexes—and thus measures of real GNP—provide any greater actual precision than such qualitative judgments as: there is no perceptible change, there is a slight change, there is a significant change, there is a large, very large, or enormous change.

1. Gross National Product and the Issue of "Double Counting": *A* Is *A* Versus *A* Is *A+*

I turn now to a subject that should be extremely straightforward and simple, but which is complicated by the most profound confusions concerning the nature of entities. Thus, while nothing should be more elementary than the fact that the axiom *A* is *A*—a thing is itself—applies to the production and purchase of commodities, it turns out that precisely this is what is more often denied than affirmed by contemporary economics. For the prevailing approach to aggregate production and aggregate spending routinely regards things as being *more than themselves*—its formula amazingly enough is that *A* is *A+*. For example, and this will be demonstrated at great length, it regards a loaf of bread as more than a loaf of bread—namely, as a quantity of flour, wheat, and labor services as well as a loaf of bread, and the purchase of a loaf of bread as the purchase of more than a loaf of bread—namely, as the purchase of flour, wheat, and labor services as well. The prevailing approach represents a systematic confusion between the contents of consciousness—that is, knowledge of connections between things—and independently existing physical entities. In effect, because its practitioners know that bread is made from flour and that flour is made from wheat, they lose sight of the fact that bread, flour, and wheat are distinct entities, and instead jumble them together as though they all represented some sort of interchangeable intellectual substance. Indeed, I will show that contemporary economics holds what can only be described as a *Platonic-Heraclitean view of the nature of entities*. That is, it holds a view of entities not as being independently existing physical objects which man's mind must grasp, but as being the *creation* of the human mind in the form of bundles of abstractions which can be put together and taken apart at will to form different entities. I call it Platonic in that it views entities as consisting of concepts or abstractions. I call it Heraclitean in that it views entities as though they represented a kaleidoscopic flux, in which a thing can simultaneously be itself and other things. This is what I mean when I say that instead of the Aristotelian formula that *A* is *A*—a thing is itself—contemporary economics goes by the formula that *A* is *A*+—a thing is itself plus more than itself.[2]

I will begin to make all of this clear by first presenting my own approach to the concept of gross national product.

Common-sense observation implies that the total production—the gross product—of the economic system in any given period of time, such as a year, is the total of all of the goods and services produced in that period of time. It is, for example, the sum of the bread, flour, and wheat, the automobiles, steel sheet, and iron ore, the tractors and auto plants, and all other goods and services produced in the year. (Previous discussion in Chapter 11, of course, makes it clear that in the context of a division-of-labor society, the production to be counted must be confined to production carried on for the purpose of earning money, because all other, merely physical production is, in actuality, consumption.[3]) This total production is obviously what should be called the gross national product.

Now much of production, of course—indeed, the greater part of it in a modern economy—is the production of means of production—capital goods—which are consumed in the process of further production. In this category fall such products as flour and wheat, and steel sheet

and iron ore, as well as the equipment and factory buildings used. All such products are productively consumed in the course of further production.[4]

When the total of productive consumption is subtracted from the gross national product, the result can appropriately be termed the net national product (NNP). Net national product, in other words, is simply gross national product minus productive consumption. Net national product represents the *gain* from production. It is the excess of what is produced over what is consumed in order to produce it, that is, over what is productively consumed.

It turns out that net national product is equal mainly to that part of gross national product which is unproductively consumed—viz., to consumers' goods and services. This is because the part of gross national product which consists of capital goods is largely netted out in the subtraction of productive consumption. For example, the part of gross national product that is wheat is subsequently productively consumed in the making of flour; the part of the gross national product that is flour is subsequently productively consumed in the making of bread. Thus, the wheat and the flour will not be counted in the net national product, for they are subtracted from the gross national product as productive consumption in the process of arriving at net national product. Only the bread will be counted in net national product, because only it, as a consumers' good—a "final product"—is not productively consumed in the production of further products.

The nature of gross national product, the process of productive consumption, and the distinction between gross and net national product, is illustrated with quantitative precision in Figure 15–1. In that figure, we have a succession of time periods depicting the production of x_1 bushels of wheat in *Period 1*, y_1 sacks of flour in *Period 2*, and z_1 loaves of bread in *Period 3*. The wheat of *Period 1* is productively consumed in producing the flour of *Period 2*, which in turn is productively consumed in

Figure 15–1
Gross Product and Productive Consumption

Period	Bushels of Wheat	Sacks of Flour	Loaves of Bread
1	X_1		
2	X_2	Y_1	
3	X_3	Y_2	Z_1
4	X_4	Y_3	Z_2

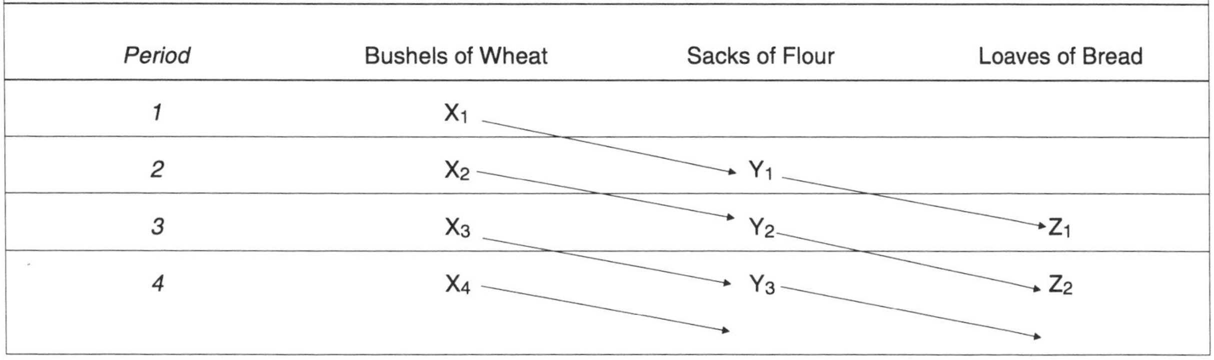

producing the bread of *Period 3*. In *Period 2*, a fresh supply of wheat, x_2 bushels, is produced alongside the production of y_1 sacks of flour. In *Period 3*, a simultaneous production of wheat, flour, and bread occurs, which is repeated in *Period 4* and, by implication, in all subsequent periods.

Now the *gross* product of *Period 3* is, of course, the sum of the x_3 bushels of wheat plus the y_2 sacks of flour plus the z_1 loaves of bread. The *net* product of *Period 3* is this sum minus the x_2 bushels of wheat and y_1 sacks of flour produced in the preceding period and productively consumed in *Period 3*. In exactly the same way, the gross product of *Period 4* is the sum of x_4 bushels of wheat plus y_3 sacks of flour plus z_2 loaves of bread, while the net product of *Period 4* is that sum minus the x_3 bushels of wheat and y_2 sacks of flour produced in the previous period. (In Figure 15–1, the productive consumption of any period is equal to the production of the period before insofar as the latter consists of means of further production.) And again by the principle that everything that is produced is produced, the gross product of *Periods 3 and 4 combined* is the sum of x_3 plus x_4 bushels of wheat plus y_2 plus y_3 sacks of flour plus z_1 plus z_2 loaves of bread. The net product of these two combined periods is, of course, this gross product minus the combined productive consumption of the two periods, which last is x_2 plus x_3 bushels of wheat plus y_1 plus y_2 sacks of flour.

Figure 15–1 confirms that the net product tends to equal little more than the production of consumers' goods alone. For example, if in *Period 3* the x_3 bushels of wheat produced merely equalled the x_2 bushels of wheat productively consumed, and the y_2 sacks of flour produced merely equalled the y_1 sacks of flour productively consumed, then the net product would be equal strictly to the production of the z_1 loaves of bread alone. This is because the subtraction of productive consumption would completely net out all of production beyond the production of these consumers' goods. Only to the extent that the production of capital goods is greater or less than the productive consumption of capital goods, does the net product differ from the production of consumers' goods. To the extent that x_3 bushels of wheat are greater or less than x_2 bushels of wheat, and y_2 sacks of flour are greater or less than y_1 sacks of flour, the net product of *Period 3* is greater or less than z_1 loaves by x_3 minus x_2 bushels of wheat plus y_2 minus y_1 sacks of flour.

It should be apparent that to the extent that the production of capital goods such as wheat and flour in a given period exceeds or falls short of productive consumption in that period, the stock of capital goods in existence equivalently increases or decreases. For this reason, the net product in such a case can be said to be equal to the supply of consumers' goods produced plus this increase or minus this decrease in the supply of capital goods. Indeed, the net product equals the production of consumers' goods plus the increase or minus the decrease in the supply of capital goods in every case, even when the production and productive consumption of capital goods are equal. (In this instance, the change in the supply of capital goods that is to be added or subtracted can be taken simply as zero.)

The concepts of GNP and productive consumption that I have just presented are essentially those of the British classical economists. For example, Adam Smith writes:

> Though the whole annual produce of the land and labour of every country, is, no doubt, ultimately destined for supplying the consumption of its inhabitants, and for procuring a revenue to them; yet when it first comes either from the ground or from the hands of the productive labourers, it naturally divides itself into two parts. One of them, and *frequently the largest*, is, in the first place, *destined for replacing a capital, or for renewing the provisions, materials, and finished work, which had been withdrawn from a capital*; the other for constituting a revenue either to the owner of this capital, as the profit of his stock; or to some other person, as the rent of his land. Thus, of the produce of land, one part replaces the capital of the farmer; the other pays his profit and the rent of the landlord; and thus constitutes a revenue both to the owner of this capital, as the profits of his stock; and to some other person, as the rent of his land. *Of the produce of a great manufactory, in the same manner, one part, and that always the largest, replaces the capital of the undertaker of the work*; the other pays his profit, and thus constitutes a revenue to the owner of this capital.[5]

The Smithian view of GNP is propounded by James Mill, another major classical economist, who states: "The whole annual produce of every country is distributed into two great parts; that which is destined to be employed for the purpose of reproduction, and that which is destined to be consumed. That part which is destined to serve for reproduction, naturally appears again next year, with its profit. This reproduction, with the profit, is naturally the whole produce of the country for that year."[6]

Indeed, there is virtually no difference between my view of the gross national product and that of the classical economists. Where I part company from them in this area is only when it comes to the question of what is to be included in the concept of productive consumption and hence in net national product. They frequently, but not always, regard the consumption of the wage earners as productive consumption, which I, of course, do not. As a result, they tend to view net national product as essentially the same as profits, while in my view, when stated in monetary terms, it includes wages as well.[7] The important ground I share with the classical economists here is that of recognizing that the gross national product—the total of what is produced in a country in a year—includes the production of everything: for example, flour and wheat as well as bread, and steel sheet and iron ore as well as automobiles. Compared with this point in common, any differences are minor.

Contemporary economics, on the other hand, presents a radically different view of gross national product. It presents GNP as the total output of the economic system. Yet it also claims that GNP is measured exclusively by the amount of *final* product, which means essentially just *consumers'* goods. In Figure 15–1, which shows the successive production of wheat, flour, and bread, contemporary economics would describe essentially only the bread as representing the gross national product! Essentially, only it is the final product. Contemporary economics dismisses goods such as wheat and flour as mere "intermediate products," which are not to be counted in the gross national product.

The treatment given by Samuelson and Nordhaus is typical. "What is GNP?" they ask. And they answer, "It is the name we give to the total dollar value of the goods and services produced in an economy during a given year."[8] And then, five pages later, they declare, "GNP, or gross national product, can be measured . . . as the flow of final products."[9] Indeed, so as to leave absolutely no doubt about it, they emphatically declare that "GNP excludes intermediate goods, i.e., ones that are used up to produce other goods. GNP hence includes bread but not wheat, and cars but not steel."[10]

Now if GNP were presented merely as the total of the final products produced in the economic system, then its measurement as such would be unobjectionable. In that case, however, it would have to be realized that what was being called gross national product was in fact a highly netted national product, that, indeed, it was virtually indistinguishable from net national product as I have described it, namely, as the gross product minus productive consumption. But this is not the procedure of contemporary economics. It advances the concept of gross national product simultaneously as the total output of the economic system—that is, as the true gross product— *and* as merely the final product of the economic system. Indeed, so ingrained is its confusion between total product and final product that it regards as an *error* any attempt even to express the actual gross national product! To include the wheat and the steel, according to Samuelson and Nordhaus, is to commit the error of "double counting." "To avoid double counting," they explain, "we take care to include in gross national product only final goods and not the intermediate goods that go to make the final goods."[11] Thus, as I say, the very act of expressing the actual gross national product—the very act of saying that the total of what is produced is the

wheat and the flour as well as the bread, the iron ore and the steel as well as the automobiles—is called the error of "double counting."

Gardner Ackley, who was Chairman of the Council of Economic Advisers under Presidents Kennedy and Johnson, expresses these views as clearly and forcefully as possible:

> National product is the economy's total current output of goods and services valued at the market prices they command . . . .

> The main difficulties in computing national product lie in the avoidance of double counting. We should not count as output the bread, the flour that went into the bread, the wheat that produced the flour, and the fertilizer that helped grow the wheat. Despite all the steps in the process, we end up only with bread—bread is the product, not bread plus flour plus wheat plus fertilizer. In other words, we want to count only "final products," excluding "intermediate products."[12]

The doctrine, so clearly expressed by Ackley, that the final product *is* the total product has truly amazing implications. Ackley himself has stated one of them when he declares, "bread is the product, not bread plus flour plus wheat plus fertilizer." True enough, bread may be all that we end up with, but bread is certainly *not* all that is produced in the course of getting to the bread. The production of the flour, wheat, and fertilizer are no less real and no less a part of total production than the production of bread; and if they were not produced, bread could not be produced. Despite the belief of contemporary economics, the production of bread does not actually represent the production of any of these things. On the contrary, in the mere act of producing bread, one not only does not produce flour, wheat, or fertilizer—one simply *consumes* flour. In order for the consumption of flour, and thus the production of bread, to be possible, there must be a production of flour. And, of course, in exactly the same way, there must be a production of wheat, to make possible its consumption, and thus the production of flour; and of fertilizer, to make possible its consumption, and thus the production of wheat. The only proper procedure is to acknowledge both the production and the subsequent productive consumption of all such "intermediate goods."

The incredible view of contemporary economics expressed by Ackley is that *it is an error to claim that all that is produced, is in fact produced*—that to do so is to claim that *more* is produced than is in fact produced. Only the bread, we are told, is produced. According to contemporary economics, to claim that the bread plus the flour plus the wheat plus the fertilizer are produced is to overstate the actual amount that is produced.

It follows, according to this view, that such usually reliable publications as *The Statistical Abstract of the*

United States are in error. For example, the 1986 edition of that publication reports on page 596 that over seven million automobiles were produced in the United States in 1984. The same publication, on page 765, reports a separate figure of over ninety million tons for the production of raw steel in the United States in 1984. *The Statistical Abstract* clearly informs its readers that both this number of automobiles *and* this quantity of raw steel were produced in the United States in 1984. And thus, according to contemporary economics, it is guilty of the error of "double counting" and of correspondingly representing the production of the United States as greater than it actually was in 1984. For contemporary economics knows that the production of the automobiles already counts the production of steel and thus to claim that both the steel and the automobiles were produced is to double count the steel. The truth, according to contemporary economics, is that only the automobiles were produced. To paraphrase Ackley, "automobiles are the product, not automobiles plus steel."

Thus, the contemporary concept of GNP is not only, in actuality, a highly netted-product concept, but it goes so far as to seek to *obliterate* both the production and the productive consumption of the so-called intermediate products. In so doing, its concept of total production denies the very existence of the far greater part of total production in the economic system.

What underlies the notion that the final product literally is the total product is a bizarre notion of what it is that an individual producer actually produces. According to common sense, the product of a baking company, for example, is bread; that of a flour mill, flour; that of a wheat farmer, wheat. According to contemporary economics, this is a mistake. In its view, what each producer produces is *not* his product, but *the difference* between his product and the means of production he uses up in order to produce it. Thus, a baking company does not produce bread, according to contemporary economics, but the *difference* between bread and flour; a flour mill does not produce flour, but the *difference* between flour and wheat; and similarly for a wheat farmer and any other producers who may still more indirectly help to make possible the production of bread. This notion is clearly expressed in the textbook of Prof. Lloyd G. Reynolds of Yale University, who writes:

> A farmer produces $100 worth of wheat, which is sold to a flour miller. The milling company, by adding labor and capital inputs to this raw material, produces flour which it sells for $150. A baking company uses this flour to produce $225 worth of food . . . .

How much has the milling company produced? Not its sales revenue of $150, since $100 of this was really produced by the farmer. The milling company's output is the sales value of its product minus its purchases from the preceding stage of production. We call this the value added at the milling stage, which in this example is $50.[13]

It bears repeating: the milling company, according to Professor Reynolds (who speaks for the whole of contemporary economics on this point) *does not produce "its sales revenues of $150, since $100 of this was really produced by the farmer. The milling company's output is the sales value of its product minus its purchases from the preceding stage of production."* Thus, for all the world to see, we have the doctrine baldly stated that *producers do not produce their products, but the difference between their products and the means of production they consume in producing them,* and, further, that the part of their products that they may naïvely believe they produce, but allegedly do not produce, is produced by their suppliers. No other conclusion is possible when it is kept in mind that the money values involved are supposed to measure underlying physical production.

Thus, according to Professor Reynolds and contemporary economics, producers do not produce their actual physical products but conceptual differences, which represent an abstract part both of their products and of the products of their customers. The wheat farmer, for example, is alleged both to produce wheat minus fertilizer, rather than wheat, and part of the flour allegedly not produced by the milling company.

It is on the basis of viewing the product of the individual producers as conceptual differences rather than actual physical products that contemporary economics arrives at the conclusion that GNP—the *total* of production—can be measured equivalently either by the value of the final product or by the sum of the values added at each stage of production. If what the baking company produces is bread minus flour, rather than bread; and what the milling company produces is flour minus wheat, rather than flour; and what the wheat farmer produces is wheat minus fertilizer, rather than wheat; and so on, back to the remotest stages of production, then the total product of all these parties combined is, indeed, the bread alone. For in adding up the sum of such differences, all items but the bread cancel out, inasmuch as they all appear as equivalent positive and negative terms. And then, of course, the value of the bread, as the value of the final product, allegedly represents the value of all that is produced.

Now let us look at the so-called value-added approach to calculating GNP. Value added, of course, is the monetary counterpart, the alleged monetary measure, of the conceptual product difference that a producer allegedly produces in place of his actual physical product. Thus, if the product of a baker really were the difference between the bread he produces and the flour (and other previously produced means of production) he consumes in order to produce bread, then the appropriate measure of his production would be the difference between the value of the bread and the value of the flour (and all other such inputs).

Indeed, all of this can be described in terms of a profound confusion on the part of contemporary economics between the concepts of gross and net product. Contemporary economics believes that what a producer produces is merely the *gain* entailed in the production of his product, that is, not his gross product but merely his *net* product. Thus its entire procedure can be described in terms of taking a highly destructive mental shortcut: Namely, instead of going to the trouble of recognizing that producers produce actual physical products and in the process engage in productive consumption, and that the gain from this process is the difference between their production and productive consumption, i.e., the net product, it attempts to leap directly to the net product, as though *that* were what producers produced. In the process it obliterates the very concepts of the gross product and productive consumption.

Despite contemporary economics, the fact is that each producer produces his product, neither less nor more. By this last, I mean that just as a producer's suppliers do not produce any part of his product, so he does not produce any part of the product of his customers. The wheat farmer does not produce any part of the miller's flour, and the miller does not produce any part of the baker's bread. The wheat farmer produces simply and only wheat, the flour miller, simply and only flour, and the bread baker, simply and only bread. Each party produces only his own product and the totality of his own product. (Interestingly, even contemporary economics recognizes this fact when it fails to urge against antitrust actions based on the fewness of producers, any presence of firms' suppliers as representing an addition to the number of producers. For example, in an antitrust action against baking companies based on alleged oligopoly, contemporary economics would not be found claiming the presence of tens of thousands of wheat farmers as producers of bread. Its inconsistency on this score is probably to be explained on the basis of what best serves the power of the state.)

The world of contemporary economics is indeed a strange one. By its logic, economics professors do not write books, but the difference between books and paper. When they go home to dinner, they find that their wives have not made a roast beef, say, but the difference between a cooked roast beef and a raw roast beef.

Indeed, the world of contemporary economics is stranger still. Its notion that producers produce conceptual product differences rather than their actual physical products, and that these product differences are present in the products of their customers, ultimately in the final products, is closely bound up with the bizarre, Platonic-Heraclitean notion of the nature of entities I referred to earlier. This is because when one conceives of a final product as being the sum of the alleged product differences of a series of producers, one no longer conceives of that product as a thing that exists independently, out there in reality. Instead, one conceives of it as though it were made up of a bundle of abstractions, namely, the alleged product differences. Thus, for example, instead of conceiving of a loaf of bread simply as the entity a loaf of bread, one conceives of it as the sum of the series of abstractions bread minus flour, plus flour minus wheat, plus wheat minus zero (zero for the sake of brevity and simplicity). As soon as one does this, one is ready to conceive of one and the same given entity as though it were a multiplicity of entities.

Specifically, one is ready to conceive of the final product as though it were the total product not merely in the sense of the sum of alleged product differences or product additions, but in the sense of the sum of all of *the actual physical entities* involved. That is, for example, one is ready to conceive of bread as being bread, flour, and wheat, and, of course, to conceive of the market value of bread as constituting the market value of flour and wheat as well. Precisely these confusions are present in the conviction of contemporary economics that the value of a final product counts the value of the so-called intermediate products necessary to its production.

The mechanism by which one conceives of a final product as more than itself—as being both itself and all of the previously existing products whose production and productive consumption were necessary to its existence—is that of an improper selective focus. One selectively focuses on different possible combinations of the alleged conceptual building blocks—the conceptual product differences—that are thought of as constituting the final product, and then one sees in each such combination a distinct entity. One then concludes that the final product is itself plus each other such entity. Thus, to continue with the example of bread (ignoring all stages of production prior to wheat farming), one selectively focuses on its alleged conceptual building blocks in three alternative ways that appear to represent distinct entities:

(1) Bread = [(Bread − Flour) + (Flour − Wheat) + (Wheat − Zero)] = *Bread*

(2) Bread = (Bread − Flour) + [(Flour − Wheat) + (Wheat − Zero)] = *Flour* + fade out

(3) Bread = (Bread − Flour) + (Flour − Wheat) + [(Wheat − Zero)] = *Wheat* + fade out

In the first formulation one focuses simultaneously on all three of the conceptual product differences that are regarded as constituting bread. The holding of all three together in consciousness is indicated by the use of surrounding brackets. In this case, bread is regarded as being bread, which is shown in italic type on the right-hand side of the equation.

In the second formulation, one regards bread as flour. One does this by allowing the first conceptual product difference, bread minus flour, to fade from consciousness, as indicated by its placement outside of the brackets. One then focuses on the combination of the two remaining conceptual product differences, which add up to flour. Again, the selective focus is shown by placement within brackets. The result on the right-hand side of the equation is *flour*, in italic type, plus a remainder that is altogether dismissed from consciousness and which I therefore describe as "fade out."

Finally, in the third formulation, bread is conceived of as wheat. Here the two conceptual product differences, bread minus flour and flour minus wheat, are both allowed to fade from consciousness, and only the remaining conceptual product difference, wheat minus zero, is focused on. Once again, the fading of a product difference from consciousness is shown by its appearance outside of brackets, while the selective focus on a product difference is shown by its appearance within brackets. On the right-hand side of the equation, the result is *wheat*—plus fade out.

In this way, a loaf of bread appears as a loaf of bread, a quantity of flour, and a quantity of wheat. And, of course, it is on this basis that the value of a loaf of bread appears to count the value of the loaf of bread, the value of the flour from which it was made, and the value of the wheat from which the flour was made.

Now as I have said, this is a Platonic-Heraclitean view of the nature of entities. It is a view of entities not as being independently existing physical objects which man's mind must grasp, but as being the *creation* of the human mind in the form of bundles of abstractions which can be put together and taken apart at will to form different entities.

It should come as no surprise to learn that the arithmetic implied by such an approach is as bad as the underlying ontology, as the example provided by Professor Reynolds clearly shows.

As we have seen in Professor Reynolds's example, in the real world a wheat farmer produces $100 worth of wheat, a flour miller produces $150 worth of flour, and a baking company produces $225 worth of bread. Professor Reynolds also includes in his example the further stage of retailing the bread to consumers for $300. Given these assumptions, he then asks:

Now, what is the total output at all stages of production? Simply adding the sales receipts of the farmer, the miller,

the baker, and the retailer would give a total of $775. This is clearly too large. *It counts the value of the original wheat four times, the value of the flour three times, and the value of bread twice.*[14]

After explaining the value-added method as the means of determining the value of the total product, Professor Reynolds continues:

There is another, simpler approach which involves only the value of final output at the point of sale. In our bread example, it's the value of bread sold by retailers. If we use this method, *we can forget about the farmer, the miller, and the baker.* Why? *Because the value of their output is already included in the retail price of bread.* The method yields $300, the same output figure as the other method [viz., the same as the value-added method] . . . .[15]

Professor Reynolds's conclusion, which speaks for the whole of contemporary economics, that the retail value of the bread counts the wholesale value of the bread, plus the value of the flour and the wheat, rests on the following mistaken procedure. First, the $300 worth of bread at retail is conceived of not as the value of the independently existing entity bread, but as the sum of the values of a series of conceptual product differences, namely: $300 worth of bread at retail minus $225 worth of bread at wholesale, plus $225 worth of bread at wholesale minus $150 worth of flour, plus $150 worth of flour minus $100 worth of wheat, plus $100 worth of wheat minus zero. Next, these value abstractions are taken apart and put together again in different combinations, to form the value of entities other than bread at retail, namely, the value of bread at wholesale, the value of flour, and the value of wheat. In the process, in violation of the nature of an equation, one or more of the constituent value abstractions is allowed to fade from consciousness to the point of totally disappearing from the right-hand side of the equation. Finally, the value of bread is taken as constituting the sum of a series of such botched equations, despite the fact that the individual equations exist only as mutually exclusive alternatives and thus are not properly subject to addition. I show all of this in the series of equations presented in Table 15–1.

In these equations, following my practice in the discussion of contemporary economics' treatment of physical entities, I depict each of the constituent value abstractions within parentheses, in order to show them as the conceptual building blocks of product values that contemporary economics deems them to be. On the right-hand side of each equation, I use brackets to depict the combination of these abstractions which is currently "on bright," as it were, that is, occupies the center of attention and thus determines the particular product value momentarily under consideration. (The particular product value is named directly below the bracketed expression.) The parenthetical expressions standing outside the brackets

Table 15–1

How Contemporary Economics Double Counts the Value of a Loaf of Bread
(and of Consumers' Goods in General)

(1)

$300 = [($300–$225) + ($225–$150) + ($150–$100) + ($100–0)]

The value of a quantity of bread at retail   The value of a quantity of bread at retail

(2)

$300 = ($300–$225) + [($225–$150)+($150–$100)+($100–$0)]

The value of a quantity of bread at retail   The value of the bread at wholesale

(3)

$300 = ($300–$225)+($225–$150) + [($150–$100)+($100–$0)]

The value of a quantity of bread at retail   The value of the flour

(4)

$300 = ($300–$225)+($225–$150)+($150–$100) + [($100–$0)]

The value of a quantity of bread at retail   The value of the wheat

are the value abstractions "on dim" at the moment, that is, the value abstractions that have been allowed to fade from consciousness.

Equation (1) in Table 15–1 shows the $300 value of a quantity of bread at retail as equal simply to the value of that quantity of bread at retail, for in this equation all four of the alleged conceptual building blocks of the value of bread are held together on the right-hand side of the equation, as shown by their placement inside of the brackets.

Equation (2) in Table 15–1 shows the value of that same quantity of bread at retail as equal to the $75 added by the retailer plus the $225 value of the bread at wholesale. In equation (2), only the last three of the alleged conceptual building blocks of the value of bread are held together, as indicated by their placement inside brackets. It is the sum of these which is $225. The first conceptual building block, the $75 added by the retailer, is placed on dim and thus allowed to fade from consciousness. Accordingly, in this equation, the value of the bread at retail is perceived by contemporary economics as representing the value of the bread at wholesale.

Equation (3) shows the value of the same quantity of bread at retail as equal now to the $75 added by the retailer, plus the $75 difference between the wholesale value of the bread and the value of the flour used to produce it—both of which are now placed on dim and allowed to fade from consciousness—plus, finally, the $150 value of the flour. This last is now on "bright," by virtue of keeping together only the last two of the alleged conceptual building blocks of the retail value of bread, which is indicated by their placement within brackets on the right-hand side of the equation. It is the sum of these

which is $150. Thus, in equation (3), the retail value of bread is perceived by contemporary economics as representing the value of flour.

Finally, equation (4) shows the value of the same quantity of bread at retail as equal to the $75 added by the retailer, plus the $75 difference between the wholesale value of bread and the value of the flour used to produce it, plus the $50 difference between the value of the flour and the value of the wheat used to produce it—all three of which are now placed on dim and allowed to fade from consciousness, as shown by their placement outside of brackets—plus, finally, the $100 value of the wheat. Only this last is now on bright and accordingly takes center stage, as shown by the placement of its value constituent within brackets. Thus, in equation (4), the value of the bread at retail is perceived by contemporary economics as representing the value of wheat.

Now what must be understood from these equations—purely as a matter of mathematics—is that it does not follow that the value of bread at retail counts anything more than *itself.* All that one is entitled to say consistently with the principles of mathematics is that the $300 value of bread at retail is equal to any one of four different *alternative* formulations of the same facts. It is equal to either (1) the value of the bread at retail, which is $300, *or* (2) $75 plus the $225 value of the bread at wholesale, which is still $300, *or* (3) $75 plus $75 plus the $150 value of the flour, which is once again still $300, *or* (4) $75 plus $75 plus $50 plus the $100 value of the wheat, which yet once again is still $300.

The importance of the little word "or" between each of these formulations cannot be overemphasized. The value of the bread at retail is equal to four different *alternative* formulations, each of whose existence precludes the existence of any of the other three at the same time. Thus, when the value of the bread at retail equals the value of the bread at retail, it does not in addition equal $75 plus the value of the bread at wholesale, or any of its other possible formulations. It is equal to just one formulation at a time. And while three of these formulations may be expressed in a way which highlights components that, considered separately, appear to represent the values of other goods or of bread at the wholesale level, still nothing may actually be omitted from any of the equations. The result is that all four formulations actually continue to represent *only* the value of bread at retail. In other words, all that is present here are four different ways of expressing the value of one and the same thing, namely, the bread at retail.

This discussion should make clear that contemporary economics commits two major mathematical errors in its belief that the value of bread at retail counts all the other values. First, after expressing the same facts in four different ways, it impermissibly jettisons some of the facts—that is, in equations (2), (3), and (4), it places value abstractions on a level of such dimness, that it simply forgets all about them. It regards equation (2) not as $75 plus the $225 value of the bread at wholesale, but simply as the value of the bread at wholesale—forgetting all about the $75 added by the retailer. It regards equation (3) not as $75 plus $75 plus the $150 value of the flour, but simply as the value of the flour, forgetting all about the first two terms. Finally, it regards equation (4) not as $75 plus $75 plus $50 plus the $100 value of the wheat, but simply as the $100 value of the wheat, forgetting all about the first three terms. It then compounds the error of these omissions by impermissibly adding up mutually exclusive alternatives—i.e., it adds the remaining elements of equations (2), (3), and (4) to equation (1), and reaches the conclusion that the $300 value of bread at retail "counts" $775 in total values. Thus, contemporary economics arrives, implicitly, at the equation

$300 = [($300–$225)+($225–$150)+ ($150–$100)+($100–$0)]

+ [($225–$150)+($150–$100)+($100–$0)]

+ [($150–$100)+($100–$0)]

+ [($100–$0)].

It is only in this way, that the value of the bread at retail can be made to count itself, the value of the bread at wholesale, the value of the flour, and the value of the wheat.

Thus, paradoxically, as this equation makes clear, *it is contemporary economics which is guilty of the error of double counting!* It counts the final product as *more* than the final product—as itself plus all the other products

which directly or indirectly contribute to its production. It is on this basis that it concludes that to count the full actual product of the economic system is to count more than is produced. If bread alone is already bread plus flour plus wheat, then bread plus flour plus wheat is more than bread plus flour plus wheat. Indeed, when one considers it, nothing could be more obvious than that contemporary economics double counts. If one believes, as it does, that part of the product—the so-called final product—is the whole product, one must be double counting that part.

2. The Role of Saving and Productive Expenditure in Aggregate Demand

The Platonic-Heraclitean view of entities and the consequent double counting of consumers' goods is present in contemporary economics' notion of what constitutes total spending in the economic system. It appears to be present no less in the way the great majority of people think about the process of spending and income formation. For it is generally assumed that in buying consumers' goods, one buys more than consumers' goods—that one buys all the means or factors of production, however remote, which have directly or indirectly contributed to the production of the consumers' goods one buys. (Because the expression "means of production" can be taken to refer exclusively to previously produced means of production and thus to exclude human labor, as when one speaks of "private ownership of the means of production," it is necessary in the present context to use the expression "factors of production," which clearly embraces labor along with capital goods.)

Indeed, the confusion is such that it is often assumed that in buying consumers' goods, one buys, interchangeably, the factors of production that have been used up *in the past* in producing the consumers' goods one buys, and the similar factors of production that the seller of the consumers' goods and his suppliers will buy *in the future,* in succeeding rounds of expenditure made with the money that one spends for the consumers' goods in question. To confuse matters even further, it is frequently assumed that in buying a given good, one buys the subsequent goods which will be produced by means of it and that in some sense one buys or pays for things that are physically unrelated to the consumers' good one buys but that the seller buys with the money one spends in buying from him.

As examples of these confusions, it is assumed that in buying a loaf of bread, one buys the flour and wheat and the labor of bakers and millers that have been used to produce that bread, or have contributed to its production. It is also assumed that one buys the further flour and wheat and labor of bakers and millers which will produce or contribute to the production of bread in the future, and which the baker and miller buy in subsequent rounds of expenditure with the sum of money received from one's purchase of bread. In addition, it is often assumed that the buyer of bread buys toast or a quantity of sandwiches, if such is the use he makes of the bread. And it is also frequently assumed that the buyer of bread buys or pays for things that are physically unrelated to the bread, such as the advertising and research and development outlays of the baking company, or its political and charitable contributions.

In sum, let there be knowledge of a connection between any two things, whether a causal connection in physical production or a connection by way of expenditure with the same physical units of money, and the things become fused together in people's minds, as though they were one and the same entity.

Such confusions grossly exaggerate the role of consumer spending in the economic system. They make it appear that consumption expenditure is the total of expenditure, allegedly incorporating the expenditure for capital goods and labor, which in reality is made only by business firms, with funds that are not consumed, but saved and productively expended. Moreover, the inability of people to see the role of saving and productive expenditure is compounded by a further set of confusions, which leads them to believe that saving is synonymous with hoarding. Indeed, with such an exaggerated view of the role of consumption expenditure as constituting virtually all spending, there is nothing left for the view of saving except to regard it as hoarding.

The result of these confusions is a "macroeconomics" that is not at all a macroeconomics, but an economics virtually of consumption alone. It is an economics that has virtually obliterated the role of saving and productive expenditure, in the conviction that all economic activity is incorporated essentially just in consumption. It is an economics fully geared to the Keynesian fantasy world in which one not only can eat one's cake and have it too, but in which one bakes one's cake in the very act of eating it.

The purpose of the present section is to set matters right by showing the enormous role of saving and productive expenditure in the generation of aggregate demand—a role which far exceeds that of consumption expenditure in size and in most respects is more fundamental than that of consumption expenditure. As an important part of this assignment, it will be necessary to present a system of aggregate economic accounting that, unlike contemporary national income accounting, reflects the full volume of production and the full volume of spending that takes place in the generation of revenue or income. This will be done in Section 3 of this chapter.

The Demand for *A* Is the Demand for *A*

The first point that must be driven home by all possible means is the proposition that *the demand for A is the demand for A*—that is, that the demand for any concrete good or service is simply and only a demand for that concrete good or service; that in buying anything, all that one buys is that which one agrees to receive from the seller and *absolutely nothing else.*

The plain fact is that in buying a loaf of bread, one buys neither a quantity of flour, nor a quantity of wheat, nor the labor of a baker, nor the labor of a miller, nor a loaf of toast, nor anything else but a loaf of bread. One buys simply and only a loaf of bread, and not anything which has contributed to its production, nor anything which the seller of the bread may subsequently buy and which may thus contribute to the production of bread in the future, nor anything into which the bread itself may subsequently be made. Nor does one make the seller's political or charitable contributions. The purchase of any and all of these items is fully as much distinct from the purchase of a loaf of bread as these items themselves are physically distinct from a loaf of bread. Their purchase is something totally separate from and *in addition to* one's purchase of a loaf of bread.

It is necessary to explain and illustrate this proposition even to the point of belaboring it, because apparently nothing less will suffice to establish it in the minds of most people. Well over a century ago, John Stuart Mill advanced the essentially similar proposition that "demand for commodities is not demand for labour." His exposition was both clear and, unfortunately, highly prophetic in its recognition that the proposition "is, to common apprehension, a paradox" and thus "greatly needs all the illustration it can receive." Mill deserves to be quoted at length on this subject:

> We pass now to a fourth fundamental theorem respecting Capital, which is, perhaps, oftener overlooked or misconceived than even any of the foregoing. What supports and employs productive labor, is the capital expended in setting it to work, and not the demand of purchasers for the produce of the labour when completed. Demand for commodities is not demand for labour. The demand for commodities determines in what particular branch of production the labour and capital shall be employed; it determines the *direction* of the labour; but not the more or less of the labour itself, or of the maintenance or payment of the labour. These depend on the amount of the capital, or other funds directly devoted to the sustenance and remuneration of labour. . . .

> This theorem, that to purchase produce is not to employ labour; that the demand for labour is constituted by the wages which precede the production, and not by the demand which may exist for the commodities resulting from the production; is a proposition which greatly needs all the illustration it can receive. It is, to common apprehension, a

paradox; and even among political economists of reputation, I can hardly point to any, except Mr. Ricardo and M. Say, who have kept it constantly and steadily in view. Almost all others occasionally express themselves as if a person who buys commodities, the produce of labour, was an employer of labour, and created a demand for it as really, and in the same sense, as if he had bought the labour itself directly, by the payment of wages. It is no wonder that political economy advances slowly, when such a question as this still remains open at its very threshold. I apprehend, that if by demand for labour be meant the demand by which wages are raised, or the number of labourers in employment increased, demand for commodities does not constitute demand for labour. I conceive that a person who buys commodities and consumes them himself, does no good to the labouring classes; and that it is only by what he abstains from consuming, and expends in direct payments to labourers in exchange for labour, that he benefits the labouring classes, or adds any thing to the amount of their employment.[16]

Inasmuch as Mill's own exposition has passed entirely over the heads of his readers, it is necessary to advance a series of arguments in favor of the proposition that the demand for *A* is the demand for *A*, that is, in Mill's words, actually to give the proposition "all the illustration it can receive."

i. Shadow Entities and Shadow Purchases

The influence of the Platonic-Heraclitean view of entities leads people to believe such a thing as that the buyer of a loaf of bread is a buyer of flour and wheat, and the labor of bakers and millers, because it leads them to believe that these inputs *physically exist in the loaf of bread* and thus that its purchase is also their purchase. Such a view, however, has absolutely no connection with the facts of reality and contradicts the law of identity.

If I wish to buy a loaf of bread *and* a sack of flour *and* a quantity of wheat, I must buy three separate and distinct items: the bread, the flour, and the wheat. Indeed, I can see myself actually going down the various aisles of a supermarket and picking up from the shelves a loaf of bread, a bag of flour, and, if there is an extensive-enough "health foods" section, a quantity of wheat stalks. My action is very different than if I buy merely a loaf of bread alone. In the one case, I have three items in my shopping cart when I reach the checkout stand, and I pay a sum of money for each of them—one for the bread, another for the flour, and a third for the wheat. I then receive into my possession the bread, the flour, and the wheat. In the other case, I have only one item in my shopping cart—the bread—and when I reach the checkout stand, I pay a sum of money only for the bread and receive into my possession only the bread. If I buy a loaf of bread alone, I do not obtain flour and wheat in addition, or pay out the additional sums required to obtain flour and wheat. The

flour and wheat I am nevertheless still supposed to purchase in the mere act of buying a loaf of bread represent, therefore, purchases of a very peculiar kind: they are purchases which cost me absolutely nothing, and purchases which bring into my possession absolutely nothing. In a word, they are purchases which simply *do not exist!* The only entity I purchase is a loaf of bread, and a loaf of bread is neither flour, nor wheat, nor anything else but a loaf of bread. Indeed, people must dwell in a world of shadows and apparitions if they believe that they obtain bread, flour, and wheat all for the price of the bread alone, all compressed within the wrapper of the bread, and—for many perhaps, best of all—all for the same calories as are present in the bread alone.

Excuse me. Did I imagine *eating* flour and wheat? That is what those who are deluded by the Platonic-Heraclitean view of entities must believe they eat when they eat bread. In their view, they obtain flour and wheat when they buy bread and so they must believe that they eat flour and wheat when they eat bread. They should stop and think what it would be like *actually* to eat flour or wheat. I can hear someone now, sputtering and coughing as he gets a mouthful of powdery flour when he takes a bite of bread, or expressing shock and anger when he realizes he is chewing on a stalk of wheat that has managed to find its way into his slice of bread. I can hear the furious denunciations of the baking company for being so incompetent as to allow such things to happen.

If the prospect of eating flour and wheat does not give pause, then one should consider what it would be like to eat fertilizer or tractor parts, which are also supposed to be contained in bread because they have been used to help produce it and which, if bought in the act of purchasing bread, must be eaten in the act of eating bread.

Incredibly, such prospects are unlikely to daunt many of today's alleged economists. For example, Prof. George Leland Bach, who at the time was a professor of economics at Stanford University, wrote in his widely used textbook: "For example, in converting the iron ore to steel above, Bethlehem adds something to the value of *the product it passes along.*"[17] The unmistakable meaning of this statement is that a steel company passes along iron ore in the steel it sells—*that somehow steel is physically still iron ore.* Similarly, Professors Alchian and Allen declare in their textbook: "For example, most steel bought from U.S. Steel by General Motors is not at that time bought by the final user, for General Motors later resells the steel as an automobile."[18] In these passages, we have the baldly stated view that entities are the means of production that have been used up producing them—that automobiles are the steel sheet from the steel mills and, indeed, iron ore, and that *that* is what automobile owners drive.

Indeed, the logic of confusing one thing with another merely because the one was used to produce the other, or merely because the matter that was present in the one now shows up in the other, implies such absurd propositions as that *ice is in steam* and *ice heats houses.* For consider. If a quantity of ice is melted into water, and then the water is boiled into steam, then on the same logic as that the wheat and flour are "in" the bread and are eaten when the bread is eaten, and that the iron ore and steel sheet are "in" the automobile and are driven when the automobile is driven, it follows that the ice is in the steam, and that ice heats houses when steam heats houses.

ii. The Need for Capital

If the demand for consumers' goods really were a demand for factors of production, then one would have to explain why it is necessary to possess capital before starting any business undertaking. Why, if the demand for consumers' goods is a demand for factors of production, is it not possible for every individual who should happen to be so inclined, to set up his own steel company or railroad line? If it really is the consumers rather than businessmen who pay for the factors of production, then why can't a prospective entrant into any line of business simply tell the workers he wants to hire and his prospective suppliers that they will be paid by the consumers of the products he will ultimately make possible, and thus should not bother him with their claims?

The truth is, of course, that before entering into any business operation, one must possess the funds required for the purchase of the necessary factors of production, for which purchases one will only *subsequently* be compensated by one's customers. These funds, of course, are the capital the firm needs and without which it cannot proceed.

Indeed, for the most part, the customers of business enterprises are *other business enterprises.* And all those business enterprises which sell to other business enterprises not only require capital of their own, but are dependent upon their *customers possessing capital.* Such enterprises are not even compensated by the consumers for their outlays, but only by other business enterprises, out of capital. The consumers compensate only those business enterprises for their outlays with which they themselves deal.

iii. Buying the Inputs OR Buying the Output

A further proof that in buying from a business one does not buy what the business buys is the fact that if one really did buy what the business buys, one would not be a customer of the business—certainly not in that transaction. If, for example, one really did buy flour and labor to bake bread, then one would *not buy bread*—certainly

not the bread made from that flour, by that labor. A real buyer of flour and the labor of a baker, compelled to buy bread that is baked from that flour by that labor, would be the victim of a robbery, for he would be forced to buy his own property! His position would be that of being presented with a check for a meal cooked in his own home, by his own housekeeper, with food he himself has paid for. In buying the flour and the labor of a baker, one obtains a natural and a legal title to the bread. One owns the bread by virtue of having bought the flour and the labor. One cannot then be asked to buy the bread.

The principle that follows is that if one really does buy the inputs, one does not buy the output. If one buys the output, it is precisely because one has *not* bought the inputs.

There is a further difficulty with the confusion that in buying the output one buys the inputs. This is the problem that the demand for the inputs—the demand for the factors of production—is a productive expenditure, while if the output is a consumers' good, the demand for the output is a consumption expenditure. In such cases, to claim that the demand for the product is a demand for the factors of production, is to claim that an expenditure which is *not* for the purpose of making subsequent sales—namely, the consumption expenditure which is the demand for the output—*is* an expenditure for the purpose of making subsequent sales—namely, the productive expenditure which is the demand for the inputs. Thus, it is to claim that one and the same expenditure is and is not a consumption expenditure, and is and is not a productive expenditure.

The Demand for Consumers' Goods and the Demand for Factors of Production as Competing Alternatives

It should now be clear that the demand for consumers' goods is not a demand for the factors of production—viz., capital goods and labor—which were employed in the past in making the production of today's consumers' goods possible. The purchase of those factors of production was made in the past, by the current sellers of today's consumers' goods and by their suppliers and by a chain of still earlier suppliers. It should be equally clear that the demand for consumers' goods is also not a demand for the factors of production which will be employed in the future, in making possible the production of possibly similar consumers' goods, and which will be purchased with sums of money received from the buyers of consumers' goods in the present. These factors of production too are purchased not by the consumers but by the sellers of today's consumers' goods and by their suppliers and a chain of further suppliers. Indeed, once the confusions instilled by the Platonic-Heraclitean view of entities fall away, one can see that the demand for consumers' goods is not only not a demand for factors of production, but is *in competition* with the demand for factors of production.

By this, I mean that to the extent that an individual consumes, he makes *impossible* the purchase of factors of production. This is because one can buy *either* consumers' goods *or* factors of production, but not both with the same money. Given the quantity of money in the economic system and thus the total ability of people to spend money, a high consumption is most decidedly not the precondition of a high demand for factors of production. If the demand for factors of production is to be high, consumption must be low. For every capitalist or prospective capitalist is faced with the following alternative: He can spend his funds either on consumers' goods *or* on capital goods, but he cannot, for example, buy a personal automobile *and* a truck for his business with the same money. He can spend his funds in the purchase of consumers' goods for his own enjoyment *or* he can pay the wages of workers who will render services in his business enterprise, and who will consume in his place, but he cannot, for example, buy a vacation *and* employ a machinist with the same money.[19]

To demonstrate as clearly as possible that the demand for consumers' goods is in competition with and at the *expense* of the demand for capital goods and labor by business enterprises, I will show how the demand for consumers' goods is capable of rising to the point of totally eliminating the demand for capital goods and labor by business enterprises. Thus, let us make the drastic assumption not only that wage earners consume the full amount of their wages but also that businessmen and capitalists, who sell goods and services, use the full amount of their sales receipts to make purchases for their own consumption. In effect, they pay themselves dividends equal to their sales receipts and go out and consume the proceeds. And to close off every last corner, let us also explicitly assume that those who introduce new and additional money into the economic system—that is, gold and silver miners as far as a precious metal standard prevails, and the government and banking system as far as such a standard does not prevail—use the new and additional money exclusively for consumption or to support consumption. In such a case, there would simply be no source of a demand either for capital goods or for labor by business firms. Whatever funds anyone took in from the sale of consumers' goods would be expended in buying further consumers' goods, or consumers' labor, and there would be nothing left with which to buy capital goods or producers' labor. Precisely this is the situation, described in Chapter 11, that prevails in Adam Smith's "early and rude state of society" and under Marx's "simple circulation."[20]

Of course, many will probably still object that the rise in consumption envisioned in this case will place additional funds in the hands of the industries producing consumers' goods, and that because of this, these industries will be enabled to make a greater demand for factors of production than before. But this objection is absolutely wrong. It fails to take into account that we are assuming a rise in the consumption of *businessmen and capitalists*, and that this includes the consumption of the businessmen and capitalists faced with the additional demand for consumers' goods—that, indeed, we are assuming that such businessmen and capitalists, along with all other businessmen and capitalists, consume the full amount of their sales receipts. Thus, there could not only be no increase in the demand for factors of production coming from the industries producing consumers' goods, but the demand for factors of production coming from those industries would actually fall to zero. Not only would each recipient of additional consumer sales receipts simply reexpend all of the additional sales receipts in the purchase of further consumers' goods, but he would also expend in the purchase of consumers' goods the equivalent of all the funds he had previously expended in any given period in the purchase of factors of production. Thus the demand for factors of production emanating from the consumers' goods industries would be zero, despite the rise in the sales receipts of the consumers' goods industries.

It is no objection to the assumption that the demand for consumers' goods rises to the point of totally eliminating the demand for factors of production, to point out that the production of consumers' goods would then also be almost totally eliminated. For example, it is certainly true that if the demand for the means of producing personal automobiles fell to zero, no personal automobiles could be produced, no matter how high the demand for personal automobiles became. If the assumption actually held that there was only a demand for consumers' goods and no demand for factors of production, it would certainly be an incalculable disaster. In that case, no consumers' goods beyond the crudest and most primitive type could be produced, and they, in the most meager quantities. But this is the conclusion to which one comes *by way* of the proposition that the demand for consumers' goods is only a demand for consumers' goods and not a demand for factors of production. It cannot be grounds for attacking that proposition. (What would happen under such conditions is that the division of labor would revert to the most primitive level. The production of products requiring any significant degree of time and temporal succession of producers would become impossible.[21])

Nor is it correct in this context to say that producers

who expend their entire sales receipts in their own consumption must disappear from the market. If all producers acted this way, then the fact that their products were primitive and few would not be sufficient to drive them out of business, because their competitors would not offer anything better.

Now not only would a rise in consumption spending in the enormous dimensions I have assumed mean a total elimination of the demand for factors of production, but every rise in consumption spending means a fall in the demand for factors of production or, as a minimum, a lesser increase in the demand for factors of production. For even when the quantity of money in the economic system and thus the total ability of people to spend money increases, making it possible for both the demand for consumers' goods and the demand for factors of production to increase together—even then, the principle holds. This is because the increase in the demand for factors of production would be greater still, if the increase in the demand for consumers' goods were less. (The same point applies, of course, to increases in the total volume of spending made possible by decreases in the demand for money for holding.)[22]

In dealing with less drastic increases in consumption spending—that is, increases in consumption spending not so great as to eliminate the demand for factors of production altogether—it continues to be necessary to keep in mind that a rise in consumption spending does not constitute an increase in the demand for any category of goods but consumers' goods. It does not increase the total demand for goods in the economic system, but merely changes the composition of that demand. Other things being equal, a rise in the demand for consumers' goods is accompanied by an equivalent fall in the demand for capital goods. And in the course of a rise in the overall demand for consumers' goods, the additional demand for many individual consumers' goods is made possible only by an equivalent reduction in the demand for other consumers' goods. Thus, for example, in order for businessmen and capitalists to pay themselves larger dividends and thus increase their expenditure for consumers' goods, they must reduce their expenditure for capital goods and producers' labor. The only effect this has on the demand for goods as such is to increase the demand for consumers' goods and equivalently to decrease the demand for capital goods, and, within the demand for consumers' goods, to increase the demand for those consumers' goods which may happen to be favored by businessmen and capitalists, and to decrease the demand for those consumers' goods which may happen to be more commonly purchased by wage earners. That is to say, a rise in consumption spending on the part of the businessmen and capitalists will, for example,

increase the demand for personal automobiles at the expense of the demand for trucks for business purposes, and, within the demand for personal automobiles, increase the demand for Cadillacs, say, and decrease the demand for Chevrolets, say. Thus, there is no increase in the total, economy-wide demand for goods as such brought about by a rise in the consumption of businessmen and capitalists, but, as I say, a decrease in the demand for capital goods, for the labor employed by business enterprises, and for the consumers' goods the employees of business firms would otherwise have purchased. The same is true in principle of all increases in consumption, because they are always at the expense of saving and productive expenditure and thus at the expense of the demand for capital goods and producers' labor.

It is necessary to clear up the confusion caused by the fact that short of every seller using the whole of his sales receipts to consume, an increase in the demand for any product by consumers tends to result in an increase in the demand for factors of production by the producers of that product. Thus, for example, if wealthy businessmen decided to withdraw funds from their firms in order to consume in the form of buying yachts, say, the effect would normally be to cause an increase in the demand for factors of production by the yacht-building industry. Nevertheless—and this is the essential point—the *total* demand for factors of production in the economic system would now be less.

For had the businessmen not withdrawn the funds in question to buy yachts, the funds would have been used to buy capital goods, such as various types of machinery or factory buildings, and to pay the wages of workers, who would have bought various consumers' goods. The demand for *these* goods—capital goods and the consumers' goods the wage earners would have bought—does not exist as the result of the use of funds to buy the yachts. Thus the demand for factors of production that would have been made in their production is not made. But it is not the case that all that happens is a shifting of demand for factors of production from the production of these goods to the production of yachts. There is *less* demand for factors of production in the economic system as a whole. There is less precisely to the extent that the demand for yachts, a consumers' good, takes the place of a demand for capital goods and labor by business.

In quantitative terms, let us imagine that the new and additional annual yacht purchases of businessmen are $1 billion. To make matters as simple as possible, let us further imagine that these yacht purchases come entirely at the expense of the demand for capital goods. To make matters even more simple, let us assume that they come at the expense specifically of $1 billion worth of tanker purchases. We can readily imagine that as the result of having $1 billion of additional sales each year, an additional demand for factors of production now takes place every year on the part of the yacht-building industry, in the amount of $900 million, say. However, we are entitled to assume that over and against this additional $900 million of demand for factors of production by the yacht-building industry, there is a $900 million per year reduction in the demand for factors of production on the part of the tanker-building industry. Thus, as far as the yacht-building consumers' goods industry is concerned, the demand for factors of production has increased by $900 million. As far as the tanker-building capital goods industry is concerned, the demand for factors of production has decreased by $900 million. The overall situation, however, is by no means mutually offsetting or neutral with respect to the demand for factors of production. This is because the outstanding fact of the case is that the demand for capital goods—the tankers—is less by $1 billion and the demand for consumers' goods—the yachts—is greater by $1 billion. Thus, overall and on net balance, the demand for capital goods is down by $1 billion as the result of the demand for consumers' goods being up by $1 billion.

Obviously, nothing of significance depends on the assumption that the demand for yachts increases specifically at the expense of the demand for tankers. The capital goods could be of any kind: factory buildings, machines, materials, etc., of whatever description. Nor does anything of significance depend on the assumption that the entire reduction in the demand for factors of production is at the expense of the demand for capital goods. We might imagine that part of it is at the expense of the demand for labor by business. Thus, for example, if $500 million of the funds required for the purchase of the yachts had come from the demand for labor rather than from the demand for capital goods, the demand for factors of production as such would still have fallen by $1 billion. The only complication introduced would have been that the reduction in the demand for labor would in turn have caused a reduction in the demand for consumers' goods on the part of wage earners and thus that part of the decline in the demand for factors of production offsetting the rise in the demand for factors of production by the yacht-building industry would have been in those consumers' goods industries rather than in capital goods industries.

What the tanker example is especially suited for illustrating is the effect of a rise in the demand for consumers' goods at the expense of the demand for factors of production, on the economic system's subsequent ability to produce. Because yachts have been produced instead of tankers, the result is simply that production in future years will have to take place without the aid of the tankers and will therefore be less. The tankers would have con-

tributed to production in the future; the yachts do not. Of course, this effect on the future ability to produce applies to every increase in the production of consumers' goods at the expense of the production of capital goods, as we well know from the last chapter. It would apply equally if the production of the yachts had been at the expense of any kind of factory or office buildings, machines or tools, or materials or components purchased by business firms, rather than specifically tankers. The increase in the production of consumers' goods at the expense of the production of capital goods always means an undermining of the ability to produce in the future.

It should go without saying that the reduction in aggregate productive expenditure that results from a rise in consumption expenditure also operates to reduce the magnitude of nominal capital in the economic system, inasmuch as nominal capital is the reflection of a series of current and prior productive expenditures. Thus while the yacht-building industry in our example attracts additional capital as the result of the rise in demand for yachts, the total capital of the economic system diminishes. The yacht-building industry does not attract as much additional capital as the rest of the economic system loses in the process.

It may be helpful to put all this in slightly different words: Namely, while every demand for goods—consumers' goods or capital goods—attracts capital and to that extent underlies an expenditure for factors of production, the amount of capital available to be attracted and the magnitude of the expenditure for factors of production that corresponds to any given demand for goods is the less, the more frequent and the larger in size is the choice of individuals to spend their funds on consumers' goods rather than on factors of production.[23] A rise in the demand for consumers' goods at the expense of the demand for factors of production increases the proportion of the demand for factors of production that is made by the consumers' goods industries while reducing the overall size of the demand for factors of production in the economy as a whole. With a big enough rise in consumption and fall in demand for factors of production, even the expenditure of the consumers' goods industries for factors of production falls and, indeed, can completely disappear, as we have seen.

Now it is certainly possible that some businessmen and capitalists who decide to step up their consumption at the expense of their capitals and demand for factors of production might merely put sales revenues into the hands of other businessmen and capitalists who choose to consume more modestly and to make a correspondingly greater demand for factors of production relative to their sales revenues. To the extent that this is the case, then the rise in the consumption of businessmen and capitalists is only passing, and disappears as soon as greater wealth comes under the control of those businessmen and capitalists who employ a relatively smaller proportion of their sales revenues in their own consumption. This circumstance, however, in no way affects the truth of the statement that consumption and the demand for factors of production move in opposite directions. For when the consumption of businessmen and capitalists rose in this case, the demand for factors of production would still fall, and only then, when the consumption of businessmen and capitalists once again declined, would the demand for factors of production return to its former level.

I do not want to be perceived as condemning in any way the purchase of yachts or any form of private luxury consumption that takes place under capitalism. Given the security of property that prevails under capitalism and the enormous degree of rationality and future orientation, such consumption takes place in a context of a far greater degree of provision for the future and capital intensiveness of production than under any other imaginable economic system. I chose the example merely in order to make the principle clear that consumption and demand for factors of production are opposites. Furthermore, it is important always to keep in mind that while a further decline in consumption relative to the demand for factors of production can always achieve further economic improvement, it can do so *only if it is uncoerced*. If the attempt were made to force businessmen and capitalists to restrict their consumption, they would lose the incentive to accumulate and maintain their capital, which would result in far greater economic loss than could possibly be gained by any restriction that might be imposed on their consumption.[24] The only truly destructive consumption expenditure that exists under capitalism (or, more correctly, under a mixed economy) is the wasteful consumption of a government that is no longer confined within the limit of its proper functions. The reduction or, better still, the total elimination of such consumption can represent an enormous economic gain in bringing about a higher relative production of capital goods and a higher demand for labor relative to the demand for consumers' goods.[25] Indeed, even the seeming beneficiaries of such consumption expenditure must end up being better off without it, when they support themselves through their own work and saving in the midst of a society characterized by economic progress.

Compatibility With the Austrian Theory of Value

It should not be thought that the proposition "the demand for *A* is the demand for *A*" or, what is virtually

equivalent, John Stuart Mill's proposition "the demand for commodities is not demand for labour," is incompatible with the so-called Austrian theory of value, according to which the prices of factors of production are ultimately determined by the prices of the consumers' goods they help to produce. The proposition is perfectly compatible with the Austrian theory of value. The reconciliation consists in the fact that the value of factors of production *relative to one another* is determined by the value of their products, ultimately consumers' goods, relative to one another, but that the value of factors of production *relative to the value of their products* is not determined by the value of their products. This is simply to say, for example, that insofar as the factors of production in question are specific and cannot be transferred between uses, the means of producing wine will be more valuable than the means of producing bread to the degree that wine is more valuable than bread; but a rise in the total value of wine, bread, and consumers' goods in general can never mean a rise in the value of the means of producing them, if there is no change on the side of money. On the contrary, if there is no change on the side of money, every rise in consumption must mean a corresponding *fall* in the demand for and total value of the factors of production.

There is nothing surprising in this. When the Austrian theory of value declares that the value of consumers' goods determines the value of the means of producing them, it is always on the assumption—either implicit or explicit—that the relationship between the value of the products and the value of the factors of production can be ignored. However, this relationship cannot be ignored when we turn to the theory of profit and interest and the concomitant question of what causes the value of products regularly and consistently to *exceed* the value of the factors of production. Then the problem is no longer one of the value of factors of production relative to each other, but *relative to the value of their products*. And here, a rise in consumption increases the margin between the value of products and the value of the means of producing them—viz., it operates to raise the rate of profit and interest.[26] The Austrian theory of value, logically considered, should be taken to mean no more than that the relative value of consumers' goods determines the relative value of the means of producing them, and this, insofar as the factors of production are specific, that is to say, not substitutable for one another in the different uses in question. As Mill himself put it, "The demand for commodities determines in what particular branch of production the labour and capital shall be employed; it determines the *direction* of the labour . . . ." To the degree that labor (or other factors of production, such as land) cannot be changed in its "direction," or cannot be changed without some loss of efficiency, then changes in the relative value of the factors of production result.

Application to the Critique of the Keynesian Multiplier Doctrine

The proposition that the demand for A is the demand for A has major application to the critique of the Keynesian "multiplier" doctrine, a doctrine that is expounded in virtually every contemporary textbook that deals with "macroeconomics."[27]

The multiplier doctrine claims that an initial increment of net investment, government spending, or any other "autonomous" expenditure is followed by successive rounds of consumption spending which serve to produce a multiple increase in national income. The proposition that the demand for A is the demand for A shows that the only incomes that could be raised by the successive rounds of consumption expenditure envisioned by the multiplier doctrine would be *profits,* not wages. As should now be clear, any rise in wages, in the demand for goods at wholesale, or in the demand for capital goods of any kind depends on what is not consumed, but saved and productively expended. This is because consumption expenditure is merely consumption expenditure. It does not incorporate productive expenditure. The demand for goods at wholesale, for materials and machinery, and for labor by business is possible only to the extent that people do *not* consume but save and productively expend. Yet the Keynesians regard saving as a "leakage" and as allegedly diminishing the amount of subsequent incomes.

It is only on the basis of utterly illusory, nonexistent, shadow purchases of the kind described earlier in this section that the Keynesians can believe that additional expenditure by consumers for the goods and services of business constitute an additional demand for the labor and other inputs bought by business. Moreover, unlike other economists who have never grasped Mill's proposition and its implicit call for the application of the law of identity to economics, the Keynesians have no escape route. They cannot claim that what they really mean when they propound the multiplier doctrine is only that an inflation-financed rise in consumer demand results in a rise in the demand for labor and other factors of production because business enterprises will spend their additional sales revenues in buying factors of production. The Keynesian analysis explicitly argues that income is raised insofar as the additional incomes corresponding to the additional sales revenues are consumed, i.e., are *not* spent for business purposes, and that the rise in incomes will be the greater, the higher is the "marginal propensity to *consume*" and the lower is the "marginal propensity to save."

Samuelson and Nordhaus propound the Keynesian doctrine in unmistakable terms. They state:

> No proof has yet been presented to show that the multiplier will be greater than 1. But the discussion up to now indicates how, when I hire unemployed resources to build a $1000 woodshed, there will be a *secondary* expansion of national income and production, over and above my *primary* investment. [Expenditure for a personal woodshed, of course, is consumption, not investment. But no matter.] Here is why.
>
> My carpenters and lumber producers will get an extra $1000 of income. But that is not the end of the story. If they all have a marginal propensity to consume of $\frac{2}{3}$, they will now spend $666.67 on new consumption goods. The producers of these goods will now have an extra income of $666.67. If their MPC is also $\frac{2}{3}$, they in turn will spend $444.44 or $\frac{2}{3}$ of $667.67 (or $\frac{2}{3}$ of $\frac{2}{3}$ of $1000). So the process will go on, with each new round of spending being $\frac{2}{3}$ of the previous round.
>
> Thus an endless chain of *secondary consumption responding* is set in motion by my primary $1000 of investment spending. But, although an endless chain, it is a dwindling chain. And it eventually adds up to a finite amount.

Upon summing up this infinite series, Samuelson and Nordhaus conclude:

> This shows that, with an MPC of $\frac{2}{3}$, the multiplier is 3, consisting of the 1 of primary investment plus 2 extra of secondary consumption responding.
>
> The same arithmetic would give a multiplier of 4 if the MPC were $\frac{3}{4}$, for the reason that $1 + \frac{3}{4} + (\frac{3}{4})^2 + (\frac{3}{4})^3 + \ldots$ finally adds up to 4. . . . In other words, the greater is the extra consumption responding, the greater the multiplier. The greater the MPS "leakage" into extra saving at each round of spending, the smaller the final multiplier.[28]

Samuelson and Nordhaus are utterly unaware that the overwhelmingly greater part of any income that could possibly be increased by virtue of the process they have described would be *profit* income. That is the only income that is earned on additional business sales revenue, and business sales revenue is the only receipt that private consumption spending generates (apart from some minor demand for domestic servants). It is also the only receipt that is generated by investment spending insofar as investment spending is for such things as the purchase of the lumber they assume in their example. Thus, for example, if I take $1,000 and go into a shopping mall and spend it in buying clothes, say, my expenditure is $1,000 of sales revenue to the seller of the clothes. The only income earned on those sales revenues is profit, not wages. (Readers who know anything about accounting should be sure to read the next paragraph.) If the seller of the clothes then decides to consume $666.67 of his supposed $1,000 of additional income, say, by going elsewhere in the mall and buying dishes for that sum, then there is $666.67 of additional sales revenue to the seller of the dishes. Again, any additional income earned is profit, not wages. If the seller of the dishes, in turn, decides to consume $444.44 of his supposed additional income of $666.67, say, in buying shoes, then once again there is only additional business sales revenue, on which the only income that is earned is profit, not wages. In this case, carrying the process to *n* stages, the effect of the "multiplier"—if it actually existed—would be that the $1,000 of initial additional spending would bring about $3,000 almost entirely of additional sales revenues and hardly any additional wage income. If the additional sales revenues represented equivalent additional net income, the only additional net income they could represent would be *profit* income, not wages. The only additional wage income would be insofar as the original investment expenditure entailed the payment of wages as opposed to the purchase of capital goods.[29]

(In the interest of accuracy, I must point out that in reality, the amount of profit income earned on my $1,000 of expenditure would be less than $1,000 to the extent that the seller had to deduct additional cost of goods sold from his additional sales revenues. The incurrence of additional cost of goods sold, as I will show later on, represents disinvestment, and would actually work to undercut any actual net investment which might have launched the alleged spending chain.[30] In order for my $1,000 of expenditure to constitute $1,000 of additional profit income, we must assume that the seller sells exactly the same total physical volume of goods he otherwise would have sold in the accounting period, but now, thanks to my spending of this $1,000, he does so for $1,000 more of sales revenue. On this assumption, my expenditure of $1,000 would constitute an additional profit income of $1,000 to the seller. A similar assumption, of course, would have to be made for every subsequent round of spending.)

It is true that insofar as business sales revenues rise from year to year, on the foundation of a growing quantity of money and rising volume of spending, the greater portion of the additional sales revenues and accompanying profit incomes is spent by business firms in paying wages and in buying capital goods. But this is a *productive* expenditure, not a consumption expenditure. It is made out of the portion of the additional sales revenues and profits which are *not* consumed, but which are *saved*—something which, as I have said, the Keynesian analysis calls a "leakage," and regards as unfortunate.

If the economic world operated in accordance with the ideals of Keynesian economics, and the greater part or all of the additional business sales revenues and profits were consumed, it would be disastrous for wage earners and for all business firms that sell to other business firms,

and even for those business firms that sell to consumers and which would have higher profit incomes. For the wage share of the national income would fall, the ratio of the value of capital to the value of output, (viz., the degree of capital intensiveness) would fall, and the relative production of capital goods would fall. In short order, economic progress would be brought to a halt and economic retrogression would commence, as capital began to be decumulated. Both real wages and real profits would steadily decline.[31] The interests of everyone in the economic system, but foremost the interests of wage earners, lie with the highest possible *productive* expenditure, which means: the lowest possible consumption expenditure on the part of those making productive expenditure.

Saving Versus Hoarding

Saving is the use of revenue or income by a business or individual for purposes other than expenditure on consumers' goods (or consumers' services). It is revenue or income that is not consumed.

Because what is saved is not spent by the saver for consumption, a popular fallacy has grown up that saving is synonymous with *hoarding*—i.e., with the retention of money in the manner of a miser. This fallacy is not so difficult to understand when committed by people with limited education, who thus know little beyond their own personal experience. Most such people are wage earners, who normally do not personally make any kind of expenditures but consumption expenditures. In the absence of wider knowledge, it is easy for such people to confuse consumption spending with all of spending and thus to conclude that what is not spent for consumption is simply not spent. But the fallacy is also prevalent in the press, which persists in equating an increase in the rate of saving with a decrease in the spending for goods. For example, whenever it is reported that some increase in the rate of saving has taken place, the press concludes that the effect must be economically dampening at the very least.

Worse still, the fallacy that saving is hoarding is prevalent among professional economists—notably the Keynesians and neo-Keynesians—who routinely describe saving as a "leakage" from the "spending stream."[32] (Such economists have taught the fallacy to the members of the press.)

Indeed, so complete has been the intellectual severance of saving from spending that for several decades it has been routinely taught in college and university classrooms not only that what is saved simply disappears from spending and depresses the economy, but also that what is invested virtually comes out of nowhere and financially stimulates the economy.[33] This is a state of confusion that would be comparable to believing that the seeds a farmer scatters simply disappear, and that the crop that later comes up, comes out of nowhere. Yet such a state of confusion is the corollary of believing that saving is hoarding. If one recognized that investment comes from saving, one would have to recognize no less that saving goes into investment—that the two are merely different aspects of the same phenomenon. In that case, one would not view saving as depressing, nor investment as stimulating.

It must be pointed out that exactly the same kind of intellectual severance of cause and effect prevails in the belief that government spending represents an increase in total spending, while taxes represent a decrease in total spending. It is not seen that the taxes do no not disappear from spending, but go to finance government spending, and that the government spending does not come out of nowhere, but, for the most part, out of taxes.[34] The objection to taxes is not that they reduce spending but that they transfer the power to spend from those who have earned it, and to whom it belongs, to those who have not earned it, and to whom it does not belong, and in the process reduce the total of what is produced.

It is not possible to emphasize too strongly that saving is not hoarding, for few fallacies are more destructive. Thus, before proceeding to show the actual positive contribution of saving to spending, which is enormous, it is necessary to show some of the fallacies that are present in the belief that there is any real or significant connection between saving and hoarding.

i. The Hoarding Doctrine as an Instance of the Fallacy of Composition

It should be realized that while any particular individual might save in the form of adding to his cash holding—that is, in the form of "hoarding"—it is not possible for the economic system as a whole to do so. Indeed, the belief that the economic system as a whole can save by means of hoarding is an instance of the fallacy of composition—the same fallacy encountered in connection with the belief that not only an individual industry or group of industries can overproduce, but that the economic system as a whole can overproduce.[35]

The reason that an individual can save by means of hoarding cash, while the economic system as a whole cannot, is because whatever cash an individual adds to his holding, some other individual has had to subtract from his holding. If I sell my goods for $1,000, say, and decide to retain that sum in the form of cash, it is true that I increase my savings by $1,000. But in the very same period of time, the individuals to whom I have sold my goods have had to reduce their cash holdings, and thus their accumulated savings in the form of cash, by that

very same $1,000. I have $1,000 more in cash and in savings, but they have $1,000 less in cash and in savings. Adding up the change not only in my position, but in theirs as well, it thus turns out that in the economic system as a whole there is no increase whatever in savings in the form of cash holdings. What some individuals save by means of adding to their cash holdings other individuals have had to dissave.

The situation of students in a classroom provides an excellent illustration of this proposition. At any given time, the members of the class have just so much cash in their possession. If the doors to that classroom were locked and that class became a "closed economic system" for an hour or so, with its members carrying on some form of production and buying and selling from one another, any individual student might increase his savings by adding to his cash holding over that interval of time. But then the rest of the class must decrease its savings in the form of cash holdings to exactly the same extent. There is no way that the class as a whole can increase its savings by increasing its holding of cash.

It follows that if there is to be saving in the economic system as a whole—that is, an increase in the savings of some or all members of the economic system that is not compensated for by a decrease in the savings of other members of the economic system—the only way it can take place is in the form of *an increase in assets other than cash.* The increase in the savings of the economic system as a whole must take the form of an increase in its capital assets, such as business plant, equipment, and inventories, or in its consumer assets, such as owner-occupied houses, personal automobiles, and home appliances. In this way, some or all members of the economic system can have an increase in their accumulated savings with no one having to have a decrease. (Consumer assets represent accumulated wealth and thus savings insofar as they retain their usefulness and a corresponding portion of their exchange value. They are consumers' goods in that they are in the process of being consumed, but they represent wealth and savings insofar as they are not yet totally consumed. Furthermore, the purchase of such consumer assets is frequently made possible by means of borrowed funds, which from the point of view of the lender are capital, inasmuch as they are the source both of their own replacement and of income as well.[36])

The only exception to the principle that the economic system cannot save by means of adding to its cash holdings exists insofar as there is an increase in the quantity of money. If, over a period of time, the quantity of money in the economic system increases, then, to that extent, there can be an increase in the holding of cash that does not imply an equivalent decrease in the holding of cash by others. But this is the only exception, and it is of absolutely no negative significance. Moreover, it is inescapable inasmuch as the new and additional money must be added to the cash holdings of someone and in that capacity will constitute part of their savings.

ii. Hoarding as the Cause of a Reduction in Savings

Even though it is impossible that everyone could succeed in increasing his savings in the form of cash holdings (except to the extent that the quantity of money increased), it is possible that many people or even everyone might attempt to do so, in an effort to become financially more liquid. The effect of such an attempt is actually to *decrease the aggregate amount of accumulated savings stated in terms of money*. This is because the effect of such action is to reduce the monetary value of land and buildings, equipment and inventories, and, of course, stocks and bonds, which are claims against such assets. For all of these things are put up for sale in unusually large quantities, in the general effort to raise cash. At the same time, of course, the expenditures to purchase such assets are sharply curtailed, in efforts to retain cash. The fall in the aggregate monetary value of these items is what causes the fall in the total of accumulated savings stated in money. The reduction in such asset values on the left-hand side of the balance sheets causes a reduction in earned surplus and retained earnings accounts on the right-hand side of balance sheets, which accounts represent accumulated savings. Thus, it should be apparent that hoarding is not only not the same thing as saving, but actually operates to *reduce* the total of what has been saved.

This discussion indicates the true nature of hoarding when it occurs on a significant scale. It has nothing to do with any attempt to save or to save more; nor does it originate with consumers. Rather, it represents the attempt of business firms and investors to convert previously accumulated savings from their usual form of physical assets or claims to physical assets, into cash, in an effort to become more liquid. The attempt takes the form both of the outright sale of existing assets and the reduction of expenditures required for their replacement. And, in the process, as just explained, it reduces accumulated savings, along with consumption and all other forms of spending, and along with all forms of monetary revenue and income.

It should be realized that in such a process, what is saved out of current income easily becomes a *negative* number. That is, not only is saving out of current income reduced, not only is it wiped out altogether, but, in such circumstances, consumption actually comes to exceed current income. (This was the case, for example, in the Great Depression of the 1930s.[37]) In part, this is because the contraction in spending that results from the desire to

become more liquid initially causes large-scale unemployment. To the extent that the unemployed have savings, they live off their savings. Even more important in terms of the size of the effect on savings, the decline in spending in the economic system reduces business sales revenues and profits. Yet even with sharply reduced profits or even outright losses, many businesses continue to pay dividends. Losses, and dividend payments in excess of profits, constitute a reduction in the accumulated savings of business enterprises. And on top of all of this is the capital losses previously referred to, which take place in connection with the sale of assets at prices below their cost of acquisition.

iii. In Defense of "Hoarding"

The fact that "hoarding," or, more correctly, the desire to increase cash holdings, operates to reduce saving no less than consumption, does not mean that it is an evil or should be prevented in any way. What the attempt to hold more cash does succeed in doing is *to increase the buying power of the stock of money*, whatever the stock of money may be. (This, of course, is if the attempt to hold more cash is not frustrated by laws interfering with the fall in wages and prices, and by fractional reserve banking in connection with checking deposits, which results in bank failures reducing the quantity of money.[38]) By virtue of driving down the prices of other assets, of goods in general, and wage rates, it operates to make any given quantity of money stand in a higher ratio to the value of other assets and to spending for goods and labor. It thus operates to increase the degree of liquidity in the economic system and finally to put an end to the desire further to increase cash holdings. To say the same thing in somewhat different words, it operates to increase the so-called quick ratios of corporations and all other businesses and to place them and everyone else in a financially stronger position, in which their cash reserves stand in a higher ratio to their current liabilities, and in which, therefore, the general state of financial solvency is better assured. (Current liabilities are reduced because the fall in wages and prices means that the sums of money owing for any given physical volume of purchases by businesses are correspondingly less.)

If, once and for all, the economic system could achieve a sufficiently high degree of liquidity, and, as a major aspect of this, the threat of mass insolvencies were thereafter removed, there would be no further basis for any contraction in spending. The economic system would operate with less spending relative to the quantity of money (i.e., the so-called velocity of circulation of money would be lower), but that lower relative level of spending would no longer be subject to reduction. From that point on, spending in the economic system could grow modestly from year to year, in line with a modest rate of increase in the quantity of money.[39]

To achieve this highly desirable state of affairs, and, by the same token, to avoid periods in which the economic system is first led into a state of illiquidity through artificial stimulus to overspending, and is thus put in the position in which it requires a financial contraction to restore a sufficient degree of liquidity, what is necessary is a 100-percent-reserve gold standard. This will be shown in Chapter 19, which is devoted to the subject of inflation.[40]

Saving as the Source of Most Spending

Apart from the case of occasional misers, revenue and income that is saved is not only spent fully as much as revenue and income that is consumed, but, in the conditions of a modern economic system, is always spent *on a far greater scale* than revenue and income that is consumed. This is because saving is the source of the demand for all of the labor employed by business firms and for all of the capital goods they buy, such as factory and office buildings, machinery and materials, components and supplies, and goods at wholesale. In addition, it is the source of the demand for all expensive consumers' goods.[41] Even when it is necessary for business firms to reduce their expenditures for the replacement of assets, in order to build up liquidity, saving—on a gross basis, that is, out of business sales revenues—continues to be the source of far more demand than does consumption.

Nevertheless, the role of saving in spending is almost entirely unappreciated. It is unappreciated even in connection with the purchase of expensive consumers' goods, despite the fact that the savings of the ordinary wage earner and of many businessmen and capitalists are normally lent to borrowers precisely for the purpose of making possible the purchase of expensive consumers' goods, notably houses and automobiles. Thus let me begin by pointing out just how dependent is the purchase of expensive consumers' goods on the existence of savings.

Virtually no one can buy a house out of current income. Very few people can buy an automobile out of current income. Most people cannot buy any kind of major appliance or any other expensive consumers' good out of current income. To buy any good whose price exceeds the income of the current pay period, or constitutes any substantial portion of the income of the current pay period, which for most people is only a week or two, it is absolutely indispensable that the buyer have access to savings—either his own or those of a lender. There simply is no other way. If a good costs the income of three years, as is typically the case with houses, then there is no conceivable way that it can be bought without savings. Indeed, if a good costs the income of three weeks, its purchase will require savings. If it costs even as much

as a third of the income of one week, it will probably require savings if its purchase is to be possible, for it probably could not be afforded if it had to deprive the buyer of so much of his other consumption for the week. Saving exists any time income of one pay period is carried over for expenditure on consumers' goods in a later pay period.

In view of these facts, it is nothing short of amazing that serious economists and the financial press could believe that saving depresses spending. Saving is absolutely essential to the spending for housing, automobiles, appliances, and every other expensive or even moderately expensive consumers' good. But these facts only barely begin to indicate the role of saving in spending.

The far greater part of the *wages* paid in the economic system are paid out of savings. In many cases—especially in manufacturing, mining, construction, and agriculture—the period of time which elapses between a wage earner's performance of labor and the readiness for sale of the product he helps to produce exceeds the period of time between the wage earner's performance of labor and the payment of his wages by the employer. For example, a wage earner is typically paid after the performance of one or two week's work. But the product he helps to produce is often not completed and ready for sale for a much longer period than that. In many cases months, and sometimes several years, go by after the completion of a given worker's work and the readiness of his product for sale. In such cases, the worker's wages are paid out of the employer's capital.

Even in those cases in which the wage earner's work contributes to the production of a product that can be sold before it is necessary for the employer to pay his wages, it is probable that the employer will not be *paid* for the product until after he has paid the wages in question. Typically, this is the case whenever the employer sells the product on any kind of credit terms, such as the common practice of giving the customer thirty days in which to pay his bill. In cases of this kind, the source of wages is again clearly the employer's capital, which, of course, represents accumulated savings.

Finally, even in those instances in which the wage earner's work contributes to the production of a product or service for which the employer is paid by the customer *prior* to the payment of the wage earner's wages—such as the case of a waiter or waitress in a restaurant whose customers usually pay in cash rather than by means of credit cards—the payment of the wages still rests on an act of saving, in that the wages are paid with revenues that belong to the employer and which he does not consume. The employer's payment of wages in such cases is still a productive expenditure, not a consumption expenditure. And to make it, the employer must not consume, but save the sales revenues in question.

The only wages in the economic system that are not paid out of savings and which are in fact paid by consumers are wages paid *not for the purpose of making subsequent sales,* i.e., wages paid not for business purposes. The leading examples are the wages of domestic servants and the wages of government officials. And even though the government's payroll is certainly grossly excessive, the proportion of total wage payments in the economic system as a whole that is constituted by consumption expenditure is relatively modest notwithstanding. This is indicated by the fact that while in the United States there are some 18.6 million government employees, whose wages represent consumption expenditure, there are over 90 million employees of private business firms, whose wages represent productive expenditure.[42]

Not only are most wages paid out of savings and constitute productive expenditure, rather than consumption expenditure, but, as I have indicated, the same thing is true of the purchase of *goods* as well. All the goods which businesses purchase at wholesale are paid for out of savings, and the funds expended constitute productive expenditure. All of the machinery, equipment, furnishings, fixtures, factories, and office buildings that businesses buy or pay to have constructed, all of the purchases of materials, components, parts, supplies, fuel, lighting and heating, and so forth that businesses make are paid for out of savings and constitute productive expenditure.

When such purchases—which, of course, must be described as purchases of capital goods—are added up, it is virtually certain that they substantially exceed the purchases of consumers' goods. For example, the sum of the purchase of groceries at wholesale by supermarkets and grocery stores, plus the expenditure for food products by the wholesalers, plus the expenditure for the various ingredients and other supplies by the food processors or manufacturers (which almost always take place at more than one stage of production), plus the expenditure for such things as feed and fertilizer by the farmers, plus the expenditure by all the parties involved for machinery, equipment, fixtures, buildings, power and light, and the like, plus the further expenditures for capital goods by the makers of these things—all these expenditures for capital goods taken together almost certainly add up to substantially more than the expenditure for groceries by consumers at the one, final stage that is constituted by retailing.

Essentially the same principle applies to the cases of clothing, housing, and transportation, and to the economic system in general. Thus, the expenditure to buy capital goods almost certainly exceeds the expenditure to buy consumers' goods. (It necessarily must do so if the percentage of sales revenues of the average business that corresponds to its costs on account of capital goods, including services purchased from other business firms, is anything greater than 50 percent. If, for example, it were 60 percent, then taking the demand for consumers' goods as 100, the demand for capital goods would be expressible as equal the sum of $.6 \times 100 + .6^2 \times 100 + .6^3 \times 100 \ldots + .6^n \times 100$, which ultimately equals 150.)

Even if the expenditure to buy capital goods by itself did not exceed the expenditure to buy consumers' goods, it would still be the case that total productive expenditure, which includes both the demand for capital goods and the demand for labor by business together, far exceeds consumption expenditure. For example, in the case of supermarkets, where the average profit margin is only 2 percent or less, the implication is that 98¢ of every dollar of sales is productively expended (which is why costs come to equal 98 percent of sales revenues). If, of these 98¢ of productive expenditure by the supermarkets, 60¢ are for capital goods whose sellers earn, say, a 10 percent profit margin and productively expend 90 percent of their sales receipts, then, already, productive expenditure equals $1.52 for every $1 of sales receipts from consumers—that is, it equals 98¢ plus 54¢. Of course, it will equal substantially more when the productive expenditures of still more remote stages are added in. Such a relationship between productive expenditure and consumption expenditure prevails throughout the economic system.

It should be realized that not only do saving and productive expenditure far exceed consumption expenditure, but also that they are the *source* of almost all consumption expenditure. The wages paid by business enterprises are the source of most consumption expenditure in the economic system, in that they provide the great majority of people with the incomes out of which they consume. They are also the source of all that consumption expenditure of the government and its employees which is financed with taxes paid out of the wages of the employees of business enterprises.

For the rest, business—in the productive process—is the source of almost all other consumption. What it does not provide for consumption in the way of wage payments, it provides in the way of dividend and interest payments and in the taxes that it itself pays. The only consumption expenditure of which business is not the source is consumption out of newly created fiat money.

From the perspective of the economic system as a whole, *consumption depends on saving and the productive process*—not only in physical terms, but in terms of the financial process of paying out and taking in money. As subsequent discussion in this section and throughout this book will confirm, from the perspective of the economic system as a whole, it is the consumers who are dependent on business, not business on the consumers. The well-known dependence of business on the consumers, which the Austrian school has done so much to demonstrate, and which I myself have elaborated upon in previous chapters, exists at the level of the individual firm and industry, where competition prevails. But at the level of the economic system as a whole, the competition of the individual firms and industries is mutually offsetting, and there the consumers are dependent on business.

The "Macroeconomic" Dependence of the Consumers on Business

As I have said, from the point of view of the economic system as a whole, it is the consumers who are dependent on business, not business on the consumers. Any individual business, any individual industry, to be sure, is always vitally dependent on its customers, and, in the last analysis, on the customers for the final products—the consumers' goods—it directly or indirectly helps to produce. But this is because of the existence of competition among the different business firms and the various industries. The consumers have the power to choose *which* individual business firms and individual industries will receive back the funds they have provided the consumers with—which will receive back more and which will receive back less. But it is nothing but the fallacy of composition to generalize from this "microeconomic" dependence of the individual business and industry on the consumers to a "macroeconomic" dependence of business as a whole on the consumers. When the entire business system is viewed at once, the consumers have no alternative but to spend. Their desire to live and enjoy life impels them to spend. And, of course, their savings, made as provision for the future, are also spent—by virtue of being spent for business purposes, by virtue of being lent to borrowers who spend them either for business purposes or for consumption, and, to some degree, by virtue of being spent for consumption by the savers themselves, later on.

Thus, at the level of the economy as a whole, the dependency is not that of business on the consumers, but, as I say, of the consumers on business. As we shall see, business is in no way dependent on the existence of any definite minimum demand for consumers' goods, for the demand for capital goods is as much a demand for the products of business as is the demand for consumers' goods.[43] At the same time, the consumers are vitally dependent on business for their physical means of survival, well being, and enjoyment. As a result, whatever cash they possess is pulled toward business with the force of a magnet, as it were. At most, it is only a question of how soon they will be drained of all the cash they possess, unless they find ways of continually replenishing their cash by obtaining fresh funds from business, in

exchange for the sale of their labor or in the form of dividends or interest paid by business. The phrase "circular flow of income and expenditure," so popular in today's macroeconomics textbooks, with its implied equality of dependence of consumers on business and business on consumers, is inaccurate. The fact is that *money comes to goods*—automatically, on the strength of people's desire to live and enjoy themselves. What is not automatic, but requires the continuous exercise of intelligence, will, and effort is the process of production.

Consequently, the consumers are dependent on business not only for the production of the products they buy, and thus for the purchasing power of the money they spend in buying them, as I showed in Chapter 13, but also for *the monetary means* of buying them. Apart from the creation of fiat money (which is always a process that tends to undermine production and thus, in the long run, the ability to consume), it is only the expenditures and disbursements of business enterprises that place money in the hands of consumers; only to the degree that one contributes to the production of products to be sold or receives money from those who do, can one obtain the monetary means of consumption.

i. Business as the Source of Its Own Demand and Profitability

Consistent with the preceding, business does not need any outside class of consumers—any deliberately created class of consumers. *It itself generates a monetary demand that is fully sufficient for the profitable sale of its products*. It does so in the mere fact of purchasing capital goods and paying wages and in declaring dividends and paying interest. In addition, the very increase in production itself operates to add further to both the real and the nominal rate of profit (the latter insofar as part of the increase in production is an increase in the supply of precious metals, with the result that under a system of commodity money the by-product of the increase in production is an increase in the quantity of money). I will show all of this in the next chapter, which sets forth my theory of profit and interest, namely, the net-consumption/net-investment theory.

The existence of depressions does not contradict the truth of any of these propositions. The wiping out of profitability that accompanies a depression is the result of a reduction in productive expenditure, which reduces the demand for capital goods, wage payments, and the consumption expenditure of wage earners. Profits are slashed because while these developments reduce the sales revenues of business, its aggregate costs continue to reflect the higher levels of productive expenditure prevailing in the past.

The reduction in productive expenditure, in turn, is

the result of a need of business firms to rebuild their cash balances relative to their outlays and revenues, which need arises because a preceding inflation and credit expansion first induced them to run down their cash balances relative to their outlays and revenues, and to incur unduly large debts besides. The problem of the decline in productive expenditure and sales revenues is compounded by the decline in the quantity of money that can occur under a system of fractional reserve banking.

The solution to the problem of monetary contraction and the wiping out of profitability it engenders is to establish a monetary system which prevents undue increases in the quantity of money, and which prevents decreases in the quantity of money. In preventing the undue increases in the quantity of money, the consequent unduly low level of demand for money for holding would also be prevented, and thus the resulting potential for sudden sharp increases in the demand for money for holding would be eliminated. (For example, in the absence of credit expansion, businessmen would not be misled into believing that they could substitute the prospect of obtaining loans easily and on profitable terms for the holding of actual cash balances. They would thus not be faced later on with the need suddenly to rebuild their cash holdings when the credit expansion was succeeded by a so-called credit crunch.) In these ways, the potential for depressions would be eliminated. Under such a monetary system, productive expenditure and sales revenues would show a modest increase from year to year, accompanying the increase in production and its by-product a modest increase in the quantity of commodity money. Corresponding to the increase in the quantity of commodity money, the nominal rate of profit would, as I say, be moderately elevated. Such a monetary system is, of course, a 100-percent-reserve gold standard.

But even without such a monetary system, business again and again recovers from the depressions inflicted upon it. Once wage rates adjust to the lower level of productive spending, and assets and indebtedness are written down, then, as the net-consumption/net-investment theory of profit will show, virtual "*springs*" to the restoration of profitability come into play, which act as a guarantee of recovery.[44]

ii. No Need for Artificial Consumption

The corollary of the fact that business is the source of its own monetary demand and profitability is that consumers have absolutely nothing of value to offer business that is apart from their contribution to the productive process. The money they spend in buying from business is of value to business only insofar as they have first received it from business, in connection with such contribution. In the case of the consumption of wage earners,

business first receives services equivalent in monetary value to the means of consumption which it places in their hands. In the case of the owners and creditors of business enterprises, consumption is a matter of those whose activity underlies and guides the whole productive process consuming a portion of their own property. If it were financed on a voluntary basis, no criticism could be made even of the government's consumption insofar as it was for the purpose of carrying out its strictly limited and indispensable functions, which are an essential safeguard of the productive process.[45]

But it is an altogether different matter when consumption takes place allegedly in order to benefit business by the very fact of its being consumption. Such consumption, which invariably takes place in the form of unnecessarily large government spending, whether financed by additional taxation or by an expansion of the money supply, can only be detrimental to business. If the government imposes additional taxes on business to finance its additional expenditures, then what it does is first reduce the cash holdings of business, and then restore them in the purchase of its products. The effect is that the government consumes without giving business anything in return. Indeed, to produce for the government's consumption, business is correspondingly prevented from producing capital goods for its own use or consumers' goods for the consumption of its employees and owners and creditors. The taxes it pays deprive it of the ability to purchase capital goods and to pay wages, dividends, and interest. The taxes thereby reduce the demand for capital goods and for consumers' goods by wage earners and dividend and interest recipients. Thus, the government's demand takes the place of these demands.

If the taxes are imposed directly on wage earners, then the government's consumption is mainly substituted for their consumption, and the loss falls mainly on them, with the likely outcome that their motivation to work is reduced.

If the taxes are imposed directly on dividend or interest recipients, the effect is largely the same as if they were imposed on business enterprises themselves, for it is to reduce the demand for capital goods and labor. Indeed, this is the overwhelming effect in both cases—that of business enterprises themselves and dividend and interest recipients—inasmuch as the consumption of businessmen and capitalists is governed mainly by the size of their capitals rather than their after-tax incomes, and will thus be reduced relatively little by the taxes, which means that the taxes will fall mainly on saving and productive expenditure.[46]

If the government finances its additional expenditures by means of an expansion of the money supply, then in return for what it consumes, it gives money. But the additional money is of no benefit to the economic system, for either in the very spending of it prices are correspondingly increased or prevented from falling, with the result that the government's added purchases come at the expense of the reduced purchases of the citizens, or inventories are drawn down, thereby leaving business with more money but a smaller supply of assets with which to carry on production. In addition, all the other destructive effects of inflation ensue.[47]

In closing this discussion of artificially created consumption, it is appropriate to quote the words of John Stuart Mill on the subject:

> It is not necessary, in the present state of the science, to contest this doctrine in the most flagrantly absurd of its forms or of its applications. The utility of a large government expenditure, for the purpose of encouraging industry, is no longer maintained. Taxes are not now esteemed to be "like the dews of heaven, which return again in prolific showers." It is no longer supposed that you benefit the producer by taking his money, provided you give it to him again in exchange for his goods. There is nothing which impresses a person of reflection with a stronger sense of the shallowness of the political reasonings of the last two centuries [the seventeenth and eighteenth], than the general reception so long given to a doctrine which, if it proves anything, proves that the more you take from the pockets of the people to spend on your own pleasures, the richer they grow; that the man who steals money out of a shop, provided he expends it all again at the same shop, is a benefactor to the tradesman whom he robs, and that the same operation repeated sufficiently often, would make the tradesman's fortune.

> In opposition to these palpable absurdities, it was triumphantly established by political economists, that consumption never needs encouragement. All which is produced is already consumed, either for the purpose of reproduction or of enjoyment. The person who saves his income is no less a consumer than he who spends it: he consumes it in a different way; it supplies food and clothing to be consumed, tools and materials to be used, by productive labourers. Consumption, therefore, already takes place to the greatest extent which the amount of production admits of; but, of the two kinds of consumption, reproductive and unproductive, the former alone adds to the national wealth, the latter impairs it. What is consumed for mere enjoyment, is gone; what is consumed for reproduction, leaves commodities of equal value, commonly with the addition of a profit. The usual effect of the attempts of government to encourage consumption, is merely to prevent saving; that is, to promote unproductive consumption at the expense of reproductive, and diminish the national wealth by the very means which were intended to increase it.[48]

Saving as the Source of Increasing Aggregate Demand, Both Real and Monetary

Saving is not only the source of most spending at any given time, but it is also a vital source of the increase in aggregate real demand. Our discussion of Say's Law has shown that aggregate real demand is determined by aggregate supply.[49] We have also seen that saving vitally contributes to the increase in aggregate supply by bringing about the dedication of a sufficiently high proportion of existing factors of production to the production of capital goods, which, in turn, makes possible capital accumulation, a rising productivity of labor, and thus an increasing supply of goods coming to market. We saw too that it contributes to the same result insofar as it raises the degree of capital intensiveness in the economic system and thereby permits the implementation of a wider range of technological advances. Thus, saving operates to increase aggregate real demand.[50]

Previous discussion has also shown that there is no fundamental scarcity of any natural resource, including the precious metals, and thus that general increases in the ability to produce are bound to result in an increase in the supply of the precious metals.[51] It follows that under a system of commodity money the effect of saving—if carried on, on a sufficient scale—is, indirectly, to bring about an increase in the quantity of money. This, of course, is the foundation for a rising aggregate monetary demand—a rising volume of total spending in the economic system—over time. Thus, saving not only does not reduce the total of what is spent in the economic system, but, under commodity money, operates positively and progressively to increase it!

As illustration of this principle, one can take the whole of economic history since the beginning of the Industrial Revolution. The massive capital accumulation and rising productivity of labor of the modern era would have been impossible without the very great increase in the degree of saving and capital intensiveness that took place in comparison with previous eras. A virtually inevitable concomitant of the process, reflecting improvements that thereby became possible in mining, transportation, and engineering, metallurgical, and chemical processes in general was a much more rapid rate of increase in the supply of the precious metals than had previously occurred. Because of its high degree of saving and capital intensiveness, the modern era surpasses previous eras in its ability to increase the supply of precious metals as well as in its ability to increase the supply of goods in general.

Saving as the Source of Rising Consumption

It further follows from the preceding discussions that saving is the source of an increase in consumption, both in real and in monetary terms.

Insofar as more saving means more production of capital goods at the expense of less production of consumers' goods, the drop in consumers' goods production is strictly temporary. Once the additional supply of capital goods comes into existence, it increases the total ability to produce in the economic system. The result is that the supply of consumers' goods begins to come back up and the supply of capital goods is further increased. The further increase in the supply of capital goods makes possible a further increase in the supply both of consumers' goods and capital goods. Soon the production of consumers' goods surpasses the level it held prior to the shift of factors of production to the production of capital goods, and with each passing year it does so by an ever widening margin.[52]

To employ the popular economic analogy of shares of a pie, the smaller is the proportion of the economic pie that is devoted to the production of consumers' goods and the larger the proportion that is devoted to the production of capital goods, the more rapidly does the total pie grow. The result is that soon, in absolute terms, the smaller consumption share of a growing, or more rapidly growing, economic pie surpasses the larger consumption share of the concomitantly fixed, or less rapidly growing, economic pie.

As an illustration of this principle, one need only consider the post–World War II economic history of Japan. Japan has achieved rapid economic progress in large part by means of devoting a greater proportion of each year's production to the production of capital goods than almost any other country. The result has been that each year the Japanese economy is able to take advantage of a substantially larger supply of capital goods than the year before and to produce a correspondingly larger output. The larger output is the source both of more consumers' goods and more capital goods. Because of its low relative production of consumers' goods and high relative production of capital goods, Japan is today able to consume vastly more in absolute terms than would have been possible otherwise.

What is true in real terms is no less true in monetary terms. The growing quantity of precious metal money that general increases in the ability to produce make possible soon increase the total ability to spend to the point that the smaller proportion of total spending that is constituted by expenditure for consumers' goods comes to surpass in absolute terms the larger proportion previously devoted to expenditure for consumers' goods. This phenomenon, of course, is reinforced by the fact that countries whose economies grow relative to the world average attract a growing proportion of the world's money supply.[53] In today's monetary conditions, Japan's rapidly growing increase in ability to produce is responsible for the fact that consumption expenditure in the Japanese paper currency now represents enormously more than it used to, both in real terms and as a fraction of total consumption expenditure in the world economy.

As a final point in connection with the relationship between consumption and saving, it should be explicitly understood that insofar as what is saved is used to pay wages, there is little or no drop in consumption spending even temporarily. For the wage earners use the far greater part of their wages to consume. Closely related to this point is the fact that most saving by wage earners is used to finance the purchase of expensive consumers' goods, such as houses or automobiles, or at least has its counterpart in the use of savings for this purpose. To this extent, as I say, saving does not represent a drop in consumption spending even temporarily. Of course, to this extent, saving also does not operate to bring about any progressive increase in production and the quantity of money, either. These results occur only insofar as saving brings about an increase in the relative production of capital goods and decrease in the relative production of consumers' goods. This occurs primarily, as we shall see, to the extent that businessmen and capitalists reduce the proportion of their sales revenues that they consume and increase the proportion that they save and productively expend.

3. Aggregate Economic Accounting on an Aristotelian Base

The purpose of this section is to reconcile national income accounting with the Aristotelian proposition that the demand for A is the demand for A, and with the consequent further proposition that most spending in the economic system is productive expenditure, not consumption expenditure. This is essential in that contemporary national income accounting gives every appearance of supporting the opposite and totally wrong conclusions that consumption spending, besides purchasing consumers' goods, pays most of the incomes in the economic system and is far and away the main form of spending. This section will demonstrate that when properly understood, national income accounting fully confirms the propositions I have advanced.

The central accounting relationship recognized by contemporary economics is that national income—consisting of the sum of all profit, interest, wage, and rental incomes—equals the sum of consumption spending plus net investment, which last sum is called the net national product (NNP). Symbolically,

$$p + w + i + r = Y = NNP = C + I,$$

where p = profits, w = wages, i = interest income, r = rental income, Y = national income, C = total consumption spending, and I = net investment.

According to contemporary economics, when depreciation allowances are added to the aggregate profit component of national income, profits are raised to gross profits and national income is raised to gross national income. When the same depreciation allowances are added to net investment, net investment is raised to "gross" investment, consisting of spending for plant and equipment plus, be it noted, the *net* change in business inventories. At the same time, NNP is raised to GNP.[54]

The reason that the addition of depreciation allowances to net investment has the above result follows from the nature of net investment. Net investment is the sum of net investment in plant and equipment plus net investment in inventories. Net investment in plant and equipment is equal to expenditure to purchase plant and equipment minus depreciation allowances. Thus, when depreciation allowances are added back in, net investment in plant and equipment is raised to gross investment in plant and equipment, i.e., to expenditure for plant and equipment. However, it is a curious and highly misleading use of terms to call the sum of gross investment in plant and equipment plus the *net* investment in inventories "gross investment." It is part and parcel of the misidentification of gross national product as the final product, which, of course, is nothing more than the *net* national product. In other words, it is an instance of the pervasive confusion on the part of contemporary economics between gross and net. As I will show, a true gross investment figure would require the further addition of *cost of goods sold*, which would raise net investment in inventories to productive expenditure on account of inventory.[55] As matters stand, gross national product is explicitly presented as the sum of consumption expenditure plus a gross investment that is actually net investment as far as inventories are concerned.

The Consumption Illusion of Contemporary National-Income Accounting

The misconceptions of contemporary economics concerning the nature of what is produced and what is purchased both profoundly influence and, in turn, are greatly reinforced by contemporary national income accounting. The equality between national income, on the one side, and consumption plus net investment, i.e., net national product, on the other, is interpreted to mean that consumption and net investment *pay* the national income. And because consumption spending is several times larger than net or even gross investment, contemporary economics assumes that consumption spending pays the far greater part of national income and constitutes the far greater part of spending for goods and services in the economic system. This view is present in every depiction of national income as being determined

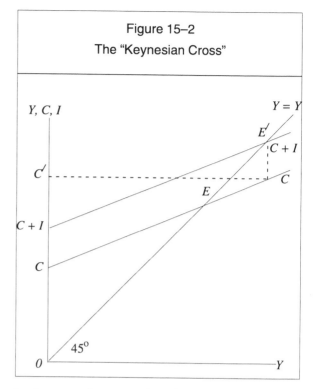

Figure 15–2
The "Keynesian Cross"

by the sum of consumption plus net investment. It is blatantly obvious in the so-called Keynesian-cross diagram of Figure 15–2, which is an integral part of every contemporary macroeconomics textbook and is faithfully reproduced there.[56]

According to this diagram, consumption pays an amount of income equal to E, if net investment does not exist at all. Given the existence of net investment, which is depicted as the vertical distance between the C and the $C + I$ lines, consumption is held to pay an amount of income equal to E' minus I. By following the dashed lines down from E' *to the $C + I$ line* and then across to the vertical axis, one can see that this amount of consumption is supposedly equal to C'.

As we have seen, of course, the actual fact is that most spending and income payments are constituted by productive expenditure, not consumption expenditure. The equality between national income, on the one side, and consumption plus net investment, on the other, represents an optical illusion, as it were, insofar as it leads to the conclusion that consumption is the major item of spending and pays most of the incomes in the economic system. Actually, most of the spending and income payments in the economic system *are concealed under net investment,* which, in effect, is the visible portion of an iceberg. For net investment, as we shall see, is *the difference between total productive expenditure in the economic system and aggregate business costs*—that is, the aggregate of the costs that business firms deduct from their sales revenues in calculating their profits.

All this becomes obvious if we take the trouble to go through a step-by-step derivation of the equality of national income with consumption plus net investment. I begin with a simplified definition of national income as the sum of profits plus wages. (I count interest income and all genuine "net rental incomes of persons" under the heading of profits. I do so not only for the sake of simplicity, but also because of their actual economic nature.[57])

Thus, we have, by definition,

$$(1) \qquad p + w = Y,$$

where p = profit, w = wages, and Y = national income.

We also have, by the common accounting definition of profit,

$$(2) \qquad p = s - d,$$

where s = aggregate business sales revenues, and d = aggregate business costs deducted from sales revenues in calculating profits.

It follows that by substituting (2) into (1), we obtain

$$(3) \qquad s - d + w = Y.$$

At this point I divide sales revenues and wage payments from the perspective of the purpose of the parties paying the sales revenues or wages, that is, from the perspective of whether the expenditures are made *for* the purpose of making subsequent sales or *not* for the purpose of making subsequent sales. My procedure is strictly in accordance with the concepts I developed earlier, in Chapter 11.[58] Thus, we now obtain

$$(4) \qquad s = s_c + s_b$$

and

$$(5) \qquad w = w_c + w_b,$$

where s_c = that part of total business sales revenues paid by consumers, i.e., paid not for the purpose of making subsequent sales; s_b = that part of total business sales revenues paid by business firms, i.e., paid for the purpose of making subsequent sales; w_c = that part of total wages paid by consumers, i.e., paid not for the purpose of making subsequent sales; and w_b = that part of total wages paid by business, i.e., paid for the purpose of making subsequent sales.[59]

I must stress that s_c, s_b, w_c, and w_b represent *revenue-expenditure subcomponents* of national income and net national product in that they simultaneously represent revenue or income, when viewed from the perspective of sellers, and expenditure, when viewed from the perspective of buyers.

Now, by substituting equations (4) and (5) into equation (3), we obtain

$$(6) \qquad s_c + s_b - d + w_c + w_b = Y.$$

The verbal meaning of equation (6) is that national income is equal to the sum of the part of business sales revenues constituted by consumption expenditure plus the part of business sales revenues constituted by productive expenditure, minus business costs, plus the sum of the part of wages constituted by consumption expenditure plus the part of wages constituted by productive expenditure—that is, that national income is still equal to the sum of profits plus wages, but expressed now in terms of their revenue-expenditure subcomponents.

It further follows that by a change in the order of addition of the revenue-expenditure subcomponents, we obtain

$$(7) \qquad s_c + w_c + s_b + w_b - d = Y.$$

Now, one should realize that

$$(8) \qquad s_c + w_c = C,$$

that is, that consumption expenditure for goods and services purchased from business firms plus consumption expenditure in payment of wages equals total consumption expenditure constituting revenue or income.

In addition, one should realize that

$$(9) \qquad s_b + w_b = B,$$

that is, that productive expenditure for goods and services purchased from business firms plus productive expenditure in payment of wages equals total productive expenditure constituting revenue or income.

By substituting equations (8) and (9) into equation (7), it follows that

$$(10) \qquad C + B - d = Y.$$

Essentially all that remains is to realize that

$$(11) \qquad B - d = I,$$

for reasons to be explained shortly.

Thus, finally, by substituting equation (11) into equation (10), we see that

$$(12) \qquad C + I = Y.$$

Consequently, we see that the equality between national income and net national product turns out to be a mathematical identity, in which the only difference is a change in the order of addition of identical terms, namely, the revenue-expenditure subcomponents and aggregate business costs.

The full statement of the relationship between national income and net national product is

$$(13) \qquad Y = p + w = (s_c + s_b - d) + (w_c + w_b) =$$

$$(s_c + w_c) + (s_b + w_b - d) = C + B - d = C + I = NNP.$$

The first formulation is national income in terms of its income components, profits and wages; the next formulation is national income in terms of its revenue-expenditure subcomponents; then, by a rearrangement of the order of addition, *net national product* in terms of its revenue-expenditure subcomponents; then net national product in terms of its expenditure components, namely, consumption expenditure plus productive expenditure minus business costs; and finally, net national product stated as the sum of consumption plus net investment.[60]

i. Net Investment as Productive Expenditure Minus Business Costs

I now must show why productive expenditure minus business costs—the same costs as are deducted from sales revenues in calculating profits—equals net investment. This, of course, is the demonstration of equation (11) above—namely, $B - d = I$.

For the benefit of readers with no background in business accounting, I offer as helpful adjuncts the essential elements both of a business balance sheet and of a business income statement. The balance sheet appears as Figure 15–3, and the income statement as Figure 15–4. In the balance sheet, our focus will be on the "Inventory and Work in Progress" account and on the three fixed-asset accounts "Gross Plant and Equipment and Other Fixed Assets," "Accumulated Depreciation Reserve," and "Net Plant and Equipment and Other Fixed Assets." (For the sake of brevity, I will often refer just to plant and equipment, though it should be realized that everything that applies to their accounting treatment applies to the accounting treatment of other types of fixed assets as well, such as office buildings, warehouses, and pipelines.) In the income statement, our focus will be primarily on the two cost elements "Depreciation" and "Cost of Goods Sold."

The reason that productive expenditure minus business costs equals net investment is that productive expenditure (viewed from the perspective of those making the productive expenditures) represents debits or pluses to the above asset accounts in the balance sheets of business firms, while business costs represent credits or minuses to those asset accounts. The difference between the sum of the pluses and the minuses is the *net change* in the asset values of business firms. This net change in the balance-sheet value—the so-called book value—of business assets is *net investment*.

Productive expenditure embraces the outlays for plant and equipment and all other fixed assets by business. It also embraces the outlays for materials, components, and supplies by business—viz., all the items entering into work in progress or inventories. These outlays represent both purchases of capital goods and wage payments. The outlays for machinery, materials and other capital goods can probably be readily understood as representing additions to asset accounts. But wage payments too are included in the items debited to asset accounts. For example, the wages of construction workers come under the heading of productive expenditure on account of plant and equipment and are debited to the gross plant and equipment account. The wages of direct manufacturing labor come under the heading of productive expenditure on account of work in progress or inventories and are debited to the inventory and work in progress account.

These productive expenditures are related to the costs of production incurred by business firms, but they do not show up directly and immediately as costs of production. Instead, as I have just indicated, they are *capitalized*—that is, debited to the plant and equipment or inventory and work in progress accounts. Only later, as the plant and equipment or other fixed assets that have been purchased *depreciate*, and when the inventories that have been purchased or that result from work in progress are *sold*, do these productive expenditures show up as costs of production in business income statements, where they are deducted from sales revenues in arriving at profits. And at that time, the costs, in the form of depreciation and cost of goods sold, represent a *decapitalization* of assets—that is, they are deducted from the plant and equipment or inventory and work in progress accounts.

The relationships can be illustrated at the level of an individual company. Thus, for example, if a company spends $10 million to construct a new factory, which will last 50 years, it certainly does not deduct that $10 million from its current year's sales revenues. Instead, the sum is capitalized, in the form of being added to its gross plant and equipment account. Depending on the particular depreciation method employed, the $10 million acquisition cost of the factory may very well show up as an annual depreciation cost of $200,000 for each of the next 50 years. And as the depreciation costs are incurred, the net value of the factory on the company's books undergoes a corresponding diminution. While its acquisition value of $10 million stays on the company's books under the heading gross plant and equipment so long as the factory is owned, each passing year is accompanied by a $200,000 increase in the accumulated depreciation reserve against the factory. Thus, each year the value shown for the factory under the heading net plant and equipment declines by $200,000. If the firm had no other purchases of plant and equipment, it would show a net investment of $10 million in the period in which the factory was being constructed, and thereafter a net *dis*investment of $200,000 a year. The principle is that the outlay is capitalized—added to assets—and the depreciation cost corresponding to the outlay represents decapitalization—a subtraction from assets.

Exactly the same principle applies to inventory and

Figure 15–3

The Elements of the Balance Sheet

ASSETS	LIABILITIES
Cash	
	Borrowed Capital
Gross Plant and Equipment and Other Fixed Assets	
less: Accumulated Depreciation Reserve	
Net Plant and Equipment and Other Fixed Assets	Equity Capital
Inventory and Work in Progress	

work in progress. For example, if an automobile company spends $1 billion in November or December to produce automobiles that it will not sell until January or February of the following year, its outlay of $1 billion does not show up in its costs deducted from sales revenues in the current year. Instead, the outlay is capitalized in its inventory or work in progress account, which is increased by that amount. Only next year, when the resulting automobiles are sold, will the $1 billion show up as a cost deducted from sales revenues. It will show up under the heading "cost of goods sold." And when the automobiles are sold, the inventory and work in progress account of the automobile company is decreased by $1

billion. In other words, the $1 billion of cost of goods sold in the company's income statement will correspond to a disinvestment of a $1 billion in its inventory and work in progress account.

Once again, the sequence is: productive expenditure, capitalization of productive expenditure in asset account, decapitalization of asset account, cost in income statement.

It should be obvious that to whatever extent any company makes productive expenditures for plant and equipment or other fixed assets that are greater than the depreciation cost it incurs in the same period of time, it experiences a corresponding increase in the value of its

Figure 15–4

The Elements of the Income Statement

Sales

Costs

    Depreciation

    Cost of Goods Sold

    Selling, General, and Administrative Expenses

Net Profit Before Taxes

plant and equipment account net of accumulated depreciation. For it has capitalized a larger sum under the heading of gross plant and equipment than it has decapitalized under the heading of accumulated depreciation reserve. To state the matter in slightly different words: The sum of all of a company's outlays past and present for the plant and equipment that is still in its possession is its gross plant and equipment account. When the total of accumulated depreciation on all of those assets is subtracted from the gross plant and equipment account, the result is the net plant and equipment account. To the extent that in any given year a company makes productive expenditures for plant and equipment in excess of that year's depreciation charges, it adds more to the value of its gross plant and equipment account than it adds to the accumulated depreciation reserve that is deducted from that account. Thus, the value of its net plant and equipment account increases to precisely the same extent. This increase in the value of the net plant and equipment account is, of course, net investment in plant and equipment.

In just the same way, to whatever extent any company makes productive expenditures on account of inventories or work in progress that exceed the cost of goods sold it incurs over the same period of time, it must have a corresponding net investment in inventory/work in progress. This is because its productive expenditures for inventory or work in progress will have added to this account a larger sum than its cost of goods sold has subtracted from it, and thus it will have an increase in the book value of its inventory/work in progress account.

It should be realized that implicit in the preceding discussion is the fact that net investment need not always be positive. It can be a negative number. This will be the case if current outlays for plant and equipment are less than current depreciation charges, or if current outlays for inventory or work in progress are less than cost of goods sold. Such conditions exist in the descent into a depression, when productive expenditure sharply declines, while costs, especially depreciation, fall to a much lesser extent, owing to their determination by productive expenditures of the past.

Now productive expenditures on account of plant and equipment and other fixed assets, and on account of inventory and work in progress, do not account for all of productive expenditure, nor do depreciation and cost of goods sold account for all of business costs. There are expenditures firms make in buying from other firms and in paying wages, which are *expensed*—that is, not debited to physical assets, but deducted as they are made, from sales receipts. Expenditures are expensed, as a rule, when they do not directly contribute to the buying firm's acquisition of tangible goods. This is the situation, for

example, with respect to the salaries of sales and clerical help, advertising outlays, and lighting and heating bills. Such expenditures can be taken as coinciding with the cost category "Selling, General, and Administrative Expenses" in the income statement of Figure 15–4.

These expensed expenditures constitute the remainder of business costs that are subtracted from sales revenues in arriving at the income-statement item "Net Profit Before Taxes." Thus, total business costs equal depreciation plus cost of goods sold plus expensed expenditures. However, because, by definition, expensed expenditures are costs which are identical with the productive expenditures constituting them, they can be added both to the sum of productive expenditures for the various fixed assets and for inventory and work in progress, and to the sum of depreciation plus cost of goods sold, without in any way affecting the difference between these magnitudes. It is a question of adding equals to unequals, which leaves the amount of the inequality unaffected. When added to the productive expenditures for the various fixed assets and for inventory/work in progress, they result in total productive expenditures constituting revenue or income to sellers. When added to depreciation plus cost of goods sold, they result in total business costs. Net investment is thus the difference between such productive spending and the business costs deducted from business sales revenues in computing profits, which is what I set out to prove.

The preceding discussion can be summarized in the form of the matrix shown as Table 15–2. In the table, productive expenditure, which equals the sum of $s_b + w_b$ and is represented by B, is broken down into $B_1 + B_2 + B_3$, where B_1 = productive expenditure on account of plant and equipment, B_2 = productive expenditure on account of inventory, and B_3 = productive expenditure that is expensed, i.e., written off as made. (For the sake of brevity, I have omitted reference both to "other fixed assets" in connection with plant and equipment and to "work in progress" in connection with inventory, and will hereafter continue this practice.) In exactly the same way, aggregate business costs d are broken down into d_1, d_2, and d_3, where d_1 = depreciation cost, d_2 = cost of goods sold, and d_3 = cost constituted by productive expenditure that is expensed. In the table, I represents total net investment, while I_1 is net investment in plant and equipment, and I_2 is net investment in inventory.

Table 15–2 shows that when all costs together—namely, d—are subtracted from the totality of productive expenditure, B, the result is total net investment, I. It shows at the same time that when depreciation cost, d_1, is subtracted from productive expenditure on account of plant and equipment, namely, B_1, the result is net investment in plant and equipment, I_1. At the same time, it

Table 15–2

Productive Expenditure Minus Costs Equals Net Investment

B	=	B_1	+	B_2	+	B_3
$-d$	=	$-d_1$	+	$-d_2$	+	$-d_3$
I	=	I_1	+	I_2	+	0

shows that when cost of goods sold, d_2, is subtracted from productive expenditure on account of inventory, B_2, the result is net investment in inventory, I_2. Finally, the table shows that when costs constituted by productive expenditures that are expensed, d_3, are subtracted from those same productive expenditures, B_3, the result is zero, inasmuch as the two magnitudes are identical. Thus, the table shows simultaneously that net investment is productive expenditure minus costs and is equal to net investment in plant and equipment plus net investment in inventory, both of which in turn are equal to specific categories of productive expenditure minus specific categories of cost.

Table 15–2 makes it possible to relate the analysis I have presented, to contemporary national income accounting. We have seen that in contemporary national income accounting, net investment is defined as gross investment minus depreciation, and that gross investment itself is defined as gross plant and equipment expenditure plus the *net change* in inventories. The analysis I have presented can be understood in terms of a concept of gross investment that is larger than that which is usually called gross investment. Call it gross gross (double gross) investment. Gross gross investment is the entire expenditure that firms make for tangible goods obtained from other firms and for labor that they directly employ in the production of tangible goods. It is gross plant and equipment expenditure plus actual, gross expenditure for inventory—in terms of Table 15–2, it is $B_1 + B_2$. Subtract from this amount "cost of goods sold," and one has what is usually called gross investment, for gross expenditure for inventory less cost of goods sold is the net inventory change. Net investment, obviously, is the difference between gross gross investment and depreciation plus cost of goods sold.

The addition of expensed productive expenditures to gross gross investment, of course, raises the latter to productive expenditure. Starting with productive expenditure, productive expenditure minus expensed expenditures equals gross gross investment expenditure. Gross gross investment expenditure minus cost of goods sold

equals gross investment. Gross investment minus depreciation equals net investment. All of this adds up to the fact that productive expenditure minus business costs equals net investment. At the same time, it helps to point the way to the integration of national income accounting with the wider, Aristotelian and classical-economics-based accounting framework of my own.

ii. Net Investment as the Tip of the Productive Expenditure Iceberg

Now that the relationship between net investment and productive expenditure has been made clear, it is possible to understand how contemporary national income accounting completely misinterprets the equality between national income and net national product. Table 15–3 provides an arithmetical example that clearly illustrates the illusion of viewing consumption spending as the main source of revenue and income payments in the economic system.

The table assumes the existence of a national income/net national product of 600 monetary units. This amount appears in the second row of the center column of the table, under the heading *Y/NNP*. The 600 is respectively equal both to a sum of 150 of profit income plus 450 of wage income, shown on the left-hand side of the table, and to a sum of 550 of consumption expenditure plus 50 of net investment, shown on the right-hand side of the table. Like the 600 of national income/net national product, these magnitudes are shown in the second row of the table, under the respective column headings for the various magnitudes, which occupy the first row of the table. (It should be observed that the table's relative breakdown of national income between profit and wages, and of net national product between consumption expenditure and net investment, approximates the actual data found in a typical year.)

In the third row, the table states the profit and wage components of national income, and the consumption and net-investment components of net national product, in terms of their identical but differently ordered revenue-expenditure subcomponents. These revenue-expenditure subcomponents, of course, were explained earlier

	Table 15–3									
	The Optical Illusion of Consumption as the Main Form of Spending									
(1)	p	+	w	=	Y/NNP	=	C	+	I	
(2)	150	+	450	=	600	=	550	+	50	
(3)	$(s_c + s_b - d)$	+	$(w_c + w_b)$	=	Y	=	$(s_c + w_c)$	+	$(s_b + w_b - d)$	
(4)	(500+500−850)	+	(50+400)	=	600	=	(500+50)	+	(500+400−850)	

in this section, in my derivation of the equality between national income and net national product. I use the same algebraic notation in the table as I did in that derivation.

In the fourth row of the table, I supply specific quantitative values for each of the revenue-expenditure subcomponents. Thus I assume that the 150 of profit income is the result of the existence of 1,000 of aggregate business sales revenues, less 850 of aggregate business costs. I further assume that the sales revenues are constituted by 500 of consumption expenditure, s_c, plus 500 of productive expenditure, s_b. I also assume that the 450 of wages are constituted by 50 of wages paid by consumers, w_c, plus 400 of wages paid by business firms, w_b. On the basis of previous discussion, I believe I am entitled to say that the assumed relative values of productive expenditure and consumption expenditure are in accordance with the actual facts.

It is obvious from the table that total expenditure and total revenue and income payments in the economic system are not the national income/net national product figure of 600, or even a gross national product figure of the 600 plus depreciation charges, but *1450*. That is, it is the sum of product sales revenues of 1,000 plus 450 of wage payments. It is also obvious that the portion of total revenue and income payments constituted by consumption expenditure is a mere 550 out of this 1450 (i.e., $500s_c$ + $50w_c$), while the portion of total revenue and income payments constituted by productive expenditure is 900 (i.e., $500s_b$ + $400w_b$).

Indeed, things are virtually the *opposite* of what contemporary, Keynesian economics believes in connection with the relative quantitative significance of consumption expenditure. Instead of consumption expenditure constituting $11/12$ ($550/600$) of aggregate spending and paying $11/12$ of national income, while net investment constitutes and pays only $1/12$ ($50/600$), the truth is that

consumption expenditure constitutes only 550 out of 1450 of total spending and pays only a mere 50 of income out of 600 of income. By the same token, productive expenditure, concealed under the head of net investment, constitutes 900 out of 1450 of total spending, and pays *400* out of the 600 of national income. (Productive expenditure pays 400 out of the 450 of total wage income. The 150 of profit income is not literally "paid" by any expenditure. Five hundred of productive expenditure and 500 of consumption expenditure pay 1,000 of sales revenues, on which 150 of profit income is earned. Accordingly, one might attribute 75 of profit income to productive expenditure and 75 to consumption expenditure. This procedure would make productive expenditure responsible for 475 of national income, and consumption expenditure responsible for 125.)

What conceals the enormous role of productive expenditure in today's national income accounts is that its presence is only implicit, in the form of net investment. Net investment, of course, is productive expenditure minus a magnitude that necessarily is always at least almost as large, namely, aggregate business costs. Thus, it is only a modest residual of productive expenditure that manages to come through in today's accounts, thereby creating the impression that most spending and income payments take place in the form of consumption expenditure. This is why, insofar as sources of spending are concerned, I have described net investment as the tip of the productive expenditure iceberg.

Gross National Revenue

The preceding discussion shows that if one wants to make the national income accounts consistent with sound economic analysis and a proper recognition of the role of saving and productive expenditure in spending and income payments, a fundamental change in procedure is required. What I suggest is taking a new, much larger

Table 15–4									
From Gross National Revenue to National Income and Net National Product									
s	+	w	=	GNR	=	C	+		B
– d			=	– d	=				– d
p	+	w	=	Y/NNP	=	C	+		I

figure than gross national product as the conceptual starting point—namely, the sum of all revenue and income payments in the economic system. This total, *gross national revenue* (GNR), would consist of the sum of business sales revenues *s* plus wage incomes *w*, on the one side, and the sum of the consumption expenditure, *C*, plus the productive expenditure, *B*, that pays those revenues and incomes, on the other side. This is shown in the following equation:

$$s + w = GNR = C + B$$

Table 15–4 shows how it is possible to begin with this equation and then go directly to national income, on the left, and to net national product, on the right, by subtracting aggregate business costs *d*. On the left, *d* is subtracted from *s*, which results in aggregate profit *p*, and which reduces the sum of sales revenues plus wages, which is gross national revenue, to the sum of profits plus wages, which is national income. On the right, *d* is subtracted from productive expenditure, which results in net investment, *I*, and which reduces the sum of consumption expenditure plus productive expenditure (also equal to gross national revenue) to the sum of consumption expenditure plus net investment.

It should be noted that if, in this procedure, one subtracts all costs but depreciation cost, one arrives at the contemporary concept of GNP. That is, one has profit gross of depreciation on the left, and "gross" investment—i.e., plant and equipment spending plus the *net* investment in inventories—on the right. (One could, of course, introduce all of the intermediate steps described earlier in going from productive expenditure to net investment.)

More on the Critique of the Multiplier

The gross-national-revenue framework provides an excellent vehicle for illustrating in precise quantitative terms what is wrong with the Keynesian multiplier doctrine. That doctrine, it should be recalled, claims that a given increase in "investment" brings about a series of further increases in consumption, thereby resulting in an increase in national income that is a multiple of the original increase in investment. For example, with a "marginal propensity to consume" (viz., fraction of additional income consumed at each round) of .75, 10 of additional net investment is supposed to result in 30 of additional consumption and thus 40 of additional national income.[61]

Now the gross-national-revenue framework necessary for the analysis of the multiplier has already been presented in Table 15–3, "The Optical Illusion of Consumption as the Main Form of Spending." Table 15–3 is reproduced in Table 15–5, titled "The 'Multiplier' in the GNR Framework." In Table 15–5 two new rows have been added to those of the earlier table. The first of these new rows, Row 3, shows the alleged operation of the multiplier in the superficial terms in which the Keynesians propound it, that is, in terms merely of net investment and consumption. Thus, in the rightmost column, the table shows net investment increased by 10, that is, to 60 from the 50 of the second row. One column to the left, it also shows consumption increased by 30, that is, from the 550 of the second row to the 580 of the third row. On this basis, in the center column, the table dutifully shows national income and net national product increased from 600 to 640. Unlike the Keynesians, however, Row 3 shows on its left-hand side that the 40 of additional net national product and national income takes place specifically in the form of 40 of additional *profit* income and no additional wage income. This is a result that the highly superficial analysis of the Keynesians is unaware of and incapable of realizing. For the ability to recognize it depends on the use of the gross-national-revenue framework, which appears in the next three rows of the table.

Of those next three rows, the first two, that is, Rows 4 and 5, are reproduced exactly from Table 15–3. Only the last, Row 6 in the table, is new. It shows, in the rightmost column, that 10 of additional net investment comes about by virtue of 10 of additional s_b, which rises

\multicolumn{11}{c}{Table 15–5}										
\multicolumn{11}{c}{The "Multiplier" in the GNR Framework}										
(1)	p	+	w	=	Y/NNP	=	C	+	I	
(2)	150	+	450	=	600	=	550	+	50	
(3)	190	+	450	=	640	=	580	+	60	
(4)	$(s_c + s_b - d)$	+	$(w_c + w_b)$	=	Y	=	$(s_c + w_c)$	+	$(s_b + w_b - d)$	
(5)	(500+500–850)	+	(50+400)	=	600	=	(500+50)	+	(500+400–850)	
(6)	(530+510–850)	+	(50+400)	=	640	=	(530+50)	+	(510+400–850)	

from 500 in Row 5 of the table to 510 in Row 6. In raising total productive expenditure by 10, in the face of an unchanged magnitude of aggregate business costs, it results in 10 more of net investment. To be precise, total productive expenditure is elevated from the sum of 500 of s_b plus 400 of w_b, namely 900, to 510 of s_b plus, once again, 400 of w_b, namely to 910. In the face of the same aggregate business costs, d, of 850, the result is a rise in net investment from 50 to 60.

At the same time, of course, inasmuch as s_b is not only a component of productive expenditure but also of business sales revenues, its new value of 510 must appear as sales revenues on the left-hand side of the Row 6. There its effect is to raise total sales revenues from 1,000, which is the sum of 500 of s_c plus 500 of s_b, to 1,010, which is the sum of 500 of s_c plus, this time, 510 of s_b. In the face of the same aggregate business costs, d, of 850, the result is a rise in aggregate profit from the 150 of Rows 2 and 5 to 160.

The rise in profits that is shown in Rows 3 and 6 is in fact much greater, namely, to 190 from 150. This is the result of the 30 of additional consumption spending that the multiplier doctrine alleges to occur on the basis of the 10 of additional net investment. The 30 of additional consumption spending constitutes 30 of additional business sales revenues, or at least something very close to 30 of additional business sales revenues. This is because the far greater part of private consumption spending is for goods and services of business firms, not for the labor of wage earners. For all practical purposes any additional demand for domestic servants can simply be disregarded.

Thus, on the right-hand side of Row 6, I show the rise in consumption as taking place entirely as a rise in s_c from 500 to 530, which has the effect of raising total

consumption from the sum of 500 of s_c plus 50 of w_c to 530 of s_c plus 50 of w_c, namely, from 550 to 580 of total consumption, C. At the same time, on the left-hand side of Row 6, the effect of the additional consumption is 30 more of business sales revenues and thus 30 more of aggregate profit. For business sales revenues are further increased from the sum of 500 of s_c plus 510 of s_b, to the sum of 530 of s_c plus 510 of s_b, that is, from 1,010 to 1,040. And because aggregate costs, d, remain at 850, the effect, as shown explicitly in Row 2 of the table, is to increase profits from 150 to 190.

It cannot be stressed too strongly that, consistent with the law of identity and the entire preceding discussion of this chapter, there is in this whole process absolutely no increase in the demand for labor by business or any further increase in the demand for capital goods subsequent to the initial 10 that gave rise to the increased net investment of 10. Furthermore, it should be realized that nothing essential is changed if we drop the assumption that all of the additional net investment is caused by a rise in s_b and assume instead that some of it results from additional w_b. If for example, 5 of the initial 10 of net investment had come about in this way, once again followed by 30 of additional consumption, the only effect would have been that the rise in profits, instead of being all 40 of the rise in national income, would have been 35, and the rise in wages, instead of being zero, would have been 5. (That is, the rise in wages would have been the wages that might have been contained in the one possible act of productive expenditure present.) Contrary to the multiplier doctrine, any rise in the demand for labor or capital goods depends—it must be said once again—on what is *not consumed, but saved and productively expended.*

4. Importance of Recognizing the Separate Demand for Capital Goods for the Theory of Capital Accumulation and the Theory of National Income

This chapter's stress on the fact that the demand for A is the demand for A and thus that the demand for capital goods and the demand for labor are separate and distinct from the demand for consumers' goods was the implicit basis of the theory of capital accumulation that I presented in Chapter 14.[62] It was only by virtue of my having recognized the separate existence of the demand for capital goods, and the separate, distinct production of capital goods, that I was able to realize that capital goods are used to produce capital goods no less than consumers' goods. It was this, in turn, that led me to realize that once additional capital goods are brought into existence on the basis of a rise in saving, those additional capital goods themselves make possible a further increase in the supply of capital goods, through their contribution to the increase in production. It is impossible to make these connections if one believes that all that is produced are consumers' goods. In that case, one believes that additional capital goods are brought into existence exclusively by means of saving. This is because the additional capital goods brought into existence by saving are held to be a source only of additional consumers' goods. To have a further increase in the supply of capital goods, further saving is thought to be necessary.

Thus, the failure to recognize the separate existence of the demand for capital goods and the corresponding separate production of capital goods prevents the development of a sound theory of capital accumulation. However ironic, it leads both to an inadequate appreciation of the role of saving in capital accumulation and to a corresponding overemphasis on the role of saving in capital accumulation. It leads to a failure to see that fundamentally saving is to capital accumulation as force is to acceleration. That is, it leads to a failure to see that a given increase in saving and in the relative demand for capital goods can be the cause of continuing capital accumulation, while a further increase in saving and the relative demand for capital goods serves to bring about an acceleration in the rate of capital accumulation.[63] The failure to recognize the separate existence of the demand for capital goods and the corresponding separate production of capital goods also prevents recognition of the role of technological progress as a cause of capital accumulation in serving to maintain the productivity of the increasing supply of capital goods. In addition, of course, it prevents recognition of all other causes serving to increase production in general as thereby being sources of capital accumulation. In effect, if one does not heed the fact that capital goods as well as consumers' goods

are produced, one must be oblivious to almost everything that contributes to their supply.

My purpose here in recalling the theory of capital accumulation I presented in Chapter 14 is not only to show its implicit dependence on the recognition of the separate, distinct demand for capital goods and the separate, distinct production of capital goods. It is also to begin to show how when that analysis of capital accumulation is combined with the *explicit* recognition of separate, distinct demands for capital goods and labor as well as consumers' goods, it serves to provide a conceptual framework for the analysis of numerous other major questions in economics, including, above all, the determinants of aggregate profit and the average rate of profit in the economic system.

My analysis of the determinants of the rate of profit is reserved for the next chapter. Here, however, as a preliminary to that analysis, by means of providing further knowledge in connection with aggregate economic accounting and the determination of national income, I must ask the reader to consider Figures 15–5 and 15–6. These are elaborated versions of Figures 14–4 and 14–5, respectively, which were essential vehicles for conveying my analysis of the role of saving and the relative demand for capital goods in capital accumulation.[64] Figures 15–5 and 15–6 take the essential information supplied in Figures 14–4 and 14–5 concerning the role played by the relative demands for capital goods and consumers' goods in the context of an invariable money and show how those two figures respectively imply definite amounts of national income.

If we examine Figure 15–5, we see that in representing the demand for capital goods as 500 units of money and the demand for consumers' goods as a further 500 units of money, Figure 14–4 implies that *total sales revenues in the economic system are 1,000 units of money.* This is because total sales revenues in the economic system are nothing but the sum of the receipts from the sale of capital goods plus the receipts from the sale of consumers' goods, which, of course, as Figure 15–5 shows, are precisely equal to the expenditures made in buying capital goods and consumers' goods. (From the perspective of the buyers, every dollar of sales revenue is an expenditure that is made either for the purpose of making subsequent sales or not for the purpose of making subsequent sales. In the first case, it constitutes receipts from the sale of capital goods; in the second, receipts from the sale of consumers' goods.[65]) A total of 1,000 of such expenditures means a total of 1,000 of sales receipts.

Furthermore, under the assumptions on which Figure 14–4 was constructed, and which, of course, apply to Figure 15–5, it follows that the demand for capital goods of 500 in each year can be taken as a *cost* of producing

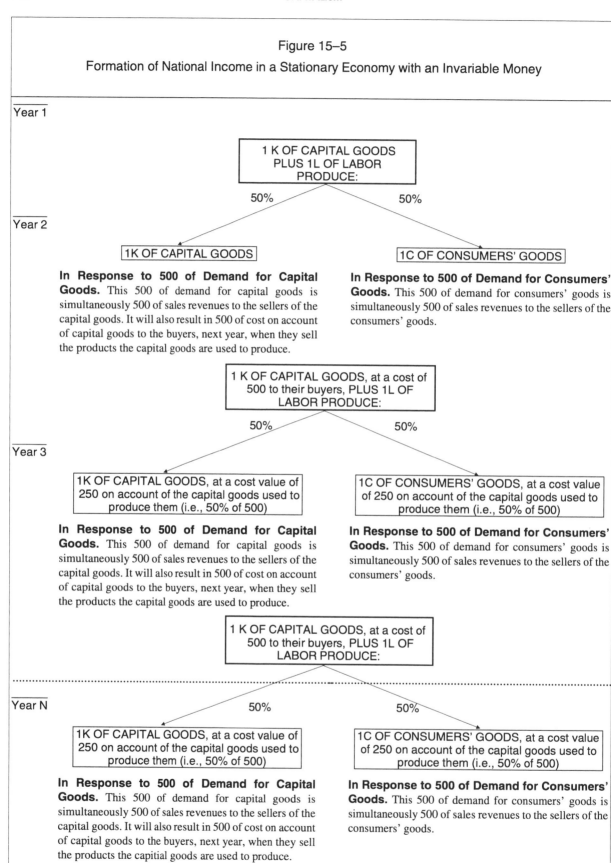

Figure 15–5

Formation of National Income in a Stationary Economy with an Invariable Money

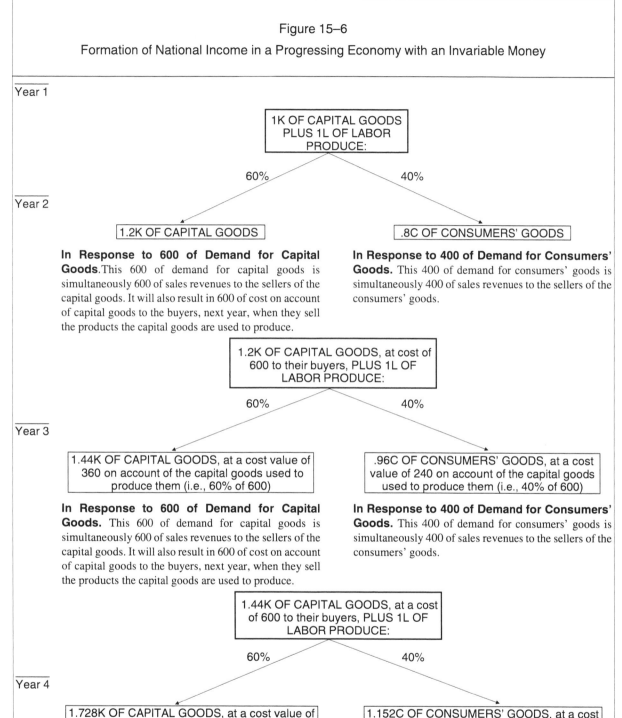

Figure 15–6

Formation of National Income in a Progressing Economy with an Invariable Money

the output of the following year. This is because the capital goods in existence at the beginning of any year are all assumed to be used up or worn out in that very same year in the course of producing the supply of capital goods and consumers' goods available at the start of the following year. Thus, the 500 of outlays for capital goods in each year are a cost of producing the output of the next year because they are made for no other reason than for the purpose of producing that output and bringing in the sales revenues obtained in exchange for it. Figure 15–5 shows this total cost of 500 on account of capital goods as consisting of 250 of respective separate costs on account of capital goods, for the capital goods and the consumers' goods of the following year, each of which comes into being as the result of the use of 50 percent of the 500 worth of capital goods and of the labor of the year before.

In sum, Figure 15–5 shows 1,000 of sales revenues in the economic system in every year and 500 of costs on account of capital goods, which costs reflect the outlays to purchase capital goods in the year before. This is so at least starting with *Year 3*, which is the first year in Figure 15–5 that follows an explicit outlay of money to buy capital goods. Thus, in Figure 15–5, we can observe 1,000 of aggregate sales revenues in the economic system and at least 500 in aggregate costs in the economic system in every year from *Year 3* on.

As I have said, this difference between aggregate sales revenues and aggregate costs which are exclusively on account of capital goods, can be taken as representing national income. This follows from the fact that costs exclusively on account of capital goods exclude costs on account of wages.[66] Costs that exclude costs on account of wages are costs *minus* those wages. Thus, sales revenues minus costs that exclude wages are equal to profit *plus* those wages, which is to say, for all practical purposes, national income. In terms of a very simple equation,

$$\text{sales revenues} - (\text{costs} - \text{wages}) = \text{profits} + \text{wages} = \text{national income.}[67]$$

The most important thing to keep in mind about national income is that it is necessarily the counterpart overwhelmingly just of consumer spending. We already know this from our derivation of the equality between national income and net national product, in the previous section of this chapter. It also follows from the fact that national income is sales revenues minus costs on account of capital goods. In Figure 15–5, of course, not only do costs on account of capital goods in any year equal the outlays for capital goods made the year before, but also the outlays remain the same from year to year—always being 500 units of money. As a result, in Figure 15–5,

sales revenues minus costs on account of capital goods also equals sales revenues minus the *current* demand for capital goods, since the current demand for capital goods is equal to the demand of the previous year and thus to the costs on account of capital goods deducted from sales revenues this year. Therefore, in Figure 15–5, national income equals only the remaining sales revenues, which represent the demand for consumers' goods alone. Indeed, in all circumstances, the national income earned in connection with the sales revenues of any year, can never exceed the consumer spending of that year by very much. The excess can be no more than the amount by which the current demand for capital goods exceeds the costs deducted from sales revenues on account of capital goods.[68]

The Inverse Relationship Between National Income and Economic Progress in an Economy With an Invariable Money

The discussion of capital accumulation in Chapter 14, in particular the role of the demand for capital goods relative to the demand for consumers' goods, and now the realization that national income is the counterpart of consumption expenditure, imply that national income and economic progress can be *inversely related*. Economists have long known this to be the case in the context of inflation, in which national income rises merely as the result of rapid increases in the quantity of money and volume of spending, which at the same time undermine capital accumulation.[69] What the present analysis shows is that in the total absence of inflation, indeed, precisely in the context of an invariable money, in which the quantity of money and the aggregate demand for the products of business remain absolutely fixed, national income and economic progress are inversely related.

This conclusion becomes obvious when Figure 15–6 is observed. In Figure 15–6, the demand for capital goods is 600 units of money in each year from *Year 2* on, while the demand for consumers' goods has fallen to 400 units of money. We have already seen how this rise in the demand for capital goods and fall in the demand for consumers' goods brings about an acceleration in capital accumulation and economic progress from zero—the stationary economy of Figure 15–5—to 20 percent a year.[70] It is only necessary to observe now that *national income in Figure 15–6 falls to 400 monetary units from its previous height of 500 monetary units*. National income is only 400, and can only be 400, because total sales revenues in the economic system are still only 1,000— the sum of the demand for capital goods of 600 plus the demand for consumers' goods of 400—while costs on account of capital goods rise to 600. National income falls, because the rise in demand for capital goods increases the costs on account of capital goods which must be subtracted from the unchanged total sales revenues. The amount by which sales revenues exceed the costs on account of capital goods, and thereby determine national income, is now only the diminished consumption expenditure of 400 units of money instead of the 500 units of money that it was in Figure 15–5. (As was the case in Figure 15–5, Figure 15–6 breaks down the total cost of capital goods into the separate portions chargeable to the respective production of capital goods and consumers' goods. Because 60 percent of the 600 worth of capital goods of each year from *Year 2* on are used up to produce capital goods for the next year, the cost of those capital goods, on account of capital goods, is calculated as 360. By the same token, the cost of the consumers' goods, representing the using of up of 40 percent of the 600 worth of capital goods of the year before is calculated as 240.)

The essential findings are shown on a year-by-year basis in Tables 15–6 and 15–7, which correspond to Figures 15–5 and 15–6 respectively. The only difference is that the tables extend the data of the figures out to *Year 5.* The tables show the demand for capital goods and the demand for consumers' goods in each year and the total sales revenues generated by the sum of these two demands. The generation of sales revenues is depicted graphically, by short lines drawn down from the respective demands for capital goods and consumers' goods in each year to a longer line drawn across and culminating in an arrow pointing up to the 1,000 of sales revenues in that year. Downward, rightward sloping arrows show the demand for capital goods in each year as determining the costs on account of capital goods which appear in the following year. National income in each year is shown as the difference between the 1,000 of sales revenues in each year and these costs on account of capital goods.

Thus, the conclusion is evident that, in the context of an invariable money, *national income and economic progress are inversely related.* Economic progress depends on the demand for capital goods, but the greater is that demand, the greater is the deduction of cost on account of capital goods from sales revenues, and thus the less that remains for national income, given aggregate sales revenues that are fixed.

This conclusion that the fall in national income is the accompaniment of more rapid economic progress must cause bewilderment to people who are accustomed to think of economic well-being and rising money income as inseparable. Thus, it is necessary to stress that the improvement in economic well-being is still fully present. It merely takes the form of *falling prices of products.* In an economic system with an invariable money—that is, once again, a fixed quantity of money and a fixed volume of aggregate spending to buy the products of business—a rise in the relative demand for capital goods and the growing supply both of capital goods and consumers' goods that it causes results in a continuing fall in the prices of capital goods and consumers' goods. Thus, from one year to the next, the diminished monetary amount of national income has a greater buying power.

If we compare Figures 15–5 and 15–6, we can observe that while national income in Figure 15–6 is only 400, in comparison with the 500 of Figure 15–5, the prices of capital goods and consumers' goods in Figure 15–6 fall every year, from *Year 3* on, in the ratio of 5: 6. This follows from the fact that, starting in *Year 3,* the same expenditures for capital goods and consumers' goods of 600 and 400 respectively, buy supplies of capital goods and consumers' goods that are twenty percent or six-fifths larger than the year before. Six-fifths the supplies,

Table 15–6

National Income in Figure 15-5

Year	Demand for Capital Goods	Demand for Consumers' Goods	Sales Revenues	Costs on Account of Capital Goods	National Income
1					
2	500	500	1,000		
3	500	500	1,000	500	500
4	500	500	1,000	500	500
5	500	500	1,000	500	500

divided into unchanged demands, result in prices that are five-sixths as great. In contrast, in Figure 15–5, where national income is 500 rather than 400, and the relative production of capital goods is correspondingly less, there is no increase in the supply of capital goods and consumers' goods, therefore no fall in the prices of capital goods or consumers' goods, and thus no increase in the buying power of incomes. In terms of *buying power,* the 400 of national income of Figure 15–6 further and further surpasses the 500 of national income of Figure 15–5.

Now it should certainly not be concluded from this discussion that there is no connection whatever between increasing production and rising money incomes. As I have pointed out several times before, there in fact is a connection. Under a system of commodity money, such as a gold or silver standard, a growing general ability to produce will almost certainly be reflected in improvements in the ability to extract and refine minerals, including gold and silver, the monetary commodities. Thus an increasing quantity of money and therefore a rising volume of spending and of money incomes will almost inevitably occur as *by-products* of the increasing ability to produce. The processes of rising money incomes and growing production will therefore be parallel to an important extent, at least under a system of commodity money. But even though parallel, the processes are nevertheless separate and distinct and must always be sharply distinguished in thought. As indicated in Chapter 12, in the discussion in which the concept of invariable money was introduced, just as a physicist or engineer conceives of the motion of objects as determined by a variety of distinct forces acting in combination and analyzes the effects of each one acting separately—for example, the combination of gravitation and air pressure,

or the combination of engine power, water current, and wind—so the economist must separately analyze the effects of changes in the relative demand for and production of capital goods and consumers' goods and the consequent changes in the rate of increase in the production and supply of goods for sale, on the one side, and changes in the quantity of money and volume of spending to buy those goods, on the other. Having done this in analyzing the process of capital accumulation under the assumption of an invariable money, we are able to recognize that, with any given quantity of money and volume of spending for the goods and services of business, the rate of capital accumulation and economic progress is in fact inversely related to the height of national income.

Overthrow of the Keynesian Doctrines of the Balanced-Budget Multiplier and the Conservatives' Dilemma

It should be realized that the recognition of the inverse relationship between nominal national income and economic progress in the context of an invariable money constitutes a substantive overthrow of the Keynesian doctrine of the "balanced-budget multiplier." That doctrine, which is propounded in almost every contemporary "macroeconomics" textbook, claims that an equal increase in taxes and government spending raises the national income by an equivalent amount—that, for example, if both taxes and government spending are increased by $10 billion, national income will also increase by $10 billion. The Keynesians, of course, assume that such an increase in national income is all to the good, and is on the order of a lesser miracle achieved by government intervention.[71]

Table 15-7

National Income in Figure 15-6

Year	Demand for Capital Goods	Demand for Consumers' Goods	Sales Revenues	Costs on Account of Capital Goods	National Income
1					
2	600	400	1,000		
3	600	400	1,000	600	400
4	600	400	1,000	600	400
5	600	400	1,000	600	400

What the Keynesians have failed to see in their zeal to overturn common sense is that under the operation of the "balanced-budget multiplier," national income rises by virtue of a form of consumption—viz., government spending—taking the place of demand for capital goods. To finance the additional government spending, the taxpayers must reduce their saving and expenditure for capital goods. If the fall in expenditure for capital goods finances the whole of the rise in government spending, then, indeed, national income will increase by an equivalent amount. This is because aggregate sales revenues in the economic system will remain the same—with receipts from the sale of consumers' goods to the government or its clients taking the place of receipts from the sale of capital goods to business—while the costs deducted from sales revenues on account of capital goods will fall. But this result, of course, is accompanied by a corresponding decline in the relative production of capital goods and therefore in economic progress and prosperity. Thus the Keynesians totally misinterpret the significance of the rise in national income that would materialize. What the Keynesians have done here is failed to heed the distinction advanced by Ricardo between "value," which can be understood as money national income in the context of an invariable money, and "riches," i.e., real physical wealth. As I have pointed out more than once, and as Ricardo pointed out in the early nineteenth century, the two are separate and distinct and can move in opposite directions.

The recognition of the inverse relationship between nominal national income and economic progress is also a refutation of the alleged conservatives' dilemma that is founded on the balanced-budget multiplier doctrine. The "conservatives' dilemma" is the alleged dilemma of having to choose between stimulating the economic system either by means of budget deficits, if one relies on the standard government-spending or tax multipliers propounded by the Keynesians, or by means of an increase in the size of government spending several times greater than what would supposedly be required in connection with a deficit. Thus, for example, it is claimed that with a government-spending multiplier of 4 and a tax multiplier of -3 (both of which allegedly follow from the same "marginal propensity to consume"), national income could be increased by a given amount, such as $10 billion, in either of three ways: by increasing both taxes and government spending by $10 billion and thus maintaining a balanced budget, or by incurring a budget deficit of $2.5

billion brought about through increased government spending with no accompanying increase in taxes or, finally, by incurring a budget deficit of $3.33 billion brought about by tax reduction with no accompanying decrease in government spending. The alleged dilemma represented by such an example is that economic prosperity requires that American conservatives choose between their two cherished principles of balanced budgets and small government. Allegedly, they must accept either deficits with relatively small government or, if they insist on maintaining balanced budgets, much greater growth in government, because one or the other is supposedly necessary for a given increase in national income.[72]

What my analysis has shown, both in this section and in my critiques of the multiplier doctrine earlier in this chapter, is that any increase in national income brought about in such ways is inversely related to capital accumulation and economic progress, because it would represent a rise in the relative demand for and production of consumers' goods at the expense of the relative demand for and production of capital goods. It would also represent a fall in the share of consumption based on wage payments, which, like the demand for capital goods, depends on saving and productive expenditure. National income is simply not the standard of economic prosperity. Any rise in national income accomplished by means of the demand for consumers' goods rising at the expense of the demand for capital goods is the same in its nature as moving from the conditions of Figure 15–6, with its national income of 400 and rapid capital accumulation and economic progress, to the conditions of Figure 15–5, with its national income of 500 and economic stagnation. Thus, American conservatives can continue to cherish both small government and balanced budgets, secure in the knowledge that both are essential requirements of economic progress and prosperity, even if in the conditions of a given quantity of money and volume of spending, they mean a smaller national income—indeed, precisely because they mean a smaller national income in such conditions.[73]

Thus, this chapter has conclusively demonstrated in every way the overwhelming role of saving and productive expenditure in the generation of aggregate demand. In the process, it has rid the science of economics of significant elements of seeming paradox and given good indication of the importance of sound ideas concerning saving and spending for the rest of economic theory.

Notes

1. See above, pp. 442–447.

2. It is appropriate to acknowledge here the profound identification made by Ayn Rand that "It is axiomatic concepts that identify the precondition of knowledge: the distinction between existence and consciousness, between reality and the awareness of reality, between the object and the subject of cognition." See Ayn Rand, *Introduction to Objectivist Epistemology*, 2d ed. enl., ed. Harry Binswanger and Leonard Peikoff (New York: NAL Books, 1979), p. 57.

3. See above, pp. 442–447.

4. On the subject of productive consumption, see above, pp. 131–132 and 443–446.

5. Adam Smith, *The Wealth of Nations* (London, 1776), bk. 2, chap. 3; reprint of Cannan ed. (Chicago: University of Chicago Press, 2 vols. in 1, 1976), 1:351–371. Italics supplied. (From now on, specific page references to the University of Chicago Press reprint will be supplied in brackets.)

6. James Mill, *Commerce Defended*, (London, 1808) chap. 6; reprinted in *Selected Economic Writings of James Mill*, ed. Donald Winch (Chicago: University of Chicago Press, 1966), pp. 128–129.

7. The classical economists were not consistent on this point. Thus, Adam Smith states: "Whatever part of his stock a man employs as a capital, he always expects to be replaced to him with a profit. He employs it, therefore, in maintaining productive hands only; *and after having served in the function of a capital to him, it constitutes a revenue to them.*" *Wealth of Nations*, bk. 2, chap. 3 [p. 353]. Italics supplied.

8. Paul Samuelson and William Nordhaus, *Economics*, 13th ed. (New York: McGraw Hill Book Company, 1989), p. 102. The only contemporary economist I am aware of whose treatment of GNP does not follow along the lines of Samuelson and Nordhaus, but rather of the classical economists and myself in recognizing the production of the so-called intermediate goods, is Mark Skousen. See his *Economics on Trial* (Homewood, Ill.: Business One Irwin, 1991), pp. 38–43, and *The Structure of Production* (New York: New York University Press, 1990), pp. 191–192. In these pages, he advances the concepts of "Gross National Outlays" (GNO) and "Gross National Output," which are similar to, though still considerably smaller than, my concept of Gross National Revenue (GNR) that is presented in this chapter on pp. 706–707.

9. Samuelson and Nordhaus, p. 107.

10. Ibid.

11. Ibid., p. 109.

12. Gardner Ackley, *Macroeconomic Theory* (New York: The Macmillan Company, 1961), p. 28. To his credit, Ackley is aware that "Final products might be limited to consumer goods and goods sold to the government (collective consumption)." (Ibid.) He is aware that the actual contemporary practice of including the production of plant and equipment in GNP represents a contradiction of the final products approach. He writes: "There is much to be said for the idea that new capital goods are not final products. They are certainly not wanted for their own sake, but only to produce (directly or indirectly) other final products. The machine services which contribute to the production of bread are essentially like the flour. Machine methods are more productive than hand methods; therefore

machinery is produced and used. But sooner or later this production of machines means that more bread will be produced than otherwise. Having counted the production of bread, this argument would have it that we should not also count the production of machinery."(Ibid., p. 29.)

13. Lloyd G. Reynolds, *Economics*, 5th ed. (Homewood, Ill.: Richard D. Irwin, 1985) p. 80.

14. Ibid. Italics supplied.

15. Ibid., pp. 80–81. Italics supplied.

16. John Stuart Mill, *Principles of Political Economy*, Ashley ed. (1909; reprint ed., Fairfield, N. J.: Augustus M. Kelley, 1976), pp. 79–81.

17. George Leland Bach, *Economics*, 6th ed. (Englewood Cliffs, N. J.: Prentice-Hall, Inc., 1968), p. 40. Italics supplied.

18. Armen A. Alchian and William R. Allen, *University Economics*, 3d ed. (Belmont, Calif.: Wadsworth Publishing Company, 1972), p. 530. Italics supplied.

19. These considerations, and the rest of this subsection, imply, of course, that the so-called accelerator doctrine of the Keynesians is completely mistaken. For the accelerator doctrine explains increases in the aggregate demand for capital goods on the basis of increases in the aggregate demand for consumers' goods. For further discussion of this error, see below, n. 22 of this chapter.

20. See above, pp. 475–480.

21. See above, pp. 140–141.

22. Perhaps the best that can be said for the proponents of the idea that increases in the aggregate demand for consumers' goods are the cause of increases in the aggregate demand for factors of production is that they confuse the effects of increases in the aggregate demand for consumers' goods with the effects of increases in the quantity of money or decreases in the demand for money for holding. Under such conditions, in which aggregate monetary demand increases, an increase in the demand for consumers' goods is probably accompanied by an increase in the demand for factors of production. But it would have been accompanied by a greater increase in the demand for factors of production if the increase in consumption were smaller. In that case saving, the indispensable precondition of the demand for factors of production, would have been greater and thus so too would have been the demand for factors of production.

23. The precise nature of this relationship will become clearer in the elaboration of the theory of profit and the role played by an excess of consumption expenditure over wage payments in determining an excess of demand for products over demand for factors of production and thus of sales revenues over costs. See below, pp. 725–736. See also below, pp. 689–690.

24. See above, p. 301 and pp. 650–653. See also pp. 653–655.

25. See again above, pp. 653–655.

26. This fact is clearly recognized in the theory of profit and interest propounded by von Mises under the name the theory of originary interest. Cf. von Mises, *Human Action*, 3d ed. rev. (Chicago: Henry Regnery Co., 1966), pp. 526–527.

27. See, for example, the extensive quotation from Samuelson and Nordhaus, a few paragraphs below in the text.

28. Samuelson and Nordhaus, pp. 167–168.

29. For elaboration of this point, see below, pp. 707–708.

30. See below, pp. 702–705, for a discussion of the nature of

net investment.

31. On these points, see above, pp. 622–629 and 631–634.

32. See, for example, Samuelson and Nordhaus, p. 168.

33. Cf. ibid., pp. 153 and 181, where investment is described as "autonomous"—viz., emanating from outside the system.

34. For examples of these errors, see again Samuelson and Nordhaus, pp. 176–183.

35. See above, pp. 573–573.

36. On the nature of consumption and capital, see above, pp. 444–447.

37. Cf. U.S. Department of Commerce, Office of Business Economics, *National Income,* 1954 ed. (Washington, D. C.: U.S. Government Printing Office, 1954), p. 164.

38. On the harmful effects of government interference with the fall in wages and prices in a depression, see above, pp. 580–594. On the deflationary potential of fractional reserve banking, see above, pp. 513–514.

39. A further significant point that deserves mention in connection with "hoarding" is that it operates to speed the adjustment process of the fall in wages and prices that is necessary to restore full employment. This is because in reducing spending, it increases the pressure on wage rates and prices to fall. See Murray N. Rothbard, *Man, Economy, and State,* 2 vols. (Princeton, N. J.: D. Van Nostrand Company, Inc., 1962), 2:691–692.

40. See below, pp. 954–963.

41. As I have already shown, revenue and income that is saved is also typically spent *faster* than revenue and income that is consumed. On this point, see above, p. 518.

42. The employment statistics can be found in *The Federal Reserve Bulletin,* September, 1993, p. A45.

43. For elaboration of this point, see below, pp. 843–847.

44. See below, pp. 778–787.

45. Such government expenditures, of course, are fully consistent with the principle that business is the source of its own demand. This is because the taxes that finance them are always paid either directly by business enterprises themselves, by wage earners and dividend and interest recipients with funds received from business enterprises, or by people who receive funds from the members of these groups, such as domestic servants.

46. On this subject, see below, pp. 739–741. To an important but lesser extent, taxes on wages also reduce the demand for capital goods and labor. They reduce it insofar as their effect is to reduce the savings of wage earners, who then either cannot finance productive expenditure to the same extent or are led to borrow savings in competition with business, in order to finance their purchase of expensive consumers' goods, such as housing and automobiles.

47. For a full account of these effects, see below, pp. 922–950.

48. J. S. Mill, *Essays on Some Unsettled Questions of Political Economy* (1844; reprint ed., New York: Augustus M. Kelley, 1968) pp. 48–49. To be fully accurate, one need only add to Mill's position recognition of the fact that production and employment can be held far below their potential limit at any given time by government interference in the monetary system and the consequent boom-bust pattern of business activity, and that such damage can be indefinitely protracted by further government interference in the form of maintaining artificially high wage rates and prices in the contraction phase. See above, pp. 580–594 and 938–942.

49. See above, pp. 559–580.

50. On the role of saving in capital accumulation and a rising productivity of labor, see above, pp. 622–629 and 631–632. See also below, p. 824.

51. For the discussion of natural resources, see above, pp. 63–66.

52. See above, pp. 622–629, especially Figures 14–4 and 14–5 and the surrounding discussion.

53. On this last point, see above, pp. 531–533.

54. See, for example, Samuelson and Nordhaus, pp. 110–116.

55. See below, p. 705.

56. See, for example, Samuelson and Nordhaus, p. 165, Figure 8–10, which is titled "HOW CONSUMPTION AND INVESTMENT DETERMINE OUTPUT."

57. Concerning my treatment of interest, see below, pp. 720–721. Previous discussion, on pp. 456–459, has made it clear that most of what is described as net rental income of persons in today's national income accounts is purely fictional in nature. It should be obvious in the light of that discussion that any actual net rental income, whether in letting rooms or apartments, houses, automobiles, computers, or whatever, is profit.

58. See above, pp. 444–447.

59. The use of lower-case s_c to represent sales revenues paid by consumers should not be confused with the previous use of upper-case S_C to represent the supply of consumers' goods produced and sold, especially since the former is actually interchangeable with the *demand* for consumers' goods, D_C. Also, I use the subscript b rather than p, to avoid confusion with aggregate profit, which is represented by p. One can think of b as standing for *business* expenditure, which, of course, is synonymous with productive expenditure.

60. It should be realized that while productive expenditure is an expenditure, net investment is not. As the difference between productive expenditure and business costs, its actual nature is that of an accounting abstraction, not an expenditure.

61. See above, pp. 690–691, in particular the quotation from Samuelson and Nordhaus.

62. See above, pp. 622–642.

63. This is the case in the context of an invariable money and its fixed aggregate demand for the products of business, which is the essential analytical framework for establishing causal relations in economics. In such conditions an increase in saving and the demand for capital goods is both an absolute increase and a relative increase at the same time.

64. See above, pp. 624 and 625.

65. See above, pp. 444–447.

66. They also exclude costs on account of interest. However, our practice, it should be recalled, is to count interest and "net rental income of persons," which are the two remaining components of national income, as part of profits. See above, this page, n. 57. Because it is not germane to the present analysis, we also omit from consideration incomes generated in the so-called consumer and government sectors, notably the demand for consumers' labor.

67. The fact that sales revenues minus costs on account of capital goods equals profits plus wages was previously demonstrated in connection with the exposition of the Marxian exploitation theory. See above, pp. 605–607.

68. I must point out that the national income earned in connection with the sales revenues of a given year includes an important component that was earned in previous years, and that an important component of the national income earned in the

current year is earned in connection with sales revenues to be brought in, in future years. For example, part of the national income earned in connection with this year's sales revenues represents wages paid in the previous year (or earlier years) to workers who helped to produce items held in this year's opening inventories. It also includes significant amounts of wages paid as far back as previous decades and generations to workers who helped to build plant and equipment in existence at the beginning of the current year. By the same token, part of the wages paid this year are credited to inventory and plant and equipment accounts and will be chargeable against sales revenues only next year and, to be sure, in future decades and generations. As a result, it does not follow that national income in any given year exceeds the consumption expenditure of that particular year exclusively by the excess of the current demand for capital goods over the costs deducted from sales revenues on account of capital goods.

69. For a discussion of the destructive effects of inflation on capital accumulation, see below, pp. 930–938.

70. See above, pp. 622–629, especially Figures 14–4 and 14–5 and the surrounding discussion. There the reader will see the basis of the derivation of the specific outputs of capital goods and consumers' goods in each year of Figure 15–6.

71. See, for example, Samuelson and Nordhaus, *Economics,* 13th ed., pp. 181–182; Willis L. Peterson, *Principles of Economics Macro,* 6th ed. (Homewood, Ill.: Richard D. Irwin, Inc., 1986), pp. 235–236; Gordon Philpot, *The National Economy, An Introduction to Macroeconomics* (New York: John Wiley & Sons, 1980), p. 81. The balanced-budget-multiplier doctrine was originated by Trygve Haavelmo, and presented for the first time in his article, "The Multiplier Effects of a Balanced Budget," *Econometrica,* October 1945.

72. See Philpot, *National Economy,* p. 81.

73. It should be realized that national income and economic prosperity are also inversely related in the case in which a rise in national income is brought about by means of an increase in the taxation of wage earners and use of the proceeds to raise the demand for labor. See above, pp. 648–650.

CHAPTER 16

THE NET-CONSUMPTION/NET-INVESTMENT
THEORY OF PROFIT AND INTEREST

THE POSITIVE THEORY

1. The Nature and Problem of Aggregate Profit

In Chapter 13, I showed how production and supply are the source of demand in the sense of purchasing power—that is, real demand. In Chapter 15, I showed how saving and productive expenditure are the source of the great bulk of spending in the economic system. This conclusion followed from the fact that they not only make possible the demand for capital goods, which in a modern economic system almost certainly surpasses the demand for consumers' goods, but also the payment of wages by business, out of which comes the great bulk of consumer spending.[1] In this chapter, I will make good on the promise I made in Chapter 15 to show how business—taken in the aggregate—is the source not only of the monetary demand for its own products, but of a *profitable* monetary demand for its products. As I promised, I will show how business "itself generates a monetary demand that is fully sufficient for the profitable sale of its products . . . in the mere fact of purchasing capital goods and paying wages and in declaring dividends and paying interest" and how "in addition, the very increase in production itself operates to add further to both the real and the nominal rate of profit." I will show, indeed, how there are "virtual *springs* to the restoration of profitabil-

ity" waiting to be unleashed whenever inflation and credit expansion bring on a financial contraction and deflation and thereby temporarily impair business profitability or wipe it out altogether.[2]

In this chapter, I will explain the determinants both of the aggregate amount of profit in the economic system and of the average rate of profit in the economic system. I will present a theory of profit which will show that in a society characterized by consistent laissez-faire capitalism, and thus free of financial contraction brought on by a preceding inflation or credit expansion, the average rate of profit is always determined at a point that is both high enough to make investment worthwhile and, at the same time, as low as the security of property and all rational provision for the future make possible. Thus, I will show—in contrast to the claims of the Keynesians and the Marxists—that the rate of profit is neither "too low" nor "too high" and that neither pretext constitutes grounds for a policy of government intervention or socialism.[3]

The theory of profit I will present in this chapter is the basis on which I was led to the development both of much of the material that I have already presented, in previous chapters, and of much of the material that is yet to come, in subsequent chapters. It is the basis of my having arrived at virtually the whole of the analysis I presented in Chapter 11 and in Chapters 13–15, from the definition of productive expenditure and consumption expenditure through the critique of the conceptual framework of the exploitation theory, the exposition of the philosophy of productionism, Say's Law, the causes and cure of mass unemployment, the productivity theory of wages, and the development of my system of aggregate economic accounting. The only major doctrine presented in those chapters concerning which I cannot fully claim my theory of profit to be the basis of my exposition, is the doctrine that the demand for *A* is the demand for *A*. This is because it was my reading of John Stuart Mill's statement of this doctrine, in the form "demand for commodities is not demand for labour," that precipitated my development of my theory of profit. My theory of profit, as I will show, rests substantially on recognition of the truth grasped by Mill in his famous proposition. Of course, in turn, my theory of profit greatly reinforces and amplifies the truth of that proposition.

In this and subsequent chapters, my theory of profit will provide both the basis of analysis of questions I have not yet considered in this book and a wider perspective and more comprehensive theoretical framework for the analysis of questions that I have already considered. It will thereby make possible both the acquisition of important new knowledge, and valuable reinforcement, amplification, and integration of knowledge that the reader has hopefully already acquired to an important degree.

Before turning to the presentation of my theory of profit, however, it is necessary to attend to a number of important preliminary matters, starting with my treatment of interest.

The Treatment of Interest

The theory of profit I will expound will explain not only the average rate of profit in the economic system but also the rate of interest. The explanation of the rate of interest will follow from the explanation of the rate of profit.

In explaining the rate of profit, my purpose will be to explain what makes possible an excess of business sales revenues over business costs that are exclusive of interest. In other words, I will continue my practice of taking profits as gross of interest cost, that is, prededuction of interest cost. The average rate of profit that I will explain will be the amount of profit thus understood, divided by the amount of capital invested in the economic system both by equity investors—i.e., stockholders, partners, and sole proprietors— on the one side, and by bondholders and other creditors, on the other. In other words, it will be the rate of return found by dividing the sum of profit income earned by business firms plus interest paid by business firms, by the sum of all capital invested in business firms. The result will approximate what many would call the average rate of return on capital invested.[4]

As I have already shown, the rate of profit taken

prededuction of interest determines the rate of interest that business borrowers are able and willing to pay. In order for them to borrow, they must expect to earn a rate of profit in this sense that is greater than the rate of interest they are asked to pay. At the same time, of course, insofar as business firms are sources of loanable funds, the rate of interest they ask as lenders depends on the rate of profit they expect to be able to make by investing the funds in question in their own operations. In these ways, the rate of profit determines the rate of interest.[5]

In addition to being the determinant of the rate of interest, it is the rate of profit inclusive of interest that must be analyzed in order to deal with all the leading questions of economic theory that pertain to the rate of profit and interest taken together, such as the effect on the rate of profit and interest of capital accumulation and of falling prices caused by increased production. It is also this rate of profit that must be analyzed in order to deal with the doctrines of Marxism and Keynesianism, which are directed at the determination and the significance precisely of this rate of profit.

As a result of these considerations, interest payments will enter into the present analysis only in the same way as do dividend payments and the draw of funds by partners and sole proprietors, that is, neither as a productive expenditure nor as a business cost, but only as a source of demand for consumers' goods by businessmen and capitalists.

The existence of financial institutions, such as banks and insurance companies, may appear to introduce an important complication into the treatment of interest payments, namely, the fact that a substantial portion of interest payments has acquired the status of business sales revenues, from which various costs are deducted and on which profit is earned. Among the costs deducted, of course, are typically further interest payments. For the sake of ease of analysis, I shall simply ignore the existence of this phenomenon and assume that all interest paid by business firms is paid to individuals, to whom it constitutes equivalent net income.

Nevertheless, this complication could easily be dealt with. In calculating the economy-wide amount of profit inclusive of interest, and the average rate of such profit, interest payments to financial institutions could be excluded. They could be treated as part of productive expenditure, as part of the business sales revenues constituted by productive expenditure, and as part of the costs deducted from the sales revenues of the firms that make the payments. This procedure would serve to reduce the sum of profit and interest income in the economic system by the magnitude of the interest payments made by business firms to financial institutions, and then to increase it by the magnitude of the profits earned by such institutions on those interest payments and by the amount of interest income those institutions paid to individuals. The net effect would be to reduce the sum of profit and interest income in the economic system by the magnitude of the costs incurred by the various financial institutions, apart from their payment of interest to individuals. The procedure would thus turn out to be tantamount to the assumption both that all interest and dividend payments were made to individuals, which, of course, is the assumption on which I am proceeding, and that their amount is net of the costs incurred by financial institutions, apart from the latters' payment of interest to individuals. It should be observed that the procedure would serve to convert part of what would otherwise be interest incomes that had to be added to profits, into literal profit incomes—namely, the profit incomes earned by financial institutions on interest revenues. However, to avoid even this much complication, I will, as I have said, simply ignore the existence of financial intermediation.

The Rate of Profit Not Based on Demand and Supply of Capital, but on the Difference Between the Demand for Products and the Demand for Factors of Production

My treatment of interest is consistent with a simplified view of productive expenditure as consisting exclusively of the demand for capital goods and producers' labor (that is, of course, labor employed by business). This makes it possible to speak interchangeably of productive expenditure and the demand for factors of production by business. The two expressions become equivalent.

If, in contrast, the payment of interest were retained as part of productive expenditure, then using the two expressions interchangeably would imply that the payment of interest was a demand for a factor of production in the same way that the demand for capital goods and producers' labor are demands for factors of production. The further implication would be that capital was a factor of production standing alongside of and in addition to capital goods and producers' labor, inasmuch as capital is what is obtained by the payment of interest.

Such a view represents a confusion of ideas. Capital in the sense of a sum of money used to make productive expenditures and thus buy factors of production, or in the sense of the monetary value of the factors of production purchased, is not itself a factor of production. It is simply the means of buying the factors of production, or it is their recorded acquisition value on the books of the firms that buy them. The actual factors of production are capital goods and producers' labor, not capital goods, producers' labor, and capital.

These considerations are extremely germane to the question of what determines the average rate of profit in the economic system. As we shall see, in no sense is the rate of profit determined by the supply of and demand for "capital." Rather, it has everything to do with the difference between two demands: the demand for factors of production by business—that is, the demand for capital goods and producers' labor—which shows up as costs of production to be deducted from sales revenues, and the greater demand for the products of business, which constitutes business sales revenues. Profit, in essence, is the difference between these two demands. Explanation of the rate of profit and interest must be geared toward explaining the difference between these two demands, not a demand for and supply of "capital," in which capital is mistakenly conceived as a factor of production.[6]

Determinants of the Average Rate of Profit in the Economic System Different fromDeterminants of the Rate of Profit of the Individual Company or Industry

Although by now it should go without saying, I cannot stress too strongly that what I intend to show in this chapter is the determinants of the average rate of profit in the economic system of a country, indeed, of the world. As I have already indicated, the determinants of this rate of profit are very different from those which determine the rate of profit of an individual company or industry. At the level of the individual company or industry, competitive factors play a major, often by far the largest, role.[7]

For example, an individual company that introduces a new and improved product is in a position to increase its profits substantially. It does so, however, by gaining sales revenues at the expense of other companies with which it directly or indirectly competes, and which now experience either an outright reduction in sales revenues or else a failure to gain sales revenues that they otherwise would have gained. As illustration, this was the case with the automobile, which competed not only against the horse and buggy and the railroads but also against industries outside the field of transportation. In the absence of the appearance of the automobile, many of these industries would have gained additional sales revenues as the result of the release of funds from the purchase of such things as food and clothing, made possible by greater efficiency in the production of such goods. Instead, the automobile industry garnered much of these funds. The same is true in all instances in which increases in profits are based on competitive factors. The accompaniment of all such increases in profits is, of course, corresponding decreases in profits elsewhere.

These observations are consistent with what I have said previously about the fact that technological progress does not raise the average rate of profit. It raises the rate of profit of those firms that introduce the technological advances or are relatively early in their adoption, and equivalently reduces the rate of profit of other firms, in the rest of the economic system. As I have shown, the only way in which technological progress can raise the average rate of profit in the economic system is insofar as it takes place in the production of the monetary commodity or commodities, namely, in the production of gold and silver under a precious-metals monetary standard, and thereby achieves a more rapid rate of increase in the quantity of money and volume of spending.[8]

Whole industries, as well as individual companies, are in a position to make higher profits or lower profits, or profits versus outright losses, on the basis of competitive factors. This occurs every time the consumers shift their demand from the products of an industry that has lost their favor to the products of an industry that has gained their favor.

The determinants of the average rate of profit in the economic system, in contrast, exclude all competitive factors. In the economy as a whole, competitive factors are always mutually offsetting. They cannot explain why or to what extent the sum of profits of the individual firms that have profits exceeds the sum of the losses of the individual firms that have losses, that is, why and to what extent there is an aggregate profit in the economic system and thus a positive average rate of profit, nor the specific height of the average rate of profit. To answer these questions, it is necessary to turn to an examination of factors that are very different than the competitive elements that are so vital to the determination of the rate of profit of individual companies and industries.

That the explanation of an aggregate profit and thus a positive average rate of profit depends on different factors than the competitive elements that loom so large in the case of individual firms and industries means that it should not be surprising if a very different significance is often to be attached to the existence of a given average rate of profit in the economic system than to the existence of an equal rate of profit on the part of an individual company or industry. It is one thing if outstanding productive innovators earn, say, a 50 percent annual rate of profit. Such a situation is consistent with the average rate of profit in the economic system being perhaps just 5 percent, and with other businessmen, who are backward and incompetent, suffering reduced profits, including outright losses, that are as large as the exceptional profits of the great innovators. Here the high profits of the innovators are due almost entirely to the improvements in production they introduce or are early to adopt. It is a very different situation if the average rate of profit in the economic system is 50 percent, with the result that even

the most backward and incompetent businessmen can earn a substantial rate of profit. In the latter situation, as we shall see, what is present is rapid inflation of the money supply and/or a state of affairs in which the great majority of businessmen and capitalists have come to value a much higher degree of present enjoyment relative to provision for the future. This situation signifies economic decline and impoverishment, while, as we well know, the former situation, in contrast, signifies economic progress and prosperity.

Critique of the Doctrine That the Interest Rate on Government Bonds Expresses the Pure Rate of Return to Which Risk Premiums Are Added

My focus on the determinants of the average rate of profit on capital invested is incompatible with the notion that the rate of interest on government bonds expresses the pure rate of return on capital, and that higher rates of return represent an addition of various premiums to this alleged pure rate, which compensate for risk or uncertainty.

I showed in Chapter 6 that it is possible, indeed, likely, that the rate of profit in the narrower sense, that is, the rate of profit on equity investments, is above the average rate of profit, while the rate of interest is below the average rate of profit.[9] It follows that the rate of interest on government bonds, being generally the lowest in any country, will be correspondingly further *below* the average rate of profit, and not in any sense represent a "pure" rate of profit.

Furthermore, insofar as a "risk" premium merely serves to offset losses on other investments of the same kind, it does not enter into the average rate of return that is actually earned. For, presumably, the losses for the provision of which the risk premium exists do in fact occur, in which case the average rate of return being earned is below the nominal rate containing the risk premium. A risk premium which is merely an offset to losses cannot constitute an element in any average rate of return which is actually earned or paid.

It is different with regard to uncertainty, however. Because of uncertainty, there may be permanent differences in rates of return actually earned. But these rates do not ascend upward from the lowest rate, which allegedly represents the "pure" rate, each containing a premium in addition to the "pure" rate of return. Uncertainty in investment is inescapable, and relative uncertainty cannot add anything to the average rate profit. All that can occur is that those investments of a relatively high degree of uncertainty will afford a rate of profit in excess of the average rate of profit, while those investments of a relatively low degree of uncertainty will afford a rate of profit below the average rate of profit.

The Path of Explanation: Net Consumption and Net Investment

In its explanation of profits, this chapter follows a path that was indicated in Chapters 13 and 14. There, under the assumption of the complete vertical integration of business and thus that business firms produce all of their own materials and equipment and buy nothing but labor services, I showed that consumption expenditure would constitute the only source of business sales revenues and that wages would constitute the only costs incurred by business. It followed that aggregate profits would equal consumption minus wages, which excess I termed *net consumption*.[10] In this chapter, I show that net consumption is *always* the most fundamental determinant of aggregate profit and the average rate of profit, irrespective of the extent of vertical integration of business firms. I then trace the phenomenon of net consumption back to time preference and show that net consumption is actually the vehicle by means of which time preference determines the rate of profit.[11]

Alongside net consumption, I also develop the very important role played in the determination of the rate of profit by the phenomenon of *net investment,* which I showed in Chapter 15 to be the result of differences between productive expenditure and costs.[12] In addition, I explain the influence of changes in the quantity of money and aggregate spending on the rate of profit, which influence I show to be integrally connected with the rate of net investment. Finally, on the basis of the knowledge gained concerning the determinants of the rate of profit, I demonstrate the existence of the virtual springs to profitability that I have referred to, which operate automatically to reestablish a significant positive rate of profit in the economic system following the end of a monetary contraction and the fall in wage rates and prices necessitated by the contraction.

The relationship between profits, on the one side, and net consumption plus net investment, on the other, is directly derivable from propositions already established in Chapter 15. In Chapter 15, I showed that profits, as sales revenues minus costs $(s - d)$, are equal to $s_c + s_b - d$, namely, to receipts from the sale of consumers' goods plus receipts from the sale of capital goods, minus costs. I also showed not only that net investment is $B - d$, that is, productive expenditure minus those same costs, but also that productive expenditure itself equals $s_b + w_b$.[13] It follows from these relationships that profits and net investment are very similar. This is because the equations for both incorporate not only the identical subtrahend d, namely, costs, but also include the identical component s_b in the minuend. It follows directly that the difference between profits and net investment is the difference between sales revenues and productive expenditure, which

reduces to the difference between s_c and w_b, that is, to the difference between receipts from the sale of consumers' goods and the payment of wages by business, which difference is net consumption. In terms of simple algebra,

$$p - I =$$

$$s_c + s_b - d - (s_b + w_b - d) =$$

$$s_c - w_b.$$

It follows, of course, that if profits minus net investment equals net consumption, *profits are equal to the sum of net consumption plus net investment.*

The rest of this chapter can be understood essentially simply as an elaboration of the concepts of net consumption and net investment and their explanatory role in the determination of aggregate profit and the average rate of profit in the economic system.

The Problem of Aggregate Profit: Productive Expenditure and the Generation of Equivalent Sales Revenues and Costs

All business activity is carried on for the purpose of earning a profit. Yet the existence of the very phenomenon of profit in the economic system as a whole, that is, an aggregate profit—an excess of the sum of all profits over the sum of all losses—can appear difficult to explain. This is because productive expenditure, insofar as it constitutes revenue or income payments, bears an equivalent relationship to business sales revenues and to business costs. This is to say, productive expenditure can be understood as generating both an amount of sales revenues equal to itself *and* an amount of costs equal to itself, which would appear to imply that as far as productive expenditure by itself is concerned, the existence of an aggregate profit would be impossible, at least in the long-run, as a permanent phenomenon.

In elaboration of these points, the reader should consider the following facts. On the one hand, one major portion of productive expenditure—the demand for capital goods—is simultaneously business sales revenues. This part of productive expenditure and this part of business sales revenues are equal by identity, just as a side of one triangle is equal to that of another by identity when the two triangles share that same side. The two are identical because capital goods are sold by business enterprises as well as bought by business enterprises. For example, the demand made for steel sheet by an automobile company, or for flour by a baking company, is simultaneously a part of productive expenditure and a part of sales revenues. From the standpoint of the automobile company or baking company, it is a productive expenditure; from the standpoint of the steel company or flour company, it is sales revenue. From the standpoint of the economic system as a whole, it is simultaneously both.[14]

At the same time, the remaining portion of productive expenditure, insofar as it constitutes revenue or income payments, is made up of wage payments, which, at least as a reasonable first approximation, can be assumed to be expended by their recipients in buying consumers' goods from business firms in the same accounting period.[15]

Thus, directly or indirectly, productive expenditure is to be understood as generating sales revenues equal to itself, and to do so essentially in the same accounting period.

In addition, however, productive expenditure generates business costs equal to itself. We know from Chapter 15 that many of these costs can appear in future accounting periods, indeed, decades in the future, insofar as the productive expenditures are made on account of plant and equipment with many years of useful life.[16] Nevertheless, what must be the result in an economic system with a fixed quantity of money? In such an economic system, it would be reasonable to assume a fixed volume of productive expenditure and a fixed volume of business sales revenues. It would also seem reasonable to assume that at some point, aggregate business costs would rise to equality with the fixed amount of productive expenditure. Indeed, even if, for example, plant and equipment is depreciated over a fifty-year period, after fifty years of the same amount of spending for plant and equipment, annual depreciation charges on fifty years' worth of such plant and equipment rise to equality with the current annual spending for plant and equipment. Thus, the proposition would appear to be supported that costs deducted from business sales revenues must rise to equality with productive expenditure in conditions in which the same amount of productive expenditure is repeated over and over again, indefinitely.

But this last, of course, would mean that costs rise to equality with *business sales revenues* insofar as business sales revenues are generated only by productive expenditure. With costs equal to productive expenditure, and sales revenues equal to productive expenditure, both must be equal to each other. Things equal to the same thing are equal to each other. Thus, it would appear that in the conditions of a fixed quantity of money, and in which productive expenditure were the only source of business sales revenues, an aggregate profit simply could not exist as a permanent phenomenon. It would further appear that the average rate of profit in such conditions would have to be zero, at least insofar as productive expenditure were the only determinant of business sales revenues. This is because a zero amount of aggregate profit would mean a zero numerator in any calculation

of the average rate of profit.

Several times in the last two paragraphs, I used the word "appear," instead of making flat-out statements. This is because things would actually not be quite as bad for the rate of profit as I have just indicated. As I will show, even with a fixed amount of productive expenditure taking place year after year, indefinitely, it would always be possible to have some positive amount of profit. There could be profit equal to some positive amount of net investment, that is to say, to some continuing excess of productive expenditure over aggregate costs.[17]

Even under such conditions, however, a major negative implication would still be present. This would be that the average rate of profit in the economic system would be *continually falling*, in the direction of zero. This implication would exist, because insofar as profits correspond to net investment, the net investment constitutes an addition to the amount of capital invested. Thus even if every year there were the same amount of net investment and profit, that constant amount of profit would have to be spread ever thinner, over a continually growing volume of capital invested. Thus, the average rate of profit would be continually falling. For example, if the total capital invested in the economic system were initially 2,000 and there were 100 of profit corresponding to 100 of net investment, the average rate of profit would initially be 5 percent—that is, $100/2,000$. In the next year, however, it would be less than 5 percent—namely, $100/2,100$—then still less, namely, $100/2,200$, and so on. This is because, as I say, the net investment of each year is added to the amount of accumulated capital.

There could be no possibility of the rate of profit holding up by virtue of net investment growing along with the growth in capital invested. This is because in the conditions of a constant amount of productive expenditure, which is the implication of a fixed quantity of money, the only way that net investment could grow would be by virtue of aggregate costs falling. To maintain a given rate of profit, aggregate costs would have to fall by ever increasing amounts—eventually, they would have to fall below zero and go on falling from there, to produce the ever growing amounts of net investment and profit that would be required to keep the rate of profit constant. But this, of course, is simply impossible.

For example, if the initial 100 of profit is the result of productive expenditure being 1,000 and costs being 900, then in the face of productive expenditure continuing to be 1,000, the only way the initial 5 percent rate of profit could be maintained would be if costs now fell to 895. This would provide 5 more of profit to accompany the 100 of additional capital resulting from 100 of net investment. Now, however, net investment becomes 105 and capital grows from 2,100 to 2,205. To maintain a 5 percent rate of profit at this point, net investment of 110.25 would be required, which means that costs would have to fall to 889.75. In order for the rate of profit to be maintained at 5 percent, aggregate costs would have to fall at a rate equal to 5 percent compounded on a base of 100. This implies that at some point aggregate costs must fall to zero and then go into minus territory. These results, of course, are absolutely impossible. At some point, aggregate costs must stabilize, if not rise. This implies a fixed or falling amount of profit, while the amount of capital invested continues to grow.

Thus, we are left with the fact that in the conditions of a fixed quantity of money, insofar as productive expenditure alone is the source of business sales revenues, the average rate of profit in the economic system, if not actually at zero, must nevertheless be continually falling toward zero.

This brings me to the first major problem that I believe the theory of aggregate profit and the average rate of profit must solve, namely, *to explain how, in the conditions of a fixed quantity of money, the existence of a positive average rate of profit is possible on a long-run, permanent basis, and is so, moreover, without the rate of profit having continually to fall.*

2. Net Consumption and the Generation of an Excess of Sales Revenues Over Productive Expenditure

The answer to the question of how a positive average rate of profit can both exist and remain constant in the conditions of a fixed quantity of money and consequent fixed volume of productive expenditure is supplied by the concept of *net consumption.*

Net consumption, which we already know is the excess of the demand for consumers' goods from business over the demand for labor by business, is also the source of an equivalent excess of the *total* demand for the products of business over the *total* demand for factors of production by business.

The total demand for the products of business is the sum of the respective demands for consumers' goods and capital goods. Both of these demands are the source of business sales revenues. They are the only direct sources, inasmuch as every expenditure to buy the products of business must be made either for the purpose of making subsequent sales, in which case it is a demand for capital goods, or not for the purpose of making subsequent sales, in which case it is a demand for consumers' goods.[18] The total demand for factors of production by business is the sum of the demand for labor by business—viz., the demand for producers' labor—plus the demand for capital goods.

Net consumption is the source of an equivalent excess of the total demand for the products of business over the total demand for factors of production by business because the addition of the demand for capital goods to the demand for consumers' goods in the minuend, and to the demand for labor by business in the subtrahend, leaves the amount of the inequality unchanged. Equals added to unequals do not affect the amount of the inequality. Thus, if net consumption is the difference between the demand for consumers' goods from business and the demand for labor by business, it is equally the difference between the total demand for the products of business and the total demand for factors of production by business. Furthermore, inasmuch as the total demand for the products of business is identical with total business sales revenues, while the total demand for factors of production by business is identical with productive expenditure for labor and capital goods, net consumption is the source of an excess of the sales revenues of business over productive expenditure for labor and capital goods.

These conclusions can be expressed in terms both of the notation for demand employed in Chapters 13 and 14, and in terms of the notation for revenues and incomes employed in Chapter 15. In terms of the former, net consumption is $D_C - D_L$. In terms of the latter, it is $s_c - w_b$. If the demand for capital goods is expressed as D_K, then the total demand for the products of business equals $D_C + D_K$ while the total demand for factors of production by business equals $D_L + D_K$. Since D_K is present in both expressions, and thus disappears when one is subtracted from the other, the difference between the two expressions remains $D_C - D_L$. Thus, net consumption can be expressed as equal to the difference between $D_C + D_K$ and $D_L + D_K$.

In exactly the same way, if receipts from the sale of capital goods are stated as s_b, then, as we already know from Chapter 15, total business sales revenues equal $s_c + s_b$ while productive expenditure equals $w_b + s_b$. Since s_b is present in both expressions and disappears when one is subtracted from the other, the difference between sales revenues and productive expenditure reduces to $s_c - w_b$. Thus, net consumption can also be expressed as equal to the difference between $s_c + s_b$ and $w_b + s_b$.

I turn now to the substantive, as opposed to the purely mathematical, nature of net consumption. Considered substantively, and essentially, net consumption is *the consumption expenditure of businessmen and capitalists,* including under the latter head, the creditors of business firms as well as the owners of equity capital. (The ranks of the capitalists, of course, also include wage earners insofar as they possess capital. To the extent that the possession of capital enables the consumption of wage earners to exceed their wages, the excess of their consumption is to be considered the consumption of capitalists and as contributing to net consumption.)

The essential sources of net consumption are the payment of dividends by corporations, the draw of funds by partners and proprietors from their firms, and the payment of interest by business firms. Of course, to the extent that such receipts are themselves saved and productively expended, they count as part of productive expenditure and the demand for factors of production by business. But some significant portion of these receipts is consumed. And to this extent, there is a demand for the products of business over and above the demand for factors of production by business, that is, a source of business sales revenues which has no counterpart in productive expenditure or costs and which thus makes possible an excess of sales revenues over productive expenditure and costs.

In the case of consumption expenditure out of dividends and draw payments, there is absolutely no counterpart whatever in productive expenditure or costs. Such payments do not represent a purchase, or even an exchange, of any kind. They are merely a transfer of funds from business firms to their owners. In the case of interest payments, there is a productive expenditure in the act of paying the interest, and this productive expenditure either immediately or later on shows up as a cost. However, these are productive expenditures and costs that, as I have explained, we deliberately ignore, in order to explain profits gross of interest cost. Consumption out of interest payments from business is a source of an excess of the demand for the products of business over the demand for actual, physical factors of production by business, that is, a source of an excess of sales revenues over the productive expenditure for capital goods and producers' labor. In this way, it is a source of an excess of sales revenues over costs on account of these physical factors of production, which, of course, is the profit we want to explain.

The role of net consumption in generating an excess of demand for the products of business over the demand for factors of production by business and thus an excess of business sales revenues over productive expenditure is illustrated in Table 16–1. The table, titled "The Components of the Demand for Factors of Production and Products," is divided into three columns. The leftmost column carries the heading "Demand for Factors of Production by Business (Productive Expenditure)," while the rightmost carries the heading "Demand for the Products of Business (Sales Revenues)." The second column of the table shows that item one under the former head is identically equal to item one under the latter head. Item one in both columns is, of course, the demand for capital goods. The second column of the table further shows that item two under the former head is equalled by item two under the latter head, that is, that the demand for labor and labor's (viz., wage earners') demand for consumers' goods are equal. This equality simply reflects the fact that the wage earners spend at least roughly the equivalent of their wages in buying consumers' goods from business. Finally, the second column of the table makes clear that item three of the third column, namely, "Businessmen's and Capitalists' Demand for Consumers' Goods," is the source of the excess of the demand for the products of business over the demand for factors of production by business, that is, of sales revenues over productive expenditure. For this item appears *only* as a source of demand for the products of business, without any counterpart in the demand for factors of production by business in column 1. Thus, it is a source of sales revenues without counterpart in productive expenditure or cost.

Table 16–2 provides a quantitative illustration of the role of net consumption in making the demand for the products of business exceed the demand for factors of production by business. Repeating the same headings as appeared in columns one and three of Table 16–1, it shows in its own first and third columns that item one under both heads, namely, the demand for capital goods

Table 16–1		
The Components of the Demand for Factors of Production and Products		
Demand for Factors of Production by Business (Productive Expenditure)		Demand for the Products of Business (Sales Revenues)
1. Demand for Capital Goods	—IDENTITY—	1. Demand for Capital Goods
2. Demand for Labor	—EQUALITY—	2. Labor's Demand for Consumers' Goods
	SOURCE OF EXCESS:	3. Businessmen's and Capitalists' Demand for Consumers' Goods

Table 16–2				
The Components of Demand Numerically Illustrated				
Demand for Factors of Production by Business (Productive Expenditure)			Demand for the Products of Business (Sales Revenues)	
1. Demand for Capital Goods:	500	—IDENTITY—	1. Demand for Capital Goods:	500
2. Demand for Labor:	300	—EQUALITY—	2. Labor's Demand for Consumers' Goods:	300
		SOURCE OF EXCESS:	3. Businessmen's and Capitalists' Demand for Consumers' Goods:	200
Total Demand for Factors of Production by Business:	800		Total Demand for the Products of Business:	1,000

and the demand for capital goods, are identically equal at 500 monetary units. It shows that item two under both heads, namely, the demand for labor and labor's demand for consumers' goods, respectively, are equal at 300 monetary units. Finally, it shows item three, which appears in column three only, namely, "Businessmen's and Capitalists' Demand for Consumers' Goods," as 200 monetary units. When the two sides of the table are added, it is obvious that this last item is the basis of the fact that the total demand for the products of business— sales revenues—amounts to 1,000 monetary units, while the demand for factors of production by business—productive expenditure—amounts to only 800 monetary units.

In making possible an excess of the demand for the products of business over the demand for factors of production by business, net consumption is the basis of the aggregate profit of business in conditions in which costs are equal to the demand for factors of production by business. This is because if the demand for products exceeds the demand for factors of production, then the demand for products exceeds costs that are equal to the demand for factors of production, and does so to exactly the same extent. If one thing exceeds another, than it equally exceeds a third thing that is equal to that other. Thus, demand for products exceeds costs even if costs are fully equal to the demand for factors of production, because the demand for products exceeds the demand for factors of production. In exactly the same way, in the terminology of sales revenues and productive expenditure, sales revenues exceed costs even if costs are fully equal to productive expenditure, because—thanks to net consumption—sales revenues exceed productive expenditure.

Net consumption is the source of aggregate profit because it is the source of the demand for the products

of business being greater than the demand for factors of production by business, and thus of an excess of the demand for the products of business over costs that are equal to the demand for factors of production by business. In the terminology of sales revenues and productive expenditure, net consumption is the source of aggregate profit because it is the source of the excess of sales revenues over productive expenditure and thus of an excess of sales revenues over costs equal to productive expenditure. To the extent that the demand for the products of business exceeds the demand for factors of production by business, to identically the same extent does the demand for the products of business and the concomitant sales revenues of business exceed costs generated by and equal to the demand for factors of production by business. Equivalently, to the extent that sales revenues exceed productive expenditure, to identically the same extent do they exceed costs generated by and equal to productive expenditure. Thus, in being responsible for the excess of demand for the products of business over the demand for factors of production by business, or, equivalently, the excess of business sales revenues over productive expenditure, the consumption expenditure of businessmen and capitalists—net consumption—is the basis for the existence of a corresponding aggregate profit in the economic system. It is the basis of an exactly equal aggregate profit whenever the costs of business equal the demand for factors of production or, equivalently, productive expenditure.

Net consumption is what explains how it is possible for business in the aggregate regularly and consistently to sell for more than it buys, even under the conditions of an invariable money. It does so because insofar as businessmen and capitalists are themselves consumers, business firms are constantly injecting more funds into the market in toto to buy the products of business than they expend for factors of production to produce those products. Receipts from the sale of the products of business in every year are generated by the *entire* expenditure of businessmen and capitalists, which includes their consumption expenditure as well as their productive expenditure; cost of production, on the other hand, tends to equal only their productive expenditure. Thus, the productive process is regularly accompanied by the existence of a demand for the products of business that is greater than the demand for the factors of production by business to produce those products. This is the cause of an excess of demand for the products of business over business costs and thus of business sales revenues over business costs.

To relate this discussion to the proposition that the demand for A is the demand for A, which I developed in the preceding chapter, we now see that the demand for products is not only not the same thing as a demand for factors of production, but regularly and consistently *exceeds* the demand for factors of production, and, in so doing, generates an amount of profit equal to that excess. The cause of the excess and thus the cause of the profit is the consumption of businessmen and capitalists. The amount of their consumption determines the amount of the excess of the demand for the products of business over the demand for factors of production by business and thus the amount of profit in conditions in which the demand for factors of production by business and the costs of business are equal.

Indeed, the net-consumption theory can be described as being contained in two propositions: (1) The entire demand for factors of production by business is directly (in the case of capital goods) or indirectly (in the case of labor) a source of demand for the products of business. (2) The demand for the products of business, however, is *not*—to the extent that it is a demand for consumers' goods—a demand for factors of production by business, but *exceeds* that demand by the consumption expenditure of businessmen and capitalists.

The role of net consumption in generating not merely an excess of demand for the products of business over the demand for factors of production by business, and thus of sales revenues over productive expenditure, but of an actual aggregate profit in the economic system, that is, an excess of sales revenues over *costs*, is depicted in Figure 16–1. This figure is an elaborated version of Figure 15–5, which showed the role of the demand for consumers' goods in determining national income under the conditions of an invariable money.[19]

Exactly as in Figure 15–5, Figure 16–1 shows a demand for capital goods of 500 and a demand for consumers' goods of 500 in every year from *Year 2* on. Thus it implicitly shows total business sales revenues as 1,000.

As in Figure 15–5, in response to these equal demands of 500, half the existing $1K$ of capital goods and $1L$ of labor are used to produce the next year's supply of capital goods, while the other half is used to produce the next year's supply of consumers' goods. Once again, the entire $1K$ and $1L$ are assumed to be used up in this way, and once again, the resulting product is shown as $1K$ of capital goods plus $1C$ of consumers' goods. Because the $1K$ of capital goods used up in production is replaced out of production, each succeeding year has the same supply of capital goods as the preceding year. And in each succeeding year, of course, the $1K$ of capital goods is joined by a fresh $1L$ of labor. As in Figure 15–5, the 500 of expenditure for capital goods each year enters into the cost of the resulting output that constitutes the next year's supply of capital goods and consumers' goods.

The only difference between Figure 16–1 and Figure 15–5 is that the former introduces the sources of the 500 of demand for consumers' goods. It explains these sources in part as 300 of wage payments by business, which makes possible 300 of consumption on the part of wage earners. To this, it adds 200 of consumption on the part of businessmen and capitalists. Figure 16–1 also points out that the 300 of wage payments by business will result in 300 of cost on account of labor in the next year. The 300 of wage payments is transmitted to the cost of the following year's supply of capital goods and consumers' goods by way of the center "production boxes," so to speak.

This is the same transmission mechanism as existed in Figure 15–5, where 500 of cost on account of capital goods alone was transmitted, though it was not named as such at the time. The only difference is that now, instead of the production box from *Year 2* on having merely $1K$ of capital goods at a cost of 500, and showing no cost for the $1L$ *of labor,* the $1L$ of labor carries a cost of 300 as well. The effect of the inclusion of the demand for labor by business is that the costs transmitted to the supplies of capital goods and consumers' goods available at the start of the following year are correspondingly larger. They are now respectively 50 percent of an 800-total outlay for factors of production instead of 50 percent merely of the 500 outlay for capital goods alone. Thus, the cost values of the capital goods and consumers' goods available at the start of *Year 3* and thereafter are 400 respectively, instead of 250 respectively, as was the case in Figure 15–5.

Figure 16–1 shows that while sales revenues in every year are 1,000, costs, which equal the productive expenditure of the year before, are only 800. Thus, an aggregate profit of 200 exists. In Figure 16–1, this is true explicitly for every year from *Year 3* on. In *Year 3*, sales revenues are 1,000, and costs, equal to the productive expenditure

Figure 16–1

Net Consumption and the Determination of Aggregate Profit

Year 1

1 K OF CAPITAL GOODS
PLUS 1L OF LABOR
PRODUCE:

50%   50%

Year 2   1K OF CAPITAL GOODS   1C OF CONSUMERS' GOODS

In Response to 500 of Demand for Capital Goods. This 500 of demand for capital goods is simultaneously 500 of sales revenues to the sellers of the capital goods. It will also result in 500 of cost on account of capital goods to the buyers, next year, when they sell the products the capital goods are used to produce.

In Response to 500 of Demand for Consumers' Goods. This 500 of demand for consumers' goods is simultaneously 500 of sales revenues to the sellers of the consumers' goods. It results from the payment of 300 of wages by business, which the wage earners consume, plus 200 of consumption expenditure by businessmen and capitalists. The 300 of wages also result in 300 of cost on account of labor next year, when the products the wage earners help to produce are sold.

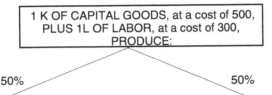

1 K OF CAPITAL GOODS, at a cost of 500,
PLUS 1L OF LABOR, at a cost of 300,
PRODUCE:

50%   50%

Year 3

1K OF CAPITAL GOODS, at a cost value of 400 on account of the capital goods and labor used to produce them, i.e., 50% of (500+300)

1C OF CONSUMERS' GOODS, at a cost value of 400 on account of the capital goods and labor used to produce them, i.e., 50% of (500+300)

In Response to 500 of Demand for Capital Goods. This 500 of demand for capital goods is simultaneously 500 of sales revenues to the sellers of the capital goods. It will also result in 500 of cost on account of capital goods to the buyers, next year, when they sell the products the capital goods are used to produce.

In Response to 500 of Demand for Consumers' Goods. This 500 of demand for consumers' goods is simultaneously 500 of sales revenues to the sellers of the consumers' goods. It results from the payment of 300 of wages by business, which the wage earners consume, plus 200 of consumption expenditure by businessmen and capitalists. The 300 of wages also result in 300 of cost on account of labor next year, when the products the wage earners help to produce are sold.

1 K OF CAPITAL GOODS, at a cost of 500,
PLUS 1L OF LABOR, at a cost of 300,
PRODUCE:

50%   50%

Year N

1K OF CAPITAL GOODS, at a cost value of 400 on account of the capital goods and labor used to produce them, i.e., 50% of (500+300)

1C OF CONSUMERS' GOODS, at a cost value of 400 on account of the capital goods and labor used to produce them, i.e., 50% of (500+300)

In Response to 500 of Demand for Capital Goods. This 500 of demand for capital goods is simultaneously 500 of sales revenues to the sellers of the capital goods. It will also result in 500 of cost on account of capital goods to the buyers, next year, when they sell the products the capital goods are used to produce.

In Response to 500 of Demand for Consumers' Goods. This 500 of demand for consumers' goods is simultaneously 500 of sales revenues to the sellers of the consumers' goods. It results from the payment of 300 of wages by business, which the wage earners consume, plus 200 of consumption expenditure by businessmen and capitalists. The 300 of wages also result in 300 of cost on account of labor next year, when the products the wage earners help to produce are sold.

of *Year 2*, are only 800. Identically the same situation applies to every year thereafter. What generates an aggregate profit in Figure 16–1 is the fact that in every year, sales revenues are constant at 1,000, while productive expenditure is constant at 800, which last means that the costs of the following year are also 800, at which time sales revenues will again be 1,000. An aggregate profit exists in Figure 16–1 because of the excess of sales revenues over productive expenditure. This fact implies an equal excess of sales revenues over costs, once costs come to equal productive expenditure, which, in the case of Figure 16–1, of course, is the very next year. To say it as simply as possible, the excess of sales revenues over productive expenditure is what explains the excess of sales revenues over costs equal to productive expenditure.

And, of course, what in turn explains the excess of sales revenues over productive expenditure in Figure 16–1 is net consumption—the consumption expenditure of businessmen and capitalists themselves. This expenditure, as Figure 16–1 further illustrates, is a source of sales revenues, but has no counterpart in productive expenditure or, therefore, in costs, which are generated by past productive expenditure, in this case, the productive expenditure of the year before.[20]

Table 16–3, which is based on the data of Figure 16–1, presents a further quantitative depiction of the role played by net consumption in determining aggregate profit. It shows that in each year, Figure 16–1's productive expenditure of 800 is the cause of equivalent costs that show up as a deduction from sales revenues in the following year. This is shown by the arrows sloping down and to the right, connecting each year's 800 of productive expenditure to the next year's 800 of costs. The table also shows each year's 800 of productive expenditure as the source of equivalent sales revenues in the same year as that in which the productive expenditure takes place. This is shown by the two straight lines, a short one going

Table 16–3

Productive Expenditure, Costs, and Sales Revenues —the Elements Generating Profit in Figure 16–1

Year	Productive Expenditure	Costs	Sales Revenues	Profit	Net Consumption
1	NA	NA	NA	NA	NA
2	800	NA	1,000	NA	200
3	800	800	1,000	200	200
4	800	800	1,000	200	200
5	800	800	1,000	200	200
. . .	. . .	. . .	. . .	. . .	. . .
N	800	800	1,000	200	200

The table above shows that the productive expenditure of each year shows up as equivalent costs in the next year. It also shows that a repetition of the same amount of productive expenditure in the next year generates sales revenues equal to those costs. Finally, it shows that the excess of sales revenues over costs is determined by net consumption, which is essentially the consumption expenditure of businessmen and capitalists. (As in Figure 16–1, on which the table is based, quantitative data are not available for *Year 1,* with the result that neither costs nor profits can be calculated for *Year 2.*)

down and a longer one going across to the right, that culminate in an arrow pointing upward to the 1,000 of sales revenues of each year. The source of the sales revenues being 1,000 while productive expenditure is 800 is clearly the 200 of consumption expenditure on the part of businessmen and capitalists in each year, which is represented by the item "Net Consumption." When the 200 of sales revenues generated by this 200 of consumption expenditure are added to the 800 of sales revenues generated by the 800 of productive expenditure, total sales revenues become 1,000. The generation of 1,000 of sales revenues is depicted by the confluence of the two vertical arrows, one representing the 800 of productive expenditure in the year, and the other representing the 200 of consumption on the part of businessmen and capitalists—the item "net consumption." (Two additional straight lines, again, a short one going down and a longer one going across, but this time to the left, connect net consumption to the second arrow pointing up to sales revenues.) Thus, what enables sales revenues to be 1,000 while productive expenditure and costs are 800 is the consumption expenditure of the businessmen and capitalists in the amount of 200. This consumption expenditure is what makes sales revenues exceed productive expenditure by 200 and thus costs by 200, with the result that 200 of profit is generated.

In order to show the determination not only of the aggregate amount of profit but also of the average rate of profit in the economic system, it is necessary to add yet some further elaboration to the diagrammatic analysis we have been pursuing since Chapter 14. This is done in Figure 16–2, which is an elaboration of Figure 16–1.

In Figure 16–2, each year is described in terms of a series of rows depicting the "Opening Assets of Business," "Transactions," and "Production," respectively. We are already familiar with all of these elements from Figure 16–1, even though they were not explicitly labeled as such at the time. In Figure 16–1, each year began with what in essence was a partial description of the opening assets of business in that year, namely, the quantity $1K$ of capital goods and the quantity $1C$ of consumer's goods. Indeed, in Figure 16–1, starting in *Year 3*, these quantities were shown as possessing cost values of 400 monetary units each. These cost values were derived on the basis of the transactions and production that took place in the preceding year. Figure 16–1 showed that starting with *Year 2*, 500 monetary units were expended in buying the $1K$ of capital goods every year, and 300 monetary units were expended in buying the $1L$ of labor that was available every year for production. The fact that 800 monetary units in all were thus paid for the factors of production in each year and that then those factors of production were used 50 percent in

producing capital goods and 50 percent in producing consumers' goods, was what underlay the respective cost values of 400 for the capital goods and consumers' goods appearing at the beginning of *Year 3* and all subsequent years.

In Figure 16–2, identically the same kind of "production box" appears in each year as appeared in Figure 16–1. The only difference is that in Figure 16–2 it is labeled as production, in a distinct row. Transactions are described graphically in Figure 16–2, whereas in Figure 16–1, they were described verbally. The only substantive difference between Figures 16–2 and 16–1 is that in Figure 16–2 the opening assets of business that are described in the first row under each year, are not only $1K$ of capital goods and $1C$ of consumers' goods, as before, but also a sum of money—namely, 1,000 units of cash. In addition, the capital goods and consumers' goods are shown bearing their specific monetary cost values, namely, 400 monetary units each, starting with *Year 1*, rather than *Year 3*. The cost values shown in the opening assets of *Year 1* are derived by treating *Year 1* as representing exactly the same set of conditions as prevailed in all the years of Figure 16–1 from *Year 3* on. In Figure 16–2, *Year 1* should be understood as representing a year following an indefinite number of previous years just like it and like those that follow it, and as being labeled *Year 1* only from the perspective of being the first year singled out for analysis.

The cash, and the various transactions that it finances, are shown in distinct, gray-colored boxes. The transactions, of course, appear in the second, transactions row under each year. They represent expenditure of the money originally held as an opening asset of business, in the first row, namely, the asset "1,000 units of Cash to Be Paid Out." This sum, and the demand for the goods and services of business that it finances every year, are both assumed to be invariably fixed at 1,000 units of money.

For the sake of simplicity, it is assumed in Figure 16–2 that all transactions take place on the first day of each year, whereafter the various parties retire to engage in the process of producing the output that will become available and will be sold on the first day of the following year.[21] Thus, it is assumed that on the first day of each year, business buys its entire supply of capital goods for the year and pays all the wages and sources of net consumption that it pays for the entire year, and that the recipients of these sums turn around and expend them on that same day in buying a year's supply of consumers' goods from business. This assumption permits dealing with all transactions in the economic system at one fell swoop and then turning to the process of production that ensues with the capital goods and labor that have been purchased. The process of production, of course, is de-

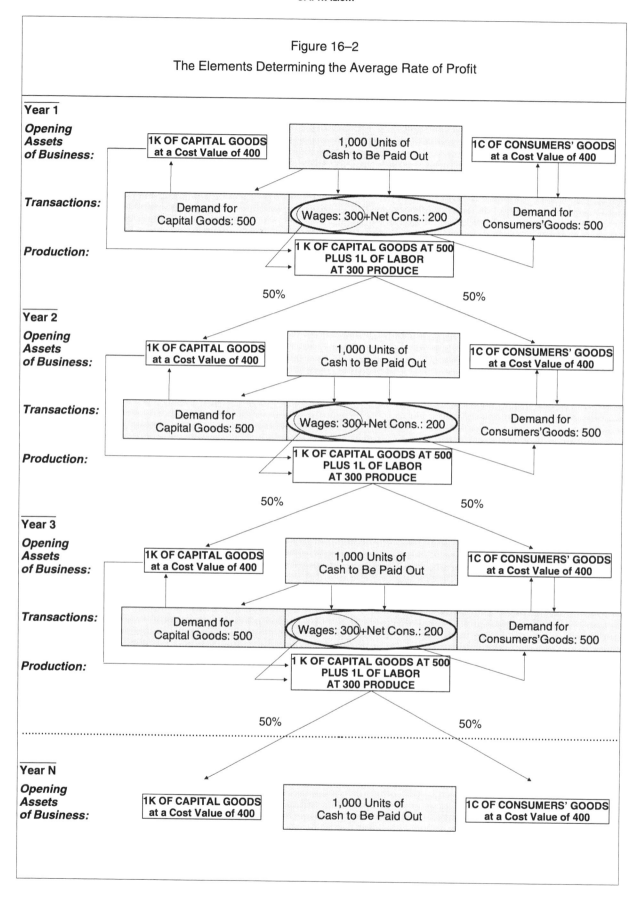

Figure 16–2
The Elements Determining the Average Rate of Profit

picted in the production row under each year, as I have already said. As in Figure 16–1, the process of production of each year culminates in the supply of capital goods and consumers' goods contained in the opening assets of business at the start of the following year. Just as before, it is assumed that all capital goods and labor used in production in any year are fully used up in producing the output that will be sold at the start of the following year. The assumption also continues to be made, of course, that the factors of production in each year are used in accordance with the relative demands for capital goods and consumers' goods that are expected to exist in the following year, and that these expectations are correct.

In Figure 16–2, in *Year 1* and in every succeeding year, 500 units of cash are expended by business firms in buying capital goods, just as was the case in Figure 16–1 from *Year 2* on. The origin of the demand for capital goods in the opening cash holding of business is indicated by the small arrow which connects the lower left-hand portion of the gray box "1,000 Units of Cash to Be Paid Out" to the upper right-hand portion of the gray box "Demand for Capital Goods: 500."

The firms that expend the 500 for capital goods receive into their possession *IK* of capital goods out of the opening assets of business. That *IK* of capital goods will then serve these firms in the process of production depicted in the production row. The conveyance of the *IK* of capital goods from the opening assets of business to their subsequent use in production is depicted by a series of three straight lines running from the box representing *IK* of capital goods as an opening asset of business, around the box "Demand for Capital Goods: 500" in the transactions row, and culminating in an arrow pointing to the production box in the production row. Thus, as in Figure 16–1, the *IK* of capital goods enters into the process of production with a cost value of 500, which is the sum of money that was paid for these capital goods in the transactions row.

At the same time that business firms are buying *IK* of capital goods for use in further production, business firms are, of course, also selling that *IK* of capital goods. Here, however, Figure 16–2 goes beyond Figure 16–1 in that it shows not only that business in the aggregate is simultaneously both a buyer and a seller of capital goods to the same extent, but also the corollary fact that from the perspective of business as a whole, insofar as the asset "cash" is drawn down in the purchase of capital goods, it is simultaneously replenished in the sale of capital goods. Thus, to this extent, the cash holding of business in the aggregate remains unchanged, and cash will be available to finance the fresh transactions of the following year. This is depicted by a combination of two arrows. First, there is the one running down and to the left from

the gray box labeled "1,000 Units of Cash to Be Paid Out" and over to the gray box labeled "Demand for Capital Goods: 500" in the transactions row. And then there is the one that runs vertically upward from this latter box to the white box representing the *IK* of capital goods in the opening-assets-of-business row. This second arrow, shows the return to business of the cash paid out by business in the purchase of capital goods.

The opening cash holding of business is also assumed to finance total wage payments of 300 units of money and net consumption in the amount of 200 units of money, which, in combination, in turn make possible the demand for consumers' goods of 500 units of money. Two small arrows running from the bottom of the box "1,000 Units of Cash to Be Paid Out" to the top of the gray box "Wages: 300 + Net Cons.: 200" indicate the origin of wage payments and the sources of net consumption in the opening cash holding of business. The depiction of wage payments by business together with net consumption as the source of demand for consumers' goods from business is achieved by means of an ellipse drawn around wages plus net consumption, to which is attached a straight line sloping downward and to the right and that culminates in a vertical arrow pointing up to the gray box representing the demand for consumers' goods. The up and down arrows running between the gray demand-for-consumers-goods box and the white consumers-goods box signify that money is turned over to business in exchange for the consumers' goods and that these goods are conveyed into the possession of their buyers.

Thus, in Figure 16–2, as in Figure 16–1, in financing both the demand for capital goods and the demand for consumers' goods, business itself is shown as the source, direct or indirect, of the entire demand for its products, that is, of all of its own sales revenues. At the same time, however, it is also shown that because the cash that business draws down in making wage and payments and in providing the sources of net consumption is returned to it in the form of receipts from the sale of consumers' goods, business will have the same 1,000 units of cash available as an opening asset in the next year as it had in the present year. This is because the 500 of cash expended in wage payments and in providing the sources of net consumption which is returned in 500 of receipts from the sale of consumers' goods, is joined to the 500 of cash expended in the purchase of capital goods and simultaneously returned in the sale of capital goods.

Thus, what Figure 16–2 shows is business making 1,000 of total outlays, on the basis of which it obtains 1,000 of total sales revenues, and, in the receipt of the sales revenues, the return of all the cash that it has laid out.

As in Figure 16–1, the *IL* of labor that business buys for its 300 payment of wages, shows up in the production box at its cost value of 300. This is depicted by the ellipse drawn specifically around "Wages: 300" and connected to the production box by a straight line sloping downward and to the left and culminating in a horizontal arrow pointing right, to the production box. Thus, as in Figure 16–1, the production box shows both *IK* of capital goods at 500 plus *IL* of labor at 300.

Figure 16–2 provides all the elements necessary for the explanation not only of the generation of 1,000 of aggregate sales revenues and 800 of cost on account of capital goods and labor, and thus 200 of aggregate profit, as did Figure 16–1. It also provides the further information necessary for a precise calculation of the average rate of profit in the economic system in every year. It does so in providing knowledge of the total value of the opening assets of business each year, which is shown to be 1,800 monetary units. This amount, which is the sum of the 400 cost value of the *IK* of capital goods on hand, plus the 400 cost value of the *IC* of consumers' goods on hand, plus 1,000 of cash, represents the total capital invested in the economic system. It is, in effect, the sum of cash together with the cost value of inventory and net plant and equipment.[22] Thus, it follows that the average rate of profit in the economic system described in Figure 16–2 is precisely 200/1,800, or 11.1 percent. This is the amount of profit earned in the economic system, divided by the amount of capital invested in the economic system, which latter, as I say, is what the sum of the asset values I have just named represents.[23]

Inasmuch as the amount of profit in an economic system with an invariable money, such as that described in Figure 16–2, tends to equal the amount of net consumption, it follows that the rate of profit in such an economic system tends to equal *the rate of net consumption.* The rate of net consumption is the rate borne by the amount of net consumption to the total capital invested in the economic system. Whatever this rate may be, precisely that is what the average rate of profit in such an economic system must tend to be. In Figure 16–2, for example, the rate of profit of 200/1,800 is precisely equal to the rate of net consumption, which is also 200/1,800. This is an essential finding of this section, to which reference will be made in subsequent pages.

Net Consumption: Its Other Sources, Wider Meaning, and Relationship to the Saving of Wage Earners

An excess of consumption over wage payments is capable of being caused by factors other than consumption out of dividends, draw, and interest payments, though these are its regular and most important sources and tend to be the only sources in an economic system with an invariable money. Consumption made possible by business firms' repayment of debt or retirement of outstanding shares of stock is also capable of contributing to consumption spending being greater than wage payments, and thus of causing sales revenues to be greater than productive expenditure and costs. Consumption out of newly created money is likewise capable of so contributing. So too is consumption by wage earners that is made possible by extensions of credit from business firms and which permits their consumption to be greater than their wages. In addition, it should be realized that to whatever extent the total consumption expenditure of wage earners turns out to be less than wages, the excess of consumption over wages is correspondingly reduced.

The term net consumption embraces *all* sources of consumption in excess of wage payments, and thus of sales revenues in excess of productive expenditure. It also takes into account any possible diminution of this excess that might be caused by the consumption of wage earners being less than wages. Net consumption is simply the total spending to buy consumers' goods in the economic system, minus wage payments by business firms. It is, as I say, the demand for consumers' goods minus the demand for labor by business.

It must be pointed out that net consumption equals not only the demand for consumers' goods minus the wages paid by business firms, but *all* of consumption, insofar as it constitutes sales revenue or wage income, minus *all* of wages. This is because the total of such consumption differs from the demand for consumers' goods only by the addition of wage payments made by consumers—viz., by the w_c of Chapter 15.[24] By the same token, the total of wages differs from the wages paid by business firms by those very same wages paid by consumers. Thus,

$$\text{Net Consumption} = s_c - w_b =$$
$$s_c + w_c - (w_b + w_c) = C - w.$$

Again, equals added to unequals do not affect the amount of the inequality.

The fact that net consumption can be stated as consumption minus wages provides further confirmation for the fact that aggregate profit tends to equal it. This is because the proposition that profit tends to equal consumption minus wages is a corollary of the previously established proposition that national income tends to equal consumption. National income, of course, is essentially profit plus wages. It should not be surprising therefore, that profit, which necessarily equals national income minus wages, also tends to equal consumption minus wages, i.e., net consumption. That is, if $p + w$ tends to equal C, then p tends to equal $C - w$. As I have said, the main sources of net consumption (and in an economy with an invariable money, virtually the only sources worth speaking about in the long run) are dividends, draw, and interest payments. In an economy with an invariable money, net consumption and the consumption of businessmen and capitalists are virtually one and the same. In an economy with an expanding quantity of money, net consumption tends to be somewhat larger than this, reflecting as well consumption spending out of new and additional money. As I have indicated, such net consumption might also include consumption spending by wage earners in excess of wage payments, which is financed by continuing net extensions of credit accompanying the increase in the quantity of money.[25]

It is almost certainly the case, however, that the influence of a growing quantity of money and therefore rising wage incomes is to lead wage earners to increase their accumulated savings, in order to maintain a certain balance with their rising incomes. In connection with this fact, it must be stressed that it would be an error to assume that consumption out of wages tends to be less than wages to the extent that wage earners save. Most of the savings of wage earners goes to finance loans for various forms of consumption, above all, home mortgage loans, which are the leading asset of savings banks and life insurance companies, which, of course, in turn are the leading vehicles for wage earners' saving. Such savings of wage earners are themselves consumed and do not in any way diminish consumption expenditure. They merely transfer it from those who earn the wages to those who borrow the savings made out of wages. The same point, of course, applies to savings of wage earners that are used to finance such things as installment loans for the purchase of personal automobiles and all the various home appliances, and to vacation loans.[26]

Of course, to an important extent, the savings of wage earners are used to finance productive expenditures by business firms, and a significant number of wage earners use their savings to launch their own businesses. But when the extensions of credit to wage earners that come from business firms—such as mortgage and installment loans financed by business firms' time deposits at commercial banks—are offset against such savings by wage earners, it is probable that the whole or practically the whole of wages has an equivalent in consumption on the part of wage earners, irrespective of the fact that the wage earners are engaged in saving.

It should be clearly understood that net consumption explains profits not only in the production and sale of consumers' goods, but equally in the production and sale of capital goods. It is not accidental that in Figure 16–2, the production of capital goods is fully as profitable as the production of consumers' goods. (With the cost value

of both the capital goods and the consumers' goods at 400 each, and sales revenue in both cases at 500, the profit in both cases is 100.) The existence of net consumption operates to make the demand for goods at every stage of the productive process exceed the demand for the factors of production required to produce those goods. This is because consumption on the part of businessmen and capitalists engaged in the production of capital goods makes the demand for factors of production at every stage of capital goods production less than the demand for the resulting capital goods at that stage.

The uniformity-of-profit principle cooperates in producing this effect. If the rate of profit is higher in any branch of production than in the rest of the economic system, then a tendency exists to withdraw capital from the less profitable branches and invest it in the more profitable branches. This results in a reduction in productive expenditure in the less profitable branches and an increase in productive expenditure in the more profitable branches.

For these reasons, productive expenditure tends to be less than sales revenues throughout the economic system, and by no means merely in the production of consumers' goods alone.

Confirming the Critique of the Exploitation Theory

It should be obvious by now that in the conditions of an invariable money, the higher is net consumption, the higher is the amount and rate of profit and that the lower is net consumption, the lower is the amount and rate of profit.

To illustrate this fact, let us assume that businessmen and capitalists, instead of expending 800 monetary units for factors of production and only 200 monetary units in their own consumption, as they do in Figures 16–1 and 16–2, reduce their expenditure for capital goods from 500 to 400 monetary units, and their expenditure for labor from 300 to 200 monetary units, thereby bringing their total expenditure for factors of production down to 600 monetary units while equivalently increasing their consumption expenditure from 200 to 400 monetary units. The demand for factors of production, therefore, is now only 600 monetary units, but the total demand for the products of business remains unchanged at 1,000 monetary units. This last is because the reduction in demand for capital goods is offset by a rise in the demand for consumers' goods on the part of businessmen and capitalists, and the reduction in the wage earners' demand for consumers' goods, resulting from the reduction in the demand for labor, is likewise offset. Thus, the difference between productive expenditure and sales revenue now rises to 400 monetary units, and, hence, aggregate profit now tends to rise to 400 monetary units. This is because aggregate business costs will fall from 800, the previous level of productive expenditure, to 600, the new, lower level of productive expenditure. This is shown in Table 16–4.[27]

Assuming an invariable money, and thus the demand for the products of business and therefore sales revenues to be unchanged at 1,000 monetary units, productive expenditure and the demand for factors of production by business could, conceivably, vary anywhere from zero to an amount not far short of the full demand for products, namely, 1,000 monetary units.[28] The height of the demand for factors of production depends on the height of net consumption. It will be the higher, the lower is net consumption, and the lower, the higher is net consumption. If net consumption—the consumption of businessmen and capitalists, who are the recipients of sales revenues—were to rise to equal the full amount of sales revenues, the demand for factors of production would fall to zero, and the rate of profit would rise to infinity. This is because in the absence of productive expenditure, the costs to be deducted from sales revenues would fall to zero. Thus the amount of profit would rise to equal the full amount of sales revenues. At the same time, as a further result of the absence of productive expenditure, the total of capital invested in the economic system would fall to zero. With productive expenditure zero, the wages paid in the production of products for sale would,

of course, also be zero. Precisely this was the case elaborated in Chapter 11, in the critique of the theoretical framework of the exploitation theory.[29] On the other hand, if net consumption were permanently to fall to as low a rate as is consistent with the existence of time preference—with the result that businessmen and capitalists consumed only the most modest portion of their sales revenues and used almost the full amount of them for productive expenditure—the demand for factors of production would rise almost to the point of sales revenues. The result would be that the costs deducted from sales revenues would rise almost to equal the sales revenues. This, together with the great accumulation of capital that would ensue, would mean that the amount and rate of profit would fall to a minimum.

Thus, it should now be apparent that in conditions of an invariable money, the rate of profit depends on the rate of net consumption. It should be equally apparent that insofar as this is the case, the rate of profit and economic progress and prosperity are *inversely related*, just as under an invariable money nominal national income and economic progress and prosperity are inversely related. This is because to the extent that the rate of profit depends on the rate of net consumption, a higher rate of profit signifies a lower relative demand for and production of capital goods. It also signifies a lower demand for labor relative to the demand for consumers' goods.

Table 16–4

A Rise in Profits Caused by a Rise in Net Consumption and Fall in Productive Expenditure

Year	Productive Expenditure	Costs	Sales Revenues	Profit	Net Consumption
1	600	600	1,000	400	400
2	600	600	1,000	400	400
3	600	600	1,000	400	400
4	600	600	1,000	400	400

The 600 of productive expenditure in the above table results from a fall in the demand for capital goods from 500 to 400 and in the demand for labor from 300 to 200, which are the consequence of a rise in net consumption from 200 to 400. Sales revenues continue to equal 1,000: while receipts from the sale of capital goods are 400 instead of 500 and receipts from the sale of consumers' goods to wage earners are 200 instead of 300, receipts from the sale of consumers' goods to businessmen and capitalists are now that much larger: 400 instead of 200. The effect is that the excess of sales revenues over productive expenditure is correspondingly increased. And since the productive expenditure of each year determines the costs deducted from sales revenues in the next year, profits are increased equivalently. In other words, the rise in net consumption results in unchanged sales revenues accompanied by equivalently lower costs of production deducted from those sales revenues.

3. The Net-Consumption Theory Further Considered

The net-consumption theory requires further elaboration. There are, first of all, a number of questions or objections not yet considered, which are almost certain to be raised against it. And then there is the necessity of tracing net consumption back to more fundamental forces.

Why Businessmen and Capitalists Cannot Arbitrarily Increase the Rate of Net Consumption and the Rate of Profit

A question that can be raised in connection with the net-consumption theory is that if the consumption of the businessmen and capitalists is, at least in part, the cause of the profit they earn, why do they not deliberately increase their consumption and thereby increase the rate of profit?

To answer this question, we need only distinguish between the effect of an increase in the consumption of an individual businessman or capitalist on the profit which *he* will earn and on the profit which *all businessmen and capitalists taken together* will earn. An increase in consumption on the part of an individual businessman or capitalist operates to increase the amount of profit in the economic system as a whole, but, at the same time, to reduce the capital of the individual businessman or capitalist in question to a much greater degree, and thereby to reduce the amount of profit which *he* will earn.

For example, let us assume that, just as in Figure 16–2, the sum of all capitals in the economic system as a whole is 1,800 monetary units and that the aggregate amount of profit is 200 monetary units, equal to 200 monetary units of net consumption. Let us also assume that in this economic system some particular individual businessman or capitalist possesses a capital of 18 monetary units. (This is obviously an enormously large businessman or capitalist, possessing as he does an amount of capital equal to a full 1 percent of the entire capital of the economic system.) If we further assume that this businessman or capitalist possesses the average degree of skill and efficiency in investing his capital, he will earn 2 monetary units in profit on his capital, for that is the product of the average rate of profit of $200/1,800$, or $1/9$, times his individual capital of 18.

Now let us assume that he increases his consumption by 1 monetary unit. In the economic system as a whole, the amount of net consumption and the amount of profit will rise to 201 monetary units, but the capital of this individual businessman or capitalist will have fallen to 17 monetary units, with the result that *he* earns a smaller amount of profit than before. This is because the now very slightly higher average rate of profit that our indi-

vidual businessman or capitalist earns of $201/1,799$, when applied to his reduced capital of 17 monetary units, yields an amount of profit of only 1.9 monetary units, as compared with the 2 monetary units of profit that he originally earned. The situation of this individual businessman or capitalist is that he now earns a profit of 17 times $201/1,799$ instead of 18 times $200/1,800$. He earns less profit because his capital falls in the ratio of 17 to 18, while aggregate profit rises only in the much smaller ratio of 201 to 200. Thus, his individual share of aggregate profit falls by more than aggregate profit increases. And if, as is more likely the case, our individual businessman or capitalist possessed a capital of one-tenth of 1 percent of the capital of the economic system rather than 1 percent, that is, 1.8 of capital rather than 18 of capital, the reduction in his profits resulting from increasing his consumption by one monetary unit would be even more pronounced. In that case, instead of earning 1.8 times $200/1,800$, he would earn .8 times $201/1,799$. His own individual capital would be cut more than in half, while he succeeded in raising the average rate of profit only very slightly.

The principle here is that while an individual businessman or capitalist can to some extent succeed in raising the general, average rate of profit by increasing his own consumption, he reduces his own individual capital to a greater degree. The effect of his action, therefore, would be to benefit other businessmen and capitalists while harming himself. Thus, businessmen and capitalists are not in a position to attempt deliberately to raise the rate of profit by increasing their own consumption.

The Net-Consumption Rate and the Gravitation of Relative Wealth and Income

The fact that businessmen and capitalists cannot arbitrarily raise their own individual rates of profit by virtue of increasing their consumption, has major implications for the question of what determines the growth and decline of the fortunes of individual businessmen and capitalists relative to one another.

In an economic system with an invariable money, the general or average rate of profit is determined by the economy-wide—necessarily *average*—rate of net consumption. Individual businessmen and capitalists, however, consume at widely varying *individual* rates—some well above the rate of net consumption and some substantially below it. If all businessmen and capitalists had the same productive ability, they would all earn the same rate of profit, as determined by the rate of net consumption. Those individual businessmen and capitalists whose consumption relative to their capitals was below average, would save and accumulate capital, while those individual businessmen and capitalists whose consumption relative to their capitals was above average would decumulate capital.

For example, in the conditions of Figure 16–2, businessmen and capitalists of average productive ability would earn the average rate of profit of 11.1 percent, which is equal to the net-consumption rate. The businessmen or capitalists of average productive ability whose own individual rates of consumption relative to accumulated capital happened to be 11.1 percent would neither accumulate nor decumulate capital. Those individual businessmen or capitalists of average productive ability whose individual rates of consumption relative to accumulated capital were less than 11.1 percent would accumulate capital. Those whose individual rates were above 11.1 percent would decumulate capital. For example, businessmen and capitalists with a 7 percent rate of consumption relative to accumulated capital would accumulate additional capital at the rate of approximately 4 percent a year. By the same token, those with a 15 percent rate of consumption relative to accumulated capital would decumulate capital at the rate of approximately 4 percent a year.

It follows from this discussion that the rate of net consumption prevailing in the economy as a whole tends to be governed by the rates of consumption relative to accumulated capital of those individual businessmen and capitalists *whose rates are the lowest*. In the nature of the case, with each passing year, these individuals tend to come into possession of a larger and larger proportion of the total capital of the economic system, while those with above-average rates of consumption progressively deprive themselves of capital. Thus the lower rates of consumption come to prevail on an ever growing proportion of the total capital of the economic system and more and more to govern the overall ratio of net consumption to capital.

This fact, incidentally, implies that even if there were somehow a conspiracy of a large number of businessmen and capitalists to raise the rate of profit by virtue of increasing their consumption, the conspiracy could not succeed for very long. This is because even if these businessmen and capitalists possessed the far greater part of the capital of the economic system and were in a position temporarily to increase their own profits by increasing their consumption, any businessman or capitalist who stood outside the conspiracy would earn that same higher rate of profit and, at the same time, thanks to his lower rate of consumption relative to accumulated capital, would be able rapidly to increase his capital relative to that of the members of the conspiracy. The effect of any such conspiracy would simply be to destroy its members and to replace them with businessmen and capitalists who consumed less relatively to their accumu-

lated capitals. Always, as far as it is governed by the rate of net consumption, the rate of profit tends to be governed by the lowest rates of consumption relative to accumulated capital.

As we already know, and shall see further, net consumption is not the only determinant of the rate of profit. The fact that it is not makes the rate of profit higher than the rate of net consumption. But even so—assuming they are of average productive ability and therefore earn the average rate of profit—those businessmen and capitalists with rates of consumption that are below the net-consumption rate tend to expand relatively to those businessmen and capitalists whose rates of consumption are above the net-consumption rate. For example, it may be that the net-consumption rate in the economic system is 3 percent, say, while the average rate of profit is 6 percent, the difference being the result of the operation of factors other than net consumption (notably, net investment). In such conditions, businessmen and capitalists of average productive ability will earn the average rate of profit of 6 percent. Those with rates of consumption relative to accumulated capital of less than 3 percent will save and invest and thus increase their capital at a more rapid rate than those with rates of consumption relative to capital of greater than 3 percent. A businessman or capitalist with a rate of consumption relative to capital of 2 percent, say, will be able to save and invest two-thirds of his 6 percent rate of profit. He will increase his capital at a 4 percent annual rate. By the same token, a businessman or capitalist with a rate of consumption relative to accumulated capital of 4 percent, say, will be able to save and invest only one-third of his 6 percent rate of profit. He will be able to accumulate additional capital at only a 2 percent annual rate. Thus, just as under the conditions of an invariable money, those businessmen and capitalists with the lowest rates of consumption relative to accumulated capital must tend increasingly to prevail, for they will steadily be increasing the size of their capitals relative to the capitals of businessmen and capitalists with higher rates of consumption relative to accumulated capital.

Of course, individual businessmen and capitalists differ widely in their productive abilities. Those with above-average productive ability earn higher rates of profit than those with below-average productive ability, which latter may actually incur losses. These differences in the individual rates of profit that are earned are no less important in determining the growth or decline of the fortunes of individual businessmen and capitalists. The full principle determining the growth or decline of the fortunes of individual businessmen and capitalists relative to one another must be stated as follows: *The relative wealth and income of individual businessmen and capitalists tends to grow to the degree that their productive ability is above average and their rate of consumption relative to accumulated capital is below average, and to decline to the degree that their productive ability is below average and their consumption relative to accumulated capital is above average.*

In an economic system with an invariable money, the wealth and income of the businessmen and capitalists of below-average productive ability and/or above-average rates of consumption would tend to decline absolutely in terms of money. In an economic system with an increasing quantity of money and volume of spending, the monetary value of the wealth and income of such businessmen and capitalists need not decline in absolute terms, but it will still decline to the same extent in relative terms. Thus, for example, instead of the fortunes of the heirs of such great businessmen and capitalists as John Jacob Astor and Cornelius Vanderbilt shrinking from tens of millions to tens of thousands, while the fortunes of new great businessmen and capitalists correspondingly rise, the decline of the former is less and the rise of the latter correspondingly greater in terms of money. If the increase in the quantity of money and volume of spending is great enough, it will be common to have cases in which there is no absolute decline in family fortunes in monetary terms. But then the rise in the fortunes of the newcomers in terms of money is correspondingly greater still.[30]

Irrespective of the nature of the monetary system, whether it is invariable or expanding, the present discussion confirms the previous discussion of economic inequality in Chapter 9 of this book, concerning the earning of fortunes in a capitalist economy.[31] Fortunes are earned on the basis of above-average productive ability coupled with below-average rates of consumption relative to accumulated capital. They are made by earning high rates of profit and saving and reinvesting the far greater part of the profits. Relative wealth and income in a capitalist economy always gravitates to those who are most productive and most provident. The further effect is the most rapid possible increase in the absolute amount of real physical wealth, which, of course, is to the benefit of all.

Accumulated Capital as a Determinant of Net Consumption

A second question or objection that may be raised in connection with the net-consumption theory is that it places the consumption of the businessmen and capitalists ahead of their receipt of profit and thereby reverses cause and effect. To be sure, this is the very opposite of the way in which one usually approaches the relationship between consumption and income. One usually places income before consumption. However, in the case of the consumption of the businessmen and capitalists, the procedure of the net-consumption theory is perfectly proper. This is because businessmen and capitalists possess not only their incomes but also, first and foremost, their *capitals*. The consumption of businessmen and capitalists is not governed by their incomes, but by their exchangeable wealth, that is, by the sum of their incomes and capitals together. At any given time, their incomes constitute only a small fraction of this total, and their capitals the overwhelmingly greater part. This is true typically even of a whole year's income. It is even more true insofar as the income earned by businessmen and capitalists is itself conceived as a sum of exchangeable wealth, which it is in the form in which it is actually obtained, such as a quarterly dividend check, or the profits of a particular month or even week or day. It is probable that a decline in the incomes of businessmen and capitalists affects their consumption only to the extent that it represents a decline in this total of their exchangeable wealth.

The consumption of businessmen and capitalists in the real world is never in fact greatly affected by the height of their current incomes. Business enterprises continue to pay interest on loans and, often, dividends on stock, even when these payments are not covered by current earnings. Furthermore, it should be recalled that in addition to dividend and interest payments on the part of business enterprises, funds for consumption can be obtained by businessmen and capitalists by means of the redemption of bond and stock issues by business firms. Imagine the case of a stockholder whose enterprise is currently paying no dividends. If elsewhere in the economic system, a bond or stock issue is redeemed, the stockholder in question can sell a portion of his holdings to these other bond or stockholders whose holdings have been redeemed, and then consume the proceeds. For the bond or stockholders whose holdings have been redeemed will almost certainly wish to reinvest most of the funds they receive, and in so doing they disperse the funds they have received to securities owners throughout the economic system and thereby provide funds for consumption even in cases in which no interest or dividend income has been received. And even apart from any current redemption of securities by business firms, there are always funds in the market available to buy the security holdings of any given individual.

In connection with this discussion, it is worth noting that in the worst years of the Great Depression—1932 and 1933—when total profit income in the United States was approximately $11 billion and $10 billion respectively, net consumption was approximately $17 billion and $15 billion respectively, the difference between profits and net consumption being accounted for by negative net investment in the respective amounts of approximately $6 billion and $5 billion.[32]

It is perfectly reasonable that the consumption of businessmen and capitalists should be governed primarily by their capitals rather than by their incomes. Imagine the case of an individual who possesses a capital of $10,000,000, and who customarily earns $500,000 in income on this capital, which, for the sake of simplicity, we assume is all available to him on the first day of the year, having been paid to him at the very end of the year before.[33] Let us assume that he is in the habit of consuming his entire income, and that suddenly this income ceases. Previously, on the first day of each year, he possessed $10,500,000, of which he consumed $500,000 over the course of the year, and employed $10,000,000 to make provision for the future, in the form of investments. Now, on the first day of this year, he possesses only $10,000,000. Will his consumption be appreciably different? Almost certainly not.

If he possesses $10,000,000 instead of $10,500,000, his consumption will be only slightly affected. He will still be a multimillionaire and will still live like one. The fact that he has no income will not have anything remotely like the significance it has for an individual with little or no capital. His loss of $500,000 of income will be taken out both on his current consumption and on his provision for the future, and probably, on average, in the same proportions as he previously consumed and made provision for the future. What is of significance for such an individual is not the decline in his income, but the much more modest decline in the total of his income as obtained plus his capital. The measure of this decline is not 100 percent, as it is in the case of his income, but something less than 5 percent. Rather than expecting his consumption to fall to zero because his income has fallen to zero, it is much more reasonable to expect that both his consumption and his provision for the future will fall in proportion to the fall in his overall exchangeable wealth, that is, in the ratio of $^{\$10,000,000}/_{\$10,500,000}$, which of course is $^{20}/_{21}$. Thus, in an average case, he would now most likely consume on the order of $475,000 over the course of the year, and employ on the order of $9,525,000 to make provision for the future. For these sums stand in the same respective proportions to $10,000,000 as do $500,000 and $10,000,000 to $10,500,000.

Thus, even if the income of businessmen and capitalists were to completely disappear for some reason, if they still possessed their capitals, their consumption would continue almost unchanged and very soon restore the rate of profit to its former height insofar as it depends on the rate of net consumption. This is because, given the existence of net consumption and its accompanying excess

of sales revenues over productive expenditure, the only way that profit could not exist would be if there were an equivalent excess of cost over productive expenditure, which is to say, if there were an equivalent negative net investment. But continuing negative net investment is an impossibility, if for no other reason than the exhaustion of assets.[34] In the absence of negative net investment, the existence of net consumption guarantees a corresponding positive average rate of profit.

There is a second aspect to the criticism that consumption should not be placed before income. This aspect concerns the genesis of what the businessmen and capitalists consume. I have said that businessmen and capitalists possess not only their incomes, but, first and foremost, their capitals. How, it will be asked, did their capitals originate, if not out of saving out of income? Here we are also involved in the question of how profit is the original form of income in the economic system.

To answer these questions, it must be realized that neither the portion of their exchangeable wealth which they devote to provision for the future nor the portion which they consume, need be acquired by businessmen and capitalists in the form of income—though, of course, in a developed market economy, they almost always will be. Incomes are generated in the process of exchange, and prior to every exchange there must be that which is to be exchanged. It is not income which is the necessary prerequisite to consumption, *but a fund of money*. This money can be acquired in the form of income, or it can be acquired by the printing or mining of new money, or by the emergence of a monetary employment for commodities already in one's possession which were acquired either by one's own labor or in barter exchange. The last two of these—that is, the mining of new money and the emergence of a monetary employment for commodities acquired either by one's own labor or in barter exchange—were the original source of consumption expenditure and of net consumption. The first incomes were generated by the spending of money, and the money which was spent could not have been acquired as income but only as a commodity produced by one's own labor or obtained in barter exchange.[35] Such is the original source of consumption expenditure and net consumption in the "early and rude state of society" described by Adam Smith, in which there is only a demand for consumers' goods and no demand for means of producing products which are to be sold.[36]

Thus, true enough, the capitals of businessmen and capitalists are accumulated by saving out of profits. But profits themselves are always caused at least in part by net consumption, whether that net consumption is based mainly on previously accumulated capital, as in the conditions of any modern economic system, or on the original sources I have just described. The essential point is that irrespective of the contribution of prior, saved profits to current and future net consumption, it is current and future net consumption that operate to determine current and future profits. Furthermore, the regress is not infinite, in that net consumption does have ultimate priority over profit in the way I have just shown.

An Explanation of High Saving Rates Out of High Incomes

We have considered the case of the effect of a loss of income on the consumption of businessmen and capitalists, and have seen that their consumption would not be diminished to anywhere near the extent to which their income falls, because it is based mainly on their possession of capital. Their consumption would tend to fall only to the relatively modest extent that the reduction in their income constituted a fall in the much larger total of their exchangeable wealth consisting of the sum of their capital plus their income as it is obtained. The same analysis applied to the case of the effect of a rise in income on the consumption of businessmen and capitalists shows that an increase in income will likewise tend to have only a modest effect. The increase in income will also tend to be consumed and saved in proportion as they employ this total of capital-plus-its-income in consumption and for making provision for the future.

For example, if the income of our hypothetical businessman or capitalist with $10,000,000 of capital rose from $500,000 to $1,000,000, his consumption would most likely rise only to something on the order of $525,000, while his provision for the future rose to something on the order of $10,475,000, for these sums stand in approximately the same respective proportions to $11,000,000 as do $500,000 and $10,000,000 to $10,500,000. Thus he would consume only about $25,000 of his additional income, and save all the rest of it. The percentage of his income that he saved would go from zero to almost 48 percent. In the same way, if the income he earned on his ten million of capital were $1,500,000, his consumption would rise to something on the order of $550,000 while his provision for the future rose to something on the order of $10,950,000. At this point, the percentage of his income that he saved would be over 60 percent.

This analysis helps to explain both why individuals with higher incomes tend to save larger fractions of their incomes than do those with lower incomes and, at the same time, why there is no tendency toward an ever rising proportion of saving out of income in the economic system as a whole, as the average level of real income rises. It is not the case that individuals having higher incomes save a larger portion of them than individuals having lower incomes, on the basis of any economic law pertaining to the absolute size of income. Rather it is the case that individuals with higher incomes are to a large extent businessmen or capitalists who earn a rate of profit that is higher than the rate of net consumption.

To the extent that this is the case, the income that is over and above what corresponds to the net-consumption rate counts merely as additional exchangeable wealth that is divided between consumption and provision for the future in essentially the same proportions as a lesser sum of exchangeable wealth consisting of capital plus its income. But this means that in the average case the only portion of the additional income that is consumed is a portion itself corresponding to the net-consumption rate, while all the rest goes to saving and provision for the future.

If these individuals were to earn the same amount of profit, however high that might be in absolute terms, and, at the same time, possessed a sufficiently larger amount of accumulated capital, they would consume the full amount of their high incomes. Let their accumulated capitals grow sufficiently relative to their incomes—in other words, let the rate of profit they earn fall to the net-consumption rate—and they will consume all of their income, however high it might be. For example, a businessman or capitalist with an income of $1,000,000 a year may well save half or more of it when his total accumulated capital is $10,000,000, but he would most likely consume all of a $1,000,000 income—and more— if his accumulated capital were $50,000,000, and most certainly if it were $100,000,000. In such a case, his saving out of income would be zero or less than zero. Indeed, on our present assumptions, he would consume all of a $1,000,000 income if his accumulated capital were just $20,000,000.

The fact that high rates of saving are to be found in connection with high rates of profit can also be explained on the basis of the fact that a high rate of saving out of a high rate of profit is the basis of building a fortune. Repeated compounding of the high rate of profit on a rapidly growing capital sum, whose rapid growth is made possible by a high rate of saving, results in the accumulation of a fortune. A high rate of profit provides both the incentive and the means for a high rate of saving, culminating in the possession of a fortune.[37]

As previously noted, apart from the connections between high rates of profit and high rates of saving out of income, Milton Friedman has shown the vital role played by expectations concerning permanent or long-run average income in leading individuals to save heavily in periods when their income temporarily exceeds their expectations of this kind. Thus, individuals such as best-selling novelists, prominent athletes, and movie stars, whose incomes in an individual year or limited period of years are among the highest in the economic system, often save heavily. The reason they do so is not because their incomes are high absolutely or relative to those of the average member of the economic system, but because their incomes are high relative to their own expected long-run average incomes and thus need to be saved heavily to make possible a more even level of consumption over time.[38]

Friedman's insight helps to explain high saving out of profits in a context in which the high rate of profit cannot be expected to continue. In this case, the profits must be heavily saved if the individual is to benefit from them in the years when his profit income will be lower, owing to the prospective fall in the rate of profit he will earn.

Friedman's insight can also be applied to understanding the disposition of previously accumulated capital between provision for the future and present consumption. Such capital will typically be regarded by its owner as having to serve his wants over a more or less extended period of the future. If the owner of a capital of $10,000,000, wishes to provide for his wants over a period of twenty years, say, and to do so evenly, then the most he will wish to consume in the present year is $500,000. If he earns no income this year, then his capital falls by that amount. In succeeding years, if he continues to earn no income, he may go on consuming $500,000 a year until his capital runs out, or if his "time horizon," so to speak, remains constant at twenty years, he will progressively diminish his consumption as his capital declines, keeping it at a constant one-twentieth of the declining amount.[39]

The present discussion makes it clear that the high rates of saving that take place out of the high incomes existing at any given time are not the result of the absolute height of those incomes. They are the result of the height of those incomes *relative* to accumulated capital or to the expected long-run average income of the individuals. Where high incomes are not earned as a high rate of profit on capital and are not perceived as higher than one's long-run average income, they are not accompanied by high rates of saving. That is to say, where they are earned in the form of a low rate of profit on a large sum of capital or where they are earned in the form of high wages which are expected to continue to be earned over the rest of one's life, the high incomes are not accompanied by high rates of saving. The businessman or capitalist with a large amount of capital relative to his income need not save, because he can look to his existing capital to provide for his future wants even if he consumes an amount equal to the whole or even somewhat more than the whole of his modest rate of profit. A wage earner who can expect to earn a high wage income throughout his life can look to his future wages as the means of providing for his future consumption. It is not necessary for him to make provision for the future beyond providing for old age and other possible periods of incapacity, and for the purchase of goods that are too expensive to be purchased out of current income.

When these facts are understood, it becomes possible to explain such things as why the average American of today does not save a larger proportion of his income than did his grandparents, even though in real terms as well as in monetary terms his income is far greater than theirs was. As has just been shown, the explanation is that higher real income as such, that is, by itself, does not cause a higher rate of saving. Indeed, owing to changes in political conditions that affect the general security of property, such as the tax system and the monetary system, and to changes in cultural values that are philosophical corollaries of the political changes, today's generation of Americans saves *less* relative to its income than was the case in the past, even though, for the time being at least, real incomes continue to be far higher than in the past. Confiscatory taxation, fiat money and inflation, and the decline of the sense of individual responsibility have all worked to reduce the degree of provision for the future relative to current consumption and thus to reduce saving out of income, despite the fact that real incomes continue at a level far higher than prevailed in the past and, at least until relatively recently, had even continued to rise. The slower rate of increase in real income that is the result of these causes is also a major cause of the reduced rate of saving out of income. This is implicit in the preceding discussion.[40]

Indeed, to maintain that individuals with higher incomes by that very fact tend to save relatively more than individuals with lower incomes, is to reverse cause and effect. This is because it is not high income as such which is the cause of high saving, but high saving which is the cause of high income, both absolutely and relatively. This point can be clearly seen in the light of the analysis we have been carrying on under the assumption of an invariable money. In this analysis, high saving and the high relative demand for capital goods that it makes possible is the cause of high and rising real income in that it is a leading cause of capital accumulation, rising production, and falling prices, which progressively increase the buying power of given money incomes. At the same time, those businessmen and capitalists who save relatively more grow in relative wealth and increase their profits at the expense of those businessmen and capitalists who save relatively less. These businessmen and capitalists have the highest and most rapidly rising real incomes, and while the monetary income of the average member of the economic system remains the same, theirs goes on rising.

The same point is dramatically confirmed by the rapid economic progress and consequent rise in real incomes of such East Asian countries as Japan, Taiwan, and South Korea. All of these countries, not so very long ago, were among the world's most impoverished nations. Their progress has its foundation largely in a very high degree of saving and provision for the future, which came into being in the midst of poverty. Their saving and provision for the future is clearly the cause, not the effect, of their high and rising real incomes.

Net Consumption and Time Preference

Net consumption is not an ultimate cause of profit. It itself reflects the operation of time preference. As explained in Chapter 2, time preference refers to the fact that, other things being equal, people value the satisfaction of their wants in the present more highly than in the future, and in the nearer future more highly than in the more remote future.[41] Time preference determines the proportions in which people devote their income and wealth to present consumption versus provision for the future. The higher the prevailing degree of time preference, the higher is the proportion in which people devote their wealth and income to present consumption in comparison with provision for the future. The lower is the prevailing degree of time preference, the lower is the proportion in which they devote their wealth and income to present consumption in comparison with provision for the future. In this way, time preference operates to establish the rate of net consumption.

This is so, because to the degree that time preference is high, and people are therefore not prepared to make provision for the future relative to present consumption, the demand for factors of production to produce products which are to be sold will be low, the amount of capital invested will be low, and net consumption will be correspondingly high. Thus the ratio which net consumption and, therefore, profit bear to the demand for factors of production, to costs (which reflect that demand), and to the sum of the capital values of business enterprises will be high. By the same token, to the degree that time preference is low, exactly the reverse will be true and the rate of net consumption and the rate of profit will be correspondingly low. Thus, one can say that the ultimate cause and determinant of the rate of profit, insofar as it depends on net consumption, is time preference.

It may be asked, what is the temporal extent of the periods called the present and the future, between which individuals divide their wealth and income? The answer is that as far as the net-consumption theory is concerned, the absolute extent of these periods is of no importance. One may consider as the present, today, the coming week, the coming month, the coming year, or any period of time extending into the future, however long or short. The reason is that every rate of profit or interest varies directly with the period of time taken as the base. For example, a 10 percent rate of profit on an annual basis is identical with a 20 percent rate of profit on a biennial basis, a 5 percent rate of profit on a semi-annual basis, a 2.5 percent rate of profit on a quarterly basis, and a five-sixths of 1 percent rate of profit on a monthly basis. And in precisely the same way that the ratio which the amount of profit or interest bears to a principal varies directly with the period of time under consideration, the ratio which net consumption bears to the sum of the capital values of business enterprises varies directly with the period of time under consideration. The ratio which the net consumption of two years bears to the sum of the capital values of business enterprises is twice as great as the ratio afforded by the net consumption of one year; this in turn is twice as great as the ratio afforded by the net consumption of six months, which, in turn, is twice as great as the ratio afforded by the net consumption of three months, and so on. Thus, if net consumption relative to the sum of the capital values of business enterprises proceeds at the rate of .0274 percent per day, .83 percent per month, 2.5 percent per quarter, 5 percent every six months, 10 percent per year, or 20 percent every two years, it is all the same. A rate of profit of 10 percent on an annual basis will be the result. The rate of net consumption and the rate of profit and interest are of the identical mathematical nature.

This explains, incidentally, why nothing essential depended on our simplifying assumption, earlier in this section, that the entire annual income on a capital sum was available on the first day of the year. It is immaterial whether one has a $500,000 annual income available at the beginning of a year and consumes one's exchangeable wealth at the annual rate of one twenty-first, or has available, say, only a quarterly income of $125,000 at the beginning of a quarter and consumes one's exchangeable wealth at the quarterly rate of one eighty-fourth.

It must be stressed that the connection between the rate of profit and time preference is not direct, but indirect. It exists insofar as time preference determines the proportions in which individuals devote their wealth and income to provision for the future relative to present consumption, as manifested in the proportion in which net consumption stands to the demand for factors of production to produce products which are to be sold and to the sum of the capital values of business enterprises. It does not operate on the rate of profit in any other, more direct way.[42]

Perhaps the simplest way to understand the operation

of time preference on the rate of profit is in terms of the concept of the "time horizon" referred to previously.[43] If time preference leads businessmen and capitalists to have an average time horizon of twenty-one years, over which they wish to make even provision for their wants, then the rate of net consumption will be one twenty-first of capital-plus-its-annual-income. Since the amount of net consumption tends to generate an equivalent amount of profit, this will operate to make the annual income on capital also equal to one twenty-first of the sum of capital-plus-its-annual-income. Thus the rate of profit relative to capital alone will tend to be 5 percent.[44]

In exactly the same way, if the average time horizon of businessmen and capitalists were eleven years, and thus they wished to consume an amount equal to one-eleventh of the sum of their capital and its annual income, the rate of net consumption and the rate of profit—as far as it depends on the rate of net consumption—would be 10 percent. If their average time horizon were 51 years, the rate of net consumption and the rate of profit—again, as far as it depends on the rate of net consumption—would be 2 percent.[45]

The fact, explained in Chapter 2, that time preference in turn is itself profoundly influenced by the degree of rationality and freedom that prevails in a society implies that as far as the rate of profit depends on the rate of net consumption, it will be the lower, the more rational and the freer a society is.[46] Special emphasis must be placed on the implication that the rate of profit will be the lower the greater is the respect for property rights and thus the security of property. This is the case because to the degree that property rights are respected and property is secure, the more are people motivated to make provision for the future relative to present consumption, and thus the lower will be the rate of net consumption and the rate of profit insofar as the rate of profit depends on the rate of net consumption. In addition, the greater is the security of property, the more will people be motivated, with any given degree of time preference, to make provision for the future in the form of the accumulation of capital rather than the accumulation of hoards of precious metals and gems. This change in the form of provision for the future, given the same degree of time preference, also serves to lower the rate of net consumption and the rate of profit. This is because it represents a greater demand for factors of production by business and the accumulation of greater sums of capital value, as opposed to the accumulation of wealth in the form of consumer assets.

It is important to realize that, however ironically, it follows from these considerations, that all the demagogues and outright bandits in the world who rail against the height of profits and who call for or actually undertake the looting and plundering of property thereby labor to raise the rate of net consumption as high as they can and thus correspondingly to raise the rate of profit. For in striving, as they do, to undermine the security of property in their various capacities of ordinary robbers, members of guerrilla bands, or officials of virtually all contemporary governments, they act to discourage saving and productive expenditure and thereby to increase the relative significance of net consumption. The message they send to businessmen and capitalists is: "Don't save, don't invest—because if you do, we will see to it that you do not benefit from doing so, for we will steal or destroy your property or tax it away. If you want to benefit from your wealth, you had better consume it before you lose it to us."

4. Net Investment as a Determinant of Aggregate Profit and the Average Rate of Profit

The equality between profits and net consumption rests on an equality between productive expenditure and the costs deducted from sales revenues in business income statements. In such circumstances, an excess of sales revenues over costs is possible only to the extent that there is an excess of sales revenues over productive expenditure. As we have seen, since both sales revenues and productive expenditure embrace the demand for capital goods, an excess of sales revenues over productive expenditure rests on an excess of receipts from the sale of consumers' goods over the demand for labor by business, that is, on net consumption. As we know, net consumption in turn is the result of the consumption expenditure of businessmen and capitalists, financed out of dividend, draw, and interest payments.

However, productive expenditure and costs need not be equal. For reasons I will explain, productive expenditure is usually greater than costs, and sometimes it is less. In these circumstances, net investment, positive or negative, exists. And at such times, the amount of profit in the economic system turns out to equal the sum of net consumption plus net investment.

Figures 16–1 and 16–2 and Tables 16–3 and 16–4 exemplify the fundamental distinction that exists between productive expenditure and costs. In these figures and tables, the productive expenditure of any given year shows up as costs deducted from sales revenues in the following year. By the same token, the costs of any given year are shown as representing the productive expenditure of the year before. Such a fundamental distinction of timing, whether of years, months, or weeks, usually exists between productive expenditure and the costs it generates in business income statements. In essence, today's productive expenditures for the most part show up as costs in the future, while today's costs for the most

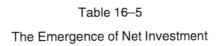

Table 16–5

The Emergence of Net Investment

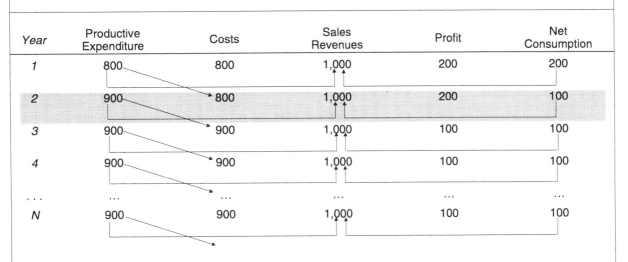

Year	Productive Expenditure	Costs	Sales Revenues	Profit	Net Consumption
1	800	800	1,000	200	200
2	900	800	1,000	200	100
3	900	900	1,000	100	100
4	900	900	1,000	100	100
...	...	...	...	...	...
N	900	900	1,000	100	100

The table above shows that in *Year 2,* profit remains at 200 despite the fall in net consumption to 100 and resulting rise in productive expenditure to 900. The reason is that the rise in costs lags the rise in productive expenditure. Only from *Year 3* on, will costs also be 900. In *Year 2,* the 100 excess of productive expenditure over cost implies the existence of 100 of net investment.

part reflect productive expenditures made in the past.

The distinction between productive expenditure and costs was explained in detail in Chapter 15. There it was shown that all of productive expenditure which is for plant and equipment or inventory and work in progress, is added to asset accounts, while the corresponding items of cost, namely, depreciation and cost of goods sold, which reflect previous productive expenditures, are subtracted from those asset accounts. On this basis, the difference between productive expenditure and costs in the economic system was shown to constitute net investment, that is, the net change in the value of those asset accounts.[47]

The continuous equality between productive expenditure and the costs deducted from sales revenues that is found in Figures 16–1 and 16–2 and in Tables 16–3 and 16–4 is the result of nothing more than the assumption that productive expenditure is the same year after year, reinforced by the further assumption that all productive expenditure shows up as costs precisely one year later. Under these assumptions, productive expenditure and costs show up as the same in amount year after year, to the end of time.

Nevertheless, if one looks at Table 16–5, one can observe an important break in the equality between productive expenditure and costs, and, at the same time, an

equivalent break in the equality between profits and net consumption. Specifically, one will observe in *Year 2* of Table 16–5 that productive expenditure exceeds costs by 100, and, at the same time, that profits exceed net consumption by 100. For in that year, while productive expenditure is 900, costs are only 800, and while net consumption is only 100, profits in the economic system are 200.

Table 16–5 is very similar to Table 16–3. Its only essential difference is that in *Year 2* it introduces a rise in productive expenditure from 800 to 900 monetary units, which is made possible by an equivalent fall in net consumption from 200 to 100 monetary units.[48] In all subsequent years, 900 and 100 monetary units remain the respective magnitudes of productive expenditure and net consumption. Total sales revenues, of course, continue at 1,000 monetary units throughout, inasmuch as 100 monetary units of additional demand for the products of business generated by productive expenditure take the place of the 100 monetary units of reduced demand for the products of business coming from the consumption of businessmen and capitalists, viz., from net consumption.[49] What Table 16–5 shows is that even though productive expenditure in *Year 2* rises from 800 to 900, costs continue to be 800, reflecting the fact that productive expenditure in *Year 1* was 800. Only from *Year 3* on do costs rise to the higher level of productive expenditure.

Because of this lag in the rise in costs to reflect the rise in productive expenditure, profits in *Year 2* continue to equal 200, despite the fall in net consumption to 100. This is the case inasmuch as sales revenues remain at 1,000 while costs remain at 800. All that has happened so far in Table 16–5 is that net consumption—the demand for consumers' goods by businessmen and capitalists—is down and productive expenditure and the demand for capital goods and/or the demand for producers' labor and producers' labor's demand for consumers' goods are up by just as much. Thus, there is no change in aggregate sales revenues and, as yet, no change in aggregate costs. As a result, profits are as yet unchanged, despite the fall in net consumption.

The unmistakable and obvious implication of this inequality between profits and net consumption is that something else, besides net consumption, determines the amount of profit in the economic system. That something else, of course, turns out to be nothing other than net investment. This is because the excess of profits over net consumption is the excess of productive expenditure over costs. Profits remain the same rather than fall to an amount equal to the smaller amount of net consumption, because, while sales revenues remain the same, costs have not yet risen to equal the larger amount of productive expenditure that the smaller amount of net consumption makes possible. If costs did equal the larger productive expenditure, profits would equal sales revenues minus the larger productive expenditure, that is, they would equal the smaller net consumption. So long as costs fall short of the larger productive expenditure, profits exceed the smaller net consumption. This shortfall of costs relative to productive expenditure, or, equivalently, this excess of productive expenditure over costs, is, as we know, net investment. For productive expenditure comprises debits or pluses to the assets of business, while costs comprise credits or minuses to those assets. Thus, to the extent that productive expenditure exceeds costs, the pluses to the assets of business exceed the minuses from those assets, with the result that there is an equivalent net change in the book value of those assets—viz., there is equivalent net investment.

In connection with this last point, it is necessary to keep in mind specifically that productive expenditure incorporates business spending on account of plant and equipment and inventory and work in progress, which represents debits or pluses to these respective asset accounts, while costs include depreciation and cost of goods sold, which represent credits or minuses to these respective asset accounts. The difference is net investment in plant and equipment plus net investment in inventory and work in progress. Insofar as productive

expenditure and costs do not comprise such pluses or minuses to assets, they represent identically equal expensed expenditures, that is, items that are not debited to any asset account, but written off—expensed—as made. Such items—for example, many advertising and research and development outlays—are simultaneously productive expenditures and costs. The subtraction of such costs from such productive expenditures nets to zero and thus leaves undisturbed the fact that total productive expenditure minus total costs equals net investment.[50]

The relationship between profits and net investment is actually very simple. Net investment is productive expenditure minus costs. Profit is sales revenues minus those same costs. The great bulk of sales revenues, moreover, is generated by and is equal to productive expenditure. Productive expenditure, recall, embraces the demand for capital goods, which at the same time literally *is* a major component of sales revenues. Furthermore, productive expenditure embraces all the wage payments by business firms, which is the source of the far greater part of receipts from the sale of consumers' goods by business. Thus, to the extent that productive expenditure exceeds costs and produces corresponding net investment, the sales revenues generated by and equal to productive expenditure exceed those same costs and thus result in profits equal to the net investment. Once again, the existence of net investment means that productive expenditure exceeds costs. At the same time, it means that the portion of business sales revenues generated by and equal to productive expenditure exceeds those same costs, and thus that profit exists at least to the same extent as net investment exists. Indeed, the only thing that prevents a perfect identity between profits and net investment is the extent to which sales revenues exceed productive expenditure, that is, the extent to which net consumption exists.

Table 16–6 illustrates the effect of net investment on profits by incorporating the data from *Year 2* of Table 16–5 into a framework similar to that of Table 16–2, which set forth the role of net consumption in making possible an excess of the demand for the products of business over the demand for factors of production by business, that is, of sales revenues over productive expenditure. The table shows that aggregate profit in the economic system equals the sum of net investment plus net consumption. It does so by showing once again the demand for factors of production by business (productive expenditure) on the left and the demand for the products of business (sales revenues) on the right. It shows total sales revenues generated equal to the sum of productive expenditure plus net consumption: specifically, sales revenues of 900 generated by productive expenditure and sales revenues of 100 generated by net consumption.

Table 16–6				
Net Investment as a Source of Aggregate Profit				
Demand for Factors of Production by Business (Productive Expenditure)			**Demand for Products of Business (Sales Revenues)**	
Demand for Capital Goods:	600	≡	Receipts from the Sale of Capital Goods:	600
Demand for Labor:	300	=	Receipts from the Sale of Consumers' Goods to Wage Earners:	300
Total Demand for Factors of Production by Business (Productive Expenditure):	900		Total Sales Revenues Generated by Productive Expenditure:	900
less:			*less:*	
Costs:	800	=	Costs:	800
Net Investment:	100		Profits Corresponding to Net investment:	100
			Receipts from the Sale of Consumers' Goods to Businessmen and Capitalists (Net Consumption):	100
			Total Sales Revenues:	1,000
			less:	
			Costs:	800
			Total Profits:	200
			Profits Corresponding to Net Consumption:	100

The 900 of sales revenues generated by productive expenditure are 600 of receipts from the sale of capital goods plus 300 of receipts from the sale of consumers' goods to wage earners. The 600 of receipts from the sale of capital goods, of course, are identically equal to the component of productive expenditure representing the demand for capital goods. The 300 of receipts from the sale of consumers' goods to wage earners are quantitatively equal to the component of productive expenditure representing the demand for labor. The 100 of sales receipts generated by the sale of consumers' goods to businessmen and capitalists are the receipts representing net consumption. Total sales revenues in Table 16–6, of course, equal 1,000, with 600 representing demand for capital goods and 400 the total demand for consumers' goods coming both from businessmen and capitalists and from wage earners, together.

Now the deduction of 800 of costs from 900 of pro-

ductive expenditure on the left-hand side of Table 16–6 results in net investment of 100. When those same costs are deducted on the right-hand side of Table 16–6 from the 900 of sales revenues generated by the 900 of productive expenditure, the result is 100 of profits corresponding to the 100 of net investment. Total profits, of course, are 200, rather than 100, because total sales revenues are 1,000, not 900. Sales revenues are generated by the sum of productive expenditure plus net consumption, not by productive expenditure alone. When the 800 of costs are deducted from this larger total of sales revenues, the total amount of profit surpasses net investment by the amount by which total sales revenues surpass the portion of sales revenues generated by productive expenditure alone, that is, by the amount of sales revenues generated by net consumption.

Perhaps the simplest way to think of the equality between profits and the sum of net consumption plus net investment is in terms of the following relationships:

(1)   profits = sales – costs.

(2)   profits = sales – productive expenditure + productive expenditure – costs.

(3)   sales – productive expenditure = net consumption.

(4)   productive expenditure – costs = net investment.

Thus, substituting equations (3) and (4) into equation (2) we obtain:

(5)   profits = net consumption + net investment.

In other words, profits are sales minus costs. They are also sales minus productive expenditure plus productive expenditure minus costs. Inasmuch as both sales revenues and productive expenditure contain the demand for capital goods, sales revenues minus productive expenditure reduces to the demand for consumers' goods minus the demand for labor, that is, to net consumption. Inasmuch as productive expenditure represents pluses to assets, while costs represent minuses to assets, productive expenditure minus costs is net investment. Thus, profits equal net consumption plus net investment.

Table 16–7 further illustrates the relationship between net investment and aggregate profit by showing a variety of possible cost values and the corresponding effects on net investment and profits together. The table assumes that productive expenditure is constant at 800 and that net consumption is constant at 200, with the result that sales revenues in the economic system are constant at 1,000. For purposes of illustration, three different values for aggregate costs are assumed: 800, 700, and 900, labeled (1), (2), and (3) respectively. Under these assumptions, when costs are 800, that is, equal to productive expenditure and to the sales revenues generated by productive expenditure, both net investment and the profits corresponding to net investment are zero. Thus, total profits equal 200, which is the amount by which sales revenues exceed productive expenditure and the costs equivalent to productive expenditure. That is, in this case, profits equal net consumption alone. All of these results are indicated by the label (1). When costs are 700 in the face of the 800 of productive expenditure and the 800 of sales revenues generated by productive expenditure, net investment is 100 and the profits corresponding to net investment are 100. Thus, in this case, total profits equal 300—the sum of the 200 of net consumption plus the 100 of net investment. In other words, they are now equal to the sum of the amount by which sales revenues exceed productive expenditure plus the amount by which productive expenditure exceeds costs. These results are indicated by the label (2). When costs

are 900, net investment is minus 100 and profits altogether are 100, equal to the sum of the 200 of net consumption plus the minus 100 of net investment. In this case, profit is equal to the sum of the excess of sales revenues over productive expenditure less the excess of costs over productive expenditure. These results are indicated by the label (3).

As we have seen, the variation of profits with net investment is produced by the fact that net investment exists to the degree that productive expenditure is greater than costs. But since productive expenditure is directly or indirectly the source of equivalent sales revenues, any excess of productive expenditure over costs is accompanied by a precisely equivalent excess of sales revenues over those same costs, which excess represents precisely equivalent profits. That is, to whatever extent productive expenditure exceeds costs and generates net investment, the sales revenues generated by productive expenditure, and equal to productive expenditure, exceed those same costs and generate profit. Thus, to the extent that net investment is positive, and the portion of sales revenues generated by productive expenditure exceeds costs, the excess of total sales revenues over costs is equivalently enlarged and profits exceed net consumption by the amount of net investment. By the same token, to the extent that net investment is negative, and the portion of sales revenues generated by productive expenditure falls short of costs, the total of sales revenues exceeds costs by less than the amount of net consumption; that is, profits are reduced by the amount of negative net investment.

It may be helpful to think of matters this way: while net investment—the excess of productive expenditure over costs—represents an equivalent excess of the part of sales revenues generated by productive expenditure, and equal to productive expenditure, over those same costs, net consumption represents a further excess of sales revenues over costs—the excess of sales revenues over productive expenditure itself. By the same token, while net consumption would generate profits even if costs equalled productive expenditure, the existence of net investment means that costs are equivalently less than productive expenditure and equivalently less than the portion of sales revenues generated by and equal to productive expenditure, and thus that profits exceed net consumption by the amount of net investment.

Under the assumptions we have been making of an invariable money and that all the capital goods and labor of any given year are used up in producing the products just of the next year, net investment is necessarily of short duration. Under such conditions, it can exist only on the strength of a rise in productive expenditure founded on a fall in net consumption, and then it can last only for a

Table 16–7		
The Relationship Between Profits and Net Investment		

Demand for Factors of Production by Business (Productive Expenditure)			Demand for Products of Business (Sales Revenues)	
Demand for Capital Goods:	500	≡	Receipts from the Sale of Capital Goods:	500
Demand for Labor:	300	=	Receipts from the Sale of Consumers' Goods to Wage Earners:	300
Total Demand for Factors of Production by Business (Productive Expenditure):	800		Total Sales Revenues Generated by Productive Expenditure:	800
less:			*less:*	
Costs (1):	800		Costs (1):	800
Costs (2):	700		Costs (2):	700
Costs (3):	900		Costs (3):	900
Net Investment (1):	0		Profits Corresponding to Net Investment (1):	0
Net Investment (2):	100		Profits Corresponding to Net Investment (2):	100
Net Investment (3):	-100		Profits Corresponding to Net Investment (3):	-100
			Receipts from the Sale of Consumers' Goods to Businessmen and Capitalists (Net Consumption):	200
			Total Sales Revenues:	1,000
			Total Profits (1):	200
			Total Profits (2):	300
			Total Profits (3):	100
			Profits Corresponding to Net Consumption (in all three cases):	200

single year, before costs rise to equal the higher level of productive expenditure. This is the situation in *Year 2* of Table 16–5. As we shall soon see, however, in the absence of these assumptions, in particular the assumption of an invariable money, net investment can exist not only as a long-standing, indeed, permanent source of aggregate profit, but also with no tendency toward diminution in its quantitative importance relative to that of net consumption.

Now it follows that since the aggregate amount of profit in the economic system is equal to the sum of net consumption plus net investment, that the average *rate* of profit in the economic system equals not only the previously described net-consumption rate, but *the sum of the net-consumption rate plus the net-investment rate.* This is merely to say, that in equalling the amount of net consumption plus the amount of net investment, all divided by the amount of capital invested, the average rate of profit equals the amount of net consumption separately divided by the amount of capital invested (the net-consumption rate) plus the amount of net investment separately divided by the amount of capital invested (the net-investment rate). This is on the elementary algebraic principle that $\frac{a+b}{c} = \frac{a}{c} + \frac{b}{c}$. In other words, the average rate of profit in the economic system can be expressed as equal to and determined by the rate of net consumption plus the rate of net investment. This formula is of great importance, and I will refer to it repeatedly in subsequent discussion.

Net Investment Versus Negative Net Consumption

Because of net investment, it would be possible for an aggregate profit to exist in the economic system even in the complete absence of net consumption—indeed, even in the face of negative net consumption.

Net consumption falls below the consumption of businessmen and capitalists to the degree that wage payments fail to be accompanied by equivalent consumption expenditures. At the crudest level of analysis, one might imagine a portion of wage payments simply being hoarded by the wage earners. To this extent, receipts from the sale of consumers' goods to wage earners would be less than wage payments, and the excess of total receipts from the sale of consumers' goods over wage payments would be correspondingly diminished. The excess of total sales revenues over total productive expenditure would, of course, also be equivalently reduced, inasmuch as it reflects merely the addition of the demand for capital goods both to the demand for consumers' goods and to the demand for labor. The addition of equals to both sides of a diminished inequality does not alter the diminution of the inequality.

More realistically than being hoarded, a portion of wage payments might be used to finance additional productive expenditures. One can imagine, for example, employee stock-purchase plans, under which a portion of wages is turned back to business firms and used by the firms for the purchase of additional capital goods (or even for the payment of wages to additional workers). The same results would follow to the extent that the savings of wage earners that were deposited in banks were used in making loans to business firms, which then expended the proceeds of the loans in these ways. If—for lack of a better description—such *secondary* productive expenditures should exceed the financing of wage earners' consumption by means of loans extended by business firms, then, to that extent, consumption on the part of wage earners as a group would be less than the payment of wages.

The implication of a fall in net consumption here can also be seen in the fact that each dollar of wage income paid by business that is used to make productive expenditures represents two dollars of productive expenditure for every one dollar of sales revenues. This is because there is first a dollar of productive expenditure in the payment of the wages, and then, to the extent that the wages themselves are used to finance productive expenditure, a second dollar of productive expenditure in the expenditure of the wages. There is only one dollar of sales revenue, however, which occurs when the wages are expended in the purchase of capital goods, or when the wage earners whose wages are paid by means of secondary productive expenditure, purchase consumers' goods.

In these cases, total sales revenues in the economic system would still be the same, but productive expenditure would be larger and net consumption, therefore, as the difference between sales revenues and productive expenditure, would be equivalently reduced. Looked at in more detail, to the extent that the wage earners' savings were used to buy capital goods, receipts from the sale of capital goods would replace receipts from the sale of consumers goods to wage earners. This fall in receipts from the sale of consumers' goods, in the face of the same wage payments, would represent diminished net consumption. To the extent that the wage earners' savings were used to employ additional producers' labor, whose wages, it may be assumed, were themselves fully consumed, the result would be that while receipts from the sale of consumers' goods stayed the same, the total wages paid by business would rise. Either way, net consumption would be reduced.

It could also be the case, of course, that the savings of wage earners that were turned back to business would make possible merely the continuation of the same amount of productive expenditure in the next period instead of a larger amount of productive expenditure in the current period. In this case, the situation would resemble the case of hoarding on the part of the wage earners, in that sales revenues in the current period would be reduced by the amount of such saving, and thus the difference between sales revenues and productive expenditure—i.e., net consumption—would again be equivalently reduced. Unlike the case of hoarding, however, business would receive back the cash it had expended, though in the form of loans or receipts from the sale of securities rather than in the form of sales revenues.

If businessmen and capitalists themselves consumed little or nothing, say, 5 or 10 monetary units instead of 100 or 200 monetary units, and at the same time there were a significant excess of secondary productive expenditure over the granting of new and additional consumer loans by business to wage earners—that is, if the net amount of secondary productive expenditure were significant—the excess of wage payments over the consumption of wage earners would mean the existence of negative net consumption. But even in such an unlikely case, a significant aggregate profit and average rate of profit could still exist in the economic system on the strength of net investment alone. This is illustrated in Tables 16–8 and 16–9.

Table 16–8 assumes that the consumption of businessmen and capitalists is zero and thus that productive expenditure is the only source of sales revenues. It further assumes that a portion of wage payments is simply hoarded. It shows that despite this, an aggregate profit can exist on the basis of net investment. Specifically, the table assumes that the demand for capital goods is 500, and that while the demand for labor is 300, the wage

Table 16–8

Net Investment as the Basis for Aggregate Profit With Sales Revenues Less Than Productive Expenditure Because of Hoarding or Saving to Finance Loans and Securities Purchases

Demand for Factors of Production by Business (Productive Expenditure)			Demand for Products of Business (Sales Revenues)	
Demand for Capital Goods:	500	≡	Receipts from the Sale of Capital Goods:	500
Demand for Labor:	300		Receipts from the Sale of Consumers' Goods to Wage Earners:	200
Total Demand for Factors of Production by Business (Productive Expenditure):	800		Total Sales Revenues Generated by Productive Expenditure:	700
			Total Sales Revenues Generated by Net Consumption:	0
			Total Sales Revenues:	700
less:			*less:*	
Costs:	600	=	Costs:	600
			Total Profits:	100
Net Investment:	200		Profits Corresponding to Net Investment:	200
			Profits Corresponding to Net Consumption:	-100
			(The -100 is the result of the assumed zero of consumption expenditure by businessmen and capitalists plus 200 of demand for consumers' goods by wage earners minus their 300 of wages.)	

earners consume only 200, because they have chosen to hoard 100 of their wages. Thus, sales revenues in the economic system turn out to be only 700 (500 + 200), while productive expenditure is 800 (500 + 300). The underlying basis of this shortfall of sales revenues in comparison with productive expenditure, namely, that wage earners consume only 200, while their wages are 300, represents negative net consumption in the amount of 100—viz., 200 of consumption minus 300 of wages. Nevertheless, even with sales revenues less than productive expenditure, an aggregate profit exists in Table 16–8 by virtue of the costs deducted from sales revenues being further below productive expenditure than are sales revenues. With aggregate costs of 600, as the table assumes, there is an aggregate profit of 100 on the 700 of sales revenues. At the same time, the subtraction of these

aggregate costs from 800 of productive expenditure results in net investment of 200. Thus 200 of net investment offsets 100 of negative net consumption and results in an aggregate profit of 100.

The excess of productive expenditure over sales revenues described in Table 16–8 could continue virtually indefinitely if, instead of the current saving of the wage earners being hoarded, which is a case so unlikely that it actually deserves hardly any consideration, they were used in financing loans to business or in purchasing securities from business. In this way, business could repeat its current level of productive expenditure in the next period.

Table 16–9 arrives at an essentially similar result to that of Table 16–8 under the assumption that a portion of wages is used to finance secondary productive expendi-

Table 16–9

Net Investment as the Basis for Aggregate Profit With Sales Revenues Less Than Productive Expenditure Because of Secondary Productive Expenditure

Demand for Factors of Production by Business (Productive Expediture)			Demand for Products of Business (Sales Revenues)	
Demand for Capital Goods:	500 + 100	≡	Receipts from the Sale of Capital Goods:	500 + 100
Demand for Labor:	300		Receipts from the Sale of Consumers' Goods to Wage Earners:	200
Total Demand for Factors of Production by Business (Productive Expenditure):	900		Total Sales Revenues Generated by Productive Expenditure:	800
			Total Sales Revenues Generated by Net Consumption:	0
			Total Sales Revenues:	800
less:			less:	
Costs:	600	=	Costs:	600
			Total Profits:	200
Net Investment:	300		Profits Corresponding to Net Investment:	300
			Profits Corresponding to Net Consumption	-100
			(Again, the -100 is the result of the assumed zero of consumption expenditure by businessmen and capitalists plus 200 of demand for consumers' goods by wage earners minus their 300 of wages.)	

ture in the same accounting period. It shows the wage earners' saving of 100 of their incomes resulting in a secondary productive expenditure of 100, which is added to the original, primary productive expenditure of 800, thereby bringing total productive expenditure to 900. For the sake of simplicity, the secondary productive expenditure is assumed to be entirely in the form of an additional demand for capital goods. Thus, Table 16–9 shows a demand for capital goods of 500 + 100 and identical receipts from the sale of capital goods of 500 + 100. By the same token, while it shows 300 of demand for labor, it shows only 200 of receipts from the sale of consumers' goods to wage earners. Thus, while productive expenditure is 900 (500 + 100 + 300), sales revenues are only 800 (500 + 100 + 200). The reason for the disparity, it must be recalled, is that the use of wages to buy capital goods adds to productive expenditure, but does not add to sales revenues; the expenditure for the capital goods merely takes the place of expenditure for consumers' goods. Because wages themselves are part of productive expenditure, the use of wages to make further productive expenditures has the ability in an extreme case such as the present, to raise productive expenditure above sales revenues.

Thus, in this case, there is again a shortfall of sales revenues relative to productive expenditure in the amount of 100, which represents negative net consumption in the amount of 100 (viz., only 200 of consumption accompanying 300 of wages). But once again, an aggregate profit exists on the strength of net investment—viz., on the strength of costs being below productive expenditure to an extent sufficient to enable them to be below the sales revenues that are below productive expenditure. In Table 16–9, net investment in the amount of 300 is accompanied by profit in the amount of 200. The net investment reflects the fact that while productive expenditure is 900, costs are only 600. Profit is 200, because even though sales revenues are 100 less than productive expenditure, costs are 300 less, which means that costs are 200 less than sales revenues. Thus, in this case, 300 of net investment offsets 100 of negative net consumption and results in an aggregate profit of 200.[51]

It must be stressed that the possibility of negative net consumption is extremely remote to begin with, since most savings of wage earners are used to finance consumption expenditures, such as the purchase of homes or personal automobiles, and to the extent that they are not, are largely or entirely offset by loans to wage earners from business for such purposes. Thus, as a practical matter, as I have already said, it is reasonable to assume that virtually 100 percent of wages has a counterpart in consumption expenditure. Moreover, to the extent that savings are used to finance loans for consumption expen-

ditures, the payment of interest on such loans represents a source of return on savings over and above ordinary net consumption—a source that may be termed *secondary net consumption.*

This is the case because the use of wages to pay interest on consumer loans not only constitutes consumption expenditure from the perspective of those who pay the interest, and, at the same time, interest income from the perspective of those who receive the interest, but also does not diminish the demand for the products of business. This last is because the recipients of the interest are able to spend the proceeds in buying goods or services from business. Thus the demand for the products of business remains the same, while the total of consumption expenditure and the total of interest income in the economic system are increased.

For example, total wage payments in the economic system could be 300 monetary units, of which the wage earners consume 270 monetary units in buying consumers' goods from business and pay 30 monetary units in interest on consumers' loans. The recipients of the 30 in consumers' interest—who could well be wage earners themselves, insofar as they had saved, and their savings had been lent to consumers—could then expend that 30 in buying consumers' goods of their own from business. As a result, everything would be the same except that 30 more in consumers' interest had been paid. The situation would be analogous to the case of the wage earners using part of their wages to employ consumers' labor—or paying taxes to the government, which uses the proceeds to employ consumers' labor.

In those cases, the effect is to increase the overall demand for labor while leaving all other spending magnitudes the same.[52] Here, the interest on consumer loans is not at the expense of the profits and interest earned on the capital invested in ordinary business firms, but stands as a further source of net consumption and thus of aggregate profit and interest in the economic system. In fact, insofar as it is equivalent to net income, the payment of such interest constitutes a direct addition to the amount of net consumption in the economic system. This is because it is both consumption and, not being wages, an addition to the amount of consumption in excess of wage payments.[53] (Of course, the rate of interest on consumer loans, like the rate of interest on loans to business firms, is governed by the rate of profit on capital invested in business. This is because investing in business or lending to business is typically an alternative for whoever lends to consumers. At the same time, if additional funds are required for loans to consumers, the sources will most likely be parties presently engaged in these activities.)

However, what is decisive is that even if negative net consumption were to exist, however unlikely that might be, its existence would necessarily be strictly temporary and would be followed by the resumption of a significantly positive rate of net consumption. As the analysis of the next subsection will show, this is because net investment can be indefinitely prolonged. As net investment occurs, the amount of capital invested in the economic system increases. So too, of course, does the volume of accumulated savings, which is comprised both of capital, which is by far its main constituent in any modern economic system, and savings invested in the financing of loans to consumers. In the context of an economic system with an invariable money, in which the sales revenues of business have a fixed limit and all other spending magnitudes are also constrained by the fixity of the quantity of money, the increase in accumulated capital and savings is not only an absolute increase, but also an increase relative to consumption expenditure and incomes. In other words, it constitutes an increase in the degree both of capital intensiveness in the economic system and in provision for the future relative to provision for the present. As a result, its effect is to provide the basis for greater and greater consumption expenditure relative to income, which puts an end to all possibility of negative net consumption.[54]

The Prolongation of Net Investment Under an Invariable Money

When the assumption is dropped that the capital goods and labor of any given year are used up entirely in producing the output available at the start of the next year, then it becomes possible to observe a number of ways in which net investment can be prolonged, and, indeed, prolonged virtually indefinitely. Understanding this fact makes it possible to understand how an aggregate profit and thus a positive average rate of profit can exist even in conditions in which net consumption might be zero or negative and, at the same time, why any such situation with respect to net consumption is strictly temporary.

First of all, insofar as a fall in net consumption brings about a rise in productive expenditure specifically for plant and equipment, which serves in producing the output of *a number* of future years, the higher level of productive expenditure will result in net investment over a corresponding period of years. This can be illustrated in terms of an individual company.

Thus imagine that a company spends $1 million per year on machinery which lasts 20 years. Even if such machinery goes into service at the very beginning of the year in which it is bought, the cost incurred on account of its use in that one year will not remotely equal its purchase price. Most likely, only one-twentieth of the purchase price of the machinery will show up as a cost

in any one year of its 20-year life. This is the result implied by the most commonly used method of calculating depreciation—the method known as straight-line depreciation—which is to depreciate an asset evenly over its entire life. Even where methods of accelerated depreciation are employed, only a fraction of a machine's purchase price is deducted from sales revenues in any given year, a fraction which is always the smaller, the longer is the expected useful life of the machine.

If the method of straight-line depreciation is followed, then the annual cost on account of the use of the machinery will be only $50,000. Only over a 20-year period will the purchase price of the machinery show up as an equivalent cost, because that is the period over which the machinery serves in production. It follows that if every year this company spends $1 million for such machinery, then only after 20 years will its total *annual* depreciation cost come to match its million-dollar annual outlay for such machinery. It further follows that until that happens, the firm's annual expenditure of a million dollars for such machinery results in net investment, which means in this case that net investment will be present for twenty years on the strength of this given, higher level of productive expenditure.

To clearly grasp this fact, it may help to realize that in *Year 2* of the present example, the firm will have 2 batches of such machinery, each incurring an annual depreciation of $50,000. In *Year 10*, it will have 10 batches of such machinery, creating a total current depreciation charge of $500,000. Only in *Year 20*, and thereafter, will it have 20 batches of such machinery, creating a total current depreciation charge of $1 million. Thus, only from *Year 20* on, will its annual depreciation cost on account of such machinery equal its million-dollar annual outlay to purchase such machinery. Until that time, the firm's productive expenditure for machinery exceeds its depreciation on existing machinery and it experiences corresponding net investment in plant and equipment.[55]

Obviously, the same relationships as just described apply to the expenditure for assets of any life. For example, if every year a business expends funds for buildings that will be depreciated over a 50-year period, then it would take 50 years for total annual depreciation cost on account of such buildings to come to equal the firm's annual outlay for such buildings. Thus, for 50 years, a given additional expenditure for such assets would result in net investment. The relationships obviously apply to the economic system as a whole. If, in the economic system as a whole, there is, say, $500 billion of annual expenditure for machinery and buildings with an average life of 25 years, then such expenditure must be repeated for 25 years before aggregate depreciation cost in the economic system equals the annual outlay for machinery and buildings. Until that time, there is net investment.

Net investment, and the aggregate profit that accompanies it, can exist not only by virtue of a fall in net consumption and rise in productive expenditure, but even with no fall in net consumption and no rise in productive expenditure. It can exist *by virtue of a change in the disposition of a given aggregate amount of productive expenditure*. For example, to the extent that productive expenditure shifts from expensed expenditures to expenditure on account of inventories, the productive expenditures involved are debited to assets instead of being instantaneously deducted from sales revenues as costs. The expenditures are added to the inventory/work-in-progress account and thereby result in an equivalent diminution of the costs deducted from sales revenues. Thus, there is net investment and corresponding profit.

To the extent that productive expenditure that is already on account of inventories or work in progress is shifted to the account of inventories or work in progress of a kind that requires a longer period of time before coming to market, there is a correspondingly greater deferral of the time before the productive expenditures involved show up as costs deducted from sales revenues. To take an obvious example, if the whiskey distilleries shift from the production of eight-year-old scotch to the production of twelve-year-old scotch, twelve years must go by instead of eight before the outlays for raw whiskey become deductions from sales revenues.

The same kind of phenomenon is potentially present in every case in which products or methods of production entail different periods of time in going from the purchase of labor and materials to a product sold to buyers. In every such case, a shift to products or methods of production requiring more such time represents a correspondingly greater period during which current productive expenditures on account of inventory and work in progress exceed the costs currently being deducted from sales revenues as costs of goods sold.

To use the whiskey example, the shifting of a given amount of productive expenditure from the making of eight-year-old scotch to the making of twelve-year-old scotch, and maintaining this shift throughout the years, means that there will be four years during which the productive expenditures being made for the purpose of producing whiskey remain the same, and the sales revenues they directly or indirectly generate elsewhere in the economic system remain the same, but in which the costs deducted from sales revenues fall, because the assets in question remain in inventory or work in progress. In all such cases, there is less aggregate cost in the economic system and correspondingly more monetary value in the form of inventory/work in progress. In other words, there

is correspondingly more net investment and profit.

In this particular case, in which the whiskey industry is assumed to productively expend just the same amount each year, the reduction in aggregate costs would occur specifically in the whiskey industry, which would withhold some of its product from the market for four years. But it could also be the case, and would be far more likely to be the case, that the shift to the production of twelve-year-old scotch would be made possible by a shifting of productive expenditures from outside the whiskey industry to the whiskey industry, rather than by a shifting within the whiskey industry itself. Thus, for the first four years in which the greater concentration on the production of twelve-year-old scotch takes place, the outlays could be financed by funds coming from outside the whiskey industry. This would leave the whiskey industry free to go on producing eight-year-old scotch during that time. Only thereafter would less expenditure be made within the whiskey industry on behalf of producing eight-year-old scotch. Only at the start of *Year 5*, would the whiskey industry shift a portion of its own funds previously devoted to the acquisition of raw whiskey that would be laid up for eight years, to the acquisition of raw whiskey that would be laid up for twelve years. Its ability to supply whiskey eight years later would not be diminished because, thanks to the previous infusion of funds from the outside, it would already be in possession of a comparable quantity of four-year old whiskey rather than raw whiskey. In this way, eight years later, just as the eight-year-old scotch came to be in reduced supply, its place would be taken by a correspondingly greater supply of twelve-year-old scotch. In this, more likely case, the reduction in aggregate costs in the economic system takes place *outside the whiskey industry*—in all those industries from which productive expenditures of a kind fairly quickly showing up as costs are withdrawn in order to finance the production of twelve-year-old scotch.

A much greater effect on behalf of net investment, of course, results from the shifting of productive expenditures from expensed expenditures and for inventory and work in progress to expenditures for plant and equipment, and from plant and equipment of a shorter life to plant and equipment of a longer life. Still more powerful effects are achieved in cases in which productive expenditures are shifted to expenditures for plant and equipment which not only last a longer time, but require a greater period of time in their construction. Productive expenditures shifted to things like bridges, tunnels, and canals result in net investment going on for a period of years equal to the sum of the construction time plus the period of useful life over which such assets are depreciated. Only when a given amount of such productive expenditure is repeated for this long a time, does annual depreciation cost come to equal such annual productive expenditure. Finally, the most enduring source of net investment of all would be productive expenditure for assets of a kind that normally do not depreciate, notably, urban land.[56]

In every case in which productive expenditure in the economic system is shifted from a point closer to showing up as a cost deducted from sales revenues to a point further removed from showing up as a cost deducted from sales revenues, the effect, for some period of time, is to bring about a reduction in the aggregate costs deducted from sales revenues. This reduction when taken relative to productive expenditure constitutes net investment. This same reduction when taken relative to sales revenues, which themselves, of course, are generated for the most part by productive expenditure, constitutes an equivalent increase in aggregate profits. Always, the net investment and profit brought about by such shifting of productive expenditure last until a period of time has gone by that is sufficient for the temporally more remote annual productive expenditure to show up in equivalent annual cost.

Net Investment as the Result of the Marginal Productivity of Capital Exceeding the Rate of Profit

The cause of a shift in the disposition of a given amount of aggregate productive expenditure to points more remote from showing up as costs deducted from sales revenue, and the creation of net investment thereby, can be found in an excess of *the marginal productivity of capital* over the prevailing rate of profit. The marginal productivity of capital in this context must be understood in a special sense—namely, as the savings of cost or additions to sales revenue that additional capital would achieve for individual business firms, relative to the additional capital in question.[57] If, for example, the employment of an additional $1,000,000 of capital would have the effect of reducing the annual costs incurred by a business firm in producing its present output by $100,000, then the marginal productivity of capital for this firm would be 10 percent. The same marginal productivity of capital would be present if the employment of an additional $1,000,000 of capital would make it possible for the firm to produce improved products at the same total annual cost as it now produces its present products, which improved products would bring in an additional $100,000 in annual sales revenues to the firm. The marginal productivity of capital in general represents the array of the marginal productivities of capital of all the individual firms, arranged in descending order. It is the array of all firms' prospective cost reductions or revenue increases that they expect to be achievable in connection with their present volumes of output, relative to the

additional sums of capital that they perceive would be required to achieve them.

Insofar as the marginal productivity of capital is above the going rate of profit in the economic system, an incentive is created to withdraw capital from existing employments to employments of the kind requiring new and additional capital, that is, to more capital-intensive employments. This is because, comparatively speaking, such a change in the employment of capital appears as the more profitable use of the capital in the circumstances. More capital intensiveness is what offers the prospect of lower unit costs through greater efficiency and/or higher selling prices because of improved quality of products.

For example, in the grocery-store industry, those grocery stores with better warehouse facilities, better buildings and fixtures, and a wider variety of merchandise offer a prospect of reduced costs and greater sales revenues compared to grocery stores lacking these improvements. If the size of these cost savings and/or revenue increases relative to the additional capital required to achieve them is greater than the rate of return currently being earned in the grocery business and in the economy generally, then an incentive is created to move capital from its present, relatively less-capital intensive employments in the grocery business into such more-capital-intensive employments, because this is where the capital in question will be employed more profitably. To the extent that the same situation obtains in other industries, the same incentive will exist with respect to the movement of capital in and between them. Thus, if automobile or steel companies with more modern factories and machinery can achieve cost savings or revenue increases relative to the necessary additional capital that are greater than the rate of profit prevailing in those industries and in the economy generally, the incentive will also exist to move capital from its present, relatively less-capital intensive employments in those industries into such more-capital-intensive employments in those industries, because this is where the capital in question will be employed more profitably. (Mergers among existing firms can obviously be highly instrumental in achieving such greater capital intensiveness.)

Now in the face of a given aggregate amount of productive expenditure, the withdrawal of capital from existing employments, where the going rate of return is being earned, to more capital-intensive employments, which offer the prospect of a higher rate of return, entails the shifting of productive expenditure from points temporally less remote from the earning of sales revenues to points temporally more remote from the earning of sales revenues. This is inherent in the nature of movement toward greater capital intensiveness. This in turn operates to create net investment in the economic system and correspondingly to raise the amount and rate of profit in the economic system. It does so by virtue of the fact that the withdrawal of capital from existing, temporally less remote investments reduces the costs deducted from productive expenditure and sales revenues before the investment of capital in the temporally more remote investments raises such costs. In the interval, there is an addition to net investment and to aggregate profit in the economic system. To take a very simple and dramatic example, the elimination of a portion of the daily expenditures of several pushcart peddlers for groceries at wholesale and its replacement with an equivalent daily expenditure for the construction of grocery stores, means an equivalent virtually immediate reduction in costs deducted from sales revenues and the passage of many years before the appearance of equivalent costs in the form of depreciation on grocery stores.

As I have indicated, the transfer of capital from less remote to more remote employments occurs between industries as well as within industries. For example, it is obvious in such cases as the transfer of capital from investment in grocery stores, say, to investment in electric utilities, say. But the phenomenon is no less present in the provision of new and additional capital for grocery stores by means of the transfer of capital from the electric utility industry, insofar as the capital being transferred is capital invested in such things as inventories and meeting expensed expenditures, while what it is being transferred to is capital invested in fixtures and buildings.

An inference to be drawn from the preceding analysis is that the existence of a marginal productivity of capital in excess of the rate of profit leads to the formation of new and additional capital. This is implied in the fact that the shifting of capital and productive expenditure to more remote employments calls net investment into being. The net investment is an addition to capital.

Despite its role in the causation of net investment and thus profit, it cannot be stressed too strongly that the marginal productivity of capital never directly determines the average rate of profit in the economic system. The rate of profit is always directly determined by the rate of net consumption and the rate of net investment.

The marginal productivity of capital is a concept that properly pertains only to cost savings or revenue increases of individual firms that are achievable by means of the employment of additional capital. Moreover, such cost savings or revenue increases by themselves need not result in corresponding actual profits even for the individual firms that experience them, let alone for the firms with which these firms compete. To say that costs are reduced or revenues increased by $100,000 by virtue of

the employment of an additional $1,000,000 of capital is not a sufficient basis for assuming even that the firm employing the additional capital earns a 10 percent rate of profit on its capital. It could well be that all that is involved is that its losses are now $100,000 less than before and its rate of loss is correspondingly reduced.

Furthermore, under an invariable money, to whatever extent lower costs or improved products on the part of this firm result in its having greater sales revenues, other firms in its industry or elsewhere in the economic system will have correspondingly lower sales revenues and thus lower profits. Clearly, there is no basis for making any direct inferences concerning the average rate of profit in the economic system on the basis of the marginal productivity of capital.[58]

The impact of the marginal productivity of capital on the rate of profit in the economic system is always indirect, through its effect on the rate of net investment. When the marginal productivity of capital is above the rate of profit, net investment occurs and the rate of profit rises. On the other hand, when the marginal productivity of capital is below the rate of profit, capital is withdrawn from temporally more remote employments to make possible investment in temporally less remote employments, which, in affording the going rate of return, by comparison now appear to offer more profitable uses for the capital in question. In the process, net investment is reduced—indeed, it might even become negative—and the amount and rate of profit are reduced.[59]

A leading implication of this discussion is that a tendency exists for the rate of profit and the marginal productivity of capital to equalize, in that when the marginal productivity of capital is above the rate of profit, additional net investment is induced and the rate of profit rises, and when the marginal productivity of capital is below the rate of profit, net investment is curtailed and the rate of profit is reduced.[60]

Another important implication of this discussion is that the marginal productivity of capital—in the sense in which I employ the term—is not a matter merely of physical or technical factors. It depends no less on factors that are ultimately a matter of value judgments and psychology. For example, if the demand of the public shifts from a good such as eight-year-old scotch to a good such as twelve-year-old scotch, the marginal productivity of capital is correspondingly increased, inasmuch as by this action the public is now willing to allow a greater premium in the price of a product requiring a greater degree of capital intensiveness in its production. The principle, of course, applies to any shift in demand from goods produced under a lower degree of capital intensiveness to goods whose production requires a higher degree of capital intensiveness.

Net Investment as a Self-Limiting Phenomenon

The fact that net investment takes place in response to the marginal productivity of capital being above the rate of profit, combined with the further fact that net investment itself adds to the rate of profit in the form of the previously described net-investment rate, implies that net investment is an inherently self-limiting phenomenon. This is because the greater is net investment, the higher, other things being equal, is the rate of profit and thus the fewer are the cases in which the marginal productivity of capital exceeds the rate of profit, and thus the more improbable is any further increase in the net-investment rate.

This inherent self-limitation of the net-investment rate operates as an important safeguard against any possibility of even the short-run interests of wage earners being unduly denied for the sake of capital accumulation.[61] This is because any undue increase in net investment would operate to raise the rate of profit relative to the marginal productivity of capital and thereby operate to discourage or even reverse the movement toward greater capital intensiveness. Thus, the extent to which the demand for labor might be reduced in order to make possible an increase in the demand for capital goods is always inherently limited.

Capital Intensification and the Tendency Toward the Disappearance of Net Investment Under an Invariable Money

As should already be clear from preceding discussion in this chapter, *a tendency exists for net investment to disappear under an invariable money.* However more remote that portions of productive expenditure may become from having to be deducted from sales revenues as costs, still, if any depreciation whatever exists in connection with such productive expenditures, their continuation year after year will eventually be accompanied by annual depreciation costs that are just as great as those productive expenditures. At that point, the net investment and profits connected with the shift to such productive expenditures come to an end.[62] And if the more remote productive expenditures are not continued until this time, then the associated net investment and aggregate profit come to an end all the sooner, because the shifting of productive expenditures back to points temporarily less remote from being deducted as costs from sales revenues results in the rise in costs to a point of equality with productive expenditure all the sooner.

Under an invariable money and its concomitant limitation on the amount of productive expenditure, the only thing which can make possible the continuation of net investment is the *continual* shifting of productive expenditures to points temporally more remote from being

deducted as costs from sales revenues. Given the existence of such continual shifting, it is possible to imagine the existence of a given amount of net investment going on virtually indefinitely. Indeed, its continuation would be positively encouraged by the falling rate of profit that is implicit in the situation, and which would operate to keep the rate of profit below a falling marginal productivity of capital as the amount of accumulated capital increased.[63] A fall in the rate of profit in this case is implied insofar as the rate of profit depends on the rate of net investment. It follows from the fact that the same amount of net investment would have to be divided by an amount of capital that continually grew by virtue of the net investment. Thus the net investment rate would fall and the rate of profit would fall insofar as it was governed by the net investment rate.

However, because of the existence of net consumption and thus a positive rate of net consumption, the fall in the rate of profit proceeds more slowly than the fall in the rate of net investment. It falls toward the rate of net consumption and can fall no lower without *negative* net investment taking place, which is clearly not in question here. Thus the encouragement given to net investment by a falling rate of profit progressively diminishes and ultimately must cease altogether.

The existence of any given positive rate of profit in the economic system, based on the rate of net consumption or on a combination of the rate of net consumption and some positive rate of net investment, makes the continual shifting of productive expenditures to more remote points in relation to their deduction as costs from sales revenues progressively more difficult. This is because the existence of any given positive rate of profit requires that to the degree that returns on investment must be postponed, they must be greater at least to the extent of providing a return equal to the going rate of profit compounded for the longer period of time in question. Thus, for example, if the going rate of profit is 5 percent per year, then a productive expenditure made one year in advance of the corresponding sale, needs to bring about at least $5 of profit; more precisely, it needs to bring about at least $5 of additional profit or reduced losses, achieved my means either of reducing costs or adding to sales revenues in the amount of $5. A productive expenditure made two years in advance of the corresponding sale, needs to bring in at least $10.25 in one of these ways, and so on, with the required amount of return increasing at a 5 percent compound rate. Obviously, the higher is the rate of profit, the greater is the obstacle presented by compounding.[64]

In the absence of a continual shifting of productive expenditures to points temporally more remote from their deduction as costs from sales revenues—which ultimately becomes impossible by virtue of the requirement of achieving cost reductions or revenue increases equal at least to those imposed by the rate of net consumption compounded for the length of time in question—costs begin to rise toward productive expenditure. The result is a steady diminution in the amount of net investment and in the amount of corresponding profits in the economic system. The ultimate result is that in the conditions of an invariable money, *aggregate profit tends toward equality with net consumption alone.*

In effect, the existence of the combination of capital accumulation based on net investment, and a positive rate of profit based at least on the rate of net consumption, sooner or later serves to bring to an end the ability of the marginal productivity of capital to surpass the rate of profit and thereby to continue to call net investment into being. The ultimate result, once again, is that the rate of profit comes to be based on net consumption alone.

The tendency toward the disappearance of net investment under the conditions of an invariable money is greatly reinforced by the fact that an indirect consequence of net investment is an increase in the amount of net consumption in the economic system and thus a corresponding decrease in the amount of productive expenditure. Thus net investment tends to disappear by virtue both of a rise in costs toward the level of productive expenditure and, at the same time, a fall in the magnitude of productive expenditure itself.

Net investment results in a rise in net consumption and thus fall in productive expenditure because its existence constitutes an increase in the amount of accumulated capital and thus of accumulated savings in general. In an economic system with an invariable money, and in which, therefore, aggregate money income does not increase, the increase in the amount of accumulated capital and savings represents a rise in the *ratio* of accumulated capital and savings to income. As capital and savings accumulate relative to income, the need and desire of people to increase their accumulated capital and savings still further relative to their income diminishes, while their desire to consume their income correspondingly increases.

Thus, individuals with no accumulated capital or savings whatever, have an urgent need to save and accumulate capital. Those who have accumulated capital and savings equal to a year's income, say, have a less urgent need to do so. Those who have accumulated capital and savings equal to two, three, or five years' income have a still less urgent need to do so, and so on. At some sufficiently high ratio of accumulated capital and savings to income, the average member of the economic system feels no need to raise the ratio of his accumulated capital and savings any further. Thus, as the ratio of accumulated

capital and savings to income rises, net consumption rises and productive expenditure falls. Any possible diminution of net consumption stemming from saving out of wages diminishes, disappears altogether, and is followed by a positive contribution to net consumption on the part of wage earners, a contribution which joins with the growing consumption of businessmen and capitalists, as their accumulated capital and savings increase. The accumulation of savings in the form of loans for the purchase of consumer assets, such as homes and the land sites they occupy, also contributes to rising net consumption and thus to falling productive expenditure.[65]

Because of the above reasons, under the conditions of an invariable money, net investment tends to disappear, thereby leaving net consumption as the sole determinant of the amount and rate of profit.

The Process of Capital Intensification

A related approach for understanding the process whereby net investment ultimately must disappear under an invariable money, is to observe just how the economic system becomes more capital intensive as the result of a process of saving. At the same time, this will provide further understanding of the fact that any possible negative net consumption that might temporarily exist as the result of saving on the part of wage earners, must also disappear.

This approach requires tracing out the process of capital intensification step by step. This is done in Table 16–10. In this table, the economic system is assumed to begin with an annual aggregate expenditure for consumers' goods of 500 units of money. The total value of the capital employed in this economic system at all stages of production combined is assumed initially to be 1,000 units of money. This sum is the value of all the land, buildings, fixtures, plant, and equipment of business firms, less accumulated depreciation reserves, plus the value of all the inventories and work in progress that business firms possess. It also includes the quantity of money held by business firms.[66] Please note that what is referred to here is the value of the capital *stock* of the economic system, not the annual expenditure for capital goods.

The ratio of accumulated capital to consumption, or, more precisely, to the sum of consumption plus net investment, is typically called the capital-output ratio. More correctly, of course, it should be called the capital-*net*-output ratio, inasmuch as consumption plus net investment represents the net product of the economic system, not the actual total output.[67] Because of the equality between net product and national income, the ratio can also be expressed as the ratio of capital to national income.[68] Its closeness to the ratio of capital to

Table 16–10

The Process of Capital Intensification
or How More Capital Is Invested When the Demand for Consumers' Goods Falls

Year	K	C	I	K/(C+I)	K₁/C1	K₂/I1
1	1,000	500	0	1,000/500	1,000/500	
2	1,000	500	0	1,000/500	900/450	100/50
3	1,050	450	50	1,050/500	945/450	105/50
4	1,100	450	50	1,100/500	990/450	110/50
5	1,150	450	50	1,150/500	1,035/450	115/50
6	1,200	450	50	1,200/500	1,080/450	120/50
7	1,250	450	50	1,250/500	1,125/450	125/50
8	1,300	450	50	1,300/500	1,170/450	130/50
9	1,350	450	50	1,350/500	1,215/450	135/50
10	1,400	450	50	1,400/500	1,260/450	140/50
11	1,450	450	50	1,450/500	1,305/450	145/50
12	1,500	450	50	1,500/500	1,500/500	
13	1,500	500	0	1,500/500	1,500/500	
...	...	...	...	...	...	...

KEY:

K is the value of the accumulated capital stock at year end.

C is the total expenditure for consumers' goods in the current year.

I is net investment in the current year.

$K/(C+I)$ is the ratio of total accumulated capital to current net national product.

C_1 is the demand for consumers' goods in the following year.

I_1 is the volume of net investment in the following year.

K_1 is the portion of existing accumulated capital employed in the production of consumers' goods to be sold in the following year.

K_2 is the portion of existing accumulated capital employed in the production of the portion of next year's NNP that is represented by net investment.

consumption makes it obvious that the so-called capital-output ratio can be taken as a measure of the degree of capital intensiveness in the economic system, alongside the ratios we have mainly used up to now, namely, the ratio of capital to consumption, wages, and sales revenues respectively.[69]

What is necessary at this point is to trace out how saving brings about a rise in the capital-net-output ratio from its initial level to a higher level. For the sake of simplicity, the example describes how the ratio is raised from an initial level of 1,000/500 to 1,500/500, or from 2:1

to 3:1. It should go without saying, that the principles contained in this example are applicable to the process of capital intensification in general, that is, to a rise in the capital-net-output ratio from any given starting level to any other given level, and for any absolute values of consumption expenditure (or consumption expenditure plus net investment) and the capital stock.

The table assumes that the process of capital intensification is brought about by a reduction in consumption expenditure from 500 to 450 for a period of 10 years. It assumes that in each of these 10 years 50 of savings out of net income are invested and added to the preexisting value of the accumulated capital stock, which means that 50 of net investment occurs in each year. It further assumes that once the value of the capital stock has been increased by a cumulative total of 500, so that the ratio of accumulated capital (savings) to income stands at 3:1, people are content with their degree of provision for the future and thus restore their consumption expenditure to 500.

The first column of the table is simply a series of years. The second column, K, presents the amount of accumulated capital year by year; the third, C, the amount of consumer spending year by year; and the fourth, I, the amount of net investment year by year. For the sake of simplicity, I follow my usual practice of assuming that all financial transactions take place on the first day of the year. In the present case, this permits dealing with the net investment of each year both as adding to the accumulated capital of that year and as contributing to the net output available at the start of the following year. Thus, for example, the accumulated capital of 1,050 shown for *Year 3* both incorporates the 50 of net investment made in *Year 3* and serves in the production of the net output that becomes available at the start of *Year 4*.

For each year, the fifth column of the table, $K/(C+I)$, presents the ratio of accumulated capital to the so-called net national product (NNP), which, of course, is equal to the sum of consumption plus net investment and to national income. Initially, NNP is equal to 500 of consumption expenditure alone, and will be once again, at the conclusion of the process. But in the interval, as the process of capital intensification takes place, NNP is equal to the sum of 450 of consumption plus 50 of net investment. Because the net product of the economic system comes to be divided into these two portions, 450 of consumption and 50 of net investment, the total accumulated capital stock of the economic system comes to be divided into two corresponding portions: the one portion serving in producing the part of the net product purchased by the consumers, the other portion serving in producing the part of the net product that constitutes net investment.

The division of the capital stock in this way is shown in the last two columns of the table, headed K_1/C_1 and K_2/I_1. It should be observed that C_1 is the demand for consumers' goods of the following year, and, accordingly, K_1 is the portion of existing accumulated capital employed in the production of consumers' goods to be sold in the following year. By the same token, I_1 is the volume of net investment of the following year, and K_2 is the portion of existing accumulated capital employed in the production of the portion of next year's NNP that is represented by net investment. (This aspect of the table

is similar to Figures 16–1 and 16–2, in which the disposition of the factors of production within each year is assumed to conform to the pattern of the relative demands for consumers' goods and capital goods in the following year. The difference is that now the disposition of the net output in the following year between consumption and net investment is taken in place of the relative demands for consumers' goods and capital goods, which categories of goods, of course, are the components of gross output.[70])

In Table 16–10, *Year 1* represents an initial equilibrium. It shows how the economic system has been operating up to this point. The value of the capital stock is 1,000, the demand for consumers' goods is 500, and the capital-net-output ratio is 2:1.[71] In *Year 2*, consumption spending continues to be 500 and saving and net investment continue to be zero. But in this year, the allocation of capital undergoes an important change, in anticipation of the drop in consumption of 50 and emergence of 50 of net investment that is to occur in *Year 3*, and which will be maintained for a total of 10 years, viz., through *Year 12*. Accordingly, in *Year 2*, 100 of capital is transferred from the production of consumers' goods for *Year 3* to the production of the part of the net output of *Year 3* that will be represented by net investment. Hence, in *Year 2*, K_1/C_1 is $^{900}/_{450}$ and K_2/I_1 is $^{100}/_{50}$. To describe matters in terms of concretes, what will happen in *Year 3* is that there will be 50 less of spending for such goods as residential housing and personal automobiles, and 50 more of spending for such goods as factory buildings, trucks, and freighters. Accordingly, in *Year 2*, 100 of capital is shifted from the production of such goods as residential housing and personal automobiles to the production of such goods as factory buildings, trucks, and freighters.

In *Year 3*, 50 of saving and net investment occur and result in a rise in the accumulated capital of the economic system from 1,000 to 1,050. This additional 50 of capital is divided between the production of consumers' goods for *Year 4* and the production of the portion of the net output of *Year 4* which is represented by net investment; that is, it is divided in the ratio of *Year 4*'s demand for consumers' goods to *Year 4*'s net investment, i.e., in the ratio of 450:50, or 9:1. Thus, 45 of the additional capital is devoted to the production of consumers' goods of *Year 4*, and 5 of the additional capital is devoted to the production of the part of the net output of *Year 4* that is represented by net investment. Observe that from this point on the employment of capital in the production of consumers' goods begins rising. Both the production of consumers' goods and the production of the goods represented by net investment become progressively more capital intensive.

The process of increasing capital intensiveness in the production both of consumers' goods and the portion of net output represented by net investment continues from *Year 3* to *Year 11*. By *Year 11*, total capital has risen from 1,000 to 1,450, of which 1,305 are employed in the production of consumers' goods for *Year 12*, and 145 in the production of the part of the net output of *Year 12* that will constitute net investment. In *Year 12*, however, the final 50 of additional capital is accumulated, and, at the same time, the allocation of capital is shifted back from the industries producing for net investment and the increase in capital intensiveness to the industries producing consumers' goods. This is because having achieved the desired higher ratio of accumulated savings to current income by *Year 12*, people once again consume the whole of their nominal incomes starting in *Year 13*.

Of course, both the beginning and the end of the process need not be as abrupt as I have described it. There could be a gradual increase in saving and net investment accompanied by a gradual shift in the allocation of capital to the production of goods representing net investment. And the later, reverse movement could be equally gradual. Nor is it necessary that the changes in the consumption/saving pattern be anticipated with the precision I have presented. Any lack of anticipation of the initial shift will result in comparatively higher profits for the capital goods industries and comparatively lower profits for the consumers' goods industries, because to this extent there will be a greater demand relative to supply in the case of capital goods and a smaller demand relative to supply in the case of consumers' goods. By the same token, lack of anticipation of the later, reverse shift will result in comparatively higher profits for the consumers' goods industries and comparatively lower profits for the capital goods industries, because now the opposite imbalance would ensue.

Under all conditions, however, at the end of the process, the net effect is that people end up with greater provision for the future (both absolutely and relatively), production is more capital intensive, the supply of goods is more abundant and can go on increasing more rapidly (thanks to the increased ability to implement technological advances that more capital intensiveness makes possible), and people restore their consumption expenditure in a condition in which they are better able to afford to do so. It thus works out to be the same as for an individual, who first saves and, as a result, later on puts himself in the position of being able to afford to step up his consumption.

And in just this way, any saving on the part of wage earners which did have the effect of bringing about negative net consumption would prove temporary. It would go on only until wage earners had accumulated savings sufficient to enable them to consume the whole of their wages, at which point, everyone in the economic system would be better off than he had been before. (To be sure, the wage earners would not only consume the whole of their wages but the whole of any profits or interest currently earned on the capital they had accumulated.)

It should be realized, although it is not stated explicitly, that the accumulation of capital and savings in the present analysis leads to a reduction in productive expenditure along with the restoration of consumption expenditure, just as in the previous analysis. This fact is present implicitly in the restoration of consumption expenditure and disappearance of net investment.

5. The Addition to the Rate of Profit Caused by Increases in the Quantity of Money

As we have seen, under an invariable money, as net investment occurs and total capital increases, the economic system becomes more and more capital intensive—i.e., capital rises relative to sales revenues, wages, and consumption. This has a profound bearing on the average rate of profit, over and above its tendency to cause a rise in net consumption and the disappearance of net investment—a bearing that applies to the rate of profit both in nominal and in real terms, and whose precise nature is the subject of this section and the next.

This further bearing on the rate of profit exists because, as we have also seen, a major effect of greater capital intensiveness is that the receptiveness of the economic system to technological progress is increased, which, in turn, can make possible continuous capital accumulation and economic progress.[72] The relevant aspects of the process of capital accumulation and economic progress are the increasing supply of commodities in general and of the monetary commodity or commodities in particular. The effects of the latter on the rate of profit in nominal terms is the subject of this section. The effects of the former on the rate of profit in real terms is the subject of the next section. The rate of profit in nominal terms, or, simply, the nominal rate of profit, is, of course, the rate of profit as ordinarily understood, that is, the amount of money earned as profit, divided by the amount of money invested as capital. The rate of profit in real terms, or simply, the real rate of profit, is the rate of profit adjusted for changes in the purchasing power of money. It is the measure of the gain in actual wealth, if any, that is the result of the earning of any given rate of profit.[73]

A growing supply of commodity money is the virtually inevitable accompaniment of a growing overall ability to produce, inasmuch as there is no lack of any chemical element in nature, not even gold or silver.[74] Thus there is nothing to stand in the way of this result once net investment has succeeded in raising the degree of capital intensiveness to the point that the receptivity of the economic system to technological progress is such that continuous capital accumulation and economic progress can in fact take place.

Up to now, of course, my discussion of profits has proceeded on the assumption that increases in production take place with no connection to the quantity of money. It should be clear that this assumption needs to be modified in dealing with an economic system whose money is itself a physical commodity, such as gold or silver. The truth is, as I have pointed out repeatedly, that under a gold or silver standard, large-scale increases in production are bound to be accompanied by increases in the quantity of money and volume of spending. I will now proceed to show that the effect of this is *the addition of a corresponding positive component to the nominal rate of profit.* (In the next section, I will show how increases in the ability to produce the mass of ordinary, nonmonetary commodities add a corresponding positive component to the real rate of profit.)

Furthermore, as I have shown, in the case of any individual country using the same money as other countries, as is the case under an international gold or silver standard, the very fact of a more rapid rate of increase in physical production in that country compared with other countries will also increase the quantity of money in that country. This is because the economy of that country will come to constitute a larger proportion of the world's economic system. As a result, it will come to hold a larger proportion of the world's supply of commodity money and thus to experience rising spending and sales revenues within its own borders.[75] The effect of an increase in the quantity of money and volume of spending occurring in this way too is to add a positive component to the nominal rate of profit.

Thus, in reality, net investment and the growing capital intensiveness it causes are inherently incompatible with the assumption of a fixed quantity of money and volume of spending, if the money is a commodity money. They necessarily break the constraints of that assumption. The assumption of an invariable money is vital for purposes of economic theory, which can effectively develop its primary propositions in no other context. But the limits of the assumption must be recognized and the effects on the rate of profit of increases in the quantity money dealt with. Only then, can the determinants of the—nominal—rate of profit be considered as fully explained.

The rate of increase in the quantity of money and, accordingly, the volume of spending in the economic system, tends to cause *an approximately equivalent increase in the rate of profit.* For example, if the quantity of money and the volume of spending in the economic system increase by 2 percent a year, that tends to add approximately 2 percent to the rate of profit. If the quantity of money and volume of spending in the economic system increase at the rate of 5 percent a year, that tends to add approximately 5 percent to the rate of profit. In other words, if the rate of profit would otherwise have been, say, 4 percent, it will now be 6 percent or 9 percent, depending on the rate of increase in the quantity of money and volume of spending in the economic system.

This relationship follows from the very nature of the rate of profit. The rate of profit is the amount of profit earned, on an annualized basis, divided by the capital invested. For example, if a businessman spends $100 for a quantity of merchandize which he sells one year later for $110, his amount of profit is $10 and his rate of profit is 10 percent. If he spends $100 for merchandize that he sells one month later for $101, his annualized rate of profit is 12 percent. If he spends $100 for merchandize that he sells two years later for $120, his annualized rate of profit is, again, 10 percent.

Now if the quantity of money and thus the volume of spending in the economic system are increasing over time, the sales revenues of the average businessman will tend to increase accordingly. If, for example, the quantity of money and volume of spending are increasing at a 2 percent annual rate, our merchant who otherwise would have sold his goods a year later for $110, will now tend to sell them for 2 percent more, that is, for 1.02 x $110, which is $112.20. His rate of profit will thus be 12.2 percent instead of 10 percent. Similarly, the merchant who otherwise would have sold his goods one month later for $101, will now tend to sell them for slightly more. In a period of one month, a 2 percent annual increase in the money supply and volume of spending will tend to raise his sales revenues by $\frac{1}{12}$ of 2 percent, i.e., by $\frac{1}{6}$ of 1 percent. Thus instead of selling for $101, he will tend to sell for 1.00167 times $101, that is, for $101.17. When annualized, his monthly profit of $1.17 yields a rate of profit of 14.04 percent, which is approximately 2 percent more than his initial profit rate of 12 percent. Similarly, our merchant who initially sold his goods for $120 two years later, will now, at a 2 percent annual increase in the money supply and volume of spending, tend to sell them for 1.02 x 1.02 x $120, or for $124.85. A profit of $24.85, when annualized, turns out to represent a rate of profit of 12.43 percent on the $100 of capital invested. Again, the rate of profit is increased by approximately the same number of percentage points as the rate of increase in the quantity of money and volume of spending in the economic system.

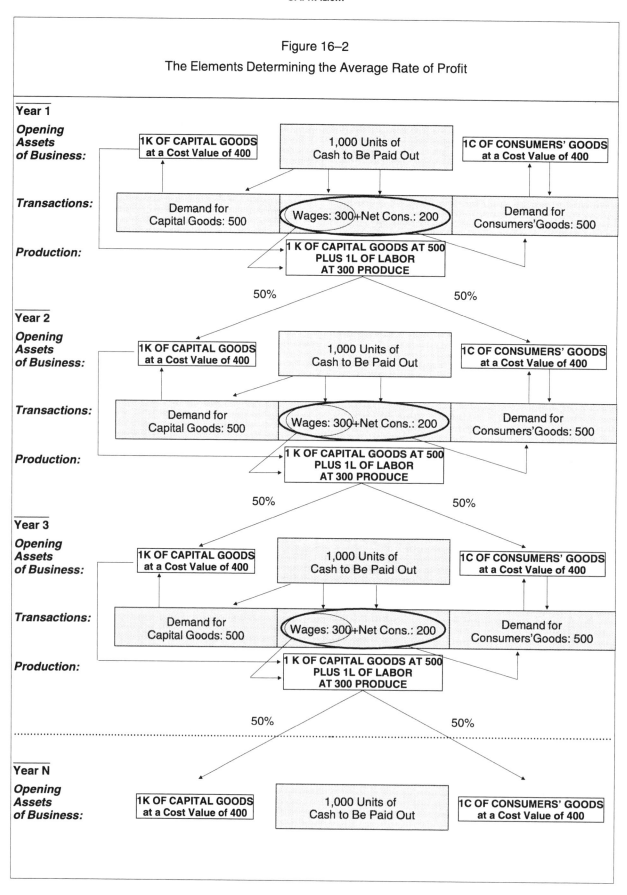

Figure 16–2

The Elements Determining the Average Rate of Profit

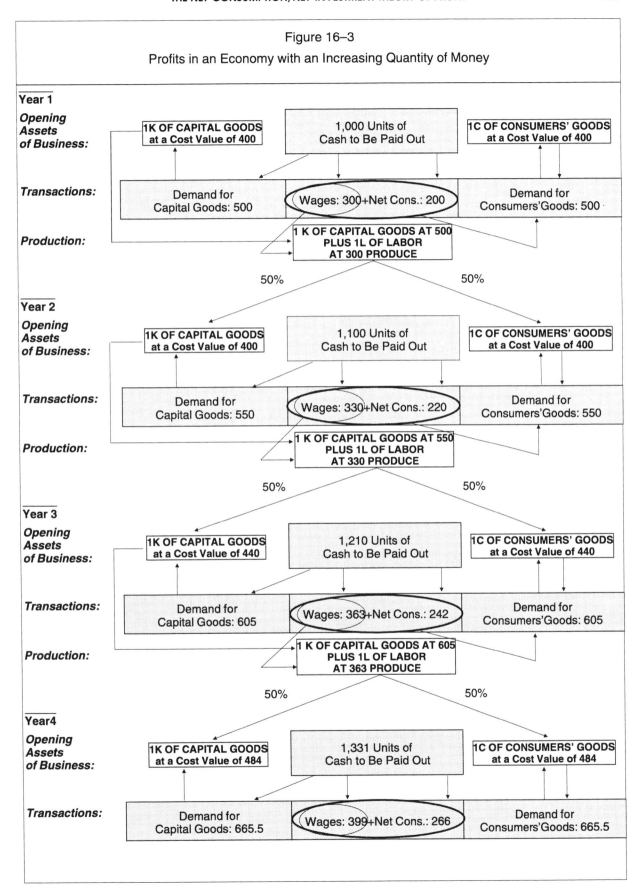

Figure 16–3

Profits in an Economy with an Increasing Quantity of Money

These results are borne out by Figure 16–3 and Table 16–11. Figure 16–3, titled "Profits in an Economy with an Increasing Quantity of Money," represents the previous Figure 16–2 but with the incorporation of the assumption that the quantity of money and volume of spending in the economic system increase at a 10 percent annual rate. (Such a large percentage increase is assumed strictly for purposes of ease of illustration. The rate of increase under a gold or silver standard would, of course, be far less.) The figure depicts a 10 percent annual increase both in net consumption and in productive expenditure, and, further, in the specific components of productive expenditure, namely, the demand for capital goods and wage payments. On the basis of the assumption that the costs deducted from sales revenues in each year represent the productive expenditure of the year before, it is possible once again to compute the annual amount and rate of profit in the economic system.

In *Year 2*, the amount of profit turns out to be 300 instead of the 200 which existed in *Year 2* of Figure 16–2, under the conditions of an invariable money. (For the sake of convenience of readers who wish to make a direct comparison between Figures 16–2 and 16–3, the former is reproduced directly facing the latter.) This is because

sales revenues, constituted by 550 of demand for capital goods and 550 of demand for consumers' goods, are 1,100, while costs, representing the 800 of productive expenditure of *Year 1*, are still just 800. In *Year 3*, with sales revenues at 1,210 and costs at 880 (the latter reflecting the 10 percent rise in demand for capital goods and labor in *Year 2*), profits rise to 330. And thereafter, the amount of profit continues to increase by 10 percent per year—that is, at the same rate as the increase in the quantity of money and volume of spending.[76]

The *rate* of profit in Figure 16–3, of course, can be computed simply by dividing the amount of profit in each year by the amount of capital that has been invested up to that year. The rate of profit computed for each year of Figure 16–3 can then be compared with the 11.11 percent rate of profit previously computed for each year of Figure 16–2. The difference will then show the effect of the 10 percent annual increase in the quantity of money and volume of spending. It should be expected, of course, that the calculations will show an addition to the rate of profit of approximately 10 percent, viz., that the rate of profit will now be approximately 21 percent instead of 11 percent.

The necessary calculations are carried out in Table

Table 16–11

The Effect of an Increasing Quantity of Money and Rising Volume of Spending on the Nominal Rate of Profit

Year	M	ΔM in %	NC	B	d	I	s	p	K	r in %	Δr in %
1	1,000	10	200	800	800	0	1,000	200	1,800	11.11	
2	1,100	10	220	880	800	80	1,100	300	1,900	15.79*	4.68
3	1,210	10	242	968	880	88	1,210	330	2,090	15.79	4.68
4	1,331	10	266	1,065	968	97	1,331	363	2,299	15.79	4.68
5	1,464	10	293	1,171	1,065	106	1,464	399	2,529	15.79	4.68

KEY: *Figures allow for rounding

M = Money Supply.   s = Sales Revenues.

ΔM = The Increase in the Money Supply.   p = Profits.

NC = Net Consumption.   K = Capital.

B = Productive Expenditure.   r = Rate of Profit.

d = Costs Deducted from Sales Revenues.   Δr = Increase in the Rate of Profit.

I = Net Investment (B-d).

16–11, which is appropriately titled "The Effect of an Increasing Quantity of Money and Rising Volume of Spending on the Nominal Rate of Profit." Table 16–11 extends the data of Figure 16–3 to a fifth year. For each year, it shows the quantity of money, M, in existence at the start of the year; the percentage rate of increase in the quantity of money, ΔM, which, of course, is 10 percent; the amount of net consumption, NC; the amount of productive expenditure, B; the magnitude of costs deducted from sales revenues, d, which equals the productive expenditure of the previous year; the amount of net investment, I, which, of course, is equal to the difference between the productive expenditure and the costs of any given year; the magnitude of sales revenues, s, which is equal to the sum of net consumption plus productive expenditure; the amount of profit, p, resulting from the subtraction of costs from sales revenues; the amount of capital, K; the rate of profit, r, which results from dividing the amount of profit by the amount of capital; and, finally, Δr, the difference between this rate of profit and the rate of profit prevailing in the conditions of Figure 16–2.[77]

It turns out that the table shows a rise in the rate of profit from 11.11 percent in *Year 1*, which represents the conditions of Figure 16–2, to 15.79 percent in *Year 2* and thereafter. This, of course, represents a surprisingly low addition to the rate of profit of only 4.68 percent, not the approximately 10 percent that previous discussion had led us to expect.

The reconciliation of this result with the reasonable expectation of a 10 percent addition to the rate of profit is to be found in the enormously large role played by the quantity of money in the calculation of capital invested. In each year of Figures 16–2 and 16–3, the quantity of money in the possession of business firms represents over half of their total capitals. This unduly large role of the quantity of money as a component of capital results from the simplifying assumption that all spending in a year takes place on the opening day of the year and is financed out of the preexisting cash holding of business.

The effect of such a large role being assigned to the quantity of money in the calculation of capital is to add a corresponding dead weight, as it were, in the calculation of the rate of profit.

This becomes apparent if the rates of profit in Figures 16–2 and 16–3 are recalculated on the basis of a provisional exclusion of the quantity of money from capital invested. If this is done, the amount of capital in Figure 16–2 turns out to be 800 in every year, as is shown in Table 16–12. Given a 200 amount of profit in each year, the table shows that the recalculated rate of profit for Figure 16–2 in every year is 25 percent rather than 11.11 percent. Similarly, Table 16–13 shows an amount of capital of 800 in *Year 1* of Figure 16–3 and a rate of profit in that year of 25 percent. It shows the amount of capital in *Years 2* through *5* of Figure 16–3 as 800, 880, 968, and 1,065 respectively. (As with Table 16–11, both tables continue to extend the analysis of Figures 16–2 and 16–3 to a fifth year.)

When these lesser amounts of capital, reflecting the exclusion of money, are divided into the respective amounts of profit of 300, 330, 363, and 399 for *Years 2* through *5* of Table 16–13, the corresponding rate of profit turns out to be 37.5 percent in each and every year. This, of course, implies an addition to the rate of profit of 12.5 percent—which is shown in the column labeled $\Delta r\%$—and suggests that the actual relationship between the rate of increase in the quantity of money and volume of spending on the one side and the addition to the rate of profit on the other, is that the rate of profit is elevated by a number of percentage points equal to the rate of increase in the quantity of money and volume of spending plus the product of that rate times the initial rate of profit. (The addition to the rate of profit of a further 2.5 percent, over and above the 10 percent corresponding to the increase in the quantity of money and volume of spending, equals the product of the 10 percent annual increase in the quantity of money and volume of spending times the initial rate of profit of 25 percent.)

Table 16–12							
Recalculation of Rate of Profit in Figure 16–2 with Money Excluded from Capital							
Year	K-M	p	r%	NC	NC/(K-M) in %	I	I/(K-M) in %
1	800	200	25	200	25	0	0
2	800	200	25	200	25	0	0
3	800	200	25	200	25	0	0
4	800	200	25	200	25	0	0
5	800	200	25	200	25	0	0

						Table 16–13					
					Recalculation of Rate of Profit in Figure 16–3 with Money Excluded from Capital						

Year	K-M	p	r%	Δr%	NC	NC/(K-M) in %	Addition to NC rate in %	I	I/(K-M) in %	Addition to I rate in %
1	800	200	25		200	25		0	0	
2	800	300	37.5	12.5	220	27.5	2.5	80	10	10
3	880	330	37.5	12.5	242	27.5	2.5	88	10	10
4	968	363	37.5	12.5	266	27.5	2.5	97	10	10
5	1,065	399	37.5	12.5	293	27.5	2.5	106	10	10

The Impact of Increases in the Quantity of Money on the Net-Investment and Net-Consumption Rates

Further examination of the data of Figure 16–3 and Table 16–11, as recalculated in Table 16–13, shows that the increase in the rate of profit corresponds to the creation of a net-investment rate of 10 percent, which is equal to the rate of increase in the quantity of money and volume of spending, plus an increase in the net-consumption rate of 2.5 percent, i.e., from 25 percent to 27.5 percent. (Both rates, of course, are calculated on the basis of the exclusion of money from capital.)

Observe. In the conditions of Figure 16–2, there is no net investment and the net-investment rate is therefore zero. In the conditions of Figure 16–3, however, net investment equal to 10 percent of capital excluding cash commences. Thereafter, the absolute amount of net investment increases at a rate of 10 percent a year, which is the same rate as capital exclusive of cash increases. Thus net investment is 80 in *Year 2*, when capital exclusive of cash is 800; 88 in *Year 3*, when capital exclusive of cash is 880; 97 in *Year 4*, when capital exclusive of cash is 968; and, finally, 106 in *Year 5*, when such capital is 1065. In other words, the net-investment rate is 10 percent in each year. In addition, a 10 percent annual increase in the amount of net consumption raises the net-consumption rate by 10 percent of the initial net-consumption rate. The net-consumption rate is elevated in this way because the amount of net consumption in *Year 2* increases by 10 percent—i.e., from 200 to 220— before there is any increase in the amount of capital exclusive of cash. And then, in *Year 3* and thereafter, as the capital exclusive of cash increases by 10 percent per year, so too does the amount of net consumption.

On the basis of this discussion, it should be clear that the addition to the rate of profit caused by increases in the quantity of money and volume of spending does not represent the creation of a new, distinct component in the rate of profit that is separate from the net-consumption and net-investment rates, but represents *an addition to those very rates*. In other words, the effect of increases in the quantity of money and volume of spending is to raise the rate of profit essentially by virtue of raising the net-investment and net-consumption rates. For the increase in the quantity of money and volume of spending operates to increase both productive expenditure and net consumption in proportion to itself. The growth in productive expenditure from year to year correspondingly elevates productive expenditure above costs, which reflect the productive expenditure of the year before. Thus, the increase in the quantity of money and volume of spending adds to or, indeed, creates net investment. In addition, it increases the amount and rate of net consumption. Specifically, the rate of increase in money and spending adds to the net-investment rate a number of percentage points equal to itself, and to the rate of net consumption a number of percentage points equal to the product of itself times the initial rate of net consumption.[78]

Increases in the Quantity of Money and the Perpetuation of Net Investment

As we have seen, the main impact of the increase in the quantity of money on the rate of profit is by way of the net-investment rate rather than the net-consumption rate. While the increase in the quantity of money and volume of spending merely adds to the net-consumption rate, it tends to be responsible for the *whole* of the net-investment rate. Indeed, it is what keeps net investment in being. For as I have shown, in an economic system with an invariable money, net investment tends to disappear.[79] It is only the increase in the quantity of money and volume of spending that makes it possible for net investment to be a regular, permanent phenomenon.

A growing quantity of money perpetuates the existence of net investment because it results in growing outlays for the factors of production, and these outlays are always ahead of the corresponding costs they generate. Imagine, for example, that because of a growing quantity of money, spending for plant and equipment by business rises at the rate of 2 percent per year, or at any given rate. Eventually, annual depreciation charges will also rise by 2 percent per year, or by whatever the rate at which productive expenditure for plant and equipment rises. But the depreciation charges will never catch up with the current spending for plant and equipment because they always reflect earlier such spending, which, in the nature of the case, was less. Thus, net investment occurs simply as a product of the increase in the quantity of money and the volume of spending.

To elaborate on this example, if the average life of plant and equipment is 20 years and the average rate of increase in the quantity of money and volume of spending in the economic system, including spending for plant and equipment, is 2 percent, then in 20 years, plant-and-equipment spending will equal whatever it is currently *times* 1.02^{20}. But total annual depreciation charges in 20 years will equal the summation of one-twentieth of each of twenty years' plant-and-equipment spending beginning with this year's plant-and-equipment spending and continuing on up to the plant-and-equipment spending of twenty years hence. The plant-and-equipment spending of nineteen of those twenty years is smaller than the plant-and-equipment spending of *Year 20*, in a compound proportion of 2 percent per year. Thus the depreciation quotas in *Year 20,* reflecting the division of each of these progressively smaller annual plant-and-equipment expenditures of the previous years by twenty, are correspondingly smaller. It is a question of comparing twenty depreciation terms ranging from $\dfrac{1}{20}$ through $\dfrac{1.02}{20}$, $\dfrac{1.02^2}{20}$ all the way up to $\dfrac{1.02^{20}}{20}$, with 1.02^{20}. Obviously the last term substantially exceeds the sum of the twenty depreciation terms. If it were broken into twenty equal parts, its excess would show up as the summation of

$$\frac{1.02^{20}}{20} - \frac{1}{20} + \frac{1.02^{20}}{20} - \frac{1.02}{20} + \frac{1.02^{20}}{20} - \frac{1.02^2}{20} + \cdots$$

$$\frac{1.02^{20}}{20} - \frac{1.02^{20}}{20}.$$

The difference is net investment in *Year 20.*

Obviously, the formula and its implications for net investment can easily be generalized to apply to any rate of increase in spending for plant and equipment of any average life, simply by substituting r for 2 percent, and n for 20 years.

It should not be difficult to see that essentially the same kind of relationship as exists between productive expenditure for plant and equipment, and depreciation cost, exists between productive expenditure on account of inventory and work in progress, and cost of goods sold. A growing quantity of money and thus rising volume of spending on account of inventory and work in progress operates to make such productive expenditures regularly exceed cost of goods sold, which reflects earlier such expenditures, which, in the nature of the case, were smaller.

The fact that the net-investment rate tends toward equality with the rate of increase in the quantity of money and volume of spending does not depend on the assumption that the labor and capital goods of any given year are entirely used up in producing the products just of the next year. Nor does it depend on the corollary of that assumption, which is that the costs of any given year are equal simply to the productive expenditure of the year before. The tendency toward equality between the net-investment rate and the rate of increase in the quantity of money and volume of spending does not depend on the number of future years that the means of production of any given year may serve or how long it may take for the value of those means of production to show up fully in the form of costs of production. These conclusions are confirmed by Table 16–14, "The Net-Investment Rate Equals the Rate of Increase in the Money Supply."

Table 16–14 assumes the existence of plant with a 10-year life. It shows that if a constant amount of productive expenditure for such plant takes place—for the sake of illustration, 500 monetary units per year—annual depreciation cost rises to equality with such productive expenditure in 10 years. At that point net investment declines to zero and the net-investment rate becomes zero. This is after gross plant has grown to 5000 monetary units, cumulative depreciation to 2750 monetary units, and net plant to 2250 monetary units. The table then assumes that starting in *Year 11*, productive expenditure for plant rises at a 10 percent annual rate (based on a 10 percent annual increase in the quantity of money and volume of spending in general). The year-by-year implications of this are presented for annual depreciation, net investment in plant, and for the respective values of gross plant, cumulative depreciation, and net plant. Finally, the rate of net investment in plant is calculated by dividing each year's net investment in plant by the value of net plant in the year before. The table shows that under the assumed conditions, the net-investment rate reaches 10 percent—exactly the same as the rate of increase in the quantity of money and volume of spending—in *Year 19*, and remains at 10 percent in all of the remaining years covered, namely, through and including *Year 25.*

Plant of any life could be substituted for the plant of

			Table 16–14			
			The Net Investment Rate Equals the Rate of Increase in the Money Supply			
Year	Productive Expenditure for Plant	Annual Depreciation Cost	Net Investment in Plant	Gross Plant	Cumulative Depreciation	Net Plant	Net Investment in Plant as % of Previous Year's Net Plant
1	500	50	450	500	50	450	
2	500	100	400	1000	150	850	88.89
3	500	150	350	1500	300	1200	41.18
4	500	200	300	2000	500	1500	25.00
5	500	250	250	2500	750	1750	16.67
6	500	300	200	3000	1050	1950	11.43
7	500	350	150	3500	1400	2100	7.69
8	500	400	100	4000	1800	2200	4.76
9	500	450	50	4500	2250	2250	2.27
10	500	500	0	5000	2750	2250	0.00
11	550	505	45	5050	2755	2295	2.00
12	605	516	90	5155	2771	2385	3.90
13	666	532	133	5321	2803	2518	5.60
14	732	555	177	5553	2858	2695	7.02
15	805	586	219	5858	2944	2914	8.14
16	886	624	261	6244	3068	3176	8.97
17	974	672	303	6718	3240	3478	9.53
18	1072	729	343	7290	3469	3821	9.86
19	1179	797	382	7969	3766	4203	10.00
20	1297	877	420	8766	4142	4623	10.00
21	1427	964	462	9642	4556	5086	10.00
22	1569	1061	509	10606	5012	5594	10.00
23	1726	1167	559	11667	5513	6154	10.00
24	1899	1283	615	12834	6065	6769	10.00
25	2089	1412	677	14117	6671	7446	10.00

Note: Because of rounding in the three columns, Net Investment in Plant sometimes deviates slightly from the difference between Productive Expenditure for Plant and Annual Depreciation Cost.

10 year life assumed in the table. In addition, any rate of increase in the quantity of money and annual expenditure for plant could be substituted. In all cases, it would be found that the rate of net investment ultimately came to stabilize at a rate equal to the rate of increase in the quantity of money and volume of spending. Furthermore, exactly the same kind of demonstration could be made in connection with net investment in inventory and work in progress.

The Increase in the Quantity of Commodity Money as an Addition to Aggregate Profit

Finally, the provisional exclusion of money from capital can now be abandoned, and money in the hands of business enterprises restored to the category of capital. With money restored to capital, the addition to the rate of profit will be found to correspond much more closely to the rate of increase in the quantity of money if we adopt the procedure of counting *the increase in the quantity of money itself* as constituting an equivalent addition to the amount of profit in the economic system. (I will provide the justification for following this procedure in the case of commodity money immediately following the demonstration of the consequences of following it.)

What I mean by counting the increase in the quantity of money itself as part of profits can be illustrated in terms of Figure 16–3 and Table 16–11. There the quantity of money increases by 100 units in *Year 2*, a further 110 units in *Year 3*, and so on, at a compound rate of 10 percent per year. What I am maintaining is that the addition to the rate of profit resulting from this increase in the quantity of money will be found to very closely approximate the 10 percent rate of increase in the quantity of money itself if the 100 of increase in the quantity of money in *Year 2* is added to the 300 of profit existing in *Year 2* on the basis of net consumption and net investment, and the 110 of increase in the quantity of money in *Year 3* is added to the 330 of profit existing in *Year 3* on the basis of net consumption and net investment, and so on.

If year by year, the increase in the quantity of money itself is added to the amount of profit otherwise existing in the economic system, this addition will be found to provide a rate of profit on the money supply of the year before precisely equal to the rate of increase in the money supply. For example, counting the 100 of additional money in *Year 2* as an addition to the amount of profit in *Year 2*, provides a 10 percent rate of profit on the 1,000 of money counted as capital in *Year 1*. The 110 of additional money in *Year 3* provides a 10 percent rate of profit on the 1,100 of money counted as capital in *Year 2*, and so on.

Thus the money supply of each year can be counted

as part of capital, and no matter how large a part—no matter how exaggerated its size relative to the rest of capital—the rate of profit will increase in accordance with the rate of increase in the quantity of money. This is because the money component of capital no longer operates as a dead weight, since its growth generates a further, additional component in the amount of profit in the economic system. For example, capital can be 1,800 in *Year 1*, instead of 800, and a 10 percent rate of increase in the quantity of money now brings about not only 80 of net investment in the next year and 20 of additional net consumption, but the 100 of increase in the quantity of money itself enters into the magnitude of profit and provides a 10 percent rate of profit on the 1,000 of the capital of *Year 1* that was constituted by money. And similarly in every following year. Thus, the monetary component of capital now has its corresponding profit component when the money supply grows, just as the nonmonetary part of capital has its net investment component in the rate of profit when the money supply grows.

This procedure and its implications for the calculation of the rate of profit, and for the increase in the rate of profit when the money supply grows, are elaborated in Table 16–15. This table is almost identical to Table 16–11. The only difference is that the year-by-year amount of increase in the quantity of money is shown instead of the rate of increase, and, more importantly, the amount and rate of profit—and thus the rise in the rate of profit—are calculated on the basis of the inclusion of the increase in the quantity of money in the amount of profit, alongside of the sum of net consumption plus net investment. The table shows that when recalculated in this way, the rate of profit rises from 11.11 percent to 21.05 percent, where it stabilizes, so long as the quantity of money and volume of spending go on increasing at a 10 percent annual rate. On this basis, the table shows that the recalculated addition to the rate of profit turns out to be 9.94 percent rather than the 4.68 percent of Table 16–11.

In addition, the last three columns of the table show, by means of a second line appearing for each year, that if the monetary component of capital were taken as the money supply of the year before, the addition to the rate of profit would conform *exactly* to the formula previously elaborated. Namely, to the formula that an increasing quantity of money tends to add a component to the rate of profit equal to the rate of increase in the money supply plus the product of that rate of increase times the rate of profit that would prevail in the absence of an increase in the money supply. For it shows that when calculated in this way, the rate of profit would rise from 11.11 percent to 22.22 percent. This rise in the rate of profit is precisely equal to the sum of the 10 percent rate of increase in the money supply plus 10 percent of the

Table 16–15

The Effect of an Increasing Quantity of Money and Rising Volume of Spending on the Nominal Rate of Profit When the Increase in the Quantity of Money Is Added to the Amount of Profit

YEAR	M	ΔM	NC	B	d	I	s	p= NC+I+ ΔM	K	r%	Δr %
1	1,000		200	800	800	0	1,000	200	1,800	11.11	
2	1,100	100	220	880	800	80	1,100	400	1,900 1,800	21.05* 22.22*	9.94 11.11
3	1,210	110	242	968	880	88	1,210	440	2,090 1,980	21.05 22.22	9.94 11.11
4	1,331	121	266	1,065	968	97	1,331	484	2,299 2,178	21.05 22.22	9.94 11.11
5	1,464	133	293	1,171	1,065	106	1,464	532	2,529 2,396	21.05 22.22	9.94 11.11

KEY: *Ignores effects of rounding

M = Money Supply.   s = Sales Revenues.

ΔM = The Increase in the Money Supply.   p = Profits.

NC = Net Consumption.   K = Capital.

B = Productive Expenditure.   r = The Rate of Profit.

d = Costs Deducted from Sales Revenues.   Δr = The Increase in the Rate of Profit.

I = Net Investment (B-d).

11.11 percent rate of profit prevailing in the absence of an increase in the money supply. It is precisely equal to the sum of the 10 percent rate of net investment that is generated plus the increase in the rate of net consumption that is brought about by the 10 percent rate of increase in the quantity of money.[80]

Now the procedure of counting the increase in the supply of money as a direct addition to the amount of profit in the economic system can be fully and readily justified in the case of a commodity money. Under a commodity money system, the quantity of gold and silver mined is the equivalent of sales revenues from the perspective of the gold and silver mining concerns. For example, the revenues of a gold mine under a gold standard are the gold it mines. Under a gold standard, a gold mine mines money, and the money it mines is for it the full equivalent of sales revenues.

Of course, gold and silver mines incur substantial costs, and these costs must be subtracted from the bullion revenues of these mines in determining their profits. Indeed, the profits of the money-mining concerns tend to be no greater in relation to capital invested than profits in any other branch of production, and thus do not remotely equal the quantity of money they mine. Nevertheless, under a commodity money, profits in the economic system as a whole do in fact tend to be elevated by the full amount of the money that is mined.

This is because to the extent that the money-mining concerns make productive expenditures and incur corresponding costs, the magnitude of productive expenditures and costs in the rest of the economic system is correspondingly reduced, and thus the magnitude of profits in the rest of the economic system is correspondingly increased. In other words, the devotion of resources to gold and silver mining, to earn the bullion revenues of these industries, equivalently reduces productive expenditure and costs in the rest of the economic system, whose sales revenues are what they are and whose profits are therefore correspondingly increased by the reduction in its productive expenditures and costs. In this way, an increase in the quantity of commodity money, in constituting revenues of the gold and silver mining concerns, constitutes in part the equivalent of the profits of these concerns and, for the rest, the equivalent of a reduction in the costs and rise in the profits of concerns elsewhere in the economic system, whose productive expenditures and costs are less to the extent that productive expenditures and costs exist in gold and silver mining.

To put matters in still a somewhat different way, the bullion revenues of the money-mining concerns represent not only the equivalent of sales revenues to them, but the equivalent of a precisely equal addition to the aggregate sales revenues of the economic system, in the face of the same magnitudes of productive expenditure and cost in the economic system. The mining of commodity money, thus turns out to be very similar in nature to the existence of a further increment of net consumption, for it is a source if not of an excess of literal sales revenues over productive expenditure, then at least of an excess of sales revenues plus the virtual equivalent of sales revenues—i.e., mined bullion revenues—over productive expenditure.

For these reasons, in the case of commodity money, the procedure of treating the addition to the quantity of money as a direct addition to the amount of profit is fully justified.

In the case of a fiat paper money, of course, it is inappropriate to add the increase in the quantity of money itself to the amount of aggregate profit in the economic system. This is because the increase in the quantity of fiat paper money is not at all analogous to the sales revenues of a business. It is the fruit of a virtual counterfeiting operation, not of any kind of productive venture. Nevertheless, it should be realized that even in this case, the deviation between the increase in the rate of profit caused by the increase in the quantity of money and the rate of increase in the quantity of money itself is far less in reality than is indicated in Table 16–11. This is because the quantity of money in the real world is much smaller in relation to capital and the volume of spending than it is in Figures 16–2 and 16–3, and thus in Table 16–11, which is based on them. As a result, the significance of the "dead weight" constituted by counting the quantity of money in capital is correspondingly reduced. The resulting rates of profit and of changes in the rate of profit, therefore, much more closely approximate those of Tables 16–12 and 16–13, in which money is altogether excluded from capital, than those of Table 16–11, in which it looms so large. For example, if the quantity of money entering into capital had been a tenth of sales revenues instead of equal to sales revenues in Figures 16–2 and 16–3 and in Table 16–11, the resulting rate of profit in each year would have approximated the rates calculated in Tables 16–12 and 16–13.

The statement, earlier in this section, of the effect of increases in the quantity of money on the rate of net consumption in terms of a strict proportionality was almost certainly inaccurate. An increase in the quantity of money would not in fact directly and immediately increase net consumption in proportion to itself, as was assumed, for the sake of simplicity, in Figure 16–3 and the various tables developed on the basis of it. The immediate effect of the increase in the quantity of money on net consumption might well be limited to the extent to which the additional money was perceived as an addition to accumulated wealth. Nevertheless, there is some effect, and one which becomes the greater and more significant, the more rapid is the increase in the quantity of money and volume of spending. The discussion of the consequences of inflation in Chapter 19 provides a variety of grounds for this claim.[81]

The fact that the increase in the quantity of money and volume of spending does operate to raise the rate of net consumption, and does so to the degree that the increase in the quantity of money is the more rapid, constitutes a powerful argument for a monetary system in which the increase in the quantity of money is strictly limited. Such a monetary system adds 1, 2, or 3 percentage points through the increase in the quantity of money to the rate of profit which would otherwise be established by the rate of net consumption alone. It thus serves to provide a sufficient incentive to invest money rather than hold it, even in the face of extremely low rates of net consumption—rates of net consumption on the order of 2 or even 1 percent. At the same time, with such modest rates of increase in the quantity of money, it does not serve significantly to raise the rate of net consumption. It thus achieves the possibly important benefits of a higher nominal rate of profit without any significant negative effects.

Such a monetary system, of course, is the 100-percent-reserve gold standard (or parallel 100-percent-reserve gold and silver standards), which compels strict limitation of the increase in the quantity of money to the modest rate of increase in the supply of precious metals.[82]

Summary Statement of the Determinants of the Rate of Profit

To summarize the determinants of the rate of profit: The rate of profit is determined by and equal to the sum of the rate of net consumption plus the rate of net investment. It can also be expressed as tending to equal, as an approximation, *the sum of the rate of net consumption plus the rate of increase in the quantity of money and volume of spending.* For the rate of increase in the quantity of money and volume of spending tends to generate an equivalent rate of net investment and, in the long run, to be the only source of net investment.

The increase in the quantity of money and volume of spending also, of course, tends to raise the rate of net consumption. While it may not do so by the product of itself times the rate of net consumption prevailing in the absence of an increase in the quantity of money, it does so at least to some extent, and one which becomes the more significant, the more rapid is the rate of increase in the quantity of money and volume of spending.

The inclusion of money in capital does not materially affect the accuracy of the proposition that the rate of profit is elevated by a percentage approximately equal to the rate of increase in the quantity of money. In the real world, the quantity of money held by business is small relative to capital and sales revenues, and thus the "dead weight" aspect of counting money in capital is minimal. Moreover, under a 100-percent-reserve gold standard, the increase in the quantity of money would itself properly enter into the calculation of total profit and thus completely offset the otherwise dead weight aspect of counting money in capital.

The amount and rate of profit is ultimately determined on the basis of time preference operating through the rate of net consumption, the marginal productivity of capital operating through the rate of net investment, and the rate of increase in the quantity of money operating through both the rate of net investment and the rate of net consumption, though primarily through the former.

6. Increases in the Real Rate of Profit Dependent on Increases in the Production and Supply of Goods

The rate of profit to which increases in the money supply and volume of spending contribute is, of course, the nominal rate of profit, i.e., the rate of profit expressed simply in terms of money. This rate of profit, as everyone should now know, is by no means necessarily equal to the actual rate of gain—the real rate of profit—that businessmen experience, that is, to the rate of increase in their ability to purchase actual physical wealth. This is because it is entirely possible, and very frequently happens, that the same increase in the quantity of money and volume of spending that raises the nominal rate of profit, equivalently raises prices, with the result that absolutely no rise in the real rate of profit occurs. For example, a 2 or a 10 percent increase in money and spending may well succeed in raising prices by 2 or 10 percent at the same time that it adds 2 or 10 percent to the nominal rate of profit. If that happens, then even if someone adds the whole addition to his nominal profit to his capital and thus becomes worth 2 or 10 percent more in terms of money than he was before, he still has not gained anything whatever in terms of buying power. His larger

nominal capital is capable of buying no more than was his original nominal capital.

Usually, these are the facts which must be stressed, so that people will realize that a nominal rate of profit of any given percentage by no means implies a corresponding increase in the ability of businessmen to buy goods. In the present context, however, what must be stressed is the fact that *under a commodity money,* the addition to the nominal rate of profit caused by the increase in the quantity of money not only can be, but typically is, accompanied by an equal or even greater increase in the real rate of profit. This becomes apparent when one realizes that the relationship between the nominal and the real rate of profit depends on the relationship between the rate at which the quantity of money and the volume of spending increase, on the one side, and the rate at which production and the supply of goods increase, on the other. If, for example, when the quantity of money and volume of spending increase at the rate of 2 percent per year, the production and supply of goods also increase at the rate of 2 percent per year, then prices on average will be stable. As our price level formula shows, 1.02 times the spending will buy 1.02 times the production and supply at an unchanged level of prices. Thus, in this case, the 2 percent addition to the nominal rate of profit caused by the increase in money and spending will also represent a 2 percent addition to the real rate of profit, because, at the same time, production and supply have increased at a 2 percent annual rate and have thus kept prices stable.

It is implied in this example that just as increases in the quantity of money and volume of spending add to the nominal rate of profit, so increases in the physical production and supply of ordinary, nonmonetary commodities add to the real rate of profit. The increase in the nominal rate of profit achieved by any given rate of increase in the quantity of money and volume of spending represents an increase in the real rate of profit only if it is accompanied by an equivalent rate of increase in production and supply. For only that will keep prices stable and thus allow the extra nominal profits to represent corresponding additional buying power.

It is no less implied that increases in production and supply can increase the real rate of profit *without* corresponding increases in the quantity of money and volume of spending, and thus without corresponding increases in the nominal rate of profit. If, for example, the nominal rate of profit were 5 percent with no increase in the quantity of money and volume of spending, and production and supply increased at an annual rate of 2 percent, then prices would fall approximately 2 percent per year. A businessman who began a year with $100 and finished it with $105 would have an increase in real wealth not of

THE NET-CONSUMPTION/NET-INVESTMENT THEORY OF PROFIT

5 percent, but of approximately 7 percent, because his $105 would go about 7 percent further than his initial $100 at prices only 98 percent of what they were at the start of the year.

What we have here is a kind of "Say's Law of Profits"—namely, that the rate of increase in production and supply adds to the real rate of profit, while the rate of increase in the quantity of money and volume of spending adds only to the nominal rate of profit. More money and spending raise the nominal rate of profit, but are accompanied by a rise in the real rate of profit only insofar as there is an increase in the production and supply of goods. On the other hand, an increase in the production and supply of goods raises the real rate of profit, whether accompanied by an increase in the quantity of money and volume of spending or not.[83]

It must always be kept in mind that the addition to the nominal rate of profit caused by more money and spending, and the addition to the real rate of profit caused by more production and supply, are separate and distinct elements, even though they are related under a system of commodity money. They certainly need not proceed at the same pace. There can be prolonged periods in which the increase in the production and supply of ordinary goods exceeds the increase in the supply of money and volume of spending. In such periods, the weighted average of prices falls, and the real rate of profit correspondingly exceeds the nominal rate of profit. If, on the other hand, the rate of increase in the supply of money and volume of spending exceed the rate of increase in the production and supply of goods, the weighted average of prices rises and the nominal rate of profit correspondingly exceeds the real rate of profit. The nominal rate of profit is always related to the real rate of profit in the following way: Namely, the nominal rate of profit plus the fall in prices or minus the rise in prices equals the real rate of profit.

A major principle which stands out is that increases in production and supply always raise the real rate of profit and, under a system of commodity money, by virtue of encompassing increases in production in mining in general and in precious metal mining in particular, also operate, at least to some significant extent, to raise the nominal rate of profit as well. The principle is that *under a system of commodity money, increases in production and supply raise both the real and the nominal rate of profit.* And it follows that the more rapidly production and supply can be made to increase under a system of commodity money, not only will the nominal and real rates of profit both be higher, but so too will be the *proportion* of nominal and real profits which is the result of increases in production and supply. In a rapidly progressing economic system that is based on a commodity

money, the greater part of profits, both nominal and real, may well be the result of nothing more than the rate of increase in production and supply.[84]

There is reason for thinking that under a 100-percent-reserve gold or silver standard, the real rate of profit would typically be above the nominal rate of profit, i.e., that the increase in the production and supply of goods would exceed the increase in money and spending, with the result that prices would normally fall. Such a situation could be expected to be typical because of the difficulties of increasing the production of the precious metals in comparison with the possibilities of increasing production in the rest of the economic system, including the possibility of adding to the list of what constitutes useable natural resources and of extending the range of products that can be produced from many of the useable natural resources already known.

A further major implication of the present discussion is that the inverse relationship that has been shown to exist between economic progress, on the one side, and both nominal national income and the amount and rate of nominal profit, on the other, does not apply to the conditions of a gold or silver money. In these conditions increases in the quantity of money appear as a by-product of the same process which increases the supply of ordinary goods, and are normally within the limit of those increases. As a result, under a gold or silver money, the growing supply of goods which represents economic progress is accompanied by a rising volume of spending, based on a growing supply of gold or silver money which itself is part of the growing supply of physical goods. It is thus accompanied both by an addition to the amount and rate of nominal profit and by rising money incomes of all types.

The inverse relationship between the rate of profit and economic progress pertains to the conditions both of an invariable money and of increases in the quantity of money at rates more rapid than the increase in the supply of a gold or silver money. It does not pertain to the conditions of a gold or silver money under normal circumstances.

Net Investment Without Increasing Capital Intensiveness

Under the conditions of a gold or silver money, the nominal net investment that results from increases in the quantity of money normally represents equivalent or even more-than-equivalent *real* net investment. For it represents an addition to the nominal capital of business firms which is accompanied either by no rise in the prices of capital assets on average or, indeed, by a fall in those prices, resulting from the increase in the production of capital goods outstripping the increase in the monetary demand for them. Such net investment is certainly real net investment, not merely nominal net investment.

Insofar as this additional real net investment represents an increase in the quantity of physical capital goods employed per worker, it can be viewed as constituting an increase in *physical* capital intensiveness. It is important to realize, however, that it does not constitute an increase in capital intensiveness in the dimension of relative monetary values—that is, in the sense of a rise in the ratio of capital expressed in money to consumption expenditure, or to sales revenues or wage payments. The relative-value dimension of the concept of capital intensiveness is the one which reflects the degree of provision for the future that is made relative to current consumption—that is, the degree to which people save and accumulate capital relative to consuming. It is the dimension to which special attention must be paid in connection with many of the leading problems of economic theory, such as whether or not capital accumulation causes or presupposes a fall in the rate of profit. The relative-value dimension, of course, is the dimension in which I have been primarily measuring capital intensiveness all along.

To be sure, the real net investment that takes place under a gold or silver money in conjunction with nominal net investment, presupposes the existence of a sufficiently high degree of capital intensiveness in the relative-value sense to inaugurate and maintain a process of rising production, including, above all, the production of growing quantities of capital goods. Indeed, my discussion of the effects on the rate of profit of an increase in the quantity of money began with the recognition that the growing capital intensiveness brought about by net investment in the context of an invariable money results in rising production, including the production of the monetary commodities gold and silver.[85] It was this which required my temporarily setting aside the assumption of an invariable money. Nevertheless, the nominal and real net investment which themselves result from the inauguration and maintenance of a sufficiently high degree of capital intensiveness in the relative-value sense do not themselves constitute the achievement of any greater degree of capital intensiveness in this sense.

In its nominal aspect, the resulting derivative net investment, if it can be called that, actually serves merely to maintain the existing, sufficiently high degree of capital intensiveness in the relative-value sense. This is because the same increase in the money supply that is responsible for this net investment, also operates to raise total wage payments, consumption expenditure, and total business sales revenues. Thus the growing nominal capital that such net investment achieves does not mean a rise in nominal capital *relative* to wages, consumption expenditure, or sales revenues. Only in the context of an invariable money does an increase in nominal capital automatically mean an increase in capital intensiveness in the relative-value sense. It certainly does not mean it in the context of an increasing quantity of money, in which the magnitudes that it must be taken relative to also increase, and do so as the result of the very same cause, namely, the increase in the quantity of money.

Along the same lines, notice that this derivative net investment goes on without any increase in the average life of the assets purchased by business. As I have shown, in an economy with a constant quantity of money and volume of spending, net investment can continue only by virtue of such things as devoting a larger and larger proportion of the outlays for factors of production to plant-and-equipment purchases as opposed to expensed expenditures and purchases of labor and materials to produce inventories, and to purchases of plant and equipment of longer life rather than shorter life.[86] However, this is not true of the net investment which is the result of a growing quantity of money and volume of spending. Such net investment is the result of growing outlays for assets of all descriptions, without any necessary change in favor of such things as spending for plant and equipment or longer-lived plant and equipment.

This net investment continues in its nominal aspect by virtue of the fact that rising productive expenditure, based on a growing quantity of money, tends always to be ahead of costs deducted from sales revenues, which costs reflect the necessarily smaller productive expenditures of previous years.[87] At the same time, in its real aspect, what is present is a growing supply of capital goods from year to year that stands in the same overall quantitative and temporal relationship to the consumers' goods it will ultimately help to produce as did the smaller supply of capital goods of the year before.[88] Thus, there is no greater capital intensiveness in terms either of the ratio of the money value of capital to consumption expenditure, sales revenues, or money wages, or of the ratio of the physical supply of capital goods to the supply of consumers' goods that will ultimately result from the supply of capital goods. The only sense in which there is more capital intensiveness is that of the ratio of the supply of capital goods to the supply of labor, and that is essentially the same as the resulting rise in the ratio of consumers' goods to the supply of labor, i.e., the same as the rise in the productivity of labor.

Capital-Saving Inventions

The fact that capital accumulation can occur without increases in capital intensiveness in the relative-value sense—namely, as the result of technological progress taking place in conjunction with a sufficiently high existing degree of capital intensiveness in the relative-value sense—should not, of course, be taken as in any way diminishing the importance of capital accumulation. Nevertheless, because the role of technological progress in capital accumulation is generally unperceived, the conviction prevails that capital accumulation is synonymous with greater capital intensiveness in the relative-value sense. Thus, when it is observed that the enormous increase in production that has taken place over the last century or more has not been accompanied by a significant increase in the degree of capital intensiveness in the relative-value sense, the conclusion is drawn that capital accumulation is of relatively little significance and that practically all of the credit for the increase in production should go to technological progress and increases in the productivity of the factors of production, *as opposed to capital accumulation.*[89] The alleged lack of need for capital accumulation to achieve economic progress is then attributed to "capital-saving inventions," which allegedly make it possible to produce more and more without additional capital or with only relatively little additional capital.

Now a capital-saving invention can mean either of two things: An invention that makes it possible to produce a given product at a reduced *expenditure* for factors of production, or an invention that makes it possible to produce a given product by employing a smaller physical quantity of capital goods. In the context of a progressing economy under an invariable money, virtually every invention would be a capital-saving invention in the first sense, for in such an economy there would be an ever greater quantity of products produced without any necessary increase in the sum of capitals invested. Little need be said about capital-saving inventions of this sort. They would simply reflect the falling prices of capital goods and the reduced quantities of labor required in the production of products of any given type. Such inventions, of course, would not in any way imply the use of a smaller quantity of capital goods. Indeed, while ever falling expenditures of money capital were made for given quantities of capital goods, the same aggregate expenditures of money capital would be made for continually increasing quantities of capital goods. However, capital-saving inventions in the second sense, that is, in the sense of a saving of physical capital goods, do require some discussion, inasmuch as it is they which are cited in order to belittle the role played by the accumulation of capital in economic progress.

First of all, it must be realized that such inventions are the exception rather than the rule. If we compare the Middle Ages or any intervening period with the present, it at once becomes apparent that the economic progress of the Western World is overwhelmingly due to the accumulation of a larger supply of capital goods per capita, and not to an economization of the same supply. It is not the case that the supply of capital goods per capita is today the same or not significantly larger than it was in the Middle Ages, only today instead of being embodied in ox carts, simple forges, deer skins, and primitive looms, it is embodied in machinery and materials of greater physical economy. The progressive rise in the standard of living has at each step of the way been made possible by an expansion in the supply of capital goods. Decade by decade, the physical supply of capital goods produced has risen. Had it not, the subsequent increases in the supply of consumers' goods could not have taken place. The increases merely in iron and steel production, in coal production, in trees felled, in wheat produced, and the indispensable role played by the larger supplies of these commodities in subsequent production should be sufficient to dispel any illusions on this score. To produce a larger quantity of iron and steel consumers' goods, a larger quantity of iron and steel capital goods is required. To produce more bread, more wheat is required. To build more and larger houses, more lumber or bricks is required.

In certain cases, of course, it is possible to discover methods of physically economizing on the use of materials. A change in women's fashions may eliminate several square feet of cloth from a dress; an improvement in the design of an automobile engine (assuming the engine itself does not require a larger quantity of capital goods in its own production) may make possible an economization of gasoline and petroleum. Household furniture may be less-cumbersomely designed. Economic progress, however, consists relatively little in making it possible to derive greater advantage from the same quantity of materials. For the far greater part, it consists in increasing the supply of materials. This is because there is a limit to how much cloth can be removed from a dress, to how much mileage can be obtained from a gallon of gasoline, and to how much wood can be removed from furniture. With economic progress, the cloth in the wardrobe of the average woman increases; motorists consume larger quantities of gasoline, requiring larger quantities of petroleum; the individual acquires larger quantities of furniture containing more wood in total. To make this possible, the production of the necessary capital goods must be increased. This principle applies even in the case of computers, where today a relatively small desktop computer has power comparable to that of a room-sized mainframe computer of a generation ago. This is because in place of a few hundred or a few thousand room-sized computers, there are now tens of millions of the desktop computers.

Frequently, what appears to be a saving of capital goods is not. One should not confuse the reduction in the physical quantity required merely of one capital good with an overall reduction in the quantity of capital goods required to produce a product. And above all, one should not confuse a reduction in the physical size of a capital good with a reduction in the quantity of capital goods it represents. It may be that the capital good now contains a more valuable material embodying a larger quantity of labor in its own production. For example, if the reduction in the size, let us say, of a machine is accomplished by reducing the iron content of the machine, but also involves the use or added use in some way of platinum wire, the machine may very well represent a larger quantity of capital goods than previously, for it may now be the product of a larger quantity of labor. Or again, even if the machine represents the same physical quantities of all materials save one, which has decreased in quantity, e.g., iron ore, but that one has now undergone a higher degree of processing than previously, no real reduction in the quantity of capital goods may be involved; for that smaller quantity of ore, in undergoing a higher degree of processing, may have had as much labor expended upon it as the larger quantity of ore which did not undergo as high a degree of processing. Furthermore, insofar as the product requires the use of more advanced capital goods in its production, that too is a case of needing a larger supply of capital goods. Thus, the tens of millions of today's personal computers require a larger supply of capital goods in their production than the comparative handful of mainframe computers of the past, not only in the sense of requiring a larger overall physical volume of materials, but also in the sense of requiring the existence of more advanced computer processors, memory chips, and so forth. Improvements in the quality of capital goods is a major aspect of capital accumulation and is to be regarded as an increase in the supply of capital goods.

Finally, even in those cases in which a genuine saving of capital goods does take place, the effect most likely is to increase the supply of capital goods. This is because insofar as capital goods are employed in the production of capital goods, the fall in the amount of capital goods needed per unit of output implies an increase in the production of capital goods. This can easily be demonstrated by using any of our illustrations of the relative production of capital goods and consumers' goods, such as Figure 16–2, and by assuming an all-round flood of inventions that save capital goods. If the same total output could be produced with, let us say, half the quantity of capital goods, then the employment of the same quantity of capital goods must result in a larger total production; indeed, on the assumption of constant returns to capital goods (at the now higher level), a doubled total production. If the relative production of capital goods is unchanged, this means the production of twice the supply of capital goods as would otherwise have been produced.

Thus, if in the absence of the capital-saving inven-

tions, quantity K of capital goods together with the fixed quantity L of labor would have produced $1K$ of capital goods and $1C$ of consumers' goods, they now produce $2K$ of capital goods and $2C$ of consumers' goods. What is present is merely nothing other than an enormous increase in the efficiency of the economic system in using existing capital goods. No more potent source of capital accumulation could be found. It follows that such capital-saving inventions as have occurred have simply further contributed to the process of capital accumulation and its overwhelming role in increasing production and the standard of living.

The studies which belittle the role of capital accumulation in increasing production commit the further error of taking the rate of return on capital as the measure of the physical contribution of capital goods to production—as the measure of the marginal net physical productivity of capital goods rather than of the marginal productivity of capital as I have used the term.[90] Such an approach ignores the fact that the supply of capital goods is responsible for well over 99 percent of the productivity of labor—for all of the additions to the productivity of labor that have taken place since caveman days, because none of these additions would have been possible without the increase in the supply of capital goods.[91]

To some extent, those who deprecate the importance of additional capital in increasing production may be led to do so because of their mistaken views concerning what constitutes an increase in output. As I have shown, using national income as the measure of output, which is the almost universal practice, leads to the fallacy of viewing a fall in the demand for capital goods and rise in the demand for consumers' goods, which has the effect of increasing national income, as the cause of an increase in output, when in fact its effect is to diminish the increase in output or, if carried far enough, cause a progressive decline in output.[92] In addition, as I have also shown, using national income as the measure of output implies that output increases to the extent that taxes are increased and the resulting increase in revenue is expended in enlarging the government's payroll, something which in reality also operates to decrease production.[93] The result of these confusions is that the very process of decline in capital formation and the increase in real physical wealth is misidentified as an increase in the efficiency of the economic system on the grounds that the amount of capital required to generate a unit of national income has been reduced.

7. The Inherent Springs to Profitability

This chapter has shown how the productive process generates its own profitability through net consumption and net investment. It has shown how net investment in the context of an economy with an invariable money, in raising the degree of capital intensiveness, lays the foundation for capital accumulation and rising production and thereby an increasing quantity of commodity money. It has shown how this last, in raising the level of spending from year to year, both perpetuates net investment and adds a corresponding positive component to the rate of profit.

What must be realized now is that these sources of profit are virtual *springs* to profitability, which operate to restore profitability whenever it might temporarily be lacking for any reason (notably, because of a financial contraction and ensuing depression). Insofar as net consumption exists—and it must exist, whenever savings have been accumulated in a sufficient ratio to income and consumption—the only thing which can prevent the existence of an aggregate profit is *negative net investment*, which certainly cannot be more than a temporary phenomenon. An increasing quantity of money and rising volume of spending, the by-product of capital accumulation and increasing production, also cannot fail to reestablish profitability.

The potential for net investment, which always exists, constitutes an even more powerful spring to profitability, one whose power increases as the prevailing rate of profit decreases. Whenever aggregate profitability is lacking, not only is net investment sufficient to restore it, but, in addition, as I will show, net investment is more and more encouraged by the fact that *the lower is the rate of return on capital, the higher is the degree of capital intensiveness that pays,* and thus the more powerful is the stimulus to the existence of net investment, as the means of achieving a higher degree of capital intensiveness. Thus, the economic system is so constituted that if the rate of profit should ever become unduly low, or disappear, that very fact encourages a move toward further capital intensiveness and thereby the calling into being of net investment, which restores the rate of profit. Once I have demonstrated these propositions concerning net investment, it will be possible not only better to understand what causes and perpetuates depressions and unemployment, but also appreciate just how alien such phenomena are to the actual nature of a capitalist economy.

In order to understand the principle of potential additional net investment serving as a spring to profitability, the context of discussion must be carefully defined. The context is the general rate of profit in the economic system as a whole. More than that, it is the general rate of profit in the economic system as a whole as determined apart from changes in the quantity of money and the overall volume of spending. In other words, it is the rate of profit insofar as it is determined by the rate of net consumption and by the rate of net investment apart from changes on the side of money.

The naming of the first proviso, that it is the general rate of profit in the economy as a whole that is under consideration, should make it possible to avoid committing the fallacy of composition and making an invalid generalization from the consequences of a low rate of profit in an individual industry to the consequences of a low rate of profit in the economic system as a whole. In the case of an individual industry, a low rate of profit means a low rate of profit relative to rates of profit in other industries. The effect of this, of course, is to discourage investment in that industry, indeed, to encourage the withdrawal of capital previously invested. But the context under discussion here is not that of a low rate of profit in a particular industry relative to the rate of profit in other industries. It is that of a low rate of profit prevailing throughout the economic system. If this is kept in mind, then it will not be difficult to see how in these conditions, a low rate of profit actually works to encourage more capital investment rather than less.

To understand this principle, let us consider a number of concrete cases from which we can abstract the essential foundations of the principle. Let us consider, first, the case of a railroad company which is contemplating whether it should construct its line straight through a mountain by digging a tunnel, or detour around the mountain. Digging the tunnel, we assume, constitutes the more-capital-intensive method in that it requires a greater initial capital investment than the alternative. But once in existence, the tunnel would make possible, virtually forever, an annual saving in operating costs, because it would reduce the time required for trains to reach their destination. In reaching its decision, what the railway company considers is how much money the tunnel would potentially save it every year on the basis of savings of train-crew time, fuel consumption, and wear and tear of rolling stock, versus how much more it must invest to construct the tunnel in comparison with the less-capital-intensive detour around the mountain.

The railroad company will decide in favor of the tunnel if the annual savings the tunnel achieves are, when divided by the extra capital its construction requires, greater than the going rate of profit on capital. It will decide against the tunnel if the savings the tunnel achieves are, when divided by the extra capital its construction requires, less than the going rate of profit on capital. For example, imagine that the existence of the tunnel would make possible an annual saving in operating costs of $1 million per year in comparison with the alternative route, and that at the same time, the construction of the tunnel requires $10 million more of capital investment than the alternative route. In this case, the railroad company will decide in favor of the tunnel if the going rate of return on capital is less than 10 percent. It will decide against the tunnel if the going rate of return on capital is more than 10 percent. This is because its investment in the tunnel will yield a rate of return of 10 percent ($1 million per year divided by $10 million). Whether or not this investment should be undertaken depends on a comparison of its profitability with the profitability of other investments. If the profitability of other investments is greater than 10 percent, then the capital that might be devoted to this investment should instead be devoted to them. If, on the other hand, the profitability of other investments is less than 10 percent, then this investment represents the better alternative, and it should be undertaken.

The essential point here is that the lower is the general rate of return on capital, the better does this particular investment appear by comparison. With a general rate of return of greater than 10 percent, this particular investment is submarginal—that is, it is insufficiently profitable to be undertaken. With a general rate of return of 10 percent, it becomes borderline. With a general rate of return of less than 10 percent, it becomes relatively attractive, and more and more so, the further below 10 percent the general rate of return falls. And as the general rate of return falls below 10 percent, still other investments become attractive by comparison. Capital-intensive improvements representing annual savings in cost equal to only 9 percent, 8 percent, 7 percent, and so on, successively become relatively attractive as the general rate of return falls below these levels. And not only in railroading, of course, but in every area of the economic system. In effect, the general rate of return operates as a standard, a test, which each particular capital-intensive improvement must pass in terms of the size of the annual cost reductions it achieves relative to the additional capital it requires. As the general rate of return falls, the standard—the passing grade, as it were—is reduced, with the result that a growing number of capital-intensive investments become relatively profitable, and the degree of capital intensiveness that pays is increased throughout the economic system. Furthermore, what applies to cost reductions applies equally to quality improvements. The additional revenues derived from these, relative to the additional capital that needs to be invested to achieve them, becomes less and less, as the general rate of return falls.

It pays to examine the same principle at work in another example. Thus, imagine a product that can be produced in a given quantity by any of three different methods of production, representing three different degrees of capital intensiveness. (The differences in capital intensiveness can be taken as reflecting different combinations of production by hand or by machine. The most-

capital-intensive method uses the most machinery. The least-capital-intensive method uses the least.) We call these three methods, simply, A, B, and C. As shown in Table 16–16, method A is the least capital intensive, but also the most costly. It requires an investment of $10,000 of capital and results in $9,000 of annual costs to produce a given quantity of the product. Method B requires $20,000 of capital to produce the same quantity of the product but enables production to take place at an annual cost of only $8,000. Finally, method C requires $30,000 of capital to produce the same quantity of the product but enables production to take place at the still lower annual cost of only $7,000.

In the conditions of this example, as the revenue derived from the sale of a given quantity of the product declines, and thus, in the face of given costs, reduces profitability, the effect is to favor methods of production of greater capital intensiveness. The stimulus given to methods of greater capital intensiveness is shown in Table 16–16 by the effects on profits and the rate of profit of three different magnitudes of sales revenues. The largest magnitude of sales revenues, $11,000, which appears in the upper portion of the table, in the row labeled "Annual Sales Revenues (1)," is accompanied by profits of $2,000, $3,000, and $4,000 for methods A, B, and C respectively, and thus by corresponding rates of profit of 20 percent, 15 percent, and $13\frac{1}{3}$ percent respectively. These results appear lower in the table, in the respective rows "Annual Profits (1)" and "Annual Rate of Profit (1)." With sales revenues at $11,000, method A, the least-capital-intensive method, is the relatively most profitable.

When sales revenues for the same quantity of product fall to $10,000, the profits of methods A, B, and C, with their respective costs of $9,000, $8,000, and $7,000, fall to $1,000, $2,000, and $3,000, respectively. This results in the three methods of production now earning the same rate of profit on capital, given their respective capital requirements. These results are shown in the rows labeled "Annual Profits (2)" and "Annual Rate of Profit (2)."

When, finally, sales revenues fall to $9,000, as shown in the row labeled "Annual Sales Revenues (3)," the profits of method A are totally eliminated. Method B continues to show a profit of $1,000, which yields a rate of profit of 5 percent on the $20,000 of capital which must be invested in that method. But method C continues to show a profit of $2,000, which represents a rate of profit of $6\frac{2}{3}$ percent on the $30,000 of capital which must be invested in it. By comparison method C, the most capital intensive of the three methods, is now favored. These results appear in the rows labeled "Annual Profits (3)" and "Annual Rate of Profit (3)."

Table 16–16			
Capital Intensive Methods and the Rate of Profit			
Method of Production:	A	B	C
Capital Required:	$10,000	$20,000	$30,000
Annual Production Costs:	9,000	8,000	7,000
Annual Sales Revenues (1):	11,000	11,000	11,000
Annual Sales Revenues (2):	10,000	10,000	10,000
Annual Sales Revenues (3):	9,000	9,000	9,000
Annual Profits (1):	2,000	3,000	4,000
Annual Profits (2):	1,000	2,000	3,000
Annual Profits (3):	0	1,000	2,000
Annual Rate of Profit (1):	20%	15%	13.33%
Annual Rate of Profit (2):	10%	10%	10.00%
Annual Rate of Profit (3):	0	5%	6.67%

This outcome should in no way be thought paradoxical. What brings it about is the fact that the more-capital-intensive methods are the lower-cost methods. As sales revenues for a given quantity of the product fall, the only way to remain profitable is by achieving lower costs of production. The way to achieve that is by investing more capital.[94]

As I have indicated, a lower rate of profit favors more capital intensiveness not only in cases in which more capital intensiveness achieves lower-cost methods of production, but also in cases in which more capital intensiveness achieves a better quality of products. An example which clearly brings out this principle is the case of thirty-year-old scotch versus eight-year-old scotch. Thirty-year-old scotch is a much higher-quality scotch than eight-year-old scotch. Its production also requires the use of substantially more capital per unit of output and is thus correspondingly more capital intensive. If thirty-year-old scotch is to be produced on a regular basis, then for every unit of scotch reaching the market in any particular year, there must be twenty-nine other units, age one through twenty-nine, in the hands of its producers. If eight-year-old scotch is to reach the market on a regular basis, there need be only seven other units—the units age one through seven—in the hands of its producers, for every unit that comes to the market in

any given year.

The rate of profit on capital invested is one of the determinants of the prices of goods. And its role is the more pronounced, the more time consuming and capital intensive the production of a product is, and also the higher is the rate of profit. If the rate of profit is 10 percent per year, then for every $100 invested in a quantity of raw scotch, the price of eight-year-old scotch must provide $214, for that is the sum required to yield a 10 percent annual rate of profit on $100 compounded for eight years. By the same token, for every $100 invested in a quantity of raw scotch, the price of thirty-year-old scotch must provide the vastly larger sum of $1,745, because that is the sum required to yield a 10 percent annual rate of profit on $100 compounded for thirty years.

Observe. In this case, with the rate of profit at 10 percent, the thirty-year-old scotch must sell for more than eight times the price of the eight-year-old scotch, so greatly does the 10 percent rate of profit influence its relative price. But now let us see what happens if the rate of profit were 5 percent instead of 10 percent. To yield a rate of profit of 5 percent compounded for eight years, the eight-year-old scotch would have to sell for $148. To yield a 5 percent rate of profit compounded for thirty years, the thirty-year-old scotch would have to sell for

$432. In this case, with the rate of profit at 5 percent, the thirty-year-old scotch need sell for only 2.9 times the price of the eight-year-old scotch, instead of more than 8 times the price of the eight-year-old scotch, which was the case when the rate of profit was 10 percent. The lower is the rate of profit, the smaller is the premium which must exist in the price of the older scotch. If the rate of profit were zero, the price of thirty or even one-hundred-year-old scotch would need to be no higher than the price of the eight-year-old scotch.

Now what is significant from the point of view of the present discussion, about the prices of the two scotches moving closer together as the rate of profit falls, is that this development is bound to favor the demand for the older, better-quality scotch. As the premium on this scotch falls, people will be able to give greater and greater consideration to its superior quality. As a result, the share of the market served by this more-capital-intensive product increases, and thus the need is created for the overall degree of capital intensiveness in this industry to go up.

This case illustrates the general principle that as the rate of profit falls, the premium in the prices of all higher-quality products whose production is relatively more time consuming diminishes, and thus the share of the market served by such products increases, with the result that a need is created for a higher overall degree of capital intensiveness in the economic system. Some further examples of the application of this principle are the comparative use of woods from trees of different growing times, the relative share of the market supplied with aged beef, and, in general, the share of the market supplied with products requiring the use of relatively more valuable raw materials further back in the production process or requiring the use of relatively more expensive plant and equipment in their production, particularly at earlier stages in their production.

The principle here sheds further light on the effects of a fall in the rate of profit on the use of more-capital-intensive methods of production in general. For example, with a rate of profit of 10 percent per year, a machine which costs $1,000 and lasts 10 years, must, if it is to be worthwhile, bring in each year the sum of $150 in the sales revenue of the product it helps to produce. This sum reflects an annual depreciation charge of $100 plus a 10 percent rate of return on the average capital outstanding in the machine over its life, which latter is one half of the initial capital invested, viz., $500. Thus, over its ten-year life, the machine must bring in a revenue over its cost of $500—i.e., 10 times ($150-$100). But if the rate of profit were 5 percent instead of 10 percent, then the machine would need to bring in each year only $125, and thus, over its ten-year life, only $250 in revenue over its cost. With the reduction in the premium in the revenue from the sale of the product that is required to make a machine pay, the value of the machinery employed in production necessarily tends to increase. And, of course, identically the same principle applies to the value of the buildings employed in production. Thus, the wider principle that capital intensiveness is favored as the rate of profit falls receives further confirmation.

In a very similar way, it can be shown that as the rate of profit falls, the growth of the more-capital-intensive industries in the economic system is favored relatively to the growth of the less-capital-intensive industries, with the result that once again a need is created for a higher overall degree of capital intensiveness in the economic system. This is shown in Table 16–17. There, Industry A, with a ratio of sales to capital of 10:1, is the least capital intensive. Industry B, with a ratio of sales to capital of 1:1, is more capital intensive. Industry C, with

Table 16–17			
Capital Intensive Industries and the Rate of Profit			
Industry:	A	B	C
Sales/Capital:	10	1	1/3
Profit/Sales:	1%	10%	30%
Profit/Capital:	10%	10%	10%
Sales/Capital:	10	1	1/3
Profit/Sales:	1/2%	5%	15%
Profit/Capital:	5%	5%	5%

a ratio of sales to capital of only 1:3, is the most capital intensive. (We can think of Industry A as representing supermarkets, which have an extremely rapid turnover of the portion of their capitals that is invested in inventories, and thus a very high overall ratio of sales to capital. Industry B can be taken as representing the automobile industry. And Industry C, finally, can be taken as representing the electric utility industry, almost all of whose capital is invested in power plants and wires underground, both with an extremely long life.)

The fact that these industries have such unequal rates of capital turnover (the sales to capital ratios) requires, of course, that they have correspondingly unequal profit margins—that is, profits as a percentage of sales—if they are all to earn the same rate of profit on capital invested.[95] Thus, in order for Industry A to earn a 10 percent rate of profit on capital invested, it requires a profit margin of only 1 percent. If it earns a profit of a mere 1 percent of sales, but its sales are 10 times its capital, it earns a 10 percent rate of profit on its capital. Industry B needs to earn a profit margin of 10 percent, if, with its 1:1 ratio of sales to capital, it is to earn a 10 percent rate of profit on its capital invested. And, of course, Industry C needs to earn profits on sales of fully 30 percent, if, with its 1:3 ratio of sales to capital, it is to earn a 10 percent rate of profit on its capital invested. All this is shown in the top half of Table 16–17.

The bottom half of Table 16–17 shows the profit margins that are required in the three industries if the rate of profit on capital invested is 5 percent instead of 10 percent. These lower profit margins are ½ percent, 5 percent, and 15 percent, respectively.

Now inasmuch as these lower profit margins are brought about by a fall in the selling prices of the products of the three industries, Table 16–17 implies that a decline in the rate of profit causes a relatively greater reduction in the prices of the products of more-capital-intensive industries than of less-capital-intensive industries. As the rate of profit falls from 10 percent to 5 percent, the price of the product of industry C falls by 15 percent, that of B by 5 percent, that of A by only ½ percent, for these are the extent of the price declines needed to achieve the respective reductions in profit margins. Because of this pattern of price reductions, the demand for the products of more-capital-intensive industries is favored, and therefore the need for capital intensiveness in the economic system is once more increased.

Thus, to summarize, a lower rate of profit on capital invested encourages greater capital intensiveness in the economic system by reducing the cost savings that more-capital-intensive investments must achieve relative to the additional capital required. This was shown in the example of the railroad tunnel. It is also accompanied by

a more rapid wiping out of the profit margins of higher-cost, less-capital-intensive methods of production than of the profit margins of lower-cost, more-capital-intensive methods of production, with the result that the more-capital-intensive methods are rendered the comparatively more profitable. This was shown in the example of the three methods of producing the same quantity of the same product. In addition, a lower rate of profit reduces the premiums in price or in revenue that more-capital-intensive products, more capital-intensive-methods of production, and more-capital-intensive industries must bear relative to less-capital-intensive products, methods of production, and industries. This was shown in the example of scotch of different ages, the example of the additional revenue required to make the use of machinery or buildings pay, and, finally, the example of the industries of different degrees of capital intensiveness. In all these ways, a lower rate of profit favors a higher degree of capital intensiveness.

If this principle is understood, then it should now be possible to understand the claim made earlier that if for any reason the rate of profit is wiped out or made unduly low, the basis exists for an automatic restoration of profitability through net investment. All one has to realize is that when confronted with an unduly low rate of profit, businessmen are motivated to divert outlays for factors of production from some of their present lines to lines representing a higher degree of capital intensiveness, because, by comparison, these will appear as more profitable lines. Thus, if most businesses are earning little or no profit with the employment of their present amounts of capital, then what they need is more capital, in order to reduce their annual costs of production and/or to increase their sales revenues by virtue of having improved products to sell. In this situation what will happen is a withdrawal of capital from some of its present lines of employment and diversion to more-capital-intensive lines, as representing a more profitable use of existing capital. For example, unprofitable retail businesses will withdraw some of their capital from the retailing trade and make it available in the loan market, where it will be borrowed and used for the construction of things like additional railway tunnels. At the same time, some of the retailers will merge with one another, in order to carry on business more capital intensively and more economically. Such retailers will themselves probably seek additional capital.

What is present here is a shifting of productive expenditures from points less remote from showing up as costs of production to points more remote from showing up as costs of production, with the result that for a more-or-less-extended period of time a reduction takes place in the costs business subtracts both from its outlays for factors of production and from its sales revenues.[96] This reduction in costs deducted is the reflection of a larger proportion of the output of the economic system being retained within business firms, instead of being turned over to customers in the sale of inventories or lost through depreciation or expensed expenditures. On the one side, it represents the accumulation of assets, which is a hallmark of net investment and the growth in capital intensiveness. On the other side, it represents an increase in profitability. Thus, the effect of the impetus toward additional capital intensiveness is a restoration of business profitability on the strength of the additional net investment entailed.

Of course, as my discussion of the sources of profit has shown, the restoration of profitability achieved by additional net investment is not confined to the existence of that net investment itself. The net investment spring presently under discussion tends to activate the other springs to profitability as well. This is because the higher degree of capital intensiveness that is brought about operates to increase production and thus, in the long run, and indirectly, the rate of increase in the supply of a commodity money.[97] The net investment spring also activates the net consumption spring in that the elimination of negative net investment immediately allows net consumption to generate profits equal to itself.[98] Moreover, in the conditions of recovery from a depression, the accompaniment of the net investment spring is a reduction in the demand for money for holding, which, in the short run, further adds to net investment and the nominal rate of profit, by raising productive expenditure and sales revenues relative to costs.

Wage Rate Rigidities and Blockage of the Springs

Given the existence of the various springs to profitability that have now been explained, the question arises of why the economic system does not in fact always spring back to profitability in the midst of a depression. One part of the answer, of course, is that the process of financial contraction and deflation must first come to an end, so that the financial losses inherent in that process can be avoided. Another essential part of the answer, which is necessary to limit the extent of the financial contraction and deflation, is that there must be a sufficient fall in wage rates. Before the critical net-investment spring can be activated, wage rates must fall to the level required for full employment in the face of the existing demand for money and quantity of money—a demand for money that is greater than it was before the depression, and a quantity of money that is very possibly smaller than it was before the onset of the depression. The demand for money in a depression is greater both because it has been deprived of the stimulus to spending

created by inflation and credit expansion, and because of the existence of the process of financial contraction itself, especially when accompanied by bank failures under a fractional reserve banking system, which serve to reduce the quantity of money.

As I explained in Chapter 13, the failure of wage rates to fall to the full-employment point causes a postponement of investment expenditures, and thus a wiping out of net investment and profitability, indeed, causes negative net investment and losses.[99] The operation of the springs to profitability comes into play only when wage rates reach the new, lower level that has become necessary for full employment, thereby eliminating the threat that present investments will be rendered unprofitable by substantial wage-rate reductions in the year or two ahead. At that point, the operation of the springs guarantees the restoration of net investment and profitability.

Capital Intensiveness and the Monetary Component in the Rate of Profit

Preceding analysis has shown that there is always need for greater capital intensiveness, that if ever the rate of profit disappears or becomes unduly low, the movement toward greater capital intensiveness acts to raise the rate of profit back up, and that the reestablished rate of profit then limits the move toward any further increase in the degree of capital intensiveness. A question now arises concerning specifically *the monetary component* that is added to the rate of profit by virtue of the more rapid increase in the supply of commodity money that a higher degree of capital intensiveness brings about. Namely, does the monetary component in the rate of profit operate to reverse the increase in the degree of capital intensiveness that brought it about in the first place, as would a rise in the rate of net consumption or a rise in the rate of net investment brought about by carrying on the process of capital intensification too rapidly?

There is some important evidence for believing that the rise in the rate of profit caused by the monetary component does not have this effect, that it does not react back, as it were, and undermine the higher capital intensiveness on which it rests. This is because there is reason for believing that the relationship between capital intensiveness and the rate of profit pertains exclusively to *that portion of the rate of profit that does not reflect the increase in the quantity of money.*

The case of the thirty-year-old scotch versus the eight-year-old scotch can be used to perform an intellectual experiment that will demonstrate this point. We have seen how a fall in the rate of profit from 10 percent to 5 percent encouraged capital intensiveness by causing the price of the older scotch to fall to a greater extent than that of the younger scotch and thus to encourage the purchase of the older, more-capital-intensive scotch at the expense of the purchase of the younger, less-capital-intensive scotch. Now what we will do is see if this encouragement to greater capital intensiveness is reversed by virtue of a more rapid rate of increase in the quantity of money that restores the rate of profit to 10 percent.

We saw that the fall in the rate of profit from 10 percent to 5 percent caused the price of the thirty-year-old scotch to fall from $1,745 to $432, while it caused the price of the eight-year-old scotch to fall from $214 to $148. This implied a fall in the ratio of the price of the older to the younger scotch from over 8:1 ($1,745/$214) to less than 3:1 ($432/$148). The test of whether or not an addition to the rate of profit by virtue of an increase in the quantity of money undermines the higher capital intensiveness on which the increase in the quantity of money rests will be whether or not the change in the relative prices of the two scotches is reversed by the more rapid rate of increase in the quantity of money.

For the sake of simplicity, we can assume that a more rapid rate of increase in the quantity of money takes place that is sufficient fully to restore the rate of profit, namely, to raise it all the way back up to 10 percent from the 5 percent to which it fell on the basis of a reduction in the rate of net consumption. If in raising the rate of profit back up to 10 percent, the increase in the quantity of money raises the ratio of the price of the thirty-year-old scotch to the price of the eight-year-old scotch back to 8:1, then we will have to conclude that the rise in the rate of profit caused by the more rapid increase in the quantity of money that is attributable to greater capital intensiveness does, indeed, work against the capital intensiveness on which it rests. If, on the other hand, we find that the rise in the rate of profit attributable to the more rapid growth in the quantity of money is not accompanied by any rise in the ratio of the price of the thirty-year-old scotch to the price of the eight-year-old scotch, then we must conclude that this kind of rise in the rate of profit does not work against capital intensiveness.

Well, what do we find? We find that if the quantity of money and volume of spending in the economic system now begin to increase at an annual rate of 5 percent (which is what will operate to raise the rate of profit from 5 percent to approximately 10 percent), the price of thirty-year-old scotch tends to be elevated by a factor of 1.05^{30}, which is an increase of 4.32 times.[100] Thus, instead of being $432, it will tend to be $432 x 4.32, or $1,867. By the same token, the price of eight-year-old scotch will tend, in eight years, to be elevated from $148 to $148 x 1.05^8, or to $218. On this basis, it may appear that the old 8:1 ratio is restored.

But this conclusion would be premature. Because what we must realize is that the more rapid rate of increase in the quantity of money and rise in the volume of spending does not stop its influence on the price of the eight-year-old scotch after eight years. It goes on influencing the price of the eight-year-old scotch *year after year*. In fact, it influences the price of eight-year-old scotch that will be available in thirty years fully as much as it influences the price of the thirty-year-old scotch that will be available in thirty years. The price of eight-year-old scotch to be available thirty years from now will also tend to be increased by a factor of 1.05^{30}—that is, by exactly the same factor as the price of the thirty-year-old scotch. Eight-year-old scotch, thirty years from now, will tend to sell for $148 x 4.32, or $639. The thirty year old scotch, at $1,867, is not eight times as expensive, but less than 3 times as expensive ($1,867/$639), just as it was with a rate of return of only 5 percent.

What is decisive in bringing about this result is the fact that the more rapid rate of increase in the quantity of money and volume of spending go on acting on the price of the younger scotch year after year. If, on the other hand, the rise in the rate of profit had been the result of a rise in the rate of net consumption, the price of eight-year-old scotch would have been increased, but the price of eight-year-old scotch thirty years from now would not have tended to be any higher than the price of eight-year-old scotch eight years from now. A rise in the rate of profit attributable to a rise in the rate of net consumption would have raised the prices of the eight-year-old and thirty-year-old scotches unequally, for it would have operated on the price of the one for just eight years and on the price of the other for thirty years.[101] But a rise in the rate of profit attributable to a more rapid rate of increase in the quantity of money is accompanied by equivalent percentage increases in both prices, because the more rapid increase in the quantity of money goes on affecting both prices year after year.

Thus, this case shows that the rise in the rate of profit that results from greater capital intensiveness bringing about a more rapid rate of increase in the supply of commodity money does not react back and undermine the higher degree of capital intensiveness. The case must be understood as demonstrating this fact as a general proposition, because every instance of greater or lesser degrees of capital intensiveness represents merely the outlay of sums of money for longer or shorter times in advance of the sale of the product to whose production the sums of money contribute. In other words, every instance of different degrees of capital intensiveness can be conceived of as the scotch case or combinations of the scotch case.

This conclusion can be readily confirmed in such cases as that of the railway tunnel. In cases of this kind, the increase in the quantity of money and volume of spending would operate to increase the annual savings in operating costs to the same extent as they operated to increase the nominal rate of profit, for they would operate to make the wages and prices that constituted the operating costs higher each year by the same percentage as they added to the rate of profit. Thus, in such cases, the higher rate of profit brought about by the increase in the quantity of money would not serve to discourage greater capital intensiveness if the greater capital intensiveness were profitable otherwise.

Nevertheless, I have not yet been able satisfactorily to verify this finding in terms of examples of different methods of production capable of producing the same quantity of a given product, and of industries with different capital turnover ratios. In these cases, looking simply at the examples themselves, it appears that a rise in the rate of profit caused by the addition of a monetary component *does* operate to discourage capital intensiveness. This is because what is present is a rise in sales revenues relative to costs and thus a favoring of less-capital-intensive methods. In view of the fact that, independently of this, the increase in the quantity of money can be shown to have a substantial effect on the rate of net consumption, and thereby without question to undermine capital intensiveness, it is clearly best if the rate of increase in the quantity of money is moderate, as it would be under a 100-percent-reserve gold standard.[102]

Capital Intensiveness Under Rapid Obsolescence

Inasmuch as I have just dealt with the question of the possible reactive effect of the increase in the quantity of money caused by a higher degree of capital intensiveness, on the degree of capital intensiveness, this is the logical place to deal with the possible reactive effect of the economic progress caused by a higher degree of capital intensiveness, on the degree of capital intensiveness. Namely, does it react back and reduce the degree of capital intensiveness?

This question arises because in the context of a rapidly progressing economy, the rate of obsolescence of machines and factories increases, necessitating more rapid depreciation.[103] It should not be thought, however, that this implies any tendency toward a diminution in the degree of capital intensiveness in the economic system. For reasons both already explained and yet to be explained, the rate of economic progress is not only positively related to the degree of capital intensiveness, but, if anything, the strength of this relationship is increased by the more rapid obsolescence that is caused by economic progress.

This is because the effect of such obsolescence is to require that a larger proportion of productive expenditure take the form of a demand for machinery and factory construction rather than a demand for labor. This is illustrated by the fact that if the average machine in the economic system can be in service for, say, twenty years, then, on average, for every twenty workers using a machine, only one machine needs to be produced in any given year. But if because of more rapid obsolescence, the average machine can be in service for only ten years, then for every twenty workers using a machine, an average of *two* machines must be produced in any given year. The effect of such a change is to increase the demand for capital goods at the expense of the demand for labor and thus at the expense of the demand for consumers' goods, which comes mainly from wage earners. Thus, the result is a rise in the degree of capital intensiveness as measured by the ratio of capital to the demand for consumers' goods or to wage payments.

This discussion, incidentally, implies the need for a modification in the measurement of capital intensiveness. Up to now, I have described capital intensiveness equivalently in terms of the ratio of capital to consumption expenditure, to wage payments, and to sales revenues. In actuality, the ratio of capital to consumption expenditure or to wage payments is a better measure of capital intensiveness than the ratio of capital to sales revenues. True enough, a rise in the ratio of capital to sales revenues does constitute an increase in the degree of capital intensiveness. But the present discussion calls attention to the fact that the degree of capital intensiveness can increase even though the ratio of capital to sales revenues remains the same or even declines somewhat. Capital intensiveness increases when a larger proportion of sales revenues is for capital goods and a smaller proportion is for consumers' goods. This change is reflected in the ratio of capital to receipts from the sale of consumers' goods, but it is not reflected in the ratio of capital to sales revenues as such. Thus, in the above example of the annual purchase of two machines with a ten-year life taking the place of the annual purchase of one machine with a twenty-year life, the ratio of net plant to sales revenues declines slightly, but the ratio of net plant to receipts from the sale of consumers' goods rises, and thus capital intensiveness increases.

This conclusion is illustrated by taking the initial amount of annual expenditure for plant and equipment as 100 monetary units. Under this assumption, with annual depreciation at the rate of 5 percent, net plant comes to equal 2,000 monetary units of gross plant minus 1,050 monetary units of accumulated depreciation, that is, 950. (Accumulated depreciation amounts to 1,050 monetary units after 20 years because that is the sum of 20 terms starting with 5 and incrementing by 5 each year until, in *Year 20*, an annual total of 100 of depreciation is reached.) If total sales revenues are 1,000 and receipts from the sale of consumers' goods are 500, then the ratio of capital in the form of net plant to sales revenues is .95 ($950/1,000$) and the ratio of capital in the form of net plant to receipts from the sale of consumers' goods is 1.9 ($950/500$). Now, in the face of economic progress and more rapid obsolescence, annual expenditure for plant and equipment rises to 200. This, together with the reduction in the depreciable life of the plant and equipment to 10 years, results in net plant coming to equal 900. (This is because gross plant comes to equal 2,000, as before, but accumulated depreciation comes to equal 1,100 instead of 1,050. The figure of 1,100 is the sum of 10 terms starting with 20 of annual depreciation and incrementing by 20 until 200 of annual depreciation is reached in *Year 10*.) In this case, the ratio of net plant to sales revenues falls to .9 from .95 ($900/1,000$). But because the rise of 100 in annual demand for plant and equipment is at the expense of a fall of 100 in the annual demand for consumers' goods, capital intensiveness as measured by the ratio of capital to consumption, rises from 1.9 ($950/500$) to 2.25 ($900/400$).

Such an increase in the degree of capital intensiveness occurs in every case in which a higher degree of capital intensiveness results in more rapid obsolescence of plant and equipment and thus in a rise in the demand for capital goods at the expense of the demand for labor.

Accordingly, it is clear that the effect of a higher degree of capital intensiveness and the more-rapid economic progress and consequent more-rapid obsolescence of plant and equipment that it causes is not to react back and reduce the degree of capital intensiveness.

PART B

THE NET-CONSUMPTION/NET-INVESTMENT THEORY AND ALTERNATIVE THEORIES

In this part, I present a critical analysis of the major alternative theories of the rate of profit and interest, namely, the productivity theory and the time-preference theory. I also trace essential roots of the net-consumption theory to the writings of Ricardo, and examine a previous very brief and unsatisfactory exposition of the combined net-consumption/net-investment theory put forward earlier in this century by Michael Kalecki and then taken up Joan Robinson.

Apart from the Marxian exploitation theory, which I refuted in Chapter 11, the productivity and time preference theories, or, indeed, as is most often the case, the two taken together in combination, are the most popular

theories of the rate of profit and interest. A leading purpose of this part is to show that to whatever extent the productivity of capital and time preference actually do determine the rate of return on capital, they do so exclusively by way of their respective influence on the rate of net investment and the rate of net consumption, and that apart from these connections they have absolutely no influence on the rate of return.

1. Exposition and Critique of the Productivity Theory in Its Traditional Form

The productivity theory can be understood in terms of a famous example developed by Roscher and then repeated by Böhm-Bawerk in preparation for his critique of the doctrine. Böhm-Bawerk quotes Roscher as follows:

> "Let us imagine a nation of fisher[men], without private ownership or capital, dwelling naked in caves, and living on fish caught by hand in pools left by the ebbing tide. All the workers here may be considered equal, and each man is presumed to catch and eat 3 fish per day. But now one prudent man limits his consumption to 2 fish per day for 100 days, lays up in this way a stock of 100 fish, and makes use of this stock to enable him to apply his whole labor power for 50 days to the making of a boat and net. With the aid of this capital he catches 30 fish a day from that time on."[104]

If we assume, as does Böhm-Bawerk, that the boat and net last for 100 days, then we have the following situation. Each day's use of the boat and net enables the fisherman using it to catch 27 more fish than he otherwise would have, or 2,700 additional fish in all. In the terminology of the contemporary supporters of the productivity theory, this is the marginal gross product of the capital constituted by the boat and net—it is what the boat and net add to the catch of the fisherman. The marginal net product of this capital is found by subtracting the cost of constructing the boat and net, which is the value of the 50 days of labor required to construct them. The value of this labor, according to the supporters of the productivity theory, is 3 fish per day, or 150 fish in total, for that is the product that must be forgone in order to construct the boat and net. (Obviously, the supporters of the productivity doctrine also support the opportunity-cost doctrine.) The marginal net product of the boat and net thus appears as 2,550 fish—the 2,700-fish-marginal-gross-product of the boat and net minus the opportunity cost of 150 fish forgone in order to construct the boat and net.

The implied rate of return on capital here is the 2,550 fish of marginal net product divided by the amount of fish representing the average value of the capital invested, which is 75 fish.[105] The resulting rate of return is 3,400 percent. And since this rate of return is earned over a period of just 150 days and thus could be earned more than twice in a year, the implied annual rate of return is over 2 times that, i.e., more than 6,800 percent.

It should be realized, of course, that the productivity theory by no means necessarily implies the existence of high rates of return. The above rates of return result merely from the particular assumptions that happen to have been used in the example. The supporters of the productivity theory are willing to concede the possible existence of very high rates of return in such primitive conditions, but argue that the law of diminishing returns quickly sets in, which operates to reduce marginal gross and net products relative to successive equal increments of capital invested. Indeed, based on the law of diminishing returns, the productivity theory implies a tendency toward a constantly falling rate of return on capital invested, as additional capital is accumulated. The major factor offsetting this tendency, in its view, is technological progress, which allegedly operates to keep up the rate of profit by creating new investment opportunities.

All of these views can be found in the textbook of Samuelson and Nordhaus, whose exposition is typical and, at the same time, even uses the very example of the fish and boat and net:

> . . . investing in capital goods involves indirect or roundabout production. Instead of catching fish with our hands, we find it ultimately more worthwhile first to build nets and boats—and then to use the nets and boats to catch many more fish than we could by hand.
>
> Put differently, we frequently forgo present consumption to increase future consumption. Fewer fish caught today frees up labor for making nets to catch many more fish tomorrow. Society thus invests, or abstains from present consumption, and by waiting obtains a yield or return on that investment. *In the most general sense, this yield—more future consumption in return for forgone present consumption—is the return on capital.*[106]

These passages clearly express the productivity theory's conception of the rate of profit as representing the physical net productivity of capital. A few paragraphs later, they are followed by the passages I quoted back in Chapter 13, which express equally clearly the productivity theory's view of the influence of the law of diminishing returns and technological progress on the rate of profit.[107]

When I quoted the passages in Chapter 13, I dealt with the productivity theory's errors with respect to technological progress. I showed technological progress to be a source of the supply of capital goods, not of "the demand for capital," and to be fundamentally neutral with respect to the average rate of profit. That is, I showed that technological progress neither raises the average rate of profit (except to the extent of contributing to the more rapid increase in the quantity of a commodity

money) nor lowers it by virtue of being the cause of alleged deflation, i.e., of falling prices. Later, I showed that in the absence of technological progress, the effect of the operation of the law of diminishing returns would be to reduce the rate of capital accumulation and economic progress, both of which would peter out in the sustained absence of technological progress.[108] This, rather than any reduction in the rate of profit, is the actual effect of the operation of the law of diminishing returns insofar as it is not offset by technological progress. In the next chapter, I will completely lay to rest the doctrine that capital accumulation causes a tendency toward a falling rate of profit.[109]

There are further difficulties with the productivity theory in its traditional form. Among them is the fact that it rests on the acceptance of the doctrine of opportunity cost, as is apparent from the example of the boat and net. Needless to say, I have also already exposed the errors of this doctrine.[110] Furthermore, even if the opportunity-cost doctrine were free of error, the productivity theory must break down in every case in which the larger quantity of the consumers' good produced is physically different than the consumers' goods forgone in order to produce it. For example, how would one calculate the rate of return if what had to be forgone in order to construct the boat and net were, say, 150 loaves of bread instead of 150 fish? How does one calculate the difference between 2,700 fish and 150 loaves of bread?

This last difficulty implies that the very concept of a marginal net *physical* productivity of capital goods is simply illegitimate when applied in the context of individual firms and industries, whose output in a division-of-labor society is always physically very different than their inputs. The only legitimate concept of marginal productivity in this context is the one I have employed, which refers to the reductions in money costs and/or increases in sales revenues to be achieved by the employment of additional capital—additional capital, it must be stressed, not in the sense of additional physical capital goods, but in the sense of a monetary value both of the capital goods purchased *and of the producers' labor employed.*

In the context of a division-of-labor society, the concept of a marginal net *physical* productivity of capital goods is legitimate only at the level of the economic system as a whole. The economy as a whole productively consumes capital goods which in turn makes possible the production of an output that replaces the capital goods consumed and more. From the perspective of the economic system as a whole, it is legitimate to view the capital goods consumed and the product produced as homogenous—at the very abstract level of units of wealth consumed and produced. Thus, at this level of abstraction, one may properly think in terms of a net physical productivity of capital goods.

It is at this level of abstraction that we will apply and analyze the example offered by Roscher and Böhm-Bawerk concerning the fishermen. When we do so, it will become obvious that the productivity theory in the form in which it is presently expounded—namely, as an attempt to explain the rate of profit on the basis of a net physical surplus in production—simply does not explain what it is absolutely essential for a valid theory of the rate of profit to explain. This, of course, is the answer to the question of just how an economy-wide surplus of *money sales revenues* over *money costs of production* comes into existence and is maintained. The existence of such a surplus is indispensable to the existence of a positive average rate of return on capital in the economic system as a whole. Without it, there cannot be a rate of profit or rate of return.

The fact that an individual fisherman or, indeed, everyone in the economic system—which is what all the fisherman taken together in the example are supposed to represent—adopts more productive methods of production and thus turns out a larger physical output does not in fact imply any addition whatever to the total of sales revenues in the economic system or any diminution in aggregate costs of production in the economic system. It thus implies nothing whatever about the average rate of profit in terms of money.

To understand this fact, let us take the case of the fishermen as the basis of an example in terms of money. Let us imagine that there is a society of 1 million fishermen organized into 1 million fishing enterprises, which initially produce 3 million fish a day, which they sell for $3 million, or at a price of $1 per fish. In other words, we take 3 million fish to represent the total physical product of the economic system and $3 million to represent the aggregate monetary demand for that product.

Having made these assumptions, still another problem arises for the productivity theory. Namely, it turns out that in such primitive conditions, in which there are as yet no capital goods and in which, therefore, the manual workers who gather the fish can be presumed simply to produce and sell their own products and not to act as capitalists, the full sales proceeds of the fishermen are profits! This, of course, follows from the fact that, not acting as capitalists, they do not make productive expenditures and therefore have no money costs to deduct from their sales revenues.[111] It also turns out that the rate of return on capital in these conditions is infinite! This last point follows because the fishermen's profit would be earned on a capital invested of zero. This is because, in the absence of productive expenditure, there can be no capital in terms of money, as well as no costs in terms of money.[112] These facts represent a serious difficulty for the productivity theory, because the theory claims to be an explanation of the *genesis* of profit and the rate of return, and here they are in existence *prior* to any capital or productivity of capital, with profit at a height in relation both to sales revenues and to capital that it will never afterwards achieve.

But we can put this difficulty aside and simply imagine that each of these fishermen is paid a wage of, say, $2.50 per day by some kind of external fishing enterprise. This assumption enables us to zero in on the central difficulty of the productivity theory in the context of an economic system that uses money and has an existing economic degree of capitalism—of buying for the sake of subsequently selling. For now we are in a position to see clearly just why the productivity theory in its present form, is simply unable to explain the determination of the general rate of profit.

What we have is the following situation. Because of the use of a boat and net, one individual fisherman produces 30 fish per day instead of 3 fish per day. All the rest of the fisherman continue as before. Thus, the output of the economic system as a whole rises from 3 million fish to 3 million and 27 fish per day. Given the same supply of money in the economic system and the same demand for money for holding, total spending to buy products (in this case represented exclusively by fish) remains $3 million. Thus, total sales revenues in the economic system remain $3 million. As a result, the price of fish declines from $1 per fish to $1 times the fraction formed by dividing 3 million by 3 million and 27.

In these circumstances, our individual fisherman with the tenfold increase in his output takes in almost ten times the sales revenue. The monetary profit of *his* enterprise is thus very greatly increased. But by the same token, the monetary profits of all the other fishing enterprises in the economic system taken together are equivalently decreased. Collectively, they take in as much less in sales revenue as he takes in more. And thus their profits are as much reduced as his are increased. In the economy as a whole, total sales revenues remain at $3 million and total costs of production remain at $2.5 million (1 million fishing enterprises, each with a wage cost of $2.50). Thus, total profits in the economic system remain at $500,000.

Nothing is changed as far as the average rate of profit is concerned if all the fishing enterprises adopt the use of boats and nets and collectively turn out 30 million fish per day instead of 3 million fish per day. So long as the quantity of money and the demand for money for holding remain the same, aggregate sales revenues remain the same. So long as the average fisherman is paid a wage of $2.50 per day, aggregate costs remain the same. And thus aggregate profits remain the same—once again, at $500,000. Whatever the money value of the capital invested in the economic system, the average rate of return on capital remains at the figure formed by dividing that amount of capital into the $500,000 of aggregate profit. All that is different is that, because of their tenfold increase in supply in the face of the same aggregate demand, fish now sell for an average price of 10 cents instead of $1. To the extent that nominal profits exist—on some other basis than that of the productivity theory, of course—real profits may be said to be increased by a factor of 10 by virtue of the 90 percent fall in prices. Real wages too are increased by this multiple. But the nominal amount and rate of profit would be unchanged, and nominal wages would be unchanged.

There are only two ways that the adoption of the more productive methods of production symbolized by the boats and nets would be capable of affecting the general monetary rate of return on capital. One would be the extent to which the more productive methods could be applied to the mining of the precious metals under a system of gold and silver commodity money. This would result in a more rapidly growing quantity of money and volume of spending in the economic system, and thus in more rapidly rising aggregate sales revenues, which last would raise the rate of return in the ways explained earlier in this chapter.[113] The other connection to the rate of return would be the extent to which the adoption of the more productive methods entailed net investment apart from increases in the quantity of money.

In the original example of the fisherman, it was assumed that 100 fish were saved up and that labor was then temporarily withdrawn from catching fish and devoted to constructing a boat and net instead, while the worker lived off of his accumulated stock of fish. That element of the example can be translated into monetary terms that have a bearing on the rate of return. Thus, let us imagine that for a time, the million fishing enterprises reduce their production of fish from 3 million per day to 2 million per day. For 150 days, they devote one-third of their labor to the construction of boats and nets (this would be equivalent to devoting their full labor for 50 days, as assumed in the original example). In these 150 days, aggregate sales revenues continue at $3 million per day, as before. But aggregate costs *fall from $2.5 million, to only two-thirds of that amount,* i.e., to $1.67 million. The fall in aggregate costs takes place because the value of the labor going into the construction of the boats and nets is not charged against sales revenues, but is debited—added—to the value of the boats and nets under construction. In other words, there is a rise in aggregate profit and the average rate of profit, insofar as net investment takes place in connection with the adoption of the more

more productive methods of production. Apart from the increase in the quantity of money, this is the only way that the adoption of more productive methods of production can be associated with the emergence of an average rate of return on capital in the economic system as a whole. In such cases, it is clear, what raises the rate of return is not the use of the more productive methods, but only such net investment as might take place in making possible their adoption.

Of course, in the context of an invariable money, the adoption of more productive methods of production made possible by a greater supply of capital goods would normally not entail any net investment in monetary terms, nor, therefore, any contribution to aggregate profit. The larger supply of capital goods would usually be the result of the greater production of capital goods that was part of the larger overall production made possible by a preceding increase in the supply of capital goods. As we have seen, this process of capital accumulation continuing indefinitely without need for further increases in the degree of capital intensiveness in the relative-value sense—which would be the necessary result of net investment in the context of an invariable money—is made possible by virtue of technological progress.[114] Thus, under a system of invariable money, while more productive methods of production can be associated with a contribution to the rate of profit, by way of the accumulation of capital necessary to adopt them, as a rule even this association will not be present.

To be sure, in reality, the adoption of the more productive methods of production that an increasing supply of capital goods makes possible is normally accompanied by net investment in monetary terms and a corresponding contribution to aggregate profit. This is in the context of an economic system with an increasing quantity of money. But here too, it is not the adoption of the more productive methods of production, nor even the accumulation of capital required to undertake them, that is responsible for any contribution to the rate of profit, but, this time, the increase in the quantity of money and volume of spending that accompany the capital accumulation and adoption of more productive methods of production.

The truth is that apart from the increase in the quantity of money that it may contribute to, the marginal productivity of capital simply has no bearing on the rate of profit except insofar as it is a cause of net investment in a context in which it results in capital intensification in the relative-value sense. Indeed, the general marginal net productivity of *physical capital goods,* when conceived in terms of abstract units of wealth, such as has been the practice of this book, is almost certainly far higher than the average rate of profit. Thus, for example, ever since the analysis of capital accumulation in Chapter 14, I have consistently assumed that the productive consumption of each unit K of capital goods results in the production of an output equivalent to $2K$ of capital goods. This implies a general, economy-wide constant marginal net physical productivity of capital goods of 100 percent. Yet the rate of profit in my examples was never even remotely this high. As we saw earlier in this chapter, when 500 monetary units were expended to buy $1K$ of capital goods, and the resulting output of $1K$ plus $1C$ (which was equivalent to $2K$ of capital goods in terms of the physical wealth it represented) was sold for 1,000 monetary units, the rate of profit was only 11.11 percent, not 100 percent. This was because, first, 300 in wage costs had to be subtracted from the 1,000 of sales revenues, along with 500 of cost on account of capital goods. And then the 200 which remained for profit had to be divided by a capital of 1,800.

We are in a position to see also that profits differ from the general marginal net physical productivity of capital goods by virtue of the difference between increases in production and increases in sales revenues. In the conditions of an invariable money, there are no increases in aggregate sales revenues, no matter how much the general marginal net physical productivity of capital goods may increase. Indeed, we have already seen this just a few paragraphs ago in the demonstration that a tenfold increase in fish production accompanying an extremely high marginal net physical productivity in terms of fish, would not imply any addition to the amount or rate of profit in the conditions of an invariable money. The tenfold supply of fish, we saw, was accompanied by an unchanged aggregate demand and thus unchanged aggregate sales revenues. In the circumstances, all that occurred was a 90 percent reduction in the price of fish, and absolutely no increase in aggregate profits in terms of money.

We can see the same phenomenon in terms of the case of $1K$ of capital goods and $1L$ of labor, by assuming that instead of producing an output of $1K$ and $1C$, they produce twice the output, namely, an output of $2K$ and $2C$. Under an invariable money, the sales revenues brought in by this doubled output would still be just 1,000 monetary units. And thus with the same expenditure of 800 monetary units for the factors of production, the amount of profit would remain 200 monetary units, and the rate of profit, 11.11 percent. This would be so even though the general marginal net physical productivity of capital goods had risen from 100 percent to 300 percent, based on the use of $1K$ of capital goods to produce an output equivalent to $4K$ of capital goods instead of equivalent merely to $2K$ of capital goods. The effect of the higher

general marginal net physical productivity of capital goods would simply be an increase in output resulting in a fall in prices. The additional 200 percent of general marginal net physical productivity would have no ability to add to profits. It would add to production and reduce prices, but add nothing whatever to monetary profits.

When the concept of the marginal net physical productivity of capital goods is viewed in the light of my analysis of capital accumulation, it becomes clear that while it is not a cause of the rate of profit, it *is* a cause of the rate of physical capital accumulation and economic progress, or at least of the determination of the height of the relative demand for capital goods that is necessary to achieve physical capital accumulation and economic progress. Taken in the context of the economic system as a whole, as it should be, the concept of the marginal net physical productivity of capital goods is simply what I have all along been referring to as the productivity of capital goods, but taken net of the capital goods used up in production. Seen in this light, its true significance relates to the ability of the economic system to produce and to accumulate capital goods, not to the rate of profit. It determines how much can be produced from any given quantity of capital goods—such as $1K$—in terms not only of consumers' goods but also of further capital goods, and thus what proportion of output must be in the form of capital goods in order to make possible the replacement of the capital goods used up in production.

In summary, when applied in its only proper context, which is at the level of the economic system as a whole, the productivity theory rests on two central errors: First, it equivocates between capital and capital goods, thereby failing to see that wages are paid out of capital. This leads it to understate the cost of production by a failure to consider that portion of the capital used up which is constituted by wage payments, and thus to confuse a percentage of the cost of capital goods with a percentage of total cost and of capital as well. This was present in its implication that the rate of profit should be 100 percent in conditions in which $1K$ of capital goods produces an output equivalent to $2K$ of capital goods, when in fact the rate of profit was only 11.11 percent. (Of course, the fact that the rate of profit was even as high as this cannot be explained by the productivity theory, but only by the existence of net consumption or, in a different context, by the existence of net investment along with net consumption.)

Second, the productivity theory ignores the relationship of net productivity to product prices. This enables it to proceed as though a gross physical product in excess of the quantity represented by the capital goods in question constitutes a larger value magnitude to the same extent. This was present in its implication that the rate of profit should be 300 percent in conditions in which *1K* of capital goods produces an output equivalent to *4K* of capital goods. Here it overlooked the fact that nothing is automatically present to increase the magnitude of sales revenues as the magnitude of net productivity increases, and that if no such thing is present, the effect is simply a fall in prices, not an addition to profits. Of course, to the extent that such a factor is present, namely, a more rapid increase in the quantity of money and volume of spending, then it is this factor—the increase in money and spending—that must be regarded as the source of the additional profit, not the increase in physical net productivity. Indeed, this criticism is applicable to the productivity theory in every context, inasmuch as the productivity theory attributes the existence of profit as such to an increase in production achieved by the employment of capital goods.

2. Exposition and Critique of the Time-Preference Theory in Its Traditional Form

The time-preference theory in its traditional form seeks to explain the rate of return on capital in the following way. Other things being equal, it argues, people attach greater importance to the satisfaction of their wants in the present than in the future, and in the nearer future rather than in the more remote future. On this basis, the time-preference theory claims, they attach a higher valuation to goods available in the present rather than in the future, and in the nearer future rather than in the more remote future, because goods derive their value from the importance of the wants they serve, and are more highly valued to the degree that the wants they serve are more important. Thus, in the words of Böhm-Bawerk, people value "present goods" more highly than "future goods" of the same kind and quantity.[115] For example, they value an apple or an automobile today more highly than an apple or an automobile not to be available to them until a year from now.

This preference for present goods over future goods supposedly enters into the valuation of the factors of production. The totality of the factors of production required to produce a product is regarded as a future good. For example, the totality of the factors of production required to produce an automobile that will be completed one year from now is regarded for purposes of valuation as a future automobile to be available in one year.

According to the time-preference theory, the fact that factors of production are future goods, which are less highly valued than present goods, is what explains the rate of return on capital. For example, the factors of production required for producing 10 apples to be available a year from today are valued as the equivalent of 10 future apples. But 10 future apples are of less value than 10 present apples. They may be of a value equivalent only to 9 present apples. Thus, the factors of production required for producing 10 future apples begin with a value equal to that of only 9 present apples. But now time passes. At the end of a year, the factors of production required for producing 10 future apples have succeeded in producing those apples. They have "matured" or "ripened" into 10 *present* apples. Thus, the totality of the factors of production required for producing 10 apples, which began with a value of only 9 present apples, has been transformed into 10 present apples, with a value of 10 present apples. In other words, profit exists because factors of production are future goods, which are purchased at a "discounted value" in comparison to present goods of the same kind and number, and then mature or ripen into present goods, which shake off that discount and sell at the full value appropriate to present goods. (This example, of course, is supposed to apply to *all* goods, inorganic as well as organic. Thus the factors of production required to produce an automobile or house are also held to begin as future goods and then to mature or ripen into the automobile or house.)

The nature of the process is clearly stated by Rothbard, who essentially does nothing more than adapt the illustration Böhm-Bawerk used against the exploitation theory and which I described in the course of my own critique of the exploitation theory.[116] Thus, Rothbard writes:

> Suppose, for example, that a capitalist-entrepreneur hires labor services, and suppose that it can be determined that this amount of labor service will result in a net revenue of 20 gold ounces to the product owner. We shall see below that the service will tend to be paid the net value of its product; but it will earn its product *discounted* by the time interval until sale. For if the labor service will reap 20 ounces five years from now, it is obvious that the owner of the labor cannot expect to receive from the capitalist the full 20 ounces *now*, in advance. He will receive his net earnings discounted by the going agio, the rate of interest. And the interest income will be earned by the capitalist who has assumed the task of advancing the present money. The capitalist then waits for five years until the product matures before recouping his money.

> The pure capitalist, therefore, in performing a capital-advancing function in the productive system, plays a sort of intermediary role. He sells money (a present good) to factor owners in exchange for the services of their factors (prospective future goods). He holds these goods and continues to hire work on them until they have been transformed into consumers' goods (present goods), which are then sold to the public for money (a present good). The premium that he earns from the sale of present goods, compared to what he paid for future goods, is the *rate of interest* earned on the exchange.[117]

It should be obvious from this quotation that the

time-preference theory in its traditional form shares with Böhm-Bawerk's critique of the exploitation theory the enormous error of regarding the wage earners as the real producers of the products, rather than, as is in fact the case, the businessmen and capitalists. The businessmen and capitalists do not buy future goods from wage earners and suppliers. *They* are the producers of the future goods and have the first and only claim to them; their obligation to the wage earners is to pay the latter for *helping* them in the production of *their*—the businessmen's and capitalists'—products.[118] But even if this error is put aside, further very serious difficulties remain for the time-preference theory in its traditional form.

First of all, the basic formula of the time-preference theory does not demonstrate what it is supposed to demonstrate. By that, I mean that the establishment of a relationship between the value of the factors of production expressed in terms of present goods, and the quantity of present goods that in the future will result from those factors of production, does not in fact convey any information whatever about the height of the rate of return. For example, the fact that 9 present apples are as valuable—in different circumstances—as the factors of production required for producing 10, 20, or 5 future apples, which, when the future comes to pass, will become 10, 20, or 5 present apples, actually says nothing whatever about the rate of return that is earned in producing those future apples. Starting with 9 present apples and ending with 10, 20, or 5 present apples a year later simply does not tell us the rate of return that is actually earned in production.

As evidence of this fact, let us assume that the price of an apple today is $1 and that, in three different, alternative cases, the price of the factors of production required for producing 10, 20, or 5 apples to be available in a year is $9. According to the time-preference theory, the rate of return implied in these three cases is 11 percent, 122 percent, and −44 percent, respectively. This is because next year, there will be 10, 20, or 5 present apples that result from factors of production bearing a value of 9 present apples of today. Thus, according to the time-preference theory, there is a gain (or loss) equal to 1, 11, and (4) units of present apples respectively, which, when divided by the initial 9 present apples, results in the three percentages of gain or loss just named.

It should be obvious that such inferences as to the rate of return rest on the unstated assumption that *the price of an apple in the future will be the same as it is in the present.* Only then would 10, 20, or 5 apples represent 10, 20, or 5 *dollars of sales revenues* and thus 1, 11, or 4 dollars of profit or loss and the corresponding rates of profit or loss implied. But in fact, there is absolutely no reason for assuming that the price of apples will stay the same over time. It will certainly not do so in the condi-

tions of an invariable money accompanied by changes on the side of production and supply. In such conditions, where the assumption that the price of present goods is constant must be abandoned, there is no way of inferring what the sales revenue, profit, and rate of return will be merely on the basis of the relationship between the value of factors of production expressed in terms of present goods and the quantities of present goods that will result from the factors of production in the future.

This point can be confirmed by means of our well-tried analysis featuring the output resulting from the use of *1K* of capital goods in conjunction with *1L* of labor. Recalling Figure 16–2, we have seen that in every year the monetary value of the factors of production required to produce the *1C* of consumers' goods of the following year is 400. We have also seen that the monetary value of the *1C* of consumers' goods sold both in the current year and in the following year is always 500. Thus, it follows that the value of the 400 worth of factors of production required to produce next year's consumers' goods, when expressed in terms of consumers' goods, is always *.8C*. That is to say, if 500 is the monetary value of *1C* of consumers' goods, 400 is the monetary value of *.8C* of consumers' goods. Consumers' goods, of course, are present goods. Thus, it is now established that in the analysis of Figure 16–2, *.8C* is the value of the factors of production of any given year, expressed in terms of present goods, that are required to produce the consumers' goods—the present goods—of the following year.

So long as everything remains stable, and thus the monetary value of *1C* of consumers' goods remains stable, the formula of the time-preference theory appears to be consistent with the monetary rate of profit, at least when it is stated as the gain in value relative to cost of production. Thus, in monetary terms, factors of production worth 400 monetary units produce consumers' goods worth 500 monetary units, and, at the same time, when expressed in terms of present goods, factors of production worth *.8C* produce *1C* of consumers' goods. As a result, whether expressed in money or in present goods, the ratio of the value of the product to the value of the factors of production used up to produce it is 5:4.

If, however, in the conditions of Figure 16–2, while everything else remained the same, the production of the economic system were to double between some particular year and the next (to choose a convenient multiple to work with), the formula of the time-preference theory would imply a very different rate of profit than the actual one. It would imply a rate of profit of 150 percent. This is because in this case, factors of production equivalent in exchange value to *.8C* of consumers' goods would produce a quantity of consumers' goods equal to *2C*. According to the formula of the time-preference theory, the gross rate of gain in value in terms of present goods in such a case would then equal *2C/.8C,* which is 2.5. When the initial capital is subtracted, this leaves a rate of net gain—a rate of profit—of 1.5, that is, 150 percent. Nevertheless, the monetary rate of profit expressed as a percentage of cost would not be 150 percent. It would still be just 25 percent. This is because in the conditions of an invariable money, the monetary value of the *2C* of consumers' goods would be no greater than the monetary value of the *1C* of consumers' goods was before. In monetary terms, it would still be a matter of 400 monetary units worth of factors of production producing a product worth 500 monetary units. The number of physical present units produced is simply irrelevant to the monetary rate of profit. The effect of their increase is merely to reduce prices, not to add to the rate of profit.

This example has provided a decisive test of the formula of the time-preference theory and has shown that the formula does not hold up. In fact, the example shows that the time-preference theory commits exactly the same kind of error as the productivity theory. Namely, both theories confuse ratios in terms of physical goods, with ratios of monetary value. The time-preference theory confuses the ratio of the present goods produced to the present-goods value of the factors of production used up to produce them, with the ratio of the monetary value of the present goods produced to the monetary value of the factors of production used up to produce them. The productivity theory confuses the ratio of the physical output produced to the physical capital goods used up to produce it, with the ratio of the monetary value of the output to the monetary value of the capital goods used up to produce it. Both theories confuse the physical product with a monetary value and take for granted that increases in the physical product mean equivalent increases in sales revenues, which is simply not the case, as analysis in terms of an invariable money conclusively shows. In contrast to the productivity theory, the time-preference theory's formula at least makes an allowance for the value of the labor expended in production, and thus the rate of profit it implies deviates from the actual rate somewhat less than does the marginal net physical productivity of capital goods.

It is perhaps not necessary to point out that in exactly the same way, under the conditions of Figure 16–2 and its invariable money, if the production of the economic system were to halve between some particular year and the next, the rate of profit would again remain the same. This, of course, is once again in full contradiction of the time-preference theory's formula, which implies that the rate of profit in this case must be in the ratio of *.5C,* which is the quantity of present goods one ends up with, to *.8C,* which is the present-goods value of the factors of pro-

duction used up to produce them. The fact is that instead of being –37.5 percent, as the time-preference theory's formula implies, the rate of profit would continue to be 25 percent when stated as a percentage of costs. This is because the *.5C* would sell for the same 500 monetary units as *1C* sold for, and thus the ratio of sales revenues to costs would still be 500:400.

Thus, in sum, the rate of return in monetary terms has nothing whatever to do with the relationship between the value of factors of production expressed in terms of present goods and the supply of present goods that will later on result from those factors of production. The difference between these two magnitudes of goods is simply irrelevant. What is relevant is the *monetary value* of the factors of production and the *monetary value* of the future goods later on, when they become present goods, that is to say, the sales revenues. The relevant relationship is that between two monetary values—the money sales revenues and the money costs—not that between two values expressed in terms of present goods. No valid inference whatever can be drawn from the quantity of present goods one ends up with to the sales revenues one ends up with. It is for this reason, that no valid inference can be drawn either as to the amount or rate of profit on the basis of differences in quantities of present goods represented by factors of production and their products.

The Contradiction Between Böhm-Bawerk's "First Cause" and the Doctrine of the Purchasing-Power Premiums

The error in the formula of the time-preference theory places the theory's supporters in essentially the same embarrassing situation as the supporters of the productivity theory and its offshoot the doctrine of secular stagnation.[119] Just as the supporters of the productivity theory, who regard technological progress as the cause of a higher demand for capital and thus, allegedly, of a higher rate of profit, are ultimately placed in the contradictory position of regarding technological progress as the cause both of an increase and a decrease in the rate of profit,[120] so the supporters of the time-preference theory are led into the contradiction of regarding increases in production as the cause both of an increase and a decrease in the rate of profit!

On the one hand, the supporters of the time-preference theory correctly perceive an increase in production as reducing the value of future goods relative to present goods, because future goods will thus be more abundant relative to present goods. Indeed, Böhm-Bawerk describes this phenomenon as "the first cause" of the higher valuation of present goods over future goods.[121] The mistaken formula of the time-preference theory then leads them to believe that the rate of profit is correspondingly increased. (The example of a doubling of production can serve once again. Thus, if the same factors of production with a present-goods value of *.8C* can produce *2C* instead of just *1C*, *.8C* of present goods is held to become the equivalent of *2C* of future goods instead of only *1C* of future goods. The implied ratio of future goods to present goods thus rises from 125 percent to 250 percent, and the rate of profit, allegedly, from 25 percent to 150 percent.)

Yet, on the other hand, when the supporters of the time-preference theory come to consider the effects of *the fall in prices* that an increased availability of goods in the future will bring about, they argue that the rate of profit and interest is correspondingly *reduced*—that it comes to incorporate a "negative price premium" that reduces it by a number of percentage points that is more or less equal to the percentage fall in prices.[122] In this way, the same cause—rising production—is held both to raise *and* lower the rate of profit.

The truth is, of course, that increases in production neither raise nor lower the rate of profit. The fall in the value of future goods relative to present goods that an increase in production brings about does not raise the rate of profit, because, other things being equal, a larger future output will be sold for the same sales revenues as the alternative smaller future output, and will thus necessarily be accompanied by a corresponding fall in the selling prices of those future goods. The fall in the selling prices of the future goods does not lower the rate of profit because, by the same token, it is the accompaniment of a correspondingly larger quantity of goods to sell. Thus, when there are *2C* instead of *1C* as the product of factors of production worth *.8C,* the additional *1C* does not add anything to the rate of profit because the *2C* sell for the same sum of money as did the *1C*. By the same token, the halving of prices when there are *2C* of product instead of *1C* does not take anything away from the rate of profit, precisely because there are twice as many units to sell at the halved price, and thus sales revenues remain the same. The rate of profit itself, it must never be forgotten, is determined by the relationship between *the amount of money* for which goods can be sold in the future and *the amount of money* expended to produce them—irrespective of the physical quantity of the goods produced, irrespective of whether that quantity is larger or smaller than the quantity produced and sold in the present, and irrespective of whether the unit price of that quantity is less or greater than the price of goods in the present.[123]

The Discounting Approach

The time-preference theory implies that one can take the prospective value of consumers' goods as *a fixed starting point*, and that the value of factors of production is then straightaway derived from the value of consumers' goods by a process of compound discount. The causal chain, in its eyes, runs from the value of consumers' goods, together with rate of discount, to the value of factors of production. This belief is stated by Irving Fisher—one of the leading advocates of the time-preference theory—in the clearest possible terms:

> The theory of prices, so far as it can be separated into parts, includes: (1) explanation of the prices of final services on which the prices of anterior interactions depend; (2) explanation of the prices of intermediate interactions, as dependent, through the rate of interest, on [the prices of] the final services; (3) explanation of the prices of capital instruments as dependent, through the rate of interest, upon the prices of their final services. *The first study, which seeks merely to determine the laws regulating the price of final services, is independent of the rate of interest.*[124]

The notion that the prices of consumers' goods are independent of the rate of profit and can, therefore, serve as a fixed base for discounting is completely mistaken. Long ago, Ricardo demonstrated that changes in the rate of profit profoundly affect the prices of consumers' goods.[125] The following example shows precisely how they can do so.

Thus, assume that a quantity of wheat ready for harvesting and a quantity of eight-year-old scotch both regularly sell for $100. If the rate of profit is 10 percent per annum, then, on the assumption that six months must elapse between the planting of the seed and the harvesting of the wheat, the value of the wheat when newly planted will be approximately $95. At the same time, the newly fermenting alcohol corresponding to the prospective quantity of eight-year-old scotch worth $100, will be worth approximately $47. (These figures are implied by the fact at a 10 percent annual rate of return, $95 is the approximate sum that grows to $100 in six months, while $47 is the approximate sum that grows to $100 in eight years.)

Now let us imagine that the rate of profit falls to 5 percent per year. According to the discounting approach, the consequence will simply be that the value of the freshly planted wheat will rise to approximately $97.50 from $95, while the value of the newly fermenting alcohol will rise to approximately $68 from $47, for at a 5 percent annual rate of return, these are the sums that grow to $100 in six months and in eight years respectively.

Nevertheless, insofar as the wheat and the scotch can both be produced by the same labor, such a result is simply impossible. This is because it would imply a much greater rise in the wages of the workers producing the scotch than in the wages of the workers producing the wheat. To see this as clearly as possible, let us substitute for the value of the newly planted wheat and newly fermenting alcohol the value of the labor required to produce them. If the wheat is produced by 95 units of labor at an initial wage of $1 per unit, while the scotch is produced by 47 units of labor, also at an initial wage of $1 per unit (the wage rates are equal because the labor is assumed to be of the same kind), then a fall in the rate of profit which had no effect but to raise the prices of the factors of production, would imply that the wages of the workers producing the wheat rose in the very modest ratio of $97.50 to $95, while the wages of the workers producing the scotch rose in the much higher ratio of $68 to $47. Yet such a development would be impossible. Any significant rise in the wages of the one occupation relative to the wages of the other occupation would cause a movement of labor out of the relatively lower-paying occupation and into the relatively higher-paying occupation.

The actual effect in this case would be a significant and approximately equal rise in the wage rates of both groups of workers. Thus the rise in wage rates of the workers producing the scotch would be substantially less than in the ratio of $68 to $48, while the rise in the wage rates of the workers producing the wheat would be substantially greater than in the ratio of $97.50 to $95. Both of these developments would be the result of a movement of workers from wheat production to scotch production.

Now the clear implication of this movement of workers from wheat to scotch is an increase in the supply of scotch and decrease in the supply of wheat, which means that in the face of the same respective demands for scotch and wheat as prevailed before, *the price of scotch falls and the price of wheat rises.* Thus, the effect of the fall in the rate of profit, accompanied by a corresponding rise in the demand for labor and in wage rates, is *a change in the relative prices of different consumers' goods.* Consumers' goods requiring a relatively long period of time to produce, such as scotch, tend to fall in price; while consumers' goods requiring a relatively short period of time to produce, such as wheat, tend to rise in price, as the result of a combination of a fall in the rate of profit and rise in the demand for labor and thus in wage rates.

Because changes in the rate of profit are thus accompanied by changes in the prices of consumers' goods, one is not justified in holding that the value of factors of production is determined by a process of discounting independently determined prices of consumers' goods. It is simply impermissible to imagine that there is the value of consumers' goods and a rate of discount, and that these two then determine the value of the factors of production. This is because the rate of profit or, better, the forces determining the rate of profit also determine the value of consumers' goods, and do so insofar as these latter re-

quire time in their production. It is not the case that the causal chain runs from value of consumers' goods, together with rate of discount, to value of factors of production. Rather, the value of consumers' goods and the value of the factors of production used to produce them are *both* determined by the forces that determine the rate of profit. That is, they are both determined by the respective supplies of and demands for products and for factors of production, including the specific supplies of and demands for consumers' goods and producers' labor.

The discounting approach is, in fact, a denial of the law of supply and demand! I say this, because it seeks to exempt the formation of the prices of factors of production from the operation of that law. In its eyes, only the prices of consumers' goods are determined by supply and demand; the prices of the factors of production are held to be determined directly by the application of a discount to the prices of consumers' goods. The truth is that the prices of factors of production are determined by supply and demand no less than the prices of consumers' goods, and that the rate of discount (viz., profit) then emerges as the result of *differences* between the demand/supply situation in the market for products and the demand/supply situation in the market for factors of production.

As an approximation, one may say that the difference between the demand for products, inclusive of capital goods, and the demand for factors of production, inclusive of capital goods, is represented by net consumption; while the difference between the supply of products and the supply of factors of production is represented by net investment—insofar as it takes place apart from the increase in the quantity of money and volume of spending. (Net investment of this type exists to the extent that the supply of products sold is less than the supply that corresponds to the factors of production previously purchased. The difference is retained within business firms as an addition to their assets and thus constitutes net investment.) As for the increase in the quantity of money and volume of spending, its effect is to make the demand for products further exceed the demand for the factors of production made in the past to produce them.

The rate of discount—of profit—is the effect of these differences in demand and supply, which, of course, at the same time are also the cause of the differences between the prices of products and the sum of the prices of the factors of production required to produce them. To the extent that the demand for products is greater than the demand for the factors of production used to produce them, or the supply of products is less than the supply of factors of production used to produce them, the prices of products exceed the sum of the prices of the factors of production and there is profit. Indeed, only to this extent is there profit.

The Disappearance of the Higher Value of Present Goods at the Margin: Böhm-Bawerk's Abandonment of the Time-Preference Theory

Yet another major problem arises for the time-preference theory in its traditional form. This is the fact that whoever has savings of any kind thereby demonstrates that he values the last unit of wealth that he devotes to the future above an additional unit of wealth that he might devote to enjoyment in the present. In other words, to this extent, at the margin, he has *a preference for future goods over present goods.* Other things being equal, for the reasons explained in Chapter 2, he undoubtedly values a unit of wealth occupying the same marginal position more highly in the present than in the future, whether it is the fifth, the fiftieth, or the five-hundredth unit.[126] Nevertheless, the fact that he regularly values *some* future units above additional present units—e.g., the fourth or four-hundredth future unit above the fifth or five-hundredth present unit—makes it incorrect to say that in the market present goods must always be more valuable than future goods. Because of the significance of valuation at the margin, there is no more reason for expecting such a relationship than to expect that water must be valued more highly in the market than diamonds. This is because there are almost always some units of future goods that at the margin are more valuable than present goods.

This was recognized by Böhm-Bawerk, and as a result of it, he virtually abandoned the time-preference theory. In a footnote to his exposition of the theory of interest, he declares:

> There are persons who are excessively well provided for in the present, or at least would be, if they wished to use up completely all the means available to them in the present, including the principal of their fortunes. In their case this relation of wants to means of satisfaction engenders a tendency in the opposite direction, that is to say, toward a higher valuation of future goods. . . . This explains one point in connection with persons who command in the present greater means than, in deference to sound economy, they may permit themselves to consume in the present. I refer to the fact that they would regularly arrive at approximate *equivalence* in their valuation of present and future goods if the first two main causes [of a higher valuation of present over future goods] alone were operative. In their case the decision in favor of present goods can be brought about only through the operation of the third main cause the discussion of which follows immediately at this point in the text.[127]

This passage is tantamount to a total abandonment of the time-preference theory by Böhm-Bawerk. This is because the "equivalence" in value between present and future goods at the margin applies to virtually everyone, since almost everyone has some amount of savings. Böhm-Bawerk confirms his abandonment of the time-preference theory by shifting the weight of his argument from his first two main causes of a higher valuation of present goods in comparison with future goods, to his third main cause of such higher valuation. As explained earlier in this section, the meaning attached by Böhm-Bawerk to the "first main cause" is the prospective more abundant provision of goods in the future compared with the present. What he means by the "second main cause" is an alleged systematic undervaluation of the importance of future wants and the means of satisfying them.[128] Böhm-Bawerk's reference to "the third main cause" as the decisive factor in the higher valuation of present over future goods refers to something that has nothing to do with time preference—namely, to an alleged "technological superiority" of present over future goods, resting on the alleged fact that the possession of present goods permits the adoption of more-time-consuming, more-productive processes of production. At this juncture, Böhm-Bawerk passes from the time-preference theory to a version of the productivity theory, which we need not consider further, since we have already fully refuted that doctrine.

Time preference, of course, does profoundly influence the rate of profit and interest, despite the fact that at the margin, future goods are preferred to present goods almost as often as present goods are preferred to future goods. The connection, as we have seen, is by virtue of its determining the rate of net consumption.

3. The Classical Basis of the Net-Consumption Theory

The role of net consumption as a determinant of profits is implicit in classical economics not only in John Stuart Mill's proposition that "demand for commodities is not demand for labour," which we have already considered at length,[129] but also in Ricardo's proposition that "profits rise as wages fall and fall as wages rise." While Ricardo's proposition is open to various interpretations, at least some of the time it can be interpreted as tantamount to the net-consumption theory operating under certain highly restrictive assumptions. For example, Ricardo declares: "If a manufacturer always sold his goods for the same money, for £1,000, for example, his profits would depend on the price of the labour necessary to manufacture those goods. His profits would be less when wages amounted to £800 than when he paid only £600. In proportion then as wages rose would profits fall."[130]

If Ricardo's proposition is interpreted to mean that under conditions of a fixed aggregate monetary demand for consumers' goods, the amount of profit depends on the amount of wages paid, which latter is to be taken as equivalent to aggregate costs of production, then his proposition is both true and fully consistent with the net-consumption theory.[131] In fact, it should be obvious that on this interpretation, the proposition implicitly presupposes the existence of net consumption, in order for the demand for consumers' goods to exceed the demand for labor in the first place.

Indeed, interpreted in this way, Ricardo's theory provides a perfectly accurate description of the determinants of aggregate profit and the average rate of profit in the example of the fishermen with the boats and nets presented in the critique of the productivity theory earlier in this chapter.[132] If, as that example assumes, a million fishermen are each paid a wage of $2.50 per day and produce a quantity of fish which always sells for a total of $3 million, then aggregate profit is $500,000, and is so irrespective of the physical quantity of fish produced and sold. What determines aggregate profit in such circumstances is wages, not the physical output of fish produced.[133]

The implicit connection between Ricardo's proposition and the role of net consumption is further reinforced when these words of John Stuart Mill are recalled, words with which Ricardo would surely have agreed: "I conceive that a person who buys commodities and consumes them himself, does no good to the labouring classes; and that it is only by what he *abstains from consuming*, and expends in direct payments to labourers in exchange for labour, that he benefits the labouring classes, or adds any thing to the amount of their employment."[134] If profits move in the opposite direction of wages, and wages in turn move in the opposite direction of the consumption of businessmen and capitalists, who are the parties who pay the wages, then profits rise as net consumption rises and fall as net consumption falls.[135]

Ricardo's theory of profit is, of course, highly deficient both in limiting itself to the case of an invariable money and in ignoring the demand for capital goods. A satisfactory theory of profit must be able to explain the determinants of profit under conditions in which aggregate monetary demand changes. Furthermore, when the demand for capital goods is taken into account, it is clear that even under an invariable money, profits and wages can rise or fall in conjunction with opposite changes in the demand for capital goods as well as opposite changes in each other, and thus that either could change and not be accompanied by a change in the other. For example, the demand for capital goods could rise at the expense of a fall in net consumption and profits, with no increase in the demand for labor; or the demand for labor could rise at the expense of the demand for capital goods, with no change in the amount of profit.

These deficiencies are at least partially responsible for

Ricardo's apostasies on the subjects of machinery and war, which he arrives at on the basis of the mistaken assumption that the interests of wage earners always lie with a higher demand for labor, even when it is at the expense of the demand for capital goods or rests on a foundation of taxation.[136] This is because the restricted confines of his theory deprive him of the ability properly to analyze these cases.

Still a further deficiency of Ricardo's theory is that it never states what it is that allows the demand for consumers' goods to exceed the demand for labor, and thus for profits to exist in the first place. The concept of net consumption is present in Ricardo's theory only by implication, not by explicit statement.

Even more serious are Ricardo's equivocations concerning the word "wages." The limited validity of his theory depends on wages being understood as total wage payments, viz., as the aggregate demand for labor, and the aggregate demand for labor in turn being understood as the aggregate demand for factors of production as such, and this in the context of a fixed aggregate demand for goods as such. Under those conditions, a rise in wages is tantamount to a fall in net consumption. Unfortunately, Ricardo uses the term wages as representing the aggregate demand for labor only some of the time. At other times, he uses it to mean the wage rates of individual workers. Thus he often argues that increases in wage rates reduce the rate of profit, when in fact their effect is to raise prices.[137] When combined with his error of believing that increases in the price of necessities cause an increase in wage rates, this confusion leads to the corollary error that reductions in the price of necessities raise the rate of profit by virtue of reducing wage rates, a notion that plays an essential role in the Marxian exploitation theory.[138] A thorough critique of Ricardo's confusion concerning a rise in wage rates as the cause of a reduction in the rate of profit appears in the appendix to this section.

Ricardo's confusion between wage rates and the total amount of wages in the economic system has also given rise to the doctrine of the so-called Ricardo effect. This is the mistaken belief that a rise in wage rates encourages the use of machinery.[139] A rise in the amount of wages, assuming it is based on a fall in net consumption, means a fall in the amount and rate of profit, hence, an encouragement to the use of machinery.[140] A mere rise in wage rates, however, has no such effect. A rise in wage rates discourages the use of machinery fully as often as it encourages it. Thus, while a rise in the wage rates of workers in employments where the use of machinery might be substituted, can encourage the use of additional machinery, a rise in the wage rates of workers *producing* machines, or anything necessary to the production of machines, discourages the use of machinery.

Furthermore, in raising the cost of production and prices of products and thus in reducing the quantities of goods demanded, increases in wage rates indirectly serve to reduce the quantities demanded of all the factors of production required to produce such goods, including the quantities of machines demanded in producing such goods. Thus, increases in wage rates not only cause unemployment and less production, but also, as part of the same process, on net balance actually reduce the overall use of machinery, along with that of all other factors of production.

Finally, even in those isolated instances in which forced increases in wage rates do lead to the greater use of machinery, the effect is in no sense a gain, but merely a diminution of the loss that is imposed. It is a fallacy to assume that in all conditions the use of machinery represents a gain. Whether or not it does so depends on a comparison of the cost of producing a product with and without the use of the machinery in question. If the cost of producing the product is less without the machinery, then there is no gain in producing it with the machinery. There is still no gain, but at most only a diminution of loss, if now a labor union artificially increases the cost of producing the product without the use of machinery, so that by comparison it becomes cheaper to produce the product by means of the use of the machinery. All that is present here is a lesser increase in cost, thanks to the use of the machinery, rather than a greater increase in cost. There is still, however, an increase in cost and corresponding loss.

Appendix to Section 3: Critique of Ricardo's Doctrine of the Falling Rate of Profit

As we have seen, Ricardo believed that the rate of profit has a tendency continually to fall. His version of this doctrine is closely connected with his errors concerning the "iron law of wages." First, he mistakenly believes, in direct contradiction of the facts, that "With the progress of society . . . one of the principal commodities [food] . . . has a tendency to become dearer from the greater difficulty of producing it."[141] Then he proceeds to the fallacy that somehow in response to this, wage rates must rise to prevent the wage earner from being deprived of subsistence. On the basis of this alleged rise in wage rates, he concludes that there is a tendency toward a continually falling rate of profit.[142]

The truth is that with the progress of society, food and everything else becomes less expensive in terms of the labor required to produce it, not more expensive. Even if, as is the case in non-division-of-labor societies, progress is so slow that population growth and the law of diminishing returns offset it, there is still no tendency for

the real cost of food or other necessities steadily to rise. Under such conditions, each fall in real cost is merely followed by a rise that pushes the average standard of living back to the level of "minimum subsistence," and at the utmost, only temporarily below it. There is never any continuing rise in the real cost of food and other necessities with the progress of society. A continuing rise in the real cost of food or other necessities could occur only as part of a process of social and economic retrogression, not progress. It would end with the collapse of society, followed by the extinction of the human race.

Ricardo is also mistaken in believing that a rise in wages must ensue in response to a higher cost of necessities. He is further mistaken in believing that if a rise in wages did ensue in such circumstances, it would reduce the rate of profit.

In part Ricardo's confusions are the result of his failure to make proper application of his own principle of analyzing economic phenomena in the framework of an invariable money. Had he rigorously adhered to his assumption of an invariable money, and conceived of it in terms of a fixed aggregate expenditure to buy the output of the economy, he might have avoided the confusions to which he fell prey.

First of all, he might have recognized that a growing supply of labor does not result in a combination of falling wages and rising prices—that it is not true that the "labourers" would be "doubly affected." Even if it were the case that because of the operation of the law of diminishing returns, more-than-proportionately-larger quantities of labor had to be applied to the production of additional quantities of agricultural commodities and minerals when population increased, the effect would still be lower prices of such commodities, not higher prices, though the fall in their prices would be less than the fall in wages. The situation would be an increase in the supply both of labor and of goods, with the increase in the supply of goods being less than the increase in the supply of labor. Thus prices would fall, but by less than wage rates.

Had Ricardo realized that the prices of agricultural commodities and minerals would fall, despite the increase in the quantity of labor required to produce them, he might well have avoided leaping to the totally unwarranted conclusion that wages would rise. He might have recognized the simple fact that in such circumstances the buying power of the wage earners would decline, and that if it declined below the point of "subsistence," the only remedy would be the extreme one implied in his own theory of wages, namely, a reduction in population followed by a consequent rise in the productivity of labor employed on land. This last would result in the prices of agricultural commodities and minerals rising less than wage rates when the supply of labor declined as the result of a higher death rate.[143]

Indeed, in the conditions of an invariable money, the pressure for a fall in wage rates would be truly overwhelming in the face of an increase in the supply of labor. This is because while the aggregate demand for the products of business would be fixed, the operation of the law of diminishing returns and growing difficulty of producing food and minerals would cause the demand for labor actually to fall. This would be the result of the ensuing growth in land "rents" displacing part of the demand for labor.[144]

Furthermore, Ricardo should have known that any arbitrary rise in wage rates that might have been secured by the wage earners would have had to result in corresponding unemployment. And precisely this is the reason why, in a free economy, it would not occur, or, if somehow it did occur, would be quickly reversed.

This is because, contrary to Ricardo's utterly mistaken implicit assumption that the demand for labor will rise in the face of higher wage rates, there is simply no source of funds for the payment of higher wage rates to the same number of workers. And thus higher wage rates must result in the employment of fewer workers and the production and sale of fewer goods. The fact that the higher wage rates would result in the production and sale of fewer goods would mean that prices would have to rise. Their not rising in the face of decreased production and a fixed aggregate expenditure to buy goods would imply the depletion of inventories, which would be the only means of maintaining the quantity of goods made available for sale. Such depletion could certainly not go on indefinitely. And when it ended, prices would have to rise.

Ricardo considers the objection that a rise in wage rates would mean a rise in product prices rather than a fall in the rate of profit, but he rejects this conclusion, largely on following grounds:

> To say that commodities are raised in price is the same thing as to say that money is lowered in relative value; for it is by commodities that the relative value of gold is estimated. If, then, all commodities rose in price, gold could not come from abroad to purchase those dear commodities, but it would go from home to be employed with advantage in purchasing the comparatively cheaper foreign commodities. It appears, then, that the rise of wages will not raise the prices of commodities, whether the metal from which money is made be produced at home or in a foreign country. All commodities cannot rise at the same time without an addition to the quantity of money. This addition could not be obtained at home, as we have already shown; nor could it be imported from abroad. To purchase any additional quantity of gold from abroad, commodities at home must be cheap, not dear. The importation of gold, and a rise in the price of all home-made commodities with which gold is purchased or paid for, are effects absolutely incompatible.[145]

Ricardo is right in arguing that under an international gold standard, the importation of additional gold from abroad is incompatible with a rise in the prices of domestically produced commodities, that, in fact, gold would be exported. However, he is incorrect in arguing that prices in general can rise only if the quantity of money is increased. They can rise even if the quantity of money and volume of spending are decreased—if production decreases by still more. Precisely this is what happens in the present case, in which wage rates rise.

This is because in this context the decrease in the quantity of money and volume of spending is itself the cause of an equivalent further decrease in production and supply. In the face of any given level of wages rates and prices, less money and spending mean equivalently smaller quantities of goods and labor demanded, which last means an equivalently smaller quantity of labor employed and thus an equivalently smaller supply of goods produced. For example, in the face of any given level of wage rates and prices, 10 percent less money and spending in a country mean a 10 percent reduction in the quantity of goods and labor demanded and thus a 10 percent reduction in employment and production. A second 10 percent reduction in money and spending means a second such reduction in employment and production, and so on. Yet, over and above the reductions in the quantity of labor employed and output produced as the result of less money and spending, there still remains the reduction in employment and production as the result of the rise in wage rates itself.

That is, once the quantity of money and volume of spending stabilize at any point, however much they may have been reduced, the fact that wage rates are higher in the face of the demand for labor that then exists means an inversely proportionate reduction in the quantity of labor demanded and thus in employment and output. Thus, with a reduction in output in inverse proportion to the rise in wage rates, prices must rise in direct proportion to the rise in wage rates, no matter what has happened to the quantity of money and volume of spending. The outcome is dictated by the law of supply and demand.[146]

The gold outflow Ricardo described goes on only until the point is reached at which the supply of products produced has fallen sufficiently to equal the smaller quantity of products demanded at the higher prices needed to cover the higher wage rates. The outcome can be viewed as the limitation to price increases imposed by foreign competition ultimately being overcome by virtue of the country's production being restricted to those goods in which it has sufficient comparative advantage to obtain the necessary higher prices. If there are no such goods, the arbitrary imposition of the higher wage rates would ultimately serve simply to destroy the country in question as a seat of production.

Ricardo advances another argument attempting to show that product prices cannot rise because of a rise in wage rates. This is the claim that to the same degree that a rise in wage rates might tend to raise the value of commodities, it also tends to raise the value of gold, with the result that product prices—the exchange ratios of commodities against gold—remain unchanged.[147]

Here Ricardo violates his normal assumption that the monetary unit possesses invariable value, and thus that all changes in the value of commodities proceed from the side of commodities, not from the side of money. He implicitly assumes that the rise in wage rates reduces the supply of gold to the same extent that it reduces the supply of other commodities, and, therefore, prevents any rise in their prices. This assumption is false, however. While a rise in wage rates does imply a reduction in the production of gold, it by no means implies a reduction in the supply of gold. This is because at any given time, the current production of gold, or any commodity money, constitutes only a small fraction of its total supply, which is the accumulation of many years of its production. A reduction in its current production would almost certainly imply merely a slowing down in the increase of its supply. Thus, the effect of the rise in wage rates would still be a rise in prices—at least in comparison with what they otherwise would have been. This would be the case insofar as the production of ordinary commodities was reduced in the face of the same or still increasing quantity of money and volume of spending.[148]

Furthermore, as I have shown, profits as such are not a source of funds for the payment of additional wages; profits are an accounting abstraction. As we have seen, the only possible actual source of funds for the payment of a larger amount of total wages in response to a rise in wage rates would be a diversion of funds from the purchase of capital goods or from the personal consumption expenditure of the businessmen and capitalists. The diversion of funds from the purchase of capital goods to the payment of wages—even if it occurred—would not serve to reduce the amount or rate of profit. It would merely serve to reduce the supply of capital goods and the productivity of labor and thus to raise unit costs and prices all the more.

There is simply no reason to expect a diversion of funds from the personal consumption expenditure of businessmen and capitalists to the payment of wages. A higher degree of saving and productive expenditure—that is, a higher economic degree of capitalism—would be required. But there is no basis for such a development taking place merely because of an approach of real wages to subsistence.

Even if, in dire circumstances, employers could be prevailed upon to increase the wages of their employees out of a sense of charity, the increase in the money paid to them would not be wages, but a charitable contribution. Any employer who appears to pay wages that are higher than those which, in accordance with the conditions of the market, he must pay, does not pay wages, but grants charity. It makes no difference whether the recipient is his son-in-law who is worth only $25,000 per year, but to whom he pays $50,000 in order to please his daughter, or any other employee or employees.

In the virtually impossible case of everyone's nominal wage coming to contain a significant component of charity, the fact would remain that the component would not be a portion of their wages, but a portion of the employer's own income or wealth which he saw fit to give away.

If it were merely their income that employers disposed of in this way, then, of course, profit would not be reduced. It would still be earned, but consumed in a different manner. Ironically, if it were not their income, but part of their capital that they chose to give away in charity, then, precisely as the result of a fall in productive expenditure relative to fixed sales revenues, the aggregate amount of profit in the economic system would actually *rise*, and so too, correspondingly, would the average rate of profit. This is because such a development would imply lower aggregate costs in the face of given aggregate sales revenues. What would be present here would be a rise in the rate of net consumption.[149]

Thus, the essential effect of an arbitrary rise in wage rates, if it did occur, and were prevented from being reversed because of a lack of freedom of competition, would be unemployment and less production. The effect of this, in turn, would ultimately have to be a rise in prices sufficient to cover the higher wage rates, not, as Ricardo argues, a decline in the rate of profit. These observations, of course, remove all remaining basis both for Ricardo's belief in the tendency of the rate of profit to fall with an increase in population and for his related belief that the tendency toward a falling rate of profit is interrupted by improvements in the production of wage earners' necessities, which allegedly reduce wage rates and thus allegedly raise the rate of profit. As I have shown, the average rate of profit in the economic system is not determined by wage rates, and wage rates, of course, are not determined by the price of wage earners' necessities. Ricardo's argument for a falling rate of profit is simply incorrect in every essential respect.

4. Other Proponents of the Net-Consumption/Net-Investment Theory

I arrived at the essentials of the net-consumption/net-investment theory in 1959, on the basis of the writings of the British classical economists and of Ludwig von Mises, and of a longstanding dispute with Murray Rothbard about whether or not the rate of profit had to fall as the accompaniment of capital accumulation.[150] At the time, and for a number of years thereafter, I believed the theory to be entirely my own, original discovery. In the course of writing my doctoral dissertation, however, in which I presented the substance of the theory and attempted to develop its leading implications, I learned that in the mid-1950s Joan Robinson had propounded, as I put it then, "a theory of profit which in form is almost indistinguishable from my own, though in substance it is much closer to Schumpeter's theory."[151]

Further investigation revealed that Mrs. Robinson, in turn, had been preceded by some twenty years by the Polish Marxist Michael Kalecki, from whose writings she had learned the doctrine. Kalecki's exposition originally appeared in journal articles in 1935 and was later presented in his book *Theory of Economic Dynamics,* first published in 1952.[152]

Apart from the fact that both of these authors are clearly in possession of the formula that aggregate profit equals the sum of net consumption plus net investment (though they do not use the expression "net consumption"), there is surprisingly little further similarity between the doctrine presented by them and the doctrine presented by me. This becomes clear even in the manner of arriving at the doctrine. I quote the substance of Kalecki's derivation of the doctrine in full:

> We may consider first the determinants of profits in a closed economy in which both government expenditure and taxation are negligible. Gross national product will thus be equal to the sum of gross investment (in fixed capital and inventories) and consumption. The value of gross national product will be divided between workers and capitalists, virtually nothing being paid in taxes. The income of workers consists of wages and salaries. The income of capitalists or gross profits includes depreciation and undistributed profits, dividends and withdrawals from unincorporated business, rent and interest. We thus have the following balance sheet of the gross national product, in which we distinguish between capitalists' consumption and workers' consumption:

Gross Profits	Gross Investment
Wages and Salaries	Capitalists' Consumption
	Workers' Consumption
Gross national product	**Gross national product**

> If we make the additional assumption that workers do not save, then workers' consumption is equal to their income. It follows directly then:

> Gross profits = Gross investment + capitalists' consumption.

> What is the significance of this equation? Does it mean that profits in a given period determine capitalists' consumption and investment, or the reverse of this? The answer to this question depends on which of these items is directly subject to the decisions of capitalists. Now, it is clear that capitalists may decide to consume and to invest more in a given period than in the preceding one, but they cannot decide to earn more. It is, therefore, their investment and consumption decisions which determine profits, and not vice versa.[153]

Not only is Kalecki's theory very different than my own in terms of its derivation, but little or no similarity can be found in the major conclusions he draws from the theory. For example, Kalecki declares that "Another long-run influence considered, rentiers' savings [i.e., the savings of businessmen and capitalists] was found to be *an obstacle rather than a stimulus to development.*"[154] Kalecki also seems to embrace the view that a high rate of profit is necessary for investment and that technological progress is necessary as a stimulus to investment. He writes:

> Inventions which occur in the course of a given period make certain new investment projects more attractive. The influence of this factor is analogous to that of an increase in aggregate profits which in the course of a given period makes investment projects generally more attractive than they were at the beginning of this period. Each new invention like each increase in profits gives rise to certain additional investment decisions. A steady stream of inventions in its effect upon investment is comparable to a steady rate of increase in profits.[155]

In Mrs. Robinson's theory, the role of net consumption, which she calls "rentier expenditure" is entirely secondary. Thus, she declares:

> So far we have abstracted from consumption out of profits and the existence of rentier income. This exclusion was made purely for the sake of exposition. Having established *the main lines of the analysis without rentiers*, [viz., without net consumption], we must now introduce them into the model. The political and social importance of consumption out of incomes derived from property is very far reaching, but so far as the analysis of accumulation is concerned we shall find that it complicates the argument *without requiring any substantial change.*[156]

In all, Mrs. Robinson devotes about twenty pages of her 435-page book to the discussion of net consumption, including all of its ramifications.[157] In large measure the concept comes up only in connection with a discussion of the wage bill paid in the "investment sector" as making possible a surplus of sales receipts in the consumers' goods industries over wages paid by the consumers' goods industries alone.[158] Of these twenty pages, only a few paragraphs constitute either a discussion of the concept itself or an attempt to prove that it is a determinant of profits. No connection whatever is seen to exist between net consumption and either Mill's proposition that demand for commodities is not demand for labor (which Mrs. Robinson frequently contradicts), or Ricardo's doctrine that "profits fall as wages rise." (Mill does not even appear in the index, and Ricardo is mentioned only in connection with the erroneous doctrine of the so-called Ricardo effect, to which Mrs. Robinson subscribes.[159]) Kalecki too seems totally unaware of any connection between the concept of net consumption and the writings of the classical economists.

In Mrs. Robinson's eyes, the primary determinant of profits is what she calls "net investment." It is not the case, however, that this means we both have the same theory but each emphasize the determinant of profits which the other treats as subordinate. For what Mrs. Robinson and I mean by net investment are two entirely different things. I mean by the term the difference between the *monetary value* of the assets purchased by business enterprises and the *monetary value* of the assets used up by business enterprises—i.e., the difference between productive expenditures and aggregate business costs. She means by the term the *physical* growth in the amount of goods between two points in time.[160] Thus her theory is in reality a quasi-productivity theory, along the lines of Schumpeter's theory.[161]

The fact that Mrs. Robinson, Kalecki, and I share the same essential formula for the determination of aggregate profit is nonetheless true, however surprising it may be, in view of all the enormous substantive differences that exist between us not only with respect to the development and application of the net-consumption/net-investment theory, but with respect to virtually every other aspect of economic theory. They are advocates of socialism, while I, of course, am an advocate of laissez-faire capitalism. Because of this, I could never conceive of cooperating with them in any manner, and thus I never attempted to contact Mrs. Robinson, who continued to be prominent in the economics profession for many years after I became aware of her theory of profit.

Notes

1. As I showed, saving is further necessary in order to make possible the purchase of all expensive consumers' goods. On these points, see above, pp. 694–696.

2. See above, pp. 696–697.

3. Concerning the Keynesian claim that the rate of profit is "too low," see below, pp. 867–878.

4. Actually, it will be somewhat larger. This is because the numerator will include profits that represent remuneration necessary to compete with the wages and salaries that the businessmen involved could earn by working elsewhere, as employees. As I have pointed out this is of particular significance in the case of small businessmen and introduces an element of permanent inequality in the rate of return on capital in favor of small business. On this point, see above, p. 186.

5. Cf. above, pp. 186–187. See also above, pp. 520–522.

6. Unfortunately, more often than not, the latter procedure is the practice today. See, for example, the discussion of the theory of capital in Paul Samuelson and William Nordhaus, *Economics,* 13th ed. (New York: McGraw Hill Book Company, 1989), pp. 720–725.

7. See above, p. 573.

8. See above, p. 176. See also above, p. 558.

9. See above, pp. 186–187.

10. See above, pp. 569–570 and 651–652.

11. For a discussion of the nature and necessity of time preference, see above, pp. 55–56.

12. See above, pp. 702–705.

13. See above, pp. 700–702.

14. There is an exception to the principle that the demand for capital goods is simultaneously business sales revenues. This is the case of the purchase of second-hand capital goods from sellers who are not dealers in the goods. For example, a restaurant's purchase of a used delivery truck from a bakery would not constitute sales revenue to the bakery. The bakery's sales revenue is derived only from the sale of the goods it is in business to produce, namely, baked goods, not its old equipment, whose sale is merely incidental to its regular operations. The same would be true of the purchase of a land site from the bakery or almost any other business: namely, the proceeds would not constitute sales revenue to the seller. Similarly, some portion of what is a demand for second-hand capital goods from the perspective of the buyers might constitute receipts to consumers, which receipts are certainly not business sales revenues—for example, the purchase by a business of a used automobile or land site from a consumer. However, little error results from ignoring all such cases. And, for the sake of ease of analysis, that will be our practice. The reason that little error is entailed in this simplifying procedure is that insofar as the purchase of such capital goods results in costs that the buyers must deduct from their sales revenues, the sellers of the capital goods are generally placed in a position in which the costs they must deduct from their sales revenues are reduced. For example, when the bakery sells its old delivery truck, it need no longer depreciate the truck. In addition, to the extent that businesses acquire capital goods by buying used goods from consumers, there are likely to be approximately offsetting sales of used goods by businesses to consumers, with the result that the effect on costs to be deducted from sales revenues should be insignificant. Insofar as such items are not mutually offsetting, it will be found that any effect that might exist with respect to aggregate profits is accompanied by an offsetting effect in the form of capital gains or capital losses.

15. This assumption is actually compatible with the existence of extensive saving on the part of individual wage earners, insofar as their savings are used to finance consumption expenditures of other wage earners or have a counterpart in consump-

tion expenditures by wage earners that are financed by funds obtained from business firms in the form of extensions of credit. For elaboration of this point, see below, p. 735. Nevertheless, even though it is probably descriptively correct, the net-consumption theory does not depend on this assumption. Concerning this fact, see below, pp. 750–754.

16. See above, pp. 702–705.

17. See below, pp. 754–756.

18. For discussion and defense of these definitions, see above, p. 445.

19. See above, p. 710.

20. Strictly speaking, I should say, no counterpart in the kind of productive expenditure and costs that we are interested in, inasmuch as a portion of net consumption, as we know, is made out of interest payments from business. However, as I have explained, we exclude cost on account of interest and the productive expenditure that generates it, because we are interested in profits prededuction of such interest.

21. This assumption has been present at least implicitly since Figure 14–4.

22. The cost value of plant and equipment is present in the cost value of the IK of capital goods on hand, together with that of all other capital goods, such as the materials purchased by business. Because all plant and equipment is assumed to be used up in a single year, the distinction between gross plant and equipment and net plant and equipment disappears.

23. For the meaning of capital, see above, p. 449.

24. See above, pp. 700–702.

25. It is possible, of course, in certain circumstances that new and additional money could be introduced into the economic system to finance dividend, draw, or interest payments.

26. The point also applies to education loans. On the subject of why education does not constitute "human capital" and why the expenditure even for vocational education should not be treated as productive expenditure, see above, pp. 455–456.

27. Table 16–4, like Figure 16–2, shows complete data for *Years 1* and *2*.

28. Later discussion will show why, in the long run, the amount and rate of net consumption must always be significantly positive, and thus that productive expenditure could not lastingly equal, let alone exceed, sales revenues. See below, pp. 750–762 passim. See also below, pp. 856–859.

29. Cf. above, pp. 475–480.

30. The increase in the quantity of money has a similar influence on the monetary value of the capital invested in particular industries and countries. Thus, in the absence of an increase in the quantity of money and volume of spending in the economic system, since, say, 1900, the monetary value of the capital invested in the automobile industry would be greater, though not nearly as much greater as it in fact is, while the monetary value of the capital invested in railroads would be substantially smaller, instead of greater. In the same way, the monetary value of the capital invested in agriculture would be much smaller now than it was in 1900 instead of being greater, while that of the capital invested in industry and commerce would be larger but not nearly as much larger as it now is. The sum of the monetary values of the capitals invested in the United States would be greater, though not nearly as much greater as it in fact is, while that of Western Europe would be substantially smaller

instead of much greater. Over the last thirty years or so, the sum of the monetary values of the capitals invested in the United States would have declined substantially instead of increased, while that of Japan and South Korea rose substantially, though much less substantially than they actually have risen.

31. See above, pp. 327–328.

32. The calculations of net consumption are based on data appearing in U.S. Department of Commerce, Office of Business Economics, *The National Income and Product Accounts of the United States, 1929–1965 Statistical Tables* (Washington, D. C.: U.S. Government Printing Office, n.d.), pp. 14, 150, 152. The amounts of net consumption were calculated by adding up the totals for proprietors' income, corporate profits before tax, rental income of persons, and net interest, and then subtracting the respective magnitudes of negative net investment which, for their part, were found by subtracting capital consumption allowances from gross private domestic investment. In the process all imputations and inventory valuation adjustments were excluded. The subtraction of net investment from profits in order to arrive at net consumption is indicated by the fact that profits equal the sum of net consumption plus net investment, as we already know. See above, p. 723. Indeed, there we saw directly that net consumption is the difference between profits and net investment.

33. Later discussion will show that nothing depends on the individual having an entire year's income available to him at the beginning of the year. Exactly the same results would follow if he had only a quarter's income available to him at the beginning of a quarter, or a month's income available to him at the beginning of a month, or even just a single day's income available to him at the beginning of a day. See below, p. 743.

34. The elimination of negative net investment must take place far short of the point of the exhaustion of assets. As we shall see later in this chapter, the lower is the general rate of profit, the more powerful is the inducement to net investment and thus necessarily the elimination of any negative net investment. See below, pp. 779–784.

35. On the origin of money cf. Carl Menger, *Principles of Economics* (Glencoe, Ill.: The Free Press, 1950), pp. 257–271. See also, above, pp. 506–508.

36. On Smith and the status of consumption and profit in the "early and rude state of society," see above, pp. 475–480.

37. Of course, in order for a high rate of profit actually to be heavily saved and in fact result in the accumulation of a fortune, the individuals in question must attach a greater value to the larger sum of wealth in the future than to the consumption which must be forgone in order to accumulate it. If this is not the case, then even the highest rates of profit do not result in the accumulation of capital.

38. Friedman's doctrine is known as "the permanent income hypothesis." See Milton Friedman, *A Theory of the Consumption Function* (Princeton, N. J.: Princeton University Press, 1957.)

39. Our previous examples concerning the consumption of businessmen and capitalists were constructed on the implicit assumption of a twenty-one year time horizon applied to the consumption of previously accumulated capital and current profit/interest income taken together.

40. Concerning the positive connection between the rate of

profit in real and in monetary terms and the rate of economic progress, see below, p. 775.

41. See above, pp. 55–56.

42. Cf. the discussion of the time preference theory in its traditional form, below, pp. 792–794.

43. See above, pp. 741–743.

44. The 5 percent figure follows from the fact that where i is the annual income on capital and equals $\frac{1}{21} \times (K + i)$, then $21i = K + i$ and thus $20i = K$. This last means that $i = \frac{K}{20}$.

45. It is not necessary, of course, that the concept of time horizon be applied in an all-or-nothing way, in which even provision is made for all the years lying within it and none at all for the years lying beyond it. It might be, for example, that one wants to make even provision for each of the next 10 years and then 50 percent provision for each of the 20 years beyond that. That would be equivalent to having a time horizon in which one wished to make even provision for the next 20 years.

46. See above, p. 58. See also above, pp. 19–21.

47. See above, pp. 702–705. See especially, Table 15–2, on p. 705.

48. Unlike Table 16–3, Table 16–5 shows complete data for *Years 1* and *2*, as did Figure 16–2 and Table 16–4.

49. It should be realized that from the point of view of the magnitude of sales revenues, it is indifferent whether the 100 of additional demand generated by productive expenditure represents 100 of additional demand for capital goods or 100 of additional demand for labor by business resulting in 100 of additional demand for consumers' goods by the wage earners of business, or any combination of such additional demands for the products of business totaling 100.

50. See above, pp. 702–705, especially Table 15–2, on p. 705, and the discussion accompanying it. It should be understood that we are temporarily ignoring taxation and thus the presence of taxes in costs.

51. Net investment and profits are 100 larger in Table 16–9 than in Table 16–8—i.e., 300 and 200 respectively versus 200 and 100 respectively—because the 100 of wage-earner saving is spent for capital goods rather than being hoarded or turned back to business in the form of loans or securities purchases to finance productive expenditure in the following period. In being spent in this way, it adds 100 both to productive expenditure and to sales revenues. In enlarging both productive expenditure and sales revenues by 100 in the face of the same aggregate costs of 600, it adds 100 to both net investment and profits.

52. See above, pp. 648–650.

53. The same principles, to be sure, apply to the use of income other than wages either to pay consumer interest or to purchase consumers' labor.

54. For elaboration of this point, see below, pp. 758–759.

55. It should be realized that the firm's annual depreciation charge never comes to exceed a million dollars, or whatever the assumed constant amount of annual expenditure for the assets in question may be. This is because once an asset reaches the end of its depreciable life, it no longer contributes to current depreciation. In the case of assets with a 20-year depreciable life, in every year from *Year 21* on the depreciation on new assets acquired in the current year merely takes the place of the depreciation of assets now 21 years old and therefore already fully depreciated and no longer subject to additional depreciation.

56. Net investment in connection with the acquisition of land usually does not have a counterpart in aggregate profit, inasmuch as the funds expended in the purchase of land generally do not constitute a sales revenue, but merely receipts from the sale of existing capital or consumer assets. Such net investment does, however, have a counterpart in a *capital gain*, to the extent that a business seller's proceeds from the sale of land exceed his own previous acquisition cost of the land.

57. This usage of the concept of marginal productivity must be distinguished from the common one, in which the concept primarily denotes a net *physical* product attributable to the employment of additional capital goods. For a detailed explanation and discussion of the common usage, see below, pp. 787–788.

58. See below, pp. 787–792, for a detailed critique of the so-called productivity theory of profit/interest.

59. Net investment will not become negative if what places the rate of profit above the marginal productivity of capital is itself the existence of significant net investment and thus the existence of a significant net investment component in the rate of profit. In such a case, the effect will merely be a reduction in the amount of net investment and the size of the net investment component in the rate of profit.

60. The equalization of the rate of profit and the marginal productivity of capital in the sense in which I have been using the concept should not be taken to imply any claim on my part that the rate of profit tends to equalize with the marginal productivity of capital in the usual sense of a marginal net physical product attributable to capital goods. To the contrary, as I will show in my critique of the productivity theory, my analysis of capital accumulation implies that the general marginal net productivity of capital in *this* sense is permanently and substantially higher than the rate of profit. See below, pp. 787–792. The mistaken belief that the rate of profit and the marginal net physical productivity of capital goods tend to equalize leads to the error of taking the rate of profit as the measure of the physical contribution of capital goods to production, which in turn leads to the error of grossly understating the importance of capital goods to production and its increase. On this subject, see below, pp. 776–778. The mistaken belief that the rate of profit and the marginal net physical productivity of capital goods tend to equalize leads to the error of taking the rate of profit as the measure of the physical contribution of capital goods to production, which in turn leads to the error of grossly understating the importance of capital goods to production and its increase. On this subject, see below, pp. 776–778.

61. Concerning the nonsacrificial character of capital accumulation under capitalism, see above, pp. 639–641.

62. See above, pp. 723–725.

63. Concerning the various ways in which a lower rate of profit operates to encourage greater capital intensity, see below, pp. 778–784.

64. The present discussion confirms the view of von Mises that time preference—here operating through the rate of net consumption—is what accounts for the fact that more productive but more time-consuming processes of production are not automatically adopted. See Ludwig von Mises, *Human Action*,

3d ed. rev. (Chicago: Henry Regnery Co., 1966), pp. 482–483, 526.

65. The contribution of wage earners to net consumption exists insofar as they themselves have accumulated sufficient savings, whether in the form of capital or consumer loans, to place them in a position to consume in excess of their wages.

66. In conformity with the actual circumstances of business life, this last can be assumed to constitute a relatively small portion.

67. On the nature of NNP, see above, pp. 675–676 and 700–702. Capital-output ratios as typically computed include in capital the value of owner-occupied housing and the land on which it stands. Capital computed in this way can be taken as an approximation of total accumulated invested savings in the economic system; a virtually exact equivalence would be achieved if the value of homeowners' equity were subtracted and the value of interest-bearing consumer loans other than home mortgages were added. (The value of home mortgages is already implicitly included.)

68. We have already encountered this expression of the capital-output ratio. See above, pp. 302 and 364, in particular in the refutation of the argument that free immigration must reduce the ratio of capital to labor.

69. Concerning the relationship between net national product and national income and the fact that both are necessarily close in amount to consumption, see above, pp. 700–702 and 712.

70. In addition, it should be recalled that net investment is not an actual expenditure, nor, therefore, a demand, as the term is used in this book. On this point, see above, p. 717, n. 60.

71. Though static in terms of monetary magnitudes, such a state of affairs is, of course, perfectly compatible with a rising physical volume of production both of consumers' goods and of capital goods, though a 2:1 capital-net-output ratio would probably be far too low to bring about economic progress in actual practice.

72. See above, pp. 631–632.

73. See above, pp. 228–230, and below, pp. 774–775. For discussion of the analogous distinctions between monetary demand and real demand, and between money wages and real wages, see above, pp. 559–561 and 618–622.

74. See above, pp. 63–66.

75. See above, pp. 531–532.

76. It should be noted that in *Year 4* of Figure 16–3, wage payments and net consumption are rounded and thus do not quite add to the demand for consumers' goods.

77. Because of limited space, all data in the table is rounded to the nearest integer, except for the rate of profit and the change in the rate of profit, which are carried to two decimal places.

78. For an important qualification concerning this last proposition, see below, p. 773.

79. See above, pp. 758–759.

80. Again, see below, for an important qualification concerning the effect of the rate of increase in the quantity of money on the rate of net consumption.

81. See below, pp. 930–937 passim.

82. See below, pp. 951–963, for the full case for a 100-percent-reserve precious metals system.

83. Concerning this aspect of Say's Law, see above, pp. 559–561.

84. These observations confirm previous discussion in connec-
tion with the critique of the demands of labor unions for the paying over of profits as wages. See above, pp. 654–655.

85. See above, pp. 762–763.

86. See above, pp. 754–756.

87. See above, pp. 768–771.

88. For a discussion of the temporal relationship of productive expenditure to sales revenues, see again pp. 768–771, above. See also, below, pp. 820–824.

89. See, for instance, Moses Abramovitz, *Resource and Output Trends in the United States Since 1870* (New York: National Bureau of Economic Research Occasional Paper, no. 52, 1956), pp. 6, 8; and Robert M. Solow, "Technical Change and the Aggregate Production Function," *The Review of Economics and Statistics*, 39, August 1957. See also, above, the quotation from Samuelson and Nordhaus on pp. 630–631, where it is claimed that the rise in the productivity of labor is due mainly to technological progress as opposed to capital accumulation.

90. See, for example, the writings of Abramovitz and Solow cited above.

91. Curiously, in a backhanded way, Abramovitz ends up conceding the actual importance of capital accumulation. After first claiming that "the input of resources per head of the population appears to have increased relatively little, while the productivity of resources increased a great deal" in bringing about "the quadrupling—more or less—of net national product per capita," he ends by acknowledging that "capital per head of the population approximately tripled." This apparent blatant contradiction of first maintaining that an increase in capital per head has not significantly contributed to the increase in output per capita, and then declaring that a fourfold increase in output per capita has been accompanied by a threefold increase in capital per capita, is left altogether unexplained. See Abramovitz, pp. 8, 10.

92. See above, pp. 712–714.

93. See above, pp. 648–650.

94. The principle that a fall in revenue relative to capital creates a need for more capital accords with my previous finding concerning the significance of high capital requirements. That finding was that far from representing any kind of infringement of the freedom of competition, high capital requirements are evidence of the existence of high competitive standards. A large capital, I showed, is necessary in order to achieve the low costs needed to be profitable in the face of the low prices charged by others. See above, p. 376.

95. On this subject, see above, Chapter 6, n. 1.

96. For an account of the various specific ways in which this can occur, see above, pp. 754–756.

97. Within the borders of any individual country, of course, an increase in the quantity of commodity money is achieved as soon and insofar as the country's increased production increases its share of world production and thus of the money supply of the world economy.

98. The significance of negative net investment in counteracting the influence of net consumption in the generation of profits is indicated by the data for the years 1932 and 1933, cited above, on pp. 739–740.

99. See above, pp. 589–590. See also the preceding note.

100. Actually, a 5 percent annual increase in the money supply raises the rate of profit to slightly more than 10 percent, in that

1.05 times 1.05 is slightly more than 1.10. This kind of result is implicit insofar as there is any induced rise in the rate of net consumption.

101. The same, of course, would be true of a rise in the rate of profit attributable to a rise in the rate of net investment that occurred independently of the increase in the quantity of money.

102. Concerning the undermining of capital formation by means of the overconsumption that inflation causes, see below, pp. 930–937 passim.

103. See above, pp. 576–578.

104. Eugen von Böhm-Bawerk, *Capital and Interest*, 3 vols., trans. George D. Huncke and Hans F. Sennholz (South Holland, Ill.: Libertarian Press, 1959), 1:74. According to Böhm-Bawerk, the original quotation is from Wilhelm Roscher, *Grundlagen der Nationalökonomie*, 10th ed., sec. 189.

105. (The figure of 75 is arrived at by taking the average of 150 fish and zero fish and of corresponding intermediate amounts; 150 fish is the capital outstanding on the last day of the construction of the boat and net and on the first day of their use, while zero is the capital outstanding at the beginning of the first day of the accumulation of capital for their construction and at the end of the last day of their use.

106. Samuelson and Nordhaus, *Economics*, p. 721. Italics supplied.

107. See above, p. 558.

108. See above, pp. 556–558. See also above, pp. 629–632.

109. See below, pp. 813–820.

110. See above, pp. 459–462.

111. For elaboration on these connections, see above, pp. 475–480.

112. See above, ibid.

113. See above, pp. 762–774.

114. Capital intensiveness in the relative-value sense, it should be recalled, refers to the value of accumulated capital relative to wages, consumption, and sales revenues.

115. Böhm-Bawerk, *Capital and Interest*, 2:259, 265. See also von Mises, *Human Action*, p. 483, and above, pp. 55–56.

116. See above, pp. 484–485.

117. Murray N. Rothbard, *Man, Economy, and State*, 2 vols. (Princeton, N. J.: D. Van Nostrand Company, Inc., 1962), 1:332.

118. See above, pp. 480–483.

119. The productivity theory implies the doctrine of secular stagnation insofar as it leads to the conclusion that the cause of a low rate of profit is a lack of technological progress.

120. See above, p. 256.

121. Cf. Böhm-Bawerk, *Capital and Interest*, 2:265–266.

122. See, for example, Irving Fisher, *The Theory of Interest* (1930; reprint ed., New York: Kelley & Millman, 1954), pp. 36–38. See also—regrettably—von Mises, *Human Action*, pp. 541–545.

123. On the errors of the belief that falling prices caused by increased production reduce the rate of profit, see above, pp. 569–573 and below, pp. 814–817. For further discussion of the specific errors in the doctrine of the purchasing-power price premiums, see below, pp. 825–826.

124. Irving Fisher, *The Theory of Interest*, p. 327. Italics supplied. A more recent statement of the same doctrine can be found in Rothbard, *Man, Economy, and State*, 1:390.

125. See David Ricardo, *Principles of Political Economy and Taxation*, 3d ed. (London, 1821), chap. 1, secs. 4–7; reprinted as vol. 1 of *The Works and Correspondence of David Ricardo*, ed. Piero Sraffa (Cambridge: Cambridge University Press, 1962), pp. 30–51. Subsequent page references to the Sraffa edition appear in brackets.

126. See above, pp. 55–56.

127. Böhm-Bawerk, *Capital and Interest*, 2:442, n. 23.

128. See ibid., pp. 268–273.

129. See above, pp. 683–685, 720–721, and 725–734.

130. Ricardo, *Principles of Political Economy and Taxation*, chap. 6 [p. 111].

131. It is relevant to note that Ricardo's chapter "On Profits," in which the above passage appears, contains an opening footnote reminding the reader that "I consider money to be invariable in value." This, of course, means the assumption of a fixed aggregate value of the consumers' goods.

132. Cf. above, pp. 787–790.

133. This interpretation of Ricardo's theory, I believe, is fully consistent with his discussion of value in sec. 7 of his chapter on that subject, and helps greatly to clarify that discussion. See above, pp. 495–496.

134. See above, pp. 683–684. Italics added.

135. Essentially the same point was made earlier, in my critique of the exploitation theory. See above, pp. 478–480.

136. See above, pp. 647–650.

137. See above, pp. 494–495.

138. See above, ibid. See also above, pp. 607–642.

139. Cf. von Mises, *Human Action*, pp. 773–776.

140. For the explanation of how a lower rate of profit encourages greater capital intensiveness, see above, pp. 779–784.

141. Ricardo, *Principles of Political Economy and Taxation*, chap. 5 [p. 93].

142. See above, pp. 494–495.

143. It must be kept in mind that the conditions being described are those of an essentially stagnant society, such as existed prior to the Industrial Revolution, certainly not those of laissez-faire capitalism.

144. Concerning the reduction in the demand for labor as the result of the rise in land rents, see above, p. 668.

145. Ricardo, *Principles of Political Economy and Taxation*, chap. 5 [p. 105].

146. The only thing that would prevent prices from rising in proportion to wage rates would be the extent to which a reduced volume of production might be accompanied by a higher productivity of labor. However, such a result is extremely unlikely in view of the greater efficiencies in a division-of-labor society that are the result precisely of the employment of a larger number of workers rather than a smaller number of workers.

147. Cf. Ricardo, *Principles of Political Economy and Taxation*, chap. 1, sec. 3 [p. 28].

148. The reduction in the production of gold would, however, imply a modest reduction in the rate of profit, inasmuch as it would mean a reduction in the rate of increase in spending of all kinds and thus in the rate of net investment. Such a reduction would be of a nonrepeatable nature inasmuch as wage rates could not continue to be arbitrarily driven up in the face of the mounting unemployment that would result. On this last point, see below, pp. 909–911.

149. For elaboration of the principles and mechanisms involved, see above, pp. 725–734.

150. As stated in the Preface, I maintained that it did not; he maintained that it did.

151. See Joan Robinson, *The Accumulation of Capital* (Homewood, Ill.: Richard D. Irwin, 1956.) See also George Reisman, *The Theory of Aggregate Profit and the Average Rate of Profit*, Ph.D. diss., New York University Graduate School of Business Administration (1963; reprinted by University Microfilms, Inc., Ann Arbor, Mich.), p. 247.

152. See Michael Kalecki, "Essai d'une Théorie du Mouvement Cyclique des Affaires," *Revue d'Economie Politique*, Mars-Avril 1935; "A Macrodynamic Theory of Business Cycles," *Econometrica*, July 1935; *Theory of Economic Dynamics, An Essay on Cyclical and Long-Run Changes in CapitalistEconomy* (1952; reprint ed., New York: Augustus M. Kelley, 1969.)

153. Kalecki, *Theory of Economic Dynamics*, pp. 45–47. Emphasis in original.

154. Ibid., p. 161. Insert and italics added.

155. Ibid., p. 158.

156. Joan Robinson, p. 247. Insert and italics added.

157. This and the following paragraph are taken with little change from my doctoral dissertation, *The Theory of Aggregate Profit and the Average Rate of Profit*, pp. 247–248.

158. Joan Robinson, ibid., pp. 43–44, 75, 255.

159. For a critique of this doctrine, see above, pp. 798–799.

160. Joan Robinson, ibid., pp. 74, 76, 255.

161. Cf. Joseph Schumpeter, *The Theory of Economic Development* (Cambridge, Mass.: Harvard University Press, 1951).

CHAPTER 17

APPLICATIONS OF THE INVARIABLE-MONEY/ NET-CONSUMPTION ANALYSIS

1. The Analytical Framework

In this chapter, I develop, or further elaborate on, a wide variety of major implications and applications of the net-consumption/net-investment theory which could not be presented in the course of expounding the basic theory itself. These concern the effects on the rate of profit (or, in some cases, lack of effect), of capital accumulation, falling prices caused by increased production, technological progress, taxation, government budget deficits, the so-called international balance of trade, and net saving. I also further develop the implications of the theory insofar as they pertain to the so-called average period of production, the relationship between capital intensiveness and technological progress, the doctrine of price premiums in the rate of interest, the process by which real wages are increased, and the theory of saving in general. In connection with the subject of saving, I develop the contrasting significance of net saving under an invariable money and under a money whose quantity increases, and thus show both the relationship between increases in the quantity of money and net saving and that the actual significance of saving lies at the gross level rather than the net level. I also develop the implications of my analysis for the critique of such prominent fallacies respecting saving as the doctrines of underconsumptionism and the alleged lack of profitable investment opportunities.

In order to develop all these implications, it is necessary to return to the assumption of an invariable money, despite the fact that under a commodity-money system the virtually inevitable effect of economic progress is to bring about an increase in the quantity of money and volume of spending. The assumption of an invariable money is necessary in order to understand the *separate connections* of phenomena to the rate of net consumption and to the rate of increase in the quantity of money—and, of course, to the rate of net investment apart from the increase in the quantity of money. Because it makes it possible to relate phenomena to the separate elements determining the rate of profit, the assumption of an invariable money is essential to the understanding of practically every aspect of the theory of profit and its applications.

For the sake of simplicity, it is also necessary to return to the further assumptions that all capital goods and labor in existence at the beginning of a year are entirely used up in producing the capital goods and consumers' goods that are available at the start of the following year and that all financial transactions take place on a single day, at the beginning of each year.

Thus, to carry our analysis further, we must turn now to Figure 17–1 "Profits in a Progressing Economy with an Invariable Money." Figure 17–1 represents exactly the same kind of analysis of assets and spending and revenue as presented in Figure 16–2, but in combination

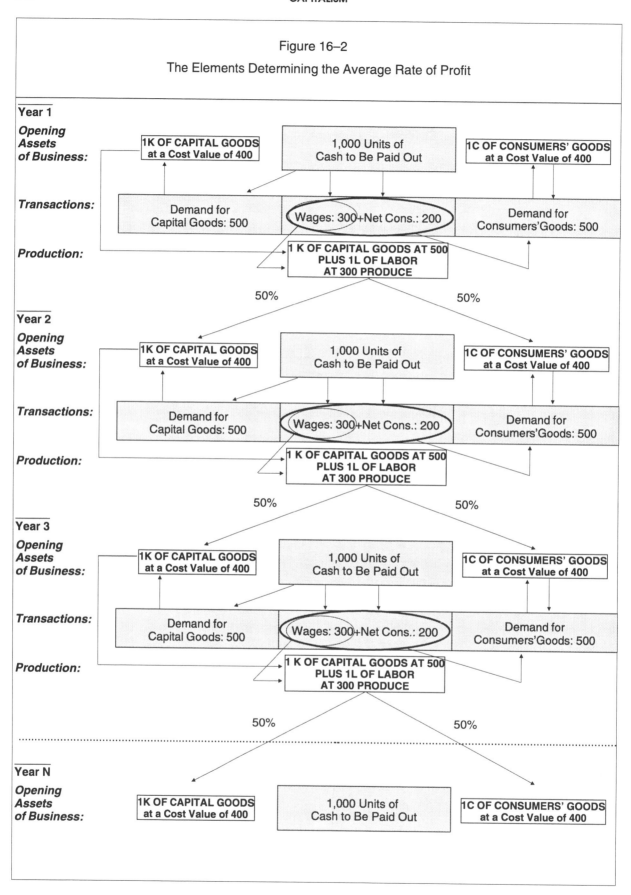

Figure 16–2

The Elements Determining the Average Rate of Profit

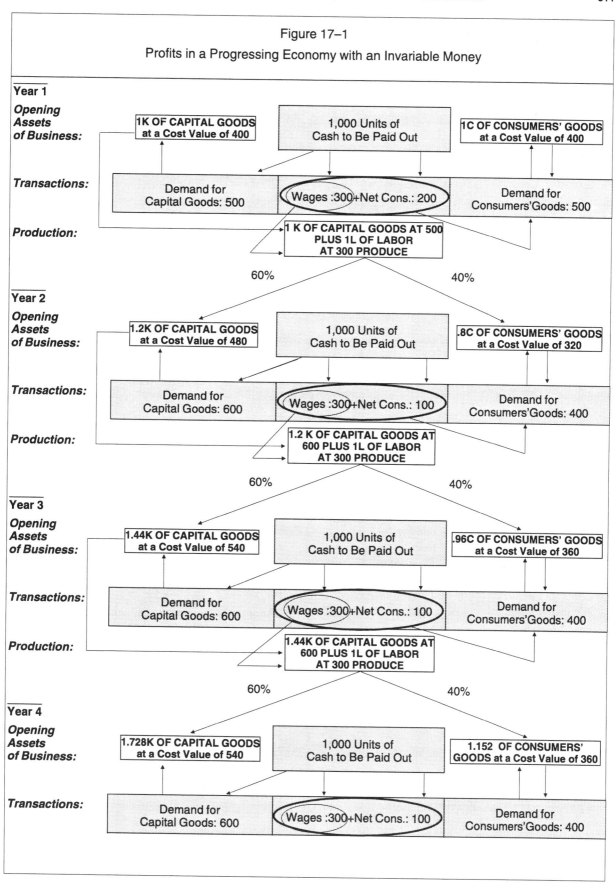

Figure 17–1

Profits in a Progressing Economy with an Invariable Money

with the capital accumulation and rising production depicted back in Figures 14–5 and 15–6. Figure 17–1 is to Figure 16–2, as Figure 14–5 is to Figure 14–4, and as Figure 15–6 is to Figure 15–5. For the reader's convenience, Figure 16–2 is reproduced preceding and facing Figure 17–1.

Strictly speaking, Figure 17–1 is somewhat more elaborate than Figure 16–2 in that, in addition to showing the course of capital accumulation from *Year 2* on, it also depicts the transition from a stationary economy to a progressing economy. *Year 1* of Figure 17–1 opens in exactly the same way as do all the years described in Figure 16–2. Even the financial transactions of *Year 1* of Figure 17–1 are identical with those of the years described in Figure 16–2. The transition to the conditions of a progressing economy begins to take place only in the production phase of *Year 1*. Here the 1K of capital goods purchased at the start of the year for 500 units of money, and the 1L of labor purchased for 300 units of money, come to be employed 60 percent in the production of capital goods and only 40 percent in the production of consumers' goods. In other words, the relative production of capital goods now rises to a level at which capital accumulation and economic progress will take place.

This change in the relative production of capital goods from the conditions of Figure 16–2 is, of course, the result of correctly anticipating the change in the relative demands for capital goods and consumers' goods which will occur in *Year 2* and remain in place thereafter. In *Year 2*, and every year thereafter, the demand for capital goods will stand at 600 units of money rather than the 500 of *Year 1* and all the years of Figure 16–2. By the same token, the demand for consumers' goods in *Year 2*, and every year thereafter, will stand at only 400 units of money rather than 500. Thus, exactly as in the earlier analysis of capital accumulation depicted in Figures 14–5 and 15–6, the 60/40 relative production of capital goods takes place in response to the correct anticipation of the relative demands for capital goods and consumers' goods coming to stand in a 60/40 ratio.

The 60/40 relative production of capital goods is sufficient to achieve capital accumulation because, just as before, it is assumed that for each existing 1K of capital goods employed in conjunction with 1L of labor, it is possible to produce combinations of capital goods and consumers' goods within the limiting extremes of 2K, 0C and 0K, 2C.[1] Thus, as in Figures 14–5 and 15–6, starting with 1K of capital goods, a 60/40 relative production results in 1.2K of capital goods and .8C of consumers' goods.

Figure 17–1 provides a direct means of understanding the relationship between the rate of profit in the economic system and all manner of other major economic phenomena. In the space of a single page, it provides an analytical framework representing the essential elements of the productive process under the conditions of economic progress. In so doing, it makes it possible to intellectually grasp their operation and mutual interconnection virtually by a process of direct observation. To know and understand, for example, the relationship between the rate of profit and capital accumulation, or between the rate of profit and falling prices caused by increasing production, such as results from capital accumulation, all one need do is look at Figure 17–1, and then explain what one observes in terms of further information either presented in the figure itself or at least readily suggested by it and derivable from it. In effect, the figure constitutes a virtual laboratory in which one captures the essential pattern of economic progress in a monetary economy in an intellectually manageable size, and is then able to look at it from every possible angle and, as it were, poke and prod it and see exactly how it responds.

Thus, the figure shows that starting in *Year 2* capital accumulation takes place at a 20 percent compound-annual rate and that, as a result, starting at the beginning of *Year 3*, the total supply of goods available for sale in the economic system increases at a 20 percent compound-annual rate.[2] Since the demands for capital goods and consumers' goods are both assumed to be fixed at 600 and 400 units of money respectively in every year from *Year 2* on, the increases in supply that take place in every year starting from *Year 3* on imply correspondingly falling prices every year, that is, prices which fall in inverse proportion to the increase in supply, namely, in the ratio of 5:6.

Observe. Even though the figure stops with *Year 4*, for lack of space for additional years, it should be taken as projecting the continuation of the relationship between *Years 3* and *4* into the indefinite future. Thus, year after year, the figure shows both capital accumulation and the implication of falling prices resulting from the increase in production caused by capital accumulation. However, it also clearly implies a definite rate of profit in each of those years, on the basis of the various monetary transactions generating sales revenues, costs, and capital values. The figure thus provides an ideal analytical framework within which to ask and answer the questions: "Does the process of capital accumulation require or cause a falling rate of profit?" and, "Do falling prices caused by increasing production reduce the rate of profit?" The answer to these and other important questions can now be found by a process of simple inspection.[3]

2. Why Capital Accumulation and the Falling Prices Caused by Increased Production Do Not Imply a Falling Rate of Profit

And just what are the answers to the above two questions concerning whether or not capital accumulation and the falling prices caused by increased production imply a falling rate of profit? On the basis of Figure 17–1, the answers are clearly in the negative. This is because Figure 17–1 shows that in every year, from *Year 3* on, while capital goes on accumulating at a rate of 20 percent and prices fall at the inversely proportionate rate of $16\frac{2}{3}$ percent, the rate of profit remains *constant* at slightly more than 5 percent.

This rate of profit reflects the existence year after year of 1,000 monetary units of sales revenues in the economic system, 900 monetary units of productive expenditure (which is the sum of 600 of demand for capital goods plus 300 of wage payments or demand for labor), and 1,900 of total monetary value of accumulated capital. These data result in an amount of profit of 100—viz., 1,000 of sales revenues minus 900 of costs generated by the previous year's productive expenditure. When this amount of profit is divided by the 1,900 of capital, the resulting rate of profit is 5.26 percent.

The value of accumulated capital from *Year 3* on is the sum of opening inventories of capital goods with a cost value of 540 and consumers' goods with a cost value of 360, plus 1,000 units of cash to be paid out. The cost values of 540 and 360 for the opening inventories of capital goods and consumers' goods derive from the preceding year's productive expenditure of 900 applied 60 percent to the production of capital goods and 40 percent to the production of consumers' goods. These cost values, when the goods in question are sold for the 600 annual demand for capital goods and the 400 annual demand for consumers' goods, imply an annual amount of profit of 100 units of money ($100 = 600 - 540 + 400 - 360$). As I say, the division of this 100 of profit by the 1,900 of monetary value of accumulated capital then gives an average rate of profit of 5.26 percent.

As promised, Figure 17–1 also contains the *explanation* of why capital accumulation and the falling prices caused by increased production take place without a fall in the rate of profit. The explanation is that the only fall in the rate of profit that is present is a one-time fall, resulting from the fall in the rate of net consumption from an initial level of $200/1,800$ in *Year 1* to $100/1,900$ in *Year 2* and thereafter, that is, from 11.11 percent to 5.26 percent. (In *Year 2*, this fall in the rate of net consumption is accompanied by the existence of 100 of net investment. Thus, the fall in the rate of profit to 5.26 percent does not take place until *Year 3*, with the disappearance of net investment.[4])

The one-time fall in the rate of net consumption is the foundation of a *permanent* rise in the relative production of capital goods to a level sufficient to achieve capital accumulation. Once the initial increase in the supply of capital goods is achieved in *Year 2*, on the basis of this rise in their relative production, *further increases in the supply of capital goods take place on the basis of the increased productive ability bestowed by the existence of a larger supply of capital goods in the current year compared with the year before.* Thus a continually growing relative demand for and production of capital goods, and the continually falling rate of net consumption (and thus rate of profit) that would achieve them, are not required for capital accumulation. On the contrary, the larger supply of capital goods in *Year 2* than in *Year 1* all by itself makes possible a larger supply of capital goods in *Year 3* than in *Year 2*, and the same holds true mutatis mutandis in all subsequent years.

This is because all by itself the larger supply of capital goods in *Year 2* than in *Year 1* enlarges the total productive power of *Year 2* as compared with *Year 1*. And thus, with the same relatively greater concentration on the production of capital goods, namely, the $60/40$ ratio, the greater productive power of *Year 2* as compared with *Year 1* results in a larger supply of capital goods as well as consumers' goods becoming available in *Year 3* as compared with *Year 2*. In exactly the same way, the larger supply of capital goods in *Year 3* as compared with *Year 2* increases the total productive power of *Year 3* as compared with *Year 2*. The result of the application of this larger total productive power in the same higher ratio, namely, $60/40$, results in a correspondingly larger supply of capital goods as well as consumers' goods in *Year 4* as compared with *Year 3*. And so on, indefinitely, with each year's larger supply of capital goods as compared with the year before, serving to increase its total productive power as compared with the year before and thus, so long as a sufficiently high relative production of capital goods continues, to further increase the supply of capital goods available in the following year.

As explained in Chapter 14, in order for capital accumulation to continue on the foundation of prior increases in the supply of capital goods, technological progress is necessary. But granted that it is present, capital accumulation continues without any further necessary connection to a fall in the rate of profit. Indeed, Figure 17–1 implies that any further fall in the rate of profit would be the result not of capital accumulation, but of factors working to bring about an *acceleration* of the rate of capital accumulation—namely, a further fall in the rate of net consumption and corresponding further increase in the relative demand for and production of capital goods.

For example, an acceleration of capital accumulation would be the result of a further fall in net consumption from 100 to 50, and corresponding further rise in the production of capital goods relative to consumers' goods to a 65:35 ratio, reflecting a 650-demand for capital goods and a 350-demand for consumers' goods. In these circumstances, the supply of capital goods and the ability to produce would increase at a 30 percent annual rate instead of a 20 percent annual rate.[5]

To be sure, if technological progress does not take place, capital accumulation cannot continue in this way. But no significant capital accumulation could then be accomplished in any case, no matter how much the rate of net consumption and the rate of profit might fall. As we have seen, in the absence of technological progress over the course of the last two centuries, no great increase in the supply of capital goods could have occurred—period. As explained in Chapter 14, an economy whose technological limits are described by sailing ships, ox-carts, and forges is simply incapable of accumulating the kind of capital that can be accumulated only on the basis of railroads and steel mills, and then airplanes and petro-chemical plants, and the continuing technological progress that all these goods presuppose.[6]

Figure 17–1 makes it possible to understand the error of the economists who believe that capital accumulation implies a falling rate of profit. The error consists, at least in part, of thinking only of what is necessary to bring about the *first* accumulation of additional capital goods in an economy that up to that point has been stationary, and then failing to consider what the effect will be of the possession of those additional capital goods on the sub-sequent ability to produce capital goods.

This failure to consider the consequences of the pos-session of more capital goods on the production of capital goods is the result of the habit of most economists of focusing almost exclusively on the production of con-sumers' goods, as though all that were produced were consumers' goods, and as though capital goods came into existence only by the allegedly very different and unre-lated process of saving.[7] As I have previously explained, this very bad habit is a result of all the utterly confused notions about aggregate production and aggregate spend-ing that I refuted in Chapter 15, notions which imply that aggregate production and aggregate spending are essen-tially coextensive with the production of and demand for consumers' goods alone.[8] This mistaken constellation of ideas leads most economists to believe in effect that all capital accumulation must take place in the same way as it does in *Year 2,* that is, on the basis of greater saving in the context of an invariable money and thus on the basis of an increase in the demand for capital goods relative to the demand for consumers' goods. If that were in fact the

only way in which capital accumulation could occur, capital accumulation would imply a falling rate of profit, because then it would almost certainly imply a falling rate of net consumption.[9]

That most economists mistakenly believe this is the only way in which capital accumulation occurs is im-plicit in their assuming that capital accumulation takes place only by virtue of an act of saving in conditions in which all other things are equal. The condition "all other things equal" includes the demand for and supply of money—that is, it necessarily implies the existence of an invariable money. Repeated acts of saving under an invariable money *would* result in a falling rate of profit. But, as we know, such acts of saving are unnecessary. Each act of saving in such conditions stands in the same relation to capital accumulation as does force to the acceleration of mass in the world of physics. Most econ-omists are unaware of this because they do not carry their analysis to the point of seeing what the effect of the additional capital goods accumulated on the basis of saving is on the further production and supply of capital goods. They do not do this because they do not even stop to realize that capital goods are used to produce capital goods. And they do not do this, in turn, because they are blinded by the mistaken belief that the only goods which are produced are consumers' goods, whose production allegedly "counts" the total of production, and that it is "double counting" to consider the production of capital goods separately.

Apart from the above constellation of errors, the no-tion that capital accumulation implies a falling rate of profit is probably the result of nothing more than the fallacy of composition, as described in connection with the discussion of Say's Law and the consequences of *relative* overinvestment.[10] Here, the fact that the rate of profit earned in any given industry falls insofar as addi-tional capital investment in it takes place *relative to the rest of the economic system*, is mistakenly taken as the basis for assuming that additional capital investment in the economic system as a whole reduces the general rate of profit.

The explanation of the ability of prices to fall without the rate of profit being reduced is first of all the fact that what determines the rate of profit under the conditions of an invariable money is the rate of net consumption. So long as the rate of net consumption is the same, then—apart from the temporary role played by net investment—the rate of profit is the same. The fact that production increases and prices fall implies nothing whatever about the rate of profit. In such circumstances, precisely as Figure 17–1 makes it possible to see, *an increase in the supply of products is preceded by an equivalent increase in the supply and or productivity of the factors of production used to produce them.* This prior equivalent increase in the supply and or productivity of the factors of production implies *an equivalent and prior reduction in the average unit costs of production,* with the result that when prices fall because of an increase in production, there is no reduction in the rate of profit.

Thus, for example, the supply of products available for sale at the beginning of *Year 4* increases in the ratio of 6 to 5 over the supply available at the beginning of *Year 3.* That is, in *Year 4* it is *1.728K* of capital goods versus the *1.44K* of capital goods of *Year 3,* which is an increase of 20 percent, and *1.115C* of consumers' goods versus the *.96C* of consumers' goods of *Year 3,* which is also an increase of 20 percent. Given that the respective demands for capital goods and consumers' goods remain fixed at 600 and 400 monetary units respectively, the inescapable inference is that prices fall in the inverse proportion of 5 to 6. However, it can be clearly seen in Figure 17–1 that this fall in prices does not represent any fall whatsoever in the rate of profit in *Year 4* in comparison with *Year 3.* The rate of profit in both years is 5.26 percent, reflecting 100 of net consumption, and thus 100 of profit, divided by 1,900 of capital.

What happens, as the necessary accompaniment of the increase in production in conditions of an invariable money and a constant rate of net consumption, is that the 20 percent larger supply of capital goods and consumers' goods in *Year 4* in comparison with *Year 3,* is the result of a *preceding* 20 percent larger supply of capital goods in *Year 3* in comparison with *Year 2,* and a preceding 20 percent increase in the productivity of labor. That preceding increase in the supply of capital goods (namely, the *1.44K* of capital goods of *Year 3* versus the *1.2K* of capital goods of *Year 2*) coming in the face of a fixed 600 monetary units of demand for capital goods, implies a preceding fall—back in *Year 3*—in the prices of capital goods in the ratio of 5 to 6, the same ratio by which the prices of capital goods and consumers' goods now fall in *Year 4.* For the rest, the ability of the same *1L* of labor to produce a 20 percent larger supply of goods for sale at the beginning of *Year 4* in comparison with the supply available at the beginning of *Year 3* implies a 20 percent rise in the average productivity of labor in *Year 3* in comparison with *Year 2,* and thus an inversely proportionate fall in unit labor costs in *Year 3* in comparison with *Year 2.* The reason that unit labor costs fall in this way, is that a rise in the productivity of labor always implies an inversely proportionate fall in the quantity of labor required to produce a unit of product. If the productivity of labor increases by 20 percent—that is, if the same quantity of labor now can produce six-fifths the output as before—the consequence is that the quantity of

labor required to produce any given unit of output is now on average only five-sixths as great as before. And thus, as is the case in Figure 17–1, with the same total wages—300 monetary units—paid to the same total quantity of labor—*1L*—and thus unchanged average wage rates, unit labor costs fall to five-sixths of their previous level. Unit labor costs, of course, are nothing but the product of wage rates times the required quantity of labor. With average wage rates the same and the required quantity of labor per unit only five-sixths as great, unit labor costs are five-sixths as great.

Thus, the fall in prices in *Year 4* is preceded by a fully equivalent fall in average unit costs of production: both costs on account of capital goods—whose prices fall in the same proportion as the prices of the products they help to produce, and fall first—and costs on account of labor—whose productivity rises in proportion to the larger supply of products it helps to produce, and whose cost per unit of product therefore also falls in the same proportion as the selling prices of the products, and falls first.

Despite the fact that average profit per unit also falls—viz., in the same proportion as the price and unit cost—the result is, of course, that the aggregate amount of profit remains the same. This is because the fall in average profit per unit is precisely offset by the increase in production and supply that causes it and that at the same time is in inverse proportion to it. The result of this is that when the reduced average profit per unit is multiplied by the inversely proportionate larger number of units, the aggregate amount of profit is the same.

And so things can continue in *Year 5* and all the other subsequent years, which lack of space makes it impossible actually to show in Figure 17–1. In each year, prices, unit costs, and profits per unit all fall in the ratio of 5 to 6, and, because this is the result of production and supply increasing in the ratio of 6 to 5, the respective arithmetical products of these quantities times the quantity of goods produced and sold—namely, aggregate sales revenues, aggregate costs, and aggregate profits—always remain constant.

Indeed, the fixity of aggregate sales revenues and aggregate costs is the starting point of analysis in most of Figure 17–1, and the constancy of aggregate profit is directly derivable from their fixity. (It is, of course, simply the difference between them.) It is their fixity that accounts for the fall in prices, unit costs, and profits per unit always being in inverse proportion to changes in production and supply, so long as their fixity continues.

It is implicit in the preceding discussion, that nothing whatever depends on any constant rate of increase in production being maintained. It will *always* work out that the fall in cost per unit—both labor cost per unit and capital-goods cost per unit—will be in proportion to the fall in prices and, of course, will precede the fall in prices inasmuch as the sums giving rise to the costs are expended prior to the receipt of the sales revenues. Thus, if it had happened, for example, that the increase in supply at the beginning of *Year 4* in comparison with *Year 3* had been only 10 percent instead of 20 percent, that is, that the production of *Year 3* had been in the ratio of 11 to 10 to that of *Year 2,* rather than 6 to 5, then the fall in prices in *Year 4* would have been in the ratio of 10 to 11, instead of 5 to 6.

At the same time, in the face of this lesser increase in output relative to the same quantity of labor, the rise in the productivity of labor in *Year 3* in comparison with *Year 2* would also have been only 10 percent. Thus the fall in unit labor costs would have been in the correspondingly lower ratio of 10 to 11, just as the fall in prices. For now ten-elevenths rather than five-sixths of the previous quantity of labor would have been required to produce any given unit of output, and thus with the same average wage rates (resulting from the constancy of the demand for labor at 300 monetary units and of the supply of labor at *1L*), unit labor costs would have been reduced to this, more limited extent.

By the same token, the 20 percent larger supply of capital goods in *Year 3* in comparison with *Year 2* would have had to be employed with a diminished productivity to result in an increase in output of only 10 percent. The corollary of this diminished productivity of capital goods is a corresponding increase in the quantity of capital goods employed per unit of product. Specifically, if six-fifths the capital goods result in the production of only eleven-tenths the output, it follows both that the output per unit of capital goods has fallen in the ratio of 11 to 12 and that the quantity of capital goods required per unit of output has risen in the inverse ratio of 12 to 11. (A rise in output in the ratio of 11:10, divided by the preceding increase in the supply of capital goods in the ratio of 6:5, implies an output per unit of capital goods of 55:60, which, of course, reduces to 11:12. When the output per unit of capital goods is only eleven-twelfths, twelve-elevenths is the quantity of capital goods required to produce the average unit of output.) Twelve-elevenths the quantity of capital goods per unit of output times five-sixths the prices of capital goods is sixty sixty-sixths, which reduces to ten-elevenths. This is the reduction in the capital-goods cost per unit of output, i.e., the same as the reduction in the price of the product.

In exactly the same way, if the increase in production and supply in *Year 4* in comparison with *Year 3* had been more than 20 percent, the correspondingly greater fall in prices would have been accompanied by a correspondingly greater productivity of labor and productivity of

capital goods, which would have resulted once again in unit costs of production falling to the same extent as selling prices, and falling first.

Thus, the principle here is that the fall in prices and the prior fall in unit costs must always be in the same proportion, when a larger output is sold for a given amount of sales revenues and is produced on the basis of a given outlay of money for factors of production. Selling prices fall because of the division of a constant amount of sales revenues by a larger output. Unit costs fall to precisely the same extent, because of the division of a constant amount of expenditure for factors of production by that *same* larger output. In terms of Figure 17–1, the relationships are that the price level of any given year equals 1,000 of sales revenues divided by the total output of the year before, which constitutes the supply available for sale at the start of the current year. The unit-cost level of any given year equals 900 of productive expenditure from the year before, divided by that same output. Thus, the more rapidly output increases, the lower becomes the price and unit-cost levels in precisely the same proportion. Aggregate profit meanwhile always remains at 1,000 – 900, that is, at 100, and the average rate of profit at $100/1,900$. [11]

In the context of Figure 17–1, of course, the productive expenditure of any year shows up as the next year's total costs of production. But the equality of productive expenditure and costs of production does not depend on this. As has been shown, under an invariable money, it tends to exist no matter how the productive expenditures of any given year are distributed with respect to production for future years. Productive expenditure and costs *always* tend toward equality, so long as the quantity of money and volume of spending in the economic system remain the same. [12]

Thus, the rate of profit is totally unaffected by the mere rate of increase in physical production and corresponding rate of fall in prices. So long as sales revenues, productive expenditure, and the amount of capital invested stay the same, the amount and rate of profit remain the same, no matter how rapidly production increases and prices fall. For it is then always merely a question of dividing two unequal expenditures or demands—viz., the demand for products, which constitutes sales revenues, and the demand for factors of production, which constitutes productive expenditure and gives rise to equivalent costs—by more rapidly growing denominators. No matter how rapid the growth in these "supply denominators," so to speak, and no matter how rapid the fall in prices, there is no effect on the amount of profit, which is the difference between the two "demand numerators," to coin another expression. And so long as the amount of capital invested is the same, there can also be no difference in the average rate of profit.[13]

Once again, in terms of Figure 17–1, the relationships are that the price level of any given year equals 1,000 of sales revenues divided by the total output of the year before—which is the supply of goods available for sale at the start of the current year—while the unit-cost level equals 900 of productive expenditure from the year before, divided by that same total output. The more rapidly output increases, the lower become the price and unit-cost levels in precisely the same proportion, for all that is reflected is the division of 1,000 and 900 by a denominator that is increased in the same proportion in both instances and, indeed, is always exactly the same in both instances. Aggregate profit meanwhile always remains at $1,000 - 900$. In sum, where S represents aggregate output (the output of capital goods and consumers' goods together), the general price level equals $1,000/S$, the unit-cost level equals $900/S$, and aggregate profit equals $1,000 - 900$. The principle, to say it yet again, in somewhat different words, is that profit depends on the difference between the demand numerators, not on the relationship between one of the demand numerators and its supply denominator. That is, profit depends on the difference between the demand for the products of business and the demand for factors of production by business, on sales revenues minus productive expenditure—in a word, on net consumption—not on prices or the change in prices.

Observe that the only fall in the rate of profit implied by Figure 17–1 occurs in *Year 3*, and that it occurs not as the result of any increase in production and consequent fall in prices, but as the result of the preceding fall in the rate of net consumption and the subsequent elimination of the net investment that took place on the basis of the fall in net consumption. Furthermore, even that one-time fall in the rate of profit, which, it cannot be repeated too often, is in no way caused by the increase in production and fall in prices, would in no way be diminished by any lesser rate of increase in production and fall in prices. If somehow the supply of goods in *Year 3* had not increased over the supply in *Year 2*, prices would not have fallen in *Year 3*. But the fall in the rate of profit would have been exactly the same. The situation then would merely have been that instead of *1.44K* of capital goods and *.96C* of consumers' goods having been produced for outlays of 540 and 360 units of money respectively, only *1.2K* of capital goods and *.8C* of consumers' goods would have been produced for the same outlays. The result would have been exactly the same rise in aggregate costs and fall in the amount and rate of profit but no increase in production or fall in prices, and, of course, no fall in unit costs of production.

Confirmation of Fact That Falling Prices Caused by Increased Production Do Not Constitute Deflation

The present analysis constitutes a full confirmation of the conclusion reached in Chapter 13 that falling prices caused by increased production do not constitute deflation.[14] Such falling prices do not reduce the average rate of profit. Furthermore, inasmuch as in the nature of the case the average seller must have a supply of goods to sell that is as much enlarged as prices are lower, it follows that there is no greater difficulty entailed in earning any given sum of money at the lower prices that prevail later on than at the higher prices that prevailed earlier. Thus, there is nothing present in falling prices caused by increased production that would make the repayment of debt any more difficult.

The only possible associated element which could temporarily make the repayment of debt more difficult is the fall in the rate of net consumption that results in a corresponding one-time reduction in the rate of profit at the same time that it inaugurates the increase in production and fall in prices. In Figure 17–1, this is the fall in the rate of net consumption that takes place in *Year 2* and which lowers the rate of profit in *Year 3*. If interest rates on loans had not been reduced in anticipation of this fall in the rate of profit, repayment of debt would be rendered more difficult until they were. But, as just shown, even this would not be the result of the increase in production and fall in prices and would not be helped in any way if the increase in production and fall in prices were less or altogether nonexistent. It would be strictly the result of the one-time, delimited fall in the rate of net consumption and thus in the rate of profit.

In fact, however, it is likely that in the period of transition to a lower rate of profit, the rate of interest would fall pretty much in pace with the rate of profit, if not in advance of the fall in the rate of profit. For one thing, in reality the fall in the rate of profit resulting from a fall in the rate of net consumption would not be sudden and precipitous, as it is in Figure 17–1. A more or less extended period of time would exist during which net investment would take place, which would both increase the degree of capital intensiveness in the economic system and to a greater or lesser extent offset the fall in the rate of net consumption. And the fall in the rate of net consumption itself would likely be slow and gradual rather than occur all at once in a single year. Thus the decline in the rate of profit would be gradual. As the rate of profit fell, it would be accompanied by a gradual fall in the rate of interest.

In addition, the very fact that the process is the result of a decline in the rate of net consumption and corresponding rise in saving operates to reduce the rate of interest immediately. This is because the rate of interest falls as soon as additional savings appear on the loan market in the face of the prevailing initial rate of profit. Because of this, it is probable that the fall in the rate of interest would actually precede the fall in the rate of profit, which, of course, for its part, would be delayed insofar as net investment went on. In addition, the declining rate of interest would give rise to numerous refinancings, thereby tending to reduce the burden of interest payments throughout the economic system. Thus, in the case of a fall in the rate of profit caused by a fall in the rate of net consumption, there would be no sudden plunge in the rate of profit in the face of a large volume of contractually fixed interest rates geared to a substantially higher rate of profit, which is what occurs in a period of deflation or financial contraction.

Indeed, the very fact that a fall in the rate of net consumption entails a rise in saving and productive expenditure, extensive net investment and the formation of new capital giving rise to a higher degree of capital intensiveness, and makes possible a correspondingly greater availability of credit, characterizes it as the very opposite of a period of deflation or financial contraction. In a deflation or financial contraction, productive expenditure falls, net investment becomes negative, capital values decline, and credit becomes largely unobtainable.

Furthermore, looking now at matters over the longer term, once we recall that a by-product of a growing ability to produce is a growing quantity of commodity money, and the effect on the rate of profit of increases in the quantity of money, it becomes obvious that the falling prices resulting from increasing production are almost certain to be accompanied by *a positive addition to the rate of profit*. They are also almost certain to be accompanied by a growing ability to repay debt, because of the growing volume of sales revenues taken in by the average seller as the result of the increasing quantity of money.[15] It should always be kept in mind that in the context of economic progress under a system of commodity money, the fall in prices is the result of a combination of circumstances in which there is an increase in money and spending, but in which the increase in production and supply outstrips the increase in money and spending.

At the same time, of course, it also becomes obvious that the fall in the rate of profit that is the accompaniment of launching or accelerating the process of capital accumulation by means of a fall in the rate of net consumption, is in part reversed by that same positive addition to the rate of profit that accompanies increasing production and its by-product an increasing quantity of commodity money. This is because the increasing production and its monetary by-product are the result of the capital accumulation launched by the fall in the rate of net consumption.

More on the Relationship Between Technological Progress and the Rate of Profit

Observe that Figure 17–1 also fully confirms the discussion in Chapter 13 concerning the alleged effects of technological progress on the rate of profit. It makes it possible to see that technological progress does not raise the rate of profit by "increasing the demand for capital," but rather prevents the fall in prices caused by increasing production from lowering the rate of profit. This is because the actual effect of technological progress is, along with increasing the supply of consumers' goods, to increase the supply and lower the prices of capital goods and to raise the productivity of labor, both of which, as shown, cause unit costs to fall to the same extent as prices and to do so prior to the fall in prices, so that when prices fall there is no fall in the amount or rate of profit. Indeed, it is only by virtue of increasing the supply of capital goods and/or the productivity of labor that technological progress serves to increase the supply of consumers' goods. And thus the fall in the prices of consumers' goods that technological progress is undeniably accountable for is inseparably connected with a preceding fall in the unit costs of production, for which technological progress bears equal responsibility.[16]

The only positive connection between technological progress and the rate of profit is by way of the increase in the quantity of commodity money that is the by-product of a growing ability to produce. Insofar as technological progress underlies a growing ability to produce, and thus a growing quantity of commodity money, it is indirectly the source of an addition to the rate of profit, namely, of the monetary component in the rate of profit. Furthermore, insofar as this monetary component is at the same time the net investment component in the rate of profit, technological progress may be said to be the indirect source of net investment and the net investment component in the rate of profit.[17]

This last connection is doubly ironic when understood against the backdrop of the prevailing Keynesian fallacies, which regard net investment not only as in no way based on technological progress, but also as requiring technological progress to offset its allegedly negative effects on the rate of profit. The double irony is the fact that the only way in which technological progress does contribute to the rate of profit is precisely in its capacity *as the source of net investment,* which, far from reducing the rate of profit, represents a major component of the rate of profit. Just as technological progress is not required as an "outlet" for capital goods accumulated merely by means of saving, but is itself the source of capital goods, so in its relation to the increase in the supply of commodity money it is not an outlet for net investment, but is itself the source of net investment. And this net investment, through the contribution it makes to the rate of profit, can in turn be described as providing its own outlet for profitable investment.

Ricardo's Insights on Capital Accumulation

The fundamental relationship between technological progress and increases in production, on the one side, and the rate of profit, on the other, is clearly understood by Ricardo, who writes:

> The rate of profits is never increased by a better distribution of labour, by the invention of machinery, by the establishment of roads and canals, or by any means of abridging labour either in the manufacture or in the conveyance of goods. These are causes which operate on price, and never fail to be highly beneficial to consumers; since they enable them with the same labour, or with the value of the same labour, to obtain in exchange a greater quantity of the commodity to which the improvement is applied; but they have no effect whatever on profit.[18]

Ricardo, of course, writes in the context of an invariable money, which for him signifies the employment of the same total quantity of labor in the economic system, while for us it means the expenditure of the same total amount of money to buy newly produced goods. And, of course, he refers to the general or average rate of profit, not to the particular rates of profit of innovators or of those who must compete against the innovators. As we know, technological progress increases the profits of the innovators and decreases the profits of those against whom the innovators compete. What it does not do is raise the general or average rate of profit—the rate of profit that is earned taking innovators and laggards together—except, of course, to the extent that it results in an increase in the supply of commodity money and thus in the volume of spending in the economic system.

With no less remarkable insight, Ricardo implicitly grasps the role of technological progress in capital accumulation and sees that in the context of an invariable money, capital can be accumulated without continuous acts of saving, that is, without continuous increases in productive expenditure and the demand for capital goods relative to the demand for consumers' goods. In his chapter "Value and Riches, Their Distinctive Properties," he declares:

> From what has been said, it will be seen that the wealth of a country may be increased in two ways: it may be increased by employing a greater portion of revenue in the maintenance of productive labour, which will not only add to the quantity, but to the value of the mass of commodities; or it may be increased without employing any additional quantity of labour, by making the same quantity more productive, which will add to the abundance, but not to the value of commodities.

> In the first case, a country would not only become rich, but the value of its riches would increase. It would become rich by parsimony—by diminishing its expenditure on objects of luxury and enjoyment, and employing those savings in reproduction.

> In the second case, there will not necessarily be either any diminished expenditure on luxuries and enjoyments, or any increased quantity of productive labour employed, but, with the same labour, more would be produced; wealth would increase, but not value. Of these two modes of increasing wealth, the last must be preferred, since it produces the same effect without the privation and diminution of enjoyments which can never fail to accompany the first mode. Capital is that part of the wealth of a country which is employed with a view to future production, and may be increased in the same manner as wealth. An additional capital will be equally efficacious in the production of future wealth, whether it be obtained from improvements in skill and machinery [viz., technological progress and or a larger previous supply of capital goods], or from using more revenue reproductively [viz, saving]; for wealth always depends on the quantity of commodities produced, without any regard to the facility with which the instruments employed in production may have been procured.[19]

All one need do to make these passages fully accord with the views I have been propounding is to substitute for the fixity of the quantity of labor as the basis of an invariable money, the fixity of the quantity of money itself and thus of the total volume of spending to buy newly produced goods. Then it is clear that in such a context, saving—viz., a fall in consumption expenditure and rise in productive expenditure—represents an increase in the monetary value of the capital employed in production, and, if productive expenditure remains at the higher level, an increase in the total cost-value of commodities. This is the way capital accumulation begins in Figure 17–1, when net consumption falls from 200 monetary units to 100 and the rise in productive expenditure increases the cost value of output from 800 to 900 monetary units. It is also clear that capital accumulation can take place without further such saving, as the rest of Figure 17–1 shows. Indeed, Ricardo argued that it is even possible for capital accumulation to take place in the face of *smaller* aggregate value of capital—in the face of a smaller relative production of capital goods. He writes in his chapter "On Wages":

> Or capital may increase without its value increasing, and even while its value is actually diminishing . . . the addition may be made by the aid of machinery, without any increase, and even with an absolute diminution in the proportional quantity of labor required to produce [the goods constituting capital]. The quantity of capital may increase, while neither the whole together, nor any part of it singly, will have a greater value than before, but may actually have a less.[20]

Such a situation can be imagined in terms of the

economic system shifting from the conditions of Figure 17–1 to conditions somewhere between those of Figure 17–1 and those of Figure 16–2. In such an intermediate situation, represented, for example, by the demand for capital goods being 550 instead of 600, and total productive expenditure being 850 instead of 900, capital accumulation would continue, though at a less rapid rate than in Figure 17–1. It would be accompanied by a reduction in the total value of accumulated capital and in the total cost value of the output produced. It would also be accompanied by a rise in the amount and rate of profit.

As the next section of this chapter will show, however, there are more or less strict limits to the extent to which capital accumulation is possible in the face of a fall in productive expenditure and the relative demand for capital goods, and thus to the case Ricardo describes. This is because the ability to implement technological advances vitally depends on the relative production of capital goods.[21]

The Rate of Profit and the Demand for Money

Preceding discussion has shown repeatedly that as far as the rate of profit is concerned, there is a fundamental distinction between falling prices caused by increasing production and falling prices caused by a falling quantity of money and volume of spending. Essentially, only the latter is associated with a fall in the rate of profit. The former is not.[22]

It is also necessary to realize that there is a fundamental distinction with respect to the effect on *the demand for money for holding,* between a fall in the rate of profit caused by a fall in the quantity of money and volume of spending—i.e., deflation—and a fall in the rate of profit caused by a fall in the rate of net consumption. Only the former operates to raise the demand for money for holding. The latter does not.

There are two reasons for this. First, unlike a fall in the quantity of money and volume of spending, a fall in the rate of net consumption cannot render the rate of profit negative. At most, it can only reduce the rate of profit to a lower positive number.[23] Second, as we have seen, in the nature of the case, a fall in the rate of profit caused by a fall in the rate of net consumption is accompanied by an increase in the supply of savings and thus an increase in the availability of credit.[24] As I showed in Chapter 12, a greater supply of savings and a consequent greater availability of credit operate to reduce the demand for money for holding. It follows that in such an environment, any tendency of a lower rate of return on capital to increase the demand for money for holding, by virtue of reducing the advantages of investing in comparison with holding cash, is necessarily accompanied by off-

setting factors that work in the opposite direction.[25]

Of course, beyond this, a fall in the rate of net consumption is virtually certain to result in a less than equivalent fall in the rate of profit, because of its indirect effects on the rate of increase in the supply of a commodity money, as we have also seen.[26] Finally, as I will show later in this chapter, the effect of any increase in the demand for money for holding that for any reason might occur is ultimately to raise the rate of net consumption and rate of profit.[27]

3. Why Capital Accumulation Does Not Depend on a Continuous Lengthening of the Average Period of Production

The analysis of Figure 17–1 has shown conclusively that neither capital accumulation nor falling prices caused by increased production imply a falling rate of profit or wiping out of profit or are in any way "deflationary."

Essentially the same analysis demonstrates the error of believing that capital accumulation implies a continuous lengthening of the average period of production or structure of production. Both of these concepts, which mean essentially the same thing, can be expressed in terms of the differing conditions of Figures 16–2 and 17–1.

In Figure 16–2, 50 percent of the capital goods and labor of each year are used in producing consumers' goods for the following year, and the remaining 50 percent, in producing capital goods for the following year. Inasmuch as the capital goods of the following year are in turn themselves used 50 percent to produce consumers' goods for the year after that, it follows that of the half of the labor and capital goods used in any given year to produce capital goods for the following year, half of that half, or 25 percent, indirectly serves in the production of consumers' goods in the year following the following year, that is, in the year after next. The implication of this is that by the end of *two* years, 75 percent of the capital goods and labor in existence in any year will have ended up directly or indirectly serving in the production of consumers' goods—50 percent in the production of the consumers' goods of the following year, and 25 percent in the production of the consumers' goods of the year after that.

By an extension of the same reasoning, it further follows that by the end of three years, the cumulative proportion of capital goods and labor in existence in any given year that will have ended up directly or indirectly serving in the production of consumers' goods will be 87.5 percent, and so on. This is because the capital goods in existence in the year after next and which reflect the remaining 25 percent of the labor and capital goods of

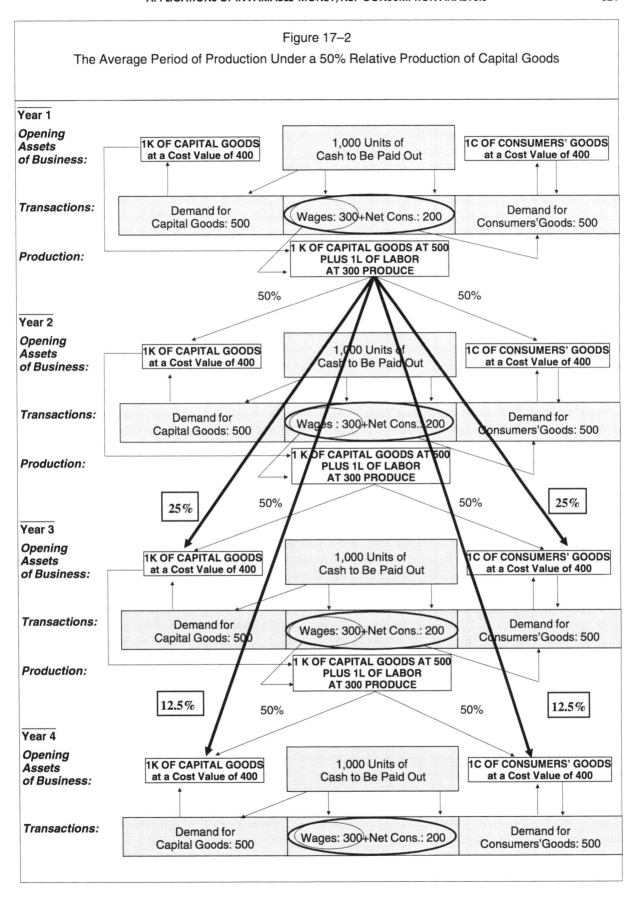

Figure 17–2

The Average Period of Production Under a 50% Relative Production of Capital Goods

two years earlier that has not yet contributed to the production of consumers' goods, are now used 50 percent in the production of consumers' goods of three years later.[28]

The cumulative increase in the proportion of the capital goods and labor of any given base year that directly or indirectly serves in the production of consumers' goods is clearly indicated in Figure 17–2, which superimposes on Figure 16–2 the connections between the supply of labor and capital goods in a given base year and the supplies of consumers' goods and capital goods of various future years. Figure 17–2 takes *Year 1* as the base year and shows the extent to which the capital goods and labor of that year not only directly serve in the production of capital goods and consumers' goods for the following year, but also indirectly serve in the production of capital goods and consumers' goods that become available at the beginning of *Years 3* and *4*.

The figure shows 25 percent of the capital goods and labor of *Year 1* indirectly serving in the production of the capital goods of *Year 3*, and 25 percent indirectly serving in the production of the consumers' goods of *Year 3*. These percentages reflect the fact that 50 percent of the capital goods and labor of *Year 1* are used up in producing the capital goods of *Year 2*, of which, in turn, 50 percent are used up in producing the capital goods of *Year 3*, and 50 percent in producing the consumers' goods of *Year 3*. (In both cases, 50 percent of 50 percent yields an indirect contribution of 25 percent.) The fact that 25 percent of the capital goods and labor of *Year 1* thus indirectly serve in producing the capital goods available at the start of *Year 3* and that these capital goods, in their turn, are used up 50 percent in the production of the capital goods that will become available at the start of *Year 4* and 50 percent in the production of the consumers' goods that will become available at the start of *Year 4*, underlies the further fact that 12.5 percent of the capital goods and labor of *Year 1* indirectly serve in producing the capital goods of *Year 4* and 12.5 percent indirectly serve in producing the consumers' goods of *Year 4*.

In this way, with the passage of years, the cumulative proportion of the capital goods and labor in existence in any base year that directly or indirectly serves in the production of consumers' goods continually grows, while the proportion continuing to serve indirectly in the production of capital goods and thus of consumers' goods in the still further future continually declines.

One can express the concept of the average period of production or the length of the structure of production in terms of how many years must elapse before some given percentage of the capital goods and labor in existence in a base year will have ended up directly or indirectly serving in the production of consumers' goods. If that given percentage is taken as 90 percent, then the length of the average period or structure of production in the conditions of Figure 16–2 is obviously somewhere between three and four years, for in three years 87.5 percent of the capital goods and labor in existence in a base year will have ended up directly or indirectly serving in the production of consumers' goods, while at the end of four years, the figure will be 93.75 percent—viz., 87.5 percent plus 50 percent of 12.5 percent, which, of course, is 6.25 percent.

Proceeding now in the same way in the conditions of Figure 17–1 (which are reproduced in Figure 17–3), it is clear that here the length of the average period or structure of production is somewhat greater. Figure 17–3 superimposes on Figure 17–1 the connections between the supply of labor and capital goods in a given base year—once again *Year 1* has been chosen for this purpose—and various future years. It shows the indirect contribution of the capital goods and labor of *Year 1* to the capital goods and consumers' goods available at the start of *Years 3* and *4* in the conditions of the higher relative production of capital goods that prevails in Figure 17–1.

Because 60 percent of the capital goods and labor of *Year 1* are used to produce the capital goods of *Year 2*, 60 percent of which are used up in producing the capital goods of *Year 3* and 40 percent of which are used up in producing the consumers' goods of *Year 3*, the capital goods and labor of *Year 1* indirectly serve 36 percent in the production of the capital goods of *Year 3* (.6 x .6) and 24 percent in the production of the consumers' goods of *Year 3* (.4 x .6). Because the capital goods of *Year 3* in turn are used up 60 percent in the production of further capital goods and 40 percent in the production of consumers' goods, the further indirect contribution of the capital goods and labor of *Year 1* to the capital goods and consumers' goods of *Year 4* is 21.6 percent (.6 x .36) and 14.4 percent (.4 x 21.6) respectively. For *Year 5* (not shown in the figure), their indirect contribution is 60 percent of the 21.6 percent and 40 percent of the 21.6 percent respectively, viz., 12.96 percent and 8.64 percent respectively.

It follows that the cumulative contribution of the capital goods and labor in existence in a base year to the production of consumers' goods over the following four years, that is, through *Year 5,* will be the sum of $.4 + (.4 \times .6) + (.4 \times .6^2) + (.4 \times .6^3)$, that is, 87.04 percent. Thus the length of the average period or structure of production in this case is greater than four years, for obviously more than four years must elapse before 90 percent of the capital goods and labor in existence in a base year end up serving directly or indirectly in the production of consumers' goods. In the conditions of Figure 16–2, of

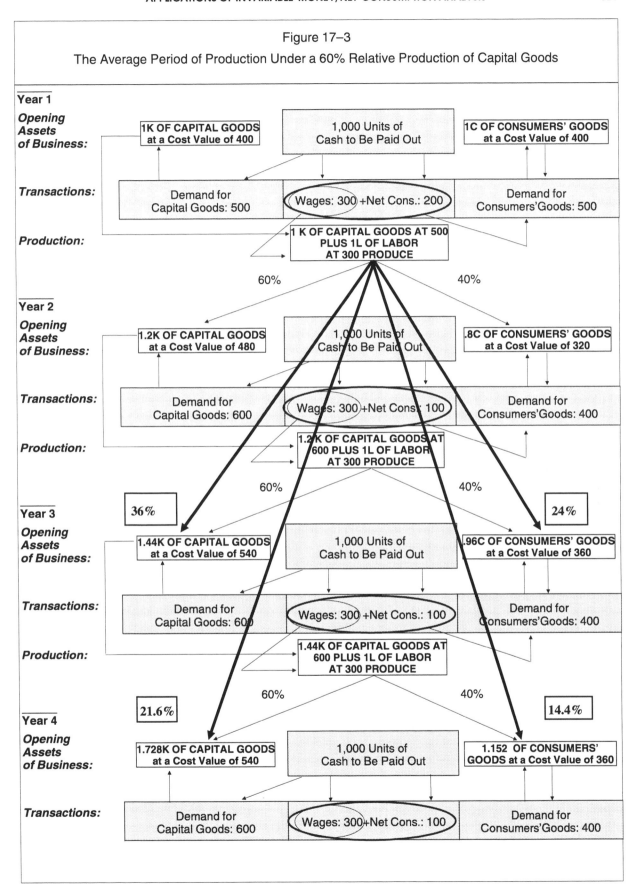

Figure 17–3

The Average Period of Production Under a 60% Relative Production of Capital Goods

course, the cumulative total of 90 percent was reached in less than four years.

Now what is essential for present purposes is merely to realize that while the length of the average period or structure of production in the conditions of Figure 17–1 is greater than in those of Figure 16–2, once that greater length has been established, capital accumulation thereafter proceeds *without any further such lengthening.* A further such lengthening of the average period of production would be identical to a further rise in the *relative production of capital goods,* which, of course, is not necessary to the continuation of capital accumulation, but to its *acceleration.*[29]

The Average Period of Production and the Limits to Technological Progress as a Source of Capital Accumulation

The concept of the average period of production sheds further light on the necessity of a sufficiently high economic degree of capitalism and degree of capital intensiveness in order for capital accumulation and economic progress to take place. At the same time, it makes clear the limits of technological progress as a source of capital accumulation. The longer is the average period of production, the greater is the foundation on which technological progress can be applied. It can be applied to a correspondingly greater extent in the production of future products requiring temporally more remote applications of existing capital goods and labor and, by the same token, in the production of present products requiring the application of relatively more capital goods and labor existing in past years.

For example, imagine two different economic systems. In one, the average period of production is such that fully 10 percent of the capital goods and labor of any given base year serves in the production of capital goods and consumers' goods that will become available in five years. In the other, the average period of production is such that less than 1 percent of the capital goods and labor of any given base year serves in the production of capital goods and consumers' goods that will become available in five years. It is obvious that technological progress that relates to the kinds of capital goods or consumers' goods specifically requiring productive activity five years in the past will be much more likely to be capable of being implemented in the first economic system than in the second. A concrete example of this might be the construction of such things as factory buildings, bridges, and tunnels with an actual construction time of five years. If hardly any of the capital goods and labor of a given year are devoted to the production of goods that become available five years later, then technological progress in the construction of such things may simply be altogether incapable of application.

Figures 17–2 and 17–3 can be used as illustrations of the differing extents to which the past can serve the present, as well as the present serve the future. In looking backward from any year, the proportions of the labor and capital goods of past years serving the production of any present year taken as a base are greater in Figure 17–3 than in Figure 17–2, and become relatively greater the more remote are the past years. For example, 60% vs. 50% for one year past; 36% vs. 25% for two years past; 21.6% vs. 12.5% for three years past; 12.96% vs. 6.25% for four years past, and so on. It is possible to implement technological advances in the conditions of Figure 17–3 which it is not possible to implement in the conditions of Figure 17–2, because of this greater contribution of the past to the present, and of the present to the future.[30]

This discussion, of course, reinforces the conclusions reached earlier about the role of capital intensiveness in determining an economy's ability to implement technological progress.[31]

It should be realized that a more-capital-intensive economic system is at absolutely no disadvantage in comparison with a less-capital-intensive economic system when it comes to implementing technologies requiring less capital intensiveness. The capacity for implementing more-capital-intensive technologies always subsumes the capacity for implementing less-capital-intensive technologies, while the reverse is not the case. It is the same in principle as the fact that a millionaire always has the ability to come down the scale and live like an average person if he wishes, while the average person lacks the ability to go up the scale and live like a millionaire.

For example, an economy that was sufficiently capital intensive to be capable of turning out thirty-year-old scotch for the mass market, would have no difficulty in turning out eight-year-old scotch for whatever part of the market might wish it. However, without greater capital intensiveness in the economic system as a whole, an economy that presently turns out only eight-year-old scotch for the mass market would encounter considerable difficulty in finding the resources to replace the eight-year-old scotch with thirty-year-old scotch.

In the same way that the advantages of living like a millionaire almost always preclude a millionaire's actually living like an average person, so the advantages of greater capital intensiveness, in terms of higher-quality products and lower-cost methods of production, preclude a more-capital-intensive economic system from actually attempting to revert to the products and methods of production of a less-capital-intensive economic system in any but the most exceptional and isolated cases.

4. Implications for the Doctrine of Price Premiums in the Rate of Interest

Recognition of the fact that falling prices caused by increased production do not reduce the rate of profit necessitates a major modification in the important economic doctrine of "purchasing-power-price premiums" in the loan-market rate of interest. According to this doctrine, the anticipation of rising prices adds a corresponding positive component to the loan market rate of interest, while the anticipation of falling prices adds a corresponding negative component to the loan market rate of interest.[32] When stated in this form, the doctrine leads to the conclusion that rapid increases in production are potentially capable of wiping out the rate of interest altogether. This is because if the rate of interest were initially 4 percent, say, and production increased by more than 4 percent a year—say, by 5 or 6 percent, with the result that prices fell by approximately 5 or 6 percent— then the doctrine would imply the existence of a negative rate of interest and thus the disappearance of any incentive to lend money rather than hold it. This, in turn, would imply the sudden emergence of a major inducement to hold money that was not present before, and thus the onset of a depression. In other words, rapid increases in production are implied to be capable of causing depressions.

On the basis of the preceding discussion, however, it should be clear that there is no basis for the anticipation of falling prices caused by increased production to result in a reduction in the rate of interest.[33] For I have shown that in the context of an invariable money, where falling prices are caused by increases in production and supply, absolutely no fall whatsoever takes place in the rate of profit as the result of the increase in production and fall in prices. Inasmuch as such falling prices do not reduce the rate of profit, they do not reduce the demand for loanable funds; nor, for the same reason, do they serve as an inducement to the shifting of funds from direct investment to the loan market, and thus they do not increase the supply of loanable funds. Since they neither decrease the demand for loanable funds nor increase the supply of loanable funds, they do not result in a lower rate of interest.

As I have shown, it is not falling prices per se that should be associated with a reduction in the rate of profit and interest, but falling prices *caused by a reduction in the quantity of money and volume of spending*.[34] Even this formulation somewhat misses the mark, because the price changes are altogether nonessential. This is because a reduction in the quantity of money and volume of spending reduces the rate of profit and interest even if at the same time prices stay the same, or actually rise.

(Prices would stay the same or rise if production and supply fell to the same extent or a greater extent as the quantity of money and volume of spending.) Deflationary reductions in the rate of profit and interest are thus not a matter of price changes at all, but strictly of changes in the quantity of money and volume of spending.

Exactly the same principles apply to the rise in the rate of profit and interest associated with rising prices: they are due strictly to the increase in the quantity of money and volume of spending and not at all to the rise in prices per se.

Indeed, I have shown that a rising quantity of money and volume of spending act to raise the rate of profit and interest even when the increase in money and spending is relatively modest and is outstripped by the increase in production and supply, with the result that prices fall. By the same token, a falling quantity of money and volume of spending act to reduce the rate of profit and interest even if accompanied by rising prices caused by a fall in production and supply to an extent greater than the fall in the quantity of money and volume of spending. Just as more production and supply do not lower the rate of profit and interest, irrespective of any fall in prices, so less production and supply do not raise the rate of profit or interest, irrespective of any rise in prices.

As I have shown, changes in the price level are related to changes in the rate of profit and interest merely by a process of association. What underlies the association and actually explains the changes in both the price level and the rate of profit and interest is changes in the quantity of money and volume of spending. As the quantity of money and volume of spending increase, prices and the rate of profit and interest tend to increase together. As the quantity of money and volume of spending decrease, prices and the rate of profit and interest tend to decrease together. The essential underlying causal element that creates the association is the change in the quantity of money and volume of spending.

Now insofar as there are changes in the supply of goods produced and sold that take place in the same direction as the changes in the quantity of money and volume of spending, the changes in the price level that would otherwise be caused by the changes in the quantity of money and volume of spending are offset and may, indeed, actually be overcome. But the changes in the nominal rate of profit and interest caused by the changes in the quantity of money and volume of spending remain. Thus, as I demonstrated earlier in this chapter, falling prices caused by increases in production and supply are actually capable of being accompanied by an *increase* in the rate of profit and interest.[35] All that is necessary for prices to fall while the rate of profit and interest is increased is that at the same time that production and supply increase, there is an increase in the quantity of money and volume of spending that is less than the rise in production and supply. In this way, the increase in the quantity of money and volume of spending adds to the rate of profit and interest, but the still greater increase in production and supply overcomes its price-raising effects and succeeds in reducing the price level.

In exactly the same way, rising prices caused by a decrease in production and supply are capable of being accompanied by a decrease in the rate of profit and interest. All that is necessary is that at the same time that the fall in production and supply raises prices, there is a decrease in the quantity of money and volume of spending that is less than the fall in production and supply. In this case, the price-reducing effects of the fall in the quantity of money and volume of spending are more than overcome, with the result that prices rise. But the negative effect of the fall in the quantity of money and volume of spending on the rate of profit and interest remains. Thus, prices rise while the rate of profit and interest is reduced.

The doctrine of the purchasing-power-price premiums is thus substantially mistaken. One should speak instead, of a positive or negative *monetary component* in the rate of profit and interest, reflecting the change in the quantity of money and volume of spending in the economic system. This would permit recognition of the fact that falling prices caused by increased production not only do not reduce the rate of profit and interest but, under a commodity money, are actually almost always accompanied by a positive addition to the rate of profit and interest resulting from the increased production and supply of the monetary commodity or commodities that takes place as a by-product of the general increase in the ability to produce. It would also greatly encourage recognition of the fact that depressions and all their negative consequences are a strictly *monetary* phenomenon, proceeding from a monetary system of a kind which makes possible sudden, large-scale decreases in the quantity of money and sudden, large-scale increases in the demand for money for holding.[36]

5. Implications for the Process of Raising Real Wages

Figure 17–1 shows the process by which real wages are increased, namely, through an increase in the supply of capital goods relative to the supply of labor, which is then followed by an increase both in the supply of consumers' goods relative to the supply of labor and by a further increase in the supply of capital goods relative to the supply of labor. On this basis, in each year in Figure 17–1, from *Year 3* on and continuing indefinitely, real wages rise, as a steadily growing supply of consumers'

goods is sold for the same 400 monetary units of consumption expenditure while total wage payments remain at 300 monetary units.

The figure makes plain the role of a lower rate of net consumption in inaugurating the rise in real wages and is fully consistent with, if it does not actually suggest, the role of the competitive quest of businessmen and capitalists for above-average profits in the continuation of technological progress, capital accumulation, and rising real wages.[37] It shows how rising real wages are possible without any continuing fall in the rate of profit, and how, in fact, the buying power of the constant monetary amount of profits is increased at the same rate as the buying power of the constant monetary amount of wages—in other words, how real profits and real wages increase together. It shows how the process of raising real wages always takes place from the side of production and supply and is fundamentally a process that in the absence of increases in the quantity of money and volume of spending would raise real wages exclusively by means of reducing the prices of the goods purchased by wage earners, not by raising money wages. Of course, along with Figure 16–2, it also makes apparent the role of saving and productive expenditure in determining the demand for labor relative to the demand for consumers' goods. In essence, Figure 17–1 can be taken as a confirmation of the entire productivity theory of wages and its applications, which I presented in Chapter 14.[38]

6. How the Taxation of Profits Raises the Rate of Profit

The invariable-money/net-consumption analysis leads to the conclusion that the taxation of profit results in a substantially equivalent rise in the pretax amount of profit and in a corresponding rise in the pretax rate of profit.[39]

The fact that the consumption of businessmen and capitalists is governed primarily by their possession of capital rather than by their earning of income implies that the taxation of profit and interest falls mainly on capital. This is because so long as their capital remains intact, the consumption of businessmen and capitalists is not substantially reduced by the reduction in their disposable income that taxation causes.[40]

It is because the taxation of profit and interest falls mainly on capital, that its long-run effect is to raise the rate of profit and interest on a pretax basis. This comes about because, in falling on capital, the taxation of profit and interest reduces productive expenditure. Funds which business firms would have used for the purchase of machinery and materials and the payment of wages are instead diverted to the payment of taxes. The government, or the people to whom the government gives the tax proceeds, spend the funds. Thus, the aggregate monetary demand for products as such remains the same. What happens is that the demand for machinery and materials by business falls, the demand for consumers' goods by the employees of business falls (as the result of the fall in the demand for labor by business), but the demand for consumers' goods by the government or those to whom the government gives the tax money rises by an amount equal to these reductions. However, while aggregate sales revenues thus remain the same, the reduction in productive expenditure brings about an equivalent reduction in the aggregate costs of production that are deducted from sales revenues in computing profits. Thus, aggregate profits increase correspondingly.

The rise in aggregate profits, of course, is only on a pretax basis. What occurs, in effect, is that costs in the form of taxes displace normal business costs in the form of costs on account of machinery, materials, and labor. If the taxes are excluded from costs, as they are in calculating profits on a pretax basis, aggregate profits rise by an equivalent amount. They rise to whatever extent tax costs, which are not counted in the computation of pretax profits, displace ordinary business costs, which are counted in the computation of pretax profits.

The process can be understood by using Figure 17–1 as the framework of analysis. From *Year 3* on, the rate of net consumption in Figure 17–1 is implicitly equal to one-twentieth of the sum of the 1,900 of capital plus the annual 100 of profit received by the businessmen and capitalists. (Expressed relative to capital alone, the rate of net consumption is, of course, one-nineteenth.) If in some year subsequent to *Year 3*, the government imposes a tax of, say, 50 percent on profit income, the effect will be to make the net-consumption rate apply to 1,950 of capital-plus-its-income rather than to 2,000 of capital-plus-its-income. Thus the amount of net consumption will fall merely from 100 to 97.5—that is, to $1/20$ x 1,950. As a result, the far greater part of the tax will fall on productive expenditure and capital, which will both decline by 47.5—that is, by the amount of the excess of net consumption of 97.5 over aftertax profits of 50. Productive expenditure and capital will thus fall from 900 and 1,900 respectively to 852.5 and 1,852.5 respectively.[41]

Since the drop in productive expenditure will bring about an equivalent drop in aggregate business costs, i.e., to 852.5 from 900, while aggregate sales revenues remain at 1,000, the further effect will be a rise in pretax profits from 100 to 147.5. If the tax rate remains at 50 percent, the process is not yet complete. This is because taxes will now rise from 50 to 73.75 (50 percent of the profit of 147.5). Net consumption will again fall modestly, while productive expenditure and capital bear the brunt of the still higher tax payments. Equilibrium will

be reached only when pretax profits are almost doubled and the aftertax portion of profit becomes high enough to cover the whole of the amount of net consumption dictated by the sum of remaining capital plus the aftertax profit.

Indeed, under the present assumptions, a precise equilibrium will be reached in the conditions of Figure 17–1 only when productive expenditure falls to 809.52, and capital to 1,809.52. At that point, a net-consumption rate of one-twentieth applied to capital-plus-the-aftertax-profit (or, equivalently, a rate of net consumption of one-nineteenth applied to capital alone) results in an aftertax profit of 95.24 and a pretax profit of double that amount, or 190.48. This pretax profit of 190.48 is regenerated in every year by the combined operation of 95.24 of net consumption plus the expenditure of tax proceeds of a further 95.24. Net consumption plus the expenditure of the tax proceeds serve to make sales revenues in every year exceed productive expenditure and thus costs other than taxes by 190.48.

These specific figures are arrived at on the basis that capital in Figure 17–1 equals 1,000 monetary units plus productive expenditure, while, at the same time, in a state of equilibrium, productive expenditure equals 1,000 monetary units of sales revenues minus an amount equal to two times aftertax profit (i.e., the sum of net consumption plus tax payments equal to net consumption), with aftertax profit itself equal to one-twentieth of the sum of capital plus aftertax profit. Thus, where K is capital, B is productive expenditure, and p is profit after tax,

$$(1) \qquad K = 1{,}000 + B,$$

$$(2) \qquad B = 1{,}000 - 2p,$$

and

$$(3) \qquad p = (K+p)/20.$$

The solution for equation (3) is obvious:

$$(4) \qquad 19p = K.$$

When $19p$ is substituted for K in (1), and (2) is substituted for B in (1), the result is

$$(5) \qquad 19p = 1{,}000 + 1{,}000 - 2p.$$

Thus,

$$(6) \qquad 21p = 2000,$$

and, therefore,

$$(7) \qquad p = 95.24.$$

Thus, the effect of the imposition of a 50 percent tax rate on profits is almost equivalent to that of a doubling of the rate of net consumption. In terms of Figures 16–2 and 17–1, it represents driving the economic system back from the progressive conditions of Figure 17–1 toward the stationary conditions of Figure 16–2. In addition, of course, in real life, the effect would also be to reduce the demand for labor by business relative to the demand for consumers' goods.

Obviously, at some point, the taxation of profits becomes capable of stopping economic progress altogether and causing economic retrogression. At every step of the way, it is diametrically opposed to the real self-interests of the wage earners, because it operates totally counter to the rise in real wages.

Insofar as the rise in aggregate pretax profits is at the expense specifically of the demand for capital goods, not only profit but also national income rises. Indeed, the present case is very similar to the operation of the so-called balanced-budget multiplier and is a further illustration of the inverse relationship that prevails under an invariable money between aggregate profits and money national income, on the one side, and economic progress and prosperity, on the other.[42]

Insofar as the rise in aggregate pretax profits is at the expense specifically of the demand for labor by business, there is no rise in nominal national income as far as it is generated in business firms. There is merely a displacement of wage payments by tax payments, with the government and those to whom it gives money obtaining funds at the expense of the wage earners. Pretax profits rise simply because the tax payments are not deducted from sales revenues in calculating pretax profits while costs on account of labor, of course, are deducted. As in the case of pretax profits rising at the expense of the demand for capital goods, the rise in pretax profits at the expense of the demand for labor is of absolutely no benefit to business firms. It signifies nothing but that they pay taxes instead of wages. Indeed, in real terms there is almost certainly a loss to business firms—and to the general consuming public, as well—just as there is when taxes rise at the expense of the demand for capital goods. The loss in this case comes about insofar as the government uses the tax proceeds to employ labor and to this extent bids labor away from business firms and thus from the production of goods and services serving the general consuming public.[43]

The Influence of the Monetary System

It must be pointed out that the rise in aggregate pretax profits does not depend on aggregate costs falling absolutely, as they ultimately would in an economic system with a fixed quantity of money and a fixed aggregate monetary demand. The rise in aggregate pretax profits also occurs insofar as aggregate costs fall in comparison with what they otherwise would have been. In an economic system with an increasing quantity of money and rising aggregate monetary demand, the effect is that the

growth in productive expenditure is less than it otherwise would have been and that productive expenditure comes to stand at any given time at a lower level than it otherwise would have achieved, even if it is able to go on rising. The effect of this, in turn, is that aggregate costs come to stand at a lower level than they would otherwise have reached. Thus, aggregate profit and the average rate of profit, on a pretax basis, are correspondingly increased.

The precise effect of the taxation of profit and interest incomes on the pretax rate of profit depends on the type of monetary system a country has. Under an invariable money or under a fiat money, the effect is clearly a rise, in the ways just explained. Indeed, under a fiat money system, it is almost certain that as a result of its negative effects on capital accumulation and economic progress, a rise in the taxation of profit or interest incomes will be followed by a more rapid rate of increase in the quantity of money and thus by a further, corresponding addition to the rate of profit. This is because the government will be tempted to print money all the more rapidly to the degree that a lesser rate of economic progress—let alone economic stagnation or outright economic retrogression—diminishes the real revenues at its disposal while at the same time increasing the demands made upon it by the public.

Under a commodity money system, on the other hand, reduced capital accumulation and the lesser increases in the ability to produce that it causes result in a reduced rate of increase in the quantity of money in a country. If the reduction in capital accumulation is sufficient to render a country's economic system stationary or, worse still, retrogressive, the country's quantity of money will be likely actually to fall, owing to its declining economic status relative to other countries and its correspondingly declining share of the world's supply of commodity money. (If economic retrogression pervades the world as a whole, the quantity of money will decline owing to a decline in the production of precious metals below the point required for maintenance of the money supply.)

Such effects on the money supply result in a diminution of the monetary component in the rate of profit and could even turn the monetary component negative. Thus, under a commodity money, the taxation of profit and interest income need not result in a rise in the general rate of profit in a country, for the reduction in productive expenditure will be followed by reductions in sales revenues, or, at the least, lesser increases in sales revenues.

Because of the intimate connection between the monetary component of the rate of profit and the net investment component, the reduction or elimination of the former means the reduction or elimination of the latter.[44] Thus, what happens in the case of a commodity money is that the effect of a tax on profit or interest is to consume funds that otherwise would have represented net investment and to more or less abort the process that would have led to continuing nominal and real net investment. As a result, under a commodity money, profits corresponding to the taxes on profits for the most part merely take the place of profits corresponding to the increase in the quantity of money and corresponding net investment, and to that extent do not succeed in actually raising the pretax rate of profit. This, of course, operates to limit the extent of the damage that taxes on profits and interest are capable of doing, insofar as it takes away the possibility of their being applied to profits and interest which they themselves call into being.

The clear implication of this section is that a principal means of bringing down the present, very high rate of profit and interest is to reduce government spending and abolish the taxation of profit and interest, and all other taxation which falls on saving and productive expenditure. Such a policy would raise productive expenditure, and ultimately costs, relative to sales revenues, thereby diminishing the amount of profit and interest income in the economic system on a pretax basis. It would also result in a rise in the amount of capital invested, both absolutely and relative to sales revenues, consumption, and wage payments. It would be the basis of a rise in the demand for capital goods relative to consumers' goods, a rise in the demand for labor by business relative to the demand for consumers' goods, and a rise in the degree of capital intensiveness. It would thus be the foundation for an acceleration of capital accumulation and economic progress, not only from a state of less rapid economic progress to more rapid economic progress, but also, and even more importantly, from a state of economic stagnation or retrogression to one of absolute economic progress. A leading feature of this process, of course, would be more rapidly rising real wages or the resumption of rising real wages.

A policy of abolishing taxes on profit and interest, or at least substantial movement in the direction of such a policy, is clearly urgently called for in the present-day United States, which is on the verge of becoming a stagnant or even retrogressing economic system. Yet it is greatly to be feared that the growing ignorance and envy of the present generation of Americans, and of their elected representatives, will prevent these necessary steps and instead carry the American people into growing poverty, and the United States ultimately into the backwaters of history.

The ignorance and envy of today's Americans are, of course, themselves to an important extent the product of the overthrow of the gold standard. The overthrow of the gold standard served to break the connection between the rate of profit and the rate of economic progress, and to lead people to regard the high profits created by taxation and inflation as though they signified the rapid enrichment of business firms and their owners at the very time that the general public came to grow rich less rapidly or not at all. Thus the implication of the preceding analysis is no less a reinstitution of the gold standard.

7. How Government Budget Deficits Raise the Rate of Profit

The invariable-money/net-consumption analysis illustrated in Figures 16–2 and 17–1 makes it possible to understand the effects of persistent government budget deficits on the rate of profit.

Insofar as they are not financed by the creation of new and additional money, budget deficits are financed by the sale of securities in exchange for funds that otherwise would have entered mainly into productive expenditure.[45] As a result, just as in the case of taxes falling on productive expenditure, the demand for capital goods is reduced, and the demand for labor by business firms, and thus the demand for consumers' goods by the employees of business firms, is reduced. These reductions in the demand for capital goods and in the demand for consumers' goods by the employees of business are, of course, accompanied by an equivalent increase in the demand for consumers' goods by the government or by those to whom the government gives money. Thus, once again, just as in the case of taxes falling on productive expenditure, aggregate business sales revenues in the economic system are unchanged.

But, just as in the case of such taxes, while aggregate sales revenues are unchanged, the reduction in productive expenditure works to bring about an equivalent reduction in aggregate business costs that are deducted from sales revenues in computing profits. Therefore, the result once again is that the aggregate amount of profit rises correspondingly. The average rate of profit is raised by virtue both of the rise in the aggregate amount of profit and the reduction in the aggregate amount of capital invested. The difference between the effect of budget deficits on the rate of profit, and of taxes that reduce productive expenditure, is that in the case of budget deficits the rise in the rate of profit is a rise in the net, aftertax rate of profit, not merely in the gross, pretax rate of profit. This is because in this case, there is no rise in tax costs in the economic system to offset the fall in ordinary business costs that results from the fall in productive expenditure.

Of course, just as in the case of a fall in productive expenditure caused by taxation, the decline in productive expenditure caused by budget deficits is inimical to economic progress, and, if carried far enough, must cause economic retrogression. In a word, the effect is once again that of moving from the progressive conditions described in Figure 17–1, in the direction of the stationary conditions described in Figure 16–2. In both cases—that is, taxes or budget deficits coming at the expense of productive expenditure—the rise in the amount and rate of profit signifies merely that in the context of an invariable money, an inverse relationship exists between aggregate profits and national income on the one side, and economic progress and prosperity on the other.[46]

Obviously, all that was said in the preceding section about the urgent need to abolish or at least radically reduce the taxation of profit and interest incomes, and all other taxation falling on saving and productive expenditure, applies to government budget deficits.

The Need to Reduce Government Spending

The vital goal of increasing saving and capital formation through balancing the government's budget and cutting taxes that fall on saving and productive expenditure can be achieved very simply: namely, by *slashing government spending*. Such a policy would be consistent with reductions both in taxes falling on saving and productive expenditure and in taxes falling on consumption, and at the same time with a balanced government budget and, indeed, with government budget surpluses. Above all, it would be consistent with preserving and enlarging the freedom of the individual to spend his own income and wealth. The failure to reduce government spending, on the other hand, makes the achievement of greater saving and capital formation either altogether impossible or possible only at the price of sacrificing the freedom of the mass of wage and salary earners to dispose of their own incomes.

It should be clear that reducing taxes without reducing government spending cannot promote saving and capital formation, but must undermine them further, even if the funds no longer claimed by taxes are overwhelmingly saved. For in this case, the government must substitute a dollar of borrowing for a dollar of tax revenues. Each dollar borrowed is a dollar less of savings available for the rest of the economic system. Thus even if a dollar less of taxes results in as much as ninety cents of additional saving, there is a significant net reduction in the supply of savings available for the rest of the economic system. In this instance, while ninety cents of additional saving takes place as the result of tax reductions, a full dollar less of savings is available to business and private consumers as the result of the government's borrowing, and thus there is a net reduction of ten cents of savings available for every dollar of such tax cuts based on

increases in the government's deficit.

Tax cuts to promote saving and capital formation which are financed by deficit increases are thus simply contrary to purpose. The fact that they are contrary to purpose remains if, instead of being financed by borrowing, the resulting deficits are financed by the more rapid creation of money. In this case, all of the destructive effects inflation has on capital formation come into play, which effects I will show in Chapter 19.[47]

By the same token, balancing the budget by means of raising taxes is destructive of saving and capital formation to the degree that the additional taxes fall on saving and productive expenditure. Ironically, it is precisely taxes that fall heavily on saving and productive expenditure that today's advocates of balancing the budget through tax increases favor. The taxes they wish to increase are precisely those which land on corporations and the so-called rich. The only way that these advocates of balanced budgets through tax increases could proceed consistently with the goal of capital formation would be by increasing the taxes of the very people they claim to favor, namely, the poor and the mass of wage and salary earners, who save relatively little. Indeed, the only way that greater saving and capital formation is possible in the absence of decreases in government spending, is by means not only of increasing such taxes to the point of balancing the budget, but also increasing them still further, to compensate for decreases in the kind of taxes that land more heavily on saving and productive expenditure. In essence, if one advocates greater saving and capital formation and yet refuses to support reductions in government spending, one is logically obliged to advocate increasing the taxes of wage and salary earners and of the "poor" in order both to balance the budget and to compensate for reductions in taxes on profits and interest and on the "rich."

But there is absolutely no reason to advocate such a downright fascistic policy.[48] Instead of sacrificing anyone to anyone, the simple, obvious solution is sharply to reduce the sacrificing that is already going on—namely, sharply to reduce and ultimately altogether eliminate pressure-group plundering and the government spending that finances it at the sacrifice of everyone.[49]

The preceding analysis makes clear that an essential flaw of so-called supply-side economics—the policy of the Reagan administration—was its failure to face up to the need to reduce government spending. While the administration's program of tax reductions—in particular the reduction of the maximum rate of personal income tax on profit and interest income from 70 percent to 28 percent—was courageous and praiseworthy in the extreme, most of the value of the tax cuts achieved was lost through the corresponding enlargement of federal budget deficits. Regrettably, the administration and its supporters lacked the further courage required to abolish government spending programs to make those tax cuts possible without deficits.

The Government's Responsibility for the Emphasis of Today's Businessmen on Short-Term Results

Among the virtually endless criticisms of business is one of relatively recent origin, namely, that American businessmen are unduly concerned with short-run results, in contrast to the businessmen of such countries as Japan, who, it is claimed, attach much greater importance to long-run results.

There is an important measure of truth in this accusation. American businessmen of the present generation are much more concerned with short-term results than the businessmen of such countries as Japan and, indeed, than American businessmen of previous generations. But the reason for this situation is not, as is apparently believed, some intellectual or moral deficiency on the part of contemporary American businessmen. Totally apart from any such deficiency, which the climate of massive government interference and all of its accompanying subsidies, regulations, and associated influence peddling might well in fact foster, there is a profoundly important, objective difference between the economy of the present-day United States and that of contemporary Japan and of the United States of the past—a difference emanating from the same quarter. This is the difference in the magnitude of the government's assault on saving and productive expenditure and the consequent artificial elevation of the rate of profit and interest.

Because of anticapitalistic tax policies, compounded by major government budget deficits and decades of inflation, American businessmen have been placed in a situation in which they must evaluate all investment projects in the light of the need to earn a pretax rate of return of 12 to 15 percent or more, in order to be competitive. This means that any possible greater earnings that might be achieved in the long run stand at a correspondingly steep discount in comparison with earnings that can be obtained in the short run. In order, for example, for earnings which come in 5 years later to outweigh lesser earnings in the present, those earnings must be greater in a magnitude of 12- to 15-or-more-percent *compounded* over that 5 year period of delay—i.e., they must be greater by 76 to 101 percent or more ($1.12^5 = 1.76$, and $1.15^5 = 2.01$). In contrast, in contemporary Japan and in the United States of the past, businessmen are or were in a position to evaluate investment projects in the light of the need to earn perhaps merely a 5 or 6 percent rate of return or less. The significance of this is

exemplified by the fact that in these conditions, in order for greater earnings 5 years later to outweigh earnings in the current year, they need only be greater by 28 to 34 percent ($1.05^5 = 1.28$ and $1.06^5 = 1.34$). It is certainly much easier to be concerned with the long run under the latter state of affairs than under the former.

The responsibility for today's inordinate rate of profit and interest in the United States is squarely that of the U.S. government. At a deeper level, it is the responsibility of the pressure groups and the demagogues who are responsible for the government's pursuit of anticapitalistic policies. Above all, at a deeper level still, it is the responsibility of the last several generations of intellectuals who, corrupted by the philosophy of irrationalism, altruism, and collectivism, have polluted the intellectual environment of the country to the point where there is little or no serious opposition to the activities of the pressure groups and the demagogues. Responsibility does *not* lie at the end of the line, in the hands of businessmen, who did not create the political-cultural environment in which they now must operate and who do not deserve this further vituperation from the intellectuals at what is in fact a consequence of their—the intellectuals—own, utterly destructive philosophy. It is perfectly consistent, however, that those who destroy, whether through ignorance or viciousness, should blame innocent victims for the consequences of their actions.

8. Profits, the Balance of Trade, and the Need for Laissez Faire in the United States

The previous section has shown that government budget deficits financed by the diversion of savings from productive expenditure to the government's consumption operate to reduce aggregate business costs to an equivalent extent—while leaving aggregate business sales revenues unchanged—and thus to raise the amount of profit in the economic system to an equivalent extent. So long as the outside world does not view the country concerned as firmly on the road to ruin, the resulting rise in its rate of profit acts as an attraction to foreign investment. This foreign investment alleviates the destructive effect of the budget deficits on domestic capital formation. At the same time, the excess of imports over exports that constitutes the foreign investment, operates to scale back the rise in the amount and rate of profit caused by the budget deficits and to spread that rise over the economic system of the countries that export on net balance to the country with the budget deficits.[50]

These results can be made plain by mentally placing Figures 16–2 and 17–1 side by side. Figure 16–2, which should be imagined to be on the right, can be taken as representing the economy of the present-day United

States—with its placement on the right indicating the relative location of the United States on a map of the Pacific rim. Figure 17–1, on the left, can be taken as representing the economy of present-day Japan, and the relative location of that country on a map of the same region. The economy of the United States is characterized by Figure 16–2 because in the United States an annual budget deficit of 100 monetary units is responsible for a reduction of productive expenditure and costs by 100 monetary units in comparison with what they would otherwise have been, while sales revenues remain 1,000 monetary units. Thus, the budget deficit is responsible for productive expenditure and costs being only 800 in the United States, while they are 900 in Japan, and thus for a correspondingly higher amount and rate of profit in the United States than in Japan. At the same time, the budget deficits are responsible for the relative demand for and production of capital goods being less in the United States than in Japan, and thus for the economy of the United States stagnating while that of Japan rapidly progresses. (In reality, of course, other major factors are also at work causing economic stagnation in the United States and economic progress in Japan, but we ignore them for the sake of simplicity.)

Now imagine that in a given year some part of the output of the Japanese economy of Figure 17–1 is loaded onto ships and sent over to the U.S. economy of Figure 16–2. For example, one can imagine that in *Year 3*, say, 5 percent of the output of the Japanese economy is exported to the United States. (For the sake of simplicity, one can assume that there are no imports into Japan from the United States.)

The effect of this movement of goods is that the supply of goods in Japan in *Year 3* is reduced from *1.44K + .96C* to *1.368K + .912C*, while the supply in the United States is equivalently increased, from *1K + 1C* to *1.072K + 1.048C*. (These figures reflect the fact that 5 percent of *1.44K* is *.072K*, while 5 percent of *.96C* is *.048C*.) What is significant for the rate of profit is that while aggregate sales revenues in both countries remain at 1,000 monetary units each, with each monetary unit in Japan representing so many yen, and each monetary unit in the United States representing so many dollars, *the aggregate cost value of the goods remaining for sale in Japan is reduced by 5 percent*, while the aggregate cost value of the goods available for sale in the United States is equivalently increased.

Instead of there being *1.44K* of capital goods at a cost value of 540, and *.96C* of consumers' goods at a cost value of 360, for sale inside Japan for 1,000 of sales revenues, there are now only *1.368K* of capital goods at a cost value of 513, and *.912C* of consumers' goods at cost value of 342. (These cost values result from the fact

that 95 percent of 540 is 513, and 95 percent of 360 is 342.) Thus, in Japan, aggregate costs are reduced by the cost value of the goods exported, namely, by 27 plus 18, and aggregate profits, therefore, are increased equivalently, viz., from 100 to 145.

On the simplifying assumption that the dollar and the yen are freely convertible into one another at the exchange rate of 1 monetary unit for 1 monetary unit, it would follow that aggregate profits in the United States would be reduced from 200 to 155 in *Year 3*, owing to the sale of *1.072K* of capital goods with a cost value of 427, and *1.048C* of consumers' goods with a cost value of 418—that is, reduced by exactly the same amount as aggregate profits in Japan are increased. The principle would be present that the cost value of the goods exported/imported represented an equivalent rise in the aggregate profits of the exporting country and an equivalent fall in the aggregate profits of the importing country. This would be because in the one case—that of the exporting country—the cost value of the goods in question would be subtracted from the costs deducted from the same sales revenues, while in the other—that of the importing country—it would be added to the costs deducted from the same sales revenues.

In reality, foreign investment will not cause an immediate addition to profits in the exporting country, and an immediate reduction in profits in the importing country, equivalent to the cost value of the goods exported/imported. Rather it will cause less net investment in the exporting country and more net investment in the importing country. However, it is still the case that foreign investment does serve to make the costs deducted from sales revenues in the importing country greater, and those in the exporting country less, if not all at once, then over time, and thus the effect is still a rise in the amount and rate of profit in the exporting country and a fall in the amount and rate of profit in the importing country. Sooner or later, the repeated export of goods means a corresponding reduction in aggregate costs and rise in profits in the exporting country, while the repeated import of goods means a corresponding rise in the aggregate costs and fall in the aggregate profits of the importing country.

It should be obvious that the fact that both countries export as well as import does not change anything of significance. The results I have described hinge on *net* exports/imports.

Thus, the unmistakable conclusion to be drawn is that the American trade imbalance with Japan serves to deflect part of the destructive consequences of American budget deficits to Japan. In effect, it helps to replace some of the productive expenditure lost in this country as the result of government budget deficits, with the benefit of part of Japan's productive expenditure. In the process, it diminishes the increase in the rate of profit in the United States that would otherwise result from the American government's budget deficits and transmits part of the elevated rate of profit of this country to Japan—and, of course, to all other countries that on net balance export to the United States. Thus, it serves to spread over the economic system of all trading nations the fall in productive expenditure and rise in the amount and rate of profit caused by government budget deficits in the United States.

The increase in the pretax rate of profit in the United States (or any other country) caused by the *taxation* of profits and interest, also serves to attract foreign investment and thus to cause an "unfavorable" balance of trade. This is the case to the extent that foreign suppliers are able to translate the higher pretax rate of profit into a higher aftertax rate of profit. This can occur by such means as foreign investors concealing part of their profits through overstating the cost of supplies they bring in from abroad.

The preceding discussion in this section did not go into the influence of differences in the rate of capital formation on the balance of trade. But it should be recalled from previous chapters that a rate of capital accumulation and economic progress that is below the world average implies that the economy of a country will constitute a declining proportion of the world's economy as time goes on, while, of course, the reverse is true of an economy with a rate of capital accumulation and economic progress that is above the world average. Of two such opposite economies, the latter will come to possess a growing proportion of the world's money supply while the former will come to possess a declining proportion of the world's money supply.[51] This process too entails a so-called favorable balance of trade in the one, and a so-called unfavorable balance of trade in the other, insofar as both countries use the same money and movements in the supply of money between them take place in conjunction with the purchase and sale of commodities.[52]

If one recognizes that the fundamental cause of America's trade imbalance with Japan is the higher rate of profit prevailing in the United States, which the trade imbalance operates to diminish, and the closely related slower rate of capital formation and economic progress in the United States, which the trade imbalance also helps to alleviate, then it follows that what will reduce or even eliminate the trade imbalance is a fall in the rate of profit in the United States, which would be accompanied by a higher rate of domestic capital formation.

If, in addition, one recalls the discussions of the two

immediately preceding sections of this chapter, then it becomes clear that what would accomplish a fall in the rate of profit in the United States and a higher rate of capital formation would be precisely the balancing of the U.S. government's budget and the radical reduction of taxes that fall on saving and capital formation. Better still, it would be the achievement of budget surpluses, accompanied by the total abolition of such taxes, above all, the corporate income tax, the progressive personal income tax, the inheritance tax, and the capital gains tax. The social security system and its diversion of hundreds of billions of dollars of savings into government consumption would also have to be phased out in favor of private saving supporting actual investment.[53] What all this requires, of course, is the abolition of the welfare state and the radical reduction of government spending in the United States.

Unless and until such measures are adopted, the United States as a whole will be in a position analogous to that of an individual capitalist who consumes at a rate above the net-consumption rate and whose relative wealth and income steadily declines in favor of others who consume at a rate below the net-consumption rate.[54] In order for the United States to retain its international position and not ultimately be relegated to the ranks of second- and third-rate nations, it is vital that its net-consumption rate fall to a point at least approximating that of Japan and the other rapidly progressing countries of East Asia. (As used in the present context, the net-consumption rate is to be understood as incorporating all elements that serve to elevate business sales revenues above productive expenditure. This includes all government consumption that is financed by means of funds obtained at the expense of productive expenditure, whether through taxes or through budget deficits. Such consumption takes place at the expense of a diminution of productive expenditure and at the same time maintains business sales revenues, thereby enlarging the magnitude of difference.) Only to the extent that the relative efficiency of the United States in using existing capital goods was greater than that of Japan and the other rapidly progressing economies of East Asia, could it afford to have a higher such net-consumption rate than they. Today, however, the United States probably substantially lags behind Japan and the others on this score too.

But the solution for both aspects of the problem is essentially the same: It is the radical reduction of government intervention in the economic system.[55] It is the coming home of the United States to full-bodied capitalism. It is the establishment of laissez-faire capitalism.[56] If this course is not pursued, then not only will the United States decline relatively, but it may also decline absolutely. The factors working to choke off economic progress by no means automatically stop at the point of stagnation. They easily go further and result in economic retrogression.

As indicated, the only alternative to laissez-faire capitalism that might be compatible with economic progress for a time is the utterly vicious one of a fascistic-style tax system that would place all or almost all of the enormous tax burden created by the welfare state on the consumption of the ordinary citizens, thereby lifting the burden that now falls on saving and capital accumulation.[57] This burden, of course, would have to be the greater, the more government intervention reduces the efficiency of the economic system in using existing capital goods. For this requires the existence of a greater relative production of capital goods and higher degree of capital intensiveness in order to achieve any given rate of economic progress. Government intervention for the purpose of actually achieving capital accumulation—notably, taxation for that purpose—would mean collecting taxes from the ordinary citizens as a source of capital, which capital would itself be used inefficiently and thus require still more such taxation. Capital accumulation under such conditions would have important features in common with attempted capital accumulation under communism.[58] It is an absurd and vicious method of capital accumulation.

At the very best, the enormous burden of taxation that must fall on the average person under the welfare state, in order for it to have capital accumulation and economic progress, means giving to people the very dubious and largely fictional benefits of the welfare state at the expense of much greater benefits they could have had without the welfare state and with the freedom to spend their own incomes as they wished. As shown throughout this book, people can have incomparably more and better education, medical care, and retirement security without the welfare state than with it, and in a measure that grows progressively greater the longer the period of time in which economic freedom exists rather than a welfare state.

Furthermore, such capital accumulation and economic progress as might be enjoyed under a welfare state are possible only if the welfare state remains stable, in the sense of not continually claiming a greater proportion of people's incomes, and only if no new government intervention adds further disabilities to the efficiency of production. But if the principle of economic freedom is abandoned and that of government intervention and the welfare state put in its place, it is impossible to assume that such stability would exist. More than likely, growing government intervention and a growing welfare state would deprive the masses of people of most or all of the benefit of the capital accumulation that took place. At the same time, a growing disparity between their relatively stagnant conditions and the improving conditions of a small upper class of businessmen and capitalists and individuals prominent in such fields as the performing arts and professional sports, would fuel growing envy, and thus ultimately lead to the imposition or reimposition of a system of taxation and government finance that was incompatible with economic progress, period. Thus, laissez-faire capitalism—acceptance of the *principle* of laissez-faire capitalism—is essential to economic progress in the long run. It is the only system in which economic progress is possible without the exploitation of the so-called common man.

9. Implications for the Theory of Saving

Previous discussion in Chapter 16 has shown that in the conditions of an invariable money, net investment tends to disappear, leaving net consumption as the sole determinant of the amount and rate of profit.[59] A corollary of that discussion is that under an invariable money, *saving out of money income likewise tends to disappear.*

Net Saving and Increases in the Quantity of Money

Under an invariable money, the constancy of the quantity of money and volume of spending implies a constancy of aggregate money income. As we have already seen, it follows that under these conditions, saving out of income not only adds to the amount of accumulated savings and capital, but also signifies a rise in the *ratio* of accumulated savings and capital to income.[60] Yet as savings and capital accumulate relative to income, the need and desire of people to increase their savings and capital still further relative to their income diminishes, while their desire to consume their income increases. This is because the future is becoming progressively better and better provided for relative to the present by virtue of such saving and capital accumulation. As the desired ratio of provision for the future relative to the present is approached, the growth in the magnitude of accumulated savings and capital relative to income operates to increase the proportion of income that is consumed.[61] This means that at some point under an invariable money, having achieved a sufficient ratio of accumulated savings and capital to income, and thereby having made sufficient provision for the future relative to the present, people stop adding to their savings and capital and consume their full nominal income.

Thus, in an economic system with an invariable money, an equilibrium is ultimately reached, in which saving out of money income and net investment in terms of money both disappear. It is an equilibrium in which the economic system ceases to grow more capital intensive in the relative-value sense—i.e., in the sense of the ratio of accumulated savings and capital to income—and in which all money income is consumed.[62]

Of course, in such an economic system, many individuals go on saving. For example, young people starting out in life must accumulate savings. But their saving is balanced by the dissaving of others, such as old people living in retirement, or people out of work because of illness or accident. In the system as a whole, there is no net saving in terms of money. Capital accumulation and economic progress in such circumstances take place exclusively in the form of falling prices.

The implication of the fact that saving out of money income tends to disappear in the conditions of an invariable money, is that *the existence of saving out of money income, as a permanent phenomenon, is the result of the continual increase in the quantity of money.* Indeed, the increase in the quantity of money operates continually to raise money incomes and thus to make necessary a continual increase in the absolute magnitude of accumulated savings and capital if any given ratio of accumulated savings and capital to money income in the economic system is to be maintained. Saving out of money income is necessary to provide the required increase in the magnitude of accumulated savings and capital in these circumstances.

For example, if people desire on average to maintain some given ratio of accumulated savings to current income, such as 3:1 or 4:1, and the increase in the quantity of money makes current nominal incomes rise by 2 or 3 percent per year, then it is necessary for total accumulated savings also to increase by 2 or 3 percent a year, or whatever the figure might be, in order to maintain the same ratio of accumulated savings to current income. This in turn implies a definite ratio of nominal net saving to current income. In the present examples, saving as a percentage of nominal net income must range from 6 percent to 12 percent, as the condition of accumulated savings continuing to bear the same ratio to nominal net income. This is because if a magnitude that is 3 times current income is to grow by 2 percent, the amount of its increase is 6 percent of current income. By the same token, if a magnitude that is 4 times current income is to grow by 3 percent, the amount of its increase is 12 percent of current income.

Thus saving as a percentage of current income appears as the product of the rate of increase in the quantity of money—and thus in nominal incomes—times the ratio of accumulated savings to current income that people wish to maintain on average. If there were no increase in the quantity of money and thus no increase in nominal net incomes, there would be no need for an increase in accumulated savings once the desired ratio of accumu-lated savings to current income was achieved. Given an increase in the quantity of money and nominal net incomes, the need for additional accumulated nominal savings is the greater, the higher is the ratio of accumu-lated savings relative to current income that people wish to maintain.[63]

Failing the increase in accumulated savings in a context in which an increase in the quantity of money and volume of spending continually raise money incomes, the effect would be a progressive fall in the degree of capital intensiveness in the economic system. For exam-ple, starting with an aggregate money income of 500, and 1,500 of accumulated capital, and thus a capital-net-out-put ratio of 3:1, a 2 percent annual increase in money income and no additions to accumulated savings would imply that in 35 years, when money income had doubled, the capital-net-output ratio would be halved. The capi-tal-net-output ratio can be maintained at 3:1, only if over the course of this period of time there is saving out of income sufficient to increase accumulated capital to 3,000. Thus, in the context of an increasing quantity of money and rising volume of spending, continual net saving is necessary not to increase, but to maintain the degree of capital intensiveness.

Why the Actual Significance of Saving Lies at the Gross Level

The realization that saving out of money income tends to disappear in an economic system with an invariable money makes it possible to understand much more fully than would otherwise be the case precisely what role saving plays in relation to capital formation—viz., to the increase or decrease in the supply of capital goods. The disappearance of saving out of money income in an economy with an invariable money does *not* mean the disappearance of capital accumulation. The supply of capital goods can go on increasing. In such circum-stances the increase in the supply of capital goods results in falling prices of capital goods, just as the increase in the supply of consumers' goods results in falling prices of consumers' goods. Each year, in these circumstances, the depreciation quotas recovered from previous invest-ments are able to buy a larger supply of capital goods than the year before. Each year, the funds recovered in the sale of inventories make possible more than the mere replacement of those inventories. In other words, the same productive expenditure for capital goods buys a growing supply of capital goods at falling prices of capital goods. This, of course, is exactly what happens in Figure 17–1, which shows the demand for capital goods constant at 600 monetary units in every year from *Year 2* on, while capital accumulation and economic progress continue at a rapid rate.

In such an economic system, the real connection between saving and capital formation becomes clear. The relationship is not one between saving out of money income and capital formation—it is not between *net* saving and capital formation. Rather it is between *gross* saving—mainly saving out of business' sales revenues—and capital formation. (Gross saving also includes saving out of net income, when such saving exists. However, saving out of sales revenues and gross saving become synonymous in an economy with an invariable money, because of the disappearance of saving out of net income.)

As demonstrated repeatedly in this book, saving out of business sales revenues determines the demand for capital goods relative to the demand for consumers' goods. It thus determines the relative production of capital goods and in this way the rate of capital accumulation. This vital aspect of saving, namely, determining the relative production of capital goods, is what is clearly revealed under the conditions of an invariable money. As far as saving goes, this aspect is what is decisive in determining the rate of capital accumulation. And while saving out of net income can certainly enter into determining the relative production of capital goods, saving out of sales revenues is capable of discharging that function strictly by itself, when the conditions of an invariable money make it necessary—that is, it does so without the existence of net saving in terms of money income.

Furthermore, as I have repeatedly shown, saving out of sales revenues is also the essential determinant of the demand for labor. The greater is saving out of sales revenues relative to the sales revenues, the higher tends to be both the demand for capital goods and the demand for labor, relative to the demand for consumers' goods, and thus the higher and more rapidly rising the level of real wages. Saving out of sales revenues, in other words, is the essential determinant of what I have characterized as the economic degree of capitalism.[64] Again, saving out of net income can make a contribution, but the essential aspect of the role of saving is independent of the phenomenon of net saving, which is essentially to say that it is independent of the increase in the quantity of money.

A closely related aspect of the relationship between saving and capital formation that stands clearly revealed in the conditions of an invariable money, is precisely that between the *ratio* of accumulated savings and capital to such magnitudes as consumption and income, on the one side, and capital formation, on the other. As previously explained, the higher are such ratios, the more capital intensive is the economic system and the greater its ability to implement technological advances, which tech-

nological advances result in an increase in the supply not only of consumers' goods but also of capital goods.[65] Insofar as net saving signifies a rise in these ratios, it again signifies an acceleration in the rate of capital accumulation and economic progress—precisely because of its implication of a greater ability to implement technological advances.

Thus, the true significance of saving that is revealed in the conditions of an invariable money is that gross saving determines the relative production of capital goods along with the demand for labor relative to the demand for consumers' goods, and in these ways the height and direction of real wages. And, as an accumulated amount relative to current income, savings determine the degree of capital intensiveness of the economic system and thereby the ability to adopt technological advances and achieve capital accumulation and economic progress. The role of net saving, which in the long run reflects nothing more than the continual increase in the quantity of money, is entirely subsidiary.

It should be realized that the appearance of a direct, one-to-one relationship between net saving and capital accumulation, which is created by the increase in the quantity of money, serves both to conceal the role of saving in capital accumulation in one respect, and grossly to exaggerate it in another respect. On the one hand, it conceals the fact that in determining the relative demand for and production of capital goods, gross saving—when accompanied by technological progress—operates as force to acceleration in the accumulation of capital goods.[66] On the other hand, in creating the appearance that for every accumulation of capital, corresponding net saving must occur, it supports the belief that saving by itself is the source of capital accumulation. In this way, it serves to reinforce all the errors stemming from the fallacy that the production of consumers' goods constitutes production in its entirety and that the causes of capital accumulation have no essential connection with the causes that increase production in general, such as technological progress and economic freedom.[67]

Net Saving and the Rate of Profit

In view of the widespread influence of the doctrine that saving (net saving) reduces the rate of profit, it is important to integrate two of the major propositions that have now been established in this chapter or the last one. Namely, that the existence of net saving as a permanent phenomenon is the result of the increase in the quantity of money and volume of spending, and that that same increase in the quantity of money and volume of spending adds a corresponding positive component to the rate of profit. It follows from these propositions that the net saving which takes place as a regular, continuing phenomenon in the economic system is the accompaniment of a rate of profit which is not only not reduced by virtue of its existence, but in fact is *elevated* by virtue of the same cause that underlies its existence. Thus, insofar as net saving goes on for the most part, it is accompanied by a rate of profit that is higher, not lower, than would exist in its absence. Indeed, precisely the elevated rate of profit is the source of most of the net saving.

10. More on Saving and "Hoarding": "Hoarding" as a Long-Run Cause of a Rise in the Rate of Profit

The fear of saving is perhaps even more widespread than the fear of production. I have already refuted one leading root of this fear, namely, the confusion of an increase in saving with an increase in the demand for money for cash holding.[68] Here it is necessary to add to that critique the observation that to the extent that people do desire to make provision for the future in the form of cash holding rather than in the form of business investment, the long-run effect, contrary to popular belief, is not to reduce, but to increase the rate of profit.

This is because insofar as net consumption takes place in proportion to accumulated savings in the form of cash holdings, a rise in the ratio of cash holdings in the economic system to capital in forms other than cash holdings means a rise in the ratio of net consumption, hence profit, to capital in forms other than cash. For example, if people wished to hold fully half of their accumulated savings in the form of cash and only half in the form of capital invested in assets other than cash, a net-consumption rate of 2 percent would generate an amount of profit equal to *4 percent* of the capital invested in assets other than cash.[69] In the most extreme case imaginable, in which *all* provision for the future took place in the form of cash holding, the rate of profit would be infinite, for there would be a demand for consumers' goods, hence, the existence of sales revenues, but neither productive expenditure, costs of production, nor capital. The effect on the rate of profit would thus be the same as if people made no provision for the future.

"Cash hoarding" operates to reduce the rate of profit only in the short-run, insofar as it represents an increase in the demand for money for holding above its previous level and thereby brings about a decrease in the volume of spending and sales revenues. Here the result is to reduce net investment and, indeed, even to turn it negative. However, once the demand for money for holding stops increasing and stabilizes at the higher level, and the economic system becomes adjusted to the accompanying lower level of spending—viz., once costs deducted from sales revenues fall to equality with the lower level of productive expenditure—then the effect of the rise in the

ratio of net consumption to capital other than cash is felt and the rate of profit rises. In other words, the negative effect of cash hoarding on the rate of profit is purely transitory. The long-run effect is to increase the rate of profit.

Implications for the Critique of Keynesianism

That cash hoarding does serve in the long-run to raise the rate of profit provides an answer to the pretended fear of the Keynesians that in a free economy the rate of profit will be too low to make investment worthwhile and will thus lead to a limitless rise in "liquidity preference"— viz., cash hoarding.[70] The answer is that if the rate of profit ever were too low to make investment worthwhile and thus did result in cash hoarding, the effect of such cash hoarding, as we have just seen, would be to restore the rate of profit to a point high enough to make investment worthwhile.

The point I have just made in criticism of the Keynesians bears a mild resemblance to the so-called Pigou effect propounded by the neo-Keynesians, a resemblance which, frankly, embarrasses me, inasmuch as I consider the "Pigou effect" to be extremely weak as a criticism of Keynes.[71] The similarity is simply that both my criticism and the Pigou effect recognize a connection between consumption and accumulated savings in the form of cash holdings and that the existence of this connection has negative implications for essential doctrines of Keynes. The difference is that while the Pigou effect claims merely that because of this connection, consumption expenditure will not fall in full proportion to a fall in wages and prices and thus that at some point a fall in wages and prices is capable of leading to full employment, my criticism here is that every increase in the relative significance of cash holdings operates directly to raise the rate of profit and thus to eliminate the central stumbling block to full employment claimed by the Keynesians, namely, the allegedly too-low rate of profit. However, as I show in Chapter 18, there are other forces operating far more directly and powerfully to raise the rate of profit when wage rates and prices fall, so that it is not at all necessary that the influence of greater relative cash holdings ever come into play. And in fact it would not, since recovery from a depression and the restoration of the rate of profit that is part of that recovery are accompanied by a reduced demand for money for holding, not an increased demand.

Indeed, contrary to the Keynesians, the truth is that apart from some short-term, relatively inconsequential funds that might be held as cash rather than lent out, as the result of a lower rate of profit, the rate of profit in a free economy can never be too low to make investment worthwhile, even in the conditions of an invariable money.

This is because in a free economy, the average rate of profit and interest must always be significantly positive, for in such an economy there is no government intervention in money and banking, thus no inflation or credit expansion, and thus no financial contractions or depressions.[72]

As we have seen, in the absence of inflation and credit expansion and thus of financial contraction and deflation, a positive rate of profit and interest is guaranteed by virtue of the operation of net consumption and net investment. Even if the saving of wage earners temporarily made net consumption negative, net investment and the consequent accumulation of capital and savings would take place to the point of sufficiently enlarging capital and accumulated savings relative to current income, to render net consumption positive once again.[73] The positive rate of profit that net consumption and net investment guarantee means that investment must be worthwhile.[74] In an economy with a commodity money, which is what any free-market economy would be, and in which, therefore, the rate of profit contains a significant monetary component, the impossibility of the rate of profit being too low to make investment worthwhile is doubly strong.

11. Critique of the Investment-Opportunity and Underconsumption/Oversaving Doctrines

Following the confusion of saving with cash hoarding, the second and third grounds for the fear of saving can be termed respectively the doctrine of lack of investment opportunity and the doctrine of underconsumption or, equivalently, oversaving. These two doctrines are similar in that both fear saving as bringing about the existence of capital or capital goods without profitable uses for them.

The investment-opportunity doctrine holds that the rate of profit and interest is determined by the supply of and demand for "capital," which last it understands interchangeably as a sum of monetary value and a supply of physical capital goods. It views net saving as the source of all additional capital and, in the face of a given demand for capital, as driving down the rate of profit, just as a larger supply of any good, in the face of a given demand for it, drives down its price. Specifically, a growing supply of capital is supposed to encroach more and more on the allegedly limited opportunities that exist for the profitable investment of capital. These opportunities allegedly reflect the net physical productivity of capital and become progressively less rewarding as the supply of capital is increased, because of the operation of the law of diminishing returns.[75] The investment-opportunity doctrine regards technological progress as es-

sential for creating new and additional investment opportunities and thereby raising the demand for capital in the face of the increasing supply of capital provided by saving. It fears that in the absence of technological progress or sufficient technological progress, the supply of capital and capital goods will increasingly use up the limited profitable opportunities for investment and thereby drive the rate of profit toward zero. Only technological progress, it maintains, can prevent this from happening and keep up the rate of profit. Technological progress, it holds, is valuable because it creates a new and additional demand for capital to keep pace with the new and additional supply generated by saving, and thus operates to prevent the rate of profit from steadily falling.

The investment-opportunity doctrine obviously derives from the productivity theory of profit and interest, which I refuted in the last chapter.[76] It is utterly confused and mistaken in virtually every respect, not the least of which is its failure to see that the rate of profit is not determined by demand and supply but, above all, by the *difference* between the demand for products and the demand for factors of production—that is, by net consumption—specifically, by the rate borne by net consumption to the total of capital invested.[77]

I have already substantially refuted the investment-opportunity doctrine in my critique of consumptionism, in Chapter 13.[78] Here it is only necessary more or less to summarize that critique and name a few additional points of criticism implied by the further knowledge provided in the intervening pages of this book.

As I have shown, the investment-opportunity doctrine's fear of an accumulation of capital goods in the face of the absence of technological progress, or of insufficient technological progress, is absurd. Without technological progress, there can be no significant capital accumulation. Moreover, as I showed, the investment-opportunity doctrine is unaware that within the framework of any existing state of technology the need for capital goods always enormously surpasses the supply of capital goods actually available or that can be made available. The need for capital goods encompasses the need for all the capital goods required to make possible the production of the best-known models of all consumers' goods, including the most expensive and luxurious—to the point of sating the desire for those consumers' goods. It encompasses the need for all the capital goods required directly or indirectly in the production of any consumers' good—at any stage, however remote—to make possible its production by means of the most capital-intensive methods of production that are capable of achieving any reduction in cost or improvement in quality whatever. Until that point is reached—which it never will be—capital goods are scarce. The investment-opportunity doctrine does not see that the real need for technological progress is to provide capital goods, not uses for capital goods—that is, to provide the goods that are physically to be invested, not opportunities for investment.

The doctrine is utterly confused in the role it assigns technological progress, namely, as a source of greater "demand for capital" and thus of a rise in the rate of profit, when in fact technological progress is the source of a greater *supply* of *capital goods* and thus of a fall in the prices of capital goods. Along with the fall in the prices of capital goods, as we know, technological progress is the source of a rise in the productivity of labor and thus of a fall in labor costs per unit. As a result of these facts, technological progress is responsible for a reduction in unit costs of production as well as being responsible for falling product prices.[79] As a further result, it is responsible for the falling prices of consumers' goods that it causes not being the cause of a fall in the rate of profit or of "deflation," which is the belief of the supporters of the investment-opportunity doctrine—in direct contradiction of their belief that technological progress is the cause of a higher rate of profit by virtue of its alleged contribution to the demand for capital.

As we have seen, technological progress simply has no connection with the average rate of profit in the economic system, apart from the contribution it makes to increasing the supply of commodity money. The rate of profit is governed entirely by the rate of net consumption and the rate of net investment, with the influence of the rate of increase in the quantity of money and volume of spending manifested almost entirely through the rate of net investment.

Ironically, to the extent that technological progress does contribute to raising the average rate of profit—through its effect on the supply of commodity money—it does so precisely in conjunction with its responsibility for the existence of net investment and net saving in terms of money. As already explained, both of these phenomena, insofar as they are permanent, are the result of the increase in the quantity of money and volume of spending. Thus, technological progress, which is supposed to be the source of a greater demand for capital that is allegedly necessary to solve the problem of an increasing supply of capital and capital goods provided by saving, is in fact the source not only of the additional supply of physical capital goods, but also—under a commodity-money system—of the additional savings and capital that are available in monetary terms. And, as we know, these additional savings and capital in monetary terms are accompanied by corresponding additions to the amount and rate of profit, rather than by any necessity of a fall in the rate of profit. The additions to the amount and rate of profit are part of exactly the same process—

namely, the effects produced by the increase in the quantity of money and volume of spending—that is responsible for the additional savings and capital in monetary terms. In this process, it is the additional net investment that is caused that provides the additional profitability, not any alleged increase in the "demand for capital" that technological progress is supposed to cause.

The reason the investment-opportunity doctrine is unaware of the profound, ineradicable scarcity of capital goods, is that it mistakenly believes, in essence, that the only use for additional capital goods is in the form of more and better machinery used to produce consumers' goods. Thus it largely does not understand what can physically be done with an additional supply of capital goods if it becomes available. At the same time, as we know, it believes—in ignorance and contradiction of everything said above—that saving, unaided by technological progress, is potentially capable of providing practically unlimited supplies of additional capital goods. It is on the basis of these beliefs that it comes to the conclusion that a danger exists of technological progress not providing sufficient possibility of using additional capital goods at the very time that saving is generating a flood of capital goods, and thus that there is simply no good use to which the additional capital goods can be put. Given its confusion between increases in the supply of capital goods, which in fact reduce the prices of capital goods and thus help to reduce costs of production, and increases in the supply of "capital," which allegedly reduce the rate of profit, the consequence of these beliefs is the doctrine of "secular stagnation." This last, as we have seen, claims that in the absence of sufficient technological progress, saving causes depressions by virtue of bringing about too low a rate of profit to make investment worthwhile.[80]

In addition to its ignorance of the vital role of technological progress as a source of capital accumulation, and of the virtually limitless need for additional capital goods within the context of the existing state of technology, the investment-opportunity doctrine, as we know, is totally unaware of the limitations of saving as a source of capital accumulation. It does not realize how limited is saving at all times, because of the operation of time preference. Nor, of course, does it see how limited would be the ability to accumulate capital goods merely on the strength of saving—that is, in the absence of technological progress—even if radically more saving took place relative to income than is ever likely to take place.

The reason for the investment-opportunity doctrine's enormously exaggerated view of the power of saving, unaided by technological progress, to bring about capital accumulation, is the continuing existence of net saving in terms of money and thus the appearance of a more or less one-to-one relationship between such nominal net saving and capital accumulation in physical terms. The investment-opportunity doctrine does not see that the continuing existence of nominal net saving, rather than reflecting any direct, one-to-one relationship between saving and capital accumulation, is actually the result of nothing more than the increase in the quantity of money. It does not see that nominal net saving takes place in connection with capital accumulation not as a fundamental cause, but merely as the result of the increase in the quantity of money and volume of spending. These go on as the by-product of the fact that technological progress and a sufficiently high relative demand for capital goods—the actual causes—bring about capital accumulation and increases in production, including the production of the good or goods serving as money. In this connection, the investment-opportunity doctrine does not realize that precisely technological progress is what allows a constant relative demand for capital goods and a constant proportion of gross saving to result in capital accumulation; and a rise in the relative demand for capital goods and the proportion of gross saving, to result in an acceleration of capital accumulation.[81] It is unable to see that net saving in terms of money simply plays no fundamental permanent role in capital accumulation. Considered as a permanent phenomenon, it is, as I say, merely a by-product of the process of capital accumulation and rising production.[82]

What the investment-opportunity doctrine does is to confuse the net saving that goes on in the world of an increasing quantity of money with the net saving that goes on in the world of an invariable money. It fails to realize that in the world of an increasing quantity of money, in the very nature of the case, virtually all of the net saving that exists is accompanied by a corresponding elevation of the rate of profit, and, indeed, takes place largely out of that elevated rate of profit. Instead, it proceeds—implicitly—as though the conditions of an economic system with an invariable money obtained, in which case every act of net saving would have to be the result of a fall in the rate of net consumption. If, indeed, those conditions did obtain, the rate of profit would have to fall with every repetition of net saving. But in those conditions, net saving in terms of money would come to an end, and thereafter capital accumulation would proceed without it. It would proceed with a given magnitude of accumulated savings and capital that stood in a sufficiently high, but not continually rising, ratio to consumption.

The investment-opportunity doctrine's errors on all of these scores are, of course, compounded by its acceptance of the prevailing confusions between the production and purchase of capital goods and the production and purchase of consumers' goods—namely, the Platonic-Heraclitean view of entities that I have so extensively described and criticized.[83] This last, by obliterating the very existence of the production of capital goods as distinct entities that exist separately from consumers' goods—especially the production of materials, components, supplies, and all kinds of semimanufactures—underlies the investment-opportunity doctrine's belief that the only use of capital goods is in the form of machinery to produce consumers' goods. It leads to its failure to see both the use of capital goods in the production of further capital goods and the extent of the use of capital goods in the production both of capital goods and consumers' goods.

This brings me to the underconsumption/oversaving doctrine, which is, perhaps, even more crucially dependent on the confusions fostered by the Platonic-Heraclitean view of entities than is the investment-opportunity doctrine. The underconsumption/oversaving doctrine fears a lack of profitable uses for additional capital because it does not understand certain essential monetary aspects of the process of saving and capital formation. In effect, it believes that saving places business in the contradictory position of spending more to produce its products at the very time that its sales receipts are reduced by virtue of the fall in consumer spending that underlies the additional saving.

The fears of the underconsumption/oversaving doctrine can be found in the following passage from J. A. Hobson, a late nineteenth-, early twentieth-century writer who is quoted with approval on the subject by Keynes:

> The object of production is to provide 'utilities and conveniences' for consumers, and the process is a continuous one from the first handling of the raw material to the moment when it is finally consumed as a utility or a convenience. The only use of Capital being to aid the production of these utilities and conveniences, the total used will necessarily vary with the total of utilities and conveniences daily or weekly consumed. Now saving, while it increases the existing aggregate of Capital, simultaneously reduces the quantity of utilities and conveniences consumed; any undue exercise of this habit must, therefore, cause an accumulation of Capital in excess of that which is required for use, and this excess will exist in the form of general over-production.[84]

Actually, this passage can be interpreted as representing the fears of both the underconsumption/oversaving doctrine and the investment-opportunity doctrine. Insofar as it can be interpreted as a complaint about an alleged physical problem of how to employ the additional capital goods made possible by additional saving, it represents the fears of the investment-opportunity doctrine. Insofar as it can be interpreted as a complaint about a reduction of consumer spending in the face of an increase in the spending for factors of production, it represents the fears of the underconsumption/oversaving doctrine.

In connection with the former, it is sufficient to observe here that Hobson is apparently unaware that a reduction in consumption spending and rise in accumulated savings serves to increase the physical volume of consumption in the future, by means of making business more capital intensive, and that the additional capital is useful in any or all of the ways I described in the discussion of the vertical dimension of the scarcity of capital.[85] He appears to believe that when people consume less and save more, they permanently reduce the physical quantity of goods they consume, while having accumulated the capital to produce a larger quantity of consumers' goods.

However, I believe that Hobson's real difficulty here is his inability to understand how a smaller volume of consumer spending can support a larger volume of invested capital in terms of monetary value and, above all, a larger volume of spending for capital goods. I believe that it is this which prevents him from seeing how the smaller volume of consumer spending can purchase the growing volume of physical output that results from the greater capital invested. This fear of how a smaller volume of consumer spending can support a larger volume of capital and capital spending is, of course, the essence of the underconsumption/oversaving doctrine, to the detailed critique of which I now turn.

The Basic Error of Underconsumptionism

Underconsumptionism fears saving because it is based on the belief that the aggregate demand for goods *as such* consists essentially just of the demand for consumers' goods. This belief, which I thoroughly refuted in Chapter 15, easily leads to the fear that saving places business in a contradictory position, in which it cannot escape from losses. For it then appears that if what is saved is to be invested, i.e., productively expended, that business is placed in the position of having to spend more for the means of producing its products at the very time that it receives less from the sale of its products. Underconsumptionism believes that consumers alone reimburse business for its outlays made in purchasing factors of production and thus that if consumption falls, the sales revenues of business fall equivalently. On this basis, a rise in the demand for capital goods made possible by an equal fall in the demand for consumers' goods must, according to underconsumptionism, place business in the position of spending a larger sum for the means of producing its products at the very time that it receives a smaller sum in the sale of its products. Indeed, once the expenditure by business for factors of production comes to equal the receipts obtained from the sale of consumers'

goods, then, supposedly, all profit is wiped out. And once the expenditure for factors of production comes actually to exceed the receipts obtained from the sale of consumers' goods, then, supposedly, losses must result. Only a sufficient demand for consumers' goods, and corresponding lack of saving, underconsumptionism holds, can ensure the profitability of business.

To illustrate the underconsumptionist doctrine in quantitative terms, if the demand for consumers' goods is 500 monetary units and the demand for labor, 300 monetary units, as is the case in Figure 16–2, then, according to underconsumptionism, business can be profitable only if the demand for capital goods is less than 200 monetary units. If, for example, the demand for capital goods is 100 monetary units, then, according to underconsumptionism, business can be profitable in the amount of 100 monetary units. For in this case, it would have total costs in the amount of 400 monetary units (300 of cost on account of labor plus 100 of cost on account of capital goods), while its sales revenues were equal to the 500 monetary units of consumption expenditure.

Underconsumptionism regards the actual conditions of Figure 16–2, and, even more, those of Figure 17–1, as placing business in the position of having to incur an aggregate loss. For it believes that with only 500 monetary units of consumption expenditure to generate sales revenues, and a demand for factors of production of 800 monetary units generating costs of production, which is the situation in Figure 16–2, an aggregate loss of 300 must ensue. According to underconsumptionism, the case is even worse in the conditions of Figure 17–1, because there a consumption expenditure of only 400 monetary units is left to cover costs generated by 900 monetary units of productive expenditure (which last, of course, is the sum of the 300 monetary units of demand for labor plus the 600 monetary units of demand for capital goods).

Putting aside the fact that Figure 16–2 is already supposed to imply major losses, the transition from the conditions of Figure 16–2 to those of Figure 17–1 provides exactly the kind of dreaded situation described by Hobson, namely, a diminution in the demand for consumers' goods and at the very same time an increase in the expenditure for factors of production, which factors of production have no other ultimate purpose but "to provide 'utilities and conveniences' for consumers." By examining this transition, it is possible to understand exactly why it is that the "exercise of this habit [of saving]" does *not* "cause an accumulation of Capital in excess of that which is required for use"—that it does not in fact result in an aggregate loss. This benevolent outcome is already apparent inasmuch as Figure 17–1 unquestionably shows that the additional saving and productive expenditure are actually accompanied by an aggregate profit of 100, despite the fact that productive expenditure rises to 900 while the demand for consumers' goods falls to 400.

The explanation is that *the demand for capital goods is a demand for goods*. It is fully as much a demand for goods as is the demand for consumers' goods. Thus business is in no way exclusively dependent on the demand for consumers' goods for its sales revenues, because the demand for capital goods is in every respect as good a source of sales revenues as is the demand for consumers' goods. When the demand for capital goods is taken into account in the respective cases of Figures 16–2 and 17–1, it turns out that sales revenues are not merely the respective 500 and 400 of demand for consumers' goods, but include as well the respective 500 and 600 of demand for capital goods. Sales revenues in both cases are *1,000*. As a result, the productive expenditures of Figures 16–2 and 17–1, in the amounts of 800 and 900 respectively, are not deducted merely from the sales revenues constituted by the respective annual consumption expenditures of 500 and 400, but from sales revenues of 1,000.

It must be kept in mind that in each year in Figures 16-2 and 17–1 there is a demand for capital goods as well as consumers' goods. Thus, when the outlay for factors of production in each year shows up as a cost deducted from the sales revenues of the following year, it is deducted from sales revenues which are constituted not only by the demand for consumers' goods of the following year but no less by the demand for capital goods which is made in that following year. In the conditions of Figure 16–2, only *half* of the 800 outlay for factors of production in each year shows up as a cost of producing the consumers' goods of the following year, for the sales revenues of the following year are only 50 percent constituted by the consumption expenditure of 500. Fully the remaining half of the 800 of productive expenditure shows up as a cost of producing the capital goods of the following year, which also bring in sales revenues 500. The fact that in Figure 16–2 fully as much cost is deductible from receipts from the sale of capital goods as from receipts from the sale of consumers' goods has been shown from the very first, in the description of each year's output as "1K OF CAPITAL GOODS *at a Cost Value of 400*" and "1C OF CONSUMERS' GOODS *at a Cost Value of 400.*" (Italics added.)

In the transition from the conditions of Figure 16–2 to those of Figure 17–1, first 60 percent of the initially prevailing 800 outlay for factors of production comes to be deducted from the 600 of receipts from the sale of capital goods. That is to say, the cost value of the capital goods of *Year 2* rises to 480 from the 400 cost value of the capital goods of *Year 1*. At the same time, only 40

percent of the initially prevailing 800 outlay for factors of production comes to be deducted from the 400 of receipts from the sale of consumers' goods—viz., the cost value of the consumers' goods of *Year 2* actually declines to 320 from the 400 of *Year 1*, corresponding to the fall in demand for consumers' goods from 500 to 400. From *Year 3* on, of course, the 100 increase in the demand for capital goods that commenced in *Year 2* shows up in the aggregate costs of production. At that point, 60 percent of this 100 addition to the demand for factors of production is deducted from the 600 of receipts from the sale of capital goods while only 40 percent of it is deducted from the 400 of receipts from the sale of consumers' goods. In other words, the cost of the capital goods produced comes to be 60 percent of the now prevailing 900 of productive expenditure, while the cost of the consumers' goods produced comes to be 40 percent of the now prevailing 900 of productive expenditure—viz., the respective aggregate costs of capital goods and consumers' goods come to be 540 and 360. All of this was shown in Figure 17–1.

The principle here is not only that the demand for capital goods is fully as much a demand for goods as is the demand for consumers' goods, but also that *the demand for factors of production is fully as much deductible as cost from receipts from the sale of capital goods as it is from receipts from the sale of consumers' goods.* Factors of production are used to produce capital goods no less than consumers' goods, and the expenditure for such factors of production is deductible as cost from the receipts from the sale of the capital goods, just as expenditure for factors of production to produce consumers' goods is deductible as cost from the receipts from the sale of the consumers' goods.

Further, to the degree that the demand for capital goods rises relative to the demand for consumers' goods, a correspondingly larger proportion of the factors of production comes to be employed in the production of capital goods relative to the production of consumers' goods, and thus *a correspondingly larger proportion of the demand for factors of production comes to be deductible as cost from receipts from the sale of capital goods rather than from receipts from the sale of consumers' goods.* And to the degree that a larger demand for capital goods represents a larger demand for factors of production in toto—that is, a larger demand for capital goods and producers' labor taken together—the addition to the demand for factors of production is allocated as additional cost of capital goods and additional cost of consumers' goods in proportion to the changed relative demands for capital goods and consumers' goods. What is present is both a shift in the disposition of a given amount of productive expenditure as between the production of capital goods and the production of consumers' goods, and an increase in the overall total amount of productive expenditure. The larger total of productive expenditure shows up as cost of capital goods and consumers' goods respectively, in proportion to the changed relative demands for capital goods and consumers' goods.

Thus, as I have said, in Figure 17–1, when the demand for capital goods rises from 500 to 600 and the demand for factors of production in toto, from 800 to 900, while the demand for consumers' goods falls from 500 to 400, there is both a shift in the disposition of the demand for factors of production from a ⁵⁰⁄₅₀ ratio in the production of capital goods and consumers' goods to a ⁶⁰⁄₄₀ ratio, and then, in addition, a rise in the absolute demand for factors of production in the production both of capital goods and consumers' goods. The transitory result is that in anticipation of the change in relative demands, the demand for factors of production to produce capital goods rises from 400 to 480 (60 percent of 800), while the demand for factors of production to produce consumers' goods falls from 400 to 320 (40 percent of 800). The permanent result, once the 100 of additional demand for capital goods actually takes place and enlarges the demand for factors of production, is that the demand for factors of production to produce capital goods rises to 540 (60 percent of 900) and the demand for factors of production to produce consumers' goods rises to 360 (40 percent of 900), reflecting both a continuation of the changed relative allocation of the demand for factors of production and its absolute enlargement.

Understanding this twofold effect of a rise in the demand for capital goods and the overall demand for factors of production accompanying a fall in the demand for consumers' goods, makes it possible to carry the critique of underconsumptionism further, in the discussions that follow immediately below.

How the Demand for Capital Goods and Labor Can Radically and Permanently Exceed the Demand for Consumers' Goods

In order to place the alleged problem of underconsumption in the clearest possible light, and then show further why, in fact, there is no problem, let us consider a very extreme case.[86] Let us imagine that in the economic system as a whole, total spending for consumers' goods each year is 200 units of money. At the same time, let us imagine that total spending for capital goods in the economic system each year is the enormously greater sum of *800* units of money, and that the demand for labor is 100 units of money. Thus, we assume that the total demand for factors of production is 900, while the demand for consumers' goods is only 200. (The 200 of demand for consumers' goods should be understood as

constituted by 100 of consumption on the part of the wage earners employed by business and by 100 of net consumption on the part of businessmen and capitalists.) Given these assumptions, it appears to the underconsumptionists that business is placed in the position of buying its factors of production for 900 units of money each year while having to sell its products—the consumers' goods—for only 200 units of money each year. It thus appears that business is locked into the position of having to sell its products at an annual aggregate loss of 700 units of money, for it regularly buys for 900, and yet just as regularly sells for only 200.

It should already be obvious that in fact the sales revenues of business available to defray its outlay of 900 for the factors of production are not 200, but *1,000,* consisting not only of the following year's consumption expenditure of 200 but, far more importantly in terms of size, the following year's *800 of demand for capital goods*. In the conditions of this example, only 20 percent of the total aggregate demand for goods is a demand for consumers' goods, while 80 percent is a demand for capital goods. Thus, only 20 percent of the capital goods and labor of each year are employed in producing consumers' goods for the following year, while 80 percent are employed in producing capital goods for the following year. Accordingly, of the 900 monetary unit demand for factors of production only 180 (20 percent of 900) are charged against the sale of consumers' goods, while the remaining 720 (80 percent of 900), are charged against the sale of capital goods.

Indeed, if matters were as the underconsumptionists believe, and the 900 of demand for factors of production were all chargeable against the 200 of receipts from the sale of consumers' goods, the resulting 700 of loss in the consumers' goods industries would be accompanied by 800 of profit in the capital goods industries, because they would have sales receipts of 800 and *zero* costs of production since no productive expenditure would take place in their production. Such a situation is obviously impossible. Any higher rate of profit in the capital goods industries than in the consumers' goods industries would result in the withdrawal of capital and labor from the latter and their employment in the former. In the circumstances of our example, equalization of the rate of profit in the two sets of industries requires the employment of 80 percent of the factors of production in the production of capital goods and only 20 percent in the production of consumers' goods. The underconsumptionists simply fail to recognize that the expenditure for capital goods represents sales revenues to the sellers of capital goods. They see the expenditure for capital goods exclusively as showing up as a cost, and because they fail to recognize that receipts from the sale of capital goods are sales receipts, they see all the cost corresponding to the expenditure for capital goods as a cost exclusively to the consumers' goods industries. They commit these fallacies because they believe that receipts from the sale of capital goods have no separate existence—that they are somehow counted in receipts from the sale of consumers' goods and that to acknowledge their separate existence would be to commit the alleged error of "double counting."[87]

Table 17–1 provides an economy-wide income statement in elaboration of this example. In the column headed "Economy as a Whole," it shows total sales revenues and total costs in the economic system, and then, in the columns headed "Consumers' Goods" and "Capital Goods," a breakdown of total sales revenues and total costs into the sales revenues and costs of the consumers' goods and capital goods industries respectively. In all three columns, total costs are broken down into cost specifically on account of capital goods and cost specifically on account of labor. (Costs in each case, of course, are the reflection of productive expenditures.) In addition, profits are shown, both for the economic system as a whole and separately for the production of consumers' goods and capital goods respectively.

Table 17–1 shows that of the 800 worth of capital goods annually purchased, only 160 are employed in the production of next year's 200 worth of consumers' goods, and *640* are employed in the production of next year's 800 worth of capital goods. (This is shown in the row labeled "On Account of Capital Goods," under the heading "Cost.") The table also shows that of the 100 worth of labor annually purchased, only 20 are employed in the production of next year's 200 worth consumers' goods, while 80 are employed in the production of next year's 800 worth capital goods. (This is shown in the row labeled "On Account of Labor," under the heading "Cost.")

Accordingly, in the production of consumers' goods, where sales revenues are 200 and total costs are 180 (160 + 20), profits are 20. In the production of capital goods, where sales revenues are 800 and total costs are 720 (640 + 80), profits are 80.

A second table, Table 17–2, goes on to describe not only how the outlay for capital goods and labor is allocated between the production of consumers' goods and capital goods in general, but also how it is allocated within the category of capital goods among the production of capital goods of various specific degrees of remove from the production of consumers' goods. The first column of the table represents a series of years, starting with *Year N* and extending on into the indefinite future, ultimately to *Year N+n*. Each year is assumed to be identical with the following year and with the preceding year, since the table depicts a continuing equilibrium under an invariable money. In the table, the column headed s represents aggregate sales revenues, while the columns headed D_C and D_K represent the respective demands for consumers' goods and capital goods, which, taken together, are equal to those sales revenues, and respectively constitute them in the form of receipts specifically from the sale of consumers' goods or specifically from the sale of capital goods. Thus far, the table does not add anything to what was already shown in Table 17–1.

Proceeding over to the right in the table, $D_C + D_K$ are shown to equal D_C plus a breakdown of D_K into a series of subcomponents: $D_{K1} + D_{K2} + \ldots$. Implicitly, the last term here should be shown as D_{Kn}, but the table goes only as far as D_{K4}, for lack of room.

In the table, D_{K1} represents that part of the expenditure to buy capital goods in any year which is specifically for the purpose of producing the consumers' goods of the

	Economy as a Whole	=	Consumers' Goods	+	Capital Goods
Sales Receipts:	1,000	=	200	+	800
Cost:	900	=	180	+	720
On Account of Capital Goods:	800	=	160	+	640
On Account of Labor:	100	=	20	+	80
Profit:	100	=	20	+	80

Table 17–1
Sales Revenues, Costs, and Profits in the Production of Consumers' Goods and Capital Goods

Table 17–2

The Demand for Factors of Production at Various Degrees of Remove
from the Production of Consumers' Goods

YEAR	s	=	D_C	+	D_K	=	D_C	+	D_{K1}	+	D_{K2}	+	D_{K3}	+	D_{K4}	+	...
N	1,000	=	200	+	800	=	200	+	160	+	128	+	102.4	+	81.92	+	...
									20		16		12.8		10.24		
N+1	1,000	=	200	+	800	=	200	+	160	+	128	+	102.4	+	81.92	+	...
									20		16		12.8		10.24		
N+2	1,000	=	200	+	800	=	200	+	160	+	128	+	102.4	+	81.92	+	...
									20		16		12.8		10.24		
N+3	1,000	=	200	+	800	=	200	+	160	+	128	+	102.4	+	81.92	+	...
									20		16		12.8		10.24		
N+4	1,000	=	200	+	800	=	200	+	160	+	128	+	102.4	+	81.92	+	...
									20		16		12.8		10.24		
...	...	=	...	+	...	=	...	+	...	+	...	+	...	+	...	+	...
N+n	1,000	=	200	+	800	=	200	+	160	+	128	+	102.4	+	81.92	+	...
									20		16		12.8		10.24		

KEY:

s = Sales revenues.

D_C = Demand for consumers' goods.

D_K = Demand for capital goods.

D_{K1} = Demand for capital goods to produce consumers' goods.

D_{K2} = Demand for capital goods to produce the capital goods to produce consumers' goods.

D_{K3} = Demand for capital goods to produce the capital goods described under D_{K2}.

D_{K4} = Demand for capital goods to produce the capital goods described under D_{K3}.

next year. This sum, as we already know, is 160, on the principle that the proportion of the total expenditure for capital goods which is for the purpose of producing consumers' goods is in proportion to the portion of total sales receipts which is obtained in the sale of consumers' goods. Receipts from the sale of consumers' goods of 200 represent 20 percent of the total sales receipts of 1,000 in every year, and thus 20 percent, or 160, of the 800 of expenditure to buy capital goods in any given year is assumed to be chargeable to the sale of consumers' goods in the next year.

By the same token, 20 percent of the 100 of total expenditure for labor, namely, 20, is also assumed to be chargeable to the sale of consumers' goods in the next year, as cost on account of labor. The expenditure for labor in each year is shown directly below the corresponding expenditure for capital goods. Thus, the 20 appears immediately below the 160. Both together represent the cost of producing the 200 worth of consumers' goods output available in the following year. In each year, a downward and leftward sloping arrow runs from the 160 and 20 of expenditure for factors of production to produce consumers' goods, to the 200 of sales pro-

ceeds brought in by those consumers' goods in the following year. This 160 worth of capital goods and 20 worth of labor can be described as representing the value of factors of production at one degree of remove from the production of consumers' goods. In the terminology of Menger and the Austrian school, they are goods and services of the second order.[88]

In the table, D_{K2} represents that part of the outlay for capital goods in any year which is specifically for the purpose of producing those capital goods of the next year which will stand at one degree of remove from the production of consumers' goods, that is, those capital goods of the next year which will be used to produce consumers' goods for the year after next. Thus, D_{K2} is the portion of the outlay for capital goods in any given year that is devoted to the production of capital goods falling specifically under the heading of D_{K1} in the following year. D_{K2} and the demand for labor that accompanies it represent the demand for capital goods and labor at two degrees of remove from the production of consumers' goods.

By way of elaboration, the fact that in each year there is 160 of expenditure for capital goods that is specifically for the purpose of producing the consumers' goods of the following year means that in each year there are 160 of *receipts* specifically from the sale of such capital goods. In each year, therefore, a specific portion of the total outlay for capital goods and labor must be viewed as chargeable against *this specific portion of next year's receipts*. In other words, some portion of the outlay for capital goods and labor in any given year is devoted specifically to the production of those capital goods of the next year which in the following year will be devoted to the production of consumers' goods. Just as D_{K1} is the specific portion of the outlay for capital goods in any given year that is chargeable to the D_C of the following year, so D_{K2} is the specific portion of the outlay for capital goods of any given year that is chargeable to the D_{K1} of the following year.

The value of D_{K2} is taken as 128 because the 160 of demand for capital goods to produce consumers' goods—viz., D_{K1}—is 16 percent of the 1,000 aggregate demand for all goods combined. It follows, on the same principle as previously applied, that the portion of the 800 demand for capital goods devoted to producing these particular capital goods is also 16 percent—namely, 128, which last is equal to .16 times 800. In the same way, the value of the labor employed to produce the capital goods of one degree of remove from consumers' goods is 16, which, of course, is 16 percent of the 100 total demand for labor. Thus, factors of production with a combined value of 144 at two degrees of remove from the production of consumers' goods produce capital goods of one degree of remove from the production of consumers' goods, which latter capital goods have a value of 160.

In every year, there is a demand for capital goods and labor of the second degree of remove, side by side with the demand for capital goods and labor of the first degree of remove. In every year, a second downward and leftward sloping arrow runs from the 128 and 16 of expenditure for factors of production of the second degree of remove, to the 160 of sales proceeds brought in, in the following year, by the capital goods of the first degree of remove that they serve to produce.

Carrying the same reasoning a step further, the 128 of demand for capital goods of the second degree of remove constitutes 12.8 percent of the total demand for goods in each year ($128/1,000$). Thus 12.8 percent of the demand for capital goods and labor in each year can be assumed to be devoted to the production of capital goods of the second degree of remove in the following year. On this basis, the third component of the demand for capital goods, D_{K3}, turns out to be 102.4 (viz., .128 times 800). The accompanying demand for labor at this point of three degrees of remove from the production of consumers' goods is, of course, 12.8, which is 12.8 percent of 100.

Thus, 115.2 is the total demand for factors of production at this, third degree of remove, and it is the cost of producing the 128 worth of capital goods that become available in the following year at the second degree of remove from the production of consumers' goods.

Finally, the table shows that at four degrees of remove from the production of consumers' goods, namely, in the column labeled D_{K4}, 81.92 worth of capital goods and 10.24 worth of labor are employed to produce the 102.4 worth of D_{K3} capital goods that will become available in the following year at three degrees of remove from the production of consumers' goods. (These amounts, of course, represent 10.24 percent of the respective 800 and 100 demands for capital goods and labor, which percentage corresponds to the percentage of 1,000 monetary units of total sales revenues that is constituted by the 102.4 monetary units of sales revenues represented by D_{K3}.)

In every year, capital goods and labor of all degrees of remove exist side by side and are used to produce capital goods of one degree of remove less for the following year; or, in the case of capital goods and labor which are themselves merely of one degree of remove, consumers' goods for the following year. At all degrees of remove in the table, arrows trace the connection to the next, lower degree of remove in the following year and thereby show how the demand for factors of production at any given degree of remove serves to bring in sales revenues greater than itself.

Thus, far from the entire outlay for factors of production being charged against the sale of consumers' goods, only that portion is charged which corresponds to the *fraction* of the total demand for goods constituted by the demand for consumers' goods specifically. Thus, in this case, not the full 900 of demand for factors of production is charged to the production of consumers' goods, but only 20 percent of that 900. The portion of the outlay for factors of production made by the producers of consumers' goods which is constituted by their demand for capital goods (160 out of 180) in turn constitutes the sales receipts of the producers of these capital goods. The producers of these capital goods in turn must make outlays for factors of production, and, in the present case, the principal portion of their outlays is for capital goods, and constitutes the sales receipts of further producers of capital goods, and so on. It is only in this manner, by cumulating the demand for capital goods made by producers at different degrees of remove from the production of consumers' goods, that the outlays for factors of production by business exceed the demand for consumers' goods.

From a mathematical perspective, the right-hand portion of Table 17–2 represents an infinite series that is repeated over and over again in succeeding rows of the table. Starting with the second term of this series in the first row, namely, the term under the heading D_{K1}, and taking each further term to the right representing the outlays for capital goods of progressively greater degrees of remove from the production and sale of consumers' goods, it is clear that each such term is covered by a larger volume of sales revenues for the corresponding product, which is represented by the term of the series just to the left, one row down. (In the case of the demand for capital goods under the head D_{K1}, the sales revenues represented by the term to the left one row down are, of course, the demand for consumers' goods, D_C.)

It should be understood that the assumption made in the preceding discussion that the demand for capital goods and labor is always strictly proportional to the sales revenues brought in, and that the two respective demands are always in the same proportion to each other, is not necessary. It has been made for the purpose of simplification. Actually, technical considerations would make the demands for capital goods and labor stand in different proportions both to sales revenues and to each other at different stages of production. Such differences, however, do not affect anything of significance. From the perspective of the present discussion, they are mutually offsetting.

It should also be realized that, beyond a point, production at the higher degrees of remove is physically indistinguishable from production simultaneously going on at lower degrees of remove. For example, it is a matter of such things as the output of steel serving in the construction of steel mills, some portion of whose output serves in the construction of further steel mills, and so on and on, indefinitely. Production at the higher degrees of remove becomes a matter of indefinite duplications of processes of production simultaneously going on at lower degrees of remove. That is, beyond a point, it differs from processes of production simultaneously being carried on at lower degrees of remove only in that its ultimate targets are more remote—for example, the steel mills that will be built from steel produced in steel mills constructed with this year's steel versus simply the steel mills that will be built with this year's steel. Thus, a rise in the economic degree of capitalism and in capital intensiveness represents an increase both in the extent to which physically different processes of production requiring the more remote employment of capital goods and labor can be implemented and in the proportions in which physically identical processes of production are devoted to temporally more remote ends.

Consumption as the Purpose of Production and the Progressive Production of Consumers' Goods Over Time

Ironically, Table 17–2 demonstrates that, if qualified by the word "ultimately," Hobson was right when he said

that the only use of capital is to aid in the production of "'utilities and conveniences' for consumers." His error was in thinking that this was incompatible with the demand for factors of production being greater than the demand for consumers' goods.

Table 17–2 shows that the entire outlay for factors of production in any year, even though enormously larger than the demand for consumers' goods (900 vs. 200) ultimately serves entirely in the production of consumers' goods, and is ultimately chargeable entirely to the sale of consumers' goods. However, the consumers' goods in question are certainly not those just of the next year. Rather, they are the consumers' goods that will come into existence to a progressively greater extent with the passage of time. For example, the D_{K1} of Year N, and its associated demand for labor, is the only part of the outlay for factors of production in Year N that directly serves in the production of consumers' goods—specifically, in the production of the consumers' goods that become available in Year N+1. This outlay is directly chargeable to the sale of consumers' goods. However, the D_{K2} of Year N, and its associated demand for labor, indirectly serve in the production of consumers' goods—the consumers' goods that will become available in Year N+2. These outlays are indirectly chargeable to the sale of those consumers' goods, for they serve in the production of the capital goods that become available in Year N+1 and which in turn serve in the production of the consumers' goods of Year N+2. Arrows trace the path from D_{K2} and its associated demand for labor in Year N to the sale of consumers' goods two years later.

In the same way, the D_{K3} of Year N, and its associated demand for labor, indirectly serve in the production of the consumers' goods of Year N+3; the D_{K4} of Year N, and its associated demand for labor, indirectly serve in the production of the consumers' goods of Year N+4; and, finally, the D_{Kn} of Year N, and its associated demand for labor (neither of which are shown in the table), indirectly serve in the production of the consumers' goods of Year N+n. Again, arrows trace the paths. All outlays for capital goods and labor are, to repeat, *ultimately* for the sake of producing consumers' goods. It is only a question of how far in the future those consumers' goods lie.[89]

Thus, in Table 17–2, the cumulative demand for capital goods that takes place in Year N and that contributes to the production of consumers' goods within four years from Year N is 160 + 128 + 102.4 + 81.92, or 472.32 out of an eventual total of 800. This is the sum of the demands for capital goods in Year N under the column headings D_{K1} through D_{K4}. The cumulative demand for labor that contributes to the production of consumers' goods within four years from Year N is 20 + 16 + 12.8 + 10.24, or 59.04

out of an eventual total of 100. This is the sum of the associated demands for labor in *Year N* under the column headings D_{K1} through D_{K4}. The combined cumulative demand for capital goods and labor together is thus 531.36 out of an eventual total of 900. If the number of years beyond *Year N* under consideration were increased from four to eleven, then it would be found that more than 90 percent of the demand for capital goods and labor in *Year N* would be accounted for as contributing to the production of consumers' goods. This, indeed, is shown in Table 17–3.

Table 17–3 compresses the format of Table 17–2. It shows one-dimensionally what the former shows two-dimensionally. Thus, it is able to depict the expenditures of a larger number of years in the same space. It shows the contribution of the labor and capital goods of *Year N* to the production of consumers' goods through *Year N+11*, both year by year and cumulatively.

Column one of the table is the series of years *N* through *N+11*. Column two lists one through eleven degrees of remove from the production of consumers' goods, with each degree of remove representing a year

of time—the time between *Year N* and the year shown in column one. The expenditures shown in columns three, four, and five represent the expenditures made in *Year N*—at the degree of remove shown in column two—on behalf of the production of consumers' goods that become available in the corresponding year in column one.

Thus, for example, for *Year N+5* the table shows that the expenditure for capital goods that is made in *Year N* on behalf of the consumers' goods that will become available in *Year N+5* is 65.54, while the associated demand for labor is 8.19; the summation of these two figures, shown in the last column, is 73.73. Similarly, for *Year N+10* the expenditure for capital goods that is made in *Year N* on behalf of the consumers' goods that will become available in *Year N+10* is 21.47, while the associated demand for labor is 2.68; the summation of these two figures is 24.15, which, as in the previous case, is shown in the last column.[90]

When these expenditures for factors of production on behalf of consumers' goods that will come into existence over the years *N+1* through *N+11* are cumulated, it turns out that 91.40 of the 100 total demand for labor serves

		Table 17–3		
		The Demand for Factors of Production in *Year N* and Its Cumulative Contribution to the Production of Consumers' Goods in the Future		
Future Year	Degree of Remove of *Year N* from Future Year	Demand for Capital Goods in *Year N* on Behalf of Consumers' Goods of Given Future Year	Demand for Labor in *Year N* on Behalf of Consumers' Goods of Given Future Year	Total Demand for Factors of Production in *Year N* on Behalf of Consumers' Goods of Given Future Year
N+1	1	160.00	20.00	180.00
N+2	2	128.00	16.00	144.00
N+3	3	102.40	12.80	115.20
N+4	4	81.92	10.24	92.16
N+5	5	65.54	8.19	73.73
N+6	6	52.43	6.55	58.98
N+7	7	41.94	5.24	47.19
N+8	8	33.55	4.19	37.75
N+9	9	26.84	3.36	30.20
N+10	10	21.47	2.68	24.16
N+11	11	17.18	2.15	19.33
	Cumulative Demands:	731.27	91.40	822.67
...	Eventual Cumulative	...	...	...
N+n	Demands:	800.00	100.00	900.00

directly or indirectly in the production of consumers' goods and that 731.27 of the 800 total demand for capital goods serves directly or indirectly in the production of consumers' goods. Thus, 822.67 of the 900 total demand for factors for factors of production serves directly or indirectly in the production of consumers' goods that will become available within eleven years.[91] This figure and the two figures from which it is derived all represent something more than 90 percent of the respective total demands for labor, capital goods, and factors of production in general. If the cumulation process were concluded with *Year N+10* rather than *Year N+11*, the accumulated sums would represent something less 90 percent of the respective total demands.

Thus conditions in Tables 17–2 and 17–3 are essentially similar to the conditions previously described in connection with Figures 17–2 and 17–3, where it was found that in both cases 90 percent of the factors of production in existence in a base year contributed to the production of consumers' goods within some period of years—less than four years in the case of Figure 17–2, and more than four years in the case of Figure 17–3.[92] Table 17–3 confirms that in all cases, irrespective of the demand for capital goods relative to the demand for consumers' goods, the entire supply of factors of production in existence in any given period of time always ultimately serves to produce consumers' goods and only consumers' goods. The effect of a rise in the demand for capital goods relative to the demand for consumers' goods is merely to increase the time interval which must elapse before any given percentage of the existing supply of factors of production results in the production of consumers' goods. All that is involved in the present, deliberately extreme case is a substantially longer average period of production. Thus only by *Year N+11* will more than 90 percent of the factors of production available in *Year N* have contributed to the production of consumers' goods.

What must always be kept in mind, however, is that even though all production is ultimately for the sake of the production of consumers' goods, the length of the period of time which must elapse before any given percentage of the production of a given base year results in the production of consumers' goods is of critical importance, insofar as that time span is determined by the extent of concentration on the production of capital goods. In the case of Tables 17–2 and 17–3, as opposed to that of Figure 17–2, four years elapse, and still the fraction of the capital goods and labor of *Year N* which cumulatively result in the production of consumers' goods is below 60 percent ($531.36/900$). Eleven years must elapse before it exceeds 90 percent. Under different conditions, this figure could be 90 percent (or even more) in just a single year. This last case would be approached if each year the relative magnitudes of D_C and D_K were the reverse of those in the present example. If D_C were 800 and D_K were 200, then 80 percent of the capital goods and labor of *Year N* would have served in the production of consumers' goods by *Year N+1*, and a further 16 percent by *Year N+2*.

Such differences make all the difference in the world. In an economy in which 80 or 90 percent of the capital goods and labor are used up in producing consumers' goods in just one year, production will be in a radically inferior state in comparison with one in which a decade or more must elapse before such a high percentage is achieved. In the latter economy, the production of each year is devoted heavily to the production of the means of production for the following year and for more remote future years. In the former economy, the production of each year is devoted only minimally to the production of means of production for the following year and more remote future years. Thus, the ability to implement technological advances will be radically different in the two economies, with the economy enjoying the longer average period of production possessing enormous advantages over the one with the shorter average period of production.[93] In its case, the likely outcome will be that its total ability to produce and accumulate capital will rise from year to year, with the result that it will enjoy economic progress and rising prosperity.

In contrast, in the economy with the radically shorter period of production, the result at best must be stagnation at an extremely low level. Indeed, insofar as an economy's average period of production is first in the process of becoming substantially shorter, the result must be capital decumulation and a falling ability to produce from year to year, in other words, economic retrogression and worsening poverty. This is because an economy suffering a substantial decline in its average period of production will not be able to maintain technologies it has previously implemented insofar as they require the employment of substantial quantities of means of production significantly in advance of the completion either of the ultimate consumers' goods or, indeed, of the production of the relevant capital goods. Economic retrogression must go on until the methods of production employed require so little in the way of capital goods that the capital goods can all be replaced just by devoting to their production the modest share of the meager output that it is possible to devote to their production in the conditions of the case.

Tables 17–2 and 17–3 show that the entire outlay for factors of production in any given base year can be regarded as covered by receipts from the sale of consumers' goods, provided only that one looks to the production of consumers' goods over an extended enough number of years. Thus, in Table 17–2, the outlays for capital goods and labor under the headings D_{K1} through D_{K4} in *Year N* can be regarded as covered by a total of 800 of receipts from the sale of consumers' goods—viz., by 200 of receipts from the sale of consumers' goods in each of the four years $N+1$ through $N+4$. By the same token, the outlays for capital goods and labor in *Year N* that would appear in a table wide enough to contain columns for D_{K1} through D_{K11} could be regarded as covered by the 2,200 of receipts from the sale of consumers' goods brought in over the years $N+1$ through $N+11$.

This understanding should not give rise to any new worry that now perhaps business somehow appears inexplicably profitable, with 2,200 of consumer sales receipts covering less than 900 of demand for factors of production. In each year, aggregate profits are no more than 100. In each year, the 200 of receipts from the sale of consumers' goods covers—accordion-like—the outlays for factors of production made not just in any one prior year, but in a whole series of prior years extending back into the indefinite past. For example, the 200 of receipts from the sale of consumers' goods in *Year N+4* covers far more than the demand for capital goods and labor made just in *Year N*. It covers successively the 160 of demand for capital goods and 20 of demand for labor made under the heading D_{K1} in *Year N+3*, the 128 of demand for capital goods and 16 of demand for labor made under the heading D_{K2} in *Year N+2*, and the 102.4 of demand for capital goods and 12.8 of demand for labor made under the heading D_{K3} in *Year N+1*, as well the 81.92 of demand for capital goods and 10.24 of demand for labor made under the heading D_{K4} in *Year N*. Indeed, the 200 of demand for consumers' goods made in *Year N+4* covers an indefinitely large number of further expenditures for capital goods and labor extending back indefinitely into years prior to *Year N*.

A relatively small amount of demand for consumers' goods is able profitably to cover such a large demand for capital goods and labor—a demand much larger than itself—precisely because, as repeatedly shown, the demand for capital goods is subdivided into successive, component parts, each one progressively more remote from the production of consumers' goods. These parts stand behind one another and can, in effect, be fitted into one another, along with their accompanying demands for labor. That is, each preceding part of the demand for capital goods is smaller than the one it precedes, just as the first and largest component part of the demand for capital goods is smaller than the demand for consumers' goods, which it precedes. And thus each prior component part is able to represent sales revenues that profitably cover the next, more remote component part along with

its accompanying demand for labor.

As illustration, the situation in Tables 17–2 and 17–3 is that 200 of demand for consumers' goods in any one year covers 900 of demand for factors of production made over an indefinitely large number of prior years. In the first instance, it covers only 160 of demand for capital goods and 20 of demand for labor—viz., the demands for capital goods and labor made at one degree of remove the year before. In the second instance, it covers the 128 of demand for capital goods and 16 of demand for labor that were made at two degrees of remove, two years before. This latter demand for capital goods and labor was directly covered by the 160 of demand for capital goods at one degree of remove. (In effect, the 128 and 16 stand behind the 160, and are covered by it, while the 160 and a further 20 of demand for labor stand behind the 200 of demand for consumers' goods and are covered by it.) The same process extends backward prior to the 128 and 16, to an indefinite number of still earlier years each of whose demands for capital goods and labor are covered by a demand for capital goods that is one year less removed from the demand for consumers' goods.

Tables 17–2 and 17–3 depict a kind of lining-up and fitting-in process as it were, by which successive components of the demand for factors of production at further degrees of remove are covered by the demand for capital goods at one degree of remove less, and ultimately by the demand for consumers' goods. A good analogy is provided by a set of luggage of the type in which all of the pieces can be successively packed into the next-larger piece, with the result that all of them ultimately fit into the single, largest piece. For example, an attaché case fits inside an overnighter, which fits inside a one-suiter, which, in turn, fits inside a two-suiter, which, finally, fits inside a three-suiter. The three-suiter is the counterpart of the demand for consumers' goods, while the remaining, successively smaller pieces are the counterpart of demands for capital goods at successive degrees of remove. The largest piece, the three-suiter, is large enough to contain all of the smaller pieces, even though the combined volume of the four smaller pieces is substantially greater than the volume of the largest piece. This is exactly how it is when the demand for capital goods, or capital goods plus labor, is greater than the demand for consumers' goods. As in Table 17–3, the demand for labor and capital goods at the eleventh degree of remove fits into—viz., is profitably covered by—the demand for capital goods at the tenth degree of remove, which, in turn, together with its associated demand for labor, fits into the demand for capital goods at the ninth degree of remove, and so on until the demand for capital goods and labor at the first degree of remove fits into the demand for consumers' goods.

The suitcase analogy can shed light on other important aspects of the process. It helps to make clear exactly how it is possible—and, indeed, under the conditions of a fixed quantity of money and total volume of spending, absolutely necessary—that *in order for the demand for capital goods to rise, the demand for consumers' goods must fall.* For if there is a fixed total amount of material that is available for the production of all the pieces of luggage in the set, then it is clear that if all of this material were devoted to the production of a single, very large, largest piece, say, to a five- or six-suiter, then absolutely no material would be available for the production of the smaller pieces. In order to have material available for the production of the smaller pieces, it is absolutely essential that the amount of material devoted to the largest piece be strictly limited. We know, of course, that it is limited, and that, nevertheless, there is no problem of its being made too small to contain all the other pieces at the same time, because each of those other pieces successively fits into the next-larger one. In just the same way, with a fixed quantity of money and total volume of spending, in order for there to be a greater demand for capital goods, the demand for consumers' goods must be correspondingly less. And however great the demand for capital goods may become relative to the demand for consumers' goods it will all still "fit into" the demand for consumers' goods because it consists of separate portions which successively "fit into" each other.

The Ratio of Demands Between Stages

The luggage analogy can be carried further. It shows not only that as the size of the largest piece in the set is reduced, material becomes available to enlarge the size of all the remaining pieces, but that the greater total volume of space now represented by the smaller pieces fits into the smaller volume of space now represented by the largest piece, by virtue of a change in the ratio between the size of the succeeding pieces. At the most extreme, the largest piece requires all of the material and has the maximum possible volume, leaving no material and no volume whatever for the smaller pieces. One can think of this case as the five- or six-suiter followed by a second piece *zero percent* as large. When the size of the largest piece is reduced to that of a three-suiter, the next-largest piece becomes perhaps two-thirds as large (the two-suiter), followed by a third largest piece (the one-suiter) having a size perhaps half as large as the second largest piece, and so on. Thus, as the size of the largest piece is reduced, it becomes capable of containing the growing total volume of space contained in the further pieces by virtue of a rise in the size ratios between the successive pieces.

It is essentially the same when it concerns the demand for consumers' goods and the demand for capital goods, only more so. The demand for consumers' goods can fall and the demand for capital goods can rise at the very same time, and yet the demand for capital goods is always profitably covered by the demand for the product, whether further capital goods or consumers' goods. All that is necessary is a change in the ratio between the demand for the product at each stage and the demand for the capital goods to produce the product. This fact can be highlighted by comparing the present case of a 200 demand for consumers' goods and 800 demand for capital goods, with the case back in Figure 16–2 of a 500 demand for consumers' goods and a 500 demand for capital goods.

In the present case, the demand for capital goods at one degree of remove from the demand for consumers' goods is 160—80 percent of the demand for consumers' goods. In the conditions of Figure 16–2, the demand for capital goods at one degree of remove from the demand for consumers' goods is 250—50 percent of the demand for consumers' goods. It follows that if the economic system made a transition from the conditions of Figure 16–2 to those of the present case, not only would the demand for consumers' goods fall, but also the demand for capital goods at one degree of remove would fall, because the fall in demand for consumers' goods would be so very great. But it should be noted that this fall in demand for capital goods at one degree of remove would be much smaller than the fall in demand for consumers' goods. While the fall in demand for consumers' goods is 60 percent (500 to 200), the fall in demand for capital goods at one degree of remove is only 36 percent (250 to 160).

And then, which may appear to be astonishing to some people, it turns out that from two degrees of remove on, the demand for capital goods in the present case begins to further and further *surpass* the demand for capital goods in the conditions of Figure 16–2, despite the fact that the demand for consumers' goods is so much lower in the present case. For at two degrees of remove, the demand for capital goods in the present case is 128 (80 percent of 80 percent of 200), while the demand for capital goods at this degree of remove in the conditions of Figure 16–2 is only 125 (50 percent of 50 percent of 500). At three degrees of remove, the difference is that between 80 percent to the third power times 200, and 50 percent to the third power times 500—viz., between 102.4 and 62.5—which is a much wider difference in favor of the present case.

Indeed, the difference between the present case and that of Figure 16–2 can be expressed as the difference between two infinite series, the first term of one of which is 200 and the first term of the other of which is 500, and with each succeeding term being 80 percent of the preceding term in the one case and only 50 percent in the other. When seen in this way, it becomes obvious that very quickly the succeeding terms become relatively larger in the case in which the first term—the demand for consumers' goods—is smaller, and then widen their lead with each succeeding term. This fact is illustrated in Table 17–4, which compares the demand for capital goods and labor in the present case with that of Figure 16–2 for eleven degrees of remove. The table shows that starting with the sixth degree of remove even the demand for labor in the present case is greater than in the conditions of Figure 16–2, despite the fact that the total demand for labor is only 100 in the present case while it was 300 in the conditions of Figure 16–2.

The general principle can be stated as follows: When the demand for consumers' goods falls and the demand for capital goods rises, the process represents the transition from an infinite series with a relatively high first term followed by a relatively rapid rate of diminution in the subsequent terms, to a new infinite series with a correspondingly lower first term and a correspondingly diminished rate of diminution in the subsequent terms. When understood in this way, it becomes obvious that in the conditions of an invariable money, in which the sum of all terms combined will always be the same, such as 1,000 monetary units, the sum of all terms beyond the first—viz., the demand for capital goods—is higher, the lower is the first term, which first term, of course, is the demand for consumers' goods.

It is worth noting a related fact. Namely, that while in the present case something over 90 percent of the total demand for factors of production serves directly or indirectly in the production of consumers' goods within eleven degrees of remove, the percentage for Figure 16–2 within the same number of degrees of remove is virtually 100 percent. The significance of this is that provision for more remote future periods continues to be substantial in the one case, after it is virtually exhausted in the other.

More on the Average Period of Production

The preceding discussion, particularly the application of infinite series, raises questions concerning the length of the average period of production. The average period of production can be understood, quite correctly, as covering a period of potentially unlimited length. To some very limited extent, the consumers' goods being produced today owe their existence to capital goods and labor employed at the time of Caesar, indeed, to capital goods and labor employed in the very earliest periods of human history. And to some extent that is also very limited, the capital goods and labor in existence today

will contribute to the production of consumers' goods in the years 5,000, 10,000, and beyond.

This is so because with the exception of the very first consumers' goods, which were appropriated directly from nature, such as nuts and berries growing wild on trees, all consumers' goods have been produced with the aid of capital goods. And with the exception of the very first capital goods, which were also appropriated directly from nature, such as rocks and sticks, all capital goods have been and will continue to be themselves produced with the aid of capital goods. Thus, the indirect contribution of capital goods to the production of consumers' goods spans a period of time that is virtually coextensive with man's presence on earth and, as far as the future is concerned, a number of degrees of remove that has no fixed limit.

Obviously, the contribution of the past to the present and of the present to the future declines exponentially as one extends the period of time under consideration. And for this very reason, I have followed the procedure of selecting a limit, in the form of how long a period of time must elapse for a given percentage of the means of production in existence in a base period to have directly or indirectly contributed to the production of consumers' goods. Applying that approach, the length of the average period of production becomes sharply delimited and independent of the absolute length of man's existence on earth either up to now or at any point in the future.[94]

Whether one takes the contribution of 90 percent of the factors of production in existence in a base period or 99 percent of such factors of production, or whatever percentage, the period of time which must elapse before any such percentage contributes to the production of consumers' goods is strictly delimited, and always remains the same, so long as the relative production of consumers' goods and capital goods is the same.

The method of measuring the average period of production employed thus far is very easy to apply in the highly simplified conditions which have been assumed, namely, that all capital goods in existence in the beginning of a year are used up in that very same year and that a year is the period of time which elapses in all stages of production. Conditions are far more complex in reality, of course. Thus, an alternative, but still relatively simple method may be appropriate for conceiving the length of the average period of production.

This is the concept of *how long a time would have to elapse for the wage payments made in a given period to grow to equality with the prevailing level of spending for consumers' goods when compounded at the rate of one plus the prevailing rate of profit*. To illustrate the concept in the conditions of Figure 16–2, it means the time that must elapse for 300 of wage payments to grow to equality

Table 17–4

Comparison of the Present, Extreme Case With That of Figure 16-2

Degree of Remove of Year N from Future Year	PRESENT CASE			CASE OF FIGURE 16–2		
	Demand for Capital Goods in Year N on Behalf of Consumers' Goods of Given Future Year	Demand for Labor in Year N on Behalf of Consumers' Goods of Given Future Year	Total Demand for Factors of Production in Year N on Behalf of Consumers' Goods of Given Future Year	Demand for Capital Goods in Year N on Behalf of Consumers' Goods of Given Future Year	Demand for Labor in Year N on Behalf of Consumers' Goods of Given Future Year	Total Demand for Factors of Production on Year N on Behalf of Consumers' Goods of Given Future Year*
1	160.00	20.00	180.00	250.00	150.00	400.00
2	128.00	16.00	144.00	125.00	75.00	200.00
3	102.40	12.80	115.20	62.50	37.50	100.00
4	81.92	10.24	92.16	31.25	18.75	50.00
5	65.54	8.19	73.73	15.63	9.38	25.00
6	52.43	6.55	58.98	7.81	4.69	12.50
7	41.94	5.24	47.18	3.91	2.34	6.25
8	33.55	4.19	37.74	1.95	1.17	3.13
9	26.84	3.36	30.20	0.98	0.59	1.56
10	21.47	2.68	24.15	0.49	0.29	0.78
11	17.18	2.15	19.33	0.24	0.15	0.39
Cumulative Demands:	731.27	91.40	822.67	499.76	299.85	799.61
. . .	. . .	. . .	. . .	. . .	. . .	. . .
Eventual Cumulative Demands:	800.00	100.00	900.00	500.00	300.00	800.00

*Summing the two columns to the left may not equal this column because of rounding.

with 500 of demand for consumers' goods at one plus the 11.11 percent rate of profit that prevails in Figure 16–2. In the case considered in Tables 17–2 and 17–3, it means the time that must elapse for 100 of wage payments to grow to equality with 200 of consumer spending at the implied rate of profit of 5.26 percent. (This last is the rate of profit implied by a 100-amount of profit—which is equal to the 100 of net consumption in the case described by the tables—divided by 1,900 of capital, which latter equals 900 of productive expenditure plus 1,000 of cash in the hands of business. Thus, the rate of profit here is

the same as the rate of profit that prevails in the conditions described earlier in Figure 17–1.)

The basis for this method of measurement of the average period of production is the fact that the price of every product is ultimately equal to a sum of profits and wage payments extending into the past, with profits compounding on the wage payments at the prevailing rate of profit, as the process of production successively approaches the present.[95] The lower is the rate of profit and the greater is the ratio of the demand for consumers' goods to the demand for labor, the longer is the average period of production. The higher is the rate of profit and the smaller is the ratio of the demand for consumers' goods to the demand for labor, the shorter is the average period of production. In the specific cases of Figure 16–2 and that of Tables 17–2 and 17–3, for example, the average period of production turns out to be 4.89 and 13.5 years respectively, when computed in this way.[96]

The reason that the length of time required for the current payment of wages to grow to equality with a sum equal to the prevailing level of demand for consumers' goods, at the currently prevailing rate of profit, can be taken as the measure of the length of the average period of production is as follows. If an invariable money prevailed for an indefinitely long period of time, along with constancy in the ratios between the demands for capital goods and consumers' goods and capital goods and labor, today's demands for consumers' goods and labor could be taken as representing the demands for consumers' goods and labor in every future year, and today's rate of profit could be taken as representing the rate of profit for the indefinite future. Today's wage payments would then be launched, in effect, toward segments of future demands for consumers' goods which in toto equalled today's demand for consumers' goods, and they would be launched with continuing "velocities," so to speak, equal to the prevailing rate of profit. The average time required for n segments of this year's wage payments to grow to equality with n segments of aggregate consumer demand collectively equal to the aggregate consumer demand of this year, at the currently prevailing rate of profit, is approximated by the time required for the sum of all wage payments this year to grow to equality with a sum equal to this year's consumer demand, at the currently prevailing rate of profit. Thus, to use the case of Table 17–3 as illustration, the average time required for the sum of $20 + 16 + \ldots = 100$ of wage payments this year to grow at a 5.26 percent rate of profit to equality with $20(1.0526) + 16(1.0526)^2 + \ldots = 200$, is approximated by the time required for 100 to grow to 200 at a 5.26 percent rate of profit, namely, 13.5 years.

To adapt this technique to the conditions of an increasing quantity of money and volume of spending, it is necessary to estimate the influence of this factor on the prevailing rate of profit and then to subtract the estimated monetary component from the rate of profit before performing the calculation.

A Rise in the Demand for Capital Goods and Fall in the Demand for Consumers' Goods: The Cross-Hatching of Production

The belief that the demand for consumers' goods by itself must cover the outlays of business for factors of production is so deep-rooted that still further discussion

demonstrating the contrary is called for. Therefore, let us consider a concretized illustration of a drop in consumption. Let us take two industries producing consumers' goods as representing all industries producing consumers' goods. The automobile and air-conditioning industries will serve. We assume that the consumption of the owners and creditors of the automobile industry manifests itself in a demand for air conditioners, the product which we employ to represent all consumers' goods which the producers of automobiles might purchase. And we assume that the consumption of the owners and creditors of the air-conditioning industry takes the form of a demand for automobiles, the product which we employ to represent all consumers' goods which the producers of air conditioners might purchase.

Now let us imagine that the businessmen and capitalists of the automobile industry reduce their consumption. Must this adversely affect the producers of air conditioners? Not at all. For the funds which the businessmen and capitalists of the automobile industry previously employed in their own consumption can now be employed in the purchase of products to be employed in their business. Air conditioners can be installed in the automobiles they manufacture, or if not air conditioners themselves, then some other product which can be produced by the air-conditioning industry and which is of use in the production of automobiles. Thus, the total sales revenues of the air-conditioning industry are unchanged. All that has happened is that now the air-conditioning industry concentrates less on the production of consumer air conditioners and devotes more of its resources to the production of something employed in the manufacture of automobiles, such as automobile air conditioners. Thus, there has simply been a shift from consumption expenditure to productive expenditure on the part of the businessmen and capitalists of the automobile industry, and a corresponding shift in the production activities of the producers of air conditioners in response to a change in demand.

If no objection can be made to our treatment thus far, then, certainly, none can be made to the assumption that instead of the consumption of the businessmen and capitalists of the automobile industry falling, while that of the businessmen and capitalists of the air-conditioning industry remains unchanged, the reverse occurs. For then it would simply be a matter of the businessmen and capitalists of the air-conditioning industry buying fewer pleasure cars and correspondingly more trucks (or cars) to be employed in their business. In this case, the automobile industry would concentrate less on the production of consumers' goods and more on the production of capital goods. This time, there would be a shift in the demand of the businessmen and capitalists of the air-conditioning industry and a corresponding shift in production on the part of the businessmen and capitalists of the automobile industry. As in the case of the air-conditioning industry a moment ago, the total sales revenues of the automobile industry would remain the same.

What is present in both of these cases is the very important physical fact that every capitalist who reduces his consumption and expands his purchases of capital goods thereby benefits his customers to precisely the same degree. This is because the buyers of his products spend no more in the purchase of those products, while more has been spent in their production. The capitalist who so acts passes on to his customers, in the product he sells, the contribution of the factors of production which otherwise would have been employed in producing for his own consumption. This is what happens when the producers of automobiles reduce their consumption. They provide their customers with more and better automobiles, because instead of buying products to be consumed, they now possess the financial means of buying better-quality materials and more and better accessories or components or more and better plant and equipment; and to their increased financial means corresponds the increased physical means of producing these products, owing to the release of factors of production from the production of consumers' goods. Exactly the same kind of result occurs when the manufacturers of air conditioners reduce their consumption: not only do they then have additional financial means of buying more and better capital goods, but also to their greater financial means correspond the increased physical means of producing those capital goods, owing to the release of factors of production from the production of consumers' goods.

It is when the consumption of both sets of businessmen and capitalists is assumed to drop simultaneously that difficulties are imagined. Yes, it will be said, the businessmen and capitalists of the automobile industry can reduce their consumption and employ more funds in their business, because the demand for automobiles has not fallen. Alternatively, the businessmen and capitalists of the air-conditioning industry can reduce their consumption and employ more funds in their business, because the demand for air conditioners has not fallen. But both together? That, it will be claimed, is impossible, because it means that the demand for the products of the two sets of producers has fallen and they are being asked to spend more at the very time that the revenues they derive from their products are less.

Nevertheless, of course, it is possible. And the revenues they derive are not any less. The automobile industry, instead of producing merely more and better automobiles by virtue of its increased demand for capital goods, now produces more and better automobiles *and*

more and better trucks, or other capital goods. And the air-conditioning industry, instead of producing merely more and better consumer air conditioners by virtue of its increased demand for capital goods, now produces both more and better consumer air conditioners *and* more and better capital goods, such as air conditioners for automobiles and trucks.

Moreover, each industry's improved production of capital goods then serves the production of the other not only with respect to the other's production of consumers' goods, but also with respect to the other's *further production of capital goods*. The automobile industry's improved production of trucks or other capital goods resulting from its increased input of capital goods, serves the air-conditioning industry not only in the production of consumer air conditioners, but *also* in the production of the capital goods produced by the air-conditioning industry, thereby making possible still further improvements in the production of both types of products by the air-conditioning industry. By the same token, the air-conditioning industry's improved production of capital goods resulting from its increased input of capital goods, serves the automobile industry not only with respect to its output of cars, but also with respect to its output of trucks or other capital goods, thus making possible still further improvements in the automobile industry's production of capital goods as well as consumers' goods. The improvements of each in the production of capital goods, in serving to improve the other's ability to produce not only consumers' goods but also capital goods, creates the possibility of endless improvement through endless feedback, with the other's improved production of capital goods serving in the further improvement of one's own production, including one's further production of capital goods, and thus in the still further improvement of the other's capital goods as well as consumers' goods.

There are three things involved: (1) A shift in the demand of each party from consumers' goods to capital goods, causing a corresponding shift in the production of the other. (2) An increase in the production of each party resulting from his possession of the additional capital goods produced by the other. (3) A disposition of the enlarged productive ability of each party in favor of capital goods, conforming to the change in demand on the part of the other.

In response to the other's change in demand, each party shifts from the production of consumers' goods to the production of capital goods. And as the result of his own change in demand, each party employs more funds—and more real resources—in producing both his consumers' goods *and* his capital goods than if the demand of the other party alone had changed. That the demand of the other party has changed results in the fact that one not only employs additional capital, but also employs a correspondingly larger proportion of one's additional capital in the production of further capital goods.

What happens as the result of this process is that production becomes cross-hatched, as it were, or more cross-hatched. That is, part of the output, or a greater part of the output, of each of the industries serves as capital goods to the other and enables the other, in turn, all the better to produce not only consumers' goods but also capital goods and thus to supply it with still more and still better capital goods, as well as its wage earners and businessmen and capitalists with more and better consumers' goods. The result in our example is that the automobile industry is able to carry on its production both of consumers' goods and of capital goods with the aid of more of the output of the air-conditioning industry, and the air-conditioning industry is able to carry on its production both of consumers' goods and of capital goods with the aid of more of the output of the automobile industry. And the output of each that serves the other benefits from a greater prior contribution of the output of the other.

What is true of this illustration based on two industries is true of the economic system generally. The greater is the demand for capital goods relative to the demand for consumers' goods in the economic system, the larger is the fraction of the output of the economic system that takes the form of capital goods and the larger is the fraction of the output of the economic system that enters into the production of capital goods. Both capital goods and consumers' goods have more prior output going into them, as well as more of current output being in the form of capital goods. The consequence of the expanded and improved production of capital goods is the possibility of endless improvement in the further production of capital goods and thus of endless improvement in the production of consumers' goods.

These results, of course, are fully confirmed by examining the data of Figure 17–1 as the transition is made to a more capital intensive economy, and thereafter. The economic progress of Figure 17–1 results from the relatively greater concentration on the production of capital goods and the employment of more capital goods in the production of further capital goods.

An implication of the preceding discussion is that the perception, over the last several decades, of flimsy and shoddy products—for example, thin walls in newer buildings compared with those constructed before World War II—as a reflection of less going into the products, is correct. Such phenomena are manifestations of a less-capital-intensive economy today in comparison with the past. Less *is* going into products, not because of any greater personal consumption on the part of businessmen

and capitalists, however, but because taxation, budget deficits, and inflation, to finance the consumption of the government, are diverting factors of production from the production of capital goods, which contribute to further production, to the production of consumers' goods for the government and those to whom the government gives money.

12. More on Why Savings Cannot Outrun the Uses for Savings

In the last chapter, I showed how the process of net investment and capital intensification operate to eliminate any possibility of the persistence of negative net consumption, which might be imagined to stem from saving on the part of wage earners.[97] Here, it is appropriate to bring forward additional considerations in support of the proposition that in the long-run at least net consumption must always be significantly positive and thus that a significantly positive rate of profit must exist even under the conditions of an invariable money.

Capital Intensiveness and Land Values

The disappearance of any negative net consumption on the part of wage earners is absolutely guaranteed by the fact that as the rate of profit on capital approaches zero, the degree of capital intensiveness that becomes economically worthwhile literally approaches infinity. Thus there is room in the economic system for incalculably more savings and capital than wage earners or anyone else can ever accumulate, and thus certainly room for wage earners to accumulate enough savings and capital relative to their incomes to put an end to any negative net consumption on their part.

The degree of capital intensiveness that pays approaches infinity as the rate of profit approaches zero, if for no other reason then because of the effect of a zero rate of profit on the value of land. (In addition, of course there is the fact that in such conditions it would pay to carry the use of capital to the point where absolutely no further reductions in cost of production or improvements in the quality of products could be achieved by the use of more capital, which itself would entail the existence of far more capital than could ever be accumulated.[98]) At a zero rate of profit, the value of land would literally be infinite. Indeed, the value even of a single parcel of land yielding a permanent net income, such as a single piece of downtown real estate in any major city, would be infinite.

A piece of land that is expected to yield a net income year after year, virtually forever, can be sold at a finite price only because of the existence of a positive rate of profit. Assume, for example, that the use of a piece of land somewhere is expected to be worth just $1,000 a year, but virtually forever. Even though there is no limit to the total income that this piece of land will eventually yield, it sells at a price that is equivalent to a relatively small number of years' income—perhaps just 10 years' income. If the rate of profit is 10 percent, that is exactly the price for which this piece of land will sell. The $1,000 annual income from the land will yield a 10 percent rate of profit only if the price of the land is $10,000 ($1,000/$10,000 = 10 percent). The existence of a 10 percent annual rate of profit thus leads to the $1,000 annual income of the land being capitalized at a purchase price of just 10 years' income.

But if the rate of profit were 5 percent instead of 10 percent, that same piece of land, yielding $1,000 per year forever, would have a price of $20,000. This is because it takes a $20,000-capitalized value of the land to make the $1,000 annual income from the land yield only a 5 percent rate of profit. If, to go further, the rate of profit were 2 percent instead of 5 percent, the capitalized value of the piece of land would be raised to $50,000, because it takes that much to make a $1,000 annual income yield only a 2 percent rate of profit. It is not difficult to see that in order for a $1,000 annual income from the land to constitute a *zero* rate of profit, the capitalized value of the parcel of land would have to be *infinite*.[99]

As the rate of profit falls, therefore, the capitalized value of land in the economic system increases in inverse proportion. And this alone has unlimited potential for raising the value of accumulated assets—and thus of accumulated savings and capital—relative to current income and consumption. It helps to explain why the accumulation of savings and capital relative to income and consumption must always stop far short of the point at which their further accumulation would still be useful. In other words, it helps to explain why capital intensiveness is always *scarce*—why more of it would always be desirable than we can ever actually have. For with the accumulation of the additional savings and capital represented in part by a growing capitalized value of land, people feel free to step up their consumption and, ultimately, not increase the ratio of savings and capital to income and consumption any further.

Because there is always room for additional capital, there is always room for further net investment. But under the conditions of an invariable money, at some point there is no further net investment. As we saw in the last chapter, this is because at that point sufficient net consumption exists to make the rate of profit high enough relative to the marginal productivity of additional capital to make additional net investment no longer worthwhile.[100]

The Housing Outlet and Consumer Interest

Saving out of profits and saving out of wages are the only sources of additional capital intensiveness. In both cases, saving is limited by time preference. For wage earners, the ability to earn wages in the future is the main source of provision for the future. Wage earners are motivated to save primarily as the means of providing for periods of inability to earn wages, such as unemployment, illness, accident, and old age. Apart from that, their motivation to save is mainly limited to saving up to buy goods that are too expensive to purchase out of a single pay period, such as appliances, automobiles, and, especially, houses. Most of the savings made by wage earners not only end up ultimately being consumed, as when one dissaves during a period of unemployment or in retirement, or when one buys the consumers' good one has been saving up for, but, as previously explained, they are probably consumed almost immediately upon being set aside, or at least are matched by current consumption. For they are mainly used to finance consumer loans, such as home mortgages and consumer installment loans, and to the extent that they are not, they are largely or entirely offset by loans for such purposes originating in business firms.[101]

This last—the extent to which saving out of wages does not finance consumption—refers to the savings of wage earners who become businessmen, or whose savings are accumulated within business firms, as in the case of many employee pension plans. As I say, from the perspective of the economic system as a whole, such savings are largely or entirely offset by loans for consumer purposes originating in business firms. Moreover, when such savings become substantial, it is often after the workers in question have begun to succeed as businessmen, in which case, from that point on their saving is saving out of profit income. And in the case of all substantial savings that wage earners accumulate within business firms, a major portion originates in the reinvestment of interest or dividends. Thus, here too the saving is largely saving out of profit income.

For these reasons, the extent of any actual negative net consumption emanating from wage earners is almost certainly not very great, if it exists at all.

It is important to realize that all of the savings wage earners would ever be likely to wish to accumulate relative to their incomes could probably easily be absorbed *just by housing alone*. Even if the average wage earner followed the conservative rule of personal finance of spending no more than a fourth of his income on housing expense, that would probably be sufficient to support an amount of savings invested in housing of five times his annual income. For example, if his income is 100 per year, and he spends 25 on housing, of which 15 represents either the interest he pays on his mortgage or is the equivalent of the profit his landlord earns on him, then at a 3 percent rate of interest or profit, he can have a house or live in an apartment that is worth 500. (If there were sufficient accumulated savings and no increase in the quantity of money or volume of spending, a rate of profit and long-term rate of interest of 3 percent would certainly be achievable.) It follows, moreover, that if the average wage earner accumulates savings of five times his income, those wage earners beginning retirement accumulate savings of ten times their income, balancing the zero accumulated savings of wage earners just starting out. Thus, with far more savings than wage earners are ever likely to seek to accumulate being so easily capable of being employed, there is certainly no problem of the savings of wage earners ever outrunning the uses for such savings just in the field of housing alone.[102]

The Automatic Adjustment of the Rate of Saving to the Need for Capital

Not only does saving out of wages constitute no threat of the supply of savings ever outrunning the uses for savings, but also saving out of profits can never constitute such a threat. This is because in an economy with an invariable money, as soon as the need for additional capital intensiveness diminishes, productive expenditures begin showing up more quickly as costs, with the result that net investment diminishes and the rate of profit falls toward the rate of net consumption. Thus, saving out of profits declines precisely as the need for such savings declines. Note: it is not that a fall in the rate of profit here diminishes the incentive to save; the fall in the rate of profit is part of a process which directly diminishes the *capacity* to save, namely, the excess of profit income over net consumption.

Furthermore, whatever savings businessmen and capitalists might ever wish to make at the expense of a reduction in net consumption can always be easily accommodated. If there were no other way, then simply the use of more expensive materials and the inclusion of more and better components and accessories in the production of products would provide an outlet for such savings and productive expenditure.[103] But, of course, such an outlet for additional saving and productive expenditure would quickly be followed by an equivalent rise in aggregate costs and fall in profits, which would, once again, equivalently diminish the capacity for further net saving out of profits.[104]

The essential point here is that in an economy with an invariable money, saving out of profits, which, in fact, is by far the main form of saving in the economic system, only exists insofar as there is a substantial need for additional capital. In the absence of such a need, produc-

tive expenditure quickly shows up as cost, with the result that profit income immediately falls to the prevailing level of net consumption and, in so doing, simply eliminates net saving and net investment.

In an economy with an invariable money, savings and capital would be accumulated relative to current income up to a point determined by time preference, and would be accumulated no further unless something occurred to make time preference fall. Capital accumulation in physical terms, of course, would go on if the prevailing degree of time preference were sufficiently low and if technological progress took place.

In view of what we shall learn of his views in the next chapter, it may be surprising that Lord Keynes himself alludes to the true state of affairs concerning the relationship between saving and the need for saving under the conditions of an invariable money, but feels free to disregard it merely because he chooses to refer to it in a way that makes its existence seem like only a remote possibility. He writes: ". . . there are no intrinsic reasons for the scarcity of capital. An intrinsic reason for such scarcity . . . would not exist, in the long run, *except in the event of the individual propensity to consume proving to be of such a character that net saving . . . comes to an end before capital has become sufficiently abundant.*"[105]

In the peculiar terminology of Keynes, what must be recognized is precisely that—under a system of invariable money—"the individual propensity to consume" *is* "of such character that net saving . . . comes to an end before capital has become sufficiently abundant." It does so by virtue of the existence of limitless potential employments for savings and capital in conjunction with the existence of time preference. Under the conditions of an invariable money, long before savings and capital can be accumulated to the point of exhausting the uses for them, which are literally infinite, time preference puts an end to further saving and capital accumulation.

Of course, the conditions of an invariable money do not exist. What exists, even under a 100-percent-reserve gold standard, is an increasing quantity of money. In an economy with an increasing quantity of money and volume of spending, net saving and capital accumulation in monetary terms exist as permanent phenomena. In this context, however, as I showed in the last chapter, they are accompanied by a corresponding *positive addition* to the rate of profit, mainly in the form of an equivalent rate of net investment.[106] In such an economy, as I have shown, the continuing net saving out of profits takes place out of a rate of profit that is elevated by the same cause that necessitates the continuing net saving and continuing capital accumulation in monetary terms, namely, the increase in the quantity of money and volume of spending itself.[107]

As we have seen, this net saving and net investment, which takes place as part of a process that increases capital and nominal income in the same proportion, does not represent any rise in the economic system's degree of capital intensiveness in the relative-value sense—that is, it does not represent any rise in the ratio of accumulated savings or capital to consumption, wages, or sales revenues.[108] Capital accumulation here goes forward both in real and in monetary terms without capital rising relative to any of these magnitudes.

Thus, for the reasons explained, in no case is the economic system ever threatened with savings outrunning the profitable uses for savings. The saving of wage earners is no problem, and saving out of profits always takes place in intimate connection with the need for such saving, the capacity for such saving being governed precisely by the strength of the need for it, whether that need is a need to increase the degree of capital intensiveness or, in an economy with an increasing quantity of money, a need to maintain an existing degree of capital intensiveness.

These facts should be kept in mind in appraising the doctrines of Lord Keynes, which I set forth in the next chapter.

Notes

1. See above, pp. 623–626.

2. At the start of *Year 2,* there is no increase in the *total* supply of goods available for sale. At that point, which represents capital accumulation achieved by a rise in the relative demand for capital goods, the 20 percent increase in the supply of capital goods is made possible by an equivalent reduction in the supply of consumers' goods.

3. Indeed, we have already applied this procedure in the critique of the productivity and time preference theories of interest in their traditional forms, by means of introducing the assumption of changes in production into the conceptual framework represented by Figure 16–2. See above, pp. 787–794.

4. The same basic facts appeared in Table 16–5, which was used to illustrate the emergence of net investment and its contribution to the amount of aggregate profit. See above, p. 745.

5. This is because the *IL* of labor and the existing supply of capital goods in each year would then be employed to produce *1.3K* of capital goods and *.7C* of consumers' goods to be available at the start of the next year for each *1K* of capital goods presently existing. Thus, with *1.3K* of capital goods produced for every *1K* of capital goods productively consumed, the supply of capital goods and total productive ability would grow in the ratio of 1.3:1. It should be understood that the outputs of 1.3K and .7C for every 1K of capital goods productively consumed are inferred by multiplying .65 x *2K* and .35 x *2C*. The multiplicands *2K* and *2C*, of course, are the outputs of capital goods and consumers' goods that would result from the employment of 100 percent of the *IL* of labor and 100 percent of any existing *1K* of capital goods in the production of capital goods or, alternatively, in the production of consumers' goods. Of course, there are conditions in which the rise in the relative demand for and production of capital goods would be followed by an acceleration in the rate of capital accumulation and economic progress that represented a deceleration in the rate of acceleration. On this point, see above, pp. 628–629.

6. See above, p. 630.

7. For a fuller account of the destructive influence of this view, see above, p. 709.

8. See above, pp. 674–699.

9. A rise in the demand for capital goods relative to the demand for consumers' goods could take place without a fall in net consumption only by virtue of the demand for capital goods rising at the expense of the demand for labor.

10. See above, p. 573.

11. Essentially the same conclusions, of course, were reached back in Chapter 13. However, there the assumption of vertical integration precluded discussion of the falling prices of capital goods. See above, pp. 569–570.

12. See above, pp. 758–759.

13. A similar formulation appeared back on p. 570. As pointed out in the note before last, however, the assumption of vertical integration that was made at the time, prevented inclusion of capital goods in the analysis.

14. See above, pp. 573–580.

15. On this last point, see above, pp. 575–576.

16. See above, pp. 557–558.

17. The nature of the monetary component in the rate of profit and its relationship to net investment is explained above, on pp. 762–774. See in particular pp. 768–771.

18. David Ricardo, *Principles of Political Economy and Taxation*, 3d ed. (London, 1821), chap. 7; reprinted as vol. 1 of *The Works and Correspondence of David Ricardo*, ed. Piero Sraffa (Cambridge: Cambridge University Press, 1962), p. 133. This passage was quoted above, on p. 495, in connection with showing the actual meaning Ricardo attached to "a fall in wages." Subsequent page references to the Sraffa edition appear in brackets.

19. Ibid., chap. 20 [pp. 278–279]. Inserts added.

20. Ibid., chap. 5 [p. 95].

21. On this point, see below, p. 824. See also above, pp. 631–632.

22. This, of course, is apart from a transition phase, during which a fall in the rate of net consumption occurs as the precondition of increasing the relative demand for capital goods and thus their relative production, and thereby getting the process of increasing production underway. On this subject, be sure to see above, pp. 817–818.

23. This is true irrespective of the extent of saving by wage earners and of the extent to which their saving serves to raise productive expenditure. See above, pp. 750–754 and 759–762. See also above, pp. 778–787, and below, pp. 856–859.

24. Concerning this fact, see above, pp. 817–818.

25. Concerning the effects of a more abundant supply of savings and credit on the demand for money for holding and thus on the velocity of circulation of money, see above, p. 518.

26. See above, pp. 817–818. See also above, pp. 762–767.

27. See below, pp. 837–838.

28. It is implicit in this example that all of the capital goods and labor in existence in any base year are always ultimately, directly or indirectly, devoted to the production of consumers' goods in their entirety. For application of this fact to the fallacy of underconsumptionism, see below, pp. 847–851.

29. The writings of Murray Rothbard present a clear instance of error on this subject and on the closely related subject of whether or not capital accumulation implies a falling rate of profit. Rothbard simply does not see how previous capital accumulation can serve as the basis for subsequent capital accumulation. Nor does he understand the role in capital accumulation of technological progress and anything else that increases the general ability to produce. Cf. Murray N. Rothbard, *Man, Economy, and State*, 2 vols. (Princeton, N. J.: D. Van Nostrand, Inc.: 1962), 2:470–496.

30. On the subject of past production serving the present, and present production serving the future, see Eugen von Böhm-Bawerk, *Capital and Interest*, 3 vols., trans. George D. Huncke and Hans F. Sennholz (South Holland, Ill.: Libertarian Press, 1959), 2:88.

31. See above, pp. 631–632.

32. See Ludwig von Mises, *Human Action*, 3d ed. rev. (Chicago: Henry Regnery Co., 1966), pp. 541–545.

33. It should be recalled that it was also previously established that the anticipation of falling prices caused by increased production does not bring about an increase in the demand for money for holding in order to take advantage of lower prices in the future. Thus it is also not deflationary by that route. See above, pp. 574–576.

34. See above, pp. 813–818 and 574.

35. See above, pp. 817–818.

36. On the implications of these facts for the case for a 100-percent-reserve gold standard or gold-and-silver standard, see below, pp. 954–959.

37. See above, p. 176.

38. Indeed, in my own intellectual development, it was the grasp of the implications present in an intellectual construction essentially similar to Figure 17–1 that led me to the development of the productivity theory of wages and to most of the other major propositions of the second half of this book.

39. It should be kept in mind that profit is taken as gross of interest, and that the analysis applies equally to interest income and the rate of interest.

40. See above, p. 740 and pp. 741–743. See also the quotation from von Mises concerning the effect of eliminating the capitalist's role as receiver of interest causing its replacement by the capitalist's role as consumer of capital, above, on p. 302.

41. In support of this pattern of outcome, see above, p. 740.

42. See above, pp. 712–714.

43. In this case, there is a rise in nominal national income to the extent that the economy-wide demand for labor is increased. To this extent, of course, the case at hand is also one demonstrating an inverse relationship between national income and prosperity. See above, pp. 648–650. for a detailed explanation of the negative effects for prosperity.

44. See above, pp. 762–771.

45. To some extent, private consumption expenditure that would have been financed by borrowing, is also reduced, such as home buying and purchases dependent on consumer installment credit.

46. In the case of taxation, of course, the rise in the rate of profit is on a pretax basis, while in the case of budget deficits, it is on an aftertax basis.

47. See below, pp. 930–937.

48. As I have shown, just such a policy has been pursued in Sweden, the model country of today's "liberals." See above, p. 310.

49. A program for the abolition of the welfare state and all government interference in the economic system is presented in the concluding chapter of this book.

50. Concerning the fact that foreign investment entails an excess of exports over imports in the country or countries providing the investment and a corresponding excess of imports over exports in the country or countries receiving the investment, see above, pp. 529–531.

51. See above, pp. 531–532.

52. If the two countries use different moneys, then with the same rates of increase in the money supply of the two countries, the foreign exchange value of the currency of the more rapidly progressing country will appreciate relative to that of the less rapidly progressing country. The relative appreciation will be all the greater to the extent that the money supply of the less rapidly progressing country increases at a more rapid rate than that of the more rapidly progressing country.

53. The replacement of social security by private saving would promote investment even though the savings of wage earners are used largely to finance consumption expenditures, such as housing purchases. This is because the availability of these savings to finance such purchases would correspondingly reduce the diversion of savings from business investment that must presently occur in order to finance such purchases.

54. See above, pp. 737–739.

55. See above, pp. 622–639, in particular pp. 634–636.

56. Strictly speaking, it would be the establishment of laissez-faire capitalism for the very first time. For an indication of the significant departures from laissez-faire capitalism even in the nineteenth century, see above, p. 28.

57. See above, pp. 830–831. See also above, pp. 308–310.

58. See above, p. 278. See also above, pp. 639–641.

59. See above, pp. 758–759.

60. For example, see above, ibid.

61. See above, pp. 739–741, 753–754, and 759–762.

62. It should go without saying that if the equilibrium capital-intensiveness in the relative-value sense is sufficiently high, the degree of capital intensiveness in the *physical sense* of the ratio of capital goods to the supply of labor can go on rising indefinitely, on the basis of technological progress, whose implementation is encouraged by the sufficiently high degree of capital intensiveness in the relative-value sense.

63. Of course, increases in the quantity of money and volume of spending operate to an important extent directly to increase the nominal value of assets, both capital assets and consumer assets, especially in the form of land. These increases must be taken into account in calculating the percentage of income that

must be saved in order to maintain the ratio of accumulated savings to current income. Their influence is obviously to lessen the percentage of ordinary income—that is, income other than asset gains—that needs to be saved.

64. On the economic degree of capitalism, see above, pp. 632–634.

65. See above, pp. 631–632. See also above, p. 824.

66. The same point applies, of course, to the degree of capital intensiveness in the relative-value sense. It too operates as force to acceleration.

67. On these subjects, see above, p. 709.

68. See above, pp. 691–694.

69. To the extent that the cash holdings were outside of business firms, the rate of profit on the whole of the capital invested in business firms, including the cash holdings of business firms, would be correspondingly increased.

70. On the Keynesian doctrines, see below, pp. 863–894. On the Keynesian doctrine of the too-low rate of profit in particular, see below, pp. 868–876. On the liquidity-preference doctrine in particular, see pp. 885–887. See also pp. 891–892. The last reference explains why I claim that the Keynesians' fears of too low a rate of profit are pretended.

71. Concerning the "Pigou effect" and its inherent weakness, see below, pp. 865–866.

72. For an account of the government's role in causing financial contractions and depressions, see above, pp. 513–516 and 519–526. See also below, pp. 938–941.

73. For elaboration of this point, see above, pp. 750–754 and 759–762. See also, below, pp. 856–859.

74. For a critique of Keynesian claims to the contrary, see below, pp. 885–887.

75. For a textbook exposition of the investment-opportunity doctrine, see Paul Samuelson and William Nordhaus, *Economics,* 13th ed. (New York: McGraw Hill Book Company, 1989), pp. 720–725.

76. See above, pp. 787–792.

77. As I previously pointed out, as far as it corresponds to net investment, the magnitude of profit is in part also attributable to the difference between the supply of products and the supply of factors of production previously purchased. See above, p. 796.

78. See above, pp. 556–558.

79. As we have seen the reduction in unit costs it achieves takes place prior to the fall in selling prices. See above, pp. 807–817.

80. On all of these points, see above, pp. 556–558.

81. The degree of capital intensiveness should, of course, also be included in the list of actual causes of capital accumulation and increases in production. I omit it here, merely for the sake of economy of expression.

82. Strictly speaking, it is a consequence of the by-product, namely, the increase in the quantity of money and volume of spending. Under a system of fiat money, the status of net saving is even less than that. Then it is a consequence not even of a by-product of capital accumulation and rising production but of a mere accompaniment of these phenomena, that is, of the accompaniment constituted by the increase in the quantity of fiat money.

83. On the Platonic-Heraclitean view of entities, see above, pp. 674–689.

84. Quoted in John Maynard Keynes, *The General Theory of Employment, Interest, and Money* (New York: Harcourt, Brace, 1937), p. 367. Along the same lines, see the quotation from Spence by James Mill in James Mill, *Commerce Defended* (London, 1808), chap. 6; reprinted in *Selected Economic Writings of James Mill,* ed. Donald Winch (Chicago: University of Chicago Press, 1966), p. 131. See also the underconsumptionist writings of W. T. Foster and W. Catchings: *Money,* Publications of the Pollak Foundation for Economic Research, no. 2 (Boston and New York: Houghton Mifflin, 1923); *Profits,* Publications of the Pollak Foundation for Economic Research, no. 8 (Boston and New York: Houghton Mifflin, 1925); *Business Without A Buyer,* Publications of the Pollak Foundation for Economic Research, no. 10 (Boston and New York: Houghton Mifflin, 1928).

85. See above, pp. 56–58. See also above, pp. 556–557.

86. The pattern of my resolution of the underconsumptionists' paradox in what follows has been inspired largely by the writings of F. A. Hayek. See in particular his essay "The 'Paradox' of Saving" in his book *Profits, Interest and Investment* (London: Routledge and Kegan Paul, 1950). See also his treatment of the structure of production in *Prices and Production,* 2d ed. (London: George Routledge, 1935), pp. 29–64. But equal or even greater credit should go to James Mill. See the latter's *Commerce Defended,* chap. 6; reprinted in *Selected Economic Writings of James Mill,* pp. 127–133.

87. Concerning double counting, see above, pp. 674–682.

88. Cf. Carl Menger, *Principles of Economics,* trans. and ed. by James Dingwall and Bert F. Hoselitz (Glencoe, Ill.: The Free Press, 1950), pp. 55–67.

89. On this point, see Eugen von Böhm-Bawerk, *Capital and Interest,* 2:77–118, for a discussion of how current production serves the future and is served by the production of the past.

90. In terms of the format of Table 17–2, these expenditures would represent the addition of further columns to the right of those in the present Table 17–2. Thus, there would be a column headed $D_{K5},$ just to the right of the present rightmost column, which is headed $D_{K4}.$ The outlays of 65.54 plus 8.19 would appear in this column and would serve in the production of capital goods that would be sold in the next year, under the column heading $D_{K4},$ for 81.92. Five columns further to the right would appear a column headed $D_{K10}.$ In this column would appear the outlays 21.47 and 2.68, which would serve in the production of capital goods that would be sold in the next year under the column heading $D_{K9}.$ A series of downward and leftward sloping arrows would connect these outlays with the sale of capital goods five years later, under the column heading $D_{K5},$ and, five years after that, with sale of consumers' goods.

91. It is possible that if he takes the trouble to check all of the arithmetic involved in the construction of Table 17–3, the reader will arrive at slightly different totals as the result of differences in rounding. My procedure has been to calculate the amounts in columns three and four year by year and then to derive from them both their totals and the respective amounts shown in column five.

92. For Figures 17–2 and 17–3, see above, pp. 821 and 823.

93. See above, pp. 824–824.

94. See Böhm-Bawerk, *Capital and Interest,* 2:79–88, for an alternative approach to the measurement of the average period

of production.

95. On the equality of prices with sums of past wages and profits, see above, p. 201. See also above, pp. 639–641 and 647.

96. Note that in the case of an infinite rate of profit accompanied by an infinite ratio of the demand for consumers' goods to the demand for labor, namely, the case of Adam Smith's "early and rude state of society" and Marx's "C–M–C," the average period of production is extremely short, despite the fact that it appears to be mathematically undefined in the present discussion. This is because the case contains no demand for capital goods and no accumulated capital. In such conditions, production is of the hand-to-mouth variety.

97. See above, pp. 759–762.

98. For a description of the virtually limitless quantities in which additional capital would be useful in reducing costs and/or improving the quality of products, see above, pp. 56–58.

99. Cf. Ludwig von Mises, *Human Action*, p. 526.

100. See above, pp. 758–762.

101. See above, p. 735.

102. Of course, it should be recalled that the payment of interest on consumer loans, such as home mortgages, represents a further source of net consumption and thus of aggregate profit and interest. See above, p. 753.

103. Along these lines, see above, pp. 854–856.

104. The use of funds released from net consumption for such purposes, of course, would occur only if there were no greater need for additional capital, such as would require the employment of the funds spared from net consumption in the making of productive expenditures that were more remote from showing up as costs.

105. John Maynard Keynes, *The General Theory of Employment, Interest, and Money* (New York: Harcourt, Brace, 1936) p. 376. Italics supplied.

106. See above, pp. 762–774, especially p. 768.

107. See above, the preceding note. See also above, pp. 825–826 and 836–840.

108. See above, pp. 775–776.

CHAPTER 18

KEYNESIANISM: A CRITIQUE

In previous chapters, I have criticized various major aspects of Keynesianism, notably the Keynesian approach to aggregate economic accounting, its negative view of saving, and the multiplier doctrine in its various forms.[1] Very significantly, I have also shown that insofar as people might choose to hold accumulated savings in the form of cash rather than income-producing assets, the effect would be to raise the rate of return on the income producing assets, thereby automatically limiting any possible preference people might have for holding savings in the form of cash and rendering impossible the limitless rise in "liquidity preference"—viz., cash hoarding—alleged by the Keynesians to exist in response to too low a rate of profit.[2] Of course, I also showed how the determinants of the rate of profit, along with the enormous abundance of profitable investment opportunities for additional capital, preclude any actual need for people in modern conditions to attempt to accumulate a major portion of their savings in the form of cash in the first place. I demonstrated that the profitability of investment, and thus the superiority of investing rather than holding cash, is guaranteed by the very nature of the forces that determine the rate of profit, including the existence of veritable "springs" to profitability.[3]

In addition, I showed that what leads to efforts to hold a greater portion of accumulated savings in the form of cash is not any lack of investment opportunities in the economic system as it is basically constituted, but undue increases in the quantity of money, which almost always take place, ironically enough, precisely in the conviction that spending needs to be stimulated. The result, I showed, is that cash holdings are driven down relative to the volume of spending and lending in the economic system—viz., business becomes illiquid—and the stage is thereby set for a financial contraction once the stimulus of the additional quantity of money comes to an end and the normal demand for money for holding reasserts itself.[4]

My demonstration that the rate of interest is not the "price of money" and cannot be permanently reduced, let alone eliminated, by virtue of the increase in the quantity of money, can also be counted as a criticism of Keynesianism.[5] This is because Keynesianism ardently embraces this doctrine and makes it central to its views on "monetary policy."[6]

Up to now, I have dealt with Keynesianism either merely by implication or on the fly, so to speak. It is difficult to do otherwise, because conceptually Keynesianism is a form of amorphous sludge, oozing its way through any possible cracks or chinks in the intellectual armor of a capitalist economy and thereby undermining as far as possible the intellectual foundations of such an economy. Before turning full face to Keynesianism, it has been necessary to set right a number of major theoretical issues that are wider than Keynesianism. Yet, from time to time, I have felt morally obliged to deal explicitly with various Keynesian positions at the earliest opportunity, just as soon as my own theoretical position was in place.

Here I turn to an exposition of Keynesianism in its best organized, strongest form, preparatory to slaying the dragon one more time, with a critique of all of the doctrine's remaining essential claims whether in the realm of economic theory or in the realm of economic policy.

This is the variant that goes under the name the *IS-LM* analysis.

I believe that my exposition of this analysis is far more compact and much clearer than those to be found in the very best of the Keynesian textbooks. At the same time, I am confident that any honest Keynesian will agree with the substance of my exposition. I consider the superiority of my exposition to be based on the fact that I have reversed the usual order of development of the doctrine. I begin with the Keynesian view of aggregate demand, whose significance can be understood immediately, and then proceed to explain the underlying doctrines on which it is based. The usual procedure is to devote chapter after chapter to subjects apparently leading nowhere, such as the "consumption and saving functions," the various "multipliers," the "marginal efficiency of capital schedule," "liquidity preference," and so on, and then at the very end pull all the elements together into the central argument concerning aggregate demand. By that time, as I will show, the reader has forgotten the essential questions and is no longer in a position to see that the wool is being pulled over his eyes. In contrast, my procedure keeps all of the elements in sharpest focus and never allows sight of the essential questions to be lost.

1. The Essential Claims of Keynesianism

Prior to the publication of Keynes's book *The General Theory of Employment, Interest, and Money* in 1936, economists had accepted the proposition that unemployment can be eliminated by a fall in wage rates.[7] This was an intellectually uncomfortable position for most economists to be in, because its obvious implication is that, in order to prevent or eliminate unemployment, the government should abstain from interfering with the height of wage rates—i.e., should not enact prounion legislation, minimum wage laws, or in any other way coerce or pressure employers into paying wages higher than those which a free market would establish.

This position, of course, was in direct conflict with the Marxian exploitation theory, which exerted a powerful influence probably over the majority even of the economics profession and certainly over the overwhelming majority of intellectuals in all other fields. For according to the exploitation theory, a free market in labor means subsistence wages, unbearably long hours of work, and inhuman working conditions. Thus, acceptance of the doctrine that a free market in labor can eliminate unemployment by means of a fall in wages placed economists in a position in which they appeared to be virtual enemies of mankind and in which virtually they alone stood in opposition to what was (and by many still is) regarded as the only possible path of social progress—namely, ever-

growing government interference and ultimately, if not immediately, socialism.

In this intellectual environment, Keynes appeared on the scene. His entire system can be summarized in a single sentence: *A free market in labor and fall in wage rates is incapable of eliminating unemployment; mass unemployment is an inescapable feature of a capitalist economic system in modern conditions.* Thus, Keynesianism held, it is pointless to fight for a free market in labor. Because even if it were achieved, it would be to no avail. On the contrary, the only solution is "fiscal policy"—by which, in essence, is meant that the government must adopt a policy of budget deficits.

In this way, Keynes's ideas filled what perhaps the majority of economists experienced as a vital need—it gave them a way out of conflict with the rest of the intellectual world and with a good portion of their own convictions. For if Keynes were right, economists need not oppose labor legislation. Indeed, they could join in the calls for expanded government intervention. This is because Keynes also gave them arguments designed to show that the more the government spends for any purpose—even for the least valuable programs imaginable, even for pyramid building—the more prosperous must the economic system become.[8]

If one considers the implications of such ideas as that pyramid building and budget deficits are economically beneficial, it becomes obvious that Keynesianism is the enemy both of common sense and the love of liberty (viz., the freedom from excessive government, which excess is fostered by the policy of budget deficits). Keynesianism is also incompatible with such fundamental economic truths as the quantity theory of money. And, if it is not already apparent, we shall see, too, how it is actually nothing more than a species of consumptionism.

The incompatibility of Keynesianism with the quantity theory of money requires some comment. Keynesianism implies that even though the quantity of money remains the same, the volume of spending in the economic system falls without limit as wages and prices fall, and thus that no connection whatever exists between the quantity of money and volume of spending. It implies this because if spending does not fall in full proportion to the fall in wage rates and prices, thus totally obliterating the connection between the volume of spending and the quantity of money, the fall in wage rates and prices must result in larger quantities of goods and labor being sold, and thus, at some point, in the elimination of unemployment. If, as the quantity theory of money in fact implies, the volume of spending tends to remain unchanged in the face of a given quantity of money, then, of course, reductions in wage rates and prices must put an end to unemployment in short order. And, indeed, as we saw in the discussion of unemployment, there is actually good reason for believing that when wage rates and prices fall to their new equilibrium level following a financial contraction, total spending in the economic system will actually increase, since it first declines in part as the result of the postponement of investments precisely to that time.[9]

The incompatibility of Keynesianism with so much of established sound economic doctrine and with the traditional Anglo-Saxon acceptance of the political philosophy of limited government, and, no less, its open flaunting of the absurd and paradoxical as newly discovered truths, deservedly aroused great opposition. Unfortunately, the critics were not able to answer the Keynesian sophistries decisively.

The reason was that in the two generations preceding the appearance of Keynes, much of the foundations of sound economics had quietly been lost, without anyone even being aware of the loss. The loss took place starting in the 1870s, in the abandonment of British classical economics in favor of the newer neoclassical economics. As explained in Chapter 11, the cause of this development was the fact that classical economics, with its labor theory of value, appeared to lay the groundwork for Marxism. Instead of eliminating the particular, localized errors of classical economics which did provide support for Marxism and then integrating the new doctrine of marginal utility propounded by neoclassical economics with the essential substance of classical economics that remained, virtually the whole theoretical body of knowledge constituted by classical economics was abandoned. What then remained were largely just out-of-context, memorized conclusions that in the absence of the necessary theoretical foundations could no longer be supported. Thus, when Keynes came along, it was only necessary for him to overturn such out-of-context, intellectually severed conclusions, not serious, living convictions. The state of underlying intellectual decay that had set in long before Keynes appeared is clearly indicated in a passage written by J. A. Hobson as far back as 1889, a passage which Keynes quotes approvingly:

> Saving enriches and spending impoverishes the community along with the individual, and it may be generally defined as an assertion that the effective love of money is the root of all economic good. Not merely does it enrich the thrifty individual himself, but it raises wages, gives work to the unemployed, and scatters blessings on every side. From the daily papers to the latest economic treatise, from the pulpit to the House of Commons, this conclusion is reiterated and re-stated till it appears positively impious to question it. Yet the educated world, supported by the majority of economic thinkers, up to the publication of Ricardo's work strenuously denied this doctrine, and its ultimate acceptance was exclusively due to their inability to meet the now exploded wages-fund doctrine. That the conclusion should have survived the argument on which it logi-

cally stood, can be explained on no other hypothesis than the commanding authority of the great men who asserted it. Economic critics have ventured to attack the theory in detail, but they have shrunk appalled from touching its main conclusions.[10]

The wages-fund doctrine referred to by Hobson, is, of course, the doctrine that holds—correctly—that the demand for labor is separate and distinct from the demand for consumers' goods, and is made out of saving and productive expenditure, not consumption expenditure. As I showed in Chapter 14, it was never actually refuted. The essential criticism raised against it was merely that changes in wage rates might be accompanied by changes in total payrolls coming at the expense of other portions of productive expenditure or at the expense of net consumption.[11] I have already explained very well how to analyze such changes in total payrolls, namely, that little or nothing can be obtained at the expense of net consumption and that what can be obtained at the expense of other parts of productive expenditure is against the long-run interests of the wage earners.[12] The possible variation of total payrolls in no way affects the essential fact that wages are paid out of saving and productive expenditure and in real terms depend on the economic degree of capitalism and productivity of labor. The wages-fund doctrine was not overthrown; it was simply left undefended. It was left undefended because it was an integral part of classical economics, which had ceased to be seriously valued and studied. As I have shown, there was—and is—no justifiable basis for abandoning the doctrine.

What Hobson was absolutely correct in pointing out, however, and which is my reason for quoting him, is that the abandonment of the wages-fund doctrine, and other such essential doctrines of classical economics, did have the effect of withdrawing the foundation for conclusions that could otherwise not be supported.

Neo-Keynesianism

In response to some relatively mild criticism levied by a colleague of Keynes at Cambridge University, A. C. Pigou, Keynesianism was succeeded by "neo-Keynesianism." According to this variant, which concedes the substance of Pigou's criticism, a fall in wage rates might, conceivably, be capable of eliminating unemployment, but the fall would have to be enormously out of proportion to any additional employment achieved. The clear implication is that in the process virtually every debtor would be bankrupted, because the grossly disproportionate drop in wage rates and prices implies correspondingly large reductions in aggregate spending and revenues and thus in the ability to repay debts. For example, if to eliminate an unemployment rate of 10 percent, wage rates and prices had to fall by 90 percent, the volume of spending in the economic system would equal one-tenth the price-and-wage level times ten-ninths the output and employment. Thus, total spending would be reduced to one ninth of its former height, or by 89 percent.

And, even if people were willing to allow such a thing to transpire, the further argument is ready at hand that a necessary condition of prices being able to fall would be the adoption of a radical antitrust policy, or a program of widespread nationalization of industry. These measures would allegedly be necessary to establish "price competition." Big business, left to its own devices, it is held, is "oligopolistic" and practices "administered pricing"— i.e., won't reduce prices. Thus, either it must be broken up into large numbers of small competitors, to approximate the conditions of "pure and perfect competition," or the government must take it over and set prices.[13] Thus, neo-Keynesianism, no less than Keynesianism, holds that a free market is incompatible with full employment. The only difference is that while Keynesianism claims that a free market in labor cannot establish full employment, neo-Keynesianism claims that a free market in products cannot establish full employment, for the free market in products allegedly results in "oligopoly" and the refusal to cut prices. Thus, according to both variants, a free economy must be accompanied by mass unemployment.

Much of the substance of neo-Keynesianism is clearly stated by Joseph P. McKenna, a supporter of Keynes, in his relatively readable textbook *Aggregate Economic Analysis:*

> Keynes's conclusions were unacceptable to two groups. The first group objected because his analysis made government intervention or continued depression the only two possible alternatives. Many members of this group opposed government intervention in principle and therefore rejected this choice as undesirable.

> The second group, the supporters of classical analysis, opposed Keynes's conclusions on logical rather than political grounds. To them, it seemed impossible that workers could not find jobs by cutting their wages sufficiently. Among this group was A. C. Pigou, who discussed the question in his article "The Classical Stationary State." He observed that price changes would alter the consumption function. . . . A decline in prices tends to raise the value of money assets and, therefore, to shift the consumption function upward. . . .

> This result satisfied Pigou. He had proved that it was always possible to obtain full employment if wages and prices fell sufficiently. As a logical proposition this conclusion was almost indisputable, and Pigou claimed nothing more than logic. (Pigou himself made it clear though that, as matter of policy, he preferred to increase demand through fiscal policy.) Strangely enough, this result also satisfied the political opponents of Keynes, who could now blame unemployment on the unwillingness of workers to accept

lower wages, for Pigou had shown that there exists *some* level of wages that would be compatible with full employment. The important practical question was an empirical one: Just how elastic is the aggregate demand curve? If the elasticity is very high, a modest change in price might produce the desired income level. If the elasticity is low, the price level that is compatible with full employment might require such a large change that the process of reaching it would be hopelessly disruptive. (Imagine what would happen if it were necessary to lower the price level to one-tenth its present level.)

The question of how much prices must change to produce a given level of income [viz., real income and employment] cannot be answered by any purely theoretical analysis. Only statistical study, concerned with the size of consumer assets and debts and the effects of these upon consumption, could offer even a tentative hypothesis. The usual conclusion is that the aggregate demand curve is inelastic, so that very large changes in prices would be required for moderate changes in income. Nevertheless, the controversy is not yet settled, and further study continues.[14]

The reason for such negative conclusions about the extent of the fall in wage rates and prices necessary to achieve full employment is that Pigou and the other neo-Keynesians are trapped in the Keynesian intellectual framework. The only mechanism they can imagine by which a fall in wage rates and prices can increase the quantity of goods and labor demanded is by virtue of its effect in increasing the buying power of the stock of money. Once in possession of a stock of money of larger real purchasing power, people will be willing to consume more, and this will create additional employment. Obviously the doctrine views an additional demand for consumers' goods as equivalent to an additional demand for labor.

Actually, Pigou's doctrine is even weaker than the Keynesians themselves recognize. For if the money of the economic system rests on a fractional reserve, and if it were the case that there must be some significant drop in total spending accompanying the fall in wage rates and prices, then there would be substantial business failures, which would result in substantial bank failures and in a reduction in the quantity of money. In such a case, the "Pigou effect" would be reduced to depending on the ability of a fall in wage rates and prices to raise the purchasing power not of a fixed stock of money (which would not be fixed, but falling) but of a much more limited fixed *monetary base.*[15]

Obviously the answer to Keynes concerning the effect of a fall in wage rates must be far more powerful than the answer provided by Pigou. After I have set forth the essential elements of Keynes's doctrine, I will provide such an answer.

In its most recent incarnation, neo-Keynesianism has

abandoned the claim that the problem is an inelastic aggregate demand curve, or, indeed, has anything fundamentally to do with a problem on the side of demand. It has given up the whole substance of the Keynesian position and retreated to the claim that wages and prices are somehow inflexible in the downward direction and that this inflexibility is what necessitates government intervention to alleviate unemployment—as though the inflexibility (and the periodic reductions in aggregate monetary demand that exacerbate it) were not itself the result of government intervention. In the most brazen misrepresentation of the views both of the classical economists and of Keynes, Samuelson and Nordhaus declare in the most recent edition of their textbook:

> The basic difference between classical and Keynesian approaches can be found in differing views about the behavior of aggregate *supply*.[!] Keynesian economists believe that prices and wages adjust slowly, so any equilibrating forces may take many years or even decades to operate. The classical approach holds that prices and wages are flexible, so the economy moves to its long-run equilibrium very quickly. . . . While the classical economists were preaching that persistent unemployment was impossible, economists of the 1930s could hardly ignore the vast army of unemployed workers . . . . Keynes emphasized that because wages and prices are inflexible, there is no economic mechanism to restore full employment and ensure that the economy produces its potential. . . . In the Keynesian model, aggregate supply slopes upward, implying that output will increase with higher aggregate demand as long as there are unused resources.[16]

Thus, what currently remains of the Keynesian position is merely an obstinate refusal to challenge the government intervention that is responsible for mass unemployment, and an insistence that the problem of unemployment be dealt with by means of still more government intervention.

In view of the virtually total intellectual capitulation of today's neo-Keynesians, it may be asked why I believe it is necessary to engage in an extensive critique of Keynes's actual doctrine when his supporters themselves have apparently abandoned it and proceed as though he never even held it. My reason is—precisely as the passages quoted above indicate—that the world abounds with prominent intellectuals who do not take ideas very seriously—who adopt them and then discard them on the basis of no more genuine intellectual conviction than stands behind a change in such fashions as the height of women's hemlines or the width of men's neckties. What has been casually discarded for the present can just as easily be pickup up again in the future. My purpose in what follows is to provide intellectuals who do take ideas seriously with the means of quashing any possible future resurrection of Keynesianism.

2. The Unemployment-Equilibrium Doctrine and Its Basis: The *IS* Curve and Its Elements

The Keynesian doctrine that a free economy cannot escape from mass unemployment, that a fall in wage rates and prices is useless, because it is accompanied by a corresponding fall in the aggregate monetary demands for consumers' goods and labor, is known as the doctrine of *the unemployment equilibrium*. This doctrine is a species of out-and-out consumptionism, as its diagrammatic exposition (provided by the Keynesian textbooks themselves) clearly demonstrates. For what is presented as the Keynesian aggregate demand curve in Figure 18–1 is nothing other than the very same aggregate demand curve we examined earlier, in Chapter 13, as representing the views of the consumptionists.[17] All that is different is the description of the horizontal axis as representing employment as well as output, and, following the customary, Keynesian practice, the use of the letter Y to denote output.

The presentation of the Keynesian aggregate demand curve DD as absolutely inelastic—as a vertical line—and the belief that as wage rates and prices fall, the aggregate monetary demands, i.e., the respective volumes of spending, fall in proportion, are mutual corollaries. If people are prepared to buy just so much in physical terms and no more, then any fall in the price of what they buy must be accompanied by a proportional fall in the overall amount of money they spend in buying it. By the same token, if as wage rates and prices fall, people reduce the amount of their monetary demand in proportion, then they are capable of buying no more at the lower wage rates and prices than they bought at the higher wage rates and prices.

The strictly limited quantity of output and employment that is depicted by DD is allegedly all that a free market is capable of absorbing in a given period of time, and thus all that it is allegedly capable of demanding. Just as in the case of consumptionism, unemployment supposedly results because (and exists to the degree that) the economic system is capable of producing more at the point of full employment than corresponds to the allegedly fixed aggregate quantity of goods and labor demanded. In the diagram, output at the point of full employment (denoted by Y_f) is indicated by the vertical line SS, which is drawn to the right of DD. In other words, Keynesianism in essence is really nothing more than the overproduction doctrine. It simply adds some peculiar twists and turns.

These twists and turns concern how Keynesianism arrives at the notion of a fixed aggregate quantity of goods and labor demanded. One route is the widely held belief, fostered by labor unions, that because a cut in wage rates reduces the ability of the individual wage earner to spend money for consumers' goods, it correspondingly reduces overall spending for consumers' goods in the economic system. This is an elementary fallacy. It does not see that the reduction in wage rates makes possible the employment of correspondingly more wage earners, with the result that the total amount of spending—the monetary demand—for consumers' goods does not fall. The basic result is the existence of the same amount of monetary demand both for labor and for consumers' goods, but because wage rates and prices are lower, the same respective monetary demands employ more labor and buy more consumers' goods.[18]

Of course, the demand for labor and the wage earners' demand for consumers' goods are not the only relevant monetary demands in the economic system. There is also the demand for capital goods and the demand for consumers' goods on the part of businessmen and capitalists, i.e., net consumption. It is entirely possible that under an invariable money, a fall in wage rates would be accompanied by some change in the demand for labor accompanied by an equal and opposite change in one of these other elements, especially in the demand for capital goods. But even if this entailed some fall in the aggregate monetary demand for labor, over and against this is the fact that in the context of the elimination of mass unemployment the fall in wage rates to their new equilibrium level almost certainly results in a rise in spending of virtually all kinds, including the demand for labor. This is because in a situation of mass unemployment the fall in wage rates brings out the investment expenditures which had been postponed, awaiting their fall. Thus, in actuality, the fall in wage rates to their new equilibrium is accompanied by a rise in the aggregate monetary

demands for labor and for goods, both consumers' goods and capital goods.[19]

Despite the widespread impression to the contrary, the fallacy that lower wage rates are the cause of proportionately less spending, is not the major argument that Keynesianism advances in support of a vertical aggregate demand curve—that is, in support of the notion that the aggregate quantity demanded is fixed. The actual doctrine it relies on is the so-called *IS* curve and the relationships from which it is derived. An *IS* curve appears in Figure 18–2.[20]

The *IS* curve is the relationship between the "marginal efficiency of capital" (viz., the rate of profit and interest), on the one side, and the volume of output and employment, on the other, for equilibria of investment and saving. (The meaning of this definition will become clearer as we proceed.) The *IS* curve purports to show that as output and employment expand, as measured along the horizontal axis, the rate of return on capital falls, as measured along the vertical axis. (Output is represented by Y and the rate of return is represented by r.) The Keynesians claim that at the point of full employment, namely Y_f and its corresponding output, the rate of return would either be negative or, if not negative, at least unacceptably low—below 2 percent is the usual estimate of what is unacceptably low.[21] *This alleged insufficiency of the rate of return that would exist if full employment were achieved is supposed to be the reason that full employment cannot exist, or if it did exist, could not be maintained.*

Observe that in Figure 18–2 full employment and the output it results in are alleged to be accompanied by a rate of return on capital of zero. The specific assumption of a zero rate of return is not necessary. Any rate of return

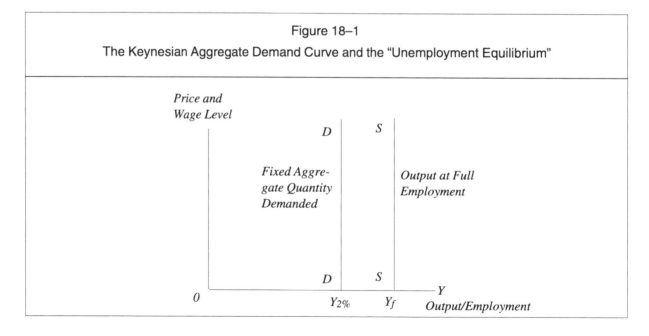

Figure 18–1

The Keynesian Aggregate Demand Curve and the "Unemployment Equilibrium"

Price and Wage Level

D   S

Fixed Aggregate Quantity Demanded

Output at Full Employment

D   S

0   Y

$Y_{2\%}$ Y_f *Output/Employment*

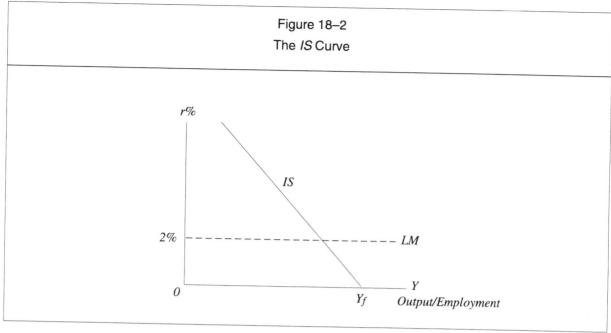

Figure 18–2

The *IS* Curve

on capital of less than 2 percent is held to be unacceptably low. At any such rate of return, the Keynesians argue, businessmen and investors will prefer to hoard cash rather than to invest. Thus, if full employment requires any rate of return below 2 percent, the existence of full employment is allegedly impossible, at least as a lasting phenomenon. And this, according to the Keynesians, is exactly what it does require and is why its existence is allegedly impossible. Full employment cannot exist under the conditions of modern capitalism, say the Keynesians, because its existence requires a rate of return on capital below the minimum acceptable rate of 2 percent, the rate below which lending and investing allegedly simply do not pay. Whether full employment actually requires a rate of return of zero, 1 percent, 1½ percent, or a negative rate of return, the rate is allegedly just too low to make investment worthwhile. And thus, if somehow full employment were achieved, say the Keynesians, savings would be hoarded rather than invested. The effect would be a drop in spending for output and labor and a reduction in output and employment below the full-employment level. This would go on until sufficient movement had taken place up and to the left along the *IS* curve to raise the rate of return on capital back up to the 2 percent figure, the alleged minimum acceptable rate of return.

(In the preceding discussion, I have not dealt explicitly with the so-called *LM* curve. The relevant portion of it is present in the horizontal line representing the alleged minimum acceptable rate of return of 2 percent, and which is intersected by the *IS* curve in Figure 18–2. As wage rates and prices fall, according to the Keynesians, and less and less money is required in the form of

"transactions balances" to provide the spending necessary to buy the same physical product at lower prices, funds allegedly pile up in "speculative balances." At a rate of return of 2 percent, the potential accumulation of speculative balances is allegedly infinite.[22])

Figure 18–3, which combines the *IS* curve of Figure 18–2 with the aggregate demand and supply curves of Figure 18–1, shows precisely how the *IS* curve is supposed to set the allegedly fixed limit of aggregate demand.[23] The horizontal axes of both diagrams are exactly the same. In the upper diagram, depicting the *IS* curve, output and employment are limited to the point marked $Y_{2\%}$. This is because that is the volume of output and employment at which the rate of return on capital is 2 percent. Any greater volume of output and employment would allegedly require a rate of return below 2 percent, which is unacceptably low and which would induce the hoarding of savings and drive the volume of output and employment back down (viz., to the left) and the rate of return back up. Equilibrium would allegedly be reached only at the respective values of $Y_{2\%}$ for output and 2% for the rate of return. This is the situation with respect to the *IS* curve, in the upper diagram of Figure 18–3.

The vertical aggregate demand curve *DD*, in the lower diagram of Figure 18–3, is drawn precisely at the point where the volume of output and employment allegedly bring the rate of return on capital on the *IS* curve down to 2 percent. *DD* cannot be one iota to the right of where it is, say the Keynesians, because if it were, the rate of return on capital invested would be below the minimum acceptable rate of 2 percent on the *IS* curve shown in the upper diagram. Thus, say the Keynesians, the aggregate demand curve of Figure 18–3 cannot possibly move to the right to coincide with the aggregate supply curve that reflects output at the point of full employment. It cannot, it is argued, because, if it did, the rate of return on capital would be zero, as shown by the IS curve in the upper diagram, at the point of output corresponding to full employment. Indeed, the aggregate demand curve allegedly cannot move so much as a hair's breadth to the right without reducing the rate of return below the minimum acceptable level, as shown by the position of the rate of return on the IS curve.

Thus the Keynesian argument is that *full employment cannot exist, because if, somehow, it did, the rate of profit would be too low.* Businessmen would then start to hoard, and the hoarding would reduce output and employment until the rate of profit was raised back up to an acceptable

level. This is supposed to be the reason why a fall in wage rates and prices is unable to achieve full employment.

The underlying problem, allegedly, is that the *physical output* corresponding to full employment imposes an unacceptably low rate of return on capital. The level of wage rates and prices is thus held to be irrelevant. Employment and output cannot get beyond where they are, no matter what happens to wage rates and prices, according to the Keynesians, because if they did, the rate of return on capital would be lower than it is, which is already the minimum acceptable rate. Thus, say the Keynesians, the only effect of a fall in wage rates and prices would be a reduction in the volume of spending for the same amount of goods and labor, not any increase in employment and output.

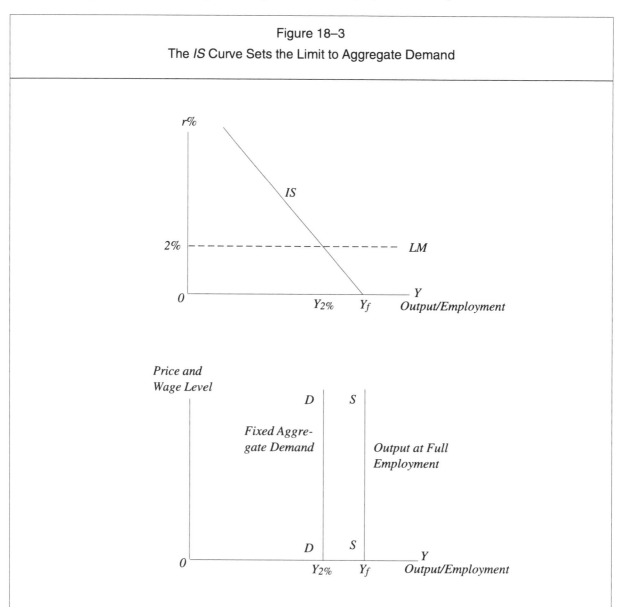

Figure 18–3

The *IS* Curve Sets the Limit to Aggregate Demand

Figure 18–4
The Derivation of the *IS* Curve

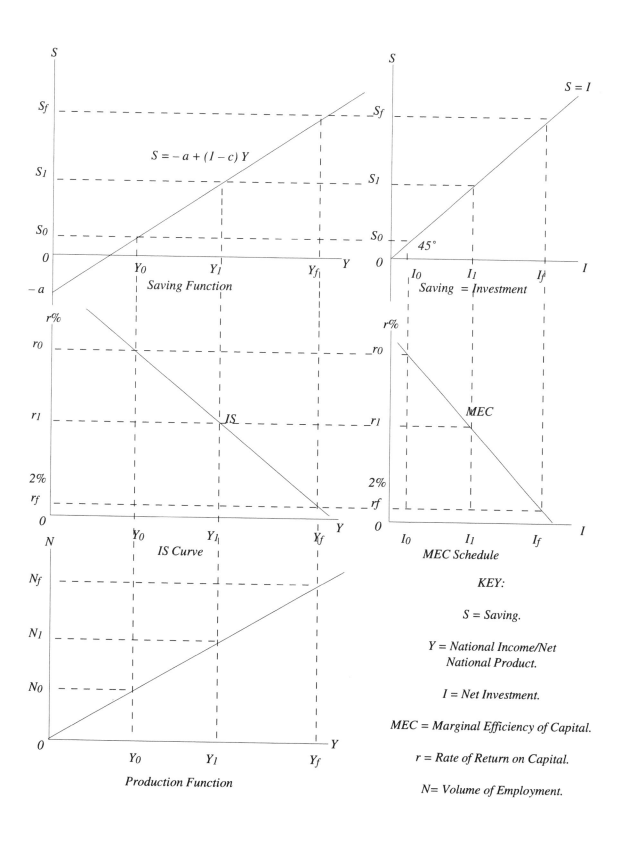

Now some people may object to the Keynesian analysis that there is no good reason for picking 2 percent as the minimum acceptable rate of return—that employment and output should be able to expand so long as the rate of return on capital remains above zero, because earning any positive rate of return is better than earning none at all. This criticism, of course, could not meet the argument that the rate of return at full employment would have to be less than zero. Moreover, the Keynesians have various arguments in favor of taking 2 percent as the practical lower limit of acceptability for the rate of return. It would be possible to present and then refute these arguments. It would also be possible to show why full employment would be compatible even with a negative rate of return (because the prospect would still exist of any given individual employer earning a positive rate of return and thereby continuing to have a sufficiently strong motive for investing). Instead, however, I prefer to challenge the *IS* curve—the very notion that as employment and output expand, the rate of return on capital falls.

In order to accomplish this, it is necessary to explain the process by which the Keynesians derive the *IS* curve from various other real or imagined relationships. These relationships are: (1) the production function, (2) the saving function, (3) an equality of saving and investment, and (4) the marginal-efficiency-of-capital schedule. All of them, and the derivation of the *IS* curve from them, are shown in Figure 18–4 as a set of five interconnected diagrams. The production function appears in the diagram in the bottom-left portion of Figure 18–4; the saving function, in the diagram in the top-left portion; the equality of saving and investment, in the diagram in the top-right portion; the marginal efficiency of capital schedule, in the diagram in the center-right portion of the figure; and, finally, the *IS* curve, in the diagram in the center-left portion of the figure.

"Production function," it should be recalled from Chapter 13, is simply the technical name given to the relationship between the volume of employment (labor performed) and the volume of output that results, given the state of technology and the supply of capital equipment. The labor performed is shown on the vertical axis, while the output produced is shown on the horizontal axis. This, of course, is a relationship that is in no way specific to Keynesian economics.[24] The use of the letter *N*, however, to measure the volume of employment is taken from the practice of the Keynesian textbooks.

The "saving function" is the Keynesian doctrine that a definite, determinate mathematical relationship exists between the level of income, on the one side, and the volume of saving out of income, on the other. In the diagram, saving is shown on the vertical axis and income on the horizontal axis. The saving function is the corol-

lary of the more widely known Keynesian doctrine of the "consumption function," according to which consumption spending is mathematically determined by the level of income. It is derived by subtracting the consumption function from income. Typically, it is presented as the algebraic formula

$$S = -a + (1-c)Y,$$

where *a* is a given amount of consumption that occurs irrespective of the level of income, *c* is the "marginal propensity to consume," viz., the extra consumption that take place out of additional income, and *Y* is national income/net national product. A minus sign appears before the constant *a* to indicate the amount of dissaving that would occur if income were zero. Since all income is either consumed or saved, and *c* is the marginal propensity of consume, *1-c* is the "marginal propensity to save."

It should be noted that there is more than a little equivocation in the way the symbol *Y* is used. When it appears in connection with the production function, it refers to *physical output*—to "real income." When it appears in connection with saving, however, it becomes *money income*, out of which cash hoarding occurs. Please note in this connection that the horizontal axis of the production function and the saving function are presented as identical, and so is the horizontal axis of the *IS* curve. *Y* is the measure of all three.

The third diagram—the equilibria of saving and investment—in the upper-right portion of Figure 18–4, shows investment equal to saving at every point. The vertical axis of this diagram is identical with the vertical axis of the saving-function diagram. Thus it too represents saving. The equality of investment, which is shown on the horizontal axis, with saving, is accomplished by the drawing of a 45-degree line through the origin. Every point on this line represents an equal distance on both axes of the diagram, and thus represents an equality of saving and investment. The purpose of this diagram is to set the stage for showing why investment cannot in fact be equal to saving when saving is substantial. Its purpose is to ask what would happen if all that were saved at every level of real income were actually invested.

The answer to this last, and very critical question is supposedly supplied in the fourth diagram, the marginal-efficiency-of-capital schedule—*mec* schedule for short—in the center-right portion of Figure 18–4. Here, the horizontal, investment axis of the diagram above is repeated, while the rate of return on capital is shown on the vertical axis. It is claimed that the greater is the volume of net investment, the lower is the rate of return on capital. This is shown by the *mec* schedule sloping downward to the right, with the greater being the size of *I*, the smaller being the size of r. (The reasons advanced in support of the *mec* doctrine will be presented shortly. For the moment, it can be taken at face value, simply in order to understand the derivation of the *IS* curve. It is important to note in this connection, that the vertical axis of the *mec* schedule and the vertical axis of the *IS* curve are also identical.)

Given the production function, the saving function, the equilibria of saving and investment, and the *mec* schedule, the derivation of the *IS* curve is not difficult. We can begin by picking a low level of employment. Let us take point N_0 on the vertical axis in the bottom-left diagram. Reading over to the production function, along the dashed line, we see that this implies a definite level of output (real income). Call that level of output Y_0. Now we read up a dashed line, all the way to the saving function. There, we find that Y_0 output (income) implies S_0 of saving. Reading across, along the dashed line, to the investment-equals-saving diagram, we find that S_0 of saving requires I_0 of net investment, if the saving is not to be hoarded. Reading down now, along the dashed line to the *mec* schedule, we find that I_0 of net investment implies an r_0 rate of return. If we now connect the Y_0 output produced by the N_0 volume of employment, with the r_0 rate of return that results from the investment of the savings generated by that level of output (income), we have a point on the *IS* curve.

Down in the bottom-left diagram, let us pick a second, higher level of employment on the vertical axis, namely, the amount denoted by N_1. Reading over to the production function, we see that this implies another definite level of output—a higher one. Call it Y_1. Again, we read up along the dashed line to the saving function. There we find a second, higher level of saving. Call it S_1. Reading across to the saving-equals-investment diagram, we find that S_1 of saving requires equivalent I_1 of investment, if the saving is not to be hoarded. Reading down to the *mec* schedule, we find that I_1 of investment implies a lower, r_1 rate of return. If we now connect the r_1 rate of return with the Y_1 level of output, we obtain a second point on the *IS* curve. This is a point of greater output and a lower rate of return. What is present here is that more employment means more output (real income), more saving, the need for more investment to prevent the hoarding of that saving, and a lower rate of return on investment, if that investment actually takes place.

Finally, let us pick a third, still higher level of employment on the vertical axis in the production-function diagram. Let us call it "full employment, and denote it by the letters N_f. Once more reading over to the production function along a dashed line, we find that the higher level of employment goes with a higher level of output. Call this level of output Y_f, the full-employment level of

output. Reading up along the dashed line to the saving function, we see that there is a higher level of saving corresponding to the full-employment level of output. Call it S_f, the full-employment level of saving. Reading over to the saving-equals-investment diagram, we see that S_f of saving, if it is not to be hoarded, requires the correspondingly larger amount I_f of net investment. Reading down to the *mec* schedule, we see that I_f of net investment is accompanied by a further reduction in the rate of return to r_f, the full employment rate of return. The r_f rate of return and the Y_f level of output constitute a third point on the *IS* curve. Unfortunately, say the Keynesians, this rate of return is simply below the minimum acceptable rate of return of 2 percent, and so full employment cannot be achieved, or if somehow achieved, cannot be maintained.

A fall in wage rates and prices is held to be useless in achieving full employment because all of the above relationships are supposed to hold true *in physical terms*. N_f of employment means Y_f of output, means S_f of saving, requiring I_f of net investment, which causes too low a rate of return. These same physical relationships allegedly hold irrespective of the wage-and-price level. Specifically, at a lower wage-and-price level, it is held, no more physical investment is profitable (yields more than 2 percent) than before.

If, for example, initially there is 250 of investment at a 2 percent rate of return and, say, approximately 10 percent unemployment, a fall in wage rates and prices to $\frac{9}{10}$ their initial level will not achieve full employment—indeed, it will supposedly not achieve any increase in employment at all. This is because investment will allegedly have to fall 10 percent to 225—that is, in full proportion to the fall in wage rates and prices. It is claimed that investment must fall in this way because all the investment that there is room for at a 2-percent-or-greater rate of return is, allegedly, *that physical amount of investment*—for example, so many steel mills, cement factories, bicycle shops, and so forth—which at the initial price-and-wage level requires 250 to purchase. At a price-and-wage level $\frac{9}{10}$ as high, that physical amount of net investment requires only 225 to purchase. Net investment cannot remain at 250 in money, because then 250 of monetary net investment would be equivalent to approximately *278* of net investment at the initial price-and-wage level (viz., at $\frac{9}{10}$ times the initial price-and-wage level, 250 would be equivalent in buying power to $\frac{10}{9}$ times 250, which is 278). This greater physical amount of net investment would mean a rate of return below 2 percent. Thus, all that net investment can be at the $\frac{9}{10}$ price-and-wage level is 225, because now 225 represents the alleged maximum physical quantity of net investment that is profitable.

In exactly the same way, if the wage-and-price level were to fall all the way to half, the monetary amount of net investment would supposedly have to fall in half—to 125 from 250. It allegedly could not remain at 250 or even at 225, because monetary amounts of net investment at those levels would now represent real, physical net investment equivalent to what 500 purchased at the initial price-and-wage level, or what 450 would purchase at $\frac{9}{10}$ the initial price-and-wage level. Such volumes of net investment would allegedly thus result in a rate of return all the more below 2 percent. At a halved wage-and-price level, net investment cannot get beyond 125 in money, it is held, because that sum now represents the maximum physical amount of net investment that is profitable.[25]

These results are shown in Figure 18–5. Below the horizontal axis in this figure are three different scales of measurement of net investment, each one corresponding to a different price-and-wage level, namely, the initial price-and-wage level, one that is $\frac{9}{10}$ as high, and one that is only half as high. Because the same maximum physical amount of net investment is allegedly all that is profitable—namely, the amount that is profitable down to a rate of return of 2 percent and no lower—the effect is that each successive scale of measurement at lower prices and wages moves correspondingly to the right. Thus, the net

investment that initially required 250 to purchase, successively requires only 225, and then only 125. Continued net investment in the amount of 250 at the $\frac{9}{10}$ price-and-wage level, and then at the halved price-and-wage level, would allegedly result in rates of return on capital respectively equivalent to those produced by 278 and 500 of net investment at the initial price-and-wage level

Thus, despite the fall in wage rates and prices, the problem that allegedly remains is that there cannot be an outlet for saving in excess of the given physical amount of net investment that is profitable (i.e., that yields 2 percent or more). And thus there cannot be a real income (output) that results in any such greater level of saving, nor, finally, a volume of employment that would result in any such level of output. The volume of employment is thus allegedly limited to that amount that results in a level of output (real income) out of which saving is no greater than is consistent with the allegedly limited physical volume of profitable investment opportunities.

In other words, according to the Keynesians, there cannot lastingly be a level of employment, output, and real income greater than what produces the limited volume of saving that can be accommodated by the limited volume of profitable investment opportunities. If the volume of employment is greater than the one that pro-

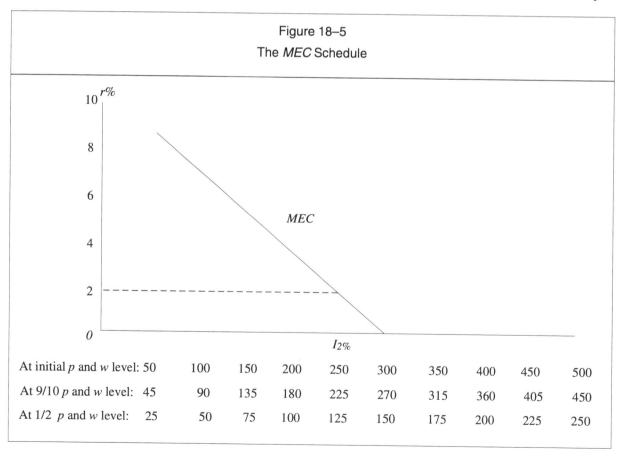

Figure 18–5

The *MEC* Schedule

At initial *p* and *w* level: 50	100	150	200	250	300	350	400	450	500
At 9/10 *p* and *w* level: 45	90	135	180	225	270	315	360	405	450
At 1/2 *p* and *w* level: 25	50	75	100	125	150	175	200	225	250

duces such a limited level of saving, then saving supposedly exceeds the limited profitable investment opportunities that exist, thereby driving the rate of return on capital below the minimum acceptable level. The alleged consequences are that hoarding results, spending drops, and sales revenues, employment, and output all decline. Their decline then represents a drop in real income. Out of the smaller real income, less saving occurs. The drop in employment, output, and real income must allegedly be great enough to reduce the volume of saving to the point where it no longer exceeds the allegedly limited profitable investment opportunities available.

In sum, full employment, or any employment beyond a fixed, given amount, cannot exist, or at least cannot be maintained, according to the Keynesians, because it would produce a physical volume of output out of which there would be a physical volume of saving requiring a physical volume of net investment that would put the rate of return below the minimum acceptable rate. In essence, the Keynesian argument is that full employment cannot exist in a free economy because if it did, the economic system would, in effect, choke on the allegedly excessive saving that would accompany full employment. Keynes himself states the essence of his position in the following words (where helpful, I insert my own clarifications in brackets):

> Perhaps it will help to rebut the crude conclusion that a reduction in money-wages will increase employment "because it reduces the cost of production", if we follow up the course of events on the hypothesis most favourable to this view, namely that at the outset entrepreneurs *expect* the reduction in money-wages to have this effect. It is indeed not unlikely that the individual entrepreneur, seeing his own costs reduced, will overlook at the outset the repercussions on the demand for his product and will act on the assumption that he will be able to sell at a profit a larger output than before. If, then, entrepreneurs generally act on this expectation, will they in fact succeed in increasing their profits? Only if the community's marginal propensity to consume is equal to unity, so that there is no gap between the increment of income and the increment of consumption [i.e., there is no additional saving]; or if there is an increase in investment, corresponding to the gap between the increment of income and the increment of consumption, which will only occur if the schedule of marginal efficiencies of capital has increased relatively to the rate of interest [i.e., either the *mec* schedule must somehow move to the right, which there is allegedly no reason for its doing, or the rate of interest must fall, which it can't do, if it is already at 2 percent]. Thus the proceeds realised from the increased output will disappoint the entrepreneurs and employment will fall back again to its previous figure, unless the marginal propensity to consume is equal to unity [i.e., there is no additional saving] or the reduction in money-wages has had the effect of increasing the schedule of marginal efficiencies of capital relatively to the rate of interest and hence

the amount of investment [Keynes means, of course, increase the amount of investment that is profitable—i.e., yields 2 percent or more]. *For if entrepreneurs offer employment on a scale which, if they could sell their output at the expected price, would provide the public with incomes out of which they would save more than the amount of current investment, entrepreneurs are bound to make a loss equal to the difference; and this will be the case absolutely irrespective of the level of money wages.*[26]

I have italicized the last sentence because if any single sentence of Keynes can express the theoretical substance of his doctrine, that is the one.[27]

The Grounds for the *MEC* Doctrine

It should be obvious that the two critical doctrines underlying the *IS* curve are the doctrines of the saving function and, above all, the declining *mec* schedule. According to the saving function, people insist on saving a significant portion of the additional real income corresponding to the additional output that results from additional employment. If they did not do so—if there were no additional savings requiring investment as employment increased, full employment might actually be achieved according to Keynes, as the passage quoted above makes clear. For the rate of return on capital would then not have to fall as employment increased. Thus, if only people were sufficiently profligate, they could be prosperous, says Keynes.

Fortunately, of course, people do wish to save. From the perspective of Keynesian economics, however, this creates the problem of having to prevent the resulting savings from being hoarded, because of the alleged decline in the rate of return on capital that results from their being invested.

It is now necessary to present the reasons Keynes and his followers advance in support of the declining *mec* doctrine—of the claim that as net investment increases, the rate of return on capital must fall. Keynes himself writes:

> If there is an increased investment in any given type of capital during any period of time, the marginal efficiency of that type of capital will diminish as the investment in it is increased, partly because the prospective yield will fall as the supply of that type of capital is increased, and partly because, as a rule, pressure on the facilities for producing that type of capital will cause its supply price to increase . . . . Thus for each type of capital we can build up a schedule, showing by how much investment in it will have to increase within the period, in order that its marginal efficiency should fall to any given figure. We can then aggregate these schedules for all the different types of capital, so as to provide a schedule relating the rate of aggregate investment to the corresponding marginal efficiency of capital in general which that rate of investment will establish. We shall call this the investment demand-schedule; or, alternatively,

the schedule of the marginal efficiency of capital.[28]

When Keynes speaks of rising "supply prices" of capital assets as investment demand increases and causes pressure on the facilities for producing capital goods, what he has in mind is the notion that more net investment constitutes additional demand for capital assets and thus raises their prices. His further belief that increasing net investment results in declining yields to capital assets is based in part on the conviction that as more productive capacity is brought into existence, as the result of the net investment, the selling prices of products will fall because of their larger supply. In addition, the yields to capital assets will allegedly fall because of the operation of the law of diminishing returns: successive equal increments of net investment, even at constant purchase prices of capital assets, supposedly result in diminishing physical returns to the successive doses of capital assets purchased.[29]

To express these ideas in terms of a simple example, we might imagine that initially the price of a machine that turns out widgets is $1,000 and that its use enables the same quantity of labor to produce 10 additional widgets every year, which have a selling price of $10 each. On the simplifying assumptions that this machine will last forever and that the cost of materials and fuel can be ignored, the implied rate of return is 10 percent per year: 10 additional widgets times $10, divided by $1,000. Now, however, there is a demand for two such machines. As a result, the purchase price rises above $1,000—say, to $1,050. In addition, the selling price of widgets will fall somewhat, because of their larger supply—say, to $9.50. Finally, because of diminishing returns, it may be possible to obtain only 9 additional widgets instead of 10 by virtue of the employment of the second machine. The operation of any one of these factors, it is held, reduces the rate of return. Their combined operation in this example must reduce the rate of return to not much more than 8 percent: $9.50 times 9 widgets, divided by $1,050. In these ways, more net investment is held to reduce the rate of return on capital.[30]

The Keynesian Solution: "Fiscal Policy"

The Keynesian solution to the alleged unemployment equilibrium of capitalism is government budget deficits (euphemistically called "fiscal policy"). The purpose of the budget deficits is to absorb the excess saving that allegedly would otherwise take place at full employment. Figure 18–6 shows the nature of the gains the Keynesians believe government budget deficits achieve.

The diagram in Figure 18–6 is the same as that in the upper-right portion of Figure 18–4—that is, the saving-equals-investment diagram. But it shows investment as

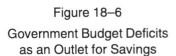

Figure 18–6
Government Budget Deficits
as an Outlet for Savings

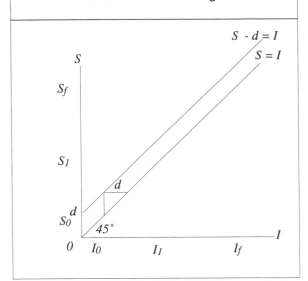

equal to saving minus the deficit, instead of saving in full. The deficit, according to the Keynesians, serves as an additional outlet for saving and thus reduces the amount flowing through to net investment. This is shown in the diagram by the drawing of a second 45-degree line, above the first one by a vertical distance equal to the amount of the deficit, which is represented by d on the vertical axis. This new 45-degree line is labeled $S - d = I$—saving minus the deficit equals net investment—in contrast to $S = I$, which is the label describing the first 45-degree line. Note that when saving equals the deficit, investment equals zero, as shown by the intersection of the new 45-degree line with the vertical axis at point d. Because both are 45-degree lines, the new line is not only above the original one by the amount of the deficit but also to the left of it by the amount of the deficit. This depicts the idea that every given amount of saving now requires an amount of investment that is less than itself by the amount of the deficit.

The crucial result is supposed to be that for any given level of employment, output, and saving, the amount of investment required to prevent hoarding is less than it otherwise would be by the amount of the deficit. Since there is less investment, the further crucial result is supposed to be that the rate of return on capital is now higher for any given level of employment, output, and saving. By the same token, it takes more employment, output and saving to achieve the same rate of return as previously. *In other words, the effect of the deficit is supposedly to shift the IS curve up and to the right.*

This result is confirmed by drawing the new saving-

Figure 18–7

How Budget Deficits Are Supposed to Promote Full Employment

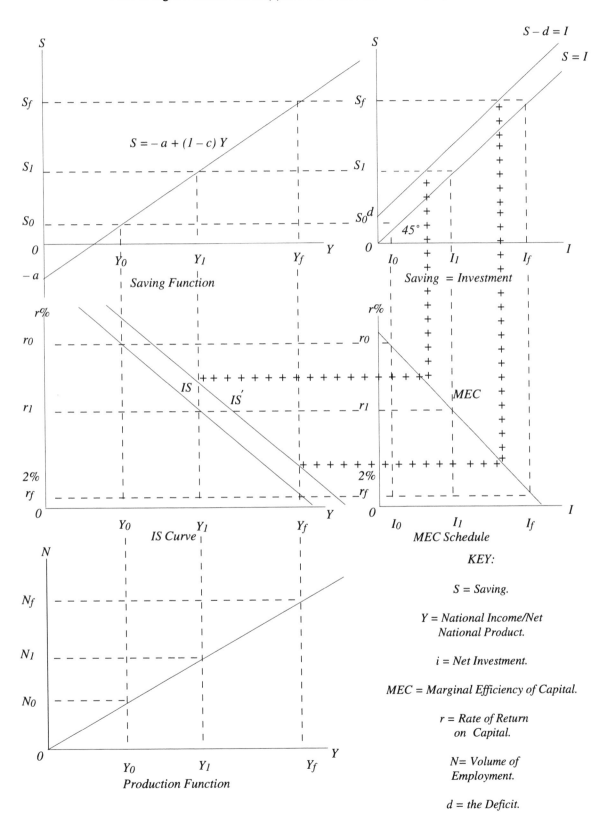

Saving Function

Saving = Investment

IS Curve

MEC Schedule

Production Function

KEY:

S = Saving.

Y = National Income/Net
National Product.

i = Net Investment.

MEC = Marginal Efficiency of Capital.

r = Rate of Return
on Capital.

N = Volume of
Employment.

d = the Deficit.

minus-the-deficit-equals-investment line in the upper-right diagram of Figure 18–4 and then examining the effect on the *IS* curve. Each N, Y, and S point will be found to go with a lower I and thus a higher r point. This is shown in Figure 18–7, which, in essence, substitutes Figure 18–6 for the upper-right diagram of Figure 18–4.

What the set of diagrams in Figure 18–7 purports to show is that, thanks to the government's budget deficit, for any given volume of employment, output, real income, and saving, there is less investment and thus a higher rate of return on capital than before. Thus, there can be more employment, output, real income, and saving before the volume of investment becomes so large as to push the rate of return on capital to the minimum acceptable level of 2 percent. With a large enough deficit, argue the Keynesians, there can be full employment.

The whole process is described by the upward and rightward movement of the *IS* curve. Following along the dashed lines, notice how the same magnitudes of employment, N_0, N_1, and N_f, continue to result in the same magnitudes of output (real income) and saving—namely, Y_0, Y_1, and Y_f and S_0, S_1, and S_f respectively. But now S_0 of saving requires less than I_0 of net investment; S_1 of saving now requires less than I_1 of net investment; and, what is supposedly critical, S_f of saving now requires sufficiently less than the old I_f volume of net investment that full employment can now take place at a rate of return above 2 percent. The new relationships to investment and the rate of return are indicated by lines composed of plus signs, which run downward from the saving-minus-the-deficit-equals-investment line to the *mec* schedule and then across, to the left, to the various values of Y resulting from the various values of N.

To describe matters verbally, one could say this: The alleged problem of capitalism, according to the Keynesians, is that full employment results in a volume of saving that the economic system cannot profitably invest. In effect, such saving is a destructive by-product of full employment under capitalism, and thus prevents the existence of full employment. It is a kind of toxic excrescence—a veritable boil on the economic body that interferes with its vital functioning. Fortunately, however, there is a doctor, and he has a cure for the problem. The doctor is the government, and the cure is a deficit in its budget. As Keynes has explained matters, the government doctor will lance the savings boil and allow its destructive juices to flow into the waiting pan of the government's deficit rather than into private investment, where it would reduce the rate of return on capital to an intolerably low level.

A different, perhaps less distasteful analogy can be used. Capitalism, we might imagine, cannot have full employment because of the existence of a hard-drink function, rather than a saving function. As employment and real income rise, people feel themselves able to afford to drink more. At the point of full employment, they drink so much that they are physically hung over on the week ends to such an extent that they are incapable of work on Mondays. This too would represent a kind of "unemployment equilibrium." Once again, a case might be made for the intervention of the good government doctor: it might siphon off people's liquor money with the sale of soft drinks, 2 percent beer, or perhaps even methadone. Or, perhaps, it might work to divert their liquor money onto ecclesiastical collection plates, in effect, buying bonds issued in the name of heaven rather than in its name.

Innumerable analogies to the unemployment-equilibrium doctrine can be created on the basis of environmentalism. That doctrine, of course, holds that economic activity is replete with self-destructive by-products.[31] On the basis of it, one could easily invent all kinds of mathematical functions analogous to the "saving function." Then all one would need to do is arbitrarily assert some fixed limit to the capacity of the world to cope with the particular by-product. On that basis, one could proceed to argue that employment and production must be limited to the point of not generating an amount of such by-product in excess of the alleged fixed limit. Indeed, this is precisely what the environmentalists are doing in the cases of carbon dioxide emissions and garbage disposal. Only instead of seeking to impose an unemployment equilibrium by forcibly holding down the volume of employment, they seek to impose limits on the productivity of labor and the volume of consumption. But just as with Keynesianism and its budget deficits, there is still an alleged need for the good government doctor (though not as often, because the environmentalists believe that human suffering is fundamentally inescapable and, indeed, desirable). In the case of the carbon dioxide emissions, it is sometimes argued that the alleged low-productivity-of-labor equilibrium might be overcome to some extent by virtue of government imposed tree-planting programs. These would play the same kind of role in the absorption of allegedly harmful carbon dioxide as government budget deficits are supposed to play in the absorption of allegedly harmful saving. The essential common element in Keynesianism and environmentalism is the belief that free individuals are engaged in essentially self-destructive activity that, if it can be remedied at all, can only be remedied by the coercive power of the state.

3. Critique of the *IS-LM* Analysis

The Declining-Marginal-Efficiency-of-Capital Doctrine and the Fallacy of Context Dropping

The critique of the Keynesian *IS-LM* analysis can be concentrated on the declining-marginal-efficiency-of-capital doctrine. The Keynesians' use of this doctrine is a prime example of a major logical fallacy identified by Ayn Rand, which she calls "context dropping."[32] Context dropping is the fallacy of denying, forgetting, or otherwise contradicting the context that is explicitly or implicitly under discussion. An example of context dropping from outside the field of economics is the following. Imagine a group of aeronautical engineers who are working on the problem of how to increase the speed of an airplane. They know that other things being equal, the lighter the weight of the plane, the faster it will fly. If, to make the plane lighter, they concluded that its engines should be eliminated, they would be committing the fallacy of context dropping. For the context under discussion is the flight of a heavier-than-air machine, which is possible only by virtue of its possession of engines. Another example of context dropping would be an esoteric discussion of the effects of living or working on the tenth floor of a building, which discussion somehow managed to deny or otherwise contradict the existence of any one or more of the lower nine floors of the building or of its foundation.

The use of the declining-marginal-efficiency-of-capital doctrine is an example of context dropping, for the following reasons. The context under discussion is the question *can a fall in wage rates and prices achieve full employment or can it not?* This question is the context which must always be kept in mind. It is the context within which the declining-marginal-efficiency-of-capital doctrine is advanced, in order to show why a fall in wage rates and prices cannot achieve full employment. Yet, as will quickly be made apparent, every one of the three grounds advanced in support of the declining-marginal-efficiency-of-capital doctrine, and which were described in the previous section, flatly *contradicts* the context under discussion.

Once again, the context under discussion is the ability of *lower* wage rates and prices to achieve full employment. This context, of course, implies lower unit costs of production, for that is what lower wage rates achieve both directly and through bringing about lower prices of materials and machinery and capital goods in general. The achievement of full employment also implies the availability of more labor in production relative to the existing supply of capital goods. In a state of mass unemployment, the factories and machinery exist in vir-

tually the same quantity as before the onset of the depression and the unemployment. But they are largely idle. The ratio of capital to labor employed is correspondingly high. As full employment is approached, and more and more workers return to the factories, the ratio of capital to labor correspondingly falls.

Now this whole context is contradicted by the use of the declining-marginal-efficiency-of-capital doctrine to show why a fall in wage rates and prices cannot achieve full employment.

The use of the declining-marginal-efficiency-of-capital doctrine enables the Keynesians to end up claiming that a *fall* in wage rates and prices cannot achieve full employment, precisely by dropping the context of a fall in wage rates and prices and rise in employment, and switching to an altogether different, indeed, *opposite* context, which could exist only if wages rates, production costs, and prices rose instead of fell. For the context to which the Keynesians deftly switch is one of a *rise* in the prices of capital assets, *no* fall in the costs of production but constant or, indeed, *rising* costs of production, and no increase in the quantity of labor employed relative to the supply of capital goods in existence, but, on the contrary, a further increase in the supply of capital goods relative to the supply of labor that is employed.

Recall that the first reason advanced in support of the falling marginal efficiency of capital was the claim that as more net investment took place to offset the additional saving accompanying the additional employment, the prices of capital assets would *rise*, in response to the increase in demand for capital assets allegedly constituted by the additional net investment. The actual fact is, of course, that in the context of the elimination of unemployment by means of a fall in wage rates and prices, the prices of capital assets would *fall*, not rise. Keynes and his followers thus totally contradict the context under discussion. They claim that a fall in wage rates and prices cannot achieve full employment, because if, *instead of falling*, as they necessarily would in these circumstances, the prices of capital assets *rose*, the rate of return on capital would be reduced.

Furthermore, it is curiously ironic that in arriving at their bizarre conclusion that the prices of capital assets would rise in the midst of a fall in wage rates and prices, the Keynesians commit precisely the fallacy that the arch-Keynesian Professor Samuelson is at such pains to warn new students of economics against. Namely, the fallacy of confusing the increase in the quantity of a good demanded that takes place in response to a lower price of the good, with an increase in the demand for the good.[33] Precisely this fallacy is what is present in the Keynesians' belief that the rise in net investment that accompanies the fall in wage rates and prices and the restoration of full employment, constitutes a rise in the demand for capital assets and thus acts to raise their prices. The fact is that the additional net investment presupposes and is in response to *lower* prices of capital assets, and can endure only so long as the prices of the capital assets are lower. It does not operate to raise those prices. And this is true even if one were to grant the legitimacy of conceiving of the additional net investment as representing an additional total expenditure of money for the capital assets. It would still be necessary to keep in mind that the larger expenditure of money was in response to lower prices and could endure only so long as the prices of capital assets remained lower.[34]

Recall that the second reason advanced for the declining marginal efficiency of capital was the claim that more net investment means more capacity in place, which means lower selling prices of products, which, other things being equal, means a fall in profitability. Here the context dropping consists of forgetting that other things—namely, the costs of production—are *not* equal. Precisely a *fall* in wages and costs is what brings about the additional production and the decline in prices. Lower prices founded on lower costs of production do *not* reduce profitability or the so-called marginal efficiency of capital.

Again, the Keynesians contradict the context. They argue that a fall in wages, costs, and prices cannot achieve full employment because if all that occurred were the fall in selling prices and *no fall in costs*—indeed, a rise in costs because of the alleged rise in the prices of capital assets—the rate of return on capital would fall. This, of course, is totally absurd. It is absurd to argue against the ability of a fall in wage rates and costs of production to achieve full employment on the grounds that if there were *no* fall in costs of production but, somehow, only a fall in the prices of the products, full employment could not be achieved. This dropping and switching of context enables the Keynesians to fail to see that the lower selling prices of products are offset and in fact more than offset by a fall in costs of production, and thus that there is not only no fall in the rate of profit (the "marginal efficiency of capital"), but an actual *rise* in the rate of profit in consequence of the fall in wages and costs of production.

Finally, it should be recalled that the third reason advanced in support of the declining marginal efficiency of capital was the claim that diminishing returns would accompany the additional net investment that was required to offset the additional saving taking place as employment, output, and real income expanded. Now putting aside the actual irrelevance of the law of diminishing returns to the rate of profit, and assuming for the sake of argument that it did have a determining effect, the truth is that in the context of a fall in wage rates and

prices and increase in the volume of employment and output, the physical returns to capital goods would *increase* rather than decrease. This is because as the economic system moves from mass unemployment to full employment, *the supply of labor employed in production increases at a more rapid rate than the supply of capital goods*. This is so because in the conditions of mass unemployment a substantial supply of capital goods previously used in production continues to exist in the form of idle machines and factories. Its existence relative to the diminished number of workers employed constitutes an unusually high ratio of capital to labor. As the workers come back into the factories and once again take up the use of these capital goods, the ratio of capital to labor sharply declines.

Such increase in the supply of capital goods as occurs as the result of additional employment, output, real income, and saving is a purely derivative phenomenon. The fundamental, primary phenomenon is the increase in the ratio of labor employed to capital goods, which implies increasing returns to capital goods, not decreasing returns. If ever there were a problem of too-low physical returns to capital goods, nothing could be a surer cure than the employment of more labor. Whatever problem might be imagined to exist, it would necessarily be less at the point of full employment than at the point of mass unemployment, or any unemployment.

As an illustration of this fact, imagine that in conditions of unemployment there are 12 units of capital goods and 3 workers employed, who produce a net output of 3 units of goods. The achievement of full employment means, let us assume, the employment of 4 workers who produce a net output of 4 units of goods. If fully one-half of the additional net output of 1 unit is saved, the ratio of capital goods to labor still falls dramatically—from 12 to 3 (i.e., 4:1), to 12.5 to 4 (i.e., to 3.125:1). And this principle continues to hold, even if it were the case that the long-term continuation of full employment and steady saving and net investment of a half a unit of net output per year ultimately resulted in a ratio of capital to labor of, say, 24 to 4 (i.e., 6 to 1) at the point of full employment. This is because in that case, with the same unemployment as before, the ratio of capital to labor would be 24 to 3 (i.e., 8 to 1). Thus, the movement from unemployment to full employment would still reduce the ratio of capital to labor and increase the physical returns to capital goods, not decrease them.

The procedure of the Keynesians, of course, is to forget the existence of the fundamental phenomenon, the increase in the supply of labor employed as the economic system goes from unemployment to full employment, and to focus on the secondary, derivative phenomenon, the increase in the supply of capital goods that results from the saving out of the net output of the additional workers employed. In this way, the Keynesians proceed to assume that the ratio of capital goods to labor rises and the physical returns to capital goods fall, at the very time that exactly the opposite is true. Thus, the Keynesians end up claiming that full employment cannot take place on the grounds that if extra employment did *not* mean an increase in the ratio of labor to capital, but somehow the opposite, namely, an increase in the ratio of capital to labor, full employment could not exist—by virtue of the too-low rate of profit allegedly resulting from the relative overabundance of capital goods. In a word, the Keynesians end up denying that full employment can exist by confusing the effects of its existence with the effects of its nonexistence.

Indeed, the whole process by which the Keynesians reach the conclusion that a fall in wage rates and prices cannot achieve full employment is nothing more than *a refusal to consider its actual existence.* Instead of considering the existence of a fall in wage rates, costs, and prices and the employment of a larger number of workers, they choose to consider the totally different and opposite case of a rise in the prices of capital assets, of no fall in the costs of production but only in the selling prices of products, and of no increase in the supply of labor employed but only of an increase in the supply of capital goods that derives from that employment. Then, on the basis of their consideration of this totally opposite and thoroughly illegitimate case, in which down has literally become up—namely, a fall in the prices of capital assets has become a rise in the prices of capital assets—and in which effects have been divorced from their causes—that is, the fall in selling prices has been divorced from its cause, the fall in wage rates and costs, and the additional net investment and capital accumulation has been divorced from its cause, which is the employment of additional workers with the capital goods already in existence—they conclude that they have proven something about the case at hand. All they have actually proven is their own capacity for confusion, if not intellectual dishonesty.[35]

The Marginal-Efficiency-of-Capital Doctrine and the Claim That the Rate of Profit Is Lower in the Recovery from a Depression Than in the Depression

There are further major criticisms which must be made of the Keynesian analysis in connection with the marginal-efficiency-of-capital doctrine. The Keynesian claim that a fall in wage rates and prices cannot achieve full employment, because at full employment the rate of return on capital would be too low, is a claim that *the rate of return in the recovery from a depression is lower than it is in the depression.*

What the Keynesians claim is that the economic system cannot recover from mass unemployment and depression because if somehow it did, the rate of return on capital would fall—which means that it would be lower in the recovery from the depression than it was in the depression. In effect, the Keynesians tell us that if we think the rate of profit is low now, in the conditions of mass unemployment and depression, we should wait and see what it will look like in the recovery. In the state of mass unemployment and depression, it is already at the minimum acceptable level (in the neighborhood of 2 percent) and at full employment it would have to be lower still, they say. Indeed, according to the Keynesians, if somehow the economic system did temporarily manage to recover and achieve full employment, it would immediately have to return to the conditions of mass unemployment and depression as the means of *elevating* the rate of profit—above the still lower level that is supposed to exist in the recovery. This is the actual meaning of the whole Keynesian argument for the unemployment equilibrium. If there is any doubt about this fact, the reader should look once again at the standard Keynesian diagrammatic relationships presented above in Figure 18–4 of this chapter and reread the extensive passage quoted from Keynes himself some paragraphs later, in which he claims to "rebut the crude conclusion that a reduction in money wages rates will increase employment."

The Unemployment-Equilibrium Doctrine and the Claim That Saving and Net Investment Are at Their Maximum Possible Limits at the Very Time They Are Actually Negative

An equally profound and closely related reversal of economic reality on the part of the Keynesian analysis is its belief that in a depression saving and net investment are at their maximum possible limits, and the problem is that full employment requires that they be carried still further.[36] This, of course, is the alleged proximate cause of the marginal efficiency of capital having to be pushed below its minimum acceptable level. The actual fact is, however, that far from being at their maximum limits, saving and net investment are extremely low or even *negative* in a depression. For example, in the Great Depression following 1929, corporate saving (undistributed corporate profits) was negative in every year from 1930 to 1936 and again in 1938; personal saving was negative in 1932 and 1933 and barely more than zero in 1934; net investment was negative in the years 1931 to 1935 and again in 1938.[37]

There should be nothing surprising in these facts. They are logically implied in the very nature of a depression and mass unemployment. When people are out of work, they must live off their savings. In a state of mass unemployment, the consumption of savings in this way is necessarily very considerable. At the same time, corporations are under pressure to continue to pay dividends to their stockholders, even though they are currently earning little or no profits. To pay dividends under such conditions, they must dip into their accumulated savings—their earned surplus accounts. Unincorporated businesses, of course, are under the same kind of pressure; they too must frequently continue to support their owners even though their current profits are insufficient to do so. In these ways, the current saving of those individuals and business firms who are still in a position to save out of income is more than offset, and saving in the economy as a whole becomes nonexistent or, indeed, becomes negative.

The fact that net investment becomes negative can be understood by direct inference, either from the fact that saving out of income becomes negative or from the fact that in a depression productive expenditure sharply declines, in particular productive expenditure for fixed assets, such as plant and equipment. A plunge in productive expenditure for fixed assets implies a fall in net investment, because at the same time depreciation charges hardly change at all, since they are based on a percentage of the productive expenditure for fixed assets made over a long period of prior years. Net investment in fixed assets actually becomes negative to the extent that current productive expenditure for fixed assets drops below depreciation charges. To that extent, the sum of the subtractions from the fixed asset accounts in the economic system exceeds the sum of the additions currently being made to those accounts, and thus the net change—the net investment—is negative.[38] Similarly, in a depression productive expenditure on account of inventory and work in progress plunges, while cost of goods sold, which reflects such productive expenditure made in prior periods, continues to hold up. To the extent that productive expenditure on account of inventory and work in progress drops below cost of goods sold in the economic system, the result is negative net investment in inventory and work in progress, because what is now signified is that the sum of the additions being made to these accounts correspondingly falls short of the sum of the subtractions. The reduction in the value of the inventory and work-in-progress accounts in the economic system is the extent of the negative net investment of this type.[39]

The Marginal-Efficiency-of-Capital Doctrine's Reversal of the Actual Relationship Between Net Investment and the Rate of Profit

We are now in a position to make what is perhaps the most decisive objection of all to the declining-marginal-efficiency-of-capital doctrine and the Keynesian analysis. And that is that our discussion of the determinants of the rate of profit has shown that the rate of profit and net investment are *positively related*. We have seen that net investment and profits move together virtually dollar for dollar, because while profits are the difference between sales revenue and costs, net investment is the difference between productive expenditure (which is almost equivalent to sales revenue) and those same costs.[40]

Thus, the actual reason the rate of profit is so low or negative in a depression is the same as the reason net investment is so low or negative—namely, that productive expenditure has fallen, taking sales revenue with it, while costs, especially depreciation costs, fall only with a lag. By the same token, in the recovery from a depression *net investment and the rate of profit both improve together*. For every dollar by which productive expenditure rises relative to costs, creating net investment, sales revenues rise relative to those same costs, creating profits. Likewise, for every dollar by which costs fall relative to productive expenditure, also creating net investment, those same costs fall relative to sales revenues, creating profits. The mathematical implication of this virtual dollar-for-dollar equivalence between additional net investment and additional profits is that the rate of profit—the so-called marginal efficiency of capital—must actually *rise* with the rise in net investment, and not fall as the Keynesians maintain.

For example, if in the depths of a depression, aggregate profit in the economic system is 10, while total accumulated capital is 1,000, then the average rate of profit is a mere 1 percent. But if now net investment increases by, say, 50, then aggregate profit increases from 10 to 60. At the same time, of course, the total accumulated capital of the economic system rises to 1,050. The average capital outstanding over the period becomes 1,025—viz., the average of 1,000 and 1,050. However much it may come as a shock to the Keynesians, the unavoidable implication of these facts is that the average rate of profit rises from 1 percent to almost 6 percent! What happens mathematically is exactly the same sort of thing as happens to the season average of a baseball team that goes on a winning streak. In the case of the baseball team, its season average rises in the direction of 1,000. A thousand is its average over the course of its winning streak—its marginal average so to speak—and thus its season average rises accordingly. In the case of more net investment and equivalently more profit, the average rate of profit rises in the direction of a mathematical limit of 200 percent, for the additional net investment is accompanied by an equivalent addition to the amount of profit and by an addition only half as great to the average capital outstanding in the economic system.

As indicated, the rise in the rate of profit that must accompany more net investment in the recovery from a depression, has its counterpart in the fall in the rate of profit that accompanies the wiping out of net investment in the descent into a depression. In the latter case, the plunge in productive expenditure not only drives productive expenditure below costs, making net investment negative, but equivalently reduces sales revenues relative to the same costs. This drives profit in the economic system below net consumption. Profit comes to equal net consumption plus a negative net investment component.

In the light of the foregoing analysis, it is difficult to imagine a more erroneous conception of things than the Keynesian notion that the rate of profit is at a depression level because of too much net investment and that the further net investment that must accompany recovery from the depression will drive it still lower. The facts are that the rate of profit is low in a depression for the same reasons that net investment is low—to the point of being negative—and will rise with the rise in net investment. In other words, among the changes that would need to be made in the Keynesian analysis, if for some reason one had any wish to retain it, is a reversal of the slope of the so-called *mec* and *IS* curves in the context of recovery from a depression and the reestablishment of full employment. But since the Keynesian system is so thoroughly riddled with errors and contradictions, there is no point in attempting to modify it or retain it in any way. The Keynesian analysis is so wrong that it is beyond redemption. The one, fundamental change that is needed is its total abandonment.

The Contradiction Between the Marginal-Efficiency-of-Capital Doctrine and the Multiplier Doctrine

It is worth pointing out the existence of a major contradiction between the marginal-efficiency-of-capital doctrine and the multiplier doctrine. When they propound the marginal-efficiency-of-capital doctrine, the Keynesians claim that the effect of more net investment is a reduction in the rate of profit. Yet when they propound the multiplier doctrine, they claim that the effect of more net investment is a multiplied increase in aggregate demand. (In their absurdly narrow view of aggregate demand, of course, this means an increase in net national product, NNP, which is equal to the sum of net investment plus consumption, which in turn allegedly pay the national income.) The additional net investment, they tell us, brings about a diminishing series of additional consumption expenditures, which increases aggregate demand by a multiple of the initial increase in net investment.[41]

Now surely, if there is an increase in aggregate demand, aggregate profit must rise. Even on the highly conservative assumption that aggregate profit maintain-

ed merely a fixed percentage relationship to "aggregate demand," instead of bearing a higher percentage relationship, as a rising demand actually implies, the greater the increase in net investment, the greater would be the increase in the rate of profit.

If, for example, profits were assumed to constitute a steady 20 percent of the national income, which, historically, is not an unreasonable figure, a multiplier of two would mean an increment of profits 40 percent as large as the increment of net investment. A multiplier of three would mean an increment of profits 60 percent as large as the increment of net investment, and so on. Even with a multiplier of only two, the rate of profit on accumulated capital would certainly have to rise as net investment increased, for it is certainly below 40 percent to begin with and would move in the direction of 40 percent on the basis of additional net investment. (Indeed, allowing for the fact that the average capital outstanding grows by only half of the additional net investment, the rate of profit would rise toward 80 percent rather than 40 percent.)

The contradiction between the multiplier doctrine and the declining-marginal-efficiency-of-capital doctrine is actually much more acute than this example indicates. For I have shown that virtually *all* of the increase in national income that would accompany the rise in consumption spending that the multiplier is supposed to bring about, would be profit income.[42] Of course, I have also shown that the multiplier doctrine itself is totally fallacious. The fact that it totally contradicts the marginal-efficiency-of-capital doctrine, which, as shown, is also entirely fallacious, further adds to the indictment of the Keynesian analysis.

A Fall in Wage Rates as the Requirement for the Restoration of Net Investment and Profitability Along With Full Employment

Not only do net investment and the rate of profit improve together in the recovery from a depression, but precisely what is required for their improvement is *a fall in wage rates*. In the context of recovering from a depression, a fall in wage rates is necessary both for the restoration of productive expenditure and thus sales revenues, and for the write-down of the value of existing fixed assets and inventories, which operation reduces the costs deducted from productive expenditure and sales revenues. In both of these ways, a fall in wage rates increases net investment and profits. Thus, it not only brings about full employment, but restores net investment and profitability as well.

To elaborate, when wage rates fall to their new equilibrium level—a level corresponding to the reduced velocity of circulation of money and the reduced quantity of money that follows the removal of the artificial monetary stimulus of the preceding boom—the costs of new investments are correspondingly reduced. In response, as I have repeatedly pointed out, investment expenditures which had been postponed, awaiting the necessary fall in wage rates and costs to the lower level, now take place, with the result that productive expenditure and thus sales revenues in the economic system are increased. At the same time, assets acquired in the previous boom at an artificially high level of costs, are written down to be competitive with the lower-cost investments that can now be made, as the result of the fall in wage rates. And this, of course, reduces the costs deducted from productive expenditure and sales revenues. In these ways, the fall in wage rates restores both net investment and profitability.

By the same token, as I have also pointed out before, the failure of wage rates to fall operates not only to prolong, but also to deepen the depression. To the extent that it causes the postponement of investment expenditures and the consequent wiping out of profitability, it adds to the inability of business firms to repay their debts. This, in turn, causes more bank failures, a further reduction in the quantity of money and velocity of circulation, and thus necessitates greater wage cuts to achieve full employment and recovery than would have been the case if the wage cuts had come quickly.[43]

Wage Rates, Total Wage Payments, and the Rate of Profit

The preceding discussion has shown that when unemployment exists a fall in wage rates operates to increase total productive expenditure. As part of this process, it is virtually certain that total wage payments increase, with the result that the fall in wage rates is actually accompanied by a more than proportionate increase in the quantity of labor demanded, and thus by a more than proportionate increase in the volume of employment. However, it should be realized that the improvement in business profitability will tend to be the greater the *smaller* is the portion of the additional productive expenditure that takes the form of wage payments. Indeed, business profitability would increase the most if the fall in wage rates were accompanied by an actual fall in total wage payments and a correspondingly greater increase in the demand for capital goods.

The reason for these conclusions is that wage payments tend to show up relatively quickly as costs deducted from sales revenues. In contrast, outlays for machinery and plant show up much more slowly as costs deducted from sales revenues. Thus, if a billion dollars, say, of wage payments were replaced with a billion dollars of spending for plant and equipment, total business profits might very well increase by almost the full billion dollars. This is because total business sales revenues would be unchanged: the demand for capital goods would rise by a billion dollars, while the wage earners' demand for consumers' goods would fall by a billion dollars. At the same time, depreciation cost, equal to a relatively small percentage of the billion dollars spent for the plant and equipment, would take the place of the much larger cost figure reflecting the payment of a billion dollars in wages. Thus, total profits in the economic system would rise—by virtue of aggregate sales revenues remaining whatever they were while aggregate costs deducted from sales revenues fell. Obviously the increase in net investment would also be correspondingly greater under these conditions.[44]

This discussion should serve further to refute the popular Keynesian and labor-union doctrine that a fall in wage rates operates to intensify a depression by virtue of reducing total wage payments and thus consumer spending. The truth is that even if the effect of a fall in wage rates really were a reduction in total wage payments and consumer spending, the rate of profit would rise all the more, for all that this effect would really mean would be a shift of sales revenues from the sellers of consumers' goods to the sellers of capital goods, and, at the same time, a reduction in aggregate costs.

Critique of the "Paradox-of-Thrift" Doctrine

Another popular Keynesian doctrine that calls for special attention is the alleged "paradox of thrift." According to this doctrine, the more people attempt to save, the poorer they become. Instead of being a principal foundation of economic progress and prosperity, saving is made to appear as the cause of unemployment and poverty. Samuelson, a leading supporter of this doctrine, states it as follows:

> In a multiplier model with unchanged investment, an upward shift in the savings function, reflecting an increase in thriftiness, will actually reduce income and output. How much? Output is reduced in a multiplied way until income falls low enough to bring people's new desired saving again into equality with investment. Thus an attempt to save more may lead, instead, to a lower income and no more saving or investment.

> Just when we have learned Poor Richard's wisdom, along comes a new generation of financial wizards who claim that in depressed times the old virtues may be modern sins.[45]

Now the paradox-of-thrift doctrine rests entirely on the central notion of the Keynesian analysis that there is room in the economic system for only a strictly limited amount of profitable investment. It is only on this basis that the attempt to save a larger proportion of income implies the necessity of a smaller amount of income. Thus, for example, if there were room in the economic system for only one unit of saving that could be profitably invested, and people sought to save only 1 percent of their income, their income could be 100 and still be consistent with the allegedly limited profitable opportunities for investment. If, however, they seek to save 20 percent of their income, then their income can be no more than a mere 5 and still be consistent with the allegedly limited profitable opportunities for investment.

It should be apparent that the paradox-of-thrift doctrine is utterly absurd. In the context to which it is meant to apply most strongly—namely, that of depression and mass unemployment—saving and investment, far from being at any kind of maximum limit, are extremely low or even negative, as we saw just a few pages ago. And, as we saw even more recently, it is precisely when saving and investment are restored, as the result of a fall in wage rates, unit costs of production, and prices, that the rate of profit is restored, along with full employment.

At all other times, as I have shown, there is room for far more profitable investment in the economic system than the power of saving can ever have the capacity to meet. One need only recall the enormous extent of the need for additional capital in its various forms, the extent of the need for savings to finance housing, and the fact that the downtown real estate of a single city all by itself provides an investment outlet for a virtually infinite amount of savings. At the same time, one should recall that the effect of a higher degree of capital intensiveness in the economic system is a more rapid rate of economic progress, including, as a by-product, a more rapid rate of increase in the quantity of commodity money and thus the corresponding addition of a positive monetary/net-investment component to the rate of return.[46] On the basis of these facts, it follows that in the absence of financial contraction caused by preceding inflation and credit expansion, the rate of return on capital can be assumed to be not only positive but sufficiently positive to make investment worthwhile for more savings and capital than people are capable of accumulating. And finally, as I have shown, to whatever extent people do or might for any reason decide to accumulate savings in the form of cash, that very fact operates further to raise the rate of return on capital.[47]

The Keynesians' preoccupation with the utterly fictitious problem of saving as a cause of poverty bears major responsibility for the very real problem of growing poverty as the result of a lack of saving. Based on their hostile economic analysis of saving, the Keynesians have brought about the enactment of correspondingly hostile government economic policies toward saving. The result has been economic stagnation and decline, whose nature and significance are captured in the words: *the rust belt*. Over a span of approximately two generations, the intellectual rot of Keynesianism has helped to bring about the physical rot of the industrial heartland of the United States.[48]

Critique of the Saving Function

The errors of the Keynesian analysis in connection with saving include its very promulgation of the "saving function." There is no such thing as saving being a mathematical function of income. Saving out of income continues to exist only because incomes continue to grow, as the result of an increase in the quantity of money. As I have shown, if the quantity of money stopped growing, saving out income would come to an end, once accumulated savings and capital reached a sufficient height relative to income.[49] Nor, as I have shown, is there any actual tendency for saving to constitute a rising share of income as income rises. The appearance of such a tendency is entirely the result of the fact that high incomes largely overlap with incomes that are saved heavily for different reasons, notably high incomes constituted by high rates of profit and high incomes that are considered transitory by their recipients.[50]

In connection with saving as a continuing phenomenon, it should be recalled once more that the same cause that brings this about, namely, the continuing increase in the quantity of money and volume of spending in the economic system, adds correspondingly to the average rate of profit and interest. Indeed, most of the saving that goes on in the economic system takes place precisely out of this elevated rate of return on capital.[51] This fact, of course, adds still a further perspective on the errors of Keynesianism with respect to saving and its relationship to the rate of return.

Critique of the "Liquidity-Preference" Doctrine

The final aspect of the Keynesian analysis that must be considered is the "liquidity-preference" doctrine. Liquidity preference or, as Hazlitt aptly describes it, "cash preference," is what is supposedly responsible for the existence of a minimum, irreducible rate of return below which lenders and investors will not lend or invest.[52] They will allegedly not lend or invest below a 2 percent rate of return because they would prefer to hold cash instead.

Now, on the basis of all that I have established concerning the rate of return, it is virtually certain that in the absence of inflation and credit expansion and the subsequent financial contraction that results, the rate of return would actually be substantially in excess of 2 percent. But even if it were not, and even if that fact resulted in a tendency toward holding savings in the form of cash, the very existence of that tendency would itself operate to raise the rate of return, as I showed in the last chapter.[53]

In addition to this, it is also necessary to question the assumption that a 2 percent rate of return is the minimum at which people are willing to lend or invest. For if for some reason it did become necessary for the economic system to operate with a rate of return below 2 percent, there would be nothing to prevent it from doing so.[54]

The Keynesians advance two arguments that attempt to show why 2 percent, or a rate not far from 2 percent, constitutes the practical lower limit to the rate of return lenders and investors will accept. In the words of Keynes himself:

> We have assumed so far an institutional factor which prevents the rate of interest from being negative, in the shape of money which has negligible carrying costs. In fact, however, institutional and psychological factors are present which set a limit much above zero to the practicable decline in the rate of interest. In particular the costs of bringing borrowers and lenders together and uncertainty as to the future of the rate of interest . . . set a lower limit, which in the present circumstances may be as high as 2 or 2½ per cent. on long term.[55]

The uncertainty as to the future of the rate of interest that Keynes refers to is the fear that it may rise from its present level and thus create a capital loss for any investor who finds it necessary to sell his investment—for example, a long-term bondholder who buys a bond when interest rates are 2 percent, and must sell it when interest rates rise to 4 percent, and who thus suffers a capital loss.[56]

Now neither of these arguments in fact supports the conclusion that people are unwilling to lend or invest below some arbitrary rate of return. At most, they support the conclusion that at lower rates of return, the demand for money for holding will be somewhat higher than at higher rates of return, and thus that the velocity of circulation of money will be somewhat lower and wage rates and prices will have to be somewhat lower in order to have full employment. The fact that there are costs of bringing lenders and borrowers together, and of otherwise investing, is always true. The existence of such costs merely requires that in order for lending and investing to be worthwhile, the size of the loan or investment, and the period of time for which it is made, be of some minimum.

For example, as we saw in Chapter 12, if the cost of making a given type of loan or investment were some minimum amount, such as $100, then at a 2 percent annual interest rate it would not pay to lend any sum smaller than $250,000 for a period as short as one week, because that would be the sum required to yield the minimum of $100 in just one week at that annual rate of interest.[57] But it would certainly pay to lend smaller sums for longer periods of time, such as $100,000, or

even $50,000, for a year. And, in fact, when the pooling of small sums is allowed for, as is accomplished every day by such institutions as savings banks, the sums which it pays to lend and invest even at a rate of return as low as 2 percent, turn out to be far less than $50,000 and for periods far shorter than a year. Indeed, even at a 1 percent annual rate of return and need for a $100 minimum amount of interest, it would still pay to deposit a sum as small as $10,000 for a period as short as a year.

The argument about uncertainty concerning the future of the rate of interest does not fare any better. If the rate of return on capital is extremely low and people hesitate to lend or invest for fear that it will rise, then either they are right in expecting the rate of return to rise, or they are wrong. If they are right, then the rate of return rises, and the alleged problem of too low a rate of return simply disappears. If they are wrong, and the rate of return does not rise, then there is no actual reason to fear the rise and they can lend and invest at the low rate of return. Indeed, if we consider the phenomenon of a rise in the rate of return on capital as such, rather than merely a rise in the rate of interest on loans, and keep in mind that what brings it about in the circumstances of recovery from a depression—namely, a recovery of productive expenditure and sales revenues—then it becomes clear that people have good reason to go ahead and invest immediately if they expect the rate of return to rise. This is because if they invest as stockholders or other categories of equity owners, they will actually *gain* from the rise in the rate of return. And if they do not expect the rate of return to rise, then they have no good reason to abstain from investing out of any fear of securities prices falling.

The liquidity-preference doctrine represents a profoundly wrong explanation of the rate of interest. According to Keynes, the rate of interest is "the reward for parting with liquidity, is a measure of the unwillingness of whose who possess money to part with their liquid control over it. . . . It is the 'price' which equilibrates the desire to hold wealth in the form of cash with the available quantity of cash . . . ."[58] And, says Keynes, "If this explanation is correct, the quantity of money is the other factor, which, in conjunction with liquidity preference, determines the actual rate of interest in given circumstances."[59]

Thus, Keynes's doctrine here is that the rate of interest is determined by the combination of "liquidity preference" and the quantity of money. And on this basis, he comes to the conclusion that if it is not already at its minimum acceptable level, the rate of interest can be reduced by the mere increase in the quantity of money, if not to zero, then at least to its minimum acceptable level.[60] And he further concludes that by means of reducing the rate of interest in such conditions, namely, where it is not yet at its minimum acceptable level, the increase in the quantity of money will serve to make possible an expansion in employment and production, a result of which will be a reduction in the "marginal efficiency of capital"—i.e., the rate of profit.[61]

Now the fact is that "liquidity preference" is not at all a determinant of the rate of interest, much less of the rate of profit. This is dramatically illustrated by conditions under rapid inflation, where the desire to hold money virtually disappears and the rate of interest, instead of approaching zero, as the liquidity-preference doctrine implies, rises to extremely high levels. By the same token, the less rapidly the supply of money increases and the correspondingly greater is the desire to hold money, the lower is the rate of interest, not the higher—again, in contradiction of what the liquidity-preference doctrine implies.

As we have seen, the rate of interest is governed by the rate of profit, not vice versa; and the more rapidly the quantity of money is increased, the higher tends to be the rate of profit and thus the higher tends to be the rate of interest.[62] The rise in prices that results from an increasing quantity of money also contributes to the rise in interest rates, in that it brings about increases in the demand for loanable funds to buy goods such as houses, land, and raw materials in the face of prospective higher prices for them. In the absence of higher interest rates, the purchase of such goods would become progressively more profitable, the more rapidly the quantity of money increased and prices rose. Interest rates must rise in the face of increases in the quantity of money, in order to limit the increase in demand for loanable funds that would otherwise result both from a higher rate of profit and, as far as they are present, rising commodity prices. As I have shown, because the increase in the quantity of money and consequent rise in spending increases the rate of profit and makes prices rise, it is impossible lastingly to reduce, let alone eliminate, the rate of interest by means of increasing the quantity of money. If carried out consistently, such an attempt would entail the continual acceleration of the increase in the quantity of money and thus the ultimate destruction of the monetary system. It would not eliminate or even lastingly hold down the rate of interest.[63]

It should not be necessary to repeat here the critique I have made of the closely associated error of thinking of the rate of interest as the price of money, which Keynes does when he describes the rate of interest as "the 'price' which equilibrates the desire to hold wealth in the form of cash with the available quantity of cash . . . ."[64] Interest is not the price of money, but the difference between the money borrowed and the money repaid, which dif-

ference tends to be the greater the more rapidly the quantity of money increases between the time of borrowing and the time of repayment.

The critique of the liquidity-preference doctrine can be combined with a further critique of Keynes's doctrines concerning consumption, saving, employment, and the rate of profit. We have seen that the problem of unemployment, according to Keynes, rests on the fact that people insist on saving. If they did not save, if they only consumed, the "multiplier" would allegedly be infinite, and full employment would exist.

It is instructive to examine Keynes's doctrines precisely in conditions in which there would be no saving whatever—no net saving out of income and no gross saving out of sales revenues. Such conditions would be similar to those which characterized Adam Smith's "early and rude state of society" and Marx's "C–M–C" sequence, but go beyond them in that there would not even be saving in the form of cash holdings, because everyone would race to consume immediately.[65]

In such conditions, not only would there be no saving, but also there would be no liquidity preference. In such conditions, according to Keynes, because there is no saving, employment must be full; and because there is no liquidity preference, the rate of interest and profit must be zero. Yet in fact, in such conditions, employment would be virtually zero and the rate of profit and interest would be infinite. This is because there would be no demand for labor in the production of products for sale, and while sales revenues would exist, there would be no productive expenditure and thus no costs to deduct from sales revenues, and there would be no capital. Thus, profits would equal the whole of sales revenues and, when divided by zero of capital invested, would yield an infinite rate of return.[66]

4. The Economic Consequences of Keynesianism

As I have shown, the essential economic policy advocated by Keynesianism is government budget deficits, which are held to be necessary to prevent or combat mass unemployment. This is the essence of "fiscal policy." Thus, it should be obvious that matters are misrepresented when fiscal policy is presented as some kind of neutral tool which now must be used to expand the economy, and now to slow it down. The underlying economic problem according to the Keynesians is mass unemployment, and that requires a continuously expansionary policy, which is believed to be budget deficits. At most, the Keynesians may be prepared to call for a reduction in the size of the deficit if the expansion in spending allegedly induced by it is greater than necessary to achieve full employment and is thus held to contribute to rising prices. In virtually no circumstances does the logic of their position permit them to call for budget surpluses.

The most effective method of achieving a budget deficit according to the Keynesians is by increasing government spending rather than by reducing taxes. This is because, as we have seen, the so-called government-spending multiplier is held to be one larger than the multiplier allegedly associated with a reduction in taxes and is therefore believed to be correspondingly more "stimulative."[67]

The increase in government spending is held to be truly wonderful. It is alleged to be not only costless but also the source of a substantial increase in real income over and above itself. It is held to be the means of absorbing the allegedly destructive additional savings that accompany full employment and thus of permitting people to benefit from all of the additional output that full employment brings over and above their additional saving. The savings the government takes allegedly costs people nothing because those savings supposedly could not even be formed in the absence of the government's willingness to take them. And, say the Keynesians, people are then able to keep for themselves all that their additional employment produces over and above those additional savings. Thus, not only is there a free lunch for the government and its clients, but also, the Keynesians believe, the government's willingness to enjoy its free lunch is the necessary basis for the producers being able to produce and enjoy most of their additional product. Thus Keynesianism is consumptionism *par excellence*. For no doctrine is more adept in claiming that parasitism is a source of actual enrichment to its victims.

As I have pointed out repeatedly, Keynesianism is the philosophy which holds that "pyramid-building, earthquakes, and even wars may serve to increase wealth."[68] With this philosophy as a starting point, there is almost no program a government could adopt that would not represent a significant improvement in comparison, since it could almost certainly be designed so that at least some people would directly benefit from it. Public housing, public transportation, public education, socialized medicine, and so forth all compare favorably with pyramid building, earthquakes, and wars in terms of their ability to provide benefits to at least some people for some period of time.

The Growth in Government

An inevitable effect of the influence of such ideas is the increase in the size and scope of government activity. As James Mill observed in criticizing very similar ideas in the early nineteenth century:

Were the exhortations to consumption . . . addressed only to individuals, we might listen to them with a great deal of indifference; as we might trust with abundant confidence that the disposition in mankind to save and to better their condition would easily prevail over any speculative opinion, and be even little affected by its practical influence. When the same advice, however, is offered to government, the case is widely and awfully changed. Here the disposition is not to save but to expend. The tendency in national affairs to improve, by the disposition in individuals to save and to better their condition, here finds its chief counteraction. Here all the most obvious motives, the motives calculated to operate upon the greater part of mankind, urge to expence; and human wisdom has not yet devised adequate checks to confine within the just bounds this universal propensity. Let us consider then what are likely to be the consequences should this strong disposition become impelled, and precipitated by a prevailing sentiment among mankind. One of the most powerful restraints upon the prodigal inclinations of governments, is the condemnation with which expence, at least beyond the received ideas of propriety, is sure to be viewed by the people. But should this restraint be taken off, should the disposition of government to spend become heated by an opinion that it is right to spend, and should this be still farther inflamed by the assurance that it will by the people also be deemed right in their government to expend, no bounds would then be set to the consumption of the annual produce. Such a delusion could not certainly last long: but even its partial operation, and that but for a short time, might be productive of the most baneful consequences.[69]

Just as James Mill anticipated, the success of the kind of ideas advocated by Keynes in gaining popular influence has indeed been followed by the most baneful consequences. Among them is an approximately fourfold increase in the relative size of government spending in the United States. Between 1929 and the present day, government spending has increased from approximately 11 percent of "national income" to approximately 40 percent. This has meant a corresponding decline in the freedom of the individual to spend his own income as he chooses and the imposition of a reign of fear of the tax authorities, as the measures taken by the government to obtain the growing percentage of income have become more and more severe. It has also meant a vast increase in the government's interference in the daily lives of the people in countless other ways as well, which are financed with the government's additional funds. And, of course, there have been other highly destructive consequences stemming from individuals' loss of control over their incomes and the accompanying growth in government regulation, most notably, the undermining of capital accumulation and economic progress.

Budget Deficits, Inflation, and Deflation

Although Keynesianism is, and must be, radically

opposed to the quantity theory of money, for the reasons explained at the beginning of this chapter, it nevertheless recognizes the need to couple its policy of budget deficits with an expansion in the quantity of money. This is because even though Keynesianism avows that what increases spending is the mere existence of budget deficits, the fact is that in the absence of substantial increases in the quantity of money, a policy of sustained large-scale budget deficits would inevitably result in the government's bankruptcy.

Bankruptcy would be the result because the government's accumulated debt would continue to grow and the burden of servicing the debt would come to require more and more revenue. Increases in taxes would at most only delay the government's bankruptcy. For they would reduce the country's ability to produce and to compete internationally (as does, of course, the government's absorption of savings when it borrows to finance its deficits). The government's tax revenues would thus be unable to keep pace with its growing financial obligations caused by the deficits. The rate of interest the government had to pay on its debt would rise. Eventually the day would come when the government had to repay a portion of its debt and found itself unable to borrow the means of doing so. At that point, it would be bankrupt in the literal sense of the term.

The fact that in the absence of the ability to create money, a policy of budget deficits leads to a country's economic and financial decline and the government's bankruptcy, means that in such circumstances a policy of deficits is actually *deflationary!* This is the case under any kind of meaningful gold standard. Under a gold standard, a policy of deficits has the effect of reducing the supply of gold that circulates within a country's borders. This is because in undermining capital accumulation in the country, the effect of the deficits is to reduce the country's share of world commerce and thus the share of the world's gold that it possesses.[70] Within the country, moreover, the threat of the government's bankruptcy, and its attendant uncertainties, must lead to a greater demand for the holding of gold as opposed to productive expenditure and investment. Furthermore, insofar as the monetary system of the country may use government debt as an asset standing behind the issuance of fiduciary media, the quantity of money in the country is further threatened. For any threat to the solvency of the government in such circumstances is a threat to the solvency of the banks that hold its securities as an asset. Thus, under a meaningful gold standard, a policy of deficits could not achieve the Keynesian objective of expanding spending, but would sooner or later accomplish the exact opposite.[71]

Although they never acknowledge the existence of conditions in which deficits would be deflationary, the Keynesians nevertheless seem to know very well that such conditions would exist under any real gold standard. And thus, to a man, they are totally opposed to the gold standard, which they do everything possible to ridicule. They oppose the gold standard because they know that if the policy of deficits is in fact to succeed in increasing total spending, the deficits must largely be financed by an increase in the quantity of money and that the government must have the power to bring about this increase. A gold standard, on the other hand, deprives the government of this power. It makes the increase in the quantity of money depend on the increase in the supply of gold.

The Keynesians' advocacy of a policy of budget deficits is an implicit advocacy of inflation. In addition, the Keynesians explicitly advocate inflation, in the form of credit expansion, insofar as they believe that it can succeed in reducing the rate of interest—that is, insofar as the rate of interest is not yet at its allegedly irreducible level of approximately 2 percent.

As Chapter 12 has shown, and as the next chapter will show more fully, the creation of money by the government, or with the encouragement of the government, is the essence of the inflation problem—inflation *is* the government's creation, or sponsorship of the creation, of money at a rate more rapid than the increase in the supply of the precious metals. And Keynesianism bears primary responsibility for it in the countries of the Western world today and since the 1930s.

Keynesianism and Economic Destruction

Thus, in appraising the consequences of the Keynesian policies, it is necessary to charge them with all the destructive consequences of inflation. This includes rising prices and the impoverishment of everyone whose income or assets are contractually fixed in terms of a definite sum of money. It includes the arbitrary redistribution of wealth and income from creditors to debtors and from those who receive the new money relatively late to those who receive it relatively early. It includes—as does a policy of deficits without resort to inflation—the impairment of capital formation and thus of the rise in the productivity of labor and real wages. Indeed, if carried out on a large enough scale, capital decumulation and an actual fall in the productivity of labor and real wages are the result.[72]

I have said that Keynesianism and its hostility to saving are responsible for the vast economic devastation conveyed in the words "the rust belt." This devastation has occurred because under the influence of Keynesianism literally several trillion dollars of savings have been absorbed in government budget deficits—an amount of savings equal to the growth in the publicly held national debt in the years since the time of Keynes.[73] Over this period, confiscatory taxation applied to large personal incomes and to corporate profits, capital gains, and inheritances have prevented trillions more of savings from being made in the first place or, in the case of inheritance taxes, being kept. Such taxation has been strongly supported by Keynesianism, precisely because the taxes fall on saving. As we shall see, inflation too, like inheritance taxes, destroys savings already accumulated, and does so on a vast scale.

Thus factories, machinery, stocks of materials and supplies, power plants, railroads, bridges, tunnels, and homes that these savings and potential savings would have made possible have not come into existence because the necessary savings have been diverted into financing the government's budget deficits, have been prevented from occurring in the first place, or have been prevented from being maintained. The result has been a sharp decline in the rate of economic progress in the United States, if not outright economic stagnation, and increasing difficulty in replacing existing capital assets when they wear out.

In connection with this last, under conditions even of modest increase in the overall supply of capital goods—let alone stagnation or outright capital decumulation—the very fact of the economic development of new areas, such as the U.S. Far West, implies the economic decline of older areas. This is the case because in such conditions additional capital for the one, or at least additional capital for the one over and above any modest increase in the total of capital, can be obtained only by failing to provide replacement capital for the other.

Ironically, as we shall see, a further consequence of the inflation inspired by Keynesianism is a wiping out of the real rate of return on capital and the creation of conditions in which people actually do find it necessary to hoard their savings—not, to be sure, in the form of depreciating paper money, but in the form of physical assets whose price can rise, above all, gold and silver.[74] Inflation ultimately destroys the private granting of credit calling for repayment in paper money, and makes impossible the writing of contracts of any kind which are stated in terms of a fixed sum of money. For a variety of reasons it has an inherent tendency to go on accelerating until the point is reached at which paper money ceases to be acceptable in commerce. At that point, if the government has prevented the development of a new money that the market would create in the form of gold and silver, inflation actually succeeds in the destruction of money altogether, and with it, of an indispensable foundation of a division-of-labor society. Along the way, inflation creates the potential for a major depression, which is actualized if the inflation is stopped, sharply slowed, or, indeed, even fails to accelerate sufficiently.[75]

Finally, it must be kept in mind that inflation is responsible for the imposition of wage and price controls, which are enacted in misguided efforts to stop it. As I showed in Chapters 7 and 8, wage and price controls create economic chaos and culminate in a totalitarian socialist dictatorship and economic collapse.

Thus, Keynesianism and the policies it gives rise to have played a leading and essential role in causing the economic decline of the United States that has become visible over the last generation and which is likely to continue. Keynesianism is a consistent assault on the foundations of prosperity: it is antisaving, antigold, antibalanced budgets, antilimited government. Ironically, what it is not anti is unemployment. It is *not* the solution for unemployment.

Why Keynesianism Is Not a Full-Employment Policy

The Keynesian policies of deficits and inflation are not only not necessary for the achievement of full employment, but *do not achieve it*. Indeed, deficits by themselves, apart from the creation of money, actually cause more unemployment, both because of their deflationary effects, explained above, and because in depriving business of capital funds, they reduce the ability of business to make productive expenditures and thus to pay wages. And, as I explained in Chapter 13, even when the deficits are combined with inflation of the money supply, much, most, or even all of the extra spending that takes place can be nullified by wage increases that are just as rapid or even more rapid, with the result that little or no additional employment is actually achieved.[76] Furthermore, as I also explained in Chapter 13, much of any additional employment that might be achieved is likely to be of little or no economic value to those whose production must pay for it, because of the inherent nature of the output of those reemployed in connection with government make-work projects.[77] Finally, the inflation and credit expansion Keynesianism leads to, and the artificial elevation of the velocity of circulation and stimulus to indebtedness that result, help to create a constant potential for renewed depression and mass unemployment.

As I have shown, what brought about full employment in World War II was not the Keynesian policies of deficits and inflation by themselves but their coupling with wage and price controls. It was this which finally established a relationship between wage rates and prices, on the one side, and the quantity of money and volume of spending, on the other, that enabled the volume of spending for goods and labor to buy all that was offered.[78] Of course, this same result could have been achieved by a free market in labor, without any of the loss of output (not to mention human life) that took place on the battlefields of the war and without any of the shortages and economic chaos caused by wage and price controls. Thus, even when applied in combination with wage and price controls, Keynesianism should not be thought of as a full-employment policy, but as the policy that succeeds in destroying the economic value of full employment.

Keynesianism Versus the Rate of Profit: "The Euthanasia of the Rentier" and "The Socialization of Investment"

Keynesianism's concern with the alleged lowness of the rate of profit at the point of full employment turns out to be nothing but a shedding of crocodile tears. As I have said, the effect of its policies is to wipe out the real rate of return on capital and actually to cause the very hoarding of savings it claims to fear. To discover how Keynesianism accomplishes this, it is not necessary to wait until the discussion of inflation in the next chapter. The fact that the Keynesian policies reduce the real rate of return on capital is implied precisely in its attempt to neutralize current savings, either by absorbing them in budget deficits that will never be repaid or by seizing them outright through taxation. The savings that are taken away, by these or any other methods, for the most part *come out of the rate of return*. They are the result of saving specifically out of profit and interest incomes. Thus, taking them away is tantamount to taking away part of the rate of return itself. For taking away savings means, at the same time, taking away the profits and interest that are the source of the savings.

The Keynesian policies are dishonest. Even if the Keynesian analysis were correct, which it certainly is not, the question would have to be asked of why it does not consider trying to raise the effective rate of return by reducing taxes on profits and interest? Only after all taxes on profits and interest had been eliminated, would it be legitimate to talk of a problem of too low a rate of return in the economic system.

The fact is, that when all is said and done, it turns out that Keynesianism *is really not concerned with any alleged insufficiency of the rate of return*. That is merely a convoluted pretext for more government intervention. Its actual belief, expressed by Keynes in the final chapter of *The General Theory*, is that the rate of return is *too high!* If this is difficult to believe in view of the diminishing-marginal-efficiency-of-capital and unemployment-equilibrium doctrines, which are the core of his book and of the whole Keynesian analysis, consider the following passages, which are in Keynes's own words. They begin with an implicit reference to the alleged paradox-of-thrift doctrine and with an expression of satisfaction that on the basis of that doctrine his analysis allegedly deprives great inequality of wealth of one of its "chief social justifications."

Thus our argument leads towards the conclusion that in contemporary conditions the growth of wealth, so far from being dependent on the abstinence of the rich, as is commonly supposed, is more likely to be impeded by it. One of the chief social justifications of great inequality of wealth is, therefore, removed. I am not saying that there are no other reasons, unaffected by our theory, capable of justifying some measure of inequality in some circumstances. But it does dispose of the most important of the reasons why hitherto we have thought it prudent to move carefully. . . .

For my own part, I believe that there is social and psychological justification for significant inequalities of incomes and wealth, but not for such large disparities as exist to-day. . . . Much lower stakes will serve the purpose equally well, as soon as the players are accustomed to them.[79]

On the next three pages Keynes goes on with his newly revealed theme that profits are actually too high under capitalism. He even adopts a style of language which sounds hardly distinguishable from Marxism:

I feel sure that the demand for capital is strictly limited in the sense that it would not be difficult to increase the stock of capital up to a point where its marginal efficiency had fallen to a very low figure. . . .

Now, though this state of affairs would be quite compatible with some measure of individualism, yet it would mean *the euthanasia of the rentier, and, consequently, the euthanasia of the cumulative oppressive power of the capitalist to exploit the scarcity-value of capital.* . . .

I see, therefore, the rentier aspect of capitalism as a transitional phase which will disappear when it has done its work. And with the disappearance of its rentier aspect much else in it besides will suffer a sea-change. It will be, moreover, a great advantage of the order of events which I am advocating, that the euthanasia of the rentier, of the functionless investor, will be nothing sudden, merely a gradual but prolonged continuance of what we have seen recently in Great Britain, and will need no revolution.

Thus we might aim in practice (there being nothing in this which is unattainable) at an increase in the volume of capital until it ceases to be scarce, so that the functionless investor will no longer receive a bonus; and at a scheme of direct taxation which allows the intelligence and determination and executive skill of the financier, the entrepreneur *et hoc genus omne* [translation: and all of this genus] (who are certainly so fond of their craft that their labour could be obtained much cheaper than it present), to be harnessed to the service of the community on reasonable terms of reward.[80]

In other words, Keynes sees the effect of his policies as that of accomplishing the just demands of Marxism—the expropriation of the "expropriators" and the redistribution of their allegedly excessive and ill-gotten wealth to the state and the population at large—but without the necessity of a violent revolution.

Not surprisingly he advocates *the socialization of investment:* "Furthermore, it seems unlikely that the influence of banking policy on the rate of interest will be sufficient by itself to determine an optimum rate of investment. I conceive, therefore, that a somewhat comprehensive socialisation of investment will prove the only means of securing an approximation to full employment."[81]

The meaning of this last passage is that Keynes thinks it unlikely that an increase in the quantity of money (which is what he means by "banking policy") will be sufficient by itself to drive the rate of return below 2 percent, and that investment by the government, which will be willing to invest at a rate of return below 2 percent, will be necessary. Keynes claims to believe that nothing momentous is involved in the socialization of investment, for he immediately adds the words: "But beyond this no obvious case is made out for a system of State Socialism which would embrace most of the economic life of the community."[82] These words in turn are quickly followed by the admission: "Moreover, the necessary measures of socialisation can be introduced gradually and without a break in the general traditions of society."[83] It should be obvious, of course, that since the total of all the capital that is accumulated is nothing but the summation of the investments of the preceding years, full socialism requires nothing more than the socialization of new investment plus the lapse of time. Nevertheless, incredibly, Keynes is touted as a man who saved capitalism.

Keynes's views in the above passages are so confused that it may well be the case that he believed 2 percent was simultaneously an excessively high rate of return, providing unnecessarily high stakes to the "players," and too low a rate of return. Or, when he complained of the rate of return being too high, he may simply have forgotten his arguments about the rate of return being too low, or perhaps he never took them very seriously in the first place. The following statement, taken from the middle of his book, appears to support this latter view:

> There is the possibility, for the reasons discussed above, that, after the rate of interest has fallen to a certain level, liquidity preference may become virtually absolute in the sense that almost everyone prefers cash to holding a debt which yields so low a rate of interest. In this event the monetary authority would have lost effective control over the rate of interest. But whilst this limiting case *might become practically important in the future, I know of no example of it hitherto.*[84]

The inescapable implication of these words is that Keynes knows no actual example of the existence of an *unemployment equilibrium* and that his entire doctrine is purely in the realm of the hypothetical. For if the rate of interest is not actually at its alleged minimum acceptable level, Keynes has no grounds, even on his own terms, of asserting the existence of an unemployment equilibrium.

Thus, it appears that Keynes's actual objections to capitalism may well have been based merely on the standard resentments against inequality and the alleged injustice of the existence of profit and interest, and that his doctrine was merely an added pretext for government intervention. The government must intervene because the rate of profit is too high, and, if that objection does not gain sufficient support, then because the rate of profit is too low, which is the argument of the body of Keynes's analysis. In any case, the government must intervene and seize more power. Any argument that serves will do. And thus Keynesianism ends exactly where it began: a piece of flotsam and jetsam from the wreckage of critical thought that is carried along by the tide of irrationalism and anticapitalism.

Notes

1. See above, pp. 673–715 passim.
2. See above, pp. 837–838.
3. See above, pp. 725–736, 744–774, and 778–787. See also above, pp. 838–859.
4. See above, pp. 519–526.
5. See above, pp. 520–522.
6. See below, p. 889 and pp. 891–892.
7. The full reference to Keynes's book is John Maynard Keynes, *The General Theory of Employment, Interest, and Money* (New York: Harcourt, Brace, 1936).
8. For evidence of Keynes's belief in pyramid building, earthquakes, and wars as sources of prosperity, see the *General Theory*, pp. 129 and 131. Also, see above, p. 544.
9. See above, p. 590.
10. Quoted in Keynes, *General Theory*, pp. 366–367.
11. See above, pp. 664–665, the quotation from John Stuart Mill, which presents the substance of the alleged overthrow of the wages-fund doctrine.
12. See above, p. 647 and pp. 650–653.
13. For a critique of the confusions concerning price competition and of the oligopoly and pure-and-perfect-competition doctrines, see above, pp. 425–437. It follows from that critique, indeed, from the whole of Chapter 10 and from the principles of price determination set forth throughout this book, that in a free market prices fall to whatever extent changes in the conditions of demand and supply and/or cost of production necessitate, and that it is only government intervention, that prevents the necessary price reductions.
14. Joseph P. McKenna, *Aggregate Economic Analysis,* 5th ed. (Hinsdale, Ill.: The Dryden Press, 1977), pp. 220–221, 223.
15. Concerning the deflationary potential of a fractional-reserve monetary system see above, pp. 513–514.

16. Paul Samuelson and William Nordhaus, *Economics,* 14th ed. (New York: McGraw Hill Book Company, 1992, pp. 464–467. Italics supplied.

17. Cf. above, Fig. 13-1, on p. 545. Also cf. McKenna, p. 281, for a standard Keynesian textbook presentation of the diagram.

18. The fallaciousness of the union argument is recognized by Gardner Ackley in his *Macroeconomic Theory* (New York: The Macmillan Company, 1961), pp. 388–389.

19. Later in this chapter, I show that to the extent that in consequence of a fall in wage rates the demand for capital goods is increased at the expense of the demand for labor, the rate of profit would be correspondingly increased, and would be increased even if an actual decrease in the demand for labor and consumers' goods resulted. See below, p. 884.

20. Cf. McKenna, p. 210. Also cf. Ackley, p. 369.

21. Cf. McKenna, p. 210.

22. See McKenna, pp. 216–220.

23. Cf. ibid., p. 219.

24. See above, Fig. 13-1, on p. 545.

25. Cf. McKenna, pp. 216–217.

26. Keynes, *General Theory,* pp. 261–262. Italics in the last sentence are supplied.

27. Another passage from Keynes that provides conclusive support for my exposition of his views is this one, which appears earlier in *The General Theory:* ". . . the position of equilibrium, under conditions of *laissez-faire,* will be one in which employment is low enough and the standard of living sufficiently miserable to bring savings to zero. . . . Assuming correct foresight, the equilibrium stock of capital . . . will, of course, be a smaller stock than would correspond to full employment of the available labour; for it will be the equipment which corresponds to that proportion of unemployment which ensures zero saving. Ibid., pp. 217–218.

28. Ibid., p. 136.

29. Cf. Ackley, pp. 465–466.

30. Ackley believes he advances a different basis for the alleged declining yields to net investment when he cites the factor of increasing capital intensiveness and the adoption of more roundabout methods of production in the sense used by Böhm-Bawerk. See Ackley, pp. 466–472. Actually, this factor is fully in the spirit of the law of diminishing returns. Indeed, the basis for claiming diminishing returns is precisely the increasing degree of capital intensiveness.

31. See above, pp. 76–91 passim.

32. See *The Ayn Rand Lexicon,* Harry Binswanger, ed. (New York: New American Library, 1986), pp. 104–105.

33. Cf. Paul Samuelson and William Nordhaus, *Economics,* 13th ed. (New York: McGraw Hill Book Company, 1989), pp. 66–67.

34. In reality, of course, it is an error to conceive of net investment as an actual expenditure. As we know, rather than being an expenditure, net investment is in fact the *difference* between productive expenditure, which is the actual expenditure present, and business costs, which are largely an accounting abstraction, based on the productive expenditures of previous accounting periods. On this point, see above, pp. 702–705.

35. This latter possibility should not be dismissed in view of the blatant absurdities the Keynesians have embraced, and which cannot be explained on the basis of any kind of intellec-

tual confusion. Keynes's endorsement of wars, earthquakes, and pyramid building as sources of prosperity are the leading example. See Keynes, *General Theory*, pp. 129–131.

36. The saving referred to is, of course, saving out of net income, i.e., net saving.

37. See U.S. Department of Commerce, Office of Business Economics, *National Income 1954 Edition, A Supplement to the Survey of Current Business* (Washington, D. C.: U.S. Government Printing Office, 1954). Data for saving appear on page 164 of this document; data for net investment are derived by subtracting capital consumption allowances, reported on page 164, from gross private domestic investment, which is reported on page 162.

38. See above, pp. 702–705.

39. See above, ibid.

40. Again, see above, ibid. See also above, pp. 723–725 and 744–750.

41. See, for example, the exposition of the multiplier in Samuelson, which was discussed above, on p. 690.

42. See above, pp. 707–708.

43. See above, pp. 589–590. See also Ludwig von Mises, *Human Action*, 3d ed. rev. (Chicago: Henry Regnery Co., 1966), pp. 568–569.

44. These conclusions are not significantly disturbed by the fact that a portion of the expenditure made on account of plant and equipment is itself in the form of wage payments—such as the payment of the wages of workers installing machinery and the wages of construction workers paid by firms that act as their own contractors. To the extent that cases of this kind exist, the reduction in total wage payments and the consumer spending it supports is less, and a portion of the reduction in aggregate costs is achieved by the fact that the new wage payments show up as depreciation cost over a long period of years rather than all at once.

45. Samuelson and Nordhaus, 13th ed., pp. 183–184.

46. On these points, see above, pp. 56–58, 744, and 838–856.

47. See above, pp. 837–838.

48. For elaboration, see below, pp. 889–890. See also below, pp. 930–937.

49. See above, pp. 758–759, 768–771, and 834–837.

50. See above, pp. 741–743.

51. See above, pp. 836–837.

52. See Henry Hazlitt, *The Failure of the "New Economics"* (New York: D. Van Nostrand & Co., 1959) p. 193.

53. See above, pp. 837–838.

54. While this might not be as easily established in the case of a negative or zero percent rate of return, the fact that as the rate of return approaches zero, land values approach infinity, implies all by itself that the rate of return must indeed always be positive at some significant level.

55. Keynes, *General Theory,* pp. 218–219.

56. Ibid., pp. 201–202.

57. See above, pp. 521–522.

58. Keynes, *General Theory,* p. 167.

59. Ibid., pp. 167–168.

60. Ibid., p. 171.

61. Indeed, insofar as the rate of interest is not yet at its minimum acceptable level and thus has room to fall, and insofar as a fall in wage rates and prices increases the buying power of

a given stock of money and can thus be likened in its effects to an increase in the quantity of money, Keynes is prepared to concede that a fall in wage rates and prices can increase the volume of employment. This alleged concession is known as the "Keynes effect." See ibid., p. 261. See also McKenna, pp. 216–220.

62. Concerning the effect of increases in the quantity of money on the rate of profit, see above, pp. 762–774. For the connection to a higher rate of interest, see above, pp. 520–521.

63. Again, see above, pp. 520–521.

64. Keynes, *General Theory*, p. 167.

65. Concerning the views of Smith and Marx in this area, see above, pp. 475–480.

66. In 1959, I showed Henry Hazlitt an early, unpublished paper that presented some of my basic views on profit and interest and that concluded with these very points. Beginning with the third printing of *The Failure of the "New Economics,"* which appeared in the following year, he very graciously found space to describe these points and credit me for them. See, ibid., p. 196.

67. See above, pp. 712–715.

68. Keynes, *General Theory*, p. 129.

69. James Mill, *Commerce Defended* (London, 1808), chap. 7; reprinted in *Selected Economic Writings of James Mill*, ed. Donald Winch (Chicago: University of Chicago Press, 1966), p. 140.

70. Depending on the relative size of the country's economy, the by-product of a decline in its ability to produce, or of any lesser rate of increase in its ability to produce, is probably also to reduce the rate of increase in the world's overall supply of gold, which, of course, depends on the ability to increase production in general. This principle is operative even if the country itself does not possess gold mines. Gold mining outside the country will be negatively affected insofar as it depends directly or indirectly on what is produced within that country.

71. For a discussion of additional deflationary consequences of government budget deficits, see below, pp. 940–941.

72. For elaboration of all of these points, see below, pp. 925–938.

73. A significant fraction of the national debt is held by the Federal Reserve System and the banking system, as opposed to the general public. The increase in this portion of the debt represents the creation of new and additional money rather than the diversion of savings. Any lessening of the diversion of savings that this fact may appear to represent, is dwarfed by the vastly larger sums siphoned off under the social security system from savings into government consumption. Furthermore, as I have said, the creation of hundreds of billions of dollars of new and additional money is the essence of the problem of inflation and the root of all of the destructive consequences for capital accumulation that result from inflation.

74. On these points, see below, pp. 930–938 and 951.

75. On these points, see below, pp. 937–940 and 942–950.

76. See above, pp. 591–592.

77. See above, pp. 591–594.

78. See above, p. 592.

79. Keynes, *General Theory*, pp. 373, 374.

80. Ibid., pp. 375–377. Italics supplied.

81. Ibid., p. 378.

82. Ibid.

83. Ibid.

84. Ibid., p. 207. Italics supplied.

CHAPTER 19

GOLD VERSUS INFLATION

INFLATION OF THE MONEY SUPPLY VERSUS ALTERNATIVE THEORIES OF RISING PRICES

1. The Analytical Framework of the Quantity Theory of Money

The quantity theory of money, as developed earlier in this book, shows that the cause of generally rising prices is an increase in the quantity of money. More specifically, it shows that the cause is an increase in the quantity of money at a rate *more rapid than the increase in the supply of gold and silver*. The increase in the supply of gold and silver, being itself a by-product of the general increase in the ability to produce, would show no tendency regularly or significantly to outstrip the increase in the supply of the mass of ordinary commodities, and to that extent would be incapable of causing a sustained significant rise in prices. In addition, since government intervention into the monetary system is what has been responsible for the quantity of money being able to increase more rapidly than the increase in the supply of gold and silver, the quantity theory of money implies that what is responsible for the problem of a persistent significant rise in prices is an increase in the quantity of money *caused by the government*.

Indeed, the quantity theory of money implies that inflation should be *defined* in terms of the increase in the quantity of money—specifically, as an *increase in the quantity of money at a rate more rapid than the increase in the supply of gold and silver or, equivalently, as an increase in the quantity of money caused by the government*. Such a definition states the essential cause of the cluster of symptoms which people identify with inflation and which must be acted upon to eliminate those symptoms. It represents a definition in terms of fundamentals and provides, at the same time, a sound guide to corrective action. Nevertheless, the great majority of people today, including even the great majority of professional economists, define inflation in terms of one of its leading symptoms. They define it merely as *rising prices*.

The definition of inflation as rising prices says absolutely nothing about any specific cause of rising prices. It implies, therefore, that inflation can be caused by anything that raises prices.

Having accepted this definition, it is no wonder that people are confused about inflation. There are a vast number of things that might raise prices in one circumstance or another, ranging all the way from bad weather causing poor crops and thus higher farm-product prices to the development of a fad for some novelty. On the basis of the definition of inflation as rising prices, people are led to consider every possible cause of higher prices as a possible cause of inflation, and thus to believe that the cause of inflation can vary from case to case.

Thus, they believe that inflation can be caused, variously, either by "demand pull," that is, by more spending outstripping the growth in the supply of goods and thus "pulling up their prices," or by "cost push," that is, by rising costs forcing up prices. (The quantity theory of money is often thought to operate exclusively in the form of "demand pull" and is thus classified by many economists under the heading of "demand-pull inflation.")[1]

By "cost-push inflation" is meant, frequently but by no means always, the arbitrary demands of labor unions, which drive up wage rates and thus costs of production and prices. This variety of cost-push inflation is called "wage-push inflation." In addition, there is supposed to be a second variety of cost-push inflation, namely, "profit-push inflation," which allegedly occurs when the greed of businessmen is supposed to drive up the prices of critical raw materials, such as steel and cement, which in turn constitute costs of production to large numbers of other producers. The term profit-push inflation is also applied to cases in which the greed of businessmen selling consumers' goods is supposed to drive up the prices of the consumers' goods directly, without any rise in costs of production. (To incorporate this type of case, the term "sellers' inflation" is sometimes used in place of "cost-push inflation.")

Yet a third variety of cost-push or sellers' inflation is supposed to exist in cases in which this or that crisis, such as the Arab oil embargo or the sale or giveaway of large quantities of wheat to the Soviet Union, disrupts the supply of one or more vital goods and so raises the costs of production of all the producers who require them. This species of cost-push inflation is sometimes termed "crisis-push inflation."

Closely related to the doctrine of cost-push inflation is the doctrine of the "wage-price spiral." According to this doctrine, prices rise because wages rise, and wages rise because prices rise. Wages and prices, it is believed, simply chase each other upward in a spiral, and that is why prices go on rising. (If a proponent of this doctrine is sympathetic to labor unions, he asserts that the process begins with an arbitrary rise in prices due to the profit-push of employers. If he is unsympathetic to labor unions, he asserts that it begins with an arbitrary rise in wages due to the wage-push of the unions.)

So-called demand-pull inflation is also supposed to take a variety of forms. In addition to being caused by an increase in the quantity of money, it is supposed to be capable of being caused by inexplicable increases in the velocity of circulation of money; by the unexplained existence of "inflation psychology"; by the growing use of credit cards, installment credit, or other forms of credit; and even by the sheer increasing greed of consumers for more goods.

The effect of believing that "inflation" can be caused by an extensive list of things that the mind has no clear-cut way of organizing or holding is that for all practical purposes people are led to regard inflation as *causeless*. Ask the average person—or even many professors of economics—what causes inflation, and at most a blur of confused bits and pieces of knowledge about what might raise prices in this or that case comes to his mind. For all practical purposes he has absolutely no idea of the cause. For he believes that to determine the cause in the specific case at hand requires a special investigation, to determine which of all the various alleged possibilities is the actual explanation. On this basis, we can observe the appointment of successive panels of alleged experts to study the problem of inflation, as though the explanation had never been found.

But this is not the worst consequence of the definition of inflation as rising prices. For that definition not only opens the door to too-wide a range of possible explanations to be of any value. It also directly and powerfully suggests one particular, extremely simple explanation, which in fact is the most popular explanation—namely, that inflation is the result of the ill will of evil, powerful people: above all, of big businessmen driven by the greed for higher profits. This is necessarily the most popular explanation of inflation, given the general acceptance of its definition as "rising prices."

This is because if inflation is defined simply as being rising prices, then it follows that inflation only comes into existence *when* businessmen raise their prices and *exists* only to the extent that they raise their prices. In other words, it follows from the current definition that inflation exists when and to the extent that someone—Jones, the corner grocer, General Motors, or whoever—raises his price. It follows further that inflation would not exist if Jones or whoever did not raise his price. In the absence of any clear-cut understanding of why Jones or whoever must raise his price, there is no way that people can avoid concluding that Jones or whoever is responsible for inflation.

The real view that most people have of inflation, therefore, is that it is something caused by the evil of private individuals, especially greedy businessmen.

This view of the nature of inflation suggests an apparent and seemingly logical remedy: the government, motivated by concern for the public welfare, should forbid the evil businessmen to raise their prices. Price controls, it appears, are the solution to inflation.

And just as inflation stands in people's minds as a causeless phenomenon born of mere ill will, so price controls are regarded as having no effects but that of stamping out inflation. In the view of most people, what we have in the matter of inflation and price controls is a causeless evil overpowered by an otherwise effectless good. To put this another way, what most people do in the matter of inflation and price controls is to begin their thinking at the point of the businessman raising his prices, and to end it at the point of the government entering the scene with a *Verbot*. All that comes before and all that follows after is a blank in their minds.

I have already explained both the effects of price controls and the actual cause of rising prices. My purpose here is to reinforce the quantity theory of money by refuting all of the other explanations of rising prices that have been advanced. I will show that all of the alternative explanations are either simply false or else, to the extent that they do contain some modest kernel of truth, constitute merely a further confirmation of the truth of the quantity theory of money. I will show that the increase in the quantity of money is not merely one possible cause of rising prices among many possible causes, but is *the universal cause of every sustained significant rise in prices*. At the conclusion of the first part of this chapter, it will be apparent, if it is not already, that as a means of furthering both our understanding and our ability to deal with the problem, inflation should not be defined as rising prices, but in terms of the universal underlying cause of rising prices. That is, to repeat, inflation should be defined either as an increase in the quantity of money at a rate more rapid than the increase in the supply of gold and silver or, equivalently, as an increase in the quantity of money caused by the government.

The Vital Demand/Supply Test for All Theories of Rising Prices

The equation, initially developed in Chapter 12, that

$$P = \frac{D_C}{S_C}$$

—i.e., the general consumer price level equals the aggregate demand (spending) to buy consumers' goods, divided by the aggregate supply of consumers' goods produced and sold—provides an indispensable conceptual framework for examining any possible explanation of rising prices and for confirming the truth of the explanation based on the quantity theory of money.

When people speak of inflation as a rise in prices, what they really have in mind is not an isolated rise in some prices here and there, offset by a fall in prices elsewhere, but a rise in the *generality* of prices. The general consumer price level is the weighted average of all consumer prices. As previously explained, the supply it reflects is the sum of all consumers' goods produced and sold, conceived of as so many units of an abstract consumers' good in general. This supply is purchased for a definite aggregate expenditure of money. The result is the general consumer price level.

The above equation, it must be recalled, shows the general consumer price level to be the resultant of a numerator, demand, divided by a denominator, supply.

The average price at which goods are sold *is* the spending to buy them divided by the quantity of them sold. It follows from this equation that there are only two *conceivable* ways in which the general consumer price level can rise. Namely, *either the demand for consumers' goods must rise or the supply of consumers' goods must fall*. If neither of these conditions is present, then it is absolutely impossible for the general consumer price level to rise. For there is simply no conceivable way that it could. Its rise in such circumstances would constitute a contradiction of the laws of arithmetic: it would be a rise in a quotient without a rise in the numerator or fall in the denominator, which is to say, an absolute impossibility.

This reduction of the possible causes of rising prices to just two does not actually rule out the existence of other possible causes, provided those other causes operate by way of producing more demand or less supply. More demand or less supply are the only conceivable proximate or direct causes of a higher price level. There is thus still the possibility of all kinds other, mediate or indirect causes of higher prices. However, the reduction to just these two proximate causes imposes a critical test on any other alleged cause. Namely, in the nature of the case, any cause of higher prices other than more demand or less supply must produce its effects by means of causing either more demand or less supply. If there is something which is alleged to be a cause of higher prices other than more demand or less supply, and it cannot be shown how it raises demand or reduces supply, then it must be dismissed as a cause out of hand. More demand or less supply are the necessary, indispensable connection between higher prices and any alleged other cause of higher prices. If they are absent, there simply is no connection between that alleged cause and higher prices.

The quantity theory of money connects the increase in the quantity of money to the rise in prices by way of establishing a connection to more demand. As previously explained, a growing quantity of money raises the demand for consumers' goods through the new and additional money being spent and respent and, as its rate of growth becomes more substantial, through bringing about a decrease in the demand for money for holding and thus a rise in the velocity of circulation of money.[2] Every other possible explanation of rising prices must pass a similar test of linkage to the growth in demand or decline in supply if it is to be considered.

The Elimination of Less Supply as the Cause of an Inflationary Rise in Prices

Our analytical framework for examining theories of the rise in prices is carried a long way forward when it is realized that *decreases in supply must be eliminated from consideration as the cause of a rising price level*, both here in the United States and everywhere else in the world. There are seven reasons for eliminating reductions in supply. They are as follows.

i. The Actual Influence of Supply Has Been to Reduce Prices

In almost every year since World War II, which is the period complained of as marked by inflation, prices have indeed risen in the United States, Western Europe, and Japan. Yet, over the same period of time, supply has actually increased rather than decreased in these places, and it has done so in practically every year. Supply has increased enormously, as the result of a larger population, and, consequently, more people working; and, even more, as the result of technological progress and capital accumulation, which have raised the productivity of labor and thus enabled each worker on average to produce a greater output.

Our formula for the general consumer price level, of course, shows that the effect of increases in supply must be to reduce prices in inverse proportion. The fact that the price level has risen, therefore, despite vast increases in supply, can be ascribed only to the influence of even more substantial increases in demand. The problem of rising prices in the United States and every other leading country over the last fifty years or more is clearly one of rising demand, not falling supply.

ii. Where Falling Supply Has Contributed to Rising Prices, Its Role Has Been Relatively Minor

Of course, there are some countries in which supply has fallen, and fallen quite substantially, at least over portions of the period since World War II. Chile in the early 1970s and Uruguay in the 1960s are leading examples. While the precise extent of the fall in supply in these countries may be difficult to estimate, it is extremely doubtful that in the worst period the cumulative decrease ever exceeded a figure of 50 percent. If, for the sake of argument, we take the figure of 50 percent, we could account for a doubling of the price level in these countries on the basis of supply reductions. I say a doubling, because our formula for the general price level shows that a halving of supply coupled with an unchanged demand must produce a doubled price level. However, as is well-known, the price levels in countries like Chile and Uruguay have not increased by a factor merely of two over any extended number of years. An increase of this order of magnitude frequently occurs in a single year in those countries. In any given decade, prices in those countries have increased probably by a factor of fifty or more. And since World War II, they have increased by a factor of many thousand. Therefore, even where supply

has decreased, the overwhelmingly greater part of the rise in prices cannot be accounted for on the basis of reductions in supply, but must be ascribed to increases in demand.

iii. Reductions in Supply as the Cause of Rising Prices Imply the Rapid Disappearance of Material Civilization

Reductions in supply could explain a sustained significant rise in prices only if material civilization were in the process of rapidly disappearing, which, of course, it is not. For the price-level formula implies that every rise in the price level ascribable to a decrease in supply requires a decrease in supply that is inversely proportionate. This is because when changes in supply are supposed to be the operative factor, demand must necessarily be assumed to be unchanged. As a result, in the case of rising prices caused by falling supply, a rise in the price level means a rise in a quotient accompanied by a fixed numerator (demand). This implies a denominator (supply) that falls in inverse proportion. Thus, for example, a doubling of prices caused by a decrease in supply requires an actual halving of supply. In the same way, a tripling of prices ascribable to a fall in supply implies a reduction of supply to one-third of its initial level; a quadrupling, to one-fourth, and so on.

If a sustained rate of increase in the price level, such as 5 percent, 10 percent, or 100 percent per year, is to be ascribed to supply reductions, it follows that in each year, supply would have to fall in inverse proportion to the rise in prices. It further follows, therefore, that if any sustained, even moderately significant rate of increase in the price level were to be ascribable to supply reductions, the virtual disappearance of material civilization would be implied within a fairly short period of time. For example, in the course of a single generation, a 5 percent annual rise in prices based on supply reductions would mean that year after year, for a generation, supply would be on the order of 5 percent less than it was the year before. This would imply a cumulative reduction in supply to about one-third of its initial level, since at a 5 percent compound rate of increase, prices would approximately triple in a generation. If falling supply is to be the explanation of a tripling of prices, the fall would have to be all the way to one-third. With the same demand numerator, only such a fall in the supply denominator is capable of raising the price-level quotient by a factor of three.

Similarly, a 10 percent annual rise in prices, based on supply reductions and sustained for a generation, would imply a reduction in supply to about one-eighth of its initial level. This is because at a 10 percent compound annual rate of increase, prices double in approximately eight years. Thus, in a generation, which encompasses more than three periods of eight years, in each of which prices double, prices must increase by more than two raised to the third power, that is, by a factor of more than eight. If falling supply is to be the explanation of an eightfold rise in prices, the fall would have to be all the way to one-eighth.

Even a mere 2 percent annual rise in prices caused by falling supply implies a halving of supply every thirty-five years and thus a reduction in supply to one-eighth of its initial level in the course of little more than a century. This is a more rapid rate of decline than was experienced by the Roman Empire in its decline. Thus it is not possible to explain a sustained rise in prices even as moderate as 2 percent a year on the basis of falling supply, without the very rapid disappearance of material civilization being present.

iv. Falling Supply Is the By-Product of Rapid Increases in Aggregate Demand

Furthermore, if we look at countries like Chile and Uruguay, which actually experienced significant supply reductions, it becomes obvious that most or even all of the reductions in supply that occurred were themselves the result of the rapid increases in aggregate demand that took place in those countries. A rapidly rising aggregate demand disrupts production. The rapid rise in prices it brings about causes widespread discontent and foments crippling strikes, and even sabotage. In these ways, and others that are more substantial, and which will be explained in Part B of this chapter, a rapidly rising aggregate demand acts to reduce production and, therefore, supply. Thus, a decrease in supply is often itself merely an indirect consequence of a rapidly rising aggregate demand, rather than being an initiating cause of rising prices.

v. Falling Supply Cannot Explain the Range of Price Increases that Exists Under Inflation

Even such supply reductions as are not themselves caused by rising demand, and which, therefore, may legitimately be said to be an independent cause of higher prices—for example, poor crops due to bad weather—should not be described as a cause of *inflation*, despite the fact that they raise the general consumer price level. This is because they do not produce the *range* of price increases that people associate with inflation. When people complain of "inflation," they have in mind more than a mere rise in the weighted average of consumer prices that is depicted in the consumer price-level formula. They have in mind a condition in which almost every individual price rises and hardly any individual prices fall. It is highly doubtful that they would complain of inflation if a large number of individual prices actually

fell, even if, at the same time, the consumer price level, in the sense of the weighted average of consumer prices, rose. Yet precisely this phenomenon of widespread price declines would be the effect of reductions in supply that were not accompanied by increases in demand. If supply fell without being accompanied by an increase in demand, the effect would be that a whole host of prices would actually fall, even though the weighted average of prices rose.

A large number of prices would fall, because the effect of a reduction in supply would be to make people poorer. As they became poorer, they would concentrate a larger and larger proportion of their limited demand on necessities and a smaller and smaller proportion on luxuries. The prices of all luxury and semi-luxury items would therefore tend to fall.

To understand this result, consider the well-known fact that decreases in the supply of necessities produce more than proportionate increases in their price. A 5 percent reduction in the supply of wheat, for example, might raise its price by 25 percent, or more, because the price of a necessity must rise steeply before people are deterred from buying it. This kind of situation implies a shifting of spending away from comparative luxury goods, to wheat, or to any other necessity or comparative necessity in decreased supply. People have the money to pay the disproportionately higher prices of necessities in reduced supply only by taking money away from the purchase of luxuries. And that acts to reduce the price of luxuries. The principle here is that a drop in the supply of any good that comparatively speaking is a necessity causes spending to shift to it from goods that comparatively speaking are luxuries. Its price rises more than in proportion to the drop in supply, and their prices actually tend to *fall*.

Similarly, if the supply of any good falls that is employed with other, complementary goods, its price tends to rise disproportionately, while their prices actually tend to fall. For example, a drop in the supply of gasoline causes a sharp jump in the price of gasoline and, at the same time, acts to reduce the demand for automobiles, motel rooms, and so on. The prices of such things, therefore, tend to fall, and actually would fall if the quantity of money and demand in the aggregate did not rise and thus hold up or even increase the demand for them at the same time that people concentrated their expenditures more heavily on the goods in reduced supply.

The phenomenon of large numbers of prices actually falling as the result of declining supplies would be a continuing one as supply fell and the weighted average of prices rose from year to year. In one year, the prices of luxury goods and various complementary goods would

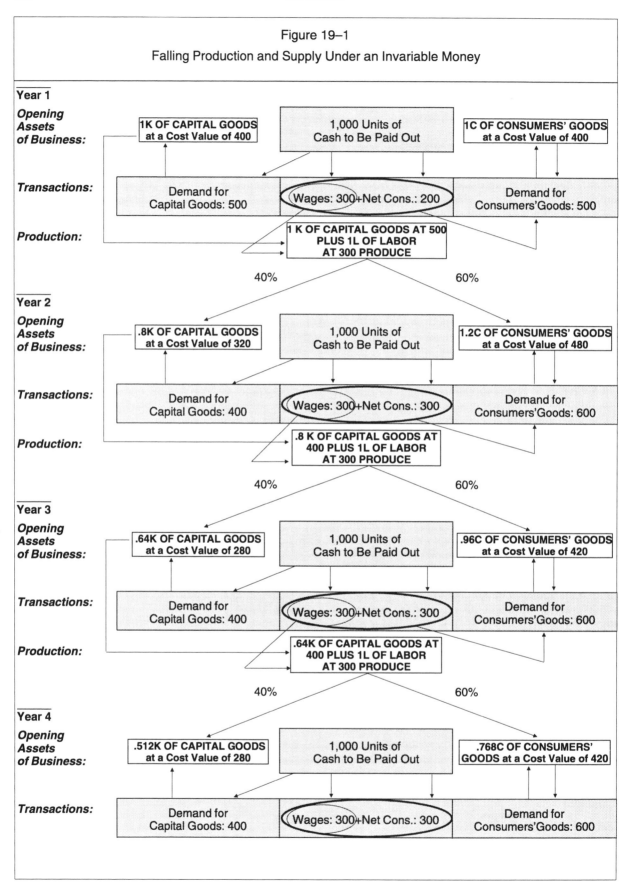

Figure 19–1

Falling Production and Supply Under an Invariable Money

fall as the prices of various necessities and certain complementary goods sharply increased. In the following year, as capital was withdrawn from the production of luxury goods and invested in the production of the necessities whose prices had sharply increased, the prices of those necessities would fall. Similarly, as capital was withdrawn from the production of complementary goods with depressed prices and invested in the production of complementary goods with sharply higher prices, the prices of the latter would come down. From year to year the rise in prices would outweigh the fall in prices, because of the overall reduction in supply. At the same time, however, numerous cases would always exist in which prices fell.

On the basis of this discussion, it should be clear that if not accompanied by an increasing aggregate demand, a reduction in supply would be accompanied by widespread declines in individual prices, even while the weighted average of prices rose. It would therefore not qualify as a cause of what most people have in mind when they complain of inflation. In order for practically every price to rise, there must be rising aggregate demand. That is the only way that the demand for some goods can increase without reducing the demand for other goods.

vi. Falling Supply Is Incompatible With the Debtor/Creditor Effects Associated With Inflation

Increases in the price level caused by supply reductions *do not produce the effects on the relations between debtors and creditors that people associate with inflation.* One of the major symptoms associated with inflation is that debtors gain at the expense of creditors. The debtors pay a contractually fixed rate of interest and are obliged to repay only a contractually fixed amount of principal. In a period of inflation, the debtors meet these contractual obligations in money of less value than they borrowed, and enjoy a gain at the expense of their creditors. For at the same time that prices rise, and reduce the purchasing power of the contractually fixed incomes and assets of creditors, the incomes and assets of debtors are free to rise without limit and generally do rise at a rate more rapid than prices. Thus debtors are enriched at the expense of creditors. The leading instance of this kind, of course, is that of stockholders—whose enterprises constitute a major category of debtor—being enriched at the expense of bondholders, a major category of creditor.

Now this phenomenon of debtors gaining at the expense of creditors, of stockholders gaining at the expense of bondholders, can occur *only if the rise in prices results from an increase in the quantity of money and volume of spending*—that is, from an increase in aggregate *demand.* It cannot occur if the rise in prices results from a

decrease in the supply of goods. It follows that if the debtor/creditor effects just described are to be regarded as an essential feature of inflation, inflation must be a phenomenon fundamentally of increases in money and spending, not decreases in production and supply.

Totally unlike the situation which prevails under inflation, the fact is that when prices rise because of falling production and supply, debtors do not gain at the expense of creditors. This can be clearly shown on the basis of Figure 19–1, titled "Falling Production and Supply Under an Invariable Money." Figure 19–1 is the virtual mirror image of Figure 17–1, which dealt with the effects of rising production and supply under an invariable money.[3] It provides the conditions for a virtual laboratory test of the effects of rising prices caused by falling production and supply on the relations between debtors and creditors, and will serve to demonstrate that in such conditions debtors do not gain at the expense of creditors.

In Figure 19–1, as in Figure 17–1, it is assumed that an existing *1K* of capital goods, when used in conjunction with *1L* of labor, makes it possible to produce either *2K* of capital goods and *0C* of consumers' goods, at one extreme, or *0K* of capital goods and *2C* of consumers' goods, at the other extreme, and that as the supply of capital goods changes, the overall ability to produce changes in direct proportion—e.g., doubling if the supply of capital goods should double, halving if the supply of capital goods should halve. Also, as in Figure 17–1, the simplifying assumption is made that all the capital goods in existence in any given year are productively consumed in that same year. Thus, as in Figure 17–1, it is necessary that the economic system devote half of its productive efforts to the production of capital goods if it is to maintain the existing supply of capital goods. The proportion of its productive efforts which it actually does devote to the production of capital goods is, of course, determined by the demand for capital goods relative to the demand for consumers' goods.

As in Figure 17–1, the initial situation, depicted in *Year 1*, is that the demands for capital goods and consumers' goods have been at the necessary 50⁄50 ratio, with 500 monetary units being spent for each, every year. Finally, as in Figure 17–1, the demand for labor is assumed to be constant at 300 monetary units per year. It is on the basis of the application of these assumptions concerning the demands for capital goods and labor to *Year 0*, which is not described in the figure, that the cost values of the capital goods and consumers' goods available at the start of *Year 1*, namely, 400 and 400, are derived. They are each 50 percent of 800, which is the sum of the 500 of demand for capital goods plus the 300 of demand for labor that took place in *Year 0*.

Figure 19–1, as I have said, is the virtual mirror image

of Figure 17–1. Thus, instead of net consumption falling from 200 to 100, as it did in Figure 17–1, it rises from 200 to 300, with the result that the demand for capital goods, instead of rising from 500 to 600, now falls from 500 to 400, while the demand for consumers' goods, instead of falling from 500 to 400, rises from 500 to 600. Thus, the relative demands for capital goods and consumers' goods change from $500/500$ to $400/600$ rather than to $600/400$, which last was the case in Figure 17–1.

The effect of this change in the relative demands for capital goods and consumers' goods is that starting with the production phase of *Year 1*, in which the changed relative demands of *Year 2* are anticipated and production adjusted accordingly, the economic system now devotes only 40 percent of its productive efforts to the production of capital goods, and 60 percent to the production of consumers' goods. The effect of this in turn is that the economic system becomes unable to produce a quantity of capital goods sufficient to offset the quantity of capital goods being used up in production. Thus while *1K* of capital goods are productively consumed in *Year 1*, only *.8K* of capital goods are produced for the start of *Year 2*, along with *1.2C* of consumers' goods. In *Year 2*, which is the second year of the changed relative production of capital goods and consumers' goods, the overall ability to produce is reduced, because of the reduced supply of capital goods available at the start of the year. The ability to produce in *Year 2*, instead of being describable by the limits of *2K* of capital goods and *0C* of consumers' goods at one extreme, and *0K* of capital goods and *2C* of consumers' goods at the other extreme, is now 20 percent less, that is, describable by the narrower limits of *1.6K* of capital goods and *0C* of consumers' goods at one extreme, and *0K* of capital goods and *1.6C* of consumers' goods at the other extreme. This is because production takes place on the foundation of a supply of capital goods only 80 percent as large, namely, *.8K* of capital goods instead of *1K* of capital goods, and can therefore itself be only 80 percent as large.

The continuation of the $40/60$ ratio of the production of capital goods relative to the production of consumers' goods results in a supply of capital goods at the start of *Year 3* of *.64K* (i.e., .4 x the limiting extreme of *1.6K*), and in a supply of consumers' goods of *.96C* (i.e., .6 x the limiting extreme of *1.6C*). Thereafter, as the result of a process of less capital goods causing less productive ability, resulting in still less capital goods, and so on and on, in every year the supply both of capital goods and consumers' goods goes on falling—in the specific conditions of our simplified example, by exactly 20 percent per year.

Now although not explicitly shown in Figure 19–1, it follows inescapably, precisely because of the 20 percent annual fall in supply in the face of a fixed aggregate demand, that the general price level both of consumers' goods and of capital goods rises at an annual rate of 25 percent from *Year 3* on. For example, in *Year 3*, 600 of demand for consumers' goods buys a supply of consumers' goods of only *.96C*, while in *Year 2* it bought *1.2C* of consumers' goods. This represents a 20 percent reduction in the supply purchased for the same money. In *Year 4*, the same-sized aggregate demand for consumers' goods buys only *.768C* of consumers' goods—that is, a supply reduced once more by 20 percent. Our knowledge of the price-level formula implies that where demand is fixed and supply is four-fifths as great, prices must be five-fourths as great, that is, 25 percent higher. And so it will be in every year beyond *Year 4*.

What is also the case in Figure 19–1 is that at no time is there an increase in the aggregate value of business assets. In *Years 1* and *2*, the opening assets of business are 1,800 monetary units. And in *Year 3* and every year thereafter, the opening assets of business are 1,700 monetary units, reflecting the rise in net consumption to 300 monetary units and fall in productive expenditure to 700 monetary units, which took place in *Year 2* and is maintained in every year thereafter.

Now the total value of business assets represents the sum of the equity and debt capitals invested in business, that is, the sum of the capitals invested by stockholders, partners, and proprietors, on the one side, and the sum of the capitals invested by bondholders and other creditors of business, on the other. The fact that nominal capital in the aggregate is fixed, or at least cannot increase (it did undergo a decrease), means that there is a loss as the result of rising prices caused by falling production and supply, not merely to bondholders and other creditors of business, *but to the owners of capital as such*. This means, it is not only bondholders and the like, whose assets are contractually fixed in money, who lose when production falls and prices rise, but the average capitalist as such—the average capitalist irrespective of whether he is a bondholder or a stockholder, that is, irrespective of whether he is a creditor-capitalist or a debtor-capitalist.

Indeed, if business had no debts whatever and there were only equity capital and thus every capitalist were in the position of being able to profit and add to his capital without any contractual limitations, the position of the *average* equity capitalist would be exactly the same as that of a bondholder. Some individual capitalists, to be sure, might gain. Not having their assets or incomes contractually fixed, they might earn extraordinary profits and accumulate nominal capital at a rate as fast or faster than the rate at which prices rose. But if the aggregate value of business assets and the average rate of profit is fixed, which are implications of a fixed quantity of money together with a fixed rate of net consumption and a given array of marginal productivities of capital, then for every individual capitalist who earns a rate of profit above the average and who can add to his nominal capital, there are other individual capitalists who earn a rate of profit equivalently below the average and who equivalently consume their nominal capitals.

What stands out as clearly as possible in this case is that from the perspective of equity capitalists as a class, i.e., on the average, the effect of rising prices caused by falling production and supply is exactly the same as it is on creditor capitalists as a class. That is, on the average their capitals and incomes are fixed, and the rise in prices caused by the fall in production and supply reduces the purchasing power of their capitals and incomes, just as it reduces the purchasing power of the capitals and incomes of creditor capitalists.

It is not necessary to assume that business has no debts and that all capitalists are equity capitalists. This is because identically the same results follow if equity capital is any lesser proportion of the total capital invested in business firms. Thus, imagine that of the 1,700 monetary units of capital that is invested in business from *Year 3* on in Figure 19–1, half represents the equity capital of stockholders and the like, and half represents the debt capital of bondholders and the like. Both halves of the capital will lose to the same extent as the result of rising prices caused by falling production and supply. The same would be true if the proportions of equity and debt capital were one-fourth and three-fourths, one-tenth and nine-tenths, or any other proportions. By the same token, whatever portion of the 300 of aggregate profit generated by the 300 of net consumption in Figure 19–1 represents profit after deduction of interest and whatever portion represents interest, the purchasing power of both portions would be reduced equally by any rise in prices resulting from falling production and supply.

Thus, what Figure 19–1 shows is that if all that happens is a fall in production and supply, then it is certainly true that prices rise and creditors suffer, because their contractually fixed money revenues and incomes buy less, as do their assets, which are also contractually fixed in money. But in that case, debtors suffer equally from the rise in prices.

If prices rise because of falling production and supply, the money revenues and incomes of debtors do not rise on the average any more than those of creditors, which is to say, not at all. Nor does the money value of the assets of debtors rise on the average any more than that of creditors, which again is to say, not at all.

If the rise in prices is due to a fall in production and supply, while conditions on the side of money and demand are unchanged, then the aggregate money revenues and incomes of the debtors are exactly what they were before the fall in supply and rise in prices. There is simply no possible basis of a rise in aggregate money revenues or incomes in the face of unchanged conditions of demand. This is because what unchanged conditions of demand mean is that the expenditures constituting sales revenues are the same and the productive expenditures giving rise to costs are the same. Thus aggregate sales revenues, aggregate costs, and aggregate profits are the same. In such circumstances, to whatever extent the average debtor sells at higher prices, he necessarily has *correspondingly less to sell*—precisely because the rise in prices is the result of less supply; indeed, as we know, in the conditions of a fixed aggregate demand, the rise in prices must be the result of an inversely proportionate reduction in supply. Thus, being able to earn no more money on average than he used to earn, the debtor's difficulty in repaying his debts can be no less than it used to be. This is illustrated in Figure 19–1 by the fact that in every year in which business debtors sell at 25 percent higher prices, they have precisely 20 percent fewer goods to sell. In other words, they are in the position of selling at five-fourths the prices only four-fifths the quantity of goods, which means they take in only the same amount of money revenue. And with the stabilization of aggregate productive expenditure and thus costs, their money net incomes also become fixed. Indeed, having to repay the same debt out of the same revenue or income in the face of higher prices for what one buys, makes the repayment of debt more difficult than it was before, because of the reduction in one's real disposable revenue or income.[4]

Similarly, to whatever extent the price of the average debtor's capital assets rises, because of a reduction in their supply, there is nothing present to increase the aggregate value of such assets or, therefore, the value of the capital assets in the possession of the average debtor. In the absence of an increase in the quantity of money and volume of spending, the rise in the average price of capital assets is merely in inverse proportion to the decline in their supply. Indeed, insofar as decreases in supply are the result of a lower economic degree of capitalism or lower degree of capital intensiveness in the economic system, the aggregate monetary value of the assets of debtors (and creditors) is less in the face of any given quantity of money and volume of spending of the kind that generates business sales revenues, because it reflects less saving and productive expenditure relative to any given amount of sales revenues. Precisely this, of course, is the situation in Figure 19–1, in which the aggregate capital invested in the economic system falls from 1,800 monetary units to 1,700 monetary units between *Years 1* and *3*.

Going still further, in the case of rising prices caused by falling supply, it is easy to imagine conditions in which individuals would be *worse off* as debtors than as creditors. Thus, for example, imagine a war, with massive bombing and shelling, which destroyed a major portion of the plant and equipment of every firm, but which was not accompanied by any change in the quantity of money or volume of spending in the economic system. In this case, production would be greatly reduced, and prices would correspondingly rise. Creditors would lose a corresponding portion of their buying power, because their money incomes and assets would be fixed. But debtors would lose even more of their buying power. This would be the case because not only would they too have to pay the higher prices, but also the money value of their assets would actually be sharply reduced, in that, as equity owners, they would suffer the full loss in the value of the assets of their firms before the creditors suffered any loss. The debtors—not only business debtors such as stockholders, but also owners of homes that were damaged and on which there were mortgages—would suffer the loss of a major portion of their monetary net worth at the same time that they faced the need to pay higher prices.[5]

In the case of rising prices caused by falling supply, it is likely that debtors would actually experience conditions closer to those of *deflation* than inflation. By this, I mean that to some extent their revenues and incomes would actually fall for a time, precisely as the result of the fall in production and supply. To understand this phenomenon, recall that back in Chapter 13 I showed that

in the case of goods with major accumulated stocks, such as housing and automobiles, in which the funds expended in the purchase of previously produced goods can far exceed the funds expended in the purchase of newly produced goods, the effect of increases in production would be to increase the size of the market for newly produced goods relative to the market for previously produced goods and thus to draw funds to the former from the latter.[6] In the present, opposite case of falling production, the size of the market for newly produced goods declines relative to the market for previously produced goods, whose accumulated stocks reflect the greater production of prior years. As a result, funds are now drawn to the market for previously produced goods and away from the market for newly produced goods. In this way, the demand for the goods and services of business firms, which, of course, are engaged overwhelmingly in new production, is correspondingly reduced.

Along the same lines, as a further irony, insofar as the effect of a reduction in production is a reduction in the production of commodity money, the result, as a minimum, is a reduction in the rate of increase in the quantity of money and volume of spending. Thus, the effect is a greater difficulty, compared to what it otherwise would have been, of earning any given sum of money and thereby repaying debt. Thus, in this way too, the effect of reductions in production and supply is directly contrary to the debtor/creditor effects associated with inflation, irrespective of any rise in prices that may result.

All of the foregoing leads to the conclusion that in

Figure 19–2

The Initial Balance Sheet of a Hypothetical Average Firm
Before a Rise in Prices Resulting from Any Cause

ASSETS	LIABILITIES
$2,000,000 representing a given quantity of plant, equipment, and inventories at a given level of prices and capable of producing a given physical volume of output at a corresponding level of prices.	$1,000,000 of debt to bondholders and other creditors.
	$1,000,000 net worth of stockholders.
	$2,000,000

order to account for the phenomenon of debtors gaining at the expense of creditors, the rise in prices must originate *on the side of money and demand, not supply*. There must be more aggregate demand, due to the increase in the quantity of money. This alone is what raises the sales revenues, money incomes, and property values of debtors as a class and thus makes debt repayment easier for them. In this case, the increase in their money incomes and money net worths can outstrip the rise in prices to the same extent as the fixed money incomes and asset values of the creditors fall behind the rise in prices.

The complete dependence of the debtor/creditor effects associated with inflation on the increase in the quantity of money and volume of spending in the economic system, can be illustrated in terms of a series of balance sheets for a hypothetical average business firm. These are shown in Figures 19–2, 19–3, and 19–4.

Figure 19–2 describes an initial state of affairs, in which the average business firm has total assets worth $2 million, $1 million of which represents capital supplied by bondholders—creditors—and $1 million of which represents capital supplied by stockholders—debtors. At the same time, the $2 million of assets reflect a given physical supply of capital goods, in the form of plant, equipment, and inventory, at a given average unit cost of capital goods.[7] This supply of capital goods is capable of producing a given volume of physical output. When the combined consumers' goods output of all such firms in the economic system is divided into a given aggregate demand for consumers' goods, the result is the initial general consumer price level.

Figure 19–3 shows an average balance sheet for conditions in which prices have doubled owing to a halving of supply. Here, because conditions on the side of money and demand remain the same, $2 million is still the monetary value of the assets of the average business firm, with the only difference being that now $2 million represents half the physical quantity of capital goods at twice the average unit cost of capital goods. In this case, the bondholders continue to have their million of capital and the stockholders continue to have their million of capital. Both classes of investors lose equally in terms of the buying power of their assets, which is cut in half because of the doubling of the price of consumers' goods that results from the halving of the supply of capital goods and thus of the ability to produce consumers' goods.[8]

Only in the conditions of Figure 19–4, where the doubling of prices results from a doubling of the quantity of money and volume of spending, are the stockholder/debtors as a class in a position to gain as prices rise. Their gain results from the fact that the increase in the quantity of money and volume of spending increases the money revenue and income of the average firm at the same time that it raises prices. Because of the rise in its revenue and income, the average firm is enabled to increase its saving and reinvestment. The result is a rise in the total monetary value of the capital assets of the average firm. This increase, of course, accrues to the benefit of the stockholder/debtors, not to the benefit of the bondholder/creditors, whose incomes and assets are contractually fixed.

Figure 19–3

The Balance Sheet of a Hypothetical Average Firm Following a Rise in Prices Caused by a Halving of Supply

ASSETS	LIABILITIES
$2,000,000 representing half of the initial quantity of plant, equipment, and inventories at double the initial level of prices and capable of producing half the physical volume of output at a doubled level of prices.	$1,000,000 of debt to bondholders and other creditors.
	$1,000,000 net worth of stockholders.
	$2,000,000

Thus, in Figure 19–4, the money value of the assets of the average firm has doubled from $2 million to $4 million. The capital of the bondholder/creditors is contractually fixed and therefore remains at $1 million. Accordingly, the $2 million increase in the value of the assets of the average firm accrues to the stockholder/debtors, whose capital thus rises from $1 million to $3 million. In these circumstances, as prices double, the bondholder/creditors, whose assets remain fixed, suffer a 50 percent loss in real wealth. The stockholder/debtors, on the other hand, whose nominal capital triples when prices double, obtain a 50 percent gain in real wealth. Exactly the same results apply to real income, inasmuch as the doubling of money and spending results in a doubling of profits gross of interest. With the amount of interest contractually fixed, the increase in gross profits accrues to the benefit of the stockholder/debtors. A doubling of prices thus represents a halving of the real incomes of the bondholder/creditors and an equivalent increase in the real incomes of the stockholder/debtors.

Of course, the stockholder/debtors will not be able permanently to gain in this way. The rise in the nominal rate of profit that is caused by the increase in the quantity of money and volume of spending sooner or later raises the nominal rate of interest correspondingly. From that point on, continued inflationary gains of the stockholder/debtors at the expense of the bondholder/creditors depend on a further acceleration of the inflation.

Before leaving the subject of debtor/creditor effects,

it is important to bear in mind that in the absence of an increase in the quantity of money, any rise in the rate of profit inaugurated by a rise in the rate of net consumption, such as occurs in *Years 2* and *3* of Figure 19–1, is accompanied by a reduction in the aggregate value of capital assets.[9] This is because the corollary of a higher rate of net consumption in such circumstances is an absolute decline in saving and productive expenditure, which serves to reduce the aggregate, accumulated value of capital assets. Thus, even if it were the case that alongside of rising prices resulting from falling production and supply, the rate of profit were temporarily to rise relative to contractually fixed interest rates that were geared to a preceding, lower rate of profit, and thereby give business borrowers a temporary advantage at the expense of their creditors, it would still not be proper to describe the situation as one of inflation. In such circumstances, precisely during the time in which the rate of profit was rising, both sets of capitalists would experience an actual decline in their nominal capitals. This, of course, is the exact opposite of what goes on under inflation, where the increase in the quantity of money and rise in the rate of profit and interest results not only in stockholder/debtors but also in bondholder/creditors adding to their nominal capitals.[10]

Moreover, the very fact that the process is the result of a rise in the rate of net consumption and corresponding fall in saving operates to raise the rate of interest immediately. The rate of interest rises as the result of a reduction in the supply of savings, and thus of available

---

Figure 19–4

The Balance Sheet of a Hypothetical Average Firm Following a Rise in Prices Caused by a Doubling of Money and Demand

ASSETS	LIABILITIES
$4,000,000 representing the initial quantity of plant, equipment, and inventories at double the initial level of prices and capable of producing the initial physical volume of output at a doubled level of prices.	$1,000,000 of debt to bondholders and other creditors.
	$3,000,000 net worth of stockholders.
	$4,000,000

credit, in the face of the prevailing initial rate of profit. Indeed, it is probable that the rise in the rate of interest would actually precede the rise in the rate of profit, which would be delayed insofar as negative net investment took place. (Extensive negative net investment is not shown in Figure 19–1, because of the simplifying assumption that all capital goods in existence at the beginning of any year are used up in that same year. It would exist in reality, however.) Thus, in the case of a rise in the rate of profit caused by a rise in the rate of net consumption, there would be no sudden surge in the rate of profit in the face of a large volume of contractually fixed interest rates geared to a substantially lower rate of profit, which, of course, is what occurs in a period of inflation. This conclusion is reinforced by the fact that the rise in the rate of net consumption would itself almost certainly be slow and gradual rather than sudden and precipitous. Indeed, the very fact that in the absence of an increase in the quantity of money and volume of spending in the economic system, a rise in the rate of net consumption entails a fall in saving and productive expenditure, resulting in negative net investment and capital decumulation, and correspondingly reduces the availability of credit, gives the situation much of the character of a period of deflation and financial contraction, despite the existence of rising prices.[11]

On the basis of all of the preceding, it should be clear that the debtor/creditor effects associated with inflation can take place only on the foundation of an increase in the quantity of money and volume of spending. A rise in prices resulting from a decrease in production and supply would simply not be accompanied by such effects. Thus, if debtors gaining at the expense of creditors is to be regarded as an essential symptom of inflation, it follows that inflation is a matter of increases in money and spending, not decreases in production and supply.

vii. Falling Supply as a Cause of Inflation Implies That Rising Supply Is a Cause of Deflation and Depression

Finally, there is still one more reason for excluding higher prices caused by less supply from the category of inflation. And that is that if they are described as inflation, it implies the absurdity that more supply—more wealth—is the cause of depressions and poverty. Because if higher prices due to less supply are inflation, then it follows that lower prices due to more supply are deflation. But deflation is virtually synonymous with a depression, which is a state of poverty. Thus, if we say that higher prices due to less supply are inflation, we imply that more supply causes deflation, depression, poverty. This is a self-contradiction, no less absurd than such *1984* notions as "war is peace" and "freedom is

slavery," because more supply means more goods, which, of course, means greater prosperity.[12] Thus, in addition to all of the other reasons I have given, we should avoid describing rising prices caused by falling supply as inflation, in order to avoid being guilty of this contradiction.

The truth is that both inflation and deflation are concepts that do not pertain to changes in the price level per se, but, at most, only to changes in the price level that originate *on the side of money and demand.*[13]

We have now eliminated reductions in supply as a cause of "inflation." We have eliminated them, first of all, as a significant factor in raising prices (points i–iii) and have shown that to an important extent reductions in supply are themselves the result of rapid increases in aggregate demand (point iv). And, to the extent we have not totally eliminated reductions in supply as a factor in raising prices, we have shown that such price increases as they do cause cannot properly be described as inflation. They cannot, because they contradict important symptoms of inflation (points v and vi), and because to describe them as inflation implies the absurdity that wealth is the cause of poverty (point vii).

This means that we have narrowed the problem of inflation down exclusively to one of rising aggregate demand, which our formula for the general consumer price level shows to be the only conceivable remaining explanation. Thus, we are now in a position to show why all of the explanations of an inflationary rise in prices other than the quantity theory of money are either totally false or must be interpreted as giving further confirmation of the quantity theory of money.

2. Refutation of the "Cost-Push" Doctrine in General

The supporters of the cost-push doctrines recognize the validity of the formula for the general consumer price level. However, they perceive the role of rising demand in a different way than do the supporters of the quantity theory of money. While the supporters of the quantity theory of money see more demand as the cause of higher prices, the supporters of the cost-push doctrines see it as the cause of greater production and supply. In their view, more demand causes correspondingly more production and supply and therefore does not raise prices. The reason the supporters of the cost-push doctrines believe this is because they see the existence of unemployed labor and idle plant capacity, and they assume that so long as unemployment and idle capacity exist, the effect of more demand is simply to enable more people to be employed and therefore for production to be increased.

The supporters of the cost-push doctrines are willing to concede that more demand is potentially capable of raising prices. But that, they say, could happen *only* in the context of an economy operating at full employment and in which, therefore, supply could not be further increased in response to more demand. At that point, they are willing to admit, more demand would not be accompanied by more supply and would thus drive up prices. The expression they use to describe this situation of more demand raising prices at the point of full employment is, of course, "demand-pull inflation." At the point of full employment, they say, more demand "pulls up" prices. This so-called demand-pull inflation is the only potential influence of more demand on prices that they recognize. To them, more demand as a cause of inflation means "demand-pull inflation."[14]

Observe how the supporters of the cost-push doctrines think. They have decided that more demand is capable of raising prices only at the point of full employment. They have decided that short of full employment, the effect of more demand is not higher prices, but more supply. These are the assumptions they bring with them when they observe that since World War II our economic system has not operated at full employment. As a result, they then conclude that they are free to dismiss rising demand as the cause of rising prices in the United States, because—as explained—they have already relegated more demand as a possible cause of rising prices to the arbitrarily limited context of full employment.

It is on this basis that they turn to the various forms of the cost-push doctrine as an explanation of the rising prices experienced since World War II. In their eyes, more demand cannot explain these price increases, because they occurred in the absence of full employment. Thus, some other explanation must be found. The reason rising costs are taken as the explanation is because, in fact, the prices of many goods are determined in the first instance on the basis of their cost of production, as I showed in Chapter 6 of this book.[15]

Of course, I also showed that all prices determined by cost of production are *ultimately determined by supply and demand*, so there is no contradiction involved in my conceding the role of cost of production in determining prices and, simultaneously, arguing that all prices are determined by supply and demand. Cost of production—and this point is relevant now—is always based on prices, including wages, which are the price of labor. For example, the cost of producing a bicycle is based on the wages of the bicycle workers, the price of the steel that goes into the bicycle, and so on. It follows that cost of production can never be an ultimate explanation of prices, but just an intermediary explanation of some prices on the basis of other prices—for example, an explanation of the price of the bicycle on the basis of the prices of the labor and steel and so forth that are used to produce it.[16]

The fact that cost of production is not an ultimate explanation of prices constitutes a major logical deficiency of the cost-push doctrine. Because what the cost-push doctrine is actually claiming is that some prices rise because other prices rise, and it is content to leave matters at that. For example, the supporters of the cost-push doctrine blame inflation on such things as the rise in the price of steel or the rise in wages achieved by various unions. They do not offer any explanation of what makes possible the higher price of steel or the higher wages obtained by the unions.

In fact, as already shown, what the cost-push doctrine boils down to is the claim that certain key prices, and this includes wages, rise arbitrarily, without any explanation other than the greed of those who raise them. The cost-push doctrine, in the last analysis, is a doctrine that tries to blame price increases on some form of arbitrary power. It tells us, in effect, that prices rise simply because some powerful people are making them rise.

Now it is true that in our present economic system, that is heavily overlaid with government regulations and controls—i.e., the so-called mixed economy—arbitrary power does exist. There are labor-union monopolies in a position to force employers to agree to almost any wages they ask. There are also some business monopolies, such as government-franchised electric utilities (though the business monopolies are generally regulated in the prices they can charge).

Nevertheless, even the existence of arbitrary power on the part of sellers cannot explain rising prices. I will explain this more fully in the specific discussions of the wage-push and profit-push doctrines that follow. But this much can be said right now: The basic reason why arbitrary power on the part of sellers is not a sufficient explanation of rising prices is that such higher prices as it might bring about *always cause reductions in the quantity of the good or service that can be sold and, therefore, act as a brake on any further such price increases.* This is closely related to an even more fundamental objection, namely, that *the cost-push doctrines are equivalent to an attempt to blame inflation on falling supply,* which we have already seen is invalid.

In order to prove this equivalence, all that is necessary is to perform a kind of mental experiment in terms of the price-level formula

$$P = \frac{D_C}{S_C}.$$

Our mental experiment consists simply of this: We assume that monopolistic sellers arbitrarily drive up prices, just as the cost-push doctrine claims. But we also assume that while this rise in prices occurs, there is no change in aggregate demand. We make this second assumption because if the rise in aggregate demand is really not a factor in raising prices, as the supporters of the cost-push doctrine tell us, then its absence can make no difference.

Thus, what we have is a rise in prices and a fixed aggregate demand—a fixed amount of spending. In terms of the elements of our formula P is up, while D_C is fixed.

Nothing could be more obvious than the result of this experiment. Namely, S_C must fall in inverse proportion to the rise in P. The higher the monopolistic sellers would drive the price level, the less would be the supply of goods they could sell—in inverse proportion.

Let us appraise the results of this experiment. We see the quantity of goods sold falling to the same extent that the monopolistic sellers force up prices. There is no essential difference between this case and the cases discussed previously in which a fall in supply raised prices—they are mathematically equivalent. A fall in supply is a mathematically indispensable condition for the rise in prices, whenever demand remains fixed. Thus, it is absolutely essential for the monopolistic sellers to reduce the supply of goods or services that are sold, if they are to drive up prices. If they did not do this, they simply could not raise prices. It is precisely because the monopolistic sellers must hold down supply to raise prices, that they want to prohibit other people from selling and to be monopolists in the first place. For example, the reason a monopoly labor union wants to control apprenticeship programs and make it as difficult as possible for people to enter an occupation is that that is a way of restricting supply and thereby making it possible for the union to drive up wages. In the face of a fixed demand, the mere fact of establishing higher wages or prices for the labor or goods that are sold serves to reduce the supply that is sold in inverse proportion. The unions and the other monopolists want to restrict as far as possible the supply that is or potentially could be offered by competitors, in order to minimize the reduction in the quantity that they themselves can sell.

The fact that the various cost-push doctrines are the same as an attempt to blame inflation on falling supply totally invalidates them. Because it means that all of the objections raised previously against falling supply as a cause of rising prices apply with equal force against cost-push as a cause of rising prices.

It is now possible to deal with each of the specific versions of the cost-push doctrine, in the light of the knowledge of what the doctrine in general implies about supply.

3. Critique of the "Wage-Push" Variant

The wage-push argument is the most plausible version of the cost-push doctrine, because what it really refers to are the activities of legally privileged, government-pro-

tected labor unions. Such labor unions possess monopoly powers in that employers are compelled by law to deal with them and either to meet their wage demands or do without labor; in addition, these unions are often in a position to resort to direct intimidation and violence to back up their demands, without fear of legal reprisal. Because of these monopoly powers, the unions are able to set wages as high as they like. Even nonunion employers must adopt the pay scales set by the unions, lest their workers decide to unionize, which they can easily do. In this way, the unions are able to drive up wage rates, costs of production, and thus prices, throughout the entire economic system.

Nevertheless, as destructive as this power of the present-day unions is and as serious as its consequences are, if this were the only factor at work—if it were not joined by an expanding quantity of money and a rising aggregate demand—it would not be possible for the unions to exert any long-run or significant influence in making prices rise. In fact, on a long-run basis, prices would probably fall in an economy such as ours, despite the activities of the unions. The fact is that it is only an expanding quantity of money and a rising aggregate demand that permit so-called "wage push," or any other form of "cost push," to go on "pushing" very far.

The reasons are as follows. If demand—spending—did not rise, if it stayed the same, any increase in the general price level brought about by "wage push" would be accompanied by a corresponding decline in the supply of goods that could be sold, as we just saw in our mental experiment concerning the effects of cost push. This decline in the quantity of goods that could be sold at higher prices would cause a corresponding reduction in the quantity of labor that employers could profitably employ. Because if the quantity of goods employers can sell falls, they obviously require less labor for production. The same conclusion follows even more directly from the effects of higher wage rates in the face of a limited aggregate demand for labor, i.e., limited total payrolls in the economy. Because the total funds available for meeting payrolls are limited, employers simply do not have the financial means of employing as many workers at higher wage rates as they do at lower wage rates.

Now this mounting reduction in the volume of employment offered every time wages and prices were increased would place a limit on the extent to which the unions would drive up wages and prices. *So-called wage-push inflation would burn itself out in mounting unemployment.* Every time a union sought a wage increase, it would have to count the number of its members it was prepared to see added to the ranks of the unemployed. The point would soon be reached where the sheer volume of their own unemployed members would stop further wage demands even on the part of the worst monopoly labor unions.

In order to appreciate just how limited would be the power of monopoly unions to raise prices without the aid of a rising aggregate demand, let us perform another mental experiment. Let us imagine that we have full employment and that aggregate demand is fixed. Now let us trace the consequences of the unions driving up the wage and price level by varying amounts. Each time they raise wages and prices, the quantity of goods that can be sold falls, the quantity of labor required in production falls, and the unemployment rate grows. The question we want to ask is: If the unions were willing to drive the unemployment rate to the height that prevailed in the worst years of the 1929 Depression before stopping in their wage demands, how much could they raise prices?

The unemployment rate in 1932 and 1933 was about 25 percent of the labor force. If it took that kind of staggering unemployment rate to stop the further demands of the unions, it would be implied that the maximum cumulative limit by which the unions could raise wages and prices would be one-third, and no more. That degree of wage and price increase would produce a 25 percent unemployment rate.

These conclusions follow mathematically, on the basis of the price-level formula. A 25 percent unemployment rate leaves a 75 percent, positive employment rate, i.e., the number of workers employed is reduced to three-fourths of the initial number. In these conditions, production and supply can be presumed also to fall to three-fourths of their initial level. (If the operation of the law of diminishing returns is allowed for, production and supply would not fall this much: the loss of the last one-fourth of the labor employed would reduce production by less than one-fourth.) The price-level formula, of course, shows that if supply is three-fourths, while demand is fixed, prices must be four-thirds:

$$\frac{4}{3}P = \frac{D_C}{\frac{3}{4}S_C}.$$

Prices of four-thirds mean a rise in prices of one-third. Hence, the movement from a zero unemployment rate to a 25 percent unemployment rate would be accompanied by a rise in the price level on the order of one-third. Or, conversely, starting from full employment, driving up wages and prices by one-third would produce an unemployment rate of 25 percent.

This rise in prices and unemployment might take place all at once, or it might occur gradually over many years, depending on how rapidly or slowly the unions forced up wage rates. But whether it occurred rapidly or slowly, one-third or some amount not much greater than a third, and probably quite a bit less, would be the maximum cumulative limit of a rise in prices ascribable to monopoly labor unions. Because the fact is that the ability of the monopoly unions to raise wages and prices is severely limited by the effect of such wage and price increases on the unemployment rate, and it can be safely assumed that even the monopoly unions would be deterred from further wage demands in the face of an unemployment rate at the level of a catastrophic depression. Indeed, the experience of the early 1980s showed that the unions were willing sharply to reduce their wage demands in the face of an unemployment of 10 or 11 percent and even to accept wage reductions in a number of cases.

Moreover, once the unions decided to stop their demands, and the unemployment rate stabilized, at however high a level, prices would probably actually *fall*.

The fall in prices would occur as the result of technological progress and capital accumulation, or any other factor that increased the productivity of labor—that is, which enabled a unit of labor, on average, to produce more. Increases in the productivity of labor, of course, mean that larger supplies of goods are produced by the same number of workers and that each unit of goods has a lower cost of production, because it takes less labor to produce it. A rise in the productivity of labor acts to reduce prices, because it means both larger supplies and lower unit costs. It is an offset to "wage-push."

To illustrate this point, let us assume that after the unions had raised the wage and price level by the limit of a third, the productivity of labor began to increase, as the result of the application to production of a series of inventions. Assume that over a period of years the cumulative effect of these inventions was to double the productivity of labor. In that case, the three-fourths of the labor force that was employed would produce twice as much as it previously did. Prices, therefore, would fall by half in comparison with the point to which the unions had raised them. And that would mean that they would actually be lower than they were before the unions began their activities. They would be half of four-thirds, i.e., only two-thirds of their initial height. In terms of our formula,

$$\frac{1}{2} \times \frac{4}{3}P = \frac{D_C}{2 \times \frac{3}{4}S_C}.$$

To the extent that increases in the productivity of labor occurred at the *same time* that the unions were driving up wage rates and creating unemployment, their effect would be to offset the rise in costs and decline in production attributable to the unions. It might very well be the case, therefore, that the unions alone would not be able to raise the price level even temporarily.

On the basis of these considerations, we must conclude that it would simply be impossible for monopoly labor unions, unaided by increases in the quantity of money and rising aggregate demand, to make any sustained significant contribution toward raising the general price level. Indeed, in the absence of an expanding money supply and rising aggregate demand, the long-run effect of the unions on the price level, and probably the short-run effect too, would most likely be not to raise it in any absolute sense, but merely to reduce the rate at which it had fallen.

Unaided monopoly unionism, or "wage push," is not the cause of rising prices but of *mass unemployment*. As I have shown, the rise in prices it might bring about would be essentially nonrepeatable, would probably be temporary at most, could never be of really major significance as price increases go, and could easily be far more than offset by increases in the productivity of labor, with the result that prices actually fell, though by less than they otherwise would have. But the unemployment monopoly unionism creates remains, and is of major significance.

The problem of unemployment leads us to the real connection between monopoly unionism and rising prices. Because what the government does when confronted with the prospect of rising unemployment *is to inject a larger quantity of money into the economic system*. The additional demand that results permits the unions to drive up wages and prices without causing corresponding additional unemployment.

The fact that the quantity of money and demand are made to increase more or less in pace with the wage demands of the unions is the only thing which permits the phenomenon of "wage push" to continue in existence, because it removes the brake that would otherwise be supplied by a mounting rate of unemployment. In other words, it is the government's expansion of the money supply that is the only thing that allows the unions to go on "pushing" wage rates and prices up very far. To put it in still a different way, no more "wage-push inflation" exists than the government is willing to provide an expanding quantity of money to finance.

The government and the economists who support it chronically evade the very necessary, critical role of the expansion of the money supply. As they describe matters, the unions simply drive up wages and prices without limit, and the government has nothing whatever to do with the mater. Its role is merely to urge the unions to exercise "restraint."

The fact is that the government's expansion of the money supply and thus of aggregate demand positively encourages the wage demands of the unions, and does so even in the midst of mass unemployment. As we have seen, it calls union wage demands into being when they would otherwise not have existed—by removing the brake on wage demands constituted by the prospect of adding further to the already existing level of unemployment; by enlarging nominal profits, which constitutes a veritable red flag to the unions and their demands for wage increases; and by causing prices of goods available only in limited quantity to rise, which, together with rising prices caused by the unions' previous wage demands, leads the unions to demand wage increases to keep pace with price increases.[17] And then, of course, the government's expansion of the money supply and aggregate demand enables the unions to go on endlessly repeating the imposition of their demands, by removing the consequence of mounting unemployment.

Thus, the government's expansion of the money supply must be regarded as the cause of the far greater part of "wage push"—as the cause of *all* of wage push insofar as the phenomenon is continuing and can be associated with a problem of inflation. To whatever extent there is an element of truth in the existence of "wage push," the phenomenon must be regarded as an extension of the influence of the quantity of money, whose increase operates not merely through "demand pull," but no less by means of making possible and, indeed, positively instigating wage push. In effect, the intellectual zone of explanation of rising prices previously regarded as belonging to the wage-push doctrine should henceforth be regarded as having been annexed by the quantity theory of money.

4. Critique of the "Profit-Push" Variant

According to the "profit-push" doctrine, prices rise primarily not because wages are rising but in order to increase the profits of "powerful monopolists" and "greedy big businessmen." It is the push for ever higher profits, say the supporters of this doctrine, that initiates the so-called wage-price spiral, because the unions, it is alleged, demand wage increases only to keep pace with price increases and the cost of living.

Needless to say, the profit-push doctrine is enormously popular with the monopoly labor unions and their numerous supporters. All things considered, it is probably by far the most popular explanation of inflation, because, as we have seen, it is directly implied by the definition of inflation as rising prices.

Now, in fact, the profit-push doctrine is subject to all the essential criticisms made of the wage-push doctrine, plus some others. It ignores the fact that in the absence of rising demand, rising prices reduce sales volume—

that is, they reduce the quantity of goods that can be sold. The prospective loss of sales volume makes even a government-protected monopolist limit his price at some point.

Indeed, let us consider precisely the case of a government-protected monopolist, because that case provides the most plausible context for the profit-push doctrine. Yet it is very easy to show that the doctrine cannot apply even there. And if it cannot apply there, it obviously cannot apply to any case in which the freedom of competition exists.

Thus, let us imagine a government-franchised electric utility that has been given the exclusive legal privilege of selling electricity in a given geographical area. Such a utility is protected from competition by law. Let us imagine further that the rates charged by this utility are not subject to any form of government regulation—it can legally charge any rate it likes. Nevertheless, even such a utility would still be limited in what it could charge by the forces of the market. It would not want to charge rates so high as to discourage large numbers of business firms from locating or remaining in its area. It would not want to charge rates so high as to discourage large numbers of home-owners from using electric heat or buying electrical appliances. Clearly, there would be a limit to what such a utility would charge, given the conditions of demand confronting it.

Now the prices charged by this uncontrolled monopoly utility might be considerably higher than the prices that would be charged under the freedom of competition or under government rate control. But what it is crucial to realize is that there is absolutely no reason why the utility would want to go on *raising* its price year after year. Such a monopoly could find it profitable to charge a very *high* price perhaps, but not a steadily *rising* price. Its interest would lie in picking the price that maximized its profits, and then *sticking to that price*. Given the same conditions of demand confronting it in the present as in the past, the monopoly would not raise its price in any given year for the same reason that it did not already charge that price in the year before—namely, it would lose too much business by doing so.

In order for the monopoly to find it to its interest to raise its price every year, the conditions of demand confronting it must be changing. People must have a growing ability to pay for its products. But how do people obtain that ability? One way might be if the prices of other things they bought were falling. This would release funds they previously required for other purposes. But observe. In this case, the rise in utility rates presupposes a fall in other prices and is strictly limited by the extent of their fall. This case, therefore, cannot be a case of a rise in the *general* price level. In this case, therefore, the problem of inflation does not even come up, but just a rise in some prices accompanied by a fall in other prices.

Another way people might be able to afford to spend more for electricity would be if they simply increased their relative valuation of electricity in comparison with goods they were previously buying. They might just decide, in other words, that they wanted to spend more for electricity and less for other things. But consider. This case means that the rise in demand for electricity is accompanied by an equivalent drop in the demand for other things. The effect of the drop in demand for other things is either to reduce the prices of other things or the supply of other things that is sold. In either event, the problem of inflation again does not come up—because we either have no rise in the general price level or one that can only be associated with a decrease in supply.

In order for the utility's rate increase to be connected with a problem of *inflation*, its customers must be in a position to enlarge their spending for electricity *without* having to reduce their spending for other things. But this means they must be in a position to make a larger *aggregate demand*. Consequently, the only possible explanation of how even protected legal monopolists could raise their prices in a way that is relevant to the problem of inflation is that of a growing aggregate demand. And this, of course, in turn depends on an increasing quantity of money.

It must be stressed that with the exception of the cases in which the government violates the freedom of competition, it is a total reversal of things to regard the quest for higher profits as a cause of higher prices. As we have seen, where the legal freedom of competition exists—that is, where the government does not stand in the way of men competing—the quest for higher profits is always the cause of more supply and *lower* prices. This is because, as I demonstrated in Chapter 6, under the freedom of competition firms can earn higher profits only by introducing new and improved products, by finding ways to cut the costs of production, and by keeping the relative production of the various goods properly adjusted to the changing needs and wants of the consumers. As I showed, all of this represents an expansion in production and, therefore, a tendency toward a lower price level. It was nothing but the quest for higher profits that developed all of our industries and built our entire economic system over the last two hundred years. The effect of this has certainly been to make prices vastly lower than they would otherwise have been, because it has radically increased supply. Thus, the profit motive is, in fact, the source of lower prices, not higher prices. This conclusion is further strengthened if we look at what is done with most large profits after they are earned. Most such profits are saved and invested. This, in turn, means more factories, more machines, more stocks of materials. And that means a greater ability to produce and, therefore, a larger supply of goods offered for sale and, consequently, again a tendency toward lower prices, not higher prices.

As I have already shown, the fall in prices that the profit motive has actually achieved is obscured by the fact that prices are expressed in terms of paper money, whose own value falls more rapidly than the profit motive can reduce the prices of goods. This is what is responsible for the rise in prices expressed in terms of paper money.[18] The situation is comparable to selecting a melting ice cube as a unit of volume and then observing that all measurements of volume persistently increase.

What complicates matters and makes the profit-push doctrine appear plausible to many people is that there is a definite *association* between inflation and a high rate of profit. However, it is not, as most people seem to believe, a rising rate of profit that raises the price level, but an expanding quantity of money and growing aggregate demand that increases both the price level and the rate of profit. As I showed in Chapter 16, rising aggregate demand raises the nominal rate of profit. Insofar as the rise in aggregate demand outstrips the rise in production and supply, the rise in the nominal rate of profit is accompanied by a rise in prices. It cannot be stressed too strongly that the rate of profit that is increased is not a genuine rate of *gain*, but merely the rate of profit *as expressed in a depreciating paper money*—that is, it is merely the nominal rate of profit that is raised, not the real rate of profit. The real rate of profit, of course, is the rate that is found after deducting from profits an allowance to cover the loss in the purchasing power of money. Indeed, in a period of inflation the real rate of profit typically *falls*.

We have already seen an excellent illustration of this fact in our discussion of the widespread ignorance and evasions that support price controls, namely, in the case of the hypothetical merchant who buys his goods at the beginning of the year and sells them at the end. We saw how inflation serves to raise the nominal rate of profit of this merchant while simultaneously reducing his after-tax real rate of profit.[19] As I will show later in this chapter, exactly the same situation applies in the case of depreciable assets, such as buildings and machinery.[20] Nevertheless, despite the decline in real profits it entails, despite the fact that it is an effect, not a cause of inflation, many people, particularly in politics and in the news media, never tire of blaming rising prices on the rise in the nominal rate of profit and implicitly or explicitly demand that government controls be imposed to limit profits.

5. Critique of the "Crisis-Push" Variant

The "crisis-push" doctrine is the attempt to blame rising prices on some sudden event, such as the Russian wheat deal in 1972, the Arab oil embargo in 1973, or the Iranian revolution in 1979, that reduces the supply and increases the price of some important good or group of goods. The doctrine rests on two basic errors. The first is the assumption that because a crisis can explain a large increase in the price of a particular good, it can explain a correspondingly large increase in the general price level.

A crisis can explain a dramatic increase in the price of the particular good in whose supply it takes place, if the good is a necessity. This is undisputed. For example, a few percent reduction in the supply of wheat or oil can cause a dramatic increase in the price of wheat or oil, as the Russian wheat deal, the Arab embargo/cartel, and the Iranian revolution all clearly showed. The inference drawn from this fact by the supporters of the crisis-push doctrine, however, was that these supply reductions could somehow also explain the less dramatic but nevertheless still very substantial rise in the general consumer price level that was taking place at the same time. That inference was an error.

It was an error because not only does a rise in the price of a necessity not explain a rise in the price of other items, but, as we have seen, it actually tends to make the prices of a whole host of other items *fall*. It has this effect because what makes it possible for people to pay the disproportionately higher price of the necessity undergoing the supply crisis is that they restrict their expenditure for other items. The prices of these other items, therefore, tend to drop. The result is that the overall rise in the general price level is relatively slight—because the dramatic rise in the price of the necessity suffering the supply crisis is largely offset in the average of prices by a mass of other prices that not only do not rise, but many of which actually fall. And because of the widespread declines in prices that would occur, even such rise in the general price level as a supply crisis could achieve would not qualify for description as a case of inflation, for the reasons already explained.[21]

This reasoning applies not only to the case in which the good undergoing the supply crisis is a consumers' good but also to the case in which the good undergoing the supply crisis is a capital good that itself enters into the production of a large number of other goods as a raw material. In the latter case, the rise in the good's price does not serve equivalently to raise the cost of production and prices of its various products, as many people appear to believe. On the contrary, the rise in its price places pressure on the prices of other, complementary factors of production to fall. A reduction in the supply of oil, for example, reduces the utility of such materials as iron, copper, rubber, and so on, and can even make them practically useless. It thus tends to reduce the prices of these raw materials. It also tends to reduce the wage rates of the workers required in the various processes of production that depend on oil. The result is that costs of production do not rise to the same extent as the price of oil, and where such other factors of production whose price has fallen enter into the production of products to a relatively greater extent than oil, costs of production actually tend to be reduced, not increased.

The second error of the crisis-push doctrine is that it confuses what is at most the cause of a transitory, delimited rise in the general price level with the cause of a permanent, repeated, and, indeed, accelerating rise in the general price level. By this, I mean that a crisis is capable of raising the general price level only in the period in which it reduces aggregate supply and only to the extent that it reduces aggregate supply. Thereafter, its ability to raise prices any further is exhausted. Furthermore, almost all supply-crises are subsequently *solved*. At that point, the effect of the restoration of supply should be to reduce the general price level to its former, precrisis level.

For example, the giveaway of a large part of our wheat to the Russians in 1972 could explain some rise in our price level in 1972 and 1973—a rise corresponding to the fall in aggregate supply that was constituted by the fall in the supply of wheat and wheat products. But in 1973 there was no repetition of the wheat deal. Therefore, insofar as it depended on the supply of wheat, by 1974 aggregate supply was restored to its precrisis level. And insofar as the supply of wheat was a factor determining the general price level, the general price level also should have been restored to its former, precrisis level.

It follows that if we want to explain why prices in 1974 were higher than in 1972, we cannot use such a thing as the crisis in the supply of wheat. The principle here is that all crises that end up being solved—and this includes the great majority of them—can be causes only of *temporary* increases in the price level.

To explain a *permanent* rise in the general price level on the basis of supply crises, one must assume that as one crisis is solved, another, of equivalent magnitude, erupts. But if one makes this assumption, one should realize that one cannot then use supply crises to explain a price level that *rises from year to year*. The effect of an annual repetition of more or less equal-sized crises that are later solved cannot be to raise the price level year after year, because the effect of each new crisis on the price level is canceled by the solution of an old crisis. Consequently, the most that could be explained would be a price level

that was higher than it would be in the absence of crises, but not a *rising* price level.

In order to explain a rising price level on the basis of supply crises, one would have to find not only replacement crises for the ones that have been solved, but additional crises as well. And in the next year, one would have to find replacements for this larger number of crises, along with still more additional crises; and this would have to go on from year to year at a compound rate. In order to explain not merely a rising price level, but one that rises with acceleration, one would have to find not only supply crises growing at a compound rate, but growing at an accelerating compound rate. This, of course, would imply the rapid disappearance of material civilization.

In the years to come, because of growing irrationality on the part of the government, it is possible that we will have growing supply crises. But the most that these crises could be responsible for in the way of a rising price level would be on the order of one or two percent a year. Nevertheless, if they come to pass, prices will almost certainly rise far more rapidly—perhaps 50 or 100 percent a year, or more. That is because a major form in which the growing irrationality of the government will manifest itself, assuming it actually does occur, will undoubtedly be an accelerating expansion of the money supply.

The truth is that operating alongside the largely self-canceling phenomenon of the eruption of new crises and the solution of old crises is the expansion in the quantity of money and rise in aggregate demand. It is this which makes the price level rise far more rapidly than could ever be accounted for by an excess of new crises over the solution of old ones.

The root of both errors of the crisis-push doctrine is a failure to think on the conceptual level—a failure to go beyond what is immediately, almost perceptually evident. We have just seen that the second error rests on the failure to extend one's field of observation back to the past and forward to the future—to see that the solution of yesterday's crises should now be acting to reduce the price level—either actually to reduce it, or at least to nullify the ability of today's crises to raise it; and that later on exactly the same point will apply to the solution of today's crises; and thus that the real cause of steadily rising prices must be something other than the transitory and self-canceling element of crises.

The first error is very similar. It consists of the failure to extend one's field of observation sideways, so to speak, to the goods whose supply is not in a state of crisis. This underlies the failure to see that supply crises act to reduce the demand for and the prices of all these other goods, and therefore could simply never account for a very dramatic rise in the *general* price level, let alone for the phenomenon of almost universally rising prices, which people have in mind when they complain about "inflation."

6. Critique of the Wage-Price-Spiral Variant

Little can be said in criticism of the wage-price spiral doctrine that has not already been said in criticism of the other variants of the cost-push doctrine. In the absence of an increase in the quantity of money and rising aggregate demand, any "wage-price spiral" that somehow came into existence would quickly burn itself out of existence in mounting unemployment and unsold stocks of goods. Even in cases in which labor unions hold the contractual right to receive wage increases on the basis of cost-of-living increases, they abandon this right when insistence upon it would add still more of their members to the ranks of an already large number of unemployed members. The experience of the early 1980s provides dramatic confirmation of the truth of these propositions.

7. Critique of the "Velocity" Doctrine

While the cost-push doctrines seek to deny the role of rising aggregate demand as the cause of rising prices, other doctrines opposed to the quantity theory of money concede the fact that more demand is responsible for rising prices. What they deny is that an expanding quantity of money is the cause of rising demand. They seek to blame something else for the growth in demand—something that will not leave a trail that runs back to government interference in the economic system.

The most important doctrine in this group is the velocity doctrine, which subsumes all of the other doctrines in the group. The velocity doctrine is the claim that the rise in aggregate demand that is admittedly responsible for the rise in prices is the result, not of an increase in the quantity of money, but of an increase in the velocity of circulation of money. The velocity doctrine has been widely taught at colleges and universities in a deliberate attempt to undercut the quantity theory of money.

To dispose of the velocity doctrine, nothing more is required than to recall the discussion of the demand for money in Chapter 12. There it was established that in the absence of increases in the quantity of money, any rise in velocity resulting from such factors as growing security of property and the development of financial markets and financial institutions would be the accompaniment of a process that increases both the complexity of production, in terms of the number of distinct stages requiring purchases and sales, and the physical ability to produce.[22] Both of these factors militate against any loss

in the purchasing power of the monetary unit. The first, it should be realized, militates against a rise in the aggregate demand for *consumers' goods* taking place as the result of the fall in demand for money, and thus against a rise in the so-called income velocity of money. It implies that the rise in spending takes place primarily or entirely in the purchase of labor services, capital goods, and securities, and thus that the rise in velocity occurs primarily or entirely in broader measures of velocity, above all, in so-called transactions velocity, which is the ratio of spending of all kinds to the quantity of money.

What causes an increase in velocity capable of substantially contributing to an increase in the demand for consumers' goods and to a rise in prices is precisely *the increase in the quantity of money*. As shown, the more rapidly the quantity of money increases, the less tends to be the demand for money for holding and thus the higher tends to be the velocity of circulation of money. (The reasons, it should be recalled, are four: First, the effect of an expanding quantity of money on the prospect for prices rising and thus being able to gain by buying sooner rather than later. Second, the effect on the prospect for being able to dispose of inventories and other assets easily and profitably. Third, the effect on the prospect for being able to borrow easily and profitably. Finally, the effect of an expanding quantity of money on nominal interest rates, which is to encourage the lending out of short-term funds that it otherwise would not have been worthwhile to lend out.[23]) To not only end the rise in velocity, but to bring it crashing down, nothing more is required than to cut back on the rate of increase in the quantity of money on which the rise in velocity rests. To the extent that that is done, all of the factors artificially reducing the demand for money for holding and thereby elevating velocity are removed, with the result that the demand for money for holding is restored and velocity falls correspondingly.

Experience of the last decade provides ready confirmation of this conclusion no less than it does of the ease with which a reduction in the rate of increase in the quantity of money can put an end to "wage push" and all other varieties of "cost push." Reduction in the rate of increase in the quantity of money both in the early 1980s and then again in 1989 and most of 1990, following years of more rapid rates of increase in the quantity of money, was on the point of so increasing the demand for money for holding and so reducing velocity, that the result both times was a major recession marked by a close approach to the precipice of a major depression. In both cases a plunge in velocity and the onset of a major depression were avoided only by the resumption of a substantially more rapid rate of increase in the quantity of money.

Thus, just as in the case of the wage-push doctrine,

and all the other variants of the cost-push doctrine, the intellectual zone of explanation previously claimed by the velocity doctrine should henceforth be regarded as annexed by the quantity theory of money. For it is the growth in the quantity of money that explains the inflationary rise in the velocity of circulation of money.

It is necessary to anticipate and lay to rest a speculation that could arise concerning the possibility of some form of "cost push" causing an increase in velocity. To understand why cost push cannot have any significant effect on velocity, we need only imagine an arbitrary rise in prices achieved by cost push—say, a 10 percent increase in prices. The reason velocity could not rise is because in order to pay these higher prices, individuals and business firms would need to increase their cash holdings. (For proof, the reader should consider the effect on his need to hold cash if his rent, food bill, and so on were increased by an average of 10 percent. In such a case he would have to hold a correspondingly larger checking balance and carry correspondingly more currency.)

Indeed, the additional need to hold cash may appear to imply that velocity would actually *fall* as the result of a rise in prices caused by cost push. However, this too would be an error. What would actually happen is that some individuals would end up holding more money to make their purchases and pay their bills at higher prices, while other individuals, who would be unemployed, would end up holding less money, in accordance with their loss of income and ability to purchase. Business firms on the average would also end up not needing to hold any more money than previously; they would need to hold more money per unit of the things they bought, in order to pay the higher prices of those things, but, at the same time, they would, on the average, buy fewer units. Thus their need to hold cash in the aggregate would be unchanged.

8. Critique of the "Inflation-Psychology" Doctrine

A leading variant of the velocity doctrine is the "inflation-psychology" doctrine. As used by its supporters, the term "inflation psychology" is supposed to refer to an uncaused primary. That is, people allegedly have an inflation psychology, and that is supposed to be the ultimate cause of inflation. *Why* people have an inflation psychology is a question that is not raised, let alone answered. They simply have it, and because they have it, they spend more rapidly.

Of course, there is such a thing as inflation psychology, but it is not a primary. It is based on the *fact* of inflation. It comes into existence only after many years

of inflation. Properly understood, what the term "inflation psychology" really refers to is the various ways in which a rapidly expanding quantity of money reduces the desire of people to hold money. Properly used, the term embraces the four connections we have traced between an expanding quantity of money and a rising velocity of circulation of money.

Inflation psychology actually refers to more than these connections between an expanding quantity of money and a rising velocity of money. It refers to more, because these connections have an effect on prices only by way of raising aggregate demand. Inflation psychology also has an influence on prices from the side of supply, because it influences the expectations of sellers. For example, if businessmen come to anticipate that in the years ahead inflation will raise the replacement costs of their plant and equipment, they may begin to raise prices today, in order to be in a position to accumulate sufficient replacement funds. Similarly, workers may demand wage increases in advance, in order to cover the rise in prices they expect to occur over the life of their employment contracts. Landlords may demand rent increases to cover the rise in prices and costs they expect to occur over the life of their rental contracts. And lenders may demand interest rates high enough to cover the increase in prices they expect to occur over the life of their loan contracts. These forces cause a rise in prices beyond the levels appropriate to the current size of demand—they make the rise in prices outrun the rise in demand by gearing this year's prices, in effect, to the expected demand of next year and beyond. These price increases operate as a kind of "cost push," but, of course, one that is entirely induced by the expansion in the quantity of money and rise in aggregate demand; and they have the same limits as any other price increases coming in the form of cost push—namely, the limits imposed by reductions in the quantity of goods that can be sold and by mounting unemployment.

Because of the widespread belief that inflation is a means of preventing and combatting unemployment and achieving full employment, it cannot be stressed too strongly that when it reaches the stage of inducing sellers to raise prices in advance of the current rise in aggregate demand, its effect is actually to *cause unemployment*. Because insofar as the rise in wages and prices outstrips the rise in demand, the supply of goods that can be sold and the quantity of labor that can be employed must fall.

Now sometimes, when the government makes an effort to cut back on inflation, and really does reduce the rate at which it expands the money supply for a while, some observers, who are familiar with the quantity theory of money, are surprised to see that prices continue to rise at a substantial rate. And they take this fact as evidence against the quantity theory, claiming that it shows that inflation psychology exists and is leading a life of its own, as it were.

The error in this reasoning is not hard to find. So long as our money is a paper money, that the government can inflate as much as it likes, there is no reason for people to believe that the government will not soon resume a more rapid rate of inflation—especially in view of the fact that the whole philosophy of the mixed economy drives it to do so. In order to convince people that it is serious in its determination to end inflation, the government must restrict its increase in the quantity of money for a protracted period. In the meanwhile, however, because people have had no reason to believe that the government will continue to limit itself, they will probably have placed themselves in even more overextended positions, in which they are operating with even lower money balances, have further increased their borrowings, and are asking still higher wages and prices—all in the expectation that inflation will come to their rescue and provide justification for their action. In this context, stopping the inflation or significantly restricting it must precipitate a crisis. And then the government must either allow the crisis to occur or, to avoid it, give in and fulfill people's expectation that inflation will resume.

It would be a serious mistake to describe this situation by saying that the government is forced to resume inflating in response to the inflation psychology of the people. It is the government's ability to inflate, and its repeated use of that ability in the past, that created the inflation psychology and that makes the consequences of finally stopping the inflation so severe.

This type of situation illustrates an inherent flaw of paper money. The fact that paper money can be inflated, and over time is inflated, causes expectations about future inflation. The existence of these expectations then makes it impossible to stop inflating without a crisis, while the threat of the crisis induces the government to resume and accelerate the inflation. Inflation psychology is an inevitable consequence of paper money and is a critical step in its ultimate downfall.

The events of the 1960s and 1970s in the United States provide clear confirmation of this process. Each time the government attempted to slow down the increase in the quantity of money, a crisis began to develop, and it quickly resumed the increase, and at an accelerated rate. The result was a growing expectation of continued and accelerating inflation. The policy adopted by the U.S. government in the early 1980s, which was carried to the point of producing a very major recession—a depression, according to many—represented the first serious interruption in the process of accelerating inflation since

1933. In 1989 and most of 1990, hardly any increase whatever occurred in the quantity of money. The effect of these two sustained reductions in the rate of increase in the quantity of money was a radical reduction in the amount of inflation psychology that existed. Indeed, the reduction in inflation psychology between 1990 and 1992 was so great that it was possible to discern a growing deflationary psychology.

It should be realized that under a gold standard, inflation psychology could not exist to anywhere near the degree to which it exists under a system of fiat money. This is because under a gold standard, it would have little or no *factual* basis. To the extent such a psychology began to develop, it would quickly run up against the fact that the money supply did not keep up with it, because it simply could not. At that point, the consequence would be that inflation psychology would disappear.

This is true even of a fractional-reserve gold standard. During the phase in which banks are in a position to expand the quantity of money more rapidly than the supply of gold, there is a limited inflation and some degree of inflation psychology develops, at least to the extent of people taking for granted the ability easily and profitably to borrow and to liquidate inventories and other assets in the face of a rising demand. But as soon as it becomes necessary for the banks to limit the rate of increase in the quantity of money to the rate of increase in the supply of gold, or less, in order to rebuild their gold reserves, these aspects of inflation psychology disappear. They are wiped out in the face of a tightening of credit and an unexpectedly low demand for goods and services.

A 100-percent-gold-reserve system would be characterized by the lowest possible degree of inflation psychology, that is, typically, by none whatever. Under such a system, the quantity of money could never increase more rapidly than the supply of gold. Under such a system, the only possible source of something akin to inflation psychology would be unduly rapid increases in the supply of gold itself, which can never occur at anything remotely approaching the rates of increase in the quantity of money achievable under a system of fiat money.[24]

9. Critique of the Credit-Card Doctrine

A second variant of the velocity doctrine is the credit-card doctrine. The supporters of the credit-card doctrine view credit cards as making possible a rise in spending without any expansion in the quantity of money. They observe, for example, that people who carry credit cards do not need to carry as much currency as previously, and they conclude on this basis that credit cards contribute to a rise in the velocity of money, by making possible more spending in relation to the same quantity of money.

The first objection to be made to the credit-card doctrine is that much of the reduction it makes possible in the need to hold money is merely apparent, and not real. This is the case insofar as credit cards are actually used in making purchases.

To prove this point, let us consider the case of cards like the American Express card, in which all charges must be paid within a few weeks. The holder of such a card need not carry as much currency in his pocket—that is certainly true. But he must have money to pay his credit-card bill when it comes due. As a result, the money that such an individual is spared from holding in currency, he must hold in his checking account, in order to be able to pay his credit-card bill.

Of course, in some cases, an individual might use his credit card and not immediately set anything aside for the payment of his credit-card bill. For example, he might decide to pay his bill out of his next paycheck, which is not to be received for one or two weeks. Even in these cases, however, it is a mistake to believe that credit cards increase the velocity of circulation. Because while the individual card holder can spend money he does not have, the credit-card company, or the supplier from whom the card holder buys, must be in possession of the necessary funds to pay for his purchases. If the credit-card company must pay the supplier immediately, then what occurs is essentially no different than if the card holder went to the credit-card company, borrowed money and then paid for his purchases with cash. If there is some delay in payment by the credit-card company, then the supplier is placed in the position of having to extend credit. But to be able to do this, he has to obtain additional financing, because while his money revenues temporarily drop, he continues to need just as much money as before to pay his own suppliers and meet his own personal commitments. Thus, he has to borrow correspondingly more; what occurs here is the equivalent of the supplier borrowing money for his customer, which the customer then spends in the supplier's shop. In either case, it is not that the credit-card holder's spending takes place without the existence of money, but that, in effect, he borrows and spends the money of a lender. Total spending in relation to the quantity of money is unchanged in these cases.

Indeed, on the basis of this discussion, we must conclude that particularly in the case of credit cards in which all the charges come due within a short period, it is probably true that the overall need to hold money is *increased* rather than decreased. This is because not only must money still be held to pay for the credit-card holder's purchases but, in addition, as we have seen, the credit-card holder needs to hold money to pay his credit-card bill when it comes due. Thus, there are now *two* transactions and a need for *two* cash holdings, whereas before there was only one transaction and a need for only one cash holding. Before the existence of credit cards, an individual who went to a restaurant, say, had to carry currency to pay his restaurant bill. Now, equivalent money must be held either by the credit-card company or by the restaurant, to finance his purchase. In addition, the credit-card holder must hold money to pay his credit-card bill when it comes due. Thus, two cash holdings are required in place of one, to effect the same purchase of goods and services. The necessary tendency of such a state of affairs is to reduce the aggregate demand for consumers' goods in relation to the quantity of money. For the situation is one of greater complexity of the productive process, with more stages of buying and selling being present and thus requiring diversion of funds from expenditures for consumers' goods to expenditures at a different stage of transactions.

Conditions are not significantly different in the case of credit cards that can be paid off gradually over many months, like the Visa card or Mastercard. In practice, of course, many people use these cards in just the same way as the American-Express-type card and pay off their credit-card balances in full each month. But insofar as the balances on these cards are paid off in modest amounts over a period of years, the effect is initially to increase the demand for money for holding by less than in the case of the American-Express-type card and then, in all the succeeding months, to increase it by more. In the first month there is a demand for money to finance the purchase of the merchandise plus a modest demand for money to pay the installment on the credit card, instead of a demand for money to finance the purchase of the merchandise plus an equivalent demand for money to pay off the credit-card balance. But in each succeeding month there is a demand for money to pay an installment on the credit-card debt, plus interest, whereas there is no such demand for money in the case of the American-Express-type card.

The aspect in which credit cards do reduce the demand for money for holding is insofar as they are not actually used but merely provide their holders with the potential for use. To this extent, they represent the possession of guaranteed lines of bank credit. That is, whoever has such a card has the right to borrow up to some agreed-upon sum to be provided by the banks involved, any time he wishes. And to this extent, credit cards can in fact reduce the amount of money that people need to hold to some degree. They do so in cases in which a person was previously holding money on the chance that he might come across something he wanted to buy and was uncertain that he would be able to obtain a loan to buy it. Such a person need not hold that money now. His loan is guaranteed in advance by virtue of his possession of the credit card and the line of credit it conveys.

But now we must ask how it happened that the banks could extend lines of credit to people who previously would have been uncertain of being able to obtain loans for specific purposes. The answer to this question brings us back once again to the quantity theory of money. The banks can extend additional lines of credit because they are in a position to expand the money supply by creating checking deposits that they can lend out. Thus, what we are dealing with in this case is nothing but the influence of an expanding money supply on the availability of credit and the demand for money. We have already seen how the increase in the quantity of money entering the economic system in this way operates to reduce the demand for money. The existence of credit cards based on this foundation means merely that the ability of the banks to expand the money supply enables consumers as well as business enterprises to attempt to reduce their holdings of money, with the same effect on the velocity of money. Thus, to the extent that credit cards do in fact raise velocity, the rise must be considered merely a further symptom of the expanding quantity of money.

The objection might be raised that even without the banks' ability to create money, credit cards would still have come into existence and might still have reduced the need to hold money on the part of the holders of the cards. That is probably true to some extent. But in the absence of the banks' ability to inflate, the extension of additional lines of credit would be strictly limited, and the only way that the banks could extend additional lines of credit at all—whether to consumers holding credit cards or to any other type of borrower—would be as a result of the availability of the necessary *savings*.

These savings could only become available either as the result of the withdrawal of savings from other uses, or as the result of an increase in the overall supply of savings. Either way, if the base of the additional lines of credit is savings, then what is presupposed at the very beginning is a corresponding reduction in spending somewhere else in the economic system. That is, either spending financed by the use of savings will be less somewhere else or, if the overall supply of savings available for use is increased, consumer demand will be less, because the existence of the additional savings is possible only to the degree that people consume less. Lines of credit based on savings, therefore, cannot be presumed to raise the overall volume of spending, because the origin of such lines of credit is a *reduction* in spending somewhere else in the economic system.

10. Critique of the Consumer-Installment-Credit Doctrine

Still another variant of the velocity doctrine is the doctrine of consumer-installment credit. According to this doctrine, prices rise because the granting of consumer-installment credit enables consumers to make an additional demand for goods.

Here, consistent with the principles presented in the preceding section, it is necessary to realize that the granting of credit out of savings represents merely a transfer of spending power from some parties to others. The savers must first reduce their consumption. Only then can the savings exist that are made available to borrowers. Or if the savings already exist and are being used, they can be made available for a new use only to the extent that a previous use is curtailed. There is no increase in overall spending whatever, but merely offsetting changes in the extent of particular types of spending, as the result of the granting of credit out of savings. To state the matter as succinctly as possible: credit granted out of savings is not inflationary. Only credit based on the ability to expand the money supply is inflationary.

The installment-credit doctrine is true only to the extent that the credit is granted out of newly created money. It is false to the extent that the credit is granted out of saved funds. Because to the extent that consumers obtain credit out of saved funds, the savers have first had to restrict their consumption before the consumer-borrowers can expand theirs, or some other set of users of the savings has had to restrict its spending. There is no increase in overall spending here, but just a transfer of spending power from one set of buyers to another.

Consequently, once again, an opposing doctrine turns out to confirm the quantity theory of money. For the only way the installment-credit doctrine could possess an element of truth is on the basis of an expanding quantity of money.

The same principle applies to every form of credit: credit granted out of savings is not inflationary. Only credit granted out of newly created money is inflationary.

This principle also applies to every form of debt. The incurrence of debt in and of itself is not inflationary. Debts incurred through the borrowing of savings are not inflationary. Only debts incurred through the borrowing of newly created money are inflationary. When applied to government budget deficits, this means that deficits financed by borrowing from the public—i.e., through the sale of securities to individuals and business firms—are not inflationary (which, of course, is not to say that they do not have other highly destructive consequences[25]). Only deficits financed by the creation of new and additional money are inflationary.

11. Critique of the Consumer-Greed Doctrine

The claim is sometimes made that inflation is the result of the consumers' "greed." Occasionally, it is the consumers' mere desire for a better life that is named as the cause of inflation, and in those very words.

The supporters of the consumer-greed doctrine appear to have in mind a case in which the consumers simply go out and overbid one another in their desire for more goods. It is possible that the supporters of the doctrine have in mind the scene of an auction in which the bidders scramble for a limited number of items and drive prices to high levels in their enthusiasm.

Such action on the part of consumers could explain how the price of a few items might rise. But it cannot explain how the general price level rises. It cannot, because it does not tell us where the consumers obtain the money to start spending more for everything. If the consumers do not have more money available in toto, then they can bid up the prices of some things only by correspondingly reducing their purchases of other things. But that implies that the prices of these other things tend to fall. No problem of inflation would exist, therefore. Nor is it reasonable to assume that "greed" somehow leads the consumers to reduce their demand for money for holding. Indeed, the only thing that could make such behavior the "greedy" thing to do, rather than continuing to maintain the same demand for money as before, would be if the quantity of money is rapidly increasing, which would provide real incentives for a drop in the demand for money. But this, of course, brings us back once again to the quantity theory of money.

Finally, it should be realized that what the consumer-greed doctrine actually cites as the cause of higher prices is people's desire for a higher standard of living. That is the meaning of their "greed." Not only is this not a cause of higher prices, but, in reality, it is the cause of *lower* prices. Because what people must do to raise their standard of living is *produce more* and *save more*. This is exactly what everyone tries to do who is seriously interested in improving his standard of living. Thus, his "greed" is the source not of more spending out of nowhere, but of harder work, more forethought and provision for the future, and thus more production and supply and therefore lower, not higher, prices.

12. The Meaning of Inflation

The preceding discussions of explanations of rising prices other than the quantity theory of money, have served further to confirm the quantity theory of money.

It has been shown that insofar as the alternative explanations contain any kernel of validity at all, it is only as an extension of the quantity theory of money. The increase in the quantity of money and the consequent rise in aggregate demand is what underlies any ability of labor unions to engage in "wage push," of businessmen to engage in "profit push," of crises to be accompanied by a general and sustained rise in prices, and of the velocity of circulation to rise in circumstances that are accompanied by rising prices. It is what underlies the existence of all so-called wage-price spirals, of "inflation psychology," and of any inflationary consequences that can be associated with the use of credit cards, installment credit, or any other form of credit, or with consumer "greed." Thus, the quantity theory of money rightfully annexes, as it were, the explanatory territory previously claimed by all these opposing theories.

The undue increase in the quantity of money that underlies the rise in prices has, moreover, been shown to be the responsibility of the government. The moneys chosen by the market were, and would be again, gold and silver. These moneys do not increase at a rate sufficient to cause a sustained significant rise in prices. Even what was probably the greatest percentage increase in the supply of these metals in recorded history, which took place in consequence of the Spanish conquest of the New World, was not sufficient to raise prices in Europe by much more than an average of 1 percent per year over the course of the next two centuries. Indeed, for long periods of time, gold and silver are capable of increasing at a lesser rate than the increase in the supply of goods and services in general, and thus, when they serve as money, of being accompanied by falling prices—as was the case in the generation prior to the discovery of the California gold fields in 1848 and in the generation from 1873 to 1896.

It was government interference over a period of more than two centuries that brought about the abandonment of the use of gold and silver as money and thus of the powerful restraint on the increase in the quantity of money that a gold or silver money entails. In the last sixty years or more, the government of the United States, like that of virtually every other country, has had unlimited power to expand the quantity of fiat paper money and has made ample use of that power.[26] Thus, the whole problem of an inflationary rise in prices reduces to an increase in the quantity of money at a rate more rapid than the increase in the supply of gold and silver or, to what is equivalent in view of its role in their abandonment as money, an increase in the quantity of money caused by the government.

All of the knowledge concerning the cause of rising prices presented so far in this chapter and in Chapter 12, can be summarized in a definition of inflation as, precisely, *an increase in the quantity of money more rapid than the increase in the supply of gold and silver*, which is to say, *an increase in the quantity of money caused by the government*.[27]

This is a definition in terms of fundamental causation, and one which explains *all* of the major symptoms of inflation: namely, a sustained significant rise in prices, a rise not only in the general price level but in the whole range of prices, debtors being enriched at the expense of creditors, high nominal profit and interest rates, and a low demand for money for holding, among others.

This definition, moreover, shows how to stop inflation: namely, stop the government from creating or sponsoring the creation of money in excess of gold and silver—viz., force the government to reestablish, and/or allow the market to reestablish, the gold and silver monetary system that the government has destroyed. This will put an end to inflation and all of its symptoms.

In sharpest contrast, the usual definition of inflation that is offered, which is "rising prices," provides no knowledge of causation. As I have shown, it perpetuates ignorance and confusion by making it possible for a wide variety of things to appear as possible causes of inflation, thereby making it impossible to be confident of the explanation in any given case. Furthermore, the definition of inflation as rising prices implies that businessmen are always the parties directly responsible for inflation, since they are the ones who decide such things as whether or not prices posted on store shelves or listed in catalogues are to be increased. And, of course, the definition of inflation as rising prices supports the corollary belief that inflation can be remedied by price-and-wage controls, since, according to it, the absence of price and wage increases that can result from such controls means the absence of inflation.[28]

Ironically, the definition of inflation as rising prices serves actually to promote inflation. It does so in part by implying that price controls are the remedy for inflation. For once price controls are enacted, the government feels free to inflate the money supply all the more rapidly, in the mistaken belief that merely because prices cannot rise, it does not have to worry about inflation—as though because the symptom was gone, the underlying cause of the symptom was also gone. The definition of inflation as rising prices also serves to promote inflation by suggesting government subsidies to keep down prices, which subsidies are likely to be financed by creating still more money. Thus, for example, in believing that it reduces inflation by keeping down the price of bread and milk, say, by means of paying subsidies to cover the losses entailed in their sale at artificially low prices, the government may very well be led to increase the quantity of money more rapidly, in order to obtain the funds with which to pay these subsidies. In this way, the government resorts to more inflation in order to fight a symptom of inflation.[29] Probably the leading instance of this bizarre practice is the pursuit of a so-called easy-money policy for the purpose of holding down interest rates. High interest rates are mistakenly believed to be a cause of rising prices, rather than the effect of the rapid increase in the quantity of money. The result of such ignorance concerning inflation is that the increase in the quantity of money is made still more rapid, for the purpose of keeping down interest rates.

In addition, the definition of inflation as rising prices makes no distinction between higher prices which are the result of more demand or of less supply. And thus it perpetuates the confusion that things which cause less supply are responsible for inflation. Finally, this definition is incapable of contributing anything whatever to the explanation of symptoms of inflation other than the rise in the general consumer price level—for example, such symptoms as a rise in the whole range of prices, debtors being enriched at the expense of creditors, high nominal profit and interest rates, and a low demand for money for holding.

The importance of determining which of these two contending definitions of inflation—rising prices or an increase in the quantity of money more rapid than the increase in precious metals—is the proper one, cannot be overestimated. The difference between them is as important as the difference between holding a right or a wrong understanding of a disease—of knowing what it is that causes all the symptoms of the disease and what needs to be dealt with to eliminate the source of the symptoms, versus attempting to deal directly with an isolated symptom. Thinking of inflation as being nothing more than rising prices is comparable to thinking of a disease as consisting of nothing more than a high temperature reading, say, which would imply that the remedy is as simple and as absurd as packing the thermometer employed to take the temperature in ice—a remedy that would be on the same intellectual level as imposing price controls as the cure for inflation. It is comparable to thinking that a problem of excessive pressure in a boiler is merely one of movement of the pressure gauge and that the pressure can be brought down by forcing the gauge to a lower reading—another solution on the intellectual level of the enactment of price controls.

Correctly understanding the meaning of inflation—that is, in terms of an increase in the quantity of money—makes it possible to realize that inflation can be present without the appearance of any of its obvious symptoms, just as a disease, such as cancer, can be present prior to the appearance of any of its obvious symptoms, and that inflation continues to be present even though some particular leading symptom, such as rising prices, has been suppressed.

Of no less importance is the fact that a correct understanding of what inflation is, makes it possible to raise questions about the causes and consequences of inflation that would otherwise simply be impossible to raise, because one would still be bogged down in trying determine the cause and consequences of rising prices in a given case. When one has finally thoroughly investigated the causes of rising prices, as we have done, and arrived at the definitive knowledge that only an increase in the quantity of money, specifically an increase more rapid than the increase in the supply of gold and silver—an increase caused by the government—can qualify as an explanation that is consistent with all of the facts, one is able to raise questions pertaining to whole new vistas of causes and effects.

For example, in the next part of this chapter, in asking the question of what are the causes of inflation, we no longer ask the question of what are the causes of rising prices. We now, once and for all, already know the answer to that question. It is cemented and conveyed in the proper definition of inflation. Thus, in asking what are the causes of inflation, we now go further and ask: *What are the causes of the increase in the quantity of money at a rate more rapid than the increase in gold and silver? Namely, what leads the government to bring about such an increase in the quantity of money?* When it is understood that inflation is, in fact, fundamentally *a government policy*, not a phenomenon of prices, the question of causation is pushed back to the plane of the intellectual and ideological influences acting on the government when it pursues that policy, and on the citizenry when it supports or calls for the government's policy of inflation.

Similarly, in asking about the consequences of inflation, we are no longer limited to asking about the consequences of rising prices. We can raise questions about *all* the consequences of the undue increase in the quantity of money. These consequences go far beyond rising prices and must be understood if one is to understand the effects of inflation, including the effects of the rising prices inflation causes.

In sum, on the basis of a sound definition of inflation, one is led to ask much more fundamental, wider, and better questions. On the basis of this foundation, it is now possible to turn to a discussion of what I have titled "the deeper roots and further effects of inflation."

PART B

THE DEEPER ROOTS AND FURTHER EFFECTS OF INFLATION

1. The Connection Between Inflation and Government Budget Deficits

Inflation as a government policy is intimately connected with deficits in the government's budget. It is not the case that deficits in and of themselves are inflationary, as is often claimed. If they are financed by selling bonds to the "public"—that is, to private individuals and nonbank corporations—there is no increase in the quantity of money or in aggregate demand. There is merely a diversion of demand: the government spends instead of private borrowers, who are deprived of the funds the government borrows and who must therefore spend correspondingly less.[30]

Indeed, under a gold standard, deficits financed by borrowing from the public can actually be deflationary, by virtue of threatening government bankruptcy and accompanying political instability, as was shown in the critique of Keynesian policies in the preceding chapter.[31] These consequences increase the demand for money for holding, cause the export of gold, and threaten the solvency of the banking system insofar as the banks hold government securities as an asset backing fiduciary media. The fact that under a gold standard deficits represent an equivalent drain of savings away from private borrowers, who, for the most part, would have used the savings for the purpose of capital investment, means that they also result in diminished economic progress and, indeed, if practiced on a sufficiently large scale, in the outright economic decline of the country. These destructive tendencies are reinforced by the increase in tax burdens to finance the growing burden of interest and principal payments entailed in a policy of deficits. As a result, the country's relative position in world commerce is impaired, which, if severe enough, also contributes to a decline in the quantity of money that circulates within its borders.[32]

What makes government deficits inflationary is *the ability to finance them by the creation of new and additional money*. When they are financed in this manner, the government can spend more and the citizens need not spend any less. Indeed, very soon—once the new and additional money begins to reach them—the citizens too begin to increase their spending. The increase in the quantity of money works its way through the economic system, and as it continues, spending increases in more and more areas, until it rises virtually everywhere. It goes on rising so long as the deficits are financed by means of the creation of new and additional money.[33]

The ability to finance peacetime deficits by means of the creation of new and additional money has existed in the United States since the abandonment of the domestically convertible gold standard in 1933. Prior to that time, the U.S. government was obliged to redeem paper dollars on demand at the rate of one ounce of gold for every $20.67 of paper. The dollars could be redeemed by anyone, including American citizens. In addition, gold reserves of at least 25 percent against National Bank notes, Federal Reserve notes, and Federal Reserve deposit liabilities were mandated by law. These requirements sharply limited the government's ability to expand the supply of currency and bank reserves and correspondingly limited the ability of the commercial banking system to increase the supply of fiduciary media. In such circumstances, it was simply impossible to rely on the creation of money as the means of financing budget deficits. This was because of an impending deficiency of gold reserves. The deficiency of gold reserves would come about by virtue both of an absolute loss of gold reserves in redemptions of paper money for gold and an increase in the amount of money against which reserves were required to be held.[34]

Even though from 1933 to 1965 the United States retained substantial gold-reserve requirements against Federal Reserve notes and deposit liabilities, these requirements ceased to be effective once the government increased the official price of gold to $35 per ounce and thereby increased its gold reserve by almost 75 percent overnight. And then, from the late 1930s until 1945, the U.S. government came into possession of a vast portion of the rest of the world's monetary gold, as many nations used their gold reserves to buy American supplies. As a result, over almost all of this period, the U.S. government was able to create additional paper money as rapidly as it wished, without being limited by a deficiency of gold reserves. When the problem of a deficiency of gold reserves began to develop—as the result of more than a decade of substantial losses of gold reserves in the London gold market and the growing gold-reserve requirements accompanying the increased quantity of Federal Reserve notes and deposit liabilities outstanding—the gold-reserve requirements were simply abolished, and, not long thereafter, the policy of holding the price of gold at $35 per ounce, as well.[35]

Prior to 1933, the government did finance wartime deficits by means of creating money. But it had to resort to extraordinary measures in order to do so. To be able to create money for the financing of deficits in the Civil War, it abandoned the requirement of convertibility to gold and issued irredeemable greenbacks. It also established the National Banking System with its National Bank notes, which made possible an increase in the quantity of money in the economic system relative to the amount of gold, as National Bank notes, backed 25 percent by gold, came to be used in place of gold coin. In World War I, the government required the banks to turn over their gold reserves to the Federal Reserve System, and to count as their reserves equivalent checking-deposit balances with the Federal Reserve System. The Federal Reserve System then used this gold to support a multiple expansion in its own notes and deposit liabilities, on the basis of which the banking system was able to expand the supply of fiduciary media correspondingly.[36]

The ability to finance deficits by means of inflation exists today at the federal-government level, but not at the state- or local-government level. Hence only federal deficits can be inflationary. And inasmuch as state and local governments lack the ability to inflate the money supply to finance their deficits, they almost always choose to pursue a policy of balanced budgets—with all of their expenditures financed by current tax revenues. They recognize, implicitly at least, that given their inability to create money to pay their creditors, a policy of deficits on their part would result in bankruptcy. To adopt a policy of deficits, a state or local government must be reckless, corrupt, or ignorant to a very high degree. The government of New York City, which came to the edge of bankruptcy in the mid-1970s before being rescued by the state and federal government, provides the only recent significant example of such a local government.

The mechanism of creating money in order to finance deficits has already been explained. It is the purchase of government securities by the Federal Reserve System, which is accompanied by the creation of new and additional checking deposits for the Treasury. When recipients of the new and additional money spent by the Treasury make additional deposits in their checking accounts, the result is additional standard money reserves for the banking system.[37] On the basis of its additional reserves, the banking system in turn can expand the supply of fiduciary media and thereby provide the Treasury with still more new and additional money to spend. (The same state of affairs exists in foreign countries. All one need do is substitute for the Federal Reserve System the name of the appropriate foreign central bank.)

The ability to create money makes it impossible for the federal government to go bankrupt in the technical sense of lacking the dollars required to pay its creditors. So long as what it owes is dollars, and it has the power to create new and additional dollars, it will always have money available to pay its debts. The fact that in the technical sense the government cannot go bankrupt under these conditions, no matter how large its debt be-comes, should not be at all surprising. An individual citizen would never go bankrupt either, no matter how much debt he incurred, if he owned a printing press and, whenever the need arose, could just go and run off whatever dollars his creditors required. Precisely this is the position of the federal government under our present fiat-money standard.

Furthermore, an important consequence of the government's creation of money is an increase in its tax revenues, for the money incomes of the citizens are increased by the inflation, and additional taxes are paid on those incomes and on the additional consumer spending that takes place out of those incomes. Indeed, the increase in taxes is almost certain to be more than proportional to the increase in real incomes. This is both because of the progressive nature of the income tax, and thus of the fact that people are pushed into higher brackets and have to pay higher rates of income tax as inflation raises their incomes, and because of the fact that inflation leads to a systematic overstatement of income subject to taxation. Under current federal tax legislation, the upward drift of taxpayers into higher brackets supposedly no longer takes place, since the upper borders of the brackets are supposed to be increased corresponding to the rise in prices each year. After decades, it is welcome to observe some remedy enacted for an obvious abuse. As we will see, however, the more serious problem of the systematic overstatement of income subject to taxation has yet to be addressed.[38]

Although, given its ability to inflate the money supply, the government can no longer go bankrupt in the technical sense of lacking the money necessary to pay its bills, it has probably long since been bankrupt in the sense of being unable to repay its debt *in the same purchasing power in which the debt was contracted.* The present national debt is the sum of the deficits contracted over all of the years since the administration of President Andrew Jackson, when, briefly, there was no national debt. Repayment of the debt in the same purchasing power in which it was contracted would require restating the debt as the sum of the deficits of all the intervening years, with each year's deficit *adjusted for the rise in prices* between its incurrence and the present. Thus, the portions of the debt which date from the First and Second World Wars would have to be adjusted upwards by a percentage that was equal to the rise in prices since those times, and similarly with the portions of the debt contracted in the 1950s, 1960s, and 1970s. Such an adjustment, of course, would result in a restatement of the debt at a substantially higher level than its already very high level.

It is extremely unlikely that such a restated debt could ever be repaid. The government would not be able to repay it through inflation, because the more it inflated, the higher would prices rise and the higher therefore would be the restatement of the debt. It is extremely unlikely that even the present national debt, let alone one restated at the substantially higher level necessary to compensate for the loss in the purchasing power of money, can ever be repaid out of taxation. Thus, in real terms—in terms of the ability to repay creditors in the same purchasing power in which they lent—the government is probably bankrupt, and probably has been for many years. For decades, the government has been paying principal and interest in money of substantially lower purchasing power than existed at the time it borrowed the money in question.

The fact that the present national debt is probably beyond the point of any possible repayment in terms of the buying power of the money lent to the government, or even in terms of the present, already sharply reduced buying power of money, may very well help to explain the prevailing high interest rates on long-term government securities—interest rates which for some years have substantially exceeded the rate at which prices have been rising. The height of these interest rates does not have to be explained merely by reference to the likelihood of a reacceleration of inflation and rising prices. Even without such reacceleration, high interest rates on government securities would have to exist to reflect the likelihood that the government is simply unable to repay its current level of debt in real terms, with or without inflation. Interest rates may be high in order to provide a risk premium as well as an inflation premium.[39]

If this description of matters is correct, then it may be only a relatively short step from the present situation to one in which it is impossible to sell long-term government securities to any buyer *but the government itself—* viz., the Federal Reserve System and the Social Security Trust Funds. For private individuals and businesses will simply stop buying such securities when they conclude that, no matter what happens, they must lose by doing so. Such a result would imply a quantum jump in inflation, because then both the entire annual deficit and the redemptions of government securities coming due would have to be financed almost entirely by inflation.

Budget Deficits and the Monetary Unit

The fact that the government has the power to inflate the money supply means, of course, that government spending is not constrained by tax revenues. In the absence of this power, it would be constrained by tax revenues, precisely because a policy of deficits would drive the government into visible bankruptcy. To avoid this specter, any semiresponsible, representative government would make a balanced budget a fundamental principle of its operation, just as almost all state and local governments in the United States do. Any federal administration that failed to do so, would soon be turned out of office.

The implication of these facts is that what is required to put an end to the present policy of deficits is to *deprive the government of the power to inflate the money supply*. Until that is done, all talk about balancing the federal budget is just so many empty words. The talk that comes from the government itself is comparable to a New Year's resolution to reduce his use of credit cards in the year ahead that is made by someone who has a license to counterfeit and thus can have no problem obtaining the money necessary to pay whatever credit card charges he runs up. When all the government has to do to pay its bills is to go and print more money, even proposals for constitutionally balanced budgets cannot be taken seriously. They have no more binding quality than written New Year's resolutions.[40]

The only thing that will ever force the federal government to balance its budget is if it loses the power to create money, and thus is put in a position in which the money it spends must be obtained from the citizens. That will happen only when the monetary unit of the country becomes something that is physically incapable of being produced at a profit except in very limited quantity, and even then probably not by the government, with all of its bureaucratic inefficiencies. That is to say, the monetary unit must be something whose cost of production is usually almost as great as its own value and, in the face of efforts to increase its production, soon rises as high and even higher than its own value. Gold and silver are monetary units of precisely this description.

When they are the monetary units, the government is *physically* deprived of the ability to enlarge the money supply beyond the rate at which a free market would enlarge it, unless it wishes to incur a financial loss and thus defeat all purpose it might have in seeking the enlargement of the money supply.[41] Thus, with gold and silver as the monetary units, the government is made dependent on the taxpayers for every dollar it spends, and is faced with the fact that every additional dollar it wishes to spend must be obtained from the taxpayers. As a result, the government simply does not have the money for spending proposals it would like to implement. It is compelled to reject proposals for a sheer lack of funds, or because their implementation would compel it to abandon other activities it considers more important. No longer is the mere "desirability" of a program a sufficient basis for its adoption. No longer can the government proceed under the delusion that its spending enriches the citizenry.

2. The Motives and Rationale for Deficits and Inflation

The Welfare State

The roots of inflation begin to become clear when it is realized that inflation is desired in large part precisely in order to make possible a policy of continuous budget deficits. Deficits, and the inflation to finance them, are the cornerstone of the welfare state. They are indispensable in order to lend the appearance of reality to the belief that the government is the source of free benefits, which belief is the fundamental delusion underlying the welfare state.

Because the government has the ability to inflate, it can pay for welfare-state programs without having to collect corresponding taxes, and without having to fear driving itself into bankruptcy. On this basis, demagogic politicians have been able to lead people to think of government programs almost exclusively in terms of their alleged benefits, with virtually no regard for their cost. They have been able to depict the alleged benefits of one government program after another—social security, public housing, farm subsidies, rent subsidies, food stamps, foreign aid, aid to education, support of the arts, support of scientific research, medicare, medicaid, child care, and on and on—as though no cost were involved. At each step, the demagogues have been able to depict the opponents of such measures as mere curmudgeons, motivated by sheer ill will toward the mass of mankind. For if the programs really were free, there could be no other motive for opposing them.

Thus, the ability to inflate is highly valued—in effect, to enable adults to believe that the government is Santa Claus.

The effect of this delusion, of course, as we have already seen, is a radical expansion in the size of the government.[42] The popularity and implementation of additional government programs would be far less if it were necessary to finance every additional dollar of government spending with an additional dollar of taxes, as would be the case if the government lacked the power to inflate and thus had to expect bankruptcy as the price of deficits. Then, every time a new measure was proposed, its supporters would be obliged at the same time to explain how its cost was to be paid. Welfare-state programs would cease to appear as free. Rather, they would be perceived as the direct, immediate cause of higher taxes. In such circumstances, the welfare state could not exist.

As matters stand, the supporters of the welfare state are actually able to use the cost of welfare-state projects as the basis for still more government intervention. The rise in prices that results from the increase in the quantity of money to finance the welfare state, is not perceived as emanating from this cause, but from the greed of businessmen. The welfare state continues to be perceived as the source of free benefits and, alongside of it, businessmen are perceived as the cause of gratuitous evil, with their quest for profits causing the impoverishment of the poor, who must pay ever higher prices. The solutions advanced are that the government must provide still more free benefits, in the form of more and larger welfare-state programs, and—sooner or later—that it must control the prices charged by the evil businessmen, so that the free benefits provided by the wonderful welfare state are not offset by the gratuitous harm the evil businessmen inflict.

Inflation and War Finance

The ability to inflate is also valued because it makes it possible for the government to finance wars which it would not be politically possible to finance through taxation. In effect, it fosters the delusion that, like the welfare state, wars can be carried on without cost. Indeed, because of their being financed by means of inflation, people are actually led to believe that wars are a source of prosperity—because everyone earns more money during a war.

Needless to say, in lending the appearance of reality to these beliefs, the ability to inflate contributes to a greater frequency and duration of wars. In the absence of the ability to finance wars by means of inflation, the prospect of war would be regarded with a dread of its financial and economic consequences no less than of its consequences for human life—because war would then be a time of sharply higher taxes and no increase in money incomes.

Inflation and the "Easy Money" Doctrine

A further root of inflation is the belief that inflation in the form of credit expansion is a means of creating capital and lowering interest rates. If new money is created by the banking system and made available as new and additional loans, then, many businessmen believe, the supply of loanable capital is enlarged and interest rates will fall.

Although held by many of the most eminent and productive members of the economic system, past as well as present, this belief is no less naïve than those of the typical supporters of the welfare state. In fact, it can be described as the businessman's version of the welfare state, in that it too implies the existence of something for nothing.

As will be shown later in the present chapter, the actual consequence of inflation and credit expansion is not more capital but less, and, along with the undermining of capital formation, the scourge of depressions.[43]

Inflation as the Alleged Cure for Unemployment

Probably the most important single root of the policy of inflation in the present day is the belief that inflation is necessary in order to prevent or combat mass unemployment. This notion is implicit in the fallacy that falling prices caused by increased production constitute deflation and thus cause depression and unemployment.[44] On this basis, one is easily led to conclude that steps must be taken to be sure that the quantity of money increases more rapidly—at least to the point of achieving a stable level of prices.

The present-day popularity of the belief that inflation is necessary to deal with unemployment stems, of course, from Keynes, and in the form given it by Keynes this belief powerfully reinforces the other motivations for inflation. The Keynesian doctrine, of course, claims that government budget deficits reduce unemployment and increase output in the economic system by a multiple of the deficits. The additional output of the reemployed workers, which allegedly could not be obtained by any other means, provides not only for the government programs but for much more besides. On this basis, additional government spending supposedly not only costs people nothing, but actually enriches them. In effect, the Keynesian doctrine claims not only that there really is such a thing as a free lunch—paid for by reemployment—but that in people's efforts to obtain it, they obtain a free breakfast and free dinner as well—namely, the benefit of the additional employment and output that is supposedly "multiplied into being" by virtue of the additional government spending.[45]

The errors of the Keynesian system have already been demonstrated, and it should already be clear why inflation is not required to prevent or combat unemployment—indeed, is incapable of doing so—and why, in fact, what is required is a free market in labor and a monetary system based on the principle of 100-percent-gold-and-silver reserves.[46] Previous discussion has also indicated how in setting the stage for financial contractions and depressions, inflation is actually the leading underlying *cause* of mass unemployment.[47] Subsequent discussion in the present chapter will confirm this fact and show how inflation is a preventive or remedy for unemployment only in the peculiar sense that more drugs are a preventive or remedy for withdrawal symptoms.[48]

The Underlying Influence of the Socialist Ideology

If matters are explored at a still deeper level, the pervasive influence of the socialist ideology becomes apparent in the support for inflation.

The expansion in government functions and powers entailed in the growth of the welfare state is a major step toward the establishment of socialism. Both the welfare state and socialism itself are advocated in the name of the alleged helplessness of the average individual and the alleged omniscience and omnipotence of the State. Inflation creates the appearance of just such a relationship between the individual and the State: on the one side stands the individual with his unmet needs, and on the other side, the State, with funds not derived from individuals, but miraculously created outside the economic system, out of thin air. Thus, it becomes possible through inflation to perceive the State in actual practice in accordance with the socialists' fundamental view of it as an all-powerful, merciful, and redeeming Father. Moreover, the advocates of socialism are none too scrupulous in their respect for individual rights (most obviously, but not limited to, property rights) nor, therefore, in the means they are willing to employ to achieve their ends. The Communists, of course, are openly willing to employ force and violence. Less extreme advocates of socialism, it seems, do not scruple to employ the deceptions of inflation to achieve their goals. Perhaps they deceive themselves as much as the voters, for inflation enables them no less than the public to perceive the State as a kindly Father who provides free benefits.

And, of course, in judging the relationship between inflation and the influence of socialism, one should not forget the famous statement attributed to Lenin, that inflation is the surest method of destroying capitalism. Its possible advocacy on this basis too should not be overlooked.

Although it predates the socialist ideology, the "easy money" doctrine is also promoted by its influence. It shares with the socialist ideology the essential conviction that free benefits can be obtained—this time, not in the form of ordinary benefits from the welfare state for ordinary helpless individuals, but in the form of the allegedly costless creation of additional capital and a lower rate of interest for helpless, needy businessmen, who otherwise could not obtain capital. Furthermore, in the hands of Keynes, the logic of the easy money doctrine was pushed to its limits and was thereby transformed into a vehicle for the virtual abolition of profit and interest income. This was Keynes's doctrine of the "euthanasia of the rentier," which was designed to achieve the goals of Marxism without the necessity of a revolution.[49]

Finally, the belief that inflation is necessary to prevent or combat unemployment is largely an indirect result of the influence of the socialist ideology. This is because the labor legislation and other government interference that creates the problem of mass unemployment in the first place is the result of the influence of the Marxian exploitation theory. In addition, the influence of the exploitation theory prevents any consideration from being given to the possibility that unemployment could be eliminated

by means of establishing the freedom of competition in the labor market, so that wage rates would be free to fall. According to the exploitation theory, freedom of competition in the labor market makes possible the exploitation of labor. With the possibility of free competition in the labor market apparently ruled out, inflation and government spending are made to appear as the only means available for solving the problem.

3. Inflation and Deficits Versus Representative Government and Economic Freedom

Since the time of Adam Smith, a fundamental conflict has been perceived between government budget deficits and the consequent accumulation of a national debt, on the one side, and the institution of representative government, on the other. Deficits oblige future generations to pay taxes for the payment of principal and interest on a debt neither they nor their representatives have any role in incurring and which their representatives cannot be present to oppose. Deficits deprive them of all choice and even voice in a matter for which they will later be held responsible. At the same time, deficits and the accumulation of a national debt are accompanied by the rise of a class of public annuitants—the purchasers of the government's securities—whose investments are guaranteed by the government and who are supported out of tax revenues, irrespective of the fact that those whose taxes must pay their incomes may well not derive even the slightest benefit from the support they must pay.

Even wars should not be financed in this manner, Adam Smith argued, because while the effect may be to make wartime taxes less than they would otherwise have been, the further effect is to encourage and prolong wars and to shorten the periods of peace and capital accumulation. The ultimate effect, Smith pointed out, is that peacetime taxes become as high as wartime taxes would have been without resort to deficits.[50]

Everywhere, the effect of deficits and the accumulation of a national debt, Smith held, is to enfeeble countries, by diverting savings from capital accumulation to consumption and by creating a need for higher and more onerous taxes later on to pay principal and interest— taxes that destroy the incentives to produce and the ability to save, and lay the citizens under a yoke of oppression, in the manner of the Spain of his day.[51] (If one thinks of the nooks and crannies into which the eager hands of the Internal Revenue Service now extend, under the pressure of our own deficits, it is easy to think that Smith was writing of our time.) And ultimately, once national debts reach a certain size, Smith pointed out, they are never fairly and fully repaid. The only release from their burden, he showed, is a government bankruptcy, either open and avowed or in the form of a pretended payment in depreciated currency.[52]

When the government has the power to inflate and deficits can be financed by the use of that power, the effect is to make government spending free of the will of the citizens and their representatives. For the government is now in a position to finance its expenditures with funds it does not obtain from the people. Even to the extent the government's expenditures have the approval of the citizens and their representatives, the approval is gained fraudulently—it is gained under the delusion that because the expenditures can be financed by inflation they are not at the expense of the citizens.

Thus, von Mises was absolutely right to describe sound money as belonging in the same category as constitutions and bills of rights, as a safeguard against despotic governmental power, and to describe the gold standard as indispensable to the system of representative government.[53] When the gold standard is overthrown and the government gains the power to spend funds it does not have to obtain from the people, a veritable revolution occurs in the relationship between the government and the people.

When the government need not obtain its funds from the people, but can instead supply the people with funds, it can no longer easily be viewed as deriving its powers and rights from the people. The ability to inflate enables the government to throw off its status as the servant of the people, deriving its just powers from the consent of the governed, and to appear instead in the guise of the Provider and Father of the people, with the people deriving their existence, powers, and rights from the government. A greater revolution in the relationship between the people and the government cannot be imagined. Yet that is the revolution that the power to inflate has operated to effect in the circumstances and in the psychology of the American people of today. Hardly a year passes but they do not willingly sacrifice some further portion of their inheritance of freedom for some imagined largess from the government.

In such a state of affairs not only does the government go on growing in size from year to year, both absolutely and relative to the rest of the economic system, but the only ultimate stopping point becomes a totalitarian socialist dictatorship, comparable to the dictatorships of Hitler and Stalin. The stage for such a dictatorship is set when the rising prices caused by inflation are suppressed by means of price and wage controls.

As demonstrated earlier in this book, the enactment of price and wage controls causes shortages and economic chaos, because it destroys the price system. This results in demands that the government seize control over the economic system by means of imposing a system of rationing and the allocation of the factors of production. In this way, the government comes to decide what and how much of each item is to be produced, and by what methods, and who is to receive the product.[54] Finally, as we have seen, the effect of this de facto socialization is to add tyranny to the chaos. The government is not able to solve the problems created by the destruction of the price system, but acquires full power over the newspapers and publishing houses, and over everyone's employment and standard of living. Caught between the chaos it has created and the responsibility for everyone's material well-being that it has assumed, its continuance in power becomes possible only by ruthless suppression of critics and the creation of an environment of fear and hysteria. Thus, life comes to be characterized by all the hallmarks of a totalitarian state.[55]

Between inflation and the enactment of price and wage controls usually lies a period of growing hostility to profit and interest incomes, which incomes inflation sharply increases in nominal terms and reduces or altogether eliminates in real terms. At the same time, inflation brings about a vast redistribution of wealth and income, in the process causing far greater impoverishment than enrichment. The victims, who are unaware of the facts, are led to believe that their suffering is the result of others' high profit and interest incomes and thus to demand price and wage controls both as a source of relief and as an act of justice.

The next two sections of this chapter will explain these consequences of inflation in close conjunction with its destruction of capital formation. Later sections will elaborate on the propositions that inflation sets the stage for traditional, deflationary depressions and that it causes rather than cures mass unemployment. They will also show why inflation possesses inherent tendencies toward acceleration, culminating in the destruction of the currency and, where the government blocks the development of an alternative currency, of money itself. The chapter will conclude with proposals for the reestablishment of a gold and silver monetary system, in the form of a 100-percent-gold-or-silver reserve against checking deposits and paper currency. It will show why such a system would be both inflation proof and deflation/depression proof, and would possess every other virtue that it is possible for a monetary system to possess.

4. Inflation as the Cause of a Redistribution of Wealth and Income

Inflation destroys the buying power of all assets and incomes which are contractually fixed in terms of a given number of dollars. In this category are savings deposits, bonds, preferred stock, life insurance policies, and annuities and pensions, as well as employment contracts, sales and rental agreements, and even fire and theft insurance. In raising prices, inflation progressively diminishes the buying power that all these contracts represent.

At the same time, inflation operates to benefit those who are obligated to pay according to the terms of such contracts. It does so by sharply increasing the sums of money they can earn with the same effort and correspondingly reducing the difficulty they experience in obtaining the sums of money necessary to meet their obligations. Thus, businessmen and corporations with debts to pay, the common stockholders of such corporations, homeowners with mortgages, the owners of inventories of commodities of all kinds that are financed with borrowed money, wage earners with personal debts, and the businessmen and wage earners who hold contracts entitling them to buy or rent on fixed terms—all of these groups of people find that the sums of money they are able to obtain from their activities tend greatly to increase and thus to make it very much easier for them to pay the interest and principal on their debts.

Inflation is capable of utterly destroying the buying power of contractually fixed assets and incomes and correspondingly impoverishing those who depend on them, and equivalently relieving from all real obligation those who are obliged to pay according to the relevant contracts. It arbitrarily changes all contractual relations at least to some substantial extent and is capable of destroying them totally. Its potential for achieving a redistribution of real wealth and income is fully comparable to that of a political revolution on the scale of the French or Russian revolutions. It is significant that in both of these revolutions, a major inflation occurred, alongside of the open confiscations and redistributions.

The destruction of the buying power of assets and incomes that are contractually fixed, and the corresponding release from real obligation of those who are obliged to pay according to such contracts, is not the only means by which inflation redistributes wealth and income. As von Mises has shown, inflation never raises all prices and wage rates at the same time and to the same extent. It raises some prices and wage rates ahead of others, or more rapidly than others. Those whose selling prices rise relatively early or more rapidly, gain at the expense of those whose selling prices rise only later on or less rapidly. Inflation shifts the terms of trade in their favor. It makes their goods and services worth relatively more of other people's goods and services and other people's goods and services worth relatively less of their goods and services. The relatively higher selling prices of their goods and services means that their revenues and incomes have risen relative to the prices they must pay. At the same time, those whose selling prices have not risen or which lag behind, find their revenues and incomes do not keep pace with the rise in prices, and they correspondingly lose.[56]

In addition to the gains inflation provides to various private individuals and groups at the expense of other private individuals and groups, it should never be forgotten that inflation always represents an unearned gain to whoever is in a position to introduce the newly created money into the economic system through his spending—and a corresponding loss to the individuals who make up the rest of the economic system. This party—most often the government or those to whom the government gives the money, but frequently also businessmen with fiduciary media to spend—is able to obtain the goods and services of others merely by virtue of the manufacture of little pieces of paper, or, indeed, merely by virtue of bookkeeping entries. Such a situation represents the receipt of something for nothing, and must be accompanied by an equivalent receipt, somewhere else in the economic system, of nothing for something. Somewhere else in the economic system, others must to the same extent consume less, produce more without consuming more, or suffer a loss in their accumulated capitals (or undergo some combination of these three), in order to compensate for the unearned gains of the spenders of the new money.[57]

Ironically, the groups which tend to lose the most as the result of inflation are the relatively poor and helpless—i.e., the very people that the welfare state claims it wishes to help. It is widows and orphans and the elderly, who depend most on the buying power of savings deposits, life insurance policies, pensions, and annuities. Similarly, institutions such as nonprofit hospitals and nonprofit colleges and universities, are also among those most dependent on the buying power of bonds and other contractually fixed assets, which, for the sake of safety of principal, must form a substantial portion of their endowments. It follows that it is inherently dishonest for the welfare state to claim that it seeks to aid these groups and institutions when its inescapable dependence on inflation makes precisely them its worst victims. The welfare state is both an exercise in futility and a fraud. By its nature, it harms those it claims to help. Its advocates have no legitimate reason not to know this.

Eventually, people come to recognize the destructive effects of inflation in redistributing wealth and income, and take steps to protect themselves from them. Thus, interest rates rise in anticipation of the rise in prices to come. The terms of employment, sales, and rental contracts are increased. Price indexing is introduced into various contracts. But these remedies are at best only partially effective, and create additional problems, namely, unemployment and/or the acceleration of inflation, as will be shown.[58]

5. Inflation and the Destruction of Capital

Inflation undermines capital formation in five major ways, which can be described under the following heads: reversal of safety, tax effects, prosperity delusion and overconsumption, malinvestment, and the withdrawal-of-wealth effect. Each of these ways will be considered in turn.

Reversal of Safety

The traditionally safest investments are high-grade corporate bonds, savings deposits, life insurance policies, and government securities. Inflation turns the safety of these investments upside down. It is capable of rendering them the least safe forms of investment. It introduces the risk that the buying power of the proceeds of these investments will be little or nothing. It makes all long-term contracts denominated in a fixed sum of money utterly meaningless, because it places the value of money totally at the mercy of government officials and pressure groups. It is as though one contracted for the delivery of so many tons of coal or board feet of lumber, without the words "ton" or "feet" having any objective meaning and thus subject to the whims of whoever might later care to assert an interest. This is the position of everyone who is contractually entitled to receive fiat money. The only thing he can be certain of is that when he receives the money due him, it will be worth substantially less than it is presently worth.

Yet contractually fixed investments are economically necessary. They are the appropriate investment vehicle for individuals not able or willing to bear substantial risk or to search out and follow more complicated types of investments, such as common stocks. As a result, the destruction of this type of investment deprives a large group of people of the possibility of benefitting from investment. To the extent that the prospect of earning a rate of return on investment constitutes a motive to save, such individuals are deprived of the motive to save. At the same time, they are largely deprived of the means of saving. They are deprived of the means of saving insofar as they are deprived of income on their investments, which income is normally a major source of further saving.

And to the extent they do continue to save, their saving increasingly tends to take an unproductive form. A leading example of the unproductive use of savings that results from inflation is the hoarding of precious metals, whose prospective rise in price in the course of inflation offers people the ability to preserve the purchasing power of their savings. Unfortunately, such hoarding does not contribute to investment.

This is certainly not to criticize the hoarding of precious metals. If the government destroys the traditionally safe investments, such hoarding is the best substitute most individuals have. And it is to everyone's interest that individuals continue to have the motivation to save, even though their saving takes the form of such hoarding. This is because if the government prevented them from doing even this, and thus totally destroyed the benefit they could derive from saving, it would deprive people of much of their motivation to work. In the absence of being able to save, people would lose the motivation to perform present labor for the sake of providing for their future wants; their only motivation to work would be to satisfy their present wants, which often would not be important enough to justify their labor. Furthermore, it should be realized that the desire to own precious metals need not take the form of hoarding. If the government permitted and enforced contracts calling for payment in precious metals, and if the tax authorities did not tax the rise in their price expressed in terms of paper money, then the precious metals could themselves be lent and so contribute to investment. But this would be tantamount to their remonetization and would mean the transformation of the whole monetary system.

In any case, it is clear that the effect of inflation is to reduce both the motivation to save and the motivation to invest productively such savings as do continue to be made. This obviously impairs the formation of capital, and not only of new capital but also the replacement of existing capital, since people are motivated to consume what they have saved in the past, or to convert it into unproductive hoards. In both ways, the effect is to raise the rate of net consumption.[59]

The prospective purchasing power of fiat money rests on a foundation that is far more precarious than the general public realizes. In the first instance, it depends on the rate of increase in the quantity of the money over the period of time that the fixed-sum-of-money investments in question are outstanding. Since the rate of increase in the quantity of fiat money is totally at the discretion of government officials, the more fundamental determinants of the rate at which its purchasing power declines are such factors as the government officials' knowledge of economics, their sense of moral responsibility, and even their method of thinking. This constitutes a truly alarming situation.

The majority of government officials today, and the majority of academic economists, whose ranks supply the advisers of the government officials, do not even firmly acknowledge the truth of the quantity theory of

money. These officials and alleged economists continue
to attempt to blame rising prices on almost everything
but the increase in the quantity of money. They talk of
the greed of businessmen and labor unions, of the price
of imported oil, of inflation psychology, of credit cards,
and the greed of consumers. In a word, they are wedded
to all the fallacies I refuted in the first part of this chapter.

Thus, those who have charge of the increase in the
quantity of money, who have the power to increase it as
much as they wish, either do not know or will not admit
the consequences of increasing it. This is a state of affairs
comparable to being in the power of someone who holds
a gun but does not know or will not admit the lethal power
of his weapon.

Among the government officials and their advisers
who do admit the truth of the quantity theory of money,
there are many—perhaps a further majority—who believe that what is true in theory is not necessarily true in
practice or who, for other reasons, are prepared to act
without integrity. In such cases, even a knowledge of the
quantity theory of money does not serve as a reliable
restraint on the increase in the quantity of money. Closely
related to this is the fact that government officials labor
under a variety of extremely powerful temptations to use
their power to expand the quantity of money. The use of
this power is the supreme vote-buying technique: it caters to all the fallacies held by the public about "free"
benefits, from free education and medical care to "easy
money," and about what must be done to prevent or
combat unemployment.[60]

In view of the enormous ignorance concerning the
nature of inflation and its effects, the widespread lack of
integrity on the part of today's public officials (and
professional intellectuals), and the extremely powerful
political motives in support of inflation, there is little
hope that, given the power to create money, the government will not use it far beyond the point of prudence.
Moreover, because of the inherent accelerative tendencies of inflation, yet to be explained, the rate at which the
government is motivated to increase the quantity of
money is steadily increased as inflation becomes more
rapid.[61]

Thus, investments denominated in fixed sums of money are in fact transformed from the safest into the most
speculative and risky from the perspective of the purchasing power they will provide. This is a situation which
must increasingly undermine saving and investment by
the broad classes of the public that depend on such
investments.

Tax Effects

As was shown earlier, inflation simultaneously increases nominal profit incomes, which are subject to tax,
and the replacement prices of capital assets. It creates
profit incomes most or all of which are required merely
for the replacement of assets at the higher prices it causes,
but which cannot be applied to replacement because they
are taxed away as though they were genuine income.

Previous discussion of this fact used an example in
terms of inventories. The example showed that despite
earning a sharply higher nominal rate of profit as the
result of inflation, the typical merchant is placed in a
position in which, after making the necessary replacement allowance for the assets needed to continue his
existing operations, his ability either personally to consume or to save and expand his business, is actually
radically reduced.[62] The following example illustrates
the same principle in application to fixed assets, such as
plant and equipment and buildings.

As can be seen in Table 19–1, I assume that a machine
(or any other form of fixed capital) initially costs $1
million and lasts 10 years. The annual depreciation on
this machine, using the common, straight-line method, is
thus $100,000. I assume that initially, without inflation,
the machine is used to produce a quantity of goods each
year that sells for $1 million. I further assume that
operating costs—the cost of the labor, fuel, and materials
required to produce these goods—are $850,000 per year.
Thus, the firm's annual gross profit (its profit before
deduction of depreciation cost) is $150,000 per year.

After deducting depreciation, the firm's net profit is
$50,000 per year. If the firm must pay a 50 percent
income tax on its profit, its after-tax profit is $25,000 per
year. If, out of that sum, it pays a dividend of $10,000,
then it has $15,000 left with which to expand its opera-
tions. This is the situation shown in the column labeled
"Without Inflation."

Now let us imagine that between the time the firm
buys its machine and the time at which it will have to
replace it, an increase in the quantity of money and
volume of spending occurs which doubles the firm's
sales revenues and operating costs, and, of course, the
replacement price of a new machine. Under these conditions, the firm will have an annual gross profit of $300,000
($2 million in sales revenues minus $1.7 million in
operating costs). However, because the purchase price of
its machine is not affected retroactively, its deduction for
depreciation on its existing machine remains at only
$100,000. Its net profit before taxes is therefore raised to
$200,000 per year—quadruple its previous net profit of
$50,000 per year before taxes. If the firm still pays the
same, 50 percent tax rate, its net profit after taxes is
$100,000 per year, which is also quadruple what it was
initially.

The apparent quadrupling of profits seems wonderful
indeed, until we consider the need to replace the machine

		Table 19–1	

Table 19–1

Effect of Inflation on the Nominal Rate of Profit and the Taxation of Profits

A machine (or any other form of fixed capital) costs $1,000,000 and lasts 10 years.

	Without Inflation	With Inflation
Sales Revenues	$1,000,000	$2,000,000
Operating Costs	850,000	1,700,000
Gross Profit	150,000	300,000
Depreciation	100,000	100,000
Net Profit Before Tax	50,000	200,000
Tax (50%)	25,000	100,000
Net Profit After Tax	25,000	100,000
Necessary Reserve for Replacement at Higher Prices	NONE	100,000
Available for Consumption or Expansion	25,000	NONE
Dividend	10,000	10,000
Reinvested Earnings	15,000	(10,000)

at a price of $2 million instead of only $1 million. When we do this, the seemingly rosy picture of enormous profits turns into something very different. For then it becomes clear that if our firm gives to its stockholders *any dividend at all*, it must impair its ability to continue doing business on the same scale, because *the whole of the firm's seemingly larger profit each year is required merely to enable it to replace its machine at the now higher replacement cost.* That is, in order to accumulate the replacement sum of $2 million, our firm needs to set aside $200,000 for each of 10 years. This sum, however, is equal to its annual depreciation of $100,000 plus the whole of its after-tax "profit" of $100,000. In the table, this is shown by means of the row labeled "Necessary Reserve for Replacement at Higher Prices," the amount of which is "NONE" in the column labeled "Without Inflation," and $100,000 in the column labeled "With Inflation." The table shows that as a result of the need to deduct this reserve under inflation, the funds available for consumption or expansion from the nominal profit of $100,000 turn out to be "NONE," while the much smaller

nominal profit of $25,000 earned without inflation is sufficient to make possible consumption or expansion to its full extent. Thus, under inflation, if the firm pays even the same dividend it previously paid—$10,000 per year— let alone the substantially larger dividend its stockholders are almost certain to clamor for in view of its sharply increased "profits," it cannot generate the funds it requires for replacement. As is shown in the table, its reinvested earnings must fall by an amount equivalent to that $10,000. (The reduction of $10,000 in reinvested earnings should be understood as being in real terms, not nominal terms. In nominal terms, if the firm pays a $10,000 dividend, its nominal capital will rise by $90,000. Its problem is that to maintain its physical capital intact, it needs to increase its nominal capital by $100,000, not just $90,000.)

Once again, therefore, we see that to the same extent that inflation provides additional profits, it also requires that those profits be devoted to the replacement of assets at higher prices. Yet this fact is largely ignored in the collection of taxes. What is involved in this case, as well as in the earlier, inventory case, is that as a result of inflation, *the firm is taxed not merely on its income, but on funds required for the replacement of its capital as well.* If its income properly begins only after full and complete allowance for replacement has been made, then its taxable income should not be viewed as $200,000, but only $100,000, since $100,000 of its apparent profit of $200,000 is actually required to be set aside for replacement. In taxing the firm on $200,000 rather than just $100,000, therefore, the government taxes the firm on the replacement of its capital as well as on its income. To say the same thing in somewhat different words, the firm should be able to deduct the item "Necessary Reserve for Replacement of Assets at Higher Prices" from its pretax income, and thus pay taxes only on the amount remaining thereafter. Instead, of course, the firm is taxed as though the funds required for the replacement of assets at higher prices were income.

In creating profits which are required for the replacement of assets at higher prices and which nevertheless are subject to taxation, inflation operates as the equivalent of a rise in income tax rates on real profits. In the above illustration, its operation is equivalent to raising the rate of income tax on real profits from 50 percent to 100 percent, because it doubles the nominal profit subject to tax, while the real profit earned remains unchanged.

The result of such increases in effective tax rates is that business finds itself with less and less ability to expand or even maintain its operations intact as inflation grows worse. Vast stretches of the Northeast and Midwest, with their abandoned factories and decaying housing, are a testimonial to this destructive consequence of inflation, as is the inability of broad segments of surviving American industry to modernize to keep pace with foreign competitors. Nevertheless, despite the visible decline of the American economic system in recent decades, inflation and the nominal profits it creates make it possible for virtual hoards of the ignorant, the envious, and the downright malicious to denounce profits as excessive and to claim that they are not taxed sufficiently!

Essentially the same principles as apply to businessmen and corporations apply to lenders, who appear to be earning unprecedentedly high rates of interest and yet are being impoverished at the same time. The position of the typical creditor in a period of inflation is that after taxes are deducted from his receipt of interest, and allowance is made for the rise in prices, his real wealth—the buying power of his principal—shrinks. Anything he consumes out of his seeming income is actually at the expense of his capital.

Imagine, for example, a lender who instead of earning a 4 percent rate of interest earns a 14 percent rate of interest. However, when he earns the 14 percent rate of interest, prices are rising by 10 percent a year. In terms of buying power, this lender is no better off than he was before, despite the much higher rate of interest that he earns. Indeed, he must be substantially worse off, because out of his seeming 14 percent rate of return, he will have to pay a substantial portion in taxes. If we assume that he pays half in taxes, he is left with only a 7 percent rate of return in the face of a 10 percent rise in prices. And to whatever extent he consumes any portion of his "rate of return," his situation is made so much the worse in terms of the preservation of the buying power of his capital.

Once more, the situation is that inflation makes the income tax operate as a tax on capital. The lender's taxable income should begin only after allowance has been made for the maintenance of the purchasing power of his principal—viz., the portion of his interest equal to the rise in prices should not to be subject to taxation. Yet he is taxed on this portion of his income, even though it represents merely the maintenance of the purchasing power of his principal.

It should be noted that inflation produces essentially the same effect in connection with capital gains taxation, despite the fact that the rate of tax applying to capital gains may be less than the rate of income tax. For it creates capital gains all of which are required for the replacement purchase of similar capital assets at higher prices, but which are nevertheless taxed away as though they were genuine gains.

Inflation plays a major role in the decline of the highways and other so-called infrastructure of a country, which is typically maintained by the government. Government officials, usually shortsighted to begin with, rarely allow for the effects of inflation on the replacement costs of the assets they manage. Thus, as inflation pours new and additional revenues into their hands, they proceed as though the revenues were available for the expansion of government activities, and neglect the need to devote an adequate portion of them to replacement and maintenance at progressively rising prices. The result is decaying water and sewage systems, subway and rail lines, and bridges and tunnels, as well as decaying roads and highways.

The Prosperity Delusion and Overconsumption

The overstatement of income that results from inflation is the cause not only of the taxation of replacement funds, but also of excessive private consumption which comes at the expense of capital formation and which would be a serious problem even in the absence of taxation. This overstatement represents what is often described as the prosperity delusion of inflation—the creation of an appearance of prosperity based on the mere increase in paper profits.

Our example of the machine clearly shows the nature of the problem. The stockholders and management of the company that owns that machine will believe that their firm is in a position to afford substantially increased dividends on the basis of its sharply increased profits. Years may go by before they become aware of the deficiency of replacement funds, and even then they may not realize that they had no genuine profit and should not have taken the dividends they did.

It must be stressed that overconsumption exists even if the owners of a business base their consumption entirely on their perception of their accumulated capital rather than their income, and at first save, or allow their firm to save, almost all of the additional profit that inflation generates for them. In this case, the effect of inflation will be an overstatement of their capital equal to the progressive understatement of accumulated depreciation, and thus an overconsumption corresponding to that overstatement of capital.

The problem of overconsumption is greatly compounded to the extent that there are stockholders and other business owners who are ready to use the occasion of higher profits as the basis for going on a "binge" of any sort. Inflation relaxes the normal competitive pressures of the market that constantly tend to minimize the economic influence of such people through the regular gravitation of capital and profit to those individuals who consume the least and save the most.[63] The existence of inflation represents giving people with the binge mentality a continual new lease on life. It continually provides them with the profit incomes they can use to indulge themselves.

The capital gains that inflation systematically creates in the purchase and sale of land and buildings of all kinds, and in commodity futures and common stocks, are also the source of substantial increases in consumption, as the beneficiaries of the process enjoy the apparent experience of growing richer. Inflation leads practically everyone to overconsume on the basis of the delusion of a prosperity that does not exist. Everyone who sells an asset at a higher price, such as a house or common stocks, almost certainly thinks he has gained something and can now afford to consume something he previously could not have afforded to consume. Yet, in reality, the same process that has produced his monetary gain has raised the prices of replacement assets and other goods on average to the same extent. If he consumes any part of that gain, he cannot replace the assets he has sold with comparable assets, nor maintain the buying power of his

nominal wealth or capital. There is no more actual foundation for additional consumption than the fact that some extra pieces of paper have been printed in a certain way or that some bookkeeping entries have been made.[64]

In some cases, indeed, individuals actually do grow richer as the result of inflation. For example, an individual who buys a $100,000 house or piece of land with a $20,000 down payment and a mortgage of $80,000, and who sells it a few years later for $200,000, makes a profit of 500 percent, since he pockets the full appreciation of the asset. Even if all other prices double along with the price of his asset, he comes out far ahead, because of the leverage of his investment.

Although the prosperity of these individuals is genuine, an overconsumption exists nonetheless, in that their gain merely represents the equivalent or even greater loss of others. For example, the individuals whose savings provided our homeowner's mortgage have a loss at least as great as his gain. This is because when the price of the house and all other prices on average double, these individuals lose half the buying power of the $80,000 they lent him. By the same token, the $120,000 equity of the homeowner represents $60,000 of buying power in terms of the original level of prices. In other words, what inflation does is equivalent to taking $40,000 from the savers who financed the mortgage, and give it to the homeowner. It is a mere redistribution of the same total sum of existing wealth, with the homeowner-gainer then consuming a substantial portion of his gain, while no equivalent reduction in consumption takes place on the part of the saver-losers.[65]

The additional consumption of the gainers from inflation is almost certain to be greater—in real terms—than the diminished consumption of the losers, because the gains go largely to people who have no special penchant for saving and providing for the future, and come at the expense of those who do. The gains from inflation come as a windfall, which the beneficiaries have not had to earn and frequently do not count very confidently on being able to keep. As a result, much of the gains are likely to be squandered. In redistributing wealth, inflation has the effect of converting previously accumulated savings and capital into an unearned current income largely of people who are bent on consumption rather than saving and provision for the future. In this way as well as others, inflation operates to raise the rate of net consumption.

In the case of a lender, it is perhaps misleading to speak of "a prosperity delusion" created by inflation, because the lender almost certainly realizes that he is falling behind. In his case, inflation serves to conceal the extent of impoverishment. It creates the illusion that in spite of his impoverishment, he still has an income, out of which he can afford to consume, when in actuality he does not. He would consume far less if, as in one of our previous examples, instead of having an "income" of 7 percent while prices rise by 10 percent, he had a monetary loss of 3 percent with no rise in prices, because then the true state of affairs would be real to him. He would directly perceive a loss instead of an "income" that somehow happened to be accompanied by a rise in prices of a greater magnitude but which he did not perceive as intrinsically connected.

Wage earners, too, are led to overconsume on the basis of the delusion of having higher real incomes than they actually do. In a period of inflation, with prices steadily rising, everyone has an exaggerated idea of the purchasing power of money, based on his past experience of prices, which, necessarily, is now outmoded. For example, his notion of the purchasing power of money rests in part on his estimate of the price of a new car or washing machine. But that estimate is based on his last experience of the prices of such goods, which may have occurred several months or even several years in the past, at which time the prices were undoubtedly lower than they are today. Thus, people consume in the mistaken belief that their incomes will enable them to afford to buy more than is actually possible at the now higher level of prices. In other words, they consume in the belief that they are richer than they really are, and thus on a scale that they cannot afford in their actual circumstances.

Malinvestment

In Chapter 12, I explained how in raising the rate of profit, inflation also raises the rate of interest. However, it must be kept in mind that the rise in the rate of interest tends to lag behind the rise in the rate of profit insofar as inflation enters the economic system in the form of credit expansion—i.e., the granting of new and additional loans out of the newly created money. The presence of these additional funds in the loan market prevents the rate of interest from rising as high as it would on the basis of the rise in the rate of profit alone. In the initial phase of credit expansion, the rate of interest actually falls.[66]

Now the artificial rise in the rate of profit, combined with the lag in the rate of interest, leads to the wasteful investment—the *malinvestment*—of the reduced capital that inflation leaves still available. Projects without genuine economic merit are made to appear profitable merely by virtue of the existence of inflation, and a relatively low rate of interest ensures that capital will be diverted to them as a result. The following hypothetical examples illustrate the process.

Thus, imagine that inflation is currently raising prices on the order of 15 percent a year. Imagine further that because much of the inflation enters the economic sys-

tem in the form of loanable funds, interest rates have thus far risen only to 10 percent. Now imagine a specific commodity, say, copper, whose price rises as fast as the average of prices. If the storage costs of copper are less than 5 percent a year, inflation in the form of credit expansion makes it profitable to stockpile copper—not because there is any real need to stockpile copper, but just because inflation in the form of credit expansion itself makes it profitable. (Without inflation in the form of credit expansion, the combination of storage and interest costs would make it highly unprofitable to stockpile copper, in the absence of some special, important need for copper that could not be met by future production.) Thus, copper is withdrawn from use, to be stockpiled, and labor and capital are wasted in the production of the stockpile.

This example shows how, even apart from the problems of taxation and overconsumption, inflation in the form of credit expansion makes a direct *loss* of wealth in an investment appear profitable all the same. For consider. Even if the price of copper rises by the same percentage as the rise in prices in general, once the storage costs are deducted from that rise, the investment in copper must entail a loss overall. If, for example, the storage costs are 3 percent a year, then the gain in money by investing in a stockpile of copper whose price rises by 15 percent, is only 12 percent. At the same time, prices in general rise on average by 15 percent. This represents a 3 percent loss in the actual buying power of the investment. But if the money for the investment can be obtained from lenders at a rate of interest of 10 percent, then the lenders suffer a loss of 5 percent in the buying power of their capital, while the borrowers, after deducting storage costs, come out with a gain equal to 2 percent of the capital invested. (The borrowers' rate of return on their own capital depends on how highly leveraged they are. If they can borrow the entire amount, their rate of return is infinite. If they can borrow nine-tenths of the capital, their rate of return is 20 percent—viz., 2 percent on the investment as a whole, divided by the 10 percent of the total investment that they themselves put up.) In effect, the loss of the lenders covers both the loss on the investment as a whole and, at the same time, provides the source of gain for the borrowers. In other words, inflation creates a situation in which one class of investors feeds off the capital of another, while the total capital of both classes of investors combined shrinks. The rest of the economy, of course, is deprived of the benefit of capital, both the benefit of the capital that ceases to exist, because it is lost, and, to a greater or lesser extent, the benefit of the capital that is malinvested.

Similar malinvestments as occur in the stockpiling of all kinds of materials, occur in the construction of housing and plant and equipment. For example, inflation makes the price of houses rise from year to year. If the rate at which the price of houses rises is higher than the rate at which mortgage money can be borrowed—because mortgage rates are held down by the fact that much of the new money enters the economic system in the form of loans—then the purchase of houses, a *consumers' good*, takes on the appearance of an investment. As a result, capital is diverted into the purchase of houses, and further capital is diverted into their construction. After purchase, the houses depreciate and suffer a corresponding loss in real value; but the losses of lenders are great enough to finance both the overall loss on the investment as a whole and a gain to the borrowers.

To use a modification of our previous example concerning housing, let us assume that while prices in general triple, the price of a given house, which grows older every year and physically depreciates, merely doubles. The overall investment in the house thus loses one-third its original buying power. Yet, if the home buyer has had to put only 20 percent of the price down, he increases his equity by a factor of 6, inasmuch as the 100 percent rise in the price of the house accrues all to him. And thus he comes out doubling his real wealth—viz., he has 6 times the equity in the face of a tripled price level. Both his gain and the overall loss on the purchase of the house are financed by the lenders, who lose two-thirds of the purchasing power of the money they lent by virtue of the tripling of prices. Using a $100,000 house for illustration, the home buyer's equity goes from $20,000 to $120,000, while the mortgage lender's principal does not rise above its initial $80,000. With a tripling of prices, the house, at $200,000, is worth what $66,667 was worth at the time of its purchase. The homeowner's $120,000 equity is worth what $40,000 was worth at the time the house was purchased. The lender's $80,000 is worth only what $26,667 was worth at the time of purchase. The loss to the lender, in terms of dollars of the original buying power, is $80,000 minus $26,667, that is, $53,333. This loss finances the loss of $33,333 on the investment as a whole in terms of dollars of the original buying power, plus the gain of the homeowner borrower of $20,000. And so it is in all cases of this kind.

The worse inflation in the form of credit expansion becomes, the worse becomes the problem of malinvestment. With a high enough rate of inflation, it may even pay to "invest" in such things as passenger automobiles, because their price as one-year-old used cars may exceed their price the year before as new cars by more than enough to cover the interest costs involved.

In order for malinvestment to occur, however, it is not necessary that inflation be strong enough to make prices actually rise or that capital be diverted into investments in which the overall rate of return is negative. As von Mises has shown, credit expansion, and the artificial reduction in the rate of interest it causes (whether that reduction is absolute or only relative to the rate of profit), creates the appearance of a more abundant supply of capital than in fact exists. That is, the mere manufacture and lending of banknotes or deposit entries does not create any actual additional capital, but only the appearance of additional capital. On the basis of this appearance, businessmen are led to undertake projects for whose execution the actual supply of capital is inadequate. Such use of capital, for purposes inappropriate to the actual supply of capital, constitutes malinvestment. Even if the use of the capital does not entail an outright loss in real terms, it still represents a diversion of capital from more important to less important uses. It is still a wasteful, inefficient use of capital, hence, malinvestment.[67]

The effect of all malinvestment of capital is a reduced overall ability to produce, since the capital required for production is used inefficiently. This impairment of the ability to produce causes a reduced ability to produce *capital goods* no less than consumers' goods. And this, in turn, represents a *further* source of diminution in the supply of capital goods in the future. Anything which, like malinvestment, impairs the ability to produce impairs the future supply of capital goods, because, as we have seen, the source of capital goods is production itself.[68]

The phenomenon of malinvestment provides an important illustration of the fact that inflation does not raise all prices at the same time and to the same extent. So long as credit expansion is capable of inducing malinvestment, it tends to raise the prices of such things as storable commodities and houses relative to most other prices, by virtue of creating an artificial additional demand for them based on the desire to take advantage of the special profit that credit expansion creates in those lines. Later, when inflation in the form of credit expansion stops, slows, or simply fails to accelerate sufficiently—with the result that interest rates rise to the point of eliminating the profitability of the malinvestments—these prices fall relative to most other prices. For then the ground is cut from under the additional demand for them. This knowledge sheds important light on major movements in the commodity and real estate markets.

The Withdrawal-of-Wealth Effect

As we have seen, the very act of spending newly created fiat money or fiduciary media must inflict losses somewhere in the economic system equal to the unearned gains of the spenders. Such spending represents an uncompensated withdrawal of wealth from producers in that the spenders draw wealth out of the system without putting wealth in. The individual businesses that receive the new and additional money may not be aware of this fact, because they can reexchange the money for the goods and service of others. But the loss must fall somewhere in the economic system.[69]

The withdrawal-of-wealth effect represents a diversion of capital to consumption insofar as the spenders of the new and additional money are consumers and probable malinvestment insofar as they are business firms. The latter conclusion is implied in the fact that the firms which depend on the creation of new and additional money have proved unable to compete for capital on the regular loan market and require the subsidy that credit expansion represents.

It is almost impossible that the withdrawal-of-wealth effect could make possible an increase in capital goods at the expense of consumption, as some advocates of credit expansion have claimed in putting forward the doctrine of "forced saving." This is because the proceeds of credit expansion are themselves largely used to finance the purchase of consumers' goods; and of the credit expansion that is used for business purposes, a substantial portion goes for the payment of wages, which, directly or indirectly, are all or almost all consumed. Thus, it is highly unlikely that credit expansion and the withdrawal-of-wealth effect could operate as a tax on consumption in favor of capital accumulation. And when placed in the context of all the other ways that inflation and credit expansion undermine capital formation, the notion that credit expansion promotes capital formation must be judged patently absurd.[70] As we have seen, the effect of inflation and credit expansion is to increase consumption expenditure relative to productive expenditure and to increase the rate of net consumption.

![black bar]

6. Consequences of the Destruction of Capital

Reduction of the Real Rate of Return

All five of the effects described have been shown to operate against capital accumulation. The reversal-of-safety, tax, malinvestment, and withdrawal-of-wealth effects also operate to *reduce the real rate of return on capital*. The reversal-of-safety effect threatens all who invest in the traditional ways with the loss of their capital and thus with the receipt of no rate of return at all, or, indeed, a negative one. The tax effect represents the taxing away of the real rate of return. The malinvestment effect represents the investment of capital in ways that are less efficient and actually loss making. The withdrawal-of-wealth effect represents the withdrawal of wealth that constitutes part or all of firms' real rate of return on capital.

It must be stressed that these reductions in the real rate of return occur in conjunction with *less* capital formation, not an abundance of capital, as the advocates of credit expansion believe. The process can be compared to the effect on the income statement of a firm, of a fire in its warehouse, or some similar calamity. It has less wealth and when it enters the reduction in its wealth on its balance sheet, it must make an equivalent charge against its income, in its income statement. Of course, none of this should really be surprising in view of the pervasive, direct and intimate relationship that we have established between aggregate profits and net investment.[71]

The Gains of Debtors Less Than the Losses of Creditors

A further consequence of the undermining of capital formation, and the accompanying reduction in the real rate of return on capital, is that the gains from inflation enjoyed by debtors are less than the losses suffered by creditors. The reduction in the overall real rate of return on capital investment as such means that there is less gain for all investors combined to share. Thus, any increase in the gains enjoyed by stockholders and other classes of business debtors must be accompanied by losses on the part of bondholders and other classes of creditors that are even greater, for the latter must provide not only the gains of the stockholders and other business debtors, but also make good the reduction in the overall real rate of return on capital as such that takes place.

The phenomenon of the gain of debtors being less than the loss of creditors is obvious in the case of malinvestments that are extreme enough actually to be loss making on an overall basis, yet turn out to be of benefit to borrowers. It is particularly glaring in cases in which *consumer* borrowers, such as homeowners, the inherent nature of whose activity is to use up wealth, are able to increase their wealth, by virtue of having borrowed at a rate of interest that is sufficiently below the rate at which prices rise. But it is present to some substantial degree throughout the economic system, whenever credit expansion takes place. And, of course, debtors, no less than creditors, bear the full brunt of the stepped-up taxation of profits that inflation and credit expansion engender, even to the point of being deprived of any real rate of return whatever. Both categories also suffer from the inducements to overconsumption that inflation and credit expansion create.

The Impoverishment of Wage Earners

Because of inflation and the rise in consumption and accompanying undermining of saving and productive expenditure that it causes, both the relative production of capital goods and the degree of capital intensiveness in the economic system are less. In addition, the efficiency with which existing capital goods are employed is less. All of these factors, of course, operate to reduce the supply of capital goods available for use in production. Since the productivity of labor vitally depends on the supply of capital goods, inflation operates to reduce the productivity of labor. This means, of course, that it operates to reduce real wage rates.[72]

Inflation operates to reduce real wages also by virtue of the fact that real wages depend on the demand for labor relative to the demand for consumers' goods.[73] And the demand for labor, of course, depends on saving and productive expenditure.[74] In raising the rate of net consumption and thereby retarding the growth in saving and productive expenditure relative to the growth in the demand for consumers' goods, inflation retards the growth in the demand for labor relative to the growth in the demand for consumers' goods, and in this way too operates to reduce real wage rates.

Thus, by virtue of its effect both on the productivity of labor and on the so-called distribution factor—viz., the demand for labor relative to the demand for consumers' goods—inflation tends to make prices rise at a more rapid rate than wage rates and thus to bring about a corresponding reduction in real wage rates.

It is important to realize that insofar as the government and labor unions attempt to resist the tendency toward the fall in real wages, by forcing wage rates to increase as fast as prices, the effect of their action is to cause unemployment. Insofar as prices rise because of a decline in the productivity of labor or because of a growth in the demand for consumers' goods in excess of the growth in the demand for labor, any attempt to make wage rates rise equivalently is an attempt to make them rise without benefit of a rise in the demand for labor. This is an important, though not the most important, way in which inflation actually causes unemployment rather than prevents or remedies it.

The Stock Market and Inflationary Depression

The fact that inflation undermines capital formation has important implications for the performance of the stock market. In its initial phase or when it undergoes a sufficient and relatively unanticipated acceleration, inflation in the form of credit expansion can create a stock-market boom. However, its longer-run effects are very different. The demand for common stocks depends on the availability of savings. In causing savings to fail to keep pace with the growth in the demand for consumers' goods, inflation tends to prevent stock prices, as well as wage rates, from keeping pace with the rise in the prices of consumers' goods.

The same consequence results from the fact that infla-

tion also leads to funds being more urgently required internally by firms—to compensate for all the ways in which it causes replacement funds to become inadequate. At some point in an inflation, business firms that are normally suppliers of funds to the credit markets—in the form of time deposits, the purchase of commercial paper, the extension of receivables credit, and the like—are forced to retrench and, indeed, even to become demanders of loanable funds, in order to meet the needs of their own, internal operations. The effect of this is to reduce the availability of funds with which stocks can be purchased, and thus to cause stock prices to fall, or at least to lag all the more behind the prices of consumers' goods.

When this situation exists in a pronounced form, it constitutes what has come to be called an "inflationary depression." This is a state of affairs characterized by a still rapidly expanding quantity of money and rising prices and, at the same time, by an acute scarcity of capital funds. The scarcity of capital funds is manifested not only in badly lagging, or actually declining, securities markets but also in a so-called credit crunch, i.e., a situation in which loanable funds become difficult or impossible to obtain. The result is widespread insolvencies and bankruptcies.

7. Inflation as the Cause of Depressions and Deflation

Inflation, especially in the form of credit expansion, sets the stage for financial contractions and deflations—i.e., for depressions. It does so in several, related ways.

It undermines the perceived need and the desire to own money balances. As a result, it causes a more rapid spending of money—a rise in the so-called velocity of circulation of money. An integral part of this process, of course, is a growing state of financial illiquidity—a declining ratio of cash holdings to current liabilities.

These results occur in large part because credit expansion creates the prospect of being able to obtain the money needed to make purchases and pay bills, easily and profitably through borrowing. The prospect of loans manufactured out of thin air by the banking system is substituted for the holding of actual money, with the result that businesses are led to draw down their cash reserves in making loans and investments they otherwise would not have made.[75] For they expect that when they need money they can readily obtain it from their banks. The fact that credit expansion, and the creation of money in any other form, causes the demand for goods and services to grow makes the holding of additional inventories also appear as a welcome substitute for the holding of money as the means of assuring the ability to make purchases and pay bills in the future, since in a rising market the inventories can be liquidated all the more easily and profitably.

These mechanisms are reinforced by the fact that after a while, inflation—even in the form of credit expansion—raises interest rates. This, of course, makes it worthwhile for people to lend out short-term sums of money that it otherwise would not have been worthwhile to lend out and would thus have remained in cash holdings. Finally, as inflation proceeds to the point of raising prices, people sooner or later become accustomed to the rise in prices and come to expect them to go on rising. When this happens, they start buying sooner, before prices rise further.

In all of these ways, inflation of the money supply brings about an even greater increase—a superinflation, as it were—in the volume of spending in the economic system, and a corresponding diminution in the size of cash holdings relative to spending and to current liabilities. Spending rises not only because there is more money, but also because the increase in the quantity of money reduces the perceived need and hence the desire to own money.[76]

The other side of spending, of course, is people's revenues and incomes, since one man's spending is another man's receipts. Obviously, in superinflating the volume of spending in the economy, inflation also superinflates people's revenues and incomes.

Inflation also does something else. It encourages people to pile up a mass of debt that they can pay only so long as their revenues and incomes hold up—indeed, only so long as their revenues and incomes go on increasing. Inflation in the form of credit expansion encourages borrowing by holding down the rate of interest in relation to the rate of profit. It makes borrowing exceptionally profitable; and the more so, the more leverage the borrowing provides. Another important way that inflation encourages debt is simply by leading people to borrow in anticipation of rising prices. Housing purchases have been a prime example of this effect of inflation. People go heavily into debt to buy houses at already inflated prices, because they expect housing prices to go on rising. The same thing happens with business spending for plant and equipment and inventories.

Thus, inflation does two critical things. It superinflates people's revenues and incomes, while making them correspondingly illiquid, and it leads them to pile up substantial debts against those revenues and incomes.

This alone must set the stage for a depression if and when inflation stops. Because then the causes of the reduced demand for money balances are removed. At that point, people start trying to rebuild their cash holdings. As a result, spending and the velocity of circulation fall, with the further result that people's money revenues and incomes fall. The effect of this, in turn, is that they cannot pay their debts. A substantial number of business and personal bankruptcies occurs.

The consequence of this, of course, is that the assets and capital of banks which have lent to such borrowers is correspondingly reduced, and many of them also fail. The failure of banks, of course, causes the money supply actually to be reduced, since the banks' outstanding checking deposits are part of the money supply. The reduction in the money supply then leads to a further decline in spending, revenue and income, and thus to still more bankruptcies and bank failures. The process feeds on itself, potentially to the point of eliminating all fiduciary media from the money supply and making the money supply equivalent to the supply of standard money alone.[77] The reduction in the quantity of money can be avoided only if the government is prepared to create additional fiat standard money to whatever extent may be necessary to guarantee the fiduciary media of the failing banks. But this lays the foundation for a still greater expansion in the supply of fiduciary media in the future.

This is the essence of the inflation-depression process. The critical factors are: artificial inducements to illiquidity and to a corresponding superinflation of revenues and incomes; the piling up of a mass of debt against these superinflated revenues and incomes; and then a contraction in spending, revenues, and incomes following the end of the inflation. The contraction phase leaves people with no means of paying the mass of debt they have accumulated, and can operate to produce a self-reinforcing downward spiral of deflation of the money supply.

The inflation-depression process is reinforced by the fact that inflation in the form of credit expansion causes malinvestments—investments which are profitable only on the basis of inflation itself. When the inflation comes to an end, the unprofitability of the malinvestments is revealed.

The onset of the depression is precipitated by the fact that inflation and credit expansion undermine the availability of real capital and thus of credit, too, in real terms. In particular, when credit expansion stops, a "credit crunch" develops. This is because the existing capital funds of many enterprises are made inadequate by the rise in wage rates and materials prices caused by the previous injections of credit in the form of new and additional money. The consequence is that firms requiring credit turn out to need more credit than they had planned on, while those firms normally supplying credit turn out to be able to supply less than had been counted on, and may even need credit themselves in order to meet the requirements of their own internal operations at these higher wage rates and prices. Thus, as the need for credit surges and as suppliers of funds become demanders of funds, or at least supply less funds, firms that had counted on borrowing money, or on refinancing their existing borrowings, find that they are unable to do so. This causes insolvencies and bankruptcies. In this environment, as it becomes clear that the funds one had been counting on from others are not available, people's demand for holdings of money rises: it becomes necessary to liquidate inventories and other assets and to curtail expenditures, in order to have the funds available to meet one's obligations. In this way, the "velocity of circulation of money" falls.

These results can occur not only when inflation stops, but also when it merely slows down or even when it fails to accelerate sufficiently. To postpone the onset of a credit crunch, it becomes necessary to provide the victims of previous credit expansion with additional funds, in order for them to be able to pay the higher wage rates and materials prices caused by the previous credit expansion. Then still further inflation and credit expansion become necessary in order to overcome the resulting inadequacy of the funds of still others, possibly including the funds of the initial recipients of credit expansion, who perhaps are now themselves faced with unexpected increases in wage rates and materials prices. If at any point, the necessary additional credit expansion is not forthcoming, a credit crunch develops. If it is forthcoming, people soon begin to borrow on a larger scale, in anticipation of the possible inadequacy of funds in the face of higher wage rates and materials prices. If that additional demand for loanable funds is not met by still more credit expansion, the result is a credit crunch at that point. If it is met by still more credit expansion, the result is a still greater increase in wage rates and materials prices, which nullifies the value of the greater borrowing and requires still more credit expansion to avoid the onset of a credit crunch. Whenever the necessary additional credit expansion is not forthcoming, some firms find that they lack the funds they require, and thus a credit crunch develops.

The failure of inflation to accelerate sufficiently can also cause the demand for money for holding to increase, and thus velocity to decrease, insofar as the demand for money for holding has become unduly low based on the expectation of a more rapid acceleration of inflation than turns out to be the case. This consideration is relevant to the fall in the velocity of circulation that took place in the United States in the early 1980s. By the beginning of the 1980s, the height of the velocity of circulation corresponded to a growing expectation that the U.S. government would begin to inflate on a scale characteristic of Latin American countries. When the rate of inflation turned out to be much more modest, the demand for holdings of money increased in the United States, and

thus the velocity of circulation fell.

Finally, it should be realized that in order to produce a "credit crunch" and the onset of a depression, it is not necessary that credit expansion result in an actual rise in wage rates and materials prices. It is necessary only—as is inescapable—that it make wage rates and materials prices higher than they would otherwise have been. If wage rates and materials prices fail to fall, or fall by less than they would otherwise have done, the effect is still to render existing capital funds less adequate than they would otherwise have been and to create a need for more capital funds than would otherwise have been the case. As a result, in this case too, firms that would have been suppliers of capital funds in the loan market must become smaller suppliers, or even demanders of such funds. Thus, the basis is still present for the unexpected deficiency of credit that characterizes a credit crunch. These considerations are of great importance in considering the 1929 Depression, which came after a decade of relatively stable or even modestly declining commodity prices.

Gold Clauses and Prospective Inflation of Paper as the Cause of Deflation in Gold

It may help to shed light on the Great Depression of the 1930s to realize that there are circumstances in which the prospect of inflation can have the seemingly paradoxical effect of producing an immediate deflation. This is the case when the prospect of inflation takes place under a fractional-reserve gold standard, such as existed in the early 1930s, and at the same time the great bulk of debt contracts contain gold clauses. (Gold clauses define debts in terms of the obligation to pay a definite sum of gold. For example, prior to April 1933, the obligation to pay $2,000 actually meant, according to most debt contracts in force in the United States, the obligation to pay approximately 100 ounces of gold, for it was explicitly stated that the dollars in the contracts were to be understood as representing gold at the rate of one ounce for every $20.67.)

In such circumstances, whenever inflation causes a devaluation of the paper money against gold to a greater extent than the increase in the quantity of paper money, it reduces the ability of the paper money supply to pay debts in gold. In this sense, it constitutes a deflation. For example, if initially there are $20 billion of paper money (including checkbook money) in existence in the United States, and these $20 billion are convertible into gold, on demand, at $20 per ounce, then this supply of paper is the equivalent of a billion ounces of gold. (Under a fractional-reserve gold standard, of course, there will not actually be a billion physical ounces of gold, backing the $20 billion of paper, but only some fraction of this physical amount. However, the supply of paper money is the *equivalent* of a billion ounces of gold in terms of current debt-paying power, so long as it is freely convertible into gold on demand at $20 per ounce.)

If now, however, as the result of prospective inflation, and of the government's refusal to redeem the paper money for gold on demand, the price of gold were to rise, say, to $40 per ounce, then the $20 billion of paper would be devalued to the equivalent of only *half* a billion ounces of gold. If we view the supply of paper money not as a supply of "dollars," but as a supply of equivalents of gold ounces, then our assumed devaluation represents a halving of the money supply insofar as the money supply is composed of paper. For the paper money supply was a billion "gold-ounce equivalents," and now it is only half a billion "gold-ounce equivalents."[78] Such a devaluation would mean radically reduced "gold-ounce" sales revenues, while "gold-ounce" principal and interest charges remained the same. The prospect of such a devaluation must obviously mean the prospect of mass bankruptcies.

The prospect of such a devaluation and of its resulting mass bankruptcies must precipitate immediate bankruptcies, for lenders with funds coming due will not reextend credit in an environment in which its later repayment is made unlikely. Widespread immediate bankruptcies, of course, precipitate bank failures and a decline in the outstanding quantity of money. What is present here can be described as the prospect of future bad money driving present relatively good money out of existence.

On the basis of these considerations, I advance the hypothesis that the depression of the 1930s was intensified by the Federal Reserve's efforts to expand the quantity of money in order to reduce interest rates and finance large-scale government budget deficits. These efforts had the effect of creating the prospect of a devaluation of the dollar against gold and thus of making the honoring of gold-clause contracts correspondingly more difficult, with the result that they precipitated greater credit contraction and thus a larger number of immediate bankruptcies and bank failures, and, because of this last, a decline in the quantity of money. Seen in this light, the budget deficits of the Hoover administration must be regarded as profoundly and radically deflationary insofar as their financing necessitated the Federal Reserve's efforts to expand the supply of paper dollars and thereby threaten their gold value. By the same token, Roosevelt's 1932 campaign promise of reducing federal spending by 25 percent and balancing the budget turns out, had it been put into actual practice, to be exactly the right prescription for combatting deflation.

I hypothesize also that the policy of inflation which was pursued around the world, and the consequent devaluation of gold-standard currencies, was responsible for the radical reduction in the volume of international trade which took place in the 1930s. For international trade had been conducted in gold or currencies regarded as equivalent to gold. This policy radically reduced the world supply of money when viewed as gold equivalents. In thus reducing the supply of internationally useable money, it reduced the volume of international trade.

(The principles present in this discussion apply to the devaluation of any currency in a situation in which substantial debts are payable in a different currency. For example, if an inflation of Mexican pesos precipitates a devaluation of the Mexican peso against the American dollar to a greater degree than the increase in the supply of pesos and spending in terms of pesos, while Mexicans owe substantial debts payable in dollars, the effect of the inflation of pesos is deflationary from the perspective of the ability of Mexicans to pay debts denominated in dollars. In the same way, the mere prospect of such a devaluation can render the Mexican government's policy of inflation deflationary from its very inception.)

8. Inflation as the Cause of Mass Unemployment

The fall in spending that takes place in the course of a depression causes mass unemployment, unless and until wage rates fall to the point of permitting the consequently reduced payroll funds to employ all who are able and willing to work. Since it is inflation that sets the stage for depressions, it is inflation that is responsible for the unemployment that accompanies them. In the absence of inflation and credit expansion, there would be no depressions and thus none of the mass unemployment that takes place in depressions, because the preconditions for a depression would simply not come into existence.[79]

Given the existence of inflation, it is true that its continuation and acceleration can forestall the development of mass unemployment. But this no more makes inflation a means of preventing unemployment than narcotics are a means of preventing sickness and debilitation. The temporarily preventative effects both of inflation and of narcotics exist only in a context in which their prior use has created a dependency on them. Had they not been resorted to in the first place, the dependency would not exist. Stop their use, and after a painful interlude, the dependency disappears. And their use must be stopped, if utter destruction is not to result. When their use is stopped, it is their *use*, not the stoppage of their use, which must take the blame for the resulting mass unemployment in the one case and for the withdrawal symptoms in the other.

As we have seen, in the face of the existence of strong monopoly labor unions, inflation is ineffectual as a remedy for existing unemployment. For the unions will seize the opportunity of rising aggregate demand to raise wage rates even in the midst of mass unemployment, and will thus prevent the growth in payroll funds from being accompanied by anything near a corresponding growth in the number of workers employed.[80] And, it should be recalled, those who are reemployed on the various make-work projects that almost always accompany any attempt to eliminate unemployment by means of inflation, are employed at a loss to the rest of the population, which must provide them with goods and services and receive nothing of corresponding value in return.[81] On the other hand, in the absence of substantial monopoly labor unions, wage rates are free to fall and unemployment can be eliminated in this way.

There is only one case in which any kind of plausible argument can be made in favor of inflation as a remedy for existing unemployment. This is when a financial contraction/deflation has begun and in which no substantial downward adjustment of prices and wages has yet been made, and when there either are no substantial monopoly labor unions or, if there are, they are weakened to the point that they will not use the occasion of a rising aggregate demand to force up wage rates significantly. In this case, inflation, or more correctly the resumption of inflation, constitutes a restoration of the status quo ante, as it were, and is capable of achieving substantial reemployment. The conditions of this case appear to have been present in recessions in the United States since the early 1980s.

Even in this case, however, the essential problem remains that the policy of inflation continues, and with it, all of its destructive consequences. And to the extent that people come to expect that inflation will be resumed in such conditions, the effect is to prevent the downward adjustment of prices and wages that would eliminate the unemployment without any resumption of inflation. What occurs is nothing more than that the withdrawal symptoms are overcome by resuming the destructive narcotic, and the knowledge that the inflation narcotic is available prevents any step toward really solving the problem.

The government's readiness to resort to a resumption of inflation as the means of combatting unemployment guarantees the continuation of inflation with only the most minor of interruptions. Inflation goes on both when unemployment is a problem and when it is not a problem. It sets the stage for a financial contraction/deflation and thus mass unemployment as soon as the government makes any serious effort to stop or reduce it, and then, because of this, no sooner does the government make such an effort than it comes under mounting pressure to abandon it and return to its policy of inflation. If inflation is ever to be eliminated, the government must lose the power to inflate even in conditions in which doing so can reduce unemployment. Unemployment must be elimi-

nated through a fall in wage rates and prices.[82]

Sooner or later, of course, even in the midst of continuing and accelerating inflation, substantial unemployment develops in any case. It occurs because of the tendency of real wage rates to fall as the result of inflation and because of efforts to prevent this fall by forcing wage rates to rise fully as rapidly as prices, without benefit of the necessary increase in the demand for labor.[83] Even more important is the fact that as inflation becomes more extreme, the potential for sudden mass unemployment is created by efforts merely to moderate the inflation, and even by the failure sufficiently to accelerate it.

For example, if the quantity of money and aggregate demand have been growing rapidly enough to raise wages and prices, say, by 50 percent a year, and the government decides that it wants to moderate the inflation to the point that wages and prices rise only by 25 percent a year, its action is capable of causing mass unemployment. This will occur simply by virtue of wages and prices continuing to rise for a time at their previous rate, on the basis of sheer inertia, as it were. In the face of a relatively "modest" 25 percent rise in the demands for consumers' goods and labor, the effect of increases in the price and wage level temporarily continuing at a 50 percent rate is a one-sixth decline in the quantity of consumers' goods purchased and a one-sixth decline in the number of workers employed. This is because $5/4$ times the demand, when divided by $6/4$ times the price or wage level, can purchase only $5/6$ times the quantities.

Similarly, in conditions in which the rise in prices and wages discounts a substantial acceleration in the increase in aggregate demand that fails to materialize, mass unemployment will result. For example, if aggregate demand has been growing at a 50 percent annual rate and wages and prices begin to rise at a 75 percent annual rate, in anticipation of aggregate demand growing at 75 percent, and then aggregate demand fails to grow more than 50 percent, a comparable degree of unemployment will be created. The same kind of results occur, of course, in conditions in which the demand for money for holding has fallen in anticipation of a degree of inflation that does not materialize, which then leads to a rise in the demand for money for holding. A situation describable by one or more of these three patterns of the development of mass unemployment in the midst of inflation occurred, for example, in Uruguay in the late 1960s, when the unemployment rate reached 28 percent at the same time that prices were rising at an annual rate of 61 percent.[84]

9. The Inherent Accelerative Tendencies of Inflation

The potentially most devastating consequence of inflation is that, once begun, the process tends to accelerate. The ultimate stopping point of the acceleration is that the inflated currency loses its acceptability. This occurs when people realize that between the time they accept it and even the earliest possible time they can spend it and thus pass it on to someone else, they will have suffered a substantial loss in buying power. At that point, they refuse any longer to accept it in exchange for their goods and services, and turn instead to barter if necessary. The inflated currency loses its character as money and ends up being dumped in the streets and down the sewers, as just so much litter.

In his seminar, von Mises used to describe the acceleration of inflation as going through three phases. In the first phase, people observe that prices are rising but still believe that the rise is temporary. They are willing to increase their holdings of money, in the conviction that prices will one day come down. In the second phase, people have come to the conclusion that prices will never come down, but will go on rising. In this phase, their attitude is described by the man who says, "I do not need a new refrigerator this year, but I will need one next year. I will buy it this year, however, in order to avoid having to pay a higher price for it next year." In the third and final phase of inflation, the attitude of people is described by the man who says, "I do not need a new refrigerator now and never expect to need one, but I will buy one nonetheless, because it is better to own anything than this rapidly depreciating money." This last phase represents what is described as the "flight into real values."[85]

Inflation tends to accelerate for a variety of reasons. One is that the underlying premises which lead to the policy of inflation in the first place—namely, the alleged helplessness of the individual and the alleged omnipotence and benevolence of the government—logically call for more and more rapid inflation as time goes on. As we shall see, two factors closely related to this are that inflation itself creates problems whose solution is perceived as requiring still more inflation, and that the stimulative effects of any given rate of inflation tend to wear off and to require a more rapid rate of inflation to maintain them.

Both of these phenomena are present in the very fact that inflation tends to raise the velocity of circulation. So long as the velocity of circulation is rising, the rate of increase in the volume of spending in the economic system is greater than the rate of increase in the quantity of money. But once the velocity of circulation stabilizes at any given higher level, the rate of increase in the volume of spending necessarily falls to that of the rate of increase in the quantity of money alone. To maintain the previously higher rate of increase in the volume of spending, a more rapid rate of increase in the quantity of money is now necessary, which, in turn, tends to be accompanied

by a still higher velocity of circulation of money, leading, of course, to the same result and the need for a still more rapid increase in the quantity of money later on. In addition, as the result of any stabilization of velocity after a sustained period of rise, the rate of profit is almost certain to fall, inasmuch as it will now reflect a lesser rate of increase in spending. Its fall, furthermore, operates to diminish the gains inflation provides to stockholders and other business debtors at the expense of bondholders and other business creditors. These gains meanwhile are also tending to be reduced by a rise in the rate of interest toward any given rate of profit.[86] Thus, an acceleration of inflation is called for to maintain the rate of profit, and a more rapid acceleration to maintain any given ratio of excess of the rate of profit relative to the rate of interest. These accelerations must be indefinitely repeated if the rate of profit is not to be allowed to fall and if its relationship to the rate of interest is to be maintained.

Of course, there is nothing inevitable in the acceleration of inflation. It can be interrupted; indeed, inflation can be stopped altogether. But in order to do either of these things, the willingness must exist to bear the temporary painful consequences. The accelerative tendencies of inflation all come down to the fact that there are such consequences. If the willingness to bear them is lacking, then inflation can be presumed continually to accelerate.

The Welfare-State Mentality

The logic of the welfare-state mentality is capable all by itself of resulting in unlimited inflation. If it is believed that the government is a real-life Santa Claus, indeed, a benevolent deity, and that its inflation-financed deficits are the source of free benefits, then there is no logical stopping point to the size of the deficits and the amount of the inflation used to finance them—given the fact that the government has the power to inflate.

If, for example, it is believed that the government has the power to provide free high-school education, then why not free college education? If it has the power to provide free medical care to people over sixty-five years of age, then why not to everyone? If it has the power to provide some people with low-cost housing, then why not more people?—why not everyone? If it can make it possible for people to retire at age sixty-five, then why not at age sixty, or even fifty-five?

Even under the Reagan administration, which appeared to manifest a substantial opposition to further growth of the welfare state, the corrupting influence of the ability to inflate never diminished. On the contrary, it thoroughly undermined efforts to end the growth of the welfare state and turned the desire for lower taxes and a stronger national defense into causes of more rapid inflation. The Reagan administration, at least in its early years, rightly regarded the proper function of the federal government as that of providing national defense, not public welfare. It espoused a philosophy of limited government and low taxes. Yet the government's ability to inflate made it possible to increase the defense budget and lower taxes without making any reduction whatever in the amount of welfare state spending. The result was that the Reagan administration simply added its increase in the defense budget, and its tax reductions, to a still growing level of welfare-state spending, and produced unprecedented peacetime budget deficits. These deficits required and received the support of very high rates of inflation—for example, a 16.9 percent increase in the money supply in 1986, following an 11.1 percent increase in the money supply in 1985.[87]

Throughout the Reagan years, the premise persisted that there is no limit to what the government can accomplish, if only it is willing to spend enough money. The great majority of people continued to believe all along that an economically insignificant city—Washington—which is utterly lacking in industry and is not a center of commerce or the performance of any other economic service, is nevertheless somehow capable of "bailing out" the economic system. "Washington" was and is thought to be capable of rescuing major companies and entire industries and undertaking the economic redevelopment of such major cities as New York, Philadelphia, Detroit, and Cleveland, and even that of whole states and entire geographic regions.

Nothing could be better evidence of the delusion inflation fosters, that it is the government that supports the people instead of the people who support the government, than the prevalence of such beliefs. "Washington" is seen as capable of achieving all these miracles for the simple reason that its ability to inflate allows it to spend money without first having to collect that money from the people. If not for this, it would be obvious that "Washington" can give nothing that it does not first take away, and thus, whenever it acts to help any individual or group, it is intensifying the hardship of other individuals and groups, and, indeed, causing losses substantially greater than any gains it may provide. For it not only takes from A to give to B, but in the process it reduces the incentive and the ability to produce.

Whatever the opposing influence of the Reagan administration, the welfare-state mentality has now been reenthroned. In the midst of massive budget deficits, and the shedding of rivers of crocodile tears over them, the last few Congresses have busied themselves with such measures as expanding the medicare system and embarking on federal support for child-care facilities. And, not very long ago, the administration of President Clinton was narrowly prevented from imposing a vast increase in government financing of medical expenses, which, had it been enacted, would almost certainly have turned out to be greater in cost than any new government program since social security.

Inflation to Solve Problems Caused by Inflation

The expressions "bail out" and "rescue" suggest what is perhaps the most important reason that inflation tends to accelerate. This is the fact that the very destruction and suffering that inflation causes makes still more inflation seem necessary and desirable. Inflation becomes the means of alleviating the consequences of inflation. It is a tool, an evil, destructive tool, but one whose immediate, visible effects for the user and for the groups on whose behalf it is used seem desirable. Thus, the more and the greater are the problems it creates, the more it tends to be used. Again, the analogy to drugs is very apt. Someone begins taking drugs as a means of alleviating his feelings of inadequacy. The effect of the drugs is soon to make him feel still more inadequate. And the apparent solution is then to increase the dosage.

The fact that major cities and industries need "bailing out"—which, of course, the government would finance largely on the basis of an increase in the quantity of money—is itself mainly the result of years of inflation and the consequent systematic overstatement of profits, leading to the taxation and consumption of funds required for the replacement of assets. It is a consequence of all of the destructive effects of inflation on saving and capital formation. Similarly, demands for ever more government aid to the elderly, and the inflation that must be resorted to in order to finance those demands, are largely the product of previous inflation, which has wiped out the value of pensions and savings. In the same way, demands for government support of the home-mortgage market, and the inflation required to finance it, are the result of the destruction of mortgage credit brought about by previous inflation.

When inflation goes far enough actually to reduce the ability to produce, the real revenues of the government begin to decline. This, together with the increasing demands being made upon the government as the result of the same process of economic decline, almost inevitably results in a still further acceleration of inflation.

The apparent need to inflate is further compounded to the degree that the rise in prices reaches the point of substantially reducing the buying power of the government's tax collections, which are largely based on incomes and transactions of the recent past. The more rapid the rise in prices, the greater is the reduction in the buying power of such tax receipts, and thus the greater the apparent need of the government to rely still more heavily on the printing press as the source of its funds. And, as previously pointed out, the apparent need to inflate is greatly increased when the day comes that private investors reach the conclusion that they must lose by purchasing government securities, and thus stop doing so, leaving the government's printing presses to make up for their withdrawal.[88]

The government is motivated to accelerate inflation not only for all of the above reasons, but, of course, also to paper over developing "credit crunches" as well as to overcome the previously described "profit squeezes" that must result from the stabilization of the velocity of money at any given higher level.[89]

Recessions as Inflationary Fueling Periods

Paradoxically, given the ability to inflate, even government efforts to end or reduce inflation can serve to accelerate it. The government begins by cutting back on inflation. But then a recession develops: insolvencies and bankruptcies appear; unemployment starts to increase. Now the government becomes frightened. Before the recession goes too far and turns into a full-scale depression, it reverses itself and accelerates the inflation. As a result, cash holdings relative to spending are built up on the basis of newly created money rather than on the basis of a decline in spending. At the same time, the injection of the new and additional money brings an end to the insolvencies and bankruptcies and mounting unemployment. Finally, once it is recognized that the danger of a depression has passed and that the policy of inflation is back in place, the money created to turn the recession around comes pouring out into the spending stream. In this way, even recessions end up serving as inflationary fueling periods.

Indexing and the Wage and Interest Ratchets

As people become aware of the consequences of inflation, they take steps to protect themselves. The use of price indexes is one very popular method.

It should be realized that price indexing does not provide any means for dealing with the problem of lags between the rise in the prices one must pay and the prices or income that one receives. At most it can enable an individual to catch up with the rise in prices. But it does not compensate people for the loss of purchasing power they experience in the intervals before catching up. Moreover, the widespread use of indexing, by operating to make prices rise automatically by the same percentage, undermines the functioning of the price system, which depends precisely on the *unevenness* of price changes.

Despite their shortcomings, inflation spawns the use of price indexes. They appear more and more in employment contracts, where they require periodic increases in wages in line with the rise in prices. Some years ago in the United States, social security payments became tied to a cost-of-living index. More recently, income tax brackets have been tied to the movement of prices: to the extent that the rise in individuals' incomes does not exceed the percentage by which prices rise, their tax bracket will not be increased. In the years ahead, it is possible that depreciation allowances will be tied to a price index. The payment of interest on government bonds and the computation of interest income for tax purposes might also some day include adjustments for the rise in prices.

All of these measures of protection against the effects of inflation tend to accelerate inflation, by creating further problems whose solution appears to be still more inflation. For example, to the extent that wages are increased merely because prices rise, that is, in the face of a given demand for labor, unemployment tends to develop. If the government wishes to avoid the unemployment that wage indexing can cause, then it must see to it that the wage increases are accompanied by further increases in the quantity of money. In that case, wages can increase and the increases can be passed along in the form of further price increases, which then serve as the basis for further wage increases. By providing the money to accommodate a wage-price spiral, the government can be led into an extreme and rapidly accelerating inflation—at each step pouring ever more money into the market in order to avoid the unemployment that would result from not accommodating the wage-price spiral. This has been the situation in Israel and Argentina and many other countries.

The indexation of the government's expenditures, such as social security payments, and the indexation of its tax revenues, operate to enlarge its expenditures and reduce its revenues. The result is a tendency toward greater deficits and thus more rapid creation of money to finance the deficits.

Even apart from wage indexing, there is a powerful tendency for inflation to accelerate in the government's efforts to avoid unemployment. For example, the labor unions may begin very modestly—seeking to raise wages by, say, a mere 2 percent above the level a free market would provide. The effect of their action is either the development of an addition of roughly 2 percent to the unemployment rate or to lead the government to choose to increase the quantity of money by an additional 2 percent, to make the demand for labor keep pace with the rise in wage rates.

If, as is likely, the government chooses to increase the quantity of money by an extra 2 percent, then no additional unemployment develops, but prices rise by an additional 2 percent. The unions now feel cheated. Their wage increase in the previous year has been eaten up by price increases. Perhaps for a number of years they will continue to ask for just an additional 2 percent. If so, the same story will continually repeat itself. Sooner or later, however, the unions will come to take a 2 percent rise in prices for granted. At that point, in order to obtain a 2 percent real improvement, they will begin to ask for wage increases of 4 percent. If the government increases the quantity of money sufficiently to accommodate this higher rate of wage increase, then additional unemployment will again be avoided, but now prices will begin to rise on the order of 4 percent a year instead of just 2 percent a year.

Once again, the scenario may be repeated several times. But eventually, the unions will conclude that prices can be expected to rise by 4 percent a year, and that in order to obtain a gain in real wages of 2 percent, they must demand wage increases of 6 percent. If the government continues to accommodate the unions by increasing the quantity of money more rapidly, their wage demands will rise to 8 percent, then 10 percent, and so on. In a word, there is an upward ratcheting of wage demands, with each higher level of wage demands (provided it is accompanied by the necessary increase in the quantity of money) serving to establish a higher level of increase in prices, on the basis of which wage demands are raised further.

At some point along the way, a process that can be described as double discounting emerges. The unions conclude that prices will not rise merely at some given rate, but can be expected to rise at an *increasing* rate. At this point, in order to obtain whatever increase in real wages they are after, they begin to demand wage increases equal not only to the rate at which prices have been rising up to now, plus the real improvement they seek, but wage increases equal to the higher rate at which they expect prices to rise over the life of their employment contracts, plus the real improvement they seek. This represents an *acceleration in the acceleration* of wage and price increases. And from here, still further acceleration in the acceleration develops, as expectations concerning the rate of acceleration start to increase. Thus, wage demands of 4 percent over the previous rise in prices are appropriate as a means of seeking a 2 percent real improvement only if the rate of price increases advances at 2 percent a year. But now, as the result of the demands for more rapid wage increases (always assuming, of course, accommodation by a more rapidly increasing quantity of money), prices will begin to rise with an acceleration of 4 percent a year instead of just 2 percent a year. Soon the unions will take such acceleration for granted and begin to accelerate their wage demands by 6 percent, then 8 percent, and so on. And thus, wages and prices begin skyrocketing upwards—10 percent a year, 14 percent a year, 20 percent a year, 28 percent a year, and on and on.

A similar process of upward ratcheting and acceleration takes place in connection with interest rates. The rise in prices that inflation causes reduces the real rate of interest received by creditors. In order for lending to be worthwhile, creditors need to receive higher rates of interest, which reflect the rate at which prices rise. But, as we have seen, no sooner do creditors begin to receive such rates of interest, than the special profit inflation provides to borrowers is removed. Moreover, inflation makes it a matter of virtual self-preservation for borrowers to gain at the expense of lenders, because if they do not, then, on an after-tax basis, their incomes cannot possibly keep pace with the rise in the replacement prices of their assets.[90] As a result, the borrowers find the rise in interest rates oppressive and demand a more rapid rate of inflation and credit expansion, both to reduce interest rates and to provide the revenues and profits with which to make any given level of interest rates payable. This problem becomes more intense, the greater inflation becomes, because the overall real rate of return on capital as such is all the more reduced, making the plight of the borrowers correspondingly more desperate in the absence of an ability to be compensated at the expense of the lenders.[91]

A succession of rounds of rising inflation and rising interest rates to compensate the creditors may ensue. But each time, the higher level of interest rates turns out to be inadequate in the face of still more rapidly rising prices. Finally, the day arrives when creditors conclude that no rate of interest, however high, will protect them, because the rate of price increase will be still higher. At that point, all private credit begins to disappear. Private citizens stop lending not only to the government but also to each other. At this juncture, a great quantum leap in the rate of inflation can easily take place. For the government may now attempt to replace the dwindling supply of private credit, provided out of savings, with credit provided out of newly created money. Indeed, this phenomenon exists, though on a comparatively small scale, as soon as any of the citizens become aware of what is happening and therefore cease to lend money. From this time on, there is a reduction in the supply of loanable funds that the government is motivated to make up for through policies of more rapid inflation.

The Current State of Inflation

As I have indicated, all of the above forces operating to cause inflation to accelerate are *tendencies*. Like anything else that is subject to human choice, their operation is not absolutely inevitable or inescapable, and certainly not in any given short period of time. Their presence very well describes the period 1933-1980 in the United States. In 1981 and 1982, however, the U.S. government refused to provide the accelerated increase in the quantity of money that the markets had come to expect it to provide.[92] Instead, it inaugurated a prolonged and severe recession—some would say the first depression since the 1930s. It allowed unemployment to increase and bankruptcies to occur to the point where people gave up the expectation of rapidly accelerating inflation and became willing to sell their goods and services at much lower rates of price increase than had prevailed before. Hence, the conviction developed that inflation was now "under control."

The result of the government's action in those years was actually to create a good deal of *deflationary* psychology. Many people came to fear that the legacy of enormous debt burdens and illiquidity left by inflation would drag the economic system into a sharp contraction of spending and successive waves of bankruptcies and bank failures, which the government would be powerless to stop. And, in truth, it must be admitted that major deflationary *potential* has existed and really does exist in the economic system. The collapse of real estate prices, the resulting failure of large numbers of savings and loan associations and savings banks, whose major asset was real estate loans, and the resulting virtual bankruptcy of the Federal Savings and Loan Insurance Corporation, all provide ample evidence of this. Further and even stronger evidence was provided by the precarious condition of many commercial banks and the virtual exhaustion of the resources of the Federal Deposit Insurance Corporation.

If, however, anything that is subject to human choice can be certain, it is that no contemporary government, with its unlimited power to create money, will allow a major depression to develop as the result of any failure on its part to increase the quantity of money. No matter how many billions or tens or hundreds of billions of dollars it takes to rescue the mass of debtors and to keep the level of spending on an upward course, the government possesses the means to create those billions.[93]

Consistent with this observation, from 1982 to early 1987, in order to prevent the debt crisis from deepening and in order to reduce the unemployment rate, the government embarked upon a reacceleration of inflation. Because the reacceleration came in the midst of a relatively noninflationary or even deflationary psychology, the result was that the new and additional money was held more tightly than it otherwise would have been. The fact that inflation psychology had been greatly diminished encouraged the government to reaccelerate inflation very sharply in 1985 and 1986, in the conviction that it could do so without experiencing the consequences of

inflation. As previously mentioned, the money supply was increased in those years by 11.1 percent and 16.9 percent respectively.[94] So long as prices were not rising rapidly and the public was thus not much concerned with inflation, the government felt free to expand the quantity of money at these much more rapid rates.

One of its objectives in rapidly increasing the quantity of money was a major reduction in the foreign exchange value of the dollar, which had continued to increase until well into 1985, as a consequence of diminished inflationary expectations in the United States. This deliberate reduction of the dollar's foreign exchange value took place in the mistaken belief that it would stimulate exports and at the same time discourage imports, thereby reducing America's allegedly "unfavorable" balance of trade. A cheaper dollar, it was believed, would make American goods correspondingly cheaper to foreign buyers, who had to buy dollars in order to be able to buy American goods. By the same token, a cheaper dollar was thought to mean that foreign goods and services would be that much more expensive to Americans, who had to buy the foreign currencies in order to buy foreign goods and services, and who now would have to pay that much more for those currencies.

What the supporters of this idea overlooked was that the virtually inevitable consequence of the much higher rates of increase in the money supply in 1985 and 1986 was an acceleration in the rate at which prices rose in 1987 and 1988. This more rapid rise in prices operated to price American exports out of the market, and to encourage imports, thereby confirming what every real economist knew from the very beginning, which was that the government's policy of inflating in order to reduce the foreign exchange value of the country's currency was contrary to purpose and an exercise in futility, precisely because it would cause American prices to rise more rapidly.

In 1987, acting no doubt in fear that it was inflating too rapidly, the government adopted a sharply less inflationary policy, which resulted in a relatively modest increase in the money supply of 3.5 percent for that year.[95] This was followed by rates of increase in the money supply of 4.9 percent in 1988, less than 1 percent in 1989, and barely 4 percent in 1990, with most of the increase in 1990 occurring in the last portion of the year.[96]

Not surprisingly, after years of having become adjusted to substantially more rapid rates of increase in the quantity of money, the extremely modest rate of increase in the money supply of 1989 and most of 1990 operated to bring about a sharply higher demand for money for holding, a correspondingly lower velocity of circulation of money, and a general inability to repay the great mass of outstanding debt—i.e., the government drove the economy to the brink of a major depression. Then, as the threat of depression became clear, the government returned to the policy of more rapid increases in the quantity of money, and brought about a rate of increase of almost 9 percent in 1991, more than 14 percent in 1992, and more than 10 percent in 1993. Overall, from the end of 1990 to the end of 1993, the compound annual rate of increase in the money supply was approximately 11 percent.[97]

In their response to the depression or near-depression of 1990–1992, the government's policy makers divided into two camps. A relatively moderate group of inflationists, led by Federal Reserve Chairman Alan Greenspan, and often mistakenly thought of as supporting "tight money," favored increasing the quantity of money at whatever rate was required to overcome the growing deflation/depression psychology that characterized 1991 and 1992. Once it became clear that that was accomplished and that signs could be found that price increases were starting to accelerate as the result of the rapid infusion of new and additional money into the economic system, this group favored going back to sharply curtailing the increase in the quantity of money. Inasmuch as this group currently controls the actions of the Federal Reserve System, it has been able to have its way, and as of October 1994, the annualized rate of increase in the quantity of money since the beginning of 1994 has been little more than 2 percent.[98] This substantial deceleration in the rate of increase in the money supply has been accompanied by a succession of increases in short-term interest rates, which the very rapid increase in the quantity of money in the face of widespread deflationary psychology had driven to levels not seen since the early 1950s.

The other group of government policy makers, which includes the president and his advisers, as well as key congressmen and senators in a position to introduce legislation concerning the Federal Reserve System, such as the chairman of the House Banking Committee, favors no substantial deceleration in the rate of money supply increase and, indeed, at least by implication, favors a further acceleration in the rate. Both of these conclusions follow from the fact that the members of this group have become alarmed at each of the increases in short-term interest rates that has taken place this year and have opposed those increases. They apparently are either unaware or unconcerned that given the rise in sales revenues and profits, and thus in the demand for loanable funds, that the increase in the quantity of money and volume of spending has brought about, the only way that interest-rate increases could have been avoided would have been by virtue of meeting the additional demand for loanable funds with a further and progressively growing increase in the supply of loanable funds provided out of

new and additional money.[99] Interest rates have risen because the Federal Reserve has been unwilling to provide the banking system with the additional standard money reserves to make that possible. In contrast, the only point at which the members of this group appear willing to consider the need for slowing down the increase in the quantity of money is when confronted with the existence of rapidly rising prices as an already established fact. Until that time, they believe, inflation is not a problem—it doesn't even exist.

Both groups of government policy makers confuse inflation with its consequence, rising prices, and are thus prepared to stop it only after it is too late. In this virtual theater of the absurd, the more extreme inflationists criticize the less extreme inflationists for seeing inflation that isn't there yet and responding to a problem that allegedly either doesn't exist at all or does not yet exist on a sufficient scale to warrant action of any kind.

When all is said and done, what distinguishes the two groups of today's government policy makers is only the degree to which they are prepared rapidly to inflate. For today's "moderate" inflationists, a rate equivalent to 11 percent compounded for three years is enough for a while. For the more radical inflationists nothing is enough, at least until prices are rapidly rising all around them. At that point, they will admit the existence of a problem. The "moderate" inflationists, it should be noted, have recently been losing ground to the more radical inflationists, as the result of appointments to the Federal Reserve Board made by President Clinton.

Whichever group prevails in the year or two ahead, the government's response to the depression or near-depression of 1990–1992 confirms that recessions and even virtual depressions nowadays do indeed represent inflationary fueling periods. Decades of inflation have so reduced the demand for money for holding and so encouraged indebtedness that all efforts seriously to end inflation serve to bring on a major depression. In the face of that prospect, the government recoils and turns the impending depression into a new inflationary fueling period. The only difference between the conservative inflationists and the radical inflationists on this score is that the conservatives hope to be able to stop the process before it goes too far. They hope to be able to keep the fuel that has already been put out there from being ignited into a major rise in prices, while the more radical inflationists do not hesitate to guarantee such ignition by continuing to pour out the fuel.

Although the conservative inflationists currently control the Federal Reserve System, it should not be expected—assuming that they are able to retain control in the first place—that they will adhere to their program of curtailing the increase in the quantity of money. That policy, when pursued in 1988, 1989, and 1990, ended up costing President Bush his reelection. It will be substantially harder to pursue the next time, even if, perhaps especially if, a conservative occupies the White House and wants to be reelected. Thus inflation must continue on a substantial scale even under conservative administrations and conservative money-supply managers. This conclusion is further confirmed by the fact that prices rising at a rate of 3 percent a year are now considered "acceptable" and as evidencing the lack of a problem of inflation, even though in a generation such an annual rate of increase must succeed in more than doubling prices and thereby halving the buying power of all incomes and assets that are contractually fixed in dollars.

Only when inflation results in prices rising rapidly enough to evoke widespread public concern and thus to become a major political issue, can the government expect to have substantial public support for a policy of reducing its inflation for any prolonged length of time and at the risk of substantial unemployment. And even then, sufficient public support is by no means guaranteed, as the experience of all the Latin-American countries shows.

Given our present monetary system, the only way the government can continue to keep inflation within the limits set by the Reagan and Bush administrations is if every few years it were willing to provoke a recession at least as severe as the last two. In essence, it would have to return to the boom-bust conditions of the pre–New Deal days, in which limited inflations were always brought to a sharp halt and followed by a depression. Then it could reinstill something of the old mentality of "what goes up must come down" in reference to prices, and of fear of becoming overextended in reference to size of debt and adequacy of cash holdings.

However, there is an essential difference between the conditions of the present and those of the pre–New Deal days. In the days before the New Deal, the existence of a gold standard *forced* the government to bring inflation to an end. Today, there is no gold standard and thus nothing to force the government to end or even limit inflation. Indeed, the gold standard was abolished precisely in order to make unlimited inflation possible. In the absence of a gold standard, it seems extremely unlikely that today's voting public will be willing to see unemployment go to 10 or 11 percent every few years in order merely to reduce the rise in prices by a few percent for a limited time.

In view of the nature of the roots of inflation and of the enormous corrupting influence of the power to inflate, it seems likely that in retrospect the 1980s and early 1990s will turn out to have been merely an interlude in the process of accelerating inflation. A real solution to the problem of inflation requires depriving the government of the *ability* to inflate.[100]

Inflation and the Potential Destruction of the Division of Labor

As I have said, the potentially worst effect of inflation is acceleration to the point of depriving the inflated monetary unit of its acceptability and thus of its character as money. If it accelerates to that point, inflation is capable of destroying a division-of-labor society and with it, the whole of modern material civilization. As explained earlier in this book, the existence of money is an essential precondition of the existence of a division-of-labor society.[101] In destroying the existing monetary unit, inflation is capable of destroying the existence of money as such.

Whether or not the destruction of a given monetary unit is tantamount to the destruction of money itself, depends on the possibility of replacing the monetary unit that has been destroyed, with a new monetary unit. A new monetary unit cannot simply be decreed into existence—it would have no better chance of acceptance than "Monopoly" money or any other play money. In order to enjoy the universal acceptability that is essential to money, the new monetary unit must already have been established as a virtual money. In order for people to be willing to accept the new money, they must have the expectation that they can easily reexchange it with others for all the goods and services that they desire. This means that the new money must already virtually be money. If such an alternative money does not exist, then the only way the destruction of the monetary unit can be followed by the emergence of a new monetary unit is on the basis of a new universally accepted medium of exchange developing out of the conditions of barter.[102] In the interval in which this development takes place, however, which could be very considerable, the economic system would be without money and thus could not sustain the extensive division of labor on which modern material civilization depends.

The collapse of the assignats in 1796, in revolutionary France, was followed by the reappearance of gold and silver coin, which had been the money of France prior to the Revolution and had continued to be the money of the surrounding countries. The reappearance of gold and silver coin also followed the earlier collapse of the American continental currency in our own Revolutionary War, and the subsequent collapse of the Confederate currency in our Civil War. The collapse of the German mark in 1923 was followed by the introduction of a new mark redeemable on demand in American dollars, which, in turn, were redeemable on demand in gold. In these cases, which can be taken as characterizing all modern hyperinflations, a new monetary unit could quickly take the place of the unit that had been destroyed, because it either was itself already established as money or was redeemable on demand in an already established money. In the case of the new marks, every German who took them knew that he could use them to buy whatever dollars could buy.

It cannot be stressed too strongly that the ability quickly to replace the monetary unit that has been destroyed has existed in all modern hyperinflations only because these hyperinflations either took place in an environment in which an alternative money already existed in the countries concerned, or occurred only in very limited areas. In the latter case, the existence of money was essentially undisturbed in the rest of the world and in particular in the areas with which the affected countries carried on extensive trade relations.

It is a different story when a hyperinflation takes place over a very extensive territory and the possibility of replacing the monetary unit that has been destroyed, with a new monetary unit, is not present. In that case, the existence of money as such is destroyed, and with it the basis of any extensive division of labor.

History appears to provide at least one major example of this kind: the collapse of the Roman Empire. A prominent history text records:

> Debasement of the Roman coinage had begun as early as the reign of Nero. But in the third century, as a result of mounting inflation, widespread hoarding of specie, and sharply reduced revenues, the emperors resorted to reckless adulteration of the imperial coinage to meet their military and administrative costs. As a result, distrust of new currency was widely manifested, by individuals as well as by banks. Ultimately the government refused to accept its own coinage for many taxes and insisted on payment in kind.[103]

Gold and silver were prohibited from reemerging as money (which they might easily have done), because of the Roman government's insistence that they not circulate at a premium over its debased coinage.[104] At the same time, all private hoards of the precious metals were subject to confiscation by the Roman government, which was eager to use them for its own, immediate purposes.

In these ways, the Roman government destroyed the existence of money in its territory, and with it the most extensive division of labor in the history of the world prior to modern times. Among the consequences was the loss of the ability to have a paid, professional army, capable of being supplied with provisions purchased with money. The impregnable legions of Rome's heyday had to be replaced with a militia of farmers, who lived along the frontier, in virtual economic self-sufficiency, and who were expected to leave their farms and go out and fight when the need arose.[105]

Given the absence of a gold and silver money ready

to take their place, a simultaneous hyperinflation of all the major paper currencies of the present-day world would have the effect of destroying money as such. Such a hyperinflation must be considered a real possibility, in view of the fact that all the countries of the world pursue deliberate policies of inflation, all of which are subject to the inherent forces of acceleration described above. Furthermore, there is a distinct pressure on each country to inflate more or less in pace with its major trading partners, in order to prevent its currency from sharply appreciating relative to theirs, thereby encouraging a so-called unfavorable balance of trade.

But even if hyperinflation did not occur simultaneously in all the major countries, it could still have the potential for destroying the existence of money in a country whose economy is as large relative to the world's economy as that of the United States. While Weimar Germany could introduce a new mark based on redeemability in American dollars, it is doubtful that the United States could introduce a new dollar based on redeemability in German marks. The reason is simply the relative size of the two economies. The currency of a vastly larger economy can serve as the foundation for the introduction of a new currency in a country with a much smaller economy. But it is doubtful that the reverse can be true. The United States had the ability economically to rescue a country the size of Germany, including the provision of sufficient dollars to back a new German currency. The provision of dollars to back a new mark neither drew away so many existing dollars from other uses, nor required the creation of so many new and additional dollars, as to create a major problem for the United States. But Germany does not have the means of economically rescuing the United States, nor therefore of providing sufficient marks in real terms for backing a new dollar. The American people could not expect, as could the German people, to be able if necessary to use their new money to obtain a mass of goods from outside the country. The resources to provide the goods would simply not be present. The provision of marks to back a new dollar would require either the drawing away from other uses of so many marks or the creation of so many new and additional marks, as to create a problem of overwhelming dimensions for Germany. The same essential points, of course, are equally applicable to Japan as a potential source of a new dollar.

Thus, hyperinflation in the present-day United States would have the potential for the destruction of money as such in the United States, and with it, the material civilization of the United States. For the modern Western World in general and for the United States in particular, inflation has destructive potential on a scale not seen since the onset of the Dark Ages.

GOLD

1. Freedom for Gold as the Guarantee Against the Destruction of Money

The solution for every aspect of the inflation problem lies in gold (and silver). The widespread ownership of gold and silver coins by American citizens, and the concomitant willingness of large numbers of Americans to accept them in payment for their goods and services, would be a guarantee against the destruction of money through hyperinflation. It would mean that a new money would be ready to take the place of the present paper money, should the latter ever be inflated into extinction.

However remote the possibility of hyperinflation and the destruction of money in the United States may appear at the moment, it should be kept in mind that the time required for such a possibility to loom as large as it did in 1979 and 1980 is no greater than the time that was required to make it recede. In other words, in the space of just a very few years conditions are capable of undergoing large and unexpected change, with the result that what may seem so unlikely at the present moment as scarcely to be worth consideration, can be upon us relatively quickly and unexpectedly. Given the nature of the present monetary system, all of the basic elements are in place that are required to make hyperinflation possible and thus to make the destruction of money possible. Because of the utter devastation that would then ensue, it is very definitely worth taking precautions against any such possibility, which, of course, is what extensive ownership of gold and silver coins would provide.

As I explained in Chapter 12, in a period of rapid inflation the market itself tends to remonetize gold and silver through their growing use as "inflation hedges." The imperishability, homogeneity, and divisibility of gold and silver, coupled with their existing high value in a small bulk, based on their utility and rarity as ordinary commodities, make them ideally suited for use as inflation hedges by most people. Their minimal costs of storage and transportation relative to their value, means that in a period of rising prices one can retain almost all of one's purchasing power simply by owning gold or silver. All that is necessary is that their price rise merely to the same extent as the average of prices. Although, if this happens, one will suffer the modest loss of having to pay storage costs, this is far less of a loss than tends to be suffered in connection with the customary forms of saving and investment in such conditions.

The customary forms of investment lose because of all of the ways in which inflation undermines capital formation. The customary forms of investment can be compared to the purchase of equipment which inflation will cause to end up as mere heaps of scrap iron. At some point, of course, as the result of inflation, even the price of scrap iron in the future will be higher than the price of the equipment today. But when it is, the prices of everything else will obviously have increased by much more. Thus the purchaser of ordinary business assets, or any form of claim to such assets, ends up, on average, a major loser. He starts with the price of equipment, and ends with the price of scrap iron, while the prices of the things he wants to buy advance more or less in line with the price of replacement equipment. The example may be somewhat exaggerated, but it is correct in describing the nature of what happens. For such is the result of the taxation of funds required for replacement, of the prosperity delusion, of widespread malinvestment, of the loss of safety of all the traditional, conservative forms of investment, and of the withdrawal-of-wealth effect.

Since the ownership of gold and silver entail a much lesser loss, their ownership becomes relatively favored, and thus, for a considerable time, their price can actually rise by more than the average of prices, as larger and larger numbers of people shift portions of their savings into them. In effect, because of their special suitability for serving as inflation hedges, the phenomenon of substantial inflation creates a new and additional demand for them, on the basis of which their value is substantially increased. (By the same token, of course, the moment inflation comes to be perceived as less of a threat, the demand for gold and silver as inflation hedges diminishes, and thus their price declines relative to the average of prices.)

It follows that if not prevented from doing so by government interference, the market itself would take all of the necessary precautions against the destruction of money, by preparing the ground for the reemergence of gold and silver as money. For the remonetization of the precious metals would readily follow from their being owned and sought as a store of value by a substantial portion of the population.[106]

A Proper Gold Policy for the Government

The process of the spontaneous remonetization of gold and silver would be enormously accelerated in the absence of various government restrictions. It goes without saying that buyers and sellers of gold and silver should not be subjected to any invasion of their privacy, such as having to report their purchases and sales to the government. The purchase and sale of gold and silver should also not be subject to taxation of any kind. The ability of people to protect themselves by means of the ownership of gold and silver from the loss of purchasing power that inflation causes should not in any way be reduced by taxes that must be paid merely because the price of gold or silver rises. In the absence of such taxes and with the ability freely to buy and sell, the ownership of gold and silver would increase much more rapidly.

In addition, the government should do absolutely nothing to prevent the importation of gold from abroad. The present quantity of gold that is owned by American citizens and by their government is almost certainly substantially below the quantity that they would want to own under a gold monetary system. The present real value of an ounce of gold is likewise far below what it would be under such a system. The ability freely to import gold now means the ability to acquire it while it is still relatively cheap.

An integral part of the process of spontaneous remonetization would be the enforcement of contracts calling for payment in gold or silver, along with the freedom of such contracts from taxation on the mere rise in price of gold or silver. Thus, for example, the law should enforce such contracts as the loan of 100 ounces of gold today in exchange for the repayment of 105 ounces of gold a year from now. At the same time, it should regard as the taxable income in connection with such a contract merely the 5 ounces of gold interest, not any increase in the paper money price of the 105 ounces of gold principal and interest.

If such a policy existed, any substantial perception of inflation as a serious problem would be accompanied by the emergence of contracts payable in gold or silver. Gold and silver capital and credit markets would develop. At the same time that people became unwilling any longer to lend paper money on a long-term basis, because they came to recognize that they must lose by doing so, they would become eager to lend gold. Provided the repayment of the principal could be assured, the receipt of any gold interest whatever would represent an improvement over the mere holding of the gold. Thus, for example, a recurrence of the conditions of the late 1970s and early 1980s, in which long-term fixed-rate mortgages were about to disappear, would mean the disappearance of such mortgages only in terms of paper money. Long-term fixed-rate mortgages payable in paper money would be replaced with long-term fixed-rate mortgages payable in gold.

The spread of contracts payable in gold or silver would powerfully promote the remonetization of these metals, because whoever came to owe gold or silver would be a willing seller for gold or silver. The existence of a growing number of sellers seeking gold or silver as a means of meeting their contractual obligations would widen the exchangeability of gold and silver beyond

what it would be on the basis of the demand merely for holdings of gold and silver. The exchangeability of gold and silver for all kinds of ordinary goods and services would soon become great enough to make everyone willing to accept them, because all would have the confident expectation of finding others willing to take them in turn. At that point, gold and silver would once again be money.

An essential aspect of gold and silver achieving a monetary role is the abolition of all restrictions on the ability of merchants to practice discrimination between units of precious-metal money and units of paper money bearing the same face value. This means, for example, that merchants should have full freedom to discriminate between an old $20 gold piece (or a contemporary restrike of such a gold piece) and a $20 bill. They should be able to accept the $20 gold piece as the equivalent of however many hundreds or thousands of dollars of paper money as its market value dictates. In exactly the same way, they should be free to discriminate between pre-1965 silver coins and contemporary coins and currency of the same face value. They should be free to accept a roll of pre-1965 silver quarters with a face value of $10 as the equivalent of however many present-day $10 bills as its market value dictates. By the same token, they should have the freedom to take gold and silver coins of a given face value as their standard of the *meaning* of the number of dollars of that face value, and to declare paper money of the same face value to be acceptable only at a discount, that is, as worth only so many cents on the dollar of precious-metal money. For example, if a $20 gold piece has a market value of $500, merchants should be able declare that the $20 gold piece is what they mean by $20 and that they accept paper dollars at the rate of only 4 gold cents on the dollar.

The existence of gold and silver moneys operating alongside of a fiat paper money, and in free competition with the fiat money, would greatly accelerate the doom of the fiat money, unless the latter were made redeemable on demand in gold or silver at a fixed, known rate, which there was no expectation that the government would change. This is because in these circumstances, people would have an alternative to the depreciating fiat money. In the face of this alternative, the demand for paper money would quickly evaporate as people shifted their allegiance to the vastly superior gold and silver moneys, which retained or increased their buying power as the fiat money declined in buying power. They would want their principal and interest, their pensions, life insurance, rental agreements, and all other contracts payable in the gold and silver moneys they could trust, and not in the depreciating fiat money. To remain in existence at all, the fiat money would have to be made into a gold-standard money—which is what it means to be redeemable on demand at a fixed, unchanging rate. These results would follow from people's direct perception, in their day-to-day transactions, of the superiority of the precious metals in retaining their buying power. They would see, for example, how a $20 gold piece came to be equivalent to hundreds or thousands of dollars of paper money, and how a silver dime or quarter came to be equivalent to larger and larger multiples of fiat money. In other words, they would directly perceive the fact that the problem of inflation lay in the paper money, which they would then turn away from.[107]

It follows from the above description of things that gold is the money of a free market and that fiat money can be maintained in existence only by the forcible suppression of the competition of gold. It should also be clear that the requirement that paper money be redeemable in gold at a fixed, known rate is not any form of price control, as some economists with inadequate knowledge of the subject maintain, but an indispensable means of keeping paper money in existence when it must compete in a free market. In a free market, there would simply be no demand for an irredeemable paper money, which in the nature of things is capable of being inflated without limit.

The government, which has done almost everything in its power to destroy the use of gold as money, could take a number of important and perfectly legitimate measures to promote the remonetization of gold.[108] For a nominal fee, and for a limited number of years, it could allow private minters, who would manufacture new gold or silver coins, to use the seal of the United States on one side of their coins, until such time as the market became familiar with their respective trademarks. It could and should also begin to collect some tax revenues in gold and silver, such as the proceeds of the tariff, and perhaps some excise taxes. This measure would immediately sharply increase the demand for gold and its value. It would immediately make payment in gold acceptable to whoever had to pay such taxes. It would be a clear indication to everyone of the course of things to come. It would also provide the government with a secure source of revenue that would be more than sufficient to maintain its essential, non-welfare-state, peacetime functions. Thus, the continued existence of the government itself would be substantially secured against the possibility of a currency collapse.

The collection of these taxes in gold would promote the highly desirable objective of the monetary demand for gold increasing as far as possible *in advance* of major financial obligations coming to be expressed in gold. This is necessary in order for borrowers of gold not to find that it is vastly more difficult to acquire it at the time

of repayment than at the time they borrowed it. A gradually increasing volume of contracts payable in gold would present no major problem, because the upward pressure on the real value of gold created by a growing demand for it to make principal and interest payments, and to buy from those seeking gold for such purposes, would at the same time elevate its value for all the new contracts being written. However, a measure such as the collection of the tariff and various excise taxes in gold, which could be phased in over a period of two or three years, would help to increase the monetary demand for gold all the more quickly, and thus correspondingly diminish any possible burden imposed by a growing monetary demand concentrated more heavily in the future. It would make gold a safe medium that much sooner in which to contract a large volume of financial obligations.

The same objective would be promoted by the government's adopting a policy of auctioning off, for gold, various assets it presently owns and should not own. These include its vast landholdings in the Western states and Alaska, the postal system, Amtrak, Conrail, the Tennessee Valley Authority and other facilities for producing electric power, and the interstate highway system. The gold taken in from the sale of such assets might be used to increase the gold stock available for the future redemption of the paper currency and outstanding fiduciary media, or, if it should prove excessive for that purpose, for the redemption of a portion of the national debt.

A further perfectly legitimate measure that the government might adopt in connection with promoting the remonetization of gold would be the enactment of a creditors' protection bill, which would make some modest portion of existing contracts, such as 5 percent of the sums involved, payable in gold, at the price of gold prevailing at the time of the bill's enactment. Such payment would be at the option of the creditor, who would elect it only in the event that the paper money due him fell below the price of the gold in question. As well as encouraging the use of gold, this measure would ensure that inflation would not be able to wipe out the wealth of creditors entirely. Depending on the extent to which the price of gold later came to rise relative to the average of prices, the measure could succeed in preserving a significant portion of the purchasing power of the contractual sums to which it applied, irrespective of the degree of inflation. For example, an outstanding contract calling for the payment of $1 million would be construed as requiring the payment of a quantity of gold presently equal to $50,000. If the prevailing price of gold were $500 per ounce, this would mean that such a contract required the payment of 100 ounces of gold at the option of the creditor. This would guarantee that no matter how great inflation became, the creditor would receive at least some significant payment in real terms. Indeed, the worse inflation became, the more would the rise in the price of gold tend to outstrip the rise in the average of prices. Thus, if, as is easily conceivable, in the course of a major inflation the price of gold rose seven or eight times as much as the average of prices, the creditor would end up at least receiving 35 or 40 percent of the real payment due him.

Neither the government nor anyone else would have to take payment in gold or silver in actual coin or bullion. Payment could be made with gold-denominated banknotes or checks. But the government could legitimately require, and indeed should in fact require, at least for the length of the period of transition and for some time beyond, that all banknotes and checks payable in gold or silver, be covered by a 100-percent-gold-or-silver reserve, as the case may be. The government itself should never accept anything but either coin or bullion or notes or deposits 100 percent backed by coin or bullion. If it accepts any form of fractional-reserve money, it places itself in a position in which it implicitly grants credit, which is not part of its proper function and which it has no right to do. The implicit granting of credit is entailed to the extent that the claim one accepts or holds is backed by debt rather than by actual money. Until one receives actual money or a fully backed receipt for actual money, one has not yet been paid, but is granting credit.

2. The Case For a 100-Percent-Reserve Gold Standard

The establishment of a monetary system that was based not only on the widespread use of gold and silver coin, but also on the principal of a 100-percent-gold-or-silver reserve against banknotes and checking deposits, would mean security not only against a possible currency collapse but against every aspect of inflation. It would be a monetary system that would be both inflation proof and deflation/depression proof.

Under a 100-percent-reserve gold standard, every unit of money *is* a physical unit of gold. The paper currency and checking deposits are merely money substitutes, i.e., transferable claims to actual money, which is gold. For example, if the dollar were defined as one-twentieth of an ounce of pure gold (which it was, roughly speaking, for most of our history), then there could be only twenty times as many dollars in the United States as there were physical ounces of gold. If, say, there were $20 billion of paper currency and checking deposits outstanding, there would have to be one billion ounces of gold standing behind them.

This example, of course, is purely for purposes of illustration. I certainly do not advocate the definition of

the dollar as one-twentieth of an ounce of gold today. Given all the inflation in the United States in this century, one *three-thousandth* of an ounce would be a far more reasonable definition, and, as time goes on and still more inflation ensues, the amount of gold in terms of which the dollar was defined would have to be still less.[109] In fact, after a period of conversion, I would advocate abandoning the very name "dollar" and defining the monetary unit simply as a weight of gold, such as the gold ounce or the gold gram. We would then speak of "ounces" or "grams" of gold as the British, French, and Italians once did of pounds, livre, and lire of silver. (All of these units originally denoted a troy pound of silver.)[110]

A 100-percent-reserve gold standard would obviously provide a guarantee against inflation. Gold is rare in nature and extremely costly to mine in anything but relatively small amounts. A gold money would increase in quantity from year to year probably by only about two or three percent, if that. Between a modest growth in population and thus in the supply of labor, and a rise in the output per worker based on technological progress and capital accumulation, it is likely that in most years the increase in the overall supply of goods would outstrip the increase in the supply of gold. The result would be that prices would show a tendency to fall from year to year. As I previously pointed out, this is actually what happened in the nineteenth century, in the generation preceding the discovery of the California gold fields, and again, in the generation from 1873 to 1896.

Falling Prices Under the 100-Percent-Reserve Gold Standard Would Not Be Deflationary

Paradoxically, it is precisely the gold standard's success in preventing inflationary increases in the money supply that is the source of much of the opposition to it. People believe that the fall in prices that would occur under the gold standard would represent deflation. And, as a result, they believe that the economic system would languish in a state of more or less permanent depression.

Amazingly, even most of the supporters of the gold standard appear to believe this in some form. They advocate a *fractional*-reserve gold standard in the belief that it is necessary to make the money supply grow more rapidly than the increase in gold taken by itself. In effect, they want each additional ounce of gold to make possible the creation of money substitutes representing claims to two, five, ten, or more ounces of gold. They apparently do not realize that if they were right, the implication of their position would ultimately be no gold standard at all. For if it in fact were necessary for the quantity of money to grow more rapidly than the supply of gold, then each year the supply of gold would represent an ever smaller fraction of the supply of money. Eventually the fraction would approach zero. If, on the other hand, gold is always to constitute the same fraction of the money supply, then it is impossible for the money supply to grow more rapidly than gold, and one may as well have a 100-percent-gold reserve. Indeed, the rate of increase in the supply of gold itself is likely to be greater under a 100-percent-reserve system than under any fractional-reserve system in which the fraction of gold is fixed. This is because the real value of gold is greatest under a 100-percent-reserve system and therefore the inducement to the increase in its supply the strongest.

Of course, it should be obvious on the basis of previous discussion, that the fall in prices that would occur under the 100-percent-reserve gold standard would not at all represent deflation.[111] In the nature of the case, such a fall in prices would be the result of an increase in production, not a decrease in spending. Because of this, it would not be accompanied by any of the essential symptoms of deflation: namely, a greater difficulty of repaying debts and a wiping out of the rate of profit on capital invested.

Under the 100-percent-reserve gold standard, total sales revenues in the economic system would in fact modestly increase from year to year, in accordance with the modest increase in the gold money supply and the volume of spending in terms of gold. The average business firm would thus find that its sales revenues modestly increased from year to year. The fact that the average business firm might have to sell at somewhat lower prices from year to year would not in any way imply a reduction in its sales revenues. On the contrary, it would have a supply of goods to sell that was larger by more than corresponded to the fall in prices, and was so to a significant degree. The fall in prices, it cannot be stressed too strongly, would be the result not of a fall in spending, not even of an increase in supply in the face of a given volume of spending, but of an increase in supply which outstripped an *increase* in spending. In such circumstances, a greater increase in the supply of goods than corresponds to the fall in prices exists to precisely the same extent as the increase in the volume of spending in terms of gold.

The context of why prices fall under the 100-percent-reserve gold standard must be kept in mind: it is because while spending rises 2 or 3 percent a year, in accordance with the increase in the gold supply, production rises 4, 5, or 6 percent a year. This kind of drop in prices is not accompanied by declining sales revenues, but by modestly rising sales revenues. The rise in sales revenues is the corollary of the rise in spending. Any business firm that increases its production in accordance with the economy-wide average increase has no greater difficulty in earning a dollar of sales revenue at the lower prices that

prevail later on than it had at the higher prices that prevailed earlier. In fact, it necessarily has a somewhat *easier* time earning a dollar of sales revenues, for the supply of goods it is able to produce and sell goes up by more than the price of its goods must fall. Because it is no harder to earn a dollar later on than it was earlier, but easier, there is not only no greater difficulty of repaying debts, as there is under deflation, but a lesser difficulty. Thus, this symptom of deflation is most decidedly not present.

Nor is the fall in prices under the 100-percent-reserve gold standard accompanied by any wiping out of the average rate of profit in the economic system, which is the other leading symptom of deflation. On the contrary, the increase in the quantity of money and volume of spending that takes place under the 100-percent-reserve gold standard represents a corresponding addition to the nominal rate of profit. To whatever extent the increase in production and supply outstrips the increase in the quantity of money and volume of spending, the resulting fall in prices is merely the measure by which the addition to the real rate of profit exceeds the addition to the nominal rate of profit.[112]

Thus, falling prices under a 100-percent-reserve gold standard simply do not represent deflation. They do not make it more difficult for the average debtor to repay his debts and they do not reduce the average rate of profit.

It is a very different story, however, when prices fall not as they do under the 100-percent-reserve gold standard, because of more production, but because of less spending in the economy. Then the fall in prices is accompanied by a decline in the sales revenues of the average seller. Then it *is* more difficult for the average debtor to repay his debts, because whether he has more goods to sell or less goods to sell, there simply isn't as much money to be taken in by him. And because sales revenues fall, the average rate of profit falls, corresponding to the lag between a fall in productive expenditure and a fall in depreciation cost and cost of goods sold.[113]

The fact is that deflation is not a matter of falling prices, but of a contraction in the volume of spending in the economy. This is what produces the essential symptoms of deflation: the general inability to repay debts and the wiping out of business profitability. If this point is kept in mind, then it becomes clear that a 100-percent-reserve gold standard not only would not cause deflation, but would actually be the best possible protection *against* deflation.

The 100-Percent-Reserve Gold Standard as the Guarantee Against Deflation

There are two basic reasons why the 100-percent-reserve gold standard would be a guarantee against deflation. First, under a 100-percent-reserve gold standard, nothing could happen that would suddenly reduce the quantity of money in the economic system. Once gold money comes into existence, it *stays* in existence. It is not wiped out by the failure of debtors, as are fiduciary media. Second, nothing could happen that would suddenly increase the need or desire of people to hold money rather than spend it, because none of the artificial inducements to a lower demand for money for holding would exist that set the stage for such an increase. It must be recalled that what creates the potential for a sudden increase in the need and desire to hold money is that first, people are misled into experiencing an artificial decrease in their need and desire to hold money. All the inducements that mislead them into this decrease are caused by the prior undue increase in the quantity of money, especially in the form of credit expansion.[114] A 100-percent-reserve gold standard would thus be a system in which the quantity of money would not decrease and the demand for money for holding would not suddenly increase. As a result, it would be a system in which total spending in the economy would virtually never contract. Thus, as stated, it would be a system that was deflation proof as well as inflation proof.

Under the 100-percent-reserve gold standard, the desire to hold money would be substantially greater than it is today and also greater than it would be under a fractional-reserve gold standard. Money would be something for which people would have great respect and would want to own in abundance. And they would succeed in owning it in abundance. However paradoxical it may seem, the 100-percent-reserve gold standard would be a system of *enormous financial liquidity*. It would be a system in which the quantity of money measured in terms of its absolute buying power and relative to such things as current liabilities, would be far greater than under any other system. It is precisely for this reason that there would be no basis for any sudden increase in the need or desire of people to own money. They would *already own* all the money they needed to.

This point may be difficult to grasp. The prevailing view is that anyone who wants to hold money is practically a public enemy, and that financial virtue, at least from a social point of view, consists of everyone spending his every dollar as rapidly as possible.

However, a different conclusion emerges if one considers a 100-percent-reserve gold standard and thinks through the effects of people wanting to hold money more tightly. Thus, let us imagine that there are only a billion ounces of gold in the world and that initially people are spending this gold fast enough to generate a five billion gold-ounce world "gross product"—in other words, the so-called velocity of circulation of money, or

turnover, is five. Now people decide they want to hold the gold much more tightly. The velocity of circulation and the world "gross product" plunge from five and five billion respectively to, say, two and two billion respectively.

At a sufficiently lower level of wages and prices, the two billion ounce world "gross product" can buy all that the five billion ounce world "gross product" bought. The only difference is that the buying power of the one billion ounce money supply will be much larger and that the money supply will stand in a much higher ratio to magnitudes such as total current liabilities and total accounts receivable. These magnitudes will fall in accordance with the fall in spending, and then stay down as wage rates and prices fall to make possible a recovery in employment and production. In other words, the result will be that the system will have *more money in terms of actual buying power and will thus be correspondingly more liquid.*[115]

Under a 100-percent-reserve gold standard, a sufficiently high degree of liquidity would once and for all long ago have been achieved and no further need would exist suddenly to increase it. The system would operate permanently in accordance with the most conservative rules of financial management and never be placed in the position of having to experience a financial contraction. As a result, the kind of example just given would not actually occur under the 100-percent-reserve gold standard. It is descriptive, however, of what happens when the artificial stimulus given to spending by inflation comes to an end.

On the basis of all these reasons, it should be clear why the 100-percent-reserve gold standard would be the solution to the boom-bust business cycle, as well as the solution to the problem of inflation.

Further Virtues of the 100-Percent-Reserve Gold Standard

Among the other major virtues of the 100-percent-reserve gold standard is that, in common with the more serious forms of a fractional-reserve gold standard, it would make possible a unified world monetary system with all its attendant advantages to international investment and the international division of labor. International investment need no longer be subject to the risk of depreciation in the foreign currency in which the investment was made. If the foreign currency is also a weight of gold, then for all practical purposes it is the same as the domestic currency.

Even more important, and with firmer guarantees than any form of fractional-reserve gold standard can provide (because of the total ban it establishes on the creation of new and additional money by the government and the banking system), the 100-percent-reserve gold standard would compel governments to operate with balanced budgets, since they would have to turn to their citizens for all the money they spent. Governments would simply no longer have the power to spend more than the taxes they collected. They could absolutely no longer finance their deficits by creating money. Nor could they hope to finance them for very long by borrowing gold, since a policy of borrowing gold would plunge a government into bankruptcy and would soon have to be abandoned, or, more likely, avoided in the first place. The consequent absolute physical need to balance the budget would in turn, of course, greatly reduce the popularity of all government spending programs, because all of them would be perceived in inseparable connection with the taxes that would be required to pay for them. This in turn would mean fewer and smaller such programs; hence, a smaller, less expensive, and less destructive government. The same principle would apply to wars, as well. Instead of being perceived as periods of prosperity, the higher taxes required to pay for them would make the public correctly identify them as periods of impoverishment. As a result wars would be less frequent and of shorter duration.

In addition, a 100-percent-reserve gold standard would provide an environment enormously conducive to saving, investment, and capital accumulation. The arbitrary redistribution of wealth and income caused by inflation would end; the future purchasing power of money would be assured; the general profitability of investment would be assured (something which fractional-reserve gold standards with their attendant depressions cannot do); and neither profits nor interest would be artificially inflated, as occurs today, and then taxed and consumed as though they were genuine gains rather than being necessary merely for the replacement of assets at higher prices. On the contrary, under the 100-percent-reserve gold standard, far more than under any form of fractional-reserve gold standard (because of the more limited potential for increase in the quantity of money), a substantial portion of profit and interest income in real terms would automatically escape all taxation—namely, all that portion which took the form of a greater buying power of the original capital funds resulting from lower replacement prices of assets. Furthermore, unlike under the fractional-reserve gold standard and its accompanying credit expansions, there would be no malinvestment or withdrawal-of-wealth effects to hamper capital formation.

The Moral Virtue of the 100-Percent-Reserve Gold Standard

What underlies the practical advantages of the 100-percent-reserve gold standard over any form of frac-

tional-reserve system is its moral superiority. It operates consistently with the law of the excluded middle and does not attempt to cheat reality by getting away with a contradiction. It recognizes that lending money precludes retaining that money in one's possession, and that retaining money in one's possession precludes lending it. The 100-percent-reserve system follows the principle that either one lends money or one retains the money, but not both together, with one and the same sum of money. In contrast, a fractional-reserve system applied to checking deposits or banknotes is a deliberate attempt to cheat reality. It is the attempt to have one's money and lend it too. It is a system fully as dishonest as all other recurring efforts that take place in one form or another in attempts "to have one's cake and eat it too."

Just as such attempts typically entail taking away someone else's cake, fractional-reserve banking applied to checking deposits or banknotes entails some parties gaining credit at the expense of other parties, and others unexpectedly being placed in need of credit. Again and again it results in financial contractions, depressions, and deflation, accompanied by widespread bank failures, which last represents the cheating coming home to roost. Again and again, individuals who believed they owned money, who would never have dreamed of lending out the money they needed to hold to make purchases and pay bills, and thus of lending to the point of their own insolvency, wake up to learn that the checking deposits or banknotes they hold represent loans that have become uncollectable.

Imposition of the 100-percent-reserve principle in connection with checking deposits and banknotes is the imposition of financial honesty. It would require nothing more than that banks ask their customers whether in making a deposit or buying banknotes their intention was to lend money to the bank or to keep their money at the bank. In the first case, the bank's customers would receive a credit to a savings account or certificates of deposit, neither of which they could spend until such time as they withdrew the funds they had lent, which would entail equivalently reducing their savings account or redeeming their certificates of deposit. During the interval the bank, for its part, could lend the customers' money out, as it thought best. In the second case, the customers would receive either a credit to their checking account or banknotes, both of which they could spend as they wished. But so long as the customers held their funds in the form of checking accounts or banknotes, the bank could not lend or spend the proceeds its customers had entrusted to it. That money would be the customers' money, which they were not lending to the bank but merely keeping at the bank.

It follows from this discussion that it is mistaken to

believe that the imposition by law of 100-percent-reserve banking in connection with checking deposits and banknotes would constitute government interference. It would constitute nothing more than the just exercise of the government's power to combat fraud—the fraud of having one's funds lent out despite the bank's deliberate creation of the impression that in making a checking deposit or purchasing banknotes one fully retained the possession of one's funds.

Shysterism in any form is always slippery. Thus if it occurs to anyone to argue that the banks' customers are not victims of fraud because they clearly know and understand that their funds are being lent out, then the answer is that in that case they would be parties to fraud. Their fraud would be the attempt to make payment to others not with money or reliable warehouse receipts for money, but with claims to debt. They would be engaged in the willful contradiction and deception of claiming to pay someone when in fact imposing on him the position of being a grantor of credit.

It should be understood that everything I have said in connection with the subject of the fraud entailed in fractional-reserve banking applies to a context in which the establishment of a 100-percent-reserve gold standard would be a real possibility. It is pointless to accuse either banks or their customers of any kind of fraud in connection with fractional-reserve banking in a context such as that of the present, in which the overwhelmingly greater fraud exists of the government's creation of a monetary standard that is utterly nonobjective and arbitrary, namely, the fiat-paper standard.

Supporters of fiduciary media and credit expansion like to argue that their effect is an increase in the volume of capital and credit that exists in the economic system. This is true, of course, only in terms of a monetary unit that is of lesser value because of credit expansion and the creation of fiduciary media. I have already shown at length how credit expansion and fiduciary media undermine capital accumulation in real terms. It is worth pointing out, however, that even if the advocates of credit expansion and the creation of fiduciary media were correct, any loss of capital and credit as might be attributable to their elimination could far more than be made up for by reduction in the national debt. As of the end of 1993, the cumulative total of loans and investments acquired by the banking system in connection with the creation of fiduciary media was approximately $738 billion.[116] At the same time, the national debt, which is the measure of the cumulative siphoning off of savings and capital into the consumption of the government, stood at almost $4.6 trillion, that is, more than six times as large.[117] Thus, even if fractional-reserve banking and

the issuance of fiduciary media, instead of undermining capital formation as they actually do, somehow made a contribution to capital and credit that could be measured as equal to the amount of debt held by the banking system as the result of the issuance of fiduciary media, the loss of such contribution could easily be far more than made good by the reduction of the national debt.

It is simply absurd for anyone to engage in sophistic speculations about how to use methods of cheating as sources of additional capital, when overwhelmingly more capital could be made available by the perfectly honest method of reducing the national debt and ultimately eliminating it. Unfortunately, there are people who like to speculate in this way because of the perverse attraction cheating holds for them.

The Monetary Role of Silver

The existence of a 100-percent-reserve gold standard would imply a major monetary role for silver. This is because the extremely high real value that would then exist for even the smallest practical-sized gold coin would make it impossible for gold coins to effectuate most retail purchases. Even at the relatively low prices of gold that have prevailed in the last decade, the smallest practical-sized gold coin has a buying power that is too high for many retail transactions. For example, at a price of gold of $400 per ounce, the smallest practical-sized gold coin has a buying power of approximately $20. (This is a coin weighing slightly less than a twentieth of an ounce of gold, which was the size of the smallest old U.S. gold coin, namely, the one-dollar gold piece.) Under a full, 100-percent-reserve gold monetary system, the buying power of an ounce of gold would be far greater, which would rule out the use of gold coin in the great majority of retail transactions.

The fact that the value of gold would be too great for most retail transactions implies that if the monetary system is to make extensive use of precious-metal coins, a major monetary role must exist for silver, which would be in use alongside gold, constituting a second, independent, parallel standard.[118] Silver was the market's answer historically to the problems posed by the very high real value of even the smallest gold coins. For many centuries it had a value of approximately one-fifteenth that of gold.

The widespread use of silver coins, rather than gold-backed banknotes or checks for most day-to-day retail transactions, is implied by the fact that under a 100-percent-reserve system, there is a substantial cost in using banknotes and checks. This is because the banks must charge fees high enough to cover the cost of maintaining and safeguarding the reserves, as well as doing whatever else is necessary in providing the services of banknotes and checking deposits. Thus the use of coins is made preferable in most such cases, but gold coins are too valuable for most day-to-day retail transactions, which leaves silver coins.

Under a 100-percent-reserve gold standard, the monetary role of silver might be so great that silver coin and bullion would constitute as much as a third of the overall supply of money. This estimate is consistent with the fact that today, paper currency in denominations of $100 and less, together with subsidiary coin, constitutes on the order of a third of the overall quantity of money, while checking balances constitute the rest. Under a 100-percent-reserve gold standard, silver coins would take the place of most of today's paper currency and would have a buying power ranging from today's $10 bills up through today's $100 bills.

This estimate of the buying power of silver coins is consistent with the assumption of an ounce of gold having a buying power of approximately $3,000 of today's money, and an ounce of silver coming once again to have a buying power of one-fifteenth as much, that is, of approximately $200. The assumption of a buying power of $3,000 for an ounce of gold follows from dividing the present government-held gold stock of approximately 260 million ounces into two-thirds of $1,150 billion, which is the approximate present money supply of the United States. It is divided into two-thirds of the money supply on the assumption that silver would constitute the other one-third of the money supply. On these assumptions, a silver coin the size of the pre–1965 dime, which contained about .07 ounces of silver, would have a buying power of about $14, while the larger silver coins had proportionately greater buying power. (Recognition that the precious metals could attain such buying power helps to explain the very low prices that prevailed in previous centuries. For example, the fact that in the mid–nineteenth century one could buy a steak in a restaurant for 10¢ or a pot of coffee for 2¢, is consistent with such high real values of the precious metals.)

With such great buying power on the part of the precious metals, even the smallest practical-sized silver coin would have too great a purchasing power for small retail transactions, namely, those of approximately $10 or less in terms of today's money. Historically, this is what necessitated the existence of a subsidiary token coinage ranging from 5 cent pieces on down to half-cent pieces. A lowly half-cent piece had a buying power comparable to 70 cents of today's money.

The case of subsidiary, token coinage represents the one proper area for the issuance of fiduciary media. On the one hand, the existence of such coinage is necessary to facilitate transactions that could not otherwise readily be facilitated. As such, it does not displace gold or silver but supplements them. On the other hand, there is no convenient way to make the issuance of such coinage profitable except by the earning of interest on the lending out of a substantial portion of any standard money received by the issuer in exchange for the token coins. To require a 100 percent reserve in this case would be to require that the token coins circulate at a premium over the gold or silver for which they were redeemable, a premium equal to the cost of providing them and of maintaining the gold or silver reserves. If the same token coins were to remain in circulation for many years, their redemption value in gold or silver would have to be progressively reduced in order to cover the on-going cost of maintaining the gold or silver reserves. Such difficulties are eliminated by providing for the costs out of interest earnings on the lending out of much of the standard money the issuer receives in exchange for the token money.

Because such coinage supplements the precious metals rather than displaces them, its issuance does not diminish their value, as does the issuance of fiduciary media in normal circumstances. On the contrary, to whatever extent the precious metals serve as a reserve against the token coinage, their value is somewhat enhanced, because now, indirectly, in the form of a reserve, they enter to an important extent into the token coinage, which they could not do directly, as circulating coin. Moreover, unlike the case of fiduciary media in normal circumstances, there is no danger of credit expansion from any excess issuance of token coinage. Whoever would seek to expand credit by manufacturing and lending out additional rolls of pennies and nickels would find that virtually all of them immediately came back to him in exchange for gold or silver, because there would be no way to induce people suddenly to increase the proportion of their money that they wished to hold in the form of minor coins. If the issuer proved unable to redeem his coins in such a case, it is unlikely that anyone's loss would be very significant if he had behaved reasonably and had accepted no more than modest amounts of such additional coins. The largest losers would probably be the customers who had borrowed the coins and who had not been able to pass all of them before they lost their redeemability.

3. The 100-Percent-Reserve Gold Standard as the Means of Ending Inflation Without a Depression

The remonetization of gold and silver on a 100-percent-reserve basis holds out the prospect of ending inflation once and for all and of doing so without causing a financial contraction or depression.[119] In order to explain how, it is necessary to begin with the following facts.

As of December 1993, the money supply of the United States was approximately $1,100 billion, and the so-called gross domestic product (GDP) of the United States was running at an annual rate of about $6,400 billion.[120] With an $1,100 billion money supply and a $6,400 billion GDP, the implied income velocity of money was somewhat less than 6.

If all that were done at this point was to stop all further inflation of fiat money, make it redeemable in gold, and permanently limit the rate of increase in the quantity of money to the rate of increase in the supply of gold, the sharply higher demand for money that would result might well drive velocity down to 4 or even 3 (its approximate level through most of the 1930s) and thus initially reduce nominal GDP to close to $4,000 billion or even $3,000 billion. In the process, of course, there would be an enormous wave of bankruptcies and bank failures, which would have the potential for wiping out the greater part of the money supply and thus reducing nominal GDP and total spending all that much further. Indeed, starting with the present velocity of almost 6, it may well be the case that the deflationary potential which exists today is substantially greater than the deflation that occurred between the years 1929 and 1933, which started in the face of a velocity of circulation in the neighborhood of 4.

All this, of course, indicates the enormous difficulties in the way of ending inflation under present monetary conditions. But not to end inflation means the continuation of all of its destructive consequences. These, it should be recalled, include: (1) perversion of the institutions of representative government by removing the financial dependence of the government on the citizenry and making the citizens appear to be dependent on the government, (2) the consequent growth in the size of government, (3) the redistribution of wealth and income, which further contributes to the growth in the size of government through its creation of impoverishment, (4) the undermining of saving and capital accumulation, which has the same effect as the previous point, (5) increased hostility to profits and interest accompanied by the threat of price-and-wage controls and thus the chaos and tyranny of socialism, and, finally, (6) the likelihood of a renewed acceleration of inflation. This last not only would make all of the destructive consequences either that much worse or more likely, but would also open up the possibility of the destruction of credit and even of money itself. In its potential for bringing about the destruction both of the price system and of money (the former through leading to price controls and socialism), inflation, as we have seen, represents a long-term threat to the continued existence of modern material civilization.[121]

This terrible dilemma, of having to choose between a catastrophic depression, on the one side, and the continual wearing down and ultimate destruction of modern material civilization, on the other, is what adoption of a 100-percent-reserve gold standard is capable of avoiding. It is, as I say, capable of ending inflation once and for all without precipitating a financial contraction or depression.

To understand just how this is possible, let us imagine that our present money supply of approximately $1,100 billion consisted of nothing but gold, and that this had been brought about by the government taking its gold holding of approximately 260 million ounces and pricing it high enough to make it equal to $1,100 billion. A price of something more than $4,000 per ounce would accomplish this.[122]

Imagine that the government physically distributed this gold to the people: It called in all the paper currency and gave out very small gold coins in exchange; and it turned the remainder of its gold over to the banks, to place their checking deposits on a 100-percent-gold-reserve basis.[123] For the sake of maximum simplicity, we can think of the money supply as now consisting of 260 million one-ounce gold coins. (Obviously, much smaller denominations would be necessary, but let's think of it this way.) Imagine that on one side of each of these coins it said "1 ounce of gold," and on the other side "$4,000." In the same way, imagine that all checking deposits were denominated both in terms of ounces of gold and in terms of dollars. The money supply could then be looked at as being either 260 million gold ounces or $1,100 billion. People would certainly want to hold this gold money supply very tightly, because the possibility of inflation would now have been definitively ended, since the money supply would actually be gold and thus there would physically be just no way for the government to increase it. People would hold the money not as dollars, but as pieces of gold.

Let us imagine that people wanted to hold this money supply so tightly that its velocity of circulation would be only 3. Thus, in terms of gold, GDP would be three times the 260 million ounces of gold, or 780 million ounces. In terms of dollars, however, the effect would be that GDP would plunge to little more than $3,000 billion (i.e., to $4,000 times 780 million), which is the very situation we wanted to avoid.

But now let's make a change in our example. While the gold money supply remains at 260 million ounces and its velocity remains at 3—because it is gold that people are holding—let us see what happens if we assume a higher price of gold imprinted on each coin. Imagine that on the dollar side of each of the one-ounce gold coins that constitute the money supply, it said not "$4,000," but "$8,000." Observe. The gold money supply remains 260 million ounces and the gold GDP remains 780 million ounces. But the dollar money supply now becomes $2,200 billion—twice as large. And the dollar GDP now becomes more than $6,000 billion—also twice as large. This $6,000 billion-plus GDP, of course, is the original size of GDP.

Now I am not in fact advocating a gold price nearly as high as $8,000 in today's circumstances—for reasons that I will explain shortly. I used it just to illustrate an important point. And that is, that in principle it would be possible to stop inflation cold with a 100-percent-gold money, and simultaneously to offset the resulting fall in the velocity of circulation of money. This last would be accomplished by making the gold supply equal to enough dollars to leave spending in terms of dollars unchanged at the lower velocity. In other words, it is possible to stop inflation cold, and yet avoid the contraction in dollars spent that would otherwise result from a greater need and desire to hold money, simply by making the gold stock equal to a large-enough number of dollars. Thus the critical factor producing a depression following the end of inflation is overcome.

It cannot be stressed too strongly here how vital is the 100-percent-reserve-coin element if gold is to be used in this way. If the attempt were made to go to gold without this element, that is, with the government continuing to hold the gold and the people using paper, the effect of a sharply higher price of gold would merely be more inflation, and an actual increase in the velocity of circulation of money. For then, people would experience merely an increase in the quantity of paper dollars, which could be endlessly repeated. On the 100-percent-reserve gold-coin system, however, what people are holding is not dollars but physical gold. The velocity of money is then determined by the fact that the pieces of money are gold. The pieces of gold are held tightly and the number of dollars the pieces are called is then unable to affect the rate at which the money is spent.

Thus, one major aspect of the depression problem could be solved—the contraction in spending that results when inflation is stopped.

What about the other aspect—the excessive debt burden? The transition to a 100-percent-reserve gold-coin system would be able to solve that, too. If there were no other way to solve it, gold could simply be priced high enough to give people an actual sudden increase in their revenues and incomes calculated in dollars. In such circumstances, the transition to the system would be accompanied by the equivalent of a last burst of inflation. Thus, for example, if the problem of an excessive debt burden exists in the face of the initial $6,000 billion-plus GDP, the price of gold could be set at the point where the 780 million ounce gold GDP represents a $7,000 billion

or $8,000 billion GDP or however high a dollar-GDP might be necessary.

Solving the problem of "an excessive debt burden" by means of inflation in any form is a reprehensible practice. Its only justification is the necessity of avoiding mass bankruptcies, which, given the inability of today's judicial system to keep pace even with its current case load, would probably take a decade or more to get sorted out. That would mean that in the interval the economy would be largely paralyzed, because no one would know just who owned what. This must be avoided.

The effect of distributing most of the country's gold to the banks, to place them on a 100-percent-reserve basis against their checking deposits must be explained. At present it would take about $700 billion in gold to do this, inasmuch as that is the amount of outstanding checking deposits. The transfer of this much gold to the banking system would represent an increase in its assets of approximately $640 billion, since its present standard-money reserves are little more than $60 billion. The addition of this much gold to the balance sheets of the banks, as reserves against their demand deposits, would permit them to take whatever writeoffs may be necessary on their existing loans and investments as the result of actual or likely delinquencies or failures on the part of their borrowers. To the extent that a substantial increase in the assets of the banking system remained, an equivalent portion of its holdings of government securities could be canceled.

Some further major positive effects of the transition to a 100-percent-reserve system would be that both the Federal Reserve System and the Federal Deposit Insurance Corporation could be abolished. They would both be rendered unnecessary and have no further function.[124]

When one allows for the fact that there is privately owned gold in the United States, and that considerably more would have come in from abroad prior to having reached the point of establishing a 100 percent reserve (provided, of course, the necessary economic freedom had been established), it turns out that a conversion price in the neighborhood of $4,000 per ounce rather than $8,000 per ounce would probably be sufficient to maintain the preexisting level of spending in terms of dollars, even with a velocity of circulation of only 3.[125] I arrive at this figure on the basis of the highly conservative assumption of a world monetary gold stock of 2 billion ounces and the further assumption that the American economy represents about one-fourth of the world's economy. As a result, I use a figure of 500 million ounces as the estimate of our potential total gold money supply. Assuming a gold velocity of 3, our gold GDP would thus be 1.5 billion ounces rather than 780 million ounces. Given today's fiat-money GDP of $6,000 billion-plus, gold would have to be priced at around $4,000 per ounce to make it possible for the 1.5 billion-ounce gold GDP to represent an unchanged dollar GDP and thus avoid a contraction in dollar revenues and incomes. Next year, of course, when the quantity of fiat money and the GDP expressed in fiat money are higher, the appropriate gold conversion price would be higher.

As before, the principle is that to avoid a contraction of spending in terms of dollars, the conversion price of gold must be set in such a way that the prospective gold-ounce GDP of the country is made at least equal to the country's GDP in dollars at the time the transition is to be made.[126]

Unilateral movement toward the remonetization of gold by the United States might at some point attract a disproportionate share of the world's gold stock. Also, a considerable burden could exist in producing the exports needed to import additional gold. Although this latter problem would be minimized through larger imports of gold while it is still relatively cheap (including imports in exchange for the sale of the kinds of government assets described earlier), a further problem could remain. Namely, the problem of the American economy becoming adjusted to the use of a disproportionate amount of the world's gold, which was then followed by other countries going over to gold. At that time, the United States might begin experiencing substantial gold outflows—in effect suffering a kind of deflation in gold.

This leads to the conclusion that it would be desirable if the conditions for the remonetization of gold could be established internationally, with the simultaneous cooperation of as many of the world's economically important countries as possible.

However, even if the United States alone moved toward the remonetization of gold, and did import a disproportionate share of the world's gold supply, the loss to American citizens as individuals would be substantially less than under the fiat-money system. Under the fiat-money system, every year the great majority of individual citizens in effect import fiat money in exchange for goods or services. For the great majority of citizens finish the year with a larger holding of fiat money than they began it, and have had to trade away goods and services to do so. This is the withdrawal-of-wealth effect I described earlier.[127] It is the necessary outcome of increases in the quantity of money, which always end up in the cash holdings of the citizens. But unlike gold, whose supply increases only modestly from year to year, with fiat money there is no end to the process short of the destruction of the fiat money in a currency collapse.[128]

If American citizens imported excess gold, not only would there be a complete end to that process, but they could probably count on later exporting the gold at a higher value, when foreign countries finally did come to move toward the remonetization of gold. Thus, their loss on this account would not be permanent. In fact, if they used most of any excess gold coming in merely to build up their gold holdings, and did not gear their normal financial activities to its presence, they would substantially benefit in the long run by their country being the first to move toward the remonetization of gold. This is because they would acquire gold at a relatively low value, when only they wanted it for more extensive monetary use, and then give it back to the rest of the world at a higher value, when everyone else also wanted it for such a purpose. And, not having geared their financial operations to its presence, they would not suffer substantial deflationary effects by virtue of its outflow.

The 100-Percent-Reserve Gold Standard, Liquidity, and the Dismantling of the Welfare State

The above proposal for the establishment of a full 100-percent-reserve gold standard in place of the present, fiat-money system has major implications for the dismantling of the welfare state—beyond the fact that it would compel the government to operate with a balanced budget. The fact that it would establish great financial liquidity, that is, large holdings of gold money relative to spending, and, of course, at the same time, reduce the burden of debt to manageable proportions, means that it would be possible radically to reduce the size of the government's budget, and the scope of government activity, without fear of causing a depression and mass unemployment.

Under present monetary conditions, if government spending were substantially reduced, the effect would be a major problem of readjustment and would probably entail a depression. This is because under present monetary conditions, the debt structure stands like a house of cards and the least failure of demand anywhere in the economic system is capable of producing a wave of bankruptcies and bank failures. But it would certainly not be true if the economic system possessed the high degree of liquidity that a 100-percent-reserve gold standard could give it.

If firms possessed both substantially larger cash reserves and smaller debts relative to their revenues and incomes, they would be able to ride out the kind of temporary, localized failures of demand that would accompany slashing the government's budget. They would be in a position of financial strength comparable to what existed in 1946.

It has been forgotten, but between 1945 and 1946—a period of just one year—federal government spending in the United States was reduced by more than *50 percent* (from $93 billion to $46 billion) and more than *ten million government employees—most of the army and navy—were dismissed!* This was the conversion from the war economy to a peacetime economy.

At the time, many people feared that the result would be mass unemployment and a resumption of the depression. The actual effect was not unemployment, but a rapid and radical change in the type of employment. The millions of former soldiers and sailors and war workers quickly changed jobs and began producing goods and services of value to the lives and well-being of individuals. The net effect was simply an enormous rise in the standard of living.

All this was possible because the tremendous financial strength of the economy—indicated by a velocity of circulation of money of less than 2 in 1946—guaranteed that as government spending fell, private spending would increase correspondingly. For there was simply no need to build up liquidity any higher than it already was.

Transition to a 100-percent-reserve gold standard could achieve comparable financial strength today. On the basis of it, the American economic system could experience a far more dramatic improvement than it did in 1946. Then, improvement came because the United States was able to disband an American army that had fought on foreign soil in the defense of the United States. Today improvement would come from the disbanding of a virtual enemy army that operates on American soil against the American people—namely, the massive government bureaucracy that redistributes and consumes the American people's wealth while doing its utmost to stop them from producing it. Disband this enemy army, and the output of goods and services in the United States will skyrocket.

Thus, the 100-percent-reserve gold-coin standard is a critical element in the economic reconstruction of the United States. It could stop inflation without depression and set the stage for the rapid and radical reduction of government activity.

Notes

1. For a typical instance of the treatment of inflation as caused either by "demand pull" or by "cost push" and the consignment of increases in the quantity of money to the demand-pull category, see Paul Samuelson and William Nordhaus, *Economics,* 13th ed. (New York: McGraw Hill Book Company, 1989), pp. 324–326.

2. See above, pp. 503–505 and 519–526.

3. See above, Figure 17–1, on p. 811.

4. The reader should note the parallelism here to my earlier refutation of the fallacy that falling prices caused by increased production constitute deflation. There, I showed that falling prices caused by increased production in the face of a fixed aggregate demand for goods do not reduce the ability of debtors to repay their debts because as the result of the same phenomenon that reduces prices—namely, the increase in supply—they have an inversely proportional larger quantity of goods to sell at the lower prices. Thus it is no more difficult for them than it was before to earn any given sum of money with which to repay their debts. See above, p. 574. And, of course, to the extent falling prices increase real disposable income, the difficulty of repaying debt is actually reduced.

5. To some extent, creditors too might suffer a loss in the money value of their assets—namely, in cases in which value of the property destroyed exceeded the value of the owners' equity. But on the whole the loss of the stockholder/debtors would be far greater.

6. See above, pp. 578–579.

7. This average unit cost, and the value of the capital as well, reflects the payment of wages no less than the purchase prices of capital goods.

8. The fact that reductions in supply would tend to be associated with a lower economic degree of capitalism and a lower degree of capital intensiveness means that if the process of capital decumulation and decline in production began subsequent to the date of the balance sheet of Figure 19–2, the total monetary value of the assets of the average business firm would be less in Figure 19–3 than in Figure 19–2. They would not be less only if the balance sheet of Figure 19–2 represented merely a point in an already established condition of capital decumulation and falling production, or if the capital decumulation and falling production were entirely the result of a fall in the productivity of capital goods rather than of a fall in the economic degree of capitalism and degree of capital intensiveness.

9. In Figure 19–1, the rate of profit and interest rise from 11.11 percent in *Year 1* (i.e., $200/1,800$) to 17.6 percent in *Year 3* and thereafter (i.e., $300/1,700$).

10. The very question of a transitional rise in the rate of profit relative to the rate of interest would not even come up insofar as capital decumulation and the fall in production were the result of a fall in the productivity of capital goods rather than in productive expenditure and the relative demand for capital goods.

11. This discussion closely parallels, mutatis mutandis, the discussion above, on pp. 817–818, concerning why no element of deflation is present in the fall in the rate of profit that results from a fall in the rate of net consumption and accompanies the early stages of the fall in prices that is caused by capital accumulation and economic progress. Also, in parallel with other discussion in the same place, it should be realized that any conceivable gain of business debtors at the expense of creditors resulting from a rise in the rate of profit would still not be the result of rising prices. If it could exist at all, it would be the result exclusively of the rise in the rate of net consumption and rate of profit, and would be capable of existing even if somehow there were no fall in production and supply and no rise in prices.

12. For a refutation of the fallacy that falling prices caused by increased production constitute deflation, see above, pp. 573–580.

13. Indeed, as I will show, in order for inflation or deflation to exist, it is not necessary that changes in the price level actually

exist at the moment. Changes in the price level are merely a symptom of inflation or deflation, not the phenomenon itself. The phenomenon itself can exist prior to and even in the absence of its symptoms, just as an illness can exist prior to and in the absence of its symptoms. On this subject, see below, pp. 921–922.

14. See above, the reference to Samuelson and Nordhaus for a typical textbook presentation of the demand-pull/cost-push doctrine.

15. See above, pp. 200–201.

16. See above, ibid.

17. On these points, see above, pp. 591–592.

18. See above, pp. 179–180.

19. See above, p. 229.

20. See below, pp. 931–933.

21. See above, pp. 899–901.

22. See above, pp. 518–519.

23. See above, Table 12–1, on p. 523.

24. See above, pp. 505–506.

25. On this subject, see above, pp. 829–831, and below, pp. 925–928.

26. See above, Table 12–1, on p. 523.

27. Rothbard originally used a similar definition. Cf. Murray N. Rothbard, *Man, Economy, and State*, 2 vols. (New York: D. Van Nostrand Company, 1962), 2:851. In his later, popular writings, however, he has come to use inflation as a synonym for rising prices.

28. On these points, see above, pp. 895–897.

29. Cf. Ludwig von Mises, *Human Action*, 3d ed. rev. (Chicago: Henry Regnery Co., 1966), p. 424. See also, idem, "Inflation and Price Control" in idem, *Planning For Freedom*, 4th ed. enl. (South Holland, Ill.: Libertarian Press, 1980), pp. 78–80. These pages also contain a valuable discussion of the semantic difficulties created by the definition of inflation as rising prices.

30. Cf. Ludwig von Mises "Planning for Freedom" in idem, *Planning For Freedom*, pp. 13–14.

31. See above, pp. 888–889. See also below, 940–941, which demonstrate an additional major deflationary consequence of government budget deficits.

32. At the same time, of course, because increases in the supply of gold are a by-product of increases in productive ability in general, the effect of any impairment of productive ability is a tendency toward a lesser rate of increase in the world's overall supply of gold.

33. Just as deficits can exist without inflation, so inflation can exist without deficits. Inflation can exist even in the face of current government budget *surpluses*. It exists so long as the quantity of money is being increased at a rate more rapid than the increase in the supply of precious metals. If, while the government operates with a current budget surplus, the central bank or the private banking system buys up already outstanding government securities or acquires any other assets by means of such newly created money, there is inflation. Inflation existed under just such circumstances in the United States in the 1920s.

34. The threat of an absolute loss of gold reserves was diminished by virtue of the existence of National Bank notes and Federal Reserve notes, which served virtually to eliminate gold coin as a normal part of people's cash holdings and thus the role of gold coin in day-to-day financial transactions. (See above,

pp. 508–509.) To the extent that gold coin is used as currency, any creation of additional paper or checkbook money is automatically followed by redemptions of paper for gold, as people seek more gold coin to keep pace with larger holdings of money overall—much as they seek more bills of the various denominations when the supply of money increases. The elimination of gold coin as a significant component of the day-to-day money supply, served to limit the loss of gold reserves to the portion flowing abroad, until such time as the citizens might become alarmed about the situation.

35. See above, p. 510.

36. See the preceding note and above, p. 509.

37. See above, pp. 504–505.

38. See below, pp. 931–933. In addition, it should be realized that as far as government debt is held by the Federal Reserve System, the payment of interest by the Treasury is largely in name only, since much of the interest is turned back to the Treasury. What this refers to is the fact that when the Treasury pays interest on debt held by the Federal Reserve System, that interest is revenue to the Federal Reserve System on which, after deducting its expenses, the Federal Reserve System earns a profit. A major portion of this profit is then turned over by the Federal Reserve System to the Treasury, just as any other government enterprise must turn over most of its profits, if any. (The Federal Reserve System is in the highly unusual position for a government enterprise of having profits because its leading product—paper money—has virtually no cost of production.) Thus, in essence, what occurs is that one department of the government—the Treasury—pays interest to another department of the government—the Federal Reserve System—on loans granted out of newly created money, and then receives much of that interest back.

39. It should not be forgotten, of course, that the economy-wide average rate of profit and interest is high precisely because of the continued existence of substantial deficits, which have the effect of raising the rate of net consumption. On this point, see above, pp. 829–830.

40. Not surprisingly, under any of the proposals for a constitutionally balanced budget, the provisions could be evaded fairly easily.

41. A loss would be self-defeating because it would reduce the government's ability to spend, while what the government wants is to increase its ability to spend.

42. See above, pp. 888.

43. See below, pp. 930–941.

44. For a critique of this fallacy, see above, pp. 573–580.

45. See above, pp. 876–878 and 887–888.

46. See above, pp. 890–891, 591–592, and 594.

47. See above, pp. 513–516 and 519–526. See also above, pp. 916–917, where the fact that inflation causes wage rates and prices to outrun the increase in aggregate demand is explained.

48. See below, pp. 938–942.

49. See above, pp. 891–892.

50. Cf. Adam Smith, *The Wealth of Nations* (London, 1776), bk. 5, chap. 3; reprint of Cannan ed. (Chicago: University of Chicago Press, 2 vols. in 1, 1976), 2:462–463.

51. Ibid. [2:461–466].

52. Ibid. [2:466–471].

53. See Ludwig von Mises, *The Theory of Money and Credit*,

new ed. (Irvington-on-Hudson, N. Y.: The Foundation for Economic Education, 1971), pp. 414, 416.

54. See above, pp. 263–282.

55. See above, pp. 282–294.

56. See *Human Action*, pp. 412–414. See also Henry Hazlitt, *Economics in One Lesson*, new ed. (New Rochelle, N. Y.: Arlington House Publishers, 1979), pp. 168–169.

57. Cf. above, pp. 554–555, where this phenomenon is discussed in relation to the doctrine of consumptionism.

58. See below, pp. 942–946.

59. See above, p. 768 and pp. 837–838. The material in the second reference explains how the conversion of savings into hoards raises the rate of net consumption.

60. See above, pp. 925–927.

61. On this subject, see below, pp. 942–950.

62. See above, p. 229.

63. Concerning such gravitation, see above, pp. 737–739.

64. On these points, cf. von Mises, *Human Action,* pp. 549–550.

65. See below, pp. 935–936, for a demonstration of the fact that the loss of the lender is actually substantially greater than the gain of the borrower in cases of this kind.

66. See above, pp. 520–521.

67. Cf. *Human Action*, pp. 550–566.

68. See above, pp. 622–636.

69. See above, p. 929. See also above, p. 555.

70. Cf. *Human Action*, pp. 548–550, 556.

71. See above, pp. 744–750, on the nature of this relationship.

72. On these points, see above, pp. 618–642.

73. See above, pp. 632–634.

74. See above, pp. 683–685 and 694–696

75. These cash reserves, of course, do not leave the economic system but return to business firms. On average, a business firm ends up with the same cash it had before, but it does so in an environment in which the volume of its financial transactions is greater. Thus, its cash reserves fall relative to the volume of its financial transactions.

76. Concerning all four of the mechanisms by which a more rapidly growing quantity of money reduces the demand for money for holding and thus raises the velocity of circulation of money, see above, pp. 519–522.

77. See above, pp. 513–514.

78. As a general principle, the deflationary effect of the inflation of paper money hinges on the gold value of the paper falling in greater proportion than the increase in the supply of paper money and thus the increase in the volume of spending that takes place in terms of paper money. This outcome is virtually certain inasmuch as the market takes into account in the present all of the prospective future decline in the value of paper money expected to result from inflation in the future.

79. Cf. *Human Action*, pp. 797–798.

80. See above, pp. 591–592.

81. See above, p. 591.

82. This does not mean that I advocate simply that the government abandon its policy of inflation in the context of our present monetary system. Such a step, taken by itself, would result in a catastrophic deflation and depression, probably worse than that of 1929. A disaster of this magnitude must certainly be avoided. It can be avoided if the abandonment of inflation is coupled with a transition to a 100-percent-reserve gold standard. On this subject see below, pp. 959–962.

83. See above, pp. 937–938.

84. Cf. Henry Hazlitt, *Man vs. The Welfare State* (New Rochelle, N. Y.: Arlington House, 1970), pp. 147, 148.

85. Cf. *Human Action*, pp. 426–428. See also Ludwig von Mises, *Stabilization of the Monetary Unit—From the Viewpoint of Theory*, chap. 1, in Ludwig von Mises, *On the Manipulation of Money and Credit*, trans. Bettina Bien Greaves, ed. Percy L. Greaves, Jr. (Dobbs Ferry, N. Y.: Free Market Books, 1978), pp. 3–16.

86. See above, pp. 520–521. See also above, p. 906.

87. Calculations based on data appearing in *Federal Reserve Bulletin,* October 1986, p. A13, and March 1989, p. A13.

88. See above, p. 924.

89. On the subject of credit crunches, see above, pp. 939–940. Concerning profit squeezes, see above, p. 943.

90. For the explanation of why not, see above, pp. 931–933.

91. See above, ibid.

92. In the discussion that follows, I frequently refer to the U. S. government rather than to the Federal Reserve System, which is merely the specific government agency charged with the formulation and execution of the government's monetary policy. I attach no great significance to the Federal Reserve's alleged independence from the government. It is, as I say, a government agency. The members of its board of governors are all nominated by the president and confirmed by the Senate. All must stand for periodic reappointment. All are subject to various political pressures. For example, many, if not all, can be assumed to have joined in various political alliances and incurred various political debts in the course of their careers prior to their appointment, debts which they can be called upon to repay during their tenure in office. In addition, of course, Congress can at any time change the law under which the Federal Reserve operates, something to which the Federal Reserve Board is very sensitive.

93. For the most part, it doesn't even actually have to create very many of those billions—its demonstrated willingness to create them is sufficient. For example, the government could create all the billions of paper currency necessary to redeem all the bank deposits in the United States. But it will never actually have to redeem any very major portion of those deposits so long as it demonstrates its willingness to do so whenever put to the test.

94. See above, this page, n. 87.

95. Calculation based on data appearing in *Federal Reserve Bulletin,* March 1989, p. A13.

96. Calculations based on data appearing in *Federal Reserve Bulletin*, March 1989, p. A13; ibid., April 1993, p. A14.

97. Calculations based on data appearing in *Federal Reserve Bulletin*, April 1993, p. A14, and July 1994, p. A14.

98. As previously noted in Chapter 12, n. 34, this calculation is based on year-end data appearing in *Federal Reserve Bulletin*, July 1994, p. A14, and weekly money supply figures as reported in *New York Times*, October 17, 1994.

99. See above, pp. 520–521, for the explanation of why increases in the quantity of money raise the rate of interest rather than reduce it.

100. By way of a postscript to the discussion in the text, I must observe that as of the early spring of 1995, the international currency markets are confirming this view. The precipitating

cause seems to be the failure of the new, Republican-controlled Congress to enact a balanced-budget amendment to the Constitution, and the interpretation of this fact as signifying continued rapid growth in the U.S. national debt and a corresponding long-term need to inflate in order to service the debt. In response to such anticipations, there is a tendency in the world market to liquidate assets denominated in dollars, and use the proceeds to purchase assets denominated in other currencies, which, for the time being, are believed to have less inflationary prospects.

As a further postscript, as this book goes to the printer in the spring of 1996, it has become clear that since the end of 1993, an important development has occurred with respect to what should be counted in the M₁ money supply. Over this time, general-purpose and broker-dealer money-market-mutual-fund accounts have rapidly become indistinguishable from ordinary checking accounts, in that requirements limiting the frequency with which checks may be written on these accounts, as well as requirements limiting the minimum-sized check that may be drawn on them, have both been rapidly disappearing. In the absence of further research, it is not possible to determine the precise amount of growth in the money supply for which this development has been responsible in the last two years. But taking it as equal merely to the increase in these accounts over this time, the effect on the rate of increase in the money supply has been substantial, even if one includes in the money supply at the end of 1993, the totality of such accounts rather than merely the fraction of them that was already the equivalent of checking accounts at that time.

Based on the data in the *Federal Reserve Bulletin* of March 1996, p. A14, the effect of recalculating the growth in the reported M₁ money supply in this way is that the percentage change between December 1993 and December 1994 becomes 3.2 percent instead of 1.7 percent, and the percentage change for 1995 becomes +4.1 percent instead of -2.2 percent. The significance of such recalculation is that it makes intelligible what would otherwise be an extremely puzzling phenomenon indeed. Namely, how the economic system can be displaying signs of inflation in the midst of fairly sustained outright deflation.

101. See above, pp. 141–144.

102. Concerning the origin of money, see above, pp. 506–508.

103. *Roman Civilization Sourcebook II: The Empire* (New York: Harper & Row, 1966), p. 440.

104. Ibid., pp. 441–442. This was like insisting today that a $20 gold coin be used as the equivalent of only $20 of paper money.

105. See James Breasted, *Ancient Times*, 2d ed. (Ginn and Company, 1967), p. 747.

106. On this point, see above, pp. 510–511 See also below, pp. 951–954.

107. This, of course, is the process of good money driving out bad money. For reconciliation of this fact with Gresham's Law, according to which bad money drives out good money, see above, pp. 510–511.

108. Henceforth, for the sake of brevity, I generally refer to gold alone. But the same points apply to silver as well.

109. One method of estimating the proper conversion price is simply to divide the government's existing gold stock into the money supply. Currently, this means dividing approximately 260 million ounces of gold into $1,128 billion of money. The resulting conversion price is thus $4,340 per ounce. When the monetary role of silver is allowed for, however, a figure of closer to $3,000 results. Concerning this last, see below, pp. 958–959.

110. On the subject of the monetary unit as a unit of weight of precious metal, see Murray Rothbard, *What Has Government Done to Our Money?* (Novato, Calif.: Libertarian Publishers), 1974, pp. 5–7.

111. See above, pp. 573–580 and 817–818.

112. See above, pp. 762–767, 774–775, 807–818, and 825–826.

113. See above, p. 574 and pp. 744–750, 762–771, and 882–883.

114. See above, pp. 519–526 and 938–940.

115. Recognition of the fact that a greater demand for money for holding increases the real stock of money and, indeed, is the only thing that can do so, can be found in Rothbard, *What Has Government Done to Our Money?*, pp. 15–16. See also above, pp. 693–694.

116. This figure follows from the fact that total checking deposits were approximately $799 billion, while bank reserves of standard money were approximately $61 billion. See *Federal Reserve Bulletin*, July 1994, pp. A13, and A14.

117. Ibid., p. A29.

118. On the subject of parallel standards, see Rothbard, *What Has Government Done to Our Money?*, pp. 17–19.

119. This section is largely a revised version of my article "Gold: The Solution to Our Monetary Dilemma," which appeared in the *Bulletin of the US Paper Exchange*, June 1980, and was subsequently reprinted in *The Intellectual Activist*, October 1 and November 1, 1980.

120. See *Federal Reserve Bulletin*, July 1994, pp. A14, A51.

121. See above, pp. 263–278, for explanation of the ways that price controls and socialism destroy material civilization.

122. For the sake of simplicity, we ignore the role of silver.

123. I am indebted to Murray Rothbard for this pattern of achieving a 100-percent-reserve gold standard, which he first presented in an unpublished monograph in the mid-1950s.

124. Ibid.

125. When the monetary role of silver is allowed for, the conversion price works out to closer to $3,000 per ounce.

126. In certain circumstances, compliance with this principle might require that the government use less than its full gold stock to redeem the supply of paper currency and fiduciary media. For example, if the U.S. government today possessed 500 million ounces of gold by itself, the conversion price implied by devoting all of it to the redemption of the money supply would be only $1,500 per ounce. This would make the gold-ounce GDP, and the volume of spending it implies, the equivalent of too few dollars to comply with the principle. In such circumstances, the government could devote less than its full gold stock to the redemption of the outstanding money supply, and use the remainder in redeeming a portion of the national debt. In other circumstances, of course, the government's gold stock might be so limited that it would be necessary to increase it before making the conversion.

127. See above, pp. 936–937.

128. The additional holdings of gold on the part of the citizens have the further distinction at least of representing an additional supply of a physical commodity, which is capable of making some actual contribution to human well-being.

EPILOGUE

CHAPTER 20

TOWARD THE ESTABLISHMENT OF
LAISSEZ-FAIRE CAPITALISM

1. Introduction

The principles and theories presented in this book call for a society of laissez-faire capitalism. (For the sake of brevity, I often refer simply to a capitalist society. In such cases, it should be understood that laissez-faire capitalism is the only logically consistent form of a capitalist society.) If such a society is to be achieved, a political movement pursuing a long-range program will be necessary. My purpose in this concluding, epilogue chapter is to describe the nature of such a movement and to offer a basic outline of the long-range political program it would have to follow, including a description of how the most difficult steps in the program might actually be accomplished. As far as I know, my effort here is the first of its kind; as such, it will undoubtedly benefit greatly from the numerous additions and refinements that I hope others will be led to make.

The Importance of Capitalism as a Conscious Goal

The first thing that those in favor of capitalism must do is to make the conscious, explicit decision that they seriously want to achieve a fully capitalist society and are prepared to work for its achievement. We need to view ourselves as active agents of change, working toward a definite goal: laissez-faire capitalism.

The advocacy of laissez-faire capitalism, indeed, of capitalism in any explicit form, has not been present in the political spectrum. In the United States, the political controversies of the last several generations have been carried on between the "liberals," who stand for socialism, and the "conservatives," who stand for nothing except what other groups, including the liberals, have managed to establish as the country's tradition.

The success of the liberals/socialists in enacting their program shows that what we need is a group of educated and articulate individuals who adopt the achievement of *capitalism* as their goal. Such individuals, dedicated to maintaining constant progress toward capitalism, would constitute a de facto capitalist political party, even if the name of such a party never appeared on a ballot. By virtue of constantly offering their own definite program for political change, they would seize the political initiative. Instead of merely attacking the socialistic proposals of the "liberals" and then yielding to them and abandoning the fight once the proposals happened to be enacted, as is the almost invariable practice of the conservatives, they would always strive to move in the direction of capitalism. As an essential part of the process of doing so, they would never tire of assaulting intellectual targets as far behind enemy lines as possible—such as social security, antitrust legislation, and public education. Never would they accept the existing state of society as immutably given and deserving of preservation merely because it exists. Always they would seek to change the existing state of society until it represented laissez-faire capitalism.

Laissez-faire capitalism would represent their fixed star so to speak. To the extent that present conditions departed from it, they would be radical in seeking to change present conditions. To the extent that conditions in the past had approximated laissez-faire capitalism, they would be reactionary in seeking to reestablish such conditions. To the extent that present conditions were consistent with laissez-faire capitalism, they would be conservative in seeking to preserve those conditions.

The program such a party would have to follow is both political and educational in nature. It is political in that it centers on the offering of specific political proposals, which, if adopted, would move the country toward capitalism. It is educational in that it views the basic problem that we face as one of explaining to the people of the United States and other countries the value of a capitalist society and the value of the specific steps required to achieve it. What people do is determined by what they think. If we want to change the political practice, there is no other way but to change people's political philosophy and economic theories. Accordingly, every political proposal that I suggest is itself intended to serve as a vehicle for educating the public and for attracting talented individuals to our cause who in turn will become capable of educating still others to the value of our program.

Needless to say, the substance of such education is the spread of the ideas of Ludwig von Mises and Ayn Rand, reinforced by the ideas of other procapitalist economists and philosophers whom I mentioned in the Introduction and elsewhere in this book. It is principally owing to the great popular success of the writings of Ayn Rand and the growing influence of the works of Ludwig von Mises that there already exists a significant and growing number of potential recruits for the procapitalist political movement that I envision. The further spread of the ideas of these two historic figures is the only possible basis for the further growth and ultimate success of the procapitalist cause.

Along these lines, I wish to acknowledge once more how important are all philosophic ideas that determine people's conception of the position of the human individual in relation to the world in which he lives. For example, so long as man is viewed as fundamentally helpless, with his destiny controlled by forces beyond his power to change, it will be next to impossible to eliminate the welfare state. People will cling to it out of a sense of helplessness. Elimination of the welfare state and the establishment of a capitalist society presupposes a view of man as a self-responsible causal agent, capable of securing his well-being by means of intelligent action. Indeed, the entire program of reform outlined in this chapter must proceed alongside a renewal of all of the philosophical foundations of a division-of-labor, capitalist society that I described in the first chapter of this book.[1] It is this above all which makes the dissemination

of the ideas of Ayn Rand so important. As the leading advocate of reason in modern times, her writings alone hold out the possibility of the necessary fundamental philosophic changes taking place in our culture, without which efforts at the level of economic theory and political philosophy are doomed to failure.

In the pages that follow, I write of political campaigns over various issues. Please understand that I am not writing merely or even primarily of campaigns carried out in connection with elections. Rather, I am writing of campaigns carried on year in and year out, as part of a process of continuous education of the public. Each of these campaigns would necessarily have to be preceded and accompanied by the writing and dissemination of an appropriate literature, ranging from books and monographs on down to handbills—a literature dealing with the specific issues at hand, but always in relation to wider, abstract principles. Indeed, the dissemination of such literature and its articulation in speeches and debates would constitute the substance of what I call political campaigns.

Further, I think that to achieve capitalism it will ultimately be necessary for a formally organized capitalist party to come into existence, whose primary function will actually be to serve as an *educational institution:* it would have one or more book-publishing houses, theoretical journals, magazines devoted to current issues, and schools turning out intellectual leaders thoroughly versed in economic theory and political philosophy. All of these vehicles would be devoted at least as much to questions of political philosophy and economic theory as to political activity.

The political proposals I make are short- and intermediate-range, as well as long-range in nature. I believe that it will take several generations to achieve a fully capitalist society, mainly because of the time required for the educational process. It will not be enough just to present our long-range goals. It will be necessary to advocate a whole intervening series of short- and intermediate-range goals whose enactment will represent progress toward our long-range goals. The major political task in the years ahead will be continuously to formulate such short and intermediate range goals, and to keep the country moving in the direction of full capitalism by means of their successive achievement. The short- and intermediate-range goals I offer are intended to illustrate principles of strategy and tactics and thus to serve as a pattern.

In the light of the preceding, it should scarcely be necessary to say that at no time should the advocacy of sound principles be sacrificed to notions of political expediency, advanced under misguided ideas about what is "practical." The only practical course is to name and defend true principles and then seek to win over public opinion to the support of such principles. It is never to accept the untrue principles that guide public opinion at the moment and design and advocate programs that pander to the errors of the public. Such a procedure is to abandon the fight for any fundamental or significant change—namely, a change in people's ideas—and to reinforce the errors we want to combat.

It is definitely not impractical to explain to people that if they want to live and prosper, they must adopt capitalism. It would not be impractical to do so even if for a very long time most people simply refused to listen and went on supporting policies that are against their interests. In such a case, it would not be the advocates of capitalism who were impractical, for they would be pursuing the only course that is capable of working, namely, explaining to people what they must do if they are in fact to succeed. Rather it would be the mass of people—perhaps, indeed, the entire rest of the society—that would be impractical, pursuing as it did goals which are self-destructive and refusing to hear of constructive alternatives. If, to use an analogy from the world of engineering and business, someone knows how to build an airplane or a tractor that people could afford and greatly benefit from, but is not listened to, such a person is not at all impractical because others refuse to listen to his ideas that would greatly benefit them. Rather it is those others, whatever their number, who are impractical. In the political-economic realm, it is the current state of public opinion that is impractical: it expects that men can live in a modern economic system while destroying the foundations of that system—that, for example, they can have rising prosperity while destroying the incentives and the means of the businessmen and capitalists who are to provide the prosperity. The advocates of capitalism, who tell people that the opposite is true and that the opposite policy is necessary, are not impractical. They are eminently the advocates of practicality—of what is achievable in, and by the nature of, reality.

It is the grossest compounding of confusions to suggest that those who know truths that masses of impractical people refuse to hear, accept error as an unalterable given for the sake of which they must abandon or "bend" their knowledge of the truth. Nothing could be more impractical, elevating as it does, error above truth and making knowledge subordinate to ignorance. The essence of true political practicality consists of clearly naming and explaining the long-range political program that promotes human life and well being—i.e., capitalism—and then step by step moving toward the fullest and most consistent achievement of that goal. That the initial effect of naming the right goal and course may be to shock masses of unenlightened people and invoke their

displeasure should be welcomed. That will be the first step in awakening them from their ignorance.

It should not be surprising that those who fear the effects of the open advocacy of capitalism are themselves highly deficient in their knowledge of capitalism. They fear to evoke the displeasure of the ignorant because they do not know enough about capitalism to know what to say in the face of such displeasure. Their ignorance on this score, I believe, is the result of an unwillingness to acquire a sufficient combination of knowledge of political philosophy and economic theory, above all, of economic theory. Remnants of the mind-body dichotomy in their thinking prevent them from fully grasping the intellectual—indeed, the profoundly philosophical—value of a subject as "materialistic" as economics. To be successful, the advocates of capitalism must immerse themselves in the study of economic theory.

The Capitalist Society and a Political Program for Achieving It

The capitalist society we want to achieve is a society in which individual rights are consistently and scrupulously respected—in which, as Ayn Rand put it, the initiation of physical force is barred from human relationships. We want a society in which the role of government is limited to the protection of individual rights, and in which, therefore, the government uses force only in defense and retaliation against the initiation of force. We want a society in which property rights are recognized as among the foremost human rights—a society in which no one is made to suffer for his success by being sacrificed to the envy of others, a society in which all land, natural resources, and other means of production are privately owned. In such a society, the size of government would be less than a tenth of what it now is in terms of government spending. Most of the government as it now exists would be swept away: virtually all of the alphabet agencies and all of the cabinet departments with the exceptions of defense, state, justice, and treasury. All that would remain is a radically reduced executive branch, and legislative and judicial branches with radically reduced powers. To the law-abiding citizen of such a society, the government would appear essentially as a "night watchman," dutifully and quietly going about its appointed rounds so that the citizenry could rest secure in the knowledge that their persons and property were free from aggression. Only in the lives of common criminals and foreign aggressor states would the presence of the government bulk large.

If these brief remarks can serve as a description of the capitalist society we want to achieve, let us now turn to a series of political proposals for its actual achievement. I group the proposals under seven headings: Privatization of Property, Freedom of Production and Trade, Abolition of the Welfare State, Abolition of the Income and Inheritance Taxes, Establishment of Gold as Money, Procapitalist Foreign Policy, and Separation of State from Education, Science, and Religion. Under each of these heads, I develop specific issues and programs each of which deserves to be fought for and which, in being fought for, would serve to promote the spread of our entire political-economic philosophy.

2. Privatization of Property: Importance of Fighting on Basis of Principles

The privatization of property is the most fundamental aspect of a procapitalist political program. In addition, its discussion is well suited to illustrate strategy and tactics applicable to the pursuit of *all* aspects of a procapitalist political program.

Privatization would ultimately require the sale of all government-owned lands and natural resources (with such limited exceptions as the sites of military bases, police stations, and courthouses), which presently include the greater part of the territory of many of the Western states and almost all of the territory of Alaska. It would entail the sale of TVA and all other public-power facilities, the sale of Amtrak and Conrail, the post office, the public schools, universities, and hospitals, the national parks, and the public highway system. It would also entail the establishment of the airwaves as private property and of private property rights under the sea and in outer space.

Those of us who work to establish capitalism must always be aware that the privatization of all of these things is part of our ultimate goal and we must be sure that all new adherents we gain fully understand and support the whole program of privatization, as well as all the other essential aspects of our program. No secret must ever be made of the full, long-range program and its goal of complete laissez-faire capitalism.

In the present situation, I believe that the most important aspect of privatization to concentrate on is that of the federal government's vast landholdings, in particular where oil, coal, and timber are concerned. Closely connected with this should be the urging of the extension of private ownership to undersea mining operations. These aspects would make it possible to link the campaign for privatization with an assault on the environmental movement, which has replaced socialism as the leading threat to material civilization. Such linkage would provide the opportunity to reestablish the rightful connection between capitalism, on the one side, and science, technology, economic progress, and the supreme value of human life on earth, on the other side. This connection has been concealed for many years because of socialism's usurpation of the mantle of progressivism. Linkage of the campaign for privatization with an assault on the environmental movement would be instrumental in reestablishing capitalism in the minds of the public as the system of progress and improvement advocated by men of reason, and the opposition to capitalism as the manifestation of ignorance, fear, and superstition.[2] A further major aspect of the linkage should be a continual hammering away at the appalling state of contemporary education and the ignorance of its graduates, including almost all of today's politicians, government officials, and journalists. The environmentalist and socialist opposition to capitalism should be portrayed as exactly what it is—a movement to return the world to the Dark Ages and a system of feudal privilege.[3] Privatization of education, of course, should be urged as an essential aspect of the rebirth of education.

Other, narrower campaigns for privatization that might profitably be conducted early on would be ones for the privatization of the post office, the airwaves, and the New York City subway system. Postal service and cellular-telephone channels are already private to varying degrees. In these two cases, privatization would merely be a matter of carrying forward something that already exists to an important extent.

The New York City subway system would be a good candidate for an early privatization campaign, because it should be relatively easy to explain how the establishment of private ownership would create an incentive for the subway's management to want to attract customers and thus to improve the cleanliness, safety, and efficiency of the system. Such a campaign would represent our going on the offensive in the country's leading bastion of collectivism and making large numbers of collectivists aware that the comfort of their daily lives depended on the acceptance of the principle of private ownership of the means of production.

Each of these individual campaigns would, of course, have to be focused on its own particular set of concretes. But if, at the same time, they were also based on the *principle* of the economic superiority and moral rightness of private ownership, the cumulative effect would be to tend to establish that principle as correct in the public's mind. Thus, provided they were conducted in the name of our basic principles and used as the opportunity for explaining those principles, success in such lesser projects would help in someday putting us in a position in which we could accomplish the objective of privatization completely.

We should certainly not expect that we would quickly win any of the campaigns for privatization, even the least among them. On the contrary, for a very long time we would almost certainly lose them all, over and over again. Indeed, we should expect for some time to be written off as cranks and even ridiculed for our views. Nevertheless, if we fight every concrete issue on the basis of correct abstract, general principles, our efforts will never be wasted. We will be successful even though we fail to win our particular objective of the moment. We will be successful because we will have propounded and helped to spread our principles. As a result, we will have gained new adherents, who will have been attracted to our principles. In addition, those who waged the campaign will have become more skilled in the defense of their principles. Thus, we will have gained the basis for conducting campaigns over the same issue, and over a wide variety of other issues, on a stronger foundation in the future. We will be embarked upon a policy of progress in intellectual influence analogous to the process of capital accumulation and economic progress.[4]

If we are successful in making continual progress in our intellectual influence, we cannot fail ultimately to possess major intellectual influence and therefore correspondingly major political influence. To achieve the most rapid possible success, our objective should be to accomplish in terms of intellectual influence the kind of rate of progress achieved economically by Japan and other contemporary East Asian countries that began in the most humble material conditions. If we could succeed in that, then even though we may begin today in the most humble conditions in terms of size and influence, within a matter of decades we would become a major intellectual force.

As part of the same point, I want to stress that a major feature of every political activity we engage in is that it must provide easy opportunities for any new supporters it attracts to become exposed to our entire philosophy. The individual campaigns, such as the ones I have just described, must not only be waged on the basis of the appropriate abstract principles, but they must also provide ready exposure to the main books and publications of our philosophy. This does not mean that handing out copies of *Human Action* or *Atlas Shrugged* is the first or most prominent thing we do in such a campaign, but it does mean that we are very interested in making every receptive individual we meet aware of the existence of these books and in getting him to read them and the rest of our essential literature.

3. The Freedom of Production and Trade

The establishment of the freedom of production and trade implies the abolition of all government interference with production and trade. It implies, for example, the abolition of all labor legislation, licensing laws, the antitrust laws, and zoning laws. It implies the abolition of virtually all of the alphabet agencies. It also implies the freedom of international trade and migration.

An important principle that I think we should adopt in fighting for the freedom of production and trade is to show how *its establishment would enable individuals to solve their own economic problems*. For example, there are few more serious economic problems than mass unemployment. As we have seen, this problem is the result of the government restricting the freedom of individuals to offer and accept the lower wage rates that would make full employment possible. The restrictions are in the form of minimum-wage laws, prounion legislation, unemployment insurance, and welfare legislation. Abolishing such legislation and establishing the freedom of production and trade should be presented as the solution to this problem—as a solution that would enable the voluntary, self-interested actions of individuals to establish the terms on which everyone seeking employment could find it.[5]

In the same vein, we must take the initiative in calling for a widening of economic freedom as the solution to the problems the United States is encountering in international trade. We must show that the inability of major American industries to compete with foreign goods is the result of government intervention, and that the remedy is not the imposition of further intervention, in the form of tariffs or quotas, but the repeal of existing intervention. For example, prounion legislation causes artificially high wage rates and holds down the productivity of labor, thereby causing an artificially high level of costs for American manufacturers. The tax system and inflation have prevented the introduction of more efficient machinery, and thus have also contributed to the artificially high costs of American manufacturers, as have numerous government regulations. Such intervention should be the target of campaigns for repeal. Obviously, this would be a fertile area for the writing of books and monographs demonstrating the general principle in terms of the specific conditions of individual industries.

Similarly, the freedom of production and trade should be presented as the means of sharply reducing the cost of housing, thus making it possible for many more people to afford decent housing. The abolition of prounion legislation, building codes, zoning laws, and government agencies that withdraw land from development (such as the California Coastal Commission) would all serve to reduce the cost of housing, as would the abolition of property taxes that support improper government activities. (As should be clear from previous discussion in Chapter 10, all of these points, of course, apply to the solution of the problem of homelessness, which is greatly exacerbated by the imposition of government requirements concerning minimum housing standards.[6])

The freedom of production and trade should also be explained as the means of sharply reducing the cost of medical care. As explained in Chapter 10, under present conditions the government restricts the supply of doctors and the number of hospitals through licensing. Its solution for the consequent inability of many people to afford medical care is then to pour more and more public money into subsidizing their medical bills. The effect of the government's spending programs is to bid the price of medical care ever higher, progressively substituting new, ever higher income victims for previous victims just below them who are added to the subsidy rolls—and, of course, to reduce the quality of medical care for all groups. The obvious real solution is to *end government interference in medical care* and thus to make possible the largest and most rapidly improving supply of medical care that free and motivated providers can offer.[7]

In sum, our theme must be the opposite of the one people are accustomed to. Instead of it being what new programs the government must undertake to solve this or that problem, it must be what *existing* government programs and activities must be *stopped*, in order to allow individuals to be able to act in their own self-interest. Instead of the question being "What can the government do?," we must explain what it must stop doing that it now does, and that has caused the problem complained of.

We need to show how abolition of the antitrust laws would mean more competition, greater efficiency, and lower prices; how abolition of the Environmental Protection Agency would mean more efficient production and thus a greater ability of man to improve the external material conditions of his life, i.e., his personal environment; how abolition of the Food and Drug Administration would mean the introduction of more life-saving drugs; how abolition of medicare and medicaid, the National Institutes of Health, and all other government interference with medicine would lower the cost and improve the quality of medical care.

While fighting against all existing violations of the freedom of production and trade, a further important principle to seek to establish is *the exemption of all new industries from violations of the freedom of production and trade*. This, in fact, was one of the principal methods by which economic freedom was established historically in England: the significance of the restrictions imposed by the medieval guilds was steadily reduced by the exemption of new industries from those restrictions.

Appropriate Compromises

It should be realized that if the immediate, total abolition of a given policy of government intervention cannot obtain sufficient support to be carried out, it is proper

to work for programs of partial liberalization as temporary compromises—provided it is done explicitly and openly, in the name of the right principles, and no secret is made of our ultimate goals, which one is always prepared to defend and whose achievement serves as the standard and purpose of any temporary compromises.

Thus, for example, while openly advocating the full freedom of the housing industry, including the ultimate abolition of all building codes, one might participate in, or even launch, a campaign for a much more limited objective. Such an objective might be that the government be required to reduce the financial impact of meeting code requirements by an average of, say, X thousand dollars per house, and that it be guided by the advice of private insurance companies, mortgage lenders, and construction contractors in deciding which code requirements to modify or abolish in order to achieve this goal. Such a step would be helpful in reducing the cost of housing. A campaign for it, properly conducted, would help to make people aware that it was government intervention that was responsible for the high cost of housing and high costs in general. If carried out under the terms mentioned, a major value even of campaigns to accomplish such limited objectives would be that government intervention, not private business, would be made the target of restriction. Government force, rather than the profit motive of business, would come to be established in the public's mind as the evil that must be controlled and progressively rolled back.

Similarly, if the immediate, full freedom of medicine cannot be achieved, then, as a temporary compromise—again, presented as such and in the name of the right principles—one might work to allow merely registered nurses and licensed pharmacists to begin practicing various aspects of medicine. Such liberalization would significantly mitigate the problem at hand and, at the same time, it would promote the essential principle that more freedom is the solution to economic problems. It would thus be an important step in the right direction.[8]

The Case for the Immediate Sweeping Abolition of All Violations of the Freedom of Production and Trade

If the public possessed the necessary philosophic and economic understanding, the ideal procedure would be the immediate and simultaneous abolition of all interferences with the freedom of production and trade. This would be both on the principle of individual rights and on the principle that pressure-group warfare is inherently self-defeating. It is self-defeating in that whatever any one pressure group gains by violations of freedom made on its behalf, is reduced by what all other pressure groups gain by violations of freedom made on their behalf, and reduced by more. For example, what the workers in the automobile industry gain in higher wages resulting from the existence of an automobile workers' union, they lose back in higher prices that they must pay for the products not only of all the unionized industries (which by itself may be very considerable), but also for the products of all industries enjoying protective tariffs or receiving government subsidies, all of which is the result of the underlying principle of government intervention. And everyone loses by virtue of the unemployment and overall reduction in the productivity of labor that result, which simply cause less to be produced and sold in the economic system. In essence what is entailed in pressure-group warfare is mutual plunder. Under such an arrangement, not only does each victim lose an amount equal to what the predator gains, but the victims produce less, with the result that there is less to plunder. The process can be pushed to the point where virtually nothing is produced and thus very little can be plundered—much less than could be obtained by honest work in a free society. The pressure-group marauders have long since carried things to the point where the real wages of the average worker are far lower than they could be.

The simultaneous abolition of as much government interference as possible would help to diminish the losses experienced by any one such protected group when its privileges were removed, and would make possible correspondingly greater gains, both in the long run and in the short run, for everyone. Thus, for example, when the wheat farmers lost their subsidy, they would be compensated by the lower prices resulting from the abolition of others' subsidies as well, along with lower prices resulting from the abolition of protective tariffs, labor-union coercion, and minimum-wage legislation. The substantial increase in production that would result would operate further to compensate them, through a fall in prices greater than any fall in the average of incomes that might result.

The special importance of abolishing prounion legislation at the same time as minimum-wage legislation, should be obvious. This is necessary to prevent unemployed workers from having to crowd into a comparative handful of occupations at unnecessarily low wages, by opening all occupations to the freedom of competition.[9]

It is important to understand that acceptance of the principle of laissez faire and the willingness to fight for that principle is the only safeguard of the public against the depredations of pressure groups. Each pressure group is in a position in which the comparatively small number of its members is able to have a potentially substantial gain. This gain comes at the expense of a relatively small loss on the part of each of the enormously larger number of people who constitute the rest of society. For example,

if the members of a pressure group numbering, say, one hundred thousand people are to receive a subsidy of some kind, that subsidy may provide each of the recipients with $100,000 per year in additional income, while it costs each of the far greater number of taxpayers only a small fraction of that sum. In this case, the total cost of the subsidy is $10 billion (i.e., $100,000 x 100,000). If there are a hundred million taxpayers, the cost of the subsidy to the average taxpayer is just $100 per year (i.e., $10 billion divided by 100 million). The diffuse interest of the taxpayers in saving $100 per year each cannot remotely compare in strength with that of the highly concentrated interest of the pressure-group members who stand to gain $100,000 per year each. Accordingly, the pressure-group members are willing to make substantial financial contributions and to engage in intense lobbying efforts in order to get their way. Virtually no individual taxpayer, on the other hand, has a sufficient incentive to do anything to counter such assaults on the country's treasury.

The taxpayers can acquire an incentive to protect themselves only when they view the depredations of each pressure group as a matter of the violation of a supreme political principle—namely, that of laissez faire—a principle whose violation by any one pressure group opens the gates to its violation by scores of other pressure groups. Taxpayers who would view the matter in terms of principle would recognize that pressure group warfare already costs them many thousands of dollars per year each in higher taxes and higher prices, and that there is no limit to its potential cost short of total financial ruin. If they could be led to view matters in this light, I believe that they could then easily be organized to overcome the pressure groups. By taking on all the pressure groups at once, they would have not only a powerful individual financial incentive, but they would also be able to play up all the inherent conflicts among the various pressure groups themselves, and thus obtain substantial support from within the ranks of the pressure-group members, a growing number of whom are also more and more harmed, the more widespread becomes the system of pressure-group warfare.

An appropriate vehicle for the establishment of the freedom of production and trade, whether all at once or gradually, would be the establishment of one last regulatory-type agency: *the Deregulation Agency.* Its powers would supersede those of any regulatory agency, the acts of state and local legislatures, and the prior legislation of Congress. In sharpest contrast to all regulatory agencies, however, its powers would be limited to the *repeal* of existing regulations and laws, including the narrowing of their scope in conditions in which considerations of political expediency prevented their total repeal. It would have no power to enact any new or additional regulation.

The mandate of this agency would be to ferret out all regulations of any federal, state, or local government department or agency, and all federal, state, and local laws, that violated the freedom of production and trade. Ideally, the agency would possess the power to render any or all of them null and void. As a minimum, the enabling legislation for the agency should require it, within a fairly short period of time, such as three years, to reduce the cost of government interference in the economic system as a whole by a minimum of 50 percent. (This figure would not apply to spending for social security, welfare, and public education, which would follow the less-radical reduction schedules explained below.) Further reductions of at least 2 percent per year would be achieved thereafter, until the full freedom of production and trade was established. If, for Constitutional reasons, the agency could not be given the power to supersede federal legislation, its tasks would include the annual submission to Congress of the necessary legislative proposals for the repeal of existing federal laws.

4. Abolition of the Welfare State

Let me now present a program for accomplishing what many people believe to be simply impossible politically, namely, the abolition of the welfare state.

Elimination of Social Security/Medicare

The social security system, together with medicare, could be eliminated by means of the following steps. First, following a grace period of perhaps two or three years, to provide sufficient warning and time to adjust, there should be an immediate rise in the age at which individuals are eligible to receive social security and medicare benefits, from 65 to 70.[10]

As compensation for the loss of these benefits, individuals in the age bracket 65 to 70 should be made exempt from the federal income tax on whatever earnings they derive from employment. The result would not only be an enormous reduction in government expenditures, but a substantial rise in government tax revenues as well. The rise in tax revenues would come about because the people in the 65–70 age bracket would now pay more in the form of sales, excise, and property taxes, as the result of their having and spending higher incomes. And they would pay more in the form of state and local income taxes as well.

If enacted today, this part of the proposal for abolishing social security and medicare would cut the costs of these programs on the order of a third.[11]

But there is more. As part of the same legislation that quickly raises the social security retirement age to 70, the age at which people are eligible to receive social security and medicare benefits should be *further increased*, say, by an additional calendar quarter with the passage of each subsequent year. Under this arrangement, individuals who wished to retire at age 70, despite the progressive rise in the social security retirement age beyond 70, would have an additional year of notice in which they would have the opportunity to accumulate additional savings to take the place of the loss of each successive three months' social security/medicare benefits.

For example, those age 64 at the time the social security/medicare phase-out began, would have an additional year in which to compensate for the rise in their prospective social security retirement age to 70¼. Those age 63 at the time, would have two additional years in which to compensate for the prospective rise in their particular social security retirement age to 70½, and so on. Possibly, the additional savings such individuals would need to make could be made tax-exempt, under an IRA-type arrangement. (Savings in the government's budget achieved by the initial rise in the retirement age to 70 would help to offset the revenue loss of making these savings tax exempt.)

All by itself, the progressive rise in the social security retirement age in this way would slowly operate to abolish the system. However, I do not believe the system's demise should be allowed to drag on indefinitely. I think that no later than twenty-five years after the initial rise in the social security retirement age to 70, the system should accept its last new beneficiaries, who would then be 76¼. By that time, everyone would have had in excess of 25 years to make provision for his own retirement at age 76¼.

It should be realized that the progressive elimination of the social security/medicare system would operate to promote savings and capital accumulation. The savings of individuals would steadily replace taxes as the source of provision for old age. The increased capital accumulation that this made possible would, of course, increase the demand for labor and the productivity of labor, which means that it would increase wage rates and the supply of goods, which latter would operate to reduce prices. Thus, real wages and the general standard of living would rise. The rise would be progressive insofar as the rate of capital accumulation was increased.

While the total abolition of social security and medicare must always be one of our long-run goals, an immediate way to begin reducing the cost of these programs would be for the government simply to make the kind of tax-exemption offer I described above, to everyone eligible to receive these programs' benefits. Namely, so long as anyone eligible to receive such benefits abstains from doing so and continues to work instead, his earnings from employment will be exempt from the federal income tax. Being enabled to keep almost all of one's earnings might make it worthwhile for many people to keep on working some years longer, rather than accept social security and medicare. Not only would the government's outlays be reduced as the result of this measure, but, as I noted before, its revenues would almost certainly increase. If enacted, this proposal would achieve some significant immediate good, and, in addition, help to prepare the ground for further reductions in the cost of social security and medicare.

It should also be noted here that the phaseout of the social security and medicare programs, or the undertaking of any other measure that would be accompanied by an increase in the number of people seeking employment, calls for an intensification of efforts to abolish or restrict as far as possible prounion and minimum-wage legislation. This is necessary in order to make it possible for the larger number of job seekers to find employment.

Elimination of Public Welfare

The public-welfare system, including food stamps and rent subsidies, could be substantially eliminated within a few years. What would need to be done is to begin reducing welfare payments for able-bodied adults and for minors above the age of fourteen by, say, 10 percent per year across the board, until those payments fell substantially below the wages of the lowest-paid workers. Aid to dependent children below the age of fourteen could be gradually abolished by a law declaring children born more than one year after its enactment to be ineligible for receipt of such aid. Henceforth, dependent children of welfare recipients would have to be supported out of the welfare payments of their parents, which would be steadily reduced. Thus within a few years, welfare for able-bodied adults would cease to be economically significant, because all such adults would be confronted with a situation in which they would be substantially better off taking even the lowest-paid jobs. Within fifteen years, aid to dependent children would cease entirely, whereupon the whole welfare program would be without economic significance.[12]

As previously noted, at the same time that welfare benefits were being reduced, legislation limiting employment opportunities would also have to be abolished or at least progressively restricted, such as the minimum-wage laws and prounion legislation.[13] In addition, restrictions on the employment of teenage juveniles would have to be eliminated in conformity with the immediate reductions in welfare allowances to teenage children.

The abolition of these restrictions on employment opportunities are necessary to provide people presently receiving welfare benefits with a realistic alternative of living by working. Finally, the reduction in government expenditures for welfare could be earmarked for increasing the personal exemption from the income tax of people who are gainfully employed. This would further increase the economic advantages of working over being on welfare.

My reason for suggesting the gradual reduction in welfare benefits rather than their immediate or very rapid total elimination, is to allow time for large concentrations of people on welfare, such as in Harlem in New York City, to move to areas that offer better prospects for employment; and, at the same time, for new industry to move into areas such as Harlem, in response to the existence of large numbers of people willing to work for low wages. The gradual reduction in welfare benefits would also allow time for private charitable efforts to develop to deal with the cases of individual suffering not caused by the fault of the individuals themselves.

Once public welfare benefits were reduced to a level substantially below the wages of the lowest-paid workers, the problem, as I have said, would cease to have much economic significance. Almost everyone would be working who was able to work. The system could then be reduced further by totally denying benefits to any able-bodied person, or to anyone suffering as the result of his own irresponsibility, such as drug addicts and alcoholics. After some years, once the government had ceased to be regarded as offering anything but the most minimal relief from want, and private charity had been reestablished in the public's eyes as the place to which the indigent must turn, the remaining public welfare system could probably be totally abolished, practically without being missed.

A vital aspect of the campaign for the abolition of the welfare system must be the conversion of intellectual opinion among the groups most affected. They must understand that the system's demise is indispensable to the genuine assimilation of all groups into American society and essential to the opportunities of every person now on the welfare roles who would like to make something of his life, and to the opportunities available to his children.

When I first wrote the above discussion of the elimination of the welfare system, I believed that the element of gradualism was necessary not only for the reasons stated but also if efforts to eliminate the system were to have any hope of gaining significant public support. On this score, it appears that I may have been wrong. For example, the state of Wisconsin now intends to remove people from the welfare rolls after two years if they turn down a job or job training, and Governor Weld of Massachusetts wants to compel welfare recipients to find work within sixty days or else lose their cash benefits or take state-provided community-service jobs.[14] It remains to be seen whether such policies, which apparently give no thought to the need to abolish the obstacles presently standing in the way of employment, can not only be enacted but also be maintained in the face of the serious hardships that are likely to accompany them.

Elimination of Public Hospitals

Public hospitals and public clinics could also gradually be abolished. Their operation and the ownership of their assets could be turned over to recognized private charities, which would temporarily receive public funds to finance their operation. But the appropriation of public funds for such purposes would steadily fall, again, say, at a rate of 10 percent per year. These charity hospitals and clinics would be empowered to charge fees to their patients, at their discretion, to help compensate for the loss of government funds. It should be expected that the elimination of government control would be accompanied by major reductions in the costs of operating these hospitals and clinics. Medicaid could be phased out in step with the reduction in the public funds turned over to the now private charity hospitals and charity clinics. (Obviously, it would be extremely desirable if this process were accompanied by the most rapid possible liberalization of the licensing requirements for entry into the medical profession and for the ownership and operation of hospitals and clinics.)

Firing Government Employees and Ending Subsidies to Business

I believe that it is possible to fire government employees and abolish government subsidies to business with the support of the groups concerned. This can be accomplished by making the termination of employment or loss of subsidy to the immediate financial self-interest of the parties. What could be done is to offer very generous severance terms, in the form of the continued payment of the salary or subsidy for a limited time, during which the parties would be fully free to change over to any alternative private, unsubsidized activity they wished.

Thus, for example, a government employee presently receiving a salary of, say, $30,000 a year and whose job deserves to be eliminated might continue to receive that salary for a full year, while being free to do anything he wished in the way of private economic activity. He would be in a position to take a substantially lower-paying job in private industry and use his severance pay to tide him over until he had gained sufficient work experience to increase his earnings to a level comparable to what they had been before. Or he could go to school and in that way

very comfortably learn the skills necessary to earn an income in private industry comparable to what he had earned as a government employee.[15]

In comparison with the present situation, such an arrangement would be very much in the self-interest of the general, taxpaying public. The financial burden of the taxpayers would certainly be no greater than it is now, and it would, of course, be reduced as soon as the severance pay of the government employees came to an end. Moreover, to the extent that the government employees are presently engaged in carrying out policies of destructive interference in the lives of the citizens, the public would enjoy the immediate gain of the end of some part of such interference. It is a comparatively minor evil to pay a simple dead weight subsidy to former government employees now engaged in other activities, when the alternative is to continue to support them as destroyers. Of course, in order to prevent anyone from taking unjust advantage of such a plan, government employees who received its benefits, should thereafter be barred from government employment (other than elective office) for a protracted period of time, perhaps for life—unless they refunded the extraordinary severance pay they had received.[16]

To the extent that the former government employees turned to seek jobs in private industry, their competition would cause the money wage rates of the average worker there to drop. This would be the case both insofar as they entered the labor market prior to the reduction in government payrolls and in taxes and insofar as, when it came, the reduction in government payrolls constituted a drop in the aggregate demand for labor. (This last would be the result to the extent that taxpayers spent the funds they no longer paid in taxes to meet government payrolls, in buying goods rather than in paying wages.[17]) A tendency toward a drop in wage rates would, of course, also be present as the result of the phasing out of the welfare system and of social security, inasmuch as both would bring about an increase in the supply of labor relative to the demand for labor.

As the readers of this book should know by now, the effect in all these cases would be benevolent. For the necessary fall in wage rates would be accompanied by reductions in prices that would be still greater. This is because the employment of more workers means more production and thus lower prices caused by more supply, as well as the saving of taxes to support the unemployed or unproductively employed.[18] The fall in prices relative to wage rates, moreover, would be a continuing one, because the effect of reduced government spending, reduced taxation, and reduced government interference in general is increased capital accumulation and thus a rising productivity of labor. Capital accumulation and the rise in the productivity of labor would be the result both of a greater relative production of capital goods and a higher productivity of capital goods. The greater relative production of capital goods would be made possible by reduced government spending and lower taxes and thus more saving and productive expenditure relative to consumption expenditure. The higher productivity of capital goods would be the result both of lower taxes and thus greater incentives to use capital goods efficiently, and of reduced government interference of other types that stands in the way of the efficient use of capital goods.[19]

It follows, and deserves to be stressed, that the long-run effect of firing unnecessary government employees is to progressively increase the economic well-being *of those employees,* along with that of everyone else, and that this is true even in the absence of any severance pay. The former government employees also benefit from the additional capital accumulation and rising productivity of labor and real wages that are made possible. They too benefit from the fact that more people now contribute to production instead of having to be supported out of the production of others, and that production is no longer held down by their activities.

Essentially the same conclusion applies to welfare recipients. In the long run, they too would be economically better off living as self-supporting wage earners in a progressing economy than as welfare recipients. Their gain would come not only from the economic progress or more rapid economic progress that abolition of the welfare system would greatly contribute to, but also, and in many cases even more importantly, from having at long last to develop and actualize their innate human potential, which the welfare system has permitted them to avoid doing. Being compelled at last to work in order to live, many of them would accept that necessity and strive to do better at it, whereas at present they need strive for nothing and thus develop into nothing.

There is absolutely no kind of magic or "free lunch" assumed here. The source of the universal gains is an increase in production. Every individual's removal from an unproductive or destructive position in government employment or on the welfare rolls, to a positive, productive position in private employment, adds to the total of what is produced and contributes to the further increase in the total of what is produced, through making possible additional capital accumulation. It is because of this increase in total production that everyone is in a position to gain, with no one having to lose. It should actually be no more surprising that former government employees end up being economically better off without their government jobs than that blacksmiths and horse breeders end up being better off without their former jobs—and that they do so, even if they must settle for a

relatively lower position on the economic scale. Indeed, it should be less surprising when one considers that the nature of so many government workers' jobs is precisely the stifling of innovation and improvement and that the loss of such jobs means precisely the opening of the way to progress and improvement. By the same token, the gain of former welfare recipients from the abolition of welfare should be no more surprising than the gain of someone needlessly confined to a hospital from his discharge and emergence into the world of life and action.

Every serious advocate of capitalism has always been able to understand such facts in connection with the so-called long run. The proposal I have made about generous severance pay for government employees makes it possible for a harmony of material self-interests to exist even in the very short run.

The principle of generous severance terms could be applied to the elimination of government subsidies to business, in the following way. As compensation for the abolition of a subsidy, the government would continue the payment of funds for a number of years equal to the profits and depreciation allowances that the subsidized enterprises would have earned had the subsidies been continued. Its payments could also cover the interest and other such contractual obligations the firms may be obliged to pay as the result of having reasonably entered into such arrangements in connection with the production of the subsidized item. Severance allowances would also probably have to be given for a time to the employees of those enterprises, equal to their wages or to a major portion of them. In addition, it would probably be necessary to some extent to provide such payments to the firms producing equipment or other supplies for the subsidized enterprises, and to their employees. For example, as compensation for the elimination of farm subsidies, not only farmers and their employees would have to receive severance allowances, but also the farm equipment industry and its employees. The total of the severance allowances in any given year, however, would not exceed what the government presently spends in buying the products concerned. The payments at each stage of production would not apply to the sales revenues received at that stage, but only to the much smaller figure of the net income earned by the various parties, plus depreciation allowances.

In this way, I believe that the businesses that are presently recipients of government subsidies, together with their employees and suppliers, could be given a powerful short-run interest in the abolition of their subsidies. They could be placed in a position in which the severance allowances they received would make the transition to producing for the free market virtually painless, indeed, even positively rewarding insofar as those allowances plus immediate earnings in the free market exceeded the income previously derived from the government.

Escaping from Rent Control With the Support of Tenants

The rental housing market, having suffered in places such as New York City from two full generations of rent control, and with no end to rent controls in sight, has devised a method of escaping from the destructive effects of rent controls, and of doing so with the support of the tenants involved. The method rests on the recognition by landlords that in point of fact the tenants have acquired a kind of squatter's rights to the apartments they occupy, "rights" which have acquired long-standing legal sanction that almost certainly will continue to be upheld by the government. Based on this recognition, the method of escape adopted by growing numbers of landlords is that of allowing the tenants to reap a substantial share of the financial gains resulting from an apartment house becoming converted to condominium or cooperative housing. This is the meaning of the fact that landlords offer their existing tenants substantially below-market "insider prices" on the purchase of the apartments they occupy, on condition that the tenants agree to the building's change from that of rental housing to condominium or cooperative status. The tenants are then free to turn around and sell their units or rights to their units for a substantial gain, which, of course, is what wins their cooperation.

This is a very sad situation insofar as it represents the fact that to an important extent a group of nonowners has managed to acquire the status and rights of property owners by means of a government-sanctioned—indeed, government-led—violent appropriation. It is the closest the United States has thus far come to a situation comparable to that of a successful feudal invasion, in which an earlier group of property owners is forcibly dispossessed by a subsequent group of property owners. Nevertheless, it is better that property rights of the appropriators finally be recognized than that property should remain indefinitely in a condition in which no one has the power to use it well. Under rent control, tenants can stay on as long as they like, and consume the capital invested in the buildings in which they live. They are succeeded by other such tenants. The result is simply the destruction of the stock of housing, inasmuch as the rent controls deprive the landlords of the incentive and, indeed, the ability, to maintain their housing. Compared with this alternative, the conversion of rental housing to a different status, free of rent controls, at least makes possible the maintenance of the stock of housing and its possible increase.

Apart from once and for all abolishing existing rent controls—however unlikely the prospect may be in many places at present—the contribution that the government could make to the process of the market's freeing itself from rent controls would be constitutionally to guarantee that once any property managed to escape from rent controls, it would never again, under any pretext, be subjected to them. This would eventually operate to reestablish an extensive market in rental housing. Such a market, of course, is vital for all those who cannot afford to buy their housing.

5. Abolition of Income and Inheritance Taxes

The total abolition of the personal and corporate income taxes and of the inheritance tax is an essential feature of a procapitalist political program. It is required by the individual's right to his own property. In addition, progress toward the abolition of these taxes helps to create the conditions required for economic progress, by increasing economic incentives and the ability to save, both of which serve to promote capital accumulation and thus a rising productivity of labor and rising real wages.[20]

It must be stressed that the more rapidly economic progress can take place, thanks to reductions in the income and inheritance taxes, the more rapidly can the relative size of the government in the economic system be reduced. The consequence of this is that the degree to which people must experience the burden of the government's exactions is correspondingly diminished. If economic progress can take place at a rate of, say, 3 percent a year, then even if government activity were not reduced at all, the relative size of the government in the economic system would be cut in half in a single generation. For in that time economic progress at a 3 percent annual rate would have succeeded in doubling the size of the economic system. Thus, the burden experienced even from supporting a government of the same size would be felt much more lightly.

These facts imply two important principles pertaining to our political program. First, in reducing income tax rates, our primary emphasis should usually be on reducing the maximum rates, until there exists only a single proportional income tax rate. Reductions in the upper brackets have the greatest impact in strengthening economic incentives and saving, and thus do the most to bring about economic progress. We need to make the public aware of how everyone benefits from these tax reductions—of how they operate to raise the demand for labor and thus wages, and, at the same time, progressively to increase the productivity of labor and thus the supply of goods relative to the supply of labor, which steadily reduces prices relative to wages and thereby steadily raises real wages.[21] Of course, once the so-called progressive aspects of the income and inheritance taxes have been eliminated, work should immediately commence on the steady reduction in what remains of those taxes, and should continue until they are totally eliminated.

Second, a closely related minimal short-run political demand we should make is that the level of real per capita government spending be immediately frozen, so that it does not exceed its current level. Such a demand would be a call not for the immediate abolition of the welfare state and improper government activity of all kinds, but a demand for an immediate cessation in their further growth. Its implementation would result in a continuing automatic shrinkage in the relative size of the government, so long as economic progress continued.

A possible way to start on the elimination of the income/inheritance tax right now would be to fight for the immediate adoption of a universal exemption of at least 51 percent of everyone's income from federal, state, and local income taxation under all circumstances. This would be in the name of the principle that the individual is the owner of his own income. The 51 percent exemption would constitute meaningful recognition of this principle. Over the years, we would work to increase the tax exempt portion of everyone's income while reducing the rates on the taxable portion, until the income tax was totally abolished. Given the drastic reductions in welfare-type spending I have proposed and the achievement of economic progress, it should be possible to phase out the income tax entirely over the course of a generation.

The same phase-out procedure should be applied to the corporate income tax. In addition, in the short-run, we should demand the elimination of the double taxation presently entailed in the corporate income tax. It represents double taxation for a corporation first to be taxed on its income, and then for the stockholders of that corporation to be taxed again on what they receive from their own corporation, which has already paid a substantial income tax. The principle of the 51 percent exemption and its progressive enlargement should be applied to the total of every individual's personal income *plus* his share of the profits of any corporation in which he owns stock.

However, the most important short-run goal that we should emphasize in connection with taxes is compelling the government to respect the ordinary civil rights of taxpayers. We should demand the abolition of criminal penalties for income-tax evasion, in the name of the principle that an individual cannot steal or fraudulently keep what is his own property to begin with. Also, just as in the case of government agencies seeking search warrants, we should demand that the Internal Revenue Service be compelled to obtain a prior court order authorizing any seizure of property or attachment of salaries and bank accounts it wishes to undertake. If it is not

possible to obtain such elementary protection of individual rights, then a compromise that at least would be a move in the right direction would be the existence of automatic judicial review of all such IRS activities. And until criminal penalties for not paying taxes are eliminated, we should demand that the Fifth Amendment rights of individuals to remain silent in order not to incriminate themselves be applied to taxpayers, i.e., that no criminal penalties exist for failure to file an income tax return. In other words, we should demand that taxpayers, who are presently subject to criminal law, enjoy the full civil rights accorded to criminals. In answer to objections that the income tax cannot work without the violation of elementary civil rights, we should reply that if that is the case, then it is further proof of why the income tax must be abolished. So long as the supporters of the income tax wish to retain it, we must demand that they accept the burden of finding ways of harmonizing it with respect for such rights.

A further principle that I believe should be applied in connection with proposals for the reform of the income tax is that no reductions of any kind should ever be made in existing tax exemptions, shelters, or so-called loopholes. Our principle should be that no one's income taxes should ever be increased over what they would be under existing law. It is true that the various exemptions, such as for interest paid on home mortgages, have some economically distorting effects by artificially encouraging some types of economic activity at the expense of other types, but those distortions will become less and less significant with the reduction in the burden of the income tax, and will disappear altogether when it disappears. We should take the position that every reform of the income tax must serve to reduce the income taxes paid by some or all people, and not increase the income taxes paid by anyone.

Still a further principle that we must uphold concerning tax reform, and one whose necessity should be obvious on the basis of all the preceding discussions concerning the role of capital formation and the consequences of inflation, is that tax reductions must be accompanied by equivalent or even more than equivalent reductions in government spending—specifically, in *nondefense spending* primarily. In view of the highly destructive effects of budget deficits, it should be clear why tax cuts must be accompanied at least by equivalent reductions in government spending of one kind or another. Deficits, it should be recalled, deprive the economic system of the benefit of the portion of the supply of savings that must be used to finance the deficits. In the absence of a gold standard, they also lead to the rapid inflation of the money supply, which, of course, also undermines capital formation. Cutting taxes without cutting government spending, therefore, is no solution for reducing the government's assaults on the economic system.[22]

The reason the reductions in government spending must be primarily at the expense specifically of non-defense spending is that defense is one of the few legitimate functions of government. Spending for defense should be cut only as it becomes genuinely safe to do so. It should be blatantly obvious that we should never advocate imperiling the defense of this country, which means, essentially, the defense of such freedom as exists in the world, in order to preserve any aspect of the welfare state. Indeed, our need for national defense exists for no other reason than to prevent the imposition of the underlying premise of the welfare state in a more extreme and more consistent form by outside military force. That premise, of course, is that some men have the right to enslave others for the satisfaction of their needs. Thus, not only must we never dream of sacrificing national defense to any aspect of the welfare state, but what we want national defense for is precisely to protect us from the logically consistent version of the welfare state that is represented by totalitarian socialism. Furthermore, what we should advocate in connection with national defense is *overwhelming military superiority* for the United States. That is our only real guarantee of avoiding war. If we have such superiority, we will not start a war, and it is unlikely that anyone else will dare to do so.

6. Establishment of Gold as Money

The establishment of gold as money is essential to the achievement of a capitalist society. (What is said concerning gold, of course, also applies to silver.[23] Furthermore, for reasons explained in the last chapter, the gold or silver money I speak of should be understood as a 100-percent gold or silver money—i.e., a 100-percent-reserve system—in which, apart from subsidiary token coinage, all money either literally *is* gold or silver or is receipts for gold or silver that are fully backed by same.)

The establishment of gold as money on these terms is necessary in order to end inflation and all of its destructive consequences. It is necessary in order to take the power to inflate—that is, to create money virtually out of thin air—out of the hands both of the government and of the banking system operating with the sanction of the government. It is necessary in order thereby to subordinate the government to the financial power of the citizens and to make people aware of the cost of government spending, and to end the arbitrary redistribution of wealth and income, the undermining of capital accumulation, the possibility of utter economic devastation either through wage and price controls or the ultimate destruction of money, and deflation, depression, and mass unemploy-

ment. It is also necessary for making possible the rapid and radical dismantling of the welfare state, by removing the threat of depression as an accompaniment of that process.

Because I have thoroughly discussed the role of gold and the methods for achieving a gold standard in the last part of the previous chapter, I will say no more about this vital subject here. However, it had to be named here at least to this extent.

7. Procapitalist Foreign Policy

In the present-day world, a procapitalist foreign policy is indistinguishable from a pro–American foreign policy. The United States is the world's leading capitalist country. It is so on the basis of its fundamental laws—its Constitution and Bill of Rights. And, not surprisingly, it is hated for it. It is regarded by much of the rest of the world in the same way that within the United States the minority constituted by businessmen and capitalists—the "rich"—are regarded by much of the rest of the American citizenry.[24] If the United States is to stand up for itself, it must learn to stand up for capitalism.

The most essential point which needs to be recognized is that to the extent that the United States is a capitalist country, its government is morally legitimate, because to that extent its government acts to defend individual rights, and the powers it exercises consist of nothing more than those of the individual's delegated right of self-defense. By the same token, governments which do not recognize the existence of individual rights, governments whose very existence is based on the premise of the forcible sacrifice of the individual to the collective, have no moral legitimacy.[25] This means, above all, that the surviving Communist regimes, such as those of mainland China, North Korea, and Cuba, and many, if not most, of the governments of the so-called third-world countries have no moral legitimacy.

The overthrow of these governments is earnestly to be desired on behalf not only of their own citizens, who are enslaved, but also on behalf of the people of the entire world, who are forcibly deprived of the benefits they could otherwise derive if these countries were free—benefits in the form of the free development of the talents of the citizens of those countries and the free development of their natural resources. A major principle here is that the violation of the rights of the individual anywhere is an attack on the well-being of people everywhere.[26]

A foreign policy based on these principles would deal with such governments as bandits and outlaws, temporarily holding power by means of force and fear. This does not mean that it would be the obligation of the U.S. government to go to war with such countries if it were not itself attacked or directly threatened by them. But it certainly does mean, as a minimum, that the U.S. government should do nothing to promote the existence of such governments. It should certainly not aid them in any way, nor provide them with any kind of forum in which to defend their crimes, nor denounce those who prevent them from expanding their power or who prevent similar regimes from coming to power in the first place.

As examples from the recent past, the U.S. government should certainly not have provided Soviet Russia or Communist Poland with free food or loan guarantees. Instead, it should have allowed them to suffer the famines that socialism causes, while at the same time explaining to the world how socialism was the cause of the famines and thus how millions were forced into starvation because of the power-lust of the Communist rulers and their insistence on the preservation of the socialist system. It should have led world opinion in demanding that the Communist rulers step down and the socialist system they had imposed be abolished, so that the citizens of the Communist countries could become free to produce and live. Had the United States followed this policy, the collapse of communism would have occurred decades earlier.

Today, the United States should withdraw all official recognition from the remaining Communist-bloc countries and from totalitarian third-world countries, such as Iran, Iraq, and Libya, and expel their diplomats and alleged trade missions. It should end all so-called cultural exchanges with such regimes. If necessary, it should withdraw from the United Nations and expel that organization from U.S. territory. The only purpose served by the presence of these individuals and institutions is spying, terrorism, and subversion. If the governments of these countries wish to continue to be recognized, the prime condition must be their formal disavowal of socialism and the adoption of a genuine plan for the protection of individual rights and the establishment of capitalism in their countries.

It should be recalled that the very fact of the United States adopting a policy of laissez faire and respect for private property rights at home would itself go a long way toward undermining the power of today's leading terrorist governments, namely, those of the Middle East. At the same time, it would cut the ground from under the resurgence of religious fanaticism in the region, which, like the arms build-up by governments in the region, is financed by money derived from an artificially high price of oil. These results would follow because a leading consequence of the adoption of a policy of laissez faire and respect for private property rights by the United States would be a great increase in the supply of domes-

tically produced oil and other sources of energy, which latter, as substitutes for oil, would cause a reduction in the demand for oil. In the face both of a substantial increase in the supply and reduction in the demand for oil, there would be a sharp decline in its price.[27] Thus, the revenues that finance the terrorists and fanatics would sharply decline.

A major obstacle to the pursuit of a proper foreign policy by the U.S. government is the incredible corruption of thought which exists not only within the United States but, to a much greater degree, in the rest of the world. This corruption was blatantly evident in the fact that throughout the so-called cold war, the state of world opinion was such that the expulsion of Communist diplomats from the United States would have been regarded as an act of aggression on our part. A call for the Communist leaders to step down and end the enslavement of their citizens would have been regarded as a transgression against their allegedly God-given right to enslave—or, as it is customarily put, "an interference in the internal affairs of sovereign nations."

The ability of the United States to pursue a proper foreign policy and the ability of foreign countries themselves to move toward the achievement of a capitalist society depends on the spread of procapitalist ideas abroad. To say the same thing in different words, both our immediate national security and our long-run goal of the establishment of a fully capitalist society throughout the world, with worldwide free trade, freedom of investment, and freedom of migration, require that we be interested in the spread of proreason philosophy and procapitalist economic theory in foreign countries as well as in the United States.

A major task in the years ahead must be to bring about the translation of all of our main books into all of the world's major languages. *Human Action*, *Socialism*, *Atlas Shrugged*, and about fifty or more other titles, should be made available in Russian, Polish, and Chinese, as well as in Japanese, Korean, Arabic, and all the other leading languages. Efforts should be made to promote the circulation of these books everywhere. I do not agree for a moment with the notion that only people brought up in the United States or Canada can readily appreciate our literature. Our philosophy recognizes only one reality and one human nature. No matter what intellectual and psychological obstacles a particular culture may create in the thinking of people, there is always some significant number who are open to new ideas. Our commitment to our philosophy and our national and economic self-interest require that we try to reach these people. As an example of the importance of doing so, just imagine the effect on our national self-interest of a totalitarian regime's someday having to deal with people who have come to realize that each individual possesses reason and has an inalienable right to life, and that their reason and their lives are being sacrificed because of nothing more than the rulers' willful refusal to abandon an irrational dogma. Imagine the effect of the regime's being infiltrated by such people.

It should go without saying that all such intellectual efforts must be undertaken privately, not as an activity of the U.S. government.

As a further point in connection with what we should be working toward in the area of foreign policy, I would like to make a suggestion for another special campaign. This would be a campaign urging newspapers, magazines, and television stations which choose to maintain officially accredited reporters in Communist or other totalitarian countries to provide a warning label on all their reports from those countries which are obtained with government sanction. The label would identify the totalitarian nature of the country and state that no reason exists for regarding the report as anything but propaganda serving the interests of the government that originated it or sanctioned it.

Freedom of Immigration

We need to make a beginning toward the establishment of freedom of immigration. A logical place to begin would be in calling for free immigration from our immediate neighbors, Canada and Mexico. There is not the slightest reason for excluding Canadians. They are virtually indistinguishable from Americans, and had one or two battles gone the other way early in our history, would in fact be Americans. By the same token, had the Confederacy won the Civil War, then, with the prevalence of today's ideas, present-day New Yorkers would probably not be able to migrate to Texas, nor Texans to California. Such restrictions, based on mere accidents of history, simply have no logical foundation.

It should not be necessary to add that the free immigration of Canadians, Mexicans, or any other nationality should not be at the expense of the immigration allowed under existing law to the members of any other nationality. As in the case of tax reduction, no one should be made any worse off than he now is, because of an attempt to improve conditions for anyone else.

The reason we must seek to abolish restrictions on Mexican immigration at the earliest possible moment is because the attempt to restrict it is in danger of making us adopt some of the most obnoxious features of the former South African regime—namely, a virtual pass law, in which people of Latin origin will have to carry identity papers to show on demand to immigration po-

lice, who, if they do not find the appropriate "papers," will have the authority to destroy the lives of said individuals by uprooting them from their jobs and homes and deporting them. Already virtually Gestapo-like conditions exist in Southern California in connection with a notorious immigration checkpoint, where fleeing Mexicans of all ages and both sexes have often run into oncoming automobile traffic rather than be arrested by officers of the Immigration and Naturalization Service. This ignominy, I must note, has now been compounded by the recent passage of Proposition 187 in the state of California, which, if upheld in the courts, will actually impose the requirement of having an official identity card that must be shown on demand to the authorities.

Furthermore, the principle of private property rights implies that the Mexicans, and everyone else, have a perfect right to come here—to work for anyone who is willing to hire them and to live wherever anyone is willing to sell or rent to them. The violation of the rights the Mexicans or any other category of immigrant is a violation of the private property rights of employers and landlords—it is telling them that other people have the right to dictate whom they may or may not employ or to whom they may or may not sell or rent their property. It is a blatant manifestation of collectivism to believe that somehow the people of the United States as a whole have the right to tell the individual, private owners of property how they may use their property—that they must use it not as they, the private owners wish to use it, but as the nation collectively, or at least a majority of those voting, wish it to be used.

As I explained in Chapter 9, in a capitalist society free immigration does not deprive those already present of the opportunity of working and it does not reduce their standard of living. On the contrary, in the long run free immigration into a capitalist society from a semifeudal one, such as Mexico's, must operate to raise the general standard of living in the capitalist society, because it means that more human beings will now live under freedom and have the opportunity to develop their talents.[28] There are Mexicans and the children of Mexicans who have the potential for making the same kind of economic contribution to the general standard of living as have immigrants from other countries before them.

The only legitimate argument against unrestricted Mexican immigration (or unrestricted immigration of any other ethnic group) is based on the existence of our welfare state. To the extent that Mexicans come here and go on welfare and medicaid, or use public hospitals and public schools, and place an increased burden on government-subsidized public transportation facilities and so forth, then, it is true, there is a genuine loss imposed on the people already here. The solution, however, is not to violate the right of the Mexicans to immigrate, but to start dismantling our welfare state.

Without immediately abolishing the totality of the welfare state, which would be politically impossible, we could simply change its terms and make all noncitizens ineligible for its programs. This, of course, is essentially what a portion of California's Proposition 187 seeks to do. However, that proposition also seeks to expel the immigrants and to deter further immigration through fear. Totally unlike Proposition 187, the mere exclusion of the immigrants from the welfare state would not impose any actual burden or disability on them. It would not be they who had to carry identity papers and prove why they should not be deported. There would be no question of that. On the contrary, it would only be the American citizens who sought the alleged benefits of the welfare state who would have to show papers and prove their citizenship.

While excluding the immigrants from the welfare state, we should simultaneously remove all government-imposed barriers to their being supplied privately with what they need. This would entail the removal of government licensing requirements in connection with meeting the medical, educational, transportation, and sanitation needs of the immigrants. As far as possible, this should be accompanied by privatization of such things as existing government-owned hospitals, schools, bus lines, and garbage-collection operations. An important result of privatization would be that the presence of the larger numbers of people resulting from immigration would be viewed as a source of more business, not more problems, as it is under the ineptitude of government ownership. In addition, in order to reduce the injustice that would exist in making immigrants pay taxes for the support of the welfare state for the native population, the immigrants should receive as nontaxable wages what would otherwise be their own and their employer's social security and medicare contributions made in connection with their employment. The ironic effect of all these liberalizing measures would be to give the immigrants more freedom than today's American citizens, and in that sense to make them truer Americans than today's American citizens. If, at the same time, the immigrants could be reached with procapitalist ideas, this might well serve as the foundation for their being developed into a major group opposed to the welfare state for anyone.

In the present circumstances, it is especially important to make every effort to exclude immigrants from the public education system. At one time, it is true, public elementary education succeeded in educating pupils of all different nationalities in the three R's. And even though its own existence represented a contradiction of the principle of individual rights, it instilled in pupils a basic respect and admiration for the United States. Today, public education teaches very little to anyone. It turns out masses of illiterates and students who have not the slightest idea of what the United States stands for. One of the last things we should want is today's public education system teaching masses of immigrants in their own language. One of the major subjects that would be taught would undoubtedly be revolutionary Marxist nationalism. Under such conditions, as far fetched as it may sound, large-scale Mexican immigration into the Southwest could well result, one or two generations later, in a widespread demand for the return of the Southwest to Mexico. Thus, an important part of any campaign for free immigration for Mexicans should be an attack on public education and its Marxist domination. It is vital that the immigrants be assimilated as English speakers who support capitalism.

It would be enormously valuable if it could be explained to the immigrants that only the philosophy of individualism and respect for private property rights made possible their immigration. It would be legitimate to require of all immigrants an oath swearing to uphold the system of private property rights and to educate their children in the English language.

It would be a very short step from freedom of immigration for Mexicans to freedom of immigration for everyone.

Friendly Relations With Japan and Western Europe

Because of their exceptional economic strength and thus their potential someday to constitute a serious military threat to the United States, a cardinal principal of American foreign policy must be the maintenance of friendly relations with Japan and the countries of Western Europe. To assure this, what is necessary on our part is a policy of free trade, freedom of investment, and freedom of immigration—in short, a policy of full capitalism with respect to these countries. If we were to follow this policy, we would eliminate any possible economic basis of aggression against us on the part of these countries.[29] And for all of the reasons shown in this book, from an economic point of view we could only gain from such a policy—probably very substantially. As I have shown, we would gain even if we alone were to follow a policy of free trade while the others clung to various protectionist measures. In that case our position would be analogous to the situation of a territory in which inbound transportation costs were lower than outbound transportation costs.[30]

If we followed such a policy toward these countries, we could reasonably ask them to undertake a larger share of the defense of the free world, in accordance with the increase in wealth and income they have experienced.

We would not have to worry that in doing so, we were encouraging potential enemies to arm, as we should presently be concerned.

Of course, the policy of full capitalism with respect to foreign relations should be applied to all countries. However, for the reasons stated, it is especially important in these two cases.

8. Separation of State from Education, Science, and Religion

Finally, it is necessary to turn to the subject of separation of state from education, science, and religion.

Abolition of Public Education

The system of public education could be abolished over the course of a generation, in a way that need not impose financial hardship on the parents of any child alive at the time of the abolition's commencement. The method would be the enactment of state laws declaring that as of the end of the seventh school year following the enactment of the law, that state and its localities will no longer be responsible for the financing of the first-grade education of any student; that a year after that, they will no longer be responsible for the financing of the second-grade education of any student; and so on, through all the elementary, secondary, and college grades. This procedure would enable the parents of children alive at the time of the enactment of the phase-out legislation to go on using the public education system if they wished; it would give prospective new parents a year's notice that they would be responsible for the cost of their children's education.

The abolition of public education should be preceded by the recognition of the right of parents to educate their own children and by the abolition of educational licensing requirements. It would also be proper if the public schools were to be made to begin charging tuition fees to those who could afford them, which would be progressively increased, until they reflected the public school system's costs. The fee system would permit steadily increasing competition and growth on the part of private schools, which would then be in a position easily and totally to displace the public schools.

One of the most immediate points to fight for in connection with the abolition of public education is the abolition of the federal Department of Education and all federal aid to education. These measures would create an immediate improvement in education by eliminating a major layer of bureaucracy and by forcing the elimination of unnecessary courses and unsound educational methods that are fostered, if not mandated, by the availability of federal funds. They would thus bring about a renewed concentration on the three R's and other serious subjects.

In the struggle against public education, an important principle to stress is that the public education system is inherently unsuited to teach any subject about which there is controversy. This is because teaching such a subject necessarily entails forcing at least some taxpayers to violate their convictions, by providing funds for the dissemination of ideas which they consider to be false and possibly vicious. On the basis of this principle, the public schools should be barred from teaching not only religion, but also history, economics, civics, and biology. In the nature of things, only private schools, for whose services people have the choice of paying or not paying, can teach these subjects without violating the freedom of conscience. The fact that barring the public schools from teaching these subjects would leave them with very little to teach, and place them in a position in which they may as well not exist, simply confirms the fact that public education should be abolished.

Separation of Government and Science

The above principle concerning the government's violation of the freedom of conscience in supporting the promulgation of controversial ideas also constitutes an argument for the abolition of practically all government support of the arts and sciences. There is great controversy concerning the artistic merit of various schools of literature, painting, and sculpture. There is significant and growing controversy even over the various theories of natural science, such as the controversy between the supporters of the "Big-Bang" theory of the origin of the universe and the supporters of the steady-state theory of the universe, which holds that the universe did not have an origin. For the government to finance any artistic or scientific activity means to compel taxpayers who hold the activity to be artistically or scientifically worthless, and perhaps immoral as well, to finance it nonetheless.

More fundamentally, our opposition to government involvement in art and science—and in education—is based on Ayn Rand's principle that force and mind are opposites.[31] Matters of truth and value can be determined only by the voluntary assent of the human mind. Yet government is essentially a policeman with a gun and club. It settles matters by means of force. This is directly contrary to the nature of knowledge. It has no place in the laboratory, the lecture hall, or the art gallery. The determination of what is true or false, or possessing or lacking in value, simply cannot properly be decided by government officials. Nor can it properly be decided by majorities in voting booths. Such a thing is further contrary to the nature of knowledge, which always begins as the discovery of just one mind, and which is as yet totally unknown to the entire rest of the human race. Governments and majorities must not be allowed to crush the isolated individual, who is the source of all new knowledge and improvement. Yet precisely this is the outcome of government support of science and art, which scoops up the limited funds available for the support of such activities and arbitrarily dictates how they are to be spent.

As to the tactics to be used to remove the government from these areas, the most important is the continuous demonstration of the contrary nature of government force, on the one side, and knowledge and value freely assented to, on the other.

An important step in reducing and ultimately eliminating government interference in science would be to require that all alleged scientific studies financed in any way by any government agency or department prominently state that fact. This might be required in the form of an amendment to the Freedom of Information Act. The requirement should extend to all press releases and public announcements made by the government or any of its employees concerning the study. In this way, the study could be easily identified as coming from the government or associated with the government. The requirement would serve, in effect, as a warning label. In addition, all information relevant to the study's being undertaken, including the initial application for a government grant, and all correspondence and internal government documents pertaining to the study, should be identified in an appendix to the study, and copies made readily available to any member of the public wishing to see them. The study should also be required to include an appendix providing an intelligible explanation of the methodology on which it was based. These requirements would make it possible to scrutinize and judge the scientific seriousness of such studies far more easily than is possible today, and thus to enable people much more readily to distinguish government propaganda from science.

An important first step in the eventual abolition of such agencies as the Food and Drug Administration (FDA) and the Environmental Protection Agency (EPA) would be a law severely limiting their powers to ban drugs and chemical substances. The law would nullify the power of the agency's adverse ruling in any case in which similar agencies in, say, two or more modern foreign countries, such as Canada, Switzerland, and Great Britain, have found no reason to ban a substance. In other words, it would subject these agencies to a form of liberalizing "peer review." In such cases, in order to ban a substance, the FDA and EPA would have to prove their case before a court of law. The principle that the FDA and EPA and their staffs are not endowed with any form of divine guidance could be progressively extended—to

the point where any *one private individual* was free to act on his contrary opinion. (After all, why should the opinions of American citizens be viewed as inferior to those of foreign bureaucrats?)

Perhaps the best way ultimately to abolish the FDA and the EPA would be to demand their conversion to private agencies, having no powers of compulsion and supported exclusively by private funds. They would then operate as advisory agencies, in competition with other such private advisory agencies, free to pronounce whatever opinions they wished about any subject, but not free to have force used to back their opinions—except when they could go before a court of law, as any other private citizen, and *prove* the existence of a danger to the lives or property of parties not willing to take the risk of such danger.

Separation of State and Church

Our opposition to government involvement in religion is based on the same foundation as our opposition to government involvement in education and science. Indeed, government-sponsored religion represents the most naked kind of use of force against the mind. Religion is based on faith. The use of force to impose it or its values is always the use of force in order to compel acceptance of what cannot be proved or denial of what can be proved.

The supporters of capitalism must take the lead in the battle against the current incursions of religion into politics and government. Nothing could be more vital to progress toward the establishment of a capitalist society. The old stereotypes of the advocates of socialism as enlightened liberals and the advocates of capitalism as religious conservatives need to be decisively broken. From now on, in accordance with the actual facts, the advocates of capitalism must be viewed as the representatives of enlightenment, and the socialists as the representatives of irrationalism and the Dark Ages.

In the 1930s and 1940s, to be sure, the seemingly enlightened Left was able to depict its opponents as virtual Ma and Pa Kettles, living on a farm somewhere, totally cut off from modern civilization, and projecting utter ignorance and contempt for science and technology. Exactly that image is what the New Left has chosen to wrap itself in, ever since it joined the ecology movement. We should be sure that the public eventually understands this fact and that it is with the New Left that those who place faith above reason belong.

Previous discussion in this book and in Ayn Rand's *The New Left: The Anti-Industrial Revolution* provide the essential basis for the transformation of the view of which side wears the mantle of Reason. They clearly show how the ecology movement, which is the last gasp of the Left, is thoroughly riddled with irrationalism and hostility to science and technology.[32] Furthermore, the whole of this book and all of the writings of von Mises, of the other Austrian and classical economists, and of Ayn Rand, show beyond a shadow of a doubt that capitalism in no sense whatever depends on the acceptance of any form of faith or denial of reason. The case for capitalism is thoroughly rational.

In view of the fact that socialism has demonstrated its failure and that as a result its advocates have largely given up the banner of reason, means that the success of a rational, capitalist political program should be all the more rapid. By the admission of both sides, capitalism is the only system to which advocates of reason can turn.

Furthermore, the projection of a rational, capitalist political program, actually capable of solving major national and world problems, will stand as a major philosophic affirmation of the power of the human mind. Thus, it can be an important source of gaining recruits for all aspects of a rational philosophy. As previously shown in connection with the ecology movement, the cultural surge in blatant irrationality that has taken place in recent decades is due in no small measure to the demonstrated failure of socialism as a politico-economic system. Socialism is what most intellectuals have regarded as the system called for by logic and reason. As a result, its failure has served to shake their confidence in reason, and thus to open the floodgates to irrationalism.[33] By the same token, a resurrection of respect for the potential of reason in the politico-economic realm will promote the case for reason everywhere.

The advocates of capitalism should take the lead in the defense of the freedoms of press and speech. At the same time that we seek to protect it for purveyors of "prurient" literature, we should seek to protect it for the writers of financial newsletters, whom the SEC wants to censor; for corporations, whom the Congress and the Federal Elections Commission want to censor by denying them the right to support political candidates of their choice; for unpopular speakers whom student thugs want to censor by denying them the ability to be heard by their audience; for ordinary citizens whom the Department of Housing and Urban Development wants to censor for speaking out against government-sponsored projects in their neighborhoods. We should demand the freedoms of speech and press for all advertisers, including cigarette advertisers.

We should place the establishment of full freedom of the press and of the more recent forms of communication, such as movies, radio, and television, in the forefront of our fight for a capitalist society. Long before the establishment of a fully capitalist society, we should seek the establishment of a fully free press and media as the pattern for all other industries later to follow. We should demand their exemption from all government regulation immediately—that is, we should demand that these industries, because of the intellectual nature of their products and services, be freed at once from the income tax, the antitrust laws, the labor laws, and every other form of government regulation and interference, so that they may advance their ideas totally without fear of punitive action of any kind being taken against them.

9. A General Campaign at the Local Level

The seven preceding sections have described various major aspects of the campaign for capitalism. Here it is appropriate to bring some of those aspects together in the form of a specific program that, over the course of less than a decade, would bring about the economic and cultural revival of America's leading city, New York. I choose to focus on New York not only because it is the country's leading city, but also because, of any major American city, it best represents the destructive economic and social consequences of contemporary American "liberalism," of which it is the intellectual home.

What would be required to restore New York to its former prosperity and greatness would be the combination of the elimination of public welfare, the abolition of rent controls, and the privatization of the city's transportation system.

The abolition of welfare, of course, would have to be preceded by the elimination of minimum-wage and pro-union legislation and of restrictions on child labor over the age of fourteen. In the absence of the outright repeal of minimum-wage and prounion legislation at the national level, it would be necessary for the city to obtain a special congressional exemption from that legislation. These preliminary measures would be necessary so that, as I have said before, the present welfare recipients would have a realistic opportunity of finding employment. As I have also said before, the elimination of welfare would need to take place gradually, say, over a ten-year period.[34] The elimination of public welfare and restrictions on employment would make possible a radical improvement in the lives of the poorest portion of the city's population, whose members would then live by working and recognize their responsibility for their own well-being, and who thus could advance to far higher economic levels than could ever be possible for them while on the welfare rolls. At the same time, and for much the same reasons, it would make an enormous contribution to the reduction in crime and thus to the improvement of the lives of the rest of the city's population, if large numbers of those who otherwise would have been out committing crimes—namely, unemployed, impoverished juveniles and the hardened criminals they grow up to become—were instead busy earning money by working.

The abolition of rent control, of course, would radically and progressively improve the city's housing stock. It would also bring about the return of the middle class to the city. [35] Another important consequence of the repeal of rent control would be a great increase in the revenues of the city government that were derived from property taxes.[36] Property tax collections would soar by virtue of bringing the value of all the housing and land in the city that is presently under rent controls, up to the free-market level. The great increase in property-tax revenues, combined with the elimination of expenditures for welfare, would make possible the elimination of much or even all of the city's income and sales taxes, which would further improve the quality of life in the city and promote the return of industry and commerce. As a result of the vast increase in the property-tax base, even the property-tax rate could probably eventually be reduced.

The privatization not only of the city's subway system but also of its bus lines, accompanied by the phasing out of restrictive taxicab licensing requirements, would achieve major improvement in the city's transportation system. This too would represent an important improvement in the daily life of the average New Yorker and serve to encourage the return of industry and commerce to the city.

No doubt, repeal of victimless crimes legislation and the consequent ability of the city's police department and judicial system to concentrate all of their resources on apprehending and punishing those guilty of crimes against the persons or property of others would be a further measure vital in restoring the life of the city.

Needless to say, success in enacting the above program in New York City would operate powerfully to promote the cause of capitalism in the entire country.

10. The Outlook for the Future

Every supporter of capitalism should take heart. All across the world, socialism is now in visible retreat and outright collapse. Its supporters are in a state of intellectual disintegration, turning en masse against science, technology, and reason, as they magnify the evidence of their own intellectual incompetence into a distrust of the human intellect as such. Having for generations pompously proclaimed the possibility of their rationally planning every detail of human life—at the point of a gun and at the price of everyone else's planning and self-interest—and somehow thereby achieving a utopia, they now

begin to see the devastation they have caused, and, their dream in ruins, they sink to the level of superstitious primitives, living in fear of the intellect and of its products science and technology. In a word, they have become "environmentalists." Safety to them now appears to lie in whatever is not man-made—in whatever is "natural," viz., tested by millions of years of blind evolution.[37]

In these circumstances, even though the world may appear to be continuing to rush on, irresistibly, to a new Dark Age, surprisingly little is needed to bring about the most radical reversal of the political currents. Just one or two victories won in the name of explicit procapitalist principle is all that is required. One or two such victories would prove that there were no irresistible currents of doom. They would serve to galvanize large numbers of people to further action, in the knowledge that rational efforts in the realm of political action actually work.

At the moment, a promising candidate for such a reversal of the currents is the defeat of efforts to establish socialized medicine in the United States, by means of showing that the actual solution for the problem of soaring medical costs is the elimination of government intervention into medicine and the corresponding widening of the zone of economic freedom in medicine. All of the necessary intellectual ammunition is present to do this—that is, all of the objective facts and logical arguments are on the side of the supporters of capitalism.[38] At the same time, with the collapse of socialism across the world, the advocates of socialized medicine have completely lost their intellectual base. Objectively, they are men without logical arguments and without an intellectual home. They are riding on nothing but inertia. On the basis of the fundamentals of the situation, there is no doubt but that they can be stopped.

Perhaps the supporters of capitalism are still too few and for the most part still insufficiently prepared intellectually to win this battle. If so, there will be numerous future occasions on which they can turn the tide. They have only to learn how to articulate their case—that is, to become intellectuals who thoroughly understand economic theory and political philosophy, and enough of more fundamental philosophy to uphold the value of human reason. If enough of them do this, their cause will be irresistible. It will be as the waves of the ocean acting on a foundation made of sand. Inevitably and irresistibly the sand is washed away and the foundation undermined. "Sand" is all that remains of the intellectual foundations of socialism and the opposition to capitalism. Let the advocates of capitalism proceed in the knowledge not only that socialism is dead, but also that what the world still needs to learn is why capitalism deserves to live.

Notes

1. See above, pp. 19–21.

2. Along these lines, see also below, pp. 987–988.

3. On these last points, see above, pp. 286–290 and 316–317. See also above, p. 668.

4. On the nature of the process of capital accumulation and economic progress, see above, pp. 622–636, especially p. 627.

5. At the same time, of course, it should be explained how the fall in wage rates that the freedom of competition would cause in the face of unemployment, would tend not to lower but to raise real wage rates. On this point, see above, pp. 584–585.

6. See above, pp. 384–385, which explain why government intervention is a leading cause of homelessness. See also above, pp. 202–203.

7. For a full discussion of the government's responsibility for the crisis in medical care, and how a free market in medical care would solve all aspects of the problem, see George Reisman, *The Real Right to Medical Care Versus Socialized Medicine* (Laguna Hills, Calif.: The Jefferson School of Philosophy, Economics, and Psychology, 1994.)

8. For an example of an appropriate compromise concerning the Food and Drug Administration, see below, p. 987.

9. On this point, see above, pp. 655–660.

10. Strictly speaking, individuals are presently eligible to receive social security retirement benefits beginning at age 62. This should be eliminated with the rise in the minimum eligibility age to 70.

11. I estimate this to be the case on the basis of data available from the U.S. government. See, for example, U.S. Department of Health and Human Services, Social Security Administration, *Social Security Bulletin Annual Statistical Supplement 1989*, p. 163.

12. A number of states are already making efforts to deny additional aid to mothers who give birth to children while on the welfare rolls. See *Los Angeles Times*, April 30, 1994, p. A14.

13. It is implicit in previous analysis in this book that the abolition of prounion legislation along with minimum-wage legislation, would make possible the employment of unskilled workers with a lesser fall in wage rates than would be the case without the abolition of prounion legislation. On this point, see above, pp. 659–660.

14. See *New York Times*, national ed., January 14, 1994, p. A12.

15. A kindred policy is already being practiced to some extent by the federal government in the form of job "buyouts." Under this arrangement, the government pays an individual up to $25,000 to retire early. See *Washington Post*, October 28, 1993, p. A21; ibid., August 22, 1994, p. D2.

16. Under the present program of job buyouts, the period of disqualification for new government employment appears to be only two years. See ibid., October 28, 1993, p. A 21.

17. On the subject of taxes and the demand for labor, see above, pp. 648–650.

18. See above, pp. 584–585. See also above, pp. 648–650.

19. See above, pp. 634–636.

20. See above, pp. 622–642.

21. See above, pp. 308–310 and 622–642.

22. For elaboration of this point, see above, pp. 829–831.

23. Concerning the necessity of using silver as money, see above, pp. 958–959.

24. I am indebted to von Mises for this observation, which he made on occasion in his seminar.

25. Cf. Ayn Rand, "Collectivized Rights," in Ayn Rand, *The Virtue of Selfishness* (New York: New American Library, 1964) pp. 135–143. Cf. also, the U.S. Declaration of Independence.

26. See above, pp. 322–323 and 362–363.

27. See above, pp. 234–237.

28. On this subject, see above, pp. 362–363. See also above, pp. 634–636.

29. See above, pp. 322–323 and 351–354.

30. See above, the discussions of unilateral free trade on pp. 190–191 and 535–536.

31. Cf. Ayn Rand, *Atlas Shrugged* (New York: Random House, 1957) pp. 1023–1024.

32. See above, pp. 76–115 passim. See also Ayn Rand, *The New Left: The Anti-Industrial Revolution* (New York: New American Library, 1971.)

33. See above, pp. 99–101.

34. See above, pp. 977–978.

35. The abolition of rent control should take place all at once, as soon as possible. For the reasons, see above, pp. 252–254. See also pp. 250–252 and 182–183.

36. See above, p. 252.

37. On this subject, see above, pp. 78–80.

38. See above, pp. 148–150 and 378–380. See also George Reisman, *The Real Right to Medical Care Versus Socialized Medicine*.

BIBLIOGRAPHY

A BIBLIOGRAPHY OF WRITINGS IN DEFENSE OF CAPITALISM

The following is a list of books and essays ranging from essential to helpful to the defense of capitalism.

1. LUDWIG VON MISES

Von Mises is by far the most important defender of capitalism in the realm of economic theory. A thorough knowledge of his writings is essential. I list his four major treatises first, and then, for the most part, his more popular works. The best way to approach the treatises is not to begin on page one, but to start with whatever chapters or sections appear to be of special interest, and then, later on, read the remaining portions.

Human Action, 3d ed. rev. Chicago: Henry Regnery Company, 1966. (The works of von Mises and those of many other authors on this list are available from The Foundation for Economic Education, Irvington-on-Hudson, New York.)

Socialism. London, Jonathan Cape, 1969. Reprint. Indianapolis: Liberty Classics, The Liberty Fund, 1982.

The Theory of Money and Credit. New Haven: Yale University Press, 1953. Reprint. Irvington-on-Hudson, New York: Foundation for Economic Education, 1971. Reprint. Indianapolis: Liberty Classics, The Liberty Fund, 1981.

Theory and History. New Haven: Yale University Press, 1956. Reprint. New Rochelle, New York: Arlington House, 1969.

Planning For Freedom, 4th ed. enl. Grove City, Pennsylvania: Libertarian Press, 1980.

Bureaucracy. New Haven: Yale University Press, 1944. Reprint. Grove City, Pennsylvania: Libertarian Press, 1993.

Omnipotent Government. New Haven: Yale University Press, 1944. Reprint. Grove City, Pennsylvania: Libertarian Press, 1993.

The Free and Prosperous Commonwealth. New York: D. Van Nostrand Company, 1962. (This book has also been reprinted under the title *Liberalism: A Socio-Economic Exposition.* Irvington-on-Hudson, New York: Foundation for Economic Education, 1995.)

The Anti-Capitalistic Mentality. New York: D. Van Nostrand, 1956. Reprint. Grove City, Pennsylvania: Libertarian Press, 1994.

The Historical Setting of the Austrian School of Economics. New Rochelle, New York: Arlington House, 1969. Reprint. Auburn, Alabama: Ludwig von Mises Institute, 1984.

Economic Freedom and Interventionism: An Anthology of Articles and Essays. Edited by Bettina Bien Greaves. Irvington-on-Hudson, New York: Foundation for Economic Education, 1990.

The Ultimate Foundation of Economic Science. New York: D. Van Nostrand Company, 1962.

Epistemological Problems of Economics. Translated by George Reisman. New York: D. Van Nostrand Company, 1960.

A Critique of Interventionism. New Rochelle, New York: Arlington House, 1977.

Nation, State, and Economy. New York: New York University Press, 1983.

Economic Policy. South Bend, Indiana: Regnery/Gateway, 1979.

On the Manipulation of Money and Credit. Dobbs Ferry, New York: Free Market Books, 1978.

Money, Method, and the Market Process: A Collection of Essays. Norwell, Massachusetts: Kluwer Academic Publishers, 1990. Despite the fact that the book's editor and publisher allowed it to go to press with a distracting number of typographical errors, the essays it contains are all of great value and eminently worth reading.

Notes and Recollections. Grove City, Pennsylvania: Libertarian Press, 1978.

A worthwhile book to have available while reading *Human Action* is *Mises Made Easier, A Glossary.* Compiled by Percy Greaves, Jr. Dobbs Ferry, New York: Free Market Books, 1974.

2. AYN RAND

The writings of Ayn Rand provide provide numerous powerful arguments on behalf of capitalism. I list her works in the order that I believe is best suited for coming to a clear and cohesive understanding of them. (Most of these works, incidentally, are available in paperback editions by Signet.)

Atlas Shrugged. New York: Random House, 1957. Reprint. New York: Dutton, 1992.

For the New Intellectual. New York: Random House, 1961. This book contains the philosophical speeches from all of Ayn Rand's novels.

The Virtue of Selfishness. New York: New American Library, 1964.

Capitalism: The Unknown Ideal. New York: New American Library, 1965.

The New Left: The Anti-Industrial Revolution, rev. enl. ed. New York: Penguin USA, Meridian, 1993.

Philosophy: Who Needs It. Indianapolis and New York: Bobbs-Merrill Company, 1982.

The Voice of Reason. New York: New American Library, 1988.

Introduction to Objectivist Epistemology, 2d ed. enl. New York: NAL Books, 1990.

The Fountainhead. New York: The Bobbs-Merrill Company, 1943. Reprint. New York: Macmillan Publishing Co., 1986.

We The Living. New York: Random House, 1959. Reprint. New York: Penguin Books, 1995.

Anthem. Caldwell, Idaho: The Caxton Printers, 1953. Reprint. New York: Penguin Books, 1995.

3. THE ECONOMIC WRITINGS OF HENRY HAZLITT

Hazlitt is perhaps the greatest popularizer of economics of all time. I regard the first two of the following works as classics.

Economics in One Lesson, new ed. New York: Arlington House, 1979. Reprint. New York: Crown Publishers, 1979.

The Great Idea. New York: 1951. Reprinted, with an important change of the ending, under the title *Time Will Run Back.* New Rochelle, New York: Arlington House, 1966.

The Failure of the "New" Economics. New York: D. Van Nostrand, 1959.

The Man Versus the Welfare State. New Rochelle, New York: Arlington House, 1969.

The Conquest of Poverty. New Rochelle, New York: Arlington House, 1973.

Editor, Andrew Dickson White, *Fiat Money Inflation in France.* Irvington-on-Hudson, New York: Foundation for Economic Education, 1960.

Editor, *The Critics of Keynesian Economics.* New York: D. Van Nostrand Company, 1960.

4. THE EARLY AUSTRIAN SCHOOL: MENGER AND BÖHM-BAWERK

Carl Menger, *Principles of Economics.* Glencoe, Illinois: The Free Press, 1950. Reprint. Grove City, Pennsylvania: Libertarian Press, 1994.

Eugen von Böhm-Bawerk, *Capital and Interest.* 3 vols., Sennholz and Huncke translation. Spring Mills, Pennsylvania: Libertarian Press, 1959. (Libertarian Press is currently located in Grove City, Pennsylvania.)

Shorter Classics of Böhm-Bawerk. Spring Mills, Pennsylvania: Libertarian Press, 1962.

5. THE BRITISH CLASSICAL SCHOOL

An indispensable part of any serious study of pro-capitalist economic theory is a thorough, first-hand knowledge of the British Classical economists, i.e., the school principally comprising Adam Smith, David Ricardo, James Mill, John R. McCulloch, John Stuart Mill, and John E. Cairnes. The ideas of these men dominated educated opinion on economic matters in the Western World in the century following 1776 (the date of the publication of *The Wealth of Nations* as well as of the American Revolution). This was the period in history most closely approximating laissez-faire capitalism, and the classical economists deserve much of the credit for it.

As I showed in Chapter 11, the writings of the Classical economists contain a number of gross errors, disastrous formulations, and major contradictions Nevertheless, the fundamental principles set forth in their writings are correct and constitute an essential contribution to economic theory. As I also showed in Chapter 11, when properly understood, their ideas, far from being the foundation of Marxism, as is generally believed, provide the basis for the most powerful refutation of Marxism, as well as lay the foundation for powerful critiques of Keynesianism and the pure-and-perfect and imperfect-competition doctrines. Much of the present book is a testimony to theimportance of their work, indeed, to the fact that their ideas are an essential part of the core around which economic science must be built.

In order to understand the Classical economists, it is necessary to read all of the Classical authors I have named, not just one or two. This entails a certain amount of repetition, but the repetition will serve to cement one's understanding. The two main Classical economists are Smith and Ricardo. Ricardo, however, is especially difficult. I suggest, therefore, reading McCulloch and the two Mills before Ricardo, or giving Ricardo a second try after reading these authors.

Adam Smith, *The Wealth of Nations.* London, 1776. Reprint of Cannan edition. Chicago: University of Chicago Press, 2 vols. in 1, 1976.

David Ricardo, *Principles of Political Economy and Taxation,* 3d ed. London: 1821. This work has been reprinted as vol. I of *The Works and Correspondence of David Ricardo.* Edited by Piero Sraffa. Cambridge: Cambridge University Press, 1962. The full Works and Correspondence contains eleven volumes and contains all of Ricardo's writings, speeches, and correspondence with James Mill and McCulloch. Its publication spans the years 1952–1973. I recommend it highly.

James Mill Selected Economic Writings. Edited by Donald Winch. Chicago: University of Chicago Press, 1966. This volume contains both *Commerce Defended* (London: 1808) and *Elements of Political Economy,* 3d ed. rev. (London: 1844). James Mill is usually greatly underrated. As I have said, he should be credited with the best and clearest exposition of "Say's Law" extant—i.e., the demonstration of the impossibility of a general overproduction. His ideas on saving and capital are equally brilliant.

John R. McCulloch, *Principles of Political Economy,* 5th ed. London: 1864. Reprinted, New York: Augustus M. Kelley, 1965. This is probably the simplest and best overall introduction to Classical economics available.

John Stuart Mill, *Principles of Political Economy,* Ashley edition, 1909. Reprint. New York: Augustus M. Kelley, 1961. (I recommend Mill with mixed feelings because of his sympathy for socialism. Nevertheless, his writings on capital, demand, value and cost, and the overproduction doctrine are brilliant. These appear in Chapters III–VI of Book I and Chapters I–VI and Chapter XIV of Book III.)

John Stuart Mill, *Essays on Some Unsettled Questions of Political Economy,* 2d ed. London: 1874. Reprint. New York: Augustus M. Kelley, 1968.

John E. Cairnes, *Some Leading Principles of Political Economy Newly Expounded.* London: 1874. Reprint. New York: Augustus M. Kelley, 1967.

Offshoots of the British Classical School

Jean-Baptiste Say, *A Treatise on Political Economy,* 1st American Edition. Philadelphia: 1821. Reprint. New York: Augustus M. Kelley, 1971. (This was the most popular economics textbook in the United States in the decades prior to the Civil War.)

Nassau Senior, *An Outline of the Science of Political Economy.* London: 1836. Reprint. New York: Augustus M. Kelley.

Nassau Senior, *Selected Writings on Economics, A Volume of Pamphlets 1827–1852.* New York: Augustus M. Kelley, 1966.

Frederic Bastiat, *Economic Sophisms.* Translated from the French and edited by Arthur Goddard. Introduction by Henry Hazlitt. New York: D. Van Nostrand, 1964. Reprint. Irvington-on-Hudson, New York: Foundation for Economic Education.

Frederic Bastiat, *Selected Essays on Political Economy.* Translated from the French by Seymour Cain. Edited by George B. de Huszar. Introduction by F. A. Hayek. New York: D. Van Nostrand, 1964. (This volume contains the justly famous essay "The Law," which demonstrates the inherently immoral nature of government intervention.) Reprint. Irvington-on-Hudson, New York: Foundation for Economic Education.

Frederic Bastiat, *Economic Harmonies.* Translated from the French by W. Hayden Boyers. Edited by George B. de Huszar. Introduction by Dean Russell. New York: D. Van Nostrand, 1964. Reprint. Irvington-on-Hudson, New York: Foundation for Economic Education.

Charles Holt Carroll, *Organization of Debt into Currency.* Edited with an Introduction by Edward C. Simmons. New York: D. Van Nostrand, 1964. This is a brilliant series of essays written between 1855 and 1879 showing how a fractional reserve monetary system causes depressions. Argues forcefully for a 100-percent-reserve gold standard.

6. RECENT OR CONTEMPORARY WRITINGS IN DEFENSE OF VARIOUS ASPECTS OF CAPITALISM

I apologize for the fact that the following list cannot be exhaustive and thus necessarily must omit some authors who, arguably, deserve to be included, and perhaps also omits some deserving titles by authors who have been included.

This category, it must be noted, includes authors who, while defending various important aspects of capitalism, hold grossly inconsistent positions. As explained in the Introduction to this book, this is obviously true of Hayek, Friedman, and Rothbard, for example. It can be safely left to the intelligent reader to detect such further cases of inconsistency on his own.

F. A. Hayek

The Road to Serfdom. Chicago: 1944. Reprint. Chicago: University of Chicago Press. Phoenix Books.

Capitalism and the Historians. Chicago: University of Chicago Press, 1954.

Prices and Production. London: George Routledge & Sons, 1931.

Profits, Interest, and Investment. London: George Routledge & Sons, 1939.

The Pure Theory of Capital. Chicago: University of Chicago Press, 1941.

Individualism and Economic Order. Chicago: University of Chicago Press, 1948.

Monetary Theory and the Trade Cycle. Translated from the German by N. Kaldor. New York: 1933. Reprint. New York: Augustus M. Kelley, 1966.

Editor, *Collectivist Economic Planning: Critical Studies on the Possibility of Socialism.* London: George Routledge & Sons, 1935. Reprint. New York: Augustus M. Kelley, 1975.

Milton Friedman

The Balance of Payments: Free Versus Fixed Exchange Rates. Coauthor Robert V. Roosa. Washington, D. C. American Enterprise Institute, 1967.

Capitalism and Freedom. Chicago: University of Chicago Press, 1962.

Free to Choose. Coauthor Rose Friedman. New York: Harcourt Brace Jovanovich, 1980.

The Great Contraction 1929–1933. Coauthor Anna Jacobson Schwartz. Princeton: Princeton University Press, 1965.

A Monetary History of the United States, 1867–1960. Coauthor Anna Jacobson Schwartz. Princeton: Princeton University Press, 1963.

James Buchanan

The Bases of Collective Action. New York: General Learning Press, 1971.

The Consequences of Mr. Keynes: An Analysis of the Misuse of Economic Theory for Political Profiteering, with Proposals for Constitutional Disciplines. Coauthors Richard E. Wagner and John Burton. London: Institute of Economic Affairs, 1978.

Cost and Choice: An Inquiry in Economic Theory. Chicago: 1969. Reprint. University of Chicago Press, 1978.

The Demand and Supply of Public Goods. Chicago: Rand McNally, 1968.

Democracy in Deficit: The Political Legacy of Lord Keynes. Coauthor Richard E. Wagner. New York: Academic Press, 1977.

William H. Hutt

The Economics of the Colour Bar: A Study of the Economic Origins and Consequences of Racial Segregation in South Africa. London: A. Deutsch, 1964.

The Keynesian Episode: A Reassessment. Indianapolis: Liberty Press, 1979.

Keynesianism—Retrospect and Prospect: A Critical Restatement of Basic Economic Principles. Chicago: Henry Regnery, 1963.

Politically Impossible—?: An Essay on the Supposed Electoral Obstacles Impeding the Translation of Economic Analysis into Policy. London: Institute of Economic Affairs, 1971.

The Strike-Threat System: The Economic Consequences of Collective Bargaining. New Rochelle, New York: Arlington House: 1973.

The Theory of Collective Bargaining: A History, Analysis, and Criticism. Glencoe, Illinois: 1954. Reprint. San Francisco: Cato Institute, 1980.

The Theory of Idle Resources, 2d ed. Indianapolis: Liberty Press, 1977.

Israel Kirzner

An Essay on Capital. New York: Augustus M. Kelley, 1966.

Competition and Entrepreneurship. Chicago: University of Chicago Press, 1973.

The Economic Point of View. New York: D. Van Nostrand, 1960.

Market Theory and the Price System. New York: D. Van Nostrand, 1963.

Perception, Opportunity, and Profit. Chicago. University of Chicago Press, 1979.

Murray Rothbard

America's Great Depression. New York: D. Van Nostrand, 1963.

For a New Liberty. New York: Macmillan, 1973.

Man, Economy, and State: A Treatise on Economic Principles, 2 vols. New York: D. Van Nostrand, 1962. This book should definitely *not* be used as a substitute for von Mises's *Human Action,* all claims and recommendations to the contrary notwithstanding.

What Has Government Done to Our Money? Novato, California: Libertarian Publishers, 1978. This booklet is a brilliantly clear analysis of government intervention into money, which, uncharacteristically, is not marred by any major contradictions on the author's part.

Hans Sennholz

Age of Inflation. Belmont, Massachusetts: 1979. Reprint. Grove City, Pennsylvania: Libertarian Press.

Death and Taxes. Washington, D. C.: Heritage Foundation, 1976. Reprint. Grove City, Pennsylvania: Libertarian Press.

Debts and Deficits. Grove City, Pennsylvania: Libertarian Press.

The Politics of Unemployment. Grove City, Pennsylvania: Libertarian Press, 1987.

Mark Skousen

Economics on Trial: Lies, Myths, and Realities. Homewood, Illinois: Business One Irwin, 1991.

The 100% Gold Standard: Economics of a Pure Money Commodity. Washington, D. C.: University Press of America, 1977.

The Structure of Production. New York: New York University Press, 1990.

Bernard Siegan

Government, Regulation, and the Economy. Lexington, Massachusetts: Lexington Books, 1980.

Economic Liberties and the Constitution. Chicago: University of Chicago Press, 1980.

Land Use Without Zoning. Lexington, Massachusetts: Lexington Books, 1972.

Other People's Property. Lexington, Massachusetts: Lexington Books, 1976.

The Supreme Court's Constitution: An Inquiry into Judicial Review and Its Impact on Society. New Brunswick, New Jersey: Transaction Books, 1987.

Thomas Sowell

The Economics and Politics of Race: An International Perspective. New York: Morrow, 1983.

Markets and Minorities. New York: Basic Books, 1981.

Race and Economics. New York: D. McKay, 1975.

Walter Williams

America, A Minority Viewpoint. Stanford, California: Hoover Institution Press, 1982.

Black America and Organized Labor: A Fair Deal? Coauthors Loren Smith and Wendell Gunn. Washington, D. C.: Lincoln Institute for Research and Education, 1979.

South Africa's War Against Capitalism. New York: Praeger, 1989.

The State Against Blacks. New York: New Press, 1982.

Youth and Minority Unemployment. Stanford, California: Hoover Institution Press, 1977.

Pamphlets by George Reisman

Capitalism: The Cure for Racism. Laguna Hills, California: The Jefferson School of Philosophy, Economics, and Psychology, 1992. An explanation of how capitalism and the unhampered profit motive achieve equal pay for equal work and operate against all aspects of racial prejudice in the marketplace, and how the unjust treatment of blacks in contemporary American society is the result of the mixed economy, not of capitalism.

Education and the Racist Road to Barbarism. Laguna Hills, California: The Jefferson School of Philosophy,

Economics, and Psychology, 1992. An explanation of the nature and universal value of Western civilization, and why the efforts to replace its teaching with "Afrocentric" and "Latino-centric" studies are based on racism and imply the destruction of education.

The Real Right to Medical Care Versus Socialized Medicine. Laguna Hills, California: The Jefferson School of Philosophy, Economics, and Psychology, 1994. This 44-page pamphlet upholds the rational right to buy all the medical care one wishes from willing providers. It shows how the displacement of this right by the pseudo-right to medical care based on need has created all aspects of the medical crisis. The pamphlet shows not only how a free market in medical care would solve the medical crisis and make medical care progressively better and more affordable, but also what specific steps need to be taken to achieve such a free market. It is full of powerful intellectual ammunition designed to enable the advocates of individual rights and economic freedom to take the offensive on this vital issue.

George Reisman is also the author of *The Government Against the Economy.* Ottawa, Illinois: Jameson Books, 1979. As noted elsewhere, this book is incorporated in the present volume as Chapters 6–8.

7. BASIC PROCAPITALIST READINGS IN POLITICAL PHILOSOPHY

John Locke, *Second Treatise on Civil Government.* Many editions. The basic political documents of the United States should be read in conjunction with Locke—i.e., *The Declaration of Independence* and *The Constitution.*

Wilhelm von Humboldt, *On the Sphere and Duties of Government.* London, 1854.

Herbert Spencer, *The Man Versus the State.* Caldwell, Idaho: The Caxton Printers, 1969.

On this subject, see also, above, Ayn Rand, *The Virtue of Selfishness* and *Capitalism: The Unknown Ideal.*

8. READINGS ON SELECTED SUBJECTS

(Note: the introductory paragraphs of Section 6 of this bibliography apply here.)

Advertising

Jerry Kirkpatrick, *In Defense of Advertising.* Westport, Connecticut: Quorum Books, 1994.

Yale Brozen, ed., *Advertising and Society.* New York: New York University Press, 1974.

The Ecology Movement

Jay Lehr, ed., *Rational Readings on Environmental Concerns.* New York: Van Nostrand Reinhold, 1992. (This volume includes George Reisman, "The Toxicity of Environmentalism" as its summary chapter.)

Dixy Lee Ray and Lou Guzzo, *Trashing the Planet: How Science Can Help Us Deal with Acid Rain, Depletion of the Ozone, and Nuclear Waste (Among Other Things).* Washington, D. C., Regnery/Gateway, 1990.

On this subject, see also, above, Ayn Rand, *The New Left: The Anti-Industrial Revolution.*

Aspects of Government Intervention

E. C. Pasour, Jr., *Agriculture and the State,* Oakland, California: The Independent Institute, 1995.

William Mitchell and Randy Simmons, *Beyond Politics.* Boulder, Colorado: Westview Press for The Independent Institute, 1994.

Tibor Machan, *Private Rights & Public Illusions.* New Brunswick, New Jersey: Transaction Publishers for the Independent Institute, 1995.

John W. Sommer, ed., *The Academy in Crisis.* New Brunswick, New Jersey: Transaction Publishers for the Independent Institute, 1995.

Richard Vedder and Lowell Gallaway, *Out of Work.* New York: Holmes & Meier for The Independent Institute, 1993.

The Monopoly Myth

D. T. Armentano, *Antitrust and Monopoly.* Oakland, California: The Independent Institute, 1996.

Yale Brozen, *Is Government the Source of Monopoly? and Other Essays.* San Francisco: Cato Institute, 1980.

Wayne A. Leeman, "The Limitations of Local Price Cutting as a Barrier to Entry," *Journal of Political Economy,* August 1956.

John S. McGee, "Predatory Price Cutting: The Standard Oil (N. J.) Case," *The Journal of Law and Economics,* Vol. 1, October 1958.

Soviet Russia

Robert G. Kaiser, *Russia.* New York: Atheneum, 1976.

Hedrick Smith, *The Russians.* New York: Quadrangle Books, 1976.

Anatoly Marchenko, *My Testimony.* New York: Dutton, 1969.

G. Warren Nutter, *The Strange World of Ivan Ivanov.* New York: The World Publishing Company, 1969.

Paul Craig Roberts, *Alienation and the Soviet Economy.* New York: Holmes & Meier for the Independent Institute, 1990.

9. NEOCLASSICAL ECONOMICS

Some of the following works, especially those of Jevons, are valuable, though badly mixed. Others are so badly muddled as to be worthless, despite their great reputations. In any case, an expert knowledge of economics requires familiarity with them.

William Stanley Jevons, *Theory of Political Economy,* 4th ed. London: Macmillan and Co., 1924. The book represents an original discovery of the law of diminishing marginal utility, but is an overreaction to the labor theory of value held by the classical economists. It claims Ricardo "shunted economics onto the wrong track."

William Stanley Jevons, *The State in Relation to Labour.* London: Macmillan, 1882. This book is philosophically corrupt. It openly abandons the principle of laissez faire and attacks arguments based on abstract principles of rights. It is nevertheless valuable for a devastating analysis of labor unions.

Léon Walras, *Elements of Pure Economics.* New York: Augustus M. Kelley, 1969. Originally published in French in 1874, this book is famous for an original discovery of the law of diminishing marginal utility roughly coinciding with its discovery by Menger and Jevons. However, it is one of the early works of mathematical economics, and thus helped to set the stage for severing economic theory from reality by introducing the needless complications of higher mathematics.

Philip H. Wickstead, *The Common Sense of Political Economy,* rev. enl. ed., 2 vols. London: 1933. Reprint. New York: Augustus M. Kelley, 1967.

Alfred Marshall, *Principles of Economics.* 8th ed. New York: The Macmillan Company, 1920. An extremely diffuse, confused book, which, among other things, helped to set the stage for the theory of "pure and perfect competition" that I criticized in Chapter 10. Marshall was the teacher of Keynes.

John Bates Clark, *The Distribution of Wealth.* New York, Macmillan, 1938. This book contains the original exposition of the theory of diminishing marginal productivity, which it propounds far more cogently than today's textbooks. Nevertheless, the basic argument is weak and its exposure is used to discredit capitalism.

Frank H. Knight, *Risk, Uncertainty, and Profit.* Boston, 1921. This work is another major source of the pure and perfect competition doctrine.

Irving Fisher, *The Rate of Interest.* New York, 1907, and *The Theory of Interest.* Reprint. New York: Augustus M. Kelley, 1954. Fisher advances a host of wrong or confused ideas about profit and interest that helped to pave the way for Keynes.

10. THE ENEMIES OF CAPITALISM

I include this group because an advocate of capitalism should have a first hand knowledge of the ideas of its enemies.

Karl Marx, *The Communist Manifesto.* Chicago: Henry Regnery Co., 1954.

Karl Marx, *Das Kapital.* vol. I, New York: The Modern Library, 1937.

J.M. Keynes, *The General Theory of Employment Interest and Money.* New York, Harcourt Brace, 1936.

Joan Robinson, *The Economics of Imperfect Competition.* London: Macmillan and Co., 1933.

Edward Chamberlin, *Theory of Monopolistic Competi-*tion, 6th ed. Cambridge, Massachusetts: Harvard University Press, 1950. This is a second source of the oligopoly/monopolistic-competition doctrine.

Benjamin E. Lippencott, ed., *On the Economic Theory of Socialism.* Minneapolis: University of Minnesota Press, 1938. Contains the attempts of Lange and Taylor to overturn von Mises's proof that economic calculation under socialism is impossible.

John Kenneth Galbraith, *The Affluent Society.* Boston: Houghton Mifflin. 1958. This book is included only because of its popularity and Galbraith's continuing influence. It is one of the least intellectually significant attacks on capitalism I know of. See my review, "Galbraith's Modern Brand of Prussian Feudalism," *Human Events,* February 2, 1961.

John Kenneth Galbraith, *The New Industrial State,* 2d ed. rev. New York: New American Library, 1971.

Joseph P. McKenna, *Aggregate Economic Analysis,* 5th ed. Hinsdale, Illinois: Dryden Press, 1977. A comparatively clear exposition of the essential ideas of Keynes. The first or second edition is the most preferable because of greater simplicity in comparison with later editions.

Paul Samuelson and William Nordhaus, *Economics.* 13th ed. or previous editions. Englewood-Cliffs, New Jersey: McGraw-Hill, 1989. This is the leading "textbook case" of the exposition of economic fallacies and anticapitalist doctrines.

Dudley Dillard, *Economic Development of the North Atlantic Community.* Englewood Cliffs, New Jersey: Prentice-Hall, 1967. If there is any fallacy that Samuelson has managed to avoid, it can probably be found in this book.

A FURTHER WORD ON READINGS

My list has omitted the names of such eminent economists as Wicksell Fetter, Edgeworth, and Pareto, and men of even greater stature, such as Adam Smith's predecessors Quesnay, Dupont, and Turgot, i.e., the French Physiocrats. The interested student will come across many references to these men as he reads the works I have recommended.

For the purpose of rounding out one's knowledge as soon as possible, it pays to read a history of economic thought early on. I recommend the one I found most helpful, and which I used shortly after beginning my own study of economics. It is:

Frank A. Neff, *Economic Doctrines,* 2d ed. New York: McGraw-Hill Book Company, 1950.

The best way to learn the history of economic thought in depth, however, is to read the great economists themselves on their predecessors, for example, Adam Smith on the Physiocrats and the Mercantilists, in *The Wealth of Nations.*

INDEX

INDEX

Note: Depending on the context, sub-subentries may refer either to the subentries
under which they appear or directly to the main entries under which they appear.

A

A is *A* vs. *A* is *A+*, 674–682
Abramovitz, Moses, 806(89–91)
Accidents, diminishing frequency of, in rational society, 107
Acid rain, 78, 80, 85, 93, 102
Ackley, Gardner, 677–678, 716(12), 893(18, 20, 29, 30)
Administered prices
  See Cost of production as immediate determinant of prices
Advances in technology
  See Technological progress
Advertising
  diminishing returns to, 471
  increases demand only to extent it increases production and supply, 555–556
  productive role of, 471–473
  results in greater gains from production and in more production, 555–556
Aggregate demand
  See Demand, aggregate
Aggregate economic accounting on an Aristotelian base, 699–708
Aggregate production
  See Production, aggregate
Aggregate profit
  See Profit, aggregate
Aggregate spending
  See Spending, aggregate
Agricultural export crisis of 1972–73, 223
Air bags
  See Safety
Air pollution, 78, 80, 83, 85
Alar, 85–86
Alaskan oil, 66, 82, 94, 112
Alchian, Armen, 1, 684, 716
Allen, William, 1
Allocation principles
  See Price system, free-market, allocation principles of
Altruism, xlvii, 281
  animal-rights doctrine, in, 114
  arguments for economic equality, in, 333–336
  economics vs., 33–34
  environmentalism reveals nature of, 103
  irrational self-interest and pressure-group warfare support, 34–35
  no basis for economic progress, 277
  no basis for solving the problem of poverty, 335
  price controls and shortages impose, as basis of relationship between buyer and seller, 239
  role of, in perpetuating mass unemployment, 589
  underlies high rate of profit, 831
  See also Profit, motive; Sacrifice; Self-interest(s)

American Indians, 38(38), 317
  inescapable conflicts among, because of lack of division-of-labor society, 317
  property rights of, 317
  why European civilization objectively deserved to prevail over, 317
American institutionalist school, 6
Ames, Bruce, 85–86
Anarchy of production
  actual under price controls and socialism, 219–282
  alleged under capitalism, 173
  capitalism vs., 138, 172–216
Andrus, Cecil, 225
Animal-rights doctrine, 112–115
  See also Ecology movement (environmentalism); Speciesism
Antitrust laws
  constitute promonopoly legislation 387
  grounds for, baseless, 376, 389–437
    alleged tendency toward formation of a single giant firm, rebuttal of, 392–396, 402–403
    cartels, 423–425
    marginal revenue and the alleged "monopolistic restriction" of supply, 408–423
    Platonic competition of contemporary economics, 425–437
    predatory-pricing doctrine, 399–407
  impair capital accumulation by reducing productivity of capital goods, 637
  rebuttal of charge that private firms "control" prices, 238
  See also Freedom, rational concept of; Monopoly vs. freedom of competition
Applications of the invariable-money/net-consumption analysis
  See Invariable-money/net-consumption analysis, applications of
Arab oil embargo
  free market vs., 188–190, 192–194, 203–204, 211–212, 213–214
  misleading news reports concerning, 192–194, 224–225, 231–237
  price controls responsible for associated chaos
    allocation of crude oil to the production of the various oil products, 263–264
    blocked spreading of loss of OPEC supplies and obtaining replacement supplies, 188–190
    geographical distribution of oil and oil products, 243–247
    hoarding of oil and oil products, 246–247
    personal distribution of oil products, 240, 243
    prevented loss of supplies being taken

out on previously marginal employments, 211–212
    prevented problems created by the loss of supplies from being solved by the thinking and planning of all concerned, 213–214
    rise in the demand for and price of OPEC oil, 254–255
    shortages of oil and oil products, 203–204
    supplies of oil and oil products in storage inadequate, 193
    supplies of oil and oil products produced in U.S. less than would have been, 222, 225, 226–227
  rational response to, 211–212, 213–214
  See also Energy crisis; Oil cartel
Argentina, 325–326, 519, 945
Aristocracy
  See Feudal aristocracy; Socialism
Aristotle, influence of, on development of economic activity and capitalism, 19
Armentano, Dominick, 1
Asceticism, 76
Atomic power, 67, 85, 88, 98, 104
  Chernobyl, 79
  disposal of radioactive wastes created by, 72–73
  Three-Mile Island, 79
  would cause further improvement in air quality, 83
  See also Ecology movement (environmentalism)
Australia, 288
Austrian economics, Austrian school, 1, 3, 7, 218(31), 414–416.
  compatibility of, with proposition that the demand for A is the demand for A, 689–690
  integration with classical economics, 3–5
  main difference with classical school, 2
  opposition to, 6
  supply curve as a vertical line, on, 163
  See also Böhm-Bawerk, Eugen von; Hayek, F. A.; Marginal utility, law of diminishing; Mises, Ludwig von; Rothbard, Murray N; Wieser, Friedrich von
Average money wage rate
  See Wage(s) (rate[s])
Average period of production
  alternative measurement of, 852–854
  extremely short in Adam Smith's "early and rude state," 862(96)
  limits to technological progress as a source of capital accumulation, and, 824
  meaning of, 820–824
  why capital accumulation does not depend on continuous lengthening of, 820–824
Average rate of profit
  See Profit, average rate of

private ownership of the means of production and the price system, 135–139, 172–295, 296–326

saving and capital accumulation, 139–141, 622–629, 631–634, 809–824

dependence of production and human life upon, 15–16

economic problem, the focal point of the ongoing solution to the, 61

efficiency with which man uses his mind, body, and nature-given environment increased by, 128

extent of, 16

    under Roman Empire, 37

framework of, makes possible counteraction of law of diminishing returns, 133

freedom as basis of development of, 27

gains from, based on independent thought and knowledge, 135

gains from, constitute objective foundation for good will towards others, 128

horizontal aspect, 141

human reason, actualization of its potential depends on, 128

implications of, for ethics, 128–129

incompatibility of socialism and collectivism with, 136–137, 267–282

influence of, on institutions of capitalism, 296–374

    economic competition, 343–371

    economic inequality, 326–343

    private ownership of the means of production, 296–326

interesting jobs, proportion of increased by, 130

late Roman Empire, leading example of decline of, 16

necessitates exchange on massive scale, 141

operates to reduce alienation, 130

production of wealth under system of, as definition of economics, 19

rebuttal of critique of, 129–130

repetitious factory work as example of rise in yield to knowledge, 127

rise in productivity of labor because of:

    benefit from existence of geniuses, 124–125

    concentration on the advantages of all individuals, 125

    economies of learning and motion achieved through: elimination of wasted motion, 126–127; rise in ratio of application time to learning time, 126; specialization in storing and transmitting knowledge, 126; subconscious automatizing of knowledge, 126

    geographical specialization, 125–126

    multiplication of knowledge used in production, 123–124

    use of machinery, which depends on, by virtue of making its use economically worthwhile through: concentrating a sufficient amount of work of same kind in same place, 127;

providing access to sufficient fund of knowledge and variety of materials needed for construction of machinery, 127; science and invention being made into specializations, 127; simplification of design resulting from reduction of work to simple steps, 127

role of, in production explains why Industrial Revolution began in England, 127

society of

    objective value of, 48–49

    recent origin and present extent of, 16

vertical aspect of, 133, 141, 824, 843–856

See also Capitalism; Economic competition; Harmony of interests; Price system, free-market; Private ownership of the means of production; Self-interest(s)

Division of payments, 140–141

"Double counting" in gross national product

    See Contemporary economics, "double counting," and

Douglas, William O., 119(119)

Du Pont de Nemours, Pierre, 1

E

Eckert, Ross D.

    See Leftwich, Richard H.

Ecology movement (environmentalism), 76–115

advocates inaction as best means of coping with nature and destruction of industrial civilization in order to avoid bad weather, 88

animal-rights doctrine and, 112–114

antihuman ethical perspective of, 80–83, 112–114

claims of

    alleged pollution of water and air and destruction of species, 83–85

    alleged threat from toxic chemicals, including acid rain and ozone depletion, 85–86

    alleged threat of global warming, 87–90

    atmosphere used as garbage dump, 91

collectivism and hysteria, appeal to, by, 92, 94–95

collectivist bias of, 91–98

    externalities doctrine and, 96–98

    irrational product liability, connection with, 95–96

    wrong judgment of responsibilities of individual, 92

conservationism absorbed by, 76

contemporary education, destructive role of, and, 107–112

cultural devaluation of man and, 112–115

damage caused by

    demand for labor and supply of consumers' goods held down by, 668

    destruction of property rights, 99

    energy crisis and rise in price of oil, 66–67, 98, 234–237

enrichment of sheiks and terrorist governments, 98

global "pollution limits" will cause international conflicts of interests, 101

land rent raised by, 316–317

needless lack of landfill areas for garbage disposal, 73

rise in costs, decline in quality of life, 98

undermines capital accumulation, 98–99, 636–639

waste of human labor in recycling, 73

dishonesty of

    claims, in, 86–87

    tactics, in, 91–92

economic and philosophic significance of, 98–99

energy crisis and, 66–67, 98, 234–237

epistemology of, vs. principle of causality and scientific experiments, 86–87

externalities doctrine and, 96–98

hatred of man and distrust of reason a psychological projection of many intellectuals' self-hatred and distrust of their own minds based on their responsibility for the devastation wrought by socialism, 100–101

hostility toward economic progress and science and technology, 79–90

individualism's view contrasted with collectivist bias of, 92–94

intellectual death rattle of socialism, as, 103

    aptly named as anti-industrial revolution, 78

    converts old unjust caricature of defenders of capitalism into accurate description of today's advocates of socialism, 104–105

    "social engineering" to the prohibition of real engineering, from, 103–104

    prominent portions of, advocate return to stone age, while advocates of capitalism are denounced as "dinosaur Republicans," because they want to return to age of reason, 105

    transfers banner of reason and science from socialism back to capitalism, 105

industrial civilization, reversal by, of facts concerning effects of, on air, water, and species, 84–85

intrinsic-value-of-nature doctrine, 80–83

    permeates claims of harm to the environment, 90–91

intellectuals and socialism, and, 99–106

irrational product liability, connection with, 95–96

irrational skepticism and, 106–107, 109

irrationalism and, 106–115

loss of concept of economic progress as preliminary to rise of, 106

loss of confidence in human reason at base of rise of, 106–115

mistaken ideas on wastefulness held by,

I

N

Y